ISBN 978-0-483-51727-1
PIBN 10786023

FB &c Ltd, Dalton House, 60 Windsor Avenue, London, SW19 2RR.
Company number 08720141. Registered in England and Wales.

For support please visit www.forgottenbooks.com

WEEKLY FAMILY AND RELIGIOUS JOURNAL.

July 7, 1898

.... 3
.... 5
.... 5
... . 6
.... 6
... . 7
.... 8
Factor in the
.... 9
R. Dungan..10
............13
.... 16
....16
............17
....17
ucation.....18
............18
.... 19
.............20
....30
.............22
Black Clay-
............22
poem)...... 24
............24
.... 24
............24
.. .. 25
.............25
.... 25
............25
.. ..14
.............15
.............20
... . .20
.... .21
.. .. 21
.... 26
.............27
es 28
.. ..29
. ...29
....30
.............32

J. H. GARRISON, LL. D., Editor Christian-Evangelist.

$1.75.

PUBLISHED BY

ISTIAN PUBLISHING COMPAN

1522 Locust St., St. Louis.

THE

CHRISTIAN - EVANGELIST

J. H. GARRISON, EDITOR.

W. W. HOPKINS, ASSISTANT.
B. B. TYLER, J. J. HALEY,
EDITORIAL CONTRIBUTORS.

What We Plead For.

The Christian-Evangelist pleads for:

The Christianity of the New Testament, taught by Christ and his Apostles, versus the theology of the creeds taught by fallible men—the world's great need.

The divine confession of faith on which Christ built his church, versus human confessions of faith on which men have split the church.

The unity of Christ's disciples, for which he so fervently prayed, versus the divisions in Christ's body, which his apostles strongly condemned.

The abandonment of sectarian names and practices, based on human authority, for the common family name and the common faith, based on divine authority, versus the abandonment of scriptural names and usages for partisan ends.

The hearty co-operation of Christians in efforts of world-wide beneficence and evangelization, versus petty jealousies and strifes in the struggle for denominational pre-eminence.

The fidelity to truth which secures the approval of God, versus conformity to custom to gain the favor of men.

The protection of the home and the destruction of the saloon, versus the protection of the saloon and the destruction of the home.

For the right against the wrong;
For the weak against the strong;
For the poor who've waited long
For the brighter age to be.
For the truth, 'gainst superstition,
For the faith, against tradition,
For the hope, whose glad fruition
Our waiting eyes shall see.

Notes From Subscription Department.

BY W. D. CREE.

Single subscriptions, new or old	$1.75 each
In clubs of five or more, new or old	1.50 "
Reading Rooms	1.25 "
Ministers	1.00 "

With a club of ten we will send one additional copy free.

All subscriptions payable in advance. Label shows the month up to the first day of which your subscription is paid. If an earlier date than the present is shown, you are in arrears. No paper discontinued without express orders to that effect. Arrears should be paid when discontinuance is ordered.

In ordering a change of post office, please give the OLD as well as the NEW address.

Do not send local check, but use Post office or Express Money Order, or draft on St. Louis, Chicago or New York, in remitting.

THE CHRISTIAN-EVANGELIST

"In faith, Unity; in opinion and methods, Liberty; in all things, Charity."

Vol. xxxv. St. Louis, Mo., Thursday, July 7, 1898. No. 27

CURRENT EVENTS.

The battle at Santiago which began about eight o'clock on Friday morning, July first, continued with increasing severity throughout the day with advantages greatly in favor of the American troops. The firing was rambling at first, but became more furious and deadly as the day wore on. The outer entrenchments of the Spaniards were taken, and at sunset on Friday evening the Americans were within less than a mile of the city. The present reports estimate the killed and wounded Americans and Cubans at four hundred, but say that there were few killed. The report says that this famous stronghold at Santiago is now in ruins and the way open for a direct attack upon Cervera's ships within the bay. Hostilities were to be resumed at daybreak on Saturday, and at this writing it is thought that the city of Santiago will be taken before the close of the day.

The railroad connecting Aguadores and Santiago fell into the hands of the American troops June 30th, with no resistance and but slightly damaged. The engines were immediately manned by American men and went to hauling troops and equipments to the front. This will not only relieve the pack trains of a great burden, but hastens the movements of the army. The horses and mules contemplated for hauling supplies to the front from the shore can now be used to haul supplies from place to place at the front. With the capture of the railroad two thousand tons of coal intended for Cervera's ships in Santiago Harbor were also captured and will be used by the American fleet. The prospect at this writing is that the big guns of Moro Castle will also be taken and used against the fleet that sought shelter under their range. The cloud over Spanish rule in Cuba thickens and the storm that is to sweep the rule of this nation from the Atlantic Ocean is already bursting upon the doomed city of Santiago, and ere we go to press we shall doubtless record its submission to the American sceptre.

The Fourth of July, 1898, is destined to be a memorable one in the history of the nation. On the morning of that day came the news of the destruction of Cervera's fleet in Santiago Harbor, by Admiral Sampson, and General Shafter's demand for the surrender of the city of Santiago. Driven to desperation by the steady advance of our army investing the doomed city, and perhaps by the bombardment of our artillery, Admiral Cervera pushed his fleet around the sunken Merrimac and came out to sea at 9:30 A. M., with a view of giving battle to our squadron, or of making his escape. The movement was at once observed by our watchful seamen, and as soon as the first Spanish ship had emerged into the open sea, it was at once engaged by our vessels, and the others following quickly, under full sail, met with the same warm reception. At 2 P. M. nothing was left of the proud Spanish fleet, of which so much had been expected, but shattered and burning hulks lying along the Cuban Coast. Only one of our sailors was killed, and two wounded. The Spanish loss was several hundred killed and wounded, and 1,300 prisoners, including Admiral Cervera. When the Spanish commanders saw that their vessels were disabled by American shells, they ran them into the shore and blew them up. The vessels thus destroyed include the entire Spanish squadron, seven in all. This news communicated by Admiral Sampson to Washington and from there distributed throughout the country added immensely to the enthusiasm of the Fourth of July celebration in progress all over the land.

The destruction of Spain's squadron puts a new phase on the situation at Santiago. The decimated ranks of Gen. Shafter's army, which might have been compelled to wait for re-enforcements before storming the city, will now have the benefit of the co-operation of the fleet in reducing the fortifications of the city. Gen. Shafter, after having demanded the surrender of the city, which demand was refused by the Spanish commander, postponed the bombardment of the city until Tuesday, July 5th, at noon, the time of the closing of our paper to go to press. This postponement was made on the request of the foreign consul to allow time for women and children and other non-combatants to get out of the city. It is not believed at this writing that the city will be surrendered until it is subjected to bombardment. The hope of receiving re-enforcements under Gen. Pando, who is approaching the city, is no doubt the cause of the refusal to surrender. Gen. Shafter and Gen. Wheeler are both reported unwell. The heat has been terrible, but in the main our army seems to be standing it well and to be in good condition.

An unusually large number of casualties have resulted from the fighting about Santiago, and Gen. Shafter has been compelled to call for additional hospital facilities. The War Department has arranged to supply this demand. The Red Cross relief corps is rendering most efficient service in caring for the wounded. We regret, for the sake of our common humanity, to learn that the Spanish, in a number of cases, have fired upon these angels of mercy while they have been discharging their offices of kindness. The number of killed and wounded is estimated at from 800 to 1,000, about 15 per cent. of this number being killed. Estimating the number of our troops engaged at 12,000, this per cent. of killed and wounded is very high, showing the destructive character of modern arms. Some of the cartridges used by the Spanish have been sent to Washington, and are found to be so constructed as to produce blood poisoning. It is thought by experts that the use of such cartridges is a violation of the rules of civilized warfare. But Spain has not limited herself to the civilized rules of warfare in this conflict. The continuation of the struggle at Santiago, when there is no possibility of saving the city from captures is a needless sacrifice of human life. This is not bravery, bnt a stupid stubbornness that disregards the consequences.

On the 29th of June, Congress passed a new national bankruptcy bill. This is the fourth bill of this kind in the history of the nation. The first national bankruptcy law was passed in 1801 and repealed two and a half years later. The second one was passed in 1841 and lived but two years. The third one was passed in 1867 and remained in force for eleven years. Many attempts have been made since 1878 to enact another national bankruptcy bill, but without success, until the passage of the present measure. The present bill is said to be a compromise between the Nelson or Senate bill, which provided only for voluntary bankuptcy, and the Torrey or House bill, which provided for both voluntary and involuntary bankruptcy. The differences were between the debtor class of the West and the creditor class of the East, but the compromise agreed upon, it is thought, will be fairly satisfactory to both classes and to all sections of the country. The bill is one of the most important ones of the present Congress outside of war measures.

General Aguinaldo, the leader of the insurgents of the Philippine Islands, has proclaimed a republic under the protection of the United States. The fear of international complications thereby do not seem to be aggravated. Reports indicate that Gen. Aguinaldo is in close touch with Admiral Dewey, for whom he manifests a a profound respect, but no official announcement has come from Dewey on that subject at this writing. Everything is awaiting the arrival of the reinforcements now over due at Manila, and no further steps toward the occupation of Manila will likely be taken until they do arrive. Before the end of the present month Governor Gen. Merritt will be on the ground and things will then be more clearly defined. The fear of international complications or interference from the presence of German war vessels in Manila Harbor, of which much has been said in the press during the last week, is subsiding. The assurances of the German Government of their intention to maintain a strict neutrality as to Spanish and American interests at Manila and elsewhere, lessens the ground for anxiety on their account.

Before going to press we learn that the first deportment of troops, with the cruiser Charleston, has arrived at Manila, and that they were followed into the harbor by a German cruiser.

The proclamation which the Philippine insurgent leader, Emilio Aguinaldo, has issued from Cavite is a state document of no mean ability. It shows appreciation of the help received and is humane in its grasp of duty toward natives and foreigners, enemies and friends, as well as due respect for order, equity, purity and liberty. The following is the text of the proclamation: "Filipinos—The great North American nation, the repository of true liberty, and therefore the friend of freedom for our nation, oppressed and subjugated by the tyranny and despotism of its rulers, has come to afford to its inhabitants a protection as decisive as it is undoubtedly disinterested, regarding our unfortunate country as possessing sufficient civilization and aptitude for self-government, and in order to justify this high conception formed of us by the great American nation, we ought to reprobate all such acts as may derogate from that conception, such as pillage, robbery and every class of outrage against persons and property. In order to avoid conflicts during the period of our compaign, I order as follows:

"Article 1. The lives and property of all foreigners shall be respected, including in this denomination Chinese and all Spanish tradesmen who have not, directly or indirectly, contributed to the bearing of arms against us.

"Article 2. Equally shall be respected those of the enemy who shall lay down their arms.

"Article 3. Medical establishments and ambulances shall be respected and persons and effects attched thereto, unless they display hostility.

"Article 4. Persons disobeying these preceding articles shall be summarily tried and executed if their disobedience leads to assassination, incendiarism, robbery or rape.

"Given at Cavite, 24th day of May, 1898."

The Indian Rights Association is making an effort to secure a more liberal allotment of lands in Oklahoma Territory to the Comanche, Kiowa and Apache Indians than that proposed in the House of Representatives' bill, which was passed May 16, 1898, relating to the opening up of their reservation to settlement. The Indian Rights Association claims that owing to the lack of rain-fall and other adverse things one hundred and sixty acres per member, of this tribe, is not sufficient and equitable, and proposes that 480 acres be allowed each member of the tribe instead, and the residue of 1,611,453 acres purchased by the United States at a price that is just, perhaps $1.25 per acre, and the same be thrown open to settlement. The fund derived from the sale of the surplus lands of the reservation, this Association thinks, should be held in trust, bearing interest, by the United States, and the interest, together with not exceeding, possibly, fifty thousand dollars of the principal fund should be available, to be expended annually for tribal benefit, at the discretion of the Secretary of the Interior. By Report of Commissioner of Indian Affairs, 1897, the population of the Comanche, Kiowa and Apache tribe of Indians is 2,828, occupying a reservation containing 2,968,893 acres.

It is intimated that a war is to be made by the new Pelloux Cabinet in Italy, against the Papacy. Some years ago the government enacted a law depriving religious corporations of the right to possess property in Italy. This largely destroyed the influence of the Papacy over the government for a time, but since the passage of that law a large number of societies have been organized, presumably for religious and philanthropic purposes, such as urban banks, co-operative bakeries, co-operative stores, co-operative soup kitchens and similar institutions and associations. These apparently secular societies, the report says, are entirely under the control of the clergy, and are a source of great influence over the masses. A strongly worded circular, which the government is about to send to the provincial authorities, declares that they are carrying on "a propaganda against the state under the mantle of elevated philanthropy," and it is on this account that Premier Pelloux has announced his intention of suppressing all societies and associations not authorized by the government.

Next in the line of importance to the great trans-continental railway of Russia is the railroad which has just come into the possession of England, extending from Cairo to within one hundred and fifty miles of Khartoum except a short break between Luxor and Wadi-Halfa. This great African railway system was purchased by an English syndicate, of which Cecil Rhodes is said to be the moving spirit. The Sultan is said to have protested strongly against this transfer of the road to British control on the ground that it was Turkish government property, but the Khedive of Egypt claims that he was forced into compliance with the demands of England by the presence of a British fleet at Alexandria. The demand of England was based on the cost of her wars in the Soudan in blood and money, and the reconquest of that country for Egypt. This road is to be extended to the Cape of Good Hope, according to intimations, thus giving to England a railway system in Africa of equal importance to that of the great trans-Siberian railway in and to Russia. England's interests and rapid developments in Africa seem to be outstripping those of all other European countries.

On Friday there was a strike declared by the Stereotypers' Union, of Chicago, and as a result the citizens of that great city were without dailies on Saturday morning. Coming at the time of the great battle of Santiago, when everybody was most anxious for news, the strike was certainly an exceedingly annoying one to the people, to say nothing of the loss to the press of that city in the enlarged sale of dailies. The stereotypers, whose union includes about 200 members, have been getting $3.25 for their day's work of eight hours. They demanded a day of seven hours and $4 pay. In case of working overtime they wanted 75c. an hour. These demands were presented to the publishers of the big morning dailies, and the latter immediately held meeting and decided to refuse the deman It was also agreed to stick together in tl fight and not issue any of the papers unle all came out. This answer was convey to the officers of the Stereotypers' Unio and they held a meeting to determine the action. It was decided to insist on tl demands, and the men were ordered ou and the city was left in intellectual dark ness as to the outside world and the w news; as not even bulletins were to be see at any of the daily offices. The pape affected by the strike were: Morning—Tl Tribune, Times-Herald, Record, Chronicl Inter-Ocean; evening—The News, Pos Journal, Dispatch. The shut-out includ not only all of the papers printed in Eng lish, but the Staats Zeitung, the Fr Presse, the Abend Post and other Germa daily papers which use stereotype plates.

Admiral Camara is not having smoot sailing on his way to the Philippin Islands. The difficulties at Port Sai which he encountered, were numerous an discouraging. He asked for coal, but w refused. He then began to coal his ship from colliers from Spain, but was notifie that he must stop. He was also told th he must leave Port Said, as the time-lim had expired. The Admiral then claime that some of his ships needed repairs, und which plea he will endeavor to prolong hi stay in that port. It is rumored that h will turn his torpedo boat destroyers bac to Spain and proceed toward the Philip pines with nine ships instead of twelve. I is also said that all of his ships are in nee of repairs and in no condition to undertak the voyage to Manila. All the coalin stations along the way are under Britis control, and this alone would make th trip an exceedingly perilous one, to sa nothing of the Indian Ocean storms at thi season of the year. The United State Consular Agent, at Port Said, had bough up all the available coal thereabout, an thus lessened the Spanish Admiral's pros pects of success. The Suez Canal tolls fo his ships was also a staggering item for bankrupt nation, and so withal it is not a all certain at this writing that the Spanis fleet under Admiral Camara will attempt t enter the canal.

Later word says that Admiral Camar coaled at sea, and has returned with hi entire fleet to Port Said, presumably t enter the canal.

The demand upon the Bureau of Engrav ing at Washington for adhesive stamps re quired by the new revenue law is some thing enormous. The requisition of collect ors under the new tariff act approximate four hundred millions, and of this numbe about one-fourth were printed and shippe to the different states before the close o business on June 29th. The Director of th Bureau, Mr. Johnson, says that seventee hundred employes are at work on stamp and that work is continued day and nigh without ceasing. In one day, from eight t eight o'clock, 21,200,000 revenue stamp from new plates were printed besides im printing one million postage stamps. An yet the demand for these war-tax stamp in the larger cities cannot be met, an much annoyance is experienced b many persons thereby. Owing to thi inability to get stamps the authori ties have been compelled to make som provisional arrangements so as not to inte fere with important business matters too severely. But this difficulty will soon be obviated, and stamps can be conveniently had in any quantity wanted. In the meantime the treasury of the government is rapidly filling up with cash from the sale of these stamps.

OUR SPECIAL OFFER.

With the view of introducing the CHRISTIAN-EVANGELIST to a large number of new readers, we are offering the paper from the time the subscription is received until the end of the present year for *seventy-five cents*. We earnestly solicit the active assistance of our old readers in making this offer known, and in extending our circulation. It is hoped that the new form in which we make our appearance this week will be acceptable to all our friends, and may be made the occasion by them of a special effort in its behalf.

PROSPERITY OF SOUL.

In his letter to "Gaius the beloved" the apostle John prays that his friend and brother may be prospered in all things and be in health "even as thy soul prospereth." What the apostle desired for his friend seems to us most desirable for all of us, namely, that our prosperity of soul should keep pace with our prosperity in material things. When this is not the case the soul is in great peril. If there be an abundance of physical health, and an increase of wealth and of power, without any corresponding growth and development of the spiritual nature, there is great danger of moral shipwreck. The reason for this is plain. With the increase of our worldly possessions there is an increase, not only of responsibility, but of temptation to luxury, to pride, to the inordinate indulgence of the appetites and to an undue attachment to material gain. Unless this temptation to evil is offset by spiritual increment, by the growth of spiritual forces, the soul is sure to be shriveled and to perish for lack of proper nourishment and care.

Most persons are much concerned about their earthly possessions, and whether their worldly condition is growing better or worse, but comparatively few are at pains to enquire into the condition of the soul and its possessions, and whether, on the whole, it is prospering or suffering loss. But on every consideration of reason and sound judgment spiritual prosperity is to be preferred to prosperity in material things. The man who is growing in faith and hope and love, in strength and symmetry of character, in moral and spiritual power, in the capacity to be useful in good works, is getting rich in a higher and nobler sense than one whose bank account is on the increase, whose stocks and bonds are advancing, but whose soul is starving.

It is amazing, when we stop to think about it, with what a small degree of spiritual prosperity many Christians are content, while the desire to increase material possessions is rarely satisfied. It is only truth to say that the average church memmember is living a poor, cramped, starved spiritual life. He is groveling in the dust where he ought to be soaring in the empyrean. He is living on less than half rations, spiritually, whereas his soul might be feeding upon all the lucious fruits that grow in the garden of God, and delighting itself in fatness.

A recent author, writing on this subject, says: "We are not straitened in the Lord, but always in ourselves. The question of the prophet, 'O thou that art named the house of Jacob, is the Spirit of the Lord straitened (Micah 2:7)?' carries with it its own answer. It is always God's way to provide more than we can use. In the natural world He has given us a water supply that we can never exhaust; He has given sunlight for a thousand worlds like this; He has stored up an almost illimitable supply of electrical power which we are just beginning to tap; He has held in reserve new forces which we are just beginning to discover. His supplies are always ahead of our necessities. So in the spiritual world, only a small portion of what has been provided is being used up. The resources placed at our disposal do not grow less, however freely we may draw upon them. They are bottomless, they are infinite, they are eternal. What folly, then, to remain poverty-stricken and live poor, pinched, hunger-bitten lives, when there are unsearchable riches at our command! Why be content to eat the crumbs which fall from the Master's table when it is our privilege, as the friends of the King, to sit at His board and enjoy the bountiful banquet which He has prepared? Why remain in a condition of spiritual pauperism? living a hand-to-mouth sort of life, expending all our strength in the effort to keep ourselves alive, when the invitation is sounding in our ears, "Eat ye that which is good and let your soul delight itself in fatness?" Why be satisfied to suck a few drops of refreshment from the shrunken wineskins of a formal faith, when we may come to the fountain of life and drink our fill? What is required is, not an increased supply, but an increased capacity of spiritual reception. Nothing could be more out of place than the prayer, "Lord, increase our supplies.' And nothing could be more in place than the prayer, "Lord, increase our faith."*

It is in view of this condition of things and the relation of the soul's desire to its prosperity that the Savior said, "Blessed are they who hunger and thirst after righteousness, for they shall be filled." It is the absence of this soul-hunger and soul-thirst that is the cause of so much spiritual leanness in the church. Too many are content with their worldly prosperity and do not realize their need of spiritual supplies. It was to this self-satisfied class of Christians that Jesus said in his letter to the church at Laodicea, "Because thou sayest I am rich and have gotten riches and have need of nothing and knowest not that thou art the wretched one and miserable and poor and blind and naked: I counsel thee to buy of me gold refined by fire that thou mayest become rich; and white garments that thou mayest clothe thyself and that the shame of thy nakedness be not made manifest; and eyesalve to anoint thy eyes that thou mayest see." Jesus means by this stinging rebuke that these lukewarm Christians of Laodicea should think less about their material gains and more about spiritual riches or the prosperity of the soul. The lesson is as applicable to many Christians in our times as it was to the members of the Laodicean church.

Our message, therefore, in this article, to all those who have been prospered in material things, is that they see to it that their souls also prosper. The proof of this prosperity will consist in their zeal for Christ and the church, and in their liberality and good works. "If thy riches increase," says an inspired writer, "set not thy heart upon them," but rather set thy heart on the Lord and upon the interests of his kingdom. So shall thy soul prosper, even as thou art prospered in earthly possessions. None of us could pray a wiser prayer than to ask the Lord that our worldly prosperity should never exceed the prosperity of the soul.

*Rev. James Campbell, in "After Pentecost—What?" pp. 87, 88.

MORE ABOUT TEXAS.

Only two states in the Union have a larger number of church organizations than Texas, and these are Pennsylvania and Ohio. The religion of the Texans is of the good old-fashioned, orthodox variety. The Baptists stand at the head of the column, with 248,523 members. And the Baptists in Texas are but little like the people who bear this name in New York. Texas Baptists are the closest kind of close communionists. They decline to sit at the Lord's table with each other away from home; that is to say, a Baptist whose church home is in McKinney will not commune in a Baptist church in Dallas. Texas Baptists do not recognize baptism administered by any other than a regularly ordained Baptist minister as valid Christian baptism. This is the closest kind of close communion. Next to the Baptists, in numbers, are the Methodists. There are of this variety of Chistians in Texas 218,890. The Roman Catholics number 99,691. According to the last United States census report there are 41,859 Disciples of Christ in Texas. But there are Disciples and Disciples. More of this anon.

The Christians who call themselves and who are called Presbyterians number 37,811. Of Episcopalians there are 7,097, or were in 1890. Universalism and Adventism do not thrive in this climate; of the former there are but 514, and of the latter 773. There are only 112 persons in the state who plead guilty when charged with being Christian Scientists.

There are about fifty colleges in the state. Some of them are called universities. Add-Ran College, under the patronage of the Christian Church, is located at Waco. It has just closed its twenty-fifth session, one of the most satisfactory in every respect in its history. This institution was founded in 1873 as a private enterprise. In 1890 the proprietors made a donation of the school and its property to a board to hold in trust for the Christian Church in Texas. It was then located at Thorp Springs. On the second day of January, 1896, Add-Ran University began work in its new home at Waco. The Waco property is valued at $120,000. This is an excellent location for a school. It is an unusually healthy place. Its artesian wells and mineral waters are becoming noted. The Paul Quinn College, a school for negroes, and Baylor University, are located at Waco. The population of Waco in 1890

ıw. Add-Ran
to the "Texas
ıtion." Much
given to Bible
e catalogue of
ced up. The
ıs a text-book.
he prescribed
y school must
rst chapter of
n the book of
ı the state of
e attention is
ered literature
customary in
. B. Sweeney
ment in Add-
ı Endeavorers
l to be used in
for the work
ts at the pres-
is loaned on
t. The breth-
of this school
before it a
iscrimination,
ex.

ı held by the
oney the first
g of unusual

the Foreign
; C. C. Smith
itative of the
ary Society;
, of the Chris-
sions. These
t of the con-

r the auspices
nary Conven-
of them were
conclusions
arratives was
fested in the
kin to that of
nnection with
ign lands. It
when pledges
he next year.
to give. M.
part of the
s simply per-
ng, coaxing,
ies were not
good humor.
There was an
The pledges
y made. As
ppeared to be

ted that the
as well repre-
uri.
oard of Mis-
The meeting
ere are sixty-
exas, with a
ndred. Two
were collect-
ies' Mission-
lian Church,
This is said
lies' society
nited States.
of the Texas
of Missions:
n, Bonham;
organizer,
D., Austin;

recording secretary, Miss Leila Fort, Paris; treasurer, Mrs. J. M. Campbell, Van Alstyne; press superintendent, Mrs. Ida V. Jarvis, Ft. Worth; superintendent of children's work, Miss Bertha Johnson, San Antonio.

The following are the officers for the ensuing year of the Texas Christian Missionary Convention: President, A. S. Henry, Blooming Grove; vice-presidents, J. J. Cramer, Lockhart, and Plummer Harris, McKinney; secretaries, J. M. Campbell, Van Alstyne, and Philip F. King, Belton.

No little interest is felt among the Texas brethren in the mission to the Mexicans at Monterey, Mexico. M. L. Hoblit is the missionary. Miss Bertha Mason, daughter of the beloved J. C. Mason, of Houston, was associated with Bro. Hoblit in this work, but on account of her impaired health is no longer actively engaged. This work was begun at Cindad Juarez. Monterey, it is believed, is a better basis for an educational and evangelistic work among the Mexicans. "Go" is the name of a paper published in English in the interest of this work. The Mexican mission owns a printing-press, which it will use in spreading abroad the good news. A paper the size of "Go," called *La Puerta Abienta*, is published in the Spanish language. Brethren from the United States visiting Monterey are cordially invited to call at the mission, which is open every day from 9 A. M. to 5 P. M., at No. 50 Calle del Roble. This work is worthy of moral and financial support. It is a mission of the Chistian Woman's Board.

The Texas state Christian Endeavor convention was held in Dallas June 7-9. The Disciples were much in evidence in this convention. They are not anxious to have their names appear on the official program. They can be heard without that formality. But in Texas, in the recent convention, their names were on the program and were also seen in the list of officers. Having shown efficiency, their official positions are continued. The Cumberland Presbyterians have 108 societies in Texas, and the Disciples have 102. The Disciples are determined to be in the lead at the next convention. In our rally money was pledged, about three hundred dollars, to the Ministerial Education Fund.

It is estimated by intelligent and conservative brethren that there are not more than 25,000 Disciples in Texas. Some who were formerly with us are now pronounced Anabaptists. They are also anti-missionary. They refuse to have fellowship with those who desire to be known as Disciples of Christ, or Christians. We are not permitted to preach the gospel in their houses of worship. This privilege is granted to Methodists, Presbyterians, Baptists, etc., etc., but not to Disciples of Christ. The reason given is that the former are consistent, while the latter are not.

These notes would be unpardonably imperfect, if they failed to call attention to Carlton College at Bonham, and the Carr-Burdette College at Sherman. The former is conducted by the venerable and venerated Charles Carlton; the latter is conducted by Bro. and Sister O. A. Carr. Carlton College has been in existence for more than a quarter of a century. The Carr-Burdette has just closed its fourth session. These schools are for the education of young women. B. B. T.

Hour of Prayer.

THE DUTY OF REPENTANCE.

(Midweek Prayer-meeting Topic, July 13.)

The times of ignorance, therefore, God overlooked; but now He commandeth men that they should all everywhere repent.—*Acts 17:30.*

This is a single statement from Paul's discourse before the idolatrous but cultivated Athenians. No amount of culture of mind or body, no amount of artistic skill, no height of intellectual attainment, precludes the necessity of repentance. At Athens idolatry and intellectual development were joined in the same people. Paul did not preach to them that they needed more art, more poetry, more literature, more intellectual development, but instead, that they needed repentance. The "unknown God" whom they ignorantly worshiped and whom Paul declared unto them was a God of righteousness and holiness, and inasmuch as all men everywhere have sinned, He commands all men everywhere to repent.

This word *repent*, in the sense in which Paul used it, was no doubt a new and strange term to these cultivated Greeks. The gods whom they worshiped were not of such a character as to create in man the conviction of sinfulness and the need of repentance. For this reason God overlooked much of the shortcomings in the Gentile world, but now that Christ had come into the world, revealing the true character of God and His will, their ignorance is no longer to be regarded as a shield for their moral derelictions, but all men are commanded to repent.

The repentance of the gospel implies at least three elements: a knowledge of God's will, a knowledge of one's own personal demerit and sinfulness, and a desire and purpose to turn away from the sins of the past and live in harmony with our knowledge of God's will and character. It was "repentance and remission of sins" that was to be preached to all nations, "beginning at Jerusalem." These are the two great key-words of Christianity. They look to the rectification of life and character, without which man cannot be at peace with God. It was a prominent requirement made known by Peter in that first sermon preached on Pentecost under the new dispensation. It has ever been and is yet an imperative demand upon all men who would come into a state of reconciliation with God.

It is evident from the very nature of repentance that its thoroughness depends upon the completeness of our faith or knowledge of God, and of our own spiritual condition. There are many Christians who need a more thorough repentance, because they are living a kind of life that is inconsistent with the highest attainable knowledge of God's will and character. As these Christians come to know God better and to see more clearly their own moral defects in the light of the high ethical standard given to us in the life of Christ, they will repent of many practices in which they indulge at present without any seeming conscientious scruples. Indeed, progress in Christian life consists largely in the clearer apprehension of God, and of our duty in the light of His character, together with the effort in our part to bring our lives up to the level of our knowledge of the divine will.

ever, the privilege of hearing the news from our army and navy on Sunday, in order to escape the evil of the Sunday paper. One of the things that make an ocean voyage so restful is the absence of all disturbing and distracting news that comes from the daily paper. After a week or ten days spent upon the bosom of the ocean without even seeing a daily paper one feels no great mental impoverishment as a result of this abstinence. A few questions as to the most important news brings one up to date without any sense of permanent loss. No doubt there is a vast amount of precious time wasted in a too careful perusal of the daily papers. They are important, and we cannot dispense with them for at least six days in the week, but we can save much time and mental dissipation by reading them discriminatingly.

Chicago is a way station between St. Louis and Macatawa. We tarried there long enough to get a glimpse of its metropolitan life and to be impressed, as we always are, with the magnitude, the energy and enterprise of this marvelous city. We took time, of course, to call at the office of the Christian Oracle, and were pleased to find Dr. Kirkham looking in better health than for years past. The Oracle of late we think shows evidence of improved health and of consequent increased mental vigor on the part of the editor. We were glad to learn that sti prospects are brightening. We took time also to visit the university, where we were hospitably entertained for the night and part of a day in the home of Bro. C. A. Young, and where we also had the pleasure of meeting Bro. H. L. Willett. Bro. Young is studying hard and will receive his degree of Bachelor of Philosophy in the forthcoming convocation. While doing a great deal of outside work he has for years been steadily preparing himself for larger usefulness. Dr Willett is of course busy, although he had just completed his examination of his classses in the university. He is a man who knows how to make good use of all his time. He and his family go to Europe in the autumn. He reports that we have a number of very bright and promising young men at the university who are likely to be a credit to the cause they represent in the years to come. We also met Bro. Gates, pastor of the Hyde Park Church, and were glad to learn that the outlook for this congregation is full of encouragement. He is proving himself to be the right man for that work.

Macatawa, June 27, 1898.

One of the things we prize about dear old Macatawa, now, is the familiar faces that we meet on our annual return hither. It is not a procession of curiosity-seekers and pleasure-hunters that come here, from year to year, but in the main those who come once come again, and the place grows on them from year to year. Already many of the well-known cottagers are on the ground, although the hotels, as yet, are meagerly patronized. Later on they will have all they can do. Among those whose names are familiar to our readers, already present, are Dr. H. W. Everest and wife, H. S. Earl and family, J. S. Hughes and wife, the family of W. F. Richardson, also the families of F. G. Tyrrell and Sydney Thomson. Brother J. H. Duncan and family, of St. Louis, are here and have rented one of the handsomest cottages in the park, fronting on Lake Michigan. The family of Bro. Smith, of St. Louis, son of our well-known Bro. B. H. Smith, of Canton, Mo., are also among the visitors here from St. Louis. Arthur O. Garrison, editor of the Pacific Christian, with his family arrived this morning from the Pacific Coast to spend the summer at Macatawa. His physician having advised him to escape the San Francisco climate for awhile on account of throat trouble, he was glad to accept our invitation to spend the summer at Edgewood-on-the-Lake, and we are glad to have the company and companionship of himself and wife, and of the little granddaughter, the patter of whose feet and the music of whose voice supply an element that was lacking in our home.

One contrast between Macatawa Park and the average city was quite noticeable on yesterday—the Lord's day. The stillness of Sunday was unbroked by the voice of the newsboy, crying the Sunday papers. By no possibility could a daily paper be secured anywhere on the grounds on yesterday. In these times of war when our boys are at the front and battles are imminent, and even in progress, one does feel some anxiety to at least look over the headlines of the news even in a Sunday paper. But we would gladly forego, for-

Questions and Answers.

How could Paul preach, as he did at Athens, that Jesus had been ordained to be the judge of the world, and that God had given assurance of this to all men by raising him from the dead, without preaching his death? It seems to me that if Paul omitted the death of Jesus, his declaration found in Acts 17:31 must have been wholly unintelligible to all his hearers. In this view of the case it is no wonder that the many mocked, but a great wonder that any "clave unto him and believed" as some did. What did they believe, if Paul did not preach so vital a point as the death of Jesus? *B. F. Manire.*

It is not probable that Luke gives us anything more than a brief synopsis or outline of the discourse which Paul delivered at Athens. There is enough given, however, to indicate the fact that Paul adapted his discourse to the condition and character of the people addressed. It is probably true that Paul did not lay as much emphasis, in this discourse, upon the death of Christ as he did in addressing the Jews, but we have never seen any reason to doubt the wisdom of his address at Athens nor its adaptability to the conditions under which it was spoken.

Does the minister who is chosen pastor of a church become an elder of the same without being elected by the congregation?

J. D. J.

The proper form of this question is, Do the pastor and the elder represent two distinct orders of the ministry in the local congregation? In other words, is the ministry of the New Testament church adequately represented by elders and deacons, or were there three distinct orders—pastors, elders and deacons? We take it that elders and deacons, or bishops and deacons, comprise the New Testament officiary. The term pastor does not refer to a distinct rank, but to an elder or bishop who devotes himself exclusively to the care of the flock. If this be correct, when a minister in selected as pastor of the congregation he is elected to its eldership or episcopate, and needs not a second election as if it were a distant office to which he was being called.

An elder in a certain church had gained the reputation of being dishonest and tricky in trade. His example had become a stumbling-block to those without. The pastor or minister of the church went to him and told him of his fault; whereupon the elder said he would have the pastor removed and went about the work at once; first attempting to circulate a petition to that effect and afterwards refusing to contribute to the church while the present pastor remained. The workers in the church are satisfied with their pastor. Should the preacher remain at the request of a majority of the members of the church, and what action should be taken against the men who circulated the petition?

D.

An elder, or any other officer of the church, who would find fault with the preacher and seek to have him removed because he had discharged his duty in telling him of his fault, shows plainly by such action that he is unfit for the office he holds. If the facts show that the opposition to the preacher is based on such cause of offence, the majority of the church would do wrong in yielding to such opposition, and the preacher should remain at their wish to carry on his work faithfully in the fear of the Lord and not of men.

As to the men who circulated the petition, if they are content to abide by the action of the majority and continue their relation to the church they should be pardoned for the mistake they made, but the "tricky" elder should be required to vacate his office, and unless he reformed in his business methods should forfeit his standing as a member of the church. So it seems to us, at least, judging from the facts stated in the communication from which the question is taken.

by saying that "whosoever is begotten of God doeth no sin" is, that he does not *habitually* or *abide* in sin, because that would be contrary to the seed of God abiding in him; but that even the children of God are sometimes overtaken in a fault, from which, however, they seek to recover themselves at once, because a life of sin is contrary to their renewed nature. In other passages in this same epistle John teaches that all men sin and need the advocacy of Jesus Christ the righteous, and the forgiveness of God.

Current Religious Thought

The Independent thinks the following from the Church Standard startling, yet true. And it is interesting and apt as well as "startling and true," we give it as quoted in the Independent, but without the Independent's comments. The Church Standard (Esiscopal) says:

Every catholic church is *ipso facto* Episcopal. Hence, the use of that word in the corporate name of our church is useless if the church is catholic, and its only purpose is to differentiate our communion, and so to emphasize our separation from Christian bodies which have not the Episcopate. Thus, like *Protestant*, the word *Episcopal*, as an ecclesiastical designation, is a word of *division*, and as such we dislike it. We go so far as to think that the Lambeth Conference committed a capital blunder in the tactics of conciliation when it made "the historic *Episcopate*" one of its four indispensable conditions of unity. If it had said the historic *Ministry*, that phrase would have meant the same thing, and while it would have been understood to mean the same, it would have been less objectionable to many non-Episcopalian Christians. In short, longing for and looking to the unity of Christ's church, which will come in God's good time, we cannot rejoice in the adoption by any church of any name or qualification which bears on its forefront the idea of division; and therefore we cannot love the name Protestant Episcopal.

Teunis S. Hamlin, D. D., has an article in The Independent, June 23rd, on "The Most Urgent Duty of the Hour," in which his perception of the same is expressed in these words:

The question of national concern, however, is, How shall we treat ourselves in this novel situation and in the face of this novel duty of loving our "enemies?" They will not suffer in person or fortune more than the exigencies of war imperatively demand; shall we suffer needlessly in our Christian character? Shall we relapse from a civilized to a barbarous temper? Shall we throw away our hardly cultivated good-will, filling its place with suspicion and enmity? It all depends on whether or not we hold ourselves to the lofty purpose of righting grievous wrongs and helping an oppressed race to that freedom which we believe to be the universal birthright of man. We must banish thoughts of revenge "Remember the Maine" must not be our battle-cry; not because that hideous wrong should not be righted—it should be, and shall be—but because revenge is a barbarous battle-cry; because the blows that it inspires fall indiscriminately, and, most of all, because it kills all Christian love in the hearts that cherish it. That love does not demand that we make war feebly; that we stifle our patriotism in apologizing for the the vigor of our national conduct; that we belittle by a breath the righteousness and the majesty of our cause; that we feel the faintest touch of indifference as to which flag finally floats over the cruelly oppressed and the dust of the starved and otherwise murdered Cubans. But it does demand that we leave vengeance to God, while we strike only for righteousness and freedom, pitying the sorrows and loving the persons of those "neighbors" whom for a time we are most reluctantly obliged to count and call our "enemies."

The distinction between the transient and the permanent in religion is evidently becoming more apparent to the religious world, as witnesseth the following from The Christian Intelligencer:

The law of gravitation did not have its origin with Newton, nor the power of steam with Watt; but as revolutionizing science and mechanics, they are barely a century old. The same is true of much that pertains to religion. What may have been eternally present in the mind of God, what form the first has been in his written Word, becomes forceful and vitalizing only when truly understood and grasped, it has all the power of novelty. Being a living force, it necessitates a new adjustment, a fitting environment.

Because of this there is a transient as well as a permanent element in religion; and the condition of life for the church is a continuous adjustment of itself to modifications imposed by its own clearer apprenension of truth and its changed environment. The church only fulfills its mission when it keeps itself in harmony with the age in which it lives—as it changes."

balance against this complicity with evil, but but were defeated. What then? Shall they, having been defeated, therefore relinquish all work for temperance in a place affording such wide opportunities for the dissemination of our principles? Such action would, it seems to us, be exactly in accordance with the enemy's desire. Such action would have made it impossible for the Woman's Christian Temperance Union ever to exist, for our Crusade mothers would have laid down their arms as soon as it became apparent to them that what they had striven for with herculean effort was not accomplished. "Where sin abounds, grace should much more abound." Because the licensed saloon is to be a feature of the Trans-Mississippi and International Exposition, there is so much the more reason why temperance forces should gather there, and why the utmost should be done to offset the iniquitous work of that licensed saloon.

After all, when one considers the question carefully, is there not a splitting of hairs on these points? If the Government of the United States protects the saloons, and we are citizens of the United States, does it so much matter whether that licensed saloon exists in Alaska or in Chicago, at an exposition, or down a back alley? It is one people, one flag, one nation, and if we were to drive the liquor traffic out of every state and city in the Union save one, the fact that it existed in that one, under the protection of the law, would be a blot upon our nation's escutcheon, and so far as we were accessories to its existence, whether through silence or through vote, the blot would be upon us as individuals as well. Perhaps we need an occasional object-lesson of this nature to show us that one spot cannot be really clean until all are cleansed, that the degradation of one becomes the degradation of all.

Our duty as a people, and as temperance workers in particular, is not to sit down and bemoan defeats, but to rise from every defeat with a strong determination to fight the saloon in the stronghold of its power, the national government itself; and when we shall have won the battle, then exposition grounds, city streets and country lanes will be alike safe and free. And to our thought one of the best ways for carrying on this warfare lies in entering every open door, in going to the places where the power makes itself most manifest, and there by distributing temperance literature, by circulating pledge-cards, by delivering addresses, and by all other means fighting till the death.

If the Woman's Christian Temperance Union goes to Omaha, it will go there to hold up the white banner of temperance and purity. Who will say that it would be better for the Exposition, and for our nation as a whole, if we were to stay away? Let him who would say this be logical, and let the plan be at once unfolded for deporting the Woman's Christian Temperance Union as a body outside the territory of the United States! Doubtless it is a matter of great importance that the sale of liquor be prohibited in such places. Doubtless, also, it is a thing of infinitely greater importance that it be prohibited throughout the length and breadth of our country. To live in America without protest and refuse to work in Omaha because liquor is sold there, reminds one strikingly of the Master's words, "Ye tithe mint, anise and cummin, and omit the weightier matters of the law."

The close relation between present character and future happiness is quite aptly stated by The Advance in the following paragraph:

Many Christians seem to think that if they can only reach heaven, they will have gained all that the soul need desire. They are disposed to indolently take refuge in the plan of salvation, saying, "I cannot gain heaven by works, so I will trust in the saving merits of Jesus, and all will be well." It is true that the reward of the Christian is of grace, and not of merit, yet there is an individual work for each Christian to do, and his future happiness will be affected by the way in which that work is done. Heaven will be heaven to all who through God's abounding grace find entrance within the pearly gates, yet in a certain sense it will not be the same heaven to all. Nothing morally imperfect can enter there, all sin will be washed away, yet, in a certain sense it will not be the same heaven to all. The redeemed will enjoy as much of heaven as they have soul to enjoy, and no more. Enjoyment will be determined by the degree in which character has developed in this or that individual towards the perfection of Christ. But will not character and capacity be developed in the other world? Doubtless they will; but during the period of earthly service we should make attainment for service and happiness in heaven, as fast and as far as possible.

CHRISTIAN EDUCATION AS A FACTOR IN THE WORLD'S PROGRESS.*

MR. PRESIDENT, FRIENDS AND MEMBERS OF THE GRADUATING CLASS:—Gathered here as we are to-day, on this anniversary occasion, on a spot which, for half a century has been dedicated to Christian education, the one theme that suggests itself more naturally than any other, is that of Christian education as a factor in the intellectual and moral progress of the world. The theme is one that might easily lead us into a discussion of the condition of the world at the coming of Christ, and of the decadent civilizations which existed before the Star of Bethlehem rose on the world. But all that may be taken for granted before an audience like this, while we attempt simply to point out the fundamental relationship of Christian education to human needs, and to the highest development of the human race. My purpose is to emphasize the value, not simply of education, but of Christian education, as an essential factor in any scheme that looks to individual, social or national progress.

If we open our ears to the voice of history, and our eyes to the lessons inscribed on its pages, we shall not make the mistake, at the close of the nineteenth century, of supposing that an education which simply stands for intellectual development, meets all the essential conditions of human progress. The history of Greece, alone, stands as an everlasting refutation of such a theory. Intellectual development reached its acme in the days of Socrates, Plato and Aristotle; but with all her intellectual greatness, in art, in literature, in logic, in rhetoric and in philosophy, there was wanting the dynamic force which lifts up individuals and nations, and starts them forward on a new career of progress.

Roman civilization added, as its contribution to the solution of the great world-problem, the value of external power in an organized government, with its center of unity and authority, and the state as the embodiment of its morality and religion. But Rome, with all its political greatness, with all its wisdom in civil administration, and with all its conquering legions, failed to furnish the basis for an enduring and progressive civilization.

Judaism made its splendid contribution of monotheism as against the polytheism and atheism which prevailed among the other nations. It presented the lofty conception of the one true and living God, infinitely holy in character, and requiring righteousness among men. And yet Judaism had degenerated largely into formalism, and at its best lacked that life-giving quality which the world needed to set it forward on an upward career toward the table-lands of a higher and purer civilization.

At the confluence of these three ancient civilizations—Jewish, Grecian and Roman—and when each of them and all of them had failed to furnish the dynamic force to lift the world out of its moral decline, Christianity was born, and reached forth its puissant hand to lift up to a new order of life and growth the sinking peoples and nationalities of earth. Its power to accomplish this for any people or nation coming under its transforming power may be seen in the contrast between the condition of the Christian nations of the earth to-day and the condition of the world at the coming of Christ, or the condition of that part of the world to-day which is without the illuminating power of the gospel.

It would seem to be entirely relevant to an occasion like this to inquire, briefly, what it is that Christianity, permeating and dominating the higher forms of education, has done, and by its very nature is fitted to do, to accomplish this renaisance for the race. It is only as we come to apprehend clearly the power of the Christian ideal, in faith and culture, to do for humanity what nothing else had done or can do to enable it to realize the purpose of the Creator, that we are prepared to make the necessary sacrifices in its behalf. It is only in the light of these facts that we are enabled to realize the greatness of the men who, here and elsewhere, have laid the foundations for Christian institutions of learning, and out of such scanty resources as belonged to those pioneer days, made sacrifices to sustain them. It is only as these truths are present to our minds that we can give due honor to that splendid army of consecrated men and women who are devoting their lives to the cause of Christian education. A clearer apprehension on the part of Christian people of the relation between our Christian institutions of learning and the advancement of the kingdom of God would do much to quicken the zeal of the churches in the endowment of such institutions.

Coming, then, to the question we have raised, as to what we have a right to expect from Christian education, and what it has done and is doing to lift up humanity to higher levels of civilization, we summarize some of these things briefly as follows:

1. As we are indebted to Christianity for a new conception of human life, and a new interpretation of its meaning, so we are indebted to Christian education for the apprehension of this new ideal of character and the power to realize it in some measure. With the coming of Christ a new force entered into human history. This new and divine force has revolutionized the ideals of the past and has changed the current of the world's thought and life. It is the province of Christian education, therefore, to interpret to us the meaning of life and to furnish us high and worthy ideals. No education that leaves out Christ as the model of human character and ignores His sublime thoughts concerning God and man, and duty and destiny, is adequate to meet the needs of humanity. To the shame of our modern civilization it must be said that there are theories of education yet extant that either give to Jesus Christ an inferior and subordinate place or entirely ignore Him as having any essential place in the scheme of education designed to fit men for the solemn ordeal of life. Be it said to the everlasting honor of the pioneers who within this grove half a century ago laid the foundation of Eureka College, that they had no such false and inadequate conception of education. They believed that Christ was the splendid and majestic pattern of a perfect man, and the highest aim of culture was to fashion men in his likeness.

2. Christianity, entering into education as a transforming force, has transferred the emphasis from the material to the

*Delivered at the Jubilee Commencement of Eureka College, June 16th, 1898, by J. H. Garrison.

spiritual. No rational system of education can be formed without a true conception of man, the being to be educated. If man be an animal only, he requires one kind of education. If he be an immortal spirit, abiding temporarily in a material body, but destined to live forever, either in weal or woe, according as his character has or has not been conformed to the will of God, then this demands a very different kind of education. As Christianity furnishes us the only true conception of the nature and possibilities of man, so Christian education is the only education adapted to the needs of man. Civilization advances just in proportion as men learn to discriminate between the material and the spiritual, and to accord to the latter the superiority which belongs to it. The age or nation that is in bondage to the sensual and the material must necessarily occupy a low place in the scale of civilization until emancipated from the prison-house of its materialism.

3. By accentuating the worth of the individual soul and the inherent dignity of human nature, Christianity has fostered the love of liberty and the growth of democracy throughout the world. Hence, our free institutions, our civil and religious liberty, are the outgrowth of Christian education. The men who brought the seed-corn of civil and religious liberty from the Old World in the Mayflower, and planted it in the virgin soil of the New World, were not only Christian men, but they were men who knew the value of liberal culture. Hence, one of their first enterprises was to establish an institution of Christian learning, which became a mighty ally of the church in the ensuing struggle for national independence. This shows that the charge of *other*-worldliness, to the exclusion of the proper regard for the duties of this present world, cannot be justly made against Christian education. It has been the steadfast champion of human rights, and the uncompromising foe of tyranny and oppression in every form. The graves of Christian scholars may be found on every battle field of human liberty. The conception of manhood which Christ furnishes us is in utter antagonism to the wearing of chains, either on the body or on the mind.

4. By bringing the moral and intellectual natures into harmony, Christianity has developed a rotundity of character and a sanity of judgment and action, which has made for human progress and for the development of the highest types of individual character. As a kingdom divided against itself cannot stand, so as long as man's mental and moral natures are arrayed against each other, there can be no healthy growth and development. When the intellect and the conscience are seen to be different aspects of the same personality, and when they enter into co-operation and cease their war against each other, we have the highest and most satisfactory results in individual character, which in turn becomes the agent for social advancement. Nothing but Christian education can effect this union of man's intellectual and moral powers. Faith without knowledge may make a bigot; knowledge without faith fosters intellectual pride and gives a superficial view of life and duty. We must look to Christian culture to save Christianity from narrowness and sectarian bigotry, and secular learning, whether in science or philosophy, from superficiality, irreverence and gross materialism. Both science and philosophy have been and are yet to be of great value to Christianity, but it is only as they are mediated by Christian thought that they can be made to serve the advancement of the kingdom of God. Without Christian scholarship there must be an impassable chasm between religion on the one hand, and unsanctified learning on the other. Christian scholarship mediates between the two, passing over into the church whatever truth, science or philosophy may disclose, and imbuing science and philosophy themselves, with Christian faith. Thus by making Christianity more rational, and science and philosophy more reverent and Christian, the chasm between the two is bridged over or closed up, and the useless war between science and religion, Genesis and geology, faith and culture, is closed by a perpetual armistice.

5. In a word, are we not justified in saying, in the light of nineteen centuries of Christian history, that we are dependent upon Christian scholarship for the true interpretation of life's meaning and purpose, and of man's place in creation, for a right understanding of history as the product of a divine force acting upon the world; for knowledge of a proper relation between the material and the spiritual worlds; for the true province of reason in religion; for the ability to lay under contribution all the results of investigation in every department of human thought and research in order to the upbuilding of a diviner manhood and the extension of the kingdom of heaven on earth, and especially for the unveiling of those treasures of divine wisdom and knowledge, found in the ancient writings of inspired men, which must needs be translated and interpreted in the light of the times in which they were written? If this, indeed, be the high function of Christian scholarship, if it be thus vitally related to advancing civilization, and to the ongoing of the kingdom of God, you, indeed, have done well in gathering here to-day in these large numbers to celebrate the inauguration of this institution of learning. It is an event altogether worthy of celebration.

It often happens that events of far-reaching importance are concealed from ordinary view by what seem to be commonplace surroundings. Perhaps the sturdy pioneers who settled in this community a half century ago, whose brains conceived and whose hands executed the plan of building here an institution of learning, understood only in part the vast import of what they were doing. They believed in God, however, and in the omnipotence of truth, and inaugurated an enterprise the scope and power of whose influence, in all the years to come, neither they nor we who are here to-day could adequately measure. Let us do honor to-day to the names of Elder Benjamin Major, who is called the founder of the institution, together with E. B. Myers, Wm. Davenport, David Deweese, A. M. Myers, B. J. Radford, Sr., Elder E. Dickinson, Elder John T. Jones, Wm. P. Atterberry and R. M. Clark, who co-operated with him in the infancy of the enterprise. Nor let us to-day forget that princely man of God who, in its later struggles, sustained the institution with his liberal gifts and with his wise counsels, the beloved John Darst. It would be a grateful service, if time permitted, to call up here the long list of faithful teachers who have labored in the institution faithfully, on inadequate salaries, because of their supreme interest in the cause of Christian education. Perhaps we ought to mention here, in this connection, the names of P. H. Murphy, J. C. Reynolds, J. W. Butler and A. B. Murphy, who were connected with the founding of Abingdon College, which subsequently became consolidated with this, and whose children have become the adopted sons and daughters of Eureka College, entitled to all its rights and privileges. Whatever may have been the causes contributing to the consolidation of the two institutions, we can but rejoice to-day in the union of our educational interests in the state of Illinois, and in the reasonable hope which this unity inspires of a brighter future for our beloved Alma Mater.

A half century is not a long period in the life of an institution, but wonderful have been the changes wrought in the world, and in our own country, since the founding of Eureka College; but every one of these changes emphasizes the value to society, to the church, and to the nation, of an institution of learning like this. We can in no way so fitly honor the memory of the noble men, who laid the foundations of this institution, as by endowing it and equipping it, so that it may more worthily accomplish the work for which it was established. As a son of Eureka, by adoption, I offer my hearty congratulations to the friends of this institution, on the success that has attended their efforts, under the present administration of the college, to lift its burden of indebtedness and give it a more adequate endowment. In what has already been accomplished we read the prophecy of larger things in the years to come. What will the next half century do for Eureka College? Those who are permitted to attend the hundredth anniversary of the founding of the institution will, no doubt, see this campus filled with stately halls dedicated to Christian learning, and filled with the noblest youth of the land, who shall come hither for that mental and moral equipment which is so essential to success in life. There will then be a large corps of teachers and tutors, supported by a liberal endowment, and enabled to give their best thought and energies to the cause of Christian education. But the Eureka College of that day may have reason to look back to the Eureka College of this jubilee occasion with proud satisfaction and grateful remembrance for what this day has accomplished. May this bright jubilee be the harbinger of that brighter centennial whose program most of us here to-day will witness from the upper and unseen galleries, whence departed spirits witness the procession of human events.

Young ladies and gentlemen of the graduating class, I am sure you will excuse me if to-day I have taken some of the time which I owe to you in speaking of the past and the future of your beloved Alma Mater. You will never cease to feel the debt of obligation which you owe to this institution, for the new light and inspiration which have come into your lives since you have been students within its halls. You will leave behind you as you go forth, a prayer for its continued prosperity, and will not fail, I am sure, to do what may lie in your power to further her interests. You will not forget, young friends, that though you close your college life to-day, you are henceforth to be regarded in an important sense as representatives of this institution. In the circles in which you move, Eureka College will be judged, in a measure, by what you are and what you have accomplished. Institutions, like trees, must be judged by their fruit. As this institution has reason to be proud of the many sons and daughters she has sent forth in the past, it is safe to assume that she will have reason in the years to come to be proud of the class of '98.

I congratulate you upon entering the active duties of life at so interesting a time in the history of the world, and of our own country. It is a great thing to be an actor in the scenes that are now being enacted on the stage of life. It is a time of wonderful possibilities. You are to go out and take your places amid these stirring scenes, and to contribute your share to the progress of civilization toward that golden age which the prophets and seers of humanity have seen since the foundation of the world. You are to illustrate in your lives the value of Christian education. Your choices in life, the tasks you assume, the spirit in which you prosecute them, the helpfulness of your lives to other lives about you, the inspiration of your example, the movements which you approve and disapprove, the causes you espouse, your continued progress or lack of progress in the knowledge and in the development of character—all these will be exponents to the world of the value of Christian education. Above all, your relation to Jesus Christ, and your success in following his sublime example of unselfish service to humanity, and of dauntless heroism in the defence of right, will be the standard by which your Alma Mater, your fellowmen and the great Judge of all will at last measure you. It is a part of the responsibility that rests upon you to refute the charge that is sometimes made against education, that it tends to create a chasm between the educated and the great uneducated masses, and to create a disrelish for that personal contact with the needy and the untaught, which is so essential to their elevation. If you have, indeed, caught a vision of the Christ, as the highest exemplification of exalted manhood, your education will but qualify you for ministering in more manifold ways than you otherwise could, to the needs of our sinning and suffering race. It is yours to show that Christian education, whatever may be true of an education that is not Christian, strengthens the bonds which bind men into a common brotherhood, and deepens the sense of mutual obligation of each to each, according to every one's ability. It is in your power to correct, to the extent of your personal influence and acquaintanceship, the misapprehension that there is anything in scholarship to antagonize faith in God, and in the eternal verities. If men have sometimes been educated out of their faith, it was because the education itself was fundamentally wrong. The ripest scholarship and the most childlike faith are often found together in the same person. It is only a "little learning" that is a "dangerous thing," and that little of the wrong kind.

The President, representing the College, will speak to you words of advice from your Alma Mater; it is only for me, as representing the larger outside community which you are about to enter, to welcome you as re-enforcements, armed and equipped to help us in the conflict of right against wrong and truth against error. May every one of you prove to be a valiant and efficient soldier in the army of righteousness. May you so fight as to win the approval, not only of your Alma Mater and of your fellow-soldiers in the great conflict, but as one by one you lay down your armor here, and pass onward and upward to another and higher sphere of action, may you receive the divine approval of Him who, in the stress and storm of life's struggles, has been your guide and inspiration.

Citizens of Illinois, Friends of Eureka, fifty years of history are looking down upon you to-day! The spirits of that heroic Company, who in faith and hope laid the foundation of this institution, must be among the unseen witnesses of this day's events. Stirred by the heroic memories of the past, and animated by the bright hopes of the future, may you achieve a victory here to-day that shall—

"Tell on ages, tell for God!"

PROTRACTED MEETINGS.*

D. R. DUNGAN.

It is doubted by some as to the good resulting from efforts of this kind. The abuse has entailed discredit upon them. Churches have been trained to live on the extra interest of these occasions. And when the meeting is over and the revivalist has gone, the Holy Spirit seems to have boarded the same train, and the church has no power left. The converts have been made largely to the revivalist; many have joined the meeting; they were swept off their feet by the occasion and the excitement. To join the church became the thing to do, and they joined the multitude. But after the enthusiasm has died out they see there are no grand evidences of spiritual uplift; they do not feel the elevation which they experienced during the revival; the assistance which they had a right to expect from those who were in Christ before them is entirely wanting, and they become discouraged and fall away, or become lethargic, and the church dies and sinks by its own weight. Many a church has gone up like a rocket and come down like a stick, leaving the space all the darker by virtue of the over brilliancy which had just preceded. Many a pastor, too, who was doing a good work before the meeting, has been counted out by the evangelist. He has poured out the stream of all his spiritual intelligence, and the converts especially are left to pine for the great preacher and the joyous time when Brother B. was with them.

If a church has been trained to live from this abnormal excitement it will be but a few years when nothing less than a spiritual whirlwind will seem to be of any avail. The work necessary before success with such a church will be its conversion. Their holiness is irregular, and they seem to be sanctified only in spots.

But we have given the unusual, the extreme; the abuse and not the use of protracted meetings. No revivalist should be employed, as a rule, who is candidating for a pulpit. He will have too many opportunities to suggest a change in the pastorate of that congregation. While most preachers are above anything of the kind, there are others who are at home in the body, and are of the earth. The preacher himself has no right to give everything into the hands of an evangelist; he should be at the helm all the time; he should take the confessions and do the baptizing, and it should be the object of the revivalist to make the pastor stronger with his people than ever before. The church should know the difference between the pet sermons which have been prepared for these occasions and delivered a large number of times, and the regular draft work of their faithful minister. And the preacher for such a people should have given them a better way, something more enduring than this fluctuating sensationalism. Religion, which is a life, not simply a heated or a sweetened atmosphere, will live. Unction and zeal and pathos are good, but if it cannot be seasoned and salted so that it will stay and be a living power, it is good for nothing.

There is still another objection to protracted meetings; the expense. There are many churches which are unable to pay an evangelist and maintain their regular work. This, however, is rarely insurmountable. If that church has a pastor for all, or even a part of the time, the arrangements can be made without the increase of expense for the meeting, and if they have not been able to support a pastor any of the time, the means will have to come from some other source. It is a missionary field.

It is said sometimes that we have a good pastor, but he has been here a good while and the people would not turn out to hear him in a series of sermons. This is basing the hope of success entirely on the attractions of the pulpit. But the success of the meeting should depend, at least one-half, on the work of the members. And that good pastor is just the man to bring about that organized effort which will insure success. It might be well, however, to exchange his time in a meeting somewhere else for help of the same kind, end in that way a new man would be found for each place. There would be but a few dollars in that case of extra expense, and they could be gathered during the meeting, which would not otherwise find their way into the church coffers.

A more serious objection comes from the condition of some communities which prevent the people from attending any meetings at night during the week. There are churches in many of our cities where not only the church members, but the people generally, especially the men, are employed as clerks, as merchants, or are in business, in which their time in the evening is required. The large number of them are not at home till seven o'clock and could not be at the church for an hour later. In the morning they are up at six, and they feel that their rest at home is a question of life or death. They must have their rest or arrange for their funerals. I feel that there are hindrances from this source in places. Though the members might make this sacrifice, the men they hope to reach would not, and so the meeting would go on without any results in the way of gain to the membership. The trouble is in such places to work up the interest to the point of bringing out those busy men who are not already Disciples. This can many times be

*A paper read before the Christian ministers of St. Louis.

done by a united effort of preacher and people.

I am ready, therefore, to conclude that while there are difficulties in the way, there are none that are insurmountable. And in the large number of places there is nothing in the way unless it is the indifference of the people who are already in the church. Of course non-members are not going to take much interest in such matters unless the church leads the way. In fact, a revival can hardly be said to have begun till the church members begin to work. But if there are a few places where a meeting of this kind will not accomplish good, they are the exception and not the rule. Nine churches out of ten could hold protracted meeting with good results. And my opinion is that all could.

It is in order now to ask what are the benefits of such efforts? If there are no evils which cannot be avoided and all can hold them, still it is a question as to their value.

1. In the first place, it is an opportunity to teach the people "what be the first principles of the oracles of God." If the pastor in his regular Lord's day ministrations should give them the teaching which even the members need, it would be regarded as tame, and it would be said that these doctrinal sermons are not called for; that not one in ten of the congregation was in need of the instruction. Perhaps that is not true, but the effect is the same; the preacher has to give them something else till a large part of the congregation do not know the difference between God's way of saving sinners and the human plans which have come in to take the place of the things which Christ commanded, and the people are left saying, "Lord, Lord," but do not his will. During the meeting, however, and especially if the preacher is some other than the pastor, this teaching will be relished, and the strangers who do not know the gospel will have an opportunity to learn.

2. In the second place, the people can be held to the study of the subject long enough to get it fixed in their minds, not only that they ought to be Christians, but how to become Christians. Those who come on Sunday, and if they are yet in the world, they will not come regularly enough to retain very much of the New Testament in any consecutive way. They may get some kind of nebulous knowledge of divine things, but like star-dust it will require a long time for such adhesion of particles that you can see that there is likely to be a new body brought into activity.

3. There are a great many men so imbedded in business that it requires a flood to wash them out; you seem to have to undermine the bank in which they are covered and let them drop in. Some one will be ready to say, "Well, how will you keep them afloat afterwards? Of course the torrent will subside a little, and the interest will abate somewhat when the meeting has closed, but if you manage to keep them in the middle of the stream for awhile they will go on well enough. I know that some of this sap-rotted timber may lodge on the sand-bars, but a great deal of it will come through all right enough.

A third question is how to make protracted meetings of greatest usefulness in the Master's cause. This is a stddy that is worthy of the best talent of the age. In my opinion, all the bad results of protracted meetings are due to bad management. There may be comparative failures, without anything in the arrangements or in the execution, deserving criticism. The elements may be indisposed, storms, floods, cyclones, or as it is many times other matters of interest come up which could not have been foreseen. Usually, however, the meeting should go right on till these oppositions give way.

In the first place, the church should be in working condition. If the meeting has to be held to convert the church, the time and strength are wasted and but little accomplished. On the other hand, if all are ready and begin at the first, the work will soon go forward, and soon will the ripened grain be brought in.

Some have accomplished a good deal by committees. I must say that I never yet received much help in that way. You can not accomplish by machinery what has to be done by the piety and faithful work of all the church. You can not so sharply define work that you can ever know what belongs to this one and what to that one. And it would be a great weakness if you should. I have known a committee on shaking hands with the people—a kind of "*smilem-up*" committee; another on prayer, and another on distribution of tracts, and so on to the end, if there is any end. If the people have been so trained that they will do one thing and nothing else, it may be the best, but it is a pity that they have been trained in that way. It reminds me of the man who had an understanding with his wife that all the affairs of the house were under her control, while he would give himself to business considerations. One day while engaged in his office, a runner announced to him that his house was on fire. He said, "Tell my wife, that department comes under her supervision!" That was a fine division of responsibility, but common sense would have done better. If cottage prayer-meetings are held during the meeting, it will be well enough to have a committee to find the places where they may be appointed and to assist in looking after the attendance at these meetings, another on advertisement; but still better, if the whole congregation should be an advertising committee, hand-shaking and invitation committee. I have no objections to the effort at this kind of organization, and yet for many years' observation I am not able to say that I have found much help in this way. If the church is all alive in the work, the preacher can easily get all the help he needs, and he is ordinarily the best committee on prayer-meetings during the revival.

Up to this moment I have never known a preacher who depended largely on the kind of organization I have mentioned who was much better than a failure. Depend rather on the piety and willingness of your people to work, know what is needed and then direct the whole affair as you proceed.

The time has something to do with the success or failure of protracted meetings. If you are in the country, and it has been wet for a long time and the farmers have a chance at last to get into their fields of corn, you can depend on it that they will be more interested in getting the fox-tail out of their fields than in the revival. So, too, in our cities, it is hard to start a meeting during the holidays. And yet, if we are waiting for everything to become perfectly favorable, we will not have a meeting. The farmer who constantly counsels with the moon and the clouds rarely has his bins full of grain. And the church can be indulged in the waiting for a good time to come until there will be found no time which will be exactly suitable, and protracted meetings will never be held.

What to preach during the meeting depends on the needs of the people. Some one says that we do not now preach so much on first principles as we did once, and our success is a great deal better. They forget that the people now listen to us because we have large numbers and much wealth, whereas when we were but a few, they could afford to despise us and neglect the meetings. The conditions much more than any change in the matter of sermons, give us a hearing. I should say from first to last, give the people the gospel of Christ. It alone is the power of God unto salvation.

If we preach as Christ did, as the apostles did, we will give offense. We can not help that. Men must know that they are sinners, they must know that Christ is the only Savior, that to be saved we must accept of the Christ and do his will. We must preach this same gospel without apology.

I recommend that a prayer-meeting be held in the church as well as in a nnmber of houses. If you cannot have this meeting at ten or eleven, have it at seven in the evening, and let this be a time for the building up in piety and devotion of those who have lately become Christians. You will come from such service prepared for better work in the pulpit. Acquaint them with the work of a soldier, and then there will not be much danger of any falling away after the meeting is over.

A good leader of song will be a great help. You can sing truth into people as well as preach it to them. I have no objection to a large number of good singers being on the platform, but what is known as a choir is rarely of much value during a protracted meeting. Provide books and get all to sing if possible. A good solo singer is a great preacher of the gospel. The people do not only hear the noise but hear the words, and are thrilled with the sentiment.

Be importunate. Ask the people again and again to accept of Christ. If you make the sermon thirty minutes in length, and to the point, make everything clear so far as you go, you will still have time for several invitations accompanied with songs. I have known strong men to come at the third or fourth invitation, who would have gone from the house without any acceptance of the Savior, and business preventing, would not have been there again durirn the meeting. Or if he should come again, the influence of that occasion would be lost, and he would go back again into his former lethargy and never become a Christian. There is a squeamishness in in such matters not born of piety or earnestness in the salvation of souls.

Last, do not stop the meeting too soon. That is the great mistake and the most common one. One or two weeks may only get up a little interest, and because some are getting tired the managers get together and decide to stop the meeting, just at the time when they could have begun to harvest the ripened grain.

ATRIOTISM.

ate services at Butler College,
obably the most impressive that
ld in the forty-three years' his-
tion. President Butler's bacca-
ɔn "Patriotism" is regarded by
as one of the greatest addresses,
of sentiment and in elegance of
red in the college chapel. The
as lifted to the highest enthu-
with the deepest devotion. The
ght to be published as a piece of
literature. Below is given an
ɪeared in the Indianapolis News.
J. D. FORREST.

ıgh made up of innumer-
ɪ one whole. Civilization,
ınging product of changing-
ıot some wild whirl of star-
rratic course through inter-
Civilization holds relation
.n of truth and answers to
There is a moving, a trans-
in the world. We cannot
ng in a day; scarcely in a
shall men be able to note
What wonder if there be
ɔt? Strange destiny is ours.
ȧn of life seems to hold so
little so weak, so purpose-
. But this thought saves:
ot of the brief present only,
ɔ, too, of all the past, and of
.rs, how many soever God's
ıin. In this way: Human-
.s an unresting march. Men
', and other men are born to
ɜes, and these, too, die and
others, succeed them, and no
ɪ knows the beginning, nor
the end. And yet, because
ne, because the life of the
nseparable from the life of
ıse the soul's breath is in the
l spirit, therefore he that is
social instinct, that rejects
ɪfuses to have faith in civili-
ɪparates himself in unbelief
'gles and the hopes and in-
is kind, he is guilty of most
he sins against himself, he
n nature, he assails his own
lty to society is, therefore,
ılf. Denial of the ascension
ımanity is denial of deter-
ıy for one's own soul.

T IS CIVILIZATION?

.k of the past as perished
civilization that it was cor-
ıd in it the seeds of inevit-
'hat its movement was ever
ɜo far, true. The sands of
ve buried ancient Egypt;
ies in undistinguished ruins
y the unbetraying seas, or
h the rank verdure of neg-
is dead. Rome's treasures
.ber's muddy bed, or labori-
l and conjecturally labeled,
in antiquarian museums to
ıs' sight-seers. So far the
never had been. But this is
ı. Civilization is not pyra-
t Parthenon. No more is
eam, or electricity, or Bes-
product of electrochemistry.
lization a microbe. Civiliza-
—the same from the begin-

vival of the fittest. Achievement destitute of high moral quality is short-lived; it perishes from the earth and from the memory of man. That survives that is of the nature of higher truth; that is, of God. And though in any age men's conceptions and acts are their own, thus does God rule in history—thus does his Spirit rule through man's spirit. This spiritual survival is the world's possession, and it unifies humanity to the end of time.

And yet, this were a cold and insufficient definition of patriotism. Patriotism means this; but it means more. It always meant more. For you to-day it means more than it ever meant for man before. What is it, then? What is it to you? Patriotism is love of country. But what does country mean? One thing to one, another thing to another, according to quality of mind and range of experience. To all it is, at bottom, a sentiment rich and full. This is elemental patriotism, the patriotism that is of the soil. The heart clings to its own. It may be barren rock in desert lands. * * * * For whether it be cold north land or sunny south; whether it be high mountain ridges, swept of winds that blow around the world, or whether it be deep valley beside still-flowing river, the heart loves its own—is in thrall to it. However long a man live and however often in later life he changes abode, I believe that he will know but one home, and that he will know that always. Who has not awaked from dreams to find that in spirit his rest had been within the wall that early sheltered him? Hard, then, it is to square one's wandering consciousness with present bearings. Such power has association.

What does patriotism mean? Why, earth, mother-earth, seems to enwrap us in her incense-laden breath; the very sod on which we rest seems to heave with the pulse of life; the beech trees, heavenward mounting, reached down benedictions on us from their drooping branches. We love our country because it is our country; because it is part of us; because the very juices of its soil seem to tingle in the blood that courses in our veins.

This is elemental patriotism, the patriotism of sentiment, the patriotism of passion—God has made us that way. Grand passion! Nature gives it to us—to all of us; none so mean as not to feel its dignity; none so proud as not to be ennobled by its possession. But though the basis, the soul, the inspiration of all true devotion to country, such feeling has its limitations. It is personal; it has to do with immediate belongings. It is short-sighted, it is sectional.

GIVE BACK THE CONFEDERATE FLAGS.

We older ones remember how a few years ago this question tried many earnest souls. viz., whether patriotism was sectional or national. They that fought for state against the National Government yielded to a sentiment misleading them, though noble always. Give back the flags. War's justification is that strife should end in peace. We fought to make our country one. Without oneness of heart and mind and purpose, North and South, our victory were vain. The union of these United States purports to be in humanity's cause and for God's high purposes—a union of brotherhood and love. So long as there remain on the one side boasting and on the other side bitterness, so long the fruit of victory is unrealized, our high profession is but hypocritical mouthing our union is false and unnatural. The brave and generous judge an honerable opponent fairly. We whom in the days of the civil war the better fortune favored in that with us loyalty to state meant loyalty to nation, we may not unduly boast the superiority of our civic virtue. It might have been otherwise with us. I make no doubt that if Indianapolis had been Atlanta, beset by

Creek, it had so rushed red with blood of Indiana's sons, arrayed in deadly war against the general government, that not all the sewage of all the cities of the earth could ever defile its sanctity.

We of this section may only thank God that in our country's fratricidal strife patriotism for us ran in the line of the higher duties of citizenship, ran in the line of his eternal purpose.

The men of the sixties in their day and generation did their part—they made us one. A third of a century has cemented our union and enriched us in material resources. God, from the beginning, did the rest for us, for he made us a people quick to fight, strong in battle and of profound ethical convictions. He has further work for us. Yesterday we were content within ourselves; to-day we are face to face with world-problems.

OUR FLAG MUST STAY IN MANILA.

For some of us who are here to-day youth began with the drum-beat and tramp of armed men. Since then the peaceful years have lengthened out till now again our times are fallen on war. What does it mean? To my ear the guns that from Manila Bay sent their echoes around the world were God's own trumpet-tones summoning his people out of its isolation into the broad arena of the world's great life—and that, not for dominion, not for possession, not for power, but for humanity's cause—for the world—extension of that principle of justice which our governmental theory embodies. The summons has come to us unsought. We began a fight to drive the dechristianized civilization of the sixteenth century out of the Western Hemisphere; we find our standard planted on the other side of the globe—it has to stay there. Does that mean larger navies; increased armament; an isthmian canal; a chain of possessions reaching round the world? Does it mean imperialism?

Whatever it means, it is not our doing; it is destiny; it is God. Young men, I want to say for myself—and now while I shall speak in the first person, please to understand me as speaking for the generation I represent—I want to say that while as I trust I appreciate this greater glory of my country and my people, yet I have to confess it, amid these preparations for war that we have been witnessing, my heart has been filled with sadness—not for precious treasures that must be spent—not for brave men that must suffer and must die—not for heart of womankind that must be anguish-torn—none of these; but when I look on the generation of my countrymen born and brought to manhood since time when we that were boys in the sixties made our fight for country and for God; when I see their serried ranks of stalwart forms, and under the slouch of brown hats catch the gleam of bright eyes; when I look along the lines of glistening steel and in the distance catch the undimmed glory of the banner that they bear—God help me, how could I but feel sad—to think that my life lies behind me—to think that while these, the men of the twentieth century, march on, proud vanguard of their country's greater glory, I can only dream my senile dreams and feel the heart-aches that women feel that wait.

Love the land that gave you birth. Is that our own section here of these United States? Nowhere shines the sun on fairer. God made it from lake to river, from mountain to "Father of Waters," made it broad, plain, sloping hillside, forest and field, and clear water course—to be the home of a prosperous civilization, of a strong, a brave, a generous people. That people you may well be proud of.

But you will love your country, then, your whole country, the union of the United States, America, for the luster of her name, for the glory of her arms, for her greatness, her power, her beneficence.

But more than that—love your country for her high aims. Love her because in her are centered humanity's hopes. Love

Our Budget.

—Great naval victory at Santiago Sunday.

—Great convention at Nashville this week.

—Great news from Santiago on Independence day.

—Smaller pages makes the demand for shorter articles more urgent.

—If you want to read some classical patriotic literature turn to the extracts of President Butler's address in this paper.

—The Jamaica Letter in this paper, coming from a country so near one of the centers of the present war, cannot fail to be of interest to our readers.

—F. M. Green, of Kent, O., furnishes us an excellent report of the Hiram commencement this week. It is somewhat lengthy, but the interest of our Ohio readers and others will not falter in it to the end.

—The New England Messenger, edited by R. H. Bolton, Everett, Mass., is a model magazine for condensed news. It shows that correspondents can say much in a few words when they try.

—The Orphan School Record, Fulton, Mo., for June, is a fine compliment to the young ladies who have contributed its literature and to the school it represents. If freed from its debt this school would soon become a great factor in the intellectual and moral welfare of the church and people of this great state.

—The New York Voice rightly insists that if the United States, maintaining its present form of popular government, is going to enter upon a new career of wider dominion and vaster territorial possessions, some political change must be made. If the saloon power is to be continued and the new territory to become simply new fields for corruptionists then our territory is already overgrown. But, if we can have just and equitable laws, strong and pure municipal and state governments, and a sound and sufficient circulating medium, the addition of a few thousand square miles will not be so hazardous.

—It will be conceded without argument that the educational interests of our country are of the foremost importance. They may not be greater than our commercial, agricultural and religious interests, but they cannot be less, and yet our government is not giving that equal portion of its attention to our National Bureau of Education which it seems to merit. We are all familiar with many of the national bureaus, but of the National Bureau of Education many, doubtless, have not so much as heard. We do not expect the government to champion any of our religious movements, although it might profit by a closer acquaintance with them, yet such is not its attitude toward our schools. It has made the plea of the popular education of its citizens one of its pillars and cannot afford criminal negligence in that direction as we fear has been the case, judging from the facts set forth in an article found elsewhere in this paper from the pen of Prof. J. Fraise Richard, of Washington, D. C. This article was written for the Washington Post, but is of such importance that we give a portion of it space in our columns this week.

—Our C. W. B. M. is to co-operate with the Y. M. C. A. of Virginia in the support of a three months' course of Bible study at the University of Virginia during the sessions of 1898-'99. The third course in this Bible study is to be given by Charles A. Young, of Chicago, beginning October 5th. This course contemplates fifty lectures. In view of the added expense of the new work the C. W. B. M. have appealed to their auxiliaries in Virginia and elsewhere to assist by increased contributions, and new liberal subscriptions for this work. Also to solicit from individuals and churches donations to the permanent endowment fund of the University of Virginia Bible Lectureship. The expenses up to a maximum of $750 will be met out of the English Bible Chair Fund; but the C. W. B. M. has assumed the entire responsibility of the three months' Bible course at the next session of the University and will need liberal assistance.

—In the absence of the editor-in-chief of this paper the office editor is responsible for the appearance of his half-tone picture on our first page this week. In view of the fact that this is the first paper in our new form it seems appropriate, and we believe it will be appreciated by our readers. W. W. H.

—A timely suggestion:

Bills come due in the summer just as in the winter. No business man lets his notes go to protest simply because trade is dull. Church members who go away for the summer and never think of paying their church debts until they return double the burdens of the pastor, the treasurer, the janitor. Just remember this, and pay before you go. True, also, of newspaper bills.—*The Standard.*

—The indifferent attitude toward religion on the part of a large number of our young men is tersely told in the following published dialogue supposed to be of recent date:

"What's yer religious persuasion?" said the sergeant to the recruit.

"My what?"

"Yer what? Why, what I said. What's yer after o' Sundays?"

"Rabbits, mostly."

"'Ere, stow that lip. Come now, Chu'ch, Chapel, or 'oly Roman?"

"I ain't nowise pertickler. Put me down Chu'ch of England, sergeant; I'll go with the band."

—The Missionary Intelligencer for July speaks encouragingly of the offerings for Foreign Missions so far this year. There has been a loss from bequests of $5,601.40 during the eight months of this year compared to the same period last year. But this shortage is more than supplied in the gain of $6,646.33 from the regular receipts from churches, Endeavor Societies and schools, and a gain of $4,800 from annuities. This is encouraging.

—The writer of an obituary of Sherman D. Reeder, who died at Stockton, Kan., failed to sign his or her name. Will the writer please supply the information wanted?

—Through the efforts of President B. C. Hagerman—who has resigned the presidency of Bethany College to accept the presidency of Hamilton College, Lexington, Ky.—$30,000 of the $100,000 endowment fund necessary for Bethany College has been raised.

—Churches taking up a special collection for a specific purpose, such as Home Missions, Foreign Missions, or other definite end, should not fail to forward all moneys so raised to the proper treasurers. To use this money for any other purpose than that for which it was raised, on the part of those into whose hands it passes, such as paying up old pledges, or for current expenses, without the order of the people by whom it was given, would be a species of deception.

—We acknowledge the receipt of the catalogue of the Nebraska State Normal and Training School, at Peru. It is a magazine of 54 pages, three full-page pictures of the buildings, and a full outline of courses of study. The students' roll shows it to be a well-attended, popular center of learning.

—We don't wonder that W. A. Jarrell, a Baptist minister of Texas, wants to emigrate from that state, when one of his own church papers, The Baptist Standard, says: "He has been known for years as a blown-in-the-bottle, dyed-in-the-wool, uncompromising, 18-karat, knock-down-and-drag-out Landmark Baptist. His ecclesiastical diet has been aboud as follows: For breakfast, Campbellite on toast, Presbyterian dressing; for dinner, Congregationalist bullion, Episcopalian fricassee and Methodists a la J. R. Graves; for supper, Lutherans cold, with Y. M. C. A. sherbet;" and the Christian Courier comes at him from another quarter, describing him as "a stalwart of the stalwarts among strict-construction-unbroken-chain-succession-anti-alien-immersion-anti-Whitsitt Baptists." We should think it about time for him to move. Grape and canister from two ways at once ought to make almost any man willing to move.

—President Jones now claims to lack but $14,000 of having funds enough to meet the debt of $30,000 now threatening the Orphan Schoool at Fulton, Mo., and urges the churches and preachers to rally to its support by subscribing for the lack, at once.

—Should the responsible position at the head of the procession of Christian Endeavor ranks ever come to the Christian Church by natural law in the spiritual world, well and good; but let us not betray a selfish, sectarian spirit in seeking the place by committee strings and religious noises.

—Optimism or Pessimism Illustrated is the theme of the Chicago Letter this week. The field on either side is amply large enough for the full activity of the largest mind during the longest life, but to become wholly committed to either side is a dangerous mistake. Every man should be optimistic enough to prevent discouragement, and yet pessimistic enough to see and rebuke sin in high places. Try to properly proportion these two unknown quantities in your nature or forces in your character.

—In the way of a rebuke for dereliction of duty in the taking and reading of a good church paper we have seen nothing better, more pungently pointed than the following from the Pacific Christian:

"What Christian paper do you take?"

"None."

"Why?"

"Hain't time to read one. Take more papers now than I can read."

"When and where is our next state convention?"

"Don't know."

"What is our foreign society doing now?"

"Don't know."

"Or in India?"

"Don't know."

"Or in Africa?"

"Don't know."

"Have we a foreign society, anyhow?"

"Think we have, but don't know for certain."

"Who is its secretary?"

"Dont know."

"What is it doing?"

"Don't know."

"Is it doing anything?"

"S'pose it is. Don't really know."

"How much money did it raise last year?"

"Don't know."

"Who are our home missionaries?"

"Don't know."

"Where is home missionary work most needed?"

"Don't know."

"What is our membership in the United States?"

"Don't know."

"What is it in this state?"

"Don't know."

"Where are we strongest?"

"Don't know."

"Who are some of our strongest men?"

"Don't know."

"Is our cause making much progress at present?"

"Don't know."

"What good are you to the church, anyhow?"

"Don't kn—— that is, I ——— well you see———."

—We have seen and heard some preachers who seem to think that a preacher's energy should exhaust itself in scolding the brethren. This is a serious error. A larger portion of this force directed toward loving the flock would produce far better and more satisfactory results. Scolding was not one of Christ's foremost characteristics—not even a visible one throughout his whole life.

—If a circular letter sent out from the "Law Enforcement Society," of Brooklyn, N. Y., now a part of Greater New York City, hints at facts, and the circular is well authenticated, we certainly cannot advise our friends to visit Coney Island during the summer. One of the mildest statements of this circular is that "it is rotten with a rottenness that is indescribable." We are glad to know that this "Law

Enforcement Society'' is to wage a war against the evils hinted at, and trust that it may be ably seconded by every law-abiding, purity-loving citizen in Greater New York; and also that a similar war may be waged against every other moral sink-hole in the land. Money spent in such a war is well invested and will return gracious benefits to society.

—Our English Topics, this week, is particularly interesting, dealing after its own lively fashion with lively topics. The question of better conditions in the industrial world is not an insolvable nor unsolved question, as some suppose, and as the first part of this letter shows. The truth is, we have the solution, but the business world, the ''on-tops,'' will not permit their use so long as they can prevent it. They are like some railroads in their attitude toward better equipments; they will not adopt them until they find that it pays to do so or the law compels them to do so; as it so often has done. We hope, however, that a few more business men like Mr. Hartely in the Topics this week, and others that could be named, will make Christian activity more popular among the business men of the world. You will also be interested in what the Topics has to say about Dimleby's prophecy of the world's end and of Andrew Lang's new book.

—The admirable treatise on ''Protracted Meetings'' in this paper, by D. R. Dungan, of this city, will bear close inspection. Coming, as it does, at this season of the year, it will be less liable to affect any protracted meeting in progress, or the prospects of any particular evangelist, but it will help churches to a wiser management of these meetings in the future. Next week we expect to publish an excellent paper on ''Ministerial Courtesy.'' As announced, we have a number of ably written papers on practical church themes to appear consecutively in our new paper.

—Cardinal Gibbons has asked President McKinley to appoint more Catholic chaplains to the army. The request, it is said, is based on the great number of Catholic young men in the army and navy and the few Catholic chaplains. It will now be in order for every other religious body in the land to make a similar request.

—The 47th annual catalogue of Christian College, Columbia, Mo., is by far the handsomest catalogue we have yet seen from that institution. It is elegantly printed on good paper and contains a large number of full-page pictures, executed in the best skill of the engraver's art. The literature of the catalogue and pictures make a book of 80 pages, and the information imparted therein ought to add many names to its roll the next school year. The tinted cover of the catalogue, with its raised gilt letters, is fine.

—The Christian Quarterly, July, just to hand, contains the following themes and authors: ''Denominationalism,'' by Joseph Franklin; ''The Apostolic Age,'' by W. M. Forrest; ''Paul's Letter to the Romans,'' Clinton Lockhart; ''Bishop Merrill On 'Buried by Baptism,''' by J. B. Briney; ''Evolution and Christianity,'' by A. M. Chamberlain; ''Machiavelli,'' by I. J. Cahill; ''Stumbling-Blocks: A Word-Study,'' by A. S. Carman. The other departments are filled with inviting literature.

—In the program of the Missouri Christian Lectureship at Carrollton, July 18-21, which we published last week, too many things appear to be in one session. We aimed to designate the hours of each session instead of the time of each lecture, but by mistake got some of the sessions run together. The program will appear again next week. It is a strong one and those who attend will have much presented to their minds for contemplation.

—Mrs. Rachel Errett, mother of Davis Errett, now pastor of the church at Canton, Mo., died June 25th. A tribute to her life, written by E. J. Lampton, of Louisiana, Mo., will appear in our next number.

Beulah Notes.

During the absence of the pastor, E. M. Smith, who is spending his vacation at his old home in Virginia, the following program for Lord's day services has been arranged by Beula Christian Church, of this city: July 3, 11 A. M., Preaching, Dr. J. H. Foy. July 3, 8 P. M., Union Patriotic Services at Mt. Cabanne Church. July 10, 11 A. M., Preaching, Dr. J. H. Foy. July 10, 8 P. M., Services conducted by Y. P. S. C. E. July 17, 11 A. M., Preaching, W. W. Hopkins. July 17, 8 P. M., Preaching, Dr. J. H. Foy. July 24, 11 A. M., Preaching, Jno. A. Owen. July 24, 8 P. M., Services conducted by C. W. B. M. July 31, 11 A. M., Preaching, W. W. Hopkins. July 31, 8 P. M., Preaching, Dr. J. H. Foy.

A new church, of which Roy L. Handley, of this city, has been chosen pastor, has just been organized in Argentine, a part of Kansas City, Kan.

The church was formed with a nucleus of thirty-eight members, and additions are constantly being made during the meeting which was still in progress at last accounts.

There is a Bible-school of fifty members in connection with the movement.

Bro. Handley is a young man held in the very highest esteem in this city for his talent, his uprightness and his energy. This is his first pastoral work, but his friends in St. Louis expect great things of the church at Argentine if the membership is nearly as faithful as the pastor.

W. D. CREE.

PERSONAL MENTION.

We are glad to report that A. M. Atkinson, of Wabash, Ind., is able to go about again; not to his work but for the increase of his physical strength. All will rejoice that the Lord has returned him to us from the very jaws of death.

R. B. Neal, of Grayson, Ky., has issued his Anti-Mormon tract No. 2. This one is entitled, ''Smithianity,'' and deals some hard blows at the pretentious claims of that pretentious people.

A sketch of the life of J. J. Haley, one of the corresponding editors of the CHRISTIAN-EVANGELIST, together with his picture, appeared in the Christian Guide last week. The picture is not a flattering one, but the loss is more than met in the sketch of his active and extended life and work.

A note worthy compliment has been paid to our brotherhood in the selection, by the Society of Pedagogy, of St. Louis, of Dr. Joseph H. Foy, principal of the Shields Public School, as Ethical Lecturer, a position fomerly occupied by Dr. Wm. M. Bryant. The society is to be congratulated on its good selection.

W. S. Wood, pastor of the church at Boonville, Mo., and Miss Susan Jones, of Milan, Mo., were recently married. The ceremony was spoken by James. S. Todd, of Galt, Mo. The newly married started for Omaha, for a trip, soon after the ceremony. May our congratulations overtake them.

Dr. W. A. Belding is in his 82nd year of life, and says he is able to preach as much as ever, if not as well.

Duncan McGregor, a man of scholarship and refinement, from the Progressive Dunkards, a preacher, united with the Disciples of Christ at Washington, Pa.

Bro. J. W. Bolton, editorial contributor of N. E. Messenger, has been called to remain at Westport and Tiverton, Nova Scotia, another year, it being his third year.

Bro. Chas. S. Medbury, pastor of the Church of Christ, in Angola, Ind., has been elected chaplain of the third Indiana Regiment and has gone to battle Spaniards.

A. C. Smithers, of Los Angeles, Cal., preached the baccalaureate sermon to the graduates of the California State Normal School, of that city, June 19, 1898. The class numbered 80. He is also to deliver four lectures on the Bible at Long Beach convention, July 7-17.

D. H. Bays, of Persia, Iowa, author of Doctrine and Dogmas of Mormonism, published by this house, has been lecturing in Ohio on that subject this summer. Dr. Bays has thoroughly mastered his subject and knows whereof he speaks. Any audience not composed of Mormons will be profited by hearing Dr. Bays lecture on that subject.

B. C. Hagerman, having been elected President of Hamilton Female College, has removed from Bethany W. Va., to Lexington, Ky.

''F.L. Hayden, D. D.,'' of Kearney, Neb., has joined in the new literary crusade against Mormonism. He is just out with a tract against this peculiar ism, and states that he will be glad to give personal aid to pastors wherever Mormon propagandists are at work. Address him for particulars.

Christian College Chronicle, Columbia, Mo., highly complimented F. G. Tyrrell, of this city, for his masterly address in Columbia on Sunday preceding the college commencement. By the way, the June number of the Chronicle is an exceptionally good one.

A. R. Adams, pastor of the church at Blandinsville, Ill., was recently pleasantly and profitably surprised by the members of his flock. Both purse and larder were largely replenished.

Mrs. M. J. Fergusson, wife of the pastor of the church at Riverside, Cal., passed through this city on last Friday, en route to Bowling Green, Ky., where she will spend the summer.

Geo. T. Smith has removed from Chicago to Albia, Iowa, where he now preaches, having accepted a call to that place.

W. E. Garrison reports a delightful voyage across the Atlantic, excepting one day of rough sea. His first correspondence—Tourist Letter—will appear in our next number.

CHANGES.

A. D. Skaggs, Cedarville, Cal., to Central Point, Ore.
Chas. S. Earley, Des Moines to Lancaster, Ia.
L. C. Swann, Des Moines to Murray, Ia.
R. L. Stanley, Atlanta to Beaumont, Kan.
Perry McPherson, Emporia to 807 Topeka Ave., Topeka, Kan.
J. V. Crawford, Waitsburg, Wash., to Enterprise, Ore.
Herbert Yeuell, Cleveland, O., to Banksville, Pa.
D. A. Brown, Bethel to Sigsbee, Mo.
A. M. Harral, Bentonville to Rogers, Ark.
W. Frank Ross, Rantoul to Champaign, Ill.
G. J. M. Morris, Auburn to Gloversville, N. Y.
J. W. Damon, Mt. Pleasant to Ottumwa, Iowa.
G. L. Stevenson, Hazel Green to Lexington, Kentucky.
J. W. Baker, Ninisila to Galvin, Ohio.
J. C. Wright, 242 LaSalle Ave., to 225 Dearborn St., Chicago.
J. U. Wiseman, Solon to Martin's Ferry, Ohio.

Correspondence.

English Topics.

BUSINESS AND RELIGION.

Some of the noblest of living Englih Christians are men deeply and lucratively engaged in life's daily business. One of these is Mr. W. J. Hartley, a great Liverpool jam manufacturer. Here is one of the most remarkable men whom the world has produced. He is one of the very busiest employers of labor in the the land, and yet he takes so much part in the religious affairs of his denomination, the Primitive Methodist, that a newspaper recently aluded to him as the Reverend W. J. Hartley. This must have greatly amused the jam-maker, as it did all who best know him. But the mistake proved the many-sided character of the man. Near his own residence is a model village, consisting of fifty houses, in which some of his workmen live. This village is a beautiful sight, with its trim gardens and pretty green lawn. Mr. Hartley says that he has never had any trouble with his workpeople, either in relation to hours or wages. He accounts for this by saying that it has been his first aim to do unto others as he would be done by. Three times within recent years the wages have been advanced unasked. Nearly twenty thousand pounds he has given to the men and women employed in profit-sharing according to the prosperity of the business. He believes that the system of profit-sharing would go a long way towards solving the problem of capital and labor. Mr. Hartley says, after the experience of years, that he does not see any solution of the difficulties of the day without the application of the spirit of Christ. In England several other great men of business are thus quietly working out what may prove to be splendid preparations for the establishment of the millennium. Mr. Lever, the founder of the wonderful town called Port Sunlight, where mountains of "Sunlight Soap" are made, is another of the princes of labor who are also leaders in the Christian community. Port Sunlight is a magnificent sample of incipient, practical Christian Socialism. Its streets of workingmen's villas, its large, handsome public hall, its literary institute and library, its baths, its gardens, all make this creation of a man who was a poor boy a real paradise of industry. Here master and men are bound together by solidarity of interests. It is so also with Huntley and Palmer, who have constructed the largest biscuit bakery in the world, at Reading, forty miles from London. These gentlemen are Quakers. The Brothers Tangye, of Birmingham, the great engineers, are known throught the land as beneficent Christian philanthropists. As employers of an army of men, they manage their works on similar lines, bringing into action the practical principles of a true Christian communism, while the dreamy dilettante Socialists of the Bellamy school, and the anarchists of the Fourier and Krapotkine models, follow Owen into the quagmire of wild and hopeless confusion. I have come to this conclusion from a long study of the different phases of modern Socialism, that only the Christian capitalists who have taken their men into actual partnership are paving the way for a better age. The splendid results they have achieved constitute object-lessons which the world will sooner or later begin to study, instead of the nostrums of the numerous fallacy-mongers who leave out of account the Bible and its economics on the one hand, and the essential faults and difficulties of human nature on the other.

SCIENCE AND THE END OF THIS WORLD.

Grim joking is being indulged in at the expense of Mr. Joseph Dimbleby and the Rev. Michael Baxter. These two gentlemen are professional prophets. They are engaged like Professor Totten in your country in reckoning up how many years, months, weeks, days, hours, minutes and seconds this poor old Terra on which we live and move and have our being has yet to exist. Now, Mr. Dimbleby has been for sometime past publishing pamphlets to show that the great cataclysm was to ensue on Easter Sunday last. Well, that was the very day when your war with Spain actually commenced as far as fighting was concerned. But the terrestrial terminus does not appear to be close at hand, and Mr. Dimbleby and his followers are in an awkward position. So is Mr. Baxter, especially as he has just taken the long lease of large business premises in which to print and publish his newspapers, which are very popular with numbers of people who crave for incessent sensationalism. But other people are making great fun of the prophet, for Michael Baxter has for many years been predicting tremendous catastrophes to come on all the earth just about this present period. The "everlasting smash" was to come for certain before the century should run out. "Forty Coming Wonders" is the title of a most appalling prophetic book at which I sometimes look for a few minutes in order to give Mr. Baxter a chance to convince me. For he argues everything from Scripture. The pictures in the "Forty Coming Wonders" are bloodcurdling and horrific. They might have been left to tell their own story with advantage, just as Mendelssohn's wonderful "Songs Without Words" are far more effective than if the musician had put language to the music. All the imaginable beastial monstrosities of the infernal menageries are depicted, and the letterpress describes all the horrors which ought by this time to have fairly started the crack of doom. My perplexity in studying this sort of literature, in which thousands of good Christians implicitly believe, is to find out how, after two or three dreadful and annihilating "Wonders" had had their turn, there could then be any of us mortals on earth left to face the next. A very few of these stupendous plagues, in which heaven and hell seem to shake hands in strange alliance out of spiteful malignity to this poor little globe, would clear off so many millions, including lots of the Baxterians and Dimblebytes, that I do not see who would be surviving to be the subjects of any of the further series of woes. Mr. Baxter is being derisively challenged in many of the newspapers to say how he could in good faith have leased fine premises for a long term of years when his predicted collapse of sublunary spheres is already a little over due. He has taken the trouble to formulate a laborious reply. The funny thing about this is that he explains that in the millennium there will be far greater need of books and newspapers than ever before, so that he is only making consistent preparation for the age to come. As his "Forty Coming Wonders," however, more than suffice to show that the earth will be swept clear of everything that has lived (for such pestilence, such earthquakes, such invasions of angels, demons, beasts with all sorts of heads, bodies, claws, jaws, crowns, stings, hoofs, tails and tongues, and dragons foul, firey, scaly and slimy, would surely make a total end of men, women and children), it is difficult for the student to understand who will be existent to read the sheets that are expected to be issued in such millennial masses from Michael Baxters's apocalyptic emporium. However, it has to be admitted that larger numbers of people than ever are greedily swallowing this kind of prophetic literature. The sillier the nonsense poured out by the old Roman augurs and vaticinators, the more eagerly Demos believed it. So it is at this day. The more audacious the soothsaying, the more acceptable to a certain large class of minds. And yet, prophecy is the finest of all studies. I take leave to say that the fooling of charlatans with this subject is in great part to be ascribed to the neglect of it by the majority of preachers. They have for the most part left it to the tricksters. Writers like Birks, Fleming, Elliott and Guinness have taught us a more excellent way, but only a few are profiting by it. In theological colleges eschatology is often openly derided.

THE EVOLUTION OF THE IDEA OF GOD.

A handsome volume has just appeared on one of the greatest controversies of our time. Mr. Andrew Lang, now accounted by many our foremost English critic, has given to the public his new work, "The Making of Religion." His main contention is that religion is born in us, not made by us. He combats at every point the views of the anthropologists. These declare in all their expositions that man derived the conception of "spirit" or "soul" from his reflections on the phenomena of sleep, dreams, death, shadow, and from the experience of trance and hallucination. First men worshiped the departed souls of their kindred, and then ghosts became gods. Finally these gods became unified, and thus arose the conception of the one God. Meanwhile man retained his belief in his own existence after death and so reached the conception of his own immortality. Thus the ideas of God and the immortality of the soul are the result of early fallacious reasonings about misunderstood experiences. This is a fair view of what is taught by anthropologists like Herbert Spencer and Grant Allen. But Mr. Andrew Lang will have none of this doctrine. He shows that certain tribes of low savages are as monotheistic as some Christians. He contends that there are two currents, the mythical and the religious, following all creeds. The religious current even amongst savages is quite distinct from the magical, ghost-propitiating habit. The other current, the mythological, is full of magic, mummery and scandalous legend. The anthropologists have kept their eyes on the impure stream, the lusts, mummeries, conjurings and frauds of the priesthoods, while neglecting the higher and purer thoughts of the people. Mr. Lang even has the courage to oppose Max Muller, and he does so with conspicuous success. He contends with great wealth of argument and illustration that in the most backward peoples known to us there is found "among men just emerged from the palæolithic stage of culture, men who are involved in dread of ghosts, a religious idea which certainly is not born of ghost-worship." In their hearts, in their moral training, we find, he says (however blended with barbarous absurdities), the faith in a Being who constructed the world; who was from time beyond memory or conjecture; who is eternal, who makes for righteousness and who loves mankind. I believe this new book will lift up Mr. Andrew Lang to fame equal to any of the greatest thinkers of our time.

W. DURBAN.

43 Park Rd., South Tottenham, London, Eng., June 17, 1898.

Jamaica Letter.

Infrequent doing of a thing makes that thing difficult to do. Letter-writing is no exception. I realize this uow as I take up my pen to put into practical effect a purpose that I have had a number of times during the past three months. However, your columns have not lacked interesting matter—probably more interesting and profitable to most of your readers than anything likely to originate in this, to them, obscure and unimportant island.* Still, we would like to have your readers interested in our circumstances and work, and interest can hardly be expected without knowledge

As regards the affairs of the island generally, there is nothing very exciting or promising in its condition to communicate. The low state of trade and the scarcity of labor for the laboring classes, the languid circulation of money and the poor price of island produce continue much the same as when I wrote at the close of last year. If there is any improvement it is

*May I take this opportunity of expressing appreciation of the great improvements that have taken place in the CHRISTIAN-EVANGELIST, especially in the addition of the C. E. Prayer-meeting and Sunday-school departments.

little; and in some districts the people are said to be in a very impoverished condition indeed. In Kingston, and two or three of the larger towns, there has been a larger influx of Cubans who have sought refuge here from the various troubles and dangers incident to a state of war. Their presence is putting some money into circulation. Out of their misfortune some good comes to us. There is scarcely a day that some American or Spanish warship or some other vessel does not run into this port. The other day the Harvard came in, and after being there twenty-four hours (the time limit), was ordered to leave. The captain reported something wrong with her machinery and his consequent inability to get away. It was commonly reported around that two Spanish warships were waiting for the Harvard outside! However, after three days she steamed quietly on her way. All our Sunday-school children had a good look at her, as we happened to be out having our annual picnic on the seashore, within about a quarter of a mile of where she passed. She seems to have encountered no opposition. Of course we are so situated that a very lively interest is taken in the conflict; and telegrams are anxiously looked for twice a day. These, however, are found to be very unreliable. We should be very thankful to hear that peace negotiations, of which there have been some rumors, are a reality.

The hard times are affecting churches throughout the island. When the Episcopalians held their synod early this year, it was found that it would be impossible to keep up their expenditures from their usual sources of income. Very considerable reductions were made all round. The Archbishop expressed his fears that the work would suffer. Two of their leading clergymen have been sent to England as a deputation to represent their case and to solicit funds to meet deficiences. This is the church of which most of the wealthy people, who are identified with any church at all, claim to be members.

Dr. Barratt and the Rev. Mr. Woods, of England, who, not long ago, where sent as a deputation, by the London Missionary Society, to the Congregational Churches here, recently stated to the Congregational Union that if funds were not devoted to the keeping up of the mission in Jamaica, the information they had led them to doubt if the mission could be continued. The Baptists are finding it very difficult to carry on their work. Their mission money has fallen off nearly one-hal,; and some of their ministers who have from 700 to 1,500 members under their care, are in great difficulties as to their support. (I may mention here, as an interesting item, that the oldest missionary in connection with this body died last week, at the age of eighty years, during fifty-four of which he labored on this island. He has left of his children, two sons and one daughter missionaries in Jamaica; one son a missionary in Burmah, and one just gone as a medical man in connection with mission work to Africa.)

In view of what I have said of the difficulties of others in this field, it will not be surprising if we have to report diminished funds. Still, we hope that these trying financial times will soon give place to something better. They say that even now there are signs of improvement. Doubtless the hard times tend greatly to prevent advance in our mission work. Many persons cannot attend the services because they have not the apparel in which they like to appear. Want of boots is one of the commonest hindrances. Still, we are making some progress. Up to the present time we have had over twenty additions to the church at Duke Street and branch this year. Bro. MacLeod expects to baptize six persons at King's Gate next Lord's day morning. The other churches are having additions also. This month we had the largest number that has ever gathered at our annual picnic. One hundred and forty went out on the cars, and had a splendid day. We have still enough to make us hope, and hope keeps us at work. We still have the droppings and plead for the showers.

C. E. RANDALL.

Kingston Jamaica, June 15, 1898.

Salt Lake City.

Temple Square, which is ten acres in area, is inclosed by a wall about three feet thick at the base and about twelve feet high. This wall rests on a foundation of masonry and is capped with stone slabs, the intermediate structure being of cemented adobe. The adobe portion is painted a straw color.

The streets are all numbered from the temple and are named according to their numbers. The streets adjoining Temple Square are known as North Temple, South Temple, East Temple and West Temple. Then come 1st South, 2nd South, and so on. All the cardinal points of the compass have their numerically named streets. This is a little confusing at first, as it is quite easy to get West 2nd South mixed with South 2nd West, although they are widely separated. West 2nd South is the west end of 2nd South, or the west end of the second street south of South Temple Street, which is the first street south of the Temple. When I say that I live at 578 East 4th South Street, I mean that I live at that number on the east end of the fourth street south of South Temple Street. A line drawn diagonally across the city from the southeast corner of the Temple would lie diagonally across the intersections of East Temple and South Temple, 1st South and 1st East, 2nd East and 2nd South, and so on. The blocks are 660 feet square and the streets are 132 feet wide. This is not peculiar to Salt Lake City. All Mormon towns and cities are and have been thus laid out. The large squares have nothing to commend them. The centres of them cannot be built upon to advantage, and space that would be valuable if it fronted on a street is rendered undesirable by being hemmed in behind lots and shut out from view by surrounding houses. The wisdom of such an arrangement is not apparent. The finger of time points out many mistakes that when born were thought to be the children of inspiration. He who builds for future generations generally builds better than he knows. He who builds no better than he knows generally builds for his own generation. If his work is seen at all by future generations it is as a moss-covered ruin—the embodiment of an antiquated idea.

At the intersection of Main and South Temple Streets stands a bronze monument of Brigham Young, standing with bared head, with his left hand resting on his cane, and his right lifted in a graceful gesture as if addressing a public assembly. His tomb is on 1st (north) between State (1st East) and A Streets. It is a grass-covered enclosure with the graves of several of his wives. It is covered with a single granite slab about six by eight feet and surmounted by an iron railing set in the margins of the slabs. The slab bears a simple inscription which embraces his name and dates of birth and death. The casket is embedded in masonry and cement twelve feet deep. There is a story—probably apocryphal—to the effect that dynamite cartridges were imbedded in the cement about the grave to prevent the stealing of the body. It was suggested by one to whom the story was told that it was a cruel thing to expose one who had been the husband of twenty-six wives to the possibility of a postmortem blowing up!

With the advent of the railroad and a large Gentile population came many changes in Salt Lake City—some for the better and some for the worse. The little ward schoolhouse, modeled after the country schoolhouse of the beginning of the century, has given place to the modern public school building, large, airy and well equipped with modern appliances. Salt Lake City has an actual population of perhaps 50,000; 12,000 being children of scholastic age. Our teachers, drawn from the ranks of both Mormons and Gentiles, are wide awake and up to date. Books are furnished free of cost. This places an education within reach of all.

With the railroad and the Gentiles came the saloon. Now many business blocks are literally honey-combed with these recruiting offices for the inebriate army, and both Mormons and Gentiles are found on both sides of the bar. Yet Salt Lake City is as orderly and quiet as the average city of its size. As in the West, Sunday desecration is so common as not to attract much attention. It is by the classes who would desecrate it anywhere.

W. H. BAGBY.

The Chicago Letter.

Shall we be optimistists or pessimists? This question is not so easy to answer as the light-headed and shallow-hearted suppose. Some of the greatest philosophers, from the writer of the Koheleth to Schopenhauer, have been pessimists. It is not always easy to say with the optimistic Browning, in the song of Pippa:

"God's in his heaven,
All's right with the world."

Yes, God is in his heaven. Let us never doubt that "all things work together for [the ultimate] good to them that love God." But does it necessarily follow that—

"All's right with the world?"

At times we must take short views in life to keep our frail hearts from breaking with their weight of woe. Again, we must look through long vistas of time to reassure our questioning hearts of the goodness of God and the ultimate triumph of truth and righteousness. Let us "be brave," and though our eyes be filled with tears because a loved boy has wandered far from home in health, or another is called home from far away on account of threatened disease, let us trust God and say with the poet of optimism:

"My own hope is, a sun will pierce
The thickest cloud earth ever stretched."

***

Shall we be optimists, or pessimists? This question not only forces itself upon the fond mother because her boy is working his way in some great city, or fighting for his native land on the high sea, but forces itself upon the noble philanthropist who sincerely struggles to ameliorate the condition of his workingmen, upon the lover of civic righteousness, upon the preacher, who prefers Christ to Kant, and sincerity to sham. It is sometimes difficult to realize that humanity is sloping upward through darkness to God by slow degrees, by more and more. The progress is so slow and there must be such constant tacking against the winds of tendency and the hurricanes of sin. Four years ago the disgraceful and demoralizing gambling at the Washington Park races aroused the public conscience sufficiently to make the mayor and public officials take steps to stop the races. Mayor Harrison's administration, however, has been trying to make gambling respectable, but like the man in the fable he finds the warmed serpent unmanageable. Indeed, as he is reported to have said that "a game of poker is good," some fear that he enjoys running a wide-open town. Nothing could be more discouraging to our optimistic hopes, that we were to have good government in Chicago, than the opening of the Washington Park races again. For over a month Chicago will be wild with the gambling spirit. Mothers, plead with your boys to shun Chicago during these days as they would shun perdition itself.

***

"Experience is the best of teachers." This is an old adage, but is it always true? I doubt whether a bad experience is ever a good teacher. The thoughtless man says: "Let the boy sow his wild oats; he will learn better by experience." Alas! there are some experiences which the dear boy cannot unlearn. And if it it is well for the boy to smoke a little and for the business man to gamble a little to learn that it is injurious to smoke and gamble, why not advise our girls to sin against their bodies and our women against all business principles? Is the girl who goes to the dance clad so as to insure a severe cold any better for an experience which puts her emaciated form under the beautiful daisies in a few months? Thirty-five per cent. of the young men who offered themselves for naval services recently were rejected because their sight was impaired, or their lungs weakened by the smoking habit. Can such an experience be construed as beneficial to our young men? While Leiter dealt in cash wheat his success was phenomenal. One month's dealing "in futures" cost him from three to five million dollars. People say: "He has learned a good lesson." I should rather say, he has learned a *bad* lesson. The habit of gambling, like the habit of drinking, grows by experience. But will not other men learn by Leiter's experience that gambling in wheat is bad business, as well as bad morals? No. There are hundreds of men, some of them deacons in Christian churches, who will read this paragraph and go on gambling; trusting their fortunes and the happiness of their wives and children to the men who run "bucket shops" in Chicago, and who call the country merchants entrusting their fortunes to them "suckers."

***

Brother and Sister J. H. Garrison passed through the city on their way to Macatawa Park. They remained over one night in Chicago and Mrs. Young and I esteemed it a great privilege to have them in our home. Such associations make us optimists.

"And all is well, though faith and form
Be sundered in the night of fear;
Well roars the storm to those who hear
A deeper voice across the storm."

C. A. YOUNG.

Our National Bureau of Education.

At a meeting of the superintendence departmet of the National Educational Association, held at Washington in February, 1866, a memorial to Congress signed by State School Superintendent E. E. White, of Ohio; Newton Bateman, of Illinois, and J. S. Adams, of Vermont, urged the establishment of a National Bureau of Education. The memorial was presented to the House by Gen. Garfield and strongly championed by him. The same course was pursued in the Senate. After some efforts and delays an office of education under the control of the Department of the Interior was established, and a meager sum set apart for its maintenance. The act securing this result was dated July 28, 1868, and took effect June 30, 1869, which is the real beginning of the bureau.

The original purpose in the establishment of this bureau was that of "collecting such statistics and facts as shall show the condition and progress of education in the several states and territories, and of diffusing such information respecting the organization and management of school systems and methods of teaching as shall aid the people of the United States in the establishment and maintenance of efficient school systems and otherwise promote the cause of education." At first the theory of state sovereignty, still entertained by those in regions most likely to be benefited, was jealous of the operations of a bureau whose purpose was confessedly just and philanthropic. It was secretly intimated that this new bureau would attempt to unify and control educational interests manifestly within the sphere and jurisdiction of the respective states. This fear, confessedly not well grounded, did much to hamper and circumscribe the usefulness of the bureau by limiting its yearly appropriations to a mere pittance, and otherwise checking the beneficent work it was intended to accomplish.

Edmund Burke said, "Education is the cheap defense of nations." That this language was given a very literal and, perhaps, unworthy interpretation is manifest when we remember that despite the most excellent work this bureau has done, and the incalculable benefits it has conferred upon the schools and school systems of the country, the aggregate appropriation for its maintenance has, after thirty years, reached only the meager sum of $57,270, distributed as follows: Salaries, $52,020; collection of statistics, $2,500; purchase and distribution of documents, $2,500; increase of library, $250.

Ten of our great battleships, viz., Alabama, Illinois, Indiana, Iowa, Kearsarge, Kentucky, Massachusetts, Oregon, Texas and Wisconsin, cost in the aggregate $32,280,000. This expense being a necessity is not unreasonable. We all rejoice at this time that they have been built, and some are doing efficient service in the present war with Spain. But stop to think of the "cheap defense" to the nation our Bureau of Education, which costs annually only about one-fiftieth part of the least expensive of these battleships, the Texas. The Bureau of Education, however imperfectly equipped it has been, and crowded in its apartments, has built up the largest pedagogical library in America, if not in the world. In its library, on the 30th of June, 1897, were 72,725 books and 150,000 pamphlets. It is doing an immense amount of educational work in the way of furnishing statistical information of great value, and it is gratifying to know that this information is being eagerly sought by schools, colleges, libraries and progressive public men everywhere. Within the last few years the publication of annual reports, previously much hindered, has been facilitated, and the management hope to see all work of this character brought up to date within the next year.

Within the next month superintendents, teachers and educational workers from all parts of the nation will visit our city in attendance upon the sessions of the National Educational Association. Probably 25,000 people will be here, the advance guard of the great hosts of educators who constitute the true standing army of the republic. It is sincerely hoped that in the near future such statesmanship will be developed in our legislative and executive departments as shall secure these results:

1. Raise the Bureau of Education to the rank of a regular department on a footing with those of Agriculture, War and the Navy—a rank which it legitimately deserves; 2. Give it an equipment in the matter of building and grounds commensurate with its importance as one of the agencies in the "cheap defense of nations;" 3. Furnish an appropriation in harmony with the value and importance of the great work it is accomplishing and qualified to accomplish; 4. Recognize the worth of talent in its management as in other branches of the public service. In that case a man of national, yea, international, reputation would not be expected to give his services at a salary which is a mere pittance of what like ability would command in other fields of intellectual activity.

When this happy day shall have arrived the teachers of the nation will, on visiting the nation's beautiful capital, be thoroughly convinced that our government practically believes the declaration of England's eloquent statesman, that "education is the cheap defense of nations."

J. FRAISE RICHARD.

Texas Letter.

The wheat and oat crop of Texas, unusually fine this year, has suffered much from recent rains—perhaps one-third. Cotton, though late, is promising, and corn prospects and hay are good, while cattle are fine. So, on the whole, the outlook is full of comfort.

J. J. Cramer, of Lockhart, is off on a well-deserved vacation. He has been at Lockhart about eight years. One of the best evidences of his good work there is the $10,000 house now being built.

L. G. Ament, who has lately come into fellowship with our "progressive" work, locates at Sabinal and will labor in the regions near there.

C. A. Mullens, an Add-Ran boy of promise, locates at Pearsall, an important place in the southern part of the state near the Mexican line.

J. H. Rosecrans, our "sweet singer," is well enough once more to enter the field. He will hold a series of protracted meetings this summer.

J. A. Tabor leaves Corsicana for Oklahoma City, Ok., where his wife will teach, while he preaches to churches adjacent.

T. D. Secrest, of Coleman, is recovering from a dangerous sickness, and our people rejoice, for Bro. Secrest is one of our purest and strongest men.

J. B. Haston, of California, returnes Texas to take up the work at Galveston. He is a good successor of Bro. E. H. Kellar, and the Island City church is fortunate.

G. B. Crenshaw goes from Taylor to San Antonio, a strong man for an important place. San Antonio's trouble has been that her men do not stay long enough; hence we hope that Bro. Crenshaw will be a fixture with them.

G. H. Morrison leaves El Paso and goes to Alvarado. He is one of our best young men, and he locates in one of the best sections of the state.

W. K. Homan is in a meeting at San Angelo. Editing the Courier is not enough for him. Occasionally he must hold a meeting to work off his surplus energy.

G. A. Hoffmann made a flying trip to Texas a few weeks since. He broke bread with us in our home and preached a sermon at the Central. Hoffmann is a success. He scented something good for the Bible College at Columbia, and he at once came, saw, and conquered about $20,000. If Missouri wants anything else from Texas, let her send down.

Miss Jennie Belle Terry, of the Central

n the Chair of Elocution
; Lancaster, and she wil
e selection.
a meeting at Sulphur
is converts is J. H. Da-
in political parlance as
e is a man of ability,
sefulness in the church.
ı slips in a sentence or
ıe of all Dallasites when
ılation at 38,067, which,
of last year, is 64,224. A
ıable maiden are much
e, one over her age, and
. Tyler's aim was good,
ancient.

M. M. DAVIS.

ıllas, Texas.

m in '98.

eeting at Hiram on com-
st closed. Thirty-one of
ent all years of the life
; the remaining years
the Western Reserve
of which Hiram College

k is always an interest-
de-awake and growing
Iiram is no exception to
laureate sermon to the
ed by President Zollars,
tenth annual sermon he
ose who are competent to
e of the very best of the
grown in power, so has
limit of growth in power
ot yet been reached by

y societies of the college
etings on Monday night.
the business of the year,
the occasion of honor-
from their halls with the
he year. This year the
exceptionally fine.
Conservatory of Music,"
of Prof. Eugene Feuch-
k within modest bounds
musical department of
surpassed by any college
ly in the United States.
equal to it, it is to be
rendering of *Rossini's*
'*Stabot Mater*,"on Tues-
ent. Sixty voices, well
s choruses. The leading
Misses Jennie M. Welch,
Dean, Lucele F. Snow,
. Addie Zollars Page, R.
. Green and Frank C.
se were imported for the
the home force, trained
Professor Feuchtinger.
atorio, so well rendered,
se the truth of Addison's

eat inspires,
ul and lifts it high,
ı sublime desires,
speak the Deity."

evoted to the "class of
meeting of the board of
terary entertainment and
c Society.
cement day, was an ideal
ot one never dawned on
ıt congregation was pre-
sentatives of the graduat-
tire class numbered 37.
eir names, each of which

.—Howard Allen Blake,
len, Will Jay Crum, Wil-
Alonzo Willard Fortune,
, Delbert Edgar Graver,

PHILOSOPHICAL COURSE.—Mary Alice Canfield, Earl Brockway Newton, Henry Wallace Murray, Elizabeth Roberts, Elizabeth Lorena Way.

SCIENTIFIC COURSE.—Clinton Mason Young.

LITERARY COURSE.—Thomas Leland Baxter Blanche Mabel Beck, Ethel Carrie Caskey, Harvey F. Fetzer, Justin N. Green, Zach A. Harris, James Johnson, Orville Titus Manley, Levi J. McConnel, Clara Worst Miller, Lorenzo Orville Packer, Esther Buckingham Patterson, Susie Letitia Rawson, Carl David Thayer, Samuel Traum, Leonard J. Wilson.

Besides these there were several who received diplomas for post-graduate work, and the degree of A. M. in course. On four persons honorary degrees were conferred as follows: The degree of LL. D. on Judge Don A. Pardee, of Louisiana; LL. D. on Hon. Andrew Squire, of Ohio; A. M. on W. H. Brett, Librarian of the city of Cleveland, O., and A. M. on J. H. Calvin, of Salem, O. These are worthy of the honor bestowed on them. The brief addresses to the graduating class by the class professors, Colman Bancroft and G. A. Peckham, and the address of President Zollars in presenting the diplomas, were gems of their kind.

The afternoon of commencement day was given up to the Alumni of the college and the old students. After the literary program had been executed, about 125 sat down at the Alumni banquet.

Hon. C. B. Lockwood was chosen president of the board of trustees, F. M. Green vice-president, and Alanson Wilcox secretary. The meeting of the board of trustees revealed the fact that the affairs of the college are in good condition. What Hiram needs now more than anything else is a large increase in its permanent endowment. About $30,000 have been added during the past year to this fund. The proceeds, however, of this addition are not yet the largest in the history of the institution. The average term attendance for 1897 and 1898 was 338. There were 421 different students during the year, of which 156 were ladies and 265 were gentlemen. Hiram makes no plea for help except on the basis of merit. It stands high among the colleges of the state of Ohio, and takes no second place among the colleges that represent the Disciples of Christ. Liberty in the noblest sense, loyalty to the Word of God, and abiding confidence in the great mission of the Disciples are characteristics of Hiram. Here any one with the form of a man, the mind of a man, and the heart of a man, is welcome no matter what the color of his skin, the character of his ancestry, or the conditions of his childhood, and until he forfeits his place by his own wrong-doing his welcome is not abridged and his tenure to the friendship of the college is unbroken. Hiram has a history, but she rests not on that only for her recognition. With dauntless face she looks into the future and promises a rich harvest to those who invest their means for her present success and her future enlargement and possibilities. Hiram is no provincial school. Her students during the year just closed came from Ohio, Maryland, Pennsylvania, Indiana, Mississippi, South Australia, New York, Iowa, Canada, Japan, Minnesota, Kentucky, Texas, South Dakota, New Mexico, Illinois, Virginia, Washington, D. C., Florida, Georgia, Wisconsin, Maine and Missouri.

Hiram enters on the new year in her history with high hope, and may her hope be realized.

F. M. GREEN.

Kent, O.

Notes and News.

The Harlem Avenue Church, Baltimore, has secured a corner lot in the northwestern part of the city and contemplates a new house of worship soon.

The annual convention of the New York Christian Missionary Society will assemble with the Church of Christ at 169th Street, New York City, N. Y., August 31, 1898 and continue to September 2nd.

The annual meeting of the Disciples of Christ on Prince Edward Island will meet at Montague, P. E. I., from July 8 to 11, 1898.

The annual convention of Disciples of Christ in New Brunswick and Nova Scotia, at Tiverton, N. S., Aug. 11-14, 1898.

Owing to the continued absence of Dr. Klapsch, superintendent of the Sunday-school at Sterling Place, it has been well managed by Bro. John R. Tuler, a faithful Disciple. The school is in a promising condition. A large donation in cash was made to assist the church. Reports show an increase of attendance over last year. Dr. Klapsch was present but one Lord's day during the year. Bro. Tuler seemed to fill his place successfully. The school adjourned last Sunday for the summer vacation until Sept. 13.

T. DE QUINCY TULLY.

Brooklyn, N. Y., June 23, 1898.

We are now in the fourth week of a meeting conducted by H. Warner Newby, of Denver, Col. Much wealth has been added to the church in heads of families. The additions to date are mostly middle-aged people. Bro. Newby is a forcible speaker. He is highly spiritual and is a power in the pulpit for good. No church will make a mistake in securing him as evangelist. I have known him personally several years and know of many hundreds of baptisms by his hands.

A. A. ARTHUR, pastor.

Washington, Kan., June 25, 1898.

Monday, June 20th, 1798, at Greeley, Ia., I had the pleasure of uniting in marriage Bro. C. L. Organ and Miss Katie G. Kleckner. Bro. Organ is the popular young minister of the Church of Christ at Greeley. This is his first work in the ministry. He is loved by all classes for his work's sake. Sister Organ is an estimable and worthy young lady, and will be an efficient helpmeet in her husband's chosen work.

W. M. HOLLETT.

Arlington, Ia.

Our Children's Day exercises were held in the church on the 17th inst. Our auditorium, which had just been refrescoed and recarpeted, was filled to its utmost capacity. Many were turned away. The collection has exceeded all all anticipations. It has reached $130.17, with others to hear from. The birthday box gave us $14.84.

W. J. MORRISON, Supt.

Bellaire, O., June 27, 1898.

During the year just closing we have added 22 to the Forest City congregation and succeeded in getting all the discords harmonized. At Bluff City we baptized six during the year. This is my mission point and the Lord is blessing our labors there. We have gathered in about 36 members there. The Forest City congregation has given me a call for another year, one-half time. The third Lord's day in this month we baptized a gentleman 53 years old at Forest City. His wife has been a member for a long time and he has been a good man. The Baptist pastor attended our meeting in January during the delivery of a series of discourses on first principles and the leaven changed the lump and Elder A. R. Hunt united with the Church of Christ at Tarkio, the third Lord's day in June. He is a young man of unblemished character. Has been the pastor of the Baptist Church here for four years. Everybody likes him and the congregation that secures him as pastor will always rejoice. Bro. Hunt is a conscientious man of good education. He is a graduate of the Baptist College of Liberty, Mo., and brings to us the experience of a six years' ministry.

W. H. HARDMAN.

Closed a meeting of three weeks last Lord's day evening at Carthage, S. D. We had only four added during the meeting, and they by letter. We found a few badly disconraged Disciples, but succeeded in locating a pastor in the person of H. C. Shipley, of Drake University. He takes the work for three months, and if suited to the field will continue. Bro. W. H. Mullins, president State Board of South Dakota Missionary Society, had been running over from Hetland and preaching to them twice per month, and had succeeded in sufficiently reviving them as to undertake the meeting. Miss Pearl Wiley led the singing. She is a good leader and a very fine soloist. She belonged to the Congregationalits, but united with us during the meeting. She is ready to sing for meetings. Churches or evangelists wanting a singer for meetings cannot make a mistake in getting Sister Wiley. Address her at Carthage, S. D. This state is a fine field and young men willing to work can find plenty to do. Most every town has more or less Disciples. Go look them up and establish a church and preach to it.

WEMPSEY A. HUNTER.

Jefferson, Ia., June 23, 1898.

Evangelistic.

MISSOURI.

Golden City, June 27.—Filled my regular appointment at Nashville yesterday. There were eight additions. Three came in the month before. Four additions here at last meeting.—W. A. WARREN, JR.

NEW YORK.

Gloversville, June 23.—I began a meeting here on Wednesday, the 22nd, in the W. T. C. U. parlor. This is a beautiful little city of about 17,000 people. I find no church organization, but 15 or 20 good people, who are loyal Disciples. Our meetings are growing in numbers and in interest. I hope to plant a good church. —J. M. MORRIS, state evangelist.

ILLINOIS.

Taylorville, June 27, 1898.—Baptized two yesterday; four additions since last report.—W. W. WEEDON.

LaHarpe, June 27.—Preached four nights at Trumbull, last week; baptized eight. There were four added at our regular services here Sunday night.—K. C. VENTRESS.

NORTH DAKOTA.

Ellendale, June 27.—We began a meeting here yesterday. W. A. Foster is doing the preaching. I am leader of song.—T. S. NOBLITT, pastor.

SOUTH DAKOTA.

Carthage, June 26.—Two additions.—H. C. SHIPLEY.

ARKANSAS.

Eureka Springs, June 28, 1898.—One confession and baptism. Summer visitors arriving and prospects brightening in every respect.—DANIEL TRUNDLE.

Kansas City, Mo.—I had a delightful visit at Newport, Ark; five confessions. Bro. J. H. Fuller is the pastor, and I have never met a young man who impressed me more favorably. Why he is allowed by our larger churches, that need strong men, to stay down there and labor largely at his own charges, can only be accounted for on the ground that they don't know him. Let some strong church that wants a man call Bro. Fuller. July and August, especially the latter, are fine months for tabernacle meetings. I want to help some congregation during these months; write me.—T. W. COTTINGHAM.

INDIANA.

Portland Mills, June 23.—We closed last night the best meeting Portland has had for 40 years. We had 37 additions. Started the congregation on a self-supporting basis and have reorganized for permanent work. Bro. Jack Ashley, of Indianapolis, did the preaching and the singing was conducted by Bro. Walter Rhodes, of Peoria, Ill.—SAMUEL MCMANUS, Elder.

IOWA.

Mt. Auburn, June 27.—Closed a short meeting here the 15th inst. Results 15 additions.—JAS. T. NICHOLS.

Stuart, June 27.—One confession here yesterday at our regular service.—E. T. MCFARLAND.

Dows, June 27.—Two additions at regular service. We organized a Y. P. S. C. E. last night. This is a new field. We will begin the Endeavor work with about 15 members and perhaps several honorary members and some associate members. Most of the members here are old people, but we hope to get the young ones interested.—F. L. DAVIS.

INDIAN TERRITORY.

South McAlester, June 27.—Meeting closed after two weeks' work. Poor preaching and no work by the members. Small collections and six additions by letter. I go to Mena, Ark., where my next meeting is.—ARTHUR W. JONES, evangelist.

TENNESSEE.

Clarksville.—A fine meeting June 26th; one confession.—A. M. GROWDEN, pastor Church of Christ.

MINNESOTA.

Evangelist A. B. Moore is now at Redwood Falls in a tent meeting with good attendance. Prof. J. Howard Sweetman is his colaborer as singing evangelist (D. L. Smith, the former singer, having been obliged to leave the state in consequence of a slight throat affection), and a good work is anticipated. But one cloud dots the horizon, and that is that K. W. White, the pastor, has resigned to leave for another field, July 6th. Another pastor will be secured at once, or at the earliest day practicable. The Austin meeting, held by Bro. Moore, continued three weeks with three additions, though Bro. Moore continued with the brethren three weeks longer in the interest of the erection of a church home. Thirty-one brethren are congregated in this town of 500 population, of whom Bro. Moore writes: "They are a plucky little band and I can't help admiring them. I have not based my standard of success on simply numbering accessions, but on service to Christ; being willing to work with and for them to the end that a church should be established that would go on. Allowing for my hopefulness, I think a chapel can be completed by winter and no bigger burden be on the congregation than it now bears in paying hall rent. People are now getting the impression that we mean to make it a success and considerable interest is manifested by some of the people outside. Offers of money in small amounts have been tendered, if we build, and this unsolicited. Regarding the meeting proper, will say that it started well the first week, but that war excitement killed it. A regiment was raised and we could not recover from the effects."—FRANK H. MELLEN, Sec.

UTAH.

Salt Lake City, June 27.—Three added here yesterday by letter from another religious body. —W. H. BAGBY.

MICHIGAN.

Algonac, June 26.—One confession here yesterday at regular service.—J. L. SMITH.

Literature.

MAGAZINES.

A master hand has pictured the life and influence of the late William Ewart Gladstone in The Chautauquan for July. Pres. Charles J. Little, of Northwestern University, has shown the "Grand Old Man" as a statesman, a man man of God and a stern advocate of justice. "Old Ironsides," by Edward S. Ellis, A. M., is a character sketch of "Commodore" Charles Stewart, who in his eighty-third year demanded of President Lincoln to be allowed to enter the service of his country.

The Review of Reviews continues strong on war topics. In the July number the editor reviews the whole campaign up to the landing of our troops for the advance on Santiago, showing the precise part which Lieutenant Hobson's exploit had in the general scheme; Dr. William Hayes Ward treats of Hobson's career as that of the typical young American student; Mr. Edwin Emerson, Jr., the brilliant young newspaper correspondent, gives notes of his adventurous journeyings in Porto Rico last month; and Dr. Max West, the statistician and economist, summarizes "Our New War Taxes" in an interesting article. "International Cartoon Comments on Our War with Spain" and the "Record of Current Events" also cover the situation up to date.

The leading article in Pall Mall for July deals with naval problems to be solved in the present war. The author, Mr. H. W. Wilson, is a naval expert and his opinions will attract a wide interest in the naval world.

The Woman's Home Companion for July is a companionable number. The patriotic articles in prose and poetry are in touch with the times, and all departments filled with fresh interesting literature.

The new features of the midsummer number of the Ladies' Home Journal makes it one of the handsomest and most interesting numbers of the year. The August number, it is announced, will be made up almost entirely of fiction. The July number is a compliment to our President.

The table of contents of the July Century is suggestive of an exceptionally interesting number. It breathes strongly of the patriotic spirit, while its numerous articles bearing directly and indirectly on naval and army maneuvers and men make a historic number of no little value. Variety in its literature, however, is not wanting. Its characteristically broad scope of subjects is as prominent as usual.

There are many seasonable features in the July number of St. Nicholas. All boys and girls will be interested in "Some Ships of Our Navy," a series of fifteen pictures of representative American war vessels, reproduced from photographs. Lieutenant Philip Andrews, U. S. N., describes the "Ceremonies and Etiquette of a Man-of-War," showing the honors with which distinguished visitors are received on board, the different kinds of salutes, etc.

The Lectureship.

The Missouri Christian Lectureship and the Missouri Christian Ministerial Association will convene this year at Carrollton. July 18-22 is the *time* and *now* is the time for you to decide to attend, if you have not already made such decision. An unusually fine program has been announced, and the church at Carrollton is anxious to entertain you. Let all who expect to attend send to me their names, that homes may be provided. Come. J. T. Ogle.

Family Circle.

A Hidden Singer.

LISA A. FLETCHER.

She sang with all the tender grace
Of one who knoweth Sorrow's face,
And beautiful of soul and strong,
Breathed forth her ministries of song.

Beauty her spirit strangely stirred,
Thrilled it with music like a bird,
Who to its winsome mate its love
Pours forth ecstatic song to prove.

Though life to her seemed unfulfilled,
Yet down the years her songs distilled
In many a heart to her unknown,
A joy responsive to her own.

Could she have seen when some sweet thought
With deep and tender meanings fraught,
Winged comfort to some soul afar,
Shining upon it like a star,

Her own heart had the happier been,
And throbbed with keener joy within;
Yet no sweeter strain had breathed to earth
Than that which drew from pain its birth.

Afar from worldly din and strife,
Patient was lived the hidden life
Of one who bore the cross of pain,
Bequeathing us the final gain.

One who in life wore not the crown,
And years have passed and years have flown,
Since meekly all life's lessons conned,
She passed into the Great Beyond.

Manchester, N. H.

JUDAS MACCABÆUS.

MARY BLACK CLAYTON.

When the conscience of Cyrus of Babylon prompted him to permit the remnant of the Jewish nation to return to the city of their love, what a joyful procession must have stretched its great length over the plain. Ezra, the Scribe, tells us that the whole congregation together was forty-two thousand three hundred and sixty, besides their servants and their maids, who numbered three hundred and thirty-seven, with horses, mules and camels innumerable. This great host turned eagerly toward Jerusalem, the holiest spot on earth, made more precious by the homesicknesses and longings of seventy years. Their joy was suppressed, however, when they came upon the desolation of the Holy City. The gates were prone, the glorious temple had been leveled, and the vineyards, olive groves and wheat fields laid barren before them. Such was their home coming, but peacefully, persistently and faithfully, they built and restored and tilled. The city gates were uplifted. The walls were partially rebuilt and fortified, but not after the impregnable manner of the days of David. A temple rose on the ancient site, which did not dazzle with gold and precious stones, and was not inlaid with such costly woods as was Solomon's magnificent pile, but within its walls the happy people practiced in peace the rites of their religion. Green came again upon the fields, and the fruits of the earth were plentiful.

The Persian kings protected the colony, the internal government being administered by the High Priest, which was an hereditary office.

Thus God's people worshiped and worked for two hundred years, making no history, and inspiring no jealousy, until, at length, the ground of Judea shakes with the tread of the army of the young conqueror of the world—Alexander the Great. Persia had fallen before his ever-victorious arms, and with it Judea had come under his dominion.

The rumor reaches Jerusalem that he, the Unconquerable One, is coming. Prayers and sacrifices are ordained by the High Priest. He clothes himself in the awful insignia of his office, the mitre upon which the name of God is emblazoned rests upon his brow, and his garments are of precious purple and blue and pure linen.

The remainder of the faithful are clad in robes of white. The High Priest leads his people, in procession, without the gates, to a high hill overlooking Jerusalem.

When Alexander reaches the Holy City, and sees the white and shining throng, and the mitre upon which flashes the name of God, he stands forth from his army, and adores the Deity of the Jews. Afterwards he gives his right hand to God's High Priest and thus taking the lead, he marches into Jerusalem followed by his soldiers, and the men of Israel.

Right gracious and gentle he was, granting the requests of the High Priest as to laws and tributes, and fascinating, by his splendor and his clemency, many of the young men of Judea who were willing to join his legions and carry his triumphal banners.

His yoke was not burdensome, but his military career was meteoric, lasting only twelve years. He died at the age of thirty-two, in 323 B. C.

Shortly after his death Ptolemy of Egypt stormed Jerusalem on the Sabbath, the Jews refusing to join battle on the holy day. Judea became the battle ground for the contending armies of Egypt and Syria.

The anguish of tyranny and destruction fell upon the devoted people of God, when King Antiochus IV. of Syria took possession of Jerusalem. His crimes against the Jews form one of the most awful stories which stain the pages of history. To begin with, he deposed the High Priest, destroyed the sacred books, stole the gold and silver vessels used in the service, dedicated God's Holy Place to Jupiter, established idol worship in it, and finally drove a herd of swine through its sacred precincts. The women and children of the Jews were carried into captivity, and a general massacre was ordered, in which, according to Josephus, 40,000 people were murdered. Antiochus also caused to be built a stony fortress upon an eminence commanding Jerusalem and the Temple, in which he placed a strong garrison of Syrian soldiers. Many of the stricken people fled to the more serene countries, Greece, Italy and Egypt. There they were peaceable and industrious, but entirely unyielding in regard to a change of religion. They carried their faith with them, and in all the large cities which gave them shelter, synagogues arose. The Apocrypha ends this story of desolation in these words: "And there was very great wrath upon Israel."

The time is ripe for a deliverer. In countries, or families, help is wont to come from Heaven when the skies grow too dark to see God's face. In Modin, near the sea, lived an old man, wise, influential, rich, named Mattathias. He was the fortunate father of five valiant and faithful sons. He was aroused to a just fury when he saw the most sacred places of his people robbed and ruined, fair Judea laid waste and his countrymen murdered for the sake of their religion. When the Syrian officers urged them to worship on the altars which Antiochus had substituted for the service of the Most High, the brave old man cried aloud with a voice like the roar of a hungry lion, "Though all the nations that are under the King's dominion obey him, and fall away every one from the religion of their fathers, and give their consent to his commandments, yet will my sons, my brethren and I walk in the covenant of our fathers!" As the words left his lips, he saw one of his people worshiping according to the commands of the wicked King. He could not control his zeal, and slew the traitor where he kneeled. While his wrath was hot he also killed the King's commissioner, whose business it was to compel the Jews to worship false gods. Roused and reeking Mattathias, followed by his sons, rushed through the streets of the city crying, "Whosoever is zealous of the law and maintaineth the covenant, let him follow me." The adherents of the wrathful old leader increased in number like the growth of a rolling snowball, and many men, women and children followed him to the wilderness. They were pursued. It was the Sabbath. The Jews refused to fight, preferring, as they said, "to die in their innocency." One thousand Jews were put to death by the Syrian army. Mattathias escaped, but was so stricken by the fate of his followers that after weighing in the balance human life, and literal obedience without reservation, he decided in favor of fighting on the Sabbath, if he should be attacked on that day. The outraged and patriotic Jews rallied around him, and, with old age upon him, he made superhuman efforts for his people. In one year he succeeded in raising an army, drove the invading Syrians from Judea, overthrew the altars of the heathen and restored the law. He did not gain his fighting material by the offer of pelf or plunder. In return for fidelity to God and country he assured his men of a glorious immortality. His last words were, "Wherefore, ye my sons, be valiant and show yourselves men in the behalf of the law, for by it you shall often glory. And behold, I know that your brother Simon is a man of counsel, give ear unto him always; he shall be a father unto you. As for Judas Maccabæus, he hath been mighty and strong even from his youth up, let him be your captain, and fight the battles of the people." Then the old man, wise in counsel, and brave in battle, went to the place set apart for heroes, at the ripe age of one hundred and forty-four years.

Judas, surnamed Maccabæus (supposed to mean hammer or hard knocks), wore the mantle of his father, and it fitted him more exactly than the mantles of most great men fit their sons.

The family name of these defenders of the faith was Asmon, but Judas, being greater and more conspicuous than his brethren, they go down in history collectively as the Maccabees.

We are told that Judas "fought with great cheerfulness the battles of Israel, so he got his people great honor, and put on a breastplate as a giant, and girt his warlike harness upon him, and he made battles, protecting the host with his sword. In his acts he was like a lion, and like a lion's whelp roaring for its prey."

Apolonius, military governor of Samaria, set forth to rid the earth of this man, so bold and rash, who, with a small and undisciplined band of men, expected to defy him—Apolonius. They clashed in battle, the hammerer hammered, and Judas the Mighty slew the military governor of Samaria, and during the rest of his career used the sword of the Syrian upon the bodies of the enemies of the Lord. It was a goodly weapon, well tempered and jeweled, and the flash of it was the last thing in sight of many men who warred with Judas. A great many of the heathen bit the dust upon the day of the sword capture, and the set showed their backs in retreat, and Judas got their spoils.

Next comes Seron, who is higher in rank than Apolonius, has more soldiers, and is commander-in-chief of the Syrian forces in Palestine. He said, "I will get a name and honor in the kingdom, for I will go fight with Judas, and them that are with him who despise the king's commandments. He chooses well his time for attack, and falls upon Judas when his following is small, and his men are weary and fasting, and appalled by the imposing array of the enemy's army. The great leader of Israel cheers his drooping soldiers by his bravery and faith in God, saying "the victory to battle standeth not in the multitude, but strength cometh from Heaven." The result justified the faith of Judas. Seron and his great army were routed. The name and fame of Judas Maccabæus became a terror to the heathen nations.

Then Antiochus, the wicked king of Syria, vowed the extermination of this rebellious horde of Jews. He gathered a mighty force, paid them a year in advance, hired mercenaries from foreign countries to help them, and vowed he would "break" Jerusalem before spring—but before that time came he had decided to break Jerusalem by proxy. He repaired to Persia to exact tribute from the various provinces, and to seize the treasures which were supposed to be hidden in royal cities beyond the Euphrates. All this plunder was to be used to trample the life out of the Jewish nation. Half his forces went with him to rifle foreign parts, and the other half were to fight under Lysias, a nobleman of princely blood, who was to be commander-in-chief, vice Antiochus, who had gone plundering to Persia. Lysias selected three mighty men of the king's household to be his lieutenants, gave them forty thousand footmen, and seven thousand horsemen, and ordered them to hunt down the rebels and destroy them.

When Judas and his brothers discovered that the eneny, in large numbers, was camping on their borders, they rallied their followers, and prepared for the greatest struggle of their lives.

The first step Judas took in preparation for the coming strife was to discharge those of his army who were newly married, who were building a house, who had planted a vineyard, or who were "fearful" lest love of life should interfere with their courage, and thus stampede the whole host. The last step he took in preparation was to ask the compassion of the God of battles, and remind his soldiers of the persecutions and sorrows of their people, saying, "Fear ye not this multitude—remember how our fathers were delivered in the Red Sea when Pharaoh pursued them with an army." Beyond the help which cometh from Above, Judas had three thousand men, badly equipped, intrenched in the mountains about twenty miles from Jerusalem. There the enemy expected to surprise the Jews and rout them. The generalship of Judas was never at fault, however, the traits of the lion and the fox being blended in his character. He discovered the plans of the foe, broke his camp, and did the surprising himself. He approached the enemy warily, and rushed his troops upon the unprepared Syrians with a force like that of the American fall at Niagara when it leaps over the cliff, the enemy showed disappearing backs, Judas pursued them, and killed three thousand of them, the number killed being as great as the size of the whole army of Judas, and took immense spoil of gold and silver, and purple and blue silk, which was hoarded for the adornment of the Temple of God.

When Lysias, the commander-in-chief, learned the awful disaster of his army he was confounded and dismayed. Nevertheless he began at once to make preparation to overpower Judea with a force so strong that it must put an end to the struggle. In the following year he attempted to carry out this plan, with the same result of utter defeat and disgrace of the Syrian arms.

This tale of war-harness, attacks, defeats, victories and pursuits, grows monotonous, and it is a pleasing variety to write that our mighty warrior before the Lord could unbuckle his armor, and between his sword flashes, go up to Jerusalem the Holy and much chastened, to purify and restore the sanctuary, which had lain desolate for five years. At the first sight of its ruin the men of war mourned, rending their garments and putting ashes on their heads. How strange this manner of exhibiting grief in the times of antiquity, seems to us, who spare our garments and our hearts are rent! Then began the sacred work, which is always better than lamentation. The altars of Jehovah were fitted for his service, the gates uplifted, the grass grown court restored, the priests' chambers prepared for them, new holy vessels were made, the front of the temple was adorned with crowns and shields of gold, and Judas protected the temple with high walls and towers which he garrisoned with soldiers, for the Syrians still held the baleful fortress, which threatened the temple and the city. With sacrifices and songs and prayers and feasting, the glad people rededicated their sanctuary, and as long as it stood, the anniversary of its restoration was held sacred and called the feast of the dedication.

Justice fell upon Antiochus, called the Great, who had gone to Persia to gather pelf with which to persecute the Jews. On his way to Judea he received news of the defeat of the army of Lysias, and the worshipers of Jehovah were in a fair way to freedom, wrought by the sword of Judas Maccabæus. Filled with overmastering fury, he was stricken with a sudden illness, which was called "distemper" by Josephus and less vaguely by Dr. Lord, elephantrasis. At any rate, he was loathsome to his friends and attendants. When he knew death was upon him, he confessed his crimes saying, "Now I remember the evils that I did at Jerusalem, and that I took all the vessels of gold and silver that were therein and sent to destroy the inhabitants without a cause." The reins of the government of Syria fell to the young son of Antiochus, whose advisers were as cruel as the arch fiend just dead.

Not yet was the sword of Judas to be sheathed. The restoration of the sanctuary of God infuriated the nations round about Judea, and they banded themselves together to restore idol worship. Truly the Jewish exiles had suffered much "by the rivers of Babylon," but this period of desecration and bloodshed was far worse. Again the Hammerer gathered his small force to make a mighty struggle against the ever-menacing fortress of the enemy. Hearing of his purpose, Syria sent into Judea one hundred thousand foot soldiers, twenty thousand horse and thirty-two elephants. Judas, as usual, with enormous odds against him, defeated the host of the heathen, but his brother Eleazer was killed in the struggle. Thinking he would strike a great blow for the liberty of his country, he watched an immense elephant who bore the royal arms of Syria, cut his way through the thick of the battle, crept under the elephant, and gave him a mortal wound. The elephant did not carry the king. It fell upon Eleazer and crushed out his life.

Enough of battle, murder and sudden death, although there is plenty of material to supply more chronicles of the same sort. At last the lion heart of Judas grows heavy. His army is dwindling on account of the great number of the men who had fallen in battle.

The fame of the Romans had reached him, how brave and strong they were, how willing to make a league of amity with all who came to them in peace, how many nations they had conquered, and how, in spite of all their glory, no one among them wore a crown. He decided to send an embassy to this far country to invoke protection for his country. The embassadors were graciously received and a treaty was made between Rome and Judea. It did not, however, prevent the hostilities of Syria.

Another great army encamped against Jerusalem. The hope of the hero was at last waning, but not his courage. His companions besought him not to give battle, but he did not heed them. Stubbornly fighting Judas Maccabæus fell, never to rise, between two wings of the Syrian army.

Thus the event is chronicled in the book of Maccabees: "Judas also was killed and the remnant fled. Then Jonathan and Simon took Judas, their brother, and buried him in the sepulcher of their father in Moden. Moreover, they bewailed him, and all Israel made great lamentation for him, and mourned many days saying, 'How is the mighty fallen!'"

His brother Johnathan kept up the fight for two years and was then treacherously murdered, being enticed to the enemy's camp under promise of amicable counsel.

Semon the wise, took upon himself the leadership. He was the son of Mattathias. He accomplished the destruction of the infamous fortress which so long commanded the Holy City for murderous purposes. He also strengthened the defences of the temple. The vine and fig tree flourished once more under his rule and the friendly alliance with Rome was renewed. He was murdered by his son-in-law in the year 135 B. C., thus ending the story of the Maccabees.

The Bravest Sailor of All.

ELLA WHEELER WILCOX.

I know a naval officer, the bravest fighting man;
He wears a jaunty sailor suit, his cap says "Puritan."
And all day long he sails a ship between our land and Spain,
And he avenges, every hour, the martyrs of the Maine.

His warship is six inches square, a washtub serves for ocean;
But never yet, on any coast, was seen such dire commotion.
With one skilled move his boat is sent from Cuba to midsea,
And just as quickly back it comes to set Havana free.

He fights with Dewey; plants his flag upon each island's shore,
Then off with Sampson's fleet he goes to shed the Spanish gore.
He comes to guard New England's coast, but ere his anchor falls
He hurries off in frightful speed, to shell Manila's walls.

The Philippines so frequently have yielded to his power.
There's very little left of them, I'm certain, at this hour;
And when at last he falls asleep, it is to wake again
And hasten into troubled sees and go and conquer Spain.

How a Warship Fights.

Before a battleship goes into action all spare gear is stowed away, and her decks are made as bare as possible. This is in order that the enemy's shot may find but little to make splinters of should it come aboard. A warship possesses three means of attack; that is, her guns, ram and torpedoes. The guns range from 110-ton weapons that throw an 1,800-pound projectile with a charge of 960 pounds of power, down to three-pounder quick-firers.

Some of the battleships carry as many as fifty-four guns, thirty-five of which are able to discharge in one broadside, thus throwing some 3,618 pounds of iron per minute at the enemy. The effective range of the big guns is over ten miles, and ten shots per minute can be thrown by the quick-firing ones. One of the big battleships fighting at close quarters with her Maxims in play would hurl at the foe about 2,600 projectiles per minute, these varying in weight from 1,800 pounds to one ounce. Some of these projectiles would be filled with high explosives, and would destroy everything for yards around the place where they exploded. As British possessions are so widely scattered that ships have to remain for a long time away from ammunition bases, they carry much more shot per gun than do other foreign men-of-war.

When a ship is commissioned, the first thing that her crew does is to practice general quarters until they are able to clear for action and be ready to fire a broadside within three minutes from the order being given. Eventually, however, the crew get to know the ship so well that they can get her ready for action in a minute and a half. This they have to do by night as well as day. Probably the captain chooses midnight when all but the watch are fast asleep to order quarters to be sounded. Immediately the bugle rings out, every man jumps from his hammock and rushes straight for the station, each one endeavoring to be at his post first. For a couple of minutes the clanging of iron doors and the clanking of chains are heard throughout the ship; then all is silent again. The bright muzzles of the guns glisten out at the ports; down in the magazines are men ready to send ammunition to the gunners on the decks above; the torpedo crews have placed white heads in the tubes, and every other preparation has been made to give battle to an enemy.

Illuminated sights are used on the guns at night. Each big gun is worked by what is termed a "crew;" that is, a number of sailors or marine artillerymen specially told off to it. The captain, or number one, as he is called, lays the gun and fires it, the other members of the "crew" stand in file to pass the projectiles and load the gun. There is also a crew to each torpedo tube. These tubes are nearly all submerged.—*Selected.*

They are slaves who fear to speak
For the fallen and the weak;
They are slaves who will not choose
Hatred, scoffing and abuse,
Rather than in silence shrink
From the truth they needs must think;
They are slaves who dare not be
In the right with two or three.

—*Lowell.*

The Supreme Moment.

Two young men recently volunteered to go to Cuba on important missions for the government. They both had left their homes, entered the army, became soldiers, were selected for special service, accepted the responsibility, sailed away, and reached the shores of the island. In these things both were exactly alike, and each as good a soldier as the other. When the supreme test of their courage came, how did they carry themselves? The one, thinking nothing of himself, and only of his mission, bravely faced danger, made his way to the insurgent chief, delivered his messages, secured important information, and returned, through many privations, amid the plaudits of his countrymen, to his place in the army. The other, on reaching the Cuban port, seeing the sad plight of the half-starved insurgents, and hearing from them of the sufferings they were undergoing, refused to land with his comrades, and on the return of the ship was found hid away in the hold. Under arrest and in disgrace he was brought back to Key West. His courage failed him in the supreme moment. Differing only in this one thing, they are wholly different ever after. The first receives the thanks of his superior officers and of a grateful country, and is advanced to high promotion; the other is dismissed in disgrace from the army and is drummed out of camp for cowardice. Having been tested and found true, the one is in line for still more eminent service; the other, having quailed in the presence of danger, will never have an opportunity to retrieve himself or serve his country.

How like life everywhere. It is the men who forget themselves in doing fearlessly the duty next to them who serve their fellows, winning probably not wealth nor fame, but surely the inheritance of heaven, and the commendation of the King of kings. It is the Christian soldier, equipped, trained, armored, experienced, and victorious, of whom the apostle Paul was thinking when he said "having done all, to stand."—*Religious Telescope.*

The Glorious Fourth.

Soon the happiest day of the year will have come! And why should it be the happiest? Because it is the birthday of the greatest and best Republic the world has ever seen—a Republic which has demonstrated for a century the power of men to preserve union and enforce laws for the public good. The people of the United States have more comfort, happiness and freedom than any nation present or past. Doubtless this results largely from our fertile and almost boundless national domain, but still more largely from the protection afforded by laws made by the people for the people and enforced by the people. There is no country better supplied, if so well, with churches, ministers, colleges, schools and missionary societies; and no country is so far advanced in temperance reformation. The nations of the world regard these United States with wonder, admiration and awe, seeing in this Republic a nation which will, ere another hundred years, doubtless be the most populous, wealthy, prosperous, and powerful in the world. In these circumstances, thankfulness for the present, and prayerfulness for the future, should everywhere abound, from the dug-out on the prairies to the White House.

Our Beloved Land.

Patriotism and piety are inseparably nited in true hearts. Whether native or dopted citizens, we are Americans, and oyal to the flag that stands as the symbol nd pledge of our republic—the church 'thout a bishop, the state without a king. o no land under the whole heavens has he tide of immigration been so strong and ontinuous as to free America. Whatever ay be true of the Old World, it is cerainly true that millions of people see nder our flag opportunities of wealth, ducation, freedom and religion enjoyed owhere else under the sun. The stranger as found welcome here, and we demand f him allegiance to the government and llegiance to God. The atheistic anarchst is not welcome in God-fearing and lawbiding America. If he has come to ndanger our property and destroy our life, he law says he must die. Nor will we olerate interference at the ballot-box, or in he halls of legislation, or with our free nstitutions. The public schools are dear o us because they are the great lever hich elevates our children to the plane of dtelligent, loyal citizenship. The flag of reedom floats over every schoolhouse. o foreign hierarchy dare lay hands upon his ark of the Lord. The world furnishes o better system of public education than s furnished in our public schools.—*Luheran Evangelist.*

New occasions teach new duties; Time
makes ancient good uncouth;
They must upward still, and onward, who
would keep abreast of Truth;
Lo, before us gleam her camp-fires! we
ourselves must Pilgrims be,
Launch our Mayflower, and steer boldly
through the desperate winter sea,
No attempt the Future's portal with the
Past's blood-rusted key.

—Lowell.

A Lesson in Manners.

Once upon a time a young man entered a railroad office where a number of other persons, all considerably older than himself, were employed. They all were so cold and selfish, so much immersed, each in his own concerns, and so indifferent to the iner amenities of life, that they were in the habit of meeting and of separating mostly in silence, and their intercourse was characterized by a certain bluff and gruff directness that must have surprised and startled the young man, although he nade no sign. The place must have been somewhat uncomfortable to him at first, for he had been carefully trained to observe all the courtesies of life, and he must have felt as though he had been suddenly ifted out of the agreeable society in which he had hitherto moved and planted in the midst of another sort of people. Young as he was, however, he had a wise head on his shoulders, and while he steadily overlooked the absence of all polite courtesies toward himself, he never omitted them in his own personal demeanor.

When any of his associates performed the most trifling service for this young fellow he invariably remarked, "Thank you." If he desired anything he prefaced his request with the phrase, "If you please." When he met his associates in the morning he bade them "Good morning," and when they separated in the evening he said "Good night." At first the practical men among whom his lot was cast, simply stared at him in silence. Then they smiled at each other. They called him "the French dancing master" or "the dude," among themselves, remarked that he was entirely too refined for the sort of company he was keeping, and in various other ways amused themselves with what they were pleased to regard his eccentricity. Nothing discouraged, however, and because it was his nature to be polite the young fellow went on observing the proprieties of social intercourse, and in the course of time, almost unconsciously to themselves, his rude associates began to say, "If you please," and "Thank you," and to manifest various other marks of good breeding and culture. The young man's example had actually won them to a cultivation of the graces of life!

The polite young gentleman no longer occupies the desk which gave him such fine opportunities for civilizing a lot of human bears. In spite of his courteous conduct and polite ways he is no drawing-room ornament, but a manly and courageous man. When the government called for volunteers to help drive the Spanish tyrant out of Cuba he was among the first to respond, and we doubt not that he will give a good account of himself, and prove as efficient a teacher of humanity, as in other fields, he has been an instructor in the graces of polite conduct. The narrative herewith given is true to the life. It has been written to show how powerful the influence of a single resolute life may be for good, and, it may be, to inspire other young men with the determination to be manly and courteous in whatever station they may be find themselves. — *Central Christian Advocate.*

Once to every man and nation comes the
moment to decide,
In the strife of Truth and Falsehood, for
the good or evil side;
Some great cause, God's new Messiah
offering each the bloom or blight,
Parts the goats upon the left hand, and
the sheep upon the right,
And the choice goes by forever 'twixt that
darkness and that light.

—Lowell.

"I want," said the excited Chicago woman at the telephone exchange, "my husband, please." "Number, please," said the polite operator. "Only the fourth, you impudent thing!" snapped back the fair telephoner; and when the operator failed to check a slightly audible smile, the bell rang off viciously.

Anxious Wife—"Do you know where my husband is, sir?" Klondyke Karl—"Th' last time I seen your husband, mum, he was goin' over the mountain." Anxious Wife—"In what direction?" Klondyke Karl (sadly)—"In all directions, mum. You see he got a can of dynamite mixed in with the corned beef he was thawing out." —*Judge.*

Teacher—"Thomas, will you tell me what a conjunction is, and compose a sentence containing a conjunction?"

Thomas (after long and solemn reflection)—"A conjunction is a word connecting anything, such as, 'The horse is hitched to the fence by his halter.' Halter is a conjunction, because it connects the horse and the fence!"—*Harper's Bazar.*

Perpetuity of the Repu

What are essential to the pe the republic? National unity remain one people, knowing South, East or West. Univer education; that man who inte this is an enemy to the republ who would divert the public s to partisan or sectarian purpose guilty of taking a stone from t tions of our national edifice. T all sects and beliefs and partie freedom is the right to differ. T tion of the nobility of labor; mission of the United States labor and honor the toiler. righteousness; "righteousness nation."

Sacred be the trusts commit care, and bright the vision of co —*Rev. T. H. Baragwunath, in t er's Magazine for June.*

When you've got a thing to s
Say it; don't take half a day
When your tale has little in i
Crowd the whole thing in a m

Life is but a fleeting vapor,
Don't take up the whole blam
With a story which, at a pinc
Could be crowded in an inch.

Boil it down until it simmers,
Polish it until it glimmers.
When you've got a thing to s
Say it, don't take half a day.

Saying Grace.

Asking a blessing upon food be was a universal custom among and was practiced both by Chr apostles (Luke 22:17-19; 26:30 35). It is a most appropriate custom, and should be universal sanctifies the act of eating, tran even more than bright conversat it "the feast of reason, and t soul." It is held by the Jews t partakes of anything witho thanks, acts as if he was steali God. Why especially over food food is the basis of life, the sou ply for all other things, so that cluded under it. The formulæ i were commonly short and simp own, such as, "May God, the ev One, bless what he has given *licott.*

Sunday School.

THE CHAMPION OF JEHOVAH.*

HERBERT L. WILLETT.

The worship of Baal which was introduced during the reign of Ahab through the influence of his Zidonian wife, Jezebel, spread rapidly through the northern kingdom and profoundly affected the character of the nation. The more important towns and cities had their local shrines and images of Baal, and these Baals, or Baalim, scattered through the land, became the objects of worship for a large portion of the people. It is probable also that as the word Baal meant "Lord" it was not infrequently the case that the features of the Baal worship were introduced into the worship of Jehovah, and the latter thus became demoralized even where it did not lose entirely its primitive character. In connection with the shrine of Baal there was generally either an image of the god or a stone pillar representing his worship. He was the god of fire and power. His consort, Astarte, or Asherah, was generally associated with him at these local sanctuaries, and her presence was denoted by a grove or tree or stake, which was called after her the Asherah. These symbols of the foreign cult possessed a sensuous meaning often found associated with religion among primitive people, and it was to this fact that the Baal worship owed it seductive character.

So far had the official sanction of Baalism gone that the prophets of Jehovah, the successors of those earlier bands or guilds of prophets associated with Samuel, were put to death or compelled to seek hiding from the fanatical enthusiasm of the foreign queen. So thoroughgoing was this persecution that when Elijah began his work, and indeed at the period of the great test on Mount Carmel, he felt himself to be absolutely alone representing the interests of Jehovah, the true God. He was afterward assured that the situation was not so hopeless as he had imagined, but that there was a remnant of the people still faithful to their ancient worship (1 Kings 19:18); and the king's steward, Obadiah, informed the prophet that he had hidden a hundred prophets of the Lord in caves (1 Kings 18:4). But practically Elijah was alone, and at the moment of crisis it was only his strong spirit that stood between the higher religious life of the nation and the prevalent and growing worship of Baal. The time of Elijah admirably illustrates that principle which all history discloses, that there is never a period in which righteousness is totally destroyed in a nation; there is always a remnant remaining, the seed of a new generation of true believers.

When the drought was at its worst the king, who had received Elijah's message of its coming with incredulity and scorn, was so harrassed by the fearful effects of the famine that he began a systematic search of his kingdom for the prophet, and when this failed he made inquiry among the neighboring nations. It was his turn to be concerned to meet the man of God. When at last they did come together Elijah met the king with bold and intrepid front, refuting the charge of responsibility for the national disaster, and in turn charging the king with being the author of all of Israel's calamities, because of his course in forsaking the worship of Jehovah. The issue was clear. Either Jehovah or Baal must be recognized as God. The nation could not live half faithful and half idolatrous, any more than a nation can live half slave and half free, or half sober and half intemperate. All the official prestige was on the side of Baal, but the prophet offered to put the whole matter to a test in one decisive moment at a conspicuous point, Mount Carmel. The king, who was probably but little concerned as to whether Baal or Jehovah prevailed, consented to the trial. The people were gathered in thousands. The four hundred and fifty prophets of Baal and the four hundred prophets of Astarte, who were particular proteges of Jezebel, were there to represent the heathen worship, while Elijah stood as the lonely champion of Jehovah. But God and one man are a majority. The heathen worship was given every advantage. Baal was the god of fire, and as his worship was celebrated by the burning of children as well as other fire-offerings, the test should be one of fire. But all day long the prophets of Baal called upon their god in a frenzy of hope and despair according to the wild practices of the ruder types of Semitic prophets. They shouted, they danced about the altar, they gashed themselves with knives to gain the ear of Baal, but all in vain. At last Elijah began to ridicule them with that biting sarcasm which the events of the day had so fully justified. It was evident that their god had gone on a journey, or was asleep, or was looking after other interests. Still he would not take advantage of their helplessness until every hope had perished that Baal would respond. At last, at sunset, after the whole day had been spent in a frantic effort to secure fire for the heathen altar, Elijah repaired the dismantled altar of Jehovah which had been the scene of earlier worship on that spot. Then after preparing his offering he drenched it with water until there could be no possibility of fraud in the appearance of fire, and poured out his soul to God in a passionate entreaty for a manifestation of power in order that the nation might be convinced of its folly in limping back and forth between adherence to Jehovah and reverence for Baal. The answer came in a shower of flame that consumed offering and altar, and brought the people to their knees in profound acknowledgment of the supremacy of Jehovah and the nothingness of Baal. Elijah celebrated his victory with swift retribution visited upon the prophets of the false religion, who perished to a man at the brook Kishon below, while the oncoming tempest compelled the king to hasten back to his place at Jezreel. The sway of Baal was broken, for the moment at least. Elijah was triumphant. Jehovah was vindicated, and the drought was at an end.

SUGGESTIONS FOR TEACHING.

There are many homes in which the altar of Jehovah which has been dismantled needs to be repaired. The same is true of individual lives where once the altar-fire of prayer arose, but where it has ceased to ascend. In all religious work the people of God are one; Elijah disregarded the divided kingdom and assumed the unity of the nation by taking twelve stones for his altar; the essential unity of Christians must be more fully emphasized and recognized; the sin of division must never be forgotten. The trial by fire on Carmel was not a foolish test of strength by Elijah, but rather a supreme appeal to God in a time of mortal danger; it is always foolish and sinful to put God to the test (Matt. 4:7); but it is just as foolish and sinful not to rely upon God to the utmost when the occasion comes for a supreme act of confidence. One need not expect miracles to-day in proof of God's presence or power; the gospel is the power of God unto salvation, and its victories are as marvelous as any miracle. Prayer that is as truly in line with God's purposes as was that of Elijah, and is uttered with as devoted and whole-hearted purpose, is certain to be answered. The miracles of the Bible group themselves about three striking personalities, Moses, Elijah and our Savior. Are there not in our own lives false gods who take the place of Jehovah and in whose interests we try to make compromise with the true faith?

*Bible-school Lesson for July 17th—Elijah on Mount Carmel. (1 Kings 18:30-39). Golden Text—And when all the people saw it, they fell on their faces; and they said: The Lord, he is the God; the Lord, he is the God (1 Kings 18:39). Lesson Outline—1. Jehovah's altar (30-35); 2. Elijah's petition; (36-37); 3. Jehovah's answer (38,39).

that we have something higher. Our light will dim theirs. The light of Asia must give place to the Light of the World. It will do no good to declare that their light is mere darkness, but it would be equally reprehensible to say that because they have an oil-lamp they do not need the arc light. The fact is that the saddest lack in the Oriental religions is the lack of life. It is morals, after all, that tells. "By their fruits ye shall know them." Religions that can foster infanticide, polygamy, child-marriage, and such, need a higher light. We need to save the heathen in this world, and God will care for the world to come. If for no other reason than to purify morals, add to human comfort and happiness and save from degradation and misery in this world, we need to send the gospel. It is the Christian life which is the strongest Christian argument. The Oriental systems preach well bnt do not practice. We preach and practice too—that is, some of the time. And here lies our warning, if we carry a more intellectual system without a pure life to the heathen, they will conquer us. We must take to them the Christ-life if we would cope with their keen mental weapons.

This is, therefore, the final superiority of Christianity—it is the religion of a person, and that Person is Christ. The world needs a center for thought and life and worship. It can find that center nowhere else so well as in a person. All other religions fail at this point and Christianity triumphs. We demand, we people, leadership. We need it in temporal affairs. We must have it in spiritual matters. We will follow a beloved leader to death. We are constituted so. So also our "heavenly vision" must be a leader, must be in the form of a man, must be endowed with the Spirit of God. Where shall we find this heavenly vision save in the Incarnation taught and lived by the Person, Jesus? With all due respect, then, and recognition for the world's religions, we say to them, "Sirs, come and see Jesus!"

Educational Conference.

The conference which has been in session two days has just closed. It is a great pleasure to be again in the atmosphere of this growing university. The meetings were held in Assembly Room, Haskell Museum, of the University of Chicago. The attendance is encouraging. Four of our leading colleges were represented by members of the faculties.

We as a people are making progress along educational lines. Prominent pastors were present from several states. Some of the points brought out were the following: The production of an educated and cultured university is our most important missionary work; more time should be given to the consideration of the college problem in our national conventions; doing missionary work that leaves out the educational question is like giving a tree plenty of air for the leaves, but denying it moisture for the roots; degrees that have a historical meaning should not be robbed of their import by conferring them for short courses of study; though it is often necessary for students to do some preaching while in the academic course; an excess should be guarded against both for the welfare of the student and the good of the congregation; the latter part of college courses may permit electives looking to the chosen life-work of the student; in the case of ministers some biblical studies may be taken; the place of the Greek New Testament is an important one in our distinctive work; many accepted theories under the keen eye of the critical Greek scholar vanish, and are replaced by more biblical and rational statements.

There was a somewhat divided opinion, not on the value of classical studies, but as to how much should give way to the demand for more room for science. Originally an A. B. meant little more than a knowledge of Greek and Latin, with elementary mathematics.

College libraries do not need to be so large as those of a university, but the books should be well selected. Not *how many?* but *what kind?* is the question. The political influence in relation to some state universities is carried to such a degree as to being an effort to cripple or destroy denominational schools. This must be resisted. The state institutions do not look after the religious side of the student's life sufficiently. We must sustain our church schools at all hazards with other religious bodies, if we would have an efficient ministry and see business life represented by Christian men and women.

After all, the *man* must be back of the book and the college to make the life of the instructed a moral force in erecting the stately fabric of a true and permanent Christian civilization. The Disciples' Club of the University gave a most delightful reception to the conference Tuesday evening in Haskell Hall. I shall leave this conference inspired with a greater determination to emphasize the importance of Christian education, and with the hope that we Disciples of Christ may be able to rise so high in the realization of duty and its performance that we shall see the threatening clouds of difficulty become — fog at our feet.

LEVI MARSHALL.

June 29, 1898.

SUBSCRIBERS' WANTS.

Miscellaneous wants and notices will be inserted in this department at the rate of two cents a word, each insertion, all words, large and small, to be counted, and two initials stand for one word. Please accompany notice with corresponding remittance to save book-keeping.

The C. E. Reading Courses.

THE LORD'S SUPPER.

F. D. POWER.

Our last Bible reading on the position of the Disciples in the light of Scripture deals with this important subject.

We read of a house of God on earth. This has been since the days of the tabernacle in the wilderness. The Most High dwells not in temples made with hands, yet he condescended to have a temple erected to himself and glorified it with symbols of his presence. Under Christ the church is called God's building, the temple of God, a spiritual house. In the Lord's house there is always the Lord's table. In the house over which Jesus presides as a Son, is a table more precious than gold as a part of its necessary furniture. It is declared to those who pollute themselves with idols, that they can not "be partakers of the Lord's table and the table of demons." Paul speaks of the cup of the Lord and the loaf as furniture of this table. Coming to this table with its divinely ordered furniture, the loaf and the cup, the loaf must be broken before the saints feed upon it and the institution of the Lord's Supper is thus called "the breaking of bread."

In accordance with apostolic usage we say "the Lord's day," "the Lord's table," "the Lord's house." Calling Bible things by Bible names we not say "the Sacrament" or "the Eucharist," but "the Lord's Supper," or "the breaking of bread." The loaf is broken. Jesus took a loaf from the paschal table and broke it. They received a broken loaf emblematic of his body once whole but to be broken for them. Eating of the broken loaf we remember our Lord's body was by his consent broken or wounded for us. So each Disciple breaks bread and holds communion with his Lord and communion with his brethren in the breaking of bread.

"They continued steadfastly in the apostles' doctrine and fellowship, in the breaking of bread and in prayers."

Now this breaking of the loaf and joint participation of the cup of the Lord, is an instituted part of the worship and edification of all Christian congregations in their stated Lord's day meetings. The first Christian congregation which was constituted by the apostles themselves in Jerusalem as steadily attended upon the breaking of bread in their public meetings as upon any other part of public worship. The apostles taught the churches to do all things our Lord had ordained. Whatever the churches did by appointment of the apostles they did by commandment of Jesus Christ, and acts of religious worship taught and sanctified by the apostles in one Christian congregation were taught and sanctified in all, as all were under the government of the same head.

Of the church in Troas it is expressly declared by Luke: "On the first day of the week when the disciples came together to break bread Paul preached to them." Two things are clear here, that it was the established custom for the disciples to meet on the first day of the week, and that the primary object of this meeting was "to break bread." Weekly observance of the first day as a day of meeting for the disciples and the weekly breaking of bread in those meetings stand or fall together. If one was fifty-two times in the year the other was fifty-two times. If one was once a month or once in three months, the other was once a month or once in three months. If they kept the Lord's resurrection fifty-two times a year on the Lord's day, they remembered the Lord's death fifty-two times a year in the Lord's Supper—he died as often as he arose from the dead. They did both—the Lord's death and the Lord's resurrection, the Lord's day and the Lord's Supper, go together.

From Acts 2:42 we learn that breaking of the loaf was a stated part of the worship of the disciples in their meetings. From Acts 20:7 we learn that the first day of the week was the stated time for these meetings and that the most prominent object of their assembling was to break the loaf. From Paul's epistles to churches in Galatia and Corinth we learn that the disciples met statedly upon every first day for this worship, for he bids them to prepare their offering "on the first day of every week" and rebukes some of them, because when they come together "this is not to eat the Lord's Supper." Nor is there any scriptural proof that any congregation of the Lord's people ever met on the first day unless for the breaking of bread, or that any congregation ever met monthly, quarterly, semi-annually or annually. Commemoration of the Lord's death should be a weekly institution in all the weekly meetings of Christians for worship. So Wesley taught: "I advise the elders to administer the supper of our Lord on every Lord's day." So Calvin declared: "Every week at least the table of the Lord should be spread in Christian assemblies," and the custom which enjoins communion once a year he denounced as "a manifest contrivance of the devil." So communion every Lord's day was universal and preserved so until the seventh century, and such as neglected it for three weeks together were excommunicated.

Do any say frequent communion makes common this otherwise solemn ordinance? So the Papist reduced its frequency, took away the cup from the laity, made Easter, Pentecost and Christmas great occasions, annexed a world of ceremonies and changed the elements into the veritable blood and body of Christ according to their claim. Did this give greater credit to the ordinance, or destroy it? Is this safe leadership? According to such reasoning once in seven, ten, twenty, fifty years would render the institution more solemn and men should pray, read their Bibles, go to church once a year or once in twenty years, because forsooth it would render the service all the more impressive and preserve it from becoming common!

We need this institution. Every week our spiritual condition demands this sacred approach to the cross. If we would follow the practice of the apostolic church we must conform to its usages. More and more God's people are coming to it and thus together.

Marriages.

CLOVER.—Mr. John H. Beck and H. Clover, both of Quitman, Mo., on 98, in Skidmore, Mo., by N. Rollo

EY—BARTON.—In Paris, Mo., C. 'n officiating, June 21, 1898, Mr. mbrey to Miss Edna Barton.

SON—TODD.—At the residence of Irs. H. H. Todd, June 26, 1898, by J. ns, Edward L. Ferguson and Miss id, of both Clinton county, Mo.

MB—CURTRIGHT.—June 23, 1898, e of the bride's father, C. H. Strawn , Mr. Daniel B. Halcomb, Cass Co., iss Ivy L. Curtright, of Monroe Co.,

N—BEEM.—At the home of the Lehigh, Ia., June 22, 1898, Dr. Harry on, of Dayton, Ia., to Miss Leona J. Dow, of Iowa City, officiating.

LS—YENOWINE.—June 20, 1898, at of the bride in Edwardsville, Ind., Dale, Mr. Jesse B. Nichols to Miss nowine, all of Edwardsville.

—BOWN.—Mr. Ulyssess Tracy, of , Mo., and Miss Ora B. Brown, of Mo., on June 15, 1898, in Graham; Davis officiating.

—WILEY.—At 451 North 7th St., ute, Ind., June 21, at 4 P. M., Mr. . Waite, of Toledo, Ohio, and Miss M. Wiley, of Terre Haute. W. ier, pastor of the Central Christian assisted by Rev. John E. Sulger, of hen's Church, officiated at the mar-

Obituaries.

ndred words will be inserted free. Above ed words, one cent a word. Please send ith each notice.]

CAMPBELL.

Gertrude Campbell was born April 3, Colusa county, California. When she ears old her parents moved to Davis Iowa, where she resided 9 years. esidence in Mitchell, Kan., of several r parents moved from there to Strong- l. On Oct. 19, 1893, she was united age to Wm. Stine, whom she leaves ttle girl of two summers to mourn her he died Saturday mourning, June 18, eceased was a member of the Old Bed- istian Church, and a devoted Christian. sermon by the writer, after which the were laid to rest in the cemetary at urst, Ill.

A. R. ADAMS.

KENSLER.

Kensler was born in Madison county, il 13, 1858, and died in the same county 1898, having lived 40 years, 1 month days. He was married to Clidona Sept. 21, 1882, who, with 2 daughters, him. Bro. Kensler became a Chris- ing the meeting held here—Winterset, ; October by the writer. He was a isband and a loving father. His sun ioon, but it went down amid the rose- ouds of peace, in the light of whose re- lory the eye of faith beholds the burn- tes of day.

J. M. LOW.

LIVINGSTON.

at her home in Kansas City, Mo., y, June 16, 1898, Kate Rush Living- ed 37 years, 5 months and 16 days. By request she was brought to Tallula, home of her childhood. She was laid a beautiful Greenwood Cemetery. Be- was carried from Kansas City Bro. Richardson, in a short exercise, read comforting passages of Scripture, and er was a benediction. Her body was the church in Tallula where in early d she had committed herself to the Christ, ever after leading the life of a nt Christian. The pastor, Bro. Be- made a short talk. By her death two ittle girls are left motherless. Her ., mother, sister and brother were

S. J.

WOODSWORTH.

Quincey Adams Woodsworth was born sylvania, Aug. 6, 1829. Died in Ma- ll., June 16, 1898, aged 68 years, 10 and 10 days. A member of the Chris- urch in Macomb for 40 years, hon- ithful, virtuous, temperate, pious. Woodsworth is left a widow. Their five l two daughters, all grown, are left s, but they are comforted by the full assurance that they can in Christ meet him where there is no death. Funeral discourse by the writer; text: Paul's words, "Comfort one another with these words."

J. C. REYNOLDS.

To the Members of the National Educational Association and Other Friends of Public Education —Annual Meeting.

WASHINGTON, D. C., JULY 7-12, 1898.

It is peculiarly fitting that the great association of teachers, from whom the American youth receive instruction, should assemble in Washington. It is likewise sufficiently important that the great American public should know that the Baltimore & Ohio Southern Railway—THE ROYAL BLUE LINE —is the premier line through the St. Louis gateway to Washington. Its superior train service, contiguity to rivers, creeks and mountain streams, which follow its tracks the greater part of the way, serve to make it the coolest, easiest riding and freest from dust of any of the lines to the Nation's Capital. Aside from these comforts entour the historic features associated with the country through which it passes are without parallel on any other line in America.

Western connections will sell tickets via St. Louis and the Baltimore & Ohio Southwestern Railway for this meeting at rate of ONE LOWEST FIRST-CLASS LIMITED FARE, plus $2.00, FOR THE ROUND TRIP. An extension of time until August 31st may be secured on payment, to Special Agent at Washington, of a nominal fee of 50 cents.

N. E. A. literature and other detailed information will be cheerfully furnished by addressing any of our traveling passenger agents, or

G. P. WARFEL,
Assistant Gen'l Passenger Agent,
St. Louis, Mo.

The Religious World.

The next national convention of the W. C. T. U. will be held at St. Paul, Minn., Nov. 11-16.

Memorial services were held at Prohibition Park, July 3rd, in memory of Neal Dow, Frances E. Willard and Mary T. Burt.

The preachers of Cincinnati recently adopted a resolution protesting against the establishment of canteens in our military camps and calling upon the government to provide our soldiers with pure water in abundance.

The Third World's Sunday-school Convention meets in London, July 11-16. The program of this convention appears in ful in the International Evangel, of this city. The first world's convention was held in London in 1889, and the second one in this city, in 1893. The work of the International Lesson Committee will be made July 14th.

All England is not pleased with the manner in which the Bishop of London is playing into the hands of the Papacy of Rome. The Christian Commonwealth recently quoted the following from a letter from Mr. Kensit to the Bishop of London with the comment following:

"I feel it my duty to remonstrate with you regarding your attendance at St. Augustine's, Kilburn, last week. What is the use of your lordship denouncing such functions to me when you go and take part in such monstrous proceedings? You told me in reference to another church, when they incensed you, that you would refuse to attend that church again. I think I have a right to ask you this question: How can you expect your clergy to be loyal to Reformation principles when you openly take part in and encourage lawlessness by your presence? Although several weeks have now elapsed since Convocation, not a single lawless practice has yet been stopped in your diocese." The Bishop of London seems to be unable to make up his mind as to what is his duty at this juncture. This is unfortunate. One of the curses of the church is the manifest division of opinion amongst the prelates. No wonder the nation is bewildered.

Thomas Morrison, of this city, who recently celebrated his 82nd anniversary, has been superintendent of the "Biddle Mission" for fifty years. He still holds the office, attends regularly, and is active in its interests. The Biddle Market Mission was established nearly sixty years ago. St. Louis was then simply a French trading post upon the edge of a great wilderness. It is said that this school has had a continuous existence since its organization.

The Council of Seventy announces a new series of reading courses, to commence October 1, to be conducted by the American Institute of Sacred Literature. These will be included under the Bible Students' Reading Guild, which for the present will drop its popular courses and present work for ministers and professional Bible students only. (It should be explained that the popular courses are dropped only for the present, and will be resumed as soon as a sufficient number of appropriate books have been published.)

No "times and seasons" will be observed in these ministerial courses. Any one of them may be taken up at any time, pursued in part or to its conclusion, as preferred. No examinations or requirements will hamper the student, but provisions for reports upon and credit for work will be made. The number of subjects taken up will not be limited; but for the present only eight are announced. The topics of these eight courses have been chosen rather as fundamental than with a view to their popularity. They are: (1) "The Historical and Literary Origin of the Pentateuch;" (2) "Old Testament Prophecy;" (3) "The Origin and Growth of the Hebrew Psalter;" (4) "The Life of the Christ;" (5) "The Apostolic Age;" (6) "The Problems Connected with the Gospel of John;" (7) "Christianity and Social Problems;" (8) "The Preparation of Sermons."

Eeach course will contain six or more books, selected first by each member of the Council of Seventy, and then by a committee of the council, who shall from the results of this composite judgment make the final choice. Upon all topics generally conceded to be in controversy the best authorities on both sides will be provided. The courses will in no case stand for a particular school of thought, but will be planned to present all sides impartially.

The books to be used in the subjects announced above will be selected during the summer. They will be loaned to those applying *in the order of their registration.* Preliminary announcements and registration blanks may be secured by addressing The American Institute of Sacred Literature, Hyde Park, Chicago, Ill.

It is reported from Sierra Leone, Africa, that a thousand persons were killed in the recent uprising in that district. One hundred aud twenty inhabitants of Freetown, most of them traders, are known to have been massacred, and other colonists were carried into the bush by the "war boys" and undoubtedly met a worse fate. Three hundred friendly natives were killed.

The whole Christian world will be interested in learning that in the house of Tiberius Cæsar, on the Palatine Hill, Rome, Professor Orazio Marucchi has discovered what he regards as a representation of the crucifixion in a *graffito*, or wall engraving. The discovery of the *graffito* created a sensation at the time. The *graffito*, by the way, is a drawing in the cement in one of the rooms which served as cells for the slaves and soldiers. Copies in photograph have already been made, and are in London. We presume they will speedily find their way to New York, where they will attract attention unless we are too busy about the war to care for anything else.

Washington & Lee University.

We call attention to the advertisement of Washington and Lee University, Lexington, Va., of which ex-Postmaster-General Wilson is now President. One professor and four regular lecturers increase the Faculty for next session.

St. Louis Letter.

Another vacation season is at hand and finds the churches in about the same condition as did the arrival of the last one. Some have their lamps trimmed and burning, while others have not. Some have grace enough to carry them through till September without a regular pastor, and some have not. Some pastors have gone on their annual trip, and others are going, but some must remain; not because they would not go if they could, but because they could not go if they would.

The writer is of course speaking of all the preachers of St. Louis, regardless of creedal distinctions; and this, after all, is about the way preachers are sized up by the people in general of any great city. About the only distinction known to the masses is that part of the churches and their pastors are Roman Catholics, while the rest are Protestants; but this distinction they know in name only. Just why or what their differences, but few can tell, while still fewer care to know. Protestant preachers are classed off by them in a "job-lot" sort of way, as a genteel set of fellows, somewhat convenient in case of sickness or death, but otherwise as social ornaments or barnacles, as they may chance to think. The respective Protestant churches, in their estimation, are but so many social centers, to which only the well-to-do or the well-appearing may go. But these do not, except on special occasions, and the rest will not, except under force of circumstances. And thus it is that Protestant churches are seldom crowded at this season of the year—on Sunday nights.

As to Roman Catholic churches, they are held in a sort of superstitious light by a surprisingly large number of apparently intelligent persons, while their priests are looked upon by the same people as sons of the "Immaculate Mary," regardless of their children-of-this-world appearence and conduct. Costly piles of masonry in a Roman Catholic cathedral are looked upon as an evidence of sound doctrine, holy worship and apostolic power, while the same thing in Protestant churches are held as indubitable evidence of hypocrisy, oppression of the poor, and enmity toward the laboring classes. Why this is thus, the writer will not attempt to explain.

In the meantime pleasure resorts, real and imaginary, harmless and harmful, are increasing in number and in popularity, so that the effects of an exceptionally fine Sunday or exceptionally hot one are more conspicuous than those of a cold or rainy one. The audiences are smaller.

Being caught in a drenching rain in the park, narrowly escaping death in a runaway or in a collision, enduring the parching heat of the sun for hours at a baseball game, pushing a wheel homeward for miles on a muddy road, or a ducking in the lake or river from an overturned boat, and many other painful, wearisome, costly experiences common to pleasure resorts seem to have no perceptible influence upon their drawing power, while the smallest accident or least inconvenience at church will settle the matter with a family for a whole year, and sometimes forever. They "will never go back to that place again." Bad men, bloated faces, lewd women, and every vicious character, who are not at all backward about improving their liberty of presence at public places, seem utterly void of influence to deter attendance at these resorts, while a single one of them suddenly appearing in a crowd of these same pleasure-seekers at church would almost cause a panic. They would be so horrified at the sight that they would never jeopardize their purity by going back again. The fear of immoral contact at church which some people have is something awful But fortunately for theaters, this dread seldom disturbs a theatre-goer. The interven-tion of diamonds, fine raiment or polished brass rails is a sufficient antidote to this danger. But I have come to deep water and must stop.

B. U. I.

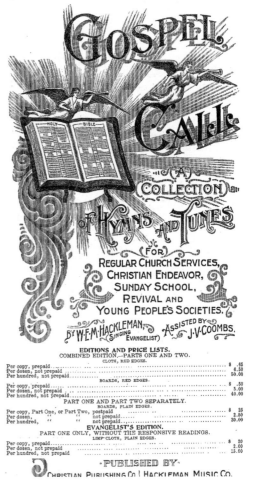

FACTS AND FACTORS.

Gen. Wheeler's advance guard cut of the water supply of Santiago, June 27th.

The new stamp act for war measures went into effect July first.

Gen. Merrett, military governor of the Philippine Islands, sailed from San Francisco, Cal., with his staff, June 29th, for Manila.

The Cuban soldiers under Garcia are co-operating heartily with the American forces in the seige of Santiago.

The cruiser, St. Paul, disabled the Spanish torpedo boat destroyer "Terror" June 28th, near the harbor of San Juan, Porto Rico.

Admiral Camara's squadron arrived at Port Said, Egypt, June 26th, purporting to be en route for the Philippine Islands.

Four of Col. Torrey's regiment of rough riders from Wyoming were killed in a railroad accident at Tupelo, Miss., June 26th.

Gen. Pando left Manzanville June 22nd with 8,000 Spanish troops, cattle, and pack train to reinforce Gen. Linares at Santiago. He is marching twelve miles per day and expects to reach Santiago, July 3rd.

Fifteen of the sixteen American soldiers killed at the battle of La Quasina, June 25th, were buried in one long trench on the ground on which they were killed. Capt. Capron's body was buried at Juragua.

The bodies of one hundred and five Spanish soldiers, killed by the rough riders at La Quasina, June 25th, were taken to Santiago. Thirty-nine dead bodies were aftewards found on the field.

Nine thousand American troops sailed from Tampa, Fla., June 29th, for Santiago, under Gen. Snyder.

A national bankruptcy bill was passed by Congress June 29th, and went immediately to the President for signature.

The eye of the vulture is so constructed that it is a high-powered telescope, enabling the bird to see objects at an almost incredible distance.

An aluminum airship, propelled by a benzine motor, rose to 1,000 feet in a recent trial in Germany, and went well until the wind became too high.

Gen. Shafter began his attack upon Santiago at 9 A. M., July 1st, at Caney, five miles northeast of the city. Gen. Lawton led the attack.

Joseph Leiter's father is arranging to borrow $7,000,000 to liquidate the indebtedness incurred by his son's venture at a wheat corner.

The monthly statement of the public debt shows that at the close of business yesterday the debt, less cash in the treasury, amounted to $1,027,085,492; a decrease during the month of $10,688,268. This decrease is accounted for by a corresponding increase in the amount of cash on hand. The increase in the cash comes largely from proceeds of the new bond issues.

THE
RISTIAN-EVANGELIST.

A WEEKLY FAMILY AND RELIGIOUS JOURNAL.

XV. July 14, 1898 No. 28.

ONTENTS.

nts......................35
e Convention...... 36
Paul to the Preachers....37
ower 37
World 39
y Chair...................39
gious Thought............40
RIBUTIONS:
-Sherman Hill....... 41
ourtesy.—Geo. L. Peters..42
n vs. Repudiation. — H.
rick............. 45
g for the Best?—Geo. T.
... .45
CE:
le Touring.................48
etter..... 49
nencement.................49
Mr. Moody...............51
the Holy Spirit....... ...51
hers of Indiana...... 52
:
f Happiness (Poem). 54
(Illustrated)................54
oice (Poem) 55
ege (Poem)...... 56
—VIII.—Spinsterhood.....56
s:
....46
ntion ... .46
ews.... ... .52
.... .53
Notes.......... 53
-school 59
actors......................59
ndeavor 60
eading Courses 61
. ... .62
... .63
....63
nts 64

scription $1.75.

WILLIAM EWART GLADSTONE.

PUBLISHED BY

CHRISTIAN PUBLISHING COMPANY

1522 Locust St., St. Louis.

THE

CHRISTIAN - EVANGELIST

J. H. GARRISON, EDITOR.

W. W. HOPKINS, ASSISTANT.

B. B. TYLER, J. J. HALEY,

EDITORIAL CONTRIBUTORS.

What We Plead For.

The Christian-Evangelist pleads for:

The Christianity of the New Testament, taught by Christ and his Apostles, versus the theology of the creeds taught by fallible men—the world's great need.

The divine confession of faith on which Christ built his church, versus human confessions of faith on which men have split the church.

The unity of Christ's disciples, for which he so fervently prayed, versus the divisions in Christ's body, which his apostles strongly condemned.

The abandonment of sectarian names and practices, based on human authority, for the common family name and the common faith, based on divine authority, versus the abandonment of scriptural names and usages for partisan ends.

The hearty co-operation of Christians in efforts of world-wide beneficence and evangelization, versus petty jealousies and strifes in the struggle for denominational pre-eminence.

The fidelity to truth which secures the approval of God, versus conformity to custom to gain the favor of men.

The protection of the home and the destruction of the saloon, versus the protection of the saloon and the destruction of the home.

For the right against the wrong;
For the weak against the strong;
For the poor who've waited long
For the brighter age to be.
For the truth, 'gainst superstition,
For the faith, against tradition,
For the hope, whose glad fruition
Our waiting eyes shall see.

RATES OF SUBSCRIPTION.

Single subscriptions, new or old	$1.75	each
In clubs of five or more, new or old.	1.50	"
Reading Rooms	1.25	"
Ministers	1.00	"

With a club of ten we will send one additional copy free.

All subscriptions payable in advance. Label shows the month up to the first day of which your subscription is paid. If an earlier date than the present is shown, you are in arrears. No paper discontinued without express orders to that effect. Arrears should be paid when discontinuance is ordered.

In ordering a change of post office, please give the OLD as well as the NEW address.

Do not send local check, but use Post office or Express Money Order, or draft on St. Louis, Chicago or New York, in remitting.

A Circuit of the Globe.

BY A. McLEAN,

Sec'y Foreign Christian Missionary Society.

This excellent missionary production is being pushed during the summer months through the various C. W. B. M. Auxiliary Societies of the brotherhood. Our sisters are making this the open door through which to replenish the overdrawn Treasury of the National C. W. B. M. If your Auxiliary has not yet received the information in reference to the plan, the terms and the excellent opportunity offered for raising a nice sum of money, write to the CHRISTIAN PUBLISHING CO., 1522 Locust St., St. Louis.

EDUCATIONAL.

EDUCATIONAL.

E CHRISTIAN-EVANGELIST

"In faith, Unity; in opinion and methods, Liberty; in all things, Charity."

St. Louis, Mo., Thursday, July 14, 1898. No. 28

NT EVENTS.

s that Admiral Cervera
the harbor at Santiago.
ort to General Blanco at
was permitted to send, he
ance with your orders, I
y from Santiago de Cuba
adron, and after an un-
against forces more than
ll my squadron destroyed
Oquendo and Vizcaya
n fleeing. I accordingly
ericans and went ashore
up." At the conclusion
re these pathetic words:
l and are necessarily de-
what makes the attempt
ore lamentable is that he
drid that the attempt was
the existing government
at home. Such obedi-
inspiration of fighting for
e hope of success in the
e from an overpowering
een very humiliating and
l to the proud Admiral of
leet.

---

on of President McKinley,
h, calling upon the people
tates, "on next assembly
ship in their respective
, to offer thanksgiving to
who, in His inscrutible
ng our hosts upon the
ed triumph, now guiding
ge land through the dread
to success, even though
now bearing them with-
oss to far distant climes,
cause and brought nearer
right and the attainment
able peace." This request
ly complied with through-
States on last Lord's day.
f a great nation, in the
conflict, pausing to recog-
God in its victories and to
edy return of peace is one
cite the admiration of the
fresh confidence in the
ple as to the ultimate suc-
efforts that are reinforced
the nation.

---

at Santiago has ended, we
h the refusal of the Span-
o surrender the city and
General Shafter. The
vacuate the city on condi-
anish troops be permitted
course promptly rejected.
ing left to do but to open
ty, and at this writing the
the army and navy is in
difficult to see what the
gain by continuing the
hopeless struggle at the cost both of property and of human life. It must be evident to even Spanish generals that Santiago is doomed, and humanitarian considerations should have permitted the surrender of the place without further bloodshed. General Shafter has already received considerable reinforcements, and General Miles, with additional reinforcements, will have arrived before this is in print. It is only a question, therefore, of a few days at most when the southern stronghold of Spain in Cuba will be in possession of the United States forces. It is to be hoped that this may be accomplished without too great a sacrifice of human life.

The second session of the fifty-fifth Congress closed at two o'clock on Friday, July the 8th. Not since the Civil War has any Congress been confronted with graver questions and greater responsibilities nor enacted laws of greater consequence. Not since 1812-'15, has any Congress had to do with a foreign war, outside of this continent, nor with international questions of a more delicate character to handle. During the session of the Congress just closed war was declared against Spain, an army of more than three hundred thousand men mobilized, the navy and coast fortifications greatly strengthened, $350,000,000 appropriated for war purposes and a war revenue law supposed to raise $150,000,000 a year enacted. During the congressional session closed the Spanish fleet at Manila and at Santiago were totaly destroyed, the city of Santiago made ready to capitulate or be taken by storm. By this Congress the Hawaiian Islands have been added to the domain of the United States, peaceably—the first addition of territory to the nation since the purchase of Alaska in 1867. By this Congress a national bankruptcy law has been enacted, the indebtedness of the Central and Western Pacific Railroads refunded and the disabilities imposed upon ex-Confederates by section three of the fourteenth amendment to the constitution removed.

After a long discussion the Senate on July 6th adopted the resolution annexing the Hawaiian Islands to the domain of the United States. The vote stood forty-two to twenty-one. The bill was signed by President McKinley, and as soon as it shall be ratified by the present government of Hawaii those islands will then be a part and parcel of the territory of the United States. These islands are about two thousand miles west of our Western Coast and lie in about the same latitude as the West Indies. It is believed that they will be of great value to us for commercial and military purposes. Its annexation is no doubt in accord with the desire of its most intelligent inhabitants. President Dole is of American birth, and it has already started a public school system after the American model. Its civilization has been created by American missionaries, and there is still work to do in this line. When in full articulation with the United States the American spirit and methods will soon prevail to even a greater extent than at present, and the real worth of the new territory will become apparent. President McKinley signed the bill at seven o'clock P. M., July 7th, and it is thought that President Dole will be the first United States Governor of the Hawaiian Islands.

Lieutenent Hobson and his fellow-prisoners of Merrimac fame were exchanged on the 7th of July. On the 3rd of June last Lieutenant Hobson and seven seamen, at the peril of their lives, sunk the collier Merrimac in the channel of Santiago harbor and became prisoners of war. Immediately upon their capture Admiral Cervera notified Admiral Sampson of their capture and praised their heroism in the sinking of the collier under the fire of the Spanish guns. They were at first confined at Morro Castle, but afterwards taken to Santiago. The Spanish Admiral proposed an immediate exchange of the prisoners, but his kind offer was interfered with at Madrid and Havana, and not until his fleet was destroyed and himself a prisoner did they consent to the exchange. Hobson had little to say in regard to his experiences except that they had been well treated by the Spaniards. He expresses high admiration for Admiral Cervera and regards his message to Admiral Sampson at the time of their capture as the act of a kind-hearted man and chivalrous officer. There was unbounded joy on land and sea at the return of these men to their freedom. This closes one of the most dramatic and daring incidents of this war and of naval warfare.

If the somwhat surprising statements of an editorial in a recent number of the Globe-Democrat on the comparative age of some of the features of our national life be true, we are in spite of our youthfulness ahead of the older nations in several matters now deemed to be of fundamental importance in government. Hugh Hastings, the state historian, of New York, is given as authority for the statement that the American flag is the oldest national emblem in the world. The oldest of the other flags is the Spanish, and this one ours antedates by more than a half dozen years. The Globe-Democrat also claims that our constitution antedates that of any other national charter in the world. Our constitutional framework, says our authority, takes precedence in age over Great Britain's present unwritten constitution, and the following figures are given in support of the statemant: "The three great franchise acts of 1832, 1867 and 1884—the first of which added 500,000 to the electorate, the second 1,100,000, and the third 3,000,-000—made a sweeping alteration of Great Britain's governmental system. Prior to the passage of the act of 1832 only one person in fifty in Great Britain was permitted to vote for members of Parliament." We have not taken time to verify these dates, but we think that the point is made sufficiently clear and strong to place America in a position to command more respect by virtue of her priority in the essential features of her government than other nations have been inclined to give her.

THE NASHVILLE CONVENTION.

The Seventeen Annual Convention of the Young People's Society of Christian Endeavor is closing its sessions at Nashville, Tenn., as we go to press. It opened with eleven public meetings on Wednesday night last, and at each of these two addresses were delivered on some phase of the general subject of spiritual enduement, followed by a brief service of prayer for greater spiritual power. Such meetings were a fit prelude to the convention.

On Thursday at 9 A. M. the old board of trustees met, completed its business and adjourned *sine die*, as the times of all its members expired. Its last act was to elect trustees under the new charter, which makes several important changes in the society. It has taken about three years to secure this new and more liberal charter, so many legal snags were encountered in the laws of Massachusetts. One of the articles under the new charter provides that each evangelical religious body shall be entitled to one trustee, and one additional trustee for every one thousand societies of Christian Endeavor in its membership. In addition to this each state president of the state union, is or becomes a trustee of the United Society. This greatly increases the number of trustees.

As we have over 4,000 societies (4,547) we are entitled to five trustees under the new charter. These were elected as follows: J. Z. Tyler, J. H. Garrison, F. D. Power, A. B. Philputt and H. L. Willett. In addition to these we have several state union presidents who also belong to the board. This arrangement gives an equal and fair representation to each religious body. The new board, as thus constituted, held its meeting immediately after the adjournment of the old board, the new charter permitting the trustees to hold a meeting and transact business outside of Massachusetts. The proceedings were marked by harmony and brotherly love.

The convention assembled in the auditorium Endeavor, on the Centennial Exposition Ground, a mile west of the city, at 3 P. M. As the attendance from abroad, owing to the fear of hot weather, was not so large as it has been at other places, admission to the hall was not limited to those having the Endeavor badge, but the doors were thrown open to the public. It was a magnificent audience that filled the great and beautifully decorated auditorium at that hour. The first incident of interest was the presentation to Pres. Clark of a gavel made by a convict in one of the jails of Kentucky, who had been led to Christ by Christian Endeavorers. An "Ode of Welcome," composed by Prof. Hinds, was then sung by the convention, led by Prof. Excell.

Pres. Clark here read the proclamation of President McKinley, calling upon the people to give thanks to God for our recent victories and to pray for the speedy return of peace. Prayer was then offered, led by Rev. Jacobs, of Columbus, Miss. The scene was most impressive. Pres. Clark read a telegram he had prepared to send to the President, and Secretary Baer read a telegram from President McKinley extendings his greetings to the convention, which was received with great applause. The audience by this time was in the right mood to sing "America," and when it was announced by Prof. Excell, it evoked great enthusiasm and was sung with much earnestness.

Rev. Ira Landrith, chairman of the local committee, delivered an address of welcome in behalf of the Endeavorers, and Rev. James I. Vance in behalf of the pastors. Both these addresses were in the happiest vein and evoked great enthusiasm. The climax of interest was reached, however, when Gov. Taylor delivered his inimitable address welcoming the Endeavorers in behalf of the state. His opening sentence was specially charateristic: "As the flowers welcome the light of the morning, as the green earth smiles welcome to the summer sunshine and shower, as the possum welcomes the ripe persimmon, and the old-time darky welcomes the possum, so Nashville gives welcome unto you." He expressed the hope that the North and the South might deliberate harmoniously in this convention, "as when Uncle Rastus held Aunt Dinah's hand in his and asked, 'Who's Sweet?' and Aunt Dinah dropped her head on his shoulder and answered, 'Bofe of us!'" It is needless to say this caught the audience. But this speech was not all humor. His speech abounded in sentiments of true patriotism and religion. When at the close of his address he expressed the wish that the earth might be girdled with Christian Endeavor, and every kindred and tribe should join in singing:

> "All hail the power of Jesus' name,
> Let angels prostrate fall!"

and started the tune himself, the scene was indescribable. The choir and platform first joined in, and then the whole vast audience sprang to its feet and caught up the strain with—

> "Bring forth the royal diadem,
> And crown him Lord of all."

The song was sung through, and at its close there was an applause that made the rafters ring. Never before, perhaps, in the history of this country has one of its governors led such an audience in such a song.

Responses to these addresses of welcome were made by members representing the East, the West, the South and the North, and Canada, all brief but hearty and appropriate. The last of these was by a Brother Grotthouse, of Dallas, Texas, who closed his stirring remarks by starting, "Blest be the tie that binds," in which the great audience joined, while many eyes were moist with tears. Then came the address of Dr. Clark, the keynote of which was, "Fruit-bearing"—bearing "much fruit." It was earnest, practical, wise, and touched upon the deeper things of the kingdom.

We have thus far only briefly sketched the opening session of the convention. It would be impossible to even mention the names of the various speakers on the program. The daily papers of Nashville
have given such spa
publication of thes
were many prominer
principal platforms,
session there was a
two large aaditorium
We can only mentic
prominent features o

PATR

The convention w
between the North a
lines were obliterate
ran high. Dr. Burre
he had heard of a N
somewhere South, bu
to find it, and he sup
ish minister on retir
with him! Saturday
to patriotism. Gene
Federal and Confede
the platform and addr
Gen. O. O. Howard
Clement A. Evans, of
Morgan, of New Yor
gerald and Arnett—
made speeches equal
to the Stars and Strip
expressing a unity of
and their equal devo
country and to our co
the heartiest applause
in this patriotic serv
Jack was draped with
over the stand on the
dian brother said w
talking of a politic
Great Britain and
Christian Endeavor h
Christian alliance, an
in order to make
formal alliance. A So
"If there had been an
tian Endeavor Society
tions in the differe
country, there would
between North and
never be another."

One of the notable
the convention was an
Dr. R. S. McArthur, c
"God's Hand in the P
was an able, eloquent
that showed how Go
nation now as in the p
most enthusiastic endo
audience that heard it

FRATER

In closing his addr
Vance, of Nashville, s
the Father, and of t
Holy Ghost, I baptize
nual convention of C
the Convention of Bro
true to its baptisma
seemed to be *immerse*
rather than merely *spr*
did denominational lin
the free interchange c
than in this conventior
sectarian feeling mar
observe it. All who
to recognize the fact t
and we are all brethr
been so profoundly co
dential mission of Ch
promote unity of fee
among Christian pe
mutual acquaintances
common platform up
workers can stand t
service.

SPIRITUAL.

In every meeting there was an undertone of spiritual aspiration which frequently found expression, but the "Quiet Hour" meetings, conducted by Dr. Wilbur Chapman, of Philadelphia, and attended by large outpourings of people each morning, were remarkable for their spiritual power and earnestness. Seldom if ever have we witnessed such intense interest, such evident desire for a deeper spiritual life, as marked these morning gatherings. We felt while listening to Dr. Chapman's talks that it could but prove an unmixed blessing if he could be secured to conduct such a series of meetings in connection with one of our national conventions. We might not approve of all his nomenclature, or even all his statements, but his penetrating, heart-searching presentation of God's Word, and his appeal for what he calls a "surrendered life," would find a most hearty response in the men and women who attend our conventions, and would prove most helpful in the real work of the convention. Dr. Clark is giving much emphasis to the "Quiet Hour" feature of Endeavor work, and we hope the local societies among us will keep it prominently before their members. These were the characteristic features of the Nashville convention: Patriotic, Fraternal, Spiritual.

OUR RALLY.

Friday forenoon was devoted to "Denominational Rallies." The members of the several religious bodies meet in places appointed for that purpose to consider matters of interest to themselves and to get acquainted. The Vine Street Christian Church was well filled with our members who were present, and Bro. Harvout, of Cincinnati, presided. A number of brief addresses were made, most of which were volunteer speeches, and all of which related to the general theme of "How We May Best Promote Unity." It was specially cheering to hear words from our brethren in the far South who, in the face of many discouragements, are holding aloft the banner of Christ. J. Z. Tyler, national superintendent of Christian Endeavor among us, presented his report, showing a great deal of painstaking drudgery on his part. We shall give our readers in a later issue the material facts in this report. Let it suffice here to say that he reports a gain of 547 societies in our churches since his last report. He has not been able to secure complete statistics. The Bethany C. E. Reading Courses are gaining ground, and over nine thousand copies of the three text-books prepared for these courses have been sold.

The following brethren represented us during the convention as speakers: F. D. Power, Philip Pendleton, J. Z. Tyler, I. J. Spencer, Chas. B. Newman, Z. T. Sweeney and J. H. Garrison. There may have been others whose names have escaped us. There were others that occupied pulpits on Sunday.

NEXT CONVENTION

Goes to Detroit. Cincinnati and Philadelphia also made application for it, but it was not their time. Chas. B. Newman was complimented on all hands for the very able presentation he made of the claims of Detroit, as chairman of the committee from that city. It will be a delightful place for such a convention, and a large attendance may be safely predicted.

Nashville did herself proudly, both in the entertainment of the convention and in the kind of weather it afforded. The local committee did its work thoroughly under the chairmanship of Rev. Ira Landrith, and their only disappointment was that more did not come. And yet this fact made it possible for the people of Nashville to get much more good from the convention. Nashville is a beautiful city, and its citizens did all in their power to make us all happy. The convention of '98 must be set down as pre-eminently the Convention of Brotherly Love.

A WORD FROM PAUL TO THE PREACHERS.

At the close of his Colossian letter Paul sends a message to Archippus, probably a young minister, which will bear repeating to all who, in our time, have received a like ministry "in the Lord:" "Say to Archippus, Take heed to the ministry which thou hast received in the Lord, that thou fulfill it." This is the advice of one of the greatest preachers in the world, and an inspired preacher, too, to all young ministers, especially who, like Archippus, have received "in the Lord"—in his name and for his honor and glory—the high calling of preaching his gospel.

The admonition suggests two points, or raises two questions, which are worth considering: 1. What is it to "take heed to the ministry?" 2. What is it to "fulfill" that ministry in the age in which we live?

I. *Taking heed to the ministry.*

One of the most essential things to do in taking heed to one's ministry is to take heed to one's self. This was Paul's idea, for he wrote to Timothy, another young preacher, "Take heed to thyself and to thy teaching." We cannot dissociate the messenger from his message. "Preaching," says Phillips Brooks, "is truth and personality mixed." As the truth is pure, so the personality of the preacher should be. The first respect, therefore, in which a preacher should take heed unto himself is as to the purity of his life and character. No man should undertake the responsibility of preaching the gospel of purity to others unless his own life be pure. Paul admonishes Timothy to "flee youthful lusts" and the love of money, and to "follow after righteousness, godliness, faith, love, patience, meekness." A preacher cannot too jealously guard his reputation against the suspicion of impurity of life, or of being influenced by mercenary aims.

Another respect in which a preacher should take heed to himself is his bodily health. Every preacher owes it to his sacred calling to give it the benefit of the soundest and most robust physical health. This involves self-mastery, the control of the appetites. Many a preacher who totally abstains from intoxicating drinks is intemperate at the table. In eating, as in everything else, the preacher should "let his moderation be known to all men." Many a preacher's health is injured, his usefulness curtailed and his mental and spiritual development retarded by gluttonous habits.

No minister of the gospel in our day can take heed to his ministry who does not study and keep up with the thought of the age in which he lives. When Paul was in prison in Rome he requested Timothy to bring him, not only the cloak which he had left at Troas, but "the books, especially the parchments." Perhaps we may understand by the "books" the current literature of Paul's time, and by the "parchments" the sacred Scriptures of the Old Testament. If Timothy could not bring both the books and the parchments, he must be sure to bring the latter. It is well for the preacher to be acquainted with the best writers of his time, but he *must* be acquainted with the Holy Scriptures if he is to be an efficient minister of the gospel of Christ. Paul was very emphatic on this point. "Till I come," he said to Timothy, "give heed to reading, to exhortation, to teaching. *Neglect not the gift that is in thee.* . . . Be diligent in these things; give thyself wholly to them, that thy progress may be manifest unto all." Paul was evidently a progressionist, and he wanted the young preachers of his day to be progressive in the sense of growing in the knowledge of truth and in the power of the Spirit. The preacher that does not grow is likely to shrivel up very soon, and complain of having reached the dead-line before he passes the half-century mark.

Once more, the preacher must give heed to his ministry by keeping himself in vital touch with Jesus Christ. He must cultivate his own spiritual life, while he is seeking to promote the spiritual welfare of others. He must drink deep of the Spirit of God, and struggle to attain the highest spiritual gifts if he is to lead others to high attainments in Christian life. It follows that he must be a man of prayer. His sermons must be conceived and delivered in the spirit of prayer. He must pray, not for himself alone, but he must be an intercessor, praying for those for whose souls he watches.

In such ways as these must the preacher take heed to his ministry. In a word, he must magnify his calling, and put his heart and soul into it. He must not seek to do too many things, but give himself wholly to the work of the ministry if he would attain to the highest degree of excellence and usefulness in his calling.

FORM AND POWER.

Form-religion is a matter of custom and habit. The Jews had been taught from infancy to reverence certain observances, and to perform certain religious rites, and these by constant repetition, in the course of time, became merely perfunctory and formal, and ceased to represent to the mind anything but the form itself. This is the origin of formalism in religion. It is natural for men to take superficial views of things, and to do as they are taught to do, and to believe what they do is all right, and as it is much easier to perform a religious rite than it is to do a moral duty, or be a spiritual person, it is equally natural to substitute the outward form for the inward life and power.

Religion consists of two things, form and spirit, or as Paul expresses it, form and power. Form is the body and spirit is the soul of godliness. It takes both to constitute a perfect religion. The form of a religion is intended to express its truth and life, and not to act as a substitute for them. Where the external form is made to do duty for the inward reality, the religion is dead and worthless. Judaism in the time of our Lord had more than six hundred ordinances. The rites and ceremonies of later Judaism had been steadily increasing for nearly four hundred years, until it had become a system of dead and dying forms, the animating spirit and inward life having gone out of it. All ritualistic and priestly religions degenerate into a mass of dead forms, and their morals are no better than those who have no religion at all. Ordinance-religions exert neither moral nor spiritual influence on the lives of their votaries any more than the false religions of paganism do, and both of them present the most incurable forms of worldliness. *A religious creed may be nothing more than a form of godliness, an intellectual form it is true, but still a form.* It is as easy to substitute a theory of religion for religion itself, as it is a sacrament or a ceremony. You may worship a religious idea and live like a heathen, just as you may worship a religious form or an idol and live like a heathen. There are men among ourselves who believe that a certain interpretation of the New Testament, and a certain conception of the church and its worship, make up apostolic Christianity, and these men compass land and sea on the same mission as the ancient Pharisees, declaring that churches using organs, and contributing their money through missionary societies for the evangelization of the world, and working through Endeavor Societies, and women's auxiliaries, and regular pastors, are not churches of Christ. On miserable theories and ignorances of this kind do these provincial gentry read us all out of the church. Their literature like their preaching is all polemic, controversial, combative, abounding, not infrequently, in abusive personalities. *This is a form of intellectual godliness that is neither intellectual nor godly.* If I were going to substitute a theory of Christianity for Christianity, a mental conception of the doctrines of godliness for godliness, I would adopt one with some sense in it, for this Texas and Tennessee provincialism is as irrational as it is unspiritual. The endless disputes of these men about trifles and questions of no vital importance remind me of a story told by Sir Samuel Baker, the great African explorer and hunter, to illustrate the extraordinary debating proclivities of some of the native tribes of Arabs. He had shot an immense hippopotamus, which when dragged to the shore was found to be covered with scars, showing that the old animal had been a great fighter in his day. Some of the men declared that his father had thus misused him, others were of the opinion that it was his mother, and the argument ran high and waxed hot. These Arabs have an extraordinary taste for argument upon the most trifling points. Baker says he has frequently known his men to argue throughout the greater part of the night and commence the same argument on the following morning. These debates generally ended in a fight, and in the present instance the excitement of the hunt only added to the heat of the argument. They at length agreed to refer it to the master, and both parties approached, vociferously advancing their theories; one-half persisting that the old hippo had been bullied by his father, and the other maintained that it had been by the mother. Baker being referee, suggested that "perhaps it was his uncle" "Wah Allahi sahe." (By Allah, it is true.) Both parties were satisfied with the suggestion; dropping their theories they became practical and fell to with knives and axes to cut up the cause of the argument. The Arab disputer has the advantage. He does not believe in his own infallibility, in the first place; in the second, he is easily squelched by arbitration; in the third place, he abandons his foolish theorizing in the end and acts on practical common sense. The question as to whether a bull hippo in Abysinia was scarred by his father, mother or uncle, is a question of more importance than some of the issues that agitate churches, because they engage the attention of a certain class of preachers. No kinds of mental concepts worked into controversial theories are anything more than a form of godliness, and nearly always without its power.

The ordinances of the church, observed with the most scrupulous exactness, may be nothing more than a form of godliness. An ordinance is a symbol and must always be distinguished from the truth which it symbolizes. It is an object-lesson, a picture, setting forth a certain truth or truths, which it is important to keep before the mind. If the inward meaning of the ordinance is not present in the mind and heart of the man who observes it, the whole significance and purpose of it is missed, and it remains a lifeless and therefore worthless form. The meaning of baptism is the cleansing of the soul from sin; it is hence the symbol of regeneration. The Lord's supper has a sacrificial significance. It means the surrender of self to God in holy sacrifice for man. It was love and self-sacrifice that transfigured the cross, and that glorifies human character. Suppose a man's body is dipped in water when his soul is not cleansed from sin, and he sits at the communion table without a knowledge of the sacrificial spirit of Christianity: the first is not Christian baptism, and the last is not the Lord's supper. When these become mere outward forms, signifying nothing, they cease to be Christian ordinances, and become hindrances more than helps to Christian character. That which makes baptism of vital importance is not water; that which makes the Lord's supper a means of grace is not bread and wine; that which makes the church a beneficent redeeming agency in the world is not the visible organization, "for our gospel came not unto you in word only, but also in power and in the Holy Spirit and in much assurance." Church membership and church attendance may be mere forms of godliness without the power.

Church membership is right and according to the will of God, and church attendance is a virtue to be commended, but like everything else good they may be perverted so as to defeat the accomplishment of the purpose for which they were appointed. When church connection is merely nominal, when it imposes no restraint, and brings no obligation, when it signifies nothing to either intelligence or conscience, it is a sin to be answered for and not a virtue to be rewarded. Any spiritual duty or privilege discharged in a perfunctory manner, from force of custom and habit, usage and fashion, is the letter that kills and not the spirit that gives life. If church membership and fellowship have no power to restrain the evil that is within us, to stimulate and cultivate the good, to deliver us out of worldliness into righteousness, they are dead cinders in which all the divine fire has been extinguished. This was the trouble with the Jewish church in the time of our Lord and for many centuries before. It had degenerated into a dead formalism that made men worse instead of better. The language that Isaiah used to describe the men of his generation Christ employs to describe the men of his: "This people draw nigh to me with their lips, but their hearts are far from me." They were still zealous for the temple service, and more punctilious in the observance of forms than they had been in the best days of their spiritual enthusiasm. Because their lives were corrupt and immoral God despised their worship, although the outward form of their service was according to the law. "Bring no more vain oblations; incense is an abomination unto me; new moons and sabbaths, the calling of assemblies—I cannot away with iniquity and the solemn meeting. Your new moons and your appointed feasts my soul hateth; they are a trouble unto me; I am weary to bear them. And when ye spread forth your hands, I will hide mine eyes from you: yea when ye make many prayers, I will not hear; [why?] your hands are full of blood; wash you, make you clean; put away the evil of your doings from before mine eyes; cease to do evil; learn to do well; seek justice; relieve the oppressed; judge the fatherless; plead for the widow." Because these sacrifices had been offered by unclean hands, and these prayers had emanated from impure hearts, accompanied by corrupt and wicked lives, the forms that God himself had commanded became an abomination to him. If these offerings had proceeded from clean hands, and these prayers from pure hearts, followed by lives of justice, mercy and kindness to men, these forms would have been acceptable to God, because joined to the power they were intended to express and promote. Church membership and fellowship are acceptable to God and beneficial to us if the Spirit is in them, and they tend to foster the life of God in our souls. The power has gone out of the form when it ceases to express a pure, earnest and consistent religious life. The greatest peril to our religion is that the dry rot of formalism may set in and lead us to substitute religious forms for the divine life and a holy character, leading us to believe when we have done the form we have paid the debt, purchased the indulgence, and may henceforth lead the life of the world and do as we please. J. J. H.

OUR SPECIAL OFFER.

With the view of introducing the CHRISTIAN-EVANGELIST to a large number of new readers, we are offering the paper from the time the subscription is received until the end of the present year for *seventy-five cents*. We earnestly solicit the active assistance of our old readers in making this offer known, and in extending our circulation. It is hoped that the new form will be acceptable to all our friends, and may be made the occasion by them of a special effort in its behalf.

s all, by which we may promote the ex-
sion of the kingdom of God. We may be able to preach sermons or write ks, but we can live the Christian life, the aid of the divine Spirit, which is ays within our reach. We can let our it shine in the several spheres in which move. It may not be a large light, but an be a *true* light, and it may make the ne, the shop, the office, beautiful with mild radiance.

Iow can we let our light "so shine that ers seeing our good works may be con-
ined to glorify our Father in heaven?" purity of life, by sweetness of temper, a cheerful disposition, by a contented id, by a sympathetic heart, by unselfish l loving deeds, by esteeming others bet-
that ourselves, by seeking to make oth-
lives brighter and happier, by seeking l embracing opportunities for doing od. Who can help loving one who ex-
its these virtues and graces? And how we fail to love and glorify Him whose ice and goodness make such a life possi-
?

What mighty results would follow this ayer-meeting, if each disciple here to-
ght should leave this place fully deter-
ned to henceforth let the light of Christ's e shine through his daily life? Why ould not this purpose be formed and why ould we not here and now seek the dine strength to carry out so high and so rthy a purpose?

PRAYER.

O Thou who art the Light and Life of men! hine Thou into our hearts, and expel hatever lingering darkness may be found ere. We thank and adore Thee that Thou st caused the light of Thy glory to shine on us, and that it is our blessed privilege reflect Thy light upon a dark world. elp us, we pray Thee, to receive, in a rger measure, Thy light into our souls, at we may be more truly light-bearers to e world. Enable us to realize as we have ver done before how much our conduct d characters have to do with impeding promoting the progress of Thy kingdom. ay we henceforth, strengthened and sus-
ined by Thy divine grace, be enabled to flect more faithfully the light we have ceived from Thee, that men may be con-
rained by our example to glorify our Fa-
er in heaven. For Thy name's sake. men!

Editor's Easy Chair.

OR LAKESIDE MUSINGS.

We were glad to have a visit, at Macat-
wa, Park, a few days ago, from our old end, Gen. Drake, of Iowa. His friends ll be glad to learn that he has dispensed th his crutches and is walking with his ne, and while his locomotion is by no ans rapid or perfect, he manages to get ong quite well. It was a pretty good test his climbing ability to ascend the stair-
ys leading up to the upper verandah of lgewood-on-the-Lake. Since the expira-
n of his term as governor he has been ving special attention to his health which, our readers may remember, was very ich impaired by his fall on the steps of e State House in Des Moines, and his alth has been gradually improving. We re glad to see him looking so robust. He recently sold his railroad interests, we former gifts to the same institution, is building him a monument there much to be preferred to the costly memorial shafts or mausoleums that mark the graves of many men of wealth. We trust he may live many years to enjoy the vast good that is being accomplished through the institution founded and nurtured by his munificence. He will probably return with his family to the Park to spend several weeks.

In making a trip from our lakeside re-
sort in the torrid zone, relatively speaking, we spent two days, including the Lord's day, in the vicinity of the University of Chicago and of the Hyde Park Church of Christ, and had occasion to note the progress of enterprises there in which our readers are interested. The Disciples' Di-
vinity House, under the deanship of Dr. H. L. Willett, is proving its usefulness and its right to be, more and more with each passing year. The number of our young men now at the University is greater, we be-
lieve, than at any previous time, and what is more gratifying is the high character and ability of those who are in attendance from year to year. They have made and are making a distinct impression upon the University authorities by their solid at-
tainments, by their clear knowledge of biblical themes and by the strength of their religious convictions. At the annual meeting of the board of trustees of the Divinity House, held while we were there, an agreement was entered into between that body and the trustees of the Hyde Park Church of Christ, by which the former will be relieved of an indebtedness on its lot and the latter will become owners of a part of same, on which they are to erect a chapel for the use of the church. It seems to us a wise arrangement, both for the Divinity House and the church. Arrangements were made by the trustees of the Divinity House to have the work of Dr. Willett carried on during his visit to Eng-
land, which will begin in the autumn and last until the early part of the following summer.

It was our pleasure to speak for the Hyde Park Church on Sunday morning, at the request of its pastor, Rev. Errett Gates. The congregation meets, as heretofore, in a hall, and the room is not well ventilated for this season of the year. In spite of this fact, however, a good congregation was present, and a very appreciative one it was. We were glad to learn that the church is making a substantial growth under the wise management of Bro. Gates, who is proving himself to be well adapted to the field. Our home while there was with Bro. C. A. Young and wife, and there are few places on earth where we could feel more at home than under their hospitable roof. Bro. Young's friends at the University and elsewhere are delighted at the fact that he has been enabled, in spite of the many calls upon his time and energy in the way of Bible lectures and work for the C. W. B. M., to carry forward his studies so success-
fully as to win an honorable and diffi-
cult degree from the University. He is still pursuing his studies, but his plans are to devote the autumn and winter months

before him a bright and useful future as a Bible lecturer." He has already gained considerable distinction in his field, especially in the South, and is continually fitting himself more fully for this kind of work. Mrs. Young and their little daughter, Helen, will accompany him during his trip South in the coming autumn and winter.

Dr. H. L. Willett is one of the busiest of men. Besides preaching on Sunday he delivers an afternoon lecture on some Bible topic in the central part of the city on each Sunday afternoon. These lectures are well attended and are developing a good deal of interest. He is to deliver a special course of lectures at Macatawa Park during the second week in August. Rev. J. M. Campbell, of Lombard, author of "After Pentecost, What?" and other works, will also give lectures during the summer. Besides these lectures, which will occur in the forenoons, there will be an address during the six evenings of the week by prominent ministers of our own people and the Congregationalists, on the different aspects of the subject of Christian Union. It is believed that we are to have one of the most interesting assemblies ever held at the Park. We would be glad if many readers of the CHRISTIAN-EVANGELIST could arrange to spend August at Macatawa Park to enjoy this among other attractions.

A great gathering of the young people, including several of the grey-headed young, convenes this week in the city of Nashville. No doubt it will be an inspiring occasion, and the editor hopes to be there to share in the enthusiasm, and if possible transmit some of it through the pages of the CHRISTIAN-EVANGELIST to our readers. This movement among the young people is too significant not to have attracted the attention of all thoughtful people. It means much to the kingdom of God. It has in it the promise and the potency of things of which many of us have not yet dreamed. It will be a pleasure to meet and greet the people of other names and creeds who love the Lord Jesus and are seeking to promote His supremacy in the world. We shall have more to say next week.

Current Religious Thought

The Presbyterian Banner incidentally gives the following excellent definition of liberty, which it denominates "a still greater height of freedom:"

The truest liberty is not outward, but inward. A man may be free outside, and yet be a slave inside. No fetters may be upon his hands, and yet there may be fetters on his mind and heart. Ignorance, prejudice, evil feelings, passion, bad habits, are forms of bondage more abject and fatal than the slave-driver's lash. A man is not really free until he is free in his soul; until he knows the truth and lives according to the laws of righteousness. The highest liberty is obedience to the right. There is no antagonism between such obedience and freedom, but the fullest harmony; the one is the means of the other. The steel track does not restrict the liberty of the locomotive, but gives it all the liberty it has. When the locomotive leaves the track its liberty is gone. So truth and right do not restrict a man's liberty, but conserve and enlarge it; when he begins to violate these, his freedom of soul is impaired. "Ye shall know the truth, and the truth shall make you free." The soul is free only when its desires coincide with duties and all its activities flow in one unbroken, unimpeded stream. Then the scul desires to do only what it ought to do, no sense of restriction binds it, all its impulses are harmonized into one music, and it enters into the glorious liberty of the sons of God.

The Independent concludes a thoughtful, timely article in a recent number, with the following paragraph on Christ's law of love:

Christ's law of love knows no exception. It embraces all that can be loved. It looks upward to God, the Giver of all good, and outward to every human being. It excludes no foreigner and no enemy; for even the enemy is to be loved as one's self. Above all it does not forget God. It recognizes him as the universal Father, the source of every blessing, the fountain of goodness and love, the author of life, temporal and eternal, through whose Son we have salvation; and it gives him the fullest love of the heart. It reaches out beyond family and neighbors and citizens to all humanity everywhere, the most ignorant and degraded, and it despises none, it loves all. It is the grandest, the most expansive of all sentiments, that which most enlarges the soul, that which brings man nearest to God. If the church by its ideals is lifting, and if it shall finally conquer the world, it is because its outreach is larger than any other that the world knows. Patriotism is noble, but Christian consecration is divine. Jesus gave the highest law, the most philosophical rule of pure ethics, nay, of pure religion, the world has ever heard, that beyond which human speculation cannot rise, when he laid down that law, not of justice nor of righteousness, on which Christianity rests, "Thou shalt love the Lord thy God with all thy heart, and thy neighbor as thyself."

Edward B. Coe, D. D., Acbury, N. J., gives expression to the following sound doctrine in an article in the Christian Intelligencer on patriotism:

What, then, does an enlightened patriotism require of us? It does not require that we should close our eyes to the evils of various kinds which are prevalent among us, or to the dangers which threaten our welfare as a nation. It does not demand that we shall go about boasting of the progress we have made in wealth and power, of our superiority to everybody else, and of the great things that we are going to do in the future. In fact, a boastful spirit is far from being a patriotic spirit. In this regard we can hardly surpass, if we try, the Spaniards or the Turks. The braggart is almost always an ignorant man, and very often a coward. He may be the truest lover of his country who sees most clearly its faults and its weaknesses. Love is apt to be blind, as the familiar proverb says, but the truest love is not blind to faults that it can correct and evils that it can remedy. A carping, critical and cynical spirit is not a patriotic spirit; but on the other hand, he does not serve his country well who is not keenly alive to whatever elements of weakness and sources of dishonor may appear in the national life. It is patriotism and not disloyalty which leads a man to seek to arrest the tide of political corruption, to allay the jealousies existing among the different classes of society, to oppose any form of organized power, whether of corporations or of politicians, by which the freedom and purity and peace of the community are threatened. It is idle for us to hope that the flag which now waves over us, and which we delight to honor, will retain its inspiring power for generations to come, if it stands for what is sordid, selfish, unjust, oppressive, instead of for liberty and truth and righteousness.

Of the larger view of the war and the new responsibilities which are coming upon this nation The Interior says:

The effect of the war, so unselfishly and so boldly waged for the rescue of Cuba from its "unsufferabe condition," has struck the alarm bell of the world and set people to thinking. It has signaled the hour for a new alignment of the Christian forces of the country, rather of the whole Anglo-American order of civilization wherever there are those who have at heart the uplifting of men into the following and redeeming fellowship of the Son of Man. These days, we may be sure, will hereafter be accounted great days in human history. It is a wise church which knows the time. Any Christian life, in high or in humble place, will now be endowed with telling power, "ages on ages telling," which shall be quick to fall into line with the divine timeliness as to the next things to be done. With such a case as we are in just now we are the last people to be caught either napping or trifling. As for the churches of America, they are either decadent and dying or else, morally speaking, they are clearing their decks for action, determined, for one thing, that this shiftless and treacherous policy of everlasting "retrenchment" along our missionary lines shall be ended. The lesson on how to do things, which Dewey has taught the world, will not soon be forgotten.

Instantly the
opened the way
in the Philippir
Christian educa
portunity. Th
one preceives, i
crisis. Wheth
or goes down, c
all-overbroodin
the light and le
it is clear that a
change the con
four hundred
empire. Alth
spoken of by I
"dying nations
way—the hour
rather turn ou
springing and
Lord's saying:
is, when the d
Son of God; an
Sought or uns
American Repu
conspicuous of a
acter of its chu
ganizations is be

In an article
antism," the S
very clearly se
of our war wit

The developme
the Western C
est sense of th
civilization and,
of the highest a
Christianity is n
armies, yet Dew
the artillery of S
ago were, uncon
ing to solve the
ress. There are
force can they be
of life; there are
scale that fleets a
their rulers com
of the fittest is a
as in nature; th
the world have c
tional affairs bec
prosper, the nati
man Catholic re
because of their a
and religious fai
with the highest
The triumphs of
are the triumphs
of civilization; t
cupation of crum
of Spanish ships;
Saxon influence
never before kno
that Protestantis
vancing with gia
the purest form c
the earth is in si

The evil of a
the New York
paragraph, can
demned. If ou
athleticism wit
better go thro
The New York

There is, howe
possible physica
letic exercises a
hosts of young
harm that com
abuses. The gre
is the sporting in
to almost all gar
hension of the g
letics seem one
gambling and dri
days have come t
substance of the
fact, such custo
on the practice
represent a mora
physical order.
orous common s
questions. Beca
for example, to t
his biceps, it doe
him to stake his
with wine, inste
that cheek whic
loved to kiss. It
country should d
sensational, com
and champion s
the road and the s
young men of .
grannies, nor sh
other hand, to h
crowd of gamest
True and fals
should be sharp

more keen and clear than other 'hey see clearly and run swiftly ers grope and fall. Men become their contemporaries than like estors or posterity. Men of the t, party or community become is claimed that if two persons ether long enough we could not h one from the other. It isn't o know as much and become as our companions, and men who same things are not long the best for each other. Hence we need to break the monotonous spell, uce new life, to chase away our

men, however, should not appear he essence of greatness, as great-lf, but as the exponent, as the ative of greatness. Accepting as the essence of greatness, as itself, leads to hero-worship, narchies possible and culminated, in the silly doctrine of the divine kings and to the accepting of such ts as "I am the state." It makes political bosses and party tyranny. nces party and custom rather than . But the accepting of great men xponent, as the representation of s, leads to truth-worship, for we gh the phase of truth which they t the greater and broader truth, they become instead of an effect, a stead of an end, a means. Their come a lens through which we see nto which we see.

men are leaders of thought in their f action and are indispensable to re of the race, for no great truth r been thoroughly established rough a great man.

is better than its great and cherish-for no stream can rise higher than e, yet the

lives of great men all remind us,
We can make our lives sublime,
nd departing leave behind us,
Footprints in the sands of time."

really great men are not needed, Gladstone was really great and was needed, his successors will tly demonstrate what his con-ries have not. He was the highest Anglo-Saxon manhood. Having sidered the place, use and charac-of a great man, let us specifically the life and work of Gladstone.

hat Gladstone did.

'itt instituted the doctrine of Eng-rvention and for years England's policy was that of might, seizing , dictating terms to other nations rally foisting her authority before ld, more in the light of a dictator n adviser. It was but an exhibi-the selfishness of man that always ndency to assert itself, especially strong, when not controlled by a rongly counteracting altruistic in-

This doctrine of selfish interven-s strongly supported in turn by lmerston, Disraeli and Salisbury. e overcame the haughty attitude ght England the Golden Rule. e's doctrine of non-intervention o its lawful end would result in the ng of standing armies, the trans-of spears into pruning-hooks, the ng of warships into ships of com-the dealings of man with man on the principles of justice, the federation of the world, the parliament of man and the ultimate brotherhood of the race.

(b) Gladstone battled for free laws, free religion and free trade. He held that men everywhere should enjoy the blessings of liberty unhampered by unjust laws. He battled for the repeal of hard, unjust and class laws. He instituted many reform laws, ignoring the distinctions of nobility and royalty. He stood as a staunch friend of men. Like George he was not a friend of the capitalist or the laborer, but of man. That unjust and favorite class legislation has wrought untold evil goes without further discussion. It has enriched the few and impoverished the many. It is a relic of Feudal days, and Gladstone smote it a deadly blow. In commerce he contended that protectionism was but a shift at self-aggrandizement at the expense of others, the truthfulness of which the evolution of the humane spirit in man will demonstrate what our obtuse reason has failed to do.

In religion he held that men should be left to their individual convictions and not to men of like passions and faults. That the church was not intended to be subservient to the state is wholly evident from the attitude of Jesus and the early church under the direct guidance of the apostles. But that they should be adjuncts, Gladstone believed and contended for. He fought for liberty, industry and religion, neither one of which can be dispensed with, and only in whose harmonious union there can come universal prosperity and peace. That he succeeded beyond measure and bequeathed to humanity a rare legacy, his record abundantly attests.

(c) He was subject to his sovereign and honored the Queen, but not in the manner that makes a crowned head a divine or better head than other heads. He did more than any dozen Englishmen to make the crown a harmless bauble. Only as recently as the time of her predecessor, in the reign of her uncle, were the votes of Parliament defied. The Queen, imbued with the desires of royalty, and not reading correctly the sentiment of her subjects, attempted to defy her lawmakers. Gladstone presented a reform bill to her for signature. Being much displeased with it, she said to him, "Sir, I am the Queen of England and I will not sign that bill;" whereupon the great Commoner replied, "And I, madam, am the people of England and the people demand you sign that bill." She scowled and signed the bill.

(d) We have been led to believe that a politician and a good man were not to be found in the same individual, but Gladstone has taught us better. There has perhaps never been a statesman who carried his Christian principles more fully into his public life and actions. He made politics a conscientious duty. He believed in doing all things unto the Lord. He did much to obliterate the imaginary line between the sacred and the secular. He verily believed that "the earth was the Lord's and the fullness thereof;" hence he could not see that a thing, though evil, was allowable because it happened to be secular. No scandal ever marred his record. He was always possessed of an eager passion to do the right thing always. Lord Salisbury was quite right when he said, "Gladstone will not be remembered so much as a minister of finance or a party leader as the great Christian statesman." But all he fully accomplished will, perhaps, not be more helpful and inspiring to us than the prominent characteristics that distinguished him.

2. *Type of man Gladstone was.*

(a) There are three types of statesmen: one who is too far in advance of his time to be duly appreciated by and of the most assistance to his contemporaries. Such a statesman was Bright. He saw the future as correctly as many see the present. Another type of statesman is too far behind his time to be of practical use to men. Such a man is Salisbury. While the most helpful, and without doubt the greatest statesman, is the one who is able to grasp the future. This sort of man was Gladstone. He was not carried away by vain visions and hopes of the future, nor retarded by the regrets of lost hopes. He realized that the future was veiled from view, and that he who acted well in the present would have few regrets for the future.

(b) He spent much time in unlearning the prejudices of his life. In this he was a prince among men. More ordinary men deemed it a weakness to admit a once cherished tenet as false; but not so with him. There is perhaps no character so great who unlearned so many things. In early life he was an ultra conservative, styled by Macaulay as the rising leader of the stern and unyielding Tories. Later he became the champion of reform and an advanced liberal party. He was a conservative protectionist, but he became a radical free-trader. He changed his views on the foreign policy and was, in his life, on both sides of the Irish question. He thought of the ministry, studied law, but gave up both and became a statesman and an author. On all questions save his religious convictions he changed his views. Yet, with all his record of altered views, no one deems him to have been a vacilating man. A careful perusal of his life will reveal the fact that every view which underwent a change was substituted for a broader and more liberal one. First, a narrow—and bigoted as they always are—conservative, then a broad liberal; first a narrow—and selfish as they must be—protectionist, then a broad and world-wide free-trader. He believed that—

"Through the ages one increasing purpose runs,
And the thoughts of men are broadened by the process of the suns."

(c) He followed duty and principle at any cost. The Bulgarian horrors brought forth from him a number of scathing criticisms that for a time threatened his success, but in no way lessened his ardor. The Armenian troubles likewise were considered by him at the expense of temporary popularity, but like Paul of old, his duty was his master, and what were impassable barriers to other men were stepping-stones for him to higher things. He, during the civil war in America, sypathized with the South, but future developments convinced him of his error, and true to his duty he urged the Alabama claims. He said of America as flattering things as Webster ever said, and wished us Godspeed from the depths of his great soul.

(d) Gladstone was the type of man for our time. Always open to conviction. Ever ready to espouse a just cause, though at the sacrifice of position and popularity and contrary to his presupposed conceptions. He was strong enough in vision to see that the problems of to-day were not to be solved by the methods of yesterday. He followed his convictions of right regardless of position or party lash. He was offered a peerage, but he chose to remain plain Mr. Gladstone. He has been an inspiration to our time and the legacy he hath bequeathed to posterity is beyond the range of earthly computation. May his ashes rest in peace, as we are confident his spirit is in the abode of paradise. Let us, while we pause beside his tomb, wreathe from our tenderest affection about the hallowed little mound a garland of purest love, and drop into its silent bosom a kind and tender tear, and thus pass on into the world he loved so much better and truer men.

Butte, Mont.

MINISTERIAL COURTESY.

GEO. L. PETERS.

That we may be the better able to apply the principles of Christian conduct to the minister in his work it will be well to ascertain the New Testament conception of the

man and his relation to his work. The modern preacher, whether scripturally so or not, does the work of both evangelist and pastor. The church expects him to preach, and it expects him to teach from house to house, ministering to the sick, both in body and soul, in meekness instructing those who oppose themselves, and exhorting to faithfulness the indifferent. If it should be necessary to warn the unruly or to exclude the impenitent, he is looked to for counsel, for instruction and generally for leadership. Should he fail to respond to the demands of either department of his work he is regarded, in a measure, as lacking in fitness for his calling.

The gospel ministry is the most sacred calling vouchsafed to man. In the wisdom of God men are the instruments through whom the devine message is to reach the world. "It pleased God by the foolishness of preaching to save them that believed." In the planning for the redemption of the race only one was permitted to join, but infinite intelligence has granted us a part in the joys of its consummation. "We are God's fellow-laborers." The commission of the risen and ascended Savior has all the sacredness and pathos of last words. His work on earth was finished. He had fulfilled all things required in the law and the prophets, and made possible the proclam tion of a message of joy and gladness, b it was not for him to proclaim it. He ha died that others might live, but the worl must hear that story from the lips of tho who had been born again. Wheth earth's teeming millions hear the story divine love or not depends upon the faith fulness of the Savior's messengers. Jesu did not call his disciples to lives of ease an and luxury, nor did he promise them place of authority in an eathly kingdom. Fa otherwise. Poverty, persecution, intens suffering and finally martyrdom were t be their lot. But their reward was to b sufficient to recompense them for all sacri fice. They were to have souls for thei hire. "Come ye after me and I will mak you fishers of men." The prospects wer inspiring, the results satisfying. Unde the wonderful power of the divine messag they saw the miser become the philanthro pist, the libertine become the puritan, th drunkard the abstainer, the bigot Jev the tolerant Christian. They rejoice that they were counted worthy to suffer i such a ministry, and Paul, ever enthusias tic in his work, wrote to Timothy, "I than Christ Jesus our Lord, who has given m power, because he counted me worthy, putting me into the ministry." To such ministry has God called us.

The minister is the central figure in the congregation. He is observed and patterne after more than any other. It is expecte that he shall "be in all things a pattern o good works." The earnest ones seek to find in him a leader who will strengthen thei own faith and draw them into a closer walk with God; the careless and indifferent are eagerly watchful for the least lapse in conduct tending to confirm them in their views of the Christian life; while the scoffer takes especial delight in reporting any seeming departure from the path of rectitude, either in faith or conduct. His life must be pure, outwardly and inwardly. The springs of his being must be purified by the salt of righteousness, that the stream of his life may be healing in its effects. He who is to exhort others to think on whatsoever things are pure must first take heed unto himself and give himself wholly to them. No mere platitudes from the pulpit will suffice. The surface of the stream may froth and foam, but the undercurrent indicates in which direction it is flowing. He must be humble. The Master of the household has givent to all talents, each according to his ability. Success crowns their use. He may be a Barnabas by whose earnest pleadings the number of believers greatly multiply, but he is exhorted to remember that he is not sufficient in himself. His sufficiency is of God, who hath made him an able minister of the New Testament. The greatest known preacher said, "I have planted, Apollos watered; but God gave the increase." The preacher must be bold. A strong ministry implies strong doctrine, and that comprehends not only what is pleasing, but what is purifying as well. There is a great temptation to seek the approval of all men by saying nice things, and there will always be those who, "having itching ears heap to themselves teachers" who will gratify their desire for fables instead of truth. Ministers are admonished to remember that the popular side is not always the safe side. It is not indictive of spiritual strength where all men

ɔf us. Sin must be rebuked, and
the salvation of the church re-
it shall be done before all. The
ıister must have the courage to
truth in love, even though he
lness for it.
ster's message is Christ. Self
lden that Christ may be seen.
.s needing Christ. Nothing else
. Philosophy and speculative
ve their place, but it is not the
personal trust in a personal Sav-
ıves. "Preach the Word," was
ıonition to Timothy. Not in-
r declamations about war; not
olutions of labor difficulties; not
quisitions about history, poetry,
t or any of the multitude of sub-
ı delight the ears and lull the
s of the unthinking ones. Bun-
that in his day "the unbelieving
ıt the Scriptures because carnal
tle the ears of their hearers with
ɔsophy and deceit, and thereby
ir hearts against the simplicity
pel and the Word of God." His
t ring out clear and strong in
ion of sin, while with tender pa-
nting Christ as the only remedy
He is Christ's evangel and he
what word of truth may be the
wer that will lead to the salvation
ıortal soul.
ıister's right to the pulpit which he
.s not absolute, but relative. The
ve a congregation is not an in-
o become dictator. It is rather a
o become leader. The evident
n of their confidence and esteem
n the call lays upon them the ob-
o respect his wishes and treat his
th higest consideration. At the
e he is not authorized to overide
ıes. They are the final sources of
They chose him, he did not choose
he relation of the minister and
e is of the closest nature. They are
in the Lord, children of the same
eirs to the same inheritance. He
eader, their spiritual instructor,
pathetic friend; the ties that bind
ether are sweet and tender; his
has heightened the joys of the
feast, and in the hour of darkness
has tenderly led them to lean
everlasting arms; they are, many
his children in the Lord, begotten
Jesus through his preaching of
l; their growth in the grace and
e of the Lord and Savior Jesus
pends upon his faithful ministry.
ıch realize their dependence upon
, the question of rights is easily

nis view of the minister and his
ıs consider his relation to a brother
in whose pulpit he may for a time
ed. There are two general cases
ıted, each involving a number of
ate ones. First, when the minister
nt; second, when the minister is
Each will be treated in its order.
e several obvious rules governing
ıct of the visiting minister which
cable to all cases where the min-
resent. From whatever source the
ı may have come, whether through
tation of a friend or the sponta-
rdiality of the minister, the visitor

tion of right demands that such courtesy shall not be violated. Every preacher has his own plans of work and his own method of conducting the services of the church. They may be crude and need changing. They may see much to critise, but his pulpit conduct ought not to indicate it. A word in private will generally be far more effective than a public rebuke or suggestion, and certainly will be less humiliating. Good-breeding would seem to suggest that the visitor lend himself in every possible way to the support of his host, but on the other hand it would also suggest that he refrain from fulsome eulogy and extravagant praise, both of the man and of his work. Such is suggestive of either insincerity or want of a proper conception of the fitness of things.

Probably the simplest case engaging our attention is the *visiting minister*, who through the courtesy of the resident minister is invited to participate in the services, either by conducting the opening exercises or by preaching. He may be visiting some member of the congregation, or the preacher himself, or he may be the preacher out of a place who has just dropped in to see the brethren. His conduct will depend very largely upon his conception of the responsibility of the public ministry. With some the reading of a portion of Scripture before an audience assembled for worship and the leading of a hundred or more hearts to a throne of grace in grateful praise or humble petition are but passing incidents. The responsibility sits as lightly upon their shoulders as the cares of citizenship upon the average politician, and the duties are discharged with about as much unction. With them an invitation to preach is evidently regarded as an opportunity for parade of their personal accomplishments, and especially if the visitor is the older and considers himself the superior preacher. But if his conception of his ministry is Pauline every duty will be so discharged as to inspire reverence for the gospel of Christ. There is a temptation to which we all are more or less susceptible in associated pulpit work, and which ought to be studiously avoided. It is what Alexander Campbell denominated "complimentary prayers, or prayers to human beings not yet deified." He was led to such reflections by observing that certain clergymen when associated with one another in public work, prayed with great earnestness for each other, but when either was absent the other asked no blessing for him. The practice of one Christian praying for another, or the one minister praying for another, is not condemned unless the nature of the petition itself indcates that it is intended for human as well as divine hearing.

It is scarcely to be expected that a preacher who has been invited to participate in the meeting of the church upon the invitation of the regular minister would use the opportunity to further his ends. But there are cases in which such opportunities become temptations to designing men. Bro. Beanblossom dwells in other places than Boomville. The minister residing in a place where he is not employed by the church will naturally be frequently called upon to assist the preacher in his public ministrations. If he is a modest Christian man he will readily see that he can mate-

of right should lead him to make his p
appearance such as to acquit him of
self-seeking.

The present prevailing custom of m
ters exchanging meetings affords occa
for the enlargement of one's field of
fulness. The primary purpose of
exchange is the saving of souls and
building up of the church. Aside fron
privilege of enlarging one's acquaint
with the people of God, the inspirati
preaching the gospel to new congregat
many of whom may be brought int
kingdom of Christ, furnishes a m
for painstaking effort not to be consid
lightly. Phillips Brooks advises prea
to occasionally go and preach to a con
gation in which they do not know a
in order that they may keep the impre
of preaching to humanity, and so to
the truth which they preach as large
ought to be. But the exchange is not
from danger both to preachers and con
gations. Contemporaneous history
probably furnish instances in which
such meetings the visiting preacher
received a call to the church, whil
pastor was compelled to seek green f
and pastors new. This may not be the
of any one in particular. It may be the r
of circumstances. The new minister
by his faithful preaching of the Word
so impressed his ability upon the pe
and they may have so recognized their
need and their own minister's inabili
satisfy it that the call followed as a m
of course. I do not speak against su
result. It is the means used to bri
about. If the call is the outcome o
cumstances for which the recipient i
responsible, well; but if it is the culn
tion of a well-laid plan such condu
despicable and merits the severest
demnation.

The evangelist probably occupies
pulpits and comes into contact with
people than any other minister. His
changing audience, making it necessa
him to dwell upon themes that move
to action, keeps vivid the impressi
preaching to the world; while his cons
ly varying associations with Christian
him the largest views of God's people.
tunately the New Testament gives
tion concerning the work of evang
Timothy and Titus were evangelists
under apostolic instructions, visite
churches, setting in order the thing
were wanting, preaching the Word, r
ing sinners and comforting saints, w
long-suffering and teaching. Their
was strong and fruitful. When an
gelist is called to hold a meeting
church, it is generally expected that h
be for the time being the leader and t
will obey his instructions. Yet is
possible for him to assume too mu
sponsibility? It not infrequently ha
that both minister and congregati
themselves compelled to follow a lead
which is not at all pleasant and whi
after effects show was not at all wise.
mitting that human nature is the
everywhere, it nevertheless is true th
faithful man of God who has labore
year or two, or more, in a certain
knows the condition of the field bette
any man can who has just come int
a few weeks' meeting, and his views

which the regular minister could not say. The people, knowing that the evangelist will soon move on and that the success of the meeting depends upon their earnest support, will tolerate from him what they would not from their own preacher. Two fundamental errors lie at the basis of this supposition. The first is that the discussion of such subjects results in permanent good, which is doubtful; and second, that the preacher's main business is to hold his job, which is entirely false. His business is to so preach the Word that sinners may be led to Christ and that they may be so taught that they will stay with Christ, and there is no subject needing public discussion that the faithful preacher of the gospel may not with the utmost propriety discuss. That men do declare the whole counsel of God and continue to grow in the affections of their people is abundantly proved by the number of long pastorates of faithful men of God among us. The apostle's instructions to the evangelists to set in order the things that are wanting are more applicable to the resident minister than to the evangelist. The same restraints that courtesy places upon one minister visiting another will apply with equal force to the evangelists.

There are some self-appointed evangelists—not many, it is to be hoped—who seem to consider that the preacher has no voice in the affairs of the congregation, and hence he is ignored and all dealing had with the church through them. This is not a fanciful case, as the following illustration will show: The writer was visited by such a brother in the second month of his ministry. He was introduced to the brethren and recommended by an old preacher who had served three congregations in that part of the country for years. It being Wednesday he was invited to preach that evening in the place of prayer-meeting. In the course of the conversation he was informed that the congregation was not in the proper condition for a meeting; that they were expecting an evangelist in a few weeks with whom they had an engagement, and they could not support two meetings so close together. He protested that he preached the gospel "without money and without price," although he had a wife and nine children at home. At the close of his sermon that evening he proposed to the congregation that he remain and hold them a meeting, and under the influence of a few friends of the old preacher who had introduced him, the majority of those present decided to have him stay. He accordingly made his announcements for the next evening, and during the eight days of his stay took complete charge of the services, condescending to permit the preacher to announce the hymns and occasionally make the opening prayer. It is needless to add that the meeting die not result in adding any to the Lord. A sensitive regard for his relation to a brother minister does not require an evangelist, or any other minister, for that matter, to compromise the truth, or to refrain from rebuking sin. He is instructed to speak the truth in love. The temptation is to leave the impression that the latter clause is forgotten. A writer in the CHRISTIAN-EVANGELIST, a few years ago, commenting upon the number of times the reports from the field assured the people that the preacher had "shunned not to declare the whole counsel of God," remarked that that usually meant a very pugnacious sort of preaching.

One more case remains to be considered under this head. It is the relation of the financial agent or missionary secretary to the minister. There is room here for an exchange of courtesies. Our great missionary causes, our colleges, orphan homes and other benevolent institutions are public enterprises, belonging to the great brotherhood, and as such are entitled to their united support. The men upon whom rests the responsibility of bringing their claims before the people must necessarily be hampered in their work unless they can have the hearty co-operation of their preaching brethren. The fact that about two-thirds of our churches are not enlisted in these great movements is evidence that such co-operation is not at present very hearty. Looking at it from the minister's point of view he naturally feels that he should be consulted by any secretary desiring to visit the congregation, both as to time and expediency of presenting the claims. And this would seem to be right. There may be circumstances known to him which would make a visit at a certain time both inexpedient for the church and unfortunate for the cause represented. On the other hand there are preachers with whom every time would be inopportune and who would never be willing to let the people hear a claim. In such a case recourse must be had to an appeal to the people. The larger interests are entitled to greater consideration.

In general what has been said of a minister's conduct in another's pulpit when his brother minister is present will apply with equal force when he is not present. The latter case, however, presents some temptations which the former does not. It is not necessary to assume that a preacher has no higher aim than to further his own interests when it is said that the absence of the regular minister furnishes a greater temptation to discourteous treatment than his presence does. A man may be confronted with temptations for which he is not responsible. A preacher ministering to a small congregation on a small salary may have an opportunity to fill the pulpit of a brother whose circumstances are so far superior to his own as to create a longing for a similar place for himself. He may even go further and be led so far as to forget his moral obligation and to let his conduct betray the confidence of his friend, without having purposed to do so. Even a literal interpretation of the Golden Rule would suggest that one minister ought to avoid unfavorable criticism of another's work, especially when he is not there to defend himself. It requires very little ability to find fault; it takes much wisdom to produce a remedy. But open criticism is not the only, nor in fact the most effective means of injuring another. Oftentimes more weight is attached to what is left unsaid than to what is said. Condemnation with faint praise is sometimes very effective. The preacher ought to do better than that. He ought to not only refrain from criticising, but he ought as he conscientiously can to give the work his whole-hearted support. He can do this and not compromise the truth in any way.

The ministers in exchanging Sunday appointments with one another is a representative case. For the time being the responsibilities of each rest upon the other. Each is the other's guest, and as neither would be guilty of alienating the affections of the wife or child of the other, no more should he be guilty of stealing the hearts of the people. It would be proper for each to ascertain beforehand the hopes and fears of the other that he might avoid things calculated to create discord, and at the same time reinforce his brother's work. If it be objected that these limitations are too great and that his conduct is too circumscribed, the answer is that he still has the gospel story with all of its sweetness and pathos to present, and that it affords a choice of subjects that will win for him the esteem of his brethren and result in the saving of souls. The conduct of the evangelist, the traveled parson, the missionary secretary, would not differ materially from the case already treated. Thus far we have only been dealing with cases in the family, if you please, or among our own brethren.

One other case demands attention. It is the exchange of pulpits by ministers of different religious bodies. To a people whose rallying cry is "a union of all Christians" every chance to get over into our neighbor's pasture and mingle with the sheep ought to be utilized and made to further the cause we plead. The most important question for the preacher to decide would naturally be, What should be the subject to be presented? Upon the character of his preaching will depend the friendly feeling of the two churches. One theme is always acceptable, namely, Christ. All can agree upon Christ as the world's Redeemer, and none need be offended in him. To choose a controverted subject for discussion would be not only unwise, but unchristian. For a Christian minister, under invitation to speak to a Methodist congregation, to choose "Conversion" or "Baptism" for his theme, unless invited to do so, or *vice versa*, would be as great an offense against good taste as it would be for a guest to insist on making a recognized question of dispute the subject of discussion in his host's parlor. If great nations can exercise diplomacy for the sake of peace, the children of light ought to profit by their wisdom. This does not imply a "wishy-washy" doctrine nor any compromise of the truth. Alexander Campbell was the prince of reformers, who never swerved an iota from the truth, and yet in his time he occupied the pulpits of Congregationalists, Methodists, Presbyterians, Baptists and others, and with but few exceptions he was free to return when he would. During our national convention at Nashville in 1892, one of our able ministers occupied the pulpit of the McEndree M. E. church, and at the close of the sermon the minister said to his congregation, "I shall never again call these people 'Campbellites.'" The truth must conquer, if the spirit in which it is presented is right.

The Savior, on the night in which he was betrayed, rising from the supper and laying aside his garments, took a basin of water, and girding himself with a towel, washed his disciples' feet and wiped them with the towel wherewith he was girded. A little later he said to them, "A new commandment I give unto you, that ye love one another; as I have loved you that ye also love one another." The twelve needed this beautiful example and this teaching. A short time previous they had been

d be greatest in the
Their conceptions
But after they were
rom on high, and the
ckened their under-
on no longer was,
" but rather, "What
They recognized the
own limitations, and
for the faith of the
no longer jealous
James, recognizing
and Barnabas, were
ld go to the Gentiles,
s went to the Jews.
they fulfilled the new
God give grace to
to manifest a like

VS. REPUDIATION.

MYRICK.

wise men; judge ye
s way Paul invited
n. Here are two fac-
revelation presented.
ng; (2) hearing, or
God's gracious reve-
Spirit-chosen words
selected to deliver his
n. The second is the
n of men seeking to
se, the actual content
in the second place,
on and application of
an needs. These are
in the revelation of
effectual working" in
men and women.
w did Paul speak?
of speech or of wis-
you the testimony of
. . . words of man's
e testimony of God,
n in words of man's
aul know this testi-
princes of this world
od hath revealed them
t." Also, as in Gal.
hich was preached of
I neither received it
it it by the revelation
the gospel is a reve-
thical growth, slowly
self-illuminated con-
seekers, groping after
ry centuries. No; it
of divine knowledge
; in words of divine
by inspiration of the
God's testimony. It
an, nor deduced from
r made known by the
ician or the winged
e philosopher. Reve-
iness, and he gave it
n by God's men.
ak? "Which things
is . . . which the
h." (See, for these
.) Again we read:
spake, moved by the
t. 1:21). We have
l unto you with the
n from heaven." Of
'They began to speak
s the Spirit *gave them*
Paul says "I speak,"
clude the following

dom or experience. It was couched in language "which the Holy Ghost teacheth;" or, in other words, was the language of inspiration. The Holy Spirit "moved" them—not caprice of man, fear of foe nor flattery of friend. The apostles did not trim their discourses, nor embellish; they neither added to nor diminished from. To contend they did is to discredit inspiration and impeach the Holy Spirit. The gospel message, in the measure of its content, is just what was needed—no more, no less.

2. "Judge ye what I say." Here is our work. Revelation is of God. We must submissively come with this conviction. These are God's words; they are final. Our work is to find out just what was said and accept, not reject. We are to interpret, not to repudiate. We are to learn human duty, not to criticise divine wisdom. We cannot retain belief in inspiration if men are to discover that the gospel message was trimmed, expurgated, softened here and there at the pleasure of the men who preached it. No; the gospel message, fully, *as far as needed*, at any time, was always spoken by the apostle, else the claim of inspiration is a farce. Christ said: "I have many things to say, but hitherto ye were not able to bear them." Paul may have refrained at times to speak of some things in the scheme of redemption, not trimming, but giving as the hearer *was able to bear*. I preached a sermon once, and one "loyal" brother criticised me because I omitted baptism. I answered that the people needed other portions of the gospel at that point. Omissions can be accounted for without impeaching either man's honor or the wisdom of the Holy Spirit.

Brethren, if we are to maintain our respect for the gospel we must "receive it as it is in truth, the Word of God." No shadow of suspicion must be allowed to fall upon it. At every place, on every great occasion, at every critical juncture, the Holy Spirit *was in charge of the work*, "moved" the men, and so just enough was always said—no more and no less. We find here the all-wise God, the illuminating Spirit, honest apostles, and hence the "Scripture cannot be broken." The bearing of this article upon recent communications is obvious. May the Lord guide us by his loving counsel.

Gentryville, Mo.

IS EVERYTHING FOR THE BEST?

GEO. T. SMITH.

Consoling if true. Would not such security lead to carelessness, and cut the nerve of effort?

One man's life is too short to determine. Some are so fortunate, always lighting on their feet, while others are rolled and tumbled through life.

The nearest the Word comes to saying so is Rom. 8:28,29: "All things work together for good." But not for everybody; for one class. It is described from above and below. From the human side it is those who love God; from the divine standpoint it is those who are the called according to his purpose. In his purpose these are called, justified and glorified. Not in reality, but in God's plan. He foreknew this class, and predestinated them to be then in body at the resurrection. For this class all things work together for good.

What is good? That is the crucial word. Our definition or God's; which shall say what is good? Not riches, but righteousness; not ease, but excellence; not comfort, but consecration; not many things, but manhood; not luxury, but life; not bodily pleasure, but spiritual profit; not earthly treasures, but the Holy Spirit, are good, by God's measure. Since it is God's purpose to people heaven with those who are fully conformed to the image of Christ, since he made the Captain of their salvation perfect through suffering, it follows that he may lead us through a sharp and stony way. Chastening (Heb. 12), pruning (John 15), trial as in a furnace (1 Pet. 1), may be essential to secure the highest good. Note the comparisons in these Scriptures: Children, vines, debased gold. So we are. We need discipline.

All things *work*, not *are*. The result is good. No chastening for the present seemeth good, but rather grievous. Afterward it yields richly. All things. But "all" is a limited word in Holy Writ. Man was created for joy. Not nerve was made for pain. No natural desire was made for pain. No natural desire was given to be a torment, or sinful if satisfied. Therefore, all good things work for good, are good at once. All evil things? Evil is of two kinds. Moral evil is not for good. It may be overruled, as Longfellow sings:

"St. Augustine! well hast thou said
That of our vices we can frame
A ladder, if we will but tread
Beneath our feet each deed of shame."

Sin does not work for good. It may be forgiven, but says Browning:

"However near I stand in his regard,
So much the nearer had I stood by steps
Offered the feet which spurned their help."

The "all things" are defined in the context. All physical evil, persecution, injustice, trials, sufferings, toil unrequited, and sorrow over others' woe—these are the things which the world laments as unmitigated evil, but which work for us a greater, an inexpressible weight of glory.

For the man without a hope in Christ every loss is an eternal regret. The marble face in the white casket is gone forever; no sweet hope and wonder of the future meeting lessen his grief. The house burned down is a permanent substraction from his means of joy; there is no consolation that for him there is a house not made with hands, eternal in the heavens. All his joy is bounded by time. At the end of life he leaves all worth having, and goes forth a pauper and friendless. For him everything is not for the best. But for you and me, "we know;" not we see. He uses "know" as Peter did on the day of Pentecost when he bade the Jews to "know assuredly;" that is, to believe firmly that Christ was enthroned. So we know, though we see not clearly through the fogs; we know that love leads and all shall be for good.

The American Baptist Yearbook for 1888 reports 43,397 churches in the United States, with 27,355 ministers and a total membership of 4,055,806. It reports 22,529 Sunday-schools with a total membership of 1,801,053. Over 5,000 of its churches have no Sunday-schools and the membership of

Our Budget.

—The war tax is on.

—The worst tax is sin tax.

—The best tax is self-imposed for Christ's sake.

—We desire to mention the article in this paper on "Ministerial Courtesy" by Bro. Peters as worthy of special attention. It is written carefully, thoughtfully and in good spirit, and deals with a practical question. We are able also to give our readers a half-tone picture of the author of the article.

—Our illustrated letter in our Family circle, this week, from Santa Cruz, Cal., is written by one who was formerly a resident of this city, but is captivated, as you will see, with the climate and country from whence he writes.

—In our next issue we shall publish the excellent paper on "Church Finance," prepared by Albert Schwartz and read before the district convention at Shenandoah, Iowa, last spring.

—Accoding to the report of the secretaries of Home Missions there was a loss of $151.04 for the week ending July 9th, over that of last year for the same week. The total for the week was $622.53, contributed by thirty-three churches, nine individuals and five otherwise. There were, however, seventeen new church contrbutors and of the former contributing for the week twelve gave increased amounts.

—Two weeks ago we stated that the Sweeney-Throgmorton debate, which had been previously announced in our columns to come off at Allen Springs, Pope, county, Ill., commencing on the 27th inst., was indefinitely postponed. This statement was based upon what we considered one of the best of reasons, viz., Bro. Sweeney's ill-health, rendering it impossible for him to perform his part. While Bro. Sweeney has our sympathy, yet we are glad to be able to say that through the persistent efforts of C. J. Kimball, of this office, an able, efficient and acceptable substitute for Bro. Sweeney has been secured in the person J. B. Briney, of Moberly, Mo., who has agreed to meet Mr. Throgmorton at the time and place originally announced, and that he (Throgmorton) has accepted the substitute; so that the discussion is expected to go on without further hitch or interruption. Remember the place and time—Allen Springs, Ill., July 27.

—Hell is filled with Catholic rich men who are damned for the good that they have neglected to do on account of a criminal indifference to the progress of God's kingdom and the welfare of souls.—*Church Progress.*

Of what use, then, is Mass for the dead?

—Do not forget the fact that the C. W. B. M. watchword is "Ninety thousand in Ninety-nine."

—The Kingdom Publishing Company has discontinued for the present all responsibilities for the publication of "The Kingdom," that responsibility having been personally assumed by Mr. H. W. Gleason, the managing editor. This step was taken in consequence of litigation with the American Book Company.

—The guerrilla fire upon passing ambulances carrying wounded soldiers from the field of battle at Santiago is a sorrowful comment upon Spanish honor, about which Spaniards have had so much to say of late.

—Dr. W. E. Garrison's first letter from England, for our columns, appears in this issue. We are expecting communications from him regularly while on his bicycle tour through England.

—The offerings for Home Missions for the week ending July 2nd was $1,099.45, a gain of $189.35. The total offerings for June were $5,267.07, a gain over June of last year of $213,20.

—We print the program of the Missouri Christian Lectureship, to be held at Carrollton, July 18-21, again in this issue.

—Another new magazine coming to our table recently is The Pulpit and Social Problems, from San Francisco, Cal. The table of contents for the June number indicates that a magazine of high order is contemplated by its founders. Practical themes are treated by prominent men, and we are always ready to welcome magazines of this class to our table. We hope the founders of this enterprise may realize their fondest expectations therein.

—The Christian Literature Co., of Buffalo, N. Y., has launched a new magazine under the name In His Steps. No. 1 Vol. I contains thirty-two pages and is filled with well-selected, short articles of a newsy, practical nature and pleasant to read. The spiritual tone of the magazine is clearly Christian, and we trust it may bear much fruit for the Master.

—It is predicted that America will soon be building 'warships for everybody.' The superiority of American warships at Manila and Santiago is now the talk of the world.

—The receipts for Foreign Missions for June are reported to be $25,814.12, a gain over June of last year of $3,295.07. The receipts since October 1st, 1897, to July 1st, 1898, amount to $83,062.95, or a gain of $9,140.00 over the corresponding nine months last year. Remember, our task is to reach $100,000 by collections only. Only three months until the books close. Ten new missionaries will sail in September. Send collections direct to F. M. Rains, Box 750, Cincinnati, Ohio.

—The new United States one-cent postage stamp shows a picture of a Jesuit priest, Marquette, in gown and with crucifix. Why not the Pope blessing the Spaniards? Now let us have Baptist, Methodist and other denominational stamps.—*American Citizen.*

—Drake University Bulletin announces the following of its students, or Alumni, now soldiers in our war with Spain: Herman Williams, '96, Chaplain of the third regiment, now the fifty-first Iowa; A. M. Slatten; H. H. Hubbell; M. C. Hutchinson; John McMillen; F. E. Gunn; Mr. Thomson; Frank West; Mr. Conriover; J. E. Shakespeare; H. B. Murray; Mr. Elgin; Mr. Keating; Allen Hickey, Medical Department, and Mark Williams, also a former student. Some have been ordered West to Manila, and some of them to Cuba or Puerto Rico.

—Among the prominent men who preached at Nashville last Sunday was F. D. Power, of Washington, D. C.

—The President's proclamation to make last Sunday a day of thanksgiving to God for victories on land and sea in behalf of freedom's cause was generally observed in St. Louis.

—Sherman Hill, of Butte, Mont., contributes an interesting article to our columns this week on Gladstone. The philosophy of greatness introductory to what he says about Gladstone is particularly interesting. The facts and characteristics of Gladstone and his life indicate good analytical mental qualities. Bro. Hill has contributed a number of very excellent thoughtful articles for our columns.

—Our obituary column this week contains the first tribute to a soldier of the present war, that of Charles B. Caton, of Terre Haute, Ind., who died at camp Alger, Va., June 25, 1898. The beautiful tribute is written by W. W. Witmer, of Terre Haute, Ind.

—The Bible has not been driven out of the public schools of New York wholly at least. In a reception program of Grammar School No. 61, that has come to hand, the first exercise stated is "Reading of the Scriptures."

—We call attention to our advertisement in this paper offering C. W. B. M. auxiliaries an opportunity to strengthen their burdened treasuries by the sale of A. McLean's "Circuit of the Globe."

—In this issue A. C. Hopkins announces over his own signature that he has leased Oskaloosa College and will reorganize it upon a broader practical basis for a larger patronage. See Notes and News page.

—We have a newsy letter from Red Oak, Ia., but no signature to it. Publication must be withheld until the writer is known.

—The interesting account of Butler Commencement is long, but appears in full this week.

—Some good resolutions and great speeches were made at the Temperance Congress at Prohibition Park, Staten Island, New York, during the first week in July, which will tend to strengthen temperance sentiment and emphasize the need for united action against the nation's greatest curse. Steps were taken in the appointment of committees to secure a closer co-operation of all the temperance forces in the United States, a thing which, if accomplished, would dispose of the liquor traffic as quickly and effectively as was the Spanish fleet at Manila and at Santiago.

—The church building at Malden, Mo., was struck by lightning during one of the recent severe thunder storms and totally destroyed. The church is cast down over their loss, but not disheartened. Steps will be taken at once to rebuild. The house destroyed cost $2,000.

—The church at Fredricksburg, Va., is asking for greatly needed help to secure a house of worship. They want churches to whom they are addressing circular letters, and others, to send at least two dollars each for that purpose. Cephas Shelburne is their pastor and is supported there by the Virginia Tidewater Board. We trust that the amount asked may be forwarded and the amount needed soon raised for a house. It will take a large number of two-dollar bills to build much of a church building.

—In keeping with the President's proclamation to observe last Sunday as a day of thanksgiving for American victories on land and sea, Archbishop Ireland, of St. Paul, ordered the "Te Deum" to be chanted in thanksgiving for the victories gained and the Litany of Jesus to be be recited for the speedy granting of peace to the nations now engaged in deadly warfare, and stated that he would preach in the Cathedral on Sunday morning. In view of the accusations of disloyalty sometimes heard against Roman Catholics, and also of the fact that the victories to be thankful for were over Roman Catholic subjects, the above act of the Archbishop becomes a matter of more than passing interest. We can hardly say that it was not issued and observed in good faith and speaks volumes for the loyalty of American Catholicism in this war.

—We are giving our readers substantial evidence that we intend the Christian-Evangelist shall be the equal, at least, of any of the religious journals in the land, and we shall expect them to show their appreciation of this fact by assisting us to add many new subscribers to our list. This will encourage us and make it possible for us to carry out our program of improvements. In order to make this an easy matter, we are making a special offer this month, to new subscribers, of seventy-five cents for the remainder of the year 1898, beginning with our first thirty-two page issue of July 7th. If you are ready to help us in the way indicated, write for sample copies at once.

—We call your attention to the letter, published elsewhere, of D. L. Moody in reference to the work of the "Army and Navy Christian Commission." We are glad that Mr. Moody is giving his personal attention to this important work, and it gives us pleasure to co-operate with him and his coworkers in extending whatever help in the way of religious instruction or consolation we can to our soldiers and sailors. It is an opportunity for doing good which should be improved to the utmost extent. We trust that the Christian people of the country generally will appreciate the value of this work, and lend it such aid as they can. Many a young man who is careless about his

me will, when exposed
n the battle field, be
mind in which he will
h. Many, too, who
ne will meet with the
fe and will need the
on of faithful religious
igious literature. Let
t home seek to supply
o go to the front.

paper by "Criticus,"
itic on the Baptism of
s written in good spirit
ng.

kes, who has labored
ex-slaves of the Chero-
Choctaw and Chicka-
fifteen years, after
scogee, Eufaula, Tahl-
ccepted the presidency
School at Muscogee,
seeking aid among the
aining to finish up the
le them to carry on the
650 more will complete
gee, and give a farm
s of good land. This
y any religious board,
ng the personal aid of
ndependent of church
his particular class of
lian Territory is prac-
ivileges, and hence his
ial mission. He called
ırsday.

ays that the drink bill
om 1890 to 1895 is $8,-
year 1896, $1,196,878,-
e simply appalling. If
had only gone for some
ent the condition of our
ave been to-day! And
ings according to sci-
hristianity! The above
ingly against our high
ngs.

isaster occurred at sea
present month. The
rtyshire and the French
irgogne, collided in a
outh of Sable Islands.
d from New York July
ired and sixteen persons
crew, bound for Havre,
rtyshire struck the La
rending a great hole in
her to sink after a few
witnessed aboard the
k were heart-rending in
the ship's company fur-
on: First-class passen-
passengers, 123; third-
ship's crew, 233; total
gers saved, 53; ship's
saved, 163; drowned,
ns to have been shown
thought to be the crew,
d. Men fought for po-
e crowded back and even
ere being launched and
This incident is one of
history, but it seems to
le. Both vessels were
l, too fast, perhaps, for
nange their course after
ime to prevent the colli-

Pope to bring peace to
as made him painfully
ency as a political factor
he earth.

n that Henry R. Pritch-
nd., is to leave to his
of a book as well as a
the ministry of the gos-
earn, from the Indiana
seventeen of his mas-
ographical sketch of his
life by Dr. B. B. Tyler, of the editorial staff of this paper.

—According to the following statement of the Indiana Christian the Christian Church in that state is about to remove one of the great hindrances and go forward. Read the following:

One thing recommended by the South Bend convention was the evangelization of Southern Indiana. This should be done at all hazzards. That part of our fair state has been too long under the blighting effects of "anti-ism," and it is time that the shackles which bind so many churches in that section of the state, should be broken and they be set free to do the Master's work. But this is not going to be accomplished without great effort. Evil influences have been at work there for years and they will not be overcome in a day, or a month, or a year. Let us put forth continuous and persistent effort to save our cause in Southern Indiana.

—The Presbyterian Banner, June 23rd, contains the following announcement:

The Presbyterian Banner celebrates its eighty-fourth anniversary and begins its eighty-fifth volume by appearing with important changes. The paper of this issue has been formed by the union of the Presbyterian Banner, founded 1814, and the Presbyterian Messenger, founded 1893, thus uniting the oldest and youngest Presbyterian papers. It is hoped that this union will be attended with the fusion of all the interests of the two papers and the merging together of their constituencies. The Rev. James Allison, D. D., will remain as editor, and the Rev. James H. Snowden will serve as joint editor. The Rev. Joseph T. Gibson, D. D., will serve as associate editor. Important mechanical and literary improvements have also been made. The paper has been reduced in size and number of pages increased, making it more convenient in form, admitting of better paper and press work, and producing a more handy volume when bound.

We shall miss the familiar face of the Presbyterian Messenger from our exchange list, but hope to find an equally companionable friend in the Presbyterian Banner.

PERSONAL MENTION.

J. S. Hughes will deliver a series of his matchless lectures on the Book of Revelation, at Central Christian College, Albany, Mo., beginning July 25, 1898. Mr. Hughes will deliver two lectures each day. Other prominent ministers will speak during the institute.

W. L. Powell has resigned his work at Bucyrus, Ohio, and can be secured elsewhere. He is highly commended by those who know him for his work's sake and any church in need of an energetic, successful preacher should address him at once. He would take a work in any part of the United States.

W. W. Sniff, pastor of the church at Gibson City, Ill., has been elected president of the fourth missionary district of that state.

Samuel Gregg closed his work at Highmore, South Dakota, July 10th, and is now at Cleveland, Minn. He reports forty added to the Highmore church under his ministry and all departments of the church actively at work.

W. E. Reeves, preacher at Denison and Round Prairie, Kansas, has his fifth Sundays at his disposal, and desires to hold some meetings during these periods. He would like to arrange, at once, for a meeting to begin on July 25th continue over the fifth Sunday to August 6th.

Bro. David Walk began work with the East Eighth St. Church in Los Angeles, Cal., in January '97, with 19 members. There are now 132.

J. P. Lucas is expected to begin work in Colorado City, Col., July 17. There are from 60 to 75 members in Colorado City, and a neat chapel has been recently erected.

J. Z. Tyler, of Cleveland, Ohio, has been visiting friends and relatives in and around Lexington since the Kentucky state convention.

In a neat tract, envelope size, under the title, "The Lost Christ and the Lost Unity," Evangelist James Small, of Wheatland, Cal., tells why he is a member of the Christian Church.

A. W. Kokendoffer, of Kansas City, Mo., is spending this month at his father's house, at Bramblet, Nicholas county, Ky.

Christian University, Canton, Mo., has elected Pres. F. O. Norton, of La Belle College, professor of philosophy, and he has accepted. Prof. Norton is said to be one of our best scholars and an experienced teacher.

A large picture of Dr. W. T. Moore appeared in the Columbia Missouri Herald, last week, as one of Missouri's distinguished educators.

We learn that the presidency of Bethany College was tendered to B. A. Jenkins, of Indianapolis, Ind., author of Christian Endeavor lesson notes of this paper, and that its acceptance was declined by him.

Edward Davis, of Oakland, California, has accepted an invitation from the church at Lygon St., Melbourne, Australia, and expects to reach his new field of labor sometime in July.

J. B. Haston now preaches for the church at Galveston, Texas.

Peter Ainslie, editor of The Christian Tribune, Baltimore, Md., is back again from his European tour. He makes no mention of having visited Spain.

A. Martin, of Muncie, Ind., will enter the evangelistic field again, August 1st. Any church wanting a protracted meeting should write to him for particulars.

E. F. Mahan, now at Salem, Ind., reports work starting off there encouragingly. He preached the annual sermon for the G. A. Rs there.

The church at Gibson City, Ill., recently extended W. W. Sniff and wife a reception. This and the preceding introductory services were tokens of the pleasure of the church at his acceptance of their call.

Sherman Hill will close his work at Butte, Mont., Sept. 1st, and desires a work more central in the United States. The high altitude of Montana and the effect of smoke from the copper mines at Butte on his wife's health make the change necessary. Bro. Hill is an educated man and an efficient pastor, and the church that secures him will secure a good helper. Since at Butte, Mont., nine months, there have been forty additions to the church. His acdress is 6 S. Idaho St., Butte, Mont.

W. A. Foster is now assisting Bro. Noblitt in a tent meeting at Ellendale, N. D.

F. N. Calvin, of Waco, Texas, will spend July and August in Chicago. His address will be 2628 Wabash Avenue. He says, "if any church within one hundred miles of Chicago would like supply a preacher, or a protracted meeting for that time, he would be glad to hear from them.

H. A. Northcutt reported 13 confessions at Sturgeon, Mo., Sunday evening, July 3rd. We are glad to see patriotism for the heavenly kingdom at the front at such a time.

James Small, of California will arrive in Des Moines, Iowa, August 1st.

L. J. Marshall goes from Huntsville, Mo., to 5473 Ellis Ave., Chicago, Ill., until August 1st. He will begin work with the church at Palmyra, Mo., September 1st.

F. O. Fannon, pastor of the First Church, St. Louis, Mo., has gone on a vacation.

T. W. Grafton and family, of Rock Island, Ill., will spend a two months vacation in Oskaloosa Iowa.

J. H. Stark, of Du Quoin, Ill., will be in Iowa two weeks in July. Pleasantville will be his address.

J. W. Elliott, of Nebraska preached in Cherokee, Iowa on June 26th. Cherokee has given him a call.

Milo G. Cummings will be compelled by the great fire in Pulaski, Iowa to change his field of lakor. Ten business houses burned.

Wm. M. Hollett, of Arlington, Iowa, is called for a fifth year.

A. M. Haggard the Iowa Secretary preached two Sundays at Marshalltown.

J. A. Seaton, of Marion, Iowa, begins a meeting in Estelline, S. D., on July 12th.

B. S. Denny, of Hampton, Iowa, is assisting Wm. Hollett in a meeting at Arlington.

E. C. Wigmore, of Charles City, Iowa, has returned from a three months' vacation on the Pacific Coast.

W. B. Clemmer, of Sloan, Iowa, held a Sunday-school rally in Sioux City with the aid of Pastor Vande Walker.

E. Edwards' gift papers the church house at Webster City.

Pres. Hardin, Eureka, Ill., desires to correspond with some young man who understands directing work in a gymnasium, who desires to recieve his tuition in Eureka College and the fees paid by students,, for his services.

From the Indiana Christian we learn that C. S. Medbury, chaplain of the 157th Indiana regiment, baptized three persons at Chickamauga and four at Port Tampa, Florida. He is Angola's missionary among the soldiers.

CHANGES.

J. L. Johnson, Missouri Valley to Farrugut, Iowa.
Lewis A. Pier, Watsonville to Santa Barbara, Cal.
Thos. Smith, Rockdale to Waco, Texas.
J. Stafford, Lexington to Georgetown, Ky.
R. J. Avriett, Woodson to Little Rock, Ark.
W. J. Shelburne, Rockwood, Tenn., to Milt, Lee county, Va.
E. F. Mahan, Bloomington to Salem, Ind.
A. L. Martin, Wichita to Mt. Hope, Kan.
O. Baker, Everton, Ont., to Colfax, Ill.
S. M. Parks, Grayville to Niantic, Ill.
Nelson G. Brown, DesMoines to Ottumwa, Ia.
A. L. Crim, Thorntown to Crawfordsville, Ind.
J. L. Palmer, Olathe, Kan., to Kansas City, Mo.
Guy Hoover; Croton to Hiram, Ohio.

What Our Friends Think of Our New Form.

Already we are beginning to receive echoes from the first issue in our new form. We give a few as the ''first fruits:''

I like your new face and new dress. May this begin a new era in your prosperity and power for doing good. G. A. Hoffmann.
Columbia, Mo.

The poet says, ''A thing of beauty is a joy forever.'' The Christian-Evangelist in its new form and dress is certainly ''a thing of beauty,'' and I hope it will be ''a joy forever'' to all who peruse its well-filled pages.
B. F. Manire.
Jackson, Miss., July 9, 1898.

I am glad you are making so grand a paper, and in its new dress it is superb.
F. M. Green.
Kent, O.

All preachers with whom I have met admire the new dress and form of the Christian-Evangelist very mvch. John A. Jayne.
Allegheny, Pa.

The new Christian-Evangelist is clear, clean, crisp and cultured. It is neat and newsy. It is sprightly, sparkling and spiritual. Its frontispiece is a good picture of a man known for grace, grit and gumption.
T. J. Williamson.
Excelsior Springs, Mo.

R. R. Rates to Eureka Encampment.

The railroads have granted a rate of one and one-third fare from all points in Illinois and from St. Louis to Illinois Christian Encampment, Eureka, Ill., August 1st to 7th. Tickets will be honored if bought not earlier than July 31 nor later than August 6. Be sure to get certificate from agent whenever ticket is purchased upon start or en route to same. Upon arriving at tabernacle show certificate to undersigned, that it may be stamped and countersigned. No one-third rate granted in returning until at least 100 have been counted. Preserve this for future use.
L. F. Watson, R. R. Sec'y.

Correspondence.

About Bicycle Touring.

To the able-bodied man or woman who is considering whether or not to go on a bicycle tour for a summer vacation, my advice is, ''Go.'' The pleasure of travel, freed from the necessity of consulting and conforming to time-tables and schedules prepared without regard to your individual convenience, not to mention the expense of railroad fare, the out-door life of a camp, freed from the possible monotony of remaining in one spot, however lovely; a means of locomotion at once swift, easy and independent; exercise and rest mingled in whatever proportions may suit your fancy; an increasing series of exhilerating incidents and wild adventures; an unrivaled opportunity for seeing the picturesque in nature and observing the life of the people—these are some of the charms of a well-conducted bicycle tour. Over and above all these, and more satisfying, perhaps, than all of them to the mind of the man who delights in activity and finds his keenest pleasure in doing things, is the sense of mastery and accomplishment which comes with the consciousness that you are doing it all yourself. When you have wheeled from the Atlantic to Lake Michigan or from the Upper Mississippi to the Gulf (and after all it is not much of a feat), you will feel that the territory covered is your own. Have you not conquered it? Have you not, in the power of your own might, overcome all the obstacles which it had to offer to your progress? There is in the process that which satisfies the desire of the heart to be doing something, in recreation as well as in business. If one cared to enter at length into the philosophy of bicycling, it might easily be possible on this basis to construct an apology for the much-abused scorcher and show that, however objectionable he may be as a member of society, he is not altogether so irrational a creature as is sometimes supposed. Of course he is a selfish creature, imperiling others for his own pleasure. Of course he sees nothing but his front wheel and hears nothing but the hum of his tires and the click of his chain. Of course he is a public nuisance. But on one truth he has a firm grip and he appreciates it, though he overworks it and thereby brings it into disrepute, as many another good truth has been brought into disrepute by being overworked. The truth is that the keenest pleasure and the best recreation are to be found, not in seeing or hearing, but in doing.

But enough of the odious scorcher. I have no desire to lose your favor and shut your ears to what I have to say, by challenging his unpopular cause. The best proof, after all, of the superiority of active over passive pleasures will be found not in a wild, muscle-wearing and heart-straining ride of a hundred and fifty miles in a day, but in a decent and moderate bicycle tour at a reasonable pace through an interesting country.

But perhaps my initial recommendation to ''go'' was too general. People can not all take the same sort of vacation any more than they can eat the same sort of food or wear clothes cut from the same pattern. A man's vacation must be made to fit him, just like his coat. Some, by reason of physical peculiarities, cannot find ready-made clothes to fit them. For others no ready-made vacation will do. A little round of sight-seeing among other sight-seers, a few weeks at a resort, a trip around the well-worn circle of European travel—these are well enough in their way, but they are like ready-made clothes which may or may not fit you. Look through the lot, and if none of them will do, then mount your trusty wheel and ride away as free as the summer breeze to make for yourself, according to your own fancy, a vacation which will fit you like a glove and will be a free expression of your individuality in the matter of vacations. Plan it all out beforehand, or plan it as you go, or don't plan it at all. It makes little difference which you do. The beauty of it is that you can do as you please. But don't forget that you are out to enjoy everything, sunshine and shower, down hill and up, smooth road and rough. You will find them all in the course of your trip, if it be a week long or more, and if you are going to allow a sudden shower, a punctured tire or a few miles of sandy road to make you unhappy, then by all means stay at home and spend your vacation weeks swinging in a hammock or playing croquet. If you can be happy only when physically comfortable, then do not risk a bicycle trip, for there will be many hours when there would be more actual comfort in the aforesaid hammock than in pushing a wheel through the sand of a country road or ploughing through the mud in the premature dusk of a rainy day to reach a gloomy inn before it is absolutely dark. If you don't habitually and constitutionally enjoy everything, then stay at home. At any rate don't, please don't, go on a bicycle tour and blame me if you fail to have a good time.

If, on the basis of these representations, you are persuaded that it is worth your while, you are hereby invited to join (in spirit if not in body) a select party of two for a nine weeks' bicycle tour in England, Scotland, Wales and Ireland. Certainly no country possesses in a larger degree than Great Britain the characteristics of good roads, picturesque and varied scenery and abundance of points of interest within comparatively short distance. The home of our ancestors is therefore exceptionally well adapted for such a trip as that which we propose to make, at least so it seems now. We will know more of it by the end of the summer than we do now, when we have not yet set foot upon the land, but are straining our eyes to catch the first glimpse of the green coast of Ireland.

The start has been propitiously made. From Chicago to Toronto by rail is a journey of an afternoon and a night. Thence by boat down the length of Lake Ontario into the St. Lawrence River, down among the Thousand Islands all one glorious morning, and through the rapids at intervals all the afternoon, landing at Montreal before sunset, is a trip sure to leave in the mind of the eastward bound traveler delightful memories and a fresh respect for the natural beauties on his own side of the Atlantic. Three good lines of steamships run from Montreal to Liverpool. It is a thousand miles from Montreal down the great river, past the wonderful Cliff City of Quebec, the only place more French than Montreal, through the gulf of St. Lawrence, past New Brunswick, along the northern edge of the Newfoundland Banks, until we pass Cape Race, our farthest point of land, and stand out to open sea. For all of this first thousand miles we are insured against rough weather, though we have more fog than we like, but for the remaining seventeen hundred (for the Atlantic is narrow so far north) we must take our chances, as passengers from New York must do for their whole three thousand miles.

What is the equipment for a trip of this sort? Not much of anything, except a bicycle suit and sweater, such a change of clothing as may be carried in a small case on the wheel and a mackintosh. We have no trunk and no valise to be sent ahead by rail; not even an extra suit of clothes, which might be convenient at times, but would be too bulky to carry. The most important item is a good bicycle—mind, a *good* bicycle—one that you can trust. Mine is a Sterling, but in this matter let every man be persuaded in his mind. Now, if you care to follow us, all you have to do is to read from week to week the narrative of such of our experiences as may be worth chronicling under the title Wheeling Through England.

Winfred Ernest Garrison.

S. S. Yorkshire.

New York Letter.

A few weeks since the New York Letter mentioned the fact that three of our brethren graduated recently from Union Theological Seminary in this city. Since that time one of them, Bro. Levi G. Batman, has accepted a call to the church at Mansfield, Ohio, and in order the more fully to equip himself for his life-work, was married on July sixth to Miss Cora Louise Dodds, at the Walnut Street Presbyterian Church, Bloomington, Indiana. This certainly is the proper thing for the young minister to do; and we sincerely wish our young brother and his good wife a long and truly blessed married life. The minister who preaches that "it is not good for man to be alone" ought himself to be an example to the flock. Bro. E. M. Flinn, another of these graduates, is at present looking over the field at Haverhill, Mass., which Bro. F. W. Henry was compelled to vacate recently on account of throat trouble. The church in that city has been forced to retrench somewhat on account of business depression, especially in the shoe trade, as Haverhill is dependent largely on the shoe factories. Notwithstanding, the work is in good condition in the several departments and the outlook promising. We hope Bro. Flinn will decide to locate with them and push the work forward without a break in the pulpit and pastoral ministrations. Bro. Henry en route to California stopped and preached acceptably at the 169th St. church last Lord's day morning. At the close of his discourse a young lady made the good confession and was baptized in the evening. We shall be glad to hear Bro. Henry's throat troubles are improving in Colorado.

***

The church at Troy, N. Y., continues to enjoy a remarkable degree of prosperity. During the past 10 months 64 persons have been added to this church at the regular services, except 17 who came in at Dr. Tyler's meeting last January. Bro. C. M. Kriedler is one of the most successful pastors among us, as the great growth of his church indicates. He constantly labors to keep up all lines of work together. Children's Day services netted $84 for missions; the C. W. B. M. has a membership of 96; the church enrollment has almost reached the 600 mark. They are now planning to open the Lansingburg Branch or outpost for work, which is a wise step to take. Local mission work is absolutely necessary to the life and continued prosperity of the church in any city. This church has begun now to pay off its debt of $4,000 at the rate of $1,000 per year, and toward the first payment the Ladies' Aid Society has just turned over $500 as the result of their labors for the year. A happy arrangement has been made for the summer services. Beginning with July and continuing till the end of August, union services will be held between the congregation and the Christian Endeavor Society from 7:30 to 8:30 P. M. on Lord's days. Bro. Kreidler is a strong Endeavor man, and in order to keep the Y. P. S. C. E. in vital touch with the church he has just concluded a series of discourses on the pledge, as follows: "Trusting," "I Promise Him," "The Rule of My Life," "A Christian Life," "An Active Member," and "Why Support Christian Endeavor?" We are glad to say many will be pleased and profited by hearing him at our Chattanooga Convention in October on "The Work of the Disciples in New York and New England."

***

A few days since a beautiful memorial window was unveiled by Joseph Jefferson, in the Church of the Transfiguration, in memory of Edwin Booth, the late celebrated actor. A distinguished company was present includinng representatives of the drama, of literature, of law and of the ministry. The memorial was the gift of the Players' Club, and represents a mediæval histrionic student sitting with a mask in his hands, having just removed it from his face. The almost life-size figure, with gaze fixed upon the mask seems to be absorbed in contemplation of his work. Below the figure is the inscription:

> As one, in suffering all, that suffers nothing;
> A man that fortune's buffets and rewards
> Has ta'en with equal thanks.
>
> —*Hamlet. iii. 2.*

Which Booth once told a friend he would choose as his epitaph if ever he should have one. In addition to these lines and just below them is the inscription, "To the Glory of God and in loving memory of Edwin Booth." This is the church known so favorably to actors in New York and from which so many have been buried. It is familiarly known among them as "the little church around the corner," and its former rector was a true friend and counselor of actors and actresses in the city.

***

The decision of several Foreign Mission boards is to follow the flag into foreign territory with the missionaries shows commendable enterprise. And in order to carry out the work in the most effective manner possible it is proposed to have a conference of the great mission boards to decide who shall enter the several fields (and perhaps who shall stay out) as a measure of economy and interdenominational courtesy. This scheme has many advantageous features especially toward those churches which have what they call the essentials of Christianity in common. But we do not see, for instance, how the Disciples of Christ could consent not to enter the Philippines, Cuba or Porto Rico because forsooth the Methodists and Presbyterians should decide to send missionaries to those islands. If these religious bodies have everything to offer that the Disciples teach certainly such difference should be shown and even more. Why should not the Disciples even support other such missionaries instead of sending their own men into these fields? Doubtless a certain degree of courtesy and co-operation may be enjoyed and should be maintained, but after all it seems each board should be free to enter any of these fields at any place and time according to its own discretion.

***

The New York Christian Missionary Society and Ministerial Association will meet this year with the 169th St. Church, New York City, August 29th to September 2nd. The program committee promise us an excellent bill of fare in each of the different features of the convention. The opening service with a sermon will be held on Monday evening, Aug. 29th, and all day Tuesday will be devoted to questions and issues peculiarly ministerial in character. The convention proper will open on Wednesday morning and close on Friday evening. The church is planning to care for all who come on what is known as "the convention plan"—provide lodging and breakfast to the delegates free of charge; delegates will pay for dinner and supper, which will be served at reasonable rates. The church extends a hearty welcome to all who may wish to attend, and urgently request all who expect to come kindly to drop us a card at once informing us of the fact, so that a place may be assigned them. Come and help in making the New York convention of 1898 the best in the history of our state work.

S. T. WILLIS.

1281 *Union Avenue.*

Butler Commencement.

The commencement at Butler Collge, Irvington, Ind., was an exceptionally joyous one this year. A spirit of hopefulness prevailed in the exercises, such as had not been felt in recent years, even in the many prosperous commencements that the college has seen. Confidence in the future development of the institution and confidence in its present high position among the colleges of the West was the prevailing feeling that made every heart strong. Professors Brown and Miller, who have been more or less disabled through illness during the past session, were seen about the buildings joining in the commencement functions.

On Sunday afternoon of June 19th a very large audience greeted President Scot Butler, who delivered his sixth annual baccalaureate address to the graduating class. These addresses have become famous in Indianapolis for careful preparation, elegant diction, and classic beauty. This year the President fell not a whit below the high standard he has set for himself. On the contrary, his treatment of the subject of "Patriotism" came at so opportune a moment and was of such large, open-minded, and yet delicately beautiful a character that his audience was charmed. Indeed some competent jndges who did not hear it, but read it when published, pronounced it to be what few addresses nowadays attain to be, viz., literature.

On Monday evening, the small but triumphant class of '98 gave its entertainment. On account of a change by which the standard of the academic department was raised one year there would, in the natural course of things, be no class of '98; but several exceptional competent students managed, by extra efforts, to complete the required work in order to be graduated at this commencement. There were, therefore, but five young men—a small but excellent class. It will be followed next year by a very large one. The senior entertainment was largely attended, and the chapel was filled to its utmost capacity. After a varied program, the evening was closed with Mr. Earl Wilfley's ever-popular stereopticon lecture on "Ben Hur." His excellent views, true to history, supported by his elocutionary powers, left the audience in the best of humor at the close of a lengthy program.

On Tuesday the final examinations were continued, and in the evening the President's annual reception was tendered to students and friends of the college. His large, roomy, cool and beautiful home was the scene of a happy gathering. The great, high ceilings, the wide verandah, the open grounds, everything on a large scale—these things make one wish for the olden days when "space was ample east and west," and where homes might spread over larger territory rather than be built straight up into the air like soldiers in ranks. But Irvington is still a suburb; there is much ground, much shade, room to breathe and time to think. Many a man or woman at the reception doubtless paused a moment at sometime during the evening upon the wide lawn to glance at a star or follow with his eye the windings of the curved street, or rather lane, and ponder the possibilities of this charming, classic place.

The Bible College held its jubilation meeting on Wednesday afternoon, after the meeting of the college board of trustees. It was a great joy to all present to see the veteran, A. M. Atkinson, restored to a large measure of health and vigor, sitting upon the platform. It was a time of joy for many reasons. The first year of the Bible College had drawn to a close under the most favorable conditions. The outlook for the year to come was of the brightest character.

The fiscal secretary, J. E. Pounds, reports that students are coming in large numbers, and he predicts an attendance for the second year about five times as great as for the first. It is not surprising, then, that a tone of the highest hopefulness pervaded all that was said at this afternoon meeting. Bro. A. B. Philputt, the new pastor of the Central Church, Indianapolis, made the address of the day. He fell most heartily and happily into the spirit of the time and of the college. All present felt that no mistake had been made when Bro. Philputt had been elected a member of the board of trustees of the Bible College; nay, that no mistake had been made in electing him president of that board. His address was followed by short impromptue speeches by A. M. Atkinson, J. E. Pounds, Prof. Benton, A. F. Armstrong and others. Dean Jabez Hall, who presided over the meeting, side by side with Prof. Benton, his colleague in the first year's teaching, gave to all confidence in the solidity of the undertaking. Some of the new members of next year's faculty were also present; but others, either at their homes or traveling in Europe, had not yet arrived upon the ground.

In the evening the Alumni reception and banquet were held in Gymnasium Hall. About a hundred guests were at the tables, presided over by Prof. Wilson, the president of the Alumni Association. Toasts were responded to by several members of the association. C. E. Thornton, of the Third Church of Indianapolis, a member of the Butler board of trustees, was chosen president of the Alumni, for the coming year. He has expressed the hope, and with the co-operation of the Alumni his executive ability will realize that hope, that next year's gathering shall be the largest and best of recent years. The decorations in the Gymnasium Hall were greatly to be commended, the dinner did credit to the ladies of the Downey Avenue Church, Irvington, who served it, and all in all, the efforts of Prof. Wilson were highly praiseworthy.

The guests departed after midnight with their hearts filled with the general joyousness and hopefulness that pervaded the commencement season.

The graduation exercises took place on Thursday morning at 10 o'clock. The address was delivered by Hon. John L. Griffiths on the topic, "Literature and Life." Mr. Griffiths, who has made for himself in recent years a reputation in this and other states as a political speaker, is also a polished gentleman of literary attainments. His address met with most hearty approbation, and his peroration, of a patriotic character, was greeted with long applause. Rev. J. A. Milburn, of the Second Presbyterian Church, at the presentation of diplomas, made a very graceful speech to the graduating class upon the "Essence of Gentlemanliness" which he considers the aim of all true culture. President Butler then conferred the degree of A. B. upon the members of the class, and the honorary degree of A. M. upon Dean Hall, of the Bible College.

A very interesting and impressive service took place on Thursday night at the Third Church, in the city, when David Rioch, of the graduating class, was ordained to the Christian ministry. Bro. Rioch is under appointment by the Foreign Board to go to India, and the service was especially interesting because of this fact, and also the fact that his young wife, who is a physician, was at that moment ill in a New York hospital, after undergoing a serious opera-[illegible]e services were under the direction of Dean Hall, and were shared by Prof. Benton, E. P. Wise, of Irvington; A. B. Philputt, of the Central and Dr. P. MacNab and the pastor of the Third Church.

Irvington has settled down into the quiet, beautiful repose that only college towns know, in the long vacation. But that repose is one filled with pleasant dreams. Her debts are all paid; her endowment, which is not great, but is better than many other colleges can boast, is secure; her faculty are all engaged for next year and are not to be excelled in this state or in the West; her Bible College has almost secured the sum it started out to raise and its future is assured; it is not wonderful, then, that her rest is peaceful and her dreams rosy. If the brotherhood rally around her everywhere as they are doing in this state, there is not the shadow of a doubt that she will be an Amherst or Williams in the West. It is of this she dreams, and there is much in dreams.

Burris A. Jenkins.

Letter from Mr. Moody.

Editor Christian-Evangelist:

Dear Friend—There are about forty Christian Commission tents at work in the army camps, and I suppose it is safe to say that the workers are touching 20,000 men every day with a positive influence for Christ. We have no means of knowing how many soldiers have been converted thus far. Unquestionably not all the seed has fallen on good ground, but thank God, much of it has. It has been cause for special rejoicing that so many of those who had accepted Christ have been prompt in confessing him and faithful in laboring for their comrades. One of the workers writing from Chickamauga says: "When I first arrived here I saw two men talking earnestly with Mr. Schiverea, and found out afterwards that they were men who had attended some of his meetings in New York last winter, and who had run away from their convictions at that time. They were greatly surprised to find Mr. Schiverea here. Both have now come out definitely for Christ, and are going about telling others about it, and thanking God that they were ever sent to Chickamauga."

We have just sent two more preachers to Camp Thomas, the Rev. D. T. Toy, of Staten Island, and Mr. Ferd. Schiverea, the evangelist. Dr. Wharton has just left Tampa after a season of great blessing.

We have at last been able to do something for the many. The hundred good books were sent to Rev. Wesley C. Holway, chaplain U. S. S. Vermont, now in New York navy yard. In acknowledging them he says: "We have no ship going immediately to Cuba, so I retain them until opportunity comes to send them where they will do special good. Meantime I have put some in the sick bags of the U. S. S., Topeka, of the Columbia, of this ship, also in the reading-room of the Cob Dock. Will also send some to the Naval Hospital. These books appear to me to be calculated to do great good, and I am anxious that not one of them shall fail of its mission. Thanking you warmly in the name of our sailor men, I am, etc."

Major Whittle writes from Chickamauga: "The interest among the soldiers has deepened since my last letter. In over fourteen meetings Sunday at least 500 men asked for prayer, and there were many decisions. Last night Maxwell and I were at 1st South Carolina, and had perhaps the most fruitful meeting I have ever held. Probably 600 men of the regiment were present. I think over 100 of them said they wanted to be Christians, and over 50 of them came into the circle around our box and knelt on the ground to be prayed for and pointed to Christ. You have no idea of the tenderness among those to whom we preach, and their sympathy with the message we bring them. We are all having the most delightful experience of our lives in preaching Christ."

All over the country the Christian people are becoming more and more aroused to the importance of this opportunity. Mass meetings are being held; the various young people's societies are taking hold of it earnestly, and also the women's societies of the different churches. I wish I could give you some extracts from letters we have been receiving with contributions. May God help us to find our places in this great movement of his Spirit.

Yours sincerely,

D. L. Moody.

East Northfield, Mass., July 1, 1898.

The Doctrine of The Holy Spirit.

The article in the Christian-Evangelist, of the 24th, by a correspondent, challenges the scripturalness of Bro. Fergusson's views in regard to the baptism of the Holy Spirit. I am not concerned to defend the writer of that noble series of articles on the Holy Spirit. So powerfully were his statements fortified with Scripture that defense is not needed. I do, however, wish to point out a few mistakes which his critic falls into in his thoughtful yet (I respectfully suggest) unscriptural response. The writer seems to have a terribly one-sided view of our relation to the Holy Spirit when he propounds the impossibility of baptism into a person, and intimates that the Spirit indwells us, and consequently it cannot be said that we can be baptized in him. Two errors are contained in those propositions. First, the Scriptures aver that we were baptized *into* Christ. Is not Christ a person? It is because the believer is baptized *into* Christ that the inspired writer adds, "Therefore we are buried *with* him" (Rom. 6:3, 4).

Secondly, while it is true that the Spirit is in us, it is none the less true that we are "in the Spirit" (Rom. 8:9), and that we "live in the Spirit" Gal. 6:25), and "pray in the Spirit" (Eph. 6:18). Hence the argument that "the Spirit indwelling the believer is not baptism," loses any force it might have, standing alone, by the counter truth that the Spirit of God is also indwelt by the Christian.

The writer, after emphasizing the "one baptism," in sad forgetfulness of this emphasis afterwards admits that there is a baptism into Christ's sufferings, whereby a place in his kingdom is gained; thereby nullifying any weight that might be attached to his first utterance.

The major matter in the article that I ask permission to dwell upon, however, is a statement so harsh and unscriptural that I wonder greatly that it should ever come from the pen of a Disciple. Does the writer readily believe that a person baptized into the Holy Spirit would be none the better for it? That water baptism would be of greater efficacy, and would be necessary to the remission of sins? I may be forgiven, for I write in love, for saying that the statement to this effect by our brother with a reference to Acts 10:48 is a glaring instance of *suppressio veri, suggestio falsi*. Not only does Acts 10:48 not endorse the statement, so rashly made, but verse 43 says that "whosoever *believeth* shall receive remission of sins." Why substitute the word baptize for believe? Do "all the prophets give witness" that whosoever is baptized shall receive remission? I fail to recall a single instance of such testimony. Peter asks, "Can any man forbid water that these should not be baptized which *have* received the Holy Ghost?" It is news to me that Disciples hold that unbelievers can receive the Holy Ghost. It is certainly not so taught in John 7:38-39: "This spake he of the Spirit which they that *believe* on him should receive." (See also 14:17.) Hence, Cornelius who *did* receive the Holy Spirit must have believed on the Christ; if he believed he did experience remission of sins (Acts 13:38-39), which he afterward showed forth in a figure (baptism). It cannot be too strongly emphasized that it is the blood that cleanseth from *all* sin (1 Jno. 1:7); that it is by the blood we have redemption (Eph. 1:7); by the blood we are justified (Rom. 5:9) and not by water, though it be baptismal water.

We do well to remember that "baptism doth now save us" in a *figure* (1 Pet. 3:21). It is a sign or seal of that which has *actually* been accomplished by the precious blood of Christ in the case of the believer.

As Alex. Campbell has it, "The blood of Christ *really* washes away our sins; baptism formally; Paul's sins were really pardoned when he believed."

In the Millennial Harbinger, page 300, volume 3, in correspondence with Dr. Fishback, the great reformer emphasizes the same trust when he tells Dr. Fishback that he (Mr. Campbell) is in agreement with him in his contention that the free favor of God by which he justifies the believer, or remits his sins, is *not* suspended till he is baptized in water.

Again, in another place, "Should I find a Pedobaptist more spiritually minded and more devoted to the Lord than one immersed on the profession of his faith, I could not hesitate in giving the preference of my heart to him that *loveth* most. Did I act otherwise, I would be a mere sectarian, a Pharisee among Christians."

This appeal to the Fathers is in marked contrast to the regrettable utterance of your correspondent to the effect that one baptized in the Holy Spirit can yet be an unforgiven sinner. "Ye are not in the flesh if the Spirit of God dwell in you" (Rom. 8:9). Such an one may be justly said to be born of the Spirit (not living in the flesh), and in regard to his case, in the matter of remission of sins Campbell say, "Those who are thus begotten of God are children of God. To be born of God and born in sin is irreconcilable. Remission of sins is as certainly granted to the born of God as life eternal will be granted to the children of the resurrection."

I hope that this criticism of a "brother beloved" may be a small contribution towards helping to elucidate truth.

I have no doubt that he is as sincere in this matter as myself.

Criticus.

To the Preachers of Indiana.

The time has fully come when the Church of Christ in Indiana should inaugurate a movement all along the line for the planting of primitive Christianity in every city, town and hamlet in all of our great state.

Every department of church work, pastoral, evangelistic, Sunday-school, Christian Endeavor, missionary, etc., should receive such an impetus, as will carry them on to grander triumphs and greater success than ever before. The people are tired of men-made religions and human theories and are crying out for the pure, sweet, simple gospel of Christ and perishing for the want of it. Everywhere the fields are over-ripe; the harvest is here; the golden grain is ready for the sickle. Is the church of the living God ready to do the work that its great Head asks it to do?

At this opportune time we have a few requests to make of the noble band of preachers in Indiana, who have heretofore made great sacrifices, and who are willing in the future to make still greater, that the old gospel may be preached. Saints strengthened and sinners converted and the church made to rejoice in the trimuphs of Messiah's kingdom.

1. Our Bethany Assembly Encampment meeting will begin on Friday, July 22, and close on Monday, August 15.

The week beginning on Lord's day, July 24, is "Preachers' Week." During that week the State Missionary Society, and State Ministerial Association will hold their convention.

The Home and Foreign Missionary Societies will have interesting exercises connected with their work.

Ministerial Relief, Church Extension, Negro Evangelization, etc., will have all their claims presented by able advocates. Indianapolis University and Butler Bible College will also have a day that week. Bro. Jabez Hall—than whom we have no riper Bible scholar among us—will deliver six lectures to preachers on living themes that will deeply interest all preachers, both old and young. Some important Assembly lectures will be delivered that week—one of the finest "Vitascope" entertainments—something entirely new will be given.

Now, what we desire to urge on our preachers is for them to make their arrangements and attend the Assembly that week. Let all the preachers come up to our great Assembly that week, and let us arrange a campaign of work such as we have never had before in Indiana. Already we have word from a goodly number of preachers from quite a number of other states, saying that they expect to attend Bethany on Preachers' Week. Preachers of Indiana, let us give them a royal welcome, and let us show them our preaching forces, and let us plan great things for God and Christ and the church.

2. We are anxious to enlist, not only the preachers—the watchmen on the walls of Zion—but the business men and women of the church as well. The preachers have their work to do, and we believe that they can be trusted to do it well. So also have the lay members of the church an important work that they alone can do. Too frequently our religious conventions are made up almost wholly by preachers. We would not have a less number of preachers in our conventions, but we would have a much larger number of lay members, especially of the business men of the church. So, among the new features of the Assembly this year is "Business Men's Day.". This is Saturday, August 6.

On that day all of the interests of the church, and especially the interests of Bethany Assembly, will be considered by the business men and women of the state.

What we ask of the preachers is that each one of them shall make special mention of this day to their congregations and urge the business men—as many as possible—to attend the Assembly that day. Would it not be well for each preacher, in bringing the matter before his congregation, to urge them to select a few of the business men of the church to attend on that day.

We will depend upon the preachers to work up a large attendance at the Assembly on August 6. And now, brethren, under the leadership of the great Captain, let us at our Assembly this year inaugurate a movement that means "Indiana for Christ."

The splendid record of the fathers of the reformation, their sacrifices and their triumphs; the fact that God has called us to be colaborers to labor for the conversion of the world; the many doors that are wide open inviting us to go in and possess the land—all these and many other reasons should induce us to make our Assembly this year fruitful of results as never before.

Let us make it the subject of especial prayer, and let us go up to fit to do brave work for God and Christ and humanity. L. L. CARPENTER,
President Bethany Assembly.
Wabash, Ind.

Notes and News.

I have resigned as pastor of the church at this place to take effect July 17, for the purpose entering Drake, next fall, after spending a month's vacation in Tennessee and Virginia.

I would like to correspond with a preacher who would like a small but growing work.
DAVID LYON.
Wheeling, Mo., June 30, 1898.

DEAR BRETHREN:—We have leased the buildings and grounds of Oskaloosa College and will open them in September as "Oskoloosa Normal College." It has been thought wise to thus reorganizethis college, and throw open its doors to all persons desiring a Literary, Practical, Normal, Scientific and Musical education. Prof. A. J. Youngblood and Mrs. Belle H. Updegraff will be my coworker in this enterprise. I shall be glad to have words of encouragement from my friends.
ALEX. C. HOPKINS,
Principal of Oskaloosa Normal College.

The sixth annual convention of the eighth Christian mission district, of Illinois, will be held with the Christian Chnrch at Du Quoin, Ill., beginning Thursday night, Sept. 8th, and continue till Monday morning, Sept. 12th, 1898. The programe which is replete with interest, will appear in due time.

J. F. McCARTNEY, Chairman Committee.

After an absence from Illinois of twelve years in the churches of the Eastern states, I desire to return to the state of my nativity to live. Any good church now or prospectively pastorless that would like to have me and my family, not only to preach and work for the church, but also to find and purchase a permanent home in your city or town, will please write me at East Smithfield, Bradford Co., Penn. S. C. HUMPHREY.

About one year ago a small band of Christians, 35 to 40 in number, four miles northwest of Mt. Vernon, Mo., "began to build a the house of the Lord," at Salem, at a cost of $800, and last Lord's day the writer had the pleasure of meeting with them in the dedicatory exercises, and after preaching to a large audience on "Our Distinctive Plea," we raised about $125, which enabled us to dedicate free from debt, with a small balance in the treasury. Because of the great sacrifices these brethren have been compelled to make in building this house, and that they may be able to purchase and pay for some furnishings, I have promised to supply them with volunteer preaching one Lord's day in each month for the next six months, and that I may be able to keep my promise with them, as evangelist of this district, I issue my first call for volunteer preachers of this and adjoining counties, who are able and willing to help these brethren. I have already one volunteer to start with—Bro. Abe Lemaster, of Aurora, who will preach for them the 4th Lord's day in July. I hope soon through the liberality of our preachers, to be able to announce preaching for the 4th Lord's day in each of the succeeding months of this year, after which time they will be able to employ some good man for one-fourth to one-half his time.

I take this opportunity of announcing that I have tendered my resignation as evangelist of the Springfield district, to take effect as soon as the board can find some suitable man to take up the work, after which I will be ready to give my time to pastoral work, and to this end solicit correspondence with churches in need of a preacher. S. J. VANCE.
Aurora, Mo., June 30, 1898.

Bro. T. A. Meredith, who recently took the pastoral charge of the Church of Christ in this village, has just closed a very interesting series of special evangelistic meetings in this place of three weeks' continuance, resulting in ten accessions to the congregation—eight baptisms and two by commendation.

Bro. Meredith is a young man, a good speaker, fearless in the presentation of the gospel truth as understood and advocated by the Church of Christ. While some take offense at his plainness of speech, all concede that he has the courage of his convictions, and preaches what he believes. He is also an efficient leader of song; his solos, prefacing each service, are especially appropriate as well as attractive. Bro. Meredith has reserved two months of the present year for the purpose of holding a few revival meetings in the state. Any church wishing such a meeting would do well to correspond with him as above. JOHN TRUAX.
Howard Lake, Minn., June 29, 1898.

State Mission Notes.

It was a pleasure to spend Lord's day at Sedalia in the great church and Sunday-school there. It was my first visit to that church in its working hours and it was a wonderful sight. That Sunday-school at work is worth going across the state to see; there was 550 present the day I was there and they said it was an off day. Of course I went into that primary room and saw that wonderful class of Bro. Dalby's. It is the largest primary class among our people in the state and the only reason it is not larger is because they won't give him any more room.

I had the pleasure of preaching at the New East Side church in the morning, where Bro. F. L. Cook is pastor. They have a beautiful edifice indeed; it is splendidly located, has a good pastor and the outlook for the future is very bright indeed.

In the evening I was at the Central Church and we had a good audience though Bro. Meyers, who notices everything, said there were more empty seats than common. They listened eagerly to what I had to say and I will tell you of the collection some other time. It is a great church and has a great future.

At California it rained. Well, I should say it did. It was wonderful how it did rain, but we had a good audience anyhow and one of the best giving audiences I have faced in a long time. But then when you have a preacher like B. F. Hill, who puts down $5 as a starter the congregation can't help it. He has done a wonderful work there in the years of his pastorate. He has proven truly that he was the man for the place. May God bless him in his work.

At night I was at Lexington where I was to deliver an address for the C. W. B. M. and I think it is the first time I saw it rain hard enough to keep the sisters from a meeting like that. But then it was one of the hardest rains I ever saw. The congregation was all torn up over the resignation of G. M. Goode and well they may be for he is a man amongst men, a preacher and a pastor to love. I was sorry to miss him. Some good church in Missouri call him quick.

k has been a hard clerical week. ıe last quarter have been sent ;et yours? Please don't cast it ırd has need of funds. It must go out of the business. Never reater calls nor more urgent. t-breaking some of them. Send ıat we may answer them.

ent out a circular letter to the ghout the state asking their rtier co-operation. I believe it e have as great a band of minis- ı shines on—some of them. I er in course of preparation to erintendents. We are looking from them. We want to reach, ry congregation in the state and in the work. We are having rts from the field now. Will hem in my next. Shall the good lend in your help.'

Yours in his name,

T. A. ABBOTT.

nter Ave., St. Louis, Mo.

:vangelistic.

MICHIGAN.

-On the evening of July 18, I ent meeting in Crooksville, Ohio, t one thousand inhabitants. We a church there, but a few faith- ıo live there have been meeting ouse for Bible study and wor- ting continued just two weeks, 13 baptisms, one from the Bap- claimed, and with those who had Christian work, we were en- ize a church with 34 members. ıptized were heads of failies— ıd are among the best families They own their own homes great help in establishing the ıster in that place. During my de my home with Brother and oper, who were formerly mem- tral Church of Christ, Colum- are ever to be counted among ɘs of earth.—W. J. RUSSELL, hurch of Christ.

FLORIDA.

2.—Am here in a meeting with by baptism. I go from here to ., in a tent meeting with J. D. open for engagement either in regular work. Address me at .—J. J. IRVINE.

ARKANSAS.

.y 7.—One baptism last night.—

OHIO.

'uly 7.—Additions here at our s, not reported, 16. Will build a on to our church house, also a onage on our church lot, at once. ıs.

ILLINOIS.

July 1.—One baptism at regular t Palmyra, last Lord's day.—

, of Gibson City reports five ad- r since he began his present min-

July 4.—Two added yesterday. number of additions since our losed.—W. M. GROVES.

o more added here the last two 3. LAPPIN.

y 1.—Three baptisms at our this week. All lines of work .. A. GILLILAND.

TENNESSEE.

-One added to membership, st, July 3rd.—A. M. GROWDEN.

TEXAS.

2.—Ten added to the Central .st report.—F. N. CALVIN.

MINNESOTA.

s, pastor, A. B. Moore, evan- H. Sweetman, singer, report in a meeting at Redwood Falls. sm.

INDIANA.

July 4.—North Park Church fessions yesterday; also three orted, since we dedicated our

INDIAN TERRITORY.

Vinita, July 4th.—Closed last night. Here nine days. Organized with 32 members. Baptized four. Organized a Sunday-school. Arrangements made for the work to be followed up. Go next to Nashville, Mo.—MORGANS AND DAUGHTER.

MISSOURI.

Skidmore, July 1.—One addition by letter and one by confession here last Sunday.—N ROLLO DAVIS.

H. A. Northcutt reported 13 confessions at Sturgeon on Sunday night, July 4th.

Sturgeon, July 1.—We are in the second week of our meeting here; 11 confessions to date.—H. A. NORTHCUTT.

KANSAS.

Abilene, July 6.—One baptized the same hour of the night here recently. The work moves on well considering everything.—N. B. McGHEE.

Independence, July 4.—I closed one year's work here first of this month with Bible-school increased; Junior C. E. of over 40 members organized, C. W. B. M. of 15 members, 36 added to church and debt of about $550 raised. We hope for great advancementin future.—Elmer T. DAVIS, Pastor.

Topeka, July 4.—Our two weeks' meeting in River View, Kansas City, was a very enthusiastic and fruitful one. There were 50 from all sources. They are well organized with all the auxiliaries and will succeed. V. E. Ridenour was leader of song. My next meeting will be with the Third Church of Topeka, Kan., F. E. Mallory pastor, F. F. Dawdy singing evangelist. These are two of the brightest and most promising young men in the state.—D. D. BOYLE.

1048 *Spruce Street.*

IOWA.

Urbana Center.—Seven added.—A. PIERSON, preaching.

Brainard.—Sixty added to date.—W. B. CREWDSON, Evangelist.

KENTUCKY.

Tyrone, June 27th.—A. B. Carpenter has just closed a meeting that we shall remember for a long time. We consider him a Christian and true to the cause which we all love.—W. T. CARR.

Lexington, June 27th.—R. B. Briney, assisting Milo Atkinson, pastor at Worthville, Ky., closed a two weeks' meeting there Sunday with 14 additions. A local preacher from the Methodist Church came, saying he was willing to accept the Bible only, and was buried with Christ in baptism.

Publishers' Notes.

DO YOU USE THEM?

We mean marriage certificates. If you do, we have just what you need. Our special catalogue of recent issue contains a large assortment of marriage certificates ranging in prices from $1.00 per dozen to $4.00 per dozen. This catalogue will be found quite convenient to have when the minister wants the marriage certificates. It gives cuts and sizes and prices of many kinds, thus enabling the preacher to select for himself. We will be glad to mail it to any minister requesting it. Write for our marriage certificate catalogue.

A POSTAL CARD

Addressed to the Christian Publishing Company, St. Louis, Mo., is all that it will cost a member of the Endeavor Society to examine our late catalogue containing a full list of Christian Endeavor supplies. It also contains a number of books giving instructions in Endeavor work, and a well-selected list of books specially adapted for Sunday-school and Endeavor libraries. Write us for this catalogue and you are certain to find something in it that will aid you in your Endeavor work.

AN HOUR

Or two spent each day can be made quite profitable in canvassing for some one or more of our books. We offer liberal terms to our agents, and will take pleasure in corresponding with those who may wish to devote a little time making a few dollars by placing good literature in the home. Young men and young ladies who are just from college for the summer vacation might engage in the canvass for the sale of good literature with much profit. Write for our catalogue, select some good book to sell, and get our terms. Address Christian Publishing Co., St. Louis, Mo.

"Wonders of the Sky, or God's Glory Exhibited in the Heavens," by W. J. Russell, is now in the press and will be ready for delivery in a few days. It calls the attention of the reader to the grandeur, sublimity, beauty and immensity of the heavens, and ultimately aims to create in the mind of the reader a greater reverence for the Creator. The book will be bound in handsome cloth, printed on good paper, and the price 50 cents.

Family Circle.

The Secret of Happiness.

Are you almost disgusted
 With life, little man?
I will tell you a wonderful trick,
That will bring you contentment
 If anything can—
Do something for somebody, quick;
Do something for somebody, quick!

Are you "awfully tired"
 With play little girl?
Weary, discouraged and sick?
I'll tell you the loveliest
 Game in the world—
Do something for somebody, quick;
Do something for somebody, quick!

Though it rains like the rain
 Of the flood, little man,
And the clouds are forbidding and thick,
You can make the sun shine
 In your soul, little man—
Do something for somebody, quick;
Do something for somebody, quick!

Though the skies are like brass
 Overhead, little girl,
And the walk like a well-heated brick,
And all earthly affairs
 In a terrible whirl—
Do something for somebody, quick;
Do something for somebody, quick!

—*Author Unknown.*

Santa Cruz.

[This article consists of extracts from a personal letter received in St. Louis from a former resident, who now lives at Santa Cruz, Cal. It was not written for publication, but through the kindness of the recipient, we are permitted to present it to our readers, believing that they will enjoy it.—EDITOR.]

If the Lord had handed me a blank sheet before I left St. Louis, and told me to write out just what I wanted in the future, I couldn't have asked for a pleasanter place in which to live, nor work more congenial than I have here. We have the bay, the ocean, the mountains, the never-failing mountain streams, the perennial blooming of flowers, and skies that outdo Italy's best in clearness and beauty, all of which are ever-enduring attractions.

The winter thus far has been colder and drier than usual. Up to this week we have had very little rain, and the crops were beginning to show the need of rain; but it commenced to rain last Tuesday, and it has been raining ever since then, and the prospects are that we will have fine crops next summer. You understand winter is the growing season in California. During the summer months we have very little rain, and yet here on the coast things never dry out as they do in the East. We have heavy dews and fogs at night, which take the place of rain elsewhere. The climate as a whole is very comfortable. The thermometer seldom goes above 75 degrees in the summer, and I believe has never been known to go below 25 degrees in the winter.

During the summer and fall months we took many trips into the mountains and along the sea coast, and spent a week's vacation at Ben Lomond, a mountain camp six miles northeast of Santa Cruz. I climbed the mountain there, and could see a landscape more extended than Moses saw from Pisgah's heights. I could see the great Pacific reaching out into infinity, and to the south was the Monterey Bay, which some say rivals the Bay of Naples, while across the bay were the beautiful Monterey Mountains. The drives here are grand and the scenery caps anything I have ever seen in the East. The mountains have a dense growth of trees of all kinds, but the stately sequoia (redwood) predominates. At Big Trees on the Narrow Gauge Railroad, six miles northeast of Santa Cruz, is a grove of those trees fenced in; you have to pay to get in and see them, but to excursions and picnics it is only ten cents apiece. Many of the trees in that grove

SANTA CRUZ.

are over three hundred feet in height, and a few giants over three hundred and fifty feet. There are large forests of such trees in the state, some of them still taller than those in Santa Cruz, but the one six miles from this city is only a short drive by conveyance over a good road. The sequoia growing on the mountains are not so tall, still there are thousands of them over two hundred and fifty feet in height. I suppose one reason trees grow so large here is because they can grow during almost the entire year, it being seldom that a tree is blown down by tide wind, or even wind-shaken. There has never been a wind in this section hard enough to blow over a light board frame house. Cyclones are unknown. The mountains are literally studded with trees, and hence are more beautiful than the bare Rockies, or the Sierras of Southern California.

Last fall, on one of our trips up into the mountains, we visited a vineyard that is located on a foothill six miles from Santa Cruz, and eight hundred feet above tide-water. It was a paradise of fruits, flowers and scenery. The owner has expended a great deal of money on it, and if his place was within six miles of St. Louis he would have big returns from it; but as it is he is not making anything out of it over and above the expenses of keeping it in order. He has the finest of grapes, and fruits of all kinds. He has over one hundred acres, all in perfect cultivation, and keeps a colony of Chinese laborers to work it. He can see Santa Cruz, the bay, and the ocean from his south and west porches, and in the opposite direction he can see "Lomo Prieta," the highest peak of the Santa Cruz Mountains (three thousand eight hundred feet above sea level), about twenty miles to the east. I left my daughter and Mrs. W. there to rusticate for a week, as it is a kind of hotel for summer boarders. Many Santa Cruzans go there to spend vacations because of the pure air and fine scenery, and the fact that one can sit out of doors at night without putting wraps on, which you cannot do down on the coast, where the cold waters of the ocean keep the temperature about 50 or 60 degrees at night all summer through. We never know any hot nights here. Wear the same kind of undercloth-ing all the year round, and the same kind of bedclothing winter and summer. Now understand me: this cold condition only obtains in the neighborhood of the ocean; that is, between the mountains and the ocean; and as soon as you enter the valleys running into the mountains, or cross over the mountains (the top of which are only fifteen miles from the coast-line), you get into a climate as hot as St. Louis in the summertime, but not near so cold in the wintertime.

The counties in the Sacramento and San Joaquin (San Waukeen) Valleys have many prosperous farmers and ranchers, who during the summer months come to the coast and enjoy the cool breezes from the Pacific, and the fine bathing at Santa Cruz and Seabright. The latter place in the "season" has a population of five or six hundred. Most of the people own their little cottages, bring their bedding and provisions along, and so can spend a month or so very pleasantly, at little expense.

But to return to the vineyard on the foothill. When we got ready to leave there, the proprietor brought out a box that would hold considerably over a bushel, and ordered some of the Jap grape-pickers to go out and pick the finest table-grapes he had. They did so and soon came back with the finest lot of grapes I ever saw, loaded them into the surrey and my wife and I drove home with them, stopping at the foot of the hill to take dinner with some picnickers that were having a good time alongside of a rapid Rocky Mountain stream. Table-grapes had no value last fall; you could have all you wanted for the trouble of picking them. Wine-grapes had a marketable value at the wineries. It does not take long to pick a bushel of grapes in a vineyard like the one I have of. The bunches are such as ade the eyes of Joshua and :. The trouble is, there is no product. There used to be ›dy went into it, but now the ›verstocked and there is sale for the over production. ›a Cruz is too small a place to the over production. Its ‹ a seaside resort. In the ›n the denizens of the ›cramento and San Joaquin) get away from their semi- Sea bathing is a big card. ‹ eighty rods of the Sea-

SANTA CRUZ BEACH.

'(which is one and a half t of the Santa Cruz Court more of a private bathing Santa Cruz Beach. There houses, mostly owned by We have access to one of ı for the horse and buggy ur part, and go in bathing [y wife likes it now, but did ffeting of the big rollers at to learn how to take them ›ock you off your feet and sand. There is an element if the undertow (the rushing ater after they have swept ach quite a ways) is too send you a photograph of : Beach, which will give you how it looks, only in the be lined with bathers. The ›nts the bay as very calm . When the tide runs high, are emphasized by the trade ill dash almost against the the left of the picture. The ıckground of the picture is of the San Lorenzo River, :harges into the bay. That ›n the cliff in the grove. taken looking east. The Mountains are off in the ›op of the mountains being ıty miles distant. The bay side of the picture, and the ıd a half to the southwest. of the city is north of the beach (that is to the left) about half a mile.

What do you think of it? Don't you think it is a picturesque little place?

I came in this morning on the bicycle, the roads having dried sufficiently to permit that kind of locomotion, but I see the rain has commenced again, and I expect my folks will have to come in after me with the rig. I would like to have the wheel at home for to-morrow afternoon if it clears off; there is no prettier ride anywhere than along the "Cliff Drive." The grade is almost as level as the ocean, except where one crosses some gully coming down from the foothills, where the grades become a little too steep for safe riding. I then dismount, and lead my machine. The city of Santa Cruz owns ten miles of road along the bay and ocean, and the road is a favorite drive. It never gets muddy, and never dusty.

The tides never let the ocean settle down to a dead calm, as the lakes sometimes do. We have been planning to cross the bay sometime on the boat. Seasickness is one of the concomitants of a trip across the bay. My wife has never been seasick, and she wants to experience that excruciating pleasure. Miss B. and I had a foretaste of it in a fearful storm on Lake Michigan once and I am not so anxious for a repetition.

Santa Cruz is certainly one of the loveliest places in California, because of the variety of scenery, and yet it is scarcely known outside of the state. It has been content to be a watering-place. It has many beautiful homes, and if it were within two hours' ride of San Francisco it would be a popular suburban place to live in. The time now is four hours. It is proposed to build a road along the ocean which would avoid the heavy grades of the roads that come over the mountains, and permit of the trip being made in two hours (75 miles). We get the San Francisco papers by nine o'clock in the morning.

Living here is much cheaper than in St. Louis. You can buy a bushel of assorted vegetables, just pulled out of the ground for about a quarter. We have two strawberry crops a year, one in May—the main crop—and the other in November, and they come down to five cents a quart. Peas picked only an hour before you get them are fine and about as cheap, comparatively, as strawberries. The Chinese and Japanese do all the market gardening here, and have driven the white folks out of the business.

Now I have told you some of the good things about California. There are drawbacks. Living so close to the great ocean develops rheumatism in some folks. I think it has been beneficial to me. I am not troubled with malaria nor insomnia. The objection I find to the climate is the everlasting monotony of it. There is not difference enough between the seasons to make the weather enjoyable. I have not heard a peal of thunder since I have been in Santa Cruz, now eighteen months, save the thunderous poundings of the waves on the beach. One kind o' loses the sense of the passage of time, when there is no marked distinctions of the seasons. H.

Hobson's Choice.

BY AMOS. R. WELLS.

[At 4 A. M. of June 3, Lieutenant Hobson and seven men ran the collier Merrimac into the ships' channel at Santiago de Cuba in the face of the fierce fire from the forts, exploded an internal torpedo and sunk the vessel, thus penning the Spanish fleet in the harbor. Almost by a miracle, all eight escaped, and are now honored prisoners of war. When call was made for volunteers to perform this daring and hazardous feat, these men were selected from the many that offered themselves.]

Darkness and midnight sea,
Blackest heart of jeopardy;
Forts that flame an angry death,
And the surer doom beneath;
Risk of life's long happiness
And the safe world's sure success;
Bellow from the mouth of hell,
Heaven—or a Spanish cell;
This, and more—he knew it well—
This was Hobson's choice.

Yes, and more, unstinted, more:
Honor waiting on the shore,
Honor even from the foe,
And where'er the word shall go,
And a wreath within the hand
Of his grateful fatherland;
Lauding lips and shining eyes,
Men's hurrahs that rend the skies,
Yes, the fame that never dies—
This was Hobson's choice.

Now no more that ancient phrase
Chattering down from Charles's days—
"Hobson's choice" of "that or none;"
He had two, an' chose the one:
Safety, danger; deck or wave;
Life or death; the sun, the grave.
Let the phrase new meaning wear
Now, henceforth, and everywhere;
Gallant choice to do and dare
Shall be "Hobson's choice."

—*Christian Endeavor World.*

Eureka College.

A Poem in honor of its Fiftieth Anniversary.

BY AARON PRINCE ATEN.

Of old in the Beautiful City,
  That sat as the joy of the earth,
Arose a bright temple of glory—
  Conception of heavenly birth.

We have read of the deep foundation
  As firm as the ancient hills;
The granite and polished marble
  Whose beauty our spirit thrills.

The cedar from Lebanon's mountains,
  The pearl from the ocean strand,
The gildings of gold from Ophir,
  And treasures of Ethiop's land.

In the book of the record is written
  How rose up the beautiful wall
With no sound of tool or of hammer,
  By the force of some magical call.

A glorious work of creation
  By the skill of some master mind,
It stood like a finished glory
  On Moriah's mount outlined.

For the honor of Jahveh builded,
  Shekinah's dread presence dwelt
In the midst of its splendid beauty
  Where the wisest of monarchs knelt.

And shall we find other motive
  Than love as the forceful thought
That kindled the kingly spirit
  That the untold treasures brought?

'Twas a concept born of the gladness
  Welling up from a human soul,
Touched deep by the Infinite Goodness
  When its waves of refreshing roll.

'Twas a grateful acclaim of spirit
  For the mercies of all the years,
And a monument through the ages,
  That the royal bounty rears.

⁂

But love in the hearts of mortals
  Finds grander expression now
Than in marble and gold and jewels
  And a temple where men may bow.

The temple on Zion's mountain
  Has crumbled to dust and death,
And its golden dome fell under
  The destroying angel's breath.

The beautiful Delphic columns
  Have passed from the earth away;
And Diana's splendid glories
  Have faded in sure decay.

But the temples for God erected—
  Not made by material hand,
But by consecrate effort of mortals,
  Through the numberless years shall stand.

When the tottering earth's foundation
  Gives way to the flood of years,
No power shall work out the ruin
  Of a temple baptized in tears.

⁂

The faith that lays hold of the future
  Looked out on the fields of earth,
Computing the wondrous mercy
  In relation to mortal worth.

Some glorious spirits and faithful
  A temple began to build,
Surrounded by leafy bowers
In a land with beauty filled.

A temple of knowledge and learning
  For the culture of mind and soul;
For the leading of spirits earthly
  Where the waters of healing roll.

The hope that inspired their courage
  Was born of the heart's desire
That a host of the world's immortals
  Might feel a diviner fire.

And so without sound of hammer,
  Through the passing of fifty years,
By faith and by prayer and courage
  And the falling of countless tears,

Arose the beautiful structure,
  As the master workmen planned
On the trestle board of their duty,
  In behalf of a world's demand.

The love of the Christ constraining,
  Foundation and dome were wrought,
As the hearts and the spirits dauntless
  His honor and glory sought.

Not marble and brick and mortar—
  They were only the outward shell
Of this beautiful temple of learning
  That the fathers reared so well—

But a building so high and so holy
  That it touches the vaulted skies;
In whose halls our children walking,
  To honor and fame arise.

In the semi-centennial closing
  This Jubilee year, we bring
A gift from our hearts' rich treasure,
  And peans of gladness sing.

May the glimpse of a coming glory
  Touch hopeful our inner sight,
For Eureka's gladsome future,
  As we bathe in its radiant light!

Hutchinson, Kan., June, 1898.

Text Stories—VII.

SPINSTERHOOD.

BY ALICE CURTICE MOYER.

And his sister stood afar off to witness what would be done to him.—*Exodus 2:4.*

"Look, Ethel, there she is now, just passing. Isn't she sweet-looking? And she is the dearest and best of teachers. There is not a girl in her class that does not feel her influence. She has such a pleasant way of showing us just what our duty is, that we can't help listening. All her girls have become Christians, and I know her influence has helped to bring it about."

"Yes, she is sweet-looking, I admit," replied Ethel, looking from the window after her friend's Sunday-school teacher, "but"—

"But what?"

"Well—of course—you see, May, she's an old maid; and you know old maids are almost always cross, and"—

"Miss Wilson isn't," interrupted May; "mother has known her for years and she has always been just as sweet-tempered as she is now."

"Well, of course, there may be exceptions, but I confess, May, I would rather die than be an old maid. How can an old maid be happy? Your Miss Wilson may seem to be what you believe her to be, but

don't you suppose that de
heart there is an unfilled
that there is something lac
there must be, and for my
to experience it."

"What is it, my dears, th
ness?" spoke up May's m
girls had forgotten was pre
it that brings such peace
unseen corner of the hea
lives with joy and gladnes
more nor less than the faitl
of duty in whatever condit
lot may be cast. No matt
duty may at first seem,
heartaches the constant fol
cost us, it will finally br
passeth all understanding,'
there will be a knowledge o
and a consciousness of t
greater the sacrifice the
the service in his sight.

"Let me tell you the
Wilson. As May says, I
for years. She is several
and was, therefore, a you
was still a little girl, but I
her. She was born of w
with a silver spoon in h
speak—but it didn't stay
the case, for you know the
slippery thing, and whe
reached the age of eigh
suddenly discovered that it
did not sit down to bem
consider herself abused,
time, for her father was
she must needs help her
him—a care which was n
for his sudden reverses hel
to that last sleep, leaving h
scantily provided for.

"Then it was that Ruth
her courage. How true it
know what we can do un
for our energies. 'Sweet
adversity,' says Shakesp
sumed the management of
fostering the small remn
tune, relieving and shieldi
mother, cheering and cor
best she could while her
breaking; for she could no
she could do was powerless
of that silent voice acros
and when, a few months a
her father, Ruth also saw

dless when 'these children' and
'en's children are all hers? How
otherwise than happy when she
she has steadfastly followed
when, in the upright lives of her
d sisters she can see her reward;
er *earthly* reward? Her's is,
rich harvest—the most bountiful
reaped this side of eternity.
's, I do not mean that it should
girls, 'Don't marry;' but I do
ght to be said, 'Girls, look well
leap.' Don't let the fear of
d urge you into hasty connubial
here the remainder of your life
ent in repentance. Take time
reflection, for prayerful con-
Take time for investigation.
) look into the character of the
e he becomes the husband.
of son is he to an aged father
ly or ailing mother? What sort
o his sister? What of his habits
tes? And what of his religious
he any? This last is not the
tant consideration. A young

attends church and has little faith in religion, but I love him.'

"'My dear young lady,' said the pastor, 'I would not assume the authority to lay down any set rule in reference to such cases, but I have lived a good while in this world and I will give you my opinion as one who has been an interested observer. Far be it from me to say that there are no honorable, upright men—men of good character—who are not Christians. But ask your own heart this question: Is it perfectly safe for one who daily prays, 'Lead us not into temptation,' to deliberately enter into a relation, the peculiar environments of which would render it a daily temptation? My dear young friend, believing as all Christians do in the oneness of the marriage relation, and believing as all Christians do in an unswerving allegiance to Christ, does it not seem a little unsafe, to say the least, to choose for a husband one who serves another master?'

"The young lady looked sad and finally said: 'But I have not told you the worst, Bro. D. It is no secret that Mr. J. is not

"'O, my young friend!' exclaimed the good pastor. 'Make no such vain sacrifice, I beseech you! Do we not see every day the sad result of this mistaken idea of heroism that has wrought such misery in the world? Time after time it has been proven that the man who will not reform before marriage, will not do so after marriage. Pardon me, but if Mr. J. will not reform now for your sake and for his own sake, he certainly will not do so after you are his wife, for the man who makes such terms will not, after having secured his prize, change his way for the sake of it. Rare indeed is it that the young woman who marries a man to reform him accomplishes her aim; indeed, a life of misery is most often her unhappy reward. To the young woman of this country, as well as to you, my friend, I would say in all sincerity of soul, Beware of such a man. Shun him as you would a plague. Daily contact with such a nature cannot but endanger purity and freshness of heart, even of the most cautious woman. Between those who are constantly together, bound by ties, there can be no compromise of relation. There is, of a necessity, either contempt or sympathy. Save yourself, my dear young lady, from the misery that such a union must surely bring. And above all, save yourself from that sorrow that none but a mother understands who cannot say to her little ones, Your father's life is worthy of your imitation; follow in his footsteps.'

"Better a thousand times, my girls, to live and die a spinster than to be held in such bonds. But I thank God that, while all this is only too true, it is but the dark side of the picture—as the happy homes all over our land will testify—but it is well that we sometimes stop to look upon the dark side. It makes us pause; it makes us thoughtful. And this is what I ask of you, my girls, be thoughtful. And I would not have you forget that there are two ways by which perfection of womanhood can be reached.

Upon the highest peak of the mountain range of noble womanhood stands forth Miriam, the patriotic old maid of the Old Testament.

At the time of our text, Miriam was a precocious little maiden of twelve years. In imagination one can see her stationed amid the palms a short way off watching the tiny cradle of bulrushes with its precious burden—her baby-brother—as it lay upon the bosom of the sacred Nile. Even at that tender age Miriam showed a brave spirit. Neither the loneliness nor the darkness of the night could frighten her from her post of duty. The story is familiar. We all know that we are indebted to this faithful little sister for the preservation of the life of the great lawgiver.

Miriam next claims our attention and calls forth our admiration as a gifted poetess—the sweet singer of Israel, where the great good done by her probably can not be estimated.

Then in the fifteenth chapter of Exodus, we hear of her as a great prophetess, to whom wonderful power was given for the foretelling of events necessary for God's people to know in that primitive time. It might be well to state here that Miriam was the first prophetess.

We next hear of her as a sinner, and as being punished for her sin when her name, Miriam, meaning bitterness, was in harmony with her dreadful fate, which was, indeed, most bitter.

However, through sincere repentance, she was enabled to gain all she had lost through sin. What a lesson of consolation there is in this for poor, faulty human beings—that through repentance we may be restored to our former position in life, and, perhaps, be better and more helpful because of the adversity. No doubt, Miriam, scourged and purified by her great sorrow, came forth from her banishment to sing and to prophesy as she had never done before. She never married; but as she journeyed through this world, she did much to aid her fellowmen in their great battle and struggle with sin. And when her summons came to join—

> "The innumerable caravan which moves
> To that mysterious realm,"

we cannot doubt but that she approached the tomb, "the house appointed for all the living," and crossed the Jordan of death to enter into everlasting peace.

The records of the church, the state, and of all benevolent societies testify to the fact that some of the grandest women of which history tells us have been spinsters. Florence Nightingale, for instance, and good Queen Bess, and a host of others.

The taunts that have been cast by unthinking people at this interesting class of society—spinsters—are as unkind as they are unwarranted. It is not necessary that a woman should marry in order to be a blessing to mankind.

Royal womanhood may be reached by a double highway.

St. Louis, Mo.

Sunday School.

THE PROPHET'S LESSON.*

HERBERT L. WILLETT.

Two dangers menace every enterprise at the moment of its first success. Ours is the tendency to consider the first victory decisive and to regard all as gained: the other is the liability to despair upon the discovery that only a partial success has been achieved, and in the reaction which is likely to follow a strong and enthusiastic effort. Very few causes are won in a single battle. Sometime an easy victory is but the prelude to a severe defeat. One must have reserve power for a second battle. Nor must defeat be permitted to discourage. It may be the best preparation and discipline for future success.

Elijah's triumph had been so signal at Mt. Carmel that he fancied all was won for the cause of Jehovah. Fire and water had obeyed him. The flame had descended upon the altar and the rain upon the land, and both in response to his prayer. He had slaughtered the priests of Baal, and been before the king's chariot on the swift return to the palace of Jezreel. Idolatry was crushed, God was surpreme in the hearts of the nation and the future was bright. Ahab was content to abide by the issue. Religion was subordinate to state policy in his mind, and the people might choose their object of worship as they would. The drought was broken and Jehovah should have the credit. But Jezebel was of a different nature. Of policy she had little, but her loyalty to the cult of her race was intense and she was not to be overcome by a desert-reared *rabi* like Elijah. At the very moment of success the prophet was thrown into a panic by the message of the queen. He knew he could not depend on Ahab's favor. There seemed to be nothing left but flight. Elijah's mistake was in the thought that one swift stroke would kill idolatry. Violent reactions are rarely permanent. The test on Carmel had been conclusive, but it needed to be followed by a long course of preaching, not by an act of vengeance like the killing of the priests of Baal, which only roused the queen, the leader of the Baal party, to a pitch of fury, and yet such violent methods were not infrequent in the lives of even men of God in the Old Testament days, and Jesus found among his disciples evidences of the same spirit which he took occasion to rebuke. Some of the darkest crimes of the centuries have been condoned by those who appealed to the Old Testament to find in the mistakes of men, who for the most part spoke the will of God, the justification for their own cruelties and errors.

Elijah was in terror when he received the message of the queen. The reaction from his intense and passionate enthusiasm came in a lapse into blank despair. He fled to the south, beyond the regions of Ahab; but even at Beer-sheba he was still in a panic of fear and left his servant, thinking that even that companionship might lead to his arrest. Into the very desert he went, and in utter discouragement sat down under a tree and prayed for death. But after sleep and food, providentially provided, had done their work, he went on to the place where he was yet to learn his greatest lesson.

Far away to the south stood Horeb, where Moses had received his call and where he spent forty days with God. To this sacred spot Elijah went. Here at last he would be safe, and here there was provided for him a message. Forty days of silence and of fasting. Forty days alone with God. Out of such a silence Moses came with those institutes which formed the basis of Israel's life. Out of this silence Elijah came with a truth which he could not learn at Cherith or Zeraphath.

Why was he here? Was there nothing to be done? Had he not been called to the prophet's work, and was this solitude the place in which to perform it? His reply in justification of himself was that he stood alone among a hostile people, and could save his life in no other way. He had tried to rescue the true faith, but it was of no avail. He had called down fire, but it seemed to have fallen on his own head. He had invoked the whirlwind, but it had swept him away. There was nothing left but to give up the unequal struggle. Then came the great lesson which the ages have yet to learn in its true meaning. It is not by whirlwind or earthquake or fire that Jehovah works. Man tries to clothe his arm with thunder that he may strike terror to his enemies. True men, weary with the sight of wrong, wish for the power of God to smite down triumphant evil. But God does not use such means. He uses a *voice*. This was the message to Elijah, and when in later days men gathered about a prophet by the Jordan and asked him who he was he responded, "A voice." Jesus himself was "the Word," and the apostle declared that it was God's pleasure to save men by so foolish a thing as preaching. This is the divine method. We see evil and demand its instant removal. This is right. But when it does not vanish we first storm and then despair. God sends a voice—a message; at first it is disregarded, and perhaps the prophet dies. But some hear; the message is borne on, and presently the world has changed front. Violence, cruelty, persecution, invective, sarcasm have all been used, and are sometimes still used by those who think to aid thereby the cause of truth, but their power is as nothing beside the effect of a great, persistent voice that speaks a message which the world needs to hear.

Elijah was not to see the changes he desired. But he was given the privilege of inaugurating them. Those changes were both political and religious. New dynasties must come, both in Israel and Syria. A line of kings more friendly to the worship of Jehovah was needed. A body of prophets who should go about as popular preachers of the will of God was required. For these changes Elijah prepared the way, though he did not live to see them. He called Elisha, and under his care the "sons of the prophets," or bands of preachers, became a moral and spiritual power, while the new dynasty of John, raised up by Elisha, overthrew the official worship of Baal and restored the true faith to its rightful place. Great victories are won by great men like Elijah. But they need to be followed up by the great and pervasive ministries of men like Elisha.

SUGGESTIONS FOR TEACHING.

One act of vengeance provokes another. Victory can only be utilized by remaining on the field, not by running away. God will strengthen his servants for every necessary work. "What doest thou here?" is the word that comes to every Christian. (1) Who has abandoned the effort to do God's will, or (2) is in evil company or places. Fear unfits one for any useful work. The greatest forces are the silent, not the noisy ones. Instruction, the voice of prophets and apostles, has always been God's means for saving the world. Elijah did not learn the lesson at once; how often we have to be taught the same truth. Elijah's purposes were consummated by Elisha: "God buries his workmen, but he carries on his work."

*Bible-school Lesson for July 24—Elijah's Flight and Encouragement (1 Kings 19:1-16). Golden Text—Rest in the Lord and wait patiently for him (Ps. 37:7). Lesson Outline—1. The Flight of Fear (1-8); 2. The Lesson and the Learner (9-12); Instruments of Reform (13-16).

SUBSCRIBERS' WANTS.

Miscellaneous wants and notices will be inserted in this department at the rate of two cents a word, each insertion, all words, large and small, to be counted, and two initials stand for one word. Please accompany notice with corresponding remittance to save book-keeping.

Christian Endeavor.

By Burris A. Jenkins.

TOPIC FOR JULY 24.

HOW TO HAVE A HAPPY HOME.

(Job. 29:1-29; Deut. 6:6-9.)

Entire frankness among the members of a family will add to the general happiness. "The unveiled face" that Paul talks about is most beautifully fulfilled in that absolute openness of countenance and heart that is now and then seen in home life. If the members of the family have few secrets from each other, if they will take it for granted that each is interested in what concerns the rest, and will impart to one another freely their opinions, hopes and interests, there will grow an intenser interest in one another. One should not be discouraged from this frank expression if received with an occasional smile or outright laugh, for these things often hide a feeling that is kindly and deeply interested.

Another source of happiness, or rather another means of avoiding misery is that rare quality which may be called nothing else but willingness to give in. It is often as hard to yield one's point in a family discussion or in a family game as it is to lose a sum in business, and a vast deal of unhappy home life is due to that stubborn disposition that stands its ground, no matter how insignificant the matter in dispute, just because the ground is its own. One can yield without sacrificing one's real opinions. Gladstone, they say, was exceedingly firm, even in boyhood, so that sooner or later all the family came to his view of things on all matters. But he gained his point in the home as in public life, not by heated contention, but by calm and kindly, even of firm, courtesy.

Such a willingness to yield, or at least to maintain a kind attitude of reserve is usually fostered by large families. The highest possible good fortune that can chance to a child is to be born into a large family; the Jews counted it the highest blessing that their families should be large. But we, in America to-day, especially in cities, are reversing this true philosophy of home life, and are counting our happiness by the smallness of our households. This is one of the dangers confronting our modern life.

Clubs are multiplied to-day, and while we are organizing clubs, a most effective one might be organized in every household. It might have for its purpose the increasing of the joy and amusement, the culture and refinement, the spiritual welfare of all its members. Its meetings might be held of evenings just as often as possible, and its engagements might take precedence over those of all other clubs—this would be a strange thing, would it not, to-day? It should engage in all legitimate amusements, celebrate all national holidays, and the birthdays of its members. It should make presents at Christmas, and be economically indulgent in fireworks on the Fourth. In short, it should be jovial and childlike in its nature, for of such is the kingdom of home. The great Froebel insisted that parents should be children with their children, and live with their children. But there is some danger that parents nowadays may become like that New York woman who recognized her baby in the park, because she knew the nurse. It is needless to say that the home club should have its musical and literary and artistic pursuits, and its religious tone and spirit.

Indeed, a deep interest in every phase and fact of life will add immeasurably to the happiness of the individual and the family. A life that is interested in but few things withdraws into itself and becomes morose. A family made up of such persons becomes silent, melancholy, dreary. But when a family has been taught from childhood to take a deep interest in everything of local, national and world-wide character, when it has been encouraged to discuss events, people, churches, birds, horses, politics, flowers, inventions, travels—in fact, all the myriad interests of humanity—that family can never grow dull or uniteresting to its members or to others.

And finally, if each member in the household will make it his resolve to seek not his own happiness, but the happiness of another and of the family in general, he shall find therein his own and the general happiness. It is love that seeketh not her own. And here we emerge upon the high ground that our Savior always occupied, and find in love the true solution for all happiness and all salvation. It is love that is to save the individual. It is love that is to save the family, which is made up of individuals. It is love which is to redeem society, of which the family is the unit. And wherever you find one who is constantly seeking the happiness of other people, doing some little deed of courtesy or kindness, you will find a savior of the home, a savior of society, a savior of himself, for such as this was the Savior of the world.

FACTS AND FACTORS.

For every man on the Spanish warships at the time of the attack our sailors recieve $100 bounty, in accordance with section 4635 of the Revised Statutes of the United States.

On July 1st and 2nd, the loss at Santiago on the American side was 231 killed and 1,303 wounded and 81 missing.

It is said that our agricultural exports this year will exceed $800,000,000.

A railroad is being built from Skaguay across White Pass to Lake Bennett.

Admiral Cervera's fleet, destroyed near Santiago, July 3rd, is estimated at $30,000,000. All lost.

Three carloads of the necessities of life were sent to the St. Louis soldiers at Chickamauga July 2nd, by their relatives and friends at home. The enterprise was managed by the Post Dispatch, of this city.

Alphonso XII., a Spanish gunboat carrying eighteen large guns and a crew of 370 persons, was destroyed July 6th, while attempting to run the blockade at Havana.

It is reported from Madrid via London that Admiral Camara has been ordered back to Spain.

A German-American regiment, organized in Chicago, has offered itself to the command of President McKinley.

The government will make an effort to save as much of Admiral Cervera's wrecked ships and armor as possible.

Leut. Peary, of the United States Navy, has started on the Windward in search of the north pole.

The first new bale of cotton for this season was sold for $100 and the proceeds sent to President McKinley for the benefit of the United States hospital fund.

William Carver, the smallest man in the world, died at Clayton, Ill., July 2nd. He was 28 inches tall.

Three vessels of Admiral Sampson's fleet sank two Spanish gunboats at Manzanillo shortly before the battle at Santiago.

Hampton Beach, N. H., was visited by a destructive tornado in the afternoon of Independence day. Seven dead and more than a hundred wounded, reported.

It is reported that the celebration of the Fourth of July in London was unprecedented in any celebration of the day that has ever taken place out side of United States territory.

News from Santiago is having a depressing effect upon the Pope. His susceptibility to fellow-sufferings seems to increase with his age. News from Cuba last year did not seem to be so distressing to him.

The C. E. Reading Courses.

PURPOSE, PROGRESS, PROSPECT.

BY J. Z. TYLER.

General Editor and Manager.

The first regular year of the Bethany C. E. Reading Courses closed July 1, and their last article appeared in this column last week. It seems a fitting time, therefore, to say a brief word concerning their purpose, their progress and their prospect.

The primary purpose of these Reading Courses is the instruction and indoctrination of the young people among the Disciples of Christ. But experience has shown that the purpose and plan ar admirably adapted to other classes. Many auxiliary societies of the C. W. B. M., for instance, have found these courses exactly suited to their needs and have increased the interest in their meetings by their use. Groups of persons, not connected with any society, have come together for the sole purpose of mutual help in taking these readings and many individuals, old as well as young, have found both pleasure and profit in pursuing these courses privately. It is being discovered that the field to be cultivated by these Reading Courses is not limited to the Christian Endeavor Societies, but that it includes all persons who need elementary instruction in its three chosen lines of study.

The progress made during this first year has been most gratifying. Between 3,500 and 4,000 readers have been enrolled. A little more than 9,000 copies of our handbooks have been put into circulation. Seven of our best papers have published articles, week by week, along the three lines of study, thus reaching a much larger number of readers than have formally enrolled at headquarters. These articles have been recognized as of superior merit, and the request has been made that they be made permanent by placing them in book-form. This, however, will not be done, since we have so much entirely new material in store awaiting publication. I wish, however, in the name of all concerned to most heartily thank the directors who have furnished these articles and the papers who have so generously given them this extensive circulation.

Perhaps no enterprise ever inaugurated among the Disciples has met such recognition as this. To use a well-worn phrase, "It meets a long-felt want." The July number of the Bethany C. E. Bulletin, published quarterly in the interest of the Bethany C. E. Reading Courses, contains most hearty and enthusiastic endorsements from a very large number of leading brethren. They characterize these courses by such expressions as "of incalculable value," "well adapted to meet our needs," "lines of study well chosen," "one of the wisest movements among us," "one of the 'hits' of the closing century," "our rapid growth calls for it," "all pastors and evangelists should advocate it," "will stop a leakage from our churches," "it is vital to our cause," "every Christian should take it," "the need is painfully urgent," "nothing more economical can be imagined." These phrases indicate the unanimous verdict of these brethren concerning the Bethany C. E. Reading Courses.

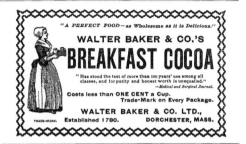

The prospects are bright. The field to be cultivated is large. All that is needed is that some one in each church shall undertake the task of giving full and accurate information concerning the movement. Wherever the people are well informed concerning it, circles seem to form spontaneously. The people know a good thing when they see it, and they are not slow to avail themselves of the advantages of such an opportunity as this. Those who wish to circulate information will be supplied, gratuitously, with the July number of the Bethany C. E. Bulletin, which contains all that needs to be known. Drop a postal card addressed to the Bethany C. E. Company, 798 Republic Street, Cleveland, Ohio, stating how many copies you can use to advantage. They will be sent to you promptly.

It is yet too early to make definite and detailed announcements concerning the second year's reading. Those who have not taken the course should begin with the handbooks prepared for the first year. Those who have taken the first year will be supplied with handbooks now in course of preparation for the second year's reading. Professor H. L. Willett is preparing a handbook on "The Life and Teachings of Jesus;" F. D. Power is preparing a handbook on "Sketches of our Pioneers;" W. J. Lhamon is preparing a handbook on "Missionary Fields and Forces of the Disciples." We hope to have these ready for delivery in September. A little later there will be issued a handbook entitled "Bible Doctrine for Young Disciples," dealing directly with the doctrinal position of the Disciples. Readers will be expected to begin the study of this about the middle of the second year. This second series of handbooks will be along the same lines as the first and will be of similar size and appearance. We shall make every effort to keep them down to the same price. More definite announcement will appear in our church papers before the opening of the second year.

Work vs. Methods.

During the recent Bible-school and Christian Endeavnr convention at Mexico, the question was raised as to what should be done in case the elders of a congregation would not allow the preacher or young people to organize a Christian Endeavor Society. Various answers were given, but none satisfactory to the questioner, and none sufficient, in my judgment, to meet the difficulties of the case.

A close study of the conditions surrounding such cases will reveal the fact that the opposition does not arise from stubbornness so much as from a desire to stand true to the faith and the simplicity of the apostolic church; and further, that the opposition is not to the *work*, but to the *method*.

I have yet to hear of an elder who is opposed to the development of our young people in Christian work, or to using the energy and enthusiasm of the young for the furtherance of the cause. But we find many who believe the method known as a Christian Endeavor Society is opposed to Bible teaching, and a step back to Rome. In such cases would it not be wise in the preacher to be content to *do the work*, using such means and methods as will not give offense? And is not the preacher as much a cause of discord if he insists on the non-essential name or form of organization, knowing it will offend, as the elder who objects to these, but is in sympathy with the work? I have known the young people's prayer-meeting to be cordially received and supported, when the Y. P. S. C. E. would be opposed. Let us be more particular about accomplishing the work, and less about the method of work. And let us take special care not to allow ourselves to become so engrossed in defending or opposing some method of work that we allow the work itself to be neglected. The command is, "Go," and nothing is said about how to go. It says, "Teach," but we are free to use such means as will accomplish that end. If there should be brethren who cannot for any reason adopt our method, let us adop theirs, and *do the work*.

J. H. BRYAN.

Shelbyville, Mo.

[We would revise the last sentence of the foregoing article as follows: "If there should be brethren who cannot, for any reason, adopt our method, let them adopt their own method, and permit us to do the same, and we will not permit the matter of method to interfere with Christian love and fellowship." It is hardly consistent to ask brethren who believe that they have learned a more successful method of doing Christian work to lay it aside for an inferior one because other good brethren are not able to adopt it. This idea has done much to injure our missionary work in the past, and it is one against which we have steadily protested. Where the Word of the Lord leaves us free to act, we are not only at liberty, but we are under obligations to act according to our best judgment; that is, to adopt the best method known to us for doing His work. The brethren who object to a Christian Endeavor Society almost universally do so because some editor whose policy it is to oppose everything that is new, has denounced it, and they take up the note of opposition without even understanding what it is they are opposing. If a mere name, these brethren need to be enlightened, and yielding to their demands would, perhaps, be the poorest way of accomplishing that end. The better way is to allow them full liberty to practice their own method, while others practice theirs, and let the results show which is the wiser.—EDITOR.]

Literature.

"The Modern Reader's Bible."

Richard G. Moulton is the editor of "The Modern Reader's Bible." He is Professor of Literature in English, in the University of Chicago. This work bears the imprint of The Macmillan Company, New York and London.

"The Modern Reader's Bible" is a series of works from the sacred Scriptures, presented in modern literary form. The work includes also selections from some of the Old Testament apocryphal books. The volume entitled "Biblical Idyls" contains the apocryphal book of Tobit. The "Wisdom Series" contains four volumes, in which is the "Book of Ecclesiasticus," and the "Wisdom of Solomon." There is a volume entitled, "Biblical Masterpieces," in which are selections from the apocryphal writings. This feature of the work is a blemish.

Each volume is about four and a half by six inches, and contains from a hundred and sixty to two hundred and seventy-five pages. They are gems of workmanship and marvels of convenience. The type is all that can be desired. A book easier to handle or more pleasant to read cannot easily be imagined. To read one of these unique volumes is a rare luxury. The common English Bible is about the worst printed book of any value in our language. There is nothing attractive about the book to a person of literary taste, in the style of printing in which it is usually presented. This defect is effectually remedied in "The Modern Reader's Bible." Its form in every way, shape, size, type, binding, etc., is unusually attractive.

The editor, Prof. Moulton, proposes to treat the Bible as literature. He is not a theologian. He is not a biblical critic, except as he finds the sacred writings in English. He is Professor—not of English literature, but—of *literature in English*, in the University of Chicago. The Bible belongs to Hebrew and Greek literature, but he finds it in English, and in this form it belongs to the department in which Prof. Moulton is a specialist. He aims to make this specimen of literature in English attractive and profitable reading to persons of culture. In this task he has become wonderfully successful. The text of "The Modern Reader's Bible" is that of the Revised Version. Prof. Moulton recognizes and accepts the work of the critics. He places "The Epistle to the Hebrews," for instance, with "The General Epistles," and not with "The Pauline Epistles."

Prof. Moulton has prepared for each volume a brief introduction in which some account is given of the writer, his time, his probable purpose, some of the peculiarities of his book, etc., etc. He does not, however, enter into a consideration of questions such as vex the souls of theologians and expositors. Prof. Moulton never loses sight of the fact that he is dealing with the literature of the Hebrew people in English. Helpful notes are found at the conclusion of each volume.

The printing is in modern, up-to-date style. Poetry, for instance, is presented to the eye as poetry. Notes of explanation, which in the common English Bible are found in the body of the text, are in this edition of our sacred Scriptures placed at the bottom of the page. The Book of Job is treated as a dramatic poem. Following the introduction are the names of the "Dramatic Personæ." The text of the work follows, printed in appropriate form.

Two volumes are devoted to the Psalms—Dr. Van Dyke calls them "the Hebrew Hymnbook." A well-arranged topical index adds much to the interest of these ancient poetical compositions. There are selections, in this connection, from "the Book of Lamentations," which Prof. Moulton calls "An Acrostic Dirge."

Volumes, especially interesting at the present time, are "The Kings" and "The Chronicles." "The Kings," as the name indicates, contains the history of the monarchs of the Hebrew people, beginning with David and concluding with Jehoiachin. The story of Saul and his reign belongs in this series, to the volume entitled, "The Judges." The Old Testament is now complete in eighteen volumes. The price is fifty cents a volume. "The Kings" and "The Chronicles" include the lessons to be used in our Bible-schools for six months, beginning July first. The volumes can be bought separately.

The New Testament will be published in four volumes. One only has appeared. This contains Matthew, Mark and "The General Epistles." The Book of Acts will contain Paul's epistles, introduced at the several points of the history to which they are usually referred, after the style of "The Records and Letters of the Apostolic Age," by Prof. Burton, Professor of New Testament Interpretation in the University of Chicago. An opportunity will thus be afforded of studying, without the interruption of comment or discussion, the continuous history of the New Testament church as presented by itself. A slight difference in the type, in the gospels, indicates the words of the Christ as distinguished from those of the historian.

It is a pleasure to call attention to and commend "The Modern Reader's Bible." Its publication is calculated to increase the interest in Bible reading and study.

B. B. T.

MAGAZINES.

To the July number of the North American Review, Rufus Fairchild Zogbaum contributes an interesting article on "The Regulars in the Civil War," describing vividly the services of these brave men, their sacrifices, prowess, discipline and fortitude; their steadiness under conditions of dismay and panic, their enthusiasm and bravery in attack, and their stubborn and courageous resistance in retreat.

The American Antiquarian, a bi-monthly magazine published at Chicago, for July and August contains an interesting article, well illustrated, on "Caves and Cliff Dwellings Compared," by Stephen D. Peet, Ph. D. There are other equally interesting articles.

Rev. Francis E. Clark has a valuable article in the Missionary Review of the World for June, "Do Foreign Missions Pay?" The advantages set forth by Dr. Clark as gains in the fields of geography, geology, meteorology, archæology, materia medica, philology and education makes a strong affirmative answer to the question.

Above
e send

er seen
entral
harles
Owen
e came
th his
ted in
Volun-
une 25.
buried
vil and
id the
e first
to free
in the
ied for
t down
Chris-
dent of
Chris-
w him.
. His
npathy

MER.

Russie
Errett,
widow
tt, one
tchers.
Errett,
rch of
rmerly
. Her
s when
ennsyl-
seph J.
tling in
re born
to the
ars old
1 sweet
years.
Errett
gospel.
ose days
ips and
iim who
s simple
rch. In
and had
npanion
e was a
a larger
ristian,
of the
a holy
he light
Never
other in
elt more
She was
ving its
gree its
pply its
omises.
e Word
r daily
'Bible-
truction
hey re-
In her
r'' was
for his
ich they
ove for
contents
er until
eavenly
eir chil-
children
left her
ke with
eritance
r. The
ren will
reward
. Such
family,
remem-
ouch of
On the
le, Pike
ience of
for her
oy Bro.
nducted
'tent,''
years of
body of
e ceme-
ay from
ie body

of one whose life comprehended what is meant by wife, mother, neighbor, friend and Christian.

E. J. LAMPTON.

Louisiana, Mo.

LUCAS.

One of the pioneers of the restoration movement inaugurated by the Campbells passed peacefully into the spirit-world last Saturday, June 25th, at his Abingdon home, having lived nearly a century. Marshom Lucas was born Sept. 5th, 1801, in Kentucky. Married Cynthia Whitman. Seven children resulted from this union. He moved to Illinois in 1829 and to Warren county in 1831. His wife died in 1837. He afterwards married Elizabeth Davidson, who bore seven children. Of the fourteen children seven survive him. He lived to see his fourth generation. For nearly 70 years he was a faithful member of the Church of Christ. His remains were brought to Monmouth, Ill., for interment, where his daughter, Mrs. W. H. Frantz, lives.

C. H. STEARNS, Pastor.

Monmouth, Ill.

SNELL.

Mrs. Eliza Arnold Snell was born Dec., 5, 1824, in Garrett county, but was reared in Madison county, Ky. They removed to Missouri in 1850. She was married to John R. Snell, June 18, 1851. She died of old age at Miami, Mo., June 25, 1898, aged 73 years 6 months and 20 days. She was a charter member of this congregation and always faithful. Her death leaves but one surviving charter member here, her sister, Mrs M. D. Pate. The latter is the last survivor of a family of 12 children. Sister Snell leaves an only daughter. We shall meet on a fairer shore.

J. W. STRAWN.

Miami, Mo., July 1, 1898.

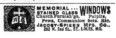

Announcements.

Illinois Convention.

The 48th annual meeting of the Illinois Christian Missionary Convention will be held at Eureka, Wednesday and Thursday, Aug. 3rd and 4th. This promises to be the best convention of years, and our people are urged to come and enjoy it. Booker T. Washington, the famous negro orator and educator, speaks Wednesday night, and it is worth the expense of the trip to hear him.

J. FRED JONES, Sec.

Nodaway Valley (Mo.) District, Attention!

The time for our county meeting is nearing. Let the boards prepare a good program. During each meeting determine where the evangelist will be wanted in the county. Let more of the paying churches use the district evangelist and thus help the treasurer of the mission work. It is hoped that every preacher in the district will help to make these country meetings a success and that our district meeting this year will be better even than last. The evangelist's report will show a good work done last year.

T. W. COTTINGHAM, Evan.

Kansas City July 7.

Program of the Missouri Christian Lectureship, Carrollton, July 19-21.

MONDAY, JULY 18.

8:00 P. M.—Lecture, "The Church and Organized Labor." Prof. J. D. Forrest, Irvington, Ind.

TUESDAY, JULY 19.

9:00 A. M.—Review of Lecture. F. G. Tyrrell, St. Louis, Mo.
—Discussion.
11:00 A. M.—Lecture, "Social Christianity." Prof. J. D. Forrest.
2:00 P. M.—Review of Lecture. James Vernon, Independence, Mo.
—Discussion.
8:00 P. M.—Lecture, "Uses of the Old Testament in the New." Geo. W. Plattenburg, Dover, Mo.

WEDNESDAY, JULY 20.

9:00 A. M.—Review of Lecture. A. B. Phillips, Fulton, Mo.
—Discussion.
11:00 A. M.—Lecture, "The Creed of the Church." Simpson Ely, Kirksville, Mo.
2:00 P. M.—Review of Lecture. M. M. Goode, St. Joseph, Mo.
—Discussion.
8:00 P. M.—Lecture, "Modern Changes in Theological Thought and Expression." J. H. Garrison, St. Louis, Mo.

THURSDAY, JULY 21.

9:00 A. M.—Review of Lecture. W. T. Moore, Columbia, Mo.
—Discussion.
11:00 A. M.—Lecture, "The Development of the Idea of God, as it Exists in Modern Thought." P. O. Powell, King City, Mo.
2:00 P. M.—Review of Lecture. Granville Snell, Trenton, Mo.
—Discussion.
4:00 P. M.—Closing business. Adjournment.

W. F. RICHARDSON,
Chairman Executive Committee.

Hughes Institute.

Albany, Mo., July 25-29, 1898, J. W. Ellis, Pres. Two lectures daily on The Revelation, by J. S. Hughes, Chicago, Ill.

PROGRAM.

MONDAY.

2:30—Devotional Exercises. J. H. Coffey, Coffeysbury, Mo.
3:00—Organization and Other Business.
3:30—Lecture. J. H. Hughes.
8:00—Devotional Exercises. W. B. Green, Bethany, Mo.
8:30—Christ Transforming the World. J. A. Smith, Osawatomie, Kas.

TUESDAY.

9:00—Devotional Exercises. Pres. Zuinglius Moore.
9:30—The True Man. E. N. Phillips, De Soto, Kas.
10:00—Conservatism and Radicalism. S. Carothers, Albany, Mo.
10:30—Recess.
10:45—Lecture. J. S. Hughes.
2:00—Devotional Exercises. Ellis Harris, Grant City, Mo.
2:30—Lecture. J. S. Hughes.
8:00—Devotional Exercises. J. S. Eldredge, Maysville, Mo.
8:30—Job, a Servant of God. Prof. J. W. Ellis, Plattsburg, Mo.

WEDNESDAY.

9:00—Devotional Exercises. J. T. Craig, King City, Mo.
9:30—Symposium—Church Discipline. W. H. Harris, Grant City, Mo.
10:00—Is Formal Withdrawal of Fellowship Taught in the Scriptures? W. A. Chapman, Rosedale, Mo.
10:15—Discussion, five-minute speeches.
10:45—Lecture. J. S. Hughes.
2:00—Devotional Exercises. A G. Alderman, Bethany, Mo.
2:30.—Lecture. J. S. Hughes.
8:00—Devotional Exercises. D. W. Martin, Bethany, Mo.
8:30—Our Distinctinctive Plea. T. H. Capp, Plattsburg, Mo.

THURSDAY.

9:00—Devotional Exercises. J. D. Oxford, Cainsville, Mo.
9:30—The Proper Attitude of our Ministry Toward the Higher Criticism. A. P. Terrell, Camden Point, Mo.
10:10—Are we a Reformation or a Restoration? J. A. Hankins, Westboro, Mo.
10:45—Lecture. J. S. Hughes.
2:00—Devotional Exercises. M. S. Gillidett, Bethany, Mo.
2:30—Lecture. J. S. Hughes.
8:00—Devotional Exercises. L. Sims, Plattsburg, Mo.
8:30—Christian Citizenship. Simpson Ely, Kirksville, Mo.

FRIDAY.

9:00—Devotional Exercises. Robert Adams, Pattonsburg, Mo.
9:30—Address. A. G. Alderman, Bethany, Mo.
10:00—Address. T. F. Kelly, Pastor Baptist Church Albany, Mo.
10:45—Lecture. J. S. Hughes.
2:00—Devotional Exercises. Rev. Grossman, Albany, Mo.
2:30—Lecture. J. H. Hughes.
8:00—Devotional Exercises. Edgar McVoy, Albany, Mo.
8:30—Address. R. J. Beard.

All the sessions will be held in the Chapel of Central Christian College.

J. D. MCCLURE,
A. L. JONES,
O. B. SEARS, } Com.

The Missouri Pacific's Camp Life souvenir booklet, complimentary to the third regiment Missouri volunteers, contains numerous excellent pictures of camp life, and the touching poem, "Just Before the Battle, Mother." Interesting references are also made to some of the noted pleasure and health resorts along this popular route South and West.

THE CHRISTIAN-EVANGELIST.

A WEEKLY FAMILY AND RELIGIOUS JOURNAL.

Vol. XXXV. July 21, 1898 No. 29.

CONTENTS.

EDITORIAL:
Current Events....65
The Nashville Convention in Retrospect....66
The Present Crisis: God's Voice....66
The Called of God....67
Editor's Easy Chair....67
Questions and Answers....68
Current Religious Thought....69
ORIGINAL CONTRIBUTIONS:
Church Finance.—Albert Schwart....70
Our Duty to Our Religious Neighbors.—Mrs. Clinton Lockhart....72
Thoughts on Applied Christianity.—Frank G. Tyrrell....72
CORRESPONDENCE:
English Topics....77
Wheeling Through England....77
Kansas City Letter....78
Myrick vs. Willett....79
Pittsburgh Letter....80
Texas Letter....80
Iowa Letter....81
Letter from Mr. Moody....81
Minnesota....82
St. Louis Letter....82
Florida Letter....83
A Union Meeting....83
Chautauqua Notes....83
Evangelistic Work....84
Not so Enthusiastic....84
State Mission Notes....84
FAMILY CIRCLE:
Hear Ye Him (Poem)....88
The Legend of Chocorua....88
Alaskan Letter....89
Language of Flags....90
Horned People....90
Short Stories....91
MISCELLANEOUS:
Religious World....73
Our Budget....74
Personal Mention....76
Notes and News....85
Announcements....86
Evangelistic....87
The Sunday-school....92
Christian Endeavor....93
A Reading Course Catechism....93
Marriages and Obituaries....94
Facts and Factors....95
Publisher's Notes....96

Subscription $1.75.

MAJOR-GENERAL WILLIAM R. SHAFTER.

PUBLISHED BY

CHRISTIAN PUBLISHING COMPANY

1522 Locust St., St. Louis.

THE

CHRISTIAN - EVANGELIST

J. H. GARRISON, EDITOR.

W. W. HOPKINS, ASSISTANT.

B. B. TYLER, J. J. HALEY,

EDITORIAL CONTRIBUTORS.

What We Plead For.

The Christian-Evangelist pleads for:

The Christianity of the New Testament, taught by Christ and his Apostles, versus the theology of the creeds taught by fallible men—the world's great need.

The divine confession of faith on which Christ built his church, versus human confessions of faith on which men have split the church.

The unity of Christ's disciples, for which he so fervently prayed, versus the divisions in Christ's body, which his apostles strongly condemned.

The abandonment of sectarian names and practices, based on human authority, for the common family name and the common faith, based on divine authority, versus the abandonment of scriptural names and usages for partisan ends.

The hearty co-operation of Christians in efforts of world-wide beneficence and evangelization, versus petty jealousies and strifes in the struggle for denominational pre-eminence.

The fidelity to truth which secures the approval of God, versus conformity to custom to gain the favor of men.

The protection of the home and the destruction of the saloon, versus the protection of the saloon and the destruction of the home.

For the right against the wrong;
For the weak against the strong;
For the poor who've waited long
For the brighter age to be.
For the truth, 'gainst superstition,
For the faith, against tradition,
For the hope, whose glad fruition
Our waiting eyes shall see.

RATES OF SUBSCRIPTION.

Single-subscriptions, new or old	$1.75	each
In clubs of five or more, new or old. ...	1.50	"
Reading Rooms	1.25	"
Ministers	1.00	"

With a club of ten we will send one additional copy free.

All subscriptions payable in advance. Label shows the month up to the first day of which your subscription is paid. If an earlier date than the present is shown, you are in arrears. No paper discontinued without express orders to that effect. Arrears should be paid when discontinuance is ordered.

In ordering a change of post office, please give the OLD as well as the NEW address.

Do not send local check, but use Post office or Express Money Order, or draft on St. Louis, Chicago or New York, in remitting.

ISTIAN-EVANGELIST

opinion and methods, Liberty; in all things, Charity."

uis, Mo., Thursday, July 21, 1898. No. 29

N ARMY ABOUT SANTIAGO AT THE TIME
ЧDER OF THE CITY.

raised over the Governor's Palace at high noon of that day, and Santiago passed forever from Spanish rule.

The newspapers and members of Congress who were disposed to criticise Admiral Sampson for not giving due credit to Commodore Schley for the destruction of Cervera's squadron at Santiago, before his official report was received, were entirely too previous in their criticism, as we believed at the time. The official report of Sampson makes proper acknowledgment of the part of Commodore Schley, in the historic action referred to, and says that the flagship, having been called away for consultation with Gen. Shafter, was "little more than a spectator" of the conflict. Commodore Schley, himself, says the credit is due to every officer and seaman engaged in the battle. It is altogether improbable that these two great naval commanders would quarrel like boys as to who was entitled to the greater honor for this great victory. It is safe to attribute most of such newspaper talk to the desire for sensationalism on the part of war correspondents. It is pleasant, too, in this connection, to notice the fine courtesy displayed by Gen. Miles who, on arriving at Santago, did not allow his presence there to eclipse Gen. Shafter, to whom the credit was due for the vigorous military operations in the reduction of that city. He has kept Gen. Shafter to the front in the negotiations pending for the surrender of the city.

It is not surprising that the talk of peace negotiations has arrived after this notable victory of our arms. The Madrid correspondent cables that the Madrid government has definitely decided to open peace negotiations without delay, proposing as a basis the renunciation of all rights over Cuba, and the immediate discussion of any "reasonable proposals the United States may make." From certain statements coming from the Spanish minister of war—Gen. Correa—it may be doubted whether Spain has yet reached a condition of mind in which to treat for peace. Our own conviction is that while negotiations may be opened on the part of Spain, the Spanish government is not yet willing to make such concessions as would justify the United States in ending the war. It is idle for Spain to talk of the autonomy of Cuba under Spainish suzerainity, and the retention of Porto Rico and the Philippines. This would have done before the war was begun, but such terms are out of date at present. War is a costly thing and somebody must pay for it. The defeated nation is generally the one that has to do it.

While the air is thus full of the talk of peace there is not the slightest cessation on the part of this government in its plans or preparations for continuing hostilities. The dispatch of a squadron under Commodore Watson to the coasts of Spain, and an expedition both military and naval to Porto Rico to take possession of that island, are among the plans for immediate execution. Meanwhile the fourth expedition to Manila has just left San Francisco, which indicates that the United States has no intention of vacating those islands and turning them over to the possession of Spain. There can be no doubt that the speediest way to the realization of peace with a government like Spain is the most vigorous prosecution of the war. That government ought to understand, however, that every day's delay in suing for peace but adds to the concessions she is bound to make in the end in order to terminate the war. But Spain is judicially blind, it would seem, until Divine Providence has accomplished, through means of this war, the purposes for which it was inaugurated.

It is reported that there are a number of cases of yellow fever in the army at Santiago. Of course these cases have been separated from the army and every precaution is being exercised to prevent the spread of the disease. And yet there is no concealing the fact that there is a great deal of anxiety through the country lest many of our brave boys at the front, who have escaped Spanish bullets, may fall victims to this yellow pest. One of the causes of rejoicing in the surrender of Santiago is the fact that it will make possible the removal of our troops to a more healthy locality and

this disease. It is not proposed, we understand, that our army shall enter the city of Santiago, but that a few regiments of immunes with perhaps some of the Cuban forces, will hold the city while the main body of our troops are taken elsewhere. Additional surgeons and medical supplies have been sent to Santiago, and no pains will be spared by the government to save our soldiers from this dreadful plague. It will give a great sense of relief, however, when it is known that the disease is under control and that our army has been removed to where it will be free from the contagion.

THE NASHVILLE CONVENTION IN RETROSPECT.

It is not in the high tide of enthusiasm, generated by a convention, that its real value is to be judged, but in the calm convictions that abide when feeling and sentiment have had time to subside to the normal level. Looking back to the Christian Endeavor convention at Nashville, we find there are certain convictions which have been deepened and strengthened by what we saw and heard while in attendance on its proceedings. We mention these in the hope that they may prove helpful to others in forming an estimate of this modern movement in the church.

1. *It seems to us to be a providential movement.* This means that there was a real need for it in the church. It means, too, that the Spirit of God gave the impulse that led to its inauguration. The wisdom by which it has been guided, on the whole, indicates that the men who are at the helm seek and receive divine guidance. Its remarkable growth, too, shows that it was not born too soon, but that the world—the religious world at least—was waiting for it. The exigencies of the church demanded this new agency, and it came in response to that demand and in obedience to the impulse of the Spirit, which abides forever in the church. If it be a providential movement having a great mission to accomplish, our duty in reference to it is clear. It is gratifying to know that our churches generally view it in this light and are using it greatly to their advantage.

2. *We believe the Christian Endeavor movement is designed to promote the unity for which Jesus prayed.* This has been doubted by some because it inculcates denominational loyalty. Waiving the point now that an interdenominational movement is impossible on any other principle, the objection to the Christian Endeavor movement on this ground is based on a false view, as we believe, as to God's method of bringing about the unity He desires. The objection assumes that it will be by the destruction of denominational walls by a force from without, and the subsequent gathering together in one ecclesiastical body of those released. But this does not seem to be God's method of promoting union. As a matter of fact we know that all attempts of that kind have resulted in strengthening denominational walls and in building them higher. God's method, if we are to judge from what we see going on before our eyes, is to deepen and widen the spiritual life *within* the various bodies of evangelical believers, and to so conform them to His own will and way, that they may be able to fraternize with each other and co-operate with each other in doing His work in the world. If all our mutual misunderstandings and prejudices were removed, we would find ourselves much closer together than we imagine. But this can be accomplished in no other way so well as through some interdenominational organization, offering a common basis of fellowship and of work. No other movement in the church, so far, has succeeded in gathering so large a number of Christians of various bodies together in a common work and with common aims, as has the Christian Endeavor movement. It is, therefore, the most potent agent known for promoting interdenominational acquaintanceship and fellowship, which must precede the unity for which Jesus prayed.

3. *It is a powerful agency for promoting a deeper spiritual life.* It is one of the keynotes of the Endeavor conventions. The "Quiet Hour" has become a feature of great prominence in the Endeavor movement. We have reason to believe that the services in connection with this morning hour at Nashville were the means of awakening in the hearts of hundreds of Christians the desire for a better and richer Christian life than they have been living, and of putting them in the way of realizing this desire. The interest of the great audiences was intense as the speaker pointed out the possibilities of the Christian life and the means of attaining these possibilities. It was no hobby of perfectionism that was presented, but the importance of surrendering our lives more fully to Jesus Christ that he may work in us his gracious purposes. Our readers will bear us witness that this has been a matter of capital importance with us for many years, and that we have sought steadily to minister to this spiritual need. Our membership is largely ready to be led into the deeper things of spiritual life. Most of our churches welcome such teaching. If this want is not supplied by those who feed the flock of God among us, our members will seek for it elsewhere, and will often find it in connection with errors of a hurtful character. The duty is upon us and cannot be evaded. We may use the Endeavor Society to good effect in supplying this need.

We need not take space here to speak of the value of the Christian Endeavor Society as a training school to prepare young people for Christian work, and to supply work for them to do. This is generally recognized. It is *in* the church and *for* the church, and is not something separate from the church. It has come to perform a mighty mission. If we be wise we will avail ourselves of it to the fullest extent. It finds a genial soil among us, and if properly cultivated it will here bring forth its choicest fruit.

OUR SPECIAL OFFER.

With the view of introducing the CHRISTIAN-EVANGELIST to a large number of new readers, we are offering the paper from the time the subscription is received until the end of the present year for *seventy-five cents.* We earnestly solicit the active assistance of our old readers in making this offer known, and in extending our circulation. It is hoped that the new form will be acceptable to all our friends, and may be made the occasion by them of a special effort in its behalf.

THE PRESENT CRISIS: GOD'S VOICE.

God is speaking to us now. He often reveals his and mind purposes in current events. His voice can easily be heard to-day if men will but give attention. In an important sense divine revelation is perpetual. New truth is seen day after day by earnest and reverent students of the Bible. New light shines forth from its pages as the years go by. Men see more in the Scriptures, much more, than they saw a few years ago. The depths of meaning contained in our sacred literature have not yet been sounded. It is more than probable that the human intellect will never reach the profoundest depths of the heaven-inspired writings. They are from God. God is infinite. His thoughts are like himself. He is infinite; his thoughts are infinite. "My thoughts are not your thoughts; neither are your ways my ways, saith the Lord." Man is finite. His mind can only compass finite things. Hence his study of the literature which, in a peculiar sense is from God, man will ever find something new. But the record of verbal and other revelations which we call the Bible, is not the only revelation that has been given to man by the Author of his being. "The heavens declare the glory of God." His love as well as his glory are declared in the volume called the Living Oracles of the Holy Spirit. It is from the Christian Scriptures alone that the way of salvation from sin can be learned. God reveals himself in history—in secular as well as in sacred. Every student of history recognizes this fact. The Word of the Lord in the Bible says that Jehovah builds and destroys governments. Who can doubt the superintending providence of God in the discovery and settlement of the New World? The birth of this republic was of God. His hand sustained it in its infancy. The same kind hand has guided it to this present hour. It is easy to see his presence in the great crisis of our history. God founded and established the North American Republic for a great and gracious purpose, and he will care for it until this is accomplished. God was as certainly present with the Pilgrims when they came to America as he was present with the people of Israel when they entered Canaan. He cared for them, and cares for their descendants no less certainly than he cared for the Hebrew people in the olden time. God is with us now. Recent events make this evident. He is directing our cause at the present time. God the Lord is our Sovereign. To hearken to his voice is wisdom; to refuse to hear him is folly. We are making history rapidly. Events of great significance crowd upon each other with tremendous rapidity. What do these events signify? What would God have us learn from them? What, specifically, are some of the lessons to be learned from the Spanish-American war?

Sin brings ruin. This thought is fundamental. Ruin is an inevitable consequence of persistent wrong-doing. This statement is as true of nations as of individuals. "Though hand joined in hand the wicked shall not be unpunished." This sentence is written in the Bible. Evidence of its truth is before our eyes. Whatsoever a nation soweth that shall it reap, is as true as "whatsoever a *man* soweth that shall he also reap." This judgment of nations is here and now. We, as a nation, have suffered for our sins. Spain is now reaping

success and become unjust in dealing with our wards?

Thank God! we are now away from questions of mere policy. There are great *moral* issues at this moment appearing above the horizon. The loving voice of our God warns us. He indicates to us the way in which we should walk. We are not left in doubt as to the things that are offensive to him. We are not ignorant of the things that are well pleasing to him. This is to us a day of crisis.

A great and effectual door is being opened before American Christians for aggressive evangelistic work. The schoolmaster and the preacher will be in demand. The peoples over whom the American flag begins to float are in dense ignorance and deep moral degradation. God calls us to preach the gospel of his grace to them. Will we be disobedient to his voice?

B. B. T.

Hour of Prayer.

THE CALLED OF GOD.

(Midweek Prayer-meeting Topic, July 27.)

But ye are an elect race, a royal priesthood, a holy nation, a people for God's own possession, that ye may show forth the excellencies of Him who called you out of darkness into His marvelous light.—1 *Peter* 2:9.

The Greek term for the English word *church* means *called*, or *called out*. The gospel is God's call to men to repent and to come out from the world into a kingdom that is not of this world. Those who respond to that call constitute the *church* or the *called*.

The apostle, in the above passage, tells what Christians are called to *be*. They are called out of the world to be "an elect race, a royal priesthood, a holy nation, a people for God's own possession." It will be seen from this what election means in the New Testament. Those who accept God's call, and come out from the world, are an elect race. This election, then, is not arbitrary, and without regard to man's acceptance or non-acceptance of the gospel, but men, as free moral agents, have to do an important part in the matter of their election. They must accept and obey God's call. God has elected the kind of character that will meet his approval, and those who seek, by His aid, to realize that character are the elect of God. This is New Testament election.

It will be further seen from this important passage that all Christians are priests in the only sense in which any Christian can be a priest. They constitute "a royal priesthood;" that is, they are both kings and priests unto God. They are priests, because they are to "offer up spiritual sacrifices, acceptable to God by Jesus Christ." They are *royal* priests because each one is to be crowned, and each one is to exercise royal prerogatives in connection with Jesus Christ. The pretense of another priesthood, different from that of the common Christian, that has exclusive rights of approach to God, is without support in the New Testament.

Christians are called to be "a holy nation, a people for God's own possession." Just as fast as the people of a nation become Christians, the nation should become "holy" in all its laws, institutions and customs. They constitute a sort of nation within themselves, a kingdom, in other words, that is not of this world. They belong to God in a peculiar sense as His ow possession, and should hold themselve ready at all times to do His will and serv His purpose.

Let it be observed that the object fo which God has called us out of darknes iato his marvelous light is that we ma show forth the "excellencies" of God. I is evident that we are to do this for th benefit of the world around us. Unbelievers should see in the lives of Christian those excellencies which characterize God But this is not all of the truth. We ar also to "make known to the principalitie and the powers in the heavenly places th manifold wisdom of God" (Ephesian 3:10). It would seem, then, that the churc is charged with the responsibility of making known the character and wisdom c God, not only to human beings, but to a celestial intelligences. God's wisdom, especially in the dispensation of the gospe is to be vindicated before the intelligence of the universe, by the church which H has called out of darkness into light.

Who is equal to this responsibility? Onl those who surrender their lives to God tha He may fill them with His own life an light. Not in our own strength, but onl in the strength that God supplies, can w form such characters and live such lives a will show forth the excellencies and th wisdom of God to all created intelligence

Beloved, if we have been "called out c darkness into His marvelous light," w ought to walk in the light, and not in th darkness of the world. If we walk in th light as He is in the light, the blood c Jesus Christ His Son will cleanse us fro all unrighteousness.

PRAYER.

O Thou infinite and eternal God, w hast revealed Thyself to us as Fath through Jesus Christ Thy Son, we tha Thee that Thou hast called us out of dar ness into Thy marvelous light, to be a roy priesthood, a holy nation, Thine own pc session, and to show forth the excellencies Him who hath called us. Help us, we pr Thee, to appreciate our high calling and walk worthy of it. May we who ha heard Thy call come out of the world a cease to be sharers in its sin and shan and walk in the light, which Thou hast sh upon us in Jesus Christ. So shall we r flect Thy glory even here, and much mc in the world to come. For Christ's sa Amen!

Editor's Easy Chair.

OR MACATAWA MUSINGS.

After a jaunt of more than a thousa miles thither and hither and mingling wi the hurrying throngs in the Internatio Convontion of Christian Endeavor, it see good to rest once more beside the peace lake. Our Easy Chair to-day is a ha mock, and it swings in full view of La Michigan, which lies to-day in dreamli repose. Not even the sound of a ripple heard. It is the very emblem of peace, it is at other times of restlessness. W a day for reading and meditation! A yet the cool atmosphere and the cool wa of the lake presents too great a temptati to the lovers of the angler's art to be lo resisted. Our yonder on the smooth lake a number of boats and men and women dropping their lines down into the c depths for perch. On a day like this, wh the blue sky bends caressingly over smooth lake, and when the stillness of t green forest is unbroken except by the sweet notes of the birds, existence seems to be a luxury. One's soul may drink in enough of the vitalizing breath of heaven in such a day to fortify it for many days of stress and storm.

Speaking of the journey southward and return, how lovely the country is at present! It never seems to us more beautiful than when the fields are full of ripened shocks of grain, and the green, young corn is rustling its blades to the passing breeze. As one rides through such states as Illinois, Kentucky, Indiana, Tennessee, Missouri, Ohio and others like them, he can but thank God for such a country and for such an abundance as it produces. As we look upon the panorama of country homes with their orchards and meadows and gardens, we instinctively feel that, after all, there is no life quite equal to that of the farmer, and that from these country homes must come in the future as in the past a very large portion of the men who are to be leaders in church and state. Somehow there is stored away in brain and brawn of boyhood in the country the vitality and energy to fit one for future success, while there are developed those traits of character such as integrity, self-reliance and reverence, which are essential to a worthy manhood and womanhood. Perhaps these country scenes look more beautiful to our eyes because they recall the scenes and associations of our own boyhood which was spent on the farm.

A concrete case may serve often to illustrate a general principle. It is a well-known fact, often mentioned, that the majority of successful men in our cities to-day were raised in the country. In our young preacherhood we preached for a village church in Illinois, which had in it one man who, more than any other, was its life and inspiration. He lived on a farm near the town and ran a small store in the village. He had several boys whom he trained in the habits of integrity, industry and self-reliance. This good brother, whose kind face is distinct before our mental vision to-day, gave us the first bank bill we ever received for preaching. He has long since gone to his reward. In passing through Chicago last week we dropped in at one of the largest and most successful business houses in the city, conducted by Chas. A. Stevens & Bros. They are the sons of our old friend and brother, Socrates Stevens. They conducted the business in the town of Colchester for a number of years after their father's death and when it outgrew the town they moved to Chicago, about nine years ago, and their success in building up one of the largest silk stores in the country has been phenomenal. They employ about 750 men in the different departments and they do a vast business wholesale and retail. They attribute their success to conducting their business on the principles of strict integrity which were early inculcated in them, and advertising. One of them is assistant superintendent of a large Sunday-school, another is an active member in one of our churches, and all reverence God and believe in truth and righteousness. Three of them own and conduct this magnificent business on State Street, between Madison and Washington, two others are connected with a life insurance company, in responsible positions, and all of them are active, enterprising, successful business men. It illustrates the possibility of the country boy who shuns evil ways and believes there is no contradiction between business success and Christian integrity. As they conducted us through their great establishment from floor to floor, and we looked upon the army of clerks and the throngs of customers, and saw what remarkable success these boys had attained while they are yet young men, we realized anew the possibilities of the country boy, and the responsibility which such success entails. These young men have influence and power. May it be that they shall use this influence and power in the same conscientious way that their good father did.

During our absence from the Park a great many newcomers arrived, and the population of this summer resort is steadily increasing. Among the latest comers are Pastor Geo. H. Combs ann family, of Kansas City, Mo., and Prof. Graham Taylor and family, from Chicago. St. Louis, Chicago and Kansas City have a steadily increasing constituency here from year to year. The Mocatawa Assembly begins here on the 7th of August. In another place in this paper may be found the program which we hope will interest a number of people and induce them to spend at least that week with us. We are constantly receiving letters of inquiry about how to reach this place. It is very easy to reach. The Holland and Chicago Line of Steamers leave Chicago, No. 1 State Street, each evening at 7 P. M., except Friday, when the boat leaves a 4 P. M., and Saturday at 9 A. M. and 4 P. M. Please clip this out. If you come by rail inquire at your railroad office for Ottawa Beach, across the channel from Macatawa and the terminus of the Chicago and West Michigan Railroad. Accommodations for board or cottages can best be ascertained after arriving on the ground.

We are grateful to our appreciative friends for their many kind words of congratulation on the new form and dress of the CHRISTIAN-EVANGELIST. They rightly regard it as a distinct step in advance in our religious journalism. While we are doing what we can to keep the paper up to the demands of a growing brotherhood, we trust our friends will feel it to be no less a privilege than a duty to co-operate with us in introducing the paper to thousands of new readers. We appeal for this co-operation on no other ground than the good influence of the journal wherever it is circulated, as a stimulator and helper in all that is best and praiseworthy in religious life and work. As a tree is known by its fruits, so must a religious journal be judged. By that test it stands or falls. We appeal to no other. If the paper in your judgment is fulfilling a useful and necessary mission among us, help us to give it the largest opportunity for doing good, and you share with us in the reward that comes to all who seek to advance the kingdom of God among men.

Rev. John Dixon, pastor of the First Presbyterian Church, Trenton, has been elected assistant secretary of the Presbyterian Board of Home Missions.

Questions and Answers.

Is the Sunday-school a child of the church of Christ, and is it a part of the church?

W. V. Boltz.

The Dalles, Ore.

Yes, the Sunday-school is the creation of the spirit of Christianity, and in that sense is the child of the church. It is also fostered and supported by the church, and is one of its most importont agencies for accomplishing its most important functions, namely, that of teaching. It is not to be regarded as distinct from the church any more than a prayer-meeting, or a sewing society or an Endeavor Society. These are but different aspects of the church, or the church engaged in different kinds of work.

(1) *Can the church or minister receive gifts from him who has been "called a brother," or is the church destined to always make cowardly compromises? (1 Cor. 5:11.)*

(2) *1 Tim. 5-11, "The younger widows refuse"—from what? If from the daily administrations, were they not to be helped except as they were 60 years old, etc.? (Verses 9 and 10.)*

(3) *A wife secures adivorce on other than scriptural grounds, when she is married to another. Is her former husband "loosed from the law" of his wife?* L.

1. Neither the church nor the minister should, of course, make any "cowardly compromise;" but they must be the judges in each particular case, as to when the acceptance of a gift from any one would be such a compromise. It is not a dignified attitude for the church to occupy, nor one calculated to win the respect of the world, for it to solicit funds to carry on its enterprises from those known to be hostile to its work, and out of harmony with its aims and spirit. The acceptance of the voluntary offerings of those who, though not church members, feel that they owe something to the support of Christian work, is a very different matter and involves no compromise.

2. The passage referred to, as we understand it, means that the "younger widows" were not to be regarded as beneficiaries of the church, to be supported by it, nor were any others who had elatives to whom they could naturally look for support. The church was not to do any unnecessary benevolent work.

3. We should think so, provided the former husband is an innocent party to the transaction.

In the 21st chapter and 27th verse of Luke, does not the word "then," in connection with the many pronouns representing the disciples, indicate that they—the disciples— were to live to see the "Son of Man come in power and great glory?"

Reader.

The passage referred to in connection with that of Matt. 16:28 would seem to refer to an event that took place in the lifetime of at least many of those to whom Jesus was speaking. The only event which meets the demands is the coming of the Holy Spirit on Pentecost and the inauguration of the spiritual reign of Christ. The destruction of Jerusalem, sometimes referred to the fulfillment of this prediction, was only the outward accompaniment of the transcendent event we have mentioned.

plain, through the
what the "unpar-
A Reader.

Christ after all the
:h a sinning against
› render the soul im-
the gospel. Every
› the commission of
ly and repeately re-
gospel against the
›nce and his better

that were to follow
Mark 16: 15-20)

any Scripture that
›romises were only
:ans of the apostolic
.everett G. Higley.

›re literal, although
hat the divine over-
into the spiritual

ecial passage that
romise to the apos-
now. The general
ıt teaching goes to
ıs events associated
›f Christianity were
eriod of the church.
er, is to be found in
fulfillment of the
no authentic record
hese sgins since the
.turally confirms the
vas given especially
were charged and
accomplish a work
tance in the estab-
ity. We believe,
gns" that follow all
e that are far more
ıpeaking with new
:pents and drinking
ical damage. The
ipirit, as love, joy,
meekness, temper-
, are "signs" that
covet.

ing forward to con-
nurred at the phrase,
saying that it was
.eginner. Is there a
formula of words
l to use on such oc-
L.

l formula. There are
the New Testament,
d seem to cover the
hing in all these
ı the acceptance of
Lord, without any
th perfect sincerity
lady in question had
as to the import of
› objected. It cer-
ıat one is to have as
ith in beginning the
rwards. It means
, full decision of the
that there is to be
between Him and
e world. It is not
recise words be em-
question asked, nor
/ question be asked
ı thing is that the

with the mouth the Lord Jesus, and in his heart accept Him as the Lord of his life. Some form of question, however, is usually desirable, and the following seems to us to cover the ground: Do you believe with the heart on the Lord Jesus Christ? Do you accept Him as your Savior and promise to obey Him in all things to the best of your knowledge and ability? The latter of these questions has always seemed to us to be important as giving an opportunity for a personal public commitment of the candidate to the Lordship of Jesus Christ. It should be impressed upon those contemplating making such confession that it is a decisive act of their lives, and that it commits them, before Heaven and earth, to submission to Jesus Christ, who is henceforth to be their Prophet, Priest and King.

Current Religious Thought

We commend the following sensible observations of the Christian Commonwealth on thoughtful preaching to the prayerful consideration of our churches and ministers:

History has taught some sharp and salutary lessons about the mind of the nation. Sanctified twaddle in the pulpit always pleases a crowd for a season. But when the season of sensationalism is over the community is lowered rather than uplifted. The preaching that has lifted populations out of degradation has always been that of students. Calvin was the most learned man of his time. Luther was a splendid Latin and Hebrew scholar. And Switerland was saved to the Reformation by the preaching of Calvin and the almost equally learned Zwingli, while the Germany of to-day is really founded on the popular preaching of Martin Luther. Knox preached before kings. The gospel which has made Scotland the most religious nation on the face of the earth did not consist of pleasant Sunday talks without hammering at the deep things. Christmas Evans was profound, poetical and imaginative, and he and the noble pulpiteers of the principality at the beginning of this century brought the Welsh people out of the horrible pit of indifference and Erastianism. A popular superficial ministry when sanctified has its proper sphere. But ministries of this school when multiplied actually injure the public mind. They minimize the glory of the gospel. C. H. Spurgeon dreaded the very thing which thoughtless people ascribed to him. He believed in scholarly preaching adapted to audiences according to their needs. The splendid success of Dr. McLaren and of Dr. Joseph Parker, lasting for half a century, must be accepted as a monumental proof of the power of men who read and think, and yet are able to touch the emotions of thousands with more than transient sensationalism. The preaching of Melvill in the last generation, and of Liddon in this, saved the Church of England from the reproach of that contemptibly small gospel which inflicted spiritual starvation on multitudes. Let scholars and students not be discouraged by the fact that a learned ministry seems to be at a discount. There is no reason why, as in the case of Wesley, Whitefield, Toplady, Newman, Manning, Wilberforce, Magee, Robertson, Sortain, Irving and the pulpit giants who have too few successors, a deep insight into truth should not acceptably accompany the popular presentation of evangelical truth.

Christian Work touched a vital point when in an editorial on "Rationalism Irrational" it gave utte1 ınce to the following language:

Then, again, note this fact, that in the name of morality these irrational scoffers despise and make light of the principle of goodness as set forth in the gospel. But how long will goodness last in any heart in which it has its own original source? How soon will be exhausted all the goodness that is in you in the midst of a world that is full of temptation and society that is depraved more or less in its every aspect? Morality cannot exist long cut off from the vital source of goodness. Morality cannot be upheld without a standard of goodness. Morality cannot be maintained without the stimulus of goodness; and all goodness is in the God of grace, as the fountain-head and source. Thus when any man deprives himself has begun his downward tendency. This is a self-evident truth, the proof of which we see all around us in every-day life. While a man who believes in Jesus Christ is improving every day in temper, in motive, in character and in life; on the other hand, the man who denies Christ is going backward and downward every day. He is conscious of it, but excuses it in himself while he observes and condemns it in others. He will bid you go talk to the drunkard or to the criminal of sins to be forgiven and infirmities to be strengthened; to those who are liable to be tempted and fall. As to himself, he does not need any special help from God. Such a spirit of pride casts aside all the influences of divine help and grace, and makes a cover for concealed sin. Our judgment of this world is oftentimes but a reflection of our own self-consciousness. While we criticise some one whom we consider a great sinner, we are often but casting the shadow of our own conscience upon him. Such men, while claiming to be rational, are constantly committing themselves to the most absurd irrationality.

Those who are inclined to look into the deep things of God may find the following analysis of the question of "The Divine Immanence," by Prof. Borden P. Browne, D. D., of Brown University, in The Independent, June 30th, suggestively helpful. The Professor says:

Three points have to be borne in mind in estimating this doctrine, if we are not to fall into speculative insanity. In the first place, we must distinguish the question concerning the form, laws and contents of the world from the question concerning its causality. The doctrine in question applies only to causality. The form, laws and contents of the world of experience can be learned only from experience; and they are the same for all, no matter what our theory of causality. The world of experience is what it is, whatever its origin; and our knowledge of that world is not vacated or made unimportant by any theory of its origin. In studying it all theorists, of whatever speculative school, meet on a common plane and have a common object. The theist and the atheist, the spiritualist and materialist, the dogmatist and agnostic have no differences here. The immanence of God, then, while doing away with nature as a substantive and self-running mechanism, in no way cancels the existence of nature as an order of phenomena, as a system of law to which we are all subject, and which is irresistibly imposed upon us in experience. Unless we bear this in mind, we shall have persons denying the facts of disease or of sense on the ground of divine immanence. Disease may not be a substance, and sense objects may be only phenomena; but as facts in the system of experience they have to be reckoned with by the most pronounced idealist as inevitably as by the most inveterate realist.

The second point to be borne in mind is that this doctrine of immanence in no way affects the contents and values of things. It simply affirms that all finite things, whatever they are, have no self-sufficient being, but depend on God for their existence. The immanence does not mean that things are in God in a spatial sense, or that God is in things in a spatial sense; it means only the constant dependence of things on God. But this dependence does not make all things alike or of equal value. It leaves things just what they are or may reveal themselves to be. Their values, absolute or relative, are not affected by this immanence. Worms and men alike have their being in God, but they are not made of equal value thereby. Even the evil will is not independent of God, but that does not make it divine. The immanence in question is a metaphysical doctrine, and throws no light on the problem of ethical relations and values. Unless we bear this point in mind, we shall proceed to identify clams and saints as alike and equally divine. Indeed, one speculator, whose mental bottle would seem to have been pretty seriously strained by the new wine of this doctrine of immanence, has announced that he has no difficulty with the doctrine of a divine man, as he believes in a divine oyster. And when a divine man eats the divine oyster, we doubtless have a divinity of the second order.

Finally, as the third point to be borne in mind, the doctrine of immanence throws no light on the problem of finite existence. This must always remain a mystery to be recognized and admitted, not a fact to be deduced or comprehended. We cannot help ourselves by any theory of pantheism. In that case we should have to declare our sense of selfhood and responsibility a delusion, and this would leave us without anyting on which to build. We should also have to attribute our folly, error, blundering, wickedness, to God himself; and this would be a very high price to pay for our doctrine of immanence. We should also have an

God himself. If we suppose the difficulty overcome which is involved in the inalienability of personal experience, and attribute our thoughts and feelings to God as his own, we are met at once by the question concerning God's relation, as thinking our thoughts, to God as thinking the absolute and perfect thought. If our thoughts are all, then God as God vanishes. If he has our thoughts as his own and another set of perfect thoughts as his own, we have many minds rather than one. In one series God is limited, confused, erring; in the other he has perfect knowledge and insight. In the one series God loses himself and does not know who or what he is; in the other he knows himself as perfect unity and perfect light. There is no answer to these questions so long as the Infinite is supposed to play both sides of the game, and no possibility of saving thought and life from utter and hopeless confusion.

How the finite can be, how it can have otherness to the Infinite and a relative independence, there is no telling. But the finite, nevertheless, is; and, by its existence, it makes possible a moral order and an intelligible, rational system. The doctrine of divine immanence must be interpreted in accordance with this fact; otherwise, we shall have to regard the brothel as a divine institution, and hold to the gospel of the divine oyster.

Yet, rightly understood, the doctrine is important, both speculatively and religiously. It cancels the hard-and-fast mechanism of deistic thought; it makes intelligible the divine omnipresence, and helps us to realize how the Infinitely Far may also be the Infinitely Near.

Marcus Dods, in a recent number of the New York Observer, concludes an interesting article on "Is Sunday a Common Holiday?" with the following excellent suggestions as to how it may and should be observed:

Sunday, then, is a great opportunity that is given to us for cultivating elements in our character which if not so cultivated do practically get stunted in the mechanical routine and thoughtless urgency of business. It is an opportunity of which every wise man will avail himself for enjoying the communion of saints, not only to that limited extent which is possible to us in church, but in that supreme and elevating degree which is possible to all who will read the inspiring thoughts of those who have lived nearest to God in all ages, and in the fellowship of whose strivings after knowledge and holiness we are ourselves purified and strengthened. It is an opportunity given to us for ministering by personal attention to the sorrowful, the wretched, the diseased, the destitute, the ignorant—a day which our Lord reminds us might be well spent in active benevolence and in an attempt to carry some share of our manifold comforts and advantages to some one or two who need them more. One day's leisure in seven—seven weeks in every year—should surely leave behind some very visible traces of our willingness to be helpful in this world, where there is such room for wise and honest helpfulness. To spend such a day in formal attendance at church, in yawning idleness that has not energy enough to think that God can not possibly prefer that to honest hard work; to spend it in gossiping levity, in a vacant weariness that hails dinner as the great event and real relish of the day, is a scandal to our common humanity. Do not let these precious hours slip through your hand without your draining them of their possibilities of imparting renewed freshness and strength to your spirit. Seclude yourself for sometime with God; make a duty of seriously considering your ways, your habits, your disposition. Let your mind rest on the great gospel facts—the life, the love, the death, the resurrection of Christ. Seek your Lord's presence and address him with the words your own thoughts of him suggest, and you will learn how reasonable and fruitful an appointment it is that from all your ordinary works that you should rest every seventh day.

The following remarks of the Religious Telescope clearly indicate some of the difficulties in the way of the enforcement of the law against "Sabbath desecration" by baseball games and other evils. It says:

But, says one, why is not the law enforced and the Sunday baseball game stopped? Yes, why? One reason is, Sunday baseball pays. The street railway lines reap large harvests from it, and the stock, much of which is held by leading members of the prominent city churches, pays much larger dividends than it would pay but for the Sunday baseball. Touch the game adversely and you touch the pockets of prominent citizens and church members; consequently, to enforce the law is unpopular.

Then, many good, law-abiding citizens, whose hearts are pained at seeing God's sacred day trampled on and anarchism encouraged by this open defiance of civil authority, say: We elect officers whose sworn duty it is to enforce the law. We pay our taxes and thereby pay those officers large salaries. Why, then, should we be asked to do anything more to secure the law's enforcement. Must we, after paying our burdensome taxes, go down into our pockets and raise large extra sums to pay lawyers to help us enforce the law, when we have already elected officers who violate their oath by neglecting to do their sworn duty?

Others are discouraged because prominent citizens who pose as being patriotic and law-abiding, either wink at this open defiance of law, or at least refuse to say or do anything to abate it, "lest it might compromise them in their business." At a public meeting called by the ministerial association of this city recently to take action for the enforcement of the law against Sunday baseball, the great majority of the citizens were conspicuous by their absence. Seeing this, ordinary men say to themselves: "If the leading citizens of the city refuse to stand out boldly in favor of the inforcement of the law, it is useless for us to attempt to effect anything in that direction. If they can afford to stand by and see the law trampled upon, and anarchy and revolution fostered in our midst, we can do so too. If the Sabbath is destroyed, the morals of the republic undermind, and our glorious Union repeats the history of the republics of Greece and Rome, the responsibility will be with them and not with us.

CHURCH FINANCE.*

ALBERT SCHWARTZ.

Church finance is a necessary element in church enterprises. It must not be over-estimated, slighted, nor abused would we have a healthy church—one that is active, growing, spiritual. It has a rightful place. True principles also are revealed which should underlie all plans. To ascertain this place, to discover these principles, and to work out a true method should be the aim of all. That these things have not been done by a large majority of Christians and churches is sufficient reason for this investigation.

I. The Place of Church Finance.

The Master came to save men, and to do this he taught them and ministered unto them. He requires the same of the church. To accomplish the work every church should have three lines of expense, viz.:

1. Local sundries.
2. Preaching at home and abroad.
3. Caring for the needy.

No congregation can work without incurring sundry expenses. Nor can it maintain efficient preaching and teaching at home and abroad unless it supports such preachers and teachers. Furthermore, no congregation can well claim the Master's spirit that neglects the call of sickness and poverty, and this demands money. To argue these points would be much like attempting to prove the self-evident. Yet we find many professed Christians and churches are very indifferent, and some even dare to reject some of these duties. And quite universally the work of the deacons as indicated in Acts 6, has degenerated into passing the emblems and the contribution basket on Lord's day and into making schemes and plans for raising money that ought to be placed at their disposal without any special effort. The church has largely lost the true work of the deacon, and as a result the lodge has risen to supply a needed work. Let the church supply the money and elevate the deacon's work to its noble place of mercy, and the lodge will fail, not because we fight it, but because we assume our much-neglected work of caring for the needy.

*A paper read before the District Convention, Shenandoah, Iowa.

II. The Principles of Church Finance.

The following are the most important principles:

1. The Master's work as indicated above must be maintained.

2. The Master's work must be FIRST in our aims and efforts.

3. The Master bought us. We and all we have belong to him. We are stewards and must use everything for his glory.

4. Love is the primary law.

5. The giving must be with liberality and according as we are prospered, or proportionately.

6. All must give.

7. Cheerful and willing giving is demanded.

8. Blessings of a spiritual nature at least attend those who do give thus.

None of these principles should be ignored in forming our standards and methods. They ofttimes are, but always with peril to spirituality.

The greatest of these principles is love. Yet, many churches think any business man is capable of managing church finance. A successful business career is often the principal reason for placing a man in church office. Yes, business is business, but not every business man can wisely direct church finance. True, some of the principles of the business world should be adhered to in the management of church finance. They are right and true. But some customs and principles must be dropped when approaching church matters. For an example, the cardinal feature of the business world—viz., competition—must be used very little if any. Some parts of business are entirely too selfish and hostile to the Bible principle or law of love to God and man. Everything Christian rests upon this one word love, nor must we think it includes love of money. Ever to remember this law and to apply it is the great duty of Christians. Its power and spirit are needed in dealing with the church's financial problems. How many are the empty treasuries that love would quickly fill! The free workings of love would remove financial methods that are unjust, unholy, and a dishonor to God. Such a doctrine is indeed very strange to many men who are used to methods of selfish competition.

Nevertheless, the first great thing to attend to in church finance is to try to enlarge the spirit of love in the congregation. That which fault-finding, scolding, worldly wisdom and scheming fail to accomplish, love will quickly do. Then, let no one forget the corner-stone—love—when attempting to frame a financial policy for a congregation.

Growing out of love is the spirit and the application of consecration in spiritual work. How could a person love God and man and not attempt to carry or send God's message of love and mercy to lost humanity? But what has this to do with finance? Very much, indeed. For the promise of Jesus, "Seek ye first the kingdom of God and his righteousness and all these things shall be added unto you," may be relied upon implicitly, not only by the individual, but also by the congregation. For the individual or congregation to doubt here is disloyalty. But many are, in fact, practically skeptics on this point. A loving or consecraned worker or church has great encouragement in this particular. This point needs frequent and heavy emphasis. Too often money-making schemes and plans are allowed chief emphasis and given much time to the neglect of love and spiritual enterprises. Consequently spirituality, church growth, and even financial interests languish.

III. Methods of Church Finance.

At the present time, methods of church finance are numerous. Some are useful, and some poor, some harmful. The Babel of methods present a strange appearance—an incongruous appearance of good aims dependent upon "the world, the flesh and the devil;" of wise ends furthered by weak, foolish, or even harmful means. Not every Christian nor every church approves and uses these inconsistent systems. Yet, so many do approve and employ methods that are evidently from the Evil One rather than from the Author of good, that it presents a sad thought to contemplate. The methods deserve attention.

Perhaps the most common method for providing for money is the subscription plan. It makes a fair degree of successs. Yet it violates some principles. It pledges on a future probability. The Scriptures ask that the offering be made according as one is prospered and this a person cannot be sure of in advance. This plan leads to many unwise pledges. Again, it sets no standard for giving. Each one according to his caprice decides his standard which very frequently means, "Give as little as you well can and yet appear respectable," instead of "as you are prospered."

While this method has done much service it must fail to reach the best results.

Another favorite method is the apportionment plan. But this also involves pledging on future probabilities. It also fails to be a system of proportionate giving; for no set of men can know the degree of prosperity of the membership, and I think none can deny that in actual practice the committee on appointment rarely attempts to make what they reasonably suppose to be a proportionate apportionment.

The usual idea is to apportion each member about all they think can be obtained. The liberal man is burdened, the close man is eased, oftimes.

A third and almost universal method is the social and entertainment plan. This is not usually resorted to for all expenses, but rather to meet deficiencies caused by other inefficient methods. Of all methods, this is the most worldly and inefficient. It has caused so much harm to spiritual growth and is so laborious and expensive that it seems strange that it is tolerated. It may not be totally depraved, but it is so much depraved that it would be well to abandon it rather than cling to it for its very few apparent benefits. It can rarely be justified as a money-making scheme; for it brings so little profit in return for the amount of time, work and money invested. Besides this it is the occasion of much strife. Any method that shows its worldly origin so clearly, that retards spiritual growth, that costs so much expenditure of labor, time and money for small returns ought to find no favor with a spiritual according to circumstances. To one who is ignorant or selfish, freewill offering may mean very little or no offering. To the intelligent and loving Christian freewill offering is pre-eminently the correct plan. Such a one understands that he is merely a steward of God's goods and not the absolue owner. Realizing this he cannot be wasteful of his Master's possessions. Nor can he be careless in investing these possessions for the best interest of the Master. As he is one who must account for these possessions he alone must decide how to use them. He understands that covetousness is idolatry and tries to keep entirely free from it. He guards against the awful deceit of personal possessions and contends against the love of money—a root of every kind of evil. He holds these possessions subject to the call of the Master.

To these ideas all agree; but in practice we find the majority of Christians fail to realize the import of all this. They are untaught, are ignorant of their obligations and blessings. Under the law of love they fail to bestow upon the Lord's work as much as did the Jew under the Mosaic law. Comparatively few Christians give a tithe of all income. They spend more than nine tenths upon themselves or hoard it for self or children. Either ignorance or perverseness must account for this; for it is hardly fitting to so use another's—the Master's—possessions.

This paper is not for the defence of tithing from the mere standpoint of law, but rather *a system of freewill offering, wherein the tenth is recognized as the very least that is consistent with Bible truth and love.*

Any church that adopts any system of finance that looks for less than a tithe of the income of each member is tolerating a system entirely too low and is thereby cultivating a spirit of selfishness and covetousness in the membership.

Such a system is practical. The Jew gave more than a tenth. He was prospered in so doing and punished when he did not do so. Many Christians here and there give a tenth or more, and almost universally they testify that it is a blessing to them in some form. Not only is this plan practical, but it is certainly scriptural—a point before referred to.

No one will doubt that the Scriptures demanded this of the Jew, and we also learn that Abram gave tithes to the great Melchisedec. But strange to say, many preachers, even, seem to think that the Christians may do less and be guiltless. They will never speak of such a system as is here advocated lest they might bind the law on Christians. They apparently forget the majestic argument of the Hebrew epistle—the argument that approves and emphasizes the good of the old law, but then shows how much grander the blessings, privileges and obligations of the new. The whole trend of the argument justifies this position. In Heb. 7 we find a strong argument showing the superiority of the priesthood of Melchisedec to the Aaronic priesthood. One of the prominent reasons for this superiority is the fact that Abram,

ham; for
honor th
type.
Again,
advocatin
apostle P
of all gos
ing. He
1. The
his own c
2. The
eats of it.
3. The
flock.
4. Oxe
was writ
as for ma
5. Th
were to li
and offer
6. "E
that they
live of th
This ar
by hard-
are mai
heart de
and in s
one?
It is no
not an ea
er. It d
do the w
can any
ordained
glorious
less offer
earlier di
"Yes."
This pl
Bible pri
stewardsh
judge the
pered."
sacrifice
spirit of
vides that
eased. It
understan
The ad
legion to
congrega
to our m
prises.
Let us
such a st
soon app
reached
hosts of h
quickly r
change w
and missi
The gosp
abroad, a
It would
sults of th
Shall w
that is e
full of ble
advocate
even very
"The g
Then eve
ways, can
cating th
Is God
out tryin

The financial side of life is the one where a large part of Christians are liable to err, and many to finally stumble, fall and be eternally lost. No greater danger besets Christians. Hence, it is clearly for our best interests to make sure of the truth in this matter and order our lives accordingly.

Shenandoah, Ia.

OUR DUTY TO OUR RELIGIOUS NEIGHBORS.*

MRS. CLINTON LOCKHART.

It is our duty to bless all our neighbors; and we believe that our religious neighbors are as good as the rest of our neighbors if they behave themselves as well. The greatest barrier to inter-denominational friendship and fraternity, both on our side and theirs, is simple prejudice (much of it very simple). There is really no good reason why this feeling should exist, and there is less excuse for it among Endeavorers than among any other class of Christian workers. The Christian Endeavor Societies are not designed to make proselytes, not even to do evangelistic work; and certainly they are not intended to carry on theological controversy. Their special aim is growth in spirituality, to which controversy and prejudice make very poor contributions. Among our own people prejudice ought to be despised as being farthest from our plea and most unsuited to our chosen work among men. Prejudice is a natural product of narrowness and a feeling of weakness. People of broad views and liberal dispositions cannot consistently entertain prejudice against their neighbors. It is our aim as Christians to bless our neighbors, not to curse them in our hearts; to love them, not to hold them in contempt. Imagine a mother prejudiced against her child! Think of one sister prejudiced against another who needs her help! The love that thinks no evil feels no prejudice. What if others do not agree with us; they only deserve our sympathy, not our disrespect.

This is a wicked, fallible world; shall we be prejudiced against a whole world? Prejudice is a narrow conceit that crowds our neighbors out of our affection, and then passes judgment againt them with an assumption of infallibility. It is an air of self-importance that angels would not dare to assert. But more than this, it is due to a feeling of weakness, and is really a compliment to the strength of one's opponent. As Gay has well said:

> "In *beauty* faults conspicuous grow;
> The smallest speck is seen on *snow*."

Our very *prejudice* is an indication that we feel an inability to cope with our antagonist, and causes us to pray in the words of Dr. Fowler's Hunter: "Lord, help me against the bear; but if you can't help me, don't help the bear." This is surely not the attitude that becomes the disciple of Christ. If we are conscious of the greatness of our cause, the righteousness of our plea and the truth of our position, it poorly becomes us to betray a cowardly and sectarian spirit; and much more as we plead for universal love, unity and confidence. We, to whose minds the whole realm of truth has access, have no reason to bar out any soul which has been illuminated with the light of the cross, or to despise any effort that is directed toward a higher spirituality or a broader philanthropy. Why should we disregard others, whose very disposition we ought to imitate? Surely it is not in this way that we shall possess ourselves of their generous impulses.

> "As a wild tartar, when he spies
> A man that's valiant, handsome, wise,
> If he can kill him, thinks t' inherit
> His wit, his beauty and his spirit:
> As if just so much he enjoyed,
> As in another is destroyed."

It is, indeed, the spirit of fraternity on our part toward our religious neighbors that we need to enable us to associate with them in every good work in which we can secure a part. Very often our greatest lack of force in preaching Christian unity has been due to our indisposition to manifest a practical willingness to unite with them in Christian work. It may be granted that in many cases such a practical unity has been impossible or inconvenient; but in Christian Endeavor conventions it is practicable to show the spirit of unity, and so to cultivate it both among ourselves and in others.

Our disposition to unity in action as well as principle is always a measure of our spirituality. The lower the light of Christian love burns in our hearts, the less will it shine into the hearts of others. The less love we have for Christ, the less we will show to our neighbors. When the tide goes out from the beach it leaves many pools with little fishes swimming about in them; and one little shrimp may be separated from another by only a foot of dry sand, and yet have no communication with his neighbor; but this is only because the tide is too low. When the tide returns and the pools overflow with water, shrimp meets with shrimp in undisturbed fellowship. Let it be so with us; let the tide of Christian love and devotion so largely overflow the Endeavor Societies of all churches that Endeavorer shall meet Endeavorer in sweetest communion.

If there were no other advantage in our Christian Endeavor Societies meeting in convention with those of other churches, the privileges of social commingling alone ought to be decisive. The social benefits of Christianity to the world are a wreath of glory to our holy religion. Un-Christian nations know nothing of our social joys; and that type of religion which looks with suspicion upon social privileges is wanting in the true character of Christianity. Moreover, it is one of the cardinal features of the Endeavor Society that it cultivates sociability among its members and thereby displaces the ballroom and other follies with the higher enjoyments of Christian sociables. Sociability in the name of Christ is always pure, ennobling and helpful. Our Canton society has no meeting that is more profitable than our social meetings; hardly excepting the consecration meeting itself. Worship is good and needful, but the very spirit of devotion itself is that which fosters the sweetest social fellowships. Let this fellowship be extended as widely as possible. It should not be limited by towns or counties or states. Let it encircle the earth, and embrace all the ages of time.

Another advantage of our broader reach of fellowship is seen in the improved methods of work and worship that we are ever learning from our neighbors. We learn how to do committee work by the better work that others do; we learn better songs by hearing others sing; we make better prayers as our hearts are led by others into a closer communion with heaven; and we can more persuasively exhort each other to higher lives after we have listened to the inspiring pleas that others make for a closer walk with God. Thus the broader our reach of observation and the more extended are our efforts and sympathies, the richer we shall be in heart and the more useful in life.

I once read an old fable of a wall that had become so weakened by age that a portion of it between two gardens one day fell down, with the result that the sun was able to pour more light into the garden on either side, so that the flowers made better growth and became more beautiful, and the perfume sweeter. "What a pity that piece of old wall had not fallen down before," said the flowers. Next, the shrubs looked over to one another, and beginning a friendly conversation they said, "What a good thing that the piece of old wall fell down; it is a pity it stood so long." Then the flowers and shrubs of each garden discovered members of their *own families* living on the other side, who had long been really near each other and had *never had any communion* because of the wall between. And finally so many benefits resulted from the occurrence that instead of a rebuilding of the part that had fallen, the remainder of the wall was pulled down to the ground; so that air and sunshine and fragrance passed from garden to garden, and near neighbors enjoyed a free friendship. So, perish forever the partisan walls that separate Christian people! "For he is our peace, who hath broken down the *middle wall of partition* between us." "Behold how good and how pleasant it is for brethren to *dwell together in unity*."

*An address read before the recent Bible-school and Endeavor convention at Mexico, Mo.

THOUGHTS ON APPLIED CHRISTIANITY.

COLLATED BY FRANK G. TYRRELL.

GEO. D. HERRON:—"The Americans are not a democratic people. We do not select the representatives we elect. We do not govern ourselves. We do not make our own laws. Our political parties are controlled by private, close corporations that exist as parasites, giving us the most corrupting and humiliating despotisms in political history. Our legislation is determined by a vast system of lobby. The people know, though they cannot prove, that our legislative methods have become the organization of indirect bribery and corruption."

ELTWEED POMEROY, President National Direct Legislation League:—"No people can be self-governed who are denied the right to vote yes or no on every law by which they are to be governed. This is direct legislation by the initiative and referendum. By the referendum, a suitable minority of the people, say five per cent., can call for the reference of any law passed by the law-making body, to the vote of the people. By the initiative, the same suitable minority can propose any law which after discussion both in the legislative body and before the people, goes to a poll of the people. This carries into law-making the principle of brotherhood and equality. Also it carries out

ıy allowing the people to
əy will take after it has
d."

.E:—"I know no country
so little true independence
edom of discussion as in

ᴡɢɪʟʟ:—"The socialistic
ɜ to stay. The socialistic
ety is partly Christian,
he existing industrial sys-
licities and injustices, so
·oduce increasing dissatis-
sm will grow if the miser-
who are pushed by the
ım into dependence and
. This multitude will in-
erculean efforts are made
improve the moral charac-
l condition of the unsuc-
The church must get down
is matter as she never has

MARKHAM:—"I prophesy
:he Social Man. There is
ngtime of the human race
ısoming of the large and
n man. Some day good
no longer be an irridescent
ıcial Man will be the divine
ɪs. He will be a man born
ıan worthy of immortality.
ı will consider the universal
ler not only those on earth,
·iads that are coming in the

ʀɪsᴏɴ:—"Our present type
many respects, one of the
hat has ever existed in the
—boundless luxury and
at one end of the scale, and
ondition of life as cruel as
. slave, and more degraded
ɔuth Sea Islander."

---

of the growth and power
corporations in the United
had from the following
ıed by The Street Railway
ement. It appears that
s than twenty-six proper-
000,000 or more; nineteen
)0,000 to $1,000,000; forty-
om $100,000 to $500,000.
ɔperties earning less than
ɔluded in the comparison.
ipts for the year 1897 were
ıion Traction Company, of
ıamely, $10,480,646. The
rated Railway Company, of
əs in second with $9,477,052;
an, of the same city, third
West End Railway Co.,
ırth with $8,719,032. Of the
ured, the Dunkirk (N. Y.)
ailway Company is the last
th receipts $26,123. One
erstand from these figures
:h a grasping for municipal
harters and why they be-
actor in local politics and
ption.

---

been passed in Congress,
hillips Bill, authorizing the
a non-partisan commission
nation and to consider and
slation to meet the prob-
by labor and immigration,

sion," and is to be composed as follows: "Five members of the Senate, to be appointed by the presiding officer thereof; five members of the House of Representatives, to be appointed by the Speaker, and nine other persons, who shall fairly represent the different industries and employments, to be appointed by the President, by and with the advice and consent of the Senate. The term of the commission is to be two years. Section 3 of this bill provides that the commission "shall furnish such information and suggest such laws as may be made a basis for uniform legislation by the various states of the Union, in order to harmonize conflicting interests and to be equitable to the laborer, the employer, the producer and the consumer." This seems to us a most sensible method of procedure, and we congratulate Hon. Mr. Phillips, of Pennsylvania, who is understood to be the instigator of the bill, and who is likely to be the chairman of the commission, on the character of the measure. Why not treat the problems presented by the liquor traffic in the same way?

The Religious World.

The German Lutheran Conference, comprising their churches in Southern Indiana, Illinois, Ohio and Kentucky, in session at Terre Haute, Ind., adjourned July 8th. Their next conference will be held at Columbia, Ind.

At the National Council of Congregationalists, in session at Portland, Ore., last week, it was ordered that the committee on union with other denominations and the denominational committee be united and continued.

D. L. Moody's 16th General Bible Conference will be held at Northfield, Mass., July 29th to August 18th.

Cardinal Gibbons prepared a circular to be read in the Roman Catholic Churches last Sunday morning, which is intended to carry out the suggestion made by President McKinley, that the people of the land unite in giving thanks for the victory of the American fleet off Santiago. The Cardinal's letter calls upon the people to return thanks to Almighty God for his blessing upon the arms of this land in the conflict with the Spanish fleet and for the victory achieved and for the escape of the Americans with comparatively no loss.

The Congregationalists have made great advance in their ministerial relief work in recent years. From August 1, 1895, to April 30, 1398, they report a total collection for this fund of $51,314.50.

The centennial celebration of the origin of Ohio Methodism, held in Delaware, O., opened June 21st and closed on the 24th.

The following interesting figures on secret societies are given in the report of the committee thereon to the National Congregational Council at Portland, Ore.: "The growth of secret and social orders during the past ten years has been rapid, both in the multiplication of societies and in members, the total annual increase in membership being rated at 250,000. In 1895 transportation, fees, banquets, testimonials, regalia and convention expenses $250,000,000 more were spent. To these items the approxmate sum of $42,000,000 was added for the rental of buildings and halls for lodge purposes, thus making a total of $941,000,000 expended in a single year by the secret societies of the United States." The position taken by the council on this report was that "the attitude of the Christian Church toward these multitudinous secret orders should be courteous and Christian, for the church cannot afford to occupy a position of prejudice or unreasonable hostility upon any question of public opinion or social habit, for such a temper at once sacrifices both the spirit and the power of the Christian faith."

OPEN-AIR WORKERS IN ANNUAL CONFERENCE.

A largely attended conference of the Open-air Workers' Association of America, was held in Boston, June 27th.

C. N. Hunt, of Minneapolis, represented the Young People's Societies. He said that young people with their winning, bright testimonies, are needed in open-air meetings. They have the best training for such work. Young people's meetings are not an end in themselves, but a means to equip workers for service outside the church.

Rev. J. A. McElwain reported the meetings he held on the steps of the late Dr. A. J. Gordon's church, where andiences of four hundred gathered on pleasant evenings. They began with a fifteen-minute song service, followed by a brief sermon and three-minute testimonies. At the close of each service a large number followed the workers into the church where, in an after-meeting, as many as six or eight would frequently seek the Lord. Similar meetings on church steps are practicable for all localities.

Dr. Alexander Blackburn, of Cambridge, recommended outdoor preaching to pastors as beneficial to their health; as giving them an opportunity to study the people, and as a school of criticism for their "fine" compositions. He said that men on the streets demand sermons on fundamental doctrines, and pastors, whose lifelong training has been in this line, should supply the demand.

Henry Varley, of Australia, advocated preaching in the market places in conformity with the example of Christ and the apostles. It cannot be denied that the working people do not care much for the churches, and the churches should overcome this barrier by going to the people.

EVANGELISTIC ASSOCIATION OF NEW ENGLAND.

7 Tremont Place, Boston.

Cotner University.

To those interested in this institution it will be of interest to know that an advance movement is being made to redeem it from debt. In addition to the successful conduct of the school during the past two years, no debt has been incurred and the redemption fund slowly increased.

Bro. J. W. Hilton has now been employed to devote his entire time to this work. He is a graduate of the institution, has a business experience and is an able preacher. Brethren, receive him and aid him in every way possible.

Our Budget.

—"The best Christian service is handmade."

—"Men need all the love, sympathy and help you can give them."

—"Human nature is not perfect, but it is the noblest thing we have here on this earth."

—"We never need to make pilgrimages to find our religious opportunities."

—"The Jericho road that we travel in our busy city life is just lined with cases that appeal to us for help."

—The above sentences are from Chas. R. Brown's new book on the two parables.

—The gate of heaven will be wide or narrow for us according to our usefulness in this life.

—The model prayer of the Christian says "give us," etc., the model prayer of the world-man says "give me," etc. This was the prayer of the prodigal son.

—The Bible-school, Central Church, Des Moines, Iowa, offering for Foreign Missions this year was $741. The banner class offering was $150. The second largest class offering was $141 and the third $127. Surely, this is splendid giving.

—A happy event in the history of the church at Steubenville, Ohio, was the laying of the corner-stone of their new house of worship, of which an account appeared at length in the Daily News of that city, July 9th. The services were participated in by other pastors of the city and were particularly enjoyable. All rejoiced together in the work. The pastor, J. G. Slaytor, was master of ceremonies.

—"Go" is the title of the bi-monthly paper started by M. L. Hoblit, the C. W. B. M. missionary at Monterey, N. L., Mexico, a copy of the first number of which is just to hand. As it contains much information about that country and people it would not be a bad idea for all who can to subscribe for it and learn about Mexico and also help to sustain the mission thereby. Ten copies to one address for a year may be had for $2.00.

—The Stars and Stripes raised in the Philippine Islands will be like the coming out of the sunlight through rifted clouds. It means the overthrow of priestcraft and the dawn of religious liberty to its benighted souls.

—The offerings for Foreign Missions received at Cincinnati for the first seven days of July amounted to $3,972.20, being a gain of $1,092.28 over same time last year. Also a gain of 64 contributing schools. This year, thus far, 317 schools have sent in an offering.

—The program of the Illinois C. W. B. M. and Illinois Christian Missionary Convention, to be held at Eureka, during the encampment, Aug. 1-7, just to hand as we are getting ready for the press, will appear next week.

—We devote an unusual amount of space to our correspondents this week and still have interesting letters which have to await another issue. Good letters and lots of church news are prominent features of this paper.

—Aside from its budget of news the Iowa Letter, this week, is somewhat critical, but for admonitional purposes. The Iowa Secretary is rather severe with his Mormon friends in Iowa, but we presume that he knows whereof he speaks. He is not alone in his convictions of deception in Mormon teachings and teachers, and there are many evidences that D. H. Bays and his book, "Doctrines and Dogmas of Mormonism," published by the Christian Publishing Co., are giving them no little trouble.

—The reference to Church Quarrels and their remedy in the Minnesota Letter, by the Minnesota Secretary, will be read and appreciated by other secretaries and our pastors in general as a timely discourse upon a shameful, yet far too frequent an occurrence in the religious world. What Bro. Mellen says upon the subject is worthy of serious attention. First, everything possible should be done to keep quarrels out of the church; and second, when they become "church quarrels" speedy steps to dissipate them should be taken by the entire church.

—If there is anything you want to know about the Bethany C. E. Reading Course, read the catechism on that subject by J. Z. Tyler in this paper. It is time now to prepare for the second reading course, to begin October first.

—You may not like the methods of the commanding officers of our army and navy, but they have accomplished that whereunto they were sent, and that is all that our country asked at their hands. It is results that count; methods are of importance only as they are effective. Even a defective method that wins is better than an ornamental one that accomplishes nothing.

—The pleasant personal remarks with which English Topics opens up this week are in striking contrast with the more stately beginnings of former "Topics," and most agreeable to us, save the excitement of our sympathy for one who longs to share the joys of a retreat from summer heat, but cannot for the want of a "lakeside paradise" within safe rapid traveling distance. The reference to England's new theological difficulty and to the row about ritualism, however, are serious enough, hinting as they do at the great undercurrents of English life and their consequent present and future problems, both of church and of state.

—The article in this paper on "Our Duty to Our Religious Neighbors" was prepared by Mrs. Clinton Lockhart and read by her before the Missouri Bible-school Convention, at Mexico, Mo., in June last. The article treats of an exceedingly practical question, after a most lucid and vigorous fashion. It strikes at the root of one of the great barriers to a better fellowship of professed Christians and should be read with prayerful attention.

—The story in our Family Circle, this week, by Minnie Hadley, entitled, "The Legend of Chocoma," is odd enough and interesting enough to hold the reader's attention to the end with unflagging interest.

—According to reports on the Manila and Santiago naval battles, the most effective factors of a war-fleet are not big guns nor torpedo boats, but the rapid-fire, medium-calibre ordnance. Similar observations have been made of the pulpit and of the church. The most effective church work is usually accomplished by medium mental and financial calibre; quick-acting men and women in the Lord's army.

—One of the most important recommendations brought before the National Congregational Council recently held at Portland, Oregon, was that "a representative council or conference of the Protestant churches in the United States and Canada be called, to meet in the city of Washington in May, 1900, for the purpose of organizing an international union, which shall meet at regular periods, and which shall serve as a visible expression of the unity of the churches, and as a common bond in their fellowship with each other and their service of the Lord Jesus Christ." Such a recommendation appeals at once to the better judgment of all who love the Lord more than they love their religious creeds. We trust that it may be fully realized in some agreeable, effective way.

—The Senate committee appointed to investigate the payment of the claim of the Methodist Book Concern and the payment to Maj. E. B. Stahlman of $100,800 as an agent in getting the claim through, finds that the Senate was deceived by the representations of Mr. Stahlman and Messrs. Barbee and Smith, the book agents, but absolves the Methodist Church South, as such, from blame in the matter. It has also found that no Senator or member of Congress received any money in connection with the claim. The testimony taken was made public. We did not expect that any blame would fall upon the church as such in this matter, and while it cannot be held responsible for the action of each of its members or implicated officials it will be compelled to deal with them according to righteous demands, that it may be exonerated before the world and become a terror to evil-doers.

—One of the underlying incidents of the historic victory of the American navy on the third of July near the harbor of Santiago is the reverent confession of faith in God made by the coptain of the Texas. It is said that when the battle was over and the exultant American crews were cheering themselves hoarse for joy, Capt. John W. Philip, of the Texas, called his men to deck, and with bared head said to them: "I want to make public acknowledgment here that I believe in God the Father Almignty. I want you, officers and men, to lift your hats, and from your hearts offer silent thanks to the Almighty." The comment on this incident by John R. Spear, author of "History of our Navy" is also worthy of being repeated here. He said: "Look on the picture of the drunken Spaniards of the Cristobal Colon and then on that of a typical American naval seaman and his crew. His crew to a man removed their hats, for a moment turned grateful thoughts to the mystery of the God of battles, and then impulsively broke into the heartiest cheers for the one who, like another typical seaman,

'Feared his foes not at all, but his God a great deal.'"

—E. J. Fenstermacher, 319 Monmouth St., Newport, Ky., wishes to inform our readers that in view of the many sick soldiers who are arriving at the Ft. Thomas Hospital, near Newport, Ky., he will be glad to hear from any who may have relatives or friends among them and will render what assistance he can in communicating with their sick, or for the soldiers in words to the homefolk. There are those no doubt who will appreciate this kindness of Bro. Fenstermacher.

—The CHRISTIAN-EVANGELIST lifts its hat to the Christian Courier for the following pleasing compliment:

> The Courier has said that the CHRISTIAN-EVANGELIST is nearer than any other paper known to us to our idea of a model Christian paper. One of its chief excellencies is that it is progressive—not afraid of improvement—and its latest step forward is a change to a thirty-two page form, a new dress and heading, a new arrangement of contents and a decidedly more attractive appearance generally. The office editor has wisely given us on the front page of the first number in the new form a good picture of J. H. Garrison, the editor. We are glad to note these additional evidences of enterprise, good taste and prosperity. We trust that some day the Christian Courier may be as good a paper as the CHRISTIAN-EVANGELIST.

There is a lot of room at the front or even at either side of us, my brother, and you are getting under good headway. So do not become weary in well-doing, but press on toward the high mark you have set for your attainment in the career of religious journalism. The CHRISTIAN-EVANGELIST bids you Godspeed in your high aims, good work and future outlook, while we ourselves groan within ourselves for still higher attainments.

—It has been announced in our city press that J. C. Creel, editor of the Church Register, Plattsburg, Mo., has sold out his interest therein to his partners, G. A. Hoffmann and R. L. Wilson, and that the plant will be taken to Kansas City, Mo., united with two or three other church papers and renamed The Christian Register. It is said that a new company will be organized to publish this paper, make it a weekly, and will start with a subscription list of about six thousand. We hope the promoters of this enterprise may succeed abundantly in all their efforts to promote the cause of primitive Christianity in Missouri and elsewhere.

.. Smith, corresponding secretary ions, Cincinnati, Ohio, reports the r Home Missions for the week end- 16th at $723.22. Nineteen new ntributed, but there was a loss for $530.45 over same week last year. the gain this week, however, will this loss or more.

ter from D. L. Moody, East North- ., expressing appreciation for our work among the soldiers at Chicka- l other camps, he says: ''Without eration on the part of the religious ork would be very difficult.'' Our ill find another letter from Mr. his paper on this work.

bate between Bro. Briney, of Mo- ., and Elder Throgmorton, of Du , begins at Allen Springs, Ill., July se who can attend will find abun- ectual entertainment and profit.

hristian Orphans' Home Board, of requests us to say that they would d good Christian homes for boys nonth to eleven years old. Also for ourteen years, who is mechanically nd would like a home with some r builder. They state that they e lot of boys for whom homes are Address Christian Orphans' Home, Ave., St. Louis, Mo.

etter from Jacksonville, Florida, in , T. H. Blenus tells us of the relig- done in behalf of the thousands of ncamped there. The interest taken s exercises by the soldiers is particu- ifying. We are thankful to Bro. r this information and for the evi- progress in the church at Jackson-

we appreciate the compliment paid the Pittsburg Letter, this week, we deeply feel the burden of the in- sponsibilities now upon us because of to give our readers what they and for which they stand rightly deserve— journal second to none in the land. vords next to a growing subscription most helpful and appreciated tonic. the Pittsburg Letter and a host of their kind words to the CHRISTIAN- ST.

xcellent article in this paper on Finance,'' by Albert Schwartz, ap- s revised form from that of its read- enandoah, Iowa. This will explain nces that may appear to those who nere. The paper was prepard during ss of Sister Schwartz, who died since ention at Shenandoah, and Bro. felt that he had not said just what he say and as it ought to be said on the nd hence its revision. The paper appreciated by the convention and that it be published in tract form for e. It will make a splendid tract on ct and worthy of wide use in all the

xcellent paper on ''Ministerial Cour- Geo. L. Peters, of Girard, Ill., eared in our issue last week, was read Illinois Ministerial Association, at April 14th, 1898. We had not this nd when the article went to press.

blish this week an appeal from the Malden, Mo., to help to replace e of worship, which was totally de- lightning, July 8th. As it is cus- divide with the unfortunate—even this—we trust that this appeal will heeded.

—The poem in our Family Circle, this week, by Cornelia P. Bozman, of Cairo, Ill., under the title, ''Hear Ye Him,'' is full of uplifting spirituality.

—The racy letter, ''Wheeling Through England,'' from Dr. W. E. Garrison, in this paper, will be enjoyed by our readers. His easy style, pleasantries and observations make this letter one of unusual interest.

—Honolulu pays a high tribute to the moral conduct of the two thousand soldiers from California and Oregon turned loose upon its streets for ten hours. It is said that ''not a trace of disorder was observed in them throughout the day.''

—Particular attention is desired to the article in this paper on ''A Union Meeting,'' by T. W. McDonald, at Des Moines, Ia. Interested parties are requested to save this paper or the article for further use and future reference.

—There is probably more reading-matter in this paper than was ever given to our readers in any other number of the CHRISTIAN-EVANGELIST in its history. Aside from the use of smaller type than in our old form there are four more pages to this number which we have used for literature instead of advertisements. And another thing worthy of mention is that the paper is printed on our New Double Cylinder Huber Perfecting Press. This press is of the most improved modern type and weighs seventeen tons. The paper is folded and covered in our new folding machine of which mention has been made. But this is the first paper from our new press, and it comes to you loaded to the guards with intellectual food, news and pleasantries.

—The Illinois Christian Missionary Convention convenes at Eureka, August 3rd, and will occupy two days of Eureka Encampment which is from August 1st to 7th. Among the notable speakers secured to delight and edify the audiences of the convention the name of Booker T. Washington, now of national fame, is announced.

—Now that the first year of the Bethany C. E. Reading Courses has closed, testimonies of the most gratifying character have been pouring in upon the managers from all parts of the country, as to its value as an educational factor. The Bethany C. E. Bulletin for July devotes several pages to these enthusiastic endorsements of the work.

—Bro. J. M. Crocker, who for sometime has been chaplain of the State Penitentiary of Iowa, has become a Missourian, as will be seen from the following note. We hope our Missouri brethren may appreciate his true worth and treat him so well that he may remain a willing captive:

DEAR BRO. GARRISON:—I am a stranger in a strange land. And I was attracted here by the high altitude and conditions favorable to physical vigor. For fourteen weeks I have clambered up and down the rock-ribbed hills of the Ozarks, breathed the pure air that whispers to the giant forests, and listened to the song of the mockingbird. Truly this is a land of fruit and flowers, sunshine and the song of birds, a delightful spot to recuperate jaded energies. And six long years' preaching to the spirits in prison with all the strain and tension upon the vital forces, is now a thing of the past, in point of fact and *effect*. Thank you—I am well. But all my life has been spent in Iowa except two years in Kansas. Of course Iowa seems like home to me, and I plead guilty to some symptoms of homesickness. I hope to get better acquainted with my Missouri brethren. I would like some work in this part of the state, if it could be had. We have bought a little home near Seymour, and would like to stay in Missouri at least for awhile.

Sincerely yours,
J. M. CROCKER.

Seymour, Mo.

—The CHRISTIAN-EVANGELIST acknowledges the kindness of a complimentary ticket to the Fountain Park Assembly, at Remington, Ind., Aug. 11-22. The accompanying program is one of the most promising along literary and social lines that we have yet seen for a pleasant and profitable summer retreat.

—The Spaniards were much more concerned about their honor in the surrender of Santiago than they were in the sailing of Camara's fleet through the Suez Canal and back again.

—The CHRISTIAN-EVANGELIST this week expresses its appreciation of the great victory at Santiago without further loss of life in battle by presenting to its readers the picture of General Shafter.

—The CHRISTIAN-EVANGELIST came to our table last week changed in form from a sixteen to a thirty-two page journal, and otherwise greatly improved in appearance. We congratulate Bro. Garrison, the editor, and the Christian Publishing Co. in view of the manifest progress that has been made from year to year in the management and conduct of this superb religious journal. The first page contains a fine likeness of the editor.

Thanks to the Christian Oracle for the above words of good-cheer and hearty appreciation of our efforts to reach the highest possible attainment of usefulness in religious journalism.

—America's war with Spain will go into history with the evidences of divine help strongly on the American side. The marvelous escape of our ships from Spanish torpedoes and Spanish guns, the remarkable escape from injury of the American fleet in the greatest naval battles of history, the capitulation of Santiago, the miraculous escape of Hobson and his men from death in Santiago Harbor, the inability of the Spaniards to sink or even to disable one of our warships, and the utter destruction of their own fleets at Manila and at Santiago are certainly things of such moment as to cause the impression that God is indeed with us. And when we hear the captain of a warship saying, as is reported of ''Bob Evans,'' of the Iowa, ''Almighty God and our gunners did it;'' and as said Captain John Philip, of the Texas, before his men, ''I want to make public acknowledgment here that I believe in God the Father Almighty. I want all you officers and men to lift your hats and from your hearts offer silent thanks to the Almighty,'' we feel like going even further and saying, God was in these men, using them for the removal of great obstacles of progress. The prevalence of the religious spirit in the army and the navy has been remarkable from the first in this war. Not the sectarian spirit,

PERSONAL MENTION.

C. L. Pickett has changed his field of labor from Harlan to Woodbine, Iowa, and reports work starting off encouragingly in his new field. He delivered the Fourth-of-July address at Manilla, Iowa.

G. C. Audrey has returned from his vacation at Stafford to his work at Burrton, Kansas, where he has been preaching acceptably for two years.

J. S. Myers, pastor of the church at Sedalia, Mo., has received a call to the pastorate of the Twelfth Street Christian Church, Philadelphia, Pa.

Ammi Fike, of Newton, Kan., has been retained to preach at Moundrige another year.

B. J. Wharton, Marshall, Mo., preached at First Christian Church, this city, last Lord's day morning.

T. W. Grafton, pastor of the Christian Church at Rock Island, Ill., and his wife are passing the month of July at Oskaloosa, Ia.

John R. Wright, pastor of the church at Hot Springs, Ark., has resigned and become a chaplain in the army. His first station will be at Chickamauga Park. His address will be Co. M., First Ark., Vol. Inf.

J. W. Baker, who recently went from Minisila to Galvin, Ohio, reports the work in his new field in a prosperous state. Galvin is a city of 9,000 souls.

E. N. Kellar delivered the postgraduate address at Add-Ran University this year. He is a graduate of Drake University, and took a two years' course under J. W. Lowber for A. M. at Add-Ran.

F. L. Davis, of Dows, Ia., reports work about to begin on their new $2,000 house of worship, and church work prospering. He asks for your prayers in behalf of the work at Dows.

F. G. Tyrrell, pastor Central Christian Church, this city, left for Macatawa, Mich., where he joins his family for their summer's rest.

J. J. Lockhart, Chancellor of Christian University, Canton, Mo., preached for the First Christian Church, of Sedalia, Mo., during the pastor's absence in the East in June.

J. K. Speer says that the annual sermon before the high school graduating class at Clinton, Mo., by J. S. Myers, of Sedalia, Mo., was the "ablest sermon of the kind ever heard" in that city.

Vernon J. Rose, of Kansas, will address the church at Blandinsville, Ill., on the Church Extension work, Sunday morning, July 31, and the church at La Harpe, Ill., on the evening of the same date.

C. E. Smith, pastor of the church at Pine Flats, Pa., has been called by the church to retain that relation indefinitely. He will preach part time for the church at Gipsy, same county.

Z. T. Sweeney's address at the Endeavor Convention at Nashville on "The Royalty of Service," is denominated one of the best of the convention, by the Evening Republican, Columbus, Ind.

The Christian Oracle this week announces the marriage of F. M. Rains, treasurer of the Foreign Christian Missionary Society, Cincinnati, O., recently, to a young lady who has been an assistant in the foreign office at Cincinnati for two years, but whose first name the Oracle had not yet learned. We join the Oracle in congratulations to Bro. Rains and his wife.

J. M. Austin preached at Havinsville, Kan., last Sunday. This was the home of W. H. Black, who recently departed this life for his heavenly home.

M. A. Carleton, formerly of Lincoln, Neb., but now of Perkins, Oklahoma, writes that he has been commissioned to travel in Russia for the Department of Agriculture of the United States, to investigate and gather seed of rust-resistant wheat varieties.

A. F. Harrall and wife, of Shawnee, Oklahoma, called at this office on last Tuesday on their way to his father's, near Ironton, Mo., where they will spend the next six weeks. During this time Bro. Harrall expects to do evangelistic work in that part of Missouri, after which they will go to some point in Texas for their future field of labor.

J. H. Fuller, pastor of the church at Newport, Ark., preached for the Compton Heights church, this city, last Lord's day. We learn that the visit was enjoyed by both the church and the visiting preacher. There was one confession.

J. N. Jessup, pastor of the church at Vincennes, Ind., has received and accepted a call to become pastor of the church at Little Rock, Ark., for a term of two years. This call was made on evidence of good work done and not on a "trial sermon." The preacher and congregation never saw one another. He will begin work there in October. He has had a pleasant work of four years at Vincennes, Ind.

Prof. W. E. Hackleman and Miss Pearl Perrine are on the program of the Fountain Park Assembly, at Remington, Ind., August 11 to 22, 1898. Of the preachers announced we mention the names of T. J. Legg, John L. Brandt, J. E. Pounds and L. L. Carpenter, all of Indiana, and J. H. Hardin, President of Eureka College.

Robt. Stewart has resigned his work at Grassy Creek Church, Pendleton county, Ky. In his ministry of eighteen months there he has held three successful protracted meetings. The last one just concluded resulted in 64 additions. The appreciation of the church for his services was shown by a gift of $12 cash and a beautiful Bible. E. S. Baker, of the Bible Collage, Lexington, Ky., assisted in the last meeting at Grassy Creek.

M. L. Hoblit, our C. W. B. M. missionary at Monterey, N. L., Mexico, has translated the tract on "The Disciples of Christ," by the editor of this paper, into their native tongue for use in his mission field. He is also publishing a little paper called Go, which he uses to create interest in the work. These he says are the first fruits of his new press. Bro. Hoblit keeps a public reading-room at his Mexican mission station and seems to be quite hopeful of good results in his Mexican field.

Frank L. Bowen and Sister Boen, of Kansas City, Mo., were sent to Nashville, Tenn., as delegates to the Christian Endeavor Convention for all of the Christian Endenvor Societies of Kansas City, Mo. This was a fine compliment to Bro. Bowen's work as an evangelist in that city, of which he makes good report in this paper.

The press of last week announced that J. S. Myers had accepted the call from the 12th Street Christian Church, at Philadelphia, and consequently has resigned his work at Sedalia, the resignation to take effect Aug. 31st. When Bro. Myers entered upon his pastorate at Sedalia the membership of the church was 425. Now it is over 1,100. The Sunday-school then had an enrollment of 200; now it has 700. Since he assumed charge a handsome $40,000 church building has been erected, and there is not a dollar's indebtedness upon it. A Second Christian Church has also grown out of his congregation. We hope to hear of an equally successful work under his skillful executive ability and able pulpit and pastoral work at Philadelphia.

Joel Brown, of Iowa, who has been appointed by the Christian Orphan's Home Board as their solicitor for Illinois, Indiana and Ohio, called at this office last week on his way to his new work and new field of labor.

W. S. Payne, of Princeton, Ky., sends us the following letter which speaks for itself: "At our union service last Lord's day, J. L. Hill pastor of the Cumberland Presbyterian church preached on Christian Union to a large audience. In the sermon he denounced creeds and denominationalism. Finally. after fully expressing his views declared his purpose to forsake the church of his father and kindred and henceforth to be known only as a Disciple of Christ and will this week be baptized and enter the Christian ministry unfettered by creeds. I have known Bro. Hill for six months, and he is very popular here with all classes. His congregations are the largest and his salary the best of any minister's in the city. He gives these up to begin again, as it were, the ministry of a freer life. He is a graduate of Lebanon University and has been preaching about ten years. Bros. Gordon and Glover, whom I know personally, both having preached here, have lately left the Cumberland church and united with us, and now that Bro. Hill has taken the decisive step it has caused no little notice. My knowledge of the Cumberland Presbyterian brethren is most fraternal, and I have known them in many relations and admire very much their deep spirituality and earnest Christian devotion. Bro. Hill will now doubtless do some work as an evangelist until he locates in some field more permanently as a pastor."

CHANGES.

A. J. Honly, Monmouth to Ashland, Oregon.
J. P. Lucas, Creston, Iowa, to Colorodo City, Col.
W. E. Johnson, Kansas City, Kan., to Kansas City, Mo., 1232 Monroe Avenue.
G. M. Read, Ogden, to Arrowsmith, Ill.
S. W. Pearcy, Hiram, O., to East Saginaw, Mich.
Wallace Tharp, Augusta, Ga., to Middletown, Ky.
M. L. Everett, Eldorado, to Topeka, Kan.
A. B. McFarlane, Hebron, to Salem, Neb.
A. L. Martin, Wichita, to Mt. Hope, Kan.
S. M. Cook, Rocky Ford, to Newark, O.
Geo. B. Ranshaw, Taylor, to San Antonia, Texas.
W. C. McDougall, Walterton, to Bridgeburg, Ontario.
W. E. Pitcher, Des Moines, Ia., to Belleville, Kan.

The Reader's Delight.

We are pleased with the way our new form is being received and think it but just to give the public a few of the many expressions of delightful appreciation which we are daily receiving from our readers. Here are some of them:

"You *had*, I thought, you *have*, I am *sure*, the best paper published by the Disciples of Christ." GEO. MUNRO.
New Cumberland, W. Va.

"The CHRISTIAN-EVANGELIST'S new costume is handsome. You deserve the congratulations of the brotherhood. It will stand comparison with any religious paper I have ever seen." B. S. FERRALL.
Watseka, Ill.

"I call attention to the CHRISTIAN-EVANGELIST with great friendly pride. It is a great paper." J. FRAISE RICHARDS.
Washington, D. C.

"Permit me to write you a word of congratulation over the marked improvement made in the CHRISTIAN-EVANGELIST. Manifestly it is seeking the highest degree of perfection in religious journalism. It commends itself to the appreciation of every intelligent reader of its columns." L. H. STINE.
Paris, Mo.

"You have accomplished a splendid improvement. The CHRISTIAN-EVANGELIST will be found in the front rank of the best papers." J. B. CRANE.
Waynesboro, Va.

"You look well in your new dress. The contents of the last number were especially good." CHAS. M. SHARPE.
Lawrence, Kans.

"I want to compliment you on the new dress of the CHRISTIAN-EVANGELIST. It is certainly, to my notion, the best paper in our brotherhood. *I hope it will experience a large increase in circulation.*" F. L. DAVIS.
Dows, Ia.

"I cannot withold my congratulations on the new and improved form in which the CHRISTIAN-EVANGELIST appears this week. The mechanical execution is second to none. As to the spirit and tone, these are acknowledged. *May your subscription list keep pace with your improved appearance.*" A. L. ORCUTT.
Indianapolis, Ind.

The *italics* in the last two quotations are ours. Improvements *must have substantial encouragement*, such as our present readers may readily and easily render by securing new subscribers among their friends and acquaintances. See our special offer of the CHRISTIAN-EVANGELIST for the six months beginning July 1, 1898, and closing December 31, 1898, for seventy-five cents. Samples for distribution, if you are willing to try.

A Call for Names!

The undersigned desires the name of every Bethany College alumnus living in Missouri; also every old student or friend of that grand institution of learning. If you are listed with either of the above, please send your name and postoffice address, as well as the names and addresses of all alumni. students (new or old) and friends of old Bethany, whom you know who live in Missouri. Please send at once and oblige Yours sincerely,

MELANCTHON MOORE.
Brookfield, Mo.

For Foreign Missions.

Comparing the receipts for Foreign Missions for the week ending July 14th, with the corresponding time last year, showing the following:

CONTRIBUTING.	1897	1898	GAIN
Sunday-schools,	219	224	5
Amount,	$7,982.97	$2,962.49	Loss $5,020.48

Send offerings to F. M. Rains, Treasuer, box 750, Cincinnati, O.

Correspondence.

English Topics.

SUMMER HAS COME.

ne weeks past, Bro. Garrison, I have
ı your ever-interesting editorial arm-
ıbrations, strong symptoms of the an-
ck of Macatawa, which never fails to
er you. We have no such lakeside
here to which to transfer the editoral
the Christian Commonwealth, and
we are obliged to be content with
ıl runs to any accessible resort, such
.te or Brighton, or else stay in Lon-
ching the beginning of the exodus of
ople. It is pleasant to hear of the
ural and constructive enterprise of
·-to-be-forgotten and dearly-beloved
. J. Haley. That masterly builder of
nons is, I perceive, designing himself a
est by that lovely lake, the descrip-
vhich from your own pen every summer
.ch romantic reading. If flying-ma-
ready made could only be pursuaded
en I would take passage and alight on
tty shore and enjoy fellowship with
ur retreat. Ever since the old Roman
ıen Ciscero wrote those delicious letters
ıs, telling of the feast of fellowship
culano meo'' (meaning ''in my villa
lum,'' where Lucullus, Horace and
nds who were cultured in all but the
vhich had not yet shown out), it has
delight of men given to processess of
often to retire from the crowded
f life's business. Well, there is one
ich many Americans have discovered.
'e found out that in summer this whole
lled Great Britain is just one paradise
st, sweetest beauty. Going last week to
.am to preach and lecture, and return-
erday, I more than ever admired the
f country of 110 miles, chiefly through
y of the Thames. The whole ride is
one lovely park. As the years roll on,
ntry will become the world's chief
nd. It is never hot and never cold
ı traveling in Europe I have met in-
and cultured people who never saw
, and who are fully persuaded that
see a sunbeam in this country, that
ınd lies steeped in an eternal fog, and
take a walk except with the umbrella
It is perfectly true that our climate
ınd uncertain, and that it does not so
ısist of actual weather as of ''samples
er'' of all sorts, as I heard a genial
ı visitor say. Some of the ''samples''
s agreeable as others, but they are all
nsient and easily forgotten when the
lish spring and summer recur. Just
early morning, with its elongated
, and the late evenings, with their pro-
and delicious twilight, are almost
. There is no country in the world in
'ork is so easy. Nowhere can the
rk so many days in the year and so
urs in the day in perfect comfort. If
et remote Britain should be commer-
ıyed out, if she should lose her great
as a nation, if her decline should fol-
.e course of history, then she will per-
oved and cherished more than in the
ıer wealth and power, for then Eng-
ootland, Wales, Ireland, the Isle of
Scilly Isles, the Channel Islands, the
, the Shetlands, the Orkneys, and all
that make up the group known as the
sles, may be known as the choicest
of the world—the lovely and romantic
les of the modern earth. And the day
d when these island realms will seem
.cans to belong to America rather than
e. For we English people are every
'e and more losing touch with Europe
racting close affinity with America.

JR NEW THEOLOGICAL DIFFICTLTY.

old one. It is ever recurring in some fresh phase. A bill has just passed through the House of Commons called the ''Church Benefices Bill.'' To the American mind it may not seem at first sight as if such a measure could be of great importance. But life in England has been for a thousand years complicated by the appalling problem of a state church. The politics of our country are at this moment plunged into a perfect quagmire by the priests. The government, pushed on against its will by the bishops, has been trying its hand at a pretended reform. Now, the Benefices Bill is to give double power to the bishops over the clergy. It is intended that in future the bishops shall have the option of refusing to induct any clergyman to a parish living if they see reason in his character or conduct for rejecting him. But this bill in one of its clauses perpetuates one of the grossest abuses still existing in the Anglican Church. It forbids the sale of next presentations, but it permits the sale of advowsons. Now, the people, the church itself, who wants to see it reformed, are specially anxious to get rid of the abominable sale of livings, called the purchase of advowsons. It is a very common thing for a parish living to be sold at the auction mart at Tokenhouse yard, where the same auctioneer who has been selling horses, sheep, cattle and houses, then proceeds to crack up a parish in a lively speech, just as he does the sheep and the pigs, and after the competition has proceeded a certain time, at a tap of the hammer the parishioners are sold to the highest bidder precisely like animals. Often the sale is arranged of the next presentation; that is to say, while the minister of a parish is yet alive, the living is put up for sale in advance, the auctioneer in most unblushing manner descants on the probability of the poor incumbent not living much longer. Then the bids go up, till the next presentation is knocked down to the highest bidder. Now, the Benefices Bill has put a stop to this last abuse, but not to the sale of the advowsons. So in one respect the Church of England is worse than the Roman Catholic Church, for Papists glory in the fact that no such thing is permitted as the sale of livings in their communion. There has been a great fight in the British Parliament over this wretched bill, for the Liberals, under the brave leadership of Sir William Harcourt, have opposed the bill in a series of splendid speeches. Although this was in vain, for the Liberals are out of power, and the obstructive and retrogressive Tories are for the time omnipotent, yet these speeches are of immense use in enlightening the public mind.

THE GREAT ROW ABOUT RITUALISM.

All the matters I have been dwelling upon are closely related to the chief of all our present English religious troubles—the advance of Ritualism in the Church of England. A Mr. John Kensit, a well-known publisher in Paternoster Row, London, some months ago boldly stepped forward in his own parish church and publicly rebuked his clergyman for the Romish rights which had been introduced into the communion service. This led to a riot, some people trying to push Mr. Kensit out of the church, and others trying to defend him. He has been repeating his protest at several such churches, and was taken to the police court after one of these occasion, by order of the clergy. But the result is that he has gained immense sympathy, and has produced a great awakening to what is going on. The Roman mass and the confessional are now practiced in about two thousand of our Protestant churches, and the bishops have quietly allowed things to drift, many of them being themselves High Churchmen, if not incipient Romanists. Mr. Kensit has been the means of constraining the Bishop of London, Dr. Creighton, to send out a circular to his clergy. He should have done this long before, and now that he has taken this step, the circular is devoid of emphasis, and is so colorless as to give Kensit is now raising a fund for a very peculiar object. He is threatening to go to work to begin a Second Reformation, by sending out, two by two, what he calls ''Wickliffite poor preachers.'' Students of the Reformation will remember that John Wickliffe, the pioneer of Protestantism, sent forth from his parish of Lutterworth in Leicestershire, in the middle of England, bands of poor preaching friars, in couples, and these scattered the truth up and down the land. Mr. Kensit means well, but he does not seem to know that there is a more excellent Reformation alread started. Perhaps we may yet enlighten him.

HANDEL HALL, CHELTENHAM.

It has been my privilege to pay another visit to our friends at Cheltenham who, by the kindness of our indefatigable brethren, J. and F. Coop, have been able at last, after long years of patient waiting, to secure a sanctuary for their own exclusive use. Ever since the cause was founded by the pioneering effort of our old evangelist, H. S. Earl, the work has been located in the public hall known as the Corn Exchange, but recently an opportunity was afforded of purchasing on tempting terms an excellent building which had been used as a musical college. Handel Hall, as it was appropriately named, is a structure capable of accommodating 500 worshipers. It is attractive in aspect, is splendidly situated in the heart of the town, has a fine series of class-rooms, is easy to speak in and is altogether what is wanted for the progress of the cause. Brother and Sister Bates, who it will be remembered came to take up this work, after long residence in Australia, are very hopeful of the influence which this new departue will exercise on the history of the church. I do not think that in all my experience I ever knew of the acquisition of a building on such advantageous terms as those involved in the purchase of this Handle Hall. There will now be a better outlook for the friends at Cheltenham.

W. DURBAN.

43 Park Rd., South Tottenham, London, Eng., July 1, 1898.

Wheeling through England.

A rainy Sunday at sea, a rainy Monday off the north coast of Ireland, and then we land at Liverpool on a rainy Tuesday morning. The immediate outlook for cycling is not brilliant, but one of the rules already laid down is that everything is to be enjoyed. Remembering this, we comment upon the beauty of all rain and the special beauty of this particular shower. Then we go out and get wet in it. It seems rather an ominous indication of a moist climate that nearly every other shop on the first street we ascend displays waterproof goods in the windows. It seems as if half the population earned its living by keeping the other half dry. I have since learned that this is a slight overestimate of the importance of the mackintosh industry in England, but my conviction of its magnitude remains. In the course of a nine weeks' tour in any civilized land one is sure to have a variety of weather, and some of it wet. If we start with the worst the next change must be for the better. On the basis of such sage considerations as these we determined to make the start at once. Mounting our wheels early in the afternoon we rode out of Liverpool in a torrent of rain, and down the road toward Manchester. It was a delightful ride of twenty-five miles, between stone walls and hedges, and through series of Lancashire villages so closely set that one never knows whether he is really in town or country. Our wheels and ourselves were candidates for a Turkish bath, but after all it was not so bad. Our waterproof capes had served us well, and the wheels, after a good grooming, were none the worse. The start had been made, and the stop that first night was at a typical English inn.

The typical English inn is an institution

To begin with its virtues, it is, if it is good enough to deserve to be called typical, scrupulously clean. It is quaint, queer and cozy. Your wants are attended to promptly and respectfully, even if you order anything so extraordinary and un-English as a glass of cold water with your meals or a cup of coffee for your breakfast, the maid endeavors, though usually without success, to suppress her astonishment. Nowhere does the "local color" seem to be applied more freely than at a good inn. But the dark side of it all lies in the fact that the inn is generally a saloon as well as a hotel. Frequently the latter function becomes insignificant by the side of the former. Many inns have no provision for entertaining travelers over night, and in almost all of them the chief source of revenue is the tap-room. Here may be seen the gloomier side of English rural life, the curse of intemperance. At the same time one need not overlook the value of the inn, and especially its tap-room, as a social center and forum for the interchange of ideas. This unpleasant side of the English inn (which, by the way, is also a characteristic of the hotels of small towns in many parts of our own country and Canada) has given rise to a system of temperance hotels, always clean, quiet and respectable, but never anything but commonplace and uninteresting in themselves.

Wednesday morning we rode on into Manchester. Just how or why it happened, neither of us has been able to make out, but we were certainly the objects of more popular attention during the three hours which we spent in that city than often falls to the lot of two modest cyclists. Perhaps it was the mere fact that we were bicycle tourists, for that is something which can never be concealed; perhaps it was the fact that we had American wheels, for every one seems to recognize an American wheel at a glance; perhaps it was the color of the wheels, for my companion's was blue and mine was green (you know the Sterling color), while nearly all English wheels are black. At any rate, the people of Manchester seemed to consider the case well worthy of consideration. If we left the wheels at the curb while we entered a shop, the sidewalk and half of the street were immediately blocked by a curious crowd. If one of us staid by the wheels, they eyed him, too, as if he were a creature of supra- (or sub-) terrestial origin. Not a question was asked, not an intelligent glance directed at any part of the outfit—just a steady, stupid, brazen stare. At first I essayed to photograph the crowd gathered about the two wheels, but no sooner was the kodak unfolded than the crowd, catching sight of it, at once moved over bodily and joined in solid phalanx again about me and the camera. That put a stop to the hope of photographing the scene. Then we went into council and devised a plan to disconcert and abash our observers. The next time we stopped the crowd gathered as usual, and we were in the center of it. The crowd gazed stolidly at us, the inner circle being about at arm's length. Thereupon we leaned upon our wheels and proceeded to discuss the peculiarities of the various individuals about us, in a good, sonorous tone. The color of their hair, the cut of their clothes, the style of their boots and their various individual characteristics of physique, gesture, gait and garb were thoroughly gone over in their hearing. Some left when they saw that they were under fire. More staid, though with evident signs of embarrassment. Still more were absolutely untouched. As a means of ridding ourselves of a crowd of impertinent gazers, it had to be admitted that the scheme was a failure, and it is my conviction still that nothing less imperative than artillery would be able to disperse a crowd of Manchester gazers. It is but fair to add, in justice both to ourselves and the English people, that nowhere else has our appearance been greeted in this fashion.

From Manchester our route lay southwest through a corner of Cheshire and that portion of Derbyshire known as the Peak District. It is our first view of English hills. What else England may have in store for us we cannot tell, but if there is nothing finer than the hills and valleys of Derbyshire all our hopes will still be realized. A road like a park boulevard winds in and out, up to the hilltop, then down to the valley. Finally, after a steady climb for eight miles, followed by a swoop into the valley, a descent of five hundred feet in a mile and a half, we reach the town of Buxton, the highest town of England, and one of the chief inland watering-places. For us it is chiefly valuable as a halting-place for the night and the starting-point for the still more delightful ride through the very heart of the Peak District. Aside from the beauty of the scenery, two points stand out vividly in this day. They are our visits to Chatsworth, the home of the Duke of Devonshire, and to Haddon Hall, an uninhabited but well preserved baronial mansion of mediæval times. The description of these two noble houses is far beyond my power and scope. It is enough to say that one represents the utmost of magnificence in present-day architecture (the house is only two hundred years old), floriculture and landscape gardening, while the other carries us back five centuries to the days when every noble Englishman's house must indeed be his castle, or he would soon have no house at all. It is pertinent at this point to remark upon the generous spirit which moves the Duke of Devonshire to throw open his park, which is nine miles in circumference, his gardens, which are a piece of fairy land, and a large part of the mansion for the free inspection and amusement of the public.

Passing Derby, we leave the region of the hills and soon enter the less picturesque but more historic county of Warwick. Coventry is a singular compound of heterogeneous elements, the old and the new. One may wander for hours among its narrow, crooked streets, meeting at every turn some sight worthy of being photographed. In fact, it is a most tempting spot for the snap-shot artist. Only one of a thousand interesting objects is Ford's Hospital, an ancient monastery of the Gray Friars, in 1529 converted to more righteous uses as a home for old ladies. The building is much older, a timbered structure of quaint design, part of which dates from the fourteenth century. What can we say of Kenilworth Castle that has not already been better said? Since Scott's Kenilworth the castle has become first and foremost the scene of the royal romance of which the leading characters were Queen Elizabeth, the Earl of Leicester and Amy Robsart. The road to Warwick is full of interest, but we must hasten, for a storm is upon us. At last we are driven for shelter to the most beautiful spot on the road, the old Saxon mill, from which there is a charming view of Guy's Cliff, a baronial residence of much interest, across the Avon. Even the rain, the cyclist's most unrelenting foe, has for this once done us a good turn. But English showers, if frequent, are also short, and we are soon in Warwick. The Prince of Wales is visiting at the castle, and we cannot enter. So, we ride on, for we are to pass this way again in a day or two. We ride into Stratford-on-Avon just at dusk on Saturday night, and here we are prepared to spend the Sunday and as many more days as need be in absorbing the atmosphere of this place.

W. E. GARRISON.

Stratford-on-Avon.

Kansas City Letter.

The few brief weeks that have elapsed since the beginning of our war with Spain have been full of surprises, not alone for the enemy, but for ourselves, and for the whole civilized world. Two such naval victories as those of Manila and Santiago are without precedent in history. Not in the fact of the sweeping defeat of Spain, but in the almost entire escape of the attacking fleets from injury to ships and men. Despite the brave and bitter struggle of the Spanish vessels, and the rain of shot and shell that fell upon the American vessels, not one of our ships was even seriously injured, and but one man killed. No wonder that brave Capt. Philip, of the Texas, after the battle of Santiago, called all hands to the quarter deck of his vessel, and with bared head thanked God for the almost bloodless victory saying, "I want to make public acknowledgement here that I believe in God, the Father Almighty. I want all you officers and men to lift your hats and from your hearts to offer silent thanks to the Almighty." The silence that followed must have been full of deep significance to the brave men, who with brows bared to the winds of heaven thus gave their recognition of the hand of God in the victory they had just achieved. Nor is it surprising that President McKinley should proclaim a national thanksgiving for the manifest providence that has attended our arms during this unhappy strife. It is but a symptom of the national feeling that we are warring on the side of right, and that our success means the enlargement of the kingdom of God among men.

But we must not press this truth of divine providence too far. To suppose that God himself directed the shells from our guns so as to make them strike the fatal spot, while he turned aside those of the enemy, and made them harmless, would be going farther than either reason or revelation would warrant us, though doubtless there are some who have about such a crude conception of the divine process. While it is *not* true, as Napoleon is reported to have said, that God is on the side of the strongest battalion, it is not safe for us to conclude that he will be on the side of the weaker one, even though its cause be just. There was perhaps never a war in which the right was more uniformly on one side and wrong on the other, than in the struggle of the Netherlands against Spain, in the sixteenth and seventeenth centuries. Philip II. and his successors were always in the wrong, their motives fairly Satanic, being none other than the stifling of conscience, the destroying of liberty and the burial of virtue beneath an avalanche of vice. The Protestants of the Netherlands were the most intelligent and virtuous of Philip's subjects, yet they were the objects of his cruelty during all the long years of his reign. Why was it that these intelligent and virtuous Protestants were defeated, in a majority of instances, by their superstitious and cruel enemies? Why were such awful tragedies as those at the sieges of Haarlem, Zutphen and Antwerp permitted? Why should the right be ground beneath the heel of wrong? Sometimes the superiority of force was on the side of one party, and sometimes the other. Was it because God withheld his hand from aiding his people? If so, why should we claim his assistance now? Are we better than the martyrs of the Netherlands?

The careful student of history will find a solution of such questions in the rational view of the divine providence, which takes into account not alone the readiness of God to aid his people, but the willingness of his people to receive and profit by his aid. In the historic example referred to, it is the saddest fact of all the sad history of the Netherland struggle, that the leader whom God raisee up for their deliverance, William the Silent, pleaded in vain for such co-operation among the oppressed states of the republic as would have made them invincible by the king. It was the lack of ıong the states that made them weak, selfishness and treachery of many of ›uld-be leaders helped on the cause of pressors.

› present conflict with Spain we have us far victorious, chiefly because we ɔt been deaf to the voice of God in the ɔne by, but have followed the path of ın civilization, while Spain has tarried athless jungle of barbarism. For this her feet are tangled in the toils of her ɑorance and superstition, and she is ying the penalty of her own willful ss. This is a contest of civilization rbarism, of typical Protestantism with Romanism, and it is inevitable that ner should win. Were it otherwise we be forced to question the very laws of ole universe, and deny the necessary between cause and effect. We are d for our marvelous success to the an faith and life of our fathers, which sulted in the quick intelligence, sturdy ty and steadfast courage so gloriously ectively displayed in the course of our e and swiftly conquering war. That a traitor to his country who, in the face simple yet wonderful lessons of these would turn the hearts of our people ·om that Christ whose holy religion has ɔossible such victories in behalf of the ·ed. Colonel Ingersoll ought to find his :ion gone, so long as the memory of and Santiago shall endure.

W. F. RICHARDSON.

as City, Mo., July 3, 1898.

Myrick vs. Willett.

that is first in his own cause seemeth ut his neighbor cometh and searcheth

an's gift maketh room for him, and th him before great men.''

gravamen in this issue so impresses me ›ut me into the critical arena, with the hat justice may not thereby temporarily The straight charge of blasphemy, made t any one, is certainly shocking.

constituents of blasphemy are the ily speaking or writing damaging, ɔptuous, foul words, expressive of such ʒs against God, Jesus Christ or the Ghost.

ıight be a fine point among critics, er this crime can be legitimately uttered intelligent man against a man. But if it applied, and associated with the Holy , the blasphemy against whom hath never eness, either in this world or in the come, surely then to pronounce against the most reckless character this most :ul malediction is bitter, indeed; but ıo against a man of fair fame and Chris- rofession, is quite far below the humane, say the Christian sensibility.

k at this thrilling, chilling, perdition- ʒning epithet, applied to the CHRISTIAN-ᵹELIST Bible-school lesson teacher! utside the writings of avowed skeptics ch a blasphemous statement be parallel-

ıristians believe Paul to have been in- by the Holy Spirit, and to them this ıtion will seem perilously near blasphem- e Holy Ghost,'' says Mr. Myrick, of Mr. :t. What was the accusation? This: Athens Paul felt so embarrassed as to he vital part of the message and trimmed ory to please his audience,'' said Mr. :t. If Paul did those things he had what ought to be justifiable reasons for doing Ie was an expert casuist, and has given evidences of that ability. Mr. Myrick ''If Paul did as Professor Willett says he 'aul was guilty of intellectual and moral dice.'' Possible? What other kinds of ıesty than intellectual and moral dis- ty are there? Mr. Myrick should have ɔy one of Paul's statements, which he M.) quotes, how Paul *qualified* his method of preaching: ''I kept back nothing that was *profitable* for them''—befitting, appropriate. On Mars' Hill Paul preached about the unknown God, and the resurrection from the dead, but omitted anything about the atonement. He thought that course profitable for his hearers, as it proved to be. Was he thereby guilty of anything? Although I need not to say anything pro or con. about Paul's course, as the criticism is upon Myrick and Willett, I may say, *en passant*, that Paul possessed that rare and valuable gift of nature which we call tact, which in the hand of its possessor is as potent as the fabled wand, or lamp, or shield, which so many coveted, but had no ability to obtain. Some persons know at a glance the befitting thing to be said or done, see the salient or the weak point, adjust the means to the end, gauge the calibre and fit the conditions for easy accomplishment of the foreseen result. Others blunder along in a hit-and-miss manner, producing effects contrary to all they intended, irritating where they designed to please and end as if they only meant to beat the air. They intended to produce great and good effects, but did only what the feeblest can do. Mr. Myrick asks, ''How does Bro. Willett know that Luke reported every word Paul spoke in Mars' Hill? Luke gives presumably but an abstract of that sermon. To charge Paul with omitting the vital part of the gospel because Luke did not report all he said, speaks poorly for the critic's discernment.'' If so, does Prof. Willett's critic not also ''discern'' that himself imagines an element into his own fabric which may topple it? ''Paul was inspired by the Holy Ghost.'' Was Luke inspired thus? ''Luke gave a mere abstract of a sermon,'' not written on the spot, given from memory, awhile after, by a non-inpsired man. An abstract is an epitomized, contracted account, drawn off by the mind apart; an account by another, a hearer of a discourse, the reporter not inspired, and in any way only abstractly making a synopsis of a discourse.

Thus we have, according to Mr. Myrick, only an abstract by a non-inspired man of Paul's transactions by Luke. This wonderfully lightens the anathema of blasphemy on Prof. Willett ''against the Holy Ghost.'' He can easily bear the stigma of being afflicted with ''an abnormal imagination.'' Notwithstanding all this Mr. Myrick is much agitated because of a sentiment he affirms ''is already wide-spread and still increasing, that the columns of the CHRISTIAN-EVANGELIST would serve its own and God's interests better by being sent out blank than by being filled with Prof. Willett's expositions of Bible-school lessons.''

This sounds quite excathedra, and is therefore out of the reach of criticism. I might suggest that the Editor and the Professor, with Mr. Myrick, should compose that triumvirate of investigation. Outsiders can but await finalities. I wish to say here that the chief personal motive I have in appearing on this evidently important issue is that I have been much interested and pleased with Prof. Willett's instructions as given in the CHRISTIAN-EVANGELIST, and glad that the Bible-schools were having prepared an appetite for the guileless milk of the Word by so judicious and gentle a feeder of them as Prof. Willett. I have had a desire to know him personally.

Hypercriticism is a perversion of criticism, which must end in a series of misfitting, meaningless jumbles of factitious attempts at putting opposites together. Your critic makes a batch of statements and then lumps them up thus: ''This charge is not a new one. It was born of Rationalism and pseudo-Christianity.'' etc. Pseudo-Christianity is as far from Christianity as any counterfeit thing is far from the true thing. There can be no such thing as a counterfeit dollar. There can be a counterfeit of a dollar, but it is not a dollar.

Rationalism is and always should be associated only with rational things. Never with anything *pseudo—lying—false—counterf* There is a good deal of mental pseudobleps false, deceptive mental vision; and beca of that condition, ''rationalism'' has b very often put in bad company by *pseu* theologians, rather theologasters, who pı of their creeds as slaves prate of their mast

Rationalism relates to reason and reas ing, and is the art and science of reasoning is the opposite of the irrational, the n reasoning, the unreasonable, the absu Did Paul ever disparage rationalism? Di ever intimate that Christianity was irratioı What part of that faith did he not pass thro the alembic of his reason? The man who a creed which leads him to fling sneers ''rationalism'' will not edify his hear but he will do for them a far worse thing t rationalize them. He will never make gı men tremble by the might of his reasoni but he may make the superstitious trem for fear of their omnipotent Friend instea showing them how to know God, who is lc by learning how to love God. There is ''counterfeit Christianity.'' There are m counterfeits of Christianity, as there are most other good things. But the counterf do not pass among rational people as th good things. Who now has any confidenc ''a profession of religion'' which any may make of being a Christian? Indeed, should they, if they know that there is but test for that profession, and that test rational one given by the Christ of Christian Jesus put no stigma upon reason, but exalted it, challenging every one ''of t ownselves to judge what is right.''

Alas for the many, and many of those high places, too, who do not seem to be abl judge what is right! They lack compreh siveness, they can run a line for a space, do not scope the periphery. Yes, ''the CH TIAN-EVANGELIST is a beautiful paper. . It easily stands at the front among our peri cals,'' as Mr. Myrick says of it. And fact made me nauseate at the nondescript of foul stuff Mr. Myrick dumped into i grewsome juxtaposition with Prof. Willett, Rev. Dr. Lyman Abbott, of New Y ''It was born of Rationalism and pse Christianity, and surreptitiously deposite the public doorsteps by Lyman Abbott a months ago. It seems that H. L. Wi discovered the spawn and was so enamor it that he immediately adopted the miseı foundling and is trying to install it in household of faith.'' Doubtless Mr. My views that as a masterly piece of caricatu two ''pseudo-Christians.'' Many of readers will see in it an attempt to coar even disgustingly, to abuse two educated refined Christian gentlemen.

Dr. Abbott has a high national and ii national repute for literary attainment, as a Bible commentator. He is an speaker, an eloquent man, ''who talks on,'' never blundering, clear as the trut sees and leads his hearers to see. As ge modest and sensitive as a well-bred youth is as serious and impressive as a Qua They are delighted to have him lecture to t as he did in Philadelphia and elsewhere the Bible. Of this theme and of himsel says: ''The one object and ambition of life is first, to understand the message of Bible, and secondly, to communicate message to others; to understand the one eminent life in which that message culmin —the life of Jesus Christ—and then appl principles and the spirit of this book oı lection of books, this ancient literature, interpreter of God, to the affairs of huma political, social, industrial, individu Now, who will elevate himself in the est tion of respectable people by attempting any way smirch that man? What impre can a tirade of fuming, bitter persiflage sardonic sneers have upon him?

Dr. Abbott is as keen as a Damascus t in criticism. He is as instructive in it as

widely informed, and as ready to learn, either by unlearning, or by learning, as when he was a boy. A man of that makeup will not die of inanity, as he is sure he does not know it all. Job taught him to speak to the earth, and God taught him to speak to himself. Thus God and this world and all worlds and all that in them is, are his teachers, and he is a willing, receptive pupil, and like him, let us all go to school. A stranger friend just writes me from New York, "Let discussion go on, clear, keen, correctly, in the spirit of truth and love, and the truth will ever come to the top." The great Paul said, "We can do nothing against the truth, but for the truth. Not that we should appear approved, but that we should do what is honest, though we be esteemed reprobates." Reprobation is one of the results pioneers for truth should look for from those who think there are no truths to be discovered. "The judgment of God is according to truth." "I will say the truth, but now forbear lest any should think of me other than that he see me to be, or that he heareth of me." JOSEPH H. MACEL'REY.

Trainer, Pa., Box 596, July 4, 1898.

Pittsburgh Letter.

The Pittsburgh brethren are very proud of the initial appearance of the CHRISTIAN-EVANGELIST in its new dress and form. It is now the neatest and most desirable of the many religious publications that come to this city. Your scribe placed the Interior, Independent, Presbyterian Banner and the CHRISTIAN-EVANGELIST side by side, and said to a practical printer, not of our brotherhood, he not knowing the object of the question, "Which do you consider the best paper from a typographical view-point?" After a rather close examination he said: "This," pointing to the CHRISTIAN-EVANGELIST. Of the subject-matter, in the paper, one can only express high praise. The subscription list ought to roll up now as never before.

A spirit of joyful optimism seems prevalent among the brethren in and around these two cities of Allegheny and Pittsburgh. It does one's heart good to hear the glowing reports of the successful work accomplished, brought in by the preachers, at their meetings. "Souls for the Master," seems to be the keynote of their work, hot weather or cold. Each preacher seems to be a bundle of concentrated consecration.

After a very successful work at Homestead, Bro. E. A. Hibbler closes his work there August first. Two years ago when he entered the work he found a body of Disciples fifty-eight in number; now there are one hundred and seventy on the roll. The debt has been arranged for through the Extension Society, and the new man as he comes on the field, whoever he may be, will find things in good condition for work.

Very recently Brother Craig of the Belleview Church took the confession of ten children. The parents of these belonged in quite a number of instances to other churches, but so thoroughly were the children grounded in "the doctrine" learned in the Junior C. E., that refusals could not be considered. It was a beautiful sight at the baptism of these "little ones," and will be long remembered.

Bro. Thurgood, the energetic, at Central, has blossomed out as a full-fledged poet. Brother Thurgood's great work is among the children. He believes, and rightly too, that the best door-bell to a man's heart is his child's love. The children going home from the Bible-school and kindergarten tell of the love of Jesus as they sit on their papas' knee, and out of that Thurgood makes this "poem:"

"My papa's knee's a pulpit,
And I am papa's preacher,
My papa prays as I do pray,
And loves to heed his teacher."

A large number of men and women, led by a little child, have witnessed the good confession at Central, proving the value of work among children.

One of the novelties of the hour presented by the war is the sight of the stars and stripes floating gayly from the upper story of the Catholic priests residence on Norwood Avenue, Allegheny. We have seen a great many flags flying from many houses in many cities, but this is the first we had noticed flying from a priest's. Of course he has a right to fly it, no one denies that, but——

Pittsburgh being the center of the iron and steel activity of the United States, the war has set in motion a great amount of new business; and, by the way, we hear very little nowadays about the inferior steel armor with which our ships were supposed to be clad. At any rate it seems strong enough to withstand Spanish shells and shots.

The following churches near here are without pastors or soon will be Duquesnes, Homestead, Johnson, McKeesport. All of them good openings for the right man.

The Western Pennsylvania Christian Missionary Society is looking for a first-class evangelist to work in this very prolific field.

The pastor of the Observatory Hill Church is reading chapter by chapter an original story, entitled David McAlister, at the midweek prayer-meeting. The attendance of young people and older ones has increased as a result.

JOHN A. JAYNE.

No. 1, Chester Ave., Allegheny, Pa.

Texas Letter.

The following lines are said to be found in Byron's Bible:

"Within this awful volume lies
The mystery of mysteries;
Oh, happiest they of human race
To whom our God has given grace
To hear, to read, to fear, to pray;
To lift the latch and force the way.
But better had they ne'er been born
Who read to doubt, or read to scorn."

Rev. Louis Albert Banks, Cleveland, O., a leading Methodist preacher, is the author of these strong words: "Many of you who hear me know enough about Christ and the gospel to be saved, but you wait and wait, as though you expected some flood of supernatural influence would rise about you and sweep you off your feet and carry you against your will into the kingdom. You may be very sure that such a thing will never happen. If it should it would do you no good, for it would not change your character. The first move must come from you. God has done everything he can do for your salvation, until you yourself act in obedience to him. The reason you do not move is because you are chained by your sins. You must break those chains so far as to accept Christ, or you will be lost forever. You are like boats fastened to the shore—there is no use pulling at the oars until the chain is unfastened."

Quite a number of small-bore skeptics should study the following utterances of Prof. Tyndall: "While I make the largest demand for free investigation; while I, as a man of science, feel a natural pride in scientific achievements; while I regard science as the most powerful instrumentality of intellectual culture, as well as the most powerful ministrant to the material wants of man; still, if you ask me whether science has solved or is likely to solve the problem of the universe, I must shake my head in doubt."

B. H. Carroll, of Waco, who stands in the front rank of the Baptist ministry, has this to say about the tongue: "The tongue is a little member, but it is set on fire of hell. The mighty boa-constrictor, crushing into pulp the bones of the bison, can be tamed. That rattlesnake in the hollow of the rocks in Western mountains, whose awful warning, whose basilisk look, and whose deadly venom make him so feared, can be tamed. That Bengal tiger, with green, glaring eyes and yellow fangs, that howling Numidian lion, whose roar shakes the forest, can be tamed. You eagle, whose eyrie has never been reached by the shaft of the bowman or the ball of the rifleman, whose wings cleave space, and whose undazzled eye looks into the glory of the face of the sun, he can be tamed. But the tongue can no man tame. Yet God keeps an account of everything it says."

These brave words, reminding us of Saul of Tarsus, are from Ellsworth Faris, a Texas boy who, with Dr. Biddle, is leading the vanguard of our missionaries into Darkest Africa. Speaking of their return from a tour of observation, he says: "When we returned here to Texas, we learned of the death of Mrs. Schrivner, a dear woman of the Baptist Society of Bolsbo. Of the missionaries we have met, five have died since we came. However, none of us came to the Congo for a health resort, and *if duty says I should die in Africa, I should be ashamed to be alive in America.*" (Italics mine.)

There are other heroes besides Dewey and Hobson. Not that I would take one leaf from the garlands which they so deservedly wear, but I would like for us not to overlook those in other fields, just as daring and deserving. Neither would I have us forget that heroism like that of Paul still dwells among the children of men.

M. Demolius, a Frenchman, editor La Science Sociale, has written a book on a living question: 'Anglo-Saxon Superiority. Here is the way he talks: "It is useless to deny the superiority of the Anglo-Saxon. We may be vexed by this superiority, but the fact remains despite our vexation. We cannot go anywhere without meeting Englishmen. Over all our possessions of former times the English or the United States flag now floats. The Anglo-Saxon has supplanted us in North America, which we occupied from Canada to Louisiana; in Mauritius, once called the Isle of France; in Egypt. He dominates America by Canada and the United States; Africa by Egypt and the Cape; Asia by India and Burma; Oceanica by Australia and New Zealand; Europe and the entire world by his commerce, industry and politcs. The Anglo-Saxon world is to-day at the head of that civilization which is most active, most progressive and most devouring. Let this race establish itself anywhere on the globe, and at once there is introduced with prodigious rapidity the latest progress of our Western societies, and often the young societies surpass us. Observe what we Frenchmen have done with New Caledonia and our other possessions in Oceanica and what the Anglo-Saxons have done in Australia and New Zealand. Observe what Spain and Portugal have made of South America and what the Anglo-Saxons have made of North America. There is as much difference as between night and day."

Fifteen years ago we had, practically, no navy. To-day we have one which commands the respect of the world. A naval officer, speaking of the first period, says: "A sense of humiliation dogged the American naval officer as he went about his duty in foreign lands. In the far East, in the lesser countries along the Mediterranean Sea, and even in the seaports of South America, people smiled patronizingly upon him, and from a sense of politeness avoided speaking of naval subjects in his presence. None but naval officers and a few Americans who happened to be abroad comprehend just how insignificant and cheap the great republic appeared in the eyes of the world." But Dewey at Manila, and Sampson and Schley at Santiago de Cuba, have turned the tide, and the smile of contempt has given place to the bow of respect. And well it may, for to say nothing of other parts of the navy, we now have afloat four great battleships, the "Indiana," "Massachusetts," "Iowa" and "Oregon;" two others, the "Kentucky" and the "Kearsarge" will soon join them; three more, the "Alabama," the "Illinois" and the "Wisconsin," are half finished, and three others have been authorized. And all this in

YEARS. Similar
h and the world
cross.
M. M. DAVIS.
'ex.

—

one hundred and
or almost a cen-
f this month has
of our national
se national days
1776, 1863, 1898.
y is never to be
sconsin town, we
ily, knowing that
n the balance at
On the fifth we
I shall proba-
ly like '63 or '98.
of untold genera-
traced backward

ex, of Des Moines,
d Abe," the war
Wisconsin—the
l scarred by three
ptation has been
was a Wisconsin
Indian boy. cap-
the tall pine tree
; I was living in
blue secured him
ont, I knew many
Visconsin. After
side in a lumber
carried Old Abe's
e fight and on the
rave Eighth Wis-
iave seemed more
Why have I yielded
e I spoken? These
eal the philosophy

Vinthrop, whom to

nore pure,
or of saint."
derwood Johnson.

! an *honest* book."
CHRISTIAN-EVAN-
, col. 3, b? This
Saint (Mormon).
one honest book?
. Williams, their
a dishonest man
e 30th, p. 408, col.
book? How can
d glass know the
, it is said, cries,
nfuse his pursuers
his Iowa Mormon
ot D. H. Bays a
his book, "Doc-
ormonism," more
s club? If it is so
gitive insinuates,
. Lambert refuse
et D. H. Bays at
VANGELIST, June
ysician (Mark 16:

Drake University,
r orators. Other
rant of his powers
age comes to me
Ia.: "Prof. Ott
rapes—before the
. It exceeded any-
ard, according to
blic. Everybody

work done by the
g is in Dennison,
e county-seat town
have been hither-
iere. There are a
nd near the town

These, with J. J. Nicholson, pastor at Union, discovered a contract for the sale of two lots on easy terms. The contract lacked but two lots on easy terms. It was a bargain not to be missed. All money needed for the first payment except $75 was raised on the spot. One member of the State Board advanced the shortage and the purchase was made. Already 50 feet of the rear ends of these lots has brought us an offer of $500, leaving us a building site 100x110. These lots are the choicest in town. They are in the same block with the residence of Gov. Shaw. His corner faces south and east; ours south and west. A tabernacle and a meeting is the next step. This week Secretary Haggard will send out to every Iowa church, known as a contributor to mission work of any kind, special literature on the state work. The Iowa board expects this year an offering from *every one of these churches*. Read what he says and respond. Here is a condensed report of the Brainard meeting, which began June 5th,—7, 23, 26, 38, 41, 45, 52, 57, 60. This is new ground. House and lot in sight. And this is but *one* out of many places we are working.

Two Iowa books will soon be from the press of the Christian Index, of Des Moines. One by John M. Van Kirk on Seventh-Day Adventism and its issues; the other, "Doctrine and Duty," a volume of sermons and addresses by Iowa preachers. G. L. Brokaw, editor of the Index, assumes the responsibilities of the publication of this book.

The Iowa State Board will arrange a series of meetings for any good evangelist in the land, unless the demand is insufficient. It is now arranging a series for Jas. Small, of California, another for Benj. F. Hill, of Missouri, and one for G. W. Elliott, of Dakota. We are expecting to do so for R. A. Omer and D. A. Hunter and D. C. Kellams and others. Write A. M. Haggard, 206 4th St., Des Moines.

H. L. Willett and his Missouri critic: I do not like Prof. Willett's interpretation of Paul, and I doubt the method of his critic. I like an intense, positive, frank spirit. But is it wise to give our brethren an occasion to play successfully the role of a martyr. Prof. Willett is too sensible to do that, but others are not. Is it scriptural to think of "censorship?" Aside from Christ and the Holy Spirit, who is wise enough to do it profitably? Is not the censorship of the Holy Spirit in the Bible a geography of free speech—showing almost unbounded latitude and longitude for the utterance of both truth and *error?* What is the best thing ever done with an objectionable doctrine? Was it not to allow it statement—separate it from its author—examine it exhaustively upon its own merits, and leave it a monument in history? What is the worst thing to do with such a doctrine? Is it not to drag a good man down to the supposed level of a bad doctrine—to forget his goodness and magnify his mistake—to thus misrepresent the man to strangers and earn the dislike of his friends—and thus to change the issues of the battle from the doctrine to the man—and in the end leave many convinced that since the man is good the doctrine is also good, and since the opponents of the doctrine are unfair to the man, they have been also with the doctrine? Is not this the way to perpetuate false doctrine? And where in the Bible is there precept or divine example for it? Fire a bullet into the thick of my body beyond the reach of the physician's probe and note the result. My flesh will treat it more wisely than Christian churches often treat a supposed heretic. A surgeon is not always absolutely essential. Freedom is not panic. Nor is freedom flabbiness. Let us learn freedom in Christ Jesus.

A. M. HAGGARD.

Letter From Mr. Moody.

TO THE EDITOR—*Dear Friend:* Every day of the history of the war tends to confirm me in the opinion that Dr. Dixon was right when he said that he believed the church had an opportunity for reaching men with the gospel such as might not come again in this generation.

Many circumstances combine to make this true, but one of the most striking things is the fact that the Spirit of God is already moving wondrously in the army camps. The fields are white already to harvest and he is leading the reapers out into them. Upon a recent Sabbath at Chickamauga, upwards of 500 men confessed Christ as their Savior for the first time. Dr. Torrey, of Chicago, who was there preaching at the time, wrote me the next day: "I never saw anything like the marvelous work going on here. There is a revival all over the camp. Men break down and cry like children." One of the other workers wrote at the same time: "The work at this place is simply wonderful. Never have I seen men so anxious for the gospel. Testimonies are coming to us day by day of the influence of the meetings upon the men. A few nights since, a man who had been at the meeting became wonderfully convicted, and about eleven o'clock called for the guard and asked him to bring the chaplain. The guard tried to talk him out of it, but he kept it up until one o'clock when the chaplain was called, and in a short time the man was rejoicing in the Lord Jesus. It would make your hearts rejoice to hear the testimonies of the men before their comrades." Another writes: "One night last week a fine-looking young man from Wisconsin got up at the close of the meeting and said: 'Boys, I came on these grounds as tough a case as ever walked. My father is a

Presbyterian minister and my mother is a God-fearing woman; but I paid no attention to them while I was at home. The night before last I came to the meeting and I accepted Christ as my personal Savior, and now I want to confess him.' '' I might give other similar incidents, but these will be sufficient to show that the fields in our army camps are ready for the reapers.

Now we cannot expect that those who are not themselves Christians will be much moved by such facts as these. Christians must realize that *this* work is distinctively *their* work. *They* are the ones to whom God has committed the Word of reconciliation. *They* are the ones who will be deeply moved by the thought that many of our brave soldier and sailor boys are not ready to die. *They* are the ones who know that the indwelling Holy Spirit can keep men from falling into sin even in the midst of terrible temptations. *They* are the ones who know that Christ can give men perfect peace in the midst of fiercest turmoil. *Those who know these things must do this work* or *it will remain undone*.

God is not calling thus loudly upon his people in vain. From every direction are coming evidences that the church is alive to this opportunity. I wish space permitted me to give extracts from some letters I have been receiving with contributions.

The President sent out his proclamation calling upon us to join in thanksgiving to God for the victories of our forces by land and sea, and we have gladly responded. Shall we not be as faithful in praising God for the wonderful victories of grace among the troops? The government is taxing us to pay the expenses of the war. We are paying them without a murmur, and shall we not just as willingly tax ourselves to carry on the battles of our Lord and Master? Yours sincerely,

D. L. MOODY.

East Northfield, Mass., July 9, 1898.

Minnesota.

The annual convention at Mankato, Tuesday, August 23rd to August 26th inclusive.

T. A. Meredith, the new pastor at Howard Lake, is in a meeting with excellent prospects, there having been eight confessions to June 18th.

E. J. Sias, pastor at Antelope Hills, writes: "Regarding our prospective meeting at Canby (Canby is the railroad station of Antelope Hills, five miles to the southward, and a town of eight hundred population), we have been keeping right after H. W. Elliott, of Dakota, till we have engaged him. Have the meeting well advertised and hope for a glorious time, beginning July 10th. Rejoice with us and pray for us."

Carey E. Morgan, of the Minneapolis church (there is but one church in this city of 200,000 population save two Scandinavian missions; take heed, O ye national boards), began his fifth year of service Lord's day June 19th, surrounded by a loyal and beloved brotherhood. In Bro. Morgan's four years' pastorate there have been 300 additions, leaving the present membership 450; and $20,000 have been raised and expended. The Bible-school has an enrollment of 200 and the Y. P. S. C. E. (Senior, Junior and Intermediate) 141. With particular satisfaction Bro. Morgan announced in his review of the incidents of the four years' service that he had married fifty couples, "and, like Alexander, 'sighed for more worlds to conquer.' " W. J. Lhamon, of Alleghany City, was Bro. Morgan's immediate predecessor, with Enos Campbell preceding him, which roll of honored servants accounts in no small degree for the unwavering growth of the Minneapolis congregation.

A LETTER.

Dear Fellow Workers in the Great Mission Field of Minnesota:—In our great state there are 81 counties, in only 21 of which is our plea represented in any way, or in one-fourth of the whole.

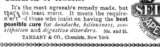

In our great state there are 1,500,000 people, among whom only have we a membership of 3,000 brethren, or one in every 500.

In our great state there occurs a yearly growth, or increase of population, of 52,000, among which only is our increase of membership 300.

In our great state there are hundreds upon hundreds of souls going to perdition yearly with no one to warn of danger, etc., etc.

Now how soon is the plea which we are making to be heralded to the other 60 counties of the state?

How soon are we to press our missionary work anywhere like unto the yearly increase of population?

How soon are we to face the obligation laid npon us to tell the unsaved of Jesus Christ and his salvation?

Face it as unwillingly as we may, yet the answer must be, *Not in a thousand years at the present rate of evangelization!*

We are but playing at missions in Minnesota! One evangelist with which to serve 40 congregations, and to evangelize the state as a whole! No church of note and influence in all the chief centres, save two or three!

How comes it that after 40 years of history in the state, there is so little to show for past labor? All because of our weak attack upon sin, or in other words, *because of lack of as great enthusiasm for Minnesota missions as for other missions.* Nearly every other missionary enterprise and benevolence receives loyal support, while Minnesota missions—the salvation of souls at our very doors, and often at our very firesides—has been made to wend its way with the halt and the blind. The services of the one evangelist could be and should be profitably spent alone in cheering the disheartened and isolated congregations, while a half dozen others should be solely kept at work raising up congregations at the chief centres.

Reform must be our watchword, or we must continue to struggle on as ineffectively in the future as in the past, content to occupy but a small portion of our possible inheritance: content to exist but in the obscure corners of the state: content to view the onward rush of population without purpose in its salvation: content to see the denominations and Roman Catholicism seize all the points of advantage. Shall we continue thus supinely to labor? No! most assuredly not, you say.

But, brother, sister, there are thirteen churches, fourteen Bible-shools, thirteen Endeavor Societies and nine Junior Endeavor Societies—almost the half of all in the state—that are having no part in this work, and what say you to this? Is your society among the number? Are you personally a non-supporter of the work? If so, you surely have not purposed thus, but have remained a non-participant through non-acquaintance with all the facts. And now the state board asks at your hands, corporately and individually, response to the needs of the work, in the nature of a pledge, to be paid before the close of the yearly accounts on Tuesday, the 16th day of August. Shall it have such a pledge? We pray you to take action now; express the good will that is within you at this moment. And above all do not in a corporate capacity present the excuse that because of some other branch of the church contributing, you must be absolved, for this would be but to discriminate. For have you not contributed to Foreign Missions and other benevolences irrespective of what the other branches were doing? Should there not be as much loyalty displayed to Minnesota missions as to other missions?

Glory to God for all missions and benevolences, and let all continue to support them; but the responsibility resting upon all to present Christ's gospel to the unsaved touching elbows with them, is equal to that respecting other missions and benevolences.

May all churches, auxiliaries and individuals, young and old, rally to the needs of the Minnesota work.

"Minnesota for Christ!"

FRANK H. MELLEN, Sec.

Box 450, *Minneapolis, June* 27*th*.

St. Louis Letter.

The war excitement has largely disappeared. When men were enlisting, and the air was full of rumors, the excitement was intense; but now that the nations have not all become entangled, the Spanish Navy is about wiped out, and the successes of the war monotonously one-sided, the excitement has largely subsided. An occasional soldier is seen on the streets, several recruiting offices still open, and the shrill cry of the newsboy announcing an extra still heard, but no excitement or anxiety about results. It is a foregone conclusion, apparently, that America will win from the shores of Africa on the East to the coast of China on the West.

Some lines of business were greatly accelerated by war maneuvers, war news and war results, while others were retarded. Building and other trades have suffered severely. This had been expected to be a year of unusual activity in real estate and building circles, but the expectants have been disappointed. Some of the idle men have gone into the army, but there is still a surplus of labor on the labor market. A tour of the manufacturing interests of the city, outside of a few special lines, reveals no unusual degree of activity. Nobody is rushed with orders. An opinion, however, prevails to the effect that a "boom is coming." When the money now going for bonds gets out into the commercial and industrial channels there will evidently be a marked change in present industrial conditions.

On the twelfth of July this city is to vote on a proposition to amend its charter so that a new debt of twenty million dollars can be incurred, presumably for street improvement. The suspicious thing about this, however, is that when it was proposed to raise this amount for improving the streets of St. Louis it was also proposed that a special commission be elected by the people to see that the money went to the streets. But the authorities would not let this feature of the proposition go before the voters of St. Louis. They were in for the twenty-million assessment, but wanted to oversee its collection and disbursement themselves; wanted it to go through the regular political officials of the city, which in itself is a suspicion sufficient to defeat the measure.

If there is any class of persons in a large city that appreciate and deserve a vacation, it is the school class—both teachers and pupils—and that blessed boon has come to them again. The schools are all out, and the children are

. on a tour,
'. Whether
the lawn or
are happy;
re than two
ks has come.
tor cars far
surrounding
lief to those
means for a
et a ride out
e of from ten
n hour or an
At many of
nds, cooling
ıds and other
r than chil-
these places
, from sinful
are largely
of revenue to
d and steam-
ar with the
especially on
present, as in

en day in St.
nce day more
observed, is
xt day. The
al Cervera's
the patriot-
the rejoicing
as filled with
to lessen the
ttraction and
Many serious
catastrophes.
city delivered
s from their
ich helped to
endence day.
the surrender
Cervera's fleet
for Dewey at
one day than
. They were
July orations
American ear.
B. U. I.

er has entered
sidered, opens
many friends
given by them
former field of
of the year in
t curtailed in
shall endeavor
ier our regular
e thousands of
ille gives the
d has brought
f the "soldier
the country to
e conducted in
plains, assist-
. A splendid
ncampment by
. Sacred con-
gs, band con-
nd recreation,
reading and
se tents. And
possible to add
The ladies of
'd in assisting
comfortable as
hospital tents.
equently, and
he writer was
ge package of
ed to the hos-
the Christian
ost thankfully
ır sisters most
ne surgeons in
r of regiments
s been a small

one. We are daily meeting members of the Christian Church among the soldiers, and would be pleased to visit and become acquainted with any young brother in any of the regiments, if his friends at home would but drop us a postal card giving the regiment and company.

Our Lord's day services, all things considered, are encouragingly attended. Our Ladies' Aid Society is in good working order. Our Y. P. S. C. E. is young, but has in it the principles of growth. Our prayer-meetings are well attended and interesting, and we are in hearty sympathy with every branch of Christian growth and progress. We are receiving encouraging and helpful words from all parts of our state. T. H. Blenus.

Jacksonville, Florida.

A Union Meeting.

The Churches of Christ in Polk county will meet in Des Moines, Ia., Sunday, July 24th, on the Chautauqua grounds, for a grand union meeting. The most enthusiastic and devout Christian men and women in Des Moines have been chosen as officers and committeemen to arrange for this union meeting. Everything has been done or will be done that will add interest to this Christian enterprise.

It will doubtless be an high day in the courts of our Lord when several thousand Disciples of Christ convene in the Jerusalem of this state to worship God as they did in the apostolic days. A very strong and satisfactory program has been arranged, as follows:

Dr. H. O. Breeden will preside at the morning service, at 10:30, in the Tabernacle.

Prof. Sherman Kirk will lead the song service, composed of all the choirs in the county.

Dr. J. H. Garrison, editor of the Christian-Evangelist, will preach the sermon.

Chas. J. Phillips will conduct the union Sunday-school at 12:15, assisted by the other superintendents of the county.

B. A. Roberts will be in charge of the music.

Dr. J. H. Garrison will conduct the communion service at 3:30, in memory of Him.

N. B. Ventress will superintend the deacon's service.

Bro. I. N. McCash will lead the Endeavor meeting at 6:15. At this great C. E. meeting it is hoped that every society in the county will be represented. Dale Stanley will be master of song. Chancellor Wm. Bayard Craig will preside at 8 P. M.

Dr. Edward S. Ames, Mrs. D. A. Wickizer, Prof. J. Mad. Williams and perhaps others will deliver short addresses.

The ushers will be directed by W. C. Cole.

At the morning service all the preachers of the county will occupy the platform; the superintendents at the Sunday-school hour; the elders at the communion service; the presidents of the Endeavor Societies at the Endeavor hour. There are more than six thousand Disciples in Polk county. You will be expecte
enjoy this spiritual feast. To this great m
ing the old, young, rich, poor, colored, wh
saint, sinner, one and all, are most cord
invited. Our preachers will feed your s
and our families will bring baskets well fille
supplyy our bodily wants.

T. W. McDonald, Sec. Adv. Co

Chatauqua Notes.

On Wednesday last, 29th June, this Ass
bly opened, and an interesting bill was be
for the entertainment of a very fair att
ance. Lectures on "Girlhood in Home
"The Quaker Laureate of Puritanism," "
of Historical Material in Romance," v
given by Prof. W. C. Lawton last week.
triotic Day exercises and evening firew
were had July 4th, and the old flag w
triumphant. "Browning's Caliban
Setebos" was the lecture by Prof. R
Moulton on Tuesday, and Dr. W. G. Ande
on "Ethical Value of Physical Culture."

To-day addresses by prominent America
librarians' meeting. Friday Mrs. Bishop
ures on "Don't Worry." To-night, ste
ticon views of the Philippine Islands.
H. L. Willett, of Chicago University,
ducts Bible study for the Assembly at 9 o'
next Sunday morning. Monday, "Reli
Liberty," by Prof. Maury; and by the tim
readers of the Christian-Evangelist see
notice, he will be speaking on Friday "Of
stoi and the Martyrs of Protestantism in
sia." On Saturday all the schools of
and lecture open, and there will be a
increase in the crowds. A lecture by Bi
Goodsell on Roman days, and a grand con
Sunday, July 17th, Bible study by Prof.
lett and sermon by Bishop Goodsell.

Dr. Pohlman lectures Monday on "Hi
Mission of Woman," and in the evening
is to be a musical flotilla on the lake ar
illumination. Your readers will get an id
some few of the many interesting things
given for the entertainment of all who
and care to have part in things scientific,
ary or religious, which center in the ple
woods of Chatauqua. We have prayer-me
on Wednesday evenings at 7 o'clock, an
pect to have service and communion
Lord's day at 10 o'clock at the headquar
Tell your friends who think of coming to
Mrs. W. J. Ford, 437 Clark Avenue I
quarters. We have good rooms in the
location at fair rates, and the money all
in to help pay for the headquarters' buil
The register shows brethren coming in f
cial and religious intercourse from variou
tions of the Union. W. J.

Headquarters Disciples, Chatauqua, July 7, 1898.

Evangelistic Work.

The writer as preacher and G. W. Adams as singer began the season's work as evangelists with a large tent, songbooks and everything complete, May 12, 1898. First meeting at Ashton, Kan., 12 miles west of Arkansas City. Continued four weeks battling with cyclones, hailstones, indifference and the devil. The order of exercises was about this way all through. Service one night and the next stormed out, etc., etc. There was only one time during the month that we had as many as five consecutive meetings. The people there all have storm cellars, and when a cloud appears, and it begins to thunder, business stops and a break is made for the cellar. This is all right for safety, but hard on the evangelists. We fortunately had a few days of fair weather to close in, for which we were thankful. Organized a congregation of 24 members, all heads of families but one. A board of three elders and four deacons. Subscription paper started to build a church and money enough in sight before the close to assure its being erected. It will be pushed rapidly to completion. Meeting closed with a firm feeling and unanimous vote from the large congregation present for us to return this year and dedicate their new church and hold them another meeting.

We went from there to Liberty, Mo., pitched our tent and opened up in this stronghold of infidelity and sin. Stayed about three weeks. Gathered together those who were disposed to work. Added from the M. E.s and the world enough to organize them into a new congregation of 42 members, officered with elders and deacons, and a good hall secured in which to hold services till their new church building is completed, which they will erect at once, a subscription paper having been started and the money secured. We are at home resting a few days. Our next meeting will be in Oklahoma, point not yet decided; three invitations. Churches desiring tent meetings may address G. W. Adams, Sheldon, Mo.

ADCOCK AND ADAMS, Evangelists.

Not so Enthusiastic.

The revolutionary resolution referred to in a late issue of the CHRISTIAN-EVANGELIST as enthusiastically passed, we are inclined to believe was not passed with so great enthusiasm as one might suppose. I refer to the resolution passed at the Mexico convention, and which looks to a division of the receipts of Children's Day between Home and Foreign Missions. It is yet to be shown that a majority of the workers present favored it. It was passed, of course, but how few comparatively voted either way! I voted against the resolution, but being a new man and not wanting to appear forward upon a short acquaintance, I took no part in the discussion. I may be pardoned now for a few lines to the point.

1. The day was set apart in national councils, not by any state convention. Hence this was not the place to set any part of its purpose aside, granting that the request of the resolution was just.

2. This day has been from the first held sacred to heathen missions. God has wonderfully blessed it. Now comes said resolution and appropriates a half interest in it without so much as consulting those who have promoted the day. The principle is wrong.

3. The vote for the resolution was almost to a vote from the preachers. A large per cent. of the vote against was from the lay delegation. The expressions from this source led me to believe that the very many who did not vote felt that the resolution was not the thing. It is not the people who oppose special days any more than the preachers. Many of these preachers who cry out against days, have never tried their people to see if they like them. When the proper course is followed these special days will be the most enjoyable of the year. We have but few national days. I tell you, if you want to cut off days begin upon these state and local days that are dawning everywhere. The national days are not too many, and we could have a children's day for Home Missions without hurting anybody.

4. I believe the result will be to cripple the foreign offerings without materially helping the home work.

5. The sentiment in this country among those who pay as well as pray, is for the foreign work. And it should be. With all the evangelical churches we have in America, I do not hesitate to say the cry of 900,000,000 pagans in six foreign fields—China, India, Africa, Arabia, Korea, Siam—should be considered more important than sending an additional force into our own land. Let no tongue set the demands of even New America against those of this heathen multitude. For the victories of our armies only multiply the reasons for foreign work.

H. A. DENTON.

Centralia, Mo.

[We have not seen the resolution referred to, but we feel sure that it would be very unwise to divert any part of the proceeds of Children's Day, on the first Lord's day in June, from that original purpose. This day has a history, and had its origin under conditions that look more like God's providence than man's devising. We would better let it alone and seek to enhance the Home Missionary interest in some other way.—EDITOR.]

State Mission Notes.

In the death of E. O. Waller, of Platte City, every enterprise of the church has lost a steadfast friend. The church at Platte City, his own family, all the poor and needy in the neighborhood gathered at his burying and poured out a tender tribute of respect in the tears of grief that ran down their cheeks. And there has lived but few men who were more worthy of such a tribute. Since his death I have received from the hand of his son, Bro. R. P. Waller, $20 which his father had requested should be given to State Missions. Thus in his death he manifested that which he had been ever since I have known him, the steadfast friend of our State Mission work. And not only has he done this, but he has set an example which is worthy of imitation. Why not, when the man has been a steadfast friend of the mission work in his life, when the hour of his departure comes, have the satisfaction of knowing that the work he has befriended in life shall still be assisted by his generosity in the years to come? Verily, such men are worthy of the encomium of the blessed Word, "Their works do follow them." Our men of means will learn in the years to come that there is a blessed joy in giving of their wealth to the service of the King. There ought to be two classes in every church, at least there ought not to be more than two, the givers and the receivers. No one but those who are objects of charity should refuse to help on the work of the Lord. This brings me to the consideration of

SOME FIGURES.

The number of contributing churches to our State Mission work last year was 104 larger than at the present time. I mean that the whole number contributing last year was 104 greater than the number so far this year. We are now near the middle of the first month of the last quarter in the year. In fact, as our convention comes one week earlier than it did last year, we are nearly within two months of the convention hour. We shall have to stir ourselves mightily if we reach the number of contributing churches of last year. But here is another figure or two. I have been working a great deal among the churches which did not contribute last year and the result is that of the number of contributing churches this year, so far, 68 of them gave nothing last year. This tells us that 172 of the churches that gave last year have not responded this year at all. Your board has depended on every one that gave last year to give this, and that we would make some gains. Now if the churches that gave last year will give this and the increase in new churches continues to the end of the year, we shall come out with flying colors.

But must have a general movement. We are in debt to the men in the field; they are needing the funds that are actually now owing to them to pay for the very necessaries of life. It is justly their due. I am sure that a great people such as we are cannot afford to have our brethren feel that they are neglected. They are doing the pioneer work for us, they are the skirmish line, they are at the post of danger, they are engaged in planting of our cause in the destitute regions, and upon their faithfulness depends our growth in a large manner in the days that are to come. What shall we do? Shall we let them suffer for the want of the very necessaries of life? I don't believe that we will. Yet to that complexion has it now come. Please send at once, that the money may be sent to these men and their families. I beg of you to hear.

Yours in his name,

T. A. ABBOTT.

1135 *Vandeventer, St. Louis, Mo.*

The Alum Heart.

Many people are suffering from some form of heart disease who have no idea of the cause of it.

Any disturbance of the digestive organs affects the heart's action, and therefore every food which interferes with digestion is responsible where there are troubles of this character.

It has been discovered that the use of baking powder made from burnt alum coagulates the blood very rapidly, which interferes with its free flow through the arteries and valves of that organ. Formerly alum was used as a specific for children's croup, but owing to its tendency from the causes named to produce heart failure, physicians no longer employ it.

In face of such facts and in view of the overwhelming testimony of scientists as to the poisonous character of this drug when used for food purposes, can there be any excuse for the ignorance or unconcern which permits any one to take from the grocer a package of alum baking powder simply for the sake of saving a few cents in price?

It is a healthful sign that many states are limiting by law the sale of alum baking powder. Very soon it will be prohibited in all states, or treated as a poison, as it should be. But for such laws, how are the alum powders to be known by consumers?

Where alum powders are not branded as such, nor their sale prohibited by law, it is better to avoid the use of any new or doubtful brand until it has been analyzed. The purity of all powders may be suspected if they are sold at a price lower than the price of the best standard brands. We know the Royal to be a first-class cream of tartar powder, and if consumers insist upon having that brand, they will be sure of a pure, healthful article. In view of a recently reported case of poisoning of a whole family living near Logansport, Indiana, from the use of alum powder, it behooves every one to use extraordinary care in purchasing their supplies. We do not hesitate to recommend the Royal to all who are in doubt as to the powder they have been using, as the United States Government tests placed that brand at the head of all the tartaric powders.

The Illinois Encampment

Will begin at Eureka, August 1, and continue seven days. The state missionary convention will be held August 3 and 4. Watch next week's papers for the program. It is important that the brethren attend these meetings in great numbers. We hope for one of the largest encampments we have ever held.

J. H. HARDIN.

Eureka, Ill.

Notes and News.

e 5th annual reunion of the Churches of st, of McDonough and adjoining counties, e Old Bedford Christian Church (Blandlle, Ill.), June 30th, was a grand success was well attended from abroad.

M. D. MELVIN.

orrespondent writes us that the church at anicsburg, Ill., will soon be out of a pas- The church will then want another cher, and the present preacher another ch.

are glad to learn that E. W. Brickert's at Red Oak, Iowa, is being appreciated that good results are coming from it. The rent activities of the church are doing efve work and our correspondent thinks that ght future is in store for the church at place.

M. Jones, an elder of the church at Pea e, Ark., wishes to say to his correspond- through our columns that the church there all, but active in faith; that S. R. Beais the pastor; that Benton county is the orchard of Arkansas; that they have a normal school at Pea Ridge, and that Ridge is seven miles west of the old Pea e battle ground and five miles west of the oad.

Indiana Letter.

is year has been a successful one in na. The state evangelist and his assishave had 2,300 accessions, raised over 0 for evangelistic purposes, and $10,400 l purposes. The corresponding secretary he districts pushed the amount up to about 00 used in missionary work in Indiana year. We have dedicated twenty church- At our state convention at South Bend, J. Coombs was re-elected evangelist, and T. egg corresponding secretary. The next convention will be held at Irvington. t year I will not confine my work to ana. I will go out of the state for a numof meetings. I can hold a tent meeting in ust.

J. V. COOMBS, State Evan.

Virginia Ave., Indianapolis.

A Beautiful Preasent.

rough the courtesy of Dr. J. W. Young, Wayne, Ind., a fifty-dollar gold medal be given to the Christian Endeavor Society h has the largest delegation at the state stian Endeavor convention of the Disciples diana, at Bethany Park, August 8, 9, 10, 1898. Junior and intermediate societies compete for it. An excellent program, in h quite an array of talent is presented, has prepared.

B. L. ALLEN,
State C. E. Supt. of Indiana.

Chesterton

country town, on the L. S. & M. S. way about twenty miles west of LaPorte, Last Tuesday night, about seven o'clock writer, in the line of business, drove said town, and seeing a tent in the sub- and a blackboard notice upon the street, de a few enquiries and learned that the stian Church was conducting a meeting. lked down and stood around like other fel-, and presently here came Bro. Coombs; a long time since we met, and my beard gone, hence he did not recognize me. I nothing until after the last amen, but ted in and took a back seat. I looked at ent and wondered whether Bro. Coobs had compaigning near the bottomless pit and ngry devil had come up and dropped a 13- shell through the roof, besides sending a four and six-pounders through its sides. I 't blame the devil at all. Bro. Coombs has bit of creating serious disturbances around Infernal Majesty's domains.

The audience was rather small, but possibly select. Reasons: Short nights, harvest time, and especially the fact that Chesterton is not noted for its piety. Besides, the meeting had only been in progress about a week, and was not likely to continue but a few evenings longer. Presently the Gospel News man announced a song and his vest-pocket organ got down to business, and I preceived that the one-armed orator had lost none of his vim; he could sing.

After awhile he opened his ammunition chest at Gal. 6:7 and brought out his gun, a 13-inch gun, and a rapid-fire at that. The slashes, gashes and rents made in his saloon business, dancing, card-playing, etc., were awful. The gunner got hot; no wonder, the devil was mad.

The good people of Chesterton doubtless hope that Bro. Coombs will have an opportunity to return and finish the job. Chesterton's Morro Castle needs storming. By the way, I think Coombs is fatter than usual; the spring chicken has appeared, you know!

J. H. LACEY.

LaPorte, Ind.

Attention!

The Executive Committee of the Benevolent Association of the Christian Church have recently determined to more vigorously push the benevolent work of their orphanage, the National Orphans' Home, located in St. Louis, Mo. To this end they have put into the field as solicitors two more brethren.

Our solicitors now are, Bro. W. B. Young for Missonri, Kansas, Arkansas, Texas and all southern points; Bro. Dempsey A. Hunter for Iowa, Nebraska, Michigan, the Dakotas and northern points; Bro. Joel Brown for Illinois, Indiana, Ohio, and all other states except Kentucky. As Kentucky has a Widows' and Orphans' Home of her own to support, we do not allow our agents to solicit in that state.

These three are all good men, and we bespeak for them the kindest treatment at the hands of our brethren wherever they may go. They will turn over all money to the corresponding secretary and make a report to the Board each month, and all contributions paid to them, or sent to the corresponding secretary in payment of pledges made to them, will be reported in the Orphan's Cry, which is issued monthly at 25 cents a year. Friends sending pledges to corresponding secretary will please not forget to state to *whom* and *when* and *where* the pledge was made, that they may be canceled without trouble. A receipt will be returned for all money so sent.

Each solicitor carries a certificate signed by the president and secretary of the board.

MRS. J. K. HANSBROUGH.

City Mission Work.

My first year's service as City Missionary for Kansas City, Mo., closes this month. I came to Kansas City, in July, 1897, from Lynnville, Ill., and was given a warm reception by the people and also the weather.

It has been a busy year and richly blessed of the Lord. We wish to commend heartily the spirit of fellowship and the co-operation manifested both by the pastors and people of the various churches and missions within the city.

I cannot fail to speak of the Endeavorers throughout the city. They have been exceedingly kind towards our work and have entered enthusiastically upon any work suggested. They have aided by prayer, offerings and by active service. Many young men have spoken at the mission when called upon and have done excellent work.

There were two missions when I took up the work. One now called, "East 15th Street Mission," the other at 24th and Vine Streets. During the year a mission was organized at Wanboe, a suburb of the city. I preach here every Friday night. Sunday-school on Lord's day at 3 P. M.

Sheffield church has come under the direction of the board and we supply preaching through our Endeavorers every Lord's day evening. Sunday-school here in the morning.

I preach every Lord's day at Vine Street and East 15th Street, also have Sunday-school, Junior and Senior Endeavor, Ladies' Aid and prayer-meeting at each place every week.

Have preached 207 sermons and there have been 145 additions during the year. There have been visits without number. Many poor families were assisted in time of dire distress. Clothing, coal, tickets on railroad, funeral expenses for the destitute, food for the hungry—these and many other calls are constantly coming to us in this general work.

Among all the helpers there is none more faithful and efficient than Sister Bowen. She is God's purpose incarnate. "An helpmeet" indeed. Ever ready to go and do wherever she is needed. With all thy gettings, get a good wife.

The future is bright with promise, the cities are the open doors—the Macedonian calls. God grant that we may enter now more fully upon this important work!

FRANK L. BOWEN,
City Missionary.

1809 *Tracy St., Kansas City, Mo.*

Eureka College Debt Fund.

The following will be of interest to those who have been watching the progress of the raising of the fund for relieving Eureka College from debt:

The finance committee of the board of trustees of Eureka College having carefully looked over the list of notes secured by Dr. J. H. Hardin and J. G. Waggoner for the purpose of liquidating the $30,000 of present indebtedness of said college, consider the notes good and sufficient, and payable according to the agreed conditions, and as an expression of high appreciation of the most valuable service rendered the college, and the entire brotherhood passed the following resolution.

Resolved, That the thanks of this meeting and the Disciples of Illinois are due to Pres J. H. Hardin and J. G. Waggoner for the persistent, able and courteous manner in which they brought the needs of Eureka College before the people and secured from a liberal public the pledges necessary to liquidate its indebtedness.

J. P. DARST, Chairman.
J. A. MCGUIRE.
N. B. CRAWFORD.

Eureka, Ill., June 24, 1898.

Idaho Encampment.

The fourth annual camp meeting of North Idaho was held at Lewiston May 28 to June 6 The Christian Church of this part of the state owns a good tent with a seating capacity of about four hundred. This was pitched in the central part of the city, and the services were well attended by the citizens generally. Near by was a little field of cottage tents, where number of families were quartered, some from remote parts as the Camas Prairie and Nez Perces countries.

Lewiston is a beautiful city of about 2,50 people, is a county-seat, and has the State Normal School. In addition to the already good steamboat navigation, a branch of the N. P. R. R. reaching Lewiston is nearing completion. The development of irrigation upon a large body of valuable land just across Snake River adds interest to the place. A town called Vineland is building up there, and will soon be connected with the city by bridge. The site of Lewiston can never be forgotten. It lies in the bend formed by the junction of the Clearwater and Snake Rivers. Just across to the north lies an immense hill, lifting itself 2,500 feet to the level of the great Palouse country. This abrupt change in the altitude gives Lewiston a delightful climate of almost perpetual summer.

The Christian Church here was formed in the home of Bro. Cantril about a year ago, bu they now meet in G. A. R. Hall, which can be rented only by the month. They began with very few members, and now have but 45, of these 15 were added during the camp meeting, mostly by baptism. Bro. J. O. Davis ministers for them half time. He is an earnest and capable young man, and the friends of the cause have reason to expect that this work will be blessed under his ministry. The visiting preachers in attendance were Bros. Daisley, of Pomeroy; Laing, of Vineland; Herrold, of Walla Walla; Smith, of Rosalea; and the writers, of Moscow and Pullman. The faithful band of disciples rejoice very much in the result of the meeting, and feel strengthened for the future.

This entire work is the outgrowth of the labors of Bro. Rogers, then of Moscow, who was holding a meeting near by, when he contracted his last illness. He died in the home of Bro. and Sister Mounce, who now stand as pillars under this work. Bro. Rogers still lives in this work, and his memory is sacred to all the people.

The camp meeting will be held next year at or near Nez Perces City.

MR. AND MRS. G. E. BARROWS.
Moscow and Pullman.

Missouri Bible-school Notes.

After one of the most interesting and successful conventions in our history, we have entered our twenty-third year, praying that it may surpass all preceding ones.

To this happy end, as in the past, I look to my preaching brethren as a chief dependence, knowing their love for Christ and the children.

Will all the schools keep in mind that the amount pledged at the Mexico convention is accepted by the board as the apportionment of your school? So that the schools so pledged need not answer the cards now going out, only as they remit the first quarter right away.

The board at its first meeting planned for some changes in the work, of which all will hear in due time, and which we are sure you will heartily and fully endorse.

Bro. D. R. Dungan remits in full his pledge for this new year, and the Marshall Endeavor does likewise. Alvah Clark, Perry, aslo sends in her pledge in full for the new year, which encourages us to believe that all, personal and school pledges, are to be paid with more promptness this year than ever. Thank these friends for such substantial manifestations of their co-operation with us.

Before the convention closed, John Giddens was arranging appointments, and immediately entered upon his work.

Brunswick, with J. P. Furnish as preacher, is pushing to the front in the Lord's work. Five years is the term of the Furnish pastorate, and the brethren seem to appreciate him today as they never did in the past. The children did not learn of the Reward of Merit Cards until near the convention, but they took right hold and have a creditable showing on the Roll of Merit in the convention minutes. The brethren handed me their apportionment for the year just closing in full.

The Marshall school, of which J. A. Gordon has been the superintendent, did not wait for the notice of quarterly dues, but remitted immediately.

Four schools have notified this office that they intend to carry the banner home from Plattsburg, one of which is Memphis, where J. T. Boone is doing such fine work, and where one of the boys carried off one of the gold medals.

We have among our county superintendents this year two more ladies, both of whom will assist us greatly. Miss Alice Potts, Lincoln, is the county superintendent of Benton, a county from which we have never had a full report in the past, but will hereafter. Mrs. Luella Hargis has kindly accepted the superintendency of Jackson, and will do for us what the others in the past have not succeeded in doing: give us a complete statistical report, with map of county, and you will see it on the wall at Plattsburg. Will some one speak for Buchanan?

At Huntsville, found I. J. Marshall just closing a successful meeting for J. A. Grimes. The school was just as prompt in meeting their apportionment as if I had worked a week for them. At Huntsville lives Miss Nora Kiernan, one of the first to volunteer her services as a county superintendent, and who has every year since given us such good reports as to come within a fraction of carrying off the banner. Aubrey Hammett is now the school superintendent, coming in from the country faithfully every Sunday; and yet people say, "Why, Bro. Davis, we live in the country," which seems to excuse all from duty. Does it?

At Arkadelphia, I sought to help a faithful band, small but devoted in service where Miss Susie Browning has taken the Normal course, solitary and alone, her grade on every book running near the 100 mark. While here it was my pleasure to unite in marriage Dr. O. R. Edmonds, Tina, and Miss Alva Creason, Avalon. Alva is a friend of long years' standing, while Dr. Edmonds is one of the rising young physicians of the state. Such unions bring happiness into the world.

To all the workers in Missouri, command us at any time for institutes.

H. F. DAVIS.
Commercial Building, St. Louis.

Will You Help Us?

DEAR BRETHREN AND SISTERS:—You have no doubt already heard that during an electrical storm, on the 8th inst., our church building was struck by lightning and was burned, and now we have no home. We had done all in our power to erect this building, and at last, with the aid of others, succeeded in relieving the church of all pecuniary embarrassments, but once again the task is before us, and we cheerfully begin the work of raising funds for another building, feeling confident that God will put it into the hearts of the people to assist us in this work. On the receipt of this my dear friends, think of the responsibility for the many unsaved souls around us, and there are many here that are still aliens from the cause of Christ, but the work is hampered. The gospel is the power of God unto salvation, men and women are willing to hear it, but we have no house to invite them to. So, in order to carry out our plans, and accomplish this work, we ask that every minister in Missouri bring the matter before their congregations, and give them the privilege of contributing something to assist us in rebuilding our church, the money to be paid on condition that we raise the amount necessary to put up the building.

All money sent by churches or individuals will be receipted for and deposited in Dunklin County Bank as a "Building Fund." In the event we fail to raise the amount necessary to insure a neat, modern brick building, we bind ourselves to return every cent to the contributors. Now, my dear friends, we sincerely ask your assistance in this matter, and feel that we will not be disappointed. May God help you to extend a helping hand to those who are so much in need of your assistance, and may God's blessing rest upon those who give cheerfully and willingly. We must have a church. Won't you help us? Address all communications to

MRS. S. A. BARHAM, Soliciting Com.
Malden, Mo.

Indian Territory Convention.

Our convention met in South McAlister at time appointed.

Attendance was small—this we expected—those who attended were well paid doubtless for their time. Arthur W. Jones, of Ardmore, was elected secretary of the convention, and made a good one. F. D. Wharton, of Bloomington, Ind., led the singing to the delight of all. A. M. Cane, of Cincinnati, Ohio, was in attendance, and delighted all with his eloquence and advice. He will be remembered many days hence. H. A. Major, of Purcell, I. T., made a strong speech on the possibilities of the convention. Arthur W. Jones, W. H. Polk and others took part in the convention. Bro. C. C. Smith disappointed us, without even sending us an apology, but we forgive him.

The report of the corresponding secretary was read and received with much interest by the convention. I submit a few facts taken from the report: Total number of additions from all sources, 532; 10 churches organized during the year; two church houses built; money for salary for secretary $556.90; moneys raised in territory for church purpose $4,000.

We ask the attention of our brotherhood throughout the land to these figures, a larger number of additions for the amount of money expended than in any other part of the country and with the exception of a few meetings had by some outside men, this work was done by the secretary, on small pay. Why will not our members living in this country we are trying to evangelize and who are contributing to outside missions help us at home? Why will not the States take an interest in this struggle we are making in this territory, and help us? Why will not the Christian Endeavor of our brotherhood in Missouri, Kansas, Illinois, Indiana, Ohio, Kentucky, Iowa and Texas and the churches as well come to our relief and help. Look over our brief figures, then act in the light of the facts.

Arthur W. Jones followed the convention with a protracted meeting at South McAlister. This leads us to say that he will hold any church a good meeting. Try him.

F. G. ROBERTS, Cor. Sec.
June 28, 1898, South McAlister, I. T.

Evangelistic.

MASSACHUSETTS.

chols, pastor of the church at Worholding a tent meeting there this

INDIANA.

olis, July 13.—Six additions to the
Christian Church yesterday.—J.
.D.

'rairie, July 11.—I began here July
vork starts off very encouragingly.
lady confessed Christ last night.
SALMON, pastor.

PENNSYLVANIA.

Point, July 8.—Four baptisms at
Church in June. The work in Indi-
is prosperous.—H. C. SAUM.

OREGON.

'une 26.—J. N. Mulkey just closed a
this place with nine additions by
hree by letter and one from the Ad-
A. E. MURPHY.

CALIFORNIA.

July 8.—We have had 52 additions
urces since June 1st; 29 were for-
bers, and 23 new additions; nearly
sm. At Capay we had 17 new ad-
l two reinstated; making a total of
itions to these congregations and 82
formerly members.—C. E. EDGMAN.

ILLINOIS.

ter, July 11.—One added since last
ro. Job Brown was with us yester-
ured $18.25 for the Orphans' Home
is. Bro. Brown's talk and work
ediction to us all. It will do any
od to have Bro. Brown with them
re with him the Christly fellowship
the children. He is a man of God.
m.—B. C. BLACK.

KANSAS.

July 8th.—Ten additions at Cran-
y baptism.—E. J. PALMER, pastor.
ooke reports two additions at Pio-
T. Bonnea, pastor. Also two ad-
Boque. B. T. Bonnea, pastor.

FLORIDA.

July 7.—S. H. Farrer, of Ocoee,
ood meeting in Orlando, which re-
ganizing a church and enlisting the
n the various departments of the
moves from Ocoee to Orlando, and
ue to visit Ocoee twice a month.
s attending the meeting demon-
t when the gospel is preached, even
st of a political campaign, excite-
war, and the summer season,
l may be accomplished. The spirit
he members of the Congregational
granting the use of their comfort-
of worship was largely due to the
of Sister W. P. Watson, by whose
the work was begun. The people
to hear, and Bro. Farrer more than
audience by his excellent presenta-
truth. Bro. H. F. Davis, of St.
l rejoice to learn of the good news.
winter in Orlando some years since,
ly spoken of. I hope to have Bro.
h us in DeLand in August.—F. J.
JR.

MISSOURI.

., July 18.—Sixty-five additions to
A. NORTHCUTT.

July 13.—One addition by baptism at
pointment at Salt River church.—
CULLEY.

s, July 18.—Four additions at the
hurch yesterday and three Lord's
us, making in all 28 added since I
work three months since. All depart-
he work are looking up. The Bible-
ranging for a patriotic emtertain-
he evening of July 28th. And on
s day evening in August will be the
e women of the church. Speakers
churchas of the city will partici-
JCE WOLVERTON.

ARKANSAS.

ille, July 15.—There were two addi-
First Church last Sunday.—N. M.

ILLINOIS.

ld, July 15.—My work here is open-
y nicely. Twenty were added dur-
nth of June at the regular services.
NN.

NEBRASKA.

, July 12.—Two confessions here last
at regular service. Will begin to

ARIZONA.

Percy T. Carnes reports four baptisms, five otherwise and a Bible-school organized at San Simon.

NEW MEXICO.

Percy T. Carnes reports one addition at Richmond and a camp meeting to begin there in August.

SUBSCRIBERS' WA

Miscellaneous wants and notices w
this department at the rate of two ce
insertion, all words, large and small
and two initials stand for one word.
pany notice with corresponding re
book-keeping.

Family Circle.

"Hear Ye Him."

CORNELIA F. BOZMAN.

I come not to the Mount,
Where smoke and flames arise,
And lurid lightnings flash athwart
The dark and angry skies,

And the loud trump of wrath
With Sinai thunder blend,
But unto Zion's holy hill,
To seek the sinner's Friend.

The spotless Lamb whose blood
Cleanses from every stain,
"Who will not break the bruised reed
Nor quench the struggling flame."

Jesus—the Friend divine
Who bore our grief and care,
Whose words of promise cannot fail,
"Give ear unto my prayer."

"Out of the depths" of sin,
I lift my cry to Thee,
Whose arm can bring salvation down,
And set the captive free.

Break every link that binds
The soul in Satan's chain—
Remove the heavy yoke and rend
His iron bonds in twain.

"To whom all power is given
In earth and heaven" above,
Who came to seek the lost, and light
A darkened world with love.

A contrite heart I bring
And count all things but loss
For Him who hath fulfilled the law
And "nailed it to the cross."

My fortress, rock and shield,
My hope, my hiding-place,
My Advocate, plead my cause
Before the Father's face.

Forgive my sins, dear Lord,
Even as I forgive
My brothers' debts, and grant me grace
As in Thy sight to live.

Walk with me day by day,
And light my thoughts on high;
Be near me when the shadows fall,
And give me grace to die.

The Legend of Chocorua.

MINNIE E. HADLEY.

"Good evening, Mr. Mulligan. Margery and I have driven all the way from the harbor to talk about closing the trade for the winter."

It was nearly dusk when the open carry-all, conveying Mrs. Bingham and her daughter, drew up to the gate of a shabby-looking farm house among the White Mountains of New Hampshire.

"Margery and I have both worked hard and economized rigidly down in our little dress-making shop in Boston, to get the money to pay for the land, but I wouldn't take it under any considerations if I thought it wouldn't make good pasture for the cows, so that we can live by selling cream to summer boarders and butter to the Harbor people in winter."

"But I've heard a strange story of the intervale since I saw you last," continued Mrs. Bingham. "They tell me that long years ago, the whites chased Old Chief Chocorua to the top of yonder ledge whence, to avoid capture, he jumped to the awful depths below, pronouncing a direful curse upon the intervale, and that all cattle pastured here soon become diseased and die."

Farmer Mulligan sat down the two pails of foaming milk which he was just carrying in from the barnyard, and brought his fist down upon the gatepost with a heavy thwack.

"If yer the sensible woman I take yer fur, Misses Bingham, ye'll not give no credit to any sech silliness. I know them tales is allers being' told about here, and some keows have died on the intervale; but its only 'cause they're not keered fur. Why look at them four keows a standin' yonder. Healthier, fatter keows ye never seed an' been feedin' on the intervale more'n two year past. My wife made heaps o' money off of 'em afore she died, and I've been amakin' it sence, till that boy Bill o' mine got to bein' careless in strainin' away the milk.

"Them summer boarder's mighty perticklar an' Bill's clean spiled me hull trade by leaving keow-hairs an' specks o' dirt an' sech like in the milk.

"But a sensible woman like you ken take them four keows yonder an' make heaps o' money off f'm the intervale. Yer too wise lookin' to be believin' any o' them fool superstitions agoin' about."

"I guess I'll close the trade with you, Mr. Mulligan. My health is failing fast in the city. The doctor says I must breathe the fresh mountain air, and the scenery about here is such a delight to Margery. If the little cottage over there at the foot of Chocorua can be vacated by Monday I think we shall move in."

"Any time that ye set, Misses Bingham. Ad' ye'll take the four keows along with the intervale?"

"Yes, we must have something for a living. Do you hear one word we've been saying, Margery?"

Margery sat as one in a dream, gazing intently at the western sky, where bold old Chocorua projected its stern, rocky front against a background of crimson red.

To her poetical nature it was a mighty revelation—something for which her soul had always longed during her short life of fifteen years, but which she had never known before in the strict confines of their little shop in Boston. She heard her mother's decision with a vague incredulousness. To live here, to breathe into her very soul, as it were, this atmosphere of marvelous beauty, was something better than she had ever dreamed of.

However, it was all settled on that very evening before the little carryall drove away, and the end of the next week found them safely lodged in the little cottage at the foot of old Mt. Chocorua.

"It all seems so strange and dreamlike, mother," said Margery, one evening as they sat on their little back porch, gazing at the smooth stone face of the mountains which, illumined by the setting sun's reflection, seemed to be glaring down upon the valley, but whether with friendship or enmity Margery could not just make out.

"Its so different from our little shop in Boston. Do you suppose, mother, that we shall be permitted to live here in peace and plenty, or will the old Chief's curse be visited upon us as it has been upon others living here in the valley?"

"Nonsense, Margery! Don't let that spoil your happiness. No special ill has ever befallen the people of the intervale that I know of, except that their cattle have sometimes become diseased and died. But I think as Mr. Mulligan says, there must have been some special cause for it. I'n sure the cows we have bought from him ar healthy enough. But what is it I see movin over there at the base of the mountain?"

"It's Bill Mulligan, mother. He's bee there all the afternoon, cleaning out th spring and sinking a box into it for ou cows to drink from. I was over there an talked to him this afternoon. He may b a good enough boy, but I don't like him mother. He wears such shabby clothe and speaks such horrible English, but i isn't that I dislike so much as the mean sneaking look he wears in his countenance I guess it was what he said that makes m uneasy. He says the old Chief's curse i still living, and that we'll find it out soo enough. He says also that more than onc the Mulligan family have sold this interval at a good price and then bought it bac again for almost nothing, because the people were glad to get rid of it. And wha do you suppose I overheard the men sayin up at the sawmill? They said it was shame for old Farmer Mulligan to rob u of our hard-earned money. They said thi patch of ground wasn't worth a cent to an one but him, and that we shall soon be gla to sell it back for little or nothing. All th people about here, in fact, seem to thin that the Mulligans have for generation back possessed a secret charm that ward off the curse and no one can find out wha it is."

"Tut! Margery! What nonsense!"

But in spite of Mrs. Bingham's seemin indifference, she sometimes felt a vagu superstitious dread of something, she kne not what, and her own feelings almos frightened her.

"If we put our trust in God and try t serve him he will certainly prosper us. I it was not his will that I should die c oxygen starvation, pent up in that littl shop, it cannot be his will that I should di here of food starvation. No, Margery, m faith is stronger than that. God will pro tect us from any wicked schemes or plots we trust him, and as for that curse it is a empty superstition."

Margery felt comforted by her mother strong faith, but resolved to shun Bi Mulligan for the future.

She positively disliked his sneakin wizard-like face, and his evil predictio only rendered her angry and miserable.

"I wonder what sort of view one coul get from the top of that low ledge?" sai Margery the next evening as she and h mother sat as usual watching the sunset o Chocorua. "I'm going to run across an see, mother, if it is growing a little late it won't take but a moment."

The next instant she was bounding ov the intervale like a startled deer. Awa she ran, bareheaded, with her long, blac curls floating out in the gentle evenin breeze.

To scramble to the top of the ledge w for her agile body but the work of a fe minutes, and she soon stood gazing dow upon a delightful portion of the inte vale which she had not yet seen. . little white, worn path was just visib in the gathering twilight. It seemed lead out from a sort of excavation under th rocky ledge on which she was standin and then to meander off through the gree grass in the direction of the Mulligan far house.

"I wonder what it's for," thought Ma

ıst be something of im-
ɔis ledge. I shall soon

ʼarf pines were growing
: the cliff to which Mar-
ɪport in her descent, and
rself at the opening of a
n under the ledge.
ueer little hollow! And
ff piled into it for?"
ɔineknots, cobblestones,
all sorts of *debris* heaped
o the hollow.
done this for a purpose.
hat it all means."
; dark and Margery al-
but she stooped down
just in the act of rolling
blestone when something
ırm and drew her forcibly

shriek Margery tore her-
grasp, and turning quick-
held the wizard-like face
. staring at her with a
ith the same evil-looking
rom under the old slouch

ι touch me!" cried Mar-
ʳ, her large black eyes
n the twilight.
Miss. 'Twas fur yer own
t know your danger.
poisonous snakes as ever
to a been bit by 'em 'ud
r'n lightning."
e *path* for?" asked Mar-
ıbdued tone.
' a lot o' men use to come
ʳ an' try ter kill 'em out
de the path. But sakes
ı use. Ten come to life
ı."
ıe near this place again,
ı for no woman."
ɔoldly answered Margery
home, in a swifter run
e.
a word of it, mother," she
after relating her story.
ɪething else under that
it has something to do
for the old Chief's curse
shall not rest until I've
is."
ver it, Margery, and don't
in," answered her mother.
it mátters to us whether
es or a den of witches so
t trouble us."
ssed quietly and prosper-
residents at the intervale,

"yer' cows are gettin' the disease that ever one o' 'em gets that pasters here, but Dan Mulligan's. That ole Indian did'nt curse this here ground fur nothin'!"

"Look 't the hair on that cow's back now!"

He reached the butt end of his whip through the barnyard gate and rubbed at a little tuft of loose hair on Brindle's back which immediately fell off.

"I know it," said Margery. "They are all getting that way; mother and I noticed it yesterday and thought they were shedding."

"Cows don't shed this time o' year. Its the curse an' nothin' else. That's the way they all git."

"No use yer tryin' ter sell any more cream an' butter in this neighborhood. Good mornin'!"

"It's upon us already," thought Margery, and as she turned toward the house the very ground seemed sinking beneath her feet.

That night she and her mother sát talking until long after midnight trying to plan what to do.

All they had was invested in this little home and now their only means of subsistance was taken away.

To go back to the city meant death to Mrs. Bingham and they both realized it, and in spite of the direful curse which seemed to hover over them from the first, both had learned to love and cherish the old mountain as a part of their lives.

At length Mrs. Bingham fell asleep in her chair.

A heavy thunder storm had come up early in the evening and it had been raining hard all night.

It was almost two o'clock in the morning when it broke away and Margery sat by the window gazing off in the direction of old Chocorua.

The moon arose and as Margery looked she saw two men approaching Snake Ledge as she had called it since her adventure.

It was Bill Mulligan and his father. Margery watched them with beating heart. Directly she saw them carrying more debris and filling up the hollow.

"If I could only reach the top of the ledge unobserved and listen what they are saying."

Seizing a light shawl she threw it around her and by a circuitous path soon reached the ledge unnoticed.

She crouched in the midst of the little pine thicket and listened. Every word they said was distinctly heard.

Suddenly her heart gave a great leap for

"And what do you suppose is ur
Snake Ledge?" she continued.
"A *spring of pure water* at which
Mulligan cows have always drank
which they have tried to choke up since
came here. They've added a fresh sup
to it this morning already owing to
heavy rain, and my little white patl
nothing more nor less than a cow pat
Scientific investigations revealed the tı
of what she said.
The Mulligans for generations back
changed the drinking places for the ca
so quietly by opening up one spring and cl
ing up the other with every transfer of
land that the simple and superstiti
country people had never discovered
fraud.
Now that it was brought to light, l
Mulligan and his son were given just
week in which to sell out and leave
neighborhood or else suffer a "tar
feathering."
Their place was soon sold to one l
Bingham's old Boston patrons for a sı
mer home.
Snake Springs as it is now called ε
restored the health of the diseased c
which were suffering from the excesı
mineral ingredients in the other one.
Sidney, Ohio.

Alaskan Letter.

We have moved a little lower down
lake in order to try our boats. They
all right, except a little small; we ar
far down as we can get until the ice g
out of Lake Marsh. We are passed
police station at Tagish and they se
everything in an outfit; they overha
our boat completely. They have a g
deal of trouble about whisky. One of
officers told Mr. Garrison that he was l
ing for whisky, but he said we had a
boat; he could not find a drop in our o
if he should hunt a month, that is
article we did not buy. They seem t
nice men, and I guess they hunt
whisky more than anything else.
It seems that I have been gone a y
and yet it is only three months. But
goes so slow up here—the days are so l
I can get up at three in the morning a
is real light and at seven or eight in
evening it is still *sunshine;* so you se
have plenty of daylight. We think we
go out of here in a week, but it is har
tell as the nights keep cool and that k
the ice so much longer than if the wi
night was warm. We sleep comfort
under two blankets, but the days are c

I am not an expert at cooking a fancy *meal.*

I see several women, but only give them a passing look, but the rest of our crowd make a great *ado*, when they lay eyes on one. But to tell the truth they are all ugly.

I am in excellent health, and feel as well as I possibly could. This is a healthy country, and there are no contagious diseases up this way. I have only seen two sick men, and they were in that condition doubtless from overwork.

We had a very nice ride in our boat yesterday except in starting. Tagish Lake in some places is very shallow, our boat draws about eighteen inches and we had hard work for three miles to get her to go. We all had on our high rubber bosts and we walked and pulled it until we struck deep water. We all got quite wet, as the wind was high and when the waves struck the boat the spray would fly ten feet high and fall on us, but the ice water seemed to do us good for we are in excellent shape *to-day.*

We are all careful as we *can* be and try to be on the safe side. Of course we do not know what is ahead of us, but I hope nothing but success is at the other end for us all. We were just one month too late in starting, for we could have gone on the ice as far as we wished to go, and as it is we lose a month in waiting, and as for the cold, we can all stand forty degrees below and work outside *all day;* a person can stand this cold and not mind it at all. Mr. Garrison wanted to come a month earlier, but his neighbors *also* said it was too early.

This has been a windy day and we did not work any. Charley Carlson and I went fishing this morning down the river in a skiff, but came back without a fish. I forgot to tell we are on Six Mile River just below the mouth of Tagish Lake about two miles, and about four from Marsh Lake which is about nineteen miles long.

We want to make one more move down the river to Marsh in order to get with another party of four; we will then lash our boats together, stretch a tent over them, so as to have a place to rest, put up sails and while one party manages the boats the other can rest; besides, in that way they will be less apt to rock and tip in a gale. My next letter will probably be written at Ft. Selkirk. A. D. BOURN.

Lake Tagish, Alaska, May 11, 1898.

Language of Flags.

To "strike the flag" is to lower the national colors in token of submission. Flags are used as the symbol of rank and command, the officers using them being called flag officers. Such flags are square, to distinguish them from other banners.

A "flag of truce" is a white flag displayed to an enemy to indicate a desire for a parley or a consultation.

The white flag is the sign of peace. After a battle parties from both sides often go out to the field to rescue the wounded or bury the dead, under the protection of a white flag.

The red flag is a sign of defiance, and is often used by revolutionists. In our service it is a mark of danger, and shows a vessel to be receiving or discharging her powder.

The black flag is a sign of piracy. The yellow flag shows a vessel to be at quarantine, and is a sign of contagious disease. A flag at half mast means mourning. Fishing and other vessels return with a flag at half mast to announce the death of some of the men. Dipping a flag is lowering it slightly and then hoisting it again to salute a vessel or fort.

Horned People.

Probably not one of our readers ever saw a man or woman with horns like a beast, and yet a number of such freaks of nature have been authenticated. A Paris journal contains an able article on the subject, and mention is made of a book in which the author describes seventy-one cases of horned human beings, the most of them being women. It is further shown that the horns of the women are usually longer than those of the men. In the British Museum is a specimen of a human horn eight inches long, and it at one time ornamented the head of an English nobleman. In the seventeenth century Mrs. Allen, c England, had a pair of horns of which sh was very proud, and wore them all her lif They attracted to her many admirer Another lady, known as the beautif Mary Davis, had her horns cut off fou times. One growth was presented to Kin Henry IV., of France. M. Lamprey, wh traveled in Africa in 1887, reports a num ber of cases of horned people. He met majestic-looking negro who had two horn one on either side of his nose. It is recorded that a Mexican was seen with a hor seven inches long, containing three branches like the horns of a stag. There ar well-authenticated cases of horns bein found on dogs, horses, and even rabbit There is mention of one case where a hor was found on a cat. These facts ar gleaned from a recent issue of the Literar Digest. In ancient times horns wer regarded as the emblem of strength. Q some of the coins which he ordered, Alex e Great had himself represented pair of horns. Michael Angelo, made a statue of Moses, pictured of the wilderness with horns as a his strength.—*The Gospel Mes-*

Short Stories.

ost says that among the specialists e government employs in Wash- s a learned gentleman who was ₃ superintendent of a Sabbath- One of the stories he tells of that of a day when a visiting clergy- iressed the school. On the very at sat a pale little boy who had Sunday-school that morning for time in his life. He watched the clergyman with almost painful The visiting clergyman was a e man, with great, dark eyes, and ike unto that of the bull of Ba- e rose.

ren," he thundered, "who made ious universe?"

ıck eyes glared fiercely at the new ıe front seat. The urchin squirmed bled.

, sir," he said huskily, "but I er do it again."

amusing stories are told of a well- professor of theology who is both ninded and short-sighted. Once ner party he took up his fork and it into the hand resting on the th of the lady at his side, saying, ad, I believe." On another occa- hat blew off and was carried by the to an adjoining garden, and away after it. He jumped over one wall, see it apparently flying over the nd so he valiantly pursued it over lozen walls, and then found out it black cat. On going back to the -place he found his hat. The same quently mixes up words in preach- or instance, "We all know what it ve a half warmed fish (half formed ıside us," he said once. And again g of the different social grades of ırtal life he added, "But when we all come to a lead devil" (dead -*Exchange.*

anted to ask her to be his ownest ıt the conventional words he had up so carefully failed him. She his purpose, but saw no chance to n out.

you read about the Manila cable?" d.

" she said. "It's cut."

was a long silence.

ıt do they do with cables that are ıe softly asked.

ɔe 'em," he answered.

gave him a timid sidelong glance. ɔke up.

s get spliced!" he hastily cried.

s," she gently answered.

the ordeal which had worried him y weeks was suddenly forgotten.— *ıd Plain Dealer.*

is an old story of a maiden who sat at, on a lake, toying idly with a ɔ of pearls. She did not notice ı end of the string had become un- l, and that the pearls were slipping, one, irrecoverably into the water, ıey were nearly all gone from her possession forever. Then she burst into tears. But a wise friend admonished her that she was permitting the moments and hours and days to slip from the strand of life, losing them forever, and urged her to a more serious and thoughtful existence, lest she become bankrupt at last in the entire loss of what is infinitely more valuable than pearls. And she awoke. It was a dream. But she was made wiser by it, and set about making her life one full of usefulness and earnest action. Then, though the days passed by, she became wiser and better, and did not lose the days, because she kept what they brought to her life.—*Christian Leader.*

Kisses for Mother.

Keep your warmest, tenderest kisses for mother's lips. What though her face is growing wrinkled, and silver threads are multiplying on her head. Away back when you were little she kissed you when no one else was tempted by your fever-tainted breath and swolen face. You were not so attractive then as now. And then the midnight kisses with which she routed so many bad dreams as she leaned over your restless pillow have all been on interest these long years. Do not forget to pay them back, principal and interest.

Profanity.

One of the most common and most reprehensible practices on earth is profanity. Most vices, in some degree at least, gratify him to practice them. But profanity is one that absolutely affords no gratification of any kind. It is simply repugnant to the finer feelings and better instincts of humanity without one single compensating feature. There is neither gain nor momentary pleasure about it, and hence it is, of all sins, the most foolish and most inexplicable. The man who is an habitual swearer disgusts all who hear him, even those who use an oath occasionaly themselves. Guard your temper and you will be less prone to profanity.—*The Messenger.*

Sunday School.

ROYAL INJUSTICE IN ISRAEL.*

HERBERT L. WILLETT.

The present study affords a glimpse of the character of Ahab's reign in relation to the rights of the common people. The whole narrative of this portion of 1 Kings deals with the contrast between Ahab and Elijah. The two men represented the opposite principles in government. Ahab was a bold, wise, far-sighted king whose ambition it was to increase the power of Israel on the line of Solomon's empire. The king was to be everything. Alliances with foreign nations would cement the power of the throne. While the worship of Jehovah was recognized as the state religion, it must not be regarded as the exclusive religion of the realm. It was more important that the friendship and assistance of the neighboring states be secured than that the ancient worship of God be safeguarded. If the best interests of Israel demanded an alliance with Phœnicia by marriage, there could be no special objection to the introduction of the worship of Phœnician gods under official sanction. With these ideas of Ahab went along the enrichment of his capital. Solomon himself was outdone. He had possessed a throne of ivory, but Ahab built a palace in which ivory was so extensively used in decoration that it was called the "ivory palace" (1 Kings 22:39). In all these things Jezebel seems to have ably seconded her ambitious husband.

But Elijah presented the opposite tendency in state and religion. He was opposed to the enrichment of the nation, because it menanced the simpler life of the people. The policy of kings like Solomon, Ahab and Jeroboam II. was always antagonized by the prophets, who perceived in it the promise of approaching danger to the true faith. But in the present study another point of opposition is developed. The kings had always respected the rights of the citizens. Among these rights one of the most cherished was the holding of ancestral estates, which were recognized as belonging sacredly to the families holding them from the beginning. This sentiment was sanctioned by established custom and found its embodiment, at least later on, in the statutes of the land (Lev. 25:18-28). The conflict of the growing monarchy with this sentiment occurred when Ahab sought to gain possession of a certain vineyard owned by Naboth, a citizen of Jezreel. The king wanted the property for a park. He could not understand why a property owner should not be willing to dispose of his field if he was offered a sufficient price, or a more desirable property in exchange. The narrative indicates that Ahab made Naboth a perfectly fair offer for his vineyard, and that the latter chose to refuse to part with his hereditary possession, which was his right. He could sell or he could refuse to sell. He chose the latter course, and Ahab knew enough of the sentiment of the people he governed to respect the will of a freeholder in Israel. No king had ever ventured to tamper with such privileges. There was nothing to do but submit, and though Ahab could ill brook the disappointment, he knew of no means of success. Petulent, thwarted and checked in his personal desires, he went to the palace, threw himself upon his bed and turned his face in anger to the wall.

But Jezebel, his wife, shared none of his scruples. She had been reared in a land where autocratic power was more firmly established, and the rights of the common people less safeguarded than in Israel. Indeed, it must ever be of interest to the student of social conditions to observe the amount of independence which was preserved to the farmers, laborers and tradesmen of Israel. This was largely due to the work of the prophets who were the tribunes of the people, and often stood between them and royal tyranny. Jezebel roused Ahab to a sense of the power he ought to exercise. Did he really rule, or was he but king in name? She knew how such things were managed in other lands when a mere peasant resisted the will of his king with pretentions to "rights" of his own. Whatever may have been Ahab's misgivings as to the success of his wife's plan, he was too much interested in getting the field to refuse her his consent. And here began the crime. Ahab would have dropped the project on its first rejection by Naboth, but led on by the masterful spirit of his wife, he plunged into open violation of right and justice. His authority was invoked to work the destruction of the honest and sturdy freeholder, Naboth. A fast was proclaimed in token of a fearful crime which was imputed to the Jezreelite. He was arrested in the king's name. At the trial false witnesses, worthless fellows, were secured to testify that he had been heard to curse God and the king. On these grounds the condemnation of the man was secured, and he was taken outside the town and stoned to death, according to the Hebrew custom of inflicting capital punishment. All this was accomplished by the magistrates of Jezreel under the direction of Jezebel. Her influence was too great to be resisted except on pain of death. It seems likely that all this had been done without the knowledge of Ahab. He had not been responsible directly for the mock trial. But he could hardly have failed to suspect the means by which his wife would gain her ends, and it could have been no surprise to him when he was told by her that Naboth was dead and the vineyard was now his.

But when the king went down to take possession of the property, the brand of murder was on his soul. His abdication of power while his wife won for him the coveted tresure could not relieve him of responsibility. One morning centuries later, a Roman governor finding himself hard pressed between his conscience and a howling mob, abdicated his judgment-seat, washed his hands in token of freedom from all responsibility, and said, "See ye to it." But the ages have held Pilate responsible for the death of Jesus, and Ahab for the murder of Naboth.

The king went to Jezreel with a feeling of satisfaction. No obstacle hindered his enjoyment of Naboth's forfeited vineyard, and no citizen would henceforth dare refuse his royal demands. But while he walked about in his new possessions he was met by Elijah, the incarnation of divine displeasure at the king's misdeeds, the indignant tribune of the people denouncing justice on royal sin. His fierce words crushed the spirit of Ahab into abject humility, and sent him back to his palace to walk with bowed head and soft tread for many days. And later years witnessed the fulfillment of those words of fire; for when Ahab was brought back from battle to die, and his blood-stained chariot was washed at the pool of Samaria, men remembered that years before on that very spot there had lain the mangled body of Naboth of Jezreel; and when Jehu entered that summer capital of the kings of Israel, his horses trampled on the form of Jezebel of Zidon, and the children of Ahab, the last surviors of his house, perished by the sword of that same fierce charioteer.

SUGGESTIONS FOR TEACHING.

Naboth was a martyr to the cause of popular liberty, and his death was an eloquent protest against the irresponsible authority of kings. No sight is more humiliating than a man who is unable to control his own bad temper. Ahab is not the last who has sulked because he could not have his own way. It was the evil advice of an unscrupulous tempter that led Ahab into crime. We are responsible not only for what we do, but for what we permit to be done when we might prevent it. The children of belial "worthlessness" live among us yet; people who by evil suggestions, insinuations, slanders and falsehoods, ruin character. The rulers of a city or state, who do corrupt and wicked things at the bidding of a party boss or commercial dictator, are as despicable as were the cringing elders of Jezereel. Sin is sure to bring its penalty.

*Bible-school Lesson for July 31, 1898—Naboth's Vineyard (1 Kings 21:4-16). Golden Text—Thou shalt not covet thy neighbor's house (Exod. 20:17). Lesson Outline—1. Ahab's disappointment (4); 2. Jezebel's plot (5-10); 3. Naboth's death (11-16).

istian Endeavor.

3Y BURRIS A. JENKINS.

TOPIC FOR JULY 31.

VILS OF COVETOUSNESS.

x. 20:17; Luke 12:13-21.)

his sin of covetousness is less spoken proportion to its prevalence, than ther. Perhaps the very fact that e above his origin in America more other country, lays us liable to in- ire. We see men's splendid homes lived in them. We hear of men's es and wonder why we might not l possess such advantages. We nd carriages, social and intellectual s, that others possess, far exceed- 'alue, and since we recognize no irth in our country, we ask why nan possess these more than an- e even covet other people's ex- -servents and maid-servants. Some ' domestic felicity—their husbands s—as if any one could be sure how little domestic joy reigns behind ors of any home. Fools that we each go home to his own little bring into it all the heaven our ig enough to carry.

that the first great evil of covetous- discontent with our lot, born of with others. The Greeks had a nce all the people of the world onted that they came together and wn his peculiar burden beside the each chose another's burden and y in life. Then, behold! the dis- v graver than ever. A great wail n all the earth, every one crying wn old burden. On an appointed ll came together again, each took lot in life and went on his way in o we know what there is behind ne fronts and oak doors of other sessions? Certainly men's hap- in proportion to the things that . Whether these things be chat- es. Heaven sits not in coin and nds or deeds, nor yet in intellect- or political opportunities. Heaven pun by that unresting little spider n vitals—the heart.

'tis better to be lowly born,
with humble livers in content,
perked up in a glistening grief
a golden sorrow!
th, I would not be a queen!''

Anne Boleyn, she was a queen, and the head that wears a crown, t crown be held in right of birth or d social leadership. When shall heed Paul's words, "I have learn- ever state I am therewith [or there- tent.''

ry close akin to malice, and there anger of covetousness bringing a in its train—hatred. We hear ers imploring the rich to make dis- r wealth, lest the people should look As if the removal of all tempta- le, or could keep one's heart right, ssible! It is impossible but that should exist; let all men, high and he most of it. It is not altogether t the high has the best. It is he has not, unless he is the best. e cousin of us all whose name was of whom it is said that he was a A friend asked him one day how form society. "Well,'' said Pat, de iverything up aquel.'' "And now, Pat, that in six weeks you'd all yours, and the rich man would it again?'' "Well, then,'' said ed first cousin, "Oi'd be in for an- e.''

h and illogical to demand that all alike in the world's goods. How etermine what are the goods and what are the bads? Riches are sometimes curses, while a hard lot often makes a soft heart. No use, then, to hate those who we fancy have fared better than we in the world's shake-up. Far better to be contented in our own little backyard, knowing that if it were not the best place for us to serve God this side of paradise, he would not have put us in it.

Covetousness sometimes even leads to crime. Many a man has been placed behind bars because of his inordinate craving for what another owned. All of us who covet are in danger of crime; if of no other crime, then the crime of covetousness. It is a crime against content, against usefulness, against cheerfulness, against ones home, against society, against God who made us and placed us here to make the most and best of our lot and of ourselves.

The C. E. Reading Courses.

A READING COURSE CATECHISM.

BY J. Z. TYLER.

General Editor and Manager.

[The following catechism contains in briefest form all necessary information concerning the Bethany C. E. Reading Courses. The questions are those most frequently sent to headquarters. Please read the answers carefully, and preserve for future reference.]

1. *Must each reader own a handbook?* It is best; yet two or more persons may be so situated that they can use one book in common without serious hindrance.

2. *Is there a discount when a number of books are ordered at the same time?* No; the books are sold to the single reader at the lowest price, so that further discount is impossible.

3. *Is it required that cash accompany each order?* Yes; we have no other means of paying the printer and of meeting other necessary expenses. Moreover, we have found that some forget to send the money at all if they do not send it with the order.

4. *To whom should money orders, drafts, etc., be made payable and how should orders for supplies be addressed?* Money orders, etc., should be made payable to the Bethany C. E. Company; the address is 798 Republic Street, Cleveland, Ohio.

5. *Must those who paid membership fee for the past year be required to pay a similar fee for the second year and what is the amount?* Yes; and the amount is still twenty-five cents a year, although we now give more than was originally intended. That twenty-five cents now pays not only for membership, but for the Bethany C. E. Bulletin for a year.

6. *Is there an enrollment of members kept at headquarters?* Yes; and between 3,500 and 4,000 persons actually enrolled during the first year.

7. *Are the handbooks and the Bulletin sent directly to each member or to the Literary Leader to be distributed by him?* That is to be just as each reading circle prefers. Perhaps it is better, as a general rule, to send all the supplies to the leader to be distributed by him to the individual readers; thus enabling him to keep the work better in hand. But supplies will be sent directly to the readers whenever preferred.

8. *May subscription to the Bulletin begin at any time?* It may be sent in at any time, but it will be credited as paying for the current volume and so will be credited to the beginning of that reading year. All subscriptions begin, therefore, with the October number.

9. *May the reading be taken up at any time?* Certainly; it is better to begin promptly with the beginning of the year. The year begins October 1, and closes July 1.

10. *When should we begin to organize a circle?* Begin early; the earlier the better. Your order for supplies would better be in at headquarters by Sept. 1, if possible. Earlier than that would be still better. If every society waits until nearly Oct. 1, it will be impossible for each order to receive prompt attention. Begin now.

11. *Are the quarterly examinations important?* We think they are. They secure definite results and aid in forming systematic habits of study. Besides, the certificate given at the close of the three years' course will be a souvenir worth having.

12. *If persons find it impossible to take all three courses may they not take one or two?* The readings are planned to be taken together, yet if persons find it really impossible to take all three they may take one or two, making their own selection. Some circles may prefer to complete the entire reading assigned to the year by giving three months, in turn, to each of the studies. This may be done.

13. *Are the articles published week by week in the "C. E. Reading Column'' of our church papers included in the required readings?* No; but any one makes a serious mistake who does not give these articles a careful reading. They have been of a high order and contain much valuable information in addition to what is contained in the handbooks. Do not neglect the "C. E. Reading Column.''

14. *In what papers does the "C. E. Reading Column'' appear, and why does it not appear in all?* During the first year this column has appeared regularly in the CHRISTIAN-EVANGELIST, the Christian Oracle, the Christian News, the Pacific Christian, the Christian Courier, Our Young Folks and the Gospel Messenger. We would be glad to publish these helps in all our papers if they would permit us.

15. *Are the second series of handbooks—the handbooks for the second year—now ready, and what are they?* No; they are not yet ready (July 1, 1898), but they are in course of preparation and we confidently expect to have them ready for delivery in September. H. L. Willett is preparing a handbook on "The Life and Teachings of Jesus;'' W. J. Lhamon is preparing one on "The Missionary Fields and Forces of the Disciples;'' F. D. Power is preparing one containing "Brief Sketches of Our Pioneers.'' There will probably be another handbook entitled "Bible Doctrine for Young Disciples,'' dealing directly with the doctrinal position of Disciples. The second series of handbooks will be along the same lines as the first and will be of similar size and appearance. We shall make every effort to keep them down to the same price. More definite announcement will appear in our church papers before the opening of the second year.

Marriages.

BRAND—WELLs.—At the parsonage of the Old Bedford Christian Church, near Blandinsville, Ill., June 30, 1898, Mr. G. L. Brand, of Blandinsville, Ill., and Miss Maud Wells, of Raritan, Ill.; A. R. Adams, officiating.

RAGSDALE—HARPER.—July 3, 1898, C. H. Strawn, officiating, Mr. Ernest O. Ragsdale, of Holliday, Mo., to Miss Annie M. Harper, of Madison, Mo.

Obituaries.

[One hundred words will be inserted free. Above one hundred words, one cent a word. Please send amount with each notice.]

PHELPS.

Margaret Mitchell Russell was born in Kentucky, October 11, 1819. When 11 years of age she came with her parents to Illinois, riding the entire journey on horsback. She was married December 27, 1838, to William H. Phelps. Her husband died three years ago, her married life covering a period of 56 years. She was the mother of 11 children, six surviving her with a number of grandchildren. She became a Christian under the ministry of A. J. Kane in 1845. She died July 7, 1898, for 53 years a pious member of the Christian Church in Macomb, Ill. Always faithful. Funeral by brother L. D. Goodwin.

J. C. REYNOLDS.

GOSNEY.

Mrs. Lucy Hawes Gosney, one of God's dear and aged saints, passed to her eternal reward on June 4th, 1898, at the advanced age of 97 years, six months and one day. "Grandma" Gosney was born in Shelby county, Kentucky, December 3rd, 1800. Was married to Alfred Gosney at the early age of 18, with whom she lived in happy union until his death, in 1862. Twelve children were born to them, of whom seven are yet living. Bro. and Sister Gosney moved from Kentucky to Indianapolis, Ind., in 1850. Here they were known, as they had been in their former home, as zealous Christians, fully committed to the plea of the Disciples, which they had both accepted at an early day in Kentucky. Sister Gosney confessed her Savior when a little girl, and united with the Baptist Church. When first the fathers of our reformation preached New Testament Christianity in Kentucky, the simplicity and beauty of their message won her heart and life, and she became an intelligent and earnest advocate of the principles for which they pleaded. Some 20 years after her husband's death, in 1882, Sister Gosney came with the family of her daughter, Mrs. S. V. Wilson, to Kansas City, Mo., where she made her home until her decease. During these latter years her sight was almost gone, and her general health was not good, so that she was deprived of the privileges of attending public worship. But her faith in God, patience in suffering, and unfailing cheerfulness of spirit were an inspiration to all who entered her presence. She was ministered to with unfailing kindness by her daughter and granddaughter and her son-in-law, who was to her all that the most affectionate son could have been. The weary years of her waiting for release from age and suffering were sweetened by their gentle and loving care. She is at rest with her dear ones who preceded her to the better land. We shall meet her again in the land of eternal youth and peace.

W. F. RICHARDSON.

Kansas City, Mo., June 6, 1898.

SARTORI.

Sister Sabra Ann Sartori was born in Marcelline, Illinois, December 21, 1842. Died in Springfield, Missouri, March 26, 1898. She was married May 28, 1868, to Matteo Sartori. Sister Sartori was one of the faithful members of South Street Christian Church. Her beautiful Christian character was a perpetual sermon. She was early surrounded with the influences of the Christian religion, her father being a minister of the gospel. Her young heart yielded easily to the gentle influences of the gospel and her entire life was but the unfolding and ripening of this seed sown in good ground. Sister Sartori was faithful unto the end and died in the triumphs of a living faith. She was laid to rest in the beautiful Maple Park cemetery, amid the evergreens and flowers, fit emblem of her beautiful and unending life. A husband, son and daughter are left to mourn this loving wife and mother.

N. S.

MITCHELL.

Sunday morning, June 26th, Mrs. Catharine Mitchell, of Monmouth, Ill., fell asleep. Catharine Miller was born in Madison Co., Ohio, 1819; married Amos Haines and lived on a farm in Pickaway Co., Ohio., until 1840; moved to Henderson Co., Ill. Her husband died in 1855 leaving seven children. In 1857 she married Wm. C. Mitchell who died in 1881. Two children resulted from the second marriage. She was a member of the Christian Church more than 40 years, living a loyal Christian life, and the Rosette Church, this state, is largely a result of her bounty.

C. H. STEARNS, Pastor.

Monmouth, Ill.

NEWCOMER.

J. S. Newcomer was instantly killed by a passing train on his farm at Falls City, Neb., the morning of July 4. Deceased was born in Fayette county, Pa., Jan. 28, 1829, where he was married May 27, 1851, to Elizabeth Stoner. From 1854 to 1881 the family lived in Stark county, Ill., and since then near Falls City, Neb. Four children have preceded him to the home above and six remain to comfort their lonely mother. He was a Christian for more than 50 years and ever faithfully led his family into the house of God. Every child born to this household early became a Christian save the one taken home to the Savior in infancy. Happy thought—a family united on earth and in heaven. Miss Annette, corresponding secretary of the Iowa C. W. B. M., was home for a short rest. Charles B. is in Berlin, Germany, where next year he finishes his four years' university course. As personal friend and former pastor the writer conducted the funeral services from the church where for 17 years the deceased had regularly worshiped God. His was a clean life. He kept the faith.

A. W. DAVIS.

Hiawatha, Kan.

FACTS AND FACTORS.

Gen. Miles sailed for Santiago July 8th.

The Havana blockade has been strengthened.

Troops are still being forwarded to Santiago.

Admiral Camara is returning to Spain with his fleet.

Five inches of water fell in St. Louis from Thursday to Friday morning of last week.

A mob at Leland, Ill., hanged the wrong negro July 8th.

A Spanish privateer was reported off the coast of British Columbia, July 8th.

The Fifty-fifth Congress adjourned at two o'clock July 8th.

Mrs. Martha M. Place, convicted of the murder of her step-daughter, Ida Place, was sentenced to die in the electric chair at Sing Sing prison, New York, during the week beginning August 29th.

A Scotchman named Morton, a Quaker, has given $1,200,000 to the Moravian Church, to be expended in the prosecution of missions.

Gen. Miles arrived at Santiago, July 11th.

The Spanish Premier, Sagasta, resigned July 11th.

Two of Cervera's wrecked cruisers and all his main batteries are likely to be saved.

Prince Victor Emmanuel, son of the late King Amadeus, who wisely resigned the throne of Spain, and nephew of King Humbert, of Italy, is making a tour of the United States, traveling under the title of Count of Turin.

Eleven men were instantly killed in a tunnel under the lake at Cleveland, O., July 12th. Cause of explosion unknown.

The Laflin & Rand Powder Co., Dover, N. J., exploded July 12th, killing eight men. Cause of explosion unknown.

Bible Institute.

Lectures on the Bible by President J. W. McGarvey, of Kentucky University, with other addresses and sermons by prominent preachers of Illinois, Iowa and Missouri, at Canton, Mo., August 1-4. Free entertainment. Visitors from a distance cordially invited.

Please to announce the above in your church.

If possible send names to Dr. R. B. Turner, Committee on Entertainment. CLINTON LOCKHART, Pres. Christian University.

Publishers' Notes.

Our complete catalogue will be sent free to any one giving us their name and address. It contains a full list of our publications and embraces a large part of the best literature of the Christian Church. Write us a card and you will have sent you a list of books which will be a perfect reservoir of good literature.

SOMETHING FREE.

Our Christian Endeavor catalogue and our marriage certificate catalogue will be sent free to those writing for them. Members of Endeavor Societies should have our Endeavor catalogue, as it contains lists and price of badges, pledges, cards, books, etc., in fact, *all* the necessary equipment for wide-awake Endeavorers. Our marriage certificate catalogue is quite convenient for the ministry. It gives cuts of a large assortment, and will enable the preacher to order according to his own taste. Address Christian Publishing Co., St. Louis, Mo.

"WONDERS OF THE SKY,"

or God's Glory Exhibited in the Heavens, by W. J. Russell, is just fresh from the press; handsomely bound in cloth, beautiful side stamp, and the price is 50 cents, postpaid. This book contains 82 pages, and the following table of contents will indicate the scope of this volume:

Preface, Introduction, The History of Astronomy, The Depths of Space, The Stars and their Number, Celestial Distances, Movements of the Stars, The Sun, Planets Farthest from the Sun, Asteroids, Are the Planets Inhabited? The Supreme Power.

The Gospel Advocate, Nashville, Tenn., says, "The author of 'The Exiled Prophet,' J. G. Encell, has spent twenty-five years investigating the Book of Revelation, and in this volume we have the fruits of his labor. In seventeen lectures the author gives what he believes to be the meauing of seven seals, the seven trumpets, wondors or signs, the first and second beasts, the returning church, the vials of wrath, the great harlot and her fate, and the millennial age."

"IN THE DAYS OF JEHU,"

By J. Breckenridge Ellis, is just in line with the Sunday-school lessons for the present quarter.

The lessons being found principally in the Book of Kings, this volume will be found a valuable aid to a thorough understanding of the Sunday-school lessons for the present quarter.

The characters of Elijah, Jehu, Jezebel, Ahab, Obadiah, Naboth and others are presented in such facinating style that the reader is both charmed and interested at the same time. The book contains 188 pages and the price is 75 cents.

Announcements.

The annual convention of the first Christian missioary district of Kansas will be held with the Church of Christ at Reserve, Aug. 23-25. Look for program later. The Church at Reserve will entertain all delegates. Let each church in the district prepare to send at least two delegates. If you expect to attend send your name to Irene Gall, Reserve, Kan.

JOHN. L. STINE,
Pastor Reserve Church.

Program of Macatawa Assembly

FOR 1898. FROM AUGUST 7TH TO AUGUST 14TH, INCLUSIVE.

The two leading features of the Assembly will be a Bible-school conducted every forenoon by Prof. H. L. Willett and Rev. J. M. Campbell from 10 to 12 o'clock—the last half hour to be devoted to discussion; and a symposium on Christian Union every evening by representatives of the Disciple and Congregational churches.

The following is the

PROGRAM:

SUNDAY, AUGUST 7TH.

The Assemly Sermon by Rev. George H. Wilson, of Paxton, Ill., at 2 P. M.

MONDAY, AUGUST 8TH.

From 10 to 12 A. M. Bible-school: Subject—The Literary Structure and Spiritual Teaching of Matthew's Gospel.

EVENING.

Symposium on Christian Union—Address by Dr. J. H. Garrison, editor of the CHRISTIAN-EVANGELIST, etc., St. Louis, Mo., on The Present-Day Movement to Union in Harmony with the Purpose of God.

TUESDAY, AUGUST 9TH.

10 to 12 A. M., Bible-school: Subject—The Gospel According to Mark.

EVENING.

Address on Christian Union, or Practical Church Federation, by Prof. Graham Taylor, Dean of Chicago Commons.

WEDNESDAY, AUGUST 10TH.

10 to 12 A. M., Bible-school: Subject—The Gospel according to Luke.

EVENING.

Address on, A Stumbling Block in the Way of Union; How can it be Removed? Rev. J. M. Campbell, Lombard, Ill.

THURSDAY, AUGUST 11TH.

10 to 12 A. M., Bible-school: Subject—The Gospel of John.

EVENING.

Address on, What are the Essential Doctrines which must form the Basis of Union? by Dr. W. T. Moore, Columbia, Mo.

FRIDAY, AUGUST 12TH.

10 to 12 A. M., Bible-school: Subject—
the Apostles.

EVENING.

Address on, The Trend of the Age—an
tion, by Prof. W. D. McKenzie, of Chica
gical Seminary.

SATURDAY, AUGUST 13TH.

10 to 12 A. M., Bible-school: Subject—
ation of St. John.

EVENING.

Addres on, The Church of the Future,
L. Willett, Dean of Disciples' Divinity S
versity, of Chicago.

SUNDAY, AUGUST 14TH.

2 P. M., closing Sermon by Prof. W. D.
to be followed by the Lord's Supper.

New Books

IN THE DAYS OF JEHU. By J. BRECKENRIDGE ELLIS. 1
cloth, 75c.

A well written and intensely interesting Bible narrative. Without sacrificing hi
cal accuracy, the author has given us a book more interesting than a work of pure fi

I have read "In the Days of Jehu" with interest and pleasure, and regard it
literary point of view, as a meritorious production. There is here shown an excep
power of constructive imagination, and at the same time a wisdom of expressic
soundness and reach of thought. Besides, the style is simple, lucid and good, s
the thoughts fall into the mind of the reader without effort on his part. I think th
opened up, in this book, a mine which will yield much good ore, whose metallurg
enhance the interest of the sacred volume.—DR. H. CHRISTOPHER, Editor *Medica*
ald, St. Joseph, Mo.

THE EXILED PROPHET; or, What John Saw on Patmos.
J. G. ENCELL. 12mo, cloth, $1.25.

The author has devoted a great many years to the study of this wonderful book.
trated with nearly forty half-tone engravings.

This is a valuable book, prefaced by an essay on Daniel by Dr. D. R. Dungan, c
ing seventy pages, and is exceedingly interesting to the student of prophecy. The s
teen chapters following on the Book of Revelation are equally as interesting and e
much research and earnestness for the truth. The author's conclusions will genera
accepted, and a careful reading of the book will awaken new interest in What John
on the Isle of Patmos.—Christian Tribune, Baltimore, Md.

For a number of years the author has been giving the substance of this bool
series of illustrated lectures. The marvel is that he has succeeded in condensin
work to its present form. It is suggestive and stimulating, and is probably as rea
and satisfactory as any small volume published on this riddle of the ages, calle
Apocalypse.—Christian Oracle, Chicago.

LIFE OF ALEXANDER CAMPBELL. By THOMAS W. G
TON. With an introduction by Herbert L. Willett. L
12mo, cloth, $1.00.

A condensed, concise and accurate account of the life of this great religious re
er, beginning with his boyhood, and following him through his trials and triumphs.
written in an attractive style. It is just the book for the busy people.

People who know nothing about Mr. Campbell, and who wish to ascertain
manner of man he was, and what he taught, can obtain from this volume the d
information. There are tens of thousands of church members who should buy thi
and read and master it.—*The Missionary Intelligencer*, Cincinnati, O.

AFTER PENTECOST, WHAT? By JAMES M. CAMPBELL, au
of "Unto the Uttermost." 12mo, cloth, 297 pages, $1.00.

This work is a discussion of the doctrine of the Holy Spirit in its relation to m
Christological thought. The following Table of Contents will give an idea of the
of the book: Introduction, The Significance of Pentecost, A Spiritual Christ, A
itual God, Spiritual Worship, A Spiritual Apprehension of Truth, An Influx of Spi
Life, The Spiritual Man, Spiritual Holiness, Spiritual Authority, The Distribut
Spiritual Operations, The Impartation of Spiritual Power, The Production of Spi
Works, The Formation of a Spiritual Society, The Inauguration of Spiritual Moven
The Establishment of a Spiritual Kingdom.

ROSA EMERSON; or, A Young Woman's Influence. A S
of the Lodge, the Church and the School. By JOHN A
WILLIAMS. 375 pages, cloth, $1.00.

Rosa represents most of the beautiful female virtues, and young Thornton is as l
and noble and fearless as a knight. Their love is strong and true, without the heart
and heartbreaks which so frequently send the Cupid-smitten unfortunates danger
near the mad-house. The whole-souluess that left no stone unturned to find the b
the estate of the father French, and succeeded at last in laying the prize on the he
Simon Bugg, who was not a bugg at all, is as wild and beautiful as the story of Py
and Damon. Here is another diamond, first in the rough, but polished, in the old
with his own dust, until Simon French Stuart, as he proves to be, comes fearfully
getting the crown of heroism. I like the fine selection of characters, with which
pose hypocrisy and sham. Faithfulness in the discharge of duty is made to rank
above sectarian orthodoxy, and to throw a white light on the miserable sectarian s
gies for religious conviction and Christian living. I hope the author will receive a l
patronage, and the book a wide reading.—D. R. DUNGAN.

Christian Publishing Company, St. Louis,

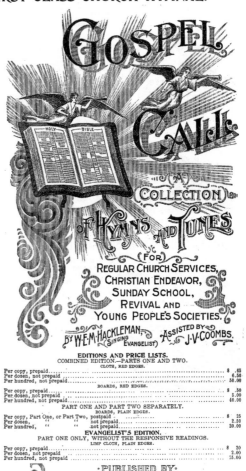

New England CONSERVATORY OF MUSIC Unequalled advantages in all departments of Music and Elocution. The Conservatory home for young women provides every comfort and safeguard.
George W. Chadwick, Musical Director.
Pupils received at any time. For prospectus address
FRANK W. HALE, General Manager, Boston, Mass.

Randolph-Macon Woman's College,

Lynchburg, Va. Endowed for Higher Education. Laboratories for Chemistry, Physics, Biology and Psychology. Gymnasium. All modern appliances. Endowment reduces cost of course to $250. Address
WM. W. SMITH, A. M., LL. D., President.

ACADEMY FOR YOUNG WOMEN. 69th Year

A high grade English and Classical School. Certificate admits to Eastern colleges for women. Beautiful location; elevating in associations; celebrated for historic names and Christian institutions.

Under same management are Illinois Conservatory of Music and School of Fine Arts, offering complete courses in these departments. Scholarships awarded to a limited number of girls of superior promise. Address
E. F. BULLARD, Pres., 206 Church St., Jacksonville, Ill.

The Woman's College of Baltimore

offers earnest, well prepared young women facilities for obtaining a college education under the direction of specialists, with abundant laboratory appliances and modern methods. Climate mild, surroundings cheerful. Total yearly expense, three hundred and seventy-five dollars.

Programs mailed on application.
JOHN F. GOUCHER, Pres., Baltimore, Md.

RANDOLPH-MAGON Academy for Boys

Front Royal, Va. (Valley of Va.). Conducted by Randolph-Macon College. Best equipped in the South. Ranks with best in U. S. Modern conveniences and appliances; gymnasium, &c. $230. Address
Wm. W. Smith, A. M., LL. D, Principal.

For Christian Education go to

Christian University,

CANTON, MO.

Classical, Scientific, Ministerial, Musical and Commercial. **For Ladies and Gentlemen.**

BETHANY COLLEGE.

Founded in 1841 by Alexander Campbell. Open to men and women. Classical, Scientific, Ministerial, Literary, Musical and Art Courses. A Lecture Association, a fully equipped Gymnasium, Literary and Reading Room. Post office, Bethany, W. Va. Railway station, Wellsburg, W. Va., on the Pan-Handle Road, reached from Pittsburg, Steubenville or Wheeling. For catalogue and particulars, address the Secretary.

AMERICAN MOZART CONSERVATORY OF MUSIC AND FINE ARTS

ANNEX TO
LIBERTY LADIES' COLLEGE. CHARTERED BY THE STATE.

Methods and Courses of Instruction same as those of Royal Conservatory of Music, Berlin, Germany. Royal Conservatory of Music, Leipzig, Germany. Royal Academy of Music, London, England. Professors full graduates with highest honors from these Conservatories.

AN UPRIGHT CONCERT GRAND PIANO, quoted by Bradbury at $1050, and other prizes at May Festival, Address **Liberty Ladies' College, Liberty, Mo.**

HAMILTON COLLEGE,

LEXINGTON, KY.,

offers to YOUNG LADIES

Thorough Courses in Literature, Music, Art, Elocution, Delsarte with Gymnasium. Terms very reasonable. For Catalogues apply to
B. C. Hagerman, President.

In This Age of practical ideas a practical education is necessary to insure a successful social or business life for your daughters.

CHRISTIAN COLLEGE,

and SCHOOL OF MUSIC,

COLUMBIA, MO.,

is a school in every way worthy the patronage of parents with daughters to educate. Located in an ideal spot, one of the most healthful in the West. It combines in every manner the advantages of a Christian home with those of a high-grade College.

A $950 Piano awarded at the May Contest.

Booklet free to parents.

Address MRS. W. T. MOORE, Pres.

HARDIN COLLEGE & CONSE

FOR LADIES.

26th year. Unprecedented prosperit sors from 8 Universities and 5 Europ tories. A $1,000 Piano to best music pu American Conservatory. XAVER S Director General, present in person Largest. Cheapest. Best. Address
JOHN W. MILLION, Pres., 23 (A St.)

University of Vi

CHARLOTTESVILLE
Letters, Science, Law, Medicine, E
Session begins 15th Septe
New Buildings. Improved
Healthful Climate.
For catalogues address
P. B. BARRINGE

MARY BALDWIN SE

FOR YOUNG LADI
STAUNTON, VIRGINIA

Term begins Sept. 1st, 1898. Located in Valley of Virginia. Unsurpassed clin and appointments. 20 States represe moderate, Pupils enter any time. Write f
Mary Baldwin S

HOLLINS INSTI

BOTETOURT SPRINGS, VI
For 175 Young Lady Boarders and most extensively equipped in Virg courses in Ancient and Modern Literature, Sciences, Music, Ar tion. 30 officers and teachers. Situ of Va., near Roanoke. Mountain S feet above sea level. Mineral waters opens Sept. 14th, 1898. For illus. catalo
CHAS. L. COCKE, Supt., H

Washington and Lee U

LEXINGTON, VA
WM. L. WILSON, LL. D., Pre

Academic, Engineering and Law Additions for next session: One profe turers; new School of Economics. Pol and History. Expenses very mode SEPT. 8. For Catalogue address the P

HIRAM COLLEGE, Hiram,

A School for Both Se

$112.00 will pay for board, room (hea for), tuition and incidental f

WE CALL ATTENTION TO

1. Four Classical Courses—Regu Ministerial, Legal and Medical. Thes degree of A. B.
2. Four Scientific Courses—Regul Philosophical, Legal and Medical. Th degree of Ph. B. or B. S.
3. Four Literary Courses—Reg Ministerial, Legal and Medical. Thes degree of B. L.
4. Five Special Courses—Teache cial, English; Ministerial, Music, Orato
5. Five Post-Graduate Courses (A three years' post-graduate course l degree of B. D.); General—(A two y course); Ministerial, Medical, Legal— class work in each).

WE LAY SPECIAL STRES

1. Upon the variety of our courses— needs of all classes of students.
2. Upon the strength of our course those of the best American Colleges.
3. Upon the strength of our Faculty— twenty-two experienced teachers inclu ors in special departments and physic
4. Upon our Location—Unsurpassed f healthfulness.
5. Upon our moral and religious surr saloons; strong religious influences.
6. Upon the fact that expenses are low, considering advantages offered.
7. Upon our splendid advantages department being in charge of a very experienced German professor.
8. Upon our excellent facilities a location for art study.
9. Upon the exceptionally strong li terial work offered.
10. Upon the professional lines of department of law and medicine.

Fall term opens Sept. 27th, 189 Catalogue to
PRES. E. V. ZOLLARS, H

A Circuit of the

BY A. MCLEAN,
Sec'y Foreign Christian Missionar

This excellent missionary producti pushed during the summer months various C. W. B. M. Auxiliary Soc brotherhood. Our sisters are making door through which to replenish th Treasury of the National C. W. B. Auxiliary has not yet received the in reference to the plan, the terms and t opportunity offered for raising a nice s write to the CHRISTIAN PUBLISHING CO. St., St. Louis.

IE

'IAN-EVANGELIST.

LY FAMILY AND RELIGIOUS JOURNAL.

July 28, 1898 No. 30.

)9
)0
)1
)1
)2
)3
)4
)4
)5
)7
10
10
11
12
12
13
13
14
6
6
20
20
21
21
22
2
22
23
23
23
8
9
9
7
8
9
4
5
6
7
7
8

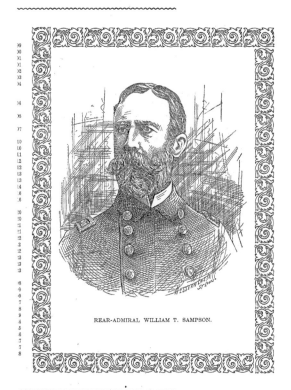

REAR-ADMIRAL WILLIAM T. SAMPSON.

PUBLISHED BY

AN PUBLISHING COMPANY

1522 Locust St., St. Louis.

THE

CHRISTIAN - EVANGELIST

J. H. GARRISON, Editor.

W. W. HOPKINS, Assistant.

B. B. TYLER, J. J. HALEY,

EDITORIAL CONTRIBUTORS.

What We Plead For.

The Christian-Evangelist pleads for:

The Christianity of the New Testament, taught by Christ and his Apostles, versus the theology of the creeds taught by fallible men—the world's great need.

The divine confession of faith on which Christ built his church, versus human confessions of faith on which men have split the church.

The unity of Christ's disciples, for which he so fervently prayed, versus the divisions in Christ's body, which his apostles strongly condemned.

The abandonment of sectarian names and practices, based on human authority, for the common family name and the common faith, based on divine authority, versus the abandonment of scriptural names and usages for partisan ends.

The hearty co-operation of Christians in efforts of world-wide beneficence and evangelization, versus petty jealousies and strifes in the struggle for denominational pre-eminence.

The fidelity to truth which secures the approval of God, versus conformity to custom to gain the favor of men.

The protection of the home and the destruction of the saloon, versus the protection of the saloon and the destruction of the home.

For the right against the wrong;
For the weak against the strong;
For the poor who've waited long
For the brighter age to be.
For the truth, 'gainst superstition,
For thé faith, against tradition,
For the hope, whose glad fruition
Our waiting eyes shall see.

RATES OF SUBSCRIPTION.

Single subscriptions, new or old	$1.75 each
In clubs of five or more, new or old	1.50 "
Reading Rooms	1.25 "
Ministers	1.00 "

With a club of ten we will send one additional copy free.

All subscriptions payable in advance. Label shows the month up to the first day of which your subscription is paid. If an earlier date than the present is shown, you are in arrears. No paper discontinued without express orders to that effect. Arrears should be paid when discontinuance is ordered.

In ordering a change of post-office, please give the OLD as well as the NEW address.

Do not send local check, but use Post office or Express Money Order, or draft on St. Louis, Chicago or New York, in remitting.

THE CHRISTIAN-EVANGELIST

"In faith, Unity; in opinion and methods, Liberty; in all things, Charity."

Vol. xxxv. St. Louis, Mo., Thursday, July 28, 1898. No. 30

CURRENT EVENTS.

The situation at Santiago, Cuba, has undergone a great change since the surrender. The population is returning, business houses are being opened, ships are unloading their commerce, the people are being fed, the city is undergoing sanitation and a general air of cheerfulness and activity prevails where but a few days ago gloom, want, fear and demoralization were the prominent features. Many business men of the city and others interested in its well-being do not conceal their satisfaction that they are no longer under the dominion of Spain. General Wood, late Colonel Wood, of the Rough Riders, has been appointed military governor of the city, succeeding General McKibbin, who was first appointed to the position. Under the assurance of a stable government, administered in the interest of the people, goods are being rapidly rushed into Santiago, and the busy scenes of trade and commerce will soon take the place of carnage and bloodshed. What is taking place in Santiago is only an indication of what will take place throughout Cuba when Spanish rule gives place to modern and improved methods of government.

A regrettable feature of the campaign in Cuba, ending in the reduction of Santiago, is the defection of General Garcia and the offering of his resignation to General Gomez. In a letter to General Shafter he explains the cause of his action. He claims that while he had been a faithful subordinate to Gen. Shafter, cheerfully obeying his orders, according to the instructions of the Cuban Republic, yet when the city of Santiago surrendered to American arms he learned of the fact through other sources that Gen. Shafter who, in all the negotiations, never conferred with or notified Garcia about the terms of surrender, and in the important ceremony of surrender he (Garcia) nor none of his staff were invited to represent the Cuban army on the occasion. This statement is in conflict with the report that he declined to take part in the ceremony of surrender because of his hatred of the Spanish who were allowed by Gen. Shafter to remain in the city, and further explanation is needed on this point. It is probable that Gen Garcia feels that he has not received the credit and honor due him on account of his long service for Cuba, but the chief cause of complaint, no doubt, is the liberal policy toward the Spanish, outlined by the President in his proclamation. These Cubans have suffered so much from Spanish cruelty that it is not strange, perhaps, that they should cherish the spirit of revenge and wish to gratify it by treating It is manifest, however, that the United States could not lend its sanction to such a method of warfare, or permit it. If the Cuban leaders lack the greatness which enables men to be generous even to their foes, it will prove a serious hindrance to the establishment of self-government in Cuba. The Cuban Junta in this country do not endorse the course of Gen. Garcia, and believe that with proper explanation the breech between the insurgents and the United States Army may be healed. Meanwhile, Gen. Garcia has retired with his forces into the interior.

Latest advices from Manila state that Aguinaldo, the insurgent leader in the Philippines, has declared himself dictator and proclaimed martial law throughout the island. Since the arrival of the American forces he has shown a decidedly hostile spirit. He has declined to see messengers sent to him by the Amercian commanders on the pretext of being unwell or asleep, until Gen. Anderson has written him a letter that will probably develop his real attitude. It is reported that Gen. Anderson's forces are moving on Manila, without waiting for Gen. Merritt. The purpose is to capture South Manila first. The California troops, under command of Gen. Greene, are in the advance, and are only two miles from the Spanish lines. It is said that the Spanish troops in Manila, who have been expecting the fleets of Cervera and Camara to reinforce them, have just learned the fate of Cervera's fleet and the destination of Camara's, and are not a little dispirited over the news.

The Porto Rican expedition, under command of Gen. Miles, the commanding General of the United States Army, is at this writing on its way to Port Rico, and the advance will have reached that island before this appears. It has been understood for sometime that after the fall of Santiago, Porto Rico would be the next objective point. The season is too advanced for campaigning in the region of Havana, and besides, it is a comparatively easy matter, now that the Spanish fleet is destroyed, to starve that city into submission while the war is being carried forward in other fields. It is *hard* on Gen. Blanco, of course, to be ingloriously starved out of the splendid fortifications he has built at such pains, without even an opportunity of winning military glory, but this war is not being waged for the special purpose of promoting the renown of Spain's captain-generals. If it were, its complete failure so far would have to be acknowledged. It is not probable that Gen. Miles would encounter very serious opposition in Porto Rico. The futility of resistance to our army and the co-operating battleships "honor" has been satisfied the island will pass into the possession of the United States, where it will probably remain as a permanent part of our domain.

A dispatch from Santiago, lacking official confirmation at this writing, reports that Gen. Garcia, after leaving Santiago, met a force of 5,000 Spaniards coming into Santiago to surrender. The Spanish commander notified Garcia that his command was a part of the forces which surrendered to Gen. Shafter, but Gen. Garcia is said to have ignored this fact and continued his attack until he was defeated by the Spanish troops with considerable loss. This breach of faith and of civilized warfare is almost incredible, and we trust there is some explanation that will relieve this incident of its present ugly appearance. Vice-President Capote, of the Cuban Republic, now in this country, expresses sincere regret at Garcia's course, and is to return at once to Cuba to see if it is not possible to explain the situation to Garcia and other Cuban leaders, so they can understand the intention and policy of the United States toward Cuba. Perhaps sufficient pains have not been taken to make these leaders understand the aim of this government and its methods of procedure.

The reverses to Spain have had the effect of awakening activity among the Carlists of Spain. Don Carlos has been in Brussels for sometime watching the course of events and biding his time to make a decisive stroke for the throne of Spain, to which he believes he is legally entitled. His friends have been active of late, and it is thought that recent events have produced the conviction that the time is ripe for action. General Weyler is believed to be in sympathy with the Carlists, and it is reported that his visit to the north of Spain on the pretense of looking after his possessions in that region, is for the purpose of joining the Pretender in his proposed struggle for the throne. A great deal of uneasiness is felt among the friends of the present dynasty as to the loyalty of the Spanish troops, and Dona Isabella, sister-in-law of the Queen Regent, has been addressing the soldiers urging them to be loyal to the Queen. Martinez Campos is exercising the power of dictator in the interest of the present dynasty. Truly Spain's ship of state is riding at present over a stormy sea, but toward what port, no one can tell.

The facility with which the government loan of $200,000,000 was taken up by the small bids of $500 and less is a gratifying indication of the faith of the people in their government, and also of the improved financondition of the country. Not only was the entire loan taken up within the time-

was asked for. The smaller bids received the preference, as was proper. The price of these 3 per cent. bonds has already advanced 103 3-8, but not many of the small investors have been tempted so far to part with their bonds. A great many banks are said to be anxious to secure these new bonds, and are willing to pay a reasonable premium for them. The eagerness to secure these 3 per cent. bonds is a striking illustration of the relation between the credit of the borrower and the rate of interest. The semi-annual payment of interest does not account for the difference in the rate of interest at which the government can borrow money and the rate which private individuals must pay. Perhaps there is some attractiveness about being a government bondholder, and we may hear less denunciation of this class in the future than we have heard in the past. The truth is, if all loans had been made popular as this one has been, there would have been less occasion for criticism.

The Carlist movement is not the only danger that threatens the present Spanish government. Republican leaders have recently declared their convictions in a circular, in which they blame the existing government for the Cuban war, and for the defeats of Spanish arms. After denouncing the policy of the government toward Cuba and toward the people of Spain, these republicans say:

> We must take to heart the lesson which our sufferings are teaching us. Spain must be governed by Spaniards. We shall lose Cuba and all our possessions in foreign seas, but out of this loss will grow up, with God's help, a free people and a free country. We must see the country prosperous and happy, the people governing themselves and the money which is spent to-day to maintain a foreign family in luxury will be used under the Spanish republican regime to reconstruct our country, naturally rich in mines and agriculture, and to educate the youth of the kingdom. This money comes now from the pockets of the workingmen. Every one pays a school tax, but it is not the children of the poor who are benefited by this money. It is to the interests of the clergy and the government to keep the masses in dark ignorance that they may not comprehend what is transpiring around them, and only the sons and daughters of the wealthy receive that education which enables them later to make common cause with the spoils people, who have gone before them.

Assistant Naval Constructor Hobson has been on a visit to Washington, under orders from Admiral Sampson to report to the authorities there the condition of the vessels of Cervera's fleet, which were sunk by our warships. He was received very cordially by officials at Washington, and received an ovation from the people whenever they got sight of him. He bore himself very modestly and seemed more intent on having some of the Spanish vessels saved to our navy than on talking about his exploit. He believes it possible to float two of these vessels, the Cristobal Colon and the Infanta Maria Teresa, provided the wrecking force be increased and new appliances be supplied at once before the hurricane season sets in. These two ships, if saved, will make a handsome addition to our already formidable navy.

Since the destruction of Cervera's fleet Admiral Sampson has been engaged in capturing and destroying Spanish gunboats, a number of which are said to infest the Cuban coasts. The expedition to Nipe, on the North Coast of Cuba, has succeeded in destroying the Spanish cruiser, Jorge Juan, which was defending that harbor, "without any loss on our part." Commander Todd, of the Wilmington, also destroyed five gunboats and two transport ships and a storeship at Manzanillo last week. It was this work of our navy that caused a little delay in furnishing the convoy to the Porto Rican expedition.

LIVING AND DYING NATIONS.

In a recent speech by a distinguished English statesman, he classified the nations now existing on the earth as of two kinds—the living and the dying. It is a most striking classification and one that seems to be justified in the light of history and of existing conditions. Lord Salisbury, the statesman referred to, did not, of course, say what nations, in his judgment, were the living nations and which were the dying, nor did he say which class outnumbered the other. It is safe to say, however, that the living nations are only a few, if by a living nation is meant one that is not only growing stronger within itself, but is imposing its language, its laws and its civilization upon other peoples and nations. It is safe to assume, also, that the distinguished speaker referred to would include Great Britain and the United States as among and perhaps as the chief living nations on the globe to-day.

The classification is one that raises an important inquiry which is worth our while to consider. What are the essential differences between living and dying nations? Or, to put the question in another form, What are the essential elements of a living nation? What are the conditions and characteristics that cause it to live? The question is certainly one in which all lovers of their country should have a deep interest. The law of the Survival of the Fittest applies to nations as well as to animal and plant life. Nations live because they are fit to live, and because they answer the purpose for which government is instituted among men. Ceasing to subserve this end, they enter into a moribund condition, and sooner or later pass away. But still the question may be pressed, as to what are the elements of power that fit a nation to live, and that enable it to fulfill the purpose for which a nation exists. This is the question that touches the very core of our national life and destiny.

In answering this question we assume the existence of a Supreme and All-wise God, from whom all governments derive their sanction and power. The state or nation is a part of the divine scheme for the education, development and well-being of the race. It is safe to assume that God, who guides the courses of the planets, whose word upholds the material universe, and whose providence is guiding the course of human history, has in view the moral discipline and spiritual welfare of mankind. So long as nations subserve this general purpose and are helpers rather than obstacles in lifting up the people to a higher plane of civilization, they are used of God in the accomplishment of his plans. But when they become engines of persecution, of oppression, enemies of human freedom and human progress, they run counter to the divine purpose, and it is only a question of time when the process of decay must set in and run its course to national dissolution. No one who believes in the sovereignty of God can doubt this proposition.

If, then, there are nations on the earth to-day that are in a dying condition, it is because they have forfeited their right to exist by failing to apprehend the divine purpose concerning man, and to work in harmony with that purpose. They have become obstructions to the execution of the divine plan for the well-being of man, and must give place to something that is better. If there are living nations it is because there are nations that stand for those things which God wishes to triumph in the earth. They will live as long as they stand for these eternal and immutable things, and thus serve the divine purpose. If they permit themselves to turn away from these high ends, they, too, will forfeit their right to live and must be classified with the dying nations.

In the light of these general principles it is not a difficult thing for the intelligent leaders of any civilized nation to tell whether the nation they represent is a living or dying nation. Does the nation stand for liberty, for freedom of conscience, for freedom of worship, for freedom to work out one's fortune and destiny according to his own judgment, in so far as he does not interfere with the rights of others? Does it hear the cry of the poor and the unfortunate? Does it relieve the oppressed? Are its laws and customs based on the principles of equity and truth? Is the government administered in the interest of the people, rather than of the governing classes? Is it seeking to promote the enlightenment of the people, and to give encouragement to all agencies and influences that make for the moral and spiritual development of men? Does it seek in its system of jurisprudence to enact such laws and administer them in such a way as will meet the demands of a righteous God? If these questions can be answered affirmatively, the nation is among the living. God has use for it. It is working along his lines and for the realization of his purpose.

On the contrary, if a nation exists for the benefit of its rulers, being based on hereditary rights, and seeks to keep the mass of the people in ignorance, lest they resist the unjust laws and restraints which are imposed upon them; if it does not permit its citizens to exercise their own free choice in the worship of God, but imposes upon them certain forms, creeds and ecclesastical usages; if it tends to build up castle walls between the people, and fails to recognize the inherent dignity and priceless worth of man as man; if it ignores the will of God as revealed in Christ, and refuses to respect the rights of all men, it is an obstacle in the way of human progress and of the divine purpose, and must needs be put away. It is a dying nation.

The principle involved in this is of universal application. It applies to men, to institutions, to churches and religious movements. The church of the future is to be the church that lends itself to God's great purposes; that lives, not for its own sake, nor its own glory, but for the well-being of man and the glory of God. The religious movement whose aim and tendency is to emphasize and promote those

re vitally
extension
re hold on
's eternal.
oever and
and abides

.

ished for?
enjoyment
onal satis-
of æsthetic
lusively or
and man.
mission of
lid we are
ld, not to
; not the
; servant;
master by
Lord him-
ire will be
f Christ in
ritual, nor
church of
y, but the
l sacrifice,
hurch that
from cor-
ight on the
an birds of
ity of God,
will sur-
of Christ.
prays and
aims about
k deep in
exist, if it
nostrils of
n. As the
rch must

vice into
s scarcely
widely ex-
l politics?
evil's own
o take the
sness into
counting-
e the Ser-
primary
take the
nsactions,
n's neces-
like him,
take ad-
gouge us?
er how it
Suppose
; and then
ake char-
s for office
party shib-
nolds was
ie answer-
Would it
ontents of
e? Do we
ich as we
ng? Yea,
s, but not
ere is any-
intry, it is
t the men.
t of Chris-
ictive par-
und of its

on character. Christ might have refused to come to this world on the ground that it was too corrupt a place for him to touch, but would that not have been a poor way to save the world? Civil government is of God, and is a human necessity; patriotism is a virtue; good citizenship is a grace; moral corruption and rascality in citizenship are a disgrace, and how can anything be purified by the refusal of good men to even make an effort to reform it? The devil gets into everything in these days. He gets into art; he paints pictures. He gets into music; he sings songs. He gets into poetry; he writes verse. He bulks to eleplantine proportions in modern literature, and runs away with the wagon in politics, and who shall go into these spheres of influence to drive "Auld Clootie oot" but good men, who cannot be bought with his money or corrupted by his wiles? There is no greater realm for Christian influence and Christian service than the purification of American politics.

Another world, and perhaps the biggest world for Christian service, is childhood. It is known to fools scarcely less than to philosophers that children are molded by the dominant influence brought to bear upon them in the plastic period of life, and the spiritual corallary of this fact makes it our business to create a religious atmosphere out of which children will grow up in the nurture and admonition of the Lord. There are more than two hundred thousand children in the Sunday-schools of the state in which these lines are written, and more than six hundred thousand not in the Sunday-schools of this commonwealth, and it is not too much to say that multitudes of the latter are growing up in ignorance and as absolutely without a knowledge of God as the children of heathen lands. In towns and cities where churches abound there are hordes of children outside the sphere of religious training and influence. There are thousands of families in all our states without Bibles, and who never by any chance get so much as a peep at a scrap of religious literature. Swarms of boys are upon our streets on the Lord's day, smoking cigarettes, chewing the filthy weed, swearing, learning to gamble, secreting pistols and bottles of whisky and visiting places where their feet take hold on hell. Do churches and individual Christians understand the responsibility that all this lays on them? With this vast field stretching before us in which the devil is getting in his work to the demoralization of the country and the ruin of coming generations, is there not something better for Christian men and women to do than to spend their days in town and their nights around the card table? The first institution God established was the family, the second was the state, the third was the church. The domestic circle is the womb of civilization, the mother of states and churches. Here the foundation of the world's redemption and of the world's evolution of a better life is to be laid. When Christ said, "Suffer little children to come unto me," he converted the family into a church and brought the kingdom of God into the family. When you bring God and Christ and the Bible and the voice of prayer and an enlightened conscience into the family you do the most fruitful and far-reaching work for God in the power of

for utterance on the great theme
tian service, but hot weather an
mand for brevity admonish me t
this point.

Hour of Praye

THE TRUE BREAD.

(Midweek Prayer-meeting Topic, Au

I am the living bread which ca
out of heaven: if any man eat of thi
shall live forever: yea, and the brea
will give is my flesh, for the life of th
Jno. 6:51.

This language of Jesus grew ou
mand made upon Him by the cavi
that He would perform some sig
that they might believe on Him.
ferred to the historic fact that M
provided their fathers with man
wilderness, and they asked Him
He would give them in order
might trust Him. Jesus tells th
ply that it was not Moses that g
bread out of heaven, but that i
Father, and that the same Heaven
gives the true bread of heaven.
which the Israelites received in th
ness was not the true bread. It se
a temporary purpose, but "the bre
is that which cometh down out
and giveth life unto the world."
them to say, "Lord, evermore gi
bread." When Jesus proceeded,
to say, "I am the living bread wh
down out of heaven," and that "
which I will give is my flesh, for
the world," they were puzzled,
and unable to understand Him.
old story of attempting to inte
figurative language of Jesus in
sense. Even many of His discip
bled at the words and went back a
no more with Him. And yet the
Jesus state one of the profoundes
revelation.

What is the meaning of the l
We understand that bread is th
life, and that it is essential to su
develop the physical life. Wh
means is that as bread satisfies th
of the body, so he came into the
satisfy the hunger of the heart,
spiritual nourishment for the sou
There is a hunger of the soul, as
the body. This hunger must be r
der to the life and growth of the
as the hunger of the body must be
for in order to its life and growt
Christ came to supply men's
needs. These needs are: the t
cerning God and man, the duti
present life, the reality of the lif
forgiveness of sin, and strength
to overcame the evils of the wo
these, with that love and sympat
the heart can find nowhere else, J
to supply.

But in order to supply what ou
ity needed, Jesus must needs d
grain of corn must fall into the gr
die, or it abideth alone. He wa
his body to be sacrificed for the s
world. It was this fact that led H
"The bread which I will give is
for the life of the world." It wa
His death that we are enabled to
height and depth of the love o
sinful men. It was by means of
that we are to be reconciled to
receive forgiveness of sins. H

We eat of this bread and drink of this blood by faith as we appropriate the teaching of Christ. Our souls are strengthened, our heart-hunger is appeased, only as we feed upon Christ, that is, believe upon Him, accept him and obey his teaching. This is to be a partaker of Christ. It is said, sometimes, that this language refers to the Lord's supper. It is truer, however, to say that this language of Jesus, and the Lord's supper both refer to the same great fact, that men live spiritually by becoming partakers of Christ, and sharers in His life. The Lord's supper sets this truth forth in symbol; Jesus here states it in figurative language.

There is no hunger so fierce as the hunger of the heart. There is nothing in all the world to satisfy it outside of Christ and His teaching. The heart cries out for the living God, for a loving Father and Helper. Jesus came to show us the Father. He came to manifest that love and sympathy for which the heart craves. He came to make possible that fellowship with God, without which man cannot attain to his highest estate, nor enjoy the greatest peace. The heart longs to know about the future, the life that lies beyond the grave. Only Christ has brought us the highest assurance of that life, and its nature. The heart longs for strength to overcome the evils of the flesh, and Jesus Christ alone supplies this strength. The human heart hungers for forgiveness and fellowship with God. Christ alone makes possible this forgiveness and fellowship.

When we come to see, as we ought to see, that in Christ Jesus all the deepest wants of the soul are met, and all its needs provided for, surely we shall be more loyal to Him and serve Him with greater fidelity. He would then, indeed, become to us "the fairest among ten thousand and the one altogether lovely." May it be that this meditation and study on this great truth—that Christ is the true bread, that alone satisfies the hunger of the heart—will lead us into closer fellowship with Him, and into more loyal and loving service for the extension of His kingdom.

PRAYER.

O, Thou loving and all-pitying Father, who hast heard the cry of Thine earthly children, and hast provided for their needs, we do thank Thee for the gift of Christ and for His ability to supply all our wants. Thou knowest, O God, what are the desires and aspirations of the human heart, for Thou hast created it. Thou knowest that there is nothing in the material world to satisfy the soul's hunger and thirst for truth, for love, for God. In order to provide for all our needs Thou didst give us Thine only-begotten Son, not only to live for us here in the flesh, but to die for us, that His flesh might become the bread of humanity. We bless Thy name that we have been permitted in some measure to partake of this bread and to rejoice in the satisfaction of soul which it gives. O that we may all partake of it more freely, to the end that we may have a more abundant life in this present world, and live with Thee forever in the world to come. And this in Christ's name. Amen!

For Foreign Missions.

Comparing the receipts for Foreign Missions for the week ending July 21st, with the corresponding time last year, shows the following:

Contributing:	1897	1898	Gain
Amount	$1,598.19	$11,123.57	$9,525.38

Of the above amount $9,690 was donated on the "Annuity Plan." There was a loss on the regular receipts of $164.62.

Editor's Easy Chair.

OR MACATAWA MUSINGS.

No book equals the Bible in its splendid similes. This splendid morning at Macatawa recalls a beautiful passage descriptive of—

"One that ruleth over men righteously,
That ruleth in the fear of God."

It is said of such an one, that—

"He shall be as the light of the morning,
When the sun riseth,
A morning without clouds;
When the tender grass springeth out of the earth,
Through clear shining after rain."

What can be more beautiful than such a morning? On yesterday evening the heavens were black with storm-clouds, whose rushing winds soon threw the lake into splendid fury. Few sights are grander than a storm approaching over the lake. At first all the tints of the clouds are reflected in the lake until the wind raises the billows and sends them like white-maned coursers chasing each other to the shore. Then came the rain, so much needed just now, in blinding sheets, blending cloud and lake into one, while the trees swayed their branches before the blast. But the clouds have passed with the night and it is—

"A morning without clouds;
When the tender grass springeth out of the earth,
Through clear shining after rain."

The son of Jesse was evidently a lover of nature, with a genius for expressing his thoughts in truly poetic language. Now that we have had an abundance of rain, our neighboring Dutch farmers will be able to continue their supply of fresh vegetables and fruits, which is one of the attractions nt Macatawa.

Religious services began here several weeks ago, Bros. Hughes, Earl and Everest occupying the platform in the order mentioned. On last Lord's day it fell to the lot of the Easy Chair Editor to preach, and he has seldom, if ever, addressed a more responsive audience. As on the previous Lord's day, the seats at the Auditorium were filled, while a number sat on the sand. One of the attractive features of the service on last Lord's day, both afternoon and evening, was a boy choir from the Presbyterian Church at Evanston, Ill., numbering about two dozen, who sang very sweetly. Last Lord's day evening we held the first of our beach meetings for the season, and it was one of the largest and best we have ever had. The unique character of these beach services attract a great many people who do not go to church. They like the large porportion of music, the short speeches, the picturesque scene of hundreds of people sitting upon the sand by the lakeshore, under the starlight, with their faces illuminated with the blazing bonfire, which is generally a feature of the meetings. It affords an excellent opportunity for sowing broadcast seeds of truth in minds and hearts that otherwise might not receive them. The freedom from all conventionality which prevails in these meetings, does not in the least interfere with the religious impressions made by these services. In witnessing the interest in these beach meetings, we have wondered whether it were not practicable for many of our churches in the cities, during the summer season, to unite their forces and hold outdoor evening services, which should take on some of the characteristics of our Sunday evening services at the beach, and whether such meetings would not be more profitable and more largely attended than the ordinary church services. The hint is thrown out for what it is worth.

The past week has been rather cool here, and as a result, perch fishing has been good. It is remarkable how many people there are; old and young, male and female, who delight in the angler's art. Greybeards and tiny children, stout dames and comely maids may be seen wending their way to the pier or the dock, carrying their poles with a look of eager expectancy on their faces. It is not an uncommon sight to see them returning with a string long enough to supply themselves and all their neighbors. The perch fishing is for the masses of the people, and all engage in it. The larger and gamer fish are caught in Black Lake, and only experts succeed in capturing many of those. The white and black bass are the great attractions here and the former are caught mostly at night. The lovers of piscatorial sport need not be out of employment here. It affords to many about the best means of mental rest which they can have, and in this respect it is more valuable by far than the actual worth of the fish caught, although fish constitutes an important feature of the menu in most of the cottages here.

The park is rapidly filling up now, and each day we see the faces of new arrivals. F. G. Tyrrell, of St. Louis, now Dr. Tyrrell by the act of the University of Missouri, is one of the latest arrivals. His family has been here for several weeks. Like ye Editor he has to unite some literary work with his outing, and the click of his reel must give place at times to the click of his typewriter. This union of literary work with fishing and boating is not a bad combination for those who are able to stand it. Bro. Tyrrell says so many of his flock are here that he felt it his duty to come up and look after them—so prone are men to seek to find conscientious motives for what they like to do! Bro. D. T. Kelley, superintendent of schools at Jeffersonville, Ind., has paid a brief visit to the park, spending last Lord's day here with a view to coming with his wife in August. He proposes conducting some nature-studies during August, to investigate the plant and animal life of this place, in connection with its geological character, provided he can secure a class. From present indications August is to be one of the fullest months for Macatawa Park it has ever had.

Macatawa Park has added a new attraction since last summer. An electric railway line, running down the south shore of Black Lake, connects this place with the city of Holland, six miles up at the head of the lake. The cars run every 15 minutes, and the people who visit Holland can now take their choice of riding on the little steamer or the electric cars. Both are pleasant methods of travel and the price of each is the same. There is naturally some rivalry betwen the two lines of travel, but since they both serve to accommodate the people of the park, and hence to promote

they may prove mutually
each other in the long run.
etition between lines of trans-
ot a bad thing for the people,
use it has proven a decided
nly in cheaper rates, but in
nodations.

Religious Thought

cis Brown, D. D., of Union
Seminary, has an interesting
Independent, July 14, on "A
e Church," the introduction
s as follows:

as God sees it, consists of those
to Christ. The ultimate test is
nion or act, but of a vital, spirit-
which each is joined to Christ,
part of the organism made up
God's Church is comprehen-
des people of widely divergent
bits, people who think quite
it great things, and people who
rent ways. The bond of union
all Christians.
en call the Church—the Church
manifest form on the earth—cer-
resemble as nearly as possible
God sees it. Its real member-
up of those who are united to
Church and man's Church
re, to be exactly coterminous.
hat they really are. The defect
n man's Church. Men are not
not see as clearly as God sees,
up the roll in man's Church
re entered which God does not
e omitted which God includes.
perfectness does not annul the
of endeavoring to make man's
ond with God's Church. What
hurch ought to contain all those
ist. It ought to be as compre-
's Church is.
the curious phenomenon of a
f human organizations, calling
urches, each of which recog-
th sincere joy, that it does not
real Christians there are—that
y truly united to Christ not
mbers—excluding those whose
it does not question, and even
to them that they join another
To one who considers the essen-
rch membership this is wholly
opinions, or usages, were the
then those whose opinions or
adjudged to be wrong might
luded. But they could not then
arded as true Christians, what-
nization they might join. How,
ion to Christ determines real
rship, can I logically drive out
h men whose *real* church mem-
nowledge? The situation is
ous. The ideal Church on earth
with this anomaly and be truly
, with ample room for difference
of religious usage—like God's
—making the one condition, that
all be really Christians.

on of members and ministers
from another in the future
become more common and in
On this subject Prof. Brown
says:

y seem remote, but it suggests
al question. In the anomalous
ich we are, what is the duty of
ganizations? The situation can
in a day, or a week. Church
oal, but what shall we do now?
luty of the different Church or-
the meantime? Manifestly, to
riers by which they are separat-
ssible under the circumstances.
to keep out as few real Chris-
le, who desire to enter it. This
ore the case. Individuals pass
ly in Protestantism from one
mination to another, without
opinions, and following their
nience in the matter of usages.
s as are imposed on the transfer
nd more, either of some formal
transfer, or of some endeavor
the individual's relation to

ion and transfer of Church offic-
ifically ministers, the matter is
simple. Various bodies have
l tests in the form of assent to
majority as to theological opinions, or both; the acceptance of certain theories, the conformity to certain practices are required. Those who do not pass muster may be highly commended for their Christian character and bidden a sincere God-speed if they turn to another organization, but as teachers and pastors in the particular one which has examined them they are rejected.

Now the ideal of the Christian ministry neither contemplates nor tolerates any such thing as this. The one necessary requirement is that the ministry which men recognize should be the ministry which God recognizes. If a man is fit to be a minister in God's Church, then he is fit to be a minister in my Church. What, then, are the tests of fitness? Obviously, the essential test of church membership is fundamental here also. The minister must be a real Christian It is right that especial pains should be taken to secure this. Besides this, for his particular work the minister needs particular gifts and attainments. It is right that he should be examined, to ascertain that he has them. But will the ideal Church exact more than this? Will she demand adherence to a standard of orthodox opinion and the adoption of an approved set of religious habits and usages? It is easy to answer this question by saying that since the minister is set to preach the truth, and to order the affairs of the Church, his adherence to the truth and to the right ecclesiastical order is, of course, to be determined before he is received into the ministry. But it is quite certain that the ideal Church will not require of *any* of its ministers, as a condition of their ministry, opinions and usages which it does not require of all. That means that the fundamental requirements of opinion and usage are few and easily defined. It is doubtless necessary that a minister should hold to certain truths and practices; in order that the force of his Christian character, and the use of his attainments and gifts may be for the increase and edification of the Church. It might not be easy to secure prompt agreement as to what these truths and practices are. But matters now confined to some fragment of the entire Church certainly do not belong to the essential requirements. The *necessary* demands are in fact common to all parts of the Church. If you recognize co-ordinate branches of the Church, it is incongruous to deny a man entrance to the ministry of one on account of opinion, while you bid him God-speed in the ministry of another. The anomalous, divided condition of Christendom has exalted this incongruity into an important principle. Sometime Christians will come to understand the Church better, and then the anomaly and the incongruity will pass away together.

After a further discussion the relation of each candidate for membership or its ministry to a Church creed Prof. Brown suggests the following possible course of conduct as a partial solution of the barriers to a closer unity. He says:

1. The Church may see to it that it scrupulously keeps its part of the contract, imposing no new and arbitrary tests, and showing itself eager to recognize all the rights of its office-bearers.

2. The Church may interpret largely and with true respect and love, the fidelity of its office-bearers to their agreement.

3. The Church may remember, always, that the form of its contract is at best a temporary one, a makeshift, due to imperfect conditions, and that severe and harsh interpretation of its requirements is out of place.

4. The Church may make it evident that the contractual element in its relation to its office-holders is not that upon which it chiefly dwells. The ministry is a consecration to high service, with divine sanction, and should be considered chiefly from the point of view of efficiency in accomplishing its divine ends.

5. The church may fix its eyes steadfastly on those ends, and never allow itself to forget that it exists, not to promote any one branch of God's work at the expense of others, but for the growth and uplifting of the kingdom of Christ.

6. The Church may be constantly in an attitude of prayer and of receptiveness, longing and waiting for new visions of truth and new endowments of power, welcoming these when they come, and gratefully honoring, as messengers of God, those by whom they come.

For every separate Church organization thus to administer its own affairs in a Christian way will not, it is true, solve all our ecclesiastical problems; but it will surely beget the temper in which alone they can be solved. And when once these truly Christian thoughts and desires are in control, we shall have made a great advonce toward that Christian comprehension which is the Church's duty and privilege and

Rev. Dr. Amory H. Bradford, of Montclair, N. J., gave an address on the "International Relations of Congregationalism," at the triennial Congregational national council at Portland, Oregon, in which he gave utterance to the following words upon the necessity for a closer unity of God's people and the supreme object of all Christian missionary effort:

Every nation and every institution have those who interpret their meaning narrowly, and those who interpret it broadly; the former are sectarians in the church, and in the state they are absolutists and ultra-nationalists. Good causes are hindered by narrow interpretations and advanced by those who have detected in them diviner meanings. If Congregationalists glorify their past in order to build higher the walls which separate them from their brethren, the sooner they cease to be the better for the world. The days of denominationalism are numbered. The international mission of Congregationalism is not different from that of any of the free churches—meaning in this country by free churches nearly all except the Roman Catholic and Episcopalian communions; and that is, the preservation and promotion of the principles of Puritanism. These are to put conscience above tradition, to insist that the Spirit of God leads men now as truly as ever, and needs no church to interpret its message. The hope of a pure church and a pure state depends upon the development of men of the Puritan type. The days of the few are passed; democracy is the order of the future. Those who face the twentieth century are thinking of a church as broad as the kingdom of God, and a nation which knows itself to exist only to hasten that kingdom. It is the large privilege of the free churches, then, to co-operate with all who have entered into an appreciation of Christ's purpose to the world.

Here we are met by the fact that the free churches exist almost exclusively among English-speaking nations. Thus their international mission is to promote harmony among all such. English-speaking people are beginning to see eye to eye, learning what to forget and what to remember. It remains for men of Christian vision to make this harmony enduring, not that we may help one another against the world, but that we may join hands in leading the world toward unity and brotherhood. To uplift this ideal is the surpassing privilege of the pulpit, the throne of power in the free churches. Just now if two great peoples will bury their differences and link hands for the peace and welfare of the world, the day will be near when one man's good shall be all men's law. We may help to bind them together, then to permeate them with the principles of Puritanism, that the democracy of the future may be a people fearing God and receiving their laws from him, to the end that the unity of the world may be realized both politically and spiritually. That is no idle dream. The world is actually coming together. When the people say that war must go, the nations will have progressed a long way, even though for a time the strife among classes is intensified. The growth of democracy will take care of that.

To the end that the free churches may help change political unity when it shall come into actual harmony between the nations, education is required, and evangelization. The foreign missionary enterprise has not yet been understood. It is not a crusade to make Presbyterians or Episcopalians out of Buddhists or Vedantists; it is the proclamation of universal fatherhood and brotherhood, that the life of the universe and the ages is the love that led Jesus to the cross. Brotherhood is the larger patriotism. It is a great thing to be an American, but it is greater to be a man. A united world with no fatherhood and no brotherhood would end in anarchy. Others will push commerce; selfishness will promote education; but the Christian church alone appreciates the importance of evangelization, for it alone deals with man as a spirit. Not to win proselytes to any name, not to induce acceptance of any creed, much less to change Buddhist bigots into Christian bigots, are we commissioned; but we are called on to preach a personal God, the Father Almighty, to teach men to love one another with the love which was in Christ, to make the future democracy a blessing by helping every individual to realize that every other man is a child of God, and that the interests of one are the interests of all.

Failures for the week ending July 7th were $1,854,394 in amount, $946,611 manufacturing and $899,763 trading. Failures for the week have been 215 in the United States against 263 last year, and in Canada 23 against 27 last year.

Questions and Answers.

A preacher stated recently, in commenting on Matt. 20:23, that if we took immersion as a mode of baptism the candidate would have to be drowned entirely before his baptism was complete. What do you think of such exegesis? *J. R. Dallas.*
Vernonia, Ore.

It is too superficial, not to say partisanly stupid, to justify refutation. If the death of Christ and the disciples mentioned was a part of the baptism of suffering, why would not sprinkling as a mode of baptism entail drowning, or death in some form? The man who is not capable of seeing that baptism is here used figuratively to indicate the intense suffering with which Jesus was to be overwhelmed, needs some primary instruction before he undertakes to be an exegete.

---

1. *What is the usual procedure among our churches when a member is being excluded from the church?*

2. *Supposing a member were recommended for expulsion by the official board, because he had committed an offense for which the New Testament requires exclusion, would it be proper to take a vote of the church on the matter? Or would it be assumed without question or vote, the law of the Lord would take effect.* *G.*

1. After the proper investigation has been made, and all efforts exhausted to bring the offender to repentance, a statement to this effect is usually made to the congregation, with the recommendation that the wrong-doer be no longer regarded as a member of the church. If no objection is made to this decision, it stands as the order of the church.

2. The acquiescence or endorsement of the congregation is usually sought in some way; either by saying, "If there be no objection this recommendation will be considered as endorsed by the church," or by a formal vote. When the vote is taken, it is not upon the propriety of following the New Testament teaching, but is an expression of the judgment of the congregation as to whether the New Testament rule is being followed in this particular case under consideration.

---

1. *Who were the messengers sent before the face of Jesus as recorded in Luke 9:52.*

2. *Did the incident recorded in Luke 9:54, where James and John wished to call fire from heaven, transpire after the feast of tabernacles or before?*

1. The messengers sent before His face were some of His disciples, probably James and John, to make arrangements for his entertainment.

2. It is probable that Jesus was going to Jerusalem for the purpose of attending the feast of the dedication of the temple. As the main question between the Jews and the Samaritans was as to the proper place for the temple—whether at Jerusalem or Mt. Gerizim—the fact that Jesus was going to attend this feast would explain the feeling of hostility on the part of the Samaritans, which made them refuse their hospitality. On this supposition it was after the feast of tabernacles that the incident occurred.

EDITOR CHRISTIAN-EVANGELIST: —What you say in a late CHRISTIAN-EVANGELIST Budget, commendatory of the monthly paper, the Boy's Friend, will doubtless meet with ready endorsement by the readers in general of its later issues; but—

1. Are you aware of the full-fledged secret society, "Knights of Character Castle," of which "order" the paper is the organ and ardent advocate; and for the enrollment of its youthful readers, in the membership of which society—with its ritual and ragalia, its grandiloquent titles and oath-taking—the paper mainly exists?

2. Inasmuch as one of the means being employed by the promoters of said society and paper for interesting and "holding" the boys is to drill and train them in the production of "plays" or dramatic performances, would it not seem that the tendency of such amateur theatricals—involving as they do the accessories of costuming, stage-settings, etc.—is to educate the boys in the direction of theater-going, if not to make some of them out-and-out theatre actors?

3. Would you advise the boys of Christian parents to connect themselves with a secret society of this or any other character, or may the cause of Christ be better subserved by them, in standing aloof from such alliances? W. P. KEELER.
Chicago, June 13, 1898.

1. We know there is some sort of organization with which the Boy's Friend is associated, and have heard that it has a secret feature in it. Our commendation, however, was of the paper alone. We are not sufficiently acquainted with the organization known as "Knights of Character Castle," to either commend or condemn it. We have no fondness for secret societies ourselves, but we would not like to condemn wholsale every organization that has the element of secrecy, as relates to passwords, grips, etc.

2. We are not able, with our meager knowledge of the society, to judge whether its tendency would be to promote a love for the spectacular and encourage theatre-going or not. We feel sure, however, that the men at the head of this organization have no such purpose in view, and do not recognize such a tendency if it exists.

3. A man's sentiments are best indicated by his action. We have never been connected with any secret society, no have we ever encouraged others to do so. Nevertheless, we have never felt that the Roman Catholic Church was justified in its war on secret societies. The best rule is to judge every society by its fruits. We would advise the boys of Christian parents to be guided in such matters largely by the advice of their parents.

NEED FOR A BETTER TRAINED MINISTRY.*

ALLAN B. PHILPUTT.

The effort now being made to enlarge the faculty and extend the course of biblical and ministerial training at this time-honored seat of learning should meet with the heartiest support.

From the beginning our people have been the friends of education. Mr. Campbell founded Bethany College for the training of men to preach the gospel. As our movement traveled westward it carried with it a zeal for learning evidenced in the attempts to found a college in almost every state where we had gained any considerable influence. Young men were encouraged to study the Bible in the original tongues as an equipment for the ministry. The higher studies were not by the founders of our movement deemed useless or dangerous.

To be sure they urged capable men to undertake the gospel ministry who had no such training. And so should we always. Learning is not the only qualification for a preacher of the gospel, nor is it an indispensable one. The church needs strong-handed, noble-hearted, unselfish men, of native ability and consecration, to herald her faith to the ends of the earth, and she can ill afford to turn away from such because they cannot read Greek and Hebrew. Collegiate training cannot make a preacher of the gospel out of a man who is not one without it. But it seems to me a most desirable acquisition if one is to attain the widest and best influence in his sacred calling. A minister to-day has no exemption over men of other callings. He will pass for just what he is worth—no more, and no less. If he is ignorant the people will know it, nor will a specious unction atone for his lack of understanding. If he is rude, uncouth in manner, discourteous and full of self-esteem, he will be despised, for such faults render a man unfit and unworthy of the high calling.

A preacher now has to face an intelligent public and treat a wide range of questions, and if he has not the equipments necessary to enable him to do this he is quickly made sensible of this lack.

1. We need better trained men to handle the questions of modern biblical scholarship. The "Higher Criticism" about which we hear so much is simply a *method* of investigating certain problems pertaining to the Scriptures. It was formerly too much in the hands of the enemies of supernatural religion and their conclusions were somewhat startling. Let us raise our own higher critics. If there is any good in this method we have as much right to it as anybody. Truth is truth, and whatsoever is not of truth will finally be sifted out and come to naught. We can, none of us, have any interest in anything that is not truth, and the Bible has a way of coming through the fires of criticism brighter and clearer than ever. This new way of looking at the Bible has come widely into vogue. Our ministry must meet it, reckon with it and use it. To this end technical training is necessary. At present many are incapable of either accepting or rejecting the conclusions of modern scholarship, for the reason that they cannot handle the data nor grasp the processes involved in arriving at those conclusions. The result is that matters involving the deepest and most patient research meet their fate at the hands of an unreasoning prejudice rather than a judicial and truth-loving temper.

A new theory may be accepted in just as ignorant and narrow a spirit as that by which it is rejected. The man who too readily accepts every new thing is less fit for leadership than the one who too stubbornly clings to the past. Oliver Wendell Holmes used to say that he preferred a conservative mellowing down to a liberal tightening up.

What we want is a ministry that shall be hospitable to new light and yet not weary of the old paths, a minister that shall hear with candor and decide with fearlessness, as far as the facts may warrant, these

*Epitome of an address delivered before the students and friends of the Bible department of Butler College, June 21st, 1898.

that trouble the surface of our
What there is in the Bible will
It cannot get away. In the end
n must say with Paul, "We can do
ig against the truth, but for the

ister of the gospel is supposed to
id and teach the Scriptures of the
New Testaments. Is this supposi-
ly to be well founded in the
of the severe discipline of study
acquaintance with the results of
nvestigation and discussion?
ministry should have a higher
in order to meet the intellectual
of their congregations. Time was
minister shared with the school-
bout all the learning there was
But that day is past. Now the
tting ahead of the pulpit. There
ly a congregation to-day where
e not some who can take the
to book if he makes a slip in the
n of current questions. Matters
science and philosophy, matters
al benevolence and ethical ques-
well as the more recondite sub-
historical and theological import,
be familiar with or his influence
ership are seriously impaired. I
cant saying, "Let him preach the
nd have nothing to do with these
." But if a man is to bring the
Jesus Christ into the life of to-
ust do it along the lines of man's
g thought and menacing prob-
difficulties. The congregation
of the pulpit a wider treatment of
han formerly, and that, too, in a
irenic spirit. The old-time cock-
about everything no longer goes
public. They prefer "sweet rea-
ss" and fairness. The preacher
gs an Indian club over his hearers
the admiration of the unthinking,
ll make the judicious grieve. He
it his themes in a modern spirit.
not proceed on assumptions which
ed to be granted or follow meth-
asoning no longer recognized as
e, and which in other provinces of
have been abandoned.
need more *first-hand* preachers,
read the Bible in the original
and who can get at the true
of correct interpretation. Too
preaching what they have heard
each. It may be true gospel, but
come by first hand, and cannot
imed with the ardor of discovery.
ers studied the Word for them-
They *hovered over* it long and
ly, and when they spoke it was
fire and conviction of prophets.
nitate their example. We must
nine anew the sacred Word, for
still much light to break forth
I am quite well aware that high
attainments and research do not
well with a busy preacher's life.
, perhaps, will keep up their
other than up on the top shelf.
cholarship is too low and we must
chools like this manned with uni-
ained men to elevate the stan-

onclusions of sacred scholarship
nger the exclusive possession of
' says Mr. A. S. Peake, in his
Biblical Study," "but have be-
of the consciousness of the age, distilled in every possible form into those subtle modes of common thought, distinctive of our time."

Those who decry schools of learning and the higher education of the ministry forget that it was scholarship of the most profound and patient kind that gave us the Bible in a tongue "understanded of the people." I once looked upon the Alexandrian manuscript of the New Testament in the British Museum, and to turn from that to a neatly printed copy of the English New Testament will give one some idea of what scholarship has done for the Bible.

He who holds in his hand a volume of the "Cambridge Bible Text-book for Schools and Colleges," has perhaps the most splendid specimen of what long years of patient and learned study can do in textual criticism, annotation, commentation, and explanation of the sacred Word. To put side by side with one of these tasty volumes the original manuscripts from which it has come is to invite a companion which will excite our wonder. The achievement is one of the greatest ever accomplished by the mind of man.

HINDRANCES TO SPIRITUAL ENDOWMENT.*

The chief characteristic of the Christian dispensation as seen by the prophets, by the forerunner of Christ, and even by Christ Himself, is the new and more copious outpouring of the Holy Spirit, and that not upon a chosen few, but "upon all flesh." The universality of this gracious gift was no less a striking feature of the new dispensation than the peculiar forms of its manifestation. The Prophet Joel, as quoted by the Apostle Peter on the occasion of the beginning of the fulfillment of his prophecy, said:

"And it shall be in the last days, saith God,
I will pour forth my Spirit upon all flesh:
And your sons and your daughters shall prophesy,
And your young men shall see visions,
And your old men shall dream dreams:
Yea, and on my servants and on my handmaidens in those days
Will I pour forth of my Spirit: and they shall prophesy."

It will be seen from this that the outpouring of the Spirit in the present dispensation is to be "upon all flesh." That is, no racial or national lines are to constitute a bar to this divine gift. Neither is it to be limited to sex, for "your sons and your daughters shall prophesy." It is wonderful how the Holy Spirit ignores our ecclesiastical rules and usages! Nor is it to be limited by age, for "your young men shall see visions and your old men shall dream dreams." Nor are social conditions to stand in the way of the universality of this spiritual endowment, for "on my servants and on my handmaidens in those days will I pour forth of my Spirit; and they shall prophesy." There is, then, no sectional line, no color line, no age line, no sex line, no social line, in the realm of the Spirit. All may claim and enjoy the benefits of that fullness of spiritual blessing peculiar to the Christian age.

It is in harmony with the prophecy of Joel that John said of his own ministry, in contrast with that of Christ, "I indeed baptize you in water unto repentance: but He that cometh after me is mightier than I, whose shoes I am not worthy to bear: He shall baptize you in the Holy Spirit and in fire" (Matt. 3:11). Again, the Apostle John attributes to Christ's forerunner the following language: "I have beheld the Spirit descending as a dove out of heaven; and it abode upon Him. And I knew Him not: but He that sent me to baptize in water, He said unto me, Upon whomsoever ye shall see the Spirit descending and abiding upon Him, the same is He that baptizeth in the Holy Spirit" (John 1:32, 33). Jesus Himself said to His disciples after His resurrection, when charging them to tarry at Jerusalem until they were endued with power from on high, "For John baptized in water; but ye shall be baptized in the Holy Spirit not many days hence" (Acts 1:5). You will notice I follow the American Revisers in these quotations. I follow the American flag, whether it be in revising an English translation or in revising the Spanish civilization! Since Christ is here designated as the one who ministers the Holy Spirit, we may infer from this fact the universality of the gift, since He is the Savior of all men. It is safe to infer, also, that this gift of the Spirit which He confers is vitally related to the progress and triumph of His kingdom.

But all do not enjoy the illuminating, life-giving and strength-imparting influence of the Holy Spirit. Not all Christians, even, have availed themselves of those gifts of the Spirit which it is their privilege to enjoy as followers of Him whose special prerogative it is to administer the Holy Spirit in such measure as each one is fitted to receive. And this brings us to state some of the hindrances to the enjoyment of the fullness of the divine power which is the spiritual birthright of all Christians.

First of all, let it be said with emphasis, that the hindrances to the reception of the Holy Spirit in such measure as to fit each one to do the duty that is laid upon him, are not upon the divine side, but upon the human. Jesus taught that His Father is more willing to give the Holy Spirit to them that ask Him than earthly parents are to give good gifts to their children. Besides, we have just seen the universality of the divine purpose in bestowing the fullness of spiritual blessings upon men in this age. We must look, therefore, to human conditions to find the hindrances to the reception of the Holy Spirit. Of course we encounter here the old problem of divine sovereignty and human freedom. But we waive it with the single remark that there is a reciprocity between the divine and human spirits, which the Scriptures everywhere recognize, and to which every man's consciousness testifies. God always and everywhere respects human volition and moves upon the human spirit in harmony with the laws of man's mental and moral constitution. If this were not so the salvation of man would be simply a question of the divine will, and that would be no question at all, for God wills the salvation of all men. But man's co-operation with God is no less necessary in the attainment of the highest spiritual blessing than in the matter of forgiveness or reconciliation with God.

It is plain that unbelief or disobedience would prove an effectual barrier against the reception of the Holy Spirit. The

*An address delivered at the International Christian Endeavor Convention at Nashville, Tenn., July 6, 1898, by J. H. Garrison.

condition of the soul out of which unbelief and disobedience arise is in such antagonism with the Spirit of Christ that reciprocity is impossible. Faith and love are the lines which connect the human soul with the divine, and along which the divine life and power are conveyed to the human spirit. The stronger the faith and the love, the stronger will be the current of divine life that flows into the human soul. The divine law of cause and effect does not cease operation in the kingdom of the Spirit. The Holy Spirit is a divine personality and we must suppose that in His dealings with the human spirit He will act in accordance with the eternal principles and established laws of the divine order. We must not attribute to Him capriciousness, partiality or moodiness of disposition, as is sometimes unwittingly done in our theories of spiritual operation.

When Peter told the convicted Pentecostians to "repent and be baptized, every one of you, in the name of Jesus Christ unto the remission of sins, and ye shall receive the gift of the Holy Spirit," he was laying down a fundamental law in the kingdom of God, namely, that an utter turning away from the sins of the past, a complete about-face, and an absolute, unconditional surrender to Jesus Christ as Lord of all, are conditions precedent to receiving, in its fullness, the gift of the Holy Spirit. Is it not probable that the lack of a thorough-going repentance, that reaches to the very core of the moral being and reverses the moral judgments, and a lurking spirit of disobedience which hesitates to make a full and open surrender to Jesus Christ are serious hindrances to the reception, on the part of many professed Christians, of the enduement of the Holy Spirit? The question at least deserves the serious consideration of every one who feels that his spiritual life is not what it ought to be, and that there are certain causes which hinder his progress in the divine life.

A wrong *motive* may vitiate our desire for the enduement with power from on high. *Why* do we desire the Holy Spirit? Is it that we may excel our brethren in this or that line of service which we have decided to enter upon and thus acquire reputation and influence among our fellows? Simon Magus wished the Holy Spirit in order to promote his own glory and gain. God does not grant His Spirit for such unworthy purposes. Are we willing to serve God in any humble sphere where his providence may place us? And are we desirous of having such measure and such particular gift of the Holy Spirit as will fit us for service in that sphere? If so we are in that condition of mind and heart which fits us to receive the spiritual gift which we need.

Perhaps we have a wrong *theory* or *unstanding* of the Holy Spirit, which hinders our reception of Him. It may be that we are looking for ecstasies and rhapsodies as the only sign of the presence of the Holy Spirit. Failing to receive this proof and refusing to accept others, we may be unconsciously rejecting the Holy Spirit. Perhaps we have been expecting such an illumination of the Holy Spirit as will free us from the obligation of studying and being guided by the Holy Scriptures. We regret to say that there are those who claim such a measure of the Holy Spirit as to render them independent, in a measure, of the teaching of Christ and of His apostles. It is very safe to say that any impulse that leads one to treat lightly any command or doctrine of Christ and His divinely guided apostles is not from the Holy Spirit, but from an *un*-holy spirit. It is as important to-day to "try the spirits" as it was in the times of the apostles. The standard by which we are to try them is the doctrine of Christ and the apostles. If any man receive not this doctrine, let him not claim to be a participant of the Holy Spirit, whose mission it is to exalt and glorify Christ and to give us an increasing knowledge of His person and work.

One of the most common hindrances, we think, to that enduement with power from on high, which all Christian workers need in order to the highest efficiency, is the lack of any high and worthy *ideal* of Christian life and Christian service. Too many of us are content with being nominal Christians and living a poor, lean spiritual life. There is no hungering and thirsting after righteousness. There is no exalted conception of what a Christian ought to be and do and suffer for the sake of Christ and the extension of His kingdom. About all that many of us aim at is to keep our lives sufficiently respectable to maintain fellowship with the church. We have not planned any hard service for the Master, any work of self-denial and self-immolation. There is a lack of that heroism in our Christian life which was so prominent a characteristic of the disciples of Jesus in the first age of the church. There are too few Hobsons in the church who are willing to sacrifice their own selfish ease and, if need be, life itself, on the altar of Christian service, in order to defeat the enemies of Christ. Such a spirit of self-abandon in the service of God would invite and insure such a measure of divine power as would qualify us for success in every righteous undertaking. If we would undertake larger things for God, and *harder* things, and things which require and anticipate the co-operation of Omnipotence to bring to a successful issue, we might well expect larger measures of divine power to accompany our efforts. God dealeth with us as with sons. What father is there among you who, if his son, for the honor, protection and welfare of the family, engage in some hard and difficult undertaking, will not stand by him with whatever measure of support he is able to render him until his task is accomplished? Not only so, but the father would feel proud that he had a son willing to engage in so difficult a task for the sake of the family and capable with his help of bringing it to successful completion. Who can doubt but that it would delight the heart of our Heavenly Father if His children here on earth, banking on His infinite resources, should engage in the largest and most difficult enterprises looking to the extension of His kingdom in the world and the redemption of the race? Who believes that He would withhold the necessary enduement of power from those who would give themselves, unselfishly and for His glory to enterprises that look to world-wide conquest in behalf of truth and righteousness?

After all this is only saying that what the church needs to-day above everything else is the utter consecration of itself and all its powers and energies to the speedy accomplishment of its divine mission in the world. If it would but lay itself out in earnest Christian endeavor to bring this world right speedily under the sway of Jesus Christ and manifest a willingness to surrender everything in its life, in its teaching or its practice that is a hindrance to the success of its holy mission, the very gates of heaven would be opened to pour out upon it such a measure of divine power as would soon make the church militant the church triumphant. The church needs to come to a clearer apprehension of its mission as the divine agent for extending the reign of God on earth. It needs to devote itself with more singleness of purpose to the carrying out of this mission in order to claim the promise of spiritual enduement and of the divine presence. The promise of Christ, "Lo, I am with you alway, even unto the end of the world," is made to a church that is seeking to make His reign universal. What vast spiritual enterprises await the aggressive action of the church! What mighty strongholds of Satan await the assault of the awakened and panoplied sons of light! Let the Church of God, like a mighty battleship, clear its deck for action and bring all its powers to bear against the batteries of sin and unrighteousness, of ignorance and superstition, if she would realize, to the fullest extent, the promise of the divine presence and experience that fullness of spiritual power and energy which God always grants to those who make themselves the agents for carrying out His beneficent purposes in the world.

It is well to hold on to the old gospel and to be zealous for "the faith which was once for all delivered to the saints;" but conservatism is a virtue which may easily degenerate into cowardice or timidity. We must take the old gospel and apply it to the new conditions of our time. Nor must we be afraid to face the new problems which have grown out of the progress of Christianity in the world. We cannot do this except our minds and hearts are opened to receive the new truths that God is revealing to us by His Spirit in the enlarging experience of the church, in unfolding pages of human history, and in the light that is shining from every department of human knowledge and research. We cannot tie ourselves to the theories and theologies which have been outgrown and which belong to the dead past and expect to receive the influx of the divine Spirit to fit us for the new tasks of to-day. The church must cut loose from everything but Christ and what Christ approves, and under His leadership and unimpeded by the ecclesiastical and theological lumber of the past go forth to face the new issues and fight new battles of our time. The church that expects to be Spirit-filled must be both progressive and aggressive.

May it not be that our divisions, our denominational rivalries and jealousies, our sectarian narrowness and party spirit, our excessive zeal in behalf of our denominational tenets and theories have prevented the outpouring of the Holy Spirit in richer abundance upon the church? Whatever may be said in justification of the origin of our denominationalism and its inevitableness under the conditions which have existed and the improbability that these denominations will cease to exist in our day, one thing at least is certain: the time has fully arrived in this closing decade of the nineteenth century when the church of the living God must put away its sectarian strifes, its small controversies, its mutual jealousies and close up its divided ranks for a united assault upon the strongholds of the enemy, if it is to hold the respect of thinking men and win the approval of Him who is its Founder and its living Head. We cannot be loyal to Christ and do less than this. Not until the church, in spite of differences of opinion and of organization, has learned to co-operate fraternally for the advancement of the kingdom of God will it be worthy to be called the bride of Christ. Not until the sacramental hosts of God shall consent to stand shoulder to shoulder, arm to arm and heart to heart against the serried ranks of the enemy and wage a united war against a common foe, will Christ's prayer for the unity of His disciples, breathed out under the shadow of the cross, be fulfilled. Not until this prayer of our divine Lord is fulfilled in a larger measure than it is to-day can the church hope to receive the fullness of the divine Spirit to equip it for the conquest of the world.

This, then, is our message: God waits to be gracious to His church. He is willing and anxious to pour out upon it the Holy Spirit in rich abundance, when it puts itself in condition to receive the blessing. But we must put away our unbelief and our disobedience before we are ready to receive the Holy Spirit. The man or the church that says this or that right thing cannot be accomplished is guilty of unbelief. To doubt that the right will triumph over wrong is practical atheism. The church must apprehend its true mission in the world and undertake it in earnest, in order to receive the fullness of the divine blessing. It can expect God's co-operation with it only as it is doing God's work. It must cut itself loose from those theologies and theories of the past which hinder its progress and must go forward, unhampered, to meet the new issues of our day. It must put away its alienations, its jealousies, its bitter controversies and close up the gaps in its columns and move forward as a united host under the leadership of King Jesus, if it is to conquer the strongholds of the enemy and win the world for Christ.

This will require faith and courage of a high order; but if we heed the voice of our great Leader we cannot hesitate as to our duty. How we were all thrilled by one of the reports of the night entrance of Commodore Dewey's fleet into Manila Harbor. When the captain of the flagship Olympia signaled, "We are nearing Manila Bay," the Commordo resignaled, "Steam ahead!" A little further on and the captain again signaled, "We are now entering that part of the channel supposed to be mined." "Steam ahead!" was the Commodore's response, and he signaled back to the fleet, "Follow me!" Soon there was a flash on the shore and the boom of a cannon from one of the forts. "We are fired upon from one of the forts of the enemy," signaled one of the captains. "Steam ahead!" was signaled once more by the brave Commodore. On went the fleet in the darkness of the night, over submarine mines and under the frowning batteries of the enemy, until it reached the very center of the harbor where, when day dawned, the squadron stood in battle array, every ship floating the stars and stripes, and the band playing "The Star Spangled Banner!" There, before them, stood the Spanish battleships and the belching batteries of Fort Cavite. Then came the onset and the victory which thrilled the world!

So the church as the old gospel-clad ship of Zion moves forward through the moral darkness of the world to accomplish her divine mission. Ever and anon the signal is given by some too conservative leader, "There is danger ahead; we are leaving behind us the old theories, interpretations and usages of the past!" "Steam ahead!" is signaled back from our divine Commander. But another timid soul cries out, "The batteries of the enemy are opened upon us, because we are threatening their strongholds. The Christian Endeavor army in its war on political corruption and the liquor traffic is drawing upon us the fire of these powerful antagonists!" "Steam ahead!" comes back the response from our great Leader. "Had we not better be content with the progress we have made, and pause here and rest upon our laurels?" suggests some timid and cautious leader in the church. "Steam ahead!" is the decisive signal waved back from our supreme Commander from the heavenly heights.

Some glad morning, not far distant, let us hope, when the mists that now obscure the issues between the church and her foes, shall have cleared away, the whole ecclesiastical squadron shall appear in solid battle array, each vessel flying the banner of the cross with the name of Christ inscribed thereon in letters of light, and all confronting the hosts of unrighteousness and the forts and batteries of Satan. Then shall come the great and decisive battle in the age-long conflict between right and wrong. Then shall Righteousness triumph in the earth and Truth shall be crowned with everlasting victory!

ALEXANDER CAMPBELL AND WALTER SCOTT AS PREACHERS.

J. B. C.

On one occasion while Mr. Campbell was addressing one of the most intelligent audiences ever assembled in Kentucky, quite a number of highly gifted and educated men arose unconsciously to their feet and leaned forward towards the speaker as if fearing to lose a single word that fell from his lips, and what makes the case more remarkable is that many of them were the public advocates of the views he was assailing, as being in his judgment contrary to the Word of God; yet such was the force, clearness and eloquence that he brought to the task, that even those who differed from him could not but pay the high tribute which we have mentioned to his admirable powers of close thought, of lofty and brilliant expression! Campbell's greatness and strength may in a great measure be realized by a careful study of his writings, and it is a wonder that a selection of his original writings on the great variety of subjects through so many volumes of the Harbinger have not been collated and published for the public. The noblest efforts of his worthy fellow-laborer, as far as the expression is concerned, perished almost at their birth; they could not be reproduced by either speaker or hearer; the impressions made on the minds and hearts of those who heard him, will never fade until all things else shall fade. But the tablets on which those memories dear and sweet are written are perishable, and when the present generation passes, or rather when the remnant of those who heard him in his prime which yet lingers shall have passed away, the world will not know anything save by dim and imperfect tradition of the wonderful eloquence of this gifted, this princely man! I claim not to have set him forth faithfully as he seemed to me and the thousands who heard him, but these few fragments, imperfect as they are, will give some idea of the man. We can safely entrust the fame of Alexander Campbell to the proofs which his writings afford of his great, his eminent abilities.

We give a quotation or transcript from the celebrated George D. Prentice, editor of the Louisville Journal. The writer was then taking the Journal and proposed to furnish said extract to Dr. Richardson who was then writing the memoirs of Mr. Campbell. From the Journal we read as now found in the second volmue the following, viz.:

"ALEXANDER CAMPBEDL.

"This venerable and distinguished man is now in our city on business connected with his college at Bethany, so recently visited, as our readers know, with a very disastrous calamity. We are gratified to perceive that neither years nor trials—and his Atlantean shoulders support a mountainous weight of both—have seriously impaired his bodily strength or dimmed, much less quenched the marvelous fire of his spirit. In all the characteristics of manhood he is still in the fullness of maturity. And long may he retain this rare possossion of his great powers.

"Alexander Campbell is unquestionably one of the most extraordinary men of our time. Putting wholly out of view his tenets, of which we of course have nothing to do, he claims by virtue of his intrinsic qualities, as manifested in his achievements, a place among the very foremost spirits of the age. His energy, self-reliance and self-fidelity, if we may use the expression, are of the stamp that belongs only to the world's first leaders in thought and action.

"His personal excellence is certainly without a stain or a shadow. His intellect, it is scarcely too much to say, is among the clearest, richest, profoundest ever vouchsafed to man. Indeed, it seems to us that in the faculty of abstract thinking, in, so to say, the sphere of pure thought, he has few if any living rivals. Every cultivated person of the slighest metaphysical turn who has heard Alexander Campbell in the pulpit or in the social circle must have been especially impressed by the wonderful faculty with which his faculties move in the . . . highest planes of thought. Ultimate facts stand forth as boldly in his consciousness as sensations do in that of most other men. He grasps and handles the highest, subtlest, most comprehensive principles as if they were the liveliest impressions of the senses. No poet's soul is more crowded with imagery than his is with the ripest forms of thought. Surely, the life of a man thus excellent and gifted is a part of the common treasure of society. In his essential character he belongs to no sect or party, but to the world!"

Our Budget.

—A sweet spirit brightens the world.

—Good literature enriches the mind.

—The heat and the burden of the day develop the soldier.

—The saloon must go some day, else God's not in his world.—*Cumberland Presbyterian.*

—The church that waits for the saloon to "go some day" will lose God first.

—The large display advertisement of Christian College, Columbia, Mo., in this paper, is worthy of special attention.

—The Christian Endeavor World, July 21, contains an excellent account of the Nashville convention, touching up all phases of it. It is a good all round report of a great convention.

—The date of the meeting of the Virginia Tidewater district has been changed from August 10-12 to August 9-11. All interested parties are requested to note this change.

—One of the handsomest pages of our large edition of the CHRISTIAN-EVANGELIST last week was the advertisement of our colleges, on the last page.

—This war ought not to pass without bringing entire destruction to something beside Spanish fleets. The whole canteen system ought to meet the doom of Cervera's ships, and will if the forces that make for sobriety in America continue the pressure already begun upon the war department.—*New York Voice.*

—James C. Creel, for more than ten years the editor and publisher of the Church Register, has retired from the editorial chair, having sold his entire interest therein to brethren Hoffmann and Wilson, as we stated last week, and will devote all his time to preaching from pulpit and house to house. The Church Register under the new management is to be removed, renamed, reformed and issued every week after September 1st.

—The catalogue of the Female Orphan School of the Christian Church, at Camden Point, Mo., for 1899, in tusean red cover, is a finely executed piece of work from the printer's standpoint and full of promise for orphan girls from the religious and philanthropic view-points. We are glad to note the increasing prosperity of this school.

—Wright & Marion have started the publication of a monthly magazine at Monett, Mo., called "Just Think." Its motto is, "Just Think on These Things;" its religion, "To do good;" and its field, "The world." Not an advertisement appears on its pages; just think! These brethren have shouldered a heavy task, but it is one of the results of their thoughts and we trust that they may succeed in their enterprise. Just Think, Vol. 1, No. 1, has some good thoughts.

—The Foreign Christian Missionary Society has received $9,690 on the "Annuity Plan" from J. Coop, Southport, England. About this time last year his brother, Frank Coop, turned over $5,000 to the society. It will be membered that these are the worthy sons of the lamented Timothy Coop, who was so generous in every good work. The "Annuity Plan" deserves the favorable consideration of those able to dispose of money in this way. This amount will be of the greatest service to the Foreign Society in providing much needed buildings on the mission fields.

—When alluding to Bro. Myers' work at Sedalia, Mo., we forgot that the splendid house in which the church worships had been built and dedicated under the ministry of M. M. Davis, now at Dallas, Texas. In round numbers the house was said to cost $40,000. The real cost of the house, we have since learned, was $37,500, including organ and furniture, and of this amount all but $5,000 was paid before the dedication. It is due both to Bro. Myers and to Bro. Davis to make this distinction between their labors at Sedalia. Both did a grand work for the church there, and both will be held in loving remembrance for the same. A second church has been organized in Sedalia and a good house of worship built for it during Bro. Myers' ministry.

—Captain Philip said the immortal words for this war: "Don't cheer; the poor fellows are dying." It is better than Nelson's, "England expects every man to do his duty," or his dying words, "Kiss me, Hardy," or Decatur's, "Don't give up the ship," or Wolfe's, "Then I die contentedly," or Grant's, "Let us have peace." They recall Bayard Taylor's, "The bravest are the tenderest, the loving are the daring." They are the passports of that Christian soldier to perpetual remembrance.—*The Interior.*

—The letter in this paper from the Statistical Burea, Washington, D. C., on our trade with China will doubtless be a surprise to our readers. When you read the article do not stop at its commercial value, but view the facts presented from a missionary view-point. The possibilities for the extension of Christ's name in China cannot be overestimated at this time.

—The following statements concerning the city of Sapphira, Montana, from Rev. Lynde Hartt in the June Atlantic is about as strong an argument in favor of Home Missions as can be produced:

Look down from the rocky crest of Mount Sapphira and ask yourself why the city looks so singularly flat and thick-set, says the Rev. Rollin Lynde Hartt in the June Atlantic. Is it because there are no trees, or, at any rate, none that rise above the second-story window-sills? Perhaps. Or is it because the houses are all so much of a size? Possibly. But there is a better explanation than either. It is because there are no church spires. Churches there are, but you must have sharp eyes to find them. They are little, they are insignificant, they are monuments of a disgraced and unpopular cause. Says Broncho Billy, "Look at them darned, contemptible churches—all-same shacks! I could buy out any three of 'em!" Out of 10,000 people, only 1,500 Protestant church-goers! Sapphira is a peculiar town, too, for in Sapphira there are classes and no masses, unless you call the Chinese merchants, mechanics and laundrymen masses. It is not the old problem of reaching the masses. It is the entirely new problem of reaching the classes. Cultured, law-abiding, progressive Sapphira has little toleration for religion. The tiny congregations in the tiny churches are made up mainly of women; a Sapphira church is a "lady chapel." A Montana business man objects to walking on the same side of the street with a church. There is still more truth than fiction in the old saying that "west of Bismarck there is no Sunday, and west of Miles City no God."

—The following letter from a soldier at Chickamauga will show the interest our soldiers take in good literature and in religious culture:

CHRISTIAN PUB. CO., ST. LOUIS, MO.:

Sirs and Brothers—I received the papers you so kindly sent, and as I could not read them all by myself I gave them to the boys. I only had enough for companys D, H and M, but what I did give out were received by all with an eagerness which shows that the Lord is not forgotten even in the army where every one is supposed to be as bad as they make them. We have a Y. M. C. A. Commission on the camp ground, and I can tell you it is a place where many of the boys hear the Word of God, and a good many have promised to lead a better life. We have services twice a week. You may send more pamphlets if you will, and I will do my best to put them in the boys' hands, and may be it will do some good, which I am in hopes it will. Before we left the barracks the Bible Society gave each soldier a Testament to keep, and the boys are making pretty good use of them.

Chickamauga, Ga., July 13, 1898.

—We are glad that Bro. Atkinson, of Wabash, Ind., has sufficiently recovered that he can send us a message again, which you will find in this paper; but we regret that he will not be able to resume his work as corresponding secretary of the Ministerial Relief Fund. Fortunately, however, an able successor to Bro. Atkinson has been chosen by the trustees of this fund, as you will see, and the work will be vigorously pushed while in Bro. Lucas' hands. Bro. Atkinson has done a grand work in behalf of aged and dependent ministers and their families, and will be held in sweet and lasting remembrance for it. And while he cannot prosecute this work farther, as he had hoped, we are glad that our gracious Father in Heaven has spared his life to his family and to the church, for many years, we trust. Even his presence with us will be an inspiration to good works and loving deeds. Note carefully his requests in his message in this paper and give Bro. Lucas your confidence and prayers, that he may prosper this work.

—All Bible-school, Endeavor and Prayer-meeting leaders should read "A Curious Incident," in this paper, and heed the implied moral. *Get others to work.*

—There were some delays in running our edition last week, due to adjustment of our new press to its work, which will explain why we were later than usual in getting to our readers last week.

—We have thought it not out of place to give our readers the picture of a few of the prominent men now leading our army and navy to victory in our war for the freedom of Cuba. This week we give an excellent cut of Admiral Sampson.

—Concerning the origin of this city, the same authority produces the following which largely accounts for its irreligious state:

The history of Sapphira is the history of the entire commonwealth. First there was gold —$30,000,000 of it in Humbug gulch. Then there were pioneers. Immediately there was a camp. Upon the vampires pounced the vigilantes. Out of vigilantism came law. With law came women. With women came civilization. With civilization came the "boom." The boom "busted" and you have Sapphira!

LOOKING FORWARD.

In view of the efforts which we have been putting forth to make the CHRISTIAN-EVANGELIST the equal of any religious journal in the land, we are expecting a very large increase in the number of our subscribers. Our progress in this direction during the present year has been steady and satisfactory.

We have endeavored to give to our readers the very best that their patronage would justify, and we feel that it is in place to thank the friends of first-class literature for the gratifying support they have given to us in this work. Our paper is now better in both appearance and quality of contents than it has ever been, and is, therefore capable of greater good in the homes which it visits.

We have no disposition to force it upon any one, but are anxious that all should have an opportunity to judge for themselves concerning its excellency and of becoming subscribers if they so desire. We have determined therefore to offer to new subscribers the CHRISTIAN-EVANGELIST from August 1st, 1898, to January 1st, 1899, on trial, for the small sum of *Fifty-cents*, barely enough to cover the expenses of sending it to them. Such subscriptions will be promptly discontinued January 1st, 1899, unless otherwise ordered by the subscriber in the meantime. We solicit the earnest assistance of all friends of the cause in this effort to place a large number of our homes under the elevating influence of good literature. We can not allow commissions or premiums of any kind in connection with this offer because of the very low price which is mentioned.

Notice!

It is desired that all students seeking to secure rooms and boarding at Lida's Wood, Eureka College, will correspond with the President of the College as below pending announcement of the new management soon to be made.

J. H. HARDIN, Pres.

Eureka, Ill.

?ERSONAL MENTION.

Briney, of Moberly, Mo., passed ıe city Tuesday morning on his way Springs, Ill., where he is to hold a with Mr. Throgmorton, editor of t News, Du Quoin, Ill. C. J. Kim- · proof-reader, being one of the s of the the discussion, also left on ıorning in company with Bro. Briney ıate.

Coggins, of Mt. Hope, Kansas, is ıis vacation in North Carolina. He to visit his mother at Asheville in

Cumingham, of St. Thomas, and Miss ı, of New Haven, Penn., were re- ried and will be sent to Japan in , as missionaries, by our Foreign Society.

Leach, of Moulton, Iowa, writes ıad the largest offering for missions ən's Day, for many years. The naking arrangements for extensive :ovements this summer. Bro. Leach the annual address for the high Moulton this year.

to be an assembly of the Gentry Crab Orchard Springs, Ky., Au- 898. The object of this meeting is gether as many as possible of the ts from the Revolutionary soldier, Gentry (who is buried near Crab prings, on the "Old Gentry Place"), r David, two sisters, Winnie and . of his uncles Martin, Watson, Wil- Moses Gentry, all of whom came from

informed that Brother Royal, of Ill., is down with what is thought to be his last sickness. Bro. Royal out a long and useful life in the ervice, and will be among those of Lord will say, "Well done thou good ıl servant."

ıroh of Eureka, Cal., extended a A. Nesbit to remain another year as He has been with them nearly four very generously tendered him a f a month on full salary.

Cassius, the colored evangelist, gan county, Okla. Ter., has publish- ; on Negro Evangelization and the ıstrial School, which he is selling at ıer copy in the interest of his educa- ıligious work at Tohee.

M. Tennyson, formerly State Sup- ıt of the Children's Home Society ıri, and more recently Field Agent ıristian's Orphan's Home, has re- position in the latter institution and h his family in California. Rev. W. , formerly a district superintendent ldren's Home Society, has been ap- fill the place in the Christian's Or- ıme made vacant by Mr. Tennyson's n. Mr. Young is a most estimable great worker. We wish him suc- s new field.—*Moissouri Children's der.*

J. Rose, of Kansas, will make the ctension address at Eureka, Friday, a.

awes' present address is Blue Bell, County, O.

Moore's present address is Austin,

arshall, pastor of the church at Mo., and his family will spend a Atlantic Highlands, N. J.

Price, who has recently removed from ., to Gibsonburg, O., would like to work for some church, hold a pro- ıeting, or assist in pulpit work.

ıoyd, of Kansas City, Mo., recently at West Moreland, Kan., on Lord's ends good report of the church there.

Hilton, of Perry, Oklahoma territory, called for his third year by the church e is the president of the ministerial Perry which is making a strong fight ressors of their municipal laws.

Ball preaches one-half time at Kan., and one-fourth time each at er and Ellendale, and reports the gressing finely at each place. The mentioned at these points by Bro. esent, is of good religious literature papers—and we are sorry ta say, this r too common among the churches

Fergusson, of Riverside, Cal., at- e Southern California convention at ch and reports it a great advance

S. W. Crutcher, of Plano, Texas, has accepted the unanimous call to preach for the church at Pine Bluff, Ark.

A. I. Myhr delivered the literary address to the graduating class of the Georgia Robertson Christian College, Henderson, Tenn.

Prof. Chas. J. Kemper, of Lexington, Ky., and his wife will spend a season at Cuckoo, Va.

E. T. Edmonds' column of church news in Christian Work shows that the church at Ft. Smith, Ark., is in a state of unusual activity for the hot season.

A. M. Haggard, of Iowa, preached at Marion, same state, on July 24. Pastor Seaton is in a meeting in South Dakota.

Romig and Dawdy lecture two nights in Marion, Ia., August 3 and 4.

Guy Martin was installed July 17 as assistant pastor in Mason City, Ia.

Joel Brown, general solicitor for the St. Louis Orphans' Home, spent Sunday, July 24, in North English, Ia., and took back one inmate for the Home.

Henry Goodacre, of Wisconsin, visited Ft. Dodge, Ia., recently.

Miss Jessie Williams, of Des Moines, Standard correspondent and office secretary of the Iowa Board, is spending her vacation in Colorado Springs.

C. C. Redgrave has located with Estherville, Ia.

J. H. Stark, of Illinois, preaches at Marshalltown, Ia., on July 31. He lectures next night.

E. C. Wigmore, of Charles City, Ia., leaves immediately for Palouse, Wash.

J. M. Hoffman, of Spencer, Ia., assisted R. J. Brondbridge, of Ruthven, in raising $110 so as to secure $400 from the Extension Board.

W. B. Crewdson, of Corning, Ia., closed his meeting at Brainard with 68 added, $400 raised on salary and $500 on building project.

R. A. Omer holds a meeting in Sidney, Fremont county, Ia., in August.

N. A. McConnell will preach next Sunday in Marion, Ia.

CHANGES.

R. L. Cartwright, Chicago to Morocco, Ind.
Wm. Branch, Centralia to Abingdon, Ill.
Samuel Traum, Wilmington to Nevin, O.
W. T. Adams, Des Moines, Ia., to Winfield, Kan.
W. H. Roach, Buda to Bradford, Ill.

From Our Exchanges.

As we have given some of the expressions of appreciation of our new form and other improvements from our readers, we will follow these with a few of the compliments which our exchanges are giving us:

The CHRISTIAN-EVANGELIST, of St. Louis, Mo., is out in a new dress. It is a thing of beauty and will be a joy forever, we trust. It now surpasses any of our papers in mechanical makeup. It is one of our leaders in thought also. May it enjoy a greatly increased circulation.—*Christian Worker.*

The CHRISTIAN-EVANGELIST, St. Louis, Mo., is out in a new form, and takes its place as one of the handsomest American weeklies. Its first page contains a good likeness of J. H. Garrison, editor.—*The Christian Tribune.*

The CHRISTIAN-EVANGELIST has joined the increasing company of weekly religious news papers which have adopted the thirty-two small-paged form, very few still retaining the large page of former years. On the first page is a picture of the editor, J. H. Garrison, who, if we mistake not, is the dean or ranking veteran among all the editors representing the plea for a return to New Testament Christianity. Of course we think the change of form improves the appearance of our contemporary. That this important journal may continue to prosper, and to improve in substance through every change of form, and that its experienced and devout editor may be granted many years yet to plead for and exemplify the motto of the paper, "In Faith, Uuity; in Opinions and Methods, Liberty; in All Things, Charity," is our sincere prayer.—*Christian Standard.*

The CHRISTIAN-EVANGELIST, one of America's most interesting religious journals, has changed its form to smaller pages and more of them. It still retains, however, the high standard of editorial excellence which makes it a welcome visitor in many homes.—*The Columbia, Mis-*

Publishers' Notes.

It is very evident that D. H. Bays, in his late book, "Doctrines and Dogmas of Mormonism Examined and Refuted," has torn down all the strongholds of the Mormon doctrine. He was for many years a powerful advocate of the Mormon faith, but seeing the errors of their teachings, he abandoned the Latter Day Saints, and has written the strongest book against their false doctrine that is now before the public. Should your community be invaded by the advocates of Mormonism, a few copies of Bays' book circulated in your neighborhood will cause them to "Fold their tents and steal silently away."

The study of "Organic Evolution Considered," by Prof. A. Fairhurst, of Kentucky University, is destined to set at naught beliefs in Atheism, Agnosticism or Materialism, or any character of scientific logic that blots God out of existence.—*The Christian Leader, Cincinnati, Ohio.*

READY FOR ORDERS.

We are now ready to fill orders for that beautiful little book by W. J. Russell, entitled, "Wonders of the Sky, or God's Glory Exhibited in the Heavens." Beautifully bound in bright colored cloth, and the price is 50 cents. No one can read this little volume without greater reverence for the Creator of the universe.

"In the Days of Jehu" will add much light to the present Sunday-school lessons.

The book will not be considered a oommentary, but is a work which treats in an exceedingly romantic and attractive manner the Bible story as found in portions of the Book of Kings. It is especially valuable just now to the large army of Sunday-school officers, teachers and workers. The reader will find that the author has taken the biblical picture of the beautiful and wicked Jezebel, and woven around it a romantic story, wonderfully interesting without the sacrifice of historical facts. After reading the book no one will regret the cost of it, which is 75 cents.

The following books will be found valuable to Christian Endeavor workers:

"The Helping Hand," by W. W. Dowling, is a book containing a history of the Y.P.S.C.E. movement, and gives instructions concerning every phase of Endeavor work. Bound in flexible cloth, price, 25 cents per copy.

"The Young People's Prayer-meeting and Its Improvement," by Cal. Ogburn, gives full details how to make the Young People's Prayer-meeting interesting, spiritual and profitable. Cloth binding, price, 75 cents.

"Ways of Working," by Oreon E. Scott, contains valuable instructions to all committees connected with Y. P. S. C. E., the author having had many years experience in Endeavor work. 38 pages, price 10 cents.

A Card from Secretary Abbot.

To the many friends who have written to inquire concerning Mrs. Abbott, I can only say that the issue is not yet decided. Her condition is very critical and only He who knows it all can tell the result of the next few days. Pray for us all. Yours in His name,

T. A. ABBOTT.

Correspondence.

New York Letter.

Chaplain H. W. Jones, of the battleship Texas, preached to an immense congregation at the Lexington Avenue Baptist Church on Suuday evening, July 17th. He was injured by a bursting shell from the Spanish guns before Santiago the day previous to the destruction of Cervera's fleet, but was privileged to see that awful sea fight. He described in interesting detail the death and burial of a number of brave American soldiers, and many were the expressions of saddened hearts as he recited the story. At the same hour of this service Lietenant Tull, of the Seventy-first New York Regiment, occupied the pulpit of the Fremont Methodist Church. He was greeted by a great throng of enthusiastic people. We are glad to know of such excellent Christian men at the front with our army and navy—men who hazard their lives for their country and who are not ashamed to stand up for the great Captain of our salvation in the midst of their commands.

***

The League for Social Service in New York, of which Dr. Josiah Strong is one of the chief executives, is gaining many strong and famous men to its practical support. Dr. Tolman, for a long time prominently connected with the Association for Relieving the Condition of the Poor, has resigned in order to work with Dr. Strong in the new society. The principle object of the League for Social Service is educational; it will issue tracts, leaflets, etc., written by specialists on the various social problems of our times in order to disseminate as widely as possible the experiences and practical knowledge of those who are giving their lives to certain sociological themes. It will maintain a bureau of information to indicate to editors, clergymen, professors, students and such like the best information on any of the topics within its sphere. The advisory counsel embraces such celebrities as Richard Watson Gilder, Washington Gladden, Chas. H. Parkhurst and Bishop H. C. Potter. Dr. Strong's leadership insures ability and practical usefulness to the League.

***

The summer relaxation in church work in New York is upon us. Many congregations have suspended all or part of their public services for the heated term, and others will do so. The church on West 56th Street has no evening preaching services through July and August. Bro. Payne will be out of town in the latter month. The preaching services at the 169th Street church and all the services at the branch on the East Side will be suspended four weeks. Sunday-school, Christian Endeavor and midweek prayer-meeting, however, will be continued right through the warm weather. Quite a lively discussion, editorial and otherwise, has been going on in certain of our great dailies recently, on the question of closing churches in New York in summer. Certainly all earnest Christian people prefer the services open all the year; but the question of support is a grave one in New York. Most of the reliable helpers in the work are on their vacation, the indifferent ones are disposed to stay at home when the weather is warm, and the result is a mere handful of good people tug and pull through an uninspiring service with little or no spiritual profit. If our church were so large that a goodly contingency could always be relied upon even in time of the country exodus we would certainly keep open house for the Lord the whole year. Many of our people going out do good in his name and coming in bring renewed vigor and life into the work at home.

***

In his little parish paper, "Upward," Bro. Lowell C. McPherson, the hard-working pastor of the Jefferson Street Church, Buffalo, says he is thinking of taking a trip across the Atlantic to visit England and Scotland this summer, to be gone about five weeks. He further says, "His plan will include feeding horses during the passage across the waters for two purposes, namely, to defray expenses and for diversion." This is just like the noble, independent, heroic man Bro. Mc. is, and we shall be glad to hear of him carrying out his plans to visit the old country and return in time to be at our state convention at 169th Street Church in August-September.

***

Just before sailing for Europe on his vacation, Dr. Parkhurst did some plain talking to his congregation on church manners. He said:

During the first twenty minutes of our Sunday morning services there is a certain amount of disorder, there is a coming and going up and down the aisles, that must be distasteful to Him in whose temple we are met. Things ere not conducted in a decent manner. I don't mean to blame the ushers. Much of the disturbance is due to the conduct of the pew-holders who come in late. The ushers don't know whether they are coming or not, and cannot seat strangers who are present. This creates disturbance and should not continue.

It is more than likely Dr. Parkhurst's church is not the only one in the land to which this language might be addressed.

***

N. C. Fowler read a paper before the Twilight Club sometime ago on "Religious Publicity." A few of the extracts from his excellent paper will perhaps be of interest. He says:

Something for nothing never has been and never will be a part of Christianity's motion. Salvation is not free. If it were free it would not be worth having. If it be a commodity, it must be handled and advertised along the better lines of developing other commodities.

He continues:

The Bible is the grandest, the most exhaustive, the most sensible, and the best written and most effective advertisement ever conceived. Every chapter of the Bible is a glorious advertisement of Christian morality and of the benefits of goodness. In every book of the Bible there are the most beautifully written, the most emphatic, and the brightest of glowing descriptions of the magnificence of heaven and of the myriads of attractions for the benefit of the blessed. The church that has stood on that peculiar composition which its members think is dignity, and has handled religion without using any of the legitimate business of methods, is but a cold monument representing something and doing nothing. Those little conventional church advertisements among the religious newspapers are not the kind that business men use to announce millinery openings. There is nothing about the ordinary religious notice to make people go to church.

The Church of Christ has something to offer to everybody, and if that something is as good as the church says it is, surely it is worth advertising so as to bring it to the attention of men. More and better advertising the services of the Church of Christ would no doubt result in great good. S. T. WILLIS.

1281 Union Ave.

Wheeling Through England.

III.

For the Shakespeare-loving pilgrim, who has made Stratford-on-Avon the center of his daily thoughts and nightly dreams from the day on which he first stepped upon British soil, there may possibly be disappointment in store when he finds himself in the midst of the actual Stratford. Here one instinctively demands a more distinct flavor of antiquity, more of the England of three centuries ago, than elsewhere. And yet the traveler, coming through Coventry, where one might live in the sixteenth century and forget the nineteenth if he wished, through Kenilworth, which seems not so much to have come down into our time as to carry us back by some pleasant magic into the days of its early grandeur, finds in Stratford not a town of Shakespeare's time, but a modern town, containing a few relics of Shakespeare and his age. The town has been rebuilt with broad and fairly straight streets, and the stream of tourists (of which we are two) has swept it clear of its atmosphere of quaintness and antiquity, except such as lingers about the Shakespeare birthplace, the grammar school and the Holy Trinity Church. These places, so long as we are not in the town, are delightful and satisfying. It is a beautiful and touching thing to behold the homage that is paid to the great dramatist, and the crowd of pilgrims who frequent this shrine is an eloquent testimonial to his fame. But one cannot help regretting that the poet's memory is made so much a matter of merchandise. Stratford obtains not only all of its reputation, but most of its livelihood from the fact that Shakespeare lived and died there. It would be interesting to know what proportion of its pupulation are engaged in pursuits directly dependent upon this fact. The per cent. would be large. Neither is it altogether pleasing to see "Shakespeare Cigars," "Shakespeare Restaurants," "Shakespeare Hotel," "Shakespeare Livery Stables," and other signs of the same sort staring one in the face at every corner. Besides this, there are abundant evidences of the demoralization which results to the residents from habitual catering to a floating population of tourists. You cannot walk the length of a street without being accosted by from two to six urchins who, for the consideration of "tuppence" are anxious to guide you to a dozen spots where you don't care to go and acquaint you with a score of facts with which (thanks to your faithful friend, Baldeker) you are already familiar. They join themselves to you and will not be shaken off. When you decline their services, they unblushingly descend to undisguised mendicancy and still clamor for the "tuppence," or perhaps with more moderation, for a penny. Yes, it must be admitted that Stratfofd-on-Avon, as a town, fails to satisfy. It is a museum. Its individual exhibits are wonderfully interesting, but they bear the same relation to the town as the contents of any museum bear to the building in which they are kept.

The best thing about Stratford, to my mind, is Ann Hathaway's cottage, the scene of Shakespeare's courtship, and one of its chief charms is that it is not in Stratford but three-quarters of a mile away, in a village of a dozen houses called Shottery. It was Sunday evening. We had attended church in the morning at the Holy Trinity, where the poet is buried, and had spent the afternoon rowing leisurely up and drifting again down the Avon, basking in the sunsnine and then seeking shelter from a sudden shower under the bushes on the bank. It cleared again with a bright sunset, followed by a long, soft, mellow English twilight, the sweetest of all twilights. On such an evening we wandered along the path which leads across the fields from Stratford to Shottery. A hedge of wild roses is on one side and a meadow on the other, while here and there a poppy flames by the path. The air is fresh and fragrant from the rain; and presently the thatch of Ann Hathaway's cottage appears at the end of the lane. Ah! Shakespeare, who could blame you for loving the girl who lived at the end of that walk? The fact that she was nine years his senior ought for sentimental reasons, to have been forgotten long ago. It seems like an impertinence even to think of it as we follow this path which doubtless the feet of Shakespeare often trod on a Sunday evening—unless the ways of men and maidens have greatly altered in three centuries. The wonder is only that a girl, the path to whose house was so flowery, wild and sweet, should not have been married to some other Stratford youth while the future dramatist was yet in grammar school. As I stood looking at the house and thinking it all over, a little girl ran up with a wild rose fresh plucked from the hedge, gave it to me, and ran away as quickly as she had come. I was sorry that she went so quickly, and yet glad, for otherwise I would never have known that it was an act of pure kindness uninvited by any thoughts of pennies that might follow.

From Stratford-on-Avon our route lay north for a few miles, back to Warwick, where a few hours were happily spent at Warwick Castle,

tive at once of ancient and modern
he Earl charges an entrance fee of
the uninvited guests who care to
le and grounds. A communicative
informed us, in answer to our
t between two and three hundred
attendants were ordinarily em-
; the castle and park, but that
'ere called in on special occasions,
ecent visit of the Prince of Wales.
arge is the family that is served
) or three hundred?" we asked.
and their parents," replied the
tor. If beauty of architecture and
surroundings could ever make a
an wish to be an earl for the sake
a castle, Warwick Castle is the
ire that unpatriotic wish.

---

as impossible as it is undesirable
nsecutive account of the English
day to day. The record could
approximately correct unless it
'om hour to hour. As a rule, each
a mixture of sunshine and rain.
factor is merely the proportion
two. Moreover, English showers
nall affairs, in space as well as in
see a black cloud about the size of
d off your starboard bow, to speak
nd coming straight toward you. It
vident that there will soon be rain
ear, but it does not follow that
t. It may miss you by a couple of
ls; or you may dash forward and
in front of it. In any case it
be over in half an hour and the
in condition to ride as soon as the
ped. Hence it was that we were
isturbed when it began to rain on
ck Castle. We simply went inoked at the Van Dyke portraits,
furniture and ancient armour for
hen rode on in sunshine to Rugby
orth.

---

h, the home and parish of John
g the last nine years of his life, is
visit. The town is nothing more
and other English towns, but the
h is one of the most interesting to
where. If the claims of the cu-
ect, part of the present structure
ed years old. The identical pul-
from which Wiclif preached evan-
tianity five centuries ago and, in
ay believe those now in charge,
ilding is substantially as it was in
e. Among the relics of undoubted
is the great carved oak communion
y Wiclif. It was made to stand
nter of the aisle instead of against
n altar according to the Roman
and now current. This usage, it
mbered, was one for which Wiclif
account by his ecclesiastical su-
i-hierarchical notions seem to have
hed in the very building, for there
the Last Judgment, two centuries
Wiclif, in which the most con-
ong the damned are a bishop with
priest with his robe and a king
wn.

---

utterworth, we returned to Rugby,
elebrated school and saw part of a
h, and then went, as many of Eng-
est men have done, from Rugby to
pping on the way at Banbury, as
e of them have done also, to make
neal on the Banbury cakes and hot
which have been known by name
rsery days. They are very good,
with milk, but are rather heavy
in quantities of more than eight
. Of Oxford we can say only
place which it is a joy to reach,
o remain in, and an agony to
) days was a time all too short
to it, but the exigencies of the
wed us no more; so we rode on, through Henley, the scene of the great boat races a few days hence; Eton, where we saw with much amusement the school-boys in their peculiar costume, short Eton jackets and high silk hats; Windsor, the home of the Queen, a vast castle, but not half so attractive as Warwick; Stoke Poges, the "country churchyard" of Gray's Elegy, and so to London.

W. E. GARRISON.

London.

A Morning Walk in Geneva.

Early one morning I was watching the bathing swans from the Pont des Bergues, at Geneva when a gentleman, evidently a clergyman, accosted me with: "Bonjour monsieur." His French betrayed the foreigner, his manner suggested the American. Replying to his courteous salutation, I added: "From Iowa; what is your state?"

"Why, I'm from Iowa, too," he exclaimed.

The reverend gentleman was not long in turning the conversation on historic subjects. "I just wanted to come out here awhile and imagine myself standing on the old bridge which once spanned the Rhone at this point and which Cæsar destroyed to prevent the crossing of the Helvetii, as he tells us in his commentaries on the wars in Gaul."

"Yes, that's a great pleasure if one has the power of abstraction highly enough developed. It requires a great deal of imagination to transform this wholly modern scene before us into that of some two thousand years and more ago, when the barbarians and Romans stood face to face on these shores."

"Quite true," he responded; "they say, too, that the old bridge of that time was probably a little farther down stream."

By means of a causeway built in the current and connected with the middle of the Pont des Bergues, we crossed over to Rousseau's Island, a favorite spot of the great author. In the midst of a cluster of trees is the sitting statue of this illustrious citizen of Geneva, whose "Emile" and "Social Contract" were officially burned before the city hall in 1762 by the hangman's hand.

A few minutes later we were walking along the Mont Blanc Quay, in view of the majestic range of the same name. The most beautiful site in the city, it boasts of the finest monument in Switzerland. It is an imitation of the Scaligeri mausoleum in Verona. It is sixty feet high and was formerly crowned with an equestrian statue in bronze. This has been removed on account of its weight and now stands on the spacious terrace. We were loud in our praises of the structure. A German, who chanced to be near and who was probably inclined toward socialism saw the matter from another point of view.

"But, do the gentlemen not find it a little strange that a man like the Duke of Brunswick known in Germany as the Diamantenherzog von Braunschweig—should have the finest memorial in the Swiss Republic?"

"We know nothing against him. The books issued by the office of Public Inquiry only say that he died here in 1873, leaving his fortune to the city, of which five million francs have been used to build the new opera house."

"True enough, it would not be politic for a city to publish the truth about its benefactors. But the Duke of Brunswick was not a Swiss, nor even a republican, nor a man above reproach, that he should be celebrated in marble, that, too, in Geneva. I find it very ironical, a curious freak of fate. The duke was a German despot, his rebellious subjects drove him from the ducal throne in 1830 because they could not endure the profligacy of his life, the tyranny and incompetency of his administration. After that he lived mostly in Paris and figured in many scandals."

A Swiss: "Our city has always been the asylum for political refugees. If they see fit to make it their legatee, it is not our place to examine too closely into their lives or their politics."

"No, to be sure," answered th
rather hotly. "The Swiss ha
seen fit to 'examine' where mon
stake. For three hundred years yo
families and your city councils were
lings of French and Italian princ
armies of Swiss rushed from their
home to fight under the flags of des
against their subjects struggling f
The Swiss went as mercenaries—
They had no other motive. And in t
of the Tuileries in 1792 more than
fell."

"But they were brave," interr
Swiss.

"Which does not alter my state
Switzerland has always been obedie
cenary motives, and"——

Leaving the two to settle their
best they could, we proceeded down t
crossed by the Island Tower and e
old city by German Street, at th
which is an appropriate shaft and
commemorating the final repulse of
of Savoy on the night of the 12th of
1602. It was a surprise, but the c
fended their walls and gained
victory, celebrated to this day as
important events in the city's his
the name of la Fete de l' Escalade.
Fourth of July for the Genevese.

Passing through Grand Street wh
seau was born, we entered the Rue
was here at numbers 11 and 13 tha
Reformer spent the years from 1541 t
is a great disappointment to find t
tories of the Board of Health quarte
property. One recalls the hours s
homes of Martin Luther, Schiller an
especially that of the latter, which h
the Goethe Meseum—and the ineff
pressions carried away. But Calvi
so; one feels like complaining of his

"Where is the tomb of Calvin?"
the janitor. He directed us to an a
longer used, but well kept cemeter
Rhone. In an obscure spot beneath
we found a little head-stone marked
There is no mound, for they do not
exact place where he rests.

"He desired to be forgotten,"
companion, reflectively. "They se
carried out his wishes literally. W
trast" he continued, "between Jo
and the Duke of Brunswick. The on
severity and imposed it on others;
noble, whatever one may justly say
philosophy of church and state; b
too somber. The world contained
him but moral verities. In dying he
be forgotten. He rests far remot
gay life of modern Geneva, so st
contrast with the Geneva of the F
days. The other seems to have b
crown in his cradle, to have lived
pleasure. In dying he gives his for
city, he orders a mausoleum and e
lates the style of it. He rests in a t
structure, in the very midst of
splendor. Thousands pass his to
The guide-books of the city devot
its description, though they do no
with a single word the place where
vin rests."

WM. H. M

Chicago Letter.

The fourth educational conference of the Disciples of Christ recently met in Chicago. The attendance was not large, but the papers were of a very high order and the spirit of the discussions was fine. Hiram, Drake, Butler and Christian (Canton, Mo.,) Colleges were well represented. During the early part of the conference a vigorous discussion arose over the following question: "Should the Consideration of Education be Admitted to the National Missionary Convention, or be Discussed Entirely in Special Meetings?" The attitude of the conference towards the secretaries of our missionary boards was sympathetic rather than critical. The concensus of judgment was that the relation of education to missions was so vital, and so thoroughly recognized by the heroic workers in the foreign field and the wise leaders at home, that our great brotherhood would demand, and the missionary secretaries would cheerfully arrange to give, ample time to the discussion of educational interests just as soon as the work of the educational board deserved such time and attention. The Chicago Letter-writer has insisted for years, and still insists, that there is no greater problem before the Disciples of Christ in this closing decade of the nineteenth century than their educational problem. The interests of our colleges should not only have a large place in our national gatherings, but in all of our state and district and county conventions. I do not advocate pleas for money in these assemblies, but addresses by Christ-filled men, prayerfully prepared, with the definite aim of giving information concerning and creating enthusiasm in the interest of all our educational enterprises, especially our Christian colleges.

***

Not only among the Disciples of Christ, but the public in general, seem to be taking a renewed interest in questions of education. The board of education in Chicago has been deeply stirred over the election of a new superintendent. E. Benjamin Andrews, the president of Brown University, who was so prominently before the public last year on account of his stand for the freedom of the teacher, has been elected superintendent of public instruction at a salary of seven thousand dollars per annum. The former superintendent, Mr. Lane, was made assistant at a salary of either four or five thousand dollars.

The speech of Hon. William L. Wilson, now president of Washington and Lee University, at the July convocation of the University of Chicago, was on "The Founders of States and the Founders of Colleges." In this address he maintained that a culture, high, broad and deep was essential to the perpetuity of our freedom and our government. Washington was the patron of the university of which Mr. Wilson is now president; Jefferson was the father of the University of Virginia; Franklin laid the corner-stone of the University of Pennsylvania, and every "North Carolina name that was signed to the Federal Constitution in 1787 reappeared in 1789 among the charter trustees of the university of that state." The drift of the address may be summed up in Mr. Wilson's quotation from a great American statesman: "Liberty is a reward reserved for the intelligent, the patriotic, the virtuous and the deserving." Dear reader, if you are a father or a mother with children to educate, remember that "*virtue*" as well as "intelligence" is essential to a true education, and choose a Christian college for a Christian training. And my brother preacher, since the only true education is the Christian education, will you not see to it that the boys and girls in your congregation who are ready for college are adequately informed concerning Hiram, Butler, Kentucky and our other worthy institutions? Work up an address on our educational interests during your vacation, and see how many students you can send our colleges next fall.

Perhaps nothing would contribute more to the advancement of all our educational interests at this stage of our progress than the employment of an educational secretary by our educational board, whose sole business would be to enlist our brotherhood in the cause of Christian education. Such a man must be broad in his sympathies and deeply in earnest himself. He must be cultured and consecrated, spiritual and scholarly, brimful of business and bubbling over with enthusiasm, tactful and tenacious, persistent and patient, a man who can preach twenty-three years for one church, if need be; who thinks more of his work than of his wages, and who realizes that there are more people in the world than there are in his parish. If the services of our ideal secretary cannot be secured for lack of funds, let our educational board do the next best thing, viz., co-operate with one or more of our colleges, or with the C. W. B. M., in having a financial secretary who will act as field secretary for the board part of the time. The C. W. B. M. has been fortunate enough to secure the services of a capable and womanly woman to represent the interests of the Bible chairs. Butler College has a noble man representing her financial interests. Let us rise above all local prejudices and trust such unselfish workers, if their services can be secured for part of the time, to represent our general educational interests. There are hundreds of noble men and women among our million members who would not only willingly, but would gladly give and give liberally to our colleges, our Bible schools and Bible chairs if the proper person were to bring our educational needs to their attention. But I believe it possible *to support the right man for all his time* in this great work if we will only arouse from our lethargy and realize that the great Captain of our salvation is calling us to go, "teaching them to observe all things" he has commanded, as well as to "make Christians of all nations."

"Let us, then, be up and doing,
With a heart for any fate;
Still achieving, still pursuing,
Learn to labor and to wait."

CHARLES A. YOUNG.

What is Death; How Destroyed.

DEAR BRO. GARRISON:—I am not a critic, neither am I called upon to stand guard over the orthodoxy of contributions to the columns of the CHRISTIAN-EVANGELIST. I would like, however, by your permission, to notice a statement or two in an article under the above heading, by W. H. Thomas, in your issue of June 23rd. It is one thing to say what the Scriptures say, and let controversy end there, and quite another thing to say what one believes, and then say the Scriptures show it! This latter method of teaching has brought the religious world into much controversy, and to the belief of many strange things.

The first statement I call in question is that Pauls shows that "the resurrection from the dead means the immediate passing of the spirit from the old material body to one that is incorruptible—one that is of a better nature and suited to our higher spiritual state." The fifteenth chapter of the first Corinthian letter is the writer's supposed basis for this statement. Verily, ideas, like individuals, partake of their environment.

Bro. Thomas says the resurrection is "the immediate passing of the *spirit* from the old material to one that is incorruptible." Paul's statement of the matter is, "*It* is sown a natural *body*, *it* is raised a spiritual *body*." It seems to me there is a discord here. Thomas talks about the *spirit*; Paul talks about the *body*. Thomas talks about the *spirit* changing from one body to another. Paul talks about the *body* being changed from one condition to another. Thomas' resurection is a transition; Paul's resurection is a transformation. Thomas' resurrection is of that which never dies; Paul's resurrection is of that which has died.

The Scriptures are plain in telling us it is that which is sown in dishonor that is raised in in glory; it is that which is sown in weakness that is raised in power; it is that which is sown in corruption that is raised in incorruption. And if these things are said concerning the spirit, then, as we follow Paul in his further statement of this same matter, we ought to hear him say; "It is sown a natural spirit, it is raised a spiritual spirit," for he would tell us, "There is a natural spirit, and there is a spiritual spirit." We would certainly think this a strange kind of spirit! We sometimes find great difficulty in fitting the plain statements of Scripture to our peculiar ideas. I should think Bro. Thomas would find it so in this case. I am inclined to credit Paul with saying what he meant to say, and also in meaning what he said. And when he says the natural body is raised a spiritual body, I confess my inclination to believe it will be that way.

Resurrection presupposes death, and only that which dies can be resurrected. The separation of thh spirit from the body, the end of earthly life, we call death. Thus using the term, we speak of the death of the body, but never of the death of the spirit. If death is a prerequisite to resurrection, and the spirit never dies, how can Bro. Thomas speak of the transition of the spirit and call it the resurrection? In his theology there is no resurrection. The use of the term is a misfit.

Again he asks, "Are we not justified in saying that much of the skepticism about the resurrection of the dead comes from the false idea that the resurrection means the returning of the spirit to the old material body?" Answering from the limit of my own general information I would say, I think not. I am not aware that such is a general idea. Per-

Thomas did not fairly state himself.
rection and the reoccupancy of the
d body are not one and the same
hat there will be a reunion of the
l the spirit is a generally accepted
: the reuniting of the body and the
ever heard called the resurrection.
les, those who believe in the reunion
esurrected body and the redeemed
ieve as Paul states: "It is raised a
body. That it is not now the "old
body, but that the body which was
ural is now spiritual. If any, even
lieve that the body is raised the "old
' body they do not believe Paul's
t of the case. Even the ingenuity of
ion gives no strength to the theory of
ıal resurrection. The flight of the
realms immortal leaves the sub-
e resurrection behind. The reunion
irit and the body depends upon the
ion of the body. A. L. ORCUTT.
apolis, July 15, 1898.

Our Trade with China.

rease of the importation of American
ures and productions into China is
the official statements of the "Re-
he Trade of China and Abstract of
s" for the year 1897, which has just
he Bureau of Statistics. This official
the returns of trade, published by the
the Inspector General of Customs, of
ives the value of articles imported
exported from China from 1890 to 1897,
quantities and values of certain im-
ırticles imported during 1896 and 1897.
ement of imports form various parts of
l shows that the United States is mak-
s in her invasion of the markets of
specially in cotton goods, metals and
oil, though in the latter article Rus-
Sumatra are proving active if not dan-
ivals.
tal value of the imports from the Unit-
s into China have, according to the
presented by this report, increased
ın 300 per cent. since 1890, the increase
rtations during that time being but
re than 50 per cent. In cotton goods
rd which the United States manufact-
d exporters made in 1897, was espec-
riking. In cotton drills, jeans and
s, importations from the United States
d materially, while those from all
untries fell off. Importations of En-
eetings, for instance, fell from 1,019,-
es in 1896 to 389,569 piecies in 1897,
om India fell from 156,709 pieces to
ieces, while American sheetings in-
from 2,251,600 pieces in 1896 to 2,418,-
897. English cotton drills fell from
pieces in 1896 to 76,202 pieces in 1897,
otton drills fell from 39,775 pieces to
ieces in 1897; Dutch from 34,334 pieces
25,862 pieses in 1897; Japanese from 9,-
es in 1896 to 1,250 pieces in 1897; while
ın drills increased from 1,228,759 pieces
o 1,531,347 pieces in 1897. In jeans
ın importations increased from 52,450
ı 1896 to 63,076 pieces in 1887. The
portations of cotton goods fell in 1897
ably below those of 1896 while, as
y the above figures, the importations
n goods from the United States in-
in every case.
ısly, the chief increase in inportations
out the entire list is in articles which
ted States supplies, while there is a
n in nearly all other articles. The
nports into China from the United
re cotton goods, cigars and cigarettes,
inseng, machinery, medicines, kero-
and timber. In practically all of these
there was in 1897 an increase in im-
ns, while in the larger proportion of
r articles imported a decrease is shown.
sene oil, for instance, the importations
United States in 1897 were 48,212,505
gallons against 33,520,649 gallons in 1896, an increase of nearly 50 per cent. Importations of timber increased from 1,182,494 haikwan taels in value to 1,321,084; machinery, from 2,064,441 taels to 2,716,737; medicines, from 106,451 taels to 136,339; ginseng, which is almost exclusively from the United States, increased from 1,619,527 taels in value to 2,149,183, raw cotton from 1,307,975 taels to 2,260,191; window glass, from 343,128 taels to 466,017 and coal, from 3,539,804 taels to 3,692,669.

American producers and exporters must, however, realize that in at least one particular their competition is sharp and increasing. This relates to kerosene oil, of which our exportrations in the year just ending amounted to $55,000,000 and of which a large proportion goes to China and other Asiatic countries. The report in question shows that while the importations of American kerosene increased in 1897 nearly 50 per cent., that those of Sumatra increased nearly 200 per cent., while in Russian oil there was also a marked increase, showing that in this important item of our exports there is sharp and growing competition in a large and important field.

That there has been a steady and marked growth in the importations into China of goods from the United States is apparent from the detailed figures of this report, while an examination of those relating to the imports from other countries shows that the imports from the United States have increased much more rapidly than those from any other country.

The following table shows the imports into China from the leading countries of the world in 1897 compared with the year 1890. It will be seen that the imports from the United States increased more than 300 per cent. and that the growth was much more rapid than that of other countries. It should be borne in mind, also, that the direct importations from the United States into Chinese ports do not by any means include all American goods entering China, as most of the articles entering Hongkong pass from that port into China, and the reports of our own Bureau of Statistics show that the exports of the United States to Hongkong have, during the past ten years, nearly equaled our direct exports to China.

Imports into China from leading countries in 1897 compared with 1890:

COUNTRIES.	1890.	1897.
	Haikwan Taels.	
United States	3,676,067	12,140,302
Hongkong	72,057,314	90,125,887
Great Britain	21,607,989	40,015,587
India	10,300,101	20,068,183
Japan	7,348,685	*22,564,284
Russia	897,826	3,442,449
Europe, except Great Britain and Russia	2,471,075	8,565,807
Macao	4,270,970	3,514,878
All other countries	3,083,273	11,497,617
	128,758,290	212,234.994

*Including 5,413,194 from Formosa.

(NOTE.—The Haikwan Tael in which the above values are expressed was quoted by the United States Mint at $1.48.8 on Jan. 1, 1890; $ .69.7 Jan. 1, 1893 and $ .68.8 July 1, 1898; the official [Chinese] report, from which the above figures are quoted, gives the average sight exchange value for 1897 at $ .72).

O. P. AUSTIN.

A Message to Men of Means.

Among our Savior's personal disciples were the rich men, Joseph of Aramathea and Nicodemus. He also loved the rich young ruler who, however, so far as we know, never became his disciple (Mark 10:22). It was not impossible, therefore, for a rich man to be a disciple of Christ, although he regarded it very difficult, saying how hardly shall they that have riches enter into the kingdom of God (Mark 10:23). He regarded riches as deceitful, (Matt. 13:22); as leading men to trust them, rather than the living God (1 Tim. 6:17); as leading men to become oppressive (Jas. 2:6); as exposing the soul to special temptations, snares, lusts, and finally to destruction and perdition (2 Tim. 6:9). So he taught the rich to give to the poor (Mark 10:21), and to be rich toward God (Luke 12:21), and not to trust in riches. For the world's good and for the salvation of the rich, the Father sent them this message (2 Tim. 6:18-19): "That they do good, that they be rich in good works, ready to distribute, willing to communicate, laying up in store for themselves a good foundation against the time to come, that they may lay hold on eternal life."

1. God recognized the prominent place of money, both in the Jewish and Christian dispensations. Achan immortalized himself by his covetousness (Josh. 7:1), the rich fool for his stinginess (Luke 12:21), Ananias and his wife for lying about their means (Acts 5:3) and Barnabas for his liberality (Acts 4:36-37). God claims the world's wealth as his own (Hag. 2:8): "The silver is mine and the gold is mine, saith the Lord of hosts." The power to get wealth is from him (Deut. 8:18): "For it is he that giveth the power to get wealth."

2. A portion, at least, of our possessions is under tribute to the kingdom of God. The Jew was said to rob God if he brought not the tithe into the storehouse (Mal. 3:8). "Freely ye have received, freely give." Let every one of you lay by him in store," are some of the instructions to us (1 Cor. 16:2).

The Lord has delivered talents and pounds to his disciples to be used and returned to him with the increase (Matt. 25:14). The time to use the Lord's gifts is now. Like servants of old, it was my lot recently to be sent to some of the Lord's children to whom he had given much goods, to receive some fruit of their riches for a most important improvement of the King's business. It is true I was not beaten, nor stoned, nor cast out as evil, and by many my mission was gladly heard and met a liberal response, to whom I am personally grateful. But others turned coldly and sent me away empty.

3. We be brethren, partners with each other and with God. The Father hath done marvelous things for his children and ha

honored them with great trusts and wide opportunities. Each disciple has his proper gift, all not the same gifts. One can preach, another make money, others do other things, yet we are all one in Christ. Paul said, "Woe is me if I preach not the gospel." This is no more true of the preacher than of the business man, who should say, "Woe is me if I give not freely of my means to promote the kingdom." He whose talent is to earn money, if uses it for the benefit of the kingdom is yielding, I believe, as valuable and faithful a service as he who can preach the gospel and does it faithfully. I wish our men of wealth would appreciate this fact and enter heartily into all the great enterprises of the church. We have here in Illinois hundreds of men who have been blessed with means and who have been blessed by the ministry that have gone out from Eureka College. A great burden rested upon the college. Everybody was cordially invited to its fiftieth anniversary last June. It was a day of wonderful moment to the great cause that we love. Some eleven thousand dollars were wanted to clear the college of debt. Had there been present a hundred men with from twenty to five hundred thousand, how easy it would have been to have distributed the burden that fell so heavily upon a few. Many of you have furnished no help to clear the college of debt; can you not now join with the trustees in building up a great college? If you would like to enter into fellowship in so great a work, drop Pres. Hardin a card and he will be glad to give you full information.

Dear brethren, ought you not to be at our great meetings? Our state convention is here the first week in August. The condition, needs and opportunities before the churches in Illinois will be spread out before the public. There will probably be no call for money, but will you not be present, get the situation and enter into whatever service you can, and be *one of us heartily*. We have a number of splendid business men now, upon whom we can always count, but the number ought to be multiplied greatly. The Lord hath need of thee. May the Lord help us all to work while it is day!

Faithfully your brother,

J. G. Waggoner.

Eureka, Ill.

Kansas Notes.

Kansas Churches of Christ never had one taken from their ranks whom they more saldly missed than her own Mrs. Hellen E. Moses. Our churches were not so familiar with any other name and face. Kansas missions never had a truer friend. By pen and prayer and voice she plead for the plan that made Kansas missionary plans unique. When called upon to help in Bible chair work, we could make no greater contribution than she. As her pastor I miss her counsel and devotion, but rejoice that the Bible chair work has found one whose sympathies for it are sure to win friends for it. The First Church feels that the C. W. B. M. has made no mistake in calling her to that important work. We heartily commend her and her cause to our brethren everywhere. Hear her plea. Sister Ora McPherson takes her place in our state board office and is proving her efficiency for the place and is making many friends. She with Bro. R. P. McPherson and Bro. O. L. Cook is doing splendid work for our state board. Bro. Cook is a workman as our field superintendent, of whom we are not ashamed. All say, "He is just the man for the place."

The First Church is moving nicely without any revival or evangelistic efforts, there having been at our regular Sunday services 35 additions from June 19 to July 17.

Bro. Mallory is doing efficient work as pastor of the East Side Church, and having additions nearly every Sunday. D. D. Boyle has olding an arbor meeting for him for two , with good attendance and two addi-

having returned from attendonce at the Endeavor Convention at Nashville, I ce seconding the CHRISTIAN-EVANGELIST'S to inaugurate a "Quiet Hour" service own National Convention, at Chatta- . Keep it going.

brethren who spoke at Nashville proved elves masters of the platform, and of they heard with delight. They were work- f whom we need not be ashamed.

M. E. HARLAN.

eka, Kan.

g People's Department of the C. W. B. M.

re was a gratifying growth in the num- f societies that made offerings to the g People's Department of the Christian an's Board of Missions, and in the amount contributions during the quarter ending June. Yet there should be remittances each of our seventy-one Intermediates ,486 Junior Societies, and 301 Mission every quarter. The work of this quar- d that of corresponding quarter last year ollows:

	1897.	1898.
r Societies contributing	321	404
on Bands contributing	162	166
nediate Societies contrib.	8	25
er of other offerings	45	82
nt contributed	$2,533.44	$3,562.06

t year the offerings made by the Young s' Auxiliaries and Mission Circles were led in the report; this year they are ed.

MATTIE POUNDS,
National Superintendent.

Why a Christian Colony?

THE REASONS WHY I CAME TO ESTABLISH THE CHRISTIAN COLONY ON RAINY RIVER, ONTARIO.

On the 25th of March I sent a letter to the Christian Publishing Company inquiring their charges for the insertion of one or two columns of matter in the CHRISTIAN-EVANGELIST on the Christian Colony in Ontario. I received a letter from J. H. Garrison dated March 29th, 1898, stating, "If it is a real estate enterprise, in which the parties managing it are expecting to make some legitimate profit out of it, we would feel justified in making a reasonable charge for such an article. If, however, it is primarily a missionary enterprise, undertaken for the good of the cause and the mutual benefit of those who enter into the Colony, I would be willing to insert the article without charge and for the good of the work."

I have written many articles regarding the Christian Colony for other papers, but I do not believe I have written one giving the reasons for its establishment. I have been so pressed with this work that I have not had time to accept the editor's kind invitation till the present. I have just returned home from visiting the Colony and will now attempt to give the reasons, or in fact, two or three of the principal reasons for its establishment.

Two years ago I asked leave of absence from the church at Bowmanville, where I had been laboring for nearly four years, to attend the General Convention at Springfield, Illinois. Since entering upon the work in the Dominion of Canada I have felt the want of association with those grand men who attend these conventions. I was much impressed with the spiritual character of this convention compared with the last one I had the privilege of attending. But imagine my surprise. I was the only representative from Canada. My name stood alone. There were representatives from China, India, Japan, men who represented Africa, in fact every nation was mentioned, and the various needs of the field discussed. I felt like a heathen among Christians. My adopted country was not worthy of recognition. In fact I grew indignant. Why this should happen I did not know. We contributed to all missionary enterprises. I felt that this great convention should manifest an interest in the evangelization of Canada. On my journey home to the northward my heart ached for this vast unknown region the broadest and the fairest, while at the same time the most available missionary field to be found in all the world. At the Indianapolis convention last year, I understand that my report was read. We asked for a representation upon the program of future conventions. I judge this request will be granted. A short time after this I wrote an article, "Canada as a Mission Field," which was published in the Christian Standard.

Another reason for the establishment of the Christian Colony: About this time I read Bro. Clay's article on Colonization in Idaho. He referred to land that could be purchased for twenty-five to fifty dollars per acre, that if it was underbrushed and irrigated it would make excellent homes for poor people. The idea struck me in this way, that if poor men had money to purchase land at twenty-five to fifty dollars per acre they could secure land nearer home at that price without traveling to the far West. I thought of Canada's vast millions of agricultural land free to all. I did not know where these lands were. I had not made a study of the free grant lands at that time. I sent to the Crown Land's Department at Toronto. I interviewed the government. I moved as on the track of destiny. I wrote several articles. I wished to get hold of something practical. Charity and feeble legislation had failed to ameliorate the material and spiritual condition of man. Christianity must free a man, but to be a Christian he must be free. No man is free unless he has a home of his own, and can assert that prerogative which is the inalienable right of man.

The best Christian men of the United States noted my articles. They could not believe that right here in Ontario 160 acres of free land couuld be obtained with plenty of wood, good water, no stones, good markets, no irrigation, no destructive droughts, and in the same latitude of all the great nations of Europe, Great Britain and Ireland, Norway and Sweden, Prussia, Denmark, Holland, Belgium, nearly all of Russia, nearly the entire German Empire and the northern part of France. Letters came from every quarter of the North American Continent. Probably no inquiry did me more good than that received from A. P. Cobb, of San Antonio, Texas. He said, "I have visited California and Texas, and even Old Mexico, looking for cheap land for a Colony such as you mention. I found land in California and Texas held at ruinous prices, while life in Old Mexico is not life, but mere existence." I asked Bro. Cobb to join me in an exploration. He came from his home two thousand miles from the Southwest, I came fifteen hundred from the East, and we met on the headwaters of Rainy River, Ontario. We were delighted with the prospect. Bro. Cobb at once purchased a fine farm fronting the river of 335 acres, also taking a free grant of 160, and purchasing the remainder of the half section at one dollar per acre.

This trip of exploration was severe upon both of us as it was taken on the first of February. It was at the risk of life. I arrived at Rat Portage on the Canadian Pacific Railway. there I had to take a trip which required six days over the ice of the Lake of the Woods and Rainy River, traveling the entire distance of two hundred miles in an open sleigh, sleeping in Indian houses and enduring the cold from day light till dark. But the work was accomplished. I then confidentially informed the people that I had land to offer them free, without money and without price. I have secured the co-operation of the Dominion and the Ontario Governments. I first asked for a township of this fine land, requested that the survey be made in order to be ready for the people on the first of May. It was done. On the first boat which left Rat Portage after the opening of navigation was found fifty happy home seekers from every quarter of the United States. They even came from California. While this land is free, it is earnestly desired that every one remember that the victory is only to those who will fight to possess it. There will be trials characteristic of the pioneer life. No one should come expecting an easy time. It means hard work and trials.

With such men as A. P. Cobb and family, Geo. W. Loman and family, of the Indian Nation, A. M. Sweany, of Oregon, G. W. Fullerton, of Nova Scotia, J. Carey Smith, of Indiana and many others of like religious character we expect to form a center from which shall radiate the everlasting gospel of Christ till Canada shall be bettered because of the advent of these noble men. These men are all helpers. Men who never owned a foot of land now say, "My home," "My land."

We have laid out a town and have named it Christiana. Nearly forty acres of lots have been sold. The Provincial Government has forty men employed cutting out a road to our town. A sawmill, business enterprises, will at once go in. Before cold weather arrives will have a place of worship erected. The Church of Christ on Rainy River, when it was less than twelve hours old, took up a collection for missions. This marvelous movement has attracted the attention of both governments. I was called before the premier of the Dominion at Ottawa a short time ago to give an account of this region and work. I prove by the fact that there are forty men at work cutting roads, and that they have placed in our hands fully nine hundred thousand acres of this fine agricultural land to be given to all who will come and avail themselves of it.

This is destined to be one of the great missionary enterprises of the century. Leading newspapers of the United States are asking for the latest developments. Just a word in conclusion in regard to the system of work. "How shall we reach the people?" I do it this way. I ask interested parties to send me twelve or fifteen cents in postage and I will send them literature which will give them the desired information regarding land and rates. This is business. I only wish persons to write who wish to help the work on, or who wish homes. My time is entirely devoted to this work, and as the responsibility is great, do not write for mere curiosity's sake. Be considerate. Take hold of this work and help some poor young man in your community, help a son or son-in-law. Give him a lift. You would like to see him a tower of strength for his family and the church. Now I feel that it is my duty to tell you about this. By availing yourself of it, it will make you independent, and place you in a condition to enjoy your religion, and to help humanity. Make helping others the thought of your life.

R. A. BURRISS.

Bowmanville, Ontario.

Missions in the "White North."

Lieut. Peary, speaking of the natives of the Arctic, says: "Poor things, why don't we send some missionaries to them and convert and civilize them?" Then in answer he says: "God willing, never either."

His reason is not far to seek. He speaks of the depraved habits of the whalers who frequent those regions, and prays that such a fate may never overtake his "faithful little tribe."

Is it not a little remarkable that this great explorer should fail to distinguish between the vice that clings like a parasite to society and the virtue of Christ's religion? These nations, he says, "properly speaking, have no religion." At best they have but a dim recognition of good and evil spirits. To the elevating, progressive influence of Christianity the lieutenant to-day owes his knowledge and liberty, yet he is averse to allowing others the same blessings. The difference between the lieutenant and his tribe is that he was born and reared under Christian influence, and they were not. Not such a great difference, after all.

Pure and undefiled religion has never yet been guilty of holding back a nation, a tribe or an individual. True, the same ship that carries out Bibles and preachers may carry rum and rum dealers, but no wise person will blame Christianity for this.

In spite of the rum and attendant evils, Christian nations are the most progressive and the most elevated.

"These nations," he adds further, "have no marriage ceremony. The wife is as much a piece of personal property which may be sold, exchanged, loaned or borrowed, as a sledge or canoe." This is a very sad commentary on their moral condition—no religion and no marriage obligations, yet he is not willing that religion should disturb them. The thing they lack is the religion of the Bible; the light they need is the light of revelation. Why should any man be unwilling that these blessings should be conferred? A higher authority said: "Ye shall know the truth, and the truth shall make you free." What else will make them free? What?

A. M. GROWDEN.

The Canton Bible Institute.

In this Institute President McGarvey will discuss the following themes:

Lecture I.—The Analytical Theory of the Pentateuch.

Lecture II.—Some Objections to this Theory.

Lecture III.—Did Jesus Know?

Lecture IV.—Did Jesus Affirm?

Lecture V.—The Prophet Isaiah.

Lecture VI.—The Book of Isaiah.

Lectures will be delivered by other prominent men. Time, Aug. 1-4. Place, Canton, Mo. Entertainment free. Come.

CLINTON LOKHART.

3.

n who is
ny church
write me
g stamp.
THCART.

ursion to
It will be
Sunday-
hes in the

BERGER.

le-school,
raise mon-
rch build-
d Soap.''
very Bible
ns of sale,
soaping''
e effort by
of soap to
needed for
stor of the
olis, Ind.,
of the Bi-

Kimberlin
a few days
mons were
heard him.
are now in
ak of it in

work, and I
t we do not
for many a

'union pa-
urch. The
E. minis-
preachers,
rt address.
upon and
s. Every-
profitably.
t the house
to be tried
I am quite

he subjects
to each:
rticipate in

everywhere

o National

.''
in complet-

nday even-
ies. These
st and giv-
iness.'' I
r the tired
HOOTMAN.

illness, act-
am obliged
rial Relief.
w, but not
an may be
will go on.
R. Lucas,
ork. Bro.
papers, and
, in behalf

ho is presi-

dent of the board of trustees, will attend to all business matters, and until further notice, all correspondence and all contributions of money should be addressed to him at 120 E. Market St., Indianapolis.

I have much joy in many holy memories of my service in this blessed ministry. The friends of Ministerial Relief can in no better way contribute to my permanent recovery than by the general support of the cause in which I came so near laying down my life.

On account of the falling off in receipts, the board was compelled to make a reduction of 20 per cent. on the July allowances. This was very unfortunate. The only way to prevent a much larger reduction on the September allowances, is by prompt and generous offerings.

Yours fraternally,

A. M. ATKINSON.

Wabash, Ind.

From The North End of Boone.

Our work prospers during the summer months. We have raised several hundred dollars for debt and repairs. All the missionary offerings have been remembered, and we have gone beyond former records in every instance. Many representative brethren have addressed us in behalf of important interests. Prof. Jones, of Fulton, for the Orphan School; Chancellor Lockhart for Christian University, Canton; G. A. Hoffman for the Missouri Bible College; C. C. Smith for Home Missions; John Sergis, of Des Moines, on Persia as a Mission field; Mrs. Alice Williams, of Cameron, for the state C. W. B. M. (not a brother, but as able as any); and others have spoken for us to the delight of all. Brethren who have known this field would be surprised if they would drop in some Sunday and hear our choir rendering one of the finest anthems; or, to hear in the announcements of three Endeavor Society meetings for one day, and this supplemented by two other society meetings and a modern teachers' meeting the following week. Instead of no organ, two; Children's Day concert taking place of regular sermon at night, pledges for Foreign Missions taken publicly, etc., etc. Shades of the apostles!

I have just returned from the Lectureship and Ministerial Association at Carrollton. I have not enjoyed any like treats more. The water got deep at times, but every now and then a paper or reviewer would give us water through which we could wade ''flat footed,'' and now and than a ''riffle'' for the little fellows to paddle in. The Ministerial Association is assuming proportions. Prof. Clinton Lockhart makes a scholarly and dignified president. The affable and energetic secretary, C. C. Hill, has done more than any one else to perfect the organization. Bro. Hill deserves the high esteem in which he is held, and the Missouri brotherhood has still better things, I doubt not, for him.

H. A. DENTON.

Centralia, Mo.

Cincinnati and Vicinity.

Vernon Stauffer is the faithful and successful minister at the Eastern Avenue Church. Reports submitted at the recent annual meeting indicate the best year in the history of the church.

E. W. Symmonds continues to make good reports from the work at Camp Washington. Bro. S. is doing a good work, and at no little sacrifice to himself.

The new mission at Fairmount, under the care and direction of J. S. Laurence, is flourishing. Bro. Wilson, district evangelist, is to hold them a meeting soon. This means a new congregation and a new house in the near future. *Our* churches in the city have been meeting in one place for a few Sunday evenings, and the arrangement has proven to be both delightful and helpful.

The Board of City Evangelization is arranging to hold an institute on city work in this city from the 1st to the 12th of next November. The purpose of the institute is to study city life and plans of church work, under the leadership and direction of some of the men of experience and who have been successful in dealing with some of the problems of city work. The following are some of the subjects that will be considered: House to House Canvass, Rescue Missions, Work Among Men, Street and Factory Preaching, Awakening and Sustaining the Evangelistic Spirit, Planting Missions, etc.

These subjects will be presented by such men as C. L. Thurgood, of Pittsburg; W. B. Taylor, of Chicago; F. G. Tyrrell, of St. Louis. The question throughout will be, not so much what can you say, but what can you do? The need of the hour is the spirit of service.

When Mr. Gladstone came down with what proved to be his last illness, the short message that was flashed over the wires, ''Mr. Gladstone has stopped work,'' is full of meaning and reveals the secret of his greatness. The working out in one's life of the convictions of a pure, strong heart, is what makes one great with God and men.

The greater America will require a change of vision. Some who have seen only America will find it necessary now to extend their vision. Others who have been talking about ''a larger outlook'' will find it necessary to learn the difference between a larger outlook and simply a *long* outlook. One may have a very extended outlook and not see very much either, because one does not see widely.

S. D. D.

California Notes and News.

California has two conventions each year. Not that she has so many Christians, but that her magnificent distances necessitate the division of the State into Northern and Southern Districts. The Southern Convention met on July the 6th, at Long Beach, the most beautiful of the many beautiful seaside watering places in California. The Northern Convention holds its session at Garfield Park, beginning July the 25th, and continuing until August the 8th. The convention program will be enriched by consecrated and able talent. Mrs. Persis L. Christian will sweeten, soften and inspire the convention as few women can. Mrs. Princess Long, the sweet singer of the Pacific, will lead the song service. No woman ever sang so sweetly our sacred songs.

Benj. L. Smith and A. McLean and George W. Sweeney will deliver the great sermons and addresses, which will make these conventions memorable in the history of the state.

WESTERN CONVENTION.

There is some agitation of a Western Convention looking toward organized, systematic and effective evangelization of the great West. Such a convention has in it possibilities worthy the consideration the churches of the Pacific slope.

Among the gratifying results of the past year's work will be the excellent reports of the Berkeley Bible Seminary and Curtener Seminary, and the enlargement of the Pacific Christian. H. D. McAneny has recently been chosen to take the presidency of Curtener Seminary. This choice is very pleasing to the friends of Curtener. Prof. McAneny has made himself indispensable to the welfare of the churches of California. He is a man whom all the coast loves and whose business ability and Christian consecration are having a very large influence for good.

Prof. S. M. Jefferson, Dean of Berkeley Bible Seminary, is very highly regarded by his students. He is laying a splendid foundation for the Seminary.

Bro. Geo. W. Sweeney, former pastor of the Oakland Church, and wife, are visiting at that place, which is really their permanent home, though they have been living for the past two or three years in Chicago, on account of Sister Sweeney's health. Bro. Sweeney has been preaching pretty generally throughout the state to large and enthusiastic audiences.

He is a favorite preacher with many of the churches of the coast. He will preach and lecture at both of our conventions. After the State meetings he will return to Chicago, which will be his home for the next few years.

Bro. Thos. B. Butler is now the much-beloved pastor of the First Church at Oakland. The church is united and prosperous under his ministry.

The Central Church of Oakland, after Bro. Davis resigned, called R. H. Sawyer to the pastorate. After three months' ministry he resigned to accept the call to Watsonville.

Bro. J. C. Day has resigned at Woodland and returned to Colorado. He was much beloved by the good people of Woodland, who very much regretted his resignation.

I have just returned to Iowa after five years' work in the West. It seems good to be once more in the shadow of Drake University.

LAWRENCE F. MCCRAY.

Des Moines, Ia.

The Home Missionary Offering.

The following shows the status of the offering for Home Mission for the week ending July 23d, as compared with the corresponding week of last year.

1897.

Number Churches Contribuing, 28.
Number Individuals Contributing, 12.
Other Contributors, 4.

Amount from Churches	$368.55
Amount from Individuals	89.00
Other Contributions	10.59
Total	$480.14

1898.

Number Churches Contributing, 28.
Number Individuals Contributing, 4.
Other Contributors, 17.

Amount from Churches	$684.10
Amount from Individuals	8.50
Other Contributions	120.54
Total	$813.14

The gain for the week is $327.00. The number of new churches contributing is eighteen. The number giving an increased amount is five.

BENJ. L. SMITH, } Cor. Sec's.
C. C. SMITH,

Y. M. C. A. Building, Cincinnati, Ohio.
July 23, 1898.

Missouri C. W. B. M.

Missouri made a fine record the second quarter; but the contributions of the third quarter were not as large as usual. The fourth quarter closes with September, and State Convention meets September 26-29. All contributions, dues and pledges should be received by Sister White, in Indianapolis, or Sister Johnson, in Chillicothe, *by Sep. 21st, at the very latest*; so that reports can be made out and sent to me; and I can have a tabulated report *printed before* I start to Nevada, on the 26th of September. Sisters, keep these facts in mind, and collect and report promptly.

Seven of the forty-five persons who pleged life-memberships this year, have paid in full. All are expected to make at least one payment before Sep. 21st. If those who can conveniently do so would pay $25 each, in one payment, between now and Sep. 21st, it would be a great favor to the cause. Twenty life-memberships, paid in full, would equal the $500 annuity gift that one sister gave the C. W. B. M. last year. All contributions made on the annuity plan bear interest, and this interest is paid to the doner so long as he lives. Thus a safe investment is made and the income secured.

Sister S. H. Gillium, the energetic manager of the Chillicothe district, and the wife of the pastor of the Hamilton Church, organized an auxiliary at Kingston, recently. We hope that all managers will be able to report new auxiliaries at the Nevada meeting.

By invitation of the sisters of the First Church, Kansas City, auxiliary, of which Mrs. Thos. Hoffman is president and Mrs. Bixby Willis is secretary, your state secretary had a part in their public C. W. B. M. service, the first Sunday in July. In the evening of the same day she attended the services of the Independence auxiliary. Brethren Richardson and Vernon are firm friends of our organization. Bro. Procter has encouraged the work in Missouri since the beginning.

Sister and Brother Felix Allison are paying for a membership in memory of their sister, Sylvia Caton, who died last winter. This is indeed a sweet memorial.

Our Sister Abbott, who has been ill so long, is growing gradually worse. The auxiliary sisters will remember her in their prayers, and extend to Bro. Abbott and his daughter, Miss Maud, their heartfelt sympathies.

VIRGINIA HEDGES.

July 14, 1898.

Evangelistic.

ARKANSAS.

C. P. Young reports 60 sermons aud 44 additions in work done on the line of K. C. P. & G. Railroad. A lot has been purchased for a house of worship at Mt. Ida, to be built soon.

Mena, July 19.—Have been here 18 days; had 46 additions. The church now numbers nearly 90 members. We may stay another week. Bro. Geo. P. Young has been for four or five months the very efficient pastor at this place. Our next meeting is at De Queen, 50 miles south of here. We desire some meetings in northern Arkansas or southern Missouri.—ARTHUR W. JONES, J. W. IRELAND.

UTAH.

Salt Lake City, July 11.—One addition by letter here yesterday—W. H. BAGBY.

TENNESSEE.

Clarkesville.—Three added to Church of Christ July 17; all by baptism.—A. M. GROWDEN, Pastor.

J. W. Zachary's meeting in the Christian Church at Nashville resulted in 22 baptisms, and his meeting at Center Point, Ark., which closed Sunday night, resulted in 21 accessions to the Christian faith; 15 of these were baptized.

NEBRASKA.

Bethany, July 1.—Three by confession and five by letter since Jan. 1, at Peru; 20 in all since I began work there in October. Eight of these were added in a meeting held by Bro. A. W. Davis, of Falls City, in October. Two others were immersed who went with the Congregationalists.—O. C. ATWATER.

KANSAS.

Cherokee, July 16.—We had three additions at our last meeting. We had one addition at our last meeting at Monmouth. The outlook is encouraging all along the line. The 30 young converts (we had at our revival) with the rest of the church at Weir City are doing fine.—J. P. HANER.

ILLINOIS.

Waverly, July 20, 1898.—Four added here Sunday.—EUGENE T. MARTIN.

Watseke, July 20.—Two baptisms here Sunday evening. Eleven pastors from the county and adjacent territory attended the regular monthly ministerial meeting in the church parlor Monday, and on the following day most of them picniced at a pleasant point on the Iroquois River, near this city.—B. S. FERRALL.

NORTH DAKOTA.

Ellendale, July 18.—W. A. Foster's meeting here closed with five additions.—T. L. NOBLITT.

INDIAN TERRITORY.

Purcell.—We had two delightful services on yesterday with two additions to the church: one by confession and one by letter.—HENRY A. MAJOR.

MINNESOTA.

Austin.—Have returned to this city, from a meeting at Redwood Falls, in which nine were added to the church; eight baptisms. This is a city of 7,000; church one year old; I expect to stay until a house is erected. The state board believes in doing permanent work. Bro. V. J. Rose organized here one year ago. The board will keep me here until they are housed. A preacher who could not work with such a band of men as compose the Minnesota board ought to quit preaching. The work in this state is great and resources limited. I have more work than four men can do. Minnesota needs the primitive gospel. Push Home Missions to the front that our land may be evangelized.—A. B. MOORE, State Evangelist.

Plainview, July 19th.—Nine added to this church since I last reported; six by confession and baptism; all branches of church prospering.—T. E. UTTERBACK.

KENTUCKY.

Lexington, July 15th.—Last Sunday night we closed a meeting at Grassy Creek Church, Pendleton county, which lasted over three weeks and resulted in 64 additions to the church. Bro. E. S. Baker, of the College of the Bible rendered valuable assistance in singing and personal work.—ROBERT STEWART.

MISSOURI.

Sturgeon, July 21.—67 additions to date.—H. A. NORTHCUTT.

Belleview, July 18.—Am beginning a meeting here at my old home—the first meeting ever held by a Christian preacher in Belleview. I am so thankful for this privilege and we are working and praying for spiritual blessings.—A. M. HARRALL.

We have organized a small congregation at Cherry Box and built a new house not yet finished.—MARY E. MCCULLY.

Galena, July 18.—Have just closed a one week's meetieg at this place, assisted by Bro. S. S. McGill, of Lebanon. Bro. McGill is a very able man and gave us the pure gospel. Two confessed Christ and were baptized. The Galena church has employed me to preach for them a year. The church has had no pastor for sometime.—G. W. HAMILTON.

Preachers Should Tell their People.

Every preacher should tell his people, and especially the young, all about the Bethany C. E. Reading Courses. Full information may be had gratis, by dropping a card to the Bethany C. E. Company, 798 Republic Street, Cleveland, O. Begin at once to plan for systematic reading among the people of your church.

There will be a tent meeting held at Fulton, Ill., a mission point in the first district, beginning Aug. 13th, lasting one week and longer if interest warrants. Disciples in adjoining territory are earnestly invited to attend. Lodging free. Meals 50 cents per day. By order of First District Board.

S. H. ZENDT, Sec'y.

Dixon, Ill.

:erature.

ND," by Miss Marguerite
ord and Works Pub. Co.,
, publishers. Price 50

. elegantly written, print-
, beautiful exhortation to
he Christian's life and
r has a strong hold upon
aith, and presents many
s about "The Home Be-

ABLES," by Charles R.
ing H. Revell, Chicago
publishers. Price $1.25.

oy practical lessons will
ook of sermons from the
les of Christ. They are
al examinations of the
adjustment, and we may
djustment, of their lessons
rs of this life. The book
, striking sentences that
: in a most pleasant and

NE," by Walter Jerrold.
evell, Chicago and New
rs. Price, cloth, 75 cents;

enient book for the busy
ing. It sketches the rise
an in easy stages from
cle unto the heights of his
an statesman. It is a very
ine of one of the world's

LF," by Mrs. N. M. Van-
stian Publishing Co., St.
publishers. Price $1.00;

g story, located at Rome
of Christianity, brings out
cts of the gospel and its
l surroundings, conflicts
This story was first printed
Young Folks, and created
emand for its publication.
ting and profitable book,
ung people.

or Book of Common Pray-
he Church Service Society
of Scotland. Fleming H.
go and New York, pub-
$1.00; 156 pages.

ok is especially valuable
e prayers, forms of service
may also be used practi-
ngregation. It contains a
f prayers suitable for all
sions.

ES TO LITERATURE," by
Arnold and Chas. B. Gil-
Burdett & Co., Chicago,
Boston, publishers.

ok is one of a series of
to meet the higher wants
n. It contains only the best
much better adapted to the
school. The authors be-
e Readers are used wisely,
plan suggested, they will
make better readers of the
chools, but will also aid in
n of studies, will cultivate
a love of good literature
rature, bring within reach
he choicest treasures of the

THE EVANGELISTIC LIBRARY, by Ashley S. Johnson, consisting of six books in paper covers, a pamphlet and ten tracts, having had a total circulation of 150,000 copies of the books at a very low price, undoubtedly has done good. The books cover the whole ground of religious discussion; the best part being "The Life of Trust" and "How to Read and Remember the Bible."

The pamphlet is a graphic story of the gradual raising of $40,000 for the School of the Evangelists and the care of one hundred young men growing into the ministry by daily toil on the school farm at Kimberlin Heights, Tenn. The enterprise at Kimberlin Heights is a magnificent labor of love to prepare young men to preach the gospel in the hills and mountains of adjacent states. The Evangelistic Library in the hands of the common people is sure to do great good. Address A. S. Johnson, Kimberlin Heights, Tenn.

W. B. YOUNG.

Lindenwood, St. Louis, Mo.

Family Circle.

Freedom's Jubilee.

What sounds are those that greet our ears, like voices swelling loud?
What means this concourse gathered here, like some fast-driving cloud?
What shouts are those, and wild acclaims, that cleave the summer air?
Hurrah! Huzza! Lift up your eyes! The flag we love is there!

* * * * * * *

On many a long and weary march those silver stars have gazed;
O'er many a hard-fought battle field those crimson stripes have blazed;
And many a triumph has been won beneath its colors bright,
By war-scarred veterans who fought for freedom and the right!
Then fling abroad that glorious flag! Set all its splendors free!
Fling out the stripes! Fling out the stars! 'Tis freedom's jubilee!

And ah, those silver stars have gazed on many a peaceful scene,
While shrined as sacred relics hung war's erstwhile weapons keen!
The bugle's voice that called to arms in shrill and martial strain,
Since then has sung the song of peace o'er many a fruitful plain;
The ruddy camp-fire shines no more on civil strife to-day,
But lights in friendly bivouac now, comrades in Blue and Gray!
Then fling abroad our country's flag! Waft it o'er land and sea!
Fling out the stripes! Fling out the stars! 'Tis freedom's jubilee!

O flag, proud flag of liberty! Though war's dark visage looms
To cast once more upon our land its terrors and its glooms,
Thy silver stars and crimson stripes shall float from freedom's dome
While beats one heart beneath thy folds to claim this land as home!
The spirits of our gallant sires have never passed away;
The blood that fired their loyal hearts throbs in our veins to-day!
Then float in majesty on high! Float over land and sea!
Fling out thy stripes! Fling out thy stars! 'Tis freedom's jubilee!

—*Helen Whitney Clark, in July Woman's Home Companion.*

Text Stories—VIII.
INDEX TO CHARACTER.

BY ALICE CURTICE MOYER.

Whose adorning let it not be that outward adorning of plaiting of the hair, and wearing of gold, or of putting on of apparel, but let it be the hidden man of the heart, in that which is not corruptible, even the ornament of a meek and quiet spirit, which is in the sight of God of great price.—*1 Peter 3:3, 4.*

We again bring to your notice our young friends, Ethel and May, whose acquaintance you made in our last Text Story. Also May's mother, who never lost an opportunity for bringing out some good thought or truth for the benefit of her daughter and her daughter's friend. It might be well to say a word here to mothers. The wise mother is the one who shares the friendships of her children; who welcomes into the friendly home atmosphere her children's friends. Aside from the fact that it gives her an opportunity to decide whom she would have her children associate with, it adds to the happiness of the son or the daughter to have his or her friend looked upon as also the friend of the family. We all know what a sweet experience it is to have a near and dear friend, whom we can trust, even with our thoughts; one who understands us and sympathizes with us; who rejoices when we rejoice and comforts us when we sorrow; who helps us to bear our burdens, thereby making them lighter. How we love such a friend. It may be a sister or brother; father or mother; husband or wife. And again, it may be one to whom we are not at all related, save by the ties of sympathy and fellowships which exist ever, between kindred souls. The heart hungers for friends and our children are going to form friendsips, with or without our help in the selection. Then how necessary that we exercise our wiser judgment and help them in their choice of companions.

But to return to our story: Ethel and May are again in the parlor of May's home, and are again watching from the window the passers-by—as girls dearly love to do—and conversing in their usual friendliness, when Ethel, catching sight of a familiar figure, exclaims:

"Look, May! There is Lucy Merritt, looking as untidy as usual."

"It does seem to me," replied May, "that she should at least have some care of her appearance on the street. It is bad enough to go to school in such fashion."

"My daughter," remonstrated the mother gently, "are you not indulging in unkind criticism?"

"I have been too well taught by you, mother, dear, for that," replied May. "I do not mean to criticise Lucy, that is, unkindly, but we cannot help noticing her untidiness, and it seems unpardonable because it is unnecessary. If her circumstances made it impossible for her to take any thought of her personal appearance, she would have our deepest sympathy, but there is really no excuse for her. And the strange part of it is, that Lucy's mother encourages her in it, saying that it is apt to make girls vain to think of dress; and that it is sinful to give so much thought to one's personal appearance. Of course, we all know that it is wrong to give one's whole thought to dress, but it also seems to me wrong to utterly neglect it."

"You are right, my daughter; it is wrong. To thinking people, this outward neglect seems almost like at least a hint of neglect within. If Lucy's mother could but understand this, surely she would not allow her daughter to say by her personal appearance, 'I am just as careless in my thoughts and motives as I am in my dress.' No mother is making a mistake to teach her child a proper regard for his or her personal appearance; rather, she is wronging the child if she does not so teach."

"You should see Lucy at school, mother, with her unkept hair, her soiled collars and her half-laced shoes. And she is just the same way about her lessons. Her exercises are never complimented for neatness or exactness, and I have sometimes wondered if it has not all come from the fact that she has been allowed to be so careless in other things."

"No doubt it is. Her mother has, without realizing, of course, the harm it may cause, allowed her to form the habit of carelessness—than which there are few more deplorable—and very probably it will cling to her through life.

"As to matters of dress, I am very sorry to say that there are some people who seem to think that the apostle meant to teach utter disregard for personal appearance when he said, 'Whose adorning let it not be that outward adorning of plaiting of the hair,' etc., but I cannot believe that he meant to advocate any such thing. I am sure that the women whom Peter had in mind were of the class who live but to make frames of themselves whereupon to display their ornaments—vain butterflies who adorn themselves with these 'outward adornings,' with but little thought for aught else. Women who live for such ignoble purpose almost deserve the contempt with which they are usually regarded, but it is the Christian's duty to endeavor to lift them to a higher plane than this mere butterfly existence, and to inspire them with a desire to fill their lives with something better than mere frivolity. A butterfly is short-lived, and nobody erects a monument to its memory.

"However, on the other hand, if a woman possesses those virtues which are in the sight of God of great price, there certainly is no reason, if her circumstances permit, why she should not wear jewels and fine fabrics. I have never been able to see wherein the wearing of these is inconsistent with religion, and I do not believe that God is going to disapprove if he sees that they are only the covering of a spirit surpassing in beauty and loveliness.

"Indeed, taste in dress may be often accepted as a sort of index to character. This, of course, is not an infallible rule, for circumstances do not always allow a freedom in the matter of dress, still it cannot be denied that we are apt to measure the mental or spiritual trend of people—especially of women—by their dress; not by the richness of quality of the apparel, but by that intangible something called taste, or a sense of the fitness of things. Everybody acknowledges that a neat print is more attractive than the richest of velvets and finest of satins, if gaudy, ill-fitting and overtrimmed. However, this is all merely suggestive—containing, of course, a certain degree of truth, but I would not like to say that it is a rule to be always relied upon.

"But while on this subject of insight to character, my dears, I want to call your attention to an index that *can* be relied upon—one that furnishes a sure insight to to the 'hidden man of the heart'—the face. In it we have a sure guide. This cannot be said, particularly, of the young face which is but an unwritten page, but of the face that bears the stamp of years. If young people could understand how truly their faces will tell of the lives they have lived, surely they would be careful as to what they write thereon. It is a fact that we all dread to grow old; and especially do women bemoan the appearance of the first sign of age. But I wish, my girls, to make you understand now, that you need not grow old—whether you do or do not, is a question you may decide for yourselves. Years may come and go, but they need not make us old; indeed, each should leave us more beautiful than before. Can we not call to mind women of our acquaintance who, though their years may be many, are yet not old? And it is because of the diary that the spirit has written on their faces. Each line tells a story of sacrifice, of silent heroism, and is so stamped with God's approval that we do not think of them as lines of age; rather, they seem like silent ors urging us to a higher and better

h a face is a sure index to a success-
e—the sort of success that cannot be
ured by houses and lands, fame or
n, but which is, in the sight of God,
ost successful and acceptable. For
all, a truly successful life is nothing
nor less than living as well as we know
and of doing, always the very best we
nd all the good we can. An eminent
r truly says: 'The life of the hum-
woman in the land, if well lived, is as
ssful as is the woman who, with great-
portunities, is enabled to make the
s of her work reach farther.'
et us, therefore, take heed what we
on this journal of ours. Our face at
y-five is the face God has given us,
ur face at fifty is the one we have
for ourselves. Let us see to it that
a face to claim the admiration and
f all honest hearts. That it be a face
ells of victories over self, glorified
e beauty and purity of the inner man
e heart, stamped with the majesty of
thoughths. In short, a face that
t grow old, for it is radiant with the
y and grace of inner adorning."
Louis, Mo.

"Mother'n Me's Partners."

sturdy little girl it was, trudging
ly by with a pail of water. So many
it had passed our gate that morning
curiosity prompted us to further ac-
ntance.
ou are a busy little girl to-day?"
es'm."
e round face under the broad hat was
ed toward us. It was freckled, flushed
perspiring, but cheery withal. "Yes'm,
tes heaps of water to do washin."
nd do you bring it all from the brook
there?"
h, we have it in the cistern mostly,
it's been such a dry time lately."
nd there is nobody else to carry the
r?"
obody but mother, an' she is
in.'"
Vell, you are a good girl to help her."
was not a well-considered compliment
he little water-carrier did not consider
e at all; for there was a look of sur-
in her gray eyes, and an almost in-
ant tone in her voice as she answered:
Why, of course, I help her. I always
her to do things all the time; she
't anybody else. Mother'n me's
ners."
ttle girl, are you and mother part-
? Do you help her all you can?—
e Worker.

A Dull Student.

ce upon a time—so the story goes,
ding to the Youth's Companion—an
priest said to his young companion:
n going away, little priest, and I leave
emple in your charge. No matter
comes, don't lend them anything."
t long after the old man left, an old
an came to worship. She prostrated
elf before the idols, and prayed and
ed until it rained. Then she said to
boy: "Your master knows me well,
come often to worship. Won't you
me his umbrella?"
o," was the prompt reply. "I cannot
anybody anything."

Upon the master's return the faithful boy related his experience; but instead of praise he received stern reproof.

"O, you stupid boy! Do you know no better than that? Why, you have driven away one of my best worshipers! You will spoil my business. You should have been polite. You should say: 'Won't you please step in and have a chair? I will steep you fresh tea and bring you little cakes. Make yourself as comfortable as possible; but I am very sorry to say my master was out in a storm one day, and it blew and it blew, and it took the skin right off his umbrella, and strewed the bones all around, and so we have none.' Say that, and she could not be angry."

"All right, sir; I'll say it next time."

Not long after this the master went away again, and there came a man who said: "Little priest, I have been high up on the mountains, and gathered a big load of kindling wood. It is too heavy. I cannot get it home. Will you let me take your master's horse?"

"Come in, sir," said the little man, "and make yourself very comfortable. I will bring you cakes and steep you fresh tea; but I am very sorry to say the old horse was out in a storm, and it blew and it blew, and it took the skin right off and blew the bones away, and we haven't any."

The man gazed in astonishment upon the boy, and turned away in disgust.

When the master returned the boy related all that had happened, and received a round scolding. "O, you small idiot! You grow worse and worse. Don't tell the same story every time. Have some sense—make your story fit. You should have said, 'I am very sorry to say the old horse was out in the field, and stumbed in a hole and sprained his leg and went lame, and we turned him out to grass, and we haven't any.'"

"All right, sir; I will say it the next time."

Again the boy was left in charge, and there came a man who said: "Your master is my dear old friend. I should like to see him."

"Come in, sir: take a seat, sir. I will bring you new cakes and steep you fresh tea. Please be as comfortable as possible sir. I am very sorry to say my master was out in the field and stumbled in a hole and went lame, and we have turned him out to grass, and we havn't any."

A Song of Water.

MRS. ALICE ROBINSON.

I will sing of pure cold water
As it flows from founts and springs,
Darkling in the depths of wildwoods,
Sparkling in the courts of kings.
Darkling water, sparkling water,
From Columbia's mighty flood
To the wondrous, mystic river
Flowing by the throne of God.

Sparkling water, darkling water,
Dips the oar and glides the boat
Where the shores are dark with willows
And the water lilies float.
O, cold water, pure cold water,
Israel's savior thou dost seem,
As they faint in Sinai's desert
Close by Marah's bitter stream.

Flashing water, splashing water,
Brimming cup for Fever's lips.
To the hidden thread of silver
Where the dainty wild bird dips.
Sparkling water, pure cold water,
O, the world owes much to thee,
From the sacred flood of Jordan
To thy waves, blue Galilee!

Dufur, Ore.

Not All a Dream.

E. O. SHARPE.

After an all-night vigil in the sick room and a weary pilgrimage of pastoral visiting I retired early to get a good long sleep, and on account of my exhaustion I did not sleep well, but dreamed troublous dreams. A strange chain of events passed through my throbbing mind as I slept, and yet all seemed so real that I am constrained to set it down here. I dreamed that while seated in my home with my children around me, there came a sharp knock at the door. On opening, there stood a young man of my acquaintance, then acting as deputy sheriff. He said, "I have a warrant for your arrest." This came upon me and my family like an electric shock. We besought him to tell us with what crime I was charged. He did not know, but I must go with him forthwith to the court, then in session. On the way thither I besought his help to escape if I was to be made the victim of injustice. He promised to have a swift horse at the court-house door and to facilitate my flight if it became necessary.

On entering the court room I beheld the judge on the bench—a stranger to me—and twelve men in the jury-box,—all chosen before my arrival. I mentally filed this as No. 1 for a bill of exceptions.

The trial began by placing *me*, the accused, on the witness stand, in spite of my protests against this injustice as well as against a packed jury, but all in vain. No affidavit was read, no charges preferred. Everything was in the greatest disorder. It seemed that every one in the court room (a large crowd was present) was permitted to ask me questions. One pert young miss asked me what I had to eat the day before, and I proudly told her "turkey with dressing and cranberry sauce." This was pressed no further, and I was glad of it, for I did have turkey, though the bird had belonged to the Presbyterian minister and had been misdelivered. This latter fact I was not aware of, however, till the turkey was in ruins. I thought an anonymous friend had sent it.

Next, an old gray-bearded gentleman, well-known as a socialistic and financial reformer took me in hand and catechised me about my preaching awhile and finally wound up by asking if I thought I was able to earn my enormous salary of $1,500 per year. I answered modestly that I was able to earn a million dollars a year if I could get it. This gave him such a shock he retired from the attorney's chair. Another person whom I did not very well know and had rarely seen at church then took the witness stand, and on examination-in-chief testified that my preaching was often irreverent, that certain anecdotes and illustrations were unbecoming so solemn an occasion and place as a sermon. In short I was sometimes irreligious and even sacriligious in my remarks, and deserved severe reprobation for my offense.

In cross-examination I was my own attorney and asked the witness to define religion since he (or she—I do not remember the sex, but it does not matter) had characterized my preaching as irreligious. Opposing counsel objected on the ground that my demand for a definition was irrelevant. Objection not sustained. Witness could not define religion. Did not know what it was, but he (or she) thought my funny illustrations were quite out of place, as they made people "laugh in meetin'." Witness did not laugh, but was horrified. Witness admitted that he (or she) did not often laugh. Did not know in what stage of the moon he (or she) was born, and could not see that that had anything to do with his (or her) missing sense of humor.

This ended the testimony, and there was a dreadful confusion, as the whole crowd tried to get up at once to make a prosecuting speech. Each one had a different fault to find in me, and what some regarded as vices others thought were virtues, so not being able to choose one of their number to speak for all, the judge commanded order and when quiet was restored he informed me I might speak for myself. I have not a very distinct recollection of all my harangue, but I called the whole trial a farce and an outrage unparalleled in the annals of jurisprudence. I said to the judge: "If your honor had a vestige of judicial equity in your head or heart you would have driven these hyenas from the judgment seat as did Gallio of old." I was just going to blast the jury with my lightning when I saw that eleven were sound asleep and the foreman had his already prepared verdict in his hand. I turned from that base crew with scorn and paid my respect to the pert young lady who had peered int my bill of fare. I think I called her a gad fly, fit for nothing but to pester her supe riors. I said she would never die, as ther was not enough to her to furnish a funeral She would evaporate and go off in thi mist and would never be missed either.

While I was dealing out these delicat compliments I saw that almost every on was choking with laughter. Then I kne it was a moot court and mock trial, an they were having sport at my expense. gave one howl of general execration an broke for the door. There stood the dep uty's horse (or some one's) and I jumpe on his back and rode him up and down th streets of M—— yelling like a wild Indian Then I awoke as tired as when I went t bed. I knew it was all a dream, but I mad up my mind that hereafter when criticise I would regard it as only a mock trial.

This was my dream, and yet it is "not al a dream."

Le Roy, Ill.

The Book of Books.

The fundamental truths of the Bible, an many of its narratives, were more or les known among all heathen nations, ancien or modern. This proves that they forme their systems of religion from that reveale by God. Let us see.

The Chinese declare that man was mad of the dust of the earth.

The Indians agree with the Bible in say ing that the first man, whom they cal Adam, was placed with his wife in a earthly paradise.

The Persians say that man and woma ought to have lived happily, but the ser pent tempted them.

The Iroquois, like the Bible, tell us o the woman who suffered herself to b tempted at the foot of a tree; of the ange of God, of his driving her out, etc.

The Chaldeans, one of the most ancien nations, tell us, like the Bible, that Go announced to mankind that he would de stroy them by a deluge; that he command ed a man to build a ship, and save himsel and his children.

The Americans, before they were dis covered by Columbus, believed some of th facts related in the Bible, because the spoke to Columbus of a universal deluge.

we find among all nations a belief n facts, not so obscured but that recognize in them the wreck, as it called, of Scripture narratives and s, we conclude that the religion of e is the source whence all others rung; that is to say, it is the one and consequently divine. While many religions, there ought to be . God would have had it thus; not. A. R. ADAMS.

insville, Ill.

A Sunbeam.

METTIE CRANE NEWTON.

a greater greatness than that which
clarion and builds monuments.
, oh, soul! In mighty deeds thy name
be writ, but in the silences
yest help on th' unfolding of God's
ns.
gest forces of the universe
tly as the stars and suns.

'ork, June, 1898.

---

noth Cave is a labyrinth of winding wo hundred miles in length, in t stories, one below another. On de there are dangers and pitfalls; Bottomless Pit, there the Mælsere Scylla and there Charybdis, he black hole" and the Dead Sea. kness is absolute; it can almost be o one can find his way without a If left behind it is not safe to A friend once got behind and was the dark, and the twenty minutes an eternity. Some of our party d behind, and then we heard them to us that they had lost their way. ld see their lights and hear their but they did not know the way to fter we had gone some little distance depths, we came to a hall called 'hurch." Here one of the guides d a high rock and called our attena short sermon he wished to preach. rmon was, "Keep close to your ' And we soon found that the only vas in giving careful heed to the sermon. And we found, too, that t place was near the guide, where d hear most plainly his descriptions ories connected with the places. our guide. He never leads us into ces or wrong doings. Sometimes es in strange ways, but always the ys in the end.—*Christian Leader*.

Cavalry Horses are Prepared for War.

r-horse is broken to be steady under tying ropes to his legs. While the is down on the ground the officer pistol and fires it close to his ear. rapid order he fires the weapon s back, under his neck, betweed his nywhere that an opening presents uring the horse's futile struggles. ntil he sinks back exhausted, all ole, and showing the whites of his oes the pistol practice cease. After three lessons of this kind it is consafe to mount him with a bridle ed with a curb bit. Up to this time se has never felt a curb. The light is still retained, and the curb bridle given a gentle pressure at first, just to let him know that it is there. is taught to stand fire from his rider's pistol or carbine.

In carbine practice the horse must be thoroughly broken, as both hands are required in using this weapon, whereas with the pistol the rider may retain the bridle with one hand.

Then comes sabre practice, and that is another trial to the horse. Again is he thrown to the ground, and when the bright blade of the sabre, with quick thrusts flashing before his eyes and cutting the air in close proximity to his ears, appears to him, he is again terror-stricken.—*Our Dumb Animals.*

Keep the Mind Clean.

Mentally, man is a house of many chambers. This house is always full of guests, who make it their inn and stopping-place, but he himself is the one who makes the conditions that attract the guests to his mental house. If he is careless and neglectful of rightly ordering his mental habitation, and remains in sensual sleep, leaving the doors and windows open to every one who wishes to enter, dirt and disease will abide in his house, vagrants and tramps will make it their stopping-place, and he will be sensible of this by the vicious ideas and mental and physical miseries that continually plague him and urge him still further on the road to ruin.

One whose mind is filled with ugly, impure thoughts is not master of his own mental house; he is the sport of demons, who use him for their own evil purposes; and, as actions are the natural sequences of thoughts, his physical body is subject to their tyrannical commands.

This is no fancy sketch. Each one can, from his own individual experience, know that it is true, if he will but look within himself. The lust, the greed, the selfishness, the destructiveness, hatred, etc., that so many exhibit, comes from slovenliness in caring for the mind. The mind has not been kept pure and clean, but has been allowed to become filthy, and has attracted that which is evil and destructive. The individual must get control of himself by cleaning up his mind, putting out all thoughts that are not harmonious, pure and true. Until this is done he is a slave; he cannot attain spiritual freedom and happiness. — *The World's Advance-Thought.*

A contradiction of terms:

"Haven't I told you," asked the father, "always to tell the truth?"

"Yes, you told me that," the young man admitted, "and at another time you told me never to become the slave of a habit." —*Pearson's.*

"My husband is so nice about explaining these war terms to me! I know I aggravate him awfully, too, sometimes. Why, only think! I had to ask him this morning what the seat of war was for!" "Yes." "Wasn't it foolish! But he is so patient. The idea that I didn't have sense enough to see that it is for the standing army to use when it gets tired!"—*New York Press.*

A Railroad Cat.

Thousands of people have heard of the railroad dog, which travels so extensively over the country and really seems to know as much about trains and time-tables as a railroad conductor does, but there is a cat in Colorado which, although not as famous as the dog in question, is certainly as remarkable in its fondness of railroad riding.

It was the pet of the wife of the engineer of a frieght locomotive, and now it accompanies the engineer on every trip that he makes. When the train has to make a long wait at a station, the cat goes off in search of mice, always returning when the whistle sounds, and at some of the junctions where numerous trains meet it is quite a pet.

When the engine is running, the cat sits in the cab or on the coal, and as its fur is jet black its beauty is not greatly impaired by its grimy surroundings.

Pussy must have traveled many thousands of miles, for it has been doing duty for several years, and has never been known to miss a trip.—*Ohio Chronicle.*

"Isn't there something in my policy," asked a caller at a La Salle Street insurance office the other day, "about having to report any change of residence?"

"Yes, sir," said the man at the nearest desk, picking up a pen; "where have you moved to?"

"I haven't moved anywhere," rejoined the caller. "I have made a change in my residence by painting it a light straw color and putting a jack on the kitchen chimney. I think that's all. Good day."—*Chicago Tribune.*

Sunday School.

THE PASSING OF ELIJAH.*

HERBERT L. WILLETT.

There are three striking figures in the history of divine revelation, figures which from certain angles overshadow all others. They are Moses, Elijah and Jesus. Of the two former it will not do to say that they are the greatest of Old Testament men. Moses, indeed, may well be assigned to a leading place. But Elijah will hardly compare in his prophetic ministry with any of the more conspicuous leaders of religious thought who appeared from the days of Amos to the close of the exile. Yet he represents the midway point of the Old Testament history as does no one else. He led a distinct movement in the progress of righteousness. About him, as about Moses and Jesus, a cycle of miracle gathers. He was the bold champion of Jehovah in a period of national apostasy: and the promise of one who should come in the spirit and power of Elijah to prepare the way for the Messiah was cherished through the closing years of the Jewish era, and was realized in the person and work of John the Baptist. Perhaps for these reasons Elijah stood with Moses on the Mount of Transfiguration to represent the authority of the prophetic age, fading before the splendors of the risen Sun of Righteousness.

The work of Elijah and his servant and successor, Elisha, occupies large space in the prophetic narrative of kings. Of the forty-seven chapters of the two books of Kings nineteen are devoted to the careers of these two remarkable men.

It has already been noted how the education of Elijah proceeded, even while he was going forward with his prophetic work. He had the native elements which were needed, but they required discipline. At the brook Cherith he was taught patience and reliance upon God. At Zarepharth he was taught humility, by being placed in circumstances most distasteful to a proud and aggressive spirit—as the guest of a poor widow, dependent upon her care for the very necessaries of life. A third lesson was that experience which followed the test at Carmel. The slaughter of the heathen prophets had, as Elijah supposed, solved forever the question of Israel's fidelity to Jehovah. But very soon the whole fabric seemed in danger of ruin. Elijah's life was in danger, and he gave up in despair. The lesson is taught him at Horeb that righteousness never wins in one contest alone, nor by the ruder weapons on which men depend. It is rather by the quiet, persistent methods of the preacher of the truth, by the "still small voice" speaking through chosen men to the nation that the work must be done. The later years of Elijah's life seem to have been spent in the work of training men for this task. The bands of prophets, who in earlier centuries represented the wilder and less restrained type of patriotism and religion, were not dispised by Samuel, but were used by him in that national reformation which prepared the way for David's reign. These bands of men played conspicuous parts in the work of Elijah, and especially of Elisha. They afforded a means of reaching the remoter parts of the nation which the great prophets could use to good purpose, and they formed the centers or schools where the prophetic teachings of the past were treasured, and from which they went forth to enrich the living generation. That these prophetic guides exibited grotesque elements is only what might be expected. The greater prophets had much to contend with in the rude and barbarous patriotism of these less inspired men. Their spirit was often far less humane than that of their great teachers (cf. 1 Kings 20:35-43 with 2 Kings 6:19-23), though even the latter reflected at times the harshness and severity characteristic of the age and of their fierce zeal for Jehovah (1 Kings 18:40).

But the end of Elijah's career drew on. Elisha had been with him as his servant and companion since the day when the man of God had cast his mantle over him as he followed his twelve yoke of oxen. It was now necessary that the task of Israel's moral culture should be left in the hands of the younger men. The divine enterprise never stops. "God buries his workmen, but he carries on his work." Moreover the time had come when the work could be done to better advantage by a man of Elisha's type. There are periods when only a figure of gigantic proportions can meet the demands of the situation; when hard blows are to be struck, and the Elijah spirit of unconquerable energy is needed. But far more frequent are the times when the world needs the quieter men of Elisha's nature, who build up where fabrics of evil have been smitten into fragments.

And Elsha had been under the guidance and discipline of the heroic prophet. The words of the latter had been repellant at the first: "Go back again (1 Kings 19:20), for what have I to do with thee?" but they were just such words as encourage an earnest nature to persevere, inviting still to service while they repel, and with such energetic words Elijah announced his final journey. At Gilgal the old man said, "Tarry here, for the Lord hath sent me to Bethel," but the tone filled Elisha with the certainty of the approaching separation. He would not stay, nor would Elijah have had him stay. As he had tested him at the first, he still tests him. His voice says "stay," but his heart says "come." Elisha needed the impress of the final scene to fix his soul in its mission to Israel, and he went with his master. Nor would he leave him at Bethel or at Jerico, for the mystery of separation was upon the man of God, and even the young man of the prophetic schools in the towns through which they passed cought the meaning of the journey, whispered it to Elisha, and some of them followed to the cliffs above Jordan to see what would transpire. The younger man had clung steadfastly to the side of his teacher, and presently his reward came. He saw Jordan cleft for passage by the touch of that mantle which he had once felt for an instant on his shoulders, when all his soul went out to that mysterious man who had faced the leagued powers of false worship in Israel, and then came the moment when he heard the question, "What shall I do for thee?" His soul was in the work to which he had been called, but he needed the wisdom, the courage, the strength of Elijah. "Let a double portion of thy spirit be upon me." He desired the portion of the firstborn, not of silver and gold, but that precious thing which Elijah alone could bestow. Again the enigmatical word in reply. Elijah's speech was always full of dark sayings. "It is a hard thing. But if thou see me when I go, it shall be so. If not, then it cannot be." If the young man could stay and face that terror of the rushing storm in which the prophet was swept away, he might well face the future with Elijah's spirit, having looked upon the awful power of God.

It was their last hour together, and they went on solemnly speaking of the past and future. "And it came to pass as they still went on and talked, that behold! a chariot of fire and horses of fire, which parted them asunder; and Elijah went up by a whirlwind into heaven." Such are the simple, sublime words which record all that later years could learn of the last movements of this strong prophet of the Lord. From the East he had come like a sudden warning voice. Into the East he disappeared from the sight of the group of prophets, and the one man who had ventured to look into the mystery of his departue saw him swept away in a whirlwind and flame.

What was there left, now that Elijah was gone? The lonely man rent his garments, and cried, "My Father, my Father! the chariots of Israel and the horseman thereof!" Elijah had been defence and strength to the kingdom. More than battlements, armies and navies to a nation are the forces that make for righteousness, the voices that speak for God.

But Elisha was not alone. Elijah was gone, but his spirit abode in the new prophet. The mantle struck confusion to the waters of Jordan as before, and when he returned to the tasks left him, the young man who saw the glory shining on his face said in awe-struck whispers to each other, "The spirit of Elijah doth rest on Elisha!"

SUGGESTIONS FOR TEACHING.

Sometimes men are tried by the obstacles that are set before them. Compare Elisha with Ruth as an example of constancy. Nature is the handmaid of God, and responds to the will of those who have his power. It is ours to ask for a double portion, a firstborn son's share of the divine Spirit. Some blessings only come as we have courage to face the dangers which surround them. The truest defenses of a people are good men and women. Strong men are taken away, but those who remain must take up their work and carry it on. God's work never fails because his servants fall in their place.

*Bible-school Lesson for Aug. 7, 1898—Elijah's Spirit on Elisha (2 Kings 2:6-15). Golden Text—How much more shall your Heavenly Father give the Holy Spirit to them that ask him? (Luke 11:23.) Lesson Outline—1. Elijah's Journey (6-8); 2. Elijah's Depature (9-12); 3. Elijah's Mantle (13-15).

THE PRIMARY UNION.

Primary Unions are supplying a need to primary workers, which is highly practical and beneficial. The members are earnest, honest workers. Not all are trained kindergarteners or educated psychologists, yet each has a place which he may nobly fill. Members may inspire others to become enthusiastic primary workers; those in the work to seek improvement, and still others to form new unions.

I. Importance of the work.

We have only to go to the words and life of Christ to realize its importance. By reading and searching the Word we shall find the pattern Christ has given.

When the disciples asked Jesus, "Who is greatest in the kingdom of heaven?" "Jesus called a little child unto him, and set him in the midst of them, and said, Verily I say unto you, except ye be converted and become as little children, ye shall not enter into the kingdom of heaven. Whosoever, therefore, shall humble himself as this little child, the same is greatest in the kingdom of heaven."

Jesus also said, "Suffer little children to come unto me and forbid them not, for of such such is the kingdom of God," and again, "Feed my lambs." We would not offend them, we would not forbid them to come, we would not give them a stone when they ask for bread, yet unless we search the Scriptures how can we know what our own duty and our whole duty may be?

Time is one of our most valuable possessions, youth is ours but once, the way it is spent is vital and the influence brought to bear upon us then can never be eliminated from our characters. Childhood is the climax of opportunity. The importance of the work may then be briefly stated.

1. Jesus has authorized it.
2. Strength of mature life largely depends upon the growth and training of the early years of childhood.
3. The influence the child of to-day will have upon the child of to-morrow.

When Gladstone was asked why he took off his hat to boys he didn't know, he said, "Because I may be speaking to the future Prime Minister of England." Primary teachers are not educating prime ministers or presidents, but greater, Christians.

II. Methods of work.

Looking again to Christ for our example we find his method to be largely through object-lessons, and those of the simplest order. He always used something known, upon which to lead to the unknown.

Another method we find is by story. When he wanted to teach the young lawyer who was his neighbor he told the story of the Good Samaritan.

We must study our children. There is a difference between child-study and study of children. The former consists of influences drawn from observations of or experiements upon many children; but hand-to-hand, heart-to-heart study of the particular child under our special care is quite a different matter.

The surroundings of the children while in Sunday-school should be most helpful and beautiful; the best pictures should hang upon the walls. Judgment must be used in selecting the objects not so many as to bewilder. The teacher ought to be filled with her lessons in a many-sided way, yet it is best to give but one thought. If we can teach how to live the lesson, we have done more than to present many thoughts and leave the mind confused.

Where it is possible, have a sub-divided class with efficient and sufficient teachers, and let them be the best. The exercises should be entirely separate, especially fitted for little children. They may include Bible verses, twenty-third psalm, Commandments, Beatitudes, books of Bible, motion exercises, birthday offerings, followed by dedicatory prayer.

The little book, "Sunny Songs for Sweetest Singers," contains much that is useful. It is published by Neal Brothers, Marion, Ind., for ten cents a copy or for five cents if fifty copies are ordered.

III. Helps afforded by primary unions.

As I know personally of the inestimable good accomplished by our Buffalo Union I will name some of the chief points.

It was established in 1892. Sunday-school workers felt the need of such an organization. Women met in the Y. M. C. A. Hall. However, only seven signed the constitution. It is generally the plan to have a paid teacher, but this one union decided not to have; a. the work done by members under the criticism of sister workers is valuable, the experiences gained is beneficial. Yet this arrangement kept some from joining at first. Last year there was an average attendance of thirty; this year it has been sixty.

Besides the regular officers there are a librarian and an assistant librarian, with nine standing committees — membership, music, publication, child-study, symbolic, finance, social, stand-table, flowers.

We meet every Tuesday at three forty-five in a chapel of a down-town church. The International lessons are followed. Besides the lesson there are special features each week. First Tuesday, business; second Tuesday, new songs; third Tuesday, motion exercise and general information; fourth Tuesday, child-study; fifth Tuesday (when it occurs), informal social.

We have learned of the relation of the Sunday-school teacher to the child, and of the child as a threefold unity, child of nature, child of humanity and child of God.

All lessons that come from the union are most practical; we have learned that teaching must be to meet every-day needs. The Bible must become a living, practical book, fitted to the every-day life of the child. Religion can ignore nothing that touches his life, so that we must consider thoughtfully his home surroundings, health, mind and character.

FANNIE CURTISS ALLEN.

Chicago, Ill.

Christian Endeavor.

BY BURRIS A. JENKINS.

TOPIC FOR AUGUST 7.

LESSONS FROM THE LIFE OF ELIJAH.

(1 Kings 18:20-39.)

Is there any lesson for a modern Western world in that wild, weird, terrible oriental figure? That man of the mountains, hairy in body and in garments, with matted beard, with leathern girdle, desert-nourished, like John of the wilderness—what is there in him for our civilized age? Much every way, for men are the same the world over and in every age. Human nature is human nature, and we shall find gentle, tender and kindly human qualities in this wild figure of a distant age.

Indeed, this very diversity of characteristics is perhaps the most striking lesson for us in his life. He combines such contradictory elements—as in fact does all human nature—that he leads us to hope for some saving traits hidden away under our own conscious imperfections. Thus we find in him a courage to defy kings and captains, to stand alone against a multitude of people and false leaders, strangely mingled with a cowardly shrinking that ran from the threat of a woman. True, she was a terrible woman, but the Elijah of the juniper and the cave is none the less a despairing, complaining coward, and God at once renders his verdict by appointing the prophet's successor. We find also in him a competence for political management that could influence kings and peoples, united with an incompetence to manage his personal affairs that made him dependent on widows and ravens for support. This is not an unusual spectacle in public men. We find, further, that his stern character—perhaps there is not a sterner, more awe-inspiring person portrayed in all the Scriptures—is softened by a tenderness that could cry to the Lord over the dead body of a little child, and could inspire in his solitary follower, Elisha, a love so great as to find utterance in no other word but "Father." What a diversified character it is! How it makes us hope that somewhere, hidden away under the cowardice, incompetence and coldness of our natures there are yet undeveloped viens of courage, competence and kindness!

A marked characteristic of the great prophet's life which it seems is sadly needed in our changeable, vacillating, mercurial age, is his firmness of purpose. His absolute loyalty to his high calling, his unswerving fidelity to God—the divine name being a part of his own name—are fixed as the polar star. Even when in discouragement he flees into the wilderness, he never for a moment loses his loyalty to Jehovah. When a whole nation follows a false track, he walks with a handful, and so far as he knows, he walks even alone, in the true one. Like Daniel, Elijah was one who dared to have a purpose firm and dared to make it known, dared to be in the visible minority which, counting God, was an invisible majority. Sometimes, even to-day, men and women are compelled to stand loyally alone.

Decision of character was another of his traits, which they say we Americans need to cultivate. He halted not long between two opinions; he pitched his tent not in the valley of indecision; the choice between God and Baal was for him quickly made. One of our American generals said the other day, when General Toral was hesitating whether or not to surrender Santiago, "the general who hesitates is doomed." And is this not true of every one else? He who hesitates in indecision never accomplishes anything. A true general would almost better make a wrong choice quickly than no choice at all; for a great leader is not one who makes no mistakes, but one who organizes victory out of many mistakes. Decide, then, lukewarm Laodiceans, neither cold nor hot, fit only to be spewed out of the mouth; be one thing or another; either for Jehovah or for Baal—how many of us try to serve God and mammon!

Finally, Elijah's trust in God is a characteristic worthy of our cultivation. "In God we trust" is our national motto, written on the coins we finger—are we true to it? To be sure, Elijah's faith was not unwavering. That is, indeed, something of a consolation to us. To find that, as James says, he was a man subject to like passions as we are, and subject to the same stormy waverings of faith, is the touch of frailty that makes the whole world kin, the sign of humanity that makes him real. Yet for the most part his faith in God was fixed, for sustenance, for strength, for encouragement and the seal of approbation. Is not God in the world as truly as in Elijah's day? Is he, like Baal, in a journey, or pursuing, talking, or peradventure sleeping? Is he not still in the affairs of men and nations? Shall we not still trust him and consign our times unto him? "My faith looks up to Thee" cannot be too often sung; "Lead, kindly light, amid the encircling gloom;" "Nearer my God to Thee"—all the hymns of faith that men of faith have uttered ought to be our frequent song. The realization that God is still in the world, and the consciousness of his presence—there can be no greater need for an age busy with things, materials.

Marriages.

SHONE—McFARLAND.—At the home of the bride, in University Place, Iowa, June 30, 1898, F. Elmer Shone, of Des Moines, to Allie, the youngest daughter of Mr. and Mrs. McFarland. D. F. McCray officiating.

Obituaries.

[One hundred words will be inserted free. Above one hundred words, one cent a word. Please send amount with each notice.]

BUTTON.

Col. Winfield Button died at Abingdon, Ill., July 6, 1898, at the ripe age of 90. He was born in Barren Co., Ky. Was married three times. By his first wife he had four children. Of these Mrs. J. B. Scheitlin alone survives him as do also three grandsons, four great-grandchildren and his last wife. In 1852 he moved to Illinois to take his family from the pro-slavery surroundings of his Kentucky home. Under the preaching of Elder Newton Mulkey, a cotemporary of the Campbells, he became a follower of Christ, maintaining his faith till the end. He was a man of earnest convictions, firmness of purpose and decision of character, exerting an influence for good wherever he lived.

J. B. SCHEITLIN.

CAKE.

Erastus B. Cake was born near Salem, Columbiana County, O., Jan. 23rd, 1837. He died at his home in Decatur, Ill., May 23rd, 1898. His death was quite unexpected, being preceded by a very few days of serious illness, though he had been in delicate health for several months. His early years revealed the strong qualities of his later manhood in his self-preparation for teaching that he might enter college. He was while quite young a classical graduate of Bethany College. He studied law and was admitted to the bar. He soon, however, turned his heart to preaching the gospel. At the beginning of the war he went as chaplain of an Ohio regiment, serving them two years. On his return home he was married to Miss Jennie Errett, a niece of Isaac Errett. To them were born seven children, four sons and three daughters, all of whom are living and the strong comfort of their mother. During his ministry, Bro. Cake preached at Salem and Mt. Vernon O. In 1869 he went to Mexico, Mo., and was state Sunday-school evangelist for three years. He was pastor at Marysville, at Clarksville and at Nevada, Mo. In 1892 he came to Decatur, Ill., preaching here for two years. He then became pastor of the church at Maysville, Ky., for three years. Since that time his home has been at Decatur, Ill., where he had the esteem and admiration of a very large circle of intimate friends. The same tender respect and high regard is betowed upon the bereaved wife and her children. Erastus B. Cake's long period of public life was unmarred by any stain. He was recognized by all who knew him as a pure man, brave and fearlessly true to his convictions without regard to the consequences to himself. His family life was ideal: calling out love in perennial tenderness from his wife and enthusiastic and reverent devotion from his children. His religious life was marked by his philanthrophy and by his love for his Father in heaven and for Jesus Christ his Savior and the Savior of the world. Funeral services were held at the residence May 25th, by the writer, assisted by Rev. W. C. Miller, of the Congregational Church.

MARION STEVENSON.

COSNER.

Mrs. Sarah Kate Cosner, of Forest Ave. Christian Church, Kansas City, Mo., died in this city July 8, 1898. She was here in delicate health on a visit to her mother and son. Was born in Woodview, O., Sept. 6, 1851, and married R. A. Cosner in Fredericktown, O., in 1869. Her age was 47. The writer spoke at her funeral last Sunday. Though a stranger, her history bore evidence of a godly life. Friends did not mourn as those that have no hope.

J. H. BAUSERMAN.

Ogden, Utah, July 12, 1898.

HARRISON.

Carlysle Harrison Murrah was born in Russell Co., Ky., May 24, 1833. In Kentucky he grew to manhood. On May 10, 1857, he was married to Melinda C. Vigus, who survives him. He lived in the states of Kentucky, Illinois, Missouri, Nebraska and Kansas. Always and everywhere he was active and zealous in the cause of the Savior whom he confessed in early manhood, being a deacon or elder in nearly all the churches where he made his home. He held fast the profession of his faith without wavering and the rejoicing of the hope steadfast unto the end. On the 15th of this month he was suddenly seized with a congestive chill, which in a few hours terminated his earth-life.

"He sleeps in Jesus, blessed sleep
From which none ever wake to weep."

He leaves a widow, one son and one daughter, the daughter being the wife of the writer. His mourning family rejoice in the knowledge that they will meet again "beyond the river."

J. ANDERSON.

Iowa Point, Kan.

HULL.

Our dear Sister, Nancy Hull, wife of the late Wm. Hull, passed away on the 12th inst., of dropsy and heart failure, and was tenderly laid to rest at Bethany. She and her late husband were each the other's companion and sympathizer in their afflictions prior to his death. They talked freely together of their hopes. Each ministered to the other in the absence of other help. Sad indeed was the separation when he was taken. She did not murmer, and though she dearly loved her children and friends, she longed to depart. Sermon text: Mark 14:8—"She hath done what she could."

C. C. DEWEESE.

Parsons, Kan., July 13, 1898.

MAVITY.

Thomas W. Mavity, died at his father's in West Lebanon, Ind., June 20, 1898. He was born in Montcalm county, Mich., April 4, 1866. He obeyed the gospel under the pastorate of our beloved E. L. Frazier, at Franklin, Ind., at the age of 14 years. He entered Eureka College in 1887, where he graduated in 1890. He attended college a short time in Butler University. In September, 1891, he was married to Miss Nettie Musick in Eureka, one of the noblest and most faithful helpers I have ever seen, in the ministry, but who died May 20, 1896, a victim of consumption. They were the parents of two daughters, Maurine and Grace, who are left under the tender care of their mother's parents in Eureka. Bro. Mavity was a most excellent young man, an able minister and a faithful pastor. He preached for the churches of New Carlisle, Ind., Washington and Onarga, Ill., resigning at the last place some 10 months before his death. He helped me much while a student here and went forth to be a blessing to many. "Precious in the sight of the Lord is the death of his saints."

J. G. WAGGONER.

Eureka, Ill.

TOWNE.

Hazel, the youngest daughter of Frank P. and Cora M. Towne, was born at Harristown, Ill., July 2, 1891, and died at Peoria, Ill, July 11, 1898. Aged seven years and nine days. Death came for this little child in a form most terrible and awful. Accompanied by her sister and mother, little Hazel came on a visit to the writer's family, and on Monday, July 11, she with other children were playing with some matches, when her clothing caught fire and she was so seriously burned that she died that night. These parents whose hearts lie crushed, bleeding and broken under the wreckage of their brightest hopes, best joys, and purest love, have our tenderest love and sympathy. May the dear Lord bless and comfort them. The funeral was conducted by the writer at Harristown, July 13, 1898.

J. P. MCKNIGHT.

Peoria, Ill., July 16, 1898.

The Religious World.

All pastors of churches, officers or members of the Woman's Christian Temperance Union, Christian Endeavorers, Young Men's Christian Associations, Good Templars, Sons of Temperance and all other Christian and temperance workers are earnestly urged to copy out the following petition at the head of a large sheet of paper, secure as many signatures as possible and send it in at once to President McKinley, that the great evils of the canteen system may be abolished before the war has proceeded further. The President has been appealed to on the subject, and it is known that he is disposed to consider favorably all protests and petitions regarding it:

A PETITION.

To the President of the United States:

Whereas, the so-called army canteen system, professedly designed to keep our soldiers from the temptations of saloons outside of camp, has in fact resulted in bringing the saloon temptation directly within the camp, exposing thereto many thousands of young men carefully nurtured in temperance principlss in Christian homes and churches;

Whereas, the amount of liquor consumed (the sales often averaging from $100 to $200 a day to the canteen) threatens seriously to injure the military efficiency of our troops and to cause wide-spread demoralization on the return of those troops to peaceful life; and

Whereas, leading army surgeons declare the use of alcoholic liquors of any kind to be extremely dangerous to the health and stamina of our soldiers campaigning in a tropical climate like that of Cuba;

We, the undersigned, do hereby respectfully petition that you will, to the extent of your authority as commander-in-chief of the army, forbid the sale of intoxicating liquors at all post and camp exchanges, or elsewhere within the lines of the armies of the United States.

The American Bible Society has received the annual report of its La Plata Agency, which includes Uruguay, Paraguay, Argentine Republic, Bolivia, South Brazil, Chili, Peru and Ecuador—a field which is over two-thirds the area of the United States. Two years after the American Bible Society was organized it printed the New Testament in Spanish, and in subsequent years many volumes were sent to various parts of South America. In 1864 Mr. Andrew M. Milne became the agent of the La Plata field, and is still there. The Scriptures have been circulated in ten languages.

The Eastern field embraces Argentina, Uruguay and Paraguay, and the Western Chili, Peru, and Ecuador. Bolivia lies between, accessible from both sides, yet with difficulty from either. Altogether they comprise an area of not far from 3,000,000 square miles, and have a population of not far from 15,000,000.

While Brazil takes fifty years to triple its population, Argentina increases at the ratio of four to one in forty-two years. Argentina is divided into fourteen states and nine territories, after the model of the United States. There are some twenty-seven normal schools for teachers and 3,700 public schools, with more than 330,000 scholars. All the religious toleration that can be desired is enjoyed. In Buenos Ayres, the Federal Capital, which has now a population of over three quarters of a million, the society has three colporteurs.

Uruguay has but 72,000 square miles of area, and is by far the smallest of the South American Republics. It has a population of 787,000, of whom one-fourth reside in Montevideo, the capital. In point of development, industry and products this country is much on a par with the province of Buenos Ayres.

During the twenty years from 1868 to 1888, when Montevideo was the headquarters of the La Plata Agency, the whole country was thoroughly canvassed. The society has had three representatives in different parts of Uruguay.

Paraguay has been called "the Garden of South America." Inclucing the unpopulated Chaco, on the west side of the Paraguay River, which may be estimated at two-fifths of the whole, it has an area of 145,000 square miles. To-day it is said to have a population of 600,000, and is rapidly increasing. Of late years it has had great accessions from immigration. The society has a depository of books in Asuncion del Paraguay in charge of Dr. Craver, a Methodist missionary, who took the oversight of Senor Bodago in the somewhat meager distribution that he was able to effect during the early part of last year.

Since 1883 fifteen men have made eighteen visits to Bolivia at the expense of the American Bible Society. Ten of these started from the Atlantic Coast and traversed to the Pacific, the others entering it from the Pacific Coast. With the exception of the city of Santa Cruz, all the chief mining districts have also been visited repeatedly. The chief mining districts have also been thoroughly canvassed. Indeed, tons of Bibles have been circulated in Bolivia, and each successive canvass brings to light some result of the former visits.

The time is near at hand when something should be done to give the Quichua Indians, of whom there are at least 3,000,000, the gospel in a form which they can understand when read to them, for thus far none of them have been taught to read, notwithstanding the oft-repeated calls of government on the state church, to set the friars to instruct the Indians.

The circulation of the Bible in Chili during the past year was 5,295 volumes.

Peru's urgent need is said to be the gospel, which the American Bible Society has proffered on its acceptance since seventy years ago.

FACTS AND FACTORS.

The Chicago Record reports the milk supply 5,000 cans short per day.

The Spanish Government sent $50,000 to Admiral Cervera and his fellow-prisoners at Annapolis last week,

Prof. E. Benjamin Andrews, president of Brown University, has accepted the position of superintendent of Chicago's public schools.

The Steamer Roanoke arrived at Seattle, Wash., July 19th from Klondike with 240 passengers and $2,000,000 in gold. Also the schooner Samoa, same date, with 36 passengers and $400,000 in gold dust.

Ten thousand rifles and 10,000,000 rounds of ammunition were surrendered to Gen. Shafter at the fall of Santiago.

Four paintings, valued at $21,000, were lost in the wreck of the La Bourgogne.

In the surrender of Santiago the captured outnumbered the captors.

The third expedition of troops from San Francisco to Manila, 4,000 strong, arrived at Honolulu, July 6th, being nine days out.

Santiago is the headquarters of three mining companies composed of United States citizens, their interests representing altogether about $1,200,000 in addition to steamers used for the transportation of the ore.

Since the beginning of the war the United States Government has bought in St. Louis for the use of the army, 2,032,037 pounds bacon, 46,188 cans corned beef, 2-pound; 2,718,252 pounds flour, 1,887,225 pounds hard bread, 90,420 pounds baking powder, 628,974 pounds beans, 26,928 cans beans, baked; 186,925 pounds rice, 63,000 pounds hominy, 1,307,500 pound potatoes, 186,550 pounds onions, 795,504 cans tomatoes, 386,035 pounds coffee, 64 pounds black tea, 34 pounds green tea, 650,818 pounds sugar, 42,339 gallons vinegar, 174,680 pounds salt, 12,900 pounds pepper, 170,580 pounds soap, 67,910 pounds candles, and 24,240 cans salmon.

A very fine butter is now made from peanuts. It is suitable for table use, for shortening, for gravies and sauces, and it is said to be superior to dairy butter. We already hear of a peanut oil factory at Norfolk, Va., capable of using up five tons of peanuts daily, and the products from five tons of peanuts will amount to 235 gallons of refined oil worth $1 per gallon, 175 gallons crude oil worth 50 cents, 3,680 pounds of flour and meal at two cents, and 3,680 pounds stock feed at 60 cents per 100 pounds, making the total gross receipts $415.90 per day, which, it is estimated, would give a yearly profit on a five-ton factory of $19,725.

SUBSCRIBERS' WANTS.

Announcements.

Convention in Idaho.

The Idaho Christian Convention will meet in Caldwell, Idaho, on September 20th, 1898. All churches in the state are earnestly requested to send delegates. It is particularly desired that the members and friends scattered through the state should attend the convention. Entertainment will be provided for all who will be in attendance.

Active, aggressive work in the state is proposed, and to that end it is important that the names and addresses of the members, and the religious conditions in the different localities of the state should be known. If it is impossible to attend the convention, it will materially assist in the work if the brethren in places where there is no organized congregation will send in their names and addresses, and whatever information they may desire to give. Come or write to B. F. Clay, Payette, Idaho, or the undersigned. JOHN C. RICE, President.

Special Notice.

The thirtieth annual convention of the Michigan Christian Missionary Association will be held with the church at Saginaw, Aug. 31 to Sept. 4. The complete program will be announced in a short time. One and one-third fare for the round trip will be granted over all the railroads, and the Saginaw church invites all of the brethren in the state who can come. The church will entertain all visitors.

Those who will attend are requested to send their names at once to A. C. Yonng, 1137 S. Warren Ave., Saginaw, Mich. ALEX. MCMILLAN, Cor. Sec.

The McGarvey Institute.

The third annual session of this Institute will be held in Windsor, Mo., Aug. 8-12th. The Windsor congregation is making all preparation to entertain all who come. A most cordial invitation is extended to our ministers and church workers. Send your name to the undersigned and you will be sure of a home and first-class entertainment.

G. L. BUSH.

Windsor, Mo.

Illinois Christian Encapment.

The 14th Illinois Encampment will meet August 1-7, in the Mission Tabernacle, Eureka, Illinois.

PROGRAM.

ILLINOIS CHRISTIAN WOMAN'S BOARD OF MISSIONS.

MONDAY, AUGUST 1.

Evening.

8:00—Informal Reception at Lida's Wood.

TUESDAY, AUGUST 2.

Forenoon.

9:00—Praise Service—Mrs. Olive Richardson, Quincy.
9:15—Reports:
State Secretary, Gussie Courson.
State Treasurer, Mrs. S. J. Crawford.
Superintendent of Young People's Department, Annie Davidson.
Conferene, led by Mrs. Edith Haigh, Peoria.
10:30—Business Hour. Mrs. J. H. O. Smith, Chicago.
11:45—Devotional. Mrs. Cora H. Lester, Belle Plain.

Afternoon.

2:00—Devotional. Mrs. John McAhan, Jacksonville.
2:15—Conference. "$90,000 for '99." Rachel Crouch.
Why?
Mrs. Fred Hagin, Pekin; Mrs. Ed. Holmes, Peoria; Mrs. Binna L. Newcomer, Maroa; Mrs. Mary Herrick, Chicago.
How?
Mrs. Emma Crow, Pittsfield; Mrs. Mary P. Miller, Springfield; Mrs. Cora H. Lester, Belle Plain.
3:15—Young Woman's Parliament, Gussie Courson, Abingdon; Ella Johnson, Chicago; Georgia May Hall, Walnut; Mamie Towne, Cobden; Mary Hoover, Sterling; Marie Hanson, Tuscola; Mary Coleman, Springfield; Stella Hendershot, Waukegan; Olive Courson.
4:00—Havest Home. Dr. Edith Haigh, Peoria.

Evening.

7:30—Devotional. Mrs. J. W. Porter, Rutland.
8:00—Address. Miss Mattie Pounds, Indianapolis.
8:30—Address. Miss Ada Boyd, Bilaspur, India.

ILLINOIS CHRISTIAN MISSIONARY CONVENTION.

Dr. J. H. Hardin, President.

WEDNESDAY, AUGUST 3.

Forenoon.

8:30—Bible Reading. Studies in the Pentateuch. Marion Stevenson, Decatur.
9:00—Preliminary Business.
Report of the Executive Board:
J. Fred Jones, Corresponding Secretary.
J. P. Darst, Financial Secretary and Treasurer.
10:30—President's Address. J. H. Hardin, Eureka.
11:10—Old Issues Restated. J. H. O. Smith, Chicago.

Afternoon.

2:00—Our State and District Work. Conference, led by W. W. Weedon, Taylorville.
(a) What it is. J. Fred Jones.
(b) What it ought to be. E. B. Barnes, Normal.
(c) How to increase its efficiency. Marion Stevenson.
(d) Five three-minute talks on last topic.
3:00—Business Men's Hour. Led by C. W. Dean, Chicago.
(a) The Busines Man as a Preacher. C. W. Dean.
(b) What makes a Missionary Church? J. A. Harrison, Stanford.
(c) The Waste of Sectarianism. L. A. Smyers, Rantoul.
Discussion of each topic.
4:00—How and Why I became a Disciple. L. D. Goodwin, Macomb.

Evening.

8:00—Popular Lecture. Booker T. Washington, Tuskegee, Alabama.
Subject: Solving the Negro Problem at Tuskegee, Alabama.

THURSDAY, AUGUST 4.

Forenoon.

8:30—Bible Reading. Marion Stevenson.
9:00—Report of Committees and other Buisness.
10:30—The Good of the Cause in Illinois. Thre-eminute speeches.
11:00—How we do it in Missonri. J. T. Ogle, Carrollton, Mo.

CRISTIAN EDUCATION.

Afternoon.

2:00—Address. What is Eureka College to Me? A. A. Wilson, Lexington.
2:20—Address. H. C. Hawk, Bloomington.

EUREKA COLLEGE AID ASSOCIATION.

2:40—Reports.
3:00—Address. Anna M. Hale, Peoria.

Evening.

8:00—Address. J. A. Lord, Editor Christian Standard, Cincinnati, O.

FRIDAY, AUGUST 5.

Forenoon.

8:30—Bible Reading. Marion Stevenson.
9:15—Address. Ministerial Relief.
10:00—Encampment Business.
11:00—address. Home Missions. C. C. Smith, Cincinnati, O.

Afternoon.

2:00—Address. Church Extension. Vernon J. Rose, Newton, Kan.
3:00—Address. Foreign Missions. A. McLean, Cincinati, O.
4:00—Sociological Conference. Leader, B. J. Radford, Eureka.

Evening.

7:30—Song Service.
8:00—Sermon. Geo. L. Snivley, Jacksonville.

YOUNG PEOPLE'S SOCIETY OF CHRISTIAN ENDEAVOR.

Russell F. Thrapp, Pittsfield, State Sup.

SATURDAY, AUGUST 6.

Forenoon.

8:30—Bible Reading. Marion Stevenson.

9:15 MISSIONARY HOUR.

H. H. Peters, Missionary Superintendent, Presiding.
1. The Diffusion of Light—20 minutes. H. H. Peters, Rantoul.
2. The Mission of the Y. P. S. C. E.—15 mintes. J. W. Kilburn, Fisher.
3. The Duty of Active toward Associate Members—15 mintues. Melvin Menges, Stanford.
4. The Y. P. S. C. E. as a Social Factor—15 minutes. S. S. Lappin, Paxton.
5. The Y. P. S. C. E. and the Local Work—15 minutes. S. G. Battenfield, Matton.

10:45 BETHANY COURSE HOUR.

L. W. Morgan, Atlanta, Bethany Superintendent, Presiding.
1. Benefits to be derived from the study of the History of the Desciples—20 minutes. Lloyd E. Newcomer, Maroa.
2. Missionary Information as an incentive to Missionary Enterprise—20 minutes. Geo. L. Peters, Girard.
3. The Importance of Bible Study in connection with the Bethany Course—20 minutes. R. L. Beshers, Tallula.

Afternoon.

2:00 JUNIOR HOUR.

Anna E. Davidson, Eureka, State Superintendent, Presiding.
Report of State Superintendent.
Methods of Work. Conference, led by Belle Smith, Cuba.
2:30—Address. Miss Mattie Pounds, National Superintendent Junior Christian Endeavor, Indianapolis, Ind.

3:30 CHRISTIAN CITIZENSHIP.

Will F. Shaw, Superintendent, Presiding.
1. The Church and the Citizen—15 minntes. W. W. Sniff, Gibson City.
2. The Christian and the Primary—10 minutes. C. B. Dabney, Mt. Pulaski.
3. Reforms Needed—15 minutes. S. H. Zendt, Dixon.
4. Pulpit Texts and Themes on Citizenship—15 minutes. B. J. Bradford, Eureka.
5. Organization and Co-operation—15 minutes. W. F. Shaw, Walnut.
4:50—Business.

Evening.

6:00—Reception to Christian Endeavor Delegates, by Eureka Christian Endeavor, at J. G. Waggoner's.
7:30—Song Service.
8:00—Address. B. S. Ferrall, Watseka.

LORD'S DAY, AUGUST 7.

Forenoon.

9:30—Bible-school.
11:00—Sermon. H. L. Willett, Chicago.

Afternoon.

3:00—Communion Service.
5:00—C. W. B. M. Hour of Prayer.

Evening.

7:30—Song Service.
8:00—Sermon. S. S. Jones, Danville.

MUSIC.—The music will be in charge of Prof. W. E. M. Hackleman.

ENTERTAINMENT.—Lodging free. Meals 25c. each. For entertainment write to J. A. Evans or J. G. Wagggoner.

RATES ON RAILROADS TO ENCAMPMENT.—The Western Passenger Association of Railroad Lines and the Central Passenger Association of Railroads, which include about all the railroads in Illinois, have granted a special rate on all lines from Illinois points of one and one-third fare, *upon certificate plan*. Conditions: Tickets must be bought not earlier than July 29th, nor later than August 4th. A certificate of purchase must be obtained from agent when ticket is bought, to be countersigned by L. F. Watson, R. R. Secretary, upon arrival at the Tabernacle. If the journey is made over more than one line and a through ticket cannot be obtained be sure to obtain a certificate for each ticket purchased. Full fare is paid going, but the return is made for one-third if 100 persons holding certificates as above are in attendance. Ministers will please explain these conditions from the pulpit at an early date.

THE
RISTIAN-EVANGELIST.

A WEEKLY FAMILY AND RELIGIOUS JOURNAL.

XXV. August 4, 1898 No. 31.

CONTENTS.

ents....131
out It?"....133
sion and Use of Property..133
venward....134
asy Chair....135
nd Answers....135
ligious Thought....136
NTRIBUTIONS:
ganism and Government.—
obbey....136
erintending Providence.—T.
s....137
a Name?—Joseph H. Mac-
....138
in the Heart.—James M.
l....139
World....139
ENCE:
pics....142
Through England....142
in Oklahoma....143
le, Florida....143
tage....144
Service....144
n, D. C. Letter....145
a Letter....145
pologizes....147
ion Notes....147
....147
ter....147
er....147
t It?....148
ristian Colony....148
rk....149
LE:
ing and Habit-Breaking
....152
herman's Son....152
gs Count....154
wart Gladstone (poem)....155
Sermon....155
ble Facts....155
y-school....156
Endeavor....157
and Obituaries....158
US:
to Our Card....139
et....140
Mention....141
ic....149
....150
Factors....151
s Notes....160
nents....160

scription $1.75.

COMMODORE W. S. SCHLEY.

PUBLISHED BY

CHRISTIAN PUBLISHING COMPANY

1522 Locust St., St. Louis.

THE

CHRISTIAN - EVANGELIST

J. H. GARRISON, EDITOR.

W. W. HOPKINS, ASSISTANT.

B. B. TYLER, J. J. HALEY,

EDITORIAL CONTRIBUTORS.

What We Plead For.

The Christian-Evangelist pleads for:

The Christianity of the New Testament, taught by Christ and his Apostles, versus the theology of the creeds taught by fallible men—the world's great need.

The divine confession of faith on which Christ built his church, versus human confessions of faith on which men have split the church.

The unity of Christ's disciples, for which he so fervently prayed, versus the divisions in Christ's body, which his apostles strongly condemned.

The abandonment of sectarian names and practices, based on human authority, for the common family name and the common faith, based on divine authority, versus the abandonment of scriptural names and usages for partisan ends.

The hearty co-operation of Christians in efforts of world-wide beneficence and evangelization, versus petty jealousies and strifes in the struggle for denominational pre-eminence.

The fidelity to truth which secures the approval of God, versus conformity to custom to gain the favor of men.

The protection of the home and the destruction of the saloon, versus the protection of the saloon and the destruction of the home.

For the right against the wrong;
For the weak against the strong;
For the poor who've waited long
For the brighter age to be.
For the truth, 'gainst superstition,
For the faith, against tradition,
For the hope, whose glad fruition
Our waiting eyes shall see.

RATES OF SUBSCRIPTION.

Single subscriptions, new or old	$1.75	each
In clubs of five or more, new or old.	1.50	"
Reading Rooms	1.25	"
Ministers	1.00	"

With a club of ten we will send one additional copy free.

All subscriptions payable in advance. Label shows the month up to the first day of which your subscription is paid. If an earlier date than the present is shown, you are in arrears. No paper discontinued without express orders to that effect. Arrears should be paid when discontinuance is ordered.

In ordering a change of post office, please give the OLD as well as the NEW address.

Do not send local check, but use Post office or Express Money Order, or draft on St. Louis, Chicago or New York, in remitting.

ISTIAN-EVANGELIST

opinion and methods, Liberty; in all things, Charity."

s, Mo., Thursday, August 4, 1898. No. 31

so far as to declare their independence. The most difficult question at issue is what moral obligation is the United States under to the people of these islands and to the civilized world, to see that a suitable and just form of government is established and maintained there. It is easy enough to say that the United States does not need these islands. It is easy, too, to declare that the attempt to govern these islands would be attended with difficulty, which would undoubtedly be the case. We may admit both of these statements, and yet the question remains, What should be done with the Philippines? Would we be justified in the eyes of the civilized world, and at the bar of our own national conscience, in turning them over again to Spain without satisfactory guarantees that the abuses which have so long cursed these islands will be discontinued? We believe an overwhelming majority of the United States will answer this question in the

a proclamation informing the people of the island that the United States forces have come "bearing the banners of freedom, inspired by a noble purpose to seek the enemies of our government and of yours, and to destroy or capture all in armed resistance." It offers to the people of the island the "fostering arms of a great people, whose greatest power is justice and humanity to all living within their fold." It announces that no war is to be made on the people of the country, but that they are to receive protection in person and property, and that it is the purpose of the government to bestow upon them the "immunities and blessings of our enlightened and liberal institutions and government." Gen. Miles does not contemplate any serious opposition in the island until he arrives at San Juan, the capital, where the Spanish troops are concentrating. He reports the country as beautiful, the troops healthful and in good

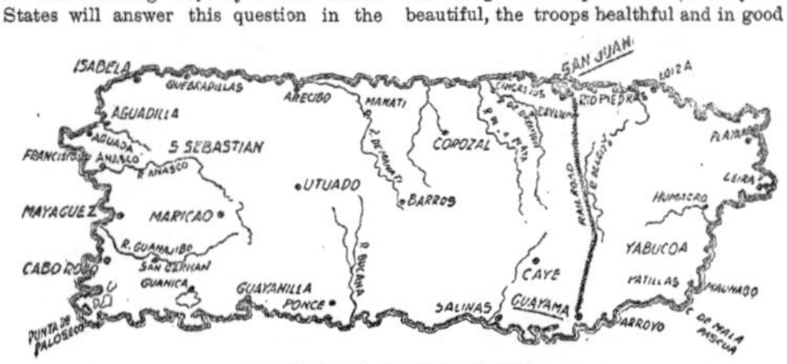

THE ISLAND OF PORTO RICO.

negative. Then the question arises, What satisfactory guarantees can Spain furnish that she will establish and maintain a government on these islands, or permit the people living there to form and maintain a government that will meet these demands? It is just at this point that the difficulty arises. It will require the greatest wisdom that our statesmen are capable of exercising to find a satisfactory solution of this

spirits. It is to be hoped that peace negotiations will be concluded in time to prevent the necessity of a battle for the capture of San Juan.

In many respects this war has been an object-lesson to the nations of the world. The rapidity with which an army of 250,000 has been mobilized and put into the field, has attracted the attention of the world.

that Spain has shown a disposition to make peace, the readiness with which the government responds to Spain's proposal, and the reasonable terms which we are sure will be offered to Spain, will show to the world that this government is as generous and magnanimous as it is brave. There is no desire on the part of this government to humiliate Spain unnecessarily, or to exact from her hard and unreasonable conditions of peace. If the great object for which the war was inaugurated can be secured, and if our obligaton toward the peoples whose interests have been affected by the war may be rightfully discharged, Spain may be allowed to have further time to show that she has profited by her experience in the present conflict. She will be a duller student of current history than we take her to be if she does not learn some lessons from this war and the causes which led to it, which will prove of great benefit to her future development. That this may be so, is the sincere wish of every American.

The rejoicing, the bell-ringing, the whistle-sounding, the shouting, the street parades and bonfires with which Honolulu and the Hawaiian Islands received the news of their annexation to the United States, is in striking contrast with the desire of the people of Cuba, Porto Rico and the Philippine Islands, to throw off their allegiance to Spain. The cause for this difference is to be found in the character of the two governments and their methods of administration. Spain seems to have regarded her island possessions as so many sources of revenue for paying her bills and supporting certain favorite officials in idleness. The question with her has been, How much will they stand? The United States seeks to give the largest measure of liberty and self-government to the states and territories within its domain, and to insure to them all equal rights and protection. There is a community of interests which makes the prosperity of every state and territory of the Union beneficial to the general government and to every other state. Not how *much*, but how *little*, can we receive in the way of taxation to meet the demands of a just government, is the question. This is why the stars and stripes awaken hope among all the oppressed of earth.

Senator Cushman K. Davis delivered an address at St. Paul on July 27th, at the laying of the corner stone of the new capitol building of Minnesota, which has attracted wide attention, both on account of the position of Senator Davis, as Chairman of the Foreign Relations Committee of the Senate, and on account of the subject he discussed. Referring to the problem of the Philippines he said that the United States must choose between alternatives. It "must become an efficient element in the the Asiatic situation, or it must entirely abstain from any participation in it, return to its own shores and cover the smallest possible share of its commercial advantages and prepare for its defense against the same aggressions which have reduced China to her present condition." Continuing his discussion of the disposition of the Philippines he said:

"It is not necessary to elaborate on the interests of the United States in the present and prospective situation. The maritime, commercial and political genius of the American people will not permit their government to be indifferent to them. It will not suffer the United States to be made the China of the west. The great question remains and comprehends the commercial and all other subjects: What action by the United States do its peace and safety require to insure to it the rightful and most advantageous results of these new international relations and adjustments? . . . It is not long since the war between Japan and China ended by depriving the latter power of her fleet, by compelling her to pay an enormous indemnity and provisionally to cede to her a portion of her territory of the greatest military and naval importance, of which Japan was in her turn deprived by the duress of Russia and Germany, only to see Russia substantially acquire the same territory and Germany make a compensatory seizure near by.

"Next to China the Pacific possessions of the United States are the most inviting objects of attack. Under existing conditions their defense would be difficult. Had Spain triumphed at Manila as decisively as did the United States her navy could have seized Honolulu and have operated from there upon the entire coast of the United States from Mexico to the Yukon. An overpowering European force in the Asiatic waters could do the same thing; so could Japan."

Referring to the Anglo-American Alliance, Senator Davis, in the speech referred to above, made a notable deliverance, the substance of which is embraced in the following quotation:

"The unpleasant relations which have existed between the United States and England for so many years were caused by a traditional aversion, which was aggravated by certain events of our civil war and by many minor irritating controversies, the worst feature of which is the fact that few of them have ever been settled. But through all this it has been felt by the people of both countries that a tie binds them together, however much they may irritate each other by straining it. Aversion and even specific controversies between peoples so related are often composed by the force of events with which their connection seems merely ideal and sympathetic. Such pacifying forces are so subtle and impalpable that they can often be perceived long before they can be described. The difficulty of indication exists in the present instance, but, notwithstanding, it is very plain that a change of sentiment, or expression and of the general contour of the relations between the two nations has taken place. The conviction heretofore only imperfectly felt, and only partially, infrequently and fitfully acknowledged, is now clearly operative, and is openly and spontaneously expressed, that the 125,000,000 who speak the English language, who have established representative governments and maintained personal liberty in every portion of the world; whose conceptions of faith, literature, morals, education, popular government and individual freedom are cognate at all times and everywhere; whose civilization, though developed, is not decadent, but is still progressive; who have heretofore taken no step backward in an expansion of influence and empire without comparison in history, are amicably approaching each other under the pressure of a great human evolution." It was not until very recently that Great Britain and the United States looked each other in the face with any sign of recognition of their political relationship. It is well for them, for civilization, for national independence and for personal freedom that they have begun to do so."

Otto Von Bismarck, the former Chancellor of the German Empire, died at Friedrichsruhe, on the evening of July 30th. While unwell for sometime he had not been confined to his bed more than ten days, and as late as Thursday previous to his death he was wheeled to the dinner table and with his family celebrated the 51st anniversary of his wedding. His death removes from Europe and the world another historic, and in many respects, great and remarkable character. Bismarck first came into prominence as a statesman in 1848 as the representative of Prussia at the congress of the confederacy in Frankfort-on-the-Main, where he obtained concessions for Prussia which Austria alone had enjoyed. In 1858 he was sent as an Ambassador to Russia. In 1862 he was recalled from Russia and sent as Ambassador to the Court of France. Ten years later he was recalled from France and made Minister of State and president of the Ministry. Germany was in desperate straits at this time and the Emperor made choice of Bismarck to steer the ship of state out of its troubles. From his entry into this office he made history rapidly, for Prussia and France felt the power of his iron will. His great work was the consolidation of the German Empire. But the new, young, ambitious Emperor of Germany rather abruptly stopped his increasing political power and career. There had come to be a great deal of friction between the young Emperor and Prince Bismarck, on which account he resigned; but he was dismissed with great honor by the Emperor. Not only the crowned heads of Europe felt the power of Prince Bismarck's influence as a statesman and a diplomat, but the head of the Roman Catholic Church as well. Some rigorous laws were enacted against the Roman Catholic Church, bearing upon the examination and appointment of the clergy under the supervision of the state, the closing of cloisters, the banishment of Jesuits from Germany, and the state supervision of Catholic schools. His opposition to the Church of Rome, in fact, partook, as many thought, of the nature of persecution—in the arrest of ecclesiastics and the confiscation of their property. But withal he showed himself to be a man of iron will and giant intellect and has immortalized his name in history. Next to Gladstone he was probably the most widely known and influential statesman of Europe, but a man of quite different spirit and temperament.

The latest word from Spain on President McKinley's peace terms, as we go to press, is to the effect that a division of sentiment in the Spanish Cabinet is said to exist. After two somewhat lengthy sittings of the Spanish Cabinet it was concluded to telegraph to M. Cambon at Washington for further explanation of some difficult points in regard to the evacuation of Porto Rico, the terms of the Cuban debt and the Philippine Islands. The demands of President McKinley, which seemed to stagger the Spanish Government, and which Senor Sagasta denominated as "severe," are reported to be "that Spain assume the municipal debt of Cuba and Porto Rico; that Spain pay indemnity to American citizens for damages suffered at the hands of the Spanish forces and authorities in Cuba." Spain is willing to concede the surrender of Cuba and Porto Rico, and to give the United States a coaling station in the Philippines, but is extremely opposed to the loss of Manila and the control of those Islands. But we shall know soon whether Spain wants peace on our terms, or to change the war from shot and shell to a war of words simply.

BOUT IT?"

title we publish else-
rather unusual com-
not know the exact
he writer, nor how far
spiritual life may be
anaticism or erroneous
life. The communica-
ests some things that
fit to our readers.
n the first place, that
unfortunate in the
ching he has received,
been laid wholly upon
has not been made to
ism, so far from being
it all," is entirely use-
sincere expressions of
desire for a better life.
course, misunderstood
aching he has listened
nt preacher among us
each, that salvation is
h. The fact, however,
any of our churches
impression from the
eard, ought to suggest
ortance of a change of
ut certainly the neces-
pains to be understood
rehension. The great
rom Alexander Camp-
time, have understood
hat without the power
od no sinner can be
e is nothing in forms
hemselves, to help the
that they are only im-
elf-surrender to Jesus
alone cleanses from

onplace truths taught
beginning is that there
r spiritual life possible
have attained to, and
d our highest privilege
to attain to this life.
, however, that suffi-
ot been laid by many
pon the necessity of
r spiritual life, and of
eans by which such a
We are now entering
religious development
is being given to this
efore. There is every-
l our churches a desire

the better it will be for the spiritual development of the churches.

This growth in the spiritual life, which must be in harmony with the teaching of Christ and the apostles, is not to be confounded with certain fanatical and unscriptural schools of perfectionists, that ignore the teaching of the Holy Spirit in the Scriptures, and that run into hurtful extremes which lead to disastrous consequences. If one avoids these fanatical errors, and sees to it that his utterances are in harmony with the Scriptures, and indulges in no vain boasting of his spiritual attainments, he will find no occasion to change his ecclesiastical affiliations in order to make all the spiritual progress that is possible to him. If he becomes a "firebrand" it is generally his own fault. If one manifests the fruit of the Spirit in his life, love, gentleness, meekness, patience, temperance, etc., he will not give offense to his brethren, but, on the contrary, they will be stimulated by his example to strive after a better and deeper spiritual life.

Our answer, then, to this brother's question, "How about it?" is, Open your heart to all the richest gifts of God and live the truest and most spiritual life possible to you, behaving yourself with meekness and patience toward your brethren and remaining where you are, seeking by your life to be an example to others. So shall you best fulfill the end of your Christian life. There was once a good man in Israel who came to believe that he was the only true worshiper of God among his brethren, and the Lord appointed his successor at once. There are many times seven thousand among us whose aspirations after a true religious life are as deep and genuine as those of our correspondent. If he be in advance of others, let him strengthen his brethren, but in meekness.

THE POSSESSION AND USE OF PROPERTY.

The Son of Man, during his personal ministry, spoke frequently and clearly on property and its use. The same statement may be made concerning his apostles. They did not hesitate to speak of wealth and what to do with it.

The possession of property was not denounced as sinful—neither by Jesus nor by his chosen embassadors. There is not even an intimation that the mere posses-

riches." He also "made silve
Jerusalem as plenteous as stor
is not space in this paper
names of the men of wealth
honorable mention in the H
They are spoken of—many
"saints." They were not
from sin. They did what th
to have done; they neglecte
they ought to have done.
named, described, denounced
they suffered. But there is n
tion that in the possessio
they sinned, Jesus spoke of
to condemn on this account.

Paul's knowledge of the g
special revelation. He was
man. This he expressly affi
teresting autobiographical p
epistle to the Galatians. Th
instructed Paul. In his doc
rectly represented his Mast
opinion of some students
Tarsus was a gentleman of
He said much about money-
abuse. In his instruction to
young preacher, he has this t

"Charge them that are rich
that they be not high-minde
uncertain riches, but in the
who giveth us richly all thi
that they do good, that th
good works, ready to distrib
communicate; laying up in st
selves a foundation against
come, that they may lay h
life."

It is the duty of the Chris
according to Paul, instead
rich men, because they poss
teach them how to so use t
"that they may lay hold on et

And this is in perfect harm
words of Jesus when he said:

"Make to yourselves friend
mon of unrighteousness; tha
they may receive you int
habitation."

The manner in which this i
explained in the latter part
fifth chapter of Matthew. In th
says that giving food to the
ing the destitute, medicine
water to the thirsty, attent
prisoned, is an acceptable se
to him—a service so well-p
that he will, as a judge, in

God, and should be used for his glory. The man who can make money, and will not, is guilty before God. He ought to use that ability for the good of those who are destitute of the talent. This he may do by giving them employment at a living wage.

Poverty and wealth are alike from God. This is the doctrine of the Hebrew Bible, "The Lord maketh poor and maketh rich; he bringeth low and lifteth up." So said Hannah, the mother of Samuel. David said unto Jehovah: "Both riches and honor come of thee." And Agur prayed: "Give me neither poverty nor riches." The Scriptures clearly teach that wealth is a gift from God and is to be used for the good of his creatures.

The man who uses his ability to make money selfishly, sins. He sins against himself. He sins against his fellow-men. He sins against God. He is a steward who has betrayed his trust. He is guilty of treason against God and man. The rich man—mentioned in the sixteenth chapter of Luke—died, and in hell lifted up his eyes, being in torment. Why? He possessed the means to relieve the poor man at his gate, but lived in selfish luxury while poor Lazarus suffered. There is only one place in all this universe for so mean a man as was Dives, and after death he went to it. It is worthy of remark that this is the only man of whom the Scriptures affirm was tormented in hell. The context shows why Jesus told the story of Lazarus and the rich man. In another place the Teacher said, speaking of such persons: "These shall go into everlasting punishment." It is quite probable that Dives was orthodox in his opinions. It is certain that he was heretical in his treatment of Lazarus—and his heresy was "damnable."

The following is from the Hebrew Hymn Book:

"Blessed is he that considereth the poor;
The Lord will deliver him in the day of evil,
The Lord will preserve him and keep him alive,
And he shall be blessed upon the earth;
And deliver thou not him unto the will of his enemies,
The Lord will support him upon the couch of languishing:
Thou makest all his bed in his sickness."

This is the general tone of Old Testament teaching concerning the relation of the rich to the poor, and the consequent obligations and blessings.

Jesus, who was thoroughly saturated with the doctrine of Moses and the Prophets, said to his disciples: "Give alms of such things as ye have." He also condemned ostentation in giving alms. Here is what he said: "When thou doest alms, let not thy left hand know what thy right hand doeth: that thine alms may be in secret: and thy Father which seeth in secret himself shall reward thee openly." And on another occasion he said: "Give, and it shall be given unto you; good measure, pressed down and shaken together and running over, shall men give unto your bosom, for with the same measure that ye mete withal it shall be measured to you again."

Nor is this duty—it ought to be regarded as a privilege—limited to the rich and well-to-do.

The Master said: "He that is faithful in that which is least is faithful also in much: and he that is unjust in the least is unjust also in much. If, therefore, ye have not been faithful in the unrighteous mammon, who will commit to your trust the true riches?" It is required of men, in every department—not merely in the department of finance—according to ability. Again and again this principle is presented in the Scriptures, "Unto whomsoever much is given, of him shall much be required." This is what Jesus said. And Paul declared that "if there be first a willing mind, it is accepted according to that a man hath, and not according to that he hath not."

How can a conscience in this duty or privilege be developed?

In the same way in which the conscience on baptism has been developed among us, that is, by the presentation of the Bible teaching on the subject of property and its use, as the doctrine of the New Testament on the duty of baptism has been presented. Let us preach and write about money and its use as we have preached and written about baptism and its blessings. In this way, and in no other, can a conscience be developed concerning the accumulation and use of property.

It is not necessary to say any other things than those that are found in the writings of Moses and the Prophets, of Jesus and the Apostles. When they speak, let us speak. What they say, let us say. What they do not say, let us not say. The blessing of God will surely attend this method.

B. B. T.

Hour of Prayer.

STEPS HEAVENWARD.

(Midweek Prayer-meeting Topic, August 10.)

Yea, and for this very cause adding on your part all diligence, in your faith supply virtue; and in your virtue knowledge; and in your knowledge temperance; and in your temperance patience; and in your patience godliness; and in your godliness love of the brethren; and in your love of the brethren love. For if these things are yours and abound, they make you not to be idle nor unfruitful unto the knowledge of our Lord Jesus Christ. For he that lacketh these things is blind, seeing only what is near, having forgotten the cleansing from his old sins. Wherefore brethren give the more diligence to make your calling and election sure; for if ye do these things, ye shall never stumble: for thus shall be richly supplied unto you the entrance into the eternal kingdom of our Lord and Savior Jesus Christ.—2 *Peter* 1-5-11.

Christian life is a march heavenward. It is not geographical, but moral and spiritual progress. To become a disciple of Christ is to enter upon a heavenly way that leads to fullness and perfection of life. This is heaven. Some of the steps in this ascent heavenward are given by the Apostle Peter in this lesson.

It is important to notice that in order to the taking of these steps, that is, in order to progress in the divine life, there must be added on our part "all diligence." Without this, spiritual growth is impossible. It is just here that a great many of us fail in our spiritual life. We do not "work at it much," as the boy said of his father's religion. Having, however, not only faith, but a desire and purpose to become Christlike, and diligent attention being given thereto, we are to advance in the following way:

"In your faith supply *virtue.*" That is, in the exercise of your faith acquire virtue or courage. It is in the use of faith, which discerns spiritual realities, that we are to cultivate courage, and we need courage to resist all the evils that beset us in our Christian life. How many of us lack the moral courage to resist evil?

"In your virtue supply *knowledge.*" I the exercise of Christian courage, we are t supply that knowledge that is essential t Christian growth. It is a knowledge tha comes from experience in doing the righ and resisting the wrong. Christians can not afford to be ignorant of moral distinctions and of great spiritual realities. It is par of our Christian business to supply knowledge and to be intelligent as to our dutie and obligations.

In the use of knowledge *temperance* mus be supplied. This means self-control Our appetites, our passions, our tempers our tongues, our ambitions, our thoughts are all to be kept in control. This is temperance in its widest sense. It is to b supplied in the right use of knowledge Many fail at this point, and failure her means shipwreck to character.

In this self-control *patience* is to b supplied. We know what this homel virtue means. We have need for it ever day. We meet with a great many thing to try our patience, and if we have not i our self-control added this grace, we shal become fretful, irascible, fault-finding an generally unpleasant. Moreover, we wil be disposed to cease our Christian effort in any direction where we ought to hold o and wait for results. What a sterling quality patience is in the home and in th church!

In patience *godliness* is to be supplied Surely it requires patience to grow i godliness. Those who imagine that godliness can be attained instantaneously hav mistaken its nature. It is our life-busines to grow like God, and it can only be done as we patiently meet and overcome th faults and weaknesses of our character.

To godliness is to be added *brotherly love* and it is in the exercise of godliness and in the growth in godliness that we come t love the brethren. We come to the lov of each other, through love of God. When we come to know God's love for us, and love Him in return, then it is easy to lov all those who love Him. Those who fail t love their brethren may well doubt th genuineness of their love to God or godliness.

In brotherly love we are to grow into a *larger and more universal love.* "God i love." He loves all men. When we become like Him we shall love all men in spite of the unlovableness of many. This is the grace which is eulogized so eloquently in the 13th chapter of First Corinthians. When our lives come to be filled with love, Godward and manward, then the end of the gospel is realized, for this is the crowning virtue of them all.

If these things are ours and we abound in them, then we shall "not be idle nor unfruitful in the knowledge of our Lord Jesus Christ." But are there not many idle and unfruitful lives? It is because these things have not been supplied, and he that lacketh them is nearsighted, only being able to see that which is near, and with no power of vision to penetrate to spiritual and eternal things. He is short of memory, too, "having forgotten the cleansing from his old sins."

In view of these facts we do well to heed the exhortation of the apostle to "give the more diligence to make our calling and election sure, for if we do these things we shall never stumble."

In supplying these Christian graces, there

hall be richly supplied unto you the en-
ance into the eternal kingdomof our Lord
ıd Savior Jesus Christ."

This is the consummation of our soul's
.preme desire—an abundant entrance into
e eternal kingdom. Such a consumma-
ɔn even in prospect should stimulate us to
r holiest and highest efforts.

PRAYER.

O, Thou who art the Author of all life
ıd being, we thank Thee that Thou hast
vealed unto us the fullness of life
rough Jesus Christ our Lord. And we
ank Thee that through Him Christian
owth is made possible, and that by the
ace He supplies we may take these steps
avenward, day by day, until we are
ınsformed into His likeness. Forgive our
st indifference, our idleness and our un-
uitfulness, and help us to be more diligent
supplying those graces through which
ıou wilt richly supply to us the entrance
to Thy eternal kingdom. And this we
k in Christ's name. Amen.

Editor's Easy Chair.

OR MACATAWA MUSINGS.

Whatever may or may not result from the
resent war, one thing of no little importance
ust be reckoned among its results. It
ay be called the recognition of God's
ınd in our national history. It is no less
an remarkable how universal the feeling
ems to be, among all classes of people,
at God's providence is over the United
ates in the present conflict. Sitting at a
ble in a Chicago restaurant recently with
ven or eight business men of the place,
e conversation turned on the war, and we
ere not a little surprised at the promi-
ence which was given to the thought that
od's hand was manifest in the remark-
ble victories that have crowned our armies.
ne would have expected this in a company
f preachers, but among hard-headed busi-
ess men, he would have looked more for
he emphasis to be laid upon the superior-
y of our battleships, our sailors and our
oldiers; but the feeling in this company
as that God was using this nation to ac-
omplish His purposes. We find this feel-
ıg very prevalent here at the Park, and it
rops out continually in the talks at the
each service, and in private conversation.
t is to be hoped that this recognition of
he divine hand in guiding our national
istory may lead to practical results. What
ıore natural than, if God is shaping our
ational destiny, we ought to recognize
His will and seek to conform our laws, our
nstitutions and our whole civil and politi-
al life, to His will? Indeed, any other
ourse would seem to be presumptuous. In
ny event, there is no question but what we
re coming to recognize, more clearly than
ver, the truth expressed by the Psalmist
nany centuries ago:

"For the kingdom is the Lord's,
And he is the Ruler over the nation."
—(Psalm 22:28).

How quiet the lake and the woods this
vening hour! The whisper of rustling
eaves and the low murmur of the lapping
vavelets on the beach, remind us of that
'sound of gentle stillness," which Elijah
ıeard in the cave at Horeb. It was in that
'gentle stillness" that God spoke to Elijah.
There is a message for us from God, no
loubt, in the tempest and the earthquake
ınd the devouring fire, but God speaks to
us oftener, we think, in moments of reverential stillness, when we are listening for His voice in the chambers of our hearts. We love the grandeur of the storm, and its conflict of the elements fills us with awe; but we love more the quiet calm of the evening or morning hour, when even nature seems to be hushed into adoring silence in the presence of God. We hope our readers will cultivate "the quiet hour" and seek to give a few moments each day to the communion of the soul with its Maker.

To-night the half-grown moon hangs on the western horizon over the lake, wearing a ruddy glow on its usually pale face. As we have been lying in the hammock watching its quiet, majestic movement through the heavens, now eclipsed by passing clouds, and now shining forth with renewed beauty, we thought of it as a fit symbol of the church and its history in the world. We can imagine that one looking upon the moon for the first time, and seeing it eclipsed by the clouds, would feel that the moon was gone, and that he would behold its bright face no more. But a little waiting would show him that while clouds pass away, the moon remains and moves along its appointed orbit. It has often happened that the glory of the church has been obscured by passing clouds of unbelief, of worldliness, of false doctrine, and men have said "The church is being permanently eclipsed and lost to the world." But anon it appears again, growing larger and brighter meanwhile, as does the moon, and shedding its beams upon the paths of men. Like the moon, to-night, the church has not as yet attained its rotundity and perfection; but like the moon, it is growing, and it is destined sometime to attain to full-orbed splendor. As God's hand guides the course of the moon and all the starry hosts, in their courses, so He is guiding the course of the church, until, in the fullness of time, it shall be presented "without spot or wrinkle, or any such thing," before the presence of His glory.

In asking for a collection on last Lord's day evening, from an audience of seven hundred or eight hundred people, sitting upon the sand on the lake shore, for the purpose of carrying on our religious work here at the Park, and particularly our Macatawa Park Assembly, in August, the writer asked why this great company of people had gathered here at this Park rather than at some other place. One prominent reason, he stated, was that Macatawa Park, in addition to its natural beauty and attractiveness, had the reputation of being an orderly, and morally clean place, where moral and religious people felt free to come themselves and bring their families with them, without fear of evil influences. It is to be hoped that this feature of the Park will be maintained in the future, as it no doubt will be, because the population of cottagers, far excels in number the hotel population, and those who own property here, who make it their summer home, are naturally interested in guarding the moral character of the place. Never have our religious services been so largely attended as during the present summer. Bro. Tyrrell, of St. Louis, delighted a large audience last Lord's day with one of his characteristic sermons. The beach meeting in the evening, conducted by Rev. Mr. Grannis, of Grossdale, Ills, was largely attended.

Among the fresh arrivals at the Park are W. F. Richardson, of Kansas City, Mo., who joined his family here this morning, and Bro. J. J. Haley, of Cynthiana, Ky., contributing editor of the CHRISTIAN-EVANGELIST, who, with his family, also crossed the lake last night. C. C. Rowlinson and his wife, of Cedar Rapids, Ia., have been here for a week, rowing, fishing and enjoying themselves generally, and might now be mistaken for Cubans, so far as their complexions are concerned. Prof. J. Mad Williams has been spending a few days here visiting Dr. Everest. Of course, he is charmed with the place, and has been looking at some vacant lots, as has also Bro. Rowlinson. Dr. Collins, of Covington, Ky., is here again, stopping at Jennison Park, as usual, and with him is Bro. Platt, of Warsaw, Ind. C. A. Young, wife and daughter, came over Saturday and spent Lord's day at the Park, and were guests at Edgewood-on-the-Lake. And still others are coming. Fortunately we have never known the fishing, and especially black bass fishing, to be so good as it is the present season, and this affords amusement and pastime to those who come for rest.

Questions and Answers.

Please say through the querists column, whether in your judgment, the practice of giving thanks for both the bread and wine, and passing both emblems to the congregation at the same time, is out of harmony with the New Testament practice? H.
Guthrie, Okla., May 27, 1898.

We do not see that the method of observing the Lord's Supper above indicated is out of harmony with the spirit and design of the ordinance as instituted by our Lord. It may not conform, and does not, perhaps, precisely, to the method given in the New Testament, but there is no intimation that we are required to conform precisely to the method given in the New Testament. If so we would have to recline around a table, dispense with the use of deacons, use barley loaves and introduce other innovations upon our present custom which would be regarded with disfavor. The main thing is to see symbolized in the emblems the body and blood of Jesus Christ, and to know that it is through his life, surrendered for us, that we live, and thus to partake of them in the same sacrificial spirit manifested by Christ in his life.

I enclose a clipping that a Dunkard brother sends me. Is it a fact that Mr. Campbell made the statement that trine-immersion can be traced to the inspired apostles. Why was the statement changed in later edition of the Campbell and Rice debate to simply immersion? We would be pleased to have you give us some light upon this through the columns of the Christian-Evangelist. G. W. Hall.
Oreana, Ill,

It is not true. It does great discredit to the candor and honesty of these Dunkard brethren to be circulating a printer's error as the statement of Mr. Campbell. We have before pointed out the fact that the word "trine" before immersion, occurred in the first edition of the book, and was afterwards corrected. The context, however, shows exactly what Mr. Campbell meant to say, and *did* say, so that no honest person, seeking for the truth, need ever have misunderstood his meaning. The clipping referred to from a Dunkard paper, contains a certificate from Mr. Spofford, Librarian of Congress, that the title page of the work from which this quotation is made,corresponds with the one in that library, which, of course, signifies nothing, since there is no dispute on this point. Mr. Campbell never made the statement, and if he had done so, it would be incapable of being sustained, and hence would be without authority. If our brethren of the trine-immersion persuasion want te maintain their reputation for being honest and godly people, even though they are not theologians, they should quit circulating this false statement.

1. What do the words "beast" and "false prophet" in Revelation 20:10 signify? and also the present tense of the verb?

2. What is the meaning of the phrase in Revelation 20:13-14. "And death and hades gave up the dead which were in them?" *I. G. Williams.*

Tower Hill, Ill.

1. We are not a specialist on the Book of Revelation, but we take it that the word "beast," as everywhere in the book stands for an earthly government, a civil power, which in this case is a world-power, because it is arrayed against him whose name is "the Word of God." The "false prophet" would indicate, on the same principle, false religion, or its personification in its leader. The present tense indicates what is stated in the twentieth verse of the previous chapter, that they had been previously overthrown and cast into the lake of fire. It is a truth that all opposing forces, whether in the form of civil government or religious systems, are being overthrown by him who rideth upon the white horse, and who is called faithful and true.

2. The language of this passage means that death and hades, or the unseen world, are to give up their dead for judgment. In other words, the language asserts that both the living and the dead are to be judged.

Current Religious Thought

What the Interior says about "The New America" and our increased responsibilities in the following paragraphs is worthy of careful reading:

The baptism of the New America is in blood, but—we say it reverently—it is in the name of the Father and of the Son and of the Holy Spirit, of a new consciousness of human brotherhood. The decisive and ruling motive which at the outset we professed, and which with every new victory we again and again protest, is honest and real. The acknowledgment of it is making a profound impression both at home and abroad. That this primary unselfishness of motive is so new in international affairs as not at once to be really understood, especially by people of other countries, is not to be wondered at. A few men in our own country, like Professor Charles Eliot Norton, of Harvard, and Professor Von Holst, of the Chicago University, have indeed betrayed their dense ignorance of the American spirit and spoken foolishly enough. And a writer of the leading article in the July Nineteenth Century, referring to our controversy with Spain, speaks of "this energetic, self-suffering nation setting out at last to be glorious," "to make history," ambitious "to be a world-power," to covet "the grandeur that was Rome's," and broadly hint that the "other powers may yet contrive to lame the wings of American ambition," and so on. But as Senator Hoar—one of the most lofty-minded and considerate statesmen of his time, declared in a very notable speech a few days ago: "There never was a people on earth who, in regard to the great subject of public conduct, were actuated by a finer, by a profounder, sense of duty and a clearer sense of justice than the people of the United States in this generation and at this hour."

With the expansion of territory, which the providential necessities of the war have made inevitable, there are thrown new responsibilities upon the American people; responsibilities which will test the inventive and original statesmanship of the country as almost never before. But more than that, the staying quality in the now aroused moral sense of the country will be tested to the fullest. And here there will be no assurance of any safety, apart from the distinctively Christian organizations and forces of the country. Navies and armies can do no more than open the door, create and secure the new opportunities. What Christian missions and Christian education and a constant Christian leadership have been doing in America itself, and have been doing for the Hawaiian Islands, will have to be done over and over again, for all the island provinces under our benign protectorate, guidance and helping, alike in the western and in the far eastern seas. Beyond a certain point, nothing is more futile, or more utterly unavailing, than are any armies or any navies. The new, the greater, America will have need of these; and will continue to have need of the same kind of heroes of public duty as those whose fame has lately filled the world with the glory of their achievement. But none of these new American provinces can add anything to the real greatness of America without the continual reinforcement of whole armies of Christian heroes along all the lines of the popular education and the civic administration. Claims and opportunities, which Spain, to its perpetual dismay and shame before all the world has forfeited, the greater America can only hold and make good by infinitely different means and methods. In Cuba, in Puerto Rico, in the Philippines, in the fullest meaning of the term, there must be "the schoolmaster abroad."

Rev. Joseph H. Bradly, in an article in Christian Work, recently, on "Eaten of Worms," administers the following severe rebuke to Christians by contrasting their low life-plane with their exalted possibilities. He says:

The civilization which exploits itself in material achievements only, is false to the age in which it exists by so much as it exalts mere intellectual and physical greatness above that which is essentially moral and spiritual. This expression may be trite, but the fact itself is none the less forever base, and, too, even though the best of mankind elect to disregard it. This fact prevails where the advantages of power and place, and dress and pleasure, are made the popular idols, even though it be in Christian households or in Christian churches. The consensus of all the wealth and virtue and "religion" on earth cannot impair, nor in any degree change, the divine ordinance.

It is not enough to ask, "Is the world prepared for anything better?" The practical and more direct question is this, "Are the Church of Jesus, and Christian men and women, incapable of grasping the fact of their duty to the world to live up to the Christian standard and true principle that "a man's life consisteth not in the abundance of the things which he possesseth?" The manifestation for which the world is always prepared, and which the church ought to provide, is the supreme glory and greatness of sincere, loving devotion to duty, and the unfailing dominance of innate spiritual principle. There is a heavenly demand for the exhibition of the fact that there is no Christian character nor honor where the everlasting power of moral and spiritual life does not act as constantly and unerringly as the laws of dynamics in chemistry and physics. They do thus act; and their due operation will show the true elevation of the spiritual life above the material. The spiritual life is so actually superior, and we are false witnesses when we do not manifest this fact, and are recreant when we do not strive by every influence in our lives to make it plain that our lives and hopes are lifted beyond the reach of worms.

While all men do not see alike as to our nation's newly acquired territory in the Pacific Ocean, it is well to have the benefit of different views for comparative values, so here is what Hon. Alva Adams has to say, in part, about the Philippine Islands in the Independent of last week:

The victory of Commodore Dewey has tied us to the Philippines by bonds we cannot break. We cannot pass title to any great Power without danger to our relations with other Governments. To give them back to Spain would be a travesty on our humanity; it would be to put fangs back in a serpent we have made harmless. We must keep them; civilization demands it, humanity demands it. True, there may be some risk. Without danger there can be little glory. We boast of the greatness of our country. We regard it as a model—an example in the evolution of man to higher political conditions. Dare we stand behind the ramparts of cowardice when our strong arm can lift up millions, and at the same time add glory and grandeur to our flag? In a community we demand more of an educated man than of the ignorant; more from the man of wealth than from the poor. The responsibility of the individual is measured by his ability and opportunities. This is no less true of nations.

The war with Spain makes the United States a world power. She is no longer a self-centered, provincial country, but an imperial nation.

The thrill of empire—of a great moral purpose, may soon impel our nation to a career more noble than has ever before directed the destinies of a people. For us to pull down the flag when once planted by our ships and soldiers would be a surrender. To permit the Spanish flag to go up again where the Stars and Stripes have floated would be to dishonor the sailors and soldiers who risk their lives to pull down the yellow emblem of brutality and oppression. When the American flag once floats over Spanish territory it should float forever. Our flag will do for the Philippines and Indies what it has done for California, Texas—for every Spanish possession that has come to us. Against these new extensions of territory there come the same protests that met Jefferson when he purchased Louisiana in 1803, against the admission of Texas, as against all Mexican cessions, and against California's and Oregon's admission as States, as against Alaska in 1867, and yet to-day the American people look upon these additions as the proudest triumphs of statesmanship.

CHURCH ORGANIZATION AND GOVERNMENT.*

BY J. E. COBBEY.

I have been asked to give a few thoughts on church organization and church government. I understand that this refers to the local organization popularly known as the church. The more thorough and more exact the business organization, the better the business of the church will be attended to and the more its business interests will prosper. When the business interests of the church are prosperous and well-managed, the church itself is a growing, prosperous church, both morally and spiritually. On the other hand, there is nothing which will so quickly destroy the spirituality of the church as poor business management. Nothing so disheartens a preacher as to have his salary come at irregular times and in irregular amounts long overdue. Nothing destroys the confidence of the world in the Christian religion so quickly as to have the bills for services rendered or material furnished the church organization laid over without action or carried in the pocket of a member until wornout or lost, and only paid after persistent dunning, when from six months to two years past due. Nothing so blunts the Christian's regard for the moral law as unreproved disregard for business rules and laws.

The failure to keep a business promise is, nine times out of ten, itself a breach of the moral law. These little breaches of the moral law, these little crimes, are too frequently but steps toward greater crimes. The incongruity of a church board disciplining a member for failure to do his whole duty, when that board is slack in its management of the business affairs of the church, may be illustrated by the case of

*Paper read before the Thirty-first Annual Convention of the Nebraska Christian MissionarySociety at Beatrice, Neb., July 3rd, 1898

o. A., who sold the church its winter's od, amounting to between twenty-five d thirty-five dollars, delivered at different ɔes between October 1st and March 1st.

In April he spoke to Brothers B. and C., o of the seven members of the board, as his bill, and was assured that it could t be paid until the board met the first onday in May. On the Tuesday after the st Monday in May he meets Bro. D. and ks if his bill was allowed. Bro. D. says: had other matters to attend to that ening and did not go the meeting, but I ppose it was, of course. You should see ·o. E., the secretary." He goes to Bro. who informs him that the board failed meet for want of a quorum, nothing can ɪw be done before the first Monday in June. ɪe first Monday in June the board meets, bare quorum being present. After conɪderable talk about the crops, trade, the ɪr and the local news, Bro. B. says: "The ood bill should be allowed," and asks if ɪy one knows how much it is. No one ɔes, but all agree that Bro. C., who is ɔsent, talked with Bro. A. and knows ɔout it, so the matter by common consent ɔes over until the July meeting. Bros. ., E., F., and G., all of the board present, ɪ clear their skirts of any remissness in ɪty, each take pains to see Bro. A. and ɪll him that if Bro. C. had been at the ɪeeting and known the exact amount of ɪe bill it would have been allowed. In ɪly, the board fails of a quorum, the ɪinority who attend, each are careful to ɪform Bro. A. that if the other members ad attended, his bill would have been alɔwed. In August they meet, and Bro. B. ɪys that eight cords of wood were deɪvered, while Bro. D. thinks it was nine ɔrds. After long discussion, Bro. D. reɪembers that Bro. A. gave him a written tatement of the account, but it was so long go that he had mislaid it and forgotten ɪe amount. So it goes over until Septemer, with the understanding that Bro. D. is ɔ get the exact amount of the bill for alɔwance at that meeting. In September, iro. D. is on hand with Bro. A.'s bill for ine cords of wood, at three dollars and fty cents per cord. Bro. B. still insists ɪat there must be a mistake, that there ʼere but eight cords, but as the other memers agree that it might have been nine, he ives up on this point, but suggests that as ʼood has been selling all summer at three ollars per cord, and Bro. A. is a good hurch member, dealing with the church, e should not ask more. This strikes the oard favorably and the matter goes over ɔ October, with Bro. B. delegated to see ɪro. A. and try for a reduction. This ɪro. B. does more promptly than he usualy does church board work. With a picnic mile on his face and a ministerial grasp of he hand he presented the matter to Bro. ʌ., who says that the wood was furnished n the winter and at the winter's price on he market, and of right ought to have been ɔaid for on delivery, but he finally agrees o the reduction because *it is the church.* n October, Bro. B. is present and the bill is ɪllowed for nine cords of wood at three lollars per cord. But Bro. A.'s troubles ɪave but begun. After four or five trips to he secretary he secures an order on the reasurer. When he presents the order to he treasurer he is informed that there are ɪo funds, that there are other bills older ·han his that of right ought to be paid first. Especially, as some of them are owing to those not members. A good, loyal member should at least take his turn. It is also suggested to Bro. A. that he might pay his subscription to the end of the year by crediting it on the bill. To this Bro. A., with some reluctance, consents, because it is the church. But here new troubles commence, as Bro. A. insists that he and his family are paid up to date. The treasurer on the authority of his books says that he is three dollars behind. Bro. A. talks to his family and then to the treasurer. The treasurer brings the matter before the board, who finally, at their January meeting, decide that the treasurer is probably correct, but that Bro. A. had better be allowed the credit, as he and his wife are positive they have paid it. Thus trying to be just and not hurt the treasurer's feelings. Bro. A., who is present with his family at this meeting of the board, asks that the rest of this bill be paid at once. All admit that this should be done, but there are still older bills to be paid, and they suggest that the pledge of himself and family for the year just commencing be credited on the bill again. To this, Bros. E. and F. of the board, object, because it would deprive the church of Bro. A.'s weekly contribution through the entire year. But here Bro. B. comes to the rescue by suggesting that Bro. A. increase his subscription by fifty per cent., thus making it large enough to cancel the bill by the end of the year, and that the bill be considered paid and the subscriptions for the year be considered paid. At first Bro. A. refuses to do this, but the board fills the room with a prayer-meeting atmosphere, and with words of brotherly love and fidelity, prevail upon Sister A. and she advises her husband that as it is the church they are dealing with, it is the best thing to do. The matter is closed up in this way, but many sore spots are left. Bro. A. says little, but feels that the church has treated him about as a highwayman who, with club in hand, called on him to stand and surrender his money. While the members of his family feel that they do not care to have business dealings with the church in any way. How can they have any enthusiasm in church work? How can they ask their friends, strangers to the church, to come in and join? How can they be expected to contribute of their earnings to the support of this organization? How can this church board have the respect of this family or of the community in which they live? What possible use is it for this board to sit in judgment on the case of Bro. M., charged with taking advantage of Bro. L. in a horse trade? Or what right have the board to cite Bro. Y. before them to answer to the charge of fraud, be it ever so plain? Such a board has by its own act deposed itself. No one in the church or out of it has any confidence in its findings. Its judgment finding a brother innocent does not reinstate him in the confidence of the members, nor does its judgment condemning him satisfy his friends that he is guilty. Their advice and admonition to erring members to reform has about as much effect as the advice of a man just convicted of petit larceny would have on an old offender arrested for grand larceny. Who of this board dare reprove Bro. A. if he fails to attend prayer-meeting regularly or to send his children to the Bible-school? But this transaction has had an influence outside of the church. Upon the strength of this sale, Bro. A., as he had a perfect right to do, promised to pay his grocer and butcher, and later his harvest hands, and still later his thrashers and corn-huskers. And each of these in turn he disappointed, and to each he had to explain that the church had failed to keep its promise to him. Though he made no complaint of their action, and from other resources redeemed his promises to pay.

The power of that church for good in that community is impaired, if not wholly destroyed. The people of that community outside of the church are moral and honest, yes, more, they are inclined to be religious, but they dread to connect themselves with an organization where financial dishonor is at a premium; with an organization whose official board at an official meeting officially approves of procrastination, repudiation and forced contributions from its own members, members whose only fault, or only crime, if you please, is that, out of a mistaken idea of respect for the church at large, they will not insist on financial integrity by the local organization in all its dealings. Such a church is tolerated, but neither loved nor respected by the community. Such conduct of its business affairs by its board raises up a barrier between the church and the outside world that is the greatest impediment to the efforts of the preacher and the evangelist. The worst thing is, that this illustration is not too strong. The statements here made are not overdrawn, but are true generally of our church organizations. In the discussion that shall follow this paper, I challenge you to show to the contrary. A want of business integrity, being then a general evil in our church organizations, and an evil so serious as to impair the confidence of the public in the church, what is the remedy? What is our duty? And, incidentally, what is the cause?

(CONTINUED NEXT WEEK.)

GOD'S SUPERINTENDING PROVIDENCE.

T. H. BLENUS.

A persuasion of the superintending providence of God is so incorporated into our very nature, so interwoven with the very principles of our being, that no nation has ever existed that has been able by any teaching or by any circumstance to eradicate the impressions of it. In all countries, savage, civilized, or semi-civilized, altars have been reared, temples have been erected and prayers to God offered, with the firm conviction of the presence of the deity, and with the firm belief that he can hear and answer the petitions of humanity. So universal a sentiment cannot be explained on the supposition of its falsity. A few men have been found who have denied it, and have made desperate attempts to substantiate the irreligious systems which reject it; but it often occurs that when the very men who are sceptical on this point are visited by some sore calamity or overwhelming affliction, their systems, like broken reeds, are abandoned, and they almost involuntarily implore the guidance and protection of the Christian's God. Even a casual review of the history of the world shows us that the special providence of God is universal. In how many and how varied ways has he interposed in the affairs of nations and peoples, so as to compel respect for his rule and divinely-appointed agencies in the development of his will and purpose? How often he displays his providence and power by the means which he employs to produce ultimate results. Sometimes he makes use of the smallest things to produce the greatest consequences; sometimes the instruments used, we would naturally suppose, would produce the contrary effects to those which they actually accomplish in his hands, and at other times using the greatest things to produce consequences which seem but casual to us.

How often do we see him proving his superintendence by bestowing on men what they desired, in a different way, and often in opposite methods to what they had planned and projected. In many instances we have seen the passions of men restrained, and a sudden change effected in their spirits for the preservation of others, or the counsels of the wise made subservient to the very ends they originally opposed. Who will say that such things are not under the controlling hand of God? He must be but little acquainted with history, and have been but a careless observer of the events that have occurred during his life, who has not remarked ten thousand such circumstances, that can only rationally be explained by the acknowledgement of the providence of God. I firmly believe that to the child of God the importance of this truth can hardly be estimated. In the sacred writings the forgetfulness of it is often mentioned as a cause of departure from God, and an occasion of sin. The wicked are represented as violating the divine laws, because they suppose "God hath forgotten; he hideth his face; he will never see it." This is also one great cause of coldness and heartlessness in our religious service. Would our worship be so languid, our prayers so meaningless and so infrequent, our praises so heartless and soulless, and our trust and confidence so feeble if we were deeply impressed with a proper sense of the universality, the watchfulness and the tenderness of God's providence? This subject is very full of comfort and consolation to all the devout children of God. Innumerable fears and anxieties must lay hold upon every considerate mind if the government of the world were left to designing men, or accident, or fate, or to mere human conduct and caprice; but these fears and anxieties vanish, and the troubled heart is at rest when we believe that though we are blind and helpless in ourselves, there is, back of all, infinite wisdom to guide, and omnipotence, omniscience, and omnipresence to be with us, over us and to defend us. We can then sing with the confidence of a blessed assurance, "The Lord reigneth; let the earth rejoice."

Jacksonville, Florida.

WHAT IS IN A NAME?

JOSEPH H. MAC EL'REY.

The great analyst of psychology said, "there is nothing in a name," and gave his meaning and the proof of his assertion by citing the fact that, "a rose, by any other name, would smell as sweet."

While these, and all similar sayings concerning the rose, and many other things, are true, there are uses to which the rose has been, like other things, applied, which could not be served if the rose and the name were therefrom diverted.

Thus, in the feuds between the Houses of York and Lancaster, the white rose was the badge of the House of York, and the red rose the badge of the House of Lancaster. The forms, colors and other qualities of those respective flowers identified certain principles and sentiments which they better expressed than words. Thus their stories were inside the lines of facts, and opinions were outside their lines—opinion about the facts cannot alter the facts.

There is something in a name, and in an emblem, and in every name. And in many names there are vitally important meanings which could be put out with some that are thereby identified and precious by inserting another word. Are any of the names by which associated parties naming themselves, or named by others, any of the diverse names by which the self-confessing disciples of Jesus have been and are known in history, names of the first and second quality, named here?

This general question seems to be an open one, and in several views of it, an indifferent one. Some desultory views upon it may be of interest to some.

In every case, of course, what is intended by the name is the essential thing in it. This is well-illustrated in the use made of names by the disciples in Corinth. They became sected, cut up, partisanized. Those of them who designated themselves by the name Christ were as partisan as those who adopted the name Paulites, or Apollosites. Their mutual intention and their wrong consisted in adopting any name, no matter what name, to distinguish them from any other members of the body of the disciples of Jesus—the body which should not be broken, rent, cut, severed, sected, bi-sected. The names they selected were honored names by themselves, and it seems, were equally orthodox. But, remarkably, they were not chosen by all the ekklesia. The names were used as party, sect badges. This was for other than selecting pastors. It was actual schismatism. Let this fact thoroughly pervade the mind, and then see where there is any escape for any one who selects a name by which to describe sectism from the sin of schism.

The general idea of a sect is that of a party breaking itself off on being broken off from the congregation of Jesus the Christ. This was not the condition existing in the Corinth Church. Paul found schism committed in the church.

The idea was that schism could not be committed out of the church, because then the party would be neither in, nor of, the church. Schism could be committed only upon, within the body, because what might be done away from a body, could not be done upon a body. Thus, St. Paul was dealing with a wounded body, a diseased body. Healing the wounded body was the idea. Excision of a part might be necessary, but he could not think of attempting the creation of a body of the exscinded part. That was cast away. It was "schism in the communion," which the apostle dreaded, in the place where the only fatal harm could be done. "That ye be perfectly united in the one mind and opinion," was his one heart-wish. It was the final prayer of Jesus. The robe must not be rent.

The freedom of Christ is fellowship with him. Not disagreement from him in dogma or opinion. Much error, many evils, and all schisms, enter and dwell here. The plea for "liberty of opinion," as distinguished from the faith which saves, are generally thought to exist far apart, but how often they are closely allied as the line which has neither breadth nor thickness. How nearer or farther are all the great opposites?

"Moved by the devil," is the criminal formula of Blackstone. "Moved by the Holy Spirit" is the divine formula of the Scripture. How far they diverge in ultimates, but how near they approach in inception! The kingdom of heaven is as the smallest of all seeds. Evil is to him who evil thinks. Good and bad are cumulatives. Opinion is mental conviction, not as clear perhaps, but therefore not less firmly fastened in the mind than if planted there by clear knowledge, and therefore all the more difficult to deal with, because laid securely up in a craggy fastness of "conscientious conviction," too sacred to be yielded up to the disintegrating processes of analysis and the risk of annihilation. "Mere opinion" is more sedulously protected than knowledge. We never hear people say they have a right to their knowledge, but we constantly hear, "I have as much right to my opinions as any one has, and no one shall interfere with them. They may be wrong, but that is my own business. I am as proud and independent in my opinions as any one." Just so. And this proves the power and sweep of mere opinion. Have opinions far wider sway than knowledge, reason, wisdom? Are they seldom based on these foundations? They would then not be opinions, merely, but clear products of knowledge and reason, the wisdom of things known, and not "merely my opinion." The multitudinous products of mere opinion have been most obstructive of human well-being. The proper names for "mere opinions," should have been, obsta, satanos, or their equivalents, as they expressed the hinderers of progress, under whatever names obstinates have ever been named.

Who has not seen the concentration of more solemn, pious-seeming, over-some gnat of "conscientious conviction" of the tweedle-dum or tweedle-dee kind, than would, if substituted to one hour of intelligent common sense examination, have converted the heads of the whole party, and done their piety and consciences more good than ever they received before? The touching of a taboo has a powerful convincing influence toward breaking down the dominion of the idol.

I wish a great multitude of this kind of religiosity would study Judges, chapter 13, Acts 10, Matthew 5:8; and take their wives with them into their debating conferences, and permit them to participate. They would then see how facts and experiences demolish "mere opinions," and how there is no piety in them, and how dangerous it is to mistake prejudice for piety, and obstinacy for orthodoxy. The sectarianisms of Christendom are the living histories of the power of mere opinions, for surely they are not witnesses for the power of the knowledge which their creators and sustainers had and have of the Bible.

Is the Bible so mysterious, enigmatical, ambiguous, that even the picked men, the profoundly learned leaders of the many colored divisions of the "universal church of Christ," as it is now the thing to style sectarianism, cannot discriminate between essentials and non-essentials, and

be be-
n lack-
ch each
the es-
tters of
e other
s of the
of the
nation-
on the
ness, of
of "the
it based
ed only
n, clear
sum it

:.

Co. 3:2.)
child of
m now.
it; he is
will be.
s heart;
at made

prouting
ughts of
ome one
elong to
iousness
of child-
of hopes
But the
n-house
g boy;"
ly vision
ecomes a
erchan-

an feels
The time
in him is
world to
mphasis
t to the
der "the
eels that
e accom-
ies with
poet? he
; is he a
ngs un-
his best
? he dies
he a man
t under-
a man's
ings for
vements,
a poor,
estion of

ere is a
he possi-
re is no
point at
n its up-
ageless
st which
han any-
n. Love
God to
the same
istakable
l quality
a social
ife is the

earthly type. The spiritual and the eternal are one. The spiritual life which Christ imparts is eternal life. It is a condition of the soul, and has no reference to time or place. It is an eternal possession, but is also something which is possessed now and here. "He that believeth *hath* eternal life." With him the ageless life of the spirit has begun.

This sense of eternity in heart makes life prophetic. It brightens or darkens the sky with premonitions of what is coming. It links the present to the future, making life all of one piece. It gives continuity to human existence, making this life and the next, parts of one realm. It makes the present the seed from which the future is evolved. "Things of to-day are deeds which harvest for eternity." Death is but an incident in the life of an immortal being. Deeply implanted in every breast are presentiments of what the future holds in store. Earnests of the heavenly inheritance are already in hand. The fires of hell are already kindled. Eternity is here.

From this sense of eternity which stirs within the heart, spring desires which time can never satisfy. As our earthly summer fades away we instinctively look for a summer that will not fade. We have a deep heart-hunger which cannot be appeased with the things of earth; we have longings for which the world has no adequate objects to offer. The things of time are perishable meat. They leave the spiritual nature unsatisfied. Man cannot live by bread alone; he cannot find his living in the things of earth. The world is a circle and the heart is a triangle, says an old writer, and as you cannot fill a circle with a triangle you cannot fill the heart of man with the world. Man is too great to be satisfied with anything short of of the spiritual or the eternal. Wherefore, then, should we spend money for that which is not bread; when in the eternal life, which is God's gift to men in Jesus Christ, and which is ours for the taking, we may find that which meets to the full the deep sense of the eternal set within the heart?

The Religious World.

On the banks of beautiful Lake Geneva, Wis., is located what is known as the Secretarial Institute and Training School of Young Men's Christian Associations, having as one of its functions a place of meeting and training for Christian service for college association men and for young men engaged as secretaries and physical directors of Young Men's Christian Associations. The success that has come to these two movements from the gatherings at Lake Geneva, has impressed the Association world with the importance of calling together annually the volunteer workers of local Associations for a ten days' conference to better qualify and equip them for the work in which they are engaged. The first of these conferences is now in session and is destined to be an epoch-making event in the history of the Young Men's Christian Association. There are now on the grounds over fifty business men and younger men from nine or more states. The sessions of the conference which take the form of class instruction and lectures, are in the forenoon and evening, the afternoon being free for rest and recreation. The scope of this gathering means the building up of an intelligent and zealous volunteer constituency which will be of value, not only to their societies, but to individual churches themselves.

JEWS IN THE UNITED STATES.

It is estimated that the Jews of the United States number about 1,200,000, although that may be somewhat in excess. Although in common with the great mass of the population they prefer the cities, they are found scattered in every section from Bangor to the Klondike, and their synagogues, which were a novelty a few decades ago, save in places like New York, Philadelphia, Charleston, Savannah and Richmond, can be met everywhere.

Chicago recently witnessed the fiftieth anniversary of its oldest synagogue—the new edifice on Indiana Avenue, with its impressive architecture, tells the story of successful growth. The new temples in Cleveland, Little Rock, Kansas City, St. Louis, Detroit, are eloquent reminders of western progress. San Francisco vies with the eastern coast-cities in the number of its synagogues. The President of the United States was present at the recent corner stone laying for the new Washington Temple, which will be worthy of the capital of our country. In New York, Philadelphia, Cincinnati and Baltimore, the synagogues are in broad places, and convey a favorable idea of American Israel. According to Rev. Dr. Carroll's statistics there were in 1897, 570 Jewish congregations in the United States, and 143,000 communicants—the last term is misleading. As a rule, the father alone counts as a member of the synagogue. Besides, in the smaller towns in which there are no regular synagogues, there will be found many Jews, and these are not included in the estimate, while a large proportion of Jewish residents of the chief cities may be unattached to any synagogue, membership being voluntary, not compulsory.—*From Frank Leslie's Popular Monthly for August.*

Response to our Card.

Recently I inserted a personal card, stating that I had agreed, at the Eureka Jubilee, to be responsible for $200 toward clearing that institution of its $30,000 of indebtedness. This pledge was made at a time when it helped materially toward securing the necessary amount of pledges. In my former card I asked Abingdon College students especially to join with me in rendering this assistance to our *alma mater*. I did not, however, intend to limit the call to such students. I regret to say that only one of the old Abingdon students, thus far, has responded. Aaron Prince Aten, of Hutchinson, Kan., writes: ,"You may count on me to assist to the amount of $5 and twice that if necessary to make up what you have pledged." We thank Brother Aten for this kind response and trust that he may be joined by many others. In addition to this, J. H. Allen, of St. Louis, whose hand is in every good work, pledges $50 to assist me in meeting the amount for which I have become responsible. This still leaves a much larger amount than I feel able personally to pay, in view of my pledges to other institutions, and the way is still open for additional pledges from other friends who are willing to help me and help Eureka College in its crisis. As the money is now due and called for, those who respond will peleas send their contributions, along with their promise, that I may pay the amount at once to the treasurer of the college.

J. H. GARRISON.

Macatawa, Mich.

Our Budget.

—There is no peace where Christ does not reign.

—The time for the offering for Church Extension is at hand.

—The vigor of our correspondents is not abating under the summer heat.

—We have received a copy of the annual catalogue, of Tazewell College, Tazewell, Va., with announcements for 1898-'99. Tazewell has many strong claims to commend its college to those seeking an education.

—The July number of the Christian Missionary Magazine gives a good report of the Bible-school convention, held at Mexico, Mo., last June, and should be freely distributed throughout the Churches of Christ in Missouri. Address T. A. Abbott, Editor, 712 Commercial Building, St. Louis, Mo.

—The camp canteens should be abolished at once. They are ruining our soldiers in purse, in health and in morals. There is no excuse for them. They are a curse to the army and a blot upon our government. Let them be abolished.

—In this paper will be found a worthy tribute to the life and memory of one of the pioneer preachers of the reformation, Bro. McPherson, of Springfield, written by Bro. Carpenter, of Wabash, Ind.

—Some one has sent us an obituary of Martha Fields Pierce, with no name attached. Will the writer please inform us of his or her name.

—It is said that two-thirds of the mail of the world is addressed in the English language. This shows the kind of people that are to become dominant in the affairs of this world.

—It sounds somewhat amusing to hear some of our exchanges which represent churches whose doctrines and commandments are so largely founded upon the Old Testament, talk about "Back to Christ." They have not yet fully come down on to Christ so how can they go back to him?

—The Chautauqua Letter in this paper came to hand on press day last week and will seem a little out of date in this paper. But as a matter of news as to what is going on at Chautauqua it is still of importance.

—Read the announcement of our Church Extension Board on the opposite page and send for literature and envelopes at once, and let your church have an opportunity to give after proper information.

—The first instalment of the paper on "Church Organization and Government," by J.E.Colby, appears in this paper. If it was not that it would be regarded personal by too many churches, we would recommend that this article be publicly read in all our churches. It goes direct to one of the chief causes of weakness in many churches.

—Chancellor Craig spent last Lord's Day in this city, and complimented this office with a short call on Monday. The Chancellor has been quietly and persistently at work since June, securing subscriptions sufficient to complete the $50,000 needed for the immediate use of Drake University. He has now $43,000, and hopes the full amount will be raised before the fall term opens in September. He reports the summer school prosperous and the cutlook good for an advance over last year's success at the University.

—There were two sermons greatly needed at the fall of Santiago. One to the Cubans from text, "ye have need of patience;" and one to the American authorities from the text, "lay hands suddenly on no man." Great allowance will have to be made by General Shafter and his subordinate officials for the Cuban mind and surroundings. We cannot expect them to square things with the usages of good government and refined courtesies at once.

—The Advance, in an editorial on "Congregationalism Stands for Something," says: "It stands for the salvation of men through Jesus Christ, the only thing in religion that is worth standing for." This is very indefinite. Each evangelical, Protestant, religious body stands for the same thing, yet the yare not Congregationalists. If all stood absolutely for this one thing then there would be no sects, and if this is the only thing worth standing for then there is no excuse for sectarianism. Brethren, if our hearts condemn us let us not forget that God is greater that our hearts. We fear that some churches will be without excuse for their exclusiveness at the last day.

—As our exchanges continue to speak words of praise for the CHRISTIAN-EVANGELIST, in its new form and dress and contents, we are placed under obligations to them for their kindly expressions of appreciation, and hereby tender our thanks to one and all for the same. We also extend our thanks to the many readers who have written us personally of their high appreciation of the paper, its progressive spirit and continual improvements. It is a great pleasure to us to know that we are not simply delighting the eye and ear of our readers, but furnishing them healthful, invigorating, spiritual food. In view of this fact we have the right to expect our readers, as they will delight to do, to do all in their power to extend the circulation of the CHRISTIAN-EVANGELIST, especially under the late, liberal offer of fifty cents for its weekly visits from August first to January first, 1899.

—Every person at all interested in the Bethany C. E. Reading Course and desiring to know more about it and its benefits should send to J. Z. Tyler, Cleveland, Ohio, for the Bethany C. E. Reading Course Bulletin, No. 4. Aside from the information contained in this bulletin, you will find the testimony of a large number of our best writers and thinkers as to the the merits of this method of study for our churches, Bible-schools and Endeavor Societies, which will command your respectful attention.

—As much as we pride ourselves in the glorious achievements of our army and navy we cannot look with any degree of allowance upon the "camp canteen" nor the governmental authority that permits it to exist. It is a thing to be deplored and opposed by every patriotic citizen in behalf of our soldiers and our country and we hail with delight the attempt to have this curse eliminated from our military camp and ranks. Would that there could be such an uprising of the good people of the land against the saloon everywhere! Petitions are being circulated, praying the President of the United States to abolish the "canteen system" and we hope that all our readers will sign and help to circulate one of these petitions, a form of which appeared in our columns last week.

—Bro. J. B. Royal, of Vermont, Ill., we are informed, passed to his reward on the 27th of July and was buried on the 28th. This brother did not dishonor his own nor his Master's name. He was a royal Christian man and was honored of God with a long life. Bro. J. C. Reynolds, his fellow-laborer and companion in Christ, will prepare a tribute to his memory for our columns.

—The four barrels of rich claret which the Guide says was presented to the First Kentucky regiment by Miss Dora Schultz, of this city, and which resulted in "several headaches" shows how even a well-intended act may intrude upon the sacred rights of others and do injury when and where not intended. We do not know that we can even say that this was unwise or indiscreet. With all the record which rich claret has behind, it borders strongly on the verge of crime. The Christian Guide well and truly says: "Not only were there headaches in camp, but many mothers' hearts were made to ache and bleed when the news reached them of their drunken boys. How much better it would have been to have given them a good, refreshing drink or two of lemonade, or better, sent some Bibles with mothers' prayers."

—The convention at Indianapolis recommended the brotherhood to raise our Extension Fund to $250,000 by the close of this century. To reach $250,000 of a permanent fund by the close of 1900 we must raise $35,000 annually. The board asks for $20,000 in the coming September offering. The board has indicated to each church what it should raise to reach this amount. Send to G. W Muckley, Kansas City, Mo., for literature and raise your proportion.

—We take pleasure in calling the favorable attention of our readers to the advertisement of Kentucky University in this and other issues of our paper. It has a full and able faculty, who do faithful work, as its hundreds of prominent and successful alumni, and a large number of students every year testify. It is one of the oldest, best, and leading colleges in the country, and affords ample means to our young men and women to obtain a good, helpful education. The location of this institution of learning and its terms afford rare advantages to all persons seeking an education.

—The placing of the statue of Pere Marquette in the rotunda of the capital at Washington and his face on a postage stamp now in circulation, are not the most harmful acts of the present Congress, and yet they are not consistent with the attitude of our government toward religious bodies, as we see things. Not only does it show the shrewdness of the Roman Catholic Church in advancing its own interests at the expense of the government, and the power of its ecclesiastics over our government to the detriment of Protestant Churches, contrary to the policy of church and state independence, but there seems to have been other men who served their country in such a way as to better deserve to be remembered.

—In this paper the reader will find an apology from Bro. Myrick to Bro. Willett and the CHRISTIAN-EVANGELIST for the spirit of an article which appeared in our columns a few weeks ago from his pen. The apology is unreserved and free-hearted, and was, we believe, prompted by the Spirit of Christ. These are brave words and we love the man the more for them. Bro. Myrick is a good writer and has delighted our readers often with the thoughtful productions of his pen. And now that he has apologized for the first appearance of the vindicative, persecuting spirit in his articles, our readers will take greater pleasure than before in reading his productions. Bro. Myrick's frankness in correcting an error is worthy of emulation by others and will be commended by everyone who hath the Spirit of Christ in his heart.

—We will be pardoned for giving this little extract from a personal letter which is appropos to our recent change of form:

I began to read the old Gospel Echo, when published, I think, at Quincy, or perhaps at Macomb, Ill. I have read it through all its changes since, until it has become that splendid cosmopolitan weekly, the CHRISTIAN-EVANGELIST. Its growth in breadth, in sweetness, in power, has recently been very marked. Now with your new and better form, scarcely anything is left to desire. May the Master bless you, and spare you long to plead the cause of primitive Christianity.

CHAS. B. NEWNAN.

177 Bagg St., Detroit, Mich.

—The time for the offering for Church Extension, the first Lord's Day in September, is drawing near, and as this is one of the important agencies in advancing the Master's work here on earth, it is time that the churches were preparing for the offering. We ask your attention to the references to that work in this paper, and to what will appear on that subject until after the offering is made. Let this notice, however, be sufficient admonition ıose churches that have not yet begun ıtions for the offering, to commence at Send to G. W. Muckley, Kansas City, ır literature.

ïeneral Miles could prohibit the use of drinks to the army in Cuba on wise s, we do not see why President McKinley not at once abolish the "camp can- for the same reason. Here is General order to the American army in Cuba:

.rmy is engaged in active service under conditions which it has not before nced. In order that it may perform its lifficult and laborious duties with the racticable loss from sickness, the utmost consistent with prompt and efficient , must be exercised by all, especially by ı. The history of other armies has strated that in a hot climate abstinence ıe use of intoxicating drink is essential inued health and efficiency.

ı following paragraph appears in the an Oracle at the close of an article en- "For a New 'Declaration and Ad- "

the members of the Garfield Park Chris- ıurch, do here and now appeal to Chris- ınd Christian Churches everywhere to with us in the program of action above y outlined. We invite correspondence ference to a "Social Christian Confer- ' to be held either separately or in con- ı with one of our general gatherings. send names, addresses and suggestions pastor, F. G. Strickland, 270 Monticello e, Chicago.

ırticle sets forth that, while we have ıuite faithful to the doctrines and ordi- of the church, "the time has fully come ıore earnest insistence on the fruits of ıpel." Hence, it recommends an earn- dy to comprehend the kingdom of God, ı social conditions of our own time, and ı "protest against the principles now ıd in society (commerce, industry, gov- ıt and all human relation) which are ry to the principles taught by Jesus. In vords, we understand the pastor of Gar- ark Christian Church and his congrega- emphasize the need of applied Chris- , in all the relations of life. We have bt but that the church of the future is ociological as well as theological.

ır esteemed contemporary, the St. Louis ian Advocate, speaks out bodly against ıpearance of evil in the official ranks of .ethodist Church, South. We give the ı paragraph of an editorial in a recent ır of that paper, appealing to the mem- f the church to refund that government ıriation, in part, at least, before they as did Achan for the golden wedge and .bylonian garment. Dr. Palmore says:

ı at once rise up and raise the $100,800, en push the Trojan horse with the entire 00 back to Washington, it will do more than if every preacher in the south preach 10,000 sermons each on "Can- "Honesty," and "Truthfulness." If ıurch, by individual contributions, will $100,000, the editor of the St. Louis ian Advocate will pay the remaining An average of 7 cents from each member ıthern Methodism will raise the $100,000. ı member is willing to give $800, the membership ought to average 7 cents ıot feel the loss, but realize a thousand- ain to a cause so dear to Christ and all ıllowers. What is money or comfort ıred with honor, purity and character! ditor had rather leave his office in tears ı out and hire to some farmer and spend ılance of his days following a plow than ıupy the greatest pulpit or tripod of a ı under any such stigma or cloud.

ıe excellent articles which have been ap- ıg in late numbers of the CHRISTIAN-EVANG- on practical themes are beginning to show ı. Here is a letter in relation to one of them will explain itself. If you agree with tter let us know and the paper will be ıted."

treatment of "Church Finance" by Bro. t Schwartz, in last week's CHRISTIAN- ıELIST, is so superior and so true to tural lines, I am constrained to suggest he same be *tracted*, and that steps be for its wide circulation among the hes. If a copy could be placed in the ly read by all, it would seem like there must result very many conversions to *the tithing plan* for raising church revenues, and a corresponding abandonment of the make-shift, semi-worldly methods of gathering moneys for carrying on the Lord's work. Were I to single out a given sentence from Bro. Schwartz' address, it would be to quote, under the last division of his subject, "Caring for the Needy"—his declaration, "Let the church supply the money . . . and the lodge will fail because we assume our much-neglected work of caring for the needy." Can we not have the tract?

W. P. KEELER.

Chicago, July 28, 1898.

PERSONAL MENTION.

E. H. Harrison, pastor of the church at Lake Charles will resign September 1st, and on account of climatic conditions, says that he wants a change. He thinks the climate of Missouri would agree with him. He says that he has had much experience in the ministry, and can furnish good recommendations.

W. F. Haman, pastor Fifth Christian Church, this city, was recently presented with a baptismal suit by his congregation.

From a statement in a local paper of Centralia, Mo., it appears that the summer heat is having no bad effect upon the audiences who attend upon the ministry of Bro. Denton. "He is a student and feeds the flock."

After visiting Yellowstone Park and the Omaha Exposition, Sherman Hill and wife will locate at Mankato, Minn., where he will assume the ministry of the Word for the church there.

A card from E. N. Tucker, pastor of the church at Greenville, Ill., says: "July 21st was a grand day with the church here. We had a mortgage burning. With the work gradually improving we feel very much encouraged with the outlook."

S. B. Moore, pastor of the church at Galesburg, Ill., and President of the Galesburg Christian Endeavor District, is spending his vacation with friends and relatives at North Middletown, Kentucky. The next convention of the Galesburg Endeavor District will be held at Cuba, Ill., Aug. 19-21, for which a good program has been prepared.

The church at Pittsfield, Ill., for which Bro. R. F. Thrapp preaches, last Sunday appropriated $50 to pay the expenses of five delegates to Eureka Encampment.

T. A. Wood expects to hold a meeting at Center School House, near Ohio, Mo., in the near future.

J. F. Sloan closed his ministry for the Central Church at Muncie, Ind., with the month of July, and has removed to Cleveland, O. Address, 502 S. Franklin St., that city.

A. P. Cobb has removed from Emo, Ontario, to Decatur, Ill., where he will answer all calls for meetings. He states that his business interests require his residence at Decatur.

H. W. White's farewell sermon at Redwood Falls, Minn., was published in full in the local paper of that city. He is now at Cando, North Dakota.

Dr. Elliott Irving Osgood, who was married on the 14th inst., to Frances Hertzog, daughter of Mr. and Mrs. O. G. Hertzog, are visiting friends at Macatawa Park for a few days, They expect to go to China in September as missionaries. They are both graduates of Hiram, and are well-fitted for the mission field.

W. T. Moore, Dean of Missouri Bible College, sailed for England on the S. S. Labrador, July 30th, from Montreal, and will return about Sept. 1st.

J. Z. Tyler, Cleveland, Ohio, and Geo. L. Snively, of Jacksonville, Ill., are expected to arrive at Macatawa Park about Aug. 8th for a brief vacation.

A. M. Atkinson and wife, of Wabash, Ind., arrived at Macatawa, July 28th, and will spend the month of August here. He is looking well considering his recent severe illness, but lacks strength yet, which we hope the Macatawa atmosphere. water and diet will supply.

Mrs. Meier, of St. Louis, one of our prominent lady workers, and President of the Orphan Home's Board, of that city, with her son, Duncan, and a party of her St. Louis friends, has arrived at Macatawa Park, and is charmed with the place.

D. S. Henkell, Pomeroy, O., who has practiced law for twenty years, and whose church relations have been until recently with the Lutherans, was ordained recently as a minister among us by Bro. G. M. Weimer, of Huntington, West Va. He desires to engage in missionary or evangelistic work, and "is not seeking a soft place." Address him as

Z. A. Harris concluded his pastorate of the church at Braceville, O., on the last Lord's Day in June. During his year and a half pastorate at Braceville there were forty additions to the church, all but six of which were by confession of faith, and mostly young people. The church held a rally the last of July, 1897, which was a season of refreshing, and was followed within a week by a series of meetings lasting eight days, which resulted in 13 additions. During all this time Bro. Harris was a student at Hiram College, from which he graduated in June, of the present year. He has now taken up the work at Bluffton, Ind., under the auspices of the State Board, where his labors will be largely evangelistic, and for which he is eminently fitted.

Knox P. Taylor, of Bloomington, Ill., preached at the First Christian Church, this city, on last Sunday morning. The First Church is doing some house-cleaning, repairing and changing in the absence of their pastor, F. O. Fannon.

We understand that Bro. J. G. Waggoner has resigned the pastorate of the church at Eureka, Ill. He went there nearly thirteen years ago, where he has preached ever since, except a year and a half in Buffalo, N. Y. The chnrch is one of the largest and most liberal in the state. There have been more than 1,300 additions during the eleven years of his ministry there. The church is in good order, thoroughly organized and in peace.

Singer A. O. Hunsaker, of Irving, Ill., is singing for G. H. Sims in a tent meeting at Defiance, O.

F. M. Branie is pushing the work at Colchester, Ill. He will hold meeting in September.

Bro. M. Ingels, of Leanna, Kansas, desires to form a partnership with a good singing evangelist, to begin work September 1st. Drop him a line.

The address of W. R. Hunt is 141 Clarendon Road, North Kensington, London, W. England.

CHANGES.

A. B. Griffith, Cleveland to Wilmington, O.

C. P. Pann, Chicago, Ill., to Riverside, Cal.

J. B. Haston, Santa Barbara, Cal., to Galveston, Tex.

E. A. Bosworth, Savannah, Ga., to Alliance, Ohio.

Tom Smith, Rock Dale, Tex., to Hermoson, Waco, Tex.

Elmer Davis, Independence to Kansas City, Kansas.

H. T. Buff, Pan Jacinte to Downey, L. A. Co., Cal.

D. A. Russell, Escondido to Berkeley, Cal.

Z. A. Harris, Hiram, O., to Creighton Ave. Church, Ft. Wayne, Ind.

D. D. Burt, Bellefontaine, O., to Beatrice, Neb.

W. T. Stephenson, Pringhar to Sutherland, Ia.

W. F. Richardson, Kansas City, Mo., to Macatawa, Mich.

C. G. Cantrell, Williamsville, Ill., to Irvington, Ind.

J. D. Forsythe, Mansing to 1356 Twenty-fifth St., Des Moines, Iowa.

R. F. Carter, Timpson, Tex., to Weakly, Tenn.

F. B. Sapp, Pine Bluff to Fayetteville, Ark.

S. M. Bernard, Broadway to 2522 Hemlock

Correspondence.

English Topics.

THE SMASHING OF DARWINISM.

The theory of evolution has had a very long run, but at last the great reaction has begun. A lecture has recently been delivered in London on the question, "What is Science?" by the Duke of Argyll. In this fine address the Duke returns to those scientific subjects which have always had such a fascination for him. He writes about such topics whenever he chooses with an intellectual vigor which is as rare as it is welcome in the aristocracy. This nobleman stands at the head of our patrician literati, and there are few scholars of plebeian rank who can equal him. The momentous part of the lecture is that in which he boldly and with terrific success attacks the assumptions of Darwinism. Now, it is only of late that there have been signs in the intellectual world of any patience with any thinkers who seem to be rebelling against the conclusions of the high priests of the evolution school. Unfortunately, large numbers of preachers and professors in religious circles have, during the past two decades, been shutting their eyes and opening their mouths and gulping down any and every absurdity enunciated by Darwinists. In England, all the broad churchmen are evolutionists. In Germany, most of the preachers and teachers of all schools are wild Darwinians. In America, the brilliant Henry Ward Beecher surrendered his great intellect at this shrine of an extreme pseudo-science. I well-remember the astonishment and regret with which I read his vivacious, but flippant, sermons on development. Strange to say, French philosophers as a body have never given their adhesion to this degrading theory. That resistance is largely due to the attitude of the greatest of French anthropologists, Quatrefages. It seemed to me some years ago that the argument of Quatrefages was unanswerable. The greatest scientist of our time in Germany, Virchow, has never been an evolutionist. This fact has had great weight in changing the current of conviction in Germany, where the reaction against Darwinism has been some time in process. The heaviest attack yet delivered on the position of the evolutionists is this by the Duke of Argyll. It will surely turn the tide. Even rationalist organs, like the London Daily Chronicle, are paying homage to the Duke's pamphlet. For Darwin himself, the Duke of Argyll, like every well-informed man, has the most profound respect. Indeed, he speaks of Darwin as the greatest naturalist who ever lived, with the possible exceptions of Linnæus and Cuvier. It appears that in the last years of his life, Darwin once called on the Duke, when a discussion took place on adaptation to special function.

MIND AS THE RULING FUNCTION OF THE UNIVERSE.

In this famous discussion the Duke said: "Well, Mr. Darwin, I cannot see any explanation of such facts except the working of mind." On this, Darwin paused for a moment, and then said slowly, "That often comes upon me with overwhelming force; but then at other times"— and he drew his hand across his eyes, as if to indicate that a vision had vanished. Now, it is on this very point that the Duke of Argyll comes into conflict with the ultra-Darwinian school; for him the vision of mind does not vanish; it offers, on the contrary, in his judgment, the only possible solution of the problem of the development of life on our planet. Cautioning his audience, in this lecture just published, against the use of vague terms like "natural selection," in which the idea of selection seems to contradict the idea of mere nature-working, for to select is to exhibit choice, and to entertain choice is to be possessed of intelligence, the Duke leads us through the several strata of which the earth is composed. He finds that there are contained in them the following clues as to the great procession of animal and vegetable life, suggesting how it has been organized and arranged. The first clue is that it had a beginning, that it has been done by steps in time. The second clue is that some forms have remained stationary, such as certain shell-fish in the Mesozoic period, while new forms have simultaneously arisen, thus showing that there was no universal necessity working. The third clue is that crowded and rapid changes have often been compressed within comparatively limited duration. The fourth clue is that the changes have followed a definite order and have "marched toward a definite consummation—namely, the establishment of higher and higher structures in the scale of organization." The final clue is that a law of mental prevision and corresponding provision is so conspicuous and all-pervading throughout the facts, that it impresses itself upon the human mind irresistibly, leading even those who sweep design from their system of thought to use words which are only intelligible on the assumption that the deliberate design of mind acts throughout the whole realm of nature. The problem, be it remembered, is whether the phenomena of nature, as we perceive them, are the products of accident and mechanical necessity or the results of the action of a free and intelligent will. As to the how of this action, the Duke of Argyll looks on the theory of natural selections as being the "most wonderful delusion which has ever imposed itself on the minds of men in the whole history of science." The assumptions of this theory are next analyzed. First, is the assumption that living forms have never been introduced save by common parentage. Now, this assumption is opposed to the very necessity of thought, for the beginning of life on this planet must have been by some other means than by common parentage. The second assumption is that while the origin of life may have been due to common parentage, that process can never have been repeated. But the Duke insists that nature is continually repeating her processes, and that the strong presumption is that she has repeated this one. Such is the argument of the Duke of Argyll against Darwinian hypothesis of natural selection based on chance and mechanical necessity. The blessed word "evolution" is too vague any longer to satisfy keen thinkers, and the reaction is fairly setting in against the most subtle form of infidelity ever known. Much of Darwin's fabric will stand because it is based on the widest observation of the facts of nature ever made. But along with these patient investigations we have a number of scientific hypothesis which have not yet been established, and some ideas which appear almost unthinkable, as students are at last beginning to realize.

THE UPWARD LOOK.

The ablest living preacher in the line of illustrations based on nature is Dr. Hugh Macmillan, whose sermons have in them more ozone, more dewy freshness, more flowery fragrance, more key-notes from the bird orchestra and more sparks from starry fires than are furnished by any other living preacher. In his new volume is an exquisite sermon on "The Oxlip, or the Upward Look." The oxlip is a favorite flower in the borders of our English gardens. It is a hybrid, produced by the union of a primrose and cowslip. The pollen or fertilizing dust of the primrose is carried by an insect to the flower of the cowslip, and that pollen works a great change upon the seed of the cowslip. It causes the young plant that springs from it to present the mingled character of its two parents. Sir George Grove, the well-known author of the "Dictionary of Music," was one day walking with Tennyson in his lovely grounds at Farringford, and the conversation happening to turn upon the changes which plants undergo by the pollen or dust of one being conveyed to the flower of another, Sir George asked Tennyson, "What is the difference between a cowslip and an oxslip?" The poet took his visitor to a corner of the garden where a cluster of cowslips and a cluster of oxlips grew near together. "Now, look," said he, "you see that the cowslip looks downward and the oxlip looks upward." Even in the Christian Church too many of us are like the cowslip, looking down to the dark soil, and like the Philippians to whom Paul wrote that they were "minding earthly things." Others, thank God, have been touched by higher and transforming influences, so that they have caught the "solar look." The Greek word for man in the New Testament is "the upward-looking." The great danger of the people of God is the materialism of the age. It is all the more perilous because it is a cultured and refined materialism. Whenever we see a bust of Julius Cæsar we notice that he is always looking up with that keen eagle glance which distinguished him from all other Romans. In no other great Roman is to be seen that same yearning gaze. Cæsar was looking beyond this world after something that he could never attain here. The gospel he never heard. But he nursed in his great soul that divine discontent which made him the greatest of pagans. All the vast heathen world is beginning to look up. The gospel of grace has sounded forth the call to this whole race, and carnal and cruel materialism hears in that call its death-knell. W. Durban.

43 Park Road, South Tottingham, London, July 14, 1898.

Wheeling Through England.

IV.

Since this is the record of a bicycle trip, it would be entirely proper to forego any attempt to detail the experiences and impressions produced by a three day's stay in London. London is better seen from the top of an omnibus than from a bicycle, and the wheels were accordingly stabled and our patronage temporarily transferred to the omnibuses. They are appallingly slow as means of transit, but are eminently satisfactory when one desires only a point of observation, in the throng and yet above it. Aside from the prevalence of omnibuses and cabs, the absence of electric and cable cars and the fact that all traffic keeps to the left instead of the right, the most conspicuous feature of any characteristic street seen in London is the vast number of silk hats in sight. The majority of business men, clerks and boys over seventeen wear nothing else (I mean nothing else in the line of hats) and are permitted by custom to wear nothing else. I was told on good authority that the clerks in many business houses were required to wear top-hats, and that on a warm day it is a common sight to see a man wearing a straw hat for comfort and carrying the required tile, to be put on before coming in sight of his place of business.

Our last day in London was the Fourth of July and it was a pleasure to see the American flag, either alone or entwined with the British emblem, flying from many business houses in Oxford Street, Piccadilly and the Strand. Never before, we were told, had the British people celebrated the Fourth of July as they did this year. When my companion and I returned to our lodgings the evening of the third, we found our beds decorated with two large American flags. So we slept that night under the double protection of the Stars and Stripes and the Union Jack, and gave thanks, not only for such ample protection, but for the kindly spirit which prompted this act of international courtesy on the part of our genial landlord. It seemed a sin against all the canons of patriotism to fail to attend the American Ambassador's Fourth of July reception, to which all Americans were invited, but it happened to be impossible for us to be present.

"Say, are you from the States? I'm from Syracuse, New York, and I'm mighty lonesome." This from a stranger who suddenly confronted us as we were walking up Ludgate

the afternoon of the sam? day, looking for cycle mechanic who could put in some re- 's on my companion's wheel. The little flags protruding from our breast pockets had the story of our nationality, and the lone- e stranger joined himself to us. "I've 1 in this country two months," he said, id I've seen everything in it. I want to go e. The last three weeks I haven't done a g but go to church to kill time. Why, do know, up here at St. Paul's they have ·ch five times every day. You haven't got atch in your pocket, have you? These lish cigars——" He had heard the morn- news of the failure of the attack on San- o, but not the afternoon news of the de- ction of the Spanish fleet. We gave him t and he seemed to feel better. Then we an to talk bicycle and found in him an ert. He took a disgusted look at the broken in which my companion carried in his pocket which bore upon it the marks of one glish mechanic's incapacity. "Oh, these :ish repair fellows. They couldn't mend incture decently. The boy that sweeps out American bicycle store knows more about a ›el than any of them." Thereupon he went n into one pocket and brought up a few s of a chain, into another and brought up a ill hammer. In ten minutes the job was e, and well-done. I happened to remark t I had lost my pump and could not find one .t my American valves. Down into another ket he goes and comes up with a pump, ere, take this. It'll fit your tires." That esome American was a God-send to us and I ik we were a happy find for him, for we t him around to Col. Hay's reception as proxy and left him looking a good deal more eerful than we found him.

Riding a bicycle through the crowded streets London, say from Charing Cross to London idge, is an exhilarating and exciting exercise, d one not to be recommended to persons of a rvous temperament. We did not do it for fun, t because we had entered London from the rthwest and wanted to leave toward the south- st. Besides, I wanted to visit the London ency of the Sterling bicycles and tell them iat a good wheel they sold. So there was no iy out of it but to ride through the city from d to end. The progress is simple enough for e most part. All you have to do is to keep the left, get in behind some omnibus and let cleave a path for you, taking care not to run it wn if it stops suddenly. Never mind the rses behind you, they will probably be all out you and over you, but if they step on u it is not your fault and the driver is re- onsible. If the omnibus sets too slow a ce, slide through the two foot space between and the hackney cab to the right, stoop and under that horse's nose, give the "'an- m'' as wide a berth as possible (for its driver tes you as a cyclist), wriggle through a hetero- neous mass of wheeled traffic, and then op in behind another omnibus. In justice to ndon streets it must be said that, while the iffic appears a continuous, crowdr? and cked procession, it never appears tangled or nfused. There is rigid law, rigidly enforced, d if you know the rules you can tell just iere every atom of the mass is going and iich way each driver will turn. So riding rough London is not a desperat? game of ance, but is in the highest degree a game of ill, having certain points in common with ess.

The courtesy of our friends at the office of e Christian Commonwealth added greatly to e pleasure and convenience of our three days London. Leaving London, the route lies rough Canterbury to Dover and thence west- of questions and observations about the war, information about his wife's relatives who lived in New Jersey, reflections on the virtues and vices of the established church, information about the goverment and international workings of cathederals, with especial reference to the sinecures enjoyed by the canons and the bishops, and a guide-book data about the cathedral. From Canterbury to Dover the road is a series of long hills, back-breaking to climb and neck-breaking to coast, but is worth the labor. We are in a land of noble cliffs along the sea and picturesque moorlands, from which the sea retired a century ago; a land rich in historical associations and relios of the Norman conquests; a land of fashionable and gay watering places, and, mingled in this sweet profusion, here and there an old dead seaport, such as Rye, deserted by her commerce, deserted by the sea itself, and left far back upon the shore as an embalmed specimen of a seaport town of the eighteenth century. Coming into Portsmouth we are again living in the present, a city full of life and activity, with harbor full of ships and streets full of sailors and soldiers. A naval officer told me yesterday that there are thirty British battleships and cruisers now in Portsmouth harbor, not to mention smaller vessels of war. From Portsmouth we cross to the Isle of Wight, for a perfect day of cycling and sight-seeing. Punctures altered our route and shortened our course somewhat, but did not mar the pleasure of the day. Then back to Portsmouth to spend the Sunday and take a fresh start toward Land's End.

W. E. GARRISON.

Portsmouth, Eng.

Our Cause in Oklahoma.

My remarks are applicable to that part of Oklahoma known as the Cherokee Strip or to Kay and Grant counties.

In Kay county we have organized at Newkirk, Ponco City, Blackwell and Bitter Creek near Rock Falls.

We have houses of worship at Ponco City, Blackwell, six miles west of Newkirk, and one now building near Rock Falls. The other congregations worship in school-houses or rented buildings. Within the last year we have built three houses of worship and finished one that was commenced the year before.

As for Grant county, we have congregations or organizations at Pond Creek, Medford, Waketa, Lamont, Orie and at Flint S. H., about ten miles southeast of Caldwell, Kan. Yes, and one at Renfrow, and I believe one or two others of which I have no definite information at present. So far as I know we have houses of worship at Medford and Orie only. We are anxious to organize congregations at Beamen, half way between Hunnewell, Kan., and Blackwell, O. T., on the railroad. Also at Nardin and Dernler, between Medford and Blackwell, on the Hutchinson and Gulf Road.

We have now four railroads in Kay and Grant with a strong probability of a fifth one.

So far as my acquaintance goes, we have seven preachers in these two counties. C. W. Prewitt at Power City, E. Backman and R. H. Walling at Medford, J. W. Hopwood at Pond Creek, —— Graham at Cleardale, Kan., J. J. Broadbent at Rock Falls, (P. O. Clare) and a "half-horse preacher," as Bro. Simms would say, at Vilott. Perhaps I ought to include Bro. Rehorn (W. S.) and Bro. C. H. Hilton (of Perry) in the list, as they bother us a little now and then. The former, I think, organized the church at New Kirk, Kay county, and at Flint S. H., in Grant county, and Bro. H. recently organized the congregation in the southwest corner of Kay. From the number of congregations and preachers mentioned above it may seem like we are strong, but such even dabble a little in politics; in fact they have done about everything that honest men can do to make a living. Perhaps I ought to say that Bro. Backman has given himself wholly to the ministry of the Word ever since the "opening of the Strip." This good brother has borne the heat and burden of the day, and I suppose has not received to exceed $200 per year until the last year. Although a comparatively young man, he has been very badly afflicted, and I understand is now forbidden to preach by his physician.

What is true of Bro. B. as to dollars is equally true of other preachers, except most of us have gone at something else for a living. For instance, Hopwood and myself have taught. Bro. Broadbent has farmed (and has succeeded) and Bro. Walling served a term in the Territorial Legislature and also has practiced medicine.

Bro. Rehorn has had to fight a contest.

Of course, none of these remarks are applicable to Brb. Prewitt, for he came here only about one year ago, just as we were entering the "financial swim" of 1897.

Of course you have heard that we had an enormous wheat and corn crop last year. The wheat averaging more than 25 bushels per acre and bringing about 75 or 80 cents per bushel on an average, and the corn about 40 bushels at about 20 cents. But you ought to reflect that we had been here three years on less than half rations—hence thousands of dollars went to pay up old scores, thousands more for houses and granaries, thousands more for machinery, wagons, buggies, etc., and some to agents, entertainments, sleight of hand performances, etc., etc., of which we have had a superabundance. For three whole years we had almost absolute rest. But with prosperity they (agents, etc.) came like the locusts of Egypt and filled the land. In another article I will mention some of our present needs and some of our hindrances.

H. W. ROBERTSON.

Vilott, O. T., May 4, 1898.

P. S.—In looking over this I notice I failed to mention a congregation of our people near Toukawa, Kay county, for which Bro. Graham preaches.

H. W. R.

Jacksonville, Florida.

There are at this writing more than twelve thousand troops encamped in and around Jacksonville. These men came from Wyoming in the north and west to the states south and east. This army corps is under the command of Gen. Lee, who has his headquarters at the Windsor Hotel. When the men went into camp here, it was determined to erect a large gospel tent on the grounds and have nightly services, conducted by the chaplains of the different regiments, assisted by the ministers of the city. It was soon found that this tent was not sufficiently large to in any way accommodate those desiring to attend, and the Y. M. C. A. Association at the north, at once sent several large tents, capable each of seating seven or eight hundred, and each under the charge of a Y. M. C. A. Secretary. This move has relieved the situation, and has continued to call into active assistance both the chaplains attached to the corps and the ministers of the city, and instead of one or two overcrowded places of meeting, there are several large tents now on the ground in which services are being conducted nightly. It was the privilege of the writer to preach in one of these tents last night. The place of meeting was crowded, the walls of the tent were folded, and hundreds sat and stood around on the outside. There were probably more than two thousand present. It was an inspiring sight and filled us with spiritual enthusiasm. I have never spoken to a more interesting audience. The time, the circum-

fellow, of Virginia, an Episcopalian, was present and aided in the services. At the close of my address, hundreds of young men crowded to the platform and expressed their gratitude for the words spoken, and scores of them asked to be remembered at the throne of grace. Quite a large number introduced themselves as members of the Christian Church from a number of different states. The discipline of the camp is very strict, and it is not an easy matter for the men to get permission to visit the city churches, but they are being well looked after, and can have the opportunity of attending divine service on the camp grounds every night of the week if they are inclined to do so. I have had the pleasure of meeting the chaplains of the different regiments here, and have found them all men of ability and fine standing in the religious bodies they represent. They have an abundance of work to do, and some of them are working very hard. Our soldier boys, as a rule, appreciate ministerial calls at the camp, and sometimes when calling on the members of some particular camp and some of whose members I have become acquainted with, pressing invitations are extended from other companies to go and see them also. It is a pleasure to meet and mingle with these dear boys, so many of them coming from Christian homes, and representing excellent families, while others perhaps never before caring about religious matters are impressed by some kindly word or little act of courtesy, and express their appreciation and almost wonder at any concern shown about them.

Our work at the new church is progressing. For the hot season we have very good audiences. Our prayer-meetings are well-attended, and some of our new members are developing good talent, all seem deeply interested, and the utmost peace and harmony reign.

The coming of the soldiers, the excitement incidental to hostilities so near, have combined to keep things stirring more than usual here in summer months. Very few have gone from Jacksonville this summer, owing to circumstances at home demanding their presence, so our city has a very animated appearance and has to-day more the appearance of a summer than a winter resort. Those coming from the north are amazed at the equableness of the climate, and the admirable weather generally.

T. H. BLENUS.

Island Cottage.

DEAR CHRISTIAN-EVANGELIST:—I greet you to-day from our happy cottage home in the northland. We have no loopholes of retreat, such as Edge-wood-on-the-Lake, where cool breezes fan the brow and hammocks rest the weary brain; but we have the sweetest island home in Hedge-Grass-on-the-Swamp, whence we

"View the busy world, and see the stir
Of the great Babel, but do not feel the crowd,
We hear the roar she sends through all her gates,
At a safe distance, when the dying sound
Falls a soft murmur on the uninjured ear."

Except the bull-frog's doleful thrum,
The busy skeeter's lonely hum

The sound of gentle stillness fills our home, and we rest in the holy atmosphere of our humble cottage in Hedge-Grass-on-the-Swamp! Around us on every hand are fields of golden grain, waving in the light of Minnesota's golden sun. In fact, the very swamp where stands our cottage home, one year ago covered with water and ducks, to-day is waving with golden grain. At our east window stands our garden of sweet and luscious vegetables and fruits—potatoes, turnips, beans, peas, tomatoes, radishes, lettuce, corn, melons, pickles, etc., etc., the finest that grow in all the land. Around our house and climbing over our windows, are sweet flowers and vines of every hue, with fragrance sweet as the incense of the Holy Place in Jehovah's temple by the brazen sea. Within is the happy, harmonious and contented family; papa writing, mamma sewing and the children making "music in the air" and filling our souls with the sunshine of love. The morning sun peeps into our chamber at three o'clock, kissing our slumbering cheeks and pouring warm entreaties into our dull ears until he rouses and leads us into the refreshing and purified breezes of day. Nor does he leave us till nearly ten at night. He really sinks to rest at eight o'clock, but O, the beautiful twilight that follows! For near two hours I can sit by the west window and read or write, in the soft light, of the beautiful night.

"Hail, therefore, patrons of health and ease,
And contemplation, heart-consoling joys,
And harmless pleasures, in the thronged abode,
Of multitudes unknown! hail rural life!
Address himself who will to the pursuit
Of honors, or 'molument, or fame,
I shall not add myself to such a chase,
Thwart his attempts, or envy his success.
Some must be great. Great offices will have
Great talents: and God gave to every man
The virtue, temper, understanding, taste,
That lifts him into life, and lets him fall
Just in the niche he was ordained to fill."

Minnesota is a land of sky-tinted waters and golden sunshine; a land of fruits and flowers and gentle showers; a land of honest occupation and health-recuperation; a land for quiet meditation, the best in all the nation; of good remuneration in almost every station, except the preacher's ration, and there it *beats creation*, to see her reputation!!

But this is pioneer work and we understand it, and prepare for it. Hence our truck patch! My father preached forty years in Illinois, and, so far as earthly remuneration was concerned, all he ever received was a pair of buckskin gloves, and they were too small for him!

So young men come to Minnesota and learn how to "endure hardship as good soldiers of Jesus Christ." I have been in this state about seven years and I think there is not now a preacher in the state who was here when I came, unless it be John Truax and William Burgess, and they are superannuated—not dead, but too old to preach regularly. I think we have never had a preacher die in the state! They either move away before they die or grow too old to die! The preacher's life in Minnesota is like a "dream," and "like a stream glides swiftly away," and the fugitive creature refuses to stay! It is now a year since I saw one of the fleeting creatures! The last one I saw, like Elijah, was on his way south! "I only am left," and I am in the top of the juniper tree—monarch of all I survey! *Sic transit gloria mundi!!* I am glad to know, however, that there are still a few in the state who have not bowed the knee to adversity. I hope to come down from the juniper tree and meet the hardy and sturdy prophets in glad convention at Mankato next month. What a feast we will have! What a joy 'twill be to see a real live preacher once more! If any of my old-time friends in the outside world would like to inhale a breath of Minnesota's health-giving atmosphere, and visit her Minnetonkas, Minneapas, Minnehahas, etc., etc., August 20-30 will be a fine time to come, and Mankato a fine place to begin your peregrinations. Ho, for Mankato, August 23-26.

This is "blue Monday" and I must close. The Lord's work in Olivia moves on apace. Two noble confessions last night and more to follow. This letter is dedicated to preachers who cannot take a vacation. God bless you.

DAVID HUSBAND.

Hedge-Grass-on-the-Swamp,
Olivia, Minn., July 25, 1898.

Intelligent Service.

The introduction of the Bethany C. E. Reading Courses was an important move in Christian enterprise. These courses have for the prime object the training of the mind. This has been a neglected field in the church. This should be a matter of regret. Thought precedes achievement. Every work is thought out before it is wrought out. Ian Maclaren says: "What one thinks to-day he will do to-morrow." The world's progress in every realm depends upon thinking men. A question is half solved when the people begin to think. "Beware when the great God turns loose a thinker upon the planet."

There is no more needy field for the full development and use of the total brain-power than in the field of Christian enterprise. It has been said that "In this world a large part of the business of the wise has been to counteract the efforts of the good." And again that "Ignorant and blundering goodness is often as mischievous as well-schooled villainy."

The Christian Endeavor movement has had certain educational features from the beginning. It has looked well to the training of the heart: that it might love him who first loved us; to the hand: that it might be used in Christian service; and to the tongue: that it might speak for the Master. As a result of this training we have zeal, works and utterance. These are all good, and the church would be shorn of much of her power without them.

But zeal without knowledge is often misdirected, and hence dangerous. Israel is an example. Peter is another. Fanaticism and intolerance have been the product in the past of zeal coupled with ignorance. This was when religious bodies were set against each other. Now that they are on more friendly terms it might lead to some unholy alliances through a compromise of the truth.

Works without knowledge are often independent of that from which they ought to spring, and by which they are made efficient, viz., faith. Faith without knowledge is superstition, or a mere acceptance of tradition. A second-hand faith is unstable. Paul said to the Corinthians, "I have not dominion over your faith . . . . for by your faith ye stand" (R. V. Marg.).

Utterance without knowledge may even more fittingly be said to be "sounding brass" or a "clanging cymbal," than tongues without love. There is much difference between having to say something and having something to say. The former may be the product simply of a pledge, the latter results from preparation.

There is need for the opening of a new chapter in Endeavor history, a chapter that will include the training of the head as well as the training of the heart, the hand and the tongue. A trained heart will give right purpose, trained hands will give skill, a trained tongue is sure to make a noise, but a trained head is necessary for direction.

The needs of our own young people along these lines are met in the three Bethany Courses. They furnish information, inspiration and intellectual equipment along fundamental lines.

Missionary information is one of the greatest incentives to missionary enterprise. We need to know what the church has done and is doing outside of the limits of our own narrow sphere. The results of Christianity as manifest in world-wide missions are the greatest evidence of its divine origin, and the surest savor for a waning faith.

As our restoration movement grows older there is the more interest taken in its study as well as the more need for its pursuit. Reminiscence is dry, history is interesting. Distance lends enchantment. There is need for this study because "those have arisen who know not Joseph." They must be informed. The work of the present is peculiar, but in order to best perform it, there must be a thorough knowledge of the past. If the house is to be refurnished, which has been swept and garnished, we must know what evil has been cast out, lest we refurnish with the same and thus make the last state worse than the first. Or to change the figure, we must know if any wheat has been uprooted with the tares, that if so, we may sow again the good seed that in the time of harvest there be no lack.

The time has come to apply our theories. The grain is ripening; we can no longer simply show our model, we must set up a live machine and go to work. To do this we must know its construction, and even be able to make

the future
the fathers
ime of con-
any move-
here. Any
t requires a

issions and
study. If
they should
curriculum.
aced as one

efitted by a
important
iples with-
guration of
ORGAN,
r Illinois.

ter.

at this sea-
ngton's ad-
spite of this
who can do
ies abandon
me the mid-
es of Christ
the heated
freshments,
out also for
doors are
l it advan-
ner months,
hus has en-
venue people
t this year
fered him a
purse. He
ous esteem
on his work
ers," which
the Bethany
r's engage-
ows: Ocean
in August,
rs, Sabina,
t 13 and 14

tern section
ccessfully as
re the Third
t was badly
arge. Much
nation of a
nsummation

ety has been
recently pur-
rch. B. A.
achers in the
services the
hem to-day.
. This new
me Board in
ization. J.
lin Heights,
t's pulpit at
absence.
sition to our
, has begun
has made a
try promises

ing promptly
rred for our
kly offerings
e we entered
s been put in
there three
additions by
ng the past

ot send many
nvention in
e gone, pre-
take the trip
Chattanooga.
agrees to put

at our disposal a special coach, or coaches, for the use of the delegates from Baltimore, Washington and points north. The route will be through Asheville, the "Land of the Sky" and along the French Broad River. A stop-over will be made at Biltmora and an opportunity afforded for a visit to the magnificent estate of Mr. Vanderbilt.

The recent meeting here of the National Educational Association brought thousands of visitors to our city. Sickness in my family occasioned my absence at this time. So I cannot write fully of the sessions of the convention. Among the preachers who were here I met George Gowen, of Lancaster, Ky., and A. E. Seddon, of Atlanta, Ga.

The brethren in Virginia are accustomed to regard the pastor of the Seventh Street Church, Richmond, as belonging to the whole state. They mapped out a tremendous lot of work for Z. T. Sweeney at their district meetings in July and August. Bro. Sweeney says: "There are some scaly fellows waiting for me up in the northwest." He goes to spend his vacation in the Lake region.

W. H. Book, the "Everywhere Evangelist," has been at work for three months in the valley of Virginia. He has added over 200 souls to the churches. He is now holding meetings in the Piedmont section of Virginia, and in September goes to Mathews County. Book's praises are upon the lips of all the preachers he helps in meetings. He not only converts sinners, but deepens the spiritual life of the members, increases the corps of active workers and strengthens the tie between pastor and people.

The writer wishes to bear testimony to the benefit derived personally and the blessing that came to his congregation from the course of study in the Bethany Reading Circle. The course for the next year is even more attractive, and thousands should take advantage of this opportunity for growth in grace and in the knowledge of the truth.

We considered the EVANGELIST of old as very near the ideal religious journal. It seems as if those in charge were not satisfied with a good paper when a better was possible. May the EVANGELIST live long and have all the subscribers its merits deserve.

EDWARD B. BAGBY.

Chautauqua Letter.

The Kentucky Mountaineer, Cram and Sacrifice Physical Life, "Mr. Creakle and Dr. Strong—Ideals of Teaching," are some of the topics for the lecture platform next week. Saturday, the 30th, Dr. Barrows gives "Observations of Popular Hinduism," and on Sunday preaches upon "The Christian Conflict in Asia." All the week following is full of interest. Confucianism and the Awakening in China, Dr. Buckley, the New York editor, on United States wars, and on Robert Emmett, will give extra force and popularity to the week.

On Wednesday, August 3rd, "What is the Bible?" and Saturday, the 6th, "What we Know About the Future," by Dr. Behrends, and then his Sunday morning service is to be followed in the evening by our Bro. Z. T. Sweeney on "Foundations." This showing is enough for one week and more.

Many of our people—Disciples, Christians, members of the Church of Christ—are coming here for a change and rest during the hot days in August. They will be anxious to hear Bro. Sweeney August 7th, in the evening, and on Monday, the 8th, again at 3 o'clock.

Some of the prosperous people who help in all good, and especially missionary work, will put in pocket an extra hundred dollars more than they need for expenses and present it to the headquarters to pay for the building, that Christian members may have a home on these grounds. Those not so able, but just as willing, will bring their part of help and the work here will be far-reaching. Isaac Errett's tract, "Our Position," is being called for and

read. Bro. Willett is doing solid Bible teaching.

Last Lord's day morning the need of a communion set was so plainly manifest when the service of the supper was over that Sister T. Roberts Harper, of Philadelphia, asked for a collection for purchase of a set. In ten minutes the amount was promised. Bro. William Bowler, of Cleveland, ordered it from New York, and in has arrived and will be used next Sunday morning. Thanks to this spirited daughter of the lamented Bro. Van Culin, of the church in Philadelphia.

Russell H. Conwell has been speaking to thousands in the amphitheatre the past hour (3 o'clock), on "Acres of Diamonds," and such a mighty teacher and preacher has kept the crowd thinking or in laughter the whole time.

W. J. F.

Myrick Apologizes.

After my criticism of Bro. Willett appeared, I was somewhat ashamed—not of the substance of it, but the unnecessarily harsh and offensive words and expressions I employed, and I privately wrote as much to Bro. Garrison. My criticism was just, but the method was unlovely. But when I read Joseph H. McEl'Rey's criticisms and reflected that my article, while not so bad, yet to a certain extent was like his, I was more than ever ashamed of the affair. And I hereby apologize, both to Prof. Willett and to the CHRISTIAN-EVANGELIST, for the harsh words and unlovely imputations contained in my criticism. It is possible to correct a statement without impunging the character of the person making it, and I promise to do so in future. When I was a boy I learned, when in a fight, to "holler enough." And I want it distinctly understood that I am doing that very thing now.

H. W. B. MYRICK.

Gentryville, Mo.

State Mission Notes.

It was recently my privilege to enjoy the association of a great quartette. I was at Nevada on Sunday morning with A. C. McKeever, and never was man treated more royally. Then at night I was at Carthage with W. A. Oldham, and everyone who knows him will feel assured that it was a pleasant companionship. The following Sunday morning I was at Odessa where that little boy of mine, S. J. Copher, ministers in word and doctrine, and at night I was with G. W. Terrell, at Blue Springs. There are days that are not very pleasant ones in my work, but these were red-letter days of enjoyment to me. I wish I had time and space to mention each as it is in detail, but I have run so far behind with my notes that I must crowd much into little.

The very next Sunday I was at Rothville to assist Bro. A. Ellett in dedicating their elegant new house. They had $600 to raise and though it took much patience and persistence, yet the amount was secured and amid great rejoicing the new edifice was dedicated to the Lord. Some men you can't help loving and one of those is J. M. Reddell; of such is the kingdom of God. It was a happy thing to met dear Bro. Ellett again.

On my way to Rothville I missed my train and had to throw myself upon the generosity of Sumner friends. Even to the extent of keeping Murph Waugh out of bed till the morning hours had come, but in the goodness of their hearts they never murmured at it at all, but actually seemed to enjoy it. God bless them.

The week was spent in attendance at the Missouri Christian Lectureship and the Missouri Christian Ministerial Association. To say that both were enjoyable, interesting and vastly profitable goes without saying.

It is to be regretted that the attendance was not larger. One cause of this is, that it was held in the hottest time of the year. This has now been remedied, as we meet next year the last of March at Huntsville. Another reason is that we are having so many other lecture courses in various parts of the state. I believe it is a thing for us to consider if this policy be the best. For my own part I doubt it very much.

The church at Louisiana has suffered a great loss in the removal of S. R. Shepherd to Louis. He has been a leader in all church work there so long, has been the pastor's right-hand man, that his removal makes a great hole in the working force of that church. He has come to St. Louis and gone into the general commission business, and I know that all who know him will wish him well. I may be clannish, but I believe that Christian men ought to patronize Christian firms who propose to do business on a Christian basis, and that is precisely what the Shepherd-Fritz Commission Co., 304 Continental Bank Building, St. Louis, will do. You can trust them in every way.

For the past two weeks the deepest shadow that can come to an earthly home has been hanging over us. Mrs. Abbott has been in the valley of death and as I write this the shadow still hangs, which way the issue will turn God alone knows. Will not the whole church pray for us in this hour of our need?

I ask also that every one invite himself to be a committee of one to see that the state treasury is at once replenished.

T. A. Abbott.

1135 *Vanderventer Ave., St. Louis, Mo.*

Dedication.

Sunday, July 17, was a memorable day in the history of the little church at Lees Summit. In 1870 the congregation was organized with twelve members. The growth has been slow since then. Last year we decided to let the world know that we were neither dead nor asleep. Bro. H. A. Northcutt was called to our assistance and our membership was doubled. The power of the congregation was ized for the first time. The money came ly and a number of our best citizens obeyed gospel.

ur old brick was soon condemned. We saw had to build. The congregation moved the Opera House and at once began the rk of building a new church home. The hful, tireless building committee, to whom church owes so much, was appointed. ver was there a more harmonious, indus-ous, liberal committee. They did the iciting—not the preacher—and set the ex-ple in giving. My task was the pleasure of olding the joy they took in the work of ing the church arise in its beauty. The ole church gave gladly, some, it seemed to , beyond their ability. At last it was shed with raised floor, circular pews—in rt with all modern conveniences. The ies carpeted the floor, the Christian En-vor Society, led by Miss Mamie Flanagan, ; in a beautiful window of cathedral glass, l Mrs. J. A. Carr gave the pulpit and com-nion table. It affords me great pleasure in ntioning these willing hearts that seemed to with each other in working for the up-ilding of the kingdom of Christ. The ptistry is elevated, and one of the most bstantial and attractive I ever saw. The ditorium is square, with Sunday-school om, opening by rolling doors, at the same gle from the pulpit.

hen everything was ready, we called Bro. O. Fannon to our assistance, whose task s to raise $1,000 and dedicate the church. his unique, matchless style he did his work riously. In the afternoon, James M. Vernon, Independence, gave us a great literary st in an address on "Our Country, its ssion and Destiny." Bro. Vernon is one of brightest men in the state and has come o Missouri to stay. Bro. Fannon was with till Thursday night and led a husband and ife to the cross whom I buried with Christ in e new baptistry, fit symbol of the new tomb Joseph of Aramathea. The congregation oves into its new home united and happy d takes another step on advancing ground. his is my third year with them, hence my joy their progress. It is due D. L. Sharr, one our brethren, to say he was the contractor d did his work to the entire satisfaction of e church.

G. W. TERRELL.

Texas Letter.

The battleship "Texas" is no longer the laughing stock" of the navy. For some ne after she was launched a series of cidents befell her. Her machinery would come deranged; in passing into or out of arbor she would frequently ground; and at nes she showed such a disposition to "wal-w in the mud," that it was feared she would nk. All manner of sport was made of her, d the people for whom she was named had most lost confidence in her. But such is not e case to-day. In the battle at Santiago, here Cervera's fleet was destroyed, she ayed a conspicuous and glorious part from art to finish, and history will mention her ong with the "Brooklyn," the "Iowa," the Oregon," the "Indiana," and the plucky ttle "Gloucester." And when the battle as over her gallant Captain Philip paraded is men, and standing reverently with un-overed heads, thanked God for victory.

R. H. Fife has returned from Kansas City Texas. He will hold a few meetings, after hich he is ready to take regular work. Bro. ife is too well-known here to need commenda-on. Let some church locate him at once. ro Hamlin has received an indefinite call to main at Palestine.

J. H. Marshall has held a meeting at Vharton and organized a church of twenty-wo members, and arranged for them to have gular preaching.

R. R. Hamlin has been at Oakwoods, a mis-on point with three members. They expect have a new house soon, and a congregation f sixty members.

J. B. Boen has done a successful work at Kingston, with a church of forty-four members organized, and Sunday-school, and money raised for a pastor. Bro. Boen is now in a great camp-meeting at Throckmorton.

A. E. Ewell locates at Wichita Falls. This is an important place, and Ewell will do great good there.

J. W. Marshall has reorganized the church at Uvalde. Their old troubles removed and a new Sunday-school, they should now go forward in the work of the Master.

Homer T. Wilson, with a batch of his church, spent a couple of Sunday afternoons at Glenwood, near Ft. Worth. Result: a new church and Sunday-school organized.

Guy Inman, an Add-Ran student, and one of the livest Endeavorers in the state, is spending his vacation in Mexico.

F. T. Denson's work at Claude is bearing fruit, as is evidenced by the fact that the lumber is now on the ground for a new house.

Philip King, of Belton, spent his vacation with the church at Itasca. His meeting was fine, resulting among other things, in wheeling the church into line on all questions of modern, progressive work.

Prof. J. B. Sweeny, of the Bible College of Add-Ran University, is in a meeting at Van Alstyne, and prospects are good.

J. V. Coombs, the Indiana evangelist, is soon to hold a meeting at Ft. Worth. All Texas extends him a hearty welcome.

E. H. Harman, of Lake Charles, La., desires, on account of health, to come to Texas. Those in position to know, speak in high terms of Bro. Harman.

Annie D. Bradley, favorably known all over the land as a versatile writer, leaves us soon for Ft. Worth. It is a case of the mother-heart following the child. We will miss her much in the Central Church.

The people of Lancaster are in earnest about Randolph College. The enterprise is only a few months old, and it has been understood that only a part of the buildings would be completed this year. But not so. Those people say that they shall all be finished.

M. M. DAVIS.
833 *Live Oak St., Dallas, Texas.*

Iowa Letter.

Suffering loss for righteousness' sake. In a fine Iowa town of 10,000 population, I was recently pricing lots for church purposes. The agent of a wealthy non-resident landowner assured me that his principal had refused three or five thousand dollars ground rent (the exact figures have escaped my memory) from the whisky business. The saloon element had the consent of the local property owners, but their plans were temporarily wrecked by this man's stalwart conscience. Of course the whisky element found other parties who took their money for rent, and this man's lots lie idle for conscience' sake. This man is known as a great lover of money; but evidently he loves one thing more than money—righteousness. He puts many church members to shame.

***

S. P. Telford, of Keota, Iowa, has a unique method of church finance in operation. On April 15th his finance committee printed and put into the hands of every expected contributor a list of apportionments. Every apportionment for the whole church is on this list. On May 1st they sent out the same list with a column added in which every acceptance of apportionment appears. I notice that some cut down the request and accept a lower amount per week, a few raise the amount and accept, and very few decline entirely. On July 1st they sent out a quarterly statement, which, on one sheet, shows the standing of every account. I copy the totals: "Pledges for the quarter. $225.09; Amount received for quarter, $165.66; Balance due, $98.47; Overpaid, $36.49; Due on former account, $142.06; Total now due, $245.48."

"A new Tract on Infant Baptism." 78 pp., lies on my table. It is by C. W. Freeman, of West Salem, Ill. Ten cents per copy, or $1.00 per doz. The author sent letters to every M. E. Bishop save two, and also to the Bishops of the U. B. Church. This is his question: "Will you kindly give me the Scriptural references that clearly teach the baptizing of infants?" The few answers received are very interesting:

"I know of no Scriptural reference that clearly teaches that infants should be baptized, nor do I recall, etc."—JOHN M. VINCENT.

"There are no particular verses of Scripture which distinctively enjoin infant baptism, or etc."—C. D. FOSS.

"I think there is no *direct* Scriptures. The proof is largely inferential."—N. CASTLE, *of U. B. Ch.*

John M. Walden's evasion is very cute and seemingly pious. Get it.

***

"A city set on a hill cannot be hid." A few years ago I organized a little band of Disciples in a large town. Recently I returned to do some soliciting for them. Among others I asked help of a man who is a member of another church. Here is his answer: "Yes sir, I have been watching a few families in your band here. It has done them good—great good. I like to help pay for work that does good in the homes of our town. Put me down on your list." On this same occasion some gave very little or none at all because they saw the dark side of life in this little band. It is a wonder that Jesus saw through the dark side of the world and gave himself on the cross to enlarge the bright side.

***

I wonder what lessons Charles Spurgeon would have found in what I saw a few days since? He was a wonderful man to see things and learn lessons. I saw a stout old wooden barrel. It was placed under the shade of a tree, the hose nozzle had been thrown into its capacious depths, and the water turned on. The filling process had gone on nicely until two-thirds done. There it halted and a battle begun. Great cracks, almost a finger's breadth, poured the water out as fast as the hose forced it in. I do not know the outcome, but after watching the contest for hours it seemed to me a hopeless task. The staves had warped so that tightening of hoops had not closed the gaping seams. The master of the house had resorted to the hose as his last and only hope in restoring the barrel to usefulness in its full capacity. A few moments thought on your part will evolve these and other lessons;

Neither barrels nor men are made to lie about empty and unused. Service is the law of our being.

Constant use means constant readiness for service and perpetual wholeness.

Neither hoops nor decalogue statutes can fully restore loss capacity. The householder and the Christ must devise something more.

A Stephen full of faith and of the Holy Spirit is a beautiful sight and a blessing to any church or any city. Our full capacity is needed.

The spiritual emptiness of our lives should not be charged up to any lack in God's grace. Back of that old barrel was a stand pipe and great engines and one of the greatest rivers of Iowa.

Partly redeemed, that old barrel was useful—worth more than for kindling wood. Use a Christian man for what he is worth. It may be that some of us are doomed to live on earth a two-thirds life because of the sins of our youth.

Is it any wonder that the Lord Jesus takes a long, long time to fill some lives when others are filled in a moment?

***

These hot days no one is working harder than Chancellor W. B. Craig, of Drake University. The $50,000 fund begun at commencement time is before him; $7,000 more will complete it. God bless him and the donors.

One of the remarkable facts which will characterize the close of this century is visible in the medical and surgical world. If you have not given it attention, you will be agreeably surprised to see how many physicians and surgeons are abandoning the use of alcohol in whole or in part, no matter in what form. Scientific experiments in Germany, France, England and America have started in the medical world what may prove to be a landslide, sweeping alcohol out of the field. Edward Hornibrook, President Iowa State Medical Society, speaking recently about our soldier boys and the canteen said: "The use of intoxicating liquors as a beverage tends to lower the vitality of the system and increase the danger of exposure to infectious diseases."

***

Professors Hopkins and Youngblood, recently of Missouri, have leased Oskaloosa College for a term of years, and will make of it a first-class Normal and Preparatory School. These men are a splendid addition to Oskaloosa and our Iowa forces. They are men of large experience in educational work, and know how to succeed. Write them for fuller information.

***

Secretary Slayton, of the Central District of Iowa, furnishes me the following data:

Membership in seven counties		11,174
Net gain for the year		1,062
Value of church property		$284,800.00
Raised for missions		5,742.21
All other purposes		54,237.42
Missions, per capita	$ .51	
Contributions, "	4.86	
Property, "	25.50	

How About It?

Editor Christian-Evangelist:—In your issue of July 7, 1898, I was very much pleased in reading an editorial entitled "Prosperity of Soul." It appeared to me that I could see between the lines that the writer is in the possession of an experience far in advance of the church which the CHRISTIAN-EVANGELIST represents—that is, what I mean by the church is the body of professed Christians who make up the congregations of that particular church.

Having been at one time a member in good standing, it appeared singular and mysterious to me that nearly every one, including their preachers, insisted that works, and works only, would qualify for the kingdom, and if immersion had taken place it was the essential thing to do, all else would follow as a consequence. That conversion was merely a turning around, and obedience to the commands would pro duce salvation. The mainspring of it all wa immersion. I could not so understand it. I seemed to me that there was something mor than merely the consent of the mind; that sinner must have applied to his soul and life more powerful agency than his own will, wit forms and ceremonies. All those things woul appeal to the mind, but it was not enough t cleanse and enable him to stand. In all tha he should do, I found him helpless, and it wa by a complete surrender that he was enabled t discover the real help necessary; in fact, th only help out of a sinful state into a pure an happy state.

This was the condition of a real sinner whose head had become gray in following afte the world and all its fancy trumpery. Thi man repeatedly said in social meetings tha the reconstruction he experienced was mor potent and effectual than water baptism, an really claimed that he had received the bap tism of the Holy Ghost, and that the blood o Christ cleansed him from all sin. In suc declarations he was told that it was not i harmony with the church, and that he wa professing too much, indeed, boasting tha he had something more than his brethren an sisters were favored with, and that the Lor was no respecter of persons. In reply, he sai that it was for all, and there was no call fo any one to feed on the husks, that divin grace was inexhaustible, and that whosoeve would hunger and thirst after righteousnes should be filled.

He was reminded again that the church o which he was a member, did not believe i Christian perfection, and that no man o woman could live without committing sin Well, then, if that be true, what is the use t try? So you see, dear Brother Garrison, tha man could not do any good among his professe friends. Now, he claimed that instead of being exercised over keeping his religion, h feels that he must have a religion that wil keep him—and that is the only kind that i worth a nickel. Walking in the light, overshadowed and enveloped in the very presenc of the Holy Spirit, he knows for himself, an not for another, that there is a divine realit in a religious experience that is dearer to hi than all the world. And so long as he is i that pathway he feels comfortable and safe and he must be on his guard and not lose it This man asks you to tell him, "How Abou It?" Must he remain in the church and be firebrand?

Yours,

LEROY CLENDENNIN.

LeRoy, McLean Co., Ills., July 16, 1898.

Canada Christian Colony.

Many inquiries have come to me respectin the Christian Colony on Rainy River, th advantages and disadvantages of this region etc.

My name has been frequently qouted as tha of one who is identified with this country These two reasons, together with the desir that those who contemplate coming here ma know something more of this country than knew when I moved here, lead me to say a fe words relative to the darker side of life here.

There are three great drawbacks here. Th first is the inaccessibility of the region. Ra Portage on the Canadian Pacific is 125 mile away. Tower, Minnesota, is the nearest rail road point, but is sixty miles distant. I takes two days and about ten dollars to ge there. We have numerous railroads coming i on *paper*. It is probable that one will b actually completed to Fort Francis, thirty mile up the river from here, by the end of 1899; bu even that is not certain. We are simply tak ing our chances on that.

A worse drawback than the absence of quic communication by rail is in the impassabl condition of the roads in summer. *Impassabl* is the only word which will honestly describ these roads. I had to bring my team an wagon from Rat Portage here by water ot been a day since my arrival that I the empty wagon to Emo, our ge. This has been the condition left the ground, and will be the til winter brings us solid founda- auling again. This is an almost burden to those who are accustomed ids in summer. And with from eet of muskeg, or swamp and moss nd no drainage in places, this con- ot be materially altered for years. st be done in winter; lumber, fire- This is not poetry; it is the rugged hose who contemplate coming here w beforehand the whole truth on t a matter to the new settler. I do hat in a generation from now the is here can compare with those of ois.

nost afflicting drawback and one aches in its burdensomeness to the gypt is that of the flies, to which indeed made in the government but so briefly and mildly made me, never formed the faintest con- the awful scourge which is sug- not described, by the statement that bad for about six weeks in sum- ould have been only fair to the settler to have told him that for time a team cannot be worked n hour or two in the early morning ght.

to have known before coming here t have dark rooms into which his tle may rush at the first attack of "bulldogs," as the large horse- e called. It is hardly enough to ; all sensible men expect flies to be countries. I was in Illinois a third ago, when it was a new country. have been in other new countries. he first time I have ever seen cattle so tormented by these truly infernal

advantages here which in the many, myself included, outweigh disadvantages; but it is not fair ective settler to tell him only the and leave him to find out for him- xpending his little all, the darker e not now, nor have I had at any- pecuniary interest in what I have ten about this region. I am not a agent as some suppose. I am not hest degree connected with any scheme here or elsewhere. I have eds of dollars of hard-earned money ting this country, and in moving ere, as well as in making an in- ere. I have bought a beautiful farm, partly improved. This is sest of those who will remain here Let those interested, ponder these if they come do, so with a better ng of the situation than I could trip in the winter which I enjoyed After setting forth these drawbacks to say that the older settlers here ing that the autumns are fine and the winters, though cold, are dry g. It is in these seasons that , etc., are done. If bad roads a part of the year, I am not sure would rather have them in summer ter; for good roads in winter mean forests, hauling of wood, hay, etc. ery one be fully persuaded in his ,

, and in the interest of truth, rnally, A. P. COBB.

ario, Canada, July 12, 1898.

---

college building of the Southern nstitute at Edwards, Miss., will be use by the last Tuesday in Septem- new building will greatly increase es of this educational institution. talogue is out and ready to mail to nts. Address Gospel Plea, Ed- s.

A New Work.

Since Bro. Atkinson has been compelled to lay down the laboring oar of the Ministerial Aid Association, some of his work has devolved upon me, and I wish in a few sentences, to take my brethren into my confience and say a few things to them.

I have never known much of the specific working of this association, though I have long known that in this attempt to restore apostolic practice that it is an application, in some measure, of that higher and better fellowship that "feeds the hungry, clothes the naked and visits the sick" in their distress. Since I have come in connection with this work I have been permitted to read the correspondence between the board and their beneficiaries, and I feel that no one could read these lines from these venerable men and women without being aroused to some thought of duty. I have just received the letters containing the receipts of the July allowances, and I want to give a few of them as specimens:

One venerable sister died before she had sent receipt, and a friend in sending account of her death says:

"Your gift was instrumental in smoothing her pathway to the grave. Her gratitude was unbounded."

Another old brother says:

"Yours most gratefully received. I am eighty-five years old; began preaching in 1836. I have no comfort like that of the love and kindness of my brethren."

Another says:

"I am grateful for your favor. It is indeed a substantial favor to me and my old helpless wife just now. God bless you."

A venerable mother in Israel whose husband was for forty years known to the Disciples in Illinois writes:

"I want to express many thanks for your help and may God bless those who have not forgotten the Lord's poor ones."

Another old sister, widow of a devoted preacher, writes:

"The money you have sent me has been such a relief to me. Without it I do not know what I would have done."

I could fill a whole page with such expressions from the correspondence I found in the office, but surely these are enough to incite a thought in the minds of those who read it as to the duty they have in helping forward this work. Don't forget to send a contribution, however small, to Howard Cale, 120 E. Market St., Indianapolis, and help forward this good cause. D. R. LUCAS.

Indianapolis, Ind., July 29, 1898.

Evangelistic.

ILLINOIS.

Eureka.—There were two confessions at prayer-meeting last week; a gentleman and his wife.—J. G. WAGONER.

Shelbyville, July 26.—One more addition to the church at Palmyra at my regular appointment last Lord's Day. My work there is being blessed.—A. M. COLLINS.

MONTANA.

Missoula, July 27.—Four baptisms here since last report.—J. C. B. STIVERS.

MASSACHUSETTS.

Worcester.—July 25.—Tent meeting opens nicely. Six additions since July 17th. Audiences average about 400. Order and attention good; interest on increase, prospects good.—ROLAND H. NICHOLS, Pastor.

Everett, July 28.—Had two additions to church last Lord's Day.—R. H. BOLTON.

OHIO.

Ashtabula, July 22.—Seven added here on the last two Lord's Days.—ROBERT SELLERS.

TENNESSEE.

Clarksville.—Two accessions July 26, to Church of Christ, by baptism.—A. M. GROWDEN.

INDIANA.

Indianapolis, July 25.—At the North Park Church; three additions.—J. M. CANFELD.

ARK.

De Queen, July 27.- closed with 64 additi tinue in Arkansas. O Amity, Ark.—ARTHUR LAND.

Eureka Springs, Jul reported.—DAVID TRU

Drake's Creek, July week's meeting at this and five added otherwi A. Bertram, (Baptist near Albany, Ky., be Zachary-Smith debat begin Aug. 29th and c W. ZACHARY.

NEB

Broken Bow, July just closed 26; present before were the meml present. Our audienc in the city, there be During the last year doubled, the church chairs, paper and f The writer has remain minister for the past flections have been ca the church, but the pa by far the happiest ar life. Our people a prestige in our city blessed our labors. I ministry, Aug. 1st, w JESSE R. TEAGARDEN,

ALA

Selma, July 22.—Ha meeting at Richmon eight by baptism.—E.

ARK

W. T. Brooks, late of Ladoga, Ind., is in Ark. We have no chu point.

KA

Washington, July 2 to July, 1898, during tions to the church; ei would like to locate a 1st.—A. A. ARTHUR,

KEN

Louisville, July 21.- ing the work with th additions there lately.

MIS

St. Louis, July 30 Fifth Church since last Pastor.

St. Louis, July 30 Second Church sin WOLVERTON, Pastor.

Rolla, July 25.—El ico, Mo., has just clos ing at this place result the church spiritually good work continue.—

Sturgeon, July 26.— in this town last nig tions to the church; 56 tism, and 17 otherwise

Nashville, July 25 audiences, 12 addition ed. Bro. W. W. Wa of the time, and is gre —MORGANS AND DAUG

Marceline, July 25. terday, 8 since last re ISOM ROBERTS.

Trenton, July 28.— ton since last report. church work doing w is the dull season o SNELL.

OKL

Tonkawa, July 29. five days ago for eva *fine*. Good attendance Expect to organize a leave.—ADCOCK AND

Literature.

BOOKS.

ORGANIC EVOLUTION CONSIDERED. By Alfred Fairhurst, A. M. Published by the Christian Publishing Co., 1522 Locust St., St. Louis, Mo. Price, cloth, $1.50, 386 pages.

I have just finished reading, under rather unfavorable circumstances, the late work of Prof. A. Fairhurst, entitled, "Organic Evolution Considered." The principal object of the work is to show that the theory of evolution, as held by Darwin and others, especially as to the doctrine of natural selection and the origin of species, is not sustained by the facts.

Though the author, in his first chapters, introduces subjects which at first glance might not appear to have a direct bearing upon the discussion, it is soon made apparent that the treatment of them was necessary to the full understanding of the objections urged against Darwin's theory. It was necessary, for example, to discuss the ordinary forms and proprieties of matter, to see its possibilities and to compare them with what are regarded as functions of mind.

The author then discusses, also, at some length, that form of matter or medium of force transmission known as the cosmic ether. It might appear to some that this reference might not be necessary, or at least available, but if the views of Haeckel are of any note, and of others inclined to give to matter in some form a potency to which it can lay no claims, the propriety of the discussion becomes apparent. Haeckel, for example, says that "religion itself, in its reasonable forms, can take over the ether theory as an article of faith, bringing into contradistinction the mobile cosmic ether as creating divinity and inert matter as the material of creation."

Now, this is unscientific vagary, and any one would suppose he had taken an overdose of absinthe, and in his exaltation of genius, gone around the world kicking up his iconoclastic heels to knock from their pedestals all of the denominational dogmas of the schools.

The professor, therefore, does well to discuss so thoroughly the properties of different forms of matter as being pertinent to the discussion, and of course the ether, the existence of which, he says, "is now admitted by the scientific world."

Its existence was surmised by Faraday, who had reason to believe, that light, electricity and magnetism were simply forms of manifestations of one force or energy which led Heinrich Hertz in 1888 to experiments that seemed to place the existence of such a medium beyond mere hypothesis.

When, however, we come to the main topic, the discussion of the theory of natural selection, for which so much is claimed, and the dependent question of the origin of species, the facts and the arguments based upon them, and the difficulties brought to view by the common sense and and originality of the author, it becomes evident that the theory of progressive organic evolution, eventuating in distinct species, is not sufficiently inclusive of the facts in the case.

On this particular branch of the subject, involving the important question of the origin of man, bearing directly upon the doctrines of the church, the professor has met the arguments advanced in support of the theory of evolution, derived from the doctrine of natural selection, from paleontology, from the existence of rudimentary organs, and from embryology with an array of difficulties, to be met and overcome, that will be seen to be formidable.

In all these divisions of his subjects, facts are given in great number, which militate against theory, and the arguments derived from them are presented with great skill.

He shows that in the geological records there are so many breaks that it is next to impossible to find any trustworthy evidence of a progressive evolution by gradual differentiation, and that the missing links, so necessary, have to be assumed hypothetically in support of the theory. In fact, one specific hypothesis after another is advanced to account for difficulties that rise up at many points.

The work being so full of scientific facts, educed to support conclusions drawn from them, their possession affords to the reader ampler opportunity to follow out his own line of thought in reasoning from them and at the same time to grasp with more ease the line of argument of the text.

The chapters on design and on agnosticism, in which the author enters the domain of philosophy and theology as well, are full of illustrations in the first case and of strong points in the latter. He gives more proofs of design from his particular branches of study than I have ever met. The agnosticism of Herbert Spencer is fully discussed, and the author shows that nature is too full of the evidences of a first intelligent cause possessing various attributes, to be relegated to the region of simply an unknowable mystery either as an object of thought or of worship.

But to be appreciated the work must be read. To thinking people it will contain enough suggestions of different lines of thought to keep their minds occupied long enough to afford something of an education, and certainly the great number of scientific facts referred to, and especially those derived from the natural history of organisms with their wonderful instincts and developments, make the work valuable even as a partial text book. C. J. KEMPER.

Kentucky University, Lexington, Ky.

"THE TWENTIETH CENTURY CITY" is a book of a hundred and eighty pages by the Rev. Josiah Strong, D. D., until recently, and for a number of years, General Secretary of the Evangelical Alliance for the United States. Dr. Strong is well-known as the author of two volumes entitled, "Our Country" and "The New Era." "The Twentieth Century City" is published by The Baker & Taylor Co., Nos. 5 and 7 East Sixteenth Street, New York. The price in cloth is fifty cents, in paper, twenty-five.

Dr. Strong attempts, in this book, both a diagnosis and a prescription. He attempts to show the essential character of modern civilization—its weakness and its peril. He suggests a remedy which, to say the least, seems to be reasonable. Experiment alone will demonstrate the practibility and effectiveness of the suggestions.

The book is divided into eight chapters. In the first the author writes about "The Materialism of Modern Civilization." In the second he writes about "A Nation of Cities." The phenomenal growth of cities in the present century is pointed out and reasons for this are given. This is not a peculiarity of the United States; it belongs to the world. In chapter third, Dr. Strong claims that our moral growth, especially in cities, has not kept pace with our material progress, and that a materialistic city is a menace to itself and so to the life of the nation. Following the statement that our moral growth has not kept pace with our material progress, place a large interrogation point. There can be no doubt that a materialistic city is a menace to itself and to the life of the nation. Our peril is still farther and more fully presented in the fourth chapter. One-half of the book is occupied with this diagnosis. There is a tinge of pessimism in these chapters, a feature, by the way, of almost all that Dr. Strong writes—a feature that is not pleasant. Of course, he protests that he is not a pessimist, and such, in the full sense of the word, he is not. Dr. Strong is by no means destitute of hope. His desires are good, and his expectation is buoyant. He believes that finally the good will triumph over the evil.

His words on "The New Patrotism," or *living* for our country, rather than *dying* for it; "Twentieth Century Christianity," that is, the Christianity of Christ, and the "Twentieth Century Churches," have a tonic effect. "The Churches," he says, "must save society, or themselves perish." But the churches will not perish. Dr. Strong thinks that the "churches have not believed in the practibility of Christ's teachings," and to a degree this statement is correct. The thought, until quite recently, has not been entertained that the church owes a duty to society as well as to the individual. More and more the thought is taking possession of the church that it has a mission to society, and this is well. "The Twentieth Century Churches" will be more practical than are the nineteenth century churches. This is a cheering thought. But the churches must not forget, nor neglect, the individual. It is by the salvation of the individual from his personal sins that society is to be made alive to holiness.

Dr. Strong, in that book, speaks of "The gospel of the kingdom," as if it is the good news that the Christ now commands his people to proclaim to the whole creation. A careful study of the expression, as it is used in the New Testament, will show that this interpretation is destitute of a substantial foundation.

The author attempts also an impossibility when he endeavors to find, as he says, an "important distinction between the church and the kingdom." The church, viewed from above, is the kingdom, the kingdom of God, the kingdom of Christ, the kingdom of heaven. This kingdom, seen from below, is the church. This is the only distinction that exists in the New Testament teaching between the church and the kingdom.

"The Twentieth Century City" is a good book. It is well worth reading. If there is a man who can speak with authority concerning the city, that man is Dr. Josiah Strong. He has been for many years a patient and diligent student of the city as a problem in our modern civilization.

Especial attention is called to chapters V., VI., VII. and VIII., in which Dr.

ders the remedies for existing · far as they are what they be. B. B. T.

/ Methods for Missionary Com- valuable compilation of infor- aissionary meetings, published H. Revell Co., Chicago and Price, cloth, 25 cts.; 76 pages.

ver has written a new version of Leviticus, just published as of the Polychrome Bible, which of Dodd, Meade & Co., New

MAGAZINES.

nprovements are to be made in plant and in all departments of s Popular Monthly this fall.

or "Summer" number of the gazine is an enlarged one, and ıg and unusually attractive table

ıt feature of the August Chautau- ng article by Rev. Anna Howard omen in the Ministry," in which women not only must equal, but cel, men in the ministry before recognized. The article is well- shows portraits of some of the men of the profession.

ı of the Woman's Home Compan- t will find many stories and arti- ıl interest.

imer's Tribe" is the name of a ə published monthly at Denver, n the interest of punctuality."

ompany, Glasgow. Scotland, have e handbooks on the health and ırts of Scotland, together with ıteresting and valuable informa- ıts and others.

nmer number of St. Nicholas is ıble and timely articles. It opens of the navy, "Margery and the y Anna A. Rogers. Mr. E. B. ı. N., contributes an article on nd Armor of Our Navy," telling pons of offense and the means of ·h are so much in evidence these ogers describes in brief the man- ; and testing guns and armor and unt of the first time that a mon- inch cannon was fired in America.

t number of The Century has a tures of special timeliness, not- which the endeavor has been up The Century's standard in en- printing. Mrs. Mary Bradford l writes a striking romance of a rican dictator, the title of her 'Sangre de Cristo." Frederick commissioner in Porto Rico for n Exposition, contributes a paper nd of Porto Rico," in which he characteristics of the land and ıd tells of the vast resources of sgood Welsh, an American sugar- gs out new facts in "Cuba as ə Inside." Both of these articles trated. Walter Russell gives the ɗ "An Artist with Admiral Samp- ' with sketches from nature of ts and the capture of prizes. Sur- l George M. Sternberg, of the ; Army, discusses "The Sanitary of Havana." Dr. Sternberg possible to stamp out yellow fever demic diseases, but that the task great magnitude and expense.

FACTS AND FACTORS.

Lieut. S. F. Massey, U. S. A., of Sandusky, O., has been appointed agent by the War Department to superintend the transportation to Spain of the prisoners of war recently surrendered to Gen. Shafter.

The steamer Charles Nelson arrived at Seattle, Wash., July 25th, from St. Michael's with 173 passengers from Dawson and gold dust estimated all the way from $1,000,000 to $1,500,000.

It has been calculated that ordinary gunpowder on exploding expands about 9,000 times, or fills a space this much larger as a gas than when in solid form. The expansion of water into steam is 1,700 times its bulk.

The personal property assessment of Iowa fell off between $7,000,000 and $8,000,000 in 1898 as compared with 1897. The principal decrease is in the items of furniture, live stock and merchandise.

A violent shock of earthquake, lasting a minute, was felt July 24th at Concepcion, capital of the Chilean province of that name, and at Taloahuano, on the Bay of Concepcion, eight miles distant from Concepcion City, Chili.

The statement is made that the population of Spain is about 17,000,000; that of these 8,000,000 could not write; that 6,000,000 could neither read nor write, and that about one-half of the whole have no sure paying occupation.

The whalers imprisoned by ice at Point Barrows are now beyond reach of want. The government overland expedition, under command of Lieut. Jarvis, of the Bear, reached its destination March 29th, having traveled 1,500 miles over a country stream, with obstacles. The expedition left Cape Vancouver Dec. 17th, 1897.

Twenty bags of mail were seized at the Santiago postoffice on the day of the American occupation. It consisted of Spanish official and private correspondence. The Spanish customs authorities asked to have the mail bags turned over to them, but the request was refused, and the matter was sent to New York by the steamer Concho.

Carroll College, Waukesha, Wis., has received from Mr. and Mrs. Ralph Voorhees, of New Jersey, a donation of $50,000 on condition that $50,000 more be secured by Oct. 1st, and that $70,000 of the total sum be set apart as an endowment, the remainder to be expended for building and equipment. President Walter L. Ranking has received pledges of $6,000 toward the remaining $50,000.

The powder mill of E. T. Johnson, at Troy, Pa., was blown up, July 28th, and the owner, who was also the paying teller in the Pomeroy and Mitchell Bank, was killed.

Gen. Shafter reported 4,122 soldiers sick at Santiago, on the 27th of July; 542 of the sick have recovered and returned to duty.

A statement of the condition of the treasury, July 29th showed available cash balance, $262,758,062: gold reserve, $189,474,535.

Family Circle.

Habit-Making and Habit-Breaking.

"How shall I a habit break?"
As you did that habit make.
As you gathered, you must lose;
As you yielded, now refuse,
Thread by thread the strand we twist
Till they bind us neck and wrist,
Thread by thread the patient hand
Must untwine, ere free we stand;
As we builded stone by stone,
We must toil, unhelped, alone,
Till the wall is overthrown.

But remember, as we try,
Lighter every task goes by;
Wading in, the stream grows deep
Toward the centre's downward sweep;
Backward turn, each step ashore
Shallower is than that before.

Ah! the precious years we waste
Leveling what we raised in haste;
Doing what must be undone
Ere content or love be won!
First, across the gulf we cast
Kite-borne threads, till lines are passed,
And habit builds the bridge at last.

—*John Boyle O'Reilly, in the Christian Commonwealth.*

Only a Fisherman's Son.

BY ALFRED BRUNK.

CHAPTER I.

"No, Ethie, I tell you I won't put up with it any longer. You are fifteen years old and it is time for you to quit all such foolishness and go to work and help make a livin'."

"Well, but pa, you know you said—"

"No matter what I said, you good for nothin' whelp. You have never earned your salt. Go 'long now, and if I ever see you makin' another picture I will whip you within an inch of your life, just as sure as your name is Ethan Langdon," and with this, Lewis Langdon stalked into the house, while his son, Ethan, a fair-haired, freckle-faced boy, started slowly and with hesitating footsteps toward the fishing boat.

"Now, Paulie," said Mr. Langdon to his wife, "I won't have any more of Ethie's foolishness. You make him ten times worse than he would be, with all your pettin' and goin' on. But I'm agoin' to break him of it, if I have to break his neck." His face was livid with wrath and he trembled with indignation.

"No, Lewis," said his wife timidly, "I have not petted him. I have my hands too full with the young ones to pet anybody. I tell him that he ought to help make the living."

"Yes, and he shall do it. I can just talk my eyes out and it don't do no good, but I'll fix him as sure as my name is Lewis Langdon. Where's the lunch? A pretty time of day to get started. We won't get no fish this time, I can tell you."

His wife handed him the lunch bucket, and he strode out of the house with a heavy step, and walked down the path to the river. Mr. Langdon looked at his son angrily, with a set determination depicted on his countenance, while Ethan drew himself as far as possible away from his enraged parent.

Many years before, when Stephen Brown was a reporter for one of the large New York papers, he had been sent on an important expedition to Italy, where he had fallen in love with beautiful, accomplished Maria Caponi, whose father was a wealthy citizen of Florence. The old gentleman violently opposed the attentions of the young stranger, threatening to disinherit Maria if she married him. This only added fuel to the flame they called love, and although her father gave them repeated warnings, the young couple were married and went to Naples, where Maria had an uncle, her mother's brother, who gladly opened his doors to them. After a year of wedded bliss, a daughter came to share life's responsibilities with them, whom they named Paulina. When Paulina was six months old, Mr. Brown was recalled to New York, and they left Italy, Mr. Caponi positively refusing to see his daughter or granddaughter. When the gold excitement spread throughout the country, Mr. Brown severed his connection with the New York paper, and with his wife and child went to California. He was not successful in the mines, so going into the valley, he purchased a farm near the Sacramento River, a few miles south of Butte City. Paulina grew up in comparative ignorance, her mother having but a slight acquaintance with the English language, and feeling that any other education would be useless in the Wild West. When Paulina was eighteen, Lewis Langdon came "a sparkin'," and while he was coarse and ignorant, yet he was strong of limb and capable of many a hard day's work. As for Paulina, she also was unlearned, and as cultivated young men were scarce in that neighborhood, her parents consented to their marriage. Almost immediately after that event, Mr. Langdon moved to a little house situated upon the east bank of the Sacramento River, and began fishing for a living. The following summer a fair-featured, blue-eyed boy came to brighten their home, and they called him Ethan. Shortly after this, Mr. Brown, wornout with his many disappointments passed away from earthly scenes. Mrs. Brown, having already learned that the manners of her son-in-law were revolting to her sense of decency and propriety, refused their offer of a home with them, and rented her farm to a middle-aged couple who had no children, she continuing to occupy a portion of the farmhouse. When Mr. Langdon had offered to share his home with his wife's mother, he hoped she would invite them to move into the farm-house and take charge of the farm. When she had politely, but firmly, rejected his offer and rented her place to another, he declared she should never set her foot in his house again, which she never did. While he did not positively forbid his wife to visit her mother, he was so cross and surly when she did go, that she very rarely went. Mrs. Brown loved Ethan very dearly and had asked his parents to let him stay with her; but her request seemed to make Mr. Langdon more furious than ever. Ethan was a bright boy and learned his lessons readily when he had been permitted to attend school.

One day, while he was attending the district school near his home, the teacher, who had no appreciation of Ethan's capabilities, sent a note to Ethan's father, stating that while he always had his lessons, yet he spent too much time making pictures on his slate. At this, Mr. Langdon gave Ethan a very severe whipping and took him out of school, declaring that if he was too lazy to study, he would put him at a task where he would be compelled t work.

Ethan continued, however, to make pic tures whenever opportunity offered. H had drawn some on the fence near th house, but being severely punished for it he sought other material for his handiwork Mary Smith, a black-eyed girl living in the community, was a perfect angel in Ethan's eyes, but that most worthy damse made merry over the awkward boy's well meant attentions.

Never mind, Mary, your day is coming

Ethan and his father had been out in th boat about two hours, when Ethan looke down the river and saw a pleasure boa coming toward them. It was a small steam boat and was the prettiest he had ever seen

"Look, pa! What a fine boat," he exclaimed, forgetting for the moment hi father's anger.

"You tend to your business or I'll fine-boat you," said his father, whose ange now burst forth beyond control, and picking up a piece of iron which lay at his feet he hurled it at the boy with all his strength Ethan quickly noted his father's actions and dodged just as the missile whizzed past his head and splashed into the wate behind him.

"Ahoy, there, and reef your sails," said a pleasant voice just down the river, and Ethan and his father looked up. The little boat had come up and was within a few fee of them. "Have you any fish aboard?" said the man who was standing by the railing of the little pleasure craft. "My daughter says she must have some fish," and as he spoke he turned toward a delicate-looking girl who was standing by his side. She appeared to be about sixteen years o age, and while not actually ill, her colorless complexion showed that she had but a feeble hold upon life. Ethan mentally compared her with Mary Smith, and it is safe to say that Mary gained nothing by the comparison.

"Well," said Mr. Langdon, "I ain't had much luck, but I've got some cats and a few 'scalers.'" The gentleman bought a few fish and then invited Mr. Langdon and Ethan to come up and look at his craft, which they did, Ethan blushing scarlet as he looked at his patched clothes and bare feet. "Henderson is my name, Dr. Henderson they call me in Sacramento," said the man, "and this is my daughter, Ethel And your name is—"

"Langdon," said Ethan's father, "Lewis Langdon, the fisherman, everybody calls me. And this is my boy, Ethan, the laziest most good-for-nothin' boy around here." As he said this he scowled at Ethan in so fierce a manner that he involuntarily drew back a few steps.

"You don't say so?" said Dr. Henderson looking at Ethan. "He looks like a bright enough boy."

"Oh, he's bright enough, just lazy. His mother's people are Italian and I expect he has got some of their fool notions."

"Come, Mr. Langdon, and look at her engines," said Dr. Henderson. "Ethel you and Ethan can stand guard while we go below," and the two men disappeared

Ethan now looked at his shabby clothes Ethel had seen his father's cruel act and she sincerely pitied this bashful, blushing boy. "Surely," thought she, "if any one was ever ground under the iron heel of oppression this boy is."

He glanced shyly at her. "She is a regular angel," thought he. At least he said afterward that he thought so, but it is doubtful whether in the confusion of that moment he thought at all.

"Do you like fishing?" she asked finally. Why should he tell a lie to that fair being, and tell her that he did like fishing? Why should he tell her the truth and have her pity him? But she had asked a direct question, he would give her a direct answer.

"No, I don't like it," and his face flushed with shame and mortification as he spoke. She noticed it, and asked gently:

"What would you like to do?"

Again he hesitated. How could he tell her the desire that was consuming his young life. Would not she laugh at him as all his acquaintances did? Yes, even Mary Smith laughed at him and called him a fool. But he would tell her the truth. Everybody thought he was crazy and she would think so, too, but he must tell her. "I want to make pictures," said he confusedly. She was surprised. She knew that he was out of harmony with his surroundings, but she had not thought of this.

"Come, Ethan, we have wasted time enough here," said his father, and they went to their own boat.

"Papa," said Ethel, as they went on up the river, "that boy is very unhappy."

"Well, well, my daughter, the world is full of unhappy people. Even my own peach-blossom has her unhappy days, and I am not sure but this is one of them. Alack, and hey-day! Don't be so pensive, Ethel."

"Now, papa, you are playing," said the girl, seriously. If that boy is permitted to stay where he is his life will be ruined. His father is repulsive and brutal, and he confessed to me that he abhorred fishing. Not because it is a dishonorable business, but because he wishes to be a painter."

"A painter!" and the doctor gave a long whistle. "A painter from the fishing-smacks of the Sacramento!" Why, Ethel, you are sentimental to-day."

"Papa, don't you remember that his father called him lazy and good-for-nothing and that his mother's people were Italian, and that he feared he had gotten some of their fool notions? Now, don't you know, papa, that no other people in the world can paint as the Italians can?"

"Why, that is true enough of some Italians," answered Dr. Henderson, "but for all that, not every Italian who is dissatisfied with his work, would make a good painter."

"Certainly not, papa, but when anybody has the intelligent look of that fisherman's son, no matter of what nationality he is, he ought to be given a chance to develop himself."

"So he should, my child, so he should," said her father, "and when we go back down the river, we will have a talk with him, and see whether he seems to have any talent."

But when a few hours later, they came to the place where they had seen the fisherman and his son, no sign of them or their boat could they see anywhere. And after scanning the river up and down, and from bank to bank they regretfully gave up the search and continued their homeward journey.

CHAPTER II.

The next two years were very hard ones for Ethan. His father became more and more severe with him, his mother dared not interfere in his behalf, and all the young people laughed at what they termed his "fool notions." He had tried two or three times to keep company with Mary Smith, but that young lady only held him up to further ridicule. It was not often that he could see his grandmother, Mrs. Brown. One afternoon, when his father was laid up with rheumatism, he stole out from the house and going to the river, took out one of the little boats and went to see her. She lived about three miles further up the river, and was always much pleased to have him come. He told her his troubles fully and freely. "Never mind, my boy, it will all come out right," she told him. "My uncle Bartolini Caponi was a noted painter in Italy. Some way will be opened to you, my dear son, so don't despair." His grandmother's words gave him great encouragement and he went home feeling more hopeful than he had for many a day. The next day "Shady" Merton, a young neighbor of the Langdons, was assisting Ethan with his work, as Mr. Langdon was unable to be out.

There, papa, as sure as I live, that's Ethan Langdon," said Ethel Henderson a few hours after the young men had gone to the river. "Now, papa, I want you to speak to him."

"So I will, my child, so I will," replied Dr. Henderson. Ethan and "Shady" had noticed the boat and bowed to the gentleman and lady whom Ethan recognized at once.

"Hello, Ethan, how are you?" called out the doctor. "Shady" looked on in surprise. That Ethan had an acquaintance, even though so slight, with such fine people as those in the other boat, he had never imagined possible.

"Come up, Mr. Langdon, and tell us how you are," said Dr. Henderson.

Ethan looked around quickly at these words, thinking for the moment that they had been addressed to his father. Then realizing that he was meant, he nervously ascended into the other boat.

"Come around on this side" said the doctor, leading him away where they would be out of sight and hearing of "Shady" Merton.

"Didn't you call that young man "Shady," just now?" he asked of Ethan. "That's a queer name, isn't it?"

"Yes, sir, said Ethan, "but I don't know what it means. Some say that he will steal, though, when he gets a chance."

"Ah, yes, that explains it, I have no doubt. Now, Ethan," continued Dr. Henderson, "my daughter tells me that when she saw you before, you were very much dissatisfied with your occupation. Is that so?"

Ethan glanced at Ethel. She had grown somewhat larger, but seemed delicate as ever. Looking at the doctor he said, "Yes, sir." Then, half ashamed, he let his eyes rest upon the rippling waters of the river.

"And what do you wish to do?" asked Dr. Henderson, kindly.

"I want to make pictures, sir," replied Ethan, half apologetically, half defiantly.

"Have you much education?" asked the doctor looking at him intently.

"Some, but not much," replied Ethan bitterly. "I didn't get much chance to go to school."

"Where is your father?" asked the doctor.

"At home, sir, laid up with rheumatis," said Ethan.

Inquiring of Ethan the way, he told the pilot where he wished to go, and soon they were at the landing near Ethan's home. Bidding Ethan to remain on the boat with Ethel, the doctor walked up the path to the house. The children had seen him coming and had scampered away to the house to tell them that "a fine city chap was comin'."

Mrs. Langdon met him at the wide-open door and told him to "come in, if you can get in for the dirt." He walked in and found Mr. Langdon on a bed in one corner of the room.

"How do you do, Mr. Langdon?" said he, "I am sorry to see you afflicted like this."

"Oh, its nothin' but this everlastin' rheumatis," replied Mr. Langdon. "It bothers me a sight here lately. But how did you ever get in here?"

"I was coming up the river with my daughter, and we saw Ethan, and he told us you were laid up with rheumatism, so I thought I would run in and see you. I know doctors are not expected to call upon sick people until they are sent for, but I count you as one of my friends, and I couldn't let you lie here and suffer, when I have a medicine which I know will cure you. I am going to have you all right in less than a week, and you will never have rheumatism again."

"I wish to goodness, doctor, I could get somethin' to help me, for it not only hurts me mighty bad, but it keeps me from my work, which is my livin'."

"Yes, yes," said the doctor, fixing up some medicine, but we will stop all that pain and make a well man of you in a week's time. Here," he held the preparation to Mr. Langdon's lips, "take this," and the sick man swallowed it. After twisting his face into various shapes, and calling for water, he settled down in a few moments and declared that he felt better already.

"Mr. Langdon," said the doctor, drawing a chair up close to the bedside, and sitting down, "I want an office boy. Can you let Ethan go and stay with me?"

Had a large wave swept up from the river and filled the room in which they were sitting, Ethan's father and mother could not have been more astonished. The children slipped out of the room, ran down to the river and called out to Ethan that "the city chap was goin' to take him away," leaving that young man very much mystified.

"We can't spare Ethan," said his father, as soon as he had recovered himself sufficiently to speak, which was a very odd thing for Mr. Langdon to say, considering that Ethan was "a lazy good-for-nothin' whelp" who never earned his salt.

But some people do say some queer things sometimes.

"He hasn't any clothes fit to wear in the city," said Mrs. Langdon, a feeling of motherly pride welling up in her bosom, at the thought that this fine-looking gentleman wished to have her son.

"That could be easily remedied," said Dr. Henderson. "If you will permit me to express myself, I will tell you something which I think you ought to know."

"Say whatever you please, Dr. Henderson," said Mr. Langdon, whose pains were greatly lessened as a result of the medicine which the doctor had given him, and consequently he felt very grateful.

"Well, it is this," said Dr. Henderson. "Ethan is not a lazy boy. On the contrary, he is bright and active and very persistent, even when the greatest obstacles are placed in his way. Is it not so, Mr. Langdon?"

"If you mean that fool notion of his about makin' pictures, it is so, and all the worse for him," said Mr. Langdon, his anger rising.

"Exactly," said the doctor, and you can't make a fisherman of him, if you were to try it for fifty years. Not because he feels that he is too good for the business, or that it is beneath him, but because his thoughts are wholly filled with the desire to be a painter."

"Then if that is the case he would be of no use to you as an office boy," triumphantly replied Mr. Langdon. "If his wantin' to be a painter crowds out fishin', it would crowd out everything else. Hi, I've got you there, Mr. Doctor," and he chuckled, as he thought how he had worsted the doctor in argument.

"Not so, Mr. Langdon, and I will tell you why. He would go into my office understanding that it was a stepping-stone on the road to success. That it would give him a chance to visit the different collection of paintings in the city. That everything he saw and heard would be training his eye and ear for his future work. Then he would have the stimulus of kindred spirits. All this would strengthen him and he could and would work with ever-increasing energy and ambition toward the one great desire of his life, namely, to be a painter. But how is it here? If he could be made to feel that every day he spent in a fishing boat he was just that much better prepared to enter his life-work of painting, he would joyfully take up the work, for he would feel that the harder he worked at fishing the sooner he would become a painter. But he has had his desire to become a painter ridiculed, while fishing has been held up before him as the only thing worthy of his serious thought, until he has become disgusted with the whole fishing business."

Mr. Langdon was silent. The truth of Dr. Henderson's words burned into his mind, and he slowly, but surely, grasped the fact, that for years he had treated his first-born son with the most cruel injustice. Rising up in the bed he clasped the doctor's hand in his own, and while tears of penitence stood in his eyes, he said:

"Dr. Henderson, I am called a hard man, and I confess to you I'm not a saint. But I will say this day, that if some one had talked to me years ago as plain as you have just now, that my life might have been different. I see now that I have treated my own boy very wrong, when I thought all the time that he was a mistreatin' me and a feelin' above his father's business. But I see it all now, I see, I see," and he sank wearily back upon his pillow and drew the sheet up over his eyes, as if to shut out the dreadful sight.

(CONCLUDED NEXT WEEK.)

Old Church, Va.

Little Things Count.

Bookkeeping has been reduced to such an exact science in the big metropolitan banks that the clerks are expected to strike a correct balance at the close of each day's work, no matter if the transactions run into the millions of dollars. When the books fail to balance, the whole force of the bank is put to work to discover the error; and no clerk starts for home until it is discovered, whether it amounts to 2 cents or $2,000. Generally a quarter of an hour will bring the mistake to light; but sometimes the hunt is kept up until late in the night.

Such a search was being conducted in a New York bank, located in the vicinity of Wall Street. Forty-five cents were missing. At 6 o'clock, not a trace of the errant sum had been discovered. Dinner was sent in for the whole force from an adjoining restaurant, and, after half an hour's rest, the search was again taken up. Midnight came, but still no clew. So sandwiches and coffee were served.

"Hello!" said a clerk. "The National Bank people are working to-night, too. Guess they're in the same box."

Sure enough, the windows of the bank across the street were brilliantly lighted. The incident was soon forgotten when the wearying hunt after the elusive 45 cents was resumed. Shortly after 1 o'clock in the morning, as they were about to give up for the night, a loud rapping was heard at the front door of the bank.

"Hello! hello! what's the matter?" called the cashier through the keyhole.

"Matter, you chumps! Why, we've got your old 45 cents! Come along home to bed!"

Outside stood the crowd of clerks from the neighboring bank. It appeared that, in making a cash transaction, one of the banks had paid the other 45 cents too much. As a result, half a hundred men had worked for nine hours, and the search was only ended then because a bright clerk, noticing the light in the bank opposite, shrewdly guessed the cause, hunted up the cash slip, and discovered the error.—*Harper's Round Table.*

tone.
TON, D. D.
; the seers,
e years;
aim,
n flame;
his voice is

led.

he free,
ea,
every wave,
their grave;
e the God
ly hero trod.

is supreme,
m;
n life's long

oom;
his 'scutch-

virtue came.
telligencer.

n.

er, but by my
h. 4:6.

great irriga-
in the valley
it made into
as an insuf-
canal. The
the machin-
Where was
r and indus-
grave. The
inery all in-
ain stood in
d not be con-
power—no

wflakes fell
here was an
vapor lying
their rocky
es wrapped
s lying fast
of their own
ater, in the
mountains,
was so much
rgy of posi-
was capable
ed an equal
r to produce
d. The old
to the north
wind blew
s, and piled
d pushed it
, and tossed
until it was
drop of water
he mill. In
in the canal
me the north

ade, the mill
to the sun.
umed disin-
ce to render
egan to pour
and snow on
te the tiny
oned, and to
available for
mill. Little
the sides of
ing, formed

larger streamlets, and these, as they sped on their way, became a river, from which water was diverted into the canal, the mill-wheels began to whir, and flour was manufactured to supply the hungry people with bread—the staff of life—and all was due to the fact that potential energy had been converted into actual force and properly applied.

APPLICATION.

The beneficent possibilities of human nature, like the potential energy of the snow on the mountains, is beyond the ability of man to measure when fully developed and properly directed. But this latent power for good cannot be made available by harsh means—"not by might, nor by power, but by my Spirit, saith the Lord of hosts." It is the truth when preached in love, as directed by the Holy Spirit, that develops the potential powers of the human heart, and makes them available for good.

Phoenix, Ariz.

Strange Bible Facts.

The learned Prince of Granada, heir to the Spanish throne, imprisoned by order of the crown for fear he should aspire to the throne, was kept in solitary confinement in the old prison at the Place of Skulls, Madrid. After thirty-three years in this living tomb, death came to his release, and the following remarkable researches, taken from the Bible and marked with an old nail on the rough walls of his cell, told how the brain sought employment through the weary years:

In the Bible the word "Lord" is found 1,853 times.

The word "Jehovah" 6,855 times.

The word "reverend" but once, and that in the ninth 111th Psalm.

The eighth verse of the 97th Psalm is the middle verse of the Bible.

The ninth verse of the eighth chapter of Esther is the longest.

The thirty-fifth verse, eleventh chapter of St. John is the shortest.

In the 107th Psalm four verses are alike—the eighth, fifteenth, twenty-first and thirty-first.

Each verse of the 136th Psalm ends alike.

No names or words with more than six syllables are found in the Bible.

The thirty-seventh chapter of Isaiah and nineteenth chapter of Second Kings are alike.

The word "girl" occurs but once in the Bible, and that in the third verse, third chapter of Joel.

There are found in both books of the Bible, 3,538,483 letters; 773,693 words; 31,373 verses; 1,189 chapters and 66 books.

The twenty-sixth chapter of the Acts of the Apostles is the finest chapter to read.

The most beautiful chapter is the 23d Psalm.

The four most inspiring promises are John 14:2; 7:37; Matt. 9:28, and Psalm 37:4.

The first verse of the fifth chapter of Isaiah is the one for the new convert.

All who flatter themselves with vain boasting should read the sixth chapter of Matthew.

All humanity should learn the sixth chapter of St. Luke, from the twentieth verse to its ending.—*Our Sunday Afternoon.*

Sunday School.

THE CHILD AT SHUNEM.*

HERBERT L. WILLETT.

Elisha has less of mystery in his character than his master. One is able to understand him better. He comes and goes continually on his tours from one center of prophetic activity to another. Carmel, Gilgal, Jericho, Samaria were places visited often by him, the last because it was the capital, where the prophet seems to have been held in high respect. He was a young man of enthusiasm, and the work left him by Elijah was great. He was of a genial and kindly nature, and drew the people to him as Elijah had never done. To be sure he was capable of sudden anger, as when he cursed the lads who ridiculed his tonsured head (2Kings 2:23-25), but he was held in such reverence by the people that his curse was popularly believed to have brought swift death to the offenders.

Among the friends he formed was a household at Shunem. The man was a landowner and evidently rich, and his wife a person of influence accordingly. She noted the prophet's frequent journeys past their home, and he accepted her repeated invitations to partake of their hospitality. She suggested to her husband the plan of making an additional chamber for Elisha's use; and soon this was done. A bed, a table, a stool and a candlestick completed its modest furnishings, and here the prophet regularly found rest, while his servant, Gahazi, was cared for without.

This "prophet's chamber," was a source of blessing to that household. How much of benediction has come to many a house in which a room is set apart to such ministries of hospitality! Those who can look back to a Christian home in which frequent visits of this kind were made by preachers of the gospel; when the meal times and the evenings were spent in conversation upon the highest themes of our holy faith, and where it was a joy to welcome the men and women who came, indeed like "angels unawares," have a treasure of memory that will be evermore precious to them. It may be feared that this old-fashioned grace of hospitality is too much neglected in these later days, as travel is more rapid and life more urgent. But is there not something lost in the change? They may well congratulate themselves whose homes were "the preachers' stopping-places," and whose fathers and mothers were saints of the old school, hospitable, charitable, lovers of the word of God.

And the blessing came to the household at Shunem. The prophet, who stood on good terms with the powers of the state, asked the woman if she desired introduction at court or advancement in rank. She modestly replied that she was content to dwell with her neighbor people of the village. Then Gahazi suggested that as they had no son, such a gift would be the greatest of blessings. No Hebrew family was content to be childless. Every woman looked forward longingly to motherhood, not alone as the discharge of a debt to her people, but as the fulfillment of her life's highest privilege. To be childless was the most dreaded of fates. We are realizing today that the duty and privilege of woman is not found in any one state of life. It is not wifehood or motherhood or spinsterhood, but *womanhood* that is needed. Nevertheless it is evident that the joy and pride, the culture and discipline, the responsibility and glory of motherhood are being evaded by too many women to-day, for fear that their social life may be hampered by these limitations. One can only look with sadness and pity on a home where there are no children, a sadness and pity the deeper if that condition is the result of deliberate choice.

When the promise of the child came to the Shunammite, she could not believe that the prophet was serious. Long years had left her hope behind. But the promise came true. The boy was born and grew to be a necessary element in that home. How much is added to the life of a family with the coming of the child! A new vision is opened, a new affection grows which strangely enough does not diminish, but deepens the old. A new schooling is begun in which the child is the teacher, and parents are the students. A new vision of God is disclosed, for the deepest meaning of his life is suggested by his fatherhood. It is a sad thing to lose a child; but it is a sadder thing not to have the experience of a parent, even if it does not last —and does it not last? Even if our own child does not abide with us, has not something entered our lives which cannot disappear, but makes us forever parental and tender to all orphaned and unloved children, teaching us that God never intended us to love only our own children, but all "his little ones?"

It was just this tragedy of death which swept into the little home at Shunem. The boy went to the fields to see the reapers, and fainting in the blaze of the harvest sun, called to his father, who, not perceiving the fatal character of the sunstroke, sent him by a servant to his mother. Upon her distress through the hours of that morning we are not to look. But at noon she took the little body to the chamber of the prophet, and feeling that even in her husband there was no help to call back the dead, she hastened to the man of God. To the inquiry of Gahazi as he met her, she would say nothing. Her message was not for the servant, but the master. Her prostration before Elisha, and her broken words told the story.

The prophet, unaware before of her trouble, thought that his servant might, perhaps, by the use of the prophetic rod, restore the child. But the woman would not leave till Elisha himself consented to go. Meantime the servant, bidden to make the utmost speed and to salute no one by the way, where salutations were so elaborate and lengthened, hastened to Shunem, only to fail. Returning, he met the mother and the prophet. As soon as the house was reached, Elisha shut himself into the room with the dead child, and then began a struggle between life and death. He was a man of God, a prophet of the Lord, but it was not for him to call back the dead with a word as Jesus was to do. More desperate was the contest. He threw himself upon the body, using all his vitality to warm it. Then walking to and fro to gain fresh warmth and power himself, he returned to the struggle. At last he seized the child in his arms and embraced him many times (see R. V. *Margin*) and at last the child came back to life. It was no easy task. The prophet had wrestled with death as with a monster of the forest and had conquered. The boy was given to his speechless and grateful mother, and a great miracle had been wrought in Israel.

SUGGESTIONS FOR TEACHING.

In our times of trouble it is only to God, and those who can speak for him, that it is worth while to go. In the midst of a busy life the prophet had time to attend to the trouble of a woman of Israel; has not God time for us? The appeal of the soul is always to the highest source of power; who should be satisfied with less than the best? It is better to have loved and lost than never to have had the object of love. When we are engaged in divine work we have no time for formalities or unnecessary trifles. Even so small a thing as a prophet's staff may at times be of mighty power. Why did Gahazi fail? Perhaps because of his own sordid nature, which was afterwards disclosed. The prophet's prayer was the first act in preparation for his struggle with death. It is only by contact that life can be given; this is as true to-day in social regeneration as then in the raising of the child.

*Bible-school lesson for August 14, 1898.—The Shunammite's Son (2 Kings 4:25-37). Golden Text—Cast thy burden on the Lord and he shall sustain thee. (Psa. 55:22.) Lesson Outline—1. The Shunammite's Journey (25-28); 2. The Servant's Attempt (29-31); 3. The Prophet's Miracle (32-37).

Christian Endeavor.

BY BURRIS A. JENKINS.

TOPIC FOR AUGUST 14.

EXALT CHRIST.

(Matt. 21:1-11.)

Jesus said: "I, if I be lifted up will draw all men unto me." How startlingly true that has proven! The attractive power of that life is greater than that of any other. And all the exaltation that is needed to bring men to his feet is simply the exaltation of uplifting. Let him once be lifted up to view, and it is sufficient to magnetize men.

Hence it was that Jesus' one great message to men was the cry "Follow *me*." He preached other things to be sure, but his principal message was to preach himself. His constant purpose was to fix men's attention on himself. When they began thinking of other men and other things, he would bring them back again to contemplation of himself. "What is that to thee, follow thou *me*." "*I* am the way, and the truth, and the life. He that hath seen *me* hath seen the Father." It was Jesus' own person that he constantly held up to view.

It is certainly striking that this egoism of the Master never becomes egotism. Perhaps there is nothing more offensive, generally, in a man's character than constant self-exaltation, and yet somehow this rule does not bear in Jesus' case. No man is ever repelled from Christ to-day because of his high claims for himself. This is convincing evidence of his supremacy and the justice of his assertions regarding himself. Even unbelievers seldom charge him with conceit. Is this not tacit evidence that his high claims are, even in the hearts of those who refuse to acknowledge him, justified? There is nothing repellant about Christ's egoism. The more he talks of himself, the more we draw closely to his feet, and look up into his eyes, as Mary did at Bethany, and hang upon his words.

Furthermore, Jesus does not tell us much about the mystery in which he was surrounded. He gave little ground for the spinning of theories regarding himself. He gave no system of theology about his person.

Perhaps this is the reason why there are so many different views of this marvelous, mysterious person. He never solved the mystery in so many words. He called attention to *himself*, and formulated no philosophical theories *about* himself. So the right attitude for us now, it seems, would be to exalt *him*, and let theories *about* him go.

"If Jesus Christ is a man,
And only a man, I say
That of all mankind I will cleave to him,
And to him I will cleave alway.
If Jesus Christ is a god,
And the only God, I swear
I will follow Him through heaven and hell,
The earth, the sea and the air."

This attitude of Richard Watson Gilder is the attitude, it appears, of our age. We are learning that we cannot penetrate the mystery of Christ's union with the Father, and that we ought to lift him up, himself, his person, his beauty, his strength, his purity, his divinity and behold *him*.

It is in this that Christianity is destined to triumph over all other religions, that it is the religion of a person. As long as we are true to that person and do not wander from him, we shall go on to the conquest of the world. It is in times when the church has been true to Christ that it has advanced. It was when the little band at Antioch became known as Christians that they began to grow. It was because Paul preached Christ that he won the Pretorium and the Roman world. On the other hand, it was when certain modern religious bodies forsook the exaltation of Christ and preached philosophy that they grew cold and dwindled. It is these religious bodies to-day which exalt the master that are drawing all men unto them. No sermon is so effective as the sermon that exalts Christ. There are as many ways of preaching him as there are preachers; but there is just one message that all the people will hear eagerly and drink of, as thirsty children in the desert, and that is the message about the Master.

"Subtlest thought shall fail and learning falter,
Churches change, forms perish, systems go,
But our human needs they will not alter,
Christ, no after-age shall e'er outgrow.
Yea, Amen! O changeless One, Thou only
Art life's guide and spiritual goal,
Thou the light across the dark vale lonely,
Thou the eternal haven of the soul."

The best way to exalt Christ is to live his life. "Herein is my Father glorified," he says, "that ye bear much fruit, so shall ye be my disciples."

Any life upon which falls the shadow of the cross, the cross of *his* uplifting, becomes glorified thereby and ever—O, think of the greatness and the wonder of it!—adds to his glory. It was only a dusty, painless, rusty old wire screen over a window in a humble cottage home. The rain was falling, but a light was shining outside—an arc-light, and the old screen with its dust and its rain-drops was lit up in a resplendent glory, while the crossing wires, beneath the strong rays of the light, formed as if in fire, the holy sign, the sign of the cross of Christ. And so can any humble life, however dusty and however poor, soiled, apparently, with rust and rain, be transformed into a thing of beauty and of brightness by the cross of Christ, the light and glory of the world.

Preachers Should Tell their People.

Every preacher should tell his people, and especially the young, all about the Bethany C. E. Reading Courses. Full information may be had gratis, by dropping a card to the Bethany C. E. Company, 798 Republic Street, Cleveland, O. Begin at once to plan for systematic reading among the people of your church.

Marriages.

ALEY—IRELAND.—At the residence of of the bride's parents, 1627 Lincoln Ave., Denver, Colo., on the evening of July 12th, Miss Anna Pearl Ireland was married to Claude B. Aley, of Wichita, Kan. F. D. Pettit, of Chillicothe, Mo., officiating.

KNOX—MOUNTJOY.—At the First Christian Church of Charleston, July 24th, Mr. Lawrence O. Knox, of Pine Bluff, Ark., and Miss Lizzie Belle Mountjoy, of Charleston, Ill., were united in marriage, the pastor, T. W. Burnham, officiating.

Obituaries.

[One hundred words will be inserted free. Above one hundred words, one cent a word. Please send amount with each notice.]

BOYDEN.

Mrs. Mary W. Boyden, youngest daughter of General W. Lipscomb, late of Lexington, Ky., was born in Madison Co., Ky., Nov. 11th, 1842, died at Slater, Mo., July 10th, 1898. She was married to J. M. Boyden, Aug. 9th, 1870, in Pike Co., Mo. She was the mother of six children, only one of whom survive her. For many years Sister Boyden had been a faithful member of the Christian Church, exemplifying the teaching of Christ by a beautiful, godly life. May the God of all comfort sustain and cheer the hearts of those who mourn her absence!

G. E. Shanklin, Pastor.

Slater, Mo., July 23, 1898.

FORD.

Amanda E. Ford died at her home in Thomas County, Kan., July 2nd, 1898; born Oct. 12th, 1854, near Lafayette, Ind., age 43 years, eight months, 20 days. With her parents she moved to Macon County, Ill., in 1863. She united with the Church of Christ at the age of 17 and continued a faithful Christian until death. She was married to S. W. Ford, Dec. 26th, 1874; to them were born five children, three girls and two boys. The family moved to Thomas County, Kan., the spring of 1887, where they now live, mourning the loss of a kind and loving mother and a faithful wife. The funeral services conducted by the undersigned.

Wm. Burkley.

FIELDS.

Byron Fields was born in Lawrenceville, Ill., and died at Morgan, Tex. His home was in Colorado Springs, Colo. He was in the twenty-sixth year of his age. He was the only son of Judge and Mrs. Margaret Fields. Three sisters mourn his untimely death. Byron became a Christian some years ago under the ministry of J. P. Lucas. At the time of his death he was employed in the building of a railroad in Texas. He fell from a caboose car when the train was in motion and was instantly killed, Friday, July 15. At the moment of his death he was in the discharge of his duty. His business position was one of unusual responsibility for a person so young, but he was faithful and efficient. The popularity of Byron Fields in his home town and where he was best known, was very great. There is profound and universal sorrow over his death. But those who mourn do not sorrow as do those who have no hope. He lived and died a Christian.

B. B. T.

GANNAWAY.

Emma Catherine Gannaway was born at Palmyra, Mo., June 27, 1844, and died at Hannibal, Mo., July 21, 1898. Her maiden name was Johnson. In 1866, at New London, Mo., she married W. R. Gannaway, who preceded her into rest last February. She leaves a daughter, Miss Lizzie, and many other relatives who will miss her counsel and companionship. In her girlhood she gave her heart to Christ, and through all life's trials and pleasures she has sustained an unfaltering faith in him. In her suffering she never complained, and, giving advice to those about her, passed sweetly into undisturbed peace.

Levi Marshall.

Hannibal, Mo., July 24, 1898.

HUNTER.

Sarah A. Smith was born near Hermon, Ill., July 21, 1857, and died at Abingdon, Ill., July 15, 1898. She was married to James W. Hunter, Nov. 16, 1876. To them two children were born, Isadora, who died at a tender age, and Charles M., who reached his eighth birthday June 29. 1898. Mrs. Hunter united with the Christian Church in early life, and never faltered in the faith. Mr. and Mrs. Hunter had just moved from Peoria to Abingdon to make the home of their old age, but within two short weeks she was called to her heavenly home. The funeral was conducted by the writer at Abingdon, Ill., July 17, 1898.

J. P. McKnight.

Peoria, Ill., July 20, 1898.

JOHNSON.

Nancy Sewell was born at Bowling Green, Ky., July 4th, married Dickson Johnson at Morton, Ind.; moved to Vinton, Ia., January, 1856. Died in the faith at Pitrodie, S. D., July 15th, 1898, was buried in Evergreen Cemetery, Vinton, Ia., July 17th, beside her husband. One daughter and three sons mourn their loss.

J. A. J.

KLEBERGER.

On Wednesday evening, July 20th, Mrs. Anna Hayden Kleberger, wife of the Rev. C. A. Kleberger, recently pastor at Ledrow, O., passed peacefully away at her home here. Her illness lasted for fifteen tedious, painful weeks. For the last six weeks she longed for rest. Her age was 39 years, two months and eighteen days. Her husband and two children, Bertha age 13 and Bruce, age 11, remain to cherish her memory. She lived a strong, helpful, Christian life. A simple funeral service was conducted at the home; no signs of mourning were seen about the house. We all know she had gone to her beautiful home.

S. H. Bartlett.

Painesville, O.

McPHERSON.

On the 5th day of July, 1898, at Springfield, Mo., the white spirit of Henry W. McPherson left its clay tenement, and went to join the general assembly and church of the first-born whose names are in the book of life.

Earth is poorer, but heaven is much richer because this eminent servant of God has been called to exchange worlds.

He was a faithful preacher of the primitive gospel, and an earnest defender of the faith once and forever delivered to the saints. He was born December 19th, 1811, and died July 5, 1898, aged 86 years, six months and 16 days. He lived to a good old age. His days and years were crowned with gospel holiness. The world has been made much better because he lived in it. In the year 1824, he removed to Fayette Co., Indiana, where he continued to reside for 11 years. When a lad, only 18 years old, he gave his heart to Christ, and united with the Baptist Church. On the 4th day of July, 1829, at the organization of the first church ever constituted in Indiana, pleading for a return to apostolic Christianity, and the reunion of all of God's people on the divine foundation, with a few others he renounced all human names and human creeds, and became a charter member of that organization. He lived to see that little band, who, on the 4th day of July declared themselves free to accept the gospel just as it had been revealed by the Holy Spirit and preached by men whose tongues were fired with the inspiration of God, become a mighty people, numbering in Indiana more than 100,000, and in the United States more than 1,000,000.

In the mighty triumphs of this blessed gospel no one rejoiced more than did Henry W. McPherson. In 1835 he removed from Fayette Co., to Liberty Township, Wabash Co., Indiana. He was one of eight persons who were the charter members of the Boundary Line Church, where he held his membership, until he removed to Springfield, Mo.

He was widely known, not only in Wabash Co., but in all the regions round-about. His name was a synonym of good wherever he was known. In the church, with other religious people, and among the world's people, all spoke of him as one of the very best men they ever knew. After many long years of happy acquaintance the writer can truly say that he never heard one person say an evil word of "Uncle Henry," as he was familiarly known. Truly he was a "living epistle, known and read of all men." Some years ago he removed to Springfield, Mo., where he continued to reside until called to exchange the cross for the crown, and to be with that Savior he loved so well and in whose service he found such sweet joy and such great delight. From Springfield comes the same testimony, concerning his godly life, and his devotion to that gospel he loved so well, and that for many years he preached so efficiently. We were not surprised when we heard that his death was a kingly triumph. He had fought a good fight; he had finished his course; he had kept the faith; and now the bright angels came to carry him to that land that is fairer than day.

"The trees of heaven rise before him, waving bright.
And the distant crystal waters flash upon his failing sight."

He lays his hand in the hand of his divine and ever adorable Guide and goes down through the parted waters of the cold river only to come up on the other side singing songs of triumph to that Savior who had redeemed him with his most precious blood.

"A holy quiet reigned around,
A calm which life nor death destroyed;
And naught disturbed the peace profound,
Which his unfettered soul enjoyed."

His aged and venerable companion and four children, with many relatives, together with the people everywhere, who knew him, mourn his death; and yet they mourn not as others having no hope. Farewell, my dear father in Israel, farewell, you have outrun us a little and gained heaven first, but by the grace of God we will meet you in that land of pure delight, where saints immortal dwell. Sweeter than the power of human words to describe, is the Master's "well-done," when our entrance is made in safety through the gates of jasper and of pearl.

The brethren at Springfield, Mo., took all that was mortal of our departed brother and covered it up in a turf-made dwelling in their beautiful cemetery, there to rest until the morning of the great day, when the redeemed shall come forth to have a body like our dear Lord, and to wear the starry crown. They will cover it over with the first sweet flowers of spring. They will remember his pure life, and will be better Christians because he lived among them.

Indiana mingles her tears with Missouri over the grave of "Uncle Henry."

"Servant of God well-done,
Rest from thy loved employ,
The battle's fought, the victory won;
Enter the Master's joy."

L. L. Carpenter.

Wabash, Ind.

NALLEY.

Died, at Elsberry Mo., July 17th, 1898, after a long, severe illness, Thomas Jefferson Nalley, in the 76th year of his age. Brother Nalley was born in Albemarle County, Va., in 1822. In 1835, came to Missouri. and in 1847 was married to Mary C. Martin, to which union twelve children were born, five having died in infancy, the others still living. More than fifty years ago he became a Disciple of Christ, and with a strong faith in God, "nothing doubting" he lived in an upper sphere, seldom attained by mortal man. Bro. Nalley did much for the cause of the Master in this county, "laboring both in faith and doctrine." Aged wife and sorrowing children, look up. God in his infinite love gave, his gift has been a benediction to you.. In his infinite goodness and mercy he has taken away; "Blessed be the name of the Lord." The writer preached the funeral, reading 90th Psalm.

R. L. Morton.

REEDER.

Sherman D. Reeder, a member of the Church of Christ at Stockton, Kan., died in the Sanitarium at Salina, Kan., June 14, 1898. He was born at Tipton, Ia., Jan. 31st, 1863. Moved to Kansas in October, 1878, was married to Lula Hall, June 29, 1884, whom he leaves with four children, a mother, three brothers and two sisters to mourn his untimely death. He said a short time before his death that his desire was that he might be spared to his little family, but if it was God's will that he should go, he was ready.

A. C. F.

nday-School & Christian Endeavor

Library + Books

he Days of Jehu. By J. B. Ellis. written and intensely interesting Bible nar- The lesson taught is that idolatry is ruin worship of God is life and peace. 189 pages. $1.00

g Saul. By J. Breckenridge Elis, f "In the Days of Jehu." As fascinating as and more interesting because it is true. The recites the history of Saul from the time s out to find his father's beasts until his t Gilboa, and so interesting is the narrative, begin a reading is to finish it. Illustrated imerous fine engravings, many of which ade esecially for this volume. Cloth $1.00

en Esther. By M. M. Davis. The ated, heroic and patriotic Queen of King is here portrayed by an ardent admirer. phic life is vividly told, and its rich lessons ssed home to the heart. Speculation and v give place to biographical and practical, the story seems as real and far more fas- than that of Joan of Arc. The book is a contribution to our literature, just now when iterest is being aroused among our Sunday- nd Endeavor Societies looking to the estab- of libraries in churches and Sunday-schools. ed with numerous engravings. Cloth $ .75

Wonders of the Sky, or, God's Exhibited in the Heavens. By W. J. Rus- 'he heavens declare the glory of God," and k leads the mind of the reader to contem- e beauty, grandeur, sublimity and wonders eavens, directing the mind to a better un- ling of the universe and greater reverence Creator. The subject is treated, not from ific standpoint, but in a popular style calcu- be easily understood by the young of our Bound in beautiful, illuminated cloth $ .50

ircuit of the Globe. By A. Mc- Illustrated. This author was sent on a tour world by the Foreign Christian Missionary . This book contains an account of the political and religious phases of the many visited by the writer. 384 pages. $2.00

oss the Gulf. By Mrs. N. M. Van- t. A story of the times of Christ. Many of at truths spoken by the Master are mingled istorical facts and traditions, showing that s the Savior of mankind. 238 pages. $1.00

ne with God. By J. H. Garrison. al of devotions, and contains forms of prayer e for private devotions, family worship and occasions. It is particularly well adapted wants of members of the Christian Endeavor . 244 pages. Cloth .... $ .75

the Rock; or, Truth Stranger than . By D. R. Dungan. The story of a struggle e Truth as it is found in Christ. It is a dis- of salvation from sin, the subject, mode ect of baptism, presented in such a way as h the understanding of the ordinary reader. es. Cloth $1.50

in Talks to Young Men on Vital By Peter Ainslie. A splendid book for to put into the hands of young men and . It abounds with wholesome advice on ng, the Theater, Dancing, Swearing, etc. .... $ .60

sionary Addresses. By A. McLean, c. of the Foreign Christian Missionary Soci- his work contains fourteen carefully prepar- esses, covering the important topics relating ions. It also contains fourteen portraits of eign missionaries. 298 pages. Cloth .. $1.00

ushtan. By Dr. J. R. Roe. A editable story, exposing the evil nature and l tendencies of the Roman Catholic Church. es. Cloth $1.00

Exiled Prophet; or, What John Patmos. By J. G. Encell. 35 Illustrations. s of lectures containing the author's inter- on of the Book of Revelation. 245 pages.. .... $1.25

Wonderful Works of Christ. By Willits. In this book the Matchless Deeds of rld's Mightiest Worker are graphically pre- many of which are appropriately illustrated. es. Cloth $1.00

us as a Teacher, and the Making New Testatament. By B. A. Hinsdale. An ting and original book on an inexhaustible , pointing out the method of instruction by at Teacher. A helpful book to every one, ess of their church relations. 330 pages. $1.25

Heavenward Way. By J. H. n. A popular book addressed to young ans, containing incentives and suggestions iritual growth, leading the young in the of life." 100 pages. Cloth .... $ .75

Studies In Acts; or, The New Testament Book of Beginnings. By W. J. Lhamon. A work that deals with things fundamental in the Christian system in a judicial spirit, among which are the First Sermon after the Ascension, First Church, First Persecutions, First Martyr, First Gentile Convert, First Missionaries, First History of the Holy Spirit, etc. 420 pages. Cloth ... $1.25

The Temptation of Christ. By J. B. Briney. An exposition of the devices of Satan and pointing out the way of escape. A capital book to put into the hands of young Christians. 154 pages. Cloth .... $ .75

Young Folks in Bible Lands. By B. W. Johnson. The story of the travels of the author in Palestine and Asia Minor, presented in such a way that the young reader may gather the facts concerning these historic countries. The book is dedicated to the "Young People's Society of Christian Endeavor." 400 pages. Cloth $1.50

Thirteen and Twelve Others. By B. O. Aylesworth. This is a story founded on the fact that a party of tourists are camping out in the Adirondacks and discover that the number present is *Thirteen*. The *Thirteen Stories* of the book show that the party had all things terminate to its advantage. It is a work of literary excellence, and the stories are highly interesting. 259 pages.
Cloth $1.25
Paper .... .50

America or Rome; Christ or the Pope. By John L. Brandt. 55 Illustrations. Contains information from authentic sources on the despotism of the Romish Church. 530 pages. Cloth $1.50

Talks to Bereans, By Isaac Errett. A series of eighteen sermons by this great author and preacher. Very helpful to those who "Search the Scriptures daily." 190 pages. Cloth $1.00

Life of Alexander Campbell. By T. W. Grafton. The life of this illustrious man written in an attractive style. The author took great pains to obtain all the facts he presents, and it is a reliable life of this great man. 234 pages. Cloth $1.00

Lessons in Soul-Winning. By E. H. Keller. This work contains many valuable suggestions in soul-winning, and will be very helpful to those who wish to aid the pastor in personal work. 184 pages. Cloth .... $ .75

Fiery Trials; or, A Story of an Infidel's Family. By R. H. Crozier. It is written in attractive language, full of dramatic interest, and teaches an important lesson. Cloth $1.50

Forty Years in China; or, China in Transition. By R. H. Graves. Illustrated. This work points out the hindrances in the past to the progress of China and details its immediate needs. Aside from the missionary features of the book it is a source of historical information. 316 pages. Cloth $1.50

Grandma's Patience; or, Mrs. James' Christmas' Gift. Illustrated. By Marie R. Butler. An interesting story, teaching a lesson of patience. 80 pages. Cloth .... $ .40

Half Hour Studies at the Cross. By J. H. Garrison. A Series of devotional studies on the Death of Christ, designed to be helpful to those who preside at the Lord's Table, and a means of spiritual preparation for all who participate. 275 pages. Cloth .... $ .75

Origin of the Disciples. By G. W. Longan. This work is more than a reply to Prof. Whitsett's book, "Origin of the Disciples of Christ." It is a broad, scholarly and dignified discussion of the fundamental principles of the movement begun by the Campbells and others. 195 pages. Cloth $1.00

The Life of Jesus. By Dr. Ferdinand Piper, Professor of Theology in Berlin. Translated from the German by Wm. F. Clarke. This is a compilation of articles presented on religious festival occasions. 310 pages. Cloth $1.00

After Pentecost, What? By James M. Campbell. One of the most quickening books on the Holy Spirit before the public, and it is calculated to dispel the error and teach the truth concerning the Spirit of God, and directing its readers into right relationship to this Spirit. 297 pages. Cloth ... $1.00

Life of Elder John Smith. By John Augustus Williams. A work of historical interest and importance. The biography of this wonderful character necessarily contains much of the history of the origin and progress of the Current Reformation, together making a valuable book for the young to study. 578 pages. Cloth $2.00

Bartholet Milon. By Fannie H. Christopher. This is a sequel to Duke Christopher. 99 pages. Cloth .... $ .40

Twenty Years Among the Mexicans. By Melinda Rankin. The experience of the first Protestant lady missionary in Mexico, told in an attractive style. 324 pages. Cloth $1.25

The Man in the Book. By Henry S. Lobingier. This is the life of Christ viewed from a poetic and philosophic standpoint, and for literary excellence is not surpassed in our church literature. 405 pages. Cloth $1.50

The Voice of Seven Thunders. By J. L. Martin. A series of eighteen well prepared lectures on the Apocalypse, giving a full and satisfactory explanation of the Vision on Patmos. 320 pages. Cloth $1.50

A Vision of the Ages; or, Lectures on the Apocalypse. By B. W. Johnson. A scholarly exposition of the Book of Revelation, showing great research and breadth of thought. 360 pages. Cloth $1.25

Autumn Leaves. By Mrs. M. M. B. Goodwin. A beautiful book containing the poems of this talented lady, so widely known among the Disciples of Christ. 176 pages. Cloth $1.00

Christian Missions. By F. M. Green. Contains historical sketches of missionary societies among the Disciples of Christ. 438 pages. Cloth $1.50

Dr. Carl Brown; or, True Success. By Mrs. M. F. Miles. This book well deserves a prominent place in every S. S. and C. E. Library, as it teaches a lesson to the young of *true success* in this life. Cloth $1.25

Edna Carlisle; or, Flossie's Violet. By L. Doyle. An elegantly written story which is pure, healthy and morally invigorating, and well adapted to the Sunday-school and Christian Endeavor Library. 390 pages. $1.50

Paul Darst; or, The Conflict Between Love and Infidelity. By D. R. Lucas. An interesting and thrilling romance, conveying a moral lesson applicable to every Christian. 206 pages. Cloth $1.00

Rose Carleton's Reward. By Margaret Frances. Illustrated. This is a story prominently bringing out the fact that true womanhood is always justly rewarded. 283 pages. Cloth $1.00

Rum, Ruin and the Remedy. By D. R. Dungan. This is a thorough discussion of the liquor traffic and the rum curse, and contains unanswerable arguments for Prohibition. 207 pages. Cloth $1.00

My Life is an Open Book. By Chaplain G. [illegible]ins. This book is to the memory of Berty G. Stover, the eloquent boy preacher of the Christian Church. The reader's own life will be much influenced by this book. Cloth $1.50

Walks About Jerusalem. By Isaac Errett. A work pointing out to the reader the landmarks, purity and glory of primitive Christianity. 212 pages. Cloth $1.00

The Divine Demonstration. By H. W. E[illegible]est. A Text-Book of Christian Evidences, presenting convincing arguments in favor of the Divine origin of the Christian religion. 401 pages. Cloth $1.50

The Story of an Earnest Life. By Mrs. Eliza Davies. An interesting account of a woman's adventure in Australia and two voyages around the world. 570 pages. Cloth $2.00

The Bible-Hand Book. By W. W. Dowling. An aid to the study of the Word of God, prepared for use by pupils and classes, and for use in the preparation of the Sunday-school lessons. 312 pages. Cloth $1.00
Boards .... $.75

Life of Knowles Shaw. By William Baxter. The history of a pure, noble and consecrated man. A careful reading of this book wil have an influence for good on the life of the reader. 237 pages. Cloth $1.25

Doctrines and Dogmas of Mormonism Examined and Refuted. By D. H. Bays. Every important question pertaining to the peculiarities of the Mormon doctrine is discussed and answered from a Biblical and philosophical standpoint. 460 pages. Cloth $1.50

Home Life and Reminiscences of A. Campbell. By his wife, Selina H. Campbell. An accurate account of this great man in his dealings with his family, and his every-day home life. 503 pages. Cloth $2.00

Hugh Carlin, or, Truth's Triumph. By J. H. Stark. A well-planned and well-developed religious story, dealing with some of the modern phases of religion in a very practical and striking manner. It takes high rank as a religious novel. 185 pages. Cloth. .... $ .75

Rosa Emerson; or, A Young Woman's Influence. By John Augustus Williams. A story of the Lodge, the Church and the School. It portrays the wonderful influence for good that a noble woman may exert on her own community. 878 pages. Cloth $1.00

ublished By

HRISTIAN PUBLISHING COMPANY, St. Louis, Mo.

Publishers' Notes.

LEARN MORE ABOUT JEHU.

The name of Jehu is prominently mentioned in the Sunday-school lesson for July 31st, of present quarter. Now is an opportune time to read that new, bright, fascinating and instructive book, entitled, "In the Days of Jehu." To many this book will be a search light thrown into the Sunday-school lessons, revealing the characters of Ahab, Jezebel and other notable persons connected with the present quarter's lessons. The book is valuable to the student of Old Testament history. The price is 75 cents.

Mrs. N. M. Vandervoort's late book, "Across the Gulf," is a story interwoven with gospel narrative and historical facts. The hero of the story is made to reject all teachings not sanctioned by the Master, and to adhere strictly to each and every commandment given by Christ. The book is beautiful in diction, unique in style and sound in morals and faith. The price of the book is $1.00.

"Organic Evolution Considered," by Alfred Fairhurst, Professor of Natural Science in Kentucky University, is highly recommended by competent judges who have carefully read this late scientific publication. Prominent among these may be mentioned Prof. W. M. Thrasher, of the University of Indianapolis, Indiana, from whose comment we give the following extract:

"A spirit of transparent candor pervades the book. The tone is judicially calm—that of a simple inquirer after truth. There is a noticeable absence of dogmatism. Concessions by opponents are fairly treated, and he makes wherever possible, the evolutionist himself draw his conclusions.

The voluminous excerpts from the best known evolutionists would alone make it instructive reading for the student.

The lucidity of arrangement, freedom from all ambiguity; the excellent literary form combine to make this volume very pleasant reading, aside from the great interest of the subjects discussed."

Our new publication, "Wonders of the Sky," by W. J. Russell, will be found interesting reading in regard to the wonders of the heavenly bodies. Aside from the information contained in this book, the reader cannot lay it down without a greater reverence for him whose glory is manifest in all the works of his hands. This little volume is bound in beautiful illuminated cloth and the price is 50 cents. We give the following Table of Contents: Preface, Introduction, The History of Astronomy, The Depths of Space, The Stars and their Number, Celestial Distances, Movements of the Stars, The Sun, Planets Nearest the Sun, Planets Farthest from the Sun, Asteriods, Are the Planets Inhabited? The Supreme Power.

IN THE DAYS OF JEHU.

J. Breckenridge Ellis, the author of this book, evinces an intimate acquaintance with both the people and times of which he writes, and he makes the good and bad qualities stand out very strikingly. The story is so well told that it is really fascinating. It freshens one's mind in the facts of history, and impresses important truths by historic examples. Jezebel, the wicked wife of Ahab, turned the heads of the nobles and made Israel bow down to Baal, and filled the land with iniquity. While Jehosaphat had some good traits of character, he committed a grievous blunder when he sanctioned the marriage of his son to the daughter of Ahab and Jezebel. Through this unholy alliance came the downfall and ruin of the kingdom of Judah. Jehu opposed Baal-worship and cleared the land of idols. He smote the idol-worshipers, but did not re-establish the worship of God. The land was stained with the blood of many wars, and there were many scenes of the most exciting character. Thus the book deals with a very important period of the Old Testament history.—*Gospel Advocate, Nashville, Tenn.*

A Curious Incident.

Once upon a time a certain good man was elected superintendent of a Sunday-school. He was far the best man for the place, and was indeed a very capable worker. If any one failed to do their part he was ready to do it. If any one backed out, he took their place. So in the process of time he came to be the principal feature of the school. In fact, it came to be that there was no school except such parts of it as he could manage and maintain. Almost no one else was doing anything. And it was not because he was selfish or self-important, for he was generous to a fault, and humble above all men. When he became the sole contributor to the school he was only sorry because he could give so little. And when he was filling nearly every office and doing most of the teaching, he merely bemoaned his inability to do more. He was sorry the rest were doing so little, but he stopped not on that account. When the end of the year came around it was so evident that he was the best man for the place, that he thought it as well to dispense with the formality of an election. The others either agreed, or seeing his great earnestness and ability were hushed into silence. After awhile the Endeavor Society came into existence, and no one else showing so great ability at managing things as he, it was unanimously agreed to elect him president. This office he has filled as faithfully as that of superintendent of the Bible-school. True not many helped in the work, but he knew it was a good work and ought to be done, and as no one else seemed willing to do it, he kept on. It soon became apparent that the semi-annual election was a farce, for there was no one else to fill the place, so this election was soon discontinued. He had long ago been elected chorister and elder without anything being said about his time of service, and his wife had become organist and President of the Ladies' Aid Society and C. W. B. M. and held them permanently. So now when the church had become so poor that they could no longer keep a pastor he was asked by some one to talk for them sometimes, and as he enjoyed talking, he accepted this added duty without more than a small show of modesty, and his cup became full to overflowing. Even now he felt so humble in his labors that he was not critical of his brethren, but earnestly strove to do his Master's will and bear his heavy burdens bravely. He was grieved sometimes when it came to his ears that some one had accused him of wanting to do all the work, for he did not want to do it, and was perfectly willing to allow every one to do their part, but rather than that the work should go undone he would do it all himself. And the work accomplished was then so small that he could honestly condemn himself for being unfaithful to the Master's cause, and often did he pray for strength that he might do more. How he finally learned that a leader's great duty was not to work, but to inspire workers, and to delegate to each his proper tasks, and how above all things he learned the necessity of submitting his position as leader to the vote of the people at regular intervals, must be told in another paper.

G. E. HARTLEY.

Bement, Ill.

Announcements.

The 10th annual convention of the Y. P. S. C. E. of the Galesburg District will be held at Cuba, Ill., August 19-21.

The annual convention of the First Christian Missionary District of Kansas, will be held at Reserve, August 23-25. An elaborate and interesting program including many important addresses and enjoyable exercises has been prepared for this convention. Each church in the district should be represented by its pastor and two or more delegates.

O. L. COOK, President.

Home Missions

FOR THE MONTH OF JULY, 1897.

Total No. Churches contributing	111
" " Individuals "	33
" " Other contributions	22
Total Am't contributed by Churches	$1,621.36
" " " " Individuals	821.11
" " Other contributions	520.31
Grand Total for July, 1897	$2,962.78

HOME MISSIONS FOR THE MONTH OF JULY, 1898.

Total No. Churches contributing	134
" " Individuals "	28
" " Other contributions	49
Total Am't contributed by Churches	$2,656.32
" " " " Individuals	103.15
" " Other contributions	435.38
Grand Total for July, 1898	$3,194.85

Number of new churches contributing, 68.
No. churches contributing an increased am't, 36.
Amount of gain for the month, $232.07.

BENJ. L. SMITH, C. C. SMITH, } Cor. Secs.
Y. M. C. A. Bldg., Cincinnati, O.

July a Good Month.

Comparing the receipts for *Foreign Missions* for the month of July with the corresponding month last year, shows the follwing:

Contributing:	1897	1898	Gain
Sunday-schools,	695	751	56
Churches,	65	59	Loss, 6
Christian Endeavor,	15	16	1
Individuals,	39	30	Loss, 9
Amount,	$14,806.65	$19,261.08	$4,454.43

The books close for the current year September 30th. Let us press forward to the $100,000 by collections only by that date. Send to

F. M. RAINS, Treas.

Box 750, Cincinnati, O.

THE
RISTIAN-EVANGELIST.

A WEEKLY FAMILY AND RELIGIOUS JOURNAL.

l. XXXV. August 11, 1898 No. 32.

CONTENTS.

ORIAL:
rrent Events........................163
e Problem of Christian Unity... ...164
uses of the Name Christian........ 165
e Refuge of the Saints.... 166
itor's Easy Chair...................166
rrent Religious Thought.. 167
estions and Answers................167
INAL CONTRIBUTIONS:
iritualism; or the Witch of Endor.—
. J. Lhamon 168
me or Jerusalem, Which?—S. K.
hellenberger 169
ganic Evolution Considered.—Robt.
. Mathews. 170
urch Organism and Government.—
. E. Cobbey .. .. .170
ESPONDENCE:
w York Letter.......... 174
heeling Through England.......... 174
naha Letter.... 175
nerating in Japan.......... 175
urch Buildings 175
ba and Porto Rico Markets.........176
tler College Day at Bethany Park..176
Glance at Michigan 177
ligious Work in the University of
Virginia...... ... .178
ES AND NEWS:
autauqua Letter....................179
Unanswered Prayer... 179
. Louis Letter.... 180
innesota.... 180
LY CIRCLE:
ter a Battle (poem). 184
ly a Fisherman's Son.......... .. 184
an Hard on Him (poem)....... 186
xt Stories...... 186
ell-Paid Authors 187
e Sunday-school 188
ristian Endeavor 189
arriages and Obituaries ... .191
CELLANEOUS:
r Budget 171
rsonal Mention. 172
angelistic.... 181
blisher's Notes........... 181
issionary 182
terature 190
cts and Factors.....................190
nnouncements 192

Subscription $1.75.

B. W. JOHNSON.
FORMER CO-EDITOR OF THE CHRISTIAN-EVANGELIST.

PUBLISHED BY

CHRISTIAN PUBLISHING COMPANY

1522 Locust St., St. Louis.

THE

CHRISTIAN - EVANGELIST

J. H. GARRISON, EDITOR.

W. W. HOPKINS, ASSISTANT.

B. B. TYLER, J. J. HALEY,

EDITORIAL CONTRIBUTORS.

What We Plead For.

The Christian-Evangelist pleads for:

The Christianity of the New Testament, taught by Christ and his Apostles, versus the theology of the creeds taught by fallible men—the world's great need.

The divine confession of faith on which Christ built his church, versus human confessions of faith on which men have split the church.

The unity of Christ's disciples, for which he so fervently prayed, versus the divisions in Christ's body, which his apostles strongly condemned.

The abandonment of sectarian names and practices, based on human authority, for the common family name and the common faith, based on divine authority, versus the abandonment of scriptural names and usages for partisan ends.

The hearty co-operation of Christians in efforts of world-wide beneficence and evangelization, versus petty jealousies and strifes in the struggle for denominational pre-eminence.

The fidelity to truth which secures the approval of God, versus conformity to custom to gain the favor of men.

The protection of the home and the destruction of the saloon, versus the protection of the saloon and the destruction of the home.

For the right against the wrong;
For the weak against the strong;
For the poor who've waited long
For the brighter age to be.
For the truth, 'gainst superstition,
For the faith, against tradition,
For the hope, whose glad fruition
Our waiting eyes shall see.

RATES OF SUBSCRIPTION.

Single subscriptions, new or old	$1.75	each
In clubs of five or more, new or old.	1.50	"
Reading Rooms	1.25	"
Ministers	1.00	"

With a club of ten we will send one additional copy free.

All subscriptions payable in advance. Label shows the month up to the first day of which your subscription is paid. If an earlier date than the present is shown, you are in arrears. No paper discontinued without express orders to that effect. Arrears should be paid when discontinuance is ordered.

In ordering a change of post office, please give the OLD as well as the NEW address.

Do not send local check, but use Post office or Express Money Order, or draft on St. Louis, Chicago or New York, in remitting.

ISTIAN-EVANGELIST

opinion and methods, Liberty; in all things, Charity."

s, Mo., Thursday, August 11, 1898. No. 32

and exaggerated reports of Spanish victories and American losses with which the Spanish press and government officers have deluded the people. At last, however, it is necessary for them to know the facts, in order to reconcile them to the situation, and this, no doubt, is the work that is now being done by the Spanish Government.

While these peace negotiations are going on, there has been no cessation as yet in military and naval activities. Gen. Miles is continuing his triumphal march through Porto Rico toward San Juan, the capital. So far he has met with no serious opposition. Nine or ten large Porto Rican cities have already capitulated, and the American flag has been hoisted in some of them even before the Americans arrived. It is estimated that about half of the beautiful island is already United States territory. Porto Ricans are welcoming the American troops with great enthusiasm, and seem delighted with the idea of having their island under protection of the American flag, instead of remaining a Spanish province. The knowledge of this fact having reached Spain tends to reconcile that country to the surrender of the island. It is reported that San Juan itself is meditating the propriety of surrendering to Gen. Miles without a battle. The Foreign Consuls there advise that course. The healthfulness and fertility of the island, together with the favorable disposition of the people toward the United States Government, give promise of a future of great prosperity for Porto Rico. There can be no doubt but that it will receive an immediate influx of population from the United States as soon as it becomes a part of the United States territory. It will be a fine field, not only for commerce, but for missionary operations, and already some of the leading religious bodies are planning for missionary operations there.

It has been known for sometime that since the fall of Santiago the health condition of our army there has been growing steadily worse. The whole truth concerning its condition, however, was not known until the generals of the army, acting on the suggestion of Col. Roosevelt in a statement to Gen. Shafter, setting forth the condition of the army and the necessity for its immediate removal to the North. This petition of the generals, now spoken of as the "Round Robin," has created considerable comment, and has led to some sharp correspondence between Secretary Alger and Col. Roosevelt. It appears from the evidence published that it was the plan of the Secretary of War to remove the army North as soon as it was believed to be safe to do so. It is probable that the letter of the generals has hastened the matter, as the War Department has ordered the ten large transports at Ponce to proceed at once to Santiago to bring Gen. Shafter's army back to this country. Some of the troops, it is reported, are already on the way, and others will follow immediately. The yellow fever patients will remain, of course, in Cuba, as their removal would be dangerous to them as well as to the health of this country. The place selected for the troops is Montauk Point, L. I., where it is thought the weary and sick soldiers will soon be restored to perfect health. Gen. Shafter has been blamed for allowing the petition of his generals to be published, but if the publication has served to hasten the return of the troops to this country, this fact will compensate for any encouragement which it is feared its publication might give to Spain to continue the struggle. Four or five regiments of immunes are expected to arrive at Santiago to hold possession of that city.

Some of the enterprising dailies of the country have been gathering a consensus of opinion from leading men on the subject of the proper disposition to be made of the Philippine Islands. As might be expected there is a variety of opinion. A large part believe that we should hold and govern all the Philippine Islands. A majority, perhaps, are of the opinion that we should content ourselves with holding the city of Manila, bay and harbor, while others would have the government take possession of the Island of Luzon, giving up the others to Spain. The question, however, is generally discussed from the point of view of commercial advantage. In most of the discussions the problem as to what can be done for the people of the Philippines to help them to a better government and a better civilization, has not received adequate attention. So far as the United States Government is concerned, the city of Manila with coaling stations, would meet her demands from a military and naval point of view. But if by the famous victory of our navy at Manila we have acquired any legitimate right to deal with the future of these islands, we ought to see to it that, whether we hold possession of them or yield them to Spain, some guarantee be given that they shall have better government than they have had heretofore, and that religious liberty shall be secured as one of the essential conditions of their future prosperity. Our responsibility in the premises is measured by our ability and opportunity to bring about a better state of things. We do not need the Philippines, further than for the purpose stated, but the people of these islands do need our civilization, and the civil and religious liberty which we enjoy. The question is, What can we do to make them sharers with us in these blessings?

Judging from the specimens we have seen, the average Porto Rican mayor is able to give lessons in rhetoric to our American mayors, especially when they are welcoming the Stars and Stripes. Here is a specimen from the mayor of Guanica, where our troops landed:

CITIZENS:—God, who rules the destinies of nations, has decreed that the eagle of the north, coming from the waters of a land where liberty first sprang forth to life, should extend to us his protecting wings. Under his plumage, sweetly reposing, the Pearl of the Antilles, called Porto Rico, will remain from July 25. The starry banner has floated gayly in the valleys of Guanica, the most beautiful port of this downtrodden land. This city was selected by General Miles in which to officially plant his flag in the name of his government, the United States of America. It is the ensign of grandeur and the guaranty of order, morality and justice. Let us join together to strengthen, to support and to further a great work. Let us clasp to our bosoms the great treasure which is generously offered to us, while saluting with all our hearts the name of the great Washington.

AUGUS BARRENECHA, Alcalde.

Guanica, Porto Rico, U. S. A., July 26, 1898.

Apropos to the remark above as to the popular ignorance in Spain of the power and resources of the United States, we give the following extract from an interview with Admiral Cervera, during which, in answer to the question by the chaplain of the Oregon as to how the naval commanders of Spain could have expected to defeat the United States, the grizzly old hero replied:

We never thought it possible, at least I did not, and neither did several of my ablest officers—two or three who visited the World's Fair in particular. We knew full well our nation's helplessness and the sure extinction our best ships were running into. We understood it could only mean in the end—barring luck and accidents that none might dare hope for—the loss of ships and our own lives. But our duty sent us out to fight, and we did not flinch. Spain is not so well informed as the advanced officers of her navy. Respecting America and its resources and fighting strength the mass of our people possess only the most woeful misconception and ignorance. The Spanish people think Americans a semi-barbarous nation, and believed our armada could wreck all the cities on your coast and then wipe out your warships wherever we met up with them. But, alas for the duty a patriot owes his mother-country when she is wholly blind! I did not dare think so many of my brave men would escape even with naked life!

The story of the foreign commerce of the United States in the year of her greatest exports has just been completed by the Bureau of Statistics in its monthly "Summary of Finance and Commerce," which presents the details of the imports and exports in the fiscal year ending June 30, 1898. It shows that the exports to all parts of the world increased both in manufactures and products of agriculture, and that while there was a great falling off in imports, the reduction was almost exclusively in manufactured articles and food products. On the other hand the exportations of manufactures, which amounted to $288,871,449 in 1898, exceeded those of 1897 by $11,586,058, and those of 1896 by $60,300,271; while the products of agriculture exported amounted to $854,627,929 in 1898 against $683,471,131 in 1897 and $569,879,297 in 1896, the chief increase in agricultural exportations being in breadstuffs. The exportations of the year increased $180,336,694, and the importations of the year decreased $148,725,253, the comparison being made in each case with the preceding fiscal year 1897. To Europe the exportations increased $160,313,645, while the importations from Europe decreased $124,100,391. To the North American countries the exportations increased $14,676,828, while the importations from the North American countries decreased $14,752,130. To South America the exportations increased but $53,325, while the importations from South American countries decreased $15,295,879. To Asia the exportations increased $5,549,363, while the importations from Asia also increased $5,300,440. Asia and Oceanica being the only grand divisions from which we increased our purchases during the year.

In no department of our industrial system has greater progress been made than in the use of electricity. Some of the marvelous strides made in this field are strikingly presented in a recent address by Dr. A. E. Kennelly, as reported in the Globe-Democrat, of this city, from which we give a few of his statements. It is estimated that about $600,000,000 has been invested in electric lighting stations and plants in the United States. The storage battery, at one time an apparently hopeless factor in electrical work, has shown remarkable advancement in efficiency and power; one installation now in active operation has 166 cells, weighs 500 tons, and has an enormous output of current. In the ten years since the first commercial trolley cars were run, electric locomotives of 1,500 horse power have made their appearance, even on steel railroad tracks. There are to-day in the United States about 14,000 miles of electric railroad, with a nominal capital of about $1,000,000,000, and employing about 170,000 men. Dr. Kennelly holds that the principal engineering value of electricity to-day lies in its adaptation to the transmission of power through mills or cities, or from some locality where power is cheap to others where it is dear. A steel rope, by its bodily motion, can transmit, with appreciable friction, and depreciation a given amount of power to a distance of some thousands of feet. A bare, quiescent copper rod, half an inch in diameter, and supported on poles, can transmit, possibly, ten times the same power for 100 miles, at an infinitesimal depreciation. A great increase in the convenience and effectiveness of the telephone has come with the general substitution of metallic circuits for ground-return circuits. People can now actually converse at a distance of 1,800 miles, and conversations at distances of 1,500 miles are common. There are now about 1,000,000 telephones connected with this country's telephone service, employing a capitalization of about $100,000,000, 400,000 stations, and about 900,000 miles of wire. Every day about 17,000 employes make on an average more than 3,000,000 connections.

As we go to press we are told by the daily press that Spain's reply to President McKinley's peace propositions is in the hands of the French Ambassador, M. Cambon, at Washington, and will be delivered during the day. There seems to be a general feeling in Washington that Spain's acceptance is full and complete, and that hostilities between these two nations will cease at once. But should there be a disposition shown by Spain to equivocate or modify the terms it is the impression that President McKinley will take some short and decisive steps to bring that foolish nation to his terms as they are, and that right speedily. But we hope that this last resort will not be necessitated.

THE PROBLEM OF CHRISTIAN UNITY

There are a great many problems i Christianity, as well as in science, tha awaits some future satisfactory solutior One of these is the problem of Christia unity. Some things in reference to thi problem are very clear. We are sure, fo instance, that it is according to the wil and purpose of God, that His church o earth should be one, in a sense that woul preclude sectarian rivalry, bitterness, waste fulness and misdirection of efforts. W know that divisions are contrary to th mind of Christ, for He prayed that Hi disciples might be one, even as he and th Father are one. We know that this unity among the followers of Christ is related t the triumph of Christianity in the world for Jesus prayed for such unity to the en that the world might believe that th Father had sent Him. We know, too that this union or unity must be in Christ that He must be its source and center; tha it cannot be effected on any platform o theology or of ecclesiastical government We know, also, that the best way t promote this unity is not by controversy, but by cultivating the spirit of fraternity with all who love our Lord Jesus Christ i sincerity, and by working with them in every possible way for the advancement of His kingdom.

These are some of the things we know, but there are other things we do not know. How long will it be until Christ's prayer for the unity of His followers will be realized? Just in what way will it be brought about? To what extent must the present forms of denominationalism give way or be changed in order to the realization of such unity? What will be the final outcome of our plea for the union of believers? These are some of the questions that many people would like to have answered, but for the answer to which they must wait. It is not given to us to know the outcome of present-day movements and efforts. If we know that Christian unity is according to the purpose and will of God; if we feel assured, as we do, that certain conditions are in the way of the realization of this unity, our duty is plain. As for the final result, we leave that to God. Most of us connected with this reformation used to feel much more certain than we now do, as to the *manner* in which Christian union would be effected. We do not believe, any less than we ever did, in the necessity of union and in the providential character of our mission as a religious body, but if we understand correctly the feelings and sentiments of the brotherhood, at present, the disposition is to do what seems plainly to be our duty in the premises, and follow the divine leadings as to future developments. We are inclined to be less dogmatic about the outcome of our efforts, or the manner in which God will bring about the unity of His sundered family, and are more disposed to commit the whole problem to God, while we seek loyally to follow the leadings of His Providence.

We doubt if the leaders of any of the great movements in history have ever known all the purposes of God which lay behind their own efforts. No one supposes that our revolutionary fathers had any conception of the magnitude and power of the great American Republic as it exists to-day. God had purposes in the founding of this nation which the fathers did not

but they were loyal to the
erty which He placed in their
is not to be supposed for a
Luther comprehended the
ts to flow from his resistance
ainst the corruptions of the
rchy. It was far from the
homas and Alexander Camp-
beginnings of their efforts to
more scriptural Christianity,
er union among the people of
y were inaugurating a move-
three quarters of a century
er a million souls, and whose
uld be felt around the globe.
id they understand how God
heir efforts in promoting the
church. When the present
Spain was inaugurated, the
d Congress and the people of
States generally, had in view
of Cuba and the relief of the
ple of that island; but no
ad in view, not only these
ds, but other and far more
ds, which were to be accom-
me of these begin to dawn
w, but it is too early yet to
all that God has in view to
in the present conflict with

true, as a general principle in
government, we ought not to
nge if it be true in reference
ment for Christian union and
thereto. It has already be-
t to many of us that our earli-
the subject were wrong, and
not working along the lines
ad marked out for Him. His
our ways, and His thoughts
thoughts; but as the heavens
ve the earth, so are the thoughts
God above those of men. We
spirit of unity is growing;
walls are neither so high nor
e, as they formerly were. We
our labors have contributed
oward the growing sentiment
union. If this be so, there was,
n for our existence. No doubt
ave been accomplished through
s movement, but it is a great
believe that God has other
ich He is using for the accom-
the same great ends, and that,
we will be able to see, as we
see, how all these seemingly
cies have worked together for
nent of the kingdom of God.
g our individual destiny, John
ot manifest what we shall be."
ing is true in reference to the
e religious movement. We
God has a great work for it
mplish. We have confidence
l take care of it and guide it to
ishment of these purposes. It
nd a sublime thing to be an
od in the consummation of His
es on earth. Let us be content
nor, and be willing to be led by
future as we have been in the
g our course, as the years go by,
x finger of the hand of Prov-
n due time we, or those who come
all see the solution of all our
If Christian unity does not
ll come in God's way, which
est way. In his faith let us go
our work, leaving the results
alone sees the end from the

ABUSES OF THE NAME CHRISTIAN.

The new name Christian was added to the old name disciple to express the higher type of character which the development of Christianity had commenced to produce. It was one of the early symbols of the *unity* of the church and the *universality* of the gospel. The church at Antioch was composed of a mixture of Jews and Gentiles, the first instance of the union of these alien races in one congregation. The middle wall of partition had been broken down by the blood of the cross, race hostilities and prejudices had given place to the unity of the Spirit in the bond of peace, and the unifying name of their common Lord was given to both in one body. This new name signified that the two races into which the world was divided, and which everything else had failed to reconcile, had become one in Christ, and that the gospel held as a sacred trust by the new church, was for the whole world, both Jews and Gentiles.

But the *spiritual and ethical significance* of the name Christian was its most characteristic mark. It has the same meaning as the name Christ. They are both derived from a Greek verb that means to anoint. The Christ is the anointed of God by the Holy Spirit. A Christian, likewise, is an anointed person, a christed man or woman, called and recognized of God, and anointed to the office of the highest character in the world, higher than the royal and sacerdotal offices of the old dispensations. A Christian is more than a follower or learner or imitator of Christ, he is himself a Christ. He is not the Christ, whose anointing was the reception of the Holy Spirit without measure, but a Christ who is limited in the Spirit's anointing according to his capacity to receive it. So the term is intended to express Christliness, not Christlikeness. It is not, therefore, similarity of qualities between Christ and the Christian, but identity of character that makes them one. To be a Christian is to be Christ, not merely to be like him. When a man is made a partaker of the divine nature by the anointing of the Holy Spirit, he is a christed man, and therefore a Christ. He says nothing that Christ would not say, he does nothing that Christ would not do, he goes nowhere that Christ would not go, for him to live is Christ, and not merely like Christ. If the truth and life of Christ are in me I do not imitate Christ but I reproduce Him. He thus multiplies, not his likeness, but himself in those who are his. A Christman, or a Christwoman is the ideal expressed in the term Christian.

In view of these facts, it is painful to reflect upon the abuse and perversion of the word in the history of the church. No term in the world has ever been more sadly misapplied, more horribly mangled in its abuses. Its New Testament sense is anointed, and consecrated men and women, conformed by the Holy Spirit to the image of God's dear Son. We apply it to institutions, to denominations, to newspapers, to church houses, to schools and colleges, and to all kinds of inanimate and non-Christian things. The application of the term Christian to a single religious body to the exclusion of the rest of Christendom, is to denominationalize and therefore to abuse the term, as we do when we call ourselves the Christian Church. The word Christian when applied to a single religious party, is just as sectarian as Baptist, Methodits, Presbyterian, or Episcopalian. You may apply the term to the individual believer, to the local congregation of believers, and to the whole body of Christ at large, and these are its three legitimate applications. The worst abuse, however, is applying the term to those who are in no proper sense of the word, Christian. State Churchism and Pædobaptism have destroyed the New Testament significance of this beautiful word. In the national abuse of the term, every man born within the geographical limits of Christendom, is without reference to moral character, a Christian. Men, women and children born in England, Germany, Canada, or the United States, who are not Jews, Mohammedans, Buddhists, or Mormons, are called Christians. They may be infidels, rogues, rascals, and political snoleghosters, and still they are Christians. In the ecclesiastical slaughter and slander of the term, all who are baptized, for the most part sprinkled in infancy, as Bob Ingersoll, Chas. Bradlaugh and Annie Besant were, are Christians. This horrible abuse of the word has brought untold reproach on the Christian name in heathen lands. Every man with a white face is known as a Christian in these lands, and hence all the villainies of white-faced humanity are put down to the credit of the Christian religion Rum, tobacco, firearms, profanity, and the nameless diseases of sexual vice, are looked upon as Christian institutions. Fancy what an obstacle this is in the way of the Christian missionary, and how long it takes him to win the confidence of the people. The unregenerate, self-seeking, rum-selling trader precedes or follows the Christian missionary, and the preparation made is commercial greed, and the civilized vices that kill the people like sheep with the rot, or hogs with the cholera, and cause them to loathe everything that bears the name Christian. Hugh Price Hughes once expressed his disgust and indignation at this dreadful abuse of the name Christian, and went so far as to propose that the churches reject it and wear in its place the name disciple. In commenting later on our religious movement, he remarked that he knew but little about it, but expressed the hope that we were worthy of our beautiful name, the Disciples of Christ. This is a beautiful name, but no more beautiful and not near as expressive of character as the name Christian, and the way to remedy the difficulty, is not to repudiate our Master's name because men have sadly abused, as they have abused every other high thing, but to teach the people its proper use, and insist on its New Testament sense. The most urgent reform, in my judgment, is the restoration of New Testament language to its New Testament significance. We had better begin with the word Christian, and first by restoring ourselves to a condition that the term Christian will fitly describe.

J. J. H.

Rev. J. H. Wingfield, for many years Episcopal Bishop of Northern California, is dead. He has been an invalid and unable to attend to his diocesan duties during the past two years.

The Y. M. C. A. of this city have recently moved headquarters into their new large, elegant Y. M. C. A. building at Franklin and Grand Avenues, this city.

Hour of Prayer.

THE REFUGE OF THE SAINTS.

(Midweek Prayer-meeting Topic, August 17.)

From the end of the earth will I call unto thee,
when my heart is overwhelmed:
Lead me to the rock that is higher than I.
For thou hast been a refuge for me,
A strong tower from the enemy.
I will dwell in thy tabernacle for ever:
I will take refuge in the covert of Thy wings.
—*Psalms* 61:2-4.

The Psalmist here gives evidence of an experience that has come to all hearts—the overwhelming of the heart, at times, with sorrow and trouble, and the desire at such times, for a stronger than a human hand to bring relief. Such experiences come to all the sons of men sooner or later. No matter in what part of the earth one may be, or how far from his place of accustomed worship, the heart, at such a moment, instinctively turns to God as its only refuge. There are many incidents and accidents of life that cause us to feel our utter helplessness and insufficiency. When we stand in the presence of death, especially if it has come near to us, or in the presence of some great and overwhelming calamity, or when, after drifting along the current of sin, we suddenly awaken to the consciousness of our guilt and of our danger and feel that no human arm can deliver us—to whom then can we go? Where is our refuge? Then the soul lifts up its plaintive cry, "Lead me to the rock that is higher than I."

It is a fault of most of us that we fail to call upon God with great earnestness unless we are in trouble. The bright days that pass by, when there is no cloud to shut out the light of the sun, and when health and prosperity attend us, we seem in a sense to be self-sufficient. We are forgetful of God. It is only when the dark cloud of calamity arises and the storm of adversity beats hard upon us, and the shadow of a great sorrow falls upon our heart, that we feel the emptiness of all earthly things, and lift up our eyes "to the everlasting hills whence cometh our strength." It would be better for us if we made God our dwelling-place continually, instead of using Him simply as a refuge in time of storm. Blessed are they who have learned to *abide* under the shadow of the Almighty and to hide under the covert of His wings!

On the desert sands a weary pilgrim, thirsty and fainting under the heat of the burning sun, is ready to perish by the way. But yonder in the desert towers a mighty rock, that casts its cooling shadow over the sand, and from its base there gurgles a fountain of cool water, which flows through green verdure, under the shadow of the rock. The pilgrim, fainting and weary, reaches the shadow of this great rock in a weary land, drinks of the cooling water, and rests under its shadow, and is refreshed for the journey. Such is "the rock that is higher than I." What such a rock in the desert is to the thirsty traveler, God is to the soul that is burdened with sorrow or with the sense of guilt.

The psalmist had experienced something like this and declares:

"I will dwell in Thy tabernacle forever,
I will take refuge in the covert of Thy wings."

There is no other place of security. There is no other place of serene and undisturbed peace. There is room enough under the wings of the Almighty for all who desire to put their trust in God. Well would it be for us if we could each, to-night, resolve, with Israel's psalmist, to take refuge under the wings of the Almighty.

The lesson emphasizes the value of prayer as the means of coming to God for refuge and help in time of need. It emphasizes, also, the importance of our living continually in such relations with God as to make our prayers effective when we call upon Him. It calls attention, too, to a life of peace and restfulness to which many of us have not yet attained. We are full of worry and care and anxiety; whereas we might take refuge from all these and enjoy "the peace that passeth all understanding." This refuge of the soul is to be found by trusting in God, abiding in Him and committing all our ways and all our interests to Him as to one who "careth for us." This kind of life is possible to all who will seek it aright. May He lead us by His Spirit into the full enjoyment of its blessedness!

PRAYER.

O God, our Father, we thank Thee that Thou art not only great, but gracious, and that in times of perplexity and trouble and sorrow, when our heart is overwhelmed, we may call upon Thy name, and come to Thee as the rock of our refuge. Thou, O God, hast been our refuge and the refuge of our fathers for generations past. Help us to abide under the shadow of Thy wings. If we have been distrustful, anxious, fretful, care-burdened, grant us such increased faith and confidence that we may seek refuge in Thee by lives of trust and obedience. Protect us, we pray Thee, from the thousand ills that beset us here, and bring us at last to be with Thee and enjoy Thy presence and the fullness of Thy peace forever. In Christ's name. Amen!

Editor's Easy Chair.

OR MACATAWA MUSINGS.

It is an important part of the philosphy of life to be able to see and appreciate the beautiful in every season, in every kind of weather, and in every environment. What more musical than the pattering rain-drops, falling from cottage roof and dripping from the eaves, and from the leaves of the trees! How suggestive of somnolence! How it calls up the rainy days of long ago in the country, when we found time to read the papers or perchance a magazine or book! Nearly all night the rain has come down copiously, gladdening the hearts of the gardeners and farmers hereabouts, and giving a newer and fresher tinge of green to all living things. We like the rain as well as the sunshine. This morning the lake has assumed one of its grander moods. The strong breeze has raised the white-caps, while cloud and sunshine, inter-mingled, are painting the billows with every shade and hue. It is a source of never-failing delight to watch the great billows, foam crested and sun-painted, sweep in majestically and break on the shore in a deep diapaison of praise to Him who holds seas and lakes in the hollow of his hand. Thank God for this great unsalted sea, and for all the beauty He has put on it and about it for man's happiness and well-being!

On the shoreline out yonder we see through our study window Old Glory, waving in the breeze, this morning, with every stripe horizontal, and its field blue standing at right angles with the st[...] from which it floats. No doubt this la[...] and these hills and canons, with their gre[...] forests, would be just as beautiful if son[...] other flag waved there, but they would n[...] seem so to our eyes. The Stars a[...] Stripes give them, to our eyes, an add[...] beauty and glory. "Forever float th[...] standard sheet" beside these inland lake[...] on the summits of our mountain range[...] over our broad, fertile prairies, in all o[...] lovely vales, on the high seas, a[...] wherever "its broad stripes and brig[...] stars" are seen, may it continue to be t[...] ensign of liberty, civil and religious, t[...] symbol of equal rights to all men and t[...] guarantee of the practicability and stabili[...] of a government "of the people, for th[...] people and by the people." The stars [...] the old banner never shone with as mu[...] of the lustre of heaven as since it has pas[...] ed through the storm of battle in an u[...] selfish war for the rights and the liberty [...] an oppressed people. Now that the sun [...] peace is about to shine upon its starr[...] folds once more, it will henceforth com[...] mand the respect and admiration of man[...] kind to a greater extent than ever befor[...] Now let the great Republic purge itself [...] all corruption, inequality and injustice [...] every kind, championing the cause of th[...] weakest and most helpless of its citizens. So shall we honor the

"Flag of the free heart's hope and home,
By angels' hands to valor given."

The gregarious habit in human being manifests itself in many ways. It is not a[...] infrequent thing here at the Park for par[...]ties to be formed for an excursion on th[...] lake, for a picnic or for some other pur[...]pose. The governing principle in the for[...]mation of these parties is friendship, o[...] geniality, based on or growing out of ac[...]quaintanceship, formed before or sinc[...] coming here. This year a large number o[...] St. Louisans are here. It was suggeste[...] that we form a little party for a picnic u[...] Black Lake. Within a few hours the part[...] grew to about sixty persons—men, wome[...] and children, including several who were no[...] from St. Louis. It was a sort of impromptu affair, each family providing for itself i[...] the way of eatables, but making a commo[...] meal of it on the grounds. A little steame[...] was chartered to take us up, towing our row boats along for use in fishing and to serv[...] as "lighters" in the debarkation of th[...] party at "Point Superior." It was a livel[...] scene—that of landing this company fro[...] the steamer, by means of row-boats—an[...] reminded us of the landing of the Pilgri[...] Fathers, though we suspect the proportion [...] children in the Mayflower was not so grea[...] as in our party. Once on the ground we a[...] became children, and spent the afternoo[...] in innocent games, and in singing, whil[...] some of the more sportsman-like wer[...] luring the wily bass. We had a great fea[...] in the evening, topping off with water melons, and then we re-embarked and ha[...] a delightful voyage home, making th[...] quiet waters of Black Lake fairly trembl[...] with our songs. It was voted to be a de[...]lightful occasion, and its repetition be[...]fore the season closes is among the proba[...]bilities.

We have perhaps remarked before upo[...] the large attendance on the religious ser[...]

tions, is for the last ten years about the same, sometimes rising a little, sometimes falling, but generally not far from 10 per cent of the whole. There is another point in this connection which is worthy of note, in the publishers' reports of American books, only two classes of publications, works of fiction and legal publications, exceed, in number, the books of a religious character. With regard to fiction it may be said that in every country where printing is done, tales and novels and romances form the largest class of publication, though it is also well to remember that quite a number of these, considering the lesson inculcated in the story, deserve to be classed with religious, while the legal publications do not represent, as a matter of fact, the original compositions of individual authors, for,. in every state in this union, the annual or bi-annual Legislature issues from one to five volumes of statutes, while the opinions of the Supreme Courts of the different states and of the United States, number from 100 to 200 volumes annually. When these and the revised statutes are abstracted from the list of legal publications, the religious list will take precedence. In Great Britain, only the class of fiction and education hold a higher place in the list than books of religion. A showing of this kind ought to set at rest a wild statement made without reason or authority. When religious books form in each of the English-speaking countries one-tenth of the whole, and when, in actual numbers, they rank third, if not second, in the United States and third in Great Britain, there is little room for the assertion that interest in religious literature is falling off.

In Robert Stewart McArthur's article on "Historic Creeds and Baptist Churches," in the Standard, Aug. 6th, he says:

If ever there is organic unity, it will begin at the baptistery. Every denomination in Protestant Christendom, and in the entire Roman and Greek churches, can agree upon baptism, that is immersion, as taught by our Lord and his apostles. The Greek Church, numbering quite 90,000,000 of adherents, has ever been a stout witness on behalf of baptism. The Roman Church joyfully accepts it, and all the Protestant churches join hands with these two great bodies. On no substitute for baptism, whether pouring or sprinkling, can all the denominations agree. We are not here arguing a point; we are simply stating an incontrovertible fact. Do men really want organic Christian unity? Are they in earnest when they proclaim this desire? Are they willing to follow Christ into the waters of baptism? Are they willing to join hands with their brethren in all centuries and in all climes? Here is the opportunity; here is the truly apostolic and catholic ordinance. If they will but follow the apostolic injunction and example, then all can say: "We are buried with him by baptism unto death;" and then there may be, if it is desired, organic union without doing violence to the convictions of any, and in acknowledged harmony with the Word of God and its recognized interpretations. On but few points is the scholarship of the world so nearly a unit as it is in regard to the meaning of the word "baptism," as practiced by the apostles and the early church. It would be easy to fill pages with the names of learned authorities on all these points, and the simple-minded disciple of the Lord Jesus, with no guide but the New Testament, comes to the same conclusion. May the Holy Spirit lead all believers into all truth!

Those who are alarmed about the growth of Romanism should read an article in a recent number of the Observer (St. Louis), on its decay in the world. It is evident from the figures presented that Roman Catholicism is rapidly losing ground in Europe and America. We quote a few statements from the Observer:

At the close of the nineteenth century all the dominant nations of the earth, except Russia, are Protestant. At the close of the Napoleonic wars in 1815 Romanism was infinitely stronger than it is to-day. In the German-speaking world Roman Catholic Austria and not Protestant Prussia was the ruling and controlling power and continued to be until the Franco-Prussian war in 1870. The triumph of Protestant Prussia over Roman Catholic France in that great war was marked by the downfall of the Roman Catholic supremacy in things German. The German Empire, consisting of 52,000,000 of enlightened, progressive people, is more than two-thirds Protestant. Romanism has lost its prestige and power in United Germany and the trend of thought and life in that country is away from Roman Catholicism. One hundred years ago France was intensely loyal to the Vatican, but to-day the heart of France is intensely anti-clerical. We do not claim that France is Protestant, but we do claim that it is not loyally Roman Catholic. It is said by no less an authority than M. Taine that less than 2,000,0000 Catholics in France are regular communicants. We could give many proofs of the statement that Romanism is decaying in the French Republic. There is even an alarming defection among Roman Catholic priests throughout France, and there is a movement, though still concealed, toward Protestantism. It is a notorious fact that every loyal Roman Catholic country is retrograding, politically and religiously. It is often contended that the Roman Catholic Church is about to reconquer Great Britian. So eminent an authority as the Methodist Times, of London, on this point says: "The actual fact is that the Roman Catholic Church alone of all Christian churches is declining all over the world. As recently as 1890 the late Cardinal Manning prepared a series of notes in relation to the condition of Romanism in England. In these documents he states there are 1,500,000 Roman Catholics in England to-day, but that only 200,000 of them are English. Of the rest we may add, 100,000 are French, German and Italian, while 1,200,000 are Irish. Now all these were Romanists, but they came to England and so represent no increase whatever. The apparent growth of Romanism in this country (England) is almost entirely due to the immense Irish immigration. If the Irish and Continental Romanists should return to their countries Romanists in England would soon disappear."

Questions and Answers.

[We insert the following questions and answers in place of the regular department this week.]

ELDER JOSEPH FRANKLIN:—I come to you for more light on the church name question. Please answer the following questions through the CHRISTIAN-EVANGELIST:

1. Is the name "Church of God" scriptural?

2. If so, is the name "Church of Christ" scriptural? Are both names applied to the same body?

3. Is it scriptural to call churches "Disciple Churches?"

4. Is it scriptural to call churches "Christian Churches," or "Churches of Christians?"

By your answers you will be helpful to many inquirers.

SEARCHER AFTER TRUTH.

The above comes to me from one who was raised among the Winebrennerians, who use "Church of God" as their denominational designation. The writer has been in New England for some years, where he often hears of "Disciples" and "Disciple Churches."

1. "Church of God" is the common form of expression in the New Testament.

2. The name "Church of Christ" is not a common form of expression in the N. T. Once in Rom. 16:16 we find the plural, "Churches of Christ." Any one of those would have been "a Church of Christ." The general church is never called, "The Church of Christ." But Jesus is "Head over all to the church, which is his body." He calls it "my church." This seems to be authority for calling it, "The Church of Christ."

3 and 4. None of these expressions are in the N. T. But in the same way that Paul (1 Cor. 14:33) said "churches of the saints," we might say "churches of the disciples," or "churches of Christians." "Church of Christ" and "Christian Church" are two forms of the same name, just as we say "Church of England" and "English Church." Neither is more "scriptural" than the other.

We may simplify this discussion if we

will abandon the fruitless search for a legal enactment affixing a title to some incorporated body. The denomination is often an incorporated body, but "the Church of God" is no more than the aggregate of the believers. When the church is called a body, reference is had to a physical body, and not to a corporation.

Again: In this endless discussion of names we are all intoxicated with denominational wine, and we are hunting after a name by which "we as a people" may be identified by a score or more of other "peoples." One "people" is separated from the others and is identified as, "The Methodist Episcopal Church." Another is known as, "The Presbyterian Church of the United States." With our thought running along this line we ask, "What is *our* proper name?" Thus put, the question means, "By what name are we to be distinguished from other denominations?" There are many parties or groups of professed Christians. Each has a name which applies to itself alone. What is "our" name?

We need not look into the N. T. for answer. The names therein apply to all Christians alike. All are "Christians," "disciples," "saints" or "believers." No designation in the N. T. serves to tell what kind of Christians any one group is and distinguish it from other groups. No N. T. name serves to classify and distinguish any one church among many professing to be Christian churches. This is the error of John Winebrenner and his co-laborers. They have adopted the name "Church of God" as the name of their church in such a way as to exclude all other churches from the use of it. In the same way a few anti-organ and anti-society leaders are trying to appropriate the name "Church of Christ" as the name of their party. Yet others are using "The Disciples," as a purely denominational epithet. Except for the capital "D" this is scriptural in form only. So is the name "Baptist." But both are unscriptural in application, because "The Baptists," and "The Disciples," are the names of two parties.

We are "Christians" or "disciples of Christ." But these names cannot locate us in any denominational connection. One church relation is that of membership in the "Church of Christ," or "Church of God." But the scriptural use of these names cannot locate us in any denominational church. JOSEPH FRANKLIN.

[This is all sound enough reasoning, except that it ignores the necessity that exists for distinguishing things that differ. As long as there are religious bodies having different creeds, different polities and distinct ecclesiastical organizations, there must be names by which we distinguish one from another, if we write about them or refer to them in any way. The wrong is, if wrong there be, in having religious bodies so different from each other as to *necessitate* different names. This is the reason why we say, "Disciples of Christ," with a capital D., because it is the least objectionable method of designating the churches of the Current Reformation when it is necessary to distinguish them from others, *as it often is*. It is perfectly useless to inveigh against distinguishing religious bodies from each other by some name. This will be done as long as these bodies exist.—EDITOR.]

SPIRITISM; OR THE WITCH OF ENDOR.

W. J. LHAMON.

"Why hast thou disquieted me to bring me up?"—1 Samuel 28: 15.

Hypnotism, clairvoyance, clairaudience, mind-reading, Christian science healing, and the phenomena of Spiritualism belong to one family of psychic forces, just as turnips and cabbages belong to the same botanical family. The species, however, in each case, are separated by such degrees that it requires the scientific mind to discover their kinship. What the botanist has done for us in showing that the turnip and cabbages are cousins, the psychologist is doing for us in showing that the above-named forces are closely related, and that their various phenomena spring from the same root.

Spiritualism, as a proposed religion, is scarcely half a century old, but hypnotics, and people with "a familiar spirit," are found far back in the dimest centuries. When mind-readers, and clairvoyants, and fortune-tellers and hypnotics were not understood, and people were incapable of a scientific study of them, they were either superstitiously courted as among the Romans and Egyptians, or peremptorily forbidden, as among the Jews. In this age we neither worship nor prohibit such things or such people; we simply put them into the crucible of scientific investigation. What is dross gets burned; the fire leaves only the gold.

Spiritualism proposes to do three things for us. In the first place, it proposes to prove for us that the spirit lives after the body is gone; that death is only transition; and that the life of the departed is, in general, more desirable than our own. It opposes materialism and annihilation, and seeks to teach us, as Whittier and all true poets do, that—

"Life is ever Lord of death,
And Love can never lose his own."

In this respect, its aims, when they do not spring from mercenary motives, are majestic. But its efforts are not needed. Christ has done this work a thousandfold better, and once for all, and without the suspicion of mercenary taint. Christ is a fact in history. He refuses to melt away in the crucible of criticism. His moral perfection equals the majesty of his spiritual claims, and both are transcendent. His resurrection is a fact, "the best established in all history." As the conqueror of death he has promised us eternal life, and his promises are final to all who trust him.

If the spirits were permitted to come back and communicate with us, would they need so much machinery about it? Would not my departed grandfather come immediately to me, rather than post off to some utter stranger, and then wait for me to hire that stranger to give him an introduction? And after the cash was paid would he still wait to be rapped up through an extension table, or smuggled out of a black muslin cabinet into a dark room, under the mesmeric influence of a piano or a brass band? In the case of old acquaintances, like that of mother and daughter, the presence of a medium with her hypnotic trance and her double slates and tables and cabinets and tests and messages and materializations would seem to be an impertinence. The necessary intervention of the medium is a presumption against the genuineness of the system. When Christ came bac[k] from the dead he needed no medium to hel[p] him into the presence of his disciples. H[e] stood before them in simple grandeu[r] and lifted up his pierced hands and said "Behold my hands; and reach thither th[y] hand and thrust it into my side; and be no faithless, but believing."

Secondly. Spiritualism proposes to giv[e] us communications from the dead. On[e] makes haste to admit that mediums d[o] many curious things, and that they tel[l] some things that must have been found ou[t] in unusual ways. One should not go s[o] far as to deny the phenomena in order to b[e] rid of the theory. That would neither b[e] brave nor honest. It may be that whe[n] the whole matter is sifted, by far th[e] larger per cent. of the doings of the med[i]ums must pass for chaff. Evidence point[s] that way. Perhaps nothing more conclusive in this line has been given to the world than the report of the Sybert commission. Mr. Henry Sybert was, during his lifetime, an enthusiastic believer i[n] spiritualism. "Shortly before his death he presented to the University of Pennsylvania a sum of money sufficient to found a chair of philosophy, and to the gift added a condition that the university should appoint a commission to investigate all systems of morals, religion or philosophy, which assume to represent the truth, and particularly modern Spiritualism." Ten men of candor and scientific ability were chosen, and of these Mr. Geo. S. Fullerton was made secretary. Mr. Fullerton declares that he began his work without any bias against Spiritualism, but on the contrary, much impressed with what he had read, and in a fully receptive attitude. The investigations were thorough and painstaking. They had numerous meetings with slate-writing mediums; they attended materializing seances; they arranged for special experiments with the best known mediums, and they gave special attention to the mediums who advertized to read sealed letters and give answers to them. In the appendix to their published report (dated 1887), Mr. Fullerton says: "I have been forced to the conclusion that Spiritualism, so far at least as it has shown itself before me (and I give no opinion upon what has not fallen within my observation), presents the melancholy spectacle of gross fraud, perpetrated upon an uncritical portion of the community." This report is no less interesting than painful. When slates were not securely tied, the mediums opened them and wrote in them. When they were absolutely sealed no writing appeared in them, though they remained for weeks with the mediums. The materializations were made of the commonest sort of human clay, talking twaddle, susceptible to flattery, tickled with a toy, and altogether too childish and human ever to have been anywhere near a graveyard. Every one of the sealed letters submitted for tests to the advertising quack mediums in Boston and New York and Columbus was opened and read—cut across the end and again carefully sealed, or cut around the seals, and afterward nicely stuck down. The answers to these letters are very funny and contradictory. The spirits do not use good grammar; they cannot spell, and their poetry is shocking.

But, we are reminded, "The spirits do tell things that nobody but spirits could

Rather, the mediums tell things
›ody but mediums could know.
different matter. The true me-
ı clairvoyant, a mind-reader, more
lept in the art. He finds a piece
ral in your pocket. How did he
was there? Did the spirits or his
'control" tell him? No, you told
ou and three other men were look-
and talking about it; the medium
that just as you have it photo-
in your memory. You carried it
ı into an office; he sees that too.
he tells you that if you invest in
e from which it came, you'll get
›s, that's just what you were think-
sn't it? What is his prophecy
Precisely what your own judgment
ı when it is overheated with the
speculation.
u have a lock of hair, over which
e cried many times; you carry it
ı, and the face of the one who wore
e a photograph before you. The
finds that lock of hair, and sees
›u see. Under the power of hyp-
ıggestion he immediately fixes you
e little story about your loved one
ery general indeed, and full of
es, precisely such as he has told to
and other people with similar locks
. Mrs. Prior found such a lock of
St. George's Hall the other even-
t seemed to me rather suspiciously
p in a clean white envelope for the
n. But we will give her credit for
it. Mr. Bishop and the "White
nas" have done more wonderful
Mrs. Prior is not a first-class
eader. Her hits and misses are
evenly balanced. Poor Annie Arm-
came one night from the spirit
wanting very much to see a dear
. Either the friend was not present,
was too cruel to respond. Surely,
'rior's audience will not soon forget
aphic picture she drew of the crip-
ımerican soldier, the "peg-leg," as
lled him, stumping down the aisle.
› one would claim him. The medium
; sight of an elderly woman, rather
with iron-grey hair; she had been
ıbout fifteen years. An impressible
.bout forty-five or fifty years old
and claimed her for his aunt; he
a prolonged and excited speech, in
urse of which he said that his aunt
ed when he was a little baby. The
ıding audience seemed not to notice
ıcrepancy as to date of death.

(CONCLUDED NEXT WEEK.)

›ME OR JERUSALEM, WHICH?

BY S. K. SHELLENBERGER.

hard to break the chains forged in
ddle ages. Unconsciously we accept
ctrines of the popes. Sentimental-
s been afraid to test the teachings of
ıthers. Age may command respect,
ıt acceptance. We take off our hats
enter the halls of antiquity, but we
at even there "all is not gold that
s," that all was not truth that was
. The finding of things ancient has
e a fad in both the literary and art
. Theology, as well, is having its
"Back to the fathers," "back to the
es," "back to Christ," "back to the
al," are cries heard from the four
of the earth. In the midst of these stirring times, sources and authorities should be looked to.

Doctrines being taught to-day are indeed ancient. Some, however, are not quite enough so. Often it is asked, "Is not the Roman, or 'Catholic' the oldest church, and therefore mother of all churches? Is not her teaching to be honored because of its age?" We answer, emphatically, "No." Jerusalem's church was the first one. Her doctrines are the most ancient, because there they began. Her teachings, by virtue of their origin, are entitled to the highest honor and respect.

The old story that Romanism preserved for us the Bible, we deny. On the contrary, it was the "woman" who "fled into the wilderness," whom the "dragon," the inspiration of the old "beast"—Romanism—persecuted so bitterly, that kept the Word for us. It was the souls of those who were slain "for the witness of Jesus and for the Word of God, who had not worshiped the beast, neither his image," that saved this precious boon from being submerged in the awful flood of the blood of martyrs. Let men stop giving the honor which belongs to him who said: "I am with you alway even unto the end," to the pope. He is a usurper. His sole ambition was, and is, to destroy the truth, and upon ignorance, to establish his own authority.

John, in the apocalypse, sees two churches, and only two. They are the *true* and the *false*. He sees them emblematically, as two cities—Zion and Babylon—and as women—the virgin and the harlot.

If the common Protestant interpretation of "the beast" of the apocalypse is true, that is, that it symbolizes popedom, (and we believe it is) then the authority of the pope comes directly from the devil; and he is therefore a stranger to anything God or Christ-like, save a stolen name. (For the inspiration of "the beast" see Rev. 13:4-11-15. If you want to know who the dragon was, see Rev. 20:2.)

Contrasted with the above-named beast, we have another, the Head of the true church. He is like unto a *lamb* and a *lion*, and received his authority from God. He is the "Lamb of God that taketh away the sin of the world," "the lion of the tribe of Judah."

The devil inspires the pope (human authority). The pope or human councils, delegates the bishops. The bishops lord it over the people, both great and small, who accept and teach and do what these human authorities have directed. On the other hand, God inspired Jesus Christ. Jesus delegates his apostles (or missionaries). The apostles rescue and save all who accept and teach and do as he, Jesus Christ, has directed.

These things being true, it is well, before lending our influence to these old doctrines, to test them. Are they from Rome or Jerusalem?

"Agonizing at the 'mourners' bench'" is readily traced to Rome's idea that God is a God of wrath instead of love. Heathenism gave the idea to Rome, and heathenism is of the devil. Laboring under this delusion, Rome instituted, first, the mediation of "Mary, mother of God." Then in their dire distress they grasped the idea of the intervention of "saints." Finally, in their deepening despair, they invented "purgatory." Willing to roast, if thereby they might appease the wrath of God. Protestantism left these methods with Rome, but brought out with her the original idea. To-day she says to the penitent, "pray and plead, and plead and pray if, haply, God's wrath may be appeased and he may be reconciled to speak peace to your soul." Why beg for a morsel when the feast is spread before you? Jerusalem says: "Come unto me *all* ye that labor and are heavy laden and *I will give you rest*." "Whosoever will, let him come and take of the water of life freely." "God so *loved* the world that he gave his only begotten Son that whosoever believeth on Him should not perish but have everlasting life."

The spending of such enormous sums of money in piles of brick and stone, ostensibly to worship God, but in reality to satisfy human ambition, is a relic of Rome. Heathenism taught that Deity could only be approached over altars surrounded by gilded walls. Rome caught the idea, confirmed it by a misunderstanding of the Jewish dispensation, and dedicated to—we will not say whom—the enormous and gorgeous temples of the middle ages. Behold the unostentatious places of meeting of the first Christians. Service, instead of show, was the moving idea. Protestants, to-day, in mock reverence, spend from one hundred thousand to half a million in a gorgeous, Christless pile, and whiningly plead poverty on missionary days. The devil and the bondholder both hold unliftable mortgages on these structures; and in their desperate struggle to pay the interest, the world, to whom God has sent us, is unthought of. Don't cry "pessimism." Statistics shockingly bear out the statement.

"Water salvation" as taught and practiced by Protestants in the sprinkling of babies, comes directly from Rome. Egyptian idolatry gave Rome the idea. Where did Egypt get it? Rome sprinkles the baby in the name of the pope and the holy Catholic Church. Then she confirms the youth in the belief that his sins are pardoned through the mediation of the pope. Perfectly consistent is she at least; for she has obeyed the pope's instructions through whom she hopes for salvation. Protestantism sprinkles the baby as per instructions of the pope, but does it in the name of Christ. Then she teaches the youth that Christ will honor the deed even to the abrogation of his own laws. Wholly inconsistent is this because of the pretense to follow Christ, while obeying the pope.

Raising money, presumably for the Lord's work, by euchre parties, charity balls, "prettiest ladies," Trilby socials, and all other such undignified and un-Christian schemes, is simply a relic of the indulgence-selling of Tetzel times. I need not tell whence came that nefarious business. The principle is now the same as then. The object was to get money to build St. Peter's at Rome and leave the peddler a handsome profit. The end justified the means. The object to-day is to build our new church or frescoe the one we have, or pay for our new pipe organ. A laudable purpose of course. Hence the ends justify the means. If one be abreast with the van of church-socialism of to-day, and if he be conscientious in the Master's service he cannot help being saddened at the growing tendency toward Rome. There is a better way, a dignified way, a respectable way, a business-like way, a Christlike way. And we rejoice to record that our *best* pastors, our *best* churches, our *best* papers, advocate that way. It is not the pope's, but Jesus' way—systematic, proportionate giving.

Human creeds are merely relics of Rome, nothing more, nothing less. For 1600 years she did little but manufacture creeds, and excommunicate, torture and slay the men who had enough Christianity in them to be heretics. Brother Disciples, we condemn written creeds; beware, lest we have an *un*written one. Glad am I, that the golden thought is being grasped, that obedience, rather than interpretation is the test of fellowship with the Master.

Putting God under obligation to us by works is another Romish idea. Works of supererogation was taught by Rome. Hence the monasticism and asceticism of the middle ages. Luther at one time thought to *merit* salvation by kissing stones trod upon by holy (?) feet. The poor, deluded dupes of Southern Colorado, New Mexico, and Mexico, to-day think to *merit* salvation by flagellations with cacti, rolling naked in cactus beds, voluntary crucifixions, etc. Protestantism follows in the rear with the same idea, but with less bravery, teaching a mechanical Christianity which is only human piety. They would keep the fourth commandment, but break the first. They would commit us to ceremonies, and rituals, and let love "soar to serener climes." They would put us under the old covenant of specifics, avoiding the new covenant of basic principles.

Such teaching leads the moralist to ask such questions as appeared in the Christian Standard, March 12, page 324. We quote it: "If a person who is not a church member is as good as one who is, will he not stand as good a chance to be saved as the church member?" Here the answer there given.

1. "It is a very great error to suppose that a person can be saved without belonging to the church, just as he can by belonging to it." *Why* is it such a "great error?"

2. "The best people belong to the church." No argument in that.

3. "A man can't live as good a life out of the church as he can in." Selfishly moral, he can. Honesty and sobriety are found outside the church as well as in.

4. "The greatest sin is to reject God's mercy." Mistaken again. See Matt. 12: 31.

5. "If a man gain heaven without Christ, then God made a mistake in the plan of salvation." What is there in this that would regenerate a man?

Where is the answer to the original question? Were I the author of that question I should now be thoroughly confirmed in my moralistic views. For both question and answer teach the old Romish idea of mechanical Christianity, namely: that by works we *merit* salvation, and God is obliged to save us. The difference between the student and teacher here is simply in the conception of the kinds of works necessary to salvation. Why not frankly say that a liar *isn't* a man, a cheat *isn't* a man, a thief *isn't* a man. The fact that one refrains from these and similar evils does not put even me, his fellow-man, under obligation to him. He has only done what any man ought to do. Upon what grounds will he merit a reward? He will of necessity go to the pope for his hope on this basis.

Works are never a means to, but a result of, salvation. The life of the peach bears peaches according to the inevitable. So the Spirit or life of Christ in us bears Christ-like deeds, fruit of the Spirit, according to the inevitable. Through or because of this Spirit we are saved. Rom. 8:11, and similar passages. To be without this Spirit is *death*. How, then, do we get this Spirit. Acts 2:38. Why not simply say in answer to such questions, "Have you obeyed? If not, then you are still an alien and 'without hope and without God in the world.'" Why not tell them plainly if they will not *march* under the "banner of Emanual" they never can claim protection under it. The only "work" that God recognizes is the fulfilling the commission. That cannot be done by trusting in one's own selfish Pharisaical works.

Let us stop dodging questions. Back to the divine original! Jerusalem is *always* right. Rome is *always* wrong.

ORGANIC EVOLUTION CONSIDERED.

ROBT. T. MATHEWS.

In making out a list of books for preachers, and in naming those on the subject of evolution, I should certainly recommend Prof. Fairhurst's "Organic Evolution Considered." On the face of it, it is the work of a live teacher. Those of us who have seen the author in the schoolroom, with his large class rising around him, will remember how swiftly the hour passed in the flow of his vital teaching. One can but feel in this cool-headed book of science the personal intentness and forcefulness of the teacher. Joubert says that the best writings of scholarship are the work of the experienced teacher. Prof. Fairhurst's volume, therefore, has this high recommendation to begin with, that it is the product of one, who, while teaching, has devoted himself daily to study and thought.

Some readers have fallen into a wrong estimate of the contents and trend of the book. It has been thought that the author is making a wholesale war on evolution in general. Strictly speaking, however, his work is a powerful polemic against atheistic evolution. By all means, let every reader "chew and inwardly digest" the "Introduction" and the chapter on "Method of Creation." Here will be found whole paragraphs of clear discriminations and balanced judgments. Let a few of these be quoted:

"It is a fact, I believe, that the propagation of the theory of evolution has decreased belief in theism. While this may be true, the fact should not be lost sight of that a belief in the former is consistent with a belief in the latter."

"At bottom the question as to the method of creation is only a dispute between theism and atheism."

"Evolution may be atheistic, but it is not necessarily so."

With this correction of some superficial readings of the book, it is then in order to recognize what a strong case Prof. Fairhurst makes out against any theory of evolution that ignores the presiding and pervasive energy of Deity. The logic of the book is to show, by the many concessions of stout evolutionists themselves, how impossible it is to account for creation apart from God. The author's polemic is none too strong, not only against atheistic evolutionists and agnostic evolutionists, but against a class, who, on account of their faint references to Deity, may be call quasi-theistic evolutionists. A thoroug interpretation of Prof. Fairhurst's argu ment still leaves the way open for a sour theory of theistic evolution.

How this can be, may be seen in th author's summation of "possible theist theories, according to which new organ forms may have been brought into exis tence."

"First, the Creator may have create each species by means of secondary agen cies alone, by the process of evolution.

"Second, he may have created each spe cies from inorganic matter by means of special fiat.

"Third, he may have created certain type of living beings from inorganic matter b special fiats, and from these types he ma have evolved, by secondary agencies, a other forms.

"The existence of secondary causes im plies a primary cause. The unity in natur shows that the primary cause is one, an not many.

"The method of creation is nothing ex cept as it bears on our interpretation of th nature of the creative power. Theisr stands in no danger from creation by sec ondary causes, for they are consistent wit the existence of an intelligent Creator Evolution may be atheistic; but it is nc necessarily so. Either of the above method of creation may be theistic."

CHURCH ORGANIZATION AND GOVERNMENT.*

J. E. COBBEY.

Of the cause first. The membership o our church boards may be, in a genera way, divided into three classes. First, thos who do not understand business methods have never used them and looked upor such methods as official red tape, the use of which is to be avoided if possible. Wh have always kept track of their own business in their heads and cannot see why th church business cannot be done in the same way.

They fail to realize that while one mar may keep track of a small business in his head and transact it without rules, a board of from seven to fifteen members cannot do the same business without a system and *de finire* rules. Second, those who understand business methods and believe in using them in the business world, but have an idea that they ought not be applied to church work. Third, a small minority who both understand business methods and believe in using them in church business but are powerless to make reforms. All o these men are honest and desire to do their duty. Meeting with the board as an advisor and helper is the pastor. The pastor usually has a prejudice against business methods, and a disinclination to advise in business matters. The board of deacons have no confidence in the pastor's advise or business matters, and feel offended if he presumes to advise them. The result is that the business of the church is so conducted that it is referred to with scorn and jeering by those both in and out of the church.

Now as to the remedy. I believe that ou people should insist that our preacher should be equipped not only with a knowl-

*Paper read before the Thirty-first Annual Convention of the Nebraska Christian Missionary Society, at Beatrice, Neb., July 3rd, 1898.

ɜ Bible, but with a thorough, ,siness education as well. Our ɪeological schools to-day should 'actical. They should instruct ɪreacher as to the best form of ɪcord. How it should be kept; ɪretary's books should be kept; ɪsurer's books should be kept; ɪim bookkeeping enough to tell ɪe work was well-done, or, if ;hat he might keep the church self. In other words, the ould be an all-around business hould be taught in these schools teps necessary to organize a ɪat constitutes the best official ɪ many deacons; how many duties of each. What class of ɪt-fitted for each position; how hould be organized; what com- ɔointed. In fact, so far as the to do with the law of the land, ɔf parliamentary bodies or of should be a legal, parliamentary ɪs expert, ready on the instant or direct. Such a man would pect from all parties and they ɪong look with coldness on his better moral or spiritual life. y, of what good is this to us, our are past? If you see the neces- ɪis class of education, you can ɪessure to bear on our Bible- ɪd theological seminaries that ɜ them to give a part of their truction in those branches. The of this generation are better han those of the last. It is our that those of the next genera- till better equipped. On the , it is no excuse for you that you ɪught on these subjects in your The last instruction of your : was that you continue to grow ɪge, and the last wish of that president was, that you might ɪrong, broad and high super- upon the foundation he had ɔu for four years in laying. If ɜdge is needed by you, if it will r power for good, you are recreant st that college reposed in you, ɪglecting your duty to the cause you hav: pledged your life, if ot provide for obtaining this at once.

ɪre that while our church organi- ave within their membership ht minds capable of organizing higher degree of efficiency, we, le, are the poorest organized of ination of church people. With ɪid material in our ranks this be discouraging were it not that attempt at organization and dis- arge number of misguided, but ɪembers raise the blood-stained ! oppression, and cry, Creed! nd the majority of our member- er at once, and with emphasis: ɪh organization! Down with hile this prejudice is non-scrip- llogic, if not positively unchris- t exists and must be considered the problems.

ɪs in mind I would suggest: That ng discuss these matters fully. nstruct your pastor in the legal ɪsary to organize a church. Let ɪg appoint a committee to pre- ɪm of legal organization which this body shall recommend to all churches. At your next meeting let each pastor report whether his church is legally organized. If not, let him give a reason, if he can, why he has not had it legally organized.

Let this meeting set apart a day for the discussion and adoption of a plan of organization for church government. Have papers prepared by your stronger men on this subject. Discuss how many trustees are best, the minimum of the three provided by statute or more? How many constitute the official board? Who are they? The trustees? The elders? The deacons? All of them together? Or an entirely separate board? How is this official board selected? Elected or appointed? How many members should it have? Should they come from the body of the membership? Would it not be better to let the various church societies, as the C. E., the Bible-school, the Aid Society, etc., name part of this board? What officers and committees should this board have when organized? Their powers and duties?

How the treasurer's book should be kept? What they should show? Enquire into the form used by the different churches; after obtaining all possible information, recommend to the churches the form, that in your judgment, is best. Then ask a report, at each yearly meeting, of the system as to its practical working.

Adopt the same plan as to the clerk's record.

Take up the subject of church finances and discuss the assessment plan, the pledge plan, or any other plan used by any church, and recommended for adoption by the churches, the plan which after investigation shall seem to you the best.

Church finances are a source of annoyance and irritation. The entire system is wrong and should be cast out, root and branch, and a new system built up. Let us teach the people how to give. Let this gathering and each of your preachers place before the people the Bible evidence of their duty to tithe their earnings for the benefit of the Lord's work. Understand the subject first yourselves, then talk it over with your board, talk it over with your members individually and collectively, then when a man has given his one-tenth conscientiously, don't at the end of the year, with a sanctimonious face say to him that the Lord loves a cheerful giver, and ask him to contribute to make up a deficiency of some one else. Don't take up an extra contribution in a public meeting where this man must either give liberally or have the finger of scorn pointed at him, for what the people unjustly believe to be his parsimony. Better go privately to those who have not paid their tenth. If you must publicly collect for your congregation, you should know who has given their tenth. Take no man's word on this. Examine their books, for such men keep books, and if asked, in a proper spirit, are glad to show them. Then say to your congregation, Bro. A. and Bro. B. have, in the past year, to my knowledge, given all that the Lord requires of them, and this appeal is not to them. If these men then choose to aid in reducing the deficiency, you can say to them, without hypocrisy, the Lord will bless a cheerful giver.

Don't hold any more church socials where members are expected to come and get acquainted at an admission of fifteen cents per head to pay for the ice cream and cake which some good mother has furnished free of charge. Don't place the best looking girl of your congregation right in front of the door with a grab-bag contrivance, at five cents a grab. And the little seven-year-old tot just beyond, to pull from your pocket the last nickel of the quarter, for a flower which your wife picked from your own garden as she took your arm to come to the church sociable.

If you need a quarter, say so, and go to the members who are in arrears to the Lord and get it. But make the church sociable free or change its name.

Let us all labor to teach our churches to live within their income. Make our church boards understand that it is just as disastrous to run a church at an expense of fifty dollars per week, when the income is but thirty dollars per week, as it is for a bank cashier to live at an expense of two thousand dollars per year on an income of but one thousand per year. The result is just as certain, and just as disreputable in one case as in the other. I know that these defects in our church business system are wide-spread and deep-rooted; that reform cannot be brought about in a day or in a year, or perhaps not in a generation, but it is none the less desirable. It is none the less our duty to make the beginning. We look to you as leaders to sound the note of alarm. It is your sacred duty to lead the way. Not blindly, not in a perfunctory manner, but with wisdom and intelligence. Will you do it?

(CONCLUDED NEXT WEEK).

The eighth annnal convention of the Baptist Young People's Union of America was held at Buffalo, N. Y., July 14-17. The receipts for the year as shown by the treasurer's report were \$70,160.18, of which \$47,159.02 was from the Baptist Union, \$12,688.70 borrowed money, and \$721.57 from contributions to the "founding fund." Sale of supplies brought in \$7,996.03. The disbursements on account of the general organization were \$5,801.89; on account of the paper, \$42,599.76; for supplies \$8,128.82. The deficit for the year of the organization as a whole, including the paper which is now self-supporting, was \$1,026,29 as against \$1,738.17 last year. A review of the seven years' history of the Baptist Young People's Union of America was given by Rev. J. R. Gow, of Somerville, Mass. He dwelt chiefly on the origin of the union as a compromise between two classes of people; those who desired an exclusively denominational society, and those who were unwilling to take any step that might lessen the interdenominational fellowship of Christian Endeavor. The critical points in the history of the union, when these two parties threatened to clash, were frankly pointed out.

The report comes from Louisville that Dr. W. H. Whitsitt has resigned the presidency of the Southern Baptist Theological Seminary and expects to retire from the position at the end of the coming school year, in May next. It has been evident for some time past, that he could not withstand the fierce opposition with which he was meeting, and it is probably for the best that he thus takes himself out of the way. He will go, bearing the respect and esteem of a large number of friends, and especially with the affectionate regard of members of the faculty and the students, as well as the graduates of the seminary. He became connected with the seminary soon after the close of the war, while it was yet at Greenville, S. C., and has been a constant quantity and power during all the years of its history since that time. His resignation will take away from many Southern Baptist exchanges their stock subject, and will compel them to skirmish about for something else to fill their editorial columns. —*Journal and Messenger*.

Our Budget.

—Peace prospects please prayerful people.

—Read Church Extension literature in this paper.

—The harvests of another summer will soon be gathered.

—We continue to receive many congratulations on our new form.

—We have had to condense many letters to get their contents in this paper.

—We have several other interesting letters which we could find no room for at all last and this week.

—The Spanish-American war will necessitate a revision of party platforms on both sides cf the Atlantic.

—The General Christian Missionary Convention meets at Chattanooga, Tenn., October 14th to 20th, and the time will soon be here.

—B. B. Saunders and E. M. Danthil report a good meeting at Garland, Texas, this week.

—Our type is smaller than formerly, and more copy is absorbed each number now than when in our old form, and yet the demand upon our columns for space is greater than we can meet.

—One brother writes that he likes the CHRISTIAN-EVANGELIST's new form because he can hold it in one hand and the baby in the other. This example of familiarizing a child in early life to the pages of the CHRISTIAN-EVANGELIST is a good one and ought to be commended to others whose babies, children and even grown-up sons and daughters who have seen nothing but their father's political-party-paper or the farm journal.

—In a letter from Prof. Charles W. Kent, of the University of Virginia, we learn that the prospects for the Bible work there next year are very fine and that they are looking forward with great pleasure to having Dr. C. A. Young, our Chicago correspondent, with them for two or three months.

—J. H. Blake, of Drexel, Mo., thinks that Port Arthur, Tex., is one of the most promising cities of the union and the country thereabout the best for agricultural purposes he has yet seen. He regards these as places offering excellent inducements to homeseekers. A special excursion train will leave Kansas City, Mo., for Port Arthur, Sept. 6th, and he urges all who can to take this opportunity to see that country for themselves. For further particulars address J. H. Blake, Drexel, Mo.

—Our Extension Fund is a necessity from the fact that in the majority of cases mission churches cannot borrow money by the ordinary means. Banks, Insurance Companies, Building Associations and money-lenders generally do not want to loan money on mission church property, because collections of interest and principal are slow, and they do not want the ill-will of people by foreclosing mortgages on mission chapels. They avoid all trouble by refusing to loan. Our Board of Church Extension, while taking first mortgage for the security of the loan, does not forclose except in a case where long forbearance ceases to be a virtue.

—W. P. Throgmorton speaks most courteously and nobly of his opponent, J. B. Briney, in the Allen Springs debate, in his paper, the Baptist News. He says:

We found our opponent a nice gentleman indeed, and we are sure that we have never had a more pleasant debate with any man; though we have had several which have been very pleasant. Bro. Briney has had experience and understands well the rules of controversy. He is honorable and fair and knows how to act the Christian gentleman. He made as able a defense of his positions as it has been our privilege to hear, taking the discussion clear through. We shall remember him with feelings of kindness and friendship, and the Allen Springs debate will always be a bright page in memory's album.

—It is reported that W. P. Throgmorton and J. B. Briney have agreed at some time in the future to repeat the discussion on the design of baptism and the work of the Holy Spirit, which they have just concluded at Allen Springs, Ill. This repetition may be oral or in writing; most probably the latter. It is then to be published in book form, so that all who are interested in those questions may have in permanent form the best these scholarly opponents have to say for the positions on them. We expect in the meantime to have a good report of their recent debate for our readers.

—A preacher of good ability, education and character, desiring to preach the gospel where it is most needed, proposes that if any member or any person will furnish him employment at fair wages in any line of work where he can earn a living, he will preach for any congregation in need for one year, free of charge; or he would be willing to give his time and labor to any church that feels itself unable to employ a preacher if it will guarantee to support him while he is among them. There are scores of congregations living on monthly or semi-monthly preaching that would do well to make an arrangement of this kind whereby they would secure the labors of a good man all his time with little or no more cost to themselves than is involved in the support of monthly or semi-monthly preaching. Any congregation addressing the editor of this paper will be put in correspondence with the preacher above referred to.

—The concentrated fire of all the church papers and pulpits is now pouring in upon the "Camp Canteen" and we hope that these vessels of dishonor will soon meet the same end that befell Cervera's fleet. They are the enemy of our army, our homes and our country.

—When Admiral Cervera learned that in the great battle in which his fleet was annihilated the Americans lost only one man killed and two wounded, struck by the marvelous disparity he exclaimed, "God willed it so."—*The Christian Endeavor World.*

There are others of the same opinion.

—The St. Louis Republic, of this city, proposes enlarging upon the feature of religious news in such a way as to be of greater interest and usefulness to the churches in the state of Missouri than heretofore. It proposes to take notice, in a more extended way, of all conventions, protracted and revival meetings throughout the state of which it can get information. This enlargement idea was the suggestion of Rev. Samuel I. Lindsay, the editor of the religious news department, and we may also say, religious editor of the St. Louis Republic. Dr. Lindsay has been a city pastor for a number of years and will understand how to use this department to the advantage of the churches and benefit of the religious world. We are glad to see our leading journals of the secular press opening their columns wider to religious news. This necessarily means less of the froth and scum of the city in their columns. We hope that Dr. Lindsay and the Republic will have the hearty co-operation of all the preachers of Missouri in this work. Send all religious news you have direct to him in care of the St. Louis Republic. Preview reports are preferred.

—W. F. Irwin, of Bronson, Mo., writes of a very destitute region thereabouts, religiously, and suggests that preachers seeking a new field for pioneer and missionary work, remember them. If our State Mission Board, however, had the money no such church-barren districts could be found in Missouri.

—J. W. Hilton, of Bethany, Neb., says that the canvass now being made to free Cotner University from debt promises to accomplish the work, by God's blessing, this present year. There will be great rejoicing to hear that there is even a fair prospect of saving this beautiful property to our people and to the cause of education. Bro. Hilton will keep us informed of the progress of the canvass.

—J. B. Sayers, Co. A, 2nd Kentucky Vol Inft., writes us an interesting letter from Car Thomas, Chattanooga, Tenn., telling of h visit to the Nashville Endeavor Convention, permission, and of Endeavor and religio work among the soldiers. We are glad read of such work and to see such faith in o soldiers. He suggests that inasmuch as sc diers can buy good literature there cheap than it can be sent, that, outside of Bible their friends should send them the cost in ca instead. As a rule this will also work bett along the line of eatables which are apt spoil en route.

—The following timely suggestion appear in an article in the Times, Washington, I C., by J. Fraise Richard:

While it is proper and stimulating that o soldiers and sailors should receive the than of the nation through the President and h Cabinet, it is equally incumbent that t President and his subordinates should equally remembered and commended for mer torious actions in whose honors all the peop participate.

—There will always be some cases where v must give money to aid neighboring mission especially until our Extension Fund ge larger. However, if the churches hasten build up this fund, they will be speedi relieved of these irregular appeals and wi have the satisfaction of making a successful managed work a great power in our growir church.

—We publish the program of the Minneso State Convention in this paper. All our sta and district programs this year appear to b prepared with more care than usual and prom ise better conventions than ever, in each stat Their composite character necessitates length programs, but these variations may preven monotony and greatly enhance their interest especially along the entertainment line. The seem to be a happy blending of business, edi fication and Christian fellowship.

—Joseph Levering, of Baltimore, Md., ha issued a circular letter calling upon churches organizations and associations of every charac ter which believes the canteen to be injuriou to the "Boys in Blue," to pass resolution setting forth that fact and petitioning th President for its removal from every camp an Soldiers' Home over which float the Stars an Stripes, emblem of protection and liberty, an to forward same to him by mail. The sugges tion is a good one and ought to flood th "White House" with resolutions.

—We have just received the Fourteenth An nual Report of the Foreign Christian Mission ary Society's Committee in Japan. Our wor began in the Sunrise Kingdom in 1883. Th report is published in Tokyo. It shows sixtee American missionaries and eight native preach ers and helpers. The membership is 484, or gain of 125 during the past year. There are 2 Sunday-schools with 690 pupils, seven day schools with 321 pupils. There are eight house of worship and 40 places of meeting. Altogethe the report will compare favorably with man state reports in this country, where the gospe has been preached so long. The report i adorned with three admirable illustrations c our missionaries and the churches and school in Japan. A card addressed to A. McLean Corressonding Secretary, Cincinnati, Ohio will secure a copy free of charge.

—The Register-Review, of Kansas City, Mo., is to hand. This new journal is the result of a combination of the Christian Review of Kansas City, Mo., and the Church Register, of Plattsburg, Mo. It is a sixteen-page journal half the size of the CHRISTIAN-EVANGELIST with G. A. Hoffmann and R. L. Wilson, firs editors. There are several departments, on of which is "State Mission Notes," edited b T. A. Abbott, Corresponding Secretary of th State Board. The paper seems to be organized editorially with a view of special helpfulnes to the different interests of the churches o Missouri and we trust that the expectation o

noters may be realized. we congratu- e Register-Review upon its neat ap-)e and newsy columns. The Register- will appear semi-monthly.

o. Kimball, who has just returned from rogmorton and Briney debate at Allen s, Ill., says that it was one of the pleas- affairs of his life. The disputants kept d spirit from first to last and their clos- narks and hand-shake before the audi- rought tears to many eyes. No bitter- as engendered among the people by their ents and the debate partook more of the of a revival meeting than a polemical gation. The sessions were well attended e kindliest feeling predominated through- that it may be said that the Baptists sciples in and about Allen Springs, Ill., ınd understand each other better than efore.

e following paragraph from a letter from E. Mitchell, a West Point cadet, is of st and encouraging in that it shows that n is not losing its hold upon all the young f our country:

will probably be surprised to learn of istence of a Y. M. C. A. at West Point. ve an average enrollment of about 320 in :ademy and about 300 of these are mem- f the Y. M. C. A. And we have leaders h to last almost a whole year without ne leading twice. And then, too, we :wo meetings each week. Cadet Boggs, honor man" of the last graduating class ur late president and Mr. Williams, so nown in football circles, was also a good '. Mr. McClure, of Kentucky, is our ıt president and is a member of the :ian Church; but in that Association de- ations are very, very seldom mentioned. ıve almost perfected church union as far efers to us.

ıe Church of Christ at Collinwood, Ohio, edicated July 31st. The services of the egan with a sunrise prayer-meeting. The ss of the day and the sermon at night delivered by President E. V. Zollars. es Darsie is the pastor. A good program .e day was carried out.

he Chicago Times-Herald publishes the of a sermon recently preached at le's Institute, Chicago, by J. H. O. ı, in which he said:

e world must recognize the rights of every whether a Southern sun has tanned his or a Northern clime has bleached him). The extension of our territory has outrun expectation and taken us by surprise, t may be a part of the divine plan that Jnited States shall extend its protectorate civilization over other lands. If so the must be solemnly accepted. Our states- will extend the arts of peace, and Ameri- Protestants and Catholics in making the ibution of a non-sectarian Christianity, ı is the only true guarantee of liberty.

PERSONAL MENTION.

B. B. Tyler, of our editorial staff, is :o be engaged with the Broadway Church xington, Ky., for a meeting in the near e.

M. Smith, pastor of the Beulah Chris- Church, this city, has returned with his y from his vacation, and resumed his pul- ork last Sunday.

s. J. R. Holdeman, our agent at Spring- Mo., has been sick for two weeks, but s to be able to resume her work soon.

W. Strawn would like to hold one or two acted meetings in Central, Mo., this Address him at Miami, Mo.

e church at Litchfield, Ill., for financial ıns is unable to keep their pastor, J. O. y, and officially commend him to any :h in need of a good, faithful, efficient r. E. M. Austin, church clerk at Litch- will cheerfully answer any questions in ion to him.

H. Bybee, of Bolivar, Mo., would like ld two meetings during October and No- ber of this year. Churches wanting a acted meeting should correspond with lirect at Bolivar.

stor H. O. Breeden is spending August in ıountains of Colorado.

W. A. Foster will assist Pastor F. L. Platt, of Waterloo, in a tabernacle meeting.

S. B. Ross, of Oelwein, Ia., is assisting in the erection of the new house at Brainard.

C. H. Van Low, Iowa's Judge Schofield, has taken unto himself a wife. One of the accomplished daughters of Iowa City has assumed with him life's responsibilities. Their home is in Marshalltown.

T. R. Hodkinson, of Clarksville, Ia., preached at Olin August 7th.

Lawrence McCrea visited Marble Rock, Ia., on same date.

R. W. Abberly, of Columbus, Ohio, will hold a meeting at Charles City, Iowa, in September.

M. S. Johnson, of Jefferson, Iowa, reports church improvements of $300.

A. W. Taylor, of Cincinnati, Ohio, is spending a month in Harlam, Iowa.

J. R. Johnson and Bro. Pardee are in a meeting at Kent, Iowa.

Vernon J. Harrington is in a meeting at Clewfield, Ia.

J. R. McIntire, of Chicago, is now in Iowa. He may locate in Tingley.

Thos. C. McIntire, his brother, has located at Atlantic, Ia.

C. C. Rowlinson will take Marshalltown Sept. 1st.

S. D. Dutcher, pastor Walnut Hills Christian Church, Cincinnati, preached at Hannibal, Mo., one of his old pastorates, last Sunday.

J. A L. Romig, will dedicate the new tabernacle at Fremont, Neb., Aug. 14th.

Howard C. Rash, of Salina, Kan., is at Portland, Oregon, for a rest.

Wallace Thrapp, of Augusta, Georgia, has accepted the call to Crawfordsville, Ind.

Marion Stevens, pastor Edwards Street Church, Decatur, Ill., holds a Bible Institute at Lewiston this month.

John J. Higgs is now preaching for the Bloomfield and Creighton churches in Nebraska. His home is at Bloomfield.

Owing to the absence of Dr. C. A. Young from Chicago, we have no Chicago Letter this week. He is in the "Old Dominion," speaking three times a day. He reports the Piedmont Assembly, which he attended, a grand success. Bro. E. M. Smith, pastor of the Beulah Christian Church, this city, also visited that Assembly and was not unmindful of the CHRISTIAN-EVANGELIST while there. Bro. Young also attended the Martinsville Convention which he says was well attended. His next point is to be the Tidewater District Convention at Mathews, Virginia.

W. H. Wilson, of Rush Springs, Indian Territory, called at this office on last Monday.

I. N. McCash, of University Place Church, is at the lakes in Northern Iowa for a month.

Melancthon Moore, pastor of the church at Brookfield, Mo., writes that he has been called to remain there another year. About forty were added to that church during the past year under his ministry.

John L. Stine, of Reserve, Kansas, writes he would like to correspond with some minsiter who can live on about $600 per year, in a field where there is a bright outlook for the future. In writing give age, experience, educational advantages and reference.

R. A Thompson, who has been preaching for the church at DeSoto, Mo., for two months, preached for the Compton Heights Christian Church, this city, last Sunday.

W. R. Jinnett, pastor of the First Christian Church, East St. Louis, Ill., has returned from a visit to friends at Eureka, Ill.

D. F. Snider, pastor of the church at Stockport, Ia., has resigned to take effect Sept. 25th. He has accepted a call to preach for the church at Creston, Ia.

J. F. King writes that he is now employed to preach for the church at Formosa, Kas., for an indefinite period of time. He was at Wellfleet, Neb.

A. C. Smithers and his wife, of Los Angeles, Cal., will spend two weeks at Chautauqua this month, then two weeks in Kentucky, after which they will return to Los Angeles, where and when Bro. Smithers will begin the ninth year of his ministry for the First Church at that place. They called at Bethany Park on their way to Chautauqua. We are sorry they could not have stopped off in St. Louis long enough to see the CHRISTIAN-EVANGELIST.

W. F. Richardson, of Kansas City, Mo., has an admirable paper in the June number of The American Home Missionary, on "Unity Among the Disciples of Christ in the Same City." This paper will bear careful study and much prayerful meditation by the pastors of all our larger cities.

B. S. Denny, of Hampton, made the address August 4th at the laying of the cornerstone at Dows, Iowa. He was assisted by Pastors F. L. Davis and W. F. McCormick.

G. A. Ragan, of Oskaloosa, visited Chicago last week, and Prof. Youngblood preached for him August 7th.

R. W. Lilly has accepted the ministry of the Word for the church at Lynchburg, Va. He was at Chicago, Ill.

G. E. Shanklin has resigned at Slater, Mo., after a four years' pastorate, to take effect Sept. 30th, and would like to correspond with any church desiring a pastor. Address him at the above place.

Through the New England Messenger we learn that Bro. A. Flower, who sojourned during fall, winter and spring in Florida, has returned to Boston and is doing some preaching in the city.

Owing to J. S. Myers' departure from Sedalia, he has disposed of The Christian, of which he was editor, to F. L. Cook, its former business manager. The Christian has been one of the freshest and newsiest exchanges that comes to our table.

On Monday evening, July the 25th, Bro. F. O. Fannon, pastor of the First Church in St. Louis, spoke to a large audience in our church. He came on a visit to some old friends and right royally were his visit and sermon enjoyed. Bro. Fannon held a successful meeting for the church here about ten years ago, and our people became attached to him and have loved him and praised him ever since. He is a man zealous for the Master, princely in bearing, noble in purpose and grandly warm-hearted. He reports his work in the First Church in St. Louis as being in every way prosperous.—*The Christian.*

E. M. Miller, of Rockwell City, Ia., writes: "We close our work here Lord's day, Aug. 14. During the two years we have been here the membership of the church has increased from about 55 to 95. It has been a great pleasure to note the growth in grace and good works among the members. The church is without a building, but a good start has already been made toward the erection of a house. A beautiful lot, in the best possible location, has been bought and practically paid for, and there is in the treasury, in pledges and cash, nearly $600 for a building. Good workers, liberal givers, good audiences and regular attendance are some of the hopeful signs of the church in Rockwell City. My successor has not yet been chosen, but will be soon if a satisfactory man can be found. I will not locate till I have taken a needed rest.

CHANGES.

J. J. Cramer, Lexington, Pa., to Denver, Ill.

E. O. Irwin, Fredonia, N. Y., to Bowmanville, Ont.

Alan G. Clarke, Seattle, Wash., to Hydesville, Cal.

C. A. Frick, Sweet Valley to Westmore, Pa.

J. D. Dillard, Cape Girardeau, to Fredericktown, Mo.

Correspondence.

New York Letter.

We are enjoying our vacation this season at Sing-Sing-Heights-on-the-Hudson, at the old camp-meeting grounds, which is the oldest camping place for religious purposes in this part of the country—this being the sixty-seventh year of the assembly. Hence the Sing-Sing camp-meeting antedates by many years, Ocean Grove, Old Orchard and other similar places. It is a beautiful little town of tents and cottages in the midst of an extensive grove of oak and pine trees, which have grown to immense proportion through these years. Of the services we hope to speak in our next letter as at this writing they are only beginning. We had only gotten into the country and settled down to rest when on the Lord's day a message came announcing the death of Sister Salina Catharine Sinclair one of our oldest and best-loved members in the 169th Street Church.

''Grandma,'' as she was familiarly called by many of us, became a Christian in her fourteenth year and was baptized in the Hudson River. At twenty-five years of age she was married to David Sinclair, a young man of spotless Christian life, who unfortunately was spared to her only about thirteen years after their marriage. This union was blessed however with six children, the first two of whom being twins died in infancy; the other four survive her. They are: Miss Nellie E., Mrs. A. H. S. Lobingier, William A., and David C., all of whom were with her until the last, except David who lives in Idaho.

Mrs. Lobingier, her second daughter, is the widow of our late and honored Brother Henry Schell Lobingier, who for four years was the beloved pastor of this church. She has lived at her mother's home since his death and here her two lovable children, Vida and Leslie, have grown up almost to maturity. Sister Sinclair's home was in a peculiar sense ''the church home'' of the congregation. There was not a member of the church however humble who did not find a cordial welcome within her hospitable home, for she, with every member of her family, had a deep ane abiding interest in the welfare of the church. She brought her children up in the nurture and admonition of the Lord. They sing in the church choir, teach and work in the Sunday-school, in the Christian Endeavor Society, the Ladies' Aid, mission band and in fact in every activity of the church they are earnestly engaged. It is largely because of their mother's influence before them. She passed away Saturday evening, July the 30th, and on Monday evening, August the 1st the funeral services were held at her late home 1280 Franklin Avenue, in the in the presence of a large number of relatives and friends, and on Tuesday she was laid to rest in the family plot in Greenwood.

She was a very dear friend to me and mine. We made our home with her family for almost a year after coming to New York, and she and her excellent family did all in their power to make us feel at home with them. Her life was one beautiful righteousness. Her death was victorious in faith and her hope was strong and steadfast to the end. To those of us who knew her well, her memory is a precious heritage. And now she sleeps the sleep of the just. She rests from her labors and her work do follow her, and through them, though dead, she yet speaks.

⁂

Bro. E. M. Flinn, who recently graduated from Union Theological Seminary in this city, has just received and accepted a unanimous call to the pastorate of the Church of Christ, Haverhill, Mass. This is Bro. Flinn's first charge and consequently he enters upon it with grave hopes and fears. He is within seven miles of Andover Seminary and within forty-five minutes of Boston, so that he has within reach excellent opportunities for educational enlargement which he expects to take advantage of as he may be able to do. We wish for our good young brother and the Haverhill church great prosperity in the work of the Lord, and may this be but the beginning of a long and useful pastorate.

⁂

Our branch work on the east side is prospering well. The 159th street church voted sometime ago to lease a lot of sufficient size on the Southern Boulevard near 167th street and build a neat chapel at a cost of about $1,000. The church has issued bonds of $10 each and is selling them now to members and friends, and we are glad to say that within a few days most all of them have been suscribed for.

The bonds are non-interest bearing and are to be redeemed by the church at the rate of two per month until the series of one hundred shall have been taken up. Among the commendable features of this scheme, one is the saving of interest to the church and the other is the distribution of the burden of this work and the fellowship among our members so that almost every one may have part therein. This also widens the interest in the branch work among our people. It illustrates one of the invariable rules of success in church work, viz., the necessity of giving each one something to do for the Lord. We hope to be in our chapel sometime in the fall, and then we are certain our work in that quarter will move forward with even more encouragement.

⁂

Bro. W. C. Payne is at Cincinnati and Bro. J. M. Philputt is at Indianapolis on their vacations. They each expect to return to the city in time to attend our state convention at the 169th Street Church, Aug. 29th to Sept. 2nd. In speaking of the convention this leads me to say again that our committee on entertainment wishes the names of all delegates to the convention before the time of the assembly so that we may be able to locate all as comfortably as possible. All who contemplate attending, therefore, and have not done so as yet, will kindly send us their names, stating at the same time how many will be present from their congregations. This will help us quite materially. We confidently expect a profitable meeting and anxiously desire a goodly representation from every congregation in the commonwealth of New York. Come, brethren, in the fullness of the blessing of the gospel of Christ, praying and planning for the advancement of the Master's cause in our beloved Empire state.

S. T. WILLIS.

1281 *Union Ave.*

Wheeling Through England.

V.

If a bicycle tourist does not make interesting acquaintances along his route, it is generally his own fault. The people with whom he cares to talk will usually care to talk with him if he goes at it right. An unexpected and apparently unfortunate circumstance detained us in Portsmouth nearly a day after we had planned to start. To pass away part of the time we took a ferry across the harbor, and on the way fell into conversation with a corporal of marines, who straighway devoted some hours of his time to the task of showing us the barracks, fortifications and harbor. Doubtless, a corporal of marines does not stand very high in the counsels of the war department, but it was pleasant to hear this wearer of Her Majesty's uniform express his hearty sympathy with the United States in the war, and his belief that British soldiers and sailors generally would welcome an opportunity to lend us a hand. If one can draw any conclusions from a series of conversations with Englishmen of the rank and file, chosen at random all through the midlands on the South of England, it would be that the English people are as desirous of our friendship as the English Government is anxious for an alliance. Since setting foot on British soil we have not as yet observed the slightest trace of animosity toward America and Americans.

Leaving Portsmouth and passing Southampton without a stop, our route lies around the head of the Solent and through the New Forest, which has been a royal hunting preserve since the days of William the Conqueror. To the historical traveler, New Forest can never quite lose the uncanny atmosphere which is connected with the mysterious death of King William Rufus, eight centuries ago, but 'Arry and 'Arriet, from the surrounding country or from Southampton, find it a merry picnicing ground and are not oppressed by thoughts of dead kings, whether murdered or killed in the hunt. To get a mental picture of this or any other of the so-called forests of England, the American reader must reconstruct his idea of a forest. New Forest happens to be well wooded, except in its high-lying moorlands, but it would be none the less a ''forest'' if it was as barren as Dartmoor. When the term ''forest'' appears on the map, look out for a tract of uncultivated land, either wood or moor, or both, used either as a game preserve or as a sheep-range. As we pass into Dorset and through the South Downs, we are in the land of sheep.

Speaking of the sheep suggests that something ought to be said about things to eat, The first and most important statement to be made in this connection is a refutation of the charge that an American must of necessity go hungry in England. This oft-repeated allegation is nothing less than calumny and slander. There exists only a shadow of excuse for it in the fact than an Englishman will often make a meal upon what we would consider merely the accessories—bread and butter, marmalade and tea. These constitute a ''plain'' breakfast or tea. In the first week of my travels, when I was green and had not yet the ripe experience of nearly a month of English life, I frankly told one hostess that these trifles were no breakfast at all, and that drinking tea in the morning was in itself a mark of utter folly. She smiled faintly, and when I tasted the cup of coffee she made me, it became evident why she preferred tea. At the great hotels, many of which are conducted on American lines for the benefit of the travelers from ''the States,'' the distinctively English features are lost—so I am told. We are not staying at these hotels, just because we cannot afford it; second, because we do not want to, since we prefer to get nearer to the life of the English people. These two considerations seem quite sufficient to induce us to choose the more humble accommodations, to be found at inns, ''temperance hotels,'' and farm houses. We have made it a point not to ask for watermelons, green corn and other distinctively American articles, but to eat and drink what is most characteristic of the part of the country where we happen to be. So in Dorset we ate mutton chops; in Devonshire we drank cider (only they spell it with a ''y,'' as they do a bicycle ''tyre'') and ate strawberries with Devonshire cream, a delectable preparation, midway between cream and butter. In Cornwall we ate fish, especially pilchard, and the meat pie, commonly known as ''squab'' or ''cornish pastry.'' The ingredients of the latter are so many, varied and unrecognizable as to give rise to a tradition that the devil dare not enter Cornwall for fear of being put in the pie. My first experience led me to believe, on the contrary, that he had entered Cornwall and had been put in the pie, but a closer acquaintance with the Cornish pastry has relieved it of the suspicion of demoniacal possession.

When the traveler reaches Exeter, he finds himself confronted to the westward with a tract of mountainous moorland, known as Dartmoor Forest. The official bicycle guides describe the twenty-five-mile ride across it as ''wild, lonely and dangerous.'' Under these ɩumstances there was, of course, nothing to out plunge into the center of it, avoiding easy road along the coast. It was an ernoon of hard work, up and down an end- s succession of steep and stony hills, but it s worth all the quiet, level rides a man ever ık. Dartmoor may almost be described as a est without a tree. In its three hundred iare miles there is only one small grove of arf oaks, in addition to the few trees along watercourses. The hills are of granite, rered with peaty soil and crowned with great ›cks of bare granite. It is a grand and ›omy scene, even under the bright afternoon ı, and much more so when the mist of ›ning begins to gather in the valleys. Then nes a giddy rush down from this highland o the town of Tavistock, a descent of five ndred feet in two miles. In the wilds of ırtmoor I lost my companion. We found ch other the next day in Plymouth, where, ›ved by a common impulse, we were both king for the spot from which the Mayflower iled for the founding of the new Plymouth in Western world.

Phe south coast of Cornwall is not a happy nd for the cyclist, unless his appreciation of e picturesque outweighs his desire for easy ling. It is a land of endless hills, and if one shes to keep near the coast he must leave e main road, and make his way over steep d stony by-ways. It is a magnificent, high, cky coast, dotted with the most picturesque hing villages, wherever a cleft in the cliffs ıves room to wedge in a few houses and drag a few boats. The most quaint and curious all is Polperro, a town without a street ıich any four-wheeled vehicle larger than a at-wagon could get through, and that only carrying it occasionally up and down steps t in solid rock. After pressing through this d a series such as this, we came for a time to the less picturesque mining section of ornwall and thence on into the Lizard, the romontory, the southern point of which, ılled the Lizard Head, is the lowest latitude ı England. We arrived in the evening and ›und quarters in a clean little cottage over- ›oking the sea. In the morning I was up at x to take a walk along the cliffs and, ambering down the face of the rocky wall, ive into the sea at the most southerly point ı England. From the Lizard to Land's End ıe coast scenery continues with increasing randeur, and finally we stand upon the Last ocks at Land's End. We are twenty-eight ays out from Liverpool and the distance ›vered is 1,013 miles. We have been as far ıst as Dover, have stood upon the most ›utherly and most westerly points in England. 'ow we are off for John o' Groat's House, the orthern tip of Scotland. W. E. G.

Land's End.

Omaha Letter.

DEAR CHRISTIAN-EVANGELIST:—Permit me to ›ngratulate you on your improved appearance, ıd through your columns to say, probably the ıost important occurrence to the Church of hrist in this vicinity in recent years, was a ıeeting at the First Church, this city, on the vening of the 26th inst., of the representa- ves of five of our congregations, for the 'orthy object of organizing a "Disciples' Inion."

There were present from Council Bluffs, rethren S. M. Perkins, A. R. Caudle, pas- ›rs of the church there, Dr. Carter and oth- rs. The First Church of this city was well epresented, their new pastor, D. D. Burt, and goodly number of representative brethren eing present. The Walnut Hill church was epresented by the pastor, Joseph Nicholls. 'he writer and others from the Grant Street ıade up the audience.

Dr. Carter was called to the chair and D. D. Burt was made secretary.

A statement by Bro. Burt of the object of the meeting was followed by the selection of a committee of six, one from each of the congregations represented, and one, Bro. Howard Cramblet, for the church at South Omaha to draft a constitution and by-laws.

After pleasant, brief addresses from a number of those present, the meeting adjourned to meet at the call of D. D. Burt, chairman of the committee on constitution.

It should here be stated that this meeting was the result of action taken by the First Church, at a recent Lord's day morning service. This move promises *great* things. Will you not join us in prayer to our God that this move may be blessed of him, to the end that it may result in permanent good?

Elmer P. Ireland, a recent graduate from Ashley S. Johnson's "School of the Evangelists," preached very acceptably in the Grant St. pulpit on the evening of the 3rd inst. We predict for this young preacher a life of great usefulness. Some church will do well to employ this Nebraska boy.

President E. V. Zollars, of Hiram College, visited your correspondent and with him visited the great exposition recently. He was greatly pleased with the display and with Nebraska.

He was the principal speaker at our recent state meeting at Beatrice. His lectures were rich in thought, in expression and in application. All who heard him felt well repaid.

The Grant St. church was well pleased on the 24th inst., to have Miss Ada Boyd, of Bilaspur, India, address them. She spoke with great interest of that far-away land, of work accomplished and work undertaken in India. She occupied the pulpit of the Grant St. church both morning and evening. She is a very fluent and interesting speaker.

Since the writing of a certain Omaha letter by our South Omaha preacher, the writer has had a number of letters of inquiry concerning a suitable place to stop while visiting the Exposition. In self-defense he would like the privilege of answering all at once in this way.

Make the Hotel Henryton, 27th and Lake Sts., your home while in our city. Why?

Because, 1st. H. O. Devries, an elder in the Grant St. church, and state superintendent of Christian Bible-schools is the landlord.

2nd. This is the official hotel of the Omaha Christian Endeavor Union.

3rd. There is no saloon near it.

4th. It is within walking distance of the Exposition.

5th. The price is reasonable.

I trust this may satisfy all inquirers and cause our brethren who attend the great Exposition to stop at this Christian hotel. In conclusion let me say, Long live the CHRISTIAN-EVANGELIST. I know of no finer Christian publication.

CHARLES E. TAYLOR.

2312 *N. 27th St., Omaha, Neb.*

Itinerating in Japan.

For a number of months I have spent a good share of my time "on the wing." It has been said "a good Methodist should have a back for any bed and a stomach for any food." It is hard for me to stand both the Japanese beds and their food. The beds are short and the covers are hard to manage, being hot in summer and cold in winter. Sometimes I find it hard work to eat cuttle fish and praise it. When I eat devil fish I feel like the devil is getting away with me rather than I am getting away with him. These are incidents; I eat cuttle fish and devil fish when I have to do so. In the mountains the food is poor, without everything, but rice and eggs. In April I started for Akita Ken for a few weeks' work there; had to travel through the mountains, over the sand for twenty-five miles, walking a good part of the way, though I was able to ride in a sled for about ten miles.

For fourteen years the work has been going on in Akita Ken. While many do not have a very accurate idea of Christianity, there is a wide-spread knowledge of the principal facts in Christ's life and the main principals of his gospel.

When I reached the Stevens' cozy home in Akita, I felt like I had reached an oasis in the desert.

An old brother, one of the charter members in Akita, died the day before my arrival. He was full of years and good report, both within and without the church. There was a feeling of joy in his victory. The Buddhist priest in charge of the cemetery insisted on performing the Buddhist ritual at the grave.

The Japanese do not have much use for Buddhism except when buried. The priests have possession of the graveyards and try to make the most of them.

However, I heard an interesting item only the other day: A Buddhist school in Niigata compels its students to study the Bible.

In Akita, we had a number of meetings which were well-attended. Persons who had years ago been in the Sunday-school are now becoming Christians, and a good many were out to the meetings to hear of Christ afresh. One inquiry meeting, attended by about twenty persons, lasted from seven to eleven P. M., and was full of interest.

At Honjo, where there had been a good deal of trouble with two unfaithful members, we had a good hearing and met a number of former Japanese friends. At the town of Iwnia, where there is a great silver mine, we had audiences of three hundred for several nights, and a good interest was aroused, the meeting could have been continued with profit, but we had to go on to the yearly meeting.

However, Bro. Stevens who took a different route from me, met me by appointment at Yokota, one of the good towns of Akita Ken. The theatre was jammed full of attentive listeners, say 500 persons, and they listened as though they were afraid they would lose a word.

It was an inspiring audience; they came forward by the score to receive literature and to be enrolled as desiring literature by mail.

Three of us, Stevens, Saito and myself were traveling at the same time in Akita Ken.

A Buddhist, sighing said: "If Buddhists had such zeal, they could take the world."

The day of open, gross idolatry is passing away in Japan.

In one address I told this story about an idol: A man fell in a river; in order to save him a friend who could not swim, tied a rope around the neck of a Buddhist idol of wood and threw it to the man in distress, he siezed it and was dragged ashore. The priest said the Buddha had miraculously saved his life. Another man fell in and was in danger of drowning when the person who had been rescued ran and tied a rope about the neck of the first image of Buddha he found and threw it to the man in the water, he siezed it as it struck the water and *went down with it*. Stories disparaging the use of idols and holding them up to ridicule are received with cheers. CHAS. E. GARST.

On a Japanese boat going from Shanai to Sakata, June 15th., 1898.

Church Buildings.

The Scriptures speak of "nine master builders," and while the passage may not refer directly to church buildings, yet it is important that great wisdom be exercised in this department of our work.

A close observation has proven to me that comparatively few churches are practicable after ten or fifteen years. Many of them are sold at a great sacrifice; others are torn down or rebuilt at a considerable loss. Would it not be better to build houses with a view to tearing them down or closing them at the end of a decade?

For illustration: Suppose a congregation in a growing town or city. They decide to build a house. They raise a certain amount for that purpose. Instead of spending a large amount on heavy stone walls, high towers, etc., that will stand for thirty years, suppose they spend one-third of their funds for a building that will last ten years, and judicially invest the remaining two-thirds, to be returned, one-third at the end of ten years, and the other one-third at the end of twenty years. In this way:

1. The congregation will be assured of a house for thirty years.

2. When the time comes to tear down the old structure no loss will be felt, for its service will have paid for all it cost.

3. The congregation at the end of ten years will be largely different from the one that built the old house, and they can now build one that will suit their tastes and meet their demands.

4. If at the end of twenty years the growth of the town shall make a removal necessary, the second ten-year structure may be abandoned or sold for some other use, and the church will sustain no serious loss.

If it is found best to rebuild on the same site, a building can then be erected according to latest improvements and the demands of the then enlarged congregation. There are many advantages in this kind of building.

1. The congregation can always have a structure that is modern, and that meets the demands of their work, both as to location and equipment.

2. The church is not burdened with a debt.

3. The members always have a local as well as general work to enlist their activities.

4. It encourages the people to keep up with modern improvements in buildings.

5. Changes and improvements are made without losses.

Of course, the illustration above given is but a sample. The amount raised and invested at any one time would depend upon circumstances.

There are three things that should always govern a building committee.

1. Location. This is vital. Always select the very best location for the work that is to be done, and change as soon as it ceases to be the best. Many an excellent work has been missed because of the location of the building. No congregation can afford to dally at this point.

2. Beauty and utility must be combined. I would not build an uninviting, prosaic, barn-like structure. Because a building is to last but ten or fifteen years, it does not follow that it must needs be homely and uninviting. But the most important requirement is that the building be suited to the work to be accomplished in it. We are now awakening to understand that the church is a working institution, and it is high time we were awakening to understand that in a very important sense the church house is a workshop, and the different departments of work to be carried on in it should be kept in mind when drawing the plans of our building.

3. Build within our means. Did you ever hear of a church being dedicated with a surplus of money in the bank? You have heard frequently of the dedicatory service being delayed because there was not enough money nor credit to complete the building. We often hear of a heroic effort being made on the day of dedication to provide for the debt. Many times congregations deliberately build handsome houses (more permanent and beautiful than practicable), and cover them with large debts and send them down together to coming generations. They seem to say to their children, "We know better than you do how to build the kind of house you will need after we are dead and gone, so we will build it now, and you can pay for it when you take up the work."

Is it any wonder that many young people forsake the church of their parents that had been provided for them in this way?

I imagine I hear the children of the future saying to us, "Build according to your present need, and pay for what you build. We prefer to have a voice in the plans of the building for which we pay. But if you wish to leave us a legacy in the way of church property, leave it in the form of money or investments, that we may utilize in erecting the kind of building that our circumstances demand."

F. N. CALVIN.

Waco, Texas.

Cuba and Puerto Rico Markets.

The markets which are likely to be opened in Cuba and Puerto Rico to American producers and manufacturers are the subject of much attention and inquiry just now. Large numbers of letters reach the Treasury Department and Bureau of Statistics asking for information regarding the class of articles imported into those islands and the countries which have been supplying these articles. This information will be given in elaborate form in the next monthly publication of the Bureau of Statistics, the "Summary of Finance and Commerce," and will show that Cuba has been, under normal conditions, buying annually about 25 million dollars worth of goods from Spain, about 4 million dollars worth from Great Britain, less than a million dollars worth from France, and less than a million dollars worth from Germany, while from the United States her purchases have ranged from 8 to 24 million dollars in value. The imports into Cuba have been of course light during the past year or more, and a fair estimate of her purchases can only be obtained by examination of the figures of the year 1896 or earlier years.

The imports into Cuba and Puerto Rico from the United Kingdom were valued at 1,478,171 pounds Sterling in 1892; 1,321,926 in 1893; 1,121,096 in 1894; 943,793 in 1895; and 729,550 in 1896. The largest of these imports from the United Kingdom in 1896 were cotton goods 233,673 pounds Sterling, linens 137,634, iron, wrought and unwrought, 78,668, machinery 43,241, hardware, cutlery, etc., 22,936, coal and other fuel 35,429.

From Spain the imports of the year into Cuba 1896 were 134,461,675 pesetas, the value of the peseta being, according to the Mint Bureau, 19 3-10 cents. The imports from Spain in the year 1896 were larger than those in any preceding year in the decade. The largest item of the 1896 imports into Cuba from Spain was flour 20,326,882 pesetas in value, shoes 17,249,760 pesetas, sandals 13,433,510 pesetas, firearms 9,361,200, wine 7,347,045, preserved food 4,742,361, oil 3,316,218, manufactures of flax and hemp 3,700,087, soap 3,176,846, wax and stearine 2,095,622, manufactures of wood 2,257,840, smoking paper 1,885,231, beans 1,878,019, rice 1,490,849, corn 1,432,815, onions and potatoes 1,205,115, pressed meats 1,581,570, soup pastes 1,435,999, saffron 1,171,260, packing paper 1,420,235, woolen blankets 1,099,356, no other articles passing the one million pesetas line.

The exports from Spain to Puerto Rico amounted in 1896 to 37,660,609 pesetas in value, a larger sum than any other preceding year in the decade. The largest item was cotton manufactures, 12,339,767 pesetas, shoes 5,380,740, sandals 3,601,380, rice 2,652,611, soap 1,255,814, oil 1,202,075, no other item reaching one million pesetas in value.

The following table shows the total exports from the United States to Cuba during the past 10 years:

1888	$10,053,560	1893	$24,157,698
1889	11,691,311	1894	20,125,321
1890	13,084,415	1895	12,807,661
1891	12,224,888	1896	7,530,880
1892	17,953,570	1897	8,259,775

The following table shows the leading articles exported to Cuba from the United States in 1893, the year of our greatest exports to that island. Only the articles amounting to $100,000 in value or more being included:

Lard	$4,023,917
Flour	2,821,557
Machinery	2,792,050
Hams	761,082
Corn	582,050
Bacon	556,747
Potatoes	554,153
Beans and Pease	392,962
Railway bars, iron and steel	327,411
Wire	321,120
Cars, passenger and freight	271,571
Saws and Tools	243,544
Steam Engines	130,652
Agricultural Implements	130,341
Cut Nails	107,002
Boots and Shoes	114,943

The exports from the United States to Puerto Rico in 1897 were $1,988,888, in 1896 they were $2,102,074, in 1892, $2,856,003. They were of about the same character as the exports to Cuba, wheat flour being the largest item, $516,188 in 1897; lard $228,051, bacon and hams $112,602, pickled pork $152,411, beans and pease $57,550, machinery $69,462, no other articles of export in 1897 reaching as much as $50,000 in value during the year. O. P. A.

Butler College Day at Bethany Park.

Saturday, July 30, was celebrated at Bethany Park in honor of Butler College. In spite of occasional showers, there was a larger attendance at the Park than at any previous day of the Assembly. A large number of persons came from Indianapolis and other parts of the state especially for the day. Quite a number of alumni were present, some having come from beyond the Mississippi, and even from the Pacific Coast.

The exercises began with an address to preachers by Prof. Jabez Hall, of Butler Bible College, upon the mutual relations of pastor and people. This was the closing address of a series that have been offered throughout the week by Prof. Hall to preachers. Any one who is familiar with the graceful and elegant diction of Dean Hall, with his wide experience as a pastor, and with his deeply spiritual view of a minister's responsibilities, can conceive what an inspiration these heart-to-heart talks have been to the brethren present.

After an hour's intermission, spent in social mingling, the audience assembled again at 11 o'clock to hear the address of the day, delivered on behalf of the University of Indianapolis, of which Butler is a part, by the Rev. J. Cumming Smith, pastor of the Tabernacle Presbyterian Church of Indianapolis. Dr. Smith is a Canadian, educated at Toronto University and Princeton Seminary. He was for some years a Professor in Philosophy at Toronto University, and is eminently qualified to represent academic ideas upon any platform. His address was upon the "Catholicity of Culture," and was highly appreciated by his audience. Dr. Smith touched upon religious culture in a felicitous manner and with such broadness and liberality that many declared afterwards that if his denomination had not been previously announced, no one would have been able to discover it.

Bro. J. E. Pounds, who presided, then introduced the college quartette, who sang selections of college songs. After dinner, and the happy hours of reunion among alumni and old friends, the assembly gathered again in the tabernacle for the Bible College session. Addresses were made in the order named, by Burris A. Jenkins, H. O. Breeden, of Des Moines, A. C. Smithers, of Los Angeles and Bro. Herzog of Hiram College. All these brethren spoke very enthusiastically of the future of Butler Bible College. Bros. Breeden and Smithers declared that the attractions to young men preparing for the ministry at Butler Bible College are unsurpassed in the brotherhood, and predicted a large gathering of students for next year.

Bro. Pounds then reported progress in the raising of funds and the prospect of students for the next session. He told of students coming from all quarters, from Texas and Missouri, from Kansas—three from Kansas—Iowa and also from the Eastern states, to study for the ministry.

The evening session was devoted to a patriotic address by Pres. Scot Butler, which was listened to by a large audience. Altogether, notwithstanding the fact the attendance thus far at the Park has not been quite up to that of recent years, the celebration of Butler Day is considered eminently satisfactory.

BURRIS A. JENKINS.

A Glance at Michigan.

word, Michigan, means "a weir for fish," ıe peninsula shape of the wolverine state a coast line to justify the Indiana ation.

higan, like Kentucky, was once "a dark ɔloody ground." Indian, Frenchman, shman, American fought in its forests n its lakes for possession, but the irre-ble Yankee came out on top, according custom. Michigan became a territory 5 and a state in 1837.

812, Congress passed a law that 2,000,000 of land should be surveyed in the terri- of Louisiana, and like quantities in s and Michigan to be set apart for the rs in the war with Great Britain.

lands were surveyed in Louisiana and s, but the surveyors reported that there ıo lands in Michigan fit for cultivation.

ordingly, Congress repealed the law so it related to Michigan and appropriated 000 more in Illinois and 500,000 in Mis- instead.

se surveyors would have "a bad taste in mouths," if they could see the country for Moses from Mt. Pisgah saw no better.

835, war existed between Michigan and overeign state of Ohio, over a strip of laimed in common by them; troops were nto the disputed territory, but happily ifficulty was settled by Congress before eads were broken.

higan consists of two peninsulas, ost surrounded by water," but numerous are found inland, and these are filled water and fish, perch, bass and blue-gill, ıe law only permits them to be taken with and line.

t is cultivated in Michigan. A member ongress from this state is known as permint Todd," because he cultivated omatic herb.

ries are a staple product. The strawberry from June 1st to July 4th. Then the erries begin to ripen and they last three . There were shipped from Benton Har- one day, 25,000 crates of raspberries. are also large fields of huckleberries and erries. The berry crop gives employment army of hands and brings in considerable y.

peach crop promises well and will last August 1st till snow flies.

re are about 8,000 Disciples in Michigan, ed among some 200 churches.

re are but four strong churches.

not as easy to make Disciples in Michi- as in Missouri. Unbelief and heresy ils to an alarming extent. The white of the Adventists are spread abroad, and prophets tell of their near coming of the Spiritual mediums tell from what l their souls are developed—cat, dog, or cow. They can make you a picture of deceased wife or your great grandmoth- pirit, if you give them an old photograph same to begin with.

re are others who teach that men are ssed with two minds each, an objective subjective mind. In most men the sub- e mind lies dormant, but when both are active we have a genius.

dicine need not be taken, let the patient t to sleep, believing that he must take ine in the morning and the subjective will produce the same effect as if the ine had been taken.

th-cure, mind-cure and Christian Science rs abound, "and my people love to have "

men preachers are numerous. Divorces asily obtained and frequent. Many be- with Betsy Bobbit:

"If women had a mice's will,
They would rise up and get a bill."

law compels a man to support his family ichigan. A poor man may marry an ss, and she can then get a divorce for non-support. She don't have to spend a single denairus of her money.

Perhaps this all flavors of the pessimistic, perhaps the evils are exaggerated. A new minister called upon one of his lady members. He remarked, "Some of the members think my sermons are long, do you think so?" The lady member replied: "They are not long, they only appear so."

There is much good in Michigan. The people are peaceable and intelligent. There is a healthy temperance sentiment. Religious people of the various sects are friendly.

Union meetings among the orthodox are frequent.

Michigan has a good school system and the influence of the great university at Ann Arbor is felt throughout the state.

The people of Michigan are proud of their General Shafter, the hero of Santiago.

The writer has been called to preach two patriotic discourses, Memorial Day and Thanksgiving Day, July 10, both union services. The people when once at church give good attention to the speaker.

Two old Disciple preachers reside in Paw Paw, Bros. Brooks and Hurd. As I have not moved my family here, I board with Brother and Sister D. Woodman. They are exemplary old people and have a delightful home.

I congratulate the CHRISTIAN-EVANGELIST on its improvement and have misgivings as to the fate of this rambling essay, but knowing that "faint heart never won fair lady," I venture the overture. J. P. DAVIS.

Paw Paw, July 20.

Michigan Grains.

L. H. Smith, minister of the Church of Christ, of Algonac, visited in Ohio during the first of the month, and the writer filled his pulpit on the 3rd of July. The work there is prospering well under the care of so faithful a man of God as Bro. Smith, who has won the hearts of the people. The congregation has outgrown the church building and we hope that a year's time will give them a start in the direction of a new building.

On the 10th of July the much-loved Bro. McCall, of Yale, was enjoying a recreation in one of the rural districts, and the writer supplied his pulpit. It was a pleasure to spend a Sunday with the Yale brethren, as I labored with them for four years. Their church building was erected during that time. When I finished my work there, which was done in my own feeble way, the church made no mistake in selecting the sweet-spirited and pure Bro. McCall, who came to us at that time from the Methodists. May the Lord bless him in his work.

On the 17th of July I was in Wovesta and Wilmot, and preached for Bro. Kean. He is doing a good work and is worthy of better support than those two weak churches can afford to give him. Bro. Kean united with our people two years ago. He came from the Free-will Baptists and dearly loves our plea and people. The church at Wilmot will erect a new church edifice during the coming year. They hope to erect one which will be a credit to our people in their nice little town.

The brethren at Durand have secured a promise from S. S. Jones, of Danville, Ill., to hold a meeting for them during the month of August. A hall has been rented for one year, and it will be used for Bro. Jones' meeting. There are just fifteen Disciples in Durand, rich in faith and of course are poor in this world's goods. We hope that at the close of Bro. Jones' meeting our number will be increased. Durand is a great railroad center and is also in the center of the state. It has a population of twenty-five hundred, and is the growing town of Michigan.

How very important it is to get our churches established in all such growing towns. It is so hard to get our work established, after the different sects have their organizations to oppose us. There are so many towns in the state of Michigan with just a few Disciples, who might meet together to break the loaf and admonish one another on the Lord's day and grow in grace and in the knowledge of the truth, if they just had the zeal and courage to do so; but instead, in many cases, they are losing their opportunity. There will be a day of reckoning and they will be the losers by not having been faithful, but those who have been loyal to the Savior will be rewarded with the crown of life. Loved ones in the Savior, think of this. If you are living in a town where there are but a few Disciples, think of this and ask with loving eyes looking heavenward, "Lord, what can we do for thee."

R. BRUCE BROWN.

All Should Take the Reading Courses.

The Bethany C. E. Reading Courses seem so wise in themselves that their plan of work is their own best commendation. To be most useful our young people must be a reading people. What better lines to fit them for usefulness than the three lines suggested in these courses?

They need to know not only more about God's Word, but how to study it; and most admirably adapted to this end is the small handbook on Bible study. They need to know more about the people and the movement with which they are connected, and hence the handbook on the Disciples. They dare not be ignorant on the subject of missions, and hence the handbook on missions. The courses are well worthy the attention of our older people, *and all our preachers could take them with profit.*

These handbooks, covering the above lines, are neat in design and are written in a clear, terse style by strong, representative men from amongst us. Our young people must leave the "iridescent" dreamland and prepare themselves for real action. To do this they must *read*. The Bethany Reading Courses come as a God-send in this hour of need. It is a mind-invigorator and gives a base of supplies for largest future usefulness.

Our young people should know more of the Bible. Here are all the main lines of Bible-thought, focusing on a few pages, making them fairly glow with concentrated heat. They should know more of missions. No book written has within the same space more fuel for missionary fire. The handbook on the Disciples is an encyclopedia of facts that lead up to our present work and standing among the reformers of the world. It was a happy day for our work when the courses were planned. Have your young people begin to form a Circle at once. Have your old people take it. *Take it yourself. It is good.*

M. E. HARLAN.

Pastor First Church, Topeka, and President Kansas S. C. Union.

Topeka, Kansas, July 21.

Form versus Life.

CHRISTIAN-EVANGELIST:—May the Lord bless you on your great mission in this world, spreading the pure light of the gospel of the Son of God, carrying light and truth to many homes and hearts. I admire the new dress and form of the CHRISTIAN-EVANGELIST. I believe this will begin a new era in the life and work of the CHRISTIAN-EVANGELIST. It is clear, clean and cultured; it is just superb! I like it more than ever. It is filled with rich spiritual food. I have just finished reading an article from the pen of J. J. Haley which, to my mind, is just grand, rich and full of truth—"more truth than poetry." I wish that all of our preachers and every member could read this one article. If heeded it would produce a great reformation in the minds of many of our people. There is too much dead formality in many of our churches. I fear "the dry rot of formalism" already has set in in many places, and many persons are substituting religious forms and theories for the divine life and holy character. I fear it is true that many believe when they have done the form they have paid the debt, purchased the indulgence and from that time on you see no change in their life. They live, act, walk and talk just like the world. There is no change in their heart (mind) hence no change in their life. The question in my mind is, have these people been baptized in the name of Jesus Christ for the remission of sins? Have they really been baptized into the name of the Father, the Son and the Holy Ghost? May the Lord save the people from dead formalism and fill them with his Spirit, love and power.

J. P. HANER.

Religious Work at the University of Virginia.

The assertion has frequently been made by those unacquainted with the facts that the University of Virginia is an irreligious institution. How utterly untrue this is, is shown by the fact that every leading denomination in the South counts among the men who fill its pulpits, edit its papers and control its counsels many graduates of the University of Virginia. Virginians take a natural pride in remembering that the Young Men's Christian Association at their University was the first Y. M. C. A. ever organized at an American college. Since the founding of the University of Virginia Y. M. C. A. in 1898 its members have gone out to fill many of the pulpits, the college and editorial chairs, and other positions of high professional and business influence in the south. "Wipe out," says Colonel Charles S. Venable, "the foreign missionaries of the Presbyterian Church who are University of Virginia men, and you almost destroy the enterprise;" and this is only one direction which the vast influence for good at the University has taken.

The problem of bringing active religious influences to bear upon the young men of our universities and colleges is one of growing seriousness. How well this problem has been solved at the Virginia University and the force of the moral and religious influence exerted there strikes the attention alike of visitors and residents. "I have never known," says Rev. Charles A. Young, National Secretary of the Christian Woman's Board of Missions, whose special work brings him into touch with student life at colleges and state universities from Michigan to Georgia and from the Atlantic to the Pacific, "I have never known a more manly Christianity than exists among the students of the University of Virginia at present. There is no show or sham in their religious pretensions." And the words of others are equally strong. Rev. John Williams Jones, known and loved throughout the south, says: "I have known the University of Virginia for over forty years and during all of that time have never heard of a case of skepticism originating there, while I have rejoiced to know of not a few cases of skepticism which have been cured by influences brought to bear upon them at the University." So much for the statement, more current in former years than now, that Mr. Jefferson founded an atheistical school.

The University Y. M. C. A., which has just closed its fortieth year of continuous work, has given out some interesting statistics for the past year. Of the four hundred and eighty-nine students at the University of Virginia last session, two hundred and fifty-eight were church members and one hundred and seventy were active members of the Young Men's Christian Association. Of the church members there were eighty-six Episcopalians, sixty five Presbyterians, forty Methodists, thirty-eight Baptists, thirteen Catholics and ten members of the Disciples Church, with others unclassified.

CHARLES W. VENT.

Notes and News.

Chatauqua Letter.

rof. H. L. Willett's work here, for this son, has closed. It has been hard, but en-siastic and earnest. People have followed . as a prophet of old, becaue he has inter-ted the Scriptures, by the internal truths the everlasting record made by the serv-s of the Lord and fulfilled in the spirit and son of the divine Son of God and his ıteousness.

ome of the thoughts gathered in conver-on are pointed and helpful.

igher criticism, when governed by the rit of Christ, is helpful to the scholar in eling mystery, and in bringing our own up he great beauty and power of the Script-s and their lessons to man.

o reach Christian union we must all get k to Christ and be controlled by his Spirit. he world is learning the Lord's prayer, that e all might be one'' and his call unto hu-ity as one great brotherhood.

hey who stand for creeds are now com-ed to make answer unto their own house-ls, who read away from theology and into pathways marked, ''Thus saith the d.'' The more the Bible is studied for , in the wants of man's better nature, more the wonderful the book is ''a lamp to feet and a light to our path.''

he quetion of baptism is where all come, there is no longer any dispute among olars. Immersion is right. The motive ch brings one to its requirements settles validity with all peoples.

he concensus of opinion is direct for Chris-ı union, and when the people reach the form their leaders will find the way of Bible is best.

o-day Dr. Burrows, of Chicago, opened wide field of Foreign Missions, in his wonderful ds on Hinduism. The thunder of the guns he Pacific Ocean is to open the doors of asteries, unchain the Bible and liberate it n papal serfdom. How the cheers went up n he spoke of a new light for Asia, ing by way of Manila, and the message of d's liberty from America!

ext week, Thursday and Friday, we have Vho is Jesus Christ?'' and ''Why did Christ ?'' by Dr. Behrends, and Dr. Burkley's stion Box.

ur own Bro. Z. T. Sweeney will have usands to hear his great argument on oundations,'' Sunday evening. This is a d mission point. People come and inquire we are, and what we believe, and they are n North and South, and many states of the ion. W. J. F.

Disciple Headquarters,
ıutauqua, N. Y., July 30th, 1898.

An Answered Prayer.

t is recorded of Adoniram J. Judson that he l: ''I never in my life prayed for a thing, nestly and persistently, that it did not at come. It may not have come in the way I ected it or when I expected it, but it cer-ly came at last.'' I quote from memory. ink this ought to be the experience of ry disciple who endeavors to work for Lord and Master. The difficulty with the jority of Christians is that they lack in the sistence which at last brings success. orge Muller prayed persistently for months enlargement in his works at Ashley Down, stol, England, for homeless and helpless hans, before he told any man or received a lling. At last the Lord opened the windows eaven and flooded him with means. Why y not this experience be duplicated by every n who gives himself unselfishly to others as ller did? Is it not a fact that prayer, per-ent, earnest and fervent, should play a far re important part in our educational and sionary enterprises? Is it not a fact that the individual in ''laying up'' what he does not need, the college in accumulating a big endowment, the missionary enterprise in accumulating property on which it can depend in an hour of pressing need, makes the ''life of trust'' in which our Father delights partly impossible, or in many cases wholly impossible?

God has expressed himself on this point in both dispensations. He gave his people bread from heaven day by day. He did this to teach them to trust him. Some of them tried to ''lay up'' for the ''rainy day'' with dastrous results: ''It bred worms and stank.'' Under Jesus his disciples are to pray for their daily bread. How many of us so live by putting our surplus into his cause that we can do this? This is to my mind, a very serious question.

I have had some experience along this line. It has been a severe test of my faith and patience, but the experience and the enlargement have and do more than overbalance the cost. I relate my experience for the benefit of ''whom it may concern.'' It began in the early spring of 1894—over four years ago. I judged from general prospects that our room would in the following fall be insufficient. I met the students in the college chapel, who were as enthusiastic as I was. I spoke of my plans for enlargement. The building I had in mind was to be three stories high and contain thirty rooms, the first story to be used as a cellar. I proposed to the students that if they would pledge the work to excavate the foundation, we would pledge the money to buy the brick. They agreed to do this. We also covenanted to meet in the chapel every evening and pray for means to complete the building. We were launching into what was to us an almost unknown sea. The young men began to dig and draw brick. We laid the corner-stone May 10, 1894. We have been working on the building and praying for means to finish it all these years. The passer-by reads on the corner-stone in imperishable marble the words of our Redeemer: "The poor have the gospel preached unto them." Last summer we finished the second story and, although we could not put in the steam, there were plenty of young preachers who were glad to live in cold rooms in order to secure an education. Volumes of prayers have gone up for the completion of this building. At last four years and four months' persistent prayer and unremitting toil have brought their reward and the building is in the hands of the painter. *And we have learned to pray! The young men have learned to pray!* The building is already wired for electric light and we are confidently looking for the money to put in the steam before frost appears. This building is and shall be opened to the poor young men of the Church of Christ. We propose to train men to be *place-makers* and not *place-hunters*. We shall have at the opening, Sept. 24, room for 140 with at least 300 applicants. Our work invites the poor young preacher to come and share its poverty, its struggles, its triumphs. It makes our brethren everywhere to invest their money in an effort that has already done and is destined yet to do much for the cause of pure Christianity. Our work does not "beg;" it is its only appeal. Two things I hesitate not to affirm: 1. We have more poor young preachers to sit at our tables than sit together anywhere else on earth; 2 A dollar and prayer invested here will never die! "Believest thou this?"

PRES. ASHLEY S. JOHNSON.

School of the Evangelists, Kimberlin Heights, Tenn.

Minnesota.

David Husband reports two baptisms at Olivia. Again please bear in mind that the treasurer's books close Tuesday (next) the 16th.

THE CONVENTION.

See the program and note the treat in store for all who attend. Of course you will be present. It will be a gem; three days and home again. The program committee had to cut much, but its "boiled-down" policy will be approved of. "Come, let us reason together" respecting Minnesota missions.

THANKS TO THE CHRISTIAN-EVANGELIST.

"A Christian paper in every home" is a taking slogan, and right persistently may the question be pressed, which introduces a word we wish to say regarding the CHRISTIAN-EVANGELIST. The CHRISTIAN-EVANGELIST has very kindly mailed gratis above 200 copies of the present issue to some two score points and in the state in the interest of increased attendance at the convention and now to put into effect the good old rule, "One good turn deserves another." What say you to "booming" the CHRISTIAN-EVANGELIST's subscription list? Will you not only personally subscribe, but circulate a subscription list about among the brethren? Scan the columns and see what a rich feast the publishers set before you. Will pastors and missionary secretaries please press the matter? It need scarcely be explained that this notice comes not at the suggestion of any CHRISTIAN-EVANGELIST attache.

VACANT PULPITS.

A matter which ought to be referred to in every letter is that at all times the secretary is in touch with preaching brethren available to the Minnesota field. Amen! Will officers of churches please bear this in mind?

EVANGELISTIC.

Evangelist A. B. Moore reports continued good audiences at Austin and satisfactory progress made in the new church building enterprise.

Evangelists Atwood and Sweetman commence a meeting at Luverne as the CHRISTIAN-EVANGELIST goes to press. These brethren come to the state believing in Minnesota and it is hoped their efforts will be blessed.

F. H. MELLEN, Sec. M. C. M. S.

Box 450 Minneapolis.

St. Louis Letter.

One of the peculiarities of a great city is the unstable character of its "*bon ton*" districts. These shift about without much regard to natural laws. The district in which the publishing house of the Christian Publishing Company now stands was once the aristocratic district of the city. On either side of "Lucas Place," now Locust Street, stand elegant stone-front mansions, once the homes of the rich, but now largely publishing, boarding, school and business houses, and what was once two magnificent church buildings. The church in which Dr. Brooks preached for so many years is now a theatre and the great stone cathedral-like stone church building where Dr. Niccolls preached to the wealth of the city so long, is now used only for mission purposes. Both of the churches have gone west, the former to Compton Avenue and the latter to Taylor Avenue. This is the second westward move of these two churches. They are following up the class of people by whom they were built and for whom they exist, and hence their change from rich to richer possessions.

When the high-tone atmosphere comes over a given district, property immediately takes on immense values. A portion of these values grow out of the class of buildings erected, while much of it is merely assumed for protective purposes—protective as to the social rank of its families. In proof of this we have only to point to the immense decline in the value of these same buildings after the high-tone atmosphere lifts and drifts to settle elsewhere. The writer has talked with men who, ten and twenty years ago, bought elegant stone-front houses as an investment which they are now offering to sell for from one-third to one-half less than they paid for them. The wealth of the district simply took wings and flew away and these men were left to wonder why they had been so short-sighted and foolish. Had they bought unimproved property farther west they might now be worth millions to their present thousands.

But the purchase of improved property has not always proved successful with investors. Many long-sighted men have bought large interest in suburban property here and there, put down costly improvements and begged and coaxed for the aristocratic swell to come, but it would not, and so their thousands are locked up in unsalable real estate. That high-tone atmosphere is an uncertain quantity. No one seems to know when it will go nor where. It lifts and splits, shifts and drifts, by some law not yet monopolized by speculators. And so the lucky ones after all, in this as in other things, are those who happened to be in the right place at the right time. Go into many of the old streets in St. Louis to-day, and the old residents of that street will tell you that it used to be "one of the swell streets of the city, but it has gone down terribly." Some families are able to follow up these social waves, but not all, and not a few are lost in the attempt.

One of the chief causes of these social, moral and physical district transformations, of course, is the growth of the city's industrial and commercial interest. As these enlarge the residence portions of the city are encroached upon and its families retreat. To get away from noise and dirt, the common people and commerce, they offer their property for sale at low figures and seek new quarters. Vanderventer Place fifteen years ago headed the society procession on the west; now it is at the foot on the east. Its historic mansions will soon become common houses as those of Lucas and other places. The advance line of this wave is now alongside Forest Park on the west, but with the extension of electric lines into the hills beyond it will not remain long at this point and the costly churches just erected in the west will be confronted with the same old problem—farther west—at no distant day.

But a more important question is, Are churches for the rich only, or for all people? That many of them are compelled to move west to retain an audience is evident, but that they move west to find a people to whom they can minister is not the case. They almost invariably move out of a more densely populated soul-impoverished district than those moved into. And why? The people will not come, they say. And why? But why should they come? Is not the command of the Lord to go? Why, then, do they not remain and minister to the intellectual, moral and physical wants of the people who surround them? The money usually sacrificed in moving a church "farther west," doubtless amounts to more than the church ever gave in the way of direct help for those in need in its immediate neighborhood, or perhaps in its history. Will the Lord not hold churches responsible for this waste of ointment in their efforts to follow the whims of fashion and fashionable society? But here again we are confronted with high mountains, and so think best to conclude our epistle.

B. U. I.

Evangelistic.

KENTUCKY.

Hebron, August 5th.—The Point Pleasant Church closed a splendid meeting last night. There were 23 additions to the church; 22 by baptism. Will begin a meeting with the South Fork Church August 15.—GEO. W. WATKINS.

TEXAS.

Garland, August 1st.—The writer and E. M. Douthit are in a very fine meeting at Garland, Texas. At the close of the second week there were 50 additions and the interest unabated. Among the additions are some of the leading business men of the town and a number of excellent young men.—B. B. SAUNDERS.

UTAH.

Ogden, July 30.—One added by letter last Lord's day. Larger congregations than before and better attendance both at Junior C. E. and C. E. Societies than at any previous meeting.—J. H. BAUSERMAN.

KANSAS.

Charles M. Sharpe, of Lawrence, reports 10 additions at regular services for July; seven by baptism, three otherwise.

Stafford, August 6.—Closed a short meeting in Macksville with two baptisms. Will try and organize this county for some good man who wishes to stay here and build up the cause. We have several good fields for proper men.—P. H. GUY, Evangelist 7th District Kansas.

OHIO.

Findlay, August 2.—In nine months 101 have been added here, over 70 being adults.—T. W. ADAMS, pastor.

Defiance, August 7.—We are assisting Pastor John Hayes and Evangelist G. H. Sims in a tabernacle meeting at this place. Meeting young and no accessions; we hope and pray for many.—A. O. HUNSAKER.

MISSOURI.

Paris, August 1.—Three additions under my labors since last report; one by relation from the Baptists, and two by baptism.—C. H. STRAWN.

Nashville, August 2.—Closed a three weeks' meeting here with 29 additions, 19 by baptism, five from the denominations and five by letter. Bro. W. W. Warren preaches here part of the time and is doing a fine work. This is a good church and the meeting was an exceedingly pleasant one to us.—MORGAN AND DAUGHTER.

ILLINOIS.

Watseka, August 1.—Three added here yesterday; one from Presbyterians and two from Baptists. 72 of our Junior Endeavorers picnicked recently on the banks of the Iroquois, near our beautiful county-seat.—B. S. FERRALL.

Arrowsmith, August 1st.—Our new pastor, Elder G. M. Read, is an efficient leader. A church rally was held yesterday. Six accessions at the A. M. service; seven during the month.—CHAS. D. HOUGHAM.

NORTH DAKOTA.

Ellendale, August 1.—Began a meeting August 3rd at Clark, S. D., under the direction of the South Dakota State Board. Our work at Ellendale is doing nicely. The church at Ellendale is the only self-supporting Church of Christ in the whole state of North Dakota.—T. S. NOBLITT.

IOWA.

Des Moines, August 1.—Baptized three young people at Lehigh yesterday. I will deliver a few sermons there this week.—L. F. MCCRAY.

Sheldon.—Four added by J. R. Mowrey.

Shannon.—Organized with 44 members.—J. R. JOHNSON.

Sioux City.—Two more.—WALTER VAN DE WALKER.

Alta.—Thirty-six gathered together.—WRIGHT AND MARTINDALE.

Kamraw.—Two added five miles south of here.—JAS. R. BELL.

Waterloo.—Four added.—F. L. PLATT.

Mt. Auburn.—One added.—JAS. T. NICHOLS.

CALIFORNIA.

Fortuna, Aug. 1st.—Two additions July 24th; baptism at the close of the service last evening.—A. B. MARKLE.

INDIANA.

Terre Haute, July 29.—At the close of our prayer-meeting, Wednesday night, July 27, six persons came forward and made the good confession and were baptized the same hour of the night.—N. W. WITMER.

Indianapolis, Aug. 1st.—At North Park Church, two additions. At the Broad Ripple Church, one addition.—J. M. CANFIELD.

Publishers' Notes.

At the beginning of J. G. Encell's book, "The Exiled Prophet, or What John Saw on Patmos," is an interesting essay on Daniel, by D. R. Dungan. This essay is intended to prepare the reader for the explanation given of the things seen by John on Patmos. The author of the work proper takes the position that the things contained in Revelation are to be understood by some one at some time. If it were not so it would not be called the "Revelation of Jesus Christ."

Those who like reading of this kind will enjoy this book. The book is one that will be read with profit by many. The author's style is clear.—*The Gospel Messenger, Mt. Vernon, Illinois.*

"The Exiled Prophet" is a late publication of the Christian Publishing Co. It is the fruit of many years' study of Revelation by its author, and contains 245 pages. The price is $1.25, postpaid.

"Across The Gulf," by Mrs. N. M. Vandervoort, published by the Christian Publishing Co., St. Louis, Mo., deals with the times of Christ, and its object is to show that out of Christ there is no remission. In the working out of the story the great truths spoken by the Master are mingled with historical facts.

It is written from the intelligent scriptural standpoint of a Disciple of Christ. Most young people will read fiction of some kind, so it is infinitely better for them to read such pure and wholesome stories as this one, even if some "traditions" have been interwoven.—*Christian Guide, Louisville, Ky.*

Members of Endeavor Societies who need books that will give them instructions concerning their work will find the following books contain valuable information along that line. The Endeavorers who will carefully read these books and be guides by the instructions contained therein will find great pleasure and profit in their work as members of the Christian Endeavor Societies. "The juvenile Revival, or The Philosophy of the Christian Endeavor Movment," by Thomas Chalmers. Introduction is by Dr. Francis E. Clarke. This book begins with the planting of the Christian Endeavor movement and follows it up through its many stages to the full fruitage. It is neatly bound in cloth and the price is 60 cents. "The Y. P. S. C. E. at Work," by Frank R. Stutzman. A pamphlet giving full instructions to various committees, the author having had many years' practical experience in Endeavor work. Price 10 cents. "The Helping Hand," by W. W. Dowling. This is a manual of instruction for the Y. P. S. C. E. covering all points concerning this work. Flexible cloth, per copy 25 cents.

Those who have read "Doctrines and Dogmas of Mormonism Examined and Refuted," by D. H. Bays, speak in the highest terms regarding the merits of the book. We give the following extract from a review of this book by the Gospel Advocate, Nashville, Tenn.: "The author was reared in the faith of Mormonism, and was for twenty-seven years a zealous advocate and defender of its peculiarities; and thus he has had a most excellent opportunity to obtain his knowledge by close relationship with all the prominent leaders of that faith. He presents the doctrines as they are defined by its leading minds, together with the biblical evidences adduced in their support, and then offers such evidences from scriptural and other sources as overthrow their arguments, and prove the entire system erroneous. It contains full proof-texts and historical references upon every phase of the question discussed, which makes it a complete handbook of ready reference. It will be an indisputable help to those who in any way have to meet Mormonism." This book contains 460 pages, is neatly bound in cloth, and the price is $1.50, postpaid.

Ohio Notes.

The annual district convention began the first of August. There are twenty-five districts in Ohio. This means five conventions. Who dares to estimate the power of these conventions in advancing the cause of Christ?

Bellefontaine dedicated her new house July 24th. President Zollars was at the helm. This is a good house, worth about $8,000. We shall expect great things from our brethren there, now that they have better tools.

Ohio soon loses one of her best young men, Bro. Plattenburg, of Ashland. He goes back to Uniontown, Pa. He has done a fine work at Ashland and they are loath to let him go. He is a strong preacher.

The church at Tiffin is without a pastor at present. This is a good church. They will no doubt procure a leader soon.

Samuel Traum, one of the recent graduates of Hiram, will preach for the churches at Fairview and Danville, Highland county. Hitherto these churches have been doing without preaching. They are strong churches in latent force and it is hoped Bro. Traum will develop them in usefulness.

Guy Hoover has given up the work at Zanesville to re-enter Hiram to finish his course. His successor has not yet been announced. He brought this church up to self-support in his two years' work there.

The Fourth Avenue Church in Columbus, only two years and a half old, is the strongest church in district No 1. Their growth is phenomenal. E. S. DeMiller is a wise and devoted leader.

The corner-stone of the new church at Steubenville was laid recently. Bro. Slater is doing faithful work there. Our brethren have the largest Bible-school in the city.

J. W. Baker has taken the work at Galion. They contemplate a house soon. The faithful few there have made a bold struggle in the years past.

W. J. Russell, formerly of Columbus, recently held a tent-meeting at Crooksville and organized a church of 36 members. They contemplate a house at once.

John S. Lawrence, the father of the North Fairmount Church, Cincinnati, was elected Corresponding Secretary of the Ohio Christian Endeavor Union. He will make a faithful officer.

The new church at Martain's Ferry is only about six months old but has a settled pastor and its own house, and 100 members. This is good work. But there are more places in Ohio where the same work could be done.

Peter Butts, of Newton Falls remembered Hiram College to the extent of $30,000. What a wonderful monument. This ought to stimulate others to a like liberality.

The North Central Ohio Ministerial Association will meet at Mansfield the fifth and sixih of September. No wide-awake preacter in reach of Mansfield can afford to miss this meeting. A good practical program has been prepared. F.

SUBSCRIBERS' WANTS.

MEMORIAL
STAINED GLASS WINDOWS
Church Furnish'gs, Pulpits,
Pews, Communion Sets Etc.
JACOBY-SPIESS MFG. CO.,
202 N. 2nd St. ST. LOUIS, MO.

BUCKEYE BELL FOUNDRY
E. W. VANDUZEN CO., Cincinnati, O., U. S.
Only High Class, Best Grade Copper and Tin
Full, Sweet Tone
Cheapest for Price
Fully Guaranteed
CHURCH BELLS

BLYMYER
CHURCH
BELLS.
UNLIKE OTHER BELLS
SWEETER, MORE DURABLE, LOWER PRICE.
OUR FREE CATALOGUE
TELLS WHY.
Write to Cincinnati Bell Foundry Co., Cincinnati, O.

Missionary.

September Fourth!

We need and must have the largest offering for Church Extension at the date just given that we have had in all the fifteen years of our work in this field. I say "must," not because of any authority in me or in our Church Extension Board, but because the exigencies of the case require the use of that word. Look at them and see.

1. We have 2,000 unhoused mission churches in this great land, 1,700 hundred of which have appealed to our Board in vain for aid in the past few years.

2. The fund on hand with which to heed the cry of our homeless brothers and sisters is so inadequate that the Board can answer but one appeal in four.

3. Our statistics show such a rapid increase of our churches that every year we are organizing more than half as many new congregations that cannot build without help, as we have been able to help through this fund in all the fifteen years of its history.

4. But fifty per cent. of our young churches can build without aid.

5. The fund must be doubled, trebled, quadrupled, quintupled before it will suffice. We could use half a million dollars right now as a loan fund.

6. Unable to reach that sum, we are trying to reach the half of it by the close of the year 1900. And with reasonable efforts it can be done.

7. Let all our churches throughout the land at once take up the watch-cry and make it echo from ocean to ocean and from the lakes to the gulf: "A quarter of a million dollars for Church Extension by the year 1900!!"

8. The fund now has in it nearly $160,000. We need to raise $90,000 in the next three years, or $30,000 a year. With reasonable effort, I say, it can be done.

9. And because it can be done it MUST be done. Duty demands it. Self-respect demands it. The exigency of the case demands it.

10. To meet this demand our churches should raise $20,000 September 4th next. Let Kentucky do her duty, and Ohio and Illinois and Missouri, all the states and all the churches, and a glorious result will follow.

GEORGE DARSIE,

Kentucky correspondent for Church Extension.

Facts and an Appeal.

Dr. Pierson said that America is the key to the evangelization of the world. In order to the conquest of the world we must conquer America. Our strength as a people is in the Ohio Valley. We must go into all the world by way of Dixie, the Pacific Coast and New England. Church Extension is of pre-eminent importance in this. It is the stay and support of all our evangelistic forces. It makes possible the completion of the works which they begin.

Less than one-fourth of the area of this country, containing 30 per cent. of its population, contains 75 per cent. of our membership. In three-fourths of this country we are a feeble folk, almost unknown. This is a missionary territory. We may plant missions, but they will die without homes. We must house them.

The Congregationalists made a strong appeal for funds in their literature last year, because they had 200 homeless churches. We have 2,500. Place one on each fifty-foot lot and they would stretch out 24 miles. Think of it! Twenty-four miles of homeless churches. We have more than 100 of these homeless congregations in Kansas. We have 5,700 preachers, 10,000 churches, perhaps 10 per cent. of them dead, and it leaves us with about 6,500 housed congregations.

A conservative Missouri brother says: "For five years past we have organized six congregation per week and built three buildings, or we have 4 per cent. annual increase in organizations and 2 per cent. in buildings. In five years we have gained 1,570 church organizations, or 19 per cent. We gained in the same period $2,745,000 in value of church property, or 20 per cent. Half of this latter was in enlargement and improvement of our older churches. Half of these 1,570 new churches are unhoused. Brethren, we must do better."

The mission of Church Extension is not so much to build churches as to boost them. Other churches have recognized the great worth and work of Church Extension.

Up to January 1, 1898, the Methodists have received $5,985,000 for church erection. They have built 10,552 buildings and their present receipts run about $10,000 per month.

The Congregationalists have a fund of over $3,250,000 and have assisted nearly 2,900 churches. During the last triennium, ending July 1, their receipts were $570,000 and built 377 churches.

The Baptists have a fund of above a million. They have assisted 1,428 churches, 91 of them last year.

The Presbyterians have largely a gift fund. The loan feature is of more recent introduction. The large part of their work in church erection has been done by donation. They have aided 6,305 churches, and the sum total of their benevolence in this direction amounts to nearly three and one-half million dollars. Last year they aided 216 churches with $126,000.

Our own fund amounts to $155,000, have built 384 churches, and 99 of them have returned their loans in full.

Some have complained, claiming that the expense is entirely disproportioned to the work done. Remember that when the fund has quadrupled, the expense will probably not have doubled. The expense of handling a small fund is proportionately much greater than for a large one. We pay our secretary less than any other board, except one, and that one does no field work and is really not much more than a clerk.

With all of these homeless churches and new organizations multiplying rapidly, and our work going forward at a constantly accelerating speed, we must have a larger Church Extension fund in order to discharge our duty as a people, and to enter the doors of opportunities that God has opened before us. We must do larger things along this line. We must strike for $250,000 by the year 1900. Let us pray and push for this result.

VERNON J. ROSE,

Kansas Correspondent for Church Extension.

Church Extension Fund.

The National Conventional at Indianapolis, last October, made the following recommendations: "Because the board can answer but one appeal in four, we recommend that *unusual effort be put forth to raise our Church Extension Fund to one-quarter of a million dollars by the close of* 1900. To this end your committee recommends that more attention be given to the September offering. Thus far we have compelled the board to raise seventy-five per cent. of this money by going into the field after it. We must raise more by annual offerings in September, and because this is the month after vacation, the month after summer sluggishness in the churches, when the pulse of church life is not vigorous, we urge that *extraordinary effort be used to work up a generous and general offering for this important work.*"

From last October we have just three years in which to lift our fund from $150, 000 to $250,000. To do this we must raise $35,000 of new money each year, the interest paying current expenses while this is being done.

To raise $35,000 annually the following plan is proposed: The board will endeavor from the collections in the churches at the September offering, asking each church to raise its fair proportion in order to secure this amount. The other $15,000 the board will endeavor to secure annually in pledges and bequests.

The board now invites the earnest help of the brotherhood at large to the accomplishment of this worthy object. "Nuggets of Truth on Church Extension" which explain the work in full, will be sent free to all churches who will notify us by card. We will also send collection envelopes to churches who desire to use them. Send in orders at once and let preparation be made in a definite and systematic manner to reach the $250,000 by the collections of the next three offerings.

A suggestion as to what each congregation ought to raise has been mailed to the churches, and it is hoped each congregation will take pride in doing its part toward raising $20,000 by the September offering.

Send orders for literature and envelopes to

G. W. MUCKLEY, Cor. Sec.,
600 *Water Works Bldg., Kansas City, Mo.*

Words of Cheer for Our Church Extension Work.

Hope for a large offering in September. Church here has an annual pledge for all missionary work. W. S. LOWE.
Manhattan, Kan.

I consider Church Extension one of the most practical means for extending the kingdom of Christ. L. F. DRASH.
Liberty, Ind.

Push the good work until all can have a good house to worship God in.
C. C. BLANKINSHIP.
Jonesville, Va.

Our people are recognizing more and more the importance of this branch of missionary activity and are learning better to appreciate the work of the Church Extension Board. Will certainly give with increasing liberality.
GUY E. WINGATE.
Anthon, Ia.

The Church Extension Fund is scarcely second in importance of all our missionary funds. I long to see a great increase in this year's offerings. Hope to increase ours here in Owosso, Mich. L. W. SPAYD.
Owosso, Mich.

Our congregation is poor and we are building a house ourselves, but we will not forget the September offering for some one in worse circumstances than we are.
GRANT E. PIKE.
Barnesville, O.

Whatever I can say or do for Church Extension will be said and done. I am a friend to this work and always have been. When thoroughly understood, I do not see how any one can be opposed to it, even by indifference. May the desire and effort you are putting forth this year be accomplished. W. E. WADE.
Vanderbilt, Pa.

The Church Extension collection is one I never fail to urge. It is our strong tower. May God prosper us that we may make it a quarter of a million dollars by the close of 1900. A. B. CUNNINGHAM.
Danville, Ind.

You may multiply our apportionment by ten.
R. F. THRAPP.
Pittsburg, Ill.

We are educating our congregation to giving. We will urge the September collection.
W. A. BRUNDIDGE.
Delta, O.

We are training the Olivia church to make an offering *each month* in the year for missions. They like it and are gaining strength thereby. We will raise an *apportionment* for *Churcn Extension* in September.
DAVID HUSBAND.
Olivia, Minn.

art is with you. We have a great e and are sadly needing just such e as you are giving. We hope to n. A. T. EDWARDS.
an, O. T.

ost permanently helpful of our mis- enterprises is the Church Extension J. C. MASON.
n, Tex.

nnot give a great amount, but will little" willingly. F. M. CUNNINGHAM.
oro, O.

You are laying a foundation for a work in years to come. E. E. CURRY.
d, O.

th in and zeal for Church Extension is only by my faith in Home and Foreign . Let us push it to the front. God urch Extension. C. A. SIAS.
e City, Neb.

God bless the work of Church Exten- : is necessary for a family to have a order to exist. May the offerings for Extension by the close of 1900 assist in many homeless Disciples. S. B. CULP.
Mills, N. Y.

und is certainly one of the greatest rs of Christianity we have. JOHN P. SALA.
lph, O.

certainly believe it is as important to urch firmly established and made self- ng as to organize it. To do this a ome is assuredly necessary, therefore t get along without a Church Extension M. S. JOHNSON.
rson, Ia.

Financial Exhibit.

aring the receipts for Foreign Missions nonths of this current missionary year e corresponding time last year shows wing:

	1997	1898	Gain
t'ing churches........	2,550	2,856	306
;'ing Sunday-schools	2,753	3,156	413
t'ing Endv. Societ's	274	380	106
t'ing individuals........	749	701	48*
....	$88,729.60	$102,324.03	$13,594.43

aring the amounts from different shows the following:

	1897	1898	Gain
s	$36,659.33	$42,755.35	$6,095.96
schools	27,951.94	31,687.31	3,735.37
r Socie's	1,840.99	1,881.56	40.57
als	6,884.90	5,960.79	924.11*
neous ...	2,171.73	2,630.42	458.60
s........	6,000.00	16,490.00	10,490.00
s	7,220.65	918.60	6,302.05*

chibit shows a gain in regular receipts 6.48; a gain in annuities of $10,490; s in bequests of $6,302.05.

t lack $15,085 of reaching $100,000 by ns only. There is time yet to reach unt. Remember the books close for ionary year Sept. 30th.

o. F. M. RAINS, Treas.
0, Cincinnati, Ohio.

Family Circle.

After A Battle.

BY HELEN A. RAINS.

A crown, a crown for the living bring,
A wreath for the noble dead;
For some let the praise of our nation ring,
For some let our tears be shed.
For some we shall stand at the cottage gate,
To greet with a kiss once more;
For some we'll no longer watch and wait,
For them is life's greetings o'er.
For some will the plume and banner wave
Anew for the brave to bear;
For some bring the bier and prepare the grave
Their place is no longer here.

A crown, a crown for the living now,
A wreath for our noble dead;
For this do the leaves of the laurel glow,
For this has the myrtle spread.
Much work is there for our hands to-night
For those that have struggled well;
Brave boys that have stood through the storm of fight,
And those who have nobly fell.
'Tis mete that our smiles with a crown should go,
Our tears with the myrtle wreath,
For one has been made for the living brow.
And one for the brow of death.

Only a Fisherman's Son.

BY ALFRED BRUNK.

Concluded.

It was arranged that Ethan should go to Sacramento and be Dr. Henderson's office boy; the doctor to come after him in two or three weeks.

Mr. Langdon speedily recovered his health and in a few days was out in his boat, fishing in the fruitful waters of the Sacramento. He was now very kind in his treatment of Ethan, and as they would spend the day on the beautiful river, drawing out good draughts of fish, and as fishing was no longer held up before him as the chief thing in the world, Ethan began to feel that there was much pleasure in it after all, and almost regretted that he was going to leave it, perhaps for life. He now enjoyed almost unlimited freedom, and often visited his grandmother. She rejoiced greatly that the door of opportunity had at last been thrown open to him.

"Work hard, my boy, and never forget your parents and your younger brothers and sisters. Make yourself an honorable name that they may have reason to be proud of you. Never let them blush for shame on your account."

The news went all over the community that Ethan was going to Sacramento and become a doctor.

"A pretty doctor he'll make," laughingly, said Mary Smith. "I wouldn't let him pull my cat's tooth," and she giggled, thinking she had made a very witty remark.

Ethan felt that he could not leave home without calling upon Mary. She received him politely and said she would be sorry to see him go, but she knew he would be back again in a few days.

"I expect to come back and visit my folks as often as I can," he said.

"Oh, yes, of course," she replied, "I expect you will. Why it won't be two weeks till you will be back here to stay,"

"I don't know," said Ethan somewhat provoked, "but I don't think I will."

"When you get down there and get to paintin' pictures, won't you paint mine?" she asked, with mock-solemnity, then laughed, and turned it off with a little cough. He saw that she was making fun of him and turned very red in the face.

"It takes a long time to learn to paint, I am told," he said quietly.

He soon took his leave, scarcely knowing whether to be glad or sorry he had called.

There was one who was genuinely sorry to have Ethan leave, and that was his mother. She had in her heart idolized him all his life, but because of the misunderstanding between Ethan and his father, she had been compelled in a great measure to hide her feelings. But now that harmony prevailed, she caressed and fondled him to her heart's content.

At last the doctor's boat appeared at the landing, and that gentleman appeared at the house with a new suit of clothes, hat and shoes for Ethan. Donning his new clothes and bidding his loved ones an affectionate "good-bye," the little vessel glides down the river, Ethan waves his handkerchief, the boat goes around a bend in the river and is lost to view.

CHAPTER III.

Ethan felt rather awkward for some time in his new place. Every-thing was so strange and different from what he had been accustomed to, that at times he became very homesick, and one night as he lay upon his bed, restless and sleepless, the pangs of homesickness so overcame him that he actually wept. He longed to see his brothers and sisters, his mother, and felt that it would be a relief if he could go out with his father in the fishing boat! Then he thought of Mary Smith, pretty, black-eyed, teasing girl. How he would like to see her. Then he remembered that she had predicted his early return home. He shut his lips tightly together. "No," said he to himself, "she shall not laugh at me this time, I'll show her what I am." And with this resolve firmly anchored in his mind he went to sleep.

Ethel Henderson and her father spent a great deal of time outdoors, either on the boat or driving out into the country, and Ethan was called upon sometimes to join them on these trips. Occasionally, Dr. Henderson would take him home for a few hours, and the respect which his own people and old neighbors showed him, served to increase his own self-respect. One day he went with Dr. Henderson and Ethel to see a fine collection of paintings and statuary on J Street. He was greatly pleased with what he saw, and looked in rapture at the various masterpieces. One especially attracted his attention; it was a Swiss landscape scene. There was a beautiful little lake, a plain stretching away into the distance, at the farther side of which rose the mountains in magnificent splendor, their hoary heads clearly outlined against the blue sky. In the midst of the lake was a small sail-boat, with a man in the act of turning the boat around. In the stern, sat a young man and young lady who were wistfully looking toward an old bare-headed man upon the shore, who was holding out both arms toward them. The name of the painting was "Called Back." Ethan called the attention of Ethel and her father to it and they thought it was indeed a masterpiece. A few mornings after that the doctor entered the office and Ethan showed him a picture which was a sketch of the painting, "Called Back." Ethan had copied it from memory.

"I must show this to Ethel, my boy," said the doctor. That young lady was very much pleased at this manifestation of Ethan's skill.

"Papa," she said, "Ethan must go to school. He has talent and it must be developed."

And so it was determined that Ethan should be sent to the city schools, assisting Dr. Henderson in his leisure hours.

As Ethel grew into young womanhood her health improved some with the years, although it was evident that she would never be strong. She was a constant inspiration to her father, who had followed her mother to her last resting-place many years before. She lived for her father as he lived for her, and each deemed it a pleasure to labor for the other. Kind and helpful to all, she was of great assistance to Ethan. He began to regard her as an older sister, and confined to her his aspirations and difficulties. She led him to the Savior and he became an earnest Christian. In such an atmosphere, is it any wonder that his noblest impulses gathered strength with the years?

After Ethan had been with Dr. Henderson about four years, the doctor said to him one day: "Ethan what would you think of a trip to Rome?"

"Why, sir, I should like it very much, but that is not possible. It takes money to go to Rome."

"So it does, Ethan, so it does, and that is just what I wish to speak to you about. If you wish to study painting, Rome is the place for you. And Ethel and I have talked it over and decided that if you desired to go, I will loan you the money."

Tears stood in the eyes of the young man. "You are too kind, sir, but I hope you will never have cause to regret it, I will accept your kind offer and go as soon as proper arrangements can be made."

Ethan had made remarkable progress, not only in school, but out of it. He had developed his powers of observation and become a good character-reader. He could detect a swindler in a very few moments.

He concluded now to spend a couple of weeks with his parents. He helped his father with his fishing and enjoyed it immensely; had some fine visits with his grandmother, Mrs. Smith. That estimable lady talked to him by the hour about Italy, and told him he must not fail to visit her old home, which he promised faithfully to do. One evening when he returned from one of those delightful trips up the river, he found Mary Smith at his father's, Mary has grown stouter, but is as lively as ever.

"Well, they do tell me you are goin' to Rome! Sakes alive! but that's a long ways off." She now tried to win Ethan's regard, but it was useless. He now saw just how coarse and ignorant she was.

Judge Harrington, so-called because in an earlier day he had been justice of the peace, was president of the Commonwealth Bank of Sacramento, his daughter Mabel, about three years younger than Ethan, attended the same school he did, and already they were very much attached to each other.

One day Dr. Henderson and Ethel came up the river and stopped at Mr. Langdon's.

"Ethan," said the doctor, "I have some important business in San Francisco that st be attended to, but you can see to it t as well as I can. So come on down h us, and you can come up and finish ır visit when you get back from San ıncisco,"

he next morning Ethan boarded the 30 train for San Francisco. Among the sengers he noticed Judge Harrington, › greeted him pleasantly. The judge ı a pretty good-natured man, but looked rply after the dollars. The day was ınsely warm and the car doors and dows were open, and the passengers e fanning themselves with fans, hats, ks or papers.

etween Sacramento and Davisville re is a long stretch of level road, with a ;ht curve upon an embankment about, ɔe miles east of Davisville. The train l slowly pulled out of the Sacramento ot, crossed the river, started out under a l head of steam, and was making the usual t time of the San Francisco Express. ey were passing around this curve when sh! bang! crash! and the cars were shing in one another and plunging n the embankment! It was a scene of greatest confusion. Men, women and dren were piled in heaps in the wrecked . Some were cursing, others praying, e were laughing, others weeping; some › loudly shouting, others silent; some bed out of the car windows, rejoicing ; they were unhurt; some were badly ised, while others were unconscious. en was on the ground unhurt. How he out of the car he never knew. He saw ; a few feet before him, Judge Harring- lying on the ground unconscious. sting his eyes upward he saw a car ınding on end upon another car, which s lying on one side at the bottom of the bankment. The first mentioned car ɔjected partly over the end of the prone e, and had already begun to fall, Ethan ısped the situation instantly. He must ıcue Judge Harrington or he would be ıshed to death. Darting toward the ɔstrate, unconscious man, he dragged n from under the falling car. Laying › judge upon the ground and gasping : breath, he straightened himself up and 'oluntarily threw out his right arm just the car came crashing to the ground.

The car came in contact with his arm ıt above the wrist, and snapped the bones if they had been thin glass. But he ew it not. Seeing that the judge was 'e, he ran to a group of people a few ps away, and singling out a young man d:

'Go, Charlie, to Davisville, and wire the icials at Sacramento! Run quick! legraph to Dr. Henderson."

No need to say any more. Charlie was ne like an arrow.

'Hello, young man! Seems you got rt," said a man to Ethan, pointing to his n. Ethan glanced at it and saw the ɔod trickling down his hand.

'It is nothing but a slight bruise," said han. "It will soon be all right."

'I hope so," said the man. "I trembled : you when you went for the judge. at's what I call grit, I do. Let's go and › how the judge is making it,"

So they walked back to Judge Harring- ı, who was now looking about him utter- confused.

'Hello, judge!" said the man, "how are u' now? Get up and shake yourself," and he and Ethan helped him to his feet. "If it hadn't been for our young friend, here, you would have been a goner. I reckon you were lying right there where that car is, and he jumped right in and pulled you out while the car was falling! Talk about pluck! If he hasn't got it, nobody has. And that's what he got for it," pointing to Ethan's arm, which had begun to swell and was getting very painful.

"So I owe my life to you, sir," said Judge Harrington to Ethan. "You have my most profound thanks and when we get back to Sacramento come to the bank and your bravery shall be rewarded."

"Thank you, Mr. Harrington," replied Ethan proudly, "but I want no reward for doing my duty."

Soon the officials and doctors from Sacramento were at the wreck, and the wounded were put on special cars and sent back to the city. Dr. Henderson gave Ethan his immediate attention.

"Come, my boy," said he, "get right on here and let us get back to town as quick as we can."

As soon as the train arrived in Sacramento, Dr. Henderson took Ethan to his home. His practiced eye soon saw that Ethan's hand could not be saved. That it must be amputated, and that at once, or he would not lose only his hand, but his life.

"Well, Ethan, my boy, I have disagreeable news to tell you, but I know a strong-nerved lad like you can bear it," said the doctor, as cheerfully as possible.

"You mean that this hand must come off, is that it?" asked Ethan.

"That's right, Ethan, that's right," replied Dr. Henderson, "but you shall suffer no pain, no, not a particle."

CHAPTER IV.

After Ethan's hand had been amputated Dr. Henderson sent for Mrs. Langdon, and the presence of his mother gave him great encouragement, in this, the gloomiest hour of his life.

Sometime after the wreck, Ethan was sitting one morning in Dr. Henderson's office, when the railroad's attorney came in and said:

"Mr. Langdon, I have called to settle with you. How much do you think we owe you for the loss of your hand."

"Well sir," said Ethan, I would not have taken $100,000 for that hand. It not only disfigures me for life, but I must give up my life's dream of being a painter."

They finally fixed on $5,000 and the money was paid over. Just as the lawyer left, a messenger boy brought Ethan a note which he discovered was from Judge Harrington, requesting his presence at the bank. Arriving at that institution he was ushered into the president's private office, and into that gentleman's presence.

Judge Harrington arose, and extended his hand. "I am glad to see you appearing so well, Mr. Langdon. Pray be seated," and going to his private safe he counted out $10,000 in crisp bank notes, and stepping up to Ethan said:

"Mr. Langdon, you saved my life and I wish to make a small return for your brave, generous act."

Ethan arose and pushed the judge's hand from him. "No, sir," said he, "I cannot take pay for doing that which was simply my duty. As for the loss of my hand the railroad company has already settled that."

"Be seated sir, I wish to have a talk with you," said the judge, going to the safe and replacing the bills, then seating himself in front of Ethan. "Dr. Henderson tells me that you were expecting soon to go to Rome and study painting, and that the accident has rendered that impossible."

"Yes sir," sadly replied Ethan, "as my right hand is gone, the desire of my life to be a painter, goes with it."

"Dr. Henderson further informed me that you have a good business education, and are apt in detecting swindlers. Well, sir, we need just such a man in this institution, and if you will consider the proposition, I can give you a position that will pay you well."

So it was arranged that Ethan should go into the bank and become general overseer, after he had acquainted himself with the workings of the institution. He then went home and spent several weeks with his parents. Nearly every one regretted his great loss, and especially did his grandmother mourn because of it.

"But it will be all right Ethan, its bound to be all right," she told him. "You do your duty and trust to God's loving care."

Mary Smith used every means in her power to once more win him to her side, and when she found her efforts unavailing she sneeringly asked, "Who would want a one-armed man, any how? And as for his makin' pictures I knew he never would."

Ethan returned to Sacramento and began his labors in the bank, and soon mastered the workings of the various departments. His keen observation was very serviceable to the managers of that institution, and he soon became a favorite with everyone connected with the bank. Judge Harrington learned to rely upon his sound judgment and kept him with him all he could. Ethan told him that he was in love with his daughter, Mabel, and received his consent to their marriage.

"Ethan met with a lucky accident when he lost his hand," said the judge one day to his daughter.

"Why do you think so, father?" asked Mabel, who was a medium-sized brunette. "I thought it was a great calamity."

"Why, if he had not lost it, he would have gone to Rome and studied painting, got himself into debt and then perhaps would have failed, for it takes a good painter to succeed nowadays. But as it is, he has settled down to business and is becoming a first-class business man."

"Well father," said Mabel, "that only shows his good sense and determination. Were it not for these good qualities he would spoil his life grieving over what might have been. But as it is, he puts the impossible behind him and goes on to success in another calling."

"Perhaps you are right," said her father and the conversation ceased.

When Ethan had been in the bank about a year, he and Mabel were quietly married, and settled down to housekeeping in a pretty cottage near the eastern limits of the city. Judge Harrington became feebler, and the care of the bank developed more than ever upon Ethan.

One day his quick eye and ear saved the bank from a heavy robbery, which endeared him more than ever to the directors of that institution.

Ethan carefully saved his earnings and became a large stockholder in the bank. One day, at a meeting of the directors, Judge Harrington resigned the presidency of the bank, on account of his increasing infirmities. Ethan was unaminously elected to fill that important position.

"Let me congratulate you, Mr. Langdon," said one of the directors, "upon your election' to the presidency of this bank. You have shown by your indomitable will, how to turn defeat into success, and that courage and perseverance will certainly reap their reward."

Old Church, Va.

Lean Hard on Him.

My inability to do
A thing that merits rich reward—
My nothingness before the Lord
Prostrates me. I would shrink from view
In this great world of workers true.
Yea, overwhelmed with sense
Of my own insignificance,
I in obscurity away
Would hie, disheartened, and lie down
And die.
How can I do his will?
How his high purpose true fulfill?
How meet the obligations of
My being? How my fellows serve?
I shrink the task to try. It is
Impossible. Too weak am I—
Too impotent in presence of
Demands so sacred and so great!
But hark! A soothing voice I hear:
"I am thy strength. Lean hard on me.
Grace, plenteous grace, 'tis mine
To give. Lean hard."
I rise, and in
His might I forward go renewed
With strength omnipotent; assured
That leaning on his mighty arm,
I all things well can do *for him*.

—*Religious Telescope.*

Text Stories—IX.

THE LITTLE ONES.

BY ALICE CURTICE MOYER.

"Oh, that I had wings like a dove! for then would I fly away and be at rest."

"I would hasten my escape from the windy storm and tempest."—Ps. 55:6, 8.

They came in seriously from their play; these two dear little ones: The sweet little daughter with brown curls all about her face and blue eyes of such a wonderful, fathomless depth, wherein there came at times, an expression as though seeing the unseen, and of holding communion with him who is invisible, and the little brother whose hand she held, two years her junior, more practical than his sister, but none the less sweet and lovable because of it. There was a world of wonder on each little face.

Evidently, there had been a serious consultation between them, and play had been put aside for its consideration; then, for its satisfactory disposition, they had to come to the supreme authority on all subjects—mother.

Stopping at her knee, their faces all serious with the solemnity of the—to them—most important thought, they asked:

"Mother, do you suppose God will allow us to choose the sort of wings we are to have in heaven?"

"Because," said the sister, "we have decided on the kind we want."

Restraining a smile, the mother gently urged:

"Tell mother what sort you have decided upon."

"If it would be just the same to God," said the serious little daughter, "I should like to have wings like a butterfly—a beautiful white butterfly, that flies about in the sunshine and seems so happy."

"And I," said the practical little son most solemnly, "would like wings like a parrot, all green and glossy and strong-looking. Do you think God will let us choose for ourselves, mamma?"

Now this mother had a way of encouraging her little ones to tell her their thoughts and of opening to her their hearts fully and freely—gently reproving if necessary, sympathizing if possible—and as a result, had so completely gained their confidence, that in their hearts there was never a thought of withholding anything whatever from her loving consideration and counsel.

Therefore, she did not say, "Don't bother mother," or "Run away and play," or "Wait until you are older," etc., but answered:

"I think, dear ones, we can safely leave that question with God. All we need to do now, is to be ready, so that when the time comes, we may be satisfied with our reward."

"But mother, we will have wings, won't we?" urged the little son.

"That is another phase of the subject, my darling, which we must be content to leave unanswered until the time when all things shall be made known to us. We can safely trust to the Heavenly Father who doeth all things well, knowing that he has planned for us, that which is best."

"And we were thinking," said the sister softly, "how nice it would be if God would take us to him now. We want to be little angels—brother and I."

The sayings of this little daughter and the strong desire she frequently expressed to be in heaven, had often raised a great dread in the mother's heart, lest this desire

ld be granted, and that the Father
:d take this pure little one to himself,
e she, selfishly, perhaps, did so pray to
her on earth. But she found comfort,
ever, in the thought she now expressed.
fy darlings, your wish is granted. You
vith God now. You are of his king-
for he has said so; and it is your
er's constant prayer that you may
r emerge from the shelter of his arms;
whatever the life of the hereafter may
ke unto, or whatever may be its con-
ns—these we can safely leave in his
s. That we may attain unto all its
es, is the question with which we have
, and with which this life is concerned.
here, in this life, that we need wings,
nere we can have them by patient
ing—wings that insure peace and hap-
ss on earth, and blessedness in the
after."

en she read to them the nine beati-
s, beginning with "Blessed are the
in spirit," explaining how the pos-
on of these requisites each bring a
ing, and how they may be likened unto
s that lift us up above all things earth-
nd which may finally "fly away and be
st."

hey that wait upon the Lord shall
v their strength; they shall mount up
wings as eagles."

e told them again, as she had often
before, how necessary it is to study
and holy living from childhood—striv-
o be "more like Jesus." And that as
allowed to come in, peace and joy
go out; and how important it is that
dear little ones whom Jesus loves,
ld early begin to cultivate a beautiful
rt-garden" wherein may grow and
om the rare and priceless plants of
and truth—taking great care that no
find a lodging-place there.

as this mother wise to speak thus
phorically? Did their young minds
her meaning? Yes. The genuine
-like child, the child unspoiled by that
cialness which consists mainly of lit-
icks and small prettiness learned by
t, take wide views, ponder deep sub-
, enjoy great books, and have large
ghts.

ice psychologists claim that it is the
r motor activities that develop first,
an understand from a philosophic point
ew why these things are. But the
beautiful theory is that given by
ridge: "In infancy, heaven lies all
t us." Whatever may be the reason,
ll know how children will leave their
to inquire into subjects that em-
ass their elders because of their in-
ty to readily answer. We have seen,
wonder, how quick they are to seize
ideas of spiritual and fundamental
ing and distinctions of great breadth.
It must be because of their purity,
nearness to heaven, that they so readi-
ad the character—see the hearts as it
—of those about them; a perception
becomes more or less dulled, perhaps,
e smaller and more prosaic things of
gradually assert their right to a place
r minds and lives. But "out of the
hs of babes and sucklings thou hast
cted praise." To merit the praise, the
and the confidence of the innocent
, is to reach a height of no small sig-
ance. A great and good man once stood
crowded street crossing in a large city,
waiting, in company with others, for an opportunity to cross over to the other side. In the waiting crowd, was a little girl. Feeling the need of a pilot, she looked into the faces of those about her, then walked straight up to this grand man and took hold of his hand. He piloted her safely across the street, and in relating the incident afterward, he said, that in all his life he had never appreciated any honor that had ever been conferred upon him, more than the confidence of that little child.

Oh, these little ones! How they get into our hearts and find firm lodgment there! When we hear men and women express a dislike for children, then may we know that there is something radically wrong with those men and women. Hard, indeed, must be the heart, that does not respond to the joy of happy childhood, or that is not touched by childish suffering, even though they be but strangers. And when these little ones come into the world as one's very own, a tiny speck of humanity, with its dependence, its wise look, its smiles and unexplained tears, it reaches a corner of the heart that has hitherto been untouched and unreached by any other love; and as we see it grow from day to day, month to month, and year to year, so should we realize in proportion our responsibilities concerning this life given into our care and keeping; and though we sigh over each transition, as from frocks to kilts, and from kilts to the "first suit," etc., of our sons, and over each lengthened tuck in the skirts of our daughters, yet we would not have it otherwise. We watch the gradual unfolding of these tender plants, and like Hannah of old, we long to lend our treasures to the Lord. We want to teach them in such a way as to lead them to see and to understand, and appreciate the possibilities of life. "It is a sad thing," says Munger, "to begin life with a low conception of it. It may not be possible for a young man to measure life, but it is possible to say, I am resolved to put life to its noblest and best use."

We cannot too early instill this sentiment into the heart and mind of a child. We cannot too early begin its training in all things moral and religious—watching, instructing, praying, guiding, with the help of the Heavenly Father, into that haven which is "safe from the storm and the tempest."

St. Louis, Mo.

Well-paid Authors.

Mr. Gladstone's price for a review was $1,000.

Conan Doyle received $35,000 for "Rodney Stone."

Ruskin's sixty-four books bring him in $20,000 a year.

Swineburne, who writes very little, makes $5,000 a year by his poems.

Browning, in his later years, drew $10,000 a year from the sale of his works.

Ian Maclaren made $35,000 out of "The Brier Brush" and "Auld Lang Syne."

Zola's first fourteen books returned him $220,000, and in twenty years he made at least $375,000.

Tennyson is said to have received $60,000 a year from the Macmillans during the last few years of his life.

Mr. Moody is believed to have beaten all others, as more than $1,250,000 has been paid in royalties for the Gospel Hymns and Tunes by him in conjunction with Mr. Sankey.

The Pall Mall Gazette paid Rudyard Kipling $750 for each of his "Barrack Room Ballads," and "The Seven Seas" brought him $11,000. He has received fifty cents a word for a 10,000-word story.

Mrs. Humphrey Ward received $40,000 for "Robert Elsmere," $80,000 each for "David Grieve" and "Marcella," $75,000 for "Sir George Tressaday," $15,000 for "Bessie Costrell."

Rider Haggard asks from $75 to $100 for a column of 1,500 words, and will not write an article for which less than $10,000 is to be paid. Two hundred thousand dollars was paid to Alphonso Daudet for his "Sappho"—the highest price ever paid for a novel.—*Exchange.*

Some of the letters dropped in the regimental letter-box by the soldiers camped around Tampa, afford much amusement for the postmaster. Large numbers of them are marked "Soldier's letter," and without the necessary stamp. A letter deposited for transmission a few days ago bore the following:

"Uncle Sam, please send this through;
I'm a soldier broke, with money due."

Sunday School.

THE CURING OF THE CAPTAIN.*

HERBERT L. WILLETT.

The kingdom of Syria, with its capital at Damascus, was one of the fragments of the older Babylonian Empire, organized into separate existance about the period of Solomon, through the encouragement offered by Egytian kings, whose policy it was to erect as many barriers as possible between themselves and the strong rival power in the Mesopotamian Valley. The new kingdom under the dynasty of the Benhadads prospered so that already in the reign of Solomon it was the cause of serious concern to Israel (1 Kings 11:14-25, and in later days entered to no small extent into the politics and military operations of both the Northern and Southern kingdoms of Palestine (1 Kings 15: 16-21; 20: 1 f; 22:1 f; 2 Kings 6:8 f; 12:17 f). War between Syria on the east, and either Judah or Israel, and sometimes the two kingdoms on the west, in league against the common enemy, was the recognized order for several generations. These wars were marked by varying success. At times, Syria was victorious, and took portions of the East-Jordan territory from her rivals; and even Samaria was reduced to desperate straits of famine on one or two occasions. The results of a successful campaign were usually a great number of captives, to be reduced to slavery or sold into service, a money indemnity, and free trading privileges in the humbled capital. This latter condition was accomplished by setting apart certain streets in the city to the free use of merchants and residents of the stronger people. When the fortunes of war reversed, the conquered territory was reclaimed; and though the enslaved captives were not restored, the trading franchises were in turn extorted from the enemy (1 Kings 20:34).

In such a period of war, as in our own day, the military class in both nations came to the front, and the most conspicuous men of the times were successful warriors. Among the most notable figures at the court of Benhadad was a certain Naaman, a hero to whose prowess Syria owed much of her recent success. He enjoyed, like Jacob under David or Benaiah under Solomon, the full confidence of his royal master. But a great affliction had fallen upon him; he was a leper. This malady was the most dreaded of diseases of the east, as it is to this day, for it was recognized as incurable. It embraced a wider variety of phases, from simple skin disorders to to the dreaded elephantiasis. One might be a leper, without hope of cure, so far as the limited therapeutics of the day could give aid, and still find the disease no especial hindrance to the discharge of his public business, save that it menaced him with increasing disorder and shortened life. This seemed to have been the case with the Syrian. Again he might be so afflicted that only seclusion, as in the case of Uzziah (Azariah, 2 Kings 14:5), or expulsion from all contact with society, as was generally deemed necessary (2 Kings 7:3 f), could suffice. These poor creatures, objects of horror to the unaccustomed eye, infested the environs of cities, subsisting upon the scant charities of pitying people. They especially appealed to the sympathies of our Savior, and there is no more notable proof of the divine likness in Christians in these later years than the work for the lepers by missionaries, in which signal ministry of tenderness our own brethren in the far lands have been not the least conspicuous examples. Such a wreck as leprosy produces, if left to work its ravages, ever appealed to the Hebrew mind as the proof of divine wrath for sin, as the stroke of God; and so leprosy as a symbol of the disasters wrought by sin has stood as a significant figure of speech in the vocabulary of the church.

Among the Hebrew slaves taken in the Syrian raids was a girl who because a servant in Naaman's family, and who had known Elisha's power as a prophet and miracle-worker. It is evident that he was not in the habit of making his power a common and cheap thing. Even the king of Israel, who is not named by the writer of the narrative, but who was probably Jehoram, did not know enough of Elisha to be saved from deep perplexity when he received Benhadads message (v. 7). But among the common people, where religious elements always have freer course than in courts, the prophet was well known, and his miracles were the cause of wonder and faith in the power of God. The maiden's frequently expressed confidence in the prophet of her God was the impelling force that set in motion the cavalcade of Naaman to Palestine, and in the end made him a notable convert of the religion of Jehovah. No position could promise less than that of a captive maiden in a foreign land, and yet no episode of the Old Testament is more interesting as a proof that God uses small instruments to accomplish great purposes, and that his love goes out to men of foreign races, as well as to those of Hebrew birth (Luke 4:27).

By the advice of his king Naaman started with a letter to the king of Israel. He had provided himself with great treasure to pay the price of his recovery. Jehoram, who was quite unconscious of the power of the prophet living in his capital, was terrified upon receipt of the letter, which be regarded as a trap, or an attempt to find a cause for war. It was then that the preacher who had seen Elijah's ascent to heaven, assumed the responsibility for the whole transaction and bade the king send the Syrian to his cottage. Here, then, began that discipline of the proud man whose sword had glittered in the foremost battle for Syrian glory. Instead of being greeted as a great guest at court, he was bidden to drive with all his train of followers to the dwelling of Elisha, among the more modest houses in the upper city (v. 24). Then when he had arrived he was not even honored with a sight of the prophet; the latter only sent word to him that he was to go dip repeatedly in Jordan in order to be heeled. And why should he go to Jordan? It was a rushing, turbulent, muddy stream; while in his own country there were beautifully clear waters—the rivers of Damascus. He had seemingly come all the way to be made the laughing-stock of a Hebrew *rabi.* It was too much to endure. He went away from the place of his humiliation in a rage. This is just the place where many men break down. The lesson of humility is too hard. The price of discipline is too great. The hour of opportunity passes, and life goes on fruitless. Many a man is asking himself why he has never succeeded better in his work for Christ. In not a few cases the true answer is to be found in his unwillingness to serve except in his own way, and with his own self-pride and importance preserved. It takes a long and severe discipline to teach one that the best of gifts and abilities may be made quite useless by a self-centered mind, which seeks great things for itself and not for God.

Fortunately, when his own pride proved his worst enemy, the love of his servants saved him. Their better wisdom prevailed, and obeying the directions of the man of God he went to the Jordan and bathed the seven times prescribed, and found his flesh restored again to freshness and health. His pride had bowed, and his blessing came. The power of God was vindicated, the prophet was honored, the captain converted, and the maiden's promise fulfilled.

SUGGESTIONS FOR TEACHING.

Riches and honors prove of small satisfaction in face of a great affliction. As leprosy blasts the physical life, so sin works ruin to the soul. God uses very humble instruments to spread his truth and accomplish his purposes. The fame of a quiet, godly life, unknown to courts, may be wide-spread among humble people who have felt its pervasive power. Men of the Elisha type find the rewards of doing good, not in money given, but in joy experienced; men like Gehazi prize the gifts. To know that there is "a prophet in Israel," that there are those who can give true counsel in times of danger, is the greatest assurance that can come to a people. The path of humility is the path of service and exaltation. "He that humbleth himself shall be exalted." The love and mercy of God are not bounded by race or distance. Obedience to divine commands always results in blessing.

:.
also
rec-
ous-
:im.
pas-
3ible
ified

is so
men
wer-
The
imes
fall
aim-
the
7ord
has
win
1, in
is so
from
and
Pas-
d to
ften
are
be
gel-
New
nple

nave
om-
ous-
is of
Com-
ath-
com-
y be
ion,
are
one
ntio
one
f the
with
est,
good
will
re is
r,''
not
less
was
, at
thus
ing,
who

ble.
ents
rse,
aen-
will
the
s of
ives
s as
are,

t in-
iklin
l the
ided
red,
pas-
The
acies
book
was
very

man who tells the story has a different selection that he declares Franklin read, and I am not sure which was the passage. This diversity only shows, however, how much of the Bible is worthy of all praise, even as literature. Many literary students are gaining respect for the Bible through Prof. Moulton's "little volumes, "The Modern Reader's Bible," published by the MacMillans. They are simply the the books of the Bible published separately in little volumes of modern form. Prof. Child, at Harvard, always had his students, in a certain course, read portions of the Bible, simply as examples of fine literature.

For *worship* the Bible is useful. For the quiet hour, when one would come face to face with the Father, and see him who is invisible, no medium is better through which to peer than his sacred Word. Our longings are expressed for us, who feel after him if happily we may find him, in no other way so adequately as through these inspired pages. The Psalms, some of Isaiah, the Sermon on the Mount, the thirteenth to seventeenth of John, the thirteenth of First Corinthians, and a world of sweet, quiet, meditative worship-words, how they express for us the inexpressible!

The best proof of the practical value of any instrument is the finding of it in every home. The sale of an article is the test of popular appreciation. Few things are found in so many homes as the sacred Book. No other volume is so widely bought.

Literature.

A Vade Mecum.

I have just finished reading a book from which I have gained much good, and I desire to say a few words in its commendation. Several considerations seem to make it unnecessary for me or any one else to commend it to others. First, its author is Phillips Brooks. Second, it dates from the year 1877, hence commands the respect due to mature years. The book to which I refer is Phillips Brooks' "Lectures on Preaching." I have read it with much pleasure and profit. I feel that any preacher who has not read it has failed to read a very helpful book—one of the helpful books that helps. It helps one at the very points at which one feels most need of help. Every young preacher should have a well-read, a well-studied, and a well-lived copy of it. The subjects of its eight lectures are as follows:

1. "The Two Elements in Preaching."
2. "The Preacher Himself."
3. "The Preacher in His Work."
4. "The Idea of The Sermon."
5. "The Making of The Sermon."
6. "The Congregation."
7. "The Ministry for Our Age."
8. "The Value of The Human Soul."

I take at random a few gems from its pages. Every page fairly glitters with them. "Preaching has in it the two essential elements, truth and personality." "It is easy to be a John the Baptist, so far as the desert and camel's hair and locusts and wild honey go." "Count your manliness the soul of your ministry and resist all attacks upon it, however sweetly they may come." "The powers of the pastor's success are truth and sympathy together." "Beware of hobbies. Fasten yourself to the center of your ministry and not to some point on the circumference." "The confidence of the minister in the people is at the bottom of every confidence of the people in the minister." "Every parishoner is a weakened repetition of the minister's ideas and ways." "The real question about a sermon is, not whether it is extemporaneous when you deliver it to your people, but whether it ever was extemporaneous—whether it ever sprang freshly from your heart and mind." "The strongest bigotry is often found among theological laymen rather than among clergymen. The pillars of the church are apt to be like the Pillars of Hercules, past which no man might sail." "When it really rains, the puddles as well as the ocean bear witness of the shower." "If you really want to drag a man out of the fire, you will not be distracted into self-conceit by his praises of the grace and softness of the hand that you reach out to him. You will say to him, 'Stop your compliments and take hold.'" "Truth and timeliness together make the full preacher." "The preacher must mainly rely on the strength of what he does believe, and not on the weakness of what he does not believe." "We anticipate a time when men shall be cordially tolerant and earnest believers at once. When that time comes it will be a new thing in the world." "Man in his mystery and wonderfulness is more full of the suggestion of God than either abstract truth or physical nature." On every page, gems of similar worth are to be found. Through every word the charming personality of the author breathes—it is the atmosphere of the book. Buy it and sell it not. Make it your *Vade Mecum.* The reading of it will make you a better man, a better preacher. It will make you love humanity more.

ROBT. G. FRANK.

Nicholasville, Ky., July 25, 1898.

MAGAZINES.

Scribner's Magazine will have each month, under the title "Episodes of the War," a collection of brilliant episodes described by eye-witnesses. They are to be brief and to the point.

The cartoons reproduced in the August Review of Reviews from Spanish journals serve to indicate the density of popular ignorance in Spain as to the facts of the present war. For instance, one cartoon shows Cervera's fleet as successfully slipping past Sampson at Santiago; another represents Cervera as having Schley bottled up; while in a third, Admiral Dewey figures as a rat caught in Spain's Philippine trap.

The most ambitious scheme in color-printing undertaken by an American magazine is the reproduction of eight full-page designs by Henry McCarter, which accompany E. S. Martin's noble poem, "The Sea is His," in Scribner's August number. The way in which the shading of color is attained is mechanically ingenious and artiscally effective. It is a novelty in color-printing, even for experts.

The Religious Review of Reviews, for August is fully up to the high standard this magazine has maintained sinde its inception, both in literary and artistic points of view. The list of contributors in this number is convincing proof of the excellence of the contents. Handsome illustrations, printed in color, lend a charm to the magazine. The leading articles are by able men and particularly interesting and timely. The departments are, as usual, filled with the best. Only topics of the livest interest are discussed in this portion of the magazine. The list suggest their contents: Current Articles of Importance, Periodicals Reviewed, Notes from Recent Editorials, The Religious World, Sermonic Review Section, Editorial Notes, Review of Recent Publications, In a Lighter Vein, and Contents of Reviews and Magazines. Published monthly, New York. $2.00 a year. Preachers, $1.50. Single copies, 20 cents.

FACTS AND FACTORS.

What is asserted to be the heaviest railway engine in the British Isles has been made for the Great Northern Co., at their Doncaster works. It has ten wheels, four being coupled, with driving wheels of six feet seven inches, and weighs 100 tons. With its tender it has a total length of 19 yards.

In 1850, Bro. Alexander Campbell delivered his great sermon in the hall of House of Representatives, at Washington City, D. C., the capitol of our nation.

A rush of business men to Porto Rico is predicted.

Up to July 20th, the money lent by the Bank of Spain for war purposes was $158,600,000.

The Hooley bankruptcy trial in London is involving many titled names in the scandal.

The citizens of Havana are beginning to suffer intensely for food. The flesh of horses and dogs is said to be the only meat obtainable in the city.

P. F. Jernegan, the supposed inventor of a method for extracting gold from the sea has fled the country to evade arrest for fraud.

The boy king of Spain, Alfonso XII. has recovered from his sickness with measles.

Larger and swifter battleships than any now afloat in the American Navy are to be constructed at once by the government.

It is claimed that there is a lighthouse to every fourteen miles of coast in England, to every thirty-four miles in Ireland and to every thirty-nine miles in Scotland.

The gross earnings of the B. & O. Railroad for the fiscal year ending June 30th exceeded those of the previous year $2,060,310.

Thirty-four passengers were hurt in a train wreck on the Santa Fe Pacific, about six miles west of Holbrook, N. M., August 2nd.

Large importations of gold from Europe to America are being reported almost daily.

The alleged misappropriation of papal funds is about to create a great sensation at the vatican. The person most seriously compromised by the scandal is said to be Cardinal Rampola.

Of the 70,000 postoffices in the United States, about 7,000 are in charge of women, and a great many of the remaining ninety per cent. might be, if the salaries were not so large as to tempt the politicians.

Only eighteen million Mohammedans are under Turkish rule, and more than one hundred and two millions are under Christian governments. Two Protestant queens, Victoria and Wilhelmina, rule three-quarters of the latter.

The emperor of China recently sent to the American Bible Society at Peking a written order for 160 books, 30 of them distinctly Christian. This was soon followed by an order for copies of all the Christian books that have been printed!

Of the 123 women students who have entered Berlin University this term eighty-eight are Germans, twelve Americans, four Austrians, and Britain, Hungary and Sweden contribute one student each.

Two new gases have been discovered and named Crypto and Neon. The discovery results from the liquifaction of air. After carefully exhausting the oxygen and nitrogen a residue remained, which was different from any known gas.

Jay Gould died in 1892, but his affairs are not entirely settled yet. The state of New York placed a tax of $587,000 on his estate, which was contested by the executors. The case is now before the court of appeals, which is probably the final step in its settlement.

The Czar of Russia, so the story runs, has among his household an understudy, singularly like him in appearance, who shows himself at the windows of railway carriages and the like when his imperial majesty does not wish to disturb himself.

It is said that the government has recently purchased 250,000 gallons of high-proof spirits for the medical department of the army and for the manufacture of smokeless powder, of which it is said to be a necessary ingredient.

member of the church at New Philadelphia, McDonough County, Ill., and was buried near that place, the writer conducting the funeral services.
C. EDWARDS.
Payson, Ill.

MARTIN.

Died, in Little Rock, Ark., July 14, 1898, Sister Huldah Tracy Martin, wife of Jas. Allen Martin, one of the elders of the First Christian Church of this city. Huldah Tracy Toncray was born Feb. 20, 1834, in Memphis, Tenn. Her father, Silas T. Toncray, organized the Baptist Church in Little Rock in 1825, and on July 4, 1832, it became the First Christian Church. Her mother was Orpah Hansbrough before marriage. Her father and mother died in Memphis; he in 1847, she in 1848. She came to Little Rock at the age of 14, and lived with her aunt, Maria Stevenson. She was baptized in April, 1850, and up to the day of her death lived the life of a devoted Christian. She was married to James Allen Martin, Oct. 21, 1852. She was the mother of nine children, six boys and three girls. Four, Silas C., Mollie O., Frank D., and James Cook, survive, all grown and married except James Cook. "Aunt Huldah," as she was familiarly called, was sorely afflicted for the past four years, and during all this time, ever manifested a loving, patient, cheerful disposition. She sleeps in Jesus.
J. B. MARSHALL.
Argenta, Ark., July 30, 1898.

McCLURE.

Bro. McClure was born in Knox County, Indiana, on the 6th day of October, 1840, and in 1853 he with his parents and two sisters removed to Oregon, locating on a farm near Eugene City, where he spent his boyhood days. In the year 1859 he obeyed the gospel and united with the Christian Church during a meeting held by Elders Gillmore, Collison, and Philip Mulkey, and for 39 years lived a devoted and consistent life. On the 13th day of November, 1864, Bro. McClure and Amanda E. Collison were united in marriage by Elder Joseph Sharp. The fruits of their marriage were 12 children, three of them having preceded their father to the spirit land. He leaves a widow, 4 sons and 5 daughters and a host of friends to mourn their loss. He lived to see all of his children obey the gospel, except the 2 youngest that are living and 2 that died in infancy, and it can truthfully be said that his house was a house of prayer. In the year 1880 he with his family removed from the state of Oregon, (to the now) state of Washington and located on a farm near Palouse City, Whitmon County, where he spent the remainder of his days. His death occurred on the 29th day of June, 1898, he being at that time 57 years, 8 months, and 23 days old. After he came to this county he placed his membership with the congregation at Eden Valley, where he was soon elected an elder of that congregation. While he was not a preacher of the gospel, in the common acceptation of the term, his mind was stored with Bible knowledge, and it can truthfully be said that by his exhortations, and wise counsel led many to the cross of Christ. During the time he was a member of the Eden Valley congregation, he was one of the pillars of that church, both from a spiritual and a financial point of view. As a citizen, he was true to his fellowman, ever ready to assist them in time of need, as far as their necessities might require or his ability would permit. He was always patriotic in his principles, and as a father one of his highest motives was to train his children up in the nurture and admonition of the Lord. He was at all times firm, but kind to his family. As a Christian he was sincere and true to his God whom he so dearly loved. We can truthfully say a soldier of Christ has fallen, but the world was made better by his living in it. Funeral was preached by the writer to a large audience, who came to pay the last tribute of respect to our departed brother. Text, Rev. 14th chapter and 13th verse. After this we laid his body to rest in the cemetery near the church house, to await the call of the Master.
E. A. LA DEW.

TRUEMAN.

Mary Helen Hope was born May 11, 1854, married George W. Trueman, Feb. 22, 1881. She died July 1, 1898, leaving a husband and four children to mourn her departure. Deceased was an affectionate wife and loving mother. Truly, she will be missed by her family, friends, the church and Sunday-school. She was a member of the Church of Christ, ever ready with a willing heart to do her part in God's service. Death came to her relief after four weeks of intense suffering, resulting from cancer, which she bore patiently. After a short service at the family residence, near Sumner, Neb., her remains were laid to rest in the Armada Cemetery.
A SISTER IN CHRIST.

WALLACE.

Sister Estelle Wallace fell asleep in Christ at her home, 1731 South 20th Street, Terre Haute, Ind., Saturday, July 16th. A great sufferer and now at rest. A short time before her death she expressed a desire to live for her husband, and Bro. Wallace replied, "It will not be long until I will be with you." Sister Wallace was buried from the church Monday, July 18, and Wednesday morning, July 20, Bro. Hartford Wallace was dead, and the next day was buried by his wife. They were both young, both Christians, lovely in life and in death they were not separated.
W. W. WITMER.
Terre Haute, Ind., July 29, 1898.

Announcements.

Minnesota Convention.

The Forty-first Annual Convention of the Minnesota Christian Churches will be held at Mankato, Minnesota, Tuesday 2 P. M., August 23rd, to Friday P. M., August 26th, inclusive. Church corner of Grove and Second Streets.

Minnesota Christian Missionary Society, David Owen Thomas, M. D., Pres., Minneapolis.

Minnesota Christian Ministerial Association, Robert Grieve Pres., Duluth.

Minnesota Christian Woman's Board of Missions, Mrs. Carey E. Morgan Pres., Minneapolis.

Minnesota Christian Bible-school Association, Prof. E. L. Sampson Pres., Howard Lake.

Minnesota Christian Young People's Society of Christian Endeavor, Ella L. Norris Pres., Minneapolis.

PROGRAM.

MINISTERIAL ASSOCIATION.

TUESDAY, AUGUST 23RD, P. M.

2:00—Devotions led by C. A. Holmgren, Minneapolis.

2:30—Annual Address by President Robert Grieve, of Duluth.

3:00—Address, H. D. Williams, Mankato.

3:40—The Ministry and the Times, A. D. Harmon, St. Paul.

4:00—Address, Carey E. Morgan, Minneapolis.

4:25—Discussion.

4:40—Address, Wm. Bayard Craig, LL.D., Chancellor Drake University, Des Moines, Ia.

TUESDAY EVENING.

7:45—Devotions, led by F. W. Mutchler, Litchfield.

8:15—Address, Wm. Bayard Craig, LL.D.

MINNESOTA CHRISTIAN MISSIONARY SOCIETY.

WEDNESDAY, AUGUST 24TH, A. M.

8:45—Praise, Scripture and Prayer, J. M. Elam, Pleasant Grove.

9:15—Committees on Enrollment and Order of Business announced.

9:25—Minutes of Last Annual Convention, Will U. Smith, St. Paul, Ass't. Rec. Sec.

9:35—Secretary's Report, F. H. Mellen, Minneapolis.

9:45—Treasurer's Report, M. R. Waters, Minneapolis.

9:48—Auditor's Report, J. W. Donaldson, St. Paul.

10:00—Appointment of Committees by the President.

10:20—President's Annual Address.

10:50—A five-minute word of welcome from our early pioneer preachers, viz., W. H. Burgess, John Truax, T. T. Van Dolah, E. T. C. Bennett, A. P. Frost.

11:25—Sermon, A. B. Moore, State Evangelist.

BIBLE-SCHOOL SESSION.

WEDNESDAY, P. M.

1:45—Praise Service, led by Lee L. Ferguson, Sharon.

2:15—Annual Address, by E. L. Sampson, State Superintendent.

2:30—How to Study the Bible, David Husband, Olivia.

2:55—What the Bible-school can do for Missions, Mrs. B. F. Shoemaker, Eden Valley.

3:05—The Importance of Teaching Temperance in the Bible-school, Mrs. A. D. Van Dolah, Rochester.

3:25—The Pastor's Relation to the Bible-school, Robert Grieve, Duluth.

3:35—The Pastor's Review, Agnes Holt, Duluth.

3:55—Preparation of the Lesson, Mrs. Alice Gadd Harmon, St. Paul.

4:05—Discussion.

4:35—Sermon, Temperance, James Crook, Madelia.

GRAND Y. P. S. C. E. RALLY.

WEDNESDAY EVENING.

7:45—Devotional, Ella L. Norris, State Superintendent.

8:15—Address, "Inspiration for Service," Carey E. Morgan, Minneapolis.

C. W. B. M.

THURSDAY, AUGUST 25TH, A. M.

8:45—Devotional Services, led by Mrs. Dora A. Weymouth, Luverne.

9:15—President's Annual Address, Mrs. Carey E. Morgan, Minneapolis.

9:30—State Organizer's Report, Ella L. Norris, Minneapolis.

9:40—State Secretary's Report, Miss Bertie Ireland, Minneapolis.

9:55—The Junior Y. P. S. C. E. and the Church, Miss Mate Maxwell, Duluth.

10:05—Junior Y. P. S. C. E. Conference, conducted by Miss Mate Maxwell, State Superintendent.

10:35—Deepening Spiritual Life, Mrs. A. A. Harmon, St. Paul.

11:00—Paper.

11:25—Sermon, C. C. Smith.

M. C. M. S. AND C. W. B. M.

THURSDAY, P. M.

1:45—Devotional, Mrs. Caroline P. Kelly, Mankato.

Parliament on Church Quarrels.—How shall the Destroyer, 'Church Quarrels,' which has wrecked a score of churches within the state, be met and overcome? Shall the present let-it-alone policy be continued, or shall a practical and scriptural policy be adopted? Shall convention action be taken?

2:15—A City Brother's Opinion, C. M. McCurdy, Rochester.

2:25—A Country Brother's Opinion, J. G. Slick, Amboy.

2:35—The Convention's Opinion. Five-minute talks from the audience, limited in each case strictly to the five-minute period of time.

C. W. B. M.

3:00—Music.

3:10—A Model Monthly Program, Mrs. C. H. Slack, Minneapolis.

3:20—Symposium: Possibilities of a Country Auxiliary, Mrs. Joh Dewar, Antrim, Mrs. Mary Sargent, Horicon.

3:45—Conference, led by Mrs. Helen E. Moses.

4:00—Election of C. W. B. M. and Junior Y. P. S. C. E. officers.

4:25—Music.

4:35—Sermon, Foreign Missions, A. McLean or F. M. Rains.

C. W. B. M.

THURSDAY EVENING.

7:45—Devotional, Mrs. Frank Marshall, Mankato.

8:15—Address, Mrs. Helen E. Moses, in charge Bible Chair Work, National C. W. B. M., Indianapolis, Ind.

MINNESOTA CHRISTIAN MISSIONARY SOCIETY.

FRIDAY, AUGUST 26TH, A. M.

8:45—Inspiration Service, Lewis E. Scott, Browerville.

9:15—Reports of Committees on Resolutions, Obituaries and Enrollment.

9:40—Report of Committees on Bible-schools, on Y. P. S. C. E. and on Incorporation.

10:05—Report of Committees on Ways and Means, on Time and Place of next Convention and on Nominations.

11:00—Complete Statistics, Secretary F. H. Mellen.

11:20—Sermon, C. C. Smith.

EVERYBODY.

FRIDAY, P. M.

2:00—Finale, H. D. Williams, Mankato.
A song of hope for the future.
A gospel battle-cry as we plunge into the new year.
Short, sweet, pithy, snappy speeches.
Stirring music.
3:30—Farewell till 1899—all aboard!

NOTES.—Pastors and others receiving copies of this program in advance of the convention are requested to distribute them judiciously.

THE CONVENTION MUSIC.—T. A. Meredith, pastor of the Howard Lake Church, will have general charge.

REGISTER.—Immediately on reaching Mankato report at the church and register. Also, at the same time leave both your delegate and railway certificate. Speakers will not only register, but please specifically notify the chairman of the committee on "Order of Business" of their arrival, that the committee may not stand in doubt respecting response to the program.

ENTERTAINMENT.—The Mankato brethren will furnish lodging and breakfast free. Dinner and supper will be provided in the church basement at 15 cents per meal. Will pastors and missionary secretaries ascertain the earliest practicable day the probable number to attend and notify Chas. H. Austin, chairman of the Entertainment Committee, Mankato, of number and day and train of arrival? This is very important, and as an act of courtesy should not be overlooked.

NOTES.—*Do not* show partiality in attendance upon any of the sessions, M. C. M. S., C. W. B. M., Bible-school, or Y. P. S. C. E. All have intensely interesting programmes, which you cannot afford to miss. Take notes and return home prepared to report upon the good things experienced.

Do not be dilatory in attendance upon any of the sessions.

RAILROAD RATES.—The railway lines of the state will as usual extend a one and a third rate, on the certificate plan. Pay full rate coming, take a receipt from the agent selling you the ticket and leave same when registering at the convention, as per suggestion above, to be given in charge of H. D. Williams, till the close, when if there be 100 certificates on hand "paying not less than 50 cents each and inclusive of clergy certificates the 1 1-3 rate will apply." There should be no difficulty in meeting these conditions. Call for the certificate on the last day of the convention. Tickets on sale three days in advance of the convention and usable two days succeeding, but passage homeward must be continuous.

DELEGATES.—"Delegates from the churches shall be elected by their respective churches within one month prior to the annual meeting of the society, and shall serve one day. Each church in the state shall be entitled to three delegates for a membership of 50 or less, and one additional delegate for each additional 50 or fraction thereof not less than 25. The election of delegates shall be certified by clerks of the respective churches to the recording secretary of this society, and the regularity of such elections shall be passed upon by the society in its annual meeting in the ordinary manner of deliberate conventions" (Sec. 2 A. of I).

THE CHRISTIAN-EVANGELIST.

A WEEKLY FAMILY AND RELIGIOUS JOURNAL.

Vol. XXXV. August 18, 1898 No. 33.

CONTENTS.

EDITORIAL:
- Current Events........................195
- What Kind of Union did Jesus Pray for........................196
- Paul on the Money Question..........197
- The Resurrection and the Life....... 198
- Editor's Easy Chair....................198
- Current Religious Thought............199

ORIGINAL CONTRIBUTIONS:
- Church Organism and Government.—J. E. Cobbey 199
- Spiritism; or the Witch of Endor.—W. J. Lhamon.................. 200
- Better Citizenship.—S. W. Crutcher..202
- Are We a Christian Nation?—F. L. Moffett 202
- Preaching Old Things.—Horace Siberell.........................203

CORRESPONDENCE:
- English Topics..........................206
- Wheeling Through England 206
- The 14th of July in Paris..............207
- Texas Letter 208
- Letter from D. L. Moody 208
- China Letter 208
- The Missouri Christian Lectureship and The M. C. M. A. 209
- Florida Letter..........................209
- The Baptism in the Holy Spirit 210
- The Bethany C. E. Reading Courses..210
- Minnesota.................... 210

FAMILY CIRCLE:
- Grown-up Land (poem)............. 216
- Text Stories—Opportunity............216
- Cervera's Fleet (poem)........... 217
- A Word to Parents and Teachers......217
- A Song of the New (poem) 218
- The Burial of Mr. Gladstone..........218
- Castilian Pride and Madness....... 219

MISCELLANEOUS:
- The Religious World..................203
- Our Budget...........................204
- Personal Mention......................205
- Notes and News........................211
- Evangelistic.......................... 214
- Publisher's Notes.................. 214
- Missionary 215
- The Sunday-school 220
- Christian Endeavor....................221
- Facts and Factors........................221
- Marriages and Obituaries 222
- Announcements 224

Subscription $1.75.

REAR-ADMIRAL GEORGE DEWEY.

PUBLISHED BY

CHRISTIAN PUBLISHING COMPANY

1522 Locust St., St. Louis.

THE

CHRISTIAN - EVANGELIST

J. H. GARRISON, EDITOR.

W. W. HOPKINS, ASSISTANT.

B. B. TYLER, J. J. HALEY,

EDITORIAL CONTRIBUTORS.

EDUCATIONAL.

RANDOLPH-MACON Academy for Boys

Front Royal, Va. (Valley of Va.). Conducted by Randolph-Macon College. Best equipped in the South. Ranks with best in U. S. Modern conveniences and appliances; gymnasium, &c. $230. Address
Wm. W. Smith, A. M., LL. D, Principal.

HOLLINS INSTITUTE

BOTETOURT SPRINGS, VIRGINIA.

For 175 Young Lady Boarders. The largest and most extensively equipped in Virginia. Eclectic courses in Ancient and Modern Languages, Literature, Sciences, Music, Art, and Elocution. 30 officers and teachers. Situated in Valley of Va., near Roanoke. Mountain Scenery. 1200 feet above sea level. Mineral waters. 56th session opens Sept. 14th, 1898. For illus. catalogue address
CHAS. L. COCKE, Supt., Hollins, Va.

For Christian Education go to

Christian University,

CANTON, MO.

Classical, Scientific, Ministerial, Musical and Commercial. For Ladies and Gentlemen.

MARY BALDWIN SEMINARY

FOR YOUNG LADIES.

STAUNTON, VIRGINIA.

Term begins Sept. 1st, 1898. Located in Shenandoah Valley of Virginia. Unsurpassed climate, grounds and appointments. 20 States represented. Terms moderate. Pupils enter any time. Write for Catalogue.
Mary Baldwin Seminary.

Washington College.

(Young Ladies)

3rd & T Sts., N. E., Washington, D. C.

Charming park of ten acres, overlooking Capitol; lovely building, beautiful rooms, elegant furnishings, good table, thorough instruction. The unrivaled educational and social advantages of the National Capital utilized in full. Schools of Music, Art and Elocution of the highest order. Rooms limited.
F. MENEFEE, President.

HARDIN COLLEGE & CONSERVATORY

FOR LADIES.

26th year. Unprecedented prosperity. 24 Professors from 8 Universities and 5 European Conservatories. A $1,000 Piano to best music pupil. German-American Conservatory. XAVER SCHARWENKA, Director General, present in person during May. Largest. Cheapest. Best. Address
JOHN W. MILLION, Pres., 28 (A St.), Mexico, Mo.

Randolph-Macon Woman's College,

Lynchburg, Va. Classed by U. S. Commissioner of Education in "Division A" as one of the fourteen first-grade colleges for women in the U. S. All modern appliances. Endowment reduces cost of course to $250. Address,
WM. W. SMITH, M. A., LL. D., President.

WOODLAND

Independence, Mo.

Easy of access; moderate expense; all departments. For catalogue address,
Geo. S. Bryant, Pres.

FOREST PARK UNIVERSITY

For women; college and preparatory. College of Music, Director Kroeger; Voice, Metcalf; Violin, Parisi; Elocution, Ashcroft. Board and tuition, $260 to $275. Day pupils, $25 to $40 half year. Take Lindell Railway. Address or call Mondays on Pres. Anna Sneed Cairns, St. Louis, Mo.

BUNKER HILL MILITARY ACADEMY,

BUNKER HILL, ILL.

A superior home and school for boys of any school age. Every equipment; College or Business. Catalogue and Book of Views on application.
COL. S. L. STIVER, A.M., B.D., Supt.

ACADEMY FOR YOUNG WOMEN. 69th Year

A high grade English and Classical School. Certificate admits to Eastern colleges for women. Beautiful location; elevating in associations; celebrated for historic names and Christian institutions.

Under same management are Illinois Conservatory of Music and School of Fine Arts, offering complete courses in these departments. Scholarships awarded to a limited number of girls of superior promise. Address
E. F. BULLARD, Pres., 208 Church St., Jacksonville, Ill.

The Woman's College of Baltimore

offers earnest, well prepared young women facilities for obtaining a college education under the direction of specialists, with abundant laboratory appliances and modern methods. Climate mild, surroundings cheerful. Total yearly expense, three hundred and seventy-five dollars.

Programs mailed on application.

JOHN F. GOUCHER, Pres., Baltimore, Md.

HIRAM COLLEGE, Hiram, Ohio.

A School for Both Sexes.

$112.00 will pay for board, room (heated and cared for), tuition and incidental fee.

WE CALL ATTENTION TO OUR

1. **Four Classical Courses**—Regular Classical Ministerial, Legal and Medical. These lead to the degree of A. B.
2. **Four Scientific Courses**—Regular Scientific Philosophical, Legal and Medical. These lead to the degree of Ph. B. or B. S.
3. **Four Literary Courses**—Regular Literary Ministerial, Legal and Medical. These lead to the degree of B. L.
4. **Five Special Courses**—Teachers', Commercial, English, Ministerial, Music, Oratorical.
5. **Five Post-Graduate Courses**—Theological (A three years' post-graduate course leading to the degree of B. D.); General—(A two years' private course); Ministerial, Medical, Legal—(one year of class work in each).

WE LAY SPECIAL STRESS

1. Upon the variety of our courses—Suited to the needs of all classes of students.
2. Upon the strength of our courses—Equal to those of the best American Colleges.
3. Upon the strength of our Faculty—Comprised of twenty-two experienced teachers including instructors in special departments and physical directors.
4. Upon our Location—Unsurpassed for beauty and healthfulness.
5. Upon our moral and religious surroundings—No saloons; strong religious influences.
6. Upon the fact that expenses are marvelously low, considering advantages offered.
7. Upon our splendid advantages in music, the department being in charge of a very competent and experienced German professor.
8. Upon our excellent facilities and favorable location for art study.
9. Upon the exceptionally strong lines of ministerial work offered.
10. Upon the professional lines of work in the department of law and medicine.

Fall term opens Sept. 27th, 1898. Send for Catalogue to
PRES. E. V. ZOLLARS, HIRAM, OHIO.

LIBERTY LADIES' COLLEGE & CONSERVATORY. Phenomenal success. Highest grade in LETTERS, SCIENCES, ARTS. Faculty specially trained in leading Colleges and Universities of America and Europe. AMERICAN MOZART CONSERVATORY OF MUSIC & FINE ARTS. Chartered by the State. Professors graduates with highest honors of the ROYAL CONSERVATORIES, BERLIN, LEIPZIG, LONDON; use the methods of these Conservatories. A fine, upright CONCERT GRAND PIANO quoted in Bradbury catalogue $1,050, a prize in May Festival Contest. Address LIBERTY LADIES' COLLEGE, LIBERTY, MO

BETHANY COLLEGE.

Founded in 1841 by Alexander Campbell. Open to men and women. Classical, Scientific, Ministerial, Literary, Musical and Art Courses. A Lecture Association, a fully equipped Gymnasium, Literary and Reading Room. Post office, Bethany, W. Va. Railway station, Wellsburg, W. Va., on the Pan-Handle Road, reached from Pittsburg, Steubenville or Wheeling. For catalogue and particulars, address the Secretary.

KENTUCKY UNIVERSITY

R. LIN. CAVE, Prest. LEXINGTON, KY.

Liberal Arts, Bible, Medical and Commercial Colleges.

Tuition for Literary $22, and Bible Course $20 a year. More than twenty teachers. $10,000 gymnasium. Thousands of successful alumni. Welfare of students receive special attention. Open to both sexes. Nearly 1000 students last year. Session begins second Monday in Sept.
Send to Pres. Cave or J. W. McGarvey for catalogue.

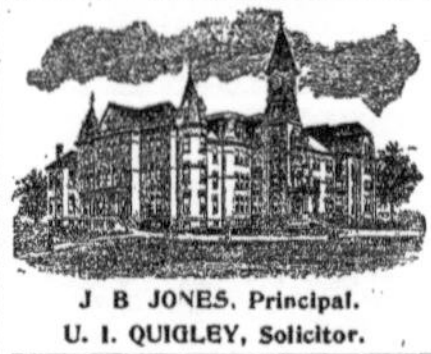

J B JONES, Principal.

U. I. QUIGLEY, Solicitor.

Christian Orphan School of Missouri,

Located at Fulton.

FOUNDED BY J. H. GARRISON, T. P. HALEY, A. B. JONES, A. R. PROCTOR, AND OTHERS.

Buildings and appointments complete. Enrollment last session One Hundred Boarders. Course of study equal to best for Young Ladies. Music, Art, Elocution, taught by skilled teachers.

Next Session begins September 1, 1898.

DRAKE UNIVERSITY

DES MOINES, IOWA.

1. College of Letters and Science. 2. College of the Bible. 3. The Iowa College of Law. 4. The Iowa College of Physicians and Surgeons. 5. The College of Pharmacy. 6. The Normal School and Academy. The Drake Business College. 7. The School of Oratory. 8. The School of Art. 9. The School of Music. 10. The Drake Summer Schools of Methods. The location is the best in the state. The University equipment is reinforced by all the resources of the city. No other school in Iowa has made such rapid and substantial growth. The last year was the most successful in its history. Next year will be better. Wake up to the fact that the best educational advantages in Iowa are right here at your door. 136 received diplomas at the last commencement. No effort will be spared to meet the needs and best interests of the student entering any of the above departments. Send for catalogue.

Drake University. Wm. Bayard Craig, Chancellor.

TIAN-EVANGELIST

and methods, Liberty; in all things, Charity."

., Thursday, August 18, 1898. No. 33

d its environs by this government garded as one of the certainties.

at the dove of peace has come to place of the vulture of war, the icians are figuring up what our ith Spain has cost us. It will be the following figures how expen- ing a modern war is. If there ther humanitarian considerations the question might well be raised there is not some less expensive f settling international difficulties. g are the estimates of the cost of war:

ar expenses, April 1, 1898, 1, 1899	$400,000,000
nditures of separate states	15,000,000
ntribution to soldiers' aid	15,000,000
nage claims against the nent	20,000,000
or of 250,000 volunteer sol- e year	100,000,000
n war debt	90,000,000
new pensions to be paid	300,000,000
he Maine	3,000,000
	$943,000,000

so near to a billion dollars that vell call it a billion. In the light igures it cannot be said, we think, government has exacted hard or able conditions of peace. On the the omission of a demand for any lemnity must be regarded as a magnanimity on the part of our ent.

the negotiations for peace have g on, the armies in the field have inactive. There have been some ents, both in Porto Rico and at uring the past week, although we the same interest now in the these battles that we had prior to of hostilities. The advance of les on San Juan has met with a osition, here and there, but no onflict. Quite a severe battle for ession of the San Juan Light- Cape San Juan occurred on the in which 800 Spaniards attempted e the lighthouse, which was by 40 of our sailors, and by some essels, as the Amphitrite, Cin- nd the Leyden. The Spaniards ven back with considerable loss. e, near Manila, our line was at- y a night sortie of the Spanish superior numbers, and after a onflict the Spanish were driven h a loss of 13 killed and 48 among our troops, and a much ality among the Spaniards. The ania troops bore the brunt of this pported by Capt. Young's battery This battle occurred the last of ough the news was only brought week. What else has occurred or r before the news of peace reaches mains to be seen. In any event Manila must now capitulate to the American forces who are to occupy the city pending the final work of the Peace Commissioners. Gen. Merritt speaks in very high terms of the courage amd discipline of the volunteers who were engaged in what will, we hope, be the last battle of the war. This battle, as we have said, took place at night while a typhoon was raging. It is reported that the insurgents under Aguinaldo rendered no assistance in this matter, but retreated at the first shot.

The following is the proclamation by the President, dated Washington, August 12th, proclaiming peace:

Whereas, By a protocol concluded and signed August 12th, 1898, by William R. Day, Secretary of State of the United States, and his Excellency, Jules Cambon, Ambassador and Plenipotentiary of the Republic of France, at Washington, respectively representing for this purpose the Government of Spain, the United States and Spain have formally agreed upon the terms on which negotiations for the establishment of peace between the two countries shall be undertaken; and

Whereas, It is in said protocol agreed that upon its conclusion and signature hostilities between the two countries shall be suspended and that notice to that effect shall be given as soon as possible by each government to the commanders of its military and naval forces;

Now, therefore, I, William McKinley, President of the United States, do, in accordance with the provisions of the protocol, declare and proclaim on the part of the United States a suspension of hostilities, and do hereby command that orders be immediately given through the proper channels to the commanders of the military and naval forces for the United States to abstain from all acts inconsistent with this proclamation.

In witness whereof, I have hereunto set my hand and cause the seal of the United States to be affixed.

Done at the city of Washington this 12th day of August, in the year of our Lord one thousand eight hundred and ninety-eight, and of the independence of the United States the one hundred and twenty-third.

By the President, WILLIAM MCKINLEY.

WILLIAM R. DAY, Secretary of State.

It is not improbable that a war between Great Britain and Russia will have to take place before the atmosphere is clear on the "Eastern Question." There seems to be a general conviction among those in a position to know the situation that this war is inevitable sooner or later. The Rt. Hon. Sir William Merriott, the British Privy Councilor, who is now visiting this country, speaking of the relations between Great Britian and the United States, is reported as saying: "We don't want an alliance," said Sir William, "but what we do want is a good understanding between the two nations. England is anxious to avoid a war with the United States as the two countries are Anglo-Saxon. Whatever differences may occur between them should be settled by arbitration. England and America with a good understanding between them should defy the world. Yes, there is a strong probability that England and Russia will soon go to war. It has been brewing for a long time and must come. It has simply been delayed by the kinship existing between the royal families of those countries. Russia will not fight quite as hard as England when the crash occurs." It is hardly possible, if this war occurs, to escape a general European war. France and Germany are deeply interested in the matter at issue between Russia and England, as it relates to the Chinese Question. The English press is becoming outspoken in its opposition to Lord Salisbury for what it calls "humiliating concessions," and it is clear that the temper of the English people is such as to support the government in a most vigorous foreign policy. England will, no doubt, have the sympathy of this country in such a conflict, as we had hers in our war with Spain.

Chicago with her usual enterprise is the first of all the cities to propose and to arrange for a grand Peace Jubilee in memory of the triumphant close of our war with Spain. A committee representing the leading business men of the city has already been appointed to arrange a programme which shall be worthy of the occasion and of the city. It is the intention to make it truly national in character. The Times-Herald of that city says: "The plans, set afoot originally for a carnival, local and commercial in its aspect, have developed into a broader and more patriotic project, and now comprehend a national celebration that will live in history. It will be an apotheosis of the soldier and the sailor—a glorious welcome to the white-winged messenger that folded its wings three months ago when the call to arms was sounded." The details of this Peace Jubilee are yet to be worked out, but it is intended to have present the naval and military heroes of the war, and if possible the President of the United States and his Cabinet. There will he a grand military demonstration, and perhaps an "Arch of Peace" constructed to remain as a permanent monument of the historic event to be celebrated. This jubilee is fixed for the month of October. It is well that the close of a war that has made so decided an impression upon our own national life, and upon other nations as well, should be celebrated in some manner, and that there should be some permanent monument somewhere to call attention to it. Chicago's reputation for doing things on a large scale is a guarantee that this Peace Jubilee will be a notable event.

This week we give our readers the picture of one of the most remarkable men of the late war, Admiral Dewey, a name now immortalized in American history. To this admiral-statesman belongs the honor not only of fighting one of the greatest naval battles in naval history, but of wisely managing some of the most delicate and intricate of international questions. An unwise move at Manila might have involved this and other nations in a greater war than ours with Spain. To Admiral Dewey also belongs the honor of fighting the first and the last battles of the war just closed. On last Saturday he bombarded Manila until it surrendered to him unconditionally. The Governor-General, Augusti, and his family escaped on the German cruiser Kaiserin Augusta to Hong-Kong. The details of his escape, why he was aided by a German cruiser, and the particulars of the bombardment and the surrender of the city have not yet been received at Washington. It seems, however, to be another of those peculiar happenings in this peculiar war in which a brave, patriotic admiral was permitted to complete his well begun victory, the capture of Manila, before being prevented by the peace protocol. It is also reported, as we go to press, that Captain General Blanco has resigned his office at Havana to avoid what seems to him to be the odium of a surrender of the city to the United States. This, however, will not effect the situation nor the results of the peace propositions. So far as can be learned, the capture of Manila does not change the situation in the Philippines. The only difficulty has been to make the American hold on the islands stronger than it would have been had the Spanish troops remained in the field. The insurgents still have to be dealt with, but the authorities are confident of the ability of Rear-Admiral Dewey and Major General Merritt to control Aguinaldo, and they don't look for any further trouble in the island of the Far East, for the present, at least.

WHAT KIND OF UNION DID JESUS PRAY FOR?

In our plea for Christian union we have rightly given great prominence to the intercessory prayer of Jesus, recorded in the 17th chapter of John. To all who have made objection to the unity of Christians on the ground of undesirability and impracticability, our reply has been, What Jesus Christ prayed for can be neither undesirable. nor impracticable. Jesus was and is the express image of God. His mind is a perfect transcript of the mind of God. There can be no question, then, as to the duty of pleading for such a unity among Christ's followers as Christ himself prayed for. It is probable, however, that we need to study more carefully and profoundly the nature of the union for which Jesus prayed. Let us look carefully at a portion of this prayer.

"Neither for these only do I pray, but for them also that believe on me through their word; that they may all be one; even as thou, Father, art in me, and I in thee, that they also may be in us: that the world may believe that thou didst send me."

Notice, first, the scope of this prayer. It is not simply for the disciples which he then had, but "for them also that believe on me through their Word." This includes all believers. The petition is perhaps made in view of the causes for dissension and division which he knew would arise in the future.

Notice, next, the *nature* of that union. "That tney may all be one, even as thou, Father, art in me, and I in thee, that they also may be in us." The unity that exists between Jesus and His Father is that which Jesus prays may exist between His disciples. How perfect that union was we know, not only from frequent statements of our Lord Himself, but from the fact that all the investigation of the ages has failed to discover any conflict between the teaching of Jesus and the will of God. Theirs was a union of nature, of life and of work. There were no conflicting aims, ambitions or spirit. They were deeply and profoundly one. The old theory that Christ came into the world to appease the wrath of the Father by His sacrifice has long ago given place to the truth that "God so loved the world that he gave his only-begotten Son, that whosoever believeth on him might not perish, but have everlasting life." Their nature was the divine nature; their life was the divine life; their purpose was the redemption of the race and the triumph of righteousness in the world.

It is a marvelous thing that Jesus should pray that such a union as this should exist between all those who believed on Him. There can be no higher illustration of the sublime possibilities of the Christian life than this, that men, different in temperaments, different in environment, alienated from God and from each other by sin and by racial and national prejudices, may be lifted up out of all their narrowness and bitterness and small envyings, and above all sectarian limitations into the larger life of God where there is unity, fraternity and co-operation. Let it be noted that this union for which Christ prays is primarily a union with Himself in the life of God, and, secondarily, as resulting therefrom, a unity between those who are thus united to Him. There can be no permanent unity among Christians that is not based on and does not grow out of a vital union with Jesus Christ. "As thou, Father, art in me, and I in thee, that they also may be in us." The union of Christians cannot take place anywhere else than "in us;" that is, in God the Father and in Jesus Christ His Son, through the agency and power of the Holy Spirit.

If this be so it seems to answer the question as to how we may best promote the unity of Christians. We can best hasten that great consummation by fostering and developing the spiritual life of Christians. Just in proportion as men grow Christlike in their character are they lifted above the things which divide and alienate brethren, and are brought into the atmosphere of love and unity. Carnality is the cause of division, spirituality of union. It is clear, too, from the nature of the unity for which Jesus prayed, that it is not to be sought for by constructing platforms of doctrines with a view to harmonizing differences. It is not an intellectual union that Jesus prayed for, and that we should plead for, only so far as intellectual unity may result from a vital union with Jesus Christ.

It is not an aggregation of men that Jesus prayed for, but for a oneness of faith, of life and of work, and similarity of character with Himself. This unity will bring about all the union that is practicable or desirable. We believe in Christian union; but only in the Christian union that is made possible by unity *with* Christ and *in* Christ. Differences of opinion, and of method, and of taste, and of temperament always have existed, and always will exist, but the unity for which Jesus prayed triumphs over all these and binds men together in a common league and under a common leadership for the accomplishment of a common end, even the conversion of the world.

These considerations make it evident

plead for the union of Chris-
be careful to exemplify in our
d work the unity for which we
at the Christian world needs
rguments in favor of unity is
on of its practicability and of
ties of achievement in Christian
e are to accomplish our provi-
ion in hastening the fulfillment
prayer for the oneness of His
e must seek the closest possible
with Jesus Christ, our Leader,
nong ourselves, and show to the
ove for Christ and love for one
y triumph over all differences
and cement us together in an
brotherhood. Our emphasis
ject of Christian union has no
ts influence in the growth of
nion sentiment. Let us see to
r congregational life, and in our
erative work, and in our rela-
ach other and with Christians
es and creeds, we do not neu-
effect of our teaching. It is
cultivate this vital relationship
Christ that we can "keep the
Spirit in the bond of peace,"
the glad day when the prayer
all be fulfilled in the unity of
es and in the conversion of the

N THE MONEY QUESTION.

bable that Paul was a man of
is certain that he belonged to a
ily. He was proud of his
In a spirit of boasting he
at he was of the tribe of Ben-
at he was a Hebrew of the
He was a blueblood—Paul was.
r possessed an excellent moral
us character, and evidently held
le, *at least* an honorable, social
He was an educated gentleman.
free-born citizen of the Roman
He knew and asserted his rights
When he became a disciple of
suffered serious loss. It is
that he was disinherited. He
ring to this matter: "I have
e loss of all things" for the sake
This remark he could not have
had not been a person of con-
means. That he was a man of
re as implied the possession of
estate by his family is evident.
sey thinks that toward the close
life he came once more into
of his property. Felix under-
Paul had means. "He hoped
y would be given him by Paul,
ight release him; wherefore he
him the oftener and communed

work as a minister of the Lord
l took an especial interest in the
had much to say about money
. Why?
pistle to the Galatians he speaks
sits that he made to Jerusalem
became a Christian. On the
of the second visit he met and
erence with James, Ephas and
om he characterized as "Pillar
' Barnabas was with him on this
participated in this interview.
"They gave to me and Barnabas
hands of fellowship, . . . only
d remember the poor; which very thing," he says, "I also was forward to do." It seems from this that Paul held a special commission from the apostolic college in Jerusalem to look after this business. This, in part, answers the question, Why? But again:

Paul's most intimate friend and companion was a gentleman of substance. His name was Joses Barnabas. He was a Jew. He belonged to the tribe of Levi. He was a native of the Island of Cypress. When he became a Christian he was an owner of real estate. After he entered the service of Christ he sold it and gave the money to the church. There can be no reasonable doubt that this "good man," as did also Stephen, the first Christian martyr, influenced not a little the character and conduct of Paul.

But for the influence of Barnabas it is not certain that Paul would have been received into the fellowship of the church. Luke says that the believers were "afraid of him and believed not that he was a disciple. But Barnabas took him and brought him to the apostles, and declared unto them how he had seen the Lord in the way and that he had spoken to him, and how he had preached boldly at Damascus in the name of Jesus." Think you that Barnabas had nothing to do in determining the character and conduct of Paul? It was this same Joses Barnabas who introduced Paul to the church in Antioch. There he was for a time assistant to Barnabas. In the Antioch church Barnabas, not Paul, was the chief minister.

It was during the Antiochian ministry that the first opportunity presented itself to render a definite financial service to the poor. This service was rendered by men who had had experience in handling money and who possessed what some preachers do not possess—business sense. The following were the circumstances:

A prophet named Agabus came from Jerusalem to Antioch and by the Spirit of the Lord predicted a famine in the land of Judea. This came to pass as foretold—came to pass when Claudius was Emperor of Rome. When the disciples of Christ heard of this impending calamity they determined, every man according to his ability, to send relief unto their brethren in the famine-stricken region, which also they did, sending the same by the hands of Barnabas and Saul. This was but a beginning.

After their visit to Jerusalem on this business they returned to Antioch and resumed their pastoral-evangelistic work; but they did not forget the poor in Judea. Paul spoke and wrote in their behalf. His interest in them seemed to increase. Certainly it did not diminish. He issued orders to the Gentiles. With clearness and courage he told men of wealth what their duty was in the use of their means. He instructed young ministers to do the same. "Charge them that are rich in this world," he said to Timothy. He issued an order to the congregations of Christ in Galatia requiring them to make a contribution every Lord's day to be used in relieving the necessities of the poor. A similar order was given to the church that was in Corinth. "Upon the first day of the week let every one of you lay by him in store, as he may be prospered, that there be no collections when I come. And when I am come, whomsoever ye shall approve, them will I send with letters, to carry your liberality unto Jerusalem, and if it be meet that I go also, they shall go with me." Now this was written "concerning the collection for the saints."

He again went up to Jerusalem with an offering for the poor. In the Epistle to the Romans he says:

"Now I go unto Jerusalem to minister unto the saints. For it hath pleased them of Macedonia and Achaia to make a certain contribution for the poor saints which are at Jerusalem. It hath pleased them verily, and their debtors they are; for if the Gentiles have been partakers of their spiritual things, their duty is also to minister to them in carnal things. When, therefore, I have performed this and have sealed to them this fruit, I will come by you into Spain."

Having arrived in Jerusalem Paul reported to James—as if James were his superior. Remember that James was one of those who at first laid on Barnabas and Paul the duty—which Paul seemed to regard as a privilege—of caring for the poor. The story of his experience during this visit resulted in his arrest and imprisonment in Cæsarea for two years, and his journey to Rome to appear before the Emperor need not be told in this place. Read as it ought to be read it is more thrillingly interesing than any romance. Shortly after his arrest, in an address to Governor Felix, Paul explained his presence in Jerusalem by saying: "After many years I came to bring alms to my nation and offerings."

It will be interesting and profitable to note some of the things that Paul said about money and its use when he was engaged in this benevolent work.

"But this I say: He which soweth sparingly will reap also sparingly, and he that soweth bountifully will reap also bountifully. Every one according as he purposeth in his heart so let him give, not grudgingly or of necessity; for God loveth a cheerful giver" (2 Cor. 9:6-7).

"For if there be first a willing mind, it is accepted according to what a man hath, and not according to what he hath not" (2 Cor. 8:12).

"For ye know the grace of our Lord Jesus Christ, that though he was rich, yet for your sakes he became poor that ye by his poverty might become rich" (2 Cor. 8:9).

Similar quotations might be continued indefinitely, but for the present these must suffice.

The foregoing is only a hint concerning the teaching of Paul on the money question. The subject is large. Study him on this question and see how much there is in it—see how large a place it occupied in his capacious mind.

A question: *In our effort to restore to the world the New Testament Christianity have we given as much attention to money and its use as we ought? Have we given as much attention to it as Jesus and the apostles?* Who will say that we have? If not, why not?

In a subsequent paper we will, the Lord willing, see what Paul says about the use of money in the support of the ministry. This paper has to do with the obligations under which Christians are to use their money in caring for the poor. May God add his blessing.

B. B. T.

Hour of Prayer.

THE RESURRECTION AND THE LIFE.

(Midweek Prayer-meeting Topic, August 17.)

Jesus saith unto her, Thy brother shall rise again. Martha saith unto him, I know that he shall rise again in the resurrection at the last day. Jesus saith unto her, I am the resurrection and the life; he that believeth on me, though he die, yet shall he live: and whosoever liveth and believeth on me shall never die.—*John* 11:23-26.

No question more deeply concerns the human heart than that which relates to the life hereafter. "If a man die shall he live again?" was a question raised, no doubt, long before it was recorded in the book of Job. Its complete and satisfactory answer is given only in Christ. He it was who brought "life and immortality to light in the gospel." With him the life beyond was as real as the life here in the flesh.

Especially does the subject of the resurrection and the life eternal interest us when we stand in the presence of death, and when one of our loved ones has been called from us. A dear friend of Jesus had died. During his illness his sisters had sent word to Jesus to come to them, but He delayed His coming until Lazarus was dead. When He came the sisters met Him with sad lamentations, bewailing the fact especially that He had not been with them during the sickness of their brother, for if so he had not died. This shows that, although they loved Jesus and had great confidence in His power, their faith had not yet reached to the sublime height which recognized Him as a Master even of death. When He told them that their brother should live again, their response was that they knew he would rise again "in the resurrection at the last day." They believed in the future resurrection, but Jesus said unto her, "I am the resurrection and the life; he that believeth on me, though he die, yet shall he live: and whosoever liveth and believeth on me shall never die." This was a doctrine of the resurrection somewhat different from that in which these sisters believed. The real resurrection, Jesus teaches in this passage, is the rising of the soul into the newness of the life eternal, which is in Christ, and death has no power over such a life. This is the eternal life, because it is the life of God in the soul of men.

In the thought of Jesus physical dissolution to one who has come into life everlasting was a mere incident. There was nothing in that to cause fear. The great thing was to come into union with God through Christ. To such death has no terrors. Jesus is the resurrection and the life. Those who believe on Him shall never die. The dissolution of the body is not death in any important sense. Real death is to be alienated from the life of God, to be dead in trespasses and in sin. "He that hath the Son hath life, and he that hath not the Son hath not life."

And then, to show the weeping sisters and all the world that He was Master of death, He approached the tomb of Lazarus, had the stone rolled away, and spoke the old familiar name, and asked him to come forth. That voice that calmed the waves of Galilee and hushed the winds, penetrated into the regions of death and brought back again from its dark dominion the friend and brother who had "fallen asleep."

The people said that was wonderful, and so it was; but through all the centuries Christ has been doing more wonderful works than that. His voice has been penetrating the regions of moral death and darkness, and calling the souls of men into life and activity. Those who have been dead in trespasses and in sins have heard the voice of the Son of God and have lived. This is the continuous and perpetual miracle of the ages. This is the proof to us that He is Master of death. He who has power to restore the souls of men into union with God, and to bring them into possession of life eternal has power to clothe these spirits with immortal bodies, adapted to the needs of the spiritual world.

Are we living the abundant life which Jesus Christ came to bring us? Or are we content with a mere starving existence? The highest assurance that we can have of life beyond the grave is the fact that even here in the flesh we have the life of Christ in us triumphing over sin and over temptation. This is the life that triumphs at last over the grave and crowns us with immortality. Blessed be the nams of Jesus Christ, who abolished death and who hath delivered us from the bondage of the fear of death and opened the gateway to the life beyond!

PRAYER.

O Thou Infinite and Eternal Father, who art the Father of our spirits, we thank Thee that Thou hast made us to live forever. We rejoice in the knowledge of life everlasting, brought to us through Jesus Christ Thy Son. We thank Thee that when we were in bondage to sin and to the fear of death, He came to deliver us from sin, and to set us free, and to give us life eternal. We thank Thee for a Savior who has conquered death, triumphed over the grave and brought life and immortality to light. Help us to live in the fullness of Thy life, that we may at last share with Thee in triumph over sin and the grave, and live with Thee forever. In Christ's name. Amen!

Editor's Easy Chair.

OR MACATAWA MUSINGS.

Given a calm, clear night with the full moon shedding its soft luster until that beautiful sheet of water known as Black Lake, or Macatawa Bay, looks like a silver sea, and a party of forty or fifty congenial people on board a little steamer for a moonlight excursion, when the party is bounded by the Missouri River on the west and Acts 2:38 on the east, and the rest can be imagined. Such an excursion we had on a recent ideal night, under the generous patronage of Mrs. Henry Meier, of St. Louis, whose advent into our St. Louis colony at the Park has added much to its enjoyment and pleasure. Our little steamer first passed out through the channel on to Lake Michigan where the swell of the waves caused more or less sensation in some of the party; but having accomplished its mission on Lake Michigan in meeting a larger vessel from Sangatuck and receiving a part of its cargo in the form of baskets of peaches, the little vessel returned through the channel, unloaded its cargo of fruit at the Macatawa Dock, barring a few baskets, which were purchased or otherwise secured, the excursion proper began, consisting of a trip to Holland and return. There was song, there was story, there was conundrum and bright repartee and laughter and conversation, and a good time generally, including the consumption of the peaches fresh from the peach orchards of
the Kalamazoo. Never did we see tl
little lake more beautiful, as it lay bathe
in the soft moonlight, and never did a mo
genial party sail over its surface than c
this occasion. A hearty vote of thanl
was given to Mrs. Meier for the pleasu
she had given us in this moonlight ri
upon the lake.

At this writing the Macatawa Assemb
is in the middle of its sessions and h
proved to be, so far, one of the most profi
able and by far the most largely attende
in the history of the Park. Bros. H. I
Willett and J. M. Campbell are giving
some fine studies in the Gospels, the o
giving us the historical aspects of tl
books and the other the spiritual teachin
with opportunity for questions and sugge
tion. The evening addresses on differe
phases of the subject of Christian Unio
are also awakening good interest, and
course meet with favor here at Macataw
where Christian union is popular. W
have never had any difficulty in living t
gether here in peace. There are abo
thirty ministers here at present, of who
twenty are Disciples, nine are Congrega
tionalists and one Dutch Reform. Ther
is a larger number of our preachers and
our members present than at any previou
time, and all who are here seem to be de
lighted, not only with the place, but wit
the people. Some of the matter presente
at this Assembly may assume a permane
form. Already one series of lectures de
livered here has been published in a boo
and is becoming widely known, namel
"After Pentecost, What?" by J. M. Camp
bell. It is hoped that in the future thi
may not only be a summer resort but
center of biblical and religious instructio
as well, which shall produce a literature o
some permanent value. What better plac
could be found for working out some of th
problems of our times? The idea of utiliz
ing resorts for religious and education
purposes is a good one. It need not inter
fere with the idea of rest, while it serves t
redeem these resorts from excessive idlene
or social frivolity.

And so Dr. Whitsitt, president of th
Southern Baptist Theological Seminar
has been forced to resign his position i
that institution, because of the continu
war made upon him by Southern Baptist
This seems to us to be a conspicuous cas
of the *odium theologicum*. The war o
Prof. Whitsitt is the result of a historic
view of his concerning the early practice
the Baptists in England on the subject
baptism. It is not charged that he ha
changed his views concerning the scriptur
teaching on that subject. It is a mere differ
ence of historical interpretation. We d
not believe Dr. Whitsitt is infallible as
historian. He made some egregiou
blunders in his treatment of the Disciple
in their historical relation to the Mormon
and to the Sandemanians. There were onl
a few Baptists who found fault with D
Whitsitt for these historical blunder
Indeed, the men whose criticism has com
pelled the resignation of Dr. Whitsitt we
the very men who extolled him for i
former interpretations concerning whic
there was a great deal less excuse than
the latter case. We regret to see thi
triumph of the narrower and less liber
element in the Baptist Church, but

course it is only a temporary triumph, for in the long run intelligence prevails over ignorance and intolerance.

It is wonderful what perennial freshness and interest attach to the gospel narratives. Our studies during this Assembly have been in the four Gospels, so far, and they have been made to stand out with their individual characteristics and peculiar coloring with great distinctiveness. When one comes into close touch with the sublime facts, the transcendent teaching and the mighty works recorded in these Gospels, the question of literary authorship takes a secondary place, and one instinctively feels that by whomsoever the facts, the deeds and the teachings were recorded, the records are true and deal with great realities. The motto, "Back to Christ," if it mean a fresh study of Jesus Christ as he is portrayed in the four Gospels, cannot fail to have a good effect in exalting Christ to his true place in the Christian system and in producing a truer proportion of faith. Christ can be seen in any of the New Testament writings, but He can be seen best in the four Gospel narratives, each of which present some true and important view of that peerless character.

We have never known Macatawa Park to be fuller than it is at present. A number of cottagers have been compelled to take in one or two boarders in order to accommodate the people, as the hotel is full to overflowing. So far as we have ascertained the following if the list of our own preachers who have been here this week: H. W. Everest, Des Moines, Ia.; H. S. Earl, Irvington, Ind.; J. S. Hughes, Chicago, Ill.; J. J. Haley, Cynthiana, Ky.; W. F. Richardson, Kansas City, Mo.; Geo. H. Combs, Kansas City, Mo.; F. G. Tyrrell, St. Louis, Mo.; J. G. Waggoner, Eureka, Ill.; J. H. Hardin, Eureka, Ill.; Geo. L. Snively, Jacksonville, Ill.; —— Dean, Harvey, Ill.; Hugh McLellan, Shelbyville, Ky.; J. Z. Tyler, Cleveland, O.; Errett Gates, Chicago, Ill.; W. E. Ellis, Nashville, Tenn.; H. L. Willett, Chicago, Ill.; Bruce Brown, Chicago, Ill.; Geo. Platt, Warsaw, Ind.; F. M. Kirkham, Chicago, Ill.; T. W. Pinkerton, Kenton, O.; F. G. Strickland, Chicago, Ill.; J. L. Darsie, Little Rock, Ark.; J. P. McKnight, Peorio, Ill.; J. W. Allen, Cleveland, O. To this might be added A. M. Atkinson who, while not a preacher by profession, preaches, nevertheless. He has been taking in these lectures and enjoying them, as also does Sister A. The attendance and interest increase daily.

Current Religious Thought

The Standard, August 13th, concludes a somewhat lengthy editorial on "The Religion of College Women," with the following practical question and its answer:

There is indeed no more important question of an educational sort than this one: What shall be the religion of the women who, passing through colleges or schools of high grade, come to rank as leaders at home? If, as wives and mothers, as helpers in the churches, as teachers, as physicians, they bear in their hands a light to lighten the darkness, to guide the young and cheer the struggling and comfort the dying, bright indeed shall be that light; and many shall walk in its radiance. But if instead they come back to their homes with the flame hidden away in their hearts, as something too rare and precious for the glare of day, living the Stoic life, scorning to show their inmost and devoutest thoughts to any but the most intimate friends, then their learning has been a curse, their religion a failure and their struggle vain. That a few have so failed is a melancholy fact which it is not well to forget; but for most earnest women the college life and the college culture have been a cherished gift, to be wisely used and not hoarded; and the college outlook upon life has, in the end, assured them more strongly than before that of all good things in this world and the next the source is the love of God in Jesus Christ.

The Missionary Review of the World in its leader, by the editor, on Spanish Movements of the Half Century, quotes from a Cardinal Archbishop of Valladolid, Spain, a paragraph that not only reveals the deplorable state of the Spanish mind, religiously, but also shows that her teachers are not all blind. The Archbishop says:

All acknowledge that the actual situation of Spain is the most critical that our country has passed through in the present generation, and can only be compared to that which preceded the French invasion at the beginning of the century. All know that we are in danger of a tempest from without, and that within a volcano is roaring under our feet. Notwithstanding, we hear of more preparations for public diversions than usual, noisy preparations for feasts, battles of flowers, bull-fights, masked balls, and the like; a paroxysm of the foolishness of carnival as out of place as it is exaggerated. In its nature carnival is a barbarous custom, nearly always immoral, and frequently sacrilegious and impious, especially so in these days of so much mourning for our insulted country, in addition to the grief of the Spanish mothers, whose sons have died in Cuba, and who, from the solitude in which they weep, can hear the loud laughter of vice as well as so much blasphemy. It appears as if the people were to be diverted to prevent them realizing their condition, to be intoxicated with pleasure that they may not feel, to bring them down to the level of the Roman decadence. We see, with the most profound sorrow, that it is intended to make the carnival this year more uproarious and, on that account, more immoral than ever. How can this phenomenon be explained? If we look at it from a natural point of view, it is repugnant to all delicate sentiments to make so much ostentatious merriment in a country and at a time when so many tears are being shed, and where there is likely to be cause for many more. More sensible have been the places, sadly few in number, that have happily agreed not to celebrate the carnival. The money dissipated on this ostentatious luxury might be used for food and medicines for our poor soldiers, or it might help to construct machines of war which would contribute to make our flag respected. We ought to reflect upon the repeated warnings which God has given to us, for has not the Lord's prophet said, "The earth is desolate because no one considered?"

The harmony between Providence and common sense is clearly and strikingly pointed out in the following paragraph from a sermon by Rev. F. M. Bristol, D. D., pastor Metropolitan Methodist Episcopal Church, Washington, D. C., on "God's Hand in the War," and printed in the Treasury:

Whether it be in times of peace or of war, Providence works in manifest alliance with the brains and hearts and hands of the most intelligent, virtuous and industrious people. There is nothing in the doctrine of Providence that excuses men from doing their duty at the plow-handle and the loom, at the anvil and the bench, in the office, study, counting-room, hall of legislation and schoolhouse; at the guns, at the ballot-box and at the altar. But when men fail to do their own duty, they are prone to lay the ill consequences on God, or persuade themselves foolishly that the results of their own delinquencies are proof positive that there is no Providence. God is on the side of good farming, good financiering, good politics, good education, good motives, good guns, good battleships, good discipline, good aim, good generalship and good causes. And if he were not, what would all your good plows, good ships and good schools avail? If he is, what excuse can a people make who fall short of success and prosperity because they have not met the conditions of an holy and invincible alliance with Providence?

On the ground that the testimony of a competent observer is of first value the folllowing from the Christian Commonwealth, London, is important testimony on the Church of England controversy:

This matter of ecclesiastical conflict between the two chief parties in the Church of England is the supreme question of the day. Undoubtedly on it hinges the issue whether England shall sink into the old Romanism again, and whether the Reformation shall be undone. But the Church of England is powerless. It is drifting and drifting the wrong way. It is easy to say, as many do, "Oh, but the great heart of the country is sound after all!" That is what some keen observers are anxious about. Thousands of our young men and women are *not* at heart in Reformation principles. They revel in gorgeous processional displays, beautiful choral music, and church millinery and costumery. And the majority of the young clergy are steeped in the Ritualistic temperament. Nonconformists, especially Congregationalists and Wesleyans, have done and are doing much to encourage the first, and to depress the second temperament. Let it be remembered that all children are Ritualists by nature, and that without a special education the first temperament must predominate in us all. The second temperament is in most people acquired through reason, reflection and instruction. It grows with a true knowledge of the gospel. It belongs to the higher and nobler nature. The martyrs were generally of the second temperament. They learnt that outward things, however beautiful, are but symbols of inward and spiritual and eternal realities. But the majority of people do not think, reason, reflet, or learn. They skim the superfices, skimming like the swallows to catch pretty insects, instead of diving like the osprey beneath the surface to grasp what is more substantial. The gospel of Christ swept away the Temple and its ritualism. The first temperament was played out. The synagogue remained, which was the predecessor of the modern chapel, with its Evangelicalism, as the Temple was of the modern church, with its elaborate ceremonialism.

CHURCH ORGANIZATION AND GOVERNMENT.*

BY J. E. COBBEY.

After careful study of the subject let this meeting recommend a plan of organization, have it printed, prepare a form for treasurer's and secretary's books. Prepare and print and make accessible to every church a model form of church government, not as mandatory, but as advisory. From your rich experience lend a helping hand to those less fortunate. I would not make of you preachers, dictators. I would not have you run the church. But I would have you make of yourselves experts, whose advice on the legal organization of the church would be as good as any lawyer's; whose advice on the business affairs of the church would be as good as any business man's. Such a man would compel the respect of the business man; respect would be followed by confidence, and confidence would open the door for conversion. This knowledge on your part can not be acquired in a day or in a year, but here is the place and now is the time for you to commence. I would make this summer school of yours a school of methods, a school of practice. Appoint a standing committee of your number on church organization and government. Such a committee would have it in its power to do more good for the cause than your secretary or any other of your officers.

It seems to me our plan of church organization is defective from the beginning. We decide to send out an evangelist to possess new fields. In selecting a man no one asks what is his business ability? Can he draw the articles of incorporation for the new church he is to found? Does he know the six things those articles are to contain according to the law of the land?

*Paper read before the Thirty-first Annual Convention of the Nebraska Christian Missionary Society at Beatrice, Neb., July 3rd, 1898.

Does he know that these articles must be recorded in the clerk's office? No one furnishes him with printed suggestions covering these points and the one hundred others which arise in the early life of every church organization, which he can leave with the young church when he goes on to other fields. How can a church whose very organization is a violation of the law of the land, and whose every day of existence is a menace to good government because a violation of the statute, appeal to honest, law-abiding citizens to come in and take fellowship? How can this church, how can any church, whose business organization is a graveyard wherein are buried every principle of business and every rule of commercial success, appeal to business men or to commercial men to come in and take fellowship? How can a church organization which has so carefully built up this barrier between itself and the business and commercial classes expect members of those classes to break down the barrier and come in? The members of these classes are wide-awake, honest and progressive. They teach the highest standard of morality. They believe in religion. They want to be members of a church organization if it is a help toward a better life. They hear the church by the mouth of its preacher bid them enter. But whenever they transact business with the church, whenever they meet in a business way any of its officers, they are repelled. No wonder so many men of these classes are trying to live religious lives outside the church. No wonder it is a standing complaint among evangelists that they cannot reach these classes. Brethren, the doors of our church organizations are closed to these classes to-day. The few from these classes who have the temerity to break in have done so at the earnest solicitation of a devoted wife or mother. The first time they attempt to give to the church of their rich experience, and place its organization in a more presentable shape, they are coldly told to stand back, this is a church, we want none of that here. The pastor probably sees the mistake that is being made. But he has been taught that he is not a business man, and that he should not know about the rules of business. The people have not been taught to look to him for business advice. He is powerless. Few of our churches are to-day legally organized. Their business methods are those they used twenty-five years ago, when composed of fifteen or twenty members.

What is to be done? I answer, Commence a reform here and now. Resolve that you will do all in your power to have the church which you serve legally organized—that you will apply the best modern business rules to the conduct of its business. If you cannot do this, I appeal to you to be honest and consistent, and before you again plead with your people, acknowledge the authority of God's law; that you hang from your pulpit in plain print the words, "I do not acknowledge the authority of the state law;" that you place back of the pulpit the words, "Church business will not be done on business principles;" that you place over the outer church-door the words, "This church was organized and still exists in violation of the state law." When you go out to establish other churches, either go equipped for your work, prepared to start them correctly, both in doctrine and in law, or if you cannot do this, drop that holy word "evangelist," and introduce yourself to them as a constant law-breaker, teaching but a part of God's law. Preachers, churches, Christians should carefully guard against deception, against appearing to be what they are not. You can't fool anybody in this day and age of the world. It is not good business, it is not good morals, it is not good religion to try. It only harms the one making the attempt, and impedes the cause in which he is engaged. Why, bless you! do you for one moment think that I am not aware of the fact that, while I am addressing the highest organization in this church, I am addressing a body without the semblance of legal organization? What excuse can you offer for this illegal existence? What excuse can I offer to my professional brethren for thus addressing you upon obedience to the state? You should be my teacher in this—not I yours. But I plead for reform in our church organization. With you more than with any one else lies the power to institute reform. Will you do it? When the Master said, "Render therefore unto Cæsar the things which are Cæsar's, and unto God the things that are God's," he meant it as he said it, not as many of us have interpreted it, that we could render unto God the things that are God's, and afterward unto Cæsar the things that are Cæsar's, if convenient. But there is still another lesson in it for us: that the man who will not render willing obedience to the proper laws of the country in which he lives, or to the rightful customs of the people with whom he is associated, is not the proper one to plead for obedience to the divine laws. In what I have said here to-day I have endeavored to speak plainly and to the point, because I recognize in you as individuals consecrated, devoted workers in a common cause, because I have the utmost confidence in your ability, honesty and integrity as leaders of the people and because I know that you have a consuming desire to live up to the full measure of Christian manhood. If I have hurt the feelings of any one, I am sorry for it. If I have reviled you or spoken evil of you falsely, I refer you to the scriptural consolation for such trials as given in Matthew 5:11.

I believe it is the sacred duty of the church to have its organization so perfect from a legal standpoint that it may be taken as a model by secular societies; to maintain its business organization at such a standard that it will be pointed to by the world as a model.

Years ago prominent Christian workers planned to make the Bible a model in every one of its parts and features. Time and money without limit have been expended for this purpose, until to-day, as an example of the bookbinder's art, it is without a rival. No finer paper for the purpose goes into any book. As a typographical job it has no superior. As to the words used, it is a standard in spelling. As to capitalization and punctuation, the best standard; as to grammatical construction and arrangement, the standard of standards. As you hold that splendid production of painstaking labor in your hand, do you for one moment think that a single item of this labor was thrown away? That those consecrated men made a mistak If not, why not make the legal and bus ness organization of our church a standa and a model also?

I have in my possession a letter writte by the final proof-reader of a publishin house in regard to a controversy over th grammatical correctness of an expressio used in a legal work. Grammars an standard English writers had been cited b each of the contesting parties. When th man, an expert among experts, cited in th Bible the place where the expression wa used as he said it should be used, sayin in that letter, that while he did not acce the Bible as a divine or inspired book, h did appeal to it as the best authority i our language in grammar, spelling an rhetoric, because it had been brought t perfection by the painstaking labor of th greatest scholars of our language. Thin of it! that Bible a Book of books in ever sense of the word. Think of it! this ma believing from his infancy in the doctrin of infidelity, compelled at sixty years o age to appeal to the Bible as the suprem authority in grammar, rhetoric and spell ing. In the sight of God not one dollar o expense, not one hour of the time neces sary to wring from that old infidel thi confession was lost. And I further say t you, not one hour of time, or one dollar o expense necessary to place our legal an business organization on the same basi will be thrown away. This old man ma never accept that Book as a spiritual guide but his power to influence others agains it is forever gone; his position, while no logically, is practically inconsistent. Th hundreds of young men who have learne their business from him cannot have th prejudice against it which he has. The cannot appeal to it as an authority in the every-day business matters, and entirel reject it as an authority in their spiritua matters. This old man has unwillingly, b the irresistible logic of events, become worker in God's vineyard.

When we shall bring our legal and business organizations up to that degree o perfection of which we are capable, n evangelist will complain that he canno reach the professional, the business or th commercial classes. They will seek fo him. This confidence in the church organization will produce friendship for it members and its teachings. This friendship will induce attendance, and attendance will result in conversions.

SPIRITISM; OR THE WITCH OF ENDO

W. J. LHAMON.

(CONCLUDED.)

Yesterday a dear friend of yours die and you knew nothing of it. You met medium, however, and he told you all abou it, giving the exact name. You couldn' believe it; but to-day you get a letter confirming the report of the medium in ever particular. Such things happen. But ho can they happen unless the medium get the knowledge from the spirit of the departed one? Students of psychology hav given us a more natural explanation. W are all endowed with a dual mind, or wit what has been called the subjective an objective mind. The objective mind is th ono we use when we are at ourselves, an when we go about our business in a sensible way. It is the every-day mind of san

ıe subjective mind is the one we p-walking, and when we are , or clairaudient, or in any way It is the mind used by al prodigies, such as Zerah Colby musical prodigies, such as and by insane people, and by irious from sickness, and by minded people generally.

jective mind is controlled by ; hence the power of the hypnotsubject and of the auto-hypnotimself. The subjective mind is hat reads other minds; it never d in a deductive way it reasons ɔt nicety of logic. Students are to concede that this mind can lerable objects that it may prole sound on a solid substance, roperly controlled it has wonderve powers. The medium, the t and the mind-reader differ from people in that they have the cquired power of bringing up at ɔres of the subjective mind into ive, or of going a step further rance or self-imposed hypnotic there of seeing clearly and of consciously, yet truly and sur- Now in the moment of death ıscious mind of your friend, freed ody, impresses the fact on your ɔus mind. The impression lies ıin you waiting to be brought to e clairvoyant, the medium, finds tells you about it. Very likely and the medium honestly think it ɔirit that did all this, whereas it the natural forces of the mind at

eported of Prof. Carpenter, that the city of Washington he put a an under the hypnotic influence a student of philosophy, and a of a leading university. He asked g man if he would like to have a . Socrates, and he readily assented. fessor said: "I will call up his ere he is now in the corner." The an approached with great rever- Professor went through the form troduction, and the young man ocrates a chair. For two hours he estions, and intrepreted to the comanswers of the imaginary spirit, g a most systematic and wonderful ıy, so that the cultured people present could scarcely but think rates was actually there. At a ıe the Professor had the same an in hand, and asked him if he ke to have a conversation with a ıic pig. He assented, and the introduced him to a pig which, him, was the reincarnation of a iest. The karma of the priest he been a little off color, but he had none of his learning. The y pig conversed in all languages the young man, and talked most upon theosophy. This story is Mr. Thomas Jay Hudson in his Psychic Phenomena," and the on is simply this: Neither nor the pig was present; the ıan in the hypnotic state was put e suggestion that they were; his e mind did all the rest, for he had the philosophy of Socrates

he lost faith, therefore, in himself and in his army; when he became a cowardly and recreant king, he sought the medium of Endor. He called for Samuel, and presently in her self-imposed hypnotic state she saw Samuel just as clairvoyants see; she saw the Samuel that Saul had hidden away in him, and of course she immediately knew Saul. Of course also she proceeded to interpret his troubled mind from the standpoint of the Samuel she saw, and to turn the king's guilty fears into a prediction of his defeat and death. This is the interpretation of the scene that springs most naturally from the facts of psychology as known to-day. This spiritualistic seance, now well-nigh three thousand years old, may stand as the representative of higher class of such performances through all the ages.

Thirdly, Spiritualism presumes to give us a new religion. It has a theology. Recently in our hearing, one of its advocates spent a half hour in telling us that Christ was divine precisely as all are divine. This is the crudest sort of unscholarly and uncritical Unitarianism. There is not a school of genuine scientists or philosophers or critical scholars in the world to-day that could be induced to assume or defend such a position. Christ is unique, and more and more the world is coming to recognize that fact, and to grant him his more than human claims.

Spiritualism as advocated recently in our city declares that "fear is the mother of worship." Then, when its advocates prayed in public (as they did) their prayers were either a hollow mockery or the offspring of cowardice. The dilemma is their own. With Christians love is the mother of worship.

Having no Christ such as the New Testament presents, Spiritualism has consequently no Savior. Its advocates very logically tell their disciples to save themselves. It is the old Buddhistic and agnostic doctrine, the time-worn doctrine of lifting yourself by your own boot-straps. But it sounds new when it comes flippantly bobbing up from some hypothetical borderland between this and the other world, where knowing ghosts range at the ready beck and call of this or the other irreverent hypnotic.

Quite logically there follows the agnostic doctrine of consequences, closely allied to the theosophic doctrine of the karma, Mr. Ingersoll being its best known advocate in America. It is simply a question of rewards for merit, of sufferings for demerit. In this system there is no room for a child's repentance, for a father's forgiveness. It is futile for a prodigal to return to his father's home, for he will find no compassion there—only a stern and awful destiny, a sort of monolithic or stone god father, who says heartlessly: "You sinned, you wretch; now suffer!"

Many spiritualists deny the personality of God, and must, therefore, be ranked as pantheists. In this respect as well as in their inclination toward occultism they are closely akin to present-day theosophists.

There are a few things about Spiritualism that should be taken into the account by students of it before they decide to take it at its own estimation.

1. The revelations of the hypothetical girl calls up Shakespeare it happens that he has forgotten his noble English, that he can't make verses, and that he is liable to spell phonetically. On the other hand, if a cultivated medium calls up Sitting Bull or Black Hawk, the old copper-colored chieftain immediately becomes a philosopher or an artist, according to the mind of the medium. Such facts indicate that after all it is the medium that speaks and not the spirit, the subjective mind of the medium, however believing itself to be the spirit, that suggestion having been made to it.

2. Spiritism has added nothing to our stock of knowledge; it has given us no invention, it has made no revelations. Were the spirits of the dead really speaking to us through the mediums we should expect wondrous things. Psalms surpassing those of David; prophecies beyond those of Isaiah; art beyond that of Raphael and Michael Angelo; flights of poetry loftier than those of Dante, Milton, Browning and Shakespeare; and a high level of religion, at least equal to that of Jesus. But we get nothing of that sort. Actually the spirits rapped up by the mediums don't know as much as some ordinary people.

3. Spiritism, aside from its false religious teaching as indicated above, has been guilty of a tendency toward free love. A few years ago its leading representatives in the United States were advocates of this species of immorality, and sad homes and many wrecked ones are the tares that have grown from that unfortunate sowing. This statement is far from being intended as an indiscriminate thrust at the morality of mediums in general, for no doubt there are pure and well-meaning men and women among them, and such also as are nobly willing to brave persecution for what they esteem to be true and right. Nevertheless, those who persist in the undue cultivation of the subjective mind should be aware of the danger they incur of disturbing both their mental and moral equipoise. Broken homes and insane aslylums are too intimately related with the history of Spiritism not to give us pause. The scientific reasons that have been offered for this are very briefly as follows: As regards insanity, that is already wrought whenever the too highly cultivated subjective mind usurps the place of reason. When that time comes the unfortunate medium or clairvoyant, lacking the adjustments to this world that come normally through the subjective mind, can find no suitable home but the madhouse. As to morality, when once the subjective mind, already under the suggestion that it is an authoritative spirit from a higher world, receives the further suggestion of "the illicit love," it very naturally returns to its owner in defiance of this poor world's arbitrary enactments a *carte blanche* for his meditated license.

Let the sincere seeker after glory, honor and immortality contrast the haphazard and uncertain results to be gotten from mediums with the sweet and gracious consolations of Jesus offered to us in words such as these: "I am the resurrection and the life; he that liveth and believeth in me shall never die;" and confirmed to us by the majestic facts of his life, death and resurrection. Let him contrast also the

with the self-sacrificial mind of him who sealed his consolations to us with his own blood, and who in resurrection, might and glory beckoned us with pierced hand to the reception of them. And finally, let him who seeks surcease of sorrow turn away from the myriad graves of earth to look by faith upon the empty tomb of the One who said: "The hour is coming in which the dead shall hear the voice of the Son of Man, and shall come forth, they that have done good unto the resurrection of life."

BETTER CITIZENSHIP.

S. W. CRUTCHER.

While admiring the skill and bravery of our soldiers and sailors we are ready to ask, Will it be possible for our statesmen to direct affairs with equal credit to themselves and to the honor of their country?

If ever we should heed the admonition of Paul to Timothy, that prayers be made "for kings and for all in authority, that we may lead a quiet and peaceable life," now is the time. New questions, difficult of solution, new policies that will be difficult of administration, are already or soon will be thrust upon us. Are we to be equal to the occasion?

We have been very far behind in dealing with the best interests of our inferior race left on us at the close of the civil war between the states. In a Southern city of perhaps 2,500 souls, the negro vote is sufficient to decide, not only municipal, but also county elections.

A man who is always at church and never misses prayer-meeting, who is very hospitable, and perhaps conceded to be one of the best men in his town or county, holds a lucrative county office—how did he get it?

He selected in the six different townships six negroes, one for each township, in whose hands he placed six fine mules, a mule to a man, saying to each, this: "If I am beaten, the mule is a loan; if elected, a gift."

The office is his; the mules belong to the negroes. This was better than working the negroes through the saloon men, as is very often the case.

I said to a preacher, "Why not close these saloons that pay into the treasury $1,200 each?" His reply was this: "You know that the larger part of the saloon money comes from the negroes, and many of the white people will approve of any plan that transfers the dimes from the negro to the white man.

We have seen the saloons voting the negroes and then getting their hard-earned pennies over their counters for their adulterated liquors during all these *post bellum* days.

Is the rum traffic to be in our way in dealing with our captured provinces, as it has been all these years in dealing with the negroes?

These are the questions that our President and Congress should consider.

Our Garfield did much to close the polygamous evil in Utah. Harrison, to the honor of religion and Presbyterianism, struck the Louisiana Lottery and all lotteries a blow from which it has never recovered; and now is the time for the more than five millions of Methodists to record that their man, McKinley, "has come to the kingdom for a time like this."

Shall rum compete with the elevating and saving influences to be used in civilizing these poor people who have had no Bibles and whose only ideas of religion is loyalty to the Catholic Church?

Our Y. P. S. C. E. and other young people's organizations ought to make themselves heard in tones unmistakable now. Party lines are so loose now and the independent voter is abroad as never before. The party lash is less feared than ever, and it is an opportune time to demand a better citizenship. Let us get our patriotism turned in the right direction. Let us show the world some of the victories of peace—a triumph of right over wrong. Preachers will join in such a work as never before. Our sectarian meanness is growing less day by day, and surely it is for some good purpose. Day before yesterday an engineer on the railroad, getting about $125 a month, got drunk. He was promptly discharged. Yesterday he attempted suicide, but failed. He is disgraced, out of work and has a dependent family. Yet Christian men by their votes and in various ways encourage this iniquity. Let us not pray less for our army and our navy, but more for a better citizenship.

ARE WE A CHRISTIAN NATION?

F. L. MOFFETT.

The question we have placed at the head of this article is not an easy one to answer. When one gets into a pessimistic mood he is disposed to answer it in the negative. None are so blind, I presume, as to think that we have reached perfection, or that the millennial reign has come; for surely our Father's will is not done "upon the earth as it is done in heaven." Yet there is much over which to rejoice. We are passing through an epoch-making period in our history. During the past three months we have been engaged in a war such as the world has never witnessed before. It cannot be explained by the word "patriotism." We have called it a humanitarian war; and so it has been. It does not have the usual element of selfishness. Brave American boys have given up their lives, and others have offered themselves as a sacrifice upon the altar of liberty. "Greater love hath no man than that a man lay down his life for his friend." These have laid down their lives for an oppressed people, but how unselfish has been this service! It has attracted the attention of the whole civilized world, and has really been an astonishment to those who are not familiar with the American type of Christianity. The success of our armies, both upon land and sea, has been phenomenal and many have come to believe, as never before, that God is operating in American history to accomplish this good purpose. Truly we can say:

"I doubt not through the ages one increasing purpose runs,
And the thoughts of men are widening with the process of the suns."

Not the least important event of this three months of history-making was the proclamation of President McKinley, requesting that the third day of July be made a day of prayer and thanksgiving to Almighty God, for the success which had attended our cause (which we trust is his cause), and that supplications be made to him that the war may be brought to a close with as little suffering and loss of life as possible. The fourth day of Jul brought us the news of the destruction c the Spanish fleet, under Admiral Cervera just outside the habor at Santiago; then after a few days' waiting, came the news c the surrender of Santiago. Our armie have had almost an ovation, at least at th beginning of the invasion of Puerto Ric and with it all comes the glad news tha very likely, terms of peace will soon b reached. Surely, God is in his world, eve though *all* is not right with it yet.

If we should write our history as th Hebrew wrote his we would give God great deal more credit than we do, fo surely our confidence has been in him. On of the most important items of the Declar ation of Independence is the statement "With a firm reliance upon the protectio of Divine Providence we mutually pledg to each other our lives, our fortunes an our sacred honor." And who would question that they had such guidance and protection?

In 1787, when the matter of formulating a constitution by which these free and independent states should be governed, was under discussion by the representatives o the states in convention assembled, the debates waxed warm—various proposals had been made, various consultations or models presented, but there was no likelihood of agreement. Dr. Franklin arose and proposed that the body adjourn for three days, and that there be free intermingling and discussion; that an effort be made to understand the positions and propositions of opponents. Said Mr. Franklin in closing: "Before I sit down, Mr. President, I will suggest another matter, and I am really surprised that it has not been proposed by some other member, at an earlier period of our deliberations. I will suggest, Mr. President, the propriety of nominating and appointing, before we separate, a chaplain to this convention, whose duty it shall be, uniformly, to assemble with us and introduce the business of each day by imploring the assistance of Heaven, and its blessings upon our deliberations." When they assembled at the close of the three-day period matters were easily adjusted, and the constitution was formulated.

In 1789, when Washington was inaugurated, there was the same recognition of Divine Providence. New York City is the place, the 30th day of April the time. "The ceremony of the day was ushered in by a salute fired from the battery. This was about six o'clock in the morning, and even at this early hour the streets were fast filling up with people. At nine the church bells rang out a merry peal. At ten they summoned the worshipers to church, each pastor devoting the occasion to imploring Heaven's blessing upon the nation's first President." At the inauguration the oath was administered by Robert R. Livingstone, chancellor of the state of New York. Washington, "bowing down, seized the Book, kissed it and exclaimed with closed eyes and much emotion, "I swear so help me God." Such were our beginnings.

Another critical period in our history comes. The country is rent by civil strife, the fullness of time has come for God to show himself visibly in the affairs of humanity. The spirit of liberty has become incarnate in Abraham Lincoln and others. The war between two civilizations has continued over two years. Lincoln is contem-

ȝ making a mighty thrust at despot- ; he watches the progress of the war. cabinet meeting immediately after ttle of Antietam, and just prior to eptember (1862) proclamation, the ent entered upon the business before by saying, "The time for the an- ation of the emancipation policy can longer delayed, public sentiment will n it, my warmest friends and support- mand it, and I have promised God would do it." The last was uttered w tone. Secretary Chase, who was near asked Mr. Lincoln if he had tly understood him. He replied, "I a solemn vow before God, that if Gen- ee was driven back from Pennsyl- I would crown the result by the ation of freedom to the slaves." › the Emancipation Proclamation, ry 1st, 1863. It might be well to have ıme of God in the constitution, but tter is to have *Him* in the thoughts ives of our rulers. In the past we been able to appeal to him for the ude of our intentions in great national es, and so have we done in our present gle, and the outcome is showing that ppeals have not been in vain. We say:

'Thou, too, sail on, O ship of state,
Sail on, O union, strong and great!
Humanity with all its fears,
With all its hopes of future years,
Is hanging bre.thless on thy fate.''

t our safety for the future will consist ving him even a larger place in our and in conforming our individual, so- nd national acts to his will. Sad d be the time, should it ever come, ı we would forget him as a nation, and e recreant to the trust which he has ›sed upon us.

the light of all our past we can say, rely he hath not dealt so with any peo- ' "Blessed is the nation whose God is Lord and the people whom he hath en for his own inheritance."

nterville, Ia.

PREACHING OLD THINGS.

BY HORACE SIBERELL.

ıe fear and dread of the average cher is that he may become too nar- that he may fall into some rut or ve, which will be the means of destroy- his usefulness. He often imagines that an avoid this by saying startling and ational things. Perchance his con- ;ation does not increase in numbers as dly as he had hoped it would. It may ıat some "wise one" of his church has ed to him that they, too, are disappoint- t the size and interest of the congre- on. The preacher begins to imagine the "old, old story" has become pro- , stale and out of date. Therefore, he ertakes to right the wrong by saying ething containing more of facy than it ı of fact, more of speculation than of real truth. If he is wise as he should e will soon see the folly of such a 'se as this; if he is not, and insist upon ›wing his proposed plan, he will only ›eed in complicating the trouble he thought to remedy.

he teacher does not hesitate to take s after class through the Binomial orem, the lawyer goes over the Law of dence again and again, the physician lies the same treatment for typoidh fever to fifty different patients, the merchant goes repeatedly over the same old account and invoice, the carpenter builds a score of houses after the same style of architecture, the farmer plows, sows and plants the same old way. And yet, none of these ever seem to fear that by doing the one thing so often they will fall into such ruts as will destroy their usefulness. Why, then, should the preacher's usefulness be destroyed and his success changed into failure because he shall constantly warn people of their sins. Should he be called an "old fogy," even if in teaching the people the plan of salvation he should happen to use the same line of thought more than one time?

It is the preacher's duty to preach the truth. He is called upon to point sinful humanity to "the Lamb of God which taketh away the sin of the world." His purpose should be to teach a few people many things, rather than many people a few things. If he has tact in his ministering unto men, a pleasing manner and delivery in the pulpit, he should count himself fortunate. Feeling, pathos, variety of expression and purity of diction are all valuable adjuncts to the preaching of the gospel, but they are by no means the gospel. They can never be made God's power for the salvation of the world.

It should not be a matter of concern whether the preacher has a large and fashionable congregation, but whether he has a congregation, no matter how few in numbers, who are zealous for good works. The preacher's congregation should not come to hear him, expecting to be entertained with some startling sentiment, which is not so much an indication of his erudition and scholastic attainment as his audacity and egotism. The preacher should be neither an entertainer or an actor for public applause. He is an expounder and teacher of the truth as found in the Word of God. His prime object should not be to "tickle the fancies of his hearers," but to instruct them in their duty to themselves, their fellows and their God. He will find that in the end he can reach more people with a few zealous Christians, whom he has taught to live earnest, consistent Christian lives, than he can with all the fine-spun theories and sensational sermons it is possible for him to prepare.

A vivid description of your feelings at first sight of Niagara or Yosemite, the relating of a touching and pathetic incident which occurred during your last visit to London, the repeating of some of the "cute" sayins of Mary and John, the "wee ones" of your household, may be more entertaining to the average audience than a clear, scholarly and scriptural argument upon the necessity of our strict obedience to the will of God. But it is doubtful if these touching, sublime or amusing things will go so far toward uplifting humanity and bringing men to a true knowledge of Christ as a few plain, wholesome truths gleaned from the Word of God.

Pickering, Mo.

For Foreign Missions.

Comparing the receipts for Foreign Missions for the first eleven days in August with the corresponding time last year, shows the following:

Contributing:	1897	1898	Gain
Sunday-schools,	86	99	13
Churches,	12	14	2
Endeavor Societies	$1,290.46	$1,497.92	$207.46

Remember the books close September 30th. Send offerings to F. M. RAINS, Treas.
Box 750, Cincinnati, O.

The Religious World.

The Sabbath Association of Maryland offers a prize of $25.00 for the best article setting forth the advantages to manufacturers, railroads, contractors, and all employers of labor, in the changing of their pay-day from Saturday to Monday; showing its tendency to reduce Sunday dissipation and a squandering of wages; the consequent physical and moral improvement of the men, and the amount and character of their service; also its tendency to improve the family life of the laboring class, and to secure a more decorous and improving observance of Sunday, as provided by actual instances where such are known. The articles must be adapted for publication in the secular papers and especially addressed to the employers of labor. Articles must not contain over 1,000 words, and must be mailed before October 12th, 1898, to Rev. Oliver Hemstreet, Secretary of the Sabbath Association of Maryland, Room 51 Bank of Baltimore Building, Baltimore Md. The prize will be awarded by the officers of the association and the money will be remitted to the successful competitor on or before November 15th, 1898. All articles sent are to be the property of the association.

The great missionary churches of the United States are already planning to plant Christianity as they preach it to the inhabitants of the Philippine Islands as pointed out by Bishop Hurst in the New York Advocate. He says:

The Presbyterian Board of Foreign Missions has already appointed a committee, which has reported. Bishop Thoburn declares that American Methodism should begin immediately at Manila, where there is a prosperous colony of Chinese. The Congregationalists of the American Board have already resolved to open work in the Philippines, and they base their action on the special and splendid opportunity which creates an obligation on all mission boards. The American Baptists have determined to begin work, and are only debating whether the home or the foreign society shall take charge of the enterprise. Some of the denominations are discussing an appeal to the government to send Admiral Dewey, after he shall have finished his work at Manila, to the Society Islands, and put an end to Spanish misrule there.

With the Spanish West Indies and the Philippines, and perhaps some smaller groups, as a new and vast field for Protestant evangelization, there should come to the American church a new inspiration. If American heroism opened this great territory, American Christianity must respond with equal energy and faith.

At the stated meeting of the American Bible Society this week an advance step was taken in respect to Bible distribution in the Philippine Islands. In view of the prospect that in the near future these islands may be open for new forms of Christian work, the secretaries were authorized to request the Rev. John R. Hykes, D. D., the society's agent for China, to visit Manila for the purpose of inquiring into existing facts and conditions, as a help to prompt and vigorous action in case there should be fit opnortunities for circulating the Scriptures. To meet the expenses incident to his journey and to such preliminary work as may seem to be advisable an appropriation of one thousand dollars was made. It was also decided to inaugurate Bible work in Porto Rico at the earliest practicable moment, and to resume the operations in Cuba which were suspended two years ago on account of the disturbed condition of the island.

Our Budget.

—Remember Church Extension Day.

—The missionary year closes September 30th.

—Hostilities between the United States and Spain have ceased.

—Only the peace that comes with destruction can stop hostilities between the kingdom of Christ and the kingdom of darkness.

—The war with Spain has greatly enlarged the possibilities and responsibilities of the United States and its churches.

—Now that the war is over, political parties and politicians are fishing up old issues and coining new ones to preserve their identity and continuity.

—In the Texas Letter this week will be found a vigorous condemnation of the saloon.

—Our English Topics this week came to us from an East Anglican seacoast retreat.

—Bro. Bently, of Shanghai, favors us with a China letter in this paper, bearing upon the political outlook of that vast ancient empire.

—The "Wheeling Through England" series of letters, by W. E. Garrison, are so interesting and so well written that they cannot fail of interest to the reader.

—The letter from Paris, by Wm. H. Matlock, gives interesting glimpses of French life and national impulses.

—The report of the Missiouri Christian Lectureship by C. C. Hill in this paper, reveals something of a rich intellectual feast which was spread at Carrolton for its guests this year.

—We publish this week another interesting letter from Mr. Moody on Christian work among the soldiers.

—M. J. Fergusson's reply to Bro. Billman's review of his article on "The Baptism of the Holy Spirit," will be found in this paper.

—See program of convention to be held in New York City, Aug. 30th to Sept. 2nd, in this paper.

—The two very interesting papers, one on Spiritism, the other on the management of churches, are concluded in this number. They are amply and ably written and full of suggestions.

—In writing to us of the death of Bro. J. B. Royal, whose obituary appears in this paper, the writer, J. C. Reynolds, of Macomb, Ill., says: "I have fallen heir to his cane. I am approaching my 73rd birthday and have never used a cane. But if I should need one I will lean upon the one my beloved brother used for years." How beautiful this figure of that staff upon which we shall all be glad to lean when approaching the valley and the shadow of death. Bro. Reynolds was probably associated with Bro. Royal more than any other preacher. Bro. Royal has gone to his reward, but we trust that his fellow-laborer, Bro. Reynolds may be spared yet many years to his friends and to the church.

—The Board of Church Extention's "Catalogue of Church Plans," is out and can be had at 50 cents per copy, prepaid, by writing to G. W. Muckley, 600 Water Works Building, Kansas City, Mo. Churches contemplating a new house of worship should consult this catalogue before adopting any plans. It might save you much money.

—B. Q. Denham, of North Tonawanda, N. Y., in a brief article in this paper, bears testimony to the excellent work done by the Bethany C. E. Reading Course last year. But this was only the beginning. Now that its mission and good fruits are known, a hundred-fold more good can be accomplished next year if the Endeavor Societies everywhere will only take up the work. Do not let such an opportunity for self-culture and increased usefulness pass unheeded.

—The Endeavor Society of the Christian Church at Chattanooga, Tenn., has published a book of views of the city, river, mountain, battlefield and other interesting and historic scenes in and about that city, which they are sending, postpaid, to any address for fifteen cents, the money to be used in assisting them to carry on their work at Camp Thomas. For the last seven or eight Lord's days they have held from two to three meetings each Lord's day and have visited the hospitals and left flowers, chicken broth, songs, smiles and hand-shakes, and doing such other work among them as they believed their Lord would have them do. As an evidence that their efforts have been appreciated they say that they have almost daily invitations to meet with them. Rain or sunshine, they have from three to four hundred soldiers assembled at each meeting, and such work needs the encouragement they ask. For the book address M. Zeigler, President Gas Co., Chattanooga, Tenn.

—The Young Men's Christian Association of the State University, Columbia, Mo., has just published the Annual Handbook for New Students. This little book contains minute directions to the new students as to boarding houses, entering the school, etc. It is invaluable to boys and girls who are entire strangers in Columbia, and unfamiliar with the management of a large institution. Any boy or girl in the country who is expecting or even contemplating entering the University, should write to the Actin General Secretary for one of these books.

—Missouri's educational exhibit at the Trans-Mississippi Exposition, with the possible exception of the educational display of Nebraska, is said to be the equal of any on the grounds. Of course Nebraska, the home state of the great Fair, has a very complete and interesting display in all departments.

—We have received a copy of the ninth annual catalogue of Cotner University with announcements for 1898-'99. We hope the effort to save this institution from its debts now being made will succeed and that it may yet attain to the proportion and influence contemplated by its founders.

—The Missionary Intelligencer for August says that we now have 2,797 contributing churches for Foreign Missions, and asks that this number be raised to at least 3,000 before the close of the year, September 30th. This is not an unreasonable request, and we hope it will be attained.

—It has been said, and is no doubt the truth, that one cause of so much beer-drinking at the camp canteens is the lack of good water. The remedy for this is lemons, lime-juice and ice-water, and systematic arrangements for supplying these articles for the soldiers ought to have been made at the start, and no doubt will yet be supplied to them. In the meantime it would be well for those sending gifts to soldiers to remember the value of lemons to them for slaking thirst and preventing fevers, and send the same in liberal quantities.

—We again call attention to the fact that the day for an offering for Church Extension is at hand. There are many living, thriving churches to-day standing as a monument to the good offices of this branch of mission work, and it only remains for us to enlarge its funds that its usefulness may be correspondingly increased. See to it, then, that an offering is made for Church Extension in your congregation on the first Sunday in September.

—The monthly bulletin of the Foreign Society for June is one of the most encouraging both from the gain in receipts and in news from the field that we have yet received. The work in the different fields is going forward without interruption and in some places many conversions to Christ are reported. The receipts for June amounted to $25,814.12 which was a gain of $3,295.07 over June of last year.

—A writer in one of our exchanges say "I know of many churches being destroyed inefficient officials." This is doubtless true, b not the whole truth. We know of ma churches having been destroyed by inefficie evangelists—and professional ones at that.

—B. B. Tyler's last editorial, Aug. 4th, "The Possession and Use of Property," h called out a number of replies excepting some of his sayings. As Bro. Tyler continu on this theme this week and promises to wri still further about it two weeks hence, we sh withhold all replies until he has concluded h treatment of the subject. Perhaps some wl have written may desire to modify some their criticisms before pressing their publication.

—Three preachers are recorded in our Obitua Column this week. First there is a tribute the memory of Joseph B. Royal, whose deat was recently reported in our columns, writte by his colaborer, J. C. Reynolds. Bro Royal was a valient soldier of the cross fo many years. Next we have a tribute to th memory of G. A. Willett, of Ionia, Mich. Br few men were better known in Ionia and i Michigan than Bro. Willett, or that will liv longer in the memory of the people and th church. And last is a tribute of respect to th memory of Henry Wright, of Stiles, Ia., by L C. Swann. These have entered that res which remains for the people of God, but thei works will live on in the hearts and lives o those who knew them, for many years.

—The time for the September offering fas approaches. Are you preparing to do your part, asked by the board in order to reacl $250,000 by the close of this century?

—Among the many signs of good cheer for ou Extension Board are the numerons requests o churches to have their department increase that we may be sure to reach this year's par of the $250,000 by the close of 1900. One church said, "Multiply our portion by ten." Many churches ask the board to double thei apportionment.

—If at all possible the churches should arrange to take the collection promptly on the first Sunday of September for Church Extension, and allow one Sunday for those who did not respond the first, and then promptly forward the money to G. W. Muckley, Co. Sec., 600 Water Works Bids, Kansas City, Mo.

—As an illustration of the folly of eliminating common sense from religious theories the Church Union relates the following story:

Whittier had a school-teacher, Joshua Coffin by name, who when old got the idea that he had been predestinated to be damned. It was a grievous burden and sorrow to the poor old man. However, he took it as the will of God, and was resigned to it. Whittier went to see him, and is said to have talked something like this with him about it: "Well, Joshua, don't thee hate God for damning thee?" "Oh no," said the old man. "It is for the good of all; it must be best." "But, Joshua, thee has spent all thy life doing good, and now since thee is going to hell, thee must be getting ready to do all the hurt thee can." "No, no; my feeling is not so at all." "Now, Joshua," said Whittier, "thee is going to hell with a heart full of love to God and everybody. What dost thee think the devil can ever do with such a one as thee?" The old man laughed heartily, and was wonderfully cheered. Some doctrines need just such a spicy injection of common sense. No amount of logical predestination will make the devil tolerate the company of a good man, even if God were of such nature as to send such a man to the devil."

—Now that the war is over we trust that there will be no political-party-glorying over the results. The organs of the party in power asked that party issues and the partisan spirit be subordinated to the one great aim of liberating Cuba and the requests, whether at their bidding or not, have been fulfilled. Any attempt now to appropriate national honor to that party would be sadly out of place and surely result to an injury to it should the attempt be made. Let the spirit of national fraternity and patriotism continue at the front.

ember that Business and Christianity ide-awake vigorous organ of the Church on Board. Send to G. W. Muckley, ter Works Bldg., Kansas City, Mo., py and post up on the magnificent work wth of the Church Extension work.

ve the CHRISTIAN-EVANGELIST; and its ss improves its appearance one hundred :. May God bless you and it and give is Spirit so you may go on to higher ents and grander results in the redemp- the world from all sin and unrighteous-

O. L. RICE.

ns, Kan.

ask special attention to an article in mily Circle this week from Josiah , on the increase of vice among the and especially among the school chil- the land. This vice, he thinks, is at- ble to the increase of bad books and e literature. However this may be the is indeed a serious one, and demands nediate, energetic and united consider- nd treatment of every parent, teacher, er, Christian and good citizen of our . The increase of sensational and im- erature and the lack of proper home- g of children about fundamental things and character are menaces to our homes, ilization and our country. The reme- iggested by Josiah Strong are both al and wise, and should not go un- . Herein lies the future work of our formers and the hope of our country.

experience and observation, during a now of nearly six years in which have the field at large in the state have led ee more and more the need of just such atic instruction, and along the exact prescribed by the Bethany Reading s. I am sure that in the Endeavor y, the most ready and fruitful soil for the sowing, is found. There is *imperative* or instruction of this order, that our people may not be ignorant of the ur of our history and the cause we I think it would be good if we could Bethany day in each society once per er. A paper read at county, district and conventions. That a drill on the order of rmal Sunday-school lesson might be ated with good results. May God bless

T. A. ABBOTT.

Vandeventer Ave., St. Louis, Mo.

foregoing card but briefly hints at the possibilities for good in the Bethany C. eading Course work. Much has been already, as Bro. Abbott indicates, but the can be greatly enlarged upon. It is an mnical, practical method for disseminat- nowledge on vital church work and inter- and the second year's reading course to double that of the first. Every avor Society of the Christian Church to take the course, and now is the time k and work it up. Do not wait until after ork of the second year begins, but begin gements now. Write to J. Z. Tyler, land, Ohio, for literature. Those who the course last year will of course want to nue in the good work.

speaking of the legalized saloon, the Louis Christian Advocate makes this ing statement:

s already the autocrat of American poli- Especially is this so in municipal nment. It holds St. Louis to-day in the ng, gasping grip of an East Indian ana- . And if the readers wish any outside nony to the truth or falsity of this state- , let them in person or by telephone, tele- or mail, interview every state officer at son City, or any ex-state officer in St. , or in any other part of Missouri.

s hard to realize that such a thing as is charged up against this city with all of urches, moral forces and courts, can be yet the fact exists. St. Louis is dom- d by the saloon. Nor is it the only city e grip of this fearful, deadly monster. uld be difficult to find an exception to the in the so-called Christian world. How shall these things continue? Here is the cate's answer:

us not listen to the wails of pessimism once said that the legalized Louisville Louisiana Lotteries could never be put down, that African slavery could never be put down. When the Church of the living God awoke to her full duty the lottery was not only banished from Louisville and Louisiana, but from our republic. When every pulpit in the North became a throne of thunder against African slavery, it had to go. And so will the legalized saloon have to go early in the twentieth century. As this red-handed murderer puts his ear to the ground to-day he hears not only the stumbling tread of a hundred thousand victims marching to a drunkard's grave and hell, but he also hears the tramp, tramp, tramp of millions of our boys and girls who have been educated to regard alcoholic drinks as poisons, and not food. In the rising generation is the doom of this awful iniquity. Long live the boys and girls! Let us train them by day and by night, and cheer them as they come.

—The Word of God is the Universal Father's Infinite, Eternal and Consubstantial Utterance of Himself in the Bosom of His own Immensity. That same Word—the Second Person of the Ineffable Trinity—was uttered in time and space when, in the womb of Mary, THE WORD WAS MADE FLESH, AND DWELT AMONG US. The individual Incarnation of the Word of God in Jesus Christ is extended, perfected and supplemented by the social incarnation of the Word of God in the Catholic Church, the Mystical Body of Jesus Christ. Jesus Christ is "God manifest in the flesh." The Church is God incarnate in society.

The only clear statement in the above paragraph, from The Church Progress, in an editorial on "The Word of God," excepting the scriptural declaration that "Jesus Christ is 'God manifest in the flesh,'" is the last sentence, and that one is of doubtful disputation. The Roman Catholic Church is meant, of course, and the history of society does not prove the correctness of the statement.

PERSONAL MENTION.

The church at Corning, Ia., has retained W. B. Crewdson, pastor, for the fourth year.

N. S. Haynes, for six years pastor at Englewood, Chicago, has resigned. He has been sick, but is recovering. He will spend a season at Eureka, Ill.

Geo. F. Hall, pastor Tabernacle Christian Church, Decatur, Ill., and his wife, called at this office last Monday while in the city. Bro. Hall reports the work at the Tabernacle in a flourishing condition. He is on a lecture tour, headed toward the Northwest. Bro. Hall now spends a considerable portion of his time in the lecture field. He was on the Mountain Chautauqua program for three lectures which he has just recently fulfilled.

On the recommendation of O. A. Bartholomew, pastor West End Church, this city, T. A. West, of Liberty, Ohio, has been called as an assistant pastor, to begin September 1st.

A. L. Drummond, though young in the ministry, is said to be doing efficient work at Smith Center, Kansas. Their new house of worship, lately completed, speaks much for him.

James Franklin King has been called to preach for the congregation at Montrose, Kas.

The church ot Chilliothe, Mo., has officially commended G. F. Assiter, of Oregon, Mo., to the churches as a scholarly preacher of excellent ability and thoroughly qualified to fill the pulpit of any church. Bro. Assiter has been preaching for the church at Chillicothe during the vacation of their pastor, Bro. Pettit, but this work will close September 1st, after which he will be available for another field. Any church in need of a pastor can correspond with Bro. Assiter at Oregon, Mo.

W. A. Gaddis, of Wayne City, Ill., writes that a young physician, member of the Christian Church, could find an opening there.

Milo G. Cummings holds two meetings to give Pulaski room to get out of debt. Good shepherds watch and keep flocks from debt.

Abram E. Cory has been sent by his physician to the Minnesota lakes for rest.

W. W. Williams, treasurer of the Iowa Christian convention was called by telegram to Illinois, where his wife lies very ill.

S. M. Perkins, of Council Bluffs, Iowa, preached 139 sermons, received 29 additions, made 620 calls, conducted 11 funerals and had 11 weddings during the year.

W. S. Johnson begins a meeting at Pleasant Hill, near Washington, Iowa, on Aug. 20.

W. B. Crewdson has accepted a fourth years' work at Corning, Ia.

Henry Brown, once of Ruthven, Iowa, a meeting near there, in the Carter sc house.

The resignation of Z. E. Bates, at S Ave. Church, Allegheney, Pa., was not cepted.

E. F. Mahan says the church at Salem enlarge its house of worship shortly. prosperous.

The East Broadway Church, Sedalia, has expressed its high regard for J. S. M services in helping it into existence and it gret at his departure for the East, in a he fully expressed set of resolutions.

J. T. Boone, pastor of the church at M phis, Mo., has gone on a two weeks' vac in Tennessee. He called at this office o way there last week.

H. Warner Newby is holding a tabern meeting at Miltonvale, Kansas. Bro. M Duncan is the pastor of the church.

G. A. Ragan, of Oskaloosa, has offere resignation to take effect October 1st. I not been accepted. A Chicago mission h vited him to take their work.

A. M. Haggard speaks at the Keota, I anniversary on Aug. 14th.

S. B. Moore, pastor of the church at burg, Ill., who has been spending his tion in Kentucky, called at this office Monday. He is on his way back to Gales but tarried in this city over Lord's day th might preach for the church at Co Heights. He is just out of a good meet Ghent, Ky., and on his way home to r work for a good, live church at Galesbur

J. S. Hughes, of Chicago, now at Maca has been devoting considerable time duri summer in giving his institutes of St. Jo he calls them. He has just closed one o at Central Christian College, Albany, where we understand his lectures made s an impression upon the preachers and p sors that they have all ordered a copy forthcoming book, and a few have orde many as ten or twelve copies for their f under the special offer for advance subscr His lectures are awakening a renewed in in this wonderful book. He says that h be obliged to all pastors who are memb pastors' associations if they will kindl him the address of either the secretary o ident of the association of which they selves are members. Address him at O., Chicago.

CHANGES.

W. M. Mayfield, Canton, Mo., to S Kan.

L. A. Smartt, Bloomington, Ind., Arlington St., Cleveland, Ohio.

R. F. Sarson, Hannibal to Ura, Mo.

Geo. E. Lyon, Weldon, Ia., to B Tenn.

Robt. Stewart, Lexington, Ky., to ville, Tenn.

S. J. McCracken, Galiad to Corsicana

W. B. Harter, Anna, Ill., to Chester,

J. S. Smith, Pennville, Ind., to Ft covery, Ohio.

J. W. Allen, Cleveland, O., to Mac Mich.

Andrew Scott, Duplain, Mich., to H ville, Mo.

T. F. Richardson, Loveland, Col., t Weston, O.

J. A. Walters, Marble Rock to Grove, Kan.

Correspondence.

English Topics.

THE GARDEN OF SLEEP.

For an all-too-brief fortnigh t I have broken away from the grip of London, that mighty octopus of our modern civilization. These lines will be penned for my American friends in sight of the elements which fascinate most of us so much, because it alone blends the suggestion of time and eternity. I am looking over the sea, a sublime picture of the infinite, but the vast bosom of that sea is heaving with fickle waves, and is moaning out the psalm that is always pitched in some minor key of music. This lovely spot on the Coast of Norfolk, the village of Cromer, is famous as being one of the few points in the world where the sun is to be seen both rising and setting in the sea. One happy way of getting far from that maddening crowd of five millions in London is to steal away to this sweet little East Anglian retreat. Hither come select batches of people who desiderate thoughtful quietude, air saturated with a bracing blend of salt and ozone, musical cadences of the murmuring ocean and enchanting permutations, combinations, variations of cliffs, moors and woods in the background. The sea is conqueror here. Five hundred years ago a town stood where the waves are rolling. Shipden, with its pier, wharves, ships and church, is sunk in the deep, which swallowed it up piecemeal, the waves corroding its foundations, as they are still steadily encraoching on portions of the East Anglian Coast. Cromer then stood a mile inland, and was in the middle ages an unknown little village. Now it is perched on the edge of the cliffs, protected at great cost by tremendous sea walls. Four miles along the coast is the "Garden of Sleep," to which I have been making a pilgrimage. The old village of Sidestrand has retreated from the crumbling cliffs against which the ocean booms when north winds are roaring. But a lovely old churchyard hangs yet on the brow over the shore. Parts of the enclosing low walls have fallen, and all the ancient enclosure is doomed. Graves and gravestones wait the time when they will go down, down, down into the abyss! In the churchyard stands a solitary tower, a curious structure. Not a tree or bush casts any shadow near it. The dead alone surround it. The deep calm is only broken by the hollow dash of the billows far below, or the occasional screech of the sea-mew. This venerable tower is perfectly circular in shape, like the famous Round Towers in Ireand, and it is all that is left of the parish church, built probably 700 years ago. It is built of rough flint stones like most of the old East Anglian churches. The "Garden of Sleep" is the name given to this dreamy, delicious spot by W. Clement Scott, who made it famous by his song, published under that title.

POPPYLAND.

The whole of this district along the northen shores of the English country of Norfolk is familiarly and poetically called "Poppyland." At frequent intervals we come across acres of country blazing with sheets of scarlet poppies. When Linnæus, the founder of botanical science, came from Sweden to England, he fell on his face in rapture before a field of yellow gorse. How would he have felt if he had found his way to Cromer, and had reveled in these pictures of glory indescribable of ocean blue, deep woodland green, and poppy crimson? I have described this locality as a delightful holiday dreamland. Truly, there is everywhere something to plunge the soul into some dreamland. On Sunday I went into the noble old parish church, of Cromer, and heard the Bishop of Norwich preach, and Sheepshanks, Right Reverend Father in God and Lord Bishop the diocese, occupied by the counties of Norfolk and Suffolk, is a man I had long wished to see and hear. His sermon was negatively pleasing and positively disappointing. It was free from the sacerdotalism which is now almost universally Romanizing the great Anglican Church. It was not tainted by any of the arrogance of priestcraft. This was gratifying. But it was also, though a very long sermon, free from any oratorical attractiveness. It was one more inducement to the mind to wander in the dreaminess of Poppyland, and dream I did. I sat dreaming of the days, 500 years ago, when the simple old villagers, all Roman Catholics, built that magnificent church. England was papist then. The Reformation did not begin till long after. In that grand old building many a mass was recited, many a confession was made to a cowled priest. And now Cardinal Vaughn, of Westminster and the Duke of Norfolk are praying to the Virgin Mary for the conversion of England, and are hoping that all the splendid old parish churches and cathederals will be reconsecrated to the Pope again. And that is just what can never be, and a storm is raising in England which will ere long convince the Ritualists that their cause is dead and their aspirations are but the mockery of real hope. But we walk a mile out of Cromer and we are set dreaming again. Along the lofty red cliffs, at the fishing village of Overstrand, where in the hush of the cornfield the poppies by myriads flaunt their gorgeous scarlet with dazzling brilliance, is a spot that has a history exactly typical of all the wonderful vanished life of old England. In the churchyard of Overstrand are two churches, side by side. One is a lonely ruin, roofless and overgrown with ivy so beautiful that many artists come to sketch it. It consist of a square flint battlemented tower, a nave and chancel, north porch and road-turret. Close by is the pretty new church, but the old one is a gem. And this village of Overstrand has a history which I recite because it is a capital specimen of the life which our forefathers led. Eight hundred years ago the lordship of Overstrand was given by William the Conqueror to Berner, a crossbowman. From him it passed to Earl Warren, who had considerable estates in the county of Norfolk, including a strong castle at Costleacre. Overstrand was held of Earl Warren, by a family named de Reymes. Agnes de Rattlesden, daughter and coheiress of William de Reymes, took proceedings against Ricter de Reymes to recover a fourth part of a knight's fee, a portion of the lordship, which he had released to Roger de Herlberge for 20 marks. Roger was called to support his title, and a waqer of battle was fought between him and a freeman on begalf of the claimant. After the fight an agreement was come to. Ah, that was a stormy old world! And now it is all past and gone, and one sometimes dreams of all its stress, and rudeness, and passion. This old church at Overstrand, in the heart of Poppyland, now a roofless but charming ruin, was built on land given by John Reymes, in the 15th century. So it is a relic of that strange time.

MISSIONARIES WELCOMED HOME.

With great joy we have shaken hands with Mr. and Mrs. Remfrey Hunt. These two missionaries have been eight years in China. It seems nothing like that time since I assisted at their valedictory service at West London Tabernacle. We and they are mourning the death of Bro. Hunt's closest colleague, that beloved friend in the same band, Albert Saw. Only two yearg ago he was among us here in good health and spirits, delighting us all with his addresses and his company. Bother and Sister Arnold will be shortly returning to China. Their visit has done good all round. Bro. Hunt will further refresh us. He was a favorite all round before he went, and we are all proud to see him here once more.

IMPS OF THE INQUISITION.

Everywhere in England excitement is steadily rising over the question about which I shall have much to say in future letters. The problem of the time is the position of the clergy. Are they to become minions of the papacy, and defy their bishops, and to play at "the mass in masquerade," as about 5,000 of them out of the 25,000 are doing, and increasing numbers are tending to do? Or are they to be compelled to make an honest choice between Protestantism in the Church of England and Popery in the Church of Rome? Riots are taking place in church after church, and the police are called in every Sunday in some of these sanctuaries to turn out the Protestants who steadily interrupt the service. We will not permit the priests to plunge dear old England back into the polluted sea of priestcraft.

W. DURBAN.

Cromer, Coast of Norfolk, England, July 29, 1898.

Wheeling Through England.

V.

To the cyclist, the northern coast of Cornwall and Devon is a land of mingled troubles and delights. One guidebook, with a commendable desire to be frank, says that the few hardy (or foolhardy) wheelmen who venture into this region of rough and hilly roads are unhappy while here and glad enough to make their escape. It is true that the hills are appallingly precipitous and continuous. It is also true that many of the roads are stony and rough as compared with other English roads. Yet the cyclist who would be unhappy while wheeling through this part of England is fit for treason, strategem and spoils! He who would not count it a matter of small concern to be compelled to toil up steep hills and down steeper, on foot, perhaps, and leading his wheel, in the midst of such beauties as those presented by this coast, knows not how to value those things for which one travels. There is before me as I write a wave-washed, purple headland whose rugged outlines are softened in the twilight; to the right are the lofty fir-covered hills which border the weird and desolate tract of Exmoor; to the left across Bristol Channel the cliffs of the Welsh Coast are clearly seen, while above all other sounds comes the surge of the rising tide, drowning even the chatter of the little river Lynn which here finishes its short and stony course. It is like a picture set to music. Who would say that it is not worth while to climb hills for such a view? Much more is it worth while to ride through a continuous panorama of such views.

By all means the most impressive and magnificent piece of coast that I have yet seen is Land's End. The rounded outlines of the Lizard's serpentine cliffs give place to the more rugged granite which rises abruptly from the sea. Looking upon this most westerly point of England, one thinks of the island as a fortified castle with the sea for its moat and these cliffs for the tower at the foremost angle of the castle wall. From Land's End there is a road, not laid down on the maps, close to the coast for twenty miles to St. Ives. Riding this road is no task to jest about, but it carries with it the satisfaction (not easily attained in England) of passing through places where bicycles are a rarity, and the further satisfaction of giving one a good view of the entire great promontory of which Land's End is the most westerly point. Within these twenty miles may be seen types of all that is most characteristic of Cornwall. The copper and tin mines of St. Just, many of them extending a long distance out under the sea, afford the best opportunity of seeing the Cornish miner in his proper surroundings and examining this important but waning industry of Cornwall. At St. Ives one sees a fishing village with narrow, crooked and quaint streets and a fleet of herring boats. About a hundred of these boats, with black hulls and red sails, were leaving the harbor for a five weeks' cruise on the Coast of Ireland as I rode out on the narrow quay. St. Ives is also a watering-place with many attractions, and so represents the newer Cornish industry of caring for tourists esorters. Many monuments of early ı and Cornish civilization are to be found ı further inland, while on the coast is al- ;o be found that most characteristic feat- ıe cliffs of Cornwall.

ving St. Ives it is convenient to drop back miles from the coast and traverse eighty or so of easier but less interesting road. e are in haste to reach the land of King r and the Round Table, and no road can ll which leads through a country over we can imagine Sir Launcelot, Sir Gala- ıd Sir Bedivere going forth to deeds of ry. I imagine that my Sterling would been little more of a surprise to those ies than it is to the "west country" shmen of to-day. The latter must have ted from their knightly ancestors the f riding heavily laden with steel, for they ler my 24-pound wheel too light by half eir roads. The town of Camelford claims istinction of being the ancient Camelot Merlin by enchantment built King Ar- s castle, but the imaginative pilgrim who ny regard for the good name of the Ar- ın legend will at once set aside this claim. uarian investigations are entirely unnec- y. The fact simply is that Camelford is p to the dignity of being King Arthur's

When one has spent half a day at Tinta- y the sea, where tradition says that Ar- was born (and this I believe), the story of uilding of the castle by enchantment will plausible enough; but no sensible wizard l have selected Camelford as the scene of exploit. It is not a bad town, only com- lace and modern. Besides, its location not fit the poet's description—and who d know how Camelot lay, if not a poet? place is not on a hill surrounded by valleys like nearly every other town in Cornwall, valley surrounded by hills. No, it will not I, for one, will never give my vote for lo- ng the legend at Camelford. Rather leave thout a local habitation. Let it hang in ir, if you like, as all good legends ought .

t in denying the claims of Camelford to be ur's Camelot we have not altogether set egend adrift in the world. Down by the six miles from Camelford, is Tintagel, a headland, almost an island, jutting bold- t and on its flat top, guarded by perpen- ar walls of living rock, offering a perfect for a knightly castle. There stand the of two castles, separated by a narrow ra- . What right have we to doubt in this ence that these are the remains of the twin es, Tintagel and Terrabil, wherein Uther ragon, King of Britain, besieged the Duke rnwall, and where Arthur was born? There e very cliff and there the narrow sands be- vhere, as a baby, he was let down from a e window, to be reared by the good Sir r under the advice of Merlin the enchanter. aps it was here that the castle was built he Round Table set up. For does the poet ay:

ear by was great Tintagel's Table Round,
l there of old the flower of Arthur's knights
le fair beginning of a nobler time."

aps it is safest as a rule not to fasten down eat a legend to one spot of earth, but when spot is such as Tintagel there is a distinct in the association.

all the picturesque coast towns of Devon is more justly celebrated than Clovelly, village which has a stairway instead of a t. A steep and narrow combe descends ptly to the sea, and in this cleft is the vil- . All wheeled vehicles stop at the top of elly street, unless their drivers or riders to carry them down. In this case we is, like a coquettish belle, rather too conscious of its charms, and it is hard to believe, though history amply proves it, that it was not built for the especial delectation of travelers and tourists who love the picturesque.

As we pass along the North Devon Coast from Clovelly, the country again becomes rough and the roads hilly, but every valley gives a view of fine encircling hilltops and every hilltop gives a view of cliffs and sea. It seems not inappropriate to call this coast the Switzerland of England. Every mile offers attractions and every village tempts us to linger, but the north beckons and the summer is passing, so our journey must be continued steadily, with an occasional stop half a day here and there, and a whole day on Sunday. W. E. G.

Lynmouth.

The 14th of July in Paris.

Tenacity is not a quality of the French disposition. They are disposed not alone to grow weary in well-doing, but to get tired of the well-done. The leading papers complain this morning (the 15th) of the lukewarmness of the celebration of yesterday. No enthusiasm was displayed in political and official circles, except a fatal tendency to glorify the army. One recalls the fable of the frogs, and the demand of the Jews of the prophet for a king. A king could renew perhaps the glory of other times; a king could avenge the wrongs of France. One ministry tumbles after another, but the army remains and increases.

The apathy of yesterday was nowhere more clearly seen than about the public edifices and in the principal streets. Not a festoon in the city. For days a stingy number of flags, dingy from too frequent use, were to be seen everywhere; the 14th did not increase their number. Many places of importance were nude of decorations. It reminded one of how the Bavarians celebrate the birthday of the German Emperor—a few flags for decency's sake. The royalists were, of course, "out of town." The aristocratic residences were alike deserted, windows barred; the few chance flags indicated, perhaps, more the patriotism of the porter left behind than of the proprietor who had gone to the seashore to avoid the annoyances of the 14th. The decorations in the laboring quarters, in the narrow streets of old Paris, as well as in the more modern tenement districts, were decidedly more numerous, more attractive and artistic. Notre Dame de Paris, the City Hall and the Tuileries did not lack for flags, and were well illuminated in the evening. The University and the Pantheon offered a sad contrast.

The feast may be said to have been civil, military and popular. The 13th and the following morning were characterized by demonstrations purely civil. The most important on the 13th was the celebration in the Pantheon of the one hundredth birthday of the French historian, Michelet. The President was present. On the 14th civic societies paraded the streets during the morning and decorated the statue of Strasburg. No orations, but cries of "Vive la France!" "Vive la Republique!" At one o'clock all the theatres and the Grand Opera were opened to the public free of charge. The crowds assembled as early as 9 A. M. in the hope of getting a place at 1 P. M.

From 10 A. M. on till 1:30 P. M. some 13,000 troops were marching through the city en route for Longchamps, in the Woods of Boulogne, the largest of the city parks and scene of the grand review at 3 P. M. The tribunes were occupied in due time by the Senators and Deputies, embassadors of the known world in costume, military attaches, and the President of France with his wife. An immense concourse of people had assembled and expected populace, right and left, at the same time as the President—a liberty which the *Figaro* denounces as too assuming on the part of the military, and as heretofore not allowed. Significant is that two generals occupying the same carriage remained rigidly immovable, the Minister of War alone violating the custom.

It is the habit, and that which makes the boulevards of this metropolis so animated, to "set the table" outdoors; that means in Paris, on the sidewalk. You will not find a "hole in the wall" so poor that it cannot afford at least one chair and a little round table with a diameter of perhaps eighteen inches. And you will often see one, two, three or a half dozen chairs only. Before the magnificent cafes and restaurants you will see hundreds of such tables arranged in rows on the sidewalk, which they occupy to the very curbing. The tables are often beautiful, even mosaic; the chairs are more comfortable than the seats in any, even the most noted of the continental churches. Along the wall is always a row of upholstered benches, calculated to hold a customer rooted to the spot. As the thoroughfares are fairly lined with places of refreshment of every sort, the promenader goes miles, not blocks, picking his way among the crowds which sit unconcernedly on the pavement. Not a boulevard in Paris that does not present, any pleasant evening, this aspect. The wider the walks the more tables, the more people, the more profits—and there are sidewalks thirty to forty feet wide in Paris. It is necessary to magnify this scene very liberally to attain any idea of the proportions reached the night of the 14th of July. Vehicles and trams of every sort vacated; Paris was on foot. Not alone the sidewalks, but the streets were occupied with tables and chairs and the happy multitude. The trees which line the avenues in single and double rows were decorated with Japanese lanterns, chiefly red; the illuminations added their light to that of the brilliant cafes. It was a scene to see and not to forget. One might say that it looked like a lawn party or ice cream social in an endless wood, with endless lawns, where all the world was present and seated at tables, or wandering bewildered and bewildering, and where one would seek in vain to escape from the throng. But more. All the principal corners and public squares had been provided with band stands. Before hundreds of drinking places, band stands! Before the "holes in the wall," in the narrow streets, some lone fiddle; before the Grand Opera an orchestra of thirty pieces! All for the people who wanted to dance. The circle of dancers extended from every musical center as far as the music could be heard. Waltzes, polkas and quadrilles followed in succession. These street balls had begun on the night of the 13th. "On with the dance; let joy be unconfined!" This was the message of the populace. A rain in the afternson, followed bp sunshine, had left the pavement in an excellent condition for the dancers. A morning paper estimates that not less than 450,000 persons took part in the street balls the night of July 14th. What shall one say of the character of such balls? of the thousands who wandered from corner to corner? It is easy to reach a false conclusion, to assume that it was simply an overflow of the slum element; but there are not probably more than 30,000 or 40,000 prostitutes in Paris. Truth is the people were largely from the provinces and adjoining neighborhood; they were country people to a large per cent. The prostitutes were lounging idly in front of the cafes. The people in the street were evidently of the laboring classes, but by no means of the more immoral element. The saloon-keepers furnished the music to sell

enchanted pavement. The latter seemed to regard a waltz in the arms of their colored colonial cousins as something not to be enjoyed every day, even in Paris. The dance continues to-night! One under my window.

WM. H. MATLOCK.

Paris, July 15.

Texas Letter.

The following eloquent and graphic strain is from Granville Jones' lecture on the Prodigal Son:

Once there was an eagle's nest high upon the mountain, where the eagles rear their young. That dread nest was fenced around with the bones of the victims that has been snatched from the green valleys below and devoured by the eagles and their insatiate young. They were objects of universal hatred, and men swore as they saw lambs from the fold and the fowls from the farm-yard carried up to that tall cliff to die, that a day of reckoning would come. It came, too, at last. Daring hunters found a way to reach that den of death. The eagles set up a cry of distress, but they were shot without mercy and fell from their dizzy robber home to die; and that foul nest, which had been the mute witness of a thousand bloody wrongs, was torn from its mooring and hurled from on high. And there is the saloon, that foul nest of every unclean and hateful bird, high upon the cliffs of human authority. Over it the aegis of the law; within it the eaglets of lust and greed and avarice, and perched upon it, like so many birds of prey, the saloon-keeper, the gambler and the harlot. With baleful eyes and bloody beak and poisonous talons, they sit and watch the homes of this land for boys. Anon a mother's cry of anguish tells to the world that her boy is taken. She stands with clasped hands and broken heart and sees him carried to that foul nest to die. She watches till she sees the beaks of the saloon-keeper and gambler and harlot tear out the heart of her precious boy, while lust and greed and avarice drink his blood, and then she falls to the ground, smitten by sorrow that can never be healed. The birds of prey flop their black wings, wipe each bloody beak and turn their eyes to other homes. Over it all floats the flag of our country, and under it all flows the ceaseless sorrow, the heartache and the grief.

But a way will be found to reach that bloody nest. Daring feet are finding a foothold on the cliffs; hands of iron hold are clutching the crevices of rock; eyes that quail not, fear not, are looking up to that place of death, and all around it now, even in the night time, can be heard the watchword of the ascending hosts. We are coming up from every side and we will meet at the eagle's nest; her black wings shall be broken, and her baneful brood shall be trodden under foot. It may not come in our day, but it will come.

The recuperating power of the South is a marvel to us all. Richard H. Edmonds, editor of the Manufacturer's Record, of Baltimore, in a revised edition of his pamphlet, "Facts About the South," opens our eyes on this subject. He shows that at the beginning of the civil war, 1860, the South contained one-fourth of the white population of the United States, and owned 44 per cent. of its wealth. Her agricultural products that year were more than half the agricultural products of the whole country. At that time we had more than 30 per cent. of the banking capital; and Georgia's wealth was more than that of Maine, New Hampshire, Vermont and Rhode Island. But the war came and swept most of this vast wealth away. During the struggle the loss was $2,100,000,000. The loss during reconstruction days was $300,000,000 more. To these amounts the loss to business by the death of her sons, and her part of the war debt are added, making a grand total of $5,000,000,000. So great was the poverty of the South, and so rapidly did the wealth shift to the North, that in 1870 Massachusetts had $1,590,000, while the entire South only had $3,000,000,000. But the period of recuperation now began. In 1880, fifteen years after the was, we had $7,600,000,000 worth of property, and ten years later this had increased $3,800,000,000, which only lacked $1,000,000 of being equal to the increase of New England and the Middle States combined. Our present annual agricultural products are about $1,000,000,000. But the South is no longer simply an agricultural country. In 1890 she had $2,500,000 invested in manufactories, and now that sum has grown to almost $1,000,000,000. She almost has a monopoly of the manufacture of coarse cotton goods, and is beginning to compete with New England in the production of finer qualities. In coal and pig-iron she seems destined to lead the world. Mr. Edmonds estimates her mining and manufacturing wealth for 1897 to be $1,200,000,000 which, added to her agricultural wealth, makes a total for last year of $2,100,000,000. Railroads have also been built since 1880 to the amount of 28,000 miles. To all this must be added the fact that one-half of the standing timber in the United States is in the South. And when the Panama Canal is built, which will be in the near future, our progress will receive a new impetus. The reader must overlook a little unpardonable pride on the part of Texas, when he learns that in all these mighty strides forward the Lone Star state has been in the vanguard.

"Summering in the South" is a rather pleasant sounding phrase, and thus far this summer it is all right for the pleasure-seeker. The weather has been delightful, and I have not heard of a single sunstroke. Rains have been frequent, but not heavy, which secures us both a pleasant climate and an abundant crop. Any one acquainted with Texas will understand the situation when I tell him that there has not been a crack in the ground this summer, and that like the man of the Scriptures, our farmers are puzzled about how to store their crops.

B. B. Sanders has just closed a great meeting at Garland with 51 additions. But he is one of our best evangelists and he had the support of a first-class church and a model pastor, C. L. Cole. Of course the Douthits were with him to sing.

Geo. B. Ranshaw is encouraged with the outlook at San Antonio. Audiences steadily increasing, with five additions the first month.

E. B. Challener, of Taylor, one of our purest and most useful men, has gone home to God. Though frail for years, he has been a hard worker in the vineyard of the Lord.

"Whitecapism" must be stamped out in Texas. This wholesale brutality to the negro must be stopped. Why shoot down women and children because some man has sinned? Why not run down the transgressor and punish him according to law? It is unworthy of the white man, and while it continues we need not be surprised that foreign capital gives us the "go by." But let the reader from abroad understand that the people of this state as a whole have no sympathy with this barbarism, and it will soon be a thing of the past. As proof of this, the Democratic party, which rules here with an immense majority, in its convention at Galveston a few days since, adopted UNANIMOUSLY a strong resolution against it.

M. M. DAVIS.

833 *Live Oak St., Dallas, Tex.*

Letter from D. L, Moody.

I would like to remind those who are interested in the work of the Army and Navy Christian Commission that the negotiations that are now going on with a view to peace with Spain by no means make the opportunity to reach the soldiers with the gospel any less imperative in its demands upon the church. The soldiers, both volunteers and regulars, are still together in the camps with the prospect that many of them will be for months to come. This will probably be the case in this country and certainly will be in Cuba, Porto Rico and the Philippines. The sailors in the navy are still perfectly accessible to the work of the Commission. It seems to me that we shall make a serious mistake if we lose our grip upon this work now. God has given us wonderful access to the hearts of men and we must hold right on.

We have sent General Howard to Cuba to arrange for work there and expect daily to hear from him, asking that workers be sent right on. We have the permission of the War Department to go there, and propose to put in some good men at once.

Mr. Ferdinand Schiverea and Rev. Dr. Hatcher, of Richmond, Va., are preaching at General Lee's camp at Jacksonville; Rev. Charles Herald, of Brooklyn, is preaching to the sailors and marines at Key West. Hundreds of them are continually accessible there and we look for a great work among them. Over twenty of the war vessels have been supplied with good literature, and measures are being taken to reach all the others as rapidly as possible.

And so the work is going right on along all lines. There is no cessation of the intense interest in the camps. Just read this extract from one of the last letters I have had from there:

Last night was one of the grandest we have had yet. I wish you could have looked in upon the scene at the 160th Indiana. It was their last night before leaving for Porto Rico. The large tent wouldn't hold one-half of them, but away back on the hill they stood through it all. At the close, when I asked all to come forward that wanted to accept Christ, there were almost 200 men came. It was a solemn and blessed scene. Just in front of me stood a young man with a broken and contrite heart. As we closed he took my hand and said, "I am a minister's son; am twenty-four years old. I have been pleaded with many times to take this step, but never have before."

One of the delegates reports:

As I came up to the hospital this morning and asked the surgeon if there was anything that I could be allowed to do among the men, he answered me most earnestly, "Yes! for God's sake go in with this woman who has just arrived and who will find her boy dying—I have not told her.' I passed into the hospital tent following a lady dressed in black, who had just alighted from the carriage which had brought her from the station. She had come from Illinois to nurse her sick soldier boy. As we stood by the cot I told her from the doctor that he was unconscious and would live but a few minutes. God helped the mother to maintain her composure and to stand with her hand upon the brow of her son as he passed away without opening his eyes to give her a last parting look. After he had breathed his last, I told the mother of my visit to the hospital the previous day, and that I had asked her son if he was a Christian, and that with a bright, happy face he had said most earnestly, 'You bet I am,'' and pointed to the badge of the Epworth League pinned upon his undershirt. I told her of my prayer with him and of the comfort I was sure he had in the presence of his Savior. The mother turned back the sheet from the form of her son and as she saw the badge still pinned where the nurse at his request had placed it, she bent over her boy with sobs that moved all our hearts; the doctor, nurses and patients sobbed with her.

I hope that the Christians will continue to pray and give for this work. I believe if we are faithful to God in it that we may see many hundreds more of our soldiers and sailors brought to Christ. I want to say also that we have some money sent us for the purpose of giving the Word of God to the Spaniards. The War Department has given us permission to work among the prisoners at Portsmouth, and we shall send them Spanish Testaments, Scripture portions, etc., at once.

Contributions sent to me at East Northfield, will be promptly acknowledged.

China Letter.

POLITICAL.

Politically, China's case seems more hopeless than that of Turkey. Russia is slicing away her territory on the north and west, France and Japan on the south and east. From present indications, her political salvation lies in moving her capital south to Nankin, and having her autonomy guaranteed by Anglo-Saxondom. For America has suddenly loosened up as a "world-power." This political question is vital to Protestant missions, for where Russia goes there goes the Greek Church and intolerance, and where France goes there goes the Catholic Church and intolerance. Protestant mission work is impossible where the former holds sway, and extremely difficult under the latter. When such ests are at stake we should like to see nment take a strong stand against the ng of China.

CHINA'S STRENGTH.

inch China is being lifted out of her f despond. For while politically she hopeless, her real strength is and moral in the lives and character ommon people. China contains the nd most contented, hard-working n of any country in the world. They to become the manual servants of the oreover, they have had centuries of in a noble system of ethics. (Noble l with non-Christian systems.) They earning and honor scholarship. *By is she will conquer.*

tiquated and evil systems are being ed by modern scientific thought and teaching and example. To these she g. And it has been predicted that she were to-day partitioned among the in one hundred years she will have red her conquerors" by the process of , so infinitely patient is she, so per- nd peaceful, and withal so massive l. These things are encouraging to is such qualities as these which make a high type of Christian character and ing church.

SHANGHAI NOTES.

l some difficulty in getting possession wly purchased building. It had been m-palace," and the dealer offered me rs a month to go on with his business. out now, and several carpenters are remodeling the building. We are eats made for the "chapel" room for 0 people. The capacity of this room y be increased to 300.

is not a good baptistery in Shanghai, lans are about completed for a good e also expect to put a brick front to ling. We hope to send a photograph ilding when completed.

ril 26 we had six baptisms.

ild in the day-school died of smallpox We have this disease ever lurking

hanghai preacher has been illl with four weeks, but is now better.

ne 14 we had two baptisms.

l have asked us to open English classes stitute.

ve many faithful attendants at regular meetings.

omen's work is encouraging.

f our members married a "heathen" it he thinks she will not remain long e fold.

to find room in the building for a "study" for myself, where I can be dquarters" all the time.

chapel at Tsaseo, twenty-five miles anghai, our preacher opens the doors enoon to any children who wish to hristian books.

the good work goes on. The lot and complete will represent about $4,000. us. W. P. BENTLEY.

ssouri Christian Lectureship and the M. C. M. A.

ps the best session of the Lectureship d in the state was the recent one at on, July 18-21. While the attendance as large as in some former years, yet ectures were of a very high order, and interest was manifested by all in at- e throughout the entire session. J. T. e beloved pastor of the Carrollton makes an admirable host, and every one de to feel at home. The principle feat- the Lectureship were the two able lec- Prof. J. D. Forest, of Irvington, Ind. lecture on "The Church and Organ- or" teemed with helpful suggestions not composed entirely of cold theoretical deductions as is usual on such occasions. His lecture on "Social Christianity" also abounded in good things, but by many it was not so highly appreciated as his first lecture.

One thing was impressed upon the minds of those present, and that is that the "up-to-date" preacher must be a student of sociological questions. Neither of the reviewers of Prof. Forest's lectures were present. Bro. C. H. Winders, of Columbia, reviewed his first lecture, and Bro. F. V. Loos, of Liberty, his second, and both did exceedingly well under the circumstances. Bro. Plattenburg, who was to have delivered a lecture on "The Uses of the Old Testament in the New," was not present, neither was the lecture as in the case of Bro. Garrison. But Bro. Ely, of Kirksville, was there with a lecture on "The Creed of the Church" that was clear, pointed and loyal to the Word of God. His reviewer was M. M. Goode, of St. Joseph, who convinced all present that if anything was contained in a lecture worthy of criticism he could certainly find it. Bro. J. H. Garrison's lecture on "Modern Changes in Theological Thought" was read by Bro. W. F. Richardson, of Kansas City. This lecture was of a high order, as was also the review of it by President Clinton Lockhart, of Christian University. Pres. Lockhart is justly regarded by the Missouri brotherhood as one of the very best thinkers. Bro. Procter attended the Lectureship, as he always does, and every now and then would regale the brethren with his advanced ideas on the religious questions of the day.

Prof. P. O. Powell's lecture on "The Development of the Idea of God as it Exists in Modern Thought"—a big subject and a big lecture. He showed much study and thought in the preparation of this lecture, though there was much in it that was not accepted by many present. Bro. Granville Snell, of Trenton, was his reviewer. Taken all in all it was a successful meeting and thoroughly enjoyed by all. The next meeting of the Lectureship will be at Huntsville and the time for holding it will be in March instead of July as heretofore. Bro. Stine, of Paris, was the presiding officer and he filled the position with grace and dignity.

The M. C. M. A. means the *Missouri Christian Ministerial Association*, that holds its annual meetings in connection with the Lectureship. This was the first meeting of the Association since its organization at Trenton last fall. The program that was prepared by the executive committee was fully carried out, and the addresses were all on live and important subjects. The first address was delivered by J. T. Ogle, his subject being "The Power of the Christian Ministry." President Lockhart's address was full of good things. So also was Bro. T. A. Abbott's, Davis Errett's and J. J. Morgan's. The Association asked that these addresses be published in the CHRISTIAN-EVANGELIST, all but Pres. Lockhart's, which was ordered printed in pamphlet form and distributed among the preachers of the state, as it fully set forth the objects of the Association. This will shortly be done, and we trust that the addresses of the other brethren will appear in our religious papers soon.

The report of the secretary showed that 96 ministers had asked for membership in the Association and at this session they were duly elected. The treasurer showed a cash balance of $27.25. Clinton Lockhart was re-elected president, J. J. Morgan vice-president and C. C. Hill secretary and treasurer. The next meeting of the Association will be at Huntsville, immediately after the Lectureship, in March.

The members and friends of the Association are much encouraged with the start it has made and with the good it has already accomplished. We trust that all members will attend the next meeting, at Huntsville, and help to push the good work along. Remember, this is not an *ecclesiasticism*, but a movement inaugurated for the moral and intellectual advancement of the ministry of the state. No good,

true minister can object to the purposes it seeks to subserve.

Brother preacher, if you have not paid your dues for 1898-'99 send them in at once (fifty cents a year) and the secretary will at once forward your new certificate which makes you credentials of which you may justly feel proud.

C. C. HILL.

Montgomery City, Mo.

Florida Letter.

For about a week the thermometer has been bobbing about among the nineties, and we have been trying to keep cool under the trying circumstances. Fortunately our warm days are invariably followed by delightful nights, which in a great measure compensate for the hot midday period. Yet if the thermometric reports published from other points be true, Florida has not suffered as much as many other more Northern states. There are now about fifteen thousand volunteers encamped in Jacksonville. The "boys in blue" have, all things considered, a good camping ground. One splendid advantage, always appreciated in a warm climate, is the fine pure water supply at the encampment. Jacksonville has a fine water system, supplied by natural flowing artesian wells. The pure liquid, clear as crystal, flows from a depth of from five hundred to a thousand feet, and is uncontaminated by any contact with surface water. Pipes bearing this precious boon have been laid throughout the camps, and water-taps and shower-baths are numerous.

In addition to the work done among the soldiers by the chaplains of the various regiments, the Army Christian Commission of the International Committee Young Men's Christian Associations are doing much for their spiritual and moral welfare. It has been my privilege to accept invitations to preach at the brigade tents, and more orderly and more attentive audiences I have never addressed. Invariably at the close of each service numbers of young men have come forward and introduced themselves as members of the Christian Church from various states. These young brethren, when off duty and when allowed passes through the lines, attend our services in the city. While on my way home from camps yesterday, and while waiting for a tram car, I was accosted by a fine-looking young soldier on sentry duty near the lines. He stepped up to me and thanked me for the service the night before, remarking that he had been present, and that he had fully decided to lead a better life. I allowed three or four cars to pass while I encouraged him to fully give his heart and service to the Lord Jesus. He had once been a Christian, he said, but had fallen back into the ways of sin. I left him, and as I cordially grasped his hand I felt to thank God that a word spoken by a humble servant had fanned in one young heart at least a spark into a flame of love and renewed determination. This is but one of many instances that might be related. God bless these dear boys! Doubtless many an anxious father and praying mother are daily petitioning the throne of grace on their behalf. I have visited and talked with many in their tents, at the request sent by fathers and mothers, brothers and sisters, and shall continue to do so, being only too glad to aid in any way in the work of Christian love, sympathy and influence. T. H. BLENUS.

Jacksonville, Fla.

The Baptism in the Holy Spirit.

Bro. Ira Billman's review of my articles on this theme does not call for more than a brief notice. I would like to say, if I could do it without discourtesy, as I certainly can without unkindness, that he does not understand what I have written. That this is not altogether my fault, the editor' note appended to his article seems to show. He did not read carefully the statements which he condemns as unscriptural, nor heed the reasons given to support them. His inaccurate quotations as well as the whole trend of his review seems to show this.

He sees clearly that the words "baptism in the Heiy Spirit" are figurative, and yet he is so in bondage to this figure he cannot see that "baptism," "coming," "receiving," etc., figuratively describe the same "plain fact." It is a "*baptism*," and therefore it cannot be a "reception," or a "coming." Surely, an intelligent student should not fall into such a vice of interpretation as this.

There are not twelve or twenty ways of receiving the Spirit, or modes of "Holy Spirit baptism." There is only one "mode" of it as far as I know, but many modes of describing this transcendent fact. It would be well to inquire what are the limitations of this figure of baptism as applied to the gift of the Holy Spirit, and how is it that so many diverse figures can correctly describe the same thing. Such an inquiry would certainly suggest that it is possible to press the figure of baptism too far, and that in our ordinary easy explanation in which we fix attention on the baptism we may have missed the point altogether. All these figures were appropriate ways of communicating the great distinctive fact of the new dispensation, and do they not deal with the fact rather than with its mode or effect?

As to the "unscriptural use of the crucial word baptism," I have sought to guard against that by showing (1) that the word is not technical, as though used to describe a peculiar and special grace, but is only one of many words having equal authority setting forth the fact of the gift of the Spirit, and is not to be honored above other inspired words selected for the same purpose, nor to have any exclusive right over them. It would be better not to use it at all than so to misuse it; and (2) that the Scriptures do not warrant such a limitation of the word in its figurative use, as is common among us, but would be appropriately applied to the gift of the Holy Spirit to all Christians. The reasons for so thinking I have freely given.

The conception of baptism in the Holy Spirit given in the review will be sufficiently disposed of when it is clearly stated. It is a spiritual state in which a man is compelled, overwhelmed, loses his power of choice, is divinely hypnotized, completely overpowered by the Holy Spirit, put in a corner and from which he received no spiritual benefit, and for his conduct during the continuance of this state there is no praise or blame. Baptized in the Holy Spirit a man would be in an ecstasy, beside himself.

If this is what the Scriptures mean by baptism in the Holy Spirit, I confess I have missed it in my writing. But this is nothing but the old mechanical theory of inspiration. I need not discuss this understanding of the subject. But it might be well to say again that baptism in the Spirit is new and peculiar to Christianity. Neither inspiration nor miracles are new. If inspiration is the essential thing nor necessarily involved in this baptism, and the baptism occurred only at Jerusalem and Cæsarea, then it would seem to follow that no one was inspired who was not a partaker in one of these baptisms. But certainly there were men inspired who were not present on either occasion. And if so were there other cases of this baptism, or was there inspiration without the baptism?

I have stated my view about as clearly as I can in my essay. A full answer to my reviewer will be found there. There is one promise of the Holy Spirit which is to all believers. There is one gift of the Spirit according to this one promise. The essential thing of this gift is the personal communication of the Holy Spirit to the sons of God. There was no ordinary and extraordinary gift of the Spirit, that is, two distinct gifts, but there were extraordinary operations or manifestations of the one gift as there was need. Inspiration and other miraculous powers, together with all benefits of the Spirit's presence in the old dispensation with the enlarged blessings of his presence under the new, are all included in this one gift, but not in every case of it, except as the special need of the kingdom required. Bu t these special fulfillments of the general promise were incidental to the essential meaning of the gift as set forth in Jno. 14:16, 17.

M. J. FERGUSSON.

The Bethany C. E. Reading Courses.

B. Q. DENHAM.

The writer has yet to hear of a Society of Christian Endeavor which has given the Bethany C. E. Reading Courses a fair trial, where the testimony is anything but enthusiastically favorable to the courses. The old saying, "The proof of the pudding is in the the eating," applies here with force. Where there is any prospect of securing an efficient leader no society should hesitate to undertake the courses, even though but few can be enlisted in the first effort. Few things are so contagious as enthusiasm. If a few can start the work and enthusiastically talk it up with their acquaintances it will soon enlist others. The success of the plan does not, however, depend upon numbers. Numbers doubtless add somewhat to the interest, but are not essential to success. The real difficulty seems to be to get a start in our many societies. A good, earnest start will mean success, though the beginning be small. Let not our C. E. leaders hesitate. Being once certain they can start with a few who are in earnest, let them launch out.

The greatest cause with which Christians have to do in this age is the effort to reunite the forces of Christendom. To accomplish this it is not sufficient to have our members converted to Christ in the sense of giving up their wills, affections and lives to him. They must be intelligently posted as to his will in regard to Christian union. They must have a comprehensive conception of the movement, and its history, that is seeking to accomplish the reunion. There are members fully converted, so that their lives are an earnest effort to follow Jesus, who know little or nothing about the plea and its history for the reunion of Christians the world over. There are such personally converted souls who know almost nothing about the great effort to preach the gospel to every creature. It is necessary that education shall follow conversion. Because I know of no method so effective, for the masses, as the Bethany C. E. Reading Courses, I heartily advocate the adoption of the plan by all our Y. P. S. C. E. organizations. Let us not forget that if "eternal vigilance is the price of of liberty," even so eternal agitation is the price of success here.

North Tonawanda, N. Y.

Minnesota.

Hurry forward the annual report!

See the program and confer with your neighbor.

Will all please bear in mind that the books close August 16th?

Do not forget the convention dates, August 23-26, and that the point is Mankato, the beautiful.

Will pastors make the best use possible of the program, published last week, laying its salient points before the congregation, and stirring up a large delegation?

J. G. Slick's meeting at Wyanette much strengthened the brethren, and increased activity may be looked for from that point. The meeting lasted but ten days and adjourned to fall because of the existing busy season.

H. D. Williams' successor at Mankato is to be Therman Hill, of Butte, Mont. Bro. Hill is highly spoken of and will be a distinct gain to the ministerial force of the state. Another important acquisition is on the tapis for one of the strongest churches.

Plans for the new church building have been drawn and ere this letter is at hand the brethren will have begun their church workshop. Bro. Moore reports audiences increasing and enthusiasm much increased.

A sister writes thanking the board and through the board the congregations of the state, for aid rendered in keeping the evangelist at that point till success is assured. Bro. Moore will remain for some weeks yet, likely.

Ho there, ye languid one! Here's the spirit carrying along one of the congregations of the state to undisputed victory (extract from letter): "All lines going along nicely. One of our girls who lives four miles in the country walked in yesterday morning (Lord's day), with the thermometer 94 degress in the shade, that she might not miss the Bible-school. I could relate many other examples of self-sacrifice equally as great."

The Canby meeting, held by G. W. Elliott, of North Dakota, continued from July 5th to July 24th with 17 confessions. The Antelope Hills congregation (five miles away) co-operated with the Iowa State Board in holding the meeting and the town was stirred as never before. The Iowa Board was presented with a sum of money by a sister at Pittsburg, Pa., for the express purpose of employing an evangelist and the board generously stepped across the line and aided in building up this co-operative work with Antelope Hills, for which will the board and the sister accept the sincere thanks of the Minnesota brethren? The Antelope Hills brethren srcrificed greatly, as might be expected, erecting the tabernacle, and dismantling their own church that there might be no question of success. E. J. Sias, of the Antelope Hills church is in charge.

F. H. MELLEN, Sec. M. C. M. S.

Box 450, Minneapolis, July 30.

Notes and News.

l' Walk, pastor Broadway Church, Los
s, reports gratifying increase and ad-
ent in the Chinese mission under his
it laments the want of devoted teachers.
bsolute loyalty and devotion of many of
Iongolian brethren,'' he says, ''would
the average Caucasian disciple.'' Of
k on East Eighth St. he says: ''It is only
ion of time when we shall have another
ing and self-supporting church in this
growing city. I am putting seven days
nights every week into the work com-
to my care.''

hurches of Christ of the Bitter Root
will hold a ''camp meeting convention''
nce, Aug. 16-20. A good list of living
ave been selected and able speakers to
them to the edification of those pres-
Every Disciple in Western Montana is
d at that convention. J. C. B. Stivers,
oula, Mont., says: ''Bring your tent
joy yourself.'' Brethren from other
will also be heartily welcomed. Florence
e Bitter Root Railroad, twenty miles
f Missoula.

E. Church, of Englishville, Mich.,
a debate recently held at Englishville,
between E. K. Evans (Latter Day
and F. G. Porter, pastor of the Chris-
urch at Ballards, Mich., in which he
ed the opinion that ''Mormonism'' in
ction hereafter will be ''a thing of the
He highly commends F. G. Porter for
arness and strength of his arguments,
lieves that he succeeded in convincing
ple generally of the errors, deceptions
aknesses of the doctrine advocated by
onent. The contrasts between the two
nts, as presented by Brother Church,
rikingly in favor of Brother Porter and
cause which he advocated. We hope
uch good may result to the people of
wm, religiously and socially, from the
.

lunkett, who has been preaching for the
at Barnard, Ind., as opportunity af-
, reports the dedication of a handsome
house, free from debt. Work on the
began April 1st. The church is five
ld, has had a hard struggle, but is suc-
g. Twelve have been added to the
under the ministry of Bro. Plunkett.
Knotts, of Zionsville, Ind., delivered the
tory sermon. We are informed that
notts' second attempt in the ministry
de at Barnard, four years ago, while a
t of Butler College. His sermon pleased
ge audience present at the dedication.
one thousand people were present. Eld.
ll, of the Baptist Church, participated
services. Eld. Stewart, an aged
er from Wyoming, was present, as was
ld. Brewer, of Danville, and O. E.
, of Roachdale. Bro. Kelley preached
afternoon. After his address Bro.
r made a few remarks, and thus ended a
ng to be remembered by the Disciples
nard. Bro. Knotts is now assisting Bro.
tt in a meeting there.

is an excellent opportunity for Endeavor
es to do practical Christian work. The
vor Society of the Christian Church at
nooga desires to organize a systematic
continuous Christian work at Camp
s for the soldiers. To do this they need
and fully equipped tent on the ground,
they alone cannot furnish. They therefore
e churches everywhere, and in our larger
especially, to assist them in the establish-
Will not each Society arrange at once to donate some part of this outfit—the tent, seats, books, communion set, etc., etc. Write at once to Mrs. J. A. Setliff or I. S. Post, Chattanooga, Tenn., what you can send, or for information of any kind about the work, or any soldier in that camp. This is an important work, and should not lack for hearty and enthusiastic support.

District Convention.

The annual convention of the Christian Churches of the 6th Kansas district was held in Phillipsburg, July 19, 20 and 21. There are ten counties in the district, viz., Jewell, Smith, Phillips, Rooks, Osborne, Mitchell, Lincoln, Ellsworth, Ellis and Trego. Representatives were present from all but Lincoln, Ellsworth, Ellis and Trego. There were fifty delegates from abroad and a goodly number from the immediate vicinity.

The program was a strong one and was well carried out, the topics in the various departments being exceptionally well handled. The addresses by Mrs. Hazelrigg, Messrs. Hilton, Drummond and Smith, were especially strong. Much good was done for the cause of Christ, the church at Phillipsburg strengthened, and the new friendships formed were of a pleasing and lasting character.

The visiting delegates were met at the trains or received by committees as they drove in and assigned to homes in the city. Meals were served at a dining hall supplied by contributions of the brethren in common. At the close of the convention those who came by train were ''brought on their way'' to the Rock Island and Central Branch, where they took leave of us for their homes.

Some important resolutions were passed by the convention. F. C. Johnson.

Missouri C. W. B. M.

The program, for the C. W. B. M. session of the Nevada convention, is completed and will be published soon. We are fortunate in securing the promise of Miss Ada Boyd to speak at the time concerning the work in India. Miss Boyd has been one of our missionaries in India for fifteen years. Mrs. Helen Moses, one of the most spiritual women of the sisterhood, will also address this convention. Sister Bantz, of St. Louis, will speak of ''Our Workers in the Field.'' Mrs. Mary Wisdom-Grant will lend her enthusiasm to the subject, ''The Significance of Missions.'' Miss Mollie Berry will tell ''The Story of a Life Membership.'' Mrs. Kate Ellis Peed will deliver the memorial address. Mesdames Vernon and Bowen and others share the program, and these with our president's address, and the reports of state workers, and the regular business, will make the C. W. B. M. session full, up to the rim. We hope that many delegates and visitors will attend and enjoy the feast.

Will the auxiliary treasurers remember, if they would receive full credit for the year's work, that they must *collect closely*, and *send promptly* all money by *Sept. 21st*, and send their reports to me on the same date? The convention meets Sept. 26-29.

Forty-seven life memberships have been pledged this year and at least *one* payment must be made on each, and we hope that the full amount ($25.00) will be paid on half of them by the middle of September. We ought to have fifty life memberships to report at Nevada and we will, if three more persons will put their hands in their pockets and draw out some of the Lord's money for this purpose.

The Kirksville auxiliary raised a large amount of money for C. W. B. M. pledges by giving an old ladies' missionary contest. Some of the elderly ladies recited missionary selections and thus instructed and entertained their audience. It was a unique entertainment, and

In the South.

There is one pleasant feature in th
here; and the same was true in many p
Texas.

We are continually meeting peop
know nothing of us; never heard a
from one of our preachers, and thes
express a willingness to know and to
stand what our position is.

This taxes our ingenuity to properly
fore these people the same things tl
fathers presented to others so effectivel
century ago. The wife of a very pr
physician said to me this week: ''I hav
heard one of you, and I confess I wo
to hear your story. This led to a short
of perhaps ten minutes in a parlor, wh
listened to by representatives of three d
religious peoples.

This will necessitate another call fron
that *rich man from New York*—rich en
send free his tracts. So with this I
card to B. B. Tyler. I gave F. G.
Errett on Our Position, and the next
saw him he was ready to give up Met
and had so told his pastor; and we wer
to go down into and come up out of the
of baptism.

'Tis pleasant to unfold such a plea
who are willing to listen, for God ha
''My Word shall not return unto me
Our success as a people must have rest
promise. We have here only a few m
but the Lord has blessed us in the past
Sapp's ministry here did much to lift
the estimation of the denominations a
many of those in the world also.

S. W. Crut

Pine Bluff, Ark.

Several Things.

Bro. H. A. Northcutt recently clo
of the best meetings in the history
church at Sturgeon. The church that
Bro. H. A. Northcutt to hold its meeti
make no mistake. He will return n
and hold another meeting for us; ther
go to Madison and hold a meeting in
1899. The writer is also pastor of this
Last Lord's day being a fifth Sunday, I
my youngest sister, who lives at Byn
Chariton county, preached Lord's day
and evening, also Monday evening,
Christian church at that place. I
Jones, evangelist for the Brookfield
preached Saturday evening. I h
pleasure of taking my sister's confess
burying her with her Lord in Christian
on Lord's day. At the close of the
Monday evening, Rev. James Ramsey
U. B. Church, came forward and was
into the Christian Church and ord
minister before we left the house. Br
sey is a young man only 23 years of
been teaching school ever since he wa
preaching in the U. B. Church for thre
He is full of the missionary spirit, st
line with the best thought of the C
Church and I believe will make
preacher. Edgar M. Rich

Macon, Mo., Aug. 3, 1898.

Of The Pekin Church.

One year ago last April the writer b
visit irregularly the church at Pekin,
that time it was almost ready to discu
some uncertainty the question, ''To b
to be.'' By the middle of August it se
be about decided in the negative. But a
or three weeks' indecision and uncert
was resolved to *try again*. My so
irregular visits were continued till Janu
after which time I was able to meet wi
and preach every Sunday morning and
with what degree of zest I was able to

church; some additions to the membership; the reviving of all departments of church work; a Sunday-school enrollment of 200; an Endeavor Society of about 50, although that feature had retained its energy well; a Junior Endeavor Society organized; an old debt to their former pastor paid off; money raised for the location of a new pastor with them. Bro. F. E. Hagen, one of our graduate students, accepted the work and was duly installed July 17. The work is starting off encouragingly even in midsummer. We shall expect to hear good things of Bro. H. and the Pekin church after awhile. She is not dead yet, although the atmosphere *is* quite malarial. It is in that district whence flows the greatest stream of "sin and death" in the world. That much the more need of her "strengthening the things that remain" and being "faithful until death."

R. A. GILCREST.

The Springdale Chautauqua.

Springdale is a beautiful little city of 2,500 souls, situated on the St. Louis & San Francisco Railroad, 343 miles from St. Louis and in the very midst of the great apple producing belt of Northwest Arkansas. On July 17th, the first convention of the Springdale Chautauqua was concluded. This enterprise is under the management of and promoted solely by our brother, Prof. Josiah H. Shinn, ex-State Superintendent Public Instruction, and is the second Chautauqua in the West to be fostered and sustained by individual capital and pluck. Among the many popular lecturers who charmed our people with their sound logic, eloquence, wit and pathos were Hon. Geo. W. Bain, H. W. Ham, Rev. Sam. W. Small. A. W. Hawkes, John Temple Graves and John J. Ingalls, while the various churches were ably represented by eminent divines from all parts of the county. On July 10th Bro. E. T. Edmonds, of Fort Smith, Ark., delivered a most excellent sermon on "The Profit of Godliness," before a large and highly appreciative audience, and on the following Tuesday, which was Christian Church Day, Bro. F. G. Tyrrell, of St. Louis, gave two masterly addresses. A great deal of credit is due to our brother, Prof. Shinn, for his undauntable energy and enterprise in bringing before the citizens of Northwest Arkansas such rare opportunities for mental, moral and spiritual improvement, and we feel confident that through his efforts there has been disseminated an influence upon the entire community which shall bring forth much good fruit in coming days. The musical feature of the Assembly was under the direction of Prof. Wm. Apmadoc, of Chicago, and this is equivalent to saying it was a decided success. The Wagner Male Quartet was with us one week and won the hearts of all by their sweet songs. We hope to hear them again next year.

CHAS. E. FREEMAN, Pastor.

Mason City Notes.

We have recently enjoyed a visit from Chas. S. L. Brown, of Washington, Kansas, a brilliant young preacher of some four years' experience, whom I baptized into Christ in 1892. Being on the lookout for a location, and hearing from Bro. Haggard that De Witt, Iowa, was needing a man, he went there immediately and has been employed for a time, at least.

Two weeks ago Bro. R. A. Martin, who with his family tried to feed on the husks of the "Rainy River Colony" in Canada, came down here with his excellent wife and three small children to stay till a suitable church could be found to employ him. He is a man in the prime of life, with a noble Christian character and ten years' successful experience in the ministry to commend him to the favorable consideration of the churches. He is a younger brother of Sylvester M. Martin, whose evangelistic labors have been so wonderfully blessed. He should have a call very soon to some good church, for I believe he will render good service, and honor the cause of Christ by his life and labors.

On Thursday, July 25th, Bro. A. B. Moore, state evangelist of Minnesota, who is giving his whole time to the establishment of the cause in Austin, Minn., came down to visit us and to present the claims of Austin to the brethren and sisters assembled at the prayer-meeting. This he did in a manner at once so wise and winning that he carried away with him the fervent good-will of those he met, and about thirty dollars in cash and pledges to help the Austin church secure a lot and a house to worship in.

Our assistant, Bro. Walter L. Martin, is proving himself the right man in the right place, and we anticipate a most fruitiul ministry for him in this ripe field.

The home department of our Bible-school is growing, and promises splendid results in many directions. We have the city assigned to ten visitors in as many districts, and we will soon have 100 scholars enrolled who pledge themselves to a regular study of the Bible-school lesson at home. I wonder more schools do not inaugurate this needy and most fruitful work. For the first four Sundays in July our Main Street Bible-school reached an average attendance of about 340. In our main school, including the home department and the baby roll, with our three mission schools, we now enroll about 900 scholars. All departments of our work is flourishing, and in spite of the hot weather our audiences are large and the interest fine. The prayer-meeting fills the lecture-room, and the C. W. B. M. now numbers over 100. The spiritual life of the church is good, and the people have a mind to work. God is blessing us, and the people are happy in Christ and glad to be used in his service. I trust I may be believed when I say that in all the elements of a true Church of Christ I record my conviction that this congregation ranks the highest of any with which I am acquainted. May the church abide faithful, and the minister always have grace and gumption to keep out of the way of their progress, even when he cannot lead them in the way of truth.

SUMNER T. MARTIN.

August 6, 1898.

Illinois Mission Notes.

The encampment just closed was the greatest in the history of our organized work. There were over one thousand people present during the week.

The secretary of the I. C. M. C., besides holding one meeting, spent from three to 10 days with a number of churches, giving such service as he was able. He attended the district conventions, nine county rallies, conducted a number church institutes, arranged 35 protracted meetings and assisted to locate 60 preachers. He visited 93 churches and collected $737.35 in the field.

A summary of this year: 30 men were employed and served 3,047 days. They held 30 meetings, preached 1,585 sermons with a results of 448 conversions and 178 additions besides. Collections by evangelists in the field were $3,328. Five churches were organized and 10 reorganized.

The recommendations of the board were unanimously adopted and they promise bettter things for all missionary interests. Churches are asked to raise a certain sum in a year for missions, that four Sundays be set apart for instruction in the cause of missions and for the making of offerings, that a thorough canvass of the congregation be made for cash and pledges before these days and that the receipts be divided proportionately among the societies, our convention receiving one-fourth of all money raised. Several churches have adopted this plan already, including the Springfield church.

The report is in the hands of the printer and will be mailed soon.

The Canton church, J. P. Litchtenberger, pastor, ran an excursion which brought 500 people from Canton and Fulton county. We shall bless Bro. Litchtenberger forever for this friendly movement, for we believe it means a host of people in attendance next year. He is not only a great preacher, but a fertile originator of sensible plans to forward the cause of his Master. He has shown the brotherhood of the state how to have an assembly worthy of a great people.

A hopeful feature of the convention was the presence of a number of business men. There were more than ever before and they brought great cheer to the hearts of their brethren.

While all on the program acquitted themselves nobly, special mention should be made of the address of J. T. Ogle, of Missouri. It will be printed and distributed among the churches.

Dr. Hardin presided with his usual dignity and grace and our people love him more than ever.

We hope to have three evangelists in the field by September 1st. It will depend entirely, however, upon the religious patriotism of brethren for our state. There is a growing conviction among the preachers that this great state should be saved for Christ and brethren should hasten to express this feeling in liberal offerings. Teach the churches to give one-fourth of all missionary offerings for the work in Illinois. The time has come to do this, and it must not be delayed. Let a strong pull be made.

Churches that are not ready to accept the plan of gathering the offerings as proposed by the convention are asked to observe Illinois Day as usual. It comes on the first Sunday in October. It is not too soon to lay your plans for a great collection now, and we urge you to do it. While 200 churches gave to state work, 400 gave to foreign missions. Is it right? Let the other 200 come to the front this year.

J. FRED JONES, Sec.

Stanford, Ill.

Ontario Christian Colony.

On Lord's day, July 10, J. L. Sharitt, of Knoxville, Ia., preached in the Baptist Church at Rat Portage. His sermon was highly appreciated by the congregation. The Baptists of Rat Portage have a gem in the person of Rev. Tapscott. A beautiful building has recently been dedicated. The Disciples always receive a hearty welcome, and many sermons have recently been delivered there. The services held by the members of the colony in this locality is the first that has been held in a radius of 500 miles of the place.

On Lord's day, the 17, Bro. A. M. Sweany, late of Oregon, preached the first sermon in the new township which was surveyed for the American colony. After the middle of August we expect to have regular services, as some special location will be arranged.

July 31, Bro. S. Baptist, late of Jacksonville, Ill., preached in the Presbyterian Church at Emo. He has filled the pulpit there very acceptably several times.

R. A. BURRISS.

Bowmanville, Ont.

Another Offer.

A written proposition has been sent me by Bro. T. E. Bondurant, of Piatt county, Ill., to be one of the twenty-five to raise another $100,000 for the endowment fund of Eureka College. He will give $4,000 if twenty-four others will give each a like sum. Bro. Bondurant has already contributed $20,000 in productive property. He desires to see the endowment fund amount to half a million. He wants this proposition met by July 1st, 1898. Now, brethren, here is the opportunity for another splendid advance. Let us do this quickly in the fear of our God!

J. H. HARDIN.

Eureka, Ill.

Missouri Bible-school Notes.

J. W. Boles, of Auxvasse, is to be our county Bible-school superintendent this year, and this assures us good reports from Callaway, while Miss Inez Terry, of Lamont, will kindly do the same for us in Pettis. But are there not others? And who will volunteer for some county from which we had no report last year? Write me.

Auxvasse shows her interest in our work by meeting the apportionment for the new year in full.

Giddens, at Delhi, has had a good meeting, with twenty-five additions; $500 for a new house, with the promise of a Bible-school as soon as the house is ready.

But in our rejoicings, brethren, let us not forget the state mission work and our beloved T. A. Abbott and family, now undergoing one of the severest trials of life. In the nearness to death of his faithful companion, who has borne with him the burdens and anxieties of this work, let us remember them at the throne of grace, asking his comfort and cheer whose presence surpasses all that of men. Then, too, as I think of them, we can show our sympathy in such a substantial way by sending in our apportionment to state missions immediately. Thank God for Christian sympathy and for its open manifestation in times of need.

At Jonesburg C. C. Hill has done one of the remarkable works of the state, so that the congregation is becoming strong and influential in the community. But he has had hearty supporters in many of the good people of the church, T. J. Mason and his devoted companion being in the lead. This is the home, too, of Uncle Jap Skinner, known and loved by all the preachers, a faithful friend of the younger men especially. Here is the benefit of the work, too, for when our evangelist, T. A. Abbott, undertook the revival of the cause at Jonesburg, good brethren shook their heads, but it was a success, and under its preacher is becoming more so all the time, and is now a regular contributor to state Bible-school work.

Illinois Bend has suffered by revivals, so that it is not so strong now as in the past; but they are still holding up the Christ, and in the school are honoring him by faithful work, as I witnessed in the teaching. Mrs. Martha McClanahan is the superintendent, the work is good and the results will be happifying. To our work those present were very generous, thanks to the leaders.

Lydia, where W. S. St. Clair is doing such good work, sends in her apportionment for this year in full, and a time when badly needed. Have never had a more ready and prompt co-operant in this work than is W. S., who leads the way in all his churches, and you know what that means.

Jno. W. Jacks has been school superintendent so long in Montgomery City that I dare not specify, and in all that time the school has not failed us. This year, as generally, I have the half of their apportionment and a promise of other assistance before the year closes, which means more than the pledge. I am told that in all the history of the school the treasury has never been empty, a record of which Brother Jacks may well be proud.

Brethren, help us this time by remitting at least the first quarter, and do not hold us off when we are needing the assistance immediately; and if possible do not send your personal checks, as they cost us fifteen cents for collection, while the exchange will not likely cost you anything, or much less.

At La Plata J. M. Smith is giving three Sundays to the work, and much time to the Bible-school and Endeavor, for so he does always. Mrs. Ernest Williams is the school superintendent, and is giving satisfaction, as all knew she would. But the church is not strong and zealous as in the past, though many faithful hearts are anxiously praying and working to see a revival in all the work there. The brethren did not see their way clear to do much for us, but a few did well. Bro. Smith, as hitherto, was ready for any part, and then gave with the others. Bless the Lord for such friendship and co-operation.

Before going to your county or district meetings, brethren, ask the schools to authorize you to notify me that the apportionment is accepted, then I make no other call for money. See? Please do this. H. F. DAVIS.

Minnesota Convention.

Did you note the program in last week's issue? If not, get the paper and look it through and plan not only to attend the convention, but to inspire others to attend. May it be made a record-breaker as well as a season of fellowship and counsel, "Minnesota for Christ" being a chief animating spirit.

A telegram from A. McLean says Dr. Butchart, of the China Mission, will take his place upon the program, which is a gratifying piece of information if Bro. McLean must needs be absent.

Were delegates chosen throughout the church and auxiliaries last Lord's day? If not, secure action next Lord's day, and forward names Monday by first mail. Notify C. H. Austin, Mankato, also. Will isolated brethren intending to be present likewise give notice?

J. G. Slick, of Amboy, and pastor of the Antrim and Willow Creek churches, who recently held a meeting at Wyanette, in the North district, thus writes of his visit to Wyanette: "Such consecration I have seldom seen. The brethren have 'grit, grace and gumption,' but lack greenbacks, and can you not visit them and induce the Church Extension Board to loan them $200, which I believe would be repaid dedication day?

F. H. MELLEN, Sec'y M. C. M. S.
Box 450, *Minneapolis, Minn., August* 13.

The New Commandment

Jesus said, "A new commandment I give unto you, that ye love one another." The practical success of the Church of Christ has always and will always depend upon the perfect obedience of this commandment. The preacher with all his literary talents, culture, oratory and society influence may attract and entertain his audiences, but if he lacks that self-sacrificing love of his Christ, he becomes to the real Christian "sounding brass, or a clanging cymbal." I said real Christian, because there are some of the other kind. A Christian in name only is far more dangerous than an infidel. The Christian in name only is a hindrance to the propagation of the New Testament Christianity. He is the devil's game.

"Love one another, even as I have loved you!" This will prevent pulpit degeneracy. It will do away with bossing elders, or officers who are in the habit of acting on the "dog-in-the-manger" policy. Such divine language enforced is the compass which guides the weary soul out of all difficulties. It gives new life to him who recognizes its divinity. Organically it wills to imitate Christ's character by perfect obedience and submissiveness. Stubborness, wickedness, covetousness, maliciousness and every evil thought and action could be cured by the obedience of this commandment. Why not live up to the command of our divine Commander? What would become of our nation if our army and navy would fail to respond to the command of our chief executive? The time has come for enforcement of divine discipline. There are men and women who have had "their own way" long enough. Heroic means should be used to bring the whisperers, backbiters, liars, etc., to repentance or withdraw from them. The new commandment is of no use to them because they willfully ignore it, and all men know, by their actions, that they are not the disciples of the Lord. To carry out the mission of this commandment would bring about prosperity. It would cause every church to employ a preacher and pay him a living salary. Old preachers would never be put on "the shelf." College students would have abundance of practice. All our missionary enterprises would so prosper that all men would find out that we are his disciples.

JOHN G. M. LUTTENBERGER.

The church at Clay Center, Kansas, is reported as prospering under the ministry of Otha Wilkison.

The 6th Kansas district churches enjoyed a convention recently held with the church at Phillipsburg.

The church at Mt. Ayr, Ia., reports a great success of their church rally and roll-call meetings. The sermons, by C. E. Wells and D. F. Sellards, were appropriate and listened to with rapt attention.

An outline of an interesting sermon, preached by J. B. Haston, Galveston, Texas. on "Territoral Expansion," was published in the Galveston Daily Aug. 8th. He distinguishes between "land grabbing" and "manifest destiny."

Evangelistic.

KANSAS.

Newton, Aug. 11.—W. E. Harlow and Miss Maud Murphy have just closed a very successful meeting of four weeks' duration with 17 accessions and church very much revived.—W. H. SCRIVNER, Pastor.

Topeka, Aug. 3.—There have been 23 additions to date in the East Topeka meeting. Will begin meeting at Holt, Mo., Aug. 7, following the dedication of their new house of worship. V. E. Ridenour, of Ft. Scott, will have charge of the music.—D. D. BOYLE.

ILLINOIS.

Rossville, Aug. 8.—Four added at all points since last report.—A. R. JACKMAN.

Herrick, Aug. 13.—I am in an interesting meeting at this place with good audiences and good attention. I begin a tent meeting at Conden, Ill., Sept. 1. We have no church there. Our aim is to build a church. We need the prayers and assistance of our brethren.—HATTRESS H. SHICK, Evangelist.

Olney, Aug. 2.—I have not forgotten the good CHRISTIAN-EVANGELIST even if it has not heard from my part of the battlefield of life for a year. My regular work has been forced to be given up because of the invalid condition of my mother, and other duties that a dutiful child will perform for parents, but I shall not leave the ministry, as I shall continue to do itinerant work, singing in meetings and evangelizing. I report 63 additions not yet reported in meetings and regular work at Robinson, Palestine and Maude. The above shall be my permanent address.—W. C. SWARTZ.

Taylorville, Aug. 12.—We have had two additions to the church at this place since last report. I will close my twelfth year's labor here the 1st of November, and it will be the close of my work here. My pastorate has been a very pleasant one. This is a good church and it occupies a prominent place in the religious work in this city.—W. W. WEEDON.

Hume, Aug. 15.—We are in a good meeting here with nine additions to date.—A. MARTIN.

INDIANA.

Indianapolis, Aug. 2.—At the North Park Church one confession, also at Broad Ripple Mission one confession.—J. M. CANFIELD.

North Madison, Aug. 10.—Three additions at the Liberty church and one at Kent. Will address the pioneer's meeting at Liberty Grove, Aug. 25, 1898. Liberty church will repair their building and rededicate soon.—O. D. MAPLE.

OHIO.

Marion, Aug. 10.—My first work as pastor of a church was from '78 to '80, in Bethany, W. Va., immediately after graduation; my last work has been here, the fourth year expiring now soon. Am open to calls; will go anywhere, but prefer remaining within 300 miles of Central Ohio. Correspondence solicited as pastor of a church or for work in some of our colleges.—A. SKIDMORE.

MISSOURI.

Martinsburg, Aug. 10.—Six confessions here last night. All young men. Meeting will continue two weeks longer.—J. C. COGGINS.

Lawson, Aug. 9.—Closed a two weeks' meeting here last night with good results. Have received calls in last 30 days to keep me in the evangelistic field for 12 months, but I can only give one month out of the year to that line of work while I continue to preach for the church at California, Mo. Sometimes my desire and these invitations almost force me to resign my work as pastor and resume the work of an evangelist. The harvest is great and the laborers few.—BEN F. HILL.

Barnard, Aug. 6.—There have been five additions since I moved from Drake University to my fields of labor, Barnard and Palestine, the first of June. Of these two, the pastor and wife, by letter to the Barnard church, two by letter and one confession at Palestine. The ladies of the C. W. B. M. gave an open program Lord's day evening. The collection was more than double any former C. W. B. M. Day collection. The pastors of Nodaway County meet in the study of pastor, O. W. Lawrence, of Maryville, the 12th inst., to plan for a county convention. I preached my farewell sermon to the church at Belinda, Ia., last Lord's day and now divide my time equally between Barnard and Palestine.—F. E. BLANCHARD.

Holt, Aug. 15.—We assisted in dedicating the new church here. We are now in a meeting with 10 additions in eight days; seven last night.—BOYLE AND RIDENOUR.

Lamonte, July 14.—We have had five confessions since last report making 35 during our seven months' work here.—KING STARK.

OKLAHOMA.

Ingalls, Aug. 5.—On last Lord's day three united with the church at our regular service by statement.—D. W. JOHNSON.

IOWA.

Stuart, Aug. 10th.—E. T. McFarland and Prof. G. A. Butler have just closed a four weeks' meeting at Luther, Ia., with 21 accessions.

Glenwood.—Two added.—A. R. CAUDLE.

Larimore.—Sixteen banded together, three baptized.—B. D. CLARK.

Alta.—Forty-two at close; $200 pledged for preaching, and $50 for hall rent.—WRIGHT AND MARTINDALE.

Dowes, Aug. 7th.—One addition since last report. We laid the corner-stone of our new church last Thursday. Bro. B. S. Denny, of Hampton, Ia., delivered an able address. Bro. W. F. MacCormick, of Iowa Falls, was with us and made a few remarks. The services were the best the town ever had, they say. We put a copy of the CHRISTIAN-EVANGELIST in the corner-stone.—F. L. DAVIS.

TEXAS.

August 9.—Fifty-two additions in R. R. Hamlin's meeting at Martindale. An aged couple 76 and 67 years old were baptized.—R. R. HAMLIN.

WEST VIRGINIA.

Huntington, August 8.—I lately baptized and ordained to the ministry Bro. D. S. Henkel, of Pomeroy, Ohio. He is a worthy man and a natural organizer. Let some city call him to take its mission, or some district its evangelistic work. Three baptized at our mission in South Huntington yesterday. One added from the Baptist Church last night.—G. M. WEIMER.

ALABAMA.

Anniston, August 10.—I held a four days' meeting with New Hope church in Cleburue county, and baptized 11 persons, also two from the Baptist Church; total, 13.—HOWARD J. BRAZLETON.

ARKANSAS.

Two additions at Pine Bluff August 7th.—S. W. CRUTCHER.

TENNESSEE.

One added to Church of Christ, Clarksville, Aug. 7th. Two added Aug. 16th.—A. M. GROWDEN.

COLORADO.

Salida, Aug 8.—Glascock and Givens have been with us for two weeks. 10 were added, 5 by baptism and confession. The pastor continues the meeting with the aid of the home forces. The interest is very good.—L. A. BETCHER.

NEW YORK.

Gloversville.—Meeting resulted in organization of a new church of 31, Bible-school of 40, C. E. Society of 15. C. W. B. M. will soon be formed. M. Gunn located as pastor. Prospects for the future are good.—J. M. MORRIS, State Evangelist.

FLORIDA.

Jacksonville, Aug. 8.—There were two additions to the new Christian church of this city at the close of the services last evening, a gentleman and his wife. Our attendance is gradually increasing. A number of men from the various regiments encamped here are always in attendance at our regular services.—T. H. BLENUS.

Publishers' Notes.

"KING SAUL."

Those who have read "In the Days of Jehu," by J. Breckenridge Ellis, will be pleased to know that his second book on Old Testament characters is now about ready for delivery. The title of this new book is "King Saul," and it fully ststains the author's reputation as a fascinating writer, and a close student of Bible history and character.

The Young Southron, of Atlanta, Ga., has given quite a lengthy review of our late publication, "Studies in Acts, or the New Testament Book of Beginnings," by W. J. Lhamon. On account of space we can only give the following extract from this commendation: "Dr. Lhamon is a clear thinker, well furnished as a scholar, and conversant with the writings of great thinkers of various schools who have handled the same themes. To these qualifications he adds a devout enthusiasm, a strong faith in the ultimate victory of New Testament truth."

This book has 420 pages, cloth binding, and the price is $1.25.

Now is a good time to begin preparations to place a library in your Sunday-school and Endeavor Society. The long evenings are approaching when one will be inclined to turn their minds to books. Our special catalogue containing a list of suitable books for these kind of libraries will be mailed on application. As the Christian Publishing Co. publishes a large portion of the literature of the Christian Church, the selections are made from this large source and are wholesome books to place before the young.

The Daily Telegraph, of Kalamazoo, Mich., has the following to say in a review of W. J. Russell's late book, "The Wonders of the Sky," which is just from the press of the Christian Publishing Co.:

"The subject is a fascinating one, and as presented in this neat little volume is one we can apply with profit in our nightly star gazing. Mr. Russell is thoroughly conversant with astronomical literature, yet the magnitude of the study has been cleverly constructed by the author into simple, earnest language that can not fail to entertain as well as instruct."

"Wonders of the Sky" is bound in beautiful illminated cloth, and the price is 50 cents.

The Christian Publishing Co. is prepared to fill orders promptly for all kinds of Christian Endeavor supplies, such as Pledges, Badges, Topic Cards and cards for Applications, Invitations and Committees. Write us and we will mail you our special catalogue giving full particulars on all requisites for Endeavor Societies.

"After Pentecost, What?" by James M. Campbell, is a discussion of the doctrine of the Holy Spirit. The book contains 289 pages and the price is $1.00. Aside from the thought of the book its literary excellence is not surpassed in recent publications. From the Christian Messenger, Toronto, Ontario, Canada, we give the following extract concerning this book: "One thing, without doubt, the author has done for us: he has set the great day of Pentecost flashing before us historically in the light of the Holy Spirit as it flashed once literally 'with tongues of fire.'"

RATES OF SUBSCRIPTION.

Single subscriptions, new or old	$1.75	each
In clubs of five or more, new or old	1.50	"
Reading Rooms	1.25	"
Ministers	1.00	"

With a club of ten we will send one additional copy free.

All subscriptions payable in advance. Label shows the month up to the first day of which your subscription is paid. If an earlier date than the present is shown, you are in arrears. No paper discontinued without express orders to that effect. Arrears should be paid when discontinuance is ordered.

In ordering a change of post office, please give the OLD as well as the NEW address.

Do not send local check, but use Post office or Express Money Order, or draft on St. Louis, Chicago or New York, in remitting.

Missionary.

Church Extension Notes.

Send at once for literature and collection envelopes to G. W. Muckley, Kansas City, Mo., and prepare for a rousing Church Extension Day in September.

The harvests are reaped, the summer is ended, God has blessed us in basket and in store, and we should be willing to show our gratitude in a large September offering for Church Extension.

Do not fail to get home from your vacation in time to aid our Church Extension work. It is your duty and the church so recognizes it.

"A suitable church building is one of the first requisites of the permanency, the prosperity and the efficiency of a congregation." So writes George Darsie, of Frankfort, Ky., whose congregation raises annually more than $300 for Church Extension.

Our Church Extension work has always appealed to good, hard American sense. As a successful work it appeals to enterprising Americans.

We have an independent church polity. Everything should be done to make strong our bond of unity. Let the strong and weak churches unite as one body in taking the September offering and the missions now wanting to build will be encouraged to put forth the best efforts to help themselves.

Every church aided by our Extension Fund will be heart and soul a missionary church. Freely it has received, freely it will give. In the day of its strength it will not forget the mother that helped it.

We should bestir ourselves and show a zeal hitherto unknown in Church Extension, because other religious bodies have long years the start of us in Church Extension and have accumulated large funds which enable them to seize points in great numbers. We should be patriotic in cur plea.

Let us clasp hands with a tighter grip as we approach the September offering for Church Extension. Let us walk as one man to our duty and raise our proportion this year of the $250,000 for 1900.

We speak in no narrow spirit, but if other religious bodies, having from our standpoint a religious plea so inferior to ours, yet excel us in zeal and liberality, must it not humiliate us to think that the leading denominations like the Congregational, Presbyterian and Methodist churches raise more in one year for Church Extension than we have in our Fund altogether?

Before our Church Extension Fund was inaugurated all our efforts at aiding mission chucrhes to build were weak and expensive. Men traveled half way across the continent in vain efforts to get money and appeals were published in our papers for aid to places we knew nothing about. Now every case is carefully looked into by our Board and, if worthy, aided at once in such a way that the loan made helps the mission to good beginnings in self-helpfulness and self-respect, and the money keeps going and coming in the same good way from year to year.

The Methodist Episcopal Church of the North leads all other bodies in results achieved in the field of Church Extension. During 1896 it aided 472 churches. In the first 32 years of its history its extension fund assisted in the erection of 10,184 Methodist church buildings, more than half the churches which that denomination to-day owns. It raised and expended in all for this purpose up to 1896 the sum of $5,725,000. GEORGE DARSIE.

W. C. Payne, of New York City, will address the church at Bethal, Indiana, on our Church Extension work, Sunday morning, August 28th.

Church Extension.

If the history of all the churches that have been organized and died, went out of existence, utterly perishing, could be written, it would be appalling. If the history of souls that have been thus ruined and forever lost could be written, it would be still more appalling.

Among the causes of the loss of these churches and souls would be found the lack of church homes, houses in which to meet and worship every Lord's day and into which to call all the people to hear the gospel preached.

Our Church Extension fund ought to be made large enough to secure the erection of a decent house in every county-seat where one is needed. Remember September 4th.

J. C. REYNLDS.

Words of Cheer for Church Extension.

In looking over date of organization of the Church Extension Boards of the different denominations, I was surprised to see the mighty strides our brotherhood has made in the cause of Church Extension. Our Board is to be commended for its untiring efforts. Mogadore will reach its apportionment in September.

D. D. FENNEL.

Mogadore, O.

Every Christian's heart should sorrow for our unhoused congregations, therefore we should give as God has blessed us to the Church Extension fund to aid the cause.

KILBY FERGUSON.

Selma, Ala.

Since coming West I see more than ever the need of a large Church Extension fund. The West is in great need of Christian work, and ought to buy a lot in every town while it is new and property cheap, and later should build a house. This is the only way to establish the cause early and permanently in any large measure. J. C. B. STIVERS.

Missoula, Mont.

We will endeavor to reach and possibly exceed our apportionment, $20.

H. S. SINSABAUGH.

Danville, Ill.

There is no more important work than Church Extension, and God will bless it.

S. H. BARTLETT.

Painesville, O.

The brethren of Swampscott desire to participate in the effort of the Board to raise $250,000 for Church Extension toward the close of 1900. EDWARD F. RANDALL.

Swampscott, Mass.

I regard Church Extension work as the "open sesame" of our Home Mission work.

N. J. REYNOLDS.

Toulon, Ill.

We can never remove the mote which obscures the vision of our brethren abroad until we get rid of the beams of ignorance and false teaching at home. O. W. MASON.

New Richmond, Ind.

I have found that good business men *who understand Church Extension* contribute for it more willingly than for any other of our benevolences. W. W. SNIFF.

Gibson City, Ill.

I sincerely and earnestly hope that you will succeed in your most reasonable desire. We will do what we can to make it possible.

J. H. MCNEIL.

Rushville, Ind.

I have always felt that Church Extension is one of our wisest and best enterprises. Will do our best in September.

THAD S. TINSLEY.

Owingsville, Ky.

This is an all-around missionary church, and will not neglect to take an offering for Church Extension while I am pastor.

HARRY G. HILL.

Hebron, Ind.

The church here is weak both financially and numerically—about thirty members — but we decided in a business meeting at the beginning of the year to do what we could for our various missions. ALBERT NEESE.

La Crosse, Kan.

Will give my earnest help to make the collection the greatest we have ever had.

C. H. MATTOX.

North English, Ia.

We must have the money to build more churches or our Home Mission work will be greatly hindered. Count on us to help Church Extension and thus to help Home Missions.

J. E. PAYNE.

Mt. Byrd, Ky. (Milton.)

Certainly, I shall do my utmost to secure an offering for Church Extension from the three churches for which I preach.

S. J. PHILLIPS.

Sugar Grove, Wis.

Statesmen differ concerning the wisdom of colonial expansion, but Christians cannot differ as to the wisdom of extending Christ's kingdom, Church Extension, Colonial Expansion.

ROBT. F. FRANK.

Nicholasville, Ky.

No enterprise of the church is so well received as Church Extension.

J. H. JESSUP.

Vincennes, Ind.

SUBSCRIBERS' WANTS.

Miscellaneous wants and notices will be inserted in this department at the rate of two cents a word, each insertion, all words, large and small, to be counted, and two initials stand for one word. Please accompany notice with corresponding remittance to save book-keeping.

Family Circle.

Grown-up Land.

Good-morning, fair maid, with lashes brown;
Can you tell me the way to Womanhood Town?

Oh, this way and that way—never stop;
'T is picking up stitches grandma will drop,
'T is kissing the baby's troubles away,
'T is learning that cross words never will pay,
'T is helping mother, 't is sewing up rents,
'T is reading and playing, 't is saving the pence,
'T is loving and smiling, forgetting to frown,
Oh, that is the way to Womanhood Town.

Just wait, my brave lad—one moment I pray;
Manhood Town lies where—can you tell me the way?

Oh, by toiling and trying we reach that land—
A bit with the head, a bit with the hand—
'T is by climbing up the steep hill Work,
'T is by keeping out of the wide street Shirk,
'T is by always taking the weak one's part,
'T is by giving mother a happy heart,
'T is by keeping bad thoughts and actions down;
Oh, that is the way to Manhood Town.

And the lad and the maid ran, hand in hand,
To their fair estates in the Grown-up Land.
—*The Commonwealth.*

Text Stories—X.

OPPORTUNITY.

BY ALICE CURTICE MOYER.

And they kept the feast of tabernacles as it is written, and offered the daily burnt offerings by number, according to the ordinance, as the duty of every day required.—*Ezra 3:4.*

The corn rows seemed to stretch out into lengths interminable, and the sun shone down with a heat so oppressive that the faint breeze was barely noticed by George Lacy, who was toilsomely following the "double shovel" plow, thus laboriously cultivating the young corn.

Strange to say, George was not whistling to-day—strange, because his was one of those happy, sunshiny natures whose hopefulness makes one feel that there is something in life after all, or at least something to look forward to. But to-day his face was troubled. The heat was oppressive and the length of the corn rows was discouraging. Not that these would, as a general thing, have worried him, but to-day he was in one of those self-pitying moods that we all know so well, and taken together with other things of which he was thinking, they had power to greatly annoy him.

"What is the use of trying?" he said, half aloud. "Or what is the use of even thinking? I am tied right here—doomed to a life of unremitting and uncongenial toil. And I *would* like to make a stir in the world—even a small ripple. Now there is Robert Long—and if I do say it myself he is no more capable than I—who is to go to college next autumn and then to some Bible School. He expects to become a great preacher, just what I have so often hoped to be some day. Surely, it must be a glorious thing to be able to so preach the gospel as to lead people to repentance and the right way of living. 'And they that be wise shall shine as the brightness of the firmament and they that turn many to righteousness as the stars forevermore.' That's what I want to do—to turn many to righteousness. I want to see my sermons in the papers and hear myself quoted on every hand. Ever since I was a very small lad that has been my ambition. But now—well, I don't mean to complain. Somebody must run the farm and look after mother's comfort, and I am all she has left." His thoughts journeyed to a grave in the neighboring churchyard wherein the husband and father had been laid to rest during the past winter. "No," he continued, "I won't complain. For so good a mother I can well afford to give up everything."

It is evident that a "small ripple" would not be sufficient to satisfy George as he tried to make himself believe. And it would seem, also, that his ambition was tinctured somewhat with a desire for the honor of men rather than the glory of God. But he was young, and we must therefore judge him leniently. And besides, he was only giving voice to the ambition of the heart, while you or I might be treasuring there an ambition no more worthy, though so secret that we would not even whisper it. Let us not condemn others while there is a mote in our own eye.

But I think we can see in George at least one most beautiful trait of character, one that may work wonders in time—that of devotion to his mother. When a lad of fourteen or thereabouts, his obedience to his mother's wishes to remain out of a school-boy escapade called forth the wrath of certain of his mates who tauntingly accused him of being "tied to his mother's apron strings." Not having the slighest suspicion that their remarks had been overheard, they were very much surprised and a great deal ashamed when their teacher said that afternoon just before dismissal:

"Boys, one of our greatest needs while journeying through this world is a guide. Your mother is your best friend, and it is no disgrace if you are tied to her apron strings. You cannot find a more gentle or a safer guide. The boy thus tied will never go far wrong. He may not know how to play cards or use profane language in a way calculated to call forth the applause of hoodlums, but he makes the sort of man that is called upon when somebody is wanted to fill a position of honor and trust. Boys, if you are tied to your mother's apron strings don't seek to untie the knot. It is an honor to you of inestimable value, and will lead you safely and surely to that supreme Guide which the psalmist had in mind when he said: 'Thou hast holden me by my right hand.'"

Somehow that little incident came back to George to-day as he followed the plow back and forth across the cornfield, and he continued:

"Yes, the teacher was right. A wise mother is her boy's best friend. I know from experience. My mother has always known the inmost secrets of my heart; and perhaps, because I never loosened the knot of her apron string, I had no secrets that I could not share with her. Any burden, no matter how heavy, cannot be grievous if borne for her sake. But it is greatly for her sake that I long to develop whatever talent I may have. How I should like to have it said of her: 'This is the mother of the great preacher, Dr. George Lacey.' How proud of me she would be!"

And then George remembered something else he had heard that particular teacher say. He had found it convenient one day to make use of that old and wise maxim, "Cut your coat according to your cloth," and then had gone on to say in his own peculiar way:

"My dear boys and girls, I want to call your particular attention to this old maxim. My understanding of it is that we had better come down a peg or two in our notions. Not that we should not be ambitious, but that we should not allow our ambitions to be so large as to completely swallow up the small opportunities that line our path. We cannot always be doing something in harmony with our condition and ability. If we would square our ideas with our circumstances, how much more contented we might all be. Happiness, that fleeting will-o'-the-wisp, might then be within our reach. It is not, after all, so much what we have or what we have not in this world that adds to or subtracts from our felicity, but the ever-present and overpowering longing for something else, and the envying of those who, as it seems to us, possess that something, and the great desire to appear in the eyes of the world as one of great consequence."

"Well," argued George aloud, as though in reply to the teacher whose voice had long been silent—thus does our influence live—"that may all be very well, and perhaps I deserve the rebuke, but how can I help it? The desire is there. I *do* want to do something noteworthy. As for the little opportunities, I do not see any along *my* path. I don't believe a search with a microscope would reveal them. I can't convert cornstalks; and Jerry and Joe," nodding to the lazy team of bays and smiling at the thought, "are about as good as horses can be. So where are my opportunities?"

"All around you," replied a voice so close that George was startled. So absorbed had he been that, unnoticed, the aforesaid Jerry and Joe had stopped under a shade tree and had been dutifully listening to the one-sided conversation of their master. But what astonished George more than any thing else, was the presence of his visitor. Who he could be or from whence he had come, he had not the slightest idea, and before he could sufficiently collect his wits to ask, his visitor continued:

"There are opportunities everywhere, my young friend, but it sometimes requires the closest scrutiny to recognize them. I went once into the studio of a sculptor and was admiring a statue which was nearing completion and which promised, when finished, to be a most beautiful piece of art. But I noticed that its face was hidden and asked the sculptor why this was so.

"'Because it is seldom recognized,' said he, 'it occured to me that position would be most appropriate. It's name is Opportunity!'

"Here lies the trouble. We so seldom recognize our opportunities. But, my friend, that does not excuse us. We are obligated to look for them until we find them. A young lady desiring to do something noteworthy, confided to her pastor that she longed to go to India as a missionary. The pastor, who knew her well, looked at her over his spectacles and said:

"'My dear, who lives in that little house next to you?'

"The young lady was surprised, but answered:

"'I have never spoke to them, but they seem to be a family of ignorant German people.'

"'Who lives in the alley back of you?' asked the pastor.

"A poor Portuguese family,' was the eply.

"'And who lives in that old tumble-own house across the street form you?'

"'O, that you know, is occupied by three r four families, but of course I do not now them."

"'Are they Christians?' the pastor sked.

"I should say not," replied she. 'They o not seem to even know when the Lord's ay comes. They do not send their chil-ren to Sunday-school, and I doubt if they re are ever inside a church themselves. hough, of course, I cannot say positively, s I have never spoken to them.'

"'My dear,' said the pastor, impressively, you do not need to cross the ocean to find he heathen.'

"It is not necessary, my boy, to go very ar out into the world to look for oppor-unities, and, as I said before, we are bligated to look for them. There is a ertain amount of obligation resting upon ach individual. None of us live for self lone. We each have a certain amount of nfluence. Our lives are for a purpose, for fe is not an incident, but is a part of the ivine plan. You and I and every other ndividual are but expressions of the)ivine Mind, wherein we have been latent ince the beginning of time; and had there ot been a reason for the expression of love s manifested in our being, our spirits ould never have been sent to dwell here in :his tabernacle of flesh. Our first and greatest obligation, therefore, is to God—seeing that we do not allow this temporary abode to destroy the soul and render it unfit to be received back to him from whence it came. Next to our obligation to God comes our obligation to our fellow-men—his creatures—and one of the most acceptable services to each is to make use of the little opportunities for doing good that are continually manifesting themselves to the earnest searcher therefor.

"We may not always be able to see God's purpose in our life; that is, all at once. But if we look for it, we will be permitted to see a small part, and by faith-fully discharging our duty concerning that minute part, we will be enabled to see something further ahead. There will be a gradual unfolding of our duties and obliga-tions and opportunities as God sees that we are prepared to meet them.

"You wonder what your opportunities are and what they can be. Well, in the first place, you have an opportunity to show whether you may become fitted for what you might call more congenial work, by faithful performance of the every-day, prosaic little duties that go a long way toward making up the sum-total of your life. Our lives, after all, are made up mostly of little duties, and if we do these well, they are just as acceptable in the sight of our Heavenly Father as though they were deeds to bring the world to our feet in homage. These little duties form a sort of discipline that goes very far toward character-forming, and unless we perform them as faithfully as we know how, we can never be ready for that to which we aspire, should God see fit to give it to us.

"In the account that Ezra gives of the quired," we can find a lesson of inestimable value.

"You say you want to turn sinners to Christ, but that your life is so restricted and narrow, and you are so tied to your daily labors that you can see no op-portunity. It may not be the sort of op-portunity you would like, still it is there. You may not see an account of how you recognized and performed it in the daily papers, but it will be recorded in the heavenly record if it is done 'In His Name.' You will remember it was not among the people of leisure where Jesus found his apostles, but among the busy, hard-working fishermen of Galilee. It is also true that it was the busy, toiling men whom God in the ancient times called into his special service. Elisha was called from the plow to become a great prophet and Moses was taken from his flocks to lead Israel.

"Another thing: Very often we forget to follow the example of Andrew who first went to find his brother that he might bring him unto Jesus. There may be some member of your family who is looking up to you and waiting for your word of en-couragement. Or perhaps there may be some one of your associates—some of your young friends—who are needing just such help as you can give. Or possibly there may be in your community some outcast whom everybody shuns because of an evil life, and who is, therefore, being allowed to sink deeper and deeper into the mire of degradation. While such characters are always repulsive, we should try to remem-ber that while our Master hated sin he loved the sinner, and that though he 'came to destroy the works of the devil,' he so loved, at the same time, the sinner, that he gave his life for him. If religion is some-thing as we believe it is, which appeals to every chivalric impulse and every noble element of the heart, then the possessor thereof should be able to see beneath sin and to recognize the nobility, a portion of which—though it may be small—is in every heart, and the longing of better things, a little, at least, of which is in every soul.

"My young friend, look about you; You are surrounded by opportunities. And remember that even the hardest labor as the duty of every day may require, if well done, is a step onward and upward, and is preparing you for whatever else God may have in store for you after you have proven yourself 'faithful over a few things.'

"And now, if you will kindly direct me to B—— I will be going, but if anything I have said may be of help to you I shall be glad that I lost my way and came myself to ask directions instead of sending my driver."

George mechanically gave the desired information and was just about to find his tongue sufficiently to ask whom his visitor might be when the stranger spoke again:

"I know how to sympathize with you, my boy. I have been over the same road. But the grace of God will help you—some-thing you can always have, for the asking and keep for the fostering—and will prove to be an inexhaustible source of strength to you. Good-bye."

George was so dazed that for a momen the forgot to look at the bit of pasteboard left Jerry and Joe were allowed to rest in the shade for sometime longer while George sat between the plow-handles and thought —thought harder than he had ever done before.

"And this from him," he finally said aloud, "whose sermons I have read with keenest delight. Whose words I have committed to memory and whose career I have longed to imitate. And he has been through it all, he says, and knows how to sympathize with me. Evidently he has won by hard work, inch by inch and step by step, the position he now occupies, while I had imagined that he was born to it or that it had been—well—sort of thrust upon him. God help me to hereafter per-form my tasks faithfully and cheerfully as the duty of each may require; and forgive me, I pray thee, my ingratitude for all the blessings thou hast bestowed upon me!"

It was wonderful how different things seemed to George in the days that fol-lowed. The sun was hot, to be sure, but he was thankful for the health and strength that enabled him to endure it. The culti-vation of the corn was toilsome and tedious, but he was glad that the rows were long and thanked God that the field was large.

The autumn harvest bountifully repaid him, but there was another and a better harvest—one that cannot be measured by gold—that came of that summer's work. And one of its results in after years was that *the great preacher, Dr. Geo. Lacey*, became a reality.

St. Louis, Mo.

Cervera's Fleet.

N. S. P.

See! they come, as sure as fate,
Out of Santiago's gate;
Spaced along in grim array,
Dashing blue waves into spray—
Glaring at the ready foe
Fleeing, battling as they go.
Hissing shot and bursting shell
Fall on them like bolts of hell,
Hot with memories of the "Maine."
Vengeance cometh, haugty Spain!
One by one their desparate reach
Falls along the Cuban beach,
Now their wrecks in grim array,
Charred and shattered, strew the bay.
Liberty, thy beacon light
Over Cuba waxes bright;
Dark oppression fades away,
Daybreak broadens into day!

—Church Union.

A Word To Parents And Teachers.

During the past year my duties as Secre-tary of the Evangelical Alliance have brought me into contact with the pastors of nearly two-score cities. In almost every city they have spoken to me of the de-plorable prevalence of vice among children and young people. Facts have been brought to light which are shocking in the last degree. I am not speaking of children of the slums whose heredity and environ-ment have both been vicious, but of the children who belong to good homes, often Christian homes, whose parents refuse to believe evil of them until confession forces conviction.

Statements have come to me from Cali-fornia, Minnesota, Michigan, Ohio,

The exceptional cause of it would seem to be the wide circulation of vicious literature. Salacious French fiction whose sale has long been a crime in England, and is now outlawed even in Paris, may *legally* corrupt American youth. But doubtless the worse source of contamination is the obscene literature, often illustrated with photographs, which, though forbidden by law, finds easy access to the mails, and is surreptitiously distributed by hand often on the platforms of railway stations, sometimes on the playgrounds of children.

One who has never seen this obscene literature can form no notion of it. A Christian imagination simply cannot conceive of it. It might have come from the cesspool of perdition. This poison has repeatedly been found in public schools, academies and colleges. In some cases every boy and every girl in these schools has confessed to having read it; and the vice which pastors are deploring is the perfectly natural result.

Two things, it seems to me, can be done and ought to be. First, let parents and teachers break the conspiracy of silence, into which they seem to have entered. Rare are the parents who do not leave their children to learn from vicious companions the most sacred facts of their physical life. I do not believe one father in twenty does his duty by his boy, in this particular. If he does not know how to speak on so delicate and difficult a subject, let him put into his boy's hand a judicious book like "What a Young Boy Ought to Know," one of a series of dollar books by Sylvanus Stall, D. D., of Philadelphia, admirably adapted to meet the needs of parents and teachers, and which has received eminent endorsement everywhere.

Secondly, the curfew ordinance which has been adopted in many western cities with admirable results would throw a shield around the children during the hours of greatest temptation.

Pastor who have seen the working of this ordinance tell me that it has wrought a great reformation where it has been adopted, and city officials are loud in its praise.

If we give our children less libetry and more light, there will be less vice.

JOSIAH STRONG.

New York.

MORE IRISH BULLS.—Two laborers set out from Wexford to walk to Bublin. By the time they reached Bray they were very much tired with their journey, and the more so when they were told they were still twelve miles from Dublin. "Be me sowl," said one, after a little thought, "sure, it's but six miles apiece; let us walk on!" During a discussion at a meeting of the Trinity College Historical Society upon the slight consideration attached to life by uncivilized nations, a speaker mentioned the extraordinary circumstance that in China if a man were condemned to death he could easily hire a substitute to die for him; "and," the debater went on, "I believe many poor fellows get their living by acting as substitutes in that way!"—*London Spectator.*

A Song of the New.

BY MAURICE THOMPSON.

There's a new swell on the sea, and a new light in the sky;
The weather freshens and sings;
A spirit of power hovers on high,
And a waft comes down from its wings.

The old time is no more; its dust is blown away;
Its broken ships went down
In a tidal wave at Manila Bay
And Santiago town.

Oh the ships have shaken the world, and the flag is soaring high
Over isles made suddenly dear
By our dead who died so valiantly,
And our heroes who hold and cheer.

Now the old may dote on the past, and the weak may pule and cry,
And shrink from the change that comes;
But the young and the strong, with their hearts beating high,
Have the pulse of the trumpets and drums.

Their guns have spoken the word, and their trumpets have borne it far
In triumph from shore to shore;
Our flag on the isles where our heroes are
Shall be held there for evermore.

Crawfordsville, Ind.

The Burial of Mr. Gladstone.

LADY HENRY SOMERSET.

In the center of the historic Westminster Hall, bound up with all the associations that have made for the greatness of England, lay the greatest of England's sons in the simple casket made of the oak grown on his own estate by the hands of his own laborers. There was no adornment, nothing to indicate the position of the man who was to be laid to rest—just the plain oak casket, the four burning candles, the gleaming cross—that was Gladstone's resting-place, whence the people came to do him homage. Away across the Thames, over the Westminster Bridge, across Parliament Street and Parliament Square to the courtyard of the House of Commons, the dense crowds stretched, representing all classes of society, from the very poorest to the strong artisan and members of the wealthier classes. They poured in one continuous stream for two days, and in the great halls there reigned absolute silence, save for the constant tramping of feet as they passed, a hundred and twenty a minute, through those long two days.

In the early morning light, on Saturday, May 28, the sunlight shone through the windows of the abbey and touched here and there the historic tombs and marble statues that spoke of the great dead that had rested there for long years. But there was one open grave to which all thoughts were turned, the last resting-place waiting to receive the greatest Englishman of our generation. Already in the gray gloom of choir and chancel, those who were privileged to obtain admittance were beginning to assemble. In little knots the distinguished visitors arrived, foreign ambassadors, the immovable Chinese, the white-haired Russian, the tall Dane. Then a vivid flash of color, and the Lord Mayor, in his robe and chain, walks up the Abbey with his attendants, and as each little group enters, keen interest is manifested by those who are waiting for the supreme event. Suddenly the whole congregation rises, and a hush steals over the crowd, which betokens that this is no ordinary greeting. Presently a tall figure in black, bowed and feeble, leaning on the strong arm of her son, walks up the Abbey. It is Mrs. Gladstone, associated through all these long years as the truest wife and the most devoted woman with whom a great man's life was ever blessed. Behind her walks the little curly-headed girl, who has been the joy of her grandfather's later years, and then in groups the sons and daughters, and as they pass we cannot but remember that amongst all the tributes that can be paid to this great man none, perhaps, is higher than the beautiful example of family life which his home always held out to the nation. By and by comes the Princess of Wales and the Duchess of York, both dressed in deep mourning, and then the silence is broken, and the solemn notes of Beethoven's Funeral March Equale breaks on the air. The slow measure gives place to Schubert's March in B minor, and then the magnificent opening chords of Beethoven's Funeral March, which seems to celebrate the triumph of life rather than to speak to us of the sadness of death. Then two heralds, both in black, arrive, to head the funeral possession, and by and by the long-trained, white-robed choristers and the clergy file past. Following comes the sergeant-at-arms, carrying the mace, the speaker in his robes, surrounded by his different officers, the members of the House of Lords, headed by the Lord Chancellor, the Archbishop of York, then the members of the House of Commons. The organ gives place to the beautiful slow chanting of the choir, and "I am the resurrection ann the life" sounds out, as it always does, the great triumph note that lifts all mourners and tells them that death is swallowed up in victory.

The supreme moment comes when the coffin is borne past, and among the pall-bearers are seen those who have striven against one another in the field of politics—the Marquis of Salisbury and Sir William Vernon Harcourt, Mr. Balfour and Lord Rosebery. All differences are laid aside now, and hands are clasped across those quiet hands folded in eternal prayer. The Prince of Wales and the Duke of York are among those who bear the dead. Slowly the beautiful service goes forward, and by and by the familiar sound of "Rock of Ages" thrills out, and a thousand voices gather up the well-known strains of the great statesman's favorite hymn. Then all is over. The great man has been laid to rest by the nation that loved him. Mrs. Gladstone is seated at the head of the grave, and then the most touching scene came upon that great audience with almost unbearable intensity. The Prince of Wales went toward her, and taking her hand in his, bent low over it and reverently kissed it. All the pall-bearers in turn followed his example, and long she held the hand of her husband's great rival, Lord Salisbuy, as with tenderness the old man paid her his respect.

Gladstone has done many great things; he has stood for the freedom of our country, he has championed the oppressed, he has believed in the good of the many against the privileges of the few; but he has never done anything greater for the home, never anything that spoke more truly of his deep sense of the oneness of the most sacred tie that God ordained, than when he made the stipulation that if the nation buried him, Mrs. Gladstone must rest by his side in Westminster Abbey.

The impression that this great pageant left upon one's mind seemed to me to be one that brought home perhaps more than any other the elementary truths which are the foundation stone of all those great lives, and through the chanting psalm and the sweet refrain of the hymns and the clear voice of the dean as he read those last solemn words, in the benediction of the archbishop—there seemed to me to run one quiet refrain, "The best thing in the world is to be good." Others have been great, others have weilded magnificent power over this great nation, other voices have been eloquent, other patriots have stood for the freedom of humanity, but in Gladstone there is on attribute which stands out pre-eminently—he was good because he loved and reverenced his God.—*Union Signal.*

A Good Weather Receipt.

St. Nicholas gives the following helpful "Weather Receipt," which all grumblers would do well to ponder:

"When if it drizzles and drizzles,
If we cheerfully smile,
We can make the weather,
By working together,
As fair as we choose in a little while.
For who will notice that clouds are drear
If pleasant faces are always near,
And who will remember that skies are gray
If he carries a happy heart all day?"

Castilian Pride and Madness.

AN ENGLISHMAN.

Why is this war prolonged, this deadly strife,
These scenes of carnage and this loss of life,
These moans and cries of wretched, mangled men,
Driven like beasts into a slaughtering pen,
And far from home surrendering their breath
On field of battle meeting bloody death?
For what is Spain contending? Can they hope
With free America in arms to cope?
Ere this can they not learn all hope has flown?
In all their struggles not one victory won.
The pride of all their navy, 'neath the waves,
Where twice a thousand seamen found their graves.
With insane madness why do they contend?
Rush onward to their ruin, to defend
What they call "Spanish honor" — effete pride,
Void of all reason, wisdom's voice denied.
Does honor say, contend unto the last
With every prospect blighted, each hope past,
Consign to fruitless death ten thousand sons,
Change songs, once full of joy, to dying moans?
Does honor bid, defy the lightning stroke,
Or stand on Etna's crater, midst the smoke
And burning lava of volcanic fire,
Curse, and defy, and in the midst expire?
To tread this path is honor's path to miss.
What honor found in folly such as this?
With chaos threatening, this sole hope they have
A feeble, tottering dynasty to save.
That young Alfonso, Christina's son,
May rule, a king, ascend the Spanish throne!
That one may be upraised, must thousands die?
That one may wear a crown, thousands must lie
In unmarked graves, upon a foreign shore;
One heart beat proudly, many to beat no more.
And what is young Alfonso? Just a boy
Like other boys, a mother's hope and joy,
And her ambition is to see him reign,
Crowned king, and sway the scepter over Spain.
That this may be, poor mothers shed a flood
Of tears as their sons shed their blood.
Yet shed in vain, for trembling to a fall
Is throne and dynasty, one ruin threatens all!
Oh, maddened rulers of a once great land,
What defense will ye make when ye shall stand
Before the bar of God, on that great day,
When justice shall be done, what can ye say
When myriads plead against you, show their scars
And gaping wounds, received in bloody wars
Ye forced them to; when all the widows' cries
And orphans' wails, against ye accusing rise?
A dark and bloody trail has marked your path,
A fearful reckoning waits, a day of wrath,
This now remains to you, and this alone,
A tarnished honor and a tottering throne.

—*St. Louis Christian Advocate.*

Some school-boys were asked to define certain words, and to illustrate their meaning.

Here are a few:

Frantic means wild; I picked some frantic flowers.

Athletic, strong; the vinegar was too athletic to use.

Tandem, one behind another; the boys sit tandem at school.

Dust is mud with the wet squeezed out; fins are fishes' wings; circumference is distance around the middle of the outside.

Sunday School.

A Young Man's Vision.*

HERBERT L. WILLETT.

The relations between the courts of Damascus and Samaria varied with the fortunes of the two nations. The Syrians were naturally inclined to warfare, like most people of Semitic stock, and when there was no more serious enterprise on hand they usually stood ready to engage in a struggle with Israel, their nearest neighbor on the west. When left to themselves the Hebrews did not seek war. They were for the most part a peaceful, agricultural people, but capable of stout resistance when beset by an enemy. The periods of war were, therefore, those in which Syria was strong.

In one of these campaigns the king of Syria whose name, as well as that of the reigning king of Israel, is not preserved by the author of the narrative, had planned to station his army at a certain strategic point, probably capable of being used for an ambush against the king of Israel as he came out to battle. The success of the plan depended on its being kept secret from the opposing side, and the utmost care was taken to prevent the movement from being discovered. But the scheme utterly failed. In some mysterious manner the king of Israel seemed to know the location of the hostile camp, and gave no occasion for advantage. This was repeated until the Syrian king was convinced that nothing but treachery in the camp could account for the skillful conduct of his enemy. Some of his trusted officers, he thought, must be secretly supplying information to the Hebrew army. He accordingly called a council of war, and charged his subordinates with the crime, demanding to know who was the guilty man. But these soldiers had learned more than their king of public affairs in the land they were invading, and had heard the marvelous stories that were told regarding the power and might of Elisha. When courts are ignorant of such things, the common people may be well acquainted with them, as we saw last week. It was easy to see that this great prophet who lived in Samaria was spoiling all the plans of the Syrians by his messages to king Jehoram, though the latter had not even known enough of him to think of his help when Naaman came to be healed. Thus the prophet of God was proving, as so often before and since, the safeguard of the nation.

The words he had applied to Elijah (2:12), and which were afterward applied to Elisha himself by King Joash (13:15), were literally true of him now. He was chariots and horsemen to Israel. No army could have been a greater safeguard to the nation than was he. It is a fatal mistake for a people to dream that its strength lives merely in military and naval equipments. Back of all these and greater than they, must be the manhood of the nation, with its trust in God; who must be "Lord of its far-flung battle line," as well as director of its quieter and more secret purposes. It is the supreme danger that God will be forgotten when success perches on the banners of a nation, victorious amid the smoke of battle.

"For heathen heart that puts her trust
In reeking tube and iron shard;
All valiant dust that builds on dust,
And guarding calls not thee to guard;
For frantic boast and foolish word
Thy mercy on thy people, Lord!"

The fact spoken to Benhadad by his officer, that the man of God knew all that passed in his most secret chamber, is in its larger significance the message that needs to be impressed upon every child, and should be borne in mind through life. God's knowledge of us, his perception of all our conduct and purpose, is at once the most blessed and most terryfying of thoughts. It is delightful to one who seeks to fulfill his highest ideals of life. No matter how unappreciated he may be, or how little there may be to show for his effort, there is ample reward in the assurance, "Thou God seest me" (Gen. 16:13). But to the one whose life is a constant defiance to the divine will the thought has terror. There is no evil purpose but what is seen by an eye that never closes, and that looks in sorrow upon the foolish refusal of any man to be led into the light. "Thou God seest me" should be a thought of delight, not dread. Whether or not it is, may be regarded as a true indication of one's relation to God.

Such a man as Elisha must not be left at large. He was too dangerous an opponent; too valuable an ally of the king of Israel. Dothan was learned to be the place of his temporary abode. His pastoral visits as a preacher of rigteousness took him to many places in Israel. Dothan was accordingly invested with a force strong enough to prevent his escape. In the morning his servant, the successor of the avaracious and leprous Gehazi, looked out with consternation upon the Syrian soldiers, who were surrounding the village. Clearly, there was no escape. The prophet was in the hands of his enemies, who would show him small favor, even though he might have claimed the protection to which his kindness to their strongest war-lord entitled him. But Elisha had no thought of pleading for himself, and he was not dismayed. Why should one who is at peace with God, and has done no evil to any man, be afraid? Nothing can injure him. He may suffer the "stings and arrows of outrageous fortune," but he cannot be harmed. Nothing that affects his external life can do him ill. Only things that endanger his relation with God are to be feared. But there was a surer defense than this. The power of God is always at the disposal of his people to serve them. It needs but the open eye to see this vision of providence. The servant saw nothing but the Syrian troops. We too often see only the dangers which threaten our cherished plans, and do no not have eyes that "look unto the hills from whence cometh our help." One needs to have his eyes opened, and to look upward. We are continually the victims of unnecessary fear. We do not believe God will keep us. Yet his message to his peopel has been evermore, "Fear not." There is no element in life more destructive than fear. We fear disease, and we are ill, not infrequently because our mental condition has invited it. We fear disaster, and we prepare the way for it to come. Who shall say how much of our sickness and trouble comes because we have fancied they *might* come, or probably *would* come, and have permitted ourselves unconsciously to assume an attitude of expectancy and invitation? Against all this the message of God is, "Fear not." The Bible is the most optimistic book in the world. Its word is, "Expect health, not disease; expect success, not failure; expect righteousness, not sin." It is the business of the Bible to open our eyes as did the prophet those of the young man, that we may see the mountains round about full of the horses and chariots of God. The gospel has no place for pessimism. It gives no bases for the theologies of despair—Romanism, Tractarianism, Millenarianism. Its message is rather, "Open your eyes, look to the hills, fear not."

The prophet was in no danger, but he proposed to use the Syrians as his captives till he could show his spirit toward them. He threw over them the spell of bewilderwment, and under the offer of guidance led them to Samaria, the capital, where they were completely at the mercy of the king of Israel. But when Jehoram wanted to use his advantage to put them to death, Elisha forbade him, and ordering them to be fed, he sent them back, humbled and astonished, to their own land.

SUGGESTIONS FOR TEACHING.

The king of Israel showed his wisdom by heeding good advice. All hearts are open to God; no secrets are hid from him. "Thou God seest me" is a word of cheer to those who love him, but of terror to those who do wrong. "Fear not" is the word of God to his children. "Perfect love casts out fear;" therefore to love God and our fellowmen is the secret of being at peace with all, and having no fear. Horses and chariots were no means of capturing Elisha; he may well represent those forces for good which cannot be destroyed. God and one man who is godlike and on the right side are a majority, and have only to wait till the rest comes over. The Christian life is the process of getting one's eyes opened to see the horses and chariots of God. "They that are for us ara more than they that are against us." Elisha exemplified the true spirit of kindness when he only used his power over the Syrians to do them good.

*Bible-School Lesson for Aug. 28—Elisha at Dothan (2 Kings 6:8-18); Golden Text—The Angel of the Lord encampeth round about them that fear him, and delivereth them (Psalms 34:7); Lesson Outline—1. The Prophet's Power (9-12); 2. The Prophet's Peril (13-15); 3. The Prophet's Protection (16-18).

Preachers Should Tell their People.

Every preacher should tell his people, and especially the young, all about the Bethany C. E. Reading Courses. Full information may be had gratis, by dropping a card to the Bethany C. E. Company, 798 Republic Street, Cleveland, O. Begin at once to plan for systematic reading among the people of your church.

Christian Endeavor.

By Burris A. Jenkins.

TOPIC FOR AUGUST 28.

"WITH YOUR MIGHT."

(Eccles. 9:10; Jno. 4:27-35.)

ıere is a great deal of our nature that never been developed. There is a vast deal of ht hidden away in every man that is like w land, never plowed and utilized. We talked so much, both sincerely and inərely, about our "mite" that we have otten our *might*. Until one gets an adee idea of his own power, even the average of us, he will never do the work he is ble of doing. Man has never learned what werful creature he is. Small as he is, he is e powerful than beasts, ocean, lightnings, anoes, for he has made ali of these his ants. Only ordinary men they are, too, are powerful enough for this. If men of monplace powers would but learn their h and exercise it, the world would see ter prodigies than it has ever seen.

pon every duty that comes to hand one's le soul should be centered. Close attento the present task is the test of success. , that is the word—*tension*. Attention teacher demands. Attention the employer t have from every employee. Tension the ician must have—just the proper tension—ery string. All these are the same thing, as they are expressed by the same word. must be tense, if it gives forth beautiful, nonious music. It must be stretched tight t *too* tight, lest it snap into fanaticism or nity, but just tight enough to be harmoniand tuneful. Every power should be aoniously called into play, every muscle ind and soul employed. Our work should ays seem to us, as we view it lying before just a trifle greater than we are able to form; for we shall find, when we shoulder :hat though it may strain every nerve, it snap none of them.

o-day's duties, too, are the ones that uld be done with our might. It is not to-rrow that our work is to be done. It is not the ıg of great things by and by, but of everyıg that confronts us to-day, that the Lord ıands of us. "Do ye next thing," was the English motto. "Live for to-day," is an ellent motto for to-day. We are so inclined ive in the future—especially we young peo—so inclined to feel that we haven't really ered life yet; that we are only waiting our ortunity, preparing ourselves for great ts; that some day we shall serve God, but to-day; that some day we shall find time to y and be religious, but there's no particular ry; so inclined, we are, to let a beautiful ıre, like a mirage, beckon us on past unilled duties. Ah, when shall we learn that s *this* life that we are living, and not the t; that it is to-day's duties we are concerned h and not to-morrow's rewards; that it is e and now we are to do with our might ıt our hands find to do, for in the grave, ther we go, there is no work, wisdom, wledge or device!

! we once learn to center our full energies what we have at present to do, we shall l it will give us courage and spirit to meet ills of life. Melancholy and unhappiness from before busy hands as ghosts before signs of the cross. Weakness becomes ıngth, fear becomes courage, fainting beıes fighting when even the most trembling l hurls itself with all its unconscious power ın its appointed work. The very exertion omes meat to eat that we know not of—ıt of joy and meat of increasing strength. more might we expend the more we gain; more we give out the more we get. There :hat scattereth and yet increaseth—and it ıight.

FACTS AND FACTORS.

The first American bank in Cuba was opened in Santiago, August 8th.

The Pope has issued an encyclical protesting against the suppression of Catholic journals during the recent insurrection in Rome.

Adolph Sutrs, former mayor of San Francisco, died Aug. 8th, leaving an estate valued at $4,000,000.

George Ebers, a famous German novelist and Egyptologist, died at Muncice, Bavaria, Aug. 8th.

Consul Walker estimates the 1897 import into Manila at $16,000,000, of which about one-half was of Spanish origin, the imports from other countries having materially fallen off in 1897, while those of Spain increased largely. The exports from Manila have, he say, increased in the past year in several of the trading articles, notably tobacco, hemp and copra, the dried kernel of the cocoanut, the value of which alone he estimates at $45,000,000, while he estimates the sugar crop at $13,000,000 and hemp at $14,000,000. He makes no estimate of the tobacco exports, but says they were larger in 1897 than in former years.

Mr. Moody is said to have already received over $2,500,000 in royalties for the Gospel Hymns and Tunes, published by him in conjunction with Mr. Sankey.

Since 1804 the American Bibe Society has issued and distributed through its agencies alone over 274,900,000 Bibles, Testaments and portions of Scriptures.

The Bureau of Education has recently reported that there are 103,785 Sunday-schools in the United States, 956,142 officers and teachers and 8,747,859 scholars.

Buffalo is to make the experiment of voting machines next fall by puting one in each ward as a test. If satisfactory they may be used in every precinct hereafter.

The Earl of Minto has been appointed Governor-General of Canada, to succeed the Earl of Aberdeen.

Artificial teeth are now being made of paper in Germany.

Mrs. Emmons Blaine has given the University of Chicago $25,000 with which to establish in the down-town district of the city a branch of the University for the higher education of public school-teachers. It is an experiment that is to be tried for five years. If it proves successful provisions will be made for its continuance.

The great Broadway cable-car line, New York City, is to be converted into a trolley electric line.

The value of church property in the United States is estimated to be $670,000,000.

It is estimated that since the birth of Christ 4,000,000,000 men have been slain in battle.

It is claimed that at the present the English language is spoken by 116,000,000 people.

The following figures represent the wealth of the leading nations of the world: United States, $81,750,000,000; Great Britain, $59,030,000,000; France, 47,950,000,000; Germany, $40,260,000,000; Russia, $32,125.000,000, Austria, $22,560,000,000; Italy, $15,800,000,000; Spain, $11,300,000,000.

Marriages.

COLLINS—NEAL.—At the home of the bride, near Salem Church, Nodaway County, Mo., Aug. 3, 1898, John Collins to Edna Neal; F. E. Blanchard officiating. Both are members of the church.

Obituaries.

[One hundred words will be inserted free. Above one hundred words, one cent a word. Please send amount with each notice.]

ROWLEY.

Sister Jane E. Rowley, who had long been a patient sufferer, passed into the life beyond at her home near Fortuna, Humboldt county, Cal., July 27, 1898. The deceased was for many years a member of the Presbyterian Church, but in 1894 she united with the Christian Church, of which the majority of her family were members. Besides her bereaved husband she left eight children, a mother 83 years of age, two sisters, four brothers and 24 grandchildren, who were all present except three. Funeral services were conducted at the Christian Church by the writer, and the remains were placed in the cemetery of the I. O. O. F., to which they were followed by a large circle of friends. A. B. Markle.

Fortuna, Cal., Aug. 1, 1898.

ROYAL.

Joseph B. Royal was born Nov. 1, 1816, near Columbus, in Franklin county, Ohio. He died at his home in Vermont, Ill., July 27, 1898, aged eighty-one years, eight months and twenty-six days. He went with his father's family in his childhood to Sangamon county, Ill., where he experienced all the privations of pioneer life. He was married there to Miss Louisa Downing August 19, 1841. She died in Vermont, Ill., January 8, 1853. He subsequently married Mrs. Elsie McHendry, who died four years ago. Four children, a step-daughter, an adopted daughter, sixteen grandchildren and six great-grandchildren survive him.

He was a patriotic citizen, a faithful, loving husband, an affectionate father; bringing up his children in the nurture and admonition of the Lord. He was honest, truthful, temperate, virtuous, benevolent and a doer of good all the days of his long life. All the above is said, and more could be said in truth of the man Joseph B. Royal. But I wish to speak of him as a preacher of the gospel. He obeyed the Lord in early life and became a preacher before the beginning of the writer's personal acquaintance with him. But I was intimately acquainted with him for more than forty years. The remembrance of that acquaintance is very precious to me now. We were friends; yea, we were more than friends—we were brothers, brothers in the Lord, brothers knit together in the bonds of Christian love. In all those more than forty years there was never an unkind act, word or even thought between us. Memory recalls nothing to mar the sweetness of those long years of friendship and love. Brother Royal was a great preacher. Yet he never thought of greatness. He simply knew the Englinsh language and the English Bible. But he knew them well. Jesus had a dwelling-place in his heart. The love of God abounded there. His soul was full of the Holy Spirit. With all his heart he himself believed all that he preached, and he had a wonderful faculty of convincing his hearers of the truth of the gospel. Many hundreds of the people did he lead to obey the Lord and to consecrate their lives to his service. He did the work of an evangelist. Yet he was not an evangelist of the more modern style, with his hired singer. He induced the people all to sing, and led them himself, if it was necessary. He did not get up a great excitement. But by his plain, common-sense, scriptural presentation of the truth, and by the purity of his own life, he led the people, without excitement, to render an intelligent obedience to the Lord. He was a man who, without seeming to know it, did let his light shine and others were thereby constrained to glorify God. Good men, bad men, all men who knew him, and he was extensively known, said that Royal was a good man. He not only led sinners to come to the Savior; he also instructed the brethren, building them up in the faith. He was a safe and wise counselor. He was a peacemaker. He was a good pastor. He planted many churches; but he did not leave them to die. He taught them, encouraged them, exhorted them, made them self-sustaining. There are many churches in Illinois that are monuments of his earnest, self-sacrificing toil. He did all this work for only small pecuniary reward. He never received a big salary in his life. He never had more than a bare competence of this world's goods. But he was rich in faith, rich in spirit, rich in heirship, and now rich in the society of the spirits of just men made perfect. Though dead, he yet speaks, and will continue to speak for generations to come. To his surviving sons, G. A. and Eugene Royal, and his daughters, Mrs. J. M. Little and Mrs. M. R. Burton, we say, Be comforted. Your father's name and godly life are a richer legacy than gold. Be as true to the Christ as he was true, and you will be crowned with him in glory. And now, my well-beloved brother, farewell for a season, only for a little while! I am in tears now. I am sad now. I will look no more, in the flesh, upon your honest face. I will no more hear your loving voice pleading with sinners to come to the Savior. I think few men, if any, loved you more than I loved you. I love you still. My affection for you is as warm as it ever was. You are not dead. To me you are living. The earthly body only is dead. You have only gone before me for a little while, dear brother! By the grace of God I am determined to "meet you in the New Jerusalem." J. C. Reynolds.

TUSSING.

Mary A. Portner was born in Fredric County Md., December 15, 1817. Was married to Isaac P. Tussing, Oct. 29, 1835. She was the mother of 14 children—eight of them with one brother survive her. She came with husband and family about 30 years ago to Neosho County, Kas., where she died August 1, 1898. She became a Christian about 19 years ago; was baptized by Bro. John W. Randall. She continued faithful until the last. We sorrow, but with hope. Many relatives and friends followed the remains to their rest in the grave at Bethany. Sermon text, 2 Cor. 5:1-4, by the writer.

C. C. Deweese.

WILLETT.

Gordon A. Willett was born in Onondago, N. Y., Aug. 23, 1835, and died in Petoskey, Mich., July 18, 1898. He came to Michigan in 1854. Was baptized by Isaac Errett in Muir in 1860. January 16, 1862, he was married to Mary E. Yates. To them were born four sons, Prof. Herbert L., who has charge of the Disciples' Divinity House in connection with the Chicago University, Arthur, pastor of the Church of Christ in Petoskey, Mich., and two who preceded their father to the spirit-land. He came to Ionia in 1867, where he was engaged in the agricultural business for about 20 years. In the spring of 1895 he went to Chicago to assist his son in the pastoral work of the Hyde Park church, and the following fall was ordained to the ministry. He was his son's assistant for about two years. During the past he has been in failing health, and during the last few months has suffered untold pain, but was patient through it all, and his faith never failed. Bro. Willett has always taken great interest in the enterprises of the church and often attended the missionary conventions. He has visited nearly every church in Michigan. Long before the C. W. B. M. established the Bible chairs at Ann Arbor he insisted that such steps should be taken. He put forth every effort to educate his sons for the ministry, and during his last illness the fact that two of them were devoting all of their time to teaching and preaching the gospel of Christ, was a great comfort to him. When he realized that he must pass away, he looked forward with pleasure to the reünion with the two sons who had gone before him. One died in infancy, the other at the beginning of manhood, when he was ready to devote his life to the ministry. On July 20 Bro. Willett's remains arrived here from Petoskey. Brief funeral services were conducted by the writer, assisted by Bro. C. A. Preston and Dr. Cope, both old friends of the deceased. The burial took place at North Plains, 10 miles from here.

Dr. Cope said at the funeral that Bro. Willett lived in advance of his age, that Ionia was the better for his having lived in it and that "well done thou good and faithful servant" might be written as his epitaph. Bro. C. A. Preston read a short address, from which we quote the following:

"I have been acquainted with him 35 years. For very many years our relations were intimate, and during that time I can truthfully say that I never saw an act of his or a spoken word unbecoming a Christian gentleman. For many years he was an elder of this church and I think gave more time and attention to its duties than any one before or since. He greatly excelled in one of the conditions prescribed as a qualification for the position: he was given to hospitality. His home was the home of nearly every visiting minister or lay member of the churches of Christ. He was very familiar with our people throughout the United States; he could tell the standing, the character and ability of the leading Disciple preachers in the Union. His knowledge of the Scriptures far excelled that of any member of the Ionia church. He studied the Scripture, not merely read it, and to all of us he was authority on Bible history, prophecy and facts, and as a Bible-class teacher he was always prepared and was always instructive. During the past four years it has been my good fortune to visit in district conventions nearly all our churches in this district. I was surprised and pleased at the general manifestations of interest and affection for Bro. Gordon Willett. He was acquainted with nearly every Disciple in this part of Michigan and during his long illness he had their prayers and sympathies.

"Bro. Willett, thou are gone! We will not deplore thee. Your works will follow after. The sons you helped to educate and prepare for the ministry are living monuments to your credit. The good they have done and are doing we cannot measure, but in their heart of hearts they will thank you over and over again. We who knew you best and appreciated your worth will see you here no more. We will remember you on warm and cold days. Your days of sickness and pain are over."

"You have heard the song of triumph
They sang upon that shore,
Saying Jesus has redeemed you
To suffer nevermore;
Then, casting your eyes backward
On the race which you have run,
You can shout, Hosanna!
Deliverance has come."

G. K. Berry.

Ionia, Mich., Aug. 3.

WRIGHT.

Henry Wrigh was born in Washington couuty, Ind., Oct. 12, 1820, and died at his home in Stiles, Ia., May 30, 1898. In 1840 Bro. Wright married Sarah Letherman, who proved a faithful companion to him during the 55 years of their wedded life. To them 14 children were born, six of whom survive them. In 1849 Bro. Wright moved from Indiana to Davis county, Ia., where he resided until his death. For many years he had been a faithful minister of the gospel, and as a pioneer preacher his influence has been widely felt. At his funeral Bro. S. B. Downing, of Bloomfield, an old friend and fellow-worker, officiated. L. C. Swann.

Announcements.

Northeast Kansas.

Churches in Northeast Kansas needing a pastor for one-half time will do well to write at once Bro. L. S. Ridenour, Highland, Kas. Bro. Ridenour gives one-half his time. He does not just preach twice two Sundays of the month and call it half the time.

JOHN L. STINE.

Reserve, Kas., Aug. 9, 1898.

A Basket Meeting.

An old-fashioned, all-day, basket meeting will be held of all churches in Tipton county, August 28th, on grounds of Hoosier State Sanitarium. Bro. L. E. Brown, of Frankfort, will be chief speaker. Any and all Disciples who can attend are invited.

E. A. COLE, Pastor Tipton Church.

Tipton, Ind.

Kansas Convention.

The Third District Christian Missionary Convention, of Kansas, meets at Cherryvale, August 30th to September 1st. A program of good things is in store for those who attend. For entertainment write to Dr. J. A. DEMOSS, 3rd Dist. Sec.

Cherryvale, Kan.

"Egypt."

Brethren in "Egypt" who desire to engage for one or more revival meetings should send in their names to the undersigned, as he purposes to visit each county in the S. I. C. M. C., and arrange for meetings wherever feasible. Our purpose is to engage the labors of the brethren who are contiguous to the locality where meetings are to be held.

Send your addresses to W. BEDALL, Cor. Sec.

Flora, Ill.

Louisiana Convention.

The second annual convention of the Disciples of Louisiana will convene at Cherryville, September 1-3. One and one-third rate on all roads in the state, certificate plan. Write J. B. Cole, Cherryville, La., that you will attend.

CLAUDE L. JONES, State Evangelist.

Program

Of conventions to be held in New York City, August 30th to September 2nd, inclusive, at the 169th Street Church of Christ.

MINISTERIAL ASSOCIATION.

TUESDAY MORNING, AUGUST 30.

9:00—Devotional, E. S. Muckley.
President's Address, S. B. Culp.
"The Preacher's Personal Preparation," F. P. Arthur.
"Perils of a Modern Preacher," D. H. Patterson.
"Modern Books of Value to Preachers," F. W. Norton.
Discussion.

TUESDAY AFTERNOON.

2:00—Devotional, Wallace C. Payne.
"How Best to Evangelize our Cities," E. R. Edwards.
Conference on Pastor's Work, J. M. Morris.
Business session.
"The Work of the Brotherhood of Andrew and Philip."
An Open Parliament, "How to Reach the Unsaved. Methods," Lowell C. McPherson.

TUESDAY EVENING.

7:30—Song Service.
Sermon, B. Q. Denham.

NEW YORK CHRISTIAN MISSIONARY SOCIETY.

FORENOON, AUGUST 31.

9:00—Devotional Service, led by W. A. Belding.
Formal Opening of Convention by President.
Address, "Our Convention Keynote," J. M. Morris.
Business.
Reports of Sunday-school Committee, Y. P. S. C. E. Committee, Junior C. E. Superintendent, Haven's Home, State Evangelist, State Treasurer and Corresponding Secretary.
President's Address.
Announcements.

AFTERNOON, AUGUST 31.

2:00—Devotional Service, led by B. A. Bower.
Sunday-school hour:
Address on S. S. Work, followed by an Open Parliament.
Christian Endeavor hour:
C. E. Address, "Practical Endeavoring," by R. H. Miller.
Free Parliament: "Needs of Our State Work and How to Supply Them," led by J. M. Morris, State Evangelist.
Announcements.

EVENING, AUGUST 31.

7:45—Devotional Service, led by S. B. Culp.
Address: "What Our Sunday-schools can do to Promote our State Work," by C. M. Kreidler, Chairman S. S. Committee.
Address, Peter Ainslie, Baltimore.

FORENOON, SEPTEMBER 1.

9:00—Devotional Service, led by C. E. Smootz.
Reports from mission points: Watertown, E. S. Muckley, pastor; Elmira, C. C. Crawford, pastor; Rochester, Second Church, J. R. Tabor, Jr., pastor.
Business—Reports of Committees, etc.
Address, "Foreign Missions," A. McLean or F. M. Rains.
Announcements.

AFTERNOON, SEPTEMBER 1.

2:00—Devotional Service, led by Jos. Cost.
Address, E. R. Edwards.
Business.
Address, "The Preaching for the Times," W. C. Payne.
Business session.
Address, J. R. Toler, Jr.
Announcements. Adjournment.

EVENING, SEPTEMBER 1.

7:45—Devotional Service, led by D. H. Patterson.
Address, "What Endeavorers can do to Further our State Work," by F. P. Arthur, Chairman C. E. Committee.
Address, E. J. Teagarden, Danbury, Conn.

FORENOON, SEPTREMBER 2.

Devotional Service, led by Robt. Christie.
Business, Reports of Committees, etc.
Address, "Home Missions," C. C. Smith or B. L. Smith.
Business, Reports of Committees, etc.
Address, "Christ's Invincible Church," Roland Nichols, Worcester, Mass.
Closing remarks and final adjournment of convention by the president.

C. W. B. M. SESSION.

AFTERNOON, SEPTEMBER 2.

Service of Prayer and Praise.
Greetings.
Reports of Secretary and Treasurer.
Report of Junior Superintendent.
"Practical Points," Mrs. R. C. Belding.
Paper, "Mahoba," Mrs. K. G. Grove.
Paper, "The Initiative," Mrs. W. C. Payne.
Exercise by children.

EVENING, SEPTENBER 2.

Devotional.
Reports of Committees.
Address, by Mrs. Helen E. Moses, National Superintendent Bible Chairs.

Suggestive Program for the Indiana District Conventions.

The purpose was to curtail the length of the fall conventions, but at the urgent request of the districts themselves, they have been set again at the regular length. However, as the program is only suggestive, the district boards will exercise their own judgment in the matter, as well as the whole program.

The odd-numbered districts hold their conventions the first half of the week, and the even-numbered districts hold theirs the last half. There will be a break of two weeks in October for the National Convention at Chattanooga.

The sermons for the evenings should be preached by some of the strong men of the district, while strength has been added to the program by such brethren as W. D. Starr, Henry R. Pritchard and D. R. Lucas.

This is the annual meeting, and it is the place where the business of the district must be adjusted for the year. Let every department of every church be represented. May your state board suggest that this is but one convention and not four, and that the district president should preside at all sessions, and the district secretary take all minutes, with the possible exception of the C. W. B. M. work.

PROGRAM FOR FALL C. E. SESSION DISTRICT CONVENTION.

FIRST DAY—AFTERNOON.

2:00—Devotional.
2:10—Symposium on "Our Responsibilities."
(a) For the organization of new societies.
(b) For the reorganization of old ones.
(c) For the enlistment of new members.
(d) For the development and training of old ones.
(e) For Good Literature.
(f) For Christian Citizenship. Each speak limited to five minutes.
3:00—Reports from societies and district superi tedent.
3:30—The Bethany Reading Circle.
3:40—The Quiet Hour.
3:50—The Tenth Legion.
4:00—Appointment of Committees and adjour ment.

EVENING.

7:00—Praise service.
7:15—Open Parliament—Our needs in C. E. work
7:45—Address by State Superintenent.
8:15—Consecration Service.

SECOND DAY—MORNING.

MISSIONARY.

9:00—Devotional, led by —— ——.
9:15—Report of District Secretaries and Treas.
9:30—Reports of County Secretaries.
9:45—Address of District President.
10:15—Address, State Cor. Sec., T. J. Legg.
10:35—Recess.
10:45—Our Associated Interests, W.D. Star, Munc
11:30—Appointment of Committees. Song. Noon Recess.

SECOND DAY—AFTERNOON.

SUNDAY-SCHOOL.

2:00—Devotional, led by —— ——.
2:10—The International Lessons, July to Janua Used in the Christian Dispensation, by— ——.
2:40—Written Reports of Schools; Number of (officers, (b) teachers, (c) classes, (d) p pils, (e) average attendance, (f) amou paid to our own State S. S. work, (g) other Missions.
3:10—(a) Points where Schools could be organize
(b) Points that need help, by —— ——.
3:20—Open Parliament; (a) Our weak points a our difficulties, led by —— ——.
(b) Our successes and what produced the led by —— ——.
4:00—Address, T. J. Legg.
4:10—Miscellaneous and Adjournment.

EVENING.

7:30—Devotional, led by —— ——.
7:45—"Amalgamated Programs," led by —— ——.
8:00—Sermon, by —— ——.

THIRD DAY—MORNING.

MISSIONARY.

9:00—Devotional, led by —— ——.
9:15—Reports of Committees.
9:45—Our District Canvass in October, by —— —
10:00—Address, Henry R. Pritchard
10:50—Ministerial Relief, D. R. Lucas.
11:40—Miscellaneous, Adjournment.

THIRD DAY—AFTERNOON.

C. W. B. M.

2:00—Devotional Services.
2:20—Annual Report of Auxiliaries.
2:40—Paper—Soul-winning.
3:00—Discussion.
3:15—Recess for Acquaintance.
3:30—Paper—Lent unto the Lord. Discussion.
4:00—Adjournment.

EVENING.

7:30—Exercise by Children.
8:00—C. W. B. M. Sermon.

SCHEDULE OF DISTRICT CONVENTIONS.

1. Hamilton, Sept. 5-7.
2. Lowell, Sept. 7-9.
3. Fowler, Sept. 12-14.
4. Windfall, Sept. 14-16.
5. Markle, Sept. 16-19.
6. Greenfork, Sept. 21-23.
7. ————, Sept. 26-28.
8. Dana, Sept. 28-30.
9. Shelbyville, Oct. 3-6.
10. Madison, Oct. 5-7.
11. Burnsville, Oct. 24-26.
12. Odon, Oct. 26-28.
13. Gentryville, Oct. 31 to Nov. 2.
14. New Albany, (Central) Nov. 2-4.

T. J. LEGG, Corresponding Secretary

THE CHRISTIAN-EVANGELIST.

A WEEKLY FAMILY AND RELIGIOUS JOURNAL.

XXXV. August 25, 1898 No. 34.

CONTENTS.

ɪAL:
ɪnt Events....227
War is Over....228
Revised Version on the Friendship
t....228
ruit of the Spirit....229
r's Easy Chair....230
ions and Answers....231
ɪnt Religious Thought....231

ɪL CONTRIBUTIONS:
ons in the Old Testament Proph-
.—G. A. Peckham....232
atopsis.—C. J. Kimball....233
Good is the Enemy of the Best.—
). T. Smith....234

PONDENCE:
ling Through England....239
York Letter....240
Chicago Letter....240
Letter....241
as City Letter....242
Bethany C. E. Reading Courses....242

CIRCLE:
'ading Summer (poem)....248
Quiet Hour....248
's Rabbit....249
On (poem)....250
Stories....250
I Live for (poem)....251
r Can't....251
Floors in Summer....251

LANEOUS:
Religious World....235
Budget....236
nal Mention....238
and News....243
gelistic....245
onary....246
ature....251
Sunday-school....252
tian Endeavor....253
and Factors....253
iages and Obituaries....254
uncements....256
shers' Notes....256

Subscription $1.75.

HIDDEN.

AARON PRINCE ATEN.

The treasures of the earth are deeply hid
Down in the depths, or the waters mid.
The golden seams that to men appear
Are the earnest of wealth that is not here.
Down, far down do the treasures lie
Beneath where the picks of the miners ply.
We can gather only the grains of gold,
While the mountains of metal are yet untold.
The diamond that glows with a flash of fire
And kindles the spark of a deep desire,
Is only one from a cave filled deep
Far down where the swirling waters sweep.
So human thought, though a treasure rare,
Is only a grain that is flashing fair—
A grain of gold from celestial source
That is stranded here in its onward course.
The love that stirs in the finite deep
Far away from the infinite fountain's sweep,
Is only a drop that descends to earth
To tell of its Author's wondrous worth.
And, too, this being that boasts its might,
And feels the flowing of earth's delight,
Is the offspring small of the glorious One,
Whose dwelling place is the Central Sun.

Hutchinson, Kansas.

PUBLISHED BY

CHRISTIAN PUBLISHING COMPANY

1522 Locust St., St. Louis.

EDUCATIONAL.

RANDOLPH-MACON Academy for Boys

Front Royal, Va. (Valley of Va.). Conducted by Randolph-Macon College. Best equipped in the South. Ranks with best in U. S. Modern conveniences and appliances; gymnasium, &c. $230. Address
Wm. W. Smith, A. M., LL. D, Principal.

ACADEMY For YOUNG WOMEN 69th Year

High grade English and Classical School. Literary, Music, Art courses. Certificate admits to Eastern colleges for Women. Correspondence solicited. For catalog address, E. F. BULLARD, A. M., Pres., Jacksonville, Ill.

For Christian Education go to

Christian University,

CANTON, MO.

Classical, Scientific, Ministerial, Musical and Commercial. **For Ladies and Gentlemen.**

MARY BALDWIN SEMINARY

FOR YOUNG LADIES.

STAUNTON, VIRGINIA.

Term begins Sept. 1st, 1898. Located in Shenandoah Valley of Virginia. Unsurpassed climate, grounds and appointments. 20 States represented. Terms moderate. Pupils enter any time. Write for Catalogue.
Mary Baldwin Seminary.

HARDIN COLLEGE & CONSERVATORY

FOR LADIES.

28th year. Unprecedented prosperity. 24 Professors from 8 Universities and 5 European Conservatories. A $1,000 Piano to best music pupil. German-American Conservatory. XAVER SCHARWENKA, Director General, present in person during May. Largest. Cheapest. Best. Address
JOHN W. MILLION, Pres., 28 (A St.), Mexico, Mo

BUNKER HILL MILITARY ACADEMY,

BUNKER HILL, ILL.

A superior home and school for boys of any school age. Every equipment; College or Business. Catalogue and Book of Views on application.
COL. S. L. STIVER, A.M., B.D., Supt.

Washington College.

(Young Ladies)

3rd & T Sts., N. E., Washington, D. C.

Charming park of ten acres, overlooking Capitol; lovely building, beautiful rooms, elegant furnishings, good table, thorough instruction. The unrivaled educational and social advantages of the National Capital utilized in full. Schools of Music, Art and Elocution of the highest order. Rooms limited.
F. MENEFEE, President.

The Woman's College

of Baltimore

offers **earnest, well prepared young women facilities** for obtaining **a college education** under the direction **of specialists**, with abundant laboratory appliances and modern methods. Climate mild, surroundings cheerful. Total yearly expense, three hundred and seventy-five dollars.

Programs mailed on application.
JOHN F. GOUCHER, Pres., Baltimore, Md.

Conservatory Life

Is most healthful and delightful. The teachers are masters; the students are enthusiasts. Everything in the equipment and environment of the

New England CONSERVATORY OF MUSIC

tends to encourage high ideals and a devotion to art.

GEORGE W. CHADWICK, Musical Director.
Send for our Catalogue to
FRANK W. HALE, General Manager, Boston, Mass.

WOODLAND

Independence, Mo.

Easy of access; moderate expense; all departments. For catalogue address,
Geo. S. Bryant, Pres.

Randolph-Macon Woman's Colleg

Lynchburg, Va. Classed by U. S. Commissic of Education in "Division A" as one of the fourt first-grade colleges for women in the U. S. modern appliances. Endowment reduces cost course to $250. Address,
WM. W. SMITH, M. A., LL. D., Presiden

BETHANY COLLEGE.

Founded in 1841 by Alexander Campbell. Open to men and women. Classical, Scientific, Ministerial, Literary, Musical and Art Courses. A Lecture Association, a fully equipped Gymnasium, Literary and Reading Room. Post office, Bethany, W. Va. Railway station, Wellsburg, W. Va., on the Pan-Handle Road, reached from Pittsburg, Steubenville or Wheeling. For catalogue and particulars, address the Secretary.

KENTUCKY UNIVERSITY

R. LIN. CAVE, Prest. LEXINGTON, K

Liberal Arts, Bible, Medical and Commercial Colleges.

Tuition for Literary $22, and Bible Course $20 a year. More than twenty teachers. $10,000 gymnasi Thousands of successful alumni. Welfare of students receive special attention. Open to both se Nearly 1000 students last year. Session begins second Monday in Sept.
Send to Pres. Cave or J. W. McGarvey for catalogue.

AMERICAN MOZART CONSERVATORY OF MUSIC AND FINE ARTS

ANNEX TO

LIBERTY LADIES' COLLEGE. CHARTERED BY THE STATE.

Methods and Courses of Instruction same as those of Royal Conservatory of Music, Berlin, Germany. Royal Conservatory of Music, Leipzig, Germany. Royal Academy of Music, London, England. Professors full graduates with highest honors from these Conservatories.

AN UPRIGHT CONCERT GRAND PIANO, quoted by Bradbury at $1050, and other prizes at May Festival. Address **Liberty Ladies' College, Liberty, Mo.**

EUREKA COLLEGE

POINTS TO ☞

FIFTY YEARS OF SUCCESSFUL HISTORY

As a justification of the invitation she hereby sends out to the Young Men and Women of America to seek their Training for Life's Work under Her nourishing care.

Location unsurpassed for Good Morals, Health and Economy.
Courses of Study cover all requirements.
Faculty Strong and Enthusiastic.
Fall Term begins Sept. 13, 1898.
For Catalogue and all particulars address,
Pres. J. H. HARDIN, Eureka, Ill.

Christian Orphan School of Missou

Located at Fulton.

FOUNDED BY J. H. GARRISON, T. P. HALEY, A. JONES, A. R. PROCTOR, AND OTHERS.

Buildings and appointments complete. Enrollm last session One Hundred Boarders. Course of study equal to best for Young Ladies. Music, Art, Elocution, taught by skilled teachers.

J. B. JONES, Principal.
U. I. QUIGLEY, Solicitor.

Next Session begins September 1, 18

DRAKE UNIVERSITY

DES MOINES, IOWA.

1. College of Letters and Science. 2. College of the Bible. 3. The Iowa College of Law. 4. The Io College of Physicians and Surgeons. 5. The College of Pharmacy. 6. The Normal School and Acade The Drake Business College. 7. The School of Oratory. 8. The School of Art. 9. The School of Music. The Drake Summer Schools of Methods. The location is the best in the state. The University equipmen reinforced by all the resources of the city. No other school in Iowa has made such rapid and substan growth. The last year was the most successful in its history. Next year will be better. Wake up to the f that the best educational advantages in Iowa are right here at your door. 136 received diplomas at the l commencement. No effort will be spared to meet the needs and best interests of the student entering an the above departments. Send for catalogue.

Drake University. Wm. Bayard Craig, Chancellor.

ISTIAN-EVANGELIST

opinion and methods, Liberty; in all things, Charity."

s, Mo., Thursday, August 25, 1898. No. 34

with the outgoing of the Spanish forces, and the incoming of the American troops. It is the purpose of the Washington authorities to send a sufficient force into these islands to maintain order as early as possible. The hatred that exists between the Spanish and the Cubans, growing out of the protracted war, and the mutual indignities they have suffered from each other, makes it imperative for the time heing that the government of the United States should interpose its strong arm between these peoples in the interest of peace and good order. It is very short-sighted and unwise for the Cubans to exhibit impatience with or opposition to this policy on the part of our government. The military commissions appointed by the Pressident will proceed at once to Havana and San Juan to exert their influence in the interest of peace and order.

The double duty of getting the Spanish prisoners shipped home from Cuba, and our own soldiers away from Santiago to Long Island, has been carried out as promptly as transportation facilities would permit, and is now about accomplished. It is a relief to know that our soldiers who exhibited such high courage in the battles about Santiago, and who survived those terrible assaults, are to have a chance for their lives by being removed from the fever-stricken island to a healthy location. It is a relief, too, to know that the Spanish soldiers who surrendered at Santiago are soon to be home again with their families and friends. No doubt a large part of our volunteer force will be mustered out of the service, and the brave men who donned the military uniform to defend their country's flag, will resume their peaceful callings again as if there had been no war with Spain. Our chief reliance in the future for our nation's defense is our citizen soldiery, who in a few weeks can be transformed from peaceful citizens into a volunteer army, drilled and equipped for efficient service.

It is to be regretted that Captain-General Blanco has not justified the good opinion which the Americans had of him when he succeeded Weyler in Cuba. His recent resignation as captain-general of the island because of the treaty of peace, and his bombastic proclamation about continuing the war, puts him in a very bad light before the civilized world. At a time when he could be of some service to his country for the humbler but not less important duties connected with the evacuation of the island. A great man shows his greatness in defeat no less than in victory. Gen. Blanco has not manifested the elements of greatness in this hour of his country's need. Like Gen. Augusti in the Philippines, he has been weighed in the balances and found wanting.

The victory at Manila, like nearly all our victories in our conflict with Spain, increases with fuller reports. It now seems certain that not only has the city of Manila surrendered, but that the whole archipelago has been turned over to the Americans, Manila being the capital of the entire group of islands. While the two governments were engaged in putting the finishing touches on the protocol, and affixing the official signatures thereto, Admiral Dewey and General Merritt were gradually investing the city of Manila, and on the day following the signing of the protocol, the day on which the news of peace reached the world, the city of Manila, with all the islands of which it is the capital, was surrendered to the American forces. As to the influence of this battle on the final treaty of peace, the Grand Rapids Herald is not far wrong in the following editorial utterance as to the controlling influence in the settlement of this question:

While opinions honestly conflict as to whether we ought to retain the islands in whole or in part, it is highly probable that public sentiment will follow pretty closely the line that Dewey lays down. If he says that we should gather in the whole archipelago, including Aguinaldo and his whistle, public opinion will very generally accept this as the true gospel of the situation and demand it. Should he hold that the island of Luzon is enough, the appetite of the most voracious land-grabber will be appeased, and a single island will satisfy. If he would confine our acquisitions to a single harbor, his opinion will be accepted. It is unusual for the American people to place so much reliance in the judgment of a single man in a matter of so great importance, but Dewey is on the spot, and has given such evidences of having a level head that it is safe to say a final public opinion will not be formed until he has been heard from, and no policy will be determined upon until he speaks. This confidence in Dewey's good judgment is as fine a compliment to him as the cheers which greeted his May-day victory, and he seems to deserve it.

The national conference on the foreign policy of the United States opened its ses-

San Francisco by 10,000 miles. That fact alone was urged as sufficient answer to all objections. Mr. Warner Miller claims that the Nicaraguan Canal, within ten years after its completion, will increase the population of the Pacific cities 10,000,000. He estimates that it can be built for $100,000,000 to $140,000,000. There were present at the conference both the Expansionists and the Anti-Expansionists. Carl Schurz, of New York, represented the views of the Anti-Expansionists, while Judge P. S. Grosscup, of Chicago, represented the Expansionists. In his speech the latter said:

> The true question is not whether Porto Rico, Hawaii and the Philippines are intrinsically worth the responsibilities incurred by their occupation; whether their resources will counterbalance the new dangers that their acquirement would introduce into our political system. For I see behind them something more than islands, nothing less than a continent. Within Asia lies the interest and opportunity that, by its largeness, dwarfs every other prospect. I favor the acquisition of Porto Rico, partly because the moral purpose of this demands that it should no longer be a political plague spot in the otherwise putrified Caribbean Sea, but because it is the gateway to the Caribbean Sea when the coast of the sea is fully developed and the Nicaragua Canal opened will, from both a naval and commercial view, become the most important water on the face of the globe.

William Dudley Bull, of Indiana, delivered an address on the "Immorality of Prize Money." The conference has not completed its sessions at this writing.

It is authoritatively announced that Secretary of State, Judge Day, who will serve as a member of the Peace Commission, is to retire, after that service has been rendered, to private life. He accepted the position at the request of the President, and has discharged the duties of the high office with a delicacy, tact and wisdom which mark him as a man of great ability. He is to be succeeded by John C. Hay, our present ambassador at the court of St. James. Mr. Hay was the private secretary of Mr. Lincoln during his administration, and has had other experience aside from his present position to fit him for the duties of the office to which he is now called. He seems to have discharged his duties as Minister to England in a manner satisfactory both to the English people and to the United States. It is generally understood that he was Mr. McKinley's orginial choice for Secretary of State, but the necessity of finding a place for Senator Sherman, in order that Mr. Hanna might become Senator, prevented his taking the position at that time. There is no reason to doubt that Mr. Hay will discharge the duties belonging to the portfolio of state to the satisfaction of the President and the American people.

In the very nature of things there will be more or less friction in the transfer of authority from Spanish to American military rule in Porto Rico, Cuba and the Philippines, but on the whole, thus far, order is being well preserved and conditions are rapidly adjusting themselves to the new order. The volunteer army will be reduced to only necessary requirements as rapidly as possible, the sick soldiers removed to better localities and some of the larger fever-stricken camps abandoned. The ports are being opened to commerce, and provision ladened vessels will soon be crowding to the wharves of the larger cities of these islands, and starving men and women relieved of the long and painful fast, and the war will soon be known only as a thing of the past.

"THE WAR IS OVER!"

This was the cry of the newsboys on Saturday morning, the 13th inst. It was a welcome sound. For three months these industrious news venders have been crying, "All about the war!" and we opened our morning and afternoon papers to find accounts of naval and army engagements in Cuba or in the Philippines. Now comes the welcome news of peace. The protocol has been signed. The President's proclamation has been issued suspending hostilities in our army and navy. Let the whole nation give thanks for this blessed consummation!

No more are our brave boys to suffer from tropic sun and Spanish mauser. They will soon be coming home. There are vacant chairs awaiting them, and hearts and hearthstones that will give them glad welcome. Those who have stemmed the red tide of battle, and those who have been undergoing the drill and discipline in camp, far from the scene of action, preparing themselves for their country's service, alike will be welcomed home by their friends and by the whole country. The part performed by these latter, although they were not permitted to fight a battle, was an important one in accomplishing peace. They have shown their willingness, their courage and their patience, in their enlistment and subjection to discipline, and preparation for their country's service.

Best of all it is peace with honor. The end for which the war was inaugurated has been gained. Cuba is freed. Porto Rico is to find a shelter under the American flag, and Spain's dominion in the Western World is ended. The Stars and Stripes are to find a place to float in Manila Harbor, and the rest remains to be determined. The war, though brief, has demonstrated the courage and efficiency of our army and navy, the superiority of our battleships and the willingness and ability of the American people to rally, unitedly, in defense of their country's flag, when its honor demands it. Thank God for the peace that comes with honor!

That Spain is to be benefited by the war, we do not doubt. She feels her honor and her pride to be stained, somewhat, at present, but it is certain that she has learned some lessons from the war that will prove of advantage to her in the future. If she will now give her attention to public enlightenment, to securing the rights of all the people under her dominion, to the enlargement of liberty, both civil and religious, to the development of her resources at home, and to economy and honesty in public administration, there will come a brighter day for Spain.

The war is over, but not our perils. We are face to face with great national problems which require the wisest statesmanship. We have enlarged our national domain and vastly increased our responsibilities. We have risen to a new height of influence among the nations of the world. There has been developed in the national consciousness a sense of wider responsibility than we have ever felt before. This makes it the more important that we shall solve the many internal problems that affect our national life, purify our own civil administration in city, state and nation, develop the different sections and classes of our own people, and so prepare ourselves for the larger and wider career of usefulness to which Providence seems to
pointing us.

This is no time for narrow sectionali
for bitter party enmities, for strife over
spoils of office, for controversy about pa
minor issues. The times demand mer
large intellectual mold, of a high sense
moral obligation and of a patriotism
wide at least as our own vast dom
Never was there a time when Christ
people needed to pray more that God n
give us wise and broad-minded statesn
to stand at the helm and guide our Shi
State safely through the perils and pr
lems which have come to us through v
tory and peace.

THE REVISED VERSION ON TH FRIENDSHIP TEXT.

He that would have friends must show him
friendly (A. V.).

He that maketh many friends doeth it to his
destruction (R. V.).—*Prov. 18:24.*

This text, as it is rendered in the
versions, illustrates in a very forcible m
ner the way in which the new translat
has played havoc with old sermons.
once had a peculiar experience with t
particular passage. One Sunday morni
in England I went into my study and p
pared a sermon on it as it reads in
common version. When I had finished
and was on the eve of starting to chu
it occurred to me that I would see how
revised version had rendered the passa
I opened the book and read to my ut
dismay and the overthrow of my serm
"He that maketh many friends doeth it
his own destruction!" Not a slight var
tion from the old text, but an absol
contradiction, apparently. One passa
says if a man would have friends, and
necessary implication is the more
merrier, he must show himself friend
the other is a distinct warning agai
having many friends, on the ground t
the man who multiplies friends does it
his own destruction! I got out of my di
culty on that occasion by extemporizin
few remarks on the latter passage by w
of introduction to the former, and by sho
ing that both passages are true. They
the two sides of a fundamental truth
human life. Is it not a fact of experie
that a man who multiplies friends does
frequently, if not generally, to his o
undoing? Never since the making of m
has one person been led astray by
enemy, or by one who cared nothing
him. All men who go wrong are led ast
by their friends, never by their foes.
are only susceptible to temptation on
side we turn to our friends. Hence
greater the number of our friends, es
cially if they be worldly-minded friends,
greater and stronger the number of tem
tations that may end in destruction. T
genial, good-hearted, magnetic young m
who is hail fellow well met with everybo
who makes friends easily and rapidly, w
find his popularity a constant peril. Wh
he walks along the streets and every ot
man he meets makes a demonstration o
him and invites him into a saloon to dri
or to play cards, he would have to
almost an angel to get through with
being swallowed up in perdition and
struction. Over millions of young m
who have gone down to premature gra
through dissipation and bad habits c
tracted from their associates, it might
justly written, "Ruined by his friend

ɔpular young men have more temptations an any other class of people, and the ore friends the more temptations. A ousand men have been ruined by friends ɪere one has been ruined by enemies. all we advise young people not to make ends? No. Tell them to be careful of ɘ friends they allow to influence them. ise men make but few friends in the ghest and best sense of that term, cause they find but few persons in life ɪom they can safely take into that intiate and almost divine relationship. There an old saying, "Be friendly with all and timate with none," but there are a few oice spirits on whom you can afford to vish all the wealth of your friendship at you may obtain theirs in return. Life thout these highest and divinest friendips would be a place of leafless woods d barren fields, but these in the short ce of human life can be and need be but w. Friendship in this profound spiritual ɜaning is more than acquaintance, more an kind feeling and well-wishing, more an neighborly interest or brotherly symthy. It is the highest human relationip. Love and absolute reciprocal trust nstitute the basis of friendship in its st sense. It is one soul in two bodies, as Greek philosopher expressed it. When u can find a person in whom you can put solute and unwavering trust, and who n repose the same in you, your souls w together and become one soul, and ou would do as much for your friend, or ɪore, than you would do for yourself. uch was the friendship of David and onathan, Damon and Pythias, Tennyson nd Hallam. Here it enters the region of ɪve and breaks into poetry, as David's legy over Jonathan, and Tennyson's In Iemoriam over Hallam.

I am distressed for thee, my brother Jonathan.
ery pleasant hast thou been unto me,
hy love to me was wonderful,
assing the love of women."

The term, however, is not used in this igh, delicate sense in the two texts I have ted. It seems to signify in both stateɪents the good-will and sympathy that we re justified in seeking from all the rightɪinking of our fellowmen. This especially is the significance of the word in the ld text, as true to experience as the other. He that would have friends must show imself friendly." Who has not seen undreds of verifications of this in their bservations of life? Who does not know ɪat the way to make friends is to show ɪrselves friendly? We may illustrate, but would be useless to argue this proposion that stands in the nature of a social ɪiom. It would be absurd for an uniendly person or an unfriendly church to ɪpect to make friends. Like produces ke. What we give out we get back. The ɔirit we manifest towards others is the one ɪey manifest towards us. If we hate we re hated, if we love we are loved, if we ɘfriend others they will befriend us. Life ɘgets life, love begets love, joy in us wakens joy in our fellows, a friendly disosition awakens friendliness in others. What you put into men and into life is will receive in kind and in quantity what he has given out. The converse of the text is true, the unfriendly man has no friends. Whether he is morose, or proud, or timid, or indifferent, the effect is the same—his friends are few and far between. Timidity is frequently mistaken for pride and lack of sociability. So-and-So is proud and stuck up, he doesn't speak to people, when perhaps there is nothing the matter with the man but timidity. He is apparently cold and unsocial, but the cause is bashfulness and self-consciousness, and not pride or indifference. Timidity is not a sin, but it is a misfortune, and a great drawback in social fellowship with men. Help the timid person by making the first advance, and do not say that people are stuck up and hateful when they are only bashful and lack confidence in themselves. Silent, timid, say-nothing people repel those who would approach them, but they do not mean to do it. They chill the atmosphere in which they live, and no one desires to breathe it. Nobody cares for them because they seem to care for nobody; but do not misunderstand them, they do not mean it that way. Their hearts are as good as yours, but they have a poor way of showing it, and you have a better way, that is the only difference. It is the duty of the timid to overcome their timidity as they would any other human weakness that stood in the way of their usefulness and happiness, for he that would have friends must show himself friendly.

J. J. H.

Hour of Prayer.

THE FRUIT OF THE SPIRIT.

(Midweek Prayer-meeting Topic, August 31.)

But the fruit of the Spirit is love, joy, peace, longsuffering, kindness, goodness, faithfulness, meekness, temperance: against such there is no law. And they that are of Christ Jesus have crucified the flesh with the passions and lusts thereof. If we live by the Spirit, by the Spirit let us also walk. Let us not be vainglorious, provoking one another, envying one another.—*Gal.* 5:22-26.

This passage is of great value in assisting us to a clear understanding of our spiritual relationship to Jesus Christ. There is little need of our singing the one time popular hymn—

"'Tis a point I long to know,
Oft it causes anxious thought:
Do I love the Lord or no,
Am I His or am I not?"

"If any man have not the Spirit of Christ," or the Holy Spirit, "he is none of His." But how are we to know whether we really possess the Holy Spirit? One of the best ways to know this important fact is by its fruit. If the Holy Spirit abides in the human heart it brings forth a certain kind of fruit, such as love, joy, peace, longsuffering, kindness, goodness, faithfulness, meekness, temperance or self-control. Having this fruit in our lives we are Christ's. In the absence of such testimony we may be sure that we have not the Spirit and are not Christ's.

Such is the nature of these dispositions and qualities of character that we need not be in any doubt as to their presence in us. Christ Jesus will lead us to seek to please them in all things, and to make sacrifices for their cause. Are we doing it? If we love our fellowmen as we do ourselves, we will be seeking to serve them and help them in every possible way. We will be charitable to their faults and not easily offended. Is this our attitude and feeling toward our brotherman?

Have we *joy* in our Christian life? Do we "rejoice in the truth," and in the triumphs of truth in the world? Do we take a joyful, optimistic outlook of things?

Are we at *peace* with God? Have we a conscience void of offense toward God and man? Do we feel that between us and our heavenly Father there is a perfect understanding, and we are at one with Him, and come what may all is well? The opposite of this is that worrying, fretful, unrestful condition that shortens life and neutralizes Christian influence.

Are we *longsuffering*, able to endure harsh criticism, misinterpretation, misrepresentation, and even slander, without loss of temper or a feeling of resentment or retaliation? The opposite of this would be a disposition to take offense easily and to resent injuries in kind.

Are our lives full of *kindness*, manifested by deeds as well as words in our relations with our fellowmen? Have we eyes for seeing opportunities for doing good to those in need, and hearts to improve these opportunities?

Have we a reputation in the community for *goodness*, which is not only the absence of that which is evil, but the possession of a positive quality that flows out in life-giving streams to others? Barnabas was a "good man, full of faith and the Holy Spirit." Goodness is, after all, true greatness.

Have we the element of *faithfulness* or fidelity, standing at the post of duty when others have deserted it, and when the cause is unpopular, and when "the love of many has waxed cold?" Can we stand for the right in the face of opposition and be true to God and to ourselves in the midst of temptation?

Are we *meek* in spirit, not seeking promotion and honor, not ambitious for place or power, not anxious to have our names blazoned abroad, but willing to occupy humble places and to do humble service, if only we may have the approval of God and of our conscience?

Are we *temperate* in all things, letting our moderation be known to all men? Are we able to control our appetites, our passions, our temper? Or are we the slaves of these appetites and passions?

These are questions which we can answer in our own hearts. We know whether these qualities exist within us, and to what degree. These are the elements of Christian character. These qualities make us Christlike. If we possess them we are Christ's and Christ is ours.

"If we live by the Spirit"—if we are indebted to the Spirit for whatever spiritual life we possess—"by the Spirit let us also walk." That is, let there be harmony between our inner life and our outward conduct. "Let us not be vainglorious, provoking one another, envying one another," but

seen—a truly Christian life. These are the elements worth striving for. Silver and gold, all forms of material wealth, earthly honors and possessions—these soon fade away, but the royal graces here called "the fruit of the Spirit," will endure forever and form a part of our eternal inheritance.

If these things be "the fruit of the Spirit," with what zeal and earnestness should we seek to possess the Spirit Himself. This is the one gift that includes all others. With what *hopefulness*, too, may we seek this divine gift, in view of the words of Jesus, "If ye, being evil, know how to give good gifts to your children, how much more shall your Heavenly Father give the Holy Spirit to them that ask Him?"

PRAYER.

O Thou most gracious and righteous Father, who art in heaven; we acknowledge our transgressions which have separated us from Thee, but we rejoice in the salvation by which our transgressions are removed far from us, and we are brought into union and reconciliation with Thee through Jesus Christ our Lord. We thank Thee that in this relationship to Thee we are promised and we receive Thy Holy Spirit as the Giver of life, as the Source of every grace and virtue, and as the earnest or pledge of the everlasting inheritance. May we come into such close relationship with Thee, and so enjoy the communion of the Holy Spirit, that our lives may abound in all true and precious things which go to make up Christian character. Forbid that any of us should live barren or unfruitful lives, but may we abound in all fruitfulness unto the praise of Thy glory, through Jesus Christ our Lord. Amen!

Editor's Easy Chair.

OR MACATAWA MUSINGS.

The Macatawa Park Assembly for 1898 has now closed, and we may look upon it and judge it as a whole. To say that it has excelled all its predecessors in attendance, in interest awakened, in the impression it has made and in the quality of work done, is only to give voice to the general sentiment of those who have attended these assemblies. Bros. Willett and Campbell seem admirably adapted to working together and their lectures supplemented each other beautifully. They have given a decided stimulus to biblical study and especially to the study of the four Gospels. The evening addresses on the different phases of Christian Union excited a deep interest, though there was little or no differences of opinion developed. The people who come to Macatawa Park and attend these assemblies seem to be pretty thoroughly imbued with Christian Union sentiment. The plan is, we believe, to publish in some form or other both the lectures on Bible study in the morning and the evening addresses on Christian Union. J. J. Haley was substituted for Dr. W. T. Moore, the latter having sailed for England, and while Bro. Haley spoke on brief notice his address was worthy of the occasion and received the hearty approval of those who heard it. It was the first time we have had with us Prof. McKenzie, of the Chicago Theological Seminary, and he has impressed us all as a man of wide culture, of profound thought, and of a splendid personality. We hope to have him with us again. As for our old standbys, Campbell and Willett, they are like wine, in that they grow better with age. They were never more highly appreciated than during the recent Assembly.

There were some special features and episodes connected with the Assembly week that deserves special mention. On Friday afternoon, there being a large number of preachers present associated with the Disciples of Christ, it was decided to resolve ourselves into an executive session for the transaction of some business of an informal nature and for mutual edification. For this purpose a little steamer was chartered and about twenty-three or twenty-four preachers, with the wives and families that were present with them, making a company in all of about thirty-five, went to Point Superior, about half way between the Park and Holland, on Friday afternoon, on a picnic. Once upon the ground under the trees, in the little peninsula that runs out into the lake, while the ladies were engaged in making preparations for the evening meal the preachers held a pow-pow, sitting on the ground like Indians in a council of war. H. W. Everest was called to the chair and H. L. Willet elected secretary. After a free exchange of opinions it was unanimously resolved to issue a call for a Congress of the Disciples of Christ to convene in April next, and a committee was appointed to arrrange the programme and to fix the place and exact time. It was the unanimous sentiment of these preachers, representing several states, that the time had come in our history when we needed a separate and independent gathering to discuss some living questions that could not well come before our National Missionary Convention. It was believed, further, that the City Evangelization Conference had accomplished its special mission, and could be well merged into and find its place in our National Missionary Convention. This was the general sentiment of those who attended the last Conference, and it was felt, therefore, that this arrangement for a congress would not interfere with any other general meeting of the brotherhood. The committee appointed to arrange the programme for this congress consists of H. W. Everest, H. L. Willett, J. Z. Tyler, W. F. Richardson and J. H. Garrison. They will hold a meeting perhaps at the National Convention at Chattanooga to perfect the plan. By the time this pow-pow had ended supper was ready, and such a meal as it was! Beautiful white cloths spread under the green boughs of the trees, decorated with ferns and with almost every good thing to eat one could think about. We adopted the apostolic method of reclining, except in the cases of Bros. A. M. Atkinson and J. Z. Tyler who, on account of their venerable appearance, were given stools. After the meal there was a reading by Bro. Atkinson, some atheletic sports by the younger preachers, some social enjoyment, and then we gathered our goods together and returned to the sandy beach to meet the little steamer that was coming up the bay to take us home. The evening was calm and the level beams of the sun converted it into a sea of glass mingled with fire. As we stood on the narrow peninsula at the water's edge we sang several of the sweet familiar hymns, while a solemn hush seemed to rest on the lake, on the woods and on the people. It seemed to be a holy hour when hearts were uplifted to God Many were affected to tears at the tranqui holy scene. Soon we were aboard the littl steamer and the singing was continued, in tercepted only by brief speeches from th brethren, whose hearts were too full fo silence. Bro. Atkinson, among others made a little talk and told us how beautifu was this scene of Christian fellowship, an how greatly he had enjoyed it, and how h hoped that this characteristic featur among the Disciples, of brotherly love would continue, whatever changes migh come. It was voted unanimously that Bro and Sister A. be invited to make thei permanent summer home at Macataw Park. They were to leave that evening and this picnic will remain with them pleasant memory of their visit. It wa agreed that among all the picnics we ha ever had this one would easily rank first and a number said it was the most enjoy able afternoon they had ever spent. Th Congregational brethren on the same after noon also chartered a launch and took ride up the lake and back. One of them i speaking of it at night said that "the Disciples took to the woods and the Congregationalists to the water," which may be regarded as a significant indication of th union of the two bodies!

On Saturday afternoon of Assembl week the ladies gave a social and recep tion to the people who had been attendin or were interested in the Assembly. Th Auditorium which, by the way, had bee neatly floored and seated for Assembl week, according to previous notice in thi column, was beautifully decorated wit branches of trees, ferns, flowers, and th American flag was gracefully draped in th rear of the platform. A programme, con sisting of recitations, was rendered wit great satisfaction to the people. The came light refreshments and the socia hour. But the crowning meeting of th Assembly was the one held on last Lord' day. The sermon at four o'clock was b Prof. McKenzie, and was a powerful pre sentation of the power of the human con science and the danger of stifling it, a illustrated in the case of Herod in his rela tion to John the Baptist and Jesus. Afte the sermon, which had made a profoun impression, came the communion service presided over by Profs. Everest and Mc Kenzie. It was a union communion servic and the Spirit of God was manifestl present, and that is always the spirit o unity. This tender service closed with th singing of—

"Blest be the tie that binds
Our hearts in Christian love."

The great beach meeting at night wa presided over by Prof. Graham Taylor, i which the theme of the Assembly was th general theme of the evening, and a num ber of earnest speeches were made on th subject of Christian unity. There mus have been 800 or 1,000 people sitting on th sand listening to these songs and talks while the bonfire on the beach added it radiance to that of the electric bulbs, an the lamps of heaven.

Somehow the feeling has taken deep roo that Macatawa has entered upon a new an wider era in its history. Its future is n longer uncertain as it was for a number o years. The tone of the place is so pre dominantly moral and religious that it i

agency for the extension of the kingdom. As some one has expressed it, "The kingdom of God is the church as seen from above, while the church is the kingdom of God as seen from below." In other words, the church is the kingdom of God objectified, in an institution, with its ordinances and officers, but its influence is affecting social life, and influencing the state and its legislation.

2. We would say to such an one that the kingdom, in its triumphant condition, is yet to be established, but that the kingdom has already been *inaugurated* and its work of conquest is going on. The confusion arises from not distinguishing between the kingdom in its present process of overcoming the world, and in its future triumphant state when it shall have put down all opposition.

3. We would cite such Scriptures as "The kingdom of God is among you," and such passages as give the conditions of admission into the kingdom of God, as John 3:5, and the fact of our translation out of the kingdom of darkness into the kingdom of God (Col. 1:13). The fact of Christ's coronation as king and the existence on earth of millions of obedient subjects, is evidence of the existence of the kingdom of God on earth.

II. CONCERNING IMMORTALITY.

1. The Scriptures which teach that man was created in the image of God (Gen. 1:26 *et al.*), show that man has a nature that survives death or dissolution of the body. Man's likeness to God is to be found, not in his material, but in his spiritual nature. Again, the teaching of Jesus, that we are not to fear those who have power only to kill the body, but rather him who hath power to cast both soul and body into hell, involves the same truth. The tremendous emphasis which Jesus lays upon the value of the soul is based upon the fact that man is a spiritual being and to live forever.

2. That God alone possesses immortality *within himself*, unconferred.

3. Eternal life may be enjoyed here, and its possession is the assurance of a blessed immortality. One is a negative term, indicating simply the absence of death, while the other is a positive term, indicating possession of life—that peculiar kind of life that persists and is eternal because it is the life of God in the soul of man. The term "immortality" has reference chiefly, if not solely, to the body, and refers to the spiritual body which believers are to have hereafter. Eternal life is the power in man that makes such an immortal body possible. It has been conjectured, not without reason, that it is the power that is now forming that body within us.

4. Taking immortality to refer to the immortal body, that is to be given to the righteous, the statement would not be incorrect, but we must not make the mistake of identifying immortality with everlasting *existence*.

5. The Scriptures shed little light upon the question as to the future destiny of the wicked; that is, the finally impenitent. The fact that they enter into "everlasting punishment" (Matt. 25:46) has been supposed to indicate that they will exist forever. The problems of eschatalogy or the Last Things, involve many questions concerning which we cannot afford to be dogmatic. The fact that man is created in the image of God would seem to indicate that he is to exist forever. If He has seen proper to withhold from us what disposition will be ultimatly made of those whom all His remedial agencies shall fail to recover from the power of sin, we can afford to wait for the revelation of the last day.

Current Religious Thought

The New York Observer thus emphasizes the distinction between Christianity and the moral maxims of Roman authors. After quoting from Terence the maxim, "I am a man; I regard nothing human as foreign to me," the Observer says:

The limping sentiment of the popular Latin author, Christianity however, takes up and surpasses both in theory and practice. Christianity is not indeed the belated inheritor of all the odds and ends of morality that have found expression in various quarters up to the time of the Christian era, but expresses in fuller and unequivocal terms, and with an originality of its own, the axiomatic moral sentiments which are of the eternal structure of things, concerning which moral teachers ventured but a few half guesses. While a Terence reckons that nothing that a man does or feels is apart from him, Christianity bespeaks a discriminating interest in our fellowmen, which will differentiate their follies from their virtues, detect the fallacies beneath their faults, and evidence the truest sympathy with their troubles, by seeking to remove the curse of sin which is the root of most of these difficulties. According to gospel teachings we are to sympathize with sinners, not with sin. The Christian conception is that what we are to share with humanity is its better life and what we are to induce it to share with us is our best morality.

Thus Christianity argues for a subtler sympathy with humanity than ever entered the brain or heart of a Roman moralist. Its teachings as to this law of sympathetic brotherliness comes to highest expression in the words and works of him of whom it could be said that, while divine, He himself became subject to a process of temptation in all points like as we are, yet without sin. The significance of this summary of the life of Christ resides as much in the last as in the first of its terms. Christianity is thus seen to take both a juster and a broader view of the needs of humanity, which revuires not alone sympathy, or a simple fellow feeling, but as well the right kind of sympathy.

Those who are inclined to doubt the progress of the world toward a higher civilization and life would do well to read an article in the Independent, Aug. 11th, by Rev. Jas. A. Miller, Ph. D., on "Slowly But Irresistably." We give one paragraph from the article. After speaking of the slow development of an individual from childhood to manhood he says:

It is altogether likely that God is the same God, whether creating a world, building up his civiliztaion in the world, or bringing in any particular sector of his circle of truth. God's day may be a thousand of our years in the proclamation of truth as in other of his works. Rapidity in the acceptance of truth is the exception, and not the rule, as is the raising of an island in a night. Haste to take on new methods of living and thinking may sometimes carry with it a justifiable touch of suspicion. Nations, as a general thing, do not accept even divine truth in a human day or a human week. It took many centuries, and a world of effort on the part of the traveler, the historian, the statesman and the philosopher, to convince the masses of the Greeks that the earth was not like a plate, with the heavens, like an overturned bowl, resting upon its upturned rim; that the rivers did not all rise in the ocean, nor all flow into the Mediterranean Sea. That which is bred into bone and muscle and blood and brain and soul does not disappear in twenty-five or even fifty years. We grossly misinterpret God's manifestation of himself in the world if we think that the Hindus or the Chinese are going to be Europeanized and Christianized within one or two generations. We believe that Christian civilization is entering, and must eventually triumph; but in ancient peoples like these it is one of the

innumerable branches to the ground to form innumerable trunks, may be felled; but we should have little faith in a workman who would promise to throw it down in an hour. Nations clinging to wrong ideas for centuries first defend them, then allegorize, then revise, then doubt, then desert, then accept the inevitable. Civilization becomes secure in the gradualness and quietness with which it permeates a section of humanity.

Probably no man understands better the international relations and problems of the Old World than George Washburn, D. D., president of Robert College, Constantinople. And, living as he does between England and Russia, he is especially qualified to speak forth the truth on the interests and relations of these two great rival powers. In an article in a recent number of The Independent on England and America he speaks on the advisability of an alliance of these two nations as follows:

No one expects us to enter into this alliance on purely sentimental grounds, although the fact that there are such grounds is not to be ignored. We shall do what we believe to be for our interest, or, if we can rise so high, what we see to be our duty to the world. It seems clear to me that sentiment, interest and duty, in this case, all point in the same direction. All must see that we can no longer pursue that policy of selfish isolation which we fell into after the Civil War. I am not an Imperialist, in the sense in which that word is now used. I have no desire to build up a great colonial empire to rival that of England; but we have our interests and our duties in all parts of the world, and we must be ready to meet them. We need friends whose duties and interests are in some measure the same as ours, and England is the only great Power of which this is true. Whenever England raises her flag there is freedom of trade for all the world, and political freedom for the people just so far as they are capable of appreciating it. This is true of no other great Power, least of all Russia, which is the coming Power of Europe. Only by an alliance between England and America can Central and South America be saved from annexation by the Continental Powers. Their designs upon China are confessed already, and we have as great an interest as England in keeping that great empire open to our merchants.

We have no concern in the special politics of Europe and no desire to meddle with its affairs. There are great questions there, such as the Eastern question, the question which is soon to come of the Austrian Empire, and the question between France and Germany. which may lead to great wars. We have nothing to do with them, and should enter into no alliance which would involve us in any responsibility for them; but in all world-questions we are interested, and for these we need an alliance with England, the great sea power. We are commercial rivals, and we shall always be such; but we only ask a fair field, and England is more ready to grant this than we are. She opens her home market to us as we do not ours to her.

In short, we have entered upon an era in our history when we need an ally strong enough to stand by us in the face of the world, and in sympathy with our ideas of government. England is the only such country, and the only one with which anything like a permanent alliance is possible.

About as clear a distinction as we have yet seen made between preachers and sermonizers appeared in the following words of President DeWitt Hyde, in the Preachers' Magazine for August. He says:

To the preacher the sermon is a means; to the sermonizer it is an end. To the preacher the sermon is an opportunity; to the sermonizer it is a task. Hence the preacher is a free man and a master; the sermonizer is a subject and a slave. The preacher has something to say; the sermonizer has to say something. The preacher bears in his heart a great, glowing ideal of what Jesus would have his people to be; he feels with tenderest sympathy and keenest sorrow how far short of this they come, and, impelled by this ideal and a burning desire to lift his people up to it, he searches the Scriptures for a text which shall express it, and draws on all the sources of his reading and his experience for argument, illustration and incident to commend it to their minds and hearts. The sermonizer carries in his head a general outline of theology, goes to his commentary for an appropriate setting, splits his thought up into the requisite number of heads, gives each a striking title, tacks on an appropriate appeal or application, and goes forth to meet his audience.

SERMONS IN THE OLD TESTAMENT PROPHETS.

BY G. A. PECKHAM.

In the Prophets we have a mine often too little explored, rich in material for sermonizing. Aside from portions recognized by the New Testament as messianic, they are filled with the application of divinely inspired truth to present-day problems, because the panacea in our age, as in that of the Prophets, for the ills of mankind, social, political and moral, is to crowd the spirit of selfishness out of men's hearts and to fill them with love for God and humanity.

Then, as now, men had their short-comings and excellencies. Among the evils of the land then, as now, were the demon of intemperance, oppression of the laborer in his hire, grinding the faces of the poor, prostitution of so-called courts of justice to the wishes of the rich and powerful, corrupt legislators enacting iniquitous laws to further their own selfish ends, cornering the grain market that exhorbitant prices might be extorted from the people for the necessaries of life, short weights and measures, false prophets whose sole object is to flatter men of position and influence and curry favor with them, preachers of error and falsehood, a ruling passion on the part of some to grab all the land in sight, adding farm to farm and joining house to house until there is no room left for people to dwell, advocates of quack remedies for the social and political ills of the nation, worshiping at the shrine of the golden calf, the sins of unchastity, hypocrisy and practical atheism, and last but not least, idle women given to wine, and living in luxury, whose vanity and thirst for finery must be satisfied at any cost. The old prophet met these evils, far more common then than now, by preaching sermons full of divine instruction, many of which are preserved in the inspired record. But the prophets see the virtues as well as the vices of humanity, and as we read we often find ourselves in the company of God's noblemen. Then, as now, but in smaller numbers, there were preachers of righteousness fearlessly proclaiming Heaven's message to men, courts where the claims of justice were sacred and the innocent man, be he rich or poor, had nothing to fear, and legislators whose only object was righteousness between man and his fellow. There was true devotion to God, true love for humanity. Indeed, human nature is very much the same in all ages. But thanks to the Word of God in the Old Testament Prophets and the Spirit of Christ, gradually taking possession of the world, never was the outlook for our race so bright as now. If we read the Prophets aright, they lift the veil of the centuries past and put us in touch with the generations which these inspired messengers of God served in such a way that they are no longer strangers and foreigners, but our fellowmen with whom we live, in whose midst we walk and whose joys and sorrows we feel. The study of the Prophets is of great value to the minister of the gospel, because they are servants of God preparing the way for the perfect revelation to come in Christ Jesus, their ideal representative, who is the goal of all prophecy. In them are seen the foundations of faith. Then, too, they give their readers enlarged views of God in history. Jehovah is God of all nations, not of Israel alone. "Saith Jehovah, Have not I brought up Israel out of the land of Egypt, and the Philistines from Caphtor, and the Syrians from Kir?" In Isaiah we read, "Blessed be Egypt, my people, and Assyria, the work of my hands, and Israel, mine inheritence." The Assyrian, with his mighty host, for a time invincible, is the staff in Jehovah's hand for inflicting punishment upon his people, but afterwards the instrument magnifies itself against its owner and suffers destruction. He hisses, and the armies of Assyria and Egypt come swarming in like bees and flies to do his bidding.

The Prophets see Jehovah interesting himself in state and city government, bringing the well-laid plans of crafty politicians to naught. It is he who taught the farmer how to carry on his occupation. In short, they bring God into the life of the common people and make him a present reality for all receptive readers. They also have the faculty of turning a man's eyes toward his own heart that he may see whether he is rendering true worship or not. If one's religion drifts into mere formalism, an evil against which the human heart has had to guard from the beginning of religious history (and, let me say, there is a possibility for as much formalism in a regular round of attendance at church, or even in public prayer, as in the sacrifices offered upon ancient Jewish altars), if it has lost its life or vigor, so that he is indifferent to the rights of the poor who work for him, or takes a *legal* advantage of a man who is in his power because "business is business," or enters an unjust combination for the purpose of enriching himself by robbing the people, or finally as a laborer he fails to give a full equivalent for the wages received, he may, if he will but pause a moment for reflection, hear God saying in his Prophets, "I hate your worship, it is an abomination to me." "Practice justice and love mercy." "I desire mercy and not sacrifice."

The Hebrew word translated *mercy* in the last quotation is a very comprehensive one. It may represent God's *grace*, or man's *piety*, and in the relation of man to his fellow it embraces the duties of love and mutual consideration. Those old preachers of righteousness touched human life on every side, and the religious teacher who makes them his companions will not want for interesting material to illustrate the great truths of the gospel and impress them upon the hearts of the people. It may not be out of place to call attention to a few books that will help the busy preacher to understand the life and work of these holy men of God. I mention "The Prophets of Israel," by W. R. Smith; "The Cambridge Bible;" "The Doctrine of the Prophets," by Kirkpatrick, and G. A. Smith's volumes of the "Expositors Bible," on Isaiah; and then the Minor Prophets. The last-named writer, in discussing the Servant of Jehovah, so human and so divine, as he is pictured in the second part of the book of Isaiah, notes the fact that one must become a servant of God before he can be a true servant of humanity. The man who fails to see in God the source of virtue is like the "savage who imagines that it is the burning-glass which sets the bush on fire, and so long as the sun is shining it may be impossible to con-

he is wrong; but a dull day
his mind that the glass can
hout the sun is upon it."
o the old Jewish division of
ment, we have the Law, the
the Writings. Not the least
Prophets.

HANATOPSIS."*

C. J. KIMBALL.

"All that breathes
destiny. The gay will laugh
gone, the solemn brood of care
ch one as before will chase
antom; yet all these shall leave
d their employments, and shall

r bed with thee. As the long

y, the sons of men—
ife's green spring, and he who

gth of years, matron and maid,
babe and the gray-headed man—
e be gathered to thy side
n their turn shall follow them."
—*William Cullen Bryant.*

ure consists of two hemi-
nay so say—the lower and the
h when taken together consti-
ll, complete, well-rounded
lives. These are sometimes
er and higher natures; or, in
our earthly, sensuous, selfish,
r, more rational and spiritual

subject of death is viewed
er hemisphere of our nature
nts to our mental vision the
ve, horrible and shocking
when contemplated from the
man's higher, more enlight-
ritual nature, we see it in a
kindlier light. But neither
spheres can be ignored or lost
would see this and all other
their true light, and if we
ur lives fully and perfectly
They must be blended into
nd beautiful sphere, as God

kness—although a real factor
ne existence, is a symbol of
anger, want, ignorance, sin
n heaven none of these things
Hence we are told that "there
night there." No night in
we ever stop to think of the
aning couched in this beauti-
Our earth-life is the night of
"abundant entrance into the
ngdom" is the soul's sunrise.
hat Miss Frances E. Willard
randest of American women—
the death of her mother at
years of age as a "glorious
rring to the sinking of the
nto the darkness of the tomb.
e to Mrs. Willard herself it
en nothing less than a mag-
plendent sun-*rise*. As in our
ghts the darkness is deepest
e dawn, so we must pass into
f death before emerging into
glories of an eternal day.
een viewed in almost innum-
nt ways, but to all of us,
e comes with the thought of death a feeling of repugnance, awe and shrinking; we feel that it is an unseen land, a land of which we absolutely *know* almost nothing till we are called upon to make the journey through "the valley of of the shadow" for ourselves. In other words, experience is the only means by which we can gain any *definite* knowledge of this "mysterious realm." Shakspeare describes it as an "undiscovered country, from whose bourne no traveler returns." It has been represented under many symbols and figures, some grim and ghastly; others beautiful and touching. We are told that among some Indian tribes there is the custom of releasing white doves over the graves of their dead, thus representing the soul as winging its way to the "Great Spirit." The ancient Greeks, we are informed, designated the soul by the word *psyche*—a butterfly—thus intimating that even they had some idea, though vague and imperfect, of the soul's immortality. Their conception of the soul seemed to be that of flight to higher and more beautiful things after being set free from its tenement of clay. Again, writers and speakers use the word "ghost" and "spirit" as convertible terms; albeit, the former is a very inelegant and almost obsolete synonym of the latter. Scholars tell us that the English word "ghost" comes from an old Anglo-Saxon term signifying *guest*, thus conveying to us the thought that the spirit is an inmate or guest of the body, and that when the visitor or guest has ended its visit it takes its departure to heaven, whence it came—"returns to God, who gave it."

The standard poetical works are full of beautiful and striking similes, tropes and hyperboles on this subject, of which my space will permit me to cite only a few examples, and but a few words from each.

"There is a Reaper whose name is Death,
And with his sickle keen
He reaps the bearded grain at a breath,
And the flowers that grow between."
—*Longfellow, in "The Reaper and the Flowers."*

"And as she looked around she saw how
Death, the Consoler,
Laying his hand upon many a heart, had
healed it forever."
—*Longfellow, in "Evangeline."*

"Death lies on her like an untimely frost
Upon the sweetest flower of all the field."
—*Shakspeare, in "Romeo and Juliet."*

"That golden key [death] that opens the palace of eternity."
—*Milton, in "Paradise Lost."*

"None return from those quiet shores
Who cross with the boatman, cold and pale;
We hear the dip of the golden oars,
And catch a gleam of the snowy sail;
And lo! they have passed from our yearning
heart—
They cross the stream and are gone for aye—
We may not sunder the vail apart
That hides from our vision the gates of day."
—*Nancy Priest.*

"Of all the thoughts of God that are
Bourne inward into the souls afar,
Along the Psalmist's music deep;
Now tell me if that any is
For gift or grace surpassing this:
'He giveth his beloved sleep?'"
—*Elizabeth Barrett Browning.*

"God's finger touched him, and he slept."
—*Tennyson, in "In Memoriam."*

"There's nothing terrible in death;
'Tis but to cast our robes away
And sleep at night without a breath
To break repose till dawn of day."
—*Montgomery.*

"One sweetly solemn thought
Comes to me o'er and o'er:
We're nearer our Father's house to-day
Than we've ever been before."
—*Alice Carey.*

"Life! we've been long together,
Through pleasant and cloudy weather;
'Tis hard to part when friends are dear—
Perhaps 'twill cost a sigh, a tear;
Then steal away, give little warning,
Choose thine own time—
Say not good-night; but in some brighter clime
Bid me good-morning!"
—*Anna Letitia Barbauld.*

To me one of the saddest things in this sad world of ours is the apparently untimely and even cruel demise of dear, sweet, innocent young children. In some deaths—such, for instance, as the incorrigibly wicked, the hopelessly diseased, the extremely aged, and even the loss of a beloved life-companion—an experience through which the writer has but recently been called to pass—we can see, although but dimly, some traces of justice, and even of mercy. But when a precious little darling is suddenly snatched from the fond embrace of loving parents and borne swiftly from their view upon the dark billows of death's rolling river—then it is we find that the light of our poor, weak, fallible, short-sighted reason is but the "blackness of darkness." This untimely setting of a sun that had but just commenced its career in the skies; this cruel blighting of a half-blown flower ere it had unfolded its beauties or emitted its sweet fragrance upon the "desert air;" this withering and perishing of a promising young tree by the early summer drouth; this hopeless failure of a thousand sweet prophecies, whispered in the ears of Faith, and Hope, and Love; this sad and unlooked-for quenching of the loveliest, purest, brightest light that burned upon the home altar—O, what does it mean? In the highest reach of intelligent Christian faith, we can only be dumb in the presence of such a calamity, and adore where we cannot comprehend.

I know a man and wife—the husband a pious, able and scholarly minister—who lost their two precious little darlings (all they had) only a few days apart. The one went in the dying agonies of the old year; the other in the birth-throes of the new. It became my melancholy duty to conduct the funeral services in both cases, and nothing in my long experience ever so unnerved me, or caused me to so keenly realize my utter weakness in the presence of death. This was their first great sorrow; and surely, dear reader, it was no ordinary sorrow. It was a *double* sorrow. They lost their *all*. When the tendrils of love and affection, so firmly entwined around those dear ones, were thus suddenly snapped asunder, it seemed to them as if the whole world were violated. They knew that we could neither change nor put aside the solemn reality; they knew that their darling ones were gone from their fond and loving embrace *forever*, so far as this world is concerned; that never again on earth would they look into the pure depths of those loving little eyes, nor listen to the childish prattle of their innocent little tongues, nor hear the pattering of their busy, industrious little feet. They

is composed of two Greek words—
ng *death*, and *opsis*, a *view*. The
signifies *a view of death*, or *reflec-*
'—*McGuffey's Eclectic Reader, Re-*

knew all this as well as I; and, looking at the matter from this standpoint exclusively, if there is any comfort, or any consolation, or any help, then I frankly confess I cannot see it. Under such circumstances how could I presume to offer any word of consolation? Mere words are so vain, so empty and so unsatisfactory; when they fall from our lips they seem to bound back upon us like echoes in some old deserted hall.

On the other hand, however — and I write for thousands who are this moment passing through somewhat similar bitter experiences—the parents to whom we have referred, whose happy home circle death had so ruthlessly invaded, as intelligent and devoted Christians could not fail to recognize the fact that their precious flowers, like some rare exotic, were too frail and tender to flourish in this cold and sin-cursed clime, and that God did, therefore, transplant them into the Garden of Paradise for the purpose of attracting them thither also; that their "sparkling jewels" were taken only to deck and beautify their "crown of rejoicing," which is "laid up" for them; that their loved ones have only "climbed the golden stair" to the "highlands of heaven"—

"Where the bright blooming flowers
Are their odors emitting,
And the leaves of the bowers
In the breezes are flitting,"

far beyond the reach of disease, decay or death, and that for this very reason their own desire to live for God and heaven is now stronger than it ever was before—so that they "sorrow not as those who have no hope;" and, as I look at it, this is really the only hope or consolation there is in such a case. But ah, what a hope and consolation this is! It is indeed "an anchor to the soul, both sure and steadfast, and which entereth to that within the vail, whither Jesus, the Forerunner, is for us entered." Without this hope we might indeed sink into unutterable and irretrievable despair. And yet, nothwithstanding all this, we are so glued to the things of time and sense; the wings of our faith and hope are so clogged by sin; our spiritual perceptions are so dimmed and blurred by daily contact with the world; the cloud is sometimes so black and the bow so dim, that it requires a long, patient and steady gaze to discern even the faintest outlines of the harbinger of hope. But of one thing we may be sure—and this it seems is all that can be said—the beautiful bow of promise still spans the heavens; it is only the darkness and the blindness of weeping that hides it from our vision; and to those who have the patience to "wait and watch" it will appear, sooner or later.

"And then you shall know that lengthened breath
Is not the sweetest gift God sends his friend,
And sometimes the sable pall of death
Conceals the fairest boon his love can send."

There are certain master-keys, so to speak, to which the melodies of all human lives are attuned, and they can no more grow old, or cease to vibrate to the proper touch, or lose their freshness and power, than the mocking-bird can forget his song; and there are some events the keen edge of which time can never dull. With us the awful presence of DEATH, that relentless disturber of all human affairs, is one. It is old as our race, and yet it is new as the perpetual dawn of the morning. And when its dark shadow settles down upon our homes we think, Surely there never was such sorrow as ours; and I would not vainly endeavor to comfort such bereaved ones by telling them that the same revelation of sorrow has come to others, any more than I would tell the young mother that there are thousands of babes just as pretty, and smart, and sweet, and precious as hers. Neither of them would believe me, and I am glad of it; for it is wrong and sacrilegious to make such holy things *common*. What, then, shall I say? Simply this: *It is the shadow of God's wing;* and in the midst of its blackness I must leave you, sorrow-stricken ones, whoever you may be, at least for the present. And those who gather around you, so eager to tender you their sympathy and condolence, probably cannot enter fully into the depths of your terrible grief. In a certain sense you must bear it alone; and yet not alone, for the Lord will be with you, "a very present help in time of trouble."

Dear reader, if you have not been subjected to such an experience as this, if your home has not been robbed of all that makes it *home* to you, press the question to your own heart and ask yourself, What if the light of *my* home should be thus suddenly and irrevocably extinguished? and you may devoutly thank God that you have thus far been spared the trying ordeal. But still, and forever, it is "*somebody's* darling," and the light of *somebody's* home. The monster will yet conquer us all. We will struggle against his power, but we will struggle in vain. He will lay his cold hand upon us and we will perish at his touch. We will feel his icy breath and fade as a leaf in his presence. There is a cry that will never be hushed. It has rung through the ages—"Rachel weeping for her children and will not be comforted, for they are not." Sometimes it is loud and boisterous, like the wild and majestic wail of the psalmist, "O, my son Absalom! my son, my son Absalom! Would to God I had died for thee, O, Absalom! my son, my son!" Again, it is low and sad, like the "far wind-harp's" dying wail. And then again, it is a *voiceless* grief, that can find no relief in word or tear or moan—the deepest and saddest of all grief. Thus, David and Rachel continue through the march of time, bearing each other company. It is still and forever true, the summer roses are changing to winter lilies. We all, as with the certain tread of fate, are moving on in the same solemn procession.

"Our hearts, like muffled drums,
Are beating funeral marches to the grave."

But even here the practiced eye can behold the bright bow of God's precious promises which, like the "old, old story of Jesus and his love," are old, yet ever new; "unto which promises ye do well that ye take heed, as unto a light that shineth in a dark place."

"There is never a day so sunny,
But a little cloud appears;
There is never a life so happy,
But has its time of tears;
Yet the sun shines the brighter,
When the stormy tempest clears."

Thus do we alternate and oscillate and vacillate between the lower and higher hemispheres of our nature, so to speak—between the grosser and more refined departments of our being. And now, as we began these cogitations with an excerpt from one of the most justly celebrated poems in the English tongue, by one of America's most distinguished poets, I deem it meet to conclude with the closing paragraph of this same wonderful piece of blank verse which, when interpreted in the light of the spirit and genus of the Christian religion, affords us the real *Thanatopsis*—the true "view of death"—and the perfect solution of the "problem of human life, here and hereafter:"

"So live that when thy summons comes to join
The innumerable caravan that moves
To that mysterious realm, where each shall take
His chamber in the silent halls of death,
Thou go, not like the quarry-slave at night,
Scourged to his dungeon, but sustained and soothed
By an unfaltering trust, approach thy grave
Like one who wraps the drapery of his couch
About him, and lies down to pleasant dreams."

St. Louis, Mo., July 20, 1898.

THE GOOD IS THE ENEMY OF THE BEST.

GEO. T. SMITH.

Man seeks good. God has promised good to those who ask him. The Book, science and our experience teach that the asking must be in the right way, the seeking must be according to law, the knocking must not be with the little finger.

Our asking is too limited. "Ask great things from God; attempt great things for God." The good is the enemy of the best. Let us illustrate. Begin low. Invited to dinner in the country; after the morning sermon we found an idiotic boy of sixteen. Dinner was delayed. He grew furious. He could not be pacified. He rushed to the table as soon as the food was put on, filled his plate, gorged himself and tumbled off to bed. Eating is good. That way is not best. Play is good. But what of the truant boy? Good antagonizes the best. Two workmen in the Philadelphia navy yard employed their leisure. One taught his dog to dance on his hind legs. That was recreation. The other devised a machine for dressing the knees of ships. That was recreation.

If time be spent on inferior pursuits, or if the aim be too low, the good is the enemy of your best. Do you read the papers? Or skimp them? If the former, what solid course of reading are you taking? In fiction, do you postpone the historical and philosophical novel for the last sensation? The good drives out the best.

The Ptolemaic system of astronomy, making the earth in the center, is yet extant. It is a foe to progress and hindered Columbus. The Copernican swept away the horizon, buried time in eternity, made the heavens known. What is the center of your life? Either this self, made of earth, or the Sun of Righteousness. If of the earth, earthy, then it checks advance and opposes our Columbus who would for you cross the Atlantic of life and return with convincing word that he would pilot your bark safely through the billows to the real Fountain of Youth, in the land where the grave is never seen. If your life-center is Copernican, then it has abolished death, made life timeless and the stars but the

Colombia, Cuba, Central America and the islands of Oceanica. Our telegraph instruments click in Japan, China, Australia, Russia and in all parts of Europe. Our wire nails go to all European countries, to Canada, British Honduras, all the Central American states, Mexico, British West Indies, Cuba, Puerto Rico, the South American states, China, British East Indies, Hongkong, Japan, French Oceanica, British Australasia, British Africa and Liberia; our steel rails and locomotives go to Australia, China, Japan, Hawaii, Central and South America, Africa and Russia. Our electrical machinery is attracting the attention of the world and during the past year Austria-Hungary, France, Germany, Italy, the United Kingdom, Argentina, Brazil, Mexico, Japan, British Australasia, British Africa and French Africa have been among its purchasers. In every country in the world and in practically every inhabited island where articles of civilized or semi-civilized use are required American manufactures of iron and steel find purchasers, and the demand for them is rapidly increasing. The following table shows the value of imports and exports of iron and steel into and from the United States since 1880:

	IMPORTS.	EXPORTS.
1880—	$71,266,699	$14,716,524
1881—	60,604,477	16,608,767
1882—	67,976,897	20,748,206
1883—	58,495,246	22,826,528
1884—	40,147,053	21,909,381
1885—	33,610,093	16,592,155
1886—	37,584,078	15,745,589
1887—	49,203,164	15,958,502
1888—	48,992,757	17,763,034
1889—	42,377,793	21,156,077
1890—	41,679,501	25,542,208
1891—	53,544,372	28,909,614
1892—	28,928,103	28,800,930
1893—	34,937,974	30,136,482
1894—	20,921,769	29,220,264
1895—	23,048,515	32,000,989
1896—	25,338,103	41,160,877
1897—	16,094,587	57,497,872
1898—	12,615,903	70,367,527

The Religious World.

The Herald and Presbyter recently gave this information to the public:

The total number of additions to our church last year, as reported in the minutes of the General Assembly, just issued, was 94,166, of whom 57,041 were on profession. Added to the whole number of communicants of last year. 960,911. This would make 1,055,077. But there were losses. Deaths to the number of 11,406 occurred. There were 56,042 who were "dismissed and dropped." The loss thus reported amounted to 67,448. Deducting this and we would have left on the roll 987,529. Instead of these figures we find published 975,877 as the whole number of communicants for this year, or a discrepancy of 11,652. Where have these gone? Should there be another column headed "Missing" for these? We find that our churches last year received on certificate 37,125 persons. The same churches "dismissed and dropped" 56,402. Supposing the dismissals and receptions by certificate to be entirely within our denominational lines, we have 19,277 who were "dropped," whatever that means. If it means a relaxing of sessional care, an end of discipline, a wholesale suspension, or an easy backdoor, it indicates that many persons are making their exit from the church by means other than certificate or death. In addition to this the 11,652 who are missing show why our sum-total of communicants is not over a million and why we are not making the numerical progress that seems possible to our church.

The will of George Alfred Pillsbury, of Minneapolis, has been filed with the pro- which half is in personal property. As was expected, Pillsbury Academy, at Owatonna, receives a large gift. He leaves $250,000 as a fund, none of the income of which is to be used for the erection of any new buildings, but entirely for apparatus and scientific appliances. Until the income from this fund is $8,000 annually, the general estate is to be taxed to make up that sum. Other endowment funds go to the Minneapolis Baptist Convention, $10,000; American Baptist Missionary Union, $5,000; American Baptist Home Mission Society, $5,000; American Baptist Publication Society, $5,000; Home for Children and Aged Women, $5,000; Northwestern Hospital for Women and Children, $10,000; New Hampshire Centennial Home for the Aged, $5,000. The will also requests that the widow shall bequeath $20,000 to Pillsbury Academy as a Margaret Pillsbury Fund, the income from half to go to the aid of worthy men and women, from $5,000 for prizes and from $5,000 for the support of the library. She is also requested to bequeath $5,000 to the Hospital Association of Concord, N. H.—*Zion's Advocate.*

About 2,500 delegates attended the World's Sunday-school Convention, held in London. They represented 24,000 Sunday-schools, 2,500,000 teachers and 25,000,000 scholars. The tone of the meetings was spiritual and evangelistic. Tender allusions were made to the missing four who went down on the lost Bourgogne. The American flag was generously in evidence, and rousing applause greeted every allusion to America. A reception and lunch was tendered by the British Bible Society. The delegates were also received by the Lord Mayor and Lady Mayoress of London. Among the most interesting addresses were those of welcome by the Marquis of Northampton, by Mr. Edward Towers, for the churches of Great Britain and Ireland, and by Rev. John Clifford, D. D., for the churches of England and Wales. Rev. Dr. Spalding, of Massachusetts, responded for the United States, and Hon. S. H. Blake for Canada. Many countries were rapresented. Bishop Thoburn, of India, spoke of 5,538 schools with over 257,000 teachers and pupils in India. Dr. Joseph Parker, of London, preached a great sermon to a packed audience on "Subdue It." The chief inspiration given by the many notable speakers and remarkable addresses was that of the value and potency of Sunday-school work.—*The Union Signal.*

In speaking of language as a medium of divine revelation, The Advance speaks thus eloquently upon the influence of the Divine Mind upon human speech:

We should rejoice that God in his infinite condescension has consented to domesticate himself with man; that he has humbled himself to use human language and to act down towards man that he might bring man up towards himself. He emptied himself of his divine reputation, his flawless perfection, for our sakes, and gave occasion for critics and philosophers to flout at him because he is the God of the populace, using plain, homespun modes of expression and terms which are obnoxious to their philosophy. But in spite of the limitations which God took on himself when he made known his will through the imperfect medium of human language, what wonderful services the Bible has performed for the enrichment of language! It is hardly too much to say that it has re-made every language into which it has come speaking the thoughts of God. It has refined and spiritualized rude languages; has enlarged small words to contain great meanings; has lifted pauper words from the dust and made them princely; has given many languages literary form which before its advent spoke illiterately from uneducated lips; has shaped and enriched the noblest literary productions of the world; has made known God's will in ways which men can understand, exhibited his character in such ways that they can worship him, and in ten thousand different

Our Budget.

—Church Extension is a personal duty.

—Chattanooga is prepering for the General Convention.

—The Missouri State Board is in a stress for funds; see Hoffmann's and Abbott's articles.

—A wave of torrid weather has prevailed here for the past three days.

—Religious and relief work among soldiers should not be discontinued because peace has been declared.

—The fallen heroes, whether from Cuban or Spanish bullets, will not be forgotten in America.

—We have a letter, care of this office, for Seimaro Kubota. Will this person please tell us where to send the letter or call in person for it?

—I. J. Cahill, of Dayton, Ohio, says that the article on "Spiritism" by W. J. Lhamon, which recently appeared in our columns, ought to be put in tract form.

—The printed official report of the 17th International Christian Endeavor Convention, held at Nashville, Tenn., in July makes a book of almost 250 pages. It is closely printed, but well illustrated with numerous full-page cuts. The leading addresses and sermons of the convention appear in full and make it a volume of more than statistical value. It is a book of spiritual energy.

—An association known as the "American Boy Association" has been organized for the purpose of raising funds to build a battleship to replace the ill-fated Maine. This plan, it is said, originated in the mind of W. Rankin Good, a pupil of the High School of Cincinnati, Ohio, and has been approved by Secretary Alger, Gen. Lee and various senators and governors. Branch offices are being formed in the larger cities to push the movement. This will doubtless prove a good thing for the arousing of patriotism in young America.

—Pope Leo's love-letter to the people of Scotland is somewhat lengthy and full of gentle reminders, but withal a strong appeal for their return to the Catholic fold. Due allowance is made for the wanderings of these people through ignorance, and the hope entertained by the Pope that they will yet see their errors and accept the papal oversight of former centuries, which thing, we fear, the Scot's will hardly do. Rome's wayward children are hard to reclaim.

—S. K. Hallam believes that Sister Moyer's Text Stories appearing in our columns should be put into a book. He thus speaks of their merit: "I consider her last two, 'Christian Love' and 'An Helpmeet,' possessed of merit of a high order. I think they are worthy of being put in a more permanent form." Another writer says: "I believe the appearance of these stories in a neat little volume would be timely and successful. I write this from convictions that were formed by experience as state evangelist for the Sunday-schools of Kentucky, believing that our children and young people need something of this kind to stimulate them to more religious reading.

—The life and vigor of the Pacific Christian seems to be unaffected by the Pacific summer, the California drouth, the close of the war, or the absence from his home of its editor, A. O. Garrison. His management from afar and the local editor, with the strong editorial force, are steadfastly maintaining its high plane and pushing it forward to greater usefulness with a zeal worthy of more abundant success.

—The Christian Standard appeared last week with additional pages and claims also to be the largest edition in its history. Much of the additional space, however, is devoted to the evidences of its growth and prosperity, all of which we are glad to note.

—If we look at God's people as a temple, Christ is the foundation; as a body, Christ is the head; as a kingdom, Christ is the king; as an olive tree, Christ is the root; as branches, Christ is the vine; as a sheepfold, Christ is the shepherd; as a moral universe, Christ is the center; as an intellectual empire, Christ is the sun (light of the world); as a family, Christ is an elder brother; as a fraternity, Christ is a friend; as an army, Christ is the captain of our salvation; as a pilgrim band, Christ is the star of hope; as a new creation, Christ is their redeemer.

—A letter from Frank Ainsley dated Whitneyville, Mich., August 7th, says: "What you said recently in your Macatawa Musings as to the practicability of city churches holding out-door evening services similar to those held at the beach I think would apply to the country as well. Suppose you suggest to some of your friends the idea of coming here and holding revival meetings this month. The ground is owned by Disciples and adjoining the ground is a hall. The lake is one and a half miles from McCord Station, which is fifteen miles from Grand Rapids, on the D. G. R. & W. R. R." For further particulars address Bro. A. as above.

—The echo of the Briney and Throgmorton debate at Allen Springs, Ill., in the Baptist News, is not unpleasant to the ear nor opposed to the spirit of fairness and of Christ. We are pleased that the Baptist News can speak of us as a religious body without the use of the term "Campbellite." We hope other denominational papers will soon learn the better way.

—Remember that the National Convention recommended that the Church Extension Fund be raised to $250,000 by the close of the year 1900, and that in order to do this it will be necessary to raise $35,000 annually. The board says that it will raise $15,000 of this amount annually in the field, if the churches will raise the remaining $20,000 each year. This does not look like a difficult task, and yet if it is accomplished it will only be by the prompt, hearty and liberal offering made by each member in all the churches. Will you see to it that this is done?

—John Logan, evangelist, Gatesville, Tex., has published a tract in which he critically reviews the points at issue between what has come to be known in the South as the "progressive and the "anti" parts of the church. It is sad to realize that the occasion exists for such a tract; but being confronted with the conditions, we commend the tract. How any one can be an "anti" after reading this tract, we cannot imagine. It is written in good spirit, yet it is an energetic and effective treatment of the case, and we hope that it will be freely distributed wherever the "anti" malaria exists.

—George Darsie's sermon on Church Extension, now printed in tract form, is a clear and forceful presentation of the claims and benefits of this home missionary enterprise and deserves to be liberally distributed throughout the churches and carefully read. It is said that the author of this sermon raises annually $350 for Church Extension, hence the charge of not practicing what he preaches cannot be laid at his feet. George Darsie, of Frankfort, Ky., believes in Church Extension and is pleading manfully for its extension: We are glad the sermon has been tracted and trust that it will be freely used as a campaign document. We presume they can be had in any quantity by addressing G. W. Muckley, 600 Waterworks Bldg., Kansas City, Mo.

—We publish this week a short symposium on Church Extension, to which we invite your attention. The articles are written by some of our best missionary preachers and express not only their convictions on the benefits of Church Extension, but the manifest moral duty of every Disciple of Christ toward its support. The articles are short, well written, to the point and well worth careful reading. It is also the duty of the preachers to present the claims of Church Extension clearly to the churches and to give the reasons why it should be supported. The day for the offering for this branch of our mission work is at hand and we trust that there will be a liberal and hearty co-operation of all the churches in this grace.

—A correspondent says: "Thanks for the sample copies of the CHRISTIAN-EVANGELIST you sent me, which I have used to good purpose. Some of them went far away, and one went to the University of Oxford, England, to my friend, Canon Cheney."

—We this week publish program of the Michigan conventions to be held at Sagamon, August 31st to September 4th, which see on last page.

—The commercial history of the fiscal year 1898, just issued by the Treasury Bureau of Statistics, can be obtained free of cost by application to the Bureau of Statistics, Treasury Department, Washington, D. C.

—In the Independent, August 11, Dr. Munhall presents some strong practical reasons why the army canteen should be abolished. Let not those who have begun a good fight against this enemy of the soldier and our country relax their efforts now that the war is over. The system is an unholy, wicked, debilitating, expensive device and should be banished from the army. Let this war go on to a finish.

—Having examined a copy of the eighth annual catalogue of the Southern Christian Institute for 1898-'99, just to hand, we hasten to mention the indications of growing efficiency and future usefulness of this institute of education. A large working faculty and a practical course of instruction are announced for the coming session, beginning Sept. 27.

—An examination of a copy of the catalogue of the officers and students of Add-Ran University, Waco, Texas, for 1897-'98, with announcements for 1898-'99, is sufficient to convince any one of the strength and efficiency of the growing educational institution in the Southwest. The book is beautifully printed and handsomely illustrated with a number of full-page half-tone views, from, in, and of the University. A strong faculty is announced.

—One of the revelations of our war with Spain was the solidarity of the United States. Not a few of the Old-World nations expected that the United States would go to pieces in this war, but they were disappointed. Never did the provinces of any empire ever articulate more fully and harmoniously with its supreme head than did each state in the Union with its government. The old proverb, "In union there is strength," has received a new and striking demonstration of its truthfulness. The supremacy of American fellowship, workmanship and generalship are matters of no small surprise and concern tothe Old World.

—In speaking of the resignation of Dr. Whitsett on account of the objection which Southern Baptists have made to his statement that the Baptists of England did not immerse only in the early part of the seventeenth century, the Herald and Presbyter makes this singularly confusing statement: "We do not see that they make their argument for immersion any stronger by this. Certainly immersion can not be proved from the Bible, and failing there, the case is hopeless. The 'apostolic succession' of immersion also breaks down. Of course, if they wish to baptize in that manner they may do so, but they can not insist upon it with the authority of Scripture or of unbroken history behind them." If these words have any logical conclusion, it is that immersion is an unscriptural practice, an innovation. They can immerse if they wish, but cannot support the practice with Scripture. Now the facts are quite contrary to this statement. Sprinkling and pouring for Christian baptism are innovations. Of course people

his if they wish, and call it baptism, practice is without scriptural author- paper of the pretensions of the Herald sbyter ought to be consistent, if not Bible, at least with its own creed.

's program of the war of the United vith Spain was so paramount that it le the imperfections and mistakes of the lesser lights more conspicuous and All men are finite, and mistakes in not wholly be avoided. Greivous mis- re no doubt made by some of the high of the army in the late war, but of one are better informed and perhaps keenly feel now as they who made But the war is over, the desired and more obtained, and so what cannot helped should be lovingly covered with tle of charity or profitably reserved for mergencies.

w effort is being made to do more re- vork among seamen than they are ac- d to see. A yacht capable of seating ındred people is being built for their is yacht will be fully equipped for hold- ious services and will go from port to ime and utility may direct. The work of an interdenominational character, e management of Geo. E. Benn, of , Mich., who is also the president of hapel Yacht Associations'' organized special work. There seems to be a itness in the move to this particular people who, because of their sea-rov- are usually overlooked in evangelistic . Dr. Benn, the promoter of this en- , bears high testimonials to his moral istian character, and seems to be wholly d in the work and we hope that he will disappointed in the amount of good e hopes to accomplish.

meeting of the national executive W. . Committee at Chicago, recently, it ided to abandon the effort to raise the necessary to pay out and own the W. . Temperance Temple, Chicago. The of this temple by the W. C. T. U. leven years ago as a monument to the spoused by this body in behalf of ood, our homes and humanity, and it regretted that they have failed in the se. The building was completed, but h a heavy debt, which they have not een able to liquidate or carry. The t of The Voice on the failure of the se, however, is perhaps about the best be taken of the matter after all. It

ends an enterprise on which a tremend- ount of toil and sacrifice has been ex- As a business enterprise, pure and it never was a wise one. It was senti- at gave birth to it, and tho the senti- as a noble and exalting one, the scheme big and has encountered too many s—including a commercial panic and a re—to admit of success. It has been ous to the union for years, and it must at relief to the general officers to feel organization is at last relieved of the

will be disappointment, but there is ace attaching to anyone because of the It was a noble effort, nobly made. ret now that it was ever made; we re- t, having been made, it failed; but we find it in our heart to censure anyone r part in it. It was a mistake of the ot of the heart.

speaking of the celebration of "The tion of the Blessed Virgin," the Progress says:

event, the Fourth Glorious Mystery of ary, is attested by the consistent tradi- the Universal Church, but there is vergence regarding its details. It took , 15 or 12 years, according to the vary- ounts, after our Lord's Ascension, and re when she was 72, 63 or 60 years of olweck's Fasti Mariania, p. 170).

wonder, in the face of such indefinite- hat Roman Catholic journals are com- g of great losses to their church in a.

—According to inquiries made by Carroll D. Wright, Labor Commissioner, Washington, D. C., more than half of the business men of the United States, in employing help, make a difference in favor of those not given to intoxicating drinks. Out of seven thousand business men addressed 1,284 of them replied that they would not employ a man who drank either on or off duty. This is a practical and valuable test of the detriment of strong drink to laboring men and of the growth and worth of total abstinence and prohibition sentiments and principles. Now let all men who value their business, their manhood and their homes, vote accordingly.

—Now that the vail is lifted from the Philippine Islands, Cuba and Spain, and the civil, social, moral and religious conditions are found to be so deplorable as they are, the more respectable class of Roman Catholic journals in the United States have undertaken the very difficult task of irreconciling these conditions to Roman Catholic influence over these islands for centuries. To Protestants the conditions and the controlling influences are somewhat consistent; but for Roman Catholics to acknowledge this incriminates the Roman Catholic Church and discount its religion, so other causes have to be sought by Roman Catholic journals et al., to account for the present undesirable prevalent state of the people intellectually, morally and religiously, in these heretofore Roman Catholic countries. The Church Progress, of this city, in a recent number expressed the opinion that these things were due to European Freemasonary. It says:

We, who are accustomed to the mild type of Freemasonary which prevails in America and England, cannot understand the virulence of European Masonary. European Masonary bears the same relation to infidelity that A. P. A.-ism bears to Protestantism. Its object is to crush out revealed religion, and the means used are political lodges, whose members alone are put into office. It is one of the mysteries of Latin politics that this should be true in France and in Italy as well as in Spain. But still this is true. These countries, inhabited by Catholics, are governed by infidels. Nothing is too sacred for these infidels to sneer at. The honor of men and the fame of women are bywords in their mouth. Their slanders against the clergy are worthy of the dirtiest preacher who ever preached for the beetle-browed. All these things have their bearing on the present condition of affairs in the Philippines. Colonies are notoriously more conservative than the mother countries. Up to some twenty years ago religion was respected by all classes in the Philippines. When the Angelus rang every one, young and old, gentle and simple, in the streets of Manila uncovered and publicly recited the prayer. The people were thoroughly Catholic and the average of crime among them was, by the confession of European observers, extremely low. But a change has been wrought within the past twenty years. Spain began to send out infidels and Freemasons as officials to the colony. They began their campaign against religion and morality. To-day the results of that campaign are evident. The Philippines are lost to Spain and Spain may thank her rulers.

This opinion is not worth much in the face of history, but it is well to see how others see things.

—Only those who have given special consideration to the subject are aware of the alarming increase of secret societies during the past ten years. The total increase is estimated at 250,000. In 1897 the expenditures in benefit gifts and claims reached the sum of $640,000,000, while in transportation, fees, banquets, testimonials, regalia and convention expenses $250,000,000 more was spent. To these items the approximate sum of $12,000,000 was added for the rental of buildings and halls for lodge purposes, thus making a total of $941,000,000 expended in a single year by the secret societies of the United States. If we compare the last-named large sum with the amount raised annually for missions, $10,000,000, the question involuntarily presents itself: "What will the outcome be? Will the manifold and diversified secret orders finally crowd out the churches, even as they are now sapping their vitality?" These are questions of no ordinary significance.

The above paragraph is from The Gospel Messenger. We do not know that the figures are correct, but there is no doubt but that lodges are costly institutions and that large sums of money are annually invested in them. The Gospel Messenger, of course, takes the dark view of these facts and figures. We are certain that there are more or less encroachments upon church funds by lodges, but we do not think that they are to be denominated the enemy of Christianity and humanity. Think of the $640,000,000 paid out in benefit claims. Think also of how the growth of lodges indicates the want of the fraternal spirit among men, and of its growth in the world. Then think once more of the argument in these facts and figures in favor of the growing doctrine of the brotherhood of man. If the churches have been delinquent in their duties along the lines of lodge work they must blame themselves and not the lodges. The truth will come to the surface somehow. The lodges are not above criticism, but this does not justify the churches for shortsightedness and delinquencies.

—Rev. T. DeWitt Talmage recently closed a sermon in Washington, D. C., on "Alleviations of War," with the following words:

Yet what the world most wants is Christ, who is coming to take possession of all hearts, all homes, all nations; but the world blocks the the wheels of his chariot. I would like to see this century, which is now almost wound up, find its peroration in some mighty overthrow of tyrannies and a mighty building up of liberty and justice. Almost all of the centuries have ended with some stupendous event that transformed nations and changed the map of the world. It was so at the close of the fourteenth century; it was so at the close of the fifteenth century; it was so at the close of the sixteenth century; it was so at the close of the seventeenth century; it was so at the close of the eighteenth century. May it be more gloriously so at the close of the nineteenth century! "Blessed be the Lord God of Israel from everlasting to everlasting, and let the whole earth be filled with his glory." Amen and amen!

—In an article in Pall Mall for September, about "Mark Twain," the writer strikingly portrays the man by alluding to the difference between the man who studies to be "funny" and the man who studies to be serious. In one instance the "fun" is ground out for the occasion; in the other it is an ever-flowing well. We wonder how many preachers there are of the machine class who grind out sermons for the occasion. The true preacher is the one from whom the words of salvation flow as the crystal water from the unfailing spring. Affectation is, of all places, least excusable in the pulpit.

—We are thankful to the Christian Messenger, Toronto, for the following words of appreciation and good cheer:

For several weeks the CHRISTIAN-EVANGELIST, of St. Louis, has come to hand in its new dress. The paper is now a thirty-two page journal of magazine form, somewhat after the style of the Toronto Westminster, but as to contents we think much superior. The series of illustrations appearing on the first page, including already portraits of Gladstone and American military and naval heroes, adds to the appearance and interest of the paper. The articles are vigorous, refreshing and helpful. The type is clear and the paper of about the same quality as that of the Messenger. The CHRISTIAN-EVANGELIST stands in the very front rank of our exchanges.

The Christian Messenger is a live vigorous journal ably advocating primitive Christianity, across our national northern border, and wortho of abounding success for which it has our hopes and prayers.

—There may be some moral effect from the sight of a church paper in the home, but far better results would obtain if these papers were more considerately read. Too many find time only to "scan" the paper; that is, to read the personals and the locals. Some even do not take the time to do this. A church paper cannot do the good that it would unless it is reasonably well read. We fear that some families take a church paper for consicence' rather than for the soul's sake. This ought not to be. If the church paper you take does not pay the time and cost of taking and reading it, change it for one that does. A good church paper is a good investment and ought not to be neglected; not even its reading.

—The Evangelist, edited by W. J. Russell, Kalamazoo, Mich., has now become the Michigan Evangelist, edited by Alex. McMillan, Ann Arbor, Mich. Alex. McMillan is the state secretary and will use the paper in the interests of the mission work and churches of the state more particularly. The paper has lost none of its many excellent qualities in the transfer from editor to editor and place to place named.

—A glance at the table of contents of this paper will certainly whet the appetite for reading. Passing over the editorials, which we are persuaded are timely, suggestive, and interesting, we are sure the reader will enjoy the vigorously writter articles in our contributor's department, of which we would especially commend Prof. Peckham's article on the Old Testament Prophets. Our correspondents also, as usual, have something to say, and say it in such an interesting way that their department in no way lags from any canse, and will be enjoyed by our readers. The other departments are full, covering a wide range of territory, persons and interests, and fill out what we are sure our readers will call "a good number of the CHRISTIAN-EVANGELIST."

PERSONAL MENTION.

James B. McIntire who has been attending the University of Chicago for a year and six weeks, writes that he will spend a few weeks at Oskaloosa, Ia.

E. M Barney is just closing his work at Drake University, Des Moines, Ia., and would like to find a field of work in the Southwest. He has been preaching for eight years and can give satisfactory references.

F. H. Cappa, singer, has lost some engagements on account of sickness, but would now be glad to assist in meetings again. Address 1221 Jefferson St., Louisville, Ky.

While at its annual outing the Bible-school of the Christian Church at Bellaire, Ohio, presented the pastor of that church, Chas. M. Watson, with a fine "Rambler" bicycle. Bro. Watson seems to stand high in the affection and esteem of that church and school.

Perry Stevenson, of Vermont, Ill., has accepted the office of the principalship of the South High School, at Abingdon, Ill., and has removed to that place from Vermont.

H. S. Gilliam, of Hamilton, Mo., preached a: Compton Heights Christian Church, this city, last Sunday.

Dr. W. Frank Ross writes that the College of Hygiene at Champaign, Ill., gives free tuition to all foreign missionaries.

We learn through the Christian Courier that M. L. Hoblit, the Mexican missionary, was married to Miss Orpha A. Bennett, at Keokuk, Ia., August 18. They have our congratulations.

The editor of this paper made a flying trip from Macatawa to Grand Rapids, Mich., on the 18th inst.

Harold Baldwin is now engaged in preaching for the churches of San Angelo and Sherwood, Tex.

T. M. Burgess, of Woodhull, Ill., has been called to the superintendency of the public school, Gardner, Ill. He has been a student of Eureka and expects to return to complete the course as soon as possible. He does not expect to cease entirely his work in the ministry.

L. J. Marshall has closed his work with the Keytesville church. He preached for them two Sundays per month for six months. There were 20 persons added to the church during that time. The Bible-school, he says, is doing well under the direction of B. H. Smith, superintendent. Bro. Marshall goes to Palmyra, Mo.

Word from T. A. Abbott this week says that his wife is no better of her sickness, and that the physician has no word of cheer for him concerning the result. This news we deeply regret hearing, and the more deeply grows our sympathy for Bro. Abbott.

W. T. Stephensen, pastor of the church at Sutherland, Ia., publishes the smallest weekly church paper, in size, that we have yet seen—about three inches square, with eight pages—but by no means barren in news, thought and religious food. It indeed contains much in small space.

J. V. Coombs, who has had charge of the evangelistic forces of Indiana for a year, now resigns that work for the general field. He states that during the year there have been 2,300 accessions to the churches of Indiana, and about $4,000 raised for evangelists.

W. L. Luck closed his work at Lafayette, Ind., July 31st. He has been there over three years, during which time there have been 350 additions. The church house also has been remodeled and improved.

A. G. Aderman, of Bethany, Mo., has accepted a call to the chair of Commercial Science, Central Christian College, Albany, Mo.

The Christian Tribune, Baltimore, this week contains the following interesting item of news: "Dr. C. A. Young, of Chicago, has been tendered the presidency of Bethany College. His wide experience in university work and his successful service in the Bible chairs eminently fit him for this important post. If he be given absolute control of the college affairs, it will mean new life for old Bethany. We hope that Dr. Young will accept."

After sixty-eight years, Harrison Jones, of Alliance, O., recently visited the church at North Royalton, O. This church was organized in 1829 and the next year Bro. Jones, then but eighteen years old, became its pastor. His visit was the occasion of many touching, pleasant and hallowed memories. J. B. Watson is the pastor of the North Royalton church who, with his congregation, extended a royal welcome to this aged veteran of the cross. Bro. Jones was chaplain of President Garfield's regiment in the civil war.

J. W. Coggins, of Benton City, Mo., paid his respects to this office while in the city last Monday. Bro. Coggins preaches for the Unity, Martinsburg and Forestell churches. He was recently assisted in a meeting at Martinsburg by his brother, J. C., which added twelve persons to its membership. These brothers in the flesh and in the Lord will hold a meeting at Forestell in October.

On last Monday we had the pleasure of a call at this office from Dr. R. M. Sargent, a well-known Congregational minister, and long resident of this city. Dr. Sargent's son, Dr. C. S. Sargent, is the pastor of the Central Congregational Church, of this city. These two ministers have very kindly feelings toward the Disciples of Christ and their greetings in presence or by word are always occasions of pleasure to us.

The Christian Index, Aug. 17th, says: "N.A. McConnell preached at Marshalltown, Aug. 14th." We are glad to hear from this veteran in the Lord's army again.

S. S. McGill, who has been preaching for the church in Lebanon temporarily for the past few months, has closed his labors there and returned to his home at Smithville, Mo. On account of financial matters the church was not able to secure him permanently. T. B. Burley, of Lebanon, Mo., says: "Any church in need of a preacher will find in Bro. McGill an earnest, thoughtful, energetic preacher of the gospel. He knows what Christianity is and is not afraid to proclaim it."

Both the official board of the First Christian Church of Sedalia, Mo., and the Board of Trade of that city have passed resolutions of appreciation of the ability and labors of J. S. Myers, for eight years the pastor of that church and citizen of that city. The resolutions commend him highly for his work's sake and good generalship, and will be held by Bro. Meyers as a valued expression of their good will toward him and of the high esteem in which he was held by both church and city of Sedalia.

The Kansas City, Osceola and Southern Railway, extending from Kansas City, Mo., to Bolivar, Mo., will, on and after Sept. 1st, 1898, be operated as a part of the St. Louis and San Francisco Railroad System. Transportation issued by the St. Louis and San Francisco Railroad will, unless otherwise limited, be honored over the Kansas City, Osceola and Southern Railway. A copy of either of the following publications will be mailed free to those who ask: "Eureka Springs," "Feathers and Fins on the Frisco," "Missouri and Arkansas Farmer and Fruitman." Please address B. L. Winchell, General Passenger Agent Frisco Line, St. Louis, Mo.

G. L. Applegate, of Wakefield, Neb., has resigned his work there to take place Oct. 1st. His work the past year has involved a travel of over 8,000 miles, going to Craig every other Sunday with one exception, with horse and carriage, and preaching five times each trip. He had 35 additions there during the year and three at Craig. He preached about 225 discourses during the year, held protracted meetings at each place of over three weeks each, and leaves the church at Wakefield about 100 strong. He will devote his time to evangelistic work for a time.

To the surprise of the church and people Perry, O. T., the pastor, C. H. Hilton, I resigned that he might accept the work of t ministry for the church at Lanard, Kas. his work at Perry the Perry Enterprise Tin says: "Rev. Hilton has been pastor of t church here for the past two years, and bei an untiring worker in the vineyard has su ceeded in building up a large and flourishi congregation and the citizens by his every-d walk and his earnest efforts for the betterme of mankind in general and Perry in particul and it is with feeling of sincere regret that shall bid him farewell." Correspondence regard to the work at Perry should be a dressed to Hon. Dick T. Morgan, of that cit

Geo. C. Myers, of Albany, Ore., sends us t following note:

"To-day was a great day for the Church Christ at this place, on account of what h transpired in our midst. Bro. Lane, who h been pastor of the C. P. Church here, preach in the Christian church this morning. H text was, 'But in vain do they worship m teaching for doctrines the commandments men' (Matt. 15:9). He started with the na ing of these on the door at Wittenberg a followed the reformatory work forward, sho ing the reason of the multiplication of denon nationalism in about the brightest, if r the best manner that the writer ev heard. He closes with an invitation to all w would to present themselves for membesshi saying that he wanted the church to consid himself as an applicant, and that he intend henceforth to preach the gospel where could do so without first fitting it to an ecc siastical gauge. He expects to subscribe f the CHRISTIAN-EVANGELIST."

CHANGES.

E. C. Wigmore, Charles City, Ia., Palouse, Wash.

Wm. H. Matlock, Lausanne Swizterland 9 Rue du Sommerard, Paris, France.

J. G. Encell, St. Louis, Mo., to 1075 W 26th St., Des Moines, Ia.

Levi Marshall, Atlantic Highlands, N. J Hannibal, Mo.

J. E. Hawes, Blue Bell, to Ada, Mo.

Walter R. Davis, Boston to Haverhi Mass.

Geo. E. Dew, Weston to Savannah, Mo.

D. A. Howe, Lanark to Eureka, Ill.

K. W. White, Redwood Falls, Minn., Lawrence, Kan.

G. A. Reynolds, Sherman to McComb Cit Miss.

G. Kervorkian, Marsivian to Tocat, Turke

W. S. Moore, Chanute to Humboldt, Kan.

John Young, Marshall, Mo., to Jonesbor Ark.

rrespondence.

ng Through England.

VI.

of "Lorna Doone" is the best enjoying and appreciating the mouth to Porlock, along the r of the wild and barren Exmoor is novel, Blackmore has inter- ery of this wild, desolate, but active part of North Devon, as is interpreted the Lake District. Lynmouth, the wheelman must n and mountaineer for a time wheel up a two-mile hill where of the question. Thence, by a nd downs, the road follows the ills along the coast, with Bristol distant view of South Wales on ne broad expanse of Exmoor on e valley of the Doones is soon does not accurately get the he novel. The little church of John Ridd was warden, and s' farm are, however, real and o satisfy any reader of Lorna Ridd in his time testified with roads in that locality had been at a rider need not entirely sink laylight, provided he be quite ent degree of sobriety is still ny traveler among these hills, bogs have been banished from The descent of Porlock Hill, a n hundred feet in a mile and a considered as the end of this ection.

ty of interest but little excite- erived from the ride through Wells, and Bath, to Bristol. al place of its kind and worthy than any of them could receive of a bicycle tour. One of the ng sights in Bristol, to one who g about ecclesiastical architec- hurch of St. Mary Redcliffe, a of perfect symmetry and elabor- lt upon the lines of a cathedral. ours when I reached it, but the s easily found and he readily low a small party of us through. the church was, the old verger ore so. The pride of his heart ent church, and all his thought ion were colored by admiration and workmen of the thirteenth ntempt for all modern methods. were the days of thoroughness; ays of quick, cheap and shoddy eople who did their work in the solid way did not need not contemptuous emphasis) to give Presently we come to a corner pty stone sarcophagus of some ury bishop was lying, with its beside it. "There now," said 'that's a coffin to last awhile. ake 'em like that now. Just of it, too. Big men in those d have to look for awhile ind a man to fill it." To the verger, I proceeded to crawl sarcophagus, and to his further t from end to end and from side fact is, that a stone coffin is not as it looks. "That's a Yankee ne verger, "aren't you from the reupon he led us away hastily to f the church to inspect a beauti- ore the light failed.

e is less than fifteen miles from ere the trip up the valley of the ut the Severn flows between and ay of getting across except by nd going through the tunnel er. The only alternative is to make a sixty-five mile ride around it by way of Gloucester. Having conscientious scruples against taking a train when on a bicycle trip, except in case of emergency, I chose the latter course. My companion, who is less sensitive about such matters, chose the train and we met the next afternoon at Hereford. The valley of the Wye is starred in the guidebooks and described as "one of the loveliest pieces of river scenery in Europe," but this expression is too commonplace to be accurately descriptive. It is not wild, rugged or overwhelming. Except at one or two points, notably at Wyndcliff, it could scarcely even be called grand. "Pretty" is too shallow and insignificant a word to use, and "magnificent" is to large. Riding up from Chepstow to Tintern at the time of day when afternoon was passing into evening, the valley of the Wye seemed to me the most peaceful spot I had ever seen—a spot where weariness and haste and feverish unrest could not exist, a spot where the cynic would regain his faith in man, the atheist his faith in God, a spot where all the problems of life seemed a little easier of solution. One is already under the spell of this scene when, rounding a curve, the beautiful ruin of Tintern Abbey comes into view, lying far below in a meadow in a bend of the river, and then the scene is complete.

The next day it rained. The Wye is a slender stream at best. Its volume would not entitle it to be called more than a creek in our country, and as I rode ten miles in the rain next morning to get into Monmouth, catching an occasional glimpse of the diminutive stream which was almost lost in the haste, it seemed (probably erroneously) that it would have taken several Wyes to make up the stream which coursed freely down the back of my neck. At least there was more water in the air than in the river just then. At this point perhaps a word ought to be said in regard to English weather. It is now six weeks since we started from Liverpool. In that time we have been inconvenienced by rain only three times. Twice we rode on through the rain and once we stopped for half a day in a place where stopping was no loss of time. There have been other occasional showers, but not of a sort to impede progress or mar the pleasure of the trip. This seems to me to be a good average to be maintained for six weeks by a country with England's reputation for rain, and grateful acknowledgment is hereby made.

It was at the close of that same rainy day, after we had ridden a good many miles through rain and a good many more through mud, and had spent the rest of the day pushing our wheels against a heavy head wind, that darkness came upon us and found us out of reach of any village. Just as the supper and bed problem was beginning to look rather dark, there appeared two wayside inns, one on either side of the road, the "Crown Inn" and the "Green Dragon." Choosing the latter, we applied for admission and were soon happy before a good supper. Somewhat later in the evening I chanced to pick up a book of stories by Beatrice Harraden, the first of which was her well-known "At the Green Dragon." The identity of the name with that of our inn seemed a singular coincidence, but nothing marvelous, for "Green Dragon," "Red Lion," "White Horse," and such are favorite names for inns. But it did seem strange when on the very first page mention was made of a Crown Inn just across the road from the Green Dragon in the story. When a little further on, Shopshire was mentioned as the county and Shrewsbury as a neighboring town, it was plainly time to make inquiries. Inquiry revealed the fact that this was the scene of the story and that the author had stopped here while writing it three years ago. I can add my testimony to that of Beatrice Harraden that the Green Dragon is a goodly inn and well worthy of being taken as the type of English inns.

Shrewsbury is a venerable place full of houses three or four centuries old, timbered structures with upper stories projecting over the sidewalk. There are inns and public houses at every corner, at any one of which one might easily expect to see the doughty Sir John Falstaff sitting before a measure of sack and discoursing of his adventures. Leaving Shrewsbury, the hills of Wales are soon in sight, and after skirting them for some miles and crossing the Welsh border of Chirk we plunge into the hill-country at Llangollen, following the valley of the river Dee. The road, with the surface of a boulevard, is a splendid piece of engineering, winding by easy gradients up and down hills, a stone wall and a valley on one side and a steep hillside on the other. As we advance the hills grow bolder. It is again twilight (all of our best views have come at that time) and at last the triple peaks of Snowdon are seen twenty miles to the west with the evening star above them still faint in the light of the setting sun. Next day we abandoned our wheels long enough to make the ascent of Snowdon. It would have been a pleasure, of course, to take the wheels along, but one can't expect to ride up a fire-escape, even on a Sterling. The ascent is a very easy one, as mountain climbing goes. It means about nine miles of walking, scrambling and climbing, but there is a path to follow all the way, and no single point of it could be called difficult. There have been several fatal accidents to climbers of this peak, but in every case they have resulted from attempts to reach the summit by going straight up the precipices or in some other strange and unusual way. The view from the top of Snowdon—what need to describe it? It is the highest mountain in a land of mountains. Nearly the whole of North Wales with its ridges, peaks and lakes, St. George's Channel, the Coast of Ireland and the Isle of Man are spread before us like a map.

We could not wait to see the sunset from Snowdon, for the descent must be made and several miles of traveling done before dark. It is thirteen miles of down grade and smooth road from the foot of Snowdon to Carnarvon by the sea—just the sort of road on which to race with the setting sun. The moon was rising over Snowdon now as we turned our backs upon her and sped away down the pass. English laws strictly demand that bicycle-lamps shall be lit at one hour after sunset and the law is enforced to the minute in the city and country alike. The time was up and we were still a couple of miles out of Carnarvon when, in passing through a village, we ran full into the arms of a uniformed policeman. There was nothing to do but to jump off and anxiously inquire the time and ask how many minutes we had left to ride. It was no surprise to learn that we had already overdrawn, but the genial "bobbie" was not above being beguiled. "I'll give you permission to ride on," he said, "and if anybody stops you, tell him that Mogan, number forty-seven, says it's all right." Happily we were not called upon to use the talismanic words, "Mogan, 47," but it is evidence of the virtue of the English police that the permission did not cost us a penny.

The day's ride from Carnarvon at the northwest corner to Hawarden at the northeast corner of Wales showed us more of the people of Wales and less of its scenery. The people tell us that it is a mistake to suppose that the Welsh language is dying out. The children learn English in the schools and English is the language of the courts, but Welsh is the language of the home, the street and the market. It would perhaps not be right to close these paragraphs on Wales without casting the expected fling at Welsh names and the generally unpronounceable character of the words of that tongue. To the ordinary traveler these names, with their ominous appearance and worse sound, are merely the subject of a passing jest. To the cyclist who must occasionally inquire his way, they present a serious problem. For example, what is a man to do when he wants to know the way to opposite Bangor on the strait of Menai of which the full name is *Llanfairpwllgwyngyllgogerychwyrndrobwllll-andysiliogogogoch!* They call this place Llanfair P. G. for short, but I did not know that at first. The best scheme I have yet developed for use in such a case is to find on a map the first town within easy name immediately beyond the one desired and ask to be directed to it, trusting to luck that the route will take you through the desired point. After a day of this sort of thing, just as we are on the point of emerging from Wales into Cheshire, we stop for the night at Hawarden, a name long familiar as the home of Gladstone. But of this more anon. W. E. G.

Hawarden.

New York Letter.

As suggested in our last letter we are summering this season at the famous Sing Sing Camp Grounds on the Hudson, some thirty miles from New York. Certain of our flock have rested here for a few summers past and through them we were persuaded to secure a tent. We did so, and are greatly enjoying the novel experience. The Camp Grounds are owned by the Methodist brethren of New York and here they have conducted "revival services" every summer for sixty-seven years. "The Camp" of the present season opened on August the 4th and continued ten days and was a revelation in the manner of methods and sustained joy. Some of the sermons were excellent, the singing was as a rule inspiring and soulful, the large choir at the main services at "the Circle" being accompanied by a cornet and piano. At the close of each preaching service "seekers" were called to the mourner's bench "in the straw," where many brethren and sisters would kneel and fervently pray for their conversion. The excitement and noisy shouting at times would lead to most any state of mind before it would make one turn to Christ in the full assurance of faith. The love-feasts held at the Circle each Sunday morning were seasons abounding in joy in the Lord to hundreds of the old campers, who in relating their Christian experience would usually tell the day and hour, and sometimes the very minute of their couversion to Christ. Among the leaders of the camp services are many who profess to be subjects of the "second blessing"—"a second distinct and definite work of grace"—as they term it. Some of them even claim for themselves sinless purity. This seems to differ somewhat from Paul who found that when he would do good evil was present with him; and from John who declares if any man says he has no sin he is a liar and the truth is not in him. But that these good brethren are sincere is quite evident, though they are in grievous error.

The religious enthusiasm was such that at times four or five services were in progress at the same time in different places. The last was high day in the camp, about 7,000 people being in attendance from all parts of the surrounding country and from New York City. It was my privilege to preach one sermon and conduct several Bible readings. The latter services, I think, were very much appreciated in view of the fact that the Bible was brought into use so seldom in the other meetings; it was rarely read, quoted or even referred to; the brethren and sisters usually confined themselves to their experience. The number of professed conversions was very small.

⁂

On one side of the camp grounds the Swedish Methodists held services in a large tent in their own language. Though we could understand but few words they uttered, their happy faces, abounding joy and evident sincerity were pleasing to all Americans who attended their services. The closing up of the camp is always interesting, when the Swedes form a procession and "march around Zion," singing hymns. The American brethren receive them with enthusiasm at the Circle, where all join together in singing, shaking hands and shouting for joy. Among the most inspiring discourses were those of Dr. Cadman, of the Methodist Metropolitan Temple, Dr. Crouch, of Beekman Hill Church, Dr. Rowe, of Purdy's Station, and Dr. Johnson, of Brooklyn. The Rev. Thomas Harrison, "the boy preacher," was present through most of the Camp, and conducted most of the after-services. He overflows with eccentric enthusiasm.

"Children's Day" and "Old Folks' Day" are always special on the programme. Many old people have been coming here for years—one sister stated that she had not missed the annual camp for fifty-four years. And the Rev. A. C. Morehouse, superintendent of the services, has been actively engaged in this work for more than fifty years. The fathers and grandfathers of many of those who now worship here in other generations sang hymns of praise and worshiped God in this leafy temple. It is to them a sacred spot.

⁂

Immediately following this issue of the CHRISTIAN-EVANGELIST the New York Christian Missionary Convention and Ministerial Association will convene with the 169th St. Church, New York City. Again we welcome all delegates and ask that those expecting to attend send us their names at once. We hope all will come early and stay through the sessions until Friday night, when the convention closes. We expect a goodly representation from most all the churches in the state, and the talent on the program assures a continuous feast of good things.

⁂

It is understood that Dr. John Hall, of the Fifth Avenue Presbyterian Church, will retire next year on the completion of fifty years' ministry in the Presbyterian Church. Just now he is in Europe on his vacation, and his pulpit is supplied by probable candidates for the Fifth Avenue Church. Dr. J. Wilbur Chapman, of Philadelphia, Dr. McKilrick, of Buffalo, and Dr. G. C. Morgan, of London, England, have supplied the pulpit, and Dr. McGregor is booked for next Lord's day. Dr. Morgan drew an immense audience last Lord's day to hear him; he made, it is reported, a most favorable impression on the congregation. It is a church with sufficient money power to attract most any minister in America, or Europe, if that were all that is necessary. The congregation usually assembled in the Fifth Ave. Church on Lord's day morning represents more than $400,000,000. The pastorate of this church entails great responsibilities also, because of its financial and social influence.

⁂

Mr. Russell, Sage one of the multimillionaires of Wall St., has just passed his 82nd birthday. His wealth is estimated at $75,000,000 and he works just as hard now as he did at 23. A reporter called on him on his birthday and said to him: "Tell the young men, Mr. Sage, how to keep young fourscore years." His reply in brief was:

"I do not use tobacco."

"I am temperate in the use of stimulants."

"I eat good, plain food and no late suppers."

"I keep regular hours and work."

"I never felt better in my life than I do to-day, and I hope to live to see many more birthday anniversaries."

He works now with as much regularity and enthusiasm as he did when he began to build his fortune. These expressions are good advice to thousands of young men all over this country And I hope that many may read and consider them. S. T. WILLIS.

1281 Union Ave.

The Chicago Letter.

Nothing has been more gratifying to all
lovers of "the land of the free and the h
of the brave" than the cordial and sym
thetic relations between the "South"
the "North," which the war with Spain
fostered and developed. In keeping with
gratifying sense of growing unity, this le
will give a resume of several weeks of hard
most enjoyable and profitable work outsid
Chicago, and chiefly in the "Old Dominior
I say "hard" work, for although many of
lectures and addresses I delivered had b
thoroughly prepared beforehand, still speak
three full hours each day and traveling most
the time at night, in the month of August,
hardly be designated *easy* work, however "
joyable" it may be. And I say "profitabl
work, (1) because I have no reason to do
the sincerity of the C. W. B. M. members
the twoscore or more of earnest, hard-worki
God-fearing preachers and the much lar
number of intelligent Christian workers, w
by their constant attention and kind wo
assured me of the helpfulness of the mission
addresses and the Bible lectures I gave;
(2) because, not only were my traveling
penses paid, besides an average of three d
lars for each lecture and address I deliver
but sufficient interest was manifested in
University of Virginia Bible Lectureship
warrant the public statement that I confide
ly hope to see such a Lectureship, with
loved and lamented John B. Cary as
founder, established. All person interested
this noble enterprise should write Miss El
Kent, State President of C. W. B. M., Loui
Va., or Mrs. Lizzie Daniel, Richmond, Va
who has consented to serve on the endowm
committee.

⁂

Before going to Virginia I spent a most d
lightful Lord's day at Macatawa Park, whe
Mrs. Young, Helen and myself were guests
the home of Bro. and Sister Garrison. Arth
who is an expert fisherman, had a plenti
supply of fine white bass and toothsome crop
on hand, which Sister Garrison cooked a
served to suit any epicure. It was a brief da
but will be cherished and often lived over
memory.

"In the world's broad field of battle,
In the bivouac of life,"

we often grow heart-hungry for the socie
and sympathy of true and tried friends. Th
a day of quiet joy in the society of those
love is rest, sweet rest. But in addition
such deep soul-satisfaction as flows from
companionship of the friends of "auld la
syne," a day at Edgewood-on-the-Lake, li
one heavenward and Godward. With Word
worth we feel that heaven lies all about us,
only in our infancy, but also in the stress a
struggle of life. The calm lake before you
now green, now amethyst, now every color
the rainbow blended; the blue sky above y
—floating the fleecy clouds shot through w
the rays of unraveled light; the tall pines
the steep slopes, and the delicate ferns
shady ravines back of you—these and ma
other beauties of nature make one exclaim w
the poet:

"Earth is crammed with heaven,
And every common bush is aflame with God.

Leaving Macatawa at four o'clock we reac
ed Chicago at eleven. As the "Soo City
steamed through the government pier into t
open lake, bathed in glorious sunlight,
thought of "the sea of glass mingled wi
fire." The coloring of the calm still expa
of water was a delightful study for my w
who has an artist's eye. As the westering s
sank lower and lower it threw an ever-expan
ing bar of golden light across the lake ea
ward, and the great ball of fire had no soon
been lost in the bosom of the lake than t
queen of the night began to throw a silver b
of borrowed light from the eastern horiz
westward. Such is life—meeting, partin
journeying homeward. Gentle reader, let

ɔ live that with Tennyson we may
ing:
evening star,
clear call for me!
iere be no moaning of the bar,
ut out to sea,
om out our bourne of Time and Place
may bear me far,
e my Pilot face to face
ave crossed the bar. . .

***

ay to the "Old Dominion" I stop-
day at Indianapolis. At the C. W.
quarters I found Miss White work-
t her post, notwithstanding the fact
d been suffering for two days with a
s other workers, except Mrs. Ford,
king a much-needed rest at home,
at their respective desks. In com-
Mrs. Helen E. Moses, our Bible
etary, I visited the home of Sister
ress, who, I take pleasure in report-
dually gaining strength. We hope
visit us in Chicago before we re-
ginia. Constrained by the love of
C. W. B. M. has been not only
, but *doing* great things for God
ity. Notwithstanding the financial
of the past few years this noble
eroic women has constantly heeded
r's great commission. Undaunted
rdrawn treasury they are steadily
the lead of their president whose
is "Forward." Sister, brother,
llar to help the board go to the
Convention in October with a
ank account.

***

iia I attended the Piedmont Assem-
rdonsville, the South Piedmont Con-
Martinsville, the Tidewater Con-
Mathews, and visited Danville and
. The first meeting of the Piedmont
was very successful. Such preach-
en as Bernard Smith, of Charlotts-
ard Bagby, of Louisa, Huston,
others, supported by such unselfish
tlike business men as Brethren
Norford, Bond and Davis, desreve
t for their excellent management of
ssembly. The program was credit-
he attendance fine. F. D. Power,
ok, Peter Ainslee, P. A. Cave, I.
r, L. M. Omer, L. A. Cutler and
ers preached soul-stirring sermons.
ocke and the writer conducted the
es and the writer also gave several
M. addresses. Dr. Charles W. Kent,
ersity of Virginia, gave an admirable
the founding of a Bible Lectureship
versity of Virginia. The C. W. B.
, which was the first open session
n the Piedmont district, was most

***

th Piedmont Convention met in the
ernacle at Martinsville. After the
the writer held a Bible Institute,
dies both in the Old and New Testa-
The audiences were fine, both in
d quantity. Despite the excessive
Tabernacle, which I was informed
n hundred people, was well filled at
sessions. Mrs. Cowen and Mrs.
e ladies who took a life membership
secure the Institute, Mr. and Mrs.
rown, who entertained me royally,
I. C. Bowen, the efficient pastor of
isville church and a score of faithful
contributed to the success of the Bible
Mr. Saunders, the treasurer of
nty and a member of the Methodist
contributed to the expense of the
nd to the endowment fund of the
of Virginia Bible Lectureship fund.
embers of the Episcopal Church took
erest in the work.

***

night. August the 7th. I preached in

efficient president of Milligan College, who had delivered an excellent address at the Martinsville convention, on "Christian Education," preached for the Danville brethren Sunday morning. The manly, godly, consecrated and sincere life of Pres. Hopwood is the explanation, in part at least, of the fact that Milligan College has turned out so many loyal-hearted, noble-minded men for the ministry, such as B. A. Abbott, W. H. Book, *et al.* After a day spent in Richmond, where A. R. Moore has been preaching during the summer, I proceeded to the Tidewater convention, stopping over night at Old Point Comfort. Here we saw a number of sick and wounded soldiers and three of the Spanish vessels, which had been captured. But this letter is already too long. I shall briefly mention the Tidewater convention and my trip home in my next letter. It is said that Cato ended all of his speeches before the Roman Senate with the words, "*Delenda Est Carthago.*" Let me end this letter with the great thought of Col. Cary's last years: "The Atlantic Seaboard for the Christianity of Christ."

C. A. YOUNG.

Iowa Letter.

Latitude is a factor in state mission work and general growth. Iowa has grown up in membership from 22,500 in 1890 to 57,000 in 1898. And her gifts for missions of all kinds from $9,000 to $20,000. *One reason* is that the churches and workers have been of one heart and one mind. Once or twice in twenty years division of sentiment has threatened, but never materialized. Why this splendid unity, this oneness of purpose? I answer, partly because the long way of our state is east and west, rather than north and south. In this we have the advantage of Illinois and Missouri. Iowa life is very nearly uniform. In the other states there are two or three kinds or strata. They lie across the westward sweeping tide of civilization; we lie parallel with it. Our geographical ontlines are our advantage.

***

Before speaking of our battleship Iowa, allow me to congratulate M. M. Davis and all Texas. The incident of thanksgiving and confesion of faith on board the Texas, July 3rd, is destined to become a monument in history. Pictures of Capt. John W. Philip and his ship lie before me. And the picture of his men with bared heads before God is a fit companion piece for Thomas Jones Barker's famous painting, "The Secret of England's Greatness." Winston Churchill, a graduate of the Naval Academy and a writer of matchless skill says: "The words of Captain Philip . . . have thrilled his countrymen and his race with a sacred feeling no writer can define."

***

On July 3rd, off Santiago, our four ships which, with the yacht Gloucester, destroyed the Spanish fleet, lay in the following order: Broklyn, Texas, Iowa and Oregon. The swift Oregon soon moved up next to the flagship, leaving the Texas and Iowa as partners in a very important part of the engagement. Cutters from the Iowa received part of the survivors of the Vizcaya. On board the Iowa Captain Eulate kissed and sadly surrendered his sword to Captain Robt. D. Evans. And tears welled up in his eyes when the American captain refused it and grasped his hand instead. The Spanish captain will never forget this nor the cheer given him by the American crew. During the action a shell exploded on her berth deck and set her on fire. Others penetrted her water line. One, especially, "found a bed in her armor without going off, a guest that caused some embarrasment when the fight was over." Her corn-pith armor, an ingenious American device, swelled at once and closed up the wounds along the water line and the fire division put out the fire. She has 140 rooms and cost over six millions of dollars and carries at least a million dollars' worth of am-

Fearn, Washington correspondent in the August Chautauquan, says: "The Iowa is to be considered the finest vessel belonging to us, and not only that, but is unsurpassed by any of the fighting ships of the world." During the administration of Governor F. M. Drake, the founder of Drake University, his daughter, an Iowa girl, christened this ship. And at the banquet which followed Gov. Drake turned his wineglass down.

***

Various denominations are crediting their remarkable growth in the past fifteen years largely to the introduction of the Y. P. S. C. E. movement. They support this claim by elaborate statistics. Whether right or wrong, the Endeavor movement is one of far-reaching importance. And none have more reason for cultivating it than the Disciples. The official state paper, the Iowa Christian Endeavor, is published in our town, Oskaloosa. Our representatives among the officers of the state union are a credit to any people. John B. White, of Adel, is treasurer. He is a Christian lawyer, a great Sunday-school worker and can preach a good sermon. His home is as genuinely literary as the typical New England home of fifty years ago. Newspapers in more than one modern language have been seen in his mail-box. He has but recently enjoyed some foreign travel. Wm. Orr, another lawyer, from Clarinda, is superintendent of the department of Christian Citizenship. Bro. Orr is Iowa's Knox P. Taylor in the Sunday-school work. His wit and his liberality are unbounded. He is famous for has convention addresses. Among the district presidents we have two, Pastor A. J. Marshall, of Onawa, and C. H. Van Law, of Marshalltown. The

is yet too young for prophet to predict all his splendid future, but he has a little of the Abe Lincoln build. Bro. Marshall has been with us but a few years from the Free Baptists. We count him one of the best prizes ever drawn by Iowa Disciples. During his pastorate the fine new house at Onawa has been erected and paid for and his congregation largely increased. Besides he is the efficient, wide-awake secretary of the northwest district of our Iowa state work. Let us hold up the hands of these our leaders.

***

Have you recently read Matthew 19:16-26? The majority of people who do, feel somehow that Jesus renders a hard verdict upon the rich young ruler. And I confess that the commentaries seem to me to present Jesus in an unfavorable light. Now let us remember a few things clearly: The young man assumed the initiative. He came to the Master, not the Master to him. He was a perfectionist and had been for years. And we must not forget that he asked Jesus *two* questions, not *one*. And that it was the second question, not the first, which got him into trouble and broke down his dream of perfection. His trouble originated in his own condition—his heart, his intents, his purposes and vows, not in Jesus' words. His first question Jesus answered substantially as he answered the same question in Luke 10:25. And there it would have ended but for the second question pushed to the front. In substance it seems to be this: *"I want to be perfect; measure me by the highest standard yuo have, and tell me, what lack I yet?"* Measured by the apostles (v. 27) what other answer could Jesus give? He had to answer as he did. And in verse 24 makes entrance to the kingdom imposible to such a character. This also he had to do, for the young man had come to complete moral collapse, as complete, at least for a time, as that of Adam and Eve in the garden. His vows are broken, his conscience dethroned, and a known standard of God rejected. If he ever enters he must be born again and is not this the meaning of verse 26? His conscience one hour was a heaven, the next it was a hell. Jesus, urged by his questions, had gone to the bottom of his character. Did he not serve notice on the ruler in verse 18 that he would go deep? This verse, so troublesome to the commentators, seems clearly to say: "I do not use words below par, with me they must have their deepest meaning. None is good but God. In this whole interview I shall take your words and you mine with full depth of reality, no surface work between thee and me this day." Like most perfectionists he had lived honest but shallow. Now in his overconfident questioning and in spite of warning he brings to his own eyes his shallowness plus a violated conscience. And Jesus, instead of being hard (save as the realities of life were hard) makes his outlined task easier by a royal promise: "Thou shalt have treasure in heaven" (v. 21 with vv. 27, 28, 29).

***

Meetings at Brainard, Alta, Van Meter, Lorimore, Boonville, New Keokuk, Nevada, Waterloo, Charles City, Sheldon, Manilla, Fort Dodge and Shannon City are in the summer program of the Iowa Christian Convention. The state meeting will be held in Des Moines, with the East Side Church, D. A. Wickizer, pastor. Dates are Oct. 3d to 7th, inclusive. It is not too early to begin selecting delegates and preparing your final offerings for state mission work.

A. M. HAGGARD.

Kansas City Letter.

Except its title, this letter will have little or nothing in it pertaining to Kansas City. Ye scribe has been absent from home for the past three weeks, enjoying his vacation beside the restless waters of Lake Michigan, at Macatawa Park, made famous by the pen of Bro. J. H. Garrison. This is becoming a notable summering-place for members of the Christian Church, more of whom are coming every year. Our preachers are discovering the rare opportunities afforded here for rest and recreation, and are returning year after year for their week or month of vacation, never failing to find physical, mental and spiritual refreshing for the year's hard service. At a recent delightful picnic of the Christian preachers and their wives, of which the "Macatawa Musings" will doubtless give an account, there were twenty-two of our preachers present, including a number whose names are household words among the Disciples of Christ. In the opinion of the writer, there is no equal to Macatawa Park as a resting-place for a tired body and brain, and the man is to be envied who is able to possess a cottage here, and occupy it every summer.

A letter received a few days ago from an elder of one of our Missouri churches affords occasion for renewed reference to the vital subject of our ministry and its relation to the churches. The letter makes inquiry as to the standing of a certain preacher whose career has been notorious for his gross immorality, brazen effrotery and unmitigated rascality in general. He had already been engaged to hold a meeting for the said church, but reports had come of his conduct elsewhere that made the elders pause and investigate before allowing him to begin. These brethren are to be commended for their wisdom. In too many instances such rumors are unheeded and the glib talker welcomed to the pulpit on the sole ground of his ability to entertain the public. But what are we to do to prevent such men from profaning the gospel ministry by their unholy lives, and using its sacred and confidential privileges, as they too often do, for the gratifying of their unhallowed lusts? We have so long been terrified at the bugbear of ecclesiasticism that we have utterly failed to provide any protection for our churches against the wolves that rend the flock. We sadly need some system of ministerial supply whereby every preacher shall be made directly responsible to his brethren, and by which his ministry shall be directed, sustained or suspended, as the interests of the kingdom of Christ may require. For one, I stand ready to enter at once into such a co-operation of the churches and ministers of any given district as will bind them together in mutual responsibility to and for one another. Only by some application of the principle of mutual responsibility can our cause be saved from the incalculable injury it now suffers at the hands of wicked men. The writer would be glad to hear from brethren who has thought upon these things, and to have our scribes treat of the question in our religious press. It is high time that we were doing something practical.

The time is at hand for the annual offering of our churches for Church Extension, the first Lord's day in September. Let our motto be, "A sermon from every preacher, an offering from every church, a contribution from every member." No higher, holier cause appeals to us to-day than that of aiding our scattered and feeble brethren to provide houses of worship for themselves and their neighbors. The calls are many and urgent. The possibilities for fruitful service are infinite. Let us give generous response to the appeal of our Lord.

W. F. RICHARDSON.

Macatawa Park, Mich., Aug. 17, 2898.

The Bethany Reading Courses.

CHAS. B. NEWNAN.

One looking over the July Bulletin of this work we cannot but be struck by the uniformly favorable witness concerning it. And yet why should it not be so? The lines of study taken up contain the very things we need to know.

I. *Know your book.* This, of course, comes first. The plan of the Endeavor pledge provides for daily Bible reading. This will, however, prove of less service than it ought, unless wisely guided. To be an efficient workman one must know his book, but he cannot know it well by simple desultory reading. Something like system and definiteness must mark his study. Says, Munhall: "God has not ordained anything to the conviction and conversion of the world except his Word." A still wiser has called it the sword of the Spirit, and designated it the one aggressive weapon of Christian warfare. Must a soldier know how to handle a sword? Then you, Oh, young Christian, must handle aright this Divine Sword, if you would fight acceptably for the Master. This drill in the use of your sword, the "Guide to Bible Study" undertakes to give you.

II. *Know your field.* One to be an intelligent servant must know his field of operations. Particularly should he know of those great heathen fields where the vanguard of God's armies is winning wonderous victories for Christ our King. We follow with eager interest each new development of this Spanish-American war, and each new victory won or act of heroism performed receives quick and ample meed of praise. Shall we be content with less information concerning the progress of Christ's war? Shall his soldiers fight unwatched? Their heroism go unrewarded by our prompt praise? Nay, rather, if souls are worth more than bodies, if Heaven means more than earth, if eternity be longer than time, shall not our interests in these things which make for eternal peace be uppermost? The book upon Missionary Fields furnishes this information.

III. *Know the forces.* No man is rightly ready for work who does not know somewhat, at least, of the forces with which he is allied.

(a) Leaders. As brave and true, as loyal and faithful as any who ever lived, you will find the men who are the leaders of this Nineteenth Century Movement for the Restoration of Primitive Christianity. You cannot estimate this movement rightly unless you know these mem.

(b) That immense and constantly growing body that is now the visible fruit of this three-quarters of a century's work: this plain, practical, earnest, consecrated brotherhood, you certainly wish to know it and to rejoice in its fellowship. It is a study in religious statistics and in spiritual dynamics well worth while.

(c) Providential location. Is there any significance in location? Do you believe in Providence? Listen! God planned it so that this movement should begin on the Eastern edge of the great Mississippi Valley, fast coming to be the mightiest valley in the world. It has the broadest and most fertile fields, the longest rivers the most splendid variety and abundance of resource.

This nation is even now coming to be what Gladstone called it: "Head servant in the household of the world." This valley is coming to dominate the nation's life. This religious movement, we believe, is under God destined to dominate this valley. Is it anything to be so closely identified with a movement so clearly indicated servant of God in guiding the world's religious life? You should know of these things, not to puff up your pride, but rather to give you a new and adequate vision of your opportunity, and a deepened sense of your responsibility. Begin at once to *arrange for a Bethany Reading Circle for this coming winter.*

Detroit, Mich.

Notes and News.

The Mississippi Christian Convention was held at Haze under a gospel tent on the 18th of this month.

The corner-stone of a new house of worship was laid at Joppa, Md., August 14th. Peter Ainslie, editor of the Christian Tribune, and W. J. Wright, both of Baltimore, were present and made addresses.

The Piedmont District Convention was held last week at the Assembly Grounds, near Gordonsville, Va. Z. P. Richardson was chairman and W. J. Hall secretary. There are forty churches in the district, and thirty of these were represented by forty-five delegates, which was said to be the largest delegation for the past fifteen years. The movement of the Piedmont Assembly seems to have greatly revived the work in the district, and it is only the mere beginning of what will come in a few years. J. H. Gordinier preached the convention sermon. Addresses and sermons were delivered by F. D. Power, L. A. Cutler, B. P. Smith and Richard Bagby.—*Christian Tribune.*

After ten weeks' hard work Evangelists Wright and Martindale organized a church at Alta, Ia., which for the present will be under the care of the pastor at Storm Lake. Lucius E. Christian, of Alta, extols Bro. Wright's ability, resources and Christian deportment in very high terms. He also writes appreciatingly of the work and responsibilities of the church.

W. Bedall, Cor. Sec. Southern Illinois C. M. C., of Flora, says: "Churches of the Disciples in Egypt—Attention! I am in constant receipt of letters of inquiry from preachers with first-class testimonials and references and splendid records as pastors and preachers. If, therefore, the congregations needing pastoral care will communicate with me, I can speedily bring these two parties together and help the cause along. I am also slating revival meetings for every county in Egypt, if you desire one. Write me."

At Home Again.

Have returned to my work after five weeks' vacation, spent in Indiana and Kentucky. Feel much refreshed. Bros. Procter, L. Z. Burr, G. W. Webb and others preached for us in my absence. Held a meeting of two weeks at my old home church, East Union, Nicholas county, Ky. Had 29 additions; 24 by confession. This was my third meeting with this church and my last. I begin a meeting at Antioch, in Clay county, a few miles north of here, August 21st. Success to the CHRISTIAN-EVANGELIST. Very truly,

A. W. KOKENDOFFER.

Forest Avenue Christian Church, Kansas City, Mo.

About Missouri Brethren.

W. S. St. Clair, the faithful, has bought a nice country home near Olivet, in Boone county, that he may be near his work, as he preaches for Olivet the 1st, at Lydia the 2nd, at Richland the 3rd, at Berea the 4th, having held his work for five years, and the end is not yet.

Baxter Waters is taking his vacation holding a meeting for the Lentner brethren, with H. F. Ritz, of Canton. In September Bro. Waters will return to Yale, expecting to complete his course this year.

W. M. Featherston, Moberly, is now preaching for Armstrong the 1st, for Liberty, Randolph county, the 2nd, for Fair View, Macon Callaway, the 2nd, at High Point the 3rd and at Warrentown the 4th. J. E. Donovan is one of the Christian University boys that is an honor to his Alma Mater, and a blessing to the kingdom of God. He is making a new church out of Danville.

J. C. Coggins, of Ottowa, Kansas, can not forsake Missouri if he did marry away from home, all wrong, too. He is now in a meeting at Martinsburg, with fine prospects for success. Is with his brother, J. W., who has been preaching for the brethren "off and on," these many years.

Geo. E. Prewitt, Schell City, will begin his work as Bible-school evangelist south of the river, and with John Giddens will make a team, though brother Prewitt will give himself largely to normal work, and it is needed, too.

North of the river, F. M. Rogers, Edina, takes up the work also, with the first of the month, and will do the work of a Bible-school evangelist in those regions, and now let us all give these young brethren and the board hearty co-operation in their efforts to build up our Bible-schools and glorify the Son of God.

Bro. H. F. Ritz, Canton, is preaching for the Illinois people who will fully and completely qualify himself for the ministry of the Word.

It will be good news to all that our schools over the state have much brighter prospects this year than last, and as a result the professors and scholars wear happy smiles all over their faces.

John P. Jesse is making his home for the present at Gower, and is serving the brethren at Faucett on the 1st, at Clarksdale on the 2nd, at Gower on the 3rd and at Dekalb on the 4th. But those good people will not hold a man like John Jesse much longer, and it is not right that they should.

Arthur Elliott, just married, and living at Kirksville, preaches for Illinois Bend on the 1st, at Maudè on the 2nd, and at Moore's Chapel on the 3rd, leaving the 4th Sunday for some brethren in Macon or adjoining counties.

H. F. DAVIS.

Florida.

The Christian Church in Jacksonville, of which the writer is pastor, gave a complimentary social entertainment August 5th to the members of the Christian Church encamped here in the Seventh Army Corps. The social was given at Bro. C. B. Smith's residence, 23 East Monroe St. Some of the best musical and literary talent of the city were present and rendered some fine music, recitations and impersonations, after which the ladies of the church provided ample refreshments. A large number of our soldier boys and friends were present and enjoyed themselves immensely, judging from their smiling faces and happy expressions. It is a pleasure to mention that the majority of the young men who are members of the Christian Church in this corps did not leave their home, but brought it South with them, and although many of them have found the churches in the Southland neither as numerous nor as influential as in the Western and Middle States, these young men have not been ashamed to show their colors. We wish we could say the same of many others who came this way to seek recreation or to escape the rigors of more Northern climes. All honor to our noble and brave soldier laddies. There are numbers of them encamped here who attend the churches of the city regularly and are actually engaged in Sunday-school and Endeavor work. The Lord willing, I expect to hold a service at the camp on Lord's day afternoon, August 14th, at which all members of the Christian Church in camp, off duty, are expected to be present, when we will observe the commemorative institution of the Lord's supper. The "boys" are working this

Letters are still coming to us from the friends of the boys, and we are listing their names and calling on them as we have opportunity. We trust we are making among them some lifelong friends.

T. H. BLENUS.

Jacksonville, Fla.

Chautauqua Notes.

The Assembly Herald said on Thursday that Hon. Z. T. Sweeney is one of the most popular ministers in the Church of the Disciples, and was twenty-six years pastor at Columbus, Ind., and at the close of his lecture here throngs of people took his hand in greeting and appreciation. His power was felt, and his wit and humor rested the hearers.

The sermon on Sunday evening was to a vast throng, and it held the people as words of truth, based on the eternal foundations of God's love, can only do. The impression of the truth in righteousness, as it has builded up the bastions of liberty for this nation, were spoken with such magic earnestness and power, that our strength is in the Bible and in the Christ of the Bible, as to make men say, "We could hear him all night."

The Governor-General of Canada was present with his wife, the Countess of Abereeen, and their family, on the platform yesterday. It was a pleasant greeting the great audience of 8,000 gave to these friendly brethren from the land north of ours.

In his words of response, Lord Aberdeen spoke very highly of Uncle Johnathan and the American cousins. He is a plain, straightforward Scotchman, and has the wiry strength of mind and body of his ancestors. The children were plainly dressed—as if we might contrast our show of style with the neat and tasty costume of an old-time nation. Headquarters house is full of people. Ten different states were represented by ladies in prayer-meeting last Wednesday evening.

W. J. FORD.

Chautauqua, Aug. 13, 1898.

State Mission Notes.

Preaching three times a day and then traveling all night, and yet one brother suggested the other day, "You don't take exercise enough!" But I enjoyed the days work if it was hard, for in the morning I was at Wellsville, where C. C. Hill is the pastor, in the afternoon at Two Mile Branch, where C. C. Hill holds forth the Word of Life, and at night at Bellflower, the new church in Montgomery county, whose existence is owing to the indefatigable, intelligent efforts of Bro. C. C. Hill, and it is always an enjoyment to be with these men of God and their churches.

Montgomery county. The house cost $1,400, of which $500 was to be raised. It was done, of course, and we had a happy day indeed.

That week I attended the Henry county meeting at Freedom and the Howard county meeting at Armstrong. In both places we had enjoyable, interesting and profitable work; indeed, these two counties are always in the very heart of the work of God in all things.

The board meeting at Kansas City was interesting because it is getting close to the end of the year. Only one more meeting till the convention at Nevada, Sept. 26-29, and we are anxious for the outcome. The receipts of the treasury were exceedingly light and were it not for the great confidence we have that the churches will bring up their opportionments we would have to call some of our workers out of their fields. This would be a calamity indeed.

Many of the churches have but one more meeting before the gathering at Nevada. This will be their only chance to raise the money so badly needed. Will they not make a special effort at the very next meeting to obtain and send the money so very much needed?

I was at Independence Sunday morning and enjoyed the visit very much. This is one of the staunch fields of our stae mission work. Never-failing, ever-sure, Bro. Vernon is getting hold of the work well indeed.

The Montgomery county meeting at Wellsville, Randolph at Liberty church; preaching one night at the McGarvey Institute, at Windsor, and one day at Red Top, in Boone county convention, brought me to Friday morning, which also brought me a come-quick message from home, on account of another dangnrous turn in Mrs. Abbott's condition.

At this writing the dangerline has not been passed. I again express my thankfulness to friends all over the state and in other states as well, for their expressions of sympathy.

Surely the prayers of so many will find audience with God.

Then I am especially grateful to so many whose sympathy has taken a practical turn in the shape of the payment of pledges. Life memberships and church apportionments and many others who are saying, "Don't worry, we will send it soon." May the dear Lord bless the hearts whose love thus comes in such helpful ways. Yours in his name,

T. A. ABBOTT.

1135 *Vandeventer Ave., St. Louis, Mo.*

State Missions in Illinois.

At our recent state convention, held at Eureka, an interesting and gratifying report of work done the past year was made by our secretary, J. Fred Jones. The report impressed us all that fidelity and wisdom had been exercised by the state board, and that all had been accomplished that we could expect with the means at command. Let this be clearly understood, in order that I may not seem to be finding fault with the secretary or with the board. I have no purpose to do such a thing. My purpose is altogether different from this.

In a very imperfect address as president of the convention, I ventured to suggest that a movement be undertaken looking to a larger increase this year of the receipts for the prosecution of this work. I desire, Mr. Editor, by means of this article, to ask the influence of your valuable paper in behalf of this effort. The movement ought, it seems to me, to involve at least the following features:

1. The enlistment of every church in the state, if possible, to take up the regular collections when called for. Every possible effort ought to be made to do this.

2. The securing from all the pastors an agreement to work up systematic, liberal and prompt offerings in all their churches.

3. This may require a personal canvass by the secretary or assistants. If it does it will pay, if wisely and energetically prosecuted.

4. Such prosecution of the work of missions in the destitute and promising fields as will assure the people that their money, when given, will bring adequate results.

Of one thing I am convinced, viz., that we are falling so far short of our ability and duty in this matter of state missions, that our shortcoming is liable to become a shame and a reproach soon, if not remedied. We must do better. We can do it if the churches are once aroused; and they can be aroused if we but go about it systematically and in earnest.

May I go one step further? I believe that what is here said of state missions in Illinois is true in a general way of the same phase of work in almost all of our other states. No better fields are afforded in the world than those in Ohio, Indiana, Illinois, Missouri, Iowa, Kansas, Nebraska, *et al.* Good and inspiring work is being done in all of them; but the time has come when a long step forward ought to be taken in all of these and many other states for evangelization. So far as Illinois is concerned, I move that we inaugurate a forward march. God will go before us if we but have faith to move at his Word. Willing hearts always find the doors opening before them. "Speak unto the people that they go forward."

The next regular collection for Illinois missions will be taken the first Sunday in October next. The board has before it many inviting fields. It cannot enter them for lack of means. The churches ought to be stirred as never before on this subject, so that means shall be in hand to send preachers to plant the cause of Christ in all of these destitute places. J. H. HARDIN.

[The CHRISTIAN-EVANGELIST has been a staunch advocate of the principles set forth in President Hardin's foregoing timely suggestions, and we hope that they will be more sacredly regarded and applied, not only by the Churches of Christ in Illinois, but in every state, than heretofore. EDITOR.]

Michigan Grains.

Bro. S. S. Jones is holding a meeting at Durand, Mich., and will organize a church and Sunday-school on Lord's day next. The meeting has been in session one week and one has already made the confession and others are interested. Bro. Jones is a very able preacher of the Word. He is spending his vacation in Michigan, and while doing so is holding the meeting which will result in a new church in one of the best towns. If other brethren coming to the state for a vacation and rest would devote their time to the preaching of the Word, there would be rejoicing at the state meeting on account of new souls being born into the kingdom of Christ, new churches organized and warm attachments formed and much good accomplished in the name of the Master. Now is the harvest; the reward will be when the Lord comes. May Bro. Jones have his reward then. He holds this meeting free of charge on account of it being his vacation.

About two weeks ago I had the privilege of going to Owosso, where we baptized Sister Lillian Wightman, of Durand. She had been a member of the Methodist Church for four years, her father being a Methodist minister. She took this step because she believed she was obeying her Savior. After her baptism Bro. Spayd extended the hand of fellowship and she took membership with the Owosso church until the organization at Durand shall be effected.

Last Lord's day I was with the brethren at Wilmot, where I found a young Adventist minister with his young wife in prayer and Bible study. I spent Monday with them in careful investigation and on Monday night he took membership with us and will leave his Sabbath-keeping a thing of the past. He and his wife are pure young people. They were both educated in the Adventist faith from infancy. It was so hard for them to give up their Sabbath-keeping that they fasted for two days before they could undertake the step. He had been well instructed in the Adventist College at Battle Creek. One month ago I was introduced to them, and at that time after prayer by myself and each of them we spent four or five hours' earnest study by ourselves, and now Bro. and Sister Hartson are Disciples of Christ. They are both capable of teaching the truth publicly and privately, and we can hope for them to have many years to spend in the Lord's service and to bring many sould to Christ.

Our brethren at High Banks will have Bro. W. D. Campbell, of Plumb St. church, of Detroit, to hold a meeting for them in September.

Bro. L. W. Spayd, of Owosso, will hold a meeting for the church at Mt. Pleasant in September and the writer will supply his place in Owosso.

Bro. add Sister Eckles, of Pine Run, have been passing through the valley of sorrow on account of the death of their estimable daughter, Mrs. Fox, of Chio, who died of heart failure.

On my way to Wilmot I called on Bro. Billman, the very efficient pastor of our church at Saginaw. I had the pleasure of meeting Bro. McCarty, of Carlton. He was visiting with Bro. Billman. In this case three made good company for an hour or two. They were both feeling greatly encouraged with the outlook in the field of labor. They are making great preparation for the coming state meeting, to be held in Saginaw, beginning August 31. As Carlton is near to Saginaw they will provide for a number of the delegates. May this be the best meeting ever held in the state, is the prayer of many Michigan Disciples making preparation to attend.

R. BRUCE BROWN.

Omaha Notes.

To-day is Texas Day. Gov. Culbertson and staff are in the city viewing the display of the resources of the great West. Appropriate services in the Auditorium, with fireworks at night, are the chief features of the day. Early in July was Southern Texas Melon Day, when all who came to the horticultural building received a large slice of melon. The display of our Southern sister in the various departments of the big fair is one of which they can well be proud.

***

Approriate to Texas Day is the presence of the Mexican National Band, which has just opened a six weeks' engagement with the exposition. These men, thoroughly trained and many of them artists who have a reputation on their own account, attract large and enthusiastic audiences every afternoon and evening. When our own Marine Band left some persons believed that ended the music of the season, but now they are ready to look for even better things.

***

Those who attended the Exposition during the first six weeks and return again can scarcely find the old landmarks. New exhibits have been entered, old ones improved and a generous rivalry engendered, till each week sees changes in nearly every building. Especially do the horticultural and agricultural buildings show an entire change. Not least among the displays is that of the landscape gardener upon the Bluff Tract. The rarest water lilies and the tenderest house plants vie with each other for the admiration of the multitudes.

August 5th one of the most gorgeous flower parades was held on the Bluff Tract. The thousands who witnessed it were unanimous in pronouncing it the best they had ever seen. Over forty carriages were in the procession, and each had a beauty of its own, till the judges were bewildered by the various visions of loveliness.

***

Many of our brethren have visited our city. Bro. J. W. Hilton, of Bethany, made an a for Cotner. Only $9,000 yet to be ›cure a $100,000 property, free from ith a clear title. Is there not some will come to the aid of this work . large subscription?

nig also gave us two very nice illus- ıres. It was a delighiful privilege s old friend and to receive the as- .at we might expect him in Omaha 'ere ready to co-operate with him. visitors and the great attractions ıly changed our audiences. Smaller :ule. But few preachers are taking now. All deem it best to be in their s. Sister C. E. Taylor and Sister rt are visiting their old homes in ıis leaves our fellow-laborers very

HOWARD CRAMBLET.

25th St., South Omaha, Neb., 1898.

State Mission Notes.

sue of the CHRITSIAN-EVANGELIST will vigerous article by the former state Bro. Hoffmann. It shows that which ; to those who love the state in which nd who are anxious for the future of . I fear there is growing up the he *need* for state mission work is the territory has already been oc- we ought to turn our attention to lds.

'as there a wider mistake. We say ıve gone into every county in the ›lanted organizations, but in twelve unties we are practically unknown— ıoolhouse organization in some of ere are nine county-seats in whi ch *organization* and *twenty-three* in ıave no building. I preached last a place in South Missouri, and the was made by one of my hearers, and 'exceptional by any means, that it *st sermon he ever heard in his life,* was no church of any kind within 25 :, on the way to that place, in a travel overland, I passed through three ıd in the first were three saloons, in the ad in the last one three more. Eight ıre men were being ruined for this at which is to come, and not a single 'e they were being taught of Jesus 're!

'e is not an isolated case, either. ›r was such need of vigorous labor as he years gone by we have gone into ıaces, and now the tough, knotty, s are to be taken for Jesus. It ·money, more faith, more consecra- ver for this. Bro. Hoffmann's figures d by the panic, but now is the time

Your board is doing all it can to destitute country. We have four ıcting as evangelist there, J. B. '. W. Warren, D. B. Warren and ey, and besides these we have mis- stors in all that region. This takes)nly one month till the state con- Such a short time in which to act! ot take up thsee matters and say by ibutions that you love Christ and his l the grand old state of which we are

you, do not pass this by. It will be as a people if we do not push with all ıergy this work of state missions. st brethren made the same mistake ›m to be on the verge of making; their state mission work; they lost uch an alarming rate that they saw er and are making a great effort to 00 for this year's work. Will we esson? God help us to see our day. ise, that apportioment *now.*

Yours in His Name,

T. A. ABBOTT.

ınerly Ave., St. Louis.

Evangelistic.

ARKANSAS.

Just closed a short meeting at Hamburg, Ark. Five baptisms—two from the Methodists. Twenty-one Disciples were gathered together and agreed to constitute a church. We have only one preacher in all that part of the state. Won't some good preacher go and take care of the Hamburg church? Write me at Ladoga, Ind.—W. T. BROOKS.

Arkadelphia, Aug. 16.—The annual camp meeting held at Mineral Springs near Okolona, was very enjoyoble. The meeting began Aug. 5th and closed Aug. 14th. There were 17 accessionn; 13 by confession. The meeting was conducted by Vernon J. Rose, of Newton, Kansas. A number of other preachers were present and aided in the meeting. Mineral Springs Camp Ground consists of 40 acres of land, held by an association of brethren. Seven mineral springs are on the ground, each one differing from the others. There are also two large freestone springs that furnish abundance of pure water for all who attend the meeting. There is a substantial tabernacle with a seating capacity of about 700. 1,200 to 1,500 people usually camp on the ground during the meeting. On Lord's day from 2,000 to 3,000 are in attendance. A large portion of Southwest Arkansas is represented at this meeting each year. The influence of this meeting is widespread, affording great opportunity for doing good.—E. S. ALLHANDS.

Bentonville, Aug. 22.—Five additions to this congregation at yesterday's morning service. Work is moving off nicely.—CHAS. E. FREEMAN, Pastor.

IOWA.

Ft. Madison, Aug. 16.—One confession last Lord's day. This makes some 25 or 26 since we began here the last of March.—R. H. INGRAM.

UTAH.

Ogden, Aug. 15.—One united by letter yesterday.—J. H. BAUSERMAN.

MISSOURI.

Warren's Store, Aug. 19.—Since we came down from St. Louis, five weeks ago, we have been constantly in the work, preaching at Belleview, Piedmont and this place. I never closed a meeting with greater interest than was manifest here last night, but owing to circumstances could not continue longer. Our efforts in this section have been strictly missionary, and we trust helpful to the many anxious hearers.—A. M. HARRAL.

Merwin, Aug. 21.—We are in another good meeting at this place; seven additions last night. Church in better condition than ever before.—JOHN M. CLAYPOOL.

Holt, July 22.—Our meeting booms; 15 days with 46 additions; we continue.—D. D. BOYLE AND V. E. RIEDENOUR.

Waynesville, August 22.—E. E. Dawson, of Dexter, Mo., and I have just closed a 19 days' meeting here, with 56 accessions; 28 by obedience.—D. B. WARREN.

Minden Mines, August 16.—Here two weeks. Organized a congregation. Had fifteen additions; eight by obedience; five from Baptists, one restored, and one by letter. Some noble brethren here. Go next to Jasper City, Mo.—MORGANS & DAUGHTER.

MICHIGAN.

Algonac, Aug. 20.—Two confessions here since last report. One a lady of 70 who has been under Catholic influences for 50 years.—J. L. SMITH.

OHIO.

Dayton, Aug. 21.—Two confessions to-day. —I. J. CAHILL.

ALABAMA.

Birmingham, Aug. 15.—R. Lin Cave, of Kentucky, has been in a good meeting with us for two weeks, with large audiences and 20 additions to date.—O. P. SPIEGEL.

SOUTH DAKOTA.

Carthage, Aug. 16.—One added Aug. 14th. —H. C. SHIPLEY.

MINNESOTA.

Luverne, Aug. 17.—Good attendance and interest. Five additions last night. Evangelist Atwood is preaching sound doctrine.—F. H. SWEETMAN, singer.

IOWA.

Des Moines, August 19th.—While visiting my old home in Kingman, Kan., I preached for the brethren last Lord's day, resulting in four additions; three by baptism. They have no pastor now, and it would be a good field for an energetic young man. I hold a three weeks' tent meeting with my own church at Sandyville, Ia., before entering school at Drake this fall.—WM. J. LOCKHART.

INDIANA.

Lowell.—Three accessions since last report, and $200 of repairs being put on our church property.—S. A. STRAUN, Pastor.

ILLINOIS.

Champaign, Aug. 16.—Baptized six at Ludlow recently.—DR. W. FRANK ROSS.

Rossville, Aug. 15.—Three added yesterday during regular Lord's day services. I am to to begin a meeting to-night with the congregation at Coal Creek, Ind.—A. W. JACKMAN.

Eureka, Aug. 15.—The church at Henry is moving quietly but steadily forward. Two persons were added yesterday by statement. I have recently preached twice in union meetings. The Ladies' Aid Society has shown commendable energy and enterprise by raising money and repainting the church. Its appearance is greatly improved and quite attractive. —M. P. HAYDEN.

Saybrook, Aug. 16.—Last Sunday at the morning service we had one confession, a fine married lady at the head of a family. On the 13th near the close of the day, mother Hudson dropped dead at her son's home here, being in her 76th year. She was well and widely known, and a daily reader of the Bible. Only the Sunday before she was in her place in the church. Funeral on the 15th, to a large gathering, conducted by the writer. Text, Rev. 14:13.—A. L. FERGUSON.

Fulton, August 22.—Our tent meeting starts off well here; four added the first week and many more are inquiring the way of life, so we hope for many more.—J. S. CLEMENTS.

Moweaqua, Aug. 22.—The first week of our meeting results in seven added. Town stirred, crowds thronging the large tabernacle. The pastor, A. R. Spicer, preaches the Word while Prof. Geo. T. Matthews leads the song services.—EDNA RICE.

KENTUCKY.

August 15.—We have just closed a series of very interesting sermons at Turkey Foot, Scott county, Ky., delivered by Bro. W. H. Willyard, a graduate of the College of the Bible, Lexington, Ky., class of '98. This meeting resulted in 20 accessions, and the church wonderfully strengthened spiritually. We wish to say to the brotherhood, as due Bro. Willyard, that after two years of service at this place he has succeeded beyond expectation in accomplishing a great work for the Master, and as he leaves us for other fields of labor it is with a feeling of deepest regret that we undergo this parting. No laborer for Jesus was ever held in higher esteem by a congregation than is Bro. Willyard.—LEONARD BARNHILL.

Athens.—The meeting here, which ended my labor, closed Aug. 5, with 60 additions. Bro. W. R, Lloyd was the evangelist. His preaching was clear, logical and strong The church has secured the services of Bro. J. T. Sharrard for the rest of this year.—ROBT. STEWART.

TEXAS.

San Antonio, Aug. 15.—One addition yesterday, making a net gain of six for the first two months of our work with this church. The signs are very hopeful for a steady and substantial improvement. Despite the summer exodus, the heat and lastitude of this season in the South, our audiences have increased to thrice their size in June, and our prayer-meetings are an inspiration both in interest and usefulness. We are publishing a weekly paper which is attracting wide att ntion in the city. This is a hard but a hopeful field and one full of strategic advantage. We need the prayers of the brotherhood.—GEO. B. RANSHAW.

Abilene.—The Rebaptism brethren here had full sway in all the country districts out west, but I am doing a good work among them by going out and preaching for them occasionally and showing them a better way. I have held a meeting at a point eight miles from town; 40 additions and much prejucice removed, as some thought we "progressives" were bad folks. There are many good people among these brethren who, if taught properly, would make good workers. The church in Abiline is doing well; 50 added since last January. Thy brother, A. J. BUSH.

The church at Mt. Vernon and at Sedro want a preacher. Can raise about $600. Towns twelve miles apart and one thousand inhabitants each. Address W. S. Crockett, New Wharton, Wash.

Missionary.

CHURCH EXTENSION ARGUMENTS.

A Wise Enterprise.

Church Extension is one of our wisest enterprises. It is a loan fund that ever comes back to the treasury in a sort of perpetual-motion way. It recognizes the fact that a church can no more grow and become an active force in the world than a bird can grow and hatch without an eggshell. Then, what can pay the donor larger profits than in this way, to lay up "a good foundation" for heavenly wealth, where they "rest from their labors" and have "their works follow" on forever and ever.

A WONDER.—Years ago Bro. Pendleton and I and Bro. Bosworth were appointed a committee by the General Convention in Cincinnati to report that P. M., and while on Bro. Bosworth's porch we looked across lots and saw a beautiful multiflora that had spread all over the gable end of a large residence, and soon guesses began as to how many buds and blooms it bore, running from 500 to 2,000, and such was the interest aroused that they were the next day actually counted and found to number about 5,000. Then, assuming that every pod held at least ten seeds, it was seen that the Savior's estimate for "good ground" of thirty, sixty, and one hundred-fold was very conservative, for in the case before us it was *fifty thousand*-fold!

We then remembered that a few years ago one little seed was dropped into the soil, and here is its product for a single year. But then it was a perennial plant, and so produced year by year. The Savior did not limit the crop to one hundred-fold, nor to annuals, but left all nature open to stir our ambition.

"CROWN OF REJOICING," 1 THESS. 2:19.—If you build or help to build a church house, it will surely be the means of saving souls, and these will be your "Crown of Rejoicing." Read the quotation above and prayerfully resolve that you will not be without some at "the Beautiful Gate waiting and watching for you."

THOMAS MUNNELL.

Carton, O.

Among the Best Enterprises of Our Times.

The mightiest and noblest impulse that moves the Church of Christ to-day is that of the evangelization of the world. It is the expression and direction of the sovereign will of God. No enlightened and thoughtful Christian man can fail to see this.

But this wonderful missionary development of the power of God has called forth inevitably the enterprise of Church Extension as a necessary element of the successful evangelization of the nations. The triumph of the kingdom of God in this great land *demands imperatively* the development of Church Extension on a scale that shall be altogether commensurate with the mighty progress (which should be) of the preaching of the gospel throughout all this vast and most inviting field.

Successful missions are not conceivable without the powerful adjunct of Church Extension. Every church, every individual Christian, should be made to understand this. Among the best enterprises of our times, so extraordinary in great and enlightened movements of men, Church Extension is one of the wisest, and one that will certainly win the approval and support of the intelligence and piety of the Church of Christ.

CHAS. LOUIS LOOS.

The Two Great Works.

What are the two great, supreme works of our brotherhood at this time? In my judgment they are Church Extension and Home Mission work. They are really the two arms of one work—the work of establishing and sustaining our plea for a return to apostolic Christianity in all this great land. Give me the money to assist in building a house of worship, and then give me the money to assist in supporting a good preacher in that field, and I can establish the cause we plead in any community in our country where there are enough people to form a congregation. Church Extension appeals to our people now. The appeal should reach every Disciple. No one should close his pocket-book against it. It offers a rich investment, perpetual and ever-increasing. Though but a poor preacher, I have fifty dollars in this fund and I count it a richer investment than a claim in the Klondike. We have thousands of brethren who can and should each give that much to this fund. There is scarcely a brother who cannot give one dollar. In hundreds of splendid fields we cannot establish our cause because we cannot build a house. In scores of other splendid fields, where we have planted our cause, we must struggle against overwhelming odds because we cannot have a respectable house of worship. I speak from personal knowledge, having had nearly five years experience in Portland and Seattle. Out of a heart burdened with such an experience, I appeal to our men of wealth and to our men in moderate circumstances to swell the Church Extension Fund. I appeal to the preachers to press this matter upon the consciences of their people. It is God's work and we dare not neglect it.

J. N. SMITH.

A Modest Sum.

I rejoice greatly in the determination of the Board of Church Extension to raise $250,000 by the close of 1900. This is not too much to ask and to confidently expect from a million members. With this amount in hand three churches can be helped to secure buildings where one can be helped now. Unusual emphasis should be laid upon the September collection. The board asks for $20,000. Thousands of churches that have made no response in previous years should heed the request of the board and contribute generously this year. Because September is not the most favorable month in the year for a collection, special efforts should be put forth that this worthy cause may not suffer. All over the land there are groups of Disciples needing and deserving help. They are unable to build without assistance. Having seen much of the good work of this board in my travels throughout the country I am in position to recommend its appeals to the favorable consideration of churches and people everywhere. Had we begun the work of Church Extension fifty years before we did it is safe to say that we would have a thousand more self-supporting churches than we have to-day.

AN EXTENSIVE TRAVELER.

The Pastor Should Help.

Bro. Muckley asks of me an article on some phase of Church Extension. But what can I say in behalf of this work which has not already been said, and how can I say it any more effectively? With the true followers of Christ there is but one side to the question. It is a work which commends itself to every man's judgment. Then why does not every Christian man give towards its support? The chief hindrances to universal support of this enterprise are stinginess, indifference and ignorance. The first is not so general, nor so obstinate as is generally supposed, although there is enough of it; but of indifference and ignorance there is a vast deal, and the latter is the mother of the former. If all our people understood the work as they might, the quarter-million mark would be reached long before 1900. But does not Bro. Muckley flood them with facts and figures, with appeals and arguments? Verily, and that, too, in most concise, readable and intelligible form. But the majority fail to read them unless urged thereto by those really interested. Pastors can do much in this way. They ought to preach upon and explain the work, and at the same time read to their flock many of the good things published by those whose minds and hearts are constantly full of it. This would do much to dispel the ignorance, and the indifference would disappear with it.

The Imperative Need.

This need seems appalling when it is remembered that only one-fourth of the calls for help in building churches can be responded to because of lack of funds. This ought not so to be. Another appalling fact is that more than one-fourth of our church organizations in the United States are without church houses. Many of them will never get houses unless aid can be rendered them from our Church Extension Fund. It will not be forgotten that the growth of our cause in the United States is intimately related to the growth of our Church Extension Fund, which often makes possible the establishment of churches which might not otherwise ever exist. Upon no one thing is a church more dependent for its perpetuity and growth than upon possessing a church building adequate for its needs. Unlike our other church enterprises, the Church Extension Fund goes on increasing with the years in power and efficiency. Our old established churches should aid mightily in this work for the progress of the cause we love so well.

A. C. SMITHER.

Los Angeles, Cal., July 6, 1898.

Benefits of Church Extension.

There are many places where it is impossible to build up without a house, and the life of any church must be considered precarious until it has a house of worship. This is more especially necessary in towns.

In new and growing towns we cannot afford to wait until the means can all be raised on the ground. Church Extension comes to our relief in a practical, business-like way. The points to be emphasized, as it appears to me, to make it most helpful, are:

1. *Keep it growing by liberal donations.* The principal advantage of special collections is that they call attention to special interests, which otherwise would be neglected.

2. Preachers should not encourage over-building, and they should consider themselves under obligations to see that the notes are paid as they become due. No matter how low the rate of interest, when the payments run behind everything connected with the church will drag.

3. No one should encourage a loan on property badly located. If the loan will not advance the cause it should not be made. I know several churches that are worthless on account of mislocation.

4. Very few churches in new towns or small villages should borrow more than $300. Then the house should be planned so it can be enlarged.

Perhaps no interest among us has been more wisely managed or energetically pushed than Church Extension, and now has more promise of good. It makes effective and gives permanency to our missionary efforts.

E. C. BROWNING.

Miss Ada Boyd at Her Old Home.

Miss Ada Boyd, late missionary to Bilaspur, India, delivered a very interesting and instructive address to a large and attentive audience at the State Line Church of Christ, Wednesday night, Aug. 10, 1898. State Line is Miss Boyd's old home. Here she confessed her Savior in her girlhood days, and a short time afterward left all behind and went into India to assist in lifting the veil of ignorance and superstition from the minds of that benighted and idolatrous people and turn them from the worship of images of wood and stone to the worship of the true and living God.

In 1882, as she was making arrangements to leave for her field of labor, the church here presented her with a beautiful copy of the

We are certainly not doing for the heathen more than we should do, but how about our own boy? How about our own state? Is our own family to be neglected? The time has come when we must face this question seriously. We are not doing for our state work what we should, and our churches are suffering the consequences. G. A. HOFFMANN.

Hard at Work

Are the committees at Chattanooga, preparing for the entertainment of the convention, October 13-21. We want to make it the greatest gathering of our people in the history of our work. But let every one bear in mind that the success of any work depends upon the individual. Let every church, C. W. B. M., Y. P. S. C. E. and Sunday-school, as well as every county, district and state convention send some one to the convention and bear their expenses. Let every church or number of churches employing a minister send their poor, hard-working servant to Chattanooga that he may catch the inspiration of this convention and returning electrify the entire membership with his renewed zeal. Let every individual member who is able to come remember that the seat made vacant by his neglect of duty will speak out against him. Let every one come who can and you will be happy to know that you contributed so much to the cause in adding to the numbers and enthusiasm of the assembly.

The Southeastern and Central Passenger Associations have granted the rate of one fare for the round trip and we feel confident that the Western Associations will do the same.

Your expenses while here will not be great. The best homes in the city will be thrown wide open at the rate of $1 per day.

The hotels, as good as we have in the South, give a rate of $1.50 and $2 per day.

Reduced rates will be given to Lookout Mountain and Chickamauga National Military Park, where from forty to sixty regiments of the patriotic sons of America have been encamped for the summer.

The trip is worth your money. The convention will be clear profit to you.

Let some one volenteer from each district in each state to work up a delegation for this great occasion. Please let us know if you are coming in due time, so that we can find a place for you. Those writing beforehand will save the committee a great deal of trouble.

Please pray and talk and work for the success of the convention from now till we are in its sessions. Yours in the work,

W. M. TAYLOR, Gen. Sec.

A Curious Wick.

Ever since lamps were made we suppose that the wick has been the bane of every housewife, and since the use of oil heaters and oil cooking stoves has become general her life has been more than miserable. Yankee ingenuity, however, has come to her help with the invention of a wick which the government has thought meritorious enough to patent, which will not clog, will not creep, and needs but little care or trimming. Smoking lamps are now a thing of the past, and cracked chimneys are unnecessary with ordinary care.

For the first time in its history the Standard Oil Co., one of the largest corporations on earth, has seen fit to give a complimentary letter. It is as follows: ''We have made a number of careful and exhaustive tests of the 'Marshall Process' Wick, and feel that we cannot speak too highly of its qualities.'' It has been adopted by all the leading lamp, stove and heater makers, including the makers of the famous Rochester and Miller lamps.

This wick, which is known as the ''Marshall Process'' Wick, is colored brown, so that you may easily identify it; in fact, it has come to be known among its friends as ''The Brown

THE

CHRISTIAN - EVANGELIST

J. H. GARRISON, EDITOR.

W. W. HOPKINS, ASSISTANT.

B. B. TYLER, J. J. HALEY,

EDITORIAL CONTRIBUTORS.

RATES OF SUBSCRIPTION.

Single subscriptions, new or old	$1.75	each
In clubs of five or more, new or old	1.50	"
Reading Rooms	1.25	"
Ministers	1.00	"

With a club of ten we will send one additional copy free.

All subscriptions payable in advance. Label shows the month up to the first day of which your subscription is paid. If an earlier date than the present is shown, you are in arrears. No paper discontinued without express orders to that effect. Arrears should be paid when discontinuance is ordered.

In ordering a change of post office, please give the OLD as well as the NEW address.

Do not send local check, but use Post office or Express Money Order, or draft on St. Louis, Chicago or New York, in remitting.

SUBSCRIBERS' WANTS.

Miscellaneous wants and notices will be inserted in this department at the rate of two cents a word, each insertion, all words, large and small, to be counted, and two initials stand for one word. Please accompany notice with corresponding remittance to save book-keeping.

Family Circle.

The Fading Summer.

HELEN A. RAINS.

The summertime, like a queen quite surfeited
With triumphs that have wrought her slow decay,
Deals tenderly with subjects that must need
Return to dust before another's sway.

The airy blooms—brief offsprings of her day,
Blue, purple, white—the fairest of the flow'rs
Are dropping, leaf by leaf; what part have they
Midst storm and blight that rule her later hours?

The sunbeams, scant and less effulgent, seem
But ghosts of what rejoiced our hearts in June,
And bear a hint in ev'ry phantom gleam
Of early frosts, e'en at the hour of noon.

She veils the lowlands in a cloud of haze,
Now steely gray—anon a snowy white—
As if to shield from cold, repellant gaze,
A vision that has been our chief delight.

The clear, cold night encroaches on her day
And saps her vital forces one by one,
And gives her realm the aspect of decay
The more apparent, now her race is run.

Harsh sounds pervade where once her wind-harps thrilled
And woke sweet intonations by the hour,
A foreign host her sacred precincts filled
And wrought these changes with sibylic pow'r.

* * * * * * *

Now reverently she lays her garb away
And tucks her flow'rs each in its narrow bed,
Quite safe, to sleep until some future day
A summons comes to wake them from the dead.

And then the heart beneath the pulseless tree
Will throb again as earth renews her trust,
And dormant forces in obedience be
In unison with the awakened dust.

Mt. Ayr, Ia.

The Quiet Hour.*

MISS BESSIE HOMAN.

This morning, as God looked down from his throne in the kingdom above upon the inhabitants of this sin-cursed world, the hearts of more than eighty thousand Christian Endeavorers were communing with their Father, and he was listening patiently to each petition, gladly recieving the gratitude of each heart and mercifully pardoning the sins of every penitent believer.

"Have you and I to-day
Stood silent as with
Christ, apart from joy or fray
Of life to see by faith his face,
And grow by brief companionship more true,
More nerved to lead, to dare, to do
For him at any cost? Have we to-day
Found time in thought our hand to lay
In his and thus compare
His will with ours and wear
The impress of his wish?
Be sure
Such contact will endure
Thoughout the day; will us help walk erect
Through storm and flood; detect
Within the hidden life, sin's dross, its stain,
Revive a thought of love for him again;
Steady the steps which waver, help us see
The footpath meant for you and me."

With a great deal of pleasure we welcome into the Christian Endeavor family another organization, bringing to us richest blessings from the Author of all that is good and perfect—comrades of the Quiet Hour—the greatest forward movement ever made by Christian Endeavorers.

The Quiet Hour was formally introduced to the world of Endeavor through the columns of the Christian Endeavor World, which paper devotes a column each week to this subject.

Not only members of the Young People's Society of Christian Endeavor, but all Christians, are urged to become members of the organization and receive its benefits, which are numerous and lasting.

Do you ask what constitutes a membership?

We are only asked to make a covenant with God our Father; he alone with his child knows whether this covenant is faithfully observed.

We make a solemn pledge to God which, though simple, is beautiful: "Trusting in the Lord Jesus Christ for strength, I will make it the rule of my life to set apart at least fifteen minutes every day, if possible in the early morning, for quiet meditation and direct communion with God."

"Trusting in the Lord Jesus Christ for strength," is a Christian Endeavor watchword. How could we attempt to do anything for him without his strength and guidance? He will never forsake us if we only trust in his wonderful love and power.

The pure and sinless Christ so deeply realized the need of quiet communion with his Father that on one occasion, "in the morning, rising up a great while before day, he went out into a solitary place and there prayed."

We are striving to follow in his footsteps and to do whatever he would like to have us do, but we very often lose the path and stray into sinful ways. Then, should we not be very grateful for the privilege of coming into the very presence of a merciful God, whose loving arms are ever extended to you and to me, though we are so unworthy of his care?

Do not promise the Savior that you will spend a few moments in talking with God occasionally, or whenever your soul is in deep distress and feels a sore need of divine aid. He woud like to have you make it the rule of your life. Be systematic in your private devotion, and it will not only be more acceptable unto God, but the blessings which you derive from the Morning Watch will be richer and sweeter.

Your spiritual breakfast will prove a strength to you throughout the entire day.

Does your sense of mere duty, even, permit you to offer to God less than fifteen minutes each day?

We must remember that time spent in communing with God and meditating upon his holy Word is always strength gained for his service.

The little trials which usually come into our daily lives will be scattered like chaff before the wind if we only take a little of our time each morning to tell the Lord all about them, asking him to stay very near to us and keep us from falling.

We never fail to give our bodies three meals a day, yet some of us think we can not find time to feed our souls upon the Bread of Life.

Our lives must never be so busy that we cannot spend fifteen minutes in gathering up spiritual food for an entire day, when our great Leader "went out into a mountain to pray, and continued all night in prayer."

If possible, let us consecrate the early morning to the observance of this sacred privilege.

How natural to open our eyes after a night of peaceful slumber and look to him whose protecting wing o'ershadowed us while the curtain of darkness hung round all his children!

How happy to thank him first of all for his protection through the night and for the beautiful dawning of the morning!

Give God the choice hour of the day. It is very unchristianly for us to go to him at the close of the day when our minds are so crowded with thoughts of the day that we find it almost impossible to lay aside everything but thoughts of God and his love. One comrade has said, "I have found that very often our waking thoughts rule the whole day. How necessary, then, that they be inspired of God! This inspiration can come only through his presence."

Let us say unto him, "My voice shalt thou hear in the morning, O Lord; in the morning will I direct my prayer unto thee, and will look up."

Spend the Quiet Hour in quiet meditation and direct communion with God. Dedicate your whole life anew each day to the service of the Master. Talk with him face to face. Give him the deep gratitude of a child's heart for his fatherly protection. Open your heart before him and ask him to purify it. Do not expect God to give you everything for which you pray, but always be ready to say, "Not my will, Father, but thine be done."

Never fail to ask him what he would like to have you do, then find his message to you in the Book.

If there is a person in this assembly who knows not the blessedness of a quiet talk with God, let him be convinced by listening to the testimonies of thousands who are keeping the covenant.

It has proved a sources of great joy to the invalid, the tired mother, the burdened father and even to the prisoner behind the bars.

Surely, you can raise no objection to this organization. The are no dues, fines nor meetings, no officers to support—simply a promise to worship God in a more satisfactory manner.

How remarkably strange it seems that we must make an effort to become quiet!

When the soul grows tired of sin and strife, it seems that it would be very natural that we should long for a quiet hour with One who is ready and anxious at all times to give us strength and courage. Yet in this age when people "never have time," when life is a continual rush for wealth, fame and honor, we must draw ourselves within our shells in order that our souls may bask in the sunlight of Heaven.

How happy this world would be if every Christian in it were a comrade of the Quiet Hour!

If even every member of the societies of this grand state should sign the covenant, the effect upon the spirituality of the society as a whole, as well as its individual members, would soon be evident.

Trusting in the Lord Jesus Christ for

*Read before the Texas State Endeavor Convention, Dallas, June 8, 1898.

let us strive to bring the Chris-
ld into the secret of his presence
the influence of the Quiet Hour.
ne is coming when all Christians
more like Jesus because they are
arer to him.
here will be a world-wide sunrise
ieeting every day. The Christian
: banner will bear the motto of the
ur, "O, satisfy us in the morning
mercy."
uls will delight to hide in the
his presence to learn the sweet
f love that enable us to resist the
ns continually thrown into our

under the shadow of his wing, we
im all our sorrows and our fears.
s ever ready to listen patiently to
ings and his lips always uttering
ords which cheer the drooping soul.
ll often reprove us, but his pure
ind within our hearts sins that we
new were there; so let us thank
reminding us of our errors and
is into the path of righteousness.

you like to know the sweetness of the
et of the Lord?
ide beneath his shadow, this shall
i be your reward;
ne'er you leave the silence of that
py meeting-place
t mind and bear the image of the
iter in your face."

w-Endeavorers, let our watchword
y-eight be, "Every Christian in
omrade of the Quiet Hour."
r, help us during the coming
draw near to thee each day by
many quiet hours in the secret of
nce, and we will love thee more
e thee forever. Amen!"

Much in Little.

llowing newspaper squib manages
y quite a cargo of information
Philippine Islands, though it is
o closely packed.
oms.
s worn.
arry at fifteen.
ves nor forks.
leep at midday.
are a cusiosity.
omen than men.
the chief product.
as small as goats.
enjoys electricity.
s bathe thrice daily.
asshopper is a delicacy.
y half Manila's hemp.
rs earn ten cents a day.
ut oil is an illuminant.
was founded in 1571.

Flora's Rabbit.

MARY COBB.

old rainy evening, in the late
ttle Flo was in the garden, care-
mining the beds in which her
ad been planted. Hearing some
ng along the road, she looked up
a man, who had just moved into
borhood. He was a kind-hearted
as he greeted her pleasantly he
his hand in which was a little
red animal, and kindly said, "I
ttle rabbit, it is cold, hungry and
ould you like to have it for a pet?"
dly accepted it, and almost for-
o thank him, she bounded into the house to show her treasure. Her mamma advised her to wrap it up in some flannel and leave it until it was warm and dry. This she did and at once began to talk about what she would call it.

After seaching her little mind an hour or more for a suitable name, she decided to call it "Bunny." Bridget said that was a squirrel's name. To this little Flo replied, after studying a minute, "I guess I'll change the style and have it a rabbit's name." Though Bridget laughed the rabbit was called Bunny.

Flo now began to wonder if the little animal was hungry. She coaxed Bridget to warm some milk and then tried to feed Bunny, but he absolutely refused to drink.

Now Flo's bedtime had come, so Bunny was put to bed in a little box and Flo also retired.

I need not tell you of the pleasant dreams she had that night, in which Bunny played an important part, but her eyes were scarcely open the next morning when she sprang from her bed and ran to the box in which Bunny slept, only to find that he believed in rising with the sun and had acted accordingly. Flo's eyes filled with tears; mamma said that he could not get out of the house and was hidden behind something. Our little girl's face brightened, and she began the long search in which the whole family joined.

After we all had become discouraged and Bridget had repeatedly declared that Pussy knew something about Bunny, if she only chose to tell it, Tom looked under the bookcase and saw a little dark-colored ball that had ears. He excitedly told Flo to see what was under the bookcase, as his hand was so large he couldn't get it under far enough to reach back in the corners.

With tears in her eyes she put her little hand under, when out something jumped, and it started across the floor. Mamma just had a glimpse of it and jumping on a chair she screamed, "There goes a mouse." A second look showed that it was only Bunny.

While papa and Tom were laughing themselves hoarse, mamma, blushing, climbed down from her place of safety and Flo danced with delight. Meanwhile, Bridget had closed the doors and after running from one corner to another she succeeded in catching the frightened little animal.

Flo was sure it was hungry now, after having such vigorous exercise, and this time her attempts at trying to teach it to drink were successful. By this time mamma's fear had subsided and she laughed heartily to see it put its little tongue out at first one side of its mouth and then the other. Seeing that it was awkward about drinking, she donated some of her young cabbage plants and Tom brought some clover leaves for it. But contrary little Bunny seemed to think he was too young for such coarse food and would not touch them.

Flo as well as Tom had great fun with Bunny and planned to go to grandma's that afternoon to show her how Bunny could drink. However, the rain just poured, so they were obliged to stay at home. This disappointed them, but Flo busied herself by laying more plans and even engaged Tom as a carpenter to build a house for Bunny.

That night Bunny was put to bed in a deeper box, so Flo was sure that he could not get out. The next morning, to her great disappointment, he was gone, and though repeated search was made, Bunny was nowhere to be found.

We could not imagine what had become of him until Bridget said that the kitchen door blew open sometime during the night and remained open until morning. This solved the mystery and filled Flo's heart fuller of sorrow than it had been of joy, the evening she received the pet.

That afternoon she climbed into her mamma's lap and, with tears in her eyes said, "Mamma, how do you suppose Bunny could run away and make me feel so bad after I had been so good to him when he was helpless?" Mamma said, "Bunny is just like people. You know we are helpless and our Father in heaven takes care of us, but sometimes we do naughty things. Then we do not love him. We are trying to get away from him, just as Bunny was trying to get away from you, when he hid under the bookcase and you know Bunny kept on trying and trying to get away and at last he succeeded. When we keep doing nauhgty things, we keep getting farther and farther away from our Heavenly Father and often succeed in getting clear away. This makes him feel much worse than you do about Bunny."

Flo was silent a long time and then said, decidedly, "I am never going to be naughty again, for I love Jesus and don't want to make him feel bad about me as I do Bunny."

Valparaiso, Ind.

Sail On.

IRA M. BOSWELL.

He who upon life's unknown sea
Some unseen danger fears
Will never great in this world be,
Nor live beyond his years.
O, youth, there's nought behind, life's ocean lies before.
Be brave, unfurl thy sails,
And lift thy anchor from the shallow shore.
Know this: True courage never fails.
Wouldst thou thy impress leave
Upon thy fellowman,
The battling waves of ocean cleave,
Depart the smilling land.
If on thy ship, O, youthful soul,
Fears and doubts in mutiny arise,
Bid hope and courage still be bold,
Press onward toward the prize.
When tempests howl and lightnings dart,
And thunders shake the sea,
Sail on, fear not, have heart,
Let faith thy pilot be.
And when the sun into the deep
Hath plunged his burning face,
Sail on, let hope not sleep;
Nor fear usurp his place—
Sail on, though night with clouds be dark,
Nor pause to look behind;
For on the troubled track of thy frail bark
The light of duty's star will shine.
When in the night no stars appear,
Then to thy task with courage bend,
The breaking day will bring thee cheer—
Thy journey soon will end.
Soon o'er the waves the sun will glow,
And in the hopeful morning clear
The floating driftwood strange will show
Some undiscovered land is near.
Sail on to where the water's blue
Break on the shore with many a laughing wave:
Reward is for the good and true;
The victory's for the brave.
Now plant thy banner deep into the soil,
Its silken folds to the breeze unfurled,
Then know: There is no gain without its toil;
'Tis work that makes the world.
When base ingratitude shall bind thee with his chains,
Have thou no fear: his purple robes will rot.
With each succeeding year thy reputation gains,
Thy name, thy deeds, shall never be forgot.
Sail on, sail on, whatever be the wind,
Give God thy precious soul;
Trust self, trust God, trust all mankind,
Through storms you'll reach the goal.

—*Gospel Messenger*.

Short Stories.

A very rich man once upon a time chanced also—strange to say—to be a very unhappy man, and offered an immense sum of money to any one that would make him happy.

A philosopher brought to him a new game that he had invented. It was a good game, and whoever invents a good game does a good deed. But in a few days the rich man wearied of the game.

Came next a philosopher who set the rich man to work sawing boards and planing them and making things; and for a time he was very happy, for labor is a great lightener of the heart. But one day he could think of nothing else to make, and of no place to put it after it was made, so that all his gloom returned.

Whereupon came a third philosopher, who set the rich man to doing things for other people. And the rich man has been happy ever since.

A little boy was going past a liquor saloon, the door of which was wide open, with his dog Sport. The dog, not knowing any better, went in, but his little master was soon after him, with the following good advice: "Come out of there Sport! Don't be disgracing the family."

Of the late French Senator Renaud, the Kolnishe Zeitung tells the following anecdote:

When Renaud first came as senator to Paris, he engaged a room at a hotel and paid a month's rent—one hundred and fifty francs—in advance. The proprietor asked if he would have a receipt.

"It is not necessary," replied Renaud; "God has witnessed the payment."

"Do you believe in God?" sneered the host.

"Most assuredly," replied Renaud; "don't you?"

"Not I, Monsieur."

"Ah," said the senator, "I will take a receipt, if you please."—*Congregationalist.*

Tho Homiletic Review tells the following characteristic story on Sam Jones:

Having been invited to hold meetings in Dr. Talmage's Brooklyn church, he called upon the latter gentleman before the fir meeting. Talmage was a little shocked the evangelist's shabby apparel, and aske him if he would accept a new suit clothes. The couple visited a clothin store, and Sam Jones was arrayed in ne raiment and decorated with a silk hat.

At the meeting Talmage introduced hi as the "Rev. Samuel P. Jones, fro Georgia."

Then the evangelist made this astonish ing speech: "Yes, the Rev. Samuel P Jones, from Georgia; and this is the ne suit of clothes and the hat your pastor ha presented to me. If your pastor had much of the grace of God in his heart as h has pride, he would convert all Brooklyn and would not need me!"

Once Spurgeon passed a stonemaso who, between every stroke of his hamme cursed and swore. Mr. Spurgeon laid hi hand on his shoulder, and looking kindly a him said, "You are an adept at swearing Can you also pray?" With another oat he replied, "Not very likely." Holding u five shillings, Mr. Spurgeon said if h would promise never to pray he would giv him that. "That is easily earned," sai the man, with a fresh oath, and put it i his pocket.

When Spurgeon left, the man began t feel a little queer. When he went hom sked him what ailed him, and he "It is Judas' money!" said the on a sudden impulse, he threw it ire. The wife found it and took l discovered who had given it to man took it back to Spurgeon, rsed long with him, warning him, gth was the means of saving him. ie an attached member of his henceforth his home became the eace.—*The Standard.*

General Grant was a boy his e morning found herself without breakfast, and sent him to borrow a neighbor. Going, without into the house of his neighbor, was then at West Point, young rheard a letter read from the son at he had failed in examination ming home. He got the butter, ome, and without waiting for ran down to the office of the ian from that district.

amar," said he, "will you appoint it Point!"

and so is there and has three erve."

ppose he should fail, will you

nar laughed. "If he doesn't go to use for you to try."

ie you'll give me a chance, Mr. ryhow."

nar promised.

t day the defeated lad came home Congressman, laughing at Uly's gave him the appointment. aid Grant, "it was my mother's of butter that made me General lent." But it was his own shrewd- be the chance and promptness to that urged him upwards.—*Chris- cate.*

deal of laughter was created in n magistrate's office one day last n excitable German, a prisoner, with some minor breach of ordi- are you a single man?" asked the

you look oud," was the indignant But don'd you try to make no me yoost because I vas Dutch . Do I look like I vas a double I look like I vas a Si'mese uh! I vas no fool if I am not long try."—*The Philadelphia Call.*

Can or Can't.

an would begin it,
an't isn't "in it"
e is work to be done.
an is awake,
an't is a fake,
way the world is run.
an is at school;
an't is a fool,
s is thinking of fun.
an is a worker;
an't is a shirker,
is up with the sun.
an is a master,
an't means disaster
ing life has begun.
an is a man;
et can't be can;
ess, then, will life's work be done.
—*Unidentified.*

What I Live For.

I live for those who love me,
Whose hearts are kind and true;
For the heaven that smiles above me,
And awaits my spirit too;
For all human ties that bind me,
For the task my God assigned me,
For the bright hopes yet to find me,
And the good that I can do.

I live to learn their story
Who suffered for my sake;
To emulate their glory,
And follow in their wake—
Bards, patriots, martyrs, sages,
The heroic of all ages,
Whose deeds crowd history's pages,
And time's great volume make.

I live to hold communion
With all that is divine,
To feel there is a union
'Twixt Nature's heart and mine;
To profit by affliction,
Reap truth from fields of fiction,
Grow wiser from conviction,
Fulfill God's grand design.

I live to hail that season
By gifted ones foretold,
When men shall live by reason,
And not alone by gold;
When man to man united,
And every wrong thing righted,
The whole world shall be lighted
As Eden was of old.

I live for those who love me,
For those who know me true,
For the heaven that smiles above me,
And awaits my coming too;
For the cause that lacks assistance,
For the wrong that needs resistance,
For the future in the distance,
And the good that I can do.
—J. Linnæus Banks.

The Floors in Summer.

I believe in bare floors in the kitchen and dining-room for summer, for they are so easy to keep clean, and so much cooler than when covered with carpet. It is a positive rest to one's eyes to see a room without chair and picture-scarfs, lambre-quins and other dust-catchers, and with only the necessary furniture and bare floors. Keep out the flies with screens, and let in the air and sunshine. Paint or oil the floors, or if they are too rough to look well uncovered, get oilcloth or linoleum for summer, but do not buy a heavy wool carpet. A few minutes' work every other day will suffice to keep them clean and free from dust.

Neither linoleum nor oilcloth should ever be scrubbed with a brush or mopped with hot water. Heat the water until it is lukewarm, and dissolve enough pearline in it to make a good suds. Now wash your oilcloth, changing the water frequently as it grows dark. Nothing causes it to grow dull and grimy so quickly as washing it with insufficient or dirty water. Mop a small place, then rinse with clean water and wipe dry; proceed in this way until the floor is cleansed and the entire surface will look bright and clear like new oilcloth. Oiled or painted floors are cleaned in the same way. E. J. C.

Literature.

"Organic Evolution Considered."

I have just finished reading this "Little Drab Book," by my friend, Prof. A. Fair-hurst, of Kentucky University, and pub-lished by the Christian Publishing Com-pany, of St. Louis. There are six things I want to say about it:

1. It is a thoroughly *readable* book. It has a breezy freshness of style, a logical piquancy of argument and a lucid force of statement which held me with absorbed interest to the close. Books on such themes the unscientific reader expects to find dry and tough as the rind of a pomegranate, but this is a marked exception. It is full of juice from cover to cover.

2. I love the *modesty* of the book. It makes no loud or boasted claims. It does not crow over the eminent men whose theories it combats. It recognizes their title to respect and honor for what they have done in the various fields of scientific re-search, while making bold to differ from some of their conclusions. The world can stand a considerable increase of this quality in books on this subject.

3. I love also its *candor*. The author has nothing of the bigot in his make-up. He is always ready to admit the force of facts which may not be favorable to his side of the case. He often announces his conclusions after pages of close and lusty argument in language far less dogmatic than they would easily bear. Such a spirit tends greatly to give me confidence in an author.

4. I was much impressed by the *strength* of the "Little Drab Book." There is nothing puerile about its reasonings. They grapple the merits of the question in a thoroughly robust fashion. The Professor's stronghold is in *handling facts*, and there are places in this book where the way he does it can be described only by the word *masterly*.

5. I must express my gratitude for the *instruction* the book has given me. Not only for the fresh conviction it has revived of the vulnerableness of the evolution theories, but for important information concerning such subjects as "Instinct," "Rudimentary Organs," "Paleontology," "Design in Nature," "Embryology," etc., which are of no small value to me.

6. And finally, I am glad to have read the book for the strengthening of my *faith*, which has come from it. My faith in a personal God, in the truth of revelation, in immortality, in miracles, in the super-natural origin of Christianity have all re-ceived fresh confirmation from this little book of 386 pages.

And what has thus been a pleasure and a benefit to me I cordially commend to others. No man can read this book without mental and moral stimulation. No preacher can read it without adding very decidedly to the equipment needful to the success of his work. George Darsie.

Frankford, Ky., Aug. 2, 1898.

Preachers Should Tell their People.

Every preacher should tell his people, and especially the young, all about the Bethany C. E. Reading Courses. Full information may be had gratis, by dropping a card to the Bethany C. E. Company, 798 Republic Street, Cleveland, O. Begin at once to plan for systematic reading among the

Sunday School.

ELISHA'S LAST WORDS.*

HERBERT L. WILLETT.

Elisha's prophetic career covers a longer period than that of any other of those great men who stood to interpret the will of God to Israel. Moses' leadership lasted for forty years; Samuel acted as judge and prophet for perhaps as long; Isaiah's ministry was of about the same duration; Jeremiah continued for half a century to proclaim the purpose of Jehovah to Jerusalem, but Elisha must have spent not less than sixty years as a prophet, and perhaps seventy-five. It was in the reign of Ahab that Elijah cast his mantle over him and called him to be his helper; his death occurred in the days of Joash, of Israel. Meantime, Ahaziah and Jehoram, sons of Ahab; Jehu, a general who put to death the whole race of Ahab; Jehoahaz, a son of Jehu and Joash or Jehoash, another son of Jehu, had all reigned.

But this long period marks a change in the position of prophecy as recognized by the royal house. Since the days of David the prophets were of small moment in the state. Solomon had elevated the priests and neglected the prophets. The kings of the northern kingdom had followed this evil example, and had even disarranged the priestly functions, putting obscure men into the sacred office. When Elijah appeared in the reign of Ahab the religion of Jehovah was in deadly danger of total extinction, and throughout his career as a prophet he scarcely gained further attention than to occasionally appear upon the scene as a reminder of the divine judgment impending over the corrupt court. This was the condition when Elisha began his work. He was unknown to the king, though he lived in the capital. But his patriotic services during the Syrian wars brought him into notice, and gradually he became known and respected, not only among the common people, but by the kings as well. When he lay at the point of death Joash came to see him, and exhibited a probably sincere affection for him, and a feeling of public calamity at his death. Elisha had spoken of his master Elijah as the defender of the state, but now it is the king himself who calls the prophet the chariot and horseman of Israel. The distress of the nation had, no doubt, assisted to bring about this result. Never did the power of the kingdom sink so low as in the reign of Jehoahaz, the son of Jehu, whose poor remnant of an army was at the mercy of the new dynasty of Hazael of Syria (2 Kings 13:7). Some little improvement was made under the leadership of the king's brother Joash, who presently came to the throne and who was able later on to make war with Amaziah, of Judah. But Israel had learned by the lesson to respect in some degree the men of God, and the work of Elisha must have prepared for that striking appearance of the prophetic spirit in the following reign, that of Jeroboam II., during which both Amos and Hosea preached.

But Elisha was essentially a prophet of the older order. With all his quiet ways and kindly feeling for the common people, he had not a little of the Elijah spirit. He had been in Damascus and seen something of the power of that kingdom with which Israel was at such odds for centuries (2 Kings 8:7-15). His spirit even as death approached was full of a fierce desire to sweep back the enemies of his nation beyond the eastern border, and he sought to infuse some of his fire into the too-easy nature of the king. The moment was opportune. Joash was touched with regret as he looked on the face of the dying prophet. Elisha roused himself and begged the king to send out his defiance against the Syrians in the characteristic fashion of the East. The king drew his bow, with the arrow pointed eastward through the open window. The prophet laid his weak hands on the king's in token that the divine blessing was on the royal challenge. Then the king shot the arrow far to the east, toward the camp of the enemy. But the prophet was not yet satisfied. The arrow was the signal that war was to be begun again, and the promise of Elisha was that it should bring deliverance. But he wanted to test the purpose of the king by having him thrust arrows into the earth. To him the action was not significant, and he was not of sufficiently energetic nature to do any more than was necessary. Elisha saw the meaning of the act. The king was not the man to be a great leader, such as the situation demanded. Aggressiveness and persistence are necessary qualities to bring to any enterprise. God can make little use of listless, easy-going people, who never undertake anything except under pressure, and have no persistency after a work has been begun. The victory could never be very decisive with such a leader.

A great man's power abides after he is dead. Even the bones of Elisha could revive the body hastily thrust into his grave in the time of panic. A story of this kind could only be preserved in a circle where the name and fame of Elisha were assured. It was a delight in later years to recount the wonderful things associated with his name. The number of these preserved in our accounts of the prophet's life shows how his story took hold of the popular mind.

But Elisha's words came true. Israel was sinful, but God was gracious. His covenant with the patriarchs could not be forgotten. Human sin is not as great as divine grace. The kingdom had sunk to a low level under Jehoahaz, but the promise to Joash was redeemed, and thrice over victory perched on the banners of Israel. Moreover, the successful war with Judah (2 Kings 14:8-16) gave the nation new confidence in itself, and prepared the way for the brilliant successes under the following king, Jeroboam II., in whose days Israel reached the pinnacle of material prosperity.

SUGGESTIONS FOR TEACHING.

A good life gets itself understood and appreciated at last. Because the prophets were often men of warlike impulses is no justification for indiscriminate fighting to-day. War is a dreadful necessity at best, and is less, and less to be justified as the nations learn the will of God. Energy and persistence are necessary factors in every successful life. The influence of a life for good or evil does not end at death. If God treated us only as we deserved, for how little could we hope! It is the graciousness of our Father that fills us with wonder and love. God always keeps his promises.

*Sunday-school lesson for September 4, 1898—The Death of Elisha (2 Kings 13:14-25). Golden Text—Precious in the sight of the Lord is the death of his saints (Psa. 116:15). Lesson Outline—1. The Prophet and the King (14:18); 2. The Miracle at Elisha's Tomb (20, 21); 3. The Three Victories (22-25).

ristian Endeavor.

By Burris A. Jenkins.

TOPICS FOR SEPTEMBER 4.

TANCE AND CONVERSION— WHAT ARE THEY?

ek. 18:20-32; Acts 26:19, 20.)

is caught in the act and is placed in
He is exceedingly cast down and
id wrong. But he is more sorry that
aught. This is not repentance. He
autious next time, but in all proba-
would repeat the offense upon a
opportunity. Or, on the other hand,
d may see that liquor is injuring his
n and impairing his business suc-
he may deliberately resolve to drink
and possible he might keep the resolu-
s is not repentance, either. Re-
is more than sorrow for a deed or a
to forsake a certain practice. It is
these two combined. Repentance is
y sorrow for wrong-doing which
the act as sinful, and which abhors
d determines to forsake it.
the repentant one may not succeed
his sin forever away. Most of us are
avoid the repetition of sins of which
repented perhaps many times. But
finitely tender and merciful. As a
es his children, so he pities us, and
ties of seventies will he forgive those
t. But the sin must not become so
with us that, grown familiar with its
rst endure, then pity, then embrace.
de must be one of continual loathing,
ul felt when he cried, "Who shall
from the body of this death?" as if
arrying a decaying corpse upon his
all the time. Then shall the comfort
as in Paul's next breath, "I thank
gh Jesus Christ!" We should not
mourning about sin, though forever
of sin. We should strive to be at
l at rest, though forever should we
sin that made thee mourn." We
ek for the Christian's calm, yet be
riving against sin. Even when we
quered, perhaps, each individual be-
, we shall still feel the general sense
ss that stands between us and God
still yearn to remove it. Is not re-
then, a state of soul which comes to
ian, not once nor twice, but many a
d may it not possibly be ever a con-
ate?
deal of mystification has arisen over
"conversion," because of a poor
n which runs all through our Author-
on, and which has been corrected in
ised Version. Every Endeavorer
n a revised New Testament. One
ight for eight cents, and he should
concordance and look up every pas-
which the words convert and conver-
rs in the King James Version and
ame in the Revised. His eyes will
, to the meaning of this simple word,
been wrapped in mystery. "Be con-
s not used in the numberless passages
it formerly occurred. The only ex-
s, "turn" or "turn yourself." And
nd in the Revised Version. Nobody
turn us to God. We cannot "be
." We must turn ourselves. We
ert ourselves from disobedient ser-
rusting and loving children. Who-
s to God performs this act of conver-
is a thing to do, not to receive. No
ves conversion, he converts himself,
turns about. He is not turned by
side hand; he turns. You are walk-
and you cross a friend's path. You
tention to him. By and by you feel
n back, speak to him and walk with
hen that friend is God, your act is
n. You turn to God. The act, of
course, is accompanied by belief in him, trust that he will receive you kindly, sorrow that you have neglected and wronged him, but the essential thing is that you *turn*. This turning in some instances may be calm, deliberate and, so far as the world sees, unaccompanied with strong emotion. In others it may be a convulsion of the whole nature by which the inmost depths are stirred. In all, a new creature, a new companion, a new child of God has been born into the world and there is joy in the presence of the angles.

FACTS AND FACTORS.

Of the 1,300 wounded at Santiago, it is said that only about 100 have died of their wounds.

About $2,000,000 have been expended on the exposition buildings and grounds at Omaha, Nebraska furnishing one-half of it.

President Harper, of the University of Chicago, announces a gift of $15,000 from Miss Katharine Gross, of New York, for the promotion of the study of astronomy.

There are more Congregational than Anglican communicants in Wales. A national church for a minority seems an anomaly.

Mme. J. Langles, of New Orleans, and her daughter, Miss Angelle Langles, who perished in the Bourgogne disaster, left among other bequests, $10,000 to the Charity Hospital in New Orleans, $1,000 to the ambulance fund, $2,000 to the House of the Good Shepherd, and $3,000 to the Newsboys' Home. Provision was also made for the erection in that city of a memorial hospital for women and children.

Boston is building the largest and finest railway station in the world.

August 15th was London's hottest day for many years past.

Of the 400,000 canary birds sold in England annually (for about $500,000) 100,000 are imported from Germany.

During the past year 1,775 new Sunday-schools were started in India, and 66,000 new scholars brought in.

The annual output of coal in Japan has been estimated at 3,000,000 tons.

The President has announced his intention to muster out from 75,000 to 100,000 volunteers.

The Navy Department will ask Congress to authorize the construction of the largest and most formidable battleships and cruisers afloat.

The City of Manila is lighted by 12,000 incandescent and 260 arc lights, has a telephone system, and is the center of 720 miles of telegraph in the islands.

Marriages.

BYBEE—BABCOX.—Aug. 11, 1898, by C. H. Strawn V. D. M., Mr. Horace Bybee to Miss Cora Babcox, both of Santa Fe Mo.

GOLDSBERRY—WOODWORTH.—At the home of the bride's mother in Macomb, Ill., Mr. Frank Goldsberry, of Colchester, Ill., to Miss Mary Woodworth, Aug. 4, 1898. I married the bride's father and mother many years ago. J. C. Reynolds.

SAWYER—MERRICK.—Married, at the home of the bride on Lord's day, July 31, by Elder J. E. Masters, Dempsey W. Sawyer to Miss Callie Merrick, all of Dorchester, Ill.

Obituaries.

[One hundred words will be inserted free. Above one hundred words, one cent a word. Please send amount with each notice.]

BUTLER.

Sybil S. Butler, wife of the late Pardee Butler, entered into rest on Lord's day morning, August 7th, at nine o'clock. The passing from the shores of time of this excellent Christian woman deserves more than a passing notice. Sybil Carleton was born in Sullivan, Ohio, July 4, 1823. On the 17th of August 1843 she was united in marriage to Bro. Pardee Butler. In 1850 they moved to Iowa, near Davenport, Bro. Bulter preaching the gospel in Eastern Iowa and Western Illinois. In 1855 they came to Kansas, settling on a farm a few miles west of Atchinson, near a village now called Pardee. Those were troublesome times in Kansas—the dark days just before the storm of civil strife broke upon our beloved land. Bro. Butler's ardent support of the Union cause, the perils in which that support placed him, his famous forced ride down the Missouri River on a raft, are events well known in all this part of the country. He was a pioneer, too, in preaching the ancient gospel in this state. The fruit of his successful seed-sowing has been gathered, and will continue to be, in the regions round about. He was an intelligent, earnest advocate of the truth as it is in Christ Jesus. He passed to his reward on the 20th of November, 1888. In all the labors and trials and triumphs of her honored husband, Sister Butler shared with splendid fidelity. Cultured, refined, beautiful in heart and life, a Christian wife and mother, training her children to know and fear the Lord, she was a queen among women. There can be no more exalted station in life than that so worthily occupied by Sister Butler. To Bro. and Sister Butler were born seven children, four of whom died when young. The three grown are Sister Rosetta B. Hastings, wife of Bro. Z. S. Hastings, a minister of the gospel; Bro. George C. Butler and Bro. Charles P. Butler, all of whom live in this county. Sister Butler's two sisters, Mrs. A. E. Riley, of Cummings, and Mrs. C. O. Dunshee, of Pardee, this county, were present at the funeral. Sister Rosetta B. Hastings has contributed much to our religious literature and is widely known. When the writer first came to Atchinson, a little more than fifteen years ago, Bro. and Sister Butler were among the first of his acquaintances and warmest friends, and many a time did he enjoy the hospitality and fellowship of their delightful home. It was Sister Butler's desire that he preach the funeral sermon, which was done at the Pardee church on Monday, Aug. 8th, at 2 P. M., the subject being, "The Positiveness of the Christian Faith" (2 Cor. 5:1), a theme deemed especially fitting, considering the firm character of both Bro. and Sister Butler and their lifelong advocacy of the principles of the Current Reformation. The services were attended by a large company of people, particularly the earlier settlers of Eastern Kansas. Bro. Claude Haskell, the pastor of the church at Pardee, had charge of the services and Bro. Marris, who had known Bro. and Sisters Butler for more than forty years, spoke tenderly of the blessed followship he had with

and three sons survive to mourn the loss of a most devoted wife and mother, and three brothers and one sister also weep that their loved one has passed away. May our Father guide these bereaved ones and bring them and all who mourn, at last, into that land where there is no death. J. P. PINKERTON.

Springfield, Mo.

KINNEY.

John Kinney died July 27, 1898. He was born in Montgomery county, Ky., near Mt. Sterling, December 25, 1829. In 1847 he was married to Caroline Wymore. After 11 years of happy home life she passed away. He served his country in the war of 1861 and in 1867 married Eliza Yocum. A short time previous to this he was converted and united with the Church of Christ at Sycamore where he resided and officiated as elder till 1869, when he and family moved first to Minnesota, thence to Iowa, and in 1871 to Nebraska; then, after 23 years, to Phill county, Kas., the place of his departure from earth. Our brother lived a peaceful life and died in the triumphs of a living faith. A wife, six children, and many friends mourn his departure to the better land.

C. K. HAZLIT.

Pleasant Green, Kas.

MORRIS.

Millie L. (Kenney) Morris, wife of Reddick Morris, died on her 25th birthday, July 31, 1898, at Kenney, Ill., where her whole life was spent. Two small boys are bereft of her motherly guidance. She is mourned by husband, aged mother and a large circle of relatives and friends. Hers was a heart which seemed not to have known doubt. She gave it, in childhood, to the Savior, whose service was her delight in life, and in whose name she triumphed.

C. B. DABNEY.

Mt. Pulaski, Ill.

A. F. H. SAW.

WHEREAS, God, merciful in his severe as in his good providences, has removed our brother, Rev. A. F. H. Saw, from his missionary labors among us to his eternal and abundant reward in the joy of his Lord, we, the members of the five societies represented in Nanking, while we submit to the will of our Heavenly Father, desire to record our deep sorrow on account of his death and to express our thankfulness for the life and work which has so suddenly ceased.

His work during the 12 years spent among us is remembered with great admiration. The fragrance of his devoted and faithful service and his meek and quiet spirit will ever remain an inspiration to us. In love and good work he was not behind those who abound in all things and we will mourn that now we shall see his face no more: We desire to record our sincere condolence with the two families so greatly bereaved by this apparent early departure of their son, our brother, and especially we would express our sympathy with her whom we commend to our God who ever careth for the widow. Also that we desire to express our heartfelt regret that our sister mission is called upon at this time in so sudden and trying way to part with a brother beloved and that the society and friends in England and America have to endure this irreparable loss of a faithful and successful missionary. We would also express the sense of our own loss to the work in the missionary work in this field from which we can so illy afford to spare from our small number one so efficient in his chosen work. And we would express further our hope that his society may make good our great loss by speedily sending a number to take up the pressing work which by its urgency as seen by our brother was no small part of the cause which makes us all now mourn;

Resolved, That a copy of these resolutions be presented to Mrs. Saw, to the family and friends of Mr. and Mrs. Saw, to the Foreign Christian Missionary Society, and that they be recorded in the minutes of our Association.

CHAS. LEAMAN,
ROBT. C. BEEBE. } Com.

Nanking, June 3, 1898.

SEYMOUR.

Jennie I. Sanford was born at Atwater, O.,

stricken by paral
patient sufferer
her death, July 2
of eight children,
Mother Vincent
ist Church from
when she united
She was a faithfu
life. Funeral se
Christian church

"Princely Knights of Character Castle."

ıe Home Light, a Boston monthly, ı the July number of which the subjoined ıle is taken, stands, as its name implies, he guardianship of the home. That it should n the "secrecy" feature of the "P. K. C. (recently noticed in the CHRISTIAN-NGELIST querist column) that which is ical to the highest interests of the boys is suprising. Presumably tha CHRISTIAN-NGELIST with its wonted spirit of fairness not hesitate to print for its readers this ɔw of the Princely Knights Secret Society.

W. P. KEELER.

ıicago, *July* 30, 1898.

"CHARACTER CASTLE."

this era of secret societies why should the be overlooked? If signs and grips and all paraphernalia of secrecy are a good thing ıis elders why not for him who is "father ıe man?"

The Princely Knights of Character Cas-' is a boy's secret society seemingly ded on the above idea. We have read fully the constitution of the Order, and several copies of The Boy's Friend, ıh is its special organ; and while we credit ɔriginators with the best of motives, the ıe Light would be untrue to its name if it ıot throw its warning search rays on any ɪnpt to solve the "Boy Problem" which lves the use of secret methods; which peals"—we quote from the official outline ts work—"to the boy's desire to learn ets, his love of banners and regalia, and lesire for entertainment."

hy think to build up in a boy a strong and ıring character by using the weakest ıents in his nature for the substructure? ən men would rear an impregnable fortress ıey use for the foundations "wood, hay, ble?" Do they build it on the sand, or on rock?

ıat the boy when he enters must sign a ge "never to use intoxicating liquor in any ı; to abstain from the use of profane or ıre language; to discourage the use of ıcco in any form; to strive to be pure in and mind"—all this is eminently praise-thy. And as to its work: "To teach boys e heroes at heart; to endure temptation not to do wrong; to have love for all man-; to be pure in morals and patriotic in ı"—what can we want more? Nothing the elimination of that secrecy which ls it all, as one crack in a costly vase lers it valueless; as one drop of poison in a of the pûrest water will make it a savor of h to him who drinks thereof.

The Princely Knights," we are told orially in the March number of The Boy's nd, "is a fraternal order of *men* that ıits boys into its membership." That e men are largely Masons, Oddfellows or ıbers of some other secret society goes ıout saying. In the April issue we find an orial strongly urging fraternity men to e it a point to join the order and thus ɔme the means of helping "tempted and perienced boys from fifteen to twenty s of age." This appeal to lodgemen is as natural and fitting as would be an əal to church members on behalf of the istian Endeavor Society, or the Epworth gue. It is right that the parent, whether rch or lodge, should support its own off-ng.

ıt let us do a little serious thinking on the ıence that boys are likely to receive at the t impressionable age, from intimate asso-ion with men who wear the square and pass, the three links, or perhaps a number secret society badges together. In our lic schools instructors are forbidden to r the peculiar garb of any religious sect rder because of the influence on the pupil. the display of these secret society blems on the persons of men and hom they are taught to look as mentors t be a constant object-lesson before eyes of the boys, leading them to the ılve that when old enough, they, too, will , and thus have a right to sport the same. at is the honor of a "Princely" neophyte ıpared to the glory of a full-fledged Mason, night Templar, or a Mystic Shriner, or ıething else that will admit of titles and hers and aprons galore? Do not the found-of the P. C. frankly admit that they eal to that part of boy nature which is ısed with such things, and supply in the of regalia and secret work just what will se it to develop along that line?

he secrecy, as we have said, is the one ure that vitiates and corrupts what might erwise be a good thing. It creates an

stand aside unrecognized if he cannot give the grip and sign. And what use for secrecy any way? It gives the lie to its professed object. Why should a purpose so praiseworthy hide away from the light as if its deeds were evil? Why should a "Princely" character be best evolved under the cover of darkness where all kinds of human vermin creep and burrow? Why should an eagle created to soar with his eye on the sun seek the habitat of the owl and the bat?—ED.

The Boys' Friend and Character Castle.

EDITOR CHRISTIAN-EVANGELIST:—Permit me to thank you for your most fraternal commendation of the Boys' Friend in a recent number of the CHRISTIAN-EVANGELIST, also for your nice and pointed reply to Bro. W. P. Keeler's letter in the CHRISTIAN-EVANGELIST of July 28th. I am grateful to Bro. K. for noting the growth and improvement of the Boys' Friend, but I regret that he so greatly misrepreseted the purpose and relations of this paper.

The Boys' Friend is the friend of all boys, whether they be in Christian or unchristian families. It stands for an *idea*, namely, *the bringing of noble and experienced men into a personal, friendly and vital companionship with all boys everywhere;* and that during the most dangerous period of the boy's life, the *adolescence*. Hence, the Boys' Friend is primarily a paper for the *friend* of the boy; secondarily, for the boy of the age named. The chief aim of the paper is to inspire in the hearts of *men* a true love for any boy as he stnds before God a *prince* most royal, "The Child of a King," meriting the friendship of friends of the Prince eternal. That this has always been its purpose may be seen from the following statements taken from the initial number of the paper:

As friend of boys we shall defend all their innocent amusements and pleasures, and in every laudable way seek to purify the joy and intensify the happiness of boyhood. Much, however, as we desire the friendship of all boys and men, we shall never hesitate to draw the sword and strike fearlessly at all forces that tend to mar or destroy the physical health, the intellectual growth, the moral purity or the spiritual happiness of our boys. [illegible]

While The Boys' Friend is emphatically non-partisan and undenominational, it is an ally of home, school, church and state; and we intend that none shall surpass us in love's labor for Christ, church, home and native land. We covet a hearty welcome in every home and the loving friendship of every boy in America.

We desire not only to make The Boys' Friend of interest and profit to the boys, but of equal profit to men. We can scarcely hope to do a better work for our boys than to turn the hearts of the fathers to their sons; to establish a more intimate and stronger friendship between good men and boys; a friendship that will place before the boy the same high standard of purity of thought, speech and life that is placed before the girl. Indeed, we plead for a friendship that will cause society to chaperone her lads as well as her lasses.

The Boys' Friend is no more the advocate of "Knights of Character Castle" than it stands ready to do any good work for boys. Whatever helps boys to nobler living will have my personal friendship and the Boys' Friend will seek to sustain the most friendly relationship to that work, whether it be secret or public, and if it has an evil tendency no one will expose it more quickly than the Boys' Friend.

The statement of Bro. Keeler, that for the enrollment of its youthful readers in the Society of Character Castle the paper "mainly exists," *is utterly false*. The Boys' Friend will exist whether an other name is enrolled in Character Castle or not. Personally, the editor of the Boys' Friend is favorable to Character Castle work, because the princely knight idea is in harmony with that of the Boys' Friend. If at any time he finds Character Castle work evil in its tendencies, at once that fact will be made known. So long as he sees the work to be pure and helpful the editor will defend it. Yours for princely boyhood.

The McGarvey Institute.

The Institute opened Monday evening with a sermon by Dr. B. E. Dawson, of Butler, Mo. President McGarvey delivered two lectures on the Pentateuch Tuesday. He contended for the Mosaic authorship, and his arguments seem to the writer to be unanswerable. The plain statements of the O. T. and N. T. writers, the belief of the Jews, the affirmation of Jesus Christ and the fact of such authorship being unquestioned for nearly eighteen centuries, was made to stand out clearly against the arbitrary analysis and guesswork of the critics. King Stark, of Lamonte, preached Tuesday evening. There were three lectures Wednesday and three Thursday; two on the knowledge of Jesus, based upon Phil. 2:5-8, and Luke 2:52, were fully met by such passages as John 1:32, 33; 3:34, 35, and Luke 4:14, showing conclusively that whatever may have been the limitation of his knowledge from the incarnation to the beginning of his ministry, this was ended when he received the Holy Spirit without measure.

Pres. McGarvey believes in one Isaiah and that his book is one book. The position of the critics was shown to be untenable and mere guesswork.

All of these lectures were heard by large and deeply interested audiences. Our church and community have been richly blessed by the presence and instruction of this servant of God. It would be a great blessing if all of our churches could hear such a course of lectures. The people of Windsor will long remember the McGarvey Institute.

G. L. BUSH.

Windsor, Mo.

Announcements.

The sixth annual convention of the Christian Missionary Association of the eighth district of Illinois will be held at Du Quoin, September 8-12. A good program has been prepared for this convention. Music will be in charge of F. A. Sword and J. S. Bobbitt.

Entertainment will be provided free by the good people of Du Quoin.

Reduced rates will be allowed on all railroads on the certificate plan.

I. A. J. PARKER, Secretary.

Lowell Convention.

Second District Convention at Lowell, Ind., Sept. 7-9. Every church in the district should at once select delegates and send word to me the number expecting to come from that congregation. Excellent program, free entertainment, with a hospitable people, eloquent and strong men as speakers, are some of the features of this convention. You will be welcome. Send us your name at once.

S. A. STRAWN, Pastor.

Palmyra Convention.

The Marion County Christian Convention will convene with the church at Palmyra, Mo., Sept. 5, 6, and 7, 1898. H. CLAY WHALEY, Sec.

Michigan Convention.

The Thirtieth Annual Convention of the Michigan Christian Missionary Conventions will be held at Saginaw, Aug. 31 to Sept. 4, 1898.

PROGRAM.

WEDNESDAY EVENING, AUGUST 31.

7:30 P. M—Devotional, President W. J. Russell, Kalamazoo, Presiding.
7:45 P. M—Address of Welcome, Prof. S. W. Pearcy, Saginaw.
8:00 P. M—Response, L. W. Spayd, Owosso.
8:15 P. M—Sermon, G. K. Berry, Ionia.

THURSDAY FORENOON, SEPT. 1.

8:45—The Cities of Michigan and How to Capture Them, E. B. Widger, Grand Rapids.
Small Towns and Country Districts, H. E. Rossell, Shepherd.
How to Capture the Country, H. C. Foxworthy, Manton.
Congregational Co-operation.
Pastoral Evangelism, C. M. C. Cook, Mt. Pleasant.
Reviving Old Churches, J. L. Smith, Algonac.
State and District Unity.
Discussion.
Report of Board.

AFTERNOON.

2:00—Devotional.
The American Pyramid, Wm. Chapple, Vandalia.
America for Christ, B. L. Smith, Cincinnati; O.
Reports of Committes.

EVENING.

7:30—Devotional.
Sermon, Prof. H. W. Everest, Drake University.

FRIDAY FORENOON, SEPT. 2.

Simultaneous meetings of the Ministerial Association and the Christian Woman's Board of Missions.
Ministerial Association—Auditorium, L. W. Spayd, Presiding.
8:30—Devotional.
8:45—The Minister as a Student, G. K. Berry, Ionia.
The Minister as a Pastor, W. W. Wyrick, Dowagiac.
The Minister as a Citizen, Dr. J. E. Cohenour, St. Louis.
The Minister and Missions, W. M. Forrest, Ann Arbor.
Christian Woman's Board of Missions—Church Parlors.
8:30—Devotional, Miss Sarah Ogden, Grand Rapids.
9:00—Reports of Secretary, Treasurer, Superintendent Young People's Department, District Managers and Committees.

AFTERNOON.

Christian Woman's Board of Missions—Auditorium.
2:00—Devotional, Mrs. F. M. Seelye, Owosso.
2:30—Opportunities for Work in the Home Land, Mrs. G. K. Berry, Ionia.
Discussion.
Symposium:
How May We Secure the Best Results in C. W. B. M. Work?
a. Importance of the Program, Mrs. Lucy H. Weeks, Ann Arbor.
b. Is State Development a Necessity, Mrs. Clara S. Williams, Kalkaska.
c. Is it Necessary to Develop a Missionary Spirit in our Young People? Mrs. M. L. Thompson, Ferris.
d. The Benefit of Missionary Education, Mrs. W. J. Russell, Kalamazoo.
Exercise by the Saginaw Juniors.
4:00—Retrospect and Prospect, Mrs. Louise L. Campbell, Detroit.
Report of Obituary Committee.
Unfinished Business.

EVENING.

C. W. B. M.—Auditorium.
7:30—Praise Service, Mrs. M. Young, Saginaw.
Sermon, E. B. Widger, Grand Rapids.
Missionary Offering.

SATURDAY FORENOON, SEPT. 3.

Sunday-school Session, D. J. McCall, Yale, Presiding.
8:30—Devotional.
The Fruits We Should Realize from S. S. Work, H. E. Rossell, Shepherd.
The Future Sunday-school, W. J. Russell, Kalamazoo.
The S. S. and Its Relation to the Church, Miss E. Bentley, Yale.
A Practical Lesson in Primary Work, Miss Flora Eccleston, Saginaw.
Discussion. Question Drawer. Business.

AFTERNOON.

Y. P. S. C. E. Session.
2:00—Devotional.
Denominationalism and Interdenominationalism, W. W. Wyrick, Dowagiac.
Address. Subject and name of the speaker to be announced later.
Address, Dr. Butchart, China.

EVENING.

7:30—Devotional.
Sermon, J. H. Garrison, St. Louis.

LORD'S DAY, FORENOON, SEPT. 4.

Sermon, J. H. Garrison, St. Louis.
Lord's Supper.

AFTERNOON.

2:30—Missionary Meeting. Address, A. McLean, Cincinnati, O.

EVENING.

7:30—Devotional.
Sermon, H. W. Everest, Drake University.
Farewell Service, G. P. Coler, Ann Arbor.

This will be a good convention. The attendance should be large. Railroad fare is one and one-third for the round trip on the certificate plan. All who wish free entertainment should send their names at once to A. C. Young, 1137 S. Warren Ave., Saginaw, Mich.

ALEX. MCMILLAN, Cor. Sec.

Ann Arbor, Mich.

The Central Christian Church, of San Antonia, Texas, publishes a local weekly paper called the Reporter.

Publishers' Notes.

AN OPPORTUNITY.

With the close of the war with Spain the world has learned much concerning the ignorance and superstition that has so long prevailed in Spain and her territorial posessions. Catholicism rules Spain and her colonies. Statistics reveal that 68 per cent. of the population of Spain can neither read nor write. This may account for the predominance of the Catholic Church and the power and rule of the Pope of Rome. Contrast Spain, an old and once powerful nation, ruled by Catholicism, with younger Protestant nations, in which there is but little illiteracy, and where gospel liberty makes them a free, prosperous, happy and intelligent people.

In the history of the world there has never been a more opportune time for Protestantism to show the errors of Catholicism. The curtain has just risen revealing a long line of misrule and oppression by the Romish Church. It only now remains for the world to look on Rome's theater of action and decide for itself on the merits of the part she has played.

The evils of Romanism are clearly set forth by John L. Brandt in his work, "America or Rome—Christ or the Pope." Now is the time for agents to place this book in the hands of readers. We are *now offering extra inducements* to agents to handle this work. People will now want to read this kind of literature, and an active agent can do well by showing and selling this exposition of the despotism of Rome. Write us for our *special inducements to agents* on America or Rome—Christ or the Pope.

Address Christian Publishing Co., St Louis, Mo.

HE
TIAN EVANGELIST
EKLY FAMILY AND RELIGIOUS JOURNAL.
September 1, 1898 No.

.....259
ı....260
.....261
f the
.... 261
.....262
... 263
.....264
..... 267

ımp-
.....265
.. 265
·bee. 267

.....270
.... 270
.....271
.....272
....272
.....273
Rus-
.... 273
.. .274
.... 275

.... 280
. ...280
.....282
.. 282
.... 282
.... 282

.....268
.....269
.... 276
.... 277
... 277
.....278
.... 283
.....284
.....285
.....285
.....286
ion..288

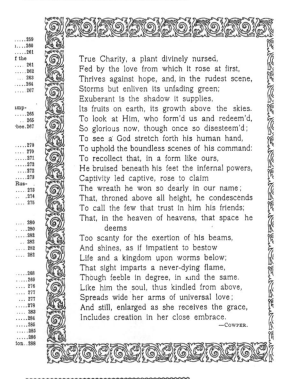

True Charity, a plant divinely nursed,
Fed by the love from which it rose at first,
Thrives against hope, and, in the rudest scene,
Storms but enliven its unfading green;
Exuberant is the shadow it supplies,
Its fruits on earth, its growth above the skies.
To look at Him, who form'd us and redeem'd,
So glorious now, though once so disesteem'd;
To see a God stretch forth his human hand,
To uphold the boundless scenes of his command:
To recollect that, in a form like ours,
He bruised beneath his feet the infernal powers,
Captivity led captive, rose to claim
The wreath he won so dearly in our name;
That, throned above all height, he condescends
To call the few that trust in him his friends;
That, in the heaven of heavens, that space he deems
Too scanty for the exertion of his beams,
And shines, as if impatient to bestow
Life and a kingdom upon worms below;
That sight imparts a never-dying flame,
Though feeble in degree, in kind the same.
Like him the soul, thus kindled from above,
Spreads wide her arms of universal love;
And still, enlarged as she receives the grace,
Includes creation in her close embrace.

—COWPER.

PUBLISHED BY
TIAN PUBLISHING COMPANY

THE

CHRISTIAN - EVANGELIST

J. H. GARRISON, EDITOR.

W. W. HOPKINS, ASSISTANT.

B. B. TYLER, J. J. HALEY,
EDITORIAL CONTRIBUTORS.

What We Plead For.

The Christian-Evangelist pleads for:

The Christianity of the New Testament, taught by Christ and his Apostles, versus the theology of the creeds taught by fallible men—the world's great need.

The divine confession of faith on which Christ built his church, versus human confessions of faith on which men have split the church.

The unity of Christ's disciples, for which he so fervently prayed, versus the divisions in Christ's body, which his apostles strongly condemned.

The abandonment of sectarian names and practices, based on human authority, for the common family name and the common faith, based on divine authority, versus the abandonment of scriptural names and usages for partisan ends.

The hearty co-operation of Christians in efforts of world-wide beneficence and evangelization, versus petty jealousies and strifes in the struggle for denominational pre-eminence.

The fidelity to truth which secures the approval of God, versus conformity to custom to gain the favor of men.

The protection of the home and the destruction of the saloon, versus the protection of the saloon and the destruction of the home.

For the right against the wrong;
For the weak against the strong;
For the poor who've waited long
For the brighter age to be.
For the truth, 'gainst superstition,
For the faith, against tradition,
For the hope, whose glad fruition
Our waiting eyes shall see.

RATES OF SUBSCRIPTION.

Single subscriptions, new or old	$1.75	each
In clubs of five or more, new or old	1.50	"
Reading Rooms	1.25	"
Ministers	1.00	"

With a club of ten we will send one additional copy free.

All subscriptions payable in advance. Label shows the month up to the first day of which your subscription is paid. If an earlier date than the present is shown, you are in arrears. No paper discontinued without express orders to that effect. Arrears should be paid when discontinuance is ordered.

In ordering a change of post office, please give the OLD as well as the NEW address.

Do not send local check, but use Post office or Express Money Order, or draft on St. Louis, Chicago or New York, in remitting.

Don't You Think

that you could secure a
few trial subscribers to the

Christian - Evangelist

From August 1, 98, to January 1, '99,

FOR

Fifty Cents?

We supply back numbers from August 1.

A Circuit of the Globe.

BY A. McLEAN,
Sec'y Foreign Christian Missionary Society.

This excellent missionary production is being pushed during the summer months through the various C. W. B. M. Auxiliary Societies of the brotherhood. Our sisters are making this the open door through which to replenish the overdrawn Treasury of the National C. W. B. M. If your Auxiliary has not yet received the information in reference to the plan, the terms and the excellent opportunity offered for raising a nice sum of money, write to the CHRISTIAN PUBLISHING CO., 1522 Locust St., St. Louis.

CHRISTIAN PUBLISHING COMPANY.
1522 Locust Street, St. Lous, Mo.

EDUCATIONAL.

THE CHRISTIAN-EVANGELIST

"In faith, Unity; in opinion and methods, Liberty; in all things, Charity."

Vol. xxxv. St. Louis, Mo., Thursday, September 1, 1898. No. 35

CURRENT EVENTS.

The Peace Commission, as arranged at present, consists of Secretary Day, Senators Davis and Frye, Whitelaw Reid and Justice White. The latter has not as yet officially notified the President of his acceptance, but it is believed that he will accept the appointment. There has been an unusual hesitancy on the part of a number of public men to accept a position on this Commission. The chief reason of this, perhaps, is not simply that the Commission will have a very difficult and and delicate work to perform, but chiefly, no doubt, from political reasons. The results of the war may have important bearings in future political campaigns, and men who are looking for political promotion are exceedingly cautious abont taking any position that may compromise them in any way in the eyes of their constituency. The persons named, however, are of such character as to give weight to their ultimate decision. The Commission is to meet in Paris as soon as practicable to begin its work. The American members expect to sail for Paris about the middle of September. The sessions of the Commission will be held in the Salon des Ambassadors, through the courtesy of the French Government. It is probable that considerable time will be required to canvass all the questions that will be involved in the treaty of peace which they are to prepare. The indications are that Spain will exhaust all her resources of diplomacy in order to gain by peaceful artifice what she has lost in war.

The custom of celebrating the return of peace or the victory of arms by a parade of the victors, reaches far back into the dim twilight of history. The hundreds of thousands of people that thronged the banks of the Hudson on the 20th inst., to welcome the return of the North Atlantic squadron, under command of Rear Admiral Sampson, were moved by the same impulse that led the people of old to celebrate the exploits of Xenophon. For three hours the steam whistles of all sizes, and small guns along the shore, shrieked and boomed the enthusiasm of the people on the return of the naval heroes with their battleships. Early in the morning of the day mentioned, the New York, Iowa, Indiana, Brooklyn, Oregon and Texas, lay in New York Bay, while the admiral in command had no idea of the preparation for the big reception that awaited him. The shouts of the people were mingled with the booming cannons as the stately ships moved out of the bay into the Hudson on the way to Gen. Grant's tomb. A correspondent describes the entire width of the Hudson River as "a struggling, fluttering, darting mass of color, confusion and cheers." The tomb of the hero of Appomattox was the center of attraction, and just as the squadron began their return from that place there was a national salute of twenty-one guns fired. President McKinley, much to his regret, could not be present to witness the pageant, but four members of his Cabinet were there. It was a memorable occasion and one that will go down in history in connection with the close of the war which it celebrated.

The severe ordeal through which our navy passed at Santiago is telling upon the health of the various commanders. Admiral Schley, Capt. Evans and Capt. Clark are all reported ill as the result of the severe strain through which they have passed. Capt. Clark's condition is perhaps the most serious, and some time will be required before he regains his health. His long journey from San Francisco to Key West with the strain which it imposed during a large part of the time, would be a severe tax on any man's nerves. The whole nation sympathizes with these naval heroes, and will rejoice at their complete recovery. The burden of anxiety and official responsibility borne by the commanders of our army and navy in the time of war makes their position a more trying one than that of the common soldier whose physical hardships and privations are greater than those of the officers. The feeling that human life, the cause at stake and the nation's honor are all involved in the campaign, or blockade, or battle, for which they are responsible, is not calculated to promote sleep or relaxation of nerves. We are glad that both officers and private soldiers are to have a chance to rest, after the dangers and hardships of the Cuban campaign.

Gen. Shafter, who was sick a part of the time during the attack on Santiago, is coming home, and has turned over the command to Gen. Lawton. In an interview on the eve of embarking he expressed himself as highly satisfied with the success of the military operations in Cuba, and said that he desired to command no better army than that which he commanded during the campaign ending in the surrender of Santiago. He has been criticised for exposing his men unnecessarily to severities and dangers in pushing his attack upon that city, but we believe, in the light of subsequent developments, that his energy and haste in securing the surrender of the city are entirely justified. With a long siege our army would have been so decimated by sickness and death that the object of the campaign may have been thwarted, while the loss of life would have been greater than it has been. We believe he pursued the proper course in pushing his campaign to a successful issue, and that history will, in the main, justify his military operations. The difficulties that had to be overcome in the way of transportation and in the movements of the army can hardly be appreciated by those unacquainted with the country and with the nature of military movements. That there should have been, under all the circumstances, lack of medicines, provisions and suitable equipments at the front to make the soldiers comfortable is not at all surprising. The disposition to criticise, especially by those who are unacquainted with the facts, has led to some injustice toward Gen. Shafter, Secretary Alger and others, which we have no doubt time will correct. The irregularities complained of were no doubt in the main such as grew out of a freshly organized army, hurried to the front, and without that experience which is necessary to bring order out of confusion. A nation that depends on making its preparation for war after war has begun must expect such irregularities.

We are glad to note that the President has found it possible to take a little vacation from his official duties. The responsibility which he has borne during the past three or four months, with the care and anxiety attendant thereon, must have made severe demands on his physical strength and vitality. He is to visit his brother, Abner McKinley, at Summerset, Pa., and will extend his trip to Cleveland, O., and will visit the soldiers at Montauk, L. I. He has signified his desire for a quiet trip unattended by official ceremony and public demonstration. In consideration of his need for quiet and rest it is to be hoped that this wish will be respected. This will be the first vacation the President has taken since the war assumed a threatening aspect. Through all the trying scenes and incidents he has borne himself with a dignity and with a practical wisdom and foresight worthy of the head of a great nation. Our readers, regardless of politics, will join with us in wishing him a restful vacation.

The threatening attitude of the Philippine insurgents, and especially of their leader, Aguinaldo, we are glad to say, has yielded to the tact and firmness of Admiral Dewey and Gen. Merritt. The situation has greatly improved within the last few days. Aguinaldo has ordered all his men to lay down their arms and to resume their agricultural pursuits. He has also voluntarily opened the waterworks which he had under his control and the city is now amply supplied. Gen. Merritt is in control as military governor, and Gen. Otis has succeeded him as Commander-in-Chief of the American forces. Business is said to be on the boom, and order is being restored.

President McKinley has telegraphed his congratulations and thanks both to Rear Admiral Dewey and Gen. Merritt, and has received grateful acknowledgments from each. Gen. Merritt has notified the President that he does not require any more troops in the Philippines, which is in itself indicative of a more peaceful outlook than existed a few weeks ago.

On the 12th of August, with simple but impressive ceremonies, the Hawaiian Islands passed under the sovereignty of the United States Government. The ceremony of lowering the flag of the Hawaiian Repulic, and raising the Stars and Stripes, was witnessed by the assembled multitude with deepest interest. There were those whose eyes moistened to see the Hawaiian flag lowered, never more to be raised, while there was great rejoicing over the hoisting ofthe Stars and Stripes, never more perhaps, to be lowered. President Dole turned over the government and all public property to the United States, and Minister Sewall accepted it in behalf of our government. It is significant that this important event took place on the day of the signing of the protocol which marked the close of the war to which the annexation of Hawaii at this time is due. For the present the same officials will administer government in these islands and the same laws will be in force. This completes the process of adding this Pacific group of islands to our national domain, and gives us standing ground for looking after our interests in the far East.

Just at a time when the flames of war seem ready to burst forth between Russia and England the Czar of Russia has surprised the world by inviting the powers to an international council for the purpose of securing a real and lasting peace. Not since the close of our war with Spain has a more surprising and significant communication been given to the world. Some of the leading journals are disposed to look upon it as a new diplomatic freak, while others regard it as the sincere wish of the Russian Emperor. The Chronicle, London, says that it is one of the most striking documents of the century. Whatever may be the hopes or the fears of any person or journal concerning this message from the Czar it must be admitted that great and cogent reasons are presented in justification of his course and call; reasons that will go to the heart of every lover of good government, peace, prosperity and Christianity. What a grand thing it would be to usher in the 20th century of the Christian era with the mind of all great nations set upon the science of good government instead of the science of war. Then indeed will men begin to believe in the verities of Christianity and the Bible. The news seems almost too good to be believed, but let us hope and pray for the realization of the Czar's prayer and of a permanent peace for the 20th century as the result of the conference. This note was written by Count Muravieff, Foreign Minister, by order of Emperor Nicholas, and its purposes certainly entitle it to rank as one of the greatest state documents ever given to the world. It is a frank acknowledgment of the evils of war and declares for a higher object than conquests as the apology for governments. We give the text as it appeared in our dailies on last Monday morning:

"The maintenance of general peace and the possible reduction of the excessive armaments which weigh upon all nations, present themselves in existing conditions to the whole world as an ideal toward which the endeavors of all governments should be directed.

"The humanitarian and magnanimous ideas of His Majesty, the Emperor, my august master, have been won over to this view in the conviction that this lofty aim is in conformity with the most essential interests and legitimate views of all the Powers, and the Imperial Government thinks the present moment would be very favorable to seeking the means.

"International discussion is the most effectual means of insuring all people's benefit—a real, durable peace, above all putting an end to the progressive development of the present armaments.

"In the course of the last 20 years the longing for general appeasement has grown especially pronounced in the consciences of civilized nations and the preservation of peace has been put forward as an object of international policy. It is in its name that great states have concluded among themselves powerful alliances.

"It is better to guarantee peace that they have developed in proportions hitherto unprecedented their military forces and still continue to increase them without shrinking from any sacrifice.

"Nevertheless, all these efforts have not yet been able to bring about the beneficent results desired—pacification.

"The financial charges following the upward march strike at the very root of public prosperity. The intellectual and physical strength of the nation's labor and capital are most diverted from their natural application and are unproductively consumed. Hundreds of millions are devoted to acquiring terrible engines of destruction which, though to-day regarded as the last work of science, are destined to-morrow to lose all their value in consequence of some fresh discovery in the same field. National culture, economic progress and the production of wealth are either paralyzed or checked in development. Moreover, in proportion as the armaments of each Power increase, they less and less fulfill the objects the governments have set before themselves.

"The economic crisis, due in great part to the system of armaments l'outrance, and the continual danger which lies in this massing of war material, are transforming the armed peace of our days into a crushing blow, which the peoples have more difficulty in bearing.

"It appears evident that if this state of things were to be prolonged it would inevitably lead to the very cataclysm it is desired to avert, and the horrors thereof make every thinking being shudder in advance.

"To put an end to these incessant armaments and to seek the means of warding off the calamities which are threatening the whole world—such is the supreme duty to-day imposed upon all states.

"Filled with this idea, His Majesty has been pleased to command me to propose to all the governments whose representatives are accredited to the imperial court the assembling of a conference, which shall occupy itself with this grave problem.

"This conference will be, by the help of God, the happy presage for the century which is about to open. It would converge into one powerful focus the efforts of all states sincerely seeking to make the great conception of universal peace triumph over the elements of trouble and discord, and it would, at the same time, cement their agreement by a corporate consecration of the principles of equity and right whereon rests the security of the states and the welfare of the people."

Our soldiers at Santiago had a new realization of the meaning of the old phrase, "The heat and the burden of the day."

EXPANSION OR CONTRACTION—WHICH?

This is one of the burning questions raised by our recent conflict with Spain. It is not usually put in this form, but that is what it amounts to. It is a law of national and individual life that we must either expand or contract. When a tree ceases to grow it is not long until the process of decay sets in. The same is true of the individual and of the nation.

So far in our history we have been an expanding nation. Beginning with a narrow strip of country along the Eastern Seaboard, our territorial domain has expanded across the Alleghenys, across the Ohio, across the Mississippi and the Missouri, across the Rocky Mountains, and the Sierra Nevada on Westward to the Pacific Coast and Southward to the Gulf. Not content with this, we have extended our possessions to the Northwest to include the new territory of Alaska. Recently we have reached out into the Pacific Ocean and have raised the American flag over the Hawaiian group of island.

The question now is whether we have reached the limits of expansion, or whether we may justly add Porto Rico, which has already been virtually added, and any part or all of the Philippines. It is a source of gratification to every true American to know that nearly all of this vast domain has been won peaceably and that the spirit of conquest without regard to the rights of others has not been the controlling factor in our national expansion. The true principle to be applied to the present question which confronts us is that of fulfilling our national destiny, and the obligations we are under to the peoples of the islands in question. If the permanent occupation of Porto Rico or any part of the Philippines be necessary for the accomplishment of the moral purposes of this nation, and essesntial to the fulfillment of our obligation to impart to the people of these islands the blessings of civil and religious liberty which God has vouchsafed to us, then we should retain them, and such expansion is not a departure from the traditions of the past, but is in perfect harmony with our national history.

The contraction which would be the result of an opposite policy is not necessarily territorial contraction, but a contraction of the high purposes and missions of the nation. If we say the welfare of Cuba and of Porto Rico and of the Philippines is no concern to us, and leave them to their own fate, we will have entered upon a policy of national selfishness which would curtail our influence abroad and exert a paralyzing influence on that "enthusiasm of humanity" among us which has been the mainspring of our recent war with Spain. A nation may suffer from the contraction of its currency or of its territory, but the most fatal contraction that can befall any country is a contraction of its moral aims and purposes.

The question is equally applicable to the kingdom of God—Expansion or Contraction—Which? The kingdom of God is destined to be a universal kingdom. It is intended to cover the earth and exert its moral sway over the life of all its inhabitants. Are we to plan our religious campaigns and mobilize our spiritual forces in harmony with this broad aim, or shall we contract our plans for only a partial conquest? The moment we lose sight of God's purpose to redeem the whole world and to fill it with righteousnes, the process of moral contraction has set in, which will soon end in spiritual impotency and death. If we say the kingdom of God must not be extended so as to cover all the vast areas of human interest—its business, its politics, its legislation, its social life—because its principles are not adapted to trade and commerce and government, then we are contractionists. Our plans and purposes at once become out of harmony with God's purpose, and only failure can result. "We can do nothing against the truth."

The same thing is true of institutions and religious movements. Concerning our own religious movement, shall we Expand or Contract—Which? One or the other is sure to take place. Either we must enlarge our sympathies, our charity, our missionary activities, our educational plans and plants, our conception of our mission as a religious force, or else the process of contraction, which has already set in in some places, will continue until it results in the irretrievable failure of a movement that has in it marvelous possibilities of good. We cannot stand still. We must go forward or backward. Our horizon must be enlarged or diminished; our ears must be attuned to hear the voice of God speaking to us in the current movements of our time, or we shall grow dull of hearing and lose the inspiration which we could have gained from catching these marching orders and watchwords for our age. Every incentive except that of moral inertness urges us onward. To the eye of faith the hands of unborn millions are beckoning us on to a mighty future, while the voice of the great Captain of our salvation calls us on to higher conquests and to wider dominion.

It should be remembered, however, that this expansion in our national life, in the kingdom of God, in our own religious movement and in our individual life, to which it equally applies, involves and demands the deepening and strengthening of moral convictions, and the intensification of our religious purposes. If we are to carry the blessings of civil and religious liberty to the world, the process of national purification must keep pace with the growth of our commerce and of our material domain. If the church is to be the divine agent for extending the kingdom of God, its life must be of such character as to commend it to the approval of God, and of all right-thinking men. It must rise above its carnality, its schisms and its petty strifes, and consecrate its resources to the accomplishment of the divine purpose. If our religious movement is to go on, increasing in numbers and influence, reaching out into new fields and conquering new areas, the inner work of deepening the spiritual life and grounding the faith of its members in the knowledge of the truth of God must keep pace with this outwark expansion. There must be the strengthening of the stakes as well as the lengthening of the cords of our Zion.

In a word, all of God's purposes concerning man, whether as nations, churches, movements or individuals, require expansion, and this expansion requires the building up of the inner and spiritual life to enable the nation, church, movement, institution or individual to accomplish their respective missions in the world.

AN ATTEMPT TO ABOLISH MYSTERY.

In another place we publish an article on the Personality of the Holy Spirit, by Jas. O. Carson. The article in the beginning speaks of "the disposition in the religious world to mystify everything connected with the Holy Spirit in his relations and intercourse with and work among men." There is a manifest disposition, in our time, to deny everything that is mysterious or miraculous, which is more to be feared than any disposition to mystify. The article referred to is a good illustration of the tendency to deny any fact or truth that is above one's comprehension. Our Savior himself taught that there is a mystery connected with the Holy Spirit and his methods of operation. Paul taught that "great is the mystery of godliness."

There has been a tendency among certain teachers connected with our own movement to banish the element of mystery from the Christian faith by reducing the facts and phenomena so as to come within the range of human intelligence. Brother Carson is not able to see how the Holy Spirit can be a person, when it is affirmed of the Holy Spirit that he dwells in every Christian. He says that the Scriptures are silent regarding the personality of the Holy Spirit. We cannot accept this statement for a moment. On the contrary the Scriptures constantly speak of the Holy Spirit in a way that implies personality; such as, "the Holy Spirit says" so and so; the Holy Spirit is "grieved" and guides, instructs and comforts the followers of Christ. Since we accept a thousand things we do not understand, we see no occasion for denying the personality of God or of the Holy Spirit, because we are not able to comprehend how a person, even a divine person, can be omnipresent.

Another illustration of this writer's tendency to discard facts which he cannot bring within the sphere of his comprehension is seen in the following statement: "Man is so constituted that he cannot take cognizance of things except through his senses. Hence it is that when God would communicate with men he does so in manners and forms that are cognizable through his senses, and *never otherwise.*" Certainly not, according to Locke's philosophy, but this writer should know that the philosophy of Locke, known as the *sensational* philosophy, is out of date. It is utterly discredited by the developments of modern science, and never was in harmony with the teaching of the Scriptures, nor with the facts of human experience.

What Bro. Carson says about the embodiment of God in the person of Christ and in the church is true enough, but it in no way disproves the larger movements of the Spirit of God, which are not limited to the methods mentioned. There is a tendency toward rationalism on the one hand and a mechanical or purely ecclesiastical conception of religion on the other, growing out of this theory when carried to its logical conclusion, which must be guarded against. No organism, however perfect, can claim any monopoly of the Spirit of God, or assume to be the sole channel of His communication with man. God does not limit Himself by these organizations. It is this theory that leads to the presumptuous claims of the Roman Catholic and Anglican Churches. They assume to be the channels through which the Holy Spirit and the grace of God alone can descend to man. On the contrary, the true Protestant theory brings every soul into direct relation with God. The one theory means despotism, the other liberty. The position that we must reject the personality of the Spirit because we cannot conceive of the personality of a disembodied being would of course lead to the rejection of God and of everything above the power of the the human reason to explain. It would empty our faith of its divine content, and there would be nothing left worth believing.

PAUL ON THE FINANCIAL SUPPORT OF THE MINISTRY.

We have seen in a former paper that the possession of property is not condemned by Jesus nor by his ambassadors. Its possion is altogether legitimate—from the point of view occupied by the Son of Man. Even the possessors of great wealth are not condemned, on this account, by Holy Scripture. How could this be, when wealth is spoken of as a gift from God? "Both riches and honor come of thee," said David. "The Lord maketh poor and maketh rich," said Hannah, the mother of Samuel the prophet. "Give me neither poverty nor riches," said Agur. "Of thine own have we given thee," said David, when he and his people made an offering for the building of the temple in Jerusalem. How could the possession of wealth be condemned by Holy Scripture, when the sacred writings speak of "riches" as a gift from God?

We have also learned that men who have business ability should use it. But, under Christ, they are not at liberty to use this talent selfishly. It is their duty to use it for the good of man. If a man can organize and conduct business, he ought to do so, that he may glorify God in helping his less fortunately endowed brethren, who are lacking in business talent. There are a few men—and only a few—who deserve to be called "Captains of Industry." It seems to be natural for some to organize and successfully conduct needed enterprises on a large scale.

Paul said: "Woe is unto me if I preach not the gospel!" He had ability to preach. The man who can make money ought to feel: "Woe is unto me if I make not money!" He ought also to feel: "Woe is unto me if I use not this money, or property, for the good of man and so for the glory of God!"

Charity—in the sense of alms-giving—has been spoken of. This is a Christian duty. Those who have ought, under certain conditions, to give to those who have not. Jesus said: "Ye have the poor with you always, and whensoever ye will ye can do them good." But good is not always done when charity is bestowed. The giving of a dollar or a dime may inflict an injury—may be a curse rather than a blessing. How to do good with one's means is a question not always easily answered. To help men to help themselves is real Christian charity.

THE FINANCIAL SUPPORT OF THE GOSPEL MINISTRY IS NOT AN ACT OF CHARITY!

How many will believe this? It is not an unusual thing to hear persons speak of *giving* to the preacher. He is looked upon and spoken of, in instances not a few, as if he were a person supported by the alms of the church. Why not regard the school-teacher in the same light? The faithful preacher renders an invaluable service to men and is entitled to at least a support. Paul put the matter in this way.

To the Galatians Paul said: "Let him that is taught in the Word communicate unto him that teacheth in all good things." From his point of view the support of the gospel ministry comes under the head of: "Bear ye one another's burdens, and so fulfill the law of Christ." Speaking of "a certain contribution for the poor among the saints that are at Jerusalem," Paul says that "if the Gentiles have been made partakers of their spiritual things, they owe it to them"—mark well the words—"they *owe* it to them also to minister to them in carnal things." Even the contributions of Gentile Christians to the Hebrew Christians, when the latter were in distress, was not mere charity—it was the payment of a debt. "They owe it to them," says Paul. Why? On what ground? Answer: "The Gentiles have been made partakers of their spiritual things." The doctrine of "reciprocity" is not a new teaching. It is certainly as old as the time of Paul and the New Testament. Nor is it a mean policy; it is justice; it is right; it is a part of religion. "Let him that is taught in the Word communicate unto him that teacheth." It is but right that carnal things—material goods—should be bestowed on those who come to us with spiritual blessings. Away with the thought that the financial support of a true minister of the Word is an act of charity!

PAUL CLAIMED THAT HE, AND THOSE WHO WERE ASSOCIATED WITH HIM IN THE MINISTRY OF THE WORD, HAD A RIGHT TO A MATERIAL SUPPORT.

"No soldier," he says, "serves at his own expense." When a man plants and cultivates a vineyard, all recognize that he has a RIGHT to eat of its fruit. If a man cares for a flock has he not a RIGHT to at least drink of the milk of that flock? Even the law said: "Thou shalt not muzzle the ox when he treadeth out the corn." Certainty, the toiling ox has a RIGHT to eat! But Paul says that this principle of the Mosaic law has an application to the support of the ministry. Does God care alone for oxen? Has he not a care also for those who preach his Word? Reasoning after this fashion he concludes: "If we"—not I, but "we"—"if we sowed unto you," who are in Corinth, "spiritual things, is it a great matter if we shall reap your carnal things? If others partake of this RIGHT over you, do not we yet more? Nevertheless, we did not use this RIGHT." Notice, please, that Paul speaks of RIGHT when he talks on this subject. He says: "I have a RIGHT, as a preacher, to a material support." He says even more than this. He says: "*We* sowed unto you spiritual things." "Is it a great matter if *we* shall reap your carnal things?" "*We*," he continues, "did not use this right." Who wrought with Paul in Corinth that he should use this plural pronoun? Silas, Timothy, Titus, Aquila, Priscilla. Who was associated with him in the writing of "The First Epistle to the Corinthians?" Sosthenes. Paul, then, claims for Sosthenes, for Priscilla, for Aquila, for Timothy, for Silas, for Titus—and by implication all who preach the gospel—material support as a RIGHT.

But when Paul preached in Corinth he supported himself by the labor of his hands. He and Aquila and Priscilla made tents. He worked with his hands during the week and "reasoned in the synagogue every sabbath." Why did not he demand from those to whom he ministered a financial remuneration? He had a RIGHT to do so. Why did he not enforce this RIGHT? He himself, fortunately for us, answers this question. He says: "We did not use this RIGHT; but we bear all things, *that we may cause no hindrance to the gospel of Christ.*" "The Lord," he says, "did ordain that they which proclaim the gospel should live of the gospel. But I have used none of these things." Why? His reply is: "That we may cause no hindrance to the gospel." How easy it would have been for his enemies in Corinth and elsewhere (and he had them) to say: "Paul is in this work for what he can make of it. He is selfish—Paul is. He is mercenary. He is, therefore, unworthy of confidence. Have nothing to do with him. Turn away from him." Do you not see how, if he had asserted and enforced his RIGHT—he called it a RIGHT—in this matter it could and doubtless would have been used in such a way as to hinder the gospel?

A similar condition existed in Thessalonica. He, therefore, labored in order to support himself while he preached in that place. To the church of the Thessalonians he said: "Ye remember, brethren, our labor and travail; working night and day that we might not burden you, we preached unto you the gospel of God." This in the first epistle. In the second he refers to this matter again and says: "For yourselves know how ye ought to imitate us; for we behaved not ourselves disorderly among you; neither did we eat bread for nought at any man's hands, but in labor and travail, working night and day, that we might not burden any of you; not because we have not the RIGHT, but to make ourselves an example unto you, that ye should imitate us." But concerning the permanent ministry in the church of the Thessalonians, and the duty of the brethren toward this ministry, he says: "We beseech you, brethren, to know them that labor among you, and are over you in the Lord, and admonish you, and to esteem them exceeding highly in love for their work's sake." These words certainly include a material as well as a moral support.

In Ephesus Paul pursued a course similar to that pursued by him in the cities named, and doubtless for similar reasons. In his farewell address to the pastors whom he met at Miletus as he was on his last journey to Jerusalem, in a review of his three years' work in Ephesus, he said: "I coveted no man's silver, or gold, or apparel. Ye yourselves know that these hands have ministered unto my necessities, and to them that were with me. In all things I gave you an example, how that so laboring ye ought to help the weak, and to remember the words of the Lord Jesus, how he himself said, It is more blessed to give than to receive."

Paul possessed business ability to such a degree that when there was a necessity for so doing he was able not only to support himself, but also those who were associated with him in the Master's service.

Paul certainly did not object to receiving financial assistance. Philippi was the first city visited by Paul in Europe. Wh[illegible] was a prisoner in Rome he address[illegible] letter to the saints in Philippi. In [illegible] epistle he acknowledges the receipt [illegible] contribution which the church sent t[illegible] by Epaphroditus. He says that it wa[illegible] odor of a sweet smell, a sacrifice, ac[illegible] able, well-pleasing to God." In this [illegible] nection he says: "Ye Pilippians know [illegible] in the beginning of the gospel, wh[illegible] departed from Macedonia no church [illegible] fellowship with me in the matter of gi[illegible] and receiving, but ye only; for eve[illegible] Thessalonica ye sent once and again [illegible] my need." Remember that it wa[illegible] Thessalonica that he worked night [illegible] day that he might not be a charge t[illegible] person in the place. He says also [illegible] when he was in Corinth he robbed [illegible] churches that he might serve the Cori[illegible] ians. "When I was present with you, [illegible] says, "and was in want, I was not a bu[illegible] to any man; for the brethren, when [illegible] came from Macedonia, supplied the m[illegible] ure of my want."

The ideal ministry in the teachin[illegible] Paul is a ministry wholly devote[illegible] preaching and to the work of caring [illegible] the spiritual welfare of all the chur[illegible] He speaks of his "anxiety for all [illegible] churches."

Paul's conception of the ministry is [illegible] fully expressed in his epistles to Tim[illegible] and Titus. To the former he said: [illegible] soldier on service entangleth himself i[illegible] affairs of this life; that he may please [illegible] who enrolled him as a soldier." He enj[illegible] on Timothy to give himself "wholly [illegible] reading, to meditation and to preac[illegible] "the Word." In this connection als[illegible] employs language similar to words a[illegible] quoted from the ninth chapter of [illegible] "First Epistle to the Corinthians"[illegible] place in which he speaks of the RIGH[illegible] the ministry to a material support. [illegible] Timothy he said: "The husbandman [illegible] laboreth must be the first to partake o[illegible] fruits."

The pedigree of Christianity runs [illegible] to Judaism. In a subsequent paper [illegible] financial system of the Hebrew people [illegible] be considered.

B. B.

"THE DISCIPLES."

The editorial paragraph following my [illegible] to inquiries, published in the CHRISTIAN-E[illegible] GELIST of August 11th, implies a misu[illegible] standing of my position. I do not hold [illegible] the disciples who comprise the Current R[illegible] mation movement are never to be thoug[illegible] or spoken of as a separate body of people. [illegible] as Bro. Garrison said once before in criti[illegible] of what I had written, my own languag[illegible] plies and even expresses such a distinctio[illegible] have just now drawn such a distinction.

But my protest is against the effort to [illegible] the distinction in Scripture language. I d[illegible] think that calling this party "The Discip[illegible] is the "least objectionable method of d[illegible] nating the churches of the Current Refo[illegible] tion." It is more objectionable than [illegible] ways, because it is so nearly scriptural in [illegible] as to really involve a perversion of Scrip[illegible] In drawing a distinction not drawn in [illegible] Scriptures, why should we *imitate* Bible [illegible] guage? There is no reason for it. We sh[illegible] "call Bible things by Bible names." But [illegible] should we call anything not mentioned i[illegible] Bible by a "Bible name?"

It may be that any protest is vain, and [illegible] this new denominational title has come to [illegible] If so, one of the "immortals" has "nodd[illegible]

A man has a thousand sheep inclosed

.-acre pasture. He builds within this
. nine smaller inclosures and pens up
.d sheep in each one. The other hun-
held only by the outside fence. He
.e pen "Methodists," another "Bap-
another "Presbyterians," etc. The
red, which are not penned up, he re-
, "The Sheep," with a capital "S."
. have got used to his whim, you can
understand him. But most people
re is a better way. And so do I.

JOSEPH FRANKLIN.

.ly point in which we misunder-
o. Franklin's position was as to the
/ and propriety of distinguishing
s as reformers from other Chris-
the use of any terms. Many who
the name, Disciples of Christ,
.t we do not need to distinguish
s and our religious movement from
We naturally supposed Bro. Frank-
the same view. It now appears
loes not so hold, and that the only
.e between us is as to how this
on should be made when it seems
y to make it. His "protest is
the effort to draw the distinction in
e language." This is strange, in
our professed zeal for Bible lan-
When a scriptural term happens
the very purpose of distinguish-
elves from others, and when it car-
. it no implied claim of exclusive-
seems to us in every way prefer-
.ny phase or term we might invent.
.ly is this true when the name is not
.ptural, but beautifully significant
.lation to Christ and to oneanother.
we should designate ourselves as
.ers," and our churches as "Re-
hurches of Christ." These are not
.l names, and would be free from
.anklin's criticism. Even waving
that they would not designate us,
.y one feel that this would be an
ment on the name, Disciples of

F. saks, "Why should we call any-
t mentioned in the Bible by a Bible
we were under the impression
rsons owning allegiance to Jesus
s Lord and Master and seeking to
t His will on earth are called "Dis-
. Christ" in the New Testament.
sense is it a departue from New
.nt usage to continue the use of that
designate those who sustain the
.lation to Christ? The answer to
Bro. F. and others, is that the
Disciples of Christ, includes many
.an those connected with our special
s movement. This is readily grant-
.urse, but it so happens that these
sciples have chosen other names by
. designate themselves, leaving un-
iated a name which we can use in
harmony with our plea for Chris-
ion and the restoration of New
.nt Christianity, and in such a way
. imply that we are the only dis-
. Christ. The matter of the cap-
.n, is a matter simply of good
r and good manners. The illustra-
ut the sheep and the pens is very
.t it overlooks some facts in the
s situation which have an important
on the question under considera-

is not the person who owns the
.at has built the pens in Christen-
t the *sheep themselves*, because they
wish to keep company with the

2. It is not the sheep-owner that has called these different groups of sheep by the names "Methodists," "Baptists," "Presbyterians," etc., but either they themselves, or some other sheep, and they have accepted the designations and use them as their proper names. Our chief concern should be to get these fences out of the way that keeps the sheep apart. When this is done the names will take care of themseves.

3. The Good Shepherd has given appropriate and significant names to his spiritual sheep, which express their relation to Him. Among these are disciples, Christians. Now, if other groups of sheep call themselves by other names, and pen themselves up, is this a good reason why the other sheep, who are content to abide in large pasture, provided by the Shepherd, with no smaller pen to limit them should deny themselves these appropriate names, provided only they do not so use them as to deny that others are Christians or disciples? We think not. If some wish to be known as Presbyterian disciples, others as Methodist disciples, etc., and we are content to be known as Disciples of Christ, the capital D. implying that we are not the only disciples, but the disciples content to be so designated, what principle is violated? If Bro. F. thinks there is "a more excellent way" let him say what it is.

Hour of Prayer.

GREAT AND PRECIOUS PROMISES.

(Midweek Prayer-meeting Topic, Sept. 7th.)

Seeing that his divine power hath granted unto us all things that pertain unto life and godliness, through the knowledge of him that called us by his own glory and virtue; whereby he hath granted unto us his precious and exceeding great promises; that through these ye may become partakers of the divine nature, having escaped from the corruption that is in the world by lust.—2 *Peter* 1:3,4.

Hope is an element of human nature which "springs eternal in the human breast." But Christian hope is based upon the promises of God in Christ Jesus our Lord. It hath pleased Him in his goodness toward our poor, weak and sinful race, to make certain promises to us which the Apostle Peter, in this lesson, describes as "precious and exceeding great." This shows that Peter himself had a very vivid appreciation of the value of these promises. It is well for us to remember, when we are inclined to complain because God hath not made known to us certain things which we should like to know, that "His divine power hath granted unto us all things that pertain unto life and godliness." We can afford to wait for the remainder until we have passed beyond the region of shadows.

Among the "all things" which he hath granted unto us "through the knowledge of him that called us by his own glory and virtue" are these "precious and exceeding great promises." Before calling attention to these promises, let us note a significant change in the Revised Version, in the text quoted, in which it is said that Jesus Christ has "called us by his own glory and virtue," instead of "called us to glory and virtue," as it reads in the King James Version. According to the revised rendering we are called into a Christian life by the glory and virtue which shine out in the character of Jesus Christ, as portrayed in the gospel. This is the power by which He draws us to Himself. Let it be noted also that it is

"through the *knowledge* of him
called us by his own glory and vir
we come into the possession of th
and precious promises. Consid
some of these are.

There is first of all the promise
giveness of sins and reconciliat
God. Who that has ever felt the
a guilty conscience, and has ta
sweetness of forgiveness, can fail
the preciousness of such a promi
value of this promise is enhance
fact that our sins when forgiven
membered against us no more
They are utterly and forever bl
This promise, of course, comes to u
Jesus Christ, whose death in our b
disclosing the goodness and love
which lead us to repentance, m
giveness possible. Not only are we
forgiveness of past sins on entering
tian life, but if we are led astray
tians and commit sin, "He is fai
righteous to forgive us our sins
cleanseus from all unrighteousness
is no need, then, that we carry abo
the burden of a guilty conscience.
obtain forgiveness through repent
confession.

Then there is the promise of
Spirit which the Lord Jesus giv
them that obey Him. This is a
promise, and exceeding great be
brings with Him a train of blessin
beautify and enrich human life.
what the fruit of the Spirit was i
lesson. When we remember that
Spirit is our Advocate whom Jesus
to His disciples on His leaving t
and that He stands by us and p
cause, teaches us how to pray an
life and power to us in our conflict
temptation and trial, we can reali
is, indeed, a great promise and a ve
ous one. How strange that any
should be indifferent about clain
seeking to realize such a promise!

The comradeship of Jesus Chri
other one of these great promises
never leave you nor forsake you.'
am with you alway, even unto t
the world." Not in prosperit
triumph alone, when the sunlight f
pathway, but in darkness and def
the way is toilsome and difficult, H
us. His rod and staff, they co
What can give more courage and
to the weary pilgrim, making
through earth to heaven, than to
he has the companionship of Jes
as Friend and Brother, who will
him in every trial and give him st
overcome every difficulty?

Then there is the great promi
everlasting. "In my Father's h
many mansions; if I were not so,
have told you." Death is only th
way from the mortal to the immor
are to live forever. We are to
Christ is, at the right hand of th
Who can measure the greatness
promise? What infinite comfo
brought to the human soul throu
toiling and struggling ages!

But, as if this were not enough,
our hope needed the fuel of anot
promise to make it blaze out th
the darkness of human life, we ar
that it is God's predestined pur
we who are called to be Christian
conformed to the image of his S

not yet made manifest, John tells us, what we shall be, but "we know that when Christ is manifested, we shall be like Him, for we shall see Him as He is." Think of such a destiny as that! How all the rewards and prizes of this earthly life fade into utter insignificance in comparison with this marvelous transfiguration into the glorious likeness of Jesus Christ! It is not given to human imagination, quickened by the power of faith, to paint the glories of such a destiny. We must wait for its fulfillment in order to the full realization of its greatness.

No wonder the Apostle Peter calls these "precious and exceeding great promises." But why are they given to us? Peter's answer is, "That through these ye may become partakers of the divine nature, having escaped from the corruption that is in the world through lust." The purpose of these promises, then, is to beget within us Christian hope, and to strengthen us in our conflicts in this present evil world, so that we may realize the purpose for which we were created and called into fellowsip with Christ.

Let us, then, keep these promises before our minds, and encourage our hearts with them, that they may accomplish the end for which they were given. Above all, let us remember that these promises are "yea and amen in Christ Jesus," and can be claimed only by those who are struggling to do His will and to be like Him even here in the world.

PRAYER.

Almighty God, our Heavenly Father, we thank Thee for the revelation of Thyself in Jesus Christ our Lord, and for the precious and exceeding great promises which Thou hast made to us through Him. We thank Thee that Thou has seen proper, in Thy great goodness, to hold up before us these wonderful promises, to strengthen us and to cheer us in the conflicts, the trials and the misfortunes of life. We thank Thee for the Christian hope that is built on these promises, and which sheds its radient light on our pathway in the darkest hours of our human experience. Help us, we beseech Thee, strengthened and girded by such promises, to turn our backs upon all the sinful allurements of this present world, and seek glory and honor and immortality from Thee. Grant us the joy of realizing the fulfillment of many of these promises, while we are yet in the flesh, and at last permit us to realize the fulfillment of our highest hopes in being with Thee and with our glorified Lord, to enjoy unbroken fellowship with Thee forever. In His name. Amen!

Editor's Easy Chair.

OR MACATAWA MUSINGS.

The editor of this paper has not seen the Apostolic Guide for some time, being absent from the office, and does not know who the present editor is. Some one, however, has sent us an editorial clipping from the paper, in which the editor takes occasion to lecture us on the evils of division and the desirability of Christian union! This struck us first as an instance of "bringing coals to Newcastle," as this has been almost a hobby with us for a third of a century; but perhaps the young man—we take his youth for granted—may have a theory of union that would need to be urged upon us before we could accept it. Some of the Kentucky brethren, however, should explain to this Apostolic editor the difference between recognizing the necessity of distinguishing things that differ and the approval of sectarian divisions. As long as love and hatred both exist it is necessary to have different names for them, for the calling of hatred by the name of love would not change its nature. What the CHRISTIAN-EVANGELIST is laboring to bring about is such a unity of Christians as will do away with the necessity of denominational names. Our special offense, which has drawn upon us this criticism of the Guide, was the position that if we are justified in assuming a distinct and independent position among the religious forces of Christendom, it is essential for us to use some name by which to designate ourselves, if we are to be intelligible. The editor of the Guide regards this as the relinquishment of our plea for Christian union! And yet, like all other critics of this school, he uses the pronoun "we" and "us" in making the very distinction which he criticises us for making!

There is a noticeable and increasing desire on the part of our ministers and other intelligent brethren to have our membership more generally read one of our best religious journals. They have come to see that those who read our representative journals are more intelligent Christians, are more in sympathy with our general interests, have a better knowledge of the brotherhood and its co-operative work, have a clearer understanding of the spirit and meaning of our religious movement and are in every way more useful members of the body of Christ. There is also increased zeal on the part of our publishers in extending their circulation. This zeal may take one of two forms: It may make increased expenditures for the improvement of our religious journals and adopt special means for bringing these journals before the attention of the Christian public; or it may take what seems to us the injurious form of cutting rates, and cheapening prices until a price is set which will make it impossible for publishers to bring their religious journals up to the standard of literary merit of the journals of other religious bodies. There are always some people who welcome the cheapening process and who hail with gladness a reduction in the price of our papers, but we are persuaded that the more intelligent membership believe that the highest interest of religious journalism among us is not served, but hindered, by this reduction in price. It is a well-known fact that the religious journals among the Disciples of Christ have always been published at a lower rate than those of equal merit in other religious bodies. This has been done at great sacrifice. Any further reduction in price we believe will tend to lower the standard of our papers more than to increase their circulation. What we wish for all our religious journals whose influence is right and good is the highest degree of prosperity and the largest possible circulation. Above all we wish for them a constantly increasing standard of excellence. A dollar paper may mean a few hundred or a few thousand more subscribers, but it must necessarily mean, in the long run, a lower grade of religious literature.

Life at Macatawa is a little more quiet since the close of the Assembly, and there is already a slight decline of the summer
population, though there are some new
rivals that partially compensate for the
partures. The summer days are pass
away too swiftly and autumn with its br
ing atmosphere will call the people hor
ward very rapidly. Never have we knc
summer days to go more swiftly than d
ing the present season. We have not b
troubled with heat, or flies, or mosqui
nor with dust, mud or *ennui*. The d
have seemed too short and the nights
not quite long enough. There is someth
in this atmosphere and in the music of
unresting lake to produce somnolence.
one looks forward with much pleasur
the idea of leaving Macatawa. Many
those who are here for the first time, t
summer, are planning to become perman
summer residents of the place. They
purchasing lots and planning cottages tc
built for the coming season. A new ad
tion of the Park has been laid out on
lake front, south of Edge-wood-on-tl
Lake, in which many are purchasing
for summer homes.

While, as we say, life here at the P
is more quiet since the close of the Ass
bly, it is anything but monotonous. Th
are a number of things going on to occ
the time and attention of the people v
are here. Recently Mr. E. C. Westerv
one of the owners of the Park, gave a f
excursion for the cottagers up Black L
and return, lasting from eight until ele
in the evening. It was a merry crowd,
there were music, recitations and impro
tu speeches, with a vote of thanks to
Westervelt for his kindness. Mr. J.
Post, another of the proprietors of
Park, has also shown many kindnesses
the cottagers, and planned a free excurs
down Lake Michigan to Saugatuck one
this week, but the rough sea preven
many from going. On last Sunday aft
noon at the close of the service, the me
bers of the Central Christian Church, of
Louis, present here in the Park, determi
to give their pastor, F. G. Tyrrell, a li
surprise on his thirty-third birthday.
was conducted by his wife, under prete
of taking a walk, into a secluded nook do
one of the wooded canyons, where
gathered the members of the Central,
gether with some of their neighbors at
Park, and there were refreshments
congratulations and a few short speech
and a happy response from the surpri
pastor. The pastor of the Central is v
popular here at the Park, and the wh
populace would have turned out if they
been let into the secret. On one even
of the past week a few families of us ga
ered on one of the sandy knolls overlook
Lake Michigan and had what is kno
here as a "corn roast." The young roa
ing ears in their husks are buried in
sand and hot coals are piled over them u
til they are thoroughly roasted; then tl
are taken out and each one takes his ear
corn, pulls back the husks carefully, a
after supplying the necessary condimer
proceeds to eat it from the cob. Of cou
there are other things to go along with
In these ways do we manage to drive d
care away and banish *ennui*. But this
plies only to the vacant hours, for after
nearly everybody who comes here, e
though they do not, like the editor, br
their work along with them, have somethi
to do to occupy a part of each day, and

things we have mentioned only serve to fill the otherwise unoccupied hours. To one who has to spend most of the time at his desk, they afford a welcome relief from the tedium of daily tasks.

Last Lord's day we were favored with another magnificent audience at the Auditorium and with an able sermon by J. J. Haley on the meaning of life. He gave the four prevailing theories of life—the Ascetic, the Hedonic, the Puritanic and the view best illustrated by the life and teaching of our Savior, who regarded life not as pain, not as pleasure, not as discipline, but as opportunity, and opportunity for the development of character, the great aim of life. Bro. Haley is now occupying his beautiful cottage, "Melbourne Heights," on Cedar Walk, which affords a splendid view, through rifts of greenery in the intervening forests, of the Great Lake. The beach meeting at night was one of the largest and one of the best. It was conducted by President J. H. Hardin, of Eureka College who, with his wife, is occupying a cottage on the Grove Walk, near the hotel. Several of our preachers yet remain on the ground, though Richardson and Tyrrell take their departure this week, and others are to follow pretty soon. Among recent transient visitors to the Park are Z. T. Sweeney, Bro. Reeves, of Columbus, Ind., Henry Meier, of St. Louis, F. E. Udell and wife, of St. Louis and Bro. Ball, of Muncie, Ind.

Geo. A. Bellamy, head of the "Hiram House," Cleveland, Ohio, who was married on the 17th inst. to Miss Marie Laura Parker, at Bedford, O., was tendered a reception at the residence of his father, Wm. Bellamy, in Grand Rapids, on the evening of the 18th. The house of Bro. Bellamy was beautifully decorated for the occasion, and the rooms and hall were filled with the throng of happy guests, mainly our church people, at Grand Rapids, to welcome and congratulate the newly wedded pair. There were refreshments and music to add to the attractions of the evening. It was in every way a most delightful occasion, and a deserved compliment to these young people, who have dedicated their lives to the elevation of the neglected population of Cleveland. The young couple will spend a fortnight at the cottage of the groom's father, at Macatawa Park, before resuming their labors. In this connection it gives us pleasure to add that the Christian people of Cleveland, recently, without regard to church affiliations, resolved to stand behind this work of Bro. Bellamy, and to furnish him proper support and buildings for carrying on the same. This speaks well both for the manner in which Bro. Bellamy has conducted his work, and for the Christian spirit of the churches at Cleveland. During our visit at Grand Rapids, on the occasion referred to, it was the pleasure of myself and wife to spend the night with the family of Ex-Mayor L. C. Stow, who have been our neighbors at the Park for several years, but on account of the sickness of Sister Stow have not been here the present season. We were delighted to learn that Sister Stow's health is rapidly recovering as the result of a recent surgical operation. They have been much missed from the Park, this season, but they hope to be here later, and during coming seasons.

Edgewood-on-the-Lake, Aug. 24.

RELIGION PRACTICAL.

NO. III.

JAS. M. CAMPBELL.

Now concerning the collection for the saints.—1 *Cor.* 16:1.

The balance of truth demands that the heaven-side of things do not overshadow the earth-side. As Socrates caused philosophy to descend from heaven to earth that it might enter into the cities and homes of men, religion must be brought down into human life as a working power for righteousness. The life beyond is always viewed in Scripture in its relation to the present. It is brought to bear as a practical force upon present duty. The charge that religion is unpractical; that it has more to do with a visionary life in the future than with the actual life of the present is a very shallow one. It is true that the church has often done a great wrong to humanity in representing the actual life as a matter of no moment, but in doing so it has misrepresented Christianity. The transference of the aim of religion from this world to the world to come is a perversion of the Christian ideal. The design of Christianity is not to prepare men for heaven, but for earth; not to fit them to die, but to live. A Christian is not to spend his time star gazing, but in faithful performance of the duties of daily life.

In the middle ages, when the world was regarded as doomed, and separation from it was looked upon as necessary to a life of holiness, there was a dwarfing of the importance of the present. It was the complaint of Tyndale in his day that men gave attention to the building of cathedrals and neglected the construction of harbors and public works. Happily the point of emphasis has changed. We do not now think of forsaking the world, but of improving it. We recognize the dignity of the common life. We inculcate diligence in business as a Christian duty. Indeed, the pendulum swings to the other extreme, and the danger is that we shall overemphasize the present life and forget its true relation to the hereafter.

Out of the future come life's deepest motives. "Earth is the battle ground of the eternities." Between the spiritual and the practical there is an intimate connection. The step between the highest doctrine and the humblest duty is a very short one. We see this illustrated in the abrupt transition of thought from the lofty argument of Paul about the resurrection and the reality of the life beyond, in the fifteenth chapter of First Corinthians, to the words of practical exhortation in the beginning of the sixteenth chapter, which stand at the head of this paper. The unfortunate break between the chapters has, however, destroyed completely the force of the apostle's appeal. His plea is this: "You as Christians believe in a glorious resurrection; you believe in eternal rewards; you believe in the recognition or all good-doings by the King of kings; then show your faith by ministering to the poor saints in Jerusalem."

The practical bearing of the future upon the present is seen in furnishing a right motive to social action. Materialism takes away all incentive to good-doing. It selfishly says, "Let us eat and drink, for tomorrow we die." Belief in a future life, by setting life in eternal relations, leads men to seek the welfare of their brothermen. It leads them to labor for the establishment of justice, and the enforcement of humanity. The times when men feel most deeply the powers of the world to come are times when their interest in others is intensified, and their efforts to benefit them are redoubled. Times of unbelief are always times of stagnation in beneficent effort. In promoting a spirit of beneficence, in stimulating high thought and lofty endeavor, in furnishing a motive to self-sacrifice, in gendering spiritual energy that expends itself in present service, the influence of the future upon the present cannot be overestimated. Am I to live forever? Am I heir of all the ages? Is my present life introductory to the ageless hereafter? how exalted, then, ought to be the manner of my life! Am I to meet my brother again at the judgment-seat, and shall I then be asked, "Have you done the right thing by him?" Then let me see to it that my conduct toward him is such as shall commend itself to the Lord of love, who will be the judge of us both.

THE HOLY SPIRIT.

JAMES O. CARSON.

The disposition in the religious world to mystify everything connected with the Holy Spirit in his relations and intercourse with and work among men, his personality, dwelling-place, the methods and means by which he influences men to righteousness and carries forward the work which he came into the world to accomplish, is to me inexplicable. Some of the teachings on this subject are so marvelous and mystical, and at the same time so at variance with established laws both in nature and in grace, as to suggest the suspicion of intent to mystify and bewilder. Prominent among these teachings and probably the most popular, are those respecting the *"personality"* and *"personal indwelling"* of the Holy Spirit. The teachers in this school of marvels and mysteries insist on the *"personality"* of the Holy Spirit, and at the same time they as strenuously insist that this personality dwells at the same moment of time in the individual body of every Christian on the earth.

A moment's reflection ought to satisfy any one that both of these teachings cannot be true, for if it be true that the Holy Spirit occupies at the same moment of time millions of other personalities like man, and scattered as they are all over the earth, then it is not true that he is a personality of which man has knowledge, or which he can form an intelligent conception.

Respecting the *"personality* of the Holy Spirit," it may be said that the Scriptures are silent; that we have no knowledge of our own, and do not possess capacity to even form an intelligent conception. As well might one attempt to form an intelligent conception of the personality of God. And yet those teachers do not hesitate to insist upon men accepting this as a fundamental doctrine of the New Testament. Personality as understood by men and as the term is applied by them in their daily intercourse with one another, and moreover the only personality of which they possess knowledge, is a person—a sensible, tangible body—having capability to think, to reason, to purpose, to devise, to execute. Contrast with this the popular orthodox mystical idea of the *personality* of the Holy Spirit, and we will agree with a brother who says: "If the Scriptures teach the personality and personal indwelling of the Holy Spirits, it must be in a mystic spirit sense, accepted by faith." This mystic idea of personality, as we gather it from orthodox teachings, partakes largely of that entertained by people who believe in ghosts. A Spirit without corporeal existence; a being whose every action is mysterious; who in his intercourse with men, in "his own good time," manner and place, and without means or instrumentalities, influences them to be good; who shines into human hearts to comfort them, even as a sunbeam shines into a drop of dew and warms it; a personality that has been in the world almost two thousand years working with and among men the works of God, feeding the hungry, clothingthe naked, visiting the sick, provid ing homes for destitute widows and orphans, and sending the gospel of the grace of God to the ends of the earth—and yet has never been seen by human eyes, heard by human ears, or handled by human hands, as was the "Word" when he was in the world doing the same works. In the absence of more specific information it is assumed that this is the idea of personality of the "mystic Spirit sense." It is certainly not a simple, common-sense idea.

But scarcely less marvelous and credulity-testing is the doctrine of the *personal* indwelling of the Holy Spirit in the individual bodies of men. According to this doctrine the Holy Spirit in his own personality dwells in each separate individual body of every Christian man and woman in the world! The simple statement of this proposition ought to be its own refutation.

One word just here in regard to the too common idea of understanding and accepting things spiritual "*in a sense.*" Respecting this we will say that God never does anything of himself, nor does he ask man to do anything for him "*in a sense,*" not even in a "mystic Spirit sense." Whatever he does, he does absolutely and requires the same of man.

But it may be asked: "Can a spirit be seen by human eyes?" Certainly not. Neither can an unembodied spirit hold intercourse with or in any wise influence men. Man is so constituted that he cannot take cognizance of things except through his senses. Hence it is that when God would communicate with man, he does so in manners and forms that are cognizable through his senses, and *never otherwise.* This is at once the reason and explanation for the several manifestations of God known to men as the "*Word* of God," the "*Spirit* of God," the "*Son* of God" and the "*Church* of God." These are *manifestations, not mysteries.* Each came for a separate, specific mission. One was to make known the "infinite power and deity of God;" another his wisdom and goodness; another his character, and yet another who is the consummation of all who have preceded him. This is he in whom we are now interested, and concerning whom we desire to learn the things that have been revealed. Fortunately, much has been revealed and in language so plain that the simple-minded can understand. Let us look at these. When Jesus was about to leave his disciples they were very despondent, and he said to them: "When I go away I will not leave you alone; I will send to you *another,* the Advocate, who is the Spirit of Truth, who when he comes will lead you into all the truth; he will bring again to your minds whatsoever I have told you, and he will take of mine and show [explain] it to you. He will convict the world of sin, of righteousness and of judgment, and he will abide with you always." Here, then, we have given to us the name of him who was to take the place of Jesus, "the Spirit of Truth," his office that of "*advocate,*" and his mission to lead the church into all the truth, and to convict the world of sin, of righteousness and of judgment.

Besides these we have been advised of the time, the place where and the manner of his coming, so that it remains only to ascertain the place in which he took up his abode, assured as have been that wheresoever he took up his abode when he came, he abides still. Concerning these the divine historian says: "When the day of Pentecost was fully come, the disciples of Jesus, numbering one hundred and twenty persons, had by appointment assembled in one place; that suddenly there came from heaven a sound as of a great rushing wind which filled the place where they were assembled; that there appeared among them tongues like unto fire which, separating, sat upon each of them; that they were all filled with the Holy Spirit and began to speak in foreign languages as the Spirit empowered them;" that when the multitude, attracted by these events, had come together, Peter and the other apostles, in explanation of these marvelous occurrences, said: "Having received a promise from the Father, he [Jesus] has sent forth this which you now *see* and *hear.*"

From this record we learn concerning the events attending the advent of the Holy Spirit to the earth, that the *church,* consisting of one hundred and twenty members, was assembled by one consent in one place; that the Holy Spirit in a visible form and miraculous manner came to this organized body and took possession of it as he did the body of Jesus of Nazareth at the time of his baptism and entry on his ministry, and the announcement in all the languages of the earth, that this same Jesus whom you crucified, God has highly exalted, having constituted him Lord and Christ, the result of all these being the addition of three thousand men and women to the list of the saved.

These are momentous events, and are in exact harmony with the promise of Jesus to his disciples and of his intercessory prayer. He said: "I pray not for these alone, but for all who may believe on me through their word, that they may be one [among themselves] as thou, Father, art in me and I in thee." And then he adds these significant words: "The *glory* which thou gavest me I have given them, that they may be one as we are, *I in them as thou in me,* that they may be *perfect* in one [body] that the world may know that thou hast sent me." The *glory* which Jesus received from the Father was the descent upon him, in visible, bodily form, of the Holy Spirit at the time of his baptism and entrance upon his ministry, accompanied by the voice: "This is my Son, hear him." This is the *glory* which Jesus said, "I have given them," and which he did give them on the day of Pentecost when, in visible, bodily form, the Holy Spirit descended
upon the assembled church and announc
through his body, in all the language
the earth, the exaltation of Jesus to
"Lord and Christ," King and Savior of
world.

Jesus needed the divine presence
help to perfect him for the work which
been given him to do, and "God gave
him the Spirit without measure."
same divine presence and help was nee
by the church to *perfect* her for the w
given her to do, and Jesus having recei
from the Father the promise of the H
Spirit hath sent this forth which you
see and hear. "I in them as thou in
is the need of the church to perfect her
the great work of bringing the world to
acknowledgment of the Christ.

The same divinity, then, that was
Jesus of Nazareth was by him transmit
to the church, and is there to-day, and
presenting to the world the same evide
of the divine presence with *her* that Je
presented to the Jews of this presence w
him. The Jews said: "No one can do
works which thou doest except God
with him," and Jesus said: "If I had
done among you the *works* which n
other did you had not sin, but now y
have no excuse for your sin." To his d
ciples he said: "Greater works than th
shall ye do when I go to my Father;" a
these greater works are now being done
the church—works which could not
done except by an organized body un
divine direction and power.

In further support of the contention t
the Holy Spirit dwells in the organi
kown as the church, the body of Chri
and not in the separate individual bodi
of the members of that church, attenti
is directed to the fact that in the N
Testament the dwelling-place of the Ho
Spirit is spoken of under the figu
of "a building," "a temple," "a body
and *always in the singular number.* T
is in exact harmony with the divine ord
both in nature and grace. "One body
one Spirit." One dwelling-place or buil
ing for one family; one temple for the o
living God. God never had more than o
temple on the earth at one time. So, the
the reputed many bodies for the one Spi
would be a monstrosity, and many templ
for the one and only living God would
idolatrous. Speaking of this "buildin
the apostle says, "It is compactly fram
together for a habitation of God by
Spirit." Concerning this temple (n
temples) he says it is constructed of t
bodies of men, which are "living stone
in which a holy priesthood may offer sp
itual sacrifice to God; and that this bo
is composed of many members, of whi
Christ is the head and the Holy Spirit
the life. So closely allied are the me
bers of this body that if a single memb
becomes diseased, the whole body is a
fected; so sacred and perfect is this tem
that if a single stone becomes defaced t
beauty of the entire edifice is marre
"There is one body and one Spirit." T
church is this "one body," and is
organism as complete as is the hum
body. In this organism the Holy Spir
as we have seen, took up his abode on t
day of Pentecost, and if so he abides the
still. By becoming a member of this bod
and in no other way, a man enters in
relationship with God and Christ and t
Holy Spirit, and becomes "a partaker

vine nature"—the Holy Spirit—who
there, and thus becomes a *partici-*
in the honors, privileges and bless-
which are inherent in the body, by
of the presence there of the Holy
, just as a member of the human
by reason of its relation to that
becomes a joint participant in the
ngs which are inherent in the body.
is no miracle or "impenetrable
ry" in this. It is natural, sensible
criptural.

Louis, Mo.

ASSOCIATED EVILS.

C. H. WETHERBEE.

re are several evils of a very danger-
haracter which are associated with
tian and church life. From many
of the country reports come that a
leal of worldliness is pervading the
hes. Correspondence with ministers
laymen, located at different and dis-
points, reveal the fact that worldly
ements of various kinds are being in-
ingly patronized by members of the
hes, and that these things are serious-
ecting the lives of these Christians.
I have been studying the situation
what and I think I see an association
ls, which seem to have significant con-
on with each other. One evil is a cer-
legree of laxity in the pulpit. For
a number of years a great many pas-
and evangelists have failed to bring
front, with any frequency whatever,
sterner aspects of both law and gos-
which are very essential to a full voic-
f God's mind concerning sinners. The
features of the gospel have mostly
ed the ground. The awfulness of sin,
he certain and eternal perdition of all
lie in sin, have not been presented
the pulpit in due proportion. This is
erious evil, which is having a mighty
on church life. Another is great
ness in receiving people into the
hes as members. It is the truth to
hat almost any one can become a mem-
f a Christian Church to-day. Only
ne go before either a pastor or a
h and say that he intends to lead a
r life or that he desires to be associ-
with God's people in a church capaci-
nd he will be received. I am far from
g that this is so in all cases, but I am
dent that it is in the great majority of
. The sad fact is, the churches are
filled with raw, unconverted material,
f this thing keeps on much longer
of the churches will not be in any
sense Christian, for the members will
be Christians; they will simply be
lly church members. Another evil is
me indifference to church discipline.
gets excluded from a church in these
of love, liberality and liberty? Very
O, this brood of church evils! A
t revival is needed among all the
ches, not to get additions, but to make
ractions.

---

nce 1871 the Broadway Tabernacle
ch, New York, has contributed to
ion and charitable causes $625,000. Be-
this, and during the same time, it
contributed toward its own support,
rd its debt and toward Bethany Mis-
$900,000. During the same period the
en of the church have contributed to
ion work, in money and boxes, $89,000.

Current Religious Thought

Rev. Geo. Matheson's articles, in the July and August numbers of the Biblical World, on "The Feminine Ideal of Christianity," are deeply interesting, alike for their originality of thought and application of some of the Beautitudes. In the opening of the second article, in the August number, he says that Christianity has done greater things for women than for any other class —"It has given her dominion." And at the conclusion of this article he tells us wherein and of what this greatness consists. We quote Dr. Matheson's concluding lines:

The greatest thing which Christianity has done for the spirit of woman is to put into her hand a microscope—to give her the power of seeing little things. The spirit of womanhood is the spirit of the new charity. It ceases to look at masses; it keeps its eye on the individual life. It regards not his price to the state; it considers not his advantage to the community; it views only his need. The strength of his claim is the strength of his necessity. The Roman dropped the protective hand where the argument of utility failed. Christianity's argument for charity only began there. It took up men because they were useless, because they were unprofitable to the state. It took them up just because the state had laid them down, and just where it had laid them down. It gathered from the highways and the hedges—from the waste places of the community. It was a new order of chivalry which it proposed to inaugurate. The old order of chivalry was to redress the wrongs of beauty. Beauty was an adjunct of the state, because beauty was power. Pagan fiction could describe the retaliation of the injury to Helen, or could tell how the last Tarquin was banished for a Roman matron's sake. Christ brought in a higher chivalry—to redress the wrongs of ugliness, to follow the ninety and nine which had no beauty, no excellence, no power. Mercy is the youngest born of the children of God, and the prerogative of mercy is this: "To seek and to save that which was lost,"

For reasons hinted at in the following paragraph the Christian Commonwealth, London, thinks any union of the Roman, Anglican and Russian Churches would be a curse rather than a blessing to the world:

What, however, are the Eastern Churches like? Are they worth uniting with? Not unless it is desired to plunge back into darkness and superstition instead of dvancing to clearer light. The Babylonian apostasy of a corrupt and fallen Christendom prevails in Eastern as well as in Western Christendom. Should the Anglican find a way of reunion in this direction, its ruin would be completed. A Russian Church is the home of endless ceremonies. There is much that is instructive, but the ritual and the symbolism have become extravagant and overwhelming. At the Eucharist two round-flat cakes are presented, united together in the baking, representing the two natures of Christ in one person. Five such cakes are used at each celebration. Each is marked on the upper side with a cross and an inscription, "IC. XC. NIKA."—*i. e., Jesus Christ conquers*. After the priest has taken the first *phosphora*, or cake, he makes on it with the spear used as a knife the sign of the cross. The piece which he now cuts off is called "the Lamb," which he cuts in half, indicating that Christ gave himself as the Lamb for the sins of the world. He then pierces it with the spear. All through he recites appropriate texts. The second cake is cut in memory of the Virgin, and the piece is put beside the Lamb. From the third nine little pieces are taken in honor of the various saints. Out of the fourth more pieces are cut, while prayers are offered for the Emperor, Synod, etc. Out of the fifth other fragments are cut, while the priest prays for deceased members of the church. All these pieces are now covered with the asteriskos (cross-star), in order to recall the star over the house where Jesus was born. Then follow other ceremonies in immense and complex elaboration, until the question arises, What has become of the simplicity of Christian worship? The same question repeats itself at every point connected with Eastern Christianity. Preaching is almost unknown. Pictures are adored in churches, homes, shops and streets. The priest enters everywhere. True, he is to be preferred to the Roman celibate priest, for he must be a married man. But the sacramentarianism and sacerdotalism which threaten to eat up Anglicanism have long ago swallowed up the Eastern Church, until now reformation is hopeless. *That* can only come from without, and at present a cruel civil despotism is allied with this corrupt and superstitious communion to crush all Nonconformity directly it attempts to propagate the truth. We repeat that only those ignorant of the real state of Oriental Christianity can excusably imagine that reunion with it would be anything but a curse.

Until the mystic enchantments of the faith-healer lose their charms the following sensible remarks of the Interior and similar criticisms will be in order. After pointing out certain historic facts, bearing on the history and nature of various cures, the Interior says:

On the whole, as we said at the beginning, it would be hard to invest a process of "cure" under which the recuperative powers of nature will not restore most of the sick provided the method be not in itself injurious. And if so be the method require abstinence from the popular patent medicines of the day, which depend for their effect largely upon the morphine or the whiskey they contain, we ought to be grateful. And we try to be. But when with this beneficent result there are spread abroad crude metaphysical speculations and monstrous perversions of sacred Scripture, it is a more serious matter. It is a sorrowful sight to see tens of thousands of good people turned aside from the simplicity which is in Christ and taught to believe that the Holy Bible is a book of so difficult an understanding that it requires an abstruse philosophy to supplement it, all because people who accept such dicta "get well." The wonder would be if they did not get well, for they have recovered under every and any system that man has ever devised, unless the system were in itself fatal.

Meanwhile, there is an honest and honorable profession of therapeutics which has approved itself by the suppression of smallpox by the arrest of cholera at infected ports, and by the stamping out of yellow fever the moment it shows itself upon our coasts. The only real test of the value of any system of medicine is when it is brought face to face with an epidemic. The science which can arrest a bubobic plague is a verity, and any that cannot check its progress is a fraud, however lofty its claims. Failing to take a common-sense view of these facts has wrecked many a believer's faith; for when the collapse comes, which is sure to come, whatsoever is built upon the theory falls with it.

There is much wisdom in the following short article in a recent number of the Standard, by Rev. Walter B. Vassar.

Whatever else a minister may or may not be, he should never be a talking machine. Ability to give utterance to his thoughts, this is one sign among others of a call to the ministry, but glibness of speech, if that is all a man can set forth as a reason for church orders, it were well the fallacy were dispelled early in his career. Greatness seldom shows itself in a great mouth. So long ago as the age of Moses, men saw that to be a herald there was a demand for easiness of speech, but if Moses had been efficient here and deficient in all else, how poorly he would have served his day and ours. Laws that never have been repealed—the Ten Words which Moses spoke—came from a man so far removed from a talking machine that his chief complaint and disquietude when called of God was, "O, my Lord, I am not eloquent, neither heretofore nor since thou hast spoken unto thy servant; but I am slow of speech, and of a slow tongue."

Taken all in all, the open mouth has done more damage than good, thus far in the centuries. "Speech was given to the ordinary sort of men, whereby to communicate their mind; but to wise men whereby to conceal it." The training not only of children, but also of ministers, to think twice before they speak, might engage the attention of faculties of instruction, who are supposed to turn out the ready-made minister. None but the wise are of the opinion—

> "I had a thing to say;
> But I will fit it—with some better time."

We hear the long sermon reprobated. It is not the long sermon, but the sermon long drawn out by word of mouth. It is this which kills devotion and makes the old refrain of Job pregnant with meaning in our own century—"Who is he that darkeneth counsel with words?" We speak of the minister, making him the pattern for all, though, alas, the responsibility.

Swift had a way of using a lash that left a smart, and none the worse for that if the medicine were needed—

> "She [he] sits tormenting every guest,
> Nor gives her [his] tongue one moment's rest,
> In phrase batter'd stale, and trite,
> Which modern ladies call polite."

Our Budget.

—The terms soldier and hardships are almost synonymous.

—Next Sunday, September 4th, is the day for the offering for Church Extension. Though last in the year, it should by no means be the least.

—The great national debts of the world are chiefly war debts. What a sad comment upon the dispositions of men! What a tremendous burden thrown upon innocent parties!

—"On to Chattanooga" is again the cry. This time it is the gathering of the hosts of Zion for counsel on things pertaining to the kingdom of heaven. See notice in this paper.

—The International Evangel, of this city, for September, contains a good account of the World's Sunday-school convention, London, by its editor, W. J. Semelroth, of St. Louis. The Evangel is a good, all-round Sunday-school journal.

—The First Christian Church, of this city, having renovated, painted, grained, frescoed and carpeted their auditorium, and in fact the entire church house, in the absence of their pastor, on last Friday night, on his return to the city, gave him an informal reception. The house, in its new electric light and new, clean dress suit, presents a fine appearance, all of which will be enjoyed alike by the pastor, church and strangers within its gates. The reception was an occasion of much joy to all present.

—"Close the all-night saloons," says the Chicago Record. And permit us to add, the all-day saloons as well. They are crime-breeding places and have no decent claims to a place among civilized men.

—The war is proving a prolific source of literature for magazines and religious journals as well as for the secular daily press. Every phase of battleship and army life, equipment, heroism and hardship has been made the theme of repeated articles, and the end is not yet.

—Our readers will find an enjoyable article in this paper from our esteemed contemporary, the St. Louis Christian Advocate. We print the editorial in full because of its exhilarating influence upon the reader as well as for its interest and facts so interestingly portrayed.

—The range finders used so successfully on our warships in the late war has suggested to the Interior the idea of suggesting to the ministry the use of such an instrument in the delivery of their sermons. The idea is a good one provided the preacher has any solid shot to send toward an enemy; otherwise it would be an expensive luxury. By the way, why don't some inventive brain suggest to preachers the propriety of useing smokeless powder in the delivery of their sermons? Many good points in a sermon are often concealed in smoke, and sometimes there is nothing but smoke!

—Some people, preachers and papers talk about the annexation and non-annexation of the Philippine Islands as some other people talk about joining or not joining the churches, as though such a step affected our responsibilities pro or con. in the case. The non-annexation of the Philippine Islands cannot lessen our responsibilities toward the people of those islands in the face of the now wide-open door. Moral obligations of this character cannot be thrown off by closing our eyes or stopping our ears to their condition and to the facts. These obligations exist whether we annex these islands or not, and if not annexed it must be for some better reason than the fear of moral obligations.

—The second number of the Register-Review, Kansas City, Mo., has not devoted much space to lengthy, learned articles, but it is brimful of state news.

—If any appointments in the Santiago campaign or at Montauk Point, N. Y., were made for political effect, as some papers have alleged, the political party making the appointment will in all probability be surprised at the result, in due season.

—At the August meeting of the Foreign Society at Cincinnati, the following appropriations were made for buildings in the foreign field: $2,000 for a lot and house in Lu Cheo Fu; $3,500 for a hospital in the same city; $1,000 for a home in Shanghai for one missionary family, and $4,000 for another. This money will be paid out of the Annuity Fund. Had it not been for the money received on the Annuity plan these buildings could not be erected. From this same fund buildings are now in course of erection in Japan and in India. Ten new missionaries leave for the field in September. Some go to India, some to Japan, some to China and some to Turkey. A special committee was appointed to take under advisement the propriety of entering Cuba and Puerto Rico. A number of men are ready to enter these fields with a view of establishing missions in them. The receipts for the month were $19,261.08. Of this amount $9,690 was received on the Annuity plan. The regular receipts for the month were slightly larger than those for the corresponding month one year ago.

—It is reported that Commodore Philip has protested to the Secretary of the Navy against his own promotion because it is made at the expense of his comrades and friends, who he believes have performed their duty quite as bravely and ably as he; but he cannot decline the promotion, for that would be equivalent to a resignation from the service. We cannot but commend this spirit of consideration for others. It is one of the noblest traits of our nature, and may be even called one of the Christian graces. Commodore Philip is not the only navy and other official who has shown this excellency of heart, but is none the less deserving of praise for it. The same principle carried into all our vocations would greatly alleviate jealousies, bickerings, strifes and other evils so prolific of friction and troubles among men.

—Allow me to express my sincere appreciation of the CHRISTIAN-EVANGELIST. I have often thought when reading it, What spiritual manna this is to me. Of the religious papers that come to my table the CHRISTIAN-EVANGELIST is much the superior. May the brotherhood support you, that you may continue to give us such a paper, so full of spiritual food.

Fraternally yours, JOHN P. SALA.
Randolph, Ohio.

—From the Missionary Voice for August and October, a number of unusual interest, we learn that the receipts for Foreign Missions now aggregate $117,324.03. It also states that more churches, Sunday-schools and Endeavor Societies have responded this than any previous year. This is encouraging; but if this amount was the least of all our different missionary department receipts for the year, instead of the greatest, we should have much greater cause for rejoicing. Since writing the above we are otherwise informed that the total receipts have now reached $120,499.92.

—President McKinley has written a congratulatory letter to the army and navy Christian Commission and expresses the hope that this good work may continue. The D. L. Moody letters which have appeared in our columns will give our readers some idea of the character and extent of this Christianly work. The interest which Christian people have taken in the moral and spiritual welfare of the soldier in our war with Spain is somewhat unusual, and betokens the deep hold of Christian influence upon the conscience of the nation.

—The knowledge of the fact that "there's plenty of room at the top" is a strong temptation to some men to get there by the shortest route. Some succeed by climbing over t wall, but these become thieves and robbe Only those who enter by the door of hon labor, real merit and a pure heart are wort of the place.

—W. J. Russell, pastor of the Church Christ at Kalamazoo, Mich., has a sh article in the Daily Telegraph of that c severely criticising the double moral standar and especially the church that refuses forgiv ness and fellowship to penitent fallen wome The article was provoked by a reported case this kind in "the Darlington Presbyteri Church," and concludes with the followi strong but just rebuke of the unforgiving spi in any church:

> That church that refuses to grant forgivene and welcome to the returning sinner has mission in this world worthy to give it existence. The curse of God rests upon such congregation. The church has something do to prepare herself for the coming Chri This spirit of unforgiveness will send to h many who profess to be Christians. It is ti to do away with an empty profession, a show to the world the Spirit of the Master, w said: "Father, forgive them." When this realized we can expect that the world will ha confidence in the church, and not until the In conclusion, let me appeal to the you women that they show "mercy" to the u fortunate of their number, and throw around t young womanhood of to-day all the help th possibly can.

—The Central Christian Church, S Antonio, Texas, believes in printer's ink. has a conspicuous ad in the Sunday Light, that city, accompanied by pregnant Scriptu quotations.

—Our first statement concerning the time the General Convention at Chattanoog Tenn., was Oct. 14-20. We now learn that is Oct. 13-21. The first statement is not error but seems to include the full tim Remember the date Oct. 13-21.

—Next Monday is Labor Day, and its o servance in honor of labor seems to be increa ing with the passing years. There is no dou but that the processional display of labore and their professional classifications has good effect upon the world. It is well f society to see occasionally how dependent it upon labor for its existence. The moral effe of the observance of such a day is also goo barring the evils of drink and some oth associated evils. The intellectuality of t laborer is manifested, and the value of go habits and good morals emphasized. A m does not lose his right to be called a gentl man because he is a laborer. Intellectuall morally and spiritually he may be as fit for t best society as the most polished autocrat the land. It is good also to show that in t field of manual labor there is a demand f every mental, moral and spiritual faculty man. Enlightened labor moves the world.

—The remark is frequently heard, "What short summer this has been." This is a com plaint most peculiar to elderly people, but th summer it is heard from both old and youn Doubtless the chief cause of this remark th year is the war which has just closed. T destruction of the Maine in Havana Harb in February threw this country into fever of excitement, and sensational even have since happened so rapid that the peop were unconscious of the rapid transit of th months. And yet there are doubtless man exceptions to this rule; many to whom hours anxious waiting for news seemed weeks dreary time; many sick and suffering soldie to whom the passing weeks were months sluggish, painful life; many sad-hearte mothers who have lived years of time in th few months in which their sons have faced th dangers of the camp and the battlefield, an many whose remaining life will be spent unde the shadow of death. How unequal, therefore are our lives, and how imcompetent the sand of the hourglass to measure either the lengt or the number of our days.

PERSONAL MENTION.

A letter from Joel Brown, field agent for the ıristian Orphans' Home, written from Goodıd, Ind., states that he is receiving conıerable encouragement wherever he has portunity to present his mission. He was pecially well received at the Fountain Park ısembly, where he was given $40.25 for the ome.

J. V. Coombs will dedicate the new church at ıring Creek, Cass county, Ind., September th.

B. S. Ferrall, pastor of the church at Watka, Ill., with his wife, has been spending cation at Lake James, Ind.

A. O. Swartwood will sing for W. A. Baker a meeting at Walnut Corner, Ill., in Sepnber.

The Baptist News incidentally pays the llowing excellent tribute to Bro. J. C. Creel: It is due Bro. Creel for us to say at this time at he is one of the most gentlemanly men we ve ever met in public debate. It is also a ct that we have met very few who were ler.''

J. T. Boone has returned to his work at emphis, Mo., from his vacation in Tennese.

F. M. Rogers, of Edina, Mo., has closed his bors for the church there in order to do angelistic work in North Missouri. He was Edina fifteen months, added thirty-three embers, and raised $197 for missions. J. T. cGarvey, of La Belle, will succeed Bro. ogers at Edina.

A. O. Hunsaker is singing for J. V. oombs in a short meeting at Princeton, Ill., here Chas. D. Purlee ministers. Large idiences and good interest in the meeting are ported.

The editor of this paper preached at Grand apids, Mich., on last Sunday. On the same y the assistant editor preached at Compton eights church in this city.

Miss Benella Davenport, a grandniece of lxander Campbell, will teach in the Sumerlin Institue, Barton, Florida, this sumer. Miss Davenport's parents were mared in Mammoth Cave, Kentucky, Sept. 29th, 68, at 9:30 A. M.

The address of T. A. Abbott, Corresponding ecretary, is now 4760 Kennerly Ave., St. ouis, Mo. Don't send to Louisiana. Be ıre and put street and number on, and your ail will reach him promptly. This is now his rmanent address.

M. S. Errett has resigned as pastor at North opeka, Kas., and has accepted the position district evangelist for the second district of ansas, consisting of eight counties along the astern boarder. He is now in a meeting at onway Springs, where Clyde Sharp is pastor ıd will begin work in the district with a eeting at De Soto, Sept. 1. E. R. Phillips is e pastor at De Soto, and reports everything ady for a good meeting. I. A. Smith, of ssowotomie, held at week's institute at De oto two weeks ago that was well received by e people.

David Husband and wife, of Olivia, Minn., ere recently made happy by the gift of a ıughter to their home.

W. H. Bybee, of Bolivar, Mo., writes that has resigned his work for the church at that ace on account of its financial burden or ress, and is at liberty to engage elsewhere. or information about his efficiency inquiring ırties are requested to write to Dr. J. R. Vinn, a member of the official board of the ıurch at Bolivar.

J. P. Davis, who has been preaching at aw Paw, Mich., for a year, will be compelled change his field of labor for want of sufficient ıpport. He is loved by the church and highly ommended for his efficient services, but they e not strong enough financially to retain him. e will be at liberty to engage for work elsehere October 1st. Correspondence may be ldressed to him at Paw Paw, Mich.

T. E. Jones, the evangelistic singer, of hicago, has been spending a week at Macatwa Park and delighting the audience with his ne singing. Evangelists desiring a fine oloist to accompany them will do well to orrespond with him at 9 Lane Place, Chicago, l.

Cecil J. Armstrong, the minister of the hurch at Edgerton and Grayson, Mo., recent' resigned there in order to attend Kentucky niversity. In 1896 he graduated in the ollege of the Bible, but now desires to ıke a more extended course. Any congregaon in reach of Lexington, Ky., desiring a reacher might secure one by addressieg Bro. rmstrong at once.

I. N. Hale writes us from Monroe, Wis., that Eld. J. H. Berkley, formerly a "Christian Adventist," together with his family, all of that city, have taken membership in the Christian Church at that place. Bro. Berkley has an extensive reputatin as a lecturer on temperance, having lectured in many states east and west and is said to be a man of great efficiency and usefulness. We trust that his field of usefulness will be greatly enlarged by taking his stand with us for Christ and for primitive Christianity.

J. H. MacNeill, pastor of the church at Rushville, Ind., recently made formal announcement of his resignation, which had already been tendered the official board. The announcement was the occasion of deep sorrow to the audience, in whose esteem Bro. MacNeill occupied a high place. His pastorate began in March, 1888, and since then 800 new members have been added to the church. His great work was the erection of the magnificent new $30,000 church house on North Main Street, and the $4,000 parsonage adjoining. His untiring zeal for the welfare of his flock is known to all.

The writer was called to Albany, Ore., on the 19th of this month to baptize Rev. C. M. Lane who, for the last three years, has been preaching for the Cumberland Presbyterians. Bro. Lane had "become tired of creed bondage and desired the liberty of Christ," as he expressed it, and is now happy in a service as full and free as the New Testament allows. Bro. Lane is a man of good ability and pleasing manner. He is a graduate of the Southwestern Presbyterian and the Vanderbilt Universities, 38 years old, married and has held pastorates in San Francisco, Oakland and Middletown, Cal., before coming to Oregon. The Christian Church in Albany was without a pastor and will be served by Bro. Lane for sometime.

MORTON D. ROSE.

Ex-Governer Mathews died at the home of Isaac Meharry, ten miles north of Crawfordsville, Ind., Sunday, Aug. 28th, from a stroke of paralysis received while addressing the old settlers of Montgomery county during the week. He was elected governor of Indiana in 1892.

B. B. Tyler, who has been spending the summer with the church at Colorado Springs, will leave that city on the 12th prox. to hold a meeting in the Broadway Church, Lexington, Ky. From there he will go the Chattanooga Convention, and thence return for awhile longer to Colorado Springs, where he is filling a temporary engagement. He reports the work there as in excellent condition, the audiences testing the capacity of the house, and the free-will offerings of the people more than meeting the current expenses. The outlook, he says, is full of ecouragement.

The Bulletin, Kent Ohio, August 13th, announces the resignation of of F. M. Green as pastor of the Christian Church at that place. He has been the preacher of the church at Kent for two years. He is also well known to the entire brotherhood as a vigorous writer for our church papers and an author. The Kent Bulletin says: "Rev. Green is a faithful and ardent worker in the Christian cause and the members of his congregation, as well as a wide acquaintance outside of the church have learned to love and respect him as a Christian man, an eloquent preacher and a genial gentleman." After a few weeks' rest Bro. Green will be available for duty elsewhere. Any church in need of a strong, efficient preacher should not lose this opportunity of securing the man they need.

J. W. Allen, of Cleveland, O., who was pastor of the West Side Church for thirteen years, and saw it grow from a small body of believers into the grand company that now compose its membership, came to preach for us last Lord's day, on his annual visit to the church he loves so well. This visit, like all previous ones, was an occasion of great joy to all the members, who fairly took Bro. Allen in their arms, so happy were they to meet again their former pastor and beloved friend. And Bro. Allen fully reciprocated this generous and true expression of love and esteem on the part of the members. He spoke in glowing terms of the solidarity of the West Side Church; its marvelous growth and perfect unity of its members, and the cordial and undivided support which they are giving their pastor. Its future, he declared, was "brighter than ever." Indeed, we have been wonderfully blessed. In the past seven months there has been added to the church ninety-two earnest, active and consecrated members, and a special service of thanksgiving will be held when the number of additions shall have reached one hundred. The Lord has helped us beyond our faith. The magnitude of our audiences and the healthy state of our finances are things which our fondest expectations hardly hoped to realize. BRUCE BROWN,

Pastor West Side Church, Chicago.

A. W. Jomes, wants to correspond with a church needing a preacher. His last pastorate was at Ardmore, I. T., where he added 85 members to the church and where he may be addressed.

Dr. Andrews, the new school superintendent of Chicago, is reported as in favor of the annexation of the Philippines, and has advised the teaching of the Spanish language in the Chicago schools.

CHANGES.

J. H. Stove, White House to Lyons, Ohio.
W. T. Maupin, Perry, Iowa, to Omaha, Neb.
C. C. Rawlison, Cedar Rapids to Marshalltown, Ia.
R. L. Stanley, Beaumont, Kan., to Princeton, Mo.
C. S. Weaver, Brook, Ind., to Martinton, Ill.
F. B. Elmore, Rich Hill to Appleton City, Mo.
J. W. Elliott, Harvard, Neb., to Cherokee, Iowa.
E. G. Rees, Diller to Filley, Neb.
W. F. Richardson, Macatawa, Mich., to 1016 Lydia Ave., Kansas City, Mo.
R. A. Burriss, Bowmanville to Port Arthur, Ontario.

Correspondence.

English Topics.

ENGLAND AND RUSSIA—WAR COMING.

Ever since I traveled in Russia I have loved the Russian people as sincerely as I have hated the Russian Government. That bureaucratic despotism is the most brutal form of tyranny now existing on earth, excepting only the rule of the infernal Sultan of Turkey, with whom your American ambassador was not ashamed to dine, according to the reports current and uncontradicted in the dreadful days of the Armenian massacres. The Sultan and the Tsar answer very well indeed, for all present practical purposes, to the two Beasts of the Revelation. Of course this is not meant, on my part, by any means as a theological interpretation, but it is a sensible and intelligible political one. The young Tsar of Russia is doubtless a very amiable fellow, but unfortunately, he is but a gilded figurehead to the hideous battering ram] which is ere long to be sent crashing with fatal impetus into the fabric of modern civilization. For the last two years the chief agents of the Tsar, Muravieff and Pavloff, have been lying and cheating in their diplomatic dealings to an extent which is perhaps only fully known by Lord Salisbury. First about Armenia, then about Crete, then about Greece, and now about China these two Muscovite statesmen have been forging unbroken chains of falsehood. In every case they have stolen a march on Europe, and they have specially aimed at deceiving England. I wish the whole world could be made to understand that there is at this moment arising in Britain a quiet, suppressed but intense feeling of anger at the astounding and cold-blooded treachery of the Russian Government in all its dealings with the international difficulties. Lest it may be imagined that I am writing from the standpoint of individual imagination, I will right here quote the words written in an English paper this week by one of the most accomplished men I know. This gentleman says, "Russia is playing so *fast* a game in China, that if she continues it, it will inevitably land her in war with us, and no personal affection of princes will avert it. If Lord Salisbury ventures now to retract his stated policy in the Lords, in his August speech, he will find the solid earth of confidence is a mere shivering morass into which he and his government will be gravitated and be swallowed up by public anger. There is no capitulation or going back now or ever any more possible. And if we are to have war it could hardly come at a better time. In ten years it could hardly come at a worse. Give Russia time to make Port Arthur another Kronstadt, and then whistle to the winds for any success ahead and they will not hear us! The true diplomacy would have been a working policy *with* Russia, but her Muravieffs and Pavloffs will respect no treaties and are bound by no promises. That line of diplomatic life is certain, and that is that Russia will never go to war with England unless she can rely on the co-operation of France and the neutrality of Germany. Unfortunately, she is fairly sure of both. I fear that at no remote date war will ensue, that it will involve all the great nations of Europe, that it will be the final crash so long expected, out of which a totally new state of things will emerge, and that the present discipline of America in her war with Spain is a Providentail warning to your great nation to get ready for the tremendous duty which will devolve on your grand republic. I fully credit the whispers that are mooted privately about, according to which it is hinted that Lord Salisbury knows too well that a great coalition is being steadily plotted by the carnal military despotisms of the continent against England, who is execrated as the representative in Europe of democratic right and civil and religious freedom. The time is approaching when the world's only hope will be in something more than a sentimental alliance between Britain and America.

PASTOR RAPKIN'S NEW BOOK.

I willingly pass on to a more peaceful topic. Our indefatigable evangelist at Margate is bravely pursuing his remarkable work. His nightly open-air preaching on the beautiful beach is again bringing friends into sympathy with our cause. He has been baptizing, as in previous summers, persons who, visiting Margate from London and elsewhere, have stopped to listen to him on the shore and have learned the truth there under the sky which they had never heard before. I have just received from Bro. George Rapkin a copy of a new book from his pen, entitled "Baptsm." It is a small work of only 174 octavo pages, but as a simple, lucid, scriptural and popularly written treatise it is a masterpiece. For Baptists who are in a muddle, as most Baptists are whom I ever heard of, and for those who are entirely opposed to the New Testament truth on the subject, this is the ideal volume, although it is not intended by the author for students who need a learned and exhaustive presentation. There is a feature in the book which makes it exceedingly pleasant and enlightening to read. In every case the texts which are referred to are fully quoted. How very desirable this is, and how few authors help their busy readers in this way! Generally we are pointed to a crowd of texts which few people have time to hunt up. But in Rapkin's pages all the verses of the New Testament on baptism are displayed before the reader's eyes as they come along in the easy and triumphat argument. The only blemish in the book is the lapse of the printer into an occasional curious misprint. You have perhaps a plethora of books on this subject in America, but if any are looking for something fresh to put into the hands of seekers after truth, they might do worse than to secure this work. It will be mailed direct to American friends from Pastor G. Rapkin, Myrtle Villas, Margate, free for 50 cents a copy, bound in cloth, or 40 cents in paper, the cash to be sent in stamps.

TOO MUCH GRANDFATHER.

The holiday vacation still proceeds with its "usual severity." Our churches are greatly depleted in the towns inland, though great congregations are assembling to rejoice the hearts of ministers of seaside churches. The English people are in one respect admirably faithful. They certainly transport their religion with them wherever they go. At Cromer, on the lovely Norfolk shore, I found that the churches and chapels of the little town were crowded out, and at the parish church, a grand and stately building, the vicar had to arrange for overflow meetings in the town hall. Moreover, I found that notwithstanding the attractions of a beach and cliff, moors and woods, were naturally supreme in their claims on people seeking well-earned rest and recreation, yet week-evening meetings were excellently attended. I have always found it so. Our Christian people for the most part act up to their profession, with all their faults. The salt has not lost its savor in dear old England. One thing at our English resorts, or at very many of them, I may mention, from which you Americans are free. It is very tiring and embarrassing in this country to be unable anywhere to get away from one's great-grandfather, who is of course an interesting old fellow, but is rather a tedious drag when we want to ramble about, forgetting the cares of the dead past and seeking only to enjoy life for a brief spell, on the "carpe diem" principle of old Horace. At almost any of our nicest watering-places we have history flung at us in a heavy volume at every corner. For instance now, take a trip to dear old Whitby, on the lovely Yorkshire Coast. Can anything be more charming? Hardly. But you soon have to learn that the history of Whitby goes back to Roman days and to 547, when Ina landed at Flamborough and founded the Saxon kingdom of Northumbria. I am very glad that it happened, but yet I think it is a little bit boring to have to venerate these musty worthy ancestors when we just want to stop our "thinkers" for a few dreamy hours, while we listen to what the wild waves are saying. However, as I mentioned Whitby, I may say that it lies on a coast which would charm any strolling American friends. The fame of the quaint little fishing town is intimately connected with its abbey and its famous abbess, Hilda. About 656 Hilda, accompanied by the king's daughter Aeflida, who afterwards succeeded her, founded a religious settlement on the East Cliff. The church was probably formed of the trunks of trees split in two, having side lights partially secured by light lattices, or boards pierced with holes. The building would be thatched with rushes. Around it were huts of the simplest character in which the nuns resided. There now! That is how religion grew up in Britain more than a thousand years ago. And that is how we poor weary Britishers have to tire ourselves out in the perpetual study of history when we go off for a holiday. Oh, what perambulating encyclopædias we ought to be! It would send Mark Twain silly. Perhaps that is why he keeps far away from our shores. Now, I envy you Americans your country for holiday making, for the most comfortable feature about the United States is that they have no history, and it will take them over a millennium longer to grow one such as we have on this side. Nobody in America has a great grandfather. What a blessed negation of Providence! I notice, Bro. Garrison, that you do not have to "get up" anything about your beautiful Macatawa, for it is not burdened with history, chronology, mythology, archæology and ecclesiology! I wish I could come there to get away for a season from too many great-grandfathers. Be very thankful for your escape—and *carpe diem!*

W. DURBAN.

43 *Park Rd., South Tottenham, London, August* 11, 1898.

Wheeling Through England.

VII.

A visit to Hawarden has two objects. One is to see the place where Gladstone lived; the other is to talk with the villagers and get their view of the great man who lived in their midst. The first-named object is easy enough of accomplishment. The park and grounds about Hawarden Castle, which was Mr. Gladstone's home, are open to the public at all reasonable hours. The grounds are of considerable extent and the mansion is such as was appropriate for the home of the great commoner—beautiful and dignified, but not magnificent like the castle of a lord. Even more interesting than the ride through the park were the conversations which we had with the people of the village, but the latter required more tact. One feels it in the air, somehow, that the name of Gladstone is not one to be lightly spoken in the presence of these people who knew and loved him. To ask them bluntly what they thought of Gladstone would be like abruptly asking a man what he thinks of his father and wife. There is a reverence and affection in the attitude of the villagers of Hawarden toward Gladstone for which it is difficult to find a parallel. One would be convinced here, if he were not elsewhere, of the goodness as well as the greatness of the man. We found accommodations for the night at the humble cottage of a dear old lady whose daughter, as we afterwards learned, was in service in the Gladstone household. Gradually, as she became convinced of the genuineness of my admiration for "the old gentleman," as he was called in the village, she spoke more and more freely of his character, his many acts of kindness to the poor of the village and to the servants of his own household. "He was such a good man," she said, "and he had so much good-will for everybody that it made us all kinder to be near him and to see him once in a while." Tears came to her eyes

! the last time she had seen him,
ıe a copy of his last picture.
ıne died, the world placed a
the grave of the statesman and
ıt the villagers of Hawarden are
the loss of a father.

---

f an hour's run from Hawarden
To the left we get an occasional
"Sands o' Dee," the estuary
ee, with its treacherous quick-
l lady told us that she almost
husband there, and her tone
ıly that the experience of later
her to be more careful with her
ıbands, and not to lose them so
ıester is a charming city, which
aintness of mediævalism with
ern virtues of cleanliness and
ipal respectability. The secret
tion lies in the fact that every-
been retained with judicious
ıd repairs, and that the new
ə been built in architectural
the old. After a stop of a few
which is utilized in walking
l the city on the top of the old
ide on a few miles into Berkin-
a ferryboat takes us across the
erpool. Just six weeks have
we left Liverpool in a rain-
distance, as we have made it,
to Liverpool by way of Dover
d, is one thousand six hundred
miles.

---

early that night in Liverpool,
an early start for a day's run
ry us into the heart of the
District, and straightway fall to
ıhimmering lakes, of rivulets
ı mountain sides and of frothy
ıe waterfalls, even in the
ə more noisy than a dream has
, and gradually, but all to soon,
stead of a visionary Lodore, I
a very real and very wet Liver-
Liverpool tin roof. It proved
tent sort of rain, the conscien-
working kind which begins its
ore sunrise and continues until
whistle blows. Obviously it was
cling; neither was it much of a
Liverpool to advantage, except
which is indoors. Accordingly
day visiting art galleries and
haps on the whole the most
e of the day was a giddy set of
church steeple or in the tower
all, which played the gay and
ich is generally designated by
the words which accompany it,
d mother were Irish." So the
ıe next day was fine, and with a
ks it was an easy ride of ninety
erpool to Bowness-on-Winder-
twilight again when we rode
of Windermere, and the scene
ace in our gallery of English
.

---

tineau, who lived for several
gion, described the climate of
ct as "moist, but not damp."
t my experience of three days
several years I would say that
rict is neither moist nor damp,
t! Perhaps this generalization
hasty, for our first day in Lake-
of the sort unparallaled in the
oldest inhabitant. A steady
in, punctuated and emphasized
lightning, left us little chance
land of Wordsworth that day,
lendid opportunity to read his
this preparation we were the
appropriate, for whenever the delight of the traveler rises above the point of mere incoherent exclamation ("Oh my!" "Ah!" "Um-m-m") it is sure to run in the channel which Wordsworth has made for it. Southey and Coleridge come to mind occasionally, but Wordsworth is never absent. He has become an element in the scenery.

The road from Bowness to Keswick, through Windermere, Ambleside, Rydal and Grasmere, is the north and south diameter of the Lake District. The total distance is little more than twenty miles, but it furnishes ground for one full day of riding, with occasional digressions on foot into the mountains at either side. Late in the afternoon, as our road is winding between the foot of Helvellyn and the edge of Thirlmere, it occurs to us that this mountain, the second in height in England, ought to be ascended to obtain a comprehensive view of the district. A stony bridlepath leads to the top, but the recent rains have transformed this into the bed of a mountain "beck," and it is more convenient to pick a path for ourselves up the green and grassy slope. It is an easier ascent than Snowden, and though it is not as high by six hundred feet, the view from the top is perhaps even more beautiful. It was dark when we rode into Keswick that Saturday night, and there we stopped over Sunday.

W. E. GARRISON.

Keswick.

Chicago Letter.

In my last letter I referred to the Tidewater convention, which was royally entertained at Mathews, where our energetic, wide-awake Bro. Walker labors. Mathews county, Va., is so indented by inlets from the Chesapeake Bay that I was informed a stob could not be driven in the ground anywhere in the county more than two miles from tidewater. Many of our best workers in the churches on the Atlantic Seaboard have gone from this county. Here J. Z. Tyler's noble soul-mate was reared. After meeting Sister Tyler's excellent mother and hospitable sisters, I can truthfully say she is a fair sample of the entire family. Here Captain Bohanan, of Baltimore, fished, plowed corn, ate fried chicken and grew to man's estate. I was entertained at the home of Judge Garnet, where I saw a watermill with a wheel which turned one way when the tide was coming in and in the opposite direction when the tide was going out. The foundation of this mill was laid before the Revolutionary War. The old colonial house, built facing the water and surrounded by century-old trees, makes a delightful summer resort. Here the Judge, Sister Garnet and their manly Christian sons regale their guests with oysters and chickens of their own raising. They keep carriages for driving through the pines, and a fine sailboat for sailing on the water. I commend this quiet retreat to those who contemplate spending a few weeks on the Bay Shore. Here I found Bro. Bagby, who writes our Washington letter. He will write up the convention.

***

No one of our preachers on the Atlantic Seaboard is working more heroically to advance the cause of primitive Christianity in that important section of our wide domain than Peter Ainslie, who in addition to the duties of a city pastorate edits the Christian Tribune. Bro. Ainslee, like the great poet Wordsworth in his day, has a sister to whom he owes much. It was my pleasure to spend a day and night on the Chesapeake Bay in the company of this pure-minded, noble-hearted brother. His brother preachers, who have known him from early boyhood, tell me that Peter Ainslie's thoughts were as pure and his language as very instructive one to me. The thousands of square miles of shoal water is the secret of its great fisheries. Oyster tonging, crab catching, poggy seining, herring netting and shad fishing are all carried on on a scale which is simply stupendous, yielding millions of dollars to the dwellers on the bay. At one landing, just as the sun was setting, I saw fourteen large sailboats, each having a crew of sixteen or more men, and all loaded with fish (I was told several thousand in each boat) from which oil could be made for the railroads and fertilizing for the farms. I did not realize before how many millions of fish were used every year in our country for fertilizing.

***

After several weeks of very hard work, speaking two or three times each day, I came direct to Chicago from Baltimore over the Baltimore and Ohio. I have hardly ever had a more delightful trip from Washington to Pittsburg over this line. At Harper's Ferry I saw many historic landmarks. At Conneccsville I saw miles of coke-ovens; at Braddock, where the memorable defeat of the general of that name occurred, are the great Carnegie iron foundries where several hundred tons of iron are turned out daily. From Harper's Ferry the road gradually ascends the mountains, keeping close to the Potomac River. Beyond Cumberland you plunge through a long tunnel and descend the Alleghenies, following the line of Washington's march along the Youghiogheny River. I paid my fare over the Baltimore and Ohio, and these lines are not written to advertise that road, but I want my friends to enjoy the rare scenic beauty and exhilarating mountain air which I enjoyed on this trip. I reached Chicago after a twenty-four hours' run, really rested.

***

The churches of Chicago usually take a rest during the summer, while his Satanic Majesty is especially active. This summer, however, most of our churches have been pressing forward in the midst of difficulties, which only workers in a great city like Chicago can appreciate. Our evangelist, E. W. Darst, has gone to Vermont for a brief vacation, but before going he planted a new congregation at Irving Park, a suburb of Chicago. The writer spoke for them last Lord's day. They have a nucleus of seventy-five good members, many of whom Bro. Darst has recently baptized. I have never known a new work in Chicago to start out under more hopeful conditions. It is an excellent commentary on the importance of city evangelization. Young Bro. Morrison is holding the fort at Monroe Street. Every one speaks highly of him and his work. His brother, Charles Morrison, will become the permanent pastor of the congregation in September. The congregation at Monroe Street are most excellent people, and with such a leader as Bro. Morrison they have a bright future before them. We regret to learn that Bro. N. S. Haynes has been ill. After a number of years of most faithful service he has resigned his pastorate at Englewood. The Englewood church has a number of noble, consecrated members. Bro. Haynes is not only a strong preacher, but also an efficient Bible teacher, and his congregation, fed upon the truth as it is in Christ Jesus our Lord, has grown strong in word and doctrine. A large number of our preachers have been attending the summer school of the University of Chicago. I had hoped to give their names in this letter. Perhaps the head of the Disciples' Divinity House will furnish me the names of those who are in residence, for a future letter. Bro. F. N. Calvin and family, of Waco, Tex.; Bro. Ellis and wife, of Nashville, Tenn.; Bro. Jno. Darsie, and many others have spent part of their vacation in Chicago.

***

lecturer was Bro. J. H. O. Smith. The previous lecturers have been representatives of various religious bodies. Bro. Smith's lecture was not only scriptural, but was also a fine literary production. It is my understanding that this series of lectures are to be published. However, I cannot pass it by without a brief notice. The three points the lecturer was asked to consider were—1. "Is Christian union practical?" 2. "If so, in what form?" 3. "What is the attitude of your denomination toward Christian union?" The paper dealt with Christian union as a union of persons rather than of denominations. First, he maintained the practicability of Christian union. This was illustrated by the history of the early church. Second, as to form, "Not a union of denominations, not a compromise, not an ironclad ecclesiasticism, not uniformity of opinion, but unity in Christ." Here the scriptural meaning of the phrase, "In Christ," was clearly brought out. As our readers are familiar with the attitude of our brotherhood on the question which has been so fully discussed under the auspices of the Disciples' Club, they will appreciate the thorough treatment Bro. Smith gives the subject when this lecture is published. In closing I shall give a brief and inadequate statement of the year's work at the People's Institute, under the leadership of J. H. O. Smith and his helpmeet.

The Union Christian Church was organized a year ago with two hundred and eighteen members. During the year the membership has grown to six hundred and fifty. The Sunday-school has grown from three hundred and seventeen to seven hundred and eighty-three in attendance, with an enrollment of one thousand. The three Endeavor Societies from 165 to 650; the C. W. B. M. from fifteen to seventy-five; King's Daughters from twenty to fifty-five; Ladies' Union from twenty-five to forty-eight, etc., etc. These facts speak volumes. They mean unceasing work and strong leadership. This is a great work to be accomplished in such a great city as Chicago.

C. A. YOUNG.

Washington (D. C.) Letter.

Since the war before the late war our cause in old Virginia has not made very rapid progress.

There has been a decided growth in Richmond and in several of the cities in the Shenandoah Valley and the southwestern section of the state. In the country districts of the Tidewater and Piedmont sections we have made but little advance. The work in the latter district for some years has been especially discouraging.

The annual Piedmont convention was slimly attended, but little money was raised and the results of co-operative work meager. Those who foresaw the possible disintegration of the Piedmont co-operation, which had once been the pride of the state, decided upon an advanced movement. This year the Piedmont Assembly was inaugurated. We believe it will mark the beginning of a new era in the history of the Disciples of the state. The site chosen is an ideal one.

In a beautiful oak grove, about one mile from Gordonsville, upon a slope commanding a magnificent view of the Blue Ridge Mountains, the tabernacle with a seating capacity of 1,500 has been built. The meetings this year were eminently successful. Some days as many as 2,000 people were upon the grounds.

The sons of Old Virginia are loyal to their mother and usually come home for their summer vacation.

The committee drafted these into service. Among the preachers present were L. A. Cutler, Z. P. Richardson and Richard Bagby, of Louisia; H. C. Garrison and L. M. Omer, of Richmond; Preston Cave, of Hagerstown, Md.; F. D. Power and E. B. Bagby, of Washington, D. C.; W. J. Cocke, of Uniontown, Pa.; Peter Ainslie, of Baltimore, Md.; W. H. Book and J. C. Dickson, of Clifton Forge; C. A. Young, of Chicago, Ill.; P. B. Hall, of Orange, Cal.; S. R. Maxwell, of Rockville, Md.; M. A. Stickley, of Strasburg; L. W. Cave, of Spotsylvania; E. R. Perry, of Virginia.

No one need doubt the loyalty of these brethren to the old plea. It seems that nearly every one who came was loaded with a sermon on Christian Union. After having three addresses on this theme the committee requested every speaker to choose some other subject.

The week following the Piedmont Assembly the brethren of the Tidewater district met in their thirty-second annual convention. One hundred delegates and visitors from the various churches were present. The 28 churches in this district report a membership of 4,370, additions during the year, 358, and $17,881 raised for all purposes. The missions in West Point and Fredericksburg were assisted. Special attention will be given to the building up of the church in the latter place during the coming year.

One of the most interesting sessions of the convention was that given to the ladies of the C. W. B. M. The reports show 21 auxiliaries with 450 members and $536.65 raised.

Mathews is not one of the largest counties in the state, but it is certainly one of the most delightful. There is not a farm in the county more than two miles from salt water. Yet in spite of this Mathews is known as a dry county. Some ten years ago the good people made an ffort to expel the saloon. There were 600 ballots cast and of these only 55 were for abolishing the saloon. Two years another effort was made and a glorious victory resulted. Judge G. T. Garnett, who entertains so royally all visiting preachers at his palatial home, Poplar Grove, gave during the convention an interesting account of this election. Both sides knew that the issue hinged upon the vote of the colored people. The negro preachers were a unit against the saloon and this meant much. There lived upon Judge Garnett's farm a colored man, Robert Brooks by name, who wielded considerable influence. The judge argued with him by the hour, but could not convince him that it was his duty to come out on the side of the temperance people. The negroes had arranged an anti-saloon meeting in White's Neck. The baser element of that section began to collect bad eggs and other missiles and said they would break up the meeting. The officers of the Westville Christian church offered their colored brethren the use of their house of worship for their rally.

At this meeting the negro leaders arranged an ingenious scheme to capture Bob Brooks. The meeting was called to order and the leader called Bob Brooks to offer the opening prayer. That settled it. Of course Bro. Brooks could not pray for the triumph of liquor, but must beseech the throne of grace for its suppression. Then this brother in black knew no better than to vote as he prayed, and many followed his example. At his precinct it was three o'clock before a vote for license was cast. The county went dry by a vote of 761. After this triumph for temperance the key of the old jail did not turn in its lock for three years. Eight out of every ten boys in the county under twenty-one never saw a drop of liquor sold.

W. G. Walker, the pastor of Westville church, has been holding tent meetings in a section of Mathews county where there is no Christian church. Twenty-four persons had been baptized at last report and the meeting continues. A new church will be the result of this meeting.

This has not been a favorable season for tent meetings. In Baltimore, W. J. Wright has been greatly hindered by thunder storms that have been of almostly nightly occurrence. Some converts have been gained, much good seed sown and the work goes on.

EDWARD B. BAGBY.

Texas Letter.

The liquor question is a living question, and good people are always anxious to know the facts about it. The department of labor at Washington has been investigating it, with some interesting results. We learn that distilled spirits are decreasing and that malt liquors are increasing. The change in the per capita consumption for the 16 years between 1880 and 1896 in spirits was from 1.27 gallons to 1 gallon; in wines from 0.56 of a gallon to 0.16 of a gallon; and in malt liquors from 8.26 gallons to 15.16 gallons. This shows that the drinking of distilled spirits fell off one-fifth in sixteen years; and that of wines about one-half; while the increase in the consumption of beer almost doubled. The production of spirits decreased about 1,400,000 gallons, notwithstanding the population increased 20,000,000, while the production of beer increased 175 per cent. Five-sevenths of the manufacturers take into consideration the drinking habit when employing men, and one-half require their men to abstain entirely during working hours. Night work and exposure does not increase the inclination to drink. This is quite opposite the popular opinion. But irregularity of work does increase the drinking habit. The custom of treating is the source of much if not most of the drinking. Thus the social instincts, a thing most harmless and desirable in itsself, is at the bottom of most of this wickedness and waste.

R. E. Grabel leaves Mesquite and takes up the work at Big Springs. Grabel is a fine fellow, but he lacks a female assistant in his work.

M. L. Hoblit, our Mexican missionary, was married to Miss Orpha Bennett, of Keokuk, Iowa, on August 18. Now we may expect better work down in the the land of the Montezumas.

A. S. Henry, financial agent for Add-Ran University, is an unqualified success. For example, he went to Midland, one of our far-West churches, a few days since, and raised $3,000! He then turns prophet and says, "You need not be surprised if this church gives $10,000 to Add-Ran within the next five years." But it must not be forgotten that he could not have done this but for the assistance of that splendid church and its brilliant pastor.

R. R. Hamlin, of Palestine, has done more fine work at Martindale. There were 52 additions; 37 baptisms. Two of them were husband and wife, aged 76 and 67. As the husband came up out of the water he said, "Thank God, it is done; but I wish it had been done forty years ago." Money was raised for a pastor half the time.

B. F. Wilson changes from Sherman to Plano. And on the threshold of his ministry the people are talking new house. That is good, for they need it.

J. B. Faulkner and J. G. Huddleston have held a good meeting at Johnson, with 22 additions. Three years ago we had almost nothing here, but now we have 100 members, and a controlling influence in the community.

J. B. Boen held a meeting last year in Meridian, a good railroad town. They have had no regular preaching, and yet they have built a tabernacle with a seating capacity of 1,000; and best of all, *every member is an active worker in the church.*

Granville Jones, our pastor at Midland, has organized a church at Granado. It was a new place and he preached several days before giving an invitation. But on Sunday morning he extended an invitation to all who desired to become members of a church modeled after the New Testament example, and to be known as "Christians," when 33 people responded. They were organized, and the meeting continued with 20 more additions. A lot was secured and more than one-third of the money for a house was raised. Rosenberg, El Campo and Edna are good towns, and it is hoped that they will also have congregations and houses soon.

ith's meeting at Farney closed with ıs. It was a success. The work at ·tant point is doing well in the hands McClendon.

Lingan reports successful work at ·. A sure evidence of this is seen ; that they expect to have a new house ıonths.

ored brethren have just closed their nvention in this city. The attend- small, and the outlook is not en-·.

M. M. DAVIS.

Oak St., Dallas, Texas.

Chautauqua Notes.

əting of ministers of all denomina- əld daily in Methodist headquarters, ¢periences, hopes and fears of a class g men, responsible for so much as ı are, to the people, makes the hour ·resting. One from the West ac- : an improvement in the schools of by teaching more of God's Word, ing for explanations of truth, Christ apostles, while a Baptist felt there thing lacking in the theological train- queried if the theological mysteries ·ful. He could not help but say, there of Scripture teaching. The modern ·angelizing, by great men of reputa- . large pay, was objected to by a t brother, and it was repeated by :hat the converts did not stay with the . A Presbyterian was deploring the family worship, and reading of the ·s, while another excused his people round that workingmen in cities left ly in the morning. One old brother nen should not be preached straight ı, but that the Word said there was a people should know it, ere it was too ıother minister laid aside all papers ; in Sunday-school class and took the :o the school Sunday morning and ·om it with gratifying results.

neetings are very interesting and the ıt feeling of unrest in the religious uses anxiety, while all stand firmly ırn to the true teachings of the Bible. I. L. Willett's straightforward work ›rought many charms, and his making truths to explain themselves from all s of prophecy, and the explanations ›istles, as helpers to those who had ıear to the life and times of Christ; ich was said in the most happy way, the Professor is master, make him an ›dged power in the class-room and on um. Bro. Sweeney had profound at- ·n Sunday evening, and the Monday ·as popular, gainingen thusiastic ap- John Miller spoke to the Grangers on ·, and in discussing his subject took ins in his masterly speech to show that ed States is sufficient unto itself for all a nation, and to hold her own place lently in the world. Dr. Kellogg, of reek, Mich., spoke yesterday on liv- ›ating food, the health of man, etc. ry of vegetables and fruits, to beat the ı, was well given. And so we have all discussed here which are healpful, and y strong spirit of union and strength ıutauqua go forward.

ost good can be accomplished here ıllest expense of money of any place :ca, and so we all rejoice in the help ›mes in to pay for the headquarters. of thinking people come here, and and ask to know us. Of the hundreds ; registered I note a few: Bro. J. W. and wife, Bro. Walker and wife, Bro. and his mother, from Kentucky; Bro. and wife, from California; the Blanks ·rom Texas; L. Darsie and family, Bro. ınd family and Bro. L. C. McPher- v York; Bro. Gable and family, from d, Mrs. Mary Cain and daughter and ·hillips and family, from New Castle, Pa. Officers at the association were all re-elected. There is still another week of the Assembly.

W. J. FORD.

Chautauqua, N. Y., Aug. 17, 1898.

A Farmer Among the Turks and Russians.

During the most frienzied fury and wildest excitement of Turkish atrocities and Armenian massacres, we made a journey through the Turkish and Russian Empires. In 100 days our passport was in greater demand than in twenty years of travel in almost every other part of the world. Before getting through Servia, Bulgaria and Roumelia, it had been *vised* three times in twenty-four hours, and when we had been aroused at various hours of the night to answer, "Whence? What? Who? Whither?" During the second night we were the only occupent of a *coupe* of an European car. About midnight we were suddenly aroused from a profound slumber as the train crossed over into the Turkish frontier. We were dazed by Oriental colors and the glitter of carbines, pistols and swords! Policeman, soldiers and censors blustering in unknown tongues and pulling at our baggage. They seized about all the books we had and took them to another part of the train. One book in the shuffle and scramble we managed to conceal, presented by Spencer Trask, of New York. The title was in big, red letters, "Horrors of Armenia!" by an Eyewitness. This book was highly prized, but we sacrificed it on the altar of prudence, by backing up to an open window and dropping it from under our coatskirt into the darkness outside the rushing train. All our other valuable books on Turkey the Government of the Sultan will probably keep until a great fleet of our battleships some day steams into the Dardenelles and demands indemnity for American losses!

In the early gloaming of nearly every morning we were in Constantinople several Armenians would be found hanging on improvised scaffolds on a pontoon bridge near our hotel. A few days after we left this hotel, 6,000 Armenians were murdered in the streets around it. Imagine a farmer sleeping in the fourth story and suddenly aroused about 2 o'clock, the still hour of the night, when all sounds are supposed to be hushed, to hear 10,000 dogs barking at once, on every key of the chromatic scale, and carrying all the parts! Leaping from our slumber and couch in confused consternation and rushing to an open window to see whether the city is on fire or whether it is being stormed by the combined powers of Christendom! Amid such a babel of human tongues by day, there was some satisfaction in finding all this army of dogs to be barking in English! Only man has had a Babylonian tongue-tangle. Every other genus of sentient life speaks the same language the world over.

While gazing from that window we thought of a night just 2,236 years preceding, when Philip, of Macedon, was beseiging old Byzantium. While he was secretly tunneling under the walls, a light in the form of a crescent suddenly appeared in the heavens, which awakened the barking Byzantium dogs, and thus the garrison was aroused and the city saved. Since then dogs have had the right-of-way by the Golden Horn and Bosporus, and the crescent on Saracen banners has floated for 455 years in Europe, Asia and Africa.

A few of the visions of life linger in memory like a renaissance or new birth. A solitary midnight stroll through the Yosemite, a day-dawn on Kinchinjunga and Mount Everest, a sunrise on Athens and the Bay of Salamis, a sunset on the Vega of Andalusia, seen from the tower of Alhambra, the Bay of Rio Janiero from the summit of Corkovada, the midnight sun from the North Cape, and our first view of Jerusalem. But for the royal richness and marvelous blending of colors, there is nothing on earth comparable to the Yellowstone Chasm and a sunset view of Constantinople from the summit of the Galata Tower. The majesty of Michael Angelo, the delicacy of Raphael, the gorgeous glow of Rubens and the sombre shadows of Rembrandt are seen at every angle from the top of this ancient tower. If all the colors of the artists of all the ages were spread upon one canvas, it could not exceed the splendor which Europe, Asia, nature, art, land and sea have here artlessly combined in one picture. The purple domes and white minarets of a multitude of mosques, the dark green of majestic cypress trees in a hundred cemeteries of six cities, red-tiled roofs toned by weeks, months, years or centuries into every conceivable shade; Jewish synagogues, Greek and Armenian churches, palaces, barracks, homes and harems of a score of nationalities; the sea of Marmora, the Bosporus and Golden Horn, on which float the many-colored flags and ships of the world, all softened, blended and glorified in the crimson sheen of the setting sun.

Over all hangs the pall of Mohammedanism, and back of it is the horrid history of Turkish terror and astrocities. But in front of this black background of history will ever flit and float two fair figures in white, like angels of mercy—Florence Nightingale and Clara Barton. In Scutari, across the Bosporus, in the edge of Asia, is a vast lemon-colored hospital with 1,000 windows gleaming in the face of the setting sun, bearing the name of the heroine of the Crimea. Here she wove the golden halo that will ever surround her musical, magical name, in softening the asperities of war, alleviating the suffering and cheering the drooping spirits of wounded heroes. Here the wounded, grateful, chivalric spirits kissed her shadow upon the wall as she ministered to them by day and by night. On the opposite shore we met the brave, radiant, heroic Clara Barton, the story of whose life in our Civil War and the Franco-Prussian War, sounds like romance. The dawning rays of a life beyond are gleaming above her brow, but the stranger would never supect that she has passed far beyond her threescore and ten. It required more real couraged to do what these two women have accomplished than it did for the Earl of Cardigan to lead the charge of the "noble six hundred" into the valley of death at Balaclava.

We were with Miss Barton and her financial agent, Mr. George H. Pullman, a short time while they were distributing $100,000 among the bleeding, starving Armenians, a few thousand of which were raised through the St. Louis Christian Advocate. Then we entered the Russian Empire, traveling about 8,000 miles in unbeaten paths, around the Black Sea, over the battlefields of the Crimea, to the old city of Tiflis, North of Mt. Ararat, across the Caucasus with horses, over the Caspian Sea and 2,000 miles up the Volga. We visited the Pan-Russian Exposition at Nishni Novgorod, traveled over a part of the great Siberian Railroad, which will be completed in the early years of the coming century, about 7,000 miles in length, and will connect Petersburg and Vladivostok. Then we visited Moscow, Petersburg and Warsaw, of all of which we will write more extensively in a book soon to be published on "What a Western Farmer Saw in the Turkish and Russian Empires."

Russia now has a law prohibiting a minister entering the empire as such. The preachers representing the British Bible Society enter as book merchants. Fortunately for us we have been identified with and supported by a farm for fifty years. We were born on a farm. The first twenty-two years of life our home was on a farm not our own. The larger part of this first twenty-two years of life we plowed and labored as a regular farm hand. For about twenty-eight years we have owned a little farm of our own. It contains only 320 acres, but it happens to be in the garden-spot of the world. The $20,000 invested in it does not yield a very large per cent. of income, but it furnishes our entire personal needs: board, clothing, educational and traveling expenses. A man may have one vocation and several avocations. What little money we have made by way of our avocations, such as merchandising, preaching, lecturing, publishing, writing and editing, we have been able to use in some other way than in personal expenses. We have ever felt a little awkward and but poorly qualified in all our avocations, but perfectly at home and thoroughly prepared for our vocation, by which we have been supported for a half century. So we did not hesitate to suspend or lay aside our avocations, and enter Russia as a farmer. We would not have attempted to preach in Russia for a thousand dollars a sermon. Had we attempted it, possibly we would now be languishing in a Siberian prison. Count Pashkoff, who was converted under the preaching of Lord Radstock, also became a great preacher, and was banished by the Russian Government. He owns a very large farm in Russia, which he is allowed to visit once a year, on the condition that he signs a written obligation not to preach while in the empire.

Some of the Russians were a little curious to know how a farmer could be so far away from his farm in harvest time. Our invariable response to this inquiry was a candid explanation of the fact that we do not cultivate our farm with our own hands, but by tenants. We stay on our farm a very small part of the time, but keep a vigilant watch of every department and detail, directing largely by mail.

—*St. Louis Christian Advocate.*

The Spirit and the Letter of the Gospel.

To one coming from the ranks of sectarianism, like myself, the difference between the legalism and the spirit is of great importance. It seems sometimes hard to determine just where the one ends and the other begins. Still, I feel that the letter adhered to in all sincerity and the spirit will not be far away. The CHRISTIAN-EVANGELIST occasionally has something to say along this line which is always of interest to its readers.

A few weeks ago the writer was asked if he could go and see a very old man who, in consequence of being burned, was not likely to live. Learning the particulars I perceived that it was a case of neglecting the great salvation, and now some one to read and pray was wanted, and this with the usual idea of death-bed repentance would be all that is necessary. Am sorry to say I felt relieved that I could not go. What sort of prayer ought to be offered, and where could I find Scripture selections to comfort a man out of Christ, and who had sinned away life's opportunities?

It was like trying to obtain a passport into heaven under false pretences. And how could I muster up courage to tell him the naked truth?

We are told that the Lord is able to save unto the "uttermost," and they that come unto him shall in "no wise" be cast out, and Jesus said, "Come unto me," etc. All true, of course, but suppose the sick man cannot "*come*" in God's appointed way, then what? I know of no recorded case of a death-bed repentance in the gospel.

Again, the man at death's door may be a believer, but the unbaptized believer does not appear to be recognized in the New Testament. The friends of the sick man may think that baptism is a nonessential, or if it is essential, sprinkling will do, or perchance God will accept the will for the deed. I fail to find such teaching.

Suppose a man, having abundant opportunities in life, whereby he might have obtained a competency, utterly neglects the same, and at last, unable to work, is in great need. We presume that no one would feel under obligation to provide him with the home and the comforts of life that a competency would have afforded, and which but for his folly might have been his. The verdict will be, that he must suffer the consequences of his own neglect.

Try a little of this "natural law in the spiritual world." How shall a man escape who has deliberately neglected this great salvation? Must God accept him because in view of approaching death he desires to be saved, and yet he has not and now *cannot* comply with the divine requirement?

In such desperate cases, which so often occur, who has the courage to quote John 3:5, or kindred passages, or say, You have deliberately sinned away your day of grace and placed yourself beyond the pale of God's mercy and must now accept the result of your own folly? The majority of professed Christians would listen to such utterances in horror. But would it not be infinitely better for the living, if awful plainness of speech should characterize such cases? It would surely tend to put a stop to the patched-up, so-called death-bed repentances — or am I too much of a legalist?

J. H. LACEY.

La Porte, Ind.

[It is not well to limit God's mercy, even against death-bed repentance. Why specify the neglected duty of baptism. Is that a more unpardonable sin than other neglected duties? If a man on his death-bed, when brought face to face with death, repents of his neglect to be baptized, is he not as likely to receive God's mercy as one who, under similar conditions, repents of his covetousness, or of his hard, unforgiving spirit, and seeks God's pardoning grace? It is not improbable that when we all come into the presence of death, we may feel the need of invoking God's forgiveness for neglecting duties and opportunities. It is always right to ask every rational man to render whatever obedience may lie in his power at the time. If one can truly repent and confess Christ with the mouth, by all means encourage him to do it, even if he can make no public confession in baptism. Why should we deny this privilege to him because he is about to die when, if he should live a score of years longer in sin, we would not deny him the privilege of repentance in health? If death itself, as it approaches, may serve to rouse a soul from the stupor of sin and lead it to repentance, let not this door of hope be closed. Much wiser is he, however, who in life and health prepares to meet God in peace than he who procrastinates till the dying hour.—EDITOR.]

ımpling Preachers.

ıes are slowly growing out of many
ious customs, one of which is the
candidates for the pastorate.
ılpit is about to become vacant a
appointed to open correspondence
of available preachers, and for
ıonths the people are regaled with
of new men, each one preaching a
or two, and without any action
on the part of the church in mak-
ion the victims are kept coming
ıtil the minds of the people are so
ıt a unanimous choice simply be-
ssible. I know one church that had
iserable custom up for five years,
ger they played at it the more im-
'as to get a man to suit them, until
eer disgust and exhaustion, they
ı the first mediocre that came along
t, were in a measure contented,
were utterly weary of their dis-
. Something like this is the style
t is usually addressed to the person
to set up as preacher for the peo-
n in competition with others who
o go on trial:

JOHN JONES:—We anticipate a.
astors. Owing to the distance, we
d to defray your expenses here, but
oming this way we would arrange
reach one or two sermons as a
ıd pay you $5 or $6 for the same,
obligation resting on us to engage
of course, you should prove our
ır pastor, a grand, good man, intel-
d spiritually, is on his vacation,
this trial the pulpit is being filled
ching brethren, with a view of em-
very soon: This is a grand field
ıt man. Especially do we need a
r," etc., etc.
ı in the faith, DEACON SMITH.

ıercial idea of competition, push,
ı self-seeking has crept into almost
so that before we know it our relig-
ast on the same lines, and without
it there is a mad scramble of un-
reachers seeking to break into a
le empty pulpits, in order to secure
e loaves and fishes it can offer. A
onal minister once said to me, "If
ounced that I were going to leave,
16 preachers would immediately file
ations for this pulpit." I think that
tdone many times in our own ranks,
ere are hundreds of vacancies that
res. A simple rule or two, it seems
operly observed, would largely cor-
ıte of affairs: 1st. Not being too
let the church take up the matter,
, with the most available man they
d settle conclusions with him alone,
e at the past record than at their
atures, melodious voices, the style
ss, the eloquence of their lips, or
'orable impression they might make
lience. The best way to do this is
committee go and see them at work
fields, with power to make a con-
eir services. The most happy en-
I have ever known were where pas-
ople had never met until he arrived
und to take charge of the work.
of men are settled every year in this
ive the very best satisfaction. 2nd. A
e preachers: Pass by all of the
and take up with the most difficult
u can find that will pay you a suf-
ry to afford a fair living. Result:
-services, more martyrs and general
of our work all over the Reforma-

J. L. D'ARSIE.

More About It.

HRISTIAN-EVANGELIST:—Noticing a
tion in your journal of August 4th

Church of Christ at this place on May 2nd, 1897, having formerly been a member of the Cumberland Presbyterian and M. E. churches, and had backslidden from the latter into a very sinful life. We gave him a hearty welcome, a helping hand, and notwithstanding his pretensions and spiritual boastings of superior gifts and powers, we bore the affliction patiently, urging upon him constantly what seemed to us to be the teaching of the Scripture concerning pardon, the Holy Spirit, perfection, etc. That he ever heard anything, either from the pastor or any well-informed member of the church, that "works and works only would qualify for the kingdom," or that "immersion was the mainspring of it all," we most emphatically deny. He slanders ministry and membership in so stating. In many sermons in his presence and in many personal conversations the truth has been told him, that salvation has a divine and human side, and that without what God has done and is doing by his Word and Spirit man could do nothing. Of course we have insisted upon immersion, following faith in the Lord Jesus Christ, and sincere repentance, as one of the conditions of pardon and citizenship in the kingdom of God on earth. This aged sinner, after having claimed to know the Christian Church many years, accepted the invitation to come to Christ, was baptized and became a member of the church here. After exploiting his theories and wondrous feelings among us for some months, he took his place again in the Methodist fold, where we bade him God-speed and wished him well. Now it seems his high state of spiritual cultivation produces false statements concerning the teaching and practices of the Christian Church. We have no desire to show up his inconsistencies, which are many, but ask him to kindly forbear criticism of those who took him by the hand and tried to help him up, when he was without favor of God or man, especially in this community. That he tried to be a firebrand while among us is perhaps true, and we may therefore be presumed to be "saved so as by fire."

G. M. CONRAD,
Chairman of Board.

N. L. HILL, Clerk.

A Phenomenal Educational Growth.

In 1872 I was the head of the Northwestern Normal School at Republic, Ohio. I advertised quite extensively. An "ad" was inserted in the Sandusky Register.

By chance, one Ira C. Hoops, of La Porte, Ind., was stopping in Sandusky City. Some of his laundry work was returned to him in a copy of the Register. Seeing the "ad" of our school, he sent to me for circulars. I sent them, of course, together with a request to join us. He did so and remained in school some thirty weeks.

While there he was a pupil in the classes of one of my teachers, Prof. H. B. Brown. He called Mr. Brown's attention to an unoccupied seminary building at Valparaiso, Ind., and aroused sufficient interest in it to prompt a prospecting tour. This Mr. Brown made in the early summer of 1873. On his return Mr. Brown and I were out riding one evening. Taking from his pocket a cut of the seminary building, he requested my judgment as to the propriety of starting a school at Valparaiso. I answered favorably, saying that it was an enterprising region, remote from all competitors and favorably near to Chicago, a railroad center.

In September, 1873, with one of my teachers and three or four of our students, he started for Valparaiso. His capital was about $300 in cash, an Estey organ worth about $40, a copy of Bryant and Stratton's Counting House Bookkeeping and two years' experience as

panic. Against all opposition
obstacles the school, known t
the Northern Indiana Norm
grown until at the close of
stands as the largest education
America, its annual enrollment
in 1897-98, the enormous numbe
ent students, representing all
Union. The plant is worth no
It has trained, during the 25 ye
over 75,000 young ladies and
fitted them for the active work

Within the past scholastic y
graduates from its various dep
lows: Teachers, 340; Commer
manship, 40; Music, 35; Elo
chology and Pedagogy, 9; Ki
Pharmacy, 67; Scientifics, 1
Law, 36; Phonography and Ty

The school started with thr
and three teachers. It has n
partments and 52 teachers.
has occurred within a quarter o
without the aid of a single do
endowment—a most remarkabl
what may be accomplished in
centration of purpose, comme
asm and untiring perseverance.

The 25th anniversary of thi
able school was celebrated on
the occasion of the annual
Hon. W. D. Owen, Secretary
diana, delivered the address, h
"Dreamers and Plodders." H
scholarly and appropriate, an
ceived.

The Northern Indiana Norn
fruit of a stray advertisement,
tution and deserving of patro
educational marvel, whose his
than fiction. It will bear ca
repay imitation in many par
true educational leaven that is
whole country. J. FR

Aug. 17, 1898.

North End of Bo

I have just returned from the
of Montgomery county, whicl
Wellsville church the 8th and 9t
It was a good meeting. Mone
assist two places last year an
at $1,500 was built and dedica
Money was pledged at the co
coming year.

Splendid sermons and addr
ered by T. A. Abbott, J. W.
Davis and C. C. Hill. Some
men who are just starting in th
good talks. Montgomery cou
pride in her young men, such
Rupert Ford, J. E. Donovan,

The writer delivered his ad
America and Heathen Missions

On the 9th dinner was served
by the Wellsville sisters.
ever glad he is in Missouri
is called to a meal prepar
women. Montgomery count
her Hills, just as Audrain cou
Robbins, and Boone to her W
to her Clay, Randolph to her B
Monroe to her Stine, as soli
hills. C. C. and Claude E. H
power in Montgomery count
wisely and unselfishly forged
the results are beginning to te

Centralia, Mo.

Notes and News.

The Christian Church at Rantoul, Ill., where H. H. Peters preaches, sent four delegates to the annual encampment at Eureka, Ill.

The Christian Church at Andrews, Ind., is to have a reunion and financial rally, Sept. 3rd and 4th. On Saturday there will be a roll-call and picnic dinner. Several former pastors are to be in attendance. Also Bro. L. L. Carpenter will speak on Lord's day morning. All brethren and friends are cordially invited to be present. Come one and all.

G. J. MASSEY, Pastor.

Closed a full week's meeting here with six baptisms. This protracted effort is the end of the first quarter of my year's engagement for one-half time. If the other half is not soon engaged, either here or elsewhere convenient to this place, I may vacate it for work in another field.

J. A. WALTERS.

Council Grove, Kan., Aug. 22, 1998.

DEAR EVANGELIST:—Our attempts to plant "the cause" in Harrisburg starts off very encouragingly, notwithstanding the continued wet weather. When the weather is taken into consideration (we were rained out entirely two nights in succession) the attendance is along with the attention almost phenomenal.

We are receiving very much substantial aid from Bro. H. F. Lutz, pastor at Le Moyne, and his good people.

"Our plea' is being well received and is something entirely new here, but how many will act on it is yet to be determined.

RYAN AND HUSTON.

Le Moyne, Pa., Aug. 20, 1898.

Wisconsin State Meeting.

The time of our state meeting draws nigh. It is to be at Pardeeville, Sept. 7-11.

This will be the best as well as the most important convention we have had for years. Six speakers from outside the state, as well as some from within the state, have been secured. The six are: E. M. Gordon, India; Miss Ada Boyd, India; Dr. Butchart, China; C. C. Smith, Cincinnati, O.; Mrs. Helen E. Moses, Indianapolis, Ind., and Prof. C. G. Hertzog, of President Garfield's old college, Hiram, O.

The brethren at Pardeeville have prepared to entertain a large convention. Please see that your congregation is represented. Send names of those who are going, to L. Z. Smith, Pardeeville. Make all this announcement at all your meetings from now on to Sept. 7. Printed programs will be sent you this week.

C. G. MCNEILL, Pres.

Milwaukee.

South Dakota.

June 23 I left my home to attend the fourteenth annual convention of the S. D. C. M. S. at Bradley. It was a grand meeting and many helpful ideas were presented by able men, but the life of the convention was Bro. C. C. Smith, of Cincinnati. He talked on Ministerial Relief, and the convention promptly gave $35 for that good work.

He lectured on his trip to Jamaica, and every one laughed till he was tired. He addressed us concerning our work among the negroes, and again concerning our general home work, and each felt his interest increase with knowledge.

He preached, and every one who had named the Savior's name went out to better service—more earnest Christian living. The debt which has hampered the state work for a number of years was paid in full, and $225 pledged by individuals for new work. The outlook for apostolic Christianity in our thriving state is most excellent.

Monday, June 27, I returned to my home to find its light gone out, my darling wife having died that morning after an illness of but twelve hours. Then came the long, sad journey of a thousand miles back to the old home in Northern Ohio, the gathering of friends to do honor to one whose every acquaintance loved her, the kind and helpful words spoken by Bro. W. H. Scott, of Ravenna, and the lowering casket, covered over with flowers from South Dakota and Ohio. So young, so helpful, so hopeful, so full of zeal in the Master's work! Truly God's ways are not our ways, nor his thoughts our thoughts.

Three weeks I tarried among the scenes and friends of other years, visiting in Randolph, where H. F. McLane baptized me, in Alliance, where I met Bro. A. M. Chamberlain, in Hiram, where I called on Prof. Snoddy, who was a Dakota boy, and on Dr. E. I. Osgood, who with his young wife goes to China next month for the F. C. M. S., in Warren, in Talmadge and other near-by towns.

Now I am back in my lonely home—gladdened, however, by my mother with whom I had not lived for eight years. In all my sorrow and heartache God has raised up for me friends that are friends indeed. I am grateful to him and them.

A. H. SEYMOUR.

Arlington, S. D., August 9, 1898.

Warning.

Notice is hereby given that one J. C. Rawlings, alias C. F. Paul, alias John Grayson Paul, etc., has been preying upon the churches of Illinois the past year, at Fulton, Mt. Auburn, etc. His past is a mystery. His present is inconsistent in name and statement with the conduct of a minister. His peripatetic habits make it difficult to anticipate his next field of operations. He is a large, heavy man of suave address and florid countenance, with reddish hair inclined to curl, a ready, fluent talker, using good language. The churches are warned against him.

By order of first district board of Illinois.

S. H. ZENDT, Sec.

Dixon, Ill., Aug. 22, 1898.

Warning.

It pains us to know that a professed minister of the gospel should prove himself unworthy the high calling and bring disgrace and irreparable harm to the cause. But Christian duty calls us to say that such is true of one R. L. Stanley, and the effect of his conduct on the cause here at Beaumont. From several persons he has borrowed money and not repaid it. It is positively known that he has partaken of the intoxicating cup while having charge of our work here. There is no question but that he is a fraud, and has no intention of paying, as he left here at night, saying nothing to any one of his leaving, and also left a small board bill unpaid, taking his grip from one of the private rooms unmolested. If he wishes to reform, let the brethren among whom he may dwell help to lift up the fallen brother, but let none again trust him with the overseeing of the flock until he has beyond question proven his sincerity in that direction.

J. L. BUTTS.
W. J. PHILLIPS.
Elders.

Beaumont, Kan., Aug. 22, 1898.

From the North End of Boone.

One phase of the social life has been giving some trouble to those in this city who desire a clear-cut religion, positive and vital, as it has in nearly every community in the state—cards and the dance. The writer addressed a union meeting of the churches of Centralia on the theme, "Upon What Ground Does the Church Object to the So-called Popular Amusement?" by request. At the close of the services the M E. South preacher offered the following as the sense of the meeting, and it was passed by a vote of five-sixths of the large audience:

1. Realizing the potency for good or evil i the social life of our people; and—
2. Desiring to discourage that which has a evil tendency; and—
3. Deploring the use of cards and the danc as a means of entertaining; and—
4. Desiring to foster a healthful and spirit ual society in our city, we, the church peopl and citizens of Centralia, Mo., agree to use al our influence to open the homes of the city t our young people and to build up a societ which will afford pastime and pleasure to al and do violence to the conscientious scruples o none."

This resolution strikes at one of the mos potent enemies of a deeper spiritual life This, to some extent, is admitted by all. W have not a minister, so far as I have heard who will not agree that it destroys spiritualit and pulls down what the spirit of Christ seek to build up. And yet it is entrenched in ou churches and commands wealth to such a extent that it is only here and there a preacher dares speak from the pulpit his views on th subject. Some say handle it privately, whic practically means not handling it at all. If i is such an evil as most all our preachers admi when talking to one another, it ought to b shown up from the pulpit, as well as come u for consideration at the meetings of the elder of the churches.

Another fact should come out: there i scarcely a girl's school in the state of Missour to which you can send your daughter one yea and have her return without having learned t waltz. There is probably no way to reach th State University, but it does for the youn men what most of the girls' schools do for th young women. It is a more serious situatio than many are willing to admit. And the day of reckoning with schools tolerating suc things is not far off.

If the church continues to entangle hersel with the prevailing and growing social customs, she will not long sustain sufficient vitality to be a power for good.

May it not now be considered time for a reformation along these line? If these thing are good and harmless, let their devotee come out with the evidence of it.

H. A. DENTON.

Centralia, Mo.

The Chicago and Northwestern Railway Company has issued a booklet illustrating the elegance, comfort and convenience of "the "Northwestern Limited" trains, one of which leaves Chicago at 6:30 P. M. daily for St. Paul and other Northwestern cities. These trains are supplied with electric lights throughout and composed of New Compartment and Standard Sleeping Cars, Dining Cars, Buffett Smoking and Library Cars and Coaches, all of which run through without change. Any business you may have with this company will receive prompt attention by addressing W. B. Kinskern, G. P. & T. A., Chicago, Ill.

Notes.

und City did
t I have not
more practi-
ents of the
haracteristic
eir minister,
t undone for
of the dele-
elist, T. W.
at could be
l one time in
the meeting
er Mitchell's
· the first to
appy in my
1876. The
Master and
her husband
Bible-school
g to all.
$15 to Bible-
school remits
good wishes.

ill begin his
r the first of
is time to all
work, espe-
f the work.
n, and give
Bro. Rogers
o make it his
rize himself
lling. Your

perintendent
Guillodd the
for year in

e anticipated
rroll County,
h persistency
ing very few
ful feature of
of parents in
g showing up
idered one of
th Missouri,
ogard and at
ainsaying the
very gener-
dies seemed
ng. This is to

ing at Wells-
f telling the
a number one
n C. C. Hill,
e county but
Bible-school
t the Mexico
t let that one
nearly all of
ork accepted

vill begin his
1st., and he
Normal work,
etter the con-
souri schools
). E. a work-
his teaching,
serving the
ith good and
ep him busy.
h side, Bro.
his efficiency
l him to your

h additional
believe their
nal funds for
orth, trusting

nd Jno. W.
heir pledge in
blessing to us
y it makes us
ays promptly

pays twice? Will not another good school lead in full that we may keep right up to date with all the expense? Will you see me at a county or district meeting, and will you not ask your school to accept its apportionment and tell me so there? Please.

H. F. DAVIS.

Commercial, Bldg., St. Louis, Mo.

Evangelistic.

KENTUCKY.

Hebron, Aug. 25th.—In a meeting with the South Fork church; meeting 10 days, and two confessions to date. Next meeting at Florence beginning Sept. 26.—GEO. W. WATKINS.

WISCONSIN.

Sugar Grove, Aug. 26.—One confession and baptism here Sunday—a young man. Six additions to the church recently. Large congregations, and many at work.—S. J. PHILLIPS, Pastor.

INDIANA.

Muncie, Aug. 27th.—Our two and a half weeks' meeting at Hume, Ill., closed with 14 additions. I am now at White Water, Ind. Go to Iowa next.—A. MARTIN.

TENNESSEE.

Clarksville, Aug 26.—One addition to Church of Christ.—A. M. GROWDEN.

TEXAS.

San Antonio, Aug. 27th.—One addition at regular services Sunday last; two at prayer-meeting Wednesday night. Our fiscal year begins September 4th and we expect to move forward with even greater results from that date.—GEO. B. RANSHAW.

ILLINOIS.

Chicago, Aug. 25th.—Our meeting at Irving Park (Chicago), by E. W. Darst, has just closed with an organization of 75 members. This will make a good church.—A. LARRABEE.

Rossville, August 28.—Five confessions and baptisms at Coal Creek, Ind., August 26th.—A. W. JACKMAN.

Moweaqua, August 29.—Meeting two weeks old last night. Twenty additions to date. Splendid interest manifested.—A. R. SPICER, pastor.

KANSAS.

Clay Center, Aug. 26.—Three took membership here last Lord's day.—OTHA WILKISON.

UTAH.

Ogden, Aug. 25.—Many things prevent the growth of the Lord's work in this land of deserts, mountains and Saints. Here Jews are called Gentiles and things are badly inverted outside of state religion. But thanks to God, this week four young ladies were buried with Christ in baptism and raised to walk in in newness of life.—J. H. BAUSERMAN.

SOUTH DAKOTA.

Sioux Falls, Aug. 23.—The Church of Christ here is wide awake and doing good work for the Master. Three accessions Aug. 14th and 17 accessions Aug. 20th; all by confession and baptism. The last-named conversions are from our mission work at the state penitentiary here; 17 strong, stalwart men confessed their faith in Christ, and the afternoon of the 20th, in the presence of the elders of the church and a few of the members, surrounded by prison walls, I baptized them into Christ. Others will follow soon. I write you these lines that you may rejoice with us.—L. H. HUMPHREYS.

MISSOURI.

Holt, August 29.—Our meeting thus far has resulted in 58 additions. Will close Wednesday evening of this week.—D. D. BOYLE AND V. E. RIDENOUR.

Publishers' N

"America or Rome; Christ o
by John L. Brandt, contains 53
illustrations. It has a copiou
list of authors consulted. It is
complete exposition of Romani
the highest authorities are quote
reliable in every particular. Co
say it is the most thorough di
doctrines, principles, spirit ar
Romanism now before the publi

Just now it is an exceedingly
the agent to handle. The war
and the United States has revea
ance, superstition and degrad
countries ruled by Roman C
public has learned a few of the n
cerning Romanism and is the b
to take hold of the additional
"America or Rome." The age
what has been revealed, togethe
given in this book, will have bu
in selling this exposition of R
are offering agents special indu
this book.

The agent would only have
condition of the inhabitants c
Rico, and the Philippine Island
effects of Catholicism. Each of
in natural resources, but left in
superstition through Rome's i
fluence.

Write us for our *special i*
agents on "America or Rom
Christian Publishing Co., St. L

FINISHED.

"King Saul," by J. Brecke
just from the press and is ready
public. This book is bound i
cloth and contains 281 pages.
$1.00 per copy. Those who hav
days of Jehu," by the same a
pleased to learn that his secon
Testament characters is just
form. This work gives the m
features of the life of King Sau
ing Bible characters an easy
study.

Ladies of Manil

Little has been said or wri
mestizos or half-breed ladies of
combine the superstition of the
grace and languor of the creole
ures of either the Chinese or Ja
favorite costume is a long, loose
hued silk, and their long, flow
their mantilla.

The illustration in another co
duced from a photograph take
1892. It was intended to form p
of National Costume cards pr
Singer Manufacturing Co: for
the Chicago Exposition, but wa
time. It now has a peculiar
women of America because of
connecting the U. S. with the
lands, where Singer Sewing M
in every other part of the wo
foremost factors of civilization.

Missionary.

Church Extension Notes.

Our collection for Church Extension begins next Sunday.

Our Extension Fund was organized to assist missions to get their first building. The money is loaned to such missions as cannot borrow elsewhere.

It is sometimes stated that our Extension Fund is not needed; that churches giving good security can borrow money elsewhere. This is not the case. Trust Companies, Building Associations, Banks, Insurance Companies and Attorneys having money to lend for others will not loan money on mission church property, for obvious reasons. The mission is slow pay and irregular in paying, and if such companies as indicated above foreclose on the property they get the ill-will of the community, and to avoid trouble these corporations refuse to loan money at all to missions. Our Extension Fund is an absolute essential to the upbuilding of our new work, and should be vigorously supported.

It is sometimes asked, "Does Church Extension pay?" Yes, it pays in manifold ways. By the encouragement of a loan to a mission in a new town it secures a lot when lots are cheap, which becomes very valuable in after years, and the churches helped by this fund generally raise from three to four dollars for every dollar loaned them.

Thus far in the ten years of its history our Extension Board has aided over 400 missions to get church houses, 100 of which have paid back every dollar of principal, with interest at four per cent. Others have paid back the first, second and third notes, and over $90,000 of principal and interest have been returned to the board. Surely, this is a successful work. Think of what our board could do with $250,000 of a fund; then think of a half a million, and finally of what a million would do when our brotherhood will be organizing 1,000 missions a year. Last year 500 new missions were organized by our evangelists and pastors.

Put words of cheer into your appeals for money for Church Extension next Sunday. Look upon the whitening fields as Christ did. Catch his encouraging words and make them ring hopefully in the ears of your congregation and you will have no trouble in even going beyond your apportionment.

Keep in mind next Sunday the 2,500 missions among us that are meeting in halls, storerooms, schoolhouses, etc., with no place they can call their own in which to spread the Lord's table; think of your own religious comforts, and then reach into your pockets for your part of the $250,000 for Church Extension by the close of 1900.

Collections for Church Extension should be sent to the writer, 600 Waterworks Bldg., Kansas City, Mo.

G. W. Muckley, Cor. Sec.

The September Offering.

The time of the year for the annual offering for Church Extension is now at hand. September is the month. For eleven months in the year our churches are thinking of other matters, and other interests. It is but right, therefore, that Church Extension, one of the most worthy of all our lines of work, should receive the hearty and undivided support of our great brotherhood for this *one* month. Not a church and not an individual should allow the month of September to pass without making a liberal offering to this work.

Listen to the recommendation of the National Convention: "Because the board can only answer one appeal in five, we recommend that UNUSUAL EFFORT BE PUT FORTH TO RAISE OUR CHURCH EXTENSION FUND TO ONE QUARTER OF A MILLION DOLLARS BY THE CLOSE OF 1900. To this end your committee recommends that more attention be given to the September offering. Thus far we have compelled the board to raise seventy-five per cent. of this money by going out into the field after it. We must raise more by annual offering in September, and as this is the month after vacation, the month after summer sluggishness in the churches, when the pulse of the church life is not vigorous, we urge that EXTRAORDINARY EFFORT BE USED TO WORK UP A GENEROUS OFFERING FOR THIS IMPORTANT WORK."

Now it is the purpose of the Church Extension Board to carry out, so far as possible, the wishes of our people as expressed at the great National Convention, last October. To do this the board should have the hearty support of every preacher in the brotherhood.

The board, composed as it is of some of the *best* men that I have ever met, has a right to expect that every preacher and every member *in every church* does his duty in September.

The board, to carry out the wishes of the convention, has a tremendous work before it, as the following will indicate:

THE WORK NOW BEFORE US.

"From last October we have just three years in which to lift our fund from $150,000 to $250,000. To do this we must raise $35,000 each year of new money, the interest paying current expenses while this is bening done."

The "how" is as follows:

THE PLAN OF THE BOARD.

"To raise $35,000 annually the following plan is proposed: The board will endeavor to secure $20,000 annually in collections from the churches at the September offering, asking each church to raise its fair proportion in order to secure the amount. The other $15,000 the board will endeavor to secure annually in pledges and bequests."

To make our work permanent and prosper as it should we *must* have a large Church Extension Fund. We should house every houseless congregation in this country. No organization without a church house in which to meet can demand the respect and accomplish the work of the Lord in any community. As well expect a *bodiless* spirit as a *houseless* church to do the Lord's work. There should be one *solid, forward* movement from ocean to ocean in the interest of Church Extension during the *only* month allotted to this work. All who are in favor of this movement, let it be known by sending a liberal offering to the board.

J. T. Ogle.

Our General Convention.

The General Convention of the Churches of Christ will be held at Chattanooga, Tenn., October 13th to 20th, 1898. The sessions of the Christian Woman's Board of Missions will begin on the evening of October 13, and continue through the 15th. The American Christian Missionary Society will meet at 9 A. M., October 17th, and continue until 12 M., October 19th. The Foreign Christian Missionary Society will meet at 2 P. M., October 19th, and continue through the 20th. The programs will be strong and helpful, the report will be encouraging, and everything points to one of the greatest conventions in our history.

RAILROAD RATES.

The railroads of the Central and Southeastern Traffic Associations have granted the rate of one fare for the round trip. This covers the territory from the Potomac to the Mississippi Rivers, and from the lakes to the gulf. The Trunk Line Association northeast of the Mississippi River has granted a fare of one and one-third fare on the certificate plan, or you can buy through the gateways of the Central or Southeastern at the regular rate, and get the one-fare rate through these gateways and return. The Western Passenger Association, west of Chicago and the Mississippi River, has not yet announced its rate, but we are urging the one-fare rate and hope we will get it. These low rates should secure a very large attendance. There could be no more delightful trip than to go to Chattanooga in October.

THE ENTERTAINMENT.

The churches at Chattanooga are making large plans for the entertainment of the convention. Rates have been secured in private houses at one dollar per day. This includes three meals and lodging. The hotels have granted special rates for delegates at the convention. The convention will be held in the great Auditorium builing of Chattanooga, which is furnished us free by the city. The Mayor of the city will be present at the first session to extend us the welcome and hospitality of the city. The program is being finally revised and will soon be published.

SEND YOUR PREACHER.

Every congregation owes it to itself and to the cause of primitive Christianity to be represented in this great gathering of the hosts of Israel to plan and pray for the extension of the Master's kingdom. An earnest invitation is given especially to our business men that they come up to this gathering to help forward the cause. Our churches should see to it that their preachers attend this convention, for the good they will give and for the greater good they will receive. The minister's preaching will be richer if he can participate in this gathering of the Lord's people. If your minister is not able to go, make it a pleasure to send him. It will cost but little, and that little will be far more than repaid to you for the blessing that will come to him.

Let every good motive appeal to our brethren to attend the Annual Convention at Chattanooga, October 13th to 20th, 1898.

Benj. L. Smith, Cor. Sec.
American Christian Missionary Society.

General Convention News.

The place of the convention is Chattanooga, the time October 13-21. Keep these well in mind.

Indications point to a large and enthusiastic attendance. Many have already begun making preparations to come.

The local committees are exerting themselves to have everything in perfect readiness. Nothing will be omitted which will contribute to the comfort and enjoyment of those present.

Are you coming? If so, drop me a card. We want to tell the people who are going to be here. This will arouse enthusiasm, and encourage others to come. Don't fail to do this at once.

And, brethren, please begin talking about what a great convention we are going to have. Help us in a campaign of agitation. Let us strive for the largest attendance ever seen at our national conventions. Why not? This is possible, and a good possibility should be made a grand reality.

The program is going to be one of the best, and the various reports will show a decided advance in all lines of missionary and educational work. These reports will fan the flame of enthusiasm and fill the heart with devout thanksgiving to God. Nothing so thrills the heart of the true soldier as news of victory from the field of battle.

"Come thou with us and we will do thee good."

M. D. Clubb.

Chattanooga, Tenn.

Christian Endeavor in the Chattanooga Convention.

Our General Christian Missionary Convention will be held in Chattanooga, Tennessee, next October. The entire afternoon session of Monday, Oct. 17, will be devoted to Christian Endeavor. This is in harmony with action had by the General Convention in Indianapolis last year. All our Christian Endeavor Societies should begin *at once* to arrange to have representatives there.

The following attractive program has been prepared for this C. E. session:

1. Annual Report of National Superintendent—10 minutes.
2. Address: "The Manifold Mission of

ın Endeavor,'' by C. B. Newnan, De-
lich.—35 minutes.
aper: ''The C. E. Society as an Edu-
l Agency,'' by Burris A. Jenkins, In-
lis, Ind.—15 minutes.
ymposium: ''How May We Best Devel-
Utilize Our C. E. Forces?'' Led by
I. Tyrrell, St. Louis, Mo.—40 minutes.
astors and our papers are requested to
in bringing this Christian Endeavor
to the attention of our young people,
secure a large attendance. *Let us give
oughtful attention to our young folks,*
s build wisely for the future.

Truly and fraternally,
J. Z. TYLER,
National Superintendent of C. E.
land, O., August 20, 1898.

Church Extension.

S THAT HAVE RECEIVED AID FROM THE
H EXTENSION FUND, THAT HAVE AGREED
TAKE AN OFFERING IN SEPTEMBER FOR
THIS WORK.

ı the Board of Church Extension sent
ers asking our congregations to pledge
the September offering, the missions
y our board were among the first to re-
In about one week one-fourth of them
led to the call to aid their less fortunate
ors. This is the greatest argument that
advanced for Church Extension. Those
ve received help are willing to aid oth-
promptly come to the rescue.
hould be and *will* be a great inspira-
the brethren who have aided this fund
l give a mighty impetus to our Septem-
ection. Others will yet be heard from.
would be too long to publish. Here is
of it:

NA.—Phoenix.
IDA.—Bartow, Inverness, Starke.
GIA.—Athens, Tallapoosa.
OIS.—Erie, Joppa, Mt. Vernon, Olney.
NA.—Corunna, Knox.
.—Des Moines (Highland Park Church),
ville, Lenox, Mason City, Rock Rapids,
n, Villisca, Wapello.
AS.—Atchison, Florence, Galena, Goffs,
gton, Lansing, Pawnee Rock, Seneca,
, Wichita.
UCKY.—Nicholasville.
LAND.—Rockville.
GAN.—Owosso, Saginaw.
URI.—Birch Tree, Carterville, Craig,
, Sheffield, Marceline, Naylor.
ASKA.—Beaver City, Brock, Chester,
gs, Lexington, Red Cloud, Wymore.
H CAROLINA.—Winston.
—Rockville.
HOMA.—Downs, El Reno, Enid, King-
Oklahoma City, Perry, Guthrie.
ON.—Coquille, Eugene, Forest Grove,
n, Tillamook.
SYLVANIA.—Lemoyne.
AKOTA.—Sioux Falls.
S.—Corsicana, Nocona, Paris, Tyler.
INIA.—Hampton, Newport News.
HINGTON.—Centralia, Medical Lake,
, Walla Walla.

h Extension With the American hristian Missionary Society.

ch Extension is that agency of the
an Church which assists needy and
ing mission churches to houses of wor-
The evangelization of this country, in a
way, our churches entrust to two
—the Board of Home Missions and the
of Church Extension. The Home Mis-
oard goes on the ground first, gathers
r and organizes. The Extension Board
e congregation a church home with a
money at four per cent., which is paid
n five years, the mission raising from
irds to three-fourths of the cost. No
ation is permanent until the house of
is secured. The church builder must
l in hand with the evangelist. No one
this so well as our mission workers in
the West and South, and in all parts of the East.

NOTE.—This is a Building and Loan Association in the Church of Christ, to help those who cannot build without borrowing. In cities where loan associations exist, young men are early encouraged to save their money and get a home. Struggling churches, knowing this fund is in existence, are encourged in their very beginning to save for a lot, knowing that when they own their own lot they can borrow money from this fund at four per cent. and build, thus getting a church home and Christian workshop two or three years sooner than they could get it themselves, and command respect in that community immediately.

PLAN AND MANAGEMENT OF THE FUND.

The Church Extension plan is to loan this money for five years to aid the mission churches in securing meeting houses that they could not get without aid from some other source. The loans are made on the following conditions: First, that the building is actually needed. Second, that the mission asking aid has done everything possible towards buying the lot and commencing the building. Third, that all debts incurred by purchasing the lot and building are paid in cash except what the loan from this fund will pay. Fourth, that the church gives first mortgage security on the property. Fifth, that they insure the house for the full length of the loan. The mortgage clause is attached to the insurance policy. In states subject to cyclones the Board requires cyclone insurance.

Every title, deed, article of incorporation and insurance policy is carefully examined by the Board. A competent man is kept in the office in the person of T. R. Bryan, secretary and treasurer, who is very thorough in the matter of these examinations, and whenever a difficult point arises in the examination on any legal document, our attorney, Mr. Bacon, passes upon it. The money is to be returned to the Board within five years in equal annual installments with four per cent. interest, payable semi-annually. It can be paid sooner if the mission church is able. Mr. Bryan also prepares all legal papers and collects loans and interest. This fund is now $160,000, and is doing a banking business. It requires all of Mr. Bryan's time to care for the fund.

Interest and principal come back to the Board from missions in small amounts. This requires bookkeeping and much refiguring of interest. Any one close to church work knows how much effort and patience are required to get collections in local church work. So it requires time and tactful men to collect these loans and interest. Bro. Bryan is really lawyer, bookkeeper, treasurer, examiner of abstracts, copier of deeds, incorporation papers and insurance policies, and is office secretary. Sometimes a week is required to examine a single abstract. Abstracts as thick as a church hymnal are frequently received. Remember, the Board gets them from thirty-seven different states and territories where it makes loans, and laws on church titles differ in different states. The Board has laws on church titles in every state and territory in the Union, and is prepared to loan money to our missions in any place in a safe and business-like way.

The Board never loans closer than one-third the cost of the house and lot, and can report thus far that not one dollar has ever been lost on loans. If a mission gets too far behind on its payments, the corresponding secretary visits the mission on his way to appointments, without much additional expense, and helps to raise the money. Loans are made in amounts of $150 to $1,000. In exceptional cases, in cities, larger amounts must be loaned, because the ground will cost more. The Board does not loan money to pay old debts, except to save a church from sale for debt.

The National Convention earnestly recommended that we increase this fund to $250,000

Family Circle.

The Garden of My Soul.

BY SUMNER T. MARTIN.

When scarce the noon of life's short day
Our weary feet have reached with pain,
'Tis hard for eager soul to say—
"I cannot reap the golden grain."

But hands of weakness are not fit
To wield Truth's sickle, Heaven-given;
With aching heart we down must sit,
Where others reap, where we have striven.

To Heaven still our prayers may rise,
For those whose strength our burdens bear,
May be our cry will will reach the skies,
And God will build a golden stair,

While, Jacob-like, our hands we lay
On stony pillow of our pain,
We hear the angel voices say—
"We'll show you field of yellow grain."

"Your souls afield has waited long
With Passion's weeds and thorns of sin
The Heavenly Father's plants among;
Make haste, O soul! and enter in."

My vision now has clearer grown,
Since lifted from the fields abroad,
And sickness' very plain hath shown
The weedy garden of my God.

With Truth's two-edged sword I slay
The tares, thick sown while I had slept;
God's grain grew riper every day,
While our my sins with prayers I wept.

He helped me grow the fruits of grace;
Faith triumphed over all my fears,
And Hope sprung up with shining face,
And Love reached out deathless years.

'Tis well to love the whole world round,
And labor for its Godward growth;
The garden of the soul ne'er found
All o'ergrown with weeds of sloth.

Mason City, Ia., Aug. 16, 1898.

Text Stories—XI.

THE USE OF THE TONGUE.

BY ALICE CURTICE MOYER.

Set a watch, O Lord, before my mouth; keep the door of my lips.—*Psalms 141:3.*

"Good morning, Mrs. Raymond. I just ran in a minute, the first thing this morning, to find out whether Deacon Smith has been to see you."

"Been to see me? Why should Bro. Smith have been to see me, Mrs. Blank?"

"Well," with a show of hesitation, "Mrs. Lane told me that somebody told her that Deacon Smith told somebody else that he considered our fair as nothing short of a desecration; that it was nothing more nor less than converting the house of God into a den of thieves, and that he intends to see that it does not occur again. I thought like as not he had spoken to you about it, you being one of the most interested parties. No, I cant sit down. I can only stay a minute. I just ran in to see if you had seen the deacon."

"No, I haven't seen him," replied Mrs. Raymond, "and it surprises me that he should speak in such a manner. I think it must be a mistake. As you know, we were careful to avoid charging fancy prices for our articles, simply because they were for the church, and we had no grab-bags or any other form of gambling. Our principal object was, in reality, of a social order, where the members might meet each other and become better acquainted—a need which we all feel. Surely, Mrs. Blank, it must be a mistake."

"O, no! It is not a mistake, as you will find when you see the deacon. He is very indignant over the affair. But I must be going. I can't stay a minute."

When Mrs. Blank declared she couldn't stay a minute she invariably staid two hours. She continued:

"Do you know that Bro. Elliot's daughter is soon to be married to that worthless young fellow whom her father picked up a few years ago, and has been trying to make something of?"

"And *has* made something of," interrupted Mrs. Raymond.

"Well, I don't know about that. When people have once been down in the world, there is always danger of their going back—not that his downfall was really his fault, I have heard people say, still I shouldn't want a daughter of mine to marry him. But of course people's tastes differ. His friend, I understand, is an admirer of your Edith. I heard a person say the other day that you had better be cautious. 'Birds of a feather flock together,' you know."

Mrs. Raymond's face flushed, but she forced herself to say calmly:

"I am cautious, Mrs. Blank. I trust I shall never be otherwise. The two young men to whom you refer are well known to me. I am familiar with the circumstances concerning the first one's 'fall' as you term it, which was not a fall at all. He was simply the victim of conditions brought about by others than himself, and Bro. Elliott, instead of giving him a push downward, extended a helping hand at the time when it was most needed; and he evidently knows his real worth, else he would not be willing to trust in his hands the welfare and future happiness of his daughter. As to the second party you mention, I have in him the same confidence that I place in the first. They are both noble, Christian young men, and well deserve the admiration of their many warm friends."

Mrs. Blank, not one whit daunted, continued:

"Well, of course they may. I really hope they do, but people will talk, you know. Did you see the disgraceful state in which our next-door neighbor came home Saturday night? He was brought in a closed carriage. Really, they could hardly get him into the house. And Mrs. L—— took the children the next morning to Sunday-school just as though nothing had ever happened. Now if my husband should come home in such a condition I should be so ashamed I wouldn't so much as put my head outside of the door."

"I think Mrs. L—— takes exactly the right course. Suppose she cared no more for her family or had no more self-respect than her husband? I honor her for her efforts to rise above all obstacles and for her determination to bring up her little ones in the right way in spite of the fact that she is unaided and unsympathized with by her husband. Many a mother has had just such a path to travel. Because Mrs. L—— has a drunken husband is no reason why she should not make an effort to save her boys from the same fate."

Mrs. Blank continued:

"Have you heard about the dreadful time they are having in the Fourth Church? The morning paper is full of it. They do say that some of the most prominent members are the most deeply implicated, and that it is liable to break up the church entirely. But I must be going, for I really haven't time to stay a minute." And she went at last, leaving poison in her wake.

Of the class to which she belongs, an eminent minister once said:

"I think among the worst of the worshipers are those who gather up the harsh things that have been said about you and bring them to you—all the things said against you or against your family or against your style of business. . . . . They bring them to you in the very worst shape; they bring them to you without any of the extenuating circumstances, and after they have made your feelings all raw, very raw, they take this brine, this turpentine, this aquafortis, and rub it in with a coarse towel until it sinks to the bone. They make you the pincushion in which they thrust all the sharp things they have ever heard about you. . . . Sometimes they get you in a corner where you cannot very well escape without being rude, and they tell you all about this one, and all about that one, and all about the other one, and they talk, talk, talk. After awhile they go away, leaving the place looking like a barnyard after the foxes and weasels have been around: here a wing, there a claw, and yonder an eye, and there a crop—destruction everywhere."

Mrs. Raymond well knew the character of her morning caller, yet her gossip had left its sting. It had robbed her morning of its sunshine. And when, early in the afternoon, she heard the gate click and beheld the familiar form of Deacon Smith, her heart was in her month, so to speak, but he was soon saying:

"I stopped to tell you, Sister Raymond, that I consider your church fair a decided success, as church fairs go. Like church festivals they are touchy things to undertake. However, I have always maintained that the two expressions, 'the house of prayer' and a 'den of thieves,' are the antipodes in meaning, and that between them there lies a wide plain which, if wisely utilized, may be rendered most helpful. I was just saying to some of the violent opposers of such things that you had struck the happy medium. The social life of the church, as we all know, is a most important factor; and if it pleases the ladies to manufacture little fancy and useful articles, I *hope* there is nothing wrong in their disposing of them at reasonable prices. Anyhow, your last fair seemed to me a success. Good-bye."

What a load was lifted from the heart of Mrs. Raymond! How foolish she had been to listen to the morning's gossip! She smiled at Bro. Smith's non-committalism on the subject of church festivals and fairs—a subject which has never yet and perhaps never will be satisfactorily disposed of.

With the burden of the first bit of gossip lifted, she could smile concerning the others, and quoted from Emerson:

"'We should be as courteous to a man as we are to a picture which we are willing to give advantage to the best light.' Knowing Mrs. Blank as well as I do, having lived beside her for so many years, I ought not to have allowed her report to worry me in the least. Still, what right have I to quote Emerson and blame myself for giving credence to the remarks Bro. Smith was reported to have made, without attempting to apply the same quotation to the reporter. Well, in justice to myself, and as an ease to conscience, I *can* say that I have tried to look for Mrs. Blank's good qualities—and she really has some—but I can't help seeing that her tongue is her greatest enemy. It seems to run away with her prudence and the result is she has few friends. It is hard to think well of such a person, yet I know it is my duty to make the attempt and to continue to pray for her. I know that I must cultivate the spirit of giving kind thoughts and of loving even my enemies, and people as trying to my patience as Mrs. Blank, if I am to be numbered among the children of the Heavenly Father."

Another visitor was announced—a woman with a face as sweet as the flowers she carried. It was a pleasure to look at her.

"I have brought you that promised book, Mrs. Raymond," she said. "I would share my roses with you, but they are for little Nellie Wayne, and I know you would rather she should have them. She loves flowers so, and her pleasures are few, poor little thing."

"It is to be regretted that there are not more of us who try to bring a little sunshine into the lives of those less favored and less fortunate than ourselves," replied Mrs. Reynolds. "I saw Nellie's mother yesterday and her eyes were full of grateful tears as she told me of all you had done for herself and for her poor, lame, little one."

"My dear friend, I am simply sharing with them the things that God has entrusted to my care to be used as he would have them used. What right have I to imagine, because I am more blessed with this world's goods than are many others, that I have the right to selfishly enjoy them all to myself instead of distributing them among others who are just as appreciative and just as worthy as I. The thanks are due to the Heavenly Father, my friend, from whom comes every good and perfect gift. We are but his servants, to whom he intrusts these things, and how careful should we be to see that we make the use of them which we know to be acceptable in his sight."

"Who is my neighbor?"

This is the question which Mrs. Raymond asked of herself after the departure of her last visitor.

"Of course," she said, "the meaning of the old Anglo-Saxon from which the word 'neighbor' is derived is 'nigh-dweller;' but the nigh-dweller is not always the neighbor. Mrs. Blank is a nigh-dweller, but she certainly does not come up to the standard which Christ laid down for a neighbor. Now my last caller lives at least two miles away, yet she is certainly a neighbor in the fullest meaning of the word to a great many people. She knows how I love books and she also knows that in this libraryless town I could not satisfy my taste for reading did not she, good Samaritan-like, give to me of the rich benefits of her own library. Her very personality is suggestive of thoughtfulness, interest and sympathy. She is never too busy to sympathize with her friends and acquaintances in times of sorrow, nor too indifferent to rejoice with them in times of gladness, or to give of her service when sickness comes to them. She seems to know intuitively who it is that finds life dull and monotonous, and how to put into that life a little variety and into the life that is very lonely she knows just how to bring a little pleasure.

"On the other hand, it is fearful to contemplate how many homes may be made unhappy and how the peace of individuals may be disturbed by the busybody—the peacebreaker—be she a nigh-dweller or far-dweller. Her influence is felt throughout the entire community. She can see further through a stone wall or a keyhole than other people can see through an open door. She can hear conversations that are being carried on in the next house. She knows all about everybody's private affairs and performs the work of the evil one so well that his Satanic Majesty disturbs himself but little concerning affairs in her community, knowing his work is well looked after."

Can we wonder that Mrs. Raymond asks, "Who is my neighbor?"

Doubtless we are all acquainted with the story of the great philosopher and his no less philosophic servant who set before his master the two dinners of tongue, but the truth it presents cannot be too well learned:

This philosopher invited some friends to dine, and ordered his servant to get the very best thing that the market afforded; and when he and his friends sat down to the table, they were served with nothing but tongue—tongue fried, tongue stewed, tongue roasted, tongue prepared in every conceivable way. The philosopher was vexed and said:

"Didn't I tell you to get the very best thing your could find in the market?"

"And that is just what I did, sir," replied the servant. "Surely the tongue is an organ most divine. It is the organ of worship. By it are expressed words of love, of kindness; the language of a pure heart. It is a most useful and blessed organ."

"To-morrow," said the philosopher, "I desire you to get the worst thing you can find in the market." And when the morrow came he again sat down to a dinner of tongue.

"Did I not tell you to get the worst thing in the market?" he asked.

"I did get the worst thing, sir," was the reply. "Is not the tongue the organ on which 'Satan plays?' the organ of lying and of blasphemy? Surely, sir, it is a most destructive organ."

O, for the right use of the tongue! the organ of which Jesus says, "It is an unruly evil, full of deadly poison." O, that we might cease our fault-finding and our criticizing! It is so easy to find fault and to see the flaws of which the world is full. It requires little brains or heart to be a critic. It is a sure sign of moral decadence to be able to see only the defects, and the man or woman who becomes a gossip, critic or fault-finder cannot but lose ground spiritually. We need an eye to see the good and the beautiful in this world. We need to pray for a loving spirit—the spirit of the loving Christ—that we may have a pitying heart and judge not our fellowmen. And without ceasing do we need to pray:

"Set a watch, O Lord, before my mouth; keep the door of my lips!"

St. Louis, Mo.

Going Back to Grandpa's.

Read by A. M. Atkinson at a Macatawa picnic, and reprinted here by request.

I'm going back to grandapa's,
I won't come back no more
To hear remarks about my feet
A muddyin' up the floor.
They's too much said about my clothes,
The scoldin's never done—
I'm goin' back to grandpa's
Where a boy kin have some fun.

I dug up half his garden
A gittin' worms for bait;
He said he used to like it
When I laid abed so late;
He said that pie was good for boys,
An' candy made 'em grow;
Ef I can't go to grandpa's
I'll turn pirate first you know.

He let me take his shotgun,
An' loaded it fer me.
The cats they hid out in the barn,
The hens flew up a tree.
I had a circus in the yard
With twenty other boys—
I'm goin back to grandpa's,
Where they ain't afraid of noise.

He didn't make me comb my hair
But once or twice a week;
He wasn't watchin' out fer words
I didn't orter speak;
He told me stories 'bout the war
And Injuns shot out West.
Oh, I'm goin' down to grandpa's
For he knows wot boys like best.

He even run a race with me,
But had to stop an' cough:
He rode my bicycle and laughed
Bec'us he tumbled off;
He knew the early apple trees
Around within a mile,
Oh, grandpa was a dandy,
An' was "in it" all the while.

I bet you grandpa's lonesome,
I don't care what you say;
I seen him kinder cryin'
When you took me away.
When you talk to me of heaven,
Where all the good people go,
I guess I'll go to grandpa's,
An' we'll have good times, I know.

—*Sioux City Tribune.*

"I'll Pay You For That."

A hen trod on a duck's foot. She did not mean to do it, and it did not hurt the duck much. But the duck said, "I'll pay you for that!"

So the duck flew at the hen, but as she did so, her wing struck an old goose who stood close by.

"I'll pay you for that!" cried the goose, and she flew at the duck, but as she did so her foot tore the fur of a cat, who was just in the yard.

"I'll pay you for that!" said the cat, and she started for the goose, but as she did so her claw caught in the wool of a sheep.

"I'll pay you for that!" cried the sheep, and she ran at the cat, but as she did so, her foot hit the foot of a dog who lay in the sun.

"I'll pay you for that!" cried he, and jumped at the sheep, but as he did so his leg struck an old cow who stood by the gate.

"I'll pay you for that!" cried she, and she ran at the dog, but as she did so her horn grazed the skin of a horse who stood by a tree.

"I'll pay you for that!" cried he, and he rushed at the cow.

What a noise there was! The horse flew at the cow, and the cow at the dog, the dog at the sheep, and the sheep at the cat, and the cat at the goose, and the goose at the duck, and the duck at the hen. What a fuss there was, and all because the hen accidentally stepped on the duck's toes.

"Hi, hi!" What's all this?" cried the man who had the care of them. "I cannot have all this. You may stay here," he said to the hen. But he drove the duck to the pond, the goose to the field, the cat to the barn, the sheep to her fold, the dog to his house, the cow to her yard, and the horse to his stall.

And so all their good times were over, because the duck would not overlook a little hurt which was not intended.

Guidance.

Being perplexed, I say,
Lord, make it right!
Night is as day to Thee,
Darkness as light.
I am afraid to touch
Things that involve so much;
My trembling hand may shake,
My skilless hand may break:
Thine can make no mistake.

Being in doubt, I say,
Lord, make it plain!
Which is the true, safe way?
Which would be vain?
I am not wise to know,
Nor sure of foot to go;
My blind eyes cannot see
What is clear to Thee.
Lord, make it clear to me!

—*Unidentified.*

A Doctor's Bill.

A good true story is told of a San Francisco philanthropist and a doctor with a conscience. A wealthy lady several years ago developed an insignificant wen on her face. In her travels in Europe she consulted an eminent surgeon as to its removal and was advised not to have it done. An Eastern surgeon of equal eminence also declined to perform the operation.

Returning to San Francisco she happened to show it to a physician and surgeon of no national reputation—a humble homœpath—but a man whose skill was unquestioned. He examined it carefully, and said there would be no trouble about it; it was a simple operation. Dreading to risk it after such eminent warning, she delayed action, but finally asked another examination and opinion. The same conclusion was reached; and the operation followed, with wholly successful results.

One day, when the doctor called, his bill was asked for. He presented it, $50 being the amount. The lady smiled and said, "Do you consider that a reasonable charge, considering the circumstances?"

The doctor replied, "That is my charge for that operation; your circumstances have nothing to do with it."

The lady went to her desk and drew a check for $500, and presented it to him. He looked at it and handed it back, saying: "I cannot accept this. My charge for that operation is $50."

"Very well," the lady replied. "Keep the check, and place the balance to my credit."

Some months after she received a lengthy itemized bill, upon which were entered charges for treatment of various kinds, rendered to all sorts of odds and ends of humanity, male and female, black and white, who had been mended at her expense. She was so delighted at it that she immediately placed another check for $500 to her credit, on the same terms, and it is now being earned in the same way.—*Pacific Unitarian.*

Pay of American Officers.

The pay of army officers is higher than that of naval officers, even when the latter are at sea. Thus a general gets $15,000 a year, an admiral $13,000; a lieutenant-general $11,000; a vice admiral $9,000; a major-general gets $7,500, a rear-admiral gets $6,000; a brigadier-general $5,500; a commodore $5,000; a colonel gets $4,500; a naval captain the same; a lieutenant-colonel gets $4,000; a commander $3,500; a major $3,500; a lieutenant-commander from $2,800 to $3,000. A captain in the army $2,500, a lieutenant in the navy from $2,400 to $2,600; a first lieutenant in the army gets $2,000, a lieutenant, junior grade, in the navy gets from $1,800 to $2,000; a second lieutenant gets $1,540, an ensign gets from $1,200 to $1,400. Even the cadet at West Point gets $450, as against $500 for the naval cadet at Annapolis. On shore the navy pay is cut down from one sixteenth to to one-fifth.

The Spanish-American war will rank as one of the shortest in the world's history. Other notable conflicts of modern times have been:

Turkey versus England and Russia—1807 to 1812, five years: estimated cost to England and Russia, $250,000,000; loss of life for all involved, estimated at 250,000.

Turkey verses England, Russia and France—1827 to 1829, two years; estimated cost to the allied powers, $150,000,000; loss of life for allied powers, estimated at 10,000.

Crimean War—1853 to 1856, two years and seven months; English loss in life, 24,000; French loss in life, 63,500; Russian loss in life (largely from camp disease), 500,000; cost to England, $205,000,000; to France, $125,000,000; to Russia, $600,000,000.

Austria versus France and Sardinia—April 23, 1859 to July 12, 1859, eighty days; estimated cost to Austria, $85,000,000; Austrian loss of life, 18,000.

Austria versus Prussia and Italy—June 18, 1866, to July 26, 1866, thirty-nine days; estimated cost to Austria, $50,000,000; Austrian loss of life, 7,200.

Franco-Prussian War—July 15, 1870 to Feb. 22, 1871; German loss of life, 127,867; French loss of life, 350,000; war expenses of France, $1,977,000,000; war indemnity of France, $1,000,000,000.

Turco-Russian war—April, 1877 to January, 1878, ten months; Turkish loss of life, 162,000; Russian loss of life, 89,879; cost to Russia, $600,000,000; cost to Turkey, $750,000,000.

The cilil war of the United States lasted four years and one month and cost this government nearly $2,000,000,000. The total loss of life on both sides was about 1,000,000. The Spanish-Americon war to yesterday had lasted 103 days, and cost this government during that time approximately $103,000,000, with a total loss of life of less than 600, exclusive of deaths in camp on American soil.—*Post Dispatch.*

Literature.

ISTIANITY AND ANTI-CHRISTIANITY, IN HEIR FINAL CONFLICT. By Samuel J. ndrews, author of the "Life of Our ord," "God's Revelations of Himself to [en," "Some Thoughts on Christian nity." G. P. Putnam's Sons, New ork and London. 1898.

his book was written for a purpose—to ain a theory. The theory is that of nillennialism—the world growing worse the church more apostate until a moral clysm transpires at the second personal earing of Christ. This gives the whole k a pessimistic tone that is neither nal nor healthy. The bugbear of the nor is pantheism, and this, culminating ome man, is the anti-Christ to which re drifting. The immanence of God in re and history, a controlling thought ur day, is with this author only a phase antheism. All tendency to Christian n and international co-operation is re-led as preparatory to the development he anti-Christ, who is to revolutionize world, overthrowing church and state. n the growth of democracy is worked his pessimistic scheme, as evidence of general degeneracy of the times.

he author seems to have hunted up the t radical and materialistic uttrances of lasses of thinkers and thrown them to-ier to describe the present condition of church. For this reason it would be a fortune for the book to fall into the ds of the skeptically inclined. They ld find food in it to feed their skepti-ı.

his would be a sad world if the outlook n in this book were the true outlook. the author has a theory according to ch things must grow worse, and all ements are interpreted accordingly. ourse it states some wholesome things, these will be neutralized by the general of the work.

RGE MULLER. By Fredric G. Wagner. leming H. Revell, Chicago, Publisher. rice, 75 cents.

in the later period of the church life e were needed an illustration of the that God is a prayer-answering God, rge Muller has helped the church to w it. The keynote of this remarkable may be told in his own words. Speak- of the orphanages established by him Bristol, he says:

But still the first and primary object of institution was and still is that God ht be magnified by the fact that the or-ns under my care were and are pro-d with all they need only *by prayer and h*, without any one being asked by me ny fellow-laborers, whereby it might be 1 that God is FAITHFUL STILL and HEARS YER STILL. That God wonderfully sed his labors is evident from the re-s. During the 63 years of his labors, re came to the orphanages about 10,000 dren. In the schools established under care about 120,000 pupils received in-ction, over 2,000,000 copies of the Bible, v Testament, Psalms or other portions he Bible were sent out, over 111,000,000 ptural books and tracts were distributed for the support of this work, over $7,-,000 came into my hands." Not a cent of was ever solicited from any individual. s is worthy our study. The story is l in simple language. The teaching is plain. The example of faith is a tower of strength.

Geo. Muller passed away on March 10th last in his 93rd year, having worked up to the last day. As one said, "He just stepped quietly off home as the gentle Master opened the door and whispered, 'Come!' "

BRUCE WOLVERTON.

DIVINE HEALING AND DOCTRINES. By J. W. Conley. Fleming H. Revell, Chicago, publishers. Price, 15 cents.

This booklet is a calm discussion of the subject under the light of revealed truth. The writer takes up the passages referring to the use of medicine, or to physicians and healing. He does not *forget* the *context*. This is a great excellence and prevents much one-sided treatment of such subjects. He does not fail to recognize the power of God in healing. The prayers of the righteous man working in accordance with his prayer is availing. He concludes "that the Bible is favorable to the use of medicines and the employment of physicians."

BRUCE WOLVERTON.

The 14th annual report of the United States Civil Service Commission, a copy of which we have just received, is a voluminous affair. Why this is so, however, becomes apparent at a glance at its pages, containing as it does so many departments, positions, rules, regulations and officers. As we could give no adequate outline of its contents without a lengthy paragraph we recommend all parties interested, especially those contemplating an examination for civil service, to send to the Commissioner at Washington, D. C., for a copy.

"The United States in Relation to the Messiah's Return" is the title of a small book recently written by Caleb Davis and published by the Knox Publishing Co. This book takes the ground that the little stone cut out of the mountain without hands in Daniel's vision signifies the United States and occupies its pages with reasons for the position. Some of these, we admit, have a fitness to the vision, but these may be coincidents only. The end of the little stone—filling the whole earth—seem to signify more than the United States has yet or will ever accomplish. However, the book is interesting and the thoughts presented deserving of careful consideration.

MAGAZINES.

Richard Harding Davis' account of the Rough Riders' fight at Guasimas leads the September Scribner's. He was in the fight actively from first to last, and this is his only elaborate descriptive narrative of it. It abounds in personal incidents. Nothing is given on hearsay. Mr. Davis describes only what he himself saw. Other articles are also devoted to scenes and events of the Santiago battle.

Everybody has heard of the Red Cross, yet comparatively few people have more than a vague idea of what it really is. Belle M. Brain, in a very interesting and timely article entitled, "The Story of the Red Cross," in the September Woman's Home Companion, tells all about this great movement, from its inception to the present day, with many illustrations.

The Chautauquan for September displays a wealth of literary matter which will find a hearty welcome in scores of homes. Subjects of general interest are treated by skillful writers, and from the initial paper on "The Literary Women of Washington," by Etta Pamsdell Goodwin, attractively illustrated with portraits of Mrs. Burnett, Mrs. Spofford, and other literary women, to "History as it is Made," with its concise account of the current events, the magazine is one of the best of the volume.

The Pall Mall for September contains a wide range of subjects for its readers from a strong paper by Sir Chas. W. Dilke on an Anglo-Saxon union to entertaining facts and popular fiction. This is one of the best numbers of the year.

Sunday School.

SINS THAT KILL.*

HERBERT L. WILLETT.

The first of the prophets whose sermons have reached us in a collection is Amos. The reign of Jeroboam II. was perhaps the most prosperous period in the history of the Northern Kingdom. Of the three monarchs whose administrations, judged from a merely political standpoint, were able and prosperous, viz., Jeroboam I., Ahab and Jeroboam II., the last was the most notable. Territories lost during previous reigns were regained, and the kingdom was greatly widened and enriched. But, as is so often the case, external prosperity was accompanied by a sad decline in ethics and religion. Growing wealth among the upper classes caused increasing poverty at the opposite end of the social scale. Religion was associated with the sanctuaries, of which there were many in the country, but the worship was mingled with elements taken from the Baal worship and had thus become corrupt, while both priests and prophets of the popular cult were men of low morals and motives, and made a mere profession of their calling. As a result the life of the common people was on a low moral level; they were not likely to rise above the practice of their religious leaders.

It was this situation which strongly appealed to a herdman named Amos, who added to his scanty income by a rather indifferent variety of fruit, such as the hilly country of Judah was able to produce. He lived at Tekoah, a town a few miles south of Bethlehem. From this region he probably took his merchandise to the market towns of both Judah and Israel. This gave him occasion to observe the low moral and spiritual conditions prevailing in Samaria, probably much worse than those in Jerusalem at the time. A man of strong religious nature, and already impressed with the awfulness of such a state of morals, he was the very man to preach the divine will to these people. Accordingly, the prophetic call came to him, and while there is no hint that he gave up his business or ceased to provide for himself in the usual way, we have the record of his prophetic work in Bethel and Samaria, which may have covered but a brief period. His contact with the merchant life of these towns gave him admirable opportunities for conversations which grew into sermons, as his listeners multiplied. He disclaimed with indignation any relation with the guilds of prophets, which may supply another hint as to the mercenary level to which their work had sunk.

The series of discourses recorded under the name of Amos discloses a nature passionately indignant at the state of affairs, and determined to register the most emphatic protest against it. The people are what they are largely because of the character of their nobles, princes, judges, priests and preachers. When these are wicked, weak or worthless men, the nation can only suffer as the result. The picture of the times as given in the lesson is graphic. The rulers in Jerusalem and Samaria, with both of which capitals Amos is familiar, are totally indifferent to any obligations to righteousness; they are "at ease." They know what right is, but do not care to practice it. Yet these men are those who are set over the people, to whom appeals for justice must be made, and from whom the pattern of conduct is derived. Israel cannot claim that her condition is the result of meagre conditions of poverty or limitation, yet the people considered that no nation has ever been blessed as has this one. Look at the great cities on the horizon. Has not Samaria been prospered as neither Calneh, Hamath or Gath? Every blessing has been hers, yet she is indifferent to God. But those other cities, rich and powerful, as they were, have perished or are perishing under the desolating power of the world-conquering Assyrian. How can Samaria escape if she continues to disregard the law of God?

Yet these men, the appointed leaders of Israel, are corrupt and luxurious men. They laugh at a day of reckoning; their court-rooms, where justice is supposed to be practiced, are seats of violence, where bribery and outrage prevail; they pass their time in effeminate idleness, in houses furnished with splendor, the fruit of their rapacity; their tables are loaded with the choicest food, which the poor have to furnish by their unjustly rewarded toil; in their revels they employ singers and dancers, and prostitute to ignoble uses the very instruments of music which David had consecrated to the holiest purposes; they drink immoderately and their debaucheries are the scandal of the land. For the real evils of the nation they care nothing. They are mere self-seeking, scheming, unscrupulous politicians, and that only, no matter how sacred the calling to which they were chosen. The result can only be national destruction. The land must suffer for its unworthy leaders. They themselves will go captive in the first deportation, and very different shall be their fate after that dreadful day. The whole land has become a stench to Jehovah by means of such practices, and their evil example has infested every rank of society. The divine law has been outraged. A process of destruction, purging, cleansing, discipline, is the only result.

In such pictures as these the condition of Israel in the eighth century B. C. is described. The striking element in these pictures is their appropriateness to our own time. We sometimes speak of the Bible as an old book, dealing with long-vanished situations; as a matter of fact, no book is so up to date as this. The problems of society with which Amos, Hosea, Micah and Isaiah had to deal are the very problems of our day; the growing distance between the rich and poor; the power of the well-to-do over the less resourceful, the avaricious spirit that lies next to its own possessions, the tendency to drunkenness in officials in county, city and state, the anarchism which breeds like a festering sore beneath the surfice of a corrupt social and municipal life. The Bible is the freshest of volumes on the social questions of the day.

The root of all reformation and the hope for the future lies in the child. Much can be done to reform, but infinitely more can be done to form at the start. The hope of the race is in the child, and the child is in the Sunday-school. To use the opportunity there afforded is to save him, and through him to save society. No one method will solve the dreadful problem of drink and the ruin it works; every effective attack must be pressed—probibition, moral suasion, restriction, reformation, education. But the greatest hope lies in the child, and his war-cry—"Tremble, monster, I shall grow up!"

SUGGESTIONS FOR TEACHING.

The man who knows how to do good and does it not is the greatest sinner. Leadership imposes the greatest responsibility; in which direction are you leading? What people have received greater blessings than we? Of whom will greater results be demanded? Wealth that is held as a trust from God and is used for his service is a blessing to the world. Wealth that is regarded as a personal possession and used selfishly is a curse to the world, and a greater curse to the possessor. "True wealth consists in laying out, not in laying up." Our use of the so-called better things of life must be regulated by the effect they produce on ourselves and our obligations to share with others. The only temperance is an abstinence which permits no danger to ourselves or evil example to others. Intemperance is not confined to drink, but may appear in eating, dressing, speech and pleasure. Some people are very careful about drink, but very intemperate in temper. The best of things, like music and art may be prostituted to evil uses. Evil conduct can but bring disaster. God is too mercifui to divorce sin from its consequences.

*Sunday-school Lesson for Sept. 11, 1898—Sinful Indulgence (Amos 6:1-8). Golden Text—They also have erred through wine, and through strorng drink are out of the way (Isa. 28:7). Lesson Outline—1. Indifference (1-2); 2. Luxury (3-6); 3. Disaster (7-8).

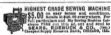

ıcavor.

:INS.

R 11.

ĘLF-DENIAL?

:16-24.)

tion comes the

it is far oftener
it is every day,
ꜱ the question,
nper and please
t?'' From the
ng, stretching,
ether to indulge
hands in sleep
ht-light, it is a
the better im-
ssible conflict:
:t—the question

the question is
will thrive. If
e the loser. If
ins. There are
tter service by
ıre that kind of
oncerned. We
em.
kind or tender,
r to himself in-
riable result of
ıat to be very
rain, to leave it
the day, and to
ly in cotton at
water—strange
lgence to a seed
Strange that he
ains, give him-
kind to himself,
imself, and yet
Strange that
cold ground and
lect is adding to
ed, but it is so.
not spare him-
and no pain,
ıt he flourishes
has so ordained
ꜱ it, and he who
ground must be
rist was pierced
us be broken in
ore we can bear
''Good-bye, be
which is, being
y yourself!''
re in themselves
hich are not, in
hing which, in
that to abstain
ellence, ''Tem-
have been burn-
es, and many in
al form of self-
in the land, but
ough its secrets,
per the tale of
n kind to them-
l both to selves
t the life-giving
ıg current, who

ıt but one of the
e which have
d homes? Are
-pride, money-
y, self-seeking,
nd unkindness—
ys in which a
r than the open
ndulgence blasts
and friends?
t ''drunkards,''
ve drink of *any*
ss that hardens
our homes un-
of our souls?

EACTS AND FACTORS.

The first of Spain's repatriated soldiers on the Alicante reached Cormma Aug. 24th.

Our school system will be established in Santiago at the opening of the schools there Sept. 15th.

Gen. Merritt found $800,000 in Spanish gold in the surrendered treasury at Manila.

A colored man recently died at Omaha whose age is said to have been 130 years.

There is trouble at Pana, Ill., between union and non-union miners.

Forty-two children were poisoned at a picnic at Dubuque, Ia., Aug. 16th, by eating canned meats. By hard work the lives of all the victims were saved.

Pensioners now on the United States pension roll number more than a million.

The American Association for the advancement of science met in Boston, August 22nd, in a two days' session.

The steamer Heligoland, of the Learner North Polar Expedition, has returned to Tromsoe for repairs. After penetrating to within 600 miles of the pole, the searchers for Prof. Andree report no trace of the explorer.

''Emperor William Memorial Church'' has cost $865,000, and is not yet completely finished; about $500,000 will be needed for the interior decorations, one-half of which sum is at hand.

An accident to the Prince of Wales will disable him from walking for several weeks.

The oldest university in the world is El Ayhar, at Cairo. It is the greatest Mohammedan university, having clear records dating back nearly a thousand years.

The longest telephone line in the world is that just being completed between San Diago, Cal., and Nelson, British Columdia. It is 2,225 miles long. Think of listening to a human voice at such a distance!

According to Appleton's Cyclopedia the gifts bestowed upon schools, libraries, picture galleries, hospitals, etc., during the last five years, amounted to $165,800,000, of which the largest annual total, $45,000,000, belongs to last year, and the smallest, $27,000,000, to the year preceding.

In 1890, 1891, 1892 and 1893 there were over a thousand railroad accidents by derailment in each year; in 1894 there were 873, in 1895 there were 810 and in 1896 the number was reduced to 792. There are not so many collisions as there were in former years. Between 1888 and 1893, iuclusive, the number ranged from 1,100 to 800. In 1894 there were 613; in 1895, 602 and in 1896 there were 514.

A mathematician has compiled the following list of speeds a second: The snail, one-half inch; a man walking, 4 feet; a fast runner, 23 feet; a fly, 24 feet; fast skater, 38 feet; a carrier pigeon, 87 feet; locomotive (sixty miles an hour), 88 feet; swallows, 220 feet; the worst cyclone known, 380; the Krakatoa wave (at the volcanic catastrophe of August 27, 1893, in the Sunda Islands), 940 feet; the surface of the globe on sea level at the equator, 1,500 feet.

Marriages.

JOHNSTON—VENNUM.—At Normal, Ill., Aug. 3, Virgil W. Johnston, of Pontiac, Ill., and Vinnie V. Vennum, of Fisher, Ill., Dr. W. Frank Ross officiating. Both are Christians.

Obituaries.

[One hundred words will be inserted free. Above one hundred words, one cent a word. Please send amount with each notice.]

FULLER.

Mrs. Maria Louisa Fuller, daughter of Abram and Nancy Darst, was born in Meigs county, O., Feb. 4, 1837. Married J. L. Fuller Dec. 13, 1858, to whom were born five sons and three daughters. She died at her home July 1, 1898, aged 61 years, four months and 27 days. She gave herself to Christ at 18 and has lived an earnest Christian life ever since. The funeral sermon was preached by the writer to a large concourse of people at her home at Shelby, Ind., July 3, 1898. She left many dear friends behind to mourn their loss.

S. A. STRAWN.

FYFFE.

Allen Herman, son of Oscar and Nettie Fyffe, born in Laurence County, Ill., March 12, 1897, and died in Stoddard County, Mo., Aug. 16, 1898. He was sick but eleven hours with congestion of the brain.

M. B. F.

HALL.

On June 25, 1998, after an illness covering a period of over a year, J. W. Hall passed away at his home in Roodhouse, Ill. In this sad event the community feels the loss of an honorable, highly respected citizen and the church a pillar of support and a tower of strength. Bro. Hall was born Nov. 7, 1826, in Rohan County, N. C., but early in life accompanied his parents to Illinois where, wi h the exception of a two years' residence in Lyons, Kas., he has since lived. On May 16, 1850, Bro. Hall united in marriage with Miss Jennie Long. To this union were born three children, John T., the oldest, who died in Dodge City, Kas., Dec. 15, 1881, Emma E., wife of Dr. J. S. Chase, of Venice, Ill., and C. C. Hall, of Milton, Ill. The two last named, with their mother, survive in deep realization of bereavement and loss. In early manhood, while yet unmarried, Bro. Hall united with the Christian Church and has ever lived a consistent Christian, sharing the burdens of the congregation and exulting in every triumph of the cause of Christ. A staunch believer in the eternal right, he was found always, on all great questions, on the side that seemed right to him. Thus the cause of religion, temperance, citizenship and charity found in him an able supporter. His death, though long expected by many, came with a shock to the community and his funeral was attended by a throng of sympathizing friends. His remains were conducted by rail to Milton, Pike County, Ill., and in the church, built forty years before by his own hands, the last sad tributes were paid. His body rests in the Blue River cemetery, while his life is held in sweet remembrance by many sincere friends. He has fought a good fight, he has finished his course, he has kept the faith. The promises of God to such as he lifts a heavy load of care from the hearts that remain.

HUGH A. ORCHARD.

Roodhouse, Ill., Aug. 22.

METZ.

Maude E. Metz was born in Pike County, Ill., April 16, 1878, and died July 23, 1898. She was the daughter of E. R. and Emma L. Metz. She died of consumption. She was sick a year. She never complained, but was hopeful. She obeyed the gospel Jan. 10, 1893. Jesse Gresham baptized her. When not sick she was present at all church services. She was an *active*, practical Endeavorer. She did what she could. She wasn't perfect, but was a good and obedient girl.

A. C. ROACH.

Chambersburg, Ill., Aug. 15, 1898.

TAYLOR.

Ella A. Taylor was born April 22, 1860, and died July 13, 1898. From a child she had followed her Savior. She was a sympathetic and devoted Christian. To know her was to love her. The writer preached the discourse at her funeral to a very large congregation of tear-stained faces. She indeed was the embodiment of the Christian character, and our loss is her gain.

S. A. STRAWN.

)SPEL CALL

N 100,000 COPIES SOLD!

POPULAR SONG-BOOK.

THAN 400 OF THE CHOICEST HYMNS AND GOSPEL
00 OF THE BEST COMPOSERS OF SACRED MUSIC.

Music, Bright, Cheerful and Inspiring.

PRAYER AND PRAISE.

24. More Like Jesus.

J. M. S. J. M. STILLMAN.

1. I want to be more like Je - sus, And fol-low Him day by day;
2. I want to be kind and gen - tle, To those who are in dis-tress;
3. I want to be meek and low - ly, Like Je-sus our friend and King;
4. I want to be pure and ho - ly, As pure as the crys - tal snow;
I want to be true and faith-ful, And ev -'ry com-mand o - bey.
To com-fort the bro-ken heart-ed, With sweet words of ten-der-ness.
I want to be strong and earnest, And souls to the Sav - iour bring.
I want to love Je-sus dear - ly, For Je - sus loves me, I know.
REFRAIN.
More and more like Je - sus, I would ev - er be.........
ev - er be,
More and more like Je - sus, My Sav-iour who died for me.

By permission of J. M. Stillman.

or Societies that contemplate buying new Song Books, will be sent Sample
od order within a reasonable time.

SEND ALL ORDERS TO

ING COMPANY, 1522 Locust St., ST. LOUIS.

Words of Cheer for Church Extension.

Church Extension is doing more for our people than any other work. Let every member put a shoulder to the wheel.
T. J. REZNOR.
Elliott, Ia.

Our duty is to evangelize the world, but there can be no church abroad until there is first a church at home. As the church at home is, so will be the other. Let us push the church at home, and the church abroad will most surely come. A. J. MARSHALL.
Onawa, Ia.

I look upon the days for our collections as the most pleasant of the year. They are days when we can practically exemplify our Christianity. HORACE SIBERELL.
Pickering, Mo.

I consider the work of Church Extension one of the most important in our brotherhood.
WM. E. ADAMS.
Fort Wayne, Ind.

Hope for a large offering in September. Church here has an annual pledge for all mission work. W. S. LOWE.
Manhattan, Kan.

I most certainly believe it is as important to see a church firmly established and made self-supporting as to organize it. To do this a church home is assuredly necessary; therefore, we can't get along without a Church Extension Fund. M. S. JOHNSON.
Henderson, Ia.

We will do what we can to help reach one quarter of a million dollars by the close of 1900. MISS MARY HILL.
Mt. Healthy, Ohio.

A work that shelters so many houseless congregations, that cultivates a spirit of independence in those it aids, and that is founded upon such business-like principles, deserves heartiest support. MARK COLLIS.
Lexington, Ky.

I have secured loans for three churches. Neither could have been built without Church Extension help. H. ELLIOTT WARD.
Pasadena, Cal.

"Put yourself in his [their] place" and then ask, "What your contribution should be to Church Extension." FRANK A. MORGAN.
La Porta, Ind.

The importance of the work your Board is doing cannot be overdrawn. I know from experience and observation that churches are being built that never would be built if aid had not been received from our Board. A loan of $300, or even $100, starts the ball rolling, and soon the house is built. J. W. JENKINS.
Hood River, Ore.

We *believe* in Church Extension, and will *work* for it. W. T. HILTON.
Beloit, Kan.

Church Extension is one of the most important of all the missionary enterprises. What even a little money can do in the hands of the Extension Board is appreciated on this field. Extension extends. J. F. GHORMLEY.
Portland, Ore.

No church can make progress as it should without a building, and we should remember we have hundreds of churches stranded on this very rock. Let's help them off.
H. A. DENTON.
Centralia, Mo.

Church Extension is the only hope of making permanent the results of evangelization.
GEORGE DARSIE.
Frankfort, Ky.

It will require a gift from each member if we house the churches that are being planted now. Such a wonderful growth requires large gifts from all. Of so great a people great things are required. L. H. FULLER.
Burlington, Ia.

First send the gospel preacher to disciple the people, then aid them to build a house where they can meet on the first day of the week to break bread. Houseless disciples often mean scattered disciples.
C. W. TURRELL.
Lampasas, Tex.

Every preacher should see that the fondest hopes of the Extension Board are fully realized.
ROBT. L. WILSON.
Richmond, Mo.

Kankakee is a mission point, being aided $100 by the district each year. Small, poor membership—no house—struggling to finish paying $800 for a lot. We will raise our apportionment and we fondly hope the Extension Board will help us build. W. D. DEWEESE.
Kankakee, Ill.

Will do all we can for Church Extension; church here needs education along this line.
J. B. HOLMES.
Panora, Ia.

Will push collection as it deserves.
J. B. CLEMENS.
Arcola, Ill.

I think the Church Extension Fund is essential to the steady advancement and future success of our movement. Hope you will attain to your ideal. W. R. MCCREA.
Liscomb, Ia.

Our people are recognizing more and more the importance of this branch of missionary activity and are learning better to appreciate the work of the Church Extension Board, hence will certainly give with increasing liberality. GUY WINGATE.
Anthon, Ia.

Our congregation is poor and we are building a house ourselves, but we will not forget the September offering for some one in worse circumstances than we are.
GRANT E. PIKE.
Barnesville, O.

The Church Extension Fund is scarcely second in importance of all our missionary funds. I long to see a great increase in this year's offerings. Hope to increase ours here in Owosso, Mich. L. W. SPAYD.
Owosso, Mich.

We are building and very much in need of aid ourselves, but feel that we must maintain our position as contributors to Church Extension. J. V. CRAWFORD.
Enterprise, Ore.

I believe in Church Extension as a part of the Great Commission and shall aid it whenever I can. L. P. BUSH.
Bethany, Neb.

No work that we have undertaken gives greater returns for the money invested than Church Extension. L. M. DAUGHTY.
Lovington, Ill.

The perpetual motion of money for Christ is like a perpetual life of righteousness—an eternal exhortation to right living. Crops are a total failure this year, but will do what we can, be it ever so humble. JOSEPH SHIELDS.
Nipomo, Cal.

This is bearing one another's burdens, and yet each one bears his own burden at last. A very good way. A. MILNER.
Cisne, Ill.

This fund is certainly one of the greatest promoters of Christianity we have.
JOHN P. SALA.
Randolph, O.

We cannot give a great amount, but will "help a little" willingly.
F. M. CUNNINGHAM.
Marlboro, O.

The most permanently hopeful of our missionary enterprises is the Church Extension Fund. J. C. MASON.
Houston, Tex.

The Church Extension work is the backbone of all missionary work in America.
A. M. HOOTMAN.
Union City, Ind.

Think we can raise our apportionment all right. Have done much better in other lines of missionary work than usual this year. Want to keep up the record on Church Extension.
E. L. MOFFETT.
Centerville, Ia.

We are in debt about $600; but will try to do something for Church Extension.
J. M. JAYNE.
Memphis, Mo.

Best wishes for your success.
R. L. BRESHERS.
Tallula, Ill.

The Church Extension Fund has greatly aided this church and, if I remain here as pastor, the church will raise its proportion for each year. It is one of the best business works in the Church of Christ. Our method of aiding churches is the best, viz., to encourage self-help. May the good work soon extend to the securing of good locations in new towns and fields. P. J. DICKERSON.
Canon City, Col.

Church Extension is the most business-like business that we have. It preaches Christ and multiplies itself at the same time.
Marion, Ind. E. L. FRAZIER.

My ministry is under deep obligations to this board. I pray sincerely for guidance to secure generous offerings for it. No other is more deserving. C. H. STEARNS.
Monmouth, Ill.

THE
[C]HRISTIAN-EVANGELIST.

A WEEKLY FAMILY AND RELIGIOUS JOURNAL.

XXXV. September 8, 1898 No. 36.

CONTENTS.

:
Events....................291
-national Peace Conference... 292
and Longevity............ 292
d in the Balances.... 293
Easy Chair....................293
s and Answers....... 294
CONTRIBUTIONS:
of Living and Dying Nations.
ur F. Crafts, Ph. D...... ..295
e and Bismarck.—Frank R.
an 297
w of Religion as Revealed in
e.—A. L. Ferguson.......... 298
Christ.—J. M. Lowe 299
NDENCE:
g Through England 303
a Letter..... 303
version of Europe....... 304
ure of the C. E.......... 305
Montana ... .305
Letter. 305
Christian Colony Notes.... 306
RCLE:
poem). 312
ries.—The Companionship of
. . .. 312
e-staying Caller..... 312
ently (poem). 313
ake Sunset 313
g an Evil .... .313
y Power 313
ry Alphabet 314
on the Coffin-lid......... ... 314
s of the War........... 315
amine that Worry 315
EOUS:
lget 300
Mention. ... .302
stic.... 307
d News............ 308
ry 310
gious World 311
day-school 316
Endeavor 317
re...... 318
es ... .319
ements 320
rs' Notes.....................320

ubscription $1.75.

LULA FALLS, LOOKOUT MOUNTAIN.
GENERAL CONVENTION, CHATTANOOGA, OCTOBER 13-21.

PUBLISHED BY
CHRISTIAN PUBLISHING COMPANY
1522 Locust St., St. Louis.

THE

CHRISTIAN - EVANGELIST

J. H. GARRISON, EDITOR.

W. W. HOPKINS, ASSISTANT.

B. B. TYLER, J. J. HALEY,
EDITORIAL CONTRIBUTORS.

What We Plead For.

The Christian-Evangelist pleads for:

The Christianity of the New Testament, taught by Christ and his Apostles, versus the theology of the creeds taught by fallible men—the world's great need.

The divine confession of faith on which Christ built his church, versus human confessions of faith on which men have split the church.

The unity of Christ's disciples, for which he so fervently prayed, versus the divisions in Christ's body, which his apostles strongly condemned.

The abandonment of sectarian names and practices, based on human authority, for the common family name and the common faith, based on divine authority, versus the abandonment of scriptural names and usages for partisan ends.

The hearty co-operation of Christians in efforts of world-wide beneficence and evangelization, versus petty jealousies and strifes in the struggle for denominational pre-eminence.

The fidelity to truth which secures the approval of God, versus conformity to custom to gain the favor of men.

The protection of the home and the destruction of the saloon, versus the protection of the saloon and the destruction of the home.

For the right against the wrong;
For the weak against the strong;
For the poor who've waited long
For the brighter age to be.
For the truth, 'gainst superstition,
For the faith, against tradition,
For the hope, whose glad fruition
Our waiting eyes shall see.

RATES OF SUBSCRIPTION.

Single subscriptions, new or old	$1.75	each
In clubs of five or more, new or old.	1.50	"
Reading Rooms	1.25	"
Ministers	1.00	"

With a club of ten we will send one additional copy free.

All subscriptions payable in advance. Label shows the month up to the first day of which your subscription is paid. If an earlier date than the present is shown, you are in arrears. No paper discontinued without express orders to that effect. Arrears should be paid when discontinuance is ordered.

In ordering a change of post office, please give the OLD as well as the NEW address.

Do not send local check, but use Post office or Express Money Order, or draft on St. Louis, Chicago or New York, in remitting.

EDUCATIONAL.

ISTIAN-EVANGELIST

opinion and methods, Liberty; in all things, Charity."

, Mo., Thursday, September 8, 1898. No. 36

by all who are seeking to promote the welfare of the race.

One of the results of the war, not usually mentioned, is the better understanding that is likely to exist hereafter between Spain and the United States. It is evident that the people of Spain, including many in high office, were entirely ignorant of the American character and of the resources of the United States. Contact with our American soldiers in the recent war has served to dispel this ignorance and to create a respect for the people of the United States on the part of Spain that she has never had before. It will be remembered that before the Spanish soldiers began their return to Spain one of their number, writing in behalf of 11,000 of his fellow-soldiers, expressed the gratitude of the Spanish prisoners of war for the kind treatment they had received from the officers of the United States. Gen. Toral, before sailing the other day for home, expressed his appreciation of the American soldiers in the following statement:

> In all my experience I have never seen soldiers fight better nor handled more skillfully. They are a credit to any nation, and quite on a par with any Continental army. Each man fought as if the issue of the battle depended on his individual exertions. I see a great future for America with soldiers of the caliber of those we met in front of Santiago.

Out of this mutual respect for the courage of the soldiers of the two governments it is not improbable that there will come more peaceable and amicable relations.

It was feared, immediately after the close of hostilities, that the insurgents in Cuba, under the deep sense of wrong which they feel toward the Spanish people, would continue a sort of guerrilla warfare against their former enemies, until they would be compelled into submission by Uuited States troops. Such a course would have been the best proof of the incapacity of the Cuban insurrectionists to establish and maintain self-government. It is assuring, however, to learn that a much better state of things prevails throught the island. A dispatch from Havana, dated August 31, says that "it is now known that the insurgents have suspended hostilities in all parts of the island. There is, therefore, complete tranquility everywhere. The insurgent chiefs of all the zones have been given strict orders to respect the rights of all citizens, no matter how hostile they may have been to the insurrection during the war. They declare they are now ready to forget the past, being secure in the guarantee of freedom, and to dedicate themselves with faith and enthusiasm to the reconstruction of the couutry." This course on the part of the Cubans will give great satisfaction to the American people, whose supreme desire concerning them is that they may demonstrate to the world their capacity for self-government.

The same *penchant* for the sensational in journalism which led a certain class of papers before the war with Spain to denounce the President for his conservative policy, and after the war began, to report imaginary strifes and jealousies between admirals, generals and cabinet officers, now that the war is over, is finding a congenial field in exaggerated reports concening the condition of the soldiers, and in reckless criticisms against the war department and many prominent officials. Recent investigation has shown that these reports concerning the condition of the army are either wholly unfounded or are greatly overdrawn. It is simply the fondness for sensationalism that has led these journals to place our government in a false light before the civilized world. It is not surprising to find in some of the foreign journals an echo of these criticisms, for they have a right to suppose that pride of country would prevent American journals from grossly misrepresenting the condition of things which have followed the war. As intimated before, in this journal, we believe these criticisms in the main to be unjust, and whatever irregularities have existed have been chiefly due to the calling out and equipping of a large army in so brief a time. If the present war shall teach the American people to discriminate, in their patronage, between yellow journalism and the higher type of daily papers, this fact should be recognized as one of the beneficent results of the war.

The joint high commission for the settlement of a number of points of disagreement between the United States and Canada is now in session at Quebec. The commissioners have met, exchanged friendly salutations and have outlined the work before them. It is understood that there are four principle subjects that will receive the attention of the commission—the tariff; bonding regulations for the trans-shipment of goods over the great trunk railroads; pelagic sealing, and the Alaskan boundary. There will be other minor questions, such as the Newfoundland fisheries and alien labor to be considered. If the commission is successful, as it no doubt will be in perfecting the treaty, it will put at rest a number of causes which have produced irritation between the two countries. There is no reason why Canada and the United States should not be good neighbors and work to each other's mutual interest. The settlement of these disputed points by a commission would be another triumph of civilization over the ruder methods which once prevailed. The annexation of Canada is not a practical nor important question at present, but it is highly important, since Providence has placed the two countries alongside of each other, that they settle all their misunderstandings amicably and cultivate the closest relationship socially and commercially.

In an article on crime, in Pall Mall for September, by J. H. Schooling, some very interesting and important tables are given, indicating the relative positions of men and women to social ethics. First we have the following table showing the ratio of women to men in each hundred convictions. The ratio is about four and a half men to one woman. But here is the table:

Nature of Crime	No. of each sex convicted, per 100 convictions.		
	Women.	Men.	Total.
Child-stealing and Cruelty to Children ...	70	30	100
Crimes against Property without Violence	19	81	100
Coining	18	82	100
Miscellaneous Crimes .	16	84	100
Malicious Injuries to Property .	15	85	100
Crimes of Violence against the Person.....	11	89	100
Robery and Extortion	10	90	100
Forgery ...	9	91	100
Crimes against Morals	4	96	100
Buglarly and Housebreaking . .	3	97	100

The influence of nationality and locality are shown, respectively, in the following table:

Country.	No. of each sex convicted, per 100 convictions.		
	Women.	Men.	Total.
England and Wales.....	18	82	100
Germany	18	82	100
France	17	83	100
Hungary......	16	84	100
Austria	14	86	100
Belgium.	11	89	100
Russia.	9	91	100
United States.........	9	91	100
Italy.	8	92	100

The investigations of the writer lead him to conclude that the number of suspected criminals at large as regards sex are also about four and a half men to one woman. The tendency to treat women more leniently in the courts may have a bearing upon these figures, but the fact seems established beyond a doubt that male criminals are the most numerous in all lands and nations. Other diagrams and tables of the writer show that the greatest number of burglaries occur from two to four A. M., and violence is offered to the person burgled in only one case out of every 336 burglaries. Best of all, however, is the table showing a marked decrease of all crimes in these last days. Here is the table:

	Per 10,000 of the population in	
	(1881)	(1895)
All Crimes	233	167
Larcenies	207	165

According to Dr. H. K. Carroll, in an article in the Forum, it requires $10,365,000 annually to pay the bills of the Protestant Episcopal Church, $23,863,000 to pay those of the Methodist Episcopal Church, nearly $24,000,000 for the expenses and contributions of the Northern Presbyterian Church, $11,673,000 for those of the Regular Baptists and $10,355,000 for those of the Congregational denomination, making an aggregate of $88,000,000 every year contributed by 10,768,000 members, an average of $8.16 per member.

AN INTERNATIONAL PEACE CONFERENCE.

The proposition of Emperor Nicholas, through Count Muravieff, his Foreign Minister, to the foreign diplomats at St. Petersburg, to hold an international conference looking to the preservation of peace and to partial disarmament, is an event of the first importance. Coming as it does from one of the most warlike nations of Europe, and one that was supposed to be preparing for an inevitable war, gives the proposal additional significance. His note to the foreign diplomats, published in our columns last week, looks as if the Russian Government had come to see what ought to be apparent to all European powers, that the way to permanent peace is not by constant preparation for war, but in coming to a mutual understanding with each other, and in cutting down their respective armaments to something like a peace footing. In this way only lies permanent peace. The Emperor goes on to argue with force that the expense attached to the constant increase in the army and navy, and in keeping up with the changes which new inventions make necessary, has become an unbearable burden upon Europe. The money and the talent of these countries are devoted to war instead of promoting national progress. The Emperor hopes that the conference which he proposes will find some way of preventing these evils, and "will be, by the help of God, the happy presage for the century that is about to open. It would converge into one powerful focus the efforts of all states sincerely seeking to make the great conception of universal peace triumph over the elements of trouble and discord, and it would, at the same time, cement their agreement by a corporate consecration of the principles of equity and right wherein rests the security of states and the welfare of peoples."

These are some of the most significant utterances that have ever come from any authorative source among European Governments. It can hardly be that the European powers will fail to respond favorably to this proposition for an international conference. The conception of a conference in which all the great powers of the world, or even of Europe, should be represented, to consider the question as to how they can live together peacefully and reduce the burdens of their respective peoples, and make life more comfortable for the masses of the people, is one that appeals strongly to Christian sentiment, and is in harmony with the best thought and feeling of our time. The world is not so large as it used to be. Rapid communication has brought the ends of the earth together. It is the more necessary, therefore, that nations learn the art of living together in peace and mutually promoting each other's welfare.

It was Victor Hugo, we believe, who spoke of the possibility in the future of "the United States of Europe." Why not United States of the world? Would it not be a sublime consummation of the progress of the nineteenth century, if at its close there could be a federation of all the civilized nations of the world, looking to peace and progress? What loftier aim could the statesmen of the world have in view than such a combination of the forces of civilization for the enlightenment and Christianization of the race and for the betterment of the condition of mankind? That this
will come about in the future we can
doubt. Such a conference as that propo
by Emperor Nicholas will hasten
larger federation of which we speak.

We hail with pleasure, therefore, t
proposition as a step toward internatio
co-operation for the promotion of pe
and the arts of peace. We regard it a
significant sign of the times—a harbing
indeed, of that brighter future.

"When the war-drum throbs no longer
the battle-flags are furled,
In the parliament of man, the federation of
world."

MORALITY AND LONGEVITY.

Nobody will dispute the proposition t
morality, as a rule, is a condition
longevity. Every one knows that
bauchery, libertinism and dissipation
disease-breeders and life-shortners. Se
any five young men from a town comm
ity, who loaf in barrooms and p
cards for drinks, and in twenty years f
of them will be dead and forgotten, and
fifth will be in his grave if he has not
good sense to quit his evil ways and g
work. I visited two sick men about t
time last year. Each of them was ab
thirty-five years of age and men of famil
They were in the same condition from
same cause, muscular paralysis brought
by youthful debaucheries. The loaths
disease contracted by these men in t
early life of sin had poisoned the bloo
their children, who were broken out
over their bodies with running so
Neither of those men will live to see fo
and if they should, all concerned will w
they had died at thirty-five.

I have just examined a list of vital sta
tics with reference to the longevity
different classes of men. It carries a g
lesson with it as bearing on the quest
before us. It is significant that preach
stand at one end of the scale and liqu
dealers at the other. The deathrate am
ministers was but little more than half
general deathrate, while that am
saloonkeepers and bartenders was ne
double the general deathrate. Engin
share with ministers the distinction of
smallest deathrate due to intempera
In both of these occupations intempera
is reported to have caused but two deat
year among 62,215 men. Nearly 2,
liquor men, 500 preachers and 603 teach
is the general proportion.

These suggestive facts show how m
temperance has to do with long l
Farmers stand second to ministers
average length of life, and school-teach
third. Preachers live longest because
a rule, they live best. Farmers are sec
in longevity because they are second
morality. Both moral and physical co
tions are more favorable in the country t
in towns and cities. Rural populati
never rise so high in their virtues, nor s
so low in their vices as those in the cent
A city is a strange combination of
highest and the lowest in human life.
tremes of wealth and poverty, educa
and ignorance, virtue and vice, relig
and irreligion meet here and live in sigh
each other. The country does not g
high as the highest, nor as low as the l
est in the city; but it strikes a be
average of moral health and soundn
because it lives in the open air and is
from the debasing influences and tem

tions of city life. The bone and sinew of a nation's morals are to be found in the country. If the moral soundness of the country did not replace the moral rottenness of the town, no nation could survive more than two or three generations. To the average young man town or city life is a death-trap and the open gateway to destruction. The minister, the farmer and the school-teacher live longer than other men because the vices that kill do not come their way, as they go the way of other classes of men.

And not only is it true that the man who lives best lives longest, but he lives happiest and is the most useful while he lives. It is a great crime for a man to die before his time as the fruit of wrong-doing. It is God's will that man shall live long on the earth, and be happy while he is here, and the only way to fulfill these ends of being is in the recognition of God's claims upon us, and conformity to the laws he has made for our guidance. An upright man has a good conscience, he enjoys the approval of God and the best that is in himself, he sets a good example before his neighbor, and vindicates the wisdom of God in making him. Is it not the great fact of the universe that right-doing pays the largest dividends? Will it pay to do wrong? Will anything pay, even in this life, but righteousness? Is not an evil practice or a vicious habit insanity, when you consider the consequences to which it leads? Is not sin both a life and a happiness-destroyer? "What man is he that desireth life and loveth many days that he may see good? Keep thy tongue from evil, and thy lips from speaking guile, depart from evil and do good, seek peace and pursue it."

J. J. H.

Hour of Prayer.

WEIGHED IN THE BALANCES.

(Midweek Prayer-meeting Topic, Sept. 14, 1898.)

Thou art weighed in the balances, and art found wanting.—*Dan.* 5:27.

God is constantly weighing men, institutions, measures, movements and nations, in the balances. It is a process from which nothing and no one escapes. Belshazzar was a king occupying a position of responsibility and power. Like many another king before and since his day, he was unmindful of the true interests of the people, and had given himself to feasting and drinking. It was during one of these feasts that there came forth the fingers of a man's hand and wrote on the wall of the king's palace some strange words. The king was troubled, for he no doubt had a guilty conscience. Daniel was remembered as having interpreted a dream for his father, Nebuchadnezzar, and was sent for to interpret the strange words. The words were, "Mene, Mene, Tekel, Upharsin," and this was the interpretation which Daniel gave: "God hath numbered thy kingdon and brought it to an end. Thou art weighed in the balances and art found wanting. Thy kingdom is divided, and given to the Medes and Persians." "This was probably a severe blow to the king's ambition, but it was God's judgment and it was inevitable. He was given a great opportunity, but he failed to improve it. He was found wanting. At a time in his nation's history when he should have been giving his clearest thought and his best efforts to promote the unity and well-being of the people over whom he ruled, he was given to banqueting, to sensual indulgences and to idolatrous practices. God weighed him in His balances and he was found wanting. It has been His verdict upon many a king and potentate.

God not only weighs kings, but He weighs every man in His balances. He gives to each of us life and endowment with a certain measure of ability and opportunity for usefulness. If we neglect to develop our God-given powers, and to use the opportunities that are offered to us, we are weighed in the balances and found wanting.

If God gives us riches, and we selfishly use them for the gratification of our pride, our ambition and our appetites, instead of regarding them as a trust from God, to be employed for the welfare of mankind, we are weighed in the balances and found wanting.

If in His providence God has placed us in a position of responsibility and influence, where our example will tell powerfully for truth and righteousness, and we hide our Christian light and refuse to let it shine, we have betrayed our trust; we have been weighed in the balances and found wanting.

If it has been given to us to preach the gospel, and we have been honored with a pulpit and a congregation, but have sought our own selfish ends and have been more anxious about our salaries than about the souls of those for whom we watch, or if we have neglected to cultivate the gift that is in us, so as to render the best service to him who hath called us into the fellowship of the gospel; in a word, if we have failed to recognize the dignity and the responsibility of the high calling, and to meet its demands upon us, we have been weighed in the balances and found wanting.

If we have been reared in a Christian home, with Christian influences about us from our youth, but have neglected the claims of Christ and the call of duty, and trusting to our own strength have made moral shipwreck of ourselves, we have been weighed in the balances and found wanting.

If a nation, planted by the hand of God, and favored above many other nations with the blessings of civil and religious liberty and the material advantages, grows rich and powerful and capable of becoming a great civilizing and Christianizing agency in the world, forgets God, becomes absorbed in money-getting, heeds not the cries of the oppressed, and the poor within its own borders, and puts forth no effort to purify itself from corruption and unrighteousness, it, too, has been weighed in the balances and foud wanting.

If the American Republic, having received special tokens of divine guidance and help in its recent conflict with Spain for the freedom of Cuba, should fail to understand the significance of this divine interposition, and not see in it a call to large and unselfish service in the uplifting of humanity, but should settle down to selfish ease and luxurious living, it, too, will be weighed in the balances and found wanting.

If our own effort to restore a simpler and purer Christianity, and to promote the unity of God's people, which has been so signally blessed of God, should lose the spirit of religious freedom in which it was born, and of high devotion to truth which has marked its history, and should degenerate into a mere sect, seeking its own glory, the sentence that will be ultimately pronounced upon it will be, "Weighed in the balances and found wanting."

These are testing times. Only those who trust in God and who make it their supreme aim to do His will can abide the test.

PRAYER.

O, Thou who art the God of nations, as well as of individuals, we beseech Thee that Thou wouldst bless this great Republic of the West which, in Thy providence, has become a lighthouse for the nations of the earth. We invoke Thy blessings upon its President his Cabinet and upon those who have been called to act as commissioners in arranging for a permanent peace, based on righteousness. May they be endowed with wisdom from on high, and seek to carry out Thy high counsel in the purposes of this nation. May all who are in authority in the nation and in the various states be men who shall fear God and love their fellowmen, to the end that this nation may be a blessing, not only to all its own citizens, but to the world. May it not be weighed in the balances and found wanting. Let Thy blessing rest upon us as individual Christians, that we may walk worthy of our high calling in Christ Jesus, and not bring reproach upon that worthy name by which we are called. Grant us grace to so live that when the testing time is over we may meet with Thy approval and be received into everlasting habitations through Jesus Christ our Lord. Amen!

Editor's Easy Chair.

OR MACATAWA MUSINGS.

Grand Rapids is 30 miles distant from Macatawa, and quite a large number of its citizens have their summer homes here at the Park. It is a city of about 100,000 population and is one of the cleanest, thriftiest and most enterprising cities of its class in the whole country. On the invitation of the members of our church in that city, we spent last Lord's day with them, preaching morning and evening. The pastor, E. M. Widger, is on a short vacation, and has been taking in some of the Northern Michigan resorts. He made us a brief visit at Macatawa, and we were all very favorably impressed with him. We found his church to be enthusiastic concerning him and hopeful of making substantial progress under his wise and energetic leadership. This church has been singularly fortunate—or wise, we should say, perhaps—in its selection of preachers. It has always had good men, and the result is that the church has good standing in the community. It has also an efficient board of officers. It is not a large church, but it contains within its membership some of the best people of the city, and its Sunday-school and Endeavor Society are among the liveliest and best we have seen anywhere. We enjoyed our visit to Grand Rapids very much, and it is always a delight to be the guest of our Brother and ex-Mayor, L. C. Stow. He explained to us the plan of their city government, which has in it some features worth studying by other cities. Grand Rapids has an intelligent class of citizens, who mean to keep their city as good as the best. As one of the great centers of the furniture manufacturing industry it has a prosperous future before it.

These are clear, beautiful, restful days here at Macatawa, and the nights are perfect poems. The moon, now at its full, turns the night into a softer day, and bathes hill, lake and forest in its silvery light. With these closing days of August, however, the exit from the Park increases, and "friend after friend departs." Each steamer that plows its way through the silver sea, these moonlit nights, carries scores of our summer population. Among the last to leave us were Bro. Geo. H. Combs and family, of Kansas City, Bro. J. P. McKnight, of Peoria, and Bro. F. E. Udell and wife, of St. Louis. Bro. Combs' departure was hastened a couple of weeks by an accident which befell his younger son, Errett, whose hands were severely burned by falling into a bonfire. He was doing well when he left, but they felt it would be better to have him where he would be under the care of a skilled physician. Bro. Combs preached a sermon at the Park last Lord's day which was a source of comfort and help to many. The people here are as much pleased with Bro. Combs and his family as *they* are with Macatawa, which is sayiug a good deal. Kansas City has given us some splendid people this year:—The Richardsons, the Combses, the Buxtons, and others; we shall be surprised if it does not send us more of the same kind next year.

Among the late arrivals who are coming for a September vacation are Burris A. Jenkins, of Indianapolis, and Bro. Davidson and wife of Fayetteville, Ark. Howard Cramblet is expected in a few days. September is a delightful month here and there is plenty of room for those who remain during that month. The air is a little cooler, fishing is livelier, and later in September the ducks make their appearance on Black Lake and vie with the black bass in affording amusement to those who are fond of the gun as well as the rod. Edgewood-on-the-Lake will not be closed for the season until about or a little after the middle of September. It is our purpose to attend the Michigan State Missionary Convention, which meets in Saginaw this week. After that we shall tarry a few days, until the September hot spell is passed in St. Louis, before we return to the city. As long as Uncle Sam's mails run on schedule time it matters little where the editor is, so closely do steam and electricity connect us with the office.

Speaking of conventions reminds us that our own national gathering at Chattanooga approaches, and it is not too early for the people to be getting ready to make this one of the greatest conventions, in numbers, in enthusiasm and in work accomplished. There are many reasons why the next convention should be a large and successful one. Its location, in the South, or at the gateway to theSouth, will make it accessible to many of our brethren who have never before had the privilege of attending one of our national conventions. It will be a source of inspiration to the whole South, and will tend mightily to remove a good deal of unreasonable prejudice that has been entertained by many good brethren in those parts against our missionary conventions. As the North and South have buried their sectional differences, politically, in a war for the oppressed Cubans, why should not Disciples North and South unite, hand and heart, in pushing forward to victory the great plea which we are making for a united church and a purer Christianity? It is high time that the little differences of the past, concerning methods of co-operation in mission work, should be buried, and we should illustrate to the world the power of union and co-operation in the work of the gospel. The historic associations around Chattanooga, the desire to benefit our brethren in the South, the demand that are upon us to increase our efforts, both in the home and foreign fields, all unite in calling for one of the largest conventions in our history. Let us begin to plan at once to make it so.

We are not surpised to learn from the Subscription Department of the CHRISTIAN-EVANGELIST that since it assumed its new form, and under its special offer, it is adding many new names to its list of readers. We would be more or less than human not to feel gratified at the expressions of appreciation which reach us continually from brethren in whose taste and judgment we have confidence, concerning both the mechanical beauty and contents ofthe paper. In neither respect has the paper attained to our ideal as yet, "but this one thing we do: forgetting the things that are behind and stretching forward unto the things that are before, we press on toward the goal" of higher excellence in religious journalism. One of the things that must go before and pave the way for all religious progress, is an improved religious journalism—freer, more independent, more devoted to truth, more intensely Christian, and commanding the best consecrated talent of the church to enrich its pages.

Questions and Answers.

There is an impression, among a number I come in contact with, that the CHRISTIAN-EVANGELIST *is not sound in the faith regarding baptism, and I must ackhowledge that I am sometimes forced to think the impression well founded, if I have correctly understood the editor and some of our leading contributors, like Haley, Tyler and others. Whether sound in the faith or not, there seems to be a marked difference from the teaching of A. Campbell, B. W. Stone, J. M. Mathes, Elijah Goodwin, J. W. McGarvey, Franklin and a host of others. In order that myself and others may understand the editor, I will ask the question, Is baptism in water in order to real remission of sins or of formal remission only?* J. N. Stone.

There has been an "impression" among a certain class of brethren who make a hobby of baptism that the CHRISTIAN-EVANGELIST is not "sound in the faith," on that subject. With these brethren, however, the relation of baptism to the remission of sins is an important item of "faith," whereas according to the generally accepted view among us it is not an object of faith, but a matter of interpretation and knowledge. No doubt, if we should attempt to enter into a philosophical discussion of the reasons that underlie baptism and its relation to remission of sins, there could easily be developed a variety of opinions among us, and if these opinions should be made matters of faith and tests of fellowship, it would be quite possible to originate a number of distinct sects on this question. This, however could never be done in harmony with th principles of our plea. All who believe i Christ, and because of that faith desire t obey him in the ordinance of baptism, ar regarded as "sound in the faith," an entitled to our Christian fellowship. A to the distinction between "real" an "formal" remission of sins, it is one tha we never made, as the Scriptures do no seem to make it. Mr. Campbell used th phrase once in defining his position in debate, but we do not see that its use tend to unity of judgment. We believe that baptism was designed by Jesus Christ to b a real help to the believer in coming to th assurance of forgiveness. As it stands fo the unconditional surrender of the believe to Christ and a solemn commitment to Hi Lordship, remission of sins is associate with it in the New Testament. Acts 2:3 and 22:16, and other kindred passages, d not readily admit of any other interpretation. It must never be lost sight of, how ever, that baptism derives all its signif icance from its being an act of faith i and of loyalty to Jesus Christ. To spea of it apart from the repentance and fait of which it is the outward expression, as i often done, tends to create a prejudic against it in some instances and in other to lead persons to attach an undue importance to the act itself. It was characteristic of Christ's teaching, as against that o the Pharisees, to lay supreme emphasi upon the inner life—the heart and it motives and purposes—and this must b characteristic of all who would seek t reproduce the Christianity of Christ. N amount of regularity in form can atone fo the absence of that Spirit without whic we are none of Christ's.

In answer to a recent question concerning the Lord's Supper you stated that "w are not required to conform precisely t the method given in the New Testament; i so, we would have to recline around th table, use barley loaves, etc." Was Jesu speaking of those things, and if not woul they enter into the argument? By the sam method of reasoning some of our preachers instead of "going down into the water" with the candidate, stay on dry footin while they are baptizing the candidate Why did not the apostle practice this wa if it was as good as any?

G. W. Calhoun.

Bro. Calhoun is not the only one wh has stumbled at our answer concernin the method of observing the Lord' Supper. A few brethren have been great ly "grieved" at what we said. We ar sorry to give offense to them or to griev any one, but we would be false to th spirit of Christianity as we understand i if we taught differently. What we sai was that we are not bound to follow slavish ly the details of the *manner* or *method* o observing the Lord's Supper. Jesu had no such thought in his mind. H adopted certain emblems to be used i remembrance of him. When they ar used in that spirit and for that purpose, th ordinance is properly observed. Whethe they be passed by deacons or handed fro member to member, whether thanks b returned for both before either is passed seems to us to be wholly a matter of taste not of law or of conscience. We migh

our querist as to the preachers not
g down into the water with the candi-
, was Christ speaking of this when he
tuted the ordinance of baptism in the
t commission? Is it enjoined any-
re, upon any one, in baptizing, to "go
n into the water" with the candidate?
does our querist know what the
tice of the apostles was in reference to
matter? It is nowhere stated in what
ner any apostle baptized his candidate
iether he went down into the water
him, or stood upon the edge of the
or stream and baptized him. The
g to be attended to is the *baptism*—
burial and resurrection of the candi-
in the likeness of Christ's burial and
rrection. The attempt to bring the
t of Leviticus over into the Acts of the
stles is to misunderstand the genius of
stianity. Commands must be obeyed,
in methods there is liberty.

———

*the production of the Holy Spirit is
joy, peace, long-suffering, meekness,
erance, fidelity, patience, what kind
pirit is it that produces war, strife,
ed and bloodshed?*

Chas. E. Delano.

irbury, Neb.

n unholy spirit, of course.

———

the CHRISTIAN-EVANGELIST of May
, 1898 (article—The Model Church),
egard to "the first church in Jeru-
n" it is said: "The fact that it con-
ed to practice circumcision, to observe
Jewish Sabbath and to keep the law of
es would place it beyond the lines of
orthodox Christianity of our day."
t. From what time and how long did
"first church" *continue* "to practice
imcison, to observe the Jewish Sabbath
to keep the law of Moses?"
d. Were "to practice circumcision"
"to observe the Jewish Sabbath"
rent from "to keep the law of Moses?"
s, in what respect did they differ?
i. Does the phrase, "Jewish Sabbath"
y that there *is* another?
i. One here denies that the "first
ch" practiced as you affirm, and to
te you argues thus: Jesus commanded
apostles to teach those whom they
e disciples *to observe all things he com-
ded;* the apostles *taught* as the Spirit
them utterance; the disciples continu-
teadfastly in the apostles' teaching:
efore, since the apostles did not *teach*
e things "the first church" did not
rve or keep any of them. Briefly show
rror.
n. May not any kind of wine, black-
y, cherry, etc., be properly used at the
l's Supper.
h. Would water do in case wine could
be had? G. C. HUTCHINSON.
lso, Wash., July 2, 1898.

It is probable that many of the Jew-
Christians continued to practice cir-
cision and perhaps other Jewish rites
o the time of the destruction of Jeru-
n and perhaps later. We known from
21:20-24 that the Jewish Christians at
salem were jealous of the law and
ticed some of its ceremonies, at least,
he close of Paul's third missionary
.

The practice of circumcision and the
rvance of the Sabbath were part of
law of Moses, but not all of it.

No. By the phrase, "Jewish Sab-
," is meant that it was the Sabbath of
Jews. There is, of course, a Sabbatic
ure in the Lord's day, but it is not
gnated as the Sabbath in the New
ament.

This line of argument would prove altogether too much. For instance, it would prove that the church at Corinth never abused the Lord's Supper nor neglected the assembling of themselves together nor committed any sin, for surely the apostles did not teach them to do these things. Unfortunately, Christians even do not always obey the truth fully, partly because they do not always understand it and partly because of the weakness of the flesh through which they are led to depart from the truth.

5. and 6. There is no need of any departure from the use of the "fruit of the vine" in the observance of the Lord's Supper. If persons were so situated that it would be impossible for them to secure the "fruit of the vine," then the question would be pertinent as to whether something else would not answer; but with proper foresight this condition of things need not exist.

A STUDY OF LIVING AND DYING NATIONS.

BY REV. WILBUR F. CRAFTS, PH. D.,
Superintendent of the Reform Bureau.

And I will cause thee to ride upon the high places of the earth.—*Isa.* 58:14.

It is of the bearing of this promise on nations that I wish especially to speak. The prophets did not, like preachers of to-day, seek the conversion of individuals as an end, but only as a means to the saving of the state. The supreme fact of living history is that the Sabbath-keeping nations are literally riding on the high places of the earth. I have not read in a year a news item so significant as the statement of that very reliable paper, the Baltimore Sun, that two-thirds of the world's mail is in the English language. That means that one-fourteenth of the world's population sends two-thirds of the mail, and that means a corresponding pre-eminence in intelligence and wealth.

On the other hand, the Sabbathless and Sabbath-breaking nations are poor—poor physically—Italy once, and France twice in ten years have cut down their standard for soldiers; poor mentally—they have the greatest illiteracy; poor morally—they have the most vice; poor financially—their workmen, despite longer hours per day and one more work-day in the week, get the lowest wages; and they are also the worst off politically, vibrating between the extremes of despotism and anarchy, while Sabbath-keeping peoples enjoy the golden mein of liberty under law.

If I should claim that the difference in nations is all due to their treatment of the Sabbath I should proclaim that I had been run away with by a hobby. Let us broadly study the "living and dying nations"—to borrow Lord Salisbury's expressive classification of the quivering map of the world as it now spreads before us in dissolving views. What a time to teach geography and history! Surely, no true teacher can fail to teach also the great lessons in civics that throng the world-map of living history to which Dr. Dewey's guns have called all eyes! Lord Salisbury did not need to specify the "dying nations." Every well-informed person thought the names of China, Turkey, France and Spain. And when he said "living nations," in every corner of the civilized world every reader was bound to admit that the British Empire and the United States belonged to the "living nations."

These "living nations," however, have some serious symptoms, and should study the dead and dying nations in order to keep out of their graveyard.

With nations once mighty dying before our eyes, we face anew as a living problem the academic question of our college history classes, "Is it necessary that a nation should grow old and weak and die?"

As a matter of fact nations have hardly averaged as long a life as the patriarchs, and there is no Methuselah among them. We are easily deceived by old names on the maps. The "body politic," the government, which bears the name to-day, may be but a young namesake of a body politic deceased that once occupied the same territory.

THE GRAVEYARD OF NATIONS.

Where are the nations of which we read in the Bible and the classics? The world-empires of the Egyptians, Hittites, Assyrians, Persians, Macedonians, Romans, died in turn. We read "Egypt" on the map, but there are no Egyptians. The word "Rome" is on the map, but there are no Romans. The word "Greece" is on the map, but alas! the recent war showed that there are no Greeks. Of all races of antiquity the only ones that survive are the great prophetic races, the Jews and Arabs, both long ago dead politically, surviving only as subject peoples.

EXISTING NATIONS YOUNG.

Turn to the map of to-day. This continent is the "New World," our own young nation, hardly older than some of its centenarian citizens, the elder brother among American Republics. Africa in its civilized governments is a yet newer world. Even Europe is new politically. The present Government of Spain is an infant in many senses. The French Republic is an epileptic child. Germany's Emperor is known as the "infant terrible," of Europe, and his empire is hardly older or more stable. The kingdom of Italy, too, is still struggling with the diseases of childhood. Great Britain's present monarchy goes back only to Cromwell, and real constitutional government only to the coronation of Victoria. Russia claims a thousands years, but it is a thousand years of savagery, and the nation has not yet borne a long test of civilization.

Surely, we shall find some nations in Asia. First, we come upon Turkey, called "the sick man," but really dead and stinking, only kept from burial by the quarrels of the undertakers. Now that we have learned to use our navy for humanity, let Turkey take care not to have any more Armenian massacres.

Japan's Mikado claims an ancestral royal line of 6,000 years, but previous to 1879 the mikadoes were popes, and the tycoons, now abolished, were the civil emperors, so that as a civil ruler the Mikado is the first of a new series. But China surely is old. Nay, the present Mantchu Empire began in 1796 and has already died and is on the dissecting table under the knives of Europe.

A NATION MAY BE IMMORTAL.

Must every nation, must our own, grow old and die? Nay, for in the very nature of the case a nation may be immortal, like a river; its drops ever passing on to the sea, but ever renewed from its mountain springs. If we maintain the Christian morality and popular education which

Washington declared to be the high sources of national prosperity, and keep unbroken on either hand the banks of liberty and law, our nation's life may go on ceaselessly, singing like the river:

"Men may come and men may go, but I go on forever."

"Arise and shine in youth immortal,
Thy light is come, thy king appears;
Beyond the century's swinging portal
Breaks a new dawn a thousand years."

But eternal life to a nation can come only through "eternal vigilance." Many who firmly believe nature goes by law, act as if history went by luck. As surely as effect follows cause Babylonian vices will produce a Babylonian fall.

IMPURITY THE DEADLIEST PLAGUE OF NATIONS.

Babylon, Greece, Rome, the Renaissance kingdoms of Italy and France, form a national series, all showing that the highest art, if it be mental culture without moral, if it be the art whose motto is "art for art's sake," the godless æstheticism of nude art that puts beauty in the supreme place instead of duty, not only cannot take the place of religion in checking immorality, but even increases it, dragging the nation down the three steps to national ruin: first, moral; second, physical; third, political decay. France is on the second step, the only civilized land in which the birth-rate is falling below the death-rate—a blazing warning on the walls of this modern Babylon of the retribution to men and nations that follows the violation of the fourth and seventh commandments.

Why should we cast aside our Anglo-Saxon traditions to welcome the nude to our literature and homes, when every nation from which we have borrowed it is either dead or dying? Since France is dying of the worst of plagues, French pictures, French plays and French novels should be quarantined like ships from infected ports.

The problem of purity is the question of life or death to nations.

As we look through history we see that nations have died chiefly of internal causes; not of free silver or free trade, but of free love.

Therefore, moral questions should be the supreme questions in politics, those that conform to Gladstone's definition of the purpose of law—"To make it as hard as possible to do wrong and as easy as possible to do right." This series of deceased empires teach also that our culture must not ignore morals. Better a man be not educated, if his conscience is not to be developed with his wits, lest he be only the more skillful criminal. "An ignorant thief may rob a frieght car, but an educated thief will steal the whole railroad."

WHAT IS THE MATTER WITH CHINA?

If France is dying through neglect of morality, why is China also dying, which has given more attention to moral teachings than any other country? China's warning is against a morality that ignores God. It is a stupendous proof of the inefficiency of agnostic ethical culture, utilitarian morality. Confucius and Buddha, the greatest of purely human moralists, are the Herbert Spencer and Felix Adler of Asia, only they had opportunity to try their theories wholly apart from Christianity and for centuries on great races with every aid of government favor. And what has been the result? When their pretty but powerless sayings were being paraded at the World's Parliament of Religions, by men of Asia, who were significantly unaccompanied by their wives, I would like to have interjected this one question: "How do you treat woman?" Like a flashlight that question exposes the failure of the agnostic ethical culture to produce those two essentials of social welfare and national prosperity, good morals and human rights. The Bible in the schools has had a great influence in producing these two great essentials in our American history. We take a great risk if we throw over this sheet anchor of our ship of state.

In the words of Wendell Phillips: "The answer to Confucianism is China; the answer to Buddhism is India; the answer to the Koran is Turkey; the answer of the Bible is the Christian civilization of Europe and America."

"Better fifty years of Europe than a cycle of Cathay."
—*Tennyson, in "Locksley Hall."*

WHAT IS THE MATTER WITH SPAIN?

But what is the matter with Spain? It is a medieval ghost, wandering about the 19th century, vainly attempting to rule its colonies by medieval methods of grasping despotism.

To those European nations that threaten to interfere with our work of deliverance we say, the Powers should have interfered long ago between Spain and her oppressed colonies and insisted on civilized modes of government. Now that we have taken up their neglected task, let them stand back till it is fully done.

Let us not approach the consideration of Spain in any spirit of revenge. The cry, "Remember the Maine," breathes the spirit of a Spanish pirate. And those who talk as if national honor were the chief thing at stake in this war are equally misrepresenting our noble motive. Not hatred or honor, but humanity is our commander-in-chief. For the first time in all history a nation has entered upon a great war to secure the independence of another and inferior people. Not the explosion of the Maine, but Senator Proctor's appeal to pity brought on the war. And let our pity not cease till every island oppressed by Spain is freed. But let not our humanity stop with the island victims of Spanish errors. Let us pity the "Peninsula," where long misrule has created the spirit of revolution. In that broadening humanity which the war has developed let us find a place for Spain's own people. But while we pity Spain let us also search out the meaning of her decline. It is not chiefly a matter of climate, for Anglo-Saxons maintain free governments in all climes. Nor is Spain's condition so much due to Catholicism as many Protestants suppose, for Germany, the home of Protestantism, has less civil liberty than Catholic South America. Spain's arrested development is no doubt largely due to the Inquisition, that killed or banished every one who believed in progress. Like the massacre and exile of Huguenots from France this was slitting the arteries and letting out the nation's best blood.

CONTINENTAL VERSUS ANGLO-SAXON INSTITUTIONS.

Why is the French Republic more in sympathy with tyrannical Spain and despotic Russia than with our Republic and Great Britain, whose government is freer than its own? The Zola trial has shown France is really a military despotism, which is also suggested by the fact that it takes ten times as many soldier police to keep Paris from revolution as it takes of civilian police to keep the larger city of London in better order. In London the Sabbath is the chief of police. We are now coming on the explanation of the great contrast between Anglo-Saxons and continentals, in which last category we include the South American Republics, strangely more in sympathy with their old oppressor than with the emancipator of Cuba. It is passing strange that so many of our people read of the constant revolutions of the childish Spanish Republics south of us and never think what they mean. These republics mostly have copied our paper constitution, but that does not make them truly American Republics in the same sense we have given the word American. See Honduras turning over its most important government functions to an American syndicate—customs, banking, railways—because it has neither brains nor character enough for self-government. And this but a sample. No nation that spends its Sabbaths in work and play has ever developed safe and stable popular government. And yet in the teeth of a whole continent of horrible examples we allow misers and prodigals to sacrifice our palladium of liberty to their selfish uses, and even the churches are doing little to prevent them. In my judgment the contrast between the despotism and anarchy of the continentals and the stable freedom of Anglo-Saxon is due chiefly to the influence of the two sets of institutions, one the continental, of which the continental Sunday if chief; the other Anglo-Saxon, of which the British-American Sabbath is the chief.

WHAT DOES "ANGLO-SAXON" MEAN?

We talk of Anglo-Saxons as if the words stood chiefly for heredity. In reality they stand more for institutions, for training, to which, it is being discovered, most of the credit belongs that was formerly given to heredity. There is something in blood, but the best born child, brought up in the slums, is likely to be a vagabond, while thousands of slum children placed in Christian homes have developed into good citizens. We call ourselves Anglo-Saxons, but most families have more than two lines of blood—my own for instance, English, French, Greek and German. A man seeking for naturalization papers was asked by the judge: "What is your nationality?" He replied: "I don't know, judge; I wish you would tell me. My father was an Englishman, my mother was a Spaniard and I was born on a French ship flying the Dutch flag. I want to make the rest of the voyage of life under the Stars and Stripes." That would make a fair analysis of what an American is—a composite British-Spanish-French-Dutchman under the Stars and Stripes, that is, under the training of Angla-Saxon institutions.

NECESSITIES OF A REPUBLIC'S LIFE.

There are three necessities of life in a republic: intelligence, conscientiousness and a spirit of equality. In order to develop these the relation of master and

week by
ath, and
ssipation
for the
of the
rved in
merican
hile the
les that
ay.
Hallam,
who says
pe have
Sunday
et under
t me put
of Bob
depend-
dive on
g shot."
-defying
nal cus-
"liberty"
niard his
y is not
the long
that is
etoscope
ge as life
national
nced by
ffalo; the
, Sunday
rom the
Anglo-
troduced
r cities.
s," is the

cities are
l institu-
eans, who
aring for
making
Santiago.
banner,
as?"

.—COM-
T.

so much
are, pro-
Truer this
ncrowned

ist of the
y fallen.
y unlike,
haracter-
ls several
in their

, preserv-
ed to the
rs of age,
when he
lic life.
pable of
ice when
youthful

d marvels
a writer,
onder and
arck, too,
was con-
emes, he
ne to read
ne noblest
est novel-

ists. Persistent vigilance and untiring industry were the price paid by Bismarck as well as Gladstone, for achievements in statecraft.

Both made statesmanship the business or main pursuit of their lives, and in this achieved the great victories by which they will be chiefly remembered by posterity.

Concentration of purpose and energy to the accomplishment of a great idea, or ideal, is a prominent charateristic in the career of each. Each was eminently though not entirely successful in reaching the goal he set before him.

Neither Gladstone nor Bismarck was obliged to struggle with poverty, that school in which so many of the world's brightest lights have developed their great qualities. Gladstone's father was quite wealthy. Bismarck inherited a goodly estate.

Let us now note some points of contrast presented in their busy careers.

The youth and early manhood of each stand out in striking contrast. Gladstone early evinced a rare precocity and his purity of life was no less marked. Bismarck, on the other hand, was a wild, reckless, dissipated youth, who up to the time of his marriage, at the age of 32, was in no wise distinguished "except in an avidity for country sports and skill in horsemanship."—[Lord, in "Beacon Lights of History."]

Gladstone entered Parliament when but 23. The example of Gladstone, as well as other great men, brands as infamous the flippant assertion that "every young man must sow his wild oats."

With respect to their records as statesmen, that of Gladstone is without a flaw, viewed from a moral standpoint. Preeminent in ability, he was greater yet as a Christian statesman. Like Sumner, he could affirm: "The slave of principle, I call no party master." In regard to Bismarck, while we must give him credit for a lofty patriotism, and even granting with his staunch admirer, Dr. Lord, that he was "conscientious in the discharge of his duties, as he understood them, in the fear of God," yet, respecting the methods employed by him in the consummation of his patriotic purposes, the same writer admits: "He considered only the end in view, caring nothing for the means; he had no scruples."—["Life of Prince Bismarck."] Bismarck was an arch-trickester; a cunning intriguer. Is it to harsh a judgment to pronounce upon him, that in his methods he showed himself the scheming politician rather than the highest type of statesman?

In one other capital point there is presented a marked contrast between these two men. While neither was by birth or early association what we call a "man of the people," yet the whole trend of Gladstone's public career was in the direction of the promotion of the welfare and lifting the burdens of the masses. Bismarck, on the other hand, devoted his life to the upholding of centralized authority and to the strehgthening of the monarchical idea.

Gladstone modified his views considerably in the course of his life, becoming the champion of reforms, investing the people with a constantly enlarging measure of liberty. When Gladstone retired to private life it was said of him that he had found England an oligarchy and left it a republic

in all but name. Bismarck,
trary, found Germany a bund
pendent states and left it
centralized monarchy, vergi
absolute. Gladstone's work v
mony with the spirit of the
century. Bismarck was Carly
man," representing the absolut
parted age.

Posterity will hold Gladsto
tionate remembrance as the
Man," while the career of B
"Iron Old Man," imparts valu
upon the power of an indomit
conjunction with indefatigable
surmount colossal difficulties.

THE NAME "CHRISTIAN"

BRUCE WOLVERTON

I desire to thank J. J. Haley
torial of Aug. 11th on "The A
Name Christian." It is exhil
and then, in the maze of contr
the "Name," and the "Anointi
"Baptism of the Holy Spirit,"
article that evinces the gleam
Clear thought, distinguishing
differ, more clean-cut stateme
showing right relationships,
in these days. It does mak
to plod along with those who s
"as trees walking." One is tem
trees rather then men. There
lief: One *can* get out from th
the trees and get a glimpse of

I once asked a person who, f
his name on the church record
conveyed by the word Christ—
It seemingly had no meaning to
thought I, are *we* also drifti
mere ritual of "mouthing" a
others to "mouth" the creed?
is too true!

Lately I listened to a series
from one said to be noted in
joining states as an evangeli
times struck with his boldne
noted with pleasure his insight
systems of teaching. Not s
note his knowledge of the Wo
were impressed; some respond
vitation. They were expected
telligently, the confession. B
came to baptism I found it nec
plain to them the faith they we
to confess. Then remembered
of those discourses, not a ray o
light had been shed upon the m
by they could know the import
"Christ," the keyword to t
sion."

Thus in my cogitations I f
the wanderings of the Discipl
this time) as *they* followed
The one thing that they nee
"by heart" was the meaning
Christ. Is it not worthy of no
not once intimated a word co
death for the sins of the wor
"disciples" had "learned" thi
heart?"

Read Matt. 16:21 (Italics m
that time BEGAN Jesus to show
ciples how that he must go un
and suffer many things of th
chief priests and scribes, and t
the third day be raised up."
as an objective reality that he
ointed One," but they themse
anointed before they were rea
WORK.

Preparatory to this they must obtain a fuller realization of the truth before they were ready for the anointing. Proof (Jno. 16:12): "I have many things to say unto you, but ye cannot bear them now."

This was *before* his resurrection. Afterwards he said, "These are my words which I spake unto you [this is what I meant as I spake by parables:] Then opened he their minds, that they might understand the Scriptures" (Luke 24:45).

Following closely upon these words came, first, (Jno. 16:13): "Howbeit, when he the Spirit of truth is come, he will guide you into all truth;" next (Luke 24:49): "And, behold, I send the promise of the Father upon you."

Again, let us distinguish things that differ. As an illustration, take Peter. We have Peter the disciple, Peter the Christian and Peter the apostle. Peter the disciple had or desired to have his own will, and mind, too. Peter the apostle spake only as the *Holy Spirit* gave him utterance. Peter the Christian blended beautifully his will with the will of the Master and both spake and acted through his own will and mind as the Holy Spirit had directed in the revealed will.

Peter the disciple was found withstanding the Lord's death, though he had confessed him as the Christ. Peter the disciple took the sword in the garden after his sound sleep in the presence of agony; followed afar off, denied thrice the Master, wept bitterly. After the resurrection Peter the disciple, while tarrying at Jerusalem, presumed with others to enter politics and fill out the Apostolic College, a transaction in the sanctioning of which the Holy Spirit is as silent as the grave.

Peter the saint, the anointed, in the language of Christ, "the [when the thou art] converted," is ready to speak the Word with all boldness. In prison he is thankful to be counted worthy to suffer in the name of the Lord. He heeds the lesson taught him at Cæsarea, that God is no respecter of persons. He stumbles at Antioch, but arises and goes on. He strives to not grieve the Holy Spirit whereby he is sealed unto the day of redemption. He writes kindly of Bro. Paul who once rebuked him, and in the same sentence evinces the fact of his character as a Christian, where he tells us of many things in Paul's writings hard (even by Peter the disciple or Christian) to be understood, and which the ignorant (undiscipled) and unsteadfast (unchristed) wrest * * * to their own destruction (2 Peter 3:16).

But Peter the apostle is another person, inasmuch as the baptism of the Holy Spirit is different from the anointing which he received of the Father. Peter the apostle preached what Peter the disciple had rejected and Peter the Christian had to study out even by revelation and memory. Otherwise, what is the import of Acts 10:16: "Then *remembered* I the word of the Lord," etc.?

The baptism of the Holy Spirit opened the door of faith to the whole world, Jew and Gentile. The anointing of the Holy Spirit comes in at that open door and finds the temple cleansed for his indwelling. And this is the only "christening." Truly are such called *Christians*.

In conclusion, shall we write it Disciples? There are two reasons why we should: It is a good *d*enominational title. "Nomen" is "name." "De" is "drawn from," or beneath, *i. e.*, lower than the name. But the name is "Christian." *So were they* called. (See Acts 11:26; Jas. 2:7.)

By all laws of definitions, as to genus and species, the lower the order the greater the extension. It gives opportunity for vast expansion in the United States Census. Let me write it U. S. Census.

Lastly, shall we write it with a big D? Then why not with a big I. Yea, why not write it with two big I's? Thus: DIscIples. It would at least be characteristic—of denominationalism!

THE LAW OF RELIGION AS REVEALED IN NATURE.

A. L. FERGUSON.

One would conclude that even the casual reader of the Bible would quickly learn that work, or Christian activity, is the great law that obtains in Christian ethics. Then, to reverse the order and note the way many so-called Christians live, one would conclude that to obey first principles and attend the service of God's house when you please, and help support the work of the church when you please, is all there is in Christian ethics. It is safe to say that there is a great deal of religious idleness in the church, and this idle element is painfully large. We now appeal to nature as a teacher of the great law that governs the spiritual life, and also for examples of indolence.

Work, work, is nature's voice to all of her children, and as a rule they yield implicit obedience to her great law. Take, for example, one of nature's noblest and bravest children, the stalwart oak, and from the day of its birth it puts forth an independent effort to live, and through the sweep of the years it overcomes all obstacles, and bravely meets and conquers a thousand storms, and finally with well-developed strength and graceful symmetry waves its green banners above the dome of a hundred years. In this monarch of the wood we have revealed the possibilities of Christian living and growth, and the same law obtains in the realm of spirit, and the Christian character that is well rounded out in the graces of strength, solidity and symmetry has yielded implicit obedience to the same law.

We now turn to that indolent element in nature for the lesson and warning it gives us. Parasites are known as nature's paupers, and they abound by the thousand in both the animal and vegetable kingdoms. They put forth very little effort in the way of independent living, but live at the expense of their neighbors. They appropriate food that is already prepared at hand. In the Southland the mistletoe and Spanish moss are seen in great abundance as they adhere to the living trees. As you ride or walk through the forests of Texas the Spanish moss looks like great vails flung over the trees, giving a sombre appearance to the children of the wood. Degeneration is the punishment that nature inflicts upon those who will not pay the price of independent living, and in this class we would point to the dodder that in time loses roots and leaves, and stands a naked stock; also the hermit crab that was once a crustacean of the sea, but now a slimy, disgusting object as it is drawn from the old shell of the whelk. Thus nature punishes by a waste of energy and a loss of organs.

The great lesson to us, intensified by revelation and experience, is to avoid becoming moral parasites, for that means degeneration and death. That ecclesiastical body that says, "Come and put the keeping of your soul and its interests into our hands, and we will care for them and insure you a safe transit from this world to the next," is a dangerous body, and its teaching militates most seriously against the essential element in the growth of Christian character. The Protestant would also make the mistake of saying, "We have discovered all essential things that relate to divine truth, and have formulated and classified them under the headings of Trinity, Atonement, Depravity, Resurrection, etc., and all we ask is that you assent to them, and you need not make research for yourselves, for they are sound and have been safely stored in the tomes of the fathers." Thus the average Christian is expected to passively assent to the statements of men relative to these and other great truths, and to conclude that there is nothing more to do or to find out about Bible truth, and the chief danger to which he is exposed is that of living at the expense of others, spiritually, and becoming a moral parasite. Then again he concludes that his pastor is employed expressly to make research and study and think for him, for he has no time for religious thought and study, and on Lord's day his sole business is to go to the house of God to be entertained and fed on the milk of the Word (for he is not able to endure strong meat) year in and year out, and his attitude is that of a consumer all his life, freely devouring all that is given him without being able to question its truthfulness, for his spiritual horizon is but a a stone's cast before him, and his development of moral power is still less. Now that we have learned the attitude of the average Christian, let us inquire relative to the results of this law as seen in the secular world.

We have the great free school system, of which we are justly proud, and supposing the parents would refuse to send their children, saying, "All things have been discovered in the way of secular truth and classified in the text-books, and it is not possible for them to add to the volume of truth, and it would do no good to send them to school;" what would be our reply? We would say, "You view things from a false premise, for the child is not to add to the volume of truth, but by close application he is to make truth already discovered his own. To do that he must through months and years be forming studious habits, and then, by walking the old beaten paths of thought, study, work, he will in time be able to analyze and digest the great principles of truth, and it is this unceasing struggle of the mind's powers with the varied lines and forms of truth that at last evolves the finished scholar."

The work of the teacher, then, is not to aid the cause of truth, but the unfolding of the child-mind, and by quickening it along the paths of knowledge it will in time learn to act independently and attain intellectual greatness that is possible in no other way. In the example now given it must be patent to even the casual observer e law governing mental growth is intellectual exercise or work, and l with its germs of power is subject ame law. Mental assent to classi- ıth as found in our religious com- ns, without any labor or research on t, is one of the evils against which ɔit voices should be raised, for its y is toward moral degeneracy, and s most seriously against the growth stian character. Classified truth is nd proper in its place, and very to the studious, but the casual derives little benefit therefrom. ve are in hearty sympathy with all elps, and would not speak lightly of ıarch of scholarly men, yet the pro- Christian man must make research self; he must patiently study, work gest Bible truth, and familiarize with the greatness of its history, t men and great events, and above irink in of the Godlike mind and f its ideal character, Jesus of Naza- He must learn that persistent, pa- il is the price the Christian pays to he higher forms of Christian excel- Indolence and indifference to Bible s alarmingly common to-day, and e soul of priceless treasures, and pits of America should warn the against these dangerous conditions so fatal to the spiritual life.

'e gives us everything, and yet we ıat corn and wheat as it comes from ıds, but it must be ground and by us for food to nourish the body, s it is with Bible truth in its rela- the soul. Everything depends on d in providing food for the soul, everything depends on us in the e of the food provided. Spiritual ment joined with unceasing activity ıtial to the growth of charaeter, who would attain the beauty and of the Christly graces must yield obedience to God's law and ut his own salvation with fear and ng."

ook, Ill.

ONE IN CHRIST.

J. M. LOWE.

lay, after a very fraternal discussion Ministerial Association, the Presby- ninister led the closing prayer. In ayer, among other things, he said Lord, we thank thee that though we fer in minor points, we are one in ' Somehow the truth of the state- orced itself upon me. Is it not Do we not differ upon minor points, e we not one in Christ? We all in the same God, in his Son Jesus in the Bible, the record of God's on in Christ, in the Holy Spirit, the ter. We agree as to the necessity rpetuity of the church, that its ces are baptism and the Lord's . We all pray to the same God in ne of the same Christ, read the Bible, and uphold essentially the tandard of spiritual life. We all he indwelling of the same Spirit ulge the some hope of eternal life. if we agree upon all these great , the points wherein we differ must l.

differ upon the observance of the Supper, upon the form and design ism, upon the operation of the Holy Spirit, and we hold different views as to the nature, origin and power of sin. We differ also about church government. I believe this comprehends the points of difference among Protestants. None of these can be said to be primary. No difference need be divisive unless it affects the practice of the church, such as baptism, the Lord's Supper and government. Belief as to the Holy Spirit, the power of sin, state of the dead, theories of atonement—none of these should be divisive. It would be a calamity if we all agreed upon them. I am aware of the unique position of the Disciples upon Christian union and in the spirit of such a position have thus written.

But should these differences, that affect practice, prevent a hearty and extensive co-operation of the different bodies of Protestant Christendom? The editorial that appeared in the CHRISTIAN-EVANGELIST several weeks ago, entitled—"Not Enemies but Allies," should be read again and again, for most certainly does it set forth the true relation Christian bodies sustain to each other. By a certain reticence upon the part of the Disciples they have postponed that glorious consummation toward which the ages are advancing. If we have the position that the Christian world must one day occupy, instead of declaring war upon all Christendom we should rather by co-operation and association so infuse Christian thought with the *spirit* of union that ere long, when a union *basis* is sought, nothing better will be found—for it does not exist—than the basis which the Disciples have for years upheld.

The objection arises at once: But many of our neighbors have never been baptized, and hence have not put on Christ; how, then, can we be one in Christ? He who would make the burial of the body in water the condition of being in Christ knows neither baptism nor the Spirit of Christ. The significant part of baptism is not the water, but the heart full of faith in Jesus Christ which expresses itself in baptism. If the man is not vitally joined to Christ before baptism, I am sure he is not afterward. That the burial of the body in *water* brings a man into *spiritual* relation with Christ is the acme of absurdity. I very frankly say that the great question is, How much of the Spirit of Christ finds its way into my life? rather than how much water was there when I was said to be baptized? What advantage, then, hath baptism, and profit is there in immersion? Much in many ways; chiefly because immersion is New Testament baptism, and beautifully symbolizes the burial of the old man and the resurrection of the new. Nor can baptism ever fall from the place it occupies as the threshold of the kingdom of heaven. Yet it must be said with emphasis that baptism is more than a burial in water. It is faith in obedience, which is a better expression than faith *and* obedience. There is no place where faith leaves off and obedience begins.

Seeing, then, that the vital part of baptism is a heart-condition upon which all agree—as to the baptism of adults at least—the statement that we disagree upon minor points is reinforced.

If we would talk more upon points of agreement we would not only get acquainted with each other's ways of thinking, but we would also have a common view-point from which to survey and adjust our differences. If one stands upon the mountain top of hyper-Calvinism, another roves around upon the plain of ultra-Arminianism, another is paddling his own canoe up the river of works and another is being blown across the sea by the winds of free grace, how can they get the same view of anything?

Winterset, Ia.

In an article in the Interior, recently, Dr. Geo. B. Russell, on "Nature in Grace," deals with a vital subject in a most reasonable way. His discussion of the theme lies along the domestic line, and what he says commends itself to sound judgment. Dr. Russell's article concludes as follows:

How the natural life thus holds real relation to the spiritual life, begotten by divine operation through the power of God in the use of human means, is not for us to analyze or explain. But the fact is here, nevertheless, to be made due account of in Christian nurture. A plant in well-adapted soil, properly nurtured, will grow to the completion of its life in due season. And a child brought up in the nurture and admonition of the Lord will just as surely develope a Christian character. If there is ever a falling short of this in some sad failures, the cause must be sought for in some defective or adverse elements of the nurturing conditions applied on the human side. God on his part, in his promises and work, never fails. His conditions are surely adequate, and his word is always made good—though every man be made a liar.

Where children of believing parents are not properly nurtured, they may fail of the grace of God. Large allowance is to be made, of course, for imperfect application and use by man of the gracious means intended of God for the soul's salvation. All children of the Christian families in the covenant, it is sad to reflect, do not manifest practically the good fruits and saving efficacy of this element of nurturing grace. A carnal heart of unbelief may make the birthright blessing of none effect. Esau bartered his away for a mess of pottage; and the pleasures of sin, which are but for a season, may nullify the good effects of Christian nuture and baptismal grace. This sad fact is one of the mysteries of iniquity. But it does not alter the other and larger factor in God's gracious means.

Still it may be held for truth, therefore, that gracious nurture in Christian families is a divine election appointed for the right training of the child for a true Christian faith and religious life. Parents are confronted here with the terrible responsibility of the duty of life in example and precept. In this they are ministering to the saving or losing souls committed to their care and charge. Daily they are doing the one or the other. All their children, in the faith and use of God's means in the plan of the kingdom, may be saved. Rightly trained and religiously educated in the piety of the everlasting covenant of grace brings them to know God and to love him and to serve him. That is true religion. Nurtured into this, they are led by the Spirit in the way to life everlasting. Such preaching of the gospel saves souls.

Material family inheritance to be left for children requires and presupposes that they be trained and prepared for what is to fall to them. If not, it will likely be no blessing. But if they are taught from early years that they must be fitted for their future position, it will grow into them. As a rule their lives will be shaped accordingly. So in the state: we educate children with a view of making them good citizens and patriots, worthy of their fathers and their country. More attention to such training would save our nation from some of its shame.

What is thus undeniably true for the family and the state is no less a condition for the well-being of the church, as the kingdom of Christ in the order of grace. For spiritual and heavenly things the analagous general law holds good, as that does which is found to be true in the domestic and political; only it is more sure in its operation, as it has more powerful aid in its behalf. True Christian nurture in God's approved way will make believers of the growing children, and thus secure the salvation of their souls. Now, if the powers of the world to come, touch us so really in the kingdom of heaven at hand here for purposes of communicating divine grace in the saving nurture of the Christian household, it is only the revelation of God's love. With the divine promise, and the sacramental seal to the baptismal covenant, there is need for a revived sence of the duty of training the children in Christian nuture for the spiritual life.

Our Budget.

—Church Extension this month.

—General Convention next month.

—September ends the missionary year.

—All pledges and apportionments should be paid in full before the convention.

—Any church that did not make an offering for Church Extension, on last Sunday should do so next.

—If last Sunday was too hot, too stormy or too anything else for an offering for Church Extension try another Sunday before the month ends.

—Special dispatch to the CHRISTIAN-EVANGELIST:

"Went beyond apportionment. Not all in; will do our best." L. T. FAULDERS.
Harristown, Ill.

—We publish the program of the Missouri State Convention in this paper. Please preserve it for future use.

—J. H. Fuller, of Burlington, Iowa, says: "Raised more than our apportionment yesterday. $250,000 by 1900 is sure.

—We hope that all our readers will read the Florida Letter this week. Bro. Blenus we know to be an impartial witness of what he relates and, in the midst of so many rumors about mismanagement in the military camps, what he says becomes of special interest.

—"The Conversion of Europe," by Wm. H. Matlock, in this paper, reflects the spirit of France and other European nations toward America before and after the Spanish war. The title itself is significant. The article is interesting.

—Rev. Howard H. Russell, Supt. Anti-Saloon League, Deleware, Ohio, has issued a circular outlining a plan for the enrollment of all who have taken or will take the pledge of total abstinance, and will work for the suppression of the liquor traffic. The plan has some good and commendable features—the closer unity of the hosts of the cause of temperance and the increase of those pledged against the saloon and the drink habit—but beyond this nothing definite is stated. No plan of action against the saloon proposed. However, to successfully enlist the friends of temperance in one army on the plan proposed means much in many ways and seems to us at present to be worthy of encouragement. Send to Dr. Russell for his circular and examine it for yourself.

—From a correspondent in Nebraska we learn that only $9,000 are now needed to save the buildings of Cotner University. We hope that being now so near landing, the remaining need will be supplied. Cotner University could be of great service to our brotherhood in the great Northwest if placed on a substantial financial basis.

—The Annual Catalogue of Christian University, Canton, Mo., with announcements for 1898-'9, outlines opportunities for an education worthy of the attention of any young man desiring to fit himself for greater usefulness in life. The fall term opens Sept. 6th.

—We publish in this paper a most deeply interesting article from Rev. Wilbur F. Crafts, Ph.D., superintendent of the Reform Bureau, Washington, D. C., on "A Study of Living and Dying Nations." Our readers will, of course, have to make allowances for his use of the term "Sabbath," etc, but they will understand this from his view-point, and not allow that to prevent them from a careful reading of the entire article, as it contains so much that is worthy of prayerful consideration.

—D. L. Moody desires to have the work of the Army and Navy Christian Commission continued and still asks for offerings for this work. Send all contributions to him at East Northfield, Mass., and the same will be promptly acknowledged. Dr. Moody says that he "never felt so sorry for a lot of men as for these here in the hospitals," and relates a few of the many instances of comfort brought to sick and dying men through this agency. Surely this is a Christian work, and our patriotism and Christianity should be combined to support it. We hope that it will, indeed, become one of the permanent associated benefactors of the army and navy.

—"The Voice Extra," Vol. I., No. 4, a folder of sixteen pages, is devoted wholly to a description of the beer saloons in the army and their effects, which have become a blot upon our nation That these saloons have been an auxiliary to the scourge of fevers which invaded every camp is almost certain, to say nothing of the sickening stories of drunken fights which have found such frequency in the newspapers. Why these saloons have not been abolished by the administration after what has transpired in the camps, and the petitions which the Christian people of the land have made, and especially after General Miles' and General Shafter's pronounced opinions and orders against strong drink in the army, is a mystery; a mystery which has called forth a strong editorial in the Voice for Aug. 25, severely arraigning the War Department for what it claims to be a criminal neglect of duty. The army canteen as seen at Chickamauga and other camps, it claims, is run in defiance of Congress and disregard for army regulations and for local option laws. That the sale of alcoholic liquors in states or territories prohibiting the same by law is in violation of a Congressional act, June 30th, 1890, is clearly made out by the Voice, and the United States army, through certain of its officers, are charged with having violated the laws of Congress and army regulations by which they are governed. There is Christian, temperance and humane sentiment enough in this nation to correct these abuses if it could only be exerted, and if such negligence and violations of law and shameful results do not arouse it we fear that we have too highly exalted the true degree of our civilization.

—The Church Versus the Minnesota Issue is a new and vigorously edited temperance journal, published monthly, from Minneapolis, Minn., by the Anti-Saloon League. We are pleased at the way this journal hurls itself against the liquor traffic, and if it shall succeed in convincing the world that the Anti-Saloon League is not a compromise institution between absolute prohibition and political party privileges for the comfort of those who have political corns on their toes it will have demonstrated its full right to a place among the living forceful journals of the day.

—The Minnesota State Convention at Mankato, recently, passed a resolution endorsing and adopting Drake University at Des Moines, Ia., as its organ of education and commended the same to the patronage of all families in Minnesota having sons and daughters to educate. They also ask for a representation on the board of trustees of Drake University. A similar step was taken by South Dakota at its state meeting last June. This ought to add materially, morally and in other ways to the prosperity of Drake University. We understand also that $40,000 of the $50,000 needed for Drake University has been raised and Chancellor Craig says, "The rest will come." The outlook of this University for a large number of new students is said to be bright. The fall term begins Sept. 13th.

—It is time now to begin to talk up the General Convention at Chattanooga, October 13-21. Are all your pledges to the various missionary societies and boards, to report at that convention, paid? If not, this is the last month. Their books will be closed September 30. The churches of Chattanooga are hard at work, preparing to entertain the convention. One fare for the round trip has been secured over nearly all the railroads for those who will attend. The brethren everywhere are urged to be there for many cogent reasons. One or more delegates from each church, Sunday-school, Endeavor Society and C. W. B. M. will be expected. Tell your church about the time, place, and of its importance.

—As many of our soldiers who volunteered to drive Spain out of Cuba were college and university students, the fortunate closing of the war and discharge of troops will enable many of them to resume their studies this fall. The need for this has been strongly urged by R. H. Jesse, president of the University of Missouri, and we trust will be heeded by all returning student-soldiers. The return of commandants of cadets is especially important that the military education of the colleges and universities enjoying these privileges be not impaired. President Jesse states that the new club house at Columbia, capable of seating four hundred men at one time, is completed and that in architectural beauty, light, heat, ventilation and comfort it is an honor to the state of Missouri.

—The July-August number of the American Home Missionary is devoted to the interests of negro education and evangelization. Particular space is given to the Louisville BibleSchool, the Southern Christian Institute, the work of Robt. Brooks in Alabama and to an address by Booker T. Washington. The history of this branch of our missionary work is given, together with the address of C. C. Smith, delivered at the Richmond convention. This excellent magazine of literature on this vital subject is valuable and worthy of the immediate and careful consideration of every Disciple of Christ. We hope that large numbers of this magazine will be procured for distribution by and in the churches and carefully read.

—The League for Social Service, incorporated in 1898, with headquarters at 287 Fourth Ave., New York City, has come into existence for educational purposes. It is strongly organized, with Josiah Strong for president, and proposes to push its work energetically. A bureau of information, lecture bureau, literary bureau and other departments have been established, and work will be directed toward the public conscience and toward legislative bodies. The leaflets on living, urgent topics and issues of the day are and will continue to be published for distribution at low rates. For sample leaflets, further information, etc., send to the "League for Social Service," United States Charities Building, Fourth Ave., 22nd St., New York City.

—The Disciples' Divinity House Circular gives a clear, brief statement of its plan, organization and work, which will be a matter of convenience for those desiring to become better informed about this particular school for Bible study and its relation to the University of Chicago.

ɔ note from the Missionary nuity Fund of the Foreign ɪry Society is making conɡring the current missionary f England, has just turned Foreign Society on the Anbrother, Frank Coop, had ɪver $5,000 to this society on ae society has also received, :om one friend, which is the ft ever received by the socils to be used in providing homes for the missionaries and other needed buildings. The society pays interest on this money during the lifetime of the contributor, when it becomes the money of the society. The receipts of the Foreign Society already aggregate $117,324.03 for the present year. The most encouraging feature of this growth is that about one thousand churches have contributed to the work this year that did not the year before, and almost as many new Sunday-schools have been enlisted. It is only a question of time when all the churches and schools worthy of the name will be enlisted in world-wide evangelization.

—Last Sunday was Church Extension Day. If for any reason you failed to make an offering for Church Extension on that day, see to it that another Sunday in this month be set apart for that purpose. There is only one collection for Church Extension asked of each church per year, and this one should not be carelessly om tted. Send all collections for Church Extension to G. W. Muckley, 600 Waterworks Building, Kansas City, Mo., as soon as taken.

—The Missionary Intelligencer writes hopefully of the missionary outlook in foreign fields. The closing year, it says, has been a successful one in amount of funds raised at home and in the increased conversions abroad. With predjudices toward missionaries in foreign lands decreasing and the missionary spirit of the churches of Christ in home lands increasing we may well prophesy greater things for Christ in the future.

—The Western Passenger Association says to the Iowa secretary that, for the national conventions, a rate of one and one-third fare on the certificate plan wi'l be granted to the eastern gates of their territory from Oct. 10th to 15th. But you must be at the borders of the Central and Southern Association Oct. 10th to 13th to get the one-fare rates.

—The Baptist News says:

"We are perfectly willing to speak of our religious neighbors always in such away as not to offend if practical. But we know a good many people for whom the CHRISTIAN-EVANGELIST stands, that will take offence at being called "Disciples" almost as readily as they will at being called "Campbellites." Will the CHRISTIAN-EVANGELIST tell us what to do in a case like that?"

The CHRISTIAN-EVANGELIST never advocated the propriety of calling any collective religious body by the term "Disciples." Such a term alone is too indefinite to hurt anybody's feelings. But if the Baptist News means "Disciples of Christ" the CHRISTIAN-EVANGELIST is not aware of standing for any that object. There are some, we are aware, that object to writing the word Disciple with a big D. They prefer it thus: "disciples of Christ." But, however written, there is a vast difference between that phrase and the term "Campbellite." It is the relationship implied that makes "Campbellite" objectionable to us as a religious name, and this objection cannot obtain in the phrase "disciple of Christ," however written. We could not consistently plead for a restoration of Christ's authority in the church and at the same time permit ourselves to be called "Campbellites." If the Baptist News knows of any who do not like to be called Disciples of Christ let him try calling them "Christians," or some other Bible name.

—We call the attention of all interested in the education of boys to Bunker Hill Military Academy, Bunker Hill, Ill. Col. S. L. Stiver, the proprietor, will take pleasure in answering all letters of inquiry.

PERSONAL MENTION.

J. C. Coggins, now in a meeting at Corinth, Mo., called at this office while in the city on last Friday. Bro. Coggins is one of our always-busy evangelists.

Lawrence McCrea preached in Oskaloosa, Ia., on August 28th.

G. L. Brokaw, editor of the Christian Index, spoke at Fort Dodge same day.

J. J. Nicholson is in Washington, Iowa, securing pledges for the purchase of a lot.

H. O. Breeden and I. N. McCash have returned from their summer vacations.

The Keokuk County (Iowa) convention was presided over by S. P. Telford. T. T. Thompson was its faithful secretary. Pastor Fisher, of Delta, made a fine impression upon his new friends. A. J. Garrison presented a masterly paper. J. A. Ragan delivered one evening discourse and A. M. Haggard the other. B. W. Petitt acted as host.

A. L. Chapman was married to Miss Mae C. Childs on the 1st of September. D. R. Van Buskirk and A. McLean officiated. The bride hails from Greensburg, Ind. Mr. and Mrs. Chapman sail on the 10th for Constantinople to engage in missionary work.

Allan B. Philputt, pastor of the Central Christian Church, Indianapolis, will deliver one of the addresses at the State C. E. Convention of Pennsylvania, to be held at Harrisburg, Oct. 4-6.

J. E. Lorton, pastor of the church at McPherson, Kan., was given a vacation with salary continued, and on his return found the present of a first class bicycle awaiting him.

The Christian Tribune announces the intention of L. M. Omer to resign the pastorate of the Third Church, Richmond, Va., and expresses a very high estimate of his ability as a preacher. Bro. Omer has been at Richmond a number of years and they will be slow to give him and his esteemed wife to other fields.

J. F. Williams' sermon on "Good Citizenship," preached at Stuttgart, Ark., Aug. 7th, was published in full in the Free Press of that city. It is a strong, healthful sermon.

C. M. Hughes, singing evangelist, can be had to assist in protracted meetings. Address Grant, Ind.

M. F. Harman has been called back to Jackson, Miss., to take the pastorate of the church made vacant by W. A. Neal's death. He spent six years there building up the church which, he says, has the best house we have in the gulf states, except one or two points in Georgia. He left there two years ago in September and will return October 1st.

G. E. Jones has located at Paris, Ark., and reports work starting of nicely there.

Miss Snowy Ditch, singing evangelist, of Ft. Scott, Kans., can be had to assist in protracted meetings.

M. L. Mum, of Wichita, Kan., is visiting his son in this city and called at this office. He has been visiting and preaching in Southwest Missouri for a few weeks.

R. W. Stancill has resigned his work for the church at Elizabeth City, N. C., for lack of sufficient financial support.

J. F. Williams, of Stuttgart, Ark., uses a monthly bulletin to assist in announcing services, etc.

A. L. Chapman's address is, German Imperial P. O., Constantinople, Turkey.

C. E. Millard, of Maysville, Mo., can be secured as a singing evangelist to assist in protracted meetings.

Earle Wilfley began his fourth year of service for the church at Wabash, Ind., on last Sunday.

The church of East Sedalia, Mo., passed resolutions of appreciation of the services of J. S. Myers in helping it into existence and for its present excellent conditions, possessions and possibilities.

W. H. Bybee wishes to say that correspondents can write to any of the official board at Bolivar, Mo., for knowledge of his efficiency and work nstead of to J. R. Winn only, as appeared recently in this column.

Isaac Selby, of Australia, is now visiting in the United States and while here will be available for lectures. His address will be in care of J. H. Fillmore, 119 W. 6th St., Cincinnati, Ohio.

Miss Mattie Boyle, who has been spending the summer at Macatawa, Mich., returned to her desk in the subscription department of this house on last Monday, greatly benefited by her rest..

Sherman B. Moore, of Galesburg, Ill., has accepted a call to preach for the Compton Heights Christian Church, this city, and is expected on the field by Oct. 1st.

J. M. Philputt, pastor of the Lenox Avenue Union Church, New York City, has been spending his vacation with his brother at Indianapolis, preaching once each for the Third Church and the Central.

Pres. E. V. Zollars will dedicate the new church building at Niagara Falls, N. Y., on September 18. F. W. Norton is the pastor.

J. W. Lowber, of Austin, Tex., preaches three times on Sundays, even during the hot weather. In addition to this he superintends a Sunday-school and attends Endeavor service. The result is, notwithstanding the fact that the membership is small, they will soon begin the erection of a fine stone church building with a seating capacity of one thousand. It is to be entirely modern and one of the best church buildings in Texas. This, he says, is needed, as the University of Texas has nearly a thousand students and many of them attend the Christian church.

A. B. Maston, manager of the Austral Pub. Co., Melbourne, Australia, who has been in the United States since April, will return to Melbourne by a steamer leaving San Francisco Sept. 27th. His postoffice address during his stay in the United States was at Larwill, Ind.

SOUTH DAKOTA.

W. H. Mullins, of Heatland, presided with credit over the Huron Endeavor convention of this state.

A. H. Seymoure, of Arlington, was elected secretary of the state Endeavor at the Huron convention.

W. P. Shamhart, of Aberdeen, at the Huron convention delivered the response to the address of welcome. He secured the state Endeavor convention for 1899 for his town also.

R. D. Cantz, of Clark, M. B. Ainsworth, of Watertown, L. W. Thompson, of Volga, and H. C. Shipley, of Carthage, also attended and participated in the "Huron '98" convention.

A. M. Haggard, of Iowa, was the only Disciple invited from out of the state.

IOWA.

Bro. Jewett, of Des Moines, recently returned from Europe, spoke at the Central Church on Aug. 21st.

Prof. Edward Ames spoke for the Central on Aug. 28th.

Carl C. Davis has located at Davenport.

C. C. Rowlison will be installed at Marshalltown on Sept. 6th. A very appropriate programme is arranged.

W. A. Moore, of Webster City, has been invited to hold his own meeting. Pastor Moore recently took his boys' brigade into camp for one week.

W. A. Foster and Pastor Platt, of Waterloo, are in a great tabernacle meeting. Capacity of the structure is 1,200.

W. S. Lemen, of Volga, is in a meeting at Graham.

J. A. Senton, of Marion, has been called to Rock Rapids.

J. A. Bennett begins a meeting on Sept. 11th at Mt. Auburn.

B. L. Kline reports ground broke on Aug. 22d for a new house at Dallas.

G. A. Ragan, of Oskaloosa, will remove to Chicago, Ill., on Sept. 1st.

A. M. Haggard is now out of Iowa for a few days. He is delivering three addresses before the South Dakota Endeavor Convention at Huron.

D. A. Wickizer is in a meeting at Deep River.

Mills county Iowa Convention will buy a tent. Brethren Caudle, Johnson, Hallam and Haggard participated in the convention.

Bro. M. G. E. Bennett, of Villison, is doing a good work.

A. M. Haggard, for five years secretary of the Iowa board, will retire at the coming state convention. Who will succeed him is not yet known.

CHANGES.

S. W. Nay, Hamilton to Fisher, Ill.
E. W. Emerson, Seneca to Holton, Tex.
A. J. Hanly, Ashland to Central Point, Oregon.
E. F. Taylor, Benham to Bay City, Tex.
S. J. Corey, Waterloo, Neb., to Rochester, N. Y.
J. K. Brown, Modesta to Wheatland, Cala.
J. A. Smith, Osawatamie to Wichita, Kan.
S. R. Lewis, Lincoln to Broadwell, Ill.
J. M. Morris, Randall, Kan., to Lexington, Ky.
G. L. Cook, Cleveland, to 180 West College St., Oberlin, Ohio.
R. F. Carter, Weakly, Tenn., to Timpson, Tex.
J. J. Cramer, Denver, Ill., to Lockhart, Tex.
Meade E. Dutt, S. Frankford, to Coe, Mich.
H. D. Williams, Mankato, Minn., to Ann Arbor, Mich.
E. M. Miller, Rockwell City to Fonda, Ia.
W. J. Burner, Pleasanton, Kas., to Irvington, Ind.
D. F. Stafford, Red House to 1816 W. Chestnut St., Louisville, Ky.
E. E. Mack, Logan, Ia., to Albion, Ind.
H. C. Shropshire, Fowler to Ukia, Cal.
A. D. Skaggs, Ashland to Independence, Ore.
Philip T. King, Belton to Hillsboro, Tex.
F. N. Calvin, Chicago, Ill., to Waco, Tex.
H. W. Everest, Macatawa, Mich., to Des Moines, Ia.
F. W. Emerson, Seneca to Holton, Kan.
A. G. Alderman, Bethany to Albany, Mo.
J. S. Hughes, Macatawa, Mich., to 6458 Stewart Boul., Station O., Chicago, Ill.
H. S. Earl, Macatawa, Mich., to Irvington, Ind.
E. C. Ford, Port Williams, N. S., to 287 Gottengen, W. Halifax, N. S.

STOCKHOLDER'S MEETING.

Notice is hereby given that the annual meeting of the stockholders of the Christian Publishing Co. will be held at the company's office, 1522 Locust St., St. Louis, Mo., on Tuesday, Oct. 4th, 1898, at 10 o'clock A. M., for the election of Directors, and for the transaction of such other business as may legally come before said meeting.

J. H. GARRISON, Pres.
W. D. CREE, Sec.

St. Louis, Lo., Sept. 1, 1898.

rrespondence.

g Through England.

VIII.

rhere we stopped over Sunday, sure that was not on the bills. a matter of course, to enthuse s of Derwent Water, to admire nmetry of Skiddaw, and quote 'alls of Lodore. These are the ictions of the place, and we highly satisfactory. But the not tell you that in a quiet k there is a sedate little board- by a sedate lady for the benefit f other sedate persons, mostly ı. And they do not say what ent can be derived from these dings by two cheerful cyclists liven up the situation. It was watch the effect of the Ameri- hese staid and sober Britons. k of wild surprise, followed by .on, as it became more clearly st had been perpetrated. This ›ded by a shocked expression, hat not only has a personal in- ceived, but the common social ı been outraged. The third or ı of the offense brings a look of .stened submission to the in- , when all hope seemed gone, first token of sympathetic re- nmistakable twinkle becomes orner of a hitherto sober eye, ; is only a matter of time until ;ers and the two elderly couples o be sedate.

—

ıodore have been extolled, per- ʳ Southey, and have been the and unmerited slander on the 'ho declare that there are more er. The fact is, the Falls of exceedingly variable quantity. 1 dry weather they are a mere but a single heavy rain trans-) a foaming torrent, the water traced far out across the peace- erwent. Passing Lodore, we weep to the west and south, nister House one of the most ses in the district. In the f the Lake District there are ads of any sort, and the mount- ! the roughest kind. To avoid wide detour west of the mount- d the lake country again at its r by Wast Water, a lake of 1idden among high mountains ipitously from its edge. We ıeart of the most rugged part of amid scenery far wilder than sssociate with the name of Again we are confronted by a ains with no road. This time asier method of going around s on our shoulders, start on the r trail up Sty Head Pass. It er the fells to Langdale Pikes, begins, and it took five hours) cover the distance. A party rhom we met half way looked at ost astonishment, as if bringing ch a place savored of the black ; entirely satisfied and all token) vanished when they observed, ›ur wheels and the accent of our were Americans. The capaci- trange and unheard-of things e of the elements of American- by most Englishmen. Just to ; crossing the mountains with a mere bagatelle, I mounted and pony-track on the mountain iendly crag shut us from their ather harder on us than it was think. At least, the Sterling bore it, as it has all the abuse to which it has been subjected on this trip, with remarkable good humor.

—

Brantwood, the home of John Ruskin, stands, as the home of Ruskin should, in a spot of peaceful and quiet beauty, on the shore of Lake Coniston. We did not see "the professor," as he is called in the neighborhood, but we had a talk with his nearest neighbor, who told us that Mr. Ruskin walks out every day and seems to be strong of body in spite of his eighty years. His mind, however, is so far lost that he recognizes no one except those who constantly attend upon him. There was a pathetic significance in the words when our informant told us of the things Mr. Ruskin used to do and say "when he was all right." Tennyson lived for a short time near Brantwood, but the place has no vital associations with the poet's life or work. Close by is the queer little town of Hawkshead, where Wordsworth went to school in his boyhood, and his name, carved in the desk by his own hand, is still exhibited.

—

Our last day in Lake-land may be considered typical of that district, as regards weather. First, it rained violently. Then it stopped long enough to lure us forth, and when we were well on the way toward Kirkstone Pass the rain came again, beating in our faces, both drenching and blinding us. We knew we were passing through magnificent scenery, for the guide-book said so, but we could no more see it than we could have seen through a snow bank or, for that matter, a savings bank, for we were in the cloud as well as in the rain. I have traveled some thousands of miles on passes, thanks to my connection with a newspaper, but I would rather pay full fare than travel again on a pass such as the Kirkstone Pass in wet weather. But, after a dozen miles of this, it cleared again and, as we rode out of the land of lakes, Ullswater was a blaze of glory and Helvellyn stood out clear against a bright western sky. We hurried at dusk across the border into Scotland, as many an eloping English couple has done in times past, and stopped at Gretna Green. This famous village never had more than a dozen houses in its palmiest days, and the only thriving industry which it ever possessed was that of marrying runaway lovers without a license. It is grievous to relate that this ancient industry has fallen into complete desuetude, owing to the operation of a cruel modern English law and the keen competition of Milwaukee in the same line of business. We have here another illustration of the invincibility of Western enterprise in the face of modern competition.

—

They say it always rains on the border of Scotland. Inasmuch as we slipped in under cover of darkness, we escaped for the time, but it caught us next morning. The middle of the morning found it still pouring, with no prospect of cessation. No one needs to be told now, since Ian Maclaren and J. M. Barrie have told us all, that one of the chief characteristics of the Scotch mind is a hatred of exaggeration, resulting in an habitual understatement of facts. Thus a Scotch mist is proverbially wetter than an English rain. On this same morning, with the weather as stated, we facetiously ask an old Scot if he does not think it may rain presently. He replies seriously, "Oh, ay, man. I canna say but that it maun be a bit weet afore the nicht." And so it was.

—

Looked at on the literary side, the Lowlands are the land of Burns and the Highlands are the land of Scott. A line from Glasgow to Edinburgh will serve as a rough boundary between the two. Coming through Dumfries, with its many memorials of Burns, to Ayr, the place of his birth and the scene of most of his poems, one cannot help contrasting the relation of Burns to these places with the relation of Shakespeare to Stratford-on-Avon. One feels awed to find himself in the place where Shakespeare was born. Somehow it does not seem that he ought ever to have had a birthplace. He, with his universal and impersonal genius, is the Melchisedek of literature—without beginning or end of days, and without obvious connection with any place or time. One is not likely to gain any new interest in Shakespeare's works or insight into them by visiting Stratford. With Burns it is different. You cannot know the genial lowlander until you have seen something of the places where he lived and where he found the inspiration and the materials for his poetry. The peasants of Ayrshire have a claim upon Burns such as the citizens of no town can ever have on Shakespeare. As a literary pilgrimage, therefore, we would say that a visit to Ayr is far more satisfying than a trip to Stratford.

—

There are various ways of looking at Scott's relation to that portion of the Highlands which he has immortalized. Sailing down Loch Katrine and fully under the spell of its wild and peculiar beauty, we fell into conversation with an officer on the little steamer, "Rob Roy." Scott was the theme and I was pleased with his apparently intelligent appreciation of the wizard of the North. At last, as we rounded a curve and the full beauty of Ellen's Isle broke upon us, while thoughts of the "Lady of the Lake" were seething in my brain, he came to the climax of his appreciation thus: "Yes, sir, Scott just made this country. Why, there are thousands of tourists who sail down the lake on this boat every year whom we could never have touched if it had not been for Scott's 'Lady of the Lake' and 'Rob Roy.'" In view of the fact that they charge three shillings and six pence (equal to eighty-four cents) for transporting a man and a bicycle six miles on Loch Katrine, it will be observed that this faithful employe's gratitude to Scott was not misplaced.

—

Loch Lomond is surely the king of all Highland lakes and the crown and climax of his majesty is the great Ben Lomond, which rises on the eastern shore. A magnificent road runs by the western edge on the opposite side of the lake. Nowhere, perhaps, will the cyclist find the ideal conditions for wheeling more perfectly realized. But if Loch Lomond is the king, Loch Katrine is the queen of the lochs, and the brightest jewel in her diadem is fair Ellen's Isle. Passing these renowned lakes and on through the Trossachs to Callander, we turn north into the less frequented but not less beautiful parts of the Highlands, and here we stop to spend Sunday at this microscopic village in the very heart of the Highlands, with great Ben Moore rising behind and bens of all sizes piled about in luxuriant profusion.

W. E. GARRISON.

Crianlarich, Scotland.

Honolulu Letter.

This is now the Far West. In fact, the Far West has finally "located" in these islands, never to change again. Moreover, henceforth these islands are to be reckoned as a part of "the home field;" for, before the message I am sending you can reach your readers, the Stars and Stripes will float over Hawaii for good and all. Does "the case being altered alter the case?" If one may judge from the many inquiries that come from the would-be settlers, the case is unquestionably in a state of being very much altered.

As to those Disciples of Christ who labor for the restoration of the faith once delivered to the saints, and who pray and work for unity among believers on the basis of unity with Christ, let us record a note at this epoch-making season. We may want it for reference in days to come.

For several years W. C. Weedon and wife, W. L. Hopper and wife and a few other Disciples prayed and pleaded and hoped that a church might be organized and sustained here. Their prayers were heard. August 5, 1894, T. D. Garvin began work in Harmony Hall, in this city. A church was formed with twelve charter members. During the past four years 140 additions have been made to the little band. Several have been baptized who could not take membership here. In November, 1895, the church then numbering thirty-nine, completed and occupied its beautiful chapel, which was paid for before the opening day. (There is still a debt on the lot.) In February, 1896, Bros. Romig and Harrell began a meeting that lasted six weeks. In September of the same year Bro. Garvin and wife returned to California on a year's vacation, during which time Bro. J. M. Monroe continued the work. In September, 1897, Bro. Garvin returned and rasumed the work, which is still carried forward. Mr. Desky, a prominent business man of the city, has given a lot which has been improved by Bro. Weedon. It is designed to erect a mission chapel thereon in the near future. Sister Alice F. Beard, of California, who has a coffee plantation on Hawaii, in addition to liberal help given to the church in Honolulu, has built a chapel on her lot in Kona, Hawaii, where she is carrying on a Japanese mission with the assistance of Bro. T. Fukao, recently from Tokyo. The brethren here are anxious to enter upon a more vigorous work among the Japanese and to begin a mission among the Chinese. The attitude of the workers here towards other Hawaiian churches, and towards the brethren and churches and boards of the brotherhood in in the states, is ideal. They deserve and have and like to have the respect of those who know them. Wherein the assistance from the more favored brethren and churches comes short of their support they cheerfully make their living by such ways as Providence opens up for them. Though they are not under the appointment of any board they gladly receive through the boards, and from the boards and local societies any help that may come to them. If this state of things could continue, and if workers thus minded could be added to the number, and they could continue to have the good-will of the brotherhood, a phase of disunion that obtains in some places would be avoided. The workers for this field can be and will be increased spontaneously. Those who are willing to labor in self-denial, as did the pioneers of every previous "Far West" outpost, will come to this the last and fairest of them all. I suggest, therefore, *if they can have the good-will of the brotherhood*, as I have intimated, let offerings in aid of this work be sent (t rough any forwarding agency the reader may like to employ) to Bro. T. D. Garvin, Honolulu, H. I. He will keep faithful records of funds contributed, and make due reports of the work. His long and faithful service in the ministry entitles him to your confidence. Besides, he and his colaborers know what should be done much better than those who have no experience in the field.

Now is the time to help the work.

Yours faithfully, A SOJOURNER.

August 6, 1898.

The Conversion of Europe.

Until now the inhabitants did not know what time had wrought. In the midst of peace a mighty empire had attained permanence and power, nor had it been founded by an emperor or sustained by an imperial force, booted and spurred. The impossible had been achieved. Liberty, equality and fraternity had been justified; while discouraging the spirit of militarism the science of war had not been forgotten; moral courage and patriotism had increased from decade to decade. The power and wish of the people had become absolute and invincible, willing and executing in its own name and under its own great seal, being alike its keeper. "We the people!"

In the eyes of Continental Europe such a government was, if not a fiasco, at least not to be feared. Above all, the political sages did not consider the opinion of the United States as having a feather's weight in the affairs of the Old World or of the great Orient. There was not a prophet among them who would have had the temerity to predict that that far-off republic, loving and serving only the dollar, would soon be in position to make its voice heard across the vast oceans which wash its coast lines and separate it toward the East from the civilized (?), toward the West from the heathen world. Europe was ignorant of America while professing knowledge. In all Europe, to be an American was, and still is, for the most part, synonymous with being either a farmer or at most a merchant. Chicagoan and pork-packer are current synomymns. Of the idealism of American life and American institutions, Europe was profoundly unconscious; the ignorance of the masses on this subject having no other source than a partisan press to draw from, could be likened only to a London fog. It is not yet three months ago that the writer heard a professor use America as an illustration of a land where patriotism did not exist in the European sense of the term. In America only a venal patriotism existed. That was in the lecture-room of a Swiss University. I quote a word from a morning paper:

"Before the war, so unfortunate for Spain, one imagined voluntarily in France [he might have said Europe] that America would be incapable of arming ships, equipping troops and organizing armies. We were accustomed to think that the Yankees were simply merchants, strangers to all conceptions of war, disdainful of glory and nearly entirely lacking in that extreme patriotism of which the old nations of Europe thought they had a monopoly."

Such being the current of opinion in France the press, in particular the conservative and royalistic papers, did not hesitate to encourage priest-b ind Spain. When Martinez Campas was replaced by Gen. Weyler—the humantarian by the brute—the French press praised the Canovas ministry and eulogized Weyler. When the United States began to talk earnestly of war, the French press held out the hope of success to the Spaniards. They recalled the inequality of the fleets in emphasizing that it would necessarily be a war on the seas. All Europe was loud in the praise of Spanish discipline, Spanish fleets and Spanish strategy. They admitted the ultimate defeat of Spain while predicting the annihilation of American ships at the outbreak, not believing in the American navy. They even spoke of America as like China—big, but not great. But it was wish rather than conviction. "'Declare war sooner than withdraw from an island which you discovered and civilized!" Such were the exclamations which encouraged Spain. To make themselves the more responsible for Spain's attitude they held out the hope of possible interference on the part of the "European Concert." Spain believed them in spite of the fiasco of last spring in Greece. To all this long-drawn eulogies on the chivalry of the Castilian race, and the patriotic duty of Spain to protect the inviolability of her territory against the insulting audacity of a race of merchants who, not loving their own country, could easily see how another could sell or barter a part of its possessions. Such a proposal was worthy of America. Spain was praised for having refused in former years the sordid proposals of a sordid race.

Spain decided haughtily in favor of war. We Americans, residing on the Continent, reading daily the unfavorable statistics as to the fleets of the belligerants, and sharing not the ignorance of our instructors, trembled for American sailors and cities, while believing in final victory. Imagine our rejoicing when the papers began to annouce the annihilation of a a whole Spanish flee before Cavite. At first they said it was a mere rumor, then it was doubtful, then probable, then it became possible and exaggerated, then—O welcome dispatch from Madrid!—it became certain.

The press reeled before the Spanish advices. An unheard-of General Dewey had committed an unheard-of act of daring and had gained an unheard of victory! Some editors were carried away for the instant with a feeling of impartiality; they even praised the American editor. But they soon saw through it all and declared the matter as a very one-sided affair. The real Spanish fleet was in the Antilles, or would be soon. Dewey became a mere butcher. His brutality would meet with summary vengeance when the Atlantic fleets should meet in Cuban waters. The pirates and would-be conquerors would receive a lesson as salutary as needed. They forgot soon the battle in disussing the Philippine question, and the audacity of beginning the war in the Pacific which Europeans had so carefully planned for Cuban waters.

The brilliant passage of Cervera across the Atlantic, the rapidity of his vessels, the safe arrival of his fleet, destined to become the second armada—all this was a proof of Spanish genius and American negligence. So they said.

One beautiful morning the wit of the Yankees informed Europe that Cervera was in a bottle, having succeeded in putting one ship after another through the neck. Americans were laughing at Spanish strategy. All the papers here began to say the Spaniards were in a bottle; the wiser heads began to see in this a possible fatality. The strategy of Cervera "fell," as they say on 'change, as Spanish papers had done. The military sense of Europe revived and discovered that it was the duty of a powerful fleet to search the enemy and give battle; not search the harbor, but the open sea. They advised him to flee by night. To his honor, be it said, he fled by day.

It was consternation which swept over the continent when the telegraph bureaus announced the annihilation of this second armada. A cry of, "Peace! peace!" went up from every newspaper office. Those who had counseled war now advised peace. Since that morning the press has ceased to talk of America in a disparaging way. Editors who went about a few days ago with editorials in their heads on the proclamation of a European Monroe Doctrine with Germany behind it, and the Continent behind Germany, are now writing on the new maritime power in the other hemisphere, the American peril, etc. The fall of Santiago, the successful expedition to Porto Rico, the constant arrival of troops at Manila, The annexation of the Hawaiian islands, the certainty that America will have, at the very least, coaling stations off the coast of the Orient and be absolute dictator in the Antilles, has completed the awakening and conversion of arrogant Europe. Continental conceit has been dealt a severe blow. The papers, even the Figaro, of Paris, pronounces the humiliation of Spain as in part a humiliation of the Continent. Some editors have been studying geography anew and have discovered that the possessions of the united Anglo-Saxon race form a festoon of fortifications about the Continent and the Orient, that in the course of time the European and all the Asiatic races have been penned in by the greatest of maritime races, that disunited Europe, lacking in outlets to the sea, and in fleets is surrounded by the united English-speaking peoples, who have gradually taken posession of a large part of the earth's surface and all the seas. "On the North," they say, "we are bounded by the Frigid Zone, on the South, the East and the West by the no less frigid Anglo-Saxons."

The conversion of Europe has been complete. There is no danger of backsliding. The Continental powers are staring bewildered at the American navy, glorified and transfigured in victorious strife, heroic in attack, equally chivalrous toward a vanquised foe. They know to-day what they denied three months ago, that there are ships and good admirals, armies and brave generals, patriotic sailors and soldiers in the Western Hemisphere, and e terms liberty, humanity and fraternity re than idle words in the Republic of the States. WM. H. MATLOCK.

;.

The Future of the C. E.

evident that the attractiveness of the ' connected with the movement has away, but great good has been accom- : and will continue to result from the ›ut forth by the young in this valued de- ›nt of religious servi·e. Those who ed the cause because they rush to any ›ork for the reason that it is new and tor changes have of course dropped out, ose who saw in it a door of entrance to ısefulness in contributing to the spirit- of the church, are brought into closer thy by experience in service, and many are attracted by the opportunity of direct help to the church by word and

›tless two reasons why some denomina- ıave withdrawn and organized on lines ·ir own are that they may emphasize ›eculiar doctrine more and that they may ıore efficient denominational leadership. ; a people can accomplish all this. by ıing in the society, and thus still hold ITS ble features. The Bethany Reading will give you ample training in "Our ' The leadership is now in the hands of ıo, with his limitations, has shown what ıt work he could accomplish were he . in a situation where he could give him- ıolly to this service. Bro. J. Z. Tyler is ıghly familiar with the needs of our people and should be persuaded to give hole time to this cause, in which he has so much interest, even to the degree of ·dizing his health from the necessity of ng a pastorate at the same time. All enominational conventions will be of the › of a rally, which is important, but what- ystematic work is planned and prosecuted ›e done by each religious body for itself. › the importance of our national leader. ; promote our leader to full time. The d of support will easily suggest itself.

LEVI MARSHALL.

Western Montana.

he western part of this state is the ful Bitter Root Valley, some ten or : miles in width and nearly a hundred in length. It is becoming far-famed for ıldness of its climate, the productiveness soil and the attractiveness of its moun- which rise majestically on either side, g a spell, as it were, over those who too long within the fertile vale.

ı here that the great copper king and ı of the turf, Marcus Daily, has his sum- ›sidence and ranch of several thousand besides owning a controlling interest in .siness of Hamilton.

look out of my window I see passing a of that fast-vanishing race, who but a ears ago roamed at will over the moun- ınd through the valley, calling it their. But they have been removed to the ation on the North, and are only per- l to pass through here on their hunting ıtions. Great as have been the changes past twenty-five years, we should look he next quarter of a century as calami- ! the changes are not greater. A merce- spirit largely rules the West. A large nt. of the people have come here seeking t anything but the kingdom of God and ;hteousness. But, thanks be unto God, not true of all. The leaven is working; It is purifying and preserving, and the is shining. Notwithstanding the ramp- ·dlessness which cares not for the meek wly spirit of the Master, and the "drink e" which hovers over the lovely garden- seeking whom it may devour, yet I believe these people are to be won to the higher life. And no unimportant factor in their salvation are the Disciples of Christ. They have had an organization since 1880, with four at the present time and a good prospect for organizing others. Last Sunday evening we closed our first "camp meeting convention," which was held at Florence. Although it came at a very busy season of the year, there was a goodly number in attendance, and an excellent interest was manifested throughout. The papers were of a high order, dealing with practical questions of church work. Bro. W. M. Jordan, our state secretary, was with us, delivering a number of most excellent addreses and encouraging us to go forward in greater things for the Master. Bro. W. D. Lear, our first located preacher in the valley, was with us on Lord's day, and spoke in the afternoon to the delight of all. To Bro. J. C. B. Stivers, pastor at Missoula, no small credit is due for the success of this meeting. He believes that Eastern ideas will work in the West, and he is busily engaged demonstrating the fact.

The churches of the valley report about fifty accessions in the last nine months; about half of these by primary obedience. The *net gain* is much smaller, as the population is still quite migratory. One hundred and twenty dollars were given by the children and Bible-schools for Foreign Missions. Florence Sunday-school raised twenty-eight dollars. There are but two ministers at present giving their whole time to the work—J. C. B. Stivers and Frederick Grim. We hope to receive sufficient appropriation so that we may increase our corps of workers during the coming year. There was one lady who made the good confession and was buried with her Lord in baptism, having come a distance of over twenty miles. A permanent organization was effected with Bro. Stivers as president; F. F. Grim, vice-president; Mary E. Doan, treasurer; and H. L. Carter, secretary. J. H. Cowan, L. D. Reynolds, Chas. Boone and Mrs. G. E. Sullenger were elected as additional members of the executive committee. Our state convention meets with Bro. McHargue at Bozeman, September 8 11.

F. F. G.

Florida Letter.

Yesterday in company with my wife I visited, for the second time this week, the Second Divisional Military Hospital in the vicinity of this city. More than five hundred men are in this hospital confined by malarial or camp fever; some are at the point of death, but the majority convalescing. While we were visiting the various ward tents, sixty more sick ones were brought in on ambulances, and were awaiting places. It is about decided in the minds of those in charge of the hospitals here that the troops are suffering from a low and slow type of malarial camp fever. The city of Jacksonville is in a very healthy condition. Never perhaps in its history has there been so little sickness among the citizens. The change of living, of diet, of general customs and habits, with probably in many cases more or less intemperance and climatic changes, have largely been the causes of the illness among the "soldier boys." Owing to the specially peculiar and often too tardy methods pertaining to military matters, it has taken much time to bring order out of chaos in arranging for the comfort and attention necessarily due the sick in such large numbers. It is a scene not soon or easily forgotten, to see the long lines of cots, each cot containing a patient. As we passed slowly from one ward to another we did what we could in the way of words of cheer and sympathy. Occasionally could be see some watchful, anxious mother who had come a long journey to sit beside a dear boy and fan him through the long and tedious hours, leaving him at night only to return and take up the motherly vigil in the returning day. As we looked into the faces of these loving mothers, our hearts were at once uplifted to God, to spare to them their precious sons.

To many of those whose fever had about left them we gave such reading-matter as we were able to take with us. I carried a number of small Testaments, kindly given to me by a friend for the purpose, in my pocket. They gladly received these and said: "We will always keep them." Some of the tracts supplied for the sick, and coming to me for distribution from some sources, I have not been consciously able to use. How much I have the need of some healthy and scriptural, consistent religious literature for this work. My congregation has kindly loaned my pastorate calls to the "boys in blue," while they are with us. And instead of losing anything by this arrangement, our services are all the better attended. To-day I had the pleasure of dining with a number of the officers of the Ninth Illinois through the courtesy of Bros. Chaplain Boles and Lieutenant Day—and a few evenings since I enjoyed the same courtesy with the offiers of the First Texas, preaching for the men of this regiment the same evening. We take this opportunity of thanking the many who have written to us so kindly in view of the limited efforts we have made to encourage and otherwise to aid socially and spiritually the boys who have been in camp "Cuba Libre." We have wished many times that it had been in our power to ameliorate the conditions, and more materially assist those far from the comforts and surroundings of home. If we were in the business we think we could easily find room for much complaint and justifiable criticism of much that has transpired through inadequate preparation and incompetency in performance in some of the military camps of the present campaign. There have been some extremely bitter experiences, and dear lessons taught. Political pulls and partisanship should cut no figure where the lives of thousands of the truest and bravest are at stake. This war has taught the average American citizen many a lesson otaer than those suggested by the victories of Dewew, Sampson and Schley.

T. H. BLENUS.

Jacksonville, Florida.

Ontario Christian Colony Notes.

A. M. Sweany, of Cottage Grove, Oregon, with his two grown sons, one of them married, arrived last May. Brother S. is about seventy years of age, and because he killed a bear from his front door and did not run, Bro. Moore, of Rushylvainia, Indiana, said: "He is the hero of Burriss township." Brother Geo. W. Loman calls him "the noblest Roman of them all."

One time, shortly after Brother Sweany arrived, he became discouraged and thought about going back. When the money arrived he had changed his notion, and asked for two more quarter sections of land. He has sent for his family and in a short time all his earthly interests will be in the colony. He and his sons will own five quarter sections of this choice land. Brother S. delivered the first sermon in the colony, and is therefore the pioneer preacher.

This township was surveyed and donated to the Christian Colony by the Ontario Government, and they have spent $2,000 constructing us a road into the town site of Christiana. Forty acres have been plotted for this town. Brother Geo. W. Fullerton, of Pictu, Nova Scotia, Canada, after visiting the colony, locating a claim and a building site in the town, wrote: "You have started a great work for the Lord, and I hope we will keep that in mind as we work together to build up a community whose influence for righteousness will be felt over the known world, and that we will not go forward in our own strength alone, but look to Him who is able to make the work an abiding success and blessing. I have every faith in the colony, for everything is there to make it a great country."

Brother Geo. W. Loman, who came from the Indian Nation, a prime man, writes: "I have an interesting little Sunday-school on my hands at the schoolhouse here." Here is a new call to the brotherhood. Here is another mission field, the first Sunday-school organized and managed by a Disciple in a radius of five hundred miles on the Ontario side of Rainy River. He asks, "Can't some philanthropic brother or sister send enough literature to supply a school of about thirty members for the next quarter? After that we will be self-sustaining." Address this mission at Big Fork, Ont.

This is the opening up of a work long desired. We have had preaching at Port Arthur, Rat Portage, Fort Frances, Emo and Christiana, and probably other points. The latter part of next month we will hold our first annual meeting. It will be necessary to hold this meeting under the shade of the trees and to mingle our voices with the birds, for we have no house of worship yet except the blue sky.

Brother J. P. Martindale, of Greeley, Iowa, wrote: "I have thought to write to you since coming home, but have been very busy. I was well satisfied with the colony and its prospects. The outlook is encouraging."

Brother Green Norris, who came from Sterling, Ill., wrote me from the colony last week: "I am well pleased with the country. The longer I stay the better I like it. The boys are all in good spirits." Bro. Norris is the son-in-law of Brother John O'Hare, of Sterling, Ill.

Sister McGill, near London, Ont., wrote me about a brother. She said: "We have a brother here who has lost all; has a large family; no better man living; have sent him to you." He came to the colony and introduced himself to me. I at once assigned him one hundred and sixty acres of land. Three months afterwards I asked him how he liked the country and how he was getting along, and he replied: "I have been at work every day and am satisfied. I have a fine tract of land." Such men, separated from their families and thus working, deserve success. These men will succeed.

One brother came and when he landed he did not have enough money to purchase his supper and night's lodging. I paid his bill at the hotel, and before the sun went down the next day he owned 160 acres of land joining his brother's and had a good job of work at $1.00 per day and board.

Brother M. Franklin Smotz, of Augusta, Ohio, writes: "Have spent ten years in colonization mission work in the jungles of India. My experience in pioneering has not been small. I have been reading your letters in the CHRISTIAN-EVANGELIST and the Christian Standard from Ontario, and from all that I can gather it is one of the best prospects for a poor man of which I know at this time in North America."

Brother J. L. Sharitt, of Knoxville, Iowa, after spending two weeks in the colony, selecting a beautiful claim and clearing a location for a house, returned home thoroughly satisfied that the country was all I had represented it to be. He writes: "Thirteen men have started from here with teams to drive through, and probably twenty-five will come through at the time of the excursion."

I believe in combining the two great enterprises, colonization and evangelization. I am glad to be known as the Christian Colony agent. It is a good work for humanity. Not every man that undertakes to accomplish an object succeeds. Not every man that comes to the colony is going to be satisfied. Many of these very men have been failures, and much of this refuse material will slip into our colony. These men were failures when they came; when they go away they will be failures, and will always fail in everything they undertake. But these failures will not deter the honest homeseeker. Every great enterprise started for the betterment, for the uplifting of humanity was opposed. Christ did not escape the opposer in his divine work. Shall frail mortals escape? Opposition does not affect the validity of its existence. We shall continue to move forward. That the governments have confidence in the work I prove by what I am able to offer good, honest homeseekers.

I am giving up my beautiful home on the banks of Lake Ontario, forty-five miles east of Toronto, and have arranged to make my headquarters at Port Arthur, Ont. Port Arthur is located at the head of navigation over the great lakes, the gateway to the ocean. We are also on the Canadian Pacific Railway, and at the point where the new Ontario and Rainy River Railway begins. This road is now under construction. The governments have given a subsidy of $9,500 per mile, and the road is to be completed in two years. Address all communications to Port Arthur, Ont.

R. A. BURRISS.

A Profitable Visit.

Browning, the corresponding secretary ;ate, was with us from Aug. 12 to Aug. ı labors resulted in great good to the church by uniting and strengthening thren. Six were added by confession tism and seven were added otherwise; ıday-school took on new life and the was enabled to employ A. R. Wallace h one half-time the coming year.

Browning went from here to spend a s at Ione, Freeman and Booth, where will be made to unite and build up the the Master. He is doing a great work eak and destitute fields.

he brethren who contribute to his sup- ept of our thanks for the blessings they nferred on us? God will continue to e labors of his faithful followers.

W. A. STREATOR.

ff, Ark., Aug. 28, 1898.

Evangelistic.

MISSOURI.

Perrin, Aug. 25.—In a good meeting here with Prof. Sears, of Albany College. Meeting one week old; five additions. Will hold a meeting at Columbus and Elm Grove.—S. J. COPHER.

T. N. Kincaid, of Holden, reports eight additions at Malta Bend. Church there re-organized.

J. C. Coggins closed his meeting at Martinsbnrg recently with 13 additions. He is now at Corinth with good outlook for additions.

Ashland Aug. 30.—Closed a two weeks' meeting here last night. 19 baptisms—three added otherwise.—W. S. St. CLAIR AND J. A. BERRY.

Appleton City, Aug. 22.—Have just closed a meeting at Freedom Church in Henry County with 11 additions; six by baptism, four by statement and one restored.—F. B. ELMORE, Evangelist of Clinton District.

Kansas City.—Closed meeting at Orbon with 15 added. Baptized an old man 63 years old who had always waited for a change of heart. He now possessses a changed heart and a changed relationship.—BRO. COTTINGHAM.

Jasper, Aug. 30.—Closed here to-night. Been here two weeks. The interest good. Seven additions. Go next to Wyaconda. Bro. Warren preaches here very acceptably, and is loved by all.—MORGANS AND DAUGHTER.

Mexico, Sept. 2.—I have just closed a meeting at New Bloomfield which resulted in 25 additions; 13 by primary obedience. I have been preaching for this congregation for nearly four years, except five months given to the Sedalia district as evangelist, and the congregation has more than doubled in that time. The Lord has greatly blessed us.—J. D. GREER.

Marceline Aug. 26.—Closed a short meeting at Salem Church, Randolph County, Tuesday night with three additions. I begin a meeting at Gosneyville Saturday night. I am expecting to be assisted by Bro. L. H. Harbord, one of the best vocal music teachers in North Missouri. I could hold a few meetings this fall. Address me for the present at Paradise, Clay Co., Mo.—B. C. STEPHENS.

Perrin, Sept. 2nd.—Closed here with 12 additions; four last night. This is a strong church. Prof. O. B. Sears is its pastor. He has been here four years.—S. J. CEPHER.

ILLINOIS.

Holder, Aug. 29.—Meeting here one week old; two confessions; meetings continue.—S. E. FISHER, Eureka; assisted by F. W. BURNHAM, Charleston.

Fulton, Aug. 22.—We erected a tent in the city park, and opened a meeting the 14th of August, S. H. Zendt, of Dixon Ill., preaching the first two sermons. Since then J. S. Clements, of Lanark, has done the preaching and will continue. So far three added by baptism and one otherwise.—C. F. GAINES.

OKLAHOMA.

Perry, Aug. 30.—Just closed a two weeks' meeting at Polk with two additions; one from the Baptists, one by statement. I will hold them another meeting soon.—WM. DUNKLEBERGER.

OHIO.

Randolph, Aug. 22 —Seven confessions here the past two Lord's days. I closed my work here Sept. 1st and am succeeded by W. J. Oram, of Wellsburg, W. Va. I go to Akron and take up the new work in the south end of that city.—JOHN P. SALA.

NEBRASKA.

J. J. Higgs, district evangelist, reports 15 additions at Bloomfield to date. No church at that place previous to this meeting of our people. F. H. Sweetman was to join Bro. Higgs to assist in this meeting as singing evangelist.

KENTUCKY.

J. M. Taylor reports 13 additions to the church at Crittenden; seven were immersed. —GEO. A. MILLER.

Turner, Aug. 23.—Aug. 14th we closed a two weeks' meeting at Morgan, where I preach the first Lord's day in each month. Bro. P. H. Duncan, of Ludlow, did the preaching and has greatly strengthened our work. There were 22 additions; 15 by confession.—WALTER P. JENNINGS.

CALIFORNIA.

Fortuna, Aug. 29th.—One baptized Lord's day, Aug. 21st. Also one last night, 28th. Our work is prospering.—A. B. MARKLE.

Santa Ana, Aug. 28th.—Four additions to-day; two by baptism.—A. H. Thomas.

Dixonville, Aug. 30.—Just closed a meeting at Yeatesville, N. C., with two additions. Organized a Sunday-school, and the church agreed to break bread every Lord's Day.—R. W. STANCILL.

CALIFORNIA.

Santana, Aug. 22.—One addition by statement yesterday. Bro. Bateman represents the Christian Church in the evening union meeting at Anaheim, as they have no pastor.—A. H. THOMAS.

ARKANSAS.

Fayetteville, Aug. 29.—Closed a nine days' meeting at Tyro on the 21st. Five confessions; two by relation.—F. B. SAPP.

Little Rock, Aug. 25.—Eleven accessions at Mangrum, Craighead county; six baptized. One at Hot Springs. Thirteen at Cardiff, Scott county; seven baptized. Thirteen baptisms, 12 accessions from other sources; total, 25 during the month. Results of one year's work: Churches organized, 14; Sunday-schools organized, 28; baptisms, 261; other additions, 353; total, 614; houses built or in process, 13.—E. C. BROWNING.

INDIANA.

Lowell, Aug. 23.—Two accessions last Lord's Day.—S. A. STRAWN.

Angola, Aug. 22.—Please report two more added at Watseka, Ill., by relation, Aug. 7.—B. S. TERRALL.

Lowell, Aug. 29.—One addition at prayer-meeting Wednesday evening.—S. A. STRAWN.

Winamac, Aug. 29.—Our annual meeting at this place on Sunday, Aug. 28, was a success in every sense of the word. C. C. Smith was with us and his addresses were of special interest to all. Our work here is in a more prosperous condition than for years. We have at last succeeded in raising the amount necessary to pay off that old debt. Have had three accessions in the last month. We go for a short vacation and a much-needed rest.—W. W. DENHAM.

Mishawaka, Aug. 29.—Since my last report there have been 18 additions to this congregation; eight by baptism and 10 by letter or statement. I have been laboring for the First Christian Church of Mishawaka for just nine and a half months, and the work is growing, not only in additions, but also in the spirit of service and unselfish devotion to the Master. Our Bible-school has more than doubled itself within the nine and a half months. We have had 220 in actual attendance. The other departments are doing good work.—C. H. TROUT.

KANSAS.

Lawrence, Sept. 1.—I baptized my father and mother on Aug 21.—K. W. White.

Lafontaine, Aug. 22.—I have been preaching here nine days with 10 additions; nine by confession. Sister Elsie Nichols, of Buffalo, Kan., has helped greatly by her singing. She is but 17 years of age.—C. W. YARD.

Topeka, Sept. 3rd.—Closed at Holt, Mo., Aug. 31st with 63 additions. Go next to McPherson, Kan.—D. D. BOYLE and V. E. RIDENOUR.

Seneca, Aug. 30.—Closed one and one-half years pastorate here Sunday, with three additions to the congregation. Want a good man for successor. Will take charge of congregation at Holton, Sept. 10th.—F. W. EMERSON.

Argentine. — Work here is getting along very well. Our audiences have been good during the summer. Will have a Sunday-school picnic next week. Bro. C. M. Mickham and Bro. R. C. Davis, a singing evangelist, are holding a meeting in the new tabernacle of the North Side Church, of Kansas City, Kan. I attended last night. They start the meeting with good audiences. B. Q. Denham will preach a part of the time. Bro. Elmer Davis, the new pastor of the Armourdale church, has moved from Independance, Kan., and is starting his work off nicely. The West Side Church in Kansas City, Mo., has secured Bro. Mills Easter, of Larned, Kan., for pastor. Three additions here this month. —ROYAL HANDLEY, Pastor.

MICHIGAN.

Durand, Aug, 24.—S. S. Jones, of Danville, Ill., has just organized a church in this place with 17 members. The meeting continues for this week.—R. BRUCE BROWN.

TENNESSEE.

Knoxville Aug. 29.—Five added to the Park Street Church in August.—ROBERT STEWART.

IOWA.

Larimore.—Nine added; seven confessions and organization of 21. Subscription started for a house.

Mt. Auburn, Aug. 29.—One baptism at regular services yesterday at Oak Grove.—J. T. NICHOLS.

Fort Dodge.—Two, G. L. Brokaw supplying pulpit.

Waterloo.—15, W. A. Foster assisting F. L. Platt.

Summitville.—24, A. F. Sanderson and Bro. Connosan.

Sidney.—Six added and 1,000 hearers, R. A. Omer, evangelist.

Notes and News.

The annual meeting of Wayne County, Ind., held at Jacksonsburg, Aug. 27th and 28th, was large and enthusiastic. Rev. Jno. T. Brown, of Louisville, Ky., and Rev. Robt. Hall, of Indianapolis, Ind., made excellent addresses. Officers elected for next year are: president, T. A. Hall; vice-president, J. T. Brown; secretary, Roy L. Brown; treasurer, J. S. Harris.

The Eureka College Aid Association, organized in March, 1897, has become state-wide. This society is composed of women, and characteristic-like is doing a good work for the college in the way of securing students and money. This society is introducing the college to the state in person and by the use of suitable literature. The membership of the society now numbers three hundred and fifty members, about one hundred of which belong to the local society. These 350 have subscribed shares amounting to $2,500. Of this $1,173 have already been paid in, besides $127 additional, raised by entertainments given by the local society. Miss Anna Hale, the well-known Sunday-school evangelist, is the field secretary of this association, which bespeaks for her a hearty reception on behalf of Eureka College throughout the state.

From a report of the Boone County (Mo.) Co-operation Meeting, held at Red Top, Aug. 10-12, in the Centralia Courier, it is evident that it was a fine convention. About fifteen churches reported. Among the preachers present who delivered vigorous addresses and sermons, were Sec. Davis, Sec. Abbott, J. C. Hall, G. A. Hoffmann, W. S. St. Clair, J. A. Berry, J. R. Linville, C. H. Winders and, we suspect, H. A. Denton, of Centralia, and others.

These are days when patriotic sentiment has become pregnant with action. Let us not forget that the cause of Church Extension is a patriotic one, inasmuch as it contributes to an intelligent and Christian citizenship. I guarantee our apportionment.

Lisbon, O. M. E. CHATLEY.

The Twin City Churches.

The two Christian Churches in the "Twin Cities," North and South Tonawanda, N. Y., have prospered greatly in the last several years. The two churches now number over 1,000 members, being about one-eighteenth of the whole population of the two places. Truly, the Lord has greatly blessed the preaching of his truth here. "Jesus and the resurrection," Paul's theme at Athens, will always, when faithfully preached. E.

Tipton County Meeting.

The county meeting of churches in Tipton county, Ind., Aug. 28th, was a great success. It was the first county co-operation meeting. Bro. L. E. Brown, of Frankfort, Ind., did the preaching. His sermons were very strong. People were charmed with the speaker and his discourses. Many not members of the Christian Churches said they did not know there was a man of such eloquence and pulpit ability among us. We feel that these meetings will do great good. E. A. COLE.

Tipton, Ind.

Regrets.

It is with regret, indeed, that I note in last week's CHRISTIAN-EVANGELIST, Bro. A. W. Conner's characterization of one of my (incomplete) statements, in a previous CHRISTIAN-EVANGELIST query regarding his paper, the Boy's Friend, and the secrety society of which it is the organ; regret that the query was so incautiously framed as to furnish my brother the occasion for classing me with prevaricators; regret instead of so phrasing the query as merly to express an opinion (my actual intent) I allowed myself to make an apparently positive assertion—for I should have added "*as it seems to me;*" regret most of all that the cause we all love should have been compromised to an extent by reason of acrimonious repartee between brethren.

W. P. KEELER.

Chicago, Aug. 31, 1898.

Those Reading Courses.

Permit me to say, in answer to numerous inquiries, that the three handbooks for the second year of the Bethany C. E. Reading Courses will be ready for delivery before the close of September; that the price, to members, will be twenty-five cents a copy; to others thirty-five cents, or the three for one dollar. Those who have not yet taken the first year should begin with the handbooks prepared for that; the price is the same as for the handbooks for the second year. Thirty-five cents pays for an annual membership, and for one year's subscription to the Bethany C. E. Bulletin.

J. Z. TYLER.

Cleveland, O., Sept. 1, 1898.

Notes from Eastern Kentucky.

"The hit hound howls." I did not expect that my tracts would prove palatable to Mormon Elders. To weaken their force some are howling that my "quotations are not correct," etc. I never write or say anything that I can not prove or take back. Hence, if some representative Mormon will point out any mistake it will be corrected. I predict that no *representative* Mormon will undertake the job.

The Mormons are circulating a very subtle tract, compiled from a work called "Mr. Durant, of Salt Lake City." I will reply to it as soon as I finish the work I now have on hand. I would like a copy of every leaflet, tract or pamphlet they are using in the field. They must be met on every point of attack.

The C. W. B. M., of Danville, Ind., sent in five dollars to aid my work. It was needed and the gift was appreciated. With it came the statement, "We are glad to help you this much and only wish that we could do more, and pray that your appeal may touch the hearts of many others."

To which we say, "Amen! and amen!" for the magnitude of this work, battling Mormonism, almost checks our efforts as we fully front it. But God is on our side and we are on the side of God in this fight, and victory will rest on the banners of truth.

Foes of Mormonism should use the county papers as much as they can. Clip everything you see that will aid in exposing the fraud and put it in your county paper. I offer my tracts No. 1 and 2 for this purpose, though one of them is copyrighted. Also any item in my paragraphs. I am trying to keep alive anti-Mormonism columns in several leading weeklies. If all papers would take hold we would soon "blockade" the efforts of the 1,700 Mormon Elders now in the field proselyting.

Received the following from a good brother who is evangelizing. How many of our readers can guess what state he is in? Some of you try it. He says:

I find the situation very much the same as in the mountains of ————. Where we have congregations in the country they are poor people and think a preacher ought to support himself and preach for nothing. Every man almost in a congregation here as in ———— who can talk some publicly, has a call to preach the gospel and will work on his farm and preach to the brethren on Lord's day once or twice a month for $25 or $50 per year. At the end of the year he may receive the half of it. I know one congregation of 75 or 80 members who engage a preacher once a month for one year. At the close they had paid him $11 of the $25 promised. Such a spirit will continually produce death in our congregations.

A remedy for this state of affairs is worthy the efforts of our best minds.

Received a letter from an old brother in Ohio who stopped two nights in the "J Smith Inn," at Nauvoo, Ill. He says Emm Smith, Smith's widow, told him that "Brig ham Young introduced polygamy after he go into the wilderness." He says Smith' widow, known in Mormondom as the "Elec Lady," had "spare features, was fairly edu cated, fairly good looking, black eyes, but ha a ghostly phiz like all persons who believe i ghosts and hob goblins." R. B. NEAL.

California State Convention.

The California state meeting is a thing o the past, but the pleasant memories of tha convocation of Christians by the sea will liv on. The attendance was fully up to an former year, and the surprise was constan that there were so many present this dry year

Reports showed that a number of preacher had sought the green pastures East of th Rockies, and left their flocks to hunt dr stubble. They will expect to be called bac when it rains and the grass starts. They wil then return for their health.

We have many others who are feeding thei flocks and living with them, sharing thei misfortunes, and "streakings of the mornin light" lead them on, and the cause is progressing.

The various departments of church wor filled two weeks full of business. The Preachers' Institute, C. W. B. M., State Missio work, Sunday-school and Christian Endeavo Days showed that California has workers fo the greatest cause in the world.

Bro. J. H. Hughes proved himself to be a convention president of the first order. H was also placed at the head of the State Board.

The presence of Bro. A. McLean, the grea around-the-world missionary man, was a

-wide
was

Bro.
The
re us
then

se of
f the
see

every
train
office
ne to

oint-
Bro.
d the
e af-

se or
r the

bol of
great

park,
time,
f our
did to
told
bride-
bride
ed the
nittee
were
made
is no

Bro.
aring
from

Sister
tell.
helped
ment.
IAM.

in our
relig-
t take
ssippi
l them
reso-
fight
y pos-
r does
lution
From
esolu-
f it by

l, wilt
ith the
ll not

great
ancient
rce to
side.
orker,
York
egalize
lligent
salem
d say,
things.
y my-
can?''
be ex-
say so;
use for
s it not

does not excuse the evil; he recognizes it, not only here, but everywhere. To close the eyes tc all the good and open them to all the evil is surely not the Christian way. Christians should search out the good and find it, notwithstanding the evil. It is the spirit of evil that directs pure hearts to see only the mistakes and magnify them, only the sins and dwell upon them. The Christ-spirit grasps the good, and ''thinketh no evil.''

> ''Alas for the rarity of Christian charity
> under the sun!''

Why not treat the great Trans-Mississippi Exposition as it justly deserves—*see and profit by all the good and pass by all the evil?*

Just this word more: It is said by those competent to judge that the Exposition is second to none in quality and only to the World's Fair in size. As President Zollars put, it: ''It is the World's Fair all over again, not so immense, but with some points of improvement.'' The fireworks he regards as the finest he ever saw.

Brethren, the Trans-Mississippi Exposition at night is beautiful as a dream of glory. To view the government display alone is worth the expense of a long journey and one week of time to properly see it.

I believe the Exposition at Omaha the most glorious sight under the sun to-day, and those who miss seeing it will go through life just that much behind the procession.

This much in the name of righteousness and in defense of our city and state.

CHARLES E. TAYLOR.

No. 2312 N. 27th St.

Homes in Arkansas.

Many inquiries are made by persons North, South, East and West concerning homes in Arkansas.

In general terms it may be safely said that the state furnishes extraordinary inducements to homeseekers. . This is true in almost every part of the state. The present paper, however, will be devoted to that part of Scott county brought into notice as the ''Streator Colony,'' and contiguous country.

1. The land is not first-class; that is, it will not produce as much corn per acre as the noted corn belt of Illinois, Iowa, Nebraska or Kansas; will not produce as much wheat as the noted wheat districts, nor as much cotton as the Arkansas and White River bottom lands.

2. Improved lands that are now obtainable at from three to ten dollars per acre, cultivated in corn, will yield as much profit when either sold or fed as an Illinois farm. Twenty-five bushels here will sell for as much as fifty there, and in the judgment of the writer, if discreetly fed, will have a farther advantage. It ought to be principally a stock country.

3. The yield of the staple crops, as nearly as I can ascertain, for the present year, is about as follows: Wheat, eight to fifteen bushels per acre; last year a little better. The crop of corn now in the field, from ten to forty bushels per acre. Oats good. Peas, the great boon to the Southern farmer, grow well. Sorghum, both for syrup and as a forage or hay crop, does well. Some farmers raise the ribon or Southern cane for syrup. All kinds of garden vegetables seem to be in their element. Irish potatoes and sweet potatoes do well, especially the latter.

In the above estimates care has been taken not to overstate anything. Fruits I do not think have been as thoroughly tested as desirable. Peaches thrive, and there is but little doubt that apples will do well on the mountains and ridges, while it is well adapted to grape culture.

4. The immediate section of the country known as the Colony is a succession of ridges and valleys, terminating in the Potean Valley, in which is situated Waldron, the county-seat of Scott county. The valleys are from forty to due west—the main Potean Valley
rection of Waldron, widening out int
ful country. The main roads do
valleys are excellent. The ridges a
at intervals of several miles by cros
thus connecting the neighborhood
communication. The ridges are
steep and rocky, but covered with a
growth of pine and other trees va
lumber.

5. Surroundings. A good roller
and planing mills are in operation
Ridge, and doing a good business.
brought to this mill for many mile
They are increasing their facilities
ing, being at present very much
though running night and day. T
situated on the main road, four or
from the extreme eastern limit of t
ment, about five miles from Waldr
which are to be found excellent farm
the best schoolhouses in the county
at Green Ridge. Several families
correspondence with Bro. Streator.
tled in the valleys east of the mill,
on the uplands; all, as far as I could
well pleased with their investment
are generally members of the
Church, and are enterprising and
people. They are from various st
every point of the compass.

Seldom have I seen more wel
people brought together in a congr
the size of that at Cardiff. They
house of worship, but will build
church at present meets in the
Schoolhouse. Bro. A. R. Wallace
ed to preach for them. They have
means. They came as ''homeseeke
brethren or other good citizens wi
comed among them and by the older
the community.

The writer was much better pleas
country and with the general outlo
expected to be. This will be a
prosperous neighborhood. Brethre
afford to investigate this matter
homes, where they will not be c
church privileges.

6. Brother Streator asked me to
''dark side.'' The only serious draw
of railway transportation. The near
station at present is about twenty-e
Waldron is a good business plac
two miles from the railroad. There
doubt that a road will be built t
county at no distant day.

On the Petit Jean River, twelve
the railroad, is another locality in
lands can be bought very cheap.
land is better than that referred to
it is doubtful whether it is as health

Brother Streator (present addre
Scott county,) can give you more
about the location of lands, price
two hours than you can learn b
around in two weeks. He will sav
than three times what his little
will cost, if you buy.

A suggestion to preachers: A pr
of course, a right with all others
home if he can secure it, but if you
from forty to seventy-five dollars
where you are, don't imagine th
come where land can be bought for
per acre, or government land can
live on your claim and receive the s
You will be disappointed. Three g
ers are already members of the litt
forty-two at Cardiff.

It is my conviction that many ho
sons could improve their situation d
coming here. From $300 to $1,000
one very comfortably.

Homesteads can be taken wher
land can be obtained in small fie
places probably offer as good opp
Scott County, if there were some
them out but, considering church
this at present would be my cho
reader thinks of investigating
write Brother Streator and come o
one on whose judgment you can re
take pleasure in showing you land
homesteads. Come not as North
Southern men, not as Eastern men
men, but as citizens of the kingdo
and of our common country, to mak
your home and help build up the
society.

E. C. E

Missionary.

The General Convention.

The most important and interesting event in the work of the Disciples of Christ that will occur in the near future will be the General Convention, which will meet in Chattanooga in October. Every individual should esteem it a sacred duty either to *go* or to *send*. This is especially true of those who live in the South and the Southwest. We should show our appreciation of the presence of the convention in our midst by attending in large numbers. Every department of the work should be represented. Churches, Sunday-schools, Endeavor Societies and auxiliaries to the C. W. B. M. should send large delegations. Make preparation at once to attend this great assembly of the saints.

"What we would do
We should do when we would,
For this would changeth."

N. M. RAGLAND.

Fayetteville, Ark.

Great events are born of travail of soul. There are indications that there will be both a new Protestantism and a new Declaration of Independence for the new century. Men of earnest minds are feeling after, if haply they may find, a better way. The lifting up of broader horizons means a larger America. The Christian enterprise of which we are exponents is more American in its genesis, development and animus than any other. In this land, so providentially guided, who knoweth whether we have come to the fore for such a time as this? Blessed are the eyes that see what we see in the open doors of opportunity and the new spheres of influence. Let the convention at Chattanooga be a vast host of representative men and women, who will devise and execute liberal things for our God. May it be our supreme ambition to give to the nation a Christianity that will Christianize, and to the world a civilization that will civilize.

H. D. CLARK.

Mt. Sterling, Ky.

$15,000.

The Foreingn Society has recently received $15,000 from one friend on the *Annuity plan*. This is the largest personal offering ever before received. This friend appreciates the importance of the work. The executive committee will now be able to furnish a number of buildings that have been needed on the mission fields for a long time. Homes, chapels, hospitals and school buildings must be furnished if the work is successful.

The Foreign Society has been compelled to pay exorbitant rents for inferior buildings which are not suited to the purposes of its missions. The money received on the *Annuity plan* will be invested in buildings at once, and the amount paid annuitants will be charged to the various missions instead of so much rent. This will insure—

1. A saving to the missions. The rents paid amount to much more than the money at a low rate of interest invested in buildings.
2. Better homes for the missionaries, and better chapels, school buildings, etc.
3. It will insure the people among whom a mission is planted that the work is to be permanent.
4. And at the death of the annuitants the society is free from further financial obligations.

Money is received in amounts of $100 or more, and the annuitant is paid interest semi-annually until death. This plan has the following advantages for the annuitant:

1. There is no care about investing the money.
2. There are no taxes to be paid.
3. There is no interest or rents to be collected.
4. The annuity is certain, and will be paid promptly semi-annually.
5. At death there is no danger of the money being diverted from the purse of the donor.

We have received $38,390 on this plan already. Others are considering it.

F. M. RAINS, Treas.

Cincinnati, O.

The Foreign Field.

INDIA: Dr. C. S. Durand, who spent seven years in India, has informed the society that, owing to the condition of Mrs. Durand's health, he will not be able to return to the field. He wishes to be in nominal connection with the society at least as long as he lives. Dr. Mary McGavran writes that the boys at Demoh are in good health; only five or six a day need any treatment. Mrs. Rosine Miller Crisp takes charge of the work at Mungeli in the absence of Mr. and Mrs. Gordon. Mrs. Crisp is an experienced missionary.

JAPAN: Miss Kate Johnson and Miss Bertha Clawson have recently made a trip into the interior. They found the people eager to listen to the gospel. By all accounts the Japanese are more willing to listen to the truth than they have been for some years. M. B. Madden, speaking of the new home, says: "It is a great blessing. It is not to be estimated in dollars and cents, but in added efficiency, power and influence in the work and better health in both body and mind. One church in Japan has decided to co-operate with our people. The advisory committee did not invite this church, but heartily welcomed it upon learning its desire and purpose." E. S. Stevens writes that he recently visited Innai and held a five days' meeting. He had a good hearing. One man signified that he was ready for baptism. Mr. Stevens adds, "The inquiry after Christianity is now reviving." F. H. Marshall reports that in the last year 125 souls have been added to the kingdom. God has kept the missionaries and native helpers in perfect peace and unity. This is the brightest page in the history of our mission. The future is full of hope. Mrs. Marshall expects to return to Japan in December.

CHINA: James Ware writes that the tutor and confidential adviser of the emperor has been dismissed from office because he sought to discourage the emperor from reading Western books. This man was the second man in the empire in power. His dismissal has caused great excitement throughout the empire and has done more to wake up the officials than the war with Japan. Not only has this man been dismissed, but the emperor has abolished by imperial edict the old and worthless system of examination for office, substituting Western learning for the classical books. Most of the new text-books have been prepared by missionaries. A. F. H. Saw, in his last letter, writes of a visit to Luhoh. The mayor issued a number of proclamations making favorable mention of the mission and calling upon the people to treat the missionaries kindly. Mr. Saw called to see the mayor. He was received very cordially by him. The next day the mayor returned the call. He showed acquaintance with Christian writings and with the geography of the world. This man comes from the most anti-foreign province in the empire.

TURKEY: G. N. Shishmanian and his family have returned to Constantinople. Dr. Kevorkian writes that he is constantly being urged by brethren in different parts of Asia Minor to visit them. When a letter does not bring him they send a man after him. The harvest truly is plenteous; the laborers are few. John Johnson writes of Smyrna that there is a great work to be done, but it is beset with great difficulties. He needs a whole-hearted helper and some machinery. He needs a school and a relief fund. Many of the people are very poor. Their mission and the national churches undertake to support their own poor. Many look to him for help, but his own funds are limited and he is not able to do as much as he would like to do.

Religious World.

ıal convention of the Missouri ıool Union was held at Carthage The attendance was large, the interesting and the report encouraging. Out of twenty-ties seventeen reported good he treasurer's report, however, encouraging, as the offerings re state only amounted to $3,-)ne of the special features ed by the financial committee every county be thoroughly within thirty days for funds. l will be asked to contrbute five ch scholar and 25 cents for each e.state work.

H. Johnson, in an article in the Chicago, almost concludes that ssociations are without an)ject for their existance. After severely, a typical Baptist As-:ogram, Dr. Johnson says:

many of our associations could better at this year's session point a committee from among versatile, active and spiritual hunt for such an object, and year. And if such an object be vriter is willing to prophesy that to do, first and foremost, with k, both evangelical and educa-ıin the local bounds of the as- The presentation of the work ·mprehensive organizations will .d merely incidental, and it will apparent loss, for the associa-ıoroughly tills its own field will st liberal toward work outside. will be held of less importance for future work, and money such work will be wasted in he utterly unimportant matter ls tne bulk of annual "minutes" associations.

---

r damages was begun on August cago, by the Rev. Father Anthony against Archbishop Patrick A. he trouble arose out of the dissat- the Polish congregation of the Church with its financial manage-accounting could be obtained from hop, and the right to have a voice gement of the church finances was e church members. This caused a oney was raised for the building of Cathedral; Father Kozlowski was ıead the seceders. A constitution and adopted for the new church, ved so satisfactory to many other Polish congregations throughout , who had had the same troubles, ıstitution was adopted by a large ıeir churches. The cardinal prin- new church is to retain church is universally the rule in Europe, ls of the church organization and ender it, as has been hitherto the lish congregations in this country, p or Archbishop. The church has ıd wide, and now numbers 120,- The breach betweed the Father and ıop grew constantly greater, and at apparently irreparable. The cul-s reached when Father Kozlowski ıunicated by act of major excom- the gravest and severest known to This is the first time that such a ento has been proclaimed in t has been read in all the pulpits Illinois and elsewhere, and its d effect explained by a priest in e to the congregation. The Arch-s letter has forbidden the faithful intercourse or communication with ıunicated one. Father Kozlowski maintains that this is in derogation of his civil rights, and amounts to a practical boycott, which would in the end make him a social pariah, and hence the suit for damages. Attorney Henry R. Rathbone, who has charge of the case for the plaintiff, was seen at his office, 610 Ashland Block, Chicago, and in answer to an inquiry, stated the nature of the case and said that it would be taken to the court of last resort if necessary, in order that the rights of citizens in such matters might be fully and finally determined. He said he regarded it as an epoch-making case, and one of the most important which had arisen for many years in this or any other country. It involved the rights of the citizen and his civil liberties in their fullest extent and the respective sphere of church and state. Mr. Rathbone is a grandson of the late Judge and United States Senator, Ira Harris, of New York, and came originally from Albany, N. Y., where his people are well known.

PROGRESS OF CHRISTIANITY.

Christianity was born in the midst of Judaism and paganism. It was obliged to obtain its followers from its opponents. It is estimated that its progress was as follows:

End of first century	500,000
End of second century	2,000,000
End of third century	5,000,000
End of fourth century	10,000,000
End of fifth century	15,000,000
End of sixth century	20,000,000
End of seventh century	25,000,000
End of eighth century	30,000,000
End of ninth century	40 000,000
End of tenth century	50,000,000
Ene of eleventh century	70,000.000
End of twelfth century	80,000,000
End of thirteenth century	75,000,000
End of fourteenth century	80,000,000
End of fifteenth century	100,000,000
End of sixteenth century	125,000,000
End of seventeenth century	155,000,000
End of eighteenth century	200,000,000
In year 1877	400,000,000
In year 1880	410,000,000
In year 1890	492,865,000
In year 1894	500,000,000

Dr. Daniel Dorchester says: "The above are probably the most reliable representations of the progress of Christianity, and show its wonderful growth in later years, far exceeding its progress. In 1,500 years it gained 100,000,000; then in 300 years it gained 100,000,000 more; then in 80 years it gained 210,000,000 more. In the last 20 years, 106,000,000. During nearly ten centuries of almost exclusive papal dominion, Christianity gained only about 85,000,000. Since the birth of Protestantism, a period about one-third as long, it has gained nearly five times as much.

"The population of this earth is about 1,500,000,000. Of these about one-third are Christian adherents, and two-thirds are non-Christian. Of the Christians about 170,000,000 are Protestants, about 210,000,000 are Roman Catholics, about 110,000,000 are adherents of the Greek Church; about 10,000,000 belong to the Armenian, Nestorian, and other Eastern churches. Of the non-Christians about 8,000,000 are Jews, 172,000,000 are Mohammedans, about 820,000,000 are pagan and heathen.

"Of the population of the earth, about two-thirds are under the rule of Christian nations. Of the 1,000,000,000 under Christian rule, about 600,000,000 are under Protestants; 250,000,000 are under Roman Catholics; 150,000,000 are under the Greek Church.

"The hopeful element of modern life is the growing influence of Jesus. Not only is the number of those who openly profess allegiance to him growing, but they are increasingly gaining insight into the meaning and spirit of his life and teaching; they are more and more perfectly carrying out his instructions—living his life. The influence of Jesus is also more powerfully felt beyond the ranks of professing Christians than ever before."—*Gospel in all Lands.*

INDIANA BAPTISTS.

The last statistics of the Indiana Baptist churches show that there are 525 churches of this denomination in the state; that in 100 years they have increased to a membership of 54,000, of which 4,000 are colored and have their own churches. These are the missionary Baptists. Their property is valued at present at $1,313,422. Their wealthiest church is at Peru; their largest congregation is that of the First Baptist Church at Indianapolis; their most modern church is at Bluffton. Other churches of the first class in Indiana are at South Bend, Wabash, Fort Wayne, Lafayette, Terre Haute, Muncie, Richmond and Seymour. It will be noticed that churches of the first class are all in Northern Indiana, except two or three. On this church membership of 54,000 falls the annual expense of $135,000 per annum apportioned for Indiana, of which $4,500 is for foreign missions, $4,500 for state missions, $2,500 for home missions, $1,500 for the publication society and $120,000 for all other religious purposes.

There are about 550 pastors in the field and Indiana has five superannuated ministers receiving benefits from the church. Ohio, Indiana, Illinois, Wisconsin and Michigan form one district for the maintenance of superannuated ministers and maintain a home at Trenton, Mich., where twenty-five men are now cared for. In all, there are seventy superannuated preachers in this district.

Aside from the funds enumerated above the Baptists of Indiana maintain their state school—Faanklin College, at Franklin—which has an unvarying attendance of about 250 students a year. It has an endowment of $400,000 placed in good land securities in Johnson and surrounding counties. An additional endowment of $75,000 is now being raised.—*Chicago Record.*

Family Circle.

Peace.

The flowers float their censers on the sated air,
The waters of the fountain foam in wanton wave,
While sunbeams, slowly streaming through the arch of palm,
Shine softly, filtered to a shaded splendor there.
And all is soothed by silence, nought is sounding save
The fountain's flow, which purls a rhythm to the calm.

And I, my soul, would soar in space supernal, still
And sated, in the calm of timeless ecstacy:
No thought, save only dreams of color-glories, blent
With lethal odors thronging. These my bliss fulfill,
While languored harmonies soft whisper peace to me.
So sleep for aye, my soul, and, dreaming, find content.

—*Marvin Dana, in September Pall Mall Magazine.*

Text Stories—XII.

THE COMPANIONSHIP OF BOOKS.

BY ALICE CURTICE MOYER.

* * * * And have no company with him.
* * * * —*2 Thessalonians* 3:14.

"I feel it my duty, sir," said the teacher, "to inform you of the fact that your son has a great liking for bad company. I am doing all in my power to eradicate this preference for evil companions, but it seems firmly rooted, and I think it right that you should know of it."

"You must be greatly mistaken, sir. Tom has very few associates. In fact, he would prefer a book, any time, to a schoolmate. He is a great reader. His evenings are spent in his room, where he reads, often till very late."

"What does he read?" asked the teacher.

"O, I haven't inquired into that. I just know that he is a great reader, and I am very glad that he is. But you see he cannot be in bad company when he is in no company at all."

"There is where you are mistaken," replied the teacher. "I insist that he is continually in company of the very worst sort. In fact, he is so engrossed with his evil companions that he has no time for his studies. I am compelled to watch him continually. Only yesterday I found him in company of the worst type, for instead of preparing himself for his recitation he held in his hand one of those vile books, whose author calls himself a realist; who takes his characters mostly from the slums and lowest walks of life, with all their coarseness of language, manner and words; who portrays human nature in all its lowest, most degraded and sickening forms. Now, if such a book is not vile company, then I do not know what vile company is. And if a boy enjoys such society in books, might there not be danger that he will seek it in its haunts? If you do not know what sort of company your boy's books afford him, it is time you look into the matter, my friend. Good-bye."

The advice of this plain-spoken but sensible teacher may, with profit, be heeded by all parents. Paul, in writing to the Thessalonians, described a certain sort of man and said: "Have no company with him."

It is most important that we consider the character of our associates—of those with whom we "have company"—and choose them as wisely and carefully as it is possible; and such choice ought not to stop with people—neighbors and friends for ourselves, playmates and school friends for our children—for if books have almost if not quite as great an influence upon our lives as we believe they do, it is equally important that we select with care all those with which we "have company." Especially should we see to it that our children, in the formation of whose characters we are so interested, read the right sort of books. The most blighting influence often lies between two book-covers, not alone of the dime novel—whose characters are so unnatural and inapplicable, while most detrimental during the period when they are believed in; soon lose their charm and are regarded with all the ridicule they deserve—but of many books that are approved by scores of readers and received into hundreds of homes which, if not disgustingly realistic are, perhaps, so sensually suggestive with their insinuating word-pictures, that they cannot but have a most undesirable influence upon the impressionable mind of the young. And the hurtfulness of it is that they may not outgrow these books as they do the dime novel. Their subtle influence remains, perhaps, through life, to the great moral and spiritual injury of the one influenced.

There are so many books—the great printing presses of the country turning out more in a day than one person can read in a lifetime, it is said—that it ought to be and is an easy matter to select many, very many, that are helpful and elevating; that feed the heart; that enrich the mind; that come under the head of "good company," and that influence in the right direction all who read them. Considering how short is life, and how precious are even our minutes, certainly we should read the very best.

First of all, we should read the Bible—the king of all books. Between its covers alone there is a library complete. It we should read first; we should read it last; we should read it all the time. Not that we should read nothing else, but that we should read it so often and be so full of it that we will have no desire for books that are bad. Christian Endeavorers pledge themselves to read the Bible every day. Surely, this is an example worthy of imitation. What other book is so simple, so pure, so full of tenderness? It speaks personally to all who will read it. It has a message for every human being who will study its pages—a message that brings such comfort as can nowhere else be found, for through it God speaks to the soul.

"My burden is greater than I can bear!" and he answers through this blessed book:

"As thy days, so shall thy strength be," and the burdened heart is comforted.

"Temptations assail me on every side," cries another. "Temptations so great that I seem powerless under their influence. Lord, help me!" And the answer comes:

"But God is faithful, who will not suffer you to be tempted above that ye are able." And the way of escape is shown the tempted one.

"There are such great enterprises to be carried forward, and such great tasks to be accomplished, and the obstacles in the way seem insurmountable!" sighs the earnest worker in the great cause of Christianity; but as he quotes from Paul:

"I can do all things through Christ which strengtheneth me," he again feels "strong in the Lord and in the power of his might," and goes on to victory.

"Lord, be merciful to me a sinner!" prays one who feels unworthy to even so much as lift his eyes to the throne of grace—who is wandering, sin-clutched, in deepest darkness. And through the gloom there comes to him, as sweetest music, the tender words:

"Though your sins be as scarlet, they shall be as white as snow."

"Lord, I have turned back after having put my hand to the plow! My backsliding reprove me! I am indeed a prodigal, and no more worthy to be called thy child!" cries another in all anguish of spirit. And the story of the prodigal son comes to him with all its comforting assurance of forgiveness, and the "lost is found."

"I have just entered thy service, Lord," prays the newly converted, "and though we know that thy commandments will bring us to thee in safety, yet fain would we have a model by which to fashion our lives." And they find their ideal in him who said:

"For I have given you an example, that ye should do as I have done to you." They come to see that he is the one model by which to mold their lives, looking unto him, the Author and Finisher of their faith.

"Father," whispers the aged one whose life has been spent in the service of his Lord; "Father, I realize that the time is drawing nigh when I must lie down to 'sleep the sleep that knows no waking.' I must leave many of my tasks and plans for thy cause all unfinished. I must relinquish the work I had laid out and entrust it to other hands. I must leave many of my hopes unrealized; and the ideal character, toward which I have ever struggled, I have not attained. But, Father, thou knowest that my motive has been true, and that my desire for Godlikeness has been sincere. And into thy hands, with all my imperfections, I commend my spirit."

And the All-pitying Eye of the Father looks upon his faithful child with infinite love and compassion, and gives his answer through his holy Word:

"Well done, thou good and faithful servant: thou hast been faithful over a few things, I will make thee ruler over many things; enter thou into the joy of thy Lord."

St. Louis, Mo.

The Late-staying Caller.

Friend Staylate makes a call in the evening. Conversation blithe and joyous, and repeated requests for him to remain yet a little while, lead him, not at all unwillingly, to prolong his visit. He looks at his watch with a gasp of genuine dismay, and hurries away slowly at last with profuse apologies for keeping us up until such an unearthly hour. "Oh, indeed, no!" choruses the entire family. "This is early for us! We never think of going to our rooms until later than this." Friend Staylate loiters a moment after he gets outside the gate. Slam goes the door; bang! wang! slam! go the shutters, calling harshly to each other, "Thought that fellow would never go!" Bang! "Why didn't he stay all night!" Slam! And the chain cries, "Gone at last!" The darkness of the dungeon settles down on the house; the fanily has gone to bed, having relieved its mind by doors and shutters that are ready to tell the truth any time they are given a chance.—*Robert J. Burdette.*

Speak Gently!

Speak gently; it is better far
To rule by love than fear;
Speak gently; let no harsh words mar
The good we might do here.

Speak gently to *the young*, for they
Will have enough to bear;
Pass through this life as best they may,
'Tis full of anxious care.

Speak gently to *the aged one;*
Grieve not the care-worn heart;
The sands of life are nearly run;
Let such in peace depart.

Speak gently, kindly, to *the poor;*
Let no harsh tones be heard;
They have enough they must endure,
Without an unkind word.

Speak gently to the erring; know
That thou thyself art man;
Perchance unkindness made them so;
Oh, win them back again!

—*Exchange.*

A Salt Lake Sunset.

W. H. BAGBY.

It was a gala day at Salt Air Beach, the beautiful breathing and bathing-place of the Emerald City of the intermountain plains, and the unique spot at which meet all the charms of mountain, plain and sea. The famous Tabernacle choir was out for a holiday, and the announcement that they would sing at intervals during the afternoon and evening had served to attract a great multitude to the charming resort; so that when our party arrived in the late afternoon, the great pavilion presented a scene of the utmost animation. About the tables in the spacious banqueting hall were gathered thousands of happy people, laughing and chatting over tempting lunches while inhaling the cool, sweet breath of the distant, snow-capped mountains, wafted to them on the wings of the wind from across the waters of the wonderful sea. To the music of laughter and lapping waves, hundreds of merry bathers were floating in the briny, buoyant waters below, while above, in the largest dancing pavilion in the world, to the sweet strains of a well-trained orchestra, multitudes of maidenly forms, clasped in the arms of manly strength, were gracefully floating through the figures of the mazy waltz, enjoying the sweet exhilaration found by happy, healthy youth in setting to music the poetry of motion. Just over the peaks of the low-lying mountains, far on the western shore of the great salt sea, clothed in splendor and clearly outlined against the edge of the azure sky, hung the great, round disc of the King of Day. Picking his way among the banks and bands of leaden clouds that hung in the western sky, he slowly and majestically descended till his nether rim touched the summit of a somber peak where he paused and laid in good-night embrace, from shore to shore across the bosom of the peaceful sea, an arm of burnished gold. Sinking slowly behind the mountains upon the lips of each tired little wave, restlessly falling asleep on the bosom of the limpid mother lake, he imprinted a good-night kiss. Climbing up the piles upon which the splendid pavilion rests and seeking a retired nook, he laid his hands of light in gentle benediction upon a head of brown and one of gold bending low over a band of gold that held a dimple finger and a dazzling gem. Stealing across the pavilion he imprinted a loving kiss on the ruby lips of a sleeping babe and touched with glory its soft, golden curls. With his last horizontal ray softened and subdued, he transfigured the two old, grey heads that bent in loving watchfulness above the beautiful child. Hastening along the city that spans the stretch of water between the pavilion and the shore, rippling across the plains to the city nestling at the feet of the mountains, he touched with golden light the pinnacles of the temple, and leaping from the flaring end of the golden trumpet of mythical Moroni, climbed up the rugged sides of the mountains that lift their heads high into the upper deep. Upon their grey heads, covered with years and crowned with the spotless snows of countless winters, he bestowed a last, lingering, benedictive kiss, and leaped to the vaulted sky. Sweeping from east to west athwart the blue dome of the heavens with his burning kisses of good-night and blessing, he set on fire every floating cloud, and they became a fleet in flames afloat on a boundless sea. Gradually the ships burn down to the water's edge and took on the red glow of flameless fire. Finally the fire died out entire y and they became floating masses of dull-gray ashes-wrecks of the upper deep.

The climax was a transformation scene. The sea below was a reproduction of the sea above. Looking toward the western horizon, we were looking between the leaves of a partially opened book, the opposite pages of which held the same surpassingly beautiful picture. Every tint of the sky was visible in the sea. The wonderful works that were done in the heavens by the sun that had set were reproduced on earth. (So should the Sun of Righteousness be reproduced on earth, for he prayed, "Thy will be done on earth as it is done in heaven.") As we stood looking, we beheld two seas. The one that spread out at our feet was shrouded in semi-darkness and the rising wind had made it rough. The islands that dotted it were rugged, steep and grim. In striking contrast with this was the beautiful scene painted on the western sky by the setting sun, in which the pale-blue sky was the sea and the clouds were the islands. This sea was rough, that was perfectly placid; this was shrouded in gloom, that was bathed in mellow light; these islands were dark and desolate, those were clothed in the glory of heaven; these waters were dark and gave back no answering outline, those were mirror-like and gave a perfect reflection of the islands and shores. Night, who had started with her sable curtain from the foot of the mountain simultaneously with the disappearance of the sun behind its peak, and had drawn it gently but surely over the sea, the islands, the golden and the gray heads, the plains, the pinnacles and the snowy peaks, then dropped it down over the western horizon and pinning it with a star shut out from vision the scene of surpassing beauty and glory. But until the curtain of a dawnless night shall be drawn over the plains and peaks of memory's realm, that beautiful scene will remain in the field of its vision, telling of a sea where storms never come and where peace, blessed peace, ever reigneth; where the islands are bathed in the light of his glory, and night never comes with its gloom.

"Where the rich, golden fruit
Is in bright clusters pending,
And the deep-laden boughs
Of life's fair tree are bending,
And where life's crystal stream
Is unceasingly flowing,
And the verdure is green
And eternally growing.
Where no sin nor dismay
Neither trouble nor sorrow
Will be felt for a day
Nor be feared for the morrow!"

Licensing an Evil.

Many Protestants denounce the Roman Catholic Church of the sixteenth century for sending John Tetzell out to sell indulgences to people to commit sin, but are we not doing the same thing in a more enlightened age, when we vote for men and parties who sell the privilege or license to erect murder mills or drunkard factories? Raising the amount of the license does not reduce the sin. If Judas Iscariot had received 300 pieces of silver instead of 30, his crime would have been none the less. Dr. Sutherland, of Canada, illustrates this folly with a fable. He pictures a donkey in a large green meadow, with beautiful lakes of water; but every time the donkey goes to one of these lakes for a drink of water he is covered with leeches, which rob him of much of his blood. In order to reduce his torture and to regulate these leeches, he levied a tax or issued a license to them, requiring each one to pay back a part of the blood which they sucked from his veins. An observing horse and ox across the meadow fence, watching the proceeding with much interest, both remarked with much emphasis, "Well, that is certainly a brilliant idea, and eminently worthy of the genius of an ass!!"—*St. Louis Christian Advocate.*

Vibratory Power.

All structures, large or small, simple or complex, have a definite rate of vibration, depending on their material, size and shape, as fixed as the fundamental note of a musical chord. When the bridge at Colebrooke Dale (the first iron bridge in the world) was building, a fiddler came along and said he could fiddle it down. The workmen laughed in scorn, and told him to fiddle away to his heart's content. He played until he struck the keynote of the bridge, and it swayed so violently that the astonished workman commanded him to stop. At one time considerable annoyance was experienced in one of the mills in Lowell. Some days the building was so shaken that a pail of water would be nearly emptied, while on other days all was quiet. Experiment proved it was only when the machinery was running at a certain rate that the building was disturbed. The simple remedy was in running it slower or faster, so as to put it out of time with the building. We have here the reason of the rule observed by marching armies when they cross a bridge, viz., stop the music, break step and open column, lest the measured cadence of a condensed mass of men should urge the bridge to vibrate beyond its sphere of cohesion. Neglect of this has led to fearful accidents. The celebrated engineer, Stephenson, has said there is not so much danger to a bridge when crowded with men and cattle as when men go in marching order. The Broughton Bridge, near Manchester, gave way beneath the measured tread of only sixty men. A terrible disaster befell a battalion of French infantry while crossing the suspension bridge at Angiers, in France. Repeated orders were given the troops to break into sections, but in the hurry of the moment and in the rain they disregarded the order, and the bridge fell.—*Professor Lovering.*

The Sanitary Alphabet.

A s soon as you're up shake blankets and sheet;
B etter be without shoes than sit with wet feet;
C hildren, if healthy, are active, not still;
D amp beds and damp clothes will both make you ill.
E at slowly, and always chew your food well;
F reshen the air in the house where you dwell;
G arments must never be made to be tight;
H omes will be healthy if airy and light.
I f you wish to be well, as you do, I've no doubt,
J ust open the windows before you go out;
K eep your rooms always tidy and clean,
L et dust on the furniture never be seen.
M uch illness is caused by the want of pure air,
N ow to open your windows be ever your care;
O ld rags and rubbish should never be kept,
P eople should see that their floors are well swept.
Q uick movements in children are healthy and right,
R emember the young cannot thrive without light.
S oap and rough towels are good for the skin;
T emperance suits the body within.
U se your nose to find out if there be a bad drain,
V ery sad are the fevers that come in its train.
W alk as much as you can without feeling fatigue.
X erxes could walk full many a league.
Y our health is your wealth, which your wisdom must keep;
Z eal will help a good cause, and the good you will reap.

—*Union Signal, June 28, 1898.*

Flowers on the Coffin-lid.

ANNA D. BRADLEY.

"Yes, he had many fine traits. I never liked him while he lived, but I always speak well of the dead."

I listened, but the words aroused a sad, hungry cry of pain in my heart, which I tried in vain to hush. We stab with cruel words or freeze with cold neglect the living, but kindle fires of gentle memory upon the silent grave, and "always speak well of the dead."

I find no fault with this. Cold and insensate, indeed, must be the one that can stand beside the coffin-bed and drag to light the one-time faults of the helpless sleeper. Over the unlovely past even the most unfriendly hand will gently draw the veil and whisper softly—"*Requiescat in pace.*"

This is as it should be. Yet sadley I ask my soul, why need we wait until the heart has ceased to throb with joy or woe before we learn to be generous? Why not now whisper words of approval? Why not today drop into the path some of the seeds of tenderness which we are reserving to piously plant above their graves?

If, as some think, the spirit of the dead still hovers about its earthly home, I can fancy it whispering sadly to its flower-strewn clay, "The gentle words, they speak tonight have lost their power to cheer. While I was with you I was often hungry for a love I did not receive; thirsty for words of approval or sympathy which I did not hear; sick and in prison of spiritual loneliness; but the hand that could so easily have removed my prison-bars forgot and let me alone. And now, oh worn out body, you are dead. You have no need for costly flowers piled high above your pulseless breast. Their fragrance and rich beauty are all unfelt by you, unneeded now by me. But oh, if on each day of our own weary journey only one simple flower had been given by them to us! The ear in which they pour their kindly words is dead; but oh, how eagerly we listened once for words which never came till now! I hear them fondly telling of kindly errands upon which our willing feet have sped; of gentle deeds our willing hands have wrought; of tender words of hope and cheer we tried to speak to other hearts discouraged. I hear them whispering of how they prized all this. Oh dear, dead clay, how priceless would have been this knowledge once! It would have made our way so much smoother; our burdens so much lighter; our words so much easier to speak. But it comes too late to-night to do us any good; for you, poor clay, lie dead, and I am now beyond all need of help!"

Oh friends, let us not wait until dea has had pity and brought rest and peace the tired heart ere we remember how faithful it is!

In every home there is always one wl bears the heaviest burdens; whose need f rest and recreation is too often overlooke It may be a father or mother; it may l only a servant. But one there is benea whose weary frame there throbs a hung heart. A tithe of the love we lavish the dead would gild with glory their dar ened life to-day. Don't wait!

A teacher in a large school recently di from mental and physical exhaustion.

Over her flower-hid coffin, how touchir were the encomiums lavished upon he Not one of all the teachers had been faithful and so true. Her beautiful lif fragrant with the incense of self-sacrific had been a stimulant to all. The impul she had given to nobler thought and pur living would never die, but grow mighti all the while, and the world would alwa be richer for this one matchless life.

I chanced to know something of the li so eulogized. Poor, worked-to-deat woman, she never once dreamed there we such stimulant to others in her life. Sh did not even know that she was genuinel liked. Many of the teachers—to who she had ever been such high inspiration, she had thought disliked her. She neve dreamed that the great school needed her she thought—poor thing!—she was barel holding her place.

How
d her
then,
) have
arnest
e she

de.d!
sick-

riking
ır war
of the
d, but

Sigs-

ready,
Ianila.
ils are
ıs.
milton
ıother.
tenant
f Cer-

ting."
Rough

ıh 'em
aodore

ıd the
Prince

:; iron
ıson to

rt lan-
Evans,

w star
of the

never
guard

; but I
ley, of

rt that
sink-
of the

Colonel

gment
ghty."

ng."—
retary
s from

long
Wain-
ıt with

ions; I
h fleet
of the

ıte.

feeds
It is a
ge.

Cross-Examine That Worry.

Are you a worry about something I can't help? If you are, what is the use of you, eh?

Are you a worry about something I *can* help! Well, then, are you going to help me straighten things out, you worry, or hinder me?

How did you come here, anyhow? Did you get in through the door of indigestion? Did that traitor, Unfaith, let you in? Was it my meddling busybody of a servant, Overwork?

How old are you? Haven't you been in court before? Haven't you been convicted of perjury about fifty times already? And you dare to come here again!

What is your name? Ernest Foresight? I know better. That's an *alias*. Your real name, you worry, is Lacktrust.

And your father? Wisdom? That's a falsehood; you are one of Beelzebub's brats.

What have you to say for yourself? That you have reason and justice on your side? I see that they *are* there, but standing over with swords to condemn you!

That all the world is dark and gloomy? Take off those blue glasses!

That you can't help feeling and acting as you do? That you were made that way? Then you made yourself that way, for to charge God with making such a thing as you would be blasphemy; and the sooner your "maker" makes you over, the better for you and all the rest of us.

Mitigating circumstances? You are not feeling well? You have taken the quickest way to feel worse. People don't understand you, don't sympathize with you? They understand you very well; that's why they don't sympathize with you.

Prisoner at the bar, you are guilty. Your sentence is severe—for you—but salutary. One month in Sunshine Parlor, and to be fed on Bible rations.—*Christian Endeavor World.*

Never Heard a Prayer at Home.

I shall never forget the impression made upon me during the first year of my ministry, by a mechanic whom I had visited, and on whom I urged the paramount duty of family prayer. One day he entered my study, bursting into tears as he said: "You remember that girl, sir? She was my only child. She died suddenly this morning. She has gone, I hope, to God; but if so, she can tell him what now breaks my heart, that she never heard a prayer in her father's house, or from her father's lips! Oh, that she were with me but for one day again!"—*Norman McLeod.*

Sunday School.

ISRAEL'S TRAGEDY.*

HERBERT L. WILLETT.

The cause of Israel's downfall as a nation may be discovered already latent in the division of the kingdom. It was practically impossible that two nations as small as Israel and Judah should survive the sundering of their unity for many generations. The neighboring people were too strong and the lack of unity within gave added cause for apprehension regarding the perpetuity of either kingdom. Especially was this true of Israel, where the rapid change of dynasties and the lack of a central and uniform worship made the danger greater. Some of the kings were strong men; but there was no continuity of power, and in the hands of the weak and nerveless monarchs, the strength was sapped from the nation's life.

But a worse disaster than any of these elements was the idolatrous worship which came in large measure with each succeeding reign and which even the earnest efforts of great prophets like Elijah had never availed to overthrow.

The early and simple worship of Jehovah, as it had been conducted by Samuel at various sanctuaries throughout the kingdon, had met every requirement of the people's higher nature; but Jeroboam changed the simple imageless worship of God into a common form of heathenism. With such a start toward idolatry the worship of Israel rapidly degenerated in the reign of Ahab through the active introduction of Baal worship at the hands of Jezebel. All the lower elements of the Semitic nature-worship came in with this foreign cult. Baal was the god of fire, and his worship was celebrated with the cruel practice of child-sacrifice. Closely related to this was the worship of Ashera, or Astarte, the female companion of Baal, which emphasized the sensuous elements of the nature cult, so seductive to people like the Israelites.

These practices of cruelty and lust, sanctioned by the name of religion, had spread throughout the kingdom. Everywhere from the loneliest outpost or watchtower to the most populous city, the symbols of Baal and Ashera were seen in the form of obelisks or stone pillars for the one, and trees or even a stake for the other. And worst of all, these symbols and their debasing ideas were associated with the worship of Jehovah in the people's mind. Under such a reigme idols multiplied. Children were sacrificed to appease the deity by being slain and burned. Still other pernicious practices relating to religion were introduced, such as the worship of the heavenly bodies and divination or Spiritism—the attempt at consultation with the dead.

But had there been no effort to check such a down-grade tendency as this? One cannot read the books of Kings without seeing that prophet after prophet had arisen to speak against such debasing tendencies. Amos and Hosea had borne witness to the truth. They had emphasized the teachings of the early prophets and lawgivers from Moses down; but the tendency to imitate other nations was too strong to be overcome. The avenues of trade were the open way for the introduction of foreign ideas of morality and religion. There was only one end to such a course of degeneracy. Nation after nation has told the same story. It seems sometimes as though in modern times nations were simply trying the old experiments over, either hoping that the laws of righteousness have changed, or utterly defying them.

The strong reign of Jereboam II. was followed in rapid succession by those of Zechriah, his son, who reigned six months; Shallum, his murderer, who reigned for a month and Menahen, who in turn conspired against him and reigned for ten years. Pekahiah, his son, reigned for two years, and Pekah, his captain, in turn rose against him and reigned for twenty years; and last of all, Hoshea slew his master and closed the list with a reign of nine years.

During all this period the kingdom of Assyria had been pressing ever more closely upon the eastern frontier of the kingdom. Its western campaigns had begun in 740 B. C., and in 732 Damascus fell under the assault of Tiglath Pilesar. Shortly afterwards the same conqueror devastated all the northern territories of Israel, and finally, in 722 B. C., after a siege of three years by Shalmaneser, his successor, Samaria fell into the hands of Sargon, the next of the kings of Assyria. The city was dismantled and the best of its people, including the king, princes and priests, were carried away into the East, leaving only the common people, without sense of unity or nationality to bind them to the land, whose character was changed by the importation of colonists from other devastated provinces. Thus the ten tribes disappeared from history. Very few of their people were ever moved from Palestine, but they were merged into another stock by reason of the importation of foreign elements, and thus lost entirely the name and character they had formerly possessed.

SUGGESTIONS FOR TEACHING.

Secret sins soon lead to open sins. The anger of God is man's way of expressing God's hatred of sin; which, however, is never separated from his love for the sinner. Whatever separates a soul from God is idolatry, whether it is the worship of golden images or of golden coins, or any other object of affection. Those who have received most instruction are most responsible, and bear the heaviest burdens of obligation. It is the most dangerous of all infidelity to doubt that the consequences of sin will be experienced by the sinner. Man is bound to worship something, and if he does no worship God he will make for himself some other object of worship. The desire to be like others, to conform to the ways of those around us by a slavish imitation, is often the cause of serious moral disaster. Cruelty and lust were the ordinary accompaniments of the worship of false gods in the olden times; with all the refinements of later times these are still the great dangers to moral life; cruelty in evil temper and the exhibition of anger and malicious speech, and lust expressed in unclean thoughts and unchaste language. Superstition always flourishes where God is forgotten; Spiritu and every other fad find fertile soil in the of those who are not true seekers after A nation or an individual that becomes u for divine purposes can only suffer rejecti

*Sunday-school Lesson for Sept. 18, 1898—The Captivity of the Ten Tribes (2 Kings 17-18). Golden Text—If thou seek him he will be found of the; but if thou forsake him, he will cast thee off forever (1 Chron. 28:9) Lesson Outline—1. Acts of Idolatry (9-12); 2. Protest against Idolatry (13-15); 3. Result of Idolatry (16-18).

ır.

NITY.

anced so
eaceful a
ohs have
lood was
pped the
orld-em-
ıbling in
ıs, as he
the air,
ıst con-
from the
Chris-
ɔy itself,
mpire of
the man-
ırned the
nd opin-
hat, too,
ns.
ɔoor—the
poor in
s in any-
he sound
tidings.
what joy
preached
s, too, is
r it is a
and cus-
dings for
d tidings
favored.
its chief
and wise
offer the
uld enter
ies. But
nes ring-
rayfaring
andoned,
n before!
s—liberty
y stripes.
las, that
of liberty
o often it
ion; too
nent has
too often
s of wor-
ne perse-
ıvariably
home in
and prej-
eathe and
the cor-
ne spirit.
of Chris-
om when,
ch, every
spiritual
God.
brought
elve went
with the
of "the
ank God,
thirsting
n sight of
in Jesus
truggling
in vain in
ght of the
ontent to
doeth all
ms which
les have
ut at all
sufficient

Once again, the triumph of Christianity it is to show that now is the acceptable year of the Lord, that if ever there is to be a kingdom of God it must begin now, that if ever there is to be a heaven it must at least open its gate and we must enter here and now, that if ever man is to be blessed he must begin to be blessed to-day—for now is the accepted time. "Man never is, but always to be blessed," has found its negative in the beatitudes, in which the present tense reigns supreme. If Christianity does nothing more for us than to turn our eyes away from the future and centre them on the life that now is, on the day and act that confronts us, it has done a great deal. Sometimes, to be sure, the church has sought to lift us unduly and prematurely out of this life into another; but this, too, is a perversion of Christianity. The real gospel proclaims the acceptable year of the Lord.

Literature.

EVERY-DAY LIFE IN KOREA. By Rev. Daniel L. Gifford. Fleming H. Revell Co., publishers. Price, $1.25.

Rev. Daniel L. Gifford was eight years a missionary in this strange Eastland, and in this book of 230 pages he has given the world an interesting collection of studies and stories about this strange people. This book is not only an interesting companion for the home circle, but is of special value as a missionary study. In this book the reader will not only see the strange customs of this strange people and the power of their native habits and religion, but also the patience and success of a faithful missionary. There is power in the gospel of Christ to remove mountains of difficulty in these non-Christian lands. The reader of this book will also find himself in possession of much history about Korea and its people that will be of value as well as present interest to him.

FELLOW-TRAVELERS. By Rev. Francis E. Clark. Fleming H. Revell, publishers. Price, $1.25.

Dr. Clark's ability as a writer is so well known in the two hemispheres that the mere mention of a book from his hand is a guarantee to the lover of good books that another interesting volume has been given to the world, and is, therefore, strongly educational in its character. Many strange facts are stated, and animating and exciting experiences related, with impressive vividness. Dr. Clark does not lose sight of the Endeavor Society and Endeavor interests at any time or place, and has a happy faculty of keeping that theme before his readers without the feeling of monotony. This book will be a valuable contribution to the Endeavor Society and literature.

W. E. GLADSTONE. By William Jerrold. Fleming H. Revell Co., publishers. Price, 75 cents.

For a convenient handbook on the life of England's great Commoner the above book is sufficiently ample for all ordinary, purposes. The development of character power and influence in the life of this great statesman are clearly shown in the orderly events selected from his life for this purpose. The book is in good style and moves along smoothly, yet with increasing interest to the end, leaving the reader in possession of the great factors of his life and new impulses to energize his own life.

THE TWO COVENANTS AND THE SABBATH. By L. W. Spayd, Owosso, Mich.

This little paper-back volume of 224 pages contains an exposition of the two Bible testaments, and is a review of a work entitled, "Two Covenants," by Elder Uriah Smith, of the Seventh-Day Adventists, and deals with the Seventh-Day Adventists' teachings in general. It is a thoroughly scriptural exposition of the Bible doctrine of the Covenants, and an able refutation of the Seventh-Day Advent teaching. In many parts of the country, and particularly in Michigan, the Adventists are exceedingly active in propagating their peculiar views, and their method of treating the Scriptures is such as to confuse the minds of many honest inquirers after the truth. The author of this little volume, living in the midst of this kind of teaching and being familiar with it, has dealt it a blow which cannot fail to be convincing to those whose minds are open to the truth. Those of our readers who live in communities where Seventh-Day Adventists are propagating their Sabbatarian views would do well to procure some copies of this little book, from the author, and put them in circulation. The work is marred by imperfect proof-reading, but the sense is always obvious. There is an index at the close giving the contents of the twenty chapters into which the book is divided.

CLERICAL TYPES. By Rev. Hames Mann. Funk & Wagnalls Co., New York and London, 1897.

The author of this remarkable series of sketches, whose real name is concealed, has given us some graphic pictures which, if not drawn from life, are so true to life as to suggest to the reader persons which have come under his own observation. The types of preachers sketched are, "A Successful Preacher;" "A Popular Preacher;" "A Transcendental Preacher;" "A Plodding Parson;" "A Spiritual Preacher;" "A Regular Hustler;" "A Modern Prophet;" "A Revivalist Preacher;" "A Liberal Preacher;" "A Doctrinal Preacher;" "A Book-Worm;" "A Fighting Parson;" "A Faith Healer;" "An Institutional Preacher;" "A ministerial Greatheart;" "A Ministerial Decorator;" "A Thorough-Paced Ritualist;" "A Priestly Priest;" "A Ministerial Wreck;" "A Ministerial Mystery."

Here are twenty types of preachers, whose portraits are drawn by the hand of a master. One recognizes familiar features in every one of them. Their faults and follies, their virtues and graces, are all set down without malice, on the one hand, or favoritism on the other. We have not read a more readable book in a long time. Each sketch seems to whet one's appetite for the next. We are not surprised to learn that the book is having a large sale, for it is just such a book as every preacher especially would like to have in his library to whet up his intellectual appetite, enliven his fancy and correct any of the clerical faults that may attach to himself. Some of the chapters excite almost a tragic interest. This is especially true of "A Ministerial Wreck," and "A Ministerial Mystery." The book constitutes a very good ministerial mirror, in which preachers may be helped to see themselves as others see them. He will be a dull learner who does not find in the work wise suggestions on many phases of church life, and ministerial conduct and character. The influence of the book cannot but be healthy, and not the less so because it is entertaining.

A story that even those who are close pressed by the duties of a very busy and practical age may pause to read with intense interest is contained in the book King Saul, just fresh from the press. It is a vivid recital of the history of the old ancient King of Israel, so told that the ages gone become reinvested with interest, and the characters appear as great in the world's history as they do in divine chronology.

King Saul is told in an up-to-date; matter-of-fact manner, with faithfulness to historical accuracy and plenty of snap, vigor and romantic details. It deserves be read as well as the histories of oth famous men who have played a part shaping the destinies of the world. As portrayal of human passions it is a maste piece.

In his preface the author, J. Brecker ridge Ellis, tells why he chose an ancie theme for his story, adding among oth things:

"A new novel has this advantage over a old history—the reader does not know ho it will turn out. But this advantage is lo after the first reading. For in taking it u again it is too often found that every in cident depends for its interest on th 'suspense' which the reader no long feels. But the calmer stream of histor not pent up in the narrow channel of single interest, ever discovers upon it way new beauties, new aspirations, ne morals, new fields of life; varying phase of love and hate which have found shelte in human beasts. Here are no dreams un dreamed."

The author begins his story with th marvelous manner in which Saul becam ruler of Israel and the transition from government by judges to that of kings.

"The people heard for the first time, says the author, "that cry which was t ring in their history for centuries to come 'God save the king!' Perhaps it woul have been better for them if they had oc cassionally varied this prayer with 'Go save the people!"

The wars, the appearance of David o the scene, the danger to the kingdom, th warnings of Samuel, Saul's double debt fo his life to David, who he tries to destroy the meeting with the witch of Endor an the passing of the crown are unfolded lik a drama. The old story is told in a magica way that brings back life to objects almos forgotten by a busy world and almost con sidered mythical by many through neglec if not actual cynicism and abuse.

The scenes in the cavern of the witch an on the battlefield of Gilboa are particular ly strong. The version of the former i extremely interesting from a spiritualisti standpoint, but is told without an argu ment.

The night scene on the battlefield of Gilboa is thus described:

" * * * And there lay the discarde bow of Jonathan as he had broken it in

stand for his life. From among ıy trees shone bright spots upon rocks—the stains of blood. And shadows white faces caught the oonbeams, and when the breeze e leaves the shadows flitted to and the gastly features as if they were : in a horrible laughter. * * * ıe dead lay the forms of the three ıd not far away another, with its ɛə market by a gleam of wealth It was the dead face of Saul, y the crown that still rested upon "

ok consists of 281 pages and is a ın to "In the Days of Jehu," which ıtly published, and has met with ɔess that the author is preparing a such works. (Christian Publish- pany, St. Louis, Mo.)—*St. Louis*

MAGAZINES.

ɔlical World for August has an ex- ticle on Damascus, by E. W. G. n, M. D. The lucid style of the nd his excellent perceptive and e faculties make this an article of interest to the Bible student. It is a rderly storehouse of historic interest h.

nposium on "The Problem of the ɜs," in the opening pages of the nerican Review for September is ıy and important as well as timely. ions exrressed are those of the Rt. Charles W. Dilke, Bart., M. P.; the n Barrett, late United States Minister and Hugh H. Lusk, and are worthy ration in any attempt to formulate a ıion on that problem.

r's for September is one of the most magazines of the year. The two ı the fight at Guasmas and Sibony, by sses, are especially interesting. The rature of this number is timely and g. There is nothing dry about it.

e story of those 278 days of suffering ıy's heroic little band of explorers in .c region has been told by General ıimself, for the first time, for the Ladies' Home Journal. For years Greeley has kept an unbroken silence fearful experience and that of his ns, as they dropped dead one by one ɘ, and it was only after the greatest n that the famous explorer was in- write the story.

non with other leading magazines for r, Frank Leslie's popular monthly considerable space to war articles. ng article, "A Warship's Battery," Harrison Lewis, tells how the great placed and worked, and is illustrated e splendid pictures of our victorious ıction at Manila and Santiago. The ɔle of contents is attractive.

.nteresting articles in the Century for ır, one is devoted to "Life and So- Old Cuba," and one to "Malay f the Philippines," the latter by Prof. Worcester, of the University of ; the former article is made up of ex- m the journal of Jonathan S. Jenkins, can painter of miniatures, written in ıth are interesting articles. Some of s in this number of the Century, bear- ɔur new territory, are especially strong ts.

nday-school Times promises its read- ɔcription of the coronation and later services of the young Queen Wil- to be crowned Queen of Holland, at ım, Sept. 7th, written by the Baro-ness of Arnheim. The article is to appear in an early issue.

In the September Review of Reviews the editor takes a strong American position in discussing the important international questions regarding Cuba and the Philippines, which must be settled by the peace commission at Paris. Plain words are also used in regard to the deplorable sanitary conditions that the American troops have suffered.

The Religious Review of Reviews for September is forging to the front of religious publications. The September number contains much valuable information for ministers and religious workers, as the list of able contributors show. A glance at the following department headings will indicate the practical character of this journal, published monthly at New York; special rates to ministers: Current Articles of Importance, Periodicals Reviewed, Notes from Recent Editorials, The Religious World, Sermonic Review Section, Editorial Notes, Review of Recent Publications, In a Lighter Vein and Contents of Reviews and Magazines.

Obituaries.

[One hundred words will be inserted free. Above one hundred words, one cent a word. Please send amount with each notice.]

BATES.

Charles M. Bates, son of Eld. W. E. Bates and M. J. Bates, was born in Council Grove, Morris county, Kan., Feb. 27, 1878. Departed this life in camp at Fernendina, Fla., of typhoid fever, on the morning of August 12, 1898, about 8 o'clock. Charlie enlisted with the Third Missouri Cavalry when the call was made for soldiers for the Cuban War. His father has for years been one of our faithful ministers of the gospel and has had the pleasure of receiving each of his children into the fold of Christ. Charlie, who was a member of the church at Trenton, became a Christian when about 12 years old. His death was peaceful and without a struggle. He was hopeful of recovery to the very last. Services were held in his memory at the Christian church in Trenton Aug. 22, Sunday morning Charlie was a promising young man, just 20 years, five months and 15 days old. His powers were rapidly developing and would have doubtless become useful in the church and society had he been permitted to live. For such trials as these the gospel of the Lord Jesus Christ becomes very precious. It is certainly true of the members of the family that they sorrow not as those who have no hope.

GRANVILLE SNELL.

BAYLIS.

John Edgar Baylis was born near Maysville, Kentucky, on the 24th of April, 1824, and departed this life at his home near Concord, Ill., on the 11th of August, 1898. He was one of five brothers and the last to pass to his reward. He came to the state of Illinois in 1850, and on March 10th, 1853, he was united in marriage to Melissa J. Green. Six children were born to this union, two of whom preceded him to the better land. About the year 1870, under the preaching of Bro. D. R. Lucas, Bro. Baylis obeyed the gospel and ever remained a faithful soldier of the cross. The funeral services were held on Aug. 15, and were conducted by the writer. May the good Father comfort the sorrowing hearts.

IVAN W. AGEE.

GLIDDEN.

Sarah, wife of T. C. Glidden, was born in Wayne county, Ind., Feb. 5th, 1836, and died of cancer of the liver August 1st, 1898, aged 62 years, five months and 26 days. Was married April 8th, 1857, in Marshall county, Ill. Went to Douglas county, Kan., in 1857, thence to Colorado Springs, Col., in 1888. She obeyed the gospel of Christ at Prairie City, Kansas, in 1882, under the ministry of Elder Gantz, and was ever afterward loyal and true to its teachings in all the relations of wife, mother and friend. She leaves an aged companion and six children, and a host of friends to mourn her departure, but they sorrow not as those without hope. The funeral services took place from the residence in Colorado Springs, August 2nd, and were conducted by the writer, assisted by Bro. B. B. Tyler.

J. P. LUCAS.

Colorado City, Col.

HOWELL.

Mrs. Miranda McGee Howell was born twenty-three and one-half years ago, and passed from her home on earth to her home in heaven, Tuesday, August 16, 1898. Her merits as a child, a young lady, a friend, a sister and a wife entitle her to more than a passing notice. In all these relations she was a pattern of fidelity. She united with the Church of Christ six years ago, and remained faithful to her Savior until death. She was married to the young and now heartbroken husband who survives her, October 19, 1897. She also leaves several brothers and sisters and her aged mother to mourn their loss in her departure; and a babe to be reared without an own mother's care and love. Her funeral, conducted by Eld. C. H. Strawn in Holliday, Mo., was attended by a large concourse of friends and relatives.

C. H. STRAWN.

MURPHY.

Mrs. Mary H. Murphy, another of the old residents of Arrow Rock, Mo., was gathered to her fathers on August 17, 1898, passing away in great peace and the full assurance of Christian faith, at the residence of her daughter, Mrs. Frank Spence. She was born in New Castle, Henry county, Ky., Jan. 11, 1813, and had, therefore, attained the age of eighty-five years, lacking from August to January. She moved with her husband, Mr. M. Murphy, to Arrow Rock in 1867, where they both spent the remainder of their lives, her husband departing this life some twelve or more years previous to her death. Of the date of the beginning of her Christian life we cannot speak positively, but she had joined the Church of Christ in Kentucky before her removal to this state in 1867. On the first organization of the Christian Church in Arrow Rock she became a charter member, and was ever an active, constant and devoted adherent, taking full part in all the work of the church until incapacitated by the infirmities of old age. Sister Murphy was one against whose pure moral character not even the vilest ever spoke disparagingly. A faithful wife, kind mother, charitable neighbor and noble Christian has been taken by the All-Father to a better world. Peace to her ashes and tears for her beloved memory. The bereaved daughter and family have the heart-sympathy of all the community. She was laid to rest in the Arrow Rock cemetery, beside her husband, till the time when her Master's voice shall call her up to the resurrection of everlasting life.

A TRIBUTE FROM A FRIEND.

Publishers' Notes.

"King Saul," the new book by J. Breckenridge Ellis, is a charmingly written history of this great Bible character. The book is just from the press, and is a handsomely bound volume, containing 281 pages and 16 illustrations.

Many who read the history of prominent men mentioned in the Bible fail to catch the many points of interest connected with their lives. Such books as "In the Days of Jehu" and "King Saul" will point out to the reader both the little and big points in the history of these prominent Old Testament characters. The price of "King Saul" is $1.00 postpaid.

H. W. Everest is certainly acknowledged authority concerning the merits of any literary work which he may have examined. After reading "Organic Evolution Considered" he expresses his opinion of the book as follows: "I regard 'Organic Evolution Considered,' by Prof. A. Fairhurst, as the strongest presentation of the obstacles in the way of evolution that I have read."

The Christian Publishing Company recently brought out this valuable book in splendid style, and the price is $1.50 postpaid.

An Offer to Agents.

The Christian Publishing Co. is now prepared to offer *special inducements* to those who will sell "America or Rome—Christ or the Pope." The book contains 530 pages and 55 illustrations. A small portion of your time can be profitably employed in selling this book. Spain and her colonies are ruled by the Pope. The war has revealed to the world the conditions of her people. The facts contained in this book are a strong indictment against the Romish Church. The author spared neither time nor means to secure only reliable facts, and what he says can be accepted as the truth.

Write the Christian Publishing Co., St. Louis, Mo., for their agents' terms on "America or Rome—Christ or the Pope."

The secular press is discovering the merits of Mrs. N. M. Vandervoort's story, "Across the Gulf." The literary editor of the Times, of Clinton, Ill., has written quite a lengthy review of this book. We give the following extract from this review:

"The plot is lain in the city of Rome, and deals with the early rise of Christianity and the persecutions of the early disciples. A most pathetic and thrilling love-story as a golden thread of fascination runs through the ever-curious and attractive details of the narrative. The authoress, with a simplicity and rythm of diction that charms either the scholar or common reader, throws the curtain back on the life of Rome and its people as history paints it; hence the work is not only attractive, but instructive also.

Announcements.

"The Saline County Christian Missionary Co-operation"

Will have their annual meeting at Marshall, Mo., Sept. 12-14, 1898. The sessions will begin on Monday night, Sept. 12, to be followed on Tuesday by a session in the A. M., P. M. and evening and on Wednesday A. M. and P. M. Addresses will be given by T. A. Abbott, H. F. Davis, G. E. Shanklin, B. T. Wharton, the writer and by others. The C. W. B. M. will have an interesting session, Tuesday P. M. There will be a good program, and a large attendance is expected and free entertainment is offered to all by the Marshall brethren.

J. W. Strawn,
G. E. Shanklin,
B. T. Wharton,
Executive Committee.

Missouri Convention.

Program of the Thirty-first Annual Session of the Missouri Christian Convention, Nevada, Mo., Sept. 26-29, 1898.

MONDAY NIGHT, SEPT. 26, 1898.

7:30—"Praise the Lord, O My Soul," a song servce. Scripture Reading and Devotion, B. T. Wharton, Marshall.
8:00—Convention Sermon, James Vernon, Independence.
8:45—Announcements, Benediction, Reception of Delegates and Visitors.

TUESDAY MORNING, SEPT. 27.

8:00—First Lecture, "Preparation of Paul," H. L. Willett, Chicago, Ill.
9:00—"Let us Draw Near with a True Heart," a prayer service, J. W. Gorrell, leader, Joplin.
9:20—Organization and Enrollment.
9:30—Announcement of committee vacancies supplied and Special Committees.
9:35—"We Bid You Welcome," Prof. Broadus, Nevada.
9:50—Report of State Bible-school Board, H. F. Davis, St. Louis.
10:00—"The Account of our Stewardship," Report of Board, T. A. Abbott, Corresponding Secretary.
10:50—Report of Treasurer, T. R. Bryan, Kansas City.
11:00—Sermon, G. L. Bush, Windsor.
12:00—Adjournment.

TUESDAY AFTERNOON.

C. W. B. M. SESSION.

2:00—Praise Service, Mrs. V. A. Wallace, Carthage.
2:10—Address of Welcome, Mrs. Gilbert, Nevada.
2:20—Response, Mrs. F. M. Lowe, Vice-President, Kansas City.
2:30—Announcements of Committees and Instructions.
President's Address, Mrs. Alice Williams, Cameron.
2:55—Report of State Secretary, Mrs. V. G. Hedges, Warrensburg.
3:05—Report of the Treasurer, Mrs. Carrie F. Johnson, Chillicothe.
3:15—Address, "Our Women in the Field," Mrs. L. G. Bantz, St. Louis.
3:35—"The Story of a Life Membership," Miss Mollie Beery, Edgerton.
3:45—"Woman's Place in the Church," Mrs. James Vernon, Independence.
4:00—Second lecture, "The Struggle with Judaism," H. L. Willett, Chicago.

TUESDAY NIGHT SESSION.

7:30—"Let all the people praise Thee," a praise service.
"My Help Cometh from the Lord," a devotional, D. W. Moore, Springfield.
8:00—Address: "Richer than Golconda," Hon. Champ Clark, Bowling Green.
9:00—Adjournment.

WEDNESDAY MORNING, SEPT. 28.

8:00—Third lecture, "The First Missionary Journey," H. L. Willett, Chicago.
9:00—"Let us Therefore Come Boldly Unto the Throne of Grace."
A prayer service, T. S. Ridge, Kansas City.
9:20—Reports of Committees.
1. Ways and Means, G. A. Hoffmann, Chairman.
2. State Missions, W. F. Richardson, Chairman.
3. State of the Cause, G. M. Goode, Chairman.
4. Literature and Colportage, S. G. Clay, Chairman.
5. American Christian Missionary Society, T. H. Capp, Chairman.
6. Foreign Missions, S. J. White, Chairman.
10:30—Missions: "Beginning at Jerusalem," B. L. Smith, Cincinnati.
11:15—Missions: "Go ye into all the world," A. McLean, Cincinnati.
12:00—Adjournment.

WEDNESDAY AFTERNOON.

C. W. B. M. SESSION.

2:00—Devotionals, Mrs. S. H. Gilliam, Hamilton.
2:10—Reports of Managers and Roll Call of Auxiliaries.
2:35—Report of Superintendent of Young People's Work, Miss Mollie Hughes, Independence.
2:45—Paper, "Junior Work," Mrs. Frank L. Bowen, Kansas City.
3:00—Address, "Significance of Missions," Mrs. Mary Wisdom Grant, St. Louis.

3:20—Reports of Committees.
3:30—Joint Memorial Hour, Mrs. Kate Ellis Pe[illegible] Warrensburg; J. A. Berry, Ashland.
4:00—Memorial Sermon, "Blessed Dead," J. Briney, Moberly.
4:30—Fourth Lecture, "The Earlier Epistles," L. Willett.

WEDNESDAY NIGHT.

7:30—Prayer and Praise Service, Mrs. Jas. Cli[illegible]scales, Carrollton.
7:45—Address, Miss Ada Boyd, C. W. B. M. Missionary in India for fifteen years.
8:20—Address, Mrs. Helen Moses, Indianapolis, I[illegible]
8:45—Harvest Home.

THURSDAY MORNING, SEPT. 29.

8:00—Fifth lecture, "The Best Years of Pa[illegible] Life," H. L. Willett, Chicago.
9:00—"Lo! I am with you always," promise servi[illegible] J. T. Ogle, Carrollton.
9:20—Reports of Committees—Continued.
1. Schools and Education, M. M. Goo[illegible] Chairman.
2. Christian Endeavor, G. L. Bush, Ch[illegible] Chairman.
3. Student's Aid Fund, Clinton Lockh[illegible] Chairman.
4. Nominations, C. C. Hill, Chairman.
5. Orphans' Home, W. B. Young.
10:45—Church Extension, Geo. Darsie, Frankf[illegible] Ky.
11:15—Sermon, J. M. Vawter, Liberty.
12:00—Adjournment.

THURSDAY AFTERNOON SESSION.

2:00—"Go ye into all the world," an obligat[illegible] meeting, E. C. Davis, Kansas City.
2:30—Final Committee Reports.
1. Resolutions, E. M. Smith, Chairman.
2. Revision of the Constitution, T. Haley, Chairman.
3. Unfinished and Miscellaneous Business
4:00—Final lecture, "Paul's Character and Plac[illegible] Christian History," H. L. Willett, Chica[illegible]

THURSDAY NIGHT SESSION.

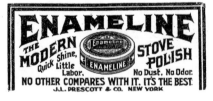

7:30—Mizpah Service, Nevada Y. P. S. C. E.
8:30—Consecrhtion Sermon, W. F. Richards[illegible] Kansas City.
Finally: "God be With You." Benediction

THE CHRISTIAN-EVANGELIST.

A WEEKLY FAMILY AND RELIGIOUS JOURNAL.

Vol. xxxv. September 15, 1898 No. 37.

CONTENTS.

EDITORIAL:
- Current Events....323
- The Heroism of Jesus....324
- The Hebrew Financial System....324
- Is Our Civilization a Failure?....325
- Peace and Prosperity....326
- Editor's Easy Chair....326
- Questions and Answers....327

ORIGINAL CONTRIBUTIONS:
- The Progress of Science.—J. W. Lowber....327
- Who Wrote the Fourth Gospel?—C. A. Young....328
- The Working of the Leaven.—R. J. Tydings....329
- Humiliation.—Joseph H. MacEl'Rey....330

CORRESPONDENCE:
- English Topics....335
- New York Letter....335
- Wheeling Through England....336
- Chicago Letter....337
- St. Louis Letter....338
- Texas Letter....339
- Jacksonville (Fla.) Letter....339

FAMILY CIRCLE:
- Take Time with the Boy (poem)....344
- Army Life in Arizona....344
- Photographed Texts....345
- What the Rumseller Knows....346
- Pointers for Teachers....347
- The Heart's Daily Work....347
- Phœbe Cary....347
- Sinim for Jesus (poem)....347
- Side Trips During Prayer....347
- The First Railroad in America....347

MISCELLANEOUS:
- Current Religious Thought....331
- The Religious World....331
- Our Budget....332
- Personal Mention....334
- Notes and News....340
- Evangelistic....347
- The Sunday-school....348
- Christian Endeavor....349
- Marriages and Obituaries....350
- Literature....351
- Publishers' Notes....352
- Announcements....352
- The Hiram College Jubilee Endowment....352

Subscription $1.75.

Lookout Mountain.
ON TO CHATTANOOGA!—OCTOBER 13-22.

PUBLISHED BY

CHRISTIAN PUBLISHING COMPANY

1522 Locust St., St. Louis.

THE

CHRISTIAN - EVANGELIST

J. H. GARRISON, EDITOR.

W. W. HOPKINS, ASSISTANT.

B. B. TYLER, J. J. HALEY,
EDITORIAL CONTRIBUTORS.

What We Plead For.

The Christian-Evangelist pleads for:

The Christianity of the New Testament, taught by Christ and his Apostles, versus the theology of the creeds taught by fallible men—the world's great need.

The divine confession of faith on which Christ built his church, versus human confessions of faith on which men have split the church.

The unity of Christ's disciples, for which he so fervently prayed, versus the divisions in Christ's body, which his apostles strongly condemned.

The abandonment of sectarian names and practices, based on human authority, for the common family name and the common faith, based on divine authority, versus the abandonment of scriptural names and usages for partisan ends.

The hearty co-operation of Christians in efforts of world-wide beneficence and evangelization, versus petty jealousies and strifes in the struggle for denominational pre-eminence.

The fidelity to truth which secures the approval of God, versus conformity to custom to gain the favor of men.

The protection of the home and the destruction of the saloon, versus the protection of the saloon and the destruction of the home.

For the right against the wrong;
For the weak against the strong;
For the poor who've waited long
  For the brighter age to be.
For the truth, 'gainst superstition,
For the faith, against tradition,
For the hope, whose glad fruition
  Our waiting eyes shall see.

RATES OF SUBSCRIPTION.

Single subscriptions, new or old	$1.75	each
In clubs of five or more, new or old. ..	1.50	"
Reading Rooms	1.25	"
Ministers ...	1.00	"

With a club of ten we will send one additional copy free.

All subscriptions payable in advance. Label shows the month up to the first day of which your subscription is paid. If an earlier date than the present is shown, you are in arrears. No paper discontinued without express orders to that effect. Arrears should be paid when discontinuance is ordered.

In ordering a change of post office, please give the OLD as well as the NEW address.

Do not send local check, but use Post office or Express Money Order, or draft on St. Louis, Chicago or New York, in remitting.

New Publications.

HUGH CARLIN, or, Truth's Triumph. By J. H. STARK. 12mo, cloth, $1.00.

"Hugh Carlin" is a well-planned, well-developed religious story, and deals with some of the modern phases of religion in a very practical and striking manner. It is the opinion of many who have read the story that it will take high rank as a religious novel in our literature.

Let all the congregations purchase a sufficient number of "Hugh Carlin," and put it into the homes throughout the land. The good it would accomplish could not be estimated.—D. N. DEJARNETT.

Such a book cannot help but have a great influence for good over the mind of any young lady or gentleman, who might have the privilege of reading it. Such grand truths presented in such a fascinating way must not be lost.—D. N. MELICK.

WAYS OF WORKING. By OREON E. SCOTT. Paper, 10c.

A Handbook of Suggestions for Wide-Awake Christian Endeavorers.

AFTER PENTECOST, WHAT? By JAMES M. CAMPBELL, author of "Unto the Uttermost." 12mo, cloth, 297 pages, $1.00.

This work is a discussion of the doctrine of the Holy Spirit in its relation to modern Christological thought. The following Table of Contents will give an idea of the scope of the book: Introduction, The Significance of Pentecost, A Spiritual Christ, A Spiritual God, Spiritual Worship, A Spiritual Apprehension of Truth, An Influx of Spiritual Life, The Spiritual Man, Spiritual Holiness, Spiritual Authority, The Distribution of Spiritual Operations, The Impartation of Spiritual Power, The Production of Spiritual Works, The Formation of a Spiritual Society, The Inauguration of Spiritual Movements, The Establishment of a Spiritual Kingdom.

ROSA EMERSON; or, A Young Woman's Influence. A Story of the Lodge, the Church and the School. By JOHN AUG. WILLIAMS. 375 pages, cloth, $1.00.

Rosa represents most of the beautiful female virtues, and young Thornton is as bright and noble and fearless as a knight. Their love is strong and true, without the heartaches and heartbreaks which so frequently send the Cupid-smitten unfortunates dangerously near the mad-house. The whole-soulness that left no stone unturned to find the heir of the estate of the father French, and succeeded at last in laying the prize on the head of Simon Bugg, who was not a bugg at all, is as wild and beautiful as the story of Pythias and Damon. Here is another diamond, first in the rough, but polished, in the old way, with his own dust, until Simon French Stuart, as he proves to be, comes fearfully near getting the crown of heroism. I like the fine selection of characters, with which to expose hypocrisy and sham. Faithfulness in the discharge of duty is made to rank high above sectarian orthodoxy, and to throw a white light on the miserable sectarian apologies for religious conviction and Christian living. I hope the author will receive a liberal patronage, and the book a wide reading.—D. R. DUNGAN.

STUDIES IN ACTS; or, The New Testament Book of Beginnings. By W. J. LHAMON, M. A. Introduction by A. McLean, Corresponding Secretary of the Foreign Christian Missionary Society. Large 12mo, cloth, 416 pages, $1.25.

This book is not a commentary; it is not a collection of sermons; but it is a volume of essays, in which the author seizes upon the most critical and interesting portions of the Book of Acts, the strategic forces, and mountain peaks of its history. These he treats with a charm of style, a vigor of thought and mastery of material that have called forth the hearty praise of many readers, though the book is but recently from the press. 116 pages at the end of the volume are devoted to Notes and Comments. A few are by the author, but for the most part they are selections from first-class authorities, and are exceedingly helpful upon many difficult and important passages.

Sent by mail prepaid on receipt of price.

CHRISTIAN PUBLISHING CO.,
1522 Locust St., - St. Louis Mo.

ISTIAN-EVANGELIST

ı opinion and methods, Liberty; in all things, Charity."

, Mo., Thursday, September 15, 1898. No. 37

week. A royal welcome was extended by the Queen City to the old soldiers. A motion to make eligible to membership in the Grand Army the soldiers who have served their country in the late war with Spain was laid on the table. Resolutions were passed endorsing the management of the war by President McKinley and Secretary Alger, and criticising somewhat severely the management of the Pension Office by the present commissioner. The resolutions declare in favor of a more liberal interpretation of the pension laws instead of refusing pensions to those who honestly deserve them, on mere technical grounds. Commander-in-Chief Gobin was succeeded in command of the organization by Col. James A. Sexton, of Chicago. Philadelphia secures the next encampment, defeating Denver in a contest for the honor.

The American commission for looking into the condition of affairs in Hawaii, and making recommendations as to suitable legislation for the islands, is on the ground and making considerable headway with its work. The members of the commission are mingling freely with the people in different parts of the island, explaining the nature of their new relations with the United States, and receiving the free expressions of the opinions of the natives as to how they regard the annexation. Public meetings are being held where the commissioners speak and where the native Hawaiians are allowed to express their sentiments. One of the questions which the natives pressed with great earnestness on Messrs. Cullom, Hitt and Frear was whether this union was only a temporary war measure, or whether it was to be permanent. Senator Cullom assured them that it was a permanent arrangement, and that so long as the American Union shall endure, so long will the Hawaiian Islands be a part of the United States of America. They wanted to know if their rights would be respected the same as Americans, or whether they were to be treated as the North American Indians. The commissioners assured them that their rights would be sacredly regarded and that they might still cherish the tenderest regards for their native land, just as the citizens of our states do not yield their love of native state because of its connection with the American Union. No doubt this mingling with the natives, hearing their views, answering their questions and removing misconceptions will have much to do in reconciling that part of the native population that was opposed to annexation.

United States Ambasador, John Hay, being about to leave England to assume the offiice of Secretary of State, was waited upon by a committee of the Anglo-American League, headed by its chairman, James Bryce, who made an address in which, after expressing regrets for Col. Hay's departure, he said:

It has been your fortune to represent your country here at a time of exceptional interest, when the war, now happily ended, gave occasion for an expression of the feelings of affection and sympathy toward the United States which the British people have long entertained, but never before have they been so conspicuously manifested. You carry back the assurance of the depth and strength of these feelings. The principle that there ought to be permanent friendship and cordial co-operation between the British Empire and the American Republic is one that all parties and all statesmen here are agreed in regarding as a fundamental principle of British foreign policy, and by it the whole people desire that their government be guided.

We rejoice to believe that in your country corresponding sentiments are entertained, and that a corresponding principle is now largely accepted. Knowing that no one holds these convictions more firmly than yourself, or can express them in clearer or more felicitious terms, we gladly acknowledge the great service you have rendered to both nations and console ourselves on your retirement by the reflection that you are called to duties in your own country even wider in their scope and graver in their responsibilities and more important in the results that they may secure.

During the past week the President and Cabinet had to consider a request from Spain that that government be allowed to send gunboats to the Philippine Islands where American authority has not yet been established in order to afford security to Spanish interests. It was claimed that Spanish subjects were being badly treated by the insurgents in various parts of the islands. The President and his Cabinet were of one mind in refusing this request, rightly supposing that to accord Spain such a privilege at this time would be to cast doubts on the sovereignty of the United States in the Philippines. This may indeed have been Spain's ultimate motive in making the request. Admiral Dewey was advised by cable that it was the wish of the government that he ascertain what outrages were committed by the insurgents and take steps to put a stop to them immediately. He was instructed to see that Spanish interests had the same protection accorded to other nations. It is believed that Admiral Dewey is able to take care of himself and to preserve order, as the squadron under his command will soon be thoroughly renovated, and has already been reinforced by the Monterey and Monadnock.

British dominion has been notably increased by the recent victory of British arms on the Nile. Gen. Kitchener, with an army of 24,000 made up of British and Egyptian soldiers, gained a decisive victory recently over the dervishes under command of the Mahdi. This battle resulted in the capture of Khartoum, or strictly speaking the site of Khartoum, for the original city has been destroyed, and the opening up of a large part of Africa to British rule and civilization. It will have important bearings, too, on the slave trade, for wherever British dominion extends the slave trade is prohibited. The campaign of which the capture of Khartoum is an incident, has for its object the occupation and control of a broad section of Africa extending from the southern cape to the mouth of the Nile. The report of the Anglo-Egyptian army in the battle above referred to, on September 2, is estimated at two hundred, while that of the dervishes was of course very much larger. The dervishes fought with great bravery, but were no match for the solid and well-drilled ranks of the British. The results of this victory of British arms in the Nile is likely to be far-reaching.

On Saturday last the Empress of Austria was murdered at Geneva by an anarchist named Luigini. The heads of the leading nations of the world immediately telegraphed their condolence to the emperor, who was almost prostrated at the news of her assassination. After an autopsy, ordered by Emperor Joseph, the body of the empress was embalmed and prepared for transportation to Vienna on Thursday of this week and for burial on Saturday. The assassination of Empress Elizabeth by an anarchist has renewed the alarm of rulers of the nations of Europe from that quarter. Not long ago an attempt was made upon the czar's life and some have supposed that the killing of the Empress of Austria is a part of a conspiracy against them; but so far no evidence has been discovered to support this theory. But the deed is none the less sinful on that account and will only increase the profound horror the nations and their rulers have for the adherents of a doctrine so dangerous to any civilization. And now that their hatred of rulers is turned toward the gentler sex and a woman of splendid attainments and record for good deeds is slain by one of that school, the horror of the Christian world of such a doctrine as nihilism will only be intensified.

The rapid gain of the United States in her invasion of the commerce of the world is shown by the British Consul at Stockholm, Sweden, by an important series of statistical tables just issued by the Swedish Government, covering the commerce and production of the world in a series of five-year periods, from 1871-5 to 1891-5. From these tables we learn that in the iron production of the world the United States has increased its output from 16.1 to 30.9 per cent., while that of Great Britain and Ireland has decreased from 46.3 to 27.5 per cent. of the world's production in the last twenty years. In the coal field, for the same period, the United States production has advanced from 17 to 30 per cent. of the world's output, while Great Britain and Ireland have decreased from 47 to 34 per cent. In the cotton consumption Great Britain has increased one-fourth, while that of the rest of Europe and the United States has doubled. In railways the increase of the United States is about eight times greater than Germany and about 23 times greater than Great Britain and Ireland. In wheat production the United States ranks one-fifth, the British Colonies about one-eighth and Germany less than one-twentieth of the total production of the world. A further analysis of the table indicates that the United States alone produces about 22 per cent. of the gold of the world, and over 35 per cent. of the silver of the world. The per centage of increase of population in the leading conntries as shown in the table places the increase in population in the United States during the last ten years at 24 per cent., the British Colonies and dependencies increased 10 per cent., Germany 12 per cent., Russia 11 per cent., Great Britain and Ireland 8.77 per cent., and France 78 per cent.

THE HEROISM OF JESUS.

There seems to be a tendency to hero-worship in all men. So far as this is the admiration of high and noble qualities which are displayed by others, it is both commendable and inevitable in good men. Why should we not admire the qualities of courage and devotion to right and patriotism, or the unselfish love of country, when we see them exemplified in a high degree in any of our fellowmen? What we call hero-worship is perhaps nothing more than the tribute which our common humanity pays to a high order of talent or genius, consecrated to high and worthy ends. To be sure, there is a lower form of hero-worship which appeals to men who are influenced by traits and qualities of a lower character; but this is by no means so universal as the admiration for the higher qualities displayed by the true heroes of the people.

Among the many elements of greatness in the character of Jesus of Nazareth we should not fail to recognize the high quality of heroism which he manifested and fully exemplified in his life. There is abundant reason why Jesus should be regarded, not only as the hero of redemption, but of humanity. Surely, no one among the sons of men has displayed a courage so lofty and unselfish as that which characterized him throughout his whole career. Consider a few of the ways in which that moral heroism was manifested.

He consented to be poor when he might have been rich because he saw that he could accomplish his mission for humanity better in that way. He became poor that we might be rich. Not many men voluntarily choose poverty rather than wealth, and when this is done in the interest of the human race, it manifests the true quality of heroism.

Again, Jesus selected the life of humiliation and suffering rather than one of kingship and earthly glory. He refused the crown when it was offered to him, and turned away from the temptation of being a great earthly ruler to tread the pathway of humiliation and lowly service. He did this because an earthly crown would have hindered him from accomplishing what he desired to do for the race. How few men reject position and power to pursue higher aims!

Jesus entered upon the work of establishing a kingdom of God whose nature and principles were out of harmony with the expectations and desires of the Jewish people. This brought him into antagonism with the religious authorities of his age. He knew this would be the case, and yet he unflinchingly adhered to his program in spite of the gathering storm which he foresaw was to break upon him. This requires courage of the highest and rarest kind. Men love to be popular. They prefer to do that which will please the people. Jesus Christ chose to do that which was best for the people, though it brought him into conflict with the Jewish leaders and resulted in his death. That is true moral heroism which pursues its goal at the cost of life.

Not only did Jesus offend the Pharisees and Scribes by his teaching and by his manner of life, but even those who acknowledged him as Master were offended at his sayings, and many of them turned away from him. There is, perhaps, not a m pathetic scene in the whole life of Jesus than when a large company of h disciples forsook him because of some his "hard sayings," and he, turning to t apostles, said, "Will ye also go away' How it must have cut him to the heart see his followers turn away from him! A yet he must tell them the truth, even if t telling of it leaves him a lone Man, witho followers and without friends. This heroism of the highest type. How oft does a preacher hesitate to declare t plain truth from his pulpit for fear offending those to whom he sustains t relation of teacher and on whom he depen for his support! What a temptation it to tone down the message so as to make agreeable to those who need it in its plai est and most direct form!

One of the greatest temptations whic comes to an editor of a religious journal to make all his editorial utterances ha monize with the views of his readers, an to "play to the gallery," instead of deliver ing the message which his readers nee The editor who has never written an edi torial which he knew at the time woul offend some of his readers and cost hi some subscribers, is not following in th footsteps of his Master, who uttered truth very unpalatable even to his friends an which cost him many of his followers We admire this heroism in the case o Christ as we look back at it across the centuries, but we deprecate it and often oppos it when we see it manifested in our ow day.

Whoever is chosen of God to be a leade of the people must, in the nature of things, if he be seeking continually the divin guidance, see certain truths and certain applications of truth sooner than a majority of others. If he lack this quality of spiritual insight, then he is not a leader of men in spiritual things. But if he see the truth and declare it not, in love and with due patience, he shows the lack of that quality which we so much admire in Jesus of Nazareth—moral heroism.

Jesus pronounced a blessing upon those who would not be offended at his sayings. He promises the same blessing to all those who are not "disobedient to the heavenly vision," but who follow the truth as God gives them to see the truth. The example of Jesus is a constant challenge to every man to be loyal to his convictions of truth, and not to shun to declare the counsel of God as the needs of men may require. May this quality of heroism in the life and character of Jesus find ample illustration in the leaders of the church of the present day!

THE HEBREW FINANCIAL SYSTEM.

The intimate historic connection of Christianity with Judaism makes the latter an intensely interesting study. The religion of the people of Israel prepared the way for the Christian religion. It is impossible to understand the principles, precepts and practices of the Christians in New Testament times without an understanding of the customs of the Hebrew people. The New Testament points back to the Old; the Old Testament points forward to the New. In our study, therefore, of the money question, from the biblical point of view, it is important for us to study the financial system of the Jews as individuals in their ancient writings.

The law of Moses was explicit and em-what it required of the people in r of finance. The law said, "Thou r tithe all the increase of thy the field bringeth forth year by ut. 14:22). "All the tithe of the her of the seed of the land or of of the tree, is the Lord's; it is the Lord. And if a man will at aught of his tithes, he shall add e fifth part thereof. And conie tithe of the herd, or of the n of whatsoever passeth under he tenth shall be holy unto the shall not search whether it be ad, neither shall he change it; change it at all, then both it and e thereof shall not be redeemed. the commandments which the manded Moses for the children of Mout Sinai" (Lev. 27:30-34).

certainly definite and emphatic. irement of Jehovah cannot be on this point. The Jew of the e knew what would please, and would displease his God in the operty. The author of the epistle brews says that "the sons of Levi" mmandment to take tithes of the But the Levites, according to were required to pay tithes of the ning into their hands. Read the :

speak unto the Levites and say 1, When ye take of the children of tithes which I have given you m for your inheritance, then ffer up a heave offering of it for even a tenth part of the tithe" :26).

nan was permitted to escape. All uired to pay a definite proportion ncome to the Lord. The law says men appeared before the Lord to "they shall not appear empty; n shall give as he is able" (Deut.

sides the payment of the annual tioned above a triennial tithe was The following is the law on this

e end of three years thou shalt th all the tithes of thine increase year, and shall lay it up within ; and the Levite, because he hath or inheritance with thee, and the and the fatherless, and the widow, within thy gates, shall come and and be satisfied; that the Lord bless thee in all the work of thine ch thou doest" (Deut. 14:28-29). s that this triennial feast was of-unusual solemnity. Its payment tter of no ordinary importance. iven this tithe to "the Levite, the the fatherless and the widow," was required to "say before the

e brought away the hallowed t of mine house, and also have m unto the Levite, and unto the to the fatherless and to the cording to all thy commandments u hast commanded me; I have sgressed thy commandments, ave I forgotten them; I have not ereof, in my mourning, neither ken away aught thereof for any se, nor given aught thereof for but I have harkened to the voice rd my God, and have done according that thou hast commanded me." After which he was required to offer the following prayer:

"Look down from thy holy habitation from heaven, and bless thy people Israel, and the land which thou has given us, as thou swearest unto our fathers, a land that floweth with milk and honey" (Deut. 26: 12-15).

But the payment of tithes did not begin with the law of Moses. Why should it terminate with the abrogation of that law? Abraham paid tithes to Melchisedek. "And Jacob vowed a vow, saying, If God will be with me, and will help me in this way that I go, and will give me bread to eat, and raiment to put on, so that I can come to my Father's house in peace; then shall the Lord be my God, . . . and all that thou shalt give me I will surely give the tenth unto thee" (Gen. 28:20-22). This was previous to the giving of the law by Moses.

Obedience to this specific and oft-repeated requirement of Jehovah was sometimes neglected by Israel. What was the result? Hear these words:

"Will a man rob God? Yet ye have robbed me. But ye say, Wherein have I robbed thee? In tithes and offerings. Ye are cursed with a curse." Why? "For ye have robbed me, even this whole nation." How were they to get rid of the curse? Answer: "Bring ye all the tithes into the storehouse, . . . and prove me now, herewith, saith the Lord of hosts, if I will not open you the windows of heaven and pour you out a blessing, that there shall not be room enough to receive it; and I will rebuke the devourer for your sakes, and he shall not dstroy the fruits of your ground; neither shall your vine cast her fruit before the time in the field. And all nations shall call you blessed, saith the Lord of hosts" (Mal. 3:8-12). This was not only the way of freedom from the curse; but it was also the way to an abounding prosperity.

The right use of money—a use of money for the good of man and so also for the glory of God—was an unfailing feature of a genuine religious revival among the Hebrew people. They did not know how to be religious without giving money. Besides the payment of tithes, at the same time, there were free-will offerings. The Lord, in the language above quoted from Malachi, speaks of "tithes and offerings"—not tithes alone, but of "tithes and offerings." Read at your leisure the account of the revival when Hezekiah was king in Jerusalem, written in 2 Chronicles 31:5-10. Examine also the accounts of revivals in the days of Ezra and Nehemiah, described in the books bearing their names. There was also a great revival when Josiah was on the throne of Judah. In all of these instances money was given in abundance.

From the foregoing quotations it is evident (1) that one tenth of the produce of the soil was assigned by Jehovah for the maintenance of the Levites; (2) that out of this the Levites were required to dedicate one tenth to God, probably for the use of the high priest; (3) that a tithe, or in all probability a *second* tithe, was to be applied to festival purposes; (4) that in every third year, either this festival tithe or a *third* tenth was to be eaten in company with the poor and the Levites. The question arises, Were there *three* thithes taken in this third year, or is the third the second only under a different description? This question cannot be discussed in this place.

Enough has been said to show claims as his own, *i. e.*, for his u tion of the income of his people I that this was not less than a te

TITHE WAS THE MINIMUM.

What was the foundation of t It was the fact that all belongs, in analysis, to God; that even the accumulate property is from hi please, the following passages:

"But thou shalt remember the God." Why? "For it is he th thee power to get wealth" (De David said, "Who am I, and wh people that we should be able to willingly after this sort? For a come of thee, and of thine own given thee" (1 Chron. 29:14). the prophet Haggai Jehovah sa silver is mine and the gold is mi 2:8). "The earth is the Lord's fullness thereof; the world and dwell therein; for he hath founde the seas, and established it floods" (Psa. 24:1-2). These words basis on which Jehovah's claim t tion of the annual income of the people rested.

But is there not the same foun a similar claim on us? Is it not that God gives ability to gain pro it not now true that the silver an belong to God? Is it not true to the earth and its fullness belong Is it not, therefore, true that whe tribute to the work of the Maste give to God a portion of what h him by an indefeasable right? therefore, who keeps all that he ing no part of it for the good of thus for the glory of God—is gu basest kind of robbery. He robs

IS OUR CIVILIZATION A FA

C. A. Conant's article in t American Review for Septemb Economic Basis of Imperialism," food for serious thought. Indi article seems to have been writte fication of the probable annexati Philippine Islands to the Unite The basis of the argument in fa advanced need of an extension of mercial interests is the need for a let for the profitable investment Mr. Conant has given his reade collation of figures to show how earnings on capital have decreas last few years in civilized natio this he attributes the present re dition of the financial world and reaching out towards uncivilized new investments. But what is Mr. Conant's view is his final as to the final outlet for capital. desire to quote his words:

There are three important soluti enormous congestion of capital in legitimate demand. One of these is istic solution of the abandonment the application of the whole earni labor to current consumption, and t of old age out of taxes levied upon tion of the community. It will be this solution will be accepted in a c sive form in any modern civilized second solution is the creation of ne at home for the absorption of ca has occurred at several previous sta world's history and is likely to c long as human desires continue expa there has never been a time before when the proportion of capital to be absorbed was so great in proportion to possible new demands. Means for building more bicycle factories than are needed; and for laying more electric railway than are able to pay dividends, have been taken out of current savings within the last few years, without producing any marked effect upon their amount and without doing more, at the most, than to stay the downward course of the rate of interest. Aside from the waste of capital in war, which is only a form of consumption, there remains, therefore, as the final resource, the equipment of new countries with the means of production and exchange.

Here, then, is pessimism, certainly, in its worst form. If this conclusion must be admitted, then is our civilization along with every other civilization, like those of the past—a failure. To prove this we have only to look forward to a time inevitably coming when there remaineth no more new countries to equip, and ask, What then? It will not do to reply by saying that the present living and dying nations will then have changed places, for that would not be progress, but history repeating itself. The weakness of this argument, however, is glaringly apparent. In the first place, we believe that it quite dangerously underestimates the extent and value of internal or home demands for capital; but the most serious fault we have with the argument and its logic is its narrowness. It limits profits on capital to an increase in its kind only. The arts, sciences, schools, trades, professions and all are set aside as unprofitable fields for the use of capital beyond their first establishment in a new country. Neither is the mental, moral and physical condition of the masses recognized in the premises by the eye of capital. Its trend is simply toward its own in kind and along the lines of syndicated investments and national loans. And furthermore it makes it the primary end of governments to seek out profitable fields for its capital, which is a prostitution of the true purpose for which all governments should exist—the mental, moral and physical welfare of all citizens. Our criticism of present governments is that they are already too much committed to just that kind of business. We do not believe in buying just to consume for the sake of trade, neither do we believe in turning our Christian civilization into a barbarous scramble for money, especially with the odds already in favor of the legally favored. Let us have more of the kingdom of heaven in our hearts, whether we add more territory to our country or not. Let us have a little more interest in an outlet for surplus labor and the question of an outlet for the profitable investment of capital will not be so difficult. One of its reasons for seeking undeveloped countries is that they abound in cheap labor. Profitable employment for laborers is one of the corner stones of our civilization and factors of progress as well as the profitable investment of syndicated capital. Our reasons for the extension of our national influence do not rest upon the interest of capital alone, nor of our own people alone, but in the welfare of our common humanity. W. W. H.

The Yearbook of the Young Men's Christian Associations of North America gives figures with regard to 1,415 associations, with a membership of upwards of 240,000, and owning real estate worth more than $20,000,000.

Hour of Prayer.

PEACE AND PROSPERITY.

(Midweek Prayer-meeting Topic, Sept. 21, 1898.)

Peace be within thy walls,
And prosperity within thy palaces.
—*Psa.* 122:7.

This psalm is an outburst of patriotic and religious devotion toward Jerusalem—the center of Jewish hopes and Jewish worship. Thither the tribes went up to their great feasts to worship God and to remember their national deliverance. They went with gladness of heart, much as our tribes now gather in their annual conventions. There was the temple, the pride of every Jewish heart and the symbol of their national unity. There Jehovah manifested his presence and made known his favor to Israel. It is not strange that concerning such a city the psalmist could exclaim:

If I forget thee, O Jerusalem,
Let my right hand forget her cunning;
Let my tongue cleave to the roof of my mouth,
If I remember thee not.

The prayer of the psalmist for Jerusalem is, that it may enjoy peace and prosperity—the peace which comes of God's approval, and the prosperity which is the reward of righteousness. There is no peace for the wicked, nor is there genuine prosperity for those who forget God and neglect his worship.

Jerusalem, or Zion, in its spiritual sense, in the Old Testament, stands for the church in the New Testament. What the psalmist asked for Jerusalem we may well ask for the church of God—peace and prosperity. We should not desire for the church the peace which is purchased at the price of truth, or compromise with evil, but the peace of God, which results from the union of the soul with God in Christ. Few blessings are more to be desired than such a peace.

We are compelled to admit that the church as a whole is not enjoying this peace. It is rent by divisions and its peace is marred by unholy strifes and jealousies. Not until the church regains its lost unity can it enjoy, to the full, the legacy of peace which Jesus left it.

Candor must compel the admission, too, that the prosperity of the church is not what it ought to be. It is moving forward slowly, instead of advancing by leaps and bounds. The hindering causes are the worldliness and carnality of the church, and the absence of that apostolic faith and zeal which enabled the early church to suffer the loss of its goods cheerfully and to endure bitter persecution for the sake of the gospel. In praying for the prosperity of Zion let us remember that we must seek to remove the obstacles to such prosperity. Not until then can we say truly,

Peace be within thy walls,
And prosperity within thy palaces.

PRAYER.

O, Thou who art the God of peace, we pray that Thou wilt give peace to Thy divided and troubled church. May its divisions and its backslidings be healed, and the peace of God which passeth all understanding abide within its walls. Grant, too, that all hindrances to its spiritual prosperity may be removed, and that it may purge itself of all sinful conformity to the world and go forward on its triumphant career, until the whole earth shall be filled with the knowledge of Thee and Thy salvation, through Jesus Christ our Lord. Amen!

Editor's Easy Cha

OR MACATAWA MUSINGS

During the past week Michigan h
welcoming home the boys it sent
front in the war for "Cuba Libre.
return has been marked by pathos
as gladness. Many of the brave
who went forth with full health and
step, came home emaciated, fever-
and weary, while others were left
nevermore to return to their hom
loved ones. It is well that the peop
received these returning heroes wit
mark of tender affection and ca
welcomed them with ringing be
shrieking whistles. They laid the
on the altar of their country, and v
in Southern camp or on Cuban batt
they have faced death for the flag
and for the extension of that lib
which it is the glorious symbol. W
to home, to parents, to wives, to
to sweethearts, and to all the bless
peace and domestic life!

Labor Day, on the 5th inst., se
have been more generally observe
usual and, as a rule, more sensib
served. Instead of a hot parade t
the streets, there was in many p
quiet rest at home with wife an
ones in the forenoon, and meetings
parks in the afternoon, when ther
music and speeches on questions
have to do with the cause of lab
laboring men. This method of obs
the day will tend to cultivate close
tions between the different classes o
and between labor and capital. S
day might well be used for culti
better relations between employe
employees. No class of men deserv
respect and kinder treatment th
great army of wage-workers, by
honest toil the national wealth is enh
and the comforts and necessities
provided. The true nobility in this
lic are those who by labor with b
brawn, or both, contribute to the wel
society and to the care of the he
Only idlers and the vicious, who pre
others, are beneath the respect of
people. Let us seek to make labo
respectable and idleness more odious

What a change a few hours can
about in the lake! This morning e
was as tranquil as a millpond or a
locked bay. But soon the blue sk
flecked with flying clouds, and the
zephyrs stiffened into a brisk breeze.
whitecaps began to appear, and
shadows from passing clouds reste
the lake in weird forms, like the sh
monsters in the upper deep, mal
marked contrast with the green s
where the sun was shining. As th
increased the waves have grown int
ing billows that are now thundering
shore, promising a lively time to tho
cross the lake to-night. O, fickle
Thou art as changeable as thou art b
ful! Thou art as responsive to the
that blow upon thee as public sentin
to the demands of Fashion, or as poli
are to the behests of the liquor
Roll on, thou great inland sea, un

roud waves are stayed by the same Almighty Fiat that put them in motion!

The abuse of the revival meeting is manifesting itself in a strong reaction against what are known as "great meetings." A pastor, writing to a brother preacher about a meeting recently, wrote: "The reason why I want you is because you do not hold great meetings. The need of many of our churches is some one to help them to recover from the effects of the great meetings they have had in the past. What green apples are to a small boy, that is what many of our protracted meetings are to the church." Too true. And yet, let us have protracted meetings, but see to it that only the ripe fruit of gospel truth be presented to church and people. First, be sure that the converts are converted to Jesus Christ and to his plan of life, then the more converts the better. But it is a sad mistake to lay the emphasis on *quantity* rather than *quality*.

Every day there are storm-shutters going up in the windows of the cottages as they are closed for the winter, and they wear a lonely, silent aspect. An uninhabited house is not an interesting object. It is the sound of human voices and the presence of human faces which makes a house look homelike. But there were never so many people here at the Park at this time in September as at present. We have been absent on the last two Lord's days, but we hear of good meetings on Sundays, with a good attendance. Still the boats are crowded each night, and sleeping berths are hard to get. We are going later, "to avoid the rush." We like these calmer, cooler days, and are trying to take a little more rest, so as to go home feeling as if we had had a vacation.

The editor of this paper had the pleasure of attending the closing sessions of the Michigan State Missionary Convention, held at Saginaw last week. Arriving at noon Saturday, most of the business of the convention had been transacted, and a majority of the preachers had returned home to occupy their pulpits on Lord's day. It was our privilege to deliver two discourses on Lord's day to large audiences. The work of the convention will be found reported elsewhere by the corresponding secretary, Alexander McMillan. The feeling was that substantial progress had been made during the past year. Converts are not made in Michigan as rapidly as in some other states, but they have staying qualities which make it worth while to push evangelistic work in that state. The preachers we met were mostly young men, but they seemed zealous for the cause. Our home was with Ira Billman, pastor of the East Saginaw church, where the convention was held. This church is finely located on one of the leading thoroughfares of the city, and the house is an excellent one. It was our first meeting with Bro. Billman, as he came among us from another religious body a few years ago. We found him a genial host, and his wife a genial hostess. Bro. B. is a poet, too, of marked ability, as a volume of his verses, "Bluebird Notes," amply testifies. The church at Saginaw seems to be prospering under his care. We greatly enjoyed our visit with the Michigan brethren, and in the house of Bro. Billman.

Questions and Answers.

What is the resurrection referred to in Col. 3:1: "If, then, ye were raised together with Christ, seek the things that are above," etc. In other words, from what were these Colossians raised? T. M. Hixson.
Hannibal, Mo.

It is the resurrection from moral and spiritual death to a new and better life, as set forth in their baptism. They were raised from their former manner of life to the life which is in Christ Jesus. "And you, being dead through your trespasses and the uncircumcision of your flesh, you, I say, did he quicken together with him, having forgiven us all our trespasses" (Col. 2:13). This verse, in connection with the 12th verse, which asserts the burial and resurrection of the believer with Christ in baptism, "through faith in the working of God, who raised him [Christ] from the dead," leaves no room for doubt as to the kind of resurrection referred to by Paul. As Christ was raised from the dead, so these Colossian Christians, being quickened by him in their moral nature, through faith in him, declared that faith in their baptism, an emblem of Christ's resurrection from the grave and of their own resurrection to a new life in him.

1. What does it take to constitute membership in the Christian Church?

2. If withdrawn from what would be the regular procedure to get back into the church?

3. Does the Christian Church govern itself by majority vote of the body, or by a board of elders ruling arbitrarily?

4. In employing a pastor is it the custom of the Christian Church to decide on the pastor by a majority vote, and instruct the elders to make terms with him, or is it the custom for the elders to employ without reference to the will of the congregation?

Yours truly, Mrs. J. C.

1. Faith in Jesus Christ, accompanied by repentance for sin, and manifested in obedience to Christ in baptism.

2. Confession of the wrong for which the person was excluded, seeking of forgiveness from God and from the church, and application for membership on this ground.

3. Each congregation is a self-governing body, but it acts ordinarily through a board of elders, or elders and deacons, who should act, not "arbitrarily," but according to the Scriptures in all things wherein the Scriptures give instruction, and in all other matters according to the spirit which the Scriptures inculcate.

4. The custom in our best churches is for a committee, usually the elders, to enter into correspondence with some minister, after having first convinced themselves of his worthiness and fitness, and if they find he can be secured his name is submitted to the church with such evidence as they have procured of his ability and character, and the church is asked to vote on extending him a call. The elders should never act finally in such matters without consulting the wishes of the church. This would be unjust both to the church and to the preacher who is called.

Will it not be quite in harmony with our plea for Christian union to work with the Baptists, in a Roman Catholic country where there are no Disciples of Christ, rather than to make one division more among the Protestant workers, whose forces are already much weakened by their lack of union? I mean join the Baptists as far as evangelical work is concerned, but keep, of course, a distinct individuality of your own as a Christian who refuses all party name and human creed. E. S.

Undoubtedly so. There is no good reason why Baptists and Disciples should not cooperate much more than they do in this country; but in a Roman Catholic country, like France, where this question originates, there are additional reasons for union of action, when such action can be had without the sacrifice of any principle. Often it is the means of extending union principles more widely than they otherwise would be.

THE PROGRESS OF SCIENCE.

J. W. LOWBER.

While the greatest philosopher of the world lived in ancient Greece, and the Greeks made many important scientific discoveries, the present age is eminently the scientific age of the world. The most important discoveries have been made within the past four hundred years. Among the ancients a knowledge of the sciences and arts was confined to the few, and the masses were overshadowed by the grossest ignorance and superstition. Since the invention of printing, everything has changed, for through the medium of the press knowledge can be very rapidly disseminated.

During the middle ages kings and nobles were almost totally ignorant of literature. Many of them were unable to write their names. The revival of classic literature in the fifteenth century changed the whole face of things. When Constantinople was taken by the Turks, Greek scholars were forced West and they gave a great impetus to the cause of civilization and to the advancement of letters. The inventive powers of man were thoroughly aroused and a glorious age of invention and discovery dawned.

The old school of scientists became very much alarmed at the new awakening. They could readily see what would, in the near future, be their doom. So they made use of the civil and ecclesiastical power to check the new doctrine. Such men as Copernicus and Galileo were rushed away to prison, and Luther was met with the most determined opposition. The excitement became so great that the fanatical rulers established that infernal court—the Inquisition. Racks, chains, scourges and thumbscrews filled its execution rooms; and the work carried on in the chambers of this horrid tribunal was calculated to strike terror to the bravest hearts. No tortures invented by untutored savages could compare to the blood-curdling horrors perpetrated by these inhuman monsters upon their victims. All Europe was for a time drenched with blood; but truth crushed to the earth did rise again.

The cruelties of the Inquisition could not stop the scientific progress of the age. Inventions and discoveries were being constantly made. America was discovered, and a new field for liberty and progress was opened. It is not surprising that the Spaniards now blame Columbus for discovering the New World. The invention of the telescope gave a new impetus to the science of astronomy. The old Ptolemaic theory fell to the ground, and the truths advocated by Tycbo Brahe, Galileo, Copernicus and Kepler were now fully established, and believed in by all thinking persons. The moon with its rugged mountains was seen coursing around the earth. Venus, the beautiful starry queen; Saturn, with his brilliant rings; Jupiter, with his belts and resplendent moons, were seen traveling round the sun. The sublime scenery of the heavens filled the mind of man with wonder and astonishment, and the reformation in science and religion went hand in hand. The Reformers were persecuted by false science as well as false religion. In fact, the old physicists stimulated both church and state to persecute the newscience.

The reformers in both science and religion were cruelly persecuted. Galileo, when an old man, was brought before the Inquisition. The tribunal, which was composed of the old scientists, pronounced him a deluded teacher and lying heretic. They intended to subject him to the severest torture and death. Galileo was an old man and could not endure such a terrible death. He knelt on the crucifix, with one hand on the Bible, and renounced all. When he arose he said to one of the attendants, "The earth does move for all that!" Science will not fortify a man for persecution as will religion. Martin Luther did not retract as did Galileo. Nothing could have forced Luther to retract. Religion develops manhood as nothing else can. We cannot endorse the conduct of Galileo, for he should have died for his convictions. The martyrs of the Reformation did much to advance the cause of truth. Religion and scientific Reformation have always gone hand in hand. In fact, true religion is the brightest science in the world. As Christianity is the pure religion, which contains the truth in all the rest, so it is the brightest of the sciences, for it is adapted to the development of the highest elements in the nature of man. The Christianity of the Bible represents the highest culture to which it is possible for man to attain.

Austin, Texas.

WHO WROTE THE FOURTH GOSPEL?

C. A. YOUNG.

I have stated the question in this form because modern biblical scholars prefer to use the terminology, "The author of the First Gospel," "The author of the Fourth Gospel" in their New Testament introductions, rather than "The Gospel of Matthew," "The Gospel of John." Furthermore, it would be unscientific to naively prejudice our conclusion by asking: "Who wrote the Gospel of John?" We must admit that the authorship of the Fourth Gospel is open to question. However certain we may be as to the didactic purpose of the First and Fourth Gospels, they are distinctively religious, rather than scientific treatises. Now in the realm of religion the famous motto, "*Credo ut intelligam*," of Anselm, borrowed doubtless from St. Augustine's "*fides praecedet intellectum*," is as cogent in this scientific age as it was in the scholastic period. But those who "walk by faith and not by sight" must necessarily base all their moral certainties, except those of consciousness, upon probable evidence. It follows, therefore, that we can only arrive at an intelligent judgment concerning any historico-religious question by weighing probabilities. The authorship of the Fourth Gospel is not only an open question, but an exceedingly difficult question. It behooves us, therefore, to avoid the dogmatic temper of mind and to pursue our inquiry in a modest spirit. There are able scholars, conservative and radical, on both sides. McGiffert, in his "Apostolic Age," says: "In John 1:14, and also in the opening words of the First Epistle of John, which was certainly written by the same hand as the Gospel, the author himself apparently claims to have been a personal disciple and a witness of the events which he records. Were it not for these passages we could hardly hesitate to regard the Gospel as the work of a disciple and a companion of John, rather than of the apostle himself. But as the matter stands, certainly either is hardly attainable."—"*Apostolic Age*," *page 616*.

The chief difficulty in the problem may be stated in the form of a brief question: "How could the author of the Apocalypse and the author of the Fourth Gospel be the same person?" The difference in the forms of thought and the great difference in the language, which is the vehicle of these forms of thought, is admitted by every student of these two writings. The first thirty-nine chapters of Isaiah are not separated from the last twenty-seven chapters by such a wide gulf in language and religious teaching as is the "Holy of Holies" of the Fourth Gospel (chapters 13, 14, 15, 16, 17) from the Apocalyptic visions of the book of Revelation. Yet few scholars hesitate to ascribe the historical prophecies of Isaiah and the "Rhapsody of Zion Redeemed" to different authors. Now the external evidence in favor of the Johannine authorship of the Apocalypse is practically indisputable. Probably the authorship of no other book in the New Testament is more certain, excepting the two which Luke wrote and the four great doctrinal epistles of Paul. Papias, Irenæus and Justin Martyr in the second century; Origen and Clemens, of Alexandria, in the third; Athanasius, Ambrose and many others in the succeeding centuries have attributed it to John the Divine. As Farrar says: "Modern criticism tends more and more to the conclusion that the Apocalypse is a genuine work of the Apostle John." Even Baur and Zellar regard it as one of the most certainly authenticated of the apostolic writings. Holding to the Johannine authorship of the Apocalypse, the difference in style, thought and language, which a student with a very superficial knowledge of Greek may easily discern, has made many of the New Testament scholars question the Johannine authorship of the Fourth Gospel. There can be little doubt that the present stage of the Synoptic problem has had an indirect influence, at least, upon those who are disposed to attribute the authorship of the Fourth Gospel to a disciple of John. For example, if the First Gospel was written by some unknown author (as it is claimed) who had as his sources the *Logia* of Matthew, the Mark incident material and other oral and written material coming from various cycles, how natural to infer that some unknown disciple of John threw the Johannine discourses into the argumentative mold in which we find then the Fourth Gospel. After fairly consi ing the probabilities against the Johan authorship of the book my recent st has confirmed my former conviction, "*the beloved disciple*," *John the apo* "*the Son of Thunder*," *wrote the Fo Gospel*. In this judgment I follow leading English rather than the Ger New Testament scholars. I trust reader will pardon a side remark to younger preachers at this point. brethren, I advise you to read the work the great German scholars. It will you to study the German language for purpose alone. But be very careful you accept the judgment of a Ger critical scholar. I find the conclusion the best English scholars far more reli than the German. There are no more ca ful, critical, painstaking scholars in world than are found in Germany. problem is too difficult for these h workers to undertake. They spend ye on details. There may be some truth the familiar story of the German who sp his life in studying a single noun, and his deathbed regretted that he had spent it on the dative case alone! T Germans are strong on analysis, and th methods of study easily drift them tow destructive criticism. English scholars is more synthetic and constructive. T Germans are experts in tearing down walls of orthodoxy. The best Engl scholars are master workmen in build strongholds of orthopisty. My reasons holding to the Johannine authorship of Fourth Gospel I will state as briefly possible.

1. The difficulty, which the difference thought and language between the Fou Gospel and the Apocalypse seems to of is not nearly so great as appears upon surface. Even accepting the Domit date of the Apocalypse, still it is not credible that both writings were by same author. The author of "Alice Wonderland" and "Through the Looki Glass" was a quiet, unimaginative p fessor of mathematics. Compare Bro ing's caricature of a type of Calvinism "Caliban upon Setebos" with the Ch tian Theism of his "Pauline." Compare first part of Goethe's "Faust" with latter part. Among New Testament writ compare 1 Thessalonians with Galatia and it will not be difficult for you to beli that John wrote both the Apocalypse Fourth Gospel, especially as there are many positive evidences in favor of Johannine authorship of both. If, ho ever, with a host of the best bibli scholars of our day we accept the Neron date of the Apocalypse, the chief difficu to the Johannine authorship of the Fou Gospel disappears.

2. The external evidence for the Joh nine authorship of the Fourth Gospe very strong. We can trace the tradit that John was the author of the Fou Gospel back to Polycarp, who was a d ciple of John himself. Irenæus, who beca Bishop of Lyons in the year 177 of our e wrote a work against the Gnos which contains about eighty quotati from the Fourth Gospel. Irenæus died 202 A. D., but in his youth he had bee disciple of Polycarp. Eusebius has p served a letter from Irenæus to Florinu in which the latter says: "I saw you wh

a youth in lower Asia with Poly-
ən you were living in scenes of
plendor, and when you were try-
ain the approval of Polycarp.
ok place then is fresher in my
than what has occurred more
' My older readers will testify to
ralness of this last statement.
e took in our youth grows up as it
ı us, and is incorporated in us.
can even now bring back to mind
place where the good Polycarp
it when he talked to us, how he
he came in and as he went out,
ived, how he used to speak to the
ow he used to allude to his inter-
th John and repeat the words of
ıo had seen the Lord, how he used
t what he had heard from their
about the miracles and the teach-
ıe Lord, and all in full accordance
written narrative." When Poly-
put to death, because he would
ınce his faith in Christ, he testi-
he had served the Lord "eighty
ears." If, as the early legends of
ch teach, John lived to be one
years old, Polycarp was the con-
y of the Apostle John for twenty
years at least. From the time of
and the fragment of Muratori, 160
which ascribes the Fourth Gospel
postle John, we have an unbroken
ı of the Johannine authorship down
present day. As Tishendorf, the
er of the Codex Sinaitacus, says:
stimony is nothing new, but it has
its due weight." He thinks the
ıy of Irenæus and Polycarp should
h all the difficulties urged by skep-
ıolars.

t the internal evidences of the
ne authorship of the Fourth Gospel
possible, even stronger than the
l evidences. In the very preface of
spel the author classes himself
the eye-witnesses of the glory of
arnate Word (John 1:14). Again,
close of his wonderfully cogent
nt proving that "Jesus is the
he Son of God," he appeals to his
ıy as an eye-witness (19:34f).
ıe appendix to the Gospel attests
edibility of the author. Weiss,
tt and others have repeatedly point-
hat we must look for the author in
cle of Jesus' three confidential
Peter is repeatedly named along
e author (12:24; 17:15, &c.), and
who died early, cannot be consid-
There remains only John, who in an
way describes himself as an eye-
of the events related in the Gospel.
hor must have been a Palestinian
iliar with the Aramæan language,
would seem that he learned his
ate in life. He is very accurate in
graphical and topographical refer-
He is not only familiar with Jacob's
t also with the traditions clinging
He reckons according to Jewish
s very familiar with the Jewish
nd customs, names particular places
usalem (9:7; 19:13) and in the
(8:20; 10:22). If space permitted I
give a resume of Luthardt's excel-
udy of the Hebraistic style of
t in the Fourth Gospel. The repe-
are so frequent that a vocabulary of
ght hundred words are used in the
book. The word "father" occurs twenty times in one chapter (8), the word "witness" eleven times in nine verses (5:31-39), the word "world" seventeen times in the seventeenth chapter. The parallelisms, cycles, etc., so easily recognized by any one familiar with Old Testament literature, can be seen on every page of what I will now call the Gospel of John. To give Westcott's summary: "The author was a Jew, a Jew of Palestine, an eye-witness, an apostle, and could be none other than St. John."

Chicago, Ill.

THE WORKING OF THE LEAVEN,
OR
The Progress of Christian Civilization.

R. J. TYDINGS.

The thoughtful student of history, if he be a Christian, can find much now to cheer him. Verily, "the mills of the gods grind slowly, but they grind exceedingly fine." The light of truth is being shed abroad, even as "the waters cover the sea."

The embodiment of all truth is the Son of God. He said, "I am the way, the *truth* and the life." That momentous truth will prevail in God's own good time. The dormant stage of the leaven may have been to us many ceturies, but to him that is but a moment, and we can begin to see the leaven at work. Lasting civilization is not the mere temporal progress we can see in our surroundings; such as our railroads, telegraphs, electrical appliances, etc., but they are the outcroppings of true and lasting Christian civilization. The transforming influence of the gospel is growing more and more apparent as the years go by. There are those who claim as high a state of civilization for ancient times as exist now. The error of that statement should never go unchallenged in the light of current events. Some ancients, I admit, made great progress in the arts and sciences, but it was genius groping in the dark, and they could but fail. Modern Christian civilization walks as the light extends, and its stability is as the Rock of Ages. Christianity is the essence of all truth, and truth will make us free. After the dark ages had rolled by, the lump of leaven, placed in the great mass of humanity by the Son of God (by the atonement), began to show signs of working in the Reformation, and the mass has never lapsed into stillness since that day. Most all the triumphs of modern civilization can be traced, at least indirectly, to the Anglo-Saxon race; a race of people who point church spires heavenward and build schoolhouses on nearly every hill. To the English-speaking people seems entrusted the great mission of spreading the truth and its magnificent attendant developments in science and industry. Wherever the light of the great central truth shines forth there is progress, and the leaven is seen to work, but when nations continue in priest-ridden ignorance, egotism and avarice, as are the Latin races, there is retrogression and national decay. It seems our mission to tear part, at least, of the veil of error away. The English-speaking people are fast dominating the world. The sun never sets now, on England's domains, and her God-fearing people have done wonders in bringing nearer that "happy coming day" when all the earth shall be radiant with the light of all truth and knowledge. Though the sun may be able to set now on our dominions, it may not
be able to do so when this present wa
Our work is alongside that of the
country if, indeed, we should not
advance of her, because of our fr
ernment and its great possibilities.
struggle the impress of Christian p
is going to be wondrously stamped
darkened spots. We will help in sp
the dawning light and the rain
promise may be discerned in the clou
sins. Our seventy millions of God-
people are fulfilling a God-given p
and the truth will be widened a
time brought nearer when it "will p
I know our boys in blue are not
but how few are those among th
have not had the fervent praye
sympathies of some loved one whi
bear fruit in their lives in God's ow
Thus we may be said to be a Cl
nation. Our people as a rule ackno
a ruling Providene, and the nati
be blessed for it. Though our s
gambling dens, race courses and
place of evil are grievous indeed,
contrast with the rest of the world w
God and take courage. God is u
for a great end. Whatever may be
the ability or lack of ability of the
or the people of the Philippines to
themselves, if the hand of this n
taken off those countries or any ot
ritory acquired by this war, before
press of Christian civilization is in
stamped thereon, then this strugg
have failed in its devine mission a
pose. I do not look for any such
The prayers and struggles of our
men and women of God of all tin
bearing fruit and the leaven is w
the day is dawning.

> "From Greenland's icy mountains
> From India's coral strand,
> They call us to deliver
> Their land from error's chain."

Sometimes war is the delivering
or is the instrument to work ou
plans.

Besides the great central truth
gospel, which is being pushed by
voted and self-sacrificing mission
foreign lands, there is another
agency at work of which we someti
sight. This is the constant deman
English-speaking people for adept
ence and industry to superintend
some work of railroad building, of e
progress or other up-to-date, time a
annihilating achievement, in a lag
tion and the cause of Christianity i
strengthened thereby. American a
lish enterprise planned and are pu
completion the great Trans-
Railway, and the Russian serf, if
knew it, is having the enterin
driven into his bonds which will
own good time split them asunder,
Russia will be free. Every leading
shortening time and space in con
tion and transportation around t
by the achievements of modern
are resultant from the spread of t
are mighty agencies for its
spread. Let us not get in the wa
tiny, but act as true coworkers
Master for the spread of all tru
truth will eventually make us
national as well as individual
thus will the whole lump be leave

So mote it be!

Washington, D. C., July 25, 18

HUMILIATION.

JOSEPH H. MAC EL'REY.

No. I.

Humiliation, which is the state of being humbled, reduced or lowered in any way, but now in the specific sense of being meekened and rendered submissive, ethically and spiritually, is an experience which may come upon one in many ways. And although not likely to be welcomed or received with exultation, yet the condition in which the experience places one will ultimately produce a state of safe exaltation if one will accept it. But it may not be of the kind one would have selected.

This is a problem which must be developed by experiences which are seldom agreeable during that process. To find ourself placed in a lower posture, so called, in our own estimation, is sad enough. But to be compelled to face that fact as it faces us in the faces of our friends, who calmly accept the fact, and that, too, without asking explanation, and not proffering even the most moderate dissent from disinterested public opinion. This is bearing two burdens of these, one being degradation. This develops an emotion which is well named mortification; because it is indeed an incipient chill, like a death-shudder, because the higher we had exalted ourself the higher we thought we were by our friends exalted. Hence to be humiliated in their eyes is more galling than to fall only in our own. We might palliate with ourself and revive self-esteem under the guise of a rapid growth of meekness or humility and thus win credit for magnanimity, which is more admired than dull humility. Many cannot live comfortably without drawing out the admiration of those who indulge their own desire to flatter the vain at the cost of honesty and the littleness of deceit for the mean fun of addling the weak-minded.

Pity any one, but be candid with the disciple who is temperamental to the virus of the fiery fever of flattery. The disciple —any one—should desire to be highly esteemed in love for his work's sake. But adulation is never loved. Self-admiration is the idolatry of selfishness. And selfishness is complete isolation from the humane. Lower than that one cannot go. The wise know that humility is preferable to pride, exaltation, popularity, or its conferments, because the affection of humility can companionate us in any condition into which love and good-will can go. Miracle you may call it, that the high and lofty One who inhabiteth eternity dwelleth either with himself there or with the humble and the lowly here to revive the humble and to restore the soul of the contrite and thus to show God to the sipirit in man. The explorer of nature finds there what nature has to disclose. What more could there be found? The humble in spirit find God the Spirit. Humility is the natal, normal spirit-attitude of God. Can the man lose the spirit-attitude in which God and the man come mutually to know each other? Can a vain, self-opinionated spirit know God? Can a man having good eyesight, but not having studied optics, either describe or understand the prism, the phenomena of colors or of light? He may have acquired much expertness in flora culture, and be a keen observer of the ways of plants. But one lesson in the revelations of light laws from the world within the recesses of the flower goddess and behind the Ægis of Ahena's eyes would reduce to a self-confessing humiliation the self-acquired knowledge which gave him feeling of creditable superiority above the many in what he called botanic skill. From whatever source the increase of our knowledge or experience may come, it is as remarkable as it is unfailing and salutary that it does bring to us normally the experience of humiliation, but which is to those of harmonious mental and spiritual composition a real uplift.

"Lord, I know not. Teach thou me!" How apt a learner will that one speedily become. Because this is the attitude of the humble, whose spirit and intellect God can educate—draw out and associate with—through humiliation: "He humiliates himself upon the throne." Is not haggle over words, although words are as necessary to sense as are other forms of things to thought and action. Get the proper words and the proper concepts and you are thoroughly secure. You thus have the teachable temper and the proper implements which put you in proper posture for knowledge and wisdom with God and usefulness with man. You can serve the Lord only with all humbleness of mind, no matter with what other attainments you may seek to know him.

The honest-hearted, true in purpose, desire and affection, and in spirit meek, holding, as Aristotle said, the resentments under good control, representing the will and the whole personality, wield power far superior to that of the impulsive, contentious and self-asserting, who can never endure meek humiliation, which will without resentment lead one into tranquil humility. Humiliated often such persons must be, but they only chafe under it as a debasing load, rather than bend and adapt their energies upon that agonic line of contest against ease to win the race essential to the triumphal crown. It is the daily and long series of ease-denying agonizings which vex the tempers and and tire the fame they toughen for the hour of contest, which are very much harder to endure than is the work of the opposing athlete in the arena. The toil of preparation and the dread of possible defeat and crushing humiliation try the stoutness of the heart far more than the actual contact. The bearing of victor and vanquished are severer tests of character than the superior prowess of the champion, because in bravery, fearlessness and gallantry the defeated may, as is often so, overmatch the winner. After defeat the foiled one generally hastens to tell the why and how of it, intending thus to lesson the credit of success. In such cases explanations are, as they must be, unsuccessful. The whole of the case is victory for one, defeat for the other. Of course there were causes for the effect. But contingencies cannot count. Each contestant did his then best. Let silence confer dignity. New facts may, if of sufficient gravity, justify another trial, but cannot change the past facts. Take defeat gracefully. Let it teach caution in the future. Success often lies in properly anticipating an opponent, but can never spring from explaining how you were beaten. Adam gave the world a standard example of that tactic. It did not touch as was intended the reason of God, because it was not a reasonable tactic. Nothing could re ably supersede the reason given by because there can be no reason abo reason of God, because pure reasonin but coincide with right and truth, an and truth and right are insepa Therefore it often is that much mo trinsic honor attaches to the humiliat defeat than to the elation of conquest. depends on the nature of the stake inv in the combat.

If the contention be of purely se difference, there may be no elemen moral right or wrong in it. If it be p a moral issue, one side must be mo right and the other side must be mo wrong. Although many and devious been the maneuverings among causis all time concerning the imperative optional ethical reason why we shall their mazes as tangly now as of ver times, to say the very least. Nor mu blame this on the refinements and de ments of modern science in any se The scientists are superior to the profe moralists. When the secular histo would lampoon the teachers of deba ethics he finds his samples among ecc astical teachers of morals.

See how many of our specialists in ci in social moralities, do by intentional or intentional propositions of specious rea ing, contrive into the vital question s minor item which they magnify into importance of the real one, as if that v the real one of the age. The true gaug "all [any] unrighteousness is sin." good man out of the good treasure of heart bringeth forth good things; and evil man out of the evil treasure bring forth evil things." These measurers all-including and all-reforming. Make tree good and all will be good. Mak corrupt and all will be so. Heart-refor God's way. Specialties are men's h bies. Out of the heart proceed the iss of life. Thought, emotion, passion, aff tion, word and action. Everything develop after its kind. Thus one thing as special and no more special than other.

Humility makes confession elevating the receipt of pardon most comforti It keeps all the faculties in equable mo ment and secures the performance of ev duty with patience and cheerfulness.

God is gracious to the humble, but m resist the proud, because pride is vaunt and inhumane. The stars of God alw shine to the lowly, as those who look from great depths see them in the ligh noonday. Humility bringeth no exc and yet is accepted of God and man. confession is whole-hearted.

One of the most if not the very m important lesson man can learn is humi tion, because it includes everything n needs that can make him useful and ha in any state or condition, obscure opulent, in any kind or way. It pla him on the line of being and doing rig from the smallest to the greatest reache ability. It frees him from every delus motive, hope and proffer of mere exaltati because every act of humble work ex him. The Rabbi washes the discip feet and the disciple confesses the Rab power to wash their heads, hands hearts.

The humblest monarchs needed body guards, because their people kı

he honest beggar
d it was thus that
es upon them and
the king could do
ɔry, in ideal, the
. guide, defender,
ity, nobility, that
ədge about a king,
.o no wrong. The
l. He was chosen
, endowed by God
man of God. The
s often been real-
has been counter-
of that we have a
n heaven through
ɔst, a holy people
and sacrifices of
.t need. We have
as royal and true
əm to witness and
s among whom "he
' That is the brief
s own." It is and
the great clouds of
Son and the Spirit
ıd. What at once
ɔ king can be done
of the king. It is
ɪry house, hospital,
nt, garret, prison,
py cottage home,
soothed, restoration
rance made easier.
can be done without
by humiliation and
into humility. To

'5, 1898.

ɔus Thought

ɪrprises which sur-
ns in our short de-
may be had from
view of the matter
ted in the Christian
ndon. This wide-
journal says:

: concerned about the
denly a great peace
med into an immense
of Europe had little
rces of the United
contest. The mighty
ɪirty years ago has
ıemory of the present
ently the European
ɪk of America as only
productive country.
ən regarded through-
mainly distinguished
operations. Now,
The American peo-
ıowithstanding their
ʳ are capable of greay
eld. It is not verd
ən war was declaret
ıtes and Spain the
ɡle thing in readiness
ittle or no standing
əagre war supplies,
ıen placed in the field
ɑt for a protracted
ɪle upon both sea and
been victorious, and
. engagements they
victories recorded in
ll this means, some-
. of the world. The
Spain and the United
ı latter territory that
tates Government to
ɡest fleets of modern
ted, therefore, that
's the United States
gland, the strongest
ɪtire world. Already
mmense power. Not

strated that however good the ships may be they are practically worthless unless the fighters can shoot and have courage and intelligence to take advantage of every strategic position.

The Christian Commonwealth thus speaks of the results of our war with Spain. The views are not materially different from those generally held in the United States, but it is of interest to note their agreement. The Commonwealth says:

What, then, is the outlook for the future? Two things have resulted from the war. First of all, the American people have themselves been thoroughly united. The old division lines between the North and South have been completely obliterated. This of itself is probably worth all the war has cost the American people. In the second place, the old sores which have so long kept England and the United States practically in a suspicious attitude toward each other have been completely removed. England's course with respect to the United States has been friendly in the extreme, and the people of the states are not slow to recognize the fact. In short, while there is as yet no definite alliance between the two countries, it is absolutelycertain that in any conflict which England might have with other European nations she could count upon the moral support of the United States, and in an emergency it is not at all improbable that an offensive and defensive alliance might be secured. In such a case it is easy to see that these two nations could practically dictate terms to the rest of the world. However, it is almost certain that Japan would be glad to come into such an alliance. This would give an immense advantage to operations in the East. It may be also further suggested that Germany would not hestitate long to join such an alliance. It is true that during the war between the United States and Spain the German interference became very irritating to the American people, but, all the same, both Germany and the United States know well enough that on almost every ground there are strong reasons why they should stand together. But whether Germany joins the alliance or not, the great Teutonic consolidation for progress will continue to develop, and is not likely to be checked very seriously, for the following reasons: First, such an alliance means a plea for human liberty throughout the world. Nothing can stand against such a righteous cause. Second, it means the dissemination of the Christian religion throughout the world. England and America are the only two countries of the world that are characterized for vigorous missionary enterprise. When they have united their forces, both moral and material, it cannot be doubted that the Bible will soon become the text-book of every nation under the heavens. Third, such a combination assures the future peace of the world. Modern warfare must be confined largely to the sea. The battles of the nations must be mainly fought during the future years by the navies. England, the United States and Japan, in co-operation, will be stronger than all the rest of the world combined. This will give them the balance of power, and as their aim is undoubtedly for the best interests of civilization, it seems to us their real mission practically assures the peace of the world for the twentieth century.

That we may know how the learned men of Holland in the 17th century held the action and design of baptism, Ford's Christian Repository, a Baptist magazine, quotes from Herman Witsius, a Professor of Divinity in the universities of Franequer, Utrecht and Leyden, 1680 to 1698, in the June number as follows:

XXVI. First, therefore, the immersion into the water represents to us that tremendous abyss of divine justice in which Christ was plunged for a time, in some measure, in consequence of his undertaking of our sins: as he complained under the type of David, Psa. 69:2. I sink in deep mire, where there is no standing: I am come into deep water, where the floods overflow me. But more particularly, an immersion of this kind deprives us of the benefit of the light, and the other enjoyments of this world; so it is a very fit representation of the death of Christ. The continuing, how short soever, under the water, represents his burial, and the lowest degree of humiliation, when he was thought to be wholly cut off, while in the grave, that was both sealed and guarded. The

the grave. All these parti
intimates (Rom. 6:3, 4).
XXVII. Moreover, bapti
those benefits which believer
and these are either present
the present, the principal is
death, burial and resurrecti
the consequence of it, viz.,
and burying of our old man
the new by the efficacy of th
of Christ. For the immersi
represents the death of the
such a manner that it can
judgment to our condemnat
dominion over our bodies, th
it in the lusts thereof.
XXIX. Moreover, as in
forth the death, burial an
Christ; but his resurrection
glorious resurrection: we ma
baptism that after being bu
the water, we directly rise
last day we shall be raised ou
eternal life. Hence Theodor
"It is an earnest of good
type of the future resurrectio
the sufferings and a particip
rection of our Lord, agrees
of Christ (Mark 16:6): "He
is baptized shall be saved.

The Religious

The World's Conference of
Christian Association was
Switzerland, July 6-10. Th
Central International Comn
in forty-four countries with
an increase of nearly 500 ass
000 members during the last
was a full representation of p
tion men, including Sir Ge
England, John R. Mott, J
others, of this country, an
from Germany, Sweden, Ital
tries. There were addresse
departments of association w
American representatives h
Following upon this was th
World's Student Christian F
nach. This federation is at
of ten national or intern
Student movements of
Great Britain, Germany, Sc
Ceylon, Australasia, South
Japan, and other scattere
mission lands. Twenty-fo
tries are covered by the
there are corresponding
lands. The unions are found
versities, colleges, etc., an
ship of fully 45,000 student
The largest growth during
been in America, and the ne
—*The Independent*.

The committee in charge
rangements for the World'
ference, to be held in N
April, 1900, has organized
L. Baldwin, of the Method
ciety, as secretary, and
work. Dr. Baldwin was fo
missionary in China, and t
this large task.

The general committee
the Rev. Dr. H. N. Cobb,
Board; the Rev. Dr. W. H
Fifth Avenue Baptist Chu
F. F. Ellinwood; also the
Brown, of the Presbyteria
Dr. A. B. Leonard, of the
the Rev. Dr. J. F. Gouch
James, William E. Dodg
Fuller.

The conference will be
missions, and features of
what has been done in m
this century, the mistak
made, and what ought to
during the century soon to
the committee is much int
the co-operation of all b
that it should be, if possib
ence of all mission agencie
Christian world.

Refusals have been recei
and the committee express
Protestant bodies will uni
ference only, and in doing

Our Budget.

—Missouri state convention, Nevada, Sept. 26-29.

—General Convention, Chattanooga, October 13-21.

—All missionary pledges should be paid before Sept. 30.

—All should remember Church Extension work before the month closes.

—We publish another of Mary Black Clayton's army stories in our Family Circle this week.

—One more article will conclude our interesting "Wheeling Through England" series, by Dr. W. E. Garrison. He is now at Macatawa, Mich.

—The cool weather for the past week has been delightful in contrast with the great heat of the previous week. We are now on uncomplaining terms with the weather.

—The annual fall festivities of the city are at hand. The St. Louis Exposition opens this week. A peace jubilee is also contemplated. There is also an election in sight and political interests are coming to the front, so that the country is not likely to suffer for attractions, even if the war is over.

—A revised sermon by Alexander McLaren appears in Christian Commonwealth, London, each week. The Christian Commonwealth claims to be the only paper in which authorized reports of Dr. McLarens sermons are published.

—See notice of the Iowa Christian Convention in announcement column this week.

—England, Russia, France and Germany have been denominated the "Big Four" in China.

—The infirmity of years seems not to hinder Pope Leo from writing encyclical letters. He has recently addressed another to the bishops of Italy.

—While China is classed as one of the dying nations, there are indications that she is about to give birth to a new life.

—Four suggestive programs appear in this paper for the observance of Forefather's Day, Oct. 23rd. There were many favorable reports from this service where observed last year, and a glance at the programs in this paper will show at once what an interesting and profitable occasion this can be made for any church or Christian Endeavor Society. Read these programs carefully and then proceed to arrange for such a meeting and the hour will not soon be forgotten.

—New York City has commenced the conversion of some of her worst tenement districts into parks under the small-park law. This is a costly but healthful sanitary and moral reform movement.

—The receipts for Foreign Missions for the first eight days of September were $2,349.30, being $314.34 more than for the same period last year. The receipts for the month of August were far below those of last year. Here are the figures: August, 1897, $6,743.02; August, 1898, $3,169.09; loss, $3,573.93. But we are glad to know that the receipts for the year will go far ahead of last year. Bro. Rains writes that the receipts to date are $122,842.42, and says they ought to reach $130,000 before the books close at the end of this month.

—Hardly a week passes that we do not have to consign one or more articles to the waste-basket for want of the writer's name. Obituaries, reports of meetings and other articles come to us frequently with no other signature than "A Friend," "Observer," or some other equally indefinite term. Sometimes there is no kind of signature whatever. The author's name does not necessarily have to appear in the paper, but it must be known to us.

—The church at Fredericksburg, Va., is making a strong effort to secure a house of worship. It is said that the one they now have "is a monument of shame to the memory of the worthy pioneers and defenders of the primitive faith and to the old historic Virginia town of Fredericksburg." Only $500 is yet lacking and the church appeals to the liberality of the brotherhood for this amount. Their pastor is sustained there only by the assistance of the American, the Virginia and the Tidewater mission boards. On the merits of the plea there is no question, and we trust that the amount asked for will soon be in hand. Address the pastor, Cephas Shelburne.

—We wonder how many Endeavor Societies not yet enlisted in the Bethany C. E. Reading Course are preparing to begin with the second year. The value of the course has now been demonstrated, and it remains for you to act. This will be a rare opportunity for profitable self-culture, and if improved will prove a blessing to the readers, the society; the church and to the world. Write at once to J. Z. Tyler, Cleveland, Ohio, for an outfit or for further information on the subject; see also an excellent article in this paper from Bro. Lynn on this present particular subject.

—The receipts for Home Missions for the month of August amounted to $1,921.05. Last year they were $1,212.18 for the same month, so that there was a gain of $708.87. We do not know the total receipts for Home Missions this year to date, but hope that they are far ahead of this time last year. The indications are now that all our missionary boards will report larger collections this year than ever before, and if so this will add greatly to the enthusiasm of the Chattanooga Convention, Oct. 13-21.

—At the request of W. R. Hunt, one of our missionaries, who after nine years of service in the Celestial Empire has been recuperating in England for a season and who expects to be present at the Chattanooga Convention, Oct. 13-21, we reprint the poem by our lamented missionary, A. F. H. Saw, entitled, "Sinim For Jesus." It is the wish of Bro. Hunt to have this poem sung at the convention for the good cheer of all our missionaries in China.

—Many of the wealthier people of the country have no conception of the amount of poverty and suffering in the land, because they are not thrown in contact with it and will not read about it. The same is true of many professed Christian families. They have no idea of the religious destitution in the land, because they are not thrown in contact with it and will not read about it in our church papers, and consequently have little or no interest in missionary conventions and missionary efforts. If some way could be found to open their eyes to see and their ears to hear, there would then be some hope for fruit in their lives, and our convention halls would have to be enlarged to contain the delegates and friends of the Master.

—Let all persons contemplating attendance at the Chattanooga Convention, Oct. 13-21, give particular attention to railroad rates. The railroads of the Central and Southeastern Traffic Associations have granted the rate of one fare for the round trip. This covers the territory from the Potomac to the Mississippi River, and from the lakes to the gulf. The Trunk Line Association northeast of the Mississippi and the Western Passenger Association, west of the Mississippi River, have granted a a one and one-third fare on the certificate plan, or you can buy through the gateways of the Central or Southeastern at the regular rate, and get the one-fare rate through these gateways and return. Last year F. M. Call, the business manager of the Christian Publishing Co., this city, arranged for special coaches to the General Convention, to the delight and financial profit of the St. Louis and Western delegates. We are authorized to state that he is making arrangements for a similar convenience this year, in which the round trip from St. Louis to Chattanooga v not exceed one fare, if not better even tl this. All persons, therefore, in St. Louis, or the surrounding country, or in Missouri, anywhere in the West, who would like to av themselves of this advantage, are requested send their names to him at once. Address M. Call, 1522 Locust St., St. Louis, Mo. T is important, that he may know how many whom to provide transportation room. Th who purchase tickets to the gateway of t Central Passenger Association must reme ber to secure certificates of the agent fr whom tickets to St. Louis are purchased order to secure the one and one-third rate fr their homes to this city and return.

—In an article in the Outlook of Aug. 27t by Dr. Amory Bradford entitled, "Whe Rolls the Oregon," he has occasion to menti the colleges in Oregon, which he does as f lows: "In Oregon there are two Methodi colleges, one Presbyterian, one Campbellit one Congregational, and so on through t list—more than a dozen in all—and added them is the State University." The use the term "Campbellite" in this connection very surprising and disappointing as we Coming from a man of Dr. Bradford's intel gence and good-breeding, and appearing in t Outlook, a paper not given to using offensi names and epithets. Dr. Bradford knows th the people referred to sometimes as "Cam bellites" not only do not acknowledge any su designation, but that such a name is in dire antagonism to their plea for union on t ground of a common name and a comm creed. We are wholly unable to account f this breach of etiquette on the part of Dr. unless it be that he imbibed something of t sectarian spirit and manners during his sojou in the West by coming in contact with some the bitter partisans who, unfortunately, ha not advanced beyond the sectarian stage religion, and can conceive of nothing broad than a sect.

—Last week we published the program of t 31st annual convention of the Missouri Chri tian churches, to be held at Nevada, Sep 26-29. The time is short and the work is grea Great because of the numerical and financ strength of the Disciples of Christ in Missou Great because of the destitution that y remains in the state in spiritual things. Mo churches, Bible-schools, Endeavor Societi pastors and evangelists are needed and the conventions represent the only systematic c operative efforts in the state to secure the Let the brotherhood of Missouri see that t convention at Nevada is made one of the be in our history and plans for greater things f the Church of Christ in Missouri than ev before. A good convention in Nevada mea great things for our cause in Southwest Mi souri.

'he Observer, St. Louis, pays the follow- 'orthy tribute to Dwight L. Moody:

e hero of the war with Spain is not Dewey, Iobson, nor Shafter, nor Roosevelt, nor ', but plain, blunt, God-fearing, God-ring Dwight L. Moody. This simple stian layman has exerted more influence lirected the religious forces of the nation more masterly skill and ability than any ral of the navy or any major-general of rmy has wielded his forces on sea or land. n the war broke out the problem of bringhe influence of the gospel to bear upon y three hundred thousand men in camp ed too great for solution. No ecclesiastical court had the wisdom or the tact to deal with the question. No purely church organization was competent to set on foot a plan to meet the emergencies of the hour. But Dwight L. Moody, with the courage of an Elijah, and the faith and zeal of a Paul, saw and seized the opportunity. He marshaled the religious forces of the country, and with as much self-command as President McKinley or Major-General Miles, set the clergy and the laity of the country to saving the young men of the army. Wherever an army pitched its camp, there Moody's men pitched their tents with every facility for worship and practical Christian work. Never has the gospel been preached with more faith or more earnestness than it has been proclaimed by hundreds of practical Christian men during the summer months now closing.

—Spain's rediscovery of America is about to become as consequential an event in her history as her first discovery.

—The Independent says that the proposal of the Czar of Russia to call a conference of the nations of the world to provide for disarmament and the preservation of peace "is like a breath of heaven blown across the open pit of hell."

—D. H. Bays has been ordered by his physician to go home (to Michigan) for two months absolute rest from all labor, mental or physical. We are sorry to hear this, but the Irving church has voted him a vacation and we hope he will return restored and ready to continue his good work.—*Christian Index.*

—The suggestion of Bro. Marshall in our last issue, in reference to Bro. J. Z. Tyler and the Christian Endeavor work among us, is exactly in time with what the CHRISTIAN-EVANGELIST has more than once suggested. It is manifestly the proper thing to do. Bro. Tyler should give his whole time to the work for which he is so well fitted, and which so much needs his wise and cautious leadership. No doubt he is a good pastor, but he is not able to do both works, and he can be better spared from his pastoral work than from the fruitful field which he has been cultivating among the young people as superintendent of Christian Endeavor and editor and manager of the Bethany Reading Courses. The convention at Chattanooga should call Bro. Tyler to this special work, and all of us should co-operate with him in making the Endeavor movement accomplish the greatest amount of good among us.

—Many hearts and homes have been made glad during the past week by returning soldiers, but our joy over the return of those released from active service should not dissipate our interest in those who are holding the fort in Cuba, Porto Rico and the Philippines, or even those still in camp in the states. Let us remember them all in our prayers and forget not to assure them of our sympathies. Let us also mourn with those whose loved ones will never return to them on this earth again. To all such this war means more than words can express. They are those who have made the greater sacrifices for their country and who most need our remembrance and our love.

—The Observer, of this city, after an eloquent tribute to Dwight L. Moody for his noble work in the army, makes this noteworthy observation on Christianity, the magnitude of which has not yet been realized nor appreciated. The Observer says:

Christianity has never displayed its spirit to greater advantage than it did during the war and is still doing. The Christian men and women who flocked to the camps to minister to the spiritual and moral welfare of the soldiers hovered around every wayward boy with a brother's or a sister's affection. It is said that never did soldiers listen to the gospel with more eagerness than they did at Tampa, Jacksonville and Chickamauga. Thousands of young men were converted, and will return to their homes better and purer men than they were when they enlisted. Alas! thousands resisted the message and went into the ways of evil. Although the war is over, the work of the Christian Commission is still greatly needed. More than a hundred and fifty thousand troops will remain after the regiments now returning shall have been disbanded. For many months to come the men will be exposed to the hardships and perils of a trying climate. The temptations will not be less, but rather greater when the men are camped on distant soil.

—We are sorry to learn that the condition of Sister T. A. Abbott, of this city, does not improve. The report from Brother Abbott to-day is that she is no better.

—RAILROAD RATES TO STATE CONVENTION.—The Mo. Pac., M. K. & T., Fort Scott & Memphis, and the Port Arthur System, which includes the Omaha, Kansas City & Eastern, Omaha & St. Louis, and the Kansas City & Northern Connection, together with their line south of Kansas City, or that portion of it that is in Missouri, have granted a rate of one fare for the round trip from all Missouri points. Tickets on sale Sept. 26-27, good to return until and including Sept. 30. All other roads have refused any concessions whatever, and you will buy local tickets to the nearest point on any of the above roads, and thence into Nevada, at the one fare for the round trip. Please see your local agent *at once* if his instructions have been received, and prepare to come for the first day.

T. A. ABBOTT.

—We have recently been informed of a new plan of insurance which has some commendable features. It is based on regular and fixed monthly dues, and having no big rents to pay, no great salaried officers to support and no costly buildings to keep in repair affords a much lower rate to the insured. The monthly dues are fixed by the regular mortuary tables according to age and are expected to meet all liabilities. Medical examinations are required, and only church members in good standing can become applicants for a policy. The organization is called The Mizpah League, with home office 712 Commercial Bldg., this city. The officers are of our substantial business men and there seems to be no apparent reason why this new enterprise should not prosper and prove a blessing to many who cannot reach the cost of a policy in one of the old line companies.

—The Gospel Messenger, Nashville, Tenn., has closed up its career and turned its subscription list over to the Christian Standard, Cincinnati, O.

PERSONAL MENTION.

J. M. Rudy preached at Cedar Rapids, Iowa, on Sept. 11th.

Pastor C. C. Rowlison and wife were duly installed in the Marshalltown pastorate on Sept. 6th. N. A. McConnell and A. M. Haggard, with the city pastors, took part. A fine musical program followed. When we remember that it was prepared for an entirely different kind of reception, apparently solid criticism should be omitted.

W. W. Blalock, of Topeka, Kansas, is in a meeting at Bartlett, Ia.

W. B. Crewdson, of Corning, Ia., is seriously ill.

Leander Lane, late of Davenport, Ia., has taken the work at Fairfield, Ia., until January 1st. For several years Bro. Lane was the Minnesota secretary and is one of the most experienced and valued men.

Mrs. B. D. Holbrook, of Onawa, such a woman as Paul would not forget to mention, has returned from her summer vacation in Pittsburg and beyond.

L. F. McCray is in a meeting at Lehigh, Ia.

D. A. Hunter is in a meeting at Minto, Ia.

A. McLean, Corresponding Secretary of the Foreign Missionary Society, called at this office on last Tuesday on his way to Columbia, where he is to spend four days in a course of lectures at the Bible College. He is looking well and speaks encouragingly of the coming report of the Foreign Society at Chattanooga.

Dr. B. B. Tyler and his wife, who have been spending the last few weeks at Colorado Springs, Colorado, expect to reach this city on Wednesday morning, of this week, on their way to Lexington, Ky., and later to the Chattanooga Convention.

H. G. Bennett, said be one of the most promising young preachers of Eureka, Ill., on Sept. 6, was married to Miss Bettie Button, of West Port, Ky., George A. Miller, of the First Church, Covington, Ky., officiating.

We have received cards announcing the 50th anniversary of the marriage of Dr. and Mrs. J. B. Crane, of Waynesboro, Va., September 17th. Dr. Crane and his wife have our congratulations on the attainment of so distant a mile post on the matrimonal highway.

Bert Van Meter, of Belle Plain, Ia., and Miss Lee, of Des Moines, formerly of West Liberty, were united in marriage on Sept. 6th; J. H. Wright, of Osceola, officiating.

W. T. Hilton, of Beloit, Kan., has begun the publication of a monthly church paper called the Kansas Evangelist. The appearance of the first uumber is pleasing to the eye and ear.

The Christian Index says that James Small, of Oakland, Cal., is to assist T. W. McDonald in a protracted meeting at the Highland Park Church, Des Moines, Iowa, beginning October, first week.

J. S. Myers' initial sermon at the First Christian Church, Philadelphia, Pa., Sunday, Sept. 4th, was based on Rom. 1:16, and a brief of the same appeared in the Public Ledger, of that city, the following day. The paper states that he was heard by a large audience.

The Vermont Avenue Christian Church, Washington, D. C., recently observed with appropriate services the 23rd anniversary of the installation of its pastor, F. D. Power. There were present of the original congregation, 23 years ago, but ten persons. His sermon was a review of the progress and events of the year and an exhortation to greater diligence and faithfulness.

The editor of this paper and his family are expected at their home in this city the latter part of this week, or first of next. They have had a pleasant and profitable vacation at Macatawa, Mich.; that is, such a vacation as usually falls to the lot of a busy editor.

Dr. W. E. Garrison, arrived at Macatawa, Mich., last Saturday, after a delightful trip through England. By his courtesy his readers as well as himself have enjoyed his trip. His "Wheeling Through England" series of letters have called out many expressions of appreciation and many fine compliments on their literature, which we take the liberty here to mention, but of which as yet we presume he has not learned.

W. W. H.

P. J. Dickerson called at this office on last Friday on his way to the district convention at DuQuoin, Ill. Prof. Dickerson has been spending the summer in Colorado, but is going to Alma to take charge of the Christian Industrial College at that place. He also informs us that the Bible department of that school will be in charge of Thomas Munnell, recently of Christian University, Canton, Mo.

J. S. Hughes is out with his new lecture on John of Patmos. Churches thinking of a lecture or lecture course should note this. Bro. Hughes' address is Station O, Chicago.

H. B. Cöen, of Mt. Ephriam, Ohio, can be had to assist in protracted meetings as a singing evangelist after Oct. 14th.

Dr. W. T. Moore, President of the Bible College, Columbia, Mo., has just returned from England. This, it is said, makes his thirty-third trip to Europe. He is reported as saying that he found the feeling of friendship toward the United States stronger than ever before.

J. P. Parker writes us from Delta, Col., that his wife died Aug. 22nd, and that he will return to Charleston, Ill.

W. G. Smith, after two years service for the church at New Castle, Ind., has resigned to take effect Nov. 1st.

Jas. S. Helm, a singing evangelist, of Marshall, Mo., would be glad to assist any preacher or church in a protracted meeting.

G. W. Hamilton writes that he has resigned his engagement with the church at Galena, Mo., on account of inadequate support, and desires another field.

The report read by Earle Wilfley, pastor of the church at Wabash, Ind., on the occasion of the beginning of his third year is an encouraging one. The anniversary services, sermon and songs were appropriate, interesting and impressive. Bro. Wilfley has an extended acquaintance and influece in that city, being loved and respected by all.

The sixtieth anniversary of the birth of J. W. Ingram, of Pasadena, Cal., was unexpectedly celebrated August 31st by the uninvited presence of about 100 members of the church for which he preaches. It is needless to add that the evening was most pleasantly spent and long to be remembered. One especially pleasant feature of the occasion was the presentation in the name of the church of a fine morocco-bound teacher's Bible. The presentation speech was made by W. H. Shell, of Washington, D. C., who was present.

Railroad Rates.

The Western Passenger Association has granted a rate of one and one-third fare, round trip, to the gateways of the Central Association, on the Certificate plan, to the Chattanooga Convention, Oct. 13-21, 1898.

Those coming from the Western Passenger Association will pay full fare to the gateway of the Central Traffic Association, and from there will get round trip tickets to Chattanooga and return, at the rate of one fare for the round trip. When you pay full fare take a certificate for the same, and after having it signed at Chattanooga you will be returned from the gateway at which it was purchased to your home for one-third fare.

Please notice that those coming from the Western Passenger Association purchase tickets twice, one at the home station for which they will take a certificate, and the second at the point where they reach the bounds of the Central Traffic Association, where they will buy round-trip tickets at the one-fare rate.

Our convention at Chattanooga promises to be the most interesting in all our history. Preparations have been making for months that it shall be the strongest Convention we have ever held. The brethren at Chattanooga have had it on their hearts the entire year, and have made the most ample preparations for the successful entertainment of this Convention.

In behalf of the Boards we desire to extend the invitation for a general gathering of the loyal Disciples of our Lord and Savior. Let us say in our hearts, "I was glad when they said unto me, Let us go unto the house of our Lord."

Come to the Convention at Chattanooga, October 13th to 21st, 1898.

BENJ. L. SMITH, Cor. Sec.
American Missionary Society.

orrespondence.

English Topics.

SPURGEON LOVE-LETTERS.

; been issued this week which will ing sensation throughout the whole rld. It is the second volume of geon's autobiography. Four vol- appear in all, so that now the 'Life of Spurgeon'' is half com- ery many respects this second in- superior to the first. The greatest reachers was not in any sense a n a lad and, therefore, the first in many respects tame and disap- t now that the work treats of his od and the real achievement of his me, all is full of the most absorb- . What must gratify and perhaps ny of the loving friends of the re- eloved subject of the work is the reserve on the part of the devoted e indefatigable private secretary intly editing the autobiography. ers of this volume form one of the ating of realistic romances ever public, for they give in open and letail the history of the ''love, d marriage'' of C. H. Spurgeon hompson. Nothing could exceed and delicate style in which this elated. Miss Thompson saw her nd for the first time on the Sunday ached his first sermons in London, rk Street Baptist Chapel. ''I do t my first introduction to him,'' purgeon. ''It is probable that he , as to many others, on that same ening; but when the final arrange- made for him to occupy the New pulpit, with a view to the perma- ate, I used to meet him occasionally e of our mutual friends, Mr. and , and I sometimes went to hear him had not at that time made any open f religion, though I was brought to d of a Savior under the ministry of . Bergne, of the Poultry Chapel, ar before Mr. Spurgeon came to He preached one Sunday evening t, 'The Word is nigh thee, even in and in thy heart' (Romans 10:8), at service I date the dawning of the n my soul.'' Mrs. Spurgeon then e afterwards became alarmed at the herself to coldness and backslid- ch dark condition she, by a great ght the counsel of Mr. William cousin by marriage. ''He may Ir. Spurgeon about me,'' she pro- t one day I was greatly surprised from the new pastor an illustrated 'Pilgrim's Progress,' in which he this inscription: 'Miss Thompson, s for her progress in the blessed from C. H. Spurgeon, April 20,

SPURGEON AS A LOVER.

striking thing about the love-letters iven in this volume is the combina- and unaffected religious sentiment affection. Spurgeon had the gift, t always allied with sincere religious of applying the higher sanctions in of the most absolute propriety to ntimate human ties. He did not trivial things with scriptural dic- ould write to his sweetheart about ity of his preaching with a genuine appealed to her, and yet with a re- satisfies fastidious taste. Even to nplace phrases which garnish the he never failed to give a certain his own abounding vitality and love Here are two letters, one from each

DOUBLY-DEAR SUSIE:—How much njoyed in each other's society! It seems almost impossible that I could either have conferred or received so much happiness. I feel now, like you, very low in spirits; but a sweet promise in Ezekiel cheers me, ''I will give thee the opening of the mouth in the midst of them.'' (This was in reference to the preparation of sermons for the Sabbath.—S. S.) Surely, my God has not forgotton me. Pray for me, my love, and may our united petitions win a blessing through the Savior's merits! Let us take heed of putting ourselves too prominently in our own hearts, but let us commit our way unto the Lord. ''What I have in my own hand I usually lose,'' said Martin Luther; ''but what I put into God's hand is still, and ever will be, in my possession.'' I need not send my love to you, for, though absent in body, my heart is with you still, and I am your much-loved and ardently loving,

C. H. S.

P. S.—The devil has barked again in the Essex Standard. It contains another letter. Never mind; when Satan opens his mouth he gives me an opportunity of ramming my sword down his throat.

75 *Dover Road, April*, '55.

To this letter Miss Thompson sent the following reply:

MY DEAREST:—I thank you with warm and hearty thanks for the note just received. It is useless for me to attempt to tell you how much happiness I have had during the past week. Words are but cold dishes on which to serve up thoughts and feelings which come warm and glowing from the heart. I should like to express my appreciation of all the tenderness and care you have shown towards me during this happy week; but I fear to pain you by thanks for what I know was a pleasure to you. I expect your thoughts have been busy to-day about the ''crown jewels.'' (He had talked of preaching on this subject.—S. S.) The gems may differ in size, color, richness and beauty, but even the smallest are ''precious stones,'' are they not?

That Standard certainly does not bear ''Excelsior'' as its motto; nor can ''Good-will to men'' be the device of its floating pennon, but it matters not; we know that all is under control of One of whom Asaph said, ''Surely, the wrath of man shall praise thee; the remainder of wrath thou shalt restrain '' May his blessing rest in an especial manner on you to-night, my dearly-beloved; and on the approaching Sabbath, when you stand before the great congregation, may you be ''filled with the fullness of God!'' Good-night. Fondly and faithfully yours, SUSIE.

St. Ann's Terrace, April, '55.

COURTING AT THE CRYSTAL PALACE.

Surely, the most beautiful building on earth is the Crystal Palace! I have taken many American visitors to that fairy land at Sydenham, six miles from London, and they have generally agreed with my opinion that it is unequaled by anything in the world. How many loving hearts have plighted their troth under that graceful roof of iron and glass! It was there that young Spurgeon and his affianced chiefly courted. ''After the close of the Thursday evening service there would be a whispered word to me in the aisle, 'Three o'clock to-morrow,' which meant that, if I would be at the Palace by that hour, 'somebody' would meet me at the Crystal Fountain.'' It was during a walk in the Palace, on the very day when it was opened, that the secret of the two hearts was mutually confessed. Spurgeon adopted a peculiar way of revealing his love. While sitting with a large party of friends at the inauguration of the glorious building, waiting for the procession to pass by, he handed the young lady a book into which he had been occasionally dipping. It was Martin Tupper's once famous ''Proverbial Philosophy.'' Pointing to some particular lines, he said, ''What do you think of the poet's suggestion in those verses?'' The lines were in the opening of the chapter on ''Marriage,'' beginning, ''Seek a good wife of thy God, for she is the best gift of his providence,'' etc. Full of profound pathos is the chapter in which Mrs. Spurgeon tells of the ripening of the perfect love between the two. But an episode comes in which shows how true it is that the course of love never runs with absolute smoothness. Mrs. Spurgeon tells how she learned a severe lesson.

THE LESSON OF THE GREAT PREACHER'S BETROTHED.

''This is the story,'' says she. ''He was to preach at the large hall of the ''Horns,'' Kennington, which was not very far from where we then resided. He asked me to accompany him, and dined with us at St. Ann's Terrace, the service being in the afternoon. We went together, happily enough, in a cab, and I well remember trying to keep close by his side as we mingled with the mass of people thronging up the staircase. But by the time we had reached the landing he had forgotten my existence; the burden of the message he had to proclaim to that crowd of immortal souls was upon him, and he turned into the small side door where the officials were awaiting him, without for a moment realizing that I was left to struggle as best I could with the rough and eager throng around me. At first I was utterly bewildered and then, I am sorry to confess, I was angry. I at once returned home and told my grief to my gentle mother, who tried to soothe my ruffled spirit and to bring me to a better state of mind. She wisely reasoned that my chosen husband was no ordinary man, and that his whole life was absolutely dedicated to God and his service, and that I must never hinder him by trying to put myself first in his heart. Presently, after much good and loving counsel, my heart grew soft, and I saw that I had been very foolish and willful; and then a cab drew up at the door and dear Mr. Spurgeon came running into the house in great excitement, calling, ''Where's Susie? I have been searching for her everywhere and cannot find her; has she come back by herself?'' My dear mother took him aside and told him all the truth; and I think, when he realized the state of things, she had to soothe him also, for so innocent was he at heart at having offended me in any way, that he must have felt I had done him an injustice in thus doubting him.'' W. DURBAN.

43 *Rock Road, South Tottenham, London, August* 26, '98.

New York Letter.

The thirty-seventh annual convention of the New York Christian Missionary Society and Ministerial Association, held at the 169th Street Church of the Disciples of Christ, in New York City, Aug. 29th to Sept. 2nd, was one of the best in the history of our work in the Empire State. In fact, Dr. W. A. Belding, one of the veterans of the cause, said it was *the* best, and he has a better right to speak on that point than any one else, as he has attended the state conventions from the very beginning. The preliminary meeting was held on Monday evening, Aug. the 29th, and though it was not as largely attended as other sessions, many delegates not having arrived, it was, nevertheless, a delightful meeting. The ladies of the church had provided light refreshments for those coming in on Monday; after they had served them in the lecture-room, an informal reception was held in which quite a number expressed words of greeting. Tuesday was occupied by the Ministerial Association, presided over by Bro. S. B. Culp, of Eagle Mills. In the forenoon Bro. D. H. Patterson, of Auburn, read a spicy and suggestive paper on ''Some Perils of the Modern Preacher.'' Not having space here to give a definite idea of it we can only say it would do good if published, in part, at least, in the CHRISTIAN-EVANGELIST. To the regret of all Bro. F. P. Arthur, of Rochester, was not present to present his paper on ''The Preacher's Personal Preparation,'' for we very much wished to hear him on that vital topic. ''Some Modern Books of Value to the Preacher'' was the theme ably discussed by Bro. W. W. Norton, of Niagara Falls, and many others followed him with timely suggestions. In the afternoon Bro. E. Richard Edwards, pastor at Syracuse, delivered a good address on ''How to Evangelize Our Cities,'' expressing among other things the opinion that we might learn some valuable lessons from our Methodist brethren in the matter of arousing sinners to a sense of their need of salvation. He thinks this one of the weakest points in our methods of evangelism.

Bro. J. M. Morris, our state evangelist, was for the first time in a New York convention, and led a helpful conference on "Pastoral Work," making emphatic the wisdom of a minister so keeping a record of his work and the names of people contemplating obedience to Christ, together with possible avenues of approach to them, that he might turn over to his successor in office, or to an evangelist coming to hold him a meeting, and thereby do much to reach and redeem men to Christ. Bro. L. C. McPherson, of Jefferson Street, Buffalo, conducted an inspiring "Parliament on Soul-winning Methods," in which a number of valuable and timely suggestions were brought forth. The sermon Tuesday evening, by Bro. B. I. Denham, of North Tonawanda, on "God in Evolution," was replete with vigorous thought and was delivered in Bro. Denham's popular style, and though some of the brethren apparantly did not accept his exegsis altogether, all seemed to listen with closest attention.

The missionary convention proper, presided over by F. W. Norton, opened on Wednesday morning; the first session being taken up with reports of the past year and the president's address. Compelled to be absent that morning at a funeral service, we missed the reports, but can say they showed one of the best if not *the very* best year's work in the history of the Empire State Disciples. The board is sustaining Bro. J. M. Morri sas state evangelist, and we are pleased to say the ministers with whom he has held meetings in the state speak in the very highest terms of him as a Christian and as an evangelist. He is faithful to his work and loyal to his Lord, and all who met him at the convention were delighted with him. He occupied the pulpit of the 169th Street Church on Lord's day evending previous to the convention and gave us a clear, strong, inspiring discourse on "Man's Conscious Need of a Redeemer." We predict for Bro. Morris a successful ministry in New York state. The board is helping sustain Bro. E. S. Muckley as pastor at Watertown where under peculiar difficult conditions he is doing a splendid work. His patience and continuous plodding are inspiring. Bro. C. C. Crawford also is partially sustained by the state board at Elmira. His field, too, is fraught with disadvantages, but he stands by his work like the hero he is. A number of other points, such as Albany, Newbury, Poukeepsie, Binghampton and Greenpoint were recommended to the board for favorable consideration. A lively discussion took place regarding the possible establishment of a mission in Albany, the capital of the state, but nothing definite was done.

I must not fail to mention the excellent work of Bro. John R. Tolar, Jr., in the Second Church, Rochester. The First Church, on Howell Street, in this city, is a child of the New York Christian Missionary Society and was planted by Bro. O. G. Hertzog, now of Hiram, Ohio, and has been watered by the faithful ministry of F. P. Arthur, who about two years ago launched the mission, which since has been organized into the Second Church, who last winter called Bro. Tolar, a recent graduate of Bethany College, to be their pastor. He is supported by his father, the church and state board. His work has grown so rapidly that now the question of enlarging their house of worship is forced upon them.

In the address of Bro. Morris, on New York as a mission field, illustrated as it was by a map showing the location of churches and hopeful points where work might be started, our beloved commonwealth seemed to cry out to us like the man of Macedonia of old, for Christian help. Bro. Morris suggested that we should employ two men in the state; one to plant churches in the cities and foster them one by one until they could sustain a pastor, and the other to do general evangelizing among the churches.

Bro. Benj. L. Smith, Corresponding Secretary of the American Christian Missionary Society, was with us and helped much in counsel and discourse. His sermon on the text, "What is in thine house?" was very fine, as was also his address on "The Work of the American Christian Missionary Society." This society puts $500 into the New York field and Bro. Smith considers it money wisely spent. We were also favored with a very pleasant visit from Sister Smith and their two little daughters, Josephine and Dorethy. They stopped at our little home during the convention. They brought sunshine and gladness with them and left the fragrance of pleasant memories when they went away.

Bro. W. J. Wright, of Washington City, came up and made the address for the Forign Christian Missionary Society. His was a strong plea. The foreign work was ably represented. Since hearing Bro. Wright we do not marvel at the success of his work at Washington. Sister Helen E. Moses, of Indianapolis, and Secretary of the Bible Chair Committe of the Christian Woman's Board of Missions, cheered our hearts and instructed our minds with eloquent words; she made two excellent addresses.

Among others from beyond our own state, whose presence and greetings were spiritually helpful to us, were Bro. E. J. Teagarden and Sisters Teagarden, Baily and Swift, of Danbury, Con. (Bro. T., the beloved pastor at Danbury, gave us one of the clearest and strongest discourses of the convention); Bro. Phillips, of Boston; Bro. S. M. Hunt, of Springfield, Mass.; Bro. W. H. McKane, J. A. Goodfeish, Plainfield, N. J.; E. M. Flinn, Haverhill, Mass.; O. G. Hertzog, Hiram, Ohio (who also occupied our pulpit Lord's day after the convention, giving us an able discourse); Sister Norrish, of Sayre, Penn., and others were with us.

Among the new ministers in the convention were Dr. J. E. Powell, of Williamsville; Joseph Tisdale, of Tulley; W. C. Payne, of West 56th Street; F. W. Troy, of Sterling Place, Brooklyn; E. C. Harris, of Pittstown. Bro. C. E. Caston represented the CHRISTIAN-EVANGELIST and Christian Publishing Co., with a fine display of books and papers in the lecture-room.

All the officers on the state missionary board were re-elected unanimously and the policy of the last year was endorsed and encouraged for the year to come. It was decided to change the time of the convention in the future so as to open on Wednesday before the last Lord's day in September. This no doubt is a nice change, though a few, especially school-teachers, may be deprived from attending, yet cooler weather usually comes with the last of September, and and with it more comfort. It was a good time to suggest such a change, for old King Sol was exercising his great power upon our delegates and making them swelter all through the convention; the people were in humor for a change.

The Christian Woman's Board of Missions held one of its very best sessions, reporting gross receipts for the year of $2,500 and a little over. This is considerably ahead of the brethren in the state. Some one said it gave a new meaning to "C.W.B.M."—now it signifies "Can Women Beat Men?" Yes it does—in some places, at some things. Mrs. Dr. R. E. Belding presided with skill. The reports were inspiring, the outlook is full of promise. Mrs. W. C. Payne, of New York, was elected president for the new year. The other officers are all continued in office.

The Christian Endeavor address was made by Bro. J. M. Philputt. The Ministerial Relief conference was conducted by W. J. Wright and the Sunday-school address was delivered by C. M. Kreider.

The place of the next convention was not decided upon, but was left to the state board: C. M. Kreider, B. D. Denham, L. C. McPherson and S. T. Willis.

It is not practicable to speak of all the excellent addresses, good measures and hopeful signs brought before us in this series of conventions, but we wish to say through this let to all who came that the 169th Street Churc grateful for your presence and help. May G bless our New York Christian Missionary S ciety and every phase of the work and all workers in our beloved state!

S. T. WILLIS

1281 *Union Ave.*

Wheeling Through England.

IX.

A week is a short time to devote to the Hig lands of Scotland, but the date of saili approaches with appalling rapidity, and t Highlands must be seen hurriedly if at a Ireland had long since been crowded out of t program, and all hopes of reaching John Groat's House have by this time been aba doned. Still, much may be done in a week the Highlands if only the weather is favorab for the roads through this mountainous cou try are engineered and constructed with a mirable skill. Most Highland scenery composed of forest, mountain and water. T combinations are infinite, but the three el ments are usually present. When you are n riding through a valley looking up at the pea about you, you are riding along a ridge looki out on a wide expanse of mountain, moor a lake. When you are not riding by the side some deep and quiet loch, about which romantic legend could seem too strange to true, you are being ferried in a skiff across o of the same sort, or perchance across son sinuous arm of the sea that winds its w inland until it is lost among the mountain For my part, I know of nothing which mo nearly approximates my ideal of perfection the conditions for bicycling than a gent undulating, shady road by the side of a la and at the foot of a mountain. Such is whee ing in the Highlands, and such, in particula is the ride from Crianlarich, where the la letter was dated and where the first Sunday Scotland was spent, westward to Oban a north along the coast from Oban to Fo William, at the foot of the great Caledonia Canal.

Speaking of ferries, there are no less tha three of them to be crossed between Oban an Fort William. When the Highland ferryma sees a cyclist loom up on the horizon h mental processes, as indicated by the seque are somewhat as follows: "Aha! and oh What have we here? Is it not even a whee man? And are not all wheelmen millionaire for how else could they afford to take bicyc trips? Go to. Is he not our legitimate pre He is minded to cross the ferry. It is wel Shall we not charge him seven prices (for it a godly number), and three more to make it a even ten? Verily, he is delivered into o hand." And so, being a guileless youth, stranger in a strange land and unfamiliar y with the exceeding "canniness" of the Sco we are rowed over the ferry. Perhaps, as Ballachulish, the distance is about a hundre yards, and there are seven other passenge and two trunks in the boat. You hold yo bicycle in your lap to make room. The othe alight, pay their two coppers and depar You ask how much for yourself and wheel, an the answer is: "Ah weel, a suppose a shilli will be aboot richt." The dubiousness of th tone leads you to believe that a reductio might be obtained by argument, but vain th hope. Pay quickly, at the rate of one-bicycle equals-ten-men, and go your way, or it ma be doubled before you can escape.

Fort William, besides being the terminus o one of the finest coast rides a man ever too and the beginning of another grand ride u the "Great Glen of Scotland," following th Caledonian Canal, is the starting-point for th ascent of Ben Nevis, the highest mountain i the British Isles. The ascent can scarcely b called climbing, for there is a well-grade path all the way, but it is a somewhat arduou ıbout six miles from the foot to the for a considerable part of which dis- surface of the path consists of sharp, .es. The view from the top is, when no clouds in the way, a map of West- and. In my case there were clouds in great billowy masses, like an ocean 's, which came seething up from the ow, parting occasionally and shifting ly so that, after all, I had the view in very direction. On the whole, the ather improved than obscured the ıd besides there was the additional ual summer amusement of throwing into a cloud.

ẓ Ben Nevis and Fort William, the ws the line of the Caledonian Canal :, a series of four long and narrow nnected by artificial waterways and communication by boat between iam on the west coast and Inverness ast. It was interesting, and to me ẓ, to find to what a great extent the ers here in the interior continue to r ancient Gælic language. About rths of the people attend church serv- ælic and there are some, though not ıo have no other language. All the however, are now conducted in and it is admitted that the language out. In Wales, on the coastway, e allied Welsh language is still the language of home, market, school ch, it is claimed that the old Celtic in no danger of becoming extinct. th regret that at Inverness our backs ned toward John o' Groat's House southward journey begun toward h, by way of Aberdeen, Dundee, l Stirling. We are no longer among tains, but in a pleasant and prosper- ng country where sheep and tourists, s of revenue, give place to oats, bar- ay. Here is a chance to develop the ər side of the trip somewhat and, roads and no occasion for long stops, easily bring us over two hundred spite of a head wind. We do not ever, to stop a few hours in Aber- city of gray granite, and in Perth. ing Stirling we begin to see that nixture of Highlands and Lowlands, even more marked in Edinburgh. a broad stretch of local, cultivated through which the Forth winds its ray—and that is Lowlands. But sud- re rises from the plain, like a rocky m a calm sea, the great rock on the of which stands Stirling Castle. On the hill is a sheer precipice, on the a gradual incline, and on this slope, ıp to the brink where the castle the historic town of Stirling is built. ngs have lived here since the days of d Wallace, but the personalties which dominant, the names with which to ere, are those of Willam Wallace and ruce. All wheelmen who know (as men do) that a cyclist's regard for a ıt has served him well is second only ection for his immediate family, will e his self-control that is needed to rom speaking a good word for my bicycle in connection with Stirling But of bicycles more anon, when the ne.

urning southward the ride has been a wrestling with head winds, and a ind is in the heavy-weight class when to wrestling. Leaving Stirling the annockburn is soon passed, where the ier Bruce defeated 'thrice their num- English. The wonder of this famous would be diminished if it were known ; (and I suspect it) that the English a wind against them as 'blew at me e field of Bannockburn.' It was even- Edinburgh was reached, not a clear, ning with early stars and a mellow twilight, but cloudy and lowering, with a drift of mist through which the lights of the city struggle with difficulty. Hurrying along, dodging pedestrians and cabs and keeping a sharp lookout for policemen (for I carried no lantern on my wheel), I was half way down Princes Street, the central thoroughfare and chief glory of the city, when a chance glance showed a light far up on the right. Its posi- tion suggested a balloon rather than anything with foundations on the earth, but a second look revealed a faint silhouette of towers against the dull sky, like a city floating in mid-air and capped by a phantom castle. It was the castle rock of Edinburgh rising from the level of the city in sheer cliffs on three sides, and with the streets of the old town sloping up to it on the fourth.

One day in Edinburgh is like one lesson on a violin—hopelessly inadequate. The difference between the two is that the one day here is a delightful experience as far as it goes, and the excruciating part is only the departure. It is perhaps not too much to say that at no place in Great Britain has the sensation of being on historic ground been so strongly marked. Its only competitors would be Oxford and London, and—well, comparisons are odious. At pres- ent we are trying our best to appreciate Edin- burgh. At any rate, if one is content to use superlatives somewhat freely and risk slight inaccuracies, it may be said with substantial correctness that Edinburgh is the most his- toric, the most beautiful and the most drunken city in Great Britain. The latter lamentable characteristic comes by direct succession from the olden times when "everybody did it." Here is an inscription which I copied this morning from a stone tablet over the door of a beershop, in the narrow old street called Cowgate. There is a bas-relief representing two men carrying a beer-barrel between them, and underneath is the devout motto: "O, magnifie the Lord with me and let us exalt his name together. A. D. 1643." Only a few doors down the street, over the door of a house which is now and always has been occupied by a wine merchant, is the pious inscription: "Almighty God, who founded, built and crownd this work with blessings, mak it to abound."

John Knox is the man of action who is most constantly before the mind of the visitor in Edinburgh, but among men of letters Scott is so far pre-eminent here that even Burns be- comes a very distant second. Setting aside the boatman on Loch Katrine and his gratitude to Scott from mercenary reasons—and, hap- pily, he is not a representative of many—there seems to be something unique in the honors paid to Scott in his native land. This is seen in the character of the monuments erected to him. In Glasgow a statue of the novelist and poet stands at the top of a lofty shaft, at the foot of which are the statues of noblemen, statesmen and warriors. In Edinburgh the Scott monument, lofty as a cathedral and graceful as a lily, marks the center of the city, and is its noblest ornament. There are many monuments in Edinburgh, and Scotland's heroes are all present in bronze or marble. But of all these effigies none pleases the Amer- ican like the bronze statue of Abraham Lincoln, which stands as a memorial of the Scottish- American soldiers who fell in our own Civil War.

W. E. GARRISON.

Edinburgh.

Chicago Letter.

Each year marks an increase in the num of Disciples of Christ who attend the sum school of the University of Chicago. Thi partly due to the location of the Universit the great metropolis of the Central States to the attractive features of the work dur the summer quarter of the University, and i partly due to the influence of the Discipl Divinity House, which corporation has rooms, both for general meetings and for cla room work, furnished them free in the Univ sity buildings. The following list may no complete, but it includes most of the stude and visitors among our own brethren: Hi Van Kirk and Erret Gates, Instructors in Divinity House '98-'99; J. Mad Willia Drake University; Hugh McClellan, Shel ville, Ky., N. U.; Henry Minnick, Lub Maine, Butler; C. G. Brelos, Tiffin, Bethany; Austin Hunter, Ada, O., Hir D. J. Marshall, Palmyra, Mo., Universit Missiouri; A. L. Chapman, missionary Turkey, Bethany; B. L. Kershner, Pittsbu Pa.; E. M. Gordon, Mungeli, India; H. Hoover, Bethany; J. R. McIntyre, Drake; W. Allen, Hiram, formerly at Buffalo, N. now preaching for the Ravenswood Church; B. Reynolds, Milligan College; A. L. Johns Ohio Normal University; E. W. Mathe Butler College; S. A. Harker, Irvingt W. F. Barr, W. S. Goode, University Missouri; N. H. Shepherd, Valparaiso, In J. D. Minnick, John Lister, J. L. Dar Little Rock, Bethany. Among the visi have been Profs. B. E. Dean and G. A. Pe ham, of Hiram College; T. N. Calvin, Wa Tex.; W. E. Ellis, Nashville, Tenn.; C. Rowlison, Cedar Rapids, Ia.

***

In the above list are well-known worker

our brotherhood, and as Chicago is already the greatest center for theological seminaries and Bible institutes in the world, the time is not far distant when several hundreds of our best preachers and teachers will be gathered annually in Chicago and its Disciple suburb across the lake known as Macatawa Park. No city in the world offers better advantages to the graduates of our colleges for advanced study in the Bible and methods of church work. Besides the Moody Bible Institute and such social settlements as the University Settlement, the Hull House and the Chicago Commons, there are more than a dozen divinity schools and missionary training schools in Chicago. Some of these, as the Chicago Theological Seminary (Congregational) and the McCormick Theological Seminary (Presbyterian) have each over one million dollars endowment. The Garret Biblical Institute is a part of Northwestern University, an institution controlled by our Methodist brethren, which has even a larger student attendance than the University of Chicago. Most of the work in all these institutions is graduate work. The importance of having the Disciples' Divinity House, where graduate students of our own colleges may form a nucleus, may be seen at a glance by those who understand the situation.

1. It would help solve our problem of city evangelization.

2. It would help solve the problem of adequately supplying the pulpits of our city churches. The best of men cannot build up city churches with country methods.

3. It would in some measure, at least, supply the growing demand among us for trained teachers, editors and authors. While "our literature" in the past, not only supplied the demand of the past but still deserves careful study, there is great need in our ranks for sane, consecrated writers and teachers who understand the conditions of to-day and who will be our leaders in the first quarter of the nineteenth century.

***

How few people realize the great crisis through which we are passing! We need to pray for wisdom from Him who guides the destiny of nations. The sermons of two leading Baptist preachers were reported in one of our metropolitan dailies last Monday. I quote the substance of one sentence from each. "Why should a campaign of one hundred days with a third-class nation make us crazy to abandon a safe national policy to launch upon an unknown sea of international diplomacy?" "Wherever 'Old Glory' has been raised she shall wave forever." But the war with Spain, with its glorious victories, is only an episode in the crisis through which we are passing. Two words may be written over the social, political and religious developments of our day, "Unity" and "Expansion;" or, as the secretary of our Foreign Society would say, "Enlargement." Think of how all parts of the world are touched by a city paper. The Chicago Record had a reporter present at the battle of Manila and paid $1,700 for his cablegram report. The Czar of Russia proposes a Peace Congress one day, and the nations of the earth express themselves against it the next day. God has called the Disciples of Christ to occupy the central place in the most strategic nation on earth. They have been preaching and praying for unity and God is answering their prayers. Shall we fail to learn the lesson of enlargement as a great brotherhood? The Foreign Society is giving us a noble demonstration of expansion. Ten missionaries sent out in one month. What a glorious act of faith and courage! The practical way to answer the above question during September is to push the Church Extension offering.

***

The writer has been absent from Chicago again. A brief visit to the old home in St. Louis County and a brief visit to Indianapolis. Dear mother is growing old. My reader, be kind to the loved ones in the old home. They need your sympathy more than your money. Don't send the dear old mother an occasional money order and think it will satisy the heart that is longing to leap for joy because you are "home again." I stopped long enough in Indianapolis to report the progress of our Bible work in Virginia to the educational committee of the C. W. B. M. I then had the pleasure of bringing Mrs. O. A. Burgess to Chicago with me. We hope the change will enable her to gain her wonted strength. Mrs. Young and I consider it a privilege to have this noble woman visit us. C. A. YOUNG.

438 57 St., Chicago, Ill.

St. Louis Letter.

St. Louis has had a prolonged wave of heat. September opened like an oven! The first Sunday was "a scorcher;" too hot to go to church, to the park, or to stay at home! A heavy shower, but of short duration, fell in the western part of the city in the afternoon, but this failed to cool the atmosphere. The heat was intense, but a cool wave came on Wednesday last and we are comfortable.

The absent pastors have all returned and the churches are now confronted with a new campaign of work. Some of the churches have not had regular preachers for the summer, although most of them have had preaching regularly. I am speaking now of the churches of Christ in St. Louis.

F. G. Tyrrell, the popular pastor of the Central Christian Church was in his pulpit again Sept. 4th, and delighted his audience with one of his characteristically "Tyrrellian" discourses, a good account of which appeared in the St. Louis Republic on Monday morning following. He is fresh from the North and full of new life from the life-giving energy of the lake and the woods.

The First Church had its house swept and garnished during the summer, and on Bro. Fannon's return from a trip to Iowa gave him a warm reception. The house has been beautifully overhauled and is now a delightful resort for lovers of God more than lovers of pleasure. Bro. Fannon came back and plunged headlong into hard work. He is always animating and vigorous, but in his absence he managed to still more deeply intensify his already highly developed religious nature in religious work, and began the new campaign with a greater determination to do greater things for the Master than ever.

Mt. Cabanne Church has abated nothing for the hot season. This church comes about as near keeping an open house for all the year as any of our churches in this or any other city. Dr. Dungan has been found so full of Bible knowlege and so willing to impart it that he has become a veritable well of salvation for the people. He is in constant demand by his church in its various activities and is too good-natured to refuse much that is asked of him not ordinarily within the supposed range of a pastor's duties in hot weather.

Beulah is one of our younger churches, and its pastor, Bro. Smith, was absent a month visiting his mother and friends in "Old Virginia," but the church did not suffer thereby. It has in it some of the non-weather, non-killable elements, and persisted in keeping an open house and in growing during the summer. Bro. Smith reports that the outlook for that church was never brighter, and the church reports that he never preached better.

The Fourth Church kept its pendulum swinging all summer. Bro. Kern is too seriously in earnest in what he does to permit even of the appearance of play. And, lest his pastoral duties might not be sufficient, or for some other good reason, some months ago he with his good wife took up the study of medicine; which, by the way, would not be a an unprofitable equipment for any city pastor. Bro. Kern reports the church ready for active service in the fall campaign.

The Second Church still stands at its pos duty as a sentinel in the presence of a g enemy. Bruce Wolverton has been preach earnestly and faithfully during the sum and has been awarded with frequent additi to the church. But this church is peculi surrounded; has great burdens to carry will need more help from other than its resources if it is to hold the fort in the another year. It has a good plant, is loc in a needy district and deserves to be uphel its fight against sin.

Compton Heights has been trying preach but it is not pleased to continue the experie It has now secured a pastor in the pe of S. B. Moore, of Galesburg, Ill., and putting its house in order for a new eff This church has lots of young energy a good general will certainly lead them to g accomplishments in that new field. Thi one of the live churches of the city.

West End Church has ventured on so thing new, but long needed by other chur in this city—an assistant pastor. So muc Bro. Bartholomew's time is taken up in b ness matters that, at his own request, West has been called to assist him in chu work. Three of our churches, the First, C tral and Cabanne, have each a lady mission employed, but this is the first of our chur in the city, to the writer's knowledge, to ploy an assistant pastor. The result will watched with interest.

The Fifth Church still lives. For years existence seemed to be a question of doubt, it persisted in living. The doubting ones t concluded that if it wouldn't die it ought t killed, but still it lives. It was voted dead the city mission board a few years ago and property advertised for sale, but it still li It was called "a rat hole" and "a sink ho er unpleasant names, but it has survived .. The Lord sent them the right man and spered, and that man is W. F. Hamann. no. preacher is better respected than amann and no church more deserving of for perseverance under trying circum- than the Fifth Church of this city.

weeks ago our brethren in Carondelet a tent that had been pitched by others an a meeting. Bro. Fannon and Bro. . began preaching there and have awakened considerable interest.

preachers resumed their Monday meet- st week. Bro. Fannon was elected it and a new program will be prepared ew committee for the fall and winter rs.

quarterly meeting of the Christian or Societies was held at the First , Sept. 5th at 8 P. M. These meetings en conducted for several years and have a fixture. They are usually well d, full of animation and a season of ng from each other's presence.

B. U. I.

Texas Letter.

is an immense agricultural territory, ne crop conditions are of general inter- he Dallas News, a great newspaper, is posted on this subject. From its I learn that wheat shows an increased and yield this year, and the corn crop argest ever raised, being fully twenty- cent. larger than last year. The cotton o, is immense. In the coast district it ction smaller than in '97, but in all ctions the yield is much larger. In the st there is an increase of ten per cent., central part the increase is eleven per n the northwest it is twelve per cent., e eastern section mounts up to fifteen t., which will foot up a grand total of than 3,500,000 bales. Moral: If you gry or naked, come to Texas.

g Saul," by J. Breckenridge Ellis, of "In the Days of Jehu," is a hand- ew volume of 281 pages. Israel's first made to stand out in a clear, simple the author, so that the reading of him the reading of a well-written novel. le of Mr. Ellis does much to make the pleasure. It combines simplicity, di- , beauty and force, and you follow him conscious effort. His familiarity with ne enables him to select the leading n the story without too much time on The Christian Publishing Company, is, sustains its fine reputation in the nce of this handsome book.

Practical Christian, edited by J. C. our Houston pastor, becomes a semi- . It is a genuine pleasure to note this tial evidence of prosperity.

. Hawkins has decided to leave New . This is to be regretted. But this s somewhat atoned for in the fact that are turned toward Texas.

outlook for Add-Ran University was etter. Good crops and easy times will our people to patronize this fine school eserves. Special arrangements have ade so that the board, lodging and e for preacher boys will not be more ght dollars per month.

F. King, after two years of good work on, goes to Hillsboro. This is one of tegic points of the state, and just such as King is needed there.

. Marshall and wife, I am sorry to say, he service of our state board and locate lor. I say "and wife" advisedly, for as good, if not a little better, than he. tulations to Taylor. Bro. M. recently a meeting at Sadler, where he organized ay-school and dedicated their new house. . Worden reports encouragingly from Eighteen months ago there were only mbers; now there are fifty-eight, with house almost paid for.

C. L. Cole, E. H. Kellar and Bro. Drew have been at work at Farmer's Branch, and henceforth we are to have a church at that place.

Blooming Grove church sent her preacher, J. B. Sweeney, to Mortens. A church of thirty-five was organized and the money for a good house was raised. Good.

Foreign Missions are growing among our people. Total receipts to date for this year, $117,324.03. A larger number of churches, Sunday-schools and Christian Endeavor Societies have fellowship in the work than ever before. Almost one thousand new churches on the roll and nearly as many Sunday-schools. Individual offerings and bequests have decreased, but the Annuity plan is increasing wonderfully. This is a new phase of the work, and yet it has reached $31,490. Let all who possibly can go to the Chattanooga convention and hear the reports from the mission fields everywhere.

M. M. Davis.

833 Live Oak St., Dallas, Texas.

Jacksonville (Fla.) Letter.

Three months ago, when we accepted the call of the Christian Church in this city, little did we think what was before us. We expected at that time to do nothing more during the hot months of summer than to maintain our regular services with decreased audiences, but the assembling of the 7th Army Corps here with its thirty thousand men, placed an open door before us, and gave opportunities for work we little dreamed of. During the early days of this encampment the Army and Navy Christian Commission began its work in the corps, with the aim of providing for the soldiers social, physical, intellectual and religious privileges, thus giving much relief from the tedium, discomforts and temptations of camp and campaign life; and with an earnest endeavor to lead the men to Christ. During the months of June, July and August, the resident ministers of this city usually take their vacations, going North to mountain and seaside resorts, leaving their churches either closed a greater part of that time or depending upon social services. We found this summer, with but two or three exceptions, thus to be the case. This circumstance alone vastly increases the duties and necessary labor of those remaining at home, as there are almost constant calls for the performance of ministerial work even from many hitherto unknown to us. Added to this we have had strong and pressing invitations to aid in the work among the soldiers, and receiving almost countless appeals from the parents and friends of the "boys," soon found ourselves not only deeply interested in the religious work in the Seventh Corps, but almost before we knew it fully installed. I have delivered a number of addresses in the various divisions, hunted up and become acquainted with a large number of those whose names have been sent by anxious parents and friends, visited regularly the different hospitals, written letters home for the sick boys, spoke encouragely to them and scattered literature among the convalescents, especially aiming to see that all physically able to read had a copy of the New Testament. The Christian Commission has quite a number of efficient and earnest workers here, holding almost nightly services. Yesterday the head of the Commission here sent for me and in behalf of the Commission thanked me for the interest I have manifested, and said he was instructed to supply me with all the New Testaments or other literature I needed in my visits. I have preferred to carry with me to the sick beds of these dear boys the Word of God, as some of the tracts and papers sent are, in my private judgment, of much less value. Yesterday afternoon, Sept. 1st, I spent entirely in the Second Division Hospital where there are more than seven hundred sick volunteers. The afternoon was spent in writing letters home to mothers and friends for the sick ones, distributing reading-matter and speaking words of cheer. A great many of these men are convalescing, while others are nearing the borderland, and in the delirium of fever are calling the names of their dear ones they will nevermore see this side the eternal world. May God sustain the loved ones at home who have been called upon and will yet be called upon to mourn the loss of some noble boy! Every regiment here has its chaplain and usually they are busy men. I have in my rounds met them and have found them Christian gentlemen; but some of them have been ill themselves, and one or two have bee compelled to go away on account of ill-health.

Regular services are held in the various regiments by the chaplains, who are more than glad to have aid from the outside.

Very few of the Seventh Corps want to go to Cuba, and the disinclination seems to be growing. The tedious delay of months in camp, with the sickness prevailing among the men and the prospects of active service removed have had a tendency to make the boys believe their mission to be at an end, and many of them long to be mustered out ond desire to return to more congenial occupations and better methods of of living.

The little work that I am daily doing is on my part purely a work of Christian duty and privilege. I have no appointment other than that from my Master, and if I have but added my mite to the alleviation of one suffering, or been the humble instrument of enlisting one volunteer for the army of the Lord, I am amply repaid and rejoice; but I must admit I have just been in a position all this summer to fail to see the glory, or at least much of it, that we read about anent this war. The work in our congregational line moves encouragely. We have omitted no service during the summer. I preach at the Fourth Virginia camp tonight, Sept. 2nd.

T. H. Blenus.

Jacksonville, Florida.

Notes and News.

Good day yesterday and more than raised our apportionment for Church Extension. The Olivia church makes an offering once each month for missions. Wife and daughter doing well at this writing.

Olivia, Minn. DAVID HUSBAND.

Special dispatch to the CHRISTIAN-EVANGELIST from M. G. E. Bennett, Des Moines, Ia., Sept. 5th, which was received too late for last week's paper, says: "Church Extension aided Villisca; we gratefully reciprocate with full apportionment."

David Walk, in his report of the Christian Chinese Mission School, Los Angeles, Cal., for the month of August, says:

Two of the pupils were baptized during the month and one, Jeu Joe Wah, will sail for his native land next week as a missionary to his own people. The field of his immediate labors will be in the city of Hoy Yuen, District of Shun Ning Province of Canton, Southern China. He is well equipped for the service whereunto he is called and the prayers of all God's people are earnestly invoked in his behalf.

His credentials on the part of the Church of Christ, under whose auspices he goes forth, are signed by Elders B. F. Coulter, W. J. A. Smith and David Walk, and on behalf of the state by United States Internal Revenue Collector Francisco and United States Senator Stephen M. White. These last-named signatures will insure him against annoyance or detention by the authorities either here or in China, and our thanks are due Messrs. White and Francisco for the cheerfulness with which they responded to our request, as well as for the flattering character of their respective testimonials.

Five new scholars have been enrolled during the month, the prospects of the mission grow brighter with each day, and with an increase of efficient teachers there will be a corresponding increase in attendance of these sons of the Orient. We thank God and take courage.

To the Clergy of Missouri.

At a meeting of the State Board of Charities and Corrections held in the capitol at Jefferson City, on September 5th, 1898, the following resolution was offered by Miss Perry, of St. Louis, and unanimously passed by the board:

Whereas, Prison Sunday has been observed more or less, in all the Northern states, but particularly in New York, Massachusetts and Michigan.

Resolved, That the State Board of Charities and Corrections, of Missouri, earnestly request all the clergy of this state to set apart the Fourth Sunday in October as "Prison Sunday," and to preach a sermon on that day bearing upon some phase of prison life.

GOVERNOR LON V. STEPHENS, Pres.
A. E. ROGERS, Sec.

Chattanooga Chair Car.

To the brethren of Illinois who expect to attend the Chattanooga Convention: The church at Spingfield, Illinois, has made arrangements to charter a special reclining chair car which will go through without change from Springfield to Chattanooga by way of the Queen and Crescent Route, through Louisville or Cincinnati, as may be determined. The arrangement, however, is on the condition that at least fifty persons shall go from Springfield. The advantages of going in a special car are many. Besides adding to the pleasure of the trip the necessity of changing will be avoided and the advantages of a reclining chair car affords practically the accommodations of a sleeper without extra charge. The rate will be one-half fare, and the car will start at 7 P. M., either Wednesday or Thursday evening, October 12th or 13th, and arrive at Chattanooga at 7 o'clock on the following evening, giving a day trip through the mountains. The church at Springfield extends a cordial invitation to all delegates in Central Illinois to come to Springfield and take advantage of the privilege of the special car. *If you can join the company, please drop a card at once* to the pastor of the Springffeld Christian Church.

J. ELWOOD LYNN.

The Chattanooga Convention.

The time of our National Convention is drawing near. We should have the largest and most enthusiastic gathering in the history of our work. Every year these conventions should grow in volume and power. To this end we urge the brethren everywhere to come. Your presence will swell the attendance, and with the multitude come the waves of enthusiasm and the shout of victory. It is in the hearts of the brethren to make this a great convention. We urge you in the name of a great brotherhood to talk about it in your churches, Sunday-schools, C. W. B. M. Auxiliaries and C. E. Societies. In every one of these select one or more delegates to attend the convention. Don't fail to do this, as we want every church in the brotherhood to be represented in these meetings. Again we ask you to announce the time and place in the secular papers in your community; this will bring the convention prominently before the people. M. D. CLUBB, Chairman.

Chattanooga the Convention City.

Chattanooga possesses special attractions as a convention city. Its transportation facilities are unrivaled. Its entertainment accommodations are adequate to any occasion. The scenery which surrounds the city is rarely equaled, never surpassed. Its historic associations are dear to every patriotic heart. A splendid convention auditorium, with all modern appointments, bearing a seating capacity of 5,000, is at the service of all conventions meeting in the city. It is not strange that Chattanooga has come to be known as the convention city. She has successfully entertained some large gatherings in recent years. At the dedication of the National Military Park, there were 50,000 visitors during the week and as many as 30,000 in one day. The next large assembly to meet here was the International Epworth League, in 1895. There were 10,000 delegates and visitors present. The Southern Baptist Association came next, with a large and enthusiastic delegation. Last year the Baptist Young People's Union were here 4,000 strong. All of these were loud in their praises of Chattanooga's hospitality. In October the General Convention meets here, and all may be assured that Chattanooga's good name will not be allowed to suffer. Everything will be done for the comfort and pleasure of the visitors. Reader, make your arrangements to come. Let nothing interfere. You can not afford to miss the delightful fellowship of this great convention. You will return to your home refreshed and strengthened and filled with a deeper realization of the power of the simple gospel to conquer the world for Christ. You will be made to understand more than ever the genius and potency of the movement with which you are identified. In short, in this great convention, from beginning to end, will be a series of mountain-height experiences that will thrill your heart to its depths and send you away to become a flaming torch in the community in which you live. Every church in the brotherhood should send one or more representatives to this great gathering of the Lord's disciples. M. D. CLUBB.

Chattanooga, Tenn.

State Mission Notes.

One of the pleasant experiences of life was the visit to Centralia, where I had the first real good chance to meet H. A. Denton, the pastor. After my association with him there I am not surprised that his people love him. They can't help it. Some of the best people on earth are in the church there, and this, by the way, can be said of Sturgeon, where I was at night. found them full of the great meeting just held for them by Brother Northcut[illegible] They were full of praise for him, and he de[illegible] serves it all, as also does their pastor, E. M[illegible] Richmond, whom they were not slow to prais[illegible]

The Pike County meeting at Clarksville wa[illegible] a great success. Bro. Dudley had gotten u[illegible] a great program, and its carrying out made [illegible] profitable meeting. But death had been bus[illegible] taking away the great ones, Sister J. J[illegible] [illegible]rrett, John Wyrick, Sister Ferguson, Dab[illegible] ney Woodson, Clem Bryson and others, so tha[illegible] it was sad to see the gaps. Yet, as I saw th[illegible] younger ones passing forward to take the[illegible] places, while our hearts were sad, we coul[illegible] still thank God.

From here we went to Carthage to the Inter[illegible] denominational Sunday-school Convention[illegible] They had a great convention, but when [illegible] comes to the matter of giving, our people giv[illegible] more than two to one for the same purpose[illegible] Indeed, I believe that where our people ar[illegible] informed they are as good givers as you ca[illegible] find. If they don't give it is because the[illegible] don't know. If a church does not give to ou[illegible] mission work, it is nearly always because th[illegible] preacher does not urge the matter upon them[illegible] Of course there are exceptions, and you ma[illegible] be one.

A message called me home, and I did not ge[illegible] away again till Sunday, when I enjoyed th[illegible] association of R. D. Chinn, of Vandalia, an[illegible] preaching to his people at night. We hav[illegible] some regular contributors to our work ther[illegible] who never fail, among whom are Sisters Sperr[illegible] and Culbertson. May the Lord bless them!

The Ralls County meeting was a great suc[illegible] cess. It was bound to be so, for J. B. Corwi[illegible] was at the throttle. No church can entertai[illegible] better than Center, and it was one of the mos[illegible] enjoyable meetings of the year. Of course y[illegible] secretary and his fellow-tramp, H. F. Davis[illegible] stopped at Hotel Wicks. *We* know the goo[illegible] places. I pleaded for an early place on th[illegible] program, and it was kindly given, and [illegible] hastened home to find Mrs. Abbott in suc[illegible] condition that I could not go to either th[illegible] Cooper County or the Maryville district con[illegible] vention. It was my loss. But all my appoint[illegible] ments now must be made subject to he[illegible] condition.

The program has been delayed, and will b[illegible] found in the next issue. It is a good one. W[illegible] are looking for a great convention. Nevad[illegible] sends invitation to all. Free entertainment fo[illegible] all who come.

Round-trip rates of one fare has been grant ed by Missouri Pacific, M. K. & T., Ft. Scot[illegible] & Memphis and the Port Arthur Route. Don'[illegible] forget these roads. We are pulling on others with what result we do not yet know.

Another thing: We made arrangements wit[illegible] the men in the field and entered into certai[illegible] obligations with them, trusting that you woul[illegible] help us to meet them. A great number [illegible] churches have not yet responded. Many hav[illegible] said, "We will come in the last month,"[illegible] Well, here it is; we are in the last month. W[illegible] need the money very, very much. Will yo[illegible] not at once take this matter up? Press it upo[illegible] your people, they will not say you nay.

Yours in his name,

T. A. ABBOTT.

4760 *Kennerly Ave., St. Louis, Mo.*

Michigan State Convention.

The 30th annual convention of the brethre[illegible] in Michigan was held at Saginaw, Aug. 31 t[illegible] Sept. 4. It was one of great importance t[illegible] our work in the state. The policy of placing th[illegible] evangelistic and executive work of the assoca[illegible] tion under the care of different persons has bee[illegible] under experiment during the year and this con vention was to show the result. As we bega[illegible] the year somewhat heavily in debt no evangel ist was employed, every effort being directe[illegible] towards putting our financial affairs upon [illegible] better basis. Before the convention closed w[illegible] reduced our debt to $38. This will probably b[illegible] cleared off in a very few weeks.

Vednesday even-
come by Prof. S.
ur former state
nd the sermon by
gave us a splen-
ısion of Thursday
ted addresses on
istic work were
3. E. Rossell, C.
Then followed
owed much prog-
s are known to
urches. Twen-
ported, but the
net increase in
sent membership
nbership in the
000. The number
). These eighty
operty value of
there are debts
They have raised
7,308.90, and for
er item promises
Several pastors
he instrumental-
ıg secretary and
avorable to much

good sermons and
Ministerial Asso-
on, L. W. Spayd
ral short address-
The C. W. B. M.
ssion. There was
n all sides to have
in their meeting
Sister A. E. H.
shown herself an
e year and has
npson, of Detroit,
old position as
M. sermon was
f Grand Rapids,

n was presided
ıle. A number of
were read and the
presented. The
ogress.
sion was intended
but after a very
ninationalism and
W. W. Wyrick,
lressed the meet-
r. Butchart also
ting his talk with
pticon views of
tion which the
; on seeing these

legates remained
warded with ser-
J. H. Garrison,
Christian char-
n us all for the

Sioux Falls, who conducted a devotional service, and A. H. Seymour, of Arlington, who had charge of the missionary session.

Bro. L. H. Humphreys, of Sioux Falls, was to give an address at the missionary session, but was not in attendance.

Bro. N. H. Mullins, of Hetland, who was president of the State Union, and is president of our own work in the state, presided throughout. Of the new officers four are of the religious body satisfied to bear simply the name of Christ. Altogether it was an interesting and inspiring convention. Next year's meeting is to be at Aberdeen.

Bro. T. S. Noblitt, of Ellendale, N. D., and Miss Pearl Wiley, of Carthage, are in a meeting at Clark.

Bro. L. W. Thompson, of Volga, baptized two candidates at Lake Oakwood on a recent Lord's day.

The church at Miller celebrates its first anniversary next Lord's day.

Bro. R. D. McCance, after a visit in Nebraska, is again in the state and looking after the work at Oldham and Elrod.

A. H. SEYMOUR.

Arlington, S. D., Sept., 1, 1898.

Minnesota.

Eureka! Minnesota has a $365 Christian. What do I mean? I mean that Minnesota has a brother who pays $1.00 per day the year round to benevolences outside of contributions to the local church. The fact came to light through the annual reports, the brother having paid an even $365 during the past year, and nowhere is there another state to show a like bit of consecration of means. The brother is not a lawyer, banker nor physician, but a farmer of ordinary means, having membership in one of the smaller churches. Glory to God for such men, and may their example be emulated.

And again, eureka! Minnesota's 3,277 brethren have, during the past year, expended $27,086.80 for all purposes, or a per capita of $8.26, and now again, what other state can show a like consecration of means? These figures are also deducted from the annual reports, which causes me to remark that it is my belief that the per capita figures given of our people by the New York Independent, $2.74, are glaringly incorrect, in that we are placed at the foot of the column in relation to the denominations, whereas we should be placed near the top, and I call for a more business-like plan of gathering statistics on the part of the state board secretaries, that we may not be further traduced. Having had training in a large business institution, where reports galore are the order of the day, I perceived, upon taking the Minnesota secretaryship, five years since, that a most unsystematic way of getting at the situation was in vogue and, securing samples of report blanks from various state secretaries, I made up an annual report blank which, in a three years' trial, has proven that

C. C. Smith, Dr. J. Butchart, Chanc
Craig, of Drake University, and Helen M
were present, cheering on and giving ecl
every session. God bless them! Next
the convention will meet with the Roch
brethren, an equally central point to Mank
The committee on enrollment reported 153
gates and numerous visitors.

Not the most memorable feature were w
of cheer from surviving pioneer preachers
wives of early preachers, who are decea
who were given a special program. A pic
of these was taken for historical purposes,
those desiring copies of same at actual
(70 cts.) can address the undersigned. Al
the entire 1897 state board was re-elected,
David Owen Thomas succeeding himsel
president. A new corresponding secretary
chosen in the person of E. T. Gadd, of
Paul (769 Laurel Ave.), to whom commu
tions should hereafter be addressed. M
Waters is still treasurer, 530 Guaranty
Bldg., Minneapolis. The state C. W. B
re-elected Mrs. Carey E. Morgan, of Mi
apolis, president. Robert Grieve, of Dul
is superintendent of the Bible-schools,
Myrtle Oliver, of Garden City, preside
the Y. P. S. C. E. F. H. MELLEN,
Ex-Sec. Minn. Ch. Missionary Societ

Church Extension Offerings.

Receipts for first seven days of September, 1898	$1,
Receipts for first seven days of September, 1897	7
Gain over last year	$

NOTE. — $940 of this year's receipts c
from a bequest, so instead of a gain from
churches, there is a loss in general receipt
The offerings that have been sent in, h
ever, in nearly every instance are doubl
amount of the apportionment. The st
weather over the West no doubt account
the loss in other receipts. The offering sh
be pushed vigorously on the third and fo
Sundays.

Many churches have sent us notices
they have reached their apportionment
gone beyond, and that the remittances wi
sent later. We hope for greatly incre
offerings over last year..

G. W. MUCKLEY, Cor. S
600 *Waterworks Building, Kansas City,*

Illinois Mission Notes.

Illinois Day comes on Lord's day, Oct.
and the cheering words from so many o
leaders show that it will be "an high d
among the churches.

Attention, brethren! Our convention
thing of the past. We should be anxious fo
future. We love our grand old state. D
love it well enough to plant the cause of
Christianity in destitute places? These p
are calling for help. Our people are ab
help them. Will we withhold from them
bread of life?

teen county-seats in Northern Illinois and nine whole counties without a single Christian Church in them. If you know of a place where missionary work is needed in Illinois more than here it would be wise to plan its evangelization at once. The field is already white unto the harvest. Laborers are few.

May God bless you in the work your are doing and helping uthers to do. I am ready to assist you in any way I cán.—G. HALLECK ROWE, Woodhull.

I will at least give you my word of encouragement. We intend again, at least, to give you our mite. We want to keep in touch with the work.—E. C. STARK, Champaign.

I am glad you are succeeding so well. I hope many more churches may be brought into fellowship with the state organization. I have my own plan for taking missionary collections and prefer it to the one recommended in the minutes. I am also in favor of the other missionary interests being brought to the front.—W. H. CANNON, Pittsfield.

The church here will be one of the churches making an offering for the work of the Lord in Illinois. I will do what I can to secure the co-operation of all the friends in this good and great work.—P. BAKER, Colfax.

After making a statement of the work and needs of the home board, a sister said to me. "I want to help this work," and gave me a dollar. This without solicitation. Let us tell the needs of the state and solicit. The gifts may surprise us.—J. B. GRAVES, Jacksonville.

One-fourth of all money raised in this state for missions is not too much to devote to the work in the state. This can and should be done without decreasing the amount given to other boards. The same amount of interest and effort on the part of our preachers and church officers in behalf of state work that is given to other enterprises will easily raise the offerings for Illinois missions to one-fourth the whole amount given annually. I do not believe that the churches of Illinois are prejudiced against Illinois as a mission field.—H. H. JENNER, Buffalo.

I am ready to do all I can to help along the state work. "Christ for Illinois; Illinois for Christ." God bless you in your efforts to evangelize the grand old state.—W. H. WAGGONER, Eureka.

I am in favor of the recommendations of the board. We will give one-fourth to Illinois.—J. E. PARKER, Waynesville.

If all of the Churches of Christ in this great commonwealth will fall in line and all of us do our duty it will not be long until all of the people in the state of Illinois will have the privilege of obeying the gospel of Christ.—H. C. LITTLETON, Sec. Third District, Astoria.

I shall do all in my power to put "Illinois missions to the front." We ought not to do less for our other missionary enterprises, but more for Illinois.—Geo. L. PETERS, Girard.

I feel deeply interested in the missionary enterprise, and shall strive to enlist the help of all connected with the Raritan organization towards bringing "Illinois missions to the fornt."—J. H. BEARD, Raritan.

I am much pleased with the general interest manifested in our state work. I think perhaps it was never so genuine and widespread before. God grant that it may continue to grow and deepen until every church, nook and corner shall feel its power! May the desert of of indifference bloom as the rose, that sorrow and sighing because of that desert my flee away.—J. B. WRIGHT, Milford.

I second the motion to push Illinois state missions clear up to the front and a little ahead, and if every congregation will adopt and carry out the recommendations of the board—four missionary days and one-fourth, for state missions—that result will be obtained. Kankakee adopts the plan, and will do her best. She appreciates the value of state and district missions.—W. D. DEWEESE, Kankakee.

Let the watchword of every preacher in Illinois be, "Illinois missions to the front!" The fields are already white to the harvest. Shall we not go and possess them?—R. A. OMER, Camp Point.

I am heartily in favor of pushing the state work and will do what I can.—L. M. ROBINSON, Mt. Pulaski.

There must be no looking backwards in Illinois. Having determined to take four collections a year for missions and to consecrate twenty-five per cent. to state work, let our battle-cry be ever onward, never backward.—W. A. MELOAN, Blandinsville.

The state of Illinois is ready for the primitive gospel. Our work is to get Christians ready to give the gospel to those who are waiting for it. The "debt of ability" must be recognized. You are taking the right plan to accomplish this. With a Christian paper in every Christian home, and a strong plea for Illinois in every paper, large results must follow. The people will gladly respond when they see victory in sight. Illinois to the front!—F. W. BURNHAM, Charleston.

Too long has our state work been neglected by some and greatly slighted by others. As the handle is to the umbrella, so is our state work to all other work. The recommendations one, two and three, made by board at the Eureka Encampment, are good ones and our preachers and churches must carry them out. —D. N. WETZEL, Farmer City.

"The sunset of life gives mystical lore,
And coming events cast their shadows before."

The twentieth century will bring wonderful events. Wars will practically cease. Character, not creed will be orthodoxy. The earth will be one neighborhood. The Fatherhood of God, and brotherhond of man will be acknowledged. Arbitration will decide national difficulties and armies disband, and so mote it be!—GEO. W. MINIER, Minier.

Preaching the gospel in its simplicity and power to our people, and to those coming from other lands is of supreme importance. Hence I always use my influence for home missions and preach two or three times a year upon the missionary work of tte church and expect to so continue while in the ministry.—P. F. YORK, Normal.

The desire to push the state missionary work by districts is in perfect harmony with the spirit and energy now being displayed in all departments of a world-wide enterprise that is straining every point to crowd into the closing years of the nineteenth century the wonderful achievements and splendid progress that God has decreed belongs to this generation.—G. W. WARNER, Mackinaw.

Our state and district boards are one in action and purpose, and this call is for both, the receipts being divided between them. Will not these earnest words of exhortation bring up every church to the support of Illinois missions? Let nothing hinder you from sending an offering.—J. FRED JONES, Sec., Stanford.

Missousi Bible-school Notes.

The Randolph County meeting only demonstrates what can be done when the right men take hold, for it was one of the very best meetings of the summer. No department of the work is growing more than that of the Bible-school and no county has a more efficient superintendent than Randolph in Miss Nora Kiernan who, by the way, has come so near the banner for four years. The schools not pledged, but accepting their apportionments, were Cairo, Liberty aud Higbee.

The Boone County meeting at Red Top was a surprise to all the brethren, being way up in "G." The Bible-schools are not in the condition that is creditable to such a county, but will be so before the year is out. C. H. Winders is the county superintendent, and he has no idea of leaving them as they are. But other schools made good reports, and of those accepting their apportionments I mention Red Top, Olivet, Mt. Joy, Dripping Springs, while Ashland always has given to this cause. At Ashland in Howard, the friends were so generous to me in their giving that I wish it were possible to mention all the names. They gave me the apportionment for the school for last year and this, and did it so cheerfully and happily and promptly that for once in my life I enjoyed the begging. Bro. Alex. Dudgeon is always putting me under obligations for kindness, but this time it is a heaping up of goodness by himself and wife. The Lord bless them and all the Ashland brethren, with their preacher, Ernest Thornquest, for such favors to the servants of Christ, who pray that the work may prosper under their hands.

In Fayette I found a union meeting at the Christian church, but it was just the same, for S. G. Clay, the preacher, and W. L. Holliday the superintendent, said the apportionment would be paid. Bro. Holliday manages the best hotel in Fayette and one of the best in the state, and yet always goes to Bible-school and Endeavor, while other brethren tell me that they cannot get away from the hotel. See?

The Lincoln County meeting at Louisville has past into history, but the reports have not come to you yet, and so I may say that the condition was reported. Good. H. L. Morton is the county superintendent, while also secretary of the county board, of which W. D. Shaw is president, and these men will not let the work lag. E. H. Lawrence and Simeon Morris have been the faithful helpers of the preachers for twenty years, always seeing that they had conveyance in and out, and this time was no exception, which is quite a gift to our work every year.

Bro. John Giddens reports that a house will surely be built at Ulman and that the work will then be on a permanent basis, and this will cause all of us to rejoice with Bro. Giddens and the Ulman brethren.

As we are giving much attention this year to the home department, will not those of the brethren having such, write me a note, giving your work and its results, as many are asking who has tried that we know, and are their circumstances something like ours, and if so, what are their encouragements? Write me.

The Monroe County meeting went back to its old-time success this year at Santa Fe, being crowded from start to finish, while the character of addresses were above the average. The work reported was not much, but it will be different this next year, or I am no prophet. In Bible-school work the county holds up well, but in reporting its work it is a failure, as was seen in M. J. Nicoson's efforts. No one ever ied harder and fared worse. The schools ind enough to accept their apportionments ere not a few, and I thank them for it.

The new men are now at work, brethren, and ou are welcome to their services, but they ill want time for arranging their dates; so rite them now—F. M. Rogers, Edina, and eo. E. Prewitt, Schell City—and if you would o us and the work a good turn, send in the pportionment or a part of it or word that you ill during the year. Let me hear from you ow.

Everybody for Nevada, Sept. 26th to 29th. nly one fare both ways. H. F. DAVIS.

Commercial Building, St. Louis.

Among the Brethren in Missouri.

A. R. Hunt, at Tarkio, is giving general atisfaction, and his work is prospering in all epartments of the church.

F. E. Blanchard, at Barnard, is having the ys of successful work to encourage and help im along. The church, Bible-school and ndeavor are all growing.

Lee Ferguson, from Drake, is now located at opkins, and is taking hold of the work like a rake would be expected to do, and the workrs at Hopkins are being revived in hopes and fe.

Geo. E. Dew will soon be under his own vine and fig tree'' at Savannah, and has alf-time at New Point and Fillmore, and will them good by thus being with each congreation two Sundays instead of only one.

D. W. Connor has resigned his work at St. e and Bolckow, and will go with wife d daughter to Pueblo, hoping to fully regain is health.

The churches of Holt County have preaching d preachers as follows: Bigelow, J. R. arlan, one-half time; Bluff City, W. H. ardman, one-fourth time; Corning, H. W. ies, one-fourth time; Forest City, H. W. ardman, one-half time; Craig, H. W. Cies, e-half time; Maitland, I. Bauserman, onealf time; Mound City, W. E. Boulton, all his me, being the only congregation in the unty with preaching every Sunday, and of urse is the most prosperous church in the unty; New Point, Geo. E. Dew, half-time; regon, Clyde Darsie, half-time; Summitt, J. . Cole, one-fourth time; Union, Clyde arsie, one-half time; Walnut Grove, J. N. ole, one-fourth time. The Nodaway Valley strict begins the new year with all debts paid full, and has over one hundred dollars in the easury. T. W. Cottingham continues as the angelist. Their money is raised by the aprtionment, so much being apportioned to e counties and then apportioned out to the urches of the respective counties.

H. T. King is giving the first and third Sunys in the month to Mt. Vernon, where he s been laboring with good results for two ars.

J. F. Hargrove, of Mt. Vernon, is giving uch of his time to the mission work of his rritory, and is doing as so many other eachers in that region—giving it without ything like an adequate support. God bless em for it, but it may be charged up to some the churches that are always pleading povty to hide their stinginess. He knows which which, and so will the other fellows some of ese days.

Good reports are coming in every week as to e attendance at the Nevada state convenon, September 26-29, and that is exactly ght, too. Make it a great occasion for all e saints in Missouri.

The friends of Brother Creighton Brooks will gret to hear that his wife happened to quite serious accident during the Santa Fe meetg, resulting in a broken limb. But all are ad to know that it is not worse.

Hurrah for Edmund Wilkes' good meeting Linn Creek, with 105 added and money for

Evangelistic.

KANSAS.

Oxford, Sept. 9.—One baptism at above place since last report.—C. HENDERSON.

McPherson, Sept. 10.—We are here with good interest the first week. It has been raining for nearly 24 hours.—D. D. BOYLE and V. E. RIDENOUR.

Independence, Sept. 5.—Nine additions at our last appointment at Lima and four added at Providence last Lord's day.—J. T. BAYS.

Howard, Sept. 5.—Four added here at morning service and one at Crescoe, six miles north, in the afternoon. Prospects are brightening. I start this evening for Tyler, Texas, for a meeting.—R. E. ROSENSTEIN, pastor.

McPherson, Sept. 3.—There have been five additions at our regular meetings since last report.—J. E. LORTON, pastor.

MISSOURI.

I held a 14 days' meeting in August for the church at Dripping Springs, Boone county. Preached 28 sermons, resulting in 11 additions, mostly by confession. Bro. B. F. Goslin labors one-fourth of his time for this church, whom I found a faithful co-worker. I found this short vacation quite restful. I am pleased with the changes made in the CHRISTIAN-EVANGELIST. Bro. G. writes me that three have made the good confession since the close of the meeting. —E. J. LAMPTON.

Troy, Sept. 9.—Closed a two weeks' meeting at Lewisville Sunday night. Four persons confessed Christ. There was good interest from the beginning to the end. Will hold a meeting here in October. The board met Wednesday and agreed unanimously to retain me at Troy for a third year, to close Sept. 1st, 1899.—E. MERRILL.

Fulton, Sept. 8.—I just closed a meeting at Hickory Grove, Calloway County, with 25 additions.—A. B. PHILLIPS.

Rolla, Sept. 9.—We held an eight days' meeting at Pilot Grove in Franklin County, resulting in four additions; also a nine days' meeting at Villy Ridge, same county, with five confessions.—R. B. HAVENER, pastor.

Frankfort, Sept. 5.—I am in a meeting with the church at Santa Fe, where I was raised. Ten added to date. My grandfather and uncle, Jno. T. and Jno. A. Brooks, have been pastors here. Their present preacher is C. H. Strawn, of Paris.—CRAYTON S. BROOKS.

TEXAS.

Denton.—A good meeting just finished in Limestone County; 58 were baptized; 20 returned to the fold. Total, 80. We tried to declare the whole council of God without addition or subtraction, and as a result we left a united body in Christ.—JNO. J. HECKMAN.

ARKANSAS.

Arkadelphia, September 5.—One of the best meetings we have ever had here closed last night with nine additions; six by baptism. Bro. Geo. Clark, district evangelist, did the preaching. Heat, sickness and politics made a strong combination against us, but we rejoice in a good meeting.—E. S. ALLHANDS.

IOWA.

Sheldon.—Several added under the labors of R. W. Aberley.

Van Meter.—Thirty-six added by D. C. Kellams, assisting C. G. Stout.

Near Madrid.—Forty-one added of whom 34 were baptized. Roy Caldwell, evangelist.

Winterset, Sept. 3.—Three subtractions here last Lord's day.—J. M. LOWE.

ILLINOIS.

Holder, Sept. 10.—Four more added here since last report. Meeting will continue another week; six in all to date.—F. W. BUNHAM, assisting S. E. Fisher, of Eureka College.

Shelbyville, Aug. 29.—One confession last night. Our audiences have been larger then during the summer months last year.—W. M. GROVES.

Barry, Sept. 9.—Baptized one last night. New meeting house going up fast; hope to dedicate in December.—N. E. CORY.

Franklin, Sept. 6.—One added by baptism at regular services, last Lord's day.—A. C. ROACH, pastor.

Moweaqua, Sept. 5.—Meeting closed after three weeks; 52 additions, 10 last night. This makes 230 additions to this work in one year. Two years ago we had nothing.—SPICER AND MATTHEWS.

KENTUCKY.

Grayson, September 5.—Ten additions to the church in August. I had three additions at Willard, and seven at Fairview; all in Carter County. I have taken the Carter County

SOUTH DAKOTA.

Ellendale, Sept. 6.—On Aug. 4th I began a meeting at Clark, under the auspices of the S. D. C. M. S. The meeting continued four weeks. Miss Pearl Wiley, of Carthage, S. D., served us throughout efficiently as organist and soloist. I was the first to present the primitive plea in the community. The location in the town was unfortunate; probably also a better time of year could have been selected. Clark has a population of about 1,000. I have held meetings in larger and smaller towns, but never before experienced such difficulty in getting an audience. Indeed, it is one thing to hold a meeting in one of the central states and quite another thing in South Dakota. Results: Eight who are willing to unite on "the Bible and the Bible alone," four by confession and baptism two others to be baptized as soon as health will permit, and a few others almost persuaded.—T. L. NOBLITT.

WEST VIRGINIA.

Huntington, September 5.—Added during August, five; added at the Mission Point, 12. —G. M. WEINER.

At the closing meeting of Bethany Assembly, Aug, 14th, its president, L. L. Carpenter, having declined a re-election, was justly honored by the hearty adoption of resolutions recognizing his untiring energies in behalf of the assembly and expressing appreciation of his patience and unselfish labors in its diversified interests and regrets at his retirement from its presidency. Concerning this meeting, these resolutions and Bro. L. L. Carpenter, Bro, Allan B. Philputt, of Inplanapolis, writes as follows: "While it was a very interesting occasion and one in which the people's esteem for the retiring president of Bethany Assembly could not be mistaken, we all felt that a much larger host, if it could have been convened that evening, composed of preachers and others scattered from the Atlantic to the Pacific, would have been glad to testify of their appreciation of L. L. Carpenter's services. The thousands that have come to the Park during the past years, and the scores of preachers that have looked into the face of the great audiences there assembled, challenging them to their best effort, can hardly think of Bethany Assembly without the tall form and kindly face of this Nestor of Indiana preachers coming up in the foreground. He greeted every one who came and gave the parting guest good-bye. Bethany Assembly has been, not a state, but a national gathering. Many noble things have gone forth from it to quicken and uplift our cause. The best speakers in our ranks have been glad to stand before the great multitudes of appreciative listeners here assembled. It has been and is the greatest thing of the kind conducted by our people. What it is, L. L. Carpenter has helped to make it. He has largely guided and controlled it, aided by the counsel of the board of directors. He has invested largely of his means and of his time. He has received not a dollar in return. It has been purely an unselfish labor. Few men have the capacity to do what he has done and still fewer have the consecration to do it for nothing. Short addresses were made at this last service oy several, to which Bro. Carpenter, unaware of the nature of the meeting before coming to it, made a fitting and tender response. At the close the ladies gave a reception, at which a light refreshment was served. Howard Cale, of Indianapolis, one of the staunch and intelligent friends of Bethany, was elected president for next year.

Indianapolis. ALLAN B. PHILPUTT.

Natives of the Philippines.

The American Volunteer, shipped to the Philippine Islands, almost half way round the world from our national capital, and seven or eight thousand miles from San Francisco, finds himself in a country where climate, vegetation, houses and people are entirely different from anything he ever saw. The cattle are only as large as goats, and the horse is almost a curiosity.

The population comprises about 200,000 Creoles and Spanish half-breeds, with a few Europeans and Americans. The four million natives, divided into many tribes, each speaking a different language, are in character and disposition very like the Southern negro. They are a peaceful, indolent people, working as field hands or day laborers when not occupied with cock-fighting. Women in the Philippine Islands are quite independent, retaining their maiden name, with the addition of "de" before the husband's name. A widow buries her husband's name with him and immediately is known again by her girlhood name.

On another page is pictured a grown man and woman, natives of the islands, each operating a Singer hand machine. The original photograph was taken on the island of Luzon by an agent of *The Singer Manufacturing Co.*,

Family Circle.

Take Time With the Boy.

A. M. HOOTMAN.

Take time with the boy, and lead him aright.
He will have many a battle in this world to fight.
Teach him kindness while young; set his young heart aglow
With the truths of manhood; let his spirit o'erflow.

Take time with the boy, and guide his young soul
Into channels of morals, where God can control.
Help him put the brakes on passion and lust,
And gird up his soul with a heavenly trust.

Take time with the boy; he needs your wise care;
The seed-thoughts you plant in him will abundant fruit bear.
Deceive not his heart with words of disaster,
But give him the TRUTH, it will then please the MASTER.

Take time with the boy, ere sorrow and shame
Crush your hopes of future and mar his good name;
Before the long night of dishonor and crime
Befoul his pure mind while yet in his prime.

Take time with the boy; for the guardian of peace
May be centered in him to give the nations release.
He sovereign and king of his manhood must be,
Ere he unshackles the slave, or sets others FREE.

Army Life In Arizona.

MARY BLACK CLAYTON.

We leave the states on the 30th of November, 1892, and after a tiresome journey of a week's duration reach the terminus of the Southern Pacific Railroad. The place is announced to us by the conductor as Ash Forks. Nothing explains the name—neither ashes nor forks to be seen—only three saloons and one residence, the latter being a deserted freight-car, and occupied by a solitary man in the employment of the railroad company.

From this interesting spot we take a stage for Fort Whipple. The inhabitant of Ash Forks, and patron of the three saloons aforesaid, informs us that the stage is usually robbed *en route* to Whipple, and we start with little hope that the rule will be varied in our favor. There are no other passengers in the stage besides our five selves and an evil-looking Jew whom I at once decide to be a highwayman who is to meet his pals on the road and unite with them in taking our money and our lives. We rattle off at four in the afternoon, and enter Hell Canon as dusk settles down upon the desert wilds. Road there is none. The stage rolls and tumbles from one great boulder to another. No one can venture a bet on the happenings of the next moment, nor form the slightest idea as to which is going to be under which, or what was going to be on top of what. Now the stage is almost down on its right side, now we expect to be dashed to pieces on the rocks at the left. Now the mules are pulling us up a place so steep that it seems as if they must fall backwards upon us, and now we pray that we may not tumble a somersault over their backs, as they rush down a place as steep as the side of a house. However, grant that the harness hold, that the mules be sure-footed, that the driver be faithful, and that he may not have sinned at the saloons of Ash Forks: the lurid light which the lanterns throw upon the wild and desolate scene does not add to the general cheerfulness of the situation. We pass many dead and ghostly looking trees, whose white branches seem to clutch at us. Hark! are we not pursued by swift hoofs?

The stage comes to a halt so suddenly that every one is thrown into the arms of their vis-a-vis. The moment, the awful moment, has come at last! We are going to be called upon to stand and deliver. Will they shoot? My children, oh my children! will they hurt them? But a merciful Providence still protects us, and we are mildly invited by the driver to alight in the darkness and scramble down a notoriously dangerous portion of our way. We tumble out helter-skelter, and the weak, assisted by the strong, feel our way down the declivity. The Arizona darkness seems lonely and a trifle dangerous, and we are glad to climb into the stage again, and persue our exciting journey.

The saloons of Ash Forks furnished only beverages and a few viands to invite thirst, which were of no possible use to our party. The pangs of hunger make themselves felt. Some one produces a can of pig's feet, a slippery comestible at the best of times, but in this stage-coach, lucky is the mouth which captures a morsel.

However, towards the small hours of the night we see light glimmering in the distance, and we finally pull up before the opening of something, which is neither a cave, a hut nor a bower, but which has a little appearance of all three. Is this a robbers' den, and is the driver in league to bring us here? We are told it is a place of refreshment for man and beast. The night has grown bitterly cold, we are not properly wrapped, and we are packed tightly in the stage, so that our limbs are cramped and aching. A glimpse of a bright fire, and the delicious odor of coffee decides us to enter, even if we are lured to our distruction. What a strange place! The shelter is constructed of mesquite boughs, with their green boughs still upon them, and its proprortions are eked out with a few yards of canvas of the tent kind. There is a little partition or screen in the center of the enclosure, and from behind it comes to us *such* good smells. Here is the warmth and light and cessation from motion. We cluster around the stove. It is made of old tin cans from base to pipe, which disappears through the bowery roof, and draws in our opinion as never a pipe drew before. We gaze with interest at a long table; it is made of rough boards and the seats are stumps of trees, but the implements for eating are laid upon it. Two Frenchmen inhabit this mansion, harmless souls, and as polite as Paris itself. They bring the good odors to the table. We eat them and drink them, and are strengthened for the remainder of this night of terror.

We did not reach Fort Whipple until six in the morning, and I look in the glass and find more wear and tear than one night usually leaves upon the human physiognomy. I am a hag! The most loyal and devoted citizen of Uncle Sam's dominions might be excused for uttering a groan, *sotta voce*, on account of having been made to endure all of the forgoing tribulations for naught. We are allowed to remain Whipple ten days, and then are ordered Tucson in Southern Arizona, which could have comfortably reached by r from Washington. Now we and our effe must be dragged through many m canons, which I am told will make H Canon seem like a paradise in comparisc

Arizona does not welcome us pleasant Its malaria takes possession of three of t family, and they shake with ague. I fo tunately am exempt and administer quini relentlessly and regularly.

When we start for Tucson we are toleral well equipped for our journey. We hav government ambulance, six trusty mul and a driver who is selected for his ability wrestle with the difficulties of canon trav We leave Whipple in a snowstorm, whi seems to have been arranged for our ben fit, as the ground is seldom whitened in th region. The invalids look sadly like t man pictured in the Vinegar Bitters a vertisement, before he took the bitte Fortunately we are journeying southwa and the sun begins to shine warmly, a the skies are blue, blue, blue. The road often rough and wild, but it is *not* as b Hell Canon. We travel only by dayligl stopping at ranches overnight. The same ranches are enough to make the ha stand on end of a person who has hithe striven to lead a cleanly and decent li The first shanty at which we tarry is bu of unplained boards. The rain con through the cracks and moistens c slumbers in the one apartment set apart the use of strangers, male and fema One quick glance at the kitchen and t cook (who is also the incumbent of the sponsible position of caring for the wants our mules) takes away all appetite, and proprietor of Big Bug, as he called establishment, made a clear gain out of o sojourn with him. Big Bug is not a m nomer, by the way!

A description of one of the ranches a plies broadly to all. At a place cal Bumble Bee the proprietress is cleaner th the rest, but she is so cross that she ala us. Why do cleanliness and crossness often combine in female human natu At another place where we stop for rep there are so many ruffians who dri swear and gamble all night long in the n room, so lightly partitioned from ours t their light shines through the cracks, a we can hear all their ungodly talk. reluctantly hear inklings of crime, p present and to come, and we keep firea close at hand with which to defend lives.

The farther south we journey the m novel and interesting the country becom The distant peaks of the Rockies take the most beautiful tints. They are m miles away, but in this clear atmosph they seem to be in walking distance. H impressive is the giant cactus! those shafts of several feet in diameter, wh rise mathematically straight as high sixty and seventy feet. They have monumental effect. They are armed fr top to bottom with straight rows of prick and sometimes they are crowned wit wreath of gorgeous red flowers. In t dry and thirsty land the birds can be s tapping them to get their plentiful sap, it is said to have saved the lives of tra ers, who would have otherwise p ished for want of water. The sli roots of the cactus are often attached to the solid rocks. Whence comes the moisture?

Some of our party enjoy the quail shooting. The meanest sportsman cannot fail to hit some, for they are plentiful and tame. They are not quite similar to their relatives, the Bob Whites of the East, nor are they so toothsome and juicy when cooked. They have a topknot.

After five days of ambulance travel, and five nights of of abject discomfort at ranches we reach Maricopa, where we send our ambulance back to Whipple. We spend one night at the "leading hotel" at Maricopa. If it "leads" we are sorry for those who occupy the hotels which follow.

It is Christmas Eve. We cannot realize that "the time draws near the birth of Christ." The weather is quite warm. The place swarms with flies. There is to be a festive gathering. The population of all the regions round about come to participate in the fete. The house is crowded with Mexicans. As we rest upon our beds we hear a great rushing through the halls, a great calling to each other in the Spanish tongue, from the different rooms. A senorita is playing a guitar. In the midst of all this foreign jabber, a true son of the Star Spangled Banner meets a dog in the hall and cries out in genuine United States lingo, "*Whose perp?*"

We feel like applauding him, but are too tired to do anything except laugh.

One more tiresome day in a slow train and we reach Tucson, and aquaint, foreign-looking place we find it. The streets are very narrow. The houses are built of adobe (sun-dried bricks), and are one story high, with flat roofs to guard against the dangers of earthquakes. There are no pavements. The sand is ankle deep. It is warm. Wraps are superfluous. The sky is light blue. The sunsets are magnificent. Is not the climate like Italy? The town itself looks oriental, not unlike what one has read of Egypt. We go house-hunting at once. There is but one in the town which can be had for love or money, and it requires a great deal of money to secure it, considering its want of alterations. It rents at seventy-five dollars a month, and is already occupied—by rats. There are five rooms in it. The paper hangs from the walls in ragged festoons. The ceilings are covered with dirty muslin. The Mexicans call this sort of ceiling "*a manta.*" The roof leaks. The landlord obligingly mends it with tar, which the hot sun soon melts, and it rains down, unimpeded by the manta, thus causing everything we eat, drink, wear, sit upon, or sleep upon to be spotted like a coach-dog.

Frequent sand-storms blow grit through every crevice, and the crevices are numerous and gaping. Mark Tapley would have been pleased here, for it is certainly a credit to be jolly.

It is impossible to fathom the wisdom of the United States Government in expending fifteen millions of dollars to purchase this portion of Arizona. It is a desert.

The Mexicans, who form a large portion of the inhabitants here, are tenacious of their peculiar manners and customs and mingle little with the American settlers. The Mexican women wear shawls over their heads, arranged so as to leave one eye for seeing purposes. The skirts of their dresses are very long, and they trail them through the sand in a manner which does not suggest cleanliness. They also sit down in the dirt on the streets or byways with a nonchalance produced by the fact that their houses have no floors, and that chairs never had any part in their domestic life. The best Mexican houses are built around a hollow square, and that enclosure is the rallying-place for the family. Occasionallly through the open gateways we catch glimpses of picturesque Mexican girls twanging their guitars under the shade of huge oleanders.

Nothing is more interesting to a stranger in a strange land than to note the manner in which the natives dispose of their dead. We are much interested in the funeral of a Mexican baby which we see pass our dwelling soon after our possession of it.

The little coffin, evidently home-made, was a box covered with bright-colored paper. It is carried on the shoulders of four little girls, who are gaudily dressed in white, with red flowers. The lid of the coffin is carried by the child's mother, who followed in her working-day clothes, but who wears upon her contenance as sad and bereft an expression as if she had been covered with black crape.

It takes no penetration whatever to point out, amidst the crowd, the Rachel who is mourning without comfort.

In May the heat comes on in force. The walled mansion we occupy becomes so heated that the withdrawal of the fierce sun during the short night does not cool it. We are confined as in a bake-oven and fear that before autumn we shall be very brown. During the day we are obliged to keep the house so dark that it is almost impossible to read, write or sew. When it is time to seek "tired Nature's sweet restorer, balmy sleep," we drag cots to the sandy corral in the rear and lie down under the silent stars, regardless of tarantulas or scorpions.

The temperature becomes endurable toward midnight, and we are compelled by motives of modesty to enter the house at daylight, for our cots are stretched in full view of passing pedestrians. Sometimes during the rainy season we weather several showers before we take up our beds and walk into our domicle, where the thermometer stands at 100 degrees all night long. In the midst of the heated term the ice factory breaks down, and the tepid, strongly alkaline water is with alteration. We buy this beverage from a wagon which comes to the house and sells sixty buckets for a dollar. It is brought ten miles. We keep our drinking water in an "olla," which is a pottery vessel made by the Indians, and which possesses wonderful sweating qualities, thus cooling the water by evaporation. This vessel is swung by ropes in the open air. Some arrangement of this same kind is used for the same purpose in India.

We buy our wood from the backs of burros (little donkeys), which are driven about the streets cruelly prodded by the sharp sticks of the Mexicans, who know no English, but insist upon receiving *cincuenta centaros* (50 cents) for enough to kindle a fire.

The streets are full of pedlers, often old women, looking like Macbeth's witches, who desire to sell us queer Mexican viands, *tortillos tomallies*, and what not, which look so strange that we have not courage to taste them. There is much cactus candy for sale, which has no taste except dead sweetness, and is disgusting.

Two boys for a compensation were willing to allow us to look at two large tarantulas fighting. The combatants are crarried in a tin can. These all vaunt their wares in Spanish.

The streets also swarm with Chinamen who do all the laundry and culinary labor for the American residents. The price for domestic services is fifty dollars a month.

We go sometimes to the rose garden of Leopoldo Carillo, where roses are cultivated by extensive and expensive irrigation and where there are baths in which we spend the few comfortable moments we enjoy during the summer of 1882. This benefactor of ours has immense stone vats into which we descend by three or four steps, and which bring to mind the baths of ancient Pompeii and Rome, making us feel as if our names might be Ione or Julia, the daughter of Diomed, or some other classic creature of a bygone age.

It is hard to realize that this interesting and foreign-looking region, with its centuries-old churches, founded by the early Jesuit missionaries, is actually a part of the dominion over which floats our almost brand-new Stars and Stripes, and that it is within the borders which resounded with the shrieks of the lately fledged American Eagle.

Photographed Texts.

"*Our old man is crucified with him*" (*Rom. 6:6*). A vision of Gough, lying prostrate in the gutter and standing manfully in the pulpit; cursing God and then preaching Christ; living a life of infamy, shame and dishonor, and then living a life of righteousness, illumines this passage with a halo of glory. The Christian, preacher, temperance lecturer Gough; the crucified, the vile, godless drunkard Gough.

***

"*A little leaven leaveneth the whole lump*" (*Gal. 5:9*). In a gloomy household there was born a bright-eyed girl, whose expression was sunshine itself. She became a child of nature. Soon the silent halls resounded with merriment, the frowning walls echoed laughter, and the once moody, morose and maunding inmates became hopeful, optimistic and vivacious. The lightsome leaven of that Liliputian fairly leavened the heaviness of the whole household.

***

"*A good name is rather to be chosen than great riches*" (*Pro. 22:1*). In an adjoining community is a widow, poor as proverbial Job's turkey, yet rich as the billionarie Solomon. To solve this paradox one must remember that often those poor in this world's goods possess a fortune of the "riches of heaven." Widow Jones' name remains untarnished; whereas, Banker Smith is branded as an embezzler; Congressman Sellvote is stamped as a pilferer of public money, while well-to-do Miss Cleopatra bears the onerous name, harlot. A "good name" is always above par in Heaven's Exchange.

***

"*And the world passeth away*" (*1 Jno. 2:17*). No truer prophetic words were ever penned by the "Beloved Apostle." The fundamental law of nature is the law of decay. Physiologists teach us that our bodies pass away every seven years. So, likewise, everything else earthly has proven mortal, transient, evanescent. Marian Harland, in her recent book of Palestine travel, "The Home of the Bible," tells us the world Christ trod is buried fifty and sixty feet beneath the rubbish of nearly a score of centuries.

***

"*His leaf also shall not wither [fade, marginal]*" (*Ps. 1:3*). Immortality is the amaranth of heaven. Milton thus speaks of it:

"Immortal amaranth, a flower which once
In Paradise, fast by the tree of life
Began to bloom; but soon for man's offense
To heaven removed, where first it grew, there grows,
And flowers aloft, shading the fount of life.
And where the river of bliss through midst of heaven
Rolls o'er elysian flowers her amber;
With these that never fade the spirits elect
Bind their resplendent locks."

Oh, the depth of love of the Christ who bore a crown of thorns that we might be invested with a crown of heaven's amaranths—a "crown that fadeth not away!"

GEORGE B. EVANS.

Kimberlin Heights, Tenn.

What the Rumseller Knows.

REV. C. A. RUDDOCK.

The Rumseller knows, yes, he knoweth well,
That the Drunkard's path is the way to hell.
He knows from the growing taste of rum,
That the tippler will soon the sot become.
He knows that sin, like a crimson flood,
Flows on, while he takes the price of blood.
He knows of the waste of valued time,
He knows of the record of daily crime.
He knows of the loss to church and state
From the wreck of manhood, small and great.
He knows of the widow's grief and tears,
He knows of the shame of infant years.
He knows of fond mother's distress untold,
He knows of the millions of wasted gold.
He knows of the blight that must surely come
To the drunkard's home, from the curse of rum.
He knows of the efforts of men to save
Their fallen brothers from drunkard's graves.
He know of the sorrow, pain or woe;
No one has a better chance to know.
But knowing all, he goes on to sell
The fiery Beverage of Hell.

—*The Minnesota Issue.*

Pointers for Teachers.

[As public schools are just opening, we give below an article containing many excellent suggestions for teachers which appeared in a recent number of the Religious Telescope.—EDITOR.]

1. As to management: Remember that the idle boy is the one whom it is difficult to manage. Hence, devise ways and means by which so to interest all your pupils in their studies and the work of the schoolroom as to keep them busy during school hours. If you cannot do this pretty generally, you had better quit teaching.

2. Recognize each child's individuality, and lead it out into habits of self-control. That is successful teaching as to behavior which develops in the child the ability to govern itself properly, and the disposition to use that ability. The man or woman who has to be controlled by another may be a fit subject for a despotism, but cannot be a good citizen of a free government.

3. So manage your school as to make it as easy as possible for your pupils to do right, and as difficult as possible for them to do wrong. Help them to learn, early and thoroughly, that right-doing is noble, elevating and happifying, while wrong-doing is degrading, unmanly and ruinous in the end.

4. Place all your pupils, as far as possible, on their individual honor. Treat them as ladies and gentlemen. Let them know that you believe them to be honest and upright in their purposes, that you trust them, that you expect good behavior of them, and that you shall be grieved and disappointed if they do mean and dishonest things.

5. Do not unnecessarily restrain their youthful enthusiasm, or curb their inclination to have a good time. When it is time to play, encourage them to romp and play enthusiastically—always, of course, in harmony with the rights, privileges and welfare of their fellow-schoolmates.

6. Do not offensively impose moral obligations; but, in a quiet, sweet, impressive manner, inculcate in their minds reverence for God, belief in the Bible as his Word, love of home, love and regard for each other, love of country and enthusiasm for the flag. Remember that "the teachers of to-day are training the Americans of the future. Therefore, teach them to act and think for themselves, under the conditions of American citizenship."

7. Remember that the kind of teaching you do will be determined almost wholly by the spirit with which you take up and carry on your work in the schoolroom. Would you have your pupils to be cultured, kind, courteous, truthful, natural, cheerful, enthusiastic and anxious to investigate the various fields of knowledge open to them? Then let all your work be marked with a spirit of culture, kindness, courtesy, truth, naturalness, cheerfulness, animation, readiness to investigate and so be and keep well informed, capable of original thought and action, having self-control and steadiness of character and purpose, patriotic, ready to co-operate with others in close touch with the parents, thus winning the love and confidence of the children.

Next to the peacher of the gospel, the teacher in our public schools occupies the most sacred and responsible position as a nt of the public. His opportunities ›nefiting the world by faithful service ıcalculable. His culpability for neg-f duty is measured only by the amount ·il he inflicts upon his pupils, and, gh them, upon the parents, the coun-ıd the world.

ıt the superiority of our country among ıations of to-day, and especially the iority of our citizen-soldiery, is al-wholly due to our public-school sys-and our religious freedom, even the t philosophers and statesmen are · to admit. And that the future ıy of our country hinges largely upon uality of work being now done in the ·ls and colleges in the land, together the work done in our Sunday-schools hurches and by the religious press, is ly true. How sacredly careful, then, d the teachers and leaders in these ıs fields discharge their duty!

The Heart's Daily Work.

› human heart is practically a force-› about six inches in length and four s in diameter. It beats 70 times per te, 4,200 times per hour, 100,800 times ay and 36,792,000 times per year, and 440,000—say two thousand five hun-and seventy-five millions, four hun-and forty thousand—times in seventy , which is "man's appointed three years and ten." At each of these , it forces 2 1-2 ounces of blood gh the system, 175 ounces per minute, ·4 pounds per hour, or 7.03 tons per All the blood in the body, which is ; 30 pounds, passes through the heart · three minutes. This little organ ›s every day what is equal to lifting ›ns one foot high, or one ton 122 feet that is, one ton to the top of a 40-mill chimney, or sixteen persons seven each to the same height. During ›eventy years of a man's life, this ›lous little pump, with out a single ınt's rest, night or day, discharges the ıous quantity of 178,850 tons of human .—*American Journal of Health.*

Phœbe Cary.

ɛbe Cary wrote, when only seventeen of age, perhaps the most beautiful of ·r poems, commencing—

One sweetly solemn thought,
Comes to me o'er and o'er,
I am nearer home to-day,
Than I have ever been before."

nding—

"Father, perfect my trust,
Let my spirit feel in death
That her feet are firmly set
On the rock of living faith."

› Rev. Russell H. Conwell, of Phila-ia, says that once visiting a Chinese ling house he found two Americans ing and gambling there, the older, vas winning all the money, constantly ʒ utterance to the foulest profanity. › the older was dealing the cards for ɛr game the younger began singing ords of the first verse, but as he sang ›lder stopped dealing, and, throwing the cards, said, "Where did you that?" "In an American Sunday-l," said the younger.

›me," said the elder gambler, getting come, Harry; here's what I have won you; go and use it for some good purpose. As for me, as God sees me, I have played my last game and drunk my last bottle. I have misled you, Harry, and I am sorry. Give me your hand, my boy, and say for old America's sake, if for no other, you will quit this infernal business."

It gave Miss Cary great happiness to learn of this incident before her death.

Sinim for Jesus.

Words by our own Chincheo missionary, the late Albert F. H. Saw.

TUNE, MARCHING THRO' GEORGIA.

Across the sea in China far,
A mighty land there is,
A land where myriads never heard
Of Life's eternal bliss;
Where millions still to idols bow,
And heavenly comfort miss,
And know not our blessed Lord Jesus.

Chorus. Awake, awake, ye armies of our God,
Awake, awake, ye bought with Jesus' blood,
And quickly pour thro' China's shores
The gospel's cleansing flood,
And take the land of Sinim for Jesus.

Oh, could you know the awful need
That still in China grows,
And hear their groans, and see the tears
That wet their mournful brows;
Oh, could you know their deepest need,
It would your conscience rouse
To quickly take Sinim for Jesus.

Cho. Arise, arise, ye ransomed souls from hell,
Arise, arise, your Savior's beauty tell;
And ere this century shall end,
The gospel chorus swell,
And take the land of China for Jesus.

And so dear Christian soldiers bold,
We thus to you relate,
Are you not touched with pitying love
For China's mournful state,
Will you not now in earnest rise?
Soon it will be too late,
And help take poor Sinim for Jesus.

Cho. Send me, send me, to join the glorious band,
Send me, send me, for Christ to take my stand,
And tell to sinners far and near
The gospel story grand,
And claim the "Middle Kingdom" for Jesus.

It may be, friend, you cannot go
To any heathen land,
But you can aid by earnest prayer
To enlarge the mission band;
And you can give your money, too,
And lend a helping hand
To take the land of China for Jesus.

Cho. Make haste, make haste, our Lord's command obey,
Make haste, make haste, our chances are to-day,
Since Christ our Lord will soon be here,
Oh, do not more delay,
But take the mighty Sinim for Jesus.

Side Trips During Prayer.

A map of the travels of an absent-minded person's thoughts during public prayer would consist of a series of elliptical dotted loops extending from the altar of prayer out toward all points of the compass and back again—if they always got back. A writer in the Christian Herald says:

"A brother rises in prayer-meeting to lead in supplication. After he has begun, the door slams, and you peep through your fingers to see who is coming in. You say to yourself, 'What a finely expressed prayer!' or, 'What a blundering specimen! But how long he keeps on! Wish he would stop! He prays for the world's conver for it? gas do has go thougl or, 'W the ba those And s after 'Amer

Tl

Gric projec States carryi Quinc water. ing b The s across rails o iron p of an crossi woode were r *Home*

Sunday School.

THREE PROPHETS: A RETROSPECT.*

HERBERT L. WILLETT.

The present study is a review of the lessons for three months, during which we have been studying the history of the kingdom of Israel, which separated itself from the kingdom of Judah at the death of Solomon, 937 B. C., and came to its close with the destruction of Samaria, its capital, by Sargon, the Assyrian king, in 721 B. C., having continued for a period of two hundred and sixteen years. The story of the Ten Tribes, which was the familiar name for this Nothern Kingdom, is after all only told for the purpose of illustrating the divine plan of operation during that period. Writers of the narratives, which are preserved in the books of Kings, were not concerned particularly with the progress of historical events, but only related them in order to form a background for the work of the prophets, who were the real makers of the nation's life.

In the lessons of the quarter, three prophets stand out with special prominence—Elijah, Elisha and Amos. These men were teachers of the divine truth and the interpreters of the Word of God to the nation in their days. They came at times when the kingdom was at its height, politically, which were also the periods of its greatest moral decline. The three occasions on which Israel arose to its greatest political and commercial prosperity were the reigns of Jeroboam. I., Ahab and Jeroboam II., The prophet Ahijah was the leader of the prophetic party in the days of the first Jeroboam; but after the long decline which followed that period the kingdom arose to power again under Ahab; but a corresponding depth of irreligion and idolatry was the result. At this moment Elijah appeared. He was from the hill-country of Gilead, east of the Jordan; was dressed in a hairy mantle, girt with a leather belt; was of intrepid and aggressive nature, a man of prayer, but the child of his age, and inclined to visit with the utmost severity any failure to perform what he believed to be the divine will. His name was soon renowned for the marvels connected with his life; among which may be named his announcement of the drought; his providential sustenance at Cherith; the unfailing supply of meal and oil at Zerapheth; the restoration of the widow's son; the fiery test on Mount Carmel; the providential supply of food in the wilderness; the vision at Horeb, and the prediction of the death of the King Ahaziah. His influence upon the ruling family was felt to the extent that his stern reproval of Ahab for Neboth's death resulted in the king's partial repentance; the stern reproval of Ahaziah for consulting a false god also struck terror to the court. The departure of Elijah in the tempest was a fitting climax to his rapid and meteoric career.

The life of Elisha, who "poured water on the hands of Elijah," or was his servant, is of even greater interest; and with him a still larger list of wonderful events is connected. Among them is the crossing of the Jordan; the sweetening of the well at Jericho; the supply of water for the army at Edom; the store of oil; the restoration of the child of the Shunammite; the cleansing of the poisoned pottage at Gilgal; the feeding of the hundred with a small supply of food; the healing of Naaman; the floating ax; the disclosure to the king of Israel of the Syrian plans; the bewilderment of the Syrian army; the prediction of the rescue of Samaria; the recovery of the corpse cast into the grave—all these show the marvelous character of Elisha's work and its deep impression upon the popular mind. In bearing and disposition Elisha partook of the character of the times, and yet was milder and more loved than Elijah; he wore the usual tonsure of the prophets of his day, and sometimes resorted to the common practice of arousing the prophetic spirit by means of music. He was followed by a servant, Gahazi, who even after his dismissal delighted to tell the marvelous story of his former master's life (2 Kings 4:8 f.). Elisha's ministry fell into the period of Israel's lowest political misfortune; but it marked the time of the greatest religious activity. When the nation was in distress and its enemies pressed on every side, the faith of their fathers was grasped with firm hand. Elijah and Elisha present the two types of prophetic work. One the stern, unbending proclaimer of judgment, the other the more accesible and friendly teacher of truth, the pastor of a nation.

The work of Amos, which came during the reign of Jeroboam II., shortly after the death of Elisha, marks a still higher revival in prophetic work. No miracles are connected with the name of this prophet. His appeal is only to the conscience and the heart. His ministry was of much briefer duration and perhaps not so effective in the transformation of the national life, but it laid the foundation for that new type of prophetic work represented by the great prophets of later days. No longer was the man of God a rough and uncouth figure, abstaining from marriage and marked by external tokens of his office, but a man of affairs, representing the ordinary life of the people; now a tradesman, now a man of leisure, now a priest and now a noble—the prophet was prepared to meet the life of the nation at its own level and bear witness to the will of God. Amos was a visitor from the Southern Kingdom, whose business brought him to Bethel and Samaria, where he denounced with all the fire of an indignant soul the corruption of the nation, and proclaimed the inevitable consequences of such conditions as he saw about him. These three prophets, Elijah, Elisha and Amos, mark the ascending steps in the progress of the prophet's work in the Northern Kingdoms, and prepare the way for the great periods of prophecy which were to follow in the days of Isaiah and the exile.

SUGGESTIONS FOR TEACHING.

1. The fundamental reason for the division of the kingdom was the opposition of the prophets to the secular character of Solomon's kingdom and the great danger to religion from increase of wealth and power. 2. Every crisis produces a man; Elijah arose at the moment when Israel needed him most. 3. The decisive command is always that which Elijah propounded to Israel—"Choose this day whom ye will serve." 4. One must never be discouraged at the seeming failure of his plans; it is only he who perseveres who can hope to succeed. 5. The sin of covetousness is just as odious when committed in small ways as in such a matter as that of Naboth. 6. The death of a great man does not mean failure of his work; others will carry it forward. 7. God, who gives life, is alone able to restore life. 8. The sin of leprosy, incurable and loathsome, is only a sign of the ravages which sin produces in human nature. 9. The hosts around us to-day are just as visible to the spiritual eye as in Elisha's day. 10. The man of God in every age is the safeguard of the state. 11. Ruin is always the result of disregard of the laws of righteousness. 12. The story of Israel with its sin and its fall is the story of every life that does not find its guidance in God.

The University of Chicago.

*Sunday-school Lesson for September 25—Third Quarterly Review: Golden Text—No good thing will he behold from them that walk uprightly (Psa. 84:11); Lesson Outline—1. The Times of Elijah (Lesson 1-6); 2. The Times of Elijah (Lessons 7-16); 3. The Times of Amos (Lessons 11, 12).

SUBSCRIBERS' WANTS.

deavor.

[KINS.

25.

[CCESS?

.)

akes life the test
m there is noth-
ld but life; nay,
ot to be weighed
Yes, it is life,
bout, as may be
in the Revised
ofit a man if he
e his own life?''

h we pant,
want.

successful in the
'e in a lifetime.
as he thrills and
excitement. O,
d not death that
when they utter
more of life,''
yearning. That
re only gratified
fe and not with
ving, then, is to

n order to make
First, we must
next, we must
In other words,
the utmost we
our utmost; we
spend ourselves;
and then give it
we have to save,
vo things done—
life is become a

much in Christ's
her's. The one
hat he has must
must never be
s he finds. God
le for what one
en he was young.
his endowments
e on he decided
the most of the
eeling sure that
or anything he
not in obtaining
is in developing
ining the whole
e, of which you

way to expand
rinciple of the
ence more won-
would save his
n every sphere.
must expend
in money must
nger who would
ath. A friend
out his love. If
n the waters it
ry one of these
tion about, and
kness, poverty,
hunger of soul
that scattereth
at withholdeth
h to poverty.''
n will never be
stands as it is

FACTS AND FACTORS.

Spanish is spoken by 42,000,000; French by 51,000,000; Russian by 75,000,000; German by 75,000,000 and English by 130,000,000.

A new planet has been discovered. Its orbit overlaps to some extent that of Mars.

The largest gasometer in the world is at East Greenwich. When full, it contains 12,000,000 cubic feet of gas. It weighs 2,200 tons, is 180 feet high, 300 feet in diameter, requires 1,200 tons of coal to fill it with gas and cost nearly £40,000.

Last year on American railways one passenger was killed in accidents out of every 2,827,474 passengers carried. That is to say, that you can take a train 2,827,474 times before, on the law of average, your turn comes to be killed. You will have traveled 72,093,963 miles on the cars before that turn comes, and 4,541,945 miles before you are injured. If you travel 20 miles every day for 300 days in the year, you can keep on at it for 758 years before your turn comes to be hurt. If there had been railways when our Savior was born and you had begun to travel on the first day of the year A.D. 1, and had traveled 100 miles in every day of every month of every year since then, you would still have (in this year 1898) nearly three million miles yet to travel before your turn.

An exchange says: The cost of the war, up to the first of this month, according to the bills published by the government, was $118,000,000, of which the largest items were: pay of troops and sailors, $27,000,000; purchase of auxiliary ships, $20,000,000; mobilization of army and navy, $17,000,000; commissary department, $15,000,000; ordnance and arms, $10,000,000, and the same amount for harbor defense; the ammunition for the Santiago fleet cost $4,000,000; the coal purchashd by the government for the use of the navy cost $5.000,000, and altogether $8,000,000 were expended in providing ammunition for army and navy.

The surface of the sea is estimated at 150,000,000 square miles, taking the whole surface of the globe at 197,000,000, and its greatest depth supposedly equals the height of the highest mountain, or four miles. The Pacific ocean covers 78,000,000 square miles, the Atlantic 25,000,000, the Mediterranean 1,000,000.

The preliminary report of the Interstate Commerce Commission for 1897 shows that last year the railways of the country paid $40,979,933 in taxes. All companies had not reported, but compared with the preceding year the report shows that on about 2,000 miles less of road in 1897 than in 1896 the railways paid about $3,000,000 more of taxes. The total dividends paid during the year were $57,290,579. Out of every 97 cents earned by the railways, therefore, above expenses, 57 cents was profit and 40 cents went in taxes. In the Central Southwestern states (Kansas, Missouri, Arkansas, Colorado, Oklahoma and Indian Territory) the taxes exceeded dividends by nearly $3,000,000. In Texas taxes exceeded dividends by over one million. In New England and the Northern and Eastern states dividends largely exceeded the taxes. The report shows that in the densely populated states the railways could pay more taxes than they do, but that in the less populous states of the Middle and West the taxes are already in excess of the profits from the business.

Marriages.

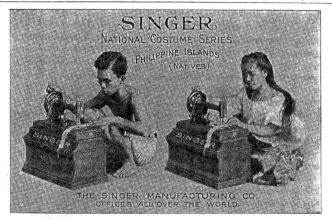

KING—GOTT.—At bride's home, near Mt. Auburn, Ia., Thursday evening, Aug. 18, 1898, by James T. Nichols, Prof. G. E. King, of Cedar Rapids, Ia., and Miss Vesta Gott.

LEMASTER—CLENDENING.—At groom's residence, near Mt. Auburn, Ia., Aug. 22, 1898 by James T. Nichols, Mr. Albert Lemaster and Mrs. Louisa Clendening, of Vinton, Ia.

ROBERTS—OVERFELT.—In Paris, Mo., Sept. 5, 1898, C. H. Strawn officiating, Mr. William W. Roberts to Miss Alzira G. Overfelt, both of Monroe county, Mo.

Obituaries.

[One hundred words will be inserted free. Above one hundred words, one cent a word. Please send amount with each notice.]

FOX.

Died suddenly of heart failure at her home in Clio, Mich., Mrs. Mary E. Fox. At the time of her death, which occurred Aug. 10th, 1898, she was 39 years, eight months and eight days old. She was born in Romulus, Mich., where she was married Oct. 8th, 1881 to Irwin Fox. She leaves two children, a little boy and a daughter of 16 years. It was said of her by every one, that she was "a lovely Chrislian lady." She has done her work well and will be worthy of a crown of life. She was the daughter of our Bro. and Sister Eckles, of Pine Run. They will haye our sympathy in this deep sorrow.

R. BRUCE BROWN.

Durand, Mich.

MINTON.

Warren S. Minton was born in Washington county, Penn., Feb. 10, 1830. His early life was spent about his father's mill, and he familiarized himself with the business in every detail. In 1855 he came to Illinois and settled in Clark county. Subsequently he removed to Edgar county and in 1864 he came to Charleston where he was actively engaged in business up to the time of the illness which, after many months of suffering, terminated in his death, Sunday, Sept. 12, 1897, at 10 o'clock P. M. On Oct. 18, 1859 he was united in marriage with Miss Maltida R. Wright, daughter of Samuel Wright. To this union two children were born, Clarence H., and Evangeline, now wife of S. E. Grove. For years previous and to the time of his death he was the senior member of the lumber firm of Minton & Sons, being associated with his son, Clarence, and his son-in-law, S. E. Grove. He has been intimately associated with the growth and development of this city. He was a man of broad information, keen insight into the affairs of men, and possessed most generous impulses. It has frequently been remarked by those who knew him best, since his death, that no worthy young man ever applied to Mr. Minton for aid in a business way and went away empty handed. His broad knowledge of men enabled him to discern the worth of a man and thus lend generous aid to worthy undertakings. In brief he was one of the old stock, now rapidly thinning by death, whose unquestionable honesty and intensity of purpose stamped their efforts indelibly on the community of which they were a part. In the broadest sense of the term he was an honest man, and that of itself is a monument more lasting than granite. For years he was a devoted and sincere communicant of the Christian Church and his walk in life was an evidence of the faith he professed. And now that he has answered the summons that awaits us all, Warren S. Minton will be mourned and remembered only as the worthy are mourned.—*Charleston (Ill.) Courier.*

WOOD.

In the death of Betsy J. Wood, the church at Cascade loses one of its charter members and Kent loses a pioneer. She united with the church at its organization in 1865; for 33 years she has lived a consistent Christian. After more than eight months' suffering she fell asleep in Jesus Aug. 25, at the age of 62 years, seven months and seven days. She leaves her husband and eight children. Funeral was held at the church, the writer using as a text Psalms 55:6.

J. JAY FINLEY.

Cascade, Mich., Aug. 29, 1898.

I Was Sick and Ye Visited Me.

Yes, I *was* sick and the board of Ministerial Relief visited me, and enabled me to obtain treatment in a sanitarium, without which I should never have been able for work again, and perhaps would not now have been living. Since I have somewhat recovered, I have done a little work, and baptized a few converts, and ere this year comes to a close I hope to be in active regular work again.

Now, brethren and friends, there is no theorizing with me about what Ministerial Relief may do, or the wisdom of making a specialty of offerings for it in all our churches. I know what it *has done*, and many of you know what it has done elsewhere, and we surely must know that it is a grand and noble work, deserving the earnest support of all.

"Sick, and ye visited me"—but what kind of visits do you make? Let us be very personal in this matter—those which bring sympathy are good, those which bring encouraging words and prayers are all right, but when a fellow is down and never expects to be up again, the visitor which brings him the means to put him on his feet, is the one he is glad to see and is the one who adopts the quickest, the best and surest way of showing real sympathy.

And then, brethren, do we remember that there are a great number of our real 'fathers in the gospel' who have given the best of their lives to upholding the Christ to the world, and have done more than you or I ever may hope to do; who, because of no fault of thei almost destitute? Who needs our sym more than they do? Do we in sympatl member them, I say? What have we d show to *them* and to the *world*, and t 'Father of Mercies' that they really do our sympaties?

My heart goes out to those who have stood by Bro. Atkinson, and supporte work. But, I believe many do not r what a great work this is, and how nobl Atkinson is laboring and how little re couragement he receives. Let us give selves earnestly and prayerfully to this just now, when it is so much needed push it to the front. Shall we not as p and evangelists, make this work *our* wor who knows just how long he may prospe just how soon he may be thankful for from the board of Ministerial Relief? T is the time. "Then shall the King say, ye blessed of my Father, inherit the ki prepared for you from the foundation world, for I was sick, and ye visited me.

ONE VISI

The foregoing is an article by a good b who received temporary aid from the bo Relief. Let every one who reads it s offering to Howard Cale, 120 E. Marke Indianapolis, Indiana, and send it at on it is greatly needed.

D. R. Lu

for God, out-and-out—he draws a good picture of John.

The cryptic theory which makes up the contents of the book on its positive and constructive side and the great travesty or pantomime theory which presents its negative side maintain the unity of the Apocalypse and its intelligibility to a degree to more than suggest the probability that the key has at last been found to the enigma of the New Testament which, when once understood, becomes a fitting close to the revelation of God to man. His publication of this volume will quicken thought and lead to a new study of the Apocalypse and to the whole history of redemption in the light of it.

J. J. HALEY.

MAGAZINES.

Self-Culture, Hebron, Ohio, comes out this month in an entirely new and very attractive dress. This magazine is now liberally illustrated, and instead of 96 pages of text, as heretofore, will in the future contain 128 pages of good reading-matter every month. This addition of 32 pages is to make room for a somewhat higher class of articles than have thus far appeared in the magazine—articles similar to those which have given the Forum and the North American Review their high standing. All the former instructive and entertaining features which have made Self-Culture deservedly popular with intelligent people will be retained, and several new departments added. This large magazine can now be had for one dollar per year.

Anything that is of practical benefit to Mothers' Clubs is, in this day and age, very welcome. The course of study published in the New Crusade for March and April, 1898, was received with much enthusiasm. The Mothers' Club Helper, issued monthly by the Wood-Allen Publishing Company, Ann Arbor, Mich., will be equally well received. It contains a well-directed series of questions upon the topics presented by the course of study, designates home readings, and presents a complete program for each meeting. It is the only complete guide for Mothers' Clubs yet published. Price thiry-five cents per copy; two dollars for one year.

STOCKHOLDER'S MEETING.

Notice is hereby given that the annual meeting of the stockholders of the Christian Publishing Co. will be held at the company's office, 1522 Locust St., St. Louis, Mo., on Tuesday, Oct. 4th, 1898, at 10 o'clock A. M., for the election of Directors, and for the transaction of such other business as may legally come before said meeting.

J. H. GARRISON, Pres.
W. D. CREE, Sec.

St. Louis, Mo., Sept. 1, 1898.

Publishers' Notes.

Many of both young and old students of the Bible will say, "I have heard and read the story of Queen Esther all my life." It is doubtless true that you are in a measure familiar with the main facts in the history of this Bible character, but have never studied her wonderful life beyond a superficial glance. What study you have already given to this remarkable person is but of an introductory nature, and now you are prepared to follow M. M. Davis as he delineates this Old Testament character in his new book, now about ready, entitled "Queen Esther." The author being a close student of the Scriptures, an eloquent writer and having an importantBible character for a subject—all combined, can but make an intensely interesting volume. The book is bound in beautiful cloth, with numerous illustrations, and the price is 75 cents, postpaid.

TWO COMPANIONS.

Our two late publications, "In the Days of Jehu" and "King Saul" can properly be called companions. The author, J. Breckenridge Ellis, has gained a widespread reputation as a vivid and eloquent writer on Old Testament characters. The former of these books has been before the reading public but a short time and has been highly praised by competent judges. The latter is just from the press and the author seems to write with a growing interest. The world needs to learn more of the traits of prominent Bible characters.

These books are beautifully bound in latest style cloth binding. The price of "In the Days of Jehu" is 75 cents, and "King Saul" is $1.00, postpaid.

LOOK UP.

Our last publication, "Wonders of the Sky," by W. J. Russell, is an interesting little book, inviting the mind to look up and see the wondors that are shown in the heavens above us. The author shows evidence of great familiarity with astronomical literature. He has so presented the subject that its greatness can be grasped by the youthful mind, and the minds of the ordinary rearders. It is truly a great subject, presented in simple and easy manner and leading the mind to a greater reverence for the Creator of the heavens, and inviting the mind to "look up through nature to nature's God." This neat little volume is just from the press, beautifully bound, and the price is 50 cents.

MORE WANTED.

We still want more agents to sell "America or Rome—Christ or the Pope." We are receiving numerous inquiries for our special terms to agents for the sale of this book, but want them in every community. Why not earn a few dollars in selling this book? It is a vigorous and reliable work on the despotism of Rome. The book contains more than five hundred pages, and is profusely illustrated. The sale of a few dozen copies in your community will aid the agent financially and will circulate a book the contents of which should be familiar to the American people. Conclude to take up the sale of this book and get the terms to agents from the Christian Publishing Co., St. Louis, Mo.

Announcements.

Iowa Christian Convention

Will be held at the East Side Church of Christ, Des Moines, Iowa, from the 26th to the 30th of Sept. Those expecting to attend will confer a favor upon the Committee on Entertainment, if you will notify the pastor, D. A. Wickizer, 918 East 12th St.; also state the day you expect to arrive. The Committee on Reception will meet all trains and direct delegates to the right street cars.

Should you fail to meet with the Committee for any cause, go direct to Street Car Depot, corner of 6th and Mulberry Sts., which is near depots, take any of the Capitol, or Fair Ground, or Walker Street cars, come to East 12th St., then walk one block north to church. In coming to the city go to West Side Depots; do not get off on East Side. Committee will not meet East Side trains.

Des Moines churches extend a welcome to the Christian workers of Iowa, or of other states, who may come to assist, or to enjoy the work of the convention. Dinners and suppers will be served at the church. Lodging and breakfast will be provided at places of entertainment. Those coming on Monday come direct to the church for your meals.

D. A. WICKIZER,
Pastor East Side Church of Christ.

Programs for Forefathers' Day, Oct. 23rd, 1898.

We give four outline programs. We think any one will make a delightful hour.

No. 1.

1. Ten minutes service of Prayer and Praise.
2. Biographical sketch of Barton Warren Stone. (5 min.)
3. Biographical sketch of Alexander Campbell and his father. (5 min.)
4. Biographical sketch of Walter Scott, the Evangelist. (5 min.)
5. A five-minute statement of the chief purpose of these pioneers.
6. Our country as a mission field. (10 min. talk, with map.)
7. Song, "My Country, 'Tis of Thee."
8. Offering for Home Missions under the auspices of the A. C. M. S.
9. Benediction.

No. 2.

Especially commended to C. E. Societies that observe the day for the first time.

1. Hymn, "I Love Thy Kingdom, Lord."
2. Scripture Reading—John 17: 20-26.
3. Prayer.
4. Short Addresses:
   a. Meaning of Forefathers' Day.
   b. The Sacrifices of the Fathers of the Restoration.
   Prayer—That we may have the spirit of sacrifice.
   c. How our movement began.
   Hymn—"Triumphant Zion, Lift Thy Head."
   d. Our present numbers and influence.
   e. There remaineth yet very much land to be possessed.
5. Song, "My Country, 'Tis of Thee."
6. Offering for Home Missions under the auspices of the A. C. M. S.
7. Closing hymn and Benediction.

No. 3.

1. "Praise God from whom all blessings flow."
2. Short prayer by pastor.
3. Hymn, "I have heard a joyful sound, Jesus saves."
4. Scripture Reading, Acts 2:37-47.
5. Prayer by president for more of the spirit of the Forefathers in our movement.
6. Short Address, "Why Observe Forefathers' Day?"
7. Short sketches of the beginnings of our movement in Ohio, Indiana and Kentucky.
8. Special selection of music.
9. Address, "Our Plea, a Restoration and not a Reformation."
10. Address, "Our Work and Workers."
11. Song, "My Country, 'Tis of Thee."
12. Offering for Home Missions under the auspices of A. C. M. S.
13. Hymn, "Blest be the tie that binds."
14. Benediction.

No. 4.

1. Opening Service—Scripture Quotations (Missionary).
2. Prayer for our movement.
3. Song, "Ho, Reapers of life's harvest."
4. "What mean ye by this service of Forefathers' Day?" (8 min.)
5. Our great editors, A. Campbell I. Errett, B. Franklin, B. W. Johnson. (8 min.)
6. Hymn, "Stand up, stand up for Jesus."
7. The strength of the plea that the Forefathers made. (8 min.)
8. Every motive that impelled our fathers to make this plea strong in the Mississippi Valley should impel us to make it equally strong all over the United States. (5 min.)
9. Song, "My Country, 'Tis of Thee."
10. Offering for Home Missions under the auspices of the A. C. M. S.
11. The inner spiritual life of Alexander Campbell. (8 min.)
12. "Blest be the tie that binds."
13. Bendiction.

Send to Benj. L. Smith, Y. M. C. A. Building, Cincinnati, O., for help and information on these subjects.

The Hiram College Jubilee Endow ment.

THE BURNING QUESTION.

We are strong in our convictions that adequate endowment of our colleges is great overshadowing question that now fronts the Disciples of Christ. Ever and certain great questions leap to the front demand the attention of the people. We firmly convinced that college endowment for the present to have the right of way. believe that this question overshadows other questions in its importance right n The reasons are not hard to discover. immense advance in educational standard the last decade or two has made it more ficult from year to year for our institution learning to meet the demands upon them w out being involved in financial ruin. We teaching in Hiram College twice as n branches as were taught twenty years Probably it is safe to say that the instru in the colleges of the country covers twi large a field on the average, as it did tw years ago. That means that college facu have had to be greatly enlarged and sequently the general expense of the col work has been greatly increased. In ord have our institutions of learning keep where in sight of the advancing educati procession, they have had to enlarge work from year to year. Our colleges meagre endowments have been compelle cover about the same field of work that o institutions around them with million endowment cover. To do this most economy has been practiced; most exac demands have been made of our teachers fact they have had to do double work on a half-pay, and even then most of our ins tions have been compelled to incur debts jeopardize their very existence. Nor ha end yet been reached. Many of our institu are compelled even now to face the questi future enlargement of work in order to com successfully with other well-endowed coll and all must face the question of gr enlarged material equipment. Somet must be done, and that speedily, f larger endowment of our colleges. question forces itself upon us at this tim never before. We must meet it now an ought to meet it in a way that will reflect h upon us as a people.

The trustees of Hiram College have d mined to make the occasion of their Ju Commencement in June 1900, the tim placing this honored institution upon a financial basis, thus enabling it to enter u new era of greatly increased usefulness. effort will be made to secure $250,000 o ditional endowment by means of a great p lar movement among the friends of the c and of Christian education in general. will undertake to enlist an army of at 50,000 people who will join together i common effort to adequately endow th stitution by giving it $250,000. True, have no precedent to warrant such an u taking. Colleges have usually been end by the gifts of wealthy people, but Hi trustees are convinced that the time is ripe great popular movement. They believe th masses of the people ought to have a h our educational work, and they furthe feel that if the proper steps are taken movement can be carried to a successful The watchword from this time on wil $250,000 for Hiram by June 1900, and the from this time forward will be to enlist an of 50,000 persons for the accomplishm this great object.

Perhaps many will ask the questio Hiram worthy of such an effort? We b that it is, but in order that all may shar faith we will publish during the next t three weeks, brief articles of a historic showing the beginning and progress o school, its work, its financial manageme present condition and its future pros We will then call for the army of volu who will give from $1,00 to $1,000 each, o more, if possible, for the accomplishm this great object.

E. V. ZOLL

THE CHRISTIAN-EVANGELIST.

A WEEKLY FAMILY AND RELIGIOUS JOURNAL.

Vol. XXXV. September 22, 1898 No. 38.

CONTENTS.

DITORIAL:
- Current Events........................355
- Expansion, of Course,—But How.....356
- Is the World Growing Worse?.... ...357
- Our Great Deliverer........ 357
- Editor's Easy Chair...................358
- Questions and Answers....... 359

RIGINAL CONTRIBUTIONS:
- Primitive Christianity.—H. W. B. Myrick.... 359
- Can I Love my Enemies?—N. J. Aylesworth............ 360
- Civilization and Religion.—Sherman Hill............... 361

ORRESPONDENCE:
- Wheeling Through England...........366
- A Bit of Dixie 366
- Los Angeles Letter............ 367
- At Fontainbleau................ 367
- Reply to Editor's Criticism............368
- Helps for Preachers 369
- Japan Letter...........................369
- Iowa Letter 370
- History of Hiram College..............370
- Newspapers in Congressional Library.371
- Nebraska Letter 371
- Christian College... 372

AMILY CIRCLE:
- To Win the World (poem)............376
- Text Stories—Where there's Drink there's Danger........ 376
- The Good as the Enemy of the Best....377
- At School and at Home 378
- Don't Hurry (poem)........ 378
- Kipling and His Work................378

ISCELLANEOUS:
- Current Religious Thought............361
- Ministerial Association of the Disciples of Christ in Eastern Ohio......362
- Our Budget. 363
- Personal Mention........... 365
- Missionary................. 371
- Notes and News.......................373
- Evangelistic.... 374
- The Sunday-school.... 380
- Christian Endeavor...................380
- Marriages and Obituaries.............381
- Literature...... ... .382
- Publishers' Notes......................384

Subscription $1.75.

Incline R. R.—Lookout Mountain.

CHATTANOOGA CONVENTIONS, OCTOBER 13-21.

PUBLISHED BY

CHRISTIAN PUBLISHING COMPANY

1522 Locust St., St. Louis.

THE

CHRISTIAN - EVANGELIST

J. H. GARRISON, EDITOR.

W. W. HOPKINS, ASSISTANT.

B. B. TYLER, J. J. HALEY,

EDITORIAL CONTRIBUTORS.

What We Plead For.

The Christian-Evangelist pleads for:

The Christianity of the New Testament, taught by Christ and his Apostles, versus the theology of the creeds taught by fallible men—the world's great need.

The divine confession of faith on which Christ built his church, versus human confessions of faith on which men have split the church.

The unity of Christ's disciples, for which he so fervently prayed, versus the divisions in Christ's body, which his apostles strongly condemned.

The abandonment of sectarian names and practices, based on human authority, for the common family name and the common faith, based on divine authority, versus the abandonment of scriptural names and usages for partisan ends.

The hearty co-operation of Christians in efforts of world-wide beneficence and evangelization, versus petty jealousies and strifes in the struggle for denominational pre-eminence.

The fidelity to truth which secures the approval of God, versus conformity to custom to gain the favor of men.

The protection of the home and the destruction of the saloon, versus the protection of the saloon and the destruction of the home.

For the right against the wrong;
For the weak against the strong;
For the poor who've waited long
For the brighter age to be.
For the truth, 'gainst superstition,
For the faith, against tradition,
For the hope, whose glad fruition
Our waiting eyes shall see.

RATES OF SUBSCRIPTION.

Single subscriptions, new or old	$1.75	each
In clubs of five or more, new or old	1.50	"
Reading Rooms	1.25	"
Ministers	1.00	"

With a club of ten we will send one additional copy free.

All subscriptions payable in advance. Label shows the month up to the first day of which your subscription is paid. If an earlier date than the present is shown, you are in arrears. No paper discontinued without express orders to that effect. Arrears should be paid when discontinuance is ordered.

In ordering a change of post office, please give the OLD as well as the NEW address.

Do not send local check, but use Post office or Express Money Order, or draft on St. Louis, Chicago or New York, in remitting.

ISTIAN-EVANGELIST

opinion and methods, Liberty; in all things, Charity."

, Mo., Thursday, September 22, 1898. No. 38

sibility for the alleged useless suffering and loss of life has been brought home where it belongs. If they are false, the Secretary of War and the heads of bureaus under him have a right to demand such an investigation as will effectually remove the suspicion which has been cast upon them.

The American Peace Commission, which was appointed to confer with a similar Spanish commission to arrange the final terms of the peace is now on its way to Paris where the sessions are to be held. After the last conference between the Cabinet and the members of the commission previous to the departue of the latter it was officially announced from the State Department that the commission would take with it definite instructions in regard to the terms of peace upon which the administration will insist. As to what these instructions are, a formal secrecy at least must be preserved until the negotiations are complete, but there is a general understanding in regard to certain points. So far as the fate of the Philippines is concerned, three points stand out with considerable certainty: The cession of the island of Luzon, on which Manila is situated, will be demanded as being necessary for the establishment of a defensible base for commercial or naval operations in the East. The other islands of the group *may* be allowed to remain under Spanish sovereignty on condition of the guarantee of a just and and unoppressive form of government. In case Spain is allowed to retain possession of

ary in the west of Ireland. He was installed pastor of the First Presbyterian Church at Armagh in 1852, and in 1858 was called to the Church of St. Mary's Abbey (now Rutland Square) in Dublin. He received from Queen Victoria the honorary appointment of Commissioner of Education for Ireland. In 1867 Dr. Hall was a delegate from the General Assembly of the Presbyterian Church in Ireland to the Presbyterian Church in the United States, and after his return to Ireland he received a call to the Fifth Avenue Presbyterian Church, New York. He accepted it and entered upon his labors in November, 1867. A new church edifice was erected for Dr. Hall in 1875, at a cost of about $1,000,000, on the corner of Fifth Avenue and Fifty-fifth Street. He was elected chancellor of the University of the city of New York in 1882."

The banking, currency, coinage and production of precious metals in the United States during the past century are presented in great detail by a series of tables just issued by the Treasury Bureau of Statistics as a part of the July Summary of Commerce and Finance. These tables, covering more than one hundred pages of this unusually large volume, present a very complete picture of the growth of the banking system and of the currency, both metallic and paper, and to this is added for comparative purposes a brief statement of the banking and currency conditions and gold and silver production in other parts of the world. An examination of

being 329; in 1840, 741; in 1850, 809; in 1850, 1,562. The decrease from 1860 was equally rapid, the number of state banks in 1863 being 1,023; in 1864, 349, and 1868, 247, while the number of national banks organized in 1863, 1864 and 1865 was 1,601. State banks again increased in numbers after 1868, the number in 1872 being 566; in 1885, 975; in 1888, 1,403; in 1890, 2,101; in 1894, 3,586 and in 1897, the number, including private banks, is reported at 3,873. Prior to 1860 the deposits in state banks amounted to but little more than half the capital stock, while since 1877 deposits have at all times been more than double the amount of capital stock, and in 1897 were $723,640,795, against a capital stock of $228,677,088.

The statements regarding the amount of money in circulation in the United States at various periods are equally interesting. The amount in circulation in 1800 is given at $4.99 per capita; in 1810, $7.60; in 1820, $6.96; in 1830, $6.69; in 1840, $10.91; in 1850, $12.02; in 1860, $13.85: in 1865, $20.57: in 1870, $17.50; in 1880, $19. 41; in 1890, $22.82, and in 1898, $24.73. The statement regarding gold production and coinage in the United States and in the world shows that the mines of the United States produced more gold in the year 1897 than in any preceding year except those of the great gold developments of California—1852-3-4. The gold production of the United States in 1897 is given at $57,363,000, while that of 1852 was $60,000,000, thaf of 1853, $65,000,000, and that of 1884, $60,000,000. Colorado is shown to have taken in 1897 first place in the rank of gold producing states, her production in that year being $19,104,200, against $14,618,300 by California; while prior to that time, California had constantly stood at the head ot the column of gold producing states.

The coinage of gold by the United States mints in 1897 was $64,634,865, which is nearly 50 per cent. greater than the average annual coinage since 1870. The statements covering the gold production of the world are also especially interesting. They show by stated periods the amount of gold produced in the world since the discovery of America. The total value of the gold produced from 1492 to 1898 (estimating 1897 at $240,000,000) being $9,023,320,600, of which amount $6,065,097,600 has been produced since 1850, the product of the last half century thus being double that of the preceding 350 years.

The second annual session of the Civic-Philanthropic Conference will be held at Battle Creek, Mich., Oct. 18 to 23, 1898, of which Rev. David J. Burrill, D. D., New York City, is president, and J. H. Kellogg, M. D., Battle Creek, Mich., is vice-president. Philanthropists, educators and ministers of all denominations are expected to participate in the conference to consider economic, hygienic, sanitary, philanthropic and patriotic questions with the hope of evolving some practical methods of reform.

"Jews who cherish the hope of ultimately purchasing Palestine and resettling it with the people of their own race convened last week at Basle, Switzerland. By a large majority the congress decided to open a colonial bank, having a central office in London, with a capital of $10,000,000. The movement for the recovery of Palestine, although it has been regarded as visionary by many prominent Jews, and has been the subject of much ridicule, nevertheless seems to be making headway."

EXPANSION, OF COURSE—BUT HOW?

The above pertinent comment is made by a thoughtful reader on our recent editorial, "Expansion or Contraction—Which?" The question refers particularly to expansion as applied to our own religious movement, in the editorial above mentioned. While we indicated in that article, in a general way, what is the nature of the expansion we need, it might be well to deal with the question more in detail.

We need more expansion *educationally*. Our colleges and other institutions of learning need more liberal endowment and better equipment to enable them to do a higher quality of work and to reach a larger number of students. This includes our Bible colleges and the biblical departments of our colleges and universities. An educated ministry is a necessity in order to any permanent or healthful expansion. Nearly every weakness or evil among us may be traced back, directly or indirectly, to the lack of a larger number of properly trained ministers to lead our churches forward in Christian growth and activity.

We need expansion among the rank and file of our membership in *biblical knowledge*. This want can only be supplied by the pulpits giving more attention to biblical instruction, and by raising the standard of our Bible or Sunday-schools. We are relying now very largely on these schools for imparting systematic instruction in the Bible, and yet the methods employed in these schools are very inadequate, the teachers are often incompetent and a large per cent. of our membership do not attend these schools. There needs to be an expansion of our ideas as to what the Sunday-school is and what it is designed to accomplish for the church and for the children. There needs to be an expansion of the sense of obligation on the part of church members to make better use of these schools for increasing their knowledge of the Bible.

We need expansion of ideas *concerning our own religious movement*—its principles and its aims. For lack of this many are sick among us and some are dead, so far as their usefulness in our special mission is concerned. The tendency is, and will be as we get older, to forget what manner of people we are, and what we are here for. If the reformation or restoration which we are pleading is a providential movement, having a mission to accomplish, nothing is dearer than that we should understand what that mission is and be loyal to it; that is, loyal to God's purpose concerning us. This work must receive special attention in our training of the young people among us. The Christian Endeavor movement among the young people affords an excellent opportunity for this training, and it is in perfect accord with the principles of Christian Endeavor that we educate our young people in a knowledge of their own principles. If it were not, then we would have no connection with it. A very wise move has been fairly inaugurated among us in the Bethany C. E. Reading Courses, under the general editorship and management of J. Z. Tyler. This should be far more generally patronized than it is at present, though the number of Reading Circles is constantly increasing. It has in it the promise of great usefulness in overcoming that ignorance and indifference which are fatal to any cause. In order to the expansion the Christian Endeavor idea among Bro. Tyler should be asked to devote whole time to this work. There must ne be expansion in our *Christian sympa* and *fellowship*. Along with a better kno edge and appreciation of our own miss there will be sure to come a growing rec nition of what God is accomplish through others, and an increasing fell ship and sympathy with all who reflect image of Christ in their characters, who are seeking to extend his domin over the world. Without this, our plea union will be as a sounding brass an clanging cymbal. It is the narrowest of provincialism, or even worse, of secta anism, for any religious people to supp that they have a monopoly of truth, that God can use no other agency for tending his kingdom. This feeling is day one of the most serious obstacles the unity of Christ's followers.

We need expansion in our ideas and practice of *Christian giving*. The idea stewardship has not taken deep root ye the minds of a large part of our memb ship. The proportion of money we give religious purposes, to that given for pu selfish or worldly ends, is lamentably sm There must be expansion, or spiritual c traction and moral shipwreck are likely result. Both the pulpit and press hav plain duty to perform in reference to expansion. Not until our wealthy men, others not so wealthy, come to feel the sponsibility that attaches to the possess of means, can our educational and m sionary interests prosper as they should

We must expand in our *missionary tivities*. This expansion must be twofo A larger number of churches and indiv ual members must be enlisted in the w of contributing missionary funds, and th who do contribute must do it with a m liberal hand. This will enable our miss boards to expand the work in new fie and give better support to missions alre established. The needs of the heat world, and of the ungospeled masses in own land, call loudly for this expansion.

Finally, we need to expand in our *fa* and in our *spiritual life*. This expans is sure to result from the expansions p viously mentioned. By education, by knowledge of the Bible, and of our c mission in the world, by charity towa others, by more consecration to the w God has given us to do in ministering the manifold needs of our race, we sh surely grow in spiritual stature and rea the end of our creation and redemption.

The Salvation Army celebrated thirty-third anniversary in London rece ly. General Booth reported that in spring of the present year the organizat possessed 15,019 officers attached to 6, corps and outposts. There were 33,662 local officers and voluntary offici 14,500 bandsmen and 1,647 officers enga in social work. This social work show woman's homes with accommodation 1,754 and 1,227 inmates; the total num admitted during the twelve months 4,769. There are 15 prison-gate homes farms, 108 slum posts, 28 food depots, night shelters with accommodation for 307; 38 work-shops, 14 children's ho and 24 other social institutions.—*The dependent.*

THE WORLD GROWING WORSE?

ccording to such books as "Caesar's ımn," and a more recent, but no less imistic production, entitled, "Chris- ity and Anti-Christianity," there is a my future in the immediate front of ıuman race. One of these authors is a ırialistic pessimist and the other is a tual pessimist, and while they go in at rent holes they come out at the same e—a disastrous future for humanity. world religious, the world social, the d industrial, the world political, and ;ary, and cosmic, and all other worlds, ıadly out of joint and steadily growing e. If one takes up a premillennialist ıal he will find on a conspicuous page, ear type, a miscellaneous collection of ı, calamities, accidents, crimes, such as ıquakes, cyclones, pestilences, fam- , strikes, riots, insurrections, battles, iers, suicides, embezzlements, robberies ıvory divorce suits and all other cosmic human offenses that can be gather- :om the newspapers, hashed up in ap- ed style, with this editorial interpreta- appended or implied—"Didn't I tell so? Don't you see that the world is g to the Devil as fast as it can?" The el pessimist, with a materialistic and ·moral conception of the universe, ng no faith in God, in immortality, in ıl responsibility, in the tribunal of cience, in the eternal order that makes ighteousness, seeing manifestations of :der in the world, and lawlessness in ıty, he is sure, in the absence of a ıl brake, and moral direction, that the machine is drifting helplessly toward rocks.

ır distinguished editor, in conveying to he request of a subscriber to write on question that stands at the head of this ır, said it always reminded him of the r question, "Is God dead?" If there living God there is a living universe, ıternal Some-One, not ourselves, that es for righteousness, and for life ever- ng. The unfailing optimism of Israel's ·hets, under the gloomiest of present ıitions, was based upon a conviction nothing could shake, that a living and God meant the world's future for his y. They looked with an unshaken ı to the far-off divine event to which whole creation moves, because they so ıly perceived the moral order of the d, and the immanence of God in all his ts, that were the sure guarantees of expected consummation. If God lives ıust reign, and the reign of God means ıltimate triumph of righteousness.

is highly probable that there is more :edness in the world than there was a ired years ago, and just as probable there is more righteoueness than at previous time, but only for the reason, ıaps, that there are more people in the d than there used to be. It is true also intensification and a bold aggression ·acterizes the activities of modern life, ıat the wicked are more wicked and the teous more righteous, than in our ıdfathers' days. But this focalization ıoral issues on burning centers, this ilization of beast-power, and the armies ghteousness for the culminating con- of the ages, is no proof that the world :owing worse. On the contrary it is a ·ful sign of the world's permanent erment, unless God is weaker than the Devil, the creed of a vile pessimism that no Christian can subscribe to. Last Sunday is the best the world ever saw, and next Sunday will be an improvement on last. There are more Bibles, more Christians, more churches, more missionaries, more Christian workers, more young people doing battle for the kingdom of God, a cleaner moral sentiment pervading public opinion than ever before. There has been more progress in science, art, education, religion, statecraft and in sociological appliances for the alleviation of poverty and the betterment of the masses, in the last fifty years, than in all the preceding centuries of the Christian era put together. As we look through the gate of the twentieth century, wa can contemplate the dying century as a hundred years of amazing fruitfulness in facilities for the uplifting of mankind.

In studying the world's moral growth we must not compare to-day with yesterday, nor this week with last, nor this decade with the one that preceded it. Long periods, centuries, cycles and millenniums must enter into the comparison. The mills of God grind slowly, if they do grind exceeding fine. Compare the closing days of the nineteenth century with the days of bad eminence, when Christ was born in Bethlehem of Judea. Compare this year of grace with two hundred years ago in the most civilized country of the world. Compare the reign of Queen Victoria with the reign of Henry the Eighth, or that of Queen Bess. They tortured heretics, burned martyrs and stuck the heads of men on iron pikes in the streets of London four centuries ago. To-day a man is fined or imprisoned for beating his horse in the streets of the English metropolis. Modern liberty has completely triumphed over the brutal despotism of the past. Look at the wars of Cromwell and Napoleon in contrast to the Hispano-American war, now happily brought to a close. Cromwell took off the head of Charles the First, and when the Royalists came into power they snatched the Protector's coffin from its tomb in Westminster Abbey, hung his moldering body at Tyburn, flung it in a hole under the gallows, and stuck his head on a pole in Westminster Hall in London. Napoleon, after Waterloo, narrowly escaped death at the hands of his captors. The Duke of Wellington voted for his execution. Admiral Cervera, while a prisoner of war, was offered a mansion in the United States for his personal safety and as an inducement to become a citizen of the land of the free and the home of the brave! Two centuries ago pirates swarmed the seas to prey on the merchant marines of the nations. When belated Spain threatened to fit out vessels for privateering and the destruction of our commerce, civilization frowned it down. On our side the late war was the most humane and generous in the history of the planet. Such magnanimous treatment of a captured foe would have been impossible a hundred years ago. The next step will be disarmament and international arbitration as the method of settling disputes between civilized nations. Slavery is gone. Polygamy is going. The saloon is doomed. The agitation for the purification of politics is spreading. Temperance sentiment is growing. The kingdom of God and its righteousness is increasingly the theme of the pulpit. Applied Christianity is the goal toward which we are forging. The kingdoms of this world are destined to become the kingdom of our Lord and his Christ.

J. J. H.

Hour of Prayer.

OUR GREAT DELIVERER.

(Midweek Prayer-meeting Topic, Sept. 28, 1898.)

He shall deliver thee in six troubles;
Yea, in seven there shall no evil touch thee.
—*Job* 5:19.

Trouble is the common heritage of man. As is stated in the same connection from which the above is taken:

"Man is born unto trouble
As the sparks fly upward."

From the universality of trouble we are justified in inferring that it has a legitimate and necessary place in the development of character. It is certain that our troubles and afflictions accomplish more toward the uplifting of men than prosperity. It may be hard for us to understand the philosophy of this, but experience and observation confirm it.

The troubles that afflict us in this life are to be considered as a part of the divine discipline by which we are to be trained for higher living. They serve to remind us of our limitations, our weaknesses and our dependence upon God. Their tendency, too, is to keep us humble and to save us from haughtiness and pride. They serve to mellow the heart and to bring us into closer sympathy with all forms of human suffering. If, in spite of all the troubles that afflict men, many of them are still proud and self-sufficient, and forgetful of God, we can imagine what would be the condition of men if they enjoyed a continual line of prosperity.

The text we are studying declares that God is with us in these troubles and uses them for our good. It does not promise us freedom *from* trouble, but that God will deliver us *in* these troubles.

"He shall deliver thee in six troubles,
Yea, in seven there shall no evil touch thee."

Seven is the perfect number, and the meaning is that God will deliver the righteous, or those who put their trust in him, in *all* their troubles.

There is no friend we prize so highly as the one who comes to us in our trouble and shares it with us and helps us to bear it. Many a minister has made a perpetual welcome for himself in some home which he has visited when the family was shrouded in sorrow, and into which he carried a message of sympathy and of helpfulness. We have many friends, so called, in prosperity, but the true and tried ones are those who stand by us in adversity, and help us to bear our troubles.

It will help us greatly in bearing trouble to know that God is with us and is using the trouble for our good. We need not suppose that He has sent the trouble directly upon us. We may have brought it upon ourselves by our misdoings; but He is *in* the trouble with us, seeking to make it the occasion of our spiritual profiting. When sorrow overtakes us and our troubles seem to be too great for us to bear, let us remember that He who was in the fiery furnace with the Hebrew children, preserving them from harm, is with us in our troubles, and He will not suffer them to crush us. He will deliver us out of all our troubles.

Our troubles, then, in this view of the case, should always draw us nearer to God instead of driving us away from Him. The man who stays away from the house of God or refrains from his religious duties because of trouble, has not yet learned the true secret of living. Their end and purpose is to bring us into closer fellowship with God, and that is the great end to be sought. Not pleasure, not freedom from trouble, anxiety and care is the end of life, but to learn to walk with God and to find our highest joy in Him. When we come to understand this we can sing understandingly—

"Nearer, my God, to thee,
Nearer to thee;
E'en though it be a cross
That raiseth me."

PRAYER.

O, God, our Father, teach us to understand that all thy chastening is in love, and that whom Thou lovest Thou chastenest. When trouble comes upon us, and our way seems dark, help us, we beseech Thee, to trust in Thee, and to be willing to walk by faith where we cannot walk by sight. Help us to remember that Thou dealest with us as with children. And if we are called upon to "walk through the valley and shadow of death," be Thou with us, even there, and may Thy rod and Thy staff comfort us. May all the troubles and afflictions of this life serve to prepare us the better for the life beyond, which shall be undimmed by sorrow and untroubled by sin, forevermore. For Christ's sake, Amen!

Editor's Easy Chair.

OR MACATAWA MUSINGS.

Macatawa Park just now reminds one of Goldsmith's "Deserted Village," though the cause of its desertion is far different from that which drew out the lamentations of the vagrant poet. There is a stillness about its shores, its shaded dells and wooded heights, its hotel and dock, that is in strange contrast with the animation and bustle which characterized the place a few weeks ago. An occasional sail is seen on the horizon, out on Lake Michigan, and a few rowboats yet disturb the placid surface of Black Lake. Nearly all the launches have sought their winter quarters to wait the coming again of bright summer days. Only a few persons now gather nightly at the dock to see friends off on the Chicago boat, for few are left. The September wind seems to moan a sort of melancholy air to-day, as it sways the branches of the forest, which harmonizes well with the dirge of the waves that are beating on the shore. To add to the sombreness of the scene, the dark clouds have been weeping copious showers all morning, as if in sympathy with the sorrow of the beautiful Park, lamenting its departing guests. But the fire burns brightly on the hearth, and with papers, magazines and books, life is tolerable yet at Edgewood-on-the-Lake. But the end thereof, for the present season, is near.

The Missouri brotherhood of Disciples will soon be sending its representatives to Nevada in annual convention. It is important for the churches to remember that these state conventions are their conventions, made up of their delegates, to consider their work. This is the theory. Too often the churches fail to send any delegates, and quite as often they fail to feel the weight of obligation resting on them to join with their sister churches in the work of evangelizing the state and in building up all our interests. Missouri has a large membership, and it is natural that our brethren in other states should expect that the work in that state should be commensurate with our numbers. Let there be a full representation at Nevada, one of the most beautiful towns in one of the greatest states of the Union. We have read the program through carefully, and cannot well see how anybody in the state who can attend will be willing to miss the rich things which it provides. Hon. Champ Clark's address and Dean Willett's lectures would of themselves pay any one to cross the state to hear. But these are only a sample of what we are to have. Let us make it a great rally and a fit prelude to the National Convention at Chattanooga.

Speaking of the National Convention at Chattanooga, that ought to be made a notable gathering of our forces. We will meet on historic ground, and we can make it a historic convention. And yet, not we, as Paul would say, but Jesus Christ, acting in us and through us by the Holy Spirit, may make it a convention long to be remembered if we put ourselves in harmony with His purpose and seek His presence and aid. Many of the delegates who go there, perhaps all of them, will wish to visit Lookout Mountain. Why not hold a prayer-meeting up there, and in another "battle above the clouds," with the invisible forces of Satan, and under the leadership of Jesus Christ win a decisive victory over our indifference, our half-heartedness, our unbelief, and give ourselves anew and more unreservedly to the carrying out of His divine will on earth, even as it is done in heaven? This would make the convention of '98 a Lookout Convention, in which we should get a clearer vision of God, of the world's needs, and of our obligations and responsibilities as religious reformers and coworkers with all who are seeking to bring this world into subjection to Christ. If each man or woman of faith among us will pray that our convention in Chattanooga may be marked by such results as these, it will assuredly be a historic convention.

R. B. Neal, of Grayson, Ky., has favored us with some of his "Anti-Mormon tracts." We have just read No. 1, entitled, "Was Joe Smith a Prophet?" It is needless to say that Neal handles this Mormon pretender without gloves, and on the very basis on which his followers ground his claim to be a prophet of God he is shown to be a willful deceiver and falsifier. It is said that there are fifteen hundred Mormon evangelists now in the field proselyting for Mormonism and deceiving ignorant people. This makes it important that such tracts as those which Bro. Neal is supplying should be scattered broadcast in communities infected by Mormon teaching. Bro. Neal is doing a most useful work in this line, and should receive the co-operation of all who would protect the people from the monstrous deception of Mormonism.

A lady writing from Kansas City wishes us to state, in this department, what is the proper pronunciation of the name of thi Park, which she says she has heard pro nounced in three different ways. We hav never seen the name in a pronouncing dic tionary, and do not pretend to spea authoritatively, but the best usage a present places the accent on th last syllable—Mac-a-ta-*wah*. It is a Indian name, of course. The place is sai to have been discovered by Mr. Hoyt G Post, now of Grand Rapids, in 1848. On September morning of that year Mr. Po made his way down from Holland ove Black Lake, in a canoe, and found th place now known as Macatawa Park, in habited by a tribe of Ottawa Indians. Th noble red man gave a cordial welcome t Mr. Post, who proved to be the forerunne of an increasing number of white popula tion that have since made this place the summer resort. The Indians have gone but they have left the lake, the sandhill the noble forest trees, the deep, dar canons and a number of their beautif names. It would surprise one of thes ancient survivors if he should revisit Mac atawa after fifty years and see the change which the white man has made in th beautiful peninsula, nestling here betwe the two lakes. No doubt another fift years will witness changes equally a great, transforming into a great and popu lar religious resort a place that was onc the home and hunting grounds of the re men of the forest.

This will be our last Musing at Maca tawa for the present year. By the tim this reaches our readers Edgewood-on-the Lake will have put on its winter blind and will be as quiet and lonely as the othe cottages that now surround it, whose in mates have gone. It has been a pleasan busy and fleeting summer, whose shinin days have sped by all too swiftly. W have not accomplished all we had hope in the way of reading and meditation, bu who ever does? It is the ideal that w aim at, and the ideal is never realize But the summer has not passed with us i vain. Its opportunities have not been en tirely neglected, and its lessons, we trus will never be wholly forgotten. We hav tried to share whatever enjoyment we cou get out of the busy days, with our reader and it is no small gratification to be as sured by many that these Musings hav helped to lighten the labor, relieve th monotony and scatter some sunshine in th lives of those who have not been permi ted to enjoy a summer outing. This h been our aim, and if it has been accon plished we are satisfied. For the presen fair Macatawa, good-bye!

A day's bass fishing in a clear, rollickin stream, flowing through romantic scener in company with Z. T. Sweeney, is a thin to be remembered. Such a pleasure w ours recently. The ex-consul gener wrote us to meet him at Grand Rapids a certain day for a little fishing expeditio Although we have good fishing at Mac tawa, his letter promised something diffe ent, and we went, accompanied by a juni member of the Edgewood household who as fond of fishing as his sire. We went Alaska, not our extreme Northwestern po session, but a small place on Thorn App Creek, about ten miles by water above th village of Cascade, on the same strea Mr. Johnston, proprietor of the Eag tel, Grand Rapids, kindly drove us to scade in his carriage, leaving at 5 A. M. er a good breakfast. If he had not been staunch prohibitionist, running a first-ss, strictly temperate hotel, he would not re inconvenienced himself so much to ommodate us. The two boats which re to be used by ourselves and our guide, F. Hall, the fish-raiser, were hauled to aska, and there we embarked and fished wnstream as the boats floated along, l when we reached a favorite bass resort anchored, and did business as long as seemed profitable, and then moved on. r guide knew every rock and log and ep hole where bass are accustomed to le, and as Bro. Sweeney had been down same stream a few times before, he had ight on to this valuable information. we put him in a boat to himself to pole own canoe, for paddles are not used on orn Apple. We reached the hotel at scade Springs about 7 P. M., with thirty all-mouthed or tiger bass. This was a pital day's sport, and after a good ght's rest at the hotel it was resumed in morning, and closed at noon in order to ke the afternoon train at Grand Rapids, miles away. Sweeney easily had the nors of the day, but then he is a fish nmisioner and is expected to excel in h sport. We were delighted with the nantic location of Cascade Springs on bank of Thorn Apple Creek, with its gant hotel and handsome cottages on grassy slope, amid magnificent forest es. It is no wonder that Bro. S. is bar-ing for the rent of a cottage there for xt summer. Mr. Holt's trout ponds, th the speckled beauties darting hither d thither, is an interesting feature of place. It was a most delightful little cursion, and for it we are indebted to o. Sweeney, whose guests we were on trip, and a more agreeable companion would be difficult to find.

Questions and Answers.

1. Why was Mary forbidden to touch sus, he having not yet ascended, while iomas was commanded to touch him?

2. We are all God's children by crea-on. Yet to enjoy his salvation we must come his by adoption. Question: Is loption to be considered a stronger rela-on between a parent and child than the lation of creation?

3. Is the term "adoption," as used by e apostle, the same as is used by us to-y in the legal transaction of taking a ild into our family? *M. W. Yocom.*

1. We do not know. We can only con-cture. The motive for asking Thomas to ndle him is clear enough. Thomas was eptical about the reality of the resurrec-on and had declared he would not believe without this tangible proof. Jesus met m on this ground and asked him to make e examination. Mary needed no such oof. She was in the act, not of testing e reality of Jesus' resurrection, but of orshiping him, and perhaps lingering in is presence, when there was urgent need swift feet to carry the glad news to those ho had not heard it. So intent was he on aking known his resurrection, that he had ot yet ascended to his Father, but was risen from the dead; and Mary must forego clinging to him, as he was foregoing ascending at once to his Father, until it was known to all his friends that he had indeed risen. This seems to be the meaning of the passage referred to in John 20:17.

2. The term "creation" does not express all of God's relation to men. He created the sea and the dry land, but they are not His children. He endowed man with His own nature, making him in His own spiritual likeness. This is the ground of the universal Fatherhood of God. "Adoption" is a legal term used by Paul to express the sinner's change in relationship to God in conversion. In its use by him it stands for the recovery of man from the power of sin and his restoration to God, in an ethical sense, by which God owns him and gives him the Spirit of adoption. The term "adoption," therefore, in this sense, stands for more, religiously, than creation and endowment, but it is based on the fact of man's creation in God's image. One is capacity for fellowship with God, the other is the actual entrance into such fellowship.

3. The Roman law of adoption, on which Paul no doubt based his use of the term, was probably different in some of its features from the law of our time, but the essential fact covered by the term must be the same—a change of relationship in which some one accepts a child—not his own—as his child, to be treated as such, and the child is held to obedience to him by virtue of this relationship. There are legal aspects, of course, which do not apply to the moral and spiritual change in man, and the likeness should not be pressed too far.

What, then, is the difference between the editor of the CHRISTIAN-EVANGELIST *and other leading brethren touchiny the method of observing the Lord's supper?* *H.*

None that we know of. Our position is that concerning details, such as whether thanks may be offered for the bread and wine both, before the congregation is served with either, or whether the distribution of the loaf should precede thanks for the cup, there is no law binding us to uniformity, and that the ordinance is rightly observed either way if the right spirit be present. No man entitled to be known as a leader among us would call in question this statement, we think, though many may feel, as we do, a preference for the customary method. We have never seen any gain in the other method, unless it be a few minutes of time, and this might be better gained, as a rule, by curtailing the sermon. But let us never transfer the emphasis from the spirit in which we commemorate the death of Jesus to the matter of method or of detail.

To decide a dispute would the CHRISTIAN-EVANGELIST *please give its opinion on this question: Are the Disciples of Christ a denomination?* *W. D. Trumbull.*
Hartford, O.

That depends on how much we put into the word "denomination." Circumstances have compelled us to assume a separate and distinct organization and place among the religious forces of Christendom, and this is all that the average man means by denomination. But as our religious movement denominations is contrary to the genius of Christianity and to the express teaching of Christ and his apostles, and as its formative or creative principle is the rejection of what is purely denominational in its character, and the acceptance of what is universally received among Christians, as constituting the common basis of fellowship, it would seem that our position among religious bodies is a unique one. To the extent that we have succeeded in finding a basis of fellowship on which all who accept Christ may be one, without sacrifice of truth or conscience, our movement is undenominational. We believe our position as understood and advocated by our representative men is catholic and undenominational; though it must be confessed that we have not all been true, at all times, to our broad, undenominational position.

PRIMITIVE CHRISTIANITY.

H. W. B. MYRICK.

Sometime ago I heard the president of one of our colleges use the above expression. I began to reflect somewhat. Why should we say "primitive Christianity?" Are there different kinds of Christianity? What is primitive Christianity?

If we consider the phrase etymologically we discover that it simply means Christianity as at first, as at the beginning. We get back to the original. As a religious people we have been pleading for a return to primative Christianity. And now, after three-fourths of a century, and after our movement in this direction is becoming popular, others are embracing the idea and voicing the same demand. A new watchword has been coined and we now hear leaders crying, "Back to Christ!" But no matter; back to Christ or primitive Christianity, the thought and the the purpose are the same. It is a clarion call to the scattered and divided hosts of God to return to their "first love," to rally around one common standard, to sink petty differences and bury unfounded animosities. It is the mighty, thrilling call to Christian union born of the needs and apprehensions of the closing years of the nineteenth century, the problems of sin, the peril of avarice, the appalling menace of the liquor traffic, the arrogance of infidelity, the cool indifference of multitudes of well-to-do people—all of these causes of defeat and humiliation confront a divided church. While we repair our sectarian fences, the devil sows tares in our most fertile fields. While we extend our denominational borders deyond some little enclosure, Satan pre-empts a whole territory. God's people are conducting a guerrilla warfare instead of a compact, well-drilled army of regulars, who ought to be defeating sin on a thousand battlefields.

The remedy for this evil condition is to go back indeed to Christ, to repossess primitive Christianity. Union upon any other hypothesis is impossible. No modern "basis," however earnest men may be in urging it, can be accepted by all parties. We must be primitive. And therein lies a great big, tremendous truth. I actually gasped with delight when I saw that truth in its relation to some fundamental problems.

Observe, we never talk of going back to

returning to primitive methods of locomotion, to exchanging locomotive engines for oxen, and palace cars for rude and creaking coaches. We are not asking for primitive methods anywhere save in New Testament Christianity.

And herein we exalt the Word. All other affairs are the inventions of men, the product of human wisdom, but Christianity is a revelation from God. Peter said, "We have preached the gospel to you with the the Holy Spirit *sent down from heaven*." Paul said, "I certify you, brethren, that the gospel which was preached of me is not after man. For I neither received it of man, neither was I taught it *but by the revelation of Jesus Christ*." Christianity, therefore, is a revelation from heaven, perfect in all of its appointments, and *final as to both its form and substance*. It needs no elimination, addition or adaptation. It came forth from God, perfect in every quality which the instrument of man's salvation needed. Teaching, warning, comfort, promise—every element of spiritual culture and right-living—are therein contained, "that the man of God may be perfect, thoroughly furnished unto every good work" (2 Tim. 3:16).

Dr. Lyman Abbott, and other good men as well, enamored of a "philosophy falsely so called," tells us that Christianity is an evolution. It is a mistake. Evolution is the very farthest removed from that which is primitive. Evolution goes forward, not "back to Christ" any more than back to the monad or to primitive star-dust. Our latest rallying-cry, "Back to Christ," is a contradiction of the assumption of modern critics, that Christianity is a development, and we say to the critic, who seeks to enlarge upon the work of Paul or Jesus, "Out of thine own mouth will I condemn thee."

No: agriculture, transportation and other temporal and material affairs are the product of human wisdom, and here we seek the latest invention as most likely the best. But Christianity is of God, a revelation, not of human devising, and here we seek not the latest speculation of man, but the earliest, even primitive things of Christ and his apostles.

Brethren, our plea for a return to primitive Christianity is the grandest imaginable. Let us be true to the primitive ideal, both in theory and practice.

Gentryville, Mo.

CAN I LOVE MY ENEMIES?

N. J. AYLSWORTH.

I.

The most serious of all forms of scepticism is that which relates to character. To disbelieve in high ideals, or to believe them impossible of attainment, is a grave unbelief. The one is moral blindness; the other is moral despair.

There is nothing in Christianity more vitally central than Christ's doctrine of love. Obscure this, and you blot out the sun. And yet it is precisely at this point that there is no small degree of scepticism, even among Christians. This scepticism takes the form, not of the denial of the excellency of this high attribute of character, but of the possibility of its attainment. There are few, even of the world, who would deny that Christ's teachings regarding love, faithfully carried into effect, would completely solve the most pressing problems of our national life; yet any effort seriously to apply them to this object would be regarded as chimerical, and the advocate of any such attempt would be considered a dreamer who had lost his hold on the practical. Some excuse for this may be found in the fact that so large a part of the body politic owns no allegiance to Christianity. But it is quite otherwise with Christians themselves. No such obstacle prevents the full realization of Christ's design with them. Yet we find the scepticism here also. "Can I love my enemies?" The answer is usually "no." Such is the reply the human heart is now making to Christ's demand. Resentment may be stifled; the fiery word may be restrained; the hand that would strike may be stayed; and, even from a sense of duty, or through love to another, deeds of love may be bestowed on the offender—but we cannot *love* him. Grass may be made to grow over the crater, but the volcano still burns beneath. The most we can hope to attain in this matter is a holy hypocrisy—the wearing of the guise of love, while the heart is ashes.

Is this the answer of the church to Christ's highest lesson, after nineteen centuries of schooling under his teaching? Some very thoughtful matter in our religious journals in the last five years has set forth this view.

Is this what Christ means when he bids us love our enemies? Would he have us assume the ways of love without loving them? When he instructs us to pray for them, does he mean a perfunctory prayer?

The answer is not far to seek. We are to love our enemies that we may "be the children" of our Father who is in heaven; that is, that we may be *like* him. Is God's love towards the evil but a chained animosity, held in check from a sense of right? We learn that he not only sends his rain and sunshine on the evil and the good alike, but that he "so loved the world that he gave his only begotten Son" that he might save it and bestow upon it the blessings of eternal life. This is not the semblance of love, but love itself; not love's deed, but love's holy passion. We have here love and love's deed standing in the contrast of *cause* and *effect*. There are in this passage two distinct statements: (1) that God *loved*, and (2) that he *did love's work*. We cannot make them mean the same thing. Take love out of this passage, and you evacuate its meaning. God's love-like deeds to a wicked world sprang from a father's heart, from a holy yearning to save and bless. Take the tender father-love out of Christianity, and it lies a corpse and powerless evermore to move the human heart. The world has been taking the love-talk of the gospel these nineteen hundred years in earnest. Has it been mistaken? If so, blessed mistake! If God's love to the wicked be a tender father-love, ours to our enemies must be a yearning brother-love, or we cannot be like him.

Christ was a revelation of God's character. Did he love his enemies? or simply perform some love-like deeds in their behalf? Listen: "O Jerusalem, Jerusalem, which killeth the prophets, and stoneth them that are sent unto thee! how often would I have gathered thy children together, even as a hen gathereth her chickens under her wings, and ye would not!" How like David's cry over Absalom is thi[s]! It is love's bitter agony. There is nothin[g] hollow here. The chalice is full and flo[ws] over with the waters of the heart. David['s] wail was over a wicked and murdero[us] enemy; Christ's over a perverse and pers[e]cuting people. This Jerusalem had murd[er] in its heart. This piteous cry was wrun[g] from love's bleeding heart.

"Father, forgive them; for they kno[w] not what they do." What mean thes[e] words? Is the sufferer instructing Go[d]? Cannot God be trusted to do right? The[y] have no meaning but of the heart. It is [a] love-cry, a heavenward yearning for th[e] bloody throng about him. Jesus *loved* hi[s] enemies.

"And he kneeled down, and cried with [a] loud voice, Lord, lay not this sin to the[ir] charge." Was Stephen acting? or was h[e] in earnest? Was not this last loud cr[y] upon earth from the heart? He has caugh[t] the holy passion from the Master, whic[h] has lit the cross through all ages.

"I say the truth in Christ, I lie not, m[y] conscience bearing witness with me in th[e] Holy Spirit, that I have great sorrow an[d] unceasing pain in my heart. For I coul[d] wish that I myself were anathema fro[m] Christ for my brethren's sake, my kinsme[n] according to the flesh" (Rom. 9:1-3). Who can doubt that this was real? Thes[e] are solemn, awful words. Paul has looke[d] within, and this is what he has found i[n] his heart—a brooding sorrow, a painfu[l] yearning of love for his deadly enemie[s] who plotted for his life and at last com[passed] his martyrdom. Few of even th[e] sublimest human characters have eve[r] been able to utter such words as these—t[o] make a sacrifice so appalling. Paul love[d] these bitter enemies with an overmastering, yearning sorrow.

The primitive church took these teachings of Christ without discount, and the[y] did not find them untrue to the possibilities of human experience.

But there is one thing which we have ye[t] to notice regarding them: this love o[f] enemies is a distinctive mark of the Christian character, and is the only one t[o] which Christ here attaches any reward. "If ye love them that love you, what reward have ye?" (Matt. 5:46.) The responsive love to those who love us and treat u[s] well, lies at the level of the worldly character ("do not even the Gentiles so?") an[d] of even the most rapacious of mankind. Even the publican loved in this wa[y] (v. 46). We may go further, and say tha[t] this species of love belongs also to th[e] brute creation, and that the capacity for i[t] is possessed by even the most ferociou[s] animals. You can win the affection of [a] tiger. This love belongs to the furnitur[e] of the animal nature, and is not even distinctively human, much less Christian. There is much in it that is beautiful, an[d] its charms may easily lead us to give to i[t] a higher rank in the estimate of characte[r] than it deserves. It is not that distinctively *human* love of which Christ speaks—the missing virtue for the lack of whic[h] the world still lies bleeding.

This question of the love of enemies is [a] very serious matter. It is a plumme[t] dropped into character to determin[e] whether it be Christian. If modern unbelief can show that such a love is impossible, it will drive its dagger through th[e]

Christianity, and there will be
left worth contending for.
st was mistaken here, where else
trust him? If we *can* love our
it is time we knew it, and were
this important part of the Sermon
Iount. To vindicate Christ's law
ı its practicability, as well as in its
y, is a task second in importance
er. On this subject we shall en-
o present a few thoughts in suc-
articles.

ILIZATION AND RELIGION.

SHERMAN HILL.

ation represents, primarily, man's
on of and relation to man, religion
ption of and relation to God.
on is the higher attribute, civil-
ie lower. They are to each other
nor and governed, as tree and fruit,
and effect.
re always in an exact ratio to each

fect religion would be a perfect
on of and relation to God. A per-
ization would be a perfect concep-
nd relation to man.
fect conception of and relation to
ld result in the perfect develop-
the individual and the thorough
tion of individuals religiously.
ect conception of and relation to
ld result in the perfect develop-
the individual and the thorough
tion of individuals socially for man,
ly or socially, is as individualistic
istic.
ost prominent ancient representa-
the foregoing were Greece and
No nations have ever attained to
inctively individualistic and social-
inence as those, and all history
no sadder pictures of the failures
n efforts.
liant individual development the
Greeks are the rivals of all time.
as at one time in Athens not less
enty men contemporaneous with
and Pericles who have come down
masters in almost as many depart-
thought.
's individual brilliancy dazzles us
her society was chaotic; she had
l organization. Her civilization as
m her partial development was
s, but from a point of real and en-
lization it was no civilization; it
partial, hence meteoric. Greece's
was in exact keeping with her civ-
. Morality was astonishingly low.
er individual development was most
there were but thirty thousand peo-
thens, and there were as many gods
e.
Greece was, China was a power-
n. She has for centuries been the
pregnable, lethargic monster. In
he individual counted for all, and
for nothing. Men were as individ-
as Ibsen would have them be. In
ciety counts for all and the indi-
r nothing. Men were as socialistic
i would have them be. But in all
ry China has not produced a great
ndividual development is as wholly
in China as social organization was
e. China's stupified solidity is to
uted to her social organization.
parison of China's civilization and

religion reveals a striking harmony; both are old, non-progressive, hopeless and socialistic. The more modern nations bear unmistakable testimony to the same truth. Mexico, Central America and South America have a civilization and religion that are in exact accord. A study of European nations exhibits the same truth. The backward social conditions of Spain, Italy, Austria and Russia are in exact keeping with their crude religion. The more advanced social positions of France, Germany and Scandinavia are accompanied by a correspondingly higher type of religion. But the highest type of civilization of our time is Anglo-Saxon, as exhibited in Great Britain and America. In these nations the development of the individual and the organization of society are in the most harmonious accord, thus far exemplified by the race, and are far in advance of any contemporaneous nation. Their religion is likewise the highest type yet exhibited. Under no system of religious faith has the individual been so perfectly developed and individuals so thoroughly organized as in the Christianity of the Anglo-Saxons. Catholicism exhibits a strong organization of individuals, but a shameful lack of individual development. Protestantism represents a marked individual development and a strong and growing organization of individuals. Men are first of all to be Christianized. As they are Christianized they will be civilized. This is abundantly demonstrated from the indisputably universal facts that no people's civilization has ever been in advance of its religion, but always the reverse, from the innumerable examples of individuals and peoples who have been Christianized and always accordingly civilized, and that the spiritual or religious nature is the antecedent and not the consequent, the cause and not the effect, the higher and governing and producing nature.

Shall we heed the language of God thus definitely woven into the warp and woof of the entire existence of the race, and so indelibly graven in the nature of every individual?

> Let us Christianize the nations,
> Change the hearts of erring men,
> Purify the source of human actions
> That the waiting hearts of men
> May see the glad fruitions
> For which the Father fashioned them.

The Outline Bible Club Course, of the American Institute of Sacred Literature, enters upon its sixth year with the first of October. The subject for the year is one of peculiar interest, namely, the *Foreshadowings of the Christ.*

The topic will at once suggest to the average mind a few isolated passages from the Old Testament prophets, such as Genesis 3:14, 15, the child-prophecies of Isaiah, and the 53rd chapter of Isaiah. The course as it is prepared by the American Institute, however, is a very different thing from the study of such individual sections, though including them also. Beginning with Genesis the whole field of Old Testament history and prophecy from Genesis to Malachi is covered in outline. At the same time all the material is selected and arranged so as to bring out the first beginnings and the continual growth of the whole Messianic idea as revealed step by step in the history of Israel. Every prophecy appears in its own peculiar historical environment. Such an addition of life and color gives new and fresh conceptions to the minds of those long familiar with the Scripture passages, and bring to the new student a real gratification of the historical as well as the religious sense.

The Institute has thousands of students from the Young People's Societies of every denomination, from churches, schools and isolated homes. The plan adapts itself to either club or individual study. It requires so little time (fifteen minutes a day) that no one who is interested need hesitate to enter upon the work. All Christians read some portion of the Bible every day. (This should be true if not.) Why not make this reading systematic by adopting some well-constructed plan? We would advise all who wish such help to address the American Institute of Sacred Literature, Hyde Park, Chicago, Ill.

Current Religious Thought

An apologetic article on "Spain and the Catholic Church," by Henry A. Stinson, D. D., in a recent number of the Independent, concludes with the following exceedingly liberal statements:

> I hold no brief for the Catholic Church, and I am sufficiently heavy-hearted over the burden which religious work in the city lays upon us all; but we must all bear witness to the success with which these, our Catholic neighbors, retain a hold upon their own people, to the immense audiences they secure, to the extent to which they exert oversight and care of their children, to their attitude towards divorce and the maintenance of the family, and to the revival now among them of the pulpit and the purely spiritual function of the church.
>
> Whatever its errors in the past, and whatever its limitations to-day, both from its traditions and what we must regard as its erroneous doctrines, it is, nevertheless, a great Christian church, almost, indeed, the greatest. We cannot, as Christians, but believe that God is in his own time and way to revive it and purify it and set its candlestick in the place which will reveal his own long-suffering, love and power. But whatever may be its ultimate destiny, it certainly is to-day one of the very greatest forces on the earth available for the Christianizing and civilizing of the world and for hastening the day we all are laboring and praying for, the day of the emancipation of all men and the bringing in of the triumphant kingdom of Jesus Christ. We Protestant Christians may be perfectly true to our convictions and true to our history, and at the same time reach out our hand to these our Christian fellow-citizens with an unreserved and grateful confidence that God is doing his work through them; and they are true to their trust no less than we, with all humility, are ourselves. If the exigencies of the war with Spain shall have this as their result to help us to show charity in our judgments, and to unite us all as Christians in hastening to do our best for the long-deferred redemption of Cuba, they will not be endured in vain.

In an article in the Minnesota Issue, on "The Duty of the Pulpit Against the Liquor Traffic," by C. H. Payne, LL. D., the following stupendous facts and weighty suggestions appear:

> 1. The first link in the chain is the incontrovertible fact that the liquor traffic is the greatest curse of Christendom and a stupendous obstacle in the way of the Christian Church.
>
> 2. Link second: This greatest enemy of man and deadly foe of Christ's kingdom will only be conquered by the agency of the Christian church. It is vain to expect the devil to strike down his strongest ally. It is useless to hope that the world will undertake the overthrow of a moral evil that the church and the pulpit hesitate to attack. It reflects honor on the church to say that the world expects and awaits its leadership in this as in all other moral reforms, and therefore this foe will go down only before the assault of the church. There is no flaw in this link.
>
> 3. A third link in the chain invites our

scrutiny. The church can cope successfully with such a foe as the liquor traffic only when its forces are thoroughly massed. A united foe, a divided church. This one sad but truthful sentence tells the story of our long defeat, tells the story of the heartsickness of our ranks and the hopelessness of our cause, if we will not learn a higher wisdom and unite for victory. And now let us test the fourth link:

4. The pulpit is the legitimate and divinely ordained agency to mass the forces of the Christian church and to lead them on to victory in this holy crusade against the liquor traffic. It would be stultifying to affirm that the church could and should undertake any work in which the pulpit might not properly act its part of helper and leader. Its voice must ring out clear and strong and unequivocal, the rallying cry calling the forces of Christ to battle. To deny this function and this duty to the pulpit is to affirm that the pulpit must be dumb in presence of society's greatest curse; must be helpless in presence of man's greatest need; must be the slave of custom rather than its liberator. If it be said that the pulpit should preach temperance to the individual, but leave unrebuked the traffic; reform the drunkard, but spare the drunkard-maker, then you ask the pulpit to belittle its own work in the eyes of all manly men by openly confessing its puerility and pusillanimity. You ask the pulpit to rescue the sufferers from incendiary fires, but be careful to speak no word against the incendiaries themselves; to bury the slaughtered victims of drink, but be silent concerning the murderous traffic and the respectable power that fosters and legalizes it. If the pulpit were to listen to this counsel it would invite the wrath of God and the contempt of all true men. It would be shorn of its strength and robbed of its respect. No, it is the plain and palpable duty of the pulpit to discuss and to conserve every interest of society, to antagonize every wrong, to encourage whatever is right. * * * * * * * * *

5. A united pulpit will soon bring a united church; the Christian forces will be massed, and the legalized traffic in intoxicating drink will be overthrown. Scarcely a moment remains to let in the light upon this glowing hope. But light there is, and hope lures us on, and courage summons us to manly endeavor.

A hundred thousand Christian pulpits united in this holy cause will bring in this millennial morn. Defections in the pew and dismissals from the pulpit may here and there occur; but when the new incumbent of the pulpit gives the same "certain sound" to the trumpet as did his dismissed predecessor the contest will quickly cease, the forces will be united, and the long-looked-for victory will have been won.

Our chain is complete. Its five links binding the hundred thousand pulpits and the many-millioned membership of Christ's church in this goodly land into a blessed unity of purpose and endeavor to destroy this ravager of human hearts and happy homes will also bind the gloomy present to a golden future, throwing a bridge of hope across the dark chasm and bidding the emancipated millions of a land redeemed from the curse of strong drink pass over to a "Paradise regained."

Prof. J. T. Bergen, in an article in the Christian Intelligencer, Aug. 31st, probably rightly holds that the naval battles of Manila and Santiago should not be classed with the miracles of the Bible. He says:

God has been our leader, our inspiration in this war; but its battles cannot be called miracles. Compare the destruction of Cervera's squadron with the destruction of the walls of Jericho. What efficient human or natural cause was there to destroy those walls? There was none. By what law did they come down? Only by the immediate hand of God. And Joshua was writing Scripture.

Our second inquiry is to the safety of holding such views as Dr. Abbott seems to maintain when he says: "If such victories had been recorded in the history of the Jews, they would have been regarded as miracles, as interpositions of God to defend his people, and they would have been rejected to-day by those who do not believe in miracles as improbable and impossible, and as pure inventions."

We have reason to believe that Dr. Abbott, with many others of his way of thinking about the Bible, accepts its historical statements as fairly accurate. But they class these events with all the wonderful occurrences of history which have been for good. Now, what is the result of this? It expands and generalizes the miraculous until its miraculousness disappears. So that they who regard these recent events as miracles and class them with the wonderful events of biblical history, need not regard those ancient events as *attesting the infallibility of the records accompanying them, nor the miracles of Jesus as proving that he was the Son of God*. This is dangerous to the extreme. It lowers the miraculous. It deadens the nerve of the great historical argument for Christianity, for it destroys the uniqueness of the biblical miracles.

In a paper on "The Moral Life a Work of Art," by Associate Prof. W. D. MacClintock, appearing by installments in the University Record, of Chicago, is this very beautiful statement of the value of the equipoise of self-knowledge and self-control. Prof. MacClintock says:

The world presents no more beautiful object than a ready, experienced, refined moral nature. The man who has assisted many other men to rise; he who has forgiven much; she who has won a thousand patiences; the courtesy that is never off guard; the gentleness that desires no vacation; the truth-telling that has become entirely instinctive—with what security, swiftness, beauty, such a nature comes among us! But we all know that it is virtue in season and out of season—*always* abounding in the work of the Lord.

The problem of the relation of spontaneity and self-consciousness seems much the same for both artists and lovers of virtue. They must know themselves, their tools, environment; they must definitely plan to create the perfect thing; yet they must be free, happy, creative, without conceit or self-seeking. Both pass through a stage of development when their self-consciousness, their analysis, their purposing alienate or destroy their spontaneity. It would be disastrous if men were always aware of their feelings, and did their good deeds in order to increase their virtues. If choice must be made one should by all means choose to be instinctive and follow his good impulses without knowing why or how. But our generation of mental analysis has taught us that self-consciousness and spontaneity are not finally antagonistic, that the notion of mere spontaneous greatness or unconscious genius is a myth. We need to know the relations, the time and place, the merit and limitations of each. In moments of activity we must act, and with all the joy and spontaneity possible. If the emotions and purposes are wholesome they will carry us over all criticism, self-knowledge and extrinsic ends. After this we pause and contemplate and learn. In the perfected soul one can be good and know it, self-controlled and understand the elements and laws of that experience. If it were not so we should always be children in virtue, with the child's uncertainty, changeableness and want of discrimination.

Perhaps at no point has the artist more to teach us than in his love of beauty for itself. He, like other men, must earn a living, must do good in the world, must win his fame. But at the moment of creation he loses sight of all these ends, and he loves his work for its own sake and loves the thing he makes. The philosophers tell us that the values of art are intrinsic and immediate.

The proposition to introduce the public school system of the United States into Cuba seriously disturbs the intellectual equilibrium of the Church Progress, this city, and in all probability that also of all other good Roman Catholic journals. Concerning this suggestion, among other things equally noisy, the Church Progress says:

The impudent preachers who gabble about the separation of church and state are always the worst meddlers in political affairs. They have always manipulated the whole machinery of government, both general and local, in the interests of heresy and separatism, so far as they have been able, by any hook or crook, to get possession of it. They have always made it a special point to control the Indian Office, for the purpose of depriving the Indians of their religious liberty. This man Morgan was one of the most notorious of the officials who have prostituted the governmental authority to sectarian ends. When he talks about "education for the common people" of Cuba he refers to the stupid, Godless, impractical public school education which teaches everything that is useless and false, and neglects almost everything that is calculated to train up efficient, teachable, intelligent, virtuous and well-bred members of the civil and religious commonwealths. When he says that without it "there is little hope for Cuba," he means little hope for the perversion of the Cuban people to the ridiculous and degrading superstitions of miserable little sects of the Baptist stripe.

We know that the introduction of religious liberty and our public school system into Cuba, Porto Rico and the Philippines hurts, but it can't be helped.

Ministerial Association of the Disc ples of Christ in Eastern Ohio.

The thirty-fifth annual meeting of the "Mi isterial Association of the Disciples of Chr in Eastern Ohio" was held September 6- 1898, with the church at Painesville, Ohi The meetings were presided over by Prof. McDiarmid, of Hiram, and the details of bu ness were carefully considered by S. Bartlett, the secretary.

A good program was prepared, of which t essential features were the address of t president on "The Resurrection;" an addr by Pres. E. V. Zollars on "The Status Education among the Disciples of Christ; three addresses by Burris A. Jenkins, Indianapolis, on "Paul and the Thirteen, "Paul's Literary Style" and "Paul's Fi Epistle — Thessalonians;" a symposium "The Pastor and His Work," conducted M. J. Grable, of Cleveland, in which t following persons took part: 1. "The Appo tionment of Time," W. J. Cadman, Clev land, O.; 2. "Duties Outside of the Parish, A. M. Chamberlain, Alliance, O.; 3. "T Pastor and the Sunday-school and Christi Endeavor Society," J. H. Mohorter, Clev land, O.; 4. "Pastoral Visiting," H. Allen, Geneva, O.; two addresses by W. Lhamon, of Allegheny City, Pa., on "T Mystery, the History and the Pauline Chara ter of the Hebrew Letter, and "The Chris ology of the Hebrew Letter;" an address Errett Gates, of Chicago, on "Some Neglec ed Elements in the Restoration of Primiti Christianity;" "Social Settlements in Ci ies," by George Bellamy, of the "Hira House," Cleveland, O.; "The Best Leng for a Pastorate," by R. W. Sellers, of Asht bula, O.; "The Responsibility of the Chur for Business Men," and the temperance que tion was presented by Mr. Wayne B. Wheele of Cleveland, O., "The Temperance Situati for '98 and '99."

Besides these addresses and papers F. M Green read a historical paper in which t history of the Association was presented as f as possible from its organization in 1863 to t present time. Only four of the original mem bers of the Association are now living, so far known—H. W. Everest, Robert Moffet, J. Jones and F. M. Green.

From the beginning there have been enroll in its membership 363 persons. Nearly all these were preachers. Nearly 100 have die and a large number of their names have bee recorded with appropriate and appreciati words in the annual records. Less than fi have proved themselves, on account of in moral and unchristian conduct, absolute unworthy of membership. A very few ha become dissatisfied with their church relatio ship, and have joined other religious bodie

The most of the lectures and addresses papers were passed as unexceptionable matter. Some of the positions taken by t speakers on the larger topics were keen criticised, but all in all not much was said th was worthy of martyrdom.

Orrin Gates and Lathrop Cowley represente the older generation of Western Reser preachers; Robert Moffet and W. L. Hayd a generation which succeeded them; J. Darsie, J. Z. Tyler and H. N. Allen a st later generation; S. H. Bartlett, A. M Chamberlain and R. W. Sellers a generati still younger.

The church in Painesville took good care the visitors from first to last.

The first meeting of the Association w held in Alliance, Ohio, and the next meetin will be held there. The sentiment seemed prevail that it would not only be pleasant, b in every way fitting to begin the second peri of 35 years where the first meeting was held.

The Association elected officers as follow President, F. M. Green, Kent, O.; vic president, E. B. Wakefield, Hiram, O.; co responding secretary, S. H. Bartlett, Paine ville, O.

It is not the purpose of this notice of t meeting to put any comparative estimate the various parts of the program. Each in h place did well, and the Association was great pleased with their presence and their work.

We hope to make next year a great year the history of the Association. We would glad if every living member of the Associatio could be present.

F. M. GREEN.

Kent, O.

Our Budget.

teadfast,
bedient,
oyal,
aring,
ıvincible,
nthusiastic,
eady.

he above acrostic was clipped from The lard (Baptist).

hurch Extension, State Convention, 'athers' Day, college openings and the any C. E. Reading Course are some of resent urgent interests of the churches of t treated in this paper.

)ur readers will discover that quite a numf pulpits are to be vacated in the near fu-

'he cool weather brings a marked increase ports from the evangelistic field. The inions are that the churches generally are ing for a protracted meeting. Let them plan for a protracted spiritual growth.

t the preachers' meeting in this office on lay, Sept. 12th, a number of preachers ted excellent prayer-meetings and two or reported what was said to be the best er-meeting in the history of their respecthurches. A good prayer-meeting is a sign of spiritual life in the church.

'he views of Lookout Mountain, appearn our first page from week to week, afford eader some idea of the magnificent scenurrounding the historic city in which our ral Convention will assemble next month. out Mountain, with all of its sacred spots, suggestions and holy inspirations will inly lend more than a charm to the conion delegates. Such a convention in the ity of such surroundings ought to touch oftiest peaks of communion with God, and roadest conceptions of his will on earth. ly, October 13-21 will mark an epoch in nward movement toward the redemption e world from sin.

'he Church Extension reports on another will bear close reading. There are many uraging things in it. The churches are g well in their aim to reach their propor- of the $20,000 sought from collections this for Church Extension. Take the collecfor Church Extension next Sunday and it thoroughly, and on Monday remit to G. Muckley Cor. Sec., 600 Waterworks build- Kansas City, Mo., so that it will reach board before the books close. They close on on the 30th.

'he Observer, a weekly religious journal his city, devoted to the interests of the berland Presbyterian Church, has just red upon the seventh year under its preseditorial management. On all living al and religious topics it has come to be idered as one of the most pronounced rs among our large list of valued exchanges. seldom miss reading its strong and vigoreditorials and are glad to know that its ent fearless, independent policy is not to bandoned. It has avoided partisanship in ics, boldly rebuking sin wherever found, is a fearless exponent of religious liberty, sparing even the errors of the church for h it stands. There is room for a few papers of this kind in the religious d. The Observer is pitched upon a high lectual, moral and spiritual tone under its ent editorial management and for its insed influence and prosperity the CHRISTIAN-NGELIST sincerely prays.

'he surprising revelation that the British Egyptian troops in the Soudan have been ng all of their wounded enemies after each le will be hard to reconcile with the claims and seemingly inhumane method, but it will be found difficult to square such conduct with the golden rule and other of Christ's sayings. When General Sherman said, "War is hell," he might have added, And hell is beyond refinement.

—The Christian, Sedalia, Mo., for September, contains the farewell sermon of J. S. Myers. The removal of Bro. Myers from Sedalia to Philadelphia leaves the Christian in charge of F. L. Cook as editor and proprietor, and it is in no way impaired by the change. It is still as neat and newsy as ever.

—"The Popular Science News says that a saloonkeeper in England advertised his beer as liquid bread. A member of the English Parliament bought a quart and paid a chemist fifteen dollars to examine it. Two per cent., about a thimbleful, was really food. Five per cent. was alcohol, and the remaining 93 per cent. water. He was arrested under the food act." In our judgment all the rest of his profession ought to be arrested under the FRAUD act.

—We are sorry to learn through Bro. J. Z. Tyler, of Cleveland, Ohio, that the enlistment of Endeavor Societies for the second year's reading course has not been as large as the merits of the work demand nor as its efficient managers had expected. It may be, however, that they are waiting until October to consider the matter. This work ought to be attended to at once and the supplies secured so as to begin actual work by Oct. 1st. Societies should not delay in the matter. Churches and Bible-schools can join in the work and would find it very helpful to do so. At all events all who are contemplating the course for the second year should send at once for further information, if needed, and for supplies. Address J. Z. Tyler, Cleveland, Ohio.

—The Christian Tribune, of Baltimore, Md., has been changed to a sixteen-page weekly, the size of Our Young Folks, and will hereafter appear from the press of the Christian Publishing Co., of this city. By this new arrangement the editor, Peter Ainslie, will be relieved of the business management and devote his attention more exclusively to its editorial demands. It is the ambition of Bro. Ainslie to greatly enlarge the influence and usefulness of the Tribune, and the steps taken and changes made will, it is hoped, open the way to that end. We are glad to have so companionable a journal as the Tribune at our side, in the same building, and of course wish it the greatest success in the Lord's field and work.

—In this paper will be found an article by J. Fraise Richard, President Normal College, Washington, D. C., containing a unique yet what seems to us to be a valuable suggestion as to the use of newspapers in our national library. As much as newspapers and other periodicals are read there is a tremendous waste of valuable knowledge for lack of systematic, practical method for classifying and preserving the same. Preachers with a little care could add many valuable volumes to their libraries by a little painstaking along the line suggested, and others could utilize them to their profit. We hope the plan will be adopted by the librarian at Washington as suggested, and in fact by all librarians, as far as possible.

—An eight-page circular has been issued by the Army and Navy Commission giving an outline of the good influences which have been brought to bear upon the soldiers in the various camps and the good results which have followed. This has been one of the most Christianly works of the Christian people of the United States during the year and they should see that it is maintained as long as the army exists. It means better soldiers, better manhood and a better nation. Pray for its success and send a contribution to Dwight L. Moody, East Northfield, Mass., for its support.

at the Christian church, Wabash, Ind., September 28th, at 6:30, have been received at this office. Friends will be received at their home 46 Manchester Ave., Wabash, Ind., after Oct. 20th. All the parties named have the congratulations and well wishes of the CHRISTIAN-EVANGELIST.

—The Baptist News says that it is willing to call us "Disciples," just this and nothing more, but not Disciples of Christ. To the last name it objects because of the "pre-eminence" it seems to imply. There is no pre-eminence in Christianity from which we as a people are lawfully excluded to our knowledge, even to the pre-eminence of wearing a name that relates to Christ. But in this implied relationship and other Christian graces, we are not exclusivists. The term Disciples of Christ signifies our leader, a fact which we are sorry to learn the Baptist News is yet unwilling to recognize. The CHRISTIAN-EVANGELIST does not ask that the people for whom it stands be recognized as the only Christians or only disciples of Christ in the land, but it does object to hearing them called "Disciples of Alexander Campbell," for historic and spiritual reasons. The Disciples of Christ have never recognized Alexander Campbell as the founder of their faith nor of the religious system to which they are committed. As congregations we claim to be "churches of Christ," and as members of his body we claim to be "his disciples." The name "Disciples of Christ" is, therefore, expressive of the relation we claim to sustain to him, and it is sufficiently distinctive for all practical purposes in the present divided state of the religious world without subjecting us to the charge of inconsistency upon the one hand or of arrogant exclusive claims upon the other; and we feel that our claims merit the respect and courtesy of all who claim to be equally related to him.

—We are requested to say that the State Convention, of Tennessee, will be held with the *Highland Park Church, Chattanooga, October 10-13.* The change from Memphis was made necessary by the quarantine in that city. All those who desire to attend the General Convention can come to the State Convention two days before and remain over. The *rates* granted by the railroads will hold for both conventions.

—A correspondent from Arapahoe, Neb., sends us the following testimonial:

One of the greatest helps to the minister, in his work of preaching to the people, is a good religious paper in each family belonging to the church. For 24 years I have done what I could to circulate Christian papers, especially the CHRISTIAN-EVANGELIST. I have given it the preference for the reason that as an all-around family paper I believe it to be superior

Elsewhere in this paper will be found a note from J. Z. Tyler, National Superintendent of Christian Endeavor, to the preachers asking them to call the attention of their Endeavor Societies to the importance of the Bethany Reading Course. Many Societies can thus be persuaded to undertake this good work which would otherwise neglect it. The time for beginning the second year's course is at hand and the matter should not be neglected. The success of the Bethany Reading Course means much for the strength and influence of the church and for every good work which it has in hand, besides the personal culture and spiritual advancement of the reader. Every preacher should, therefore, urge his Endeavor Society to take the course.

—The Union Signal says: "A brewer of Milwaukee has received orders for 60,000 car loads of beer to be shipped to the Philippines." Is this the commencement of the new civilization proposed for these islands? Behold, how alert the Devil and his agents! By and by the world will be wondering what is the matter with the Philippine Islands. Behold, "while men slept his enemies came and sowed tares among the wheat and went their way."

—With this number we begin the publication of a series of articles from the discerning, analytical pen of N. J. Aylesworth, Auburn, N. Y., on the involved and almost universal question, "Can I Love My Enemies?" We feel assured that the name of the author and the personal nature of the theme will insure for these thoughtful articles a wide and careful reading.

ıst get out of the disease and then
ke the disease out of us,'' is a
ıich the Christian and Missionary
aches much significance, and if
Alliance argues, takes away the
f the mystery of "divine healing."
ɜn, after all, two sides to this ques-
ine healing,'' and on the human
ng more than prayer is essential to
. In commenting on the impor-
above remark the Alliance says:
et out of your sickness, get out of
l consciousness, get out of the at-
your morbidness and misery, and
n cause your face to shine with the
is countenance and your life to
the fullness of your strength.''
done the way is then clear for
lo the rest, without the use of
ɔower.

Crutcher, of Whitesboro, Texas,

THER:—The article, "Conversion of
f issue of Sept. 8th, is worth the
paper for a year. I write this from
so "excuse writing." The CHRIS-
ELIST improves with each issue.

ɔer that F. M. Call, business man-
Christian Publishing Co., this city,
d for special coaches from St. Louis
oga and return, in which the fare
d trip will not exceed one-way fare
re rate. All who expect to avail
of this rate in these special coaches
their names to him at once. The
s and comforts of special coaches
a factor in your trip to Chatta-
return. Other particulars will be
next issue.

actical Christian, a well-edited,
d, newsy paper, edited by J. C.
ouston, Texas, now comes to us
month instead of monthly as before.
s as an evidence of growing pros-
history of the Practical Christian.

Cabanne Bible Club will celebrate
anniversary on Tuesday evening,
with appropriate services. Certif-
ng forth work of the club for the
given to each member of the club.
icates will contain a picture of F. M.
ird president of the club, and also of
Meador, who was one of its most
mbers and its first to fall asleep in
is organization will complete its
e in one more year.

er from Hyndman, Pa., writes:

N:—I wish to express my apprecia-
most excellent paper. I especially
he article, "A Word to Parents and
' of Aug. 18th. I can say with Jo-
that this is the need of the day.
g, and my prayers go with you.

lar freak of human nature and one
s strongly in favor of the need of
n appears in the following state-
the Peculiar People, a Christian
evoted to Jewish interests. This
s:

gular fact, that all the enlighten-
eedom of modern Jews, and all the
ey enjoy under such a Christian
as that of England, for instance,
ught them toleration for those of
en who join the Christian Church.
sserted by them that they do not
onverts; but this only means that
, as a rule, an organized persecu-
every missionary knows and every
ew painfully feels that converts are
ut off from intercourse with family
, often separated from their wives
n, deprived of their property, shun-
, and in some instances, where
nstances allow it, imprisoned on
es and beaten. It is a strange and
pectacle; Jews persecuted by Chris-
se they are Jews, and, on the other
persecuting converts because they
ans.

PERSONAL MENTION.

C. B. Scott, one of the trustees of Bethany College, and the father of Orien E. Scott, of this city, has been visiting his son here for a few days and forming the acquaintance of our people in this city. He favored this office with a pleasant call while in the city.

We are sorry to learn of the sickness of C. S. Medbury, of Angola, Ind., and hope that he is well-nigh recovered ere this writing.

J. H. Lawson, of White Right, Tex., in company with Bro. Atkinson, of the Fourth Church, of this city, and Miss Susie and Miss Ollie Threkeld, of Mexico, Mo., called at this office on day last week. They were on their way to Licking, Mo., where they were to begin a protracted meeting on last Saturday. The Threkeld sisters are vocal music teachers and will have charge of the song services during the meeting.

Rev. Charles Campbell, of Sanford, Florida, would like to have the address of C. J. Hayes, the singing evangelist.

J. M. Rudy, of Quincy, Ill., has received a unanimous call from the church at Cedar Rapids, Iowa, and will accept. The Cedar Rapids church sent a committee to ascertain the standing and influence of Bro. Rudy as a preacher and it was their favorable report that led to his enthusiastic call to Cedar Rapids. Bro. Rudy is an energetic and faithful minister, and the church at Quincy will reluctantly consent to his removal from their presence.

A. B. Moore, State Evangelist of Minnesota, informs us that two young preachers who could live on a salary of four or five hundred dollars each could be located with two country churches in that state. Bro. Moore's address is at Austin, Minn. We are sorry to learn that the wife of Bro. Moore has been quite sick. She has gone to her people in Ohio, where she hopes soon to regain her health.

A. P. Cobb is assisting W. L. Ennefer in a meeting at Blue Mound, Ill., with fine prospects. One addition Sunday night.

Bro. W. L. Ennefer will close his second year's work at Blue Mound, Oct. 9th. He is open for engagements elsewhere.

E. E. Pierce, of Fields, Ohio, will close his work there Oct. 1st, and solicits correspondence from churches contemplating a protracted meeting or wanting a pastor, in which work he has had eight years experience.

During the summer months, Singing Evangelist J. E. Hawes has been working with the Anti-Saloon League. But from now on through the winter season he is open to engagements in the evangelistic field. Write him at Ada, Ohio.

C. P. Evans, Arapahoe, Neb., is ready to make engagements either for regular work or protracted meetings.

F. M. Anderson, pastor of the church at Danville, Virginia, who has been visiting his old home and friends at Steelville, Mo., called at this office on last Monday, on his way back to Virginia. Bro. Anderson is deeply impressed with the need for more workers and work in Crawford and adjoining counties, and hopes that the state board will soon be able to send pastors and teachers into that field. We presume the wants of Southwest and Southeast Missouri will be properly emphasized at the Nevada convention next week.

Seeing that J. G. Waggoner, of Eureka, Ill., is determined in his purpose of closing his work for the church there, the church has officially expressed its high appreciation of his continued ministry of eleven years there and its sincere commendation of his whole-hearted, faithful services wherever his lot may be cast, in a strongly written resolution.

J. T. Ogle will address the Missouri State Convention on Church Extension, instead of George Darsie, as announced in the program.

J. N. Murphy, of Windsor, Mo., writes us that he has recovered his health and that of his family, and he is now permitted to engage his whole time in ministerial work.

Thos. J. Thompson writes that he has decided to close his work at Lathrop, Mo., Jan. 1st, 1898. That means, of course, that Lathrop will want another preacher and that Bro. Thompson will become available for another field or church.

On account of poor health M. R. Shanks has declined a call for another year, so the Church of Christ at Monticello, Iowa, is now ready to engage another man.

John L. Stine, of Reserve, Kan., writes that he will be at liberty to hold one protracted meeting beginning about the first of November, and prefers to hold that meeting with some weak church.

J. T. McDowell has changed his address from Magnolia, Ia., to 6643 Lyric Street, East Pittsburg, Pa. He says that he will be in the East for several months.

B. H. Hayden has changed his address from Chicago to West Madison Ave. Church, Cleveland, Ohio, and of course wants the CHRISTIAN-EVANGELIST to follow him.

C. G. Blakeslee, pastor of the church at Roseville, Ill., has resigned and is now ready for another field. He was at Roseville three years, and reports the church "in excellent condition." The church gave him a farewell social last week, leaving a handsome purse of silver and other evidences of their esteem for him and for his services.

J. G. Slick has removed from Amboy to Litchfield, Minn., and says, "Don't let me miss a number of the CHRISTIAN-EVANGELIST." He is pleased with the outlook in his new field.

From the Herald, Quincy, Ill., we learn that H. L. Stine, of Paris, Mo., is likely to be the successor of J. M. Rudy, who has been called to Cedar Rapids, Iowa, already mentioned in this column. Bro. Rudy goes into a good field, with a strong church, large house and favorable surroundings for a fine work. Bro. Stine will also find himself strongly supported at Quincy, Ill.

P. B. Hall, of Charlottesville, Va., would like engagement to preach for some church in the middle states. Remember the address.

W. E. Garrison, the only member of our editorial staff who went abroad this year, having returned resumes his regular work again on this paper. He will also be engaged in teaching in the Bible department of Butler University, Irvington, Ind., this year, and to this work he went direct from Macatawa, Mich., without calling at this office. We are pleased to note that after a fine trip he is in fine health and enters upon his manifold duties with renewed energies.

On last Sunday evening Geo. F. Hall, of Decatur, Ill., delivered a temperance sermon or lecture to a large audience in the tabernacle at Decatur.

W. H. Williams, having preached for the church at Elmore, O., for nine years, has resigned and removed to Prairie Depot, O.

There is an opening at Hyndman, Pa., for a music teacher. Address, Herbert Carpenter.

Evangelist J. V. Coombs, with Singer A. O. Hunsaker, is in a meeting with J. H. Jones at Garden City, Mo.

E. S. Conner, after five years of service for the church at Noblesville, Ind., resigned. During his work there the church built a $16,650 house and its membership has been more than doubled. The church board officially says that "his work has been characterized by energy, earnestness, ability and discretion. Under his labors the church has grown in spirituality, liberality and good works, and now occupies a stronger position and has a greater influence than before." While Bro. Conner has thus prospered the church at Noblesville he desires a change and becomes available as a good man for some of our stronger churches. Of course, he will not have to search long for another field. Such men are soon picked up by churches in search of efficient preachers and pastors.

C. H. Plattenburg has removed from Ashland, Ohio, to Uniontown, Pa. His congregation at Ashland were sorry to lose him, but the larger field opened for him at Uniontown overruled their wishes. During his three years at Ashland nearly 200 members were added to the church, and the church debt paid.

F. S. Pettit, who went from Chillicothe, Mo., to Alcott, Col., some time ago, for the recovery of his health, writes that he is improving but that it will be several months before he will be able to do regular work again. He has resigned his pastorate at Chillicothe and will remain in Colorado for a season. Bro. Assiter is his successor at Chillicothe.

CHANGES.

W. B. Harter, Chester to Clay Center, Neb.
W. H. Willyard, DeSoto to Murphysboro, Ill.
T. N. Kincaid, Holden, Mo., to Hot Springs, Ark.
E. P. Grow, Goshon, Ind., to Grayson, Ky.
W. S. Hayden, Chicago, Ill., to Richland, N. Y.
G. F. Assiter, Oregon to Chillicothe, Mo.
A. B. Jones, Colorado Springs, Col., to Liberty, Mo.
Noah Garwick, Oakland to Des Moines, Ia.
N. R. Davis, Skidmore to Maryville, Mo.
G. W. Hemry, Ashley to Angola, Ind.
C. S. Weaver, Martinton io Eureka, Ill.
J. P. Sala, Randolph to Akron, Ohio.
J. W. Allen, Macatawa, Mich., to Cleveland, Ohio.

Correspondence.

Whe ling through England.

X.

It had long ago been decided that London should be the terminus of this bicycle trip, and Friday noon had been fixed upon as the last possible moment for reaching that goal. Leaving Edinburgh with four hundred and forty miles to go and four days and a half in which to do it, this final section of the tour necessarily degenerated into something of a race against time. But if one must hurry, this was the best place in England to do it, for the roads are level and, although it is an interesting ride, there are comparatively few points of picturesque or historic interest which absolutely demand that the traveler shall linger long in contemplation. Perhaps the most attractive spot on the route is that bit of Scottish borderland which contains, within a few miles, the galaxy of Abbottsford, Melrose and Dryburgh Abbey. The present proprietors of Walter Scott's home, Abbottsford, have devised a most ingenious system for exhibiting to the visitor just those few rooms which they care to exhibit and shooting him out again into the road, admiring but dissatisfied. But at Melrose one may pause and muse and meditate to his heart's content upon the most beautiful ruin in Scotland. There is something peculiarly satisfying about a good ruin, especially one like Melrose, whose every stone is a monument to the patient labor and artistic skill of those who carved and placed it. In elaborate buildings of more modern date one cannot but doubt occasionally whether the result, beautiful as it may be, is worth its cost of toil. There are cathedrals which, by their grandeur and magnificence, suggest that there has been a vast waste of both capital and labor, a terrible misapplication of resources. This is particularly true of new cathedrals. But it is different with a ruin. Here, in the nature of the case, one is forbidden to query whether it is worth its cost. The process of construction is here lost sight of in the distance, and there remains only the product, exquisite even in decay.

The line between Scotland and England (the river Tweed at this point) was again crossed without the traditional rain, but a worse thing befell me within a mile after crossing the line—a broken crank. This would have been bad at any time, but it was really serious when the schedule for these few remaining days demanded an average of a hundred miles a day. A telegram to London summoned the extra part to meet me next morning at Morpeth, forty miles from the scene of the accident. The rest of the afternoon was spent in the interesting exercise of learning how to ride against the wind and over an undulating road, with one pedal and the stump of a crank. It is possible, but not pleasant. No one who has not tried it will appreciate the thrill of delight which I received on finding the new crank at Morpeth next morning. Perhaps it will also be hard fully to appreciate the bitterness of the disappointment on finding that the new crank was of the wrong pattern, and therefore useless. It meant another day of riding with one leg. But this day's ride was broken by long stops at Newcastle-on-Tyne and Durban. Of the many English cathedrals visited on this tour some produced such an impression as Durham, standing with a Norman castle at its side, on a commanding height, overlooking the river and town. A satisfactory repair of the crippled wheel was effected at Durham, and there seemed to be still a chance of reaching London on time, stopping to see a few more cathedrals on the way besides.

But alas for the vanity of human wishes! Two hours out of Durham, and making lively time before a friendly breeze, there came a sickening crash. It might have been a broken leg, but as it happened it was nothing worse than the breaking off of a pedal. London seemed very far away, and it was not altogether easy to take a hopeful view of the case. There was no chance of getting a repair, but the days preceding had afforded some experience in the art of riding with one leg, and in that lay the only hope. I have a deep-seated aversion to the idea of finishing a bicycle trip on the train. The outcome of the matter was that the remaining two hundred and sixty miles, including two "century runs," were ridden with only one pedal, and London was reached on schedule time, before noon on Friday. But there were interesting points to be visited before London was reached. For the lover of cathedrals no part of England can offer attractions equal to those of the strip from Durham to London. The cathedrals of Durham, York, Peterboro, Lincoln and Ely, not to mention St. Paul's and Westminster Abbey in London, will furnish to the student of ecclesiastical architecture abundant food for thought.

In the midst of these splendid monuments of the religious establishment, it is pleasing to find a spot where the mind can dwell upon the heroes of Independency and the early champions of religious liberty. It is not many miles from York—the seat of the archbishop of the North—to Scrooby, the English home of our Pilgrim Fathers before their migration to Holland and then to New England. The cathedral at York is, in its proportions at least, the most imposing of Anglican temples; at Scrooby the oaken beams of the low building in which the little band of Independents worshiped now form the roof of a stable. Scrooby is not much frequented by sightseers, although the present occupant of the manor house, as he showed through the ancient edifice by candlelight, assured me that they had a great many visitors—that, in fact, somebody came almost every week in summertime. I spent a night in Scrooby, and employed most of the evening in trying to discover whether any of the villagers were familiar with the names or the deeds of their eminent fellow-townsmen of two centuries and a half ago. Not a man could be found, except at the manor house, who had ever heard of the Pilgrims. I inquired particularly about William Brewster, but none of them could remember that any family of Brewsters had ever lived in the community. If it be not too harsh a thing to say on observation limited to a single night, I would characterize the Nottinghamshire peasants of the locality of Scrooby as an unusually dull and insensible set, little likely to be roused to deeds of heroism. Perhaps the stock has degenerated in these latter days; or perhaps, as I prefer to believe, the Pilgrims in Scrooby, before they began their pilgrimage, were men of this same sort—heavy and stolid, and what a passing stranger (like myself) might have called stupid. If so, it shows how the touch of divine fire and the possession of a divine truth may make heroes out of peasants.

It was a comfort to be assured by the guidebooks that Cambridge is inferior to Oxford in interest and beauty, for the stop there must be short, too short to admit of more than a hasty outside view of the principal colleges. One twilight and two moonlight hours gave me all the impression of Cambridge which I was permitted to get. Next morning an easy fifty-mile run brought me into London and completed a ride of three thousand and eighteen miles in sixty-six days. A few days remain for seeing London, but the bicycle trip is at an end. At the end of the tour I find several beliefs confirmed, most notably the conviction that, in such a country as England, the bicycle is the best means of vacation travel yet devised. The pride which I took in my bicyle when it was new, perfect in enamel and nickel-plate, but yet untried, has given place to a genuine affection, now that it is know[n to] be sound within, though scratched and sca[rred] without. No accidents have befallen my S[...]ling, except such as were due to circumstan[ces] over which neither it nor I had control. [The] end of the whole matter is that, to those [who] are contemplating a bicycle trip in Englan[d I] would reiterate the advice which I offere[d in] the article preliminary to this series: "G[o]."

W. E. GARRISON.

London.

A Bit of Dixie.

East Tennessee is proverbially a land of [pic]turesqueness. Writers have often likene[d it] to "the Switzerland of the South." Pen [and] easel alike pay just tribute to this "land [of] the skies." Like Cæsar, "I came, I saw," but unlike him, *I am conquered*—Tennes[see] has captivated me; at her feet I bow in rev[er]ence. God has been good to her!

Prairie-born, my first real mountain v[iew] was of that historic landmark, Lookout Mou[nt]ain, as the Chattanooga, St. Louis and Sou[th]ern car swept into the Tennessee River Vall[ey].

Forgetting its historical associations—[and] it has many, including the famous "Battl[e of] the Clouds" in which Grant, Sherman [and] Hooker largely figured—Lookout yet deser[ves] and demands more than a passing menti[on]. From its peak six states may be seen; w[hile] spread out beneath in panoramic fashion [may] be seen old Missionary Ridge on which Chic[ka]mauga National Military Park is locat[ed], where so recently thousands of "blue" b[oys] in blue were stationed; the graceful, glist[en]ing windings of the Tennessee, as it rou[nds] Moccasin Bend; a bird's-eye view, or m[ore] strictly speaking, a roof view of Chattanoo[ga], spire melting into turret and steeple into cu[po]la; and, in the dim distance, the pale pur[ple] outlines of far-away mountain ranges.

Don't miss coming to the convention [at] Chattanooga! You will miss a treat if you [do]. Come and see where Gov. Bob Taylor breat[hed] inspiration for that breezy Nashville Endea[vor] address. Come and see where "Old Hickor[y]" started on the bottom rung to clime at last [to] the President's exalted chair. Come and [see] where James K. Polk and Andrew Johnson [fol]lowed suit with the same happy result. Co[me] and see a typical Southern state.

Perhaps it is patriotism makes Gov. Tay[lor] believe "the sky is bluer, the rivers clear[er], the grass greener," etc., in his native st[ate] than elsewhere; but, nevertheless, so or not, Tennessee possesses a matchless climate. [Gov.] Bob may not be so far off after all, for a fri[end] of mine from Indiana once said, "The st[ars] seem to shine brighter down here than up [in] Hoosierdom."

A bit of Tennessee history might not be [out] of place. It was the sixteenth state admitt[ed], so did not miss much of being one of the th[ir]teen original. The spring of 1796 chronic[led] its advent and thus added a bright star to [the] blue depths of Old Glory's folds. It w[as] named Tennessee from the Indian "Tenassee," meaning "river of the big bend." It w[as] first settled at Watauga in 1769 by English s[et]tlers.

The area of the state is 42,050 sq. mi. [Its] population in 1890 was one million seven hu[n]dred and sixty-seven thousand. Memph[is], Nashville and Chattanooga are its metropolis[es].

In many respects the state, in sections, is [an] oddity. Progress evidently ossified somewh[ere] back in the time when this country was in [its] teens. The same old rough-hewn log ca[bin] with stick and mud chimney that proved [a] domicile to the early pioneer still shelters [his] great-grandsons. Youngsters go hunting ra[b]bits with muskets that would easily be mist[ak]en in the dark for old-time "blunderbuses;" the "whirr" of an occasional *octogenari[an]* spinning-wheel startles you; while flai[ls,] cradles and numerous other such farming i[m]plements proclaim the fact that they have n[ot] forsaken the "path of their fathers" for su[ch] new fangled innovations as threshers a[nd]

rork in America. My recent trip East has ιasized afresh in my mind the importance ınting our great cause in the magnificent ı of this country. There can be no greater ꞉o this than a large Church Extension .

A. C. SMITHER.

ꞩ *Angeles, Cal.*

At Fontainebleau.

'o hours from Paris. A ride through gar- and harvest fields. Bountiful harvests, itive methods, silent fields! The click of mower and binder are never heard; but are not odorless. All that poetry about eet fields'' needs revision in countries 'e the price of fertility is excessive fertiliz- ı.

rest of Fontainebleau! What a transition the boulevards of Paris! It is not large. ldier could march around it between sun- and sunset. But it is most beautiful in .ce. It has no elevated places, no mount- , though it has some hills with beautiful pects. The Tower of Denecourt in the ı part, the Rocks and Gorge of Franchard, Gorge of Apremont in the west part, and ıin localities in the south, are constantly ed; yet the most ravishingly beautiful ɜs are far aside from these popular centers h are more curious than artistic and nat- . He who penetrates a foot into the remote .ons will find himself in the midst of trees, h, oak and birch, worthy of the name. r have been carefully watched over. Nature the forester have accomplished wonders hese quiet nooks. Compared with the k Forest of Southern Germany, Fontaine- u would suffer greatly. The comparison ld be ruinous indeed.

ntainebleau has its temple, its cult, its , its idolatry as well as its oaks and hes. Its temple is one of those chapels h one sees by the score and by the hundred 'yrol, where roadside idolatry is equal to of Spain, India or China. The forest of ꞉ainebleau has but one such roadside ɔel, but that one is interesting. It stands he broad Route of Mulun, just at the en- ce of the street which leads through the ı to the palace of the kings of France, in a ain sense also a temple sacred to the mem- of the gods dethroned, and where the ager goes up to worship. The pilgrimage inues all summer.

ıt the chapel proper. Large enough to mmodate two or three persons in a kneel- posture. A marble altar some twelve es high, within doubtless a consecrated ɜr. But you do not kneel there. A great excludes the intruder while allowing him ɜe the object, or the medium, if you will, of levotion. (Object and medium are probably ɪs unknown to peasants.) Above, a statue he Virgin. Nor is it a work of art. A ɜk portal. Before this a Greek porch, ı, supported by pillars on the sides. Fifty ons might kneel beneath it. The ceiling lorned with a large painting. A mighty fills the field. A steed, frightened, is in act of stopping. The rider, a cavalier of l7th century, is prone on the ground on his : with one foot in the stirrup. Mary ɜars in the lower branches of the tree with ild in her arms. It is the babe of Bethle- .

ı either side of the Greek portal, he who may read, if he can read French, a large er, blue, printed, official, stamped, pro- ɜd beneath a trellis of wire, giving the 'igin of the Chapel of Notre-Dame-de- -Secours,'' of which Bædeker takes no ꞉e. I made on the spot a translation, h proves too long to forward to the ISTIAN-EVANGELIST. I cannot resist insert- ı few passages:

In 1661, toward the end of November, M. ɔeron was returning to the court of Louis ., when his horse threw him and dragged downhill to this point. Without doubt he was about to suffer a most cruel and tragic death. With an extraordinary devotion toward the Mother of God, the pious cavalier raised his eyes supplicatingly to heaven and called upon the august Mary to succor him. Immediately the horse stopped, still trembling with fright. M. d'Aberon could not find a single wound, though he had been dragged over stones.

"In gratitude, M. d'Auberon caused an image of the Virgin to be blessed, etc., May 3, 1662. The same day, M. Durand, pastor, carried the image in procession and fixed it on an oak where the horse had been miraculously stopped. An authentic recitation of the facts on parchment in Latin accompanied the image, etc.

"M. Grenet, a later priest, built an oratory on the spot where the oak fell with age and time. A painting adorned the front.

"The revolution of '93 did not spare this edifice, so highly venerated by the districts about, etc.

"In the calm which followed those mournful days, M. Philippeaux, archpriest of F. and honorary canon of Meaux, conceived the idea of rebuilding the ancient chapel. M. Hurtault, the king's architect and member of the Institute (highest dignity conferred in France), drew the plan and directed the work. M. Blondel, an excellent painter, volunteered to reproduce the miraculous event.

"Such is the monument dedicated by the priest of F. Sept. 30, 1821, in the midst of all the civil and military authorities in grand uniform * * * * !''

Another passage relates the organization of the now widely known cult under the name of "Notre-Dame-de-Bon-Secours,'' which received a special supply of indulgences from the Pope July 2, 1820.

A prayer to the Virgin closes the historical sketch. Solomon's temple was not able to set more dignitaries in motion than this niche by the roadside, one of a system of roadside oratories dedicated to the saints, especially Joseph and Mary, and to be met with wherever the red cap of a cardinal is in authority. The statues sometimes remind one vividly of the heathen gods in the oriental departments of the museums, so terrible is the art and handicraft displayed. The Greeks had idols, but they were works of art. In Italy the Christians have not lacked in works of art, whether in painting or sculpture, but the roadside idols, especially in Tyrol, are excelled in ugliness only by those of the Orient.

In the presence of such "authentic miracles'' one cannot help recalling the misfortunes of the poet Gringoire, in Victor Hugo's "Notre-Dame de Paris.'' It so happened that this renowned verse-maker was knocked down in a street incident one night in the year 1482, and fell in a gutter near a statue of the Virgin. It came to pass also that a merchant round the corner died. The street Arabs got the castaway straw bedd ng of the deceased and threw it down by accident on the half-senseless rhymester. They were going to build a bonfire, for it was winter and the night of the Feast of Fools. Gringoire had the good fortune to regain consciousness, sprang up and fled. The gamins, frightened by the apparition, cried aloud and spread the report that the merchant, or his soul, had come to life and fled from the tick. "All on account of the mere presence of the statue of the Virgin,'' said the clergy, and they bore away the straw tick with honor to the church of Sainte-Opportune, where it is said to have remained till the year 1759, to the great profit of the Sacristan and for the healing of the multitudes.

Fontainebleau is a town of some 14,000 inhabitants. The chief industry in summer and fall is to welcome the strangers and make them pay more per day than at Paris, an honor of which the city is justly proud.

The palace, or chateau, of Fontainebleau is chiefly interesting on account of being the country seat of the kings and emperors of

France since the reign of Francois I. You are shown rapidly through the ancient Chapel of the Trinity, where Louis XV. was married, and where Napoleon III. was baptized in 1810. From here you enter the apartments of Napoleon I. and visit the cabinet where he signed his abdication in 1814. The council chamber and throne room are elaborately furnished and decorated. From here you pass into the boudoir of Marie Antoinette, which contains some rare vases in ivory. The library or gallery of Diana has 30,000 volumes. The gallery of Francois I. is remarkable for its decorations and for a jewel casket in porcelain. A certain suite of chambers were occupied by the Pope as prisoner from 1812 to 1814. But the great historical personages who have passed through these buildings from century to century is that which makes them the object of so much attention. It was here that Louis IV. signed the revocation of the edict of Nantes in 1685; it was here that Napoleon I. divorced Josephine in 1809; it was in the Court of Farewells that he took leave of the grenadiers of the guard in 1814; here that he reviewed them on his return from exile, 1815. The guide gives you no time for musing and no time to examine closely a decoration, a tapestry or a painting.

If you leave for Paris by a late train, the last thing you do is to eat your supper on the sidewalk, a terrace or veranda, and then walk through the park to the station. You will sometimes chance to hear a bit of conversation. This evening a well-dressed American, who loved red wine, was engaged in a chat with the restaurant keeper. Perhaps it was the wine, the heat; perhaps a package of important letters had been returned from the last stopping-place to the states, or perhaps he had been reading a Paris editorial on the war. No matter, he was out of humor. He had the appearance of a man who delights in the naked truth, and who was not in the habit of sugar-coating his opinions.

"How do you find our little city?" asked the restaurateur.

"Forest magnificent, palace rich in historical souvenirs. The town? It's a convent," was the laconic reply.

"Your pardon, Monsieur, your pardon a thousand times; but have the goodness to explain."

"Not difficult. I say the town is a convent. Walls, walls everywhere. Your streets are but corridors, with stone walls and iron doors through which you enter into your homes like a monk into his cell. One might think the town was full of nuns and priests, like Manila."

"But Monsieur surely noticed that many have lowered their walls to three feet—"

"Have substituted a system of iron pickets of the height of the parts removed. Iron spears as large as pitchfork handles and as long. Would do excellently for a state's prison. Look like the spears of the middle ages, only these are not so heavy. But they are better than non-transparent stone. The homeless stranger can at least admire the pretty little gardens before the doors."

"Our pretty little gardens!" exclaimed the restaurateur, with a gesture of delight. "To protect them and to have security for life, property and privacy, the walls are necessary."

"Some of your generous citizens seem to have had an attack of penitence. They have trained vines and ivy over the spears in order to regain their precious privacy. Streets are deserted enough most of the time, are they not? Do you think your homes would be vandalized and your roses stolen by the strangers who come in summer? Are your cottages all government mints? Do they contain plans and specifications of the fortifications of France? The castles of the fourteenth century were not better walled in than your—rosebeds."

"But the security of life when one is asleep? Our children? It would be too much like the insecurity of American towns if we had no walls and iron gates. They say one is not safe there neither by day nor night."

"Which is a European falsehood. Go to the deserts of Arizona, where there are more Indians and Mexican half-breeds than pale-faces. The people of Phœnix dread nothing but mosquitoes. They sleep in their yards indifferently, or on their porches. Even the invalids sleep out of doors. Your life is as safe there, and safer, than at Paris."

The face of the restaurateur turned pale at the thought of sleeping out of doors. He regained his natural color in concluding that he had been listening to an American yarn. Having never heard of Arizona, he at once denied its existence. By this revelation of ignorance he raised himself to the level of many school-teachers on the Continent who prate about the inefficiency of American schools. My fellow-countryman was in a predicament. I came to his relief by drawing from my handsack a splendid folding map in color of the United States, probably the first the restaurateur had ever seen; and which had done me good service in the presence of more than one disciple of Thomas. We proceeded at once to give the restaurateur his first lesson in the geography of North America.

When I left for the train my compatriot was still continuing his harangue:

"Not only your houses from each other and from the street, but also your kitchen gardens, with nothing but cabbage on one side and potatoes and beans on the other, are separated by walls of brick and stone. I have no doubt but that there is waste material enough in the useless, senseless walls of your town to add another story to every dwelling-house in the place, and your streets would gain as well in width and beauty; the stranger would feel more at home and less like he was in a convent. But I presume it will take you people eight or ten centuries more to see through such a simple, economic proposition and to appreciate the beauties of a civilization without stone walls and sheet-iron gates. In America we are accustomed to see such things around convents, but not about residences."

WM. H. MATLOCK.

Reply to Editor's Criticism.

The editor of the CHRISTIAN-EVANGELIST mistakes my purpose and overestimates my ambition in characterizing what appears in the last number of that paper under my name as "an effort to abolish mystery." The writer of the paper was not impelled by any such purpose or ambition, but by a simple desire to contribute in a small measure to the removal of the rubbish of mysticism which has so long obstructed the way and impeded the work of the Holy Spirit among men. The editor seems to have read my paper under the influence of super-excited imagination, to have discovered in it "a disposition and tendency to deny everything mysterious and marvelous, and every fact and truth that is above one's comprehension." Not only this, but he construes my declaration, that the Scriptures do not speak of the *personality* of the Holy Spirit, into a denial of such personality. If one would declare that the Scriptures are silent respecting the *personality* of God, would that be evidence that such an one did not believe in the *existence* of God? Every intelligence in the universe is an embodiment, a personality, but some of these possess *spirit-bodies*, concerning which we have no knowledge, or means for acquiring it; may we not, therefore, believe in the existence of such bodies?

For the enlightenment of Bro. Garrison and my own vindication I will restate what I said on this point: "If it be true that the Holy Spirit occupies, at the same moment of time, millions of other personalities like man, and scattered as they are all over the earth, *then* it is not true that the Holy Spirit is a personality, *of which man has knowledge, or of which he can form an intelligent* conception," and then I made the statement, that "respecting the *personality* of the Holy Spirit," the Scriptures
are silent; that man, of himself, possesses
knowledge, and does not even possess capaci
to form an intelligent conception," and I sta
by this statement and at the same time decla
my belief in the personality of the Holy Spir

But the subject of this inquiry is not spir
nature, or spirit-being; of these we cann
form even an intelligent conception. We a
looking for him whom Jesus told his disciples
would send to *take his place among then*
Men and women have become weary heari
of and waiting for an invisible, intangible, i
comprehensible Comforter. They want
Comforter who is more tangible than an ide
more comprehensible than a mystery, mo
reliable than an emotion. They want a Con
forter and Advocate to whom they can go
the disciples went to Jesus for instruction, f
advice, for sympathy, for help. They want
know where he took up his abode when
came to the earth, assured that where he to
up his abode there he abides still.

But to return to the criticism of Bro. Ga
rison. He objects to the statement, that "m
is so constituted that he cannot take cogni
ance of things except through his senses," et
Will he kindly give me an instance in whi
God communicated with man, or that m
communicate with others, by manners a
means not cognizable by the senses? H
simple denial of the statement is not satisfa
tory. Again, Bro. Garrison "accepts as tr
what Bro. Carson says about the embodime
of God in the person of Christ and th
church," but says, "This in no way disprov
the larger movements of the Spirit of Go
which are not limited to the methods mentio
ed." This to me is an extraordinary stat
ment. Paul says that in his effort to save me
through Christ, God "emptied himself," e
hausted himself of means and methods. B
according to Bro. Garrison, Paul was mi
taken. The Spirit is engaged in larger mov
ments now, in which he is not limited
the methods of Christ and the church. Surel
this must be accepted, if at all, in "the myst
spirit" sense.

JAMES O. CARSON.

St. Louis, Sept. 6, 1898.

[1. If Bro. Carson will read more carefull
our strictures on his article he will discov
that we do not attribute to him "a dispositic
and tendency to deny everything mysterio
and marvelous," etc., but we mention that
a characteristic of a certain class of thinker
and this tendency, we said, was more to b
feared than the opposite one which he critici
ed.

2. To say that the Scriptures are silent co
cerning the personality of the Holy Spirit i
in our judgment, equivalent to saying that w
have no ground for the belief in the persona
ity of the Holy Spirit for, as concerning th
nature of the tripersonality of the Godhead, w
are shut up to revelation.

3. Bro. C. confuses personality with em
bodiment, whereas they are entirely dis
tinct conceptions. A person may or may n
have a body. In a certain experience of Pa
he did not know whether he was in the body
out of the body, but he was conscious durin
that time of having seen and heard wonderf
things which it would not be lawful for him t
repeat.

4. If the Scriptures reveal the personalit
of the Holy Spirit as a fact, then we hav
"knowledge" of the fact. We are not ask
as finite beings, to *comprehend* the personalit
of God, whether as Father, Son or Holy Spiri
but we can, as a matter of faith accept revea
ed facts and truths that transcend the limits
our reason and knowledge. We accept chee
fully Bro. C.'s declaration of belief in the pe
sonality of the Holy Spirit, and we have n
doubt but that his faith is grounded on th
statements of the Holy Scriptures.

5. Bro. C. says, "Men and women have becom
weary waiting for an invisible, intangible, i
comprehensible Comforter." Does he mea
by this to assert that the Holy Spirit is a *visi*
ble, tangible and *comprehensible* Comforte

the Holy Spirit does manifest himself ;h the church and through individual ians is a glorious truth; but it would be ıge mistake to identify the Holy Spirit he body or the individual through which nifests himself. For ourselves, we would ı it an infinite misfortune to have the Comforter, whom Jesus promised, trans- 1 into a visible, tangible and compre- le being. That would rob him of his and hence of his ability to meet the old needs of men.

We do not limit God to the five senses efforts to reach, comfort and strengthen ildren. This would cut the nerve of :? Who pretends to know by what God will fulfill His promise to hear and r prayer. Which one of the five senses prophets and apostles received divine tion from God, or inspiration? When :. prays in the midst of trouble and sor- nd a great peace steals into his heart—a which ''passeth understanding''— ;h which one of his five senses does this come into the soul? Ah! how much are our needs, often, than our theories ne operation.

Bro. C. considers our remark, that the nents of the divine Spirit are not limited church and to methods that we call ian, as an ''extraordinary statement.'' God have nothing to do with the heathen ? Is He not also working through the relationships, through the state and by ovidence to make this world better and 1 men to forsake their evil ways, and to uer lives? Do let us cease to limit the hty and thank Him rather that by so voices He is calling the race onward and d to a higher destiny.

. C.'s exegesis of Paul's remark about lf-emptying of Christ is an entirely new ne of the *kenosis*, and can hardly stand st of examination. It was not God ex- ng Himself in Christ, but Christ dis- ; himself of divine glory to become man ie Savior of men. EDITOR.]

Helps for Preachers.

eive many letters of inquiry respecting a of study for preachers who have not the or the means to attend school. Others, ho have graduated in the classical, but done but little work in any course pre- ry to the work of the ministry, feel the f help for their calling as a minister of ospel. Many have committed the mis- of supposing that if they have passed a able examination in the sciences and s, therefore they have made about e preparation needed for the ministry. ame course would prepare them just as r medicine or law. After they begin the of a minister they begin to realize their of Bible study and their need of helps. he brother who has not had the advan- f college I would say, first of all, you need very familiar with your Bible. If you it without references or concordace, all tter. Too many study simply for sermons, ever have more than a concordance-ac- ance with God's Book. Study its history, ronology, its geography, its prophecy, w, its practice, its promise. Study the h Bible; the Revision by all means. e familiar with it, commit it to memory uid say ''to heart.'' Read and study it would any other book, expecting to find aning by an analysis and synthesis of its words, clauses, sentences, paragraphs, ns, chapters, books. As for comment- they are good on easy questions. As a , ''the Bible Commentary'' on Old and Testament is about the best. For practi- lue in the study of the New Testament, I v of nothing better than Barnes' eleven es. As for the works written by our own , I very heartily commend McGarvey on ew, Mark and Acts; Lamar on Luke; Johnson on John; Lard on Romans; Milligan on Hebrews. But there is nothing so profitable as a careful study of the Book itself. A thorough study of Hermeneutics—the principles of Exegesis—will greatly assist. To know the methods and rules of interpretation will assist more than a knowledge of many commentaries.

You say you want to know something of the Greek New Testament, and that you have not the time to go to school, and have no teacher. Well, you might get a Greek reader, a kind of first book in Greek. This will lead up to a grammar and a lexicon and enable you to do something in translation. As a lexicon, Liddell and Scott is the best. But a very convenient small work is the Noble and Hind Greek and English Dictionary, 4 Cooper Institute, New York. It is much cheaper than the other and contains all the words and they are sufficiently defined. This is based on the Liddell and Scott, but does not give the classical occurrences of the words as does the larger work. It is much cheaper, as it costs but two dollars, with the second part in it, which is English into Greek. This is a great help to students. I have tried it and found it a favorite with the best scholars and teachers. It is coming to be a test book in many schools.

If you delight in sermon books, I recommend that you read them for their thought and literature. For, let me say, the written sermon is the highest order of literature in the country. But, above almost everything else avoid preaching other men's sermons. Use them as helps to thought, and diction too, for all that, but in the sermon be yourself. David can do better with his sling than with the armor of the king. To use a figure, if you must borrow a coat, do not get one too large nor too snug, you might get it on and not be able to get it off.

Read works of the best English, of the best thought and of most moral and spiritual worth. Sensational books or magazines are for the most part a waste of time; they may make you glib in fashionable gossip, but they will empty your head and heart of the things which the people have a right to expect of you. Enough for the present. D. R. DUNGAN.

Japan Letter.

In looking over one of the Tokyo papers this morning two facts of great importance struck me. The first was

A MOVE IN THE RIGHT DIRECTION.

In 1871 the Educational Department passed some regulations with the intention of regulating the freedom of speech among schoolteachers. They were not allowed to indulge in public discussions of anything which had even a semblance of political connection. They were also denied the right of having anything to do with religion, for fear in so doing they would infringe the liberties of the students. The new Minister of Education, Mr. Ozaki, upon assuming the duties of his office deliberately scratched these musty laws from the statute-books of the Educational Department. In doing so he has taken a long step towards the longed-for liberty of speech. Not only so, but he has shown that by denying the students and teachers the right to partake of the religious spirit of the times they have broken the law of religious freedom, which has so recommended Japan to the world. The old must give way to the new. To still cling to a suit of clothes, full of holes and dirty with age, simply because they have ''become a part of us,'' so to speak, is a thing we would not think of doing. Yet we are apt to cling to old customs and forms simply because we have been used to them for so long a time. Japan is putting off the old and putting on the new. In the language of Scripture, she is going forth. ''When that which is perfect is come that which is in part shall be done away.''

CHRISTIANITY PRAISED.

The following note will explain itself: ''According to the returns up to June last there are fourteen women's magazines published in Japan. Of these four are in the interest of Buddhism and the rest in that of Christianity. This fact alone is significant, and shows how actively the Christian propaganda is pushing the work of evangelization, in strong contrast to the Buddhist priests. The fact, also, that Buddhist ladies are relatively poorer in mental culture than their Christian sisters must also be taken into account.''—*Japan Times*.

The ignorance of most of the Japanese women is asteunding. They do not have any idea of literature, and know nothing of the great outside world. They thrive mostly on scandal and low chattering. It is a high tribute, coming as it does from a paper decidedly anti-Christian, to make such a statement as the above. The unseen leaven of Christianity is beginning to affect the whole of Japanese society. Even those in high places are beginning to recognize in Christianity a power not to be overlooked. ''The kingdom of heaven cometh not by observation.''

OUR WORK HOPEFUL.

Good reports are coming in continually from the workers in the interior. Fukushima reports two immersions. Sappora reports five. One young man has decided for Christ in Tokyo. What we need now is more men to go into the evangelistic work and urge the people ''to come in.'' The name of Christ is not unknown. The people are familiar with many Christian truths. They only need to be urged. It seems to me, as I have more to do with this direct work of preaching the gospel, that the time is not far distant when we will not have to wait and count our converts by ones and twos, but when we may count them by the hundreds. Faith in God and the anointing of his Spirit will bring us the victory. "No man can come unto Christ unless it be given unto him of the Father." H. H. GUY.

Tokyo, Japan, August 13, 1898.

Iowa Letter.

God is continually putting in stitches—binding the nations together. In this instance it is Iowa and Germany. Under date of August 8th an Iowa writer for the CHRISTIAN-EVANGELIST penciled me these lines: "I am just on the eve of starting to New York City to put my thirteen-year-old boy on the Hamburg steamer, by which he is to go to his uncle at Berlin to make his future home. His uncle is court dentist, and will raise Charlie and make a dentist of him." In the present war the German Government has not endeared itself to the American people. Yet the two lands are knit together by untold ties of great strength. My own mother was born on the Rhine.

It is a good thing for us to see ourselves as others see us. A level-headed, pious-hearted man, who lately left the people among whom he was raised and joined his fortunes with the Iowa Disciples of Christ, thus writes to a friend who does not know us so well. It was not written for publication, and is here inserted without names and without the consent of the writer or the party addressed: "As to the type of evangelism we find among the Disciples, it strikes you as it did me, and you take the same view of the case. The lack of religious fervor, rather *feeling* or *emotion*, seemed to me very marked and almost painful, and in many cases I feel it so yet. But I have studied the case so much and discovered so many compensating equivalents that I feel much more reconciled. I find a truer knowledge and interpretation of the Word of God, for one thing. This goes a good way. I find a staying power in the membership which is very remarkable for another—a zeal to save and a fellowship among my brethren that pleases me much. There is less trust in prayers and less spiritual fervor than there should be, no doubt. As to the type of moral life, I am persuaded that it is equal to other churches of the best types. Our evangelists are fishers of men, and do leave, as a rule, very much for the pastor to finish up. The difference, however, is mainly this, a really better system of distributed labor. The evangelist dwells mainly on *first principles* and in setting forth the distinctive position of the reform movement. He dwells but very briefly on second principles or the daily life duties of the Christian—such matters as moral conduct, prayer, seeking spiritual gifts, etc. This is left to the pastor. A wise pastor after every series of meetings will take up these matters in sermons and at prayer-meetings, and complete the work."

A. J. Garrison, of Iowa City, recently picked up this precious bit of Baptist wisdom. On the cars a Methodist preacher pressed upon his Baptist brother—a preacher—this question: "Why, when so many of your own brethren are opposed, do you Baptists hold on to close communion?" You cannot guess his answer. Hear it: "It is about the only thing left to distinguish us from other churches, and *we have to hold on to it!*"

This reminds me of a few words recently spoken to me by Russell H. Conwell, the famous Philadelphia pastor and lecturer. I met him just before his lecture in a live Iowa town. "I do not understand these Western Baptists," said he; "I fear it would be hard for me to fellowship them." I asked him why. "This close communion business. That's not Baptist doctrine. We don't practice it in the East. Roger Williams' old church don't practice it. These men out West are hardly orthodox."

We have been compelled to change the date of our state convention on account of the great carnival at Des Moines. The new date is September 26th to 30th. Let all take note and be present. Do not forget your railroad certificates if you want to return at one-third fare. One of the items of interest is the election of a new secretary to succeed the writer of these notes. A splendid program is prepared. Write D. A. Wickizer, so that entertainment will be provided for you. Address him in East Des Moines, Ia. W. E. M. Hackleman will have charge of the music. Dr. Butchart, assisted by H. O. Breeden, will open the night sessions, on Monday night, September 26th, with a fine display of stereopticon views. Frank G. Tyrrell, of St. Louis, Mo., will close with an Endeavor address on Friday night. Let us make it a great convention. The year's work will surpass that of last year in two or three important lines. Come one, come all. A. M. HAGGARD.

History of Hiram College.

PART I.—THE ECLECTIC INSTITUTE.

The Western Reserve Electic Institute (now Hiram College) has almost completed its semi-centennial. It was founded in 1850, or properly speaking its first session was held in the fall of that year, although the initial steps toward its founding had been taken more than a year earlier. The religious body known as the Disciples of Christ was rapidly growing throughout Ohio and an urgent need was quite generally felt for a school of academic grade that should be under the influence and control of this people. The school came very nearly being placed at North Bloomfield, Trumbull County, O., but was finally located at Hiram. The reasons for this were partly the healthful and accessible location and partly because Hiram had a very flourishing church. The aims of the new school were clearly defined and seem to have been to provide a sound scientific and literary education; to temper and sweeten such education with moral and scriptural knowledge, and to educate young men for the ministry. Many schools have arisen among the Disciples since the old Eclectic, but it will be a long time before the large body of ministers in whose memory it figures will have passed away.

Of course, the religious aspects of the school were exactly what might be expected from the nature of the Current Reformation. The Disciples believed that the Bible had been in a degree obscured by theological speculations and ecclesiastical systems. They desired that a large place should be given to the study of the Bible, and hence the charter of the Eclectic Institute declared the purpose of the institution to be: "The instruction of youth of both sexes in the various branches of literature and science, especially of moral science as based in the facts and precepts of the Holy Scriptures."

Rev. A. S. Hayden was the first president of the new seminary. Railroads were few in those days and Hiram hill had to be reached from various directions by stage-coach. Many students came to Ravenna, thence to Garrettsville and the old tavern at Hewitt's Corner, from whence a two miles walk or ride brought them to the seat of learning. The school rose at once to a high degree of popularity. A commodious brick building of two stories, which at that period was considered a large and model structure, had been built in a corn-field on the very summit of the hill. The beautiful campus into which this field has been transformed bears little resemblance now to the primitive surroundings of that early period.

Eighty-four students were present at the opening of the school. This number soon arose to two or there hundred per term. Under President Hayden's administration the work went steadily on and the Eclectic more than fulfilled the expectation of its patrons. The range of this patronage was wide. Ohio furnished the largest number of students, but there were some from Canada, New York and Pennsylvania, while no small number came from parts of the South and the West. These students differed widely in age, ability, culture and wants. Some received grammar-school instruction; others high-school instruction; while others pushed on far into the regular college course. Classes in the higher branches were organized and taught as they were called for. No degrees were conferred and no students were graduated. A course of study was published in the catalogue after the first year or two, but it was a list of studies taught as they were called for rather than a regular curriculum. Students were encouraged to push on their education into schools of higher grade and many of the old Eclectic finished regular college courses in the East. Among these were James A. Garfield, William Hayden, Warren Hayden, J. H. Wilbur and others. Williams College, in Massachussets, seemed to be a favorite finishing-place for students of the institution. The war found the Eclectic in a flourishing condition, but like all the colleges of the country, the student ranks were rapidly depleted when the call came to take up arms. Many of the boys followed President Garfield into the army, some never to return to resume their work on the old hill.

Among the early teachers of the Eclectic there were (aside from the revered president A. S. Hayden) Norman Dunshee, Thomas Munnell, James A. Garfield, Almeda Booth, J. H. Rhodes, T. E. Sutlief, Cortentia Munson, Harvey Everest and others who figured more extensively in the college era. These men and women, teaching at a ridiculously low salary, depending for this entirely on the meagre tuition receipts, were a hard-working, self-sacrificing band who made the name of the Eclectic honored and revered wherever it was known. Some are dead and the rest are scattered, but the work they did cannot be measured. For many years the Eclectic held a high position among the schools of Ohio. It did not die when it was rechartered as Hiram College in 1867. Its principal features are still to be discerned in the college preparatory department, while its inspiring spirit continues to be the life of the institution. P.

Newspapers in Congressional Library.

The value of the newspaper as a means of public education and enlightenment is being appreciated more and more as time rolls on. The period is not remote when the public speaker was the medium of enlightenment on all public questions. Then the orator was regarded as a superior being, deserving almost the adoration of the common people. Times have changed. Now the newspaper is the power behind the throne. It molds and controls popular sentiment. The public speaker finds the masses quite as thoroughly informed upon current topics as he himself is. He may inspire and create some form of enthusiastic action, but in a majority of cases the people have made up their minds on matters of public import, for they have gleaned the facts from the press.

One valuable feature in the Congressional Library is the preservation, in bound form, of the leading newspapers of the country. The advantages are numerous.

1. Newspapers are the best index possible to the condition of the public sentiment at the time of their publication. One of the most interesting books the writer ever read touching revolutionary history is a large volume made up of clippings from the Tory papers of that period. It reflects the true sentiment of the time.

2. They afford the real material out of which history is made. While it is sometimes true of these publications, as it was of the conversations of Gratiano—"He speaks an infinite deal of nothing: His reasons are as two grains of wheat hid in two bushels of chaff; you may seek all the day ere you find them, and when you have them they are not worth the search" —yet they are treasures of incalculable value. Some of our metropolitan journals took special pains and spared no expense to preserve the leading characteristics and events of the present war with Spain, as some of them did in the war of the rebellion in 1861-5, with the view of collecting all in bound form as a complete history of the period.

3. These newspapers, if carefully indexed, afford proper subject-matter for those who have occasion to investigate certain specific questions. This use of them is an important one and should be encouraged on the part of pupils in all grades of schools. It trains an essential element of their educational career—the wise, judicious selection of appropriate material from the great mass presented.

The writer desires to make a suggestion or two, and trusts that Col. John R. Young, the efficient librarian, will take the matter into favorable consideration.

1. Let newspapers throughout the country be requested to send to the library one or two copies of each issue for its special use.

2. Let additional help be employed, if necessary, to select carefully from these papers matter for a series of scrapbooks in science, biography, history, politics, poetry, theology, mathematics, language, etc., etc. The subject-matter needs to be carefully classified and put into separate volumes; according to the most approved methods of forming such scrapbooks.

3. Let all these scrapbooks be properly indexed, so that a person desiring information upon any subject can have, in addition to all that he can secure from encyclopedias and special treatises, what the newspapers of the country have gathered on the same line. For example, during the current war all our newspapers have had from time to time very important articles on the inhabitants, resources, productions, climate, characteristics, etc., of Cuba, Porto Rico, the Philippines, Ladrones, etc. This information was often secured at heavy expense and much labor on the part of correspondents, and is of immense value.

4. The initiation and prosecution of such a plan on the part of the Congressional Library, in addition to its direct benefits to its immediate patrons will be serviceable in stimulating throughout the country the practice of individuals of using in scrapbooks the important material which is found in such great abundance in all publications, daily, weekly, monthly and quarterly. The accomplishment of this desirable result will be the attainment of a most important end. The language of Jesus to his disciples is specially appropriate: "Gather up the fragments that remain, that nothing be lost." Let the Congressional Library take the initiative in this matter.—J. Fraise Richard, *in Evening Star, Washington, D. C., Sept.* 12, 1898.

Nebraska Letter.

The affable editor has asked me for occasional Nebraska letters. It was a surprise. Somebody wants to know about Nebraska? The reason at last occurred to me: The Christian-Evangelist wants to know where Nebraska is! Now for the answer.

Geographically, Nebraska is in the center of the universe. She shares with Kansas the central position in the United States, and everybody knows—even Spaniards, now—that Uncle Sam's stool is a revolving chair set on the pivot of the universe.

Politically, I cannot tell you where Nebraska is until November 4. She is either Republican, Democratic or Populist—she is certainly not Prohibitionist. I have lived in several states, prohibition and open, and plain facts have convinced me, one hundred to zero, that prohibition is an *instrument*, not automatic, but adequate, when used by Christian citizens—even in the minority—to drive out the rum fiend. I have personally engaged, as pastor of churches in two prohibition states in arousing my flock to their duty, and in both places saloons, run in public or secret violation of the law, were entirely banished. Why is it not in the range of gospel themes, without even indicating one's party preferences even on real civic issues, to demand in the name of our Master that the Christian shall think and pray first, and then carry his Master with him to the polls. When Christians do this the power of the Christian vote will be regarded in the caucus as well as that of the saloon and the banks.

Educationally Nebraska is, of course, a new state. Its University and Normal School have been a close study to me. I have the statistics of all American colleges in numbers—the very least element in rating a school, and in annual working funds the greatest item—for prices are nearly the same and money will bring the best professors, the most books for library, and the best apparatus. I have compared these with those of hundreds of other colleges and am convinced that Nebraska's University ranks as peer of those of Kansas, Missouri and Iowa. Of course we do not claim the means at present of the great institutions of the older states. But look out! Times change.

Religiously our state's location can be stated by one word—where? The answer will be given in the next generation. It will depend on the faithfulness of the Lord's workers of this generation. The standing (numerical) of the various churches is, I presume, in this order: Methodist, Presbyterian, Disciple, Baptist, Congregational.

The membership of our own fellowship is perhaps fifteen thousand. Reckoning, as some statisticians estimate, the total might be made twenty-five thousand. I have certainly given the very lowest.

It is difficult to give the number in the ministry, so slight is the division in the minds of some between local talkers and regular preachers. There are certainly over one hundred in the state who devote all their time to and receive their whole support from preaching the gospel. Less than one hundred and fifty could honestly be counted under any system of reckoning.

Nebraska has about 175 churches meeting regularly.

We have had several losses to our ministry within a year. Bro. A. D. Harmon, followed A. R. Moore, in the pastorate in St. Paul, Minn. Bro. J. M. Vawter left the First Church in Omaha, to become pastor of the church in Liberty, Mo., and now we are losing Bro. Elliott, of many years' faithful service in the state, who leaves the church at Harvard to labor in Iowa. May the Lord bless these brethren, even if they are not in Nebraska!

My next letter will assume that the reader already knows all about Nebraska, and tell of the current work and conditions.

Albert Buxton.

Fairbury, Neb., Sept. 9, 1898.

Austria-Hungary (Tyrol).

Tyrol is a prosperous county of Austria-Hungary; it is a mountainous region, containing about 800,000 inhabitants, of which one-half are German-speaking people, about 200,000 speak Italian, and the rest some form of the Slavonic language. Agriculture, forestry, mining, and the production of silk, form the chief pursuits of the thrifty people.

Every householder has his own piece of cultivable land, and clothes himself and his family with stuffs spun and woven at home from the wool and flax produced in the neighborhood.

To form from this material the quaint costumes which are pictured on another page from a photograph taken in the Tyrol by an agent of *The Singer Manufacturing Co.*, the Tyrolese women find the Singer sewing machines most satisfactory.

Christian College.

Christian College opened its forty-eighth collegiate year Wednesday morning with the usual exercises. Mrs. Moore in a few well-chosen words heartily welcomed the young ladies to the college and then gave way to Dr. W. T. Moore who delivered one of his characteristic addresses, bubbling over with good humor and feeling, which acted like a tonic upon the home-sick girls in his hearing. Dr. Moore has the happy faculty of saying the right thing at the right time.

Miss Morse gave a reading, Miss Hunt an instrumental selection, and Mrs. Cora Elgin Reid sang one of her sweetest songs.

In truth Christian College has begun a most prosperous year. More students are enrolled than ever before; several young ladies were turned away on account of lack of room. The teachers are all enthusiastic; the young ladies contented, and everything points to a happy and useful session. There would have been no trouble in securing two hundred young ladies, had the college possessed living space for them.

It is to the interest of the citizens of Columbia, irrespective of church affiliations, and to the Christian brotherhood of this state, that a suitable school, with the prestige of an honorable history be maintained for the education of young ladies; and with this in mind, we believe that the scarcity of room will be corrected before another year. It is surely a good fortune that, in spite of war taxes, and the innocuous desuetude into which prosperity has sought refuge from political assassins, nearly one hundred Missouri girls have signed the muster-roll of old Christian College. Mrs. Moore's administration represents not only culture of mind and deportment, but fine business capacity, and the tact to make every circumstance contribute to the success of the college.

Columbians will learn with pleasure that Mrs. Luella W. St. Clair, ex-president of the college, and Mrs. Moore's immediate predecessor, will reside in the college this year. She will not be actively engaged in work, but her influence and example will be worth much to the young ladies who meet her. She is a well-educated, big-hearted, charming woman —just what every young lady ought to be in time.—*Missouri Statesman.*

Andrew County Convention.

The annual convention of the Christian Churches, of Andrew County, Missouri, was held at Fillmore, Aug. 24-25. There were present seven preachers and over 100 delegates and visitors. Sermons were preached by I. Bauserman and R. M. Dungan. Reports were received from all the churches of the county. The condition of the work may be understood from the following summary: Number of churches in county 13, of which one is a mission; number of pastors, nine; houses of worship, 12, the aggregate value of which is $24,800; membership, 1071, with an increase during the year of 85. There are 12 Bible-schools, with an enrollment af 737. There are six Y. P. S. C. E. Societies, with a membership of 148. Junior Societies four, with a membership of 103, and one Auxiliary to the C. W. B. M. with a membership of nine. The entire amount contributed from all sources, $4,502, of which $284.80 was for missions.

This was one of the best and most profitable conventions ever held in the county. We hope for a forward movement on the part of all the churches during the present year.

I. R. WILLIAMS, Pres.
GEO. E. DEW, Sec.

Pastors Should Inroduce the Reading Courses.

Every pastor who has been prayerfully anxious for the Christian growth and education of the young people whom he has seen come into the church, has again and again wished for some printed courses of simple yet comprehensive lessons along just the lines the Bethany C. E. Reading Course follows. The Sunday-school lessons do not cover this field, pulpit instruction cannot take the place of personal research, and the method of the C. E. Course best adapts itself to this need that every pastor feels.

This method commends itself, not only to every Endeavor Society in our brotherhood, but it is a suggestion from which the entire Christian Endeavor world will profit. It is plainly the duty of every pastor among the Disciples of Christ to introduce these courses of study among his young people, of every paper to give ample space for the presentation of their claims. A day of power will dawn when we can say, "Every Christian Endeavorer among the Disciples of Christ is a student.

J. E. LYNN,
Pastor Church of Christ, Springfield, Ill.

Notes and News.

Scott, of Alliance, Nebraska, says e is room for thousands of our brethren Platte Valley, in Scott's Bluffs and e County, Neb., where splendid homes y be had.

ittsburg (Pa.) Times, Sept. 12th, says: st anniversary of the dedication of its ch building was celebrated yesterday ngregation of the East End Christian south Highland Avenue and Alder Rev. T. E. Cramblett, the pastor, his anniversary sermon at 11 A. M., his text Deuteronomy 8:2. During year 120 new members were added to h roll and only eight were lost by re- nd death, leaving a net gain of 112. e membership is unanimous in the be- this has been in every way the best e history of the congregation. The membership of the church is 354. Dur- ear the Sunday-school has doubled in ce, and every department of the work is in excellent condition. The tion is thoroughly united and the best prevails throughout the entire mem- At the evening service a platform was held, at which addresses were Col. Samuel Harden Church, Dr. der Evans, Prof. W. C. Lyne and J. ton, officers of the congregation, who in a most interesting manner "The Present and Future of the Church."

inios District Convention.

nvention of the seventh district of ill be held at Fairfield, Oct. 4-6. A gram has been prepared. A number preachers who will address the con- re announced. All churches in the re requested to send delegates and all are requested to notify N. J. Odell, ild, one week in advance of their Entertainment free.

ee Christian Missionary Convention

eet with the Highland Park Christian Chattanooga, Tenn., Oct. 10-13. Free ment will be furnished the delegates urch and friends. The railroads give of one fare for the round trip. Let aren in Tennessee turn out *en masse* this the greatest convention possible. st you no more to come in time for our k and then you will be better prepared the National Convention.

. M. TAYLOR, Pastor and Gen. Sec.

The Kansas Convention.

nsas State Convention will be held at on, Oct. 3-7, and preparations are de to make it one of the largest and s history. A good program has been and a one and one-third railroad rate rtificate plan secured. O. L. Smith stor of the church and an attractive over his signature says that every Kansas should be present at that con- and that every congregation in the ould send one or more delegates. E. Ridenour, of Ft. Scott, will be r of song. We sincerely hope that as churches will have an inspiring, nvention.

A Final Appeal.

TIAN ENDEAVORERS—*Greeting:*

peal was made at the beginning of ionary year for five thousand dollars Endeavor Societies for Foreign Mis- Ve have given less than two thousand, eal is lagging, our offerings are wan- ought to give the amount asked. e is short, but if every Endeavorer is this will give 25 cents, or have his society to give two dollars, *at once, the goal will be reached.*

Send offerings to F. M. Rains, box 750, Cincinnati, Ohio. Let us hasten, for we have barely a week. One grand universal effort and the deed is done.

Yours for "C"hristianity "E"xtended,

CLARENCE H. POAGE.

Chattanooga.

It was the writer's good fortune to spend a part of 1892 in Chattanooga, with the church that is to entertain the convention of the Disciples in October. This ministry, though a temporary one, is remembered as among the most enjoyable experiences of his life. With these people one finds, not only Southern hospitality, but what is better, *Christian* hospitality.

Let no one hesitate for a moment to attend the coming convention out of a fear of a "cold reception." No city in the country of the same size entertains more conventions than does this picturesque, historic and hospitable "gateway city."

S. R. HAWKINS.

New Orleans, La.

State Convention Notes.

Next Monday night opens, we trust, the greatest convention in all the history of our people in Missouri. It ought to be, because we are a greater people than ever before. We must have conventions in harmony with the numbers we have or people will be very skeptical in regard to the numbers.

We have 160,000 people in Missouri. If ten per cent. of these would go to the state convention we would scare the Nevada people badly! If only one out of each hundred would go we would have 1,600 and the number would be too great, but if we have that great a number of people we ought to have not less than 1,000 in attendance at Nevada.

Is your preacher going to the state convention? Have you asked him? Suppose you do. He may tell you that he is too poor, and that would be a good time for you to raise the money for him to go and meet with his brethren and get inspiration for another year's work.

We need to impress the people of Southwest Missouri that we are indeed a great people; that the plea we present is winning its way with a rapidity and power that is in harmony with the claims we have made. A great convention down in that section of the state will be of wondrous benefit to us, while a lukewarm, indifferent one will do us incalcuable harm. It is the solemn duty of every Disciple of Jesus who can possibly do so to attend that convention and make it a great power for good.

We are not so great in convention as we ought to be. Our religious neighbors are finding out the value of these gatherings and they are working them to a great purpose. The Methodist Conference, the Baptist Associations, are being multiplied and enlarged. There is something about the coming together of great bodies of men and women, inspired with one great purpose, that impresses the observer as nothing else can do; and, besides, the influence on our own hearts and lives, is by no means insignificant. No one can come to the convention at Nevada and enjoy its sessions without going home better and stronger therefor.

This is the first time we have had one of our Missouri "laymen" on the program for an address of any great moment, and certainly we could not have had one more distinguished than our brother, Champ Clark, of Bowling Green. As an orator he has no superior and but few equals in our state. It is said that when a Missourian hears his address he feels a foot taller than he was before! We owe it to Champ Clark to give him the greatest audience a Missouri convention ever had. Remember, he speaks Tuesday night.

Bro. Willett delivers his first lecture on Tuesday morning. You don't want to miss that. Certainly none who heard him at Trenton will willingly miss his Nevada lectures. They were easily the most attractive feature of that convention.

The presence of Miss Ada Boyd, for fifteen years a missionary for the C. W. B. M. in India, should call for such a gathering of the sisters of Missouri as never was seen before. Surely, when you think of all that is on this program, the wonder is how such a feast could be obtained, and that any one would stay away. Let everybody come to Nevada. Remember, the one-fare round-trip tickets can only be bought Sept. 26-27.

Yours in His Name,

T. A. ABBOTT.

Forefathers' Day.

Forefathers' Day falls this year on Oct. 23rd. Pastors and presidents of our Christian Endeavor Societies should begin at once to plan for its proper and profitable observance. The day may be made one not only of benefit to our young people and of help to the American Christian Missionary Society, but of great interest and profit to our churches and the communities by which they are surrounded. In not a few of our churches there is need of a clear, strong presentation of our peculiar mission and our special message.

To aid in a wise preparation for the observance of Forefathers' Day I venture to make the following suggestions to our Christian Endeavor Societies, and to all whom it may concern:

1. Have the missionary committee or a special committee begin to arrange at once to secure offerings on that day from all the members, these offerings to be sent to Benj. L. Smith, Y. M. C. A. Building, Cincinnati, O. He is Corresponding Secretary of the American Christian Missionary Society.

2. Take for your subject in the C. E. prayer-meeting, Sunday, Oct. 23rd, "Forefathers' Day, Its Lessons and Its Call." The topic list published by the United Society makes this a missionary day, and names "Go or Send" as its subject. This easily gives an opportunity to speak of the work of our forefathers in going forth to proclaim the gospel in its purity.

3. Have at least three five-minute biographical sketches of our prominent pioneers prepared and read in the C. E. meeting by members of the Society. The pastor will cheerfully aid his young people in preparing these sketches. I suggest as suitable subjects the Campbells, Stone, Scott, Rogers and Smith.

4. Have some one give, with the aid of a map, a ten-minute talk on the work of the American Christian Missionary Society. A sketch of this society may be found in our "Handbook of Missions," prepared for the Bethany C. E. Reading Courses by W. J. Lhamon. If further information should be desired, write to Benj. L. Smith, Y. M. C. A. Building, Cincinnati, Ohio.

5. Ask your pastor to preach that day, October 23rd, on "The Plea our Fathers Made." This sermon should be given at the regular church service, either morning or evening, and the young people should make special effort to secure a large audience.

Should some such plan as the foregoing be followed, I am sure the observance of Forefathers' Day will prove very happy and helpful. Let all our Christian Endeavor Societies take this matter in hand at once with their characteristic enthusiasm, and let all pastors and church officers give them encouragement and cordial support. In every aspect of it, Forefathers' Day merits a prominent place.

Should it not be convenient to observe the day on the date named, October 23rd, please arrange to observe it as soon thereafter as possible. The date is not important, the day is. Let no Christian Endeavor Society among us neglect its observance.

J. Z. TYLER,
National Superintendent.

Cleveland, Ohio.

Evangelistic.

NEW YORK.

Pompey, Sept. 13th.—Our meeting is nine days old with 23 confessions. Audiences are large and growing. Seven last night. The prospects are good.—J. M. MORRIS, State Evangelist.

MISSOURI.

Kansas City, Sept. 16.—The writer assisted Jas. E. Dunn two weeks at Antioch Church, Clay County, in a meeting, preaching at night only, save Lord's day, closing Sept. 3rd, with nine added. Bro. Dunn preached the following day, with three more; two splendid young women by confession and baptism, making a total of 12 additions.—A. W. KOKENDOFFER, Forest Avenue Church.

Balm, Sept. 10.—Began at my regular meeting at Pleasant Day, St. Clair County, Aug. 27, and continued each night until Sept. 4th. Immediate result, four baptisms; three heads of families, the fourth a noble young lady.—J. N. MURPHY.

Canton, Sept. 17.—J. H. Cail, of Perry, Mo., has just closed a successful meeting at Mount Joy church, Monroe County, of which I am pastor. Five confessions, all over 18 years of age. Bro. Cail is one of the able young men in the state.—J. P. MYERS.

Stephens' Store, Sept. 12.—Our meeting of 13 nights with Lydia church here has just closed with 20 additions.—C. H. WINDERS AND W. S. ST. CLAIR.

Two recently added to Lydia church by confession and one by letter. One added to the Olivet church, Harg, Mo., from the Baptists.—W. S. ST. CLAIR.

Canton, Sept. 18.—Three added here last month. One added at our prayer-meeting service Wednesday evening. Our work is progressing.—D. ERRETT.

Rolla, Sept. 19.—Two confessions at our regular services last evening; also two at the Union Schoolhouse six miles north of Rolla.—R.B. HAVENER.

Lone Jack, Sept. 17.—Closed meeting at La Mine Aug. 29th with 24 additions; had the assistance of Bro. Popplewell most of the time. Have been preaching a few nights here. Go next to "Cyclone," near to Lee's Summit. Bro. Popplewell preaches for these brethren and is in high esteem.—W. E. HULET, Albany, Mo.

Lamonte, September 19.—Five additions here since last report; one Catholic, one Lutheran, one Methodist, one by letter and one from the world. Verily, Christian union is flourishing here.—KING STARK.

ILLINOIS.

Rantoul, Sept. 13.—One addition Sept. 11th.—H. H. PETERS.

Murphysboro, Sept. 12.—At Russel's church I held a two weeks' meeting with 10 confessions, and one reclaimed; 11 in all. Large audiences and great interest.—W. H. WILLYARD.

INDIANA.

Wabash, Sept. 13.—Six nights at Monument City, Ind., 14 persons added to the church, all married people. On Lord's day more than 1,000 people witnessed the baptizing in the beautiful Salamonie River. I greatly regretted that the meeting could not have continued.—L. L. CARPENTER.

Valparaiso, Sept. 22.—Four additions at Hammond yesterday; one by confession, two by letter and one by statement.—WALTER L. ROSS.

NEBRASKA.

Bloomfield, Sept. 12.—Preached at Creighton last Lord's day morning and evening in the Baptist church; large congregation at both services; one addition in the evening; will hold a meeting there in October. Closed a very successful tent meeting at this place recently. At the close of the meeting a church was established with some 40 members. From here I go to Belden to continue the good work.—JOHN J. HIGGS, District Evangelist.

TEXAS.

Waco, September 12.—J. B. Sweeney, Dean of Add Ran University, Waco, spent seven weeks of his summer vacation in evangelistic work. Ninety additions were made to the churches, one church organized, a house built and one minister located.

Sulphur Springs, September 10.—Baptized two young men at our prayer-meeting last week. One brother who had been out of duty was reinstated last Sunday morning, and a young lady made the confession Sunday night and we baptized her the same hour of the night.—M. M. SMITH.

ALABAMA.

Selma, Sept. 15.—One addition from the Methodists at last Sunday's service.—E. V. SPICER.

IOWA.

Sheldon, September 11.—Thirteen additions to date here; eight by baptism, three by letter, and one from M. E.'s and one Seventh Day Adventist. J. R. Mowry is pastor. F. H. Sweetman came Thursday to assist in the singing.—R. W. ABBERLEY, evangelist.

Davenport, September 13.—Began a meeting in the Spring Street Chapel last Sunday night. This is an old house, used for thirty years as an M. E. Sunday-school mission, and where we spent over twenty years of our mischievous boyhood days. Will state later whether that old proverb is still true about the prophet and his country. The people come now from sheer curiosity. Hope they soon may not be able to stay away for a better reason. The Davenport church has just secured Bro. C. C. Davis as pastor. He is a Drake man, and a good one. He has been attending the services at Spring Street with a force of helpers, and is getting acquainted with East Davenport folks and will gain a strong foothold with them soon by it. Those people like to have the "city pastors" come up and see them. Will report developments as they arise, as we have only started. Others wanting me for meetings write me here.—MILO G. CUMMINGS, evangelist.

Bedford, Sept. 19.—Our fourth annual convention of Taylor County convenes this week at Lenox from Friday evening to Sunday evening. Chancellor Wm. Bayard Craig, of Drake University, will address the convention Sunday P. M. and evening. All Disciples of Taylor County are urged to be present. Three accessions since our last report. We are now in the second month of the second year.—S. WILL WALTERS.

University Place.—Seventeen added to-day (Sept. 18th). One confession. These represent five states. The communion season was very touching and the sermon by I. N. McCash, pastor, as thoughtful and helpful.

Redfield.—Eight added in a short meeting by Fred Williams.

Sandyville.—Twenty-two added in a two weeks' meeting by W. J. Lockhart.

Nevada.—Two added in the Wright and Martindale meeting.

Van Meter.—Forty added in the meeting held by D. C. Kellams.

Waterloo.—This meeting, carried on by W. A. Foster and G. F. Devol, reports 22 added.

Sidney.—Thirty added. R. A. Omer evangelist. And $1,000 pledged on new building.

NORTH CAROLINA.

Middletown, Sept. 19.—Evangelist W. O. Winfield held a series of meetings for us with 68 additions; 59 by baptism. This is the largest meeting ever held in Hyde County.—M. S. SPEAR, pastor. [illegible]

OKLAHOMA TERRITORY.

Perry, Sept. 15.—Closed a week's meeting at Lawson; two additions by baptism. Will hold another meeting there the first of October.—WM. DUNKLEBERGER.

TENNESSEE.

Chattanooga, Sept. 12.—Just closed a two weeks' meeting at Arlington; 45 added to the church; 28 by baptism. Am now in meeting at McMinville, Tenn.—W. M. TAYLOR, pastor Highland Park Church.

TENNESSEE.

Clarksville, September 18th.—One added to Church of Christ.—A. M. GROWDEN, pastor.

VIRGINIA.

Beech Springs, Sept. 15.—Closed a meetin[g at] Mt. Olivet (Lee County) with 25 addition[s] and one at Cedar Hill with 20 additions in seve[n] days. The work here is "booming." Ou[r] growth during the last twelve months has bee[n] over 70 per cent. in this district.—J. W. WES[T], district evangelist.

OHIO.

Farmer, Sept. 14.—We started our season['s] work at this place last Lord's day. Eig[ht] confessions last night; four the night befor[e]; 14 to date. Great crowds and interest. W[e] go next to Greenford, O., then to Hoopston, Ill., then Buchanan, Mich. Miss Nona Mc Cormick (aged 15), of Indianapolis, Ind., [is] with us and her power over an adudience wit[h] her solos is *most wonderful*. She exceeds an[y] soloist that I have ever heard. Last year ou[r] meetings ran seven months and three days, an[d] added 1,101 to the church. For this we prai[se] Him from whom all blessings flow, and are as[k]ing for even greater results this year, and h[is] name move forward.—SCOVILLE AND SCOTT.

Ashtabula, September 15th.—Evangelis[ts] Putman and Harrell, recently from Californi[a] held us a meeting, during which 16 were adde[d].—ROBT. SELLERS.

KANSAS.

Coffeyville, Sept. 17.—The brethren he[re] have just completed a new house of worsh[ip] having a seating capacity of seven hundre[d]. W. E. Harlow, of Parsons, is with them in meeting, with 12 additions to date. He wi[ll] dedicate the church Sept. 25.

Missionary.

Church Extension Collection.

Church Exten sion Receipt
For Completi ng Chapels.
For week endin g sept. 10, '98
From Churches, $ 258.28
From indiv dual's, 1,715.69
Tota $1,973.97
Last year, from ch's $262,78
From Individuals .. 846.60
Gain, $881,59

analyzing the above receipts, it will be ›ed that for the same time last year the ches sent $262.78, which is $4.50 more than he same time this year. However, last thirty-six churches contributed the $262.78 e fifty-five churches contributed $4.50 less that amount this year. We gained nineteen ributing churches, but lost in amounts. individual receipts up to September 10th, year, shows a gain of $869 over last year. e very encouraging thing is that churches reaching their apportionments, with but few exceptions.

Churches reaching the largest amounts written that they are holding their col- ons in order to increase them.

Churches that have been asked for the ıst amounts are working hard to reach amounts.

We start into the month of September $500 ahead of last year.

The corresponding secretary has already hed the $15,000 he agreed to raise this year will probably reach $17,000.

llections should be completed on the th Sunday and remittances made the fol- ıg Monday, as the books close on Friday, . 30th, at twelve o'clock.

Remit to G. W. MUCKLEY, Cor. Sec.
Waterworks Bldg, Kansas City, Mo.

"Pray for the Conventions."

is word is from F. D. Power. It is a most opriate message. The conventions will be in Chattanooga, Tennessee, October 13- Of course, if it is at all possible you will iere; you cannot afford to miss this great ıal convocation of Disciples of Christ. Be- at once, if necessary, to prepare to attend 'orty-ninth annual meeting of the Disciples hrist in the United States. Speak to your ıds about the approaching meeting. En- 'or to excite an interest in the conventions ıe part of those who are now indifferent. say "conventions?" Why not say "con- ion?" For this reason: The annual ting of the Christian Woman's Board of ions, the Foreign Christian Missionary ety, and the American Christian Mis- ary Society will be held at the time and e above mentioned. The Board of Church nsion, the Board of Ministerial Relief and Board of Education will present reports. e is reason to believe that the reports of ocieties and boards will exceed in interest reports that have been made in the past. want to attend and hear, in person and 'ourself, these reports. An exhibit will be made of our work with the young peo-

ie conventions are held in the interest of kingdom of righteousness—a kingdom of and peace. The work is God's. Let us to him for wisdom, guidance and bless- "Pray for the conventions."

Pray for the conventions" in the midweek rer and conference meeting. Make the roaching conventions a subject of special 'er. Do this, not once nor twice; do not fear that you will "pray for the conventions" too much. Speak to our Father about this great assembly. In the home, at the family altar, "pray for the conventions." Let us in our private devotions remember this general assembly of the Disciples of Christ in the United States.

F. D. Power is president of the American Christian Missionary Society. It is peculiarly appropriate that he should issue this call: He is himself a man of prayer. He knows what it is to bear great burdens. He is not ignorant, in his personal experience, of the source of strength. In this case he has a sense of grave responsibility. Human wisdom is not sufficient. For the task to which we have been called human power is inadequate. Hence the message: "Pray for the conventions." Wisdom from on high is needed. We must have the strength which God alone can give.

The work in which we are engaged is great—very great—greater, more important far than the average man among us realizes. The longer I live and the more I know of this movement the more wonderful seems its magnitude and importance.

This is enough. Whether you go or whether you stay, do not fail to heed Bro. Power's earnest call to "pray for the conventions."

B. B. TYLER.

Encouraging Words for Church Extension.

"We raised our apportionment. May God speed the far-reaching work of Church Extension. I hope it may be so strong some day that no congregation need go without a comfortable and beautiful house of worship. Such a work is Christianity in action."—P. J. DICKERSON, Canon City, Col.

The Old Bedford Church (Blandinsville), where A. R. Adams ministers raised their apportionment for Church Extension.

"We raised our apportionment, $10, and a little more. If all do as well as we have done, we will reach the $250,000 by 1900."—J. N. SMITH, Seattle, Wash.

"Our offering for Church Extension was $41.80, which is $11.80 more than our apportionment. We hoped to make it $50."—SUMNER T. MARTIN, Mason City, Ia.

"It was rainy on the first Sunday, but we expect to raise our apportionment, $100, the following Sunday."—O. W. LAWRENCE, Maryville, Mo.

"We raised our apportionment, $20, for Church Extension."—J. T. OGLE, Carrollton, Mo.

"I agree to take several public collections for Church Extension Fund."—KILBY FERGUSON, Richmond, Ala.

"The church at Reeve, Ia., just doubled their apportionment and next Lord's day we expect to do better at Robertson."—W. F. MCCORMICK, Iowa Falls, Ia.

This good work should continue until the $20,000 apportioned among the churches is raised. G. W. MUCKLEY, Cor. Sec.
Kansas City, Mo.

Do It the First Sunday in October.

Every preacher among us, if he has not already done so, is earnestly requested to call the attention of all his people, and especially all his young people, to the importance of taking up the Bethany C. E. Reading Courses at once. These courses enable the people to have systematic instruction concerning the entire Bible, concerning missions and concerning our plea for a return to the old paths. It is suggested that the matter be presented in all our churches on Sunday, the 2nd of October. In churches where it may be impossible to present the matter on this day, let it be presented as soon thereafter as possible. Full information may be had gratis by sending a postal card to me.

J. Z. TYLER,
National Supt. of C. E.
Cleveland, Ohio, Sept. 14, 1898.

SUBSCRIBERS' WANTS.

Miscellaneous wants and notices will be inserted in this department at the rate of two cents a word, each insertion, all words, large and small, to be counted, and two initials stand for one word. Please accompany notice with corresponding remittance to save book-keeping.

TEACHER of Bookkeeping, Typewriting, Stenography, wanted. A lady teacher of the above subjects, a member of the Christian Church, who would like a position in a first class female school, is requested to communicate with,
M. COLLIS, Lexington, Ky.

AGENTS WANTED.—In all parts of the United States to sell the best acetylene gas generator yet invented. Very simple in construction, cheap in price, absolutely safe, and less trouble to operate than an ordinary coal oil lamp. Will save at least one half the cost of lighting, and give a light almost equal to sunlight. Liberal terms to agents. For full information address the inventor and patentee., Rev. Cal Ogburn, 775 W. 9th St., Riverside, Cal.

BAPTISM.—The doctrines and practices of the modern church compared with those of the early apostolic. By Geo. Rapkin, Pastor of the Christian Church, Margate. Mailed free. Cloth boards, 50 cents; paper, 40 cents. Each copy signed by the author. From Geo. Rapkin, Margate, England.

STOCKHOLDER'S MEETING.

Notice is hereby given that the annual meeting of the stockholders of the Christian Publishing Co. will be held at the company's office, 1522 Locust St., St. Louis, Mo., on Tuesday, Oct. 4th, 1898, at 10 o'clock A. M., for the election of Directors, and for the transaction of such other business as may legally come before said meeting.

J. H. GARRISON, Pres.
W. D. CREE, Sec.

St. Louis, Mo., Sept. 1, 1898.

Family Circle.

To Win the World.

GRACE PEARL BRONAUGH.

How shall we win the world to Christ?
Have our words availed, have our gifts sufficed?
Have our prayers and pleadings been enough?
O, the way is long and the road is rough!
We may sit at the summit of Wisdom's peak
And call to the climbers who toil and seek
For the summit of Truth. We may rise and throw
A rope of gold to the souls below,
But unless we give them our strong right hand,
Unless we are willing ourselves to stand
On the perilous steep which their feet have trod,
We never can win him to Christ—to God.
When the rich no longer oppress the poor,
When the mighty and fortunate cease to lure
The feeble and fallen—when great and good
Are bound in a cable of brotherhood,
When the haughty grow humble, the bitter sweet,
The world will turn upon hastening feet,
Willing and glad to be led again
By the way of truth which has made *us* men!

Fair Haven, Vt.

Text Stories—XIII.

"WHERE THERE'S DRINK, THERE'S DANGER."

BY ALICE CURTICE MOYER.

Woe unto him that giveth his nieghbor drink, that puttest thy bottle to him and makest him drunken.—*Hab.* 2:15.

Ralph Lawrence awoke the morning after commencement with a most delicious consciousness of having come off with flying colors the day before. He had received the degree for which he had worked all these happy college years. He felt himself to be fully equipped for his chosen profession. Life lay all before him.

"But I am in no hurry to get down to work," he had said to his friends. "I must see a little of this big world before settling down to business. Plenty of time for work after I have had a little fun."

He was thinking about it this morning while going over the events of the day.

"Guess I'll run over to C—— for a visit to Tom Layton," he said. "I'll send a line to the folks at home, saying they may look for me when they see me coming. Of course they will be disappointed, but they oughtn't expect a fellow to never have any fun."

Then he thought of another—one who had faithfully waited for his return and was impatient that, in imagination, he could see two blue eyes looking at him almost reproachfully because of his delayed home-coming.

"Effie must wait too," he said. "I must see something of life first of all, and Tom is just the fellow to liven me up after all these years of 'digging.'"

Two years later, therefore, he was being initiated into what his friend, Tom Layton, called "having a good time."

They had stopped on ——— Avenue and Ralph was saying:

"Well, perhaps I wouldn't object to taking a little wine, but to be seen going into a ———"

"O, pshaw!" broke in Tom. "Don't let a little thing like that worry you. However, until you are a little more accustomed to it, we need not go into a regular drinking-place, but will stop at this drugstore. And you certainly must have something stronger than wine."

"I didn't know that drugstores were licensed to sell liquor," said Ralph.

"Bless the dear innocent!" cried Tom, mockingly. "Of course they are not licensed, but that is no hindrance if they want to sell it. They can find plenty of patrons, for many like you object to being seen to go into a regular drinking-place, yet are themselves regular drinkers. Unscrupulous druggists, therefore, reap a rich harvest. But what care we, just so we get what we want and have a good time."

The drugstore proprietor, whose smiling demeanor hid a soul as black as the windows through which it looked, so many had he helped on to perdition, chanced to be in, and recognizing Tom, came forward himself to wait upon them. They were invited into a room in the rear. Tom gave the order, and presently a glass was placed before each.

Ralph hesitated, but only for a moment. Conscience was trampled upon. He was in for a good time.

"Wait here a moment, Ralph," said Tom. "I saw a friend as we came in that I want to speak to."

Ralph was glad to sit down. The "something stronger than wine" had gone to his head, and somehow he could not help wondering what Effie and the folks at home would think if they knew just what a "good time" he was having.

A young man of shabby appearance, whom he had noticed when he first came in, rose from his chair and approached him:

"You are from the country, I take it," he said.

"Yes," Ralph answered; "that is, I was raised in the country."

"And have come to the city to see something of life before settling down."

"How do you know?" Ralph saw that no offense was meant and was, therefore, not offended.

"I guessed it from the first," replied the shabby young man. "And I want to tell you that Tom Layton is not the right sort of company. He is a *moderate drinker* and his influence is by far more dangerous than that of the drunkard in the gutter. Nobody wants to be a hopeless inebriate, but many young men seek to imitate the moderate drinker, and few—very few—are strong enough to remain one. Five years ago I was just where you are now. I started out to have a good time. Tom Layton took me under his wing and was my friend as long as my money lasted. Friend! What is a friend? Is it he who rides with us when we have a carriage and turns another way when we walk? Is it he who helps us spend our money while it lasts and when it is gone has none to lend us? After I got down in the world, Tom Layton had no more use for me. Like you, I did not start out with the intention of becoming a common drunkard, yet I have done so. The future spread out before me with all the brightness that it does to you at the present, yet now I see nothing ahead of me save misery and degradation, each year of a deeper dye. I know that the gutter is not far distant. And of the world that is to come, I dare not stay sober long enough to think. And when I see others in a fair way to become what I am, when I see them trampling upon conscience and turning away from the better impulses of thei nature, I long to warn them before the reach a point where the nobler impulse are deadened and the still, small voice o conscience is not heard. When I saw yo come into this vile den of outside seemin respectability and witnessed what followed I felt that I must speak a word of warning; and particularly would I war you against Tom Layton. None but hi victims ever come to know him fully. H belongs to a fast set who calls themselve society. He is a man of the world and *moderate drinker.* One such man alone while damning his own soul can send mor other men to perdition than ten preacher can reclaim."

At that moment Tom returned. H frowned as he saw the shabby young ma moving away, but said cheerily:

"Hurry up, Ralph! we yet have time t drop in at Miss A.'s hop!"

"But I know nothing about dancing,' replied Ralph, as he followed Tom out The words of the shabby young man wer with him, and he was wondering whethe he hadn't better tell Tom plainly, tha he——.

His half resolve had gone no furthe when Tom spoke again:

"But I want you to meet some of m acquaintances, old fellow. You don't nee to know how to dance. I only want t have the pleasure of introducing you t my friends."

Ralph made no further protest. Surely such a jolly, happy fellow as Tom coul not be bad. The shabby young man mus be mistaken.

The hop was at one of the most fashionable homes in the city. Tom was evidently a favorite and his friend was mos cordially received. Indeed, he was quit flattered by the attentions showered upo him. And when dark-eyed Beauty smilingly volunteered to teach him to waltz, h unhesitatingly placed his arms about he and after a few initiatory steps Ralph naturally graceful and full of music, wa whirling about as gaily as the others.

The music, the surroundings, the conditions withal, were most seductive. Ralp was under a spell—intoxicated with th feelings and sensations awakened withi him, and when Beauty gracefully offere him, with her own hands, "wine in th cup," he was powerless to refuse. The on the way home in the "wee sma' hours, when Tom suggested that they stop at public drinking house, he made no furthe objection. Already his better impulse were being numbed.

Hand in hand with drink, there are othe vices which, to record, would disgrace th pen. Suffice it to say, that Ralph becam thoroughly acquainted with them all in hi endeavor to have a good time. Friend gathered around him. He laughed an the world laughed with him.

The days lengthened into weeks an the weeks into months, and still Ralph wa not ready to go home. The pleadings o parents had no longer any influence though he knew he was breaking thei hearts and filling their lives with sorrow As to Effie, the vows he had made in al sincerity when life was bright with hig resolves, had long since been forgotten.

He was on the downward path, and th farther he traveled it the more smoothl it seemed worn. Daily it became mo

›pery with sin, and he sped on the more idly to destruction.

'wo sad messages came, to him not many nths apart, but he made no effort to r himself away from his associates, that might be present when the earthly ntle of his parents was laid in the :rchyard. Their death had little power affect him, so despoiled had his heart ome of all its natural tenderness and ıpathy.

ioon, very soon, his inheritance was ıe—swallowed up in riotous living—and ınds (?) one by one forsook him.

'You are such a fool," Tom Layton said. ow *I* can drink or not drink, just as I ı." And he closed his door in the face of *friend* whose hospitality he had accept- whose luxuries he had shared while money lasted.

'ive years later there was a funeral from workhouse. The remains of a poor briate lay hidden in the wooden box. blotted, ragged wreck, babbling and -eyed, stood near, and as he looked, a of intelligence came to the mind and realized that the body of Ralph Law- ce was soon to be consigned to a dis- ıored grave in the potter's field. He ked up to the wagon and touched the ıden box.

Good-bye, Ralph," he said. "I, even I, soon be with you. I, the *moderate nker*. How sure I felt of myself while perilously near the edge. 'At last it ıth like a serpent and stingeth like an ler.'"

leason was again gone, and the once lliant Tom Layton, so sure of his own ıngth, was led away by an attendant, le the body of Ralph Lawrence, who a years before started out to "have a d time" was carted away to the potter's l.

The wages of sin is death."

t. Louis, Mo.

The night has a thousand eyes,
The day but one;
Yet the light of the whole earth dies
With the setting sun.

The mind has a thousand eyes,
The heart but one;
Yet the light of the whole life dies
When love is done.
—*In Family Messenger.*

›Good as the Enemy of the Best.

GEO. T. SMITH.

[an seeks good. God promises it to ›e who ask him. Science, experience the Bible agree that the asking must n the right spirit; the seeking, accord- to law; the knocking, at the door. It ain to pray for health so long as the s of health are ignored, to seek knowl- e listlessly, or to knock on the gates of ortunity with the little finger.

ur asking is too limited. The good is enemy of the best. It is right to be ›tous, to be ambitious, to secure the :. We are too easily content. We note ances where the good drives out the :. We begin low.

ıvited to walk out a mile, after the ning sermon, we found an idoitic boy ixteen. Dinner being delayed, he grew ıblesome. He yelled. He rushed to the .e, filled his plate and crammed. Then rolled off to sleep. Eating is good. the quieter, social repast is best.

Play is good, especially for a boy. But the truant? His good is enemy of the best.

Two workmen in the navy yard at Philadelphia had leisure evenings for six months. One taught a dog to stand on its hind legs and even to dance. That was good. It was recreation. The other invented a machine, during the same time, for dressing the knees of ships. That was creation. Do you read a newspaper? Good. All of it? Sitting down? Skimping it is better. Reading books is best.

Do you read fiction? Sensible. Always, omitting the philosophical and historical novelists? The best is crowded out.

There are two systems of astronomy. The Ptolemaic made earth the center, hindered progress, chained Galilee, burned Bruno, obstructed Columbus' way. The Copernican swept away the horizon, swung the earth around the sun, brought the stars near and buried time in endless ages. Which is your system? Do you make this little body of yours the center of your thoughts and works? Or do you make the Sun of Righteousness the magnet which holds you steady in the orbit of duty, while the gems of the sky are the beaconlights of your pathway to the throne of God? If Ptolemaic, you have good. But you sail around in a tub, you refuse the offer of the soul's Columbus who would steer your bark across the stormy Atlantic of life to a land of fadeless day. Your good is commonplace. The cream of life you never taste. You are sprouting no wings.

Eating we adjudged good. But if to the thoughtful and pleasant company at the table the apostle comes with his benediction, saying that God has created these things for our enjoyment, that they are sanctified by his word and prayer, you may worship God in eating. You can make a meal a thankful sacrament.

What moment of sweeter bliss than the first kiss of avowed love? Happy the man for whom its fragrance never dies. But how inexpressibly sweeter is its pure joy if, then and afterward, the thought comes to the man and to the woman, "My love is a Christian; this union is forever."

"But we are already Christians; we can be no more." What grade? There is no more difference between the primary tot and the college athlete than between those called Christians. The Spanish are Christians. "Spain" is in the New Testament. But they are yet in the kindergarten. Their bullfights are the feeble copies of the gladiatorial show of the Coliseum, and Weyler, the "butcher," is in true apostolic succession from Nero.

"Ye who are spiritual restore such a one." Are we of this grade? Are we satisfied with what we are? Then the good is the enemy of the best.

Here we reach the Scripture which gave rise to these thoughts. It is the temptation of Christ. How did he win the battle which I lose? By choosing the best, not the easiest. He did not daly, nor rely on his own strength nor wisdom. He placed God between him and every temptation. He overcame and assures me that I may.

Oh, Thou who art so covetous of human love that Thou didst purchase us by the costly sacrifice of Thy heart's blood, help Thy brothers who yet abide in the clay. Forbid that we should be content with less than Thy best gifts. Thy fullness lead us to seek till Thou shalt possess us completely and we shall be altogether the children of light!

At School and at Home.

My teacher doesn't think I read
So very special well.
She's always saying, "What was that
Last word?" and makes me spell
And then pronounce it after her,
As slow as slow can be.
"You'd better take a little care"—
That's what she says to me—
"Or else I'm really 'fraid you'll find,
Some one of these bright days,
You're 'way behind the Primer class."
That's what my teacher says.

But when I'm at my grandpa's house,
He hands me out a book,
And lets me choose a place to read;
And then he'll sit and look
At me, and listen, just as pleased!
I know it from his face.
And when I read a great, long word,
He'll say, "Why, little Grace,
You'll have to teach our deestrict school,
Some one o' these bright days!
Mother, you come and hear this child."
That's what's my grandpa says.

—*Elisabeth L. Gould, in July St. Nicholas.*

He Stopped the Train.

Train No. 20 on the Indianapolis & Vincennes Railroad in charge of Conductor F. W. Russe, of Indianapolis, was tearing along toward Indianapolis the other evening fifty miles an hour. The train was loaded with passengers, and was behind time. East of Edwardsport Engineer Dorsey saw on the track far ahead a dog that was jumping about and acting in a peculiar manner. The dog's actions looked suspicious and, as a measure of caution, Dorsey shut off the steam, so as to have his train under control. When the train reached a nearer point the dog stood and barked at it, and then with a yelp, started for the woods.

Then it was that Dorsey saw that there was something red between the rails, and he threw on the emergency brakes and opened the sand-box. The train came to a standstill within ten feet of a pretty flaxen-haired baby in a red frock. The child was about two years old, and had been playing with the dog. The train crew ran forward and Baggageman Franklin picked up the child, which laughed and crowed and patted his face in glee.

About eight hundred yards distant was a farmhouse, and toward it Franklin started with the baby, to meet a man running toward him like an insane person. It was the child's father, who had missed the baby just as the train stopped and supposed that the little one had been killed. How it got so far away from home and into such a dangerous place no one could understand. The passengers were considerably jolted by the sudden stopping of the train, but no one was hurt, and when they learned the cause of it they clustered about Engineer Dorsey and congratulated him on his caution. — *Philadelphia Times.*

Kipling and His Work.

One of the interviewers of Rudyard Kipling during his visit to South Africa writes of him in the Cape Times: He takes his work hard. He is tremendously in earnest about it; anxious to give of his best; often dissatisfied with his best. He is quite comically dissatisfied with success, quite tragically haunted by the fear that this or that piece of work, felt intensely by himself in writing, and applauded even by high and mighty critics, is in reality cheap and shabby in execution and will be cast in damages before the higher court of posterity. When Rudyard Kipling had written "The Recessional," which two hemispheres felt to be one of the very truest and soundest pieces of work done by any writing man in our day and generation, he was so depressed by its short-comings of his private conception that he threw the rough copy in the wastepaper basket. Thence Mrs. Kipling rescued it. But for Mrs. Kipling we should have had no "Recessional." For his best patriotic poems he has declined to accept any pay.—*The Standard.*

Don't Worry.

Don't worry, dear; the bleakest years
That clog the forward view,
Each thins to nothing when it nears,
And we may saunter through.
The darkest moment never comes,
It only looms before;
The loss of hope is what benumbs,
Not trouble at the door.

Don't worry, dear; the clouds are black,
But with them comes the rain,
And stifled souls that parch and crack
May thrill with sap again.
The burden bear as best we can,
And there'll be none to bear;
Hard work has never killed a man,
But worry did its share.

—*Youth's Companion.*

The Women of the Bible.

MARY E. WARE.

What a diversity of characters is found in the Bible! Even Shakespeare, with all of the brilliancy of his unrivaled genius, has given us no such a study. In his portrayal of women lies his greatest strength, yet even here he is excelled by the writers of Hebrew literature.

Each woman, through illustration, quotation and association has become a type—Eve, of childish curiosity; Sarah, of personal vanity; Hagar, of a woman fleeing from the consequences of her guilt; Rachel, of beauty and innocence outwitted by a designing father; Ruth, of loyalty to assumed obligations; and Jezebel, of wickedness.

In the time of Jesus of Nazareth, Martha is typical of a woman busying herself about the temporal wants of her guests; Mary, of a woman mindful only of spiritual things.

Poor Martha! How her good reputation has suffered in these days! Especially by those who want to shirk from the small drudgeries of life. They even tell us that Christ condemned her. If he did so, it was only relatively. Is there not rather a ring of compassion in the words, "Martha, Martha, thou art careful and troubled about many things?" Just as though you would rour tired mother not to do so much ›ur physical comfort.

said that Mary had chosen the "good ' because sitting at the feet of the ; Teacher and listening to the words vine truth is higher and better than ng one's self about the cares of the ,. Because this is the better part it is ecessarily a condemnation of Martha's For the house must be kept clean, ihildren must be trained and the com- f the guests must be attended to.

, no; Christ does not condemn the do- f these things. If he condemned any ; was the woman who did nothing; the whose whole existence is passed in ss, frivolity and vanity; the one who ices nothing and grasps at everything vill contribute to her sensuous pleas-

comparison with such women, Martha's in life is good, Mary's is better, but er is the best.

› best part is found in the life of such n as Florence Nightingale, Clara Bar- ad Frances Willard. Such women not attend to the temporal wants of the but give their very life-blood in ad- tering to their spiritual needs. Great rand as the women of the Bible are, are none of this type to be found in They lived up to the best that was in age. Nineteen centuries of Chris- y has made this larger, nobler woman- possible.

e principles of the "Sermon on the it" still go on, enlarging the hearts nnobling the minds of women. Each ıry will see a higher development of nhood.

we are no better than Mary or Martha because we have not lived up to our rtunities. For Christianity ever holds progressive ideal before us: "Be ye fore perfect, even as your Father h is in heaven is perfect."

nsas City, Mo.

No Time for Trifles.

Ve teach the children Danish,
'rigonometry and Spanish;
'ill their heads with old-time notions,
.nd the secrets of the oceans,
.nd the cuneiform inscriptions
'rom the land of the Egyptians;
'each the date of every battle,
.nd the habits of the cattle,
Vith the date of every crowning;
Read the poetry of Browning,
Make them show a preference
'or each musty-branch of science;
'ell the acreage of Sweden,
ind the serpent's wiles in Eden;
ind the other things we teach 'em
Make a mountain so immense
'hat we've not a moment left
'o teach them common sense.

—*London Standard.*

Heathenism Doomed.

ıme of the most interesting pages in ›ry are those which describe the siege ities. The walls of the beleaguered are surrounded on all sides by men ıg to force an entrance. Some make len onsets on the gates. Some plant ers against the walls and fight hand to l with the defenders. Everywhere e is noise, and tumult, and capture, death, the shouts of the fighters and

digging and mining under the very wall of the city. They are undermining the foundations of the city ramparts—the city is doomed.

I sometimes think that this is the work which our Christian schools and colleges in heathen lands are doing. We are sapping the foundations of heathenism. The city is strong and ancient; its walls are thick and ugly and deep. But it is doomed. In our hands God has put an ax, and we are digging, digging; and in the end, through the darkness we shall reach the light.—*Rev. John Lendrum, in the Endeavor World.*

Short Stories.

Mrs. Fadde, Christian Scientist: "How is your grandfather this morning, Bridget?"

Bridget: "He still has the rheumatics mighty bad, mum."

"You mean he thinks he has the rheumatism. There is no such thing as rheumatism."

"Yes, mum."

A few days later:

"And does your grandfather still persist in his delusion that he has the rheumatism?"

"No, mum; the poor man thinks now that he is dead. We buried um yisterday."
—*Selected.*

Down in Maine the other day I sat on the rocks chatting with an old fisherman who was cleaning "a mess of fish" for dinner. Fish-cleaning in that part of the universe is exclusively within the sphere of masculine activity. No man ever takes fish home without cleaning them and cutting off their heads. He generally performs this duty as soon as he reaches land.

My old friend had been answering my inquiries concerning the affairs of the neighborhood in a quaint, philosophical way, when a summer girl, paddling a birch-bark canoe, passed under our vision.

"Do you like them cockeley boats?" he asked.

"They are very pretty and graceful," I answered.

"Waal, I'm not a church member and I've got the rheumatiz so bad I can't swim, so I jes' natchelly don't like to have nuthin' but a thin piece of birch bark betwixt me

He thought a minute before speaking and then answered, "Waal, my wife has been a teasin' me to for ever so long, and I calculate it's about time I was attending to it."—*Chicago Record.*

A tax-collector one day came to a poor minister in order to assess the value of his property and determine the amount of taxes. The minister asked the man to be seated. Then the latter took out his book and asked: "How much property do you possess?"

"I am a rich man," answered the minister.

The official quickly sharpened his pencil and asked intently: "Well, what do you own?"

The pastor replied: "I am the possessor of a Savior who earned for me life everlasting, and who has prepared a place for me in the Eternal City."

"What else?"

"Healthy and obedient children."

"What else?"

"A merry heart, which enables me to pass through life joyfully."

"What else?"

"That is all," replied the minister.

The official closed his book, took his hat, and said: "You are indeed a rich man, sir, but your property is not subject to taxation."—*In Christian Leader.*

Sunday School.

ROYAL REFORMS IN JUDAH.*

HERBERT L. WILLETT.

The lessons of the fourth quarter of 1898 deal with the Kingdom of Judah, which remained to the house of David after the disruption of the united Kingdom of Israel at the death of Solomon, 937 B. C. The material of these lessons is found in the books of Chronicles, Isaiah and Jeremiah with occasional lessons in Kings, one in Proverbs and one in the Gospel of Luke. The sources from which most of the lessons are taken are the Chronicles, which take their name from the court records, upon which our biblical books of Kings and Chronicles are based. The character of our books of Chronicles differs considerably from that of the Kings, although they treat in general of the same events. One can see the contrast in their character by comparing the two narratives as they run along together. This can be done without other help than the Bible, or more easily still by the use of such a Harmony of Kings and Chronicles as that recently published by Crockett. One notices in studying the two particular narratives that the authors of Chronicles deal almost exclusively with the Southern Kingdom; that they emphasize the priestly element in the national life, mentioning frequently the work of the priests and the Levites and the honor paid to them by the kings, who as a result were blessed in their administration. Sin, in the eyes of the Chronicle writers, consists not so much in moral transgression, which seems to be the standard in the narrative of Kings, but rather in departure from the ecclesiastical program of the nation, which centered in the ritual of the temple. The date of Chronicles, in some measure, accounts for this difference in tone and treatment. The record of Kings was probably compiled during the Exile period, up to which it reaches in its study of national life. The books of Chronicles, however, with their continuation in Ezra and Nehemiah, which were evidently originally part of the same narrative, reaches down into the history following the Exile, and describes the time when the Hebrew nation had passed over into the Jewish church, and the whole type of thought was colored by ecclesiastical and liturgical considerations. This history given in the Kings is written from the standpoint of the prophets, and emphasizes the disasters which fell upon the nation because of the disregard of the law of God, which is the law of righteousness and justice. Chronicles were written from the standpoint of the priests, and emphasize external and ceremonial ideas, and point out the successes of those kings who were most careful to maintain the temple worship in all of its splendor.

The Southern Kingdom had one decided advantage over its Northern neighbor in the matter of religion, and that was the presence of a central sanctuary at Jerusalem where the recognized worship of Jehovah went on in near approach to its original purity and imageless character, as taught by the early prophets like Moses and Samuel. The high places continued, as in former years, to attract large numbers of worshipers, and their type of worship was not deemed derogatory to the character of Jehovah. In the early period of the kingdom it was felt that Jerusalem was the center, and here the worship was represented at its best, but the local shrines were revered. To the capital, however, came in numbers the Levites, who sought the more remunerative service of the sanctuary, and thus left the provincial altars in increasing danger of degeneracy, and the better kings saw the need of gradually centralizing the worship at Jerusalem, and finally suppressing entirely the provincial sanctuaries, which was accomplished by Josiah.

Another striking contrast between the Southern and Northern Kingdoms is seen in the fact that the rise of political prosperity in the North was always accompanied by a corresponding depression of religion, so that the lowest moral levels were reached at the time of the greatest national grandeur, under such kings as Ahab and Jeroboam II. Exactly the opposite was the tendency in the South, where the most successful kings, like Asa, Jehoshaphat, Uzziah, Hezekiah and Josiah were the monarchs under whom the greatest religious reforms were instituted; in other words, religion and politics stood at opposite points in the Northern Kingdom, but co-operated in the Southern Kingdom where church and state were united.

The reign of Asa was one of these periods of success and reform. It was begun with a period of ten years' peace, after the wars between the two kingdoms. The attempt was made to undo the evil of theearlier times by the destruction of foreign altars and the debasing nature of the worship which had crept in from the north and from the neighboring kingdoms. These with the sun images of the Babylonian cult were swept away by the reforming zeal of Asa. The Chronicles even insist that he suppressed the high places, but the authors of Kings acknowledge that these were undisturbed. The kingdom reached a degree of strength under Asa which it had not enjoyed since the break with Israel. The more important towns were fortified by the building of walls which were pierced with gates, defended in the usual manner by bars and towers. A standing army, numbering more than half a million was raised and drilled; it consisted of spearmen from Judah and bowmen from Benjamin, these being the hereditary war methods of those tribes. Against Asa and his kingdom came the reigning king of Egypt, a usurper of Ethiopian blood, who brought an immese army with a large chariot force into the lower provinces of Judah.

Strong in the confidence of his righteousness and depending upon God, Asa went forth to meet him expecting victory, and with a prayer for success upon his lips. The narrative records his complete overthrow of the invading army and the gathering of enormous spoil from the forsaken camp. The remaining years of Asa's long reign were passed in the npbuilding of his kingdom, in which his regard for the worship of God seems to have played an important part. The ministry of a prophet named Oded is mentioned as strengthening Asa in his pious purposes; even the assults of Baasha king of Israel were turned back, although here Asa did not depend so fully upon divine help but secured the assistance of the king of Assyria. On the whole, his reign seems to have been one of ability and success in which the people prospered and the worship of Jehovah was given a prominent place in the nation's life.

SUGGESTIONS FOR TEACHING.

The condition of peace in a nation is the surest ground for growth and prosperity; war is expensive and dangerous; peace is constructive and encourages the highest elements of national life. Strange altars are erected, not alone in lands where heathen gods are worshiped, but sometimes in Christian lands where God is forgotten. The law of God, by which is meant all that has been disclosed of his will through the prophets, apostles and the Master himself, constitutes the basis for all individual and social progress. A nation needs to provide defences, not only of armament, but of character. The consciousness of doing one's work in the sight and fear of God is the source of limitless strength and confidence. The environment of the divine presence and the certainty of divine approval make life rich and fruitful. Prosperity comes just as surely today by obedience to the divine will as in t[h]
life of Israel. One need not expect to avo[id]
attacks, but he may always be able to me[et]
them with confidence and courage in t[he]
strength of God. What are the attacks whi[ch]
one may expect in these days?

LITERATURE.

Kent: History of the Hebrew People, Vol. [I]
The Divided Kingdom. (Scribner's.) Croc[k]ett: Harmony of Samuel, Kings and Chron[i]cles. (Eaton and Maines.)

The University of Chicago.

*Sunday-school lesson for Oct. 2, 1898—Reformation Under Asa (2 Chron. 14:1-12). Golden Text—Help us, O Lord our God, for we rest in thee (2 Chron. 14:11). Lesson Outline—1. Asa's Reforms (1-5); 2. Asa's Defences (6-8); 3 Asa's Victories (9-12).

Christian Endeavor.

BY BURRIS A. JENKINS.

TOPIC FOR OCT. 2.

TRIALS, AND HARD TO BEAR THE[M]

(Isa. 41:8-20.)

There are ways in which it is quite evide[nt]
that trials should not be borne. It goes with
out saying that they should not be borne wit[h]
weakness and complaining, for then, in rea
ity, they are not borne at all. Shoulde[rs]
that sink can bear no load. A reed shak[en]
by the breeze cannot stand against storms [of]
wind and wave.

Nor, on the other hand, should trials be bor[ne]
with granite-like hardness and stoical resis[t]
ance. Brutus, hearing of his wife's deat[h]
and smiting his forehead in a single gestu[re]
of stony grief, turning back to his considera
tion of maps and field campaigns, is no [f]
example for bearing trials, however wonderf[ul]
and even awe-inspiring is his self-conrtol. N[o]
no. Grief has its purpose, pain its missio[n]
Rebel as we may against the thought that th[is]
specific bereavement or that particular anguis[h]
is sent by the hand of God, nevertheless w[e]
must all agree that he made this world, ev
and all, and that in the end this and all sorro[w]
must have its beneficent purpose. Hearts
therefore, are not meant to be stone. The
are made to be soil. They must feel the plow
share and melt beneath the rain.

It is ours, then, to open our hearts to God, t[o]
bring him our sorrows, tell him of them an[d]
ask his help to bear them. This is the tru[e]
attitude of the Christian toward trials. It [is]
not a weak complaining nor a stoical indiffe[r]
ence. It is a gentle-hearted endurance, n[ot]
without a cry sometimes to God—for does n[ot]
a single groan sometimes help us to bear
pain? Does not the telling of our sorrow to
friend often decrease the ache? Did not th[e]
psalmist cry out to God from the depths of h[is]
sorrow? Did not Jesus pray, "Father, if it b[e]
possible, let this cup pass from me; neverthe
less, not my will but thine be done?" Christ'
attitude in trials is the Christian's true att[i]
tude.

Thus it is, then, that *with faith* we are t[o]
meet the trials of this life. The very wor[d]
trials is indicative that they have a purpose. [Is]
there an evil in the city and the Lord hath n[ot]
done it? Is there pain in the world and God'
law in some wise has not produced it? Whe[re]
avoidable, then, let us avoid it. Where th[e]
pain is due to our outraging of God's laws-
and a very large part of it may be so; sin [is]
the most painful of all things; the way of th[e]
transgressor is hard—let us turn and ob[ey]
him. But where the sorrow can be traced t[o]
no transgression of our own, it is ours to bea[r]
it as calmly and with as much faith as we can

"Trials must and will befall,
But with humble faith to see
Love inscribed upon them all—
This is happiness to me."

With work also we may overcome much [of]
life's pain. When Jesus sat by the well wear[y]
and tired, a soul presented itself to him tha[t]
needed his care. He seems to have forgotte[n]
his fatigue, his thirst, his hunger, in th[e]
enthusiasm of ministering to that needy soul
and when they bade him eat he said: "I hav[e]
meat to eat that ye know not of." To do hi[s]

her's will, to accomplish his work—this ; his meat and drink. And how often shall likewise, find in the heat and dust, the ɹriness and pain of this heavy-laden life, t our ease and refreshment shall be found the enthusiasm of our work. "No brave ɿ," says Carlyle, "needs any more happiɜ than just enough to get his work done." ny trial weighing heavily upon your heart, ɔw-Endeavorer? Press forward and do r work. Is any thorn eating and festering your flesh? "My grace is sufficient for e," press forward and do your work. Is great, aching void in your heart? Press ward on the lonely road, try to fill your rt with your work, *his* work, and he will you. Work for him, work in whatever do as unto him; work in the consciousness his presence; work with the feeling that the drudgery of this narrow occupation, ch seems so monotonous and mean, is gned by him and is watched and approved, n well done, by him, and the trial will grow mphant.

inally, *with the promises* which he has given can bear the ills of life. "Fear thou not; I am with thee; be not dismayed, for I am God: I will strengthen thee; yea, I will thee; yea, I will uphold thee with the t hand of my righteousness," are the ds of our Scripture lesson, spoken to disraged Israel, and they have rung down the rs to comfort the Israel of God ever since. l how numerous are the precious promises ken by our gentle fellow-sufferer, the ter of Galilee, to us directly: "Come unto all ye that labor and are heavy-laden and I give you rest." "Lo, I am with you ay, even unto the end of the world." owing tired heads upon his breast, clasping le hands in his strong grasp, supporting k forms by his mighty frame of brotherli-, guided in the dark by his seeing eye, e we not sufficient assurance from this our r brother, our friend that sticketh closer a brother, that we shall not faint? God is ching over us, guiding us with his eye; and never leave us nor forsake us. Whatever be the cloud, his face is behind it.

My life is cold and dark and dreay;
It rains and the wind is never weary;
My heart still clings to the moldering past,
The hopes of youth fall thick in the blast,
And my life is dark and dreary.

Be still, sad heart, and cease repining!
Behind the clouds is the sun still shining;
Thy lot is the common lot of all;
Into each life some rain must fall,
Some days must be dark and dreary."

Marriages.

GIBSON—WELCH.—Married, at Chrisman, Ill., Miss Jessie M. Welch and Mr. Thos. H. Gibson, of Jonesville, Va., at eight o'clock P. M., Sept. 7th, at the Christian Church; F. W. Burnham, of Charleston, officiating.

C. E. EVANS, pastor.

HYSKELL—TAYLOR.—In Macomb, Ill., by J. S. Gash, Sept. 5, Mr. Fred T. Hyskell, of Burlington, Ia., and Miss E. P. Taylor, of Macomb.

MATHEWSON—DILLS.—In Macomb, Ill., by J. S. Gash, Sept. 14, Mr. Charles Mathewson and Miss Hattie Dills, both of Bushnell, Ill.

PEARSON—GENGELBACH.—At Plattsburg, Mo., Sept. 7, 1898, by J. W. Perkins, Joseph D. Pearson and Miss Dorah A. Gengelbach, both of Clinton county, Mo.

SMITH—GROSS.—In Macomb, Ill., by J. S. Gash, Aug. 2, Mr. C. F. Smith, of Galesburg, and Miss Marie Gross, of St. Louis, Mo.

WILLIAMS—WILLIAMS.—In Macomb, Ill., by J. S. Gash, Aug. 24, Mr. Roger Williams and Miss Creole Williams, both of Colchester, Ill.

Obituaries.

[One hundred words will be inserted free. Above one hundred words, one cent a word. Please send amount with each notice.]

BORROUGHS.

Margrette Elizabeth Borroughs, who died at Berkeley, Va., Sept. 5th, was born at Shelbyville, Ind., April 5, 1872, and was 26 years and five months old. She has been in frail health for several years, but her illnesss did not assume a serious phase until last April. Since then her decline has been rapid, and her sufferings have been extreme, especially during the last few days of her life; but she bore her afflictions with patience and fortitude, never complaining, but always cheerful. In early life she gave herself to Christ, and has been a consistent church member, a daily reader of the Bible, a dutiful daughter and a kind sister. She expressed a wish that she might live in order to do all the good possible, but was ready and willing to go if it were the Lord's will to take her. Her career was a religious triumph, and her memory is a bright monument or the sweetest virtues and most enduring accomplishments. "Lizzie," as she was affectionately called in the home circle and church, was the elder daughter of our venerable and beloved Doctor Borroughs, and to him and the stricken family goes out the heart of the church and whole community.

C. O. WRIGHT, U. S. N.

Norfolk, Va., Sept. 10, 1898.

BROWN.

Mary Maranda Brown was born in Morro county, Ohio, May 12, 1840, and died in North English, Iowa, Aug. 20, 2898, aged 58 years, three months and eight days, leaving husband, one daughter and four sons to mourn her loss. She was a member of the Church of Christ 28 years. She patiently bore her intense suffering for weeks. The church here loses one more of its faithful members, but heaven is the richer. Just one year ago to a day her daughter Media preceded her to the promised land.

C. H. MATTOX.

North English, Iowa.

BUTLER.

L. Madison Butler, daughter of Mr. and Mrs. Geo. H. Butler, was born in Whiting, Jackson county, Kansas, Nov. 20, 1884; died Aug. 30, 1898; aged 13 years, 9 months and 10 days. She united with the church May 15, 1897. She was buried with Christ in baptism by Rev. A. N. Lindesy, of Canton, Mo. She was a beautiful Christian and ever ready to work for her Master. She was faithful in all things and by her bright, cheerful disposition won the affection of all who knew her. The whole community mourns her death. The funeral services were conducted at the family residence, Sept. 1st at 11 A. M., by Rev. H. C. Ventress, of LaHarpe, Ill.

MRS. T. F. WOODSIDE.

Stronghurst, Ill.

GROVES.

William Groves passed into the spirit-life August 9th, 1898; aged 42 years. He was an earnest and consecrated disciple of Christ and will be sadly missed in the church. He leaves a wife and son who have a precious memory of him. For 13 years he was captain of the ferryboat at Hannibal. He had ferried many persons across the Father of Waters; then, as if to rest him, the Heavenly Father ferried his ready spirit across the river of death into the spiritland. In the absence of the pastor on his vacation, Bro. S. D. Dutcher, his old pastor, conducted the funeral service in an impressive manner.

LEVI MARSHALL.

Hannibal, Mo., Sept. 8, 1898.

LINDSAY.

Mrs. Nannie Lindsay (*nee* Browning), of Sweet Springs, Mo., was in her 29th year at the time of her death. At the age of sixteen she gave her heart and life to the Lord and soon developed those Christian graces that made her so much beloved. July 31, 1893, she was married to Mr. John Lindsay, who survives her. Her early death, to those who regard death as calamitous, was peculiarly sad, because they loved her so tenderly. Were we able to view death from the other side we would not weep, but rejoice because of her new-found joys. While her suffering was great, her patience was able to bear all things, knowing that He in whom she had trusted could and would do all things well.

C. A. HEDRICK.

Rich Hill, Sept. 10, 1898.

PHILLIPS.

On June 26, 1898, with her husband and three daughters at her bedside, Mrs. Mary Eleanor Phillips fell asleep in Jesus. Mary Lindsey was born in Christian county, Ky., Dec. 3, 1832. She was the eleventh child of a family of twelve, six sons and six daughters. Three sons, James, Alfred and John, were Christian preachers. She became a member of the Christian Church at the age of thirteen. After attending school in Eureka she finished her course of study at Berean College, Jacksonville, Ill., and became a teacher in the public schools. In 1859 she was married to James E. Phillips and moved to Tremont, from which place they moved to Lilly and then to Normal. On Jan. 29, 1896, Sister Phillips had a paralytic stroke. For two and one-half years she was an example of patient suffering and sublime faith. As she was unable during this time to take her place in the house of the Lord, her own room became the "house of God and the gate of heaven." She was laid to rest in the family cemetery south of Lilly. Besides the husband and the three daughters there are one sister, Jean L. Linn, and two brothers, William and Felix, left to mourn her loss. 1 Thes. 4:13-18.

E. B. BARNES.

Normal Ill., Aug. 25, 1898.

PORTER.

Lizzie Porter, daughter of Mr. and Mrs. W. S. Porter, died Sept. 3, 1898. She had just passed her fourteenth birthday. Two years ago she became a Christian. The right way of life was pointed out to her by her parents and she accepted it. Anxious ones watched and cared for her tenderly, but her young life gradually slipped away from time limitations and went into the eternal. She was faithful to her Christian profession, and the influence of her life will continue to speak to her associates in the flesh.

LEVI MARSHALL.

Hannibal, Mo., Sept. 8, 1898.

Literature.

Mrs. Humphrey Ward's New Book.

There can be no doubt that Mrs. Humphrey Ward is one of the ablest writers of the present age. She has more than talent; in her pages the discriminating reader finds the subtle and indefinable marks of genius. The literary instinct is true, the wealth of diction surprising, the thought large and luminous, the analysis and interpretation of motives deep and comprehensive, and the complete effect of her work striking and impressive. It is obvious that the gifts of the Arnolds are highly developed in her, that she is saturated with Oxford culture, that she has made a careful study of the various problems with which the greatest souls of our country are occupied, and that she is conscious of a mission and a message. Wide open are her eyes, keen and receptive her mind, eager and ambitious her spirit. As she goes through the world she sees clearly what men and women are doing, what are the causes which produce in them laughter or tears, what are the principles to which they yield themselves from day to day, and what are the ideals towards which they are striving. Hardly anything escapes the sweep of her vision. And because she is a serious woman she deals with the serious things of life and paints them as they appear to her with a skillful and masterly hand.

"Helbeck of Bannisdale" is far above the ordinary novel. I do not think that it is equal to "Sir George Trenaby." But if it lacks the virility, the strong intellectual grasp, the witchery of movements, the breadth of conception, the uniqueness of execution of the latter book, it has a distinctive and peculiar charm of its own. There is not much plot in it—no more than is necessary to bring into proper relief the different persons who figure in it. Indeed, Mrs. Humphrey Ward is pre-eminently a religious, or as perhaps she would prefer to be called, an ethical teacher. Therefore, she does not waste her time or her energies on what has no direct bearing on the questions of the soul, or the claims of theology, or the hopes of the churches, or the aspirations and dreams of humanity. If she turns aside to speak of the beauties of Wordsworth's country it is that she may may show its moral value in the education of those whose lives she is endeavoring to make real to us. The bracing air of the uplands, the rugged mountains capped with fleecy clouds, the vines winding through the valleys where the cattle feed in blissful content, the woods casting their shadows in the lakes and the moss with its tendrils clinging to the massive rocks, the light playing on the larches and sycamores and making the larks to sing their joyous lays, the millions upon millions of daffodils glorifying the lovely fells of Windermere are to her a revelation of the eternal righteousness. The influence of nature combined with the influence of heredity and environments are responsible for what we are.

The chief characters of the book are not particularly attractive. Helbech, the hero of the story, lacks many of the qualities that are the distinguishing signs of the true child of God. In spite of his longing for holiness, his self-sacrificing kindness to the poor, his gentle and courteous demeanor to others and his untiring devotion to what he conceives to be for his everlasting welfare, he is a morbid and uncompromising bigot. When he exanines his conscience he depreciates himself a thousand times more than ever Jonathan Edwards did, and the mention of the building of an Anglican church near his home provokes in him a slumbering hatred of Protestantism and an intense hunger for its destruction. Laura, who is the heroine of the tale, is the daughter of a deceased Cambridge professor who had married Helbeck's sister and spent his life in revolt against Christianity. She inherits the religious opinions and prejudices of her father. A creature of contradictory impulses, wholly ignorant of the ways of life, and yet loyal to the memory of her agnostic parents, she says and does some very strange things. In her we have a splendid girl spoiled for the want of training. Mrs. Fountain, stepmother to Laura and sister to Helbeck, is certainly a weakling. Catholicism she abandons before her marriage, and her husband's eyes are scarcely closed in death ere she regrets what she has done and takes to her beads and rosary again. Father Bowls, the parish priest, is a sly, easy-going, hypocritical specimen of the ancient faith. His manner is offensively pious, his heart not engaged with supernal facts, his conscience not quickly disturbed by the voice of the Lord. The Jesuit Father Leodham is of another type. Refined, scholarly, urbane, with a considerable acquaintance of the world, he is specially adapted to win the wayward from the path of error. But he is a convert from Anglicanism, and consequently has all the faults of the convert, such as excess of zeal, intolerance of the convictions of his quondam friends and neighbors, a readiness to compass heaven and earth to gain the ends of the Romish Church. Brother Williams is low-born and cannot rise to the standard of a gentleman. He tries Catholicism for awhile, alienating from him his nearest relatives, and leaves it unceremoniously complaining of its exactions. And the Masons are a coarse, vulgar family. They are peasants to the tips of their fingers and view everything from the peasant's standpoint. In them the evangelicalism of the Church of England manifests itself at its worst. So it is all through the story. There is not a single individual that we spontaneously and unreservedly admire and love.

Mrs. Humphrey Ward in this book pays almost no attention to the free action of the human will. It seems to her that it is overborne by forces that lie outside it. Again and again she pictures it contending with the traditions of the past, with the superstititions of religion, with social customs and habits, with the wild and stormy passions that beat around it as the angry waves beat around a ship at sea. With inimitable delicacy and vividness she describes her men and women struggling for freedom, contending with the enemies of national liberty and fighting for the privilege of ushering in the kingdom of "sweetness and light." But these creations of her pen have not much part in the working out of their salvation. They are mere automata, enmeshed in a complicated web of invariable and inflexible laws and molded and shaped without their voluntary choices or consents. This, however, is not the teaching of the Bible or of experience. From the dawn of Jewish history until now, countless multitudes have declared that the children of God can determine their own weal or woe. We do not, for we cannot, admit that we are the puppets of powers that are entirely beyond our control.

And Mrs. Humphrey Ward is not fair to Christianity. She takes as its representatives persons who do not worthily embody it. In the case of Helbeck it is set forth in its worst material and dogmatic forms; in the case of Augustina in the sickliest and inanest aspects; in the case of Cousin Elizabeth and Polly in its crudest and boldest symbols, and in the case of Daffady it reveals itself in the cant and vanity of a spurious Methodism. With Christianity as thus outwardly expressed Laura is contrasted. Original in her mental processes, quick in meeting difficulties and emergencies, having at her command numerous sententious utterances of her father, and bright and sparkling in her speech, she is more than a match for the believers. And though she promises to wed Helbeck out of pity for his wretched condition, and because her own heart is torn with grief at the prospect of being left in the world alone, yet she commits suicide rather than accept the faith of her lover and become guilty of intellectual dishonesty. But we have a right to demand a juster presentation of the Christian religion. It is a conspicuous illustration of a violation of the golden, and exhibits an amazing blindness to the wonderful sanity and activity of the followers of Jesus in the realms of the noblest thought and life. If Christianity is not reasonable, then there is nothing reasonable in the universe or in the annals of our race, for apart from it we can discover no adequate explanation of mind and matter, no remedy for sin and no endless satisfaction for the infinite pleadings and hopes of our souls. S. LINTON BELL.

Publishers' Notes.

MARY ARDMORE,

Or a Test of Faith, by J. H. Stark, will soon be issued from our press. Many were delighted with this author's former volume, "Hugh Carlin," and they will be pleased to know that "Mary Ardmore" promises to be much more interesting. The characters that make up this story are aptly chosen, the incidents are very lifelike and the great truths are brought prominently before the mind of the reader. The book will be ready in a short time.

SENT FREE.

We will send a full set of our Sunday-school supplies to any Sunday-school workers desiring to examine them. The last quarter of 1898 begins with October and, if any school is not using our literature, we suggest that some of your officers write us for samples. We want your school to see what kind of Sunday-school supplies we publish.

KING SAUL, BY J. B. ELLIS.

"In the Days of Jehu," issued from the press but a few months ago, was written by the same author. The general satisfaction given by this former book warrants a good sale for this new candidate for public favor. Its conception is good, and the diction is excellent. Some of our readers may not agree with the author in thinking that Abner was the uncle of Saul. But whatever the relation the story is well written and full of interest.

Saul himself has not worth of character enough to warrant a work of 278 pages, but fortunately, David lived in those times, and his life was so interwoven with the reign of Saul that it seems well enough to borrow from him character sufficient to make one of the most readable and profitable books yet placed on the market. Like all the productions of the author, it deserves well and will evidently receive a large patronage. D. R. DUNGAN.

WANTED IN EACH COMMUNITY.

An agent to sell "America or Rome—Christ or the Pope," by John L. Brandt. We are now prepared to offer *extra inducements* to those who will sell this book. The volume contains more than 500 pages and 55 illustrations. It is acknowledged to be the best work on the despotism of Rome now before the public. It is reliable, because the author has sustained his statement by evidence from numerous unimpeachable sources.

A glance at the book, will cause a desire to know its contents. An agent would not have much trouble to sell this book, and our terms are such that we pay the agents well for the time he devotes to its sale. Write us for our terms to agents on "America or Rome—Christ or the Pope." Address Christian Publishing Co., St. Louis, Mo.

MORMONISM EXAMINED.

It is acknowledged by competent judges that D. H. Bays has presented in his late book the strongest arguments against Mormon doctrine that has yet been published. He calls his book "Doctrines and Dogmas of Mormonism Examined and Refuted." He has attacked all the strongholds of Mormonism, closely examined all their doctrines, and has refuted every argument on which they rely to sustain their beliefs. The author of this book is acquainted with the Mormon doctrines from the very inside, having been a strong advocate of their faith for many years. To those who have the question of Mormonism to meet, we commend this work to them as being a strictly reliable refutation of the teachings of Mormonism. It is a book of 460 pages, and the price is $1.50.

A story that even those who are close pressed by the duties of a very busy and practical age may pause to read with interest is contained in the book "King Saul," just issued from the press. It is a vivid recital of the history of the ancient king of Israel, so told that the ages gone become reinvested with interest, and the characters become as great in the world's history as they do in divine chronology. "King Saul" is told in an up-to-date, matter-of-fact manner, with faithfulness to historical accuracy and plenty of snap, vigor and romantic details. It deserves to be read as well as the histories of other famous men who have played a part in shaping the destinies of the world. As a portrayal of human passions it is a masterpiece.

The author begins his story with the marvelous manner in which Saul became ruler of Israel, and the transition from a government by judges to that of kings.—*St. Louis Star, St. Louis, Mo.*

FACTS AND FACTORS.

EVENTS.

A debate took place on the currency question in the Auditorium at Omaha, Neb., last week. There were prominent men on both sides of the coin question.

In the late battle of Omdurman it is estimated that 10,800 dervishes were killed, 16,000 wounded and 4,000 taken prisoners.

The Eastern squadron has been disbanded and its commander, J. C. Watson, assigned to duty at the Mare Island Navy Yard.

A destructive hurricane swept over the British West Indies last week, killing 150 persons and doing immense damage to property.

The United States Peace Commission sailed from New York City, Saturday, Sept. 17th, at two o'clock, on Steamer Campania.

The battleships Iowa and Oregon and 7,000 troops have been ordered to Honolulu, en route to the Philippine Islands.

The Empress of Austria was assassinated at Geneva, Switzerland, Sept. 10th, by an anarchist named Luigini.

Mary E. Hart, of Troy, N. Y., has given $150,000 for a library building in her city as a monument to her deceased husband.

The U. S. revenue cutter, Bear, reached Seattle, Wash., Sept. 13, with 116 whalers, rescued from a whaling fleet wrecked by an ice pack off Point Barrow in 1897.

The U. S. protocol was adopted by the Spanish Cortes in session at Madrid, Sept. 13. The vote stood 151 votes for and 48 against it.

FACTS.

British soldiers in the Soudan are forbidden the use of intoxicants.

The cotton yield of the United States for the cotton year 1897 was 11,180,960 bales.

Our war with Spain cost us $105,000,000, and Spain nearly $400,000,000 besides the loss of her navy and islands.

The salary of the Archbishop of Santiago has been reduced from $18,000 to $6,000 per annum by the U. S. authorities.

Meridian, Miss., has adopted the curfew law.

Mt. Vesuvius is in a state of eruption. Three streams of lava are issuing from its crater.

The Omaha Exposition has been pronounced a financial success.

The highest meteorological station in the world is located on the summit of a peak known as El Misti, near Arequipa, Peru. Harvard University is the maintainer of the station. It is 19,200 feet above the sea level, and is one of the eight operated by the University at Arequipa, the lowest being at a point 55 feet above the sea level, while two others are situated at 13,400 and 15,700 feet elevation respectively.

OPINIONS.

George J. Gould thinks that this country is on the eve of an unprecedented era of prosperity.

Mrs. Carse still believes that the W. C. T. U. can redeem the "Woman's Temple," Chicago, from debt.

General Gomez thinks that the annexation of Cuba to the United States is an impossibility.

General Aguinaldo thinks he is entitled to be placed at the head of an independent government over the Philippine Islands.

It is thought that M. Zola will reappear in Paris and issue another manifesto on the Dreyfus case.

ABOUT NOTED MEN.

Senator Gray declined a place on the Peace Commission.

Li Hung Chang has been dismissed from China's Foreign Office.

Emperor William attended the funeral of the Empress of Austria, Sept. 17th.

Admiral Cervera left a very pleasing note for the President on his departure for Spain.

It is reported that General Gomez has resigned his position as commander-in-chief of the insurgents of Cuba.

"Fighting Bob Evans," at his own request, has been relieved of the command of the battleship Iowa.

General Miles is confined to his bed at his home in Washington, D. C., with a touch of fever.

President McKinley dined the Peace Commissioners on the eve of their departure for Paris, F.ance.

M. Munkacsy, the eminent Hungarian artist is now adjudged to be hopelessly insane. In late court proceedings instituted by his wife for the management of the property, the fact is divulged that his real name is not Munkacsy, but Lieb. It appears he took the name of Munkacsy from the place of his birth in Hungary.

Last Word to Iowa Churches.

Our convention meets Sept. 26th to 30th—one month later than usual. We must pay for 13 months' work with 12 months' income. Our receipts at convention have usually been $650. To come out even this year we must make them not less than $1,000. Let all in arears take note. Come and bring your pledges in cash. A. M. HAGGARD, Sec. I. C. C.

THE
ISTIAN-EVANGELI

A WEEKLY FAMILY AND RELIGIOUS JOURNAL.

September 29, 1898

NTS.

.....................387
blem........... .388
f the Jerusalem
.....................389
s.....................389
.....................390
rs....... 391

s:

Chamberlain... 391
sterial Office.—J.
....393
:. D. S. Henkle.394

.....................399
.....................399
. . ..400
.....................401
.....................401
ť 402
.....................403
....403
ain...............404
uild..............404
. Notes...... 404

(poem)..........408
r in the Social
.....................408
.....................409
.....................409
poem).... 410
.....................410
....411

ought............394
....395
....398
.....................405
.....................406
.....................407
.. ..412
.....................413
aries.............413
.... :....415
.....................417
.....................416

n $1.75.

ALEXANDER CAMPBELL.

PUBLISHED BY

IRISTIAN PUBLISHING COMPANY

1522 Locust St., St. Louis.

THE

CHRISTIAN - EVANGELIST

J. H. GARRISON, EDITOR.

W. W. HOPKINS, ASSISTANT.

B. B. TYLER, J. J. HALEY,

EDITORIAL CONTRIBUTORS.

What We Plead For.

The Christian-Evangelist pleads for:

The Christianity of the New Testament, taught by Christ and his Apostles, versus the theology of the creeds taught by fallible men—the world's great need.

The divine confession of faith on which Christ built his church, versus human confessions of faith on which men have split the church.

The unity of Christ's disciples, for which he so fervently prayed, versus the divisions in Christ's body, which his apostles strongly condemned.

The abandonment of sectarian names and practices, based on human authority, for the common family name and the common faith, based on divine authority, versus the abandonment of scriptural names and usages for partisan ends.

The hearty co-operation of Christians in efforts of world-wide beneficence and evangelization, versus petty jealousies and strifes in the struggle for denominational pre-eminence.

The fidelity to truth which secures the approval of God, versus conformity to custom to gain the favor of men.

The protection of the home and the destruction of the saloon, versus the protection of the saloon and the destruction of the home.

For the right against the wrong;
For the weak against the strong;
For the poor who've waited long
For the brighter age to be.
For the truth, 'gainst superstition,
For the faith, against tradition,
For the hope, whose glad fruition
Our waiting eyes shall see.

RATES OF SUBSCRIPTION.

Single subscriptions, new or old	$1.75	each
In clubs of five or more, new or old. ...	1.50	"
Reading Rooms	1.25	"
Ministers ...	1.00	"

With a club of ten we will send one additional copy free.

All subscriptions payable in advance. Label shows the month up to the first day of which your subscription is paid. If an earlier date than the present is shown, you are in arrears. No paper discontinued without express orders to that effect. Arrears should be paid when discontinuance is ordered.

In ordering a change of post office; please give the OLD as well as the NEW address.

Do not send local check, but use Post office or Express Money Order, or draft on St. Louis, Chicago or New York, in remitting.

ISTIAN-EVANGELIST

opinion and methods, Liberty; in all things, Charity."

Mo., Thursday, September 29, 1898. No. 39

is almost solidly Roman Catholic. As to the establishment, there is, of course, only one thing to do. It will cease to exist, naturally, inevitably and without a struggle. Hitherto the church and its various institutions in these provinces have been supported in part by subsidies from the state. Henceforth, if any of these places become American territory, the Roman Catholic Church will shift for itself there as here. From this it will inevitably follow, especially in the priest-ridden Philippines, that there will be a large reduction in the number of Spanish priests in the islands. Indeed, considerations of personal safety have already induced by far the majority to return to Spain. It is estimated that out of 11,000 Spanish priests in the Philippines not more than 500 remain. It does not speak well for the influence of the church that the lives of its priests are not safe from attack by its laity when civil authority is relaxed. It is reported that the Archbishop of Manila is in favor of annexation to the United States, which would guarantee protection, though it would not give support to the church, and believes that the religious orders, Dominicans, Augustinians, Franciscans, Benedictines and Capuchins ought to be expelled. Their jealousies among themselves and the hatred of them all by the people make them a disturbing element, and doubtless the archbishop is right in believing that their removal would simplify the situation with which he has to deal.

By perseverance and persuasion the President has almost succeeded in securing the necessary quota of the right sort of men to constitute the commission for investigating the conduct of the War Department. Invitations were issued to a number of men whose names were not in the original list and seven have accepted the appointment. It is still hoped that the number may be increased to nine, but in any case the investigation will proceed without further delay. Meanwhile, Secretary Alger is making a ten days' tour of inspection among the camps and hospitals in the South and, presumably, is preparing himself to prove, if called upon to do so, that the conduct of his department as regards care of men, both sick and well, has been satisfactory and exemplary.

The cordial relations existing between the Cuban insurgent leaders and the American officers in Cuba was evidenced thereby completing the task at which the Cubans had long labored. This is in brilliant contrast with the cheerful manner in which Aguinaldo alludes to the successes in the Philippines as a victory won by himsel and his fellow-insurgents. There have been many exasperating delays in the evacuation of Cuba by the Spanish forces. Instructions have been sent to the commission which is dealing with the matter to hasten the departure of the Spaniards. The protocol says "immediately," and that is a word which does not include in it the idea of any delay. The case has been quite different in Porto Rico. There, to the surprise of all concerned, the Spanish have not manifested their usual genius for inventing pretexts and excuses for delay, but have proceeded in a straightforward manner to prepare to leave. American troops are already in Porto Rico in sufficient numbers to preserve order, and within a few days the extra troops to be sent to occupy Havana and the neighboring provinces will be ready to embark.

One of the foregone conclusions of the coming state election is the retirement of Roger Q. Mills from the Texas senatorship. It was expected that the election of the legislature would turn upon the fight between Mills and Culberson for the senatorial seat now occupied by Mr. Mills. At the very outset of the campaign Mr. Mills declared that his rival had control of the machine and without a struggle retired from a contest in which he could see no hope of victory. The circumstances which made the situation seem to him so obviously hopeless was the rigid criterion of Democracy adopted last January by the Democratic state executive committee, whereby eligibility to participate in the party primaries was limited to those who had voted the straight ticket, both state and national, in 1896. As Mr. Mills was opposed to the free coinage of silver, it was naturally expected that much of his support would come from Democrats who had not voted the straight ticket in 1896, and the exclusion of the primaries was a serious blow to Mills' chances. The downfall of this former idol of the Texas Democracy is not, however, without causes of long standing. His intimacy with the second Cleveland administration cast an odium upon his name in the minds of the large number of Texans who never loved Mr. Cleveland. His real or supposed vast influence with the President in the distribu-

and Culberson's connection with the Chicago platform, there is a probability, as near certainty as a political prognostication can be, that Gov. Culberson will soon succeed Senator Mills in the United States Senate.

There are plenty of influential Republican politicians in Michigan who are cordially opposed to Gov. Pingree and his ideas, plans and methods, but that did not prevent his renomination for governor by the Republican State Convention, nor did it render the outcome of the convention very dubious before the event. Together with the many faults which he may possess and the eccentricities which he undoubtedly does possess, he also possesses the confidence of the people in his integrity as a man and in his sincere devotion to popular interests. Knowing this, Pingree's political enemies within his own party could not leave him off the ticket without inviting defeat for their own candidate. Besides the policy of reform within the state, for which Gov. Pingree stands preeminently, the platform on which he is now renominated includes endorsement of the national administration, the conduct of the war by the President and of the War Department by Secretary Alger, the Dingley Bill and the St. Louis currency platform.

It has been commonly believed that the moral sentiment of the country has won such a victory over prize fighting that no attempt was likely to be made to "pull off" a big fight in the very heart of the country. Promoters of championship fights and the most prominent exponents of the manly art of self-defense have been compelled to seek some quiet, sequestered spot in Nevada or the Mexican border in which to give their exhibitions, and it is somewhat surprising to learn that an attempt is being made to arrange for a big heavyweight match to be held within thirty minutes' ride of Cincinnati. This may mean either Indiana, Ohio or Kentucky. Accordingly, the governors of these three states, at the first appearance of the rumor, made official statements which will have a tendency to discourage the enterprising promoters. The proclamation by Gov. Mount, of Indiana, is particularly clear-cut. He says: "There will be no prize fight in Indiana if I can prevent it. If local authority is not sufficient, the resources of the state will be drawn upon for ample force to suppress lawlessness and drive out the intruders if anything of the kind is undertaken. The persons so engaged will be treated as criminals from the time they cross the border line. Prize fighting is a disgrace to our boasted civilization, and ought not to be tolerated anywhere. It certainly will not be tolerated in Indiana while I am governor."

The death of Miss Winnie Davis, the daughter Jefferson Davis, has created profound sorrow throught the South. Miss Davis was born at the executive mansion of the Confederacy, at Richmond, during the war, this, together with the fact that she was her father's favorite daughter and accompanied him on many of his journeyings, brought her prominently before the public as "the Daughter of the Confederacy." She was known and loved all over the South.

On October 4, at Newport News, the battleship Illinois will be launched. She is built upon lines somewhat different from those of our other battleships, and will therefore have a distinct inidviduality of her own. The new vessel will be equal in fighting equipment to any boat now in our navy. Preparations are being made to have a large number of representative men from Illinois present at the launching in recognition of the honor done to the state in giving its name to the new battleship.

OUR EDUCATIONAL PROBLEM.

Many of the best minds among us have come to see, with a clearness of conviction not hitherto manifest, the transcendent and primary importance of our educational interests. For a long time our institutions of learning did not seem to be of sufficient importance to have any place on the program of our national conventions. It has only been a few years since the idea of an educational board was deemed practicable, and even yet the value of such a board and its special function have not dawned upon many of us. But many have come to see that back of nearly every other problen connected with our future growth and usefulness lies the educational problem, demanding solution. This has been the contention of the CHRISTIAN-EVANGELIST for many years, and we feel special gratification that there is a revival of interest on this subject.

There are many questions that go to make up the composite problem which we have called our educational problem. Some of these questions are as follows:

1. *How shall this reviving interest in the welfare of our colleges become more general throughout the brotherhood, so that they may receive the sympathy and support they require?* Of course, the religious press has an important duty to perform here, and the pulpit cannot be left out of any scheme that looks to the enlightenment of the mass of our membership on any subject. But it would greatly facilitate this work of awakening a general interest in our institutions of learning if there should be an educational day, or college day, on which the whole question of our educational interests could be brought before the brotherhood, by press and pulpit. The matter of lifting a collection for colleges on such a day might be omitted. Let the day be devoted to giving information concerning our colleges, emphasizing the importance of their work, and prayer for them. The fact of a whole brotherhood uniting in considering our colleges and praying for them would be a source of strength and inspiration for them. Let us have an educational day.

2. *How shall we secure adequate endowment for our colleges?* The need of such endowment is not a question. But how to raise an endowment that will enable our institutions to cope with the difficulties in their way and to meet the demands upon them is a most vital and practical question. It is one that has not received adequate thought among us. Shall we ask the churches, as such, to endow the colleges, or shall we rely upon the individual membership, or shall our appeal be to the wealthy? We see no reason why all these methods may not be tried. But still the question recurs, How shall we so place the needs of our colleges upon the consciences of those who have the ability to he them as to secure liberal gifts to that en This is a question that needs prayerl study. The uncertain future of our colleg has been a deterrent to men of weal putting money into them. But several our institutions have passed the exper mental stage, and it is only a queston the *extent* of their usefulness. The m who proves to be a success in securi money for endowing our institutions learning will have earned the gratitude the whole brotherhood.

3. *What is the relation of our colleg to the churches?* Is the relation a vital a reciprocal one, binding each to the oth in the bonds of a common destiny? Or a they wholly independent of each othe The former, of course, is the true relatio but how many churches act upon the latt suggestion! Christian colleges can on thrive where there are Christian churche and Christian churches can only thri permanently where there are Christi colleges, training young men and wom for Christian work and to carry Christi truth and faith into all the higher callin of life. This relationship should beget mutual interest in each other's welfar Churches should support the colleges, an colleges should educate to meet the nee of the churches. Nothing is clearer to a educated mind than that no religious bo can win or hold leadership among intell gent people without a high standard scholarship in its ministry and oth leaders.

4. *What do our colleges need besid endowment?* They need students, the need the sympathy and prayers of Chris tian people, they need thoroughly equippe teachers. Perhaps some of them need mo extended courses. No doubt all of the would welcome more religious enthusiasm and a more earnest religious atmospher Parents are asking, "Is it necessary for m to imperil the moral and spiritual welfa of my children, in order to give them inte lectual training?" The question is bo out of some sad experiences. Every inte ligent believer knows that there is no co flict between the highest intellectual trai ing and the deepest religious faith. A yet the latter often suffers in the effort gain the former. It is only fair to say our own colleges that they are general pervaded by a religious atmosphere, a that students who enter them as unbelie ers or religiously indifferent are much mo apt to become Christians than are those e tering as Christians to lose their fait But a more positive and all-pervading r ligious enthusiasm, that includes pure mo als, is a desideratum in all colleges.

5. *What obligations do we owe to t State Universities where so large a per cen of our young people are going for the education?* We have only recently awa ened to the fact that here is a vast fie practically unoccupied by the church. would be difficult to exaggerate the o portunities that are open to us in conne tion with these institutions. We are b ginning to do something in this directio and there is no more important branch our educational work than this. In th connection we call attention to an artic elsewhere, which we reprint from the A vance.

The relation of colleges to universities the one hand and to preparatory schools

ınother one of the many ques-
ke up our educational prob-
t time that these were fully
ılt with in an intelligent and
.on as becometh those champ-
ianity as a rational system
ıate its claims at the bar of
ı? Let us give our educa-
ts proper emphasis at the
onvention.

OLENCE OF THE JERUSA-
LEM CHURCH.

rs of the first church of Christ
This fact will explain some of
rities. Their moral and re-
ıg had been protracted and
efore they became Christians
ply religious—they were thor-
ıt according to the require-
aw of Moses. The specialty
of Israel was religion and
hey were the most religious—
ntelligently religious—people
heir religion, unlike the re-
Greeks and Romans, included
ıis was an essential feature of
ligion. They were thorough-
ı knowledge of their duties
and toward their fellowmen.
tament records are cited in
ıis fact. The change experi-
Jews in Jerusalem in becom-
s was chiefly in their concep-
ture and official character of
ıreth. They were led, by ap-
lence, to believe in him as the
nised by the Holy Spirit in
s. When they came to under-
ı was the promised Messiah,
ı in him as such, they placed
right relations with him by
ed. In this significant rite
recognized him as their sov-

ı of the church in members
ly rapid. In a brief period of
mmunicants numbered many
With the manner in which they
tians we are familiar. In our
has been made prominent and
hey heard the message of the
, they believed the story, they
ıeir sins, they put their trust
d Christ, they practically and
gnized his Sonship by being
is name. But this was not all.
y the beginning. They con-
ıstly in the apostles' doctrine,
ship, in the breaking of bread
er. They did not fall from
as the big meeting came to a
in brief, is how the Jews in
came disciples of Christ.
erusalem" has been our rally-
the beginning of our work.
ısalem" has, to us, a familiar
n a sense, and to a degree, a
ness. The man who can say it
tone and with suitable em-
nd—he who cannot do these
e at least suspected of heresy.
Jerusalem" usually means no
is: Let us in thought and im-
"back to Jerusalem" that we

cious administration of Jesus Christ our Lord. This is probably the usual meaning attached to the familiar words, "Back to Jerusalem." And this is well. But the call ought to mean, to us, much more.

We are, in the good providence of our God, set for the restoration, to the church and the world, of the Christianity of Christ—its creed, its ordinances, its life. The creed can be learned by a study of the history of the Jerusalem church. The ordinances—their number, names, and nature—can be learned also in Jerusalem. But we can learn as well in "the City of the Great King" much concerning the primitive Christian life. Let us endeavor to do so.

It was a life of fraternity. The church in Jerusalem, the first Christian church on earth, possessed ten peculiarities of a household. The members of that congregation realized that they were brothers, not in name merely, but in deed and in truth. They loved as brothers love. There was among the members of that church real fellowship. They bore each other's burdens "and so fulfilled the law of Christ." No man said that aught of the things that he possessed was his own." "They had all things in common." The members of the Jerusalem church were genuinely benevolent. They lived for one another.

Theirs was a life of benevolence, because it was a life of fraternity. The work of restoring primitive Christianity will not be complete until we learn to live for each other as did the members of that first church. Compared with them our most generous men are positively stingy! Is this not true? "They sold their possessions and goods and parted them to all according as any man had need." "As many as were possessers of lands or houses sold them, and brought the prices of the things that were sold and laid them at the apostles' feet." "Joseph Barnabas . . having a field sold it, and brought the money and laid it at the apostles' feet." This is one of the distinguishing peculiarities of the Jerusalem church. Have we attained to their degree of benevolence?

The Epistle of James was written in Jerusalem, and in the midst of these scenes. Hence the conception of religion presented in this section of our New Testament. James said, "Pure religion and undefiled before our God and the Father is this, to visit the fatherless and widows in their affliction, and to keep himself unspotted from the world." Hence also the test of faith, or the evidence of faith, found in this epistle. On this point James, the bishop of the Jerusalem church, said: "What doth it profit, my brethren, if a man say he hath faith, but have not works? Can that faith save him? If a brother or sister be naked and in lack of daily food, and one of you say unto them, Go in peace, be ye warmed and filled; and yet ye give them not the things needful to the body; what doth it profit? Even so faith, if it have not works, is dead in itself." The members of the Jerusalem church excelled in benevolence.

Of course, there was unity of thought and affection in that church. The historian tells us that "the multitudes of them that be-

They did not say that their posses
belonged to them. All things, they u
stood, belonged to God. This was
thought. They had been trained i
faith while they were yet members c
church of Moses—the old Hebrew ch
All things belong to God and are su
to his call. This is primitive Christia
To restore this conception of propert
its use is a part of our work.

The task is difficult. The membe
the Jerusalem church had been in tra
for years—even for centuries in the
sons of their ancestors—for the wond
liberality described in the first chapt
the book of Acts.

We have examined in these paper
Hebrew financial system. This syste
plains, in part, the benevolent spirit
conduct of the members of the Jeru
church. If the task before us is hercu
all the greater is the reason why we s
enter upon it at once and prosecute it
all diligence and persistence. Let
"back to Jerusalem" that we may
how to use the means with which Go
entrusted us.

"Do you think that Christians ough
to do as did the disciples of Jesus in
salem?"

Why not? Jesus by his official r
sentatives, approved of the conduct of
disciples. Dare we pronounce again
Is it not a fact that we belong to Chri
it not also true that what we call our
erty really belongs to him? These t
we confess in our prayers and hymns.
we mean what we say when we enga
these pious exercises? Or do we obse
form merely? Our confessions are
enough—our practice can be improve

Circumstances made it necessary fo
members of the Jerusalem church t
their possessions that they might give
cumstances may make such a course n
sary for us if we would show that v
genuine disciples of him who became
that we by his voluntary poverty mig
made rich. This demand is certainl
upon us now; but it is required of u
we shall consider our property as, not
but his. "The earth is the Lord's."
silver is mine and the gold is mine,
the Lord." The time has come in
we ought to form this habit of though
begin to use our property in this spiri

B. B

Hour of Prayer.

ABOUNDING CHRISTIANS.

(Midweek Prayer-meeting Topic, Oct. 5, 1

Therefore, my beloved brethren, be ye
fast, unmovable, always abounding in the
of the Lord, forasmuch as ye know that
labor is not vain in the Lord.—1 *Cor.*

It was Paul's custom to "hitch his
to a star," to use an Emersonian p
If in his argument he soared int
empyrean, it was to discover a new r
for fidelity in the every-day duties o
With him the highest thought an
noblest work were indissolubly w
The life which he lived in the fles
lived, as he tells us, by faith in the S

practical exhortation like the above. In view of the great fact of Christ's resurrection and, growing out of that, the resurrection of all those who sleep in him, he exhorts the brethren to steadfastness and unmovableness in their Christian faith, and not only to do the work of the Lord, but to *abound* in such work.

This exhortation suggests to us different kinds of Christians. There is the steadfast and immovable kind, of which Paul himself was a splendid type, and there is the opposite of this class—those who are zealous for a season, perhaps during a revival meeting or immediately following it, and then their ardor cools down and they gradually relinquish Christian work. They warm up again at the next meeting, and so are trying to get to heaven by fits and starts. Every church has one or more of this kind, but every church also has a few faithful ones that, through heat and cold, in season and out of season, are always to be found at their posts.

And then there are Christians who are always about the same, but they are content with doing a very little religious work. They do not lay themselves out to do all they can for the Master, who died for their sins and rose again for their justification. They are not *abounding* Christians. They do just enough to maintain a respectable standing in the church and are satisfied with that. Then there are others whose hand and heart are in every good work. It is surprising how much time they can find to do kind, helpful things for others, especially for those in need of sympathy and social recognition. They help all departments of the church, support our missionary treasuries and assist in benevolent work and in endowing colleges. They *abound* in the work of the Lord. The future of the church depends on the abounding kind of Christians.

The reason assigned for this fidelity and liberality in good works is the fact that we know our work in the Lord is not vain. If done in the right spirit and from the right motive it is as certain to yield its reward as that God is true and cannot lie. We sow our seeds here, looking for an earthly harvest, but often our expectations are disappointed. Not so with those who "sow to the Spirit." They shall surely reap everlasting life. And the law of the spiritual harvest is, "He that soweth sparingly shall also reap sparingly, but he that soweth liberally shall also reap liberally."

Inasmuch, then, as Christ has risen from the dead, and that we, too, are to be raised in his glorious likeness and rewarded according to our works, why should we not abound in the work of the Lord the little while that remains to us here? In a few years we shall not be here. It will matter little then whether we have been rich or poor, whether life has been full of the sunshine of prosperity or shadowed by adversity; but it will matter infinitely whether we have been faithful in the use of our opportunities for developing character and doing good.

PRAYER.

O, Thou eternal God, our heavenly Father, we thank Thee for a risen Christ and for the blessed hope of being raised from the dead in his likeness. May this hope purify us, even as he is pure, and may it stimulate us to abound in the work of the Lord during our brief earthly pilgrimage. Forbid that we should be loiterers in Thy vineyard when Thou art calling us to do Thy work. Strengthen us mightily, O Lord, by Thy Spirit, that we may devote the remainder of our lives to Thy loving service, to the praise of Thy name, and be among the number that shall follow Thee on the mountains of God forever! For Thy name's sake. Amen!

Editor's Easy Chair.

Our last day at Macatawa was one of those mild, Indian summer days, that come in the autumn season. A purple haze filled the atmosphere and softened the rugged outlines of the landscape; the lake lay as quiet as an infant in its mother's arms, only breathing softly as a sleeping child breathes. And yet, as we walked along the shore we heard a sort of deep undertone that came in under a placid surface and seemed to tell of a conflict of elements far out from shore. At about ten o'clock we bade good-bye to the few friends left to "accompany us to the ship," the good "Soo City," and were soon out through the channel on the broad bosom of the lake. We had not been in our berths long, however, until we began to feel the swell of the lake, as if some mighty giant was underneath its depths, lifting the waves and vessel upon his huge shoulders. This action of the vessel, gently undulating at first, increased until the vessel was pitching and rolling alternately. It is the rolling motion of a vessel that gives greatest uneasiness to passengers. This is caused by the vessel quartering the waves instead of meeting them squarly or at right angles. Under such circumstances, in trying to court sleep, one is apt to try to comfort his mind with such reflections as the strength of the vessel in which he is sailing, the large proportion of the vessel that is beneath the level surface of the water, the skill of the man at the wheel, the faithfulness of the engineer, and that beneath all are "the everlasting arms." With such reflections we fell asleep at last to find that daylight had driven away the mists of the night, and the city of Chicago lay out before us clearly visible in the early morning light. The vessel had gone out of its way, as good navigators know how to do, to avoid the force of the waves and give their passengers as little discomfort as possible at the expense of a little time.

Chicago was busy, asusual. It was tending to its fall trade, reaching out its vast tentacles into all parts of the country after business, making preparations for the great peace jubilee and a thousand other things that have to do with the life and development of a great city. After a pleasant visit with Dr. Kirkham, at the office of the Christian Oracle, we had the pleasure of dining at the Quadrangle Club, at the University of Chicago, with a half dozen genial friends who made the hour a very pleasant and profitable one. It is always a pleasure to meet with such men as McClintock, Willett, Young, Ames, of Butler, who was passing through; Campbell, Gates and others, and a good lunch adds to the social enjoyment of such a meeting. These busy professors and pastors and Bible lecturers are full of their plans of work, and all of them seem ambitious to do the greatest good for the common cause. They are all impressed fully with the fact—as what Chicago citizen is not?—that Boston may be the "hub" of New En[g] Chicago is the real commercial, educ[ation]al and religious "hub" of the U[nited] States. There can be no doubt bu[t] there is concentrating in that great m[etrop]olis a vast aggregation of those [forces] that make for civilization, as w[ell as] much of the lower forces that make [in the] opposite direction. When these issu[es are] fully joined in conflict the end can[not be] doubted. Where else in all the wor[ld can] the student of social and religious [prob]lems find a better field in which to [study] the operation of the complex forc[es of] modern civilization?

It seems good to be back again [at our] old desk, to dust out the pigeon [holes,] renew the ink in the inkstand, excha[nge the] rusty pen for a fresh one, meet with [famil]iar faces and drop into the regular [routine] of things. The beauty of a chan[ge of] base in the summer season is not m[ore in] the novelty of going away than in t[he] coming back. It makes two chang[es in]stead of one. But, after all, there['s no] place where one can do his work wi[th the] same ease, other things being equal, [as in] his accustomed place of work, and esp[ecial]ly do we believe this to be true of an e[ditor.] There is no place in which one can [edit a] paper so effectively as at the editorial [desk,] where he daily comes in contact wi[th his] readers and where his hand is conti[nually] on the pulse of the people. Much [as we] enjoy Macatawa, if experience ha[d not] taught us that a change was a necessi[ty for] us, we would prefer to remain the [year] round at our desk, for when one lov[es his] work, the highest pleasure that h[e can] have in this life is the doing of that [work] and in the constant effort to do it [more] efficiently. Nevertheless, as human [nature] is constituted and as the present or[der of] things is constituted, we believe it [is] highly important for a large numb[er of] people, at least, to secure the benef[it of a] change at least once a year.

Our esteemed contemporary, the Jo[urnal] and Messenger, in an editorial en[titled] "Baptism Into What?" says that "[though] the present writer, in his earlier mi[nistry,] thought it proper to use the prepo[sition] 'into,' he has become convinced o[f his] error." This comment is draw[n out] by the statement of a correspo[ndent] that he had heard a Baptist minist[er, in] good standing, in baptizing a can[didate] say, "I baptize thee 'into' the name [of the] Father and of the Son and of the [Holy] Ghost." The editor is convinced th[at this] is wrong. He admits that he is agair[nst the] revisers in taking this position, a[nd he] might have added with equal truthf[ulness] that he is against the original Greek. [We] have always regarded this as one o[f the] most important renderings in the R[evised] Version. It carries with it treme[ndous] consequences. It makes baptism, [both in its] outward action and in the inward pr[epara]tion—which alone gives baptism vali[dity]— a *transitional* institution. In that a [man] comes into formal citizenship in the [king]dom of God, and of course this p[resup]poses the qualifications for citize[nship.] Does not the Journal and Messeng[er see] that this rendering at once renders i[nfant] baptism null and void? In such case[s it is] not transitional, for the subjects of

citizenship in the kingdom of
gret to see our Baptist neigh-
er a stronghold of one of its
its from the morbid fear, which
ptists manifest, of overdoing
baptism. There is no need for
this direction as long as we
m mean what it meant in the
the apostles, and keep it in
ith faith in Christ.

ns and Answers.

nd there is a disposition on ome of our churches to aban- rnational Sunday-school Les- ou think this a wise policy in act that we advocate Christian are supposed to be broad and uld you advise such a course, you not think it would be a iscussion at our next Nation- n? Do you not think it best t believe it wise to take such a t await the action of our con- e giving up the International
Lee D. Martin.

io.

we know, the disposition to International Sunday-school ery limited among us. In the is an opposition series being hich its advocates claim to be mony with modern methods of y. The general feeling, how- hout the religious world is that ;es of a uniform series of les- weigh the benefits to be gained ion of some other series. No hat the International Sunday- ons are chosen with infallible hat there may not be improve- in future as there have been in stead of abandoning the Inter- ies of lessons, it seems to us wiser course would be to graft ies whatever good points may d by any other series, when approved themselves to the judgment of the majority of aders. It would be entirely is subject to receive consider- Sunday-school feature of our onvention, but to make such n profitable it should receive l thought beforehand by some competent to treat the subject.

---

xplain in the CHRISTIAN-EVAN- *llowing passages of Scripture: 1:44; 2. Luke 18:8?*
S. A. Q.

irst passage reads: "And he on this stone shall be broken ut on whomsoever it shall fall, tter him as dust." The lan- t of our Savior in conversation ws who opposed His claims. referred them to the Scriptures

which the builders rejected,
s made the head of the corner.''

igure of the stone that leads to e, the meaning of which is our querist. If one falls on a likely to be bruised or broken the fall; but if the stone be a nd should fall on a person, it a sudden end of him. The one who stumbles over Christ and becomes offended at Him and refuses to receive Him, is certain to be broken to pieces; but if his attitude toward the Son of God be such as to call down upon him the anathema of Christ, he will not only be broken, but ground to powder. It is a difference, we take it, in degrees of punishment, growing out of different degrees or phases of oppo- sition to Christ. Whoever puts himself directly in the way of the progress of the kingdom of God is certain to be ground to powder. The stone which the builders re- jected and which has been made the head of the corner, is sure to fall upon every such one with tremendous power.

2. The second passage quoted is as follows: "Howbeit, when the Son of Man cometh shall he find faith on the earth?" The marginal reading is "the faith." This language is part of the parable spoken by Jesus to his disciples "to the end that they ought always to pray and not to faint." The parable is that of the unjust judge. As this unjust judge was led by the continual importunity of the widow to avenge her of her adversary, so it is argued, "Shall not God avenge his elect which cry to him day and night, and he is long-suffering over them?" The answer of this question is: "I say unto you that he will avenge them speedi- ly." Then comes the question of our Lord quoted above, as to whether the Son of Man when he cometh shall find the faith on the earth. As this avenging was to be done "speedily," we may suppose that the coming of the Son of Man referred to in the passage was also to take place speedily in connection with that avenging. Perhaps the same coming is here referred to that is spoken of in Matthew 16:28: "Verily I say unto you, there be some of them which stand here which shall in no wise taste of death till they see the Son of Man coming in his kingdom." This coming was at a time when the Jewish nation, as such, had rejected Christ, and when there was only a few of His faithful followers who received Him, and even they did not understand Him nor enter into sympathy with His large plans, until after Pentecost. With- out being dogmatic we are inclined to be- lieve that this is the coming to which Jesus refers in this passage, and that He cannot mean to raise the question as to whether He will find faith upon the earth at the final coming in the kingdom of His glory.

An evangelist who smokes cigars was asked, "Is it sinful to use tobacco?" He answered from the rostrum in substance: "The Scriptures do not condemn its use. If you think it sinful you had better not use it, for that would be sin for you. But if others think it not sinful and wish to use tobacco, it is none of your business." Would not the same reasoning apply to dancing, card-playing and the use of in- toxicants? *A Learner.*

It could be said concerning the "use of intoxicants," at least, that there is scriptural prohibition, but the line of argument adopted by the evangelist is not an entirely safe one. It *is* our business to seek to win our brethren from habits which we believe to be hurtful to themselves and unpleasant to others. Of course we must observe Christian courtesy in this as in everything else. The question was not put, perhaps, in the best form to the evan- gelist. If he had been asked, "Is the use of tobacco consistent with the highest type of Christian character?" or, "Would you discourage it in the use of young converts as an evil habit which had better be avoid- ed?" it would have been more difficult for him to answer without compromising his own position. However we may seek to justify our ourselves in the use of tobacco, it would shock our sense of the fitness of things to find out that Jesus was a smoker of the weed, or that any of the apostles were given to its use. We would not by any means say that no Christian uses to- bacco, but are we not justified in saying that smoking or chewing is not consistent with the highest ideal of Christian life? Ought we not to strive after the highest ideal?

In a revival meeting one accepts the invi- tation, makes confession and asks to be baptized in the river (about half a mile from the chapel). The evangelist and pas- tor urge the use of the baptistery as being more convenient. The candidate refuses to be immersed in the baptistery, contend- ing for his preference of places. The evangelist and pastor refuse to go to the river, holding that his refusal to use the baptistery is evidence that he is not peni- tent enough to receive baptism. How about it? *Disciple.*

We think it would have been more in harmony with the Spirit and teaching of Jesus if the evangelist and pastor had accommodated themselves to the weakness of their brother, and have gone with him to the river and baptized him there. They could have trusted to time and to an in- crease of spiritual understanding to have removed the objection to the baptistery. "He that is weak in the faith, receive ye, but not to doubtful disputation."

JUSTIFICATION.

A. M. CHAMBERLAIN.

To the categorical question, "Does God deal in realities, or figments?" the enlight- ened Christianity of any age unhesitatingly replies, "Realities." Yet, philosophers have oft constructively attributed to the Godhead figment rather than reality in the development of theological systems.

In our English Bibles are several words— just, righteous, justify, justification, right- eousness—used to translate words framed in Hebrew and Greek from roots found in the Hebrew "*tsaddig*" and Greek "*dikaios*." In the New Testament the same word, "*dikaiooma*," besides one or two other renderings, is four times translated right- eousness, and once justification. The two other occurrences of "justification" in our version are found as renderings of the Greek "*dikaiosis*." The adjective "*dikaios*" is rendered right, righteous, just (once meet). The verb "*dikaio-oo*" is rendered, with few exceptions, justify.

It is not necessary to define for the average intelligence such terms as just and righteous; and that same intelligence, if left to itself, and undazzled by speculative sophism, would quite certainly affirm that just and justify, "*dikaios*" and "*dikaio- oo*," are intended to express close and real relationship. To justify is to show *to be* just. But turn to the dictionary, or appeal to the learned, and you will apparently find that the average intelligence is not a safe guide upon such delicate questions. The Standard Dictionary informs us that in theology to justify is "to regard and treat as righteous and lawfully free from the penalty of sin, on the ground of Christ's mediatorial work." The new Universal Dictionary is, perhaps, even more specific. According to it, "justification is a forensic act by which God declares the sinner righteous and acquits him of all guilt, on account of the meritorious life and atoning death of Jesus Christ, the Redeemer, imputed to the sinner and received by faith alone."

After conning these deliverances of theological wisdom, the average intelligence will undoubtedly begin to puzzle. Does God, then, regard as righteous, and declare to be righteous, those who are not righteous? Go into court and, if you hear justification pleaded in reply to an offence charged, you find that "justification," in so far as it consists in plea of counsel and decision of judge or jury, is simply the expounding and establishing by adequate evidence *of pre-existent facts*. Are we to believe, then, that on the contrary God's Word makes a thing true apart from the fact, or rather that God's Word is always in accordance with the facts? In other words, when we say, "God's Word is always true," do we bear tribute to his power, or to his probity? The first hypothesis seems to lead into interminable confusion of thought as to God's nature and the verities of life.

The question is, assuredly, not of little importance. The prevalence of this "theological" conception of justification is responsible, who shall doubt, for low ideals of Christian life. Christ's mediatorial work is considered, not as the revolution of sinful life, the establishment of true and just ideals of obligation and the inspiration of a fervor for holiness, but it is a piece of chicane by which the eyes of God are self-blinded, and by processes akin to incantation and necromancy the soul is garbed to masquerade in an alien righteousness. Happy result! The penalty of sin has been escaped; but how about the sin itself? This is ritualism, the righteousness of the Scribes and Pharisees, no more, while the words of the Master are, "Except your righteousness exceed the righteousness of the Scribes and Pharisees, ye shall in no case enter into the kingdom of heaven."

In the application of common terms to the working of the human and divine, it is not to be overlooked that, in the nature of things, the larger application will pertain to the divine. Slight examination will show in regard to this term justify an almost generic difference in breadth in its application to the action of God and man. Man, in general, justifies or attempts to justify himself as to his past, but God is ever looking to justify humanity in regard to its future. Isaiah 53:11 declares, "By his knowledge shall my righteous (*'tsaddig'*) servant jusifty (*'tsaddig'*) many." Surely, this is the promise of a real work to be accomplished in the souls of men, a partaking of the divine nature to be theirs, a transformation into the likeness of his Son, which God purposed for his children. Of similar purport is the statement of Paul in the fifth chapter of the Roman letter, "For, as by one man's disobedience many were made sinners, so by the obedience of one shall many be made righteous." Unless we are ready to hold that the sinning was only an appearance, or accounting, or imputing, it would seem we are shut up to the conclusion that the righteousness to be established is as real as the righteousness of God. In the same direction points the language of the Roman letter, 3:25, 26, saying, "Being justified as a matter of gift by his favor through the redemption that is in Christ Jesus, whom God set forth by his blood, a herald of reconciliation through faith, in order to reveal God's righteousness in passing over in forbearance the sins of past generations [cf. Acts 17:30: *'The times of ignorance, therefore, God overlooked,'*] as looking toward the full revelation of his righteousness at the present time, purposing to be both righteous himself, and to render righteous the soul born of faith in Jesus." The writer assumes whatever of responsibility is involved in a new rendition of a passage of no little intricacy. Not stopping for lengthy exegesis, we may note in passing that no explanation of the closing statement can satisfy thoughtful men which practically makes God the slave of some abstraction known as "offended justice." It certainly comports much better with the language and with God's revelation of himself to men to judge that the justice for which he was solicitous in himself in the eyes of men, was absolute impartiality as between Jew and Gentile, and paternal regard for all his children whose sin was of ignorance. By the same logic, because God has shown himself dealing in realities, the righteousness of the soul born of faith in Jesus, is to be taken as a real righteousness, an abandonment of the sin which had sullied the old life, and not some figment of "imputation."

The natural tendency of that widely current "imputation" conception of "justification by faith in Christ" is to put a premium on sluggish Christian life. Not asserting that this is the sole cause of widespread lethargy, it may freely be affirmed, from the personal experience of many, that there is nothing in such concept to inspire a battle against the evils that sadden life. It may produce resignation, but not resolution. No assertion is intended or implied, that modern theology ignores the question of personal holiness, the burden, was it not, of Christ's ministry; but it may be truthfully affirmed that to-day, in many instances, "the holy life" is made subsidiary to the main proclamation of a salvation constructively formal and ritualistic. We are saved and accepted of God primarily on account of certain observances and professions (our own or even our parents'), as a result of which a righteousness not ours is graciously attributed to us and the doors of heaven are unbarred. As a sequence of this acceptance it is presumed that a measure of gratitude will prompt to a greater or less imitation of the virtues of Jesus, but the impression is indubitably left on many minds that a passive receptivity will suffice if an active zeal for holiness does not spotaneously arise. May not the day of judgment reveal at last that the awful apathy of the modern church in face of ravage of rum and grip of greed in social life is the outgrowth of low trains of thought whose roots are concepts of past centuries of stupendous ignorance and but formal allegiance to Christ?

One need scarce hesitate to assert that
while refinements of doctrine have ch
and systems of theology have been m
in recent generations there is, aft
not a primary concept of religious
which has not been carefully preser
hallowed entirety in the form which
acquired a half millennium ago, und
molding influences of an age of into
tyranny, vicious administration and w
ing ignorance.

But, lest charge be brought that
statements are iconoclastic, smacking
arrogance of an irreverent age and
and presumptious scholarship, it m
well to review briefly the changes i
concept of "justification" which have
place in the long centuries of Ch
thought. To be sure, there is th
Bible, and to that some appeal ha
ventured that such is the nature
mind, and this brief historical glan
not be without value in giving
balance to our considerations.

Among the first of the "Fathers
Church" to give large attention to sy
atic theology was Augustine, Bish
Hippo, who lived in the latter part
fourth and the early part of the fift
turies. His concept of the meani
justification was practically that
preceding argument. For exampl
says, "God justifies the ungodly, no
by remitting the evil he has done but a
imparting love, which rejects the ev
does the good." And again: "The ung
justified by the grace of God; *i. e.*,
being ungodly, is made righteous."
idea received the greater em
from Augustine, because in his own
his acceptance of Christ had beer
abandonment of a vicious and licen
life; and, indeed, it retained its theor
vitality undiminished for at least a
sand years. To this day it persists,
modified at bottom, in the dogmatics
Roman Church.

Likewise, Martin Luther who, wh
great reformer, was not a great theolo
whose theology at least as gathered fro
writings, was not always clear nor co
ent, held to the vital development o
Christ in men as the essential eleme
justification. At the same time it is
admitted he held that Bernard's state
of the imputation of Christ's righteou
to men was a correct exposition of
teachings. Abelard, in the twelfth cen
and Socinus, and Osiander, about the
of the great Reformation, also gave
phatic expression to their opinions
the reality of the righteousness
Christ was to work among and in men.

In spite of modern claims of antiq
the idea of the imputation of Ch
righteousness to men dates as a recog
factor in theology, only a few cent
before the time of Luther. An
Aquinas and Bernard, the product o
age of the cloister, were its peculiar c
pions. With such a history it ma
asked, how comes the wide acceptanc
day of the doctrine of "justification"
"imputed righteousness?"

Two things have conspired to pr
this effect. In the first place, alongsi
the theory of the Roman Church, w
asserted the actuality of the reform
effected in human character by Ch
denominating it justification, develop
widespread belief in the doctrine of su
erogation. This idea was based on b

y God as
exceeded
ngs who
law and
d service
uity" of
interest
with the
ly minis-
ceived as
titute for
ance, by
d against
sedly in-
true, no
med the
ned great
more as
rupt age.
vas prac-
eousness
imputa-
st to men
was the
ak of the
s not in
ly minis-
ghteous-
ed in as-
of Christ
mystical
he era of
thout af-
tification

ck to the
rlier, was
otal de-
nal sin."
was pro-
f in his
was held
the race,
ndividual
om God.
nputed to
arked, in
mpts to
int, how-
ning that
rthly life
deliberate
e. After
ctrine of
idea be-
imputed
ld make
f Adam.
mon ideas
s to con-
le that an
save it.
om reali-
r. There
d or not,
lam's, but
ness our

t church
st of con-
a refor-
rist. As
nearly all
ent attest
the other
with the
which has
Protest-
n is an
de. The
ationship,

but it is the part of the other to develop and mold the life.

In view of these apparently natural relationships, there is a charming *naivete* in the surprise of some modern theologians, sure of their own infallibility, at the "*odd*" inversion of terms which marks the writings of the early "Fathers," and at the peculiar way in which they "*confounded*" justification with sanctification.

In conclusion, let it be noted that an exception to the ordinary translation of "*dikaio-oo*" as "justify" occurs in Rev. 22:11 which, there being no possibility of giving it a hypodermic injection of "theology" has been rendered into the vernacular, "He that is righteous let him be rigtteous, let him be righteous still." Inasmuch as we are English and readily understand the Saxon tongue, would we lose anything if we heard less of justifying and more of making righteous?

DANGERS OF THE MINISTERIAL OFFICE.*

BY J. J. MORGAN.

It is not the aim of this address to mention all the dangers of the ministerial office, nor to fully discuss those herein mentioned. The discussion which is to follow is expected to cover these points.

The Century Dictionary defines a gentleman, "A man of good family; a man of gentle birth." The sixth definition is, "An apparatus used in soldering pewter ware." Between these two gentlemen, the one of gentle birth and the one used for soldering pewter ware, is room for great variety.

The same is true of the ministerial office. In it there is great variety. We may range all the way from the sexton to the bishop. But I wish to confine this address to the ministry of preaching, and even here there is great variety. In the city of London at the same time Liddon and Spurgeon, Joseph Porter and Newman Hall preached the Word. What a variety the ministry of our country and our church presents! We cannot have before us any one person as a model for all. Indeed, the first danger to the ministerial office is the tendency in some souls to mold all in one pattern. In the Established Church in England all the ministry dress and drawl alike, which makes the ministry tediously monotonous. The chief charm of the Disciples is the variety there seen. The apostles were not made into one mold, even under the personal influence of Jesus.

The second danger is a very marked disposition to undervalue the ministerial office on the part of the ministry. It is not an unusual thing to hear unappreciative comments made by them, which shows the low esteem in which it is held by them. We often hear it said, "I can make a living at something else;" *i. e.*, I am in it for a living. It is more than a mere occupation. "That a man stand and speak of spiritual things to men." Said Carlyle, "It is beautiful. It is among the beautifulest, most touching things to be seen on earth. Whom have we to compare with him? A man making endeavor to save the souls of men. No public functionary is worthier than he."

Dr. John A. Broaddus, that princely man of God, said: "I do not envy our senators or legislators; I do not envy our statesmen or warriors; I do not envy our President or rich men, but I do envy your pastors. I would rather be pastor of a church than anything else." And Paul said, "I magnify mine office."

The next danger I mention is that the minister will undervalue himself. "We have this glory in earthen vessels." "The vessel is nothing; the minister is nothing; the message is all." This leads men sometimes to live a little below the best it is possible for them to attain. "What you are," said Emerson, "speaks so loud I can't hear what you say." The message is greatly affected by the messenger. He who preaches should be a superb man. He owes it to his people; he owes it to himself; he owes it to his fellow-ministers and to his Master to make the best of himself possible in every attainment, in purity, in knowledge, in spirituality, in goodness. "How beautiful are the feet of them that preach the gospel of peace!"

Many years ago this act was passed by the Massachusetts Legislature: "A man should be converted and show some signs of spiritual life before he is licensed to preach the gospel." It ought to be in force still. Our Lord said to Peter, "When thou art converted, strengthen thy brethren."

A danger not so common as the last needs mention here. It is the danger of over self-esteem. I do not think this is common, but I have heard of some cases. A young man last winter was invited to dine with a preacher. He afterward reported the conversation: "He did nothing the whole time but compare himself with other ministers, and he always got the bouquet." This is very injurious to one who stands as the representative of Jesus, and leads to many vain and foolish things. He will appeal to the populace and to the galleries and seek his own exaltation. It is dangerous, fatally so, to the minister of the gospel. We are glad it is so very rare.

Another danger against which I wish to warn you is a tendency to exaggerate statement of facts in the pulpit. It is not a new weakness, but it is none the better for its age. It seems to be a law of nature that bad things grow worse and good things better with age. Jeremy Taylor speaks of a city of fifteen millions population! Daniel Webster said: "Not one in fifty can state a thing as it occurred, without exaggeration or diminution." And Burke said: "Every word in a sentence is one of the feet on which it walks. To lengthen or shorten one may change its course." Correct statement is difficult to obtain, but it is worth the effort.

Closely allied to this is the danger of extravagance of expression—high, overwrought language and extravagant imagery. Did you ever hear Isaac Errett or J. S. Lamar draw a scene? It was beautiful, chaste. Said Bro. Errett to the speaker just before his death: "I do not want to live till I am in the way of young men. I looked out at my window the other day, and I saw little leaves peeping out [it was spring] on some twigs. But old leaves were hanging on to other twigs and the young leaves had to push them out of the way."

Did any of you ever hear J. S. Lamar in his sermon on "Lights in the World" tell of the candle he read by in time of the war? "As it burned on, great sentinels

---

*Address, delivered at the Ministerial Association in Carrolton, Mo., and requested for publication by the Association.

stood round the light; the wick burned till it turned down and curved round all, obstructing the light, till I took the snuffers and trimmed them away. Brethren, keep your lights trimmed and burning." These were chaste and master-strokes. But too many daub the scene with overwrought language and tremendous physical effort. It is the mark of mastery to be chaste, reserved. Many years ago, Mr. Beecher said: "He who would be heard must paint pictures or tell stories." But remember, it is a gift to paint or tell stories. A story badly told or a picture badly painted detracts from the sermon, obscures the thought.

One says of Renan: "He very skillfully undermines Christianity by profusion of praise. He comes to the tomb of the Savior, not to weep and worship like the women of the gospel, but to stifle with profusion of spices. He does not deal a blow. No, he embalms, but the effect is the same."

One danger is the use of hackneyed, commonplace phrases, that detract from the sermon by giving it an antiquated appearance. I saw a little miss dressed up in her mother's wedding dress. She looked very antiquated. "Too much of the preaching of to-day seems to be the preaching of yesterday, in the language of yesterday." It will repay the minister to take the pains to rid their sermons of these set phrases.

I note another danger which, though not common, as I see it, sometimes appears and strews destruction in its path. I speak of unwholesome rivalries, sometimes running into jealousy, or close to it. Sometimes symptoms appear when we would least expect it. I only mention this, for it is too coarse to have a place in the heart of even a half-cultured ministry.

The failure to realize and rightly use its powers is one of the dangers of the ministry. If the consciousness of the power latent in the ministry now could be aroused, what could it not do in his name?

Like our fathers, ignorant of the powers that lay in the electricity about them, they did not summon it to service, so lies the unrealized, the undiscovered power of the ministry of Jesus Christ. "Nothing vice so dreads, nothing the knave so hates, as the ministry," said Parkhurst. "Not the press, not the publication, but the pulpit must clear the atmosphere." When we know we are right a sort of omnipotence takes possession of us and devils flee away.

This power carries with it tremendous responsibilities. The wrong use of power has wrought devastation in the world. O, what ruin lies in the wrong use of this God-given power of the ministerial office! Worse, if possible, than the disuse is the misuse of the power we hold. To you is this power essential, but examples, be it sadly said, are not wanting in the history of the ministry, of the grossest use of it. We believe, happily, the wrong use is fast passing, and we see to-day a solid front presented by those in the ministerial office in the uplifting of depraved and fallen, struggling humanity toward the image and likeness of the perfect man, Christ Jesus.

Warrensburg, Mo.

University Church and the main building of Drake University have been frescoed. Over five hundred students are already enrolled in all departments of the University and more expected.

THE CROSS VERSUS CHRIST.

D. S. HENKLE.

A great majority of nominal Christians worship the cross more than the Christ. The cross is lifted up, and exhibited to the public gaze, while Christ is totaly obscured by the shadow of the cross. The doctrine of a redemption purchased as a sort of commodity on the cross, by Jesus Christ, has laid the foundation for this species of idolatry. The cross, as a symbol of this form of salvation or redemption has been in a measure substituted for the *living* Christ, who alone can save the soul. Faith in the *doctrine* of the blood of Christ as an atonement for sin can be professed by the vilest sinner on earth; and a profession of this faith may admit him to baptism and church membership. Expectation of reward or fear of punishment has caused thousands of persons to make a profession of this faith. Thousands of ministers of the gospel have no other conception of the religion of Christ than an acceptance of approved creeds, dogmas and doctrines. They do not receive the things of the Spirit of God, for they are foolishness unto them, neither can they know them, because they are spiritually discerned.

The religion of Christ is a religion of *life*—spiritual life, God-life. No man can get the religion of Christ outside of Christ. Christ is the religion himself. His religion is eternal *life*. He is that life. Spiritual life, without which no one can be saved, is the direct product of God. The Word is the seed of life, Christ is the type after whom this life is formed, the life thus formed is Christ. This Christ-life is multiplied just as many times as there are children born from above. Christ was "the first-born of every creature." He was the grain of wheat (John 12:24) that fell into the ground and died, that it might bring forth much fruit. This *fruit* is the *life* begotten in the heart of the believer. This is the "new creature" of which Paul speaks. This is the life that Paul lived by the faith of the Son of God. This is "*Christ in you* the hope of glory." This is the answer to the prayer of the Master (John 17:21), "That they may all be one, as thou Father art in me and I in thee." There is no salvation outside of Christ, nor can doctrines concerning Christ be substituted for him. He is the way. No man can go to the Father except through him. The *plan* of salvation, then, is Christ. *He* "is made unto us wisdom, and righteousness, and sanctification, and redemption." These graces are only to be had *in him*. His work is internal. He is revealed *in* the Christian, not *by* the Christian. The life that the Christian lives is the life of Christ. The "old man" has been crucified with Christ, and buried with him; the "new man" *is the resurrection* life of Christ. The process of salvation, then, is not a lifting up of the *cross* but of *Christ*. When Christ is found in the heart, *he lives* the subject into eternal life.

Those who try to *imitate* Christ, to act like Christ, and to look like Christ, will be miserable failures. The Christian is either *a christ* or a base counterfeit of *him*. The Christian is not *the* Christ who was anointed with the fullness of the Spirit, but a christ, the product of the same life that constituted his person. By living in *Christ* and Christ living in us we have as a result perfect *unity*—not union *with* him, but
ity *in* him.

When this high standard shall have l
reached, both in doctrine and in prac
we shall have one Lord, one faith,
baptism, and sectarianism shall be bani
into eternal oblivion.

Current Religious Thou

Of the very simple, appropriate,
pressive address delivered at the funer
Prince Bismarck, by "Pastor Westph
published in the New York Observer,
reproduce the following paragraphs u
their merits:

Not yours alone, beloved, has been this l
How the whole German land, with our h
ored emperor at its head, is united in the
row that mourns over this bier! And yet, wh
we sorrow over this painful separation, h
we not great cause for thankfulness as
stand beside the dead hero, this veteran
fourscore years and three? Must we not g
God thanks at the close of such a life as t
which God hath followed with his goodness
mercy, and thus marvelously gathered
scattered threads of so long a life into
rounding out of his gracious plan toward
man, and the perfecting of his Christian ch
acter? Did not his life, according to the wo
of the psalmist, become noble and precio
because it was filled with labor and sorr
Has not his life been manifestly under the g
cious guidance of God, so that in view of it
may well say, "The counsel of the Lord
good, and endureth forever?" Has not
man on the battlefield of life achieved victo
and gathered laurels as few have done? W
the triumphs and burdens of his most resp
sible office were laid aside, did he not by
side of his most beloved consort, and in
circle of his own household, find again t
happiness and well-earned repose? And a
God had crowned with blessing his work
purposes for the beloved fatherland, did he
grant to him a quiet eventide of life in his c
beloved Friedrichsruh? That restful event
was indeed clouded by loss of the faithful pa
ner of his joys and sorrows. Nevertheless
was made glad by the precious family life t
circled round him, it was beautified by the l
of those who were left to him. It was m
glad by the honors which his imperial ma
ever and anon showered upon him. It
made glad by the reverence of the gr
multitude who delighted to pay him the tr
ute of their gratitude. As an old ailm
broke out anew with intensest pain, and
was to be feared that life's last days wo
bring him a fearful and prolonged wrestle w
death, he drew near to God with earn
prayers for deliverance. He begged for a qu
death, a sweet release. Without any mo
agony he has gone to a better world. He
died peacefully in his own Sachsenwald, he
fallen asleep in the presence of his whole
sembled household. Therefore do we g
thanks unto our God this day and say,
hath done all things well.

But would we not still have cause to mo
if we could in such an hour thank God for te
poral blessings only? Were it not poor co
fort if, when we lost our dear ones, we did
know that the immortal explains the mor
That should be recognized by us here and n
Did not light eternal illumine his earthly l
The impression which the Christian nurtur
his father's house made upon him in his yo
he carried with him to his life's end.
without a certain regard to the Christian d
trine of the Trinity did he choose for his mo
In trinitate robur; and in a firm faith in Je
Christ, our Lord and Savior, he has depar
from us and rests with God. That faith
parents strove to impart—that consciousnes
the dependence of God which a Schleiermac
strove to deepen—that he himself has told
upheld him in carrying the fearful burden
responsibility laid upon him. In this soil g
the graces that seemed to us not only wond
ful, but most attractive. What was it but
fear of God that made him fearless before m
What but his recognition of the will of G
that standeth firm and fast, made him firm
unyielding in holding by that which he
lieved to be right and good? Was it not
trust in God that lent him that truthful s
cerity? Was it not out of his Christian c
sciousness that his humility grew, which m
him so friendly and gracious toward the co
mon people? His personal piety, which
one who came near to him could question, i
did not manifest itself ostentatiously, yet
wrougut in him that men felt themselves
only in the presence of a great man, but w
was better, a man of the highest Christ
character.

—One of the best known of the younger pastors, who has been recently called from one important field to another writes, "I am very thankful that the —— church sent a committee to —— to ascertain the influence and effect of my preaching and pastoral work here. It is one of the joys of a minister's life that when he stands boldly for what is right the people will stand by him. I wish our churches would more generally follow this example. We preachers would then stand or fall according as our influence in any community has been felt for good or for bad or not at all." We join with this pastor in the wish that the example of the congregation referred to would become the general custom. In all cases where the preacher is not personally known to the congregation, it is far superior in every respect to the custom of inviting preachers to follow each other in a long procession of "trial sermons." A wise committee, on the ground where the preacher has lived and labored any length of time, will discover more as to the real character and ability of the preacher than they would receive from any number of "trial sermons." Such a practice would lead to longer and more satisfactory pastorates.

—P. A. Seguin, an ex-priest, whose membership is now in the University Place Church, Des Moines, Ia., has for some time been endeavoring to establish a home for ex-priests and ex-nuns, but is not succeeding as he would like. In a letter from F. L. Davis, of Dows, Ia., on this subject, he suggests to the churches of Iowa that the matter be taken up by the state board as a part of their missionary work, or that a special day be set apart for offerings for this special work. While there is no doubt as to the need for such a home and the goodness of the enterprise it is not certain that either of the suggestions made by Bro. Davis is practical. However, he has made the suggestion for the Iowa brethren and we are sure that they will deal justly and wisely with it if brought before them.

—The CHRISTIAN-EVANGELIST thinks that "party names are a necessity," and so think those who believe in denominations.—*Christian Leader*.

The statement of the Leader omits an important qualification. The CHRISTIAN-EVANGELIST "thinks that party names are a necessity" *as long as parties exist*. Does not the Christian Leader believe this? If not, why does he say, in the same editorial, that "a Baptist editor in debate with a Disciple, quoted the CHRISTIAN-EVANGELIST," etc.? Why this distinction? Why did not Bro. Bell say that "a disciple editor in debate with a disciple preacher," etc.? He wanted to be intelligible, and in order to be so he must make the very distinction he criticises the CHRISTIAN-EVANGELIST for making! Such are the inconsistencies of the anti-distinction craze.

—If the doctrine of repentance after death is a Baptist doctrine we have not read in the past as we ought. Yet it has come to us by way of the grapevine telegraph that the head and front of one of our leading Baptist colleges announced himself in a public address before a Sunday-school gathering, not very long ago, as believing such a doctrine. As soon as we get the facts spelled out and the notes all in, "we'll print 'em."—*Baptist News*.

Look out for a heresy trial in the columns of the Baptist News! By the way, what *is* the "Baptist doctrine" concerning eschatology? Where will we find it formulated? We take it, from the foregoing, that there must be some well-defined position on the subject among Baptists from which they are not likely to depart. Will the News tell us where that position is stated in an authentic form?

—Hiram College has started out to find the names of 50,000 persons who will unite in an effort to find for it an endowment, and the articles appearing in our columns each week from its president, E. V. Zollars, are preparatory to that work. This is a great movement and if successful will mark a new epoch in the history of that institution.

—The CHRISTIAN-EVANGELIST, of St. Louis, is one of the very best of Disciple papers, but it is not satisfying all of its constituency, because it is suspected of being a little shaky on the subject of baptismal remission.—*Journal and Messenger*.

We would regret to know that we are "suspected of being a little shaky on the subject of baptismal remission." We repudiate it as promptly as we do baptismal regeneration. So does every other intelligent advocate of our religious position. We have never uttered an uncertain note on this question and should not be considered "shaky" on it. Only God can forgive sins. To thrust an ordinance to the front, where Christ ought to be, is one of the mistakes of Christendom. We believe that a convicted sinner, seeking for a "good conscience" and the assurance of remission of sins, should submit to baptism as a command of Christ (1 Pet. 3:21), and as one of the commands on which he promises remission of sins (Mark 16:16; Acts 2:38, *et al.*). But this is not *baptismal* remission any more than it is *repentance*-remission or *faith*-remission. Indeed, faith-remission would be less objectionable, because faith includes the other conditions. But we would not give even faith this place. It is only the channel through which God acts in the pardon of sin. Let us give Christ the pre-eminence in all things.

—Prof. B. A. Jenkins has been spending the month of September at Macatawa, dividing his time about equally between steering a sailboat over Macatawa Bay and studying the New Testament in Greek, preparatory to his work in Butler Bible College. If he proves as successful in his professional chair in guiding his students through the problems of New Testament exegesis as he is in managing a sailboat in a stiff breeze, his boys need not fear theological shipwreck.

—The Sunday-school Union, of this city, is organizing a class to be composed of pastors, superintendents and teachers of the Sunday-schools, of this city, for Bible study, and has secured D. R. Dungan, pastor of Mt. Cabanne Church, for its teacher. The first meeting of this class will be in the Holland Building, West Side, 7th St., between Olive and Pine Streets, on Saturday, October 1st, at 3:30 to 4:30 P. M. This is an important movement, and the selection of Dr. Dungan for the teacher is not only a compliment to him and to our people in this city, but also a selection that means much for the class and for the Bible-schools and churches of the city.

—The venerable John G. Fee, of Berea, Ky., writes: "I am pleased beyond power of expression with your reply to the question of J. S. Stone as presented in your issue of Sept. 8th. There is a simple basis for union—faith in Christ and baptism in his name. God give you strength to stand ever for this simple but true basis of union."

—While there is much trash, slush and villainy in the newspapers of the land, yet in them appear valuable articles on all subjects, scientific, moral and religious, and if these could be preserved and systematically arranged in a scrapbook the reader would soon be amply rewarded for his trouble in the unique and valuable books he would be able to add to his library.

—Persons who love to do little deeds of kindness for invalids have an opportunity in the Invalid's Visitor, formerly the Shut-in-Visitor, a monthly published by Kate Sumner Burr, at Williamson, N. Y. The unique feature of this paper is its letters from invalids in each number, in which they comfort and cheer each other. Of course you will send them the CHRISTIAN-EVANGELIST and Our Young Folks in addition to the Visitor for their comfort. What a grand work it would be to see that all shut-ins or invalids were thus regularly supplied with all three of these journals.

—The Cumberland Presbyterian, Sept. 22nd, says that an elder in the Ushigome church, Tokio, Japan, who became convinced t only immersion is baptism and so taught in Sunday-school, was removed from his of for the offense by the session and the act was sustained by the Presbytery and the Syn and yet in the same article it is insisted t "the mode of baptism shall not be made essential!" Why then was the elder remo from his office? In teaching immersion he scriptural, catholic and safe. Sprinkling Christian baptism is unscriptural, secta and dangerous.

lor, of Chicago, who writes so
in this issue of our paper con-
thany C. E. Reading Courses,
ssed as one of the very earliest
important educational enter-
was the one who moved the
a committee by our C. E. rally
City, in 1896, to carry out the
e by our National C. E. Super-
is was the very first formal
to inaugurate these Reading

ition made in July and August
C. W. B. M. auxiliaries is still
be for the next two or three
president or secretary of your
ot yet brought the matter be-
ty, call their attention to it at
ng. If they have not yet re-
osition write for it at once. A
unity is offered your auxiliary.
depleted treasury. Educate
ng missionary lines. Address
shing Co.

ng story, which appeared in a
of the Religious Herald, is re-
cunning and crafty use of the
d shows how incompetent any
en is to pass judgment upon the
tual state of those professing to
o Christ. It takes the fiery
fe to reveal the true heart of
is story was told the Religous
J. C. Hiden, of Richmond,

was once preaching in a meet-
onsiderable interest was mani-
umber of persons confessed their
In those days it was common
for baptism to tell their experi-
number of candidates had told
e and been received for bap-
nan in the gallery—a wild, wick-
low—said to a companion sitting
Pshaw! that is all foolishness.
ere to that bench, and give in
rience as any of them.'' ''No,
said his companion. ''Well,
dollars that I'll do it.'' And
en. It was some little time be-
vitation was given; and mean-
nion had contrived a note to the
g him of the bet. When the
given again, the young man
and was at once confronted by
who held the note in his hand.
ke that bet?'' ''Yes,'' said
n, ''and that bet was the
onviction. When I began to
rible wickedness of my conduct,
med with grief, and I am here
sin, and to accept Jesus Christ
' He acted all the signs of the
ce, was received and baptized,
e dollars. Upon the whole, I
the most daring piece of wick-
eard of, and I was not surprised
addus told me the young man
serable death.

we publish a paper by J. J.
Dangers of the Ministry,'' which
reading. Bro. Morgan is a vig-
nd writer and knows the short-
chief points of his subject.

lsewhere an article on Chautau-
attle, of Virginia, clipped from
Herald. Our readers will enjoy
the high compliment paid by a
Baptist minister, of conservative
H. L. Willett, of the Univer-
), but because of its excellent
Chautauqua, and the fair, frank
e article manifests.

ition made by J. Fraise Richard,
City, in our last number, in re-
ystematic arrangement of peri-
e in our national library, is a vast-
e. A great stack of journals on
ing object to one in search of a
le in some unknown number,
ssification of the articles from
would not only facilitate the
t, but would stimulate the search
. It seems to us that the sug-
ractical one and susceptible of
on.

—A. M. Chamberlain's study of ''Justification'' in this paper will be read with interest, being a somewhat vigorous criticism upon the orthodox doctrine of ''Imputed Righteousness.''

—We want to say, "Them's my sentiments,'' and add a loud amen! to the following plain words from the New York Observer, of Sept. 1st:

Alcholism ruins the constitution and character of the individual, and thus inevitably undermines the vigor and virtue of the state. Sapping the strength of the republic, by just so much it renders progress more difficult and success more uncertain.

Therefore, there is nothing either patriotic or sacred in the rum traffic. ''Prejudice'' against it may well continue to grow. It is un-American as well as ungodly. A barroom in this city bears the name of, ''The American Flag.'' Another calls itself ''The School.'' But what right has the saloon as saloon, in other words as the destroyer of the nation's best interests, to the proud symbol of nationality and freedom? And what sort of a ''school'' must that be where glasses rattle over a bar and youth learns lessons of disorder and riot? The truth is that Americanism is in peril most of all from alcoholism. And the proper thing for our people to do is to declare of this pernicious evil with a mighty emphasis, ''We cannot longer afford it!''

—The article in this paper on the frequent abuse of the phrase ''Cross of Christ'' should not be overloooked. Just such gross ideas as are here pointed out are great hindrances to the growth of spirituality in any life or church.

—A. B. Maston, editor of the Australian Christian, writing of his visit to Lexington, Ky., while in this country last summer, says:

While in the city I have come in contact with the leaders in the educational enterprise, and have been deeply impressed with the great influence which they in this institution must wield. Bro. J. J. Haley came from Cynthiana to visit with me and attend the commencment exercises. Like the rest of humanity Bro. Haley shows slightly the ravages of time, but his heart and mind remain young. We visited together the most of one day and talked much of men and things in Australia. Bro. Hugh McLellan made a journey to Lexington to see me. Bro. McLellan has become a ripe scholar and a useful, progressive preacher in the very best sense. Better than that, he is not satisfied with past attainments, but his motto is, ''Onward.'' Will Edmonds also made a journey to see me. Bro. Edmonds is now preaching and is doing a steady, quiet work. To meet and talk with some of the leading minds of the Reformation has been a great joy to me.

—The following editorial advice of the Chicago Record to political parties and politicians is wise, just and timely and we trust will be heeded. It ought to be the intuitive, conscientious duty of every true American:

The war that recently has come to a close was not a Republican war nor a Democratic war. It was an American war, and as such it received the united support of the American people. The effort to make such a war an issue in politics, therefore, is likely to redound to the disadvantage of the party that tries to degrade patriotism into partisanship. The war is over. It was supported by all parties and by citizens regardless of party while it lasted. Now that it is a thing of the past the people will not relish having it made a cause of dissension and party bickering. Naturally a successful war tends to benefit the party in power. Let the Republicans consciously attempt to make party capital out of the war, however, and the people will resent it, and the natural tendencies will be more than counterbalanced by the revulsion in sentiment. Let the Democrats, on the other hand, pursue a nagging policy and make it manifest that their chief concern about the war is the fear that it may be productive of benefit to their opponents and their fears certainly will be fulfilled in liberal measure. That party will profit most from the war spirit that is in reality most patriotic in its attitude toward the war and that shows the least disposition to make it serve partisan advantage. Now that the war is over the candidates should return to the discussion of questions that should naturally constitute the issues of the campaign had there been no war. The party that is quickest to do this, and to turn entirely away from the war as a matter having anything to do with politics, will strengthen itself in popular favor. The people doubtless will be glad to honor with their votes any individual war horoes who may chance to be candidates, like Roosevelt in New York and Wheeleer in Alabama, but they do not care to have the war spirit played upon by stay-at-home politicians for their own personal and partisan benefit.

—The Standard, Chicago, says that a clergyman of that city received the following reply, along with many others, to a question sent out asking the business men and professional men of all classes why they did not attend church. It is worthy of careful thought:

The church is a dead place. It is too slow. Literary clubs talk books, athletes talk athletics and politicians talk politics in a way that makes one believe that they mean business. But the people of the church have not spirit enough to exchange ideas with their fellow-members. They can get excited over pink parties and ice cream socials, but that seems to be their limit. Now if the church people cannot get interested in religion, why should they expect us to show any interest in it?

—The Literary Digest quotes the following scathing remarks of the Belfast Witness (Presbyterian) on the present state of the evangelical churches:

The Belfast Witness is convinced that the victory of the evangelical over the sacerdotal is ''delayed if not hindered by the miserable divisions and subdivisions of the Evangelicals,'' and that ''as matters now stand, Presbyterian, Congregational, Methodist, Baptist, are overlapping each other like weasels, competing with one another like rival shopkeepers, countermining one another like armies at war; proselytizing and sheep-stealing instead of making aggressions on the unsaved.''

—In answer to a question in the CHRISTIAN-EVANGELIST of Sept. 8th, the following statement occurs: ''It is nowhere stated in what manner any apostle baptized his candidate—whether he went down into the water with him or stood on the edge of pool or stream and baptized him.'' How about the following Scripture: ''And he commanded the chariot to stand still: and they went down both into the water, both Philip and the Eunuch, and he baptized him' (Acts 8:38.) Homer nods sometimes.

C. P. EVANS.

As the Philip who baptized the Eunuch was not an apostle, however, the Homer who nods in this particular instance is not the editor of the CHRISTIAN-EVANGELIST.

—The Missouri state convention is in session this week, at Nevada, Mo. All the indications are favorable to a great convention. The editor in chief of this paper left Monday night for Nevada. Some of the St. Louis pastors will be present. But we are sorry to learn that the condition of Sister Abbott is such that Bro. Abbott will not be able to attend. Her departure is hourly expected at this writing. This will be sad news for the convention and a doubly deep sorrow to our secretary. But God can sanctify all our sorrows to our good and to the glory of his name.

—A partnership advertising club has been formed by the School of Evangelists, Kimberlin Heights, Tenn., somewhat after the chain letter method, for the purpose of selling Pres. Johnson's books to sustain the school. The new hall for this school has been completed and was dedicated Sept. 24th. About $400 indebtedness is on the building, for the payment of which Bro. Johnson is hoping and praying. To meet this he is making extra propositions on his books. As souvenirs of the dedication of the new hall beautifully printed cabinet size pictures of Bro. and Sister Johnson are being given to all inquiring friends and patrons of the school, which now has one hundred and forty students enrolled.

—Dr. F. M. Kirkham, editor of the Christian Oracle, will announce this week that he has sold his stock and entire interest in the Christian Oracle to J. H. Garrison, the editor of this paper. Dr. Kirkham, in the trade, takes the stock in the Pacific Christian Publishing Co. owned by J H. Garrison, and will remove to the Coast early in October, to take charge of the Pacific Christian. The Christian Oracle is to be continued, but fuller announcements will be made soon as to the plans which are now in process of maturing. Of course this arrangement in no way affects Bro. Garrison's relation to this paper nor to the Christian Pub. Co.

PERSONAL MENTION.

W. H. Cowell, Downing, Mo., is evangelizing in Scotland County, with good results.

R. E. L. Prunty, Unionville, began a meeting for J. T. Boone, Memphis, Mo., Sept. 19th, and the outlook is good for a fine meeting.

Allen Bridges, Humansville, Mo., is preaching for Arcola, the first, Walnut Grove the second, Aldrich, the third while he evangelizes the fourth Sunday in each month. Is now in a good meeting at Aldrich.

Isaac W. Bridges, Dunnegan Springs, Mo., is preaching at home the first, at Edison the second, at Mt. Tabor the third, while the fourth Sunday is being used in evangelistic work, having had good meetings at many points in Polk and Cedar Counties.

W. W. Witmer has closed his work at Terre Haute, Ind., and would be glad to visit or correspond with any church wanting the services of a preacher. Bro. Witmer is an efficient man.

L. H. Stine, of Paris, Mo., has accepted the work at Quincy, Ill., and will enter upon his work there soon.

F. G. Tyrrell and Bruce Wolverton each have briefs of one of their Sunday sermons in the St. Louis Republic, Monday morning. F. G. Tyrrell is the pastor of Central Christian Church and Bruce Wolverton pastor of the Second Christian Church in this city.

A reception is to be tendered to S. B. Moore, the new pastor of Compton Heights Christian Church, this city, on Friday evening of this week. Bro. Moore comes to this city from Galesburg, Ill.

C. C. Davis, pastor Christian Chapel, Davenport, Ia., was recently ordained to the ministry of the gospel. T. W. Grafton, pastor of the Christian Church at Rock Island, conducted the ordination ceremony. The ordination sermon was preached by I. N. McCash, of Des Moines Ia. Bro. Davis graduated from Drake University in June last and enters upon his first pastorate at Davenport.

A. C. Corbin, of Kansas, visited Odel, Ia., recently. His old Iowa friends in other parts of the state regret not seeing him.

Prof. P. O. Powell, of Missouri, has taken the chair of English Literature in Drake University.

Milton Brown, of Garden City, Kan., a member of the Kansas State Board of Christian Missions, called at this office last week on his way East to meet his wife. He expects to be at the Kansas state convention at Wellington, next week.

F. G. Tyrrell, of this city, is announced to preach the opening sermon of the Iowa state convention, at East Side Church, Des Moines, on Monday night of this week.

R. A. Thompson, who has been preaching at DeSoto for a few months as a temporary pastor, concludes his work there this month and is open to engagement for protracted meetings or for regular work with some church in need of an efficient regular minister. His home is at Odessa, Mo.

R. L. Cartwright, who preaches for the church at Morocco, Ind., and who has been visiting his people in Pettis Co., Mo., paid his respects to this office on his return to Morocco, last week. While in the city he visited the Orphans' Home and other places of interest.

S. W. Brown has resigned his work at Evansville, Ind., and will leave the field on the first of November, at which time this congregation will be in need of a preacher. Correspondents will please address J. R. Ferguson, Evansville, Ind.

Cards are out announcing the marriage of Miss Hattie Genevieve, daughter of Mr. and Mrs. W. P. Dorsey, to Mr. Edwin C. Cook, at Laddonia, Mo., Sept. 27th, 8 P. M. The CHRISTIAN-EVANGELIST extends congratulations to all the parties named.

Wallace Tharp, the new pastor at Crawfordsville, Ind., has been extended a hearty welcome to his new field of labor. Large audiences greeted his first discourses.

Isaac Rowyer, Milton, Ia., is now preaching for Prairie View the third, for Salem the fourth, both in Scotland County, Mo., while he is evangelizing half the time. Bro. Rowyer is just up from a very severe spell of sickness.

A. H. Williams, Canton, Mo., is preaching the first Sunday at Lawnridge, the second at Granger, the third at Darby, the fourth at Bently, Ill.

G. A. Ragan leaves Oskaloosa, Iowa, for the work of the ministry at the Irving Park Church, Chicago, Ill.

J. A. Grow, Downing, is now preaching the first Sunday at Bible Grove, the second at Coffey, the third at home, the fourth at Antioch, Scotland County, and is now in a very interesting meeting at Antioch.

The many friends of Gilbert Park, Mt. Zion, Mo., will regret to hear that he is preparing to move to Kansas, but it will be to the profit of Kansas.

F. M. Hooten, Bolivar, is now preaching for the brethren at Cave Springs the first Sunday, at Stockton the second, at Polk the third, and evangelizes the fourth.

C. C. Condra, Half Way, Mo., is preaching at home the second Sunday, at Concord the fourth, at Independence the first, while the third is used in evangelistic work.

The church at Ft. Recovery, Ohio, being unable to retain its pastor, J. S. Smith, for the reason of financial inability, commends him to any church wanting a preacher as a thoughtful young preacher worthy the esteem and confidence of any church to which he may be called.

Dr. H. G. Welpton sailed from San Francisco for Chu Cheo, China, on the 2nd inst. Dr. Welpton is a graduate of Drake University. He spent six months in New York taking special courses and qualifying himself for work in China.

Dr. Elliott I. Osgood and wife sailed from San Francisco on the 2nd inst They go to Lu Cheo Fu, China. Dr. Osgood is a graduate of Hiram College. After completing his course in Hiram he took his medical degree in Cleveland. Dr. Osgood will give most of his time to evangelistic work. Mrs. Osgood is a daughter of O. G. Hertzog. She also is a graduate of Hiram.

Mr. and Mrs. A. L. Chapman sailed from New York for Turkey on the 10th. Mr. Chapman is a graduate of Bethany College. He is a great-grandson of Thomas Campbell. Recently he has spent a year in Chicago University. While in the University he was pastor of the church at Evanston. Mrs. Chapman is also a graduate of Bethany. She taught for some time in the High School at Greensburg, Ind., her home. Subsequently she took the nurses' course in Louisville, Ky.

Miss Mildred Franklin and Dr. Ada McNeill left for India on the 10th. Dr. McNeill goes out under the auspices of the Foreign Society. Miss Franklin has two sisters already in India. She expects to labor in Hurda. She will take the place left vacant by the death of Miss Judson.

Mr. and Mrs. David Rioch have postponed their departure for one month. They did this at the request of the students and faculty of Butler College. The College proposes to give them a farewell reception.

Mr. and Mrs. W. D. Cunningham are under appointment as missionaries to Japan. Their sailing was delayed by sickness.

Teizo Kawai expects to leave Tacoma for Japan on the 25th. He has been in Drake University for three years. He goes back to preach to his own people at Akita, Japan.

N. A. Walker, of Ft. Wayne, Ind., recently spent a couple of weeks in Toledo, preaching on Lord's day for Bro. Huffer. He reports the two churches there doing a great and successful work. They are jointly starting a new mission. He also expects to attend a reunion of the churches in Wayne and Holmes Counties, Ohio, where he preached forty years ago.

W. T. Brooks, of Lodoga, Ind., writes that a church has asked him to find for it a preacher. The salary, first year, will be small.

W. E. Crabtree, of San Diego, Cal., was presented with a wheel, Aug. 10th, the anniversary of his 30th birthday, by his church.

B. B. Byler, of our editorial staff, writes that his meeting at Lexington, Ky., starts off encouragingly. The audiences are large and the interest manifested is good.

John B. White presided at the Dallas County Iowa convention.

Chancellor W. B. Craig delivered the chief address at same convention.

P. N. Nystron, pastor at Odel, did much to make this convention profitable and enjoyable.

Mary Holland, of Denver, sister of B. W. Johnson, with her daughter, spent a week recently in Iowa.

Miss Carroll Johnson, daughter of R. H. Johnson, of Springdale, Ark., is an Iowa visitor.

Prof. Edward S. Ames, of Indianapolis, Ind., who has spent the summer in Iowa, will return to his home and his college classes on Sept. 19th. He spoke at the Dallas County convention on Sept. 11th and at University Place church on Sept. 18th.

J. Madison Williams has resigned h professorship in Drake University.

Ex-Gov. F. M. Drake on Sept. 17th sent the treasurer of Drake University his chec for \$26,390. \$14,000 completes the endowme of a chair named for his deceased wife a \$12,000 is for the general endowment. Th generous man has paid to the University n less than \$100,000 since its founding.

The boad of officeres of the Church of Chri at Knightstown, Ind., have had published i the Knightstown Banner some statements a affidavits greatly reflecting upon the condu of one A. J. Cheeseman, who claims to be minister of the gospel. For further particula address the official board or send for a copy the Knightstown Banner, Sept. 23rd.

Brother and Sister F. P. Smith, of India apolis, Ind., spent several days in this cit including Sunday, Sept. 25, the special gues Bro. W. W. Dowling and family. They a tended the Sunday-school and church servic at Mount Cabanne, on Sunday, which was "high day" at that church by virtue of its b ing Rally Day. They paid their respects this office and looked through the establis ment, and expressed themselves as surpris at the magnitude of the business done. Br and Sister Smith are prominent members the Central Church, where Bro. Smith is t teacher of a large adult Bible class.

The Foreign Christian Missionary Societ takes pleasure in announcing that B. F. Cl has been engaged as field secretary, with head quarters at Kansas City, Mo., to begin Noven ber 1st, 1898. His field will be Missouri, Kan sas, Nebraska, Iowa and the Southwest. H will take pleasure in visiting the churches a Sunday-schools and district and state conve tions. Mr. Clay is well and favorably know among our churches generally. He serve successfully as corresponding secretary Kentucky Missions for a number of years, a besides he raised a considerable endowme for the College of the Bible, Lexington, Ky His work at Salt Lake City as a missionary the American Christian Missionary Society i well known. He has always been a thorugh going missionary man. He brings to the wo a deep and growing interest in missions and large and varied experience. We bespeak f him the cordial support of the churches a preachers. He is ready to do their bidding i creating a larger interest in worldwide mi sions.

A. MCLEAN, Cor. Sec.

A. R. Adams has published in tract form history of the Old Bedford Church, ne Blandinsville, Ill., written by Frank Woodside This church was organized by Milton Dodge a schoolhouse on Huston's Creek, April 7t 1850. A. R. Adams, of Blandinsville, is t present minister since October, 1896.

J. G. M. Luttenberger and his wife, of Do chester, Ill., paid this office a visit while i the city last week. Bro. Luttenberger is candidate for Representative on the Prohib tion ticket in his district and will take a active part in the canvass this fall. He hope for the strength of the Prohibition party a all lovers of the temperance cause in his di trict.

C. W. Dean, pastor of the Christian Churc at Harvey, Ill., recently delivered an addre at a union temperance meeting in that cit that excited much admiration, enthusiasm a comment during the week. Bro. Dean is th youngest preacher and pastor in that cit Harvey is one of the cities of Illinois th makes a strong fight against the saloon a does not permit it to gain a footing within h borders.

R. E. Dunlap, of Seattle, Wash., Chairma of the Prohibition State Committee, and C. I Haggard, brother to the Iowa secretary, a also of Seattle, have issued a vigorous circul calling upon all prohibitionists in that state t assemble in mass meeting for the purpose nominating two candidates for Congress a two for the Supreme Court.

J. C. Howell, of Sweet Springs, Mo., calle at this office last week on his return from a tw weeks' meeting at Liberty, Ralls county, M While there were but six additions, he fee that good results were accomplished for th church in the elevation of its fellowship a spirituality.

CHANGES.

Joseph Grimm, Belle Center, O., to Lookout St., Allegheny City, Pa.

A. M. McLain, Potwin, to Sedgwick, Kan

C. S. L Brown, Washington, Kan., DeWitt, Iowa.

Edgar D. Jones, LaBelle, Mo., to 95 W. 4 St., Lexington, Ky.

T. L. Read, Johnson, Neb., to Emo, Ont

P. Kruger, Franklin to Fairbury, Neb.

W. S. St. Clair, Stephens' Store to Columbia, Mo.

G. W. Hall, Oreana, Ill., to Canton, Mo.

;pondence.

Cruz Letter.

ivaled sea-bathing attrac-
Cal., has "Chautauqua"
yearly becoming mere and
is a favorite convention
.nd religious gatherings.
stand in the forefront in
ave their annual gather-
from four to six hundred
far and near to spend two
her in the consideration of
fing the salt air from the
ack doors. Their meetings
Tabernacle, which is situ-
he electric car line of this
lf miles southwest of the
e Baptists hold their an-
vin Lakes, a little village
utheast of Santa Cruz, on
re they also have a large
odate the Baptists as they
; and gain new strength,
physical. The Catholics
round at Hotel Del Mars,
ast of Santa Cruz, on the
pleasure-seekers ensconce
Cruz, Seabright or Capi-
ts have their Chautauqua
the other side of the bay,
y considering the advisabil-
akes and coming to Santa
p with the country. We
their way clear to do so,
n good, but for the intel-
s stimulus that it would
.

more particularly of the
and surroundings. I took
rfield Park one Thursday
t on my wheel, first past
el, then up over the hill
et, passing a number of
," which would strike a
ng out of the usual order.
s is peculiar. It is a vig-
when trimmed back will
til the foliage is a dense
.. The people here have a
the dense tops into hay-
pyramids and grotesque
The cypress is also exten-
edge. In this form it is
out three feet in height,
t in width, and the thick
se and smooth that a per-
a laprobe on top and lie
a mattress.
would look strange to you
would the eucalyptus and
ange trees, not seen in the
not stop to look at the
Cowell's Warehouses stand
nd we have to run around
ishop Warren's fine resi-
, known as "The Break-
overlooking the Harbor of
the good Methodist Bishop
ations, studying theology
nature. We soon pass a
and residence known as
," and then by the Light-
e the bay ends and the
re the road turns to the
d it is, both for driving and
own as the "Cliff Drive."
acific Ocean with its rest-
ling the cliffs, and some-
y high into the air. That
ilding about half a mile
; is at the terminus of the
and the locality there is
e l'Eau" ("View of the
er words, "View of the
lding has been erected with
ws, and is two stories high,
sort in the stormy days of

winter when tide and wind unite to get up a display of waterworks that knocks Niagara silly, and makes the spectator conscious that he stands in the presence of the mightiest power on the globe—the old ocean in a storm. It is worth going to see, but such exhibitions never come this time of the year, for the weather in California is governed by law; in the summer it never rains, and in the winter it rains when it listeth, but not inordinately. Nevertheless, there are days and days when it goes at it in earnest, and then it is the time, generally, when the ocean raves. To see the great rollers crawling up on to the ledges of the cliffs, and the next moment exploding into spray, and then pouring back into the ocean like giant cataracts, and the performance continually repeated, is a sight once seen never to be forgotten.

Now from this pagoda if you will look up the street toward the north (distant about 80 rods), you will see Garfield Tabernacle, which looks as if it stood athwart the street, but it does not; the street (on which the street car line runs) goes around the tabernacle. The tabernacle is octagon in form, and stands in the center of a circular plot of ground containing five acres, more or less, which plot is laid out in walks and flower beds. The tabernacle fronts toward the ocean, and vistas of ocean can be seen from the park in several directions. It is an ideal place for any kind of a convention, and more particularly so for a religious gathering, where one's thoughts are readily directed from the contemplation of God's works to God's Word.

A high range of hills can be seen through the windows to the northwest, about a mile distant. These look unimportant to the observer who is not in the secret of their usefulness to Santa Cruz. They lock out the too cold winds from the ocean, which otherwise would sweep through our fair city and make it as uncomfortably cold in the summer as San Francisco, where the wide gap between the mountains permits the Bay of San Francisco to come inland, and opens wide the Golden Gate to the raw, cold winds from the ocean.

But to return to Garfield Park. The land was originally donated by Santa Cruzans to the Christian Church of the state of California for religious purposes, with the understanding that lots be sold, and the money so raised be appropriated in the erection of cottages and the tabernacle. The prices of the lots ranged from $105 to $150, and the cottages were to cost not less than $400 each. As a matter of fact none of the cottages have cost less than $500, and some of the buildings erected are fine residences, and are permanent homes for the owners. The first year fifteen cottages were erected, and every year has seen additions to the number. These are for the most part owned by private parties, and are occupied by them during the "season," while many are for rent at from $4 to $10 for the season.

The attendance at annual meetings is from all parts of the state of California, save the southern portion—perhaps one-fourth of the state. They come by ocean, and rail, and wheeled conveyance, and even by the now almost omnipresent "bicycle." Some of the visitors camp in their wagons, and do their own cooking on the grounds, thus making the vacation quite inexpensive. A temporary grocery is established on the grounds where provisions, etc., can be obtained at Santa Cruz prices. There is also a dining tent on the grounds, where people who do not care to be bothered with cooking can get their meals at popular prices—five meal tickets for a dollar. In addition to the cottages there are tents for rent at very reasonable prices, and on the whole this place furnishes a splendid outing for the people from the interior who need just this kind of a vacation to counteract the depressing influence of the long, dry, hot summers which are almost as bad as you have in St. Louis.

The convention is called the "Christian State Meeting," and included in this are the following: the Ministerial Association, the Sunday-school Convention, the Christian Endeavor Convention, the Church Convention—which latter embraces reports of the various organizations of the Christian Churches of the state. The attendance this year was not up to the average, owing to the fact that this has been a bad year for the farmers and fruit growers. I was told that there were about 400 persons in attendance from abroad. The meetings last over two weeks, but many of those who come stay longer than that to enjoy the fine climate of Santa Cruz and the exhilerating sea bathing.

The sessions are held in the forenoon and at night, leaving the afternoons open for committee work, if needed, and fishing or bathing in the bay, driving into the mountains, visiting friends or the Big Trees and other attractions which are lying around loose all over Santa Cruz County. A bonfire near the ocean front one night during the sessions attracts a large crowd, and with its illumination, singing, stories, speeches and experiences, furnishes a scene long to be remembered.

The Christian Church in the state numbers about 1,800, and is increasing in numbers very rapidly.

The writer was present on the forenoon that had been set apart for passing "resolutions." The minister who had been appointed to deliver the sermon kindly gave way to permit a fuller consideration of the various resolutions. To illustrate how near Christian denominations come to each other there was not one of the resolutions but that might have been offered at almost any of the denominational conventions, and the writer, Congregationalist as he is, could have heartily supported and voted for each and every one of them—provided, of course, that the local application for some of them would have to be apropos. In fact, at one stage of the proceedings he forgot that he was only a spectator, and voted a rousing "aye" upon the "Anti-saloon Resolution," with all the rest of the audience. God grant that Christian denominations may cling closer to Christ, and let go their sectarianism whenever they can.

H. C. H.

English Topics.

MEN OF THE HOUR—JOHN KENSIT.

One of the foremost of the men of the hour in this country is Mr. John Kensit. Indeed, Mr. W. T. Stead calls him "the Protestant hero of the hour." He well deserves the appellation, for he has taken up the sword of Puritanism and has gone forth to war with indomitable valor against the Ritualists, who are threatening to effect the conversion of England to the Pope. He is a Londoner, who was born in 1853 and has never been away from London, except for a few days, in his life. He is a well-known bookseller of Paternoster Row and is also a conspicuous temperance worker. Strange to say, when a lad of 15 John Kensit was a member of a Ritualistic choir, at St. Lawrence, Jewry, near the Guildhall in the heart of the city, under the stormy rectorship of the Rev. B. Morgan Cowie, now Dean of Exeter and one of the Queen's chaplains. At this time he became convinced that Ritualistic services are essentially Popish. When Dr. Creighton was appointed, not long since, Bishop of London, Mr. Kensit boldly went to Bow Church and publicly protested against the confirmation of the new prelate on the ground of alleged Ritualistic practices. This incident made an immense sensation in London, and it was the opening of the present exciting campaign, in which Kensit is the renowned leader. He accused the new bishop in public of a desire to undo the glorious work of the Reformation, which Ridley, the then bishop of London, and a noble army of martyrs, laid down their lives to accomplish. Bishop Creighton replied by wearing both cope and mitre in St. Paul's at his first ordination of candidates for the ministry. Thus the spiritual war began which is convulsing the country. There have during the summer been lively riots in churches and in the open air. These proceedings are not always to the credit of the Protestant party, who are somewhat unfortunate in their allies. They go in bands to Ritualistic churches to carry on the "Kensit Crusade," but they have been receiving the undesirable assistance of the "Gideonite Band," which consists of a lot of roughs who have offered their services simply from delight in being mixed with public disturbances. In several parts of England, when the clergy have appeared to begin service, arrayed in vestments like the priest of Baal, an uproar has instantly commenced and the scenes ensuing have been such as to baffle description. Books and cushions are flung about on such occasions and the clergy have even been spat upon! In consequence, threats of retaliation are now heard on the other side and Mr. Kensit is warned that he will be shot at with revolvers if he repeats his exploits which created such a sensation at St. Ethelbarg's, Bishopsgate and St. Cuthbert's, Kensington. At the latter he performed his celebrated feat of snatching the cross from the altar when it was being kissed and adored by the clergymen. On that occasion there was a fight in the church to the accompaniment of hysterics and fainting on the part of ladies, and Kensit was taken into custody by the police. He was brought up before the court on the charge of brawling and was fined and then released on the promise that he would do nothing further for two months, during which he would wait to see if the bishops would exercise their authority in checking the Popish pranks going on in Anglican Churches. The time is past, the bishops have done nothing at all except to put forth a few platitudinarian manifestos, at which the country is laughing, and now Kensit is brandishing the ecclesiastical tomahawk and is starting on the warpath with fiery declarations of hostility. He sent out in advance a cloud of skirmishers in the shape of seventy "Wicliffeite preachers," for whose support he has collected a large sum of money. These are now going through the land in all directions, proclaiming the principles of the Reformation and scattering literature of Kensit's publication. Public feeling is rising high and stormy scenes are feared at the approaching church congress, to be held at Bradford.

ANOTHER MAN OF THE HOUR—THE SIRDAR.

Sir Herbert Kitchener is at this moment the talk of the earth. In him another great general has arisen amongst our men of war. You Americans have lately concluded a war in which you have done the human race the beneficent work of ridding fair territories of the accursed domination of Spain. But Mahdism was even more infernal, and it has fallen to the lot of Britain to crush it to death on the desert sands out of which the sceptre sprang up. There is a curious analogy between the two wars. The enemy has in each case been wiped out with infinitesimal loss to the Anglo-Saxon side. The viper of barbarism has in each case been stamped on by the heel of Christian civilization. But there will be a very serious sequel, also, in each case. America has to deal with grave problems in the disposition of the future for Cuba and the Philippines. She had simply better keep them under her absolute control. England has to face that crucial question of the control of Egypt. She will never get out of Egypt, let the rest of Europe say what it pleases. But Europe may have a great deal to say. The destiny of England is to clear a road for civilization from Alexandria to Capetown, and she will have to do it, whether she may wish to undertake the stupendous task or shirk it. Nations are not their own arbiters or umpires. France played both the coward and the fool when she left both Egypt and England in the lurch in the hour of trouble over the rebellion of Arabi Pasha, and vainly will she now fret and fume at the continued occupation of the basin of the Nile by British troops. Seated on both banks of the Nile and seated there for all time as long as the present era of history lasts, she must remain. This is part of the mighty program of Anglo-Saxon advance to the supremacy of the world in which America is beginning to take her vast share side by side with Britain and her wonderful colonies. But England's trouble will come. The carnal "Beast" Powers, those great military despotisms have shown their claws and teeth in grim array during the tragic period of the sufferings of Armenia, Greece and Crete. God has not done with the infernal Sultan, although the sanctimonious kaiser was not ashamed to pat that colossal murderer on the back and to send him a gallery of nice German family portraits. Providence will exact a heavy reckoning from the pious German despot. Meantime, England pursues one folly, which must also cost us dear. We have taken Omdurman, avenged the "Hero of Khartoum," and our army has, on the Sunday after that wonderful victory, chanted Gordon's belated requiem to the hoarse accompaniment of nineteen minute guns. But we are blundering on in the muddle of the Concert of Crete, and now we hear this morning that the beautiful Turks have gone mad with religious frenzy and have murdered our consul and several soldiers at Candia. The Eastern question smoulders all the time. That Cretan tragedy, though it is on a small scale, will spoil all the profit which Lord Salisbury would have reaped from the victory of Sir Herbert Kitchener. Before this letter reaches my American readers the question may be settled, "Where is the Khalifa?" He has dropped on the sands of the Soudan many of those 400 wives who formed his harem. He it was who after Gordon's death ordered the massacre of men, women and children in Khartoum. The only society in this world fit for such a perfect hell hound is that of the butcher of the Bosphorus. But there seems to be no atonement in this world for such crimes as those committed in Armenia, the Soudan and Cuba.

IS ARMAGEDDON POSTPONED?

Americans seem to be taking the same view generally as Englishmen of the now famous rescript of the Tzar. The demand for a congress to consider the possibility of universal peace is probably due to a double initiative. There is a beneficent power behind the throne in the case of Nicholas II. in the person of his beautiful Anglo-German wife, the Empress Alix, who is well known to be determined to be a guardian of peace. Britain and Russia will never fight while she lives, if she can prevent war. But, although this beautiful irenicon does infinite credit to the heart of the Tzar, is it for a moment possible to believe that the high official advisers of the Emperor of Russia are simple and sincere in their sympathy with him? Not a statesman now living in the world has been more deceitful, arrogant and provoking than Mouravieff, the very minister who puts forth this rescript on behalf of his imperial master. Russian statesmen care nothing for the lives of the common people. Some of these gentlemen said in cold blood at the time when the last Russo-Turkish war began, that they calculated on spending the lives of thirty thousand of their own soldiers in forcing the passage of the Danube! It is not the sacrifice of hecatombs of victims that these beautiful bureaucrats care at all about. Russian, German and French officers are generally alike reckless of the spilling of blood and the waste of precious lives in honor of the Moloch of war. The world will realize that soon enough. But one thing has lately happened which shocked the political ruffians and nearly broke their diplomatic hearts. When you Americans were at war with Spain the four great Continental Powers had concocted a lovely plan for preventing the United States from reaping the fruits of th expected victory, just as Russia, Germar and France had succeeded in robbing Japan the reward of her victory over China. B England was not caught a second tim When overtures were made to our governme to join this delectable conspiracy, Mr. Balfo from the Foreign Office (Lord Salisbu being out of England), categorically a sternly informed the Powers concerned that t immediate action of England would be to p the British fleets at the disposal of Americ I may tell you that wherever I go, all t Englishmen I meet are proud of that messag It has established Mr. Balfour in paramou esteem with his countrymen. And now wh has this to do with the Tzar's rescript? Ve much. His ministers have been rough awakened by the terror of any sort of re alliance between England and America; tha whatever shape it may take, it is a sort threatening of the day of judgment for t despots who are throttling all liberty of t people on the Continent. Yes, this is real why Russia desires peace. I love the Russi people, knowing them well. But the bru diplomacy of Russia I abhor with a pure a perfect hatred. Let us not imagine that t Great Grizzly Bear has become suddenly tran muted into an Angel of Peace!

A. DURBAN.

43 *Park Road, South Tottenham, Londo*
Sept. 9, 1898.

New York Letter.

On Saturday, Sept. 10th, Bro. and Sist A. L. Chapman sailed from this port to Co stantinople as missionaries, and on Saturda the 17th, Miss Mildred Franklin, of Bedfor Indiana, and Dr. McNiel, of Des Moine Iowa, sailed away on the good ship A choria, of the Anchor Line, for their field labors in India. These young ladies spe several days in New York, and on Sund evening, the 11th, occupied the pulpit at t 169th Street Church, to the great delight our congregation. They go with the wel wishes of a host of Disciples of the Lord in th city, who will not forget them at the throne heavenly grace.

***

The time for our great Chattanooga conve tion is almost at hand. Let all who read t New York Letter prepare to go if possibl and if you can't go, get ready to send some o to represent you and your congregation in th convocation of the saints. Every preach among us ought to go. It will rest him, f him with zeal and strengthen him for nobl endeavor for months to come, and will be blessed memory in all the future. I lived a preached in Chattanooga at one time, and c testify that it is a delightful place in which sojourn. Chattanooga is all historic groun its scenery is beautiful and its people hospit ble. The people of the East and North shou go down in strong numbers; their presence the South will do much good toward the i spiration of their brethren in that section the country. May God bless this conventi and make it the greatest and best in the hi tory of our work!

***

In the death of Dr. John Hall at Bangor, Ireland, on the 7th, one of the most promine and honored of American preachers was tak away. If he had lived until in the autumn would have completed fifty years in the mi istry, and he had about decided to retire fro the Fifth Avenue Presbyterian pulpit at th time. He began to preach before he w twenty years of age. He came as the co missioner of the Irish Presbyterian Church the American General Assemblies in 1867, a after occupying the then vacant pulpit of th Fifth Avenue Presbyterian Church in this city he was called as its pastor; hence he w pastor of that church thirty-one years. Wh he came to New York his salary was fixed $6,000 in gold (gold being worth $1.30) and

was increased to
has been $15,000.
salary, but the de-
heavy and he fre-
liberal hand. A
several years ago
)0 on him, and his
brought his annual
over $20,000. His
presents $400,000,-
ty at Fifth Avenue
e than $1,000,000.
ion the charities of
widespread. They
and institutions of
York, besides giving
ionary work. His
$30,000 a year to
's strong point was
r and clear and loyal
is work was heavy
ld a large place in
rk; his memory is

chools reopened on
reased attendance.
n and the Bronx on
pupils, and admitted
ing a total register
ool sittings for 227,-
e congestion of the
ns some schools are
re not full. Conse-
refused admission
nto half-day classes
This compels 14,621
oughs to be turned
nto the streets, and
s of the city where,
should not be com-
ts. This will result
ny a child. Other
ld be postponed if
h the improvements
sary for the accom-
f school age in the
t is a crime against
ization—against the
e church of God.
e country should be
Schoolhouses should
and every child of
elled to attend and,
ld be taught in our
ational security and

of Count Tolstoi was
ening, Sept. 8th, at
about one hundred
ziger presided and
of divorcing litera-
g to the remarkable
age of peace to the
the Czar of despotic
doubt that it was in
of the life and work
eakers were R. W.
eph Jefferson, Hall
H. Crosby and I.
ll said one of the
e owed gratitude to
moved the last trace
t was only a kind of
se the public. This
oted author: "One
ing in your honor,

new pastor of the
ciples of Christ at
into his work with
s. We sincerely de-
ious old church may
ding the Redeemer's

of the 56th Street
nning to organize an
about October 1st in that church. He thinks there is a large field for such an enterprise in that community. We rejoice in this forward movement and hope for its success. Sister W. C. Payne, our new C. W. B. M. state president, and Sister Jennie Encell, the secretary, organized an auxiliary of twenty-four members at the Lenox Avenue Church on Lord's day evening, Sept. 18th, and are going to Green Point, Brooklyn, this week, to organize one there. The outlook for the work at 169th Street is bright this autumn. We expect a season of good work.

***

The 10th was set apart by the church at Niagara Falls for the dedication of their new house of worship. Bro. F. W. Norton, the hard-working pastor, and his congregation, are to be congratulated on the success achieved in this excellent enterprise. We rejoice with them. Here are congratulations to you, Bro. Norton, and to your flock. October 16th is the appointed time for the opening of the new church at Brockton, Mass., where Bro. G. A. Reinl has toiled so heroically for several years. This band of Disciples of Jesus has sacrificed, and great have been the sacrifices of their pastor, to build up the cause of Christ in that New England city. We are glad to know they are so soon to enter into the fruit of their labors.

S. T. WILLIS.

1281 *Union Ave.*

Texas Letter.

September 7th was a red-letter day in the history of Lancaster. On that day Randolph College opened her doors for the first time for the reception of the ambitious youth who desires an education. As our train neared the good old town the main building, a splendid modern structure, loomed into view, with "Old Glory" floating as proudly from the tower as if it had been a frowning fortress, filled with men and munitions of war. And why not? Are not our schoolhouses rather than our fortresses the safeguards of our nation? Are not our teachers rather than our generals to lead the way into the greatest battles and secure for us the truest victories? Are not the permanency, purity and power of our great Republic dependent upon the true education of our children? If so, let the flag float over every school.

This main building is flanked by two others, "The Girls' Home" and "The Boys' Home," which are also models of their kind. They are not simply boarding houses, but homes for the students. These buildings are on a campus of eight acres, sloping gracefully eastward, as if to greet the rising sun, fit emblem of a vigorous and hopeful young school. All this, costing $25,000, is the princely gift of the liberal people of Lancaster.

At ten o'clock President Randolph Clark, his strong faculty, the business board and invited guests from the chapel rostrum looked into the faces of a splendid audience. After prayer I had the honor of making the opening address, and if it was not a good speech it was not the fault of the occasion and the audience, for both were full of inspiration. Other speeches followed, closing with a capital one from Bro. Clark. I had never heard him before, and had no idea that he could do it after that fashion. He is not only a teacher, but a logician and orator.

These exercises over, a sumptuous dinner was served, and then began the work of enrolling the students. This was by far the most satisfactory part of the proceedings, for Bro. Clark felt assured that he would open with forty boarders and one hundred day pupils. Hence all signs must fail, or Randolph College is a success.

The church at Lancaster is a good one. Baxter Golightly, their pastor, on account of a sick wife, was just leaving them for Eastland, and President Clark will take up the work, and it will not suffer in his hands.

Add-Ran University, Waco, also opens most hopefully. Financial Agent Henry has met with unexpected success, and that old curse of a debt promises soon to b
This promise inspires its
courage, and students a
Addison Clark, a brothe
Randolph College, is at th
and has, like his brother,
help him.

Our state mission work
encouraging: Men employ
sermons, 546; additions,
ized, 4; Sunday-schools,
ties, 4; money raised, $2,

"The Divided Church,"
one of the best tracts of th
a living issue in a strong
spirit, and it will do good
Courier, Dallas, Texas, a

F. N. Calvin, of Waco,
visit of two months with h
Colby Hall preached accep
the absence.

The Austin work is stea
J. W. Lowber and wife a
ly. The contract for a ne
seating capacity, with all
er, of one thousand, ha
substantial evidence of th
ing.

Prof. J. B. Sweeney,
sity, has spent fifty-three
in protracted meetings,
and money raised to build
there another vacation re

John Logan, late of New
ville, is proving himself a
His last two meetings, at
sulted in more than seve
Rosecrans assisted him
meetings.

The Third Church, Ft.
Wilson as pastor, will soo
It will be of the tabernac
plain on the outside, but
with a capacity of 1,500.
for the work of the institu

833 *Live Oak St., Dalla*

Pittsburgh

After a season of rest a
various pastors and work
Pittsburgh and Alleghen
their fields, and have tak
with redoubled ardor an
churches have been close
months, but the services
shortened and, in some
meetings, with good resu
Additions to the churche
in spite of the intense h
hundred being reported at
ing held September 5th,
gust. The preachers of th
summer as well as all-win

After a pleasant season
on the Atlantic Coast, B
returns to his work, and b
workers to greater zea
anniversary of the dedica
Church with a short se
which some of the newe
pated, doing the preach
ago this beautiful edifice
God, honor Christ, and t
has been glorified there
evidenced in the fact tha
ministry of Bro. Crambl
twenty have witnessed
thus honoring Christ, w
been theirs. Three thous
been paid on the church
thousand dollars in all
missions.

The historic First Ch
comes with Bro. W. J. L
for Christ with renewed v
Lhamon spent his vacatio
for his congregation and
book for the Christian

Course. At the First Church Bro. Fred Fillmore and his noble wife have charge of the music, with most encouraging results. Bro. Fillmore is also clerk of the board and looks after collections and delinquent members. So well does he do this that the summer collections have been nearly doubled this year as compared with those of last.

At Central Bro. C. L. Thurgood was made the recipient of a very nice present. A ticket for himself and wife, and entertaiment for a ten days' sojourn at Ocean Grove. During the last few weeks a complete renovation has been made in the church edifice, so that the good brother and his wife come to their fall campaign with many encouragements.

Over at Knoxville the brethren have secured the services of Bro. M. H. Wilson, who is hustling things. Although in the field but three months, he has so encouraged the membership that they have spent over twelve hundred dollars in rearranging and beautifying their house Bro. Wilson reports good audiences with frequent accessions.

Still the march of improvement goes on. At Hazelwood Bro. C. M. Iams has with the assistance of the Ladies' Aid Society succeeded in wiping out the old debt and remodeled the building. New carpets, pulpit furniture, change of organ loft, and paint have made the building a thing of beauty, while the gospel as preached by Bro. Iams is a joy forever.

Another brother who found Ocean Grove a place of recuperation is Bro. O. H. Phillips, of Braddock, who returns to his work with little if any more avoirdupois, but a heart warmed with souls for the sake of the Master. Bro. Phillips the Jonathan of the Pittsburgh preachers; "the heart of the Davids do knit to him."

But in the midst of general rejoicing there are some notes of sorrow. Bro. Z. O. Doward, after heroic work at Lawrenceville, Forty-third Street, is leaving the field. Bro. Shelenburger is leaving Beaver, and we are in fear that our brother J. Z. Bates will also bid us adieu. Vacancies there are in the pulpits at McKeesport, Duquesne, Homestead and Johnstown. Alas, that it should be so. May God in his mercy help these to find the right men to work in fields where much work is to be done.

Bro. Craig, of Belleview, and Bro. Hanna, of Carnegie, have been among the stay-at-homes. But as each are young bachelors and passionately fond of lawn tennis, and are looking for love and finding it (love is a tennis term, your scribe has been told,) the summer for them has not been unprofitably spent. Bro. Hanna's work at Carnegie is flourishing and is showing the wisdom of the brethren there in calling and retaining him, while of Bro. Craig, hustling for a new church building in Belleview as he is, only kindliest words may be said.

The annual convention of the Western Pennsylvania Christian Missionary Society convenes in Connelsville the 20th of this month, the session lasting three days. That it will be a season of spiritual blessing there can be no possible doubt. A good program has been prepared and many are planning to attend.

The work at Observatory Hill is moving along well. Never has it been the good fortune of your scribe to work with a more genial and pleasant body of men and women than he has found there. A small congregation, but full of faith and good works, serving the Lord with one shoulder; that is, all in a united service. During the year closing October 1st there have been thirty-five accessions by letter and confession. Bills and salaries have been paid promptly, and when the church receives its renovation of new carpets, furniture, paint and additional room which even now is being carried on, it will be hard to find a sweeter, cosier building and a better body of workers than on the hill.

JOHN A. JAYNE.

No. 1 Chester Ave., Allegheny, Pa.

At Chautauqua, N. Y.

In all the world, I suppose, there is no other place just like this. There are many imitations, each having certain excellent resemblances to the prototype; but the venerable mother, now just entering upon her twenty-fifth year, sits in queenly dignity on an emerald throne, among her one hundred blooming daughters. "The great and original Chautauqua" presents to the eye of the visitor, crossing the beautiful lake from which the place derived its name, a vision of exquisite loveliness. The picturesque pier, reflected in the limpid waters of the lake; the beautifully kept lawn, with noble trees and plots of rare flowers; the roads and walks glittering in their whiteness; the magnificent Hotel Athenæum, crowning the elevation; the countless artistic cottages seen by glimpses through the trees; the touch of higher life supplied by thronging men, women and children—make a picture of grace and beauty worthy of a poet's dream.

But this world-famed summer city does not find its chief attraction in that which appeals to the eyes. It is a great system of schools, patronized by many thousands, from every state in the Union and many parts of Europe, who come in quest of better equipment for the serious and sacred business of life. Many of the most noted speakers of the world are engaged for the lecture platform. Here is a list for the present season, containing (among many others) the names of the Earl and Countess of Aberdeen; Professor Gaston Bonet-Maury, of the University of Paris; Professor C. Rene Gregory, of the University of Leipsic; Rev. Russell H. Conwell, of the Temple, Philadelphia; Professor B. Rush Rheese, of Newton; Dr. John Henry Barrows, of Chicago, Hon. Murat Halstead, Mr. Will Carleton, Commander Booth-Tucker, Mrs. Emma P. Ewing and Hon. Wallace Bruce. One hundred courses in study are offered by seventy instructors from leading institutions, and could you see the hundreds of earnest men and women (nearly all of them preachers or teachers) hurrying on their way, with notebook and pencil in hand, to lecture or to recitation, you would catch a glimpse of the real life and power of Chautauqua.

But somebody wishes to ask, "What about that teaching—is it orthodox?" Well, that depends—just as the answer to such a question must always depend. I presume the instruction in English, German, French, Latin, Greek, Mathematics, Psychology, Music and Fine Arts is quite orthodox, and of the very best; and, if it is not, I am not sure that I could prove its incorrectness.

Oh, you mean the study of the Bible? Well, that study of the Bible is, for me, the chief charm of Chautauqua. And do you know why? Because it is so thorough, so bold and so reverent. I tasted, then I became a pupil, and for three weeks drank full and deep draughts from the great fountain of consecrated learning. I do not hesitate to say that, according to my judgment, Professor Willett, of the University of Chicago, is one of the ablest and most helpful instructors in the study of the Bible that this age affords. But he is scientific to the core, and more than once I have felt constrained to take issue with him upon his conclusions. His lecturing in the classroom (where I had the honor to be the guest of the Professor) was just of the character I desired to hear—the latest deductions of the most thorough scholarship, uttered by a man who reverently accepts the Bible as the Word of God and Jesus of Nazareth as the Savior of the race. In special interpretations (as of portions of the 53rd of Isaiah) we did not agree; but we stood together upon the foundation, "which is Jesus Christ." I owe Professor Willett much. He annihilated some of my pet texts, but he made the dear old Bible dearer and more wonderful to me. He brought the historic Christ closer to my every-day life. Before that divine form, which the exquisite genius of Matthias Claudius loved to call "The Star in the Night," all at Chautauqua, in one way and another, bow and worship.

Dr. Willett has left, and the gifted Professor Rush Rheese, of Newton Theological Institution, will now conduct that department of Bible study. I have heard Professor Rheese but once. He instructed and delighted me. With not so much personal magnetism as Professor Willett (few speakers can compare with the Chicago professor in this respect), I am inclined to think that his vision is more comprehensive, and that, upon controverted points, he will be found to be more in accord with what is ordinarily accepted as the orthodox belief. And, after all, do not such differences constitute a distinct advantage in the Chautauqua course for the mature mind?

The public devotional services have been most helpful and inspiring. A number of very distinguished ministers are here, and are being used for the general good. The first Sabbath after my arrival, I heard Rev. Russell H. Conwell, of the Temple, Philadelphia, in the morning, at the great amphitheatre, which seats 8,000. It was a wonderful sermon from a wonderful man, and held the multitude as if spellbound. At the evening service it was my privilege to preach to a vast multitude, hundreds of whom stood outside the building, unable to get in. (It is estimated that 15,000 people are now at Chautauqua.) The next Sabbath I heard Dr. John Henry Barrows, of Chicago, preach at 11 o'clock. Dr. Barrows is, perhaps, best known to the general public as the head and front of "The Congress of Religions," held in connection with the World's Fair. I confess that a distinctly unfavorable impression of that noted "Congress" had for me shadowed its champion. But the ow is gone, and he now stands before my 's eye in the clear light, one of the great- ad best men of this age. As he spoke for , from his rich stores of thought and ob- tion, one could not fail to admire the und learning, the discriminating judg- , the sympathetic nature, the evangelical ; and the passionate earnestness of the ent pleader. I have not heard a nobler ore powerful plea for foreign missions. a hand that did not falter, he tore all of salvation based on heathen philosophy eathen living into shreds, and exalted the as Heaven's only provision for a lost l. It recalled the lamented Ellis when at best. In the evening, Bishop Vincent m to know is to honor and to love) gave discourse so solid, so tender, so loving, it must have accomplished—penetrated as s by the unction of the Spirit—the very est mission of preaching. The third Sun- of my stay I heard the famous Dr. A. J. ehrends; and, judging by that sermon, I d say he deserves to be famous, in the sense of the word. Many will say, "No er;" but it seems to me that it *does* mat- and matter *much*. In the afternoon, a inian lectured.

will be interesting to Southerners to learn there are 400 or 500 most excellent people from the South. Georgia leads in num- , but Virginia, the Carolinas, Alabama, essee, Kentucky, Mississippi and Texas well represented. They are here and, as ways the case, are winning golden opin- . Every vestige of bitter sectionalism s to have forever passed away, and no e is greeted with more universal or en- iastic applause, when thrown upon the n, than that of Fitzhugh Lee. The fact am tempted, from all I have recently seen heard, to believe that Fitzhugh Lee is to- as popular at the North as at the South. e writer was invited to speak for the South the night of the celebration of Chautau- s "Quarter Centennial." I shall never et that occasion. The magnificent illum- ons, the splendid fireworks, the gorgeous rations and the audience of 12,000, reach- ar beyond the great amphitheatre. As an ence of the generous spirit of the place y be permitted to say that the audience tuated almost every sentiment of the hern speaker with the most enthusiastic ause, and at one point, when the enthusi- had reached, it seemed to me, the highest a possible, the members of the band seized pieces and the thrilling strains of xie" swept out on the torrent of applause. ver expected to witness such a scene in York; but—thank Heaven—we are now people, with one God and one destiny!— *Henry W. Battle, D. D., in Religious ald.*

St. Louis Letter.

ews is accumulating so rapidly on these tiful autumn days that we fear our inabili- keep within the bounds of an "occasional r" from this city to the CHRISTIAN-EVAN- ST, granted by the editor. At the opening e summer just past the city was all excite- t over the war with Spain. Young men enlisting, troops were parading the ets, camps were growing and everything taken on a military aspect. The war is now, but the excitement of returning ps is almost as intense as was their enlist- t and departure. The returning regiments being received with open arms, and their fort made the first and foremost of all es. And while there is great rejoicing the return of husbands, fathers and sons ome and friends, the unreturned ones are forgotten.

ext to the excitement of returning soldiers St. Louis Exposition has become an object traction. One of the chief factors of the osition, the popular Sousa Band, was on d at the opening, and this alone is a guar- e of the loyal support of St. Louis, which loves to boast of its musical taste and talent. The new attraction this year is the large oriental garden in the Coliseum, and the reproduction on canvas of some of the great naval battles of the late war. The art galleries are said to be as fine, as attractive and as popular as ever. The attendance at the opening on the 14th instant was estimated at twenty thousand persons, which is a strong evidence of the popularity of this prominent St. Louis attraction for its citizens and their guests.

In religious circles the probable loss of Dr. John Mathews, a popular minister of the Methodist Episcopal Church South, by removal to another field, is the occasion of much talk, many comments, some agitation, a few tears and many regrets. Dr. Mathews has not ceased to be a drawing card, but the iron-rule government of his church compels him to go. He has lived out the longest possible measure of time allowed under the creed which he has decreed to live up to and support, and must go. The Centenary Church and a large crowd of outsiders who by several turns of opportunities have succeeded in holding him as long as they have lament his going; but he talks about the will of the Conference as though it were the will of God, and has exhorted his brethren and friends to be reconciled to its commands. Dr. Mathews is an interesting man, always attractive and one of the few preachers of St. Louis who seldom lack a large audience to hear his address or sermon. He is also one of the few men who can repeat an old story as often as he pleases; and some he has told a great many times without being too severely criticised therefor. Dr. Mathews is not a very profound theologian nor critical scholar, but he is a good generalizer, always entertaining and a fearless spokesman against the evils of the day. He is vigorous in his delivery of sermons, comes at men with his points by the shortest method, and is strictly orthodox according to the oldest Methodist tradions, except on the question of a state of absolute sinlessness in this life, which he confesses freely not to have yet attained, and advises his brethren not to provoke unnecessarily nor too severely at any time. Just what estimate is to be made of his long ministry in St. Louis, on moral and spiritual grounds, we do not profess to know, but on the score of popularity he certainly ranks high.

Our Christian preachers have again broken over the rules of past methods as to their Monday meetings, and introduced another innovation. Instead of their devout, dignified meeting at the office of the CHRISTIAN-EVANGELIST each Monday at eleven o'clock A. M., as their custom was, they have started out on a series of promiscuous informal gatherings. Two weeks ago, on Monday, they with their good wives met at Forest Park where they were to lunch, talk or play as the spirit moved them. In these Monday meetings it is now proposed, we understand, to visit various places, houses, shops and districts of the city to see men as they are through the week and to learn how to come into closer touch with them. The idea may be a good one, but we prefer to await results before venturing an opinion on this subject. Of course a number of them will attend the state and general conventions, and until these are over, together with the city's fall festivities, the fall campaign of the city churches can hardly be said to be opened.

B. U. I.

Christian Science.

The growth of the religious fad called Christian Science can be explained on the following grounds:

1. *The eagerness of invalids to be healed.* The fact that sick people will swallow anything in the hope of regaining their lost health is amply attested by the millions of gallons of swill in the shape of patent nostrums, sold annually in the United States, to say nothing of the rest of the world; and the ease with which they can be convinced of the virtue and effectivenesss of these same nostrums is as fully attested by the millions of pages of testimonials with which the country is being constantly flooded. In view of these facts and of the claims made by this new science, it is not surprising that it should find a large following among sick and morbid people. As it is impossible to brew a nostrum too nasty for some people to take (people actually took Vinegar Bitters while it was on the market!) so it is impossible to formulate a creed too absurd to win a following.

2 *A false notion concerning the proof of the Spirit of Christ.* The apostle John, in 1 Jno. 4:1-6, teaches that there are two spirits operating in the world, the Spirit of Christ and the spirit of Antichrist. He gives the sure rule by which to discriminate between them. Many, probably most people make the mistake of thinking that the spirit of Antichrist appears only in his true character. They are indebted to Milton and not to the Master for this idea. John's admonition to try the spirits indicates that it is no easy matter to distinguish between them. The fact is, the spirit of Antichrist is trying to appear like the Spirit of Christ, so as to get himself mistaken for him. In this he succeeds so well that "if it were possible, the very elect would be deceived." With this sinister end in view he may use a beautiful life. Therefore, a beautiful life is not proof conclusive of the possession of the Spirit of Christ. The person who lives the beautiful life may be deceived as to the true character of the spirit that dominates him. This is clearly implied in the passage cited above. As Jesus found innocent children possessed of demons while here on earth, so there are now conscientious people who are being led astray by the spirit of the arch deceiver. Healings are not proofs positive of the Spirit of Christ as their author. Jesus will say to many who offer teese in evidence at the last day, "Depart from me, for I never knew you!" The spirit of Antichrist does all of the works of the Spirit of Christ that are possible for him to do, in order to deceive the people. Therefore, no work that can be done by the spirit of Antichrist can be cited as positive proof of the identity of the Spirit of Christ. There is but one absolutely infallible test, and John gives it in these words: "Every spirit which confesseth that Jesus Christ is come in the flesh is of God: and every spirit which confesseth not Jesus is not of God." The one thing above all others that the devil wishes to prevent is the confession of Jesus as the Christ. The one thing he cannot do is to move a man to make the good confession. The good confession, sincerely made, cannot be prompted by any other than the Spirit of God. Here is the point at which the evil spirit is stript of his disguise and revealed in his true character. The hand that stopped the mouths of demons that would confess him while on earth is laid on the lying lips at this point. Satan must not destroy Satan, but evil must be overcome by good. Truth must triumph over error, light over darkness, life over death.

Christian Science denies every fundamental fact of the gospel. It denies that Jesus Christ came in the flesh, for it denies that there is any such thing as flesh; denying that there is any death, it denies that Jesus died, that he was buried and that he rose again; denying sin, it denies John when he cries, "Behold the Lamb of God that taketh away the sin of the world," and Paul when he says, "It is a faithful saying and worthy of all acceptation, that Jesus Christ died for sinners."

The best that can be said for these people is that they are earnest and sincere, but are being led by the spirit of Antichrist, by a flowery way, to the destruction of the very citadel of Christianity. "They know not what they do."

S. L.

Princely Knights Again.

DEAR BRO. GARRISON:—As one of the founders of Princely Knights, and as its present secretary, I desire to say a few words in reply to the criticisms of its "secret" feature which have been made by Bro. Keeler, first in an article of his own, and second by a clipping from a Boston paper.

The sum of both criticisms is that "the good in the society is destroyed by the secrecy." Does it make every good thing bad to have anything secret about it? We keep secret the preparations we make for a "surprise party," or for a "birthday surprise." The secret does not make all the good worthless. Why? "He who surprises another for his good is always counted a friend." Often to keep a thing secret until it can be made known in the best way is a duty. The Master charged his disciples not to tell the vision of the mountain top until the Son of Man be risen from the dead. The keeping of *that* secret was not "a crack in the costly vessel that made it worthless." "If he had anything good why keep it a secret?" To keep a good thing secret until it may be made known with the best result is wise—the Master himself thought so. This is all the Princely Knights aim to do in having a secret institution. Lessons can be most impressively taught to many—to *most*—men and boys when they are given in an initiation that teaches the lessons in the "surprise" it contains. The initiate could not be surprised if the ceremony were not a secret to him. This is the chief—almost the only—value or purpose of the secrecy in the initiation. To keep this secret from those who are not members of the lodge is, of itself, no more reprehensible than it would be for Bro. Keeler to keep secret his plan to make his best friend a valuable present, or for the editor of the Boston paper to keep secret his plan to give something good to his readers until his arrangements are completed.

I regret these criticisms, but if they shall cause any one to investigate the results of P. K. work I shall be content. To give all an opportunity to find out whether our work is "evil because it is secret" I will agree to send to any Christian, who is a *true lover of boys*, a copy of the ritual, on the condition that I be given satisfactory assurance that it will *only be used "to help boys build, adorn and defend a good character for themselves."* This is the only object we have and he who will *so* use our secret work ought to have the opportunity to do so.

S. M. CONNER.

Irvington, Ind.

"Take Heed How Ye Build."

A young girl said to me in the presence of her parents, "I never did have as good a time in my life, as I did at that tent meeting. I wish we could have another." When she had gone, her father said, "I can't tell you how that meeting demoralized our daughter. She has taken less interest in the Christian Church, to which she belongs, ever since; she has been clamorous for something sensational at church, and far less disposed to listen to any advice or warning from her parents."

This led me to investigate further. For weeks before that meeting the pastor, at whose bidding the evangelist came, was loud and fulsome at every preachers' meeting. It was going to be *immense;* all get ready for a blessing. When the evangelist was gone, the silence at the preachers' meeting was a noticeable as had been the noise before.

Not many moons have passed since a pastor said to me, "I wish I knew how to let go this fellow who is trying to preach and can't. I opposed his coming, but was overruled by my officers, and they all see the mistake. This Boanerges was suddenly impressed while out on the road as a commercial traveler, that he was called and sent to preach, so he sent in his samples and gave up his lucrative job and hired him a singer from another denomination and entered the ministry. While listening to him I was reminded of the little boy who whispered to his father during the sermon thus: "Is that so, or is it just preaching."

He illustrated the unimportance of baptism, by the story of Sweeney's and Jarrel's frogs, each of which escaped being swallowed by a snake by jumping into and swimming across a pond—the Disciple frog when across croaked *saved*, while the Baptist frog croaked *non-essential.*

In towns where we are strong we are "Christians," where we are weak we are "Campbellites."

One of strongest and wisest evangelists wrote me, "What is to be done to stop this craze for numbers?" The imitators of Sam Jones have made this style of evangelism so odious that the late General Conference at Baltimore has stamped its disapproval on the whole business in most emphatic terms. I hope the day for these peripatitics is well-nigh over, and when we take hold of a church that has had two or three great ingatherings and can't find half a dozen who will take hold and work with us, the pastors ought to see the remedy and apply it. I am an evangelist as well as pastor, but it is false methods and untempered mortar that needs yet to be looked after.

Compare, if you will, the reports of these sensational preachers with those of Luke in Acts, and you will have learned the lesson.

S. W. CRUTCHER.

Pine Bluff, Ark.

Missouri Bible-school Notes.

Of the Audrain county meeting I have much to say, but the space is not to spare. The Bible-school reports were not so good this year as last, and every school making a poor report was followed by a poor church report, so that all saw that a poor school report made a poor church report. When will the brethren learn this to their reformation in Bible-school work? Laddonia and Mexico made remarkably good school reports, showing work worthy of them, while County Bible-school Superintendent P. W. Harding worked hard for good reports from all schools.

Now comes Central, St. Louis, with one-half their annual pledge remitted promptly, which means much for us and the fieldmen. Thanks to all of them. Who next?

The Barnard Bible-school is another friend in time of need, and a good friend in meeting the apportionment as it falls due, with words of cheer. Am sure our schools do not know how much we depend on their acceptance or rejection of the amounts asked of them, or they would respond more promptly. Brethren, won't your school consent to give us the mite asked of each for this good work, and will you not be good enough to notify me right away? We would like to put a man in the southeast district if we could only feel sure that the schools would give us the meager sums asked of them. What do you say, friends, and say right now?

The Nevada Bible-school, under Prof. W. O. Broaddus, with his efficient corps of assistants, is worthy of model. In their opening the pastor, A. C. McKeever, and his assistant, Mrs. McKeever, were right to the front, and the song service was a delight. In the class work there was much to compliment, while their class arrangements were better than is usual. In offerings the school excels, so that they can give largely toward the church debt and also to our work, $30. Am now telling other schools about Nevada's good points, hoping to help them in their methods.

Bro. Giddens has organized a new Bible-school, and is now at Ulman, hoping to raise the money for the new house so long and badly needed. If it can be done, we all believe that John Giddens will do it. Over $300 for it on hand at this time.

A new Bible-school has been organized in the Antioch (Marion county) neighborhood, christened Willow Bend, and with a good membership. You will hear more of such work in North Missouri, now that F. M. Rogers is in the field, for he works.

At Virginia we had a great day and happy work, and so all were happy. John Jones is a yokefellow with whom one delights to labor, while the co-operation of the church membership will quicken one's best efforts. The basket lunch may have drawn some, but all took hold of the work happily, so that every moment was profitably spent, and the institute was followed with a meeting. A good offering, too.

At night, my old-time friend, C. B. Lotspeich, gave way at Passaic, and the friends gave fine hearing and the change they had for this work, $1.70. This is one of the pleasant fields for a true servant of Christ, the brethren paying promptly at every meeting, but having no Bible-school of their own in a union house, do not feel obligated to this work as they will some day. All appreciate the preacher.

The Honey Creek (Grundy county) friends will help us as long as the leaders are with them, and Miss Lyda Evans sends the first quarter promptly, as usual. It is the only school in Grundy county giving to our work this year as reported.

What a time your servant had getting to Hickman Mills, but what pleasant greeting when he did arrive! Had it not been for "Uncle" Jerry Robertson's wife and her horse and buggy, would not have made it, and then by the help of Brother B. Z. Palmer I was enabled to go on promptly, so that no miss was made in my appointments at all. The new house is a "thing of beauty," and the presence of the older people in the school did me good, while the brethren, without one moment's hesitation, said, "We will give to your work from now on." Thanks to them and God bless them. Brethren, you never will know, without experience, what a feeling of pleasure comes with your kindness to the fieldmen, nor how we appreciate it all in His Name.

Your servant declined an appointment to the Omaha Bible-school conference, for it came at the time of our state convention, Sept. 27-30, and no Missouri worker ought to neglect the Nevada convention for anything. Hear? Well, that is exactly my sentiment, and there is something wrong if you do. The rates, one fare, the entertainment, free, the program, fine, ought to enlist you if nothing else. Come!

H. F. DAVIS.

Commercial Bldg., St. Louis.

---

tes and News.

ıpt. 25th, was rally day at the Church, this city. All of the the church had special services n and night.

.l Christian Church at Pueblo, issued a very neat church direc- ımber of names enrolled is 469. ı is the pastor.

Christian Lectureship will meet le, Nov. 14-17.

by, of Perry, Oklahoma terriory, .s seeking a home to remember still much room in that country. couragingly of the climate, soil ctions. He says we have 6,000)klahoma or more than any other '. Those wanted are Disciples of ırse.

ıays that excellent homes can be county, Colorado, where conse- tian stockgrowers are wanted. doing some evangelistic work in ınd speaks highly of the oppor- ı for homeseekers. He says that ırties may address J. L. Ellis, :er or Lewis Breeze, at Craig, , Colorado.

ıs at Beech Grove, Williamsport, shed through the sacrifices of ker and Clark, and the voluntary ıe people, are now entering upon ear, and are in prosperous state.

N. A. W.

field evangelist'' spent three Arbor, Mich., during the com- ! its great university, with 3,337 llment. Of the graduating class 300 were attorneys at law. Bro. ıis well-improved intellectual op- ʒood house and grand member- ıg the leaders in the right way.

N. A. W.

per County Meeting

ty, Oct. 27-29; a good program. 'eachers of the county remember 'me out, brethren, and let us find cause is in Jasper. Delegates ɔointed by every congregation in

W. A. OLDHAM,
County President.

Logansport, Ind.

second year's ministry with this ınday. The church has paid an old hundred and eighty-five dollars. furnace at a cost of one hundred ıllars and paid for it. Gave one ırs for missions, and it was not ıugh *one* society. Fifty persons led to the church without the aid *evangelist*. The preacher has ull every week. *I am not seeking d*." The church and the Lord d to me; I wish I were more m. I will try to be. The church man anything, love excepted. o better this year. As our faith work be. Christianly,

H. C. KENDRICK.

398.

ıgton City Convention.

ınd, Deleware and District of sionary Convention will be held Street Church, corner Ninth and Northeast Washington, D. C., ıd 7, 1898. S. R. Maxwell, A.]. Smith and Mrs. Helen Moses ıe principal addresses.

Minnesota Notes.

Have been making a trip among some of the churches of this state; the evangelist could profitably spend two months in this way. Pastors are on the run; several churches pastorless. I might locate two faithful young men who could work at a moderate salary. Pleasant Grove, one of the oldest churches in the state, is wide awake in good works under J. M. Elam's ministry. David Overend, one of the oldest Disciples in the state, lives here; he has done much to build up our cause in Minnesota and still gives liberally.

Visited Horicon and Willow Creek, country congregations; they will co-operate in employing pastor. These churches are at peace and wield a strong influence on the surrounding country.

At Garden City I received a warm welcome by W. H. Rust, pastor, and the congregation. The church is strong and vigorous. It was our privilege to meet Sister Marshall, our missionary from Japan, now visiting her parents, Bro. and Sister Waite, who reside here. She will return to Japan in November.

Some time ago I visited Mason City, Iowa, where S. T. Martin ministers, and Walter Martin assists. The membership is 800; three Bible-schools with 900 pupils. No mean growth in six years. They are prospering abundantly under the Martins. I presented the Austin (Minn.) work and they responded with an offering of $26 for the building fund.

We have one of the most beautiful building sites in Austin. We are planning to have the congregation housed before winter.

Minnesota is a difficult field, but many places are ready for the harvest, and faithful work is being rewarded.

I think the time for a forward movement has come and that henceforth the progress will be more rapid. More funds for our home board and the work can be done. Send an offering to B. L. Smith, fellowworker, to help take America for Christ.

A. B. MOORE,
State Evangelist.

Austin, Minn.

Bethany C. E. Reading Course.

In our plea for apostolic Christianity we have emphasized some points to the overshadowing of others. We have read that part of the commission which says "*teaching* them to observe all things whatsoever I have commanded, I am with you." The office of the teacher in the church has been overlooked. It has seemed to me for years, in fact since I began my ministry, that we would have many more competent workers and teachers if we did as much teaching as was done in the apostolic church.

Every year since I left college I have conducted classes in Bible study and I know of no preacher of my age who has more sons in the ministry. I once asked a young man to speak to a friend about his salvation. The young brother said: "I have long wanted to, but I confess ignorance of my Bible; I don't know what to say." We conducted a class that winter on "The Early Days of Christianity." This brother took the course, began to speak to his friends of the way into the kingdom and is now a promising young preacher.

The Bethany C. E. Reading Courses are especially fitted for such needs of the younger people of our churches. First, a systematic study of God's Word, a study of missions and the needs of the world, then the inspiration of the lives of missionaries and our own pioneers to encourage them to be true to their convictions and the truth as it is in Christ Jesus.

There is a joy in proclaiming the gospel that is not known in Christian service except in living the gospel, and no person can live or tell the truth until he himself has learned it. The person with average memory listening to the average sermon in the average congregation, having preaching twice per month, would be a long time learning enough

To say that a young Christian should study his Bible as in the beginning of our movement is not enough. They have not the same incentive now that they had then. Our position is not assailed now as when the fathers began to plead for the undeniable position we occupy. That study, however, was liable to be textual and incomplete, but seemingly, to me, the plan of study in the C. E. Reading Courses is more comprehensive and valuable. Every church and Christian Endeavor Society should become a school in which the man of God should be thoroughly furnished unto every good word and work.

W. B. TAYLOR.

1234 *Montana St., Chicago*.

How Goods are Ordered by Mail.

Few people have any idea of the vast amount of goods that is being shipped by freight, express and mail direct to the farmer and the home, and few people have any idea how easy the great mail-order houses have made buying at wholesale, and how great are the inducements they offer to secure orders.

This office is just in receipt of Catalogue No. 107, issued by Sears, Roebuck & Co., of Chicago, a vast department store boiled down, so that you can sit down at your desk or table in your own home and select just such goods as you want, and everything is made so plain by large, handsome, clear illustrations, plainly written descriptions and prices in plain figures, that every one can order by mail; have the advantages of such a vast variety to select from and such very low prices that it certainly is not strange that these big department stores which issue these big catalogues are attracting the attention of buyers everywhere in the walks of life. Sears, Roebuck & Co.'s Catalogue is certainly a merchandise encyclopœdia, a book of 1120 pages, weighing nearly 4 pounds, and while it requires 30 cents postage alone to mail it, they send it postpaid to any address on receipt of only 15 cents to help pay the postage. Everything you will find in the largest department stores, everything that is offered for sale in any kind of a store anywhere, is found complete in this catalogue, and so plainly illustrated and described, and the price so low, that it is not strange that people are so anxious to get this book, and that so many send to this house for their goods. We are informed that it requires seventy carloads of paper to print their fall edition of this catalogue, fifty large printing presses running night and day to print them and $150,000.00 in postage stamps to mail them. Only from such stupendous figures can it be comprehended to what extent people everywhere are sending in their orders to this house

Chattanooga Convention.

RAILROAD RATES.

All roads belonging to the Central Passenger Association and the Southern Passenger Association sell tickets to Chattanooga and return for one fare. No certificate is necessary. The passenger buys a round-trip ticket, and it is good until the 24th of October. These tickets are for sale from the 13th to the 17th of October.

The roads belonging to the Western Passenger Association will sell tickets to Chattanooga on the certificate plan. The passenger pays full fare going, and takes a certificate. This certificate is signed at the convention, and entitles the holder to return for one-third fare. Those who live near Chicago and St. Louis would do well to pay full fare from their homes to these cities and then buy a round-trip ticket from there to Chattanooga. Those living at a considerable distance from these cities would do well to buy their tickets clear through to Chattanooga and take a certificate.

The Trunk Line Association sells tickets the same as the Western Passenger Association. Those who go to the convention must take certificates. The gateways of this Association are Buffalo and Pittsburg.

Ministers in the Western Passenger Association territory, having permits, should buy their tickets on their permits as far as either Chicago or St. Louis and then buy a round-trip ticket from there on.

ENTERTAINMENT.

It is understood that all who go to this convention pay for their own entertainment. The committee in Chattanooga has secured homes where persons can be entertained for $1 a day. The hotel rate is $2 a day. A. McLEAN.

Railroad Rates.

The Western Passenger Association and the Trunk Line Association north-east of the Potomac River has granted a rate of one and one-third fare, round trip, to the gateways of the Central Association, on the Certificate plan, to the Chattanooga Convention, Oct. 13-21, 1898.

Those coming from the Western Passenger Association and the Trunk Line Association north-east of the Potomac River will pay full fare to the gateway of the Central Traffic Association, and from there will get round-trip tickets to Chattanooga and return, at the rate of one fare for the round trip. When you pay full fare take a certificate for the same, and after having it signed at Chattanooga you will be returned from the gateway at which it was purchased to your home for one-third fare.

Please notice that those coming from the Western Passenger Association and the Trunk Line Association north-east of the Potomac River purchase tickets twice, one at the home station for which they will take a certificate, and the second at the point where they reach the bounds of the Central Traffic Association, where they will buy round-trip tickets at the one-fare rate.

Our convention at Chattanooga promises to be the most interesting in all our history. Preparations have been making for months that it shall be the strongest Convention we have ever held. The brethren at Chattanooga have had it on their hearts the entire year, and have made the most ample preparations for the successful entertainment of this Convention.

In behalf of the Boards we desire to extend the invitation for a general gathering of the loyal Disciples of our Lord and Savior. Let us say in our hearts, "I was glad when they said unto me, Let us go unto the house of our Lord."

Come to the Convention at Chattanooga, October 13th to 21st, 1898.

BENJ. L. SMITH, Cor. Sec.
American Missionary Society.

Evangelistic.

KANSAS.

Kimball, Sept. 22.—Am in a short missionary meeting here. My next meeting is with Bro. Henry Martin at Selma, Kan. Those desiring good meetings should write me here at once.—M. INGELS.

IOWA.

Des Moines, Sept. 20.—Closed a meeting Sept. 18 at Weldon with seven accessions.—GEO. E. LYON.

MISSISSIPPI.

Elzy, Sept. 16.—Just closed a meeting of seven days with four additions. Bro. Tally is our preacher. This is the first time the Christian people ever preached in this country, and great interest is taken by everybody. Hope to be able to organize soon. May the blessings of God abide and the good work go on.—E. PARKER.

VERMONT.

West Rupert, Sept. 19.—We have just closed a grand tent meeting, conducted by E. W. Darst, of Chicago. There was an intense interest from the start, and the large audiences present at all services displayed a notable enthusiasm. Bro. Darst's preaching was effective, and his sweet, kindly spirit won the admiration and respect of all who heard him. Twenty-nine persons were added to the Lord by baptism, and others are considering their spiritual duties as they never did before. Many are on the verge of surrender and will doubtless come at our regular services. A striking feature of the meetings was the large number of elderly persons who made the good confession. At least 10 of the number ranged from 50 to 80 years of age. The church is strengthened and each individual member quickened to a deeper sense of the spiritual life.—THOS. G. PICTON, pastor.

NEW YORK.

Rochester, Sept. 21.—My eighth year of service in Rochester opened Sept. 1st. In our annual meeting, held last week, we reported over 80 accessions to the membership in the city last year. Forty-four of these were received into the First Church. There is an increase of devotion and earnest endeavor in all departments of the congregation. The Second Church is duly launched into a promising future under the efficient ministry of J. R. Tolar, Jr. We are more hopeful for strength now than for numbers. Pray for us, brethren, that our strength fail not.—F. P. ARTHUR.

NEBRASKA.

Fairfield, Sept. 16.—Two added recently by letter.—GEO. LOBINGIER.

NO STATE MENTIONED.

Thirty-four additions was the result of our three weeks' tent meeting at Sandyville. The last Sunday afternoon four confessions were taken in the water. Every one of the 34 were grown.—WM. J. LOCKHART.

MISSOURI.

Tarkio, Sept. 21.—Seven additions the first week here.—H. A. NORTHCUTT, evangelist; A. R. HURST, pastor.

Charleston, Sept. 19.—Fourteen added in a two weeks' meeting at Bertrand. Oscar Rogers, of Paragould, Ark., assisted. The people were greatly pleased with his preaching.—A. F. HOLDEN.

STOCKHOLDER'S MEETING.

Notice is hereby given that the annual meeting of the stockholders of the Christian Publishing Co. will be held at the company's office, 1522 Locust St., St. Louis, Mo., on Tuesday, Oct. 4th, 1898, at 10 o'clock A. M., for the election of Directors, and for the transaction of such other business as may legally come before said meeting.

J. H. GARRISON, Pres.
W. D. CREE, Sec.

St. Louis, Mo., Sept. 1, 1898.

Dedication.

On Lord's day, Sept. 18th, it was my privilege to preach the opening sermon and dedicate the new and beautiful house of worship just completed by the church at Giffin, Ind.

Many more people were in attendance than could get into the house. We raised $200 more money than was necessary to pay all debts. The house is built in modern style, and is beautifully finished and furnished. It is a beauty. Bro. G. W. Ford is the pastor of the church at Giffin. To him is largely due the success of this enterprise. God has greatly blessed his work. L. L. CARPENTER.

Wabash, Ind.

Missionary.

Church Extension Receipts
For Completing Chapels.
For week ending Sept. 17, '98
From individuals, $ 572.25
From churches, 705.34
Total . . $1,277.59
Last year from ch's $344.49
From individuals ...316.36
Gain $113.54

will be seen by the above statement
ed in church collections and lost in
ontributions. We rejoice in this
e churches. The record with the
compared with last year stands as

tributing churches,	85.	Amt. $	705.34
tributing churches,	55.	"	347.49
buting churches	30.	Amt.	$357.85

ng words are coming in from all
e country in reference to reaching
nts. Many collections are held
to double or increase the amount
by the board. It should be noted
nly the report of the second week
. The largest amounts will come
o weeks. With the gain thus far
oard has great hopes of reaching
y collections from the churches.
hat do not get their collections to
the 30th, at the date our books
hasten their offerings to the board
o to the National Convention to
rt. All collections that come in
1st to the 13th will be put into a
y report.
the watchword for the next three
Quarter of a Million Dollars for
nsion by the close of 1900.
nces should be sent to

G. W. MUCKLEY, Cor. Sec.
vorks Bldg, Kansas City, Mo.

llowing the Recommendation?

the Board of Church Extension
ut one appeal in five, we recom-
nusual effort be put forth to raise
Extension Fund to one quarter of a
s by the close of 1900. We must
y annual offerings in September,
that extraordinary effort be put
up a generous and general offer-
mportant agency."
note that many preachers are en-
owing out this recommendation.
Sept. 20th, all the churches that
ings either reached or exceeded
ionments, with the exception of
and that one came within 85 per
hing its opportionment.
has asked no congregation for
and a vast multitude of poor and
hurches that sent sums, formerly
89, $1.53 and odd sums like that
to their apportionment of $3 and
ances gone beyond it. The only
is this: Shall we have a sufficient-
ber of churches who will put forth
ary effort" to reach the reasonable
the $20,000 *asked* of them by the
s year.
be kept in mind that unless we
,000 from the churches this year
dly make it up next year or the
g, and will therefore fail to reach
by the close of 1900.
understands that September is an
month for collections in view of

the fact that people have either not returned from their vacations, or having just returned are out of money, and that church life is not active during September as it is during other months. In view of this fact we trust that, for the sake of the work, churches will use October and November, if necessary, in order to reach their proportion asked by this board. It is too important to pass by with a light collection. Calls are pressing on all hands. About one-third of our congregations have no place to worship they can call their own. Over 500 new churches were organized last year, 43 were aided by this board to build, about 150 built without our aid, and 300 of last year's organizations are left houseless and homeless.

Remit to G. W. MUCKLEY, Cor. Sec.
Kansas City, Mo.

History of Hiram College.

PART II.—THE COLLEGE.

The board of trustees on February 20th, 1867, changed the name of the Eclectic Institute and clothed it with collegiate powers and responsibilities. As Hiram had become widely and favorably known as the seat of the Institute, the name now chosen was Hiram College. It was believed that this action would add to the usefulness and influence of the school and that a stronger financial basis could be secured thereby. June 19th, 1872, the board in pursuance of the statute for such cases made and provided, increased the number of trustees to twenty-four. It should be added that a convention of friends of the institute, held in Hiram, June 12th, 1867, endorsed the action by which it was made a college. The college began its work Aug. 31st, 1867.

The change in the name and rank of the institute did not essentially change its aims and spirit. The work formerly done has gone on all the same. It was the addition of a college to an academical and preparatory school. The announcement put forth in 1867 declared the aim of the college to be "to furnish a course of training as thorough as any in the country;" "to bestow careful attention upon the classical languages," and especially "to give a fuller course than is common in those branches which are modern and national."

The first president of the college was Dr. Silas E. Shepard, A. M., now deceased. He resigned at the close of one year, and was succeeded by J. M. Atwater, A. M. Pres. Atwater resigned after two years' service, and B. A. Hinsdale, A. M., was elected to the position in 1870. He had previously been a teacher in the Eclectic Institute and had served one year in the college as professor of history, literature and political science. Mr. Hinsdale continued to discharge the duties of president until the close of the college year 1882, and retained his nominal connection with the college until June 1883. At the beginning of the college year 1882, B. S. Dean, pastor of the church at Hiram, was elected vice-president of the college and empowered to act as president for the year. At the annual meeting of the board in June, 1883, G. H. Laughlin, A. M., who for some years previous had been president of Oskaloosa College, Iowa, was called to the presidency of Hiram. Pres. Laughlin resigned in 1886 and for one year Prof. Coleman Bancroft served as acting president of the college. In 1888 the board called Ely V. Zollars, then of Springfield, Ill., to the presidency, and he is the present incumbent.

The year 1878 was marked by the building of the tabernacle. For all ordinary public entertainments the college chapel was sufficient, but the commencement exercises had been held under a large canvas tent, erected on the grounds or in the neighborhood. The inconveniences attending this arrangement led to a discussion of the feasibility of erecting a building to meet the needs of the commencement period. With the aid of the board of trestees, the literary societies and the citizens of Hiram, such a building was erected, having a seating capacity of 1,200. The first exercises were held in it June 20th, 1878.

On the 11th of June, 1879, the board, then in annual session at Hiram, received a petition signed by forty-five ladies of the village and vicinity, that steps be taken for the erection of a ladies' boarding hall. The proposition was favorably considered and a building committee appointed. Further steps were taken at two subsequent special meetings. The property known as the Smith property on the north side of the campus was purchased and upon it was erected a substantial brick boarding hall, which was thrown open to students in December, 1879.

The commencement of 1880 was of unusual interest, owing to the presence of General James A. Garfield, who a few days before had been nominated for President of the Uuited States. It was also the year for the regular meeting of the College Reunion Association. This meeting was held the day after commencement, and was presided over by the distinguished man. The news of his election the ensuing fall was received with great joy in Hiram. On the 4th of February, 1881, he made his last visit to the village, when he made a short but touching address to the citizens and students in the college chapel. It is safe to say that from no point on the continent was the ebb and flow of his life during the eleven long weeks of his sickness watched more closely than from Hiram Hill, nor was his death anywhere more deeply mourned.

As time went on, after the organization of the college the need of more room began gradually to be felt. In the earlier days of the Eclectic Institute three literary societies had been founded: The Olive Branch, in 1853; the Delphic, in 1854; the Hesperian, in 1855. The libraries of these societies, together with that of the college, rapidly increased. Recitation rooms had always served for society halls. Added to this the great advance made in late years in the field of the natural sciences demanded better facilities for teaching them than Hiram afforded. Rambling talk of a new building was heard at times, but the school was not financially strong, and the consummation of an end so much desired was thought to be far in the future. Notwithstanding, work was begun on this building on the 8th of June, 1886. It was pushed so rapidly that the corner stone was laid on commencement day, June 17th, with appropriate ceremonies. A large concourse of people was present on the occasion. The traditional box containing papers, coins, etc., was deposited under the stone. Speeches were made by Dr. I. A. Thayer, B. J. Radford and Wm. Bowler. Abram Teachout concluded the exercises in an appropriate manner. The contract called for the completion by Sept. 28th of so much of the building as would accommodate the regular classes, and the whole was to be completed by December 1st. The first classes recited in the new building Jan. 12th, 1887. On the 11th of January the structure was dedicated.

Begining with the year 1882, several important changes were made in Hiram's course of study. At a meeting of the State College Association, held at Denison University, Granville, O., in the last week of December, 1881, a resolution was adopted requiring all colleges that wished to retain membership in the association to make their course of study equal in point of time and amount of work done. This was the beginning of the extension of the curriculum and of the numerous and excellent courses of study that Hiram now offers.

With the administration of Pres. E. V. Zollars the third era of Hiram College begins. He began his duties with the fall term of 1888, and the history which follows is that of the very progressive and successful decade ending with the present year. P.

Family Circle.

A Game of Childhood.

J. BRECKENRIDGE ELLIS.

When two years old, my little Fay
Had one game she loved best to play.
She'd hide her face upon my knee
And whisper, "*Now* you can't see me!"
When I pretended great surprise,
While still she hid her little eyes,
And cried, "Where-is-my-little-dear!"
She'd laugh and answer, "I am here!"
Or else she'd crouch behind the door
And—"You can't see me any more!"
Or, lay her little golden head
In deep, dark shadows of the bed;
Hard then my task, deep my distress,
To find her in her wilderness!

How strange the silence of the home
That echoed once a cherished tone—
A voice now hushed! I lived apart,
And bitter doubt crept in my heart.
Yes, I began to doubt that Power
Which strips earth of its fairest flower.

One night I wandered 'neath the stars,
Feeling grief press like prison-bars,
When suddenly upon my ear
A childish voice seemed to ring as clear
As in past days, as fresh, as free,
Crying, "Papa, you don't see me!"
I knew it was a fancy, born
Of hopes destroyed and a home forlorn,
But a hope dawned bright as a morning new,
As I whispered: "Darling, *where* are you?"
From above the stars I seemed to hear
A voice ring gladly—"I am here!"

Plattsburg, Mo.

Text Stories—XIV.

DANGER IN THE SOCIAL GAME.

BY ALICE CURTICE MOYER.

And they crucified him, and parted his garments, casting lots.—*Matt. 27:35.*

"Dear, now that we are married and have a home of our own, wherein we may be a sort of law unto ourselves in a few social matters and customs, let us throw these into the grate," and my wife held a pack of cards over the blaze; but I caught her hand and took the cards, saying laughingly:

"Don't be extravagant, my dear. If you burn these I shall have to purchase more." And seeing how anxious she was, I continued:

"I think you are overscrupulous, my Mary. What harm can there be in these bits of pasteboard?"

"In *themselves*," she replied, "of course there can be no harm. But any game, whether played for amusement or otherwise, in which there is danger that it may lead to the gambling habit, ought not to be practiced. And to be a gambler!" She shuddered at the thought, but I laughed again and said:

"What an anxious little woman you are! Do you fear that your husband will become a gambler because he invariably carries off the prize at our euchre parties?"

Mary did not answer, but presently said: "Henry, did you ever think of how it might look to outsiders to see a company of professed Christians gathered about a card table? More than half of the members of our euchre club have their names on the church record. Now what must the other members think of them? It seems to me there should be more distinction between the worldly and the professed Christian. How are we to recognize the Christian unless his fruits testify for him and distinguish him from the world? It seems to me that the professed Christian at the card table is simply lending his influence against the Christian life as it ought to be. You say you can play a social game with your friends, without wishing to go farther, and I sincerely hope you can; but there may be those that will seek to imitate your example who cannot resist the temptation of going farther and yet farther, until the habit has grown upon them to such an extent that all will-power is gone, or is not sufficiently strong to break off the habit. We—you and I—when we sit down to a social game of cards with our friends, are lending our influence to the wrong side, even though it may do us no harm."

But I would not listen, and said, jestingly:

"What a prudent wife I have! I only hope she will not convert her husband just yet, for he does enjoy a game of euchre; and, by the way, the club meets here next week; I hope you will bury your foolish scruples, my dear, and let us have a good time."

Mary said nothing, and as I was too selfish to take any heed of the quivering lip or the beseeching eye, the matter was settled. The club met on the following Tuesday evening, and we had a merry time. I won the prize, as usual, much to my delight and to the envy, real or pretended, of the other members. We had refreshments, and then spent an hour or two amusing ourselves in various ways. Miss Hill sang for us, and Jack Long told one of his famous stories—something that had happened to himself, as he always declared. To hear Jack's side of it, he had had more thrilling experiences and hair-breadth escapes than any other man on earth. We all knew that Jack drew largely upon his imagination, but it amused us, and we always encouraged him with our appreciative attention. We were too thoughtless to heed the fact that Jack was reaching a state wherein he hardly knew when he was speaking the truth—to such an extent had he drawn on his imagination. When the ladies were not present it was his custom to punctuate his remarks with profanity at times; and on this evening, in his excitement at a thrilling crisis in the narrative, he forgot the presence of the fair ones, and fell into his old habit. Somehow it was awkward getting on after that, and presently they went.

As the door closed on the last departing one, I turned to look into the eyes of my wife.

"It goes hand in hand with the rest of it," she said calmy. "Swearing, lying, gambling and drinking are boon companions. For my part, I have never been able to see anything amusing in Jack's stories. They are simply untruths, and an untruth is only a polite name for a lie. The Father of liars has many children, of which Ananias and Sapphira were not the greatest. This age is an age of liars. There is the business lie, the social lie, the unkept promise and the suppression of truth, which are but other forms of lying. The world is full of deception; and when we encourage any form of it, however innocent it may at first seem, we are paving the way for a soul to receive the heritage of the 'lake that burneth with fire and brimstone,' of which God has said, 'All liars shall have their part.'"

"Gracious!" I exclaimed in mock surprise. "Who would imagine that my wife is a preacher!"

"And I am not yet through," she answered, "but I wish I could say also to Jack what I feel on the subject of cursing and swearing. Cursing, it seems to me, is the expression of a wish that evil should befall something or somebody; then why use the name of God in such connection—God who is the kind Father to whom we owe life, health, strength, everything? He has given us this beautiful world; he sends the rain; we are his children, and are by far more dependent upon him than is the child upon the earthly parent, and he does not withhold his good gifts. In view of all this, how can we fail to lift up our hearts in praise and thanksgiving, rather than to use his name in a manner which is really a sort of prayer to Satan—if there could be such a thing? Swearing is to use this kind Father's name and the name of his Son, Jesus Christ, as well as other things sacred, in profanity. To the shame of Americans, be it said, they are particularly noted for this wicked practice—this disgusting and degrading habit, so offensive to the refined ear and sensitive soul. It is not only intensely vulgar, but altogether senseless. Never does a man seem more idiotic than when indulging in the profane use of God's name; never does he seem less a man; in fact no gentleman will stoop to this senseless evil, than which there are probably none more demoralizing to society. The swearer is of the same class as the drunkard, the liar and the gambler, all of whom are adepts in this senseless art. God has given us a voice that we may praise him, and as the Father of all mankind he certainly has a claim upon us."

I said but little now, for my conscience was ill at ease. My wife had not yet discovered that I was somewhat given to profanity when out among the boys. I acknowledged the truth of what she said, feeling exceedingly small. She continued:

"And, my husband, as the swearer has his seat with the gamblers and liars and drunkards, so must the gambler have his seat with the drunkards, the liars and the swearers; and the seemingly harmless game of cards may lead to gambling. I noticed to-night the flush of excitement that you could not force back when the crisis of the game was nearing. I cannot help seeing how the love of card-playing grows upon you. Oh! my husband, I beg of you to desist before it is too late!"

But I only laughed and, kissing her, assured her that she need have no fears for me; that I played only for amusement, etc., etc.

Ten years have passed. Is it only ten? Yes, it must be, but it seems centuries. I look at my hands, so weak, and white, and nerveless; I glance at my clothing and shudder, even yet, to see the stripes; I place my hand on my head to feel the short stubble that has for so long held the place of the brown waves that my Mary was once so prone to caress. The warden tells me my stubble is streaked with gray. I glance from my window, but the bars so mar the beauty of the view that I turn away shuddering. In a prison-cell! O, God! A convict! How vividly it all comes back; and with each fresh memory

I pray God—yes I have learned to pray—for strength to bear it all until he sees fit to release me. But before I go I could wish to impress upon the young men of this great land the urgent necessity of "calling out the sentinels of the soul," bidding them watch; of avoiding the appearance of evil; of trusting not in the arm of flesh. How sure I felt of myself in those old days; but the fascination grew. There is a fascination about cards which *does* get a very strong hold upon the player. Sin is very pleasant at first; its delusive charms are most alluring. Heedless of my wife's protests, sure of my own strength, and my ability to give it all up at any moment I chose, before I realized it the gambling habit was so firmly fixed upon me that I had not the will to turn from it. At least I had not the moral power to exercise it.

I saw my possessions grow less and less; I saw our home go; at last I saw the very furniture of the house we occupied taken away—all to pay gambling debts.

Then came a blow. A tiny babe had come to us during the first year of our married life, and—incongruous as it may seem that one so despoiled of morals could love—I loved that little piece of humanity; I would curse myself that I could bring my little one to beggary, and then go out to make such beggary more complete. Then God in his mercy took her to himself. As I stood by the casket that held the form of our darling I made a vow that henceforth I would live an honest life. My friends encouraged me, and as time passed, and I resolutely kept my pledge, I was entrusted with an office in which a large amount of public money passed through my hands; it was here that the old temptation came back. I fought against it, but it was a demon in strength, and I was but a poor, weak mortal, without the help of him who giveth strength to overcome the tempter. I yielded; the money entrusted to my care followed in the wake of my own money and my home, and I was imprisoned for embezzlement. Soon, very soon, my wife was laid beside our little one, and I knew I had broken her heart. I seemed a murderer in my own eyes, and would have ended my miserable existence had I had an opportunity; but I was closely watched, and thereby saved from a double crime.

Then followed days, weeks and months of such wretchedness as I trust none other may ever know. Finally, for lack of other reading-matter, I began a study of the Bible, and found that even the worst of sinners might receive God's pardoning love.

The memories of the past will ever sadden, and the thought of all the years lost when I might have been working in the interest of God's kingdom will ever cause me deepest regret; yet, if there may be in another world any way by which I can atone for the past, and make up for my ingratitude on earth, I trust the good Lord will permit me to serve him, even in the humblest capacity. I know my time here is short; I know I shall never see the light of day again in this world, save through these bars.

And the beginning of all this was the social game of cards, where I learned the first principles of prize-winning, which after all was but a form of gambling; and it seems to me that any game of chance may tend to cultivate the spirit of gambling. Is it *not* gambling? What difference is there in the principle of the thing, from the cold-hearted murderers who sat under the shadow of the cross and cast dice for the tunic of the dying Savior, to the belles and beaux of modern society who give progressive euchre parties and offer prizes to the winners. In either case it is getting something without giving in exchange an equivalent. No man has a right to a penny that he does not earn honestly.

The gambling habit has a most peculiar effect upon its victim. Like the drunkard, he becomes corrupt in morals; his finer sensibilities are blunted; he is robbed of his respectability; sooner or later he is clothed in rags, and his wife and children become beggared, broken-hearted, disgraced.

Young men, because I am interested in you, and know your temptations and your weaknesses, I want to say to you this: On the great battlefield of the human heart where the thought and the purpose may become your worst foes, put on the whole armor of God, and with Jesus as your Captain, *fight*. Put the low propensities of your carnal nature to flight; make them your servants. Do not waver in the conflict, for your success in life hinges upon your victory in these battles.

Choose with care your associates, for if you associate with the tippler you will likely tipple or look mildly upon the habit; if you associate with the curser or swearer you will likely curse and swear; if with a liar, you may become untruthful; if with the gambler, you are almost certain to be fired with the unholy desire for ill-gotten gains. But search the Scriptures; learn how rich is the life of the Christian as compared with that of the worldling; enlist with the cause of righteousness in the Young People's Society of Christian Endeavor, Young Men's Christian Association and other organizations of similar character; work; look up to Jesus as the model by which to fashion your life.

Finally, "fight the good fight of faith," and Jesus, your elder brother, will stand by you and help you; for he was tempted in all points like as you are.

St. Louis, Mo.

Queer Salaries.

Probably few people to-day know that the original name of the state of Tennessee was "Franklin," or that in 1788 the salaries of the officers of this commonwealth were paid in pelts; but the following is a correct copy of the law:

"Be it enacted by the general assembly of the state of Franklin, and it is hereby enacted by the authority of the same: That from the first day of January, 1788, the salaries of the officers of this commonwealth be as follows, to wit:

"His excellency, the governor, per annum, 1,000 deer skins.

"His honor, the chief justice, 500 deer skins.

"The secretary to his excellency, the governor, 500 raccoon skins.

"The treasurer of the state, 450 raccoon skins.

"Each county clerk, 300 beaver skins.

"Clerk of the house of commons, 200 raccoon skins.

"Member of the assembly, per diem, three raccoon skins.

"Justice's fee for signing a warrant, one muskrat skin.

"To constable, for serving a warrant, one mink skin.

"Enacted into a law the 18th day of October, 1787, under the great seal of the state."—*Christian Endeavor World.*

Short Stories.

A Richmond pastor, who is fond of frolicking with children, recently encountered a six-year-old with the question: "What is the physical conditton of your corporeal organization, with reference to the matter of salubrity?" And the child at once replied: "I'm not German." That chap has a right to be smart; hisname is Montague. —*Exchange.*

Sunday-school class was on the ninth chapter of Acts, and the teacher asked one of the boys: "What is meant by the words in this thirty-first verse, 'Then had the churches rest throughout all Judea and Galilee and Samaria?'" And the youthful interpreter, who had not consulted Meyer, nor Hackett, replied: "I reckin they didn't have no preachin'." He was not a success as an exegete; but he was no failure as an observer.—*Exchange.*

They are telling the story that William M. Evarts was going up once in the elevator at the State Department, which was loaded with applicants for the ministerships and consulships. Turning to a friend who accompanied him, Mr. Evarts said: "This is the largest collection for foreign missions that I have seen taken up for sometime."—*Exchange.*

It is one of the school laws in Boston, as in other cities, that no pupil may come from a family any member of which is ill with a contageous disease. One day recently Willie K—— appeared before the teacher and said: "My sister's got the measles, sir." "Well, what are you doing here, then?" replied the teacher, rather severly. "Don't you know any better than to come to school when your sister has the measles? Now you go home and stay there until she is well." The boy, who is a veritable little rogue, went to the door, where he turned with a twinkle in his eye and said: "If you please, sir, my sister lives in Philadelphia."—*Harper's Bazar.*

The Father's Love.

GRACE PEARL BRONAUGH.

When God's children stand aloof,
Angry at His just reproof,
He must yearn to call us back,
Take us up, supply our lack,
Soothe our sorrows, make us well.
How we grieve Him, who can tell?
We may feel the barrier sore,
But I think He feels it more.
Greatest love feels greatest loss;
Human love is mixed with dross;
Men have turned from God, nor seen
Half the sorrow it may mean.
God, who loves and knows the cost,
Losing, grieves more than the lost!

Clara Barton.

MARY BLACK CLAYTON.

The gratitude of the whole country to the great woman, whose name is at the head of my page, should be given without stint in view of her able and conspicuous services in our recent calamitous war.

Her wonderful executive ability and her untiring devotion to humanity shine in bold relief against a background of governmental "mistakes" during this gloomy summer.

An account of her efforts to establish the Red Cross Society in the United States cannot be out of place.

The Red Cross once carried by the crusaders when they set forth to shed the blood of the infidel in the name of the Peaceful One has become an emblem of a better cause.

Wherever that sacred banner floats, aid is to be found for human beings in the extremity of distress. It no longer leads marching armies, but it follows their track after their bloody business has done its horrid work.

It is also the ensign of hope wherever floods, famine, pestilence or other overwhelming disaster prevails.

M. Henri Dumont, of Switzerland, is entitled to the honor of having first planned the modern confederation of the Red Cross. The idea came to him as he looked at the horror of the battlefield of Salferina in 1859. He proposed to ameliorate the condition of wounded by establishing relief societies in times of peace to prepare for the emergencies of war, and a system of neutrality between the nations by which hospital supplies, nurses, surgeons and wounded should be protected in time of war by wearing one uniform badge. He published a book setting forth his idea and most of the civilized world read and responded.

An international conference was held on the 26th of October, 1863, and fourteen governments were represented, including Great Britain, France, Austria, Prussia, Italy and Russia. The propositions then drawn were accepted as an international code by a congress which met at Geneva, Aug. 8th, 1864, and they were soon accepted by all civilized powers *except* the United States.

In every battlefield of the Franco-Prussian war the sacred standard was unfurled, bringing help and healing to the wounded and Christian comfort to the dying.

This glorious Christian Republic of ours waited to sign this human treaty until thirty-one other nations, more or less civilized, had given their sanction.

Their duty, plainly presented to our officials by accredited representatives of the international committee for the relief of wounded in war, was entirely neglected until the matter was taken in hand by Clara Barton, a woman frail in body, large of heart and brain, of immense executive ability and braver than all the generals of earth, past, present or to come.

She was sent to Europe by her physicians in search of the strength which she had lost by her humane exertions in the field hospitals of our civil war. In Switerland she was asked why her government declined to follow the good example of the rest of the world. She answered, "If I live to return to my country, I will try to make my people understand the Red Cross Treaty." She then gave a practical illustration of her own understanding of the matter by following the Red Cross through the war between France and Prussia, which was declared a year after she left America in the pursuit of health.

She returned to her country in 1873, apparently hopelessly worn out. After five years of suffering, during which, as she has said, she "forgot how to walk,"

After the first eight or ten minutes of the battle I was not cognizant of the fact that steel missiles of death were flying all about us. The whistling of the shots I heard no more, just as you say. I suppose that is the way it should be in battle, and that a kind providence had made it so.'

"Just then a junior lieutenant of the Spanish line, who was an English scholar and had been taking in everything that was said, broke the silence he and his fellows had maintained since their capture:

"'I think I may explain that of which you have been talking,' he piped. 'We did not fire any shots after the first eight or ten minutes. You drove our men from the guns.'

"Captain Bob looked at Captain Taylor. They looked at each other. They changed the subject."

Sunday School.

THE GOOD SON OF AN ABLE FATHER.*

HERBERT L. WILLETT.

It is not often the case that a father who has the qualities of an able and wise administrator is succeeded in the kingship by a son of equally good character. This was true in the case of Asa and Jehoshaphat. The long reign of the former had prepared his son to understand the effect of the king's policy, and happily he threw himself with ardor into the undertaking of still further strengthening the kingdom. Asa had been successful in his wars with the surrounding nations, including Israel, and usually it had been his custom to rely upon divine favor in the conduct of his plans. Jehoshaphat adopted the same policy and proceeded to take advantage of the forward movements which his father had begun by fortifying the cities of his kingdom and garrisoning them with royal troops. These included as well the cities of the Northern Kingdom, which had been taken in the intertribal wars.

But Jehoshaphat did not resemble his father merely in his able and statesmanlike administration of public affairs, but as well in his religious zeal. His ancestry did not terminate with Asa, but ran back to the great name of David, and this fact must have made its impress upon his mind. All that was inconsistent with the traditions of his house must be banished. He saw the evil effect of a departure from the norm of righteousness as witnessed in the affairs of the Northern Kingdom, where false worship and immorality crept in to overthrow the simple primitive worship as established by Moses and Samuel. He determined that his kingdom should be purged from all those influences which tear down rather than build up. The effect of this course was apparent in the prosperity which he enjoyed. His court became the center of admiration and wealth. He had sought first the kingdom of God and his righteousness, and all things else were added to him. A feeling of exaltation possessed him. He was borne up by a consciousness of his relation to God and had the satisfaction of seeing the influence of his wise course reflected in the conduct of his people. The tokens of evil worship seen in the groves and pillars of heathen worship were removed.

Perhaps the most notable contribution of Jehoshaphat to the moral upbuilding of his kingdom is to be seen in his campaign of education, which he inaugurated in his third year. Regarding this part of his work the earlier narrative in Kings is silent, but the testimony of the Chronicler is of interest, and the circumstantial form of the narrative which sets forth the names of those employed in the undertaking gives it additional value. It was from the earliest days the business of the priests not only to minister in the affairs of the sanctuary, but as well to be the religious teachers of the people. This had been the purpose in view when the tribe of Levi was set apart for the ministry of the sanctuary. Unhappily, it was not always the case that the Levites concerned themselves in the religious education of the nation. Too frequently they occupied themselves with the offices of the sanctuary to the exclusion of those duties which they owed to the intellectual and spiritual life of the people at large; but in this instance at least the true function of the order was revived, and with it was combined a ministry of the princes in the same direction, which must have been novel for the members of a court which could look back to the traditions of Solomon's time, when the characteristics of the courtiers were far removed from a religious tone. Jehoshaphat sent out the princes in company with the Levites and priests. These men were instructed in the law which formed the norm of Israel's religious and civic life—that law originally given by Moses, at least in its simplest form, and amplified through the growing life of the nation, needed to be brought to all classes; and these men went forth on teaching and preaching journeys, very much as the disciples of Jesus went in the days of his earthly ministry, and as the apostles went out into further regions in the later years of the first century. Theirs was a ministry of education in the highest sense; they traveled from place to place like friars in the Middle Ages, and gathered the people together wherever they could reach them, instructing them in the teachings of the prophets and sages who had interpreted the will of God. The results of this campaign were far-reaching; a new consciousness of the presence of God came to the nation; a sense of solidarity was fostered, and as Israel became more intelligent, it improved in ethical and religious life. Such a policy could not fail to make its impress upon the surrounding peoples. A trained nation is a power in war, as well as in peace, and Jehoshaphat found himself at the head of an organized and able body of people whose efficiency had been increased many-fold by their larger knowledge of the law of God.

One may question Jehoshaphat's wisdom in his later affiliations with Ahab, of Israel, but evidently the earlier years of his reign were keyed to the higher notes of national life and his influence in his own and other lands was great.

SUGGESTIONS FOR TEACHING.

Sons of a good father ought themselves to be good. The presence of God is as possible to us to-day as to the prophets and kings of old. The avoidance of the evil example of others is one of the ways of fortifying the moral life. Jesus promised what he knew would come to pass when he made the early seeking of the the kingdom of heaven the condition of obtaining all other needed blessings. Cleansing the heart of all impurities is as necessary as cleansing a city of defiling images. No permanent good can be reached until people are educated to true ideas of justice and righteousness. The work of providing teachers is fundamental to all national prosperity, and religious and political leaders may well cooperate in so holy a cause. The law of God is a collection of all the divine truth revealed through prophets, apostles and the Master himself. A nation that fears God is a nation that will command respect.

The University of Chicago.

*Sunday-school lesson for Oct. 9, 1898—Jehoshaphat's Good Reign (2 Chron. 17:1-10). Golden Text—In all thy ways acknowledge him and he shall direct thy paths (Prov. 3:6). Lesson Outline—1. Strengthening the Kingdom (1:2); 2. Divine Favor (3:6); 3. A Campaign of Education (7:10).

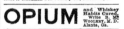

stian Endeavor.

'y Burris A. Jenkins.

TOPIC FOR OCT. 9.

PATRIOTISM.

(Psa. 33:1-22.)

patriotic enthusiasm has but just
our country. Now that it has
ubsided, it is quite appropriate
ld pause and reflect whether this
as been of the true sort or not.
well aware that a great deal of
vagance and nonsense has been
y yellow newspapers and yellower
t as to the great multitude of our
heir patriotism been shoddy, or of
?

this we must ask, What is true
and the reply to this question
not so much from the Scripture
iis subject, although the reply is
ence, as from the attitude of our
; was Jesus' patriotism? He un-
ved his people and came to the
his own nation first. But was he
all things else? Was he for his
t or wrong? Did he not come to
nly as a means to a larger end?
visions of a larger nation? The
eaching quickly swept the hearer
the confines of a single nation.
ever'' and his "all ye" were
idaism. He came to seek and to
lost. His love was a love for all
ut you say Jesus is no real test
t of to-day. Jesus *is* the test for
onditions and all positions. And
truest patriots that the world has
followed Jesus in this, that they
heir country for the sake of the
u Ben Adhem loved his fellowmen
loved his God. The true patriot
llowman and thereby loves his

y, then, we see by such a test as
surdity of such cries as, "My
t or wrong!" Immediately we
t sometimes, for the good of our
must oppose our country. Some
n quit their country for the good
ry—and not all of them criminals,
ne have expatriated themselves
' loved their country and their
Tyndale became a voluntary
country whose rulers hated him,
he might give to his countrymen
s in the English tongue. One may
might and main, the whole policy
ment and yet stand ready to die
e country. Such a thing did
ch has many another patriot done.
loves his fellowmen is the man
country. Lowell asks:

is the true man's fatherland?
'e he by chance is born?
the free-winged spirit scorn
cant borders to be spanned?
s fatherland must be
ue heavens, wide and free."

, then, as an instrument of God!
s a means of enlightening and of
of saving men! This is the object
tic love.

we stood this test in recent
s our fervor been stirred simply
s *our own* country that was con-
e sober reflection that comes to us
believe that we have failed of
some small degree our Savior's
not for *our* country that we went.
oppressed and suffering men and
was not love of our nation alone
orth in indignation till it culminat-
-flame. It was not simply because
had been sunk at Havana Harbor;
because a tyrannous government
ch outrages on Cubans or Ameri-
e, that our people rose as one
s love of men, love of right for

man, that caused our nation, hitheto stigmatized as a money-loving, crafty, commercial people, to pour out money like water and blood, more precious than money, for an unselfish purpose. At all events, a true American is glad to believe that these were our high motives. If any possessed motives below these, such motives were not true patriotism.

And in the years that are just before us, in the difficult and strange responsibilities that rest upon us, the true patriot will not wish his country to draw back or shirk for its own selfish sake, but he will wish it to do, for the love of men everywhere, that which will best serve for their enlightenment and uplifting. In politics, home or foreign, let us never say that the Golden Rule has no place. In the years immediately before us it is ours to be actuated, not by what is best simply for these states, but for mankind.

Marriages.

BONDURANT—SCHAEFFER.—Sept. 7, at the residence of the bride's parents in Normal, Ill., Mr. Frank L. Bondurant, of Paxton, Ill., and Miss Elizabeth Taylor Schaeffer were married; Walter Scott Priest brother-in-law of the bride, and E. B. Barnes, pastor at Normal, officiating.

STITH—FGSTER.—Sunday, Sept. 18, 1898, near Holliday, Mo., C. H. Strawn officiating, Mr. Roscoe S. Stith to Miss Sula Foster, both of Monroe County, Mo.

Obituaries.

[One hundred words will be inserted free. Above one hundred words, one cent a word. Please send amount with each notice.]

FIELD.

Mrs. Weltha Sexton Field was born Nov. 1, 1811. After an illness of three months she died at her home, near Ballards, Mich., on Aug. 30, 1898. She had been a widow eight years. One son died in 1875; two sons and two daughters mourn her loss. She with her husband united with the Church of Christ in 1862, having formerly been a member of the Baptist Church. She was a woman whom to know was to love.

Abby Field.

MOORE.

It is with the deepest sorrow, but sweetened with the brighest and strongest hope, I chronicle the transition of our dear Sister Eva Moore, wife of our beloved Bro. C. A. Moore. After an illness of some three weeks our dear sister quietly and peacefully fell "asleep in Jesus" at their home on Carroll Street, Nashville, Tenn. Her leave-taking was on the morning of August 30th, surrounded by the little family—her loving husband and dear little boy. Funeral services were held the next day afternoon in South Nashville Christian church. Almost the entire congregation was present, besides quite a number of visiting brethren and sisters, to share as best they could the sorrows of Bro. Moore. Sister Moore left a little babe—a sweet little girl—only about 10 days old. Oh, how sad for a child not to know the love, care and caresses of a fond mother! She leaves also a bright boy, Paul, about eight years of age. Sister Moore committed these two treasures, of course, to Bro. Moore, who will lovingly care for them and bring them up in the nurture and admonition of the Lord. Some two years ago their then baby-boy, Van, was taken from them to join the great army of little children who are in heaven. Jesus loved little children while upon earth, and often pronounced a blessing upon them, and we are sure he loves them none the less in his heavenly home. Mother has gone to be with little Van, while father remains to care for Paul and the baby-girl. Sister Moore's maiden name was Thompson. Her mother died when she was but a child. Her father died last year, near Mt. Sterling, Ky. Sister Moore was 35 years of age, and had been been a member of the Church of Christ for 20 years. She was a member in the highest and truest sense. It has scarcely ever been my pleasure to meet one with all the Christian graces so beautifully developed as in Sister Moore. Her open expression and kindness drew every one to her. She was a close student of the Bible and ready for every good work in the church. She was a coworker with her husband in the ministry, in that she rendered him every possible encouragement, and often accompanied him in his visitations to the sick and other work of the church. She was a woman of strong and decided convictions, therefore matters in which she was interested she weighed well and reached her own conclusions, and was not swayed from them by every wind of doctrine. Her faith was strong in the Christ, and it was her greatest pleasure to attend the services of the church. Her faith never wavered, even in the greatest and strongest trials. Such an heritage left to the family, church and the world, is certainly to be prized. Let us imitate such a life, that when we are called we, too, can leave a similar heritage. We can but sorrow over the loss of one like Sister Moore, but our tears are sweetened with the thought that our great loss is her infinite gain. I am sure the entire brotherhood, and especially those who know Bro. Moore, not only in America, but also in Australia, his native country, will unite in love, prayers and sympathy for him. May God bless this dispensation of his providence to the good of us all!

J. C. Martin.

PARKER.

Myrta, wife of James R. Parker and daughter of of Brother and Sister G. W. Henry, was born at Louisville, Ill., in 1873. She came with her parents to Lake City, Col., 1877 and to Delta County in 1887. She became a Christian under Bro. Parker's preaching in 1891. She was married in 1896 and accompanied her husband to Charleston and Berlin, Ill. Losing her health at latter place she returned to Delta last November. Here after more than a year's patient suffering she died at her parents' home Sept. 2, 1898, her 25th birthday, lemented by friends and relatives. Hiram W. Williams.

A Serious Situation.

It concerns the brotherhood to know that the cause of Ministerial Relief is seriously embarrassed and that longer indifference to its claims invites dishonor. On account of falling off of receipts, we were obliged to reduce the July quarterly allowances twenty per cent., which was a serious matter to the worthy and needy brethren whose better care we seek to secure. I am advised that there is now on hand—available for present use—only $500. The quarterly allowance requires $1,000. Shall these claims be reduced *one-half?* The October payments are in many cases the chief reliance of their recipients in their slender preparations for the coming winter. Must they be disappointed and be allowed to suffer for the small comforts they so well deserve? Does not the situation appeal strongly to our sense of justice and honor? God grant that your answer may be prompt and generous! "I was hungry and ye fed me."

A. M. ATKINSON.

Wabash, Ind.

The Religious World.

ccording to the estimate of a writer in :kwood's Magazine, there are 9,000,000 s in the world, of whom 5,000,000 are ıd in Russia, 2,500,000 in Eastern and stern Europe, 1,000,000 in America, 000 in North Africa and only 70,000 in estine.

---

t a session of two full Presbyteries, a weeeks ago, at Birmingham, Alabama, as decided to go over to the Northern byterian Church at the earliest opporty. It will be remembered that a sepe Southern Presbyterian Church for red people was organized at the Gen- Assembly of the Southern Presbyte- Church at New Orleans some months It would seem from the action of the Presbyteries at Birmingham above d that the colored people of the South ıot think favorably of the separate ch for colored folks plan and propose eek more congenial quarters in the byterian Church North.

ıe twenty-fifth annual convention of the onal Woman's Christian Temperance on will meet in the People's church, St. l, Minn., November 11 to 16, 1898. will be the first convention of this t body of temperance workers since the h of its great leader and will be a mem- convention. A strong appeal has been d by the acting president, L. M. N. ens, and corresponding secretary, K. Stevenson, calling for a large attend- and arousing the enthusiasm of the C. T. U. women to greater things in divine mission. Let all women and ıers heed their call and pray for the ess of their cause.

'e had learned that Christianity was ing rapid progress in Japan and exert- wide influence over the people of that ıd, but we had not yet thought of its t influence upon its government, and quite surprised by an article in a re- number of the Independent, from M. ordon, telling us of members of the who were Christians. The president he Diet, Mr. Kenkichi, Dr. Gordon , is a well-known member of the Pres- rian Church, and Mr. Soroku Ebara, her member of this body, an earnest hodist. In a recent election in Japan, Gordon says: "The Constitutional y have elected 258 out of 300 members e Diet. For some local reason un- wn to me Mr. Ebara was not re-elected; in Mr. Kataoka's district only two votes cast in opposition. And other Chris- have been elected. One of these, Mr. ara, a trusted member of the Kumi-ai rch, was chosen by a large majority."

---

rchbishop Ireland has said that the ıan Catholic Church in Porto Rico, a, and the Philippine Islands will not se the plan of the new administration hose islands, but will conform to the conditions, which of course means the ration of church and state. This will ssitate a readjustment of their affairs ose islands, but as the Roman Catholic rch has had considerable experience in adjustments it will of course under- d just what is necessary in the case. It will have to find its own finances for its bishops, priests and secular schools.

What seems like a successful if not a model church is the Bethany Church, Philadelphia, Pa., for which Wilbur Chapman preaches. The membership of Bethany church numbers over three thousand, and the Sunday-school has on its register over six thousand names. The last report states that for congregational purposes the sum of $32,500 was raised, and $12,000 in addition for miscellaneous benevolent purposes. And yet who but God knows the resources and responsibilities of such a body. Perhaps if the wealth of its membership was known and the amount of unused energy, idle factors, etc., its record might not look so brilliant. And yet we rejoice in what this church and its great preacher has done and is doing for humanity.

The present position of Evangelist B. Fay Mills in the religious world has raised a new question, which may yet assume considerable importance in the relative attitude of orthodox churches toward each other in the future, that of a membership in two or more denominations at the same time and on this question the Independent speaks as follows:

The carrying on of discipline and the removal of unworthy ministers is, we suppose, an ecclasiastical necessity. The duty occasionally has to be done. Yet it is the smallest part of ecclesiastical service. It is not what should control the government of a denomination; it is only occasional and subsidiary. Other things are of vastly more importance, the evangelistic work of the church, and the loving fellowship of its parts. If any evangelist, like Mr. Mills, or Dr. Pentecost, or Mr. Moody, working with equal delignt in different denominations, wished to be a member of two or more of them, the advantage to be gained thereby should not be prevented by the fear that he might by and by be disciplined for murder or slander. The double membership expresses beautifully the fellowship of the churches. It brings them together. It is a fascinating illustration of the worthlessness of the things which divide them, and of the importance of the things in which they are one; and it is a promise of closer fellowship in the future. This is a vastly more important matter than the consideration of discipline, which at the same time is not at all affected. Our business, as Christians, is not to bring people together, not to keep them apart; and a rule which forbids a member of one denomination to join any other comes very near being unchristian, in being exclusive. At any rate it makes that the chief consideration which should be the least.

While war is going on there must be court martials; but armies are organized for war rather than court martials, and who wants to bother with them when there is fighting to be done? With its sword of faith the Christian Church fights to achieve that *placidam quietem* which the motto of Massachusetts looks for, and which we love to call the millennium. It is for peace and good-will that the church must seek, for fellowship and union in its ranks; and the more intimate the interlacings that hold it together the closer and more blessed will be its unity. Let those that must organize its courts and be jury over its offenses; but its better work is to be teachers in its schools, and to cultivate the oneness of its citizenship, and the privileges of its common citizens in all its states.

Austria (Hungary).

The Magyars of Asiatic origin in the 9th century are to-day the dominating race in Hungary, consequently the Magyar is the official language. The Mongolian origin of the people is shown in their love for quick, passionate dancing, the accompaniment to which is familiar to most music-loving people. It is further shown in their fondness for bright colors and rich embroidery.

In another column is pictured a country tailor of the district of Heyduke as he sits at a Singer Sewing Machine applying heavy, bright-colored braid to the gala costume of a Magyar peasant.

Literature.

REMINISCENCES. By John Aug. Williams. F. L. Rowe, Cincinnati, O., Publisher. Price, 75 cents.

It is a real pleasure to open the pages of the above book. The style of the writer, the themes treated and the opportunities afforded for contrasts and comparisons in the progress of society combine to make it a book of more than passing pleasure. The author of this book has not only afforded his readers a literary treat in this volume, but much valuable information about the ways of society, its various freaks and forms in Kentucky during the first half of the present century, which may also be utilized as data from which to draw conclusions on ethical, civil and religious customs. One cannot help enjoying the book as he reads its pages.

"The Divided Church," is the title of a tract written by John Logan, Evangelist, Gatesville, Texas, and published by the Christian Courier Company, Dallas, Texas. This tract claims to be a critical review of the "progressive" and "anti" controversy in the Christian Church. Evidently the tract was written to meet a condition in Texas. It meets the condition in that state admirably. But the positions and arguments of the writer have a much wider application.

The use that is made of Paul's conduct in Jerusalem, described in the twenty-first chapter of Acts, read in the light of Acts, fiftcenth chapter, the decree of the Jerusalem council, is, so far as I am informed, new in this controversy about instrumental music, Christian Endeavor Societies and Sunday-schools; but the position is impregnable.

A distinction is made between "union" and "uniformity" which ought more frequently to be made in our preaching and teaching. B. B. T.

The Whiting Paper Company, Holyoke, Mass., one of the largest manufacturers of fine writing papers in the world has published a booklet in very attractive and artistic style on "The Evolution of Paper," in which some very interesting facts are related. The booklet is for free distribution.

The Illinois Steel Company has published an outline history of their vast plant, at Chicago, in a most attractive and finely illustrated book. One who has not visited such a plant cannot realize the magnitude and complications of such an enterprise, and this book will be found useful in helping one to realize what a factor such a plant has become in our civilization. The book reveals some astonishing information in machinery and productions of this plant. A copy may be had free.

MAGAZINES.

John Kendrick Bangs' newest stories are to appear in the Ladies' Home Journal. They are called "Stories of a Suburban Town." There are several, and each will relate some droll incidents in the life of a small town which every "suburbanite" will instantly appreciate and enjoy laughing over.

"Causes Affecting Railway Rates and Fares" is the subject of a paper by Dr. Walter E. Weyl, which has recently been published by the American Academy of Political and Social Science, of Philadelphia, Pa. Dr. Weyl, has studied the subject of transportation, both at home and abroad, and his paper is an interesting and valuable contribution to the literature in this field.

"Oscillations in Politics" is the subject of a paper by A. Lawrence Lowell, Esq., that has lately been published by the American Academy of Political and Social Science. Mr. Lowell, who ranks among the foremost writers on political questions, shows in this paper that there is a tendency in democratic countries like the United States and England to an oscillation in politics, by which one great party succeeds the other in power at more or less regular intervals.

Publishers' Notes.

The Outlook, of New York, in its issue of Sept. 24th, 1898, gave a short review of Prof. A. Fairhurst's late book, "Organic Evolution Considered." The following is an extract from the above-mentioned notice: "It is admitted that there are objections to the theory of Organic Evolution, as there are to the theory of gravitation. To present these objections is the aim of 'Organic Evolution Considered,' by Prof. Fairhurst, of Kentucky University, who has marshaled them in formidable show." This work is a book of 386 pages, and the price is $1.50, postpaid.

Such authority as the Sunday-School Times, of Philadelphia, has the following to say concerning "In the Days of Jehu," by J. Breckenridge Ellis:

"The story traverses the history of Israel from the reign of Baasha to the death of Jehu. * * * * This book will be useful in enforcing upon the minds of the young the stirring quality of the history of Israel in those days."

"In the Days of Jehu" is hansomely bound in cloth, and contains 188 pages. The price is 75 cents, postpaid.

QUEEN ESTHER

By M. M. Davis, pastor Central Christian Church, Dallas, Texas, is now complete and ready for delivery. It comes from the press beautifully bound in latest style cloth, printed in clear type, and is appropriately illustrated.

This book contains the story of the life of this beautiful Bible character, told in an interesting and attractive style. The book brings to the mind of the reader the beoutiful traits in the character of this great and pure woman.

This book should be placed in the hands of the young men and women of our times, because of the good influence it will have on the minds and hearts of this class of readers. The book is 12 mo. in size, contains 136 pages and the price is 75 cents, postpaid. Send for "Queen Esther," and place it before you sons and daughters.

BEGIN NOW.

The season of the year is now at hand whe people will begin to spend their evening around the reading lamp. They will wa good books to read, and will be ready soon buy them. The agent must be prepared meet this demand of the reading public. Ma persons would be glad to use some of the a proaching long evenings in carefully readi "America or Rome—Christ or the Pope," John L. Brandt. The agent is the person supply the demand for this book. The read wants the book, and we can furnish them agents at such a figure as will repay him for h labor in canvassing for it. We want an age in every community. Write us for our tern on "America or Rome—Christ or the Pope. A glance at the book is followed by a desire read it through.

A SUNDAY-SCHOOL LIBRARY.

It is the duty of each Sunday-school that financially able to provide, in addition to t Bible, good books for use by the school.

The time of the year is now approachi when the minds of the young will eagerly ta hold of reading matter. Nourishment for t mind should be selected with as much care that for the body. Many Sunday-schools a able to purchase a few books which, kept circ lating among their pupils during the winter, w do a vast amount of good.

A small, well-selected library, thorough read, will be a power for good in any commu ity. We can offer special inducements Sunday-schools and Endeavor Societies th want to commence this good work. A doze or so good books will not cost a large sum an will do well for a beginning. Additions ca then be made as your needs require. Prepa how to make room for these good companio in your school.

THE CHRISTIAN-EVANGELIST.

A WEEKLY FAMILY AND RELIGIOUS JOURNAL.

l. XXXV. | October 6, 1898 | No. 40.

CONTENTS.

)RIAL:
rent Events........................419
Forthcoming National Conven-
ons...... 420
New Day 420
Were a Millionaire.................421
Nevada Convention..............421
Path of the Just............ 422
tor's Easy Chair...................422

NAL CONTRIBUTIONS:
Campbellian Reformation........ 423
Us Return.—F. M. Cummins. ...425
I Love my Enemies?—N. J. Ayles-
orth......... ....:......425

ESPONDENCE:
cago Letter 430
shington (D. C.) Letter.......... 430
Omnibus Rebus............ 431
Church and the State University..432
norial of A. F. H. Saw............433
len, Utah 434
isiana Convention.................434
tory of Hiram College...... 435
w to Make the Bethany Reading
ircle Go...... ... .: 435

Y CIRCLE:
Two Selves (poem)................440
White Queen Club 440
to Chattanooga (poem).............442
Effective Sermon....................442
umn..................................442
nes...................................442
ssandphret........ 443
Bird's Trust.............. 443
wledge Vs. Education.............443

LLANEOUS:
rent Religious Thought......... ...426
Religious World..................426
Budget. 427
sonal Mention......................429
es and News.........................436
ngelistic.... 437
sionary..............................438
Sunday-school.... 444
vs Items 444
istian Endeavor.. 445
riages and Obituaries.............446
lishers' Notes.......................448
ouncements............ 448

Subscription $1.75.

FREDERICK D. POWER, LL. D., WASHINGTON, D. C.

PUBLISHED BY

CHRISTIAN PUBLISHING COMPANY

1522 Locust St., St. Louis.

THE

CHRISTIAN - EVANGELIST

J. H. GARRISON, Editor.

W. W. HOPKINS, Assistant.

B. B. TYLER, J. J. HALEY,

Editorial Contributors.

What We Plead For.

The Christian-Evangelist pleads for:

The Christianity of the New Testament, taught by Christ and his Apostles, versus the theology of the creeds taught by fallible men—the world's great need.

The divine confession of faith on which Christ built his church, versus human confessions of faith on which men have split the church.

The unity of Christ's disciples, for which he so fervently prayed, versus the divisions in Christ's body, which his apostles strongly condemned.

The abandonment of sectarian names and practices, based on human authority, for the common family name and the common faith, based on divine authority, versus the abandonment of scriptural names and usages for partisan ends.

The hearty co-operation of Christians in efforts of world-wide beneficence and evangelization, versus petty jealousies and strifes in the struggle for denominational pre-eminence.

The fidelity to truth which secures the approval of God, versus conformity to custom to gain the favor of men.

The protection of the home and the destruction of the saloon, versus the protection of the saloon and the destruction of the home.

For the right against the wrong;
For the weak against the strong;
For the poor who've waited long
For the brighter age to be.
For the truth, 'gainst superstition,
For the faith, against tradition,
For the hope, whose glad fruition
Our waiting eyes shall see.

RATES OF SUBSCRIPTION.

Single subscriptions, new or old	$1.75 each
In clubs of five or more, new or old.	1.50 "
Reading Rooms	1.25 "
Ministers	1.00 "

With a club of ten we will send one additional copy free.

All subscriptions payable in advance. Label shows the month up to the first day of which your subscription is paid. If an earlier date than the present is shown, you are in arrears. No paper discontinued without express orders to that effect. Arrears should be paid when discontinuance is ordered.

In ordering a change of post office, please give the OLD as well as the NEW address.

Do not send local check, but use Post office or Express Money Order, or draft on St. Louis, Chicago or New York, in remitting.

ISTIAN-EVANGELIST

opinion and methods, Liberty; in all things, Charity."

is, Mo., Thursday, October 6, 1898. No. 40

formulated a platform of which the chief plank is a declaration in favor of the free coinage of silver, and named as their candidate for Governor young Henry George, whose father's death last year brought him into sudden prominence as a candidate for Mayor of Greater New York.

On Thursday of last week a general plebiscite was held in the Dominion of Canada to obtain the answer of the people to this question: "Are you in favor of the passing of an act prohibiting the importation, manufacture or sale of spirits, wine, ale, beer and cider and all other alcoholic liquors for use as beverages?" Such an act had not been passed, nor was one pending, and this vote of the people had no immediate legislative power. The purpose was merely to get an official statement of public opinion on the subject of prohibition as a guide for future action by the administration and the Dominion Parliament. The result of the vote was a small majority, about 18,000 out of 800,000, in favor of prohibition. This result is not satisfactory to the temperance people, who had hoped for a much larger majority, and it is generally believed that the administration will not feel justified in proposing and pushing a prohibition measure on the basis of this slight majority. The various provincial plebiscites on this question which have been held during the last four years have resulted in much larger votes in favor of prohibition. The heavy falling off in Ontario is partly accounted for by the fact that women voted in the previous case, but not in this. The strongest temperance sentiment seems to be in the maritime provinces of Nova Scotia, New Brunswick and Prince Edward Islands, but their combined majority in favor of prohibition was only equal to the adverse majority in the province of Quebec where, under the influence of the Roman Catholic clergy, and owing also to the natural predilections of the French Canadian character, the opposition was strongest. Altogether, the outcome was decidedly indecisive, and the agitation will probably subside with no definite results for the present.

The American Peace Commissioners have arrived at Paris, and the work of turning the temporary prntocol into a permanent treaty of peace has been begun. The French Minister of Foreign Affairs has quainted. Having brought the two commissions together in this informal fashion, and having offered to them the hospitalities of the Salon for the sessions of the conference, it is announced that the French Government will "efface itself." So far as one can see, a strictly neutral and impartial attitude is being preserved by the French Government.

The War Inquiry Board is getting down to its work. It has addressed comprehensive lists of questions to Secretary Alger, the adjutant general, the quartermaster general, the surgeon general and the commissary general. Some comment was excited by the fact that General Miles was not at first asked to testify, but this omission has been supplied, and he will furnish his testimony to the board, although he says he would rather give it to Congress, and thinks that congressional investigation would be more satisfactory. There is a general belief that General Miles has a knife up his sleeve for the Secretary of War, and that his evidence may be of a sensational sort. It is certain that there is a difference of opinion as to the proper relations between the commanding general and the executive head of the department, and the limits of the authority of each. The sessions of the War Inquiry Board are secret, and all reports of their transactions, except as officially announced, must therefore be accepted with due allowance.

Rumors have been current for more than a week to the effect that the Emperor of China has met his death, either by assassination or suicide. While there is still no news more definite than "it is reported" and "it is believed," there is a growing tendency to place confidence in the report of the Emperor's death. At any rate, the Dowager-Empress, aunt of the Emperor Hwangti, is now in charge of affairs. The dismissal of Li Hung Chang, which was interpreted as a triumph of British influence, has been more than counterbalanced by the Dowager-Empress' accession to power, if not actually to the throne, and the dismissal of Chang Yen Hoon, who is a partisan of the British, as Li Hung Chang and the Empress are more favorable to Russia. The British demand for the dismissal of Li Hung Chang was honored, but the cause of the demand remains. In the matter of railroad concessions in the north-

seriously interfered with, and her commercial interests jeopardized.

The French Cabinet has definitely and formally decided that a revision of the Dreyfus case must be undertaken. This decision has seemed inevitable ever since the discovery was made that his former conviction was based on forged documents, but it was not reached without a severe struggle and threats of resignation from one or two members of the Cabinet. Here, then, endeth the first part of this long struggle. Dreyfus may be innocent or guilty. The fight up to this point has been to prove that his conviction was illegal, and that therefore a new trial should be granted. The new trial will be granted, but the Minister of Justice has announced that legal proceedings for libel will be taken against any one who ventures to attack the army in the course of the trial. To a civilian it appears that something must be wrong with an army whose honor has to be so carefully protected by threats of legal proceedings.

OUR FORTHCOMING NATIONAL CONVENTIONS.

As this is a case of one in three and three in one, we might with propriety use the word "Convention," in the singular number. These three societies have one work—the spreading of the gospel and the building of the kingdom of God on earth. They have practically one constituency—the churches of the Reformation which these societies represent. It would be better, in our judgment, because simpler, if there were but one convention in form, having in charge these three distinct branches of work. This is particularly true of the Home and Foreign Societies, as we have before pointed out. But this, by the way.

A very common question now among the brethren as they meet and greet each other is, What kind of a convention are we going to have at Chattanooga? The answer to this question is very largely yet to be furnished. So far as it is modified by location and the time of holding it, its character is determined, but these are only modifying, not determining factors in the convention. What the Chattanooga convention is to do and be is to be largely determined by the following facts:

1. The number of people having at heart our general interests, who shall determine, even at the cost of personal inconvenience and personal loss, to attend the convention, and give it the benefit of their presence and influence in every possible way. Scores, and perhaps hundreds of people who read this editorial, have not yet determined definitely whether they will go to Chattanooga or not. The kind of a convention we are to hold there, let it be distinctly understood, is going to be determined in a measure by the number of those who shall decide that it is their duty to go, both to impart and receive benefit and encouragement. There is a power in numbers which cannot well be dispensed with. We beg the readers of the CHRISTIAN-EVANGELIST, who have it in their power to attend this convention, to do so, and we guarantee beforehand that if they do, and will make good use of the opportunities which it offers for new inspiration, for larger information and for a wider outlook upon the world's needs, they will never regret the decision they made. Of course, the main reasons for going to Chattanooga are those which we have mentioned—the benefit of our missionary work and other interests there represented and the spiritual benefit to those going—but there are patriotic reasons that might well induce American citizens to visit the historic scenes around Chattanooga. It is perhaps the opportunity of a lifetime to visit the place under conditions and surroundings that would make the visit a most profitable and memorable one. Decide now to go to Chattanooga.

2. Another important factor in making the convention a great and profitable one is the character of the reports and addresses that will be made before it by the men selected for that purpose. Nothing should be presented to that great assembly that has not passed through the crucible of the most severe and critical examination, and that has not been steeped and saturated in prayer. The degree of enthusiasm that shall be awakened, the high resolves that will be formed, the liberal plans to be devised, will depend much upon the keynotes sounded by these addresses. There should not be one single slovenly, ill-digested speech, long or short, made before that convention. It is a great responsibility to be laid upon any man to address such a gathering as is assembled in one of our National Conventions. There is reason to believe, from the ability of the men chosen to address the convention, that there will be many notable speeches, which it will be vastly worth while to hear, and which will exert a lasting influence upon those who do hear them. Reports of secretaries should be so clear-cut, incisive and definite in their aim and meaning as to point directly to the ends to be attained. They should lift the standard under which the forces are to rally. They may be relied upon to do their work well.

3. In conventions as well as in legislation, much of the work is done by committees. There is nothing more time-saving and discussion-avoiding than a well-digested report of a committee. Chairmen of committees are held responsible for the character of the committee reports, and they should see that the particular work committed to them is thoroughly considered, and presented before the convention in such form as to receive intelligent consideration. Many a precious hour has been wasted in our conventions over reports of committees which contained unfortunate expressions and doubtful recommendations. Let us have thorough work on the part of the committees, even if it involves, as it often does, missing something that we would like to hear.

4. It takes two elements to make a great convention—the human and the divine. Nothing but the power of God can lift a convention of men and women to the height of moral and spiritual greatness, but this divine power must act through human agencies. The treasure is in earthen vessels, but the earthen vessels must be placed at the Master's disposal. It is possible to have a respectable, orderly convention without much prayer, but if we are to have a great convention, marked by a high degree of spiritual fervor and consecration, there must be much prayer on the part of the churches and the individual members before the assembling of the convention. Let
us go to Chattanooga on our knees, figu
tively speaking. Let us realize that in t
divine enterprise of evangelizing the wo
we are in copartnership with God, and th
it is only as he works in us and throu
us that our labors are effective. If t
conviction is deeply fixed in every hea
and we earnestly invoke the Spirit of G
to be present in the convention, and
guide it in its deliberations and actions
shall doubtless have a great convention.
will be one that will send us home, as fr
some mount of transfiguration, where
have seen the glory of the Lord, and
strengthened thereby for the conflicts a
labors of the years to come.

The Chattanooga Convention, then, is
be what under God we decide to make
If it fail in any measure to accomplish
purpose, the responsibility is on us. I
succeed in its purpose, the praise a
thanksgiving are due unto Him whose
are and whom we serve.

OUR NEW DAY.

Forefathers' Day by our Christian E
deavor Societies in behalf of Home M
sions is a wise and happy thought. W
a splendid "Trinity" of aim, agency a
method, and what a prophecy of good!

It is of very great importance that
people, and for that matter that all of
people should be kept well acquainted w
the origin and growth of this great
ligious movement in which we are engag
and that we should comprehend well
spirit and aim. To know well the fath
who projected this Reformation and
faithful band of immediate successors w
pushed it to such rapid and marvelous su
cess, to comprehend the nature and mag
tude of the work which they planned;
walk with them in their brave strugg
with popular error and religious bigot
to breathe with them afresh the spirit
loving loyalty to Christ and his inspi
works; to see with them through the mi
mysticism of superstition and creed ba
to Jerusalem, and to build with them ag
the broken walls of Zion, is to comprehe
better the mighty work God has commit
to our hands, and to become equipped a
inspired for its more speedy completion.

The study of our church literature, a
especially the study of the lives of
prominent pioneers of this Reformati
should meet with the most hearty endor
ment and encouragement from every pas
and teacher in every church of the Dis
ples. Avoiding the extreme of Rom
tradition and saintship, we have go
rapidly toward the opposite extreme of
ignorant and ungrateful oblivion of
heroic deeds of the fathers of this resto
tion movement.

We need to revive our study of the pi
eers and their splendid work for primit
Christianity. Forefathers' Day is an
portune time for this study. Observe
day in your C. E. Society.

Forefathers' Day should be a red-le
day in the history of the C. E. Socie
among the Disciples of Christ. The sp
of missions, our instinctive devotion
noble ancestors and a patriotic consec
tion to the highest interests of our c
country should combine to make it a gr
day. Let officers of the C. E. Socie
confer with the officers of their local chu
in arranging for this day, and let all ur
to make it a day abundant in blessin

ignorance and the fear of a bread famine. Scholars should be free to speak truth and fearless in announcing their conclusions. It is hardly a satisfactory state of things when every ignoramus and bigot in the country is perfectly free to utter himself, and only the men of brains and culture are gaged into silence by sectarian clamor.

I would give money to emancipate a true ministry from the fear of a half converted pewdom. Like Diogenes, but not in the same manner, I would go in search of men. There are plenty of bipeds that wear clothes and live on cooked food, but men are exceptional in the family of the *genus homo*. We must seek for a man, and when we have found him we have found the pearl of greatest price. Hope of the world's redemption lies in the regenerate personality, as free from human prejudice and the fear of man as it is from sin and the service of the devil. I would seek men of capability and conscience, courage and deep conviction, consecration and common sense. I would lay no restrictions upon them, and fetter them with no creed, and give them no orders, except that they were to go forth into the harvest field of the world and preach the truth of Christ as God gave them to see the truth, without fear and without favor. They would need no other commission, for all men of sense see the truth substantially alike when they are freed from the fear of men who do not see the truth. I would endow such men with an ample support for life, and thus free from dependence on selfish churches and the unmanning fear of the "rainy day" of poverty and old age. It is more than questionable if any institution can be reformed by its paid officials. A selfish, ease-loving motive at the base of it makes all officialism conservative, timid and averse to change. Reformation must come from without, from the initiative of free men. He who contributes most to the independence of a sound spiritual ministry, faithful to the ethics and life of the gospel, will do most to bring in the time of the regeneration.

Before my money gave out—the million at the head of this paper is five million in American money—I would endow a great religious newspaper. I would call it THE CHRISTMAN, and the most Christly man I could find should be its editor. He would be free from sectarian bias and the whole denominational conception of Christianity. The Scribes and Pharisees would not send their contributions to this paper, nor would their names be found on its subscription list. Its policy would not be dictated by any partisan constituency. Its fundamental principles would anchor themselves in the teaching of Jesus. All questions would be discussed in the light of the mind of the Master. It would not be so much a religious paper in the character of the themes discussed, as a paper that handled all questions, social, industrial, political, ethical, philosophical and religious, from the standpoint of the kingdom of God, and as far as possible in the spirit of Christ. The editor would be absolutely free to advocate the truth; neither business interests nor the subscription list should have any more dominion over him. Playing to the galleries would not be one of his pastimes. The shrieking brotherhood of intolerants who shout, "Stop my paper!" if the poor editor dares in the most modest way to call in question an opinion of one of these infallible popes, having been relegated to the shades of innocuous desuetude, would trouble him no more forever. The CHRISTMAN would have no hobby to ride, no fad to air, no axe to grind, no selfish end to serve; its only apology for existence, its only claim for readers, would be the interests of the kingdom of God and its righteousness. Such an enterprise would be a great business success, but nobody would care a fig if the balance came out on the wrong side of the ledger, so the great ends of the paper were being accomplished. If anybody wishes to risk me with a million or two I stand ready to assume the responsibility as indicated in this paper. J. J. H.

THE NEVADA CONVENTION.

The annual meeting of the Missouri Christian Co-operation was held at Nevada, on Monday evening of last week, and closed its sessions on Thursday evening. In numbers it was not a representative Missouri convention. The excessive heat and the distance of Nevada from the bulk of our membership in the state were, we presume, the chief causes of the diminished attendance. Many of the strong churches of the state had no representatives in the convention. We can see no good reason or justification for this neglect. Our leading churches should certainly feel a sufficient interest in the evangelization of the state, and in the general welfare of our cause in the state, to send delegates to these annual meetings, no matter in what part of the state they may convene. Our co-operative work will never assume the dimensions that it should until this obligation is recognized by the congregations in the state.

In spite of the diminished numbers, however, the convention at Nevada was a very good one, and the reports of the work during the past year were very gratifying. We give a few figures from the report of the board:

The state board has had in its employ during the year past 28 men, who have organized 25 churches and 28 Bible-schools, and who report 1,262 additions; 723 of them by baptism. They assisted in raising pastors' salaries to the amount of $9,690,85; building and repairs, $15,601.94; other purposes, $9,627.27; making a total of $34,-831.17. This only represents eleven months' work. Adding the report of the Bible or Sunday-school work to the above, the total number of churches orgrnized is 42; Bible-schools, 81; baptisms, 978; total money raised, $45,626.26. Including with the above the district work, we have the number of churches organized, 62; Bible-schools, 104; baptisms, 1,771; other additions, 1,507; making the total number of additions 3,286; pastor's salaries, $19,485; church building, $32,830.94; other purposes, $13,990. Total amount of money raised in mission work in Missouri, $65,191.26. Under the head of

GENERAL BENEVOLENCE

are the following figures:

State Mission Work	$43,829
Supplemental to State Mission Work	9,690
Church building in State Missions	17,555
" " " Bible-school Work	6,000
" " " County and District Work	11,300
State Bible-school Work	3,512
County and District Missions	5,765
Total	$98,151

MISSIONS OUTSIDE STATE.

Foreign Missions	$ 9,488

C. W. B. M.	6,500
Church Extension (report incomplete)	828
American Christian Missionary Society	4,096
Total	$20.870
LOCAL CHURCH WORK.	
Bible-school support	$ 45,000
Incidental church expenses	47,000
Church building and repairs	81,878
Ministerial support	355,000
Total	$528,373
ORPHANAGES, SCHOOLS AND ENDOWMENT.	
St. Louis Orphans' Home	$10,000
Educating orphan girls	6,000
Endowment	75,000
Total	$91,000
GRAND SUMMARY.	
Missionary work, Home and Foreign	$ 595,567
Local Church Work	528,873
Orphanages, Schools and Endowment	91,000
Total for religious purposes in Missouri	$1,214,940

This is not a bad showing for a year's work in Missouri. It may not be entirely accurate in every detail, but it is approximately correct, no doubt. Church Extension is the weakest item in the list, but that is to be accounted for partly by the fact that the secretary had not received full reports at the time of the convention.* He has already received several hundred dollars since that report was made, but even then it will appear that the churches in Missouri have been remiss in their duty to this important feature of our work.

As to the proceedings of the convention, we have not space to give a detailed account. We were not present at the opening of the convention, and did not hear the opening discourse by Bro. Vernon, of Independence, which we heard spoken of as an eloquent religious and patriotic address on expansion. We were favored with the presence of Bros. B. L. Smith and A. McLean, of the Home and Foreign Societies, who each gave a stirring address on the demands of their respective fields. It was gratifying to notice, however, that neither one was blind to the importance or needs of the field which the other represented, but they recognized their vital connection and essential oneness. We are certainly fortunate in the quaternion of secretaries, urging the claims of our general missionary work at home and abroad.

The lectures of Prof. Willett, of the University of Chicago and Dean of the Disciples' Divinity House, were a most interesting feature of the convention. He gave four lectures on the life and labors of Paul, which were highly appreciated by the large audiences which heard them. Bro. Willett is to sail with his family, early in October, for Europe, where he is to spend several months in study.

The address of Hon. Champ Clark, of Bowling Green, Mo., on Tuesday night of the convention, was worthy of the eloquent Congressman, and of the large audience which greeted him. He dealt with the Bible chiefly as a literary mine, and of its value in molding one's literary style, widening the intellectual horizon, and fitting one for his duties in the present life. He quoted the testimonies of great writers, poets and statesmen as to their indebtedness to the Bible, and in conclusion paid his respects, in his characteristic way, to the passing of Mr. Ingersoll as a lecturer. Mr. Clark received a most hearty welcome from the convention, as well as a most hearty response to his eloquent lecture. We trust it will not be the last time we shall hear his voice lifted in defense of the Bible in our missionary conventions.

*We have since learned that the receipts to Church Extension from the state of Missouri, from Oct. 1, '97 to Sept. 30, '98, are $1,809.71.

CHRISTIAN WOMAN'S BOARD OF MISSIONS.

The secretary of the C. W. B. M. will perhaps make a fuller report of the convention of the ladies. Their work has prospered during the year past, and the report of the secretary, Mrs. Virginia Hedges, was full of encouraging results. Mrs. Hedges was anxious to retire from the work, after four years of arduous and successful service, but her sisters rightly decided that they could not dispense with her yet, but they gave her an organizer to assist her in the work. Mrs. Williams, of Cameron, who is the president, gave a most admirable opening address, and presided throughout with queenly grace and dignity. She was also retained as the president, as was also that faithful and efficient servant of the C. W. B. M. in Missouri, Sister Johnson, of Chillicothe, as treasurer. The addresses before this convention by Mrs. Lowe and Mrs. Boen, of Kansas City, Mrs. Mary Wisdom Grant and Mrs. Bantz, of St. Louis, which we were privileged to hear, were such as to do credit to Christian womanhood, and compared favorably with anything in the convention of their brethren.

The addresses of Miss Ada Boyd, returned missionary, and of Mrs. Helen Moses, on Wednesday night, were listened to with deep interest.

The memorial hour was a joint session between the two conventions, in which beautiful tributes to the dead were read by Mrs. Hedges and Mrs. Bantz for the sisters, and Bro. J. A. Berry for the brethren. These were followed by a very beautiful and tender memorial address by F. V. Loos, of Liberty.

Mrs. H. M. Meier, of St. Louis, president of the Christian Orphans' Home, was allowed 15 minutes to present the claims of this benevolent work, and she did it most effectively. A resolution was unanimously passed recommending the national convention to give this national benevolence a hearing.

Some of the more important actions of the convention were the appointment of a committee to arrange for an educational conference to consider our educational needs in the state, which is to convene at Mexico in the late autumn or early winter. It was felt that there was no time in the convention for the proper consideration of these important questions. We shall have more to say of this later on.

The time of holding the convention was changed back to the first week in October. The state board was instructed to consider the propriety of having our conventions convene on Thursday evening, and hold over the following Lord's day instead of meeting on Monday evening, as heretofore. This, it is believed, is the only remedy for the lack of time now so sorely felt. We have been in favor of this change for years, and we hope that the state board will give us an opportunity to test it.

Bro. Kokendoffer, in the absence of the president-elect, W. M. Roe, presided over the convention, to the satisfaction of all.

THE NEVADA CHURCH.

We cannot close this report of the convention without expressing our gratification at the unanimity and zeal manifested by the church at Nevada, whose guests we were. Their entertainment was all that could be desired. The editor, together with T. P. Haley, was entertained at the home of the Baptist minister, Bro. A. E. Rogers, and we could desire no better illustra genuine Christian hospitality than ceived at their hands. Our assoc with Bro. Rogers and his good wi very delightful. All the delegates to be equally well pleased with their tainment. It was especially gratify hear from all sides that the union between the two congregations has a genuine one, and that the church i knit together in the bonds of mutu and under the strong leadership of C. McKeever is now ready for a stea vance along all the lines of Christian The brethren throughout the state rejoiced to hear this, and we take pleasure in mentioning the fact.

The next convention goes to Je City, Mo., which being in the cent of the state will attract, no doubt, convention. J. P. Pinkerton, the pastor of the church there, in an e astic speech of invitation, assur brethren that not only the homes city were at their disposal, but t State House and even the penit would be open to them. We will e large convention at the Missouri and our W. H. McClain, of St. Lou preside over the convention.

Hour of Prayer.

THE PATH OF THE JUST.

(Midweek Prayer-meeting Topic, Oct. 1

But the path of the righteous is as the dawn,
That shineth more and more unto the day.
—*Prov.*

We have adopted the marginal of the Revised Version in the abo substituting "the light of dawn" f shining light," which is in the body text. We do this because the pa more intelligible by this rendering, figure employed is more beautiful pressive.

There is a time in our religious ence when we see truth and duty in fused sort of light in which there an element of darkness. Like th whose eyes Jesus opened, we "see trees walking." The conflict betw lower and the higher nature often t obscure the intellect and to prev from seeing clearly the things we o do; but if one desires to know th and to do the truth, and if he obey as he learns, the path of duty will constantly clearer as he advances.

This is the fact which is set for poetically in the passage above Just as the early morning twilight its intermingling of light and s grows into the rosy dawn, and then into the full-orbed day, so this writer affirms the path of the just wi brighter, until it is illuminated by th fect day. Who has not watched with est the first signs of approaching day the eastern horizon begins to blush w first tints of the morning light, an how the mists and shadows of th receded before the brightening path coming sun? The spiritual expe which is illustrated by this phenome nature, is also an interesting one. seems to have used the same figure, speaking of the "voice from the ex glory," which he had heard on the said, "Whereunto ye do well that y heed as unto a lamp shining in

wn, and the day-star

sages the thought is
ht in the path of the
lk in the light. This
truth. It is a truth,
ed by the experience
lds his mind open to
s to live in harmony
is in harmony with
who said to the Jews
, "If ye abide in my
ly my disciples; and
h, and the truth shall
8:31, 32). It is also
that other saying of
willeth to do his will
teaching, whether it
I speak from myself."
stian doctrine is here
ill to do His will; that
e of a man's heart to
he will soon come to
s, and to be assured
hat he can walk in a
trine" here referred
tes to our character

eaching is such as
every honest-minded
to do right. This
ens that the path of
tians in very humble
with meagre attain-
hen it is obscure to
r pretensions. "The
with them that fear
he pure in heart, for
These passages teach
sson, namely, that
se, earnestness of
rt, are essential con-
cernment. Many of
at puzzle men would
hese conditions were

rim, the way grows
ward travel. We are
etting sun. It is the
o the Christian, and
eveningtime it shall
walketh in the path
our salvation nearer
lieved." A glorious
ine down upon our
he heavenly portals,
r, yea, we *can* hear,
the whisperings of
s that we are nearing
g light. Press on,
and in due time the
vill open wide the
nto the land where
ore night," but the
he glory of the Lord.

ER.

source of life, and
at Thou hast called
light by the gospel
ank Thee that Thou
en, when the way is
mble Thou dost lift
ntle hand, and lead
heavenly way. We
that Thou hast so
grows brighter with
sence as we journey
l. Help us, we be-
in the light as Thou
e light, that we may
ht; and when at last
ended, and we leave
may it be ours to
hy presence forever,
ur Lord. Amen!

Editor's Easy Chair.

Great interest centers in the Peace Commission, which sits in Paris. It has a most difficult and delicate problem on its hands. We can imagine the almost painful interest with which the Philippinos await the result. With them it is not a question of expansion or contraction, but it is a question of "to be or not to be" a free and independent people. Are they to be turned over to the tender mercies of Spain, to endure the same oppression and injustice which has hitherto characterized Spain's treatment of them, or will this great American Republic, whose remarkable victory at Manila makes them an arbiter of the destiny of the Philippines, say to Spain, "Hands off! Let this oppressed people go free?" This is the question in which they are most deeply interested, and all the world sympathizes in their desire to be free.

But, unfortunately, the desire for freedom and the capacity for freedom do not alwas go together. It may be that the Philippinos will have to undergo a process of tutelage, under the direction and protection of the American Government, to fit them for the responsibilities of self-government. If so be, what better business can this great nation engage in than teaching the art of self-government to the struggling and aspiring peoples of the earth? We are debtors to the barbarians as well as to the cultured nations of the earth, and this debt can only be discharged by imparting to them all that we have that is good which they are able to receive.

October should be a month of intense activity in religious work as it is in the business world. The absentees, who have generally returned in September, have by this time gotten on the harness, the enervating heat of summer is past, the cooler weather of autumn imparts new energy, and the season is propitious for aggressive Christian work. Let us hope that all the churches will avail themselves of the benefit of these conditions, and press forward in all their religious enterprises. Not until the church puts the same enterprise and energy into its Christian work that men of the world—and church members, too—put into their business operations will the church occupy the place it ought to hold as a controlling factor in the life of the community, of the nation and of the world. In our business enterprises we do not ask, Is it convenient or agreeable to do this or that? but, Does my business demand it? Would it not be a good idea to apply the same question to the interests of the Master's kingdom?

This brings us to say another and perhaps a final word about our National Convention. Remember, the question is not whether you can conveniently attend, but whether your own highest interest and that of the kingdom of God does not require you to go. No question is settled right that is not settled in the light of our obligations to the kingdom of God. So our Lord teaches when he says: "Seek first the kingdom of God and his righteousness, and all these things shall be added unto you."

What an age of travel this is! One can almost live on wheels now, and carry on his regular work. The writer has spent four nights during the past week on a sleeping-car, doing his traveling by night and his work by day. This mixing and intermixing of people, not only of the same nation, but of different nations, is bound to produce important results in the direction of the unification of the race. Water courses, mountain ranges, national lines, continental boundaries, leagues of ocean no longer separate the peoples of the earth. Steamships, railroads, telegraphs, oceanic cables have obliterated distance and brought the whole world together. This must ultimately do away with race prejudices, foster a worldwide patriotism, promote unity of interests, dispel darkness and superstition, and hasten that sublime consummation when the kingdoms of this world shall have become the kingdom of our Lord and of his Christ.

It is not probable that the Jews could have maintained their national unity as long as they did without their great religious feasts, which brought them together, and which promoted unity of sentiment and of feeling among the various tribes. It is hardly probable that any religious body to-day, which is widespread over the country, could maintain practical unity of faith, of teaching and of practice without these national gatherings that promote mutual acquaintanceship, that make common property of the best thoughts of the time and that weave the subtle cords that bind them into a common brotherhood. Our national conventions, therefore, have a mission apart from their chief aim—that of enabling us to keep the unity of Spirit in the bond of peace.

THE CAMPBELLIAN REFORMATION.*

Having an intense aversion to the expression, "The Campbellite Church," I cannot get the consent of my own feelings to use the above somewhat similar sounding term without a word of explanation.

The church is a divine institution, divinely constituted and divinely named. Hence the application to it of human name is dishonoring to the great Head of the church, whose name should be, with all men, above every name. But a reformation is simply a human movement under the leadership of men, and it is both inevitable and right that it should be known in history under the name of him who was the chief promoter.

Standing in the midst of a cluster of hills it is very difficult or likely impossible to pick out the highest, but out upon the prairie a few miles away the tallest hill stands out in bold relief above its companions.

So, fifty years ago, standing in the midst of the pioneers of the religious Reformation of the 19th century, but few could pick out the chief in leadership; but to-day, looking back across the prairie of fifty years, there towers above all his companions the magnificent face of Alexander Campbell.

Therefore, it seems to me a very proper thing to style the great religious reformation of this century, "The Campbellian Reformation," and I believe it will be a much-used term inside the next twenty-five years.

1. *What is the Campbellian Reformation?*

*An address read before the Minnesota Christian Ministerial Association at Mankato, Minn., Aug. 23, 1898, and by vote of the Association ordered published.

It may seem quite needless to broach such a question, here, but it is a vastly important question and the answer needs to be often attempted, though it will hardly be fully given for several decades yet. The answer I shall attempt involves some history.

The apostolic church was corrupted by its contact with Judaism and Paganism in the third and fourth centuries. There was the curious amalgamation of Judaism, Paganism and Christianity, resulting in the Roman Catholic Church, which abides to this day as mostly Pagan, less Jewish and only nominally Christian. That amalgamation changed vitally both the *doctrine* and the *government* of the church as ordered by inspiration. In the New Testament church the doctrine was this: faith in and obedience to Jesus as the Christ, the Son of God, as set forth by inspired men. That simple doctrine was corrupted by adding to it certain speculations from Pagan philosophy and certain concessions from Jewish tradition and theology, which practically nullified the original simple doctrine.

Now the government in the New Testament church, I choose to say, was the same as its doctrine—faith in and obedience to Jesus as the Christ, the Son of God, as set forth by inspired men. The doctrine and the government of the apostolic church were the same thing. The creed of the church was its government. Jesus the Christ was both *creed* and *head*. Hence when the apostles went out to carry out the great commission given them, they did not go organizing churches; the commission did not then nor does it now read, "Go into all the world and organize churches." The apostles went preaching the gospel, and when they had planted the divine creed in the hearts of a community, there they had a church. The divine creed in the hearts of men brought them together, kept them together and worked them together for the spread of the truth as it is in Christ.

Nearly the whole of medieval and modern theology is constructed as if the apostles first went forth and organized churches and at some later day went around and gave them their doctrine. It is a mischievous error, because it prevents people from seeing that the creed of the New Testament church is also its government. In that church Jesus was "all and in all." He was "Head over all things." He was all faith and all authority. The New Testament church was simply the aggregation of those who believed on the Christ and were constrained by that faith to obey him in all things. It was an aggregation of individuals called out from other men and called together and worked together by the power of faith in the Christ.

But to the Pagan world such an institution was no institution at all. Paganism did not believe that men were ever loyal and true except for selfish reasons. Hence it considered that any society depending for promotion upon the voluntary devotion of its members was simply leaning upon a broken reed and was bound to fall. To it a faith-controlled organization was a dead organization. The only powers known to it to unite and move men were physical force and selfish interest, and any society not using one or both of those powers was not worthy of recognition. So when Pagan influences flooded the church and corrupted its doctrines in their estimation they found no church government, and hence proceeded to make one after their own model, and the new church government was as different from the old as Peter's sword was from Paul's love—the new compelled from without while the old constrained from within; authority in human hands was the conservator of the new while faith in the Christ was the conservator of the old. So the great apostasy did these two things: added to the matter-of-fact, personal creed of the New Testament a lot of the abstract speculations of Pagan philosophy and Jewish tradition and changed the principle of church government from the inspiration of faith and love to the compulsion of force and fear.

Now when Luther came in the 16th century and hurled himself against that mountain of error called the Roman Catholic Church, he saw, to some extent, the first work of the apostasy, but not the second. He saw much that he considered wrong in the government of the Roman Church, but he did not see that it was fundamentally wrong and diametrically contrary to apostolic teaching and practice. He was so imbued with the spirit of scholasticism that he, too, saw no church in the New Testament and felt that there was no church till there was an institution that could exercise religious authority. He was badly confused on the question of ecclesiastical authority and could not right himself because he would not give up the old Pagan-descended notion that somewhere in the church there had to be a man or a body of men to pronounce judgment on men and doctrines. He raised the cry, "Back to the Word of God"—the very cry that should have been raised; it was the ideal watchword for the occasion. But he was hindered from making the whole distance by the fact that he held on to his old notion of church authority. In all his theological advances he adjusted everything to the old idea of ecclesiastical authority, and hence he could no more learn the complete Christian system than to-day a man could learn astronomy while clinging to the old Ptolemaic error, that the earth is the center of the universe. It worked as follows with Luther: Whenever he cried, "Back to the Word of God," the Romanist retorted, "No; out into religious anarchy!" and the retort made Luther wince every time. With his idea of religious authority, going out from the old Roman institution into liberty to find new truth was a very dangerous business. He went out as 13th-century sailors went out on the Atlantic ocean, fearing to go too far lest they come to the "jumpinging-off place!" He wanted new truth, but disliked to tear away from old authority. And every now and then in his search for new truth, in his going back to the Word, he would stop and say, "We are now there; we are now back to the Word; let us build our temple and call the tribes to worship." And he was led to do so, not so much because he believed he was absolutely right in doctrine as because he believed it his duty to establish religious authority among the reformers. But whenever Luther proposed to stop the search for truth—to end the journey back to the Word and formulate his doctrines and set them up as a religious standard—there was a vigorous protest among his associates. They pr
because they could not agree with th
Luther in many things. So the b
of the new temple was postpone
time to time, hoping to find some
building it in unity and harmony.

At length, however, the Romani
the situation. They clearly perceiv
if Luther could be led to formul
doctrines and to organize an eccles
institution around them, the re
would be badly divided. Hence it w
Charles V., at the instance of the
called the Diet of Augsburg in 15
demanded by civil authority an aut
tive statement of doctrine from the r
ers. The statement was written by
and Melancthon, who flattered the
that Providence was affording th
needed opportunity to establish r
authority among the reformers.
said, the reformers will not agree,
has used the Papal Emperor of Gerr
demand of us what we should hav
willingly.

The Augburg Confession at once
the authoritative standard, the
creed of the Reformation, and a
would not sign it were declared no
among the reformers. As intended
the Romanists, it divided and
weakened the reform forces. The
burg Confession was thus the p
bread which the Romanists laid
which the reformers ate. From th
to this Protestantism has been con
subjected to schismatic spasms, ind
credal poisoning. Previous to the
burg Diet, the reformers studied th
to find out the truth; henceforth, th
sacked the Bible to justify their op
At Augsburg, Luther and his fo
ceased to be true reformers, and fr
day on never gave the world a new t

Three hundred years later God ra
a man to take up the thread of
where Luther dropped it. This m
raised the cry, "Back to the Word o
and being a man who was not ha
with the old Pagan-descended no
ecclesiastical authority—a man
spurned all human authority in rel
he made progress. He said, "If
going back to the Bible, let us st
Pentecost and thence follow the m
under the direction of the Holy
first preached the gospel and fi
churches in order; let us follow
example." That man was Al
Campbell, and the work, which is
progress, is the Campbellian Refor

The difference between Luth
Campbell was chiefly these: Luth
deeply imbued with the spirit and r
of scholasticism. Accordingly, he c
ed the Bible simply a book of dat
which to construct a theological
and his conscience almost the voic
spiration within him. Also he co
possibly find any church in the New
ment. He thought he must find
doctrine and true church son
between Pope Leo X. and the las
apostles. He declared it wrong to
the theology of the fathers and the
of the fathers. Campbell flung sc
cism, the theology of the fathers
church of the fathers, to the win
found his theology sufficiently for
and his church completely organize
New Testament. Said he, "Let us

ring apostolic
ent." Luther
the road from
newhere along
authoritative
" Campbell
time on that
Jerusalem, but
Jerusalem, for
the divinely
nely delivered

ove on the old
Reformation
h as described

EEK.)

—

N.

Ohio are re-

y their atten-
politics and a
n various ways
constitutional
action.
ndividual from
orrespondingly
schemes have
ition party is
ecured enough
ate ballot, and
s found itself
or power in the

er of the Anti-
that greater
ve individuals
t, and the Good
ers in the field
ening old or-
new ones.
the failure of
sult in laying a
on upon which
nument to the
ibition.
es here learn a
dulged in the
g the world for
doing so were

n God that has
kings of Provi-
any millions of
offered in the
of evil and the
ood people have
ave neglected
recommend the
world they have
ve toned down
unduly magni-
God, until many
ner has felt that
by professing
s have winked
ongs that con-
gantic crimes of
ney contributed
been made to
s the pall which

assed land and
and neglected
neir own mem-
ck? What aid
n? None. The
ay render assist-

ance, but not the church. Is he out of employment? What account is the church to find him a place to work? A preacher may wear himself out in the service of the church. Does it defend him in his helpless age from poverty and the poorhouse? No. Do church members exempt one another from killing competition in business, from unjust dealings, from fraud, from the scramble for office and its spoils? No.

The churches are divided. They squander their means in extra machinery and in promoting one of the most enormous crimes against God—the crime of dividing his forces and thus furthering the cause of his foes. Can such a type of Christianity conquer the world? Would it make the world any better than it is if it did conquer it? It is of itself of the world, worldly, and is a failure as a redemptive agent. Let us return to first principles. Let us stop this sin of numbering Israel and work for principles instead of popularity.

The world lies in wickedness just as it did in the days of John and is a devouring, tyrannical, lascivious beast as it was in the vision of the Revelator. It is at enmity with God and truth and right, and is not to be won over by silly attempts to popularize religion. Let Christians band together to take care of their own interests both spiritual and material and make the kingdom of God a real thing of inestimable value to every citizen of it and not a metaphysical abstraction.

"Class interest" is a term which has fallen into disrepute, but if Christians will attend strictly to their class interest they will affect the general world tenfold more than they do. The class interests of Christianity are the perpetual teachings of Christ and the moral and material welfare of his disciples.

These secured and guarded with invincible power, then the church can become the Savior of the world, and not until then.

Marlboro, O.

CAN I LOVE MY ENEMIES?

N. J. AYLESWORTH.

II.

In the last article we saw that Christ demands that we love our enemies—not simply that we shall treat them well, abstaining from all acts of injury, nor even that we shall do them good, but that we shall *love* them. We saw that the reciprocal lives of social life, however beautiful their manifestations, or complete their development, can never fill out the measure of that love which Christ demands, or attain to the rewards of the Christian life—that the love which characterizes the Christian spirit is of a far higher and nobler quality; that it is found in the character of God, was exemplified in the life of Christ, and was possessed by certain of his followers. Yet this love is now often thought to be impracticable, or beyond the reach of the capabilities of the human heart. So far is this from being true that—

(1) It is entirely possible to love one's enemies.

(2) It is often done.

(3) It is *natural* to do so. I trust this will appear as our investigation advances.

Let us note, first, that *it is often done.*

When Gen. Grant received a communication from Gen. Lee offering to surrender,

*This article was written before the close of the war with Spain.

he was much elated in view of the success
of the Union arms and at the prospect oi
the termination of bloodshed; but when he
met the Southern General in conference and
proceeded to fix the terms of surrender, he
was "sad and depressed." He "felt like
anything rather than rejoicing at the
downfall of a foe who had fought so long
and violently and had suffered so much for
a cause, though that cause was," as he
believed, "one of the worst for which a
people ever fought and one for which there
was the least excuse." He sat down to
write out the conditions of surrender and
made better terms than he had formerly
offered, without any request that he should
do so from Gen. Lee. He spared the
Southern army, so far as it was possible
every indignity and every loss. Gen. Lee
at the interview, repeatedly expressed his
sense of the generosity of this treatment
and the South never forgot it. When the
news of surrender reached the Union lines
the men began firing a salute of one hun
dred guns in honor of the victory. Gen
Grant stopped it. There could be no exul
tation over a fallen foe.

What was all this? It was the spirit o
brotherhood. Here is pain and sorrow in
the hour of triumph over the fallen, there
are privileges granted which had not been
asked for or expected. The celebration o
victory hurts the conqueror, because i
hurts the conquered. The hero of thi
hour *feels* for this dejected and wasted
people. He feels their pain, their disap
pointment, their disaster. It is brother
love that presides at this scene; and her
is struck the first blow of a new conquest-
the conquest of the heart. It was well tha
this Christian-hearted man sat in th
White House for the next eight years. A
man of similar spirit followod him, an
while the narrowness of the politician ha
often sought to mar the result by fannin
anew the flames of animosity, the govern
ment has always acted in a fraternal spirit
and within a single generation this peopl
has been loved back to us. The wound i
healed, and the nation is one in heart as i
form. The people of the North turned fro
the bier of their dead to extend the han
of forgiveness and fellowship to those wh
had slain their sons. It was the Christ
spirit which healed this national wound.

A guaranty of all this was to be found i
what had gone before. The war was direct
ly and ostensibly for the preservation c
the Union; it was really a war of love
Sympathy for the crushed manhood c
some of the humblest of our race was be
hind it all. The "irrepressible conflict
was a storm of irrepressible brother-love
The years of that gathering storm wer
noble years; they were years of heavenl
anger. The white heats of those storm
times were purifying fires. Blessed th
nation that shall pass through such a bap
tism, even though it be sealed with bloo
It was all for love—love which spanned th
chasm of race, the distinction of color an
the vast remove of civilization to find
brother in the lowliest of mankind, to wee
over his calamity, to kindle in gloriou
anger in his behalf, to bleed at his sid
and at last to place on his dusky brow th
diadem of manhood. What wonder tha
this spirit should turn to his conquered op
pressor and say, "My brother!" It would n
have been itself if it had not. The peop
of this country had an agony. They ma

not have known just what possessed them, but God knew. They did not get through it without loving the enemy. It was one of God's lessons written in red.

We have now another war, a strange war, a war without hatred, an enemy without enmity. We do not hate Spain. Poor, misguided Spain! That is the way we feel. It hurts us to strike her. How long that Christian in the White House tried to avoid it! When Spain struck us in the sinking of the Maine we did not get angry. It was as when a child strikes a mother. We forgot the Maine in another sorrow. We heard only the cry of poor Cuba. It is a war of love, and love will not let us hate Spain. Nay, with the best of our people a sympathy goes out toward her. In the great brother-love which spans the race, and whose pulses we feel, Spain is not left out. We love her too, and feel a sorrow for her. It is another lesson in red. We are in God's high school of love; and as we go down on our knees over our dead, let us learn well the lesson of that love which sweeps into its arms, not only the downtrodden and oppressed, but the enemy.*

There is another kind of enemy—the criminal. How do we feel towards him? Some years ago the writer was escorting a highly cultured Christian lady through the Auburn Penitentiary. We paused at the portal and looked upon the convicts as they filed into the messroom. As she gazed into the one thousand hard, sullen faces she burst into tears. It is the spirit of our country toward its criminals. The judge pronounces the sentence of doom with pain, as if striking a son. To learn of any abuse or cruelty to those criminals in prison kindles our indignation second only to an assault on innocence. We will tolerate no injury and the infliction of no unnecessary pain upon them. If they are to suffer the death penalty, the state governments have sought with earnest solicitude to discover a means of absolutely painless death. Not a pang that can be spared them must be inflicted. Penal science is now wrestling with an anxious problem—how to give these criminals back to manhood and to the blessings of a worthy citizenship. The spirit of the nation toward its criminals is fraternal—nay, almost maternal. It is love pitying, sympathising and yearning to help. We love these enemies; but it is, as befits, love weeping, bending in compassion, striking with pain. And all this is done, not from a cold sense of duty, but at the bidding of the heart. Nor is this love weak: it is the controlling force in all our dealings with this class.

How far have the most Christian nations traveled toward the sermon on the mount! The old Assyrian kings flayed alive captives taken in war. The Romans crucified their criminals or threw them to the beasts for their own delectation, or pierced their sides with iron hooks and fastened them to posts on rafts and sent them out to sea. The torture of criminals or captives of war was enjoyed as a pastime. Now, quivering nerves run from us to them. If we strike them, we are hurt; if they suffer, we must weep. We cannot help it. The Christ-spirit has got hold upon us, and is hurting us with all the sorrows of the world. We have climbed high enough in the scale of manhood to find that it is *natural* to love enemies, and to find ourselves wrestling in the pangs of love for them.

Between the Atlantic and the Pacific there rolls another and a kindlier sea—a deep, sweet sea of the spirit of brotherhood. It has its storms and its anger, and sometimes its waters are like blood, but its tempests purify the heavens. As by fountains in the earth, it is fed from the bowels of Christianity; and as we slip across the line of another century, the tide is still rising. Watchman, what of the night?

Through the travail of the ages the love of enemies has already arrived and has possessed a vast area of human hearts. The larger love is already upon us with its agonies, its anxieties and its joys.

I do not forget that we have not spoken of *personal* enemies—the hardest task set for the human heart. This must be reserved for succeeding papers.

Current Religious Thought

A recent number of the Central Baptist gives the following good definition of an all-round practical preacher:

The best preacher is one who presents the broad side of a full man to his congregation. If he is intellectual, just that and nothing more, he addresses himself only to the intellectual element of his hearers. If the ethical predominates in his nature, he formulates his sermons in terms of conscience and his preaching is a system of morals. Should he possess in an unusual degree a glowing imagination, then to this he subjects all his other faculties and kindles in his hearers glowing pictures and gorgeous images. If he is endowed with exceptional emotional nature his preaching will abound in the pathetic, and will move his hearers to frequent tears. The best preacher combines in proper proportion all these elements. The keyboard of his heart has its octaves and register full, and his hands sweep from the highest to the lowest key with equal facility. Only thus can he touch cords which awake similar responses in the minds of those who listen. A very curious performance is that of making passable music on one string of a violin, but the best music needs four strings. Somewhere in this region is an explanation of the fact that the preachers who have most profoundly moved general audiences were not men of remarkable intellectual attainment, but rather men who embodied in themselves in fair proportion all the elements of universal manhood. A good preacher is not a freak; he is not peculiar; he is not a man of one idea; he does not play on one string; he preaches all the preaching which God commanded him, and addresses with equal directness all the hearts to whom God sends him.

The following reply to those who think that Christianity is losing its power in the world, made by the Observer, this city, is worthy of consideration:

As we see it, the church is more fruitful now than ever before in its history. Fifty years ago church work was done almost entirely by the ministry. The life of the church ran in a narrow channel, and the stream was dry a great part of every year. The annual revival was about the only season when the church showed any signs of activity or life. Often a whole year rolled round without the addition of a member. In the interval the church was in a state of suspended animation. Nothing was done to win men and women to holiness, and nothing to impress upon the community the life and power of the gospel. In those times the forces of the church were unorganized and unused. Many forms of Christian activity now so rich in blessing to society were then unknown. Indeed, the Christians of those days regarded the church as a thing separate and apart from daily life. Religion had but little to do with business, with society or with civil affairs. It was thought that the sole mission of religion was to save men and women from sin and prepare them for heaven. Feeling was the chief evidence of conversion, and the exercises of religion consisted largely in spiritual visions and rapturous anticipations. But a marked and salutary change has come over the church. The stream of life has widened and deepened, and has swept into its broad and mighty current the whole of man's interest and destiny. The mourner's bench is gone, the revival of those times is fast vanishing, the spiritual manifestations of the fathers are unknown, but the life of the church is deeper,
truer, grander than it ever was. New
of working have taken the place of the
adapted to those times. In scores of wa
life of the church is now daily exerting
upon society. * * * In the first part
century the life of the church flowed i
channel, in the last part of the century
flowing in scores of channels. Every de
ment of human life is feeling the influe
the gospel. Look at the countless benev
organizations that fill the land. While
of them are not actually under the directi
the church, they are doing the work o
church, and we rejoice in them all. Chris
ity is a mighty force in the world. Its
derful history, its mighty organizations
worldwide conquests, its numberless wor
its boundless wealth and its noble-he
missionaries in all lands are imperishable
nesses of its greatness and its glory.
vitality of the Christian religion is inexh
ible, its impress is on the thought, the m
ity and the activity of our times. The
nations that profess its creed are the con
ing nations of the globe, and they carr
banners, its principles and its laws e
where. No, Christianity is neither dead
dying. It has a great past, a greater pr
and a still greater future. Its aspiration
infinite, its labors boundless, its hopes i
ishable and its promises rich and unfailin

The Religious Worl

Work Still Going On.

In spite of the confusion in the army ca
consequent upon their breaking up and mo
to other locations, the work of preachin
gospel to the soldiers has gone steadily on,
the omission of but very few services.
Christian Commission workers have foll
the troops to Huntsville, Lexington and
tauk Point, and from all these places
come reports of sustained interest and
conversions. It is especially gratifyin
hear that the men who were converted
months ago at Tampa are giving a clear
mony for Christ and showing good evid
of a genuine work of grace in their hearts

Dr. Dixon writes from Montauk: "I pr
ed last night to a tent packed full of sold
and it was a joy to find among them so
whom I had seen at Tampa. The converts
far as I can learn, have remained true. S
of them whose names and faces I remem
were killed at Santiago, or died of fever.
fine fellow who attended our meetings
Tampa gave his heart to Christ in the tren
at Santiago, and took his first commu
just after the battle, and has been a fait
soul-winner ever since. As I have g
through the regiments, it has been like v
ing old friends, and last night several ot
accepted Christ and confessed him. It
add no little to the joy of living to meet t
men again here and there in the future,
find that they have been faithful to Ch
The indications are that this camp will soo
broken up, but other camps will remain
the evangelistic work should be kept up."

One of the workers at Huntsville wri
"Our work goes splendidly forward. Sold
are accepting Christ every day. We hold
daily services, one at 2:30 and the othe
7:15 P. M. I believe it is the biggest movem
yet in the army work. Yesterday aftern
the pastor of the Baptist Church was com
down the street and a soldier stopped h
saying, 'I have been reading one of th
books the Christian Commission are distrib
ing. I am all wrong; can you help me?'
pastor went to his church with him; the sol
accepted Christ, and was in the meeting
night rejoicing in the new-found life. We
use 7,000 of the books at this camp."

When the Commission workers arrived
Lexington they found nearly seven hund
men in the hospitals and began work am
them at once, besides holding their reg
tent meetings every day.

Taking into account the great numbers
men reached and the wonderful success that
attended the preaching of the word am
them, the work with the soldiers for the p
four months seems to me to be most rema
able, and to call for hearty thanksgiving
God. The response to the appeal for fu
made through the religious press has b
most hearty; the thousands of dollars nee
for the expenses of the work have been fre
provided and the money continues to come.
But better than the money have been the
pressions of deep interest with which it
been accompanied, and now this abund
grace bestowed in answer to prayer sh
"through the thanksgiving of many, redou
to the glory of God."

Contributions sent to me at East Northfie
Mass., will still be used to give the gospel
our soldiers and sailors, and when the work
ended, a full financial statement will be ma
public.

gold.
ıe gift.
›ath.
ıdlords.
the classes.
ıde for the
ıtituted for
for preach-
; established
ever become
ı or monop-
this paper a
, Ill., which
l who attend
nooga, Oct.
that stops at
'reek, Blue-
ı, Kicker's
rn, Murmur
:-absorbing,
the second
ng Courses,
' Fields and
has just ap-
sty glance at
convinced of
rses. There
in this little
study of our
of books are
ance at their
Endeavorer
ıd to J. Z.
of the books
t.
is paper an
ı V. Updike,
ıe Churches
ıich we are
ers owing to
at direction.
his religious
s important
people must
e conditions
theories and
ead Dr. Up-
n convention
d convention
ıdid program
sas and Mis-
this year in a
each state.
ı of the field
Home, went
e purpose of
ıe Orphans'
rches. Bro.
e interests of
ıf years and
them in the
g on our first
'ho is to pre-
ıe American
Chattanooga,
:wenty years
:tian Church,
ıached by the

more deserving of that honor than I.'' But the committee did not think so, and the convention ratified its opinion. He will make a model presiding officer.

—When the play at a ''standard theatre'' gets so immoral that a secular paper has to call it down and severely reprimend its managers for an offense to good morals and public taste as well as for bad business, it is certainly bad; and yet, this is what happened in one of the newest leading theatres in this city last week. The reprimand appeared in a leading Sunday paper. This proves the danger to young people in theatre-going despite the society distinction between what it calls high and low theatres. The imoral miasma may be more dense in the ''low'' than in the so-called ''high'' theatres, but it is by no means confined to them, as the case cited shows. The fact is that the financial success of all theatres depends upon this moral poison. Sometimes an overdose is administered and the public offended, but so long as it is not too glaringly flaunted the public applauds it. The fact is that they are all dangerous in their influence upon young people.

—The one shadow that rested on the Missouri Christian Convention was the absence of Bro. Abbott, the corresponding secretary, on account of the serious illness of his wife, who has since passed away. He was tenderly remembered by the convention in prayer, and a message of sympathy sent to him.

—At a recent meeting held by the State Board of Charities and Correction in the state capitol, at Jefferson City, the following resolution was offered by the vice-president, Miss Perry, of St. Louis, and unanimously passed by the board. It reads as follows: ''Resolved, That as Prison Sunday has been observed more or less in all of the states, that the State Board of Charities and Correction request all of the ministers in the state of Missouri to preach a sermon annually on the fourth Sunday in October on some phase of prison life.'' As prison reform has come to be one of the foremost of reform questions the request of the State Board of Charities and Correction is not only reasonable, but just and timely. It is such a deep and far-reaching question that no minister need be at a loss of material for a useful gospel sermon. That radical reforms are needed in our penal institutions is evident from a Christian standpoint, and the creation of public sentiment against medieval methods will hasten their departure; and the observance of Prison Sunday will greatly strengthen public sentiment on this question. ''This is sensible and practical Christianity.''

—In a personal letter from Bro. M. D. Clubb, chairman of the executive committee on preparation for the convention at Chattanooga, Tenn., he writes: ''I have never worked harder or prayed more earnestly for anything than for this convention, and somehow I feel that the good Father has great things in store for us. I believe it will be a great convention, marked by its good cheer, enthusiasm and far-reaching results. The work of preparation is almost completed, and our hearts are raised in silent prayer to God, that his Spirit may guide us in all things, so that when this great convention assembles we may stand before him as one man asking, 'Lord, what wilt thou have us to do.''' If this spirit of the Chattanooga brethren prevails throughout the brotherhood, we shall doubtless have a great convention. He adds: ''I like your idea of a prayer-meeting on Lookout Mountain, and will try to arrange for a Lookout prayer-meeting.''

—Good entertainment at moderate prices will be provided for all. The two leading ho-

ters at the Read House, where he will be glad to meet and greet his friends during the convention, and confer with delegates on matters relating to the Master's work.

—The following notice of the death of Thomas Munnell, clipped from the Plow and Hammer, published at Alma, Ill., and sent us by Bro. J. H. Smart, of Centralia, Ill., is the first news we have received of the decease of this widely-known brother, who has filled so large a place in our missionary annals and whose contributions to our literature placed him at one time among our chief writers. We hope some one who knew him well, and who can give us further particulars of his death, will send us a suitable notice of his life and work:

The sudden death of our good brother, Thomas Munnell, who was to become the instructor in the Bible College, brings sadness to the hearts of his many friends and acquaintances, and all interested in the college. He taught Garfield his first lessons in Hiram College, being one of its first instructors there when it opened. He has taught in Kentucky University and other institutions. He came to Alma College from the college at Canton, Mo. We feel the loss of his services in the college. Bro. Munnell was 75 years of age. He lost his wife some years ago. He was beloved by all who knew him. His daughter was summoned to her father's side, and came to see him laid to rest after a very active, useful life. The Christian Church at Alma mourns its loss, having called him to be its pastor. His remains were laid to rest in the cemetery near Alma.

—An exchange, referring to the forthcoming convention at Chattanooga, says: ''The Disciples are an inland people, having the bulk of their membership between the Allegheny and Rocky Mountains.'' Now, we may be ''an inland people,'' but we have never been charged, so far as we know, with having any aversion to water, fresh or salt. On the contrary, like our brethren of the ancient order, we believe in ''much water'' for baptismal purposes. True, we do not make as much of water as some people do who use less of it than we do, but we are going to cultivate the coasts and ride the oceans, and become a *maritime*, as well as an ''inland people.'' Keep out of the way!

—Some one has asked for the address of the Christian Orphans' Home. It is 915 Aubert Ave., St. Louis, Mo.

—On Saturday morning we received the announcement of the death of Sister Abbott. For days and weeks she was a great sufferer, but she is now beyond the reach of pain. The struggle is over and she has gone to her reward. During her sickness, severe as it was, she was unwilling that Bro. Abbott should omit any of his great duties on her account.

—Business in Christianity has a new illustration of perpetual motion. The Church Extension Society is built on the perpetual motion theory and this number of this magazine which, by the way, is an unusually interesting number, has the theory illustrated. It is a puzzling looking diagram, but there is no question about the machine working. The main wheel is so large and revolves so fast that objects in the shap of meeting-houses are thrown off from its periphery and scattered broad cast all over the land. It is a mavelous machine and worthy of careful examination or study in the light of this magazine and by the aid of its perpetual motion diagram. Address G. W. Muckley, Kansas City, Mo., for a copy.

—The eighteenth annual conference of the Christian Association and C. W. B. M., of Great Britain, is in session this week at Margate, England. W. Durban, the writer of our "English Topics," is the president of the executive committee of the association. President of the C. W. B. M. executive committee, Mrs. J. Coop. The program contains a vast amount of important and intere matter to be presented for edification, sideration and progress in the Master's

—Prof. E. M. Hackleman and E. B. Sc have bought out W. T. Sellers, of Indi olis, Ind. Bro. Sellers was the agent Christian Publishing Co., at Indianapolis had built up quite a large business. Bro Hackleman and Scofield will succeed hi these interests. Bro. Scofield is the Su school Evangelist of that state.

ɔur issue of last week there was a mis- ade with respect to the railroad rates to- ıooga. The roads in the Western ger Association and the Trunk Line As- ɔn will sell tickets on the certificate far as the gateways of their territory. ;ateways in the West are St. Louis and o. In the East they are Buffalo and ırgh. Those who go to Chattanooga pay full fare as far as the gateways and certificate. This certificate is to be at the convention in Chattanooga and ıble the holder to return from the gate-) his home at one cent a mile. The rn and Central Traffic Associations sell trip tickets for one fare.

› Eureka College Pegasus for Septem- ıe first number for the present school eems to be pitched upon a higher plane full of the new spirit by which the col- s been inspired with its new life. We he Pegasus and the college a happy, ous year.

card just to hand from H. Goodacre, ry of the State and National Secretar- ssociation, Red Wood Falls, Minn., ıces the following change in the time of ɔeting of this association at Chatta-

various reasons, chiefly (1) because a r of our memoers have requested it and ause the state convention of our breth- Tennessee will be in session Oct. 13th, ecutive committee have deemed it ıry, since the issue of our excellent m and call for meeting on the 13th, to the date to the 15th, at 8 A. M., in the t Street Church, Chattanooga, Tenn. ust this change will not inconvenience d that you will be on hand.

› program of the American Christian ıary Convention in this number. It be difficult to see how it could be im- upon for timeliness, importance of s, presentation of interests to be con- , etc. Read it carefully and study the ssibilities and powers it contains. It is ıble storage battery of spiritual energy, ıtilized in running the convention on a ane and to a glorious end.

ose who read J. Fraise Richard's arti- the proper and orderly preservation of le newspaper articles, recently repub- in this paper, will appreciate the follow- d from him on the fruits of his effort:

se accept thanks for the republication of ticle on "Scrapbooks in the Public y," and the sensible editorial notice called attention to same. A letter just d from Librarian Young returns thanks suggestion, and says it is being con- l and adopted. Commissioner W. T. , Bureau of Education, expresses same ent. The leaven is at work. The press wer. A similar letter of mine 18 months sulted in the opening of the library from P. M. J. FRAISE RICHARD.

hington, D. C., Sept. 24, 1898.

following report of a district convention alia, Mo., appeared in one of our city :

stian Churches of Pettis County con-

PERSONAL MENTION.

Evangelists Boyle and Ridenour are at McPherson, Kan., in a meeting with 24 additions to date.

H. F. Davis, Dr. B. F. Slusher and Bro. Miner were visitors at our preachers' meeting here on last Monday. Bro. Miner has been doing missionary work down in the Indian Territory.

J. W. Carpenter, of Augusta, Ill., has been called to serve the church at Washington, Ill. He will begin work the fourth Sunday in October. J. T. Alsup began work for the fourth district in Illinois, Oct. 2nd, at Dana. The meeting will continue indefinitely. All communications concerning the work should be addressed to S. S. Lappin, district secretary, at Paxton, Ill.

S. G. Clay began the sixth year of his pastorate at Fayette, Mo., on last Sunday. It is said that there was not a dissenting vote or voice to the continuance of his ministry at Fayette.

J. C. Wilson, who was at one time a minister in the Baptist Church, but who came to us from the Baptists, and was for awhile a preacher among us, but who has in recent years been engaged in secular work in this city, on last Sunday placed his membership with the Second Church here. He now states that he desires to return again to the work of the ministry of the gospel.

The Indiana State University invited Allan B. Philputt, of Indianapolis, to preach the opening sermon Tuesday, Sept. 27. This university is located at Bloomington, has devotional exercises with a sermon on Tuesday of each week and has about 1,000 students. It is also Bro. Philputt's Alma Mater. The University Reporter says: "His talk showed careful preparation and was delivered in an easy manner. He is an interesting talker and the students appreciated the chance of hearing him. Such men always please the students and draw them to the chapel exercises."

The church at New Orleans, La., has expressed its appreciation of S. R. Hawkins, who was for three years its pastor, in official resolutions which were unanimously adopted. The resolutions commend Bro. Hawkins as an efficient and earnest preacher of the gospel.

B. A. Abbott, of Baltimore, preached at the dedication of the new $10,000 church house at Wilson, N. C., last Sunday. Numerous copies of the CHRISTIAN-EVANGELIST were distributed at the meeting.

E. S. Conner, who has just closed his work at Noblesville, Ind., of his own accord, in a letter to us on the subject says: "I will reside here for awhile or until my future work is fully outlined. Yesterday was my closing day. At night the auditorium and lecture room were full of people—between 900 and 1,000. There were eight additions during the day and three at our last prayer-meeting, making a total of 11 at our closing services. The people have been good to us here and we regret to leave them. W. D. Starr will succed me here."

After Jan. 1, 1899, I will be free to hold two or three revival meetings. Have an anxcellent singer to assist. Will come for the voluntary offerings. Any desiring evagelistic work may address me at Middletown, Iowa.—R. C. OGBURN.

H. H. Rama, of Bloomfield, Iowa, says that for some time he has been disabled from preaching by sickness, but has recovered sufficiently to resume work. He would like to correspond with any church wanting a protracted meeting or a regular preacher.

Chas. Traxler, of Akron, Ohio, b city last week on business; paid hi to this office.

B. F. Maniere, of Jacksonville visiting his daughter, Mrs. W. B. Lindinwood, this city. He will go to the convention at Chattanooga.

W. H. Boles, of Alma, Ill., ca State Treasurer made a rousing speech at Irving, Sept. 28.

Evangelists Coombs and Hunsaker Worth, Tex., in a meeting with Pas Pherson.

A. O. Garrison, editor of the Pa tian, and his family have been spen days in this city. As his father has his interest in the Pacific Christi Christian Oracle, he (A. O. Garri all probability change his editorial the Pacific Christian to the Christi

Henry A. Morgan writes that he his work at Purcell, I. T., and acc to preach for the church at Bullin During the year closed at Purcell been 25 additions to the church. B wants his CHRISTIAN-ENANGELIST to into Texas on the ground that it i his work and that he cannot do with says that the church at Purcell will another preacher at present.

J. E. Masters, of Dorchester, Ill. visit to a point west of Hillsboro, M County, where he says he preach sermon, 36 years ago. Also the tow mis, where he says we once had a church. But since the death of Bro er he says the congregation has gon the church house, once a good one, dilapidated state. It is a brick str and $200 he says would put it in g He thinks the Illinois state board after this at once, as the location is one.

L. R. Thomas, preacher for the Pine Creek, Ill., since April 17th, re ditions; seven were baptized by Bro. church has raised $401.45, of whic Eureka College $117.50, and to missi besides C. W. B. M. contribution

CHANGES.

W. A. Baldwin, Rising City to Uly
D. F. Snider, Oskaloosa to Crest
E. T. Dougherty, Franklin to Ind.
K. W. White, Lawrence to Potw
J. H. Lacy, La Porte, Ind., to Mich.
F. H. Bentley, Nortonville, Kas comb, Tex.
Baxter Waters, Canton, Mo., to Yale, New Haven, Conn.
R. A. Morton, Emo, Can., to Bri
W. H. Kendall, Storm Lake, Ia., ton, Ind.
A. B. McFarland, Salem to Aub
A. Montgomery, Perry to Rossvil
S. B. Moore, Galesburg, Ill., to Mo.
G. A. Ragan, Oskaloosa, Ia., Park, Chicago, Ill.
H. L. Atkinson, California, Pa., sity of Chicago.
W. A. Wood, Eugene to Rosebu

SUBSCRIBERS' WAN

Miscellaneous wants and notices will b this department at the rate of two cents insertion, all words, large and small, to and two initials stand for one word. P pany notice with corresponding remitt book-keeping.

Correspondence.

Chicago Letter.

The gallant First Regiment of the Illinois U. S. Volunteers were received amid cheers and tears when they came home. Chicago turned out *en masse* to welcome them. Less than eight hundred out of the thirteen hundred who went to Cuba were able to march. Two hundred and sixteen came home sick several of whom have been dying every day since coming home. A long list of names have written after them, "Died before Santiago," "Died at Siboney," "Died at sea," etc. After the large number of sick and wounded soldiers had been conveyed to homes or hospitals in carriages and ambulances, the rest of the regiment, with Col. Turner, who had lost 40 pounds in this brief summer campaign, marched like the true soldiers they are to the armory amid the cheers of thousands upon thousands of enthusiastic Chicagoans. They marched straight to the armory where the iron doors shut them in from the surging crowds. Here, away up in the topmost gallery, a single cornet played "Home, Sweet Home," and "The Old Folks At Home." Tears came into the eyes of many of the brave soldier boys as they seemed, for the first time, to realize that at last they could sing:

"Home again, home again,
From a foreign shore."

Since the return of the regiment, many homes in Chicago have been made sad by the frequent deaths of the soldier boys. Near where we live a cultured widow lady, once in affluent circumstances, has been earning her livelihood and educating two fine looking boys. For nearly two weeks she has been anxiously waiting to hear from young Blake, her son, who was left behind on account of fever. This morning the papers announced his death. It was the first intimation the fond mother had received. Another boy seventeen years when he enlisted last spring could not hold his head up when he was brought home. This morning the papers announced his death. Not a day has passed since the brave volunteer regiment came home which has not chronicled several deaths among their ranks.

⁂

During the month of September the Christian Churches in Chicago have taken on new life and have entered seriously and enthusiastically upon the winter campaign "for Christ and the church." The ministers' meeting shave been largely attended. They now meet every Monday at the Palmer House, in parlor O. The subjects for discussion during the next three months will be on various phases of the Person of Christ. It promises to be a very thoughtful and profitable series of papers.

Brethren passing through Chicago and remaining in the city over Monday should not fail to attend these meetings. Last week John L. Brandt, pastor of the church at Valparaiso, where J. H. O. Smith had such a long and successful pastorate, read a paper on "Conscience." Those who passed favorable comments upon the paper spoke of the changed attitude by modern psychologists. Last Monday the writer read a paper on "The Importance of the Bible in a Symetrical Education."

Brother Brandt reported nine additions so far during the month of September to the church at Valparaiso. The pastor and his wife recently gave a reception to the members of the official board and their wives. Bro. Brandt was recently elected president of the district board of Northwestern Indiana. He reports a large attendance at the Normal School including five of our preachers, namely, Melnotte Miller, who preaches at Gate's Corners; W. L. Ross, who preaches all his time at Hammond, and three others. M. E. Bogarte makes an excellent Sunday-school superintendent and has 28 fine teachers under him.

⁂

The following are some of the preachers who were present at the ministers' meeting last Monday: George A. Campbell, W. B. Taylor, Charles C. Morrison, who has taken the pastorate of the Monroe Street Church, where his brother Hugh T. has been supplying through the summer; J. H. O. Smith; F. G. Strickland; Bruce Brown; C. W. Dean, a noble, energetic business man who is doing excellent preaching at Harvey, Ill.; J. S. Hughes, our recognized authority on the Apocalypse of St. John the Divine; F. Nelson Glover; H. J. Hill, whose fine physique is as robust as his abiding faith in our divine Master; Errett Gates; W. F. Shearer; A. Larrabee, the father of many missions in Chicago; E. W. Darst; Wm. Oeschger;——Kershner, and the writer. The West Side Church has had 99 additions since the first of February. They are planning for a thanksgiving service when the number reaches one hundred without waiting for a proclamation from the President. Their envelope collections now pay all expenses and enable them to accumulate a building fund. They expect to complete their building next summer. It will doubtless be the best building, when completed, owned by our brotherhood in Chicago. The fine foundations laid by Bro. John W. Allen will enable them to put up a fine superstructure. Bro. Brown has proved himself the right man in the right place. There have been 15 additions to the Union Christian Church in the last two weeks. Over $5,000 has been pledged for next year's work. J. H. O. Smith stands up excellently under what is doubtless the heaviest burden borne by any of our preachers in Chicago. W. S. Good will continue his work at Antioch, where we have a small membership, but with a good church building and no indebtedness. We have 38 members at Curnee, where C. B. Reynolds, a student at the University of Chicago from Virginia, is doing excellent work. The church at Joliet was organized about one year ago by Bro. Williams, a member of the West Side Church. Bro. Geo. T. Smith took hold of this little nucleus of a dozen members and by faithful and efficient preaching at a very meager compensation increased the number until they now have about 40 resident members. Bro. C. G. Brelos, who is pursuing graduate work in the University of Chicago Divinity School, has been preaching for them since the first of June. Brethern of Illinois, Joliet, a city of 40,000 inhabitants, and especially this noble struggling band of Disciples in the midst of that city, should not only have your sympathy, but substantial aid in Christian work.

The work of Hugh T. Morrison, of Des Moines, with the Monroe Street Church deserves special mention. He began his work the first Sunday in June and acted as supply until his brother Chas. C. of Perry, Iowa, assumed the pastorate. During his short ministry the church was encouraged and his preaching is spoken of in the highest terms. Even during the heated months the audiences steadily increased until the last day of his service the morning audience was larger than it had been for a long time. The Sunday-school attendance for that day was 203 and the Endeavor Society is again beginning to flourish. More than passing notice should be given to Evelyn Marston Gordon, one of our missionaries in the employ of the Foreign Society, who is pursuing the study of Sanscrit and other special studies at the University of Chicago. He was born in Bombay, India (where ArchDeacon Farrar was born), 1870. His people were Baptists for four generations and his grandfather was an English Baptist missionary. Even before he had ever heard of the Christian brotherhood, he would invariably call himself a Christian rather than a Baptist. He made the acquaintance of Morton D. Adams in Poona, seven years ago. At that time our mission station needed a supply and Bro. Gordon, though a Baptist then, was employed. His wife is a medical missionary and as a physician could make more than she and her husband are paid together, but "the love of Christ constraineth them." An illustration of the wide range of the University of Chicago library was manifested in the fact that Bro. Gordon found the Ramayan, the great epic poem of India, in the Hindi language which he speaks. It was an addition which he had never seen in India. Bro. Gordon entered the summer school of the University of Chicago expecting to attend one of our colleges during the winter, very probably Hiram, but the literature in the University along the line which would be especially beneficial to him in his work in India was so ample that he is thinking of planning another quarter at the University. His wife, who is now on the Atlantic, will soon join him.

⁂

Dr. H. L. Willett and family start for Europe early in October. Dr. Willett's wide circle of friends in and around the University will miss him. Dr. E. S. Ames, wife and son Van Meter are spending a few days in Chicago with Mr. and Mrs. Northup at Emlhurst. Prof. W. D. McClintock says the young man has high aims. The last I heard of him he was with his mother at Marshall Fields', shopping. We congratulate Dr. Ames and his good wife who have many friends in Chicago.

Mrs. O. A. Burgess, after spending two weeks in Chicago, has returned to Indianapolis. The Chicago trip benefited her, and we hope she will gradually gain her wonted strength. The writer and family leave for Virginia in a few days. This letter has been written at the C. W. B. M. headquarters in Indianapolis, where we found all well and busy. Miss Abbey Fields, one of the faithful office workers whose good mother recently went home to God, is again at her post. C. A. YOUNG.

Washington (D. C.) Letter.

The residents of the capital city are now in high anticipation of the opening of the Library of Congress in the evenings after October 1. The magnificent resources of the library have not been available to most of our citizens because the building has been closed after office hours. The construction of this home of books was planned with a view of its use at night. It is fireproof. There is a complete electric plant. Each reading table has its lights, while access to the shelves is as easy as during the day. The night opening will necessitate the employment of an extra force of twenty-five persons. For these positions there are already two thousand applications on file. The old problem of placing a thousand pegs in a hundred holes is one with which Librarian John Russell Young is now wrestling. What makes the matter more difficult is the fact that some of the applicants most earnestly recommended by congressmen could be appropriately designated as "sticks" rather than pegs. Doubtless many of those selected will fit in the places assigned them, and for years to come will grow with the library. Among these new men may be found successors to such veterans as A. R. Spofford, the father of the library; David Hutchinson, chief of the reading-room; Louis Solyou, expert in languages, and James C. Strout, for thirty years employed in the copyright division.

Speaking of Mr. Strout reminds me that he has a fad. It has possessed him for twenty years, and has resulted in untold benefit, both intellectual and spiritual, to the youth of our city. This fad is the building up of a model Sunday-school library in the Assembly Presbyterian Church of this city. It is Mr. Strout's custom to take his stand near the door of the church on Sundays. Every member knows why he is there. As they pass, many a coin and sometimes bills are dropped into his hand. When funds received in this way have not sufficed he has given of his own salary. But his contributions of money have been insignificant in comparison to the brain work he has put into this enterprise. The result is a library of some 5,000 volumes, probably the largest of its kind in the world. No effort has been made to have it big, but the aim has been to attain the highest standard of quality. Here may be found the products of the brightest minds—volumes of poetry, essays on science and natural arts, pages devoted to electricity and a description of the many ways in which it is used, volumes of sermons, biographies of missionaries, statesmen and famous soldiers, histories of all nations and religions, volumes of encyclopædias, stories by America's best fiction writers, etc. The relatives of this man of God need not trouble themselves about a monument for him when he dies. He has built his own monument.

The opening of the library at night does not mean that this splendid institution is maintained chiefly for the benefit of the reading public of Washington. The preservation of literature and historical data for future generations is the chief aim. Of great benefit to the future historian will be the scrapbooks containing notes of current events. In a recent interview Librarian Young said:

"When Mr. Gladstone and Prince Bismarck died I instructed our London agent to collect everything pertaining to them in the English, French and German press. As soon as the material arrives it will be classified, indexed and bound, and as such go on the library shelves. It should be of value to the historian as covering so large a part of the history of Germany and England.

"The library is having the early history of the Klondike prepared from material sent by Mr. Brainerd, newspaper extracts, manuscripts, maps and so on. As a rule it is never amiss to send anything to the library. We reject nothing. The trash of to-day may be the classic of the next century.

"The other day I had a broadside containing a proclamation of Jefferson Davis from the press of the Richmond Enquirer mounted. We are ever on the lookout for literature of the Southern Confederacy. We hope to have the best collection of Confederate literature in the world. Whatever concerns America is welcome—and by this I mean Presidential campaign literature, Mormonism, anti-Masonry, Knownothingism, woman's rights, reconstruction, special religious developments, like the Campbellite movement—whatever pertains to the growth of American thought."

A gentleman who has collected eight hundred volumes on the subject of Mormonism has offered to sell them to the library. It is probable that the books will be purchased. If so, the future historian will have a better opportunity to write up Mormonism than what Mr. Young calls the "Campbellite movement." Members of the Bethany Reading Circle of the Ninth Street Church sought in vain at the library last winter for books helpful in the course of study. F. D. Power in the preparation of "Sketches of the Pioneers" has found the library of no practical value. As an illustration of the deficiency in this respect, there are none of the journals and religious publications of our people except one volume of the Christian Baptist, that of 1827; four volumes of the Millennial Harbinger and the Christian Standard for 1895. While lacking the older publications of our people, the library is well supplied with books published since the act of Congress requiring all copyrighted books to be represented in the library.

Edward Everett Hale in a recent number of the Outlook tells of Dr. John Gorham Palfrey, the hospitable and courteous gentleman who with his family made their home such a delightful resort for students at Cambridge sixty years ago. One of these students after a visit there one Sunday evening said, "Palfrey makes you think that you are the best fellow in the world—and, by Jove, he makes you think that he is the next best!" It is a great pleasure to endeavor to produce this impression. When I escort a visiting brother who happens to have written a book through the library I reserve the best for the last. Taking him into the reading room, which is the crowning glory of the whole edifice, I go to a clerk and write a few lines upon a blank application. As the clerk puts this in a leather pouch and the pouch in a pneumatic tube and touches a button, I explain how it has gone to the proper bookstack and the attendant there has been called to receive it. Presently a disc by the side of the button pressed shows white, which tells us that the attendant has received our application. In a few minutes the book-carrying apparatus dumps out a volume. An attendant brings it to us, and lo! it is the book which my friend himself has written, the offspring of his own brain, kept with the lore of the ages, preserved for the enlightenment of future generations. Nothing in the library pleases my friend so much as this.

EDWARD B. BAGBY.

De Omnibus Rebus.

AN OPEN LETTER TO THE EDITOR.

I have just been reading your "Macatawa Musings," and they started me to musing a little on my own hook. I will give you the results for the CHRISTIAN-EVANGELIST, as a light reading during the hot weather may be acceptable to your readers who have not had the opportunity of visiting a summer resort during the scorching days through which we have been passing.

I was specially interested in your fishing experiences, but before I finished reading your account I felt really sorry for you. I could see that you were trying to work up a case that would look like you and Bro. Sweeney had done something worthy of being recorded. I thought, furthermore, that one could almost read between the lines a sort of free advertisement for "Cascade Springs," and consequently I felt it my duty to warn your readers against being seduced to the banks of "Thornapple Creek," with any hope that the "speckled beauties" will rise to every fly that is thrown to them. Anyway I protest against catching these *tame* trout and then calling it sport. It is downright murder, and you and "Zack" Sweeney ought both to be tried and heavily fined for your unsportsmanlike conduct. I know that Bro. "Zack" is a "fish commissioner," and consequently he has a sort of pre-emption right to use his own methods in his own way. But I decidedly object to too much freedom being allowed even to a fish commissioner. It is like shooting quails when they are sitting in coveys. It won't do. I know Bro. "Zack's" failings as well as his good points. I fished with him in Palestine and Syria, and saw him land several old-fashioned Kentucky "suckers," and then pass them off upon the unsuspecting tourists for genuine trout! While doing so he would look out of the corner of his left eye at me and with a peculiar shrug of the shoulder he would seem to say, "People who know nothing about fishing deserve to be imposed upon whenever one feels disposed to do it!"

Now, *I* had an experience at fishing this summer. I was on the St. Lawrence, in the heart of the *Thousand Islands*. The fish are all wild there. There are no "trout ponds" where you can catch them by throwing salt on their tails; but the fish are corralled in the great rock piles which are to be found in numerous places along the river bed. There is not much difficulty in getting them to bite provided you understand how to tempt them. It must be remembered that the water is so clear that the fish may be easily seen many feet below the surface. This enables a scientific angler to "pick and choose." He does not need to lose his minnow with a rock bass, perch or some other undesirable "bait stealer." Nor need he fill up his basket with "small catch." All that is necessary is to throw your minnow to the fish you want to take in, and he immediately accommodates you by testing the quality of your line and your skill with the reel. Talk about sport! Bro. Garrison, you have not been in it. You have allowed that "fish commissioner" to fool you, and I have a half suspicion that your "catch" were chiefly *suckers*. Let me test your nerves a moment. Think of a hundred and fifty black bass—real wild ones—taken within three or four hours, and then think that these were only such as you selected, without disturbing the numerous "small fry" which clamored for your approval! Then think of bass for breakfast, bass for dinner, bass for supper, and a dream about bass all night! Why, Garrison, your fish story is tame—it's a real "back number."

Passing from fish to whales is not a very unnatural transition. Well, I had a whale experience during my last crossing from Liverpool to Boston. Not far from the banks of Newfoundland we came upon a school of whales which extended for several miles. Our ship passed very close to some of these, and one big fellow seemed to take us for a Spanish war vessel, and consequently with true loyalty to his American nationality he determined to investigate what it all meant. Anyway he "laid for us," and we ran our ship within ten feet of his tail, which he had evidently "planted" with the view of sinking us in case our colors were not right. Just at the crisis-moment he seemed to discover that we sailed the British flag, and then perhaps remembering the recent friendly relation between John Bull and Uncle Sam, he decided to give us the right of way without molestation. The passengers gave him a hearty cheer as he moved off in search of the enemy's fleet!

We also had an experience of icebergs, which was not altogether agreeable. We came into the region of about a hundred, and soon a heavy fog settling upon us we were compelled to stop for about eighteen hours. During this time we found that we were between two vessels, and in front of us, not more than fifty feet away, was an iceberg. I am telling this story for the benefit of those who do not like the warm weather we have been having. Most of us would have preferred almost any kind of heat rather than the cold we experienced during the eighteen hours of our waiting.

Much of life is made up of extremes. We live by contrasts. I have reached the extreme end of my paper, so will close.

Yours for a real fish next summer,
W. T. MOORE.

[We are pained to see from the above that our distinguished brother failed to distinguish between the trout which were in the ponds and the bass that were wild as deer in Thorn Apple Creek. It was the latter we caught, not the former. Besides, an expert fisherman should have known that September is not the month for trout. Our Bible College Dean asks us to "think of a hundred and fifty black bass taken within three or four hours!" We are glad he does not ask us to *believe* that he did anything of the kind. He does not even *claim* that he did. He only asks us to *think* of it. That's easy!—EDITOR.]

The Churches and the State Universities.

BY EUGENE G. UPDIKE, D. D.

There is no more important question just now for the churches to consider than their relation to the state universities. This is especially true in the West, where state universities have had such a remarkable growth and where they assume so conspicuous a place in the matter of higher education. The articles which have appeared in the Advance recently have been timely. This question needs to be discussed in a fair way until some important facts are lodged in the consciousness of the churches. The question is not with us in the North-Middle states as to the respective merits of church and state schools; but as to the responsibility, if any, which the church has for the life of state universities. At present there is reason enough for all the higher institutions of learning conducted by both state and church. It is as much out of place to discuss the question of the right and duty of the state to establish higher institutions of learning as it is to discuss the question of the separation of church and state. State universities are here. They are logically the outgrowth of the common-school system. They are in most cases a great success. Hundreds of millions of dollars have been put into them. Some of them have as fine an equipment as money can buy. Their growth in the West has been about twenty-five times greater, for ten years past, than the growth of church schools. They are free to all classes. They are universities in the real sense, covering the widest possible range, and they are here to stay. They are attended more largely by young people from Christian homes than by any other class. In the University of Wisconsin 57 and one-half per cent. of the students are members of evangelical churches.

It is not a theory, then, that confronts us, but a condition. The state cannot teach religion, and we do not want it to. It can invest its millions for intellectual culture, and the church can supplement its work.

The separation of church and state was not a mistake. Christianity must now do its work by influences. It does not need to have organic connection with an institution to Christianize it. If the churches can do nothing to help in the religious life of our state universities because they are not organically related, then they can do nothing for the state or the municipality. They can do nothing for any interest outside of themselves, and the kingdom of God must be simply commensurate with the church. Christianity is a failure if it cannot go beyond the church. This is the narrowest and falsest interpretation of it.

Prof. Merrell, referring to the address of President Adams, says: "The appeal to the churches is to gather around in some well-defined fashion and toss loaves of the bread of life over the university fences. This will hardly satisfy the sound sense of a Christian people." This is not a fair or true statement of the case. If the loaves the churches have to give are stale—formulated statements of a traditional theology, and not an expression of the life and experience of to-day—they would have to be thrown over the fence if they found their way into a modern university; but if they are true statements of the living gospel of Christ, they will be most gladly received.

He says further, "The appeal is not to endow chairs of Christian evidence in the universities; neither to build chapels and Christian society halls on the university grounds; neither again to preach gospel sermons therein, nor to teach the truths of the Christian Bible." But this is exactly what the appeal is, not, perhaps, to do it in university buildings, but to do it in conjunction with the university, where it may be just as effective.

The appeal of the friends of the University of Wisconsin is for money to build a Christian Association hall on ground owned by the Association and most admirably located. The appeal is for representative men of the church to speak in this hall exactly as they would do in any church school. Each denomination ought every year to furnish a course of lectures by some of its best men on great Christian themes. Each denomination ought to establish a religious centre for its own students, and place in the field a man whose business it should be to teach the Bible to students in the light of the learning and experience of to-day. If such a man were the intellectual equal of the professor in the university, and had great spiritual power, he could do incalcuable good. Studies taken under such a leader, if thoroughly done, could be substituted for other work in the university as its intellectual equivalent.

There is no wall about any of our state institutions to shut out true religious influence. Christianity does not depend on decisions of the Supreme Court for an opportunity to do its work. It can go wherever there is need, or the men that profess it are at fault.

Suppose some man of wealth were to endow a ladies' hall in connection with some great state university, placing in charge of it one or two wise spiritual leaders who could give special attention to the religious culture of young women, is there any reason why the work could not be as thorough as in any girls' school, and why, at the same time, all of the intellectual advantages of the university might not be secured? The same could be accomplished by endowing dormitories for young men. The religious supervision could be as direct and thorough as in any church school.

Mansfield College loses nothing of its distinctive power by being at Oxford; but gains all there is in such an atmosphere, and at the same time has corresponding influence on the ministry. A Christianity that is afraid of becoming secularized by coming in contact with the institutions of the state is a poor copy of the real thing, and would be quickly repudiated by Christ if he were here.

Professsor Merrell quotes some Unitarian as saying that the state universities are fine fields for liberalism, which illustrates the very point. Unitarianism has had the good sense to see the importance of such strategic fields and has been in the habit of putting its missionary money into churches located at university centers, and helping in their support. If Congregationalism is to be felt here, let it do the same. The last canvass in the University of Wisconsin revealed the fact that there were more students who gave their membership and church preference as Congregational than there were Congregational students in both of the colleges of that denomination in the state. Is it good Christian sense to ignore such a fact as this, leaving it wholly to the local church to care for this most important work, while those who ought to be in better business are standing off—talking about secularizing education and doing not one thing in this particular field to Christianize it? Is it according to the methods of Christ to say to those who need help, "Come where we are and accept what we have to give, out of a spoon made in our particular fashion, or go elsewhere and look out for yourselves?"

Twelve state university presidents came together recently for a conference, and they represented fifty thousand students. A large proportion of them were out of Congregational families. What are we going to do about it—quibble about whether the state has a right to care for the higher education, or go where they are and help them all we can?

I undertake to say this is the greatest unoccupied field to-day before the churches. A college is not to be measured by the number of students that go into the ministry. There is quite as much need for Christian lawyers and doctors and men of science as for clergymen. The kingdom of God will come when the whole social organism is spiritualized.

Congregationalism has been the great pioneer in education. It has done and is still doing magnificent work. But it must be broad enough to see that its responsibility is not limited to its own schools. It should be the first to make itself felt at these great state educational centers. More and more its young men and women will go where there is the best equipment, and it must go after them and care for their religious culture wherever they are.

When the presidents and faculties and regents of such institutions are saying, "We ıt your help,'' we cannot make our religion ıing to command the highest respect if we not respond. A president of a Southern te university, himself a clergyman, said to : ''I am forced to believe that there are ıe church people who do not want state uni-sity work Christianized. It seems to put m in a position of inconsistency, if this is omplished, and they refuse to believe that h a thing can be done, or to help in doing ' Let us hope the number is very limited. › day will come when the denomination that ıot in the forefront of this work will feel dis-ced.—*The Advance*.

Memorial of A. F. H. Saw.

.. F. H. Saw was born in London, June 2, 5. He had a Christian training through his ther from childhood. When about thirteen fourteen years of age she became anxious ›ut his salvation, and although he could ʼer look back and tell the day he he decided Christ, he knew that about that time he ›ame a Christian. He was an earnest work-in the Band of Hope, and early in his Chris-n life became a soul-winner. When about een years old he went one night to hear Gen. ›th and sat in the gallery; when the invita-n was given to reconsecrate themselves to d, the General looked up and, although ; knowing Mr. Saw, said: ''Zacheus, come wn!'' It seemed to him like a voice from d, and like one in a dream he came down and ve himself to God for service. Soon he in-med his parents and received from them ›ir consent to become a missionary, and ›rtly after he entered the Baptist Church. l through his Christian life his strong con-entious nature and gentle, loving disposition re the prominent features of his character. › had entered an architect's office and was a ›st successful student, making it also a point ring these years to try and turn those in siness to Christ. One day going up to Lon-n he noticed a young man reading his Bible, he was also doing; this led to their becoming quainted, and it turned out to be the late Mr. ›arnden's brother. He informed Mr. Saw ıt there was a training class for missionaries be started in his church and he invited him join. He did so and in a year or so it re-lted in his being appointed, on a month's no-e, to China. At the age of 21 he landed in ına.

On Sept. 26, 1891, he was married to Miss la Funk.

While home on furlough he had an opportun-' to study for two years under Dr. Legge, at :ford, and although he was heard to say at it was one of the greatest self-denials of › life to give up this opportunity, his love for › work and for souls in China led him to give up feeling, as he often said, that he would ther the Lord found him in China than at :ford when he returned.

His last public testimony was praise to God : sending him to China and giving him love : these Chinese; real love for them, so that it ıs a pleasure to work with them. His last ying at the convention was, ''Brethren, it a grand thing to have divine forgiveness, and ›eautiful and noble thing to forgive.'' His vorite Bible portions were the 103rd psalm, e 15th of First Corinthians and the 8th of Ro-ans. He said once, if every portion of Script-e had to be taken from him, he would ask keep the 8th of Romans.

After his death we found the following ayer written the 11th of May, six days besore s death: ''O, Heavenly Father, thou knowest l about thy servant, and why this sickness ıs come upon him, thou art full of pity and ›st not willingly afflict the children of men, ıou knowest also my many duties at this con-ıntion; dear Father, look down upon thy lit-› child. However, dear Lord, 'though thou ıy me I will trust thee.' I would not dictate thee; but claim and receive what I believe ›ou hast in store for me. I believe! Help

thou my unbelief and magnify thy great name and the name of Jesus, for his sake.''

We have met here to-day, my Christian friends, to render a tribute of respect to the memory of a fellow-laborer, a constant and intimate friend, a beloved brother in Christ whom God our Father has taken unto himself; what shall this tribute be? The words we may be able to speak can but feebly express the sorrow that fills our breast that we shall see his face no more in this life, or the joy that lifts us up as our faith lays hold of the promises of a triumphant meeting in the life to come. It is a glorious thought that we sorrow not as those that have no hope.

How black the blackness of that night into which no light of hope comes! How unspeakably good the loving kindness and tender mercy that can dispel the darkness of the blackest hour that the enemy of the race is capable of sending upon human hearts!

As we meet here to-day, in the shadow of this great sorrow, we call upon our souls and all that is within us to bless his holy name for the solace of his Word, the comfort of his love, and the joy of his salvation. This service, then, is a service of love.

We lay him away tenderly and we strew upon his tomb evergreens and roses. We fain would have heard that always sincere and tender response to those who did him a kindness, but the sealed lips have ceased to respond and our joy is the memory of what has hung upon them in the days gone by.

We think of him this day, and what are the memories that come in upon us this day? I have known him for nearly eleven years. Shall I say intimately? Yes, for he was one of us. In business scrupulously honest; in his work most unselfish and thoroughly in earnest; in his private life constantly in communion with God; in his public work so full of love for souls that this was a theme upon which he dwelt continually. Were I to sum up in one short statement what comes to me as an epitome of his character I should express it in these words: ''A man of God, who loved his fellowmen and gave himself for them for Jesus' sake.'' When my time to go from this sphere of labor comes, I crave no more glorious epitaph upon my tomb than that which I could thus sincerely inscribe upon the monument of my brother Saw.

The character of Bro. Saw was one which it is soothing to remember. It comes over the mind like the tranquilizing breath of spring. It asks no embellishment, it would be injured by a strained and labored eulogy. All the elements of a noble character were tempered in him kindly and happily. He passed through the storms, tumults and collisions of human life with a benignity akin to that which marked his Guide and Exemplar. This mild temper spread itself over the whole man. His manners, his understanding, his piety, all received a hue from it just as a soft atmosphere communicates its own tranquil character to every object and scene viewed through it.

With his peculiar mildness he united firmness. His purposes, while maintained without violence, were never surrendered but to conviction. His opinions, though defended with singular candor, he would have sealed with his blood. His piety had struck through and entwined itself with his whole soul. In the freedom of conversation I have seen how intimately God was present with him, but his piety partook of the general temperament of his mind. It was warm, not heated; earnest, but tranquil; a habit, not an impulse; the air which he breathed; not a tempestuous wind, giving an occasional violence to his emotions.

A constant dew seemed to distill on him from heaven, giving freshness to his devout sensibilities, but it was a gentle influence, seen, not in its falling, but in its fruits. He felt strongly that God had crowned his life with peculiar goodness, and yet, when his blessings were withdrawn or withheld, his acquiesence was as deep and sincere as his thankfulness.

His firm and abiding faith in God as his Father and Jesus Christ as his Savior were marked in every detail of even his social life. He could not look upon frivolity or idle words with any degree of allowance. With him everything said and everything done must savor of Christ and the Word of his grace; so characteristic of him that his opinions had become in some measure a standard, so to speak, among his most intimate friends.

No one ever doubted sincerity in any advice

he gave or any deed he performed. One thing may be safely said of him in his relations to the natives: he loved them with all the ardency of his consecrated soul. No sacrifice was too great for him to make for them, and when his life went out from among them they lost a friend, a true brother, whose place will be exceedingly difficult to fill.

What shall I say of his peculiar love for children? None of us have forgotten how he always had a word for them when he had charge of the public services. His peculiar love of little children was a faithful index to the simple and genuine love which filled his soul.

I read a number of letters from his parents; I think I can understand where many of his beautiful characteristics had their origin. His home must have been a model home. Simple trust, abounding love, abiding faith—homes with such pillars for their support produce such men as our Brother Saw. The mission of which he was a member feel that they have suffered an almost irreparable loss. God knows best; we shall submit and bless the hand that holds the rod.

I shall never forget his last words to me. Only the day before it was announced that he had that most malignant disease I saw that he was struggling, oh so hard, to throw off the spell that bound him. I asked him how he was getting on; the response was, "I am reaching forth unto those things that are before." I did not think so much at that time as I have since of the strength of those encouraging words of Paul. What was there in the present to one in the embrace of such a terrible disease, if it were not for the things that are before? What could give such an one courage but this hope? There is life and joy and peace in such an hope.

What can I say to those so near whom he has left to mourn his departure? The life he led is more to them than any form of encouragement, couched in words, could possibly be. There is not a single doubt in their minds that he this day joins in the chorus of praise around the great white throne.

He was certainly a grand young man. Would that God would send us many such to this and all mission fields; strong in body, fervent in spirit, loving and faithful in every good work. He was a combination of all the finer qualities that the human race possesses; he was a specimen of a true English gentleman; of a Christian gentleman as we Americans have learned to know them; a gentleman in all circumstances, under all places and trials. He was fond of all that was good, all that was beautiful and true. What overcame and subdued all other fine tendencies of his being was his true Christian spirit. Whereby, when called to his attention, he immediately devoted himself to the service of the Lord in a true and living consecration, which has resulted in ten or more years of the beautiful life among us.

[The above excellent tribute to a noble man was forwarded to us for publication by A. McLean, Cor. Sec. Foreign Christian Missionary Society, Cincinnati, Ohio.—Editor.]

Ogden, Utah.

Christian-Evangelist:—Lately I received a letter from a sister in Atchison, Kas., containing money for pledges that she and two others had made to John L. Brandt when he was traveling and soliciting funds to build a meeting house in Ogden, Utah. She stated that the delay in paying the pledges was due in part to negligence and partly because she did not know to whom to send the money until she saw my name as pastor of the church.

Beyond doubt there are hundreds of dollars pledged and unpaid by brethren of financial standing. Times have been hard, in many places crops have been poor, they have not had the address of Ogden brethren and the matter has been neglected. Lately crops and prices have been good, money is easier, they have my address and that of John T. Hurst, treasurer, and it is desired that these pledges be paid immediately. They are for small amounts, were made in Kansas, Nebraska, Missouri and other states.

We have a $1,200 lot on a principal street in the city paid for and about $700 in cash. If balance of pledges were paid, then with the amount that could be raised here, we could build at pleasure.

At present we use the Congregational church in union work free of rent. It is suitable and well located. We move along harmoniously in all lines of work. They were not in condition to secure and keep a pastor and came to us saying: "You furnish the minister, we will furnish the house and we will work together." This was very kind in them and greatly to our advantage. In the past nine years we have not been so well situated. This is a difficult field, but in this we have an open door and success is attending our labors in interest and additions nearly every week. There are no restrictions and we preach and conduct services as if the work was entirely our own. We use our lesson papers and their Sunday-school papers. There is harmony and good will in the C. E., Junior C. E., Aid Societies and elsewhere during the five past months.

This is all good while it continues, but in time we shall need a church home of our own, and now call on brethren who have pledged assistance to kindly pay. Will ministers and church officers urge this where Bro. Brandt secured pledges? The Woman's Board aids this church.

In His name,
J. H. Bauserman.

Louisiana Convention.

The state convention, which was held at Cheneyville Sept. 1-5, was a marked advance in both attendance and enthusiasm over the convention of last year. The few Disciples of Louisiana are getting better organized and more determined on aggressive work than ever before. The perfect cloud of discouragements which has so long enveloped them is shifting, and there is a spirit of hopefulness which means much for the future. Our greatest need at this time is that of preachers—earnest, active men, who would carry with them to the work the spirit of missions.

Cheneyville, where our late convention was held, is near the central part of the state and is in one of the richest sections of the South. Bro. Campbell, on one of his tours in the interest of Bethany, visited Cheneyville and preached a few sermons in the elegant brick church which had not long been completed. At that time the congregation of Disciples numbered two hundred—one hundred whites and one hundred servants—who in worship occupied opposite sides of the building.

During the Civil War the church went down, and for many years there was no regular preaching. For the past year J. B. Cole has had charge of the work and has done much to revive it and give it permanency. He is much beloved by his membership and the entire community. The writer has recently located at Shreveport, one of the points where the work was established this year. At present our membership is small and poor, and we are forced to begin in a small way. Shreveport is the second city of Louisiana, and a thriving place. Many immigrants are coming in and the city boundaries had to be enlarged recently. Being located on high hills and very healthful; many Northern people prefer it as a home to the low country in the southern part of the state. It is certainly a fine location for the energetic business man who has some money to invest. The commercial future of Shreveport and its location is such as to make it very important to get the cause firmly established here at an early date, and the earnestness and zeal of our little membership is prophetic of success.

Claude E. Jones.

Railroad Rates.

The Western Passenger Association and the Trunk Line Association north-east of the Potomac River has granted a rate of one and one-third fare, round trip, to the gateways of the Central Association, on the Certificate plan, to the Chattanooga Convention, Oct. 13-21, 1898.

Those coming from the Western Passenger Association and the Trunk Line Association north-east of the Potomac River will pay full fare to the gateway of the Central Traffic Association, and from there will get round-trip tickets to Chattanooga and return, at the rate of one fare for the round trip. When you pay full fare take a certificate for the same, and after having it signed at Chattanooga you will be returned from the gateway at which it was purchased to your home for one-third fare.

Please notice that those coming from the Western Passenger Association and the Trunk Line Association north-east of the Potomac River purchase tickets twice, one at the home station for which they will take a certificate, and the second at the point where they reach the bounds of the Central Traffic Association, where they will buy round-trip tickets at the one-fare rate.

Our convention at Chattanooga promises to be the most interesting in all our history. Preparations have been making for months that it shall be the strongest Convention we have ever held. The brethren at Chattanooga have had it on their hearts the entire year, and have made the most ample preparations for the successful entertainment of this Convention.

In behalf of the Boards we desire to extend the invitation for a general gathering of the loyal Disciples of our Lord and Savior. Let us say in our hearts, "I was glad when they said unto me, Let us go unto the house of our Lord."

Come to the Convention at Chattanooga, October 13th to 21st, 1898.

Benj. L. Smith, Cor. Sec.
American Missionary Society.

History of Hiram College.

PART III.—THE NEW HIRAM.

m 1867 to 1886 Hiram struggled along nding with that difficulty of most small colleges—the lack of money. The want per buildidgs was a serious drawback in period, but buildings alone do not make ls and Hiram's teachers made the little e a power at home and abroad. Pres. .. Hinsdale's well-known ability and arship carried the name of Hiram far and during the twelve years of his administra- It is common to speak of the college 1886 as the new Hiram, although the tive really denotes no change in the aims pirit of the school. It denotes, rather, npetus given to the institution by friends about this time came forward with much- d financial help. This help was made ent first in the new college building al- mentioned.

sident Zollars began a vigorous adminis- n in the fall of 1888. Possessed of the nistrative and executive faculty so desir- in the college president of the present he began at once to enlist the churches of isciples in wider sympathy with Hiram. esult of his efforts were soon seen both in ollege and its environment. Although n had always aimed to afford some min- al education, yet Pres. Zollars gave to ork a special emphasis without destroy- however, the other long-standing features school.

1888-'9 the college presented four standard es of study, viz., classical, philosoph- ministerial and scientific. To these were l a legal course and a medical course in In 1891 a short literary course of four and a ministerial course of the same h were added to the curriculum, and were soon followed by a short legal and a medical course. These four-year courses been of great service to the college in ing students who commencing with them been led to undertake and complete some of the longer courses. Several special es were added also from time to time after or the benefit of teachers of ministerial nts whose time and means were limited, or those who desired further work after nation.

attendance of the college gradually in- ed, the enrollment by term growing from 1887-'8 to 1,015 in 1897-'8.

strengthening of the college courses and ased attendance of Hiram called for er teaching force, and Prof. E. B. Wake- was called to the chair of law and politi- ience in 1890; Miss Cora M. Clark to the of modern languages in 1891; A. W. nore to the chair of English in 1893; Dr. I. Page to the chair of medicine in 1894; McDiarmid to the chair of New Testa- introduction and Christian doctrine in E. E. Snoddy was made assistant pro- r of Greek in 1896-'7 and has since been ted to the rank of full professor, and E. J. h was made assistant professor of mathe- s in 1896-'7. Other teachers were also d in nearly all the departments. Prof. pbell became the head of the business rtment, but resigned after an administra- of two or three years and was succeeded rof. S. W. Pearcy, who left us last sum- o take a school in Michigan, C. G. Phil- being now in charge of the department. 88 Miss Addie Zollars (now Mrs. Page) charge of the music department, and after w years she gave up the work and was eeded by Prof. Harshman, and he by Mrs. F. Pearcy. In 1897 the Hiram Musical ervatory was established and Prof. me Feuchtinger, formerly of Bethany ge, placed at its head.

e rapid development of Hiram called also ther and better facilities for taking care e students. In 1889 another large and modious hall, since known as Miller Hall, was built. In the same year the boarding hall which had been opened in 1879 was remodeled and a large addition built to its front. This hall was christened Bowler Hall, owing to the munificent assistance of Mr. Wm. Bowler, of Cleveland. This gentleman, together with his friend, Mr. Abram Teachout, of the same city, has been highly instrumental in aiding all the recent improvements in Hiram. In 1893 a music hall was added to Hiram's other buildings and 1896 saw the completion and occupation of the beautiful structure known as the Y. M. C. A. Building. This edifice with its excellent equipment is justly the pride of Hiram. The village soon began to show the influence of the rapid development of the college. The means for reaching it from the railroad stations at Hiram Station and Garrettsville were greatly improved. In 1890 the former place, generally known as Jeddo, was improved by the addition of a side track and a new station house, thus transforming it from a little country crossing to a station of some dignity. An excellent pike road was built to this station in 1892 and the following year another was built to Garrettsville. Pres. Zollars succeeded in having a regular hack line established to both places, and excellent hacks now run regularly, meeting every one of the eight passenger trains that stop at Hiram or Garrettsville.

Private residences were built very rapidly in the village in this decade. Almost all of these were of modern style and has added greatly to the appearance of the village and to its greater facilities for accommodating students. The crowning glory of the village improvements, however, is the excellent system of waterworks, completed in 1897, and now in full operation. By this system Hiram village is supplied with pure, clear spring water in great abundance for every purpose. An electric light plant was established in 1892 and the streets lighted by electricity. These improvements followed for the most part upon the incorporation of the village. P.

How to Make the Bethany C. E. Reading Circle Go.

What pastor has not been grieved by lack of loyalty among church members? Going along with this absence of loyalty and causing it, is lack of information and conviction. Supply a knowledge of the gospel, of mission fields, missionaries and missionary enterprise, of the history and distinctive teaching of our people and the most formidable mountain facing the pastor is "removed and cast into the sea." Many pastors who recognize the value of a course of study like the Bethany course, yet organize no reading circles. Why not? Faith, a plan and energy are required. Have you faith to undertake the proper edification of the church, and begin the removal of this "mountain," now that the summer vacation is over?

Have you a plan so that your people may set about doing what most of them will at once admit should be undertaken? Are you willing to supply this energy to push to success your plan?

"The Bethany Course would meet an urgent need in our congregation. But how can we get our people to undertake and make successful a reading circle?" say many pastors.

1. BEGIN RIGHT.—As antecedents to organization I shall name first some "don'ts and then some "do's."

Don't "go it blind," or "feel your way," or "be governed by circumstances." Set clearly before you what will be done. Don't urge a work without giving a plan of doing it. Depend not upon the plan, but upon persons, particularly the "first person, singular."

After the proposal and endorsement of the plan don't wait for volunteers to take the initiative. Have some one pledged to take it or move at once yourself.

Make a preparatory canvass. Don't depend upon public announcement only to make things go. Make a canvass (*a*) to show the people the relation of the Bethany course of study to the healthy growth and effectiveness of the congregation; (*b*) to make apparent the advantage of a good course of study, wisely supervised, over haphazard forays into literature in chance direction; (*c*) to take into counsel those most ready to help and give a chance to volvnteer without pressure; (*d*) to secure a list of persons pledged to support the enterprise.

Awaken interest by a brief series of sermons on related topics embraced in the handbooks. Make frequent, definite, detailed announcement of the work proposed, and of meeting for organization. Exhibit the interest of others by announcement by proxy.

Previous to organization, through a period of three weeks, bear on this line in your church paper, in the Sunday-school, in the Endeavor meeting, in public, in private, in session, etc. Be patient. Interest is usually a slow growth, rarely a sudden creation.

2. ORGANIZING.—Be careful in launching. Do not allow the management to be delivered into incompetent hands. Have no figureheads. The existence of each officer and every committee should be made known by their work. Assign much work. Supervise all work assigned. Follow up all workers until the last one has reported on the last item of work assigned him. Be shy of plans that do not individualize responsibility. The lecture-teacher does all the work, but he kills the class.

Have frequent meetings. Once a week will secure a better attendance than once a month. Have a fixed night. Do not move your night up or down the week to avoid other things. Begin and close on time. See to it that the nature of the work and the obligations of membership are well understood at the beginning.

3. HOW KEEP GOING.—Frequently, and in a variety of ways, bring the work of the course to the attention of the congregation. Once in three months the circle members may present the quarter's accumulation of knowledge and enthusiasm at the evening service. Omit the preaching. Have five or ten-minute addresses and special music. Exhaust all available ingenuity to put variety into the meetings. One evening a catechism, another a contest, another brief talks on assigned topics, another a lecture by outside talent, etc. Make frequent reference to the supplementary reading matter. Sustain interest in the work of the circle by a perennial effort to add names to the membership roll. M. J. GRABLE.

Cleveland, Ohio.

Notes and News.

The dedication of the rebuilt house of worship of the Christian Church at Thornton, Ind., occurred on last Sunday. The sermons of the day were preached by L. Brown, of Frankfort, Ind.

A church wanting a good pulpit man and pastor should address Bro. J. P. Davis, 605 South Fourteenth St., Terre Haute, Ind.

A young minister of Eureka, Ill. desires to correspond with churches within a radius of 100 to 150 miles of Eureka, Ill., that are in need of a preacher. Will preach all or part of his time. Address box 379, Eureka, Ill.

Hon. Hale Johnson is announced to speak at Christian Tabernacle, Decatur, Ill., next Sunday night, Oct. 9. The pastor of this church, Geo. F. Hall, claims that they have the largest Sunday evening audiences outside of Chicago and the largest choir in America except the Mormon Temple, Salt Lake City, and the Baptist Temple, Philadelphia.

On a postal card from W. H. Kendall, Storm, Lake, Ia., he says: "Closed my three years' pastorate here. Church grew from 40 to 160 during this time, also mission point of 40 established at Alta. Church has built and paid for its church home. Expenses for coming year are provided for and Elder Clark Batemen, of Cromwell, Ia., called to the pastorate, beginning Oct. 1. I go to Irvington, Ind., to take post-graduate work at Butler. Am ready to supply churches in that region."

Ashland, Oregon.

I am located here as pastor of the little church here, lately reorganized by Bro. J. B. Leister, state evangelist. We shall proceed to build a house of worship soon. This is a fine opening for a church. Ashland is 1,900 feet above the tide and is beautifully located for scenery and blessed with fine climate and water. Land is very cheap here, no better place can be found for a home. J. F. TOUT.

Kansas City, Missouri.

I have been in West Side Christian Church, Kansas City, seven weeks. During this time ten have been added to the church. Our C. E. holds the banner for best per cent. of attendance at Local Union meeting. All lines of work are growing. B. M. EASTER, Pastor.

To Whom it May Concern.

Any one knowing of a good place, a town of some size to warrant the establishment of a mission, please address as below; also, any one desiring to help the cause of city missions can send it to the address below. Any one desiring mission meetings in Eastern Ohio can write me. REV. J. W. MYERS,

State Superintendent City Missions.

Homeworth, Ohio, Box 36.

Illinois Endeavorers.

The twelfth annual state convention of the Illinois Christian Endervor Union will be held at Peoria, October 6-9, 1898. Ministers and Endeavorers among the Disciples of Christ should take note of this and plan to be present. We should have a larger representation than ever before. The convention city is in a region where our people are strong. The program is a good one and the Disciples are well represented by some of our strongest men. The logic of our plea for union should lead us to co-operate heartily in these conventions. LESLIE W. MORGAN,

Illinois Supt. C. E., Disciples of Christ.

Atlanta, Ill.

Dedication.

Sept. 11th I dedicated a new church at Spring Creek, Ind. The church is an elegant brick building. About two hundred dollars more than was needed was raised in about thirty minutes. This makes eight churches that I have dedicated within a radius of one hundred miles. My next meeting will be at Fort North, Tex. Bro. A. O. Hunsaker is my singer, and I have never had a better worker. We can be secured for meetings after Dec. 1st. J. V. COOMBS.

15 *Virginia Ave., Indianapolis, Ind.*

Wanted.

A pastor for the church at Picton, N. S., Dominion of Canada. Any person desiring the position can obtain full particulars by writtng to W. A. BARNES, Secretary

Missionary Board.

228 *St. James Street, St. John, N. B.*

District Convention.

The eighth district convention, at its recent meeting, Sept. 4-6, elected I. A. J. Parker, of Vienna, for its president, and J. H. Stark, of DuQuoin, corresponding secretary for the ensuing year. The convention glowed with the fervor of evangelism and closed its sessions in a white heat of enthusiasm. The executive board took immediate steps to push the work of evangelism in the district. Elder Parker was requested to travel through the territory, hold meetings and arrange for pastors to pastorless congregations, and in every way to strengthen the weak churches. He is to cooperate with the corresponding secretary and evangelist of the S. I. C. M. C. in all things helpful to the work.

Preliminary arrangements were made for holding a preachers' institute next year during the hot season. It will be held at Metropolis City. Bro. J. F. McCartney, of that city, generally volunteering to provide places of entertainment.

The next convention of the eighth district is to be held at Benton.

W. BEDALL.

Indiana Convention.

Fifth district Indiana Christian missionary society convened at Markle, Sept. 18th, and continued over Lord's day. The convention was a grand success from beginning to end. Much interest was manifest, and an earnest determination to push the work of the district was the single thought of every one.

A very interesting program had been arranged, and though one or two of our speakers disappointed us, their places were very acceptably filled by those who were present.

Bro. Rice, of Ft. Wayne, our district president, a man never behind time and one who is always up to date in every good work, was on hand and opened the first service of the convention.

Among the preaching brethren present were Bros. E. Wilfley, of Wabash; C. E. Wells, of Huntington; P. J. Rice, of Ft. Wayne; Bro. Stanley, of Marion; Prof. Adams, of Ft. Wayne; E. D. Long, of Huntington; Bro. Aspey, Bro. Goodykoontz and Bro. Harris. Also, Bro. Legge was with us and made the Sunday evening address.

The special work of the district for the year is the establishment of a church at Bluffton.

The district evangeltst, assisted by J. H. Dodd as singer, conducted a two weeks' meeting at Bluffton which resulted in opening up the work for our people. Terms were agreed upon by which we became the possessors of the Universalist Church property, one of the best located properties in the city.

The good people of Markle did their part in a very admirable way. The church at Markle is wide awake and up to date in every good work. This church under the management of Bro. Goodykoontz has had a wonderful growth during the present year, and with the unanimity that is very apparent between pastor and people, the outlook for the future is very bright.

The missionary and progessive spirit among the people of the fifth district is growing and in the coming years we expect to accomplish much for the Master.

ZACH. A. HARRIS, Sec.

Springfield (Tenn.) Convention.

The county meeting of the Disciples of Christ in Robertson county, Tenn., met with the Springfield Christian church, Sept. 24, 25. This was the first meeting of the kind ever held in Robertson county. The meeting was well attended and proved in every way a successful and delightful gathering. A most interesting program was rendered. Bros. Ellis and Reynolds, from Nashville, and Bro. Myhr, the state evangelist, was with us and contributed largely to our program. The field reports were most excellent. Within the last 18 months two congregations have been organized and our membership increased 140 per cent. A most promising feature of our work in this county is its growth among the young people. The outlook is bright for the future.

LOUIS D. RIDDELL.

Springfield, Tenn., Sept. 26, 1898.

Wisconsin Convention.

The state convention of the Church of Christ and Foreign and American Missionary Society was largely attended the past week. The representatives from abroad were numerous, among whom were J. H. Berkey, from Monroe, one of the best orators in the state. President McNeil, from Milwaukee, who presided with gentle dignity throughout the meeting, winning numerous friends by his conservative, Christian manner. C. C. Smith, of Cincinnati, enthused the audience with his vivid description of the Jamaica Islands, and his sermon, "America for Christ," and the sermon by Prof. Galpin, of Waupun, was appreciated by all. The description of Foreign Mission Work by E. W. Gordon, a native of India, whose commanding appearance and more especially his address won him friends. Dr. Butchart, who has labored for seven years with heathen China, also Miss Ada Boyd, seventeen years a missionary in India; Mrs. Helen E. Moses, of Indianapolis, Ind., president Christian Woman's Board of Missions; Mrs. E. W. Lucker and Mrs. Hanson, of Milwaukee; Miss Ida Lown, of Waupun; State Superintendent D. G. Wagner, West Lima; S. J. Phillips, of Sugar Grove; Miss Meta Monroe, of Monroe and Mrs. E. M. Pease, of Richland Center; president of C. W. B. M. and E. Barstow, of Werley, were among the earnest and capable workers present. There were others whose names we have not learned.

The delegates were unanimous in their praise of Pardeeville's hospitality, and we feel it is well they were here. IDA A. TRIPP.

Pardeeville, Wis.

Who Will Support an Orphan Child?

The Christian Woman's Board of Missions have made arrangements for the opening of an orphanage at Deoghur, India. Dr. Olivia A. Baldwin, who did such efficient service in India for five years as a medical missionary, will go back to that country this fall to take charge of this new orphange. Seventy-six girls who were probably saved from death by starvation by the British Government in one of its orphanages that is now closed have been given to our missionaries. They have been taken care of for some time by the missionaries of the Foreign Society at Damoh, but will now be removed to Deoghur.

As the C. W. B. M. is unable to make an appropriation from its general fund for the maintenance of these children, it is hoped that arrangements can be made at once for their support by individuals or societies in this

thirty dollars per
:essities of each of
ll be assigned to
year, a term of
elf-supporting, as
thus "adopting"
ble to continue its
l to give up the
:hs' notice to the
. W. B. M.
t every one of our
ade stewards over
l each support one
would be richly
housands of our
.ot organized for
doing little or
gospel to those
ey should gladly
portunity to do an
s. Ladies' Aid
Circles, Sunday-
sses and other or-
his work. Those
needed to support
or one-third the

an expense to our
begins a new mis-
esire to assign the
pported from that
help in this work
MATTIE POUNDS.
dianapolis, Ind.,

) News.

in each month as
time the claims of
ans are especially
lded to the church
September. We
ry (1832-1898) of
ay, Oct. 2nd. At
s other interesting
the church each
In the evening the
Alexander Camp-

car from Spring-
nesday night, Oct.
ga, arriving there
the way of Cincin-
scent Route. The
rip, from Spring-
who expect to go
Lynn pastor, at
J. E. LYNN.

stic.

leeting two weeks
ons up to date, two
evangelist; Master
T. NICHOLS.
ng closed at Sidney
200 raised for re-
g. Now at Lake

and church closed
place with 24 addi-
y baptism, two by
e reclaimed. Seven
llies. The church
l. Pastor rejoices
ecome *hot*.—U. G.

additions to date.
r stone of a house
CK.

meeting with S.
o, Cal. Wonder-
y hand. We have
ever been known
mark last night.
the meeting and
er.—ELMER WARD

here were four ad-
on last Sunday;
nversions.—N. M.

TENNESSEE.

Clarksville.—One added here Sept. 25. Miss Lura V. Thompson occupied the pulpit here Sept. 25 and delivered a beautiful address to the edification of a fine attentive audience. God bless the C. W. B. M.—A. W. GROWDEN, pastor Church of Christ.

Knoxville, Sept. 26.—Two subtractions by letter, from the Park Street church in September.—ROBERT STEWART.

Clarksville, Sept. 30.—Work program at the Church of Christ: 16 additions at regular services in last three months.—A. M. GROWDEN.

KANSAS.

Hutchinson, Sept. 29.—Three confessions at our service last Lord's day. All departments of the church here are in good working order and the outlook for the furture encouraging.—A. P. ATEN.

Topeka, Sept. 24.—Closed meeting at Meriden the 18th with 30 additions. Began meeting at Mayetta the 23rd, with good prospects. Between meetings I visited Miltonville (my first pastorate), preached two nights with one addition. The church is doing nicely with Bro. Melvin Duncan in the pulpit (his first pastorate).—I. T. LEBARON, state evangelist.

The meeting at Coffeyville continues with increased interest. Meeting three weeks old, with 61 added. Bro. W. E. Harlow is doing splendid work. Meeting continues indeffinitely.—S. W. BROWN, pastor.

MISSOURI.

Palestine, Sept 26.—Began a meetinfi here the 28th inst.; five accessions last night; four to be baptized and one reclaimed.—F. E. BLANCHARD.

La Monte, Sept. 26.—Ten additions here since last report, all by confession; six of them men.—KING STARK.

Tarkio, Sept. 29.—Five confessions last night; 28 additions to date. My next meeting will be in Stanford, Ky., with Bro. F. W. Allen.—H. A. NORTHCUTT.

Louisiana, Sept. 26.—Last night Bro. J. B. Mayfield and his wife and two daughters united with the church here, having recently moved here from Clarksville where he had been pastor of the church for four years. We are glad to have so excellent a Christian family associated with us. Bro. W. T. Sallee is now in a meeting at Pierson, Ia.—E. J. LAMPTON.

Laddonia, Oct. 1.—My debate at Farber, Mo., with J. S. Allison, of Kirksville, was a success. I held a two weeks' meeting after the debate, with 20 additions; five from the denominations.—W. P. DORSEY.

Wallace, Oct. 10.—Have just commenced a meeting here. Prospects bright. Will hold meetings the rest of the year. The program is already arranged.—JOHN P. JESSE.

Dye, Sept. 30.—I recently held a good meeting with Old Union Church in Buchanan county, with 14 additions by primary obedience. This was my second meeting with this church in the last three years. I am now assisting Bro. A. P. Terrell in a meeting at Salem Church in Platte county, with 22 additions to date, and with fine andiences and a hopeful outlook for a great harvest. I will continue evangelistic work till the end of the year. Churches and pastors desiring my assistance in meetings address me at Olathe, Kas., my permanent address.—R. H. FIFE.

INDIANA.

Indianapolis, Sept. 26—At North Park Christian Church, thee additions.—J. M. CANFIELD.

Valaparaso, Sept. 27—Two additions at Hammond, Sunday. One confession and one by letter.—WALTER L. ROSS.

State Line, Sept. 26.—Report of our meeting at Walnut Corner, Ill.: Three to date, with crowded house. Splendid attention and great interest manifested. A full report later. Yours respectfully.—BAKER AND SWARTWOOD.

ILLINOIS.

Barry, Sept. 26.—Our house would not hold our audience last night; one young man made the good confession.—N. E. CORY.

Watseka, Sept. 26.—Another addition here yesterday, by letter. An officer in our county-seat has declared his intention of being baptized. The County Ministerial Associrtion will meet here to-day.—B. S. FERRALL, Pastor.

Shelbyville, Sept. 27.—We had one more confession Lord's day morning at Palmyra; an influential young lady.—A. M. COLLINS.

Taylorville, Sept. 29.—I closed my 12 years' pastorate in this cily last Lord's day; had four additions during the day's service. Will move to Williamsville and take charge of the work there Nov. 1st.—W. W. WEEDON.

Stronghurst, Sept. 29.—We began our meeting here with five additions the first day. Eight confessions up to date.—ARTHUR N. LINDSEY.

Casey, Oct. 3.—Three additions yesterday by baptism. Church work prospering.—E. E. BOYER.

KENTUCKY.

Junction City, Sept. 24.—Our meeting closed Sunday night with 13 additions.—IRA BOSWELL.

ALABAMA.

Citronville, Sept. 27.—One addition Sunday, the 25th, at Fairhope, by baptism. Brethren, pray for the success of the gospel in Southwestern Alabama.—Eugene R. Clarkson.

Missionary.

Church Extension Receipts
For Completing Chapels.
From Sept. 1st to 24th, '98:
From individuals, $1,948.70
From churches, 3,134.18
Total $5,082.88
Last year from ch's $1,274.53
From individuals ...3,206.46
Gain $601.89

Note.—A further analysis of our receipts shows the following for the first twenty-four days of September as compared with last September:

A loss in individual receipts of $72.28.

A gain from church collections of $674.17.

A gain in the number of contributing churches of 64.

Remittances should be sent to

G. W. MUCKLEY, Cor. Sec.,

600 Waterworks Bldg., Kansas City, Mo.

Meeting of General Board of Managers American Christian Missionary Society at Chattanooga.

The General Board of Managers of the American Christian Missionary Society will meet in annual session in the Walnut Street Christian Church at Chattanooga, Tenn., Oct. 15th, at 2:30 P. M.

BENJ. L. SMITH, Cor. Sec.

The Chattanooga Convention.

No Southern Disciple who can get the money to go on and spare the time can afford to miss this great National Convention of Disciples of Christ in Chattanooga, Oct. 13-21. We shall meet men and women whose names have been household words with us all our life. It will be the greatest possible inspiration and encouragement to meet with them. They are our brothers and sisters in our Father's cause. Let Alabama, Georgia, Mississippi, Tennessee and other Southern states roll in delegates by the hundred. It will be a long time before we have another such opportunity in the South.

O. P. SPIEGEL.

Birmingham, Ala.

"I Cannot Afford to Go."

"I would be glad to attend the Chattanooga Convention, but really I cannot afford the expense." I wonder how many of our brethren and sisters all over the land are thinking that. "I have often felt that I could not afford to attend these great annual conventions," said the lamented O. A. Burgess, near the close of the great Richmond Convention, twenty-two years ago, "yet each year has witnessed my presence; and now, as I look back over my life, I cannot recall a single financial investment that has brought me such gratifying returns. It pays to attend." I now recall this saying of this wise man as a suggestion to hundreds who are hesitating to attend the great convention at Chattanooga because they feel they cannot afford the expense. Those who are in the habit of attending will very heartily concur in the opinion that it is a good investment. Many of their noblest inspirations, many of their largest visions, many of their dearest friendships and holiest fellowships, many of their most precious treasures, held sacred by memory, are intimately associated with these great annual gatherings. They feel they are broader and better, that they are stronger and more efficient, that they are more happy and more hopeful, and that the fruitage of their life will be richer and more abundant, because they have gone each year to these great national gatherings of their brethren. You may feel you cannot afford the expense of going; I am certain you cannot afford to remain away.

J. Z. TYLER.

Cleveland, Ohio, Sept. 17.

A Great Year.

When the books of the Foreign Christian Missionary Society closed, Sept. 30th, 1898, the receipts during the year for Foreign Missions amounted to $130,925.70, a gain over the year before of $24,703.60. The receipts "from collections only" amounted to $97,363.10. We came near reaching the "$100,000 by collections only." The number of contributing churches is 2,907, a net gain of 321. The number of contributing Sunday-schools is 3,186, a net gain of 370. The churches as churches gave $45,650.20, a gain of $6,081.92. The Sunday-schools gave $34,334.97, a gain of $4,307.73. There was a loss in the receipts from the Endeavor Societies and from individual offerings amounting to $4,056.05.

Eleven new missionaries have been sent out during the year. This has been the greatest year in the history of the Society. Praise the Lord!

F. M. RAINS, Treas.

Box 750, Cincinnati, Ohio.

Convention Benefits.

An incalcuable benefit of our missionary conventions or ministerial associations is their stimulus for one's mind and heart. Any preacher who regularly attends them is prepared to give special testimony of this blessing. No studious habits at home, nor even the inspiration of a large field of labor, nor yet the hearty appreciation of one's ministry in a congregation, can give all that every preacher needs for learning and growth. Our national conventions are just now having a development of interest that is marvelous. Not for doctrinal decisions nor for ecclesiastical administrations, but directly and always for the progress of the gospel in the world, they enlist and elicit necessarily an enthusiasm at once full of light and power; they bring one into the very heart of fellowship in Christ; they inspire in one a new consideration for service. The brethren at Chattanooga are to be congratulated on their enticing preparations to receive our national gathering this year. Such faith and diligence will not fail of its reward.

ROBT. T. MATHEWS.

Louisville, Ky.

All Aboard for Chattanooga!

We are as busy as bees getting in shape to meet you and give you a cordial welcome. when you step off the train look for a party of Christians, with badges pinned on them, on which is the word reception. They are your servants, *use them*. The depot is but a short distance from the Auditorium. Be sure to put yourself in the hands of the reception committee, so that you can secure boarding rates at the uniform price of $1 per day, in the best homes, and $1.50 to $2.00 per day in the best hotels. There are plenty of cheap boarding houses in the city, but we will send no one there, except it be the preference of the delegates, as we desire to give you the best this Chattanooga affords. If the $1 a day rate does not suit you, we can get you good rooms at 25 cents up, and board for $5.00 per week, but we cannot place on that our guarantee except in few instances. Let us know in time what you want and we can meet most any request. We want no one to be cut off on account of expense. Come one! Come all! We have heard from at least 500 people who are coming, and yet it is three weeks till the convention. The S. E. P. A. will sell tickets at one fare for the round trip, from Oct. 12-17 inclusive. They will be good to Oct. 24. Please inquire of your own Passenger Associations, the date of sale of tickets, at one-fare rate. Our Tennessee Christian Missionary Convention will be the guest of Highland Park Christian Church Oct. 10-13. Let those who have written me about entertainment not grow impatient waiting for a reply. I am waiting on the entertainment committee to report to me, and as it is an assured fact that we can get all the houses we want, on short notice, they have seen fit to wait till near the time, so there will be no disappointments. Some people who are not acquainted with our city, are inquiring about the health. If they will look at the reports given by the statisticians they will find that it stands in point of health sixth in the United States. We have the finest drainage, and sewerage system in the South, and no epidemic has ever struck Chattanooga since she has been a city. The convention comes in the most beautiful and healthful part of the year. You can't afford to stay away. We already have sufficient evidence that this will be the beginning of a new epoch in our conventions and missionary work, but we ought to have no less than ten thousand of our church people here. Don't allow anything to get between you and the convention, Oct. 13-21, 1898. We shall, as much as power in us lies, make everything congenient, comfortable, and to suit your purse.

Yours faithfully,

W. M. TAYLOR, Gen. Sec.

A Liberal Offering.

The Angola church set apart the third Sunday in September as "Home Missions Day." Service was conducted by Bro. G. W. Hemry, who is ministering to the congregation till the writer fully recovers from sickness. Offering of the day in excess of $200. Total Home Missions offering of the year was $300, apportioned among the different boards.

CHAS. S. MEDBURY.

Angola, Ind., Sept. 30, 1898.

Collection.

ıurch Extension, $40.50. ular services yesterday. ion held here last Sunday.

R. F. THARPP.

:. 3, 1898.

ıe Annuity Plan.

stiạn Missionary Society wing sums during the past lan:

tis, Ohio.........	$ 1,000
.. ..	2,000
'alo, N. Y........	200
Smet, S. D......	100
ia, Ohio..........	500
....	15,000
tockport, Ia	100
Thompson, West	1,000
ɔman, Carthage, ...	500
Barnhart, Dowaj-	500
, Rochester, N. Y	1,000
England.........	9,690
ıuth, Ohio........	1,000
....	$32,590

received since the fund r is $39,390. This money ings on the mission fields. itants according to their tural lives, and at death is relieved from further ɔf the annuitants very ıeir annuities when they ven liberally for the regu- ıe society, however, pays r when it is due; this is al than to pay the high heathen lands.

F. M. RAINS, Treas.

ıst Word.

hurches of Chattanooga, Council, the Chamber of Young Men's Business lial invitation to the Dis- ɔrywhere to attend the issionary Conventions to tober 13 to 21.

·The Central and South- have granted the rate of ıd trip. This covers the ɔtomac to the Mississippi lakes to the gulf. The ın and the Western Asso- a rate of one and one- vays of the Central Asso- icate plan. When those tions purchase tickets at certificate for the same, signed at Chattanooga from the gateway home Please notice that those unk Line and Western e tickets *twice*, one at for which they take a second at the point ɜ bounds of the Central hey will buy the round- ɜ-fare rate. Date of sale thwestern Association is h inclusive, good to the ır agent the date of sale The rovnd trip from all 80.

anted those coming from i River.

ɔllowing the instructions , a rate of one dollar per will be given. This in- d lodging. Special rates t the best hotels in the :.00 per day. Everything ɔmfort and enjoyment of

convention, Missionary ıetery, Lookout Moun- National Military Park, No more delightful trip

could be arranged than to Chattanooga in October.

FINAL WORD.—Already indications point to a great convention. If we mistake not it will be characterized by good cheer and boundless enthusiasm from beginning to end. We urge upon our brethren everywhere to make it a subject of prayer and conversation. Talk the convention up. Secure as large an attendance as possible from your church. Send names of all who are coming, that we may know how many to provide for. "Come thou with us and we will do thee good."

M. D. CLUBB, Chairman.
W. M. TAYLOR, Sec.
Local Executive Committee.

Annual Convention Christian Church (Disciples of Christ) and Auxiliary Convention, Chattanooga, Tenn., 1898.

Christian Church (Disciples of Christ) Oct. 13th to 21st.

Christian Woman's Board of Missions, Oct. 13th to 15th.

American Christian Missionary Society, Oct. 17th to 19th.

Foreign Christian Missionary Society, Oct. 19th to 20th.

We have arranged for the sale of tickets from St. Louis, Mo., at one first-class fare for the round trip on Oct. 12th to 17th, inclusive, good to return until Oct. 24th, 1898.

The Louisville & Nashville trains leave Union Station, St. Louis, daily at 7:56 A. M. and 8:55 P. M., and the time of the journey en route is about 18 hours. The equipment is first-class and has Pullman cars on all trains.

It is expected that all railway lines west and north of St. Louis will sell through tickets for these meetings, but if passengers cannot purchase tickets from their home stations, they should buy to St. Louis, and without the loss of any time you can repurchase tickets in the Union Station at St. Louis through to Chattanooga, and to secure the best accommodations and time, see that your tickets read via the Louisville & Nashville Railroad.

In case you desire any further information or wish to reserve sleeping car space on any of the dates specified, please write to any of the undersigned.

Geo. B. Horner, Division Pass. Agent, 206 North Broadway, St. Louis, Mo.

C. H. Fitzgerald, W. Pass. Agent, Room 10, Exchange Building, Kansas City, Mo.

Family Circle.

My Two Selves.

IRA BILLMAN.

A mortal mixed with dual clay,
And each attempered for a different way;
Two ill-assorted travelers I,
Yet one cannot the other's presence fly.

Thus, on the narrow path of life,
These twain in discord move, and endless strife;
Not hand in hand, but back to back,
As one proceeds, the other cramps the track.

What one approves the other scorns,
O'er things that one exults the other mourns,
And soon as one its work has planned,
The other hastens, envious, to withstand.

Thus, while pursuing simple truth,
I'm swayed by party prejudice, forsooth!
And while one self all good inspires,
The other self is full of base desires.

One self I love, as love I God,
And o'er each hest bend my approving nod.
The other I with passion hate,
And its demands all question and debate.

Oh! if my better self were free,
Then would it rise to all eternity—
My higher self, the self I love—
All stormy seas, bleak mountain heights above.

But ah! 'tis here my mortal grief
Beyond all earthly balsam or relief;
That by its false companion crossed,
Its just applause my higher self has lost.

Sangamon, Mich.

Selected from St. Nicholas for October, for our Family Circle.

The White Queen Club.

BY IDA KENNISTON.

One evening I went over to Uncle Rob's, and found the whole family sitting around the fireplace, with no apparent occupation but that of eating peanuts.

"You are just in time, Winnie," exclaimed Molly, jumping up to take my hat and wrap. "We were just about to have a meeting of the White Queen Club."

"The White Queen Club!" I said. "What in the world is that?"

"The Impossible Club," suggested Aunt Emma, with a smile.

"The Paradox Club," said Uncle Rob.

"The True Liars' Club," added Tom; but Aunt Emma shook her head at him in gentle reproach.

"You have quite aroused my curiosity," I said, sitting down in the easy-chair that Tom brought forward for me, and accepting a share of the peanuts. "What is the object of this club with many names, and what must one do to belong?"

"Every one who joins must tell a story," explained Molly; "a story that is realy true, or at least possible, but told in such a way as to make it seem impossible. Then, when every one has told a story, we begin again, and each gives the explanation of his story, if the others have not already guessed it."

"I don't see how one can tell a true story so as to make it seem untrue," I said; "but I am all ready to be a listener, at least."

"Well, who would like to begin?" asked Uncle Rob.

"Oh, let me!" exclaimed little Bob, eagerly. "I know a lovely story—truly I do, papa."

"All right," said his father, good-naturedly; "we are all ready to hear it."

"Well, once upon a time," began Bobby, soberly, sitting up straight, with a very solemn face, "one day last winter, I was in Boston, and I saw—I saw—I saw a 'lectric car run right over a man!"

There was a half-suppressed "Oh!" from some of his hearers, that seemed to gratify Bobby immensely. He went on with a solemn air: "The car, the great heavy 'lectric car, ran right over both his legs, just about *here*;" and Bobby indicated a place on his own chubby person about three inches above the knee. "Well, when the car rolled off, the man just got up and walked away as if it had n't hurt him at all!"

"Why, Bobby Everett!" exclaimed his mother.

"Well, I'll tell you how 't was," said Bobby, in an ingenious tone, as if he were about to make all clear. "You see, the man was reading a newspaper, and was so int'rested in what he was reading that he never knew the car went over him.

"Why, Bobby Everett!" it was now my turn to exclaim. "I thought the stories were to be true."

"That's really true, Winnie," said my uncle with a grave face, but with a little twinkle in his eye; "that's really true, because I was the man."

"Oh, were you, papa?" exclaimed Bob, with a delighted giggle at this unexpected confirmation of his astonishing tale. "I didn't know that."

"Well, next!" said Uncle Rob.

"My story is very short, and I'm afraid you'll all guess it at once," said Molly. "Once upon a time there was a man who lived in the country, and one Fourth of July he decided to fire off an old cannon that he owned. It was a very small cannon, but he knew it could be depended on to make a big noise. He loaded it with a generous charge of powder, and scattered some powder about the little hole on top.

"Just as he had it all ready to light, he discovered that he had no match in his pocket. He didn't want to go into the house to get one, so as he was quite nearsighted he took off his spectacles and fired the cannon with them."

"Why, how could he?" asked Bobby.

"That's the point," answered Molly; "but he realy did. Only—he couldn't have done it if it had been a cloudy day."

"Oh, I see!" I exclaimed. "I've guessed one 'impossible' story, at least."

"That reminds me of another cannon story, said Tom—"one that I read last week. I'll tell that for my yarn.

"Once upon a time—we all like the old-fashioned beginning, Cousin Winnie—once upon a time there was a wonderful cannon. It was one that had been used in the Civil War, and many a huge cannon-ball had rushed forth from its mouth on a mission of destruction. But the war was ended, and the old cannon was no longer used save, perhaps, on some national holiday, when it thundered forth to celebrate the glories of the nation it had helped to save. Ahem! Well, one day people were surprised to see that, instead of balls being fired from its mouth, if they were brought near the old gun, they leaped to meet it, they hung upon it, and it took a strong man to pull them away. One day a soldier walked in front of the old cannon, and stood motionless about a foot from its mouth. The ground around him was strewn with cannon-balls and iron spikes. Presently the spikes began to leap up and attach themselves to the soldier. Then the heavy iron balls lifted themselves from the ground and hung upon him. So many were the spikes that the soldier bristled with them like a huge porcupine with iron quills. The weight of the spikes and balls was much greater than the man could have carried, yet he seemed to feel no inconvenience. Presently he began to walk away, and the balls fell from him, and the spikes dropped to the ground."

Tom began to eat peanuts once more, as if his story were finished.

"The cannon might have been magnetized," suggested Molly; "but I don't see how they could magnetize such an immense thing as a cannon, and I don't understand why the balls should have hung on the man."

"We'll keep explanations until our stories are all told," said Uncle Rob. "I'll tell mine now.

"Once upon a time," began uncle, "some men were building a railway in the Western part of our country. Oh, by the way, Winnie, you know our stories are not always *literally* true. For instance, if I wanted to tell of some of the wonders of electricity, I might speak of that strange force as a giant or as a magician; or, if I wished to tell the story of a colony of bees, I might call them brownies, and then you would have to guess the real name of the giant or the brownies.

"Well, as I said, these men were building a great railroad. For a part of the way they were working as large a force as might be, anxious to get a certain number of miles done by a certain time. The surveyors were going before the working party, marking out the lines; only two or three miles behind them was a force of laborers preparing the road-bed, laying the cross-ties and the heavy iron rails, and spiking them securely together.

"As fast as the railroad was completed, an engine and special train came over the newly laid track, bringing rails and other supplies to the workers.

"One day, Sir What-you-call-him, of the surveyors' party, came to Prince Thing-um-bob, who was superintending the work, and said: 'Your Highness, the work cannot go on.'

"'Why not?' demanded Prince Thing-um-bob, in a terrible tone.

"'Our magic box is bewitched,' answered Sir What-you-call-him, 'and will no longer serve us. Without the aid of our magic box we cannot make our lines straight and true.'

"'Have you been to the Wise Man?' asked Prince Thing-um-bob.

"'We have, your Royal Highness.'

"'What does he say?' demanded the Prince.

"'He says, your Royal Highness, that we must search until we find a little brown witch, so small that she might be hidden in a walnut-shell. The little brown witch knows how to spin a thread that is finer than silk and stronger than steel. If she will spin us some of her magic thread for the magic box, then all will be well, and the building of the road may be resumed.'

"'Tell all hands, from the highest to the lowest, to quit work, and search for the little brown witch,' commanded Prince Thing-um-bob.

"So all the men left their work, and began to hunt the little witch who was so small she could hide in a walnut-shell, and who knew how to spin a thread that was finer than silk and stronger than steel.

"They hunted and hunted, but at first without success. In about an hour, however, one of the men gave a shout of triumph as he spied the little brown witch. He carried her straight to Prince Thing-um-bob.

"'Command her to spin,' was the Prince's next order.

"But the witch wouldn't spin. The coaxed her; they offered her dainties; they threatened her. But the little witch was obstinate; she wouldn't spin, and she didn't spin.

"Not all the score of men that stood around anxiously could force the witch to spin her magic thread.

"The men stood helpless. Unless the witch would help them, work on the great iron road could not go on."

"Uncle Rob," I intrrupted, "how much is true, and how much is a fairy tale?"

"It is all true," said Uucle Rob, seriously. "The incident, barring names, really happened when one of our great Pacific railroads was being built.

"Well, after some hours the little witch consented to spin for them. The men watched her eagerly, and when she had spun enough of the wonderful magic thread, they gathered it up, and carefully placed it in their magic box. Then all went well. The magic box aided them as before. The men went zealously to work, and, thanks to the little brown witch, the work of building the great railroad went on once more.

"Next!"

"My story must be short," said Aunt Emma. "One day last summer I was at the summit of Mount Washington. I heard some men talking of the view to be seen from there. They tried to count the number of mountain peaks that were visible, and, failing in that, began to estimate the greatest distance one could see from the summit. Some placed the greatest distance that could be seen with the naked eye at thirty miles, some at fifty, and some said sixty miles. At last a gray-haired gentleman, who up to this time had taken no part in the discussion, asked one of the party how far away he supposed the Rocky Mountains to be. 'Oh, two or three thousand miles,' replied the gentleman addressed, carelessly. 'You don't suppose you can see *them*, do you?'

"'perhaps not,' answered the old gentleman, reflectively; 'but I *have* been here when the air was so clear that I saw mountains even farther away than the Rockies.'"

"Oh, what a story!" exclaimed Bobby—somewhat impolitely, it must be confessed.

"It was really true, Bobby," said his mother, with a smile.

"Well, all our stories are told now," said Uncle Rob, "so I move we begin again, and each explain his yarn—that is, unless Winnie has a story for us."

"Oh, no," I said. "Please excuse me for to-night; and I shall be very glad to hear any reasonable explanation of the extraordinary yarns I have heard. I assure you, my credulity has been taxed to the utmost."

"All right," said my uncle, in high good humor. "Now, Master Bobby, tell us about the poor man that was run over by a car, and didn't know it."

"Well," said Bobby, promptly, "you see he was in a steam-car, and the steam-car went under a bridge, and a 'lectric car went *over* the bridge at the same time, and of course it rolled right *over* the man, only he didn't notice it."

"Oh, of course!" I said. "Why din't I think of that?"

"Well done, Bobbins," said his big brother Tom. "I confess your story puzzled me."

"Now, Molly, said uncle, when we had all metaphorically patted our youngest story-teller on the back, "now, Molly, tell us about the man who fired off the cannon with his spactacles."

"Well," said Molly, "he just held them in the sun, like a burning-glass, and focused one of the lenses on the powder until it exploded and discharged the cannon."

"Why, *how?*" asked Bobby.

"Don't you remember, Bobby," explained his sister, "when we were at grandpa's last summer, we used to take his reading-glass and hold it in the sunshine, and see what a little round bright spot it would make?—and when we held it so the bright spot would come on your hand, it would *burn?*"

"Oh, yes," said Bobby. "But what makes it burn? Why is the sun any hotter when it shines through spactacles than when it shines throug window-glass.

"I'll tell you about that to-morrow, Bobby-boy, said his father, kindly. "I don't believe we will have time to-night.

"Now, Tom, I confess that *your* cannon story puzzled me. Was it only a possible story, or was it really a fact?"

"It was really a fact, sir," replied Tom. "Molly partly guessed it when she said the cannon might have been a magnet. Captain King of the United States army took the old gun (it was sixteen feet long) and wound ten miles of copper wire around it. Then he connected the ends of the wire with an electric battery. He found this made the cannon the most powerful any one had ever seen."

"But what made the balls and spikes cling to the man?" asked Molly.

"Because he was between them and the cannon," answered Tom. "The electric current was not turned on until he was in position, and then the force made itself felt through him. You know, when we were playing with Bobby's small magnet, we tried holding it above a sheet of writing-paper, and we found that pens and needles would jump up from the table and cling to the under side of the paper. The magnetic force was able to act through the paper, just as in the other case it exerted its power through the body of the man."

"How simple it is," I exclaimed, "when we once understand it!"

"Ah, but do we understand it?" asked my uncle, quickly. "You say it is magnetism that explains it; but how much do we know of what magnetism *is?* You ask what is the power that attracts iron to iron, and and we say magnetism; but all we have done is to give a name to an unknown force. Why can't we mrgnetize gold so that it will attract gold—or silver to attract silver?"

We were silent a moment, thinking over these remarks; and then Aunt Emma, with a glance at the clock, said:

"We haven't time for outside discussions to-night; it is past Bobby's bedtime now; so let us finish the stories as soon as we can."

"Has any one guessed my story?" asked uncle.

"The little brown witch may have been a spider," said Molly, "but I don't see how a cobweb can help build a railroad."

"It really does," said Uncle Rob. "In the telescopes of astronomers, and in the instruments that surveyors use, the spider's thread plays an important part. It is necessary to have two cross-hairs, as they are called, to mark the horizontal and perpendicular lines in the field of vision, and to give a means of getting the right angle. It is necessary that these lines be very smooth. The instrument magnifies so much that a piece of cotton thread would look like a cable. Even a hair or a shred of silk would make a broad, black line, too wide and with too jagged edges to permit of delicate measuring. It was found that the only thing that would give satisfaction was a spider's thread, which is really much finer than the thread of the silkworm."

"But you said it was stro nger than steel," said Tom.

"So it is, in proportion to its size," said his father. "It takes from four thousand to seven thousand spider threads, put side by side, to measure an inch. Threads sufficient to equal in size a bar of steel an inch in diameter would sustain a much greater weight than would the bar of steel."

"A good motto for your club would be 'Live and learn,'" I said. "I am sure these facts are as new to me as they are to Tom and Molly."

"Now, mamma," said Molly, "tell us about the mountains you can see from the summit of Mount Washington."

"You have seen them often," said Aunt Emma, "and so has Bobby."

"Why, mamma, where?" said Bobby.

"If I tell the others how far away the mountains are," said his mother, "it may help them to guess. They are just about two hundred and forty thousand miles away."

"Two hundred and forty thousand!" said Tom, slowly. "Oh, I know. The mountains in the moon!"

There was a hearty laugh at this simple explanation of an "impossible" story.

"I shall probably see those mountains on my way home to night," I said; "and that reminds me that it is time for me to be going.

"I have enjoyed your club meeting ever so much, Molly, and I hope you will let me come again."

"It is a favorite game with us," said Uncle Rob. "We shall be glad to have you join us any time; but you must come to our next meeting prepared with an 'impossible' story of your own."

"One more question," I said, as I was putting on my hat. "Why did Molly call it the 'White Queen Club'?"

"You have read 'Alice in Wonderland' and 'Through a Looking-Glass,' haven't you?" asked Molly.

"Of course!" I said. "Why don't you ask me if I ever heard of Mother Goose?"

"Well," replied Molly, with a smile, "you remember the White Queen practiced until she was able to believe as many as six impossible things before breakfast!"

On to Chattanooga.

J. H. STARK.

(Tune: "Marching Through Georgia.")

More than three decades ago the boys in "blue and grey"
Met upon the battlefield in deadly, grim array;
Now they meet upon the ground to sing and pray,
Down in fair old Chattanooga.

Chorus: All hail! all hail! This glorious gathering!
All hail! all hail! We'll make the welkin ring
To the praise of Christ our Lord, our princely Priest and King,
Whose cause is marching to vic'try!

This mighty host comes from the North and South and East and West—
These soldiers of the Lord, they come to plan for what is best,
For the Kingdom of the Master, and His righteous Word's their test,
As they meet in Chattanooga.

Chorus: All hail! etc.

The "Gulf" that stood 'twixt North and South for many weary years,
Thanks to our God, has now been filled, and banished are our tears;
So shout aloud our songs, our greetings, and our cheers,
As we meet in Chattanooga.

Chorus: All hail! etc.

With "helmet of salvation" bright, with faith our only shield,
The Word of God our only arms, we'll this with courage wield.
"Christ is our Immanuel, and all the world our field,"
We will sing at Chattanooga.

Chorus: All hail! etc.

Then come, my brethren, one and all, let's pledge anew our vow,
"To Jesus Christ our King be true, to Him alone we bow;
He'll save us at the close of life, He saves us oven now,"
We will sing at Chattanooga.

Chorus: All hail, etc.

Du Quoin, Ill., Sept. 20, 1898.

An Effective Sermon.

A young man, in company with several other gentlemen, called upon a young lady. Her father was present to assist in entertaining the guests, and offered wine, but the young lady asked:

"Did you call upon me or upon papa?"

Gallantry, if nothing else, compelled them to answer: "We called on you."

"Then you will please not drink wine. I have lemonade for my visitors."

The father urged his guests to drink, and they were undecided. The young lady added:

"Remember, if you called on me, then you drink lemonade; but if upon papa, why, in that case I have nothing to say."

The wine glasses were set down with their contents untasted. After leaving the house one of the party exclaimed:

"That was the most effectual temperance lecture I ever heard."

The young man from whom these facts were obtained broke off at once from the use of strong drink, and holds a grateful remembrance of the lady who gracefully and resolutely gave him to understand that her guests should not drink wine.—*Ex.*

Autumn.

Now gently falls the fading light,
The Autumn's sunset veil,
While dusky grows the wavering flight
Of whippoorwill and quail.
The grain is bound, the nuts are brown
On every wooded hill;
The light is softened on the down,
And silvered on the rill.

The partridge drums; the plover's call
Salutes the sportsman's ear,
And just above the waterfall
The fisher sets his weir.
The reddened leaves, with withered wings,
Sweep lightly to the sod,
And Autumn walks the land, and sings,
With rustling sandals shod.

—*W. H. Dierhold, in Woman's Home Companion.*

Home.

Here is a greeting for those at home—the home which many of us possess, some of us have missed, but for which each of us longs. The wretch who makes the doorstep his bed does not desire it more than many a luxurious wanderer in foreign lands, whose very prosperity, it may be, has divorced him from the place he once called by that dear name. The child who strays from the familiar door weeps till he finds it again; the man who leaves it feels himself a suppliant to Fate till he can once more speak the words "my home;" and to the woman it is a concomitant of life. Deprived of it, she misses her best happiness and her finest dignity. Even her beauty suffers, for it is true (is it not?) that part of a woman's loveliness lies in her environment, and that in her chosen and fit surroundings she has a charm which is lacking when she is otherwhere. Home is, moreover, her field of achievement, her jousting ground, the place where she properly tests her strength and her abilities, as men test themselves in business or in battle. However brilliantly she may succeed elsewhere and in other things, if she does not succeed at home she is, in a sense, a failure, nor will her heart let her deny this fact, however passionately she may protest against it.—From the new department, "Woman and the Home," in *Self Culture* for September.

Phussandphret.

lave you heard of the land called Phussandphret,
Vhere the people live upon woes and regret?
ts climate is bad, I have heard folks say;
'here's seldom, if ever, a pleasant day—
Tis either too gloomy from clouded skies,
)r so bright the sunshine dazzles one's eyes;
Tis either so cold one is all of a chill,
)r else 'tis so warm it makes one ill;
'he season is either too damp or too dry,
ind mildew or drouth is always nigh.
'or nothing that ever happened yet
Vas just as it should be in Phussandphret.

ind the children—it realy makes me sad
'o think they never look happy and glad.
t is, "Oh, dear me!" until school is done,
ind 'tis then, "There never is time for fun!"
'heir teachers are cross, they all declare,
ind examinations are never fair.
Each little duty they are apt to shirk,
Because they're tired, or 'tis too hard work.
Every one is as grave as an owl;
ind has pouting lips or a gloomy scowl;
'he voices whine and the eyes are wet,
n this doleful country of Phussandphret.

Now, if you ever find that your feet are set
)n the downhill road into Phussandphret,
'urn and travel the other way,
)r you never will know a happy day.
'ollow some cheerful face—'twill guide
'o the land of Look-at-the-Pleasant-Side.
'hen something bright you will see,
No matter how dark the day may be;
You'll smile at your tasks and laugh in your dreams,
ind learn that no ill is as bad as it seems.
So lose no time, but haste to get
As far as you can from Phussandphret.

—*M. C. Advocate.*

A Bird's Trust.

ALFRED BRUNK.

One day at Williamstown, while I was resting, I heard a sound as of a bird in distress. Turning my eyes in the direction of the sound I saw a sparrow sitting in the open window. In a few moments it flew upon the bed where I was. I took it in my hand and again placed it in the window. It was evidently frightened, for it soon flew back to me. While it is true that the sparrow, and especially the house sparrow, frequents dwellings, yet this bird was evidently from some cause considerably frightened.

O, sparrow, thou with quivering breast,
Dost seek the human's frail abode,
Contented there, thou fain wouldst rest,
Tho' fierce thy foeman's anger glowed!

Upon the ground thou shalt not fall
Without our Heavenly Father's care.
E'en trembling bird, whose strength is small,
His condescension still shall share.

O, mighty man, with glowing sheen,
Look up by faith and see thy God!
With visage soft and sober mien,
Learn now thy worth; with peace be shod.

Your very hairs are numbered all,
Your every pulse-beat, too, he hears;
His hand upholds, ye cannot fall;
Then drive away your craven fears.

Your spirit is a jewel rare;
Your sin-scarred body shall arise;
Yourself his image there shall share,
And sing his praises in the skies.

Newman's, Hanover County, Va.

Knowledge vs. Education.

And finally, what can this ideal woman in an ideal home do for humanity? She can lessen vice by her voice and presence in the home; neglected households lay the surest foundations for crime. If the thought, time and work which women now devote to the bread-winning effort were expended upon the home—aiming for artistic decoration, scientific cooking, and, in general, better modes of living—the households of the land would be lifted to a plane that would insure the conservation of what a nation holds dear. They can seek paths of usefulness in their leisure time; for example, in charitable lines: there are wrongs to right, a suffering world to help, humanity to uplift, opportunities to even some of the irregularities of life. The world is theirs to make it what they will; and when lifted out of their present unnatural position, and placed in their proper setting, the benefit to them will be mental, moral and physical; further, the effect upon mankind in general will be vast. Thus our "new" or future women will find for themselves and others perpetual peace and happiness, making for all time "an age on ages telling, in which living is sublime."—*From "A Conservative View of the Woman Question," by I. E. Turner, in Self-Culture, for September.*

Sunday School.

THE MINISTRY OF MONEY.*

HERBERT L. WILLETT.

The reign of Joash was the first which followed the usurpation of Athaliah. The evil influences of the house of Ahab in Israel had appeared in the disastrous events which followed the good reign of Jehoshaphat. We have already seen in the lessons of the last quarter the earlier effects of the introduction of idolatrous worship, which came to its fullest expression in the days of Ahab, through the influence of his queen Jezebel, daughter of Athbaal, an ex-priest who had seized the throne of Zidon. She not only secured the prevalence of idolatry in the Northern Kingdom, but her spirit was carried into the South in the person of her daughter, Athaliah, who was married to Jehoram, the son of Jehoshaphat.

How much further the evil effects of this family line would have gone it is impossible to say, had not the reforming zeal of Jehu cut it short in the Northern Kingdom and Athaliah herself came to her death through the courage Jehoiada, high priest at Jerusalem. The evil course of one vicious person may be perpetuated through many generations of a family and become a moral pestilence to the whole community. It was fortunate for both kingdoms that vigorous measures were taken to exterminate this cruel and evil stock. Ahaziah, the successor of Jehoram, came to his death at the hand of Jehu who murdered him in company with Jehoram of Israel at Jezreel. Instantly when the news of this tragedy reached Jerusalem, Athaliah seized the kingdom for herself and put to death, as she supposed, all of the children who might be heirs to the murdered king; but one was saved by the care of the high priest and his wife, and was brought up with a view of one day overthrowing the cruel woman who was a foreigner in every characteristic of her nature. When the moment of opportunity arrived he summoned the court officials and temple guards and, preparing against surprise by guarding the temple gates, he brought forth the boy-king and proclaimed him in place of the usurping Athaliah. The queen hearing the tumult came from the palace only to meet death at the hands of the troops, and Joash was crowned as the rightful monarch. He led the people in the work of reform, overthrowing the temple of Baal and putting to death Mattan, the priest of the false worship. Thus much of the evil of Athaliah's reign was counteracted.

In all these affairs the courage and wisdom of Jehoiada stand out in bold relief. No man who was not full of purpose and resources would have dared to incur the danger necessary in seating Joash on the throne. But the interests of an uninterrupted dynasty of the house of David demanded just such courageous action. If the high priest had failed at this point the Messianic hope of the Son of David would have perished, and the kingship would have passed into the hands of a foreign and usurping line of sovereigns.

Some years later the king saw that there was need of repairing the temple. That building, erected by Solomon more than a century before, had fallen somewhat into decay and had been stripped of much of its beauty by the sacrilegious vandalism of the idolatrous princes. During the reign of Joash the influence of Jehoiada again asserted itself, and under his instruction the king saw the need of rising to meet the emergency. Money was needed for the enterprise and the revenues that came regularly into the hands of the priests and Levites were not sufficient to serve the purpose. So a crusade of the kingdom was determined upon in the interest of the work of repair; but the responsibility for this work had been placed upon the Levites, who were not particularly interested in it, since they thought they needed all the money for themselves. Their delusion was just that under which many a preacher labors to-day, who imagines that if he raises offerings for missionary purposes in his congregation he will cut the supply for his own support. These men could not understand how it was possible to ask for more money than was being paid by the people into the Lord's treasury and not find that the additional funds would decrease the regular offerings for the temple. When after a time the king was made aware of this delinquency he called Jehoiada to account for the matter and pointed out the laxity of the Levites in performing his will.

It was at least possible for them to raise the poll tax, which was the rightful debt of every man, and even this was not being secured under the present circumstances. The revenues of the house of God had been sadly broken into by the unscrupulous conduct by the court of Athaliah. Not alone was she a wicked woman; but her sons followed her footsteps, and the presents that the people had brought—gifts of gold and silver for the use or adornment of the temple, had been carried away to enrich the shrines of Baal.

The king chose a new method of reaching the desired end and had a chest placed at the gate of the temple where it would attract the attention of all the people who passed into the sacred enclosure. The offerings of these gifts for the repair of the temple was not made compulsory, but simply depended upon making known the need and obligation. The people were left to offer free gifts, and they proved as always on such occasions that when an opportunity is given they will respond. Nothing is more interesting than the effect of right leadership and proper teaching in a congregation. Those churches where the ministry of money is taught and where insistence is laid upon this as well as other graces of the Spirit are not only the happiest, but the most useful churches. The people are glad to give when they know for what purpose they give, and their interest is aroused in the good cause that is to be assisted. Nothing emphasizes the right kind of leadership more than the largeness of offerings that come from certain churches.

The result of the king's policy in giving the people an opportunity to share in the work and of sending out a proclamation to that end brought the happiest results. The people were delighted to assist and the amount of money was ample. For all the work needed in repairing the temple artisans were secured and soon the house was restored to its former strength and beauty.

The University of Chicago.

*Sunday-school Lesson for October 16, 1898—The Temple Repaired (2 Chron. 24-4-13). Golden Text—And the men did the work faithfully (2 Chron. 34:12). Lesson Outline—1. The Royal Command Slighted (4-7); 2. Generous Offerings for the Temple (8-11); 3. The Work of Repair (12-13).

NEWS ITEMS.

A severe earthquake was felt at Yaukton, S. Dak., Sept. 16

The great Busk-Ivanhoe tunnel at Hagerman Pass, Col., costing $1,500,000 has been abandoned.

Wolfe's comet, of 1884, has been seen again.

The Scully Steel and Iron Co., Chicago, has been given a contract for 2,500 tons of steel plates to deliver at Victory, B. C., for use in the construction of five British steamships.

The National Council of Education has appointed a committee of 15 eminent educators to report at its next session on the establishment of a national university.

The catacomb of St. Calixtus is already lighted by electricity, and the system will soon be extended to all catacombs.

The longest plants in the world are seaweeds. One tropical and sub-tropical is known which, when it reaches its full development, is at least 600 feet in length.

The St. Louis Car Co. has received from the Japanese Government a contract for 250 street cars, to be shipped within 90 days, at a contract price of $300,000. This is the first order of the kind ever received in St. Louis from Japan.

Mr. Perkins, of Middleboro, Mass., mistook the remains of a murdered woman at Bridgeport, Conn., for the body of his missing daughter. The daughter appeared at home during the preparation of supposed remains for burial.

A German inventor at Berlin is said to have discovered a fire that cannot be quenched by water or earth. It burns with a brilliant flame, exceeding big searchlights, and it can be sunk under water or under ground, and when brought to the surface instantly bursts into flame at any desired point.

The first section of the Jungfrau railway is now complete as far as the Eiger glacier station, 7,600 feet above sea level. The entire length of the road beyond Eiger glacier will be cut through the mountain, the tunnel, which will be about five miles long, having an ascending gradient of more than 1,000 feet to the mile. The station at the summit will be 12,600 feet above sea level.

This is the fiftieth year of the reign of Francis Joseph upon the throne of Austria.

The first American flag was raised over Havana an the 20th of September.

CURRENT OPINIONS.

An eminent Russian linguist predicts that in 200 years from now there will be only three living languages—Russian, English and Chinese.

The Interior thinks that the increase of "Peoples'" churches in the larger cities indicates a class discontented with churches of regular orders.

The order for certain regiments to proceed to Manila some international lawers think is likely to complicate an already delicate situation.

Mrs. M. L. N. Stevens, acting president of the W. C. T. U., says that in giving up the "Woman's Temple," Chicago, the W. C. T. U. has nothing to lose, but much to gain.

The Journal and Messenger thinks that Roosevelt's Rough Riders will always be prominent figures in the history of the present war because of the remarkable combination of men. There were a number of millionaires and sons of millionaires among the privates, many university graduates, with cowboys and Western scouts and educated Indians. The remarkable thing is the comradeship which existed between these most diverse elements.

ABOUT NOTED MEN.

President McKinley will visit the Omaha Exposition, Oct. 12th.

Aguinaldo is proceeding to organize an independent local government for the Philippine Islands.

Bartolemo Maso, President of the Cuban Republic has formally announced the end of the Cuban struggle for liberty.

Secretary Alger is still visiting and inspecting military camps.

It is said that no man has ever seen the Empress Dowager, of China, except the Emperor and the eunuchs of her court. Li Hung Chang has never looked upon her face. When he visits her she always sits behind a screen.

Prof. Berson, of Berlin, Germany, and Mr. Spencer, an aeronaut from Crystal Palace, London, recently reached an altitude of 27,500 feet in a balloon.

Philip D. Armour, Marshal Field and Norman B. Ream have obtained control of the Baltimore and Ohio Railroad.

Col. Theodore Roosevelt has been made the choice of the Republican party in New York for the next Governor.

Gen. Joseph T. Haskell dropped dead at his post, at the Barracks, Columbus, Ohio, Sept. 16th.

Prof. Willoughby C. Tindall, emeritus professor of mathematics in the Missouri State University, died at Kansas City, Sept. 17th.

Rev. Thos. Apple, D. D., LL. D., one of the most eminent theologians of the Reformed Church, died Sept. 17th.

Miss Winnie Davis, daughter of Jefferson Davis, died at Narragansett Pier, R. I., Sept. 18th, after an illness of several weeks.

An artist friend who has just seen Ruskin at his home in Brantwood, Coniston, says that he sits for hours speechless and motionless, a picturesque figure indeed, with his long, white beard falling over his breast, but only the pitiful wreck of his former strong personality. He has lost all interest in—and, indeed, almost all knowledge of—literary life and work and converses only at long intervals, and then only about the merest trifles.

Christian Endeavor.

By Burris A. Jenkins.

TOPIC FOR OCT. 16.

OUR SOCIETY WORK AND HOW TO BETTER IT.

(Judg. 7:1-8; 19-22.)

This subject comes at a good time, when the Endeavor movement is as it were sitting down to meditate over its past and its prospects. Our Endeavor movement is something older than it has ever been before—more mature. Something of its froth and effervescence has gone, like the twenty and two thousand who turned back from Gideon, but much of steadiness and calm and strength has been gained. It is a good time to take stock, to think back and look forward.

As we think of our great Society and of our individual Societies, of what they have done and to what that is new they can turn their hands, the mottoes of past years and the good causes which have been emphasized come trooping up before us—Good Citizenship, Deepening of the Spiritual Life, the Quiet Hour and all the others—and each one of these should have its new emphasis in this meeting of retrospect and prospect. But there is one other cause which seems especially ripe for Christian Endeavor to champion, and as we look about for new worlds to conquer, here is a world awaiting us—it is the cause of popular education.

As yet education is an unsolved problem among the Disciples of Christ. Our colleges are not what they ought to be, and they never will be until the rank and file of our people are educated to demand higher things. Can not the Christian Endeavor Society, which is the hope of the church of to-morrow, take firm hold of this educational problem of ours and solve it? Among the many ways, therefore, of bettering our Societies' work, this is the one way which there is room in this article to suggest.

Every Christian Endeavor Society in the brotherhood should be educational. It should establish such classes for our young people as will give them a larger outlook on the world of culture. Any form of literary effort should be encouraged, and especially should some more adequate ideas of the history and aims of our movement, of the work accomplished and yet needed in the mission fields of the world and of careful and scientific Bible study, be provided in every Society. Such provision, indeed, is already at hand in the Bethany C. E. Reading Courses which are being rapidly established in many of our Societies. For these courses handbooks are provided by such writers as J. W. McGarvey, H. L. Willett, W. J. Lhamon, F. D. Power, under the general direction of J. Z. Tyler, and other reading in addition to the handbooks is suggested for the courses. These books are sold at cost price, and the whole object of the Reading Courses is to foster educational development, which is so sadly needed. Send at once if your Society has no Reading Course, to J. Z. Tyler, Cleveland, O., for information regarding the details of the Bethany Courses.

A new day is dawning in the educational history of the Disciples. The first step has been taken, viz., the feeling of the need. The most hopeless condition one can be in is not to be conscious of one's actual need. The diabolical condition of not wanting things is characteristic of the savage. But when one begins to feel his lack, there is hope of supplying the deficiency. Such is now the condition among our people. We begin to see how much in the educational realm is yet to be accomplished by us. We begin to see how inadequate are our present resources. This vague longing and unrest has caused the birth of one agency after another, like the Bethany Reading Circle, the educational board, the congress which is being arranged for next spring, and other efforts yet unborn will be caused by this same dissatisfaction with any educational forces we now possess. Meanwhile, the duty of the Endeavor Society is clear, viz., to turn its full strength toward making its peculiar educational force—the Bethany Reading Courses—a thoroughgoing success.

It was the peculiar glory of our brotherhood in the elder day that it was a movement of the greatest intelligence. Our leaders were scholars, and they sought to introduce sane, scholarly, cultivated conceptions of religion. One does not like to feel that we have in anywise degenerated, but certain it is that unless we hold hard by the high standard of our fathers, and present to the world an intellectual, refined and cultivated bearing in a day of increasing intelligence, refinement and culture, we shall lose our influence and fail of the high calling wherewith we are called. Where are the Endeavorers who will stand for education? Where the Gideon's band for this new-old work? Let us do our best for education, and education will better our Society's work.

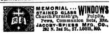

Marriages.

BROWN—GRIMES.—Married at the home of the bride's parents, near Palestine congregation, Mo., Thursday, Sept. 15, 1898, F. E. Blanchard officiating, Mr. Gaines Brown to Miss Tora Grimes.

FICKES—ATKINSON.—At Fairfield, Neb., Sept. 18, Mr. John Fickes and Miss Fannie Atkinson, both of Fairfield; Geo. Lobingier officiating.

SHAFFER—HOLLENBEAK.—At the home of the bride's parents, Payson, Ill., Sept. 20, by C. Edwards, Mr. Thomas Shaffer, of Chicago, to Miss Grace Hollenbeak.

WHITTIER—ATKINSON.—By the same, on same date, at same place, Mr. Burton W. Whittier and Miss Winifred M. Atkinson.

YOUNG—LITTLETON.—At the home of the bride's mother in Holliday, Mo., Sept. 21, 1898, C. H. Strawn officiating, Mr. Dennis B. Young to Miss B. Pearl Littleton.

Obituaries.

[One hundred words will be inserted free. Above one hundred words, one cent a word. Please send amount with each notice.]

BROWN.

Millard Austin Brown was born in Rosetta, Ill., Oct. 14, 1878, and died in the hospital at Camp Presidio, Cal., Sept. 17, 1898. He was a son of Dr. M. F. and Mrs. Lou R. Brown. The name of Mrs. Brown will be recognized by many, as prominent in our state and national C. W. B. M. work. The deceased confessed faith in Christ and became a member of the Christian Church, in the winter of 1895. Last June he enlisted in Company I 51st Iowa Volunteers. Thus another young life has been sacrificed for humanity. The funeral was conducted with military escort and honors, in Lenox, Sept. 25. Christian faith is enabling the bereaved ones to bear their grief.

W. D. RYAN.

Lenox, Iowa, Sept. 26, 1898.

DUDLEY.

Born in Kentucky, March 5, 1806, Livisa Ann Ashmore. Most of her life was spent in Illinois and Iowa, where, at Nora Springs, in the latter state, she died Sept. 16, 1898, aged 92 years, six months and 11 days. In 1830 she was married to Wm. G. Dudley, who died in 1870. She survived all but three of their ten children. Left to remember and love her, 38 grandchildren and over 60 great-grandchildren, a total of one hundred living descendants. She was indeed a Disciple of Christ. Funeral from church, by writer, Sept. 18.

W. W. WHARTON.

Nora Springs, Ia.

ENGLE.

Isaac Engle, a father in Israel, died at his home in Stark County, O., July 29, 1898, in his 75th year. On April 16th, 1846, he was married to Fietta Schiner. To them were born nine children, six of whom and Sister Engle remain. At 17 was immersed by Israel Belton, a Baptist preacher, Bro. Belding assisting in the meeting. In 1860 he united with the Christian Church of which his wife was already a member. He was a very earnest man, honest and kind, loved and respected by all. We miss him in all our services. He knew no Savior but Jesus and recognized no authority but his Word. "He came to his grave in full age like as a shock of corn cometh in his season."

R. L. LOTZ.

Mapleton, O., Sept. 26, 1898.

HOBBS.

William Franklin Hobbs was born in Shelby County, Ky., March 21st, 1826, and died near Kensington, Kan., Sept. 10, 1898, aged seventy-two years, six months and eleven days. He removed to Platte County, Mo., in 1850, where he married Miss Sarah Williams. Eight children were born to them, three sons and five daughters. One daughter preceded him to the spirit-land. In 1850 Bro. Hobbs gave his heart to God and united with the Christian Church, of which he remained a faithful and consistent member till God called him up higher. I never met a man that had more faith in God's Word than Bro. Hobbs, nor a brighter hope of immortality. I saw him a short time before his death, and he told me he was ready and waiting for God to call him. He had no fear of crossing the dark river of death. He was ready. He left a wife and seven children to mourn his departure. Bro. Hobbs came to Kansas in 1872 and settled on a farm, where he remained till his death. He was an elder in the church over 25 years. The funeral services were conducted by Bro. Drummond, of Smith Center.

L. STOCKMAN.

Kensington, Kan.

McKINNEY.

Jas. Wesley McKinney, born Nov. 30, 1841, was called from earthly toil to heavenly rest Sept. 18, 1898, aged fifty-six years, nine months and nineteen days. Bro. McKinney has lived a devoted Christian since early life. He was married to Amanda Grimes, April 30, 1867, and leaves her and his two sons, Hugh and Archie, to mourn the departure of a most faithful husband and father. The Church of Christ has lost a true member and the community a useful citizen in his death.

C. H. STRAWN.

Paris, Mo., Sept. 20, 1898.

LAWRENCE.

Alice Lawrence was born Feb. 9, 1865, in Adams County, Ill. She united with the Christian Church Feb. 3, 1878. Since which time she has been an active and efficient member, helping in every good work and encouraging others to do the same. She had been sick more than 15 months, during all that time manifesting a remarkable degree of Christian patience and fortitude. She passed away Sept. 4, 1898, aged thirty-three years, six months and twenty-three days. Her work was finished, and she has gone home to wear a crown that will never fade.

C. EDWARDS.

Payson, Ill.

POWELL.

On my return from a wearisome summer journey I found a letter announcing to me the tender words from a sister's heart the death of one of the best friends I ever had, Bro. E. L. Powell. He died suddenly at his home in Boone County, Mo., on the 8th of May, 1898, stricken by paralysis. He was born in Kentucky in 1840, and was married to Miss Virginia Daniels, of Harrodsburg, Ky., in 1865. She was a graduate of Daughters' College, a schoolmate of Mrs. Carr, and a noble Christian. Her old time friends, the boys and girls of long ago, scattered over the earth, would love to comfort her and her four sons in the sad bereavement. I would love to speak the praises of Bro. E. L. Powell, had I fitting words. While he lived, as I had opportunity I told the people of his worth. Now that he is gone from the earthly life and I was denied the pleasure of association with him during the last few years and the sad privilege of even placing a flower on his grave, I hope that what I write will serve the living and be a comfort to dear Sister Powell and her four sons. I knew Bro. E. L. Powell well, and believe that "none knew him but to love him," and I am quite sure that I heard "none name him but to praise." It was truthfully said: "He lived a pure, Christian, humble, unobtrusive life." Indeed, he was one of the few men who seemed to be in the world but not of it—not contaminated by it, as most men are.

I recall diistnctly his form, his feature, his very walk when as a fellow-student at Harrodsburg, Ky., I knew him. Of medium height, quick, bright eye, lips delicately chiseled, of ample forehead, his appearance was that of a good-hearted, refined gentleman. Modesty characterized his behavior at the university and through life. He shrank from publicity, and seemed not to know his power, but the professors knew, and the boys who called on him for help to read their Latin and Greek and solve their problems knew his ability as a student, and when the time came to divide the honors of the class there was no division; all the honors were given to E. L. Powell. I supposed he never mentioned this, so free was he from vanity, and I hope to be excused for mentioning it. When he came to Missouri he engaged to teach the country school. I thought he was out of place, that he ought to be in a professor's chair in some college or university, but he had no inclination to place himself there and nobody did this for him, though many a less worthy and less capable person has occupied that position. We often talked together of his diffidence, at which I wondered, and tried to push him forward out of it. He was induced to superintend the Sunday-school and to preach occasionally. Naturally his brethren looked to him and he became an elder of the congregation. His ability as a teacher, his good judgment, and even his modesty, together with his own good works and his orderly family, made him almost the model elder.

Mrs. Carr and I have just talked over the genuine pleasure we had in his household, everything so tidy, so well ordered, and his children so obedient and helpful, revealing the mother's tender care and the father's guidance and companionship. His children never outgrew the Sunday-school as long as I knew them. He and Sister Powell took them there regularly and taught them in class with others. With parents and children this seemed to be a sacred obligation and a real pleasure. His words were well chosen. He had few words in prayer and his preaching never revealed the scholar that he was. reverence and his modesty showed the de earnestness of the man. I am sure th he could have but little sympathy wi the flouncing up of boys, and even of girl to pronounce a prayer in public, or to s a sentence turn about and thus fill up t program. When Bro. Powell spoke, t people were impressed that it meant a gre deal, even more than his best chosen wor could tell. As a business man the world wo call E. L. Powell a failure, for he did not l up treasures here, he laid them up in heave His name was never pronounced that I kn of in high places, as the world thinks of hig ness, but I believe it was written in heave In honor he preferred his brethren, and believe he would have done so at the sacrif of himself. Indeed, he did sacrifice himse and lived an unselfish life, as nearly as mort could be expected to do and live at all in t greedy world.

As I think of my departed brother c Savior's words come into my mind: "Bless are the pure in heart, for they shall see God. I recall not one unpleasant thought or feeli during my intimate association with Br Powell, nor do I remember that I ever hea him speak a word that was unbecoming Christian or do an unworthy deed. I think his life as a most wonderful success. Jesus sai "If a man serve me, him will my Fath honor." Our Father was honored, and call to himself my beloved friend and brother Christ, and while I mourn his loss and deep sympathize with his family in their sorrow pray that the good angels may hover arou that humble home and that they may all brought at last to the happy union in the ho eternal—

"Where we shall find the joy of loving as
never loved before—
Loving on, unchilled, unhindered—lovi
once, forevermore."

O. A. CARR.

SNYDER.

Sister Rebecca Snyder, wife of Dennis Snder, maiden name Ryder, died in Sta County, Ohio, Aug. 23, 1898, in her 33rd yea She was married, Aug. 26, 1883. She w converted under the preaching of Rev. Fra Findley in 1895. Bro. Snyder was also co verted at the same meeting. She leaves large family of small children dependent Bro. Snyder for their daily bread. Funer services conducted by the writer at the Indis Run Church. May the Lord bless the husban and motherless children.

R. L. LOTZ.

Mapleton, O., Sept. 26, 1898.

SPONHAUR.

Joseph Spohaur died at his home nea Sparta, Stark County, O., Sept. 4, 1898, in h 70th year. He was married to Anna Russel April 20, 1871. He leaves three children—on son and two daughters—all members of th church at Sparta. He was a member of th Church of God, but attended with his fami while health permitted. He was a schoo teacher by profession, a man of moral and in tellectual worth. Suffered much, and passe peacefully away. The funeral services wer held in the Christian church at Sparta.

R. L. LOTZ.

Mapleton, O., Sept. 26, 1898.

Publishers' Notes.

"ACROSS THE GULF."

Mrs. N. M. Vandervoort is the clever authoress of a new book entitled, "Across the Gulf." It is along the alignment of "Quo Vadis," and is infinitely better because understood. The writing is in a pleasing vein and free from the innumerable and senseless Latin terms that mar "Quo Vadis." Mrs. Vandervoort is from Hepworth, and bids fair to become famous in the world of letters. Her "Across the Gulf" is laid in the time of the Nazarene on earth, and is historical as well as brilliant and intensely interesting. A fascination runs through the ever-curious and attractive details of the narrative. The authoress with a simplicity and rhythm of diction that charms either the scholar or the common reader throws the curtain back on the life of Rome and its people as history paints it, hence the work is not only attractive but instructive also.—*Sunday Eye, Bloomington, Ill.*

A study of the lives of the great women mentioned in the Bible is always profitable and interesting. Queen Esther stands high among the great Bible characters. M. M. Davis has recently written a book which he has entitled "Queen Esther." It is a book which brings out the grand and noble traits of this wonderful woman in an impressive manner. Many points in the life of this woman is brought to the mind of the reader that are overlooked by the ordinary student of the Bible. This new book is beautifully bound in cloth, containing 132 pages, and the price is 75 cents.

A SPLENDID BOOK.

"Plain Talks to Young Men on Vital Issues," by Peter Ainslie, is a charming little book, and one which every young man and young lady should secure and carefully read. In clear and forcible language the author denounces in successive short chapters the evils attending Gambling, The Theater, Dancing; Swearing, Lying. The last chapter is entitled, "Christian Services," and is well worth the price of the book, which is 60 cents.—*The Youth's Instructor, Chicago.*

KING SAUL.

This is not a "new novel," but a volume giving the life of this king as found in the Bible without altering or inventing one fact. The author is J. Breckenridge Ellis, who is author of "In the Days of Jehu." He has given us a very readable book, and one that will increase interest in Bible study and serve as a commentary on the Old Testament. The book has given a clear interpretation of the passage relating to the Witch of Endor. 281 pages. Cloth, price $1.00.—*Christian Index, Des Moines, Iowa.*

Announcements.

South Kentucky Convention.

THE TWENTY-FOURTH ANNUAL MEETING OF THE SOUTH KENTUCKY CHRISTIAN MISSIONARY AND SUNDAY-SCHOOL ASSOCIATION WILL BE HELD AT TRENTON, NOVEMBER 8, 9 and 10, 1898.

PROGRAM.

TUESDAY EVENING.

7:30—Devotional Exercises.
(NOTE.—The devotional exercises at the beginning of each service will be led by H. D. Smith.)
Address of Welcome, Dr. R. R. Grady.
Response, Prof. A. C. Kuykendall.
Foreign Missions, A. McLean.

WEDNESDAY MORNING.

9:30—Devotional Exercises.
Announcement of Committees.
Report of General Evangelist.
How Best to Enlist the Churches in South Kentucky Work. W. H. Ligon.
11:00—Address, T. A. Lisemby.
11:20—Address, L. H. Echols.

WEDNESDAY AFTERNOON.

2:00—Devotional Exercises.
Reports of Committees.
Present-day Problems in the Sunday-school, J. M. Gordon.
Present-day Problems in Christian Endeavor Work, J. W. Mitchell.

WEDNESDAY EVENING.

7:30—Devotional Exercises.
Address, W. H. Pinkerton.
Announcement and adjournment.

THURSDAY MORNING.

9:30—Devotional exercises.
Reports: Committee on Obituaries, Time and Place, Treasurer.
Preachers and Preaching, J. L. Hill.
Missions as a Means of Spiritual Culture, R. H. Crossfield.
Orphans' Home—Address, Prof. Milton Elliott.

C. W. B. M. THURSDAY AFTERNOON.

2:00—Devotional Exercises.
President and Secretary's Message.
Report from Treasurer and Field.
C. W. B. M.—What it Has Done for the Church, for the World—What It Wants to Do (or Must Do) in the Future, Mrs. Nannie B. Rees.
Song and Prayer.
Woman's Debt to Christ and Humanity, Miss Eugenia Parham.

THURSDAY EVENING.

7:30—Devotional Exercises.
Where Are We? E. J. Willis.
The Evangelist—His Authority and Work, T. D. Moore.
Report of Committee on Resolutions.
Final adjournment.

SPECIAL NOTICE.

1. Send all unpaid pledges to Treasurer George P. Street, Elkton, Ky.
2. All who expect to attend should send their names to J. W. Ligon, Trenton, Ky., at least ten days before the conveneion.
3. The music of the convention will be under the leadership of Prof. Leonard Dougherty.
4. The railroads will carry delegates at full fare to the convention, and one-third fare returning; provided, certificates are procured at starting-points where tickets are bought. This is absolutely necessary in order to obtain reduced rates.

J. W. GRANT, Secretary,
Elkton, Kentucky.

American Christian Missionary Society.

MONDAY MORNING, OCTOBER 17.

9:00—Service of prayer and Praise, led by E. L. Shelnut, Atlanta, Ga.
9:30—Address of Welcome, E. Watkins, Mayor of Chattanooga.
9:50—President's Address, "The Holy Spirit in Missions," F. D. Power, Washinton, D. C.
10:25—Annual Report of Board; Statement by Corresponding Secretary, Benj. L. Smith.
10:45—Business. Appointment of Committees.
10:55—Address, "Our Opportunities for Mission Work in the City," R. S. Latimer, Pittsburg, Pa.
11:25—Announcements.
11:30—Hour of Prayer for America, led by S. D. Dutcher, Cincinnati, O.

MONDAY AFTERNOON, OCTOBER 17.
Christian Endeavor Session.

2:00—Superintendent's Report, J. Z. Tyler, Cleveland, O.
2:10—Address, "The Manifold Mission of C. E."
2:45—"The C. E. as an Educational Agency," B. A. Jenkins, Indianapolis.
3:00—Address, "Home Missions to the Front," H. F. MacLane, Toleo, O.
3:15—Symposium, "How May We Best Develop and Utilize Our C. E. Forces?" F. G. Tyrrell, St. Louis, Mo.

MONDAY EVENING, OCTOBER 17.

7:30—Praise Service, led by S. R. Hawkins, New Orleans, La.
8:00—Address, "The Church Building," S. E. Cooper, Cincinnati, O.
8:30—Address, "Education: Its Importance and Status Among the Disciples," E. V. Zollars, Hiram, Ohio.

TUESDAY MORNING, OCTOBER 18.

8:30—Praise Service, led by M. F. Harmon, Montgomery, Ala.
9:00—Report on Education, Mrs. A. A. Forrest, Irvington, Ind.

9:10—Church Extension Report, G. W. Muckley
9:25—Report of Statistical Secretary, G. A. Hoffmann, Columbia, Mo.
9:45—Report on Ministerial Relief, D. R. Luc Indianapolis, Ind.
10:15—Address on Ministerial Relief, Jabez H Irvington, Ind.
11:15—Business. Reports of Committees.
11:40—Closing Prayers, led by Robert G. Fra Nicholasville, Ky.

TUESDAY AFTERNOON, OCTOBER 18.

2:00—Praise Meeting, led by T. A. Reynolds, Nasville. Tenn.
2:30—Report of Negro Education and Evangeliztion, C. C. Smith.
3:00—Address, "What We Owe to the Negroes Our Country," B. F. Manire.
3:30—Sunday-school Report and Statement, Kn P. Taylor, Bloomington, Ill.
3:45—Sunday-school Address, "Children's Ral for Home Missions," G. A. Hoffmann, Columbia, M
4:15—Reports of Committees. Business.

TUESDAY EVENING, OCTOBER 18.

7:30—Praise Meeting, led by Justin Green, Cincinnati, O.
8:00—Address, "The Paramount Urgency of Hon Missions," George Darsie, Frankfort, Ky.
Address, "A New Star in the Crown of Our Ki —Porto Rico for Christ," J. A. Erwin.

WEDNESDAY MORNING, OCTOBER 19.

8:30—Praise Service, led by L. C. McPherso Buffalo, N. Y.
9:00—Final Reports of Committees.
9:30—Address, "The North is Ripe for the Havest," A. B. Moore, Minnesota.
9:50—Address, "The South as a Mission Field," P. Spiegel, Birmingham, Ala.
10:10—Address, "The West Holds a Ripe Harvest W. H. Bagby, Salt Lake City, Utah.
10:30—Address, "The Call From the East," C. Kreidler, Troy, N. Y.
10:50—"Open Parliament," conducted by John Pounds, Irvington, Ind.
11:50—Closing Prayers of Consecration.

Island of Marken.

The quaint fisher-folk of Marken, two whom are pictured on another page, are loy subjects of the recently crowned Queen the Netherlands. They are a simple, sobe industrious people, ever struggling to sa their flat, marshy island from the encroachment of the sea.

This island was once a frontier or mark the mainland, but was separated from it by a outburst of nature in the 13th century. Th people yet retain the style of dress worn at th time. The loose, sombre garb of the me showiag no linen, is lightened only by th silver clasps and buckles which are usuall family heirlooms. Unlike their countrywome of the main land, who hide their tresses unde close-fitting caps, the women of the Isle allo their blonde curls to hang about the face. T Marken wives, who, though robust, are gau and lean of visage, with high color and dar hollows under their big blue eyes, this a rangement of hair gives an air somewh savage.

Because of the absence of the men on th ocean, the daily duties of the women fishe folk cover the whole range of outdoor work an indoor work. Thus the Singer Sewing Machin has proved a great blessing in their busy live and has become deservedly popular.

THE
ISTIAN-EVANGELIST.

A WEEKLY FAMILY AND RELIGIOUS JOURNAL.

October 13, 1898 No. 41.

NTS.

..................451
ction............452
Vicinity.........452
n.... .... .453
....454
s 454
ught........ ...455
:
hing.—Robt. T.
....459
rmation. 460
—T. H. Blenus..461

....462
. ...462
....463
.................464
l................464
....464
................465
....466
ion 466
... . 467
nvention........467
the Christian...468
.................468

poem)...........472
n Trial 472
....472
ch....... 473
. ...473
emonies.........474

....456
....458
.................460
................471
.. ...:..... 471
. ...476
.................476
....478
ies.............479
uation 480
st Cities........480
.................480

n $1.75.

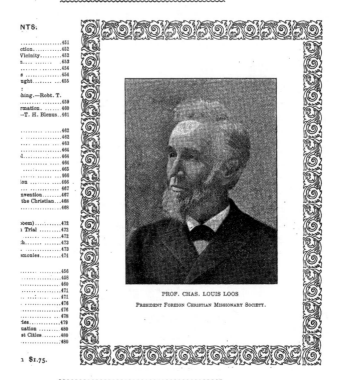

PROF. CHAS. LOUIS LOOS

PRESIDENT FOREIGN CHRISTIAN MISSIONARY SOCIETY.

PUBLISHED BY

RISTIAN PUBLISHING COMPANY

1522 Locust St., St. Louis.

THE

CHRISTIAN - EVANGELIST

J. H. GARRISON, EDITOR.

W. W. HOPKINS, ASSISTANT.

B. B. TYLER, J. J. HALEY,

EDITORIAL CONTRIBUTORS.

What We Plead For.

The Christian-Evangelist pleads for:

The Christianity of the New Testament, taught by Christ and his Apostles, versus the theology of the creeds taught by fallible men—the world's great need.

The divine confession of faith on which Christ built his church, versus human confessions of faith on which men have split the church.

The unity of Christ's disciples, for which he so fervently prayed, versus the divisions in Christ's body, which his apostles strongly condemned.

The abandonment of sectarian names and practices, based on human authority, for the common family name and the common faith, based on divine authority, versus the abandonment of scriptural names and usages for partisan ends.

The hearty co-operation of Christians in efforts of world-wide beneficence and evangelization, versus petty jealousies and strifes in the struggle for denominational pre-eminence.

The fidelity to truth which secures the approval of God, versus conformity to custom to gain the favor of men.

The protection of the home and the destruction of the saloon, versus the protection of the saloon and the destruction of the home.

For the right against the wrong;
For the weak against the strong;
For the poor who've waited long
For the brighter age to be.
For the truth, 'gainst superstition,
For the faith, against tradition,
For the hope, whose glad fruition
Our waiting eyes shall see.

RATES OF SUBSCRIPTION.

Single subscriptions, new or old	$1.75	each
In clubs of five or more, new or old.	1.50	"
Reading Rooms	1.25	"
Ministers	1.00	"

With a club of ten we will send one additional copy free.

All subscriptions payable in advance. Label shows the month up to the first day of which your subscription is paid. If an earlier date than the present is shown, you are in arrears. No paper discontinued without express orders to that effect. Arrears should be paid when discontinuance is ordered.

In ordering a change of post office, please give the OLD as well as the NEW address.

Do not send local check, but use Post office or Express Money Order, or draft on St. Louis, Chicago or New York, in remitting.

ISTIAN-EVANGELIST

opinion and methods, Liberty; in all things, Charity."

, Mo., Thursday, October 13, 1898. No. 41

of horrors as it has been depicted. The only shortage in supplies at Santiago which is admitted was in the supply of medicines, but even this was not serious, and the only deficiency in the service was in transportation, on account of which the tents and siege guns which were on the transports could not be brought up where they could be used. General Wheeler is of the opinion there was never a campaign in which the soldiers were more bountifully supplied with the necessities and even luxuries of life. He had not seen or even heard of such a thing as a sick or wounded man dying from lack of care. These statements do not purport to cover the whole ground, but to indicate the conditions which fell under the eye of this one commander. There may have been a worse state of affairs elsewhere, but there is no man in whose word the men of both parties would more readily place their confidence than in General Wheeler's, and the evidence which he has given will inevitably tend to lesson the confidence of people in their premature adverse judgments of the War Department.

A sensation was created last week by the issue of a warrant for the arrest of Senator Quay, of Pennsylvania, on the charge of conspiracy to appropriate state funds for private speculations. Implicated with the senator and included in the warrant are his son, Richard R. Quay, ex-State Treasurer Benjamin J. Haywood and Charles R. McKee. Last March John S. Hopkins, cashier of the People's Bank in Philadelphia, committed suicide, and when the condition of the bank was examined subsequently its credit was found to be seriously impaired. At this time the bank had on deposit $505,000 of state funds. The bank went into the hands of a receiver, and the president, Mr. McManes, agreed to be personally responsible to all creditors. The state received from him the full amount of its deposit. The charge against the parties above named is that they conspired with the cashier of the bank to deposit the funds of the state in the bank and then to draw them out privately to use in stock speculations. The It will go hard if a stronger line of defense than this cannot be found. Return of stolen goods after detection does not save the thief from prosecution and punishment.

The war is over for the present and the resumption of hostilities cannot seem to be more than a very remote possibility, but it is not to be understood that there is no longer a need for the maintenance of troops in addition to the regulars. For the present it is not solely a question of what necessities, in the way of a standing army, may be forced upon us by the adoption of an imperial policy, but a question of maintaining order temporarily in those places from which the Spanish forces are being removed. As soon as active hostilities ceased there began to be a strong desire on the part of a large proportion of the volunteers to get out of the service. Soldiers for whom military life had lost its charms and friends of enlisted men began to exert pressure to secure the discharge of individuals, and congressmen and others who are supposed to have influence with the administration have been flooded with petitions of this sort. It has been announced that no more troops will be mustered out now in view of the need of forces in Cuba and Porto Rico. Three regiments have been ordered to Porto Rico, and some of the commissioners appointed to arrange for the evacuation of that island are sanguine enough to believe that the last of the Spanish troops will have sailed before October 20. Sites are now being selected for winter camps in the Southern States. There is little hope that the evacuation of Cuba by the Spanish forces can be accomplished before Christmas and, if the present dilatory tactics are continued, it may be much later.

The work of peace commissions always is and of necessity must be carried on in secret and, accordingly, it is probable that for the time our information concerning the important business which is being transacted in Paris will be limited and hypothetical. There seems to be ground, however, for a surmise that all is not going smoothly in the progress of negotiations.

best possible terms. They will begin, of course, by asking for more than they expect to get. Doubtless they have so begun and this will be only the first of a long series of hitches in the negotiations.

Henry George, who was nominated for Governor of New York on a free silver platform by a seceding Democratic state convention, has refused the nomination. In his letter of declination he says he is not a believer in the free silver doctrine, but believes as his father did, in paper money and credit. Like him, too, he supported the Chicago platform in spite of its advocacy of the free coinage of silver, not on account of it, and because he thinks it on the side of the poor against the rich. He could not, therefore, conscientiously accept a nomination on a platform of which free silver is the essential and distinguishing feature. Besides, he is at work on his father's biography and does not care to enter politics at present.

FULFILLMENT VS. DESTRUCTION.

The statement of Jesus that He came to fulfill the law, and not to destroy it, is one of deep significance. It contains the philosophy of His life work as a reformer of the life of mankind. Many reformers, so called, are simply destructionists. They can tear down, but have no talent for building up. They are iconoclasts, who destroy shrines and images, but who rear no altar at which men can worship.

Jesus of Nazareth was not a reformer of this class. He had too deep an insight into human nature and into the needs of the world to pursue a purely negative and destructive policy. Here was the law given through Moses. It was a divine law. It was perfect for the purpose for which it was given. It was adapted to the needs of the people for whom it was enacted. Jesus Christ was born under the law. It represented the highest religious thought and life of men at that time. It was not adequate to meet all the wants of man, and was never designed to be. Its function was that of a pedagogue, to lead the world to the great Teacher when He should come.

Now that the promised Teacher, the Messiah, has come, what attitude will He assume toward the law? Will He attack it and destroy it, or will He recognize its divine origin and seek to fill it with a larger meaning than the Jewish people had ever given to it, and ultimately to supersede it by a new and higher form of religion, which should take up into itself all that was useful and permanent in the Mosaic law and become a universal religion, casting off all local and national limitations? The latter course was the one He chose, and its wisdom is confirmed by the experience of all the subsequent ages. This divine method is one that must be followed in all successful efforts to improve the religious condition of the world, and to give it a purer and higher type of Christianity.

We cannot break with the past. On the stalk of the religious life and thought of the present must be grafted the newer and broader and deeper conception of God and of religion which are to dominate the future. There is a true sense, therefore, in which historical continuity should be recognized. We do not invent a new gospel; we do not establish a new church; we do not originate new truth; we cannot sacrifice the past, with all its struggles and bitter experiences, in seeking to realize the ideal. On the contrary, we take the old gospel and seek to give it a larger and better interpretation; we accept the old church, established by Jesus, and seek to free it from the accumulated errors in doctrine and practice, and make it conform more closely to Christ's ideal; we accept the truths revealed through "holy men of old," and especially those declared by Christ, and seek to apply them to the new conditions and problems of the times in which we live. This is the true spirit of reformation. It seeks to destroy the old only in so far as it is false and prevents the acceptance of the truth.

It is in this spirit that our own reformatory work must be carried forward. We should do ourselves great injustice not to recognize our debt of gratitude to the moral and intellectual struggles of the past. It would be evidence of the narrowest kind of sectarianism to shut our eyes to the noble achievements which have been wrought by those who have gone before us in their efforts to promote the progress of truth and righteousness, or of the men and women of to-day who, though they see not with us, are, nevertheless, according to their measure of light and faith, working heroically for the world's redemption. We have not come as a religious body to destroy the work of the past, or the ideals of the past, which other reformers have wrought out, but to carry this work forward toward completion, and to fulfill it.

There are those among us who, recognizing the existence of evils which we have not yet overcome, and crudeness of ideas which are incident to all religious movements, grow discouraged and turn away from the divinely appointed task of giving to the world a truer and worthier embodiment of Christian life and fellowship. They do not understand that if the germinal and fundamental principles of our movement are correct, our continuous effort must be to fulfill these ideas and principles in an ever-progressive work of reformation and restoration. "Not that we have already attained, or are already made perfect, but we press on, if so be that we may apprehend that for which also we were apprehended by Christ Jesus."

LEXINGTON (KY.) AND VICINITY.

The recognized capital of the world-famous Blue Grass Region is a sort of mecca for the Disciples of Christ. It was in Lexington, in 1832, that the "Christians" and "Reformers" came together in a permanent union for worship and work. The disciples who had been taught by B. W. Stone were called "Christians." Those who had been instructed by Alexander Campbell were, in those days and in Kentucky, called "Reformers." This union was the result of a protracted correspondence and of personal conferences, in which it was found that Stone and Campbell and their friends were seeking the same end, for the same reason, and by substantially the same methods. The end was the union of believers, the reason was that the world might be led to faith in the Christ, the method was by a return to the religion of the New Testament. From the time of this happy union the Christian Church in Lexington has been strong—numerically, morally, socially, financially strong. The great men in our history have preached i Lexington—the greatest and the least hav been heard in this place. It was here tha Alexander Campbell and N. L. Rice, i 1843, engaged in a public oral discussio for eighteen days. Henry Clay acted a moderator. This debate decided our stand ing in Kentucky.

It was in Lexington that B. W. Ston and his friends, in the Presbyterian Churcl were tried for heresy. When they saw tha their condemnation was determined upor they retired to a private garden, the prop erty of a friend, and there prayed, com mitting themselves and their cause to Go They withdrew from that Presbytery an organized what they called the Springfiel Presbytery. After a year this Presbyter dissolved. Mr. Stone and his friends com mitted themselves unreservedly to the Bibl as possessing authority in all matters per taining to the Christian religion and de termined, by God's grace, to be, and to b known, simply and only as Christian. The first church established on this princ ple was organized in June, 1804—bor twenty-eight years before the union spoke of above.

It is probable that more men have bee trained for the ministry in Lexington tha in any other place. This is the home the College of the Bible. It owns a build ing well adapted to its work, and is prac tically free from debt. It has an endov ment of seventy thousand dollars. J. W McGarvey is president. Associated wit him are B. C. Deweese, I. B. Grubbs an J. C. Keith. There are more than or hundred young men in attendance th year.

There are five congregations of th Christian Church in Lexington.

The Central Church was formerly know as the Main Street Christian Church. Th old place of worship, in a dilapidated cor dition, still stands. Now that the soldie are here the upper part of the building used as a guard house. A painted woode sign indicates that the lower part is use for Salvation Army meetings. This is th building in which the Campbell and Ri debate was held. The new Central Churc is the finest house of worship in Lexingto and one of the most capacious and elegar church edifices owned by the brotherhoo I. J. Spencer preaches in this churcl His congregations uniformly fill the splen did audience room, Sunday after Sunda to the extent of its seating capacity.

The Broadway Church is on the corn of Broadway and Second Street. Ma Collis, a native of London, brought up i Australia and educated in Kentucky Un versity, is the pastor. He is the man f the place. It would not be an extravagan of speech to say that he is an ideal pasto The house is modern. One thousand pe sons can be comfortably seated within t walls. The singing in this church is a attractive feature in its worship. Th organ is not used. There is no music instrument of any kind. There is a larg and well-trained chorus. Mr. Aldrich the musical director. If he cannot find a arrangement of music to suit a given occa sion he makes it! The church is unite and aggressive. It is the purpose of th congregation to establish another chur in the near future.

The Chestnut Street Church is a child the Broadway Church. John S. Shouse

probably $50,000. There are 36 acres of ground with buildings. There is a well-invested endowment fund of about $180,000. The income from this fund does not pay expenses. Contributions from churches, Sunday-schools, Societies of Christian Endeavor and individuals assist in paying the necessary expenses. The young women in this school are so trained that they are sought after as teachers in the public schools. Money is needed. The work could be indefinitely enlarged if the board of trustees had the means. Additional buildings are needed. The faculty should be increased. The attendance would then be larger. The business of this institution is so well conducted that all bills are paid at the close of each year. There are no debts. There will soon be added a business department in which bookkeeping, stenography and the use of the typewriter will be taught.

Lexington is the natural center of a remarkable region. The beauty of the landscape and fertility of the soil cannot easily be exaggerated. It is indeed a wonderful country. But Lexington is the center of such a group of Christian Churches as can not be found anywhere else on the face of the earth.

Thirty-four miles distant is the town of Cynthiana, where lives J. J. Haley, who ministers to a large congregation in holy things. Paris, the capital of Bourbon, is only nineteen miles distant, where is a strong church, in which J. S. Sweeney has held the pastorate for twenty-eight years. His father, G. E. Sweeney, lives with him at the advanced age of ninety-two years. H. D. Clark is the preacher in Mt. Sterling, distant thirty-four miles. The Christian Church in Mt. Sterling is the church of the town. Its pastor is recognized as the best preacher in the place. It is but nineteen miles to Winchester, where lived and labored, for years, the lamented W. S. Keene. This congregation is, at present, without a pastor. J. S. Kendrick is our preacher in Danville, distant from Lexington thirty-five miles. This town is Presbyterian headqurters in Kentucky. There is a strong Christian Church in the place. Danvile is a prohibition town; Lexingtion is not. Fayette, of which Lexington is the capital, is a prohibition county. When one sees the aweful ruin wrought by strong drink in Kentucky it is difficult to understand why the people of the state do not raise up *en masse* and drive the infernal business from the commonwealth. Some things seen in a recent visit to Kentucky cannot, in this place, be told. The manufacture and use of whiskey in Kentucky is a fearful blot on the otherwise fair fame of the old commonwealth. This hellish business is at the bottom of almost all that is bad in the state. But to resume:

Frankfort, the capital of the state, is distant less than thirty miles from Lexington. Here George Darsie has preached for twenty-two years. The church was comparatively weak when he became its pastor; it is now one of the strong congregations in the state. Harrodsburg, once famous as the seat of Daughters' College, under the presidency of John Augustus Williams, is distant thirty-four miles. The church in Harrodsburg is without a pastor. Victor W. Dorris preaches in Georgetown, twelve miles from Lexington. Nicholasville is distant same number of miles. R. G. Frank preaches in Nicholasville. Shelbyville is forty miles away. The pastor of the Christian Church in Shelbyville is Hugh McLelland. Forty-one miles distant is the town of Richmond, where W. R. Lloyd is pastor. W. B. Taylor serves the congregation in Versailles, about thirteen miles from Lexington, Walter M. White is our bishop in the town of Midway, fourteen miles from this center—Lexington. In all the places here named the Christian Church is strong and possesses great influence.

It is not, therefore, an extravagant speech to say that Lexington is the center of such a group of Christian churches as cannot be found anywhere else on the face of the earth. The congregations in the towns only are mentioned—and not all of them. Nothing is here said about the strong country churches in this region. There is not space in this article to write their names. B. B. T.

Hour of Prayer.

THE GOSPEL INVITATION.

(Midweek Prayer-meeting Topic, Oct. 19th.)

A certain man made a great supper; and he bade many: and he sent forth his servant at supper time to say to them that were bidden, Come; for all things are now ready.—*Luke* 14: 16, 17.

In this way did Jesus make known to his disciples, and to all the people who heard him, the fact that his mission in the world was for the benefit of all, and all were invited to share in its benefits. Under the figure of "a great supper" he would emphasize the richness and fullness of the provisions made in the gospel to meet the needs of our human nature.

When one contemplates the sublime disclosures of God's character as a Father, the strength and tenderness of His love, the revelation concerning His will and man's duty and destiny, contained in the gospel—all of which are so essential to man's well being, he can understand that it is indeed a great feast of spiritual things to which we are invited. On the other hand, when we consider man's spiritual condition, "without God and without hope in the world," ignorant of God and of his will, alienated from Him by wicked works, and living largely in the lusts of the flesh, dead to all the higher and holier things, and yet with an everlasting hunger in his heart for something better than this world can offer we can understand man's need of just such a feast as is offered to us in the gospel of the Son of God. We are prepared, too, to appreciate the graciousness of the invitation to come and partake.

It was at a feast to which Jesus had been invited that he spake this parable. He saw how readily men responded to an invitation to a feast to satisfy the hunger of the body, and he could but contrast this with the extreme reluctance which the people manifested in accepting the invitation of Heaven to a spiritual feast. There is no accounting for this strange contrast without taking into consideration man's depraved and perverted moral nature and his blindness to those things which relate to his highest interests. It is a fact, however, which every religious teacher has observed, that one of the chief and most difficult tasks he has is to bring men to the consciousness of their spiritual needs and moral bankruptcy. Without the sense of hunger men do not care to eat. Without the consciousness of their moral and spiritual poverty men do not avail themselves of the riches of grace in Christ Jesus.

In this parable men are represented as making all sorts of absurd excuses for not attending the supper, when it is apparent that the real reason they do not go is that they do not *want* to go. We see the exact counterpart of this in all religious work. Men are prone to make excuses for not being Christians, none of which are satisfying to their own conscience. Once the soul hungers and thirsts after righteousness there is no obstacle on earth that can keep it from accepting Christ and his salvation. Why, then, do men decieve themselves in trying to deceive others with their flimsy excuses for not becoming disciples of the Lord Jesus? Nor does this excuse-making end with conversion. Even Christians are prone to make excuses for not becoming better Christians, and for not assuming burdens and responsibilities in the work of the kingdom. Many have formally accepted the invitation, and have tasted gingerly of the viands prepared, but have never yet availed ourselves of the richest and most precious things prepared for us in the gospel. Are we justified in denying ourselves the supreme joy and the higher Christian power which would come to us from a fuller participation of the spiritual blessings of the gospel?

As Jesus extended this invitation to all the hungering and starving sons and daughters of man, so he has laid upon each one of his disciples the duty of carrying the invitation to all the needy of earth. This is the meaning of our missionary organizations. They have for their object the preaching of the gospel at home and abroad. These messengers of Jesus Christ, who go out into the pagan world, and into the destitute portions of our own great country, repeat the invitation of the Master, saying: "A great spiritual feast has been prepared to meet the needs of the human soul; come, for all things are now ready." And so the word has gone out into all the world that Christ has come to minister to the world's hunger.

It is worth while for each one of us here to-night to ask ourselves what part we have in this blessed ministry; what are *we* doing to extend the invitation of Jesus to all the tribes and peoples of earth? We have a responsibility that cannot be evaded, and for neglecting which we can have no justifying excuse. "Let him that heareth say, Come."

PRAYER.

Our gracious Heavenly Father, accept our thanks for the rich provision Thou hast made in the gospel for all our manifold wants. We thank Thee especially for Christ, whom Thou didst send into the world, not to condemn the world, but to bind up its wounds, to feed its hunger, to open its prison-doors, to comfort its sorrow and to lead it to a higher and better life. We praise Thee that through Him Thou hast extended the gracious invitation to all who hunger to come and partake of the spiritual food which Thou hast prepared in Him. Incline our hearts more and more to feed on Christ, and to bear His blessed invitation to all who are perishing of hunger. And may it be ours, at last, when our earthly conflicts are ended, to sit down with Abraham, and Isaac, and Jacob, and with the prophets and apostles, and the heroes of the faith of all ages, at the great marriage supper of the Lamb; to enjoy the fullness of Thy blessing forever more. In His Name. Amen!

Editor's Easy Chair.

"Times change and we change with them." This is well. It is the condition of progress. We were reading a few days ago a splendid and deserved tribute to one of our great leaders who, years ago, laid down his Cross for the Crown. We knew the brother, whose labors and whose heroic devotion to the larger truth which he saw are recognized and properly valued in the article referred to, quite intimately for twenty years. We were of one mind and one heart as touching the great principles of the Reformation which we plead. But he was misrepresented, charged with unsoundness, and often bitterly criticised in his day and time, but he was true to the right as God gave him to see the right, and died in faith, not hiving received the approbation of all his br thren. As the most prominent leader of the type of thought which he represented, it was his lot to receive most of the blows that were delivered by the opposition. But the hands that stoned him then are ready to assist in building him a monument now. So has it ever been:

"Truth forever on the scaffold,
Wrong forever on the throne;
Yet that scaffold sways the future,
For behind the dim unknown
Standeth God within the shadow,
Keeping watch above His own."

Not long ago we sat upon a platform at a great national convention by the side of an ancient veteran who, in the strength and power of his younger manhood, stemmed the current of popular disfavor, was ostracised, persecuted, threatened with death, and his life often imperiled because of devotion to what he believed to be right and truth. His name was mentioned with honor in the convention for his long and loyal service, and the great audience gave him an ovation, as he stood before them, venerable in years and bearing the battle-scars of his long and faithful service. Reaching him a hand as he sat down, we said: "It comes late, sometimes, but it always comes!" His heart was too full for response, as his memory ran back across the years, and he contrasted the then with the now. How much nobler is it to live such a life than to float along the smooth surface of popular favor, antagonizing no wrong, making issue with no falsehood, giving battle to no evil!

It was so in the time of our Lord. Men were then building the tombs of the prophets and quoting their utterances as final authority, while they were the sons of those who had stoned the prophets for seeing farther into the heart of things, and having a truer and worthier conception of God and of worship than they had. The prophets were always giving trouble to kings, and to idolators, and to the advocates of popular wrongs, by denouncing the wickedness of their times, the heartless formality of the worship, and by pointing to a more spiritual religion. But many of them paid the penalty of their devotion to right with their lives. While the men of Christ's day were building tombs for them and honoring them with words, they were giving the very same treatment to Christ that their fathers had given to the prophets. Oh, dull eyes that cannot see and recognize the heroism of men who stand for the larger and th better truth while they are yet among u

"Strange we never prize the music
Till the sweet-voiced bird has flown."

Strange we cannot understand the m who blaze out the way for the world's prog ress until they have gone, and then cor and lay our belated garlands on the graves. It is saddening to think how mar of those who are crying, "Hosanna to J sus!" to-day, had they lived in the time his earthly ministry would have joined the crowd who cried, "Crucify him! Cr cify him!"

We are thinking of an unmarked gra in Missouri, that holds the dust of as true moral hero as ever walked to martyr-fir to lay down his life for the cause he love He used to write us in the stress and stor of criticism which some of his utteranc provoked, saying: "My appeal is to th future. I am willing to bear the calum of the present, in the hope of that vindic tion which I am sure will come when I a gone." Noble man of God! Loyal ser ant of Jesus Christ! He needs no mon ment, on his own account, to mark his qui resting-place. For the eye of God watch over his ashes; and the children of the f thers will build his tomb, and will wri upon it an epitaph that will honor his mem ory and honor the name of Jesus Chris And so it is that the world moves forwar and the tombs of its martyrs are the mil stones that mark its progress.

Questions and Answer

Editor CHRISTIAN-EVANGELIST:—*I wi you would give your position on the desig of baptism, as I think you are misrepr sented here by a brother who says "yo and the preaching fraternity of the chur teach that the baptism of a believer in t name of Christ is not for, but because o remission of past sins.* *T. A. Foster.*
Sparta, Mo.

The "brother" referred to does not, course, read the CHRISTIAN-EVANGELIST, b he doubtles *does* read some paper who editor feels it his duty to define the positi of the editor of this paper and of th "preaching fraternity." The scriptur passage, "Repent ye, and be baptiz every one of you, in the name of Jes Christ unto the remission of your sins (Acts 2:38, Revised Version), cannot pos sibly be rendered "*because of* the remis sion of your sins." This passage, as we as many others of similar import, show that remission of sins is an object *towar which* repentance and baptism look. I what *sense* baptism looks toward remissic of sins is an open question, about whic honest men differ; but that it is mentioned i this passage and other passages as a con dition precedent to the remission of sins i *some* sense is what every Christian schol is bound to admit. We do not give th passage a meaning that brings it into an tagonism with the doctrine of justificatio by faith. We believe that faith is th principle of justification, and that both re pentance and baptism spring out of faitl We look upon baptism as a gracions ad aptation or human need, to aid us in com ing to the knowledge of remission of sin and not as a hard exaction or price to b paid for pardon. When does faith justify? When it leads the believing soul to surrender itself to Jesus Christ, as Savior and Lord. But in what *act* shall this surrender be indicated or manifested? Baptism was instituted, according to our view, to meet that question, and to serve as the mark of a surrendered life. No other view, it seems to us, can account for the importance that is attached to this ordinance in the New Testament Scriptures. It was, during the apostolic ministery, "the seal and sign of pardon" because it was the "seal and sign" of self-surrender to Jesus Christ, the only Savior of sinners. Some other act, doubtless, might have been selected by divine authority to serve this purpose, but it is impossible to think of one more impressive or more appropriate than the simple and solemn act of being "buried with Christ in baptism," and and raised again therefrom "in the likeness of His resurrection." Baptism, then, is *for* or *unto* the remission of sins, because it has been ordained by divine authority as the overt act in which the believing soul openly surrenders to Jesus Christ and formally swears allegiance to Him, and because remission of sins is predicated on this surrender to the Lordship of Jesus.

A brother (M. T. Cooper, Ipava, Ill.,) takes exception to our answer in a previous issue of the CHRISTIAN-EVANGELIST to the inquiry concerning the course of the evangelist and pastor who refused to accommodate themselves to the "weakness," as we call it, of the candidate who insisted on being baptized in a stream of water rather than in a baptistery. His objection is that the "weakness" referred to belonged to the evangelist and pastor, and not to the man who wished to be baptized as was his Master, in the open stream. He expresses a similar preference and says, "We believe our faith is just as strong in God and in His requirements as the editor's, and a great deal stronger than that of this pastor or evangelist."

We did not say that this brother's faith in God or Christ was "weak." We did not use the term "faith" in this sense, but rather in the sense in which Paul uses the term when he says: "But him that is weak in faith receive ye, yet not to doubtful disputations. One man hath faith to eat all things; but he that is weak eateth herbs." Faith here is used in the sense of *moral discernment* as to the things that grow out of or have to do with faith. In this sense we would have to insist, notwithstanding the courteous protest of our correspondent, that the man who seemed to think that his baptism in a pool of water would not be valid, indicated a "weakness" in spiritual discernment, which is sure to give way in time to a better understanding of the gospel. It is that "weakness" which makes a mere *incidental* feature of an ordinance of the nature of an *essential*. There is no remedy for this confusion of things that differ but spiritual growth.

How do you account for the success of the Mormons in gaining proselytes to a system that is so monstrous as to shock the sensibilities of refined people? *Occident.*

1. By the zeal which they display in proselyting, which is as marvelous as the absurdity of their claims.

2. By their system of sending out evangelists who go at their own charges, living off the people. They have 1,500 such men in the field.

3. By their appeals to the lower motives and lusts of men.

4. By the strange fact, which Barnum observed, that the people loved to be humbugged.

Current Religious Thought

In an interesting article on "The Newer Education and the Ministry," by William Jewett Tucker, D. D., president Dartmouth College, Hanover, N. J., in the Biblical World for September, there is a distinction of methods made that is very suggestive and helpful. We give the last two paragraphs of President Tucker's article:

And when we turn to our social problems, we find ourselves under no less a necessity for painstaking and thorough study. The difference between the old philanthropy and the new, or between the lower and the higher, has been well put in the statement: "The lower philanthropy tries to put right what social conditions have put wrong. The higher philanthropy tries to put right the social conditions themselves." The difference is immense. It is the difference between the charity which expresses itself altogether in relief and rescue, and the charity which expresses itself in restraint and precaution, in the effort to recover the rights of the individual, and in the greater effort to effect at some vital points the readjustment, if not the reconstruction, of society.

To whatever department of theological training we turn, it is found to be impossible to ignore or disallow the method of the newer education. The subject-matter of the old education must hold a chief place in the preparation for the ministry, but the subject-matter of the new has an increasing value, and its method is imperative in the reconstruction of theological science. And for the practical work of the pulpit we have the right to expect of the education which takes a man up on his way to the ministry that it will accomplish these three things: First, that it will develop and furnish the man as well as specialize toward preaching; second, that it will give him contact with the mind of his time; third, that it will give him access to the truth, and not simply the technical means of access, but the strenuous spirit of search.

In an address before the Baptist Ministers' Conference, New York City, recently, by Robert Stuart McArthur, D. D., an abstract of which was published in the Religious Review of Reviews for September, are some terse and timely sayings. In speaking of "Realism" as one of the characteristics of the the present times, Dr. McArthur said:

Another characteristic of the time is what is here called realism. This word is not used in its philosophical sense, nor in some of its theological senses; but simply as equivalent to reality, to truth or truthness. We are seeking for truth, no matter from what quarter it comes nor by what messenger it is brought. We have little concern for the new theology or the old theology as such; what we want is the true theology. Baptists have no creeds, in the technical sense, to come between them and the truth. They are not fettered to the cemeteries of dead theologians. Every generation must do its own thinking. We are better able to make creeds than those who make the so-called ecumenical creeds of the church. Creeds made by men in one generation can be remade or entirely unmade by men in another generation. It is far more difficult, often, to interpret the creeds than it is to explain the Scriptures on which the creeds are supposed to be based.

We must love truth more than we do our prejudices, our traditions, our theological systems. Creeds have often been unsightly scaffolds which have largely destroyed the symmetry of God's temple of truth; the falling of the scaffolds reveals the beauty of the temple in its heavenly perfection and radiant glory. Truth is the daughter of God, the heir of eternity, and the queen of heaven. The true spirit of realism, as here defined, strikes a vigorous blow at the claims of churchianity. The doctrine of so-called apostolic succession is groundless historically, and worthless doctrinally. In the very nature of the case the apostles could not have successors, in the sense in which the term is often used. Realism hates all pretension; it wants facts. Why should a creed be called the "Apostles' Creed," when the last apostle was in heaven about four hundred years before it was made, even in its substance; and the last apostle was in heaven for nearly or quite seven hundred years before it took the form it now has? It may be said that this title simply implies that this creed is a truthful compound of apostolic doctrine. But it was given with the idea that its clauses were actually contributed by the apostles. So Rufinus the compiler and traditionalist of the fourth century teaches; but no historical student to-day attaches importance to his testimony. Why should a creed be called "Athanasian," when the great Athanaasius never heard of it, and was in heaven hundreds of years before it was really known. These are examples of what Dr. Swainson, a good authority on creeds, calls "pious frauds." Such titles are akin to the "False Decretals," and the "Donation of Constantine." Such shams in religion tend to make infidels.

We want truth, not pretention, not tradition, not asumption. Truth against the world. Let no one fear the criticism of the time so long as it is seeking and finding truth. But let us be quite sure that it is truth which it gives us, and not some old error with a new face. If we are sure that it is truth, we want it, and it will make us free indeed.

The Christian Commonwealth, London, contains a statement formulated by Dr. Rade on what German working men think of Christianity. Dr. Rade had made an investigation of the religious state of working men in Germany for the National Evangelical Social Congress, recently held in Berlin, and this is the substance of his report. It presents much for reflection and study, especially as these views are by no means uncommon to working men in this country. The information is in the form of replies to certain questions. Dr. Rade says:

1. Concerning the Church and the clergy. The radical, social, democratic working man considers the church a hindrance to true culture and progress, and a means in the hands of priest and pastor for the benefit of the privileged classes. Clergymen are either stupid or hypocrites. The more moderate class of working men, some even with Christian convictions, are quite suspicious of the State Churches, and think that their method of government is adapted to the needs of the ruling classes, and only in exceptional cases are these working men willing to have confidence in the clergy. These ideas prevail even among the evangelical working men's unions, organizations especially established for the purpose of counteracting anti-Christian tendencies among the laboring classes. 2. Concerning Church rites. The social democratic element regard these as perfectly useless, maintained only through the force of social customs and the influence of women. These rites are only dead ceremonies. The more conservative class of working men demand that in the administration of these rites no distinction be made between the rich and the poor. Compulsory baptism of infants is strongly condemned, and confirmation is both ridiculed and approved. Church funerals are also condemned even by this class of men. 3. Concerning Christ. Of all the answers received, only one ventured to deny His existence, and to claim that He was an ideal creation. It is strongly maintained that the Christ of history is not the Christ of the Church. What Christ sought and His doctrines as since perverted are as different as day and night. Most of the working men regard Christ as a very prominent man who took a firm stand for the emanicipation of the oppressed, and if He were living to-day would belong to their party. Some of the men, however, in their replies, still retain a religious devotion to the Lord and acknowledge His entirely unique character, and do not deny the possibility of the miracles ascribed to Him. 5. Concerning God and creation. God is regarded by many as an impossibility. Nature is God. The fact of creation seemed to perplex many of the respondents. They say that the world was not created, but it came into existence. The word "evolution" solves the problem for them. They are advocates of Darwin's theory. The Biblical account of creation is unscientific and an offense to conscience and a hindrance to a higher type of faith. Even the Christian class of working men do not stand on a much higher level. They do not accept the Biblical account as it stands, but understand it symbolically.

Our Budget.

—On to Chattanooga!

—Take a health certificate with you.

—This certificate is not for publication, but as evidence of good faith.

—Nothing worse will be caught at Chattanooga than an attack of missionary zeal.

—Blessed are they who are not scared at rumors, but who put their trust in God and go forward in the path of duty.

—The lesson of falling leaves is before us again.

—The General Convention, at Chattanooga, begins on Thursday of this week.

—Approaching winter brings renewed opportunities for applied Christianity.

—The lengthening evenings raise the question of intellectual food for the winter.

—Are you doing all that you can do for the welfare of the church of which you are a member?

—Do you not think that you could induce your neighbor to subscribe for the CHRISTIAN-EVANGELIST?

—A forward movement all along the line means more than simply a line of protracted meetings.

—The most descriptive, realistic, appropriate prayer that some people who join the church could pray would be, "Now I lay me down to sleep," etc.

—The present year will record a new high-water mark in our missionary offerings and successes. This ought to be a matter of rejoicing and encouragement to the churches, even if not what they ought to be, as yet.

—If there are conditions in the church, the church to-day, that are dark and discouraging, are they not to be attributed, largely, to past causes? The fruits of present methods are not yet apparent.

—Rev. Samuel I. Lindsay, a Presbyterian minister of this city, read an interesting paper to our preachers in this office on last Monday on City Evangelism. The chief point of interest in the paper was the assertion that the time for united action of all evangelical churches against sin in our great cities had come. The doctrine of a confederation of forces was endorsed by the preachers who heard the paper.

—The League of Social Service, New York City, is certainly doing an excellent work. The literature sent out by this league upon moral, social and religious themes is vigorously written, yet unsectarian and non-partisan as to religious and political parties. One of the ablest writers on moral and economic questions that this country has produced, Josiah Strong, is president of this league. An annual membership in this league, which is one dollar, will carry with it the receipt of one copy of every leaflet issued during the year of membership and the use of the information bureau. Others who co-operate financially to the extent of five dollars or more in one year will be sustaining members. Further information and sample leaflets may be procured on application to the League for Social Service, United Charities Building, Fourth Avenue and Twenty-second Street New York.

—The influence of many preachers of the gospel is ruined by the spirit in which they go about their work. A pastor or an evangelist ought not to assume dictatorial power in and over a congregation. This course is sure to create opposition and to make enemies. If Paul could lay aside his apostolic power and say, "I beseech thee," how much more should the evangelist or the pastor refrain from the exhibition of authority in the Lord's house. No man has a right to lord it over God's heritage. Every preacher should rule by love. Nothing sooner destroys a preacher's usefulness than the exhibition of authority. The church of Christ has no use for a dictator or autocrat.

—Not all who put themselves forward in church work are qualified for the place sought. All such ought to know that they offend good taste by so doing, and bring reproach upon the cause. On the other hand even the most competent when forced to the front are often most severely critised. This, too, is an evil under the sun, especially in church work. But of the two evils the former is the greater. A proper tribunal to pass upon the competency of every member of the church for any particular work seems to be one of the urgent wants of to-day in church work, and this tribunal every church ought to have in its pastor and elders.

—The October issue of the Christian Quarterly, number eight of their new series, is out and presents an inviting table of contents. The titles of the leading articles are: (1) The Trend of Modern Religious Thought, by the editor of this paper; (2) Religious Humbugs, by H. W. Everest; (3) The Supply of Preachers, J. W. McGarvey; (4) Alexander Campbell and the Mellennial Harbinger, F. M. Green; (5) Isaac Errett and Our Later History, A. M. Haggard; (6) Human Volition and Responsibility, M. C. Tiers; (7) The Law of Analysis and Synthesis Applied, D. A. Wickizer. In the book department quite a number, of important books are reviewed. There is one important because always interesting feature of the Quarterly missing in this number, and that is the lack of editorial notes and comments, caused by the editor's absence in England, and the pressure of his college duties after his return. There is not likely to be any complaint of this number, however, for the want of variety, as the leading articles cover a wide range of thought. The appearance of this number is attractive and creditable alike to the publisher and editor, and we are sure will be appreciated by the reader. We only regret that so worthy an enterprise is not more generally supported by our preachers and others.

—The Endeavor World recently contained an article on "Pocketbook Openers" and mentioned the "joke," the "sneer," "pathos," "pride," the "appetite" and "principle," but singularly forgot to mention love. When men love they give. No other power affects the purse like love.

—The friends of Cotner University will be interested in J. W. Hilton's statement of its present financial condition in this paper. We are glad to see that considerable headway has been made toward the liquidation of the debts of the institution and hope that the amount yet needed to free it from debt may be raised. We hope that Bro. Hilton's appeal to the brotherhood will meet with hearty response.

—In this issue we publish one of several articles we have received, called out by Bro. Tyler's editorial on "The Possession and Use of Property." We will publish another of these articles next week which will doubtless fully cover the ground in Bro. Tyler's article to which exception has been taken. No one will have any trouble in understanding just where Bro. Garst stands on this question by his article in this paper and think his views worthy of due consideration. We do not regard the single tax doctrine a cure-all for all industrial diseases, but we do believe that it strikes at the root of one of the great evils of our industrial system.

—From the 7th annual report of the principal of the Tuskegee Normal and Industrial Institute, at Tuskegee, Alabama, we learn that notwithstanding the war and other unfavorable conditions, considerable headway has been made. During the present year 1,047 students have been enrolled and $58,000 added to the plant which is now estimated at $300,000. But like all great institutions, much more money is needed by its founder, Booker T. Washington, to reach his ideal of an industrrial school for his people. The sum of $25,000 is needed once for properly heating, lighting and wate ing the present buildings. The report clos with an optimistic outlook for the future this now wonderful enterprise.

—We are glad to furnish our readers th week an excellent likeness of Prof. C.] Loos, of Kentucky University, who is also t president of the Foreign Christian Missiona Society. He was the successor of Isa Errett, in this position, and has given mu time and thought to the subject of Forei Missions. Few men are as vigorous in r i and body as is Prof. Loos at his age. May] be spared to us yet many years, to help a vance the cause he has served so long and faithfully.

—The serious sickness of Admiral Sampso reported last week, following so closely up the sickness of Captain Clark, Captain Eva and other naval officials is indicative of t intense mental strain to which they were su jected in the late war. Sometimes people inclined to think of such men as overpaid a overpraised political pets, but they do always know the facts in the case. It appe that the strain borne by high officials on battleships has not only cost the life of Capt Gridley, but seriously affected the health others, and perhaps has shortened their li many years.

—The following card will call out the sy pathy of hundreds of friends who know a love Bro. Reynolds:

MY DEAR BRO. GARRISON:—It is with a heart that I write this card to tell you that sainted daughter, Mrs. Lucy Wetherho died this morning at two o'clock. Oh how I bear up under this terrible blow. We n your sympathy and your prayers. Y broken-hearted brother, J. C. REYNOLDS

Macomb, Ill., Oct. 7, 1898.

We had learned of Sister Wetherhold's ness and are not surprised to hear that she passed through the change that awaits mortals. The editor has known the decea from her girlhood, and a truer and m affectionate daughter and wife we have ne known. We tender our profound sympath to Bro. Reynolds and other members of family in this sad bereavement. He kn how to lean on the everlasting arms. He been making his home at his daughter's some time, where he received from her and husband every mark of affectionate regard care. We commend them to God whose co solation alone can comfort us in such trials.

—In our issue of September 8th we rep lished an article from the Ladies' Home Jo nal, "The Late-Staying Caller," by Robt. Burdette, without credit to that journal. T omission of the credit was an oversight and matter is here mentioned with our complime to the Ladies' Home Journal for the pleas of the article.

—It is wise to do all church work in a systematic way, and as far as possible to classify duties; but these classifying lines should not be so rigidly fixed that any church member or officer may not work anywhere that necessity demands. It is all very nice to say that it is the duty of the deacons to look after the secular affairs of the church, the elders the spiritual and the pastor the pulpit work, but there are times, places and conditions when this order cannot be observed. The elders and the preacher should not be above doing the secular work of the church when the deacons are absent or need assistance. Some successful preachers have served as deacons, elder, preacher and janitor coetaneously in their time.

—The following clipping is not from the Funny Column of the Baptist News, but is intended for a sober editorial utterance, but we can trust our readers to see the unconscious humor in it:

When the returns are all in and Dr. Hulbert has heard from all the associations which have declared against affiliation of Baptist schools with the University of Chicago, he will have enough to keep him amused all winter. So far as heard from the rock-ribbed order of Baptists continue to resolute. Certainly they have no thought of shutting up the great University, but they warn against it as against other giant evils.

—Foreign Missions, Home Missions, Church Extention, Sunday-schools, Christian Endeavor work, C. W. B. M., Bethany Christian Endeavor Reading Courses, Negro Evangelization and educational interests are the great themes about which a great people are in conference this week at Chattanooga, Tenn.

—We acknowledge the receipt of complimentary tickets to the full course of lectures for the season, to be given at Christian Tabernacle, Decatur, Ill.

—T. W. Grafton, pastor of the church at Rock Island, Ill., has an interesting article in the Christian Oracle, of last week, on "The Life of John Smith." Such a life as this stands out in striking contrast to that of the ordinary preacher of our times and acts, or should, as a stimulus to greater energies by our preachers for the cause they are pleading. It will do our younger preachers good to know more about the pioneer preachers of the restoration movement.

—We are requested to make the following correction in the song, "On to Chattanooga," by J. H. Stark, in our issue last week. In the third line of the first verse after the word "ground," the words, "this time," should be inserted. And after the first word in the third line of the third verse insert the word, "we," so that it will read: "So we shout aloud our songs, our greetings," etc.

—Some splendid meetings are reported in our evangelistic columns this week.

—This number of the CHRISTIAN-EVANGELIST contains an unusual number of short articles. This is what our readers like. They admit of so much greater variety in a paper. We wish that all contributors would have more regard for the beauty of condensed articles.

—Concerning the recent victory for prohibition in Canada the Voice, for Oct. 6th, says:

We see no reason for yielding one fraction of the moral effect of the victory in Canada. It was a magnificant triumph, and though it is not conclusive, in the sense of having any legislating power, it ought to result in the prompt enactment by Parliament of a Dominion prohibitory law. Prohibitionists of Canada must not be robbed now of the victory they have so nobly won.

—If you would know the splendid lines of reading outlined for Bethany C. E. Reading Courses this year send to J. Z. Tyler, Cleveland, Ohio, for a copy of the Bethany C. E. Bulletin for October. The information contained in this Bulletin ought to make even a disinterested person hungry for knowledge.

—At last a report has been published by the Society for Psychical Research which professes to have obtained experimental evidence of immortality. Dr. Richard Hodgson, who has been spending years in experiments with a medium, after his exposure of the frauds of Madam Blavatsky and Eusapia Pallandino, has announced his conviction that he has facts to make immortality an easier hypothesis than any that can be opposed to it. The report in which he states this conclusion and the facts alleged to substantiate it is one of the most amazing pieces of work that I ever read. It must produce a crisis in the study of this phenomena. There may be no outburst of excitement respecting the question, but all who have followed the work of the society, whether near or from far, must recognize that students of it have come to the parting of the ways; and even if they can still suspend judgment on the main issue, they must begin to feel the tremendous nature of the conclusions involved, whatever theory is adopted to account for the facts.

The above is a paragraph from an article in the Independent, last week, by Prof. J. H. Hyslop, of Columbia College, N. Y., on Dr. Hodgson's study of the report of the Society for Psychical Research, and his conclusions. We have not seen the report to which Prof. Hyslop refers, neither the study of it by Dr. Hodgson, but we are far from being convinced of his claims from the article in the Independent. As to a physical basis for a belief in the existence of the spirit of man after death, we do not see how we could well have better attested facts than those of the Bible, and as to *intercommunication* between spirits in and out of the flesh, we are of doubtful disputation, but not beyond the reach of clear testimony. The dangers of such a doctrine, however, are in the already too large accumulation of acknowledged chaff and rubbish, deception and fraud that have gathered about it as well as the absence of a clearly defined purpose in its promulgation. So far this doctrine has been unfortunately so associated with oriental mysticism that it is difficult to regard the usual so-called phenomena of spiritualism seriously. In fact, in the same number of the Independent we have another article on the same phenomena from the pen of another professor—E. E. Slosson, of the University of Wyoming—in which he stands extremely opposed to the claims of Prof. Hyslop. Here, for instance, is a paragraph from Prof. Slosson's article:

One of the commonest of mediumistic manifestations is light. It is a poor "psychic" who cannot make a ball of fire or a phosphorescent hand appear in a dark room, and we have Professor Crook's photographs to show the objective character of this light. Now if this radiant energy will decompose silver bromide on a sensitive plate why should it not decompose nitrocellulose in the magazine of a Spanish warship. Probably no single person would have sufficient force to project the psychic spark far enough, but a battery of mediums could be located on some prominent point, and connected so as to secure the greatest possible voltage.

In the secret service department supernatural powers would be invaluable. An astral form should have been kept in Sagasta's Cabinet at all hours, and perhaps a similar watch at Paris and Berlin. All languages are alike to such messengers, so a knowledge of foreign tongues would be as unnecessary to them as to an American Minister at a European court. The projection of astral forms seems quite easy from the descriptions of the process. It is simply a kind of applied calculus, first differentiation into infinitesimals and integration at the required place. Telepathy is getting so dreadfully common nowadays that there ought to be no difficulty at all in finding out the plans of the enemy, provided he has any.

PERSONAL MENTION.

T. W. Grafton, pastor of the church at Rock Island, Ill., was in the city last week attending the stockholders' meeting of the Christian Publishing Co., and visiting old friends.

A half tone picture of the vice-president of the C. W. B. M., Mrs. A. M. Atkinson, appears on the first page of Missionary Tidings for October.

John Fuller, minister of the church at Randall, Kan., in company with his sister called at this office on Thursday of last week. Bro. Fuller is returning from an Eastern trip and an absence from his people of one month.

We have learned that F. N. Calvin, minister of the church at Waco, Tex., has resigned to take effect Dec. 1st, and that he is entertaining the idea of special evangelistic work in the interest of the spiritual welfare of churches. However, he may accept a new pastoral work. Bro. Calvin has been seven years with the church at Waco. He says that he has had an average of nearly two accessions per week in his regular work for over eleven years. This is a good record.

George Lipscomb, of Maryville, Mo., says: "After a very successful six months of labor with us Bro. James G. Eldredge has resigned and entered the University Medical College, Kansas City, Mo., where he will graduate in the spring. He has added 46 to the church in DeKalb County and organized a new church. Our church is in a prosperous condition and is out of debt."

J. H. Bergman and son, of Bloomington, Ill., called at this office on Thursday last. Bro. Bergman had not visited St. Louis since 1848, and finds it quite unlike the village of that year. The town has grown somewhat since that day. Bro. Bergman speaks well of Bro. Gilliland and his work at Bloomington, and the church is showing its appreciation of his labors by repairs on its house of worship to the amount of about $5,000.

T. A. Abbott has changed his residence in this city from 4760 Kennerly Avenue to 4144 Westminster Place.

H. L. Atkinson, minister of the Church of Christ at California, Pa., has removed to Chicago, Ill. His address is University of Chicago, 146 Divinity Hall.

J. M. Lowe, minister of the gospel at Winterset, Ia., has resigned his labors for the church at that place, the resignation to become effective on or before Jan. 1, 1899.

J. H. Fuller, minister of the gospel at Burlington, Ia., who has been visiting and preaching at Barberville, Ky., for a season, called at this office last week on his way back to Burlington.

G. W. Hamilton has moved back to Rob[illegible] Mo., his old home, and is ready to answer a[illegible] call for a protracted meeting.

S. B. Moore, the new pastor at Compt[illegible] Heights Christian Church, this City, took [illegible] place as a member of the Christian Preacher[illegible] Association, of St. Louis, at its meeting [illegible] this office on last Monday.

J. W. Strawn, of Miamai, Mo., announc[illegible] his readiness to serve churches wanting [illegible] protracted meeting.

A. C. Roah will preach one-half time for t[illegible] church at Mason City, Ill., during the comi[illegible] year.

R. A. Thompson began a protracted meeti[illegible] at Gilman City, Harrison Co., Mo., Oct. 9t[illegible]

Thos. J. Jones, of Chicago, Ill., has gone [illegible] New York City to continue his musical studi[illegible] under Prof. F. X. Arens. Bro. Jones is o[illegible] of our best soloists.

A card from Bro. J. C. Reynolds, Macom[illegible] Ill., dated Oct. 7th, announced the death [illegible] one of his daughters, Mrs. Lucy I. Wethe[illegible]hold, on the morning of that day.

Frank J. Nichols, of Mokane, Mo., paid [illegible] respects to this office while in the city la[illegible] week.

T. A. Abbott, Cor. Sec., for Missouri Mi[illegible]sions, was present at the preachers meeting [illegible] this office, on last Monday, and received t[illegible] personal expession of sympathy of all the mi[illegible]isters present for the deep sorrow throu[illegible] which he is now passing in the recent death [illegible] Sister Abbott.

On the 4th inst. we received a telegram fro[illegible] Jas. F. Stewart, announcing the death of Mr[illegible] Stewart, on the previous evening, at San Palma, California. Proper notice of her li[illegible] will be furnished us later for publication. W[illegible] extend our sympathy to Bro. Stewart in th[illegible] deep sorrow.

J. F. Merriman, one of the active membe[illegible] of Mt. Cabanne Christian Church, this cit[illegible] has just returned from a trip to New York a[illegible] other Eastern cities. While abroad he attend[illegible] the Maryland and District of Columbia conve[illegible]tion, held in the new 9th Street Christi[illegible] Church, in Washington City, D. C., and pr[illegible]nounces it one of the handsomest chur[illegible] buildings he ever saw. Its symmetry, conve[illegible]ience and beauty he thinks are about ideal, a[illegible] the cost marvelously low for what they have.

J. W. Lowber, of Austin, Tex., is delive[illegible]ing his third course of lectures in the intere[illegible] of the students and faculty of the Universi[illegible] of Texas. It is said that Pres. Winston e[illegible]courages these lectures in every way he can.

J. P. Davis has closed his work at PawPa[illegible] Mich., and returned to Terre Haute, In[illegible] He had to leave the church at PawPaw f[illegible] lack of financial support, but it is said that [illegible] made many friends while in that city and l[illegible] followed by the best wishes of the church a[illegible] the community. Here, then, is an efficie[illegible] minister of the gospel available for so[illegible] church.

A. R. Hunt, pastor of the church at Tarki[illegible] Mo., says that the influence of Bro. Nort[illegible]cutt's recent meeting there, for good, cann[illegible] be told in words. He was there two days ov[illegible] three weeks, with 36 additions.

C. E. Millard, singing evangelist for J. [illegible] L. Romig, and others, while en route for t[illegible] Chantanooga Convention, took in the Misso[illegible] State Meeting, at Nevada. On the last eve[illegible]ing of the convention he was publicly eul[illegible]gized by F. V. Loos and others for the swe[illegible] solos with which he had enlivendd the sessio[illegible] of the convention. W. T. HACKER.

T. H. Kuhn, who was the minister of t[illegible] church at Kokomo, Ind., resigned and is no[illegible] doing the work of an evangelist. He is in [illegible] meeting at present at Williamstown, Ky[illegible] where he may be addressed by corresponden[illegible] for two weeks.

Mention having been made in this paper[illegible] Dr. H. L. Willett's trip to Europe we w[illegible] state here that his address until further noti[illegible] will be Berlin, Germany, Care Red Star Li[illegible] Office, 49 Friedrichstrasse.

CHANGES.

Geo. W. Watkins, Hebron to Constanc[illegible] Ky.
G. L. Surber, Payett to Boise City, Idah[illegible]
A. C. Roach, Chambersburg to Mason Cit[illegible] Iowa.
B. F. Shepherd, Mendon to Marceline, [illegible]
E. A. Bosworth, Alliance, O., to Savanna[illegible] Ga.
G. F. Devol, Olin to Waterloo, Ia.
W. D. Starr, Muncie to Noblesville, Ind.
T. P. Reid, Brentwood to Madison, Y[illegible] Co., Cal.
J. C. Bass, Johnson City to Allenton, Ten[illegible]
J. N. Jessup, Vincennes, Ind., to Litt[illegible] Rock, Ark.

Original Contributions.

PHILLIPS BROOKS' PREACHING.

ROBT. T. MATHEWS.

In making out a list of books for a preacher's library I have mentioned, among four types of preachers to be read, Phillips Brooks. Of no preacher can it be more truly said that his sermons are the flower of his thought, the index of his experience, the revelation of his ideal. Phillips Brooks did not fall into the mistake of publishing too much. Hundreds of sermons are a power in the pulpit at the time of delivery, but shrink almost into skeletons when printed. The sermons that really stir as well as teach the reader are a peculiar product—a union of vital thought and appropriate style, the secret of their freshness thus both personal and literary. Phillips Brooks' sermons have these educating qualities. There has evidently been a careful selection of what has been published, both before and after his death.

Of each sermon or lecture it can be truthfully said that it has a distinct attractiveness of manner as well as pith of matter. There is not too much repetition in these printed discourses. One can but smile that some enthusiastic admirers in reciting the pulpit praise of a local celebrity should say that he was never known to repeat a sermon. Only in the narrowest of narrow senses can this statement be true, even of great preachers. Even the greatest preachers have their horizon of thought in teaching "truth as it is in Jesus;" and in all preaching there is more or less repetition of the larger, inspiring ideas, to say nothing of familiar developments and practical applications of gospel doctrine. Thus far in Brooks' discourses and lectures the appreciative reader can see "the master light of all his seeing," and can mark how this supreme note is echoed and re-echoed in different sermons, now a well-known division reappearing, then an intense conviction breathing forth its strength once more, here a homely matter of daily experience lit up by a precious Scripture, there some dire struggle of mind or heart instructed and comforted by the inexhaustible truth that has done a like service before. This is the reason that his sermons are read and reread, and by no other class more than by preachers themselves. Each published discourse bears all the marks of ripeness; it is felt to be full of the personal ideals of the preacher, not in wearisome, belittling autibiography, but in those rich generalizations that interpret the heart of humanity. For, to be read aright, he must always be read in the supreme yet customary lights that shine over and through every deliverance. On account of this fact, however, Philips Brooks preached to the ear of men in the mass, the most illiterate hearers feeling a thrill of cheer and help from the lightning rapidity of the magnetic speaker, still the circle of his habitual readers will belong rather to a class. His sermons cannot be duly read piecemeal. He does not indulge in colloquial hits and hats. He does not aim to strike off a brilliant paradox for its own sake, nor to fire a stinging epigram for a sensation in the audience. Even his most exquisite illustrations "look before and after." In the fullest sense of the method he preaches in a train of thought. So vital and central is his thought that often formal divisions and mathematical headlines are necessarily swallowed up in the vitality and glow of his doctrine. Each sermon, therefore, must be read as a whole, attentively, even critically, if its full power for good would be known and felt.

So much may be said of his discourses from a literary and personal point of view. From a doctrinal standpoint it is sufficient to say that the sum and substance of his preaching was the revelation of God in Christ. But this is saying a great deal more than is commonly understood by such a statement. The Trinitarian can honestly profess that belief; so can also the Unitarian. Dr. Hodge and Dr. Channing both recognized and taught the revelation of God in Christ; but both differed radically in their doctrine of it. It is reported that Unitarians numerously attended Brooks' ministry and gratefully acknowledged, not not so much dogmatic agreement with the preacher's utterances as the comfort and help to their souls conveyed in his living sermons. One need not be surprised to hear this report, as one can easily observe the arid sands upon which, now historically, Unitarianism is gathered here and there in shallow pools. But no attentive listener, on the other hand, could fail to catch from the pulpit of Trinity Church, Boston, notes and echoes of the great catholic creed as regards the person of Jesus the Nazarene. The simple explanation of all this is that Brooks held thoughtfully and taught vitally the supreme Bible doctrine of the *organic relation of Christ both to God and man*. So could he, in thoughts that breathed and words that burned, make the man Christ Jesus a real, present, living object of faith to all hungry hearts. But so could he, for instance, in one of his Trinity Sunday sermons, declare in the old-fashioned simplicity of the primitive creed, "the divinity of Father, Son and Holy Ghost, this is our gospel;" or, "that is our faith in the trinity—three persons and one God."

In this respect Brooks is one of the best exponents of the best thought of the age in its centering more and more on the person of Christ. Here he stands along with a dogmatic theologian like Dorner or with a versatile teacher like Maurice—one, in short, with the broadest and deepest trend of thought as it grasps and sets forth in rich, endless variety, the truth of the relation of the historic Christ to the whole creation of God. In this largest light of God's Word "the light in which we see light" sheds itself into mind and heart. Whether in some hour of toil at the student's desk, or in some tragic experience of life as the sufferer "thinks thereon," it will always prove itself to be the master force of the ministry of pulpit and parish. As the preacher knows—knows in all his studies and duties; knows in a growing unity of thought and living, "the mystery of God, even Christ, in whom are all the treasures of wisdom and knowledge hidden," will his ministry be encouragingly fruitful. Such a truth vitally held in mind and heart will supremely guide and shape one's service in the gospel. It will restrain controversy, it will temper zeal, it will test purposes and methods. Much more, it will stimulate the highest ideal of manhood and ministry together, so that in thoroughness and roundness the minister will be a man, and the man will be a minister. So also was Phillips Brooks. He thought and lived in the knowledge of God in Christ. So also was his ministry. He studied and taught in endless variety and richness the inexhaustible truth of the relations of Christ to God and man. In this master light of all his seeing may his discourses and addresses be read appreciatively. Take any of the sermons with their distinct subjects and distinct texts, and this great Pauline truth is the secret of them all.

One may study them on their more doctrinal sides—"A Good-Friday sermon," "An Easter sermon," "A Trinity Sunday sermon"—discourses on the Atonement, the Resurrection, the Trinity. Phillips Brooks in more than one trenchant passage in his writings scorns the hard and fast separation of doctrine and practice. He would have spurned the complaint that he was not doctrinal, a dogmatic preacher. But how practical, how glowingly practical, are those three sermons! He teaches the doctrine, not in cold, logical form, to prove a thesis or to carry a point, but with his eye steadily on the relation of doctrine to life, and Christ the light, the secret, the wisdom, the power of it all.

Or, one may look at these sermons on their more practical sides—"The Choice Young Man," "The Beloved Physician," "New Experiences." Still the old apostolic creed in its simple succinctness, or in its manifold suggestiveness, shines through them all. Or, one may examine these discourses for some of their more philosophical bearings—"The Mystery of Light," "The Eye of the Soul," "The Mind's Love for God," "The Priority of God," "Identity and Variety," "Nature and Circumstances," "Destruction and Fulfillment." Here are sermons that betoken the most athletic discipline of the intellect, along with the widest readings of the history of schools of thought; but we may be sure that they were preached, or that they may be read and read again, unto edification, as the perfect life of the Nazarene in their homiletical secret and power.

But in heartily appreciating this master personality of the pulpit of the nineteenth century one need not be blind to his shortcomings and limitations. For instance, with all his extraordinary grasp of the apostolic creed, he lacked the genius of a Campbell to preach to Christendom the "one faith" as the annulment of sectarian tenets and denominational tests, in the far-seeing, patient responsibility of an organic and constructive enforcement. This latter is not only the trial of a great truth, but the trial even more of the teacher of that truth. What he might have done in his new office of bishop will never be known. That he would have come into conflict there, where only a Moses-like or a Paul-like hand of decision and action will suffice for the need, cannot reasonably be doubted. The evidence is in several of his sermons that he did not feel deeply the call, nor see at all clearly the way, to the organic reunion of Christendom. But in the bishop's office, with his views of doctrine and dogma, he would have been forced to some kind of action relative to this movement of the age. Or, again, to consider what seems a serious doctrinal deficiency, we read nowhere in his published sermons full, round, certain sounds of the Scripture doctrine of retribution. There are ominous refrains, some dying echoes of a possible result of sin, but no warnings of the judgment of hell as it stands out in the teaching of Jesus, nor of the prediction of eternal destruction according to the explicit doctrine of Paul. Indeed, Phillips Brooks' preaching at this point has a double deficiency—an insufficient grasp on Scripture doctrine and a blindness to actual, mammoth, devilish iniquity of both person and circumstance. In this respect the great preacher falls short of the temper and tone of Jesus. One thing, however, he does, let it be fairly said: he exposes and interprets the sins of the heart, and brings light and comfort to the child of God in the stress and storm of the battle with evil.

There is not a living preacher, young or old, who cannot sit at the feet of Phillips Brooks and learn rich lessons in the ministry of the gospel. He may be read critically for his power of comprehensive thought, his profound logic in searching endeavors to mediate the opposite truths of revelation, his firm grip of the difficulties of modern doubt, his steadily constructive applications of doctrine to human character, his fluent and glowing style, all in the light of the Incarnation of the Son of God. The great Boston preacher would undoubtedly have confessed with Browning:

> "I say, the acknowledgment of God in Christ
> Accepted by the reason, solves for thee
> All questions in the earth and out of it."

But Phillips Brooks may also be read devotionally. It has occasionally been said of this or that minister, "He is a preacher for preachers." But in a broader, deeper sense can it be declared of Bishop Brooks, "Pastor pastorum"—"a shepherd of shepherds." He is this, all of it, because he was a shepherd of souls, who could guide and feed "all sorts and conditions of men"—the prodigal child coming to himself, the student with a burdensome problem, the hard-pressed wage-earner, the enthusiastic young man, the broken-hearted Rachel weeping by a new-made grave. He is "pastor pastorum," "a shepherd of shepherds," because, as fellow-preachers read him attentively and intently, marking the master truth of his ministry, feeling his whole-hearted loyalty to Christ, impressed by the vigor of his intellectual discipline, breathing the fragrance of his literary culture, tracing the secret of his homiletical method, admiring the fittingness of a figure or charmed by some delicate allusiveness of word or phrase—always, more than all, they are taught "truth as it is in Jesus," and are fed with "the bread of life."

Broadway Church, Louisville.

THE CAMPBELLIAN REFORMATION.*

H. D. WILLIAMS.

(CONCLUDED.)

II. *What has the Campbellian Reformation accomplished?*

In the first place, it has actually restored the apostolic church. Other movements have attempted it, but it remained for this movement to do it. All other attempts at it have worked on the supposition that the apostolic church is not described at all in the New Testament, but this movement will call nothing apostolic that is not found in the New Testament. With that idea of apostolicity, the Campbellian Reformation has restored the apostolic church.

Once upon a time a staunch and able advocate of apostolic succession and church infallibilty listened patiently to a description of what he supposed was only somebody's ideal of an effort to restore the New Testament church, but which was in reality an explanation of the purpose of the Campbellian Reformation. The description ended, the man of the historic episcopate promptly declared that such a thing would be an utter impossibility; that a church with no more organization than can be found in the New Testament could not hold together thirty days. On being told that such a movement had been in progress nearly seventy years and had built up a great brotherhood of over a million people, he apologized for his ignorance and declared that it was to him like accomplishing the impossible. But it has been done, and it can never be undone.

In the second place, this Reformation has given the world the most striking example of religious growth and development known since apostolic days. What has already been accomplished in this particular is likely only a prophecy of still greater accomplishments, for the movement is full of the active spirit of the primitive church.

In the next place, the movement has helped to popularize the cause of a united church. Other religious movements have aided in the same direction, but perhaps none more than this. It has also aided largely in the destruction of the spirit of sectarianism and the cultivation of the spirit of fraternity and toleration among Protestant bodies. It has also been a leader in exalting the Bible to the place it now holds as a book of more authority than any human creed or ecclesiastical organization.

But perhaps the greatest result of the Reformation so far is the more scriptural preaching that prevails throughout America. Formerly it was theological, fatalistic, mystical and irrational. The Current Reformation has compelled an appeal to Scripture on the part of the pulpit. That appeal has gradually modified the preaching until the Protestant pulpit in America to-day rides roughshod over its formulated doctrines and theological standards. Do no understand me to say that the Current Reformation should have all the credit for such result; I only give it the major part of the credit.

Though this movement has restored the apostolic church, though it has had much to do in popularizing the plea for union, and also in exalting the Bible above human creeds; though it has cultivated an appeal to Scripture; though it has been intensely active and evangelistic, and though it has been championed by an exceptionally able ministry it has never yet been directly and frankly credited with accomplishing anything by what is known as the theological world. In the theological writings of the day we search in vain for any direct and frank recognition of Mr. Campbell or any of our ablest men. Others, far less able and influential, are frequently recognized, but the promoters and champions of the Reformation, never. This lack of recognition is due to two facts: one is that the theology of this Reformation is fundamentally in direct conflict with the conglomerate theology of Protestanism; th
other is that the movement has not y
produced the second great, comprehensiv
overmastering theologian who was als
able to impress himself on the world.

III. *What has the Campbellian Reformation yet to accomplish?*

In the first place, it has to keep right o
making Christians and building churche
after the New Testament pattern. I
should be remembered that its work is t
restore the gospel and the gospel church
Sometimes we hear it said that its fir
work is to unite Christendom. I do no
like the expression. I prefer to say it
work is to restore the gospel so the churc
can unite on it. A divided gospel ha
divided the church and a united gospel wi
unite the church. Once get Christendom
to accept the gospel direct from apostoli
hands and the church will unite as sure a
water seeks its level. All diplomatic effort
at union will come to naught. Any unio
arising from agreements and concession
can not abide, but will at length b
shattered by differences regarding the con
ditions of salvation.

A united church is desirable. It is th
great desideratum of the age, but anxiety fo
it should not lead to any speedy and super
ficial accomplishment of it at the sacrific
of fundamental demands. It should not b
forgotten that, desirable as a *united churc*
is, a *united gospel* is even more desirabl
and that the *united gospel* once restored t
all Christendom, the united church will b
inevitable.

In the next place, the Campbellia
Reformation must do one thing in th
future which it has not done in the past
The restored church lacks one thing whic
must soon be supplied if it is to find fav
before God and in the eyes and hearts
men. I frequently contemplate the follo
ing picture: Jesus standing watching th
various parties of Christendom, eac
represented by a man or child. A very ol
man stands for the Greek Church, a
equally old man stands for the Roma
Church, a man not quite so old represen
the Lutheran Church, and so on unt
nearly a thousands persons, ranging in ag
from decrepitude to infancy, represe
as many different parties among the pr
fessed followers of the Prince of Peac
As the Master with pathetic face studi
the picture before him there steps fro
the crowd a young man, somewhat ove
grown, but withal handsome and rugge
the representative of the restoration mov
ment of the 19th century. Approachin
near this youug man says, "Master, wh
more must I do to inherit eternal life,
and the Master responds, "Doest thou n
know the gospel?" Whereupon the youn
man says, "Master, I have observed it fro
my youth, I believed on thee, I repented
my sins, I confessed thee before men, I w
buried with the in baptism, I have not sin
neglected the assembly of the saints,
have honored thy resurrection day a
ceased not to break bread in memory
thee. Moreover, Master, I have urged a
thy people to do the same, to sit at thy fe
and receive instruction direct from thee a
preserved for us in thy Word, to call n
man Master but thee and to know n
authority but thine, to wear no name b
thine and to keep the unity of the Spirit i
the bond of peace." Then Jesus beholdin
him loves him and with all the tenderne

*An address, read before the Minnesota Christian Ministerial Association at Mankato, Minn., August 23rd, 1898, and by vote of the Association ordered published.

of divine love says, "One thing thou lackest: go thy way, sell whatever thou hast and give to the poor and thou shalt have treasure in heaven." And at that saying of the Master the young man drops his head and there he stands in sad reflection. I have never finished the picture. I do not know how. Shall I have the young man go his way and sell and give to the poor and then return and receive the tenderest embrace of his Master? Or shall I have him go his way and look upon his treasures and be mastered by them? May the God of all mercies, whose providences are too good for us to comprehend, finish the picture with divine skill!

The "Campbellian Reformation" has restored the apostolic church in all its forms and principles, but not in the spirit of devotion and sacrifice. This defect must be remedied. If not, the movement will be like a river flowing out into the ocean—its fresh waters will soon be lost in the briny deep. If remedied, the movement will be like the salt that savors the sea—it will permeate and purify the whole mass of Protestant Christendom.

For seventy-five years the plea has been sounded forth in this country for a restoration of apostolic Christendom—apostolic theology, apostolic preaching, apostolic ordinances, the apostolic church and apostolic fruits of Christianity. It has been ably sounded—led by one of the mightiest intellects of all time and the profoundest theologian since Paul, and championed by many of the keenest minds and purest hearts possible among men. It has accomplished wonders; its growth stands unparalleled; it bears the unmistakable mark of divine approval. But so far it has been a theological conquest. Doctrinal preaching, the preaching of plain Bible truth, of a "thus-saith-the-Lord" gospel, has done it. That alone, however, will neither convert the world nor influence Protestantism very fast in the future. It should be faithfully continued, but something more will be necessary. In the past the world and Protestantism have been asking, "What does this movement believe?" They have been ready for the answer and the answer has been a satisfactory one. In the future it will not be so satisfying. We are on the threshold of an age that will not ask, What do you believe? but, What do you do?—an age that will not inquire of a man's faith to learn his life, but will investigate his life to learn his faith. I think no man understanding the sociological and socialistic tendencies, the practical bent and moral evolution of to-day, can differ from me regarding this spirit of the age. In the past the churches of the Reformation have been thronged by people ready and anxious and yearning for a plain, simple, direct, matter-of-fact faith. They have been abundantly satisfied and in the future they need and must be given the same faith, but they will not listen to it and consider it unless it be commended to them by works. Christian people may continue to reason from faith to works, but henceforth the world will reason from works to faith. A man said to me recently that he did not believe in immersion as baptism to the exclusion of everything else, because he could not see that it made any better people. In that saying lurks a very cunning sophism, but it is practically the present position of the world and of Pedobaptist Protestantism regarding baptism.

The same attitude is occupied regarding the Campbellian Reformation. It claims to be a return to Christ, to his church, his creed, his confession, his ordinances, his Word, his authority, and henceforth it must face the test, "If you are nearer Christ than others, show it by your works." The day has come when the world will crowd those churches that do most toward the application of the Christian ethics to practical affairs of human society; it will throng those churches which manifest in the highest degree the spirit of sacrifice for humanity, which is the Spirit of Christ. Logically, theologically and chronologically the churches of this Reformation should fill that place and perform that service. If they do not, inside of fifty years the Campbellian Reformation will have lost its identity in the great sea of Protestantism. If they do it, if they rise to the magnanimity, to the breadth of love, to the depth of devotion and the sublimity of faith that will give to the world an individual and social life commensurate with its theology —if they will do this thing, which God commands and the world asks, the gates of hell shall not prevail against them.

PAUL AS A MISSIONARY.

T. H. BLENUS.

The more the student of the Bible follows the line of life of the apostle to the Gentiles, the more is he filled with admiration at the splendid accomplishments, marvelous zeal and immense labors of this wonderful man. When we consider the means and methods of transportation of his times, the lack of direct and immediate communication between the various countries in which he labored, we are astonished into what various and distant places he bore the banner of the cross. The most celebrated and populous cities of Athens, Ephesus, Corinth and Rome acknowledged him as the herald of salvation. Countries and states most remote from each other—Arabia, Greece, Illyria, Asia Minor, Macedonia, Syria, Epirus and Italy—resounded with his gospel preaching. He utilized all situations and opportunities, signalizing them with his unquenchable zeal. He preached Christ in Jewish synagogues and in the assemblies of believers, before philosophers, in the Areopagus at Athens, to the courtiers of the Pretorium and in the palace of Nero, in prison to the jailer and his family and before Festus, Agrippa, Bernice and all their retinue, "in season and out of season," everywhere and constantly he testified of the gospel of the grace of God.

His constant journeyings and long and painful voyages gave him neither opportuity nor time for relaxation of mind or body. He had but one thought, and that was to advance the kingdom of the Redeemer. His heart seemed moved within him, constantly with sorrow, and at times with indignation when he looked about him, and everywhere saw such striking proofs that the highest cultivation of the human mind, as well as the lowest ignorance, were alike consistent with the grossest idolatry and superstition. He not only addressed himself to the Jews in their synagogues, attempting to lead them to the Savior they were rejecting; he labored most diligently also among those whom he met in the chief places of public resort. Again and again this mighty man of God had for a recompense the taunting insults of an infuriated populace, while his own countrymen at times endeavored even to take his life. He is accused by Festus of being a lunatic, the Athenian philosophers treat him with scorn and contempt, at Lystra he is stoned till he is apparently dead, at Philippi he is scourged and imprisoned; yet, ever undaunted, he continues his labors of love. A missionary life so generous, so varied and so filled with persecution should be an inspiration to-day to a people whose whole professed desire is to proclaim a pure faith in the Son of God. Wherever this man went, he was persecuted by those who were not converted. The preacher of to-day treads no new path if he be a faithful teacher of the truth as it is in Jesus. Enmity toward the plan of salvation still exists. There are many self-sufficient philosophers still who, elated with the conceit of their own speculations, sneer at the doctrine of the cross.

There seems to be something in the pride of worldly wisdom, of wealth and of office that so engrosses the heart of man as to indispose it to the humble and self-abasing teaching of the doctrine of the gospel. It has always seemed hard for one, filled with the conceit of his own knowledge, to confess a willingness to sit at the feet of the lowly Nazarene. It was so in Paul's time, it is so to-day. The philosophers who looked down with a supreme contempt on this humble, yet wonderful man, as one scarce worthy their momentary regard, have with their systems been long since swept into oblivion by the lapse of rolling ages, while untold millions have accepted and will ever rejoice in the faith of the Son of God.

In the latter part of his splendid ministration Paul was for two years in confinement. During this time his voice is not silent, as he instructed all who came to see him. He also profited by this forced retirement and wrote those excellent epistles to the Ephesians, Philippians, Colossians and Hebrews, in which, in addition to his admonitions and exhortations to all Christians, he appears to be lifted above all fears of death, and in which he expresses all the triumphs of a victorious Christian. We can bless God for Paul's chains. When liberated again for the short space of two or three years, he again with undaunted zeal started on a missionary tour to Spain—it may be to France, and also to the Asiatic churches which he had founded. Returning again to Rome, he is once more cast into prison, where in the immediate prospect of death he wrote his Second Epistle to Timothy, which contains his calm and deliberate views of an approaching eternity. Heaven now seems to be "let down into his soul," he pants to be at home and at rest in the bosom of his beloved Master, and exclaims, in view of the breaking dawn of an eternity of joy, "I am now ready to be offered, and the time of my departure is at hand, I have fought a good fight, I have finshed my course, I have kept the faith. Henceforth there is laid up for me a crown of righteousness which the Lord, the righteous judge shall give unto me."

Jacksonville, Florida.

Correspondence.

English Topics.

THE MOST POPULAR BISHOP.

By far the most beloved and honored of living bishops of the Church of England is Dr. William Boyd Carpenter, Bishop of Ripon. The finest classical scholar amongst the prelates is Dr. Brooke Foss Westcott, Bishop of Durham; the foremost theologian is Bishop Stubbs, of Oxford; the greatest ecclesiastical statesman is Dr. Temple, Archbishop of Canterbury; the most progressive and liberal is Dr. Percival, Bishop of Hereford; the sturdiest Protestant is Dr. Ryle, Bishop of Liverpool, but the most versatile and the finest preacher is the Bishop of Ripon. This clergyman stands at the head of all the English clergy for oratorical power. He is the Spurgeon of Angelicanism. His only rival in the pulpit amongst churchmen is Dr. Moorhouse, Bishop of Manchester, formerly so famous in Melbourne, but even he is hardly considered equal as a preacher to Boyd Carpenter. This distinguished man is the son of the late Rev. Henry Carpenter, Vicar of St. Michael's, Liverpool. He was born very near the spot which was the birthplace of Gladstone. He studied at Cambridge and was for some years a curate in various London churches. Eloquent curates are abundant in the Church of England, in which indeed a good preacher only comes forth by accident. In all the Dissenting churches good preaching is the rule, for a man who cannot preach at all does not attempt to enter the ministry, seeing that he would have to starve. The eternal bread and cheese question regulates even spiritual things on the side where there are points of contact with the material. But in a church the pulpit is always relegated to the side of the building, the praying desk standing on the opposite side. In a Non-conformist chapel, as we call a sanctuary not belonging to the Established State Church, the pulpit is invariably placed conspicuously in the center of that end of the building where the minister conducts the services. This well symbolizes the difference between church and chapel preaching in England. It is nearly everything in chapel, to which the people go chiefly to hear the gospel, rather too much forgetting the worship, which should after all be thought most of. In the Church of England the other extreme prevails. There worship is all in all, and the preaching is generally a brief, tedious, affected, sanctimonious, driveling drawl, lazily and monotonously read from a worthless manuscript. Yet from fashion and custom thousands of excellent people go to church every Sunday to listen to this miserable sort of pious twaddle, after asking God a great many times in the Litany to "have mercy on us miserable sinners," and after harkening to long prayers and seeing elaborate ritual parades. Therefore, a live preacher of even ordinary power is a real wonder in the Established Church, who, however, generally in his early ministry has to shift from one curacy to another, through the jealousy of his vicar.

BOYD CARPENTER PREACHING.

The best judges in the Church of England seem to agree that the Bishop of Ripon is the finest preacher in the world. This may be saying too much, but it is certain that there is not at this hour a more popular preacher in this country, in any denomination. His last curacy was at St. James' Church, Holloway, in North London, the district where I myself reside. The whole district still rings with the echo of his preaching in those days. He came to take charge of the parish during the last sickness of the old vicar, the Rev. W. B. Mackenzie, who was one of London's greatest evangelical preachers, and who sustained a congregation of 2,000 people for no less than 37 years. For nine years Boyd Carpenter shone in that pulpit as the leading pulpit light of North London. He drew such immense crowds that his fame became national. He used to preach, as he still does, in the purest extempore style, never using a note of any kind. In 1879 he removed to Christ Church, Lancaster Gate, and so became at once a fashionable West End preacher. In the same year he was appointed one of the Queen's chaplains, and he quickly became Queen Victoria's favorite preacher, being to her in England what dear old Norman McLeod was in Scotland. You are aware that our Queen has two religions. When she is in England she is an Episcopalian and would not dare to go into a Non-conformist chapel. But when she goes north of the Tweed, then she would not dare to look at an Episcopal church, because she changes her faith directly her train rolls into Scotland and is transmuted into a Presbyterian. Oh dear, what a strange muddle State Churchianity all is! Erastianism is one element in the spiritual tomfoolery of which this world is so full. Through her Majesty's influence Dr. Boyd Carpenter was elevated to the Bishopric of Ripon at the early age of 43. It is to be noted that the Queen is a great lover of good preaching and that she is a first-rate judge of it. She is a Presbyterian at heart and all her favorite preachers have been decided Evangelicals.

PRESIDENT OF THE CHURCH CONGRESS.

A curious proof of the Queen's regard for the Bishop of Ripon was furnished in connection with her jubilee in 1887, for at her own command he was chosen to praech the jubilee commemoration sermon before Parliament, the two Archbishops of Canterbury and York being thus passed over to universal astonishment. The discourse was one of the most splendid ever delivered from an English pulpit. Even the eloquent statesmen who listened were carried away by that torrent of rhetoric, hemmed in as it was between banks of logic. It was as profoundly spiritual as it was glittering in style of language and thought. A fine proof of his oratorical genius was given by the bishop when he presided at the Church Congress at Wakefield. He gave a magnificent address, amazing and delighting the great and learned assembly by delivering it impromptu. This was the first extemporaneous presidential address ever given at a Church Congress in this country.

A MUSCULAR CHRISTIAN.

Dr. Boyd Carpenter has the finest physique amongst the bishops. He is a great cyclist and pedestrian. On the first Sunday after his ordination as Bishop of Ripon he came from the West End of London to preach to his old hearers at Holloway. As he refuses to ride on Sundays he walked all the way before service, a distance of nine miles. He displayed in the sermon not the slightest sign of fatigue. The sight in the streets that day will not soon be forgotten. Thousands of people vainly sought entrance into the church to hear their former pastor. One peculiarity of the bishop is that he refuses to wear the grotesque garb of an Anglican prelate. He likes to dress like an ordinary citizen, and he often tells how he in traveling gets into conversation with people who have no idea that he is a minister at all. Lately he related at a meeting with considerable glee how he had been chatting with a man in a train who drifted into a bitter tirade against parsons, declaring that nobody dressed as a clergyman should ever come under his roof. The man little imagined that he was talking to the most popular bishop in England. In his London days Boyd Carpenter used often to be seen plodding about his large parish late at night amongst the poorest cottages. He was adored by the working classes. It was a familiar sight to note him button-holing some bricklayer or laborer for the purpose of close and sympathetic exhortation. As the genial and witty Dr. Hole, of Rochester, is the "people's Dean," beloved of working men, who crowd any place where he is to speak, so is Dr. Carpenter the "people's Bishop." He would be a foremost man in any sect, denomination or community. He is to preside again at a Church Congress, which is about to meet at Bradford in Yorkshire, in his diocese. He is a wonderfully versatile scholar. Perhaps he is to be reckoned the best Dantean scholar living in this country. His Italian essays are amongst the most delightful productions in fugitive magazine literature. I was recently delighted with his "Essay on the Geryon of Dante," in a magazine called The Minister. He has had the rare honor of being both Bampton and Hulsean lecturer. Also he has been select preacher before both Oxford and Cambridge Universities. And yet this great and distinguished man was the other day seen in Ripon stopping his carriage to call up to sit beside a poor old laborer, whom he at once drove to his destination, going out of his way to do so. It is his habit to take hold of a bundle or parcel from any old and infirm man or woman whom he comes across when he is walking in the streets of Ripon. In his relation to the lower classes he is like the late Bishop Fraser, of Manchester. Such characters are very phenomenal amongst our right reverend lord bishops and fathers in God, who are peers of the realm, with thrones in the cathedrals and seats in the gilded houses of the lords. The Church of England, with all its wonderfully beautiful and romantic history, its glorious antecedents, its heroic martyrs, its noble cathedrals and its ancient abbeys; its twenty thousand beautiful sanctuaries which fill the air with echoes from their belfries, its old ivied towers and happy parsonages, is, alas, being doomed to destruction by the pirates called Ritualists, who take Protestant pay and are doing the Pope's work! And for this impending fate the bishops are to blame. They are supine, lordly, arrogant and indifferent to their supreme duty. But there are one or two noble exceptions. And the brightest of these is William Boyd Carpenter, the beloved, honored and eloquent Bishop of Ripon. Not long ago a disaster happened which occasioned great sympathy and concern. The bishop was playing in one of his few leisure half hours on his lawn with his children, when he slipped on the grass and broke his collar-bone. But he has rapidly recovered and will preside at the Congress, much to the edification of the grand assembly who will listen to his presidential address. He has an arduous duty before him, for burning questions have to be considered and a terrible crisis has come upon the church through the outrageous proceedings of the High Church party.

W. DURBAN.

43 Park Road, South Tottenham, London, Sept. 23, 1898.

New York Letter.

Now that the United States is extending her dominion into the islands of many seas, the condition of the different peoples to be brought under the flag is of national interest. The Presbyterian, Methodist, Congregational, Baptist, Episcopal, Disciple and other mission boards have already appointed special committees, charged with the collecting of information concerning social, educational and religious conditions in Cuba, Porto Rico, the Sandwich Islands and the Philippines. Recently the Church News Association, of New York, discovered that certain gentlemen were in the city who through long residence in Cuba were thoroughly conversant with the situation of affairs on that island. A conference was arranged with these gentlemen at the mission rooms of the Presbyterian building on Thursday, the 22nd of September, at which Gen. T. J. Morgan, secretary of the American Baptist Home Missionary Society, presided. Dr. Enrique J. Verona, professor of literature and philosophy in the University of Havana; Dr. Aristides Ayurer, teacher of science and

would soon see the necessity of law and order. Without law and order no community can live. Anarchy is hades. Law is of God. America must keep anarchists out. True religion is a cure for all social ills. In true religion we shall have liberty, equality and fraternity, and every other blessing which the human heart needs and which our weary world requires.

***

MISSIONARY FIELDS AND FORCES OF THE DISCIPLES OF CHRIST, is the title of the booklet written by W. J. Lhamon, to be used as one of the handbooks of the Bethany C. E. Courses. It is a gem of rare worth and should be studied by every Christian Endeavor Society among the Disciples of Christ. The book is clear, brief and comprehensive, giving a bird's-eye view of all our missionary enterprises, including the fields of labor, the missionaries and the mission boards. It also presents a good chapter on each of the following: Religious Conditions in England; Hinduism; Confucianism; Buddhism, and Mohammedanism. The imperative need of our people just now is missionary enthusiasm. The only way to engender it is to fill our people, and more especially our young people, with a true knowledge of the missionary problem. Let all our C. E. Societies and C. W. B. M. auxiliaries take up this work at once and push it with vigor. The other books for this year's study are "Life and Teachings of Jesus," by H. L. Willett, and "Sketches of our Pioneers," by F. D. Power. These three books and the Bethany C. E. Bulletin (quarterly) will be sent to any one for $1.00, by writing Bro. J. Z. Tyler, National C. E. Superintendent. The reading courses are very important and should be followed by thousands of young Disciples of Christ.

S. T. WILLIS.

1281 *Union Ave.*

The Atlantic States.*

The time has come to claim more seriously the attention of our great brotherhood in the West to the Atlantic states as a field ripe for the sickle of the primitive gospel. It is wonderful how Dr. Strong's book, "Our Country," turned our faces from the rising to the setting sun in missionary effort. It was even urged that our Home Board be removed from Cincinnati to St. Louis, to be nearer our missionary fields. Granting that what has been done is for the best, I submit the following problem:

Given $50,000 for Home Missions, by 1,000,000 disciples, 80 per cent. of whom live in the Mississippi Valley, to determine how the money may be invested to the best advantage under present conditions.

Postulates: 1. With some exceptions in localities the American people are remarkably uniform in intelligence, education and ability to receive the truth.

2. It costs less to establish a church in the country than in a city.

3. A church planted in a center of population has an unlimited field.

4. A city church is a radiant point for missions in surrounding regions.

5. It was apostolic wisdom, guided by the Holy Spirit, to plant the church in commercial and national centers, as were Jerusalem, Antioch, Ephesus, Corinth and Rome.

With these self-evident truths I submit a series of facts. The following table gives the per cent. of the American people dwelling in cities of 8,000 and more in 1890:

North Atlantic	States	52	per cent.	in	195	cities
S.	"	" 16	"	"	36	"
N. Central		" 26	"	"	152	"
S.	"	" 10	"	"	37	"
Western		" 29	"	"	23	"

The following table shows the distribution of our churches in these cities:

		With Churches	Without
N. Atlantic	States,	28	167
S.	" "	17	19
N. Central	"	112	40
S. "	"	34	3
Western	"	15	8

SUMMARY.

All the Atlantic States	45	186
All other states	161	51

Of the 51 cities without Churches of Christ in the other states 30 of them are in Michigan and Wisconsin. But it is urged that in the West the people have moved to new homes, and may be more easily reached. The same is true in the *cities* of the East. From 1880 to 1890 the city population increased as follows:

N. Atlantic	States	9	per cent.	and	58	cities.
S.	"	" 4	"	"	13	"
N. Central		" 9	"	"	57	"
S.	"	" 3	"	"	17	"
Western		" 7	"	"	12	"

Of the 157 cities that crossed the line of 8,000 population, 71 are in the Atlantic states. It is also urged that the cities of the West are new. The same is true of many cities of the East. The manufacturing, mining and commercial interests of the East are essentially city building interests. I have recently organized a church at Gloversville, N. Y. A few years ago where 17,000 people now live there was a small village and a large cow pasture. There are 25 leather mills and 300 glove factories in the town. That is a sample of growth of many Eastern cities. The religious interests of these cities are, more largely than in the West, supplied by a few of the great denominations. In nearly all of these cities may be found a section, usually new, where there is an opening and a demand for an energetic evangelistic church. In these Eastern cities can be found about *one loyal Disciple of Christ for every thousand people,* enough in nearly every city for a vital nucleus of a church.

Here is another series of facts:

1. The Disciples of Christ are making in the Atlantic states a larger per cent. of growth than in the rest of our country.

2. Our growth in the Atlantic states is largest in the cities.

3. The financial returns per member for Home and Foreign Missions is greater in the Atlantic states than in the rest of America.

4. This is a day of Bibles and Bible reading. The Chautauqua circles have stimulated associate study and comparison of views. The W. C. T. U., the Y. M. C. A. and the Y. W. C. A. have given Bible readings. The Christian Endeavorers have promised to read the Bible every day. The Sunday-schools have taught a general view and systematic study of the Bible. There are many independent Bible classes. All these have prepared a field for our plea for New Testament Christianity.

In my meeting at Watertown a bright man had heard three sermons. He said, "I never knew about you people before; but let me tell you that thousands of people in this country are waiting for a church that teaches as the Bible reads." He obeyed Christ. Last week a woman said, "The Sunday-school lessons on the apostolic church last year made me hungry and thirsty, and I wondered why we do not have the same now. Imagine my surprise when I heard Bro. F. P. Arthur, of Rochester, preach." At Gloversville a union worker said, "I have seen these difficulties arising from the divisions in the church, but did not know what could be done. You are preaching the truth, and your plea is of God."

CONCLUSION.

From all these facts, figures and conditions our conclusions must surely be: *That the time has come for our American Missionary Society to enlarge its missionary investments in the Atlantic states.* I would not take a cent nor a missionary worker from any section of our common country. Let us place the facts and

of battle, the ridge of destiny. Let us make this the best year of our lives. Souls demand and God commands, *That we do our best*.

Against error, prejudice and sin,
Armed with God's own might
Of truth, and love, and right,
Let us forward in the fight
That can but win.

Fear neither foe nor strife,
Nor loiter by the way
For dawn of brighter day;
Press on till Christ shall say,
"A crown of life!"

Roses From Scotland.*

EDITOR CHRISTIAN-EVANGELIST:

Dear Brother in Christ—In sending you the enclosed question, I cannot refrain from spreading some little flowers of gratitude on your editorial path. Exiled from my spiritual home—the West London Tabernacle—the CHRISTIAN-EVANGELIST has indeed become, more than ever before, a friend to me, as well as the best of teachers, giving the finishing touch, so to speak, to the religious training I received at the feet of that prince of teachers—Dr. W. T. Moore.

Besides, it makes one feel quite at home with our American brotherhood and its work. I only wish it were more known and read among our English brethren, who are lacking precisely the strong special education and enthusiasm for our plea your paper gives. I am sorry I did not succeed in communicating enough of my love for it to some of them to make them subscribers, but I make large use of it to interest in our principles one of my own countrymen, a French evangelist, who says that had he heard of it he would certainly have joined such a movement, some eight years ago, when his prayerful study of the apostolic church made him leave his former religious associations. He thought there was room for a new reformation, but not willing to divide any more the few scattered Christian workers in France, he joined the ranks of the Baptists where has at least perfect freedom to work as he thinks right. All the new little churches he succeeds in forming, in his evangelical tours, take only the name of Christian, or evangelical church, but they are included in the Baptist denomination. For what I have seen and heard in France, lately, I am convinced that many minds are ripe for our unsectarian principles, should these be wisely dealt with, and come to them, not from a separate body of Christians, who want to antagonize their views, but as friends and allies, who come to share their work of making disciples in this hardest of all fields—France. I should myself like to go and help, should the Lord open the way.

It is worth noticing that the leaders among Baptists, in Paris, hold many different views, yet they work most harmoniously together for the one aim of spreading the gospel. Their success among Roman Catholics is marvelous. Those new converts need teachers as much as heathen do, and more!

But, dear Bro. Garrison, don't you think you have made a mistake in transforming the CHRISTIAN-EVANGELIST into such a nice weekly magazine? If it was already a work of real self-denial to cut the old ones in pieces for the sake of feeding others with our abundance, it becomes now quite impossible to separate from the new ones, either in part or in whole. You will have to bear the responsibility of making paper-misers of your readers.

Yet—just a little thorn with my roses. I was hoping that the welcome image of the Editor-in-Chief was but the first one of quite a picture gallery of the leading brethren—sisters included—of our own brotherhood. It is very disappointing to get now but faces of people of this world, who have all the illustrated papers at their disposal to make themselves known around the globe.

Yours sincerely, in the bond of Christian love and esteem, ELIZABETH SCHWEIGHAEUSER.

Balcaskie, Pittenweem, Scotland, Aug. 20, 1898.

*This letter was probably not intended for publication, but it contains matter that will be of interest to our readers, and we feel sure our correspondent will pardon us for giving it a wider publicity than she perhaps intended it to have. The "thorn" in her handsome bouquet of roses, is not unwelcome, as indicating a desire for what it was and is our purpose to supply on our front page.—EDITOR.

Eugene Divinity School.

The Eugene Divinity School (Oregon) commenced its fourth year's work September 20th, with an enrollment of 17 students. At least three more are expected in the near future.

This young but thoroughly established school has an extremely bright future. Its dean, E. C. Sanderson, A. M., D. D., is a man of unusual talent, splendid education, untiring effort and natural tact. His consecrated character and firm yet gentle disposition make him the students' friend—one worthy of imitation. The school's origin, like its life, rests largely in the ceaseless efforts of the dean. By him the great task of organizing the institution was commenced in 1895 when the dark clouds of financial depression were hanging low over all the land. But God blessed the work and it succeeded. In the fall of 1895 a commodious dwelling near the present site of the divinity school was rented and the first term commenced with five students. It was a small school, but a good one.

A half block, immediately west from and adjacent to the Oregon State University campus, was purchased by the board of regents and the construction of the building, shown by the accompanying cut, was commenced and finished in time for dedication Oct. 31st, 1897. The structure is strongly built throughout, and the rooms are conveniently arranged and neatly finished. The foundation is made of Oregon sandstone and was laid by the Endeavorers of Oregon, Washington and Idaho. The building is practically free from debt, the funds being raised through the churches of the Northwest and by individual subscriptions. The chapel, "Cowls Memorial Chapel," is named in memory of the late Judge Cowls, of McMinnville. Mrs. Judge Cowls has recently given an endowment note of $2,500 to the school. The building is heated by hot air and contains the modern conveniences. The library contains several hundred volumes and the students have free access to the University library of several thousand volumes.

The two schools work most harmoniously and each is a source of great good to the other. The young men of the Divinity School are a part of life to the University Y. M. C. A., which order is recognized by the faculty of University as very helpful to them in th work, as well as to the students. Christ young men and young men from Christ homes are hunted up by the society, and so as possible are brought into close relation w church influences. The life-line is also thro out to all others. Thus the young men of Divinity School are doing a vast good am their college associates. Their influence good is also greatly felt in the church.] church here has a membership of 425 and steadily increasing under the pastorate of R M. L. Rose, who is also associate professor the Divinity School. The school stands f for Home and Foreign Missions with J. Handsaker as leader in missionary history biography.

The Christian Northwest is proud of the stitution, and right well might she be, for i a signal of Christian freedom and surety for spread of primitive Christianity. Connec with the University as it is, it is already superior to any sectarian college in the W and equal to many colleges of the East.

Where God is success must be. His prese has been ever manifest through the history this institution. May such continue forever

HARRY BENTON

Iowa Letter.

I have just finished and closed up five yea work as corresponding secretary of the Io Christian Convention. These years form important chapter in our nation's history I hope in our history as a state mission society. To me they have been filled with religious romance of faith, with new mo ments of friendship and with the hardest k of labor and the joy of service. Like Mos when called I tried to escape, but my breth forced the work upon me and now when I la down many and urgent are the protests. be chosen five years in succession, to se with five boards—picked men of Iowa—to t over to a worthy sucessor my work out debt after five hard years, is to me a chapte life not to be forgotten. Brethren, you h conferred upon me honors for which I th you and praise God.

***

Extracts from report of the Iowa board m at the Des Moines convention Sept. 28, 189

Twenty new houses dedicated at a cos $58,000.

A net increase of 40,000 to our members in Iowa for the year, 1,000 less than for 189

One thousand three hundred and eleven ad to those churches aided by our board, of wh 869 were baptized. In 1897 the additions w

95 each month; this year they were 101.

New Sunday-schools, congregations, Aid and Endeavor Societies organized, 12 of each, and one C. W. B. M.

The receipts in cash were increased so that with 12 months income the expenses of 13 1-2 months were paid and the new year began without debt.

We have in Iowa 447 churches and 84 unorganized bands. We have 344 preachers in active service.

The year's work (13 months), translated into terms used in neighboring states, is equal to that of 10 men, five located and five in the evangelistic field. The five located men each averaging for the year 171 sermons, 30 added to the church, $700 secured on salary, $1,731.00 reduction of local debt, $3,190.00 in church property secured. Each of the five evangelists averaging 234 added, $731.00 raised on his own salary, $657 in pledges to the I. C. C., $4,975.00 in pledges for local work.

For every $25.00 going through our treasury we can show the following results: Over seven additions, 10 sermons preached, $29.10 pledged for I. C. C., $39.30 collected by evangelist for self-support, $190.50 pledged for local work. This takes no note of organization of all lines of church work, counsel in trouble, and a splendid system of convention work and bureau of information for churches and preachers.

***

In speaking of the year just before us I must use the plural number and say, "my successors in office." Barton S. Denny, of Hampton, is the new secretary. He is a graduate of Drake University and for five years or more he has been pastor at Hampton and district secretary of the northeast district of Iowa. He will at once move his family to Des Moines and take up his work. It is hardly necessary to bespeak for him the hearty support of any Iowa worker. All have made it their duty and their pleasure.

D. A. Wickizer, pastor of the East Side Church, Des Moines, is chosen and elected as state evangelist, with instruction to make the Endeavor and Sunday-schools first in his work. Bro. Wickizer is also a son of Drake University and was pastor at Oskaloosa for five years. In each of these pastorates he has become known as a builder of church houses. With the Sunday-schools and Endeavor Societies back of him and such a yokefellow as Bro. Denny and a bright future before us all, I predict great things for Iowa in 1898 and 1899.

***

The new board for the Iowa work is as follows: H. O. Breeden, president; M. S. Johnson, vice-president; H. J. Prussia, recording secretary; B. S. Denny, corresponding secretary, and W. W. Williams, treasurer. In its first session it selected our splendid office secretary, Miss Jessie Williams. Her perfect knowledge of Iowa and Iowa work just now when there is a change of men on the field will be worth her salary for a year. By the way our busy convention could have done a graceful thing by thanking our treasurer for a whole lot of hard work and the free use of office room for the I. C. C. It is no easy thing to take in and check out four or five thousand dollars of current funds and loan out and care for ten or twelve thousand in permanent funds. No salary and no thanks does not make service higher or fidelity more lasting.

***

My readers all know that I am a prohibitionist, of cubical mold, one who can't be upset, and of course I watch with more than ordinary interest the side of our conventions which abuts near the saloon. For some reason I missed the report of the committee on resolutions and hence do not know what they have said. For a few years past they have spoken in whispers and made sentences on the whiskey question out of twine strings, and one year they were silent! Two things in the recent convention were better than any resolution. One was a season of prayer on the fourth day, Sept. 29. While the ballots in the Canadian plebiscite were falling and winning a victory for prohibition, our prayers for that victory were going up to God. Another was the presence of Matilda B. Carse in behalf of the W. C. T. U. Temple in Chicago and ex-Gov. Drake's interest in her work. He introduced her to the convention and he gave her $1,000 towards lifting the debt thereon. Nothing that F. M. Drake has done in the last five years has given me the joy that I have from this incident. I have worked with him on our board much of the time since 1880 and I know him better than the mass of our brethren. I grieved sorely and sincerely when my hero went into eclipse. When others counted it the setting of the sun *I believed that it was only an eclipse*. Now I have seen with my own eyes the bright, widening limit of that eclipsed sun. God grant that the closing chapter of this great life may be a clear demonstration of its deep, strong enmity to the saloon. What better heritage could he leave the Iowa Disciples? What better endowment can he bestow upon our university?

***

Time and space fail me. I cannot mention half the good things. The visit of our Iowa Methodist governor and what he said when informed that we had bought a church lot in his own home town and in the very block where he lived.——The great addresses by our invited guests, J. M. Rudy, of Quincy, Ill., (soon to locate in Iowa), and Frank G. Tyrrell, of St. Louis.——The educational address by Chancellor Craig and the educational symposium.——The splendid C. W. B. M. program.——The lecture by Dr. Butchart and the views shown by him.——The hospitality of the churches—all these must pass with a word.

A. M. HAGGARD.

Minnesota.

OUR PER CAPITA.

In a recent letter I referred to the fact that the 3,277 brethren of the state contributed $8.26 per capita to all purposes the past year, and now I wish to present an honor roll showing by churches ten of the principal givers and naming them in relative order viz., Plainview, per capita, $18.46; Olivia, per capita, $15.92; Luverne, per capita, $15.20; Minneapolis, $14.08; Rochester, $14.02; St. Paul, First Church, $13.03; Duluth, $11.79; St. Paul, Central, $11.66; Willow Creek, $10.76; Belle Plaine, $8.56. As stated previously, these figures embrace in each instance, not only church giving, but auxiliary giving, and are reliable, care having been taken in the matter of possible duplications. And, indeed, the figures are under rather than over the true showing, for it has been quite out of the question to get at much of the personal giving to benevolences; hence the true per capita is quite likely nearer $9 than $8. These are expenditures only, and do not take into account balances in treasuries, which can only show properly in another year's annual report as expenditures for that year. Which leads to a homily, brother, sister, upon—

PASTORS' SALARIES.

A splendid record has been made; but what proportion of this per capita, think you, the pastors received? The state per capita is $8.26; of this just $3.45 or 24 per cent. went to the support of our beloved leaders, and what shall we say of ourselves? The average salary for the year was $595 which means that many struggled along under much less remuneration, and God forgive the mark! Intellectual, self-respecting, pushing men stood by us for this pitiable salary. Aspirations for culture, ambitions for family advancement, desire to be in the forefront of all that makes for leadership, had to go by the board because of the niggardly support rendered when abundance was all about. We are not a poor brotherhood; our farming brethren are well situated and our city and town brethren are well able to add the necessary modicum for the proper remuneration of the brethren, and yet we chose to depress, to dispirit and to wrong as we did.

I say the necessary modicum, by which I mean that it is not a new proposition that is before us, but a proposition to add slightly to an obligation already assumed, and $200, it is safe to say, is the minimum which should be added to all salaries. In general terms it may be stated that "one gets what he pays for," and though the present preaching force may be excepted conversely from the rule, yet the truth embraced holds good that if just remuneration be not provided a degenerated ministry is to ensue, for intelligent men are in demand at increased salaries in other states and will not come to nor remain in Minnesota to experience needless sacrifice, when equal work can be done elsewhere under comfortable circumstances. And especially so when the sacrifice is uncalled for. And another phase of the question is this, that if an unintelligent ministry prevail, influence upon the world is to be practically nil and a resultant, intellectual deterioration in membership, is to take place till the church sinks below the consideration of thinking people, for intellectual people will not sit under unintellectual speaking.

The pastor should be the intellectual equal if not the peer of the flock or the community to which he ministers. No half-educated, unimpressive man, no matter for his good intentions, can fill the place. Goody-goodyism is out of date. Now shall we sit idly by and allow matters to approach this crisis? Never! Minnesota is too rich a prize to let slip thus.

Our little 3,277 band must arise to the occasion. It must have leaders competent to cope with the situation. A state crusade must be inaugurated. Now possibly not another soul in the church may view this letter, so limited is the circulation of our literature, and hence I would that I could impress upon you—*you*, YOU THE READER HEREOF—the importance of your taking action in the premises. Will you take the question of increasing your pastor's salary before the church, before the official board, before the prayer-meeting, before the individual members and agitate, agitate, agitate till a just salary is raised? Will you enlist for the war? Will you be one for raising the standard of the brotherhood?

With a justly paid and intellectual ministry, Minnesota can be brought into the fold; then let us at the proposition.

The official board will not act of itself; it will need pushing, need rousing; then elbow your way, undauntedly holding up the proposition till the entire membership is alive to the importance of it. The responsibility is yours. A higher standard!

FRANK H. MELLEN, Ex-Sec. M. C. M. S.
212 W. 27th St., Minneapolis.

A Good Ministry.

It is but little more than a decade since this church had its birth, and for most of the period, N. S. Haynes has been its minister, he having entered upon his seventh year last March. From the first of his pastorate the growth of the church was so pronounced that scarce a year had passed when the original chapel was moved back and a new building placed on the front of the lot, the two structures forming one auditorium and the seating capacity being nearly thribbled. At the beginning of his term the membership was 160; accessions during the time 508; which, with the usual decrease from all sources leaves the present membership about 375. Attendance upon the Sunday services has shown a steady and healthy growth. The church has kept fully abreast of the advance lines in its observance of the general benevolences of the Disciples, and has led all of our Chicago churches in continuous contributions to our city evangelization work.

Until recently the church had not succeeded in freeing itself from its (moderate) property debt, but this last spring Bro. Haynes planned a movement—himself leading with a characteristically generous subscription—and conducted it to a successful issue; securing in gilt-edged subscriptions the entire amount, something over $3,000, payable in installments, running to June '99. With all our financial obligations thus provided for, the material outlook for the church is very promising, and yet our beloved pastor of these years has deemed it best to let this latest, effectual undertaking to clear the church of its debt be the crown and close of his ministry among us, and a goodly number of us have sat uninterruptedly under his preaching through the entire time.

Custom is to heap adulations upon the departed soldiers of the cross who have finished their earthly labors and lain their armor by; but do we often enough speak the appreciative word of the living warrior on life's battlefield! I trow not, and so make free to record such word of Bro. Haynes. No church could be blessed with an undershepherd truer to the best interests of the flock than he, nor one setting a more godly example in all holy living, liberal giving and fidelity to the teachings of Christ and his atoning sacrifice. Devout, industrious, studious, he seems in the very prime of his powers intellectually—if he has passed, by a few years, the half-century mark—and his sermons come fresh-forged every week from the gospel anvil, with an earnest gospel invitation at the finish, almost literally never omitted.

A marked characteristic of his ministry has been an ever-readiness to lead his people in the paths of prayer, to mark out for and educate them in special Bible study and investigation, and the utilization of expedients and lines of endeavor for winning souls. Spiritual minded himself, his constant aim has been to avoid all sensationalism and clap-trap, and to give forth spiritual truth—that "pertaining to the spirit and life of God in the soul of man." It goes without saying that one of whom all this can be spoken could never compromise in any sense the cause of Christ or the church with which he labors, or give occasion for any member of the body to hang the head. Hence it is that the Englewood Church of Christ has standing in the community and a reputation than which none ranks higher. In keeping with his uniform record in all of his former charges—as is testified by those who know—Bro. Haynes leaves this church at peace and with the best of feeling prevailing. Action upon the resignation has been deferred, but will probably be taken at an early day. While absent from us most of the summer, he returned and filled our pulpit on a recent Sunday and will likely do so again, as his farewell address has not yet been delivered. Many are the expressions of regret over the severance of the tie that has bound pastor and people in loving fellowship, and individual voicings of sorrow abound at the thought of parting with our brother and his faithful companion who, in the well-nigh ceaseless grind of these years, has been to him a helpmeet indeed; and to the congregation a continual benediction. Englewood will remain their home for an indefinite time to come. Our prayers will follow him and his, that God will more and more abundantly own their consecrated labors.

W. P. KEELER.

Chicago, Sept. 26, 1898.

Butler College Affiliation.

From the time when postgraduate study first began to occupy a prominent place in the scheme of higher education the need has been felt for some means of facilitating the student's passage from the undergraduate work of the college to the graduate work of the university. For those whose whole course is taken at one of the universities, beginning in the undergraduate department and ending with the attainment of one of the higher degrees, the process is simple enough. But difficulties arise when the beginning of graduate study means a transition from one institution to another which is wholly out of relation with the first, and organized and administered without reference to its curriculum and requirements. Yet, the fact remains that in most cases the aspirant for special study and a higher degree must and ought to seek them outside of his *Alma Mater*. A more perfect understanding of the reciprocal relations existing between the college and the university has suggested to educators certain plans for obviating the difficulties mentioned. The most notable of these is the plan of *affiliation*, whereby a university and a college enter into such mutual agreements that the path of the student from the latter to the former is made straight and easy, and inducements are offered for the pursuance of courses of study after college graduation.

The articles of affiliation recently agreed upon between the University of Chicago and Butler College have this for their object, and it is believed that the items of the agreement are such as will bring about this desired effect in a measure hitherto unattained anywhere. In the nature of the case the concessions must be made, for the most part, by the university, the college merely taking such steps as will guarantee to the university its worthiness to co-operate with it on the proposed terms. The University of Chicago agrees—

1. To read all answers to examination questions set by the faculty of Butler College and passed by the college, and to give all students whose work is of the passing grade credit for the same as though they were matriculated in the University.

2. To confer at each commencement of the College the Bachelor's degree of the University upon that member of the graduating class of the College who shall be designated by the College as having sustained the highest average rank during the whole college course.

3. To confer at each commencement of the College upon every member of the graduating class that receives the Bachelor's degree from the College a certificate showing that its possessor will be entitled to the Bachelor's degree of the University upon completing one quarter's (twelve weeks') study at the University, subsequent to completion of the course for the Bachelor's degree at Butler College.

4. To give to all Bachelors of Butler College, who become candidates for the corresponding degree of the University of Chicago, free tuition for one quarter at any time within twelve months of graduation from the College, and to grant the Bachelor's degree of the University upon completion of such study in accordance with the provision of clause 3.

5. To grant annually *three* fellowships affording free tuition for one year to graduates nominated by the faculty of the College. The holders of these fellowships may take advantage of the pledge in clause 4 in addition to the fellowships, thus securing from the University free tuition during four quarters.

6. To grant free tuition in the graduate schools at any time to members of the faculty of the College under regular salary.

7. To consult through the heads of corresponding departments with the faculty of the College upon all questions respecting methods and standards of work upon which mutual understanding is desirable.

8. To consult through the president of the University and the president of the College, or some other officer duly empowered by either party, upon all cases of appointment or removal of instructors, before nomination is made to the trustees of the College.

9. To elect the president of the College to membership in the University council. By virtue of such membership he becomes also a member of the University Congregation.

10. To give to the College all the other privileges which are incident to the general plan of application as set forth in the register of the University.

The College, for its part, agrees to send to the University examiner copies of all quarterly examination questions prior to their use; to send also the examination papers after they have been marked at the College; to pay the actual cost of reading the papers at the University; and in general to allow the University such oversight as will assure it that the quality of the work done in the College is kept on a par with corresponding work in the University.

In entering into such an agreement as this the College in no sense forfeits any independence which is worth preserving. It abrogates the right to lower the standard of its work, the quality of its courses or the quantity of its requirements, and it surrenders the privilege of appointing to positions on its faculty instructors without sufficient qualification. In exchange for the surrender of these doubtful privileges it secures for its students recognition from the University, as before specified, gives its graduates an assured standing with which to begin more advanced work in the University, and secures for them free tuition to the extent and under the conditions above mentioned. If this shall prove to be a bad bargain the agreement may be dissolved by either party. No educational institution in the country has ever been more conservative and careful in the distribution of its degrees than has the University of Chicago, and this recognized fact gives increased weight to the generous propositions above quoted, both as evidence of the present high grade of work done by Butler College and as assurance of profitable and intimate relation between and the foremost educational movements the day.

W. E. G.

ɪr.

ı city has been
e prides herself
her guests; but
ıey get, and in
ly for it. There
s recreation and
ity, but there is
ıal profit is with
ɔartly atones for
ıcy from all over
e special attrac-
ıent and delight
:hings, but after
lls. It is doubt-
o get away from
fe and feel the
sations such as a
ɜ as a special at-
ize that a large
ıard earnings for
naught by these
nay be pleasure,
ıtter of business.
ads, merchants,
irs, thieves and
ıe entertainment

ing the so-called
he only game for
ıble for one who
ıs many "gawk-
led Prophet from
. And, what is
ɜm on such occa-
ided, hard seats,
arter, half or full
from the country
ıride and of inex-
ıey will stand for
ɔourse city folks
stare at our tall
bout city people,
is only half the
ly know how un-
s about country
ly silly" some of
:y things are to
ɔerhaps not be so
expense of people
visit the city and
ken—that is, the
ıke things on the
s that it is about
ɪple to take in the
eqple to take in a

ne features about
l Fair that rank
ɔular only. They
ıave educational
from the country
ıarers. At least
ımentally. With
ıe opportunity to
sition is made the
ınd little interest
'herefores of any-
s band. When
rn to their homes
ut for the next six
ıs all such things
begin to wonder
ɜ anything worth
What they have
ir guests and dis-
ɔ, leaving an im-
ıat we verily feast
lers from year to
arms and become
d sometimes even
ɜ time wasted in
come to the face.
visit of some are
eless.
t over; the people
(distant) homes,
and the mourners
ut the streets.

The tall buildings that have been looking down into sentimental faces gazing up at their dizzy heights will have to stand through the long months of another year without the sight of a human face, except an occasional visitor, unless they conclude to break the monotony with an occasional fire. But how sad it must be for these great monuments to look down upon a people whose eye is continually fixed upon the almighty dollar, or whose nose is continually on the grindstone, or whose feet are ever hurrying to some new attraction. And our churches, too, are left to wonder why they were neglected or passed by so indifferently by the throngs who have come and gone perhaps without a visit to the place where they might have been most deeply impressed or most happily blessed. B. U. I.

The Iowa Christian Convention.

The twenty-ninth session of the Iowa Christian Convention and the eighteenth session of the Iowa Woman's Board of Missions, also the Bible-school and Endeavor Societies, held their yearly conventions at the East Side Church of Christ, in Des Moines, Sept. 26-30. A. D. Wickizer is the pastor of this church. The generous-hearted people of the East Side, assisted by the other churches of Christ in Des Moines, entertained the delegates royally. The ladies of the church served excellent meals at noon and night in the basement of the new church.

The C. W. B. M. occupied the first day of the convention. Their reports showed increased work. No state auxiliary is better organized or more efficiently officered than the Iowa C. W. B. M. All the officers are wise, talented and active. The president, Mrs. Ella M. Huffman, of Prescott, told in her splendid annual address of the good work accomplished in the past year by the state and district officers. The auxiliaries paid into the national treasury $4,771.70, an increase of more than $300 over last year. This increase was up to July 1st. For the national year to Sept. 1st it is over $700. This increase was made by societies doubling their dues and by contributions for the Dr. McNeil Fund. One hundred and fifty-three auxiliaries are reported. The Bible Chair Fund reached $509.04; $213.50 was from life memberships. To July 1st $305.29 was contributed to the Dr. McNeil Fund. This was largely increased by other contributions before the Doctor sailed. The receipts on C. W. B. M. Day were $283.87; from all sources, $6,189.94, every member paying $2.25. Eight auxiliaries raised over $100, seven raised over $70 and twenty-four over $50. The C. W. B. M., of Iowa, have a right to "think highly of themselves" and the work they are doing. We shall hear still better reports from next year.

The first session of the Iowa Christian Convention was given to Home Missions, Church Extension and Ministerial Relief. Dr. McCash, of Des Moines, spoke in behalf of the American Board under the theme of "Our Country." He said: "This country Christianized will be God's power to civilize and save the world. The needs and opportunities of Home Missionary work are so many no man can number them." G. W. Muckley, of Kansas City, Mo., our "Hobson," brave, determined, fearless, poured out his soul in eloquence in behalf of the Extension Board's work. Dr. Lucas, of Indianapolis, whom all Iowa loves for his goodness of heart and loyalty to the Master's service, enthused the convention with his pathetic plea for Ministerial Relief.

Prominent among the visitors at the convention was Miss Hattie Pounds, of Indianapolis, who pleased the convention with her address on "Woman and the Kingdom." Miss Pounds is endowed with a felicitous combination of high gifts of soul. The Christian Church may well be proud of those of her women "who labor with us in the gospel." They have intellectuality without masculinity.

Frank G. Tyrrell, of St. Louis, ad
convention on "What do Ye Mor
ers?" This sermon was a stron
Christian people should be cons
their own profession. If we are
better than the denominations in d
in ordinance, should we not do
others" in all Christian enterpri
"more than others" in high think
living. E. R. Dunlap, of Seattl
the convention about the needs
West. L. W. Rose, a former
Iowa, but now of Eugene, Ore., '
at the convention. J. M. Rudy, t
tor at Cedar Rapids, Ia., deliv
thoughtful address on "Present
lems, and How to Meet Them."

Secretary Haggard's report sh
houses dedicated during the past y
$58,000. Membership of Iowa inc
net gain of 4,000, making our pres
ship 56,000. One thousand, three
eleven were added to the church
the I. C. C. It also showed tha
Iowa 447 churches and 84 unorgar
432 Bible-schools, only 15 congreg
out schools. There have been 12
gations, and 12 Bible-schools, and
Societies, and 12 Aid Societies, an
iary to the C. W. B. M. organize
344 preachers in active service.

Treasurer Williams' report s
receipts to be $3,449.40, and a bal
of $85.86. The secretary in his
that this was an off year; while
not been neglected it has in a m
way, while "the God of battles
the iron dice of destiny." The
the coming year are most encou
officers elected for the new yea
Breeden, president; S. M. Jo
president; I. N. McCash, recordi
B. S. Denny, corresponding se
W. Williams, treasurer, and A.
state evangelist. This office is
one. Heretofore the secretary u
rection of the board looked after
and employed special evangelists
Evangelist Wickizer, in addition
of an evangelist," will be supe
Bible-schools and Endeavor Socie
if he can hold or cause to be h
Endeavor institutes in every c
state.

Governor Drake refused on acc
health to serve as president of
He has been president of the I.
years. His farewell address, th
torical, was eloquent with a t
that aroused feelings akin to tho
by the last words of Moses and
address of Washington, and t
Clay when he bade the United S
adieu. Bro. Drake has liberally
of our benevolent and missionar
He is, I believe, the most liber
brotherhood. His gifts and d
aggregate nearly $100,000, pe
During the convention he gave
Chicago Temperance Temple Fu
"The saddest thing in all the w
manner men gave to support th
Lord. I have borrowed mone
pledges, and given till I felt it;
I felt mighty good over it. I hav
pered as I have given."

Governor Shaw, the present
Iowa, favored the convention w
ence. He is an ardent member
Church. He is at present supe
the Bible-school at the Central M
Des Moines. He said that he r
fact that the denominations w
quarreling as they were wont to
the Governor sees the reason
can not say, but thank God, hi
true. And it is true because all
to love Christ more and denomin
Chancellor Craig's report of I
sity was gratifying. It showed re

additions to the library, apparatus for the biological department, faculty increased by P. O. Powell and M. R. Woodman, the business college reorganized and placed under Dean Belle, and that $44,000 of the $50,000 has been secured. The report declared that this is the most important work in Iowa. One hundred and forty men were preparing for the ministry last year. The future of our cause in Iowa depends on the character of our leaders, and the character of our leaders depends on the equipment and work of Drake University, and the equipment of Drake University depends on the generosity of our brotherhood, whom God has blessed with much wealth.

LAWRENCE F. MCCRAY.

1322 *24th Street, Des Moines, Ia.*

The Spanish War and the Christian.

The return of our emaciated, sallowfaced soldiers from the Spanish War is entirely too full of suggestion to be passed carelessly by. May be they look a little worse through the smoke of the great war scandal that follows their coming back, like the smoke that came with the locusts of John's fifth trumpet.

Poor fellows, their patriotism is unquestioned. They have merited our love, but they are victims of blundering officials and a murderous avarice and of partisan fanaticism.

The close of this strange war is an ominous and pregnant hour. The drum-beat of mustering out is pierced by a cry for peace from a quarter the least expected. The powers of the Old World had some months before our late conflict began agreed to establish a court of peace, of arbitration and of reference, to which all international disputes might be appealed. They presented this most humanitarian and most Christian measure before our nation for its acceptance, but our boasted Christian Republic declined. Our Senatorial House of Democratic lords refused it and I believe almost without a protest from the Christian press and pulpit of the country—to our shame be it said.

Closely upon the heels of this benign proffer came the declaration of war with Spain on the humanitarian(?)ground that a hundred thousand or more of Spain's own subjects had died from privation and confinement, etc. To reach this island of suffering with our sympathy we had to look over the tops of two hundred and fifty thousand saloons, which kill about sixty thousand of our own citizens every year, and as it is believed above the heads of more than a million victims of our own sweatshops; and now, in the close of this war, in which we have won a conquest over territory which may be many times the trouble to us that Ireland has been to England, we hear the trumpet from the Almighty coming from the greatest and most warlike nation on the earth crying, "Peace on earth and good-will to men!" God has spoken to us through the Czar of Russia in the midst of our hypocrisy and shame. Had we accepted the offer of the powers and established a court of peace for the world the trouble between us and the Spanish nation might have been referred and settled without the blood and wreck and ruin which so well illustrate John Sherman's definition of war.

How broad and inconceivably great would be the educational effects upon the nations of the world should such a question as that be brought to the thought of their citizens for free discussion. Three months of such widespread discussion would do more to prepare the world for the kingdom of God than all the wars of the world and all its legislative acts combined. Why was our own nation among the last to abolish slavery? Why the last to refuse a world's court of peace? It is out of the weak side of democracy. That is the dead-level spirit of a false and tyrannical democracy which cuts down every man who raises his head above its dreary level. They do it with such wordy weapons as "ultraist," "radical," "cranky," etc., as effectually as a French guillotine could do it.

The only independence we have is our national independence of other nations, well protected by the great waste of waters, but no personal independence above the malarial, sickening level of public opinion, which stands over our heads with scorpion whips to bring us into subjection to this giddy, fickle majority.

In England a citizen may stand well with his own class and have an independent opinion, but we are one class in America, and that is not a Christian or educational, but a strictly political class. Our religion takes second place and our churches are echoes of politics. We surrender everything to our politics and our politics is blind and partisan. Whether it is war or peace or license or superstition of vice, the pulpit and religious press are a weak and sanctimonious echo of it and feebly says, "Amen." How came we to hear this peace trumpet from Russia? It is because Russia has something greater than a Czar, greater than a republic—it has a great, true man, a Tolstoi, who has dared to utter braver words for the true meaning of the religion of Christ than any man in America for a generation. Tolstoi's emperor seems to have caught this greater spirit and is at least able to utter it from a world point of view.

What sound is this we now hear, that "where our flag goes up, there it must stay?" It means no less than the turning away of the mind of the people from the most vital issues that confront us to a new and benevolent (?) scheme of evangelizing the world with gunpowder and bringing it under the benign sway of avarice, commercialism and licensed doggeries! It means the waste of a billion of dollars yearly, spent to create vice under the permission of Congress and by the votes of church members at the ballotbox. God bless the Czar and Tolstoi, and send us some missionaries who who can stand up for Christ against immoral politics and a false democracy. If this nation is to be judged by its opportunities and its professions will it not be more tolerable for Sodom and Gomorrah in the day of judgment than for us?

J. S. HUGHES.

[So far as this article condemns the attitude of the political parties, and of many professed Christians, to the liquor traffic, it has our hearty approval; but we cannot see the wisdom or justice of associating a righteous war, a *necessary* war, with the nation's shortcomings in other respects. This government, however, has never rejected any proposal for a court to decide disputes between nations, for no such proposal has ever been submitted to it. Our Senate refused to ratify an Anglo-American treaty of arbitration, and in this we think it acted unwisely; but the principle of arbitration was not objected to. Tolstoi had precious little to do with the Czar's proposal for a peace conference. The venerable novelist is a litterateur of some distinction, and a man of kindly impulses, but he is a rationalist who rejects Christ's claims of divinity and accepts only such of his moral teaching as commends itself to his judgment. Men of a very different mold are needed to save this nation.—EDITOR.]

Northwestern Colorado.

J. C. Hay, of Clarksville, Tenn., who has been preaching in Northwestern Colorado, and who knows of the condition of our cause in that region, and also of the country and climate, its possibilities and profits, says:

Brethren contemplating migration to Northwestern Colorado can place the fullest confidence in whatever Bro. J. L. Ellis states about that country. I spent three months this summer in gospel labors in Routt County. Hoping to attend the General Convention at Chattanooga, I shall be pleased to give any interested brethren who may be there the results of my observations. Bro. Ellis' address is Craig, Routt County, Colorado.

Thomas Munnell.

I have just received the sad news of death of this servant of God. I knew him l and well. For some years he had not t prominently before the brotherhood. This doubtless his own fault, though I think brethren were not altogether free from bl with respect to the matter. There is a te ency among many churches to shelve the men. As a rule, a preacher passes the de line when he reaches the age of forty. some cases this is a righteous retribution know preachers who struck twelve before t were twenty-five. Their ministerial gro has been like the inverted view of a telesc The big end is nearest the eye.

But this was not the case with Thos. M nell. He was a student up to the last da his life. He may not have kept abreast o the living questions of the day; for being so what outside of the conflict he probably not feel the need of a close touch with livi issues. Nevertheless, he did not cease *think*, and even to write upon current qu tions.

He was a careful, critical and earn student of the Word of God. In my judgme he was the most forceful writer in our ranks questions related to Christian ethics; and I not hesitate to affirm that the Christi brotherhood are indebted to him more than any other man among us for right conceptio of the relation of the law to the gospel. was more than a writer; he was a *think* Perhaps his greatest mistake in life was imagining himself a man of affairs. He h little capacity for details. He occupied seve positions which he could only fill idealisticall Our misssionary work was too low in his d for him to make practical his high conceptio as to what it ought to have been. Howeve his work as corresponding secretary was, af all, useful in opening up the way to bett days. Still, this position was not the one ought to have filled in life. He was a bor college man. His own education ought t have been the highest attainable, and then h ought to have filled a place where he coul have impressed himself on a class of student capable of following a great mind

He was not appreciated at his true valu He did not move in the procession where popu lar favor is the reward of timely serving. few friends knew him, understood him an appreciated him. Some of the things he wro will live in our literature. His article in th first number of the old Christian Quartely en titled, "Indifference to Things Indifferent," is the best thing of its kind in the Englis language. It has furnished the key to many public teacher to unlock questions of casuistry and in it has also furnished texts for many sermon on Christian ethics.

It is hoped that some suitable sketch of hi life and work will be prepared by a capabl hand. But my personal relations to Br Munnell will not allow me to wait for th sketch. I, therefore, send these few lines as small tribute to the memory of one of the true and best men among us—a man of singular fine intellect and a culture considerably beyon that of our average educated men.

W. T. MOORE.

Columbia, Oct. 5, 1898.

Notes and News.

David Walk, minister of the church at Los Angeles, and superintendent of the Chinese missions of that church, in his monthly report to the church, says:

Jeu Joe Wah was with us for the last time, Sept. 5, before sailing for China.

Chung Sing, one of the oldest and most faithful of our Chinese brethren, was given a farewell reception on the evening of the 26th. He returns to his native land as a herald of salvation to those who sit in darkness and in the shadow of death.

His credentials were signed by W. J. A. Smith, C. H. Owen, B. F. Coulter and David Walk. Mr. A. W. Francisco, Collector of Customs, gave him a handsome testimonial of a nature calculated to obviate any difficulty in the way of his returning to the United States.

An interesting and affecting feature of the occasion was the presentation of an elegant edition of the Bible, inscribed as follows:

"For other foundation can no man lay than that which is laid, which is Jesus Christ" (1 Cor. 3:11).

"Presented by the following named teachers of the Christian Chinese Mission: David Walk, superintendent; W. J. A. Smith, C. H. Owen, Sadie Lapin, Mrs. Lipscomb, Mary Lipscomb, Jens Johnson, Theo. U. Lawson, L. F. Berkey, Fannie Collins, C. O. Goodwin, Emily Hambleton."

Los Angeles, Cal., Sept. 26, 1898.

Missouri District Convention.

The fifth annual convention or the Dexter District Christian Co-operation will be held in Charleston, Mo., Nov. 1-3, 1898. A good program is being arranged and a good convention is expected. A. F. Holden, Sec.

Charleston, Mo.

Thanks to All.

To the many kind friends, far and near, who sent messages of love to Mrs. Abbott while yet alive, and which sent so many rays of light down into the valley of shadows in which she walked so long, and to the great number who have sent such tender messages of sweet sympathy to us since our great loss, we want to return our most grateful thanks. We cannot write to you all individually, yet we want you to know how much we appreciate your loving words. May God bless you all.

T. A. Abbot and Daughter Maud.

4144 *Westminster Place.*

Kansas City, Kan.

Since our coming to the Northside Christian Church, May 15, we have built a tabernacle for permanent use with a seating capacity of 400. Bro. B. Q. Denham, of North Tonawanda, N. Y., dedicated it with $65 more money than was needed to pay all indebtedness against the church, and we have added to the membership 46, nearly all of whom are helpful additions, almost doubling our strength, both financially and as a working force. We had seven additions Sept 11, day of dedication, from two to four every Lord's day since, and we are praising the Lord for his goodness toward us. Let the brethren rejoice with us.

C. M. Wickham, Pastor.

A New Era for Bethany College.

At a meeting of the trustees of Bethany College, held in Pittsburgh, Sept. 30, plans were perfected that are expected to work out very promising results for Bethany's future. Campbell Jobes is to continue his work in the field where he has been so successful in soliciting funds and students. His address is Claysville, Penn.

J. L. Darsie was also elected to the work in the interest of the college, with headquarters at Bethany, W. Va., and Chas. A. Young was tendered the presidency of the institution. It is not yet known whether Bro. Young will accept or not, as he has reserved his decision, but Bethany's friends are hard at work and very encouraging results are already apparent.

In a few days we hope to present a financial exhibit that will be a surprise to all who have, by injurious reports, been led to suppose that the college was about to suspend.

A fine attendance of students this year, with promises of many more who will doubtless come in soon, may put the present session far above the average.

For further information address

J. L. Darsie.

Bethany, W. Va.

Explanation.

Dear Bro. Garrison:—The cause of my absence from the state convention at Nevada was sickness. I was sick in bed under the care of a physician. I so notified Bro. Abbott, but the condition of his wife kept him away from Nevada.

We are now nicely located in a splendid new parsonage. Come up and occupy the "prophet's room." J. T. Ogle.

Carrollton, Mo., Oct. 2, 1898.

Wanted.

The church at Gravett, Ark., would like to receive a donation of three dozen hymnbooks that have been laid aside by some church. Send them by freight to Mary E. Justice, Gravett, Benton county, Ark.

John Friend.

Washington Convention.

Brethren of Washington, our state convention will be held at North Yakima, Oct. 26-28, 1898, and we hope it will be the best ever held in the state. Let us make it such by all attending who possibly can. The church here will entertain free all the delegates who come. As all the trains arrive in the night, be sure and send your name and the time you will arrive to me, so that ample provision may be made for you. L. F. Stephens,

Pastor of the Church of Christ.

North Yakima, Wash.

A New Entertainment.

About the latest thing in the way of entertainment for Endeavorers of which we have heard is the tomato peeling contest. By special arrangement such a contest took place at the Tomato Canning Factory at Lebanon, Ind., by the Endeavor Society of the Christian Church, recently. The prizes awarded and won netted the society $11.82 for their evening's work. Some of the most prominent women of the city, it is said, entered the contest.

South Dakota Remarks.

Your scribe is, perhaps, rather young to be giving advice to those matrimonially inclined, but he has at least known what it is to have a happy home and a loving wife, who was a true helpmeet.

Not long ago I warned a friend against marrying a girl unless he truly loved her. I quote from his reply: "You are getting love out of its proper place. It is husbands who are to love their wives as Christ loved the church and gave himself for it. Nothing is said about boys loving their best girls. Look at the people who marry just because they love each other, and how do the live? The family life of the heathen who never sees his wife until his wedding day puts them to shame." How is that for an exaltation of heathenism? I was dumbfounded. He concludes, "I believe a preacher can do better work married to a godless woman than a single man can do." That is scarcely Pauline, is it?

"Our Cause at Chicory," by R. C. Barrows, is a little book containing much truth concerning the introduction of apostolic Christianity into the Northwest. It is well worth perusal.

Another book which I dare say very few of our younger brethren have read is "Hadji in Syria," by Mrs. Sarah Barclay Johnson, daughter of our first Foreign Missionary. This was published by James Challen & Sons, Philadelphia, in 1858.

As superintendent of C. E. I have been calling the attention of our pastors and Endeavor Societies to two important matters: the Bethany C. E. Reading Course and the observance of Forefathers' Day, Oct. 23. "Amen!" to the suggestion that Dr. J. Z. Tyler be induced to give all his time to the interests of our C. E. Societies.

In my humble opinion it is not the best thing possible that the country is being flooded with Endeavor Bibles of the Authorized Version when the Revised Version is so much better. Don't misunderstand me: an A. V. Bible is infinitely better than none at all, but a R. V. Bible ought to be in the hands of every young person. Our fathers are wedded to the verses as they learned them; let us learn them as they are in the light of recent study.

What's the matter of Des Moines for our general missionary conventions next year? It would be a blessing to our brotherhood in the Northwest to have a convention so near that we could at least get daily papers telling about it.

L. W. Thompson will remain a second year with the churches at Volga and Pleasant Valley.

A. Erichstone, a Scandinavian evangelist for the churches of Christ, is spending a few days in this part of South Dakota. His home is at Seattle, Wash. A. H. Seymour.

Arlington, S. D., Sept. 23, 1898.

Some Reasons for Observing Forefathers' Day.

1. Most people shape their lives by others; our prominent forefathers were heroic; we should keep their heroism before those whose characters are forming.

2. The greatness of our forefathers was largely due to their self-denial; this should be kept before the eyes of our young people that they may be willing to deny themselves.

3. We should be grateful for all good things; many of these we have obtained through our forefathers to whom our gratitude should be directed.

4. We claim to be a progressive people; we should study the lives of our forefathers and see how much we have progressed.

THE PURPOSE OF FOREFATHERS' DAY.

The purpose of Forefathers' Day is two-fold; to make the young people among the Disciples of Christ familiar with the purposes and achievements of our pioneers, and to enlist them in a co-operative effort to evangelize every part of our own country through the agency of the American Christian Missionary Society.

The young people among the Disciples should become familiar with the names of such men as Barton Warren Stone, Thomas Campbell, Walter Scott, Alexander Campbell, Benjamin Franklin, Isaac Errett and others who have wrought for the restoration of New Testament Christianity.

Brief biographical sketches of such men should be read before our C. E. Societies on Forefathers' Day.

The minister has no more enthusiastic helpers than Christian Endeavorers. He should bind them to him with hooks of steel by co-operating with them in their religious work. No better means of getting deeper hold and giving needed help can be suggested than Forefathers' Day. We earnestly recommend that it be made a great day in the church—a day of prayer, of song, of reminiscence, of renewing zeal in the distinctive work of our brotherhood. It should be a day of education, of prayer, of rejoicing in victories won, and in preparation of greater victories.

B. L. Smith.

The Kansas State Convention.

It was held at Wellington, near south line of the state. Notwithstanding, the attendance was comparatively large—much more so than some supposed it would be. It began Monday night, the 3rd inst., with an address by Sister Helen E. Moses, of Indianapolis, and ended the 7th inst., with an address by Bro. W. T. Moore in the City Auditorium. Brethren B. L. Smith, of Cincinnati, O., G. W. Muckley, of Kansas City, and W. S. Priest, pastor of the church, Atchison, Kas., each delivered an address in the same auditorium.

There were numerous day addresses by sisters as well as by brethren, some of which, and all the better for it, were in manuscript. By motion Bro. Hilton, of Beloit, and Sister Mattie Titus were requested to have theirs published.

It occurred to me that the program was rather too much crowded, but it was executed, however, from start to finish, in a commendable manner, under the admirable rulings of those who presided respectively at the sessions of the C. W. B. M., Y. P. S. C. E., B. S. and K. C. M. S.

It appeared that our common cause has been injured no little in Kansas by immoral preachers. Elders and deacons are required to be men of "good report," yet a man who is reputed as a drunkard is allowed by some congregations to occupy their pulpits. And why? "To reform them," we are told. The pulpit, my brother, is not the place to reform a man from drunkenness or any other immorality.

"Tell me I hate the bowl?
Hate is a feeble word;
I abhor, I loathe,
And my very soul is stirred
To its deepest depths,
Where'er I see or hear or tell
Of this dark beverage of hell."

The thought that other religious bodies are troubled more than we are with unworthy ministers is no reason that we should excuse drunkenness or any other immorality of any one in the church, especially of a preacher. But our cause in Kansas is onward. Was surprised to learn that only one Protestant body has a larger membership in this state. We may ere long be first in that regard.

O, that not only here, but everywhere we might be first in holines, and in all that it takes to constitute a real Christian in a full-orbed, or gospel sense.

Would like to report more, but fear that this is already too prolix. J. A. WALTERS.

Council Grove, Kas.

Another Victory for Eureka College.

Last night, at the meeting of the Inter-collegiate Oratorical Association, of Illinois, the representative of Eureka College, H. G. Harward, won the first prize in oratory over the representatives of five other colleges, of the state of Illinois. The colleges represented were Knox College, Wesleyan University, Monmouth College, Blackburn University, Illinois College and Eureka College. The contest was held at Galesburg, and the Association was a guest of Knox. Mr. Harward is from Melbourne, Australia, and is one of our most devoted and promising young preachers. We rejoice greatly in his success, which was at the same time a splandid triumph for our college.

J. H. HARDIN.

Eureka, Ill., Oct. 8, 1898.

A Glorious Plea.

The plea of the Christian Church is to restore primitive Christianity with all of its doctrines, ordinances, fruits and practices. This is a plea both to the world and to the various religious bodies. There are millions in our country who have never heard of this plea, and who would accept it if they could hear it, but how can they hear unless we send them preachers?

When this glorious plea is properly presented to American citizens they accept it with great joy. During three years of labor in Virginia I preached it in new fields and it was welcomed. I spent six years of my ministry in the far West and found it welcome there. I have spent five years in these great middle states and have found it welcome here. I have made side trips to Pennsylvania and Massachusetts to preach it and it was received with joy amongst these conservative people. I can testify with other evangelists and pastors that it is just the plea the world is needing. The field is ripe. Yes, brethren, millions are waiting in the North, East, South and West for you to send them the primitive gospel.

JOHN L. BRANDT.

Missouri County Convention.

County meeting of Jasper County, Oct. 26-29, will be held at Webb City. All churches are requested to send delegates. All pastors are invited and urged to come. Springfield district convenes at Carthage Nov. 28-30. A good program in both cases. All the churches in the fourteen counties are earnestly urged to send representives.

W. A. OLDHAM, Dist. Pres.

Carthage, Mo., Oct. 3.

Missouri Bible-school Notes.

The Hickman's Hill preacher is Geo. W. Terrell, and whenever he begins work with a congregation they begin co-operating with us if they had not done so before, and it seems that self-preservation would urge me to do all possible for such brethren; don't you think so?

Mt Cabanne, St. Louis, is one of the model schools. Their preacher is a natural teacher of teachers and has a Bible class of nearly thirty. Their superintendent has been in the vanguard of Bible-school teachers for lo! these many years, and is to-day, through the helps of the Christian Publishing Company, teaching, training and making more teachers than any other one person in all the brotherhood. I would love to mention the many good points which I noted for use for the schools of the state, but space forbids. F. M. Call, business manager of one of our greatest publishing interests, is assistant superintendent, and there is Barclay Meador, assistant secretary of the Y. M. C. A., in this city, leading the music, while there are a multitude of chief men and women giving their ready assistance to the success of the school. Why, they have a Bible club, under the inspiration of J. F. Merryman, one of the busiest and best lawyers in the city, and the club is just entering on its fourth and last year. Then they have a Bible-school missionary, Miss Mattie Spillman, who makes over two hundred visits a week (think of it!) in this great work of Christ. Why, of course they are friends of state Bible-school work, and with all the other doings of the schools you will hear from them in this respect during the new year.

Walker, where J. H. Jones leads, gave George E. Prewitt a hearty welcome and promp assistance, the sum being $10, then sent him away with a cheery God-speed. Such congregations are on the highway to prosperity and great success.

At Marshall, the Saline county meeting began at the close of a 28 hours' rain, so that the representation from the county was not good. Preachers present: J. W. Strawn, J. S. Russell, G. E. Shanklin, Ransom Cole, B. T. Wharton, H. F. Davis, W. B. Young, G. A. Hoffmann, E. J. Wright, Edmund Wilkes. In our Bible-school conference many took part, and from the interest it seemed that all were pleased and benefited, especiall that practical man, J. A. Gordon, in whose home we discussed the work from start to finish. He has put the Marshall school to the front among the Missouri workers, sparing neither time nor money to make it a success, and it is in such co-operation that Saline is in such hearty accord with us in state work.

Cowgill, where Mrs. Frank E. Goodnow is in the front, send us the first quarter on their apportionment, with some good pointers as to improved methods introduced.

The Waverly brethren have no thought o giving up their work. Though depleted by death and removal, their school is reported as in better working order this year than usual, while the apportionment will be paid in full.

At Jacksonville Mrs. N. D. Conely has been in the work for many years and the school has always been in touch with our work, this year being no exception, for the remittance is made in full, thanks to all the leaders.

Knobnoster is one of the smaller schools in the state that no more think of neglecting this work than of trying to do without helps; so that their prompt response was not new to us, but was cheering as usual, as it is the only school in Johnson county that has accepted their apportionment for this year.

At Schell City, for the first time in years, one of our evangelists made a plea for this work and the brethren responded real well, considering, but the friends at Berea are not slack to help us, and so let G. E. Prewitt see, when he was with them last week, but happily responded to the call; thanks.

But now why not hear from some of the better schools in the state? H. F. DAVIS.

Commercial Building, St. Louis.

North Carolina.

While "Our Plea" has not made the strides in North Carolina which have characterized the "movement" in the West, the slowness of our growth may be easily accounted for. Many difficulties have and do beset our forces which would discourage less resolute workers. With supreme faith in God they overcome obstacles which seem insuperable. Prof. Dawson, one of the most godly men I have ever met, works very hard, having visited about eighty of the one hundred and twenty churches in the state within the present missionary year. North Carolina is a great mission field. Stretching out over a territory five hundred miles from east to west, and about three hundred miles from north to south, she has within her vast domain a number of cities and towns, bustling centres of business and influence, which have never yet been reached by the grand plea for an apostolic Christianity. How any one whose soul is on fire with zeal for truth can look over the state and behold her as she extends her arms in an appeal to "come over and help us" and be indifferent to her need is one of the unexplained mysteries of the human heart.

Some six or seven houses of worship are being erected this year by our brethren. Winston is building a splendid house, the forces there being led by H. C. Bowen. Wilson is building a magnificent house. Bro. B. H. Melton is the popular pastor of that church. Bro. Dawson is superintending the construction of the houses at Plymouth and Ayden. The North Carolina Christian College is located at Ayden. Prof. A. F. Moon is the principal, and I hear he is doing a good work. The policy of the state board for the present year is to strengthen the weak places, and they are helping to support seven preachers at needy points.

Death has been mowing down some of our best workers in the old North State. J. L. Winfield, late editor of the Watch Tower, the wife of H. D. Harper and J. J. Harper's wife have passed away within the present missionary year.

The veteran preacher of the state is J. R. Winfield, of Pantego, who is about eighty years old and is awaiting the Master's summons to pass into the great Beyond.

ALFRED BRUNK.

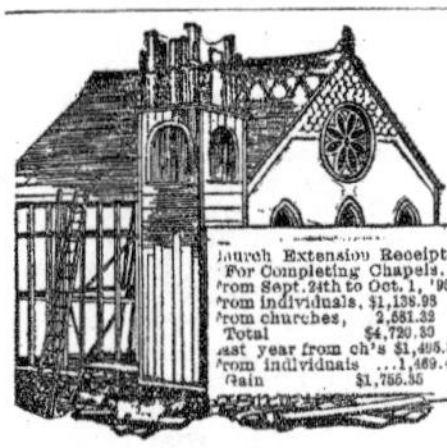

Missionary.

Extracts From Annual Report.

NOTE.—A further analysis of the receipts shows the following:

A gain of 22 churches over last year and a gain in receipts from churches of $1,085.85.

The year closed September 30th, with a net gain over last year of about $900. The receipts aggregate as follows:

From church collections	$ 6,442.34
Individuals	11,848.00
Bequests	2,848.00
Annuities	1,500.00
Advertisements	204.25
Interest	4,800.59
Total new receipts for the year	$27,498.18
Collected on loans	13,766.75
Total receipts, from all sources	$41,264.93

FUND STATEMENT TO SEPT. 30TH, '98.

Amount in Extension Fund	$167,243.03
Loans collected since beginning	66,987.14
Interest paid to date	25,115.28
Number of churches aided	389
Number of churches having paid back their loans	104
Number of loans outstanding	285

THE PREACHERS' PERPETUAL VOLUNTEER LEAGUE is still increasing in favor and numbers. Thus far over 800 have joined the League, representing over 1,000 congregations. To join the League is simply to agree to take a collection annually for Church Extension, wherever you may be preaching.

ANNUITY FUNDS FOR CHURCH EXTENSION.

The National Convention at Des Moines, Iowa, in 1890, made the following recommendations to the Board of Church Extension: "We request the board to consider and adopt, if practicable, the Annuity feature in raising funds for Church Extension, believing that it will prove, as in the case of other churches, a successful method of raising money for this fund.

The board began to receive annuities for the first time this year. The board pays six per cent. on annuities, loaning the money out at six per cent. to mission churches that cannot be helped from our general fund. The board gives an Annuity bond to the person giving his money, and at the death of the annuitant, the gift becomes the permanent property of the Church Extension Fund, without further obligations on the part of the board.

LOANS MADE FOR THE YEAR.

During the year 47 loans were made, aggregating $23,230. Other loans have been promised to the number of 53, aggregating over $25,000.

CATALOGUE OF CHURCH PLANS.

The convention at Indianapolis recommended that the Board of Church Extension get out a Catalogue of Church Plans, varying in price from a $500 chapel upwards. In the January-March issue of Business in Christianity a catalogue consisting of 72 strictly up-to-date church and chapel designs was published by the board. The advertisements secured will pay for the extra expense of publication. This catalogue is strictly up-to-date, is gotten out by the best church architect in the country and is already beginning to meet a long-felt want. The catalogue can be secured by a remittance of ten cents upon application to the board at Kansas City.

$250,000 BY THE CLOSE OF 1900.

The board is still seeking to carry out the recommendation of the convention at Indianapolis. $20,000 was asked from the churches this year. This amount was apportioned among the churches. 85 per cent. of the churches that have been heard from sent in their apportionments. However, we still lack $13,557.66 of reaching the $20,000 on the 30th of September. Collections are still coming in and we trust the churches will have commendable pride in helping to reach this amount.

Make all remittances to

G. W. MUCKLEY.

600 *Waterworks Bldg., Kansas City, Mo.*

Evangelistic.

INDIANA.

Fowler, Oct. 3.—I am holding a meeting at Bethany Chapel, nine miles east of here with 11 accessions so far. Large audiences and a great interest. I baptized six young men yesterday and took the confession of four more. A great day and a great victory for Christ.—LEE TINSLEY.

Vincennes, Oct. 4.—I closed a meeting in Davis County, Oct. 2, resulting in 22 additions; 17 by confession and baptism.—P. C. CAUBLE.

Wabash, Oct. 5.—One addition last Sunday; two the Sunday before. My third year begins with good prospects. Old debts incurred before my time are being paid off; nearly $1,800 in the past two years. Better methods and greater faithfulness are promised. Will have several representatives at the Chattanooga Convention.—EARLE WILFLEY.

GEORGIA.

Atlanta, Oct. 3.—Began my eighth year of copartnership here yesterday with three additions at the morning service; 15 added since Aug. 1st, nearly all of whom are by primary obedience. Field enlarging continually and growing whiter and whiter to a glorious harvest. Eighteen added in last three weeks in a tent meeting held by M. F. Harmon, of Alabama, with fair prospect of another organization.—C. P. WILLIAMSON.

OKLAHOMA TERRITORY.

Britton, Oct. 3.—Meeting here resulted in 14 additions and the reorganization of church They have been somewhat belligerant in the past, but all seems to promise peace. I go to Wellington, Kan., to attend state convention this week.—ARTHUR W. JONES.

ARKANSAS.

Fayeteville, Oct. 4.—There were six additions to the First Church last Sunday; one by letter and five conversions.—N. M. RAGLAND.

Arkadelphia, Oct. 4.—Four additions here last Lordsday; three by statement and one by baptism.—E. S. ALLHANDS.

IOWA.

Sheldon, Oct. 4.—Our meetings closed with 28 additions, the result of the four weeks' effort. Baptisms, 12; by primary obedience, nine; from the sects, 13; by renewal, two; males, four; females, 24; parents, 10; adults, 23. Could we have held Bro. Abberley a week or 10 days more I believe a great victory might have been won over the sinners and sects, but much good seed was sown by the able preaching. Prof. Sweetman conducted the singing services.—PARSON MOWRY.

ILLINOIS.

Stanford, October 7.—Victor W. Dorris, of Georgetown, Ky., this evening closed what is probably the best meeting Stanford has ever enjoyed. The best that can be said is that he knows the Book, loves the truth and preaches Jesus. This church loves God and hates sectarianism more because of his preaching. Fifteen baptisms and five added otherwise; one confession where baptism was prevented by bigoted parents.—MELVIN MENGES.

Saybrook, October 8.—Meeting at Fairview closed last night; result: 98 confessions, seven reclaimed and five letters from other churches. This is the result of work done in this church by John H. Swift.

KANSAS.

Abilene, Oct. 3.—One reclaimed here yesterday. I close my work here and go to California to locate for my wife's health by advice of her physicians.—N. B. MCGHEE.

KENTUCKY.

Grayson, October 7.—Please report four additions to the church in Carter County since last report. Work prospers.—E. P. GROW.

Hebron, October 8.—Am in a meeting with the old church at Florence. Baptized four yesterday. Next meeting will begin at Bullittsville, Oct. 17.—GEO. W. WATKINS.

MISSOURI.

Center, Sept. 8.—One addition here since last report; a man over 60 years old. Am now in a meeting here with some interest.—W. D. MCCULLEY.

Belton, Oct. 8.—Updike-Easton meeting closed here with 62 added. Rain and sickness hindered the first 10 days. Meeting satisfactory to all and church in good condition.—L. H. OTTO.

Tarkio, October 3.—Closed a three weeks' meeting in this place last night; 36 additions, 6 additions last day. Bro. Hunt, the pastor, is doing a good work here. I go from here to Stanford, Ky.—H. A. NORTHCUTT.

Civil Bend Oct. 5.—We have just closed a very interesting meeting at Old Union, Daviess County, with four baptisms and the brethren aroused to duty. We also report a new organization of about 25 members, all of which are reliable farmers of the true type. We extend an invitation to our preaching brethren to give us a call at any time they chance to pass this way. The writer is employed here another year one-fourth time.—Z. MITCHELL.

Springfield, Oct. 5.—I have just closed another protracted meeting at Bruner. There were 23 additions; 13 by confession and baptism, 9 by relation and one from the Methodists. There were three additions by baptism in my August meeting that were not reported, making 26 in all.—E. P. TRABUE, General Evangelist.

St. Louis, Oct. 10.—At our preachers' meeting, on last Monday, F. O. Fannon reported 13 additions at the First Church since last report, S. B. Moore one baptism at Compton Heights and Dr. Dungan four baptisms at Mt. Cabanne.

SUBSCRIBERS' WANTS.

Miscellaneous wants and notices will be inserted in this department at the rate of two cents a word, each insertion, all words, large and small, to be counted, and two initials stand for one word. Please accompany notice with corresponding remittance to save book-keeping.

SOMETHING WONDERFUL! Diarrhea and Flux cured in one MINUTE! Learn this most important process of mastering these affections. Enclose $1.00 in a letter directed to Dr. A. P. Davis, 638 Jackson Boul., Chicago, Ill., and receive full instructions how to use it. It is not a medicine. Always on hand, and never costs you any more money.

BAPTISM.—The doctrines and practices of the modern church compared with those of the early apostolic. By Geo. Rapkin, Pastor of the Christian Church, Margate. Mailed free. Cloth boards, 50 cents; paper, 40 cents. Each copy signed by the author. From Geo. Rapkin, Margate, England.

WANTED.—Position in school or private family. English, Mathematics, Latin, French, Piano. Harmony taught. Six years experience. Testimonials from Peabody Conservatory of Music and other sources. MISS A. P. RICHARDSON, Louisa, Virginia.

WANTED.—To hold a two weeks' meeting (free) in congregations where a Christian library can be placed. Library consists of ninety-one (91) cloth-bound volumes selected from the Christian Publishing Co. publications, fifty (50) yearly copies of THE CHRISTIAN-EVANGELIST, and fifty (50) copies of Gospel Call (Evangelist's edition) song books. Write for particulars. ELDER S. J. PHILLIPS, Sugar Grove, Wis.

Family Circle.

The Temple of Song.

MRS. ALICE ROBINSON.

Like a pearl in the midst of the city of light,
Like a shining pearl stands a temple white,
By the side of the mystic, running river,
That rolls down the golden height forever.
Thro' its aisles a softened radiance glows,
Thro' its air a flowery perfume blows,
And solemnly, gladly, all day long,
Its arches ring to the service of song.

On the height above the banners unfurl,
And ensigns are waving o'er gates of pearl,
And the wonderful light is that alone
Which in radiance shines from the great white throne.
There worshipers throng the golden street,
And messengers hasten with willing feet,
And ever the earnestly hurrying throng
Near the music that swells from the temple of song.

In the starlit silence when earth is at rest,
Molding her millions asleep on her breast,
The spirit leans out with an ecstasy strong
To catch the far notes of the angelic throng.
Down from afar—half felt and half heard—
Like the song of the stars or a paradise bird,
Solemnly sweet and grandly strong
The organ tones roll thro' the service of song.

Text Stories—XV.

JESUS ON TRIAL.

BY ALICE CURTICE MOYER.

What shall I do with Jesus which is called Christ?—*Matt.* 27:22.

"Hello, Tom! What's the matter?"

Tom Mayhew looked up to behold the familiar face of his friend, Frank Collins, whom he would have passed without seeing in his abstraction.

"What's the matter," he repeated absently, and then asked:

"Did you know, Frank, that Harry Loomis died last night?"

"No; did he?"

Tom nodded, then spoke seriously—more seriously than Frank had ever heard him speak before:

"And do you know, Frank, I was just thinking—well, you know, it might have been some one of the rest of us," and he shuddered at the thought.

"That is true," replied Frank, "but Harry's friends have this consolation, he was prepared."

"Which is more than can be said of some of the rest of us—myself, for instance. Somehow it has brought the thought mighty close—this death—and I was think- that if it had been—well—myself, it might have been different, you know."

"Have you seen Harry?"

"I was there all night, have just left, and Frank, it was wonderful how he died; he hadn't the least fear. And his folks, although grieving because of their loss, actually seem almost to rejoice for his sake. Surely, there must be something in religion if it can rob death of its terrors."

Frank now put his arm round the shoulders of his friend and turned to walk with him. So often he had tried to say a word to him on this subject, but as often Tom had evaded it; he had almost given up the effort, but now the longed-for opportunity had come.

"Rest assured, Tom, there *is* something in religion. Christians *do* have a hope that takes away the terrors of death. They know that it is but a change from this material body to one that is suited to the spiritual state. And this 'king of terrors' that men call death is really a friend to those who are ready to meet it. Harry's relatives know that in his case 'to die is gain.'"

"It must be a blessed thing to be a Christian, and such things as death, especially when it comes to one whom I know, makes me wish to be one myself, only I am not yet quite ready."

"You believe on the Lord Jesus Christ, and want to be a Christian, and are yet not ready?"

"And yet not ready," replied Tom. "When I become a Christian I want to be prepared to withdraw from all things worldly. I want be ready to retire from business and from all contact with the ungodly. I want to be prepared to live a purely spiritual life, far above all public matters."

"And are these your reasons? Is it possible, Tom, that you actually have such ideas of a Christian life? Why, my friend, that would be the old morbid sort of Christianity that has long ago gone out of fashion because of impracticability. The spirit of true Christianity is not the sort that causes one to hold himself aloof from all public affairs. Of all people, the Christian should be the most interested in such things, for of necessity these matters affect the welfare of the human race. As to contact with the ungodly, we are told that it is not the whole that need a physician, but they that are sick. Christ was not above eating with sinners, and if Christians are to let their light shine, it should certainly shine in the dark places of earth, where it will do the most good. And as to business Christianity is, in itself, a business, and a business that will harmonize with any other that is honorable and legitimate. When we hear a man say that he cannot harmonize Christianity with business, then may we know that there is something wrong with that man's calling. If we would but take our Christianity with us in to our regular, every-day affairs it could not but have its influence. Then would we be less prone to crush our brother in our hurry to get rich, then would we be more humane in the treatment of those who toil for us and more generous in remunerating such toiling ones. In fact, we cannot afford to bar out our religion from every-day affairs, for our soul must starve without the daily bread that God alone can give."

"But," argued Tom, "one must give up so many pleasures to become a Christian. I am too young yet to give up all the pleasures of life."

"Pleasures of life!" exclaimed Frank. "Why, my friend, such pleasures as you have in mind, are as naught compared with the joy of the Christian; the joy that passeth all understanding; that endureth forever; that satisfieth the soul. Surely, the Christian, because of the hope he has within him, has the right to be the happiest of all creatures. On the other hand, I ask you to answer me honestly. Do you not in the midst of your so-called pleasures, have everywhere and all the time a consciousness of the soul unsatisfied? the life unfilled, incomplete?"

"It is true!" Tom answered. "Almost thou persuadest me to be a Christian." And his friend replied:

"Would to God that it were not onl almost, but altogether. 'Behold I stand a the door and knock, if any man hear m voice and open the door I will come in t him and will sup with him and he wit me,' said Jesus in his message to th church at Laodicea. But, althoug primarily addressed to a lukewarm church it is likewise a message to every impeniten heart, from which Christ is barred by dis obedience. 'Behold, I stand at the door an knock.' How ready he is to enter! Ho lovingly he asks admission! But it i necessary that we respond to this knock ing. We are free moral agents, and Chris will not thrust himself into any heart if it possessor is unwilling; but, 'It any ma hear my voice and open the door I wil come in to him and sup with him and h with me.' He wants to be our Friend; t have mutual fellowship with us. He i knocking at the door of your heart to-day Tom. Ask of yourself the question tha Pilate put to the accusers of the sinles Son of God: 'What shall I do with Jesus? Jesus is still on trial. The great questio before the world to-day is, 'What shall do with Jesus which is called Christ?' W can not preserve a neutral ground concern ing this question. The mere washing of ou hands will not free us from the responsibil ity of decision. We cannot say, 'I find n fault in him,' and yet shrink from hi service without casting our influence wit his enemies. He that is not for him i against him. We are crucifying him ane each time we hear the still small voice an the gentle knock, and yet refuse to receiv him and to yield loving and loyal obedience to his commandments."

Frank and Tom had now reached the home of the latter; after a fervent handclasp Frank would have passed on, but his friend detained him:

"Come up to my room, Frank, I want you to pray."

A moment later they knelt reverently and Frank approached the throne of grace in earnest prayer:

"O, God, thou gracious Giver of all good gifts, we do thank thee for the unspeakable gift of thy Son, who gave himself a ransom for our sins; and who is now standing at the door of our hearts, seeking admission. O, may we listen to thy gentle voice, pleading with us so tenderly. And may we, through the memory of all thy goodness to us, open our hearts and no longer refuse entrance to thy sinless Son who seeks such entrance, that he may establish a right relation with us, that through such relation we may be transformed into his own image. Grant, O, God, that we may enthrone him in our hearts, thereby answering most fittingly the question that has to do with each soul: 'What shall I do with Jesus?' For thy name's sake. Amen!"

St. Louis, Mo.

"Inasmuch."

She had once been beautiful and pure. Now she was ugly and steeped in sin. Reeling across the waiting room, she fell in a senseless heap in the entrance. There were plenty of people near—elegantly dressed young ladies, gallant young men, loving mothers, so-called Sisters of Charity, and many others representing the easier walks of life, but not one extended a helping hand. Even the large-bodied colored woman whose function it was to look after the comfort of lady patrons of the various railroads centering there, straitened herself up to her full height and, with a curl of the lip, touched a bell and summoned a policeman. A big, burly fellow, club in hand, soon made his appearance, and the poor unfortunate was loaded into the patrol wagon, and, amidst the jeers of the ever-present small boy, the significant glances of the idler, and the scornful looks of society generally, driven roughly to jail. None followed, for none cared. The young ladies sauntered off home, white parasols in hand. The young men sauntered along. Mothers met their incoming friends, or bade them good-bye with many a loving kiss. The tall man with the Prince Albert coat, white tie and flowing burnsides took the train for his appointment, earnestly meditating upon the text he had chosen for his Sunday morning sermon, "Inasmuch as ye did it not to one of the least of these, ye did it not to me."

But better far it is to speak
One simple word which now and then
Shall waken their free nature in the weak
And friendless sons of men.

—*Lowell.*

GEO. F. HALL.

Decatur, Ill.

Bitter-Sweet.

GRACE PEARL BRONAUGH.

This world is bitter in a sense,
But sweet is Heaven's recompense
To all who walk with willing feet,
The bitter first and then the sweet!

Advance To Full Growth.

C. H. WETHERBE.

In Heb. 6:1, R. V., are these words: "Wherefore, let us cease to speak of the first principles of Christ and press on unto perfection." A marginal note renders the word "perfection" thus: "Full growth." The latter part of the quoted verse, as amended by the margin, would read: "Press on unto full growth." There is no doubt that this is the apostle's precise thought. The meaning of the word "perfection," in this instance at least, is evidently that of fullness of growth in Christ. In the last verse of the preceding chapter Paul says, according to the revised version, that "solid food is for full-grown men, even those who, by reason of their senses, exercise to discern good and evil." Here the word "full-grown" is rendered in the margin "perfect," which indicates that, in the apostle's mind, the two words are, in this connection, the same in meaning. He would say that the full-grown Christian is a perfect Christian; he is completely rounded out; he is fully, perfectly developed. We need to bear in mind the spiritual condition of the Hebrew Christians at the time that Paul was writing this epistle. They were mere babes in Christ; at least many of them were. There was no need of their being such at that time, for Paul says: "For when, by reason of the time, ye ought to be teachers, ye have need again that some one teach you the rudiments of the first principles of the oracles of God." They were stunted spiritual babes, far from being in the perfection of Christian manhood, and the apostle reprimanded them for being in such a state. In substance he said to them: Get out of your imperfect, baby condition and press on unto perfect manhood. Press quickly on unto full-grown men and women in Christ. This threw the burden of responsibility on each Christian. It was a perfection with which each had much to do. It was not a "second work of grace," to be performed by God, but a steady work for each to do for himself. Simply to pray for perfection was not enough. A child cannot at once become a man by prayer, however earnestly it might pray. There must be appropriate exercise and proper food and time for growth. Nor can a young babe in Christ become a full-grown man in Christ in an instant; but he can hasten fast toward that state; he can and should "press on" unto this most desirable condition. Are you still a Christian baby?

Alice Cary.

MARY E. WARE.

Sweet Alice Cary! Her body was too frail for her intellect and her intellect was never strong enough to express the fine emotions that vibrated through her soul. Is there anything more pathetic than to feel the throes of great emotions and yet not to have the power to express them?

Not long since, during a trolley party, in Cincinnati, one of the company pointed northward and said, "The home of Alice and Phœbe Cary lies about one mile from here."

Little dreamed they, in their girlhood, that their neighboring town would grow until it would one day reach their farm-house door! When that day comes, Cincinnati will surely do herself the honor of buying it and converting it into "Cary Park."

As you look at that grand old forest, with its magnificent trees that seem almost possessed with souls, you do not wonder at its being the scene of her most beautiful poem—"Pictures of Memory."

Nothing that she has written more truly reveals her sweet, shy self, her love of nature, and her capacity for sorrow. The poem is full of the pathos that tinged everything that she wrote.

She recalls the birds, the flowers, the butterflies and the sweet, affectionate companionship of her brother during their childhood. It begins in this simple way:

"I once had a little brother
With eyes that were dark and deep.
In the lap of that olden forest
He lieth in peace asleep."

Her memories of this brother are tender and beautiful. In her "Order for a Picture," which she thought her best poem, he is the hero, though the family history is somewhat disguised.

Early in the 50's she and Phœbe went East, with the intention of locating themselves where they could earn their livelihood with their pens. After many visits and inquiries, New York was selected.

Their open, frank and ingenuous ways appealed to older and more experienced people. Publishers became interested in them, men of letters like Whittier and Greeley, aided them with their advice and their influence.

One of the most beautiful metrical tributes in our language is Whittier's "Singers." In this he says of Alice Cary—

"The crown of pain that all must wear,
Too early pressed her midnight hair."

and again:

"All felt that behind the singer stood
A sweet and gracious womanhood."

Their modest home on Twentieth Street, their informal Sunday evening teas and their scholarly guests all suggest the ideal that Wordsworth had in mind when he spoke of "plain living and high thinking."

A great shock came to her loyal, trusting heart before she left her Western home. A man of wealth, culture and college education came into her neighborhood on business. He was surprised to find such a lovely, gifted young woman amid such plain surroundings. His surprise deepened into interest, and that into affection.

After they became engaged he returned to his Eastern home to make ready for their marriage. It is the same old story that the novelist uses so often, because it is so true to human nature. A proud, rich family insisted that he give up his rustic sweetheart, and a weak man yielded to their influence.

In her quiet way she once said to an intimate friend: "I waited for one who never came back. Yet I believed he would come till I read in the paper of his marriage to another."

Strange, strange what destinies are woven by the Fates for some of the truest, purest, and noblest of mortals! Yet compensation is always the golden thread woven in the fabric of their lives.

The love that was denied Alice Cary by one individual was given to her a thousand, thousand times over by her personal friends and her devoted readers. The grace, beauty and harmony which she would have carried into her own home have been scattered abroad to make all homes, where the music of her poetry has been heard, more harmonious.

She was greatly interested in Dr. Deems and his work. When told that Commodore Vanderbilt had given him Mercer Street church she wept for joy.

She was sick at the time and tried so hard to get well enough to attend the first service. It was not to be. When she did go, it was on her bier.

Her death, like that of Frances Willard, bowed the whole nation in grief.

"The clear blue eye, the tender smile,
The sovereign sweetness, the gentle grace,
The woman's soul and the angel's face"

had, at last, found their resting-place.

Kansas City, Mo.

Truth.

GRACE PEARL BRONAUGH.

"The truth shall make you free," the Savior saith;
The courage born of truth has conquered Death.
O, to be brave, no matter what the cost!
O, to be true, tho' all save truth be lost!

He Careth for Me.

IDA B. DAVISON.

In life's brightest moments, when all is at rest,
And all things about me seem happy and blest;
In nature about me, God's presence I see;
For I am his child and he careth for me.

When dark is my pathway and over my soul
The dark sea of sorrow, in great billows roll,
Then close to my Savior I ever would flee;
For, oh, blessed thought! He careth for me.

Dear Lord, I entreat thee, that close by thy side
I ever may keep, whatever betide.
In joy or in sorrow, thine ever I'd be,
For thou art my Father and carest for me.

Eureka, Ill.

Curious Wedding Ceremonies.

In different ages and nations there has always been a wide variety in marriage customs. But all these marriage ceremonies are capable of a threefold division: 1. Marriage by capture; 2. Marriage as a religious ceremony; 3. Civil marriage.

In many lands it seems to be a tradition or form of etiquette that no woman should willingly give herself to any man. This notion prevails among those barbarous or semi-civilized peoples where the lot of woman is peculiarly one of hardship. It is concluded that a refusal must inevitably meet an offer of marriage, and as the desired bride can on no account permit herself to marry peaceably, her lover captures her.

The fashion of wife-capture, based on the theory of woman's natural aversion to marriage, has been in many countries followed as a historic method, or commemorative of some great event in the national history, long after the original reason for the capture passed out of existence. The story of the capture of the Sabine women by the Roman bachelors is well known to us all; also the capture of the Shiloh women by the wifeless Benjaminites. The Greek myth of the Centaurs, who seized the daughters of the Lapithæ, is probably a poetic account of the conflict of two early barbarous races, where the men of one tribe stole for wives the daughters of the other tribe—the homo-equine nature of the Centaur merely expressing some Scythic race of horsemen. Among the Patagonians, Australians and Bedouins marriage is still by capture. In many cases the marriage capture is only a form, the contract of marriage having been carefully arranged. The Greeks and Romans pretended to capture their brides after all the preliminaries, especially the financial contracts, had been settled. The practice of lifting a bride across the threshold of her husband's home is a remnant of the capture plan.

In Australia the stealing or capture of wives is a fact attended by bloodshed and cruelty among many of the native tribes. If the poor girl is considered a beauty, she is often wounded or nearly killed in the strife of her suitors, and a murder or two of rivals in the melee is not uncommon.

Among the Circassians the bride, duly appareled and waiting, is noisily stolen by night—after the wedding contract is signed and the dowry paid! In Khurdistan the bride is captured in the daytime, her young friends making a furious defense of her. The more biting, screaming, slapping, scratching, kicking and stone-throwing that is done by the damsels the finer is the style of the affair! Among the African tribes the bride is generally carried off forcibly, even when the respective families have amicably exchanged wedding gifts some days previous to the seizure. Among almost all Tartar, Slavic and Scandinavian races marriage has been until modern times, or is now, by capture; as, for instance, among Mongols, the Caucasus tribes, the Kalmucks, Kirghiz, and anciently in Poland, Sweden, Finland and Muscovy. Two centuries ago in Prussia the young man always stole his wife, his father having straitly charged him whom to capture. This sapient parent then went to the maiden's sire and begged that his dear boy might be allowed to keep his booty. The parents signed the contract, and a grand wedding followed.

We are told that in Ireland, even in 1802, "marriage was but a lame exploit" in the hilly counties unless the groom showed himself of spirit sufficient to run away with his bride. This gave the groom fine opportunity for the national delight of "quietly arguing the matter with sticks."

l districts of Scotland, England there are retained wedding hich are plainly relics of old ions of bride-capture.

all civilized countries marriage anied by religious forms. In lands marriage is regarded as tract, made in the presence of witnesses, and is entirely valid accompanied by religious cere-, for instance, marriage by a . It is equally valid if perform- accredited minister of any n some sections of the country must be licensed by the state can perform marriage ceremo- her states the groom must ex- he parson a license, obtained ppointed authority, before he ried.

n Catholic countries marriage with the sanctity of a strictly eremonial. The Roman Church arriage a sacrament, and does e of the intermeddling of civil with the rite. This has given ch conflict in Italy and France, nsisting upon a civil ceremony magistrate, without which the legal and the children are ille- The state in these cases is quite to the question of a religious before or after the civil contract. Revolution in France religious at espousals were forbidden, urely civil marriages were legal. y a civil marriage is required ference to the religious cele-

the early Christians marriage ed as a civil contract, the chief being the leading of the bride w home in the presence of wit- radually, to prevent disorders, al and marriage were required in church in the presence of a ny of the wedding ceremonies ristian church were developed customs of the Greeks and the use of the ring, the making d the priestly benediction. In Church marriage-candles are ors of the nuptial torches of the holy water is the ancient *aqua* e marriage-mass takes the place , sacrificed by the Latin pontiff. 300 A. D. the church began to in regard to marriage.

ebrew nation the betrothal was as the marriage, and the a "betrothed or espoused wife" became by the later ceremony wife." Thus the Virgin Mary 's "espoused wife." For the s great splendor of dress as was the partiess was *en regle*. The the bridegroom" arranged all his behalf. The groom went to claim his bride. He was d by torches, music and troops The parents with much pomp he maid to her lover, and her ends joining the procession of nts, they set out, walking or the future home, the pair going

The feast lasted sometimes 14 days, being longer for a maid than for a widow.

A modern Jewish wedding is famous for its splendors. Lavish gifts are made. For the ceremony the bride and groom stand under a canopy, upon a special square of carpet called a *taleth*. On the *taleth* stand also the parents and the rabbi. The canopy is of crimson velvet, belongs to the synagogue, and is brought and returned by the servants of the synagogue. The guests hold the corners of the canopy during the ceremony. The drinking of a glass of wine and the breaking of the glass yet remain part of the Jewish nuptial ceremony.

An ancient Greek marriage was begun by betrothal, dowry and bridal gifts. Then sacrifices were made to Pollux, Hera, Artemis and the Fates. To the latter the bride gave a lock of her hair. The ceremony was at a temple, and the bridal pair were crowned with ivy. After nightfall the bride was placed in a chariot drawn by oxen and carried to her husband's home, where youths and maids met her with torches and wedding hymns.

Among the Latins augury for the marriage was first made. Then the bride's hair was rolled *a la Diana*, her robe was white wool with a purple border and a girdle of white wool; her wreath was of verbena, her veil yellow, her shoulders covered with a cloak. The bridal pair stood upon a sheepskin at the house door. A woman dressed as *Juno Pronuba* stood by the bride, the vestal virgins near at hand held oil, cakes, salt, wine. Ten witnesses were required; the bride held three ears of wheat. The friends of the groom lifted the bride over her husband's threshold, and her husband presented her with vases of fire and water. When she had touched these he gave her a kiss and the household keys, thus investing her with domestic authority.—*Julia McNair Wright, in the Voice.*

Sunday School.

A YOUNG MAN'S VISION.*

HERBERT L. WILLETT.

Far and away the most important of the prophets whose life story has been preserved to us is Isaiah. When the brilliant reign of Uzziah (Azariah) came to its close in 737, B. C., he was a young man living in Jerusalem, educated, moving in high social circles, admitted freely to the court, perhaps not distantly related to the royal family. He had no thought of being a prophet, did not belong to the prophetic guild, had been given no training to prepare him for such a ministry. But the call of God came to him and he began to preach the doctrine of the holiness and righteousness of God and the duty of the nation. Years passed and the people had given but little heed. They did not like to be reproved for following their own devices, and moreover they found themselves prosperous and felt no need to change their conduct at the voice of one who so constantly repoved. At last they demanded his authority for preaching as he did, just as Amaziah, of Bethel, had done when Amos preached there; just as the Scribes and Pharisees were to do when Jesus gave them disquiet regarding their own influence centuries later. What right had Isaiah to preach as he was doing? Who gave him authority to rebuke as he did? Then at last the prophet opens the door into an inner chamber of his own soul and permits them to see the origin of his message. While, therefore, this is not the first of his discourses to be given utterance, it was certainly the earliest of prophetic experiences, and constituted his call to service.

The description is graphic. In the death-year of King Uzziah the prophet, who was no prophet at that time, says he saw, either in a vision of the night or in a day-time vision what seemed an epiphany in the temple or palace. At the further end of the hall appeared the divine form, seated upon a lofty throne, the skirts of his mantle filling the forecourt. On either side appeared a group of shining attendants, each having six wings. With two he shielded his eyes from the intolerable brightness of the divine presence; with two he covered his person and with two he moved. The two divisions of this antiphonal choir were chanting responsively the Trisagion, ascribing praise and glory to God, and so mighty were the voices of the angelic singers that the very pillars of the court trembled as the song rose, while the incense ascending from the golden altar in front was gradually filling the house with its heavy perfume.

It was the vision of the glory of God, and its effect was most singular upon the young man. Taught to believe that no one could see God and live, he became all at once conscious of his imperfections. He who had lived the happy, careless life of a courtier felt the first profound conviction of sin. The vision of the perfect life had melted into a vision of his own utter unworthiness to stand in its presence. Nor does the consciousness of sin come otherwise. Men are not often scolded into virtue. But when they are pointed to the life of God in Jesus Christ they become conscious of their own utter imperfection before him. Isaiah cried out in self-abasement, "I am a man of unclean speech and I dwell among such a people; I shall instantly perish, for I have seen Jehovah." But the vision of sin melted into a vision of forgiveness as one of the seraphim came to signify by the touch of the living coal that his sin was cleansed. Nor does any soul ever cry in vain to God. The whole message of the gospel is one of forgiveness and love. God only wants to pardon, but he cannot pardon till the soul is ready.

And now the young man is thrilling with the joy of a great deliverance. Life itself will be but a small compensation to God for such an experience as this. At that moment a question is asked by the divine voice. The nation of Israel is stubborn and disobedient. There is no promise of repentance. Yet new efforts must be made. Who will go and proclaim God's will? Who will seek to turn the sinning people to righteousness? Among the angels there is no response. No one seeks so ungracious a task. But Isaiah has heard and with all the enthusiasm of a soul in which the vision of forgiveness has melted into a vision of service he cries, "Here am I, send me."

This is the genesis of all true service. God has as much need of prophets to-day as then. They are not called to the same service, but it is as important. They are not called in the same way, but after all their experience is the same. No one is prepared to serve God who has not passed through just the process here described in the life of Isaiah. There must be the vision of God, beheld in the face of Jesus Christ, and understood sufficiently to make all life beside seem paltry and worthless without that divine possession—only such a vision of God can bring an adequate conception of the awfulness of sin. Then when out of this darkness the soul has emerged into the light of forgiveness through the power of the gospel, the first and growing desire will be to render a worthy service to God—any ministry will then seem worthy of all effort. To find oneself without the motive to service is to be aware of a flaw somewhere in the process of our salvation.

The closing verses of the chapter refer to the divine warning to Isaiah, that though he should preach the people would not be willing to listen. He tells the nation that he had been warned of their stubborness, and he tells it as though it had been actually a part of his work to make them so. But this is only to heighten the effect of his statement that their attitude is no surprise to him, and that its inevitable consequence is going to be the almost total distinction of the nation, with the survival of but a remnant. But this remnant is the hope of the future. It was a hard message, but needed for the times. From the day of this inaugural vision to the close of Isaiah's career was more than forty years of constant service as a prophet.

SUGGESTIONS FOR TEACHING.

A single event may turn the tide of a life into an entirely new channel. The man who has never seen God spiritually will be able to bear no message for him. The service of man is greater than that of angels. The anthem of every life should be ascription of praise to God. We shall never greatly prize our salvation unless we realize the terrible nature of sin, from which we have been saved. God is more ready to forgive than we are to request it. The word of every truly converted soul is, "Here am I, send me." When it is only "Here am I send *him*," we may know there is some imperfection in our gratitude. When the gospel is refused the heart grows harder and more difficult to reach again. There is always a remnant of righteousness left as the hope of the future.

The University of Chicago.

*Bible-school Lessons for Oct. 23, 1898—Isaiah called to Service (Isa. 6:1-13). Golden Text—I heard the voice of the Lord saying, Whom shall I send and who will go for us? Thou said I, here am I, send me (Isa. 6-8). Less n Outline—1. The Vision of Holiness (1-4); 2. The Vision of Sin (5-7); 3. The Vision of Service (8-13).

Christian Endeavor.

BY BURRIS A. JENKINS.

TOPIC FOR OCT. 30.

HELPFULNESS.

(Ex. 17:8-13; Gal. 6:1-5.)

It takes sometimes but a very small matte to help one very far along upon his way. Per haps this is because it takes such a very smal matter to hinder one a great deal upon hi way. One is very much discouraged some times by a very small trifle. Perhaps we ge up in the morning and within the first hour o the day something goes awry—we scarcel know what it is. A whole day is ruined for u because of that mishap. Again, on the other hand, it often happens within the early mo ments of the day some light matter occur which we could not lay our finger upon o analyze, which lightens our spirits throughout the livelong day. We are like swimmers in the water. A very small thing will help; a very small obstacle will hinder. How careful ought to be our bearing towards those about us; for it may be a single word, or a single look, a gesture, a frown or a smile will affect a whole day in a lifetime for some one with whom we are thrown in contact. We should be very careful to show the right side of our natures to the world, and the right side is the bright side. Express packages come marked, "Right side up." Upon every life should be stamped the label, "Bright side up." Let us keep the darkness hidden away as much as possible, and let us show the better side, which is forever the brighter side of our lives, to others. Only to our very intimates should we dare to show the darker, sadder phases of our lives, and even to them not in such a way as to cloud their lives.

Moreover, the mutual character of helpfulness is one of the striking facts about it. We are dependent upon each other. We are like shocks of grain where each bundle helps support the rest. "Bear ye one another's burdens, and so fulfill the law of Christ," said an apostle who felt very keenly his fellowship with man. "Brethren, if a man be overtaken in a fault"—what a tender and beautiful word is that word, "brethren!" Paul uses it so frequently, showing that he appreciates the mutual element in our lives.

Who are those, then, whom we can help by the way? Naturally, first of all, those with whom we are most closely associated, our home ones. It is so easy to make life bright and sweet for those about us, and it is so easy to make it hard and dreary. One bright, cheerful talker at a home table, one unselfish, attentive, thoughtful disposition in a home circle can brighten a whole family's life. But alas! such a one is too often wanting about the fireside and at the breakfast table. Each Christian Endeavorer should resolve from now on to make his life a helpful life in the home circle.

We can be helpful, also, to those whom we

are associated with in business life or in the school or on the street. It was said the other day of a business man that he had helped many a young man to a career of usefulness. Few better things could be said of any business man. As J. E. Pounds says, "The only thing you can give a man in this world is a chance; you can not give him an education, you can only give him a chance to get an education." So among the highest and best gifts that any one can place in the way of a young man is a chance. Some men are helpful to all whom their lives touch—even to agents, book agents, sewing machine agents. Agents are human beings, and it is possible to be courteous, and kind, and helpful even to them. Poor agents! It is very seldom, no doubt, that they get a smile or a kind word. In our strict Endeavor work there are many who need our help; the president, the corresponding secretary, the chairman of the committee to which we belong—how much these would appreciate a volunteer offer of your service, fellow-Endeavorers. And the pastor, who can say how his heart is cheered by an occasional, really sincere and honest attempt to help him in his work. Indeed, who is there about us who does not need our help? The writer once came under the influence of a certain one's life whose constant aim it seemed to be to seek some one who needed help, even in very small affairs, and to bestow that assistance; and the fragrance of that memory has not departed to this day, but will live throughout the years of memory.

Literature.

"Organic Evolution Considered."

In writing of the volume of Professor A. Fairhurst on the subject of "Organic Evolution," I dare not undertake to speak of the question considered on its merits. Want of knowledge has more than once occasioned timidity.

The book, however, leaves an impression, and I may at least tell of that. The author has undoubtedly studied deeply the question in hand. There is no fumbling, uncertain touch. His tread is that of a man who knows that he has feet, unlike Melancthon, of whom Luther said, "He is trying to walk on eggs without crushing them." I like an author who has a grip and who can say in good English, "This is what I mean."

And yet, in Professor Fairhurst's book there is the utmost courtesy and fairness in dealing with those who hold an opposite view. There is no fierce denunciation, no attempt to drive his opponent out of court by the use of hard names—infidel, heretic and the like. The spirit of the book is altogether admirable.

One need not read very far to recognize the method of the teacher in this production. The style is simple; the plain facts, without ornamentation, are stated; the argument is made and the reader is left to draw his conclusions, and that, too, without any penalty attached, should the said reader happen to think that the conclusion is unsound. When our author chooses, he can take a flight into the empyrean, but for the most part he prefers the terra firma of ergis.

The book is a storehouse of information and will repay the careful perusal of any earnest student. I am glad that in the reading of these pages on a scientific subjec, the reader will receive no such solar plexus blow as meets him in Herbert Spencer's famous definition of evolution—"A charge from an indefinite incoherent homogeneity to a definite coherent heterogeneity through continuous differentiations and integrations"—concerning which, to quote from Drummond, the Contemporary Reviewer remarked that "the universe may well have heard a sigh of relief when, through the cerebration of an eminent thinker, it had been delivered of this account of itself." The book of Professor Fairhurst calls for thought, but it does not demand that the brain shall be wrecked in trying to understand it.

I take very great pleasure in commending "Organic Evolution Considered," and wish for it a wide circulation.

E. L. POWELL.

Louisville, Ky., Sept. 19, 1898.

OCTOBER MAGAZINES.

The sensational article in Scribner's for October is an account of the battle of San Juan, by Richard Harding Davis. Mr. Davis is a vigorous writer, and he does not hesitate to relate what he sees or thinks. He believes that this battle was fought without adequate preparation, and that many lives were unnecessarily sacrificed, and does not hesitate to tell why and how it all happened. His criticisms on some of the heads of departments are severe, while his eulogies for the men who fought and won the battle are strong and eloquent. The article is of historic value and the things stated should command the immediate attention of the government.

The leading articles of the Woman's Home Companion for October cover a wide range of thought and research, and the department articles fairly sparkle with their brightness, variety and attractive illustrations. The seasonable cover was designed by Wilcox Smith, and adds greatly to its attractiveness. The poems are of good quality and pleasant to read.

Two of the contributed articles in the American Monthly Review of Reviews for October deal with the serious lessons of our recent war with Spain. Dr. Carroll Dunham presents a calm and exhaustive survey of the nation's experience of the past six months in its medical and sanitary aspects. He shows where the failures in army administration occurred and what steps should be taken to prevent the recurrence of such costly mistakes. Lieut. John H. Parker, of the Thirteenth Infantry, who commanded the Gatlmg gun detachment at Santiago, explains from an officer's point of view the nature, cause and bearings of some of the defects revealed in the course of that campaign, and also summarizes the advance in our knowledge of the value of machine guns in battle as compared with heavy artillery.

The Pall Mall for October contains a good selection of articles for the magazine reader. One of the leading articles of this number is a discussion of English and American literary experiences by Mr. William Archer, which will be found of great interest to literary and historic minds. The Pall Mall record for fine illustrations is not broken in this number, neither its selection of fiction and poems.

An article commanding interest is that on "Electrical Manufacturing Interests" in the October Chautauquan. The facts it gives concerning the growing uses of electricity and its commercial value are gratifying and reliable, coming from the pen of Thomas Commerford Martin. Equally authoritative is Prof. L. H. Batchelder's scholarly paper on "The Growth of Chemical Science." In the same impression Eugene Parsons reviews "English Colonization in the Western World," and Mary H. Krout writes of "New Zealand and Its Resources."

Frank Leslie's for October is a seasonable, up-to-date number of this popular magazine. Beginning with the next (November) number, Frank Leslie's Popular Monthly will be changed in form and dress. Its price will be reduced to ten cents per copy, one dollar per annum. Mrs. Frank Leslie will direct editorial control of the magazine. The changes proposed will be in the line of development of the popular pictorial and literary features which have characterized it heretofore. At the same time, various novelties will be introduced.

The Treasury of Religious Thought for October, 1898, is an attractive number to a working pastor, as well as to the general Christian reader. Its frontispiece is an excellent portrait of the Rev. Samuel Zane Batten, of the First Baptist Church, Morristown, N. J., who has become widely known by his active connection with the Brotherhood of the Kingdom, the "Kingdom" newspaper, and, more recently, by his able discussion in book form of the problem of Christian brotherhood. Mr. Batten gives a stirring sermon on "The Greatest Change in the World," and a pleasant sketch of his own church, while a short notice of his life is given by Rev. S. S. Merriman, of Trenton. The first illustrated article is a full description and history of "Hawaii: Our New Territory," showing how great reason Christian Americans have for interest in that island possession. There are able sermons by Mr. Moody, and Dr. Burdett Hart; and suggestive outlines of sermons by Rev. Frank M. Ellis, Principal Gerrie, Pres. Patton, Dr. John Clifford, and others. Dr. Robert S. MacArthu contributes a fourth of his able discussions "Bible Difficulties," taking this time "Th Destruction of the Canaanites." There is fresh article on "Northfield and its Conven tion," by Rev. Dwight M. Pratt. The Rev Frank J. Mallett discusses "The Financi Problem." Prof. Small gives his review o "Movements Among the Churches," Dr Hallock gives the "Prayer-meeting Topics." There is a sketch with a portrait of Dr. Joh Clifford, the London Baptist who has supplie Tremont Temple pulpit during September (on of his sermons there being given in synopsis) and all the minor departments of the magazin are well maintained.

Marriages.

ARMFIELD. — Mr. Crawford
ss Anna Armfield were married
an Church, at Newcastle, Wy.,
day, Sept. 20th, 1898; A. San-
officiating.

IARSHALL.—At Plattsburg,
8, 1898, by J. W. Perkins,
rter and Miss Mary E. Marshall,
County, Mo.

Obituaries.

words will be inserted free. Above
ds, one cent a word. Please send
h notice.

EDMONDS.

Edmonds, well known to our
mphis and in St. Louis, died at
of his daughter in Woodford
on September 22nd, 1898, in the
age. Dr. Edmonds was born
nty, Ky., July 28th, 1822. He
faith in Christ at the age of 20,
l the subsequent years he never
is attachment to the church of
his faith in Christ. He was a
ominence in Memphis, Tenn.,
He moved from that city to St.
n occupied a prominent place in
ofession in this city, being con-
he homeopathic school and a
eir medical college here. He
h the power of graceful speech,
prayer-meeting and on social
much enjoyed. As a physician
shine with him into the sick
was always thoughtful and con-
patients. He was a reader of
and was deeply interested in all
terests. His health failed him
a resident of St. Louis, and he
cky a few years ago, where he
at the time of his death. He
him his daughter and his faith-
ife, who mourn the loss of an
ther and husband. Mrs. Ed-
sister of Mrs. Enos Campbell,
is a woman of rare beauty of
ur tenderest sympathies are
oth wife and daughter in this
reavement. Hundreds, we are
with us in this expression of
and sympathy. G.

HARRIS.

rris, the beloved wife of D. M.
sleep in Jesus at her home in
Sept. 26, of heart failure, aged
months and two days. She
n her departure her husband and
all of whom were present ex-
., who is in the 20th Regiment
eers at San Francisco. We will
D. M. HARRIS.

HASKIN.

ne H. Haskin, widow of Leonard
ged 67, died at the home of her
. Haskin, in Granville, N. Y.,
She was born at Pittstown, N.
h the church at an early age,
married in 1850. She has since
enville, N. Y., Petersburg, Va.,
Fla., Quincy, Ill., and Granville,
survived by two sons, Walden
nd. Her life was one of devo-
and her chief happiness was in
others. X.

HOUSTON.

Houston, *nee* Curtis, was born
, in Carter County, Tenn. She
ay 9th, 1869 to George Houston.
he mother of fourteen children;
d six girls. Two boys preceded
ath's stream. Sister Houston
e Church of Christ in 1868, and
follower of the meek and lowly
gently fell sleep in Christ Sept.
e leaves to mourn her departure,
of friends and relatives, three
e sisters, six daughters, six sons
d affectionate husband, who is
eacher of the gospel. On Thurs-
th, a 3:30 P. M., the remains
by a vast throng to Sparks'
ere interment took place. Elder
y conducted the burial services.
s preached on the fourth Sun-
ber by the writer, a large con-
ple being present. "She is not
peth." W. C. WILLEY.
o., *Oct.* 1, 1898.

McDONALD.

Sister Orpha K. McDonald died of consumption in Denver, Col., where she had been taken by her devoted husband with hope of recovery, Sept. 27, 1898. She was the youngest daughter of the late John and Cordelia Allison, born near Eureka, Ill., June 17, 1872. She obeyed the gospel under the writer's ministry Feb. 20, 1887, and faithfully trusted and served the Lord until the end. On July 11, 1889, she became the wife of Bro. C. C. McDonald. Unto them were born four children, three of whom are still living. The family lived in Fairbury until last spring, when they came to Eureka. It was a most devoted family, thoroughly Christian and full of true culture. The remains were brought back for burial beside her mother in the Mt. Zion cemetery. The writer preached the funeral sermon from Matt. 25:21: "Well done, good and faithful servant." May the Lord bless and comfort the bereaved. J. G. WAGGONER.
Eureka, Ill.

STUTZMAN.

My mother, Amanda M. Stutzman, fell asleep in Jesus at her home in Summerset, Pa., on Sept. 21, in the 74th year of her age. She closed her beautiful Christian life with expressions of serene confidence in her Redeemer. Her companion of 51 years survives her. Besides the writer there remain of sons and daughters: C. H. Fisher and Mrs. Emma Cook, of Summerset, Pa.; Mrs. Lillie Brown, Baltimore, Md.; Mrs. Lou Hoye, Sang Run, Md.; Mrs. Anna Boardman, Trumansburg, N. Y.; Mrs. Cora Johnson, London, Ky.; E. S. Stutzman, Washington, D. C.
F. R. STUTZMAN.

Hiram's Financial Situation.

In the three preceding articles the history of Hiram has been placed before our great brotherhood. We believe Pres. Garfield was right when he said, "Hiram has done more with the money she has had than any institution in the U. S." Whether this be true or not, it certainly is true that Hiram has accomplished a marvelous work with the small means at her command. The magnificent work done has been accomplished under disadvantages that no one can fully appreciate except those closely connected with the college. It remains now to briefly sum up the financial situation and then submit the case to the great brotherhood for action. Hiram has gradually accumulated a small endowment. If space permitted we would be glad to mention some specific gifts that she has received, but we have not room for this at the present time. Suffice it to say that her endowment has gradually increased from year to year until she has at present about $100,000 of productive endowment and probably $50,000 more that will become productive in the not distant future. She has never lost any of the money that was given to her, but has carefully guarded it and used it wisely and well. The great enlargement of its work, made necessary by the continually advancing standard in education and the continually growing demands upon the college has outrun the very gradual growth of the endowment. To show how greatly the work has increased we will say, that in 1883 thirty-nine classes recited each day; in 1898 eighty classes recite per day. In this comparison we estimate the work of the special teachers. In 1880 fifty-seven credits were necessary in order to graduation from the strongest courses; in 1898 sixty-eight credits are required. It will be understood that a credit means twelve weeks' work in a given study. In 1880 Hiram offered five courses besides the irregular and eclective work; in 1898 she offers twenty courses besides the irregular and elective work. In 1880 Hiram employed seven teachers. not counting student tutors. In 1898 she has twenty instructors, not including physical directors.

To keep out of debt under such circumstances has been a herculean task and it has only been done by the most rigid economy and by supplementing the income from tuitions and endowments by the gifts of individuals and churches. We must greatly enlarge the endowment. To cut down the work would be disastrous. In fact it is a question of enlarging rather than decreasing the work. Hiram's board has decided to make an appeal once for all to the people, for the college that has in a very emphatic way been a college of the people. Hiram's Jubilee Commencement in June 1900 is to be made the occasion for adding $250,000 to the endowment, thus placing the institution once for all on a solid foundation. The call is for at least 50,000 persons who will unite in the accomplishment of this great object, and why should not a college like Hiram, that has offered its blessings to thousands of worthy young people, be endowed by the people? Tuitions have been marvelously low and expenses have been kept down in every way. Every encouragement has been offered to struggling young people who have thus been enabled to secure an education. Hundreds and hundreds have gone forth from Hiram well equipped for the work of life that could never have received an education at all if it had not been for the advantages in the old college on the hill.

In next week's issue of the paper our great formal appeal will be made. Keep your eyes open for this appeal and read it carefully and then send your name in at once as one of the 50,000 who will join in this great movement. You can at least give one dollar and thus be enrolled in the Hiram army. Many can give much more. Let the friends of Hiram join hands in this movement and the work is done.

Z.

The Gospel in our Coast Cities.

Within the next few years there will be an immense and unprecedented growth in the foreign commerce of the United States. The Spanish war has called vivid attention to our foreign relations. We now really enter the field of a wide foreign trade. The possession of Cuba, Porto Rico and other West Indian territory of the Sandwich Islands and of interests, at least, in the Philippines, would of itself greatly increase our external commerce. Our business firms already have their agents on the grounds in our various prospective possessions. But our new business will not stop with this increase only. Our people are now reaching out for a wider trade in all directions. English ships are now carrying a large part of the foreign trade of this country. But this shall not be always so. The late war has called attention to our ships and our navy, and we shall from this time become more a maritime nation. Our own citizens will carry our own trade and their families will live in our seaports.

It is easy to see that we are upon the eve of a large growth in our seaport towns and cities. As exports and imports increase under this mighty impulse, the work of transfer and shipment will require a large working force and population in our coast cities. Especially will our Southern and Southeastern coast cities, in growing proximity to the great agricultural region of the West and Southwest that sends a considerable portion of its products to foreign lands be subject to a great increase in growth. In fact, quite a considerable growth, without the expansive influence of the late war, has already been manifest within the past few years.

During the last six years this city of Galveston has shown a striking growth in foreign trade; the value of exports has increased in instances as follows: Cattle, 1894, $900; 1898 an increase to $95,500. The exports of corn were in 1893, 186,000 bushels, having a value of $118,000, and this has increased to 4,762,000 bushels in 1898, having a value of $1,870,000. During the same period the value of wheat exports has increased from $859,900 to $10.159,000. Cotton seed oil exports have increased from $21,250 to $1,529,000; lumber from $12,700 to $606,300; zinc from nothing to $890,000 in 1897; while the total value of exports has doubled. Imports have increased one-half in the same time.

I, therefore, brethren, submit the conclusion, that we are called upon to spare no effort or money in establishing strong churches in these centers of future influence.

Jesse B. Haston.

Galveston.

Publishers' Notes.

Sir William Dawson of the McGill Univer sity, Montreal, Canada, gives his opinion "Organic Evolution Considered," as followi "I think the book may do much good in mee ing the difficulties of young naturalists per plexed by the sophistries if agnostic or spon taneous evolution."

Prof. G. P. Coler, of Ann Arbor, Mich. says concerning "Wonders of the Sky," b W. J. Russell: "One of the good things abou this book is that it is brief, containing onl eighty-two pages. These pages are cramme full of interesting information and inspirin thoughts." The price of this little book is 5 cents, postpaid. The book is bound in beati ful illuminated cloth.

"Queen Esther," written by M. M. Davis has just been issued from our press. Th book is bound in beautiful cloth, and the pric is 75 cents.

The book recites Queen Esther's career an brings out grand lessons from her eventful life The book can but have an ennobling and re fining influence on the minds of its readers The young men and young ladies of our time should carefully read this new publication. Th style of the author is fascinating and th thoughts are inspiring.

Those who are not acquainted with th biography of Alexander Campbell should rea "Life of Alexander Campbell," by Thoma W. Grafton. This work is a condensed his tory of this great religious reformer, be ginning with his boyhood and following th events of his life to its close. Every membe of our church should be acquainted with th history of Alexander Campbell. A carefu reading of this late book will give one all th important events in the life of this great man It is a book of 234 pages, and the price i $1.00.

Announcements.

We have accepted the work at Hot Springs, Ark. the famous health resort. We will take pleasure in giving our brethren any information desired concerning this place if they write with stamps. We desire you to visit our church while here. The church is located at the end of the Ouchipa car line Address W. H. Connell, elder or myself.

T. N. Kincaid.

Hot Springs, Ark.

Missouri District Convention.

Brookfield district convention convenes at Brunswick, Mo., Oct. 25, 26, 27, 1898. Addresses are expected to be made by T. J. Ogle, J. W. Davis, T A. Abbott, H. F. Davis, R. E. L. Prunty and others. C. W. B. M. session Wednesday afternoon and evening, Oct. 26. A general invitation to attend is extended to all who are interested; to brethren of the district especially.

S. G. Clay, Pres.
J. A. Grimes, Sec.

Railroad Rates.

The Western Passenger Association and the Trunk Line Association north-east of the Potomac River has granted a rate of one and one-third fare, round trip, to the gateways of the Central Association, on the Certificate plan, to the Chattanooga Convention, Oct. 13-21, 1898.

Those coming from the Western Passenger Association and the Trunk Line Association north-east of the Potomac River will pay full fare to the gateway of the Central Traffic Association, and from there will get round-trip tickets to Chattanooga and return, at the rate of one fare for the round trip. When you pay full fare take a certificate for the same, and after having it signed at Chattanooga you will be returned from the gateway at which it was purchased to your home for one-third fare.

Please notice that those coming from the Western Passenger Association and the Trunk Line Association north-east of the Potomac River purchase tickets twice, one at the home station for which they will take a certificate, and the second at the point where they reach the bounds of the Central Traffic Association, where they will buy round-trip tickets at the one-fare rate.

Our convention at Chattanooga promises to be the most interesting in all our history. Preparations have been making for months that it shall be the strongest Convention we have ever held. The brethren at Chattanooga have had it on their hearts the entire year, and have made the most ample preparations for the successful entertainment of this Convention.

In behalf of the Boards we desire to extend the invitation for a general gathering of the loyal Disciples of our Lord and Savior. Let us say in our hearts, "I was glad when they said unto me, Let us go unto the house of our Lord."

Come to the Convention at Chattanooga, October 13th to 21st, 1898.

Benj. L. Smith, Cor. Sec.
American Missionary Society.

THE
CHRISTIAN-EVANGELIST.

A WEEKLY FAMILY AND RELIGIOUS JOURNAL.

XXXV. October 20, 1898 No. 42.

CONTENTS.

:
Events....483
ple of Constructive Teaching...484
of the People....484
g the Ministry of Christ....485
mpathizing Friend 486
e Work Among the Churches. 486
s Easy Chair....486

CONTRIBUTIONS:
n Union.—John G. Fee.... 491
rmon-Christian War.—R. B.
....491
glected Ministry.—T. H. Kuhn.492
ower of Littles.—James M.
bell....493

NDENCE:
gton (D. C.) Letter....494
rk Letter....494
Letter....495
session and Use of Property..495
University....495
tinople Letter....496
s Jubilee Endowment 497
Letter.... 497
berly Educational Conference..498

RCLE:
r (poem)....506
pel Message to Childhood and
of Presenting it....506

NEOUS:
Religious Thought....487
dget....488
l Mention....490
igious World.... 493
ad News....499
istic....501
ymposium....502
Report of the Foreign Chris-
Missionary Society....504
day-school....509
lby....510
re....510
es and Obituaries....511
Experience....512
rs' Notes....512

ubscription $1.75.

A. McLEAN,
SECRETARY FOREIGN CHRISTIAN MISSIONARY SOCIETY.

PUBLISHED BY
CHRISTIAN PUBLISHING COMPANY
1522 Locust St., St. Louis.

THE

CHRISTIAN - EVANGELIST

J. H. GARRISON, Editor.

W. W. HOPKINS, Assistant.

B. B. TYLER, J. J. HALEY,

EDITORIAL CONTRIBUTORS.

What We Plead For.

The Christian-Evangelist pleads for:

The Christianity of the New Testament, taught by Christ and his Apostles, versus the theology of the creeds taught by fallible men—the world's great need.

The divine confession of faith on which Christ built his church, versus human confessions of faith on which men have split the church.

The unity of Christ's disciples, for which he so fervently prayed, versus the divisions in Christ's body, which his apostles strongly condemned.

The abandonment of sectarian names and practices, based on human authority, for the common family name and the common faith, based on divine authority, versus the abandonment of scriptural names and usages for partisan ends.

The hearty co-operation of Christians in efforts of world-wide beneficence and evangelization, versus petty jealousies and strifes in the struggle for denominational pre-eminence.

The fidelity to truth which secures the approval of God, versus conformity to custom to gain the favor of men.

The protection of the home and the destruction of the saloon, versus the protection of the saloon and the destruction of the home.

For the right against the wrong;
For the weak against the strong;
For the poor who've waited long
For the brighter age to be.
For the truth, 'gainst superstition,
For the faith, against tradition,
For the hope, whose glad fruition
Our waiting eyes shall see.

RATES OF SUBSCRIPTION.

Single subscriptions, new or old	$1.75	each
In clubs of five or more, new or old.	1.50	"
Reading Rooms	1.25	"
Ministers	1.00	"

With a club of ten we will send one additional copy free.

All subscriptions payable in advance. Label shows the month up to the first day of which your subscription is paid. If an earlier date than the present is shown, you are in arrears. No paper discontinued without express orders to that effect. Arrears should be paid when discontinuance is ordered.

In ordering a change of post office, please give the OLD as well as the NEW address.

Do not send local check, but use Post office or Express Money Order, or draft on St. Louis, Chicago or New York, in remitting.

THE CHRISTIAN-EVANGELIST

"In faith, Unity; in opinion and methods, Liberty; in all things, Charity."

Vol. xxxv. St. Louis, Mo., Thursday, October 20, 1898. No. 42

CURRENT EVENTS.

The event which is at this time most vividly present in the national consciousness is President McKinley's triumphal progress through the central states, en route to the Omaha Exposition and return. The tour has been one unbroken ovation—a general peace jubilee. The cheers which have everywhere greeted the appearance of the President have not been in any considerable degree cheers for the currency doctrine for which he stands or for the protective tariff. But, besides being tokens of his personal popularity, they have been expressions of approval of the way in which he has preserved our national honor in the late war, and in a more or less general way, approval of his conception of the duties which grow out of our victory. The President's visit to the Omaha Exposition was an exceptional opportunity for an ovation and the most was made of it. His sojourn of a day in St. Louis was a return to the place where he received the presidential nomination and where he was certain to meet with a reception marked by no ordinary degree of enthusaism. The climax is expected to be in Chicago where he will participate in the peace jubilee which is to be celebrated in that city during the present week. Evidently war is not the normal condition of this nation. We enter upon it reluctantly, acquit ourselves in it honorably, and great is our rejoicing when it is over. We have two causes for thanksgiving: victory and peace.

Since the days of the Homestead strike and riot there has not been a more threatening situation of that class than the one which developed among the coal-miners at Virden, Ill. The strike among the employees of the Chicago-Virden Company has been in progress for some time, but the acute s age was not reached until the company attempted, to make good its threat to supply the places of the strikers by negroes imported from the Southern states. The strikers, being forewarned of this attempt made armed resistance to the landing of the negroes from the train. The company, being likewise forewarned of the probability of armed resistance, placed upon the special train which brought the negroes a force of forty or fifty of Pinkerton's men armed with Winchesters. The result of the attempt to disembark the men at Virden was a pitched battle between the strikers and the guards, resulting in fourteen deaths and the injury of thirty or forty more. The strikers carried the day and the train drew out as soon as it could, carrying the imported laborers on to Springfield. The militia of the state have been called out to restore order and they have done so by co-operating with the striking miners in preventing the landing of the imported laborers. The situation is at present peaceful but still critical, for the operators of the mines announce their determination to bring in negro miners at all hazards and the troops are at hand with orders to prevent the landing of any that may arrive.

The peculiar and noteworthy feature of this case is the attitude assumed by the Governor of Illinois, who tacitly justifies the action of the strikers in taking up arms to prevent the filling of their places by imported laborers, but charges the officials of the Chicago-Virden Company with murder in employing armed men, most of whom were not citizens of Illinois, to protect their imported laborers, who were also not citizens of Illinois. The point with him seems to be that the imported negroes are a lower and cheaper grade of labor than the average in Illinois and are altogether an undesirable class of citizens. So long as he is governor, he says, he will not permit the importation of cheap contract labor from other states into Illinois, and accordingly he is now employing the militia of the state to prevent the landing of the negroes. Gov. Tanner is forced to admit that there is no law on the statute-books of his or any state prohibiting the migration of labor under contract from one state to another, and that consequently he is employing the armed force of the state to execute a law which does not exist. In explaining his measures in opposition to "the pernicious system of importing labor," Gov. Tanner says: "Perhaps in placing an embargo upon imported labor I am a little in advance of statutory enactment. However, sometimes in the interest of society it becomes necessary to enforce a law in advance of its statutory enactment." This, in our humble opinion, is a most extraordinary doctrine and a dangerously liberal interpretation of the function of the state executive. We are not prepared to give an opinion as to the merits of the original controversy between the miners and the operators. Probably the miners had good reason to strike and are deserving of our sympathy. Two facts, nevertheless, remain. First, that the action of both sides in taking up arms and turning the dispute into a battle was equally criminal. Second, that in calling out the militia to prevent the importation of contract labor solely on the ground that it is in his judgment a "pernicious system," Governor Tanner is invading the legal rights of the Chicago-Virden Company and is laying up for himself all kinds of trouble.

It is by no means assured that the trouble with the Chippewa Indians in Minnesota is satisfactorily settled or that it will be settled without more fighting. The offenders, whom the deputy marshal was trying to arrest, have not all been surrendered. The tribe is assembled and is in council, and the authorities are giving them a reasonable amount of time to consider the consequences of continued opposition, but it is hard to tell whether they are seriously deliberating about the surrender of their erring brethren or getting on their war-paint. General Bacon is prepared for the latter contingency and if the Indians are obdurate there will be bloodshed in the reservation.

One of the bills to come before the next session of the present Congress, we are informed, will be one authorizing the government to issue Post Cheques for fractional currency uses. One of the strong reasons for the issue of these cheques is for the convenience of all persons who have occasion to send small amounts by mail to other parties. The inconvenience of the present method of sending small amounts, whether by express, draft or registered letter, is familiar to all, to say nothing of the disproportionate cost of the same. C. W. Post, of the Postum Cereal Co., Lim., at Battle Creek, Mich., has placed before a few well-known merchants, and also before Secretary of the Treasury Gage, a form of postal domestic currency that is the best solution of the problem yet offered. The demand is for currency in general circulation that can be instantly made safe for transmission by mail, and free from the present annoyances. The Post Cheque is no more nor less than fractional currency in everyday circulation, while the spaces on the face are left blank. They are intended to replace the silver coin, either partially or wholly. When the individual desires to send a small amount of money through the mail, he takes from his pocketbook perhaps a fifty-cent piece and a one-dollar piece, without more ado fills in the name of the firm or person to whom he desires the money paid, gives also the name of the city and state, then affixes a two-cent postage stamp in the square indicated, and thereupon signs his name in ink, the signature traversing and canceling the stamp. By this act pieces of money that up to that moment have been negotiable and have passed from hand to hand are instantly transferred into pieces of exchange, payable only to the payee named, and the toll or fee must be paid by the sender and canceled by his signature. It is then ready for enclosure in a letter, and cannot be made use of by any dishonest postal clerk or other person than the one named as payee. This plan would also dispense with the need of money order clerks and the red tape attendant upon the present clumsy methods.

It is proposed to issue the Post Cheque in five, ten, twenty-five and fifty cent pieces, also in one, two and five-dollar notes, their faces printed in suitable form to allow of proper entries in ink by the sender, and their backs in suitable treasury note form. The faces will indicate in large figures the denomination of the note. The Post Cheques are to be redeemable at any post-office. The postmaster pays out new Post Cheques when he redeems the old ones, and this method serves an excellent purpose in keeping the notes fresh and comparatively clean, as is the case with Bank of England notes. As long as unsigned the cheques pass as ordinary currency. Just what Congress may think of such a bill, or how they would secure such currency, we are not informed, but it looks feasible, and we are sure would be a greatly appreciated convenience.

The condition of affairs in the Far East is as much of an enigma as ever. Even yet it cannot be said with certainty whether the emperor is dead or alive, but only that the empress is at the head of affairs and that the condition at Peking is critical. Foreigners resident in Peking have been subjected to indignities which have rendered it necessary for both Russia and Great Britain to introduce small bands of marines into the city. The crisis may result in a joint occupation of Peking by the powers. The Europeanization of the Orient is the end toward which all events point, but by such outbreaks as this China is only bringing upon herself more speedily the inevitable end. Little by little, European nations have been allowed to acquire interests in China and these interests, involving the lives and property of their subjects as well as the prestige of their governments, the powers must protect. In recognition of our interests in China and our right to protect them, Secretary Long has ordered two American warships, the Petrel and the Baltimore of the Philippine squadron, to proceed to Chinese waters and approach as near as possible to Pekin. The river upon which the city is situated is not navigable for boats of this size as far up as the capital, but our two warships will proceed to the lower waters of the river and be ready for any emergency. This movement is unanimously approved by the British press since it gives hope of Anglo-American co-operation in settling the Chinese question. Our interests in the East are identical with those of Great Britain and if we are drawn into the fray it would be scarcely possible to avoid an alliance with her even if we wanted to. With our military and naval forces in the Philippines, which could be available on short notice if necessary, the United States is now almost if not quite the strongest Western power in the Orient.

The net gain of the Presbyterian Church last year, the Herald and Presbyter says, was 14,966. One-third of this gain was in Pennsylvania. In New York there was a loss of 1,370. The Herald and Presbyter is by no means pleased with this report. It had expected this year's additions to raise their membership to a million in the United States, but it is still short of that number by 25,000.

A SAMPLE OF CONSTRUCTIVE TEACHING.

In an article last week we commented upon the statement of Jesus, that He came to fulfill the law and not to destroy it as indicative, not only of His own method, but of the method that must be observed by all who would advance the cause of religion on earth. It may be well to give an illustration from the New Testament of how this principle was carried out by the inspired writers. Perhaps there is no better example of this than the letter to the Hebrews.

We do not know who the author of the Hebrew letter is. The view that it was written by Paul is very generally abandoned now by biblical scholars. Some ascribe it to Barnabas, but more perhaps to Apollos, the eloquent Alexandrian. But whoever the author was his method was constructive, not destructive. He saw Judaism and Christianity coming in contact with each other and contesting the ground for supremacy. His purpose seems to have been to show that Christianity is not something opposed to the Jews, but that it was a fulfillment of principles, truths and worship, which are found in germ in the law which the Jews revered.

God did, indeed, speak in times past unto the fathers in the prophets, he says, and you Hebrews are right in claiming that your religion was divinely given; but it is also true that He has spoken again unto us in these days in His Son, and this message through His Son is more important than the former one, by so much as the Messenger Himself being none other than the express image of the Father and the very effulgence of His glory is superior, not only to the prophets, but even to the angels through whom the law was said to be given on Mt. Sinai. For this reason "we ought to give the more earnest heed to the things we have heard" from Christ and His apostles. For if disobedience to the law spoken through angels received its proper punishment, what possibility of escape is there for those who neglect "so great a salvation" as that which has been made known to us through the message of Christ, and has been confirmed to us by the testimony of His apostles? Notwithstanding the divine majesty and glory of the Son of God, it was necessary that He should become a partaker of flesh and blood, in order that He might be like His brethren, and enter into full sympathy with them in all their temptations and trials.

Now as to Moses, he was, indeed, "faithful in all his house as a servant." He was the great and good man which you believe him to have been; but Christ comes, not as a servant, but "as a Son over His own house." Some of your fathers would not believe Moses nor accept his leadership, and they perished in the wilderness. You would do well to take heed lest you also should fail through unbelief in Christ.

Aaron was a high priest, called of God, and filled his position as well as any mere human being could, but our real and perpetual High Priest is Jesus Christ, who is a priest, not like Aaron, not after the manner of the Levitical priesthood, but a priest after another order—that of Melchizedec This High Priest does not need to make an offering for His own sins, for He is sinless, but He made an offering once for all, of His own blood, through which we are cleansed from our sins, and they are remembered against us no more forever.

And so the writer goes on with his ar
ment, pointing out that the "ordinance
of divine service," which were under
first covenant, find a completer fulfilln
in Christ and His worship, and that
law contained only "a shadow of the g
things to come." Then follows the ro
the heroes of faith, who are all recogn
and honored; but after all God had "
vided some better things concerning
which is made known in the gospel.
same faith which enables these men of
to achieve their triumphs under the
should lead us now to "look unto Je
who is the Author and Perfecter of
faith," and through whom we have
ceived "a kingdom that cannot be shak

How well this line of argument is ca
lated to favorably influence those who
inclined to be held in the bonds of Juda
and to lead them on to something hig
and better than the law could furn
How much wiser this course was tha
the writer had made war on the Jewish
ligion, indescriminately pointing out
defects, but failing to recognize the t
there was in it! By recognizing all
was true, and divine, and praisewo
under the law he opened the heart
those Hebrews to receive his message
cerning the "better things" of the
covenant given through Jesus Christ.

This is the divine method. It mus
recognized in our work in pagan la
where our missionaries come in con
with pagan systems of religion, and in
land, where we are seeking to present
to illustrate the New Testament typ
Christianity as against the more or
perverted forms in which it has come d
to us. We have not always been loyal to
method, and to the extent that we have
the cause of truth has suffered at our ha
To seek to do Christ's work, in Chr
method and spirit, is the sure road to
cess.

DEFEAT OF THE PEOPLE.

Dr. Amory Bradford, in a sermon de
ered last year during jubilee week in Pl
outh Church, Brooklyn, and publishe
The New Puritanism, calls attention
some of the evil tendencies that thre
the future of the American Repu
Among the characteristics that imperil
New Democracy he enumerates a w
spread and growing tendency toward
effacement of the feeling of individua
sponsibility to God; a misconception
what is meant by intellectual and spiri
freedom; a dimming of the lines w
separate virtue and vice, right and wro
and, most painful of all, we are living
republic compelled to witness the defe
the people. This, in Mr. Bradford's o
ion, is the most ominous and perilous
in American history. The fundame
principle in modern civilization is
right of the people to rule, but the pe
in this country, we are told, do not r
Two illustrations are given to show that
fundamental principles of democracy
being systematically overthrown in
land of the free and the home of the br

"In a small town the question is ma
one of the granting of a franchise t
trolly company. The people say: 'Rest
and safeguard, and let it come;' but out
monopolies, thinking only of divide
either buy up a council, or procure spe

egislation and drive through their own chemes without the slightest regard to the rishes of those who own the property, rhose homes are invaded, and whose life-urposes are ruined. Thus the people are efeated."

The other instance is the defeat in the Jnited States Senate of the arbitration reaty between this country and Great Britain. "Two great nations, after glaring t each other for more than a century, conlude that they have shaken fists long nough, and that they had better clasp ands and prove themselves the brothers hat they are in blood and language, in istory, in religion; and the people in both ations lift such a cry of gladness as has ot been heard for a quarter of a century. This is the people's business, and they have right to be heeded. But no; the mahinery of government is straightway inoked that prejudice may rule, and the eople be humiliated and disgraced. Thus overnment of the people, for the people, nd by the people has failed almost before he echoes of Lincoln's oration have died way. Most of our cities are ruled by corupt oligarchies; most of our states are in he hands of selfish politicians; and interational problems, instead of being solved y representatives of the people, are helved by those who misrepresent them."

These illustrations of the defeat of the eople under a so-called democracy might, rith little trouble, have been indefinitely nultiplied. "Satan's Invisible World Dislayed," in Tammany politics, in the meropolis of the United States, the rottenest ivic government this side of perdition, rould have been a fruitful instance for the onsideration of the preacher. For years, nmolested, Tammany and his harpies, fed t the public crib, and laid under tribute aloons, brothels, gamblidg hells, and all he doings of darkness, to line the pockets f its rogues, preserving institutions of evil was sworn to suppress, for self-revenue nly. At last a reaction came and the peole in their wrath smote the thieving Boss, nd turned the money-changing rascals out f the municipal temple, and New York, ke the swine-herding prodigal, to all apearances, had come to itself. But how ong did the people's will prevail? Till the ext election. The boodle-ringing Boss nd his horde of civic thieves were on the lert, as the minions of Satan always are. The corrupt oligarchy is again in the sadle, and the people are unhorsed. No inonsiderable majority of the voting poputation of the metropolis registered themelves against the reinstatement of Tamiany rule, but the Boss went in all the ame, and the people are powerless to help hemselves. A more undemocratic proeeding that the civic administration of New York has never been known in the istory of mankind. The people do not, nd it seems cannot, rule in their own afairs in this great city. The democratic xperiment, the rule of the people, is a ailure, if New York City is to be accepted s the criterion of judgment.

The American people do not believe in nonopolies to enrich the few at the expense f the many, to the impoverishment of not few, but they are seemingly powerless o prevent it. Equalization of the burden f taxation so that the expenses of govrnment shall be equitably borne by inividual citizens in proportion to their wealth, is a fundamental doctrine of modern civilization, believed in by every loyal American, and yet the fact is well known that a millionaire in the United States pays less taxes than a man worth fifty or a hundred thousand dollars. The Almighty Dollar and the corrupt political Boss have the American people by the throat. To this combination the liquor power ought to be added. Nothing does more to defeat the people, and to hand over their interests to Satan and Boss rule, than the saloon. Last year a petition was circulated asking for a local option vote in the county in which this is written. The saloon element got wind of what was being done, sent round a counter petition in the town, asking for an election in the town precinct, to forestall the county election, which would entrench the saloon for three years. The judge of the county court decided in favor of the saloon petition for the minority of the saloonists against the majority of the people, ordered the election in the town, where it was known the liquor interest would carry against the majority in the county, where in all probability it would have been defeated. We ask in vain the privilege, in this county, of voting on the question of whether we will have the retail liquor traffic or not, because the saloon does not want us to. This is a specimen of American democracy under the rule of the saloon. An adjoining county carried on local option two years ago by a majority of over 500; it was thrown out by the courts on a technicality. Last year the question was again submitted to a vote and the saloon was knocked out by over 700 majority, and the saloon is running as though nothing had happened! We tried last year to get a fair and reasonable measure to both sides, through the state legislature, so that a county as a whole could vote on the question of local option, so that the individual precincts could not remain wet or dry because they happened to vote that way, against the majority in the county. This was democratic and fair, and put the power in the hands of the people. But it did not suit the saloon and whisky-soaked county towns, and again, and quite as a matter of course, it was defeated. There is no democracy and no rule of the people as long as the saloon is permitted to exist. With corrupt politics, the saloon, and the subordination of government to selfish ends, the downfall of democracy and the defeat of the people is permanently assured.

J. J. H.

FULFILLING THE MINISTRY OF CHRIST.*

II. *What is it to "fulfill" the ministry of Christ in this age?*

Archippus was exhorted to give heed to the ministry which he had received in the Lord to the end that he might "fulfill" it. No man can fulfill his ministry, as a preacher of the gospel, except he have some worthy and adequate conception of what that ministry should be. It is to be feared that many take upon themselves the work of the Christian ministry without an adequate idea of its scope, of its responsibility and of its vast importance to the well-being of the race. One of the secrets of Paul's greatness, as a preacher, was the high conception which he had of his calling. What is it to worthily fulfill such a ministry as that of the gospel of Jesus Christ?

1. It is first of all, is it not, to have a clear grasp of the fundamental truths of the gospel, an adequate appreciation of their supreme value, and then to preach them with all the earnestness and power one can command. The gospel has a definite message. It consists of facts of tremendous importance, of truths most vital to human welfare, of commands and promises that have to do with the present and eternal interests of men. The preacher whose mind does not seize these sublime facts and truths, whose divine power and energy have been tested in his own life, and deliver them to men with a moral earnestness born out of his own experience of their supreme value, cannot fulfill the ministry of Jesus Christ. To philosophize, to speculate, to expatiate upon the sublimities and beauties of nature is not to preach the gospel which is "the power of God unto salvation to every one that believeth."

2. No preacher can fulfill his ministry who relies wholly upon preaching to his congregation from the pulpit. He must see them in their homes, in their offices and in their shops. The great preacher whose advice we are studying said to a church with which he had labored in the gospel, "Ye yourselves know from the first day that I set foot in Asia, after what manner I was with you all the time, serving the Lord in all lowliness of mind, and with tears, and with trials which befell me by the plots of the Jews: how that I shrank not from declaring unto you anything that was profitable, and teaching you publicly, and from house to house, testifying both to Jews and Greeks repentance toward God and faith toward our Lord Jesus Christ." It was this sort of ministry that enabled him to say to the elders of this same church, "Wherefore, I testify unto this day that I am pure from the blood of all men." No minister to-day can dispense with hand-to-hand and house-to-house work if he would have his ministry crowned with success.

3. The man of God who would fulfill his ministry must know the age in which he lives. He cannot live in the seventeenth or eighteenth century and serve the present generation. He must know the thought of his times. He must be acquainted with the problems of the age. He must seek to apply the old gospel to the new conditions of his own age and country. He must not only know the Scriptures, he must know the people among whom he labors, if he is to greatly benefit them. He must know how to apply the gospel to the daily needs of men; otherwise, the people will turn away from him to find something which is of some practical interest to them.

4. A preacher who would fulfill his ministry must keep his mind and heart open to all the new light that shines from every source to illuminate God's Word and God's world. He cannot grow without this, and to cease to grow is to *die* as a preacher. No preacher can long maintain the confidence and respect of thoughtful people, when he gives evidence of having closed his mind to the truth, and in his blindness opposes the truth, because it is new, and because he has not taken pains to investigate its claims. The man who is the servant of any system of theology which

*The following article, written several weeks ago as the second one on Paul's admonition to Archippus was crowded out, and has been patiently waiting for a place until now.—EDITOR.

men have made, and who feels it to be his duty as a preacher to maintain and defend such a system of theology cannot fulfill the ministry of Christ to-day. He must be a free man in Christ Jesus. He must know no master but Christ, and must seek to follow him whithersoever he leadeth.

5. *Finally*. He must enter into fellowship with Christ—fellowship with his great plans and purposes, fellowship with his sufferings and his joys—in order to minister to the manifold needs of our poor sinning and suffering humanity. He must know Christ and seek to convey his tender message of sympathy and love to sinning, sorrwinig and suffering men and women. He must hold up before the world the perfect ideal and model in Jesus Christ, and urge men toward the attainments of this ideal.

By so doing those who are ministers of Christ's gospel may hope in some measure to fulfill their ministry, and at last to receive from the hand of our Lord the crown of everlasting rejoicing.

Hour of Prayer.

THE SYMPATHIZING FRIEND.

(Midweek Prayer-meeting Topic, Oct. 26, 1898.)

Jesus wept. The Jews, therefore, said: Behold how he loved him!—*John* 11:35, 36.

Few stories are more familiar than that associated with the beloved family at Bethany, consisting of Lazarus and his two sisters, Martha and Mary, where Jesus used to visit so often. By some spiritual quality in their nature they were able more than most others to apprehend the real character of Jesus, and to love him with a tenderness seldom manifested toward him in his earthly ministry. In his absence on one of his preaching tours, Lazarus sickened and died. Jesus had been sent for, but did not arrive until four days after the death of his friend. The weeping sisters poured into his ear their sorrow and grief. The Man of Sorrows was touched by their tears, and he wept with them.

"Jesus wept." Precious words! They bring this noblest and highest born of all the sons of men, this King of humanity, into the fellowship of the great company of the sorrowing and suffering ones of earth. We feel, instinctively, that he is brother-man with us. Those tears are evidence that he has a heart that can be touched with human sorrow. He made the sorrow of these orphan sisters his sorrows, and mingled his tears with theirs. He is the same "yesterday, to-day and forever."

Where, in all the annals of history, can we find a friend who is at once so strong and yet so tender; so omnipotent in his power to help, so sympathetic in his regard for others? Truly may we sing—

"What a friend we have in Jesus,
All our sins and griefs to bear!"

The strange thing is that so many of us have not appreciated nor cultivated the friendship of Jesus. We have had worldly friends who have deceived us, and we have had friends in prosperity who have deserted us in the hours of adversity. We have also had true friends who have done what they could for us, but who could not meet the deepest need of our soul. But here is a Friend "who sticketh closer than a brother." He is a friend in adversity as well as in prosperity. He is a friend who can minister as none but he can, to the hunger of the heart.

There are friends, so called, whom we do not care to have with us when the shadow of death comes into our homes. Somehow we feel that they cannot help us. There are other friends whom, when sorrow overtakes us, we like to have visit us. Jesus was such a friend. "If thou hadst been here," the sisters at Bethany exclaimed, "our brother had not died." Who of us does not want Jesus to come into our home when death has invaded it, and when we—

"Sigh for the touch of a vanished hand,
And the sound of a voice that is still?"

He is pre-eminently the Comforter in the presence of death; but he is also the Helper in every temptation and in every trial.

Let those of us who have never made the acquaintance of Christ seek his friendship; and let those of us who have been his disciples cultivate his friendship more than we have ever done, and seek to be more worthy of it. "Ye are my friends," said the Master, "if ye do whatsoever I command you." Jesus is our friend. Are we the friends of Jesus according to his own test? "Behold how he loved him!" Does he not also love us? Let Gethsemane and Golgotha answer.

PRAYER.

O, Thou Lord of Life, who did taste the bitterness of death for our sakes, and who by all Thine acts of self-denial and condescension and tender love hast shown Thyself the truest friend of humanity, accept the homage of our hearts for all the marks of Thy friendship to us. Help us, we beseech Thee, to manifest our friendship for Thee, by doing those things which Thou hast commanded us to do, and by manifesting that spirit which Thou didst manifest when Thou wert here in the world. May we be tender and true and sympathetic to those in trouble, as Thou wert, that we may alleviate the sorrows and sufferings of our fellowmen. Do Thou go with us, dear Master, and be our sympathizing friend in all the sorrows and struggles of life, and bring us at last to be with Thee to share in Thy glory and Thy friendship forevermore. Amen!

INSTITUTE WORK AMONG THE CHURCHES.

F. N. Calvin, of Waco, Tex., who is to close his work in that city Dec. 1st, writes concerning a matter in which we feel the churches are generally interested. We take the liberty of copying the following extract from his letter:

I have thought of going into the general field to hold revival services in the churches. What I mean is, to try as a *special work* to revive the churches rather than to baptize people. I believe that if the churches will do their duty, and conduct their work so as to maintain the respect and attention of the community, sinners will gladly come to be baptized. I have made a special study of pastoral work for over twenty years, and I believe I understad it pretty well. If I should do that work I would go to a place and take up such subjects as Church Organization, Church Officers, Church Finances, The Pastor and the Church, Church Buildings, Church Committees, The Institutional Idea as Applicable to our Churches in Towns and Smaller Cities, etc. In short, I would hope to cover in two or three weeks as much as possible of the ground of the church as a business and spiritual institution. My work would be specially to help the pastor and workers to carry on a larger and more aggressive work after I get through. I am the pastor's friend. I know the little annoyances which often retard his work and dampen his ardor. I woul hope during my stay to get as many of thes out of the way as possible. I could settle difficulties among the brethren, help to rais church debts, show them about special committee work, where such instruction is needed, etc.

Then, in addition, I would preach one regula sermon each day. In some places I could hol my special work during the day, and preach a night. In others I could give the first week t my Institute work, and follow that up with week or two of straight preaching.

We do not hesitate to say that there is nee for the very kind of work which is here described, and we believe, too, there will b a demand for it as soon as its usefulnes can be demonstrated in a few such meetings. We hope that Bro. Calvin will b encouraged to undertake this kind of wor among the churches.

Editor's Easy Chair.

We often receive letters from men, an women, too, breathing a spirit of moral heroism that shows that the same fait which made heroes and martyrs in the pas is present yet in the church. Here lie before us a letter from Bro. A. H. Seymour, of Arlington, S. D., which, after expressing his appreciation of "Macataw Musings" and the CHRISTIAN-EVANGELIS in general, adds:

"I cannot go to Chattanooga. I hav had no vacation, except a long, sad, lonel trip back to Northern Ohio to lay the bod of my beloved wife in the soil of her nativ county. Day after day, and week afte week brings hard work and perplexity and heartache. I had been growing almost jealous of the brethren who can go on a vacation trip or attend some summer school to gain some new inspiration, but one day I began to count my blessings, not the least of which is the privilege of reading the interesting and inspiring accounts of others' vacations. There was a bit of help in your last Musings when you said you had not done all the reading, etc., you had planned to do. I had come to think no one but myself fell short there."

It would tend to prevent jealousy of others very much if we would do as Bro. S. has done—stop to count our own mercies—and, in addition to that, if we could only remember that others have their burdens and sorrows that we know not of, just as others know not of ours. The main thing in this life is not the pleasure we get out of it, but the good that we can do to others and the advancement we can make.

"Not enjoyment and not sorrow
Is our destined end and way;
But to live that each to-morrow
Finds us farther than to-day."

Has this age turned itself against gray hairs? Not in law, not in medicine, not in statesmanship, not in any of the higher callings of life, so far as we know, except in the ministry. But one would think that above all other places the ministry would have especial need for the experience and maturity which come with gray hairs; and yet the testimony seems to be that in all religious bodies gray haired preachers are at a discount. Bishop Merrill says: "The embarrassment in all our Conferences is what to do with the old men." Dr. Jackson, Presiding Elder, Rock River Conference, says: "It has come to pass in this as in other Conferences that when a man's

ırn gray people ceasé to
ʼs anything." Another
states that he has diffi-
ıreachers over forty years
of a few men among us
nisfortune to turn prema-
ʼho, in the zenith of their
ficult, and in some cases
ıre employment that will
ıood. There lies before
one of our ministers, of
cter, who is several years
editor of this paper—
half-century mark—who
airs—being permaturely
o his employment by the
vould seem to be ridicu-
ot pathetic. A man can
ed to have reached the
ıwers at the age at which
l on the shelf.

of course, in every case.
nen so full of vigor, vim
gray hairs do not count.
cases where men cease
they fail to keep their
fertilized with the new
of the times, and they
so much because they
as because they do not
the gray matter of their
does not wholly account
ɔn on the part of church-
with gray hairs. There
n unreasonable prejudice
t class. We believe it to
ymptom, the cause and
should be studied. We
the young men who are
work, but surely we
dispense with the richer
maturer wisdom of men
l beyond. Many of our
ering to-day for lack of
aching and pastoral care
y preachers could furnish
me the churches should
uestion of age in connec-
achers?

no plea for the incom-
will not toil with their
their hearts fresh and
g in touch with the best
in which they live, and
ıods of work, they must
he consequences. What
hat men who have lost
ɔetence and are able and
ıd plan and work for the
ɔt be laid on the shelf
they have gray hairs.
book which say: "The
rown of glory if it be
ɔf righteousness." Our
e influence of men of
ınd of experience and of
hem safely through the
d them. We say of our

Current Religious Thought

The Outlook of Oct. 8th has an editorial addressed "To the Clergy," which we believe the preachers of all religious bodies would do well to heed. Speaking of the temptation to turn aside from the real work of the pulpit to discuss the public issues of the day, it says:

Nevertheless, the community as well as the church is a loser when the preacher yields to this temptation, and ceases to be a preacher of righteousness and becomes an instructor in politics or sociology. For the latter function he has no special equipment. His library is not rich in political and sociological departments. He has no expert knowledge and no special information. He is as dependent as his congregation for the knowledge of the facts on the daily papers, and generally also for his understanding of principles. He is either much more or much less than the average man if he is not subject to partisan prejudices, is not a Republican, a Democrat, a Populist or a Prohibitionist. It is not safe for him to assume that he is superior to those prejudices which are common to humanity; and if he is unprejudiced because he is indifferent, he is unfit to be a teacher. The fact that the press will report his political sermon and no other is rather a reason against preaching it than the reverse. For the kingdom of God cometh not with observation; and he who preaches for the newspapers rarely preaches with real effectiveness to his own congregation.

On the other hand, if he turns aside from his specific function of illuminating and inspiring the individual life, there is no one else in the community to take up his work. And his work is by far more important than that which beckons him away from it. It is far more important that the individuals in the community should be inspired by habits of self-control than that the state should have any particular form of legislature on its statute-books; that the citizens of all parties should be educated to abhor that which is evil than that political power should be transferred from one party to another; that Americans should govern themselves with honor in their individual lives than that they should assume the government of a new and distant people. For the solution of all political and sociological problems depends on this spiritual illumination and inspiration of the individual. Without it there will be the grossest licentiousness and self-indulgence in spite of laws on the statute-books; political reforms will only transfer the state from one set of robbers to another, and the expansion of America will be the expansion of selfish and corrupt misrule. Reforms which are simply changes of form are of very little value. The state may become Democratic in form, but if the love of despotic control is left dominant in the few and the love of political ease is left dominant in the many, the despot will reappear with the change of mask, and the old bureaucracy will be reconstituted with a new nomenclature. Feudalism may be abolished, and freedom of control established. But if the individuals who constitute society are still actuated by the principle of "Get all you can and keep all you get," industrial servitude will reappear under competition, and the victory once won for freedom will have to be won again by a new battle around a new strategic center.

The article gives some further good reasons why the minister should keep close to his high calling, as follows:

During the summer new and exciting political issues have arisen. Preacher and people are both interested in them. What more natural than that the minister should make his pulpit instructions bear directly upon these public themes? But we are convinced, and we should like to convince our clerical readers, that they should do so very rarely, if at all. This is not at all because the congregations are divided in sentiment on these questions, nor chiefly be-[illegible] reform, law enforcement, sociological discussion and educational progress, misses the opportunity which the peculiar privilege of the pulpit gives to the preacher. This is an opportunity to add to the sum of life rather than to direct life into any particular channel. To interpret to men their own restlessness, their half-conscious sense of need; to pierce the armor of their self-conceit and awaken in them a divine discontent where it does not already exist; to set before them in the life of Jesus Christ a type of human excellence, and so inspire in them an ambition to be better than they are; to arouse in them a spirit of loyalty to him, obedience to which is the sum of human duty; to recover them from that dull despair whose end is death, by showing them in the free gift of God a power to do all and be all that the highest aspiration sets before them; to put into their exhausted lives a new heart of hope and love—this is the function of the ministry.

The reports at the recent conference of the International Committee of Y. M. C. A. indicate a prosperous year in their work. Ten Y. M. C. A. secretaries are now employed on students' work, having nearly 600 associations under their supervision. The Railroad Department has increased its force to six secretaries. The railroad corporations during the past year have given $150,000 to this work among their men. The Y. M. C. A. sustains a colored and an Indian secretary. There are now nearly 50 Indian associations. In the Educational Department good progress has been made. The committee now supports 12 secretaries in Foreign Mission lands, where considerable progress has also been made. It is said that thousands of young men in missionary lands devote the first half hour of each morning to prayer and Bible study, and many have volunteered for missionary work among their own people. In no previous year has this work been so helpful and received the support of missionaries as during the past year.

The Student Volunteer Movement is in organic relation with this committee. It has now over 3,000 students pledged to go as missionaries, as the denominational boards find opportunity to use them. Twelve hundred missionaries have already gone to the foreign field as a result of these efforts. The committee is also closely allied with the student movements in Great Britain and the Continent, through which some 1,600 students have volunteered for missionary work, nearly half of whom are now on the field. One of its secretaries is the secretary of this Worldwide Student Movement.

The latest and most interesting feature of the work of the committee is that of its Army and Navy Christian Commission, which was organized immediately after the declaration of war. It had at one time some seventy tents with one hundred and fifty secretaries in charge, located in all the camps in this country, Porto Rico, Cuba and the Philippine Islands. Each tent is a Young Men's Christian Association for soldiers. This work has added very materially to the comfort of our soldiers and

Our Budget.

—Some men know too much to be useful.

—Some men know too little to be called men.

—The spiritual barometer is highest over Chattanooga, Tenn., this week.

—The cooler weather and white frosts of last week will stop the invasion of the yellow fever in the South.

—Now that church conventions and city festivities are over for a season the churches should settle down to an active, aggressive campaign against sin.

—It is not too late for Endeavor Societies that have not yet enlisted in the Bethany C. E. Reading Courses to do so, but the sooner the better now that the second year has begun.

—The last quarter of each year is probably the best season of the year for recruiting Bible-school classes and every teacher should improve the opportunity. Now is the time to increase the attendance.

—The usual article on Christian Endeavor topic by Bro. Jenkins failed to reach us this week. We mention this to explain its non-appearance in this paper.

—We have a report of the district convention held at Mondamin, Iowa, September 16-17 to which the writer's signature is not attached.

—Some men have ceased learning, hence are not growing. Their past knowledge is their working capital.

—We acknowledge the receipt of an excellent picture (11x14) of Commodore W. S. Schley, from Keeler and Kirkpatrick, Philadelphia, Pa.

—The 23rd day of October is Forefathers' Day this year. If that is not convenient, then take the earliest convenient date. The day is being widely planned; it gives promise of being the best Endeavor day of the year. It is going to be helpful in starting the new mission in Puerto Rico. Don't fail to observe it. Write to Benj. L. Smith, Y. M. C. A. Building, Cincinnati, O., for help on programs. Remit all money collected on Forefathers' Day to the same address.

—If a preacher would occasionally lead his audience in the worship of God instead of always entertaining them with a sermon the effect might be more satisfactory to the church and to the Lord.

—The Y. M. C. A. is doing a great and good work in their night-schools. Schools under the auspices of the association are now conducted in 350 cities in which 1,250 teachers are giving instruction to about 26,000 young men. These students, it is said, are on an average twenty-three years old, are employed in the day time and in the majority of places but for these facilities would be denied the educational opportunities they thus have and need. These schools supplementing as they do the work of public schools are rapidly increasing in popularity and efficiency. Through the system of standard courses maintained by international examinations, students in these schools can prepare for college without further examinations. Sixty leading colleges and universities now accept international certificates. Last year 750 certificates were won.

—Word has come to the rooms of the Foreign Society that Dr. Harry N. Biddle, of Africa, died last Saturday. He had fever a number of times. When he wrote last he was not well, but was improving rapidly. He was visiting with some friends. He wrote about their kindness and goodness. No particulars are at hand. It will be remembered that Dr. Biddle went out with E. E. Faris in March, 1897. They have been on the Congo for more than a year. In this time they have been trying to find a place and get consent to begin operations. They have found a number of places, but the officials are Catholic and try in every possible way to exclude Protestants from that part of the world. What they do is done diplomatically. They are courteous in their bearing toward the missionaries, but it is quite clear that they do not wish the pure gospel preached in that part of the country. Some one will have to be sent right way to take Dr. Biddle's place. A competent medical missionary ought to be started for the Congo within a few weeks at the farthest. It will not do to permit E. E. Faris to remain there alone.

—In the CHRISTIAN-EVANGELIST of Sept. 8th J. M. Lowe, of Winterset, Ia , in his "One in Christ," says, "That the burial of the body in water brings a man into *spiritual* relation with Christ is the acme of absurdity." I think not one claims the burial alone does this. However, Peter says, "Repent and be baptized every one of you in the name of Jesus Christ for the remission of sins and you shall receive the gift of the Holy Spirit." Sometimes in the argumentative spirit we over state ourselves. I think this point is unfortunately overstated in both directions at times. Bro. Lowe is a successful minister and an old colaborer.

Fraternally,

F. H. LEMON.

Lake City, Ia., Sept. 10, 1898.

—On last Friday this city was honored with a visit by the nation's Chief Magistrate and other high government officials, and gave to them a most cordial and royal welcome. Throughout the entire day the streets were thronged with people anxious for a sight of the President of the United States. The President is making some model speeches on his tour, which are loudly applauded wherever delivered. They are noteworthy for brevity, broad patriotism, grasp of facts, high moral tone and religious bearing, and will greatly increase his popularity as a broad-minded, impartial magistrate. Some of his allusions to industrial conditions may appear to be somewhat previous to some, but perhaps he speaks in the light of his anticipations for the immediate future. At all events, he has given satisfaction as a war President, and is not without the high appreciation of a united people.

—Of the closing years of the century and of the relative position of the United States in the world's procession of nations, Dr. Vance in a recent sermon at Nashville, Tenn., said:

The last years of the century are going out in a blaze of events as startling in their character as they must be widespread in their influence. The great Chinese Empire, after more than 3,000 years of national continuity, seems on the brink of dismemberment. Russia is forging across Siberia for the Eastern Sea and has reached her goal at Port Arthur. The last vestige of Spanish power has been swept from the Western Hemisphere, and her hold weakened, if not entirely broken, in the Pacific. Great Britain has conquered Khalifa and acquired the Soudan. English-speaking people have learned that they are friends, and must confederate for the world's good. The powers have at last spoken out, and ordered the Sultan to withdraw every Moslem soldier from Crete. The Czar of Russia has asked for a conference lookidg to the disarmament of nations, and the arranging of terms for universal peace. What does all this mean but that God is building here on the summit of the century a throne of unsurpassed privilege and unexampled power? It is a great time in which to live. It is a royal era for national greatness and opportunity. Whatever the outlook may be to the citizens of other countries, the vision which breaks upon American citizenship, as it looks backward and forward from the top of the century, is as fair a picture as the lavish hand of a generous God ever painted on the sky of a nation's hope.

—The Emperor and Empress of Germany are on their way to the Holy Land via Constantinople, and the trip is exciting much comment in various parts of the world. His own people have objected to this visit because of the unsettled state of international relations and the unnecessary exposure of his life at the hands of anarchists. The Roman Catholics are objecting because of the influence it will give to Protestantism in his own country and in the Holy Land. And some, we are told, are objecting because of the expense his by-the-way call at Constantinople will be to the Sultan of Turkey, while the superstitious are predicting evil results because of the fact that he is accompanied by the Empress. But, withal, the Emperor has a mind of his own and is pushing ahead according to program. What will come of the trip we shall see by and by, but at present we are inclined to think that his call at Constantinople will neutralize any influence that he can exert for Protestantism by going on to Jerusalem.

—One of the results of the work of the American Relief Committee in Armenia, in behalf of the Armenian orphans, will be the enlistment and education of many of them in a purer Christianity. The sympathies of many have already been enlisted by the interest of Protestant churches in America in their welfare, and their influence will hereafter be on the side of evangelical Christianity. Many of them will become missionaries among their own people. In an address by Geo. P. Knapp, of Barre, Mass., a former missionary, and secretary of the American Relief Committee on this subject, he says:

About 4,000 of these orphans, or something less than 10 per cent., have been rescued by foreign agencies. The greater part of them are under the care of our missionaries, and the funds for supporting half of them have gone from America. But while Europeans are extending their work, it is with difficulty that we are able to continue the support of those whom we have rescued. The Germans have recently taken 100 orphans from the city of Diarbekir, where there are 5,400 widows and orphans, 400 of the latter having neither father nor mother. They have just opened a fifth orphanage in Oorfa, making the total number of children, with those supported by us, less than 450 in a city where there are 12,000 widows and orphans. In Hajin our missionaries have rescued 140 orphans out of a district containing about 1,000, and rather than turn any of these children back into darkness and degradation, they are struggling for another year with an increasing debt of $1,500. When it costs on an average but $25 a year to support one of these orphans, when he gets a Christian education and learns a trade, is it not a great pity to place our missionaries under the burden of a debt for carrying on such promising work?

Here, then, is a great opportunity for doing good that should not be overlooked, but it requires money to do this work. This committee, therefore, again appeals to the liberality of a great nation of great churches for funds to carry forward this work. Money should be sent directly to Messrs. Brown Bros. & Co., 59 Wall St., New York City.

—The Register-Review thinks we erred in placing Wellington in the Southwestern part of Kansas. Well, perhaps we did; but when we visited that city fifteen years ago it seemed to us to be in that part of the state, and if it was not according to geography it was according to population.

Special Dispatch to the CHRISTIAN-EVANGELIST.

The Chattanooga Convention.

CHATTANOOGA, TENN., OCT. 17.

CHRISTIAN-EVANGELIST, St. Louis, Mo.:

The city of Chattanooga has been stormed, not by yellow jack, but by the gathering clans of our missionary hosts, to whom the city has surrendered. Over twelve hundred delegates have already arrived at this writing, and it is believed the number will reach fifteen hundred before the day closes. The weather has been all that could be desired—clear, cool and bracing. The Christian Woman's Board of Missions has closed a successful and harmonious convention. Total receipts for past year $78,-364,32, with a balance instead of a deficit. This amount is an increase over all previous years. Mrs. A. M. Atkinson presided in the absence of Mrs. Burgess, whose illness prevented her presence. Yesterday (Lord's day) was a glorious day. Pulpits of the city and suburbs were filled by our preachers, morning and evening, while a great audience, of about 2,500 people, joined in the communion service at the Auditorium in the afternoon. Both the Foreign and Home Boards have held their meetings, heard and approved of the reports of their secretaries, and the conventions follow this week. Both societies report decided gains. All things considered, this is one of the most remarkable annual gatherings in our history. The feeling of the convention is displayed in a canvas motto: "Jubilee Convention '99, Cincinnati, 10,000 delegates and a Million for Missions."

—For a full report of the American Christian Missionary Society's work for the year just closed send to B. L. Smith, Cor. Sec., Cincinnati, O., for a copy of the American Home Missionary for October. A copy of this report should be secured and read by every Disciple of Christ. It is the record of success and the prophecy of a grand work for the coming year. The Home Society is beginning to get under headway and will soon accomplish marvelous things.

—Announcement is made this week in the Christian Oracle of the reorganization of the Oracle Publishing Co., of Chicago, Ill., by which J. H. Garrison, of St. Louis, Mo.; W. F. Black, of Chicago, Ill.; W. S. Broadhurst, of Louisville, Ky., and A. O. Garrison, of San Francisco, Cal., were constituted a new board of directors. W. S. Broadhurst, who has purchased an interest in the Oracle Publishing Co., and who was elected business manager of the reorganized company, will soon remove his entire business from Louisville, Ky., to Chicago, but the company will retain a branch office at 163 and 165 Fourth Ave., Louisville, Ky. A. O. Garrison has become the managing editor of the Oracle, but no change in its appearance, make-up, or plans, will be announced until the close of the present year.

—The tendency of the times toward liberality in civil and religious laws and customs has received renewed and additional strength in the new marriage and divorce law recently passed by the General Conference of the Protestant Episcopal Church. The law proposed for adoption absolutely forbade the remarriage of any divorced person during the lifetime of the other party. But this law was rejected, and by a majority of one vote a law permitting the remarriage of the innocent party divorced for the cause of adultery and the innocent party of a cause arising before marriage was enacted in its stead. This measure is probably more in harmony with the teaching of Jesus on this subject, but there is danger at both ends of the line. The almost wide-open door to divorce and remarriage in many states is a sufficient warning to any religious body or community of the dangers of too great liberality. On the other hand the commitment of all regulations of marriage and divorce to ecclesiastical authorities would not be without its dangers. We do not believe, therefore, that the Protestant Episcopal Church has lowered its standard on this question by this act, while it has certainly better adjusted itself to the state and to enlightened public sentiment on this question. If the state would now come forward with a more stringent and uniform law on this question we would be doubly assured of a forward movement of our civilization and its general religious caste.

PERSONAL MENTION.

J. S. Hughes, of Chicago, will hear a limited number of engagements to hold protracted meetings, devoting the first week to the Revelation, which draws a hearing from all quarters by its newness, and then follow it up with a call for recruits.

J. L. Smith, of Algonac, Mich., will close his second year's work there Dec. 25th. He says that the church there has had a rapid growth at regular services during his ministry. He now desires another field, and churches in need of a pastor are requested to address him at Box 198, Algonac, Mich.

N. S. Haynes, of Chicago, will succeed J. G. Waggoner as minister of the gospel for the church at Eureka, Ill.

The Miami County Record has this to say of Bro. Fillmore's work, Peru, Ind.: "Last Sunday Rev. C. M. Fillmore began his sixth year as pastor of the Central Church in Peru. When he came here there was no organization of his people, and his first enrollment was 13 members. During the five years the number has amounted to 293. They have an excellent piece of property, as well located as any church in the city, and almost free from debt. The membership includes some of the most substantial people of the town."

W. H. Bagby, of Salt Lake City, Utah; N. M. Ragland, of Fayetteville, Ark.; S. M. Martin, from Dallas, Texas; J. B. Corwine, of New London, Mo.; G. A. Hoffmann, of Columbia, Mo.; Knox P. Taylor, of Bloomington, Ill., and Sumner T. Martin, of Mason City, Ia., are some of the preachers who, passing by way of St. Louis to Chattanooga, honored this office with a call. There were others whose names have escaped our memory at this moment, but whose presence was equally appreciated.

W. A. Meloan has closed his work for the church at Blandinsville, Ill., and announces his desire to hold protracted meetings for a season. Write him as above.

R. B. Havener has resigned his work for the church at Rolla, Mo., to take effect Nov. 1st. After that date his address will be Windsor, Mo. While at Rolla eighteen months, the membership of the church was raised from 40 to 100. He asks for correspondence with churches in view of a future field of labor.

W. E. Spicer closes his work for the church at Lewiston, Ill., Jan. 1st. J. P. Lichtenberger, of Canton, Ill., recommends him to any church needing a live, energetic pastor. Write to him at Lewiston.

N. Rolla Davis, who was four years with the church at Skidmore, has moved to Maryville, Mo., that he may have the benefit of her schools for his children and would like to work for churches within reach of that city. Churches wanting a preacher should note this opportunity.

From one of our city papers we learn of the sad death of Chaplain T. S. Freeman. On Sept. 1st, in a fit of despondency and delirium from a fever, he jumped from the transport Zealandia, at Nagaskia, into the sea. He was chaplain on the Baltimore of Dewey's fleet. He was a Nova Scotian, born 30 years ago. He graduated from Bethany College, and after preaching in Texas for a year went to Logansport as pastor of the Christian Church. Mrs. Freeman has arrived there from Yokohama and the body of her husband will be shipped home for interment, although it has not yet reached San Francisco.

James Small and his wife are again at Des-Moines, Ia., for a permanent home. The churches and people of DesMoines and of Iowa have extended them a hearty welcome back to their city and state.

M. Pittman, for two years minister of the church at Washington, N. C., has resigned. During his ministry $2,220 was raised and a church mortgage for the same burned. His pastorate at Washington is pronounced one of the most successful in the history of the church. He was also state superintendant of the Christian Endeavor Societies of the Christian Church and raised them to the second place on the list in the state. He is now engaged in a protracted meeting at Elizabeth City, N. C., with crowded audiences. The meetings are being held in the courthouse. The church there we understand will try to secure him for regular work after the meeting.

Henry A. Major has changed from Purcell, I. T., to Ballinger, Tex. This change was mentioned last week, but by error the name was given as "Henry A. Morgan" instead of Henry A. Major. He says that the church at Ballinger numbers only about 30 names, but that several copies of the CHRISTIAN EVANGELIST are taken and the work is in a prosperous condition. They hope soon to double their numerical strength.

L. W. Kemker, of Peabody, Kan, is assisting C. E. Pomeroy in a protracted meeting at Marion. He reports the church at Peabody in a more prosperous state than formerly.

Jas. S. Helm, singing evangelist, is assisting the pastor of the church at Hennessay, Okla., C. W. Van Dolah, in a protracted meeting held in a tabernacle.

Bro. Louis Jaggard, of Howard, Kan., filled the pulpit of the church at that place acceptably during the absence of the pastor, R. E. Rosenstein, at Tyler, Tex., in September.

CHANGES.

A. E. Ice, Downey, California, to Lawrence, Kan.

J. M. Morris, Niagara Falls to 198 Laurel Street, Buffalo, N. Y.

J. R. Crank, Kentland, Ind., to Mendon, Ill.

H. C. Shipley, Carthage, S. D., to Ionia, Kan.

C. P. Pann, Riverside to San Barnardino, Cal.

M. J. Ferguson, Riverside to Compton, Cal.

J. D. Forrest, Bedford, O., to Irvington, Ind.

I. K. Shellenberger, Beaver, Pa., to Madelia, Minn.

Jno. Young, Jr., Jonesboro, Ark., to Marshall, Mo.

Wallace Tharp, Middletown, Ky., to Crawfordsville, Ind.

E. M. Barney, DesMoines, Ia., to Mishawaka, Ind.

T. B. Knowles, Akron to Columbus, O.

R. E. Stevens, Picton to Willow Park, Halifax, N. S.

J. K. Speer, Iowa Point to Winthrop, Kan.

W. T. Allen, Woods to Salem, Ore.

The Apostles' Doctrine.

"They continued steadfastly in the apostles' doctrine."

This was the action of the whole church at its birth in Jerusalem; nor did trouble enter until a departure from the "apostles' doctrine" had entered the congregations some years later. If, therefore, in our day, when so little is known of the "apostles' doctrine," our preachers would study and present that doctrine to their congregations, would there not be a steadfast continuance in it by those who would gladly receive it? A failure to teach the apostles' doctrine is at the bottom of the so-called religious trouble. No one can teach what he does not know, and he cannot know the apostles' doctrine until he has learned it from the same fountain head from which it came to them at Jerusalem. Their doctrine was contained and found in the Father's revelations to his former servants, the prophets, and expounded by his Son and brought to the apostles' mind at Pentecost by the Spirit. What, therefore, God had revealed concerning his purposes through Moses and the prophets Jesus and the Spirit impressed on the minds of the apostles, which became their doctrine, the belief of which gladdened the hearts of the multitudes on that great day for the church. Let us all return to the study of the apostles doctrine if we desire to have such congregations as the old Jerusalem church. There is salvation in no other church on earth, nor in any other name than that of his Son Jesus.

J. K. SPEER.

Clinton, Mo.

Contributions.

;TIAN UNION.

HN. G. FEE.

ıee and feel the importance
ıuch union.
s, What is the *basis* for

is union is professed faith
by baptism in his name,
ɔɪ: . ɹide.
ımed by our Lord in his
, "Go disciple all nations,
ı the name of the Father,
› Holy Ghost, teaching
all things whatsoever I
you."
ɪn is to express faith by
conditions by overt acts.
of Abel by the bloody
aith of Abraham by cir-
faith of the true believer
)tism in the name of the
, and the Holy Spirit.
act of discipleship and
ctual disciple the relation
national constitution does
ɪd citizen—it is the com-
wever loyal in heart the
ɔwever orderly as a mem-
y, he is yet not an actual
all the immunities and
citizen,—cannot have the
ges or responsibilities of
hall have performed the
-signed the constitution.
plan.
act must not be of man's
he may choose or such as a
ırch may decree; but that
as commanded.
The word 'baptize' means
and it is certain that the
entirely immersing was
ɪd in the church;" and
ɔncession he affirms the
ıe church has reserved to
ɔ change the form some-

ght to change the form,
the overt act commanded,
ɔ consecration in *any way*
ɔient, but implying the
ptism is a definite, specific
mmands are enjoined by
: words enjoining specific
"drink," as used in the

, chosen by the divine
fitly symbolizes the de-
n baptism—a symbol of
ıy of sin (Acts 22:16);
· "death to sin and our
newness to life" (Rom.
of the burial and resurrec-
l (Rom. 6:4; Col. 2:12);
of our own resurrection
Nothing, then, short of
ɔr can be Christian bap-
ı in symbol these cardinal
spel plan; and thus, aside
of the original word the
ıptism, as a symbol, show
ıptism is and must be as
l shall be proclaimed.
Word teaches by symbols
'ords, and with this ad-
ıls never change in im-

therefore, set forth the facts of the gospel by symbols. To ignore or subvert these symbols is treason to the gospel plan.

Under the old dispensation God kept the symbols intact—the spotless lamb, the holy incense, the hallowed fire. These external symbols were the unchanging language of what the inward, the spiritual, should be. So under the new. We may suffer diversity of opinions, "doctrines," and maintain unity; but in faithfulness to God's plan we may not suffer the rejection of the very seal of discipleship, the symbol of the fundamental facts on which the gospel rests.

No plan of union, therefore, can be entertained that thus ignores or supplants the very seal of discipleship, the divinely appointed symbol of the facts on which the gospel stands. (See 1 Cor. 15:4.)

Further, there is no need of chisms over this ordinance. All men admit that the immersion of a true believer in water in the name of the Father, the Son and the Holy Spirit is valid baptism. They can adopt this and not sin. Also, they may not ask that others co-operate with them whilst they are ignoring or subverting the very seal of discipleship, the symbol of Christian experience and the burial and resurrection of our Lord—the great fact on which the gospel stands. Further, what we in close fellowship, organized relationship, do through others, we do ourselves—we are part and parcel of the body doing the deeds.

Then, as a basis of union we must have that which was first ordained—faith in a person—Christ; baptism in his name and the Bible as our guide in matters of instruction and discipline. To this no man can object. Here all can unite.

THE MORMON-CHRISTIAN WAR.

R. B. NEAL.

The Mormons keep a standing heading to their "ad" in the Florida Philosopher; I reproduce it:

"THE MORMONS."

Have you heard about the "Mormons?" If so, through whom did you hear: from them or their enemies? The Apostle Paul said, "Prove all things, hold fast that which is good." Solomon, the wise man, said: "He that answereth a matter before he heareth it, it is folly and shame unto him." After hearing from our enemies and learning that their arguments consist of "mob violence," "slander" and "persecution," will you listen to our side of the argument? In the days of Christ and his apostles they were everywhere spoken evil of, and Paul said: "Yea, and all that live godly in Christ Jesus shall suffer persecution." Therefore, if you are looking for Christ's gospel do not go searching for a fashionable church. The following are a few of the many publications we keep, and they are post free upon receipt of price.

The Kinsman, of Salt Lake City, a valiant, intelligent and fearless anti-Mormon paper, that "beards the lion in his den," keeps the following standing ad *free* in its columns:

"DON'T BELIEVE THE GENTILES!"

No need of it. Read the the Mormon works; get your facts first-hand.

Pearl of Great Price	50
Catechism	20
Key to Theology	50
The Gospel	75
Book of Mormon	1 00
New Witness for God	1 [illegible]
Mormon Doctrine	[illegible]
Why we practice Plural Marriage, by a Mormon wife and mother	2

The very best weapons to use agains this great religious fraud of the nineteent century are their own books. I am pre paring a list of them to advertise in m next tract. The tracts, leaflets an pamphlets they circulate free with such liberal hand do not reveal the *real inward ness* of the system.

While the "ism" may shrink, yet it cannc *refuse* to be measured by yardsticks.

Joseph Smith, Jr., was brimful o "revelations," so called. He could revelat about most anything or anybody on short est notice. He was a great "translator;" translated the Book of Mormon, the Bool of Abraham and "translated and corrected" the Bible, our Bible. In my tract No. 2 "Smithianity, or Mormonism Refuted b Mormons," I give some rare and ric facts about that work. In his "translatin and correcting" of the Bible he did no tinker with the Apocrypha. He explain this singular omission by a "revelation;" received the revelation March 9, 1833, a Kirtland, O. Here it is:

1. Verily, thus saith the Lord unt you concerning the Apocrypha, There ar many things contained therein that ar true, and it is mostly translated correctly.
2. There are many things containe therein that are not true, which are inter polations by the hands of men.
3. Verily, I say unto you, that it is no needful that the Apocrypha should b translated.
4. Therefore, whoso readeth it, let hir understand, for the spirit manifesteth truth
5. And whoso is enlightened by the Spiri shall obtain benefit therefrom.
6. And whoso receiveth not by th Spirit cannot be benefited, therefore it i not needful that it should be translated Amen.—*Doctrine and Covenant, Sec. 91 page 327, 1891 edition, published a Liverpool by Brigham Young.*

They have had so many editions an made so many changes in this so-claime *inspired* book, that a critic has to be care ful to give date, page, section, etc., o some feeble-minded Mormon will clain that the book is *misrepresented.*

In an edition published at Lamoni, Ia. 1880, by the "Josephite Church," I find th same words, Sec. 88, page 248. Botl wings agree that this was a genuine *revela tion* by Joseph and give *the reason* wh the Apocrypha was not translated b Joseph, and of course why it should not b by any one.

Reread this precious revelation. Mak the first verse the major premise and th second the minor premise, and the conclu sion in the third verse couldn't be reach ed by the longest pole of logic ever invent ed!

More, the reason given *for translatin* the Old and the New Testaments is that ther were "many things not true" in them.

Note the attempt to give a crippled logi a crutch in the fourth verse. Why not "th Spirit manifest the true from the false," when a man reads the Bible as well as whe he reads the Apocrypha?

Ponder the cyclone logic of the last verse If the reader would permit himself to be en lightened by the Spirit when reading th book he would obtain benefit—know th true from the false. If he would not per mit himslf to be enlightened by the Spirit if it was *altogether* translated correctly, h needful that it should be translated!"

There is something akin to this logic in the reply of the Caliph when Alexandria was captured and he was asked what disposition should be made of the great and valuable library? His answer was, "If the books are like the Koran we don't need them, if they are not like it we don't want them, therefore *burn them.*"

Now for a list of this revelation. Will a Mormon elder step forth and claim that he *knows* the *true* and the *false* in the Apocrypha? Did one ever make such a claim? If not, why not? Will one of them make the attempt to point out some of the "many things" in it "not true?"—to put his finger on one or more "interpolations" in it? If those of them who have read the Apocrypha, or any part of it, can not do this, they must face the inevitable conclusion that Joseph Smith was a pretender revelator.

If you know anything of Mormonism you know that they are great on "keys;" have so many religious "keys" that it takes a great big "*ring*" to hold them! It was, and no doubt is, quite a problem with the Mormons to tell the true from the false messengers and revelators. So many wanted to revelate that all, even Oliver Cowdery, were given a back seat with the statement, "Thou shalt not command him (J. Smith) who is at thy head and at the head of the church, for I have given him the KEYS of the mysteries and the revelations which are sealed, until I shall appoint unto them another in his stead." Doctrine and Covenant, page 114. In other words, Joseph had a revelation that he only held the keys and only he could revelate. Now it is very important to be able to distinguish between good and bad angels and good and bad spirits. Mormonism gives us—

"THREE GRAND KEYS,"

Sec. 129, page 459, Book of Doctrine and Covenant:

Three grand keys by which good or bad angels or spirits may be known. Revealed to Joseph, the Prophet, at Nauvoo, Ill., Feb. 9, 1843.

1. There are two kinds of beings in heaven, viz., angels who are resurrected personages, having bodies of flesh and bones.
2. For instance, Jesus said, "Handle me and see, for a spirit hath not flesh and bones as ye see me have."
3. The spirits of just men made perfect —they who are not resurrected, but inherit the same glory.
4. When a messenger comes saying he has a message from God, offer him your hand and request him to shake hands with you.
5. If he be an angel he will do so, and you will feel his hand.
6. If he be the spirit of a just man made perfect, he will come in his glory, for that is the only way he can appear.
7. Ask him to shake hands with you, but he will not move, because it is contrary to the order of heaven for a just man to deceive; but he will still deliver his message.
8. If it be the devil as an angel of light, when you ask him to shake hands he will offer you his hand and you will not feel anything, you may therefere detect him.
9. These are three grand keys whereby you may know whether any administration is from God.

Reader, what think you of the "three grand keys?"

Suppose the devil had sense enough to refuse to shake hands—and if he hasn't that much sense he hasn't sense enough to be the devil—what then?

He comes as "an angel of light," and how is he to be told from "the spirit of a just man made perfect?"

Of course, Mormons have tried these keys. If useless, unused, they are in no sense "*grand* keys." It was a useless revelation. What elder will step forth and tell us that he has *felt the hand of an angel?* What elder will step forth and tell us that he has shaken hands with the devil, and how he knew it?

These are keys and three grand ones, to unlock Joseph Smith's pretentions and expose the folly and falsity of Mormonism! I have more along this line if our readers want it.

Grayson, Ky.

OUR NEGLECTED MINISTRY.

T. H. KUHN.

There is a class of men in our ministry who stand close to the throne and have power with God, but not with man, who on account of age and gray hairs are not sought by the churches. For want of a more systematic ministry among the churches of the Christian brotherhood, the accumulated knowledge and religious influence of these spiritual worthies are practically lost to the church. Besides, many of these noble men who have spent their lives in self-sacrificing study and toil, are absolutely dependent upon their service in their chosen calling as a means of support in their old age. They have fought bravely and well many of the hard battles of life, agitating and defending in puldit and public debate the great principles of the Reformation. Living on meagre salaries, toiling with their hands by day, they burned the midnight oil in biblical research, that they might preach in wisdom and power the gospel of Jesus to a dying race. Having left in the background secular interests, these princely knights purchased for themselves a rugged intellectual character and undying fame. These are now the only gifts they have to place upon the altar of churches which have now entered into the fruit of *their* labors. It was impossible under such circumstances for them to accumulate wealth had they possessed such a disposition.

But it has been imputed to the ministry that a preacher has no financial sense. Let it be so. Men usually excel in but one point. I have known men in the possession of gaeat financial ability who had no preaching sense, who, if their lives depended upon it, could not preach a sermon. Why condemn the minister for lack of financial sense and acquit with innocence the financier utterly devoid of preaching sense? The one is just as consistent as the other. The man who, during forty years, has given his entire time and talent to the study and work of the ministerial profession, bearing the burdens and the cares of human hearts with their groanings and tears, patiently and meekly enduring the godless indifference and heartless criticisms of formal church members and a mocking world, at the same time toiling and struggling to instruct ignorant humanity and give them a higher conception of life, duty and destiny, can no more expect to succeed in financial undertakings than the man who during the same number of years has given his time and talents to bus ness can hope to succeed in the ministry.

But in the Christian dispensation, where the children of God should meet on acommon level, it is the duty of the one to bear the burdens of the other. The minister should labor to impart spiritual instruction to the financier, and the financier should so manage his possessions as to impart financial support to the ministry. In this way the progress of human society is made possible.

One of the grave questions confronting the Church of Christ to-day is, How shall these heroes who, with bent forms and minds enriched from God's battlefield, be employed regularly to the advantage of the ministry and the church, so long as they are able for active service. They do not want charity thrust upon them; "they cannot dig; to beg they are ashamed," and the church would be disgraced. They want active service, by which they can maintain themselves. It were indeed unkind for a great church to thrust upon these bent forms the troublesome, busy, active cares of pastoral life; yet, because unable to bear these burdens they are practically retired from the ministry without the means of support in their declining years.

Some of the sectarian churches, as they are denominated, have what the Christian Church has not—a fund for the relief of superannuated ministers, whereby they are enabled to keep their aged men in employment profitable to both church and ministry so long as they are able to do active service. After this they are placed upon a salary and spend their last days on earth in ease and comfort.

We have been taught to despise ecclesiasticism and religious hierarchy and to contend earnestly for simplicity of faith and church management. Yet, a system of faith and religious principles so simple that it will not accomplish the good and reach all the conditions intended to be regulated through the divine economy of the kingdom of heaven does not fulfill the divine standard. Many of these churches, through a system which may seem to partake of religious hierarchy, are accomplishing some good things, which the Christian Church, through simplicity of faith, is not accomplishing. Now a question: Which is the greater sin before God, reaching and overcoming evil conditions in human society and doing good to humanity under what may seem to you to be a religious hierarchy, or failing to reach and overcome these evil conditions? Both may be wrong, but of the two evils give me the former. But, brethren, are we not great enough, broad enough and possessed of sufficient mental and spiritual culture to take hold of this question as children of God and solve it in the interest of humanity and the church?

"Young men for war, but old men for counsel." All of our young men, many of whom in this age of opportunities are in the possession of college degrees, may profitably sit at the feet of these aged fathers in Israel and imbibe heavenly wisdom.

The churches in the states, for the most part, are divided into groups. Could not these ministers be sent to each of the churches in their respective districts once or twice each year at a great advantage to the churches and the ministry in the district? These churches individually could readily pay for their services, thus rendered, which probably would not exceed one or two Sundays per church each year. In this way these preachers might be kept in profitable employment and supported by the churches for whom they have spent their lives. The churches and the younger ministers would in turn be blessed, edified and built up. What say you, brethren?

Kokomo, Ind.

THE POWER OF LITTLES.

JAMES M. CAMPBELL.

"If the prophet had bid thee do some great thing, wouldest thou not have done it?" asked the servants of Naaman of their petulant master. No doubt he would! We are all ready for the great things. We slight the ordinary for the extraordinary. Nowadays no work is accounted worthy of notice that does not assume large dimensions. Many are unwilling to be "a lamp in the chamber," if they cannot "be a star in the sky." The smallest man wants the largest platform upon which to perform.

'Fain would he make the world his pedestal,
Mankind the gazers, the sole figure he.''

Let us to-day bring down our thoughts from the lofty and imposing aspects of Christian life to a consideration of the service of God in little things.

I. *Life is made up of little things.* The great events of life are few. Take any single year. How few things stand out as mountain peaks against the sky! In retrospect it seems a long, level highway. On and on we go, through the same round of daily duties. Sometimes we wish that something would happen to break up the ceaseless monotony of things. It is, doubtless, the best kind of a life for us. In nature God attends to details. He finishes the insect's wing; he polishes the crystals of the snowflake; he rounds a dew drop as carefully as he does a world. The life of Christ was made up of the performance of the common duties that fall to the lot of man. Thirty years were spent in the quiet home and workshop of Nazareth, and only three years in public life. He made no display of his power. He performed miracles sparingly. His kingdom came not with observation. Let us learn from him not to wait for the great occasion, but to perform with fidelity the humble duties that come to us day by day.

II. *The moral value of things depends upon what is expressed by them.* The events and actions of life are not to be estimated by outside measurement. A seemingly trivial event may involve important principles and interests; the simplest act may be informed with spiritual qualities which make it great. We measure an action by the motive, the purpose, the spirit that fills it. Some actions, apparently great, mean little; some actions, apparently small, mean much. The widow's two mites were a small gift, but they meant much. They meant sacrifice, they meant trust in God for the morrow. The woman who had been a sinner and who washed the Savior's feet with her tears and wiped them with her tresses, gave a gift as precious as that other woman who bought an alabaster cruse of costly ointment, which she poured upon the Master's head. God notices little things and puts upon them their true value. A cup of cold water given in the name of a disciple shall not lose its reward.

III. *Little things are great in their sum-total.* According to an eminent French naturalist, were all the insects collected together they would, as to bulk, outmeasure the rest of the animal creation. Though small individually they would, in virtue of their astounding numbers, prove greater than all the birds, beasts and fishes combined. From this we learn the power of littles.

The immense cables that support the bridge that stretches between New York and Brooklyn are made up of hundreds of single wires twisted together. Singly, they are weak; unitedly, they are strong. "Holland would probably be washed away were it not for the creeping roots of certain trees that bind the coast together."

Nature is content to work little by little. The plant grows not by leaps, but by slow and imperceptible degrees. Education is obtained little by little, step by step. The mind is like a vase with a narrow neck: pour upon it little or much, you will never get a great deal in it at a time. It is by line upon line, precept upon precept, that knowledge is increased. Everything great is made up of littles.

IV. *Little things supply the truest test of character.* You cannot judge a man by what he does on great occasions, for then he is on the watch, knowing that he has a part to sustain. Little, unconscious acts tell what the real man is. "He that is faithful in that which is least is faithful also in much." But the reverse is not always true.

It was easy for Peter to flourish his sword; it was hard for him to keep his temper before the mocking tongue of a servant maid. It is easier for a martyr to burn at the stake than to be roasted day by day in the slow fire of ingratitude, jealousy or hate.

A servant girl, in furnishing evidence of her conversion, said that she now swept in the corners under the sofa, whereas before she had not. A satisfactory testimony! Perfection comes from attention to little things. It is in little things that we are all apt to come short. Be watchful of the little things and the big things will take care of themselves.

The Religious World.

The new German Church in Jerusalem, just now receiving its finishing touches, will be dedicated on October 31, and the ceremony will be the central event in the visit of the German Emperor to the Holy Land. The visit is expected to be attended with much pomp and circumstance, the German Princes and other notables having been invited to attend. The date fixed is historic and appropriate, being the anniversary of the event which began the Reformation—the nailing of his famous theses by Luther to the church door in Wittenburg.

The church is, as far as possible, a restoration of the Church of St. Mary the Great. The richly ornamented doorway, with its round arch composed of twelve stones carved to represent the months, was found standing and in good preservation, and has been raised and built into the new structure. The foundations of the old church were found to rest on the debris of former overthrows, and, at great expense, the rock-bed was at last reached at a depth of about 50 feet for the new foundations. The new building is about 120 feet in length by 80 in breadth, while the massive stone tower, of some 150 feet high, overtops all surrounding domes and minarets, and is now perhaps the most conspicuous object seen in a bird's-eye view of the city. Behind the church is the old cloister in good preservation. Behind that again is a space to be occupied with a new hospice for pilgrims, and beneath this are vast subterranean chambers.

The entire plot of ground forms the east half of the celebrated Muristan, or Hospital of the Knights of St. John, and was the center of that famous order. It was presented by the Sultan to the German Emperor, William I., and taken possession of by the Crown Prince Frederick William when he visited Jerusalem on the occasion of the opening of the Suez Canal in 1869.

[The above account of the new German Church at Jerusalem was clipped from one of the daily papers of this city.—EDITOR.]

The following announcement of an interesting meeting to be held in this city, this month, was made in a recent issue of the St. Louis Republic:

The western section of the Pan-Presbyterian Executive Committe, which includes the United States and Canada, will meet in St. Louis, Oct. 27. It will be in session one day. A banquet at the Southern Hotel will conclude the session. This committee represents ten brahches of the Presbyterian faith. Of these ten branches of the Presbyterian faith, the same authority says:

"The Canadian Presbyterian Church, one of those represented, dates from about the middle of the eighteenth century, and is the leading denomination in the Dominion. Its first minister was Rev. George Henry, chaplain of a Scottish regiment, stationed at Quebec in 1765, and its first congregation was organized in 1787 by Rev. Alexander Spark, sent over from the Kirk of Scotland. The first Presbyterian Church in Montreal was erected in 1790, and in 1803 the first Presbytery was organized. In 1831 the 'Synod of the presbyterian Church of Canada' was formed, and in 1875 there was a general union formed of the four great divisions of the Presbyterian family in Canada. The standards of the Canadian church are the Westminster Confession of Faith and the Catechisms. At present it has 919 churches, 1,077 ministers and a membership of 740,000.

"The first Presbyterian church organized in America, according to the best authorities, was that of the Reformed Dutch Church of New Amsterdam, N. Y., in 1828. Probably the first English-speaking Presbyterian Church was that founded at Rehoboth, Md., by Rev. Francis Makemie in 1683. The first Presbytery was held in Philadelphia in 1705, and the first Synod in 1718. After dissensions the Presbyterian Churches were reunited in 1758, and steps taken to extend the organization in the United States.

"The first General Assembly met at Philadelphia, May, 1789, at which time the Westminster Confession of Faith was readopted, with three slight alterations, and the Larger and Shorter Cathechisms with but one change. This Assembly included 17 Presbyteries, 419 congregations and 180 ministers. In 1834 the Associate Reformed Church was merged into the Presbyterian Church. In 1838 this was divided into the Old and New School Presbyterians, but in 1871 they were reunited. During the separation both churches grew rapidly in numbers and educational interests, so that their union constituted the strongest Presbyterian organization in the United States, having 7,631 churches, 7,129 ministers and a membership of over 950,000.

Correspondence.

Washington (D. C.) Letter.

The number of delegates and visitors in attendance upon the twenty-first annual convention of the Maryland, Delaware and District of Columbia Missionary Society at the Ninth St. Christian Church, Washington, D. C , Oct. 5-7, was nearly double the number present at any previous convention. This is an evidence, not only of the growth of the Disciples of Christ, but of an increasing interest in co-operative missionary work.

J. A. Hopkins presided at the first day's session, which is known as Preachers' Day. The programme included the following: "A Working Church," by P. O. Cave; "Men for the Ministry," Peter Ainslie; "Soul-winning," D. M. Austin; "The Preacher as Pastor," W. J. Wright; "Doctrinal and Practical Preaching," H. J. Dudley; "Systematic Study of the Bible," B. A. Abbott, and the "Education of Preachers," F. D. Power.

The report of the churches given on Thursday morning showed a gratifying increase numerically and spiritually. The spiritual condition was not stated, but as the offerings, especially for missions, show that the churches are being liberalized, we take it as an indication that they are being spiritualized.

The twenty-six churches report a membership of 4,050, with 513 additions during the year and contributions for Foreign Missions, $1,221.69; for General Home Missions, $824.96; for state missions, $1,505.37; for local missions, $1,596; for all purposes $32,818.75; value of church property, $200,000.

That our Western churches may have the opportunity of comparison with our Eastern churches I give a table of statistics containing the reports of seven of our best churches for the past year:

Church	Membership	Additions	Contributed all purposes
Baltimore			
Harlem Ave ...	523	34	$5,859
Calhoun St.	443	23	2,984
Beaver Creek..	253	33	1,632
Hagerstown 1st.	405	43	2,520
Washington			
Vermont Ave...	627	60	5,900
Ninth St ..	621	74	8,001
Third Church..	210	124	1,543

The delegates were much encouraged at the results of their missionary work. W. J. Wright, the evangelist, had confined his labors for the greater part of the year with the Third Church, Washington, where there is now a congregation of two hundred and ten members. He held meetings at three new points, Herndon, Southeast Washington, and North Baltimore. He delivered two hundred and one sermons and addresses and added one hundred and forty persons to the churches. H. J. Dudley had been employed as evangelist for the eastern shore of Maryland, strengthening the weak congregations and planting the cause in new places. The report of the board says, "About the first of July a new mission work was begun in Baltimore. A tent was pitched and for six weeks W. J. Wright and Hezekiah Trail conducted gospel meetings. The brethren in Baltimore greatly assisted in the work. As a result the Fourth Christian Church will be dedicated in November. The Harlem Avenue Church has secured the lot on North Fulton Avenue and ground has been broken for a new house of worship to cost about $2,000. The field is a good one and the indications are that in a few years it will be a strong church."

The Third Church, Washington, hopes soon to begin building operations. Upon October 4, 1898, their second birthday, the Church Extension board remembered them with the handsome loan of $4,000 for the purchase of house and lot provided this sum was not more than two-thirds cost of the same.

The treasurer's report showed receipts from churches, $1,520.56; from the American Christian Missionary Society, $250; from collections in the field, $430.73; total from all sources, $2,232 29. All bills were paid and a balance of $50 remains in the treasury. The convention decided to continue their support next year to the Third Church, Washington; Eastern Shore, Maryland; Mission in Baltimore, and in addition put an evangelist in the field. It is expected that the Home board will assist us to the extent of $500. The educational committee reported $314 received and two young men assisted at college. Though the churches have put at the committee's disposal only $1,380, by wise management and plan of loaning this money to students, nine young men have been prepared for the ministry.

The one great shadow that fell upon this convention was the retirement of F. D. Power, who for twenty-one years has faithfully served the society as president. The delegetes would never have consented to releasing him had it not been known to them that by relieving Bro. Power of some of his duties he would be the longer spared to us for active service.

Hardly second to the loss of Bro. Power from the presidency was the retirement of W. S. Haye, of Beaver Creek, Md., from the office of corresponding secretary. The present success of our convention work is due in no small measure to the untiring, self-sacrificing labors of this good brother. B. A. Abbott, of Baltimore, and J. A. Hopkins, of Harford County fills the vacancies. Bros. Power and Haye are continued as advising members of the board.

Space will not permit me to tell of the delightful sessions of the C. W. B. M., Sunday-school and Christian Endeavor Societies, nor of the great camp meeting we are going to establish on the Maryland shore of the Atlantic, which is destined to be a rival of Ocean Grove, of the magnificent addresses of S. R. Maxwell, C. C. Smith, A. McLean and Z. T. Sweeney, etc.

The Sunday-school at Jerusalem, Harford County, Md., secured the prize banner. The convention meets next year at Beaver Creek, Maryland. W. R. Watkins, an undenominational evangelist, was received into our fellowship.

EDWARD B. BAGBY.

New York Letter.

On Tuesday evening, Oct. the 4th, Bro. J. S. Myers, the new pastor of the First Christian Church, Philadelphia, was appropriately installed in the presence of a large congregation. The attendance represented not only the Disciples of Christ in Philadelphia, but also those of Washington, Indianapolis and New York. F. D. Power, the good Bishop of the National Capital, came over to deliver the charge to the congregation. A. B. Philputt, for ten years the faithful pastor of the Philadelphia flock, but now of the Central Church, Indianapolis, was present to charge the new pastor, his successor. S. T. Willis went over from New York to preach the sermon. G. P. Rutledge, pastor of the Third Church, Philadelphia, conducted the devotional service and Chas. Bond, of the Christian League, of the same city, pronounced the benediction. Dr. E. E. Montgomery, one of the deacons of the congregation presided, and the choir discoursed sweet music. Toward the close of the service Dr. Montgomery read letters of commendation from the First Church and the City Board of Trade, of Sedalia, Mo., expressing most fittingly the high esteem in which Bro. J. S. Myers is held by Christians and non-Christians alike, in Sedalia, where he has labored for eight years. Samuel Troth, senior elder, made a few beautiful remarks, and followed by the other elders, extended the hand of fellowship to Bro. Myers and his family. The church at Sedalia enjoyed a remarkable degree of prosperity under the leadership of J. S. Myers. During the eight years of his ministry there the church grew to a membership of eleven hundred and a mission church of five hundred was planted and substantially housed. He baptized one thousand people in that city. We sincerely hope a sin lar growth may result from his ministry Philadelphia. It is his purpose to inaugur a strong forward movement in the city Brotherly Love. He has a splendid churc well located in a large field to back him in t enterprise and it is sincerely desired that vigorous, aggressive campaign may be inaug rated. Success to the cause of Christ in Ph adelphia, our neighboring city!

We heard only good reported of Geo. Rutledge, the new pastor in West Philadelph who a few months since succeeded Wallace Payne in that field. Chas. Bond, a preacl of good ability among the Disciples of Chri as secretary of the Christian League, is wa ing a good warefare against many of the ev of social corruption in that city.

***

New York Disciples have just been favo by a visit from our beloved missionary, Bi C. E. Randall, of Kingston, Jamaica. T Christian Woman's Board of Missions, un whose auspices he has labored in that isla for twelve years, granted him a richly meri vacation last summer, which enabled him visit once more his old home in England, s his only living sister there. On the ret trip he came via New York. We had t pleasure of a few days' visit from him in o own home, through which he was endeared us very much. Evidently he is a man w walks with God. His conversation is such becometh the gospel of Christ. On Lor day morning, the 9th, he preached a g discourse at the 169th Street Church and ga us many interesting facts relating to the land of Jamaica. He said one of the great needs of our work there just now is a sm printing press with which to issue a mont paper, as a means of intercommunicat among the Jamaican churches. The 16 Street Church was the first appealed to a responded gladly. He spoke at 56th Str Church in the evening and there received aslo. No doubt the work in Jamaica woul greatly assisted by such a journal as is p posed. We should provide the press at on

***

The Disciples' Club, of New York, is plann for the fall and winter meetings with the h of doing a larger, broader work than last ye The program committee is making ou good bill of fare, which we hope to give in CHRISTIAN-EVANGELIST soon. The papers not be quite so "churchy" as they were l season, but will deal more with literary, ciological and critical questions. It was cided at the last meeting to file in the archi of the club a copy of every paper read bef the association. Bro. R. C. McWane's "Barton W. Stone" being the first so honor The club also decided to hold all regular m ings in the future at the 56th Street Chu because it is more central in the Greater York than any other of our churches.

***

Dr. H. L. Willett and family, of Chic were in the city a few days recently, prio sailing (on the 12th) for Germany, wher goes to prosecute certain advanced stu along his chosen line of work. We trust scholarly professor may be so enlarged strengthened by this extended course of st that he may be even an abler expounder of divine truth as it is in Jesus than he is n He occupied the pulpit of the 56th St Church last Lord's day morning where, s he supplied there three months in the sum of '97, he is heard gladly. We have booked for a sermon at 169th Street Churc his return from Europe.

***

The Boux Burough Sunday-school Asso tion held a large meeting at our church on evening of the 6th and organized a Prin Teachers Union, which will hold weekly m ings to teach the lessons to their classes, the best methods of teaching songs to the li ones. Mrs. H. E. Foster, state organize

the
tings
t im-
and
an is
ught
hods
be a
rches
class
its of
ourse
ctive
bs of
od at
ns.
ople
ob-
and
thus
iver-
stian
very
mons
past
ring
Bro.
made
has
been
TIAN-
on to
ueen
l and
or all
urch
.500.
rvice
ser-
ed at
have
and
large
y no
f the
tails
antly
fre-
lems
great
ssful
antly
keep
d the
igent
vor
erves
stu-
f the
ssful
and
roine
In a
ntly,
Uni-
mber
eek.
nor
e the
aist-
some
ave,
state
our
aude
the
and
e of
l not
l, I.
Bal-

B. F. Wilson, of Plano, is doing much the same in his new field. Audiences growing, additions multiplying and $3,600 raised for a new house.

J. B. Boen is assisting G. D. Smith in a meeting at Oak Cliff. The hearing is good, with about 20 additions. The little church is encouraged, and one result of the meeting will be a new house or an enlargement of the old one.

Bros. Bradley, Miller and Reynolds, three of the boy-preachers of Add Ran University, have held a good meeting at a mission point in Waco, with 16 additions.

J. C. Eubank, of Denison, has been doing some work at Pottsboro, resulting in the organization of a church of 35 members. They have a "spirit to work," and will build a house at once.

Edward C. Boynton, after a three years' service at Plano, returns to his old home, Hamilton, and will devote h s time to the churches there and at Comanche.

Miss Fannie Malone is now in the employ of the Central Church as my assistant.

M. M. Davis.

833 *Live Oak St., Dallas, Tex.*

"The Possession and Use of Property."

Bro. B. B. Tyler wrote an article on the above subject, which to my mind does not exactly suit present conditions, for which reason I would like to add a little to what he says:

"There is not even an intimation that the mere possession of worldly goods—even to the point of great wealth—is in itself sinful." Over against the above quotation from Bro. Tyler's article, I want to call attention to Matt. 6:19, where the disciples were forb dden to lay up treasures on earth. This is a direct command forbidding the storing of wealth; the whole tenor of the remainder of the chapter is to the same effect. "Property and wealth are alike from God." They may be, and they may not.

Men often steal themselves rich, and likewise they are often robbed poor. The poverty mentioned in Scripture is generally spoken of in connection with oppression. The soothing words about giving alms to the poor may fit some cases, but they come with a bad grace at this time. If Bro. Tyler had defined property we could tell his meaning better and would be better able to judge whether he is right or wrong. I think property has been well defined as the *result of labor*. A man can own no property that has not been produced by labor. Land is not property, or if it is, it is God's property. So far as I am acquainted with the current thought on riches and poverty, the question is not so much as to the use of property, as it is on the honesty of getting wealth.

Solomon says, "The profit of the earth is for all;" in modern language: Land rent belongs to the community. If this be true, and I believe it to be so, then the landlords by taking $1,600,000,000 per year rent for the land of the United States simply rob the people of that much.

I have never seen a man who could tell of any service the landlord performs corresponding to the rent he collects, either to the tenant or to the community. Landlordism is a violation of the law of love as given by Christ.

The problem that must be solved is the relation of *wages, interest* and *land rent*. If we do not go to the bottom of the matter we may do more harm than good, as I believe Bro. Tyler's article does. The prophets and apos-

The amount of wages is fixed by accessibility of land, which is determined by the tax system. The labor question is really the land question. When the land question is settled, the use of property will be easily determined.

"Who made the land?" God.

"For whom?" "For all the people."

"Who collect the land rents?" The landlords.

"What service do they perform that corresponds to this rent?" They perform no services.

I use the term land as it is used in economics, as the bare land, excluding all improvements. The great question of the age is that of economics, and the great question of economics is that of *land rent*.

When we get a Christian conscience on this subject it will be thrashed out and we will get the golden grains of truth.

When the church gets hold of the solution of the land question we will have a reformation that will eclipse that of Luther and Campbell.

I need hardly add, that in my opinion, Henry George is the religious reformer of the 19th century, the John the Baptist of the age of economic justice.

It has also been well said, the age of justice must precede the age of benevolence.

Tokyo, Japan. C. E. Garst.

Cotner University.

There is no work being pushed with more vigor among the Churches of Christ just now than the work of education. The time is at hand for a great people to awaken to their duty. Our leaders in education with the aid of the press and ministry are urging with great persistence this imperative need. A few are being aroused to give liberally to this great cause. But how many thousands of the Master's wealth are being withheld? Every college we have should be endowed. To this end our educational leaders are working with untiring zeal to place our colleges upon permanent foundations financially. This God demands. The greatest work now claiming the attention of our people in the Northwest is the securing to the cause of Christian education the beautiful and substantial property of Cotner University. The trust fund now growing is being increased every week and is being pushed constantly forward by my field work. The claims against the property are held principally by four banks in Lincoln. Some years ago they offered to give us the property if we would pay the one-half of their claim $2,500. At the close of college in June, 1898, the committee appointed by the church visited the banks and received a proposition from them in writing that was a surprise to all. Their present demands are as follows:

Amount required by banks including ins		$ 26,000
Contributed by the banks		12,000
Amount required now including ins......		14,000
Amount raised in cash and pledges 1897 vacation	4,000	
Amount raised in cash and pledges since July, 1898	1,444,	5,444
Amount needed to obtain clear title......		8,556

We earnestly ask our brethren to contribute to the trust fund that is to be held in trust to cover this demand. Money is already laid away in a safety deposit vault in Lincoln for this purpose, and contributions are now coming in quite frequently for the fund. In addition to the above there are claims to the amount of $3,000 that have already been arranged in part, without a cash demand. When we consider that for this sum a property consisting of one of the finest college buildings

Our work and workers are appreciated by one of the best state universities in the land. Upon urgent invitation Pres. Aylesworth has taken the Hebrew in the State University of Nebraska, and recently members from the classes of '96, '97 and '98, after submitting their courses taken in Cotner University to examination, entered for the Master's degree without additional requirement.

Some new families have purchased homes here and others are arranging to come later.

The prospects are very promising for a good increase of students in the winter term.

Brethren, pray for this grand work in one of the most strategic fields of our country, and send me directly your pledges and cash to increase the growing trust fund. This work must be accomplished this school year. Act quickly. Ask for any information desired.

J. W. HILTON,
Financial Secretary Cotner University.
(Bethany) Lincoln, Neb.

Constantinople Letter.

EDITOR CHRISTIAN-EVANGELIST:—I write from our Eastern home, we having arrived ten days ago. The journey from the Blue Grass Region to the Levant, although long, was a pleasant one. At different points on the way during the first half of the trip we worshiped with God's people in Washington, New York and Liverpool, besides a delightful day at that ancient and most picturesque city, Chester, on the River Dee, and at Eaton Hall, a country residence—but a whole city in itself—of the Duke of Westminster, whose ancestor came over with William the Conqueror, and who is said by some to be the richest man in England. We were in company with Bro. and Sister Wholley's family and a few of their friends, ending the day with tea in their hospitable home in Chester. The last Disciple to bid us Godspeed was Sister Wholley, standing in the front of her own door—such a happy, cheerful spirit that we carried away some of with us. We regretted that we could not make a brief visit to Southport to see the families of Bros. Joe and Frank Coop, who are so well known and beloved by hosts of Christians, at whose lovely homes we were so nicely entertained when on our way to the United States last fall, and also to see other members of the church there. But time was pressing us onward and we were becoming more eager each day to reach the end of our journey. We had had almost a year's recreation in the home land with relatives and friends. Had the privilege of seeing and appreciating the growth of the churches, and had made the acquaintance of many earnest, whole-souled workers for the Master and had been strengthened and encouraged thereby. Had enjoyed Kentucky, Indiana and Missouri hospitality to such an extent as to wonder if we ever would be content again to live in a foreign land.

The parting with dear ones is too sacred to dwell upon. As I write many a sweet face appears between the lines, and there is for each one the kindest, most grateful and loving remembrance.

Crossing the English Channel from Dover to Calais we had a bird's-eye view of Northern and Eastern France, also of Switzerland, our train stopping long enough for us to see something of the city of Bale. Then again at Zurich, and the ride along the Lake of Zurich, then the Alpine scenery on through the Tyrol as far as Innspruck surpassed anything we had seen. We wanted to look out of the window without saying or hearing a word, or to go from side to side for fear of losing some of the lovely sights. It was such a piece of good fortune that we were passing this most interesting part by day light, entering Austrian territory at evening and arriving at Vienna next morning. We had been on the train since Sunday morning; then it was Tuesday. There being yet two days travel before us, it was decided to stop over a day, send a telegram to Johnie Shishmanian at Sophia, Bulgaria, to be ready to join us at that place; also send a post-card ahead to Constantinople, that we were coming.

The way from Vienna lay through Buda-pest, Hungary, thence through Belgrade, the capital of Servia, and was without interest except the River Danube and the Francis Joseph Canal, it was also without incident, unless it was that the call for passports began at Belgrade. We had come from the United States, passed through England, France, Switzerland and Austria and not a word had been said about "passports," but to pass through these petty kingdoms passports had to be ready at a moment's warning, and on entering and leaving the country.

We recognized our approach to Sophia by seeing the form of our son on the platform of the station. With a bound he was on the train and in our car, and the year's separation was forgotten. His companion and schoolmate, accompanied by his mother, followed, and there was a joyful meeting. Mrs. Djibaroff requested me to allow Johnie to remain a few days longer, as he and her son had just returned from a long trip to the Balkans, and she added: "They are tired; Johnie's things are not ready also." We could not refuse the request altogether, she had been so kind to him and made him feel so welcome during his visit to Bulgaria, and now spoke as if she was asking a special favor of us. She agreed to send him on next day.

Leaving Sophia, then Bulgaria, behind, the entrance into Turkey was forcibly impressed upon us by the remark of a Jewish lady who was also bound for Constantinople. The stations all along the route had been lighted by electric or other bright lights, but those of Turkey had the old oil lamps and very few at that. Looking out she exclaimed, "See, see, darkness begins; we are in Turkey!" There seemed to be perceptible change, the train ran slower, the stops were longer and more frequent. There was no longer any water in the dressing-room where one could wash off the dust from blackened faces. Men in red fezzes and soldiers in big boots walked up and down, looking in and staring at us once in a while. A German consul came in with his wife and a Karass. Officers *with lanterns* came to look at the passport. Custom officers came to examine (carefully) each handbag, a piece of United States bunting attracting special scrutiny in one of our valises. The second night passed and morning's light revealed the welcome sight—the clear waters of the sea of Marmora. We began to name the towns as we passed: "St. Stephans," "Makri Kevy," "Samtia"—then we passed two small stations within the city limits; both equal distances from our house. But we did not see any one we knew. Then we rounded Seralio Point, a place rich in historic memories, the site of Byzantium, afterwards Constantinople, more than two thousand years.

As we steamed into the central station, we were all alert to see some one to meet us. It was still early and we drove through the streets, and to our door without meeting any one of our people; evidently they had not received our post-card. Thus we took them by surprise, though they were expecting us sometime during the week.

The house was in order, Miss Isgohi, one of the teachers, her mother and sister, with other assistance, had been busy for sometime "cleaning house," and there was a feeling of grateful contentment to find everything as it was left a year before. In a short time breakfast was ready and we had not left the table when callers began to welcome us back. They inquired of our relatives and friends, many of whose names are familiar to them, of the condition of the churches, then of the war with Spain.

One or two brought flowers, another sent two ars of "sweets" of her own make. On the wall in the hall were the words in green, "Welcome Home." In my bedroom piece of handwork, the industry of the sc[hool] girls under the direction of Isgohi. We w[ent] over the house, the yard, then the schoo[l] playground, quite satisfied to be home aga[in].

Some of the children came in that first saying they were impatient for the sch[ool to] begin. When the school opened, Sept. there were 68 names; others are being rec[eived] daily.

We are somewhat disappointed that [there] are as yet no new desks for the repaired ro[oms]. The desks which Mr. Shishmanian [...] fifteen years ago are old and dingy; also, seats are without backs. They are so [...] and out of place, and look so badly t[o one] fresh from the United States. Beside[s, we] were anxious to have the rooms look tidy [and] inviting to Bro. and Sister Chapman [when] they arrive.

There were no empty seats on Lord's [day] and the sermons in Armenian sounded w[ell to] my ears. But the wily priests still are at [work] to keep the people away from school and [...] ices. Yesterday a neighbor was telling [...] their doings. We will put renewed en[ergy] into our efforts. For we are encourage[d by] the return of children that had been t[aken] away, and the words of an old lady patr[on of] the school who was present at Sunday-sc[hool] for the first time. She said at the c[lose]: "The Lord bless every word that has [been] taught these children, and may you con[tinue] to so teach them until it is so rooted in [their] hearts as to bear much fruit to the Lord."

LUCY M. SHISHMANIA[N].
Constantinople, Sept. 15, 1898.

their own way in life.
has shown wonderful vitality. For
patronage has been steadily increas-
it occupies a continually growing place
fections of the people.
is characterized by a liberal, catholic
such peculiar strength and power that
se, "The Hiram spirit," has come to
synonym for genuine earnestness,
nindedness and freedom from cant,
y and sectarian bigotry.
has always drawn the highest class of
ge. Its students are a well-natured,
and brainy class of young people; self-
industrious and persevering. They
y they are in college. Most of them
istinct purpose in view. They are not
sent to college, they go to college.
ral and intellectual quality of the
tudent body cannot be too highly spoken
ne of the best platform speakers in the
States after standing before the Hiram
body have declared it to be remarkable
urity and intellectual acuteness as
ed in its ability to grasp and appreci-
est thoughts presented.
anything more be said? If ever an in-
by hard work, faithful management
earying devotion to the interests of the
as won the right to be heard, Hiram is
titution. We confidently expect 50,-
le at least to speak out now and deat Hiram shall be endowed. Let the
cement in June, 1900, see this work
Then we can turn our attention to
eat interests. Do not say there will be
o do this without you. You are needed.
our name at once among those who are
forward in this last and supreme effort
ndowment of one of the most honored
thy institutions of our great brother-
Praying for the blessing of God upon
rt, I remain
brother in the work of our common

E. V. ZOLLARS.

---

ey in the head is cured by Hood's Sar-

Virginia Letter.

During the next three months we shall give the CHRISTIAN-EVANGELIST readers a bi-weekly letter from the "Old Dominion." Our first intention was to write an Atlantic Seaboard letter, but quickly calling to mind our most worthy correspondent from New York City, Washington, D. C., and elsewhere we concluded 'twere better to be modest and head our letter with the caption "Virginia Letter" while located at Charlottesville, Va., the seat of the University of Virginia, and a "Georgia Letter" during the months we shall teach at Athens, the seat of the University of Georgia. We hope preachers, laymen and all Christian workers will send us items of interest from Virginia and Georgia especially for these letters.

⁂

Just before leaving Chicago I attended a most important meeting of the workers interested in the Chicago City Mission work of the Disciples of Christ. A special committee had been appointed by the American Christian Missionary Society to attend this meeting. The committee consisted of J. A. Lord, editor of the Christian Standard, B. L. Smith, Secretary of the Home Board, and S. M. Cooper, one of our successful business men who is deeply interested in the city evangelization of Cincinnati. The meeting was a representative one and the city mission work was frankly and thoroughly discussed. All present rejoiced over the great work which has been accomplished during the last three years under the leadership of E. W. Darst, our superintendent of Chicago city missions.

⁂

Nearly every church in Chicago was represented in the meeting mentioned in the last paragraph. Bro. George A. Campbell and others felt that we had planted so many new churches in Chicago during the past three years (eight in all) that we should wait until the new organizations were housed before organizing any more *through the direction of the City Mission Board*. He was willing for the churches individually to plant new missions

But he thought the funds which pass through the hands of the treasurer of the City Mission Board could be expended wisest in supporting pastors who would house the new missions; *i. e.*, "strengthen the stakes" rather than "lengthen the cords."

***

There were others in this meeting especially representatives of the latest and perhaps most successful mission which has been planted by the superintendent of city missions, who felt that the wisest thing to do was to keep the superintendent of city missions constantly employed in selecting locations and wisely planting new missions. There were some, among whom was the writer, who believed in the *via media*—both lengthening the cords and strengthening the stakes. We were all agreed that no more important work is now before our Home Board than city evangelization, and that the work in the city of Chicago deserves and must have the hearty co-operation of our entire brotherhood.

***

We think it worthy of mention that the Hyde Park in Chicago has declared its intention of relieving the Home Board of any further financial responsibility. Bro. Errett Gates, who succeeded Dr. Willett, and has builded on the fine foundation for Christian work he laid, has more than doubled the financial strength of the congregation during his first year's ministry. He possesses fine organizing ability. The Hyde Park Church has not only declared itself self-supporting, but will before long purchase a lot and build. The example this congregation has set under the leadership of Bro. Gates is worthy of emulation by other mission churches. Until we have a local habitation the Hyde Park Church will be our home. The work in Chicago is advancing nobly under great difficulties. The preachers' meetings under the leadership of brethren Brandt, Oesgcher and Campbell are the best in the history of our Chicago churches.

***

Mr. and Mrs. C. M. Wakeley, with whom we had recently been making our home, and Mr. Hitchcock, saw Mrs. Young, Helen and myself to the train. We took the B. & O. for Wheeling, West Virginia, where Mrs. Young and Helen visited Mr. and Mrs. Clement and their two daughters, Eva and Elsie. Bro. and Sister Clement were faithful workers in our Ann Arbor church. They were some of the fruits of the C. W. B. M. work in that city. After a brief stay with our friends in Wheeling I visited Bethany, of which noble institution I shall have some things to say in my next letter. One day was spent in Pittsburg, one in Washington, where we met Bishop Power. My wife is a most excellent judge of preachers and she says Bro. Power is "the right man in the right place." We are now at the University of Virginia. Its noble dome, beautiful lawns, long arcades and the new buildings which cost a quarter of a million dollars, make it one of the noblest and most attractive universities in America from the architectural standpoint. In my next letter I shall give a brief report of the Virginia state convention at Charlottesville, which the limits of this letter will not permit me to do. I must, however, mention the crowning success of the C. W. B. M. state convention. Miss Ellen Kent, the State President, arranged a rare treat for the fine audience. Several of the leading professors of the University of Virginia made speeches endorsing our Bible work, and Dr. Charles W Kent announced that that the University of Virginia Bible Lectureship, founded by Col. Jno. B. Cary, would have a foundation of at least $10,000. This splendid announcement which filled all our hearts with joy, was followed by a most thoughtful and spiritually uplifting address, "The Divine Enterprise," by Mrs. Helen E. Moses. The outlook in Virginia is most promising for the work of the Disciples or Christ.

C. A. YOUNG.

Charlottesville, Va., U. of Va. Station.

The Moberly Educational Conference.

As already reported in our papers, the recent Missouri convention, at Nevada, ordered an educational conference to be called at Moberly, beginning Tuesday evening, Nov. 1st, to which all who are interested in the cause of Christian education in Missouri are invited, and in the deliberations of which they are asked to take a part. As this conference is the direct result of the annual report of Christian University to the convention, it is proper to make the facts known.

For four years a few men and women in the faculty of Christian University have carried the burden of its work and met its expenses, giving out of what would be called very meager salaries about $4,000 a year. A few people in Canton, generous above their ability, have given some help, donating in the past few years probably not less than $15,000 to endowment, buildings and expenses.

The results are an attendance last year of 125, of whom 47 were ministerial students; a correspondence Bible class of more than 100, of whom about 40 were preachers—a class of students so useful to the cause that during the year 1897, although attending college, they added over 600 to their churches, and an increased attendance the present year, with prospects of unlimited usefulness if the work be continued.

Each year our people in Missouri keep in college about 100 young men preparing for the ministry. Of these about one-half are here, many in Kentucky, some in Iowa and a very few in state institutions. Our sacrifices here have been made that this very fact might be tested. It now seems demonstrated that the young people most valuable to the cause will attend colleges of our own church, if not in this state, they will go to another. This proves that we must maintain a university of our own.

The growth and power of Christian University, although with too meager faculty and no money, establishes the fact that it can be made a great university, in every way worthy of this great Missouri brotherhood. To prove this beyond question has been another object of our labors here. The old objection that this location is off in a corner of the state is proved vain by the fact that students either come here or go entirely out of the state to find what they want. In this age of cheap and rapid transit, students disdain distance in their search for disirable instruction. As regards the natural features of the site, there is certainly no finer in the whole state. Every weakness can be obviated and every element of strength secured for a university here by ample endowment.

We have here four buildings and grounds that are so well adapted to university purposes that they might be reasonably estimated at $40,000, against which there are no mortgages. The endowment is now nearly $17,000 of which $8,000 are loaned on real estate, as safe as investments can be made. The rest is in the form of uncollected notes, the greater part of which bears interest collectible every year. Nearly all of these notes can be collected when due. This is a foundation for a university, not imaginary, not on paper, but real and unincumbered. The Christian people of Missouri are numerous and wealthy enough to put on this foundation an endowment of $500,000. In due time this would grow into a million dollars, and would from the first be the strongest university among our people. It does not seem worth while to call for pittances for such a work, when only thousands will maintain our self-respect. Indeed, there is little doubt that our people are ready to give thousands more promptly than fives and tens.

If in this matter we have been behind our brethren in other states, we can by prompt, hearty and united action sweep quickly to the rout. Whatever is to be done ought to be done at once. The present faculty cannot reasonably be asked to continue their work unsupported. Indifference of the brotherhood toward the work already done would give them no encouragement to go on; and they would regard their task accomplished at the end of this session. They would feel constrained to accept work where permanent results could be achieved, and it is not probable that another faculty would find encouragement to take up this work. If there has ever been an opportune time to act in this matter, it is now. How would posterity explain our destructive delay?

CLINTON LOCKHART.

Notes and News.

E. R. Rollins, of Ardmore, I. T., says that they now have a deed for a church lot and are ready to receive money for the erection of a church building.

A Prospering Church.—The Christian Church, Des Moines, Iowa, has given for expenses the past year, $5,114.50; missions, $3,170; for man's work $234.00; S. S., $317.00; making a grand total of nearly $9,000.00. One hundred and forty-one have been added to the church during the year, 74 by baptism.—*Christian Index.*

The Church of Christ at Watson, Mich., will celebrate its first anniversary Oct. 20-23, with appropriate service. A good program has been prepared.

A New Church Building.

A faithful little band here of only thirteen brethren, ten of whom are sisters, built a beautiful modern house, the finest in the town. We dedicated it yesterday clear of debt. We raised every cent of the money and dedicated clear of any incumbrance. Many shed tears for joy. This was the day of their triumph. Bro. Richardson, of Ridgeway, Bro. Gillett, of Bethany, and Bro. Bryant, of Cainsville, were here and assisted us. We will follow in a short meeting.

Morgan Morgans and Daughter.

Mt. Moriah, Mo., Oct. 3, 1898.

Another Dedication.

On Sept. 25th the new house of worship at Wilson, N. C., was dedicated. B. A. Abbott, Baltimore, Md., was the chief speaker of the day. B. H. Melton is the pastor of the newly homed church. The day was ideal, the audience immense, the services impressive and the offerings liberal. The church cost $9,000; of this the citizens of town gave $800, the congregation contributing the $8,200.

Kansas District Convention.

Report of the convention of the Church of Christ of the 9th district of Kansas, held at Atwood, Kansas, Sept. 27-29, 1898. The president being absent, O. L. Cook presided. Number of counties in the 9th district, twelve; number of counties represented, seven; number of delegates present, fourteen; number of ministers present, five.

We had a splendid convention, much enthusiasm. Six of the deligates drove across the prairie 110 miles that they might be present.

Many interesting papers were read and discussed, especially the paper on "Christian Endeavor Work: Its Place and Importance," by Mrs. Kate Marshall, of Colby. The paper, "The Duty, Manner and Purpose of Giving," by Rev. Walter Menzies, of Dresden, and the paper, "The W. C. T. U. and Its Work," by Mrs. C. T. Price, of Atwood, were of great interest.

On the call of committees they all responded with reports laden with suggestions for the upbuilding of the Master's cause. The committee on district work recommended: 1st. The need of county organization; 2nd. The need of a district evangelist; 3rd. A county mission fund to be used by the county committee.

A gain of 248 members over last year was reported.

The convention was spiritually alive as all could testify who attended. Much business was brought before the different committees and disposed of with energy and ability.

The convention closed by tendering a vote of thanks to the citizens of Atwood, who so royally and hospitably entertained the delegates while in their city and hoping to meet them all at the convention in Hill City next year.

Ernest Petty, Reporter.

More Success.

Dear Bro. Garrison:—Am right in it; building a meeting house for our congregation; here will almost complete it next week. I found a struggling little band here about ready to give up. We have bought the finest church site in the city and will soon have a comfortable place to meet it. God has helped me in this work, for which I feel very grateful. They did not think it could be done. Immersed one here last week. A. B. Moore.

Austin, Minn., Oct. 5, 1898.

Progress at Sloan, Ia.

W. B. Clemmer, pastor of the church at Sloan, Iowa, 11 additions, $42.96 for missions, one Junior C. E. and one C. W. B. M. organized and many improvements of a substantial nature, including the building of a parsonage, during the year. They will observe Forefathers' Day and are organizing a Bethany C. E. Reading Circle. Six graduates in the Iowa State Normal Course. Diplomas conferred in public graduating exercises.

Indiana District Convention.

The annual session of the 12th Indiana district of the Christian Endeavor Society, Christian Woman's Board of Missions, Indiana Christian Missionary Society and District Sunday-school Convention, will be held at Odon, Oct. 26-28. A fine program for each has been prepared and every minister, Sunday-school superintendent and church worker in the district is especially requested to be present. Each church is expected to send reports from church, Sunday-school, Christian Endeavor and Woman's Board of Missions. A rate of one and one-third fare will be given over all railroads, when single fare is 75 cents or more. Certificates will be furnished by railway agent on purchase of tickets and must be endorsed by T. A. Cox, secretary, at convention before return. You will reach Odon over the Southern Indiana Railway, making close connection with all trains from North and South at Elnora and points east of Odon.

Christian Church, Connellsville, Pa.

The Church of Christ was organized in Connellsville about the year 1830, under the leadership of Lester L. Norton, Abram Shallenberger, Joseph Herbert and others, its nucleus being formed by a few persons previously Baptists, but who had become dissenters from the doctrines of that church and adooted the views and teachings of Alexander Campbell, who often preached in Connellsville. Services were first held in private houses, with preaching by James Darsie, J. B. Pratt, —— Young, and others. A stone church building was erected about 1840. It was sold to the Lutherans in 1874, and a church edifice was built on Pittsburg St., at a cost of $10,000. This church was sold and the present magnificent house was dedicated June 26, 1898. Among the preachers who have ministered for the church have been A. Campbell, G. D. Benedict and others. The present minister is W. R. Warren who with his people gave the convention a warm welcome.—*Lighthouse Supplement.*

A Voice from Arizona.

Please give prayerful attention to the following reasons, why the Christian Church should give special attention to Arizona at this time.

1. The work in Arizona has been overlooked by our people in the past, while other religious bodies have been wide awake and active in its interest.

2. It is a new field and has all the advantages that usually belong to a new field.

3. Arizona is a rich country and is growing richer every year. Whoever commands its wealth will be able to command many good things—to build meeting houses, asylums, orphan schools, orphan homes, etc., and to send the gospel to the destitute at home and abroad.

4. Arizona is not only a rich country, but a large country—as large as all the Philippine Islands together. To come nearer home, it would make fifty-five states as large as Delaware and have 270 square miles left, or ninety states as large as Rhode Island and 520 square miles left. In all this vast rich region we have but three small churches and but one small, indifferent house of worship and but one feeble preacher.

5. This is to be the home of many of the enterprising sons and daughters of the East. In helping Arizona, then, you will be helping your own sons and daughters, and will be providing them church homes that will prevent many of them from falling away and being lost, and many others it will save to the work of the Christian Church.

6. Tempe is the strategic point of the territory. The Territorial Normal School is here and is always to be here, and with its tuition free it will always be full. The large, fine brick building was not completed till this year, and there were 168 matriculations (not counting the small children) and 17 graduates this session. The number, no doubt, will increase from year to year.

7. Last, but not least, by any means, Providence seems to be leading in the work and richly blessing the efforts that are being made at this time. This is the golden opportunity. Some say the only opportunity they ever had. By the aid of a benevolent man we have a lot paid for in a fine location, but we are not able to build upon it without aid from abroad. Who will come to the help of the Lord? Who will help us in our time of need?

Our Father in heaven, bless this paper, bless the eye that reads it, the ear that hears it, the heart that feels its power and the hand that helps in the glorious work. I ask in Jesus' name. Amen! R. A. Hopper.

The only preacher among the Disciples in Arizona.

State Mission Notes.

It was my great misfortune not to be able to attend the convention at Nevada, and I have been trying to get an insight into all that was done, and I find some things that I must at once bring to your attention. For instance: it was recommended by the committee on Ways and Means that State Mision Day be changed from the first Sunday in January to the first Lord's day in November. I must say that this meets my most hearty approval. The month of January is usually so cold and bleak that the country church very often fails to meet at all. It is just after the holidays when the people have spent a great deal in the festivities and are feeling uncommonly poor. But the month of November is a good-weather month, and it is the month of thanksgiving and praise. It is exceedingly fitting, therefore, that we make it the state mission month of the year.

The only thing I fear is that it will take us some time to get used to the change, and especially this year, because it will seem like taking two collections for state missions in one year. This is not true, however, as our convention year ends in September. It, however, will take heroic efforts on our part to get ready for it; the time is so short. But the greater the need of energetic work the more we ought to be ready to undertake it. For Missouri Disciples to back out from anything because it was hard to accomplish would be a new thing under the sun.

But in order to make the matter a success we must have the co-operation of all. I must ask first of all, the hearty co-operation of the county superintendents. Won't you please at once, either make a canvas of the churches in person, or address a circular letter to the churches and preachers in the county and endeavor to get them to bring this matter to the attention of the people? Can you not call for a conference of the preachers of your county and discuss the matter till they shall be full of interest in this matter? I believe that the ministry of Missouri can make this a success if they will. I have that much confidence in our people, if the need of this work is properly placed before them. I have not a single instance among all our churches where they refused to contribute at all when they were told of the need.

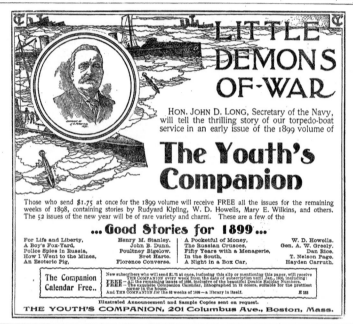

Therefore, I ask for the hearty co-operation of the ministry. Our money now must come from the churches as never before. I am sure that not one of our preachers in the state wants that the church should take second place in the list of Protestant Churches in the state. Yet, there are two other churches who are perilously near to us. And it will only be by the exercise of the greatest diligence that we shall be able to keep the place of honor which the providence of God has bestowed upon us. The destiny of our people in Missouri is wonderful if we but have the courage to persue it to the end. Our history is one full of inspiration; it should incite us to deeds of heroism that will hesitate at no sacrifice if only thereby the destitute places of our state are entered and captured for our King. As long as there is a place where we can plant a Church of Christ; as long as the divided condition of the church is before us; till the prayer of the Master for a united church is realized, we can't afford to lay our armor by.

I ask you, therefore, that you make Missouri Day a great day among us. Put your heart, your soul, your mind, your strength in it and our God shall give us the victory. Remember Missouri Day, the first Lords' day in November or as soon thereafter as possible.

Yours in his name. T. A. ABBOTT.
4144 *Westminster Place, St. Louis, Mo.*

Hope for the Sick.

A few days since I got a letter from the president of a large college in which he said he was very sick and had been for months hardly able to be out of bed. He was so thoroughly tired of medicine that he quit all medicine and drugs. He also quit drinking tea and coffee; ate meat only once a day; quit using pepper, vinegar and mustard; drank large quantities of hot water between meals and took an ordinary bath twice a week. He immediately began to recover rapidly, and is now strong. He tells his students that if they get sick not to take medicine, but to quit eating for a day or two, take a hot bath to make them sweat, and rest, and they will soon be well. His college has over two thousand students.

The president of another college which has about three hundred students wrote me recently that he was suffering from obesity, nervousness and kidney troubles. I told him to do as the other college president did. He did so and in one month wrote me he had greatly improved and had lost ten pounds of his excessive fat.

Nine cases of every ten of sick headaches are cured by doing as the above college presidents did. Don't laugh at the remedy, but try it.

When I was in London, England, the celebrated Dr. T. R. Allinson told me that any disease could be cured, was cured, by very simple hygiene rules.

Most cases of constipation are cured by drinking a glass of cold water half an hour before each meal, eating plenty of fruit and eating graham bread instead of white. Medicine alone never cures constipation.

The sore throat and tender throat of preachers and orators are cured by wearing a cold wet towel around the throat at night and gargling hot water in the throat.

I am sure that half the sickness in the world comes from the use of tea, coffee, condiments, rich foods and excessive use of meats. Sleeping in bedrooms without ventilation is a great evil. For further information address the writer.

W. FRANK ROSS, A. M., M. D.
Champaign, Ill.

The Relation of Prayer and Results.

Last night.—I heard Prof. W. E. Newell remark to an audience of 1,500 or more (the initial session of his Monday evening fall and winter Bible class in Englewood) that the secret of the phenomenal success last season and the promising greater success during the coming months of these five classes conducted by himself in various parts of our city is that two years ago he was led to address—and secured the sought-for co-operation—about 300 Christians in our own land and in the old world, known to be mighty in prayer, and requested them to *pray* for this special effort, then first entered upon, to enlist the people of Chicago in Bible reading and study.

This Morning.—I read in the CHRISTIAN-EVANGELIST, from the pen of its editor, these lines concerning the Chattanooga Convention: "Many of the delegates who go there will wish to visit Lookout Mountain. Why not hold a *prayer*-meeting up there, and in another 'battle above the clouds,' with the invisible forces of Satan and under the leadership of Jesus Christ win a decisive victory." Why not, indeed! Do it brethren—and as farther suggested, "let each man and woman of faith among us *pray* for the convention."

W. P. KEELER.
Chicago, Sept. 27, 1898.

Evangelistic.

WEST VIRGINIA.

.tington, Oct. 10.—Two added yesterday. on the three previous Lord's days.—G. EIMER.

NEBRASKA.

raska City, Oct. 12.—Our tent meeting the 9th with 30 additions to the church. interest manifested. A. B. Hurkins, eat temperance singer, led the music.—F. NG, preacher.

UTAH.

H. Bagby reports one confession at Salt City since last report. On his way to the anooga convention he preached at Colo- Springs, Col., Oct. 9th and had one con- n.

TEXAS.

tin, Oct. 8.—There were five additions ord's day and five two weeks before. We ptizing right along and additions every s day.—J. W. LOWBER.

KANSAS.

vard, Oct. 12.—One confession Sunday ig.—R. E. ROSENSTEIN.

vnee Rock, Oct. 15.—Our meeting is now ays old with six additions. My brother h and in Christ, from Princeton, Ill., is the preaching and I am leading the song e. Audiences are splendid despite the hat our M. E. brethren are running a ng at the same time in a town of 300 in- ants. But the Word will prevail.—C. D. LLIS PURLEE.

ll, Oct. 13.—I closed my work at above last Lord's day with two additions. There been 19 additions during the year at reg- ervices, increasing the congregation over hird in membership.—C. HENDERSON.

ena, Oct. 10.—Just closed a meeting of veeks four and one-half miles south of Had four additions; three by baptism one reclaimed. The congregation was a mixed multitude. Many were astonished doctrine. So good was the attention no one left the room during the two weeks' ng. Would like for any church in South- rn Kansas to correspond with me at Ga- Kas.—H. C. McNABB.

sing, Oct. 15.—Since last report we have zed three at Walula and two at Little ger.—H. C. BALLOU.

OKLAHOMA TERRITORY.

ry, Oct., 10.—Just closed a 10 days' ng at Lawson with three additions by sm. I go next to Polk, O. T., to hold a r three weeks' meeting.—WM. DUNKLE- ER.

rshall, Oct., 9.—We have just closed a neeting four and a half miles from Mar- 16 were added, two reclaimed, seven the denominations and seven by primary ence. Money, grounds and work were ed for a church building. The brethren t to have the house built by Christmas. egin a meeting next Saturday at Medford, —W. S. REHORN.

ud Chief, Oct. 8.—I have just closed a weeks' meeting at Oak Dale, of this y. The results were a good Sunday- l started and a church of 51 members or- ed: one from the Baptists and 11 by tive obedience. I expect to give them of my time.—A. L. TAYLOR.

MINNESOTA.

veland.—Our meeting is one week old, nine additions; one a former U. B. her of high standing. F. H. Sweetman y leading the song service. We go to ueur at close of meeting here.—SAMUEL G.

KENTUCKY.

ersontown, Oct. 12.—We have just d a good meeting at Fairview. There ut one addition, but much good was done ter lines of church work. Bro. Shouse, xington, Ky., did the preaching. It was g and helpful.—J. W. ROGERS.

ington, Oct. 14.—Bro. B. B. Tyler has with us at Broadway for three weeks. His has been very enjoyable and helpful to the egation. Two services a day were held. fternoon Bible readings were on such sub- as The Mission of the Holy Spirit, Prayer, Books of the Bible, etc. They were the instructive services we ever had in our h. Some great gospel theme was dis- d each night, the speaker injecting his personality in a most delightful manner a most lucid and scriptural presentation of ubjects. The meeting will be long remem- l by our people. There were 35 additions. RK COLLIS.

ARKANSAS.

Fayetteville, Oct. 11.—There were four conversions at the First Church on last Sunday.—N. M. RHGLAND.

MISSOURI.

Marceline, Oct. 10.—Just closed a 12 days' meeting at Twinn Grove, Ill., with six addition.—ISOM ROBERTS.

Mexico, Oct. 11.—I recently closed a short meeting at Boydsville, with eight additions to the church. Will begin a meeting at Friendship, Boone County, the 12th inst.—J. D. GREER.

Monroe City, Oct. 10.—Our meeting with the church in McPherson, Kan., closed with 28 additions. These are an excellent people and Bro. Lorton is a pastor worthy of all confidence. I am now in Monroe City, Mo. Fine audiences both A. M. and P. M. Sunday. Bro. Nicoson, the pastor, has everything in readiness for a good meeting.—D. D. BOYLE.

Maryville, Oct. 7.—Our meeting, which began Sept. 6 and closed the 29 of the month with the church at Skidmore, resulted in 20 additions; 14 new converts, two from the Cumberland Presbyterians, one from the Missionary Baptists, two by statement and one by letter. The writer did the preaching for the first week and Bro. W. H. Harris, of Grant City, Mo., the remainder of the time. He did splendid preaching and is a fine evangelist. We enjoyed his help very much indeed. This is my fourth year with the Skidmore congregation, and the church board sometime since extended me an invitation to stay with them another year. We were very sorry to leave them, but we have moved to Maryville that our children may have the advantage her superior schools. I would like to say to any congregation in reach of Maryville by team or rail which will be needing a minister for 1899, that I will be glad to serve them if suitable arrangements can be made.—N. ROLLA DAVIS.

Liberty, Oct. 15.—We have had four additions the first week of our meeting.—V. E. RIDENOUR, assisting Pastor J. M. Vawter.

NORTH CAROLINA.

Dixonville, Oct. 11.—Have just closed a meeting at Roundtree with 26 additions; 21 by confession and immersion and five otherwise. Also added 29 new members to the Y. P. S. C. E. Also held a meeting in September at St. Clans Creek with three additions.—R. W. STANCIL.

INDIANA.

Franklin, Oct. 11.—Eleven added, nine at Fillmore; eight by confession and one from the Baptists. Two were baptized at Christian Chapel. The old soldiers of Mooresville and vicinity were addressed by me on Lord's day Sept. 25, at 3 P. M.—WILLIS M. CUNNINGHAM.

Milroy, Oct. 10.—Bro. C. H. De Vae has just closed an excelent three weeks' meeting here with 10 accessions. His preaching was plain but forcible, and much good seed has been sown.—W. F. FOLKS, pastor.

Jeffersonville, Oct. 14th.—We are in a successful meeting here with C. C. Cline singing for us, and many additions. Our next meeting will be at Georgetown and New Washington.—T. M. MYERS.

Muncie, Oct. 15.—Have just closed at Fairview, Ia., with 13 additions. Begin to-day at Spartansburg, Ind., and at Mt. Vernon, Ind., in November. Any church wanting me in December should write at once.—A. MARTIN.

IOWA.

Oelarin, Oct. 10.—Ten baptisms, four by statement and two confessions not yet baptized since last report. Our prospects are better and our working force increasing. May God bless the workers in all the field.—SAM B. ROSS.

Lehigh, Oct. 10.—I began a meeting here on August the 17th, assisted by G. A. Butler, of Mound City, Mo., as singing evangelist. There had once been quite a flourishing church at this place, but like all things human it has had its adversities. As is usual when a church gets stranded, a few faithful women kept the ship afloat until it could be floated off the rocks. They needed help, sympathy and encouragement. We did not receive much encouragement in undertaking to "set things in order." After the meeting had been in progress three weeks it was decided to disband, and reorganize at the close of the meeting. From the day the church disbanded the interest grew; 75 have come forward to take up the work in the new organization; among them a number of confessions. The church has taken on new life, and is well equipped for good work. We will reorganize the church, with all its auxiliaries, and close the meeting on Oct. 16th. The church will need a good pastor. We will raise his salary and get all things ready for him.—L. F. McCRAY AND C. A. BUTLER.

M. R. Shanks reports 14 confessions at regular services, Oct. 2, at Monticello. Bro. Shanks has closed his work there that he may take a course of study in Drury College, Springfield, Mo.

CALIFORNIA.

Fortuna, Oct. 4.—Accompanied by Mrs. Markle and Sister C. P. Cone, of Hanford, we took the vacation proffered us by our congregation, by going back into the mountains 60 miles. While there we held a meeting resulting in a little organization of 18 members, 10 by confession and baptism, four from the Baptists and four who were formerly Christians. We also organized a Y. P. S. C. E. and Ladies' Aid Society. We will return the 17th to arrange the purchase of a church building from the United Brethren. Our camp was on the banks of Eel River and we spent the day casting the fly for trout and climbing the hills for deer, of which we had an abundance during our four weeks' stay, and a fine "spike buck" to carry home with us.—A. B. MARKLE.

ILLINOIS.

Stronghurst, Oct. 9.—Meeting will close next Tuesday evening. There have been 20 additions.—A. V. LINDSEY, Canton, Mo.

Stronghurst, Oct. 12.—Elder A. N. Lindsey, of Canton, Mo., closed a two weeks' meeting at this place last evening evening with 22 additions to the church.—L. A. WILSON.

Pittsfield, Oct. 10.—Seven more added yesterday. Have a Bible class for the study of the Life of Christ numbering 65; meet on Monday evenings.—R. F. THRAPP.

Blandinsville, Oct. 10.—Have just closed a two weeks' meeting at New Harmony, Pike Co., Mo., with 10 additions; nine by confession and one restored. Am now in a meeting at Jonesburg, Mo.—W. A. MELOAN.

A. O. Swartwood reports a 19 days' meeting at Walnut Corner, by W. H. Barker, with 12 additions; 11 baptisms. A. O. Swartwood was song leader.

C. E. SYMPOSIUM.

[The following symposium on our Christian Endeavor Societies was read at the National Convention at Chattanooga, on Monday afternoon of this week.—EDITOR.]

What Others are Doing for their Young People, and How they are Doing it.

There are five ways of solving the problem of the young people:

1. Do nothing for them.
2. The strict denominational society.
3. The open denominational society that gives free fellowship to other organizations.
4. The general Y. P. S. C. E. without any organization within the denomination.
5. The Y. P. S. C. E. with special organization within the denomination for oversight of the work of the Endeavor Societies.

Of ten denominations, of which information has been gathered, three have the strict denominational society; four have the open denominational society; two have the general organization of Y. P. S. C. E. with special denominational organization for oversight.

Only two of the ten have no organized method of oversight. These two rely upon addresses in conventions and conferences.

Aside from this work of guidance churches do two things for their young people:

1. They instruct them.

Seven of the ten denominations have reading courses which cover some three of the following subjects: The Bible, Missions, Denominational History and Polity, Science, Literature and History.

Of the seven denominations who have distinctively denominational organizations, either open or close, six give financial support to a man who superintends the young people's work.

Of the three who have simply Endeavor Societies, not one gives support to a leader in the work.

2. They *use* them.

Every one of the ten takes collections from the young people assiduously. This is right. But he that soweth bountifully shall also reap bountifully.

We should do great things for our young people. The church of God has fallen upon great times. It is an era of gigantic enterprises; in commerce, trusts and monopolies that touch every inhabitant of the land; in mechanics, achievements of stupendous power, whose very conception is dazzling; in war, tons of steel are hurled every minute, ceasing not until the enemy is utterly overwhelmed.

The church must partake of this spirit. We would stultify ourselves to do less than the greatest for our young people. Give them the best. Give it abundantly. Give it freely. Let them be full, rounded, large-hearted, broad-minded Christians whose spirits shall be stirred within them as they see the world given to iniquity and who will find no rest till this great wide world shall be wholly turned to the Lord Jesus Christ. I. J. CAHILL.

How may we best Increase the Religious Intelligence of the Christian Endeavor Societies?

One of the most blighting curses of the world is ignorance. It has filled more hearts with hatred, it has crimsoned more hands with blood, it has closed more eyes to the gleams of beauty and stopped more ears to the appeals of wisdom; it has done more to retard the progress of the race, and has contributed more largely to the misery of man than any other one thing of which I know. He is, indeed, a benefactor who contributes ever so slightly to banishing this withering curse from the world.

The church's progress has been retarded by nothing so mush as by ignorance. "When by reason of the time ye ought to be teachers, ye have need again that some one teach you the rudiments of the first principles of the oracles of God." Christ has often been "crucified anew" through ignorance. Long ago Christ should have triumphed through the wisdom of his people, and yet even now he must suffer partial defeat because of their inexcusable ignorance.

Blessings of incalculable worth will come to the world where ignorance is supplanted by knowledge. Solomon says of wisdom:

"She shall give to thine head a chaplet of grace;
A crown of glory shall she deliver unto thee."

And a greater than Solomon has said: "If ye know these things, blessed are ye if ye do them;" and again, "Ye shall know the truth, and the truth shall make you free." The people of God shall be one again; the world shall believe that Christ was sent of God; "the wilderness and the solitary place shall be glad, the desert shall rejoice and blossom as the rose," the "knowledge of the glory of the Lord shall fill the earth as the waters cover the sea."

To tell how a result so necessary and so beneficent as is the increasing of religious intelligence and the consequent diminishing of ignorance is to be attained is not so difficult a task; but the doing of these things—"Aye, there's the rub." "Every one of us knows better than he practices, and recognizes a better law than he obeys."

Having only hinted at the pressing necessity of increasing religious intelligence, and having but pointed to a few of the beneficent results of so doing, I shall wholly omit the mention of the many means by which we may *help* increase the religious knowledge of the young people, and address myself to telling how, as it seems to me, we may *best* increase their religious intelligence, and thus prepare them for the doing of those duties which shall soon devolve upon them. That you may remember what I say just here I shall revert to the question as stated in my subject. It is, "How May We Best Increase the Religious Intelligence of the Christian Endeavor Societies?" I answer unhesitatingly, "By the widespread, persistent and thorough use of the Bethany Christian Endeavor Reading Courses."

If I have correctly diagnosed the case, and if I value at its true worth the remedy just mentioned, I should give the prescription to every Christian Endeavor Society, and the direction should read, "To be taken every day until the patient is dead." Here is a field of untold richness in which to sow "the good seed of the kingdom." In the classes of these Reading Courses the preacher becomes a teacher, and the listener becomes a learner.

This method is best because it is the most systematic. It is a difficult task to preach systematically—to preach so that each sermon leads up to its successor, and each successor leads back to its predecessor. And even if the preacher do this systematic preaching he must contend with the systematic forgetfulness of his hearers. It is quite time that he who learns all he knows of the Bible from the sermons he hears gets almost no systematic knowledge of the sacred Scriptures. In the classroom, however, the preacher teaches and the listener learns systematically.

Again, the method is best because it is thorough. "Precept upon precept, line upon line, here a little, there a little," is a splendid motto for the teacher, but the preacher must work in a more general way. Here one can be as painstaking as the importance of the truth he is teaching demands. Here the preacher can teach more thoroughly than he can from the pulpit, and here also the pupil can learn more thoroughly than he can from the pew.

Surely, that preacher is "blind and cannot see afar off," who does not see in the Bethany Reading Courses his golden opportunity for increasing the religious intelligence of the young people of the church to which he ministers. Thousands of young people are praying—

"Open thou our eyes, that we may behold
Wondrous things out of thy law;"

and it seems to me that the preacher can hel answer their prayers in no way so well as b gathering them into these classes, and "teaching them the way of the Lord more perfectly."

ROBT. G. FRANK.

Nicholasville, Ky., Sept. 22, 1898.

How may we best Develop and Utilize ou Christian Endeavor Forces?

1. We must cultivate a feeling of responsibility and sympathy. The church is alway reponsible for the wise training of the young Their welfare and the church's future are involved. The Lord is saying to the church a Pharaoh's daughter said to the mother o Moses, "Take this child and nurse it for m and I will give thee thy wages." The exten of the church's responsibility and power in th nurture of the young is indicated by the ol proverb, "Youth and white paper take an impression" and by the fact of commo observation, that youth is the formativ period of life, when most is done to determin destiny. You cannot put the oak back int the acorn, the eagle back into the shell. Lik a fond mother, the church must brood over he young until Christ be formed in them.

Her responsibility is in no wise diminished but rather increased by the coming of the Y. P S. C. E. It has aroused the latent forc among the young, organized it and brough them into new and sometimes trying relations How shall this new engine be directed? Wha works shall it perform? Who shall guide it We can do nothing without sympathy. Happy indeed, is the man who though furrows wrinkl his brow and snow crowns his temples remembers that he was young, and knows well wha it is to be young, because he has sympathy A well-known minister in a crowded omnibu expostulated with some wags who were makin sport of a drunken Scotchman. The tips fellow appreciated it, and said in a loud voic as he finally left the omnibus: "I see ye ke what it is to be drunk yersel!"

2. We must see to it that the young people get to doing things. The talking machine has passed through a wonderful evolution in our time, but we do not want the Christian Endeavor Society to be one of its stages. The danger with the Society is that it will become a school for talkers, rather than a camp for doers, and so find its best description in Romeo's sneer to Mercutio, "A gentleman nurse, that loves to hear himself talk, and will speak more in a minute than he will stand to in a month." Let us engage hands as well as tongues. Give the young disciple a taste of actual service. When emotion all evaporates at the mouth, it leaves the soul limp and powerless. There can be too much talk; we want enough for stimulus, but beware how you allow any one to become spendthrift with his tongue.

Visit the sick, the absent, the indifferent. Carry flowers and music to the hospital and to the prison. Distribute judiciously food to the hungry and clothing to the naked. Scatter good literature until the community is sown ankle deep with its white leaves of healing. "Sampson is fighting, not talking," said the secretary.

3. We should also try to see the possibilities of Christian Endeavor. Said our tireless national snperintendent, "I believe in Christian Endeavor, not for what it is, but for what it may become." It has boundless possibilities for good. May we not look upon it as the beginning of a time when the world shall be blessed with a higher type of Christian character? "Not more Christians," wrote the contemplative and philosophic Drummond, "but better Christians!" Surely the proper fruitage of Christian Endeavor will be greater delicacy of moral insight and greater conscientiousness.

The church must become more beautiful and glorious. This high tide of youthful devotion and enthusiasm will float any old hulk off the shoals into the deep water of Christian enterprise. Christian Endeavor puts the emphasis in the right place, and will eventually produce a church which will not spend so much on its own shepherding. It will inscribe upon helmet and brow, "Ich dien" (I serve), and grope its way into the crowded court and along the dark alley and down the winding stair. It will stand by the wretched and the unfriended, and speak of love and mercy and forgiveness. Wherever population is denest, wherever shadows are darkest and the need is the sorest, there the church will go, bearing balm and sympathy and succor. Then will the church be "the union of all who love in the service of all who suffer." Even Buddha declared, "Never will I seek or receive private salvation, never enter into final peace alone; but forever and everywhere will I live and strive for the univeral redemption of every creature."

Among the magnificent possibilities of Christian Endeavor in its influence direct and reflex upon the church is the accomplishment of much of its work. The time is coming when there shall be no more wars to drench the earth with blood; when there shall be no more shadows of ignorance and phantoms of superstition; when the red carnations of sinful passion shall pale into the lilies of celestial purity, and the world will be Eden-clad again. Armies shall flee away and shepherds shall tune their lutes. Every stagnant pool of corruption shall be dried up and fountains shall murmur and rivers sing. The nations shall bring their diadems and twist them into one magnificent crown for the luminous brow of Immanuel, and the universe, redeemed from sin and thrall, multitudinous and innumerable will rise like a mighty congregation and sing—

"All hail the power of Jesus' name,
Let angels prostrate fall!
Bring forth the royal diadem
And crown him Lord of all."

FRANK G. TYRRELL.

Missionary.

Home Missions.

AMERICA FOR CHRIST.

When the books of the American Christian Missionary Society closed Sept. 30, 1898, the receipts during the year for Home Missions amounted to $39,016.05, adding to this amount the collection in November for the Board of Negro Education and Evangelization, $2,329.62, we have a total of $41,345.67, which shows a gain over the combined collection of last year of $3,446.40. We have gained 316 in the number of contributing churches and $6,352.30 in the offerings of the churches. The gain in the number of contributing Christian Endeavor Societies is 190, many having sent in offerings to the "Romig Tabernacle Fund." The year shows a loss of $2,872.55 in bequests and a loss of 340 in the number of contributing individuals.

We believe our offering from the churches would have been much larger but for the waves of war excitement which was sweeping over the country when the offering was taken. War was declared against Spain the 23rd day of April; our offering came the 1st day of May, and our ministers found it hard to get the attention and interest of the people to Home Missions in that great time of war excitement.

Great advances have been made in the work of Home Missions, many new fields have been entered, and now the board has decided to follow the flag and preach the gospel of the New Testament in Porto Rico.

Next year is the jubilee year of the American Christian Missisnary Society, and we should make it the greatest year in the history of our Home Mission work. The Home Board proposes $100,000 for Home Missions. This is the least we should plan for the jubilee year. We earnestly appeal to our brethren everywhere to help us in this holy crusade. Help us to come to the jubilee of the American Christian Missionary Society with $100,000 for Home Missions.

BENJ. L. SMITH, C. C. SMITH, } Cor. Secs.
Y. M. C. Bldg., Cincinnati, O.

Started on the New Year.

Comparing the receipts for Foreign Missions for the first ten days of October with the corresponding time 1897 shows the following:

Contributing	1897	1898		Gain
Churches	10	11		1
Sunday-schools	9	8	Loss	1
Individual offerings	11	8	Loss	3
Amount	$607.52	$6,373.57		$5,766.05

Of the above amount received $5,951.76 came from a bequest.

F. M. RAINS, Treas.
Cincinnati, Ohio.

Church Extension Receipts.

For completing chapels for week ending Oct. 8, 1898:

From churches	$399.89
From individuals	410.53
Total	$810.42
Last year, churches	$682.15
Individuals	400.25
Loss	$271.98

NOTE.—A further analysis of our receipts shows that we gained $10.28 in individual receipts, while we lost $282.26 from the churches. We also gained two in the number of contributing churches, 59 having sent during the week ending Oct. 8th this year, while 57 sent in the same time last year.

Collections should be pressed vigorously by the churches all through October. Remittances should be made to

G. W. MUCKLEY, Cor. Sec.
600 Waterworks Building, Kansas City, Mo.

Memory Notes for Home Missions.

The Home Field is the reservoir from which the stream of beneficence must flow to all our future work. We must not let that reservoir grow smaller, but rather enlarge it.

The best expenditure of means that our brotherhood could make would be to put one hundred thousand dollars in Home Missions next year. All our enterprises would feel the stimulus at once.

"I believe it is fully in the hands of Christians in the United States, during the next twenty years, to hasten or retard the coming of Christ's kingdom hundreds of years."

The better day is dawning for Home Missions. The largest growth of the next few years will take place in this department of our work, because we have neglected it and it has fallen behind, and because there is no more fruitful field of effort, and because every mark of divine leading calls upon us to push Home Missions to the front.

The Home Board organized the work in many states; as, for instance, Nebraska, where D. R. Dungan and R. C. Barrow under the direction of the American Christian Misssonary Society, began the work and organized 122 churches. The missionaries of the Home Board have organized more than 2,100 churches in the United States.

Both good and evil have a longer leverage in the United States than anywhere else in the world. . . . He does the most to Christianize the world and to hasten the coming of the kingdom who does the most to make thoroughly Christian the United States. I do not imagine that an Anglo-Saxon is any dearer to God than a Mongolian or an African. My plea is not, save America for America's sake, but save America for the world's sake.—*Josiah Strong.*

God led Israel to Kadesh-Barnea and their spies came back and reported a land of milk and honey, but they feared the giants and refused to enter into the promised land. God leads us to view the great land of America; in our marvelous growth, in our successful evangelization, in our simple gospel of the New Testament, God is saying, "You are able to win this land." There are giants of sectarianism and sin, but if true to our Lord Jesus we can win.

Forefathers' Day.

Our Christan Endeavor Societies will celebrate Forefathers' Day on Oct. 23rd, 1898.

It should be a red-letter day for the study of the lives and works of the fathers of the Restoration movement.

Attractive programs have been prepared and will be sent on application. Let all Endeavor Societies prepare and plan for a great day. Begin now.

For information and program address

BENJ. L. SMITH, C. C. SMITH, } Cor. Secs.
Y. M. C. A. Bldg, Cincinnati, Ohio.

Annual Report Foreign Christian Missionary Society.

The past year has been the best in the history of the society. There has been a decided gain in the amount contributed and in the number of contributors. Several new stations have been opened. Reinforcements have been sent out into four fields. The workers report that God has dealt graciously with them.

Finances.—The receipts for the year amount to $130,925.70. This is a gain over last year of $24,703.60. The contributing churches number 2,907. This is a gain over last year of 321. The churches as churches gave $45,650.20. This was a gain of $6,031.92. 960 churches contributed this year that did not do so last. 667 churches that gave last year gave nothing this. Churches that raised their full apportionment or more, 752. The Sunday-schools gave $34,334.97, a gain over last year of $4,307.75. The contributing schools amount to 3,180, a gain of 370. Schools that raised their full apportionment, 926. Churches that either gave or raised as much as $1.00, 5,868. Schools that now use the Birthday Box, 1,221. The Endeavor Societies did not do as well this year as last. The amount received from them is $2,127.76, a loss of $1,270.57. From bequests only $975.60 was received this year. As compared with last year this is a loss of $7,615.55. On the Annuity plan the society received $32,390. Last year the watchword was $100,000 *for Foreign Missions by collections only.* It was proposed to raise this amount from annuities and bequests. The sum was not quite reached. The receipts aside from annuities and bequests amounted to $97,363.10. This is an increase over regular receipts of $6,529.15. In five years the number of contributing churches, Sunday-schools and Endeavor Societies has been more than doubled. The receipts also have been more than doubled. The missionary force in the field has been greatly increased.

The Missionaries.—At the time of the last convention Miss Hattie L. Judson died. She had been in India for five years. In May last A. F. H. Saw, of China, died of typhus fever. Gulali, a native evangelist, and Amiabai, the wife of Sampson Power, a helper in the hospital in Hurda and Jagannath, an Indian evangelist, went to their reward. Miss Oldham and Miss Rioch, of Japan; E. M. Gordon, of India; Dr. Butchart and W. R. Hunt and family, of China, came home on furlough. Dr. C. S. Durand and wife felt compelled to sever their connection with the society, on account of Mrs. Durand's health. John Johnson, of Smyrna, was married to Miss Ellen Allen. E. E. Faris and Dr. H. N. Biddle have spent most of the year in searching for a place to begin work in Africa. It is possible that Bolengi, on the Congo, will be their first station. The missionaries have enjoyed as good health as usual. They have done everything in their power for the furtherance of the gospel.

New Buildings.—In the past year the society has appropriated $22,492 for buildings. Two homes have been erected in Japan. Money was granted to help to build two small chapels, one at Innai, the other at Akozu. The believers at those places propose to pay back the money when they are able. Money was granted for a home for the young ladies in Nankin, China, and for a chapel in the same city. Also for a second home in Chu Cheo. The committee granted money for a lot and building in Shanghai, for a school and chapel, and also enough to put up two homes in that city. Money was granted for a hospital in Lu Cheo fu and also for a home. The Municipality of Hurda, India, gave a piece of ground to the mission for a girls' school. A building is in course of erection for a home for young ladies of that place. This money has been taken from the Annuity funds. Had it not been for the money received on the Annuity plan, these buildings could not possibly have been erected.

New Missionaries.—Since the last convention the following have been appointed: Dr. E. I. Osgood and wife and Dr. H. G. Welpton, to China; Miss Mildred Franklin and David and Dr. Minnie Rioch, to India. Miss Franklin will take up the work laid down by Miss Judson. Mr. and Dr. Rioch will probably open a new station. A. L. Chapman and and wife have gone to Constantinople. They will be associated with G. N. Shishmanian and family. Miss Bertha Clawson went to Japan. W. D. Cunningham and wife have been appointed to labor in Japan. On account of sickness they have not yet started for the field. Teizo Kawai has gone back to work at Akita, Japan. W. E. Gordon and S. McMullen have been appointed to aid in the work at Bilaspur, India. F. E. Stubbin has been sent from Queensland, Australia, to help in the Industrial Work at Damoh, India. He will be supported by the churches in Australia.

REPORTS FROM THE FIELD.

India.—At Hurda and the stations round about, there were forty-two added in the year; present membership, 104. In the Sunday-school there are 360 enrolled; in the day schools, 140. The number of baptisms is much larger than in any previous year. This is due, in a measure, to the relief given to the people in the famine. The gospel has been preached far and near by Mr. Wharton and his associates. Dr. Drummond reports 6,976 patients treated. In the hospital at Timarni there were 2,128 patients. G. W. Coffman has taken charge of the education of the boys. He is teaching the common branches and the Bible. Fourteen lepers were baptized during the year. Nathoo Lall has preached in 42 villages. He reports 24 baptisms at Charwa. M. J. Shah teaches two Sunday-schools, one in Timarni, the other in Rahatgaon. There are 70 children enrolled. Dr. John Panna preaches the gospel and heals the sick. A hospital and a dispensary have been built in the year. Also the bungalow in which he and his wife live. He has a Sunday-school of 25 amomg the lower caste of people.

Bilaspur.—M. S. Adams reports 24 baptisms in the year. The present membership is 66. Sunday-school attendance 80. The church has made very substantial progress. The house is usually well filled at the services. The Sunday-school is encouraging. Mrs. Adams has had charge of the food and clothing of the orphan boys at that point. S. McMullen has served as an evangelist. He has spoken at home and in the surrounding villages. The people say while listening to him, "Our deities are only stone." W. E. Gordon has worked among the boys. He is the headmaster of the school. Part of every day is given up to scriptural lessons.

Mungeli.—E. M. Gordon states that the membership at Mungeli has been almost doubled. The pupils in the day-school numbered 30; in the Sunday-school, 176. Dr. Anna Gordon has treated 6,265 patients. There are 20 lepers in the aslyum at this point. Dr. Gordon has prepared a number of women to help in the mission.

Damoh.—John G. McGavran's time has been largely given to orphanage, famine and building work. In the year about 730 children passed through the orphanage. At the present time there are about 225 boys and 93 girls. He supplied seed to the farmers of about 75 villages. He reports that the missionaries in Damoh have built a school and church costing about $400. There were 13 baptisms in the year. The church now has 34 members. A site has been secured for the ladies' bungalow. It will be finished about the close of the present year. The people are open to the gospel as never before. There is more reason than ever to hope for the conversion of many. W. E. Rambo has had charge of the orphanage since his return. He is teaching the larger boys trades. Some are taught dairying, some poultry culture, some gardening, a few tailoring. The Industrial School is conducted in the belief that a training in improved methods will contribute to a sturdier Christian charac ter. The boys are being prepared to suppor themselves, and not only so, but to introduc improved methods of work among the lowe people. Mrs. Rambo has given out about 80 garments. Nearly 200 of these she brough with her. She has made on her own machin most of the coats for the little boys. Sh visits the orphanage every morning an teaches the children Bible verses and simpl songs. Miss Josepha Franklin has spent mos of her time in the orphanage. She has looke after the food, clothing, bathing and genera cleanliness of the girls, and has cared for th sick. She spent $1,270 in relief work durin the year. She has now oversight of the girls school. She spends five hours daily in th schoolroom, and knows every child. A hal hour daily is given to the study of the Bible The children are required to learn a few verse by heart each week. Fifteen new boys hav made the good confession and been baptized On Sundays she sings hymns and teaches th people in four or five zenanas. Sometimes a many as 20 or 30 women gather in one house She is greeted in the town by, "Come in an sing;" after singing the people say, "No teach us wisdom from your Bible." The door for the gospel are open. We have only t enter. Dr. Mary McGavran reports 4,62 persons treated. In the dispensary, in th girls' orphanage and other outside work 2,030; making a grand total of 6,654. Dr McGavran needs a hospital. Miss Stell Franklin has used $350 in famine relief work She has helped to care for the small boys i the mission orphange. She has also taught i the schools. She has gone out with her help ers into the villages. She has visited th women in their homes. On Friday evening she has a class for the native Christia helpers.

Japan.—C. E. Garst has preached th gospel in Tokyo and in many towns and vil lages throughout the empire. He has held a number of protracted meetings for th churches that have been organized. Mis Johnson has conducted two Sunday-schools, two women's meetings, the weekly prayer meetings and the Junior Christian Endeavo meetings. She has taught an English clas for boys twice a week, and one for women tw afternoons of each week, besides an Englis Bible class. In addition to her other dutie she has acted as treasurer of the mission. Miss Mary Rioch reports a steady growth i most departments of the work. In one schoo it has been necessary to squeeze in four more desks. The school is crowded. The Bible is taught a half-hour daily. Some work is done among the mothers of the children. She has taught English two hours a week in the English school connected with the mission. The Sunday services, prayer-meetings, women's meetings, show a gradual increase in attendance and interest. H. H. Guy and F. H. Marshall have spent most of the year in the training school. Mr. Guy has taught Old Testament history, New Testament history, life of Christ and Paul, New Testament Greek, and has given lectures. In addition to this he has preached in one of the churches and has made a number of trips into the country. Mr. Marshall has taught New Testament exegesis, church history and New Testament Greek. He has taught English four hours a week. On Sunday evenings he has conducted an English Bible class, which is well attended. Mrs. Guy reports that a house has been bought in a thickly settled neighborhood for a school. She has been working in this district ever since she came to Japan. A little band of Christians has been gathered there. Wherever she goes she has an opportunity o talking the gospel to people. E. S. Stevens has preached and taugh regularly. Five men are taking a course in general history, Old Testament and New Testament history, miracles, parables, geography and church history. He has taught some classes in English to break down preju-

ı among the people. patients treated. t in the home and rage attendance of n's meetings. All household duties, care for the needy. goodly number of ıny saw a Christian He has the over- ı and vicinity. He se places. He has panese Christians. 6 young men came eir desire to learn rs. Madden reports l; one near their he city. She has omes of the people. n welcomed. The quite difficult. No mission unless she a. R. L. Pruett esults. The gospel mber turned to the ıe faith they once ople in their homes lks to them on the ı in his home. He urrounding towns, s and tracts. Mrs. school with 44 en- the little ones are are nine organized which meetings are were 129 additions. ay-schools number studying for the e making a special

reports a lot pur- ı American Settle- is a two-storied ll serve as a school e for some of the has taught English omen's meetings. l in Shanghai, also ıing. He has been ost of the year. In ped to translate the lect. C. E. Mol- the best in his mis- ı not been without used these to prove There are at present ı at Wuhu, and 33 F. E. Meigs has ear in school work. preaching regularly ed as much time to l. The school has ı not flagged. Dr. ents at the dispen- The medical work ıat he does. Every class with the in- ıe out-patients. vice. Three after- out into the country ı. Over 6,000 por- been sold or given ital. He has pre- c Garrett has taken o. He has taught a ege. In the hospi- every day with the privilege to baptize ıs gone to the girls' and talked to the isited some in their English some in the ı Lyon states that wth in spiritual life n girls have shown ıatever they could. school classes, oth- en who came, and house. The pupils know a great deal about the Bible. They say they will not worship idols. Miss Lyon has charge of the women's meetings, Christian Endeavor Society, and superintends the Sunday-schools. Dr. Daisy Macklin has acted as a nurse and as a physician. She has held prayers in the wards. Some of those who came to the clinic were treated by her. She has attended others in their homes and has assisted her brother in his operations and performed some herself. Miss Kelly has spent the year working among the women. She has visited Chu Cheo and Yu Ho Tze and some other places. W. R. Hunt has preached in the market place, in the chapel, dispensary, villages, cities and homes. He baptized five persons in the year. Mrs. Hunt has accompanied her husband at times on his tours. She has gone to the homes of Christians and inquired and talked with them. Mrs. Saw made a number of trips to Lu Hoh and to the north-gate and one to Yu Ho Tze. Dr. Butchart opened work in Lu Cheo fu. He treated 2,550 patients in all. The in-patients numbered 96. A church of 12 members has been organized. Mr. and Mr. Titus have gone to Lu Cheo fu and have established themselves there. Thus far most of their time has been given to the study of the language. They address the people through an interpreter. They have assisted Dr. Butchart in his operations and in caring for the sick.

It will be of interest to know that the increase in the three great heathen fields is as follows: India, 60 per cent., Japan, 34 per cent.; China, 46 per cent.

Scandinavia.—Dr. Holck reports 15 added in Copenhagen and the present membership is 175. The church has lost several by death and by emigration. The work is moving along smoothly and is in good condition. In the church in Sweden there has been a net gain of 15. The present membership is 25. The Swedes are open to conviction and religiously inclined. The present membership in Norway is 886; scholars in the Sunday-school, 102, preaching stations, 26; contributed for self-support, $977. The reports from Norway are incomplete. On their face they show an apparent decrease. This is owing to the fact that it has been difficult to get full statistics from all the churches. Had all the additions been reported, there would have been an increase instead of a decrease.

Turkey.—Dr. Kévorkian reports for six places. The aggregate membership for these is 199. The churches have lost members by death, by emigration and by various other causes. In the Sunday-schools there are 135 children and in the day schools 96. Turkey, like Scandinavia, greatly needs more qualified men. G. N. Shishmanian reports for eight points. There are four unordained men preaching the gospel; two male teachers and three female. In the eight organized churches there are 387 members. In the day schools there are 121 boys and 79 girls.

England.—The churches report 395 baptisms and 112 other additions. There are 15 churches in all. For self-support and benevolent purposes these churches paid $15,820; for missions, $1,460. In the Sunday-schools there are 2,641 enrolled. In the Christian Endeavor Societies there are 306 members. The Cheltenham church has bought a property of its own, and, though heavily encumbered with debt, this building is a great advantage. Aside from indebtedness the buildings in England owned by the society are worth $98,307. The reports from the several churches are very encouraging.

CONCLUSION.

We record with gratitude that the churches are growing from year to year in interest and liberality. More men and women are volunteering for this high service. More money is given for their support, and more prayers on their behalf are offered. The missionary spirit is urgent need of recognizing that all that we have and all that we are belong to our Redeemer, and must be used for his honor and glory. In our churches and colleges and in our literature this cause must have a larger place than it has had hitherto. Its claims must be pressed home to the hearts and consciences until the knowledge of the glory of the Lord shall cover the earth as the waters cover the sea.

A. McLean, Cor. Sec.

Family Circle.

A Prayer.

IDA B. DAVIDSON.

As a bird that is wounded,
 Dear Lord, would I fly
To thy care and protection—
 Thy covert so nigh.

And in peace and contentment
 With thee would I rest;
While with blessed assurance
 I lean on thy breast.

For the way oft seems dreary,
 The path seems so long;
And a night dark and starless
 Comes down without song.

But beyond all the darkness
 And pain and distress,
Is a brightness more glorious
 Than tongue can confess.

So on thee all my burdens
 In trust I will lay;
And will live for thee ever
 Till dawns that bright day.

Eureka, Ill.

The Gospel Message to Childhood, and Ways of Presenting It.

LESLIE W. MORGAN.

If there is a gospel message for children it goes without saying that we should know what it is and how to present it. For in proportion as there is such a message, and in proportion to its faithful presentation, will there be live, healthy Christianity to-morrow. President David Starr Jordan says: "Our greatest duty may not be to save the parent, but to see that the child does not walk in the parent's footsteps." It is, indeed, true that if we can take care of the coming generation, time will attend to the present one. It is surprising to think how simple would be the solution of the problems of crime and intemperance if only we could stop the supply. The children occupy the field for operation, and the gospel is the power of God unto their salvation. That the gospel has a message for children, and that in some measure at least it has been presented, is evident from a comparison of the condition of children in Christian and non-Christian lands. The heritage of the majority of children in heathen lands is degradation, misery and want. Victor Hugo says: "He who has seen the misery of a woman has seen nothing; he must see the misery of a child." The three plainest footprints of Christianity are those that mark its influence on the three closely related realms of womanhood, childhood and the home.

The first question that we will consider is—

WHO SHALL PRESENT THE MESSAGE?

The message must be presented to the child through the medium of the parent, the teacher and the minister of the gospel.

1. The parent has a part because of what must be done before the child is born. When Ezekiel denied the proverb, "The fathers have eaten sour grapes and the children's teeth are set on edge," he was not denying the scientific facts of heredity, but the unreasonable doctrine that God would arbitrarily punish the innocent for the guilty. The influence of heredity is beyond dispute, and he who fails to reckon with this influence has left out of his calculations one of the prime factors in the determining of human destiny.

But a child may be ever so well born and yet its character, like the seed sown broadcast, will depend upon the soil and the nourishment given it. If heredity is the first factor in determining human destiny, environment is the second. If the color of a bird's feathers may be determined by the kind of food it eats, what of the coloring of the child's soul by its moral diet? For the nature of this diet the parent is largely responsible. The world never forgets that the mother rocks the cradle, whether it receives from her hands a Jesse James or a James A. Garfield. This is responsibility. The scepter must be assumed early. The hand that rocks the cradle will not rule the world unless it first rules the cradle. An iron hand may not be necessary, but a pure atmosphere is indispensable.

2. In one sense the parent is becoming less responsible for the early environment of the child. For if even the first eight years of a child's life may determine its course, there is another, besides the parent, who has an important mission to fill, even during these early years. The public school-teacher and kindergarten instructor have charge of the child three and in some cases five years of this time. The mother's work is to get the child up in the morning, give him his breakfast and send him to school; receive him at night, give him his supper and put him to bed. The teacher is the child's patron saint. There can scarcely be an over emphasis of the teacher's responsibility. She may supplement or even overcome the influence of the home, whether for good or evil. As one has said: "To study in Paris is to be born in Paris." Such is the influence of the school. There is some truth in the claim of Victor Hugo that, "there are no bad plants or bad men, but only bad cultivators." The new education is not making a mistake in laying emphasis on the fact that the real business of education is to teach men to live. In proportion as this is realized is the standard for teachers raised. The time was when the slave who was good for nothing else was given charge of the child. We have passed far beyond this point. But we have yet to learn, with Matthew Arnold, that "conduct is three-fourths of life," and contrary to him, that religion is morality touched, not simply by emotion, but by God. The state needs to realize more fully that the teacher is training citizens, and that the true citizen must have moral stamina as well as intellectual power and an active conscience as well as an active brain, and that otherwise his education will prove a curse rather than a blessing to his nation and his fellowmen. We have no sympathy with that law which banishes the Bible from the public schools, and much less with that rigid interpretation of it, as was recently the case in the capital city of the state of Missouri, where it was held that the children should not even be allowed to join their voices in saying, "Our Father." And this, too, in view of the fact that in the recent World's Congress of Religions, Catholic and Protestant, Jew, Mohammedan and Pagan, joined their voices daily in that universal prayer, "Thy kingdom come, thy will be done." And all assembled in the spirit of the motto: "Have we not all one Father? Hath not one God created us?" It shoul not be thought for a moment, however that the teacher cannot convey a gospe message because the Bible is taken fro her desk. There are many ways left i which moral and spiritual truths may b impressed on the child-mind. And suc lessons, more or less desirable, are bein impressed; hence the necessity of care i the selection of teachers: that they b faithful, cultured and moral.

3. It goes without saying that the minis ter of the gospel has an important part i the presenting of this gospel message He not only has a direct relation to th child, but also an indirect one through th parent and teacher, especially the teache in the Sunday-school. He is the teache of both parents and teachers in spiritua things. This is a difficult position to fill It is often more difficult to invent machin ery for the manufacture of tools to be use in the manufacture of other machinery which has already been invented, than i was to make the original invention. So o the teacher of teachers—he is a rare an difficult product.

(1) The minister should be in touc with the home life of the parent, and henc with that of the child. The parents' re sponsibility should be impressed from th time of the child's birth. The ministe should be a comparatively early caller i the home where a young life has bee ushered into the world.

The question of infant dedication sug gests itself here, and is open for fruitfu discussion. While it is almost as much a one's ministerial head is worth for a minis ter among the Disciples to champion suc an innovation, some are doing so. If solemn pledge and a beautiful and impres sive service would increase the parent feeling of responsibility, and if it woul not, by counter influence, decrease th natural responsibility that is felt by th parents, then welcome to the dedicatio service. Under any circumstances it shoul be impressed on Christian parents that i is their duty to raise their children fo God. And the child should be impresse with the fact that this is the parents desire and the chief burden of thei prayers. It is not desirable, however, t establish any system that will cause th child to regard itself as a member of th church without any act on its own part, a is largely the case in the Roman Catholi and Episcopal Churches. Jesus taugh that men are not sons of Abraham b virtue of birth, but by virtue of choice nor sons of God by virtue of his Father hood, but by virtue of loving, childlik obedience to his will. The child shoul grow up, not in the church, but into th church. Its membership being conditioned not on birth, but on rebirth. It should b borne in mind, however, that the child tha is well born the first time, and that is wel trained, will be more readily "born again." It is folly to suppose that it is necessar for a child to wander into sin in order tha the work of regeneration may be mad possible or complete.

(2) Sunday-school teachers should b carefully selected and trained. In th education of children the state utilizes fiv days of the week, and the church on twenty-fourth of one; and too often thi one hour is worse than wasted by untrained teachers in an attempt to pan off

for relig-
: ahead of
: efficient
ous person
is all that
sidered an
or of the
dent of a
nly would
When by
teachers,
ach you."
lic school,
the meth-
taught by

irect rela-
: through
l consider

re the at-
e Sunday
Various
ccomplish
:ess. The
rough the
desirable,
sful, is to
e gospel.
o Jesus to
ought his
missioned
. Lambs
be placed

ossible to
; even the
rtion may
need and
n-minute
liscourse;
at stated
designed
or black-
impress-
both ear
nses that
he inter-
common
iel at one
, divided
the one-
ner third
r third to
, he said,
potter's
lace near
reached a
king the
e of the
us sayeth
l I break
reaketh a
prophets
ds of in-
Jesus to
l God to

spake as never man spake. So may the minister of to-day draw lessons of wondrous beauty and impressiveness from the common objects of nature and the every-day occurrences of life.

The ordinances of the church—baptism and the Lord's supper—are suggestive of the same methods being used of God to keep before the mind gospel truths to impress their significance.

But by whatever means the truth may be brought before the child's mind there must be observed certain—

PRINCIPLES OF INSTRUCTION.

1. The appeal should be made, not to the memory simply, but to the reason as well; and the acceptance of any principle should not depend alone upon the authority of the teacher, but upon the reason and experience

There is no more powerful branch of Christian evidence than that of experience. One class of religious teachers seeks to produce an abiding faith by teaching the pupil to believe. Another class, on the other hand, seeks to keep the pupil on the side of truth by teaching him to think. The true position is between these two and is found by recognizing the true aim of the true teacher, viz., to teach how to live. One who believes either because of authority or because he has "thought it out," that "it is more blessed to give than to receive," may be easily moved from his position, but one who knows it from experience cannot be moved. One who recognizes this principle will not seek to force the creeds and traditions of the past on the rising generation, simply because they are hoary with age, but will rather first seek to determine

in action by heredity or environment, except as he voluntarily yields his will to their influence. Liberty is one of the great messages which the gospel brings to the world. And it is a message which needs emphasis in dealing with the childhood of to-day.

The theological doctrine of predestination has lost its influence, but its counterpart, the philosophy of fatalism, is very much alive indeed. This, as Dr. Van Dyke calls it, is "Calvinism with the bottom knocked out." The influence of heredity should undoubtedly be taught to the parent and that of environment to both parent and child, but not in such a way as to discourage personal effort. As Dr. Van Dyke asks, in his "Gospel for an Age of Doubt": "What could be more dispiriting than to doubt the reality of all effort, to deny the possibility of self-conquest and triumph over circumstances, to find heroism a delusion and virtue a dream? What could break the spring of life more completely than to feel that our feet are entangled in a net whose meshes were woven for us by our ancestors, and for them by tailless apes and for them by gilled amphibians, and for them by gliding worms and for them by ciliated larvæ, and for them by amœbæ, and for them God does not know what? It does not help the case in the least to do as some theologians have tried to do and bring back into the theory, by the aid of certain misconstrued and very much overworked passages of Scripture, the aid of a supreme Deity who has constructed the loom and devised the pattern of the net and decreed the weaving of every loop. The chain of fate is not made less heavy by fastening one end of it to the distant throne of an omnipotent and impassive Creator. . . . To baptize fatalism with a Christian name does not change its nature" (p. 216).

No teacher of children can fulfill his mission who believes in total depravity or predestination, or who champions the false philosophy of fatalism. To succeed he must have an overpowering faith in the possibilities in human nature. And he must inspire his pupils with the same thought. But few children are born either on the mountain peak or in the valley below, but on the mountain side, from whence they may either ascend to the summit and there build a tower or descend to the valley and there dig a pit. Each is the arbiter of his own destiny. The human will is the greatest factor in the determining of human destiny. It is the mission of the gospel to strengthen this will and inspire with hope. There is no message so well calculated to do this as the message of the gospel. It raises up an ideal before the mind, encourages to effort and insures victory. Ian Maclaren says, "Possess the soul with an ideal and one need not trouble himself about action."

There is one word more to add to what has already been said viz.:

TEACH THE TRUTH.

This may seem axiomatic, and therefore unnecessary of mention. Nevertheless, it is not only not axiomatic, but some may even deny that the truth ought to be taught in the sense that is meant.

1. The child should be taught the truth in regard to his own being. This is often withheld, and even falsehoods told in order to escape telling the truth. As if the truth would not come out in the end—and yet, perhaps, too late to save from error and possible sin. Better that the child should hear the truth from the pure lips of a discreet mother than from the foul breath of an older companion in the street or back alley.

2. Again, the child should be taught the truth concerning God and his revelation. No false impressions should be given, either by direct statement or by implication. The gospel teacher, above all others, need not be afraid of the truth. And above all others he ought to be afraid of falsehood. All that is taught that is not strictly true will either have to be unlearned, thus endangering the faith that is dependent on the falsehood, or it will remain as a part of the foundation and weaken the superstructure by so much. The child, therefore, should be taught an up-to-date theology, or perhaps it would be better to say, an up-to-date gospel. Old creeds and theories should not be forced upon the child simply because they are old or because it is feared that the child is not capable of receiving the new. What is good for the man is good for the child as far as the truth is concerned. Do not misunderstand me. I am not making a plea to have the mere speculations of the critics presented to the child, but that whatever has been established as truth should be faithfully taught. True, men do not agree as to what has been established as the truth. But for what we plead is that the truth shall not be withheld from the child simply because he is a child, and that the teacher teach the truth as he is led to see it, that the rising generation may have the full benefit of the truth discovered by the passing one.

It would be unwise, perhaps, to cite many examples where this principle should be applied, for as I have said, we do not agree as to what is the truth. But perhaps we can agree on this: That the world will be long enough in getting over the delusion of a huge black devil with black horns and a long tail, and an eternal hell burning with literal fire and brimstone, without our making use of these in order to frighten the children, and older people, too, for that matter, into the kingdom of heaven. The child should be fed, certainly, on mild, not on strong meat, but it should be the "sincere milk of the Word," pure and unadulterated.

Atlanta, Ill.

ınday School.

IE GOLDEN AGE.*

HERBERT L. WILLETT.

nations the "golden age" is in
st, and to it men look back with
time never to come again. The
vever, looked to the future with
ope. It was the dream of proph-
that in the future, more or less
should be a time of victory and
God should be near his people.
esson affords a graphic sketch of
ge by Israel's greatest prophet.
n of the future was not unrelated
it out of which it came. The
not rhapsodists, who dreamed
ıd left their thoughts for future
to discover written on parch-
e secret place. They were men
o struggled with unhappy relig-
cial conditions, who attempted
eir own age, and who denounced
vine wrath on the heads of offend-
raged the faithful with pictures
et to be. Of such prophets, whose
n told, Isaiah occupies the fore-
His call to service we studied a
hat was in the year that King
737 B. C.). Nearly forty years
, and during that time Jotham
ve ruled over Judah, and Heze-
he throne. Many things have
change the current of events.
Empire, which began its career
bout the time Isaiah received his
steadily westward toward the
n coastlands, those coveted terri-
n the highway between the rival
pt and Assyria. These coast
luded Syria, with its capital at
rael, with Samaria as its chief
ıdah with its chief center at
In 739 B. C. the Assyrians took
Arpad, two strong cities on the
ler of Syria. In 732 B. C. Da-
nto their hands, and the inde-
Syria ceased. In 722 B. C., ten
Samaria was destroyed, and the
gdom came to an end. By these
fulfilled the prophecies of Isaiah
speedy downfall of the two allied
combined against the terror-
in 733 (see Isa. 7). Still later, in
istine territories were subdued,
ne Assyrians under Sennacherib
ng at the gates of Jerusalem.
before the siege of the city began
reached the series of sermons to
sent lesson belongs. For forty
d foreseen the distress of the
nder the Assyrian invasion, and
his fellow-citizens to escape the
pendence on God and a thorough
n morals and politics. But they
le heed to his words, and were
to doubt whether Assyria would
em, and if she did they believed
difficult enterprise to secure the
and drive back her armies. So
to impress the people with the
the coming trouble, which he re-
divine chastisement upon the
. In less than a year Ariel
would be brought low (ch. 29).

is only the divine instrument, though quietly unconscious of the fact (10:5-11). When God has used him as a means of discipline for Israel, but himself shall be humiliated (12-19). Israel shall not be destroyed, but purged; a remnant shall remain (20-23). Therefore do not fear, Israel, for your oppressor will depart (24-27). But now he is near. He is coming swiftly across the mountains of central Palestine. The cities in his path fly at his approach, or are crushed by a blow of his enormous hand (25-32). But his destruction shall be sudden and without remedy (33, 34). Thus Isaiah preaches that the enemy shall come to the very gates, but shall be overthrown, and after this there shall be a time of peace and glory. The description of that happy time, to follow soon upon the departure of the Assyrian, is in strict keeping with Isaiah's whole ministry as a prophet. He had four ideas which he emphasized in every sermon. 1. Israel has sinned; 2. Israel shall suffer punishment, and destruction shall come upon her; 3. Not all shall be destroyed—a remnant shall remain; 4. The future will be glorious; the nation will be pure; strife will cease; God will dwell with his people.

It is the fourth of these ideas which the lesson presents. The glorious future was always associated with the reign of a great king, who was to be of the stock of David. That was the royal line, and it was believed that in its perpetuation the hope of the people lay. This king was to be an ideal ruler, wise, careful of the interests of his kingdom, blessed of God with a wise and discerning mind, incapable of rendering perverted judgment or listening to the wrong side of a case of litigation. His rule would be full of blessing for the poor and the weak, but of terror to the evildoers. Girt with righteousness and true to his word, his reign would be a time of prosperity and glory.

But the most significant feature of this coming age of gold was to be the universal peace which should prevail. Not only were nations to be at one with each other, but the old antipathy between man and beast was to pass away. The most bloody and ravenous prowl-

illustrate the prophetic n
figures, which were imp
their realistic and startl
prophet no more expect
would come to pass in ba
blooming gardens and
were actually expected in
highway of the returning
in these terms were cloth
tions of the prophet for
compelled to use the
could understand. They
labor for an ideal which
hend. For one merely a
they would not work s
understand it. In literal
the prophet have not com
will. In deeper reality,
met and are continually
fulfillment. The king wh
saw, but of the time of
uncertain, came not as a
Davidic line, but as the
world. The era of peace,
is progressively being r
age of peace has not yet
vances are being made u
gospel that we can begi
plishment of that hope
realized in its fullness wh
be full of the knowledg
waters cover the sea."

SUGGESTIONS FO

Jesse's family was not
but from it came the m
history—that of Jesus o
have a perfect king, a m
ideal government; but
heaven we have such a k
power and holiness mak
With such a king there
of justice nor with those
The sway of love is not
severest chastisements u
gospel becomes dominant
evil purposes, and all will
are men to-day for whom
ization can be found th
wolves, leopards, lions

Isaac Selby.

It may not be generally known among our churches in America that there is in this country this noted preacher and lecturer of Australia. For ten years Bro. Selby was associated with the Freethought movement in Australia and for seven years was an accredited lecturer and writer on Freethought topics. In 1889 he embraced Christianity, and for seven years been a preacher and lecturer on Christian subjects. For five years he has been preaching for one of our largest churches in Melbourn, succeeding J. J. Haley of that church. Bro. Selby was led to Christianity largely through a debate with one of our preachers, Bro. Green, of Australia. As he himself said a few evenings ago in one of his lectures, when in this debate he spoke of the cruelties perpetrated by Christians in the middle ages, Bro. Green replied that he was not basing his argument upon so-called Christians, but Christ. When he found fault with the creeds and opinions of men, again came the reply, that they were not debating what men had taught about the Bible, but the Bible itself. This led Mr. Selby to read the Bible with the new object to learn what the Book itself taught, and as a result of this study became a believer.

During this week Bro. Selby has been giving a course of lectures in the First Christian Church of this city on the general theme, "From Atheism to Christianity and What I Learned on the Way," and I have never listened to a finer series of lectures o. any subject. Mr. Selby is thoroughly acquainted with all the arguments against Christianity, having since becoming a Christian debated with the leading secularists of Australia, such as Joseph Symes, W. W. Collins and Wallace Nelson. His argument is forceful, his thought is profound and his language beautiful. I have heard many of the great thinkers and speakers of the present, but Isaac Selby ranks with the foremost along these lines. He has done our church and this community inestimable good. He should not be idle a day while in America. If you desire your church to be established more firmly along these lines, if you have infidels in your community, if there is a current of unbelief amongst the people, send for Isaac Selby to lecture for you a week and give these Freethinkers a chance to ask questions at the close of the lecture, and if theories are not scattered to the winds, and the truths of Christianity more firmly established, it is because people will not be convinced by reason. The lectures besides being convincing are also popular and will hold a mixed audience throughout the course. His stereopticon lecture on "Picturesque Australia, or Life Under the Southern Cross," if rightly managed, will pay the expenses of the entire course. Mr. Selby is at present making his home in this city, where he can be addressed; or, address Bro. J. H. Fillmore, of Cincinnati, O., who will make engagements for him. You will not make a mistake by securing Bro. Selby.

GEORGE A. MILLER.

Covington, Ky.

Literature.

QUEEN ESTHER. By M. M. Davis. Christian Publishing Co., St. Louis.

This Company is presenting the public with a series of Bible storybooks. I believe the above book is the third one in the list. They do the work well. Bro. Davis is one of our best writers, and the book of Esther is one of the most interesting stories ever read. Its place historically is between the sixth and seventh chapters of Ezra. The story loses nothing in the hands of Bro. Davis. All will continue to the close, who begin to read it. All will be delighted and benefited. The great worth of the work would warrant twice the space given it. The deductions of the author are worth many times the price of the book. It is a story which the child can follow with delight, and from which the preacher can add many sermons to his stock. Here is philosophy, psychology and sociology illustrated. The integrity of Mordecai, the judge of the gate, shown to be the hero of the age, and Haman, the premier, is the best possible illustration of that political shrewdness which draws the line only at personal success. That descendant of Agag knew as well as Mordecai that one or the other must fall. But God, who makes the wrath of man to praise him, destroys the last of the old enemies of the Jews through the heartless cunning of one of their own number.

D. R. DUNGAN.

The Netherlands.

There is much interest just now in the Netherlands, or lowlands of Europe, where Wilhelmina, a beloved girl of eighteen, has recently assumed the duties of a queen. She rules over a rich, well peopled land, saved only by watchfulness and energy from being entirely flooded by the sea.

The country was, by nature, a wide morass partly protected by sand hills on the coast. This natural embankment is now further strengthened by artificial dykes. The scenery is made charming by the many tree-lined canals crossed by picturesque bridges, the solidly constructed windmills, and the flowers and trees, for the raising of which the people have become famous.

Although generally wealthy and living well, Dutch make little display, being by nature steady and frugal. The men are usually of middle height, strong built and fair complexion. They smoke much and drink strong liquors, but intoxication is rare. The women, tall and handsome, are world-famed for their domestic virtues and scrupulous neatness. A Dutch house reaches the acme of order and completeness; it usually contains a Singer Sewing Machine, thousands of which are sold annually to the thrifty Dutch housewives. Such a one, seated at her machine, is shown in the photograph reproduced in another column.

The report of the Interstate Commerce Commission shows that last year the railways of the United States carried over 13,000,000,000 passengers one mile. They also carried 95,000,000,000 tons of freight one mile. The total amount paid in dividends on stock was $87,603,371—call it $88,000,000. Of the total earnings of the railways about 70 per cent. came from freight service and 30 per cent. from passenger service. Let us assume, then, that of the $88,000,000 paid in dividends, 70 per cent., or $61,600,000, was profit on freight service and $26,400,000 was profit on passenger service. Let us drop fractions and call it $62,000,000 from freight and $26,000,000 from passengers. By dividing the passenger profit into the number of passengers carried (13,000,000,000) we find that the railways had to carry a passenger 500 miles in order to earn one dollar of profit—or five miles to earn one cent. Their average profit, therefore, was less than two-tenths of one cent for carrying a passenger (and his baggage) one mile.

By dividing the freight profit into the freight mileage (95,000,000,000) we find that the railways had to carry one ton of freight 1,530 miles in order to earn one dollar, or over 15 miles to earn one cent. The average profit, therefore, was less than one fifteenth of a cent for carrying a ton of freight (besides loading and unloading it) one mile.

CHAPTER.
I. The Search.
II. God Save the King.
III. Saul Delivers a City.
IV. The Kingdom Divided.
V. He Who Knows Not How to Wait.
VI. The Hero of Gibeah.
VII. On Making Rash Vows.
VIII. One More Opportunity.
IX. How Saul Improved The Opportunity.
X. Music and Madness.
XI. The Hero of Bethlehem.
XII. Too Many Thousands.
XIII. The Daughter of the King.
XIV. David's Narrow Escape.
XV. A Prince Yet a Friend.
XVI. The Madness of Jealousy.
XVII. "Next to Thee."
XVIII. In The Cave.
XIX. Abigail.
XX. Saul's Spear.
XXI. Abigail is Abducted.
XXII. A Spirit from the Dead.
XXIII. David Rescues Abigail.
XXIV. The Battle of Gilboa.
XXV. How Are the Mighty Fallen.

Marriages.

;OODWIN—BROWNING. — Near Paris, ., Oct. 6, 1898, by C. H. Strawn, Mr. mes F. Goodwin, of Sprague, Mo., to Miss ılla M. Browning, of Monroe County, Mo.

ɬARTIEN—CAMPBELL.—In Paris, Mo., t. 5, 1898, by C. H. Strawn, Mr. Charles H. ɾtien to Miss Clara M. Campbell.

ɬcGEE—CHAPMAN.—In Paris, Mo., Oct. 1898, C. H. Strawn officiating, Mr. Joseph McGee to Miss Lucy J. Chapman.

[HOMPSON—RISSE.—At the home of the de's parents in Vernon Township, near ws, Ia., on Wednesday, Sept. 21, at eight :lock, were married Mr. F. W. Thompson d Miss Mae Risse, both of Vernon Township; L. Davis officiating.

JLERY—PRUNTY.—At the residence of the de, J. W. Strawn officiating, Mr. John R. ery to Miss Eliza Prunty, on Oct. 6, 1898.

/AUGHN—NUGENT.—At the home of the de's parents near Paris, Mo., Oct. 5, 1898, C. H. Strawn, Mr. Robert T. Vaughn to ss Bessie M. Nugent.

Obituaries.

)ne hundred words will be inserted free. Above hundred words, one cent a word. Please send ount with each notice.]

ABBOTT.

)ied in St. Louis, Mo., the morning of Sep- nber the 30th, 1898, Mrs. Josie B. Abbott, fe of Eld. T. A. Abbott, Corresponding Sec- ary of the Missouri Christian Missionary ciety. Sister Abbott was the daughter of . and Mrs. Benjamin B. DePue. She was rn near Chain-of-Rocks, in Lincoln Co., Mo., ptember the 27th, 1850. After her mother's :ond marriage, which was to Mr. Chas. For- sh', t e family moved to Sap au Sris where ɘy resided until after the Civil War. The st school that Sister Abbott attended was ıght by Eld. Denis Grandfield, at Highland airie. Her education was obtained in pub- and private schools. Not far from the ırch of Corinth in Lincoln Co., Mo., she ɘw to womanhood. It was in this church d under the preaching of Bro. Abbott ıt she, in September, 1880, confessed her th in Christ, and by him was baptized into rist. On the 24th of November following was united to Eld. T. A. Abbott in mar- ge by Bro. R. L. McHatton, now of Cali- nia. It is a singular coincidence that at the ɘe of her death these two brethren should be lding the same relation to the missionary rk of their respective states. To those who ew Sister Abbott I need not say that she was evoted wife, seeking as best she could to p her beloved husband in his chosen work. ielding herself was not in her make-up, but ɘr disregarding her own personal ease, she ıght and labored to be what God had said, helpmeet.'' Lucretia like, she lived with- t a shadow falling across her faithfulness. r home and its work absorbed the energies her quiet, industrious and Christian life. owing her intimately as friend and sister in rist, I can say truthfully, the last year of her was one of suffering, incr-asing in inten- y as the days and weeks passed by, which patiently bore, ever looking forward to the ward that awaits those who lovingly trust in rist. To Bro. and Sister Abbott was born child (a daughter named Maud Ell), on the ıth of September, 1881. To this daughter r thoughts turned with a special anexiety as neared the "dark river." Among her last rds she said, "Let me kiss my baby good- ," then calmly left earth for her home th Christ. For Bro. Abbott and his now otherless daughter many a tear of sympathy s fallen and prayer gone up to God for his ssing to rest upon them in their lonely ırney through life. On the first Lord's day

me say, pluck every fragrant flower from your mother's life, and there were many, and bind them into the boquet of your own life, that your mother may ever be honored by your life.

E. J. LAMPTON.

ALLEN.

Alberta Tunis Allen, daughter of Johnson and Marie Allen, of Danville, Ky., was born May 31, 1898, and died Sept. 10, 1898. Death rests upon her as does an untimely frost upon the sweetest flower of the field. Oh, broken-hearted father and mother, let Faith, eagle-eyed and eagle-winged, bear you up, far up, until the dark veil shall in God's own sunlight become transparent, and a loving, bright face, with its soft eyes, shall reveal to you *garnered immortality!*

FRANK W. ALLEN.

Stanford, Ky., Oct. 5, 1898.

JAMES.

Mary Watson James was born in Carlton County, Ohio, in the year of 1820, and united in marriage to William H. James in the year 1837. Of this union 11 children were born, five of whom survive her. She was one of 14 children, all of whom have passed on before except one sister, Mrs. Anna Foy, of Glenwood, Iowa, who is nearing her 82nd birthday. Mother James united with the Christian Church about the year 1834, under the preaching of Alexander Campbell, and has lived an exemplary Christian life. She survived her husband about 13 years. Mary James departed this life Sept. 26, 1898, at Sheridan, Mo., being 77 years, 11 months and 27 days old. Funeral services were conducted at Powell, Neb., by Earl E. Boyd, pastor Christian Church at Belvidere, Neb.

E. E. B.

MILLER.

Diether Miller was born near Sturgeon, Mo., May 30, 1842, and died of paralysis, Aug. 25, 1898, at Excelsior Springs, Mo., where he had gone for his health. Thought to be improving, his sudden death was a great surprise to his family and friends. He was married, May 7, 1877, to Miss Nancy E. Malone, who survives him. To this union there are four sons and a daughter. This with his aged and saintly mother, four brothers and four sisters and a host of friends mourn his loss. He was a deacon in the Sturgeon Christian Church, and freely gave of his time, money and influence to promote the cause of Christ. An enterprising citizen, a kind neighbor, a loving husband and father, he will be greatly missed. He came

Publishers' Notes.

All students of the Old Bible know that it contains many romantic narratives, but even those most familiar with the ancient Scripture are unprepared for the fascinating story developed from the life of King Saul, by J. Breckenridge Ellis. This latest literary work of the author is a charming illustration of his thoroughly individual style. "King Saul" abounds in masterly description.—*The Leader, Plattsburg, Mo.*

The little volume, "The Wonders of the Sky," is a very pleasing and helpful little book, beautiful in thought and reverent in spirit.

FRANK V. IRISH,
Author and Educator.

A SPLENDID BOOK.

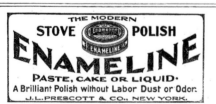

Plain Talks to Young Men on Vital Issues. By Peter Ainslie, editor of the Christian Tribune.

This is a charming little book, and one which every young man should secure and carefully read. It would make a very appropriate gift for the holidays.

In clear and forcible language, the author denounces, in successive short chapters, the evils attending (1) Gambling; (2) The Theatre; (3) Dancing; (4) Swearing and Cursing; and (5) Lying. The last Chapter is entitled "Christian Service," and is alone well worth the price of the entire book.

In the following introductory words, Mr. Ainslie shows some of his reasons for writing such a book:

"Though briefly, I have spoken plainly in the pages following, and at times my words may even appear a little harsh; yet when we consider that there are seventy-five young men out of every hundred who never go to church; ninety-five out of every hundred who are not members of any church; and ninety-seven out of every hundred who make no pretensions to lead Christian lives—I say when we consider these facts, no language could be too harsh and no voice could be too loud against those alluring paths in which our young men are blindly walking and against those influences that scorch like hot breezes, withering human hearts and blasting immortal hopes."—*The Youth's Instructor, Chicago, Ill., Sept.* 29, 1898.

A NEW BOOK.

All the students of the Old Bible know it contains many romanctic narratives, but even those most familiar with the ancient Scriptures are unprepared for the fascinating story developed from the life of King Saul by Prof. J. B. Ellis. This latest literary work of the author of "In the Days of Jehu," is a charming illustration of his thoroughly individual style. "King Saul" abounds in masterly description, and is withal so terse in its concise simplicity. One of the secrets of this book's charm is artlessly revealed by the author in his preface, thus: "I have not suffered myself to be beguiled into laying down the burden of my narrative in order to take up the cudgels of a controversy. In the history of King Saul the road passes over several smoldering volcanoes where commentators have poured forth in times past. One of these dangerous places is found at Endor where once lived a witch. But after carefully considering the various theories which relate to different epochs in Saul's life, I have in each case chosen one and then proceeded as if the others had no existence. It may be thought I am ignorant of these conflicting theories because I do not refresh myself with the pleasures of an argument. But I will cheerfully surrender all claims of a scholarship as obscure as it is profound, if I succeed in interesting the reader, not in theories, but in the facts of the Old Bible."

"King Saul" is such an unqualified success that its many readers ars impatiently awaiting "King David," the next of the series promised by the author.—*The Leader, Plattsburg, Mo.*

Spain's Experience.

"With what measure ye mete it shall be measured to you again."

Spain is learning a lesson. See how retribution is visited upon a nation.

She has always been tyrannical and despotic; to-day she is subdued by a superior power.

She took gold from helpless subjects; to-day she is bankrupt.

She inflicts cruelty, and insurgents put the fear of death into her subjects.

She starves others; now her people cry for bread and die in her streets.

She forces religion upon her subjects, while to-day she is religiously dispossessed.

"With what measure ye mete."

So to-day every unjust deed, every act of religious persecution, every plan of iniquity shall receive its just recompense of reward. God hears. God sees. God knows.

"Vengeance is mine, saith the Lord."

He has declared he will break the teeth of the ungodly. Prosperity does not follow ungodliness.

It is vain to try to cover sin—to look pious and say, "Why, what have we done?"

God's law will bring retribution. God is not mocked. His judgment is as sure as it is severe, and is visited upon nations and individuals alike.

A. M. GROWDEN.

Clarksville, Tenn., Sept. 30, 1898.

Senator R. Q. Mills, of Texas, has withdrawn from the political race for re-election.

George A. Fowler, of Kansas City, has given $21,000 to rebuild the agricultural shops of the University of Kansas, recently destroyed by fire.

THE CHRISTIAN-EVANGELIST.

A WEEKLY FAMILY AND RELIGIOUS JOURNAL.

Vol. XXXV. October 27, 1898 No. 43.

CONTENTS.

EDITORIAL:
- Current Events 515
- Our National Conventions 516
- The Chattanooga Convention 517
- Editor's Easy Chair 518
- The Day of Salvation 520

ORIGINAL CONTRIBUTIONS:
- The Noonday of the S ul.—L. H. Stine 524
- Monumental Evidence of Scripture.—T. Darley Allen 525
- Is the World Growing Worse?—T. Davis 526
- Supernaturalism.—J. W. Lowber 527
- "Not as the World Giveth, Give I Unto You."—T. H. Blenus 527

CORRESPONDENCE:
- English Topics 528
- Are We Overloading? 529
- Christian Science in India 529
- Missouri Bible School Notes 531
- Missouri C. W. B. M 531
- The St. Louis Letter 532
- Reminiscences 532

FAMILY CIRCLE:
- Truth (poem) 536
- A True Story 536
- Nina 538
- The Infinite (poem) 539

MISCELLANEOUS:
- Current Religious Thought 520
- Our Budget 521
- Personal Mention 523
- Notes and News 533
- Evangelistic 535
- Honored Servants 540
- Christian Endeavor 541
- Hiram College Jubilee Endowment 541
- Literature 542
- Marriages and Obituaries 543
- Publishers' Notes 544

Subscription $1.75.

J. Z. TYLER,

NATIONAL SUPERINTENDENT CHRISTIAN ENDEAVOR.

PUBLISHED BY

CHRISTIAN PUBLISHING COMPANY

1522 Locust St., St. Louis.

THE

CHRISTIAN - EVANGELIST

J. H. GARRISON, EDITOR.

W. W. HOPKINS, ASSISTANT.

B. B. TYLER, J. J. HALEY,

EDITORIAL CONTRIBUTORS.

What We Plead For.

The Christian-Evangelist pleads for:

The Christianity of the New Testament, taught by Christ and his Apostles, versus the theology of the creeds taught by fallible men—the world's great need.

The divine confession of faith on which Christ built his church, versus human confessions of faith on which men have split the church.

The unity of Christ's disciples, for which he so fervently prayed, versus the divisions in Christ's body, which his apostles strongly condemned.

The abandonment of sectarian names and practices, based on human authority, for the common family name and the common faith, based on divine authority, versus the abandonment of scriptural names and usages for partisan ends.

The hearty co-operation of Christians in efforts of world-wide beneficence and evangelization, versus petty jealousies and strifes in the struggle for denominational pre-eminence.

The fidelity to truth which secures the approval of God, versus conformity to custom to gain the favor of men.

The protection of the home and the destruction of the saloon, versus the protection of the saloon and the destruction of the home.

For the right against the wrong;
For the weak against the strong;
For the poor who've waited long
For the brighter age to be.
For the truth, 'gainst superstition,
For the faith, against tradition,
For the hope, whose glad fruition
Our waiting eyes shall see.

RATES OF SUBSCRIPTION.

Single subscriptions, new or old	$1.75	each
In clubs of five or more, new or old. ..	1.50	"
Reading Rooms	1.25	"
Ministers	1.00	"

With a club of ten we will send one additional copy free.

All subscriptions payable in advance. Label shows the month up to the first day of which your subscription is paid. If an earlier date than the present is shown, you are in arrears. No paper discontinued without express orders to that effect. Arrears should be paid when discontinuance is ordered.

In ordering a change of post office, please give the OLD as well as the NEW address.

Do not send local check, but use Post office or Express Money Order, or draft on St. Louis, Chicago or New York, in remitting.

THE CHRISTIAN-EVANGELIST

"In faith, Unity; in opinion and methods, Liberty; in all things, Charity."

Vol. xxxv. St. Louis, Mo., Thursday, October 27, 1898. No. 43

CURRENT EVENTS.

Instructions have been issued from Washington that the evacuation of Cuba by the Spanish forces must be accomplished not later than December 1. At that date the American authorities will assume control of the island and when that limit shall have been passed, Spain will be without a possession in the Western Hemisphere. The protocol said that Cuba was to be evacuated "immediately" and the Spanish can scarcely complain that this term has been construed too rigorously when they have been allowed nearly four months. One of the curiosities of diplomacy is the pretext which the Spanish commissioners have alleged for not abiding by the terms agreed to in the protocol, namely, that the agreement was made under coercion. We should say it was! The whole war was nothing more nor less than the exercise of the coercion necessary to induce Spain to agree to do certain things. If she does not do them there will be some more coercion. Every treaty of peace signed by a vanquished power is the result of coercion by the victorious power. We did not appeal to force and arms in this matter until the possibilities of moral suasion had been exhausted and no method remained but coercion. For Spain's representatives to attempt to establish an analogy between this situation and the case of a contract between individuals, in which case proofs of coercion nullifies the contract, is nonsense of the purest Castillian type.

The report of the plot to overthrow the present French Government by a military *coup d'etat*, which was frustrated by its timely discovery, is almost incredible by reason of its magnitude. The story is that Gen. Boisdeffre was at the head of the conspiracy and that his associates in it were Gen. Zurlinden and other officers whose interests have been adversely affected by the reversion of both public and official opinion in regard to the Dreyfus case. It is even said that there is evidence of President Faure's implication in the plot to overthrow his own ministry and perhaps destroy the republic. The *gendarmerie*, or provincial police, which is the most loyal part of the French army and is directly and solely subject to the demands of the Minister of the Interior, has been concentrated in Paris during the past ten days. This extraordinary action was before understood as a precaution against violence in connection with the serious strike of the building trades, but it is now believed that Minister Brisson, having information of the plot through some of the secret agents of the French Government, had summoned these forces to forestall any *coup d'etat* which might be attempted. In either case it has succeeded, for there was no attempt to carry the plot into execution, and there was little violence in connection with the strike, which is now happily on the way to settlement.

Emperor William and the Empress are on a tour to the Orient, the chief objective point of which is Jerusalem. Out of this simple fact have sprung a large number of discussions. The greater part of this copious stream of newspaper talk on this topic relates to the question of the Emperor's personal safety in taking such a trip at such a time as this, and to the dire posibilities if anything should happen. No regent has been appointed to direct affairs of state in the absence of the Kaiser, Prince Henry, upon whom that duty would naturaly devolve, being absent with the German squadron in Chinese waters. It would, in truth, be a very awkward time for anything to happen to the Emperor, in view of the many international complications which are now threatening the peace of Europe. The Kaiser's trip is also commented upon as being somewhat extraordinary as a Protestant pilgrimage to the ancient shrine of mediæval Catholic pilgrimages, and every effort has been made to give the trip the flavor of a religious pilgrimage. But this Protestant pilgrimage begins with a visit to the Sultan, the common and traditional foe of all Christendom, and is to be continued into the Sultan's dominions more or less definitely under his auspices. The Kaiser will be, in a sense, the guest of the Sultan at Jerusalem. An emperor's travels are expensive and it is estimated that this tour will cost Kaiser Wilhelm 5,000,000 marks for general traveling expenses and three or four million more for presents, to say nothing of the sum which the Sultan will spend for his entertainment.

Wednesday, October 19, was the day set apart for observance in schools and colleges all over the country as Lafayette Day. On that day the services of Lafayette to the colonies in the Revolutionary War were celebrated and funds raised for the erection of a monument to him to be unveiled in Paris on July 4, 1900, which is to be "American Day" at the Paris Exposition. The cause is a worthy one and in every way deserving of success. October 19 was the anniversary of the surrender of Lord Cornwallis at Yorktown, a victory in which Lafayette rendered valuable assistance and which practically ended the War of the Revolution.

The present relations between Great Britain and France contains all the elements for procuring a first-class disturbance. True, the immediate matter in dispute, the French occupation of Fashoda, is not worth a serious dispute, but this is not the whole matter; there is the special sensitiveness of Great Britain to invasion of her rights in Egypt and the constant annoyance which France experiences in seeing Great Britain in possession of the valley of the Nile. there is the sense of humiliation which would come to France in withdrawing from Fashoda, as if confessing either error or weakness; and there is Russia, apparently standing ready to make the quarrel of France her own and the promise of alliance, encouraging her to enter upon a conflict the prospect of which would otherwise have more terror than temptation in it. The Paris Municipal Council has passed a resolution calling upon the government to make any honorable concessions rather than go to war over the possession of Fashoda, and pointing out the fact that the commercial interests of Great Britain and France are so nearly identical that their relations abroad should never be anything but friendly. The French populace, as judged from the tone of the French press, has remained fairly sane in reference to this matter until recently, but has become much excited by a speech made by Sir Michael Hicks-Beach during the past week, which is interpreted as a threat against France. In consequence of this it is reported that the feeling is much more warlike. In England there has been general approval of Lord Salisbury's firmness, but also a disposition to let France down easy and allow her to withdraw from Fashoda with as little humiliation as possible.

Heavy financial interests are involved in the relations of France and England. On the one hand Russia, who is sorely in need of a large loan to carry on the work on the Siberian railway and her other Asiatic enterprises, and who, having failed to raise money in Germany, is now trying France, discovers that French capitalists have become suspicious as to the stability of the Franco-Russian alliance. They have already invested large sums in Muscovite securities, but show no disposition to advance any more cash until there is some assurance that the alliance is something more than a Russian scheme to get hold of French capital. The Russian Ministers of Foreign Affairs and Finance are now in Paris trying to give this assurance, and the best way they can find to do it is to declare the willingness of Russia to aid France in a struggle against Great Britain for Fashoda. This makes for war. On the other hand, Egyptian bonds to the value of $800,000,000 are held by French investors. These bonds are now above par. If Egypt were to pass out of Great Britain's hands, the bonds which are not guaranteed would without question drop as low as they were in 1882, namely, 36 below par. Naturally this state of affairs imposes a restraint upon the bondholders, whose pa riotic desire to vindicate the honor of France is more than offset by anxiety about their Egyptian dividends.

OUR NATIONAL CONVENTIONS.

The fear that the yellow fever scare would ruin our national conventions at Chattanooga proved to be groundless. No doubt some were kept away by the very measure designed to protect the people of Chattanooga and the state against any possible danger, namely, the quarantine regulation requiring persons going to Chattanooga to carry a certificate that they had not come from an infected region. For that reason people living in Mississippi and Louisiana were prevented from attending the convention. But in spite of these drawbacks there was a great convention—one of the greatest in our history, all things considered. At the very first meeting of the convention a resolution was passed declaring all fear of danger from yellow fever or from quarantine regulations groundless, and asking the Associated Press to publish same. We do not think it was published, however. If it had been a notice of the pulling off of a prize fight, it would have found space no doubt.

CHRISTIAN WOMAN'S BOARD OF MISSIONS.

On Thursday evening a large number of delegates assembled at the Auditorium—a spacious hall with a wide gallery extending around the building and connecting with the platform in front—where the various sessions of the convention were held. No special program was prepared, but some committees were announced, a few letters of regret read by the corresponding secretary from persons who could not be present, and the rest was social. We think it would be better to utilize this introductory evening by a social meeting of prayer and praise, closing with the announcements, and followed by a period of fraternal greetings. Every convention would thus begin with a prayer-meeting.

Mrs. A. M. Atkinson presided over the convention of the Woman's Board in the absence of Mrs. Burgess, whose detention at home on account of ill health was much regretted. Those who know Mrs. Atkinson need not be told that she presided with great ability and to the entire acceptance of the ladies. A message of sympathy was sent to Mrs. Burgess. The report of the work during the past year was quite satisfactory, showing a gain in receipts over the previous year, and a balance on hand of over $1,000 in the general fund instead of a deficit of over $8,000, as was the case at the last report. The women had a good program and some of the papers read before their convention were among the best things in any of the conventions. The address by Mrs. Jessie Brown Pounds was not excelled in style or sentiment by anything we heard at Chattanooga. The motto of the women for next year is, "Ninety Thousand for Ninety-nine." This means ninety thousand women enlisted in the work, as well as $90,000. They will probably reach it, though this means a remarkable gain both in membership and contributions.

SUNDAY SERVICES.

Lord's day has come to be one of the most interesting days in our national conventions. It was an ideal day in Chattanooga, and the churches generally opened their pulpits to our ministers, and there were large audiences, the delegates dividing to hear their favorite preacher or to hear a new preacher. We heard flattering reports from a large number of these sermons. In the afternoon there was a union communion service at the Auditorium. It was not hoped to equal in numbers the communion service at Indianapolis, but a vast host, estimated at from 2,500 to 3,000, assembled at the time and place to participate in this impressive service. Bro. M. D. Clubb, of the Walnut Street Church, Chattanooga, presided, and our venerable brother, Robert Graham, of the University of Kentucky, made a brief address on the significance of the occasion and the institution. Thirty-six deacons waited upon the great congregation with the utmost order. While they were passing through the audience appropriate hymns were sung in low, subdued tones, which added to the impressiveness of the occasion. The concluding hymn, "All Hail the Power of Jesus Name!" was sung with great earnestness and spiritual fervor.

THE HOME MISSION CONVENTION.

The American Christian Missionary Society began its 49th convention Monday morning at 9 o'clock. The hour previous had been occupied with a lecture by Prof. B. A. Jenkins, of Indianapolis, on "Paul's Literary Style." This was the second of two very able and interesting lectures by Bro. Jenkins, the first of which drew a contrast between First Thessalonians and Galatians. In both of these lectures he manifested rare gifts as a Bible lecturer. The lecture on Friday morning was to have been by Prof. Jenkins, but owing to the delay of the train he did not arrive in time, and his place was filled by Bro. C. A. Young, who conducted a very interesting study on "The Gospel of John." It is very gratifying to note that a number of our younger men are fitting themselves for lecturing upon Bible themes and upon books of the Bible, and that these lectures are eagerly enjoyed by the people. It shows that the Bible is a living book and that when men enter into its spirit, familarize themselves with the historical settings of its various books and have the power to present its facts and truths clearly and forcibly, they are listened to with the greatest attention.

President F. D. Power, of Washington, D. C., called the convention to order at 9 o'clock, and introduced Mayor Watkins, who delivered a very happy address of welcome to the convention, offering the delegates the freedom of the city and even proposing to resign his Mayorship if the convention would select some one of its delegates to fill the office during their stay in the city. President Power responded briefly and appropriately to this address of welcome, and then delivered his presidential address. It was a strong and timely address on the topic, "The Holy Spirit and Missions."

The report of the board which followed, through its corresponding secretary, Benj. L. Smith, showed a good year's work, the most successful, perhaps, in the history of the society. We have made such extracts from the report of this board as will give our readers at least a bird's-eye view of what has been accomplished. The motto, "Home Missions to the Front," which B. L. Smith adopted on his entrance upon the work of corresponding secretary, seems to have become something more than a mere motto in the minds of a large number of our people, who are coming to see the supreme urgency of this work.

JUBILEE CONVENTION.

On the announcement of the appo
ment of the committee on time and p
of the next convention, President Loo
the Foreign Society, suggested that
question be settled at once, without
usual preliminaries, and moved that
convention convene in Cincinnati, in 1
in its semi-centenary convention. A.
Harvout, of Cincinnati, and Geo. A. Mi
of Covington, made neat and happy speec
urging this invitation, and the motion
carried by a unanimous rising vote.
understand that Music Hall has been
cured for the convention, and the aim
rally 10,000 delegates and to make
total contribution for missions $1,000,
This is a large program, but it will d
harm to work towards its realization.

Time and space fail us in an attem
follow in detail the proceedings of this
vention. Among the good things
vided for us on Monday was an addres
R. S. Latimer, of Pittsburg, on "Our
portunities for Mission Work in the Cit
"The Hour of Prayer for America,"
ducted by S. D. Dutcher; Report of
tional Superintendent of Christian
deavor, J. Z. Tyler; address on "The M
ifold Mission of Christian Endeavor,'
C. B. Newnan, of Detroit; "The Chris
Endeavor as an Educational Agency,'
B. A. Jenkins, of Indianapolis; "H
Missions to the Front," by H. F. McL
Toledo; a symposium on "How May
best Develop and Utilize our Chris
Endeavor Forces," by F. G. Tyrrell,
Louis. In the evening after praise ser
conducted by S. R. Hawkins, New Orle
there was an able address on "Educat
Its Importance and Status Among the
ciples," by E. V. Zollars, president
Hiram College, and another by S.
Cooper on "The Church Building."

Tuesday we had a Report on Educat
by Mrs. A. A. Forrest, Irvington, In
Church Extension Report by G.
Muckley; Report of Statistical Secret
G. A. Hoffmann, Missouri; Report on Mi
terial Relief, by D. R. Lucas, Indiana, w
a talk on same by A. M. Atkinson, follo
by an address by Jabez Hall, of Bu
Bible College. The report showed a l
of funds to meet the present wants o
number of beneficiaries of this fund an
liberal collection was lifted to meet t
deficit. Of the above addresses and
ports we were only permitted to hear t
of Bro. Hall, which was a maste
presentation of the value of the Christ
ministry and of our obligation to sup
it, even when the minister from infirmi
of age or misfortune is unable to sup
himself. After a brief praise service
Tuesday afternoon, led by T. A. Reyno
of Nashville, Mrs. H. M. Meier, of
Louis, was given ten minutes to pres
the claims and explain the object of
Benevolent Association of the Christ
Church. In a word, its object was
plained to care for the orphans and
homeless children, and also for the he
less and homeless old people among
members. The method was to hav
central board with state auxiliaries, wh
shall co-operate with this board in look
after the benevolent work in the vari
states, and when practicable establish
homes in these states for the care of ho
less children and old people. "Give t
women of the church," Mrs. Meier s

"the orphan children and aged and homeless old people among us to love and care for, and you men may do the voting and look after politics." Mrs. Meier's address was heard with deepest interest and created a most favorable impression for the Benevolent Association.

C. C. Smith made a ringing address, as he always does, on the subject, "Negro Education," and was followed by an able paper by B. F. Manire, of Mississippi, upon "What we Owe to the Negroes of our Country." The remainder of the afternoon was occupied with the report of the Sunday-school work by Knox B. Taylor, of Illinois, and an address on "Children's Rally for Home Missions," by G. A. Hoffmann, of Missouri. The evening session brought us two stirring addresses, "The Paramount Urgency of Home Missions," by George Darsie, of Kentucky, and "A New Star in the Crown of our King—Porto Rico for Christ," by J. A. Erwin. The urgency of our Home Mission work perhaps never had an abler presentation than that which Bro. Darsie gave it, and J. A. Erwin enlisted our hearts as he told us how Porto Rico, to which country he went immediately from the convention as a missionary, should be won to Christ.

OUR WIDE FIELD.

Wednesday forenoon was occupied, aside from the reports of committees, with the the claims of the different sections of our great country. A. B. Moore, of Minnesota, told us "How the North is Ripe for the Harvest;" O. P. Spiegel, of Alabama, told us of "The South as a Mission Field;" W. H. Bagby, from the dominion of Brigham Young, showed "How the West Holds a Ripe Harvest," and "The Call from the East," was presented by C. M. Kriedler, of New York. An "Open Parliament" was conducted by Jno. E. Pounds, of Indiana. Fitly enough this session closed with prayers of consecration. Surely, the needs of these great fields in our country demand a deeper consecration on the part of Christ's followers. The sum-total of the impression made by the sessions of this convention was that we have a magnificent field, making mighty demands upon us, and that we have scarcely begun to realize the magnitude of our obligations, much less to respond adequately to these demands.

THE FOREIGN CHRISTIAN MISSIONARY SOCIETY.

This society began its 23rd annual convention on the afternoon of Wednesday, President C. L. Loos in the chair. Secretaries A. McLean and F. M. Rains presented synopses of their printed reports, showing a decided gain over the previous year's work. This gain is in the amount of money contributed, number of churches organized and in the number of churches and Sunday-schools enlisted in the work. The gain in money over the previous year was $24,703.60. The gain in the number of contributing churches is 321 and in the number of contributing Sunday-schools 370. Less than 3,000 churches and a little over 3,000 Sunday-schools now participate in the annual offerings to Foreign Missions. It shows that there is much land yet to be conquered in the way of enlisting our forces in the enterprise of world-wide missions. After praise and thanksgiving for the success of the past year, the convention heard two very striking addresses, one by W. J. Wright, of Washington, D. C., on "Missions the Heart of Church Life," and the other, "The Preacher's Responsibility to Missions," by Geo. H. Combs, of Missouri. These men had put time and thought upon their addresses, and presented something which it was not only worth while to hear, but to go a long distance to hear. The evening of Wednesday was occupied by a single address by F. M. Rains, the treasurer of the Foreign Society, upon "The success of Modern Missions." The speaker was considerably hampered by his manuscript and did not awaken the degree of enthusiasm which he is capable of exciting when he speaks without manuscript, as he usually does.

FOREIGN MISSIONARIES.

We were favored by the presence of a number of foreign missionaries in the convention. On Thursday forenoon a number of these were to address the convention. "Mission Work in Japan" was to be presented by Miss Lavinia Oldham; "Missionary Experience in China," by Dr. Jas. Butchart; "My Work in India," by E. M. Gordon. W. R. Hunt, of China, was also a visitor in the convention and was to speak. It was the writer's misfortune to be confined to his bed during that session of the convention and unable to hear the addresses. Indeed, we were compelled to leave the convention before its close and our enjoyment of the sessions throughout was marred by ill-health. The addresses on the afternoon of Wednesday on "Children's Day," by W. A. Harp, and "Giving for Foreign Missions," by J. L. Brandt, we were also deprived of hearing. The last evening was to be occupied by two illustrated lectures, "Missions in China," by Dr. Jas. Butchart, and "Missions in India," by E. M. Gordon.

SUMMING UP.

Perhaps we are justified under all circumstances in saying that this was a very successful convention. There were some drawbacks, chief among which were the number of people absent from the convention during the day, visiting Lookout Mountain and Chickamauga Park. This was to have been expected, however, as the historic associations of the place were presented as one reason for taking the convention there. The other unfavorable circumstance was the large number of people that were temporarily ill during the convention, caused, perhaps, by the water. This was especially true of those who stopped at the Read House. This hotel entertained a large number of our delegates, and few of us we think will cherish pleasant recollections of our stay there. The people who were entertained in private homes fared much better, and are generous in their praise of the treatment they received. But in spite of these drawbacks, the attendance was fine, considering the location. The spirit of the meeting was admirable, most of the speeches were worthy of the occasion, the work accomplish showed a decided advance, and altogether the outlook for the future is hopeful and inspiring.

It is a fundamental mistake to suppose that church members are not needed in the Sunday-school. They should make the best of Sunday-school scholars in attendance, in deportment, in class studies, in teaching, in proficiency and in general duties. The Sunday-school is not for children only.

THE CHATTANOOGA CONVENTION.

These notes are prepared in the midst of the confusion and enthusiasm incident to a great assemblage of our people.

It cannot be said of this grand assembly of the Disciples of Christ that it is the greatest meeting in their history. It is not; but it is a great meeting, and a good.

Brotherly love is dominant. The spirit of the meeting is devout, reverent, enthusiastic. The addresses are uniformly of a high order. It is evident that the speakers, as a rule, have thought—have carefully and closely thought—on the topics on which they address the people. There are but few, strictly speaking, extemporaneous addresses. This does not mean that the speakers *read*. The speakers generally *speak*. Some of them read their addresses, but some of the most thoroughly prepared addresses were delivered without the use of a note. This feature of this general assembly of the Disciples is worthy of heartiest commendation.

The reports of work done, moneys collected and disbursed, and known spiritual results secured, indicate an advance over anything attained in previous years. But present attainments do not satisfy. There is a desire for better results. Out of this desire, generated by the successes of the past and present, has been born a determination to make the future in every way an improvement on the past.

These notes do not deal with statistics. Our readers will obtain an abundance of information of this character in other departments of our paper and in other issues. It is sufficient to say here that the amount of money collected and disbursed by the American Christian Missionary Society and the Foreign Christian Missionary Society exceeded by several thousand dollars the collections and disbursements of former years. The report of the Christian Woman's Board of Missions shows that the national missionary organization of our women is in a healthy, perennial condition, and that the good work of our God in the hands of these devoted servants of the Most High receives marked evidences, and continual, of the divine approval. Church Extension gains steadily year by year. There ought to be no serious difficulty in placing a quarter of a million of dollars in the treasury of the Board of Church Extension before the year 1900. The enterprise appeals with peculiar force to level-headed business men. It is a fine illustration of business in Christianity. The only note of discouragement sounded during the convention related to the work of Ministerial Relief; and in this sacred ministry, as Bro. Atkinson so felicitously styles it, there is no real ground for discouragement. His ill health accounts satisfactorily for the diminished receipts for the last year. He was able to serve the board only about four months during the year. It is a great pleasure to his friends—and their name is legion—to have him present and able to participate in this convention. D. R. Lucas, of Indianapolis, will now plead the cause of Ministerial Relief before the brotherhood. Such a ministry ought not to require a plea. It ought to be regarded as a privilege to minister in material things to the veterans who have faithfully ministered to us the glorious gospel of the blessed God.

There is an unusual attendance of those

who are called evangelists in this meeting. The use of the words—"those who are called evangelists"—is not intended as a slur upon the good men who spend their time and strength in protracted meeting work. Why the word evangelist should be applied to them exclusively is not apparent. Our pastors generally do evangelistic work to a greater or less extent. Not a few of them are among our best evangelists.

There has been a drifting apart of the men who are called pastors and those who are spoken of as evangelists. One or two meetings have been held by the evangelists who are here, and some of the pastors. These meetings were in the nature of conferences, were in good spirit, and can but result in a better mutual understanding and more cordial co-operation. It was determined to hold similar conferences at the time of the General Conventions in Cincinnati next year. It is understood that these conferences will be quite informal and that their purpose will be mutual acquaintance, mutual improvement, and the attainment of greater efficiency in the work to which pastors and evangelists are alike devoted—the salvation of men.

The place of Christian Endeavor among us, and the care of our young people, received thoughtful attention. A paper was read in which a summary statement was made of what other Christian people are doing to promote the spiritual welfare and efficiency of their young people. It is evident that the Disciples are in the very front ranks in the training of their young people to serve wisely and well the one Lord. Christian Endeavor has reached such a magnitude among us as to require the entire time and strength of one man. An effort will be made, it is understood, to secure the services of a competent man for this important work. There is no service among us of greater importance than that of directing the energies of our young men and young women in such a manner as to make them efficient servants of the Christ. The church of the future is involved in this enterprise. Let us in this, as in all else, seek the wisdom that comes from above.

It is apparent that the Disciples are growing in every direction. Their numerical increase has been great, but better than their growth in numbers is their increasing unity. They are rapidly becoming a united people. The spirit of unity and union is on the increase. The bitterness, the strifes, the contentions of the past have disappeared, let us hope, to return no more. There is also a marked increase in the general intelligence of the people. They do not understand "the way of salvation" one whit better—if indeed they understand it as well—than did those former generations, but their general intelligence and culture are superior to the intelligence and culture of those who have gone before. This fact is full of encouragement. We are beginning to know how to use the wealth with which God has entrusted us. The word "beginning" is used in this connection with deliberation and purpose. We are only at the beginning of an experience the end of which no man can see. Gen. F. M. Drake handed B. L. Smith his check for $5,000 a day or two ago, the income from which will be used in general evangelistic work. This is well; but there are others who could give in a similar way —with equal generosity—and they will. We are moving in the right direction in this matter. The time is not far distant when our prosperous business men will contribute of their means by the ten thousand to extend the kingdom of righteousness and peace. The meaning of stewardship is beginning to dawn upon us. The following quotation presents the duty of preachers in this matter:

"Charge them that are rich in this present world, that they be not highminded, nor have their hope set on the uncertainty of riches, but on God, who giveth us richly all things to enjoy; that they do good, that they be rich in good works, that they be ready to distribute, willing to communicate; laying up for themselves a good foundation against the time to come, that they may lay hold on the life which is life indeed."

Do such conventions as this in Chattanooga pay?

The answer must be, on the part of those who attend, an emphatic affirmative. It pays in every way. They promote unity of thought, of purpose, of speech, and of effort. They cultivate a spirit of intelligent evangelism. The grace of benevolence is increased. Faith is augmented—confidence in our brethren, in God and in the special message with which we have been entrusted. A spirit of catholicity is also promoted, broader views are gained. The needs of the world are considered and how to meet them. One is saved from the narrowness encouraged by the treadmill life of the parish. In every way it pays to hold such conventions as this Chattanooga Assembly.

To experience the intellectual stimulus and spiritual uplift afforded by the morning meetings for Bible study is itself a sufficient return for all expenditures incurred in attending this convention. There are those who will never forget those meetings. Their influence for good was extensive and permanent.

On to Cincinnati in '99 is now our cry. It is not too soon to begin to prepare for that—our jubilee—convention. Fifty years ago our organized work began in Cincinnati. What changes have taken place in that time! Surely, God's hand is on us for good!

In our preparation for Cincinnati in '99 we must not forget to assist in the collection of $100,000 for Home Missions. Home Missions to the front *this* year. One of the mottoes on the wall of the Auditorium in which the Chattanooga Convention is held is $100,000 for Home Missions this year. Just above it is this motto: One hundred thousand souls for Christ this year! ! Note well this motto. It is not 100,000 church members this year, but—and this is a very different matter—100,000 souls for Christ. To aid in securing souls for the Savior is one of the ways in which to prepare for Cincinnati in '99. God help us!

B. B. T.

—Nov. 13-19 has been appointed a week of prayer for young men by the American International Convention of the World's Conference of the Y. M. C. A. During this week all ministers are asked to preach a special sermon for young men and to mention the work of the Association in their behalf. Also to point out to young men the part they play in the family, the church and the state. All of these fields of work demand healthy, strong, Christian young men. A good program has been prepared by the associations for the entire week, and it is hoped that the week will be generally observed and attended, especially by our young men.

Editor's Easy Chair.

CONVENTION ECHOES.

The Easy Chair cannot do otherwise than fall into line with the general trend this week and pay its respects to the great annual convention at Chattanooga. Instrumental, as we were, in having the conventions go to the Mountain City, we feel special gratification at their success. Several had already begun to say to us in anticipation of failure, "I told you so;" but nothing of that sort was heard after the convention got under way. The truth is, we have reached a point, not only in numbers, but in zeal for our general interests, that neither distance nor fear of pestilence nor self-support while there nor, even fourth-class hotels can prevent a large attendance at our National Conventions.

We doubt if the brethren in any city where our conventions have previously met have given as much time, anxious thought and labor to make suitable preparations for the convention as were given by the brethren in Chattanooga. They felt that the demands upon them would be very great and they organized their forces thoroughly and worked systematically, and all that could be done on their part to make our stay there pleasant and profitable was done. We sincerely trust that they may realize from the convention that permanent good for which they hoped and which their unselfish labors for the convention so well deserve. The executive committee, together with the committees on reception, finance, entertainment, pulpit, press, local excursion, auditorium and hospital seem to have anticipated all the possible needs of the convention. If the convention was not all that they had hoped for in the way of numbers we trust that it made up in quality what it lacked in quantity.

It was good to see the familiar face of ex-Governor F. M. Drake, of Iowa, present once more in our annual conventions. His donation of $5,000, to the general mission fund of the Home Board, is an expression of his interest in the evangelization of our beloved country. Other prominent business, as J. H. Allen and F. E. Udell, of St. Louis; W. S. Dickinson and S. M. Cooper, of Cincinnati; W. W. Williams, of Des Moines; A. M. Atkinson—preacher, business man and philanthropist combined—Howard Cale and Amos Clifford, of Indianapolis; R. S. Latimer, of Pittsburg, besides others whom we do not now recall, were present as participants in the work of the convention. We could wish that this class could be more largely represented in our conventions. We believe it would tend to benefit our conventions in many ways if they were present in larger numbers and had more to do in shaping the course of things.

A pleasant episode of the convention was the presentation by W. M. Taylor, one of the local preachers of Chattanooga, of a gavel made out of wood from the Chickamauga battlefield, with its handle entwined with red, white and blue, to President Power, in a happy speech, in which he referred in eloquent terms to the union of the North and the South during the late war with Spain—a union which he believed d be perpetual. President Power re- ded in suitable terms, accepting the l and returning his thanks to the r in behalf of the convention. At this ;ure the song entitled, "On to Chatta- a," by J. H. Stark, printed in the STIAN-EVANGELIST a few weeks since, reprinted on slips and scattered ıgh the convention, was sung to the of "Marching through Georgia." The ulty of matching the meter to the tune st sight prevented the song from being :ided success as a musical performance, he sentiment more than covered this :t, and it was followed by enthusiastic ause.

---

e lack of time to suitably discuss ;ures of importance that come before onvention is always sorely felt, and)egrudges all the more any time that be wasted in a speech or sermonette has no special bearing on the subjects the convention. There were some nmendations voted down during the ention which we cannot doubt, could have been thoroughly discussed, would been adopted. Perhaps there were adopted which might have been voted . if there had been fuller discussion. recommendation of the committee on nations, that the president of the ign Board and the president of the ign Society be not the same person,)ased on reasons so apparent that we ler that it was voted down without any .ssion, or even without an inquiry as e reason of the recommendation. The od of the American Christian Mis- .ry Society in this respect is much :, and should be adopted in the Foreign ›ty. There may not be the slightest er now, and there is not, in having the .dent of the board that conducts the :onary operations all the year appoint ;ommittees that are to consider and upon its action. But there may come ae when the impropriety of this ar- ement would become manifest, and ıwhile it would be well to avoid any icion of a close corporation. It is ult to see why the Educational Board aot allowed to have a secretary to look its business provided it was willing to for his services. We have no more rtant board than this when its place ıs to be properly recognized.

.e following paragraph from the report .e Board of Education will be gratify- e friends of the colleges:

ɜ *resume* of the year's work would not be lete without mentioning the good fortune ı has fallen to Butler, Drake, Hiram and ka Colleges. It is really a misnomer to it good fortune, since it is due to the nt labor of the men who have been devel- : these institutions. Hiram has secured tate of $30,000, upon conditions that an ity be paid the donor during his lifetime. suggests a way by which benevolent per- can benefit institutions more securely by bequests; for inheritance taxes are .ed, and the possibility of breaking the s entirely removed, while a fair income is ed the donor during his lifetime. Drake ecured $38,000 to pay off floating indebted- Eureka has received $30,000 for a like ɔse. This relieves Eureka of a burden h has been pressing upon it for several ı, and puts the institution in a position to al to the brotherhood for increased en- ıent on a business basis. The newly organized Bible department of Butler has been assured of support for three years; and steps are now being taken to secure a permanent endowment for the four new professorships that have been added.

The scope and the value of the work of the National Superintendent of Christian Endeavor may be seen from the following opening paragraph of the Christian Endeavor report:

During the past year I have aimed (1) to secure a better enrollment of our Christian Endeavor Societies; (2) to bring them into more general and more efficient co-operation with all our missionary enterprises; (3) to provide for the systematic instruction of all our young people, and (4) to bring our brotherhood to recognize the latent and still undeveloped possibilities of Christian Endeavor.

In the closing paragraph of the same report the National Superintendent, J. Z. Tyler, under the head of "Backward or Forward—Which?" after giving the numerical strength of Christian Endeavor among us, adds:

But the greater possibilities of Christian Endeavor still lie latent and undeveloped. I believe it has a possibility of usefulness of which few of us have ever dreamed. I am thrilled when I think of what, by wise management and the divine blessing, it may yet become and what it may yet accomplish. But present methods cannot secure further progress. I speak out of an experience in which I have seriously hazarded my health when I say that it is impossible for me to longer continue the double duty of the pastorate and of the superintendency of Christian Endeavor. While my heart is more devoted than ever to this good work, and while its possible future seems to me more promising than ever, I am yet compelled, by considerations of health and the demands of duties elsewhere, to ask that you release me from the office of National Superintendent of Christian Endeavor.

It is safe to say that no man among us understands the spirit and true scope and possibilities of the Christian Endeavor movement more thoroughly than J. Z. Tyler, nor do we believe there is another man in all the Endeavor ranks that has been a wiser leader and a more faithful and unselfish worker in this field than he has been. Accepting as true the above statement of the superintendent, that he can no longer do the work of pastor and that of National Superintendent of Endeavor, the convention, nevertheless, felt unwilling to part with his valuable services, and recommended that the board of managers retain him for his whole time to cultivate this promising field, provided it could find a way for his support, either directly from its treasury or through the Endeavor Societies. We are sure that the Home Society would find it highly remunerative to their treasury to secure his work in stimulating missionary zeal in the Endeavor Societies, and we are sure, too, that if the societies are asked to contribute, say $1.00 each per annum, to a fund for the general interest of Christian Endeavor, and extending it in new fields, they would readily do so. In one of these ways let Bro. Tyler be continued as our standard bearer in Christian Endeavor, until we become, not third or second, but first in rank among the religious bodies of Christendom.

The daily papers of Chattanooga treated the convention with great courtesy, not only printing the proceedings of the conventions quite fully each day, but even giving the pictures of some of our handsomest men and women in their columns. Sometimes the pictures had the wrong names under them, but this made little difference. We notice the picture of the venerable president of the Foreign Society appeared with the name of the president of Hiram College underneath. The Mayor, in his speech, complained that too few pictures of the women had appeared in the papers, but added with characteristic Southern chivalry: "The faces of your fair women will remain photographed upon our hearts long after the pictures of your men have faded from memory." This, of course, compensated the ladies for any slight they may have felt in not being pictorially presented to the people of Chattanooga. Many of us never know how great men we are until we see ourselves written up in the personal column of these convention reports in the daily papers. It is evident from these columns that there are no small men who attend these conventions. This is as it should be. The convention needs our largest men.

The social feature of the Chattanooga convention was one of its best features. No one gets more out of this side of the convention than does the editor. It is his best opportunity for getting acquainted with people who have known him for many years and whom he has never met. The hearty hand-grips from those who have read his paper and have been strengthened by it into a larger and better religious life, and who have been comforted by it in times of sorrow, and encouraged by it in moments of weakness and fear, together with their words or even looks of appreciation, is no small part of an editor's compensation for his ceaseless toil and unremitting care. We never met more of these kind friends than at Chattanooga, and the remembrance of their hearty greetings and words of encouragement will be a source of strength to us through all the on-coming days.

In looking back at the conventions we have a feeling, which we think many share, that after all there was something lacking —a something, too, that is essential to a sense of satisfactoriness and completeness. There was not that point of spiritual enthusiasm and devotion that has sometimes been reached in our conventions. Perhaps the size of the hall had something to do with it, but the consciousness of hurry and rush did most to interfere with the devotional feature of the conventions. There was a lack, as it seems to us, of spontaneity, or, perhaps we should say, of the *opportunity* for spontaneity in the devotional service. There was no meeting that we now recall that was thrown open to the whole convention for volunteer prayers or exhortations. It may be said that this is impracticable in the present plan of running our conventions. Might we not, then, modify our plan so as to give an hour for the overflowing of hearts in voluntary praise and thanksgiving and exhortation? Brevity, of course, is a good thing, and a zeal for running on time is also to be commended when it does not assume the form of a menance to all spontaneity and unfettered devotion. The "Quiet Hour" feature of the Christian Endeavor Convention would add not a little to our conventions.

Hour of Prayer.

THE DAY OF SALVATION.

(Midweek Prayer-meeting Topic, Nov. 2.)

For he saith,
At an acceptable time I hearkened unto thee,
And in a day of salvation did I succor thee;
behold, now is the acceptable time; behold, now is the day of salvation.—2 *Cor.* 6:2.

This parenthetic clause, thrown in in the midst of one of Paul's celebrated climaxes, states a truth of transcendent importance. Quoting from Isaiah the word of the Lord to Israel of old, saying, "In an acceptable time have I answered thee, and in a day of salvation have I helped thee" (Isaiah 49:8), the apostle adds, "Behold, *now* is the acceptable time; behold, *now* is the day of salvation." There is a tendency in human nature to look forward to some future time as more favorable for amendment of life than the present. We are all prone, more or less, to procrastinate. It is easy to find in our present condition and surroundings what seem to us obstacles hard to overcome in entering upon a new life. "Some other time," we say, "will be more acceptable; some other day will be a better day for accepting the great salvation than to-day."

This is a delusion of Satan. Not the future, but *now* is the acceptable time. Not to-morrow, but *to-day* is the day of salvation. There has been and is yet, to some extent, current an idea among religious people that people must wait until God's "good time" before they can turn to the Lord. Under this kind of teaching earnest seekers after truth and salvation have been kept waiting in darkness through weary months and even years for God's good pleasure to grant them salvation. To all such waiting souls this word of the apostle comes sounding the note of good news, saying, "Now is the acceptable time; now is the day of salvation." No time is so acceptable to the Lord for a sinner's return to him as the present, and no day has the promise of salvation but the present day.

The truth has larger application than to waiting penitents, who are hesitating about throwing themselves upon the mercy of God, and entering into the joy of forgiveness of sins. It applies also to that class of Christians who promise themselves that after awhile, when times are better, when they have gained more leisure, they are going to devote more time to religious thought and religious work. "In some acceptable time," they are saying, "we are going to enter upon a broader and richer and fuller Christian life. We are not satisfied with what we are and with what we are doing, but the time is not convenient for us to begin the struggle after higher and better things." It is the same old mistake. Paul is saying to all such: "Now is the acceptable time; now is the day of salvation."

How often do we hear Christian people say that when they get older, and have accumulated more of this world's goods, they are going to be less in bondage to material things; they are going to give themselves more time for reading, for study, for travel and for the development of their higher nature. This, too, is an illusion. There are no better days than the present, and none so good for beginning this very work of self-development, and of living in the higher region of our nature. It is pitiful to see so many church members spending most of their lives engrossed with material interests, with a mere rift in the clouds on Sundays, until their souls have well-nigh lost the capacity for soaring into the higher regions of thought and aspiration and enjoyment. A sort of moral and spiritual atrophy prevents them from ever realizing the dreams which came to them in their earlier years.

Of all the mistakes which mortal men make, none seems to us more pitiful than that of men passing along through life to its swift close, postponing until some future time the joy and blessedness that might be theirs to-day; walking under brazen skies instead of under a starlit dome that stretches away into the infinities; slaves to their daily tasks and in bondage to pursuits that minister only to their lower natures, when they might be freemen in Jesus Christ, rejoicing in the liberty of the children of God; moaning out lamentations because of their hardships, their burdens and their disappointments, instead of singing jubilant songs of triumph along the pilgrim way that leads to the delectable mountains; deluding themselves with the idea that sometime in the future will be a better time for them to open their souls to Heaven's light and peace than to-day, instead of early entering into fellowship with God and walking all the way in the sunlight of his presence, their paths growing brighter until they enter the Celestial City.

Let not this mistake be ours. Let us be admonished by this word of the apostle and to-day begin that larger and better life to which God is calling us and to which our souls in their higher and better moments respond.

PRAYER.

O, Thou who art the God of patience and of tender compassion, how great is Thy mercy toward the children of men! How patiently hast Thou waited with outstretched hands for Thy wandering children to come to Thee and accept the rich gifts which Thou art so willing and so ready to bestow! Forgive us, dear Father, for delaying our return to Thee so long, and forgive us, too, that we have not come closer to Thee and received more of the infinite treasures of Thy grace and love. Forbid that we should postpone to some future time the acceptance of that grace and mercy and peace which Thou art ready to bestow upon us to-day. May these meditations lead many faltering ones to commit themselves to Thee, and many who have been living too far from Thee to accept a fuller salvation, through Jesus Christ our Lord. Amen!

Current Religious Thought

In an editorial on "Conduct by Proxy," in the Advance for Oct. 13, in which numerous dangers are pointed out in the use of this method of doing business, a good explanation of the failure of temperance and other good laws is incidentally given. The editor says:

'One common form of conduct by proxy is undue dependence on legal enactments. Here is some great evil, like the liquor traffic, or gambling, which is at war with the public welfare, and good citizens who love law and order come together and say, "Let us pass a law which will prohibit or restrict this evil." Very good; but the law when enacted, be it ever so good, does not lift from one citizen interested in it one iota of his responsibility for its enforcement. It is a rule for action, but as a statute there is as little action in it as there is in a street car dynamo which has no connection with the power house. Conduct by proxy is the dangerous shoal on which hundreds of excellent prohibitory laws have gone to pieces. Who will enforce these laws after they have been enacted? Too many citizens think that they have done their whole duty when the have secured the enactment of a law and hav committed its enforcement to certain dul elected officials. But the lawbreakers ar merely put on their mettle by a new law, n matter how strict it may be in provisions an penalties. They regard it as an antagonist and they begin to plan how they may overcom or evade it. "It looks formidable," they say "but has it teeth and claws? Yes, it ha teeth and claws, but is it a dummy figure stuffe with virtuous but innocuous ballots, or is ther *life* in it?" The only thing that can endow with life and keep it healthy and active vigilant citizenship. Lawbreakers are nc one bit afraid of legal enactments, and the are not very much afraid of officers of the law for they can often make terms of peace wit these which are mutually satisfactory; bu they are desperately afraid of aroused citizen —in sufficiennt numbers—who are bent o having the right done. "Died from condu by proxy," might be written over every dead letter law.

In the Biblical World for Septembe Prof. Geo. H. Gilbert, D. D., Chicag Seminary, has an article on "The Apostle Creed Revised by the teaching of Jesus. After an examination of the creed, articl by article, Prof Gilbert concludes that i the light of the personal teachings of Jesu it should read as follows:

I believe in God as the Father of all men who so loved the world that he gave his Son t die for it, and who freely pardons every peni tent sinner.

I believe in Jesus as the Messiah and Savio of the world, who lived a perfect life of trust obedience and love; who in his character an teaching gave a perfect revelation of the will o God; who founded the kingdom of heaven upo the earth; who was glorified by the Father i his death and resurrection; who sitteth at th right hand of the Father, and who is also i vital spiritual connection with his disciples o the earth.

I believe in the Holy Spirit, who takes th place of Jesus with his disciples, who show unto us the things of Jesus, and inspires t Christian service.

I believe in the holy kingdom of Jesus entered through faith in him, manifest where ever his spirit is manifest, extended by per sonal witness to Jesus, triumphant and ever lasting.

I believe in the forgiveness of sins throug Jesus, the life of consecration to the will o Jesus, the reception of believers by Jesus i the hour of death, and their perfect felicity i the perfected kingdom of God the Father.

In an article in the Church Union fo October on "A Wrong Emphasis," by H C. Hayden, D. D., are these sayings:

It is a significant fact that the Higher Critic of England and America, in spite of or as result of their investigations, find the Bibl no less an inspired book—not less full of God nor less authoritative over the conscience tha their brethren who decry their work. And i is at least possible that the rest of us, if w took the same pains to get at their standpoin that we do to suppress them, might also com out into a large place, with a greater wonde in our hearts at God's footsteps in history an a greater delight in the book we cherish as the veritable "Word of God"—a phrase which Dr Robertson Smith himself declined to swap of for the equivocal, "Contains the Word o God."

* * * * * * * * * *

How much grander and more Christian i would be if, instead of crowding our saintly honest and reverent scholars out, they wer met in their own field by other scholars, hones and saintly, who go at least part of the wa with them, but not all, and together, reverent ly searching, have mutually helped each othe into the light, tell the rest of us that we too ma walk in it. The church is in no danger of set tling down on the dictum of any man, or an one school of men, dogmatize and asseverat as they may. To the consensus of scholarshi she must submit herself. For this, in som things, we wait.

This surely will go on, whatever we do. I ought reverently to go on. Then let us giv comprehension and elasticity enough to ou ecclesiasticism to allow our devout scholars t abide within the fold, not under the ban of dis trust and with the stamp of odium upon thei brows, but with confidence in the truth, and charity for those whom we believe Christ ac cepts, even though to us they seem in thei search for truth to be putting themselves and us to needless trouble. Let Erasmus say t the twentieth what he said to the sixteenth century: "By identifying the new learning with heresy you make othodoxy synonymous with ignorance."

us hearts.
apology.
ss increases

in heaven
hly losses.
er organiza-
es.
een unusual-
al things.
week to the
ou also may

Goss Carter,
ublish in this
stories. Miss
ich language
The word-

s Christ en-
'—*Dr. Lori-*

an excellent
parent and
hat contains
But the chief
We fear that
neglected on
h public and
n either case,
pon the child.
the title of an
Pew (from the
y discrimina-
. But while
n indicated it
church is no
for all and
of the com-
en laid upon
istribution of
nd the things

mployers will
strong drink
the interests
rce may drive
enlightened
for the neces-
squelch the
the family,
ater, to say
ls.
ringing arti-
ls and Hopes.
of the Reform
nd under the
trong reform
congressional
fts says, the
e, votes and
could soon rid

big Thusrday. About one more visit would have changed him from an optimist to a pessimist. He was half converted as it was. Is not this the true position for Christ's soldiers after all? Has not the doctrine of optimism been pressed too far? Why try to make things seem what they are not? Or to think they are all right when they are not? This is the nature of Christian Scientists' philosophy and is unsound. Facts are facts and the truth will out. It is time—high time—that the army of the Lord was mobilized for battle. It is no use to cry peace, peace, when there is no peace with sin, crime and moral evil.

—We are glad to give the following commendation of the portrait of Alexander Campbell, recently given on our front page, from so competent a judge:

I wish to express my commendation of the portrait of Alexander Campbell. found on the first page of the CHRISTIAN-EVANGELIST of September 29. I think it is unsurpassed if equaled in accurate delineation of his features by any *printed* picture I have ever seen. In the earlier days of my portrait painting, in 1852 I spent two weeks at the Bethany mansion having personal sittings from Bro. Campbell for the portrait that I then painted, which, although crudely executed, was at that time certified to me in writing by himself as the best that had been painted. This print in your paper has more resemblance to it than any other I have seen. I desire a copy myself, as I wish to paint the face again with my original and this photograph to aid me, seeing I have had 46 years' experience since the original was painted.

M. C. TIERS.

913 *Forest Ave., N. Y.*

The photograph referred to above can be had by writing to Eugene Goodrich, Grand Rapids, Mich., enclosing bare cost of reproduction—fifty cents.

—The Religious Telescope last week began an editorial as follows: "The Word of God rests upon an impregnable foundation of evidence." We had thought and are still inclined to think that the Word of God is in and of itself *impregnable*. It is its own foundation and must endure forever quite independent of any evidence rallied in its support by man. It is men's theories of the Bible that need proping up with evidence; or rather that need impregnable foundations; not the Bible. The increase of substantial testimony only reveals to man more clearly the impregnability of the Word of God.

—In an editorial suggested by the welcome extented to President McKinley on the occasion of his visit to this city the Observer last week said:

Perhaps no city in America so fully represents both the Northern and the Southern elements of our population as St. Louis, and it is safe to say that in no other city has the President of the whole country been more cordially and sincerely received than he was in the great metropolis of the Central West. It is a matter for national gratitude that we have a President who is honored, revered and loved by the whole people. Chicago tried to lift the President above the people by bestowing upon him the doctor's hood and the doctor's degree, but he is still the great American commoner whose proudest honor is that he is an American citizen. Our Washington University might have bestowed degrees and honors on the President, but he is greater and grander as

the commentary series from his hand. It
especially commended for its analytical
its collation of sidelights, its frequent i
tions and its terse comments and s
applications. The book is out in good
for the new year and all may be sup
good time. There is also time to do som
missionary work by extending the use
book among the pupils, officers and teac
your school and of introducing it int
schools.

—Leslie J. Perry concludes an inte
article on "An Alliance with England"
Independent, with the following optimi
claration:

The moral and physical effect upon th
of such a union will be immeasurable.
will be for good can hardly be doub
will mean that Anglo-American liberty,
gence, prosperity and happiness shall
with the English language and overspr
earth. Occasionally some benighted
out of the past, like Spain, will att
obstruct this march, but without avail
haps in some remote, hide-bound spo
cardinal virtues will have to be plant
the aid of Anglo-American fleets and a
the sound of Armstrong and Gatling g
the ameliorating effects will be none
efficacious or permanent. Salisbury'
nations will be absorbed and rejuvenat
the whole human race elevated.

The writer of the above paragraph, h
thinks that England should and will
everything on this continent except a f
ing stations in order to secure the
We fear that Mr. Perry's optimistic
has somewhat blinded his eyes to the c
of national nature; especially to British

—From a copy of the third annual
the Board of Ministerial Relief we le
the donations from friends to this fun
the year has been but $3,629.11. Ther
hand, Oct. 1, 1897, $1,682.08. There
collected interest on loans $427.73.
mortgage loan returned to the treasury
making a total of funds for the yea

—We will send the CHRISTIAN-EVANGELIST on trial until the end of this year for twenty-five cents; or from time order is received until Jan. 1st, 1900, for one dollar and seventy-five cents.

—The leading editorial in the Christian Commonwealth, London, Oct. 6th, is devoted to a backward and forward look of that journal, which has just completed its 17th volume. While the editor's ideal has not yet been attained, the journal does not feel disposed to change its course, plans or policy, except to insist more vigorously for a purer Christianity and a clearer presentation of "the old Jerusalem gospel." This is a splendid mission for such a paper in the world's metropolis, and we heartily wish the Commonwealth another 17 years of life in that city on this work.

—Sister Hallam, of McKinney, Texas, writes to tell us of the location of a sister recently locating in this city, that she may be properly acquainted at the nearest church. This is a good plan. Every one knowing of the removal of any member of the Christian Church anywhere to this city should notify us, or the pastor nearest the location, of the fact. Many of our people could no doubt be saved to the cause if they were thus carefully cared for.

—An exchange says that "motion has in it a terrible power." This is a very indefinite statement. A body in motion has power against resisting obstacles, but this is modified by the volume, density and velocity of the moving body. Something analogous to this may be witnessed in the church. This is one of the natural laws of the spiritual domain.

'. C. McDougal, who has recently re- l from Bridgeburg to Winger, Ontario, la, and who expects to return to Hiram ;e, Hiram, Ohio, next fall, says: "Your ent paper must follow me where I go, for ıot afford to do without it. I speak a good for it at every opportunity." We ap- ıte all such kindly words and assistance, would be glad if many more of our rs would be at the same pains to extend irculation of the CHRISTIAN-EVANGELIST. doing you benefit yourself, your neigh- nd the cause for which the CHRISTIAN- 'GELIST stands.

'ards are received announcing the mar- , on Nov. 9th next, at Ocala, Fla., of Minnie Eliza Thompson, daughter of Mrs. ;aret Ross Thompson, to Mr. Charles rson Powell.

V. F. Richardson, Kansas City, Mo., :hosen president of the American Chris- Missionary Society, and will preside at innati over the Jubilee Convention.

'here remains yet some fragments of news the Chattanooga Convention, which will ar next week.

No article on the Sunday-school lesson ap- s this week on account of Dr. Willett's ıge to Europe. He had intended writing d for the trip, but was prevented by duties preparations for the voyage. This will be ıappointment to our readers who have come ıgard these articles as a substantial help, Dr. Willett promised that on his arrival at werp he would forward notes in advance another break might not thus occur.

Our frontispiece this week presents a face is familiar to Christian Endeavor workers ughout the United States. Bro. J. Z. r's active relation with the Christian En- 'or movement and his zealous labors in its ılf, even to the probable permanent im- ment of his health, have made him a gnized leader of this modern movement ng the young people. His labors in prepar- ınd managing the Bethany Christian En- 'or Courses have earned him the gratitude l who understand the latent possibilities of istian Endeavor among us. We are glad dd his picture to our portrait gallery of nguished men.

We understand that the Christian Asso- ion of Great Britain is likely to want a good for an important field in that country in the ng. This is a good opening for some ng preacher among us who would like to r for a few years in England and assist our hren there in establishing churches and ıagating principles in harmony with the ' Testament teaching. E. M. Todd, 28 mwell Grove, West Kensington Park, don, is the secretary of the English com- :ee who have the selection of the man. Of :se, only brethren of established character reputation as ministers of the Word would ligible.

The Central Christian Advocate strikes at uch-needed reform in the following intro- ion to an editorial on "Political Vilifica- ," in a recent issue. If it wasn't for ıing the country of secular papers we feel saying that all newspapers that indulge in kind of political currency ought to be cotted:

very time the American people engage in a tical campaign of any magnitude—and means once every two years—the press platform become rivals as reputation- rchers. It has become so well known a of American political life that he who ires to public office must expect to have motives questioned and his reputation as- ed, that many a sensitive soul resolutely lines even to consider the propriety of en- ng the public service, although the views of y may call in that direction. The country lost the services of some of its best citizens ıure of this odious peculiarity.

If this paper reaches you who are not a GELIST readers. Our special offer of $1.75 from now until Jan. 1st, 1900, ought to satisfy you. You may try it until Jan. 1st, 1899, by sending your name and address, together with twenty-five cents. If you appreciate the improvements which we are constantly making in the CHRISTIAN-EVANGELIST we should be pleased to have you secure your neighbor as a subscriber. *Substantial* encouragement at this end of the line will also be appreciated.

—If you are going to say anything, by voice or pen, you must know beforehand what point you are to aim at. What you need at the start is not ideas, but an idea. If one thing possesses you, and you want to convey it to others, words will be at your call to express it. But if you have words in abundance, and try to think of ideas which can be expressed in those words, neither words nor ideas will be worth much to you or your hearers. If the best navigator in the world starts out on a voyage he must decide, to begin with, where he wants to go. Otherwise his charts, his compass, the tides, the currents, the winds, and his nautical knowledge are of little use to him. Your first need in speaking is to be possessed by an idea and a purpose.—*Sunday-school Times.*

Educational Conference at Moberly.

Remember the Educational Conference to be held at Moberly, Mo., Tuesday, Nov. 1. It is important that the friends of education in the state be present at that conference.

PERSONAL MENTION.

C. R. Hudson, of Franklin, Ind., has gone to New Haven, Conn., for a postgraduate course in Yale University.

W. J. Russell, of Kalamazoo, Mich., has been tendered a unanimous call to preach for the church at Rushville, Ind.

Cards announcing the wedding of Mr. J. A. Briggs and Miss Bertha Widman, at Chattanooga, Tenn., Oct. 15th, have been received at this office.

The British Weekly says that Dr. Lorimer began his great sermon before the Baptist Missionary Society, at Nottingham, England, "with closed eyes, level voice and measured utterances." He did not open his eyes, it seems, until he was well into the depth and spirit of his sermon.

A farewell reception was tendered to Dr. F. M. Kirkham and wife and their daughter, Grace, in the parlors of the Central Christian Church, Chicago, on Friday evening, Oct. 14. About one hundred and fifty persons gathered to say good-bye to the departing ftiends. Short addresses were made by Bros. Black, Dr. Kirkham, Arthur O. Garrison, Bros. Hester, Palmer and others.

Bruce Wolverton, who for the past 6 months has been preaching for the Second Christian Church of this city, has returned to Portland, Ore. The Second Church had to give him up for want of sufficient finances for his salary and its current expenses and debts. While at the Second there were 40 additions under his ministry. The church found Bro. Wolverton to be an efficient, active pastor. As the church will arrange with its own forces to conduct its services, for awhile at least, no preacher need apply for the pulpit.

The following excellent testimony to appreciated worth and labor which appeared recently in the Courier-Journal, will be readily seconded by all who know the parties named and who have read their excellent books: "One of the most scholarly and interesting books that I have recently seen is 'The Song of Songs,' by Prof. J. W. Ellis, of Plattsburg, Mo. His translation and arrangement lend such a charm to the book that the student of the Bible must read it with greatly intensified interest. J. Breckenridge Ellis, of Plattsburg, is a worthy son of his father, and to his other publications he has added one of greatest interest, a book entitled 'King Saul.' It is one of those rare books that one can scarcely down after he begins reading it. Send to these authors and procure a copy of these books. You will not be disappointed. Our brethren should hail with delight such cultured and scholarly works coming, as they do, from our own people."

On last Friday, Bro. Muckley, of Kansas City, Mo., our Church Extension secretary, paid this office a flying visit. His face was still aglow with the spirit and fervor of the

C. E. Pomeroy, of Marion, Kan., is assisting L. W. Klinker at Peabody, Kan., in a series of gospel meetings instead of as stated iu this column last week. These brethren expect to continue there four weeks, then go to Marion to hold a meeting. Bros. Klinker and Pomeroy, the pastors at these places, are exchanging meetings and Prof. H. D. Funk, of Borner, Kan., is to lead the song services.

CHANGES.

D. D. Burt, Beatrice to 3159 Farman St., Omaha, Neb.
E. S. Ames, DeSoto, Ia., to Irvington, Ind.
C. E. Hudson, Franklin, Ind., to New Haven, Conn.
S. M. Cook, Newark to Weston, O.
Benj. Burchett, Sandusky to Diswood, Ill.
L. C. Swan, Murray to 1315 26th St., Des-Moines, Ia.
L. H. Stine, Paris, Mo., to Quincy, Ill.
A. Clark, Waco to Hermoson, Tex.
W. C. McDougal, Bridgeburg to Winger, Ont. Can.
R. J. Arnitt, Little Rock to Jewell, Ark.
J. S. King, Formosa, Kan., to Scottville, Ill.

THE HOME DEPARTMENT.

Great attention is now being given to the Home Department of the Sunday-school. It is intended for all persons who for any reason cannot attend the regular sessions of the school, yet who desire to study the International Bible Lessons, and keep paee with the great Sunday-school movement.

The Supplies.—The supplies necessary for the Home Department, in addition to the Lesson Annuals, Quarterlies or Papers that may be used in the school, are as follows:

1. Application Blanks for membership in the class to be signed by the applicant and filed with the Secretary of the Department.

2. The Home Register, containing full explanations for conducting the Department, with ten Test Questions on each lesson of the quarter, followed by blank spaces for writing the answers.

3. Certificates of Proficiency, to be given to members at the end of the quarter, signed by the Superintendent and Secretary, based on the written answers to the questions on the lessons of the quarter.

Price List.—The prices of these necessary supplies are as follows: *1. Application Cards*, 10 cents per dozen; 50 cents per 100. *2. The Home Register*, 5 cents per copy, or in packages of not less than ten copies, 3 cents each. *3. Certificates of Proficiency*, 25 cents per dozen, or $1.50 per 100.

Order your supplies for the Fourth Quarter of 1898 immediately and start the good work.

CHRISTIAN PUBLISHING CO.,
1522 Locust St., St. Louis, Mo.

Original Contributions.

THE NOONDAY OF THE SOUL.

L. H. STINE.

I.—THE POTENCY OF LIGHT.

Light is the countenance of the Everlasting. Its effulgence is the garment of the Almighty. Holy light was the first "offering of heaven"—the one in which God built himself into the world, and it became the sublimely beautiful symbol of the "true light" that, in the process of time, would enshere the soul of man and would irradiate his mind through all its noble organs. It is the likeness of the Eternal and, with its "burning head" lifted aloft, lights one "deep into the Deity." Light went went before all things as the precursor of Cosmos, and it played the first part in the history of the world. Light was the prelude of creation's destiny. The creation hymn begins its lofty narration of "almighty works" with the birth of light. That eternal beam that shot forth from the hand of God to penetrate primeval gloom, to raise the infant world from its cradle of chaos, and to guide it over the highway of vast geologic time to the sunlight of things, demanded the first note of praise. "Let there be light" is the first recorded word of the determining will of God.

The vision of the dayspring from on high, and of the rising of the Sun of Righteousness in victorious struggle with unsuccessful darkness, forms the prologue of the "sweeping acts" of the imperial gospel theme.

The ringing imperative of cosmical history is the world's first need, whether in evolving cosmos from chaos, or in conforming the soul to the image or the Christ. When the day grew dark on the scene of his desperate fight, from morning until evening, the "prayer of Ajax was for light." "The soul of his century," the literary idol of his time, Goethe, on whose meditative mind, in one of its inspired moments of dreamy revery, dawned the brilliant generalization that all the parts of a plant, from the seed to the blossom, are "mere modifications of a leaf"—a bold generalization of rare ingenuity and beauty that revolutionized the science of botany, this "master of histories, mythologies, philosophies, sciences and natural literatures" (Emerson), this poet that strikes the "harp with the hero's strength and grace," when dying called for "Light! O, for more light!" Having professed to seek the truth all his life, and having written much on Christian themes, Feuerbach expired with the confession of bewilderment and despair on his lips: "Truth! O, truth! where is it?" Sheridan, the brilliant parliamentarian, screamed in his dying hour: "O, I am absolutely undone!" These stars, and others, such as Hobbes and poor Goldsmith, that shone with the lustre of stars of the first magnitude in the firmament of mind, passed forth into the night at their setting. Had the light of literature, of science and of philosophy—true image of the "true light" that blazed from the enthusiasm of their genius—disappeared in the refulgence of the "light of life," as a star hides itself in the splendor of the day instead of sinking below the horizon of hope, resting on a soul winged for its ascent to be with God, it would have gleamed forever in the lordlier skies.

Beams of light are God's creative luminaries and the sacred instruments he handles for the accomplishment of his purpose and for the effectuation of his decrees. The Creator commissioned them to proclaim the evangel of the day and they gave to the world the "bridal of the earth and sky." Their gleams wreathed the face of nature with radiant smiles on the rose, on the tender violet and on the "fields until they laugh and sing." They tune the summer's silent organ for its throbbing chant of love and praise. Their invisible touch opens the courtly tulip and their summer's glow crowns the year with its coronet of golden corn. Speeding on their way through the dark shower that fronts the crimson west, they expand high on the evening sky the brightening bow of promise and change its harmonious colors with a revelation of God.

One day while holding a spectacle lens in each hand, Hans Lippershey directed them toward the steeple of a neighboring church when a "flashlight" out of the infinite revealed to him the future telescope. Sporting along the line of a spider's web, a sungleam made known to Sir Samuel Brown the principle of the suspension bridge. A beam of light exposed to view the behavior of a shipworm perforating a piece of wood, and suggested to Sir Marc Isambard Brunel the copy of the Thames tunnel. Piercing the long rows and proud tops of European pines, where dwelt the spirit of Odin and Thor, beams of light suggested to the Northern imagination designs for the "long-drawn aisles" of Christian temples and patterns for the gorgeously painted cathedral window. A friendly beam playing about a swinging chandelier in the Cathedral of Pisa revealed to the youthful mind of Galileo the long-hidden secret of the pendulum.

They were beams of light that revealed to the lawgiver the pattern of heavenly things which should serve as the model of things on earth, and that taught the accomplished artist how to conform to the true model in idealizing the heavenly. They opened the prophet's eyes to the "infinite book of secrecy" and inflamed the spirit of his poets with the feeling of momentous truths. They guided the holy apostle in the use of the mystic keys designed to unlock the kingdom of the Son of Man to the nations sitting in darkness, and they wove rich hues of promise for the reformer and martyr of the better life beyond their conflict and their desolation. Young Saul, resolute in defending the honor of the ancient faith, stricken to the earth by a legion of victorious beams, arose to his feet the "perfectest herald" of the new evangelism. They led the mind of Savonarola, the prophet of Florence, into his deep sense of the divine presence and awoke the slumbering energies of Luther for the epochal action of the reformation. "The glory of the Lord" hung like a transfiguration cloud over the land of the Cæsars and "while the Roman Empire was invaded by open violence or undermined by slow decay, a pure and humble religion quietly insinuated itself into the minds of men, grew up in silence and sobriety, derived new vigor from opposition and finally erected the banner of the cross on the ruins of the capitol" (Gibbon).

Waves of light not only evoke the tend germs of plants from the earth, and gener ate the chlorophyll within the leaves plants and the tissue of muscular and nerv ous fibres; not only give color to the fra grant blossoms and generate the electro magnetic activity of the earth's crust; bu in varied gradations of intensity and dura tion are "mysteriously connected with th intellectual susceptibilities, and the melan choly an cheerful tone of one's feelings' (Von Humboldt). One is consciousl aware of the sensible difference produce in one's moral nature by a dark day or bright one. Every ray of sunshine distil a balm to mitigate the pains of life, and cordial of hope flows in every beam to de light and exhilerate the delicate feelings o the soul. Light gives zest to the spirits vivacity and joy to the heart, and crowd the mind with cheerful ideas. It is the lif of the soul as well as the soul of the uni verse. Light conceals an occult power o enchantment and fascination that tranquil izes one's feelings, composes one's thought and inspirits one's heart. "The sun chase sadness from the sky, and dissipates th clouds that darken the human heart' (Pliny the elder). This is king David' idea in his beautiful epithet—"the LORD is my light." Light is a figure for comfort In a strain of confidence and hope he sing of the providence of the Lord of light wh makes plain the way of salvation. It i the function of light to dispel the shadow of doubt and fear, and to create faith and trust. Recognizing the inspiring effects of light on one's moral nature, one can appreciate the feelings of the cynical philosopher, Diogenes, who ordered an intruder to stand out of his sunshine. His morose temper craved the sunlight. No other power could successfully counteract the sombreness of his nature. Many a man having degenerated into the sullen disposition of a misanthrope would be led into a more assuring faith in the goodness of God, into a serener apprehension of the future, and into a more comprehensive view of the humanity, philanthropy and patriotism of man by a restoring, lubricating and balmy bath of sunshine.

The wonderful discovery in natural science that "no substance can be exposed to the sun's rays without undergoing in time chemical change," furnishes a forcible illustration of the transfiguring power of the "light of the gospel of the glory of Christ" (2 Cor. 4:4), as it is diffused through the civic and religious structure of society. One is told that a sunbeam is one of the most powerful agencies of nature. With a magic force it breaks up the strongest chemical affinities, and creates a myriad combinations that tend to the harmony of the world. In the Bible it is said the sun is the emblem of God. It is the glowing lamp of the world—*lucerna mundi*, as Copernicus was wont to name it. Such a symbol of God conveys an impressive truth when one thinks of the sun as the source of light and heat. A new conception of the sun's energy is imparted to the emblem, however, when one learns from astronomy that it is the center of attraction, and when one, in addition, takes in the generalization that the sun is the ultimate physical source of every form of power that exists in the world. The winds waft the commerce of every nation over the seas, but it is the heat of the sun that rarifies the air and sets the winds in

ne running stream yields a
grinds one's grain, turns one's
rks one's looms and drives
but it is because the sun has
the vapors from the bosom of
the "mother of life"—that fall
and are now meandering back
ce from whence they came,
e surface of nature in their
the forms of exquisite beauty.
ive energy of steam propels
, but the fire with which it
ocked up in the coal—the re-
inct forests stored away among
derived from existing forests.
rimeval and existing forests
substance from the sun. It is
l force resident in the sun's
disengaged their carbon and
as a source of power for fu-
The animal exerts a force by
ontraction, but he draws it
etable on which he feeds; the
erives it from the sun whose
and heat determine its growth.
one lifts his arm or takes a step
the power the sun gives him.
teps into a railway carriage, or
ean steamer, it is the power of
hurries one along. The gentle
fan one's cheek when the days
and the restless tornado that
in its fury are obedient serv-
un (Prof. Green).

ear Muse of Arts, plenties, and
s," is winning her victories
most Christian nations, and is
a beautiful calm the thirsty
l sword; but it is because the
lustrated in the life of Jesus
t the man at arms to serve upon
Christendom witnesses with
delight the joyful coronation
, and with gladsomest carol and
em celebrates the sacredness
but it is because Jesus shed his
e a "celestial benison" on the
dhood, anointed the child-life
of the spiritual race, erected
is glory into the standard of
and made its "virtues of sim-
ility and worldliness" (Chrys-
condition of entrance into his
grace. Every child brings
ld with it the image of the per-
l the work of the Christ is to
that image where it has not
l by sin, or to restore it where
ost. Woman is no longer the human nature with the sterner virtues of man. The exemplification of the delicate graces of woman in combination with the masculine attributes of character was the sublime miracle of the life of Jesus. He was mighty in word and in deed, because the tenderer and finer virtues of human nature rose in his life to the full measure of their power. This extraordinary union in one person of the weak and the strong as the old civilizations regarded these two poles of human nature, is the distinguishing mark or sign of the Christianity of Christ. Neither an arc lamp, telephony, phonography, telegraphy, science, philosophy, art nor literature indicates the true progress or an age, but the gradation that woman records in the scale of civic and religious life and the honor man pays to her salvation in its broadest sense, is the positive assertion of the charming excellences and supernal powers of sweet sympathy, patient kindness, heavenly pity, prevailing gentleness, native simplicity, vestal modesty and endless trust, and it is the light of Jesus that evokes these divine attributes from the human breast and develops them into the perfect man.

The potent beam that formed in the brain of Isaiah his "odes of silver tone, of which the ear is never weary," or thrilled the soul of King David when his lyric melodies were begotten; that imparted to Sampson his herculean strength, or endued Elijah with royal power for triumphant miracle; that enlivened the artistic taste of Bezaleel with a "clear perception and a strong, bold hand," to beautify the sacred tent, or animated the talent of Hiram, the Tyrian artist, to engrave precious metals for the embellishment of King Solomon's temple, came from the same fountain, illumining alike the natural and the spiritual talent. Light has a common centre of power. The light has prepared the mechanical skill of Aholiab to work in blue, in purple and in scarlet, moved the genius of Raphael to create the "Transfiguration" for the embellishment of the cathedral of Narbonne; that guided the talent of Gideon in his military exploits, inspired the genius of Wellington to join his sword to the providence of God for the overthrow of Napoleon, and for the reversion of the march of Eureopean events toward the "glories of the Possible;" that illumed the faculties of Paul in the midst of the Areopagus, inspired Luther at the Diet of Worms; that streams like a celestial tide through the

and the violen
his feet on th
ing his soul
death, were n
is conceiving
and is enfoldi
white. This
prophecies is
like a clock,
powerful spri
he entered u
shining now
first it tinted
means of the
the fields with
nal verities."
seashore whe
the soul of
Apollo's hand
of God." It
Ruth and aw
Miriam. From
drama of Job
It revealed to
a child of G
heart of Lyd
things which
beams in the
of truth and
testimony of
creating a p
shining thro
last, blazing
devoted love,
bers that are
with the char
the beautiful

—

MONUMENT

The argum
tinually gaini
in the East.
late years to
history conta
have been f
which, prior
believed to be

In the earl
the Old Test
very slight te
the greater p
productions
have come do
could deny
Testament s
without any
shown to be

chief value lies in the fact that it overwhelmingly refutes the claim that infidels so often urged, that the Jewish people of the royal period were rude and barbarous. The inscription shows that the Jews of that time were a remarkably cultured and literary people.

A well-known critic referred, a few decades ago, to the Hittites as a "mythical nation of ancient times, for the existence of which there is no extra-biblical evidence." To-day, however, every critic admits that the Hittites were among the most powerful races of people of remote antiquity, monumental evidence, discovered in 1879, showing that they were able to cope with the mighty nations of Assyria and Egypt in the fourteenth century before our era.

The Old Testament references to Ahab, Tiglath-Pileser, Shalmaneser, Sennacherib, Cyrus and other kings find illustration in the discoveries of archæologists. The names of the cities of Palestine conquered by Shishak, king of Egypt, still to be seen upon the temple walls at Karnak, and the Jewish faces of his captives are still visible, although sculptured many years ago in the days of Rehoboam. The history given in 2 Chronicles 12:1-8 is, therefore, shown to be perfectly true by evidence that even infidels must accept. The explorer has also unearthed Pithom, the treasure city which the Israelites built, and bricks made without straw are still to be seen there. The ruined palace of Pharaoh-hophra, at Tahpanhes, whither King Zedekiah's daughters fled for refuge (Jeremiah 43), has also been discovered.

The remarkable evidence of the truth of Old Testament history afforded by archæological researches, strong as it is to-day, may double its strength through the discoveries of the next few years. Many able scholars are devoting their lives to the investigation of Oriental antiquities, and there is every probability of a great deal of fresh light being thrown upon the scriptural history.

"IS THE WORLD GROWING WORSE?"

T. DAVIS.

The CHRISTIAN-EVANGELIST of Sept. 22, 1898, contains an article from the pen of Bro. J. J. Haley under the above caption. In that article Bro. Haley seems to have departed from his usually clear and analytical style of thought and diction. Many of his statements seem to me to be misleading. On many of his statements and inferences there are many who, like myself, desire instruction. Bro. Haley, by implication, censures certain authors for their pessimistic tendency of thought regarding the present and future condition of the world, and then, after repeating the editor's question, "Is God dead?" declares that the optimism of the prophets of Israel was based on a clear conception that the moral order of the world and the immanence of God in all his works were the sure guarantees of the ultimate triumph of righteousness.

It is on the question of the immanence of God, or what is the same thing, the general and special directing providence of God in the affairs of the world, that I—and I am sure many others—desire enlightenment, not merely as an abstract problem in theology or metaphysics, but because of its intimate connection with the unfortunate condition of about nineteen-twentieths of the human race. If it is true that the stupendous and for the greater part sickening panorama of life, from the time history first reveals it to us down to the present time, is but the visible manifestation of the controlling power of God in the affairs of history, then I see no good reason why we should question the truthfulness or reasonableness of the old saying, "Whatever is to be will be, and whatever is, is right."

Does Bro. Haley mean to affirm that all the events of history, even to the most insignificant thoughts and actions of men, are under the immediate direction of God, and in fulfillment of a universal plan or purpose formed in the infinite mind from all eternity?

If God exercises a universal and special providence, can it embrace less than every thought, volition and action in the world? Is this what men mean when they talk about "divine providence," "providence o God," "divine purpose," etc.? Is God's providence directive and compelling as well as permissive? If yes, does that fact affect in any degree our volitional freedom, and to what extent? Also, to what extent does it affect our accountability? If no, then I would like to be told exactly what men mean when they talk of God's overruling providence? (See CHRISTIAN-EVANGELIST, Aug. 4, 1898, p. 137.)

Again, if God's providence, or plan, or moral order, each of which we are told is directed to the accomplishment of the final triumph of righteousness, does not embrace in its working every minutia of life, how are we to determine the limit of its action? It occurs to me that there are many wholly unwarrantable things said concerning the providence of God. For instance, it has been repeatedly asserted, with the confidence of almost absolute certainty, that our great naval victories over the Spaniards were directly ordered by providence. Let that be admitted for a moment while we ask whether God in his providence assisted Turkey in her wars against the Greeks and Armenians. Who that is not destitute of the commonest feelings of fairness and humanity will assert that he did? If the doctrine of the divine immanence be true, who dares to deny that he did?

And if this doctrine be true I see no escape from the conclusion that all the crime and misery and suffering that have ever cursed humanity are but so many of the factors which God ever has been and still is employing in the solution of the great problem of life. What can be more horribly revolting to any one possessing the feelings and endowments of a proper man?

Finally, why should we believe in the "divine immanence?" Can the belief in such a doctrine contribute in any degree towards making people wiser or better? It is a question on which we reasonably hold different opinions, therefore there is nothing certain known about it. And I am utterly unable to see how such a belief, with all it implies, can increase one's reverence, not to say respect, for the Creator.

Our good brother makes sundry statements to show that the world is not growing worse, some of which I wish to notice briefly.

1. As regards the appliances for the relief of poverty, I suppose it is the proper thing for the millions of hungry wretch in the world to be thankful for sm favors. Doling a scanty charity to relie present suffering is no justification for social condition which compels men a women to drag out weary lives of men toil; lives as destitute of real enjoyment those of beasts. Whatever amelioration suffering has come to the laboring class a product of force exerted in the face danger of death or imprisonment, and t church, as a unit, has no right to claim or iota of credit for it; for she has ever bee as now, a passive spectator in the conflic I will say in this connection, that it will l in order to boast of the civilization whic protects the horse from the brutal trea ment of his driver when there are la made and executed that will effectual protect the laborer and tenant from tl worse than brutal treatment of mast (employer) and landlord.

Here is the proper place to notice wh our brother says about disarmament—th pleasing but delusive dream. Dulusiv because so long as there are so man millions of struggling human beings t writhe and groan and contend against th oppression of mammon, just so long will be convenient for those whose wealt shapes legislation to use bullets an bayonets to hush the mutterings of discon tent and to reduce the refractory to obedi ence. Nations will not disarm, becaus nations are ruled directly or indirectly b those whose interests it is to maintai armies.

2. "Modern liberty has completel triumphed over the brutal despotism of th past." I think the facts hardly warrant so positive an assertion. But let that pas while we reflect for a moment. What does our brother mean by *modern* liberty? Was it not liberty that inspired Miltiades and Leonidas and Judas Maccabæus and the heroes of all times, who raised their arm against the usurpations of tyrants?

But how did this fact called "modern liberty" become such a factor in the world? Did tyrants in every form, political and ecclesiastic, touched by the cries of suffering, grant willingly, peaceably, to the victims of their cruelty the right and privilege to enjoy unmolested the swee boon of liberty? Is it not rather the produc or achievement of long ages of the mos fearful and persistent conflict? Rivers o blood, prisons, tortures, racks and scaffolds sufferings unutterably horrible, are a few o the items in the terrible price paid fo liberty up to the present time.

I challenge any one to point to a singl case in history wherein the "powers tha were" granted peaceably one solitary righ to the masses. Are there still some con cessions to make? Have all an equa chance to-day in the terrific struggle fo existence? And does the sweet angel o love and fraternal fairness pervade th hearts of those to whom want and wretched ness kneel in tearful supplication, i sufficient strength to impel them to rela their inhuman grasp without more blood shed? Time alone can tell.

3. I do not know our brother's age, bu if he is as old as I am, I am at a loss t know why he should go back to the wars o Cromwell and Napoleon in his search afte exhibitions of savage brutality in war Our own civil war furnished examples b the thousands that would call forth th

itten about the semi-miraculous hs of Christian civilization in these f ours is wholly unauthorized by the n the case, and is, therefore, mis- ; and harmful. Also, that the prime in the perpetuation and extension of great modern evils is the power and wealth. All of which goes to prove ere remain many adequate reasons complaints of the "vile pessimists."

dward, Ia.

SUPERNATURALISM.

J. W. LOWBER.

rnatural literally means above na- It may not be unnatural, but above linary laws of nature. When under- he supernatural is as much governed as what we call the natural. A aturalist has said the laws of nature thoughts of God. When we know s we are known the distinction be- the natural and the supernatural isappear. The established order of is not to be violated by any who is a t of the laws of nature. None ex- he Author of nature has a right to re with these laws. If it can be shed as a fact that these laws have nterfered with even by higher law, here can be no doubt about the ex- of a supernatural Author who es over and governs the natural

of the most eminent of modern cal philosophers was the celebrated acé. This great man claimed that the ility of the continuance of the laws ure is superior to any other evidence, the best established historical facts. position claims that the probability perpetuity of the natural law is or to the evidence of the senses, to idence of testimony; in fact, to all ce. This difficulty comes up against gument of the skeptical philosopher: does he know anything about the of nature except through the testi- of the senses? We cannot make ss in anything and ignore the testi- of the senses. It is also impossible philosopher to get along and deny torical evidence. No man lives long h and has enough personal experi- o talk about the permanency of the f nature. It is only upon historical ce that he can base any such claims. science is against the doctrine that hing has continued from eternity as is. Geology teaches that the earth nce in a chaotic state. Since that ew laws have been added to nature e old ones have been greatly revised. Nebular Hypothesis claims that the system of nature was once in a neb- state. This gaseous state, which is ost refined state of matter, was not ermanent state, for matter did not ue in that state. As matter is inert r could have reached that state with- pernatural agency. It is impossible ount for the origin of life if we reject pernatural. Whatever may have he law by which the first man and n were produced, they were miracles; such law continues in operation at resent time. It ceased to operate he origin of man, and the purpose of fies to the existence of the miraculous. It is the law of nature that cold contracts; but when it reaches the freezing point this law is reversed, so ice is lighter than water. The Author of nature here introduces a new law for the welfare of man. The prophecies and miracles of the Bible cannot be accounted for without a belief in the supernatural. It is not surprising that the great skeptic, Rochester, became a believer when he had studied carefully the fifty-third chapter of Isaiah. I cannot see how any candid student of the book of Isaiah can otherwise than believe in the Christ of prophecy. Every conscientious student of the Bible and of nature must reach the conclusion that the Christianity of the Bible is a divine institution.

We all have our mother tongue, and linguistic science certainly teaches that the first man and woman had a teacher. Whatever may be true in reference to the law of evolution, like Mother Earth it is in itself dumb, and if like the other laws of nature it is the thought of God; then, after all, it is the Father in heaven who taught our first parents. The supernatural is, therefore, required in order to make man a speaking being. Language is of divine origin, and God not only made use of it in the creation of the heavens and earth, but also in giving man a revelation of his will. The Word was in the beginning with God, and the Word was God. The same Word became flesh, and dwelt among us. While the incarnation is not unnatural, it is the greatest manifestation of the supernatural.

Austin, Texas.

"NOT AS THE WORLD GIVETH, GIVE I UNTO YOU."

T. H. BLENUS.

The customary salutation of the Jews, both in saluting friends and bidding them farewell, was by the use of a term equivalent to "*Peace be unto you.*" The Savior alludes to this custom when he says to his disciples, "Peace I leave with you," but to show that he is not merely using a common form, and in a common manner, he adds the remark so worthy our attention, "Not as the world giveth, give I unto you." In the first place, the men of the world are unable to confer the peace which in their salutations they desire to bestow upon their friends, but the wishes of Christ were not thus impotent. The world's peace is transitory and often visionary, but the peace of Christ will endure forever. When the world proclaims peace to us the exclamation often wants the principle of sincerity. It is not difficult to find many whose words instead of being the unequivocal ineterpreters of their heartfelt sentiments are in direct opposition to them. There are many who cultivate with assiduity the wretched art of concealing the most unworthy and unscrupulous designs, by an imposing and extremely affectionate exterior, who with a cruel dexterity dissemble the true emotions of the soul that they may abuse the unsuspecting sincerity of those with whom they come in contact, who decorate and adorn with beautiful and sweetly scented garlands the victims they are leading to the slaughter. How often, while the whole heart is rankling with envy or aflame with anger, do the lips utter professions of regard and attachment. This is

cerity. Thousands will accede to what we have written who, deceived by vain assurances of affection, by feigned expressions of respect, supposed that they had found warm and true friends, but who in the hour of trial have found these pretended friends, on whose pretentions and caresses they confidently relied, cold, distant, and unheeding to the voice of their needs, and in the hour of trial treacherously abandoning them. Thousands will attest its truth who have been the dupes of those whom they imagined were attached to their interests, whose confidence has been betrayed by those in whom they supposed it was most firmly placed, but who have found by sad experience that the professions of the world are generally a strategem which selfishness and self-love employ for the accomplishment of their designs. Not so with the expressed attachment of the Lord Jesus. Disgusted with the world's treachery, indignant at its falsehood, we turn our thoughts to the words of our Lord—"Peace be with you;" "Peace I leave with you." There is no falsehood here, no dissimulation of friendship. These words drop from lips that never knew guile, and come welling up from a heart into which deceit never entered. Reproving all sin, Christ's indignation was yet peculiarly excited by fraud, deceit and double-dealing, either in word or action. If ever there were times when Jesus laid aside his meekness and lamb-like gentleness, it was when he directed his thunders and pronounced his woes upon the Pharisees, whose outward deportment and language were in opposition with their inward sentiments. Christ never deceived a hope, never betrayed the confidence of a single soul that relied upon his assurances and trusted in his Word. That is an unhappy man, indeed, who has no other reliance than a world which perpetually dupes, deludes and disappoints, but thrice happy are they who have found in the Savior a friend who will never frustrate their expectations, and who will in the hour of trial and adversity justify his sincerity by the most clear and unequvocal proofs. In the midst of the fluctuations and trials of this life we need some sure support on which we may confidently and with the assurance of confidence lean, some faithful bosom companion on whom we may unreservedly rely. An insincere, insecure world is not calculated to be such a support. Too often do we find as Amasa found in Joab, treachery approaching us with the accents of peace on its lips, while it firmly grasps the deadly, hidden dagger of death. A sincere, faithful, supporting, guileless, comforting Jesus is the one who, ever near to us, "is able to do abundantly above what we ask or think."

Jacksonville, Fla.

Correspondence.

English Topics.

HOW PEOPLE LOVE TO BE HUMBUGGED.

One of the chief topics of the hour in England is the history of M. Louis de Rougemont. During the last two months this gentleman has been amazing the world with reports of his personal experiences as the new Robinson Crusoe. He has succeeded in fascinating that immense section of the public who were so faithfully characterized by Barnum as "delighting to be humbugged." To my own mind we are gaining another illustration of the effect of faith, which is simply belief in testimony. If the testimony is false, then the faith is false also, and yet it may be most sincere. Now, M. de Rougemont is testifying to such wonders as the world never heard of before, and multitudes are being bewitched by his extraordinary record. He solemnly declares that he has spent thirty years amongst cannibal savages in unknown regions of Australia. Sir George Newnes, the Baronet editor of many popular magazines, and one of the members of our Parliament on the Liberal side, was so impressed with the veracity of the adventurer that he at once ordered his staff to supply him with everything that he needed, and he undertook to publish the account of Rougemont's sufferings and achievements. Truly this is a specimen of simple faith on the part of one of our cleverest public men, the most successful publisher of our time, and as simple faith is invariably contagious, the enthusiasm for Rougemont has spread in the most wildfire fashion. For instance, at the recent meetings of the British Association of Science, perhaps the most learned assembly in the world, Rougemont was actually invited to deliver an address, and although a few men plainly expressed their convictions that he was imposing on public credulity and attempted to put him through a heckling from which he at once shrank, he was received with the most cordial and childlike confidence. Now, this sort of faith is very different from that required either by the law or the gospel, whereby testimony is demanded from the mouth of not less than two or three witnesses. We are not asked by the New Testament to believe on the testimony of any one eyewitness that Jesus rose from the dead. Many of the testimonies are presented to us, and it is the convergence of testimony from men and women of all temperaments and all ranks which overwhelms unbelief and slays doubt at the empty tomb of the Redeemer. We are being asked to believe in a series of miraculous incidents in connection with Rougemont, simply on his own individual and unsupported testimony, and many people who can never believe the multitudinous proofs of the truth of the Christian religion, instantly and greedily swallow anything marvelous which an unknown pretender is pleased to offer them.

WHAT LOUIS DE ROUGEMONT SAYS.

One very serious matter is that Rougemont's backers are trying to form a syndicate to explore and open the wonderful fields where this king of the Cannibals declares that he found crude gold besides many a gem of purest ray serene. This means that many gullible persons are about to be swindled out of their money, as so many have been in every country at all times by pretentious impostors. I fear we are about to witness the perpetuation of one more gigantic fraud. What sort of tales is M. de Rougemont telling us? A man who relates how he buried a tomahawk in the head of a giant alligator whose scaly hide would turn the edge of one of your Kentucky axes is not to be complimented on the air of veracity worn by his narrative. A man who has paced the length of a dead whale and made it out one hundred and fifty feet must not be surprised if people tell him they do not believe
him. A shipwreck adventurer who dis
seawater into fresh out of one kettle for
years and gets enough out of it all the t
for a large dog and himself, strains the fait
his readers not a little. He reaches breal
point when the same kettle is made also t
duty for his savage guests for months on
and during a lengthy sea voyage in an c
boat. A residence of two years on a sa
spit only seven or eight feet above high w
in midocean is another patent impossibil
There is no region in the world where
ocean waters would not again and agair
such a space of time wash over and overwh
such a refuge. That all this farrago of n
sense should be gravely presented as a c
tribution to geographical and ethnograph
science, and should be seriously received e
in a learned conclave is exciting great indig
tion in the minds of the men most intimat
acquainted with the part of the world refer
to. Mr. Carr-Boyd is one of these. He
man of acknowledged repute as an explor
a magistrate, and a Fellow of the Royal G
grahical Society. He has been offering to
de Rougemont some awkward questio
which that gentleman says he is not
enough at present to deal with. But he
been well enough to perpetrate one very
reputable blunder. He has sneered at
Honorable David Carnegie as a mere diletta
traveler, notwithstanding that Mr. Carneg
dangerous, adventurous and romantic marc
known and authentic and its achieveme
were astonishing.

THE PARLIAMENTS OF THE CHURCHES.

Religiously speaking, this is the most int
esting period of the year in this country,
during the latter part of September the gr
denominations hold their conventions. L
week the Baptist Union met in strong force
Nottingham, under the presidency of my
friend Samuel Vincent, of Plymouth, one
the foremost of living preachers. But at t
meetings at Nottingham the most promine
speaker was not an Englishman, but
American visitor, very familiar to us on th
side of the water. Dr. Lorimer, of t
Tremont Temple, Boston, gave more than o
oration during the week, but his most striki
utterance was on "The Preservation of Prim
tive Christianity." Now, when I read t
program and saw this subject notified,
thought that either you American Disciples
Christ had been converting Dr. Lorimer
pentecostal and primitive Christianity, or el
that he had been stealing our thunder. B
now that his address has been published I pe
ceive that it does not denote either of the
contingencies in a complete sense, and yet
an approximate degree it is true that th
eloquent and eminent American Baptist is o
of us. He is certainly a Baptist in form and
name, but he is wonderfully unsectarian
spirit. Who amongst the most ardent
Disciples could speak more appropriately th
Dr. Lorimer did in the following passage: "
change is imperatively needed. If society is
be regenerated and the soul sanctified, we mu
go back to primitive Christianity. A gener
movement in that direction would abate irrit
tion (created by recent criticism), would
received with satisfaction by the workin
masses and would restore a dynamic which
the first was equal to the overthrow of paga
ism and the subjugation of barbarism. To y
belongs the initiative. It is for you to inau
urate the

RESTORATION OF PRIMITIVE CHRISTIANITY.

Not enough is it," Dr. Lorimer went on
say, "for us to insist that we have been i
custodians; we must justify our assumption b
evincing as never in the past its generous an
gracious attitude. We should go all throug
Great Britain proclaiming primitive Christia
ity." Now, after this extraordinary delive
ance form a denominationalist, I think th
when Dr. Lorimer returns to Boston yo
American Disciples should invite him to act

his own theories and join you who are actually doing in the United States what he wants done here. His speech is a welcome sign of a change of thought setting in amongst the Baptists.

DRAGGING ENGLAND TO KISS THE POPE'S TOE.

The great Church Congress has been held at Bradford, Yorkshire, at the same time as the assembly of the Baptists in Nottingham. The most eloquent of the English bishops, Dr. Boyd Carpenter, the Queen's favorite preacher, was president, and he had a very difficult task. The Church of England is divided into three great camps. The High Churchmen are crazy; the Low Churchmen are lazy; the Broad Churchmen are hazy. And the crazy, lazy and hazy parties met in conclave, not in order to settle their differences, as the English people are expecting them to do, but to enter into a sort of conspiracy to suppress all real discussion and to let all things drift on as they are. But this means that if the Anglican Church is not stirred to amendment and reform, then it will be captured by the determined Ritualists, whom the bishops are all affraid to attack, and it will lay itself down in a Chinese ''kotow'' at the feet of the wily old Pope, who last year administered such kicks to Mr. Gladstone and the High Churchmen, when they abased themselves at the Vatican to beseech the Holy Pontiff to be so very condescending as to recognize the validity of Anglican orders. The church met in a vast crowd, but the policy of ''laissez faire'' reigned throughout the week. The Bishop of Ripon actually went out of his way, in a style altogether foreign to him and unworthy of so truly great a man, to sneer at those who are going into hysterics about the mere lighting of a candle, or the color of a surplice, or the position of a lectern. This is a tremendous snubbing for the Evangelicals from their own most trusted leader. So that Churchmen are crying peace where there is no peace, except the peace which prevails with portentous hush before the breaking of a terrific storm. Steadily on towards a stupendous crisis is the great Established Church drifting. When that crisis arrives it will result in the greatest change in the history of England since the Reformation.

W. DURBAN.

43 Park Road, South Tottenham, London, Oct. 6, 1898.

Are We Overloading?

The contrast between what Jesus said of his yoke and what is expected of church members to-day, by the church, is we think sufficiently marked to justify the question at the head of this paper. If we may draw a conclusion from ecclesiastical history we believe that the tendency of present religious organization is to increase the burdens of their communicants. We will cite some noted instances cited in support of this view.

(1) The religious system inaugurated by Moses seems to have been a very simple affair at the first, but as it grew older it became so burdensome in its demands and exacting in its service that no man could meet all of its requirements. Rites, ceremonies, ordinances and tithes were added until it become a yoke which no man could wear. No Hebrew of Christ's day had the time or wealth to fully meet its requirements. Jesus saw this and severely denounced the authorities for a condition of things that had become unbearable. He accused those who sat in Moses' seat of having bound burdens upon the people that were grevious and of refusing to remove them or even of helping to bear them. And so in order that the people might have their liberty again, he set the whole thing aside and gave to the world a new system in its stead, the yoke of which was easy and its burden light.

(2) One of the most marked features of Christ's religious system at the first was its simplicity. During the first century it was remarkably free from cumbersome ordinances, rites, ceremonies and tithes. But, like the system of which it was the substance, it also increased its exactions of men until it became as complex and as ponderous as Judaism. Its adherents became its slaves. Their possessions, talents and time were at the command of the authorities of the church. Under the ponderous weight of the church the light, life and joy of the home and of nations was crushed out. A few men in the 15th and 16th centuries saw these unjust exactions of ecclesiastics and their oppressions of the poor, and hence the Protestant Reformation.

(3) In the Protestant Reformation religious liberty was not fully restored to the people, but the contrast between Protestant and Catholic Churches in this respect became very marked. But, unfortunately, as we think, this breach, which should have widened, seems rather to be closing up. The trend of Protestant Churches to-day seems not to be toward lighter but toward heavier burdens. The increase of societies, clubs, bands, meetings, missions, sociables, entertainments, lectures, schools, benevolences and collections has been so great that it has about become impossible for a man to keep the whole law. Church members are already staggering under their burdens, and the end is not yet. As things are now, but little if any of a man's time, talent or possessions is left for himself, his family or his friends. Perhaps some are ready to say that this is as it ought to be, but so said the doctors of the law and the bishops of the Papal system in their day.

Perhaps we should illustrate our meaning. Under the Roman Catholic religion in its palmiest days the people's money was gathered ostensibly ''for the Lord;'' but in reality for high livings and costly cathedrals. What was the result? Let the ignorance and poverty of their peoples answer. And yet, in the face of these facts Protestant Churches are committing the same error—increasing the burdens of their communicants and traveling toward the same end—oppression.

At first a sinner is told that salvation is free. After he becomes a church member he is then told that it is his duty to support the church. By and by he is told that he ought to have a hand in every good work; a principle which, by the way, is nowhere recognized in the business world as either practicable or sound; this is an age of specialties. Then, if he becomes a liberal giver, he is exhorted to donate all that he has "to the Lord." And some even are admonished to borrow on the unpromised and unknown future—another unsound business principle—and offer that ''as a sweet-smelling odor unto the Lord.'' Then, if he should show a disposition to hold back his gifts ''unto the Lord,'' he is charged with being ''afraid to trust God,'' ''a nominal Christian,'' ''a figurehead'' or some other chilling epithet, calculated to either extort money from him or drive him from the church. The aforesaid epithets and accusations, bear in mind, are simply the Christianized methods of torturing non-submissive church members. They are the torture-machines of medieval times modernized with but little loss to their severity and effective features.

In most of the so-called churches to-day, but few crimes are more emphasized than that of non-giving. No other qualities of soul are sufficient to offset this lack.

It may be true that all a man has and is belongs to the Lord, but not in the sense nor for the purpose in which this claim usually comes from the church. It is yet difficult for some men to believe that the taking of hard-earned wages, upon which a whole family is depending for daily bread, to put into a costly church edifice, or to make up the salary of an expensive ecclesiastic, is ''giving to the Lord.'' Or if this saying is true and the preacher who makes it would hate to be accused of trying to obtain money under false pretense, and the Lord so uses that money, they then conclude that ''the Lord is a mighty poor financier, and not the friend of the poor that he claimed to be.''

But it is not about the increasing demands of the church for money alone that we complain; there are other burdens. The demands upon an average church member's time are becoming equally oppressive. There are so many meetings, sociables, societies, clubs, bands and other church activities that it is almost if not quite impossible for the laboring church member to keep up with the procession. And yet, if he misses one of these his example is held up as a bad precedent and he is indirectly twitted and tormented over the matter until he becomes sour and don't care whether he goes to church at all again or not. And so things seem to be going from bad to worse. The burdens of the churches are becoming oppressive and the people are rebelling. They will not submit, and hence the empty pews. That these conditions are driving thousands of men from the church and keeping tens of thousands from hearing the gospel is the belief of your writer, and the apology for this paper. What think ye on this subject, O ye scribes and editors? In the meantime, let us not forget that the increase of burdens divided the kingdom of Israel, overthrew Judaism, devitalized Christianity, and to-day is one of the causes that has set ''the masses'' at naught with the churches. Not the increase of pure and undefiled religion, but of the mercenary, worldly, selfish demands of ecclesiasticisms and religious organizations.

F. T PEW.

Christian Science in India.

NOTES OF A RECENT ADDRESS BY THE PANDITA RAMABAI.

After a four months' stay in America I have become more than ever impressed with the words of Solomon: ''There is no new thing under the sun.'' With all the advancement of the nineteenth century I am surprised and shocked to find that ancient philosophies are making their appearance in the United States under the guise of Christian names. It is a sad sight to one who is acquainted with the results of heathen philosophy and superstition, to see educated people, who enjoy all the privileges of a Christian civilization, being deceived by the glamour of a new name.

On my arrival in New York last spring I was told that a new philosophy was being taught in the United States, and had already many disciples. The philosophy was called Christian Science, and when I asked what its teaching was, I recognized it as being the same philosophy that has been taught among my people for four thousand years. It has ruined millions of lives and caused immeasurable suffering and sorrow in my land, for it is based on selfishness and knows no sympathy or compassion.

But what has shocked me most has been the report that there are women in America who are not deceived by the name of ''Christian Science,'' but are confessedly studying and adopting the philosophy of the Hindus. As I was born and educated in the philosophy, having taken my degree of Pandita in it, I am acquainted with both its literature and its influence upon my people; and I want to witness to its degradation. To study Indian philosophy one must go to India and see its results and learn to read the Shasteas in the original. It is all very nice to read pretty translations, where much that is base and degrading is expurgated; but the original is quite another thing.

INGRATITUDE FOR GOD'S BLESSINGS.

The difficulty is that these American disciples of Hinduism have never appreciated the good things God has done for them. They are not interested in God's Word because they do not study it, and ignorance is at the root of all their infatuation. They are ignorant of the goodness of God, and they are wise in their own eyes. Many of them have had a university education, just as the men have had. They have clubs of their own, and many other privileges, but in spite of all this they have become foolish. I do not say so, but the Bible says so. Now, if you want to have a philosophy that will be useful to you in your life and will allow you to be useful to others, study the philosophy that you will find in the Gospel of John and the First Epistle of John.

These people are dissatisfied and want something better, something grand. Some of them told me they found so many "grand things" in the Hindu religion after they studied these translations. They received that knowledge in the English language and they say those books are "full of grand thoughts." I can tell you many of those "grand thoughts," for I have studied the same books in the original tongue. I thought I could find something happier and something higher in the philosophical works of my people, but I only found large words. The philosophical language is "very deep and very grand," therefore it is fine to make long sentences, and these sentences fill perhaps two or three or six pages. When you have got to the end of a sentence you do not remember what is said on the first page, and so you find it "very grand and deep." You know it is very grand when you do not understand it, and that is just what this philosophy means. It is a philosophy when you do not understand it. I can tell you I have sounded the depths of that philosophy, and what did I find? I will give you an idea in my own language. It means just this:

THE PHILOSOPHY OF NOTHINGNESS.

You are to take the whole universe as nothing but falsehood. You are to think that it does not exist. You do not exist. I do not exist. When you realize that, that is philosophy. Can you realize it? There was once upon a time a great being called Brahma, and that person was no person at all, but something like air, full of joy and knowledge! I cannot understand it, but philosophy tells you that you have to believe that this being, full of joy and knowledge, without any personality, existed once upon a time. That being had no mind. It did not want to say anything or have anything near it, and therefore, of course, it did not understand anything. Then there came another being just like himself, and that being was nothing but darkness. It was all falsehood. Now this air united with that darkness and assumed personality. It became male and female, and as that person has formed all things, the logical inference is that everything is falsehood. The birds and beasts that you see do not exist. You do not exist. When you realize that you have no personality whatever, you have no life, no knowledge, nothing, then you have attained the highest perfection of what is called "yoga," and that gives you liberation and you are liberated from your body and you become like him, without any personality. You draw on the blackboard zero, plus zero, minus zero, multiplied by zero, divided by zero, and it equals zero! It is just that—nothing more.

ITS FRUITS.

And what has that philosophy done for the people of India? A tree is judged by its fruits. An appletree can not bring forth a pear, but it will bring forth its own kind. The grandeur and beauty of that philosophy must be judged by its fruit. You are a people of some feeling. Everything is real. You feel that when other people are starving you ought to give them something to eat, but out in India they do not feel that. Men do not feel any sympathy for others. They do not feel for people who are starving or being killed in war. In our late famine our philosophers felt no compassion for sufferers and did not help the needy. For why should they help when they claimed the suffering was not real, neither were the dying children real. The first result, then, of the philosophy is the basest cruelty and selfishness; no compassion for sufferers, and supreme egotism.

WHERE TO STUDY HINDUISM.

To study Hindu philosophy it is best to visit India and experience it. Plenty of opportunities are afforded even if you go only to Bombay. That city is very large, and it is very hot there; but that will make no difference to philosophers who never experience heat at all. The people of India and the philosophers who have studied with the learned men ought to feel alike towards all people and all beings; but they never show a particle of kindness to the women, and their lives are made so unbearable that they want to kill themselves. These philosophers have shown mercy towards all lower animals. They have established hospitals for animals, but they have never established hospitals for women. The preachers who have come over here to preach Buddhism to the American people have established a hospital for animals in Bombay. In that hospital there is a ward devoted to bugs, and a man is hired to feed those bugs on his blood every night. They never take any thought of the women who are dying under the weight of this philosophy, but they just show their charity towards the bugs. I recommend that hospital for the edification of American students of Buddhism. Let them stay one night in that bug ward. That will pay them for all their labors in studying that philosophy!

The Hindu women have been made slaves, and it is the Christian people who are now bringing them the liberty of Christianity. Our philosophers have never established schools for our women and girls, but they have taught that it was a religious duty to burn thousands of widows alive. The women are very necessary in order to cook the food and care for husbands, but when the husbands die they are good for nothing. When I was in Calcutta I was asked by some of the philosophers to speak on something of the religion of the Hindu women. They tried to make a preacher of me. If I had become a preacher of the Hindu religion I do not think I could have remained a Hindu a single day. I was told, in the first place, by our learned people, that the women must never study the holy books of the Hindus. The men of India think that the very study of the books gives them salvation; but if the women study these books they are lost. What is good for men is not good for women in India. That is their belief. I just overstepped that rule a little and made a study of the religion. What do you think that I found woman's religion was? This religion said, You must never read or write, and knowledge is not the thing that is desirable for women. Women are naturally wicked, and if they get knowledge they become worse and worse!

THE HINDU WOMAN'S RELIGIOUS DUTIES.

The next duty of a woman is that she must be married, no matter how old or how young she is. You can find not many unmarried women in all that country. The religious books teach that unmarried women are going to hell, to be doomed to eternal punishment, and so the first care of the parents is to get a girl-baby married. As soon as a girl-baby is born in the family, the father begins to think where he can get a husband for her. When she is about nine or ten months old, he goes to a neighbor and says, I have a daughter, and would like your son to get married, and will he marry my daughter?" And so they are married. The two men fall in love with each other, and the contract is settled between them! That is marriage under Hindu philosophy, and it is binding.

Perhaps there are 700 girls in 1,000 that are married under ten years of age, for no girl is allowed to remain unmarried after she is twelve years of age. It is only the low castes who allow them to remain unmarried until they are fourteen or fifteen; high-caste men get their girls married before they are ten years of age.

What happens after? If the man dislikes the woman, why, he has the divine right of marrying as many women as he likes, for the man is considered the incarnation of the god Vishnu, and that god had 6,000 wives in this life! A man can get married to severa women at a time. There are some high-caste people who get so high as to marry 100 or 150 wives at a time. They do not have a very good memory, and so they keep a directory of their wives and children. As the husband is immortal, the Hindu religion says that a woman must never marry again when her husband dies. If they want to get to heaven, and do not stop anywhere else, then they must burn themselves alive. Seventy years ago the women used to be burned alive with the dead bodies of their husbands, but now that is stopped by law. Now the women are taught to cast themselves in the sacred rivers, or to take opium, and go to heaven, where they may find their husbands.

WHERE A HINDU WIFE IS FREE.

The husband is considered a god, and in heaven, my countrywomen are taught that they must be the servants of their husbands the same as on earth. On earth or in heaven the Indian woman can never be free. The third place open to her is hell. The man does not go there to trouble her, and that is the only place where she can be free! That is what the Hindu religion says regarding women, and that is the only religion that is given to her.

The Hindu woman's religious duties consist in household cares and the worship of her husband. After rising early and attending to the cares of her house her next duty is to put her head on the scared feet of her husband and worship him. When he comes home from business with bare feet her duty is to take warm water and wash those beautiful feet and drink the water in order to purify herself. Woman is naturally unholy, and drinking that dirty water is what scantifies her! That cleanses her from all sin, and there is nothing else, and in this way she is to live all her life. I wonder how many of these American disciples of Hinduism would like to realize that religion?

SINLESS LIES.

The philosophy of India teaches that there are five sinless lies, and among these are lies told to women. It does not matter whether it is to a mother or sister or wife or daughter. They must be met on their own standard, and so the man tries to deceive them.

That is how the women are treated, and if the American women think that they would like that philosophy, I wish they would feel it before they forsake the Bible and take it up. India is the best place for the study of the results of Hinduism. Go out there and see what it has done for women, and you will know what the religion is!

I want to tell you about the widows of India. There are 23,000,000 of them, and probably one-fourth of the whole number are under twenty-five years of age. We have probably 70,000 little children who are doomed to live in widowhood, and there are 13,000 under four years of age. They have to work without much food being given to them, and they have just one meal a day. The people think they ought to be punished for being widows. Many of these poor little creatures are committing suicide. Many of them want to go away and take liberty, and that liberty is taken to their own destruction.

INDIA'S WIDOWS AS MISSIONARIES.

Reader, thank God for everything you have, and think of the 140,000,000 women in India who do not have the light or liberty, but are doomed to be miserable all their lives and die like dogs and cats. Now I have come to be a Christian, I can never be thankful enough to God for the things he has done for me. I think it is our highest pleasure to do something for our women in India, and I pray that the Lord will give me a little more strength to do something for my countrywomen. It has pleased the Lord to give me 300 childwidows who are in my school in Poona. There are over 275 who are Christians, and preparing themselves to work for their own countrywomen. They are learning the Bible, and I hope that there

ırry the Bible to their
ıes.
ly pray for the widows
out to India, make the
ɔject; for if the widows
hed to them they will
the widows, I think,
vangelize India. They
'eatures, but God can
ıtures and-make some-
. us pray for them and
as we can, and thank
ıas done for us.—*Rec-*

ɘ-school Notes.

: in your Bible-schools
, concise manner gives
he first principles of the
ı order a good supply of
ıe New Testament," by
dleton. I have not ex-
clet in a long time that
atisfaction, and I would
classes formed in every
ıate of Missouri, for in
the children and youth
but it will be a good
s.
ɔurg gave me some good
other parts of the state.
he Normal school is a
he same methods in the
intendent. They have
l are working for 500. Of
tudents. What a great
ıg out the truth! There
ng whom are such as
Dutcher, Dr. and Mrs.
Johnson, with an army
ıuld gladden any heart,
nday not a teacher was
them taught the lesson
ny help save the Bible,
ed to do likewise. This
above all else. Their
ıd on attendance and
, works well, while their
e average of the state.
ools that have never cut
Bible-school work one
, year, and promised the
:h such promptness that
ıem for it. The school
ıyer, and then under a
assed out of the building
that I am anxious to see
. J. J. Morgan is giv-
ɔn as pastor, one of the
ıe was remarkable in the
preaching, doing noth-

hool, W. A. Fite minis-
ır Geo. E. Prewitt such
and ready co-operation,
that the evangelist would
offering was $15 in cash
ɔh W. A. Fite was as
as the workers. Our
etter, truer or more con-
most of the Missouri

ıe good books coming to
ɔopular address, another
ul," by J. Breckenridge
ear testimony that there
preparing oneself for the
ıtament than by reading
purchased and read now
viewing when our lessons
and times, while there
of spending the winter
:h company, and I plead
ɔd reading, all the Bible-
yourselves and present
ɔh as "King Saul."
ppened into Fayette at
ɔ, for the church was to
en deacons and decide on

their minister for another year. In choosing their eld͡ɔr, without any opportunity of knowing who was going out, the brethren re-elected Solon Smith, and also the same brethren for deacons, so that no changes were made, all to the credit of those serving the church and the Lord. Brother S. G. Clay was continued for his sixth year without one dissenting voice, speaking in stronger terms than any words the appreciation of the pillars and supporters of the work in our brother and God's servant, every act of which those of us knowing him and his good wife fully endorse.

In my institute at Grayson the work on the part of those attending was better far than I have had otherwhere this all. Mrs. M. B. Culver is the superintendent, but all seem to be workers, so that the school membership is larger than that of the congregation. The teachers have not yet come to where they can leave the helps on the seat and teach the lesson, but am sure they will. By removal the little band has suffered, but in their zeal they know no such word as fail, and the meeting to follow will manifest the good results of such work. The entire fellowship were as kind to me as could be, while their offering to the work was unusually good in view of their losses, even beyond their ability.

H. F. DAVIS.

Commercial Building, St, Louis.

Missonri C. W. B. M.

A number of district and county meetings were held in September, and most of them did fine work. The Nodaway district is never behind, and Sister Hosmer has been their efficient manager for years. Sister Dew is to have the work next year.

Miss Kittie Johnson, the manager of Marion County, arranged a good program and liberal contributions were made. Bro. Davis Errett suggested that the wife of the pastor of the Palmyra church be made a life member of the C. W. B. M. The amount was easily raised and will be paid in the name of Sister Marshall. Another life membership will be taken for a brother, for his wife, in the near future.

More than once has your secretary enjoyed the hospitality of Bro. and Sister M. McDonald. They give to Christians a friendly salutation and a kind reception; and they give much more—they give sympathy and interest in the cause which cannot be expressed in words,

Pettis County had a good convention and a life membership was started by Bro. Henry Davis, complimentary to Sister Stark, the wife of the LaMonte pastor. The LaMonte church is second to none in missionary zeal.

The state convention, at Nevada, fulfilled its promises. Only one person absent whose name was on the C. W. B. M. program. Sister Williams is an admirable presiding officer. Sister Gilbert gave us a warm welcome, and Sister Lowe's response was a beautiful expression of our thanks for the royal entertainment of the Nevada people. Mrs. Bantz had carefully gathered and arranged the facts concerning the lives of our missionaries now in the field.

Miss Mollie Beery's "Story of a Life Membership" was a true story. Sister Vernon read an excellent paper. Mrs. Bowen gave some valuable suggestions on Junior work. Mrs. Grant delivered a soul-stirring address on the "Significance of Missions." She is a speaker of great power and wields her audiences as she wills.

Miss Ada Boyd is the best speaker among our missionaries; and we saw India through her descriptions as we had never seen it before. The address of Mrs. Helen Moses was classical. She will visit the Missouri auxiliaries soon and all who desire may hear her.

The report of Miss Mollie Hughes, the superintendent of Young People's work, was very gratifying. It will be better when the auxiliaries determine to mother the Y. P. S. C. E. and Juniors in missionary endeavors.

The Missouri C. W. B. M. sent this year to national and state treasuries, $6,634.55. This amount will be increased by Sept. 30, and will equal the total of last year.

Fifty life memberships were pledged this year, the largest in our history of one year. How many can we secure for our Honor Roll next year? We begin with three.

The officers were re-elected. Your secretary asked to be released from office. Her request was denied, but she was excused from field work. An organizer will be put in the field after Christmas.

There were fewer delegates than usual present and less money was pledged. But the auxiliaries will report their usual pledges this quarter and all will do their best for this great cause—the extension of Christ's kingdom on earth.

VIRGINIA HEDGES.

Warrensburg, Mo., Oct. 1, 1898.

The St. Louis Lꞇtter.

The recent unlooked-for cold wave has revealed the fact that there are many people unprepared for the approaching winter. But there is nothing strange in this. There are always some people who seem never to prepare for anything. But the cold wave did more. It revealed the fact that there are still many men out of employment. Men who want work at any price, but cannot get it. There may not be as many men out of employment now as one or more years ago, but that there are still large numbers of enforced idlers to be seen on the streets is undeniable. In proof of this let any reliable business man or house advertise for a man and he will be appalled at the applications for the place. In a St. Louis suburban town the marshal, recently, was killed; before he was buried there were fifty applicants for the place. In some instances the ratio of applicants to the places open are even greater than this.

A little further investigation will also reveal the fact that a large per cent. of those who have work are working for wages on which they can eke out only the leanest kind of an existence.

It is furthermore evident that these conditions are not confined to common laborers. Men of experience, men of education, men who have held high places in their day, men who have been prominent in public life, professors, educators, writers, teachers and preachers are known to have offered their services for work and at wages which in other days they would have spurned. A man who has traveled extensively in many states and is widely known as a preacher was heard to say recently that the churches were generally complaining of hard times and their preachers were living at a shamefully small salary; some of them, he said, were disheartened. They could not educate their children and some could scarcely keep themselves in decent clothes for the pulpit.

A similar condition prevails among store clerks and mechanics. Those that have work generally haye wages on which they are barely living. Shops are not increasing their winter forces, much less raising wages. Some are shutting down; some are running on short time; others are reducing their force. Strikes are still in the land. One strike is scarcely settled in one place until another occurs somewhere else.

There are doubtless some who will not admit these facts. In their judgment any man who is out of employment does not want employment; that he is a knave, a tramp, a hobo, too lazy or too dishonest to work. They say that work is plenty and there is no honest excuse for idlers; that the banks are full of cheap money and the stores are full of cheap goods. You may point out the conditions complained of to them, but they steadfastly refuse to see them. They talk about government credits, balance of trade, per capita capital and other big things known only to corporations, trusts and syndicates, as though every laboring man in the land shared in their profits.

Why are we as a nation so troubled about markets abroad when our own people would consume the products of our factories if they had work at living wages? Our stores are full, but our homes are empty. There is a surplus of capital, and there is also a surplus of labor. And yet the government is seeking foreign markets at enormous cost, and our capital is going into other lands.

"But you can't compel men to invest their money by law," say some. Perhaps not. But there is a law higher than statutory enactments. Money needs no law to compel it to seek investment. Men who have money want to invest it. There is no more natural law in the universe than this. What drives money from the field is competition. Small capitalists are afraid of trusts and syndicates. They prefer to hide or hold their money. There are also other reasons, which we cannot give here and now. The editor would not permit it.

But the law of humanity, of brotherhood and of brotherly acting is a religious question within the precincts of a religious journal, and we will follow that line. Christian men, Christian corporations and Christian capitalists do not have to follow the ways of the world in these matters. They could if they would (and true Christian men would) be a law unto themselves in these matters; or, better still, they would follow the law of Christ, and this would greatly help to solve these questions.

In the first place, they could if they would organize a bank which would loan small sums of money to laboring men on household goods or other personal security at reasonable interest rates. This would save thousands of men from soulless money sharks and their families from suffering.

Second, they could if they would pay a little better wages to their employees than non-Christian men and houses pay. As it is some of the foremost men in the churches have the reputation in labor circles of being the hardest taskmasters in the city. Why should they not set an example of liberality in these things? Why should they not show that they are actuated by their Christianity, and not by mercenary motives even in the matter of wages? A profit-sharing system would be better.

Third, they could if they would provide some public work which would give to every man that asks work, even at the lowest wages, until he could get work elsewhere or money enough to take him to other parts, as is often the only favor asked.

Fourth, they could if they would assist many worthy families to colonize where they could in due time become independent and return the money used to the colonizing company with interest. There is still plenty of land to support all who are unemployed, and who thereby could and would willingly earn their own living if properly helped.

Fifth, they could if they would exert a much more effective influence through municipal, county and state governments against poverty-producing causes, and thereby save many from idleness, crime and destruction. But why go further? The facts stated have already discredited the church as the friend of the helpless, and so the enforced idler is left to look out for himself and his family as he can, without help and without sympathy.

B. U. I.

Reminiscences.

Mr. Editor, allow me through your valuable paper to relate a few memories of the events of the first years of the introduction and struggles of the Reformation in the state of New York.

First, I note that Eld. Jeffries, a popular and gifted Baptist preacher at the village of Throopsville, pastor of a large and influential church, upon taking and reading the Christian Baptist, a monthly paper, edited and published by Alexander Campbell, of Bethany, Va., accepted and approbated the views of Reformation as pleaded by Mr. Campbell in said paper, and preached them to his large congregation. This resulted in the withdrawal of some seven of his most intelligent and liberal-minded members from the Baptist Church and the organization of a church of reformatory views. The names of most of these men we can give: Mr. Allen, Sr., of Clarksville; Col. J. Barnum, Capt. J. Crane and Mr. Crull, of Centerville; Mr. Freer, Mr. Green and Mr. Wilkerson, of Skaneateles. These men were the leading, substantial ones of the Baptist Church. This was then supposed to be the second church of like faith and order in the state: the other one, or First, being in the city of New York. Eld. Jeffries entertained the same views of reformation that these leading men did, and had preached them to his congregation; but in that early day (about 1830), from the strictures in the Christian Baptist upon a hirling clergy, they were opposed to a salary being paid to the preacher and hence Elder Jeffries did not see fit to joi them. Therefore, he remained as he was pastor of his own Baptist Church. The organiz ation remained for years, doing their ow preaching and edifying themselves, as the had men of much talent among them. In fact they had the cream of the Baptist Church Eld. J. J. Moss, of Ohio, was the first o about the first preacher of the Reformatio that visited them on his first visit to th Empire state. The writer heard Eld. Mos say that this company was so afraid of preach ers that they talked so roughly to him becaus he was preaching, that he wept like a child i their presence. Such were their views of th hirling preacher, and such were their views fo a long time. As they had to pay nothing for preaching it seemed to be a doctrine to them very full of comfort. Years afterward I have known them to postpone a funeral with the corpse in the house and Eld. Bartlet to preach the funeral, till after the elders attended to the exercises of the first-day meeting! Hence the church never grew any under such regimen. Fortunate for the cause of truth that the Heavenly Father transplanted all with such views in due season to a better climate.

Such was the beginning of the Reformation movement in that early day and in that part of the state. How wonderfully God can bring marvelous things out of seeming impossibilities! With all these hindrances, yet that same church, after years of agony, became the mother-church of several others. Little did the writer think when he attended there for years with Dio Lewis, the Goodriches, the McCarthys, and Waites, and Clapps, that she would ever be such a blessing to the world as she has been. How true that God's ways are past finding out! Clarksville and finally Auburn and South Butler and a host of others can call her mother. It did not, of course, flourish much till those who entertained the anti-preacher idea (and they would preach hours against preaching) preached themselves into such unsavory welcome as to lose all their influence, or God in his infinite mercy translated them from mortality to immortality. But against years of such struggling and anti-missionary spirit and action, still how true that "truth though crushed and trodden under foot—despised—will rise again, for the eternal years of God are hers." There are several churches in the West that can rightfully call her mother—the one at Paw Paw was built up by the members of this same old church, at Thorn Apple, Albion, Marshall and others we do not now remember. All glory to the old Throopsville Church, after all. She was, after her severe agonies, cultured and watered by Elds. Moss, Hayden and other preachers from Ohio, and Shepherd, Bartlet, I. Errett, Hunter, etc., etc. It would be pleasant to mention the main pillars of the old church, those who have stood by it in its adversity and prosperity. Most of them have gone to their long rest and now their labors do follow them, those who were busy actors up to A. D. 1840. How I would like to preach to the Throopsville Church now!

J. B. Crane.

Waynesboro, Va.

otes and News.

ıren at State Line, Ind., presented
suit to their pastor, A. O. Swart-
ord's day, Oct. 16, to show their
n of his earnest efforts in the
ause. The work is moving along
. W. H. Baker, of Robinson, Ill.,
A. O. Swartwood in a meeting at
which continues from Oct. 6th.

—Pastor for West Side Church of
ira, N. Y. A young man who will
$500 or $600 per year preferred.
ell recommended and able to hold a
l meeting. Address
CHAS. F. LILLEY.
N. Y.

'ch at Detroit, Ill., will want a
an. 1st, 1899. Address Newton
sent pastor.

ch at DeSoto, Mo., we have heard,
call S. J. Copher, of Odessa, Mo.,
cher.

ch at Hematite, Mo., has called J.
formerly of Cape Girardeau, Mo.,
ths.

lson, of St. Louis, Mo., preached
Mo., last Sunday.

Another Dedication.

Side Christian Church, Pasadena,
ated their new church home on last
A very appropriate program had
nged for the occasion. A. C.
of Los Angeles, was to preach at
g service. Also short addresses by
stors of the city were to be made.
gram, pastor of the First Church in
was to deliver the sermon at the
vice. H. Elliott Ward is the pastor
ishing congregation. The dedica-
followed with a protracted meeting,
by R. H. Bateman, of Santa Ana.
s 48x50, with vestibule, class rooms,
ms and baptistery. Cost, $1200.

District Convention.

-annual convention of the fourth
Nebraska convened at Beldon,
o Oct. 2. The convention was well
ad a success from beginning to end.
ting program was rendered. Bro.
, of Forrest, district president for
years, was re-elected for the en-
. He is a wide-awake man and an
ristian worker. He has proven
be the right man in the right place.
wood, of Creighton, corresponding
nd treasurer for the past year, was
ted. Bro. Elwood is one of those,
feel a deep interest in the cause of
'e has done a noble work during the
The most interesting feature of the
was the report read by the corres-
cretary. It showed the excellent
by the district board. But the best
owed that the district was entirely
and $20 in the treasury. During
ar a large tent was purchased, an
employed and meetings conducted
fields and for churches that were
nable to pay for a meeting. Among
ing brethren present were Bro.
of Wakefield; Bro. Shoemaker, of
o. Harrison, of Bancroft, and John
of Bloomfield. Sister Applegate, of
district president of C. W. B. M.,
hat their society, though few in
as heart and hand in the great mis-
work, and through their untiring
uxiliary was organized at Creighton
The Wakefield auxiliary, she said,

send the gospel to heathen lands in the near future. Auxiliaries will be organized at Bloomfield and Oliver's Grove. Thomas Rollings, district president of the Y. P. S. C. E, gave a thrilling talk upon The Relation of the Y. P. S. C. E. to the Church. We were sorry more Endeavorers were not present to hear their relation to the church. It was a splendid discourse. Sermons were preached by Bros. Applegate, Shoemaker and Higgs. John J. Higgs was appointed distrct evangelist for the coming year. The convention was one long to be remembered, and we believe every delegate went to their homes resolved to do more the coming year than they have done during the past. The convention recommended that we drop the name Sunday-school and adopt the name Bible-school, being more scriptural. We are glad to report that the missionary and progressive spirit is advancing rapidly among the Disciples in this fourth district. And our aim is to do a greater work in the coming year for Christ and the church than we have in the years gone by.

JOHN J. HIGGS, District Evangelist.

Oct. 11, 1898.

A Visit to Kentucky.

We left home Sept. 26th for a few days' visit with our dear mother and grandmother, who lives a Barbourville. I reached St. Louis at 3:45 P. M. that day, and called at the rooms of the Christian Publishing Company and found every one busy. The editor of the CHRISTIAN-EVANGELIST looked rather warm for a man who had been cooling all summer. We reached our destination at 5 P. M. the 27th. I had not reached the home after getting off the train till a messenger came after me to preach the next evening; so I said yes, and for seven days I tried to rest and preach. It was not much rest and poor preaching, I guess. I did not meet Bro. Dickson, the preacher at Borbourville. He lives at London and preaches at B. once per month. Those good people seemed to appreciate our preaching, and showed it by giving a nice purse of silver. We have some most excellent Christians in that town and community. I met my brother, A. L. Fuller, of Bentley, Kan., whom I had not seen for eight years. My grandmother has passed her 90th milestone, and still reads her Bible without glasses. We hope to visit these good people again sometime. The CHRISTIAN-EVANGELIST will visit several of their homes there for one month now. We called again as we came back and took in the Fair at St. Louis on St. Louis Day. Reached home in time for prayer-meeting Thursday evening.

J. H. FULLER.

Burlington, Ia.

The Martin Meeting at La Junta, Colorado.

For one who has never worked in the West and does not understand the conditions, it would be difficult to form an idea what success here really means. Satan has absolute control, and runs things generally to suit himself. A city of 4,500 population, with five saloons and four drugstores, each deriving its support from the sale of liquor, will give some idea concerning the religious sentiment of the place. There is, among the few moral pe ple we have, a feeling of total indifference as to their souls' welfare. In the entire city and surrounding country, which represents 6,000 people, there are about three hundred who attend church.

To enter such a community and succeed, the church knew, requires a man of unusual ability, great tact and power to preach the old plea, all of which we believed Bro. S. M. Martin possessed, and we have not been disappointed.

For five weeks he has held such audiences as have never before been witnessed in this part of the state, many times passing the six-

have been done I would have said it w
possible, and I know of no other man
believe could do it. The good accom
in this community by his great meeti
take years to measure. It has been my
ure to hear the greater evangelists of t
i. e., Sam Jones, B. Fay Mills, Dwi
Moody and others, but I rank Bro.
above them all. He has a much finer d
and his sermons are far more intellectua
Brethren, if you are in a city with a p
tion of or over 10,000 you can make no n
in engaging Bro. S. M. Martin to hold
meeting. He goes from here to Dallas,
to hold a meeting for M. M. Davis a
great church. ELMER WARD CO
Pastor Church of Ch

Thanksgiving Service.

The West Side Church, Chicago,
Brown, pastor, recently had a thank
service that all present seem to have
enjoyed. A good program for the occasi
been previously arranged, and the uplift
fluence of the occasion was felt by the c
Of this meeting and the church the
writes as follows:
"There have been 100 new members
to the West Side Church since Feb. 1
at the service Wednesday night we sta
the second hundred. No one has been c
who has not become actively identifie
the work. I mean by that, non-resident
ple from mission points and people who l
far away to attend services regularly.
number of these three classes have bee
tized, but we do not count them in the 1

La Harpe, Ill.

On last Thursday occurred the jubi
annual meeting of the church at this pla
Just before the annual meeting each
if it is necessary—the church makes a
effort to raise money and settle up all ex
and any indebtedness that may be outsta
We then call in some neighboring preac
former pastors of this congregation an
all-day services with roll-call of the
bers, and annual reports from the officers
various societies of the church, such a
day-school, Y. P. S. C. E., etc. Di
usually served at the church, by the s
and part of the day is observed in a g
social visit with each other.
This is a day looked forward to and enj
all in attendance, and is considered be
in more ways than one.
The treasurer's report showed $1,564,
during the year for all purposes, inc
missions. There were 25 additions duri
year, and six dismissals by letter and
deaths, leaving a net gain of 16. Total
bership now is 236. Bro. K. C. Vent
now in his seventh year's work with us,
getting along nicely with the work.
church is prosperous and we have a ve
cient Sunday-school under the leaders
Dr. W. O. Butler.
H. S. DICKSON, Cl
Oct. 17th, 1898.

Dedication at Indianapolis.

We are quite happy. Sunday, Sept.
dedicated our new house—the Seventh
tian Church of Indianapolis—and sur
even our most sanguine hopes. Bro. J
Pounds preached the sermon, then pro
to raise money as though he were an old
an at the business. The result was that
the day was over our pledges overr
mark, which in the morning seemed
sible of attainment.
Our improvements cost $4,200. To
shrinkage, provide for further expense
we placed the pledge mark at $5,000, an
than covered it. For a poor congregati
is a noble showing, and required self-sa
A no less pleasing feature of the day v

manifested toward us. The long-felt need of a closer relationship in the work of the whole city is about to become a reality.

This church was organized in 1884, by Bro. J. M. Canfield. Those who have ministered to it since are Bros. A. Plunkitt, J. W. Crews, James Conner, S. M. Conner, Aaron Walker, E.M.Egolph and the writer, who is nearing his third year's end. The growth of the church has never been phenomenal, yet always upward. Schemers, in times past, have here tried their infamous work, but God has preserved the church intact. Selfish men and women, who knew (or thought they knew) the form of godliness, but who knew not its power, finding no congenial atmosphere in it, were compelled to withdraw, where they could manufacture surroundings favorable to their ends. They are doing it, too, by the way, with a vengeance. Though they have involved some good men, yet as a whole it has been a great blessing to the church that they were not with it.

The new church is capable of accommodating 1,000 people. Seating capacity of 800. It is brick veneered. The auditorium is 44 by 51 feet, inside measurement. The lecture-room is 30 by 45 feet. The two rooms are connected by sliding doors. From the open porch in front, doors lead into a vestibule, 10 by 12 feet, on either side. From the west vestibule, stairs ascend to the bacloony. The floor inclines toward the pulpit. It is heated by a furnace, lighted by electricity and seated with modern pews.

We are expecting beter things.

R. W. CLYMER.

Michigan Grange.

Bro. Chapple, of Vandalia, is engaged in a meeting at Hill's Corners. He has been engaged to preach for the churches at Vandalia and Hill's Corners for another year, with an increase of salary.

Bro. J. H. Lacey, of LaPort, Ind., has taken up the work at Duplain.

Bro. Spayd, of Owosso, has closed his meeting at Mt. Pleasant with ten added to the Lord. He had to close the meeting on account of the illness of Sister Spayd. May it be the Lord's will for our consecrated Sister Spayd to be fully restored to her health. She has been very ill, but all her friends will be glad to hear that she is some better at present. I would like to say a great deal about Bro. Spayd's new book, "The Two Covenents and the Sabbath." Brethren, it ought to be circulated widely. Send twenty-five cents to L. W. Spayd, Owosso, Mich., and he will send you a copy by mail. It is just what you need in meeting the Seventh-Day Adventist. Two have been added at Durand since last report.

Bro. McCall begins his fourth year at Yale. His audiences are larger than they ever were.

The people of Michigan will be pleased to learn that Bro. W. A. Ward began his evangelistic work once more, with this month. You may expect to hear of some grand meetings.

We are pleased to hear that Bro. McMillan, our state secretary, has gone the way of all the living, by taking unto himself a wife. We congratulate him ad wish him success and happiness. May the Lord prosper him in his work. More again. R. BRUCE BROWN.

Bethany.

At Chatianooga the alumni and friends of Bethany met and conferred. The results of that meeting may have a very important bearing on the future of this worthy old institution. Already restored confidence is asserting its sway. It has begun to dawn upon most thoughtful people that, come what may, Bethany has yet a great future before her.

It was the unanimous opinion of all present that the graduates and patrons of Bethany should form local organizations in the larger cities and centers of influences, through which help could be extended to her in many ways, especially in moral and financial support. A plan, with this as a result, is soon to be put into operation. There are nearly one thousand graduates of the college scattered throughout the United States and British Provinces.

The financial outlook steadily grows brighter, although it is only about a fortnight since the board of trustees started out on the present *new departure*. Bro. McLean remarked in the meeting at Chattanooga that after a careful and thorough investigation he was fully satisfied that the administration of Bethany's affairs had always been strictly honest, however great may have been the misfortunes that may have overtaken them. If errors have been committed, they were not inspired by dishonest purposes.

There is scarcely an educational institution in the land that has not at some time in its history been so near the brink of failure that it required extraordinary help to save it from ruin. This can scarcely be said of Bethany now, however much she needs funds, and it is doubtful if she ever was in a worse condition than at present. What other college has ever had such vitality? J. L. DARSIE.

Bethany, W. Va.

Revised Report.

[In our report recently, of the Missoure state work for the year at the Nevada convention the wrong punctuation of a number caused a mistake in the grand total of money received for all purposes. And as other items in the report were only approximately given we have secured from the secretary, T. A. Abbott, a revised statement which we here give.—EDITOR.]

Contributed to state missions	$ 5,555
Supplemental to state mission work	10,498
Church building in state mission work	16,856
State Bible-school work	3,512
Church building in Bible-school work	6,000
Contributed in county and district missions	5,985
Church building in county and district work	11,300
Total	$59,706

MISSIONS OUTSIDE STATE.

Foreignn Missions	$ 9,448
C. W. B. M.	6,500
Church Extension	1,809
A. C. M. S.	3,095
	$20,832

PAID FOR LOCAL CHURCH WORK.

Bible-school support	$ 45,000
Incidental church expenses	47,000
Building and repairs	81,370
Ministerial support	355,000
	$528,370

ORPHANAGES, SCHOOLS AND ENDOWMENT.

Maintaining Orphans' Home	$10,000
Educating orphan girls	6,000
Endowment	75,000
	$91,000

GRAND SUMMARY.

Mission work, Home and Foreign	$ 80,538
Local church work	528,370
Orphanages, schools and endowment	91,000
Grand total	$699,908

T. A. ABBOTT.

Convention Miscellany.

The Chattanooga Convention proved that it takes something worse than yellow fever to scare the Disciples of Christ, or keep them from their annual assemblage.

The weather, excepting only the rain of Monday, was splendid. It was clear, cool and bracing; the air was fragrant with the breath of the magnolia and the rose, and the rain had laid the dust.

Nobody with whom I met before the convention expected a thousand people; the enrollment must have reached nearly 1,400. And they were splendid people. There were no growlers, no kickers, no critics. The proceedings were full of "go" from start to finish.

One of the veterans remarked two features that particularly impressed him: first, the "old stagers," who have always been making their big speeches, were jostled off, and a program had been made with new timber; second, the addresses were rather better than usual at our National Convention. Doubtless the young men have been learning from the old.

On the whole the program committees are to be congratulated. Their work is exceedingly difficult, to secure variety and ability and acceptability. It was remarked that if they persist hereafter in placing two speakers on the evening program, the humane society ought to interfere. After an entire day of convention work the evening session ought to be made one of uplift. The devotional service, the singing, the announcements and items of business that overflow from the day's sessions, with one address, ought to be enough to satisfy anybody. It is better for both speaker and audience. But if the wealth of talent is so great and the themes so numerous that two speakers are indispensable, limit them both, and knock them down when the limit is reached; if they are too big, sing them down!

Two new days were added to the calendar of special offerings for such churches as choose to observe them. Children's Day for Home Missions, in November, and a day for Ministerial Relief, the Sunday before Christmas. The report making these recommendations was voted through by less than three hundred people, and not more than one-third of them voted either aye or no. Some of our churches have already abolished all special days; all of them that co-operate at all with the boards are struggling to adjust things so as to leave at least one-half the Sundays free for plain preaching, without begging.

Through the courtesy of C. C. Smith the Benevolent Association had a hearing of ten minutes, Mrs. H. M. Meier, president, being the spokesman. There were occasional stretches of vacuity in the program that could have been much better occupied with a full and fair presentation of the work and methods of this new National Association than with the items that were scheduled. However, imperfection marks all things human.

The convention was a surprise to Chattanooga, a stimulus to every delegate and visitor, and a real uplift to our cause. There were several finished addresses, and several times a finished audience. The hotel fare was not the best, but the arrangement in private homes was entirely satistory.

FRANK G. TYRRELL.

National Perils and Hopes.

BY REV. WILBUR F. CRAFTS, PH. D.,
Superintendent of the Reform Bureau, Washington, D. C.

Twelve cyclonic clouds of moral evil darken our national sky: The pro rata increase since the civil war, of liquor consumption, murders, divorces, lynchings, labor riots, municipal misrule, Sabbath-breaking, impurity, corrupt journalism, brutal sports, negro criminality and respectable lawlessness.

These clouds should be the chief concern of Congress and the churches alike, for they are more perilous to the nation, in the light of history, than any foreign foe. To remove or reduce these clouds we must remove or reduce the causes, which are, in part: the civil war, for war, however just, always increases intemperance, impurity and Sabbath-breaking, lowers the sacredness of life and impropriety; the lager beer invasion, which came under cover of the civil war; immigration; excessive commercialism; impersonal business, the "soulless corporation," that in public thought can neither cheat nor be cheated; luxury; the relaxation of belief in future retribution, which always multiplies hells on earth.

These evils are as much weaker than the moral forces of the churches as Spain is weaker than the United States, and will be defeated whenever the united churches really attack them. First, the churches must recognize that the gospel has to do with personal and social ethics as much if not more than with theology; and, second, the forces now divided into one hundred and fifty sects must be sociologically united to save society as well as souls. That these clouds can be dispelled is betokened by the fact that clouds as dark have been dispelled in this generation by the unitedaction of Christian citizenship—dueling, slavery, Mormon polygamy, the Louisiana lottery, the spoils system, to which may be added three other reforms so nearly complete that we may count them as done, which are, scientific temperance education in the public schools—but four states out of the union on that—and the Australian ballot—only three states haven't that in some degree—while the Anglo-Saxon international treaty of arbitration is now practically assurred, and promises to be the beginning of the end of international war. The other clouds also are to be dispelled when the churches unite their forces, a grand army of 23,000,000, which becoming really the "church militant" will become the "church triumphant."

Church Extension Receipts.

For completing chapels for the week ending Oct. 15th, '98:

From churches	$285.17
From individuals	845.40
Total	$1,130.57
Last year, churches	200.77
Individuals	820.32
Gain	109.48

NOTE.—A further analysis of our receipts shows a gain of $25.08 in receipts from individuals; a gain of $84.40 from the churches, and a gain of five in the number of contributing churches.

Collections in the churches should be kept going through November. We still lack $13,000 of reaching the $20,000 from collections this fall.

Remittances should be sent to

G. W. MUCKLEY, Cor. Sec.
600 Waterworks Bldg., Kansas City, Mo.

Evangelistic.

OHIO.

Cincinnati, Oct. 17.—There were three baptisms last Sunday night, Oct. 9th. There was one confession yesterday morning. Walnut Hills Church was never in a more flourishing condition than now.—S. D. DUTCHER.

MISSOURI.

Wallace, Oct. 17.—Our meeting here two weeks old and eight added; church united, people interested, prospects good. Our hindrance, very bad weather. I go next to DeKalb, Mo.—JNO. P. JESSE.

Center, Oct. 15.—Closed meeting here Wednesday with five additions. The church built up in zeal I trust. Begin at Spaulding tonight. Hope for a good meeting there.—W. D. MCCULLEY.

Frank L. Bowen, City Missionary in Kansas City, is conducting a meeting in the hall occupied by the Ivanhoe Park Christian Sunday-school at Thirty-eighth and Woodland Avenues in that city, and reports the outlook for a new church there to be good. The first five days' work, ending Oct. 15, resulted in three confessions and one addition by letter. This work is in one of the most rapidly growing sections of Kansas City, and it is important that a rallying point for our work there be firmly established.

1519 Tracey Ave., Kansas City, Oct. 22.—Recently closed an eight days' meeting at Bethel Church, Buchanan County, assisting W. A. Nickell. There were five additions. The church is in perfect harmony and splendid working condition. Have seldom seen a country church doing such fine grade of work. I wanted to say this for church and minister. —A W. KOKENDOFFER.

Trenton, Oct. 22.—One addition at Trenton recently. All departments of the work moving along reasonably well.—GRANVILLE SNELL.

Mt. Moriah, Oct. 20.—Notwithstanding the storm the interest in our meeting is good. Eleven additions and fine audiences. Bro. Gillidet, of Bethany, has been with us part of the time. We go next to Princeton, Mo.—MORGAN & DAUGHTER.

OKLAHOMA TERRITORY.

Oklahoma City, Oct. 17.—J. V. Coombs and Hunsaker will begin a meeting with O. P. McMahan here Oct. 23.—O. P. Mc.

KENTUCKY.

Stanford, Oct. 19.—Seventeen additions to date.—H. A. NORTHCUTT, evangelist; F. W. ALLEN, pastor.

INDIANA.

Indianapolis, Oct. 18.—Three additions at North Park Church; one at Broad Ripple.—J. M. CANFIELD.

IOWA.

Ottumwa, Oct. 19.—The meeting at the Oak Grove Church closed after 16 days with 13 additions; nine by obedience. Jas. T. Nichols and the writer conducted the meeting. Bro. Nichols has been laboring for Mt. Auburn and Oak Grove Churches, but Mt. Auburn needs all his time and he has arranged to stay all time with them while the writer continues his work here. The Oak Grove brethren love Bro. Nichols and give him up with reluctance.—A. L. CRILEY.

Clarinda, Oct. 16.—Have just returned from holding a 12 days' meeting at Little Hickman Church, near Nicholasville, Ky. Five years ago we held a meeting for this church, and hence it was quite a pleasure to be there in another meeting. The meeting resulted in 14 additions and the organization of a splendid Endeavor Society.—C. H. WHITE.

Winterset, Oct. 20.—One baptism recently. I begin my third meeting here next Lord's day with J. Will Landrum singer.—J. M. LOWE.

Milo.—The Milo meeting, which has been in progress for five weeks, closed last Lord's day. This meeting, which was in a new field, was under the auspices of the churches of Warren County and conducted by Bro. Dempsey A. Hunter, of Jefferson, Iowa. Bro. Hunter is a strong man in the Lord and a very effective speaker. He is a very clear, concise talker, and by his kindly spirit won the hearts of many. Although some may say the meeting was a failure, there has been good seed carefully sown that will bring forth much fruit in the future. There were two confessions, and a church organized of 10 members. Plans were almost completed for the coming year. A building being secured for services and arrangements being made by which they will secure a student from Drake University to preach for them next summer, when another meeting will be held and large ingathering of the Master's flock is expected. The town is so full of sectarianism that it will take some time to overcome it, but right will triumph.—IDA PAYNE.

ARKANSAS.

Bald Knob, Oct. 17.—Our meeting at this place closed last night with 30 additions, mostly by baptism. The writer has been with this church for seven years and will contiuue indefinitely. Our meetiug was conducted with our home force and all are happy, praise the Lord.—M. A. SMITH.

OKLAHOMA.

Hennessy, Oct. 13.—With the assistance of Singing Evangelist Jas. S. Helm I am holding a meeting at this place which is two weeks old with five additions. Yesterday was a bad day, almost stormed us out. I sent for Bro. Helm after reading the notice of him in the CHRISTIAN-EVANGELIST. I am by no means disappointed. The CHRISTIAN-EVANGELIST is to me the most trustworthy and helpful weekly visitor.—C. W. VAN DOLAH.

TEXAS.

Waco, Oct. 19.—My work with the Central Church this city is closing with additions at nearly every service. I baptized three last Sunday, and had two other additions during the day. One to be baptized later.—F. N. CALVIN.

ILLINIOS.

Lincoln, Oct. 17.—Our meeting commenced yesterday. Two additions to begin with; one by confession. The prospect is very good. The regular minister and the church have things in charge. Lincoln Church will be in line again not manv days hence.—ALBERT NICHOLS.

Rantoul, Oct. 21.—One addition last Sunday. The church here and at Bethany, which is our mission point, gave $38 to Illinois missions.—H. H. PETERS.

SUBSCRIBERS' WANTS.

Miscellaneous wants and notices will be inserted in this department at the rate of two cents a word, each insertion, all words, large and small, to be counted, and two initials stand for one word. Please accompany notice with corresponding remittance to save book-keeping.

WANTED.—To hold a two weeks' meeting (free) in congregations where a Christian library can be placed. Library consists of ninety-one (91) cloth-bound volumes selected from the Christian Publishing Co. publications, fifty (50) yearly copies of THE CHRISTIAN-EVANGELIST, and fifty (50) copies of Gospel Call (Evangelist's edition) song books. Write for particulars. ELDER S. J. PHILLIPS, Sugar Grove, Wis.

Family Circle.

Truth.

The only amaranthine flower on earth
Is virtue; the only lasting tresure, truth.
But what is truth? 'Twas Pilate's question put
To Truth itself, that deigned him no reply.
And wherefore? will not God impart His light
To them that ask it?—Freely: 'tis his joy,
His glory and His nature to impart.
But to the proud, uncandid, insincere,
Or negligent inquirer, not a spark.
What pearl is it that rich men cannot buy,
That learning is too proud to gather up;
But which the poor and despised of all
Seek and obtain, and often find unsought?
Tell me, and I will tell thee what is truth.

—*Cowper.*

A True Story.*

In the village of Valadimir was a young merchant by the name of Aksenov, who owned two stores and a dwelling. Of prepossessing appearance was Aksenov, with blond, curly hair. He was fond of gaiety and songs. In his youth he drank freely, and when under the influence of liquor would become very boisterous. But after his marriage he drank only occasionaly.

One summer day Aksenov decided to go to the market town, Nijni-Novo-gorod. As he bade adieu to his family his wife said to him:

"Ivan Dmitrievitch, do not go there today. I have had a bad dream about you." Aksenov laughed good-naturedly and said:

"You are afraid I will do something foolish at the market."

His wife responded: "I scarcely know myself of what I am afraid. Only I have had a bad dream. I saw you coming home, your head bare and your hair entirely white."

Aksenov laughed all the more and said: "Ah, well! It is a good sign. I will be successful in my business and will bring you some beautiful presents."

He took leave of them and departed. About midway to the market town he met a merchant whom he had known and stopped with him for the night.

They took tea together and retired in adjoining bedrooms. Aksenov was not a great sleeper. He arose at midnight, that he might travel at his leasure in the cool of the morning. He aroused the postboy and gave him orders to harness his horses. Then he entered the hotel, paid the landlord and departed.

After he had gone about twenty miles he stopped to let his horses eat again and to rest at the tavern. As he sat on the steps waiting for dinner he took a guitar and began playing. Suddenly there arrived a carriage; an officer and two soldiers alighted from it. They approached Aksenov and demanded of him what his business was and from where he had come. Aksenov answered their questions and invited them to eat with him. But the officer continued to press the questions—

"Where had he spent the past night? Was he alone with the other merchant? Why had he left the tavern so precipitately."

Aksenov, surprised by their questions, told them all, then said: "Why do you question me so closely? I am neither a thief nor a brigand. I am attending to my own business and no one has a right to question me."

Then the officer called the soldiers and turning to Aksenov said: "I am the sheriff. If I question you it is because the merchant with whom you passed the night has been slain! Soldiers, search him."

They enter the tavern, taking his trunk and knapsack with them, which they opened and looked through. Suddenly the sheriff pulled from the knapsack a knife and exclaimed:

"Whose dagger?"

Aksenov looked and saw a knife covered with blood. It was from his knapsack they had drawn it and terror seized him.

"And why was blood on the knife?" Aksenov tried to answer but he could not say a single word.

"Me—I—er—do not know—I—a knife! It does not belong to me."

Then the sheriff said: "The merchant was found this morning with his throat cut. No one but you could have committed the crime. The house was securely fastened from the inside, and in it no one but you. Here, moreover, is a knife covered with blood, and found in your possession. Besides, the crime is pictured on your countenance. Confess all—how you slew him and how much money you have stolen."

Aksenov swore he was not the guilty one, that he had not seen the merchant since they took tea together, that he had no one's money but his own—8,000 roubles—and that the knife did not belong to him. But his voice was choked, his face was pale and he trembled from fear as one guilty.

The sheriff having called the soldiers, ordered them to bind him hand and foot, and to put him in the carriage.

Aksenov crossed himself and wept. They took possession of his baggage and his money and carried him to prison in a neighboring village. They made inquiries in Valdimir. All the merchants and inhabitants declared that Aksenov, whom they had loved to drink with and be entertained by was an honorable man.

Then the case was taken before the judges. He was accused of having murdered the merchant, from Riazon, and of having stolen from him twenty thousand roubles. Aksenov's wife was heart-broken and knew not what to think. Her children were small—one of them a baby-in-arms. She took them both with her and went to the village where her husband was imprisoned. At first they refused to let her see him. Then when she had entreated them they granted her permission.

On seeing him in prison clothes, bound and huddled with criminals she swooned and fell to the floor, and did not come to herself for some time. When she did she put the children away from her, was assisted to a cot by Aksenov and then gave him an account of the family affairs and asked him to tell he all that had happened to him. When he had told her all she asked:

"What are your chances now?"

"A supplication must be sent to the tsar," he responded. "For it cannot be that the innocent should suffer punishment."

His wife told him she had already sent a supplication to the tsar, but it had done no good.

Aksenov was overcome with grief and made no answer.

The wife said to him: "It was not in vain, that dream I had, you remember, in which I saw you with white hair, for truly your hair has become white because of sorrow. You should not have gone that day."

Then she placed her hand upon his head, and said: "Ivan, my dear, tell the truth to your wife. Was it not you who murdered him?"

Aksenov said, "And you, my dear, also believe it!" He covered his face with his hands and wept bitterly.

A soldier appeared and informed the woman it was time for her and her children to retire. Then Aksenov bade farewell to his family for the last time.

When his wife had departed he went over in his mind the conversation which they had just had. In recalling that his wife believed it of him also and that she had asked if it was he who had murdered the merchant he said to himself: "God alone knows the truth. It is to him I must cry. I must rely upon his mercy."

And from that moment he ceased to send petitions to those in authority. He shut his heart against hope and did nothing but pray to God.

The judges sentenced Aksenov to the knout first and afterwards to hard work. They beat and bruised him at the knout and after the wounds had healed they sent him with other convicts to Siberia.

There he remained twenty-six years. His hair became as white as snow, his long gray beard fell out. He lost all his mirthfulness. He vowed he would never laugh and talk again, but devote himself to prayer.

In prison Aksenov learned the shoemaker's trade. With money thus obtained he bought a martyrology which he read while there was light in his cell. On feast days he went to the chapel, read the psalms and sang in the choir. He still had his musical voice. The officers loved him for his gentleness, his companions held him in high esteem and called him "grandpa" and "man of God."

When the prisoners had a favor to ask, it was always by Aksenov that they presented their request, and when they had disagreements with each other it was Aksenov again whom they chose as arbiter.

No one wrote to Aksenov from home. He did not even know if his wife and children were living.

One day they brought a band of new convicts to the prison. That night the old ones asked the new ones from what cities or villages they had come, and for what crimes they had been sent here. Aksenov approached them and with head downcast, listened to their conversation. One of the new convicts was an old man, about sixty years of age. He related the circumstances of his condemnation.

"It is this way, my brothers," said he. "They sent me here unjustly. I had just unharnessed a horse from a sleigh when some one seized me saying I had committed robbery.

"I have committed no offense, said I. I am not running away. You see I have unhitched the horse. Besides, the postboy is my friend."

*"*A True Story*" was written by Count Leo Tolstoi, translated by Halpirine Kaminsky into French and translated from the French into English for the CHRISTIAN-EVANGELIST by (Miss) J. Goss Carter, of Canton, Mo.

"'Not so,' said they; you have stolen the horse." But they could not say where nor from whom I had stolen him. Most certainly I have committed misdeeds which should have brought me here long ago. But they could never take me on that charge. And to-day they have brought me here in spite of the law. But wait; I have been in Siberia before, and I am not going to stay here much longer."

"And from where have you come?" asked one of the others.

"I am from the city of Vladimir. I am a shopkeeper in that place. My name is Makar Semivnovitch."

"Oh, Semivnovitch, have you not heard spoken of in Vladimir some merchants named Aksènov, and if so are they living yet?"

"How then! They are rich merchants, although their father is in Siberia. For without doubt he has sinned like the rest of us."

Aksenov did not like to speak of his sorrow. He sighed and said: "It is for my sins that I have been here these twenty-six years."

"And for what sins?" asked Makar Semivnovitch.

"It is what I deserve," Aksènov answered simply. He did not care to say anything more. But his companions related to the new ones why he had been placed there; how during his journey some one had assassinated a merchant and concealed in his possessions a knife covered with blood and how on account of that evidence they had sentenced him unjustly. On hearing this Makar Semivnovitch looked at Aksenov, slapped his knees with his hands and exclaimed:

"Oh, what a miracle! What a wonder! Ah, you are indeed old, little grandfather!"

They asked him why he was so astonished and where he had seen Aksenov. But Makar did not answer them. He simply said:

"A miracle, my friends, that Fate should have brought us together here."

By these words Aksenov thought that this man might be the real assassin; so he said to him:

"Have you heard that affair spoken of? Or indeed, Semivnovitch, have you seen me somewhere outside this prison?"

"How then! I have heard it spoken of. *Even the walls have ears!* But it has been a long time since it happened, and what they told me I have forgotten," said Semivnovitch.

"Perhaps you have learned who killed the merchant," said Aksenov. Makar laughed and said:

"But what about the sack in which they found the knife? It, without doubt, belonged to him who was the murderer. How could any one else have put it in your sack? You had it under your pillow—you would have known it."

Upon hearing these words Aksenov felt convinced that he was the very one who had murdered the merchant. He arose and went away. All that night he could not sleep. Presently, however, he fell into a deep trance and dreamed he saw his wife as she had looked when last she was with him. He saw her still living, her eyes, her face; he heard her laugh and talk. Then his children also appeared to him as they had been, both small; one wrapped in a fur robe, the other in its mother's arms. He saw again himself as he was then; gay, young and playing the guitar on the porch of the hotel where he had been arrested. He recalled the horrible place where he had been flogged and the villains who had flogged him, the crowds standing by, and the convicts and his twenty-six years in prison. When he awoke he thought of his old age, and he longed for death to end it all.

"And all of this on account of that scoundrel!" thought he. He felt such intense hatred for Makar that he wished for the moment to slay him in order to avenge his wrongs. He prayed all night without being able to calm himself. During the day he would not go near Makar Semivnovitch. Thus passed five days. At night Aksenov was unable to sleep. He became a victim to insomnia. One night as he was walking in the prison he perceived that one of the bunks had fallen from the side of the dungeon. He stopped to see what had caused it, when Makar Semivnovitch sprang up quickly from under the bunk and beheld Aksenov with an expression of dread. Aksenov wished to appear as if he had not seen him. But Makar seized him by the arm and told him how he had dug a hole in the wall, how every day he carried some of the dirt out in his boots to empty in the streets when they were led out to work, and he added:

"Only keep silence, old man; I will take you away with me. If you betray me I know they will beat me almost to death, but you will pay for it to me, for I will murder you!"

On seeing him who had blasted his life Aksenov trembled with suppressed rage. He withdrew his arm and said:

"I do not want you to free me, and you have no cause to slay me. You have already killed me years ago. As to exposing you or not, it is God who will decide that."

On the morrow when the soldiers were going over the prison they found the excavation. All the convicts denied having any knowledge of it. Those who knew did not care to betray Makar. They knew he would be beaten half to death. Then the chief addressed himself to Aksenov.

"Patriarch," said he, "you are a just man; tell me, before God, who has done this?"

Makar Semivnovitch remained impassive, looking steadily towards the chief, and not once turning to Aksenov. As for Aksenov his arms and his legs trembled, and he could not utter a word.

"I will keep silence," thought he, "but why spare him, since it is he who ruined my life? Let him pay me for my torture. It is true he would be beaten almost to death, and even if he is not the assassin whom I think, what would he do to relieve me?"

The chief reiterated his command. Aksenov looked towards Semivnovitch and said:

"Your Honor, I can not tell. God does not allow me to make it known. I will not tell you. Do to me what you choose. It is in your power."

In spite of the chief's efforts Aksenov would say no more. They could not ascertain who the culprit was. The following night as Aksenov was falling to sleep on his bunk he heard some one approach him and stop at his feet. He looked in the dim light and beheld Makar. Aksenov said to him: "Have you further need of me?" What are you there for?" Makar Semivnovitch did not answer. Aksenov arose and said: "What do you want? Tell me, or else I will call the guard."

Makar bent over very near to Aksenov, and said in a low voice:

"Ivan Dnitriecvitch, forgive me!"

"Why! For what must I forgive you?" asked Aksenov.

"It was I who slew the merchant, and it was I who hid the knife in your sack. I intended to kill you also, but at that moment I heard a noise in the yard. I placed the knife in your sack and made my escape through the window."

Aksenov knew not what to say. Makar Semivnovitch crept from the bed, prostrated himself before Aksenov and said:

"Ivan Dnitriecvitch, pardon me. In the name of God forgive me! I am going to declare to the authorities that I murdered the merchant. They will give you back your liberty, and you will return to your home." Aksenov responded:

"That sounds well, but I have suffered here a long time. Where would I go? My wife is dead. My children have forgotten me. I have nowhere to go."

Makar remained on his knees. He brushed the dust from his head and said:

"Ivan, forgive me. Had they beaten me at the knout it would have made me less unhappy than to see you thus, and to think you still have pity upon me! You have not exposed me! Pardon me. In the name of Christ, pardon a cursed malefactor!" And he commenced sobbing. When Aksenov saw Makar was crying he himself cried and said:

"God will pardon you. Perhaps I am a hundred times worse than you."

Aksenov suddenly felt a great joy overspread his whole soul. He ceased to mourn for his home. He did not care to leave the prison, and did not dream of its being his last hours there.

Makar Semivnovitch did not heed Aksenov, but declared himself guilty.

When the order came to release Aksenov it found him—dead!

Whose House is Nailed.

When people own the house, they drive
Each tiny tack with greatest care;
But when they rent it—sakes alive!
They slam a spike in anywhere.
—*Christian Work.*

Nina.*

STELLA STRAWN.

Nina was a queer child, not like most other children. Heaven and Jesus was very near to her, and she had some very strange ideas. Perhaps the reason was because she was not very strong, and that her mother had gone to heaven.

One day she said to grandma in her serious way, "I'm always going to remember what mamma said before she died, about how I must always take care of little brother and be a good girl and teach him to be good and pretty soon I'll die and go to heaven."

One day Cecil (who was about six) was playing with a little cart and broke it. He began to cry. Nina came up and said:

"Don't cry, Cecil, I'll try to fix it, but if I can't, just remember that mamma's in heaven, and that before long we'll go to mamma and Jesus, and up in heaven toys are never out of fix. This world is ful care and trials, but it is not long before all over, honey."

With these cheerful remarks it is wonder that Cecil's mind was very ful sober thoughts.

Cecil started to school in the spring. was six years old. It was about one-hal a mile to school across the fields, but was a hardy boy and Nina always cared him. But this story is to be about Nin

One cool March day Cecil was kep after school to recite a lesson he had miss and Nina waited for him. He was o kept a few minutes, but the other child were all gone.

"Come, Cecil," said Nina, "let us hu home. It is cloudy and it will get d early, and it looks like rain."

So taking her brother's hand Nina h ried along across the fields in the well-w path. Away they went through the fie till they came to the brook. Here th stopped in dismay, for the board on wh they expected to cross had floated away. dry weather this stream was usually d but wet weather had swollen it till it v now a little torrent of ice-cold water.

"Oh, how can we cross?" cried Cecil.

"It's awful cold, but I guess we can wa It can't be very deep," said little Nina.

"No, no, no; I won't, I can't, no, nc cried Cecil, pulling at Nina's arm.

"It's too late to go back to the road, a I don't want to be out after dark, and i going to rain, too," said Nina.

There was a moment's silence, then Ce said, "well, I can't wade; it's too deep a cold."

"Come, Cecil," said Nina; "I know, wade and carry you."

"You'll let me fall, I know," whimpe Cecil.

"No, I don't think I will," said Ni "It's all we can do, so there."

So saying, Nina sat down and pulled her shoes and stockings, and put them her satchel, and put the satchel around h neck, and taking her brother in her ar said, "Now be still and don't scream, a you'll be all right; you had better h your eyes on my shoulder so you can't the water and be scared."

Nina put one foot in the water; s could hardly bear it, but resolutely s stepped in and waded bravely forward. grew deeper and deeper, until it was to h knees; and her dress skirt was wet. S was frightened, but soon it began to gr shallow, and soon she was on the oppos

*The writer of this story is but 13 years old.—EDITOR.

legs were trembling and she was cold. Wringing out her dress, ıer feet on it and with great dif- ›eeded in putting her stockings p feet. Then it began to rain, an home as fast as they could; hing grandma's, they told their

rave," said grandpa.

ugh to kill her," said grandma, ning it would kill her.

want any supper," said Nina; :hes, and I feel chilly."

immediately tried her home ›ut to no good, so grandpa went tor. It proved that Nina had Several days after she had been said she wished to see Cecil. ›rought in. He had strict orders quiet, so he approached her tim-

r, darling, come near to me," "I want to talk to you, to tell think. I think I shall die soon you to be a good boy. I often rth is full of sorrow and pain, t long before we go to heaven if esus. You are young, brother, I, but you can understand. You ; and serve him and soon you will to heaven, and mamma and papa be there, for heaven is not far Ve don't remember papa, but id he was a good man. But I'm Cecie; promise me you will al- ›od; will you?"

es, I will," cried Cecil bursting for he had been swelling up all Nina was speaking. "But don't on't; I can never live without ny Nina, my Nina, don't, don't!" ndma came and led him away, d him by saying it was only be- was despondent she spoke so, but eart was full of trouble and anx-

ver saw Nina alive again, though t die for several days; he was not the sick room again.

a's eleven years' sojourn on earth en in vain. For we never fail to we follow the footsteps of our er, who was humble and lowly, despised little things. And if the footsteps of our blessed Sa- all reap a reward, and we must our pilgrimage on earth is short

not the slightest word or deed,
eem it void of power;
fruit in each wind-wafted seed
waits its natal hour."

Mo.

Barroom Has a Bank.

osit your money—and lose it.
ıe—and lose it.
aracter—and lose it.
alth—and lose it.
ength—and lose it.
nly independence—and lose it.
f-control—and lose it.
me comfort—and lose it.
fe's happiness—and lose it.
ildren's happiness—and lose it.

The Infinite.

BY GRACE PEARL BRONAUGH.

If we of earth could draw aside the pall
Shrouding the chasm, would we dare to fall?
Who shall be free from terror or from shame?
Shall he of tainted life or tarnished name?
Launched on the Sea of Silence, who is sure?
The wise, the great, the mighty? No; the pure!
For whom shall Heaven's secret be unsealed?
To whom shall Heaven's beauty be revealed?
Who, rising from Earth's clash and crash of wars,
Shall hear the trump of triumph from the stars?
Not he whose god is gold, whose creed is lust,
Who grinds his fellow creature in the dust.
When soars the soul in undiscovered space
Above the world, beyond the reckless race
Which laughs and eats and sleeps and has no care
For the eternal secrets of the air,
What soul is there which shall be safe or sure?
Who on the Sea of Silence shall endure?
To-day we sleep, and if we dream at all,
Our dream is of delight. But soon will fall
Upon our ears voices of the vast
Regions of Mystery—on our sight be cast
The awful vision of Infinity.
Who then from shame or sorrow shall be free?
When, seeing sin by daylight, by the dawn
Of Heaven's truth and glory, we are drawn
To hide ourselves in darkness—when the light
Makes us to shrink and sicken at the sight
Of our own souls; how much we weep too late
And weeping, shudder at the face of Fate!
For whom shall Heaven's beacon beam afar?
For whom shall Heaven's gate be flung ajar?
From whom shall Hell's foul phantoms flee, dismayed,
As floating fearless thro' the field of shade
The spirit passes? Who shall be secure?
Lo, he whose hands are clean; whose heart is pure!

Fair Haven, Vt., Oct. 3, 1898.

Endeavor Badges.

The accompanying cuts are exact representations of the genuine Christian Endeavor Badge, as adopted by the societies. All profits from its sale are used in spreading the movement.

Size No. 1. *Size No. 2.* *Size No. 3.* *Junior.*

PRICES.

Size No. 1.

Solid Gold Scarf or Catch Pin	$1.00
" " Charm	1.50
" " Face Button	1.25
Coin Silver Scarf or Catch Pin	.25
" " Charm	.35
" " Button	.50

Size No. 2.

Solid Gold Scarf or Catch Pin	.80
" " Charm	1.00
" " Face Button	.95
Coin Silver Scarf or Catch Pin	.22
" " Button	.40
" " Charm	.25

Size No. 3.

Bible Lesson Annuals.

The Lesson Primer.

A Book of Easy Lessons for the Little Learners of the Primary Classes, in Simple Stories, mostly in words of one syllable.

PRICE—Single copy, prepaid, 20 cents; per dozen, not prepaid, $2.00.

The Lesson Mentor.

An Aid for the Junior Classes, containing the Scripture Text, Lesson Story, Lesson Lights, Lesson Pictures, Lesson Words, with Definitions and Explanations, Lesson Questions, Lesson Thoughts, and Suggestions for Home Study and Work.

PRICE—Single copy, prepaid, 25 cents; per dozen, not prepaid, $2.40.

The Lesson Helper.

An Aid for the Senior Classes, containing carefully selected Daily Readings. Geographical, Biographical and Chronological Notes, Lesson Summary, Lesson Outline, Lesson Comments, Lesson Questions and Lesson Thoughts, with practical suggestions for Home Study and Work.

PRICE—Single copy, prepaid, 35 cents: per dozen, not prepaid, $3.60.

The Lesson Commentary.

A Book for Advanced Pupils and Teachers, containing a careful Analysis of each Lesson, with Introductory, Geographical, Explanatory, Illustrative, Applicatory and Practical Notes, with Suggestions for Teachers and Pupils on each lesson. The Text is printed in both the Common and Revised Versions, for the purpose of comparison, in parallel columns.

PRICE—Single copy, cloth, prepaid, $1.00; per dozen, not prepaid, $9.00.

CHRISTIAN PUBLISHING COMPANY, ST. LOUIS

Sunday-School Literature

THE matter of Sunday-school Literature is one of very great importance. For, whether it should be so or not, the fact is that the character of the instruction given in nine-tenths of the Sunday-school classes throughout the country is determined by the contents of the Lesson Helps they use. This being true, and the fact that first impressions are most lasting, how important that Pastors and Superintendents of Christian Sunday-schools see that their Schools are supplied with Christian Periodicals. If the children are taught that one church is as good as another, that certain divine commands are of little or no importance, or can be changed or set aside by man, what effect will it have on the church of the future? "Think on these things."

We understand a FEW of our schools are using sectarian or union (so called)

Honored Servants.

DEAR BRO. GARRISON:—I am down here in the interests of a son stricken with typhoid. I wish to say a few words of surrounding conditions. When the troops came here I wrote our dear Bro. T. H. Blenus of several of our boys who were members of the church. He visited them promptly, made their acquaintance, secured their friendship and strengthened them against the temptations that surround the loose life of a soldier. My son among the many was taken down with typhoid fever. Bro. Blenus gave him immediate attention. Many are the individuals who have received the personal attention of Bro. Blenus, while they lived, and funeral services when he died. The benefits received by the devotion of this godly man and his estimable wife, can never be measured. I am glad God sent him here in time to meet in some measure the terrible exigencies of the times that have fallen on the soldier's life in this community. I wish to state that, with all the appliances now in use, no better place or surroundings could be found than the field hospital tent for the recovery of the sick soldier. All medicines, ice, milk and everything needed for the sick or convalescent are in abundant supply. To measure the tireless devotion and assiduous attention, by day and night—all the time—of the army of trained lady nurses, cannot be done. My son is recovering. Thanks to Bro. Blenus and all these, with the prayers of my Christian brotherhood.

LEROY WILEY.

Jacksonville, Fla., Oct. 17, 1898.

[C]hristian Endeavor.

By Burris A. Jenkins.

TOPIC FOR NOV. 6.

THE GOOD FIGHT.

(1 Tim. 7:11-16; 2 Tim. 4:7, 8.)

e is such a thing as a good fight. Our y has just fought one in behalf of truth, ghteousness, and freedom. Our young ave unselfishly and gloriously stepped d in defense of the great principle of liberty, and some have paid the forfeit ieir lives. And yet we all agree that the such fights there are the better. The as made a suggestion which should be by every voice that can be raised in of peace. The other day one of the it thinkers of this country was asked, Procter, what to you think of the Em- Nicholas' proposition that all Europe disarm?'' Instantly he replied in that l, striking way of his, ''It will make mortal!'' And it is true. Think of the ess of the idea, that all Europe—many nore populous and wealthy than Amer- ishing with arms as the sea glitters with l waves, crowded with bivouacs as our ire crowded with shocks of grain, that eat armed camp should turn its atten- om militarism to industry, and should s swords into plowshares and railroad ! It is one of the greatest thoughts of itury. Three men, if they would agree, inaugurate the reform, and one of them posed it. Every preacher and religious l, every lover of peace and progress in land should raise his voice in a hearty amen! to the conscientious, peace- monarch's proposal. Long live the ian Czar!

after all, the figure of the fight serves illustration for the Christian life in a at no other figure can so well do. Paul again and again. The battle between nd spirit, the struggle between inclina- d aspiration, the fight with that great ror of conquerors, Self—nothing can this war of extermination except the ght. It is the best battle ever on. It is great, good fight.

e have been men who conquered the and then there is a great world-con- who has conquered them. Greater is o ruleth this greatest of conquerors e who takes all cities. Alexander the once visited the poor philosopher who n a wretched home. ''Diogenes, what o for thee,'' asked the emporer, he who the world. ''Please,'' answered the l scholar, ''Please to stand out of my it!'' There's an emperor greater than der who daily comes to us all with the question. He is ruler of the world, Self st, Self the Great, and he asks each one t can I do for thee?'' O, if we all only courage to say to him, ''Stand out of my ne!'' and then if necessary fight him till s.

is the only fight in the world worth aking, it is the only good fight, it is the f faith, to be fought with armor of God, of the Spirit, and it is without quarter, to ath. Either Self will win and the Spirit l within us will be quenched, or Self rish gradually, finally, and God and be all in all, reigning in us the hope of Blessed is he that overcometh! The vill end in peace! After the struggle the quiet, after the storm sometimes me the calm. This self of sin—''Who eliver me from the body of this death?'' k God through Jesus Christ!'' There Ally who will turn the tide of battle in avor, vanquish the all-powerful con- of kings and say to our souls that strive y, ''Peace be still!''

Hiram College Jubilee Endowment.

The great popular movement has begun. Hiram College is to be endowed by an additional sum of $250,000 on the occasion of its jubilee commencement in June, 1900.

The army of 50,000 persons who will accomplish this grand work is forming. We publish our first list of names, consisting of several hundred persons. Let every friend of Hiram and every friend of Christian education send in his name. All we want now is your name, which identifies you with this great movement. You can give one dollar or more, the definite amount to be named later. If you can give but one dollar, send in your name with as much freedom as if you could give a thousand.

We here give a copy of the enlistment card. Send us your name and we will write it on the card; and do not fail to give your address, street and number.

HIRAM COLLEGE JUBILEE ENLISTMENT CARD.

Whereas, the friends of Hiram College are uniting in a movement to add $250,000 to the endowment of the institution on the occasion of its fiftieth anniversary in June of the year 1900, and whereas an effort is now being made to secure the names of 50,000 persons, more or less, who will make a donation of from one dollar to one thousand dollars each for that purpose, I do hereby agree to join in this movement by promising to pay one dollar or more and will name the definite amount of my donation and the time of payment when called upon to do so.

Name............

Postoffice. ... .

Street and number ....

Date..... .... 189-......

Mrs. N. Dyson, E. V. Zollars, E. O. Zeigler, J. P. Reed, H. H. Angle, P. A. McKinley. M. B. Wood, M. O. Carter, O. R. Sine, J. J. Angle, A. McDaniel, Mrs. W. F. Ford, E. J. Smith, Mertie B. Smith, E. S. Smith, W. C. Oliver, L. McDonnald, Lulu E. Kistler, C. C. Spencer, G. Black, G. A. Vincent, O. McCully, L. Fuller, C. E. Linsell, Jennie M. Shanower, Mabel L. Alden, Ina M. Gibbs, P. B. Rudolf, W. N. White, G. C. Wallace, E. F. Burch, C. A. Pearce, W. C. Massey, T. L. Van Voorhis, Maud M. Rowland, W. D. Ward, W. F. Rotherberger, A. B. Crafts, L. D. Carter, Guy Hoover, Cora Gehrett, R. T. Williams, C. H. Frick, T. C. Brown, S. H. Calend, Myrta M. Bennett, H. W. McMahan, C. E. Alden, R. W. Moore, C. W. Wells, J. T. Trowbridge, O. L. Carter, F. M. Field, Bessie Moss, Flora M. Borne, A. W. Cinniger, O. L. Mercer, Mrs. G. M. Stockberger, Mrs. C. H. Westland, Kate Teachout, G. S. Stage, Elsie Jackson, Mrs. Frost, A. P. Frost, Kate S. Parmly, Ila B. Williams, J. H. Taylor, Mrs. E. H. Hill, E. E. Sands, C. E. Merkle, C. M. Clark, R. R. Kahle, J. B. Kahle, C. Hunt, A. E. Taylor, Ollie Johnson, J. Slimp, R. Duckey, H. A. Deihl, Mrs. Wm. Dudley, Alice Udall, Albert Udall, H. B. Hazzard, Lizzie Longanecker, Lida Longanecker, Lena J. Feuchtinger, Sara Feuchtinger, Eugene Feuchtinger, E. E. J. Feuchtinger, J. Sietzer, B. F. Rohrer, H. H. Emmerson, Hattie Parker, F. C. Richardson, Lee Nichols, G. G. Richardson, Carl Nichols, C. Moore, M. A. Sanda, W. Logan, H. F. House, Florence Hathway, A. S. Mottinger, C. S. Berry, Mrs. J. F. Futcher, C. Bancroft, Mrs. L. Cook, Mrs. W. S. Fortune, Mrs. M. Van Voorhis, Josie Miller, H. F. Miller, M. G. Craft, Clara Darsie, Bernice L. Johnson, Mrs. E. M. Nebb, Miss Edwards, P. L. Green, H. I. Weaver, S. M. Shattuck, Mrs. E. Fetger, Rhoda Whitacre, Alice Turner, Mary Woodward, A. G. Woodward, G. H. Colton, Mrs. Floy Riegle, H. B. Garber, Blanch B. Kent, C. M. Allyn, Ava Skidmore, A. E. Sheriff, Ada M. McCormick, Josephine Carter, Ada L. Wilment, Mary B. Colton, Mrs. G. H. Colton, W. F. Riegel, Mrs. A. Wildon, C. McDonnald, D. N. Lee, L. W. Lee, L. E. Chase, Mrs. A. Bishop, Mrs. L. E. Chase, W. L. Bruehlman, F. C. Rulon, Mrs. J. Hunt, J. B. Oliver, Mrs. G. A. Peckham, G. A. Peckham, Mrs. W. C. Russell, H. Herrick, S. E. Oliver, E. H. McConoughey, Anna Lee Russell, H. McDiarmid, Mary C. McDiarmid, E. W. McDiarmid, N. L. McDiarmid, Ethel M. McDiarmid, W. L. Parsons, Yetaro Kinosita, A. H. Alden, F. M. Longanecker, Mrs. N. E. Rowland, Mrs. Y. W. Warren, Mrs. J. W. Allen, J. G. Smith, J. J. Line, F. H. Dilley, Effie Phyllis, Claudia Z. Page, Mrs. E. V. Zollas, Mrs. H. M. Page, H. M. Page, Mary M. Williams, E. A. Henry, C. H. Patterson, P. P. Rider, C. W. Colgin, Mary B. Patterson, Jane E. Wheeler, Winona Bradley, W. C. Sage, D. B. Grubb, Marcia Henry, S. S. Dill, Clara Hale, T. O. Allyn, Annie I. Holmes, A. Holmes, Diantha L. Alden, B. K. Kooms, H. M. Garn, G. M. Knox, Alanson Wilcox, G. H. Brown, M. L. Pontius, Mrs. M. L. Churchill, B. L. Averill, C. Young, Mrs. W. A. McCartney, Ellen Wheeler, Adaline Hunt, Florence Oliver, F. E. Taylor, C. S. Smith, Q. R. Hall, F. M. Udall, Harry Reed, Alice M. Witmer, T. L. Wolfe, Josephine Dustin, Mrs. C. M. Allyn, Mae Rowland, Mrs. H. J. Munn, L. Longcoy, N. V. Lindsay, Estella Spencer, W. Rounds, L. B. Gary, Beatrice A. Wolley, Louise Hoagland, H. Reed, Bertha Allen, H. H. Elwinger, H. W. Heritage, E. M. Neal, Effie M. Wright, Ella McMahan, N. T. McMahan, L. Grace Mitchell, Emma O. Rider, C. E. Harris, L. G. Scherlitz, L. S. Parker, B. K. Kaufman, F. G. Carpenter, J. G. Henry, F. A. Turner, Mrs. W. L. Bruehlman, Mrs. F. B. Hillman, Mrs. J. W. Smith, J. W. Smith, Mrs. G. O. Line, Julia Bythewood, R. B. Chapman, C. C. Ryder, F. C. McCormick, P. Davis, J. G. Hays, Ella M. Shupe, F. R. Carlton, Jesse Turner, Mrs. Hattie Wakefield, E. C. Dean, Clara Bancroft, C. D. Russell, Mrs. L. J. Miller, W. P. Chamberlain, Maud Tilton, W. Z. Ballard, E. L. Hall, Mrs. E. L. Hall, W. Bellamy, C. G. Phillips, Ruth N. Phillips, Sadie B. Phillips, Mrs. C. Young, C. M. Young, G. E. Osborn, C. L. Hall, R. F. Hall, C. L. Burkley, Lydia Berkley, Josephine Line, B. D. Wray, F. C. Lake, C. D. Harvey, Jeanette Evans, W. Hatcher, R. D. Gates, W. C. Muman, Nellie L. Walker, N. R. Walker, Mrs. N. R. Walker, Paul Wakefield, Vesta V. Schummacher, J. E. Peck, O. C. Arndt, Mrs. L. Bennett, Nellie S. Spencer, A. Ransom, Sylvia Kenner, Laura Hoffman, Mary Leach, D. R. Alden, Mrs. M. Ransom, J. C. Price, S. M. Leach, Mabel G. Crosse, E. Squire, Mrs. F. Squire, W. M. Dudley, Grace S. Dudley, S. A. Shupe, A. Mugrage, Ella Hertzog, O. G. Hertzog, A. Mae Barber, E. Woodward, Miss LaFontaine, Mrs. J. Folks, W. F. Shwartz, Craig Shwartz, Alta Miner, H. M. Rice, Lee Thrice, W. J. Ford, C. S. Hertzog, D. E. Mitchell, W. W. Templin, J. N. Green, Mary Hescock, T. G. Gardner, W. Hertzog, J. R. Ewers, Mrs. W. E. Hayes, C. M. Heiges, F. B. Messing, E. B. Collister, A. A. Turner, Ellen Patison, Bertha Ferguson, B. O. Ferguson, A. Robinson, Miss Hill, Mrs. M. L. Mull, Mattie Schwartz, Ruth M. Wheeler, E. Hill, Lois Hurd, Harry King, Nellie Kent, G. Coe, H. E. Yoder, Olive C. Lindsay, W. E. VanVoorhis, G. J. Thompson, H. J. Turney, Elizabeth Carlton, Deedie Vance, Nellie Shriver, M. Lawrence, E. A. Cook, N. B. Neiter, W. C. Carlisle, C. C. Wisem, W. G. Gibbs, H. M. Leach, Mabel C. Erb, Marce Barber, Merl Clark, Mrs. H. B. Pratt, E. Blackburn, Orah Haight, Mrs. N. B. Dyson, J. C. Archer, R. L. Rice, E. W. Allen, A. M. Maeder, J. A. Egbert, J. L. Rice, G. G. Hertzog, Mrs. G. G. Hertzog, S. Rowley, Mary N. Folks, Mrs. H. H. Elwinger, G. W. Edmondson, H. R. Thayer, Katie Weeks, W. E. Ransom, C. E. Pickett, C. Young, James I. Myers, Mrs. J. I. Myers, Marie E. Ballou, Nellie J. Stull, Jane E. Wheeler, Mark Peckham, J. O. Bridwell, Edith M. Bridwell, E. E. Snoddy, J. L. Garvin, A. E. Hanham, Amy Asher, Leland Bradley Snoddy, Mina Bradley Snoddy, Arthur L. Bancroft, Amy B. Dickinson, Lizzie VanVoorhis, Cora Clark, Jennie Britton, Mabelle Gore, James E. Couch, A. L. Bancroft, S. J. Tilden, J. H. Beatty, Alfred Willman, Fred S. Linsell.

E. V. Zollars, Pres.

Literature.

THE MAN IN THE BOOK. By H. S. Lobingier. 450 pages, Cloth, $1.50. Christian Publishing Co., St. Louis.

"This is doubtless the choicest work in our church literature, from the standpoint of literary excellence, poetic fancy and philosophic insight. 450 pages, 12 mo. Cloth, $1.50." The above quotation is taken from the catalogue of books and periodicals published by the Christian Publishing Co., St. Louis, Mo.

Through the kindness of Dr. A. Steward Lobingier, M. D., of Denver, Col., a brother of the author of the above book, H. S. Lobingier, I have enjoyed the great pleasure of reading and *studying* this charming book. I want to give my testimony to the merits of this wonderful work. I have read every life of Christ published in the English language, and I do not hesitate to say that "The Man in the Book" surpasses them all. Every minister in the Christian Church should have this book in his library. Surely, this gifted writer was so near the Man in the Book when he wrote that he was under his inspiring influence. The book in its present form is very cheap at $1.50, but it is the belief of the writer that a paper edition should be issued that every family may possess this literary and Bible gem. Every purchaser of this work will add to his library a book of great excellence, and at the same time aid the family of one of the purest, sweetest of God's servants.

J. W. INGRAM.

Pasadena, Cal.

"GLIMPSES OF GOD." By Rev. B. G. Newton, Cleveland, Ohio.

This is a book of nine sermons, preached by the Rev. B. G. Newton, pastor Franklin Ave. Congregational Church, Cleveland, Ohio, and published by request of his congregation as a means of assisting in the payment of a debt on their church building. The sermons are readable and worthy of this form quite apart from the primary purpose for which they are published and sold by the author and his church.

"THE STATE." By L. T. Chamberlain. The Baker & Taylor Co., Publishers, 5-7 E. 16th St., New York. Price, in cloth, 50 cents.

This book is an excellent essay on the nature, origin and function of the state, and well worthy of careful reading. The writer denies that the origin of the state is artificial, and that it exists only to punish evil-doers or to regulate commerce alone. It has its origin in the nature of man, and is supreme in its right to exist, govern and develop the race. But he holds that it must take cognizance of the individual as well as of the body collective, and the reverse. The state cannot yield its rights to govern, neither can it justly be partial in its benefits and favors. Much stress is also laid upon individual character as a determining factor of the purity, power and blessings of civil governments.

H.

"LIGHT AMID THE SHADOWS." A book of poems, by Annie Clarke. Fleming H. Revell Co., Publishers. Price, 50 cents.

The sentimental and religious poems of this book will afford very pleasant reading for various minds, moods and occasions.

"YOUNG MEN IN HISTORY" is the title of a little book by Frank W. Gunsaulus, D. D., that will bring good cheer to any aspiring, ambitious young man. The book is published by Fleming H. Revell, Chicago, and may be had for 25 cents.

"THE MAN WHO WANTED HELP" is a word of helpful admonition to the man of opportunity, by Jas. G. K. McClure, D. D. This little book is also published by Fleming H. Revell, Chicago, and may be had for 25 cents.

TRACTS.

We acknowledge the receipt of the following tracts:

"Faithfulness and Romanism," by J. W. Zachary, Gospel Advocate Publishing Co., Nashville, Tenn.

"The Lord's Day," by Edward Evans, 5, The Woodlands, Birkenhead, England.

Reprint Munnell's Article.

Dr. W. T. Moore, in the CHRISTIAN-EVANGELIST of Oct. 13th, states that the late Thomas Munnell's article, "Indifference to Things Indifferent," printed in the first number of the old Christian Quarterly, "is the best thing of its kind in the English language."

Would it not be wise to reprint this article in the New Christian Quarterly, or in the CHRISTIAN-EVANELIST at least? Many of the younger men in our ministry have not read it. Such reprint would be a small but appropriate tribute to the sainted Munnell.

JESSE B. HASTON.

[Nothing could be more appropriate than the republiction of the article referred to, and we are sure Bro. Moore will gladly give it a place in the Christian Quarterly.—EDITOR.]

Edwards Davis.

To the Churches of Christ Everywhere:—We the Christian ministers of California assembled in mass meeting at Santa Cruz this August 1, 1898, desire to inform you of the unanimous action taken by us in regard to Edwards Davis, of Oakland, Cal., who having been charged with immoral conduct by the Central Christian Church of Oakland, was excluded from its fellowship. He afterwards confessed to the Ministerial Union his guilt and that he was justly excluded. Therefore:

Resolved, That although he was restored to the fellowship of said Central Church and granted a letter of recommendation, yet since this act of restoration was premature and was the act of one of the board of the church and not of the congregation, we most emphatically affirm our conviction that he should not be recognized by any of our churches as a minister of Jesus Christ, nor permitted to preach in their pulpits until such time as he shall have given conclusive evidence of genuine repentance and reformation of life.

Resolved, That we deeply regret the necessity laid upon us for taking this action and do now and s all continue to pray for him that he may yet become a true Christian minister, filled with the Spirit of Christ.

Resolved, That this action be published in our church papers and in the Oakland and San Francisco dailies. We take this action in mass meeting because Mr. Davis, not being a member of our State Ministerial Association, is not subject to action by that body as such.

J. H. HUGHES, Chairman,
J. F. TOUT, Secretary.

The foregoing notice came to us a few weeks ago, but its publication has been delayed pending some correspondence with the secretary of the meeting which passed the resolution. Whatever irregularity there may seem to be in the proceedings in this case, it appears that this action of the ministers was necessary to protect their good name and the reputation of our common Christianity. We regret exceedingly the necessity for such publication.—EDITOR.]

Marriages.

UCH—DAY.—Married at Fillmore, Ind., 2nd, 1898, Wm. S. Couch and Edith S. both of Fillmore; W. M. Cunningham ating.

LL—PARRISH.—By N. Rollo Davis, at esidence in Maryville, Mo., on Sept. 27, Mr. Alfred A. Gill, of Maryville, and Martha M. Parrish, of Skidmore, Mo.

'ERFELT—BARTON.—At Firth, Mo., 11, 1898, C. H. Strawn offiiciating, Mr. ll Overfelt to Miss Anna Gertrude Barton, olliday, Mo.

ГCHER—HUBBELL.—At the residence e bride's parents in Howard, Kan., Wed-ay, Oct. 12, 1898, W. Eugene Pitcher, or Christian Church, Belleville, Kan., and Anna Hubbell; R. E. Rosenstein officiat-

ΙΙΤΗ—ADKINS.—In Clearmont, Mo., on 28, 1898, Mr. Lee H. Smith and Miss . Adkins, both of Clearmont; N. Rollo s offici.ting minister.

Obituaries.

e hundred words will be inserted free. Above undred words, one cent a word. Please send nt with each notice.]

GRIDER.

ntie May Grider, wife of John T. Grider, of the elders of this congregation, died . 27, 1898. Sister Grider was born and ated in this place. She was married to . T. Grider Oct. 2, 1889. There can be no ter, purer character than hers. She was ig the faithful in all the work of the ch. For a long time she was organist . Every one is made better by being ainted with one so spotless. She left us r 30th year. Bro. Grider and dear little e, now in her 7th year, have the heartfelt athy of many friends. T. F. WEAVER.

llivan, Ill., Oct. 10, 1898.

HART.

aude Garfield, youngest son of Elder E. J. Sarah Hart, died Sept. 27, 1898, aged 20 s, after a brief illness with typhoid fever. n but 13 years old he obeyed Christ, and faithful until death. He was a consecrated ter in all the activities of his Master's e. We all feel that a great worker has to his reward. A host of friends remain ourn his early death. S. G. NAYLOR.

heeling, W. Va.

JOURNEY.

ed in the city of Quincy, Ill., Oct. 8th, r Caroline Journey. Sister Journey was of the charter members of the Christian rch at Payson, Ill., and was at all times of its most helpful members, helping with neans as well as by her good counsel and lar and cheerful attendance. She was be-l by all who knew her, for she was ever y to extend the helping hand to the needy distressed. She was 71 years, 11 months 23 days of age. She leaves three sons and daughters, besides a host of friends to rn their loss. She was buried at Payson, the undersigned officiating.

C. EDWARDS.

yson, Ill.

SEWELL.

September 11, 1875;
August 30, 1893;
March 22, 1898;
September 30, 1898.

ese four dates note the birth, the accept- of gospel truth, the marriage and the h of Lettie, daughter of Mr. and Mrs. es Kirby and wife of Eld. E. W. Sewell, derson, Tenn. *Is Mrs Lettie Sewell dead?* ian knowledge replies, "She is;" but he sed Word kindly whispers, "She is not dead, sleepeth." In the purity of girlhood she ngly placed herself in the Savior's care; in blooming young womanhood she united t and life with one who was faithfully try-o lead sinners to a better mode of living. he started out in evangelistic work her r, strong voice and musical attainments ed a great assistance. She was willing to ell her part, and encouraged him greatly is labors. When we thought they were ready to begin life's work in earnest, and d see a beautiful field opening before them, submissively responded to the Master's "Come up higher." Lettie was tender-ted and affectionate; had a bright, cheery disposition with which she made friends wherever known; sang well, one of her favorite songs being, "Blessed Assurance." Even while one by one the silver threads of life were severed by the raging, burning fever, she continued to sweetly sing, "Blessed assurance, Jesus is mine." This "Blessed Assurance" was well founded, for she tried to live prepared to "enter the pearly gates at Christ's command." May the hand of love touch with gentle healing the hearts of her devoted parents, sisters, and husband. Think not of Lettie as slumbering in the silent city, but as sweetly slumbering in the arms of eternal love.

MOLLIE L. MEEKS.

Henderson, Tenn.

STEWART.

Died Oct. 3rd, 1898, Flora Hopkins Stewart, aged 44 years, two and one-half months. She was a woman of rare ability and culture. The wife of Bro. J. F. Stewart, pastor of the church at Santa Palma, Cal. She was a faithful assistant pastor for 20 years, in which work she was supremely happy and never thought of self while laboring to save others. She labored even beyond her strength and gave her life for others. She leaves with her heartbroken husband two daughters, 18 and 14 years and a son 12. All of whom she saw baptized into Christ. She was married to Bro. Stewart July 30th, 1878, by E. J. Hart, at Louisville, Ill., at which time she resigned the position of 1st assistant teacher in the public schools, of Flora, Ill. She began public life as a teacher at the age of 16, serving in that capacity eight years. Her health failed in Oregon, where they were in the employ of the General Missionary Board. By the advice of physicians she came to Southern California, where she regained her health for a time, but it was only temporary. In addition to her arduous labors as a home missionary while in Oregon she served the C. W. B. M. as state president three years, during which time the work in the state was greatly enlarged. It was said of Bro. Stewart, "He is a good preacher, but Sister Stewart is a better one." Truly, she has done what she could. She rests from her labors and her works follow her. Bro. Stewart says he has been a subscriber for the CHRISTIAN-EVANGELIST for about 25 years.

F. T. B. VALE.

Publishers' Notes.

By the time this reaches the reader our new publication, written by J. H. Stark, will be ready for delivery. The author has given this new work the title of "Mary Ardmore." This is a high-class religious story based on religious convictions and holding fast to such convictions until they are proven false. The characters are well chosen and each is made to carry out their part to great perfection. The book is handsomely bound in colored cloth and the price is $1.00, postpaid.

QUEEN ESTHER.

M. M. Davis is one of our best writers, and the book of Esther is one of the most interesting stories ever read. The story loses nothing in the hands of M. M. Davis All will continue to the close who begin to read it. The deductions of the author are worth many times the price of the book. It is a story which the child can follow with delight, and from which the preacher can add many sermons to his stock. Here is philosophy, psychology and sociology illustrated.—D. R. DUNGAN.

"Queen Esther," by M. M. Davis, has just been published and is beautifully bound in latest style cloth. It has many illustrations specially prepared for this book. The price is 75 cents, postpaid.

When I commenced "In the Days of Jehu," by J. Breckenridge Ellis, I read it through with much interest and pleasure. The author has taken the facts from the Bible, leaving out genealogies and all that is not necessary to the narrative. I consider this a valuable book. I am glad the author has taken up the life of Saul in the same way. We need more sermons, articles and books on the Bible that are narrative and expository. Such books should be freely put into the hands of the young.—*A. E. Ewell, in Christian Courier, Dallas, Tex.*

The Bloomington (Illinois) Daily Pantagraph, of recent date, has the following notice concerning our late publication, "Across the Gulf:"

"Mrs. N. M. Vandervoort, of Heyworth, has written a little volume which is deservedly attracting much attention from literary people. It is entitled 'Across the Gulf: A Story of the Times of Christ.' It deals with the persecutions of the early Christians in Rome under the reign of Tiberius Cæsar, and is graphically written. The chapters are all strongly drawn, the chapters regarding the reception of Ptokia, the Christian, in paradise, and of Plutos, the unbeliever, in hades, being especially dramatic. Mrs. Vandervoort has talent of a high order."

The Christian Church Department of the American Benevolent Association.

The attention of the members and friends of the Christian Church is earnestly invited to the consideration of the plans and purposes of the Christian Church Department of the American Benevolent Association, organized for the purpose of creating an endowment fund for the benefit of the missions of the church, such as Church Extension, Home and Foreign Missions, Orphans' Homes, etc. The purposes and plans of the Association are receiving the endorsement of practical, thinking business men, as being right in principle, a plan to enlarge and prosecute in a practical way the work and mission of the church. The Association desires to secure County and State Superintendents, to whom liberal compensation will be afforded. To that end correspondence is invited from church workers in the Christian Church, men or women, from all parts of the country.

Address at an early date American Benevolent Association, 240 Wabash Ave., Chicago, Illinois.

Talks to Churches.—I.

I. *Do You Know* that special arrangements have been recently made with the Christian Publishing Company by which every member of your church may receive the CHRISTIAN-EVANGELIST one year free, and that every church in the land can afford a Christian Library, composed of the best books of the Christian Church?

II. *Do You Know* that this library contains ninety-one books that cover every possible phase of our doctrine and work, fifty copies of one of our best songbooks, The Gospel Call, and fifty yearly copies of our very best church paper, the CHRISTIAN-EVANGELIST?

III. *Do You Know* that for a Library club of fifty members (each member paying a membership fee of $2.75), you can obtain this entire Library? or, that for small clubs, the Library will be proportionately divided?

IV. *Do You Know* that the founder will gladly visit your congregation, preach to the people until an interest is awakened, then personally assist in placing the Christian Library, *provided* his traveling expenses are paid?

V. *Do You Know* that churches placing their own libraries will be allowed a discount of twelve and one-half per cent. on all money collected from membership fee? Finally,

VI. *Do You Know* that one of the libraries placed in your church building would greatly *enlighten* your church membership, *enhance* the efficiency of your S. S. and C. E. and church work and *increase* the interest and attendance at all your services?

If You Know These Things, write for fuller particulars. Address the founder,

S. J. PHILLIPS.

Sugar Grove, Wis.

For the World of the Destitute.

The great questions of how to assist the thousands of the unemployed poor might be settled by the government:

1st. Appropriating public land for a plantation.

2d. Supplying suitable managers.

3d. Conveying all able and willing to work of the unprovided poor to the land.

4th. Enabling them to (irrigate it, if necessary, and) produce and make by hand all the necessaries of life.

5th. As soon as they have earned enough to take up land under the homestead laws and farm, or to go into other independent business, helping them, or paying them sufficient, to do so.

6th. Causing the laborers on the government plantation to receive the overabundant products of discharged farmers, in return for overabundant hand-made necessities on the plantation, and to receive the necessary handiwork of the discharged unable to farm, in exchange for articles needed, from the government plantation, and all this as long as necessary to the welfare of the discharged, and only as far as agreeable to the same. If the destitute have a right to life, which includes a right to whatever is indispensable to life, and if the United States Government has what is indispensable to their life, is it not the duty of the government to supply it to them, as muc as is necessary to enable them perpetually t supply themselves?

[The above unsigned circular is worthy o consideration. It would be a humane, eco nomic and wise measure for the goverment t act on this suggestion, at least until some thing better could be established.—EDITOR.]

The best way to avoid sickness is to kee yourself healthy by taking Hood's Sarsaparilla the great blood purifier.

THE CHRISTIAN-EVANGELIST.

A WEEKLY FAMILY AND RELIGIOUS JOURNAL.

Vol. XXXV. November 3, 1898 No. 44.

CONTENTS.

EDITORIAL:
Current Events....................547
Highest Authority....................548
The True Church United....................548
A Divine Mission—What?....................549
The Love of God....................549
Convention Afterthoughts....................550
Editor's Easy Chair....................551
A Printing Press for Jamaica....................551
ORIGINAL CONTRIBUTIONS:
"Spiritism:" Other View-Points.—Joseph H. Mac El'Rey....................554
Can I Love My Enemies?—N. J. Aylesworth....................556
CORRESPONDENCE:
New York Letter....................557
Pittsburg Letter....................557
Kansas City Letter....................558
A Resting Spell....................558
The Other Side....................559
Iowa Letter....................559
The Bible College at Columbia....................560
A Love Feast of Evangelists....................560
Are We Overloading....................561
Texas Letter....................562
The Bethany C. E. Reading Courses....................562
The Rainy River Colony....................563
Seventh Anniversary....................563
FAMILY CIRCLE:
Let Me Try (poem)....................568
Text Stories—The Obedient Test His Promises and Find Them True....................568
Just Laura Ann (poem)....................569
The Slanderer....................569
A Geographical Rhyme....................570
The Influence of Flowers....................570
King of England....................570
Strong Testimony for Prayer....................570
Scientific Philanthropy....................571
MISCELLANEOUS:
Our Budget....................552
Notes and News....................564
Evangelistic....................567
With the Children....................572
Literature....................573
Christian Endeavor....................574
Marriages and Obituaries....................575
Personal Mention....................576
Publishers' Notes....................576

Subscription $1.75.

B. B. TYLER, D. D.

PUBLISHED BY

CHRISTIAN PUBLISHING COMPANY

1522 Locust St., St. Louis.

THE

CHRISTIAN - EVANGELIST

J. H. GARRISON, EDITOR.

W. W. HOPKINS, ASSISTANT.

B. B. TYLER, J. J. HALEY,
EDITORIAL CONTRIBUTORS.

What We Plead For.

The Christian-Evangelist pleads for:

The Christianity of the New Testament, taught by Christ and his Apostles, versus the theology of the creeds taught by fallible men—the world's great need.

The divine confession of faith on which Christ built his church, versus human confessions of faith on which men have split the church.

The unity of Christ's disciples, for which he so fervently prayed, versus the divisions in Christ's body, which his apostles strongly condemned.

The abandonment of sectarian names and practices, based on human authority, for the common family name and the common faith, based on divine authority, versus the abandonment of scriptural names and usages for partisan ends.

The hearty co-operation of Christians in efforts of world-wide beneficence and evangelization, versus petty jealousies and strifes in the struggle for denominational pre-eminence.

The fidelity to truth which secures the approval of God, versus conformity to custom to gain the favor of men.

The protection of the home and the destruction of the saloon, versus the protection of the saloon and the destruction of the home.

For the right against the wrong;
For the weak against the strong;
For the poor who've waited long
For the brighter age to be.
For the truth, 'gainst superstition,
For the faith, against tradition,
For the hope, whose glad fruition
Our waiting eyes shall see.

RATES OF SUBSCRIPTION.

Single subscriptions, new or old	$1.75 each
In clubs of five or more, new or old ...	1.50 "
Reading Rooms	1.25 "
Ministers ...	1.00 "

With a club of ten we will send one additional copy free.

All subscriptions payable in advance. Label shows the month up to the first day of which your subscription is paid. If an earlier date than the present is shown, you are in arrears. No paper discontinued without express orders to that effect. Arrears should be paid when discontinuance is ordered.

In ordering a change of post office, please give the OLD as well as the NEW address.

Do not send local check, but use Post office or Express Money Order, or draft on St. Louis, Chicago or New York, in remitting.

New Publications.

LIFE OF ALEXANDER CAMPBELL. By THOMAS W. GRAFTON. With an introduction by Herbert L. Willett. Large 12mo, cloth, $1.00.

A condensed, concise and accurate account of the life of this great religious reformer, beginning with his boyhood, and following him through his trials and triumphs. It is written in an attractive style. It is just the book for the busy people.

ACROSS THE GULF. By MRS. N. M. VANDERVOORT. 12mo, cloth, $1.00.

A wonderfully interesting and instructive story of the time of Christ.
The reading of "Across the Gulf" will awaken thought, strengthen faith, and stimulate the life of the reader to nobler service.—N. S. HAYNES.

IN THE DAYS OF JEHU. By J. BRECKENRIDGE ELLIS. 12mo, cloth, 75c.

A well written and intensely interesting Bible narrative. Without sacrificing historical accuracy, the author has given us a book more interesting than a work of pure fiction

WAYS OF WORKING. By OREON E. SCOTT. Paper, 10c.
A Handbook of Suggestions for Wide-Awake Christian Endeavorers.

ORGANIC EVOLUTION CONSIDERED. By ALFRED FAIRHURST, A. M., Professor of Natural Science in Kentucky University. 12mo, cloth, 386 pages, $1.50.

This is a very thorough and scholarly discussion of Organic Evolution by one who has had many year experience as a teacher of science.

CHRISTIAN PUBLISHING COMPANY, 1522 LOCUST ST, ST. LOUIS, MO

THE CHRISTIAN-EVANGEL

"In faith, Unity; in opinion and methods, Liberty; in all things, Charity."

XXXV. St. Louis, Mo., Thursday, November 3, 1898.

CURRENT EVENTS.

minds of unprejudiced and thinking may still be much perplexed in at- ng to judge of the responsibility of ar department for the alleged mis- ement of the Cuban campaign. The ce received by the investigating ission has all tended to establish aim of Secretary Alger, that there ittle or no suffering among the :s, except such as is necessarily in- to war in a tropical climate, and that asonable measures were promptly to operation to relieve the suffering sick and wounded. The commission w making a tour of the Southern investigating in detail the present ion of the camps, and the results are most part satisfactory. On the other there are the reports of certain cor- idents, who are known to be intelli- and trustworthy, who are still g positive and specific allegations of nagement, the burden of which must ne either by General Shafter or by ary Alger, or by both. Even those rish to make light of these charges speak of Richard Harding Davis George Kennan as "irresponsible lists," and the explanation that their es are invented for the gratification ir private grudges is not even plausi-

orge Kennan's Story of the War," lished serially in the Outlook, con- es one of the best current histories of te war, if not the very best. The ree articles of this series (published issues of Oct. 8, 15 and 22) on the iago Campaign" and "The Wrecking Army by Sickness," are the most serious and specific arraignment of ar department that we have seen. er the universal joy of the nation a victory won in spite of these de- cies nor the cheerful generalizations se whose devotion to the administra- renders them blind to the possibility ious faults in certain parts of it will as an answer to these charges and as these. When we ask whether there not a great deal of sickness which have been avoided by reasonable ations, we must not be told that while of landing them there was not an exhibition of gross mismanagement and lack of fore- sight, resulting in the loss of much valu- able time and many lives and endangering the whole expedition, we must not accept as an answer the patriotic generality that the victory is ours and that the joy of our triumph should not be marred by discord- ant clamor of carping critics. What we want is a definite answer to definite criti- cisms. There is little need to take evidence as to the condition of the army before Santiago. General Shafter's official tele- grams to the Secretary of War contains evi- dence enough to last us for a while. Let there be an explanation of some of the con- ditions which he sets forth. Let us see whether those conditions were inevitable or not, and if not, who is to blame. At present the official investigation does not appear to be approaching this point very directly or very rapidly.

The general election, to be held on Tues- day, Nov. 8, will determine the complexion of both national and state politics for some time to come. All the states except Maine, Vermont and Oregon will elect representa- tives to Congress. Eighteen states will elect governors. In thirty-four states new legislatures or parts of legislatures will be elected. There are thirty United States Senators whose terms of office expire March 3, 1899, and for not more than five of these senatorial seats is the succession yet de- termined. Hanna, of Ohio, Money, of Mississippi, and Proctor, of Vermont, have already been chosen as their own succes- sors; McComas will take Gorman's place as senator for Maryland, and the Maine Leg- islature, which has been already elected will doubtless support Hale. The remain- ing twenty-five seats will be filled by the legislatures now to be elected. In view of these conditions, it is manifestly impossible for the campaigns in the several states to be conducted exclusively upon state issues. It is a national campaign, for the outcome of it will determine the attitude which the Federal government will assume in regard to the weighty problems of national policy which must be solved within the next two years.

Just at the moment when both foreign and domestic affairs were wearing the most ing against Dreyfus and t inet had decided upon re no means unanimously, a sion which is the occasi Gen. Chanoine, Minister excited speech in the Cha concluding with his res the premier, M. Brisson, cure a vote of confidence tion, and the failure of thi lowed by the resignation inet. It is probable that culty will be experienced of a new Cabinet. App has declined an offer of th the task of forming a been entrusted to M. Duj

The Cuban Assembly h on Monday of last week a body of delegates repre army, and the presence o delegate makes it probat the ruling spirit in the temper of the assembly, a is to maintain the Cuba strength until all outside as well as Spanish, are Cuba is left to herself t career as an independen Cuban anti-annexationis because it will insure C betrayed by her friends nexation. Incidentally, leaders observe with m when the first bunch of republic are being dist stand a better chance of if they are on hand with under their command.

The relations of Fra which were already su may become still more result of the present ch the French Government try continues in office formed, but it is doubtfu will care to treat with death warrant is already successor may repudiat It is reported, however resignation M. Delcasse of Foregin Affairs, had a the British demand for arrangement allowing the surrender of Fashoda under these pretexts and leaving the question of a French station on the banks of the Upper Nile open for future settlement is said to be entirely satisfactory to the French people, who do not want war, but only want it to appear that their actions are not controlled by the fear of war. There is an unconfirmed report that Great Britain is about to establish a formal protectorate over Egypt,in place of the present irregular and indefinite system of control. This would involve a recognition by the powers of her right to be there, which France has never recognized, and if carried through successfully, would render impossible a repetition of the Fashoda episode or anything like it.

The publication of Admiral Sampson's report to the Navy Department gives to the public the inside history of the naval operations of the late war from the beginning of May until the destruction of Cervera's fleet at Santiago, July 3. One fact which is brought out by the report is that Commodore Schley made a serious error in judgment in locating the Spanish fleet and that he was so sure of his opinion that he came dangerously near to disobeying orders to follow it out. When Cervera's fleet had mysteriously disappeared, Sampson correctly located it at Santiago, while Schley thought it must be at Cienfuegos and spent several days in blockading that port, thus affording Cervera ample time to recoal his ships and escape. Why he did not seize the opportunity nobody knows, but that he failed to do so was not due to Commodore Schley. When the Commodore had exhausted to the utmost (if not more) the discretion which his orders allowed him, he proceeded to Santiago in accordance with imperative orders from Admiral Sampson, and there, by his brilliant service at the time of the sortie of the Spanish fleet, vindicated the judgment of those who had kept him in command of his squadron in spite of his one serious blunder.

By a recent decision of the United States Supreme Court, the Joint Traffic Association, composed of thirty-one of the leading railroads in the country, is declared illegal on the ground of violating the anti-trust law. The avowed purpose of the association was "to establish and maintain reasonable and just rates, fares and regulations on state and interstate traffic;" in other words, to prevent cut rates, railroad wars and ruinous competition. The Trans-Missouri Association, founded for similar purposes, but on a smaller scale, was condemned by the United States Supreme Court last year as a violation of the Sherman anti-trust law and the interstate commerce law. The court held that this case was substantially equivalent to that of the Trans-Missouri Association, that the Joint Traffic Association was a trust, and that it operated to the prevention of competition and therefore in restraint of trade or commerce. The case has attracted much attention in the legal world and in railroad circles.

Another legal decision of interest is that of the Illinois Supreme Court in regard to the Pullman Palace Car Co. As is well known, this company owns property and performs functions which do not appertain directly to the manufacture of cars. The town of Pullman, where the company's works are located, is owned by the company, including the homes of 12,000 people, the streets and alleys of the town, the waterworks, gas plant, sewerage system, schools, churches, hotel, theater, market, etc. The court held that, in holding this property, and further in exercising in the town of Pullman functions which belong to the municipality, the company is acting in excess of the powers granted to it in its charter and, therefore, in violation of the law and contrary to good public policy.

A DIVINE MISSION—WHAT?

It is commonly believed among us and is often affirmed that the religious movement which we are urging has a divine mission to accomplish; that it is one of those providential agencies which God ever and anon in the history of the church inaugurates for the accomplishment of his purposes on earth. To destroy this belief would be to destroy at the same time our confidence in the value, necessity and ultimate success of our plea. There is a very general acceptance of the proposition laid down by Gamaliel, that whatsoever is of God will prevail in spite of all opposition, and whatsoever is not of God will come to naught sooner or later.

This belief in the divinity of our plea, and in the fact that God was in its origin as He has been in the history of the movement, may not be in harmony with certain very generally accepted views of God's relation to man and to human history, but we believe it to be in entire harmony with the biblical doctrine of the divine immanence, which is now receiving confirmation from the best scientific and philosophic thought of our day. Any view of God's relation to his world that excludes the possibility of divine intervention at any time to advance the interests of the kingdom of God is, in its last analysis, a species of rationalism, that is as unbiblical as it is unphilosophical.

We believe in the presence of God in nature, in history, and especially in the ongoing of the kingdom of God. Because we believe this, we believe in the divine origin of our religious movement. We believe that the Spirit of God impelled the leaders in this movement to make their protest against existing abuses in the religious world, and to raise their voices for a return to a simpler and purer religious faith and practice, and to the unity of the apostolic church. We believe, further, that as God was in the beginning of this movement, so has He been in its continuous progress, guiding the course of its development so as to accomplish the purpose which He had in view in its inauguration. Believing this, we cannot believe otherwise than that there is a great destiny before us if we are faithful to the divine leading.

There is, in this view of our origin and mission, nothing to inflate our vanity or self-conceit, or to inflame us with spiritual pride. On the contrary, there is much in it to teach us the lesson of humility, and to impress us with a sense of our personal unworthiness. If God has seen proper in His wisdom to make us custodians and defenders of certain truths and principles which need emphasis in our day, what manner of people ought we to be, that these truths
and principles be not hindered by
blindness, our narrowness, our lack of
secration to the high purposes for w
God would use us? Whatever excell
there may be in our position is not of
selves, but of God. Whatever failures
have attended the progress of our
are due to our own weaknesses and
faithfulness. Had we been more loy
God's great purpose, had we given
selves to it with greater self-abandon
truer consecration, the truths we hold,
principles we advocate, would have gai
a far wider acceptance than they have t
far gained. A sense of profound humi
tion should come over us whenever
compare the supreme value and the irres
ible power of the plea we are making
what we have achieved. Great as
progress has been we cannot doubt but
it would have been many fold greater
we been worthy instruments in so migh
movement in behalf of a return to
Christianity of Christ and to the unit
his church.

Believing that we cannot keep too ste
fastly in view this special work to w
God has called us, and feeling that wi
views as to the nature of this work h
done and are doing much to retard its pr
ress, we purpose, in a series of editori
to point out what seem to us to be G
purposes in this religious movement.
task we feel to be as difficult and deli
as it is important, and we do not enter u
it without a profound sense of our
worthiness to deal with it adequat
Relying, not on our own wisdom, but se
ing that which cometh down from ab
we shall seek to guide our readers o
more, as we have often done in the past,
a series of studies concerning these vi
matters which we hope may help them t
larger appreciation of, and a more act
participation in, the work to which God
his providence has called us.

THE TRUE CHURCH UNITED.

A notable conference has been held
England between "Church" and "D
sent." Representative Churchmen a
Nonconformists assembled in Bradford
discuss in fraternal spirit and unconve
tional form the Banquo question of trini
This, most significantly, is a step
advance. Ten years ago the most libe
of Churchmen would have declined to m
on terms of equality or in a spirit of mut
fraternity any body of Nonconformists
the discussion of any question whatsoev
The middle wall of partition of bigo
and prejudice has commenced to crumb
. The chairman and chief promoter
this meeting, Dean Fremantle, of Ripon
man of catholic sympathies, gave expr
sion to several noteworthy sentiments
his opening address. "Beyond any c
organization," he said, "was the gr
church of God, which consisted of all w
owned Jesus Christ as the Lord of th
lives, and who were willing to follow hin
Recognizing the Christian faith and chara
ter of his dissenting brethren, he decla
that the congress was there assembled '
give a message from the Christian chu
as a whole to the nation, speaking w
one voice and one heart from vario
points of the ecclesiastical horizon." O
of the Dean's most significant utteran
sounded the keynote of one of the m

ions of Christian union in
s. "There was much more
g Christians," he asserted,
was division; they had one
namely, to build up the char-
n after the image of Jesus
ne great message—the love of
The great need of the times
the faith in Christ and his
itial in every sphere—the
, the nation and the empire.
d of primitive Christianity
atory: 'Go into all the world
e gospel.'"
of Bristol, the distinguished
ster, struck a decisive blow
l in answer to the question,
e sin of schism?"—"I hold
is committed whenever a man
from any soul or souls in
wells." This sentence should
ally before the eyes of every
Christendom, and should be
the face of the church clock
anctuaries. This is getting
pearance down to the essence
very church that stands aloof
in which God dwells, that
wship or membership to such
hismatic church—it lacks the
depth of the New Testament

ost comprehensive, scriptural
basis of unity put before the
as that of the illustrious Dean
e true church, he declared,
itself to what Christ taught.
mple and brief indeed: "God
er—love him; Christ is your
ve in him and walk in his
oly Spirit is sent into your
not prefer the lusts of the
this message was the true
h there were tendencies to
the Dean's own church), as
umbers of Christians said that
f salvation almost depended
ng to our particular commun-
e church meant the blessed
all who loved the Lord Jesus
erity and truth. The church
led in its duty; but if it was
he teaching of Christ, and
ole energy into the ameliora-
orld, then it would have noth-

Norton said that patriotism
an all the differences between
ies; and similarly Christian-
per than all the differences
stians. We believe, after all,
could be essential to the being
h which was not essential to

study the simpler and profounder theology of divine immanence that makes everywhere for human solidarity. A recent eminent writer among us who touched upon this universally accepted idea of the divine immanence in the universe, called out the alarum of the frightened watchman on the walls of Zion, who understood that said writer was advocating the Pantheism of Lyman Abbott! Well, Lyman Abbott is doubtless a naughty boy, and Pantheism is doubtless a bad thing, but the Pantheism of middle-age theology is worse than either! A little deeper thinking and a little clearer insight would save us a great deal of trouble! The thing most needed is not the creation or even the promotion of Christian union, but the recognition of an already existing unity in vital things. There is an inward spiritual quality of the union with God through Jesus Christ, that the saints of all times and climes possess in common, that makes them one despite ecclesiastical vanities and theological dogmas. Read again Dean Farrar's platform for unity in the teaching of Jesus. J. J. H.

HIGHEST AUTHORITY.

In a recent paragraph in the CHRISTIAN-EVANGELIST we quoted from the Baptist News a paragraph serving notice on some brother who had uttered an uncertain note on the question of future punishment, and inquired of our Baptist contemporary, "What is the Baptist doctrine concerning eschatology, and where can we find it formulated?" The Journal and Messenger has answered our question, and the Baptist News quotes and approves the answer. Both these Baptist papers refer us to the "New Hampshire Articles of Faith," Articles 3, 18 and 19. We need not quote what these articles say, as it is the generally accepted view among orthodox people, but by no means the universally accepted view, even among Baptists. The point is that these representatives of the Baptist press refer us to the "New Hampshire Articles of Faith" and say, "Now it seems to us that our contemporary ought to find in those statements what it desires to know of the belief of Baptists relative to the final doom of the ungodly."

In a murder trial Gen. Butler and Senator Hoar were on opposite sides. The theory of the defense was that the act was committed in self-defense. Said Gen. Butler, attorney for the defense, "We have it on the highest authority that 'all that a man hath will he give for his life.'" Senator Hoar replied: "It has long been a mooted point as to what is 'the highest authority' with Gen. Butler, but he has now settled

theologi
own thi
creeds t
ecumeni
made by
or entire
tion. It
creeds th
which th
This,
from D
him the
tist Ne
substan
ment of
which t
Baptists
what m
concern
hold a
their po
would b
quoted i
in harm
far as th
cerned.
Havin
Journal
on us
EVANGE
ciples b
cannot
have be
our vie
them to
and to
books i
express
about a
can be
Baptist
the teac
the sub
for our
slightes
tation
other w
these p
the futu
race.
in the
the futu
factory
lems t
world.
case, a
contem
hope.

(M

down as a general proposition. Some one has said that we can only understand Shakespeare according to the measure of Shakespeare we have in us; that is, it is only according to the measure of our ability to understand poetry that we can estimate his ability as a poet. This is more profoundly true in reference to our knowledge of God. If He is Love, as John declares, then no one that does not love can understand His nature or know Him. That is John's proposition. It is a far-reaching one.

If John was the profoundest theologian among the apostles it was because he loved the most. No man, according to John's declaration, no matter what his theological training may be, understands God if he does not love. We are to know God through the heart rather than through the intellect. Many of the great creeds of Christendom have been formulated by the intellect alone, while the heart has not been allowed to exert its molding influence; hence many things have been attributed to God and affirmed of God that the heart which loves has never approved. The much talked-of revision of a certain creed had for its object the elimination of certain features that are obnoxious to those who understand God better through their hearts than their fathers did through their intellects.

"God is Love." Magnificent truth! Glorious revelation! Cornerstone of all true theology! Basis of all true optimism! Ground of human hope! Motive of Christian service! These three words are worth more than all the tomes of theology that have ever been formulated by human wisdom. It throws more light on the dark problems of life than all the world's science and philosophy. It paints a rainbow of hope on the sky of every human life, and gives songs in the night to the children of sorrow and affliction.

If God is Love, if the hand that guides the courses of the planets and holds in balance the infinitude of shining worlds is the hand of the Father, prompted by love, why should we not dismiss our fears and anxieties and commit ourselves lovingly, trustingly, to His care? Love does not forget its own. Love does not permit its own to suffer, except for their own good. Love is stronger than death and mightier than the grave.

If God is Love, of *course* He "sent His only-begotten Son into the world that whosoever believeth on him might not perish, but have everlasting life." It is just like love to do that. It is always stooping down to lift up the lowly and the fallen. It is always seeking to save. It is always leaving the ninety and nine safely in the fold to go out upon the dark mountains in search of the lost one. The whole gospel is easily understood on the basis that "God is Love." Gethsemane, with its unutterable anguish, and Calvary, with its suffering and shame, are comprehensible in the light of the truth that "God is Love." Love is always suffering, and pleading, and sacrificing for the welfare of others.

"Beloved, if God so loved us, we also ought to love one another." Hereby let us test our hearts before God. Do we respond to God's love? Do we really love Him as He is manifested to us in Christ? Are we manifesting that love by deeds of self-sacrifice for His sake? Do we love one another? Are we willing to forbear one another and to forgive one another? Do we bear each others' burdens, and so fulfill the law of Christ? Are we seeking to do unto others as we would have them do unto us? If not, then, according to this apostle, we know not God, for "God is Love." What a candle this text is by which to examine our own hearts!

PRAYER.

O, Thou whose name is Love, we thank Thee that Thou hast manifested Thy love for us in the gift of Thy Son. We rejoice that Thou hast revealed Thyself to us as the God of Love. Forgive us, we beseech Thee, O Father, for our lack of love for Thee and for all Thy children. Help us to love Thee more that we may serve Thee and one another more acceptably. Shed abroad in our hearts Thy love by the Holy Spirit, and transform us through the power of love into willing and obedient servants here, that we may share in Thy glory hereafter. And this we ask in the Name of Him who was Love incarnate, even Jesus Christ our Lord. Amen!

CONVENTION AFTERTHOUGHTS.

That Lookout Mountain prayer-meeting never materialized. The program committee left no room for it and made no arrangement for any special time for the delegates to go there. The result was that they went each day without standing on the order of their going. Most of the delegates took in this view at one time or another during the various conventions. We had intended arranging for an independent meeting in the tavern on the brow of the mountain, but sickness prevented, and so between not having time in the early part of the convention and being knocked out by the Chattanooga artesian water and the Read House menu, we were denied the pleasure of the view from this mountain of vision. The place would have lent inspiration to such a meeting, and it would have been well worth while to have arranged for it, but we will perhaps attend to that the next time we go to Chattanooga.

***

We did take a half day off sight-seeing, however, and it will form a very pleasant picture in our memory of the Chattanooga Convention. One bright forenoon eighteen of us took a wagonette, with a colored historian as driver, and took in Chickamauga Park, about ten miles distant. It was a delightful day, a most delightful company, the roads were Uncle Sam's best make and the scenes and associations most interesting and historic. Here on this historic battlefield "Greek met Greek" in one of the great battles of the war. The monuments that stand thick over this ground tell where heroes fought and died. Yonder on Snodgrass Hill stood the brave Thomas, "the rock of Chickamauga," fighting when the rest of the army had fallen back, and saving the day from disaster. To him on this hill came the lamented Garfield, in that daring ride in which he dashed through Confederate lines to carry a message from Rosecrans to Thomas. On this hill stands an observatory, from the summit of which the whole battlefield lies beneath. We returned by way of Mission Ridge, from whose summit we have a fine view of Lookout Mountain, lifting its bold head above the valley, and the Tennessee Valley and the city of Chattanooga. On this ridge was fought later another one of the great decisive battles of the war. Yonder on Orchard Knob stood Grant with glass in hand, directing the moveme of the army, and watching the Union fo storm the heights of Mission Ridge, driv back their brave foes. This spot, mar by Federal and Confederate monume will ever remain historic ground, and of distant generations will come to v the place made sacred by the sacri of so many heroic lives on the altar patriotism.

***

Quite a number of our leading evangeli attended the Chattanooga Conventio men who have made a national reputati by their success in winning souls to Ch and in planting our banner in new fiel These, with a number of our state eva gelists and evangelistic pastors, held so meetings to consider questions of inter connected with their work. One of th expressed to us the feeling that our ligious papers were not as friendly formerly to evangelistic work. We vent the suggestion that this is a mistaken i pression. To make disciples of all natio including our own, is the great work of t church, and the men who are most succe ful in this work will ever hold a high pla in the esteem of the brotherhood. It only truth, however, to say that some cesses or extremes in connection with th evangelistic meetings have produced a s of reaction against what is called " meetings." An excessive zeal for numbe it is believed, in many cases has led to t baptism of many who have not been co victed of sin or made to realize their ne of salvation. This in one danger. A other is the manifestation of a belligere spirit and attitude toward other religio bodies, which arrays the religious forces the community against each other a prevents their mutual co-operation in goo works. These two dangers guarded again and the evangelists will have no reason complain of the lack of appreciation on t part of their brethren. Let men be co verted] to Christ and not to any theory any party. Let truth be preached in lov with a brotherly appreciation of all that true and good in our religious neighbor and the more meetings we have of this ki the better.

***

We were glad to see so many of o colleges represented. No class of m among us are exerting a profounder infl ence upon our cause than the teachers our colleges, who come in direct conta with the young men and women who are be leaders in a few years. Kentucky Un versity was represented by President Ca and Professors Graham and Loos. Bethan was represented by its financial agent, L. Darsie, and some of its trustees, wh were zealously pleading its cause. Hira College was represented by its presiden E. V. Zollars, who delivered the address education—a strong presentation of t value of education and its relation to Chri tian work. Butler was ably represented b Jabez Hall, president of the Bible Depar ment, and Prof. B. A. Jenkins, of t Chair of New Testament Theology, both whom won additional renown by their a dresses. Nor can we omit Jno. E. Pound financial agent of Butler, whose sermon the Walnut St. Christian Church on Su day morning called out the highest prais Eureka College was well represented by i president, J. H. Hardin, who presided ov the meeting of the Home Board, and who preached a strong sermon on Sunday night at the Walnut St. Christian Church. Drake University was not represented by any of its teachers, but Gen. Drake, the founder, was present, and H. O. Breeden and perhaps others of its board of trustees. Add-Ran University, Waco, Tex., was represented by Prof. J. B. Sweeney, who has had much to do with the later prosperity of the institution. The Bible work in connection with the state universities was represented by such men as C. A. Young who, by the way, made a strong address on the value of such work before the C. W. B. M. Convention, Bro. Forrest, of Ann Arbor, and Hiram Van Kirk, now associated with the Divinity House of the Disciples in the University of Chicago. The convention could ill have spared the presence of these men from its proceedings.

***

Two steps were taken at the convention which look in the direction of greater unity and closer co-operation. One of these was the agreement of the secretaries of the various states on a uniform day for State Missions, the day selected being the first Lord's day in November. This action was ratified by the convention, and we hope will be generally ratified by the churches. Our general work cannot succeed if the state work be neglected, and the setting apart of one day for the collection in the various states will be certain to call more attention to the state work and secure for it the attention which its importance demands. The other step to which we refer was the appointment of a committee to arrange a uniform series of mid-week prayer-meeting topics for use in our various papers and publishing houses, with a view to their securing their adoption by the churches. We believe this is a step in the right direction. Such a uniform series, we believe, will tend to the improvement of the mid-week prayer-meeting, doing for that meeting what the uniform series of Sunday-school lessons has done for the Sunday-school. This committee is to take action at once, and have the new series of topics ready and published before the beginning of the new year. The topics issued by the Christian Publishing Company and used in this paper have been widely adopted, and calls are coming in for the next year's series. We shall be glad to co-operate in this union movement.

***

The adoption of Cincinnati as the place for the Jubilee Convention was done, not only with unanimity, but with enthusiasm. There was but one mind on that subject. We rise, however, to remark that the time to begin for that Jubilee Convention is now. If it is to realize what it ought to realize for the cause it represents, plans should be laid at once for the entire year's work. Let there be distribution of labor and responsibility, giving to each man his work and to each state its special task, if we would come up to the measure of our hopes. It should be a remarkable year in our history that will set the pace for the coming years. It has not yet entered into the heart of any of us what we could accomplish by united and universal effort. This year ought to be a revelation to us of the latent possibilities of our brotherhood. Let our leaders lead, and the rest of us will follow.

Editor's Easy Chair.

After a little flurry of winter, autumn has come with its blue sky, its hazy atmosphere, its hoary frosts, its bright colors, its falling leaves. What a strange and subtle relation is that which exists between sound and sentiment, or melody and mental images! Sitting in the parlor a few evenings since, listening to the tones of the sweet melody, "Woodland Echoes," as they rippled from the keys of the piano, we had but to close our eyes and the parlor became a vast woodland, the foliage of the trees wearing its autumnal tints and the autumn wind sighing through the branches of the trees. We seemed to hear the music of running brooklets and the sound of far-off waterfalls. We could hear the noise of the falling nuts, the chatter of squirrels laying in their winter store and the "caw" of the crow flying by on lazy wing in search of some of its ebony companions. And all this troop of mental images and sounds were born of a few notes of music! Who but a master of melody can thus join sound and sentiment in an everlasting wedlock?

The fact mentioned in the foregoing paragraph should receive far more consideration than it does in the matter of Christian worship. Music has a most important part to play in calling forth the purest and best sentiments of the heart, and in opening the mind to all holy and blessed influences. Some good people have imagined that there is no sort of connection between worship and what they call "mere sound;" but the truth is, there is no such thing as "mere sound." Sound is vocalized sentiment. All the birds and beasts of the field understand this, even if some good religious people do not. This being true, it should have a decided influence in the selection of tunes and melodies to be used in the public worship. What does it matter to put religious words to the air, "The Little Old Log Cabin in the Lane?" It is a musical misfit. The song will ever carry with it its old-time associations and sentiments. The religion is not all in the words. Even "Rock of Ages" sung to the tune of one of our modern ditties would lose all its religious value. Much remains yet to be done in the field of religious music to furnish a hymnology that will cultivate and be a fit expression of spiritual devotion and inspiration.

There is an astonishing amount of superstition, among even enlightened people, which influences their conduct in many ways. A great many people will not undertake a journey or inaugurate a work of any kind on Friday, believing it to be an "unlucky day." The number 13 is regarded by a great many intelligent people as an "unlucky number," and many refuse to sit down at a table if their presence makes the unlucky number. On a recent trip to Chicago and return, the Easy Chair editor, securing his berth late in the day, went and returned on successive nights, occupying lower 13. A friend coming on another road the same night, and securing his berth late, had lower 13. These facts seem to indicate that many people avoid that number, so that it is the last one chosen. Of course, this is the baldest kind of superstition, and no one could begin to give a reason for this prejudice against the number 13. But there it is as a force in modern life, influencing the actions and choices of men. Like all other kinds of superstition it should be discouraged, and, if possible, banished. It has no legitimate place, in civilized and especially in Christian society. The man who finds himself the victim of these superstitions should face them with the two-edged sword of faith and reason, and show them no quarters, until they are exterminated.

There is probably no better test of character than the manner in which one behaves under criticism. It cuts some people to the quick to have their statements called in question, and when their motives are impugned by some reckless scribe they are miserable and disconsolate. Is there not a good deal of intellectual or spiritual pride in this restiveness under adverse criticism? Why should it be thought to be so serious a matter that our theories are questioned, and our conclusions denied? Are we so infallible as that? There is always a bare possibility that our critics may be nearer right than ourselves. If, however, we feel a perfect confidence in the correctness of our position which has been assailed, why should we fret? If we are right, time will develop it. If a man does not love truth more than he fears criticism he is not likely to benefit the world much by his thinking. We long ago determined not to love a brother less because he differed from us or criticised our teaching, and not to be deterred from presenting any truth which we believed should be presented, through fear of criticism.

A Printing Press For Jamaica.

One of the conspicuous figures at the Chattanooga Convention was the man who has stood at the head of our missionary operations in the Island of Jamaica for several years, C. E. Randall. He is a heavy-built, square-shouldered specimen of the Anglo-Saxon race, his hair and full whiskers grizzled with gray, and his eyes bright with an intelligent and kindly glow. He has shown himself to be a man of unwavering fidelity and of practical wisdom in the management of the missions in Jamaica. He made an encouraging report of the progress of the work in the island, and of its outlook for the future. He also made a strong appeal for a cheap printing press which he could use to good purpose on the island in the dissemination of necessary information among the churches there. Some of his members could be easily trained to set the type, manage the press and do the necessary printing. He desires very much to make arrangement for this press during his visit in this country and to have it shipped before he returns. We have promised to assist Bro. R. in securing this press, which we are sure will be a most useful auxiliary to the work in Jamaica. On inquiry here we find that such a press can be secured for a very moderate sum, say from $200 to $300, and if necessary a second-hand press that will probably answer the purpose can be secured for even a less amount. We will be glad to receive donations from a number of our readers to assist Bro. Randall in the purchase of this press. Let those who feel disposed to assist in this enterprise report to the undersigned at this office at once, and we will agree to receive the funds, make report of same and assist Bro. Randall in the selection of a suitable press. Let us act promptly, and give Bro. Randall this assurance of our appreciation of his faithful services as the representative of the Christian Woman's Board of Missions in the Island of Jamaica.

J. H. Garrison.

1522 Locust St.

Our Budget.

—Discouragement is an element of weakness.

—Fellowship in suffering is an element of strength.

—Self-denial is an element of the divine nature.

—Nobody cares to take passage on an overloaded ship.

—There are other calls as divine as the call to preach.

—Christians cannot be whipped (scolded) into working harness.

—If men were more concerned about a good conscience and less about wealth, the world's condition would not long remain as it now is.

—"What to Eat," says that Dewey is about the only prominent American commander in the late war that "hasn't slopped over;" that is, talked too much for his own good.

—If some men in the religious world had as much "Holy Ghost" in their lives as they have in their religious language they would be ready for translation soon.

—If Christ were here on the Sabbath day would he attend church, or go to the park?—*Living Words.*

As to some of our city churches, if Christ's life on earth may be taken as a sign, he might prefer the park.

—In the recent death of Dr. C. E. Felton, at De Funick Springs, Fla., the Methodist Episcopal Church has lost an able, consecrated, godly man. We had the pleasure of knowing Dr. Felton in this city 14 years ago and have not forgotten his kind looks and words at the meetings of the Evangelical Alliance. Dr. Felton was a man loved by all who knew him and a benediction to any city or community.

—Bishop Chapelle, the newly appointed papal delegate to Cuba and Porto Rico, says that "as a thoroughly loyal American I may be able to help our government in the work of reconstruction." We wonder if our government has appealed to Mr. Chapelle or the Pope for assistance in this reconstruction business? We had naturally supposed that he was going to Cuba to help the Roman Catholic churches instead of "our government."

—Another artist has been heard from anent the late picture of Bishop Campbell. R. J. Tydings, Washington, D. C., writes that he was so struck with the picture that he sent to Bro. Goodrich for the original daguerreotype and has about completed a life-size oil painting which, he adds, "'If I do say it myself, as oughtn't' (to quote Josiah Allen's wife) is, I think, something nice." We are glad to have helped in the multiplication of the portrait of this great reformer of the 19th century.

—"Can I Love my Enemies?" by N. J. Aylsworth, of Auburn, New York, is resumed this week. This is a vital question, and those who know Bro. Aylsworth's ability as a writer know how deeply interesting and profitable he can be on the spiritual side of a hard question.

—Our Subscription Department is in receipt of a letter from Thos. V. Elmore, who forgets to give his postoffice address. Will he kindly supply this office with the missing information?

—Just as we close this paper news comes of a notable triumph of the gospel at Clarksville, Tenn., where Evangelist Romig is holding a meeting. The church, which has been divided for some time, has been happily united, all differences healed, and there is great joy among the saints in that place. Fuller particulars later.

—H. W. Everest, Dean of the Bible College of Drake University is again in the hands of his physicians for a season and A. M. Haggard, A. M., of Oskaloosa, has been called to assist Dean Everest for the remainder of this term of college work. Bro. Haggard will fill all of his previous engagements, reaching into the new year, except his meetings. These he will turn over to others. Teaching is not new work for Bro. Haggard. Since his 25th year he has taught nearly eight years in Iowa and Minnesota. He is our Iowa correspondent of the CHRISTIAN-EVANGELIST.

—Discouragement is everywhere recognized in God's Word as a source of weakness and of loss in the advancement of his kingdom. The apostles, following their Master, seek to infuse hope and confidence into the disciples of that early day, and to minimize the weight and force of whatever tends to take life and spirit out of God's people.—*Sunday-school Times.*

—The Christian Worker, published weekly at Kinston, N. C., has doubled its size. It now has eight pages and they are well filled with news items and religious literature. We much prefer to hear of the increase than decrease of one of our well-edited church papers.

—We wish all parents, Bible-school teachers and other readers of the CHRISTIAN-EVANGELIST to call the attention of the children to the "Children's Column" in this paper. The writer of that column this week, J. Breckenridge Ellis, has outlined a plan whereby the children may be both amused and instructed if they will only join his band and follow his instructions, which we are sure they will gladly do when they read and see what he proposes for them. It is for this reason that we ask the older readers to call the attention of the children to this article and have them read it.

—Christian Work, a monthly paper published formerly by J. S. Shibley, Paris, Ark., is now edited and published at Siloam Springs, Ark., by L. C. Wilson, formerly of Iowa. The salutation pledges the paper to both the voice and the silence of the Bible. The paper has been and doubtless will continue to be the organ of the Arkansas State Mission Board.

—Bishop Chapelle, the newly appointed papal delegate to Cuba and Porto Rico, is reported to have said, "The Holy Father will welcome in the new territories the happy order of things under which the church has prospered in the United States. He believes in religious liberty before all things." We wonder why the present Pope and his predecessors never thought of introducing this happy order of things in Cuba and Porto Rico some years or centuries ago. Again, the Bishop says: "The United States will readily understand that their political and economical interests, as well as the honor of the country amongst nations, require that this work of reorganization shall be carried out with justice and equity to all." It will be amusing to watch and see just what the Bishop will ask of President McKinley under this plea of "justice and equity." A bid for the "temporary" support of the priests from the public treasury has already been made. But how much time may be pressed for under cover of this word "temporary" remains to be seen.

—We complain of pastorless churches and churchless pastors and attribute the condition, sometimes, to a lack of an adjusting machine. But here come churches blessed each with an episcopacy or other regulating board making the same complaint. May it not be that the cheapest man at the cheapest place and the poorest preacher at the poorest church, a plan that obtains generally in the religious world, is partly at fault. An oversight that would distribute preaching talent on a broader Christian basis might obviate some of the things complained of, especially as to cities. If a strong church would go to pieces under a poor preacher, how can a weak church be expected bear up under him.

—According to figures given by the Voice, the Raines law is not so much of a reform measure after all. It has shut up some of the lesser liquor stalls, but without decreasing the amount of liquor consumed in the state. And not only this, but the figures given by the Voice show an increase in arrests for drunkenness and other crimes directly attributable to this evil. If men mean what they say when they talk of controlling and curtailing the liquor traffic, why do they not enact a law that secures the result desired? It is the sheerest political nonsense to talk about reducing the "doggeries" and yet leave the way open to enlarge the traffic and its crimes. Some politicians talk about the liquor traffic as though it was the most sacred thing outside of heaven.

—Temperance is the Reform Bureau's topic for November. The Bureau's topic a month course is being widely adopted by the Y. M. C. A., W. C. T. U. and various clubs.

—In this paper you will find an article on the Bethany C. E. Reading Courses introductory to the second year's reading. An article will follow each week, as last year, from the authors of the handbooks—brethren Willett, Lhamon and Power—in their turn.

—DEAR BRO. GARRISON:—Am just up from my first delightful dip in waves rolled hitherward from the Chattanooga Convention by the CHRISTIAN-EVANGELIST, and I am on my feet to say that the Endeavor Society of the First Church of this town will pay $1.00 or more to the support of Bro. J. Z. Tyler as National Superintendent of C. E. It's the thing!

W. S. PRIEST.

Atchison, Kas.

—The Fourteenth Annual Report of the Bureau of Animal Industry gives the number and value of horses, mules, milch cows, oxen and other cattle, sheep and swine in the United States for the years 1867 to 1896, inclusive, and by states for the years 1870 to 1896, inclusive. These statistics, with those on the imports and exports of animals and animal products for the years 1892 to 1896, inclusive, make the volume valuable to all who desire to have such facts in form for ready reference. This volume is published by order of Congress for distribution by Senators and Representatives, to whom all requests should be made. It will be available for distribution about December 1, 1898.

—A distinguished member of a Baptist church, writing from New England, says: "I see evidence of religious progress here in the East, not so much a direct advance as a recognition on the part of Baptists and others that their traditional positions are unscriptural." By the "traditional positions" our correspondent, no doubt, means those little denominational peculiarities which have served to perpetuate divisions and impede religious progress, in the past, and which in certain minds have assumed more importance than the fundamentals of Christian faith. It is, indeed, a sign of progress that these are coming to be recognized as unscriptural traditions.

—The Journal and Messenger believes in the salvability of "the chief of sinners." It does not believe that any human soul ever went so far in sin that the grace of God could not reach and save it.

Of course not, since the grace of God reaches even the totally depraved. But if all men start life at total depravity, how can a sinner get farther away from God in sin?

—The article in this paper entitled, "A Love Feast of Evangelists," by Geo. F. Hall, is an interesting and important document because of its reference to a supposed breach or growing chasm between pastors and evangelists. Such a chasm or even coldness cannot exist except to the detriment of the church and its cause; but we have not understood that such a chasm or even the suspicion of one existed. The war, if such has been waged, has been against some of the methods used by evangelists to draw crowds and to get additions and not against evangelists as a class of workers in the Lord's vineyard. Objections have likewise been made against pastors for resorting to sensational methods in their work. Probably

sts nor pastors, as a class, are
in this respect and we make
eep the issue on its merits.
nt need in these days for th
'"preach the word,'' and to
ine for the conversion of men
on of the church.

page this week will be found
. B. Tyler, than whom but few
brotherhood are better known
yler has not only been before
for many years as a promi-
pastor and evangelist, but also
d contributor to our religious
several years he has been on
aff of the CHRISTIAN-EVANGEL-
no introduction to our readers.
arned the art of keeping him-
he sunny side of life and in a
h all men. He has been doing
rist great good by his spiritual
ng the churches during the past

ention to the admirable article
-haired Pastors'' in this paper.
written in a most lovely spirit
at wisdom which is from above.
not give his full name, is not
ither a citizen of the United
is a citizen of the heavenly
lder in Israel and a teacher
ful.

abolish canteens and other
uor selling, now on the House
avorably reported, ought to be
next session of Congress. A
ing this wish in the matter sent
congressman and also to one of
will materially assist in the en-
a law. The bill is known as
H. R. 7,937, to abolish liquor
teens,'' immigrant stations and
uildings. The same course
taken for the Hepburn bill, H.
bid the transmission by mail or
merce, of pictures and descrip-
ights. This bill has also been
ted to the House and ought to

a time we had a statesman in
es Senate who declared that the
ents and the Golden Rule had no
and that the idea that they did
ce was an ''iridescent dream.''
tired to the shades of private
odore Roosevelt, one of the can-
ernor of New York—a state in
' Platt and ''Boss'' Croker
respective parties—comes for-

In Germany to-day no woman can control property; she cannot even control her own actions; whatever of value she has acquired in any way belongs to her father, her husband or her son, and the law requires her to obey their orders. Germany is the only country on earth that pretends to be civilized where the rights of women are so restricted. When a woman marries all her property passes into the ownership of her husband forever. He has the legal right to use or dispose of it in any manner he chooses, regardless of her wishes or protests. If they are divorced the property remains with him. When she assents to the marriage vow she forfeits independence and confers upon him absolute jurisdiction over her mind, body and esta e. He can compel her to work or do anything else that is lawful for women to do, and she has no relief or protection except in public opinion. Some of the American heiresses who have married German barons have learned of this law to their sorrow, and others who may have an opportunity to assist in supporting the German army and restoring ancestral estates should look into the matter very carefully before they appoint the wedding day.

—If a man is a Baptist at all, should he not be a Baptist all over and all through and everywhere and all the time? Is it possible for one to be too much of a Baptist? Should not a Baptist be a straight Baptist and a sound Baptist and a strong Baptist? Of course a man may be a fool and prate and boast, but it is not the Baptist that is in him that causes him to do foolish and offensive things.

The above statements from the Word and Way raises some serious questions. For instance, if all were ''a Baptist,'' then where were the Christian? Is madness (''a fool'') one of the dangers of being too much of ''a Baptist?'' Why does not ''the Baptist that is in him'' drive out the fool? Who are the crooked, the unsound and weak Baptists implied in the third query? Will ''a straight,'' ''sound,'' ''strong'' Baptist admit that there is salvation in any other name? Will such a Baptist commune with one of another name? Is there any reason for a man being ''a Baptist at all'' in order to his salvation?

The State University and Skepticism.

In a circular sent out by President Clinton Lockhart, of Christian University at Canton, Mo., he says:

I have the undisputed report from many people, and especially from students of the State University themselves, past and present, that they find it almost impossible there to maintain even faith in God, and much harder to hold their zeal or their membership in the church. Now inasmuch as the church cannot now, and never will, have the power to select professors in state institutions, the question becomes a very plain one. Shall the Church of Christ fold its hands and leave the state to turn by wholesale our brightest minded and best educated young people into infidelity? If not, we must have our own university, and

in the form
hart cannot
from going
endow in a
Bible Colle
counteractin
may be at
men to Chris
Christian
tion in the st
by disparag
Bible Colleg
students wit
education.
mate fields,
be assisted b
is not the sli
any war upo
is meeting,
tive obligat
its students.
begin it ea
more liberal
with the peo
understand

Th

[Unfortun
ling, is not
impression
Czar's prop
is England
must be ju

Original Contributions.

"SPIRITISM:" OTHER VIEW-POINTS.

JOSEPH H. MAC EL'REY.

"I have a bias, but I can be just." What the perspicuous and versatile Goethe said of himself is comprehensively true of the mass of our people in the fairness they accord to all in exercising the personal prerogative of their "bias," or opinions, in their own way. When they criticise they are supposed to do so in the best spirit and knowledge they possess, being willing to be measured by the same rule. The public desire plain statements, rather than tedious details; explanation of the principles involved, the presentation of the facts for clear conclusions, and thus to obtain sound instruction. The public wish to see justice done. Assertions without proofs, none but the merely biased, who do not wish to be just, will accept. It is dangerous for persons to appear in print, even after they have studied the pros and cons of their theme sufficiently to protect themselves from discovering the unwelcome fact that they are more ignorant than they thought they were. This is the guantlet those must run who will venture criticism or dogmatism upon important topics which they desire to promulgate.

The present writer has been an observer of "isms" in the past, and is likely so to be. Therefore, the most notable "isms" of the present century has attracted a fair share of his attention, as it has of many who wish to possess an up-to-date intelligence concerning one of the earliest displays of the many mysteries of man, and almost constantly in some degree developing in every age and place, and now remarkably spreading, and thought to be worthy the study of the ablest students of nature, science, history, art and man, is constantly being more and more searchingly examined upon the several alleged phases of this protean ism. It has concreted into a religion as well as a philosophy, which challenges domination of the present common and by many termed "miscalled Christianity and Christian ethics."

These issues are anything but trivial, and it is a great mistake so to rate and treat them, when they are so frequently occupying large space in most widely read daily papers, and also in high-grade monthly and quarterly periodicals, by able critics, leading clergy, M. D.s, jurists, university professors and noted scientists of many specialties.

An able critic recently had, quite properly, ample room in your liberal columns to discuss "Spiritism" in every variety which his taste inclined him to pursue. Hence he "briefly" but severely assailed Spiritualists, and Spiritualism, and Christian Science healers upon every item of their ethical, psychological, speculative, philosophical, religious and moral views and deportment, but particularly so upon this latter item—their *moral* conduct. This is always a dangerous item to attack successfully in aiming to fasten general moral discredit upon a whole fraternity, and also the odium theologicum—the enmity peculiar to religionists.

It is all as far-off proper tone in a philosophical, psychological analysis of spiritual, occult, psychic forces, "requiring the scientific mind properly to exploit them," as for a genius in such studies, where in the Empyrean abodes of divine Zeus and the other supreme gods, after imbibing with them their own ambrosia and saturating his superior faculties with their sublime inspirations, to suddenly and ingloriously plunge into the dark earth-levels of the Empyreuma, there to sense the fetid exhalations of decomposing "cabbage, turnips, leeks and onions," as among which Mr. Lhamon mixes himself up in his peculiarly conglomerated effort at associating and disassociating the vegetable and animal genera and species, "with hypnotism, clairvoyance, mind-reading, Christian Science healing, Spiritualism and witchcraft," all in one heterogeneity, such as he admits "requires the scientific mind to discover their kinship."

True, indeed, and Mr. Lhamon may discover that such a scientific mind has not yet materialized, or that if he has, he has explained far more to be mere "psychological unconscious cerebation," and nothing more than Mr. Lhamon and millions more are ready to accept on their present basis of Bible spiritism, spirit intercourse, dreams, trances, inspirations, experiences and faiths. But as I do not propose to "hypnotize" the reader by any art of "suggestion," that assumed talisman of hypnotic, clairvoyant, mesmeric witchery, we will enter as speedily as the obstructions Mr. Lhamon has placed about it, "the crucible of scientific investigation" of these isms, at the mortal risk of appearing after that fusion only "as dross." "Every work shall be tried by fire." "It is already kindled." Although Mr. Lhamon did not say in what degree of authority he uses the Bible as a test of "Spiritism and kindred fallacies and delusions," I think it well for me to positively state what my view-points for criticism of his production are. I shall deal with the Bible as plenarily inspired of God, and in which there is no mixture of error. I shall not argue this position, but assume it, as the basis for everything it contains on faith and morals especially. I do not know how to be more explicit than this. I shall use Spiritualism as it develops itself, and shall treat what is passing for Christianity in a similar manner.

If as Mr. Lhamon states it, "Spiritualism or witchcraft and Christian Science healing," are all of one, they are too immense now to be slurred, sneered, ridiculed, ignored, or as a last resort persecuted out of existence. Indeed, Mr. Lhamon must be aware that those treatments have been through many centuries tried on every kind of spiritism and have not annihilated them, and as he admits cannot now be used upon them. Nothing but the scientific crucible can be used now. Hail to this inestimable freedom!

As regards the moral status of the organizations assailed by Mr. Lhamon, I shall treat that comparatively, of course, with other religious and ethical organisms on the commonly accepted view that this and other countries called Christian are uninfluenced perceptibily for good or bad by the superstitious, inane degenerates Mr. Lhamon thus esteems. Let their degraded characteristics define and distinguish them. They cannot be those to whose immoralities the public press makes reiterated reference as a few following items indicate.

Mr. Lhamon accepts the postulate tl this is a Christian country, ignoring t isms he has characterized. Very we "Crime is increasing in all Christian cou tries and so is poverty, beyond the increa of the natural populations." "Over seve teen thousand killings in this country t year before the present, and one hundr and three legal executions for those hom cides." High-toned editors, like t Philadelphia Ledger, ask: "Have old-tin commercial integrity, the honorable di charge of moral duties, the keeping business promises, been retired to the dai recesses of moral desuetude? This is tl general query on the outlook over the epidemics of financial and moral (alls institutions and men thought to be invul nerable."

Take a broad, wholesale case, in that o the "Methodist BookConcern," lately befor the investigating committee of senators The fiducial engineer of the claim agains the government for money damages did as it appears, some very crooked work amounting substantially to perjury Replying to questions, he said he did no act under the motive of obtaining an money reward, but only for the good of th "Book Concern" of the church. He ha not done worse than some Bible characte who were pardoned, like Peter, Paul an others, who repented and were pardone through the merits of Jesus' blood, etc Now, I do not censure the whole church witl this crime, but the legal rule is that th act of the agent is the act of the employer, and it appears that the church got the money claimed and thus endorsed the act of their agent. The vicarious-atonement doctrine has, it seems, a commercial value in some churches as well as a spiritual value. Since "going astray," as it is now termed, has become so common in financial concerns as not to be shocking, the question has often been asked through the papers, "What churches do they belong to?" As the reports of their falls came out, one paper took to ferreting out for reply and said, "We find Mr. ——— a ruling elder in Dr. ———'s church. Mr. ——— is Sunday-school superintendent in the ——— church. Mr. ——— is a deacon in the ——— church, and Mr. ——— is local preacher in Grace M——— church, and Mr. ———is a man of the world and yet in his sins." I of course reserve names. "The secular press" is not afraid to call a spade a spade. A very prominent sacred paper lately, did "sadly lament the avidity of the general press for spreading the weaknesses of otherwise worthy people, before the eyes of the young!"

Even His Holiness lately begged the press to cease publishing their daily catalogues of crimes, and particularly not to put church troubles upon the wings of the printing press. Well, it is not pleasant, although it should be powerfully instructive reading! Crime exists among Christian communions in proportions larger according to their claims of orthodoxy and zeal in propagating themselves. The cool retorts of criminal court records and prison statistics are generally admonitions to the champions of the superior moralities of Christian professors not to boast too loudly of their practice of our most excellent Christian theories. The smaller religious bodies—Untarians, New Jerusalem, Universalits, Old Christians, Free

:en, Reformed
Disciples of
ristian Science
are superior in
ed by the self-
to mingle with
'he "orthodox"
if offensive to
ng men. They
by "faith," as
t.
nation, practic-
:s and imbeciles,
in it. What it
se. Specialists
t if Christians
n and admitted
and "*the* social
ristian countries
Thus, whatever
be, the applied
is this a Chris-
Without works?
such faith, and

drunken as any
one Christian?
might or would
tianity we have
1 out that, what
moral condi-

tems taken near
tual belt of the
erning the eth-
nd cities of the
. I quote "An-
of our State at
City"—disgust-
taxpayers of the

'ays disgraceful,
; Cortland, been
ever. Incorpor-
state, the pro-
itures are ever
has, in the char-
und the carrying
gathering, fully
The Slum City.'
of these 'meets'
beforehand that
un 'wide open.'
won the honor
on, as the latter
g too high up in
ns, of this city,
his speech pro-
he happy time of
that, in his own
pton would give
wanted of every
udge particular-
plain to quote.
s been kept, and
he great conven-
at Binghampton
rk: Two weeks
there was an
'the perennial
lge Downs. The
ve drink saloons
to the elegant
d many times
ial accommoda-
away all furni-

Residing for many years near to beautiful Binghampton, it was thought then to be a Christian city, and there were very few spiritualists or witchcrafters in it. It has several costly and wealthy churches, hotels and saloons, theatres, dance halls, etc. There is a fine inebriate asylum near it and an insane asylum. I visited them several times, and found a fair proportion of Christians and preachers, legal and medical inmates there, but no Spiritualists, although there are many Spiritualists in the state of New York.

Of the progress of Christianity in New York City and surrounding cities, the most wide-awake clergy there tell us that the profession does not, *per capita*, hold its own, and that the iniquities of "the cities of the plains" of Bible-making times were purity itself compared with the mature, gigantic and multitudinous infamies of those many-hued, festering, cankering, cancer-eating Sodoms, and even in the one termed, as if in caricature, "the city of churches," their every-day crimes and their spiritual wickedness in high and low places are not behind any of the cities. "The whole state has been permeated by the virus of viciousness in the metropolis." Well, does it mitigate the condition of the entire case a whit to blame it on other parts of the Christian compact? When I went West I was told at DesMoines that "there was very little Sabbath west of the Mississippi." I said, "Well, this is supposed to be a Christian nation." By and by I found salesmen for most prominent church leaders in Philadelphia selling their wares by sample in the hotels on the Sabbath days. I saw it done. None of the parties were Spiritualists or Christian Science healers. One agent, knowing me in Philadelphia, came to hear me. Calling that afternoon I was ushered into the sale rooms, and found my friend with other agents and quite a company of retail buyers at work. My friend said, "This is our best day. . . . Yes, our pious employers at home know that." Now, of course Christianity is not blamable for all or any of these things. But are those calling themselves Christians and teachers of Christianity blamable? Christianity in theory is as like Christianity practiced as merchandising in theory is like merchandising practiced. Neither is worth anything in only theory. Put the two together.

Select a collection of those Mr. Lhamon has set at naught for everything but duplicity, and if between their profession and their moral conduct they create a chasm as wide and deep as Christians thus create, let them fall into it, because they but cumber the land!

Mr. L. will admit that Christianity has no more power in this world than is exerted by the mediums, and that is true of all powers or forces. Causes are known only through their effects. We will not quibble or higgle over nothings. The facts will do us. The tree is known by the fruit. We have thousands of names of persons distinguished in every department of learning and leadership in all the world who have been convinced that the phenomena Mr. Lhamon terms witchcraft are done by persons in this world, because negations are nothings. The doctrine of the sphericity of the earth stood a twelve hundred years' campaign against Christian Scientists like Eusebius, Lactantius, Cosmas and everybody's St. Augustine. Their scientific weapons were mighty enough to drive men to death, and as they believed, to eternal hell. The "infidels" finally triumphed. The earth is round now to all. But next, it was infidel to say the earth revolved. It now revolves. It is instructive to read the uses they made of Scripture to prove that the earth does not revolve, that it is flat, that the sun passes around it, etc., that "nothing could live under it except damned souls!"

The canons of our now science were then as absurd to the theologians of that time as are the experiences of those now "whose efforts are not needed" to help overcome the materialism of this age.

Luther said, referring to the destructive doctrines of Nicholas Copernick: "People gave ear to an upstart astrologer who strove to show that the earth revolves, not the heavens and the firmament, the sun and the moon. Whoever wishes to appear clever must devise some new system. This fool wishes to reverse the whole science of astronomy. But sacred Scripture tells us that Joshua commanded the sun to stand still, and not the earth." The mild Melancthon, too, was as harsh in this instance as his chief in slandering Copernick, putting the sting into his heart: "It is dishonest and indecent to assert openly the pernicious deception that the earth revolves, when our eyes are witnesses that the heavens revolve in the space of twenty-four hours. It is the part of a good mind to accept the truth of God and acquiesce in it."

Things come by contrasts and opposites. To know one history with its philosophy you must study two histories of the same events.

Christian saints and Bible defenders who knew nothing of any science but that of the metaphysics of logomachy and abuse of whatever they did not like, thus by mental affinity took to such defenses of the Bible and religion as seemed to agree with their lack of natural science and the scientific trend. Cosmas thus defended the Bible against "the astrologers" (he could not use the respectable word astronomers) by diagraming "the table and ark of the covenant," etc. He took to the Jew trend, who never displayed mechanical skill, and could not construct their own temple. The abusers of the scientists called them atheists, Pythagorean and Zoroastrian infidels, lovers of heathen philosophers, etc. (See Jowett's Plato, Timæus 62, Phædo 449; Cicero, Acad.; Whewell, Ind. sc. v. 1,185.) These men had the idea of rotundity and antipodes. To the Christian Fathers these ideas were damnable (Leckey, Hist. Ref. N. T. v. 1, 279). Mr. L. says, "Egyptians and Romans courted clairvoyants and fortunetellers. Jews peremptorily forbade them." Much so. "Thou shalt not suffer a witch to live." As if in regret for lack of the power to be "peremptory" he adds, "In this age we neither worship nor prohibit such things." "I will not kill thee

CAN I LOVE MY ENEMIES?

N. J. AYLSWORTH.

III.

We have seen that the spirit of human brotherhood has grown to be, especially in this country, a mighty force, and that it embraces in its activity not only the down-trodden and depressed, but even certain classes of enemies. It still remains true, however, that the usual attitude toward a *personal* enemy is one of hatred. The reason of this is to be found in the fact that human sympathy in this case comes into more dirct conflict with self-love and self-interest, for which it proves no equal match. A closer inspection, however, will reveal the fact that there has been a change of feeling even towards the personal enemy. Precisely what this is can be best understood by considering another fact of our mental experience.

Our feelings are generally composite. Especially with the civilized man it is rarely that any particular occurrence, with the emotion it tends to excite, has complete and undivided possession of the soul. Memory and foresight are ever yielding a varied fund of motive. The event which tends to excite a particular emotion has its connection with the past and future or with some deeper insight of the present, and out of these there arise various incitements to feeling, blending with and modifying the original emotion. It is not the single tone of the lute, but the modern music of many parts. That complex of feeling making up a man's spirit is often a symphony of emotion. As colors are often the composite of many shades, some strong and others of such delicacy of tint as to be scarcely perceptible, yet modifying the general result, so is that color of the soul called *the spirit* woven of many pigments.

This is less so with the unreflecting savage, who abandons himself without reserve to the the passion of the moment, and least of all with the animal creation, whose reasoning powers cannot take them out of the present; but with the intelligent man a wide world of circumstances is ever playing its motives upon his heart.

Some of these incitements to feeling are of a contrary nature, and act with a restraining power upon each other, struggling for ascendency. Such are love and revenge, or hatred. Philosophically speaking, a man may love and hate an enemy at the same time. You may resent a wrong and feel like retaliating, but you do not feel like crucifying the offender, and your whole heart would revolt against any inhuman act of torture. This is because the humane feeling—which is a species of love—has not been extinguished even toward this enemy. This feeble love does not exert a controlling influence in your mind or on your conduct, but is consumed in restraining your hatred. It is here that there has been a vast change in the attitude toward the personal enemy. He is still hated, but in the face of a struggling human sympathy, which weakens the virulence of hate and transforms it often into a composite of many contending emotions. The growth of human love, which has reached such remarkable efflorescence in many departments of modern life, has not failed to reach even the personal enemy, and is exerting a powerful influence on our feelings and conduct toward him. When an object falls to the earth we see the action of gravity, which is the controlling force in the result, though the air resists in some measure and retards the fall; but when the cyclone lifts objects from the earth and bears them aloft in its fury, gravity is not seen as acting, though it is doing so quite as much as before, and its power is expended in limiting and restraining the force of the tornado. In this sense of a masked sympathy there are few who do not now love their enemies in some degree, but this does not fill out the measure of Christ's requirement. He demands that this love shall be the controlling force in feeling and the shaping force in conduct. Yet the situation is one of vast encouragement. That we have already stepped on the first rung of the ladder reveals both the possibility and the method of ascent. We need but rise higher in the same direction and the summit will be reached.

If the first step in the loving of an enemy is taken when the heart can say, "I cannot inhumanly torture him," the next step is taken when you can say, "I wish him no harm." If you wish your enemy no harm, you do not desire to *do* him any harm, and your revenge has disappeared. A burning sense of wrong may be felt and an anger with him, but you do not desire to injure him, though your heart may not prompt you to go farther. "Let him go his way, and I will go mine, I do not feel like having anything to do with him." The general benevolence of your spirit has brought you to this point, but this is not called loving your enemy, because love is not in evidence as the controlling force. Yet, let us give it due credit for what it is. It may not command our admiration, but it is love scoring a victory, and driving hatred within its intrenchments. The man whose heart lets him say this has traveled far towards Christ's ideal; and I believe there are many who can to-day say this very thing.

Are there not many who can take another step and say, "I wish him well?" If you can sincerely say this, you have reached a point where you can put that wish into a prayer and pray for your enemy (Luke 6: 28), and into an act and do him good (v. 27). If you can do this you have reaced Christ's goal, and your spirit is Christian.

Such a state of mind is not incompatible with a keen sense of the wrong done and indignation at it; nor does a struggling feeling of resentment entirely exclude it. There is sometimes a well-nigh evenhanded contest between the two passions. At times, as the greatness of the wrong done passes in review, the spirit of resentment rises, soon to be subdued by the kindlier feelings born of nobler reflections. To deny these facts would be to be untrue to the life of the human heart as it is. The human soul is not a statue, whose features know no change. A mother, weary and vexed, may strike her child unkindly. Does she love it? Let danger threaten, and she will rush to lay down her life for its safety. Equanimity of spirit is a virtue to be cultivated, but flitting resentments do not prove that there is not love in the heart. They are the breaking wave caps on the surface of the sea fretted by the gusts of incidents, but the great quiet ocean sleeps below. Let love hear its summons, and it rises to the occasion and moves the mighty wheels of life.

It is often said that men are liable to be deceived regarding the deeper motives o the heart, and to think themselves right eous while they are, in their deeper life selfish and unworthy. But the truth ha another side; the deeper heart may b nobler than we think. What we *do* is th best test of this deeper life.

I may say in passing that this strugglin feeling of resentment in the heart is no wholly an evil. It is the relief agains which our love of enemies becomes sub lime. A character so servile and spiritles as to feel no recoil against injustice o abuse does not command our admiration but a man smarting under a keen sense o wrong inflicted and still rising up to bles the foe that smote him presents a sublim spectacle. It is because it costs us something to love our enemies, that it is so noble. It belongs to the heroisms, and that is why, like all other heroism, it thrills us, and moves with such transforming power upon the object of its exercise. The offender sees in the other party a man of like passions with himself rising above the lower instincts, and returning blessing for cursing, kindness for injury, and it awes him and subdues him to a nobler spirit. But let him see in all this a mere weak servility, and he despises his victim. It is only as he sees in the other all that belongs to his own nature *plus* something grander that he is smitten. He bows to a crowned king wielding that strange sceptre—heroic love.

It should be further said that we must not make the mistake of supposing that all love evidences itself as a glowing and pleasurable emotion. The eye cannot see itself, and there are some feelings so much a part of our inmost selves that we are scarcely aware of them. This presence is to be determined by suitable tests. Nor is love always pleasurable. If the object loved suffers, love is pain—sympathy; that is, *suffering with* another. If he is fallen in character, love may be compassion. The love of complacency is never possible toward an enemy; for we cannot be pleased with his wrongdoing against us. This is not the love that Christ requires; for our love is to be like God's, who does not look with complacency on the wicked. The love of the enemy is always love with a thorn in its breast. But it *is* love. It is a yearning desire to bless; it is the outgoing of the heart towards an erring brother.

In speaking of the "Jews at the Close of the Century," the Menorah, a Jewish monthly, says:

The prosperity of the country not only does not suffer by the competition of the Jew, but is enhanced by his enterprise, energy and push. What if, occasionaly, a hotel keeper or the proprietor of a residence who caters to the spirit of aristocratic snobbishness refuses to admit the Jew? "There are others," the ordinary citizen would reply, "who are glad of the patronage of the Jew." If anybody works into the hands of the anti-Semites, it is the short-sighted, misled leader of the Zionistic movement. If anything would please the hard-boiled anti-Semite, it would be the establishment of the Jewish state. They know that they would fight among themselves a more bitter fight than anti-Semites ever offered them. Is not the Greek nation an example that should be a warning to those who attempt to set up another petty nationality? The Greeks are on classical grounds, they own a country and nevertheless are a constant apple of discord to even their Christian friends. Anti-Semitism, in spite of the picture of Dr. Nordau, drawn gray in gray, is not by far as gloomy and disheartening as it is painted. It could not be expected that the incomparable success of the Jew since he left the Ghetto should be accepted with equanimity by thosewho are distanced by him in the struggle for existance. But the same force which has achieved the success and has maid the Jew in every civilized country an equal among equals, a power in the land, will also bring about his social equality; the name of that force is education.

Correspondence.

New York Letter.

The program of the Disciples' Club, of New York, is just out, giving the outline of work for the entire season. The Club meets the fourth Tuesday evening in each month from October to May (except December, when it is moved back one week), in the church of the Disciples on West 56th Street. Perhaps the items of the program may be of interest to many. They are as follows: Oct. 25th—"Current Events," Clarence M. Aden; Paper: "European Armament and Disarmament," Col. A. C. Fisk; Book Review, Mrs. E. B. Grannis. Nov. 22nd—"Current Events," S. W. Hoke; Paper: "Imperialism," J. H. Banton; discussion led by G. W. Kramer; Book Review, Chilton Dean. Dec. 20th—"Current Events," Isaac Van Beuschoten; Paper: "Critical Study of Isaiah," W. C. Payne; discussion led by J. M. Philputt; Book Review, F. Applegate. Jan. 24th—"Current Events," R. E. Carpenter; Paper: "Cardinal Newman," H. S. Buller; discussion led by F. W. Troy; Book Review, W. F. Stevens. Feb. 28th—"Current Events," R. B. Koontz; Paper: "The Resurrection: Doctrines of the Ancients Surviving in Christianity," J. L. N. Hunt; discussion led by F. H. Moore; Book Review, M. C. Tiers. March 28th—"Current Events," W. H. Harrison; Paper: "Education among the Disciples as Compared with other Religious Bodies," S. T. Willis; discussion led by A. S. Heaney; Book Review, Charles E. Colston. April 25th—Annual Dinner. May 23rd—"Current Events," W. A. Sinclair; Paper: "Martin Luther," R. C. McWane; discussion led by Robert Christie; Book Review, F. M. Johns.

***

The last will and testament of the late Dr. John Hall, of this city, has just been filed for probate in the surrogate's office, and presents some items of interest to preachers and church people generally. A close friend says the estate is worth about $100,000. To each of his six brothers and sisters he bequeathed £100, and to each of his stepsons a similar amount. His watch and books he gave to the Rev. Thos. C. Hall, and his real estate in Kansas he bequeathed to his son, Robert W. Hall. After the distribution of minor bequests to relatives and friends, Dr. Hall gives the residue of his estate to his widow, Emily Hall, during her life. At her death her estate goes to the five children in equal parts. Dr. Hall received a salary of $15,000 a year, and his handsome home on Fifth Avenue was owned by the church, and was rent free. In the course of his life he received many valuable presents, and the sums he received as wedding fees and other presents were notable, although the amount given to Dr. Hall in this way has been exaggerated a great deal, so it is said. When William Sloane, who was the treasurer of the church, died he left to Dr. Hall $30,000. Alexander Stewart also left to him $10,000. Mrs. Ford left to him an annuity of $3,000 a year as long as he lived. Dr. Hall received similar presents, but of less value. It is the general belief that $100,000 will be near the amount of the estate.

***

Hundreds of Disciples in these days are living in the pleasant memories of the great Chattanooga Conventions, which in many particulars were better than all that have gone before. Home Missions certainly did come to the *front* this time with tremendous enthusiasm. We are beginning to see the imperative need of turning America to Christ. It is absolutely necessary in order to evangelize the whole world. And more than this, we are awaking to the fact that the conversion of America means the evangelization of our cities. But to reach our Eastern cities, at least, we must employ the common-sense methods of patiently teaching the gospel. There is no better mission field to-day in the United States than the city of New York, but cyclonic evangelism would not avail anything here. These people must be reached. if at all, by the hand-picking process. Perhaps the best and surest way to reach New York, and especially the North Side, is by planting Sunday-schools as branches of church work. We rejoice at the unmistakable dawning of a brighter day for American missions.

***

The sessions of the Foreign Christian Missionary Society were none the less enthusiastic. The reports of the past year exceed by far every record of the past. The splendid addresses following these reports led us to the very mountain top of Christian experience and blessed fellowship as coworkers with God in the salvation of the world. One of the most delightful features of the Foreign Missionary Convention came to us in the presence and greetings of so many of our heroic workers from the field: Mr. C. E. Randall, Miss Olivia A. Baldwin, Miss Oldham, Mr. and Mrs. Gordon, Dr. Butchart and Mr. R. W. Hunt. These all delighted us with their evident joy in the service of the Lord. Unquestionably our convention was of one mind as to the efficiency of all our secretaries; they are doing noble service for the Lord, and we take just pride in the success of their work. The standard for this year is $150,000 for Foreign Missions! For American Missions the work set before us is $100,000! Beloved, these works are easily within our reach. Let us ever go far beyond them in the grace of giving to the Lord's cause—the salvation of men. We must not fail, either, along the line of Church Extension. That $250,000 *must* be in this fund by the end of 1900. It was shown by the reports that the Disciples of Christ, with their comparative paltry sums, are doing relatively seven times more in turning men to the Lord than any other people in this country. If the simple gospel as the Disciples preach it wins men so readily, should we not support that gospel even more liberally than ever before?

***

The Christian Woman's Board of Missions showed the best year's work of their glorious history. Their missions are all prospering and hopeful. Their work is constantly growing, both in America and foreign lands. Greater emphasis was laid upon their English Bible Chair work than usual, which was a natural result of the substantial encouragement recently given to that work at the Virginia University. Bro. Cary, of Richmond, son of the late Col. John B. Cary, of blessed memory, has given recently $10,000 toward a fund of $50,000 for the support of the English Bible Chair work at Charlottesville. This fitting monument to the memory of Bro. John B. Cary, the foundation of which is laid by a grateful son, should be speedily completed. We are glad to hear of this good work at Charlottesville. It will do our cause good throughout Virginia.

***

One of the most blessed of all the General Convention privileges is the spiritual and social fellowship afforded those in attendance. The old-time acquaintances are renewed, and new ones are formed, which in succeeding conventions will be sweetened and strengthened. The Chattanooga Convention was especially delightful to me because of having lived and labored in that city as pastor at one time. Many friends of former days were there, but some have gone on before to the general assembly and church of the first born in heaven. Chattanooga entertained the convention right royally. Cincinnati says we must have 10,000 delegates at the semi-centennial in 1899. S. T. WILLIS.

1281 *Union Avenue.*

Pittsburgh Letter.

The annunl convention of the Disciples of Christ in Western Pennsylvania was held in the bustling little city of Connelsville, Sept. 20 to 22. Owing to your scribe's typewriter being out of repair the report has been delayed, but hope it will be none the less acceptable even at this late date.

The Pittsburgh contingent, about sixty strong, left Pittsburgh in a special car headed by the ever energetic and Christly hearted president of the society, Robert S. Latimer, assisted by the imperturbable W. H. Hanna, of Carnegie, who hustled the tickets and change as though he had never preached a sermon or sung a gospel solo. The delegation was met at the train in Connelsville by representatives of the church who took good care of each and all, so that when the evening session opened, every one was safely housed and homed with the warm-hearted Connelsvilleians. Hearts and homes of these good people were alike open and the days of work and intellectual and spiritual feasting will long be remembered.

The Connelsville church edifice is a thing of beauty, a joy forever. It has only recently been completed, at a cost of nearly $30,000. From a small, struggling congregation the church has grown to be a power in the community. Great preachers have ministered here. Men who have entered into their rest, but who, being dead, still speak. Alexander Campbell won much of his fame in this district and made for himself the honored name and memory that follows him. Bro. W. R. Warren, a graduate of old Bethany, now labors here and is doing heroic work in what is known as a hard field.

The convention opened with an address by Herbert Yeull, of Banksville, with the suggestive theme: "The Coming Church: Its Relation to the Social Problems." Bro. Yeull made a strong and radical address, showing wide reading and careful preparation. He said the church of the future will be a New Testament church, on broadest line, reaching and helping all classes, even as did the Lord Christ in the days agone.

Bro. Warren, in the evening of that beautiful first day of the convention, gave as the keynote John 16:14, glorifying Christ.

An address by O. H. Philipps on "The Strength and Weakness of the Disciples" was, from a literary standing point, most masterly and scholarly. With careful conservative thought he pointed out the strength of the Disciples in their loyalty to the Word and their evangelistic spirit and obedience to the commands of Christ. No less carefully did he speak of our weaknesses. His address must have been prepared while in the spirit of prayer.

Your scribe then had the pleasure of presenting a stereopticon sermon on baptism.

Wednesday morning President Latimer made his annual address. For ten years he has been president of the W. P. C. M. S. In that time over 40 churches have been organized, with over 5,000 additions as a result.

The reports of Financial Secretary Bullard and Treasurer Errett were received, showing that during the year there has been a total of $1,690 raised for work in the district. Nine mission points have been established, of which seven, with an approximate membership of 787, raised over $10,000 to carry on their work. The report showed that 94 cents of every dollar contributed to the work is applied directly to the field, the remaining six cents being used for car fare, postage, etc., by the financial secretary.

During the year four new buildings have been erected and dedicated—Confluence, Scotdale, Beaver and Connelsville.

Dr. I. A. Thayer gave a timely address on the making of a preacher, that fairly bristled with good points.

Wednesday afternoon was devoted to the C. W. B. M. The ever faithful secretary, Mrs.

C. L. Thurgood (thoroughly good, some people call her) reported a membership of 1,005, representing 54 societies. Reported $1,937.61 sent to Lois White and Mrs. Julia A. Evans. The Junior Bands, through Mrs. F. F. Bullard, presented an interesting report, showing 1,590 enlisted in the work and 90 added to the church during the year. The sum. of $895.31 was raised by the Juniors for the work, both state and national.

The old board of officers, consisting of Mrs. T. W. Philipps, president; Mrs. C. L. Thurgood, secretary; Mrs. F. F. Bullard, superintendent of Mission Bands; Mrs. Julia A. Evans, treasurer, was re-elected.

Wednesday evening Bro. W. L. Hayden, the veteran, who was present as a happy bridegroom, and introducing to all his bride, made a great success with his now widely known address on Alexander Campbell.

Thursday morning Bro. Marshall, of Belle Vernon, enthusiastically told the story of the devotion of the Apostle Paul to his work, inciting his hearers to emulate the noble example of the great missionary of the cross.

The Y. P. S. C. E. and the Sunday-school sessions were great features of the convention, and many valuabie suggestions were made as to the furtherance of the work.

The convention closed on Thursday evening with ringing addresses by W. H. Hanna, on "The Quiet Hour;" C. L. Thurgood, on "The Tenth Legion," and W. J. Lhamon, on "Americanism and the Endeavor Movement."

The following officers were elected: President, R. S. Latimer; vice-presidents, T. J. Allen, D. C. Evans, W. H. Graham, T. W. Philipps, John Barge; secretary, J. H. Craig; treasurer, W. R. Errett; corresponding secretary, W. H. Hanna; superintendent of Bible-school work, John A. Jayne; superintendent of C. E. work, Mahlon H. Wilson; superintendent of Children's Home Mission work, Miss May Netting; chairman program committee, W. J. Lhamon.

Two preachers have taken unto themselves brides recently and were present, W. L. Hayden, of Edinburgh, and E. A. Hibbler, now located at Johnstown.

The enrollment committee presented their report, showing 144 present as delegates and 35 places not represented.

PITTSBURGH POINTS.

The Knights' Templar Conclave was a great success, from an artistic, electric and financial standing point. More than 2,000,000 people were estimated to be in the city the day of the great parade. Pittsburgh knows how to handle a crowd.

J. H. McSparren, formerly of Glouster, begins work with the W. P. C. M. S. as evangelist, with a meeting at Scotdale.

O. H. Richards, of Beaver Falls, has returned from the Klondike.

F. A. Wright has taken up the work at Homestead, while J. F. Futcher has gone to Duquesne.

John L. Darsle has taken up the work of raising funds for Bethany College.

JOHN A. JAYNE.

No. 1 Chester Ave., Allegheny, Pa.

Kansas City Letter.

If any readers of the CHRISTIAN-EVANGELIST have missed my accustomed letter for the past month or so (and what scribe does not try to persuade himself that his silence is noted?) they will perhaps be interested in knowing that I have been laid up for a few weeks by a severe hurt to my right knee and ankle. The accident came just in time to prevent my attendance at our state convention at Nevada, and national conventions at Chattanooga. I have been rejoiced to learn of the goodly attendance, splendid reports and unbroken harmony that characterized both these gatherings.

I have not spoken for some time of our local affairs, and it will be in order to report progress in our Kansas City churches. Bro. Geo. H. Combs is steadily leading his splendid church at Sixth and Prospect, up to higher ideals and accomplishments. This church has now the largest membership of all our congregations. Bro. H. A. Northcutt begins a meeting with them in a week or two, and they are hoping and praying for large results.

Bro. A. W. Kokendoffer has been for many years the beloved pastor of Forest avenue church, and each year seems to strengthen the bone between him and his people. His church is steadily growing, and is the second in point of membership among our churches in this city.

Bro. E. W. Thornton is proving the right man in the right place, in his work with the South Prospect church, and the good people of that congregation are learning to esteem him very highly in love, for his work's sake. There is every reason for encouragement as to the future of his labors here.

Bro. T. P. Haley has been serving the Springfield avenue church as pastor during the past year, to their unbounded joy and profit. This is one of the mission churches of our city whose history has been one of constant struggle for existence. The strong leadership, wise direction and inspiring preaching of Bro. Haley have given new heart to the faithful workers, and the membership has already been substantially increased. Their outlook is brighter than ever before in their history.

The West Side church is being ministered to by Bro. B. M. Easter. perhaps the youngest pastor that Kansas City has ever had. He is doing a very fine work there, and is developing much power as preacher and pastor.

Our City Missionary, Bro. F. L. Bowen, has done a wonderful work during the past year, and our three missions are constantly growing in every way, through his ministry. He has added over a hundred by baptism during the year. We expect to continue his work next year, and anticipate yet larger results.

Bro. T. J. Dickson has been preaching for the Westport and Sheffield churches for a few months, and the interest is growing at both places. They anticipate an excellent winter's work.

Our brethren across the state line, in Kansas City, Kansas, have five congregations, including the suburbs of Armourdale and Argentine. Three of these have houses of worship, and all have or expect very soon to have pastors. Bro. J. M. Kersey, of Washington, Pa., has been secured as pastor by the Central Church, and begins his work December 1st. Bro. C. M. Wickham has just dedicated a new chapel on the north side of the city, and his congregation is rapidly growing. The Armourdale church, so long and acceptably served by Bro. W. H. Embry, is now enjoying the ministry of Bro. Elmer Davis, whose labors promise to be entirely satisfactory. Bro. Hanley and Bro. Phillips are preaching for the Argentine and Riverview churches, and we hear good reports of their work. All in all, the cause of primitive Christianity seems full of promise in these twin cities.

The State Christian Endeavor Convention was held in our city last week, the sessions being held simultaneously in the First Christian and First Congregational churches. Much of the time both churches were crowded to overflowing, and the spirit of the meetings was all that could be desired. The societies of our own churches were well represented, and brethren A. B. Phillips, of Fulton, C. M. Chilton, of St. Joseph, and W. H. McClain, of St. Louis, filled creditably their places on the program. The state secretary reported 254 societies of the Christian Churches, the Presbyterians following with 153, the Cumberland Presbyterians with 97, and the Congregationalists with 60, placing us easily in the lead. But it is known that we have at least 400 societies in this stase, and nearly this number have reported to our own state secretary, Bro. F. R. Stutzman. If all these would have reported to the interdenominational secretary, our showing would have been correspondingly goo There are 1,226 C. E. Societies reported in t state, 436 of which are Juniors. No doubt t full number would reach over 2,000, if all r ported. The feature of the report received wi greatest enthusiasm was the conversion 2,763 associate members during the year. Wh a blessed spiritual influence going out from o Endeavor Societies does this fact suggest!

W. F. RICHARDSON.

Kansas City, Mo., Oct. 25, 1898.

A Resting Spell.

During the session of the district missionar convention in this city last week I hear among many good things, an experience relate by Eld. C. C. Smith, of the American Chri tiad Missionary Society, in his address befo the convention, which will bear repetition. was the occasion of the would-be resting spe of his, of a few days, on one of our Norther lakes, but I will endeavor, as well as I can re member, to quote Bro. Smith's own words, an I will only add that if his *active* spells were a effective in proportion as the *resting* spell Bro. Smith must be a power for the promulga tion of the "doctrine once delivered to th saints:"

"I was just starting off," Bro. Smith be gan, "on a little trip up the lake for a brie rest, and the steamer started pleasantly an gaily on her way. The day was superb, th scenery sublime, and all nature combined t render the occasion delightful to me. I kne nobody on the steamer and I was just no thankful for this fact, as you know, brethren we are sometimes. I sat down on the dec resolved to take my ease, and to indeed le things go as they might—

'The world forgetting
And by the world forgot.'

In a few minutes an old gentleman cam along by me and pushed a small paper in m hand saying, 'Read that.' I did not take to this disturbance of my was-to-be rest very much, but I took it and glanced at the title, which was, 'What Ingersoll has to say about the Presbyterians.' Well, with a sort of unexplained perversity which will sometimes impel humanity to seek to find out what somebody has to say about their neighbors I read it. After awhile the old gentleman came along again, and seeing me asked, 'Did you read that paper?' 'I did,' I answered. 'Well, what did you think of it?' querried he. 'Well, it's about like all emanations from Ingersoll,' I answered, 'a little truth mixed in with a great deal of error.' 'What! where is any error in that, sir?' snapped out my pumping interlocutor. Well, I saw I was in for it, and that I must meet the issue. I began with all the earnestness I could to show the fallacy of Ingersoll's reasoning, and the impregnable foundation of Christianity, and I suppose before I was scarcely aware of it I was hammering away pretty lively. Anyway, in a very few moments I discovered that I was backed up against the outside of the cabin and was surrounded by nearly the entire number of people on board the little steamer, some two hundred or upwards, who stood around with evident and opened-mouthed interest. When I saw that my rest for the time, at least, was thus knocked into smithereens I told the old gentleman that as he had started me into this thing he had to give me half an hour in which I would tell what Jesus and his gospel had done for humanity, and then I wanted him in another half-hour to tell what Ingersollism or infidelity had done for the people. He agreed, because he saw from the looks of the bystanders that it would be best to do so, and I put in my best licks for that time in doing so, and to a most attentive audience. When I got through the old gentleman used but very little time. He didn't seem to have as much to say as he thought he had. Most all he said was of a sneering and sarcastic nature concerning creeds, their human origin, hypocrites, etc., and finished by asking with best attempt at withering scorn, 'Now t's *your* creed; I know you've got one?' :hren, didn't I feel good just then? Here when our noble plea stood me well in 1, and I endeavored to use it for all it was th. 'I have no creed,' I answered. An est confession of faith in the Lord Jesus ist and obedience to his commands is all I or my people ask, and a plain, common-ie interpretation of the New Testament is cient for every intelligent human being to vell informed as to his duty.' My audi- crowded around me with questions as to my rch or my people whose tenets seemed en-ly new to them, and I verily believe there was another person on board that vessel that was iainted with the Disciples of Christ save elf. I answered all to the best of my ity and after a while, when the crowd had ut dispersed, the old gentleman who started affair came along back by where I was sit-', glanced at me and said: 'I had a con- awhile ago on religion with a fellow up here leck and I want to see him again.' 'Well,' l I, 'I guess I am the fellow.' 'Why, I i't know ye,' said he; 'you've got your hat ' Then I realized that I had been doing all talking and preaching with my *hat on!* said he wanted to show me the pictures of two little grandchildren and to tell me that ioped that I wouldn't think him in every ect bad. Ah, my hearers, my heart e a leap for the cause of the blessed Jesus ch I had tried to uphold. Ah, thought I, onscience is galled from his late experience rying fo belittle all that is good of this day age, and he is trying to make amends for I looked at the pictures and talked to him best I could to make a friend instead of a of him, and I think I succeeded, for at the nent of separation, at the landing, where were all to disembark, he took me to one and asked me to advise him about a board-house and the best way to use a few spare s, etc. From that hour's talk until the of the two or three days' voyage my time taken up with explanations of our plea, and naking many new acquaintances, quite a iber of whom were pleasant indeed; but my ing spell was completely used up in the old t's assault on me, but I do not look back n that experience with any degree of regret t such was the case."

R. J. TYDINGS.

Vashington, D. C. Oct. 11, 1898.

The Other Side.

here is a large and increasing class of read- of the CHRISTIAN-EVANGELIST who will not satisfied with the sentiments expressed by B. T. under the caption, "The Possession Use of Property," in the CHRISTIAN-ANGELIST for Aug. 4.

et it be understood that we esteem B. B. as a brother beloved and a father in our iel, but at the same time maintain with mness that his sentiments regarding the do not answer to the urgent call of prop- reform.

'Abraham," says he, "was rich, Isaac rich, Jacob was rich. Their descendants possess enormous wealth. The obituary David in the Holy Bible reads as follows: of the gospel came by special revelation. H was not taught by man. The Lord Jesus in structed Paul. In his doctrine he correct represented his Master. It is the opinion some students that Saul of Tarsus was gentleman of ample means. He said muc about money—its use and abuse."

Poor Paul! We were shocked recently being told that in Athens he "trimmed" h discourse to suit his audience, and now, for purpose, he is classed with the rich—a millio aire, perhaps! It may be that he had a m nopoly of supplying the Roman army wi tents and got immensely rich by a wi "management." Hear his words of burnin sarcasm and indignation:

Already are ye filled, already ye are becon rich. Ye have reigned without us. Yea, an I would that ye did reign, that we might al reign with you. For I think God hath s forth us the apostles last of all, as men doome to death. * * * Even unto this prese hour we both hunger, and thirst, and a naked, and are buffeted, and have no certa dwelling-place; and we toil, working with o hands (1 Cor. 4:8-12).

As poor, yet making many rich; as havin nothing and yet possessing all thing (2 Co 6:10).

This is the "gentleman of ample means; and listen to what he says:

Godliness with contentment is great gai for we brought nothing into the world, f neither can we carry anything out; but havin food and covering we shall be therewith co tent. But they that desire to be rich fall in temptation and a snare and many foolish an hurtful lusts, such as drown men in destructi and perdition. For the love of money is th root of all kinds of evil; which some reachin after have been led astray from the faith, an have pierced themselves through with ma sorrows. But thou, O man of God, flee the things. (1 Tim. 6:7-11).

Hear James, who was also instructed by th Lord Jesus:

Hearken, my beloved brethren, did not Go choose them that are poor as to the world be rich in faith and heirs of the kingdo which he promised to them that love hin But ye have dishonored the poor man. I not the rich oppress you, and themselves dr you before the judgment seats? Go to no ye rich, weep and howl for your miseries th are coming upon you! Your riches are co rupted and your garments are motheate Your gold and your silver are rusted, and the rust shall eat your flesh as fire (Jas. 2:5, 5:1).

And to quote the writer, "This is in perfe harmony with Jesus when said:"

Woe unto you that are rich! for ye have r ceived your consolation. Woe unto you th are full now! for ye shall hunger (Lu 6:24, 25).

We make these quotations of Scripture show how easy it may be to plead on both sid of a question if we choose to pursue the [suc methods. It is an improper use to make of t Bible, and no one should know this bett than the venerable brother who has thus us it in making a special plea.

The great need of the day is not an apolo for wealth or an eulogy on poverty, but t earnest and complete preservation of God truth touching social and economic righteo ness, that a public conscience may be creat which will undo so much of the present ind trial system as makes it possible for a few m to become immensely rich at the expense the laboring people. And it will never done by mild repetitions of commonplace p

friends and relatives. I have known Bro. Dunlap since 1882. It was a great privilege to renew our acquaintance. He is a famous man in prohibition work as well as in other gospel work. He preached one sermon in Oskaloosa, which was greatly enjoyed.

Last week Mrs. Geo. Turner, of Marshalltown, passed away. This is a great loss to a beautiful and a hitherto happy home. She leaves a noble husband, a lovely daughter and a promising son to mourn her departure. A host of friends will mourn with these. But a beautiful hope—a hope as strong as beautiful—will sustain them.

Mrs. C. C. Rowlison, of Marshalltown, will conduct a great Sunday-school rally in Oskaloosa on Oct. 30th. A. M. HAGGARD.

The Bible College at Columbia.

Are the members of the Christian Churches of Missouri awake to their educational opportunities? It is difficult to believe they are. What are the facts?

It is not my purpose to call in question the usefulness of other colleges, or to interfere in the slightest degree with any support they may command. Indeed, I should like to know that all our colleges in the state are in a most prosperous condition. There is no need for rivalry with respect to any of our institutions. There is room for all; and there is use for all, provided they can secure the necessary support. But it must be apparent to the merest tyro in educational matters that too much division, in this respect, is as bad as too much division in anything else. It is better to have one or two good colleges, thoroughly equipped and liberally sustained than to have fifty half-manned and half-starved. Nevertheless, the plea which I am about to make has little or nothing to do with the other colleges of the state. The "Bible College of Missouri" occupies a unique position. Its work does not come in conflict with other colleges at all, but practically supplements them. This will appear evident to any one who will take the trouble to investigate the facts of the case. The time has come when these facts should be clearly made known.

During the two years and a half of the Bible College's existence 467 pupils matriculated, without counting the present year's enrollment. At the close of the present year the grand total will not be less than six hundred. This, I venture to say, is the best showing ever made in a similar institution; and yet this number might have been increased very largely, if I had encouraged the attendance of young men who wished to take the Bible study, but who were not sufficiently advanced to enter the University, or else did not care to take academic studies at all. I could have had a hundred young men at this time in the Bible College studying for the ministry on the following conditions:

(1) These young men to be allowed to enter the Bible College without taking academic work at all, or else taking only a partial course in the University.

(2) These young men to be supplied with preaching stations, or else some other means secured by which they could pay their way while at Columbia.

(3) These young men to be guaranteed the Bible College diploma within two years, provided they should make reasonable progress.

Now I want the brethren of the state to know that I have rigidly set my face against this whole business, and expect to discourage it as long as I occupy the position I do. Indeed, I do not hesitate to say that I prefer to have one single student each year studying for the ministry, who will at the same time take the academic course in the University, than to have a hundred less than half-educated young men who are seeking the advantages of the Bible College as a sort of introduction and recommendation to a ministry which must, in the present age, be largely a failure, though it may answer the ends of an ambition which has neither the courage nor the insight which is necessary to eminent success.

These remarks must not be construed as in the slightest degree reflecting upon the brave, earnest and useful preachers who have done so much to make our reformatory movement wha it now is, notwithstanding many of them have had little or no academic education, such as is within the reach of every young man who now aspires to the ministry. The men who served the past generation cannot serve the present one. We must now have an educated ministry or we cannot hold our place in the van of religious movements.

What, then, can be said in favor of the Bible College at Columbia? This much if nothing more: It has placed at its disposal, for academic purposes, a University with an equipment which would cost at least *five millions of dollars*. Now, if it can be shown that the use which we may have of this University serves us better than if we owned it ourselves, surely that fact alone ought to justify the location of the Bible College near to it. If we owned the University we should have to find the money and the men to keep it going; we should have all the anxiety of investment, management, discipline, etc., etc. But none of these things trouble us now. We have all the advantages with none of the disadvantages. If there are any blessings we have these "without money and without price;" if there are any troubles the University authorities must dispose of these as best they can—we have nothing at all to do with them.

It is simply impossible to provide a University like this unless we have millions of dollars to invest in it; and yet, without something equal to it in educational facilities we cannot educate our young men for the ministry in a manner commensurate with the needs of the age. The time for our little half-equipped colleges has passed. We have reached the day of great universities. Whoever does not understand this fact fails to perceive the most prominent characteristic of the age.

What, then, will our brethren in the state do? The usefulness of the Bible College could be almost immeasureably augmented if we had suitable buildings erected upon the lot which has been purchased for that purpose. Considering the number and wealth of the brethren in this great state it is difficult to understand how a problem like this can remain unsolved for a single day. It seems to me that there ought to be a spontaneous contribution of at least a hundred thousand dollars to this enterprise the moment our brethren in the state can be made to understand its importance. Other religious people are already planning to take possession of this important field. The Presbyterians and Baptists may soon be here. *We are already on the spot.*

Possession is not only nine points in law, but it is more than nine points in this case. We must not lose our opportunity. What do our brethren in the state say to these things?

W. T. MOORE..

Columbia, Mo., Oct. 21, 1898.

A Love Feast of Evangelists.

DEAR EDITOR:—I wish to tell you about a love feast which was held in the Chamber of Commerce, at Chattanooga, one night, after the regular convention session. It was one which will make history. Evangelists were the participators, principally, but there were many sympathizers present.

It is well known that for years past our papers have permitted thrusts at evangelists to appear from time to time. No names, of course, have been mentioned, but in some instances the references were too plain to be mistaken. The word "professional" as applied to evangelists has become a common club which numerous disgruntled pastors use with evident delight. The result is seen in a widening breach between pastors and evangelists. It is worthy of note in passing that not one of our leading evangelists has ev written one word for publication detrimental any pastor or the pastoral relation, but on tl other hand hundreds of "write-ups" ha appeared from their pens commendator There is no doubt now and then an unwortl evangelist. But are there not unworthy pa tors? And because some weak brother beli his profession occasionally, must the mar noble men who have given the best years their lives to the rallying of thousands of sou to the cross be branded wholesale as a cla that will bear watching?

Again, there is a little fad springing up favor of what is termed spiritual revival No additions, but a good, sweet little tin with the church folks, pastors of other churcl es participating, etc. Such meetings alwa have and always will prove failures, not ev accomplishing their advertised purpose many instances. Any pioneer preach among us can vouch for the statement th there is nothing in this world that will so edify congregation in every way as a genuine, ol fashioned protracted meeting, with scores additions.

But, arguments aside, a number of us car to the conclusion that if evangelists were excrescence, fit only for the pruning knife public opinion, or to change the figure, expensive piece of unnecessary furniture in tl house of God, the sooner we all quit the fie and assume pastorates the better. Ma have already done so from various reason and the rest are willing to do so if it is wror to continue the work they have been trying do. In order to arrive at some understandi of the situation, a meeting was called at tl Walnut Street Church for four o'clock Monday afternoon, at which all evangelis and those interested in evangelists we

dly number attended
ı now recall J. V.
F. MacLane, Victor
C. C. Browning, C.
tenberger, W. J.
erger, E. W. Darst,
ngham, G. A. Hoff-
l O. P. Spiegel. J.
the chair and Geo.
ary of the meeting.
in a general discus-
ame quite warm. A
inally appointed to
n and report at the
ioned in the first
ee, which consisted
MacLane, Victor W.
net and deliberated,
ed that it seemed to
nother organization,
nly accentuate the
widen the breach
is urged that the pas-
it to get together at
and talk over their
ter understanding of
ion of warmer ties of
e sense of all present
presentation on each
ple are pre-eminent-
and our evangelists
an any other class of
erests of all depart-
e work, and yet an
an unheard-of thing
gatherings. S. M.
the following resolu-
animously:
his meeting that we
nutes on the annual
Convention for the
it of evangelism by
ul evangelists.
retary of the Home
doubt hereafter our
rge that we would be
sections, and he saw
not have a half day
or open parliament,
an arrangement may
ee Convention next
of the meeting ex-
l the feeling prevail-
bygones, and evan-
d fully realize that
). Smith proposed a
d them—petitions of
of our common Mas-
ve feast. Long will
remembered by those
vas to be present.
that hour continue to
rk of the consecrated
ıded in the Lord's
.
ır afternoon meeting
collection and put up
ı—"100,000 souls for
." The money was
nner looked down on
next morning. It is
re that two years ago

Are We Overloading?

In a previous article we pointed out what seems to be a dangerous tendency in evangelical churches. In some of these churches it sometimes requires as much time to make the announcements for the week as it formerly required an apostle to preach a gospel sermon. One of the results of this crowding process we think is to dishearten church members and to scare away sinners. A few saints may have grace enough to stand the pressure, but the ordinary church member and common laborer whose time from Monday morning to Saturday night is required to earn bread for his family will not likely keep spiritually warm under the load. But we have other burdens than those mentioned, to which we invite attention in this paper.

We mention, first, the care of the poor. Somehow it has come to be generally believed that it is the duty of the church to assume the entire care of the poor, the sick, the unfortunate, the widow and the orphan. This is certainly a dangerous doctrine. Much of the poverty, distress and suffering in the land comes from bad legislation and legalized evils. To make the church a dumping ground for the results of corrupt legislation and corrupt governments has not the shadow of righteousness in it. And for godless politicians to run governments in such a way as to grind out a continual stream of paupers, dependents, widows, orphans and others, expecting churches to care for them and then decry Christianity should they not care for them is a species of audacity too brazen, base and barbarous to be for a moment conceived of as a part of any civilization, much less of Christianity. The state should care for its own products, and if the burden is too great, let the proper steps be taken to decrease it and not put its bad results on the church under the name of charity. Such a doctrine let loose would soon of itself become a burden which all the churches combined could not carry.

That such poor ones should be cared for until such conditions can be prevented is unquestionable, and that church members should share in the burden as citizens of the state is just, but that the church should assume the whole burden of caring for all that the operations of unjust laws or legalized evils have made poor, sick, unfortunate, husbandless and fatherless in the land, is neither reasonable nor just. This is the function of the state, and the churches have burdens enough of their own without assuming these at present alarming ones. The churches should inculcate that spirit in the hearts of their communicants and of all people that builds homes, hospitals, institutes, schools and other charitable institutions for the unfortunate, but they ought not to be expected to assume the entire cost of building and maintaining such institutions. Neither should the churches be made cities of refuge for those reduced to penury and want by the oppression of capital, syndicated or otherwise. For organized capital to press wages to a point below living expenses and then expect the churches to supply to these

unable to work from sickness
to the sweet charity of the chu
community. For humanity's sa
es assume burdens of this kind, b
morally bound to play the role
for the convenience of capital, n
able to carry the load. The ch
more helpful to the world in othe

Another danger that sho
observation in this discussion is
incompetent preachers who ar
living off the churches. Some
a rule of hiring the cheapest
comes along, and this becomes
for men who cannot earn a livi
else to preach. It is a commo
ignorant and lazy men seek the n
a man is an imposition upon
community. Some of them ar
doubt, but sincerity is not the on
needed for a successful ministry.
will leave his family in destitute
to preach the gospel violates o
laws of nature and of the gosp
imposition upon any church or
have to support such a man and h
greatest burden of these men to
however, is not the salary they r
as it is their hinderance to the
put Christianity in a humili
before the world.

These remarks apply also t
preachers. Men should not go
try for a living. It is an impo
churches and a hinderance to
There are other callings as
ministry.

Next to an excess of incomp
fessional ministers carried by
the overproduction of denomin
They are generally called colleg
and universities, but many of
rank with the public high scho
in which they are located. B
have a living endowment; mos

bearers, but burdens in their hinderance to the cause they profess to have espoused. This burden upon the churches is enormous, and unless leavened or thrown overboard may lead to serious results. And now we leave the question, Are we overloading? for you to answer. We have tried to present the situation as it is seen and discussed in the lower ranks. In our next we shall point out another from this point of view, seemingly hindering cause, to wit, harmful antagonisms.

F. T. PEW.

Texas Letter.

F. N. Calvin, of Waco, after a long pastorate in that important city, resigns his work. There is some talk of his leaving the state, which we hope is not true, for we need just such men in this new field.

B. B. Sanders takes the field as financial agent under the state board. His former success in this sphere inspires the hope that our mission work will now receive a new impetus. Sanders is a strong man, well known and much loved, and we expect this hope to be realized.

J. V. Coombs, of Indiana, is assisting C. McPherson, of the First Church of Fort Worth, in a good meeting. We are glad to have a new man from that region come down into "Dixie," and we hope he will come again.

The death of Dr. Henry Biddle, our medical missionary to Africa, is a sad thing to all, but especially to us down here in Texas. His companion, Ellsworth Faris, a Texas boy, and son of a Texas preacher, is now left alone in the heart of the Dark Continent; and yet he is not alone, for God is with him. Our prayers go out for the sorrowing ones who have lost a loved one, and for the brave, consecrated boy, bereft of his colaborer.

J. F. Newton, pastor of the First Baptist Church, of Paris, has resigned and united with the First Christian Church, of that city. He is a young man of twenty-two years, and graduated at Hardy Institute in 1893, and at the Southern Baptist Theological Seminary, of Louisville, Ky., in 1897. Bros. Faris and Holsapple, who know him well, speak in high terms of his character as a man and of his power and promise as a preacher, and say that his investigations after truth have led him to take this step. We bid him a hearty welcome and wish him the greatest success in his new field.

At Georgetown recently an old man went forward and grasped the hand of the preacher, Bro. Naylor, his own blind son, and made "the good confession." It was a most affecting scene. This reminds me that my father made this confession after he had passed his threescore and ten years.

The San Antonio church, under the direction of their pastor, Geo. B. Ranshaw, has organized a Gentleman's Aid Society, which holds regular prayer-meetings for men only. The ladies of the church abbreviate the title, and smile when they call it the G. A. S. Society.

Miss Bertha Mason, of Houston, becomes C. W. B. M. organizer in place of Dr. Olivia Baldwin, who returns to the foreign field. Miss Bertha is popular, consecrated and industrious, and hence will succeed.

R. B. Harwood, one of the Central deacons, has a godly house. He and his Christian wife train their children in the nurture of the Lord. A beautiful evidence of this was seen in the Sunday-school a few days since. The baby was taken to the school the first time. She was much interested and seemed somewhat disappointed, and after gazing all about the room, she looked into mamma's face, and asked, "Mamma, where is Jesus?" She had heard so much about Jesus in connection with the Sunday-school and church that she expected to see him there.

S. M. Martin, the beloved evangelist of California, is in his second meeting with us at the Central Church. He was here six years ago, and we had a fine meeting. We are hoping for a better one now, and it begins well.

D.

The Bethany C. E. Reading Courses.

The management of the Bethany C. E. Reading Courses takes pleasure in announcing that the second year of its regular work is opening under very favorable auspices. Although there have been some unavoidable delays in issuing the books for the second year's readings, they are now ready for delivery, and they will sustain the high standard set by the handbooks for the first year. In planning these reading courses, the attempt is made to give a bird's-eye view of each field, in the introductory handbook for each course, and then to take up in each field for special study the subjects of most value and interest to our own people; just as an intelligent traveler visiting Boston, for instance, would first ascend the Bunker Hill monument to secure a bird's-eye view of Boston and the bay and the surrounding towns, and then descend to give special attention to points of special interest.

In pursuance of this plan, our introductory book to Bible study entitled, "A Guide to Bible Study," gives a bird's-eye view of the entire Bible, from Genesis to Revelation. Its sixty-six books pass in rapid review under the skillful hand of Professor McGarvey. Our introductory book to the study of missions, prepared by A. McLean and entitled, "A Handbook of Missions," gives a bird's-eye view of Christian missions from New Testament times to the present. It is a masterful condensation and presentation of this profoundly interesting subject. It has been pronounced by competent judges the best book of its kind in the English language. Our introductory handbook to the study of our own plea for a return to the old paths, gives a bird's-eye view of the religious conditions necessitating the plea, the heroic pioneers who made it, the principles which guided them, the success which attended their labors, the subsequent rapid growth of the movement and its present status. This handbook was prepared by B. B. Tyler and is entitled, "Concerning the Disciples." It is an excellent snmmary. These are the three books with which all readers should begin. One dollar pays for a year's subscription to the Bethany C. E. Bulletin, a sixteen-page quarterly, and these three books. All orders should be sent to the Bethany C. E. Company, 798 Republic Street, Cleveland, Ohio.

The handbooks of the second year, present subjects of chief interest in our three chosen fields. In our Bible study, for instance, we take up the life and teachings of Jesus, and use the handbook bearing that title, prepared by Professor H. L. Willett. The handbook is divided into two equal parts: Part I. presents the life of Jesus in its outward activities, and Part II. presents a summary of his incomparable teachings, grouped under such titles as "Jesus' Teachings Regarding God," "Jesus' Teaching Regarding Man," "Jesus' Teaching Regarding Himself," "Jesus' Teaching Regarding the Kingdom," "Jesus and Judaism," "Jesus' Teaching Regarding the Future," "Jesus' Teaching About the Holy Spirit."

The mere mention of the subjects ought to awaken a widespread desire to read this handbook. In our study of missions for the second year, we have a handbook entitled, "Missionary Fields and Forces of the Disciples of Christ." This handbook has been prepared by that devout student of missions, our own W. J. Lhamon. This handbook tells what we are doing, where are doing it, through whom we are doing it, and how we are doing it in every department of our missionary enterprises at home and abroad. Never before in our history have we had such a complete and concise presentation of our missionary fields and forces. In addition to its charming narrative concerning our own work, it has five brief but admirable chapters on the various forms of religious faith and superstition which confront our forces on foreign fields. In our study of the Disciples for the second year, we have

a handbood entitled, "Sketches of Our Pioneers," prepared by F. D. Power, of Washington City, and who among us is better fitted to write such a handbook? It is a graphic rehearsal of our heroic period. Before us pass Stone, the Campbells, Walter Scott, followed by John T. Johnson, John Smith, Samuel Rogers, the Creaths, Bently, Henry, Raines, Hayden, O'Kane, Goodwin, Hoshour, Mathes, Allen, Hopson, Lard, Burnet, Richardson, Shepard, Pendleton, Bullard, Coleman, Shelburne and Isaac Errett. How important that all our people, old as well as young, cherish the memory of these eminent servants of the Lord! Who can estimate the value of such a study to our young people and to the cause which they must soon represent before the world? These handbooks and the Bethany C. E. Bulletin are sent to any address for one dollar. All orders should be sent to the Bethany C. E. Company, 798 Republic St., Cleveland, O.

It would be a great mistake to limit these readings to our Christian Endeavor Societies and to our young people. They are suited to all. They deal with subjects concerning which all our people should be informed. These handbooks are meant to create a demand for larger and more exhaustive works. They are placed at the lowest possible price, in order to put them within the reach of all. The plan of reading undertakes to utilize the spare moments in busy lives so as to enrich them with definite knowledge. Even where circles cannot be formed, these readings can be successfully carried on. Many pastors are finding it very helpful to preach on the subjects presented in the handbooks, and thus sustain the interest of the members of the churches in their private reading. In many places the C. W. B. M. auxiliaries takes oversight of the work. In a few places the Bible reading is carried on in connection with the Sunday-school. The management of those courses has no stereotyped plan to suggest, but prefers leaving that

ose con-
hurches.
the first
ken up at
take all
t one or
done so
ter to the
nd then,
r reports
Republic
TYLER.

'Quite a
asked me
ur Rainy
ack. In
be many
enumer-
es (we all
ome is a
their feet
hungry.
and the
quer this
prefer to
fruits of
pposition
are some
ey think
Galileo's
capital),
y by the
y broad-
pt things
xpect the
expenses
hey have
ad of the
to culti-
the flies
vork, by
and seek
heir fail-
'' in dis-
ttention,
a great
a great

for a kit
tools, or
and some
ch'' at a
voods are
all need,
objection
coming
boats and
forest is
t thereof
to paint

o off dis-
erzealous
them to
ving been
ful, level
uch like
e mowed
they see
other new
prairie is
nothing
re on the
over the
l means,
when he
s bad as
e almost
edes and
exas, for

they almost wish they could do as the Quaker did when he laid aside his broad brim and gray coat till he whipped a man that told him a—falsehood. But be patient, dear brother. When that promise was made the promiser really hoped to have these things, but those of us who have had the work to do have had our hands full helping to make the roads and get a little clearing done so as to put up our houses. We have made the start and the line is ready for the hack, and the boarding house is in process of construction, and we *hope* to have the sawmill in the near future. There is a great future for this country, and *we* ought to take advantage of this opening to make ourselves *felt* as an important factor of that future. To this end we should be very careful not to make any mistakes. Don't come for selfish purposes alone, and if we can't ''endure hardness as a good soldier'' we are not fit for a new country. Neither should we become so zealous as to overstate anything in connection with it. The plain, simple truth is what we as a people plead for, and when that is told every honest, industrious man will know he can have a home on the best of soil in a country very suitable for such an enterprise, with a climate as fine as can be desired.

Yours in Christ, J. CAREY SMITH.

Emo, Ontario, Sept. 17, 1898.

Seventh Anniversary.

Last night the members and friends of the Main Street Christian Church, Mason City, Ia., gathered to celebrate their seventh anniversary. The house was full, the enthusiasm high, the rejoicing great, and never did a church have more reason for devout joy and gratitude. The year has abounded in blessings and peace, and good-will and activity has reigned supreme.

The report showed an increase of 237 new names during the year, 27 letters have been granted and six have passed over the river; net increase of 204. There were 693 names a year ago, making a total membership now of 897. Of these, 175 are non-residents. The clerk's report showed a steady and rapid growth since the organization, October 25th, 1891.

The treasurer's report showed that a little more than $3,500 had been raised and about $150 was paid to missions, not going through the regular channels. This is an increase of contributions of about $1,000 over last years. Added to this the amounts collected by the different departments of the church—Bible-school, C. W. B. M., Junior and Senior Endeavor Societies and Aid Societies—swells the offerings to a grand total of over $4,200, or an average of over $80 each week for the whole year, or about $5 from each man, woman and child in the congregation.

This is the more remarkable when it is remembered that there is not a rich man in the church, but that nearly all are in very moderate circumstances. The auditing committee reported the books and accounts of the clerk and treasurer carefully examined and everything found correct.

The Bible-school report showed an average attendance of officers 90 per cent., of teachers 82 per cent. In these two facts is the secret of much of the success the school has achieved. The total attendance for the year was 11,493, an average of 297 per Sunday. Ninety persons on an average carried a Bible each Sunday and the same number studied the lesson. The total receipts of the school were $291.83, or nearly $6 each Sunday.

The home department was organized in January, with 10 visitors, in as many districts. They have secured 109 scholars who agree to study the lesson at home. These have given

under one year, twenty-one under two and twelve under three years, and four have passed their fourth birthday and w ready for the primary class next year. babies have contributed $1.04.

The three missions under the fostering of the church were then reported. Walter L. Martin, the pastor at Lincol Burchinal, reported these. The Lincoln gregation has contributed $193.82 their organization December 26 with fort members.

The Southside mission Bible-school reported by the secretary and treasurer, Ida Poyfair. The school was organized M 20, 1898. There has been an average at ance of sixty-two and an average weekly off of 71 cents. Other money was received socials, picnics, etc., making a total of $ for the seven months of the schools exist

The assistant pastor, Walter L. Ma made some appropriate and feeling remar this point, explaining that his health mad resignation imperative. He expressed high estimate of the church, and his e ment in its services. He leaves next wee his home in Kansas; then he goes to Vaca Cal., to begin his new work, the third L day of November. There is universal reg his departure. His character and ser have endeared him to the whole church.

Mrs. Jennie Long sang a beautiful after which Mrs. Hastings read the rep C. W. B. M. The auxiliary has ninety members and has contributed $150 for mis this year.

The Y. P. S. C. E. was reported by secretary, Lola M. Martin, and shows a m bership of ninety-one and $62.61 raised.

The Junior C. E. report was read by Drake. It was of the most cheerful na showing a membership of one hu and twenty-one, the largest in Iowa, offerings for missions, Home and Forei $46.47. Mrs. Height is the efficient sup tendent.

The two ladies' aid societies reported $1 raised, besides a large amount of chari work done among the poor. Their lates to the church was the railing around th pit platform, and a most elegant set of p furniture.

The pastor's report showed 150 ser preached, 10 lectures delivered away home, two protracted meetings held, pastoral calls, 203 persons baptized, 35 rec by letter, 13 marriages and 17 funerals. A $500 was contributed for missions. It i lieved the church was never in better c tion. He urged redoubled diligence fo coming year, and that the church sh advance on its knees, with its hands i hand of Omnipotence.—*Mason City Times*

A Preacher Wanted.

Bro. W. T. Henson, who has served church here for the past five years has resi to take effect with the close of the year. U his able ministry the church has prosper all departments. Never in the history c church has it had a preacher that was popular with church and people. We reg lose him and his faithful wife. The ch will be open for engagement with some man for one-half his time.

J. M. SETT

New Franklin, Mo.

Sulphume has a vaporous and vol sound to it, and it certainly seems destin ''blow up'' many of the nostrums that ar cepted as remedies by this confiding pu

Notes and News.

Texas Christian Lectureship

With the Main Street Christian Church at Waxahachie, Texas, Monday, Nov. 14, to Thursday, Nov. 17, '98. Reduced rates on railroads. Free entertainment. The best program yet presented. Prof. J. W. McGarvey discusses themes of vital importance. Come. Send your name to E. H. KELLAR.
Waxahachie, Texas.

A Minister Called.

The church here has called Bro. W. H. Coleman, of Carlisle, Iowa, as its pastor. He will begin as soon as he can make the change. I write this that many others who have sent in applications may take notice and govern themselvs accordingly. J. F. FISHER, Elder.
Rossville, Ill.

A Growing Church.

The church here has engaged for the coming year Bro. C. A. Hill, the present pastor. He is doing a grand work here. The church is in a very prosperous condition, both spiritually and financially. Pay pastor and all bills promptly every week. J. D. JOHNSON.
Canton, O.

A New Circular.

David Husband, pastor of the church at Olivia, Minn., has designed a new circular for advertising a protracted meeting which they are just beginning with C. M. McCurdy, State Evangelist, preacher, and T. A. Meredith, song leader. The circular contains the names of all kinds of business in the form of a cross, with Christ over all, and Scripture references to principles upon which each should be conducted. It is unique and suggestive. It illustrates applied Christianity.

Jacksonville, Fla.

The Christian Church in Jacksonville, Fla., has recently secured a most excellent lot in a central part of the city, and will enter upon preparations to build in the near future. The lot procur-d is a very valuable one and most admirably located. It has a dwelling on it which will be remodeled and used for the present as a place of meeting and until the church is ready to build. Although but six months old, this church is manifesting much enterprise and is already wielding a marked influence in Jacksonville. There is a constant increase in attendance and the most favorable comment is heard from those attending the services. The church will be known as the Adams St. Christian Church.
T. H. BLENUS, Pastor.

Dedication.

On Lord's day, Oct. 16, I preached the opening sermon and dedicated a new and beautiful house of worship at Glen-Easton, Marshall county, W. Va. We raised money enough, cash in hand, to pay all debts, besides a handsome list of pledges, which can be used for church purposes. It was a day of mighty triumphs for the church at Glen-Easton. Several other new houses are being built in this part of West Virginia. A bright day has dawned upon the cause of primitive Christianity in West Virginia and the churches are making commendable progress.
L. L. CARPENTER.
Wabash, Ind.

Nebraska District Convention.

The meeting of the 10th Nebraska district was held at Gering, October 14, 15. This is a large district; some 17 counties, with but few churches and fewer preachers, so that the cause is not in the best shape. The attendance was small, but we have a few good workers. The convention went off smoothly. The office of corresponding secretary was left to be filled by the board when a suitable person can be found. Bro. B. F. Thomas, of Crawford, was selected as district organizer. Gering, Neb., is in need of a preacher. Bro. J. M. Eads has resigned and expects to go to Denver. This would be a good place for some young man who could accept small things and be willing to grow up with the cause.
GEORGE LEAVITT.

Palmyra Progressing.

Our work here is moving along nicely. We have just put a new carpet on our church floor, removed the chairs and seated our auditorium with handsome new pews. We have organized a Bethany Reading Circle. Our Endeavor Society will observe Forefathers' Day, October 23. Two additions by letter this month.
L. J. MARSHALL, Pastor.
Palmyra, Mo.

Sound Preaching.

The Pike County Democrat, Pittsfield, Ill., speaks of the line of fruitful work being done by R. F. Thrapp, pastor of the Christian Church of that city:

The series of evening lecture sermons now being delivered by Elder R. F. Thrapp, of the Christian Church in this city, is attracting large audiences and proving of special interest to those who hear them. The general subject of the series is, "The Land and the Book." They deal with a new line of evidence to the authenticity of the Bible. Last Sunday evening he showed the exactness existing between the physical characteristics of the land and the statements of the book. Those to follow will deal with some of the wonderful discoveries made in Palestine, corroborating the facts of the book. They exhibit wide reading and much research in the realm of scientific discovery.

Those Church Institutes.

EDITOR CHRISTIAN-EVANGELIST:—Dear brother, it is not often that I write for publication, but a short article in the CHRISTIAN-EVANGELIST of Oct. 20, by Bro. F. N. Calvin, of Waco, Tex., entitled "Institute Work Among the Churches," attracted my attention in a special manner. I have for years observed the chaotic condition in which many of our churches have fallen. We have congregations of several hundred members without influence and hardly capable of doing any good in their present condition. The "big meetings" we have been having for more than a decade have added numbers to the faithful, but have failed to add force to the churches in proportionate measure. The rocks have been quarried out by the blast, but they have not been builded together and fitted in the great temple. Builders, and not hewers; drillmasters, and not recruiting officers is the present need of the church.

I have for a number of years practiced law and preached in the neighborhood on Sundays. And while doing that I took an active part in politics, and have learned to appreciate the wisdom of organization and order. I have been preaching regularly for these last two years, and feeling the necessity of a more complete organization in the churches I have prepared a series of discourses along the line suggested by Bro. Calvin.

I hope that the successful Waco preacher may soon launch himself out on this new phase of the Lord's work and that others may follow.
J. C. FRANCE.

Board of Education.

The cause of education among us never did receive more or livelier attention than at the recent national convention in Chattanooga. The acting board of directors and the general convention supported the board's request for more representation on the state and national convention programs. Hereafter one full session (that is, a morning or afternoon or evening) will be devoted to the discussion of educational problems among us. This, as stated in the report, is not out of harmony with the original plan of Mr. Campbell, who felt the need in his own day of a common meeting-place where the cause of education, together with the cause of missions, would be defended. If this need was felt in that early day when all educational interests centered in one college under Mr. Campbell's personal supervision, how much more imperative is the need to-day when our colleges are scattered all over the country under varied conditions, and in accordance with various demands. The convention also felt and President Zollars in his address adequately proved that education is fundamental to missions, and is therefore appropriate to a missionary convention. The educational board appreciated the support which was given by so many of our prominent men in the attempt to give education its rightful place among our other interests.

Then the board was allowed a day in which to have the interests of education presented to the public through the pulpits of our people. *The board has selected the first Sunday in July as Educational Day.* Special literature preparatory to this day will be sent to all preachers and a general attempt made to "educate our people upon the subject of education." The early part of July is especially good because just then the men of the college faculties are free to go out in behalf of education and at the same time, the young people are making arrangements for the fall school work. All of this organization and agitation means much work now and ultimately a man to devote his whole time to the work.

The new board at its first regular meeting appointed Mr. Hiram Van Kirk as secretary. During the summer he carrted on this work during the absence of the regular secretary and is therefore well acquainted with the purposes of the board. Mr. Van Kirk's extensive training and successful experience as a preacher make him especially capable both to conceive large things for education and to wisely bring these interests before our people. The board bespeaks for him the hearty support of all our preachers in any attempt he may make to help the cause of the Disciples by more fully bringing to our attention its educational interests.
ALBERTINA ALLEN FORREST.

Decatur Push.

The Christian Tabernacle, Decatur, Ill., Geo. F. Hall, pastor, has a full-page advertisement of eight entertainments for the season. These are to consist of lectures, readings and music. Season tickets good for the eight entertainments are announced at one dollar.

Hiram College Jnbilee Endowment.

The great popular movement to adequately endow Hiram College on the occasion of its fiftieth anniversary, through the courtesy of our religious papers has been inaugurated. The call for the army of 50,000 persons who will give from $1, to $1,000 for this great object] has been made. The claims upon which this great call is based have been fully presented. In view of Hiram's past history, its work, its financial management and its traditions it is certainly worthy of all that it calls for; and the indications strongly point to a successful issue of this great movement. Already several hundred names have been secured. We confidently expect that before this article appears the first thousand milepost will have been passed. Do not neglect this matter or put it off for a more convenient season; send in your name at once. You can decide on the amount that you will give later, and if in the end you only choose to give $1, you will still have the satisfaction of feeling that you have given your name and influence in one of the most important movements that has been presented to our great brotherhood. The adequate endowment of our colleges is the most pressing matter that is before us at the

No money given in the line of ll yield such returns in good ac- Send us your name. "He who speaks twice."

E. V. ZOLLARS.

ndeavor Work.

or Society has taken it upon t our nice church building, and ays we will enter upon the erec- parsonage, next lot from the

L. SWINDLE.

al.

New Watchword.

tchword coined by the Chatta- tion for the Foreign Christian ciety is: $150,000 *for Foreign Mis, the Jubilee Year.* The re- r were $130,925.70, or a gain of gain this year of $19,074.30 will i0,000. Let us make the Jubilee le by large offerings for world- . It is not too soon to begin ach the $150,000. The friends of ould send personal offerings at church, Sunday-school and En- will rejoice to have fellowship nterprise during this glad year. ny thousands of dollars will be o the Foreign Society on the

F. M. RAINS, Treas.

0, *Cincinnati, O.*.

rful Endeavor Meeting.

at Murphysboro, Ill., is taking was called here five weeks ago very busy during this time in arranging our forces for work. it 175 members in all, some of rown cold, which is but natural h is without a preacher. We ithful and earnest workers as I they are strong in "the faith." splendid church building, fully all of the modern conveniences. ach separate week to some one ents of our work.

as given to the Endeavor work. d dwindled to 21 members. In added 32 more to our number, n more names would have been for sickness. Sister Lena Rey- ident of the society, proposed he last meeting. Next Sunday less than 15 more. We are now otracted meeting and intend to rd's day. Pray for us and the may have a large ingathering.

W. H. WILLYARD, Minister.

te Mission Notes.

nportant actions of the Chatta- ition was the appointment of a Mission Day, so that every state will take its offering at the same S STATE DAY IS THE FIRST SUNDAY

this was a wise action, as it tends ion of our work, and it ought to ch an awakening on the impor- te Missions as will push this to a much greater prominence ins. We *must* interest the peo- r the ministers; we must interest le, not simply a few. More and eing compelled to depend on the from the churches. When in utions for State Missions reached er mark of $11,104 $2,450 came berships alone. Bro. Quigley gent and collected $2,467.48, and general evangelists in the field ons were included in the money ate Missions, and this was $2,- was also in that year $662.45 State Mission treasury as being e, making a total of $5,108.33.

Then there was the annual members and the money raised at state convention, and district and county co-operations, so that the amount coming from the churches at large was not so great as it is now.

Now we have no financial agent; we employ no evangelists, whose collections swell the aggregate of the funds. Attempts to obtain life members are often met with the statement that they are paying through the churches, and the county and district conventions are, some of them, saying the same thing when asked for a collection for our work. Our receipts from life members last year is only a little over $600. We have no credits from St. Joe, like we had in 1892-'3, yet we raised more money than we did last year.

But the amount raised is totaly inadequate to the work to be done and we must enlist a larger number of our churches in the work of State Missions. Think of it: one church in Tennessee, and it is not a wealthy one, gives $500 for State Missions and to other missions in proportion. But it is not the large sum from the few that we are so anxious to obtain as a contribution large or small from every member of every congregation in the state.

Hence this National State Day has been appointed, and it is a good thing that it coincides exactly with the action taken by the Nevada convention, which recommended that the Missouri State Day be changed from the first Sunday in January to the first Sunday in November. Now let the preacher arm himself with facts concerning our great work and go

Light Bearers, gifts by individuals in behalf of a Band or Society, or other moneys, *when sent to the Builders' Fund*, be credited toward the payment of the shares apportioned to a Band or Society.

That a certificate of membership in the Builders' Fund, on which shall be inscribed the number of shares paid for during the year, shall be awarded to each organization paying for one or more shares.

That our young people be urged to make "a silver offering for the silver anniversary," giving their money toward their shares in the Builders' Fund; and that every young person giving one dollar for this work shall be awarded a certificate which shall be prepared for this purpose; and that the names of those securing these certificates be published in Junior Builders.

That the National Banner be awarded to the state that pays for the greatest number of shares above its apportionment; or, if no one succeeds in going beyond the apportionment, that the banner be awarded to the state that comes nearest reaching it.

That the basis of enrollment upon the Roll of Honor, *i. e.*, that a Society or Band make a larger offering to our missionary work during the current missionary year than it did last year, remain unchanged.

That the Junior Builders be enlarged so that each number shall contain twenty pages, the size of its present page.

That the support of the children in the new orphanage be recommended to the Intermediate Societies especially; and that all the young people be urged to bring this important work to the attention of Aid Societies, King's Daughters' Circles, Sunday-school Classes, and similar organizations; and also that they urge individuals who are able to do so to undertake the support of one of these children.

That the orphanage, schoolhouse and sick-ward building at Deoghur and the dispensary at Mahoba, India, be builded as soon as possible; that the needed repairs in Jamaica be granted, and that the $1,500 asked for for the chapel at Oberlin be allowed if $300 additional be raised on the field; and that such other needed buildings be erected as the Builders' Fund will provide for.

That great attention be given to the work of organizing new Societies and Bands, and that untiring efforts be put forward to win those already existing not co-operating with the C. W. B. M. into fellowship with the Young People's Department, and that earnest efforts be made to secure a greater interest on the part of the Auxiliaries in the work of the young people.

MATTIE POUNDS, National Superintendent.

306 *Delaware St., Indianapolis, Ind., Oct.* 22.

Our Gray-haired Pastors.

EDITOR CHRISTIAN-EVANGELIST:

Dear Brother—With great pleasure I observe that the attention of the brethren is being called to the existing condition of things in our midst with regard to our older pastors. The fund for the assistance of these tried and faithful pioneers of the Restoration movement, is practical evidence of our interest in and thought for them, and it certainly deserves greater prominence and larger support from our brethren. God bless the dear old men who have done so much to prepare the way for us to do more, and imbue us with the grace of giving to their assistance. But it is of the pastors referred to in your last issue (Oct. 20), gray-haired but unimpaired for Christ's service that I wish to write here. The disposition complained of, to shelve older men and to call in younger men to the pastorate, is neither local nor peculiar to any body of Christians, but rather to the present age in all Christendom, with, of course, a few happy exceptions. That it is unscriptural and un-Christlike, we all know, who give the matter due consideration, but a remedy for the wrong it is not perhaps easy to prescribe. Might it not be well, however, to search for the cause, finding which we may be better able to determine the best method of dealing with the trouble. There are perhaps two reasons why young men are in such demand, the first of which is economy. Many congregations are seeking a pastor, or rather a preacher, without having adequate means to support one, hence they call a young man, who either has not prepared himself for the work, or has just emerged from college, because they can secure his services cheap. The churches partake very much of the spirit of the times, and want their religion, like their drygoods, done up in bargain lots, and young untried men are eager to make an engagement at a salary that would not support a pastor with a family. But the second and chief reason for the neglect of older pastors for younger ones, even though the latter should dearer than the former, is the preponderance of young people in official positions and in the councils of our congregations. While it is true that the church for centuries sadly neglected the young people, it is equally true that the church of to-day has gone to the other extreme and given the young people undue prominence and importance, to the serious injury of the church as a whole. I do not lay the blame for this state of things at the door of the young people; it is probably the result partly of a reaction from the former condition, and partly of apathy and indifference among the older brethren. But from whatever combination of causes it comes, the result is an unevenly balanced church, and the result of this result is that the young people who largely control the congregations, will not have any but their own style of men for pastors, hence the neglect of the older men. Is there a remedy for this state of things? Undoubtedly there is. How is it to be accomplished? By getting more of the love of Jesus in our hearts, so that all, both young and old, will readily submit to whatever is for the honor of Christ's name and the advancement of his cause. How shall we secure this spirit of love? By thinking constantly of all that Jesus has done for us, of his great love to us; and then by thinking of the service that these older men have rendered, and the invaluable experience they have acquired. We shall be led to recognize their true work as pastors, and to continue them in the work until they are totally disabled. Another feature of this question is that many men are really worn out before they ought to be, because they commenced work too early. They were too impatient of training time, and the church was not careful for them. I honestly believe that for every year that a young man spends in active preaching before he is twenty-five, he loses two or even sometimes more years after he is forty. Let us begin to take more care of our young students, and instead of calling them to preach, give them full time and opportunity to prepare for their life work, and the next generation will rise up and call us blessed, for having preserved to them pastors of rich and ripe experience combined with vitality and power. Yours, J.

Over in Kansas.

DEAR BRETHREN:—I am taking a vacation from my home (Eureka, Kan.) congregation for a few weeks to attend the Kansas state meeting and to do a little work under the direction of the Kansas state board. I find Kansas conventions, boards and field superintendents, especially O. L. Cook, fully abreast of the times and wide awake. Am endeavoring to save the cause at Arkansas City—big debt, no pastor and a bad case of blues. One confession last night. Give us your prayers. Yours in the faith,

DANIEL TRUNDLE.

Arkansas City, Kan., Oct. 29, 1898.

Jasper County Convention.

The churches of Jasper County met together two evenings and a day, Oct. 26th, 27th, at Webb City. Bro W. T. Hacker, the pastor, and his charge entertained royally, and there was a joyful time and a profitable. Bro. Abbott infused much of his "missionary conscience" into the meeting, and as always, was just the man for the emergency. The second evening the house was crowded and a deep interest manifested. The young people were in charge, all were enthused. Next meeting at Jasper City. District convention here Nov. 28th-30th. Fourteen counties, don't forget.

W. A. OLDHAM.

Carthage, Mo., Oct. 28.

Changed Churches.

On last Lord's day, 23rd inst., the Rev. John A. Copeland, a prominent Methodist minister, was baptized by Bro. A. R. Miller, pastor of the old South Side Christian Church, Tonawanda, N. Y. The following local notice of the event appeared in the Evening News, of this city:

Rev. John A. Copeland, formerly a Methodist, was baptized last evening by Rev. A. R. Miller, of the South Side Christian Church. Rev. Copeland preached a very acceptable sermon to the congregation. He is well known as one of the most eloquent ministers in Western New York. He will enter the missionary field.

Bro. Copeland expects soon to visit the Middle and Western States, and it is hoped that the brethren will accord to him that Christian greeting due to his calling in the Lord's work. E. EVANS.

SUBSCRIBERS' WANTS.

Miscellaneous wants and notices will be inserted in this department at the rate of two cents a word, each insertion, all words, large and small, to be counted, and two initials stand for one word. Please accompany notice with corresponding remittance to save book-keeping.

Evangelistic.

INDIANA.

Ladoga, Oct. 24.—Our meeting one week old. House crowded and many turned away. One confession to date. We expect a grand meeting. My singer, Prof. C. M. Hughes, can be had for another meeting before the close of the year. We have a large chorus class, with piano and cornet, and the music is one of the interesting features of the meeting. —W. T. BROOKS.

Jeffersonville, Oct. 25.—M. Myers has just closed the most interesting meeting in the history of our church during which a number of our most prominent citizens were baptized. Bro. C. C. Cline led the music. Bro. Myers is now holding a meeting at the Clifton Heights Church in Louisville.—HAYES L. SEWING.

Seymour, Oct. 27.—Our meeting here goes grandly on over all opposition. Voted last night to build at once. Will be here for two or three weeks longer. Last week I was called to Lexington, Ky., to solemnize the rites of matrimony between Mr. Jessie, of Bowling Green, Ky., and Miss Maye Taylor, sister to W. B. Taylor, of Chicago, and niece to the writer.—H. C. PATTERSON, state evangelist.

Morocco, Oct. 24.—There were two more additions to our church last Sunday afternoon. Our cause is growing rapidly in this commuuity; 22 members have been added by baptism since we began our labors with this congregation in June, and 70 during the preceding year. We have not arranged definitely for our meeting in Morocco this fall, but expect to have it in November. The church house will no longer accommodate our Sunday-school, so we contemplate building in the spring.—R. L. CARTWRIGHT.

Franklin, Oct. 28.—Eight were buried with Christ in baptism at my last visit to Mt. Gilead. Our young people organized a Y. P. S. C. E. The first collection taken for Church Extension. Twenty have been buried with Christ during the month at the three churches for which I minister.—WILLIS M. CUNNINGHAM.

CALIFORNIA.

L. Swindle, of Glendora, reports 24 additions to the church at that place during the past year.

MICHIGAN.

Shepherd, Oct. 25.—Just closed a three weeks' meeting at Clay Hill with 20 additions; five from Methodists and Methodist families. Left work in a prosperous condition.—MEADE E. DUTT, district evangelist.

MISSOURI.

Trenton, Oct. 23.—Three additions here since last report. I declined to entertain a call from the church here for another year. My work close with the year. The church is united and a good field for a good man.—GRANVILLE SNELL.

Lamonte, Oct. 24.—There have been six additions here since last report.—KING STARK.

DeKalb, Oct 24.—Our meeting at Wallace, Mo., was closed by the blizzard. Commenced meeting yesterday; one confession at morning service and one at night. Hope for large results.—JNO. P. JESSE.

Macedonia, Oct. 24.—Just closed a good meeting of two weeks, which resulted in 18 accessions; 13 by baptism and five from other churches. The preaching was done by Eld. W. A. Hopkins, of Liberty, Mo., and was with power and sympathy.—RICHARD OWINGS.

Paris, Oct. 23.—I held a ten days' meeting with the church at Illinois Bend, Adair Co., but had to close on account of bad weather. Have just received a telegram calling me back to continue the meeting; will return on next train. We had 31 additions up to the 15th Oct.; 25 by confession.—JACOB HUGLEY.

Bro. Winders, of Columbia, is assisting Bro. Phillips in a protracted meeting at Fulton, with large audiences and 14 additions to date.

Kansas City, Oct. 28.—Our meeting in Sheridan is booming; 70 additions and prospects fine for more. This is in the Nodaway Valley district. Bro. E. E. Lowe, who will graduate from Drake University in June, is pastor, and is aiding. His work has made such a meeting possible. I hope to give this district the best years of my life.—T. W. COTTINGHAM, district evangelist.

OKLAHOMA.

Oklahoma City, Oct. 24.—Coombs and Hunsaker are assisting O. P. McMahan in a meeting here.—A. O. HUNSAKER.

UTAH.

Ogden, Oct. 24.—We had one addition this week. Our work in this difficult field is doing reasonably well.—J. H. BAUSERMAN.

ARKANSAS.

Hebron, Oct. 20.—There were three added to the church at Gurdon in a meeting just closed.—E. S. ALLHANDS.

Springdale, Oct. 27.—At the morning service on Lord's day, Oct. 23rd, there were nine accessions to this congregation; three by letter and six by confession. At prayer service last night there were three confessions and seven baptisms. We have recently added a splendid brick baptistery, which was largely the gift of our brother, Prof. J. H. Shinn. We are greatly encouraged to go on.—CHAS. E. FREEMAN.

ILLINOIS.

Colchester, Oct. 23.—Our meeting closed after four weeks with 25 additions; 20 were by baptism. Bro. D. J. Elsea helped me the last two and a half weeks, and I recommend him to any one wanting the assistance of singer.—F. M. BRANIC.

Watseka, Oct. 26.—Four have been added to our numbers here during the last two weeks. The mission Sunday-school in West Watseka is full of promise; S. F. Swinford is superintendent and L. F. Watson assistant superintendent; both splendidly equipped men.—B. S. FERRALL, pastor.

Champaign, Oct. 28.—Baptized two at Ludlow recently.—DR. W. FRANK ROSS.

Clay City, Oct. 24.—Am in a meeting here two weeks old. House full of people, town full of prejudice, and myself full of rheumatism. Sixteen baptisms to date.—W. E. HARLOW.

Sumner, Oct. 27.—I closed a 10 days' meeting at Bone Gap, Ill., on the 26th with 13 accessions; 10 were heads of families.—FRANK S. HALTONE.

KENTUCKY.

Junction City, Oct. 22.—My meeting at Junction City resulted in 31 additions. The preaching at Mt. Vernon resulted in 19 additions. I am now in a meeting at Petersburg.—IRA M. BORWELL.

Stanford, Oct. 29.—Twenty-six additions to date. My next meeting will be with Bro. Geo. H. Combs in Kansas City, Mo.—H. A. NORTHCUTT.

KANSAS.

Council Grove, Oct. 24.—One confession yesterday. We will protract over 30th if not longer. Much better prospect for success than we had in our eight days' meeting in August, which resulted in six baptisms. The membership here is 12 larger than at the begining of my work, early last June. O. L. Cook will be with us 26th, 27th and 28th.—J. A. WALTERS.

Mina, Oct. 20.—F. L. Pettit held a meeting for us closing, Oct. 2nd, with 11 additions. We generally had a full house, especially at the close. Bro. Pettit held a meeting for us about a year ago with 21 additions.—H. F. DETWEILER.

NEBRASKA.

Arapahoe, Oct. 28.—I spent the third Lord's day in October with the brethren at Stanford in Harlan County. Had two additions; one from the Baptists and one confession. I am now ready for protracted meetings wherever I may be called. Address Arapahoe, Neb.—C. F. EVANS.

MINNESOTA.

Cleveland.—Our meeting closed last night with a full house. Results of meeting, 25 added by letter, statement and confession besides results that cannot be estimated. We go to Le Sueur.—S. GREGG, T. H. SWEETMAN.

Family Circle.

Let Me Try.

Wise Duty moves me to believe
'Tis noble only to achieve;
Attempting draws a blessing nigh
To brave the hearts of all who try.

What if life-storms dissolve in air,
Our luring prospects growing fair?
There's peace defeat cannot deny
To bless the unknown souls who try.

One's great as what he tries to do,
And good as his conviction's true;
Men gauge us by the heights we scale,
But God by what we try, tho' fail.

If others soar the topmost height,
And we've not wings for lofty flight,
Let's climb the summit ere we die,
And learn God helps the weak who try.

No earnest effort proves in vain,
For e'en through failure's fires we drain
The dross that cankers sterling worth,
And leaves the purest coin of earth.

If marble shaft do not proclaim:
"He lives immortal here with Fame,"
This nobler tribute's not denied
To any striving soul: "He Tried!"

—*Andrew M. McConnell, in Alkahest for October.*

Text Stories—XVI.

THE OBEDIENT TEST HIS PROMISES AND FIND THEM TRUE.

BY ALICE CURTICE MOYER.

And being fully persuaded that what he had promised he was able also to perform.—*Rom.* 4:21.

"Standing on the promises that cannot fail,
When the howling storms of doubt and fears assail,
By the loving Word of God I shall prevail,
Standing on the promises of God."

The clear tenor of the young lawyer, whose office joined that of Judge Black, was most pleasing; but the judge smiled at the sentiment of the song.

Then came the chorus:

"Standing, standing,
Standing on the promises of God my Savior;
Standing, standing,
I'm standing on the promises of God."

"Standing on the promises of God, indeed!" exclaimed the judge. "I wonder what Smith has gained by it. I have never stood on them and yet I am called a successful man. How much of my wealth did God help me to gain? Not one cent. I have stood alone. I am under obligations to neither God nor man. I have earned every penny I possess alone and unaided. I ask no favors and extend none."

"Foolish man!" whispered the still, small voice of the soul. "To whom do you owe the health, strength and ability by which you have been able to gain these possessions?"

The judge shrugged his shoulders, and at this moment there was a tap at the door and his young neighbor, whose custom it was to consult with his elder and wiser friend on knotty problems of the law, entered.

The judge looked up, saying: "You seem happy this morning, Smith."

"I am always happy," was the reply.

"I believe you are. Would you mind telling me the secret of such happiness?"

"Not in the least. I don't believe I ever was one of the gloomy sort; but the date of my real joy began when I attended a funeral several years ago."

"A funeral!" echoed the judge.

"Yes; the funeral of Old Man Sin."

"Oh, I see!" said the judge, smiling. "You mean that your happiness comes from being a Christian."

"I do."

"Well, Christianity may be very well in its way. But what is there to be gained by it?"

"Life eternal."

"Oh, pshaw, Smith! You know what I mean. What is there to be gained from a worldly point of view? What have you gained by it? You are not rich."

"Not in the treasures of this world; no."

"You are unknown."

"Save to him who said: 'I am the good Shepherd and know my sheep, and I am known of mine.' "

"Are you Christians not rather conceited to feel so sure of your footing?" asked the judge.

"We are told to be ever ready to give an answer to every man that asks a reason of the hope that is within us."

"Oh!" said the judge; and then, after a moment's silence:

"Speaking of reasons, let me hear some of your best personal ones for being a Christian. I have plenty for not being, but I am willing to hear your side of the case."

"Well, some of the reasons that now come to my mind are, because I cannot live without Christ in this world of sin and sorrow and disappointment. I need his Spirit to keep me joyous and sweet-tempered and to give me patience in cross-bearing; because it would be dishonoring the Heavenly Father to refuse to accept the salvation he has provided for us; because religion makes me a kinder husband, a more affectionate father and a better citizen; because the Christian life is the only truly successful life and the only life that will lead me to eternal happiness. I may be always unknown; I may be poor always; but what will it profit a man to gain the whole world and lose his own soul?"

"You talk like a preacher, Smith; and I believe you are sincere, but it must require a great deal of faith to believe all this."

"Faith is one of the great Christian requisites. Indeed, we must have faith; without it we can do nothing. But believing that God's promises are sure, he will do according to his Word to them that keep his commandments. Knowing this, the Christian does not fear to undertake anything wherein he sees that good may come of it. By faith he removes mountains of difficulties; through faith he steps right out on the promises of God, and of course he cannot fail. Like Solomon he can say, 'There hath not failed one word of all his good promise.' To wholly believe in him is to sojourn in the 'land of promise' where, through faith, we are led on and on, reaping the bountiful harvest that faith alone can yield."

"Well, Smith, I can but admire your sincerity. No doubt you believe all you profess, but you are simply laboring under a delusion. I cannot see wherein I am remiss; I have never cheated anybody out of a penny; I am not a willful liar; I am a moral man. What more can you ask?"

"One thing yet thou lackest — obedience."

"And that is something I will not render if it means all this nonsense and fol-de-rol that it takes to get into the church. I stand on my morals, and when the time comes I expect to fare as well as anybody else."

The young lawyer's face flushed with feeling. Judge Black was a valuable friend. Dare he risk the loss of his friendship, the loss of his influence? Could he risk all in the defense of the cause he loved? Feeling that he must speak, 'though the heavens fall,' he said:

"My dear sir, you have been a good, true friend to me, and I thank you for it, but I must speak, and I trust you will understand that I mean no disrespect. First of all, I must tell you that the old theory of standing on our morals is worn threadbare—too threadbare to call forth the arguments that always destroy it. Second, that the expression of such a sentiment not only involves the utter lack of any consciousness of ill desert, but shows forth a most deplorable narrowness and shallowness of nature. What must be the condition of the man who is content to measure himself by his fellows, who rests perfectly satisfied in the belief that he is just as good as the rest of them, and expects to fare as well in the world to come? What a despicable display of self-righteousness! The Pharisees are not all in the church, my friend. Good-by."

Desperate cases require heroic remedies. All the argument on earth, as his young friend well knew, would not have had half the effect on this arrogant, self-sufficient man that these few words of righteous indignation had.

He sat perfectly quiet for a time, feeling decidedly small. Then, stepping to the door and locking it, he began a mental introspection of himself. He held himself up in all his littleness, and saw himself in all his narrowness. He weighed himself in the balance and found that he was sadly wanting.

"Smith is right," he said as last. "I acknowledge it. Strange I never saw it before. 'As good as other people,' indeed! What flimsy excuse! How little I must seem in the eyes of broad-minded people! How little I seem in my own eyes! However, as there is no convenient augerhole in which to conceal myself, the next best thing I can do is to become so large with new resolves as to burst this old shell of Pharisaical self-satisfaction and to come forth into the light of a broader life and of future usefulness. If the good Lord will accept me at this eleventh hour and will show me what to do, henceforth I, too, will stand on his promises." Then, for the first time since childhood, a prayer passed his lips:

"Lord, consecrate me to thy service.
Whate'er I have is no longer mine;
My life, my all, henceforth shall all be thine."

The sequel can be easily guessed. When we reach a point at which we can sincerely say, "Here, Lord, take me; let me no longer be a cumberer of the earth," we are going to do some good in the world. Like Judge Black, we are going to dig up our talents, rusty from long burial, and use them in the service of the Lord.

Even though our faith at the beginning may be small; as we try God more and more and find that he is indeed able to perform all that he has promised, our mustard seed of faith will grow until it is like unto a great tree of spreading, fruit-laden branches, inviting the passer-by to find shelter thereneath and influencing all who come near to consecrate themselves—their wealth, talents, occupation—to the great cause of Christianity; to sojourn in the "land of promise."

St. Louis, Mo.

Just Laura Ann.

J. BRECKENRIDGE ELLIS.

It's not because she's pretty,
And it's not because she's good—
For I've known her, at times, to rouse the neighborhood—
It's not the golden in her hair,
The heaven in her eyes—
Though sometimes you can see it dawn, a sweet surprise—
Not for this I love her well,
For no reason I can tell,
Except that she's
Just
Laura
Ann.

I have three other children;
The oldest one is ten—
As steady as the government is Ben;
And Fanny minds the baby well,
And never does complain,
Though she's but eight—when sitting long is pain.
The baby dosn't cry,
And that's the reason why
It's strange how I began
Loving so much
My
Laura
Ann.

She cried straight from her birthday,
Till she was two years old;
Then all the sicknesses in town took hold.
And she destroyed more furniture
Than any other tot—
Needed more spankings which she never got;
Tore, broke, and would declare
She didn't care!
Till it was strange a man
Could put up with
Bad
Laura
Ann.

When she gets so very headstrong
That she won't obey command,
The neighbors look they'd like to lend a hand.
And she's got the name of being
The worst child in the town,
For five years old, and has the crossest frown.
The kinfolks say how Ben
Will make the best of men,
And the baby—only wait!—
Will be famous in the state.
And they kiss my little Fan,
But no word for
Poor
Laura
Ann.

But when the day is over,
From labor I am free,
Who do you think comes, climbs upon my knee?
Who puts her arms about me
And shows the last sore place—
Tells how she fell into her last disgrace?
With head upon my breast,
Says she loves "papa" best,
But "mamma" just as well—
s there any need to tell?
No other than
Just
Laura
Ann.

Plattsburg, Mo.

The Slanderer.

J. W. LOWBER.

Evil-speaking, which is the language of the Bible for slander, is a crime of the deepest dye; it is cruel and properly ranks with theft and murder. We frequently hear these epithets, describing its malignity: "To rob one of his good name;" "to stab one's reputation;" thus stealing, slandering, stabbing, are closely associated in guilt.

In the slanderer you will always find the presence of a malignant spirit. It is a premeditated purpose to work ruin of character. The slanderer does not appreciate character as he has none of his own. He is extremely shy of his nefarious conduct. He shrugs the shoulder, and secretly acts out the villainy which he has not the courage to utter. He will quietly pour into your ear vile and detractive language, which is calculated to injure another, without letting you know the wicked intent. There is nothing meaner than the effort to injure another without the possibility of benefit on your part.

The slanderer frequently does his cruel work under the guise of friendship, as Iago proceeds to awaken suspicions on the part of Othello. The foul aspersions of the serpentine Iago against the guiltless Desdemona, so graphically pictured by the great dramatist, are realized almost every day in the drama of human life. The demoniacal person under the guise of disinterested friendship, stimulated with base envy, will sometimes cause great injury to the most innocent persons. It was through envy that the Son of God was slandered and delivered up to be crucified. If the Master was thus slandered, it is not surprising that his disciples meet with a similar fate.

The slanderer has not even one redeeming feature in his character. His work is one of selfishness, maliciousness and evil intent. A young man starts with fair prospects in life, but the slanderer determines if possible to defeat him. All at once, in a quarter vital to his prosperity, some adverse influence begins to operate. It is some time before he discovers that the poisoned breath of the secret slanderer has been doing the work. It is difficult for me to form a conception of a worse demon than the man or woman who, through envy, will secretly try to injure another.—*Christian Courier.*

A Geographical Rhyme.

The brewers should to Malta go, the Boobies all to Scilly;
The Quakers to the Friendly Isles, the Furriers to Chili;
The little crying, caroling babes, that break our nightly rest,
Should be packed off to Babylon, to Lapland or to Brest.
To Spithead cooks go or to Greece, and while the miser waits,
His passage to the Guinea Coast, Spendthrifts are in the Straits.

Spinsters should to the Needles go, Wine-bibbers to Burgundy,
Gourmands to lunch at Sandwich Isles, Wags to the Bay of Fundy,
Bachelors to the United States, Maids to the Isle of Man;
Let gardeners go to Botany Bay, and Shoeblacks to Japan.
Thus emigrate and misplaced men would then no longer vex us,
And all who are not provided for had better go to Texas.

—*Church Union.*

The Influence of Flowers.

Flowers not only are nature's "sweetest gift to man," but their fragrant presence quickens all the better impulses of the human heart. Philosophic students of natural laws are coming more and more to recognize the importance of the part played by environment in the drama of life, and of all the softening influences which may be found along mankind's rugged pathway, none possesses quite the power which it is given to flowers to wield.

The rythmic ripple of the smooth-flowing river charms never so soothingly as when its way lies between banks overhung with foliage and flowers. As the same river becomes a raging torrent, rushing madly through mountain gorge and canon, in impatient haste to reach its mighty destiny, the sea, suddenly its turbulence is quelled as it glides, none the less swtftly by reason of its noiselessness, through some flower-bedecked plain.

And so we find the mightier current of passion and desire which flows from every human heart yielding to the holy influence of flowers as it will to nothing else in all its environments. The man so fortunate as to have the fragrance of a flower-garden among his boyhood memories may be touched and softened through the medium of flowers, whatever the bitterness and iconoclasm the weary way of life may have forced into his heart. Even death, the universal conqueror, loses his arrogance as he sees the sting of his victory relieved by the flowers offered as the last tribute of love for the departed.

Flowers are always evidence of the rpesence of the spirit of kindness and purity, and the homes in which they are grown are homes where refinement and happines reign. The constant increase of interest in floriculture is the strongest possible argument in support of the belief that the world is growing better.

"The mission of flowers is to ennoble and unlift," we are often told, and it follows that those who extend in any way the borders of the floral kingdom are engaged in work that will tell forever for the benefit of human kind. Remember, then, that the pleasure you derive from your flowers is by no means the full measure of the good they may do. Whether it is in the crowded window of a poverty-stricken tenement or in the magnificent conservatory of a mansion, a collection of flowers is ever the source of an iufluence of purity, kindness and justice, which will extend afar, like sound-waves, if it is but given the opportunity.

"Not useless are ye, flowers, though made for pleasure,
Blooming in the field by day and night,
From every source your presence bids me treasure
Harmless delight.

"Your voiceless lips, O flowers, are living preachers;
Each cup a pulpit, every leaf a book,
Supplying to my fancy numerous teachers
From loneliest nook.

"Were I, O God, in churchless lands remaining,
Far from all voice of teachers or divines,
My soul would find in flowers of Thy ordaining,
Priests, sermons, shrines."

—*How to Grow Flowers.*

Kings of England.

Those who have once learned this jingle, which gives the names of England's kings and queens since the Conquest, have, no doubt, found it very useful. We suggest to teachers especially the helpfulness of such aids to memory as this old rhyme:

First, William the Norman, then William, his son;
Henry, Stephen and Henry, then Richard and John;
Next, Henry the Third, Edwards one, two and three;
And again, after Richard, three Henrys we see.
Two Edwards, third Richard, if rightly I guess;
Two Henrys, sixth Edward, Queen Mary, Queen Bess;
Then Jamie the Scotchman, then Charles, whom they slew,
Yet received after Cromwell, another Charles too.
Next, James the Second ascended the throne;
Then good William and Mary together came on;
Till Anne, Georges four, and fourth William all past;
God gave us Victoria—may she long be the last!

—*Zion's Herald.*

The Bridge Was Done.

Spurgeon was fond of this story, tak from our Civil War:

Once when the Union soldiers were r treating from the Valley of Virginia, th burnt a bridge over the Shenandoa Stonewall Jackson, who wanted to purs them, sent for his old bridge-build "Sir," he said, "you must keep men work all day and all night, and finish th bridge by to-morrow morning. engineer shall give you a plan." Old Mil saluted and withdrew.

Early the next morning the general se for Miles again. "Well, sir," said Jac son, "did the engineer give you the pl for the bridge?"

"General," said the old man slowly, "th bridge is done; I don't know whether th picture is or not!"

Now that is the kind of bridge-builde Mr. Spurgeon says we want in the churc —men to go right ahead with their ow work, no matter what their neighbors a doing.

Strong Testimony for Prayer.

I have found prayer a blessing far be yond my power to describe in the afflictio and sorrows of life. I can truly say th from a child God has sweetened many bitter cup, sanctified to me many a dee distress. If I had my life to live ov again I would not hesitate to commit it the same God, who has so graciously car for me.

If I could write the most charmin poetry, and the most fascinating music, could not produce a song fit to sing th praises of God's goodness to me in trial an affliction. No tongue can tell the wonde of God's grace displayed to his childre in answer to prayer when the night w dark and the storm beat hard. If the cu was bitter, it mattered less to know th this dear hand held it to our tremblin lips. If the way was long and hard, it w made a thousandfold more pleasant to kno that, though invisible, the Master walke at my side. And when the way led dow among the death-shadows and through th vale of tears where the heart ached, and th spirit was heavy with grief, and where w laid to rest the loved ones to whom o lives were knit with love, it helped us say, when he drew near in answer to pra er: "The Lord gave, and the Lord ha

be the name of the h I walk through the of death, I will fear rith me; thy rod and t me."—*Rev. A. S. ard.*

n Deeds."

easured by years,
ls we have done,
issed of their tears,
self we have won.
fe to its full,
been many or few,
nd loved by one soul
e tender and true.
in Alkahest for Oct-

ilanthropy.

CRAFTS.

form Bureau, Washing-
. C.

ome a science, but ard. The capitalist housands, of skilled oduction, but seldom ant to aid him in the e wealth God gives guments against the of wealth is that a imes as much to dis- .00,000, has even less it can be used most nly scientific aspect ne-giving, which is less than a tithe of From the days of God has taught men ime and one-tenth of gainst selfish uses. both, but that much is God's part as our himself ultimately, y, our nobler selves, therhood. "Liberty rely does not mean ian the Jews. How is not a new struggle draft on "the Lord's

sumed that the prob- has decided to give *what?*" is a ques- . One preacher has s of sermons to prove e whole tithe should mination. If in our s, as in the Jewish f all the education rms there would be n, but to-day much is done and by its one by Christians of nitedly. One's own ome first in the giv- national resolutions ments. Shall Chris- bute nothing to such k as the defence of overthrow of drink? k as the crusade of

Parkhurst's society is the only bequest worth mentioning to any reform society in a dozen years. Let us make our distribution cover the whole gospel as Christ preached it at Nazareth, which included social reform. In giving to philanthropic movements those who follow ruts without thought often bestow everything in charity and nothing in reforms, overlooking the fact that *reform is preventive charity.* When Mr. Roosevelt closed the saloons of New York on Sunday he thinned out the hospitals, reduced the calls for relief and increased the deposits in savings banks. If by more vigorous reform work we could stop or greatly reduce drinking, gambling, lust and Sabbath breaking, most of the hospitals and asylums could be turned into schoolhouses, of which we are short because preventable vices call for so many shelters that it uses up our taxes. It is easier and wiser to prevent than to repent.

Chenille Rugs.

ELSIE GRAY.

There is nothing that will improve the appearance of a room so much as several pretty rugs. It requires very little skill to get a good combination of colors, and when that is done very pretty and artistic effects may be produced. The rug I shall describe is a woven one, twenty-seven inches wide and one and one-half yards long. It is made of soft woolen pieces, scraps from the sewing basket, little bits that were left after piecing woolen quilts, children's old dresses and other things that could be used in no other way. They were cut in bias strips one and one-half inches wide and gathered through the middle on coarse thread. It is not necessary to sew the pieces together; simply lap the edges and gather through them. This twists upon the thread and looks like chenille. When one thread is gathered full another is tied to it and the work proceeds as before. It is better to cut all the rags and mix them thoroughly before any sewing is done, so the colors will be nicely blended. When you the colors required with diamond dye, and although it has been used constantly for several years, it is as pretty as when new. Light colors may be beautiful in themselve, but they should not be mixed with the rich dark shades, but gathered together and used for another rug. A pretty rug has a plain brown center, with a border composed of two shades of red and green on either end. Other combinations may be used to correspond with the furnishings of the room.

Pray for Others.

Have you grown weary of prayer, young Christian? Have you become careless? If you have, you are making the greatest mistake of your life.

Perhaps your selfishness has been developed by your praying; that is, you have prayed for yourself, prayed for your own needs, and confessed your own sins so much that you have grown more selfish. Begin to pray more for others. You have a desire to help others, and prayer is a successful way to do it.

"More things are wrought by prayer
Than this world dreams of. Wherefore, let
thy voice,
Rise like a fountain for me night and day.
For what are men better than sheep and goats,
That nourish a blind life within the brain,
If, knowing God, they lift not hands of prayer,
Both for themselves and those who call them
friend?
For so, the whole round earth is every way
Bound by gold chains about the feet of God."

With The Children.

Who Will Join?

Children, are you listening? That's right, because I am talking to you, and not to grown up men and women. Who of you would like to join the Advance Society? You don't know anything about it. Of course not. But I am going to tell you. It is a curious kind of society; you don't have to go anywhere to meet together; it doesn't matter if there is only one member in a town, and you are that member. There isn't any president or treasurer;]there are secretaries, for every member is a secretary. This is how it is:

Any one wishing to join must make five resolutions. He determines to—1. Read five pages of history or biography every week—textbooks do not count; 2. Memorize every week a quotation from a standard author; 3. Read once a week a poem of not less than thirty lines; 4. Read a verse of the Bible every day; 5. Have a blank book in which to record the amount of work done—in other words, be one's own secretary.

There you are—five resolutions. You merely say, "I will try." If you forget or neglect to do the work one week there is no great harm done. You can begin the next week. You can choose your own history, poem, biography or quotation; you may read in the Old or New Testament. You see you are not bound down by hard rules as in some societies. And when you have kept these resolutions for three months, send me your names, stating what books you have read and how many pages, and I will have your names printed in this paper in our list of honor. Now, remember, it is not fair to skip one week and then double your work the next. The aim of this society is to make people regular in reading and to get them to read the kind of books they ought to read. When you have kept the resolutions faithfully for twelve weeks, let me hear from you. It doesn't matter how much more you do than is required, but never do less. You will be surprised to find how much you can accomplish — good, solid reading, that will fit you to become wise and good and regular in thought.

While the society is for children, any one may join. You know there are grown-up people who always *feel* that they are grown up. They have forgotten how to play. That is the kind I meant when I said I was not talking to grown-up people. Now, children, you have seen big persons spend many hours with novels, who would be dreadfully bored over a history. That is because they did not get used to reading history when young. The Advance Society is to keep us from growing up just that way. Storybooks are all right. I like a good story when nobody dies at the end of it. But I take for granted you will read stories. No use to resolve to do that. And don't imagine the Advance Society will take your mind away from your studies. It won't take long to do everything required. Just an hour or so every seven days. That is not much to spend in training our minds for high things. Just as soon as you read this send me your name and age, telling me you will join the Advance Society. I will enter your name on the list of members in my own book. This is a society where no money is asked. If you want to make any suggestions or ask question, write to me, but be sure to enclose a stamp. I would like to hear from a hundred children in the next ten days. Will you not be one of these soldiers of progress?

But it is not all work in the Advance Society. We are going to have fun, and this is the way we are going to do it: I will name a subject for the members to write on, and those who care to will send me short articles on that subject. I will select from these and get up a splendid column or so in the CHRISTIAN-EVANGELIST out of their pieces, giving credit, of course, to each author. Here is our first subject: "The Funniest Thing that Ever Happened." I want all members to write me a brief sketch, telling me about the funniest happenings or the funniest speech they know of; something they or their friends have seen or heard. Won't that make a fine piece? I will pick out the very funniest of the stories sent us, put them all in one article and have it printed in paper.

Now, children, don't write too long a piece. But don't fail to write. If you never knew anything funny to happen—the idea!—at least you have heard your little brother or sister say something that was funny. I know something that happened that was so funny, just to think of it makes me laugh aloud, even if I am hungry! Now, everybody look out for that first essay of the Advance Society, "The Funniest Thing that Ever Happened!" It will come out in a few weeks. And perhaps I will tell my funny story with the rest.

Who will join in the fun, the work and the play? A member doesn't have to write for our column unless he wishes to, but he will enjoy what the others write. Let me hear from you at once. Address

J. BRECKENRIDGE ELLIS.

Plattsburg, Mo.

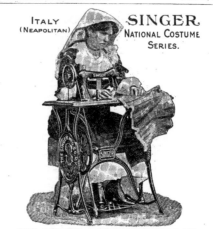

; Besant's South London and Tuna Fish-, by H. A. Vachell, are some of the in-esting themes and strong writers of the ent number.

he Living Age for October 22 translates n the leading Italian review, Nuova Anto-a, a striking article on the Present Condi-of Italy, which gives a vivid but despond-presentation of the social and political blems with which Italy is at this moment fronted.

the series of articles on the problems of opean nations appearing in the American thly Review of Reviews, "Ouida" con-utes a chapter of eloquent censure entitled n Impeachment of Modern Italy." In the e number of the Review (November) Signor chia publishes a defense of the Italian Gov-nent on the various charges specified by uida."

. going "From Denver to the Pacific," lter A. Wyckoff, in Scribner's for Novem-, reaches the end of his long journey across continent as a day laborer. This install-t, which closes "The Workers—The st," describes his adventures in the Colo-) mining camps and across the plains, and greatly extend its circulation. The leading articles in the new form are interesting.

The Youth's Companion, Boston, Mass., is probably the only periodical in the world seventy-two years of age whose first subscriber is still living and still a constant reader of the paper. The subscriber who enjoys this unique distinction is Mrs. Hannah M. Parsons, of Brooklyn, New York, now in her 85th year. She was the little sister of a friend of Nathanael Willis, father of N. P. Willis, the poet, and founder of the Youth's Companion. When Mr. Willis had resolved upon publishing a new paper for young people, his friend had him put down his sister's name as the first subscriber. The Companion's first issue was dated April 16, 1827, and for more than 70 years this first subscriber has continued to read and enjoy it. The volume for 1899 will be the best the Companion has ever published.

Christian Endeavor.

By Burris A. Jenkins.

TOPIC FOR NOV. 13.

CHRISTIAN RECREATION.

(Isa. 35: 1-10.)

Many people imagaine, especially perhaps young people, that in order to relax from work and welldoing, and to have a "good time," they must do something a little wicked. "Stolen fruit is sweetest," is a vicious saying. It is responsible for many a wrong, and many a heartache. It is never recreation to do wrong. Recreation is creating over again. When nerve force is spent, when tissue is burned up with work, then we need to be created over again, made new. But wrong-doing will never do this. Sin cuts nerves, pours out life force, brings weakness, lassitude and pain. One never commits a sin, but it tells on his physical life, and the wages of sin is death here and now. In proportion as we do evil, in that proportion we sow death. Wrongdoing is the opposite of recreation, it is destruction.

It follows naturally, then, that welldoing is recreation. Time need not be wasted or misspent in order that a worked-down frame may be made over. It is the most useful activities of life that are the pleasantest. It is the employment of our faculties in useful work, in welldoing that is most exhilarating. Nothing gives a child more pleasure than to race and run, to swing his arms and shout with his lungs, until the blood surges through his viens and all his body is aglow, and nothing could be more useful to him. It is his recreation and it is his work.

The most healthful thing a Christian can do for recreation, then, is to change from his usual vocation, to some avocation that will employ his powers, physical and mental, in some new way. Every Christian should have some chosen avocation to which he can turn in leisure hours for recreation, and turn eargerly. Some book should be kept near at hand which forever attracts us; some musical, athletic, photographic or other pursuit should always be waiting to allure our leisure into healthful activity. Evil thought will then find no roomt vicious and degrading amusements will not attract us.

With such wholesome activities, a life otherwise dreary or monotonous may be brightened. The wilderness and the solitary place may be glad for them, and the desert bloom and blossom as the rose. In this modern day when all things are furnished ready to hand for wholesome activity, no life need be tame or dull. "The joy of the working," as Mr. Kipling calls it, is the one great, abiding joy of life. The little poem with which he closes his volume of "The Seven Seas," is a healthy, exuberant expression of the belief that this joy is to be the keenest delight of heaven:

"When Earth's last picture is painted, and the tubes are twisted and dried,
When the oldest colors have faded, and the youngest critic has died,
We shall rest, and faith, we shall need it—lie down for an aeon or two,
Till the Master of all Good Workmen shall set us to work anew.

"And those that were good shall be happy: they shall sit in a golden chair;
They shall splash at a ten-league canvas with brushes of camel's hair;
They shall find real saints to draw from—Magdalene, Peter and Paul;
They shall work for an age at a sitting and never be tired at all!

"And only the Master shall praise us, and only the Master shall blame;
And no one shall work for money, and no one shall work for fame;
But *each for the joy of the working*, and each in his separate star
Shall paint the thing as he sees it, for the God of ings as they are."

Mr. Kipling throws himself very earnestly into life. His very recreation is a change of work. He spent a summer vacation once, flat of his back under the trees, reading the dictionary. This might not be an advisable procedure for most Endeavorers, but it shows the spirit with which one should throw himself into his employment. Earnestness in working! Dr. Thomas Arnold, when he assumed charge of old Rugby school, had all the old, time-honored boards, bearing the rules of the school, chopped down. The other masters held their breath. Such desecration, to them, was awful. But Arnold said to the boys, "Remember, boys, from now on there is but one rule at Rugby, 'Be Earnest.'" The boys were happy under that rule, and they loved its author with an ardent love. To be earnest in our work is to enjoy it. To give our whole selves to our employment is recreation in itself. Many a man has been kept alive by his work Many a man has rusted out and died, because he has retired from work. To take a new lease of life, to be *recreated*, then, is to make a change in one's work.

NOTED EVENTS.

The degree of LL.D. was conferred upon William McKinley, President of the United States, by William Harper, President of the University of Chicago, in Kent Theatre, Chicago, Oct. 17th.

The Emperor and Empress of Germany arrived at Constantinople Oct. 17th, on their way to Jerusalem. The Sultan of Turkey extended the Emperor of Germany a royal welcome.

The Dowager Dutches of Sutherland was robbed of her jewel-case containing gems, the intrinsic value of which is placed at $200,000. The robbery was from a railway coach between Calais and Paris.

FACTS AND FIGURES.

The universal demand for wire nails, a product of American workmen, is shown by the fact that they go to every grand division of the globe, and to practically every country. Germany, France, Belgium, Netherlands, the United Kingdom, Canada, Central America, the West Indies, all the South American States, China, Japan, Asiastic Russia, British Australasia, French Oceanica, British and Portugese Africa; in fact, it is difficult to find a spot among the civilized and semi-civilized people of the globe where this recent product of American invention and American labor does not find a place. The exportation of wire nails from the United States has grown from 1,547,078 pounds in the fiscal year 1888 to 22,894,099 pounds in the fiscal year 1898.

Italy (Naples).

This province on the western coast of Italy has, since its formation more than 300 years B. C., belonged to many nations, and is therefore one of the most cosmopolitan divisions of the Italian kingdom.

The capital city, Naples, the most densely populated city in Europe, vies only with Constantinople as being the most beautifully situated city in the world. "See Naples and then die" has been the sentiment of many visitors who find no other place in the world combining, within the same compass, such natural beauty with so many objects of interest.

A most undesirable feature of Naples is the number of lazy mendicants, but they are gradually disappearing as manufactories and schools increase. On another page is shown a Neapolitan woman, in the provincial dress, using a Singer Sewing Machine in corset manufacture.

The Singer Manufacturing Co. has 70 offices in this sunny clime, its sewing machines being extensively used both in the family and the factory. Typical Italian women from other parts of Italy will be presented hereafter in this series of National Costume illustrations.

Marriages.

UGH—SORBER.—At the parsonage Ind., Friday evening, Oct. 21, 1898, ie W. Ashbaugh, of Germantown, Miss Ella J. Sorber, of Milton. performed by Rev. T. A. Hall.

)RISCHEL.—At the parsonage in d., Saturday evening, Oct. 22, 1898, Feir and Miss Minnie Drischel, both ige City, Ind. Ceremony performed . A. Hall.

—HAYNIE.—At the Christian :iami, Mo., J. W. Strawn officiat- Walter K. Grady to Miss Ida M. The former from Lee's Summit, the Miami, Mo.

R—BOYER.—At the residence of mother, near Paris, Mo., Oct. 19, J. F. Kesner, of Granville, Mo., to Boyer; C. H. Strawn officiating.

)N—CHENOWETH.—I went back rsburg, Oct. 11, '98, and united in Mr. A. L. Newton, of Concord, Ill., Maud Chenoweth. A. C. Roach.

—SMITH—At Spokane, Wash., John P. Perrin and Miss Clydia L. e united in marriage by Elder S. B. They will reside at Medical Lake, on.

Obituaries.

[red words will be inserted free. Above words, one cent a word. Please send each notice.]

ALLAN.

V. Allan was born in Lubec, Me., 34 died at Kalamazoo, Mich., Oct. ged 64 years, five months and four leaves a wife and five children to departure. Bro. Allan became a 31 years ago. When the Church of organized in Kalamazoo he became nember and served as deacon until He took especial interest in the hool, of which he was superintendent ırs. He loved Christ and his church. tered into the rest that is for the God. We will meet him on the other river. C. M. Keene.

BRIGGS.

inerva Briggs died in Stockton, Cal., 898, in her 74th year. She was born ty and came to California in 1863. was married to R. L. Briggs, of ty. At an early age she became a under the preaching of Thomas Allen Thomas. The surviving members ily are Wm. H. Foreman, of Paris, A. L. Chapman, of Santa Clara, and . Montgomery, of Stockton, Cal. A Israel has passed away. She came re in full age, "like a shock of corn his season." A. M. Elston.

CONYERS.

lina Talbot Conyers, the subject of , was born in Boone County, Mo., 1823. When 14 years of age with her mother to Monroe County, was married to Jno. S. Conyers 840. She and her husband obeyed under the preaching of Bro. Henry 1841. They were for many years useful members, and always liberal, and hospitable. Many of our in days agone have enjoyed their home. Among the number were ob Creath, D. P. Henderson, Alex. ıd T. P. Haley. This noble couple ldren, but helped to raise and edu- al orphan girls. They were members gregation at Paris many years, where right lives and liberality they left ion for good that will never be ob- rom the minds and hearts of that This noble couple adopted, in 1860, ne Collier, then but a child of tender she has ever since made her home dopted parents. Miss Pauline Coll- married to Jno. W. Irvine. This blessed with two daughters, who omanhood, yet the tie of love seemed own stronger all these years. These of the foster-grandchildren, and again gloom spread over this dear family. Only three of the household now remained, yet they were knit together by the ties of love. Sister Conyers now had reached a good old age, and was loved by every one who knew her on account of her beautiful life, and the lovely traits that adorned her character. In the quietude of her home in Paris, surrounded by relatives and dear friends, she calmly breathed her last Oct. 5, 1898. Thus closes the life of a pure Christian woman. While the relatives mourn on account of their loss, I trust they will never cease to praise God for this beautiful life and the heritage left them. The only brother and sister—D. H. Moss and Mrs. Kittie Edwards—were present at the death of this good woman. Sister Edwards has already reached her fourscore and seven years. Bro. Moss is much younger, but as time flies it will not be many years before this good man and this faithful woman, with all the consecrated relatives and friends will meet the loved one in heaven.

Jacob Hugley.

ECCLES.

Richard Laughlin Eccles was born in New Orleans, La., Oct. 14, 1856, and died in Metropolis City, Ill., Aug. 20, 1898. He became a member of the church in the fall of 1890, and was faithful in every good work from that time until the close of his life. He leaves a wife and three children. He has been called from life's toils to his reward while yet young in years. He will be greatly missed by his home congregation, but his works will still live. Albert Nichols.

Lincoln, Ill.

GORDON.

Rosetta S. Waters was born at Aledo, Mercer County, Ill., April 24, 1861, became the wife of Mr. J. B. Gordon, May 12, 1886, and departed this life Oct. 14, 1898, leaving a husband and four children and a host of friends to fondly remember her gentle life. One of the family, a little boy, a few years ago led the way to the better land, where the mother now awaits the divided family. Her departure was sad, as a babe but a few weeks old was left to be cared for by other hands. Sister Gordon united with the Christian Church five years ago. The family has the sympathy of a host of friends. The writer conducted the funeral services at the Dimond Grove cemetry, at Jacksonville where the remains were interred.

D. F. Seyster.

Lynnville, Ill.

HURST.

Sarah Lewis was born south of Centerville, Ind., Oct. 29, 1826. She gave her life to Christ at the early age of 17 and was baptized by Eld. A. Harland. March 23, 1848, she was united in marriage to Dixon Hurst. She was the mother of three children, Alice, Horace Lewis, and Mary. Her husband departed this life Jan. 12, 1857. For the last few years she has been almost a helpless invalid and a great care to her faithful daughter, Mrs. Alice Gresh. Death came as a sweet relief Oct. 18, 1898. The funeral service was conducted in the Milton Christian church by the writer.

T. A. Hall.

Milton, Ind.

JOHNSON.

James Perrin Johnson, a faithful member of the Christian Church at Hanibal, Mo., passed to rest in his home in that city, Oct. 15, 1898, aged 38 years. He leaves a wife and daughter and brother in the old home into which he always brought cheer and encouragement. Though in delicate health for years he discharged the duties of a responsible position and always looked on the bright side of life. He was loved and esteemed by all who came into touch with his life. He was a very companionable man, and will be sadly missed in the community. The family have the Christian hope. Levi Marshall.

Publishers' Notes.

"Plain Talks to Young Men on Vital Issues," by Peter Ainslie, is a book that parents should place in the hands of their sons and daughters. It speaks out in clear and forcible language concerning the evils attending Gambling, The Theater, Dancing, Swearing, and Lying, and closes with a chapter on Christian Service. It is handsomely bound, and the price is 60 cents, postpaid.

The story of the beautiful life of Esther has recently been written by M. M. Davis and published in a book by Christian Publishing Co., St. Louis. The title of this new work is "Queen Esther." It is bound in beautiful cloth, and the price is 75 cents postpaid. In this book the author has told the story in such a manner that the child will read it with delight, the parent will find much instruction, and the preacher material for sermons. It is bound in the latest style cloth, and it is 75 cents, postpaid.

Superior to Any.

Under date of Oct. 14, 1898, we have the following commendation of the Gospel Call song books: "We have received the Gospel Call song books ordered and our church and Sunday-school think them superior to any we have ever used. I think your advertisement, 'Superior to any book now on the market,' is every word true." A. L. Moore, Cornetist.
Queen City, Mo.

In a recent issue of Public Opinion, New York, the editor gave a review of "Organic Evolution Considered," by Prof. A. Fairhurst, of Kentucky University. Not having space for the full article, we give the following extract from it: "We commend his work to the examination of students of biology because of its judicial spirit and good temper." 386 pages. Cloth, price $1.50.

If your Sunday-school expects to give a Thanksgiving entertainment, send to the Christian Publishing Co., St. Louis, for the "Harvest Home" concert. This is an appropriate concert for that occasion, and consists of familiar songs without the music, Scripture selections and recitations. It is easy to render and very entertaining. Price, single copies, 2 cents; or 25 cents per dozen copies, postpaid.

Ready for Orders.

"Mary Ardmore" is just from our press, and shows a high order of the mechanical art. This is the latest work by J. H. Stark, author of "Hugh Carlin." "Mary Ardmore" is a strong moral and religious story of a high class. Its characters are all well chosen, and the story is unique in its plan, beautiful in thought, and charmingly interesting from beginning to close. It will please all, as it contains love, morality and religion. It is elegantly bound in high colored cloth, has 328 pages, and the price is $1.00 postpaid.

PERSONAL MENTION.

Bruce Brown, pastor West Side Christian Church, Chicago, Ill., has adopted the method of announcing his sermon themes a month ahead in primer type on large (8x10) cards.

Prof. J. W. McGarvey, of Lexington, Ky., is announced as the chief lecturer of the Texas Christian Lectureship to be held at Waxahachie, Nov. 14-17. The railroads will offer special rates and entertainment will be free for all that attend.

H. C. Patterson, state evangelist, has located at Irvington, Ind., to which place he asks all correspondence for him to be addressed.

B. F. Manire, who returned to St. Louis from the convention at Chatanooga, on account of the yellow fever at his home, Jackson, Miss., left last week for Memphis, where he will await the opportunity to return home.

C. B. Black, Salem, Ill., desires to change his field of labor, and will enter into correspondence with churches looking to this end. Bro. Black is highly recommended by the brethren who know him as a minister of a clean record and good ability as a preacher. Address him as above.

W. H. Bybee, of Bolivar, Mo., has been commended by the official board of that church as an earnest preacher. He desires a new field of labor and asks correspondence with some church wanting a preacher.

S. G. Battenfield has closed his ministry at Mattoon, Ill., and is free to engage for protracted meetings or a new pastorate. While at Matoon, two years, there were 82 additions to the church and other benefits along moral and spiritual lines.

S. M. Martin is now in a protracted meeting at Central Chrisitan Church, Dallas, Texas. The preacher is a large man, the audiences are large and large results are expected.

We find this in the Christian Courier, Oct. 27th: "Arthur O. Garrison has become editor of the Christian Oracle, of Chicago, his father, J. H. Garrison, having purchased a controlling interest in the paper. F. M. Kirkham, formerly of the Oracle, becomes editor of the Pacific Christian, having purchased the paper. The Pacific Coast was not favorable to A. O. Garrison's health. He is a vigorors and entertaining writer and the Courier wishes for the Oracle great prosperity under his editorial management. Wm. O. Broadhurst, a most capable man for the place, becomes business manager of the Oracle."

J. C. Stark, of Du Quoin, Ill., author of "Hugh Carlin," was in the city last week and gave us a call. He is doing a good work at Du Quoin.

E. G. Shanklin, of Slater, Mo., and J. W. Blalock, of Stanbury, Mo., will exchange fields of labor for the year, beginning Nov. 1st. Bro. Shanklin has been preaching at Slater for over a year, and is greatly beloved for his work's sake. He had a unanimous call to remain at Slater indefinitely, but thought best to make a change. They go to Stanbury highly commended by the church and friends at Slater. The same is also true of Bro. Blalock and his work at Stanbury, and he goes to Slater with the esteem of all his people.

T. A. Wood, Rock, Mo., would like to engage with some church to preach part or all time for the next year.

Lawrence McCrea, of Iowa, is in a good meeting at Burnside.

A. J. Marshall, of Onawa, born on a foriegn mission field, is presented to the Home Board by his Iowa friends as a suitable man for our new mission work in Porto Rico or Cuba.

A. E. Cory taught Dean Everest's classes for one week.

A. M. Haggard, of Oskaloosa spent three days in Chicago last week.

T. C. McIntire, of Montezuma, Ia., preaches Oct. 30th at Garden Grove, Minn.

B. W. Pettit, of Avery, Ia., will preach at Oskaloosa on Nov. 6th. On 23rd this pulpit was filled by J. D. Gutherie.

B. S. Denny, the new Iowa secretary, is taking vigorous hold upon his work.

Mrs. B. W. Johnson, of Oskaloosa, Ia., is spending a few weeks in Northwest Missouri with her sister. She was also a St. Louis visitor recently.

F. N. Calvin, of Waco, Tex., will begin a three months' ministry for the church at Kankakee, Ill., Dec. 1st.

Geo. W. Campbell, of Chicago, recent filled the pulpit at Perry, Ia.

Dr. Albert Buxton, pastor of the church Fairfield, Neb., paid his respects to this offi on his way home from the Chattanooga Co vention, via Milligan, Tenn., and Canton, Mo at each of which places he lectured.

The Columbia Herald, Columbia, Mo recently complimented the author of "In t Days of Jehu," as follows: "J. Brecke ridge Ellis, of Plattsburg, takes us back Hebrew history in his new work 'In the Da of Jehu.' It is the story of sacred W brought in modern fashion, a story of absor ing interest, however told, and Mr. Ellis is mean story-teller. Ahab and Jezebel, Elij and Jehu, are brought more vividly before us this pleasant, profiting story. Mr. Ellis fi out the narrative where the Books of Kin give but a line. He has done his work car fully and well."

W. Bayard Craig, Chancellor of Dra University, is being prominently mention for President of the State University of Iow of which he is an alumnus. Chancellor Cra would make an almost ideal university pre dent, but we should regret to see him tak from the place which he is now occupying wi such excellent results to Drake University.

W. H. Waggoner has just concluded his 30 institute in behalf of systematic Bible stu and world-wide missions, at Bedford, Ind the home of Bro. Joseph Franklin, who pastor of the church in that city, of whom a his work Bro. Waggoner speaks most favo ably.

We regret to learn that Bro. W. F. Ric ardson, who was prevented from attendi both the Missouri Convention and the Natior Convention at Chattanooga by an accident his knee, is still on crutches and will probal be for several weeks. It is to be hoped that permanent injury will result from the accider Bro. Richardson is a man who is alwa greatly missed from the councils of l brethren.

M. L. Hoblit, C. W. B. M. missionary Monterey, N. L. Mexico, has changed t name of his missionary paper. It is now call "The Memorandum" instead of "Go." Th paper is published as a means of obtainin funds to keep his mission press at work prin ing gospel literature in the Spanish languag Subscription money and contributions to t press fund will be devoted to that object.

R. E. L. Prunty recently received an en thusiastic call from the congregation at Unior ville, Mo., to remain with them another yea this being his fifth year with this exceller body of Disciples.

The official board of the First Christia Church, Beaver Falls, Pa., testifies to th very acceptable and able manner in which Eld J. L. McDonald, of Hiram, O., conducted th services of the church during the eight months absence of its regular pastor, Eld. O. A Richards, in Alaska. It says: "Bro. Mc Donald is a conscientious, faithful man; we read, a deep thinker, thoroughly conversar with God's Word and will do a good work fo any church requiring the services of either pastor or evangelist."

W. C. Dimmitt has permanently located a Benjamin, Texas.

J. G. M. Luttenberger, Prohibition nomine for representative of the 36th Illinois congres sional district has issued a campaign documer bristling with prohibition facts and intempe ance figures. It ought to be a good eye-opene to any voter. Bro. Luttenberger's home is a Dorchester, Ill.

T. H. Kuhn, of Kokomo, Ind., is now in meeting in Ingalls and calls for sample copi of the Christian-Evangllist.

E. O. Sharpe will remain at Le Roy, Ill. another year at the request of the church.

Changes.

P. D. Gunter, Fortuna to California, Mo.
C. H. Plattenburg, Ashton, O., to Unior town, Pa.
J. H. Hughes, San Jose to Chico, Cal.
H. F. Detweiler, Axtell to Mina, Kan.
H. P. Atkins, Cincinnati, O., to Harrod burg, Ky.
E. B. Scofield, Columbus to 323 N. Del. St Indianapolis, Ind.
C. W. Anthony, Grandview, Ia., to 16(Lathrop St., Omaha, Neb.
N. S. Haynes, Chicago to Eureka, Ill.
F. E. Haughey, Chester, Neb., to We Grove, Davis County, Ia.
J. L. Ellis, Craig to Maybell, Routt County Cal.
C. S. Earley, Lancaster to 1320 25th St. Des Moines, Ia.
Richard Bagby, Louisa to 307 Market St. Charlottesville, Va.
W. W. Weedon, Taylorville to Williams ville, Ill.

THE
[CH]RISTIAN-EVANGELIST.

A WEEKLY FAMILY AND RELIGIOUS JOURNAL.

XXV. November 10, 1898 No. 45.

CONTENTS.

ents....579
Mission—What?....580
he Home Mission Office....581
Rally for America....581
asy Chair....582
ness of Sin....582

NTRIBUTIONS:

Rationalism—Speculation.—
ierce....587
y of the Disciples, the Christ-
the Bible.—L. D. Goodwin..587

ENCE:

opics....589
for the Remission of Sins..590
h and the World....590
on-Christian War....591
rewell....592
C. W. B. M....594

LE:

em)....598
ds and His Great Round
....598
Hymn (poem)....600
ills....60
f Mexico....601
ains....601
m is there in Card-playing?.602
poem)....602
Sermons....602

OUS:

ous World....583
et....584
News....595
ic....597
Children....603
....604
Endeavor....605
. E. Reading Courses....605
hool....606
and Obituaries....607
Mention....608
' Notes....608

bscription $1.75.

J. J. HALEY, CONTRIBUTING EDITOR CHRISTIAN-EVANGELIST.

PUBLISHED BY

CHRISTIAN PUBLISHING COMPANY

1522 Locust St., St. Louis.

THE

CHRISTIAN - EVANGELIST

J. H. GARRISON, EDITOR.

W. W. HOPKINS, ASSISTANT.

B. B. TYLER, J. J. HALEY,

EDITORIAL CONTRIBUTORS.

What We Plead For.

The Christian-Evangelist pleads for:

The Christianity of the New Testament, taught by Christ and his Apostles, versus the theology of the creeds taught by fallible men—the world's great need.

The divine confession of faith on which Christ built his church, versus human confessions of faith on which men have split the church.

The unity of Christ's disciples, for which he so fervently prayed, versus the divisions in Christ's body, which his apostles strongly condemned.

The abandonment of sectarian names and practices, based on human authority, for the common family name and the common faith, based on divine authority, versus the abandonment of scriptural names and usages for partisan ends.

The hearty co-operation of Christians in efforts of world-wide beneficence and evangelization, versus petty jealousies and strifes in the struggle for denominational pre-eminence.

The fidelity to truth which secures the approval of God, versus conformity to custom to gain the favor of men.

The protection of the home and the destruction of the saloon, versus the protection of the saloon and the destruction of the home.

For the right against the wrong;
For the weak against the strong;
For the poor who've waited long
For the brighter age to be.
For the truth, 'gainst superstition,
For the faith, against tradition,
For the hope, whose glad fruition
Our waiting eyes shall see.

RATES OF SUBSCRIPTION.

Single subscriptions, new or old	$1.75 each
In clubs of five or more, new or old. ...	1.50 "
Reading Rooms	1.25 "
Ministers ...	1.00 "

With a club of ten we will send one additional copy free.

All subscriptions payable in advance. Label shows the month up to the first day of which your subscription is paid. If an earlier date than the present is shown, you are in arrears. No paper discontinued without express orders to that effect. Arrears should be paid when discontinuance is ordered.

In ordering a change of post office, please give the OLD as well as the NEW address.

Do not send local check, but use Post office or Express Money Order, or draft on St. Louis, Chicago or New York, in remitting.

America or Rome? Christ or the Pope?

With the close of the war with Spain the world has learned much concerning the ignorance and superstition that have so long prevailed in Spain and her territorial possessions. Catholicism rules Spain and her colonies. Statistics reveal that 68 per cent. of the population of Spain can neither read nor write. This may account for the predominance of the Catholic Church and the power and rule of the Pope of Rome. Contrast Spain, an old and once powerful nation, ruled by Catholicism, with younger Protestant nations, in which there is but little illiteracy, and where gospel liberty makes them a free, prosperous, happy and intelligent people.

The evils of Romanism are clearly set forth by John L. Brandt in his work, "America or Rome—Christ or the Pope." Now is the time for agents to place this book in the hands of readers. We are *now offering extra inducements* to agents to handle this work. People will now want to read this kind of literature, and an active agent can do well by showing and selling this exposition of the despotism of Rome. Write us for our *special inducements to agents* on America or Rome—Christ or the Pope.

Price, in cloth, $1.50.

Sent prepaid on receipt of price.

CHRISTIAN PUBLISHING CO.
ST. LOUIS, Mo

Popular Series TEACHERS' BIBLES

At Very Low Prices

We can furnish any of the following STANDARD EDITIONS in this Series:

Oxford · Nelson · Bagster

OXFORD Popular Series, containing References, Concordance, Self-pronouncing Dictionary of Proper Names, Maps, &c,—nearly 300 pages of Handy Helps. Minion, 8vo, size, 7¾x5¼ inches.

No. 40403	Egyptian seal, divinity circuit, round corners, red under gold edges...	$1 25
No. 40408	Egyptian seal, divinity circuit, round corners, red and gold, linen lined.	1 50
No. 40404	Egyptian seal, divinity circuit, red under gold, leather lined......	1 75

NELSON'S Popular Series, containing the Combined Concordance, Indexed Bible Atlas and Popular Helps, with 68 Illustrations from Illustrated Bible Treasury.. Minion, 8vo, size, 7¾x6 inches.

No. 7001	Egyptian seal, divinity circuit, round corners, gold edges	$1 25
No. 7002	Egyptian seal, divinity circuit, round corners, headbands, red under gold edges..............	1 50
No. 7004	Egyptian seal, Divinity circuit, leather lined to edge, round corners, red under gold edges..............	1 75

BAGSTER'S, containing Concordance, References, Maps, &c, with 17 Full-page Illustrations. Minion, 8vo, size, 8½x5½ inches.

No. 3805	American seal, divinity circuit, red under gold edge............	$1 25
No. 3805½	American seal, divinity circuit, red under gold, linen lined, silk sewed..	1 50
No. 3806	American seal, divinity circuit, red under gold, leather lined....	2 00
No. 3808	American seal, divinity circuit, red under gold, leather lined to edge, silk sewed........	2 50

We will send prepaid on receipt of price as above.

☞We also carry a large line of Self-Pronouncing Teachers' Bibles and Text Bibles. Send to us for a New Illustrated Catalogue which we have just issued.

Christian Publishing Company, St. Louis, Mo.

Xmas Concert Services.

We have a great variety of Services for Christmas, among which are the following:

1. **The Wonderful Child.** By W. W. Dowling. Just from the press, and one of the best ever issued. Consisting of Bible Readings, Recitations, Class Exercises and Songs with music in full.

2. **The Unspeakable Gift.** By F. S. Shepard. With music in full.

3. **The Old, Old Story.** By L. E. Jones and F. S. Sheprrd. Readings, Recitations and Songs, with music in full.

4. **The Sweet Old Story.** By W. W. Dowling. A Service in Scripture Story, Poetry and ng without music, introducing in costume Angels, epherds, King Herod, and the Magi, with parts many special speakers.

5. **Tidings of Joy.** By J. L. B. and L. E Jones. New music and well-arranged Readings and Recitations.

6. **The Guiding Star.** By W. W. Dowling. A Service arranged for all classes, composed of Poetical Recitations, Bible Readings, Solos, Quartettes and Choruses without music, all of which point to Jesus as King of Israel.

7. **The Story of Jesus.** By W. W. Dowling. A Service in Poetry, Scripture and Song without music. It begins with the expulsion from Eden, and noting the prophecies of Christ's coming, his advent, scenes in his life, his betrayal, his crucifixion, his resurrection and ascension, closes with his coronation as King of kings.

STYLES AND PRICES

The above services each contain 16 pages, neatly printed, stitched and trimmed. The price of those which have the music printed in full is 5 cents per copy; 50 cents per dozen; $3.00 per hundred. The price of those which have the words of the songs without the music is 25 cents per dozen; $2.00 per hundred.

☞No free sample copies, but a sample of each of the above will be sent for 25 cents.

Christian Publishing Company, 1522 Locust St., St. Louis, Mo.

HE CHRISTIAN-EVANG

"In faith, Unity; in opinion and methods, Liberty; in all things, C

xv. St. Louis, Mo., Thursday, November 10, 189

URRENT EVENTS.

ly begun to look as if England
might be guilty of the un-
olly of going to war over the
of Fashoda. Preparations for
en going on actively, and Eng-
lly has been making a some-
itious display of her readiness
rue, Major Marchand had al-
ashoda, but it was still a debat-
n whether or not his personal
plied his recall and the aban-
the position which he had
matter is, however, very mate-
ed by Lord Salisbury's speech
et given at the Mansion House
Gen. Kitchener, the new hero
an. The prime minister stated
hat, although there were still
f opinion between France and
regard to their respective rights
et the immediate cause of fric-
n removed by the decision of
Cabinet, that the possession of
ould bring to France more
d expense than advantage.
there will be many discussions
but a somewhat acute and dan-
e of differences has been re-
r the wise determination of
bandon Fashoda. In his speech
banquet, Gen. Kitchener thus
assets that remain to England
ome of his Egyptian expedi-
hundred miles of railway, gun-
illa of sailing craft and— the

---

sbury's speech may dispose of
a incident as a possible *casus*
still leaves unexplained the ob-
hat extraordinary preparations
are being made in both army
If the French occupation of
e Egyptian station is not the
these preparations, then there
e more important and serious
. There could not well be one
ificant. The report came only
go that the ships of the British
; Wei-Hai-Wei had been or-
ar for action. But even this, if
ot afford any indication as to
of the enemy or the cause of
for a war between Great Britain
her of the European powers
nly involve naval operations in
ers. The only solution of the
ch immediately presents itself
t Britain is, as reported, about
a protectorate over Egypt, and
to meet with force any possible
hich may be made in any quar-

and in anticipation of such an attempt he is already beginning to throw obstacles in its way by granting to France privileges in Egypt which will bring France still more directly into collision with any British protectorate which might be established. Great Britain will probably have plenty of need for her warships cleared for action.

The new French Cabinet formed, not without difficulty, by M. Dupuy as Premier, is as follows: M. Lebret, Minister of Justice; Dupuy, Premier and Minister of the Interior; De Freycinet, War; Lockroy, Marine; Delcasse, Foreign Affairs; Peytral, Finance; Leygus; Public Instruction; Deloncle, Commerce; Guillaine, Colonies; Vigier, Agriculture; Krantz, Public Works. The retention of the Minister of Foreign Affairs in the late Cabinet in the same position in the present Ministry is an element of strength. He will be likely to preserve pacific relations with England and the other powers if any one can. The new Minister of War is a civilian, and may be expected to exhibit a higher degree of sanity than his predecessor did, in his consideration of the "honor of the army" as affected by the revision of the Dreyfus case. Meanwhile, the work of revision is going on. The hopeful feature of the present situation is that the Court of Cassation, which has just begun a retrial of the Dreyfus case, is a civil tribunal, and therefore not, as the court-martial was, in bondage to the phantom of French military honor.

In spite of the official secrecy which surrounds the work of the Peace Commissioners now in session in Paris, we receive almost daily detailed reports which purport to give an accurate account of all that transpires in their meetings. Much of this, probably most of it, is doubtless the product of the fervid imagination of the enterprising correspondents, whose lack of authentic information is no check upon their zeal for the enlightenment of the public. Public opinion has to be molded, and as good a way as any to do it is to put into the mouths of the Commissioners the words which these molders of public opinion think ought to be said. However, it cannot be doubted that, along with much political exhortation, dressed in the garb of sober narrative, a grain of truth does occasionally filter through from the secret session to the general public. It is probably true that our Commissioners have filed a demand for permanent possession of the whole Philippine group, and that the only concession that has been offered in return is that the United States will reimburse the Spanish Government for her expendi-

Spain to pay
rection there.
that Spain wi
gestion. The
been no thre
tions, and the
gives Spain n
gain anything
pean powers.

Considering
tempts at reg
out Europe, it
one of the po
toward a conc
pression of ar
ment has issu
State a procla
ernments whic
tatives at Ron
pate in a ge
common syst
forever the sc
of anarchy."
of the Italian
can be too s
check this
Obviously, ex
protect societ
the spirit of
The ordinary
no force over
to forfeit his
ing a blow at
of a king.
anarchist, as
who fell befor
dan, a fanat
which breeds
punishments
individual. I
exhibition of
ple. It wou
criminal. W
this country
ating sort.
sentative of
derous idiocy
two have mar
must be supp

Early in th
Nicaragua Ca
discussion in
which is alre
represents th
Canal Compa
government
guaranteeing
Company is c
and has conc
and the Cos
concessions f

desirability of a canal connecting the Atlantic and Pacific Oceans, or who have a financial interest in opposing any project, as the transcontinental railways have. The railways which connect our Eastern and Western coasts will exert all their influence to keep out this new line of competition. *Second*, opposition will come from those who believe that the canal is needed, but that it ought to be constructed, owned and controlled solely by the government, ignoring the Maritime Company and all other private schemes. Of this class Senator Turpie is a representative, a friend of the canal, but of the plan for its construction proposed in the Morgan bill. *Third*, there will be those who will favor the claims of other companies. The Government of Nicaragua has been somewhat prodigal with its concessions. An English corporation, the Atlas Company, has received exclusive concessions which conflict with those held by the Maritime. Besides this, there is a report that within the past week concessions have been granted to another American company, to come in force at the expiration of those granted to the Maritime and thereby preventing their renewal. The Panama scheme is not dead yet either (see two interesting articles in the Forum for November), and there will be some to favor the abandonment of the Nicaraguan route and co-operation with the French Government for the construction of the canal by the shorter Panama route. A commission appointed by the President has spent the past six months in going over the ground with the services of more than fifty engineers, and its report, to be presented soon after the opening of the session, can be made the basis Congressional action.

It had been commonly assumed that polygamy among the Mormons in Utah was a thing of the past. The custom was formally abrogated with the most solemn pledges by the leaders and representatives of the Mormon Church, a few years ago, as a condition of the admission of Utah to statehood. There is reason to believe, however, that the pledge was not made in good faith, and that it is not now observed. Mr. Roberts, a high officer of Mormonism, and one of the chief authorities on its doctrine, is now a candidate on the Democratic ticket for a seat in Congress. Evidence is presented to prove that this high Mormon official and would-be congressman is a polygamist, and that he is so by consent of the church. He has not denied the charge, and the managers of his campaign have defended him only by making a counter-charge that some of the nominees of the opposing party are guilty of the same offense. No specific evidence has been adduced, however, in support of the latter charge. As the matter stands, polygamy is practically a political issue in the campaign in Utah. If a man of so much prominence in the church has more than one wife, it can be assumed that the leaders of Mormonism know about it, and do not object. The outcome of the election will show whether or not they dare to declare themselves openly in favor of polygamy.

Dr. Lorimer has been given a royal welcome back to his church in Boston after a summer spent in England.

A DIVINE MISSION—WHAT?

I. CHRISTIAN LIBERTY.

Accepting as true the principle stated in a former article, that God's immanence in history is shown by the providential men and movements by which his kingdom is advanced on earth, and regarding the current movement urged by the Disciples of Christ as coming within the general scope of this principle, the inquiry as to God's purpose in this movement is pertinent and by no means irreverent. Nothing is more becoming God's rational creatures than an effort to understand the meaning of his dealings with them, and the nature of the work to which he has called them. The question which Saul of Tarsus asked when he was arrested on his way to Damascus by the manifestation of Christ, "Lord, what wilt thou have me to do?" is a question which not only every Christian, but every body of Christians may well ask.

In seeking to ascertain what purposes God had in view to accomplish through the agency of this reformation of the nineteenth century, three sources of information are open to us: (1) The Bible as the literary record of God's revelations to men; (2) the conditions and needs of the religious world at the beginning and during the progress of this reformation, and (3) the history of the movement itself. The first of these will furnish the norm or the unchanging principles and truths by which all religious work must be guided; the second will suggest the application of these principles demanded by existing conditions, and the third will afford us that light without which we cannot understand God's will and way aright—the light of experience.

Putting ourselves back now in the beginning of the present century, what are the prevailing religious conditions? If the history of the period may be believed, it was a time of intense sectarian bitterness and strife. The various religious parties emphasized inordinately the peculiarities of their doctrinal beliefs, making them tests of fellowship and of communion. Men's minds and consciences were in bondage to church traditions and the speculative beliefs of their respective parties. The free, untrammeled, creative spirit which marked the first era of Christianity and which had been reproduced in a measure in various periods of reformation in the church had degenerated into a spirit of contentiousness about small things and to slavish conformity to the utterances and practices of other men in other times. As might be expected under such conditions piety was at a low ebb, and infidelity and irreligion prevailed to an alarming extent. Especially was this true among the young and educated classes.

If we turn the light of the New Testament on this condition of things, which was not unlike that which prevailed among the Jews in the time of our Savior, and also the light which subsequent history throws back upon the situation, the conclusion seems to be irresistible that God desired, first of all, to break the fetters of partisan bondage and assert once more the great principle of Christian liberty. Men must be made to feel free to think before the prevailing errors of the time, both ecclesiastical and theological, could be corrected. Liberty is the essential atmosphere of religious reform.

We feel justified, therefore, in sayi that one of God's purposes in the reform tion of the nineteenth century was to gi a fresh assertion of the principle of Chri tian liberty. This did not mean liberty reject truth or to ignore its claims in li and conduct; but it meant freedom fro party tyranny; freedom from the authori of human creeds and traditions; freedom look reverently into the Word of God ascertain for themselves the way of li and salvation; freedom to stand erect und God's blue heavens and call no man mast but Christ. It meant also freedom to be Christian without wearing the collar badge of any sect in Christendom.

This was a most astounding claim to t great body of religious people of that da It is difficult for us to estimate the amou of moral heroism which was involved in t taking of such a position at that tim The idea that men could with impuni reject the venerable symbols of fait which had come down from former gener tions, and undertake to read and unde stand the Bible for themselves, seem sacrilegious in the eyes of many go people who had thoroughly identified the respective systems of belief with Christia ity and were unable to make any distin tion between them. And yet, weari with the petty strifes and partisan conte tions, and with the bondage of hum opinions which everywhere prevailed, t men of God who inaugurated this reform tion did issue a declaration of independen from all human authority in religion a asserted their purpose to henceforth guided solely by divine authority in the religious faith and practice.

Loud and long as were the denunciation against this course, it is now apparent i the light of nearly a century of histor that it was the only possible remedy fo the evils that afflicted the church, an must have been the initial step in an religious movement that looked to th betterment of these conditions. Whe religious leaders come to exalt their tradi tions and speculative opinions to an equal ity with the Word of God and seek to mak them binding on the consciences of men and when the ecclesiastical lash is applie to any man who dares to think differentl from these formulated opinions, it evident that the time has come for a re former to arise. There can be no religiou progress without it. Such a time was th early part of the present century, and God who is never taken by surprise, had pre pared human agents by which he woul free the church from its bondage to huma creeds and traditionalism, and start it o a new career of freedom and of power.

Priceless to the church and to humanit is this boon of religious liberty. All hono to the men who, at the call of God, wer willing to sacrifice personal popularity, th good opinion of their religious friends their former religious associations, place of honor which might have been their and devote themselves with single-hearted ness to the advocacy and defense of principle so unpalatable to the times i which they lived, but so vital to the inter ests of the church of God. It is throug their labors and sacrifices that we have th privilege to-day of being Christ's freemen wearing no man's name, acknowledgin allegiance to no human creed, owning n man as master but Christ, and claiming

ıd their helpers—are pictures of Alexan-
ɘr Campbell, Isaac Errett and R. M.
ishop. A Disciple, born and bred, feels
uite at home in this place.

This office is no place for loafers. The
ıen and women in it are busy persons.
remendous interests occupy their minds
nd employ their hands. The offices of our
iissionary secretaries are veritable work-
ıops. The twenty-fourth day of October,
ıe force was found hard at work preparing
ɔr Children's Rally for America, the new
ay appointed by the Chattanooga Con-
ention, in which to instruct our children in
Iome Missions, both state and national.

It was a privilege to look into the mail.
Ixtracts from some of the letters will not
e out of place at this point. A lady, a
hysician, wrote: "I wish to enlist to win
'uerto Rico for Christ. Enroll me in the
rmy of invasion, and do not mind a part
'ith the advance guard of the Rough
Riders. I am a physician, a Harvard
raduate, have had experience in treating
ellow fever, and can make myself under-
tood by Spaniards. Hoping to be called
ıto this service, I am yours in Christ."
ınother wrote: "I am a member of the
Christian Church, and an officer in 'the
olunteers of America,' under Ballington
Booth. My wife and I have given ourselves
o the service of the Master wherever he
alls. Can you use us anywhere? We
vould be willing to go. I am in charge of
he volunteer post here." How can we use
hese persons for Christ? What would
ou do? How would you do it? Write to
Benj. L. Smith about this. But here is
nother letter. Let us read: "We have called
Brother —— to be our pastor. Our only
ifficulty is the financial one and we want
he Home Board to solve that. Will you
ay half the salary?" Would you say
'yes" without investigation? But investi-
ation takes time, labor, expense. Nor
an half the salary be paid if money is not
ent in for the purpose. Have you sent a
ontribution? How much? "Jesus sat over
gainst the treasury." He sits there now.
Ie knows what is done and who does it.
But let us continue to examine this mail.
t contains revelations. A faithful minis-
er of the Lord Jesus writes: "My helper
ı the work for Christ and humanity passed
way on the third instant. I feel so weak
lone, but I know his promise to be with
ıe. My wife's health failed while in the
mploy of the General Board. She was
ever happier than when working for the
hurch of our Lord. We think the best
ıonument we could erect to her memory
'ould be a church at —— and we ask
our help." God bless them and give them
church building! do you say? But who
'ill furnish the money, or even a part of
:? Wm. F. Cowden writes: "I have lo-
ated Bro. G. L. Surber for three months
t Boise, Idaho. Bro. Davis is at Lewiston,
'here they are about to build. F. B. Sapp
ives splendid satisfaction as our new state
vangelist. I dedicate at Enterprise, Oreon, soon; then to the Willamette Valley
› assist Bro. Sicafoose. We need a num-
swer, favorably, not more than a thi:
the urgent, worthy appeals made to t
The call of ONE HUNDRED THOUSAND
LARS FOR HOME MISSIONS is timely. I
could spend a day in the office of the A
ican Christian Missionary Society and
the pulse of the mighty demand for
you would be fired with missionary ze
never before. This amount of mone;
be raised if we have a mind to give it.
wealth is in our hands. We are a mi
people. How will we use our wealth'
what direction will we exert our might

B. B.

CHILDREN'S RALLY DAY FOR AMERICA.

The Convention at Cattanooga re
mended that the Sunday prece
Thanksgiving be observed in our Sun
schools as Children's Rally Day for A
ica, the offering to be divided bet
Church Extension, State Missions an
American Christian Missionary Soc
One-fifth to be given to Church Exter
and two-fifths to the State Board in w
state the Sunday-school is located and
fifths to the A. C. M. S. This is ex
right. The State Boards have long
they had some right to claim an intere
the Sunday-school offering and to c
the attention of the children to the r
of their own state; but in the multipl
of days and interests this was exceedi
difficult. Again, it did not seem right
the young in our churches should hav
education concerning the need of Am
for missionary work. How many of the
dren in the more favored part of our
know of the mighty mission field
America? Do the children know tha
Home field includes all the United S
(only in a third of which have we
strength) and Canada and Alaska
Mexico and now, after our victories
Spain, many islands of the sea? Th
Rally Day, not for the United States a
but for *America*, and yet it does not fo
the claims of the beloved state in w
the school is located and the funds are
not only to send messengers with
gospel, but to build church houses
chapels.

Then again, many of our wise men
for sometime felt that there has not
sufficient unity in our missionary w
This, then, is a movement in the :
direction. The work of the Ame
Christian Missionary Society and o:
State Boards and of the Church Exte
Society is alike in that it seeks to li
the standard of primitive Christiani
America, and this unity of hands is h
with satisfaction by all the friends of I
Missions.

Again, this seems a fortunate choi
days. It conflicts with no other int
and how appropriate that we teach
children to express their thanksgivin
the blesings coming from the protec
peace and prosperity vouchsafed by
government, by giving to their be
land the greater blessings found alo:

of field, forest and orchard. What more appropriate than to bring to the eyes of the children the blessings which God has given them and teach them that their own offering is but an expression of thanksgiving for the blessings which their eyes behold. Make America's Day a great day this jubilee year.

"America" never meant so much to Americans and to the world as it means today. The stars on our flag never shone with quite so great a lustre as they do today. The Bible—the bedrock of our civil and religious liberty—was never so clearly recognized as being the source of all our nation's greatness. Let these great truths be impressed on the minds of the children on the "Children's Rally Day for America" —Lord's day, Nov. 20th.

Editor's Easy Chair.

Looking from my office window one day, not long ago, out upon a cross street, we beheld a sight which filled us first with pity, then with indignation. A man and a woman, presumably husband and wife, were engaged in a contest over a small boy, perhaps six or seven years of age. The father was trying to get the boy to go with him, but the little fellow clung to his mother and refused to be parted from her. The mother was pleading, the father was storming, the child was crying. At length the father seized the child in his arms, tore it from its mother's clasp and started down the street, the mother following and pleading and the little boy making vigorous efforts to extricate himself from his father's hold. Seeing he could not carry him farther, he let the boy down rather unceremoniously on the walk and began to kick him. Just as we were about to leave the office to interpose a man came along and engaged them in conversation, and after a few moments the three passed around the corner out of our sight, and we know not what was the end of the domestic tragedy. Let us hope that the poor little fellow was permitted to remain with his mother, and that whatever evil influence may have brought discord and strife in that family may be removed.

It has occurred to us, as we have thought upon that sad scene, that it is only a striking symbol of what is going on continually, especially in our towns and cities. There are two opposing influences contending for our boys. On the one hand there is parental love and on the other Satanic influences are seeking to draw them from the paths of virtue, of righteousness and purity into the downward way that leadeth to destruction. Satan wants the boys, and he cannot run his kingdom without them; and yet the home, the church and the state all require the boys, out of which to mold men that are to decide their future destiny. What a contest this is that is going on! How all heaven must be interested in it! Every saloon, every gaming table, every brothel, every ungodly home is an agent of the devil to entice our boys into his service. One of the problems of the age is how to overcome these evil forces and save the boys for the church, the state and the home. How poor and inadequate seem our methods and our zeal for the salvation of the boys, in view of the perils that surround them and the agencies seeking their ruin!

An agitation is now in progress in St. Louis, under the leadership of Mr. Hoagland, in favor of the enactment of the curfew ordinance, requiring boys and girls under fifteen years to be off the streets after eight o'clock. This ordinance has been tried in many towns and cities, and has worked most beneficently in the way of decreasing crime and promoting good order. It is one of the ways in which civil law can co-operate with the religious agencies to save our boys and girls from the snares of the evil one. It is to be regretted that many homes exercise little or no restraint in this direction, and it is all the more important that an ordinance of the city should reinforce the discipline of the home, both in preventing crime and in protecting the young. We trust the ordinance which has already passed through one branch of our city government may receive the approval of the other and become a law.* It will then become the duty of all good citizens to cooperate with the city authorities in its enforcement. The devil probably has no more successful school of vice than the streets of our cities and towns after nightfall.

He was a bright-faced, manly little fellow of eight or nine years of age who stood on the corner of the street on last Sunday morning, with his Sunday-school book in his hand, waiting for the car to carry him from the western part of the city to a down-town church. "Where do you go to Sunday-school?" we asked. "To the Compton Avenue Presbyterian Church," he replied. "That is a long way to go to Sunday-school," we said. "Here is a church just on the corner; why not go there?" "That is a Catholic Church," he replied, as if that were reason enough why a Presbyterian boy should not go there. "But there are other schools in the neighborhood," we said. "Yes," he replied, "*but I have been so long a member of that church that I feel more at home there than anywhere else!*" Just then the car came along, and we both stepped on board, each of us going to the Sunday-school where we would feel most at home. There was a boy who had religious convictions, and who had a love for his church and Sunday-school, and who had fixed habits of attending religious services, at the age of about eight or nine years. That boy is comparatively safe, even amid the temptations of city life. He is already anchored to home and church and school, and these anchors will probably hold him amid all the temptations and trials to which he may be exposed. It was an object-lesson on the value of early religious training. Ordinarily, we do not begin soon enough to plant the seeds of religious truth, and to weave the strands in the cable of good habits, which are to hold our boys and girls in the storms that are to overtake them later on.

Since the foregoing paragraphs about the boys were written, we took occasion, passing up Olive Street returning from our noon lunch, to study the faces of the people who throng that busy street at the noon hour. What a variety of types, and how varied the histories written thereon! There were comedy and tragedy and plain bestiality. How few young people stop to think that they are writing their biographies on their faces! You hide your deeds behind scre do you, and under cover of darkness? no, young man. You are writing th and even your thoughts, all over your co tenance. One of the men into whose we looked, had almost white hair, and well dressed; but his face looked as i fire would light a match, and upon e feature was written the dominance of fle ly appetites, the supremacy of the b passions. Does he imagine his secret is known only to himself and a few i mates? It is written in letters of fir over his face, and he that runs may rea Learn it early young friends: there is beautifier of the face like pure thoug high ideals, noble, unselfish deeds. Be now to prepare for a beautiful old age.

*The ordinance has passed both houses and is now in force. The hours are eight in winter and nine in summer.

Hour of Prayer.

AGGRESSIVENESS OF SIN.

(Mid-week Prayer-meeting Topic, Nov. 16th.

But evil men and impostors shall wax w and worse, deceiving and being deceive 2 *Tim.* 3:13.

It is a fact taught in Scripture and c firmed by observation and experience, t while good men grow better evil men g worse; that sin as well as righteousnes aggressive when it gets its seat in the he of man. We believe it may be said v equal truth that, because of the weaknes the flesh and the depraved nature of me appetites, sin makes headway more ea than does righteousness. It is easier float down stream than it is to swim agai the current. The context of the pass above quoted would seem to indicate t this is the apostle's thought. He had j been referring to his trials and persecutio and added, "Yea, and all that would li godly in Christ Jesus shall suffer persec tion. But evil men and impostors sh wax worse and worse, deceiving and bei deceived." It is not intimated that t latter class suffer any persecution. T world in which they live and move is co genial to their character and aims. Th mistake the suspension of divine judgme upon their conduct for divine indifferen and go on sinning with impunity, waxi worse and worse.

Two classes of persons are here said wax worse and worse, namely, "evil me and "impostors." By the first we suppo is meant those who are open and abov board in their wickedness, making no pr tensions whatever in the way of religio Impostors are men who pretend to be wh they are not. They have chosen "t livery of heaven to serve the devil in They are professors of Christianity, b not possessors. They are Christians "f revenue only," or for a baser purpo They are hypocrites, a class of men co cerning whom Jesus uttered his mo scathing denunciation. Of both th classes it is affirmed that their wickedn is of an aggressive character. They "w worse and worse."

It is easy to see why this is so. Bo these classes of men are acting contrary their own convictions of right and tru They ignore the voice of their conscien reproving them, until these conscienc have become seared. They have resist the higher promptings of their natu until that nature has become hard a callous. Few men are aware of the awf consequences to their moral nature sinning against light and knowledge. Fe

is nature of
to the heart,
ence, unless
whole moral
f the story of
ie camel only
put its head
y it drew its
lowly dwell-
to the Arab
for both, the

re of sin. It
ing a part of
and actions,
on complete

r, that these
eive others in
their wicked
es deceived.
He promises
penury. He
st gives dis-
He promises
ives dishonor
promises life
the wages of
of Satan.
y easy: Re-
sin. Refuse
you have felt
u have found
at Physician.
ience. Every
ness makes it
ward step and
self. Do not
to free your-
abit, but seek
rs, and in his

ink Thee, not
Thy love in
lation of Thy
We thank
pel, by which
on of sin and
d come into
lp us, we be-
ful of the in-
ful ravages of
nating power
omplete bond
g worse and
ot, under Thy
e and more
until we shall
His image.
!

World.

iew by Rev. E.
appeared in the
published here
int bearing on a
wide attention.

Herzl, the
n.

ite that piece
e, the Votiv-
eit, the organ
nt to solve an
Dr. Theodor

meet a small copy of Michael Angelo's Moses, or a copy of my own image of Jeremiah; instead, I found a man with the face and bearing of a king, who repels one by his reserve, but fascinates by the dignity of his bearing and by the classic beauty of his figure and face. The fire of Sinai is in his eyes, though he bears none of its rugged features. The prophet's sadness has drawn its lines upon his face, but unlike our conception of the prophets, he is dressed in the height of fashion, and is surrounded by the comforts and luxuries of life.

Dr. Herzl is a lawyer by profession, but has chosen a literary career, in which he has been very successful. He is one of the editors of the Neue Frei Presse, one of the best German newspapers in Europe. He is the author of many books, and a dramatist of great promise.

"I am at your disposal," he said, throwing himself into a comfortable arm-chair, and in spite of his readiness to be interviewed, I was not very ready with my questions, and so he began:

"I suppose you would like to know what made me write that book."

"Yes," I said, "that's one of the questions I would like to ask you."

"That book wrote itself," he replied. "It forced itself upon me. I fought it, for it meant for me to show my colors, and to force the Jews of Europe to show their colors, and for a Jew in Austria to show himself a Jew, especially if he be a literary man, is dangerous to his reputation as an author, and still more perilous to the publication with which he is connected. The Jews here have played the game of hiding a long time. We have hidden our Old Testament names behind those of our New Testament enemies. We have shunned the synagogue, and have sprinkled ourselves with holy water, and have kept from our children the dreadful secret that their parents were Jews—and yet we were persecuted. We wanted to be Austrians or Germans; we delighted to mingle with our Gentile neighbors, but "Juden raus" was the cry in Germany. It was echoed in Austria, it was realized in Russia, and in Poland they are beating them to death by thousands. If we are to go, whither shall we go? If we cannot be citizens here in the land of our birth, where shall we be citizens? They can't kill us off. They have tried it for thousands of years; they have not succeeded; let them give us a land, no matter how small, but let it be our own land, where we may not only carry the burdens, but also have the privileges of citizenship."

"Do you think," I asked, "that the Jews will be willing to go to Palestine, even if you get the land?"

"No, not all at once," he replied. "The poor Jews of Russia and Poland will certainly be willing to go immediately. They will be the pioneers. They will till the soil, build roads and telegraphs, and then the merchants, manufacturers and artists will come of themselves."

match factories, whe
about twenty cents a da
mines; they manufac
the peasants' dress, bu
wagon grease—anythin
do. The reason they
fields is simply this: Th
with the native laborer
still smaller pittance th
"The Jew is in the m
shops of the world. If
er, and if he can do not
least do that in Palest
he can sell his clothes
can from London or Vi
"Have you any hope
of the Jew in Europe v
with the growing civili
"No, indeed not," h
"It will grow worse e
France, which shelte
everybody else persec
to ten years ago hadn
Semitism. See to wh
portions it has grown
where they are very pr
horrors will repeat the
ten years. In Austria
is ruined; many hotel
are closed against the
as social relations w
unheard-of thing. In
against the Jews is
Germany—cultured Ge
as hard a condition to
the world."
"Do you think the S
to sell Palestine to the
"No, not just now;
ing themselves in such
give us hope that he
some neutral power ha
stance, the journey of t
to Jerusalem. It is tu
of the Powers to this li
doesn't like it a bit, a
doesn't like it a bit be
anything. Austria do
but doesn't care to sa
Pope—well, you may
thinks about it. The
able to the Jews, in
might ensue, will be o
the Jews in their old
1,000 birds with one sto
tions of the German
of the vexing Jewish q
"What if you fail in
you yourselves?"
"What if we fail?
cannot be a failure. I
ed, or recreated the J
caught the drifting, t
given him a state if on
has brought him back
his God, and that is
we have taken. But i
may, in this generatio
live until it is realized.
needs. It is what God
"Just look at the me
gathered: Max Nord
Bernhard Lazarus, R
dozens of other men f
world. Our coming
bring together a large
brated Jews than have
the balmy days of Jud

Our Budget.

—This is State Mission month.

—Has your church made its offering to this cause?

—Are you planning for such an offering during the present month?

—Do you vote for Christ and his righteousness?

—Is your own election to the kingdom of God sure?

—Did you study your politics from the Christian view-point?

—Is your Christianity founded on sound business principles?

—What does it take to constitute a Christian nation? is still a proper question.

—Truth cannot be created, and that that is is indestructible.

—"Christian Science" is not the only doctrine that is founded upon an eddy.

—The biblical instruction, to "lay hands suddenly on no man," is strictly adhered to in relation to the liquor traffic.

—The refusal of Roman Catholic authorities to endorse the plan for a congress of religions at the World's Fair in Paris in 1900, such as was held at Chicago, shows of what spirit they are where they have control.

—Some of our churches are planning to unite "Children's Rally Day for America," Nov. 20th, with the State Day for Missions in the church. This is a good plan where the offering has not been made.

—This combination is the more natural because a part of the children's collection goes to State Missions, and the whole of the church collection. It is all Home Missions. It brings the school and church into line on the same day in behalf of the same cause.

—The Word and Way asks, "Is your Christian work shaped after the right pattern?" How many patterns of Christian work are there? we should like to know.

—Next week we will offer our readers a symposium on the methods of conducting our National Conventions, and of the best means of making the Jubilee Convention a success. You will be interested in it. Look out for it.

—The qeestion is not so much, What shall we do with the Philippines? as, What shall we do with the Fillipinos? That is, it is not a question of getting more territory, but having the territory in our possession. Can we leave the inhabitants to Spain or to themselves? Are we not under obligations to help them to a better civilization and a better government? This seems to be the point of view of the administration, and it is one which the American people will approve.

—At the preacher's meeting held, in this office on last Monday, there were present as visitors, C. C. Smith, Cor. Sec. Negro Education and Evangelization, of Cincinnati, O.; J. J. Haley, Cynthiana, Ky.; J. L. Darsie, of Bethany, Va., and W. A. Meloan, Blandinsville, Ill. C. C. Smith made a brief talk on the outlook of Home Missions, and enlarged work in our larger cities. J. J. Haley is on his way to Columbia, Mo., where he is to deliver a course of lectures on "The Crucial Tests of the Bible." Bro. Meloan was at East St. Louis Christian Church on last Sunday and was on his way to Litchfield where he is to hold a protracted meeting. The preachers listened to an excellent paper from Dr. Dungan on "How to Preach First Principles." The preachers' reports of meetings all encouraging. In all about twenty additions were reported.

—The Christian Oracle announces that with the Thanksgiving special number it will appear in new form and its future announcements for the coming year. The price of the paper is to be reduced to one dollar per year.

—The Annual Report of the Foreign Christian Missionary Society has been mailed. Those desiring a copy can have one upon application. This is the most interesting report ever issued by the Society. Address A. McLean, Cincinnati, Ohio.

—The Interior says, "There is no reason why there should not be, in effect, a confederation of Christendom." We should like to add, upon the other hand, that there are many reasons why there should be such a confederation, at least of all evangelical church. The times are ripe for such a movement.

—A gentleman in this city is reported to have recently filed suit for a bill of divorce from his wife on the ground that she is "a religious fanatic." He alleges that his wife's religious propensities have become unbearable; that she has inaugurated daily prayers in the family, compelling the children to take part, and in her supplications held him up before the children as a sinner and a madman, alienating their affections from him, and that she neglects her household duties to attend the religious services of the divine healing school. It is certainly remarkable that a man should make his wife's religion the ground for a bill of divorce, and the case will hardly be pressed to an issue in the courts on that ground; but it is easy to see how religious fanaticism may be made an occasion for complaint against all religions by unreasonable, irreligious and indiscriminating men. It is very seldom that a man objects to his wife's religious habits, even to daily family prayers, but the neglect of household duties for religion goes beyond the province of reason. A woman no less than a man who will not provide for her own household is worse than an infidel. Had the above husband, however, been more considerate and had any just ground for complaint and known the difference between pure and undefiled religion and the divine healer's religion he would probably have placed his wife under the care of some physician having a reputation for the successful treatment of nervous disturbances instead of making use of her to offend Christianity.

—The Sultan is opposed to the Zionist movement and has forbidden the sale of any land in Palestine to Jews, even if they are Turkish subjects. Perhaps Emperor William can molify the Sultan's mind on this subject in behalf of his own subjects and prospective interests in Palestine and in Syria.

—While we have taken no part in the criticisms of the Santiago campaign and felt no desire to detract in the least any glory justly due to Gen. Shafter for the management and results of the battle we do not think that the method of meeting the charges of inefficiency or neglect which have been so freely and so boldly made against him and others by comparison with other battles where losses were greater exactly the square thing. It is a question whether there was the neglect of anything within human forethought previous to the battle that would have reduced the fatalities of the battle? The slaughter of men in battle is bad at best, but if due to inefficient management or neglected factors or movements it is infinitely worse.

—We wish to again ask you to call the children's attention to their column in this paper. They will find the writer a most pleasing companion and enjoy his plans for their amusement and profit.

—The dedication program of the new Central Building of the Y. M. C. A., at Grand and Franklin Aves., this city, occupied five of the evenings of last week. Monday, Oct. 31, was contributor's night; Tuesday, business men's night; Thursday, young men's night; Friday, young people's night, and Saturday, student's night. There was a fine program for each night and a fine audience for each program. This city now has one of the finest and best equipped Y. M. C. A. buildings in the West, and under one of the best managements.

—In the Family Circle this week will found a short article from Mexico and picture of two of its greatest cathredals. article is from O. Curtis Omer, Mexico C Bro. Omer and his wife are anxious that Disciples of Christ open a mission in that at once. While he has heard of but one ot Disciple of Christ there he thinks the field for mission work. The following extract f his letter we think, worthy of the attentio our Foreign Mission Board and the Disciple Christ in the United States:

The opportunity here I think is all that co be desired if the work could only be start The first thing to do would be to open a sion school for those who have no means getting an education otherwise. In this they could be brought up in the church learn the ways of truth and thus becom great help in bringing others to their o people into the work. There are many g people, but poor who would be only too gla turn their children over to a mission so t they might get an education and become be men and women. It would be a hard matte describe the poverty and ignorance of the m of Mexico's inhabitants. All over the repu and at every railway station there are m beggars and hence the need of Christi n kno edge and education. It is true, lexico making a great stride towards reforming th conditions, but why cannot the Christ Church lend a helping hand so that they have a grand footing when the great refor tion is accomplished?

—The town of Pullman has not prospe since its encounter with Debs, and now tha is found guilty of exceeding the limits of corporate charter by the courts it will proba cease its real estate experiments. Retribut sooner or later overtakes all that is evil.

—President Harper, of the University Chicago, has recently made charges agai theological seminaries that are likely to aro no little discussion and self-examinati Theological as well as other institutions m fall behind the times in their confidence of p sessed truth and long-continued methods, a therefore need an awakening on the subj such as President Harper's declarations a calculated to produce. We will quote Pre dent Harper's words as published in the Ce tral Christian Advocate, of this city, la week, but as we have no theological seminari to look after, further comments on what says are unnecessary:

The theological seminaries are not in tou with the times. They do not meet the d mands of the times. They are not prepari men for the ministry who are able to grapp with the situation in which the Christi church to-day finds itself. These men a prepared, perhaps, to solve the problem rural parishes, but they are for the most pa unfitted to deal with the urban problems.

The old and artificial distinction betwe Old Testament exegesis and New Testame exegesis, ecclesiastical history and dogmatic is one which cannot be maintained. The O Testament student takes up no problem th does not require of him the use of the N Testament, and the New Testament stude cannot deal intelligently with a single subj who has not considered that subject in all i details from an Old Testament point of vie The introduction of biblical theology as di tinguished from dogmatic theology has pr duced confusion in the organization. On third to one-half of the time of the theologic student is wasted in this vain effort to acco modate himself to the requirements of t so-called departments, involving artifici distinctions which exhaust his patience and h time. A new order of things is demanded a the indications seem to point to the introdu tion of this new order of things in the openi years in the coming century; but meanwhi we are drifting, and precious time is bei lost.

I raise the question whether our divini school may not be one of the pioneers in rea justing the work of training men for the mini try to the new conditions which exist to-da To do this will require courage and great ski I do not have in mind the question of creed doctrine. My thought relates exclusively the form and method of work, the extern situation which has developed and the eradic tion of what seems to me to be the high-scho method now employed in most of our divini schools and the substitution of a true unive sity method.

has just come to us that J. B.
Waynesboro, Va., one of the co-
f the fathers of the Restoration
has gone to his heavenly reward.
obituary will appear in our next
Ve extend our sympathy to Sister
er sorrow.

tuary of one of the victims of the
t, Oct. 12th, at Virden, Ill,, appears
er. Also in the same department a
ce of the ilfe and death of J. J.
of our efficient and fathful ministers
el. Bro. Wright has written briefly
tly of his departure.

ter signed by "A Friend," recently,
ollar to be forwarded to Church Ex-
cretary. The letter indicated that
was a member of one of the churches
n Des Moines, Ia., and closed with
at the offering "was one hundred
stead of one." This indicates how
tension is appreciated even by those
ive only small amounts.

terior advises those who are capa-
n, in a friendly way, of those follow-
he Christian Science delusion, what
it that commends it to them. We
the attitude of the Interior toward
h of psychic phenomena. In this
vestigation and discovery it is not
penly condemn any new thing as a
antagonize it as an enemy until the
he case have been brought to light.
r that the tree is known by its fruits.
ion in Christian Science lies in the
xalt it above Christianity, whereas it
ranch of psychical science. There is
al want in an awakened heart that
e supplied by Christianity.

has abolished the distinction made
nale and female teachers in her public
regards their salaries. All teachers
me grade are to be paid the same
gardless of the question of sex. The
el that they have thus scored a vic-
heir fight for equal rights, but the
en are wondering what the effect of
will be upon their opportunities for
. Perhaps it will enable women to
husbands. At all events, right is
women should not feel that they are
to marry for a support in life. The
en of Iowa will have to move their
s up a notch or so to keep up
procession.

meeting of the Board of Church Ex-
n November 1st, a great deal of im-
usiness was transacted. The corre-
secretary's report showed $3,718.36
for October. Of this amount 147
sent $1,240.36; individuals, $1,903,
uest was received amounting to $575.
urer also collected $557.97 of interest
de a total of new receipts, amounting
33. There was returned on outstand-
, $975.31. This shows a healthy gain
s over October, 1897, and there is a
utlook for Church Extension this com-
The amount now in the permanent
ver $170,000. At this meeting, the
nted the following loans, which will
t the completion of the church build-
eville, Mo., $250; Monroe City, Ind.,
art, Ia., $400; Riverdale, Neb., $350;
n, Mo., $500; Sac City, Ia., $800;
Falls, Wis., $250; Scottdale, Pa.,
ontiac, Ill., $300; Joppa, Md., $250;
Pa., $2,000; Winston, N. C., (in-
700; Bakersfield, Cal., $400. This is a
hirteen loans, amounting to $7,800. It
tly hoped by all our missionary breth-
the aggressive work of our Board of
Extension will receive most hearty
No missionary church should fail to
ffering to this important work. Re-
s should be made to G. W. Muckley,
, 600 Waterworks Bldg., Kansas City,

—Any article or communication of any kind sent to this paper for publication at the same time that it is sent to one or more other papers, without any notice to the editors that a duplicate has been sent elsewhere, must be regarded as an effort to take advantage of us, and to cause us to do what we would not do with a knowledge of the facts. It is a rule in this office, as it is in other well-regulated offices, not to publish articles that are sent to other religious journals, unless they be of the nature of an official notice. We are constantly declining articles from our contributors for a lack of space, and it is not fair to them nor to our readers to publish matter that is to appear in our other religious journals. We hope our writers will remember this rule and act accordingly.

—There are some Germans who evidently do not believe that the character of Emperor William's visit to the Holy Land is in keeping with the spirit of Christianity and its founder. Here is the opinion of a Teuton as expressed in a recent number of the Observer, as follows:

There are not a few patriotic Germans who are incensed at the grandiose proportions which this pilgrimage has assumed. They think that even a mighty German kaiser visiting the early cradle of Christianity where its Founder could not find a place to lay his head might approach those holiest spots on the earth's surface with more of evident humility, with less of the trappings of circumstance and authority. Warships to accompany him, soldiers before and behind, servants in gold embroidered liveries, bishops and canons in their milinery, salvoes of artillery and blowing of trumpets—these are not the accompaniments which many honest German patriots and Christians like to see, but they have not given public utterance to their thoughts.

—We learn from a note from Bro. W. S. Broadhurst, of Louisville, Ky., that his large printing plant on Broadway, in that city, was destroyed by fire on Monday evening, 31st ult. We regret to hear of this loss, though we understand the establishment was insured so as to cover the larger part of the loss. Bro. Broadhurst was about changing his headquarters from Louisville to Chicago, where he expects to remove in a short time to assume the duties of business manager of the Oracle Publishing Co.

—We have received clippings from the local press giving account of the dedication of the new church edifice being erected by the Disciples of Christ at Brockton, Mass. The paper states that "the building has been completed as the result of untiring effort and considerable self-sacrifice on the part of those who will attend divine service therein and the hard and ceaseless work of the pastor, Rev. G. A. Reinl, who since he came here two and a half years ago has, with but little means at the disposal of himself or congregation, bought and paid for a lot of land, and built thereon an edifice which, while not as large and handsomely decorated as some similar institutions, is sure to prove the means of bringing many a wandering sinner from the temptations of the outside world into close and profitable communion with God." The building is said to be a two-story structure of Gothic architecture, the entrance being by two doors, one on either side of the building. These doors lead into cozy vestibules. The church is handsomely decorated and furnished. The architect was our Brother G. Wilton Lewis, of Everett, Mass. The dedication sermon was preached by Roland A. Nichols, of Worcester, and Bros. R. H. Bolton, E. C. Davis, S. M. Hunt and the pastor, G. A. Reinl, assisted in carrying out an interesting program. There were ordination services in the afternoon, with a sermon by Bro. E. C. Davis. We are glad to note this addition to our forces in the East, and extend our congratulations and best wishes to Bro. Reinl and flock at Brockton.

—In another place we publish a sermon by Bro. Ragland, of Fayetteville, preached on the occasion of the departure of Miss Annie Agnes

Lackey to join the American missionaries in India. It was a notable occasion in the church at Fayetteville. Indeed, in a letter from Bro. Ragland, he says: "This is the best day our church in Fayetteville has ever seen." Bro. Ragland agreed to become responsible to the C. W. B. M. for the raising of $1,000 to pay Miss Lackey's passage to India and her salary for one year. This was a brave and generous thing for Bro. R. to pledge. As to the outlook for raising it Bro. R. writes as follows:

When Miss Lackey received the appointment at Chattanooga, Miss Withers, of Florida, arose and said: "Bro. Ragland, I want to be the first to give $20 to Miss Lackey's passage money to India;" then Sister Teachout, of Cleveland, O., said: "I will gladly give $25." This was followed by Sister F. L. Sutton, of Litle Rock, who said: "I will give $50." Last week I had a letter from the auxiliary to the C. W. B. M. in Minneapolis saying, $15 dollars had been sent to Miss Lois A. White to apply on the fund for Miss Lackey. Only a day or two ago a letter came from Sister Walden, of Fort Worth, Tex., telling the good news that she had just sent a draft for $200 to Miss Lois White for Miss Lackey. Last Sunday I presented the matter to my own congregation, and within ten minutes almost $100 was subscribed. So you see how God is blessing me. I am so ashamed that I even doubted that the whole amount could be raised.

We think it is only necessary to publish these facts to enlist the interest of our Christian women and others in this good word. Bro. Ragland should receive the assurance soon that the whole amount will be provided.

—"Of course, we all have our ideas about running church papers. I have mine. I think Sunday-school Departments and Endeavor Departments in our church papers are a nuisance. I am sorry the Register-Review has adopted this fad.—*Simpson Ely, in Register Review.*

It might be well to raise the inquiry as to whether the above represents the sentiment of any considerable number of our own readers. We have supposed that these departments representing practical lines of church work would be found helpful to our readers and would be appreciated by them. If, however, we are mistaken in this, we would find it more economical to omit them. The "Hour of Prayer," too, designed to aid the midweek prayer-meeting and to promote personal piety, can be omitted if it is failing to accomplish its purpose. We hope our readers will feel free to express themselves concerning the utility or inutility of any feature of the paper.

—The German Emperor is said to have been the first "Christian" that has been permitted to enter David's tomb at Jerusalem since 1187. The German Emperor seemed to have the right of way through all Mohammedan institutions, their most sacred tombs not accepted. We wonder if his entrance to and exit from this "sacred shrine" will shed any new light on sacred history.

—The young people of the church in Eureka, Ill., gave a royal farewell reception to the retiring pastor, the evening of Oct. 28. It has been his effort to be helpful to all classes and has given especial attention to the young, the appreciation of which was shown by a purse of money and a splendid study chair.

—Our frontispiece this week presents the face of another one of our editorial staff and one whose contributions are always read with interest. Bro. Haley is pastor of the church at Cynthiana, Ky. He spent eleven years in Australia and four and a half years at Birkenhead, England, in each of which places his work was highly appreciated. Bro. Haley is this week delivering a series of lectures before the Bible College at Columbia, Mo., on "The Old Book in a New Crucible." He stands equally high as a preacher and writer, and is now in about the full prime of life. He is a Kentuckian by birth, and a graduate of Kentucky University.

—Last week we announced the news of the healing of the division that had existed in the church at Clarksville, Tenn., for some time. We have received clippings from the local papers containing full accounts of the proceedings. It is sufficient to say here that the preachers, J. C. Hay, who was ministering to one of the congregations, and A. M. Growden, who was preaching for the other, acted nobly and unselfishly in the matter, and manifested the Spirit of Christ in the course which they pursued. By mutual concessions and mutual forgiveness the breach was healed. We congratulate the two pastors, the united church and Bro. Romig, under whose labors the union was consummated. It was a signal triumph of the gospel and the spirit of brotherly love and unity over whatever discordant elements had temporarily gained ascendance. These brethren have all given additional evidence of their loyalty to the Master in the course they have pursued. We can only hope that the spirit which prevailed in bringing about this happy condition of things in Clarksville may be permitted to have its way in all congregations which have been similarly affected.

—Dr. H. L. Willett writes us from Antwerp. He wrote his article on Bible-school lesson after going aboard the ship at New York, intending to send it back by the pilot, but missed the pilot by a few minutes, and so had to wait until across the Atlantic before another opportunity to send it to us came. Three articles came from him this week, but two of them are too late to be of present use to our readers, and so we omit them. The one that appears in this paper is the one in its regular order, and we presume that the others will now follow without intermission.

—We have already noted with pleasure that Gen. Drake has given five thousand dollars to our Board of Home Missions (Benj. L. Smith, Cor. Sec.) to be a permanent fund with which the Home Board agrees to maintain a missionary all the t me. We are glad to see our brethren taking up the work of Home Missions especially in this the Jubilee Year of the American Christian Missionary Society. We hope many and large gifts will be sent to the Home Society this year that we may realize the motto of the Chattanooga Convention—"One Hundred Thousand Dollars for Home Missions in the Jubilee Year."

—In the recent death of Dr. Samuel A. Mutchmore the Presbyterian Church has lost an able, scholarly editor and preacher. He was the editor of the Presbyterian and pastor of the Memorial Church, Philadelphia, Pa. "His religious life was one of consecration, both of his strength and of his means. His abilities and services were recognized by the church in his election to the Moderatorship in Saratoga, 1894."

—The Santa Cruz Daily Sentinel, Santa Cruz, Cal., contains the following singular answer to prayer. The answer, however, evidently did not come from heaven. We glean only the facts from the Sentinel, omitting the unsavory details:

Pastor McHatton, of the Christian Church, is a firmer believer in the efficacy of prayer than ever, if that be possible. He prayed for $300 with which to complete his church on Lincoln St., and his prayer met with a responsive chord when Joseph Fleiss, or Fleisher, listened to it. Fleiss was not a member of the church, but happened to attend services when the pastor, whose heart and soul are wrapped up in the completion of the structure, prayed for financial assistance. The donation came about in rather an unexpected and tragic manner, for the giver lay cold in death when a check for the amount was handed to him. A wound in his right temple, a pool of blood on the lounge where his head rested and a pistol on the floor with one chamber empty told the story of the suicide. The right temple was powder burned, showing that the pistol had been held close to the head. On the bed was a typewriter. When the trunk of the deceased was opened two typewritten letters were found. One was addressed to the pastor of the Christian Church, containing two checks, one for $300 and the other for $80. Both checks were properly stamped, and drawn on the Bank of Santa Cruz Co. The other letter was addressed to Geo. Nicol. Fleiss did not commit suicide because of lack of means, for he had government bonds amounting to $1,000 and $380 on deposit in the Bank of Santa Cruz Co. There were two causes that impelled him to his rash act. One was that he was a sufferer from heart trouble, which caused him to be melancholy. The other, according to those who knew him, was due to a love affair he had in the East. He was in love with a young lady who had died since he came to Santa Cruz. Over this he brooded constantly. After her death he lost interest in his surroundings.

In a letter which he left he says:

I hereby give and bequeath to the First Christian Church of Santa Cruz, as per check enclosed, $300, hereby authorizing the pastor (I don't know what his name is. It might be Beans, for that comes nearest to being mine of anything I know of now), or any one in authority of the First Christian Church, to cash or collect the same. If the First Christian Church refuses to accept same, owing to my rash act, any other denomination may have same by applying for it; and if no other denomination, I guess some one will call for it. I have no particular reason for giving the same to the First Christian Church, only, perhaps, the same is in construction and incomplete for lack of funds; and whether I go into a hole in the ground or any place else I cannot take any of it along anyway. I do not suppose I belong to any denomination, and if I did claim to I would be no credit to any one anyway, for I don't think any one would care to recognize me after this act.

Educational Conference in December.

We print elsewhere the report of the Educational Conference held at Moberly, last week, by one who was in attendance. The time was too short to arrange any definite plans for such a conference, and we are not surprised that no definite action was taken. It will be seen, however, that another conference has been arranged for and called to meet at the same place, Moberly, Mo., on Tuesday, the 6th of December. This gives a little less than a month to get ready for that conference, and there is no time to be lost. The object of the conference is of such pressing importance that it should call out a representative assembly of the brotherhood of the state.

It is recognized by all of us that Missouri is not doing her share of the educational work of the brotherhood, and is not meeting the responsibility growing out of our numbers and resources. The question to be faced and to be solved is, *What is the best thing to do under existing conditions, and at the present time, to further our educational interests in Missouri?* Shall we endow the Bible College at Columbia to meet the obligations we owe to that institution, as the leading religious body in the state, and to our own boys and girls who are going there as students? If so, shall we also utilize the other institutions that we have in the state in the fields where they are located, and seek to make the most out of them? Or, shall we undertake an independent educational enterprise, and seek to concentrate the brotherhood of the state in one educational effort? This latter plan has been tried without any practical result, except to demonstrate its impr
ability. It seems to us, therefore, that
remaius nothing else for us to do but tc
the friends of these different institu io
give them better financial support, and
plans by which they may be endowed.
these are questions of such far-reachin
portance as to demand the best thought
wisest men we have in the state.

In order both to form and to formula
sentiment of the brotherhood of the sta
this subject we invite a condensed stat
of opinion from such as feel an interest
educational work in the state, on the foll
question: *What ought the brotherhoo
Missouri to undertake to do now to mee
educational demands that are made upo*
Let the answers be very brief, that we
hear from many on this question. Let
be specific, too, that they may be unders
Above all, let them be *practicable*, poi
out something that lies within the ran
possibility and reasonable probability.
them come promptly, for the time is shor

How We Look from an Australi Point of View.

Our good brother, A. B. Maston,
Australia, after telling the people of
country about the good points of the chu
in the antipodes, is now telling the peo
Australia, through the Australian Chri
his impression of things in this country
the article now before us entitled, "In
Land," he gives an account of his vi
Tennessee. Referring to the positic
David Lipscomb, of the Gospel Advocat
says:

He thinks the New Testament contain
revelation from God, and that it is comple
itself, and that we can neither add to or
tract. In theory that is what we all beli
but Bro. Lipscomb insists upon putting it
practice.

This announcement might be appropri
headed, "Important if True." If this re
sents Bro. Maston's sentiments we may ex
him, on his return to Australia, to patter
paper after the Gospel Advocate, so far a
teaching is concerned, and devote much o
time and space to opposing what the re
the brotherhood are doing along mission
educational and benevolent lines.

Concerning our "Bible colleges and theol
cal schools generally," he says it is his "
did judgment" that they "are turning c
class of men who preach because they are
instead of because they are impelled by a g
and unquenchable desire for the salvatio
men and the glory of God." He admits t
are exceptions to this rule, but this is the r
That is about the harshest judgment of a c
of men who have given themselves sp
training for the ministry of the Word
remember to have seen from any respect
source. We are compelled to say in the l
of these statements, that in our "ca
judgment" Bro. Maston has suffered seve
in loss of Christian charity, and in breadt
view and sympathy by his associations on
other side of the globe.

CHANGES.

W. L. Shouse, Shelbyville to Shelbina,
M. J. Maxwell, Bellville to Greenwich, O
L. F. Stephens, N. Yakima, Wash., Corvallis, Ore.
A K. Wright, Catlin, Col., to Beth Neb.
F. A. Sword, Benton, Ill., to Montic Ia.
E. M. Miller, Fonda to Schaller, Ia.
H. F. Martin, Freestone to Farmers, Ky

nal Contributions.

—RATIONALISM—SPECULATION.

B. W. PIERCE

knows all of anything. We
ed an ordinary lamp, and yet all
and editors could not, we pre-
ribe every process in the manu-
that useful article. If we have
ated their ability we might in-
ıer, Of *what* is a lamp made?
Yes. But what is matter?
that occupies space and is
ıle." Yes. Is the *form*, or *weight*,
pace-occupancy, or all these and
bined the *matter* out of which
is made? Possibly some one
gest the term substance—that
s under and gives tangibility to
l forms. But what is *that?* God
lon't. God gives the material,
ınics make the lamp, and men of
ase can light the lamp and use it
do sages. Light the lamp and
haps you may solve the mysteries

informed that "man is so con-
at he cannot take cognizance of
ept through his senses," and
is deduced the remarkable con-
ıt "when God would communi-
aen he does so in manners and
; are cognizable through their
d never otherwise." In other
l always, in communicating ideas
erates as man operates—through
angible symbols. He so respects
stitution that he always, in com-
g ideas to man, uses symbols ad-
man's outward organs of sense.
rue, the claim to a divine revela-
from nature falls to the ground.
, then, becomes the interpreta-
outward symbols. Either the
ıind operating upon external
;ives man religion; or the divine
ating through outward symbols
ı religion. In the one case we
e deism, and in the other a sort
ism almost identical with skepti-
w should we distinguish between
ı and divine?

s a wide difference between two
ne of whom is searching for
ruths through outward symbols,
ther receiving those same truths
he same symbols *selected and*
by a divine teacher. But the one
's the spiritual truth and pre-
differs widely from either. The
ul's natural man. The last is his
man. The second, of course, is
o whom the gospel came. Now
ual man did not come into the
ı of his spiritual ideas through
ymbols. As proof of this we cite
These truths it is the province
rit to reveal, and is above and be-
an reason.

rit of prophecy is not the product
reason or foresight. Neither is
t-matter of prophecy deducible
symbols. One may see the
l not know its meaning. Another
g the Spirit may interpret the
nd through the symbols. The
nay not be found in nature, and
not presented to the senses from without, but the divine mind operates from within. He is not limited to the use of natural symbols in communicating with men. The symbols in the case have no definite meaning till *interpreted* in vision or by a man empowered by the Spirit to do so. Here, then, in vision and in prophecy, the spiritual man stands on a higher plane than the natural man.

It must be observed, further, that such prophecy and teaching of the Spirit has no private interpretation. It deals with truths belonging to the entire race. The relation between the divine mind and the spiritual man is direct and primary; between the spiritual man and they to whom the gospel comes it is indirect, through words of the Spirit or other symbols. (Read Heb. 1.)

Just how the Spirit operated on the minds of the apostles so as to show things to come, or to enable them without thought to make their defense, is a mystery. That it did so operate is a matter of record, and not of observation. Through the preaching of the gospel by men who spake as they were moved by the Holy Spirit the church was established; and by the proclamation of that same gospel the church has come down through the ages. That the Holy Spirit was in the apostles before operating through the Word is evident from the Scriptures. That Christians did not come into possession through belief and obedience of the Spirit in that degree of fullness the apostles possessed it, is evident from the fact that the apostles laid hands on early Christians that they might receive the Holy Spirit. But that Christians do come into possession of the Spirit is evident from Peter's language to the Pentecostians: "And ye shall receive the gift of the Holy Spirit." This was *not* "the Word of the gospel" they were to receive. "Have ye received the Holy Spirit since ye believed?" After baptism in the name of the Lord Jesus Paul laid hands on them and they received the Holy Spirit. This, of course, was not the Word. To the Galatians Paul writes: "Because ye are sons God hath sent forth his Spirit into your hearts crying, Abba, Father." This surely was not the Word of the gospel. "If any man has not the Spirit of Christ he is none of his."

Now the question of the direct relation between the Holy Spirit and the spirit of the Christian, it seems to me, is already established by the above and especially the following Scriptures: "God will not suffer you to be tempted above that you are able bear, but will with the temptation make a way for escape." No man has ever been able to tell how God would make that promise good without admitting a direct relation between the Spirit of God and the Christian in temptation. Let some one try his powers at this point.

No man has a right to claim that relation who refuses to obey the gospel as set forth by the apostles of Jesus Christ. "He that heareth you heareth me." The Christian will not conduct himself out of harmony with the revelation as set forth in the New Testament.

Bear in mind one thing more. This spirit which is in the Christian is not there to teach him to neglect the gospel given of the "common salvation," not to give new revelations to the world. Its mission is not general, but to the individual. "God works in each Christian to will and to do of

his g
keep
which
prope
apost
fanat
on a
claim
posse
indiv
comn
Spiri
as ar
any
here
for th
to the

THE
THI

Th
Chris
Chris
Bu
the s
of C
range
in th
Re
exten
giver
giver
comp
scien
He
but h
tema
arrar
this
Go
trine
doctı
we l
huma
rang
Sy
usefı
In a
centı
and
shall
W
faith
of G
the
Aı
scrip
sove
the
Lord
Cl
thro
thro
Chri
canr
son.
Sa
ive
theo
This
our
emp

Tl
Old
by J
mea
is th

*A
Ph.D
the s

and they must be interpreted by his person and work.

Out of the wreck and ruin of paradise God points to a future Deliverer. Abel offers a lamb upon the altar and his faith embraces the Lamb of God who shall take away the sin of the world. Noah sees the promised One in the rainbow that spans the peaceful heavens and pitches his tent under the protection of its arch. Abraham rejoices to see the day of Christ, sees it, and is glad. When Jacob is dying he looks down the long line of centuries and sees the long-promised One.

"The sceptre shall not depart from Judah, nor a lawgiver from between his feet until Shiloh come, and to him shall the gathering of the people be." A great leader and lawgiver leads the nation from bondage, but a prophet greater than Moses shall arise; him we shall hear in all things.

David looks forward to the reign of his greater son. The prophets speak of the sufferings of Christ and the glory that shall follow. Isaiah prophesies that a child shall be born and a son given, who is the Everlasting Father and the Prince of Peace. The same prophet declares that he shall be a root out of dry ground, despised and rejected of men, yet bearing in his own body the sins of the world.

Daniel sees a great kingdom over which the Messiah rules. In the New Testament all this finds its realization. Type has been succeeded by antitype, shadow has grown to substance, prediction has been consummated in fulfillment and the Christ of prophecy has become the Christ of history.

But what is the interpretation that the New Testament writers put on the Old Testament conception of Christ. The apostles and evangelists are certainly safe interpreters of the Old Testament.

First of all, the Jesus of the Gospels is the Christ. The Messiah of the Old Testament is the Christ, the anointed of the New Testament. He is the long-expected One for which they waited and for which the ages were the preparation, the King of Israel, "the desire of all nations," the Prophet, Priest and King of humanity.

But he is more than the Messiah; he is the Son of God. He is the Word incarnate, was in the beginning with God and was God. The revealer of God, God manifest in the flesh. "All things were by him and without him nothing made that was made." "He was before all things and by him all things consist." He is the Head of the body, the church, both Lord and Christ. Has been exalted to the highest heavens and is to be honored and worshiped. He is the long-promised Messiah and the Son of God.

We are now prepared to understand the place Christ occupied in the thought of the early church. To them he was Redeemer and Lord. They trusted in his blood for forgiveness of sins, were reconciled to God through his cross, and when groaning after immortality they embraced his resurrection life.

Any system of theology that claims to be Christian must give Jesus Christ the preeminence in all things. It is my purpose to show that our position as Disciples is in harmony with the biblical conception of Christ.

PLACE OF AUTHORITY.

There must be a standard of appeal. What is it? The Unitarian says the reason. The Roman Catholic, the church. The Protestant appeals to the Scriptures. The real authority in religion is Jesus Christ. He said himself, "All authority is given unto me in heaven and in earth." Every appeal must be made to Christ, as he has expressed himself in his Word. The Christ is infallible; beyond him there is no appeal. Before the incarnation he was the Word of God. He revealed himself as Lawgiver and Prophet. "He was the true light that lighteth every man coming into the world."

The Spirit of Christ was in the prophets when they spake beforehand of the sufferings of Christ and the glory that should follow. The Word of God before the incarnation was the revealer of God. He came to lawgiver and prophet and gave them their message. Thoughts are clothed in words. Jesus Christ is the word that expresses the thought of God.

To the pre-incarnate Christ we must attribute the moral sense of the heathen, the wisdom of the philosopher, the genius of the poet. The utterances of the prophets have value because they are inspired by him. The incarnate Christ reveals the Father, discloses the heart of God, expresses the thought of God.

Referring to the Old Testament as authority in religion, Jesus said: "You seach the Scriptures, and in them you think you have eternal life, and they are they which testify of me." "The Scriptures must be fulfilled." "The Scriptures cannot be broken." Their moral failures were due to their ignorance of the Scriptures. "You do err, not knowing the Scriptures nor the power of God."

But this Spirit that was in the prophets would take possession of the apostles and guide them into all truth, take the things of Christ and show them unto us. Now the final authority in Christianity is the Lord Jesus Christ. The mind of Christ has been revealed to prophets and apostles. This is recorded in the Scriptures; to the Scriptures we must appeal to find the mind of Christ. In the Scriptures his will is recorded. All the authority in reason is because Christ enlightens the reason by his Spirit and Word.

If the church speaks with authority it is because the body is united to the head, or because the building rests upon Jesus Christ, the one foundation, and is the repository of divine truth.

This being true, we should be deaf to every other voice but the voice of the Son of God. Beyond him there is no appeal. If prophets and apostles are to be heard it is because they speak his Word. "This is my beloved Son, hear ye him."

FAITH IN CHRIST.

The faith of the gospel is faith in the personal Christ. Or, in other words, the faith required in order to salvation is not doctrinal, but personal. Not faith in a creed, but a personal trust in the person of the Lord Jesus Christ.

It is stated thus: "Jesus is the Christ, the Son of the living God." The faith that saves is personal. It has Jesus for its object. Theories about Jesus, belief in doctrines, however true, have no saving vitality. A sinner, conscious of his ruin, needs a personal Savior. Such a Savior i Jesus Christ. No human system of doc trine can be the object of faith. "Believ on the Lord Jesus Christ and thou shalt b saved." This was the faith required in th preaching of the apostles.

Says Bishop Phillips Brooks: " there is one change above all others th has altered our modern Christianity fro what it was in apostolic times it is this, substitution of belief in doctrine for loyal to a person as the essence and test of th Christian life." "Christ is Christianity and to follow him and to love him is to be Christian. There are two ideas of Chris tianity: one magnifies doctrine and it great sin is heresy; the other magnifie obedience and its great sin disobedience.

The faith of the gospel rests upon Jesu as the Son of God. The sinner, consciou of his sin, turns away from every fals hope, flees for refuge and lays hold on th hope set before him. He finds salvation i the Son of God. Jesus Christ satisfies th intellec and masters the heart. This ma be a simple creed, but it is divine an possesses real saving vitality. It is faith i him who is our Prophet, Priest and King who is the Son of God, who died for ou sins, and rose again for our justificatior This belief of the heart will produce love t Christ.

There will be a real personal attachmen to Jesus. Such a faith produces obedience It is not a mere passive belief, but a livin faith that leads to an obedient life. Th soul that really believes in Jesus receive him as a Savior, Master and Lord. Bu this means to accept his authority. Th believing soul seeks to do the will of Christ, listens to the voice of Christ, and bows tc the authority of Christ. So Christians come to be called by the name of Christ. If Jesus is the object of faith, the Lord and Master, would it not be the natural thing to call his followers by his name? "Let every one that names the name of Christ depart from iniquity." The church is built upon Jesus as the one foundation. He is the Head of the church, Redeemer, Shepherd and Lord. Ought not his church to be called by his name? To give a human name to the people of God is to rob Christ of what is his own. It is to give his glory to another.

RELATIVE VIRTUE OF OBEDIENCE.

The ordinances of the gospel are administered by the authority of Christ. The command of Jesus is: "Go ye, therefore, make disciples of all nations, baptizing them into the name of the Father, Son and Holy Spirit." This is the authority for baptizing. It is the command of our Lord. We cannot set it aside without disobedience to the Head of the church.

This is equally true of the Lord's Supper. Says Jesus, "This do in remembrance of me." The Apostle Paul, in referring to the Lord's Supper said, "I delivered to you that which I also received of the Lord." These ordinances symbolize the great facts in the gospel of Christ. The Lord's Supper symbolizes his death. In this institution we see Jesus dying for our sins, his body broken and bruised and his blood poured out for our redemption. "As often as ye eat this bread and drink this cup, you do show forth the Lord's death until he comes." Baptism symbolizes the burial and resurrection of Christ. "We are

into death."
the glory of
ized in bap-
and rise with
on life.
osely related
aptism of the
on Christ, is
Its value
he ordinance
ie person in
s have been
ave put on
ete surrender
esus Christ,
g penitent in
ord's Supper
not an un-
ans of grace.
, the love is
ristian life is
we break, is
dy of Christ;
not the com-
"

N.

after which
e conformed.
His earthly
ciples. "If
let him deny
is and follow
by obedience
ssion to him.
y following
engaged all
od. It should
Christian to
which should
s not exstatic
eriences, but
y man serve
Tot every one
rd, shall in-
, but he that
The Christ-
ie Christian.
rit of Christ,
istian knows
ut after the
eliever. He
He has the
g made like
Christ. As
ayer, so the
e prayerful
t doing good,
s daily life to
lled with the
sing to man-
ith an enthu-
passion for
the church is
ist; thus will
hy with the
men and will
nkind.

essor of Old
University of
a course of
on of Israel
ne Exile," at

osphate.
, says: "I have
indigestion and
actory results."

Correspondence.

English Topics.

THE ANGLO-AMERICAN WRECK.

The wreck of the Mohegan has set the heart of England thrilling with many emotions. This fine steamship belonged to both England and America. It was the property of the New York Trans-Atlantic Company. It has been lost on the dreadful reef of rocks off the Coast of Cornwall, called the Manacles, near the city of Falmouth, and not far from the rugged Cape called Lizard Point. Many an American traveler remembers the Lizard and the grand but dangerous cliffs of Cornwall which are stormed at by the tempestuous billows of the mighty Atlantic rolling in for 3,000 miles. The Mohegan was a fine new ship, going out on her second voyage from London to New York. Many American passengers were on board. These had just sat down to dinner in the saloon when that horrid, grating sound vibrated through the vessel which told that the great and beautiful ship had gone crashing on the ribs of death. In half an hour, amidst heart-rending scenes of farewell between loving friends, the Mohegan had settled in her deep sepulchre, the shrill requiem of shrieks and cries being accompanied by the hoarse bass of the billows. No fewer than 107 souls perished in that awful thirty minutes! But now come some lessons which ought to be stereotyped on the consciousness of several nations. Let Englishmen and Americans take courage. Let Frenchmen and some other Continental peoples take warning. When a few months ago we were all shocked by the tragedy of La Bourgogne, the civilized world was outraged by the records of hideous cowardice and cruelty on the part of the French crew and the Italian steerage passengers. Not a woman was saved, nor yet a child. Now mark the contrast! The crew, officers and passengers of the Mohegan were all Americans and English people. And in the appalling scene in which the majority met their end not any approach to panic occurred. Every man was a hero, and every woman played the heroine. The very first cry was, "Save the women!" Captain and officers died at their posts. These people on the Mohegan did not belong to any of those nations which have cast out the Bible and expatriated God. The Anglo-Saxons know how to die when the grim enemy suddenly summons them to the eternal presence.

BRITAIN AT BAY.

Lord Salisbury has put down his foot. That is the most important announcement made in this country for the last seven years. But no man knows what it may involve. Hitherto our Prime Minister, who is also Foreign Minister, has, whenever he needed to put down his foot, elevated it as high as a skirt dancer. He has been for years pampering France with concessions which neither Gladstone nor Rosebery would have allowed. And now a momentous crisis has arrived. Nobody really believes that it means war with France, but everybody in this country has made up his mind that war with France must be risked this time. Major Marchand must quit Fashoda, and England must control the whole region of the Nile Basin. I have never known my country so compactly united as on this question. Parties have vanished in reference to the determination that France must yield. If she will not, then she must expect the whole power of the British Empire to be launched against her. This is a fearful alternative, but I am bound to say that this nation has calmly made up its mind to face the worst, if the worst is to come. And here let me ask a question: If France, great though her navy may be, cannot find to man it sailors of a better type than those panic-stricken specimens who formed the crew of La Bourgogne, how is she going to fight our fleets, every ship of which will contain scores of men as cool and brave as the heroes of the Mohegan?

OUR OWN CONVENTION.

In this country we love a convention of religious minds as much as you Americans do. But we generally call it a conference. Our brothers and sisters representing our beloved Churches of Christ have been enjoying our Annual Conference of the Christian Association of Great Britain, which assembled at Margate. I have already in my letters sounded the praises of Margate as a lovely seaside resort. It is famous for the iodine which impregnates its atmosphere from the masses of seaweed on its wave-washed sands. It is historically interesting as being in the district which was the cradle of British Christianity. Close by is the landing-place of Augustine. At about the same spot the first Saxons under Hengist and Horsa landed. The Romans also built their first British fortress close by, called Richborough, whose wonderful ruins are a first-class archeological curiosity. And within an easy walk is Minster, which is in some respects the most interesting church in the world, for it is British, Saxon, Roman, Norman and English, all in one. The only other building equally composite I have ever seen is York Minster. A little farther on is wonderful old Canterbury. These are amongst the very first and chief places which an American visitor ought to see, yet they are the very places which the majority miss in favor of inferior sights. I sometimes wish I could afford to make myself guide and lecturer to American Christians visiting this country. Our conference was the very best we ever had. This was the common verdict. May I remark that it was in no small degree brightened by the strong American contingent we now have again with us regularly in the great work. It may sometimes be wondered why we want this element and never seem to get along so well without it as with it. I will tell you. The new Egyptian army has fought and won simply because stiffened by a small proportion of Englishmen. This is exactly analogous to the case I am dealing with. The new Reformation was introduced into this country by American Evangelists. They brought some of us English Christians on to the right line, and formed a little army of such of us as they could enlist to fight for the simplicity of the ancient gospel. But these are early days still with this movement here. Therefore, this little army needs stiffening by a contingent of American evangelists, and the time has not come for us to dispense with them. Now, at Margate we had with us E. M. Todd, of West London Tabernacle; Mark Collins, of Chester; Mr. and Mrs. Bicknell, of Liverpool, as well as that type of the best American sisterhood, Mrs. Frank Coop, who hardly knows whether she is American or British. She is ever with us, but is about to visit you for a season. You will see Brother and Sister F. Coop on your side this winter. Thus, we have at work on this side picked soldiers from your side. There is room for as many more as you like to send.

OUR PROGRESS.

Does this movement advance in England? Yes; it is moving on as things do move in this grand old land. Slowly and surely we creep on. Every church reported an increase with the single exception of Cheltenham, which showed a decrease of five; but even in that case the deficiency was made up by conversions between the date of the returns and the conference. In point of fact there has not been a single church without a gain. This has never happened before. Our numbers have shot up by over three hundred this year. This is not a big figure, but considering the conditions in this country it is a wonderful sign of encouragement and of coming success. All who attended the conference were full of hope, thankfulness, joy and confidence. God is in this work. It has had to suffer all that the virulent opposition of sectism could inflict on it, but it has come to stay, and it has begun to conquer. Remember that for some time we have to endure misapprehension in England. We are everywhere to a large extent misunderstood. But our day is at hand. The pioneering is being faithfully done, and it has to continue sometime yet. If our American friends would regard this English enterprise as a work of faith, and would be content to encourage us to pioneer still, waiting God's time for the grand season of success, they would be gloriously rewarded in due time. Bro. Rapkin and his faithful wife, our happy German sister, and the members of the church at Margate, all shone out in their zeal and hospitality in welcoming the delegates, who came from all parts of the country. It was good to see ministers of the different sects in Margate come into meeting after meeting. I discovered from some of these gentlemen that they had learned some lessons. Our churches are now exciting surprise by their vitality. It used to be assumed that they would either fizzle out or be snuffed out. But it is coming to be felt that even the least of these churches has no need to say, in the words of a text adopted by a candidate for the Methodist ministry, ''I pray thee, let me live!'' The conference is invited to assemble next year in the beautiful old cathedral city of Gloucester. How joyously Brother and Sister Spring would welcome a goodly contingent of American visitors! We will give good notice of the event, hoping that many will take Gloucester on their way when touring in England. W. DURBAN.

43 *Park Road, South Tottenham, N., Oct.* 22, 1898.

Is Baptism for the R mission of Sins?

When are the sins of the alien actually remitted? At what place, stage or time can the alien coming to Christ and into his kingdom have the assurance that his sins are forgiven?

If it had been said to me twenty years ago that I should some day write a paper to convince my own brethren on these points I would not have believed it. It seems, however, that some of the old battles are to be fought over again. The time has come when those who are not of us can not learn clearly from our preaching and from our papers what we believe and teach concerning this. Even our good Brother Garrison, editor of the CHRISTIAN-EVANGELIST, is not understood. His position on baptism for remission of sins is not understood, and by others he is suspected of unsoundness.

I wish to be heard, for I have something to say, and it is something that ought to be said at this stage of the proceedings. I wish to be heard in two papers. The first will be a John the Baptist for the other.

The first is a paper on justification by faith. I think a large part of the difficulty lies in a want of knowledge as to the part that faith does in bringing the alien to the forgiveness of sins and the assurance of it.

Let us take up the old text, Rom. 5:1: ''Therefore, being justified by faith we have peace with God through our Lord Jesus Christ.'' This statement is clear and full. There is something by which we are justified. That something of itself is sufficient for our justification. Nothing else is required. Anything in addition to it would be superfluous. Whatever that something is, *is* absolutely necessary to our justification. Nothing else is necessary to our justification. He who has this something *is* justified, and having this may be assured that he is justified. Whatever is included in this something and is part of it is necessary in order to justification. Nothing else is necessary. We are in no doubt as to what the name of that something is. The difficulty arises in not understanding it when we know its name. Paul says, the Spirit says, God says, that something is faith. Faith it is, then, that justifies. What is faith? What is faith in this text? Mr. Moody says, and Mr. Jones says, and the great Methodist Church says, and the whole system of mourner's bench, or penitent form, or altar service, says it is the act of believing, a mental act. That it is taught that this is a soul-act, a heart-act, etc., does not affect the argument. It is the opposite of a physical act. Not matter, nor yet mind and matter, but mind or spirit. Baptism is a physical act, therefore baptism has nothing to do with it. Consequently, since baptism follows this act, and this act brings justification, baptism is not for justification. The *actual* remission of sins takes place when this mind-act, soul-act, heart-act or spirit-act is performed. This is the position of Moody, *et al.*

B. B. Tyler, J. H. Garrison and others among us *seem to adopt* this position, but add this, that in baptism the alien receives assurance of pardon already granted. I submit this proposition: If Moody, *et al.*, are right in their understanding of what the ''faith'' mentioned in Rom. 5:1 is, baptism has absolutely nothing to do with remission of sins, or the assurance of remission. See the next verse. It is declared that by ''faith'' we have access into this grace wherein we stand.

Let Paul say what this faith is. Gal. 2:16 explains the matter perfectly: ''Knowing that a man is not justified by the works of the law, but by the faith of Jesus Christ, even we have believed in Jesus Christ that we might be justified by the faith of Christ and not by the works of the law, for by the works of the law shall no flesh be justified.'' We have two things mentioned, the works of the law and the faith of Christ. In other words, the law and the gospel. It is plain. Faith stands for the whole system of the Christian religion. Gal. 3:2: ''Received ye the Spirit by the works of the law, or by the hearing of faith?'' Judaism and Christianity. Gal. 2:5: ''He, therefore, that ministereth to you the Spirit and worketh miracles among you, doeth he it by the works of the law, or by the hearing of faith?'' There is no mistaking this. I challenge any man to place Rom. 5:1 and Gal. 3:11 side by side and read them. ''But that no man is justified by the law in the sight of God is evident, for the just shall live by faith.'' The same ''faith'' in each meaning the gospel. It may safely and truly be said we are saved by this faith only, but it is not the faith James speaks of (Jas. 2:17-26).

Again read Gal. 3:23-25. Here two things are mentioned. One is called law, the other is called faith. Before faith came we were kept under the law. It is the same faith of Rom. 5:1, and means the gospel.

But why multiply texts? Many more might be given. Suffice it to say, then, there are two meanings to the word faith as used in the New Testament—the gospel of Christ and the act of believing. The latter precedes repentance, and baptism, and turning to the Lord, and all Christian living and obedience, and leads to all these. The first includes the latter and repentance, baptism—all obedience and Christian living.

While the apostles lived and preached, and the New Testament history was being made, there were in that country three separate classes: pagans, Jews and Christians. When a man left the pagans or Jews to become a Christian he was called a believer, which meant a Christian. To believe meant to become a Christian, and involved the whole process. One faith—believing—precedes baptism. Of the other faith—the gospel—baptism is a part.

If ye know these things, happy are you if you preach and write as if you knew them. In my next I will speak of baptism for the remission of sins. E. L. FRAZIER.

Marion, Ind.

[If there is to be a rediscussion of this subject it would be well to enter into a definition of terms. What is faith in its New Testament sense? Is it a mental act or a certain attitude of the soul toward God? Is it an objective system by which Paul declares we are jus[illegible] fied, or a subjective principle—the principle loyalty and submission to God? What is ba tism? Not in its external form, but in [illegible] totality? What is meant by ''remission sins?'' Is this merely absolving from guilt, does it include deliverance from the power a the habit of sin? We would request Bro. not to state our position except in our o words. No one has antagonized more stea fastly than we have any conception of fai that divorces it from obedience and surrend to God. But we do not think Bro. F. h attained Paul's point of view in his doctrine justification by faith. ''The faith'' do sometimes mean the gospel, but Paul does n mean in Rom. 5:1 that we are justified by t gospel. Abraham was justified by faith b fore the law was given and before the gosp was published.—EDITOR.]

The Church and the World.

It seems to be held in orthodox religio ranks that the relation between the church a the world is that of belligerents and unchang able. That such a relation existed betwe Christians of the first century and the preva ing spirit of the world at that time, and shou still exist as to all that is evil, is true. But affirm such an attitude of the church towa the world in an unqualified and an unchangea sense is to go beyond the bounds of reason, t facts of history and the demands of revelatio

The things to which Christianity stood o posed in the mind of the apostolic school we not the earth and its elements, nor the esse tial social and civil institutions of the worl nor with the people, but with their sins a the spirit that caused them. If they oppos civil and religious institutions it was becau of the moral evil in them. If they oppos existing social and industrial conditions it w because they were founded on lust, injusti and unrighteousness. If they opposed weal it was because of its dangers. If they oppos rulers it was because of their wickedness. Ar if they spake disparagingly of the earth and i elements it was because they were not as im portant and enduring as the human spirit.

The writers of the Holy Book nowhere attri ute the source of moral evil to the material un verse. They could not consistently do this ar at the same time predicate a portion of God glory upon it as in the 19th psalm. To ho the earth and its physical elements in contem would be equivalent to an attitude of unfrien liness if not of enmity toward God.

The indiscriminate condemnation of all ex isting institutions in the world, of whatsoev character, other than the church, is equal faulty and injurious. There were many thin in the world which Christ and his apostles re ognized, other than the church, as original from heaven, and essential, even, to the welfa of the church. There was the family, th state, the arts, the sciences, commerce, indu tries, and other factors essential to civiliz life against which no word of condemnation found from their pen and against which th church founded by them was not arrayed. An for want of a proper recognition of this fact th church has since committed some most grie ous and humiliating blunders, having earne for itself the unenviable reputation of being th enemy of enlightenment, education and prog ress.

But this is not all nor the worst of this false applied theory. Bible-schools, Christian En deavor Societies, literary societies, benevole societies, missionary societies, secret societie religious societies, temperance societies, a classed as worldly institutions and to be hate by the church. Such, then, are some of th results of a wrong conception of the relation the church to the world. Some men will n cast a ballot because the state, in their judg ment, is Satan's empire. Some even do n recognize any good thing outside of the relig ious body to which they are joined.

Even if we admit that the apostolic churc

ing institutions
s a whole, in its
'rom the nature
at this attitude
If so, the mis-
lained failure.
e that the atti-
world should be
ring the latter
ve not then ad-
ailed, thus far,
iission? Is not
not its gospel
world?

t seems to us,
extent that the
tter, or coming
in that respect
belligerency of
church, there-
onsistently op-
l of the world
t moral, intel-
The progress
fore, naturally
f its relation to
relation of ne-
e church to the
church is ever
will be, its re-
become that of

elligerent atti-
as not against
y and essential
that was in the
that was even
his respect the
ain the attitude
well as toward
not only dissi-
, but stultifies
position before
ecome indiffer-
within its own
vigorous war-
world that are
than that they
ie position of a
'et swallowing
that makes the
ous and repul-

rasts between
urches, and to
y, is in and of
od as belliger-
h the apostolic
se of the pres-
ions, medieval
urches became
is particularly
o idolatry, to
in high places,
, to social dis-
her pernicious
condemned by
many churches
ome instances
preached and
all heard men
as—a church to
t opposition to
ching? But we
here and now.
he subject of a
st upon is that
church should
essential insti-
is in the world;
o far as human
are the better-
he enemies of
he church—the
of the living
so recognized,
ly needed; of
time.

F. T. Pew.

The Mormon-Christian War.

Jacob, brother of Nephi, was born to Lehi and Sariah, their firstborn in the wilderness after they had started from Jerusalem to what is now known as the United States of America. They started on this journey 600 years before Christ was born.

So says the "Book of Mormon." Mormons admit that their "ism" stands or falls with this book as a divine or a human book. Jacob was a preacher; his talent run to exhortation. Some of these phrases sound very "modern" to have been written over 2,500 years.

"Wherefore, we labored diligently among our people, that we might persuade them to come unto Christ and partake of the goodness of God, that we might enter into his rest, lest by any means he should swear in his wrath that they should not enter in, as in the provocation, while the children of Israel were in the wilderness."

Jacob says that under the "second king" the people "began to grow hard in their hearts and indulge themselves somewhat in wicked practices, such as like unto David of old, *desiringmany wives* and concubines, and also Solomon, his son."

Jacob determined to let them have it. He says: "And we did magnify our office unto the Lord, taking upon us the responsibility, answering the sins of the people upon our own heads, if we did not teach them the Word of God with all diligence; wherefore *by laboring with our mights* their blood might not come upon our garments; otherwise their blood would come upon our garments and *we* would not be found spotless at the last day."

That's pretty good. I predict if some one will find Sidney Rigdon's barrel of old sermons he will find that Jacob, 2,500 years before Sidney was born, used a great many pet expressions of Sidney who, of course, at the time he petted certain phrases, didn't know of Jacob and Joe Smith's gold plates. When I quote Jacob I am presumably quoting from those gold plates.

Jacob says to his audience: "And it supposeth me that they have come up hither to hear the pleasing Word of God; yea, the Word which healeth the wounded soul. Wherefore, it burdeneth my soul, that I should be constrained because of the strict commandment which I have received from God, to admonish you according to your crimes, *to enlarge the wounds* of those already wounded, instead of consoling and healing their wounds," etc.

He charges them with polygamy and says: "For behold, thus saith the Lord, This people begin to wax in iniquity; they *understand not the* SCRIPTURES, FOR THEY SEEK TO EXCUSE THEMSELVES *in committing whoredom*, because of the things which were written of David and Solomon, his son. Behold David and Solomon truly *had many wives* and concubines, which thing was *abominable* before me, saith the Lord. Wherefore, thus saith the Lord, I have led this people forth out of the land of Jerusalem, by the power of mine arm, that I might rise up unto a righteous branch from the fruit of the loins of Joseph."

By an easy exegesis "the fruit of the loins of Joseph" can be made Joseph Smith's descendants, and the "branch" the Mormon Church of to day.

Jacob continues: "Wherefore, *I the Lord God* will not suffer it; *this people* shall do like unto *them of old.*"

That is, that the Mormons of to-day shall not have wives like David and Solomon. If it does not mean that doesn't mean anything. Jacob says further: "Wherefore, my brethren, hear me, and harken to the Word of the Lord, for there shall not *any man* among have save it be ONE wife, and concubines he shall *have none.* For I the Lord *delighteth in the chastity of women.* And whoredoms are an abomination before me."

If this does not teach monogamy and pronounce polygamy unchaste and whoredom,

language cannot be handled to so exp
When I called the attention of a Utah
what Jacob said he looked at me a
"*Have you read the next verse?*" I r
verse 30—here it is: "*For I will*, s
Lord of Hosts, *raise up seed unto me*
COMMAND MY PEOPLE: otherwise the
hearken unto *these things.*"

That is, if I the Lord command you
to be "unchaste," and you men to
"whoredom," though I "delight
chastity of women," and the polyg
David and Solomon was "abominable
must be "unchased" and "abominable

What a book and what a God the M
have! The world has been giving the
Mormon great credit for being *opp*
polygamy, yet it indicates that, in full
edge of its "abominations" and in
bitter *denunciations* of it, it will be pr
in the name and by the command of th

The Book of Mormon I have before m
me by a footnote to the Book of Doctr
Covenants, Sec. 132. Here it is, th
infamous document of any age. The
TIAN-EVANGELIST can give it in installm

R. B. N

[The quotations from the "Spiritua
System" of Mormonism is too ridiculo
to say revolting, to reproduce here.
work and read it if you are intereste
subject.—EDITOR.]

A Last Farewell.*

TEXT—I heard the voice of the Lord, saying, Whom shall I send? and who will go for us? Then, said I, Here am I, send me.—Isaiah 6:8.

"My soul is not at rest. There comes a strange
And secret whisper to my spirit, like
A dream of night, that tells me I am on
Enchanted ground. Why live I here? The vows
Of God are on me, and I may not stop
To play with shadows, or pluck earthly flowers,
Till I my work have done, and rendered up
Account. The voice of my departed Lord,
'Go teach all nations,' from the Eastern world
Comes on the night air, and awakens my ear,
And I will go."

The most authoritative word that is ever heard above the confused noise of this changing world is the voice of God in the soul, saying: "Go into all the world and preach the gospel to every creature." This is at once both a high command and an exceedingly great and precious privilege. The call was made a while ago to the young men of the country to enlist in defence of the flag and in the cause of humanity. Thousands came forward and placed their lives on the alter of liberty. The brave soldiers esteemed it both an honor and a privilege to go to the front either for service or for sacrifice in a holy cause. The mission that engaged the sailors and soldiers at Manila and Santiago was one of "confused noise and garments rolled in blood." The high service to which this dear girl has been called is one of peace on earth good will among men. It is the same mission that brought the Savior from heaven to earth and sent the holy apostles into every part of the great Roman Empire. Only a soul filled with love and the Spirit of Christ ever undertook such a task as this. Such a scene as you witness to-day is one of rare and radiant interest. In this unworldly place, at this sacramental feast, angels must love to stay their waving wings and pause to hear the consecration vows of a soul espoused to Christ and about to go forth to join the American missionaries in the East.

"I may no longer doubt
To give up all my friends and idol hopes,
And every tender tie that binds my heart
To thee, my country! Why should I regard
Earth's little store of borrowed sweets? I sure
Have had enough of bitter in my cup,
To show that never was it His design,
Who placed me here, that I should live in ease,
Or drink at pleasure's fountain.
Henceforth, then,
It matters not if storms or sunshine be
My lot—bitter or sweet my cup;
I only pray—'God fit me for the work.
God make me holy, and my spirit nerve
For the stern hour of strife.' Let me but know
There is an arm unseen that holds me up,
An eye that kindly watches my path,
Till I my weary pilgrimage have done;
Let me but know I have a friend that waits
To welcome me to glory, and I joy
To tread the dark and death-fraught wilderness."

The beautiful service of the missionary was defined by the Master as he stood in the synagogue at Nazareth on that long-gone sabbath day and read from the prophecy of Isaiah:

"The Spirit of the Lord is upon me, because he hath anointed me to preach the gospel to the poor; he hath sent me to heal the broken-hearted, to preach deliverance to the captives, the recovering of sight to the blind, to set at liberty them that are bruised, to preach the acceptable year of the Lord, to comfort all that mourn, to give them beauty for ashes, the oil of joy for mourning and the garment of praise for the spirit of heaviness."

The coming of Christ brought both a new force and new ideals into the world. In the Empire of Rome, where Christianity was born, there were sixty millions of slaves, forty millions of freedmen and only twenty millions of free citizens. The ideal life among such a population was one either of vaulting ambition or elegant leisure. Christ taught both by example and by precept that this was wrong. He was the image of the invisible God, the firstborn of every creature. By him were all things created that are in heaven and that are on earth—visible and invisible—whether they be thrones, or dominions, or principalities, or powers. Yet he made himself of no reputation and took upon him the form of a servant and was made in the likeness of men. It was his chief joy that he was in the world as one who served. His was a varied life, yet all was concentrated in a single sentence: "He went about doing good." His final word to all who ask if he is really the Christ, is this: "The blind receive their sight, the lame walk, the lepers are cleansed, the deaf hear, the dead are raised, the poor have the gospel preached to them, and blessed is he whosoever is not offended in me." These holy ministries are still in these last days the best evidences of Christianity.

"Follow with reverent steps the great example
Of Him whose holy work was doing good;
So shalt the wide earth seem our Father's Temple,
Each loving life a psalm of gratitude."

The history of modern missions is an added chapter to the Book of Acts. It is a fulfillment of the Master's promise of his continued presence with his disciples in every generation till the end of time. Lift up your eyes and look on the world wherever the missionaries of the cross have gone. There the wilderness and the solitary place are glad; the desert rejoices and blossoms as the rose. The parched ground becomes a pool and the thirsty land springs of water. The eyes of the blind are opened, the ears of the deaf are unstopped, the lame man leaps as an hart and the tongue of the dumb sings for joy. The cheering reports that come from the foreign field are the divine call to increased devotion to the cause of world-wide missions. The need of the hour is more of the Spirit of the Man of Galilee "who, although he was rich, yet for our sakes he became poor that we through his poverty might be rich." Many are converted, but few are consecrated. It is one thing to come into the fellowship of the church, but it is another and very different thing to take up the cross daily and follow Christ. In the days of his earthly ministry multitudes pressed upon him to see his miracles and to hear his teaching. Some followed because of the loaves and fishes. A few, however, were with him in Gethsemane, before Pilate and at Calvary. It costs a great deal to be a blessing. The dross must be consumed and the gold refined before one can be fashioned into a vessel of honor, sanctified and meet for the Master's use. This can be realized only through the fires of affliction. Many pass through strange experiences before coming into the larger fellowship of the gospel. Christ is constantly leading his people by a way they know not. What he does now we may not understand, but we shall know hereafter. Paul prayed for a prosperous journey to Rome, but he realized the very opposite! It was a path all rugged with rock and tangled with thorn. When, at last, he reached the gates of the Imperial City, he entered as a prisoner bound with a chain. It is a beautiful grace that enables one to satisfied with his lot wherever placed. Pa learned by long and varied service, in wha ever state he was, therewith to be conten A contented mind is a continual feast. T secret of the great joy of the missionaries their lives of toil and sacrifice in pagan lan is in the consciousness that they are ju where God would have them be, and doin just what God would have them do.

" There is a secret in the ways of God
With his own children which none others know,
That sweetens all he does and is such peace,
While under his afflicting hand, we find,
What will it be to see him as he is,
And past the reach of all that now disturbs.
The tranquil soul's repose? To contemplate
In retrospect unclouded, all the means
By which his wisdom has prepared his saints
For the vast weight of glory which remains!
Come, then, affliction, if my Father bids,
And be my frowning friend; a friend that frowns
Is better than a smiling enemy."

Any one who leaves home and friends an native land at the call of God, as did Abraham and goes out into the wide world, not knowin whither he is going, deserves to be called hero of the faith. The missionaries of th cross in every age have linked their name with that of the father of the faithful as the have gone over the winter seas and into th dark places of the earth in search of a countr that God would show them. Their name deserve a place among the splendid compan of believers mentioned in the eleventh chapte of the Epistle to the Hebrews. Nothing bu the grace of God in the heart can sustain on in the determination to go to the foreign field "As thy days so shall thy strength be" is precious promise that has reassured many sinking heart in the hour of trial. Sooner o later every trusting soul comes to realize tha God's grace is sufficient for every experience The saintly Robert Murray McCheyne, in th shadow of death, thanked God for strength i the hour of weakness, for light in the time o darkness, for joy in the time of sorrow, an for comforting us in all our tribulations.

The motives for engaging in the missionar enterprise are many and various. We cann be followers of God as dear children withou having the Spirit of Christ, who was the fir missionary to a world that had gone far awa from God. Christ loved the church and gav himself for it that he might sanctify an cleanse it with the washing of water by th Word, and present it to himself a gloriou church without spot, or wrinkle, or any suc thing. He came to seek and to save the lost If any one will be his disciple he must den himself and take up the cross and follow Christ even into the darkest corners of the earth The gospel is a balm for every wound, a cor dial for every woe, and the only remedy fo the evils that afflict the world. Dr. Jno Stewart Blackie says: "Christianity is strong medicine to knock down a strong dis ease." For centuries on centuries the paga philosophers have been trying to solve th

*A sermom preached by Rev. N. M. Ragland in the First Christian Church, Fayetteville, Ark., Sunday, Oct. 30, 1898, on the occasion of the departure of Miss Annie Agnes Lackey to join the American missionaries in India.

problems of human life and destiny. Without the light of revelation this is a hopeless task. It has been well said that the answer to Confucianism is China, the answer to Buddhism is India, the answer to Mohammedanism is Turkey. A tree is known by its fruit. Men gather neither grapes of thorns nor figs of thistles. Christianity rests her claims to the serious consideration of thoughtful men on the record she has made in every age and in every clime. Grea Britain and the United States are the noblest fruitage of our holy religion. Dr. Jno. Henry Barrows says of his recent trip around the world:

"I have found the American name beloved and trusted where other names failed to awaken any happy and affectionate feeling. The brightest light which shines on the Syrian Coast beneath the shadow of the Lebanon mountains flashes down from an American college, and the darkness which broods over the pyramids and the tombs of the sacred bulls would be far darker but for the American Presbyterian schools and colleges stretching through the whole length of the land of the Nile. Throughout India, from coast to coast—and I crossed the continent five times—while I saw many things to depress the mind and bring before me the shame of Christendom, my heart was filled with pride over the good name which American Christians have given to their country."

Christianity is to be tested by its influence on individual life and character. An ancient poet once excited the applause of the theatre when he said: "I am a man; nothing that belongs to a man is uninteresting to me." The gospel individualizes the race. It regards every one—whether Christian or pagan—as of equal importance in the sight of God. Compared with the value of the soul everything else is as dust in the balance. The Jews, after they had made the law of God of no effect by their traditions considered the strict observance of the sabbath of more importance than an act of mercy to a fellowman. It was left for the Man of Sorrows to teach the great lesson that the sabbath was made for man and not man for the sabbath. He suspended the holy day till the poor man at the pool of Bethesda was healed. Blessed are the merciful, for they shall obtain mercy.

"Go to your bosom, knock there,
And ask your heart what it doth know
That's like thy brother's fault;
If it confess a natural guiltiness,
Such as his, let it not sound
A thought upon your tongue,
Against thy brother's life."

William Carey went out from England a hundred years ago to preach the gospel in India. His thoughtless countrymen laughed when Sydney Smith referred to him as a "consecrated cobbler going out on a fool's errand to convert the heathen." Carey lived out his life in the shadow of India's need, and died at the age of seventy-three years. When on his deathbed he was visited by the Bishop of India, the head of the Church of England in that country, who bowed his head and invoked the blessing of the dying missionary. The British authorities had resolutely denied Carey a landing-place on his first arrival in Bengal. But, when he died, the government dropped all her flags to half mast in honor of the man who had done more for India than any of her generals. The disciple is the light of the world and the salt of the earth. His light should shine and his influence should be felt on every continent and in every island of the sea. This is possible only to those who have fellowship in world-wide missions. There is only one alternative for the disciple who respects Christ's commission. He must either go or send. Only the few have the disposition to go, and they are mostly women. Now, as in the days of his earthly experience, Christ's truest followers are women. Strange to tell, for every man who offers himself for service on the foreign field there are seven women who say: "Here am I; send me." This is a magnificent tribute to woman's faith and to woman's love. In the little mission in the city of Deoghur, to which Miss Annie Lackey has been appointed, there are five women and not one man. The church is the salt of the earth, but the women are the salt of the church. It is a suggestive remark that "Columbus discovered America, but a woman discovered Columbus." The great need of the hour is more men like the saintly Earl of Shaftsbury, who said: "When I feel how old I am, and know I must soon die, I hope it is not wrong, but I cannot bear to go and leave the world with so much misery in it." It is a strangely indifferent heart that is not deeply moved by the petition that comes on every breeze that blows from beyond the seas:

"Hark! what cry arrests my ear?
Hark! what accents of despair?
'Tis the heathen's dying prayer;
Friends of Jesus, hear.

Man of God, to you we cry,
Rests on you our tearful eye,
Help us, Christians, or we die—
Die in dark despair!

Hasten, Christians, haste to save,
O'er the land and o'er the wave,
Danger, death and distance brave;
Hark! for help they call.

Africa bends her suppliant knee,
India spreads her hand to thee,
Hark! they urge the heaven-born plea,
Jesus died for all."

While the missionary makes great sacrifices in going to live in the darkness of heathenism, there are also great compensations for this labor of love in the Master's name. The richest joy the spirit knows is the consciousness of having guided an immortal soul out of darkness into light. To convert a sinner from the error of his way is to save a soul from death and hide a multitude of sins. There is joy in heaven over one sinner who repents whether he be in the home land or on the banks of the Ganges. The one who wins souls is wise. This is a better investment than bonds and bank stocks. Blessed is he who sows beside all waters. Sometime far in the future and up from the dust of the dead he shall shine as the brightness of the firmament and as the stars forever and ever. For every one there is a day coming when he will wish that the moments devoted to soul-winning had been multiplied into years, and that the pence given to missions had been increased a thousandfold. The privilege of fellowship in preaching the gospel in all lands is the best opportunity for profitable investment. It is the pearl of greatest price. One who has come into the possession of this heritage has no greater joy than to tell others of the treasure he has found. A little girl once said:

"I wish I were the little key
That locks love's captive in,
And let him out to go and free
A sinful heart from sin."

This dear young woman goes out under the direction of the Christian Woman's Board of Missions to labor among the children of India. She will teach in the orphanage in the city of Deoghur, two hundred miles west of Calcutta, in the province of Bengal. It is a great joy to her friends that she is to go in company with Miss Olivia A. Baldwin, who spent several years in India as a medical missionary, and now returns to her home beyond the seas to resume the work she so much loves. Seventy-five children in the orphanage at Deoghur await the coming of these two gifted, cultured and consecrated women. In the children of India there is a soil genial almost to a miracle. They are the home of the gospel in that land of idols. A Hindu said to a missionary: "I expect to live and die a Hindu, but I have no doubt that my grandchildren will all become Christians. So we want missionaries to come to India and explain all about the religion of Christ, for it is sure to prevail." The orphanage affords the best field for sowing the good seed of the kingdom. Miss Baldwin said at the Chattanooga Convention: "The orphanage work is progressing encouragingly. We now have five and will soon have six orphanages in that land. India's little ones are sweet and impressible, and their beautiful innocence is destroyed at an early age. We are putting these children into the orphanage and they will be educated for home missionaries. They can receive no home influences. The women of India are slaves. Besides being slaves forty millions of them are prisoners. The poor, uneducated people are more easily reached by us than the educated class, but we must reach all. This educational work in Bengal has been going on year after year, and our work is meeting with success. We have done nothing with young India as yet. Have we no message for such? Young India is not Christian, but may become so. Our force of missionaries in that country is not adequate. It has been said that mission work is not inadequate on account of lack of money, but for want of love. I willingly return to India, but the burden is too great. We need assistance. Friends, pray for this great work."

Beloved, I beseech you by every consideration that is high and holy, help these noble young women who are about to leave our shores to bear the burden and the heat of the day under a tropical sun. Is there a sacrifice too great, a gift too good to be made in behalf of these who have forsaken all to follow Christ? A tie is forged this day that binds our hearts to India in constant devotion and unchanging affection. Henceforth, a heavy draft will be made on our faith, our love and our prayers. May every member of this church, which God has so highly honored, have a double portion of the spirit of good Andrew Fuller, who said: "There is a gold mine in India, but it seems almost as deep as the center of the earth. Who will venture to explore it? 'I will venture to go down,' was the instant reply of William Carey, 'but you,' addressing Fuller, 'must hold the ropes.' 'This,' said Fuller, 'I solemnly engage to do, pledging him never to desert him as long as I shall live.' "

And now, my dear sister, there is only time for a final farewell and a parting blessing. It is an unspeakable pleasure to the heart that has known you long and well, to testify to the purity of your life, the beauty of your character, the fervor of your piety and the singleness of purpose with which you have devoted your life from childhood to the cause of foreign missions. A great company both in heaven and on earth rejoices with you that your fondest hopes are realized. This is a day for which you have waited long. The call that has come to you is a call from God. You have made patient preparation both in mind and heart for the work you go to do. You go out from the bosom of a family and a church who have carefully guarded you along the paths of peace over which your feet have come. For this constant care you have made a rich return. As we send you forth this day to India's whitening fields, we lay upon the altar of Foreign Missions the best sacrifice that love can prompt, and the most precious gift we have to make. The breaking of this alabaster box moves the heart of the gentle Christ as it was moved on that long-gone day in Bethany. Now, as then, he accepts the sacrifice and approves the deed. He will be nearer to you both on land and sea because of the offering you have made. "The crowded hour of glorious life is worth an age without a name." Reginald Heber, the second Bishop of Calcutta, after a day of toil in India, said to a friend: "Gladly would I exchange years of common life for one such day as this." Alas! that was the last day he ever spent on earth. He went to his room, and an hour later the the author of the great hymn—

> "From Greenland's icy mountains,
> From India's coral strand,"

had gone to God as the dew goes up to the sun. To-day you leave your native land, henceforth to live under the protection of the British flag, the proudest ensign, next to the Stars and Stripes, that floats on sea or land.

> "Where England's flag flies wide unfurled,
> All tyrant wrongs repelling,
> God make the world a better world
> For man's brief earthly dwelling."

> "The Lord bless thee, and keep thee;
> The Lord make his face to shine upon thee,
> And be gracious to thee;
> The Lord lift up his countenance on thee,
> And give thee peace.
> The Lord hear thee in the day of trouble;
> The name of the God of Jacob defend thee:
> Send thee help from the sanctuary,
> And strengthen thee out of Zion;
> Remember all thy offerings,
> And accept thy burnt sacrifice;
> Grant thee according to thine own heart,
> And fulfill all thy counsel.
> We will rejoice in thy salvation,
> In the name of our God we will set up our banners."

May the Eye that never sleeps and the Hand that never tires guide you safely over land and sea till your eager feet come at last to rest on the soil you have so long sought—

> "Fearless ride the stormy billows,
> Fearless every danger dare,
> Onward in your steadfast purpose,
> We will follow you with prayer.
> Glorious mission!
> 'Tis the cross of Christ you bear!"

Tennessee C. W. B. M.

EDITOR CHRISTIAN-EVANGELIST:—Just learning from the proceedings of our General Convention, which recently convened at Chattanooga, that the C. W. B. M. of Tennessee had no recognition in our National Convention because of having received no recognition in our State Convention, which also met in Chattanooga, I ask that you publish this letter as a "call to arms" as it were, of all the Christian Churches of Tennessee. Sisters of Tennessee: Can we afford to sit idly by when there is such a glorious opportunity for us to work in our "Master's vineyard," when there is such an imperative call to us to be up and doing? Can the women of the Christian Church of Tennessee be content to go up to our state and general conventions and be debarred the privilege of being recognized as coworkers in this great movement of sending out the gospel of our Lord?

The C. W. B. M. is now nearing its twenty-fifth year of active life, having passed successfully over the trials and dangers attendant upon all infant life, reaching the years of maturity in great strength of character and purity of purpose, it now has only to go bravely forward to the glorious destiny awaiting every soul or organization that is working for the Master. This is a missionary organization, "pure and simple," and should appeal to every Disciple of our Lord Jesus. If I know anything of our plea we are missionary people, but I fear some of us are laboring under the impression that we are living under the first commission, when our Savior sent the apostles forth to preach and teach in Judea.

This commission is not to us, but the last, the great commission: "Go ye into all the world and preach the gospel to every creature"—given after our blessed Savior had tasted death that we through him might have life eternal; just before going to the Father he left us this command. Not to the apostles, nor to the preachers of all succeeding ages alone, but to us, to you, to me, to every one who wears the name of Christ.

This commission does not say, Go into Judea, to your own city, or state, or country, but "into all the world." This command is world-wide in its embrace, extending through all time and to all Christians—none are exempt. It is this voice speaking to us through all the ages, linking the present to the past, taking us back to the resurrection morn, when our blessed Lord broke the bands that enslaved woman. Sisters of the Christian Churches of Tennessee, rouse from your indifference and do your duty! Listen to the voice of our Savior: "If ye love me, keep my commandments." We cannot all go as missionaries, but we can by united effort contribute our mite in our quiet and humble way to sending the gospel in our own and heathen lands, never forgetting that we are working for Jesus when we "give a cup of cold water to one of his little ones."

Let every Christian woman not forget that the gospel of our blessed Savior would have died at Jerusalem had it not been for the missionaries. Who can picture the degradation of womanhood to-day, had the missionaries who spent their lives and the Christians who gave their talents, means and time to spreading the gospel of Jesus Christ remained listless and indifferent as we who are content to do a part but not all our duty? Let every church in Tennessee begin at once and organize a C. W. B. M. and next October, when our convention meets, let us be there and see that our state is enrolled as a state filled with the missionary spirit and hence filled with the spirit of Jesus Christ, our first missionary. I am a woman with a life of cares and time is precious, yet I feel that my life, my time, my all belong to my Savior, and he being my helper I shall try more earnestly to do whatsoever my hands find to do for the advancement of his kingdom, not looking to man, but to him who gave his life for me to say, "Well done thou good and faithful servant."

The three Christian Churches of Memphis are united in one C. W. B. M. organization with Sister W. D. Rice, the wife of the pastor of the Linden Street Church for our president, our secretary being from the Mississippi Avenue Church and our treasurer from the Third Church. The ministers of the three churches are members in "good standing;" they meet with us, encourage and help us by their counsels and pay their dues promptly and cheerfully, not asking for any part in our deliberations. We meet monthly, the meeting alternating between the three churches, thu in sweetest Christian love and harmony ou three churches as one C. W. B. M. are work ing together to fulfill, as best we can, ou Lord's commission, looking to his approval "she hath done what she could" as our onl reward. A MEMBER OF LINDEN ST. CHURCH.

Memphis, Tenn., Oct. 31, 1898.

Notes and News.

Another Debate.

A discussion has been in progress here for week between Bro. Jas. Anderson, of the hurch of Christ, and W. E. Peak, of the eorganized Church of Jesus Christ of L. D. S., nd to say that Mormonism—so far as this ebate is concerned—has been utterly wrecked s to put it mildly. Bro. Anderson is now howing in his affirmative proposition from od's Word the divine nature and character f the church of which he is a member. The utlook is fine. The entire community is tirred. A full report will be sent when the ebate closes. E. S. CHAMBERLAIN.

Brownville, Neb., Oct. 31, 1898.

A Growing College.

The attendance at Christian College, Columbia, Mo., this year, is unprecedented. The oarding department is full and runuing over. A number of applicants have been refused. However, it is encouraging to know that our rustees are wide awke to the importance of providing for the emergency. At a recent neeting of the trustees it was decided to begin at once to erect additional buildings. Accordingly, a new and commodious extension will be nade which will provide ample space for at east 50 more girls. The building will be ready for occupancy before the beginning of the next collegiate year.—*C. C. Chronicle.*

October a Good Month.

Comparing the receipts for *Foreign Missions* for the month of October with the corresponding month last year shows the following:

Contributing	1897	1898	
Churches	23	20	Loss 3
Sunday-schools	17	20	Gain 3
Endeavor Societies	42	6	Loss 36
Individuals	32	19	Loss 13
Amount	$2,207.20	$8,294.40	$6,087.20

About $6,000 of this amount came from a bequest; $1,200 was received on the *Annuity plan.* Remember, $150,000 is the mark for the year set by the Chattanooga Convention.

F. M. RAINS, Treas.

Box 750, *Cincinnati, O.*

Eureka's Representative.

It give me great pleasure to announce to our brotherhood and to the public generally that J. G. Waggoner has been appointed to work among the people in the interest of Eureka College. We feel that in him the college has a representative of whom any institution might be proud. His acquaintanceship is very wide, his interest in the college profound and his knowledge of its needs thorough. We ask the brethren everywhere to receive him cordially and to co-operate with him in whatever good things he may undertake among them. The writer will continue to be much among the people, while at the same time teaching certain classes and taking care of the internal workings of the institution.

J. H. HARDIN, Pres. and Chn. Ex. Com.

Eureka, Ill., Nov. 2, 1898.

Jubilee of Home Mission Society.

Accepted the Call.

I have just been employed as pastor of the Church of Christ at this place and begin labor at once. The field promises a fruitful harvest, and that "our plea" shall be the leading power in this place for Christ. E. M. BARNEY.

Perry, O., Oct. 31, 1898.

Does It Pay?

In the CHRISTIAN-EVANGELIST'S editoria notes, by B. B. T., Oct. 27, he asks, "Do such conventions as this in Chattanooga pay?" and immediately says, "The answer must be, on the part of those who attend, an emphatic affirmative." I want in behalf of many who could not be there to say, please do not limit your affirmation to those present. We do not want our brethren to feel that we were absent from our own choice, nor will we permit for one moment the thought that because absent in person we were not interested in everything done there and partakers of the fellowship. I looked eagerly for my papers containing the reports, and when they came everthing else had to give way while I so far as possible looked in upon the deliberations and partook of the feast of rich things brought to me. I am sorry I could not be there, but I feel an uplift from the reports that I fear I could not have gotten in any other way.

When I think of what a great host of consecrated Christian men and women we have, all working together harmoniously, sympathetically and lovingly for the same purpose, I am made stronger and better prepared for the work in my little corner of God's vineyard, and with Paul I can say, "I thank God for this fellowship from the first day even till now."

Yes, such conventions pay, not only those who are present, but those who can attend only in spirit, as they read of what has been done and the plans of the larger conquests in the future. F. N. CALVIN.

Waco, Tex.

P. S.—I want to have some part in helping to raise that $100,000 for Home Missions, and in bringing the 100,000 souls to Christ in 1899.

Educational Conference at Moberly.

Pursuant to call the conference authorized by our State Convention at Moberly met on Nov. 1st. On account of a misunderstanding as to whether this was the time for the committee meeting or a meeting of the conference the attendance was not as large as expected. It is possible that we did not secure all the names of those present, but as near as we could ascertain J. B. Jones, C. H. Winders, H. A. Denton, Z. Moore, H. A. Buckner, J. W. Strawn, J. W. Robbins, S. G. Clay, T. P. Haley, W. G. Surber, G. A. Hoffmann, M. J. Nicoson, J. J. Lockhart, Clinton Lockhart, Davis Errett, Levi Marshall, W. M. Featherston and F. O. Norton were among the teachers and preachers in attendance. The following business men were also present and took quite an interest in the discussions: W. H. Dulany, Hannibal; J. W. Alexander, Gallatin; J. W. Barnett, Sedalia; Jerome Bryant, Middle Grove, and Daniel Boothe, O. C. Clay, L. H. Condit and Dr. R. H. Turner, Canton. There were also students from the school at Canton as follows:

schools would present the
of the different schools the
tian University, the Orp
Christian College, Christi
Bible College were prese
and conditions discussed.
conference it was decided
ing until Dec. 6th at 3 P.
Moberly. It was also d
conference would take u
tablishing and endowing
colleges at the next m
seems to be that somethi
to make our educational i
to humanity and especial
Christ. The coming conf
a very important meeting
form a new epoch and m
the progress of our educa
state. Every church in
lowed a vote in the next n
200 members and less tha
gations having over 500 n
All schools are allowed
preacher in attendance
Churches all over the s
send delegates that there
sentation. This educatio
question and full of impo
the issue like men. Let u
thought necessary for a
righteous salvation.

Then and

"Eight years ago to-
official here, "Pine Bluff
we have 17. Then the r
and city was $40,000 from
it was $10,000, and the l
increased." There seems
uplift of some kind—a hig
To go about such places
spectable all the time.
his children who were goi
Rock, "Don't tell anybo
a saloonkeeper. Tell the
keep pipes, cigars and tob
that really *belong to the g*

I had a full house to wh
fathers' Day sermon. H
good seems to be right,
kin to hero worship. If t
hear of Davis, Lee, the
son, or Grant, Sherman,
as, we want the people
bells, Stone, Scott, Smit
of Jerry Black and Garfi
weary of the burden of t
was in the interests of u
of the sinfulness of divi
among the followers of C

There was a time when
est men hardly knew w
to state, or to the nation
is a close kinship betwee
loyalty to country. A
very poor specimen of
these with drawn weapo
near here to wait on the
the station and let them
by the time Uncle Sam
heroes, they like Spain
respectful to the auth
States.

Weyler and Blanco ca

Another Convention.

The churches of Christ in Elk County, Kansas, will hold their convention at Grenota, November 16, 17. A good program has been prepared for the occasion.

THE SECRETARY.

Reopening.

The Christian Church in Ligonier, Ind., having repaired their old church building and added parlor, dining-hall; which can be opened into main room; kitchen, pantry and vestibule—addition containing 2,200 square feet of floor—new seats, furnace, etc., will reopen on Nov. 20, 1898. Pres. E. V. Zollars, of Hiram College, will be master of ceremonies on this important occasion.

The annual meeting of the Disciples of Christ in Noble County will be held at the same time, commencing Nov. 18 and continuing over Lord's day. An invitation is extended to pastors and churches. GEO. MUSSON.

Dedication.

Our new church building will be dedicated Lord's day, Nov. 13. The brethren in this state are invited to attend the services. Our new state secretary, Bro. B. L. Denny, will have charge of the services. Will follow the dedication with a meeting, with Bro. J. A. Bennett helping the writer by doing the preaching. Pray for our success.

F. L. DAVIS.

Downs, Ia., Nov. 4, 1898.

Announcement from Bro. Clay.

EDITOR CHRISTIAN-EVANGELIST:—As previously announced in the columns of the CHRISTIAN-EVANGELIST, I have been appointed by the Foreign Christian Missionary Society as its Western Field Secretary, with headquarters at Kansas City, Mo. I now beg the privilege of addressing the brotherhood of Missouri, Kansas, Nebraska, Iowa, Arkansas and Texas through your paper. I am in Kansas City as your fellowservant, and am ready to assist any and all of our pastors and churches in their efforts to send the gospel to the unevangelized nations of the world. I shall be glad to receive calls from the brethren for my services in assisting them in their preparations for the March Offerings and Children's Day collection. I am ready to come to you and speak for you *free of cost* to you and your church.

We are just entering upon the Jubilee Year of our organized missionary work. It will soon be fifty years since our people organized for aggressive missionary work, and sent out their first missionary to a foreign land. It is proper that we should celebrate this semi-centennial of missionary work. In Cincinnati, Ohio, preparations are being made for the greatest convention ever held by our brotherhood. Music Hall has been engaged as the place of meeting and 10,000 delegates are expected from the churches. This must be made a great year in all respects. The watchword for the society is, $150,000 for Foreign Missions in this, the Jubilee Year. We believe this sum can and will be raised. To do it, however, every church and state must increase its offering for Foreign Missions. Systematic effort should be put forth by every church and pastor to make this a Jubilee Year for themselves. Every church should be enlisted, and, as far as practicable, every member. An offering from every soul redeemed by the Christ for the world's salvation should be our aim. Time and again we have tried to secure this, but this year we must try again and succeed.

It will be my pleasure to attend district and county conventions, and to speak on Foreign Missions to the churches wherever I am wanted west of the Mississippi River. And I shall be especially glad to assist churches in rallies for the March Offerings. Letters addressed to me at Kansas City, Mo., will receive prompt attention. Truly yours, B. F. CLAY.

Missouri Bible-school Notes.

Nelson brethren are no more in the union school, but have organized one of their own, as ought to have been done some time ago, as the Interdenominational Association advises wherever practicable. Some one is responsible for one, while no one cares to stand good for the other; hence its failure to do the work. The Nelson school is going to join us in this good work, too, and that's right.

The Scotland County meeting at Memphis was good, brethren Grow, Rohrer, Williams and Boone having good representations from their respective schools. The program was intensely practical and all seemed to enjoy it. Simpson Ely gave us the keynote the first night, as he can do, and those hearing it declare that it was helpful to every one, but that is the way he does it. In Bible-school work I had hearty co-operation and such a financial response as made me rejoice, Memphis alone contributing in cash and pledges $18.13; but this is through J. T. Boone and J. M. Jayne, two of our best friends. Among the younger people of the church Brother Boone is doing a great work, while the membership is growing in all features of the work.

Of the Polk County meeting you have heard, but the Bible-school growth is a delight to such as myself. There were ten churches represented, and the preachers are all sacrificing to preach the Christ to the people, living in the plainest manner that they may continue in their respective fields, though offered better salaries in other territory, and God is blessing them in their work.

Brethren Rogers and Prewitt are visiting among the schools in their district, getting acquainted with the conditions of the work, that they may the better do that which is desired at their hands, and the schools are very generally coming to their support, so that they will not waht for anything, but co-operation.

John Giddens continues in his good meeting at Stoutland, and will report a good congregation at this important point, with money for a house and a good Bible-school at work. In pioneer work he is in his element.

The Pettis County meeting, as usual, was fine, being held with one of the best congregations in the state, Lamonte; in charge of J. N. Dalby, the meeting had to be good. The reports showed some needs which are to be seen to immediately, especially the Bible-school work. Preachers present, F. L. Cook, J. W. Felrell, Phil Stark, D. C. Peters, H. F. Davis, J. J. Morgan, Mrs. Virginia Hedges, King Stark, J. Stark. The interest in our work was shown by the giving to it, while the general interest is largely due the influence of King Stark, whose devoted wife was made a life member of the C. W. B. M. by those present. The entertainment at the church was fine, every consideration being the comfort of their guests. Lamonte school and Endeavor are with us this year as usual. King Stark's meeting, the second or third of the year, went right on, there being three confessions the last night of our meeting, and all the church seemed harnessed for work in earnest. Brethren Cook and Dalby, who love the Bible-school work, give me every assurance that their respective schools will soon be with us in this effort for the children.

Have you seen "Esther," by our fellow-worker, M. M. Davis? If not, you are missing a treat in the line of interesting Bible characters, and in the happiest vein of this godly man. I have concluded reading with the determination that all the young people especially should possess themselves of a copy, while the older ones will find in it much to cheer them on the way. The style is very free and easy, and you become so taken up with the character that you will regret the brevity of the book. It is from the press of the Christian Publishing Company, but can be had of any, and you will thank me for calling your attention to it.

The second quarter is now upon us, and the notices are going out. Remit us promptly, as we are behind with the force. Send it in now, please. H. F. DAVIS.

A Lovely Character Translated.

DEAR BRO. GARRISON:—I know you will be pained to learn of the death of Sister Hieronymus, wife of Prof. R. E. Hieronymus, of this city. After an illness of four years, Sister H. fell asleep in Jesus Thursday evening, Oct. 27. She was one of the loveliest characters I ever knew.

To calmly turn her face from a devoted husband and three lonely little children and, without a tremor, walk into the arms of death, requires a courage that can only be born of the religion of death's conqueror. Without doubt she was the most uncomplaining sufferer I have ever known. She was pre-eminently a woman of faith, hope and love. The funeral was conducted by the writer, assisted by Prof. Edwards, president of the University, at 10 o'clock Saturday morning, Oct. 29. The funeral was largely attended and the sympathy deep and sincere. Many of the professors and teachers from the State Normal School, where Prof. Hieronymus taught last year, were present.

The floral offerings were most elaborate, and beautiful beyond description.

Captain Franz, who won distinction with the Rough Riders at Santiago, a brother of our deceased sister, arrived at her bedside only a few moments before her departure. Surely the Lord permitted her to tarry long enough to enjoy the great satisfaction of this meeting.

J. W. INGRAM.

Pasadena, Cal., Nov. 2, 1898.

Evangelistic.

OKLAHOMA.

Perry, Oct. 31.—Just closed a two weeks' meeting at Polk with 15 additions; 14 by statement, one by baptism. Arrangements are being made to build a meeting house there.—WM. UNKLEBERGER.

WISCONSIN.

Sugar Grove, Oct. 31.—One addition here yesterday and one two weeks ago. Work prospers. We are getting ready to entertain the state convention next year.—S. J. PHILLIPS, pastor.

INDIANA.

Lawrenceburg, Nov. 3.—We just closed a meeting here Sunday that was generally a success; 11 were added; all by baptism. Work here moving splendidly. At the unanimous call of the brethren I remain here for another year.—WILL G. LOUCKS.

NEBRASKA.

Norman, Nov. 1.—Meeting at West Point is progressing nicely with increasing interest. Bro. E. E. Francis is the faithful minister here and much appreciated.—S. W. GLASCOCK.

KENTUCKY.

Earlington, Oct. 30.—For the 19 days past Bro. Jas. C. Creel, of Plattsburg, Mo., preached the gospel of our Master with great power and fine effect. Visible results 12 additions. Much good was accomplished otherwise. —I. H. TEEL.

Lexington, Oct. 31.—Bro. C. K. Marshall has just closed a meeting with the church at Little Rock, Ky., which resulted in 29 confessions, one from the Baptists, one from the Methodists and two by letter. The preaching was of a high order and greatly enjoyed by all. Here is a brother that has done valiant service for the cause, and is vigorous and strong in body and mind, yet at present without regular work. Some of our best pulpits in Kentucky and Maryland can testify of his faithful ministry, and some of our leading churches that are without a man will make a mistake in not knowing Bro Marshall as a pastor. The writer closed a meeting with the Berea Church, Fayette Co., Ky., on the 14th of October with 11 confessions.—R. H. LAMPKIN.

MISSOURI.

La Belle, Oct. 31.—Closed a two weeks' meeting here with four added; three confessions. Go next to Plevna, Knox Co., to hold a meeting for J. H. Bryan.—W. F. TURNER.

Paris, Nov. 2.—Fourteen additions to the church under my labors since my last report; 7 by baptism, 3 by statement and 3 reclaimed.—C. H. STRAWN.

Bro. A. B. Elliott and I have just closed a meeting at Illinois Bend, with 46 additions, 38 of whom were by confession and baptism.—JACOB HUGLEY.

Rolla, Oct. 30.—Closed my work here to-day with three additions. Will begin a meeting at Labadie, Nov. 2nd. My address in the future will be Windsor, Mo.—R. B. HAVENER.

Trenton, Nov. 3.—One confession here Sunday, making four accessions to the congregation in the last month. Expect to close our work here with this year. We have been called for for the sixth year, but feel that it is best for all concerned to close our work here. We expect to leave the church free from debt and with one thousand dollars on interest with $800 pledged for a new organ.—G. SNELL.

KANSAS.

Howard, Nov. 4.—Preaching at Creso, a

KANSAS.

Olathe, Nov. 2.—I have just closed a
meeting at Weston, Mo., with 23 additi
18 baptisms and the rest by statement or le
The meeting was greatly hindered by the
and snow.—R. F. FIFE.

Council Grove, Oct. 31.—Closed last nigh
eight days' meeting here with three bapt
and two other additions to this church.
O. L. Cook, of Topeka, preached Wedns
Thursday and Friday nights for us and o
the new recruits was gained during his
with us.—J. A. WALTERS.

TEXAS.

San Marcos, Nov. 2.—I closed my work
South Butler church last Lord's day wit
accessions to the church; 10 by baptism and
by statement. Have had 82 added since I b
the work there about three years ago. Chur
in Texas needing protracted meetings or
toral work can address me at San Ma
Texas.—C. E. SMOOTZ.

IOWA.

Rock Valley.—No organization here.
in a 10 days' meeting by J. M. Hoffmannn
Bro. Rust, of Wisconsin, three were bapti

East Side Des Moines.—Melvin Putnan
California, has begun a meeting of w
and reports one confession.

Nevada.—The Wright and Martindale m
ing closed with 18 added and a $300
purchased.

Highland Park, Des Moines.—Jas. S
assisting T. W. McDonald closed his mee
on Nov. 3rd, with 27 added.

Kellarton.—L. P. Kopp closed a good m
ing here with nearly a dozen added to
Lord.

Creston, Oct. 31.—We had a grand ch
rally yesterday. Much enthusiasm was ge
ated, great hope inspired and better
assured. It was a blessed day for both pa
and people. Since our first visit here in J
five have been added by letter and state
and four by baptism. God be praised for
tories won and for his great promises.—D
SNIDER.

ARKANSAS.

Fayetteville, Nov. 2.—There were four a
tions to the First Church last Sunday; one by
ter and three conversions.—N. M. RAGLAN

ILLINOIS.

Blandinsville.—An audience of over
listened to A. R. Adams lecture on "Cowa
at the Old Bedford Christian Church Su
evening, Oct. 30. At the close of the se
three young ladies came forward, made
"good confession" and were baptized.

Blandinsville, Nov. 2.—The great s
closed our meeting at Jonesburg, Mo., o
10th day. We had three additions. W
next to Litchfield church for one month's
from Nov. 6.—N. A. MELOAN.

Murphysboro, Oct. 31.—There were
additions to the church here, during the
week of our protracted meeting. Our End
or Society had 16 more names proposed
memership at its last meeting. This ma
total of 66 additions in the last three w
and still others to come.—W. H. WILLY
pastor.

Sidney, Nov. 2.—I began my meeting
last Lord's day and have two additions
four sermons preached. Interest runing h
The U. B. preacher has held four weeks
and one addition. Send me a bunch of pa
and will distribute.—C. H. BERRY.

Hoopston, Nov. 1.—Thirteen added ye
day and thirteen the day before and
grand men and women to-night; 81 in
to date. Meeting continues. Bucha
Mich., next.—CHAS. REIGN SCOVILLE, eva
ist; S. R. SCOTT AND NONA MCCORMICK sin

Family Circle.

Divine.

AARON PRINCE ATEN.

Bright spark of heaven's celestial fire,
Imprisoned from thy high desire!

Within an earth-born cell confined,
Thou offspring of Eternal Mind!

Be still and know that thou art part
Of Spirit's omnipotent heart.

For thee goes out Eternal Thought,
For thee, with endless blessing fraught.

Not lost art thou from heaven's ken,
Though hid within the sons of men.

A part of God, his image grand,
Within his presence thou shalt stand.

The fires that in thy being burn,
To him ascending, shall return.

A part thou art though small or great,
Of light that pours through heaven's gate.

Returning, shall reunion be
With that great Light that shines on thee.

Triumphant thought, O spirit mine;
Though of the earth, yet still Divine!

Hutchinson, Kan.

Mr. Davids and His Great Round World.

BY MARY F. M. BALDWIN.

Mr. Davids "took summer boarders." The *menage* of his establishment was cast upon strictly rural lines.

"No frills, no city fixin's; if folks wants country board and country livin' I'll give it to 'em straight. That's me, Billy Davids."

This announcement, uttered in stentorian tones, constituted the leading feature in the welcome he extended to me at the beginning of my two months' stay at his comfortable farmhouse. Having fairly settled down, I soon found a congenial associate in a Mrs. Joy. This lady was decidedly my senior in years, and also, as I soon discovered, my superior in worldly wisdom. She got on famously with our eccentric and outspoken host, and easily brought about a few needed amendments in our bill of fare. Fortunately for me she shared my liking for long walks. Together we thoroughly explored the country near at hand, and discovered the best points from which to view its fine scenery. We escaped from cows, and were frightened by snakes. We sat on fences, paddled in brooks, picked flowers and berries, and in general lived the sort of life which rests the soul—and also secures a favorable report from the platform scale. Instead of lapsing into that paganism to which city people take so kindly when away from home, we regularly dropped our mites in the collection-box of a rather distant church, going and returning with our host, behind a pair of beautiful black horses, feeling, as the spirited animals gladly took us over hill and vale, that there are times even in this troublesome world when virtue has its just reward. Our life, however, was not wholly an outdoor one. Occasionally we could sympathize with the young men at one of our great universities, of whom one of their number, a Japanese, innocently remarked: "When it rains the students read books." The reading of books, however, was not our only resource on a rainy day; for at such times our host would tarry a while at the table, setting forth his views of matters and things in a manner that was at once original and striking, his favorite topic being the flatness of this world; his chief authority, a mythical spelling-book.

"Yes, ma'am," he said, addressing Mrs. Joy, as if assured of her approval, "I can almost see it now, the way it was in the back part of that old, yaller-covered spellin'-book (it's round the garret somewhere, now). 'This world is square and p'ised on a pinnacle.' I always believed it and do yet. What's your idee about it, Mrs. Joy?"

"Well," said she, "your theory is worthy of consideration. It is a decided improvement on the notion that the world is carried on the back of a tortoise."

"Tortoise!" he exclaimed, contemptuously; "why that's a kind of a turkle, isn't it? Now that's some furrin notion, I'll warrant. I tell you, Mrs. Joy, these furriners is a thousand years behind the age. Don't it beat all what idees some people do have? Turkle!—huh!"

Too full for further utterance, Mr. Davids took his pipe from the mantel and left the room.

The next day was fine, and we took our usual leisurely course along the road, finally stopping to rest under a widespreading chestnut tree. Here some kindly soul, mindful of the needs of his fellowmen, had provided a rude but comfortable seat, while near at hand a large watering trough received its abundant supply through a wooden pipe that rose abrubtly from the ground. The cool shade and the soft murmur of the flowing water contrasted most gratefully with the heat of the glowing highway beyond.

We had comfortably settled ourselves and were beginning to realize that these things were largely designed for our especial comfort and enjoyment, when the sound of approaching wheels warned us that possibly others might be cherishing the same delusion. The newcomer proved to be Dr. Blake, Mr. Davids' pastor, to whom we had already been introduced. While this worthy and affable gentleman was watering and resting his horse a conversation very naturally began, and as naturally followed the line of current parish life, our host and his peculiarities receiving their due share of attention. One thing led to another until, before the interview ended, it was arranged that Mrs. Joy's nephew, Dr. Harris, a young physician and amateur astronomer, who was visiting in a neighboring county, should give a talk on his favorite science as soon as the necessary arrangements could be made. Dr. Blake suggested that it might be possible to secure the use of a large barn upon which Mr. Davids' nearest neighbor, Squire Hood, was just putting the finishing touches.

"I shall try," said he, gathering up the lines as a hint to Dobbin that the journey was to be resumed—"I shall try to have my young people let Mr. Davids alone in this matter. They are rather disposed to make him a butt for their ridicule, although his ready wit generally gives him the victory. Still, the thing has been quite overdone, especially in the matter of the 'yellow-covered spelling-book.' "

As he said this Dr. Blake raised his hat, tightened the reins, and the horse slowly moved away from the welcome shade. Events moved smoothly on, and in a few days the arrangements for the lecture were complete. It then naturally became the chief topic of conversation in the neighborhood, but Dr. Blake's desire that the matter should not be intruded on Mr. Davids' attention was so well carried out that that gentleman, far from being pleased, was rather annoyed by the lack of attention. He kept his own counsel, however, until shortly before the time set, when one day at dinner he abruptly said:

"I hear they're going to have an astronomical lecture Thursday night over to Squire Hood's barn." As no one made any response to this rather belated information, he continued: " 'Pears to me they're keepin' the thing mighty close."

"Why, no," said his wife; "it's been give out in church twicet; an' the Ladies' Aid Association is makin' quite some count on it for a new heater to put in the basement."

"Well, now here, Hanner! that ain't what I'm a-drivin' at at all; if I didn't want to go to the blamed lecture they'd all be a-pesterin' on me to buy tickets; but now they've got something I'm really interested in, narry a one of 'em has offered me the fust ticket. I know what it's all for; it's for the sake of bein' contrary. If there's anything that gets me riled up, it's havin' to do with folks that's always pullin' 'tother way. But I'm goin to be there, an' don't you forget it!"

The eventful evening at length arrived. Mr. Davids was not at home at supper-time; his wife informed us that he had "had a snack early," and gone off on "considerable of a drive." "He allowed," she added, by way of explanation, "that he'd be back in time for the lecter."

When we set out in the early twilight no inconsiderable part of the people round about were on the move. As we looked down into the valley the road, as it occasionally came to view, seemed filled with a constant succession of stylish turnouts—family carriages, wagons and buggies, while a few determined cyclists bent to the pedals and toiled up the steep ascent.

Squire Hood not only granted the use of his fine new barn for a lecture-hall, but also threw open to the attending public a large adjoining field, which having been recently mowed and being now covered with the fresh, springing grass, had quite the effect of a great lawn. A constant succession of vehicles streamed through the single broad entrance, while the scene was most animated. Everybody was in good spirits and seemed to know everybody else; and the chatter of the young, and the more formal but hearty salutations of their elders filled the air with a continual hum. As the twilight deepened the women gradually made their way toward the barn, while the men, with a skill born of long experience, carefully arranged for the security of their horses. Moving in and out among the crowd were many bright-faced damsels who hardly needed their ribbon badges to point them out as members of the young ladies' auxiliary. It was they who marshaled the audience and collected the tickets; and it was by one of them that we were conducted to two of the best seats in the house. But where was Uncle Billy Davids? This was not only our query, but, so far as we could judge, was the uppermost thought of those about us. We did not, however, remain long in ignorance, for soon there was heard a whoop and a "hooray." Uncle Billy having driven up, had found the gate closed; a state of affairs upon which he proceeded to comment in no uncertain tone.

there! What's the matter with
e boss told you to shut the gate,
ell, I tell you to open it—mighty
! A fine lot you are, a-tryin' to
the best part of your aujence.
ere, Cesar! Steady, boy! Look
! these hosses is gettin' cross;
used to no sich foolin' as this."
with a dash came the splendid
am of dapple grays. Turning
ur seats and looking out through
t doorway we saw Mr. Davids
ound his equipage in a masterly
present to us the rear of a long,
lumber-wagon. Then came a
orders and demands.
you young fellers, git them hosses
; tie one to each wheel. Hold
Clarke, you wait a minute. Here,
bring out one of them chairs.
re's the ticket committee? Well,
off; I'm payin' for the hull out-

dience, which by this time had
faced the rear, awaited with the
pectancy the entrance of the out-
; as we judged from the remarks
ispering and tittering neighbors,
been gathered together as the
considerable thought on the part
avids; for its members were all
f marked individuality. It is but
y that the audience paid for its
it by securing for the late comers
e most eligible seats.
light having given place to dark-
improvised lecture-hall was well
y several rustic candelabra sus-
rom the rafters by strong cords,
sses and festoons of wild flowers,
arranged, everywhere met the

ture was an unqualified success.
s not only had a clear and forci-
f stating new facts, but had also
rare talent which enabled him to
inite shape, acceptably, many of
y and ill-defined notions of which
iformed people have so large a
ut while all others were pleased
is was unhappy. As the lecture
d, his square world became more
unsteady on its pinnacle. En-
room at the rear, he had grad-
ked his way along one side to-
front, each round of applause
him a seat or two forward until,
pled look and parted lips, he came
hin view of the audience. As
we could judge, his mental state
set forth by a broad-shouldered
r us who whispered to his com-

ok at Uncle Billy; why, he's all
"
vids proved, however, that his
still at command, for the chorus
' which expressed the thanks of
nce had hardly ceased, when he
his feet, and with outstretched
ointing finger said:
fossor! I want to ask one ques-
w kin a man find out for sure that
is round?"
" replied the lecturer; "if the
could once stand on the sea-
see a ship, hull down, behind the
g mass of water his doubts would
be at an end."
ase by this simple statement, Mr.
once turned to the congenial

task of getting his team in shape. His turnout was soon ready, and if surprised we were also pleased when we heard his urgent invitation to take our places on the front seat for a ten miles' drive in the moonlight. The route was to us, for the most part, a new one, so that much sooner than we expected we had turned the most distant point and found ourselves well on the way homeward.

Mr. Davids, who up to this time had been fully occupied in guiding the spirited team, had also kept up a lively inward wrestling with his great problem, and so remained for the most part silent; but now as the team, once more on familiar ground, jogged steadily along, its master voiced some of his reasonings as follows:

"That air lecture was fust-class. I kinder think that young feller might 'a' been right. The moon's round, ain't it? and so's the sun; and why hain't the world got just as good a right to be round, too? Anyhow, I'm goin' to find out, and mighty soon, too."

The second morning after the lecture we learned that Mr. Davids had taken an early train and was well on his way toward Asbury Park. He returned late that evening, evidently in good spirits, for his hearty laugh as he entered the house awoke us from our first sound sleep; and when we met, the next morning, at breakfast, our host was overflowing with the zeal of a new convert, and it was not an easy task to bring him down to a connected narrative of the previous day's adventure.

"It's all settled, Mrs. Joy," he began, in a tone of mingled relief and exaltation. "Yes, ma'am! the world is round for sure; there ain't no more room for doubt on that subject, 'cause I've seen the hull thing with my own eyes. I got down to the shore all right. About the last thing I met a gent on the train, and he give me a lot of information—just what I wanted for a good start. Very soon after we landed I was a-standin' at the foot of a telegraph pole a-bucklin' a pair of climbin' spurs onto my boots. I had slung around my neck what the gentleman that lent it to me called a binocular. Well, the lineman I hired the spurs of"—

At this point, Mrs. Davids, whose curiosity had finally gotten the better of her awe, said: "What kind of spurs was they, Father? hoss spurs?"

"No, no, woman; like rooster's spurs."

"But," she persisted, "a rooster never climbs with his spurs."

"Now don't interrupt me no more; let these ladies," he added, with an air of extreme dignity, "hear how it come to get settled whether the world was round or not. Sometimes," he continued, impressively, "we have to let small matters go while we're a-settlin' the great fac's of the universe. Well, as I was a-sayin', I was strappin' these spurs onto my boots when the lineman he says: 'Bein' as you're a begginner, you want to dig them spurs in middlin' hard.'

"When I was all ready to start I took the binocular and sighted on some kind of a vessel, and there it was sure enough, the poles a-stickin' up out of the water; but somehow it didn't look like it was sunk. 'Thunder!' I says to myself, 'that ere water don't look like I thought it would; but here, this ain't business!' So I dug in one spur; then I dug in the other one,

hevin' a good grip around the pole with
left arm and a-holdin' on to the binocu
with the other hand like grim death; a
up I went. But the mischief of it w
that not bein' used to the business a
havin' my nose middlin' close to the po
I kind o' sidled around so that when I
the binocular up to my eyes again, al
could see was a lot o' housen; there wa
no ocean 'tall where there ought to be o
So I had to stick the binocular back in t
case ag'in and grab the pole with bo
arms and get up a kind of a' Injun wa
dance till the ocean come round to wh
it belonged. It sounds funny to tell o
but you'd better believe that between be
afraid I'd drop the binocular and then lo
my footin' and drop myself, I tell you fo
minute or two I had a pretty busy time
it. But when I sighted on that ship ag'i
there she was, the hull of her, on top of t
water. I wa'nt exactly satisfied, for y
see I couldn't know what those fellers h
been a-doin' when my back was turned
'em. Well! by this time I got the hang
them climbin' irons, and I saw the rig
thing to do was to keep a climbin' up a
down drawin' a steady sight onthe boat
the while. So up and down Iwent, and t
first genuine round trip I made, *the wh
thing was settled*.

"I was 'most struck dumb to see th
great, big, green ocean a-bublin' up th
way. I tell you, Mrs Joy, it looked powe
ful. So up and down I went, the idee
gittin' more and more wonderful all t
while. But all of a sudden I heard t
lineman holler: 'Say, boss! time's up;
got to go to work in ten minutes.' So
looked down and there was a crowd b
enough to fill a meetin'-house, and peo
a-flockin' from all directions; some on
walk some on a run, but all making fu
class time. 'Hello!' I says to myse
'what's all this? I must have struck
camp-meetin'; but see how the folks is
runnin.' I've hear tell all my life of peo
a-comin' under good influences, but this
the fust time I ever seen 'em comin' a
hand-gallop.'"

"Perhaps," suggested Mrs. Davids, "
was the salt air made 'em so spry; they s
it's powerful strenghthenin'."

"Salt air! salt nothin'. It wa'nt
camp-meetin' 'tall; it was a curiosi
meetin'. Feelin' pretty good myself
wasn't hurt much by the kinder p'inted
marks they was makin' about me. So
kept agoin' down the pole, slow and eas
and takin' it all in. By the time I w
pretty near down, one of 'em says:

"'Tommy, gir some hoss liniment; s
how stiff he is in the j'ints.'

"At this the crowd give a yell, and ju
then I felt one of them blamed spurs giv

way, and down I come kerplunk, partly onto the sand and partly ag'in a fat man and two boys that stood there a-gawkin at me. Well, nobody wa'nt hurt much, the trouble bein' kinder distributed round, which I calc'late on the hull is about the best way to take trouble, and accordin' to Scriptur', too. As soon as I got on my feet a policeman come up and says:

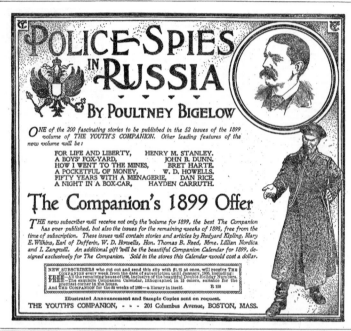

"Here, Cap; 't won't do to get such a big crowd together here.'

"'All right,' I says; 'I'll fix 'em.' You see it just run across my mind about the Life Savin' Service; so I shifted half a dollar into my vest pocket and up I clumb about six foot, when they all stilled down expectin' to have more fun, I reckon; then roared out:

"'Is there any one here who would like to contribute to a noble object?' Well, in spite of their bein' on sand, I could hear a general shuffle, and all of a sudden everybody seemed to have business on hand. As soon as I see I got a move onto 'em, I hollered out ag'in louder than ever:

"'When the storm's a-roarin' outside an' we're a-lyin' comfortable in bed a-listenin' to the rain a-beatin' onto the pane—an' the bough a-scrapin' ag'in' the house—a little band of heroes is a-breastin' of the billow for—to—save—*life*.'

"By this time there was a clear circle twenty foot wide all 'round the pole; and seein' that the movement was under full headway I crep' down, an' while I was unstrappin' the irons the policeman tapped me on the shoulder, an' said: 'I say Cap, that was a quick job.'

"Just then, by good luck, up druv the gentleman that lent me the binocular, so I returned him his property and give him the half-dollar for the Life Savers; then I had a good dip in the bulgin' sea, and come home."

Here our worthy narrator moved back from the table, slapped his hands on his knees, and, slowly wagging his head, said: "I reackon I was middlin' well up to that crowd even if they was brought up on salt air." Saying this he arose and went out to his work.

The remaining weeks of our stay with Mr. Davids passed rapidly, he meanwhile airing his newly acquired knowledge in many quaint statements. It was quite evident, however, that a desire to grapple with other deep problems had been fully aroused by his recent experience, and I imagine some of our answers to his questions showed more skill in dodging than depth of scientific knowledge. Mrs. Joy's favorite resource, when too hard pressed, was a promise to refer the matter to her nephew; and as a natural result our host soon formed a plan for a course of lectures by Dr. Harris which should embrace the whole field of human knowledge. And it so happened that when, in due time and with renewed health and strength, we took our places on a departing train one beautiful September morning, Mr Davids called after us in tones which were easily heard above the clanging of the bell and the rumble of the wheels: "Tell him he's *got* to come; this here Science has got to be settled."—*The Independent.*

Morning Hymn.

Ps. 18:1, 2; 15:1, 2; John 3:16;15: 4, 7, 12, 13.

I only wish, my Lord, to know
Why Thy dear heart doth love me so;
A love so pure, so strong, so sweet,
It brings me to Thy blessed feet.

My joys, my hopes, my cares are Thine;
O'er my whole life Thy glories shine.
Thou art my Star, my Sun, my Shield;
To Thee I bow, to Thee I yield.

Thy blessed service claims my soul;
I give it all to Thy control.
Before no other gods I'll bow,
But ever love and praise Thee now.

My Sun, my Shield, my Staff, my Guide,
With Thee I'll evermore abide;
Strong Fortress mine, to Thee I flee,
And ever hide from storms in Thee.

Alcohol Kills.

The Evangel for October contains an account of some experiments made by Dr. Frederick W. D. Evelyn, of San Francisco, California, for the purpose of determining the effect of alcohol upon animal and vegetable life, from which we reprint the following "facts:"

I find that an onion growing in pure water will at the end of 30 days have grown a sprout 7 inches high, one in water containing 5 per cent. of alcohol 6 1-4 inches, one in 10 per cent. alcohol 5 3-4, in 15 per cent. alcohol but 2 1-2 inches, and the onions in water containing 30 per cent. or over, of alcohol have not only refused to grow, but the sprouts have withered and the body onion lost over 28 per cent. in weight. In each case the onions had grown sprouts an inch in length before transplanting. . .

I have experimented not only with vegetables grown in water in which a percentage of alcohol was presented, and noted results, but I have carried the investigation further and planted a variety of vegetables in soil. These I watered with a percentage of alcohol, and while the restricted growth was not quite so noticeable, yet the effect upon the cell life was the same. I found that under these conditions a potato, onion, carrot or turnip would still show signs of life when the water-food contained as high as 50 per cent. alcohol. It required almost 60 per cent. to cause death within thirty days. I attribute this change of condition to the fact that the soil modified the effect of the alcohol upon the plant. The soil acted as a filter for the first few days, or until such a time as it became surcharged with the alcohol.

In the above experiments but little change was noticeable in the color of the sprouts or stalks until after the fifteenth day. From that time on the decay was more pronounced. However, the soil that had been used in the experiments for the high percentages was immediately used again and with marked results. Soil that had been saturated daily with 50 per cent. alcohol, when used for new growth caused the death of all plant life within 12 days. The 40 per cent. soil killed a healthful growth of potatoes in 16 days.

A pigeon fed with three tablespoonfuls of whisky a day died on the twenty-first day. A carefully conducted autopsy disclosed the fact that the direct cause of death was gangrene of the stomach, brought about by dehydration of the stomach. Food which had to my knowledge been eaten at least five days before was still undigested.

To sum up the results of my investigation, I have concluded that there is one common element opon which life depends, and that is water. Whatever tends to lessen the normal amount or condition of the water provided by nature interferes with life.

The Czar—I will build two big battleships.
John Bull—I will build four.
The Czar—I will build eight.
John Bull—I will build sixteen.
The Czar—Let us have peace.—*Hamilton (Canada) Spectator.*

CATHEDRAL OF GUADELUPE, CITY OF MEXICO, MEXICO.

CATHEDRAL OF MEXICO, MEXICO CITY, MEXICO.

The City of Mexico.*

The City of Mexico is very pleasantly situated on a high plateau surrounded by hills. To the east there are two mountain peaks which are continually covered with snow, and can be plainly seen from the city almost every day in the year. Mexico is a city of churches, there being over 130, but mostly Roman Catholic. There are but five or six of the Protestant faith. We attend the M. E. Church, which is doing a great work all over the republic. There are many beautiful parks and plazas in and around the city, one of which is the national park at Chapultepec which surrounds the National Palace, or White House of Mexico. This house sits on a very high natural mound. The Alameda, in the center of the city is where, at 11 A. M. on Sundays, all the wealthy people promenade, and the young ladies get to see their sweethearts (dulce corozones) who are always on hand, they not being permitted, here, to visit at the young ladies' homes, ordinarily, without being engaged.

The flowers bloom at all times here and every day in the year the noted flower market is filled with the most fragrant flowers which always find ready buyers. This market is near the great cathedral and at the north side of the zocolo, the central plaza of the city.

Many suburban villages surround us, all connected by the great street car system of Mexico. One of these villages is where the noted church of Guadalupe is situated.

The Cathedral of Guadalupe, of which we send you a picture, was built in honor of the Virgin of Guadalupe, whose image is so much adored by the Roman Catholics. The picture shows one of their fiestas, the 12th of December, when they gather from far and wide to pay homage to her and ask for forgiveness. On these days they gamble and have all kinds of oddities for sale. It is a beautiful cathedral, having been over 200 years in building.

The next picture is that of the great cathedral of Mexico, covering a whole square. Its location is in the center of the city, and it is surrounded by a beautiful garden of verdure and the central plaza or zocolo.

*Extracts from a letter from O. Curtis Omer to W. D. Cree, Mgr. of our Subscription Department.

Lace Curtains.

There have been many complaints recently concerning the durability of lace curtains, for after they have been sent to the laundry a few times they seem to literally "drop to pieces." This is not due to the inferior quality of the curtains when purchased, but to the strong chemicals that are often used in cleaning them, and the housekeeper who does this work at home not only saves the laundry bill, but her curtains will last much longer. It is not a difficult tast, and one who understands the proper method and is willing to devote the necessary time to the work is sure to succeed.

When the curtains are taken down shake them thoroughly to remove the dust, and if any small holes or broken threads are visible, darn them carefully before they are put in the water. When this work is neatly done it will show very little if any when the curtains are laundered. Heat the water until it is almost boiling hot, dissolve a little borax in it and enough soap to make a good suds. Pour this over the curtains and allow them to soak half an hour. Rub them gently between the hands and work them up and down in the water for ten or fifteen minutes, then fold each curtain separately, wrap a clean white cloth around it, and pass it through the wringer into the second suds prepared just as the first was. The amount of borax required varies with the kind of water used, as more will be needed for hard water than for soft. They will seldom need boiling, and after they have been washed in the second suds they will be ready for rinsing and starching. Rinse through two waters, then dip in a very thin boiled starch, which should be slightly tinged with blue, if a clear white is desired. Adding cold coffee to the starch will give it an ecru tint, or saffron tea will make them a delicate cream color.

If you have no curtain frames and cannot get them, do not be discouraged, for your curtains can be dried very satisfactorily without them. Spread several sheets out upon the floor of a spare room, stretching them smoothly and securing them by tacking them to the floor at intervals. Spread the curtains upon them, drawing them tightly and pinning every scollop in place. Open the windows so they will dry quickly, and when taken up you will find them as pretty as new curtains. They will not need ironing.

E. J. C.

"What Harm is there in Card-Playing?"

The harm (1) of handling the tools of the gambler. (2) Of learning the methods of using these tools. (3) Of coming under the influence of the tendency towards the tricks and trickery that so commonly go with the use of those tools. (4) Of entering even the outer circle of the kind of people who use such tools, and of coming under the influence of the tendency to be drawn into the circles that are nearer and nearer the wicked vortex of such things. (5) Of becoming familiar with and a party to the lowering of the principle of the lot commonly called "chance," but really predestination (or providence) to the uses of mere recreation. (6) Of risking the tendency toward the waste of time in prolonged play. (7) Of venturing into the danger of not doing whatsoever one does to the glory of God, in the name of the Lord Jesus. (8) Lastly, even though it would do you no harm, there would be the harm it would do to others in any of these ways; and your daily petition, "Lead us not into temptation," makes it incumbent upon you not to lead any one into temptation or to lead temptation to any one. —*London Christian Endeavor.*

Eternity.

BY WILL H. DIXON.

Strange we seldom miss the the moments till
the day is past and gone;
We seldom prize God's sunshine till our lives
are cast in gloom;
We scarcely learn life's lessons until the
latest breath,
When the shadows fall around us and we close
our eyes in death.

O, let us heed the precious moments, then and
work while life shall last,
For time's clock will strike no more the hours
that have passed;
Soon the angel, Death, will call us from out
life's narrow sea—
Far beyond this life of toil and time, TO THE
GREAT ETERNITY!

Rock Island, Ill.

Illustrated Sermon.

CAL OGBURN.

Text: For as we have many members in one body, and all members have not the same office: so we, being many, are one body in Christ, and every one members of another.—*Rom.* 12:4, 5.

The eye cannot say unto the hand, I have no need of thee; nor the head to the feet, I have no need of thee. Nay, much more those members of the body, which seem to be more feeble, are necessary.—*1 Cor.* 12:21, 22.

SERMON.

While winding my watch the other night I imagined the various parts that enter into its construction were engaged in a very animated discussion. I listened, and heard the mainspring say in a complaining mood: "I am shut up here in this prison and can only pull and pull to make the rest of you go, and I'm getting very tired of it. I am the essential part of any watch, and I protest against such treatment from my inferiors."

At this seemingly unprovoked attack the balance wheel chimed out, "I am quite as necessary as you are," laying a great deal of emphasis on the personal pronouns, "and here I am being constantly jerked from side to side till I am so dizzy I could not stand alone, if I had the privilege of trying. It is too bad."

This explosive speech from the somewhat unbalanced wheel gave the delicate hairspring occasion to relate her grievances, which she did in very plain language. "Do you mean to insinuate," said she, "that I am the cause of all your annoyance? You are forever determined to go to one extreme or the other, and I am so tired trying to keep you in your proper place that I think I shall certainly have an attack of nervous prostration. Will you not hereafter conduct yourself as a balance wheel should? And please do not insinuate, at least while you are so eccentric, that I am of little importance. If it were not for me, delicate as I am, a watch would not be a watch."

Then the second hand accused the minute hand of being lazy, and the minute hand retorted by saying, "I am not lazy, I would have you know. You certainly have forgotten that I have a greater distance to travel than you have, and that my work is much more important than yours, for while you tick off the seconds I count the minutes. Besides, I perform twelve times as much labor as my neighbor, the hour hand, for he travels around the face of this dial but twice in twenty-four hours, while I go round twenty-four times. I've a great mind to sue you for slander or accusing me of being lazy."

Before the minute hand had finished his harangue the hour hand interrupted him by saying, "The insinuation you have just made to your noisy little neighbor that I am not doing my duty is false and ridiculous. It is my business, as you very well know, to mark the hours as they go by, while it is your business"—and this was spoken in such an emphatic way as to convey the impression that the minute hand was inclined to meddle with the business of others—"to tell off the minutes. This duty I have done faithfully and well. It requires sixty minutes to make an hour, therefore I am sixty times more important than you. I am come to bear witness to the truth."

Just then the watch suddenly stopped, and the combined efforts of all the hands and of all the springs could not move a wheel. The conference assumed a different aspect, and upon due inquiry it was found that a very small cog had been broken out of a very insignificant little wheel—presumably by the bickering and contention that had prevailed—rendering the watch practically useless.

APPLICATION.

Unfortunately, there are egotistic, disparaging, contentious church members as well as self-centered, hypercritical watch springs, hands and wheels, and the one is as ruinous to the church as the other is to the watch. Let us strive to realize that "those members of the body which seem to be more feeble are necessary," and as Christians govern ourselves in harmony therewith. Nothing more quickly destroys the usefulness of a congregation than for the spirit of fault-finding and disparagement to prevail. Keep selfishness without by keeping love within.

775 West 9th St., Riverside, Cal.

With The Children.

Getting Started.

Children, I have already told you something about this department, but when anything new is started you know there must be a good deal of talking. So I must say more about it. For this column is a new thing—there is not another corner in any magazine or paper just like it. And I want you to understand all about it from the beginning. This place in the CHRISTIAN-EVANGELIST is given up to the children, and it is for them, and not for their parents. Grown people can read it if they want to, but children will read it because it is for them, and they can't get anywhere else what they will get here. You know what young folks' departments generally are—places where mothers are told how to raise their children; or sermons to boys and girls about not losing a minute of time, or throwing away a string; or a little story about somebody who was so good that he died of it.

Of course we all want to be good, but we want to live and enjoy it. And when we have a children's column we want something in it that will interest children and make them anxious for the next paper to "come out." How will I know what you want in this column? Am I going to guess at it? No, I am going to leave it to you. What would you like to read in your column? I invite you all to write to me and tell me just what you want, and you shall have it. Isn't that fair? This is why this column is different from any other in the world. The children are asked to make it a success. Write to me at once and tell me what you think it ought to be. Do you like continued stories about boys and girls—sure enough, live, happy, healthy boys and girls? Or do you like short stories for children? Or do you like poetry? And what about facts? And are you going to join the Advance Society?

I told you about that society last week, but perhaps you missed the paper. I will tell it again in a few words. Anybody can join who makes five determinations: 1. To read weekly five pages of history (not a text-book); 2. To memorize weekly a quotation from some standard author; 3. To read 30 lines of poetry weekly; 4. To read a verse of the Bible daily; 5. To keep an account of how much you read in a notebook. And at the end of twelve weeks if you have kept all these resolutions write to me, saying so, stating what you have read and how much, and your name will be printed in this column on the List of Honor. Remember, you are not allowed to skip one week, then make up the next. Regularity is what we want. You can begin any day, and if you miss a week you must begin all over. If you didn't see what I said about this last week hunt up the paper and read it now. We want members from all the states, and from foreign countries. Write, saying you will join; and give me your age, and tell me about yourself, and give us advice about making this column a great big success. I will keep all your names on my book, and we will all come close together and feel a good deal like kinfolks. Not the kind of kinfolks that tell you to make less noise, however, just because it is a habit with them—and I can make good use of your letters, and give the good things out to the rest.

Another new thing about this society—every once in a while we will write upon a given subject, and I will put all your pieces into one article, with your names after what you write. Not subjects like "The Pyramids" or "Time," but something you won't have to dig out of books, and then harrass yourselves by trying to say it in a different way. Do you know our first general subject? It is, "The Funniest Thing in the World." Ever know of any thing funny happening, or ever hear of any funny remark by a boy or girl? Write at once and tell me about it. Now, you don't have to do this unless you wish, but I hope you will wish. And tell your friends about this piece; it will be printed in this column in about two weeks. Tell them to get ready to laugh! Make your stories just as short as you can, but don't leave out the point. Always write your age. If you don't want me to publish it draw a circle about it. In that case I will keep it a dark secret. Nobody shall get it out of me! If you are real old, and ashamed of having lived so long, you needn't give your age. But send that funny story. We all want to hear it. When I insist that this column is not for old people, don't suppose I mean to be unkind to them. Here's a story that will show just what I mean, and it's a story you never heard before.

THE ROBINS AND THE OWLS.

There was a certain yard where some robins lived as happy as robins can be. All day long they chattered and sang as they went about their daily household duties. They skipped back and forth in the sunlight, because they knew the yard was plentiful of big, fat worms; and the trees threw down twigs and leaves for them to make into nests. And they were glad they were robins, and not ostriches or any other kind of bird, and they were willing to enjoy their corner of the world and let God manage the rest.

One day some owls flew into the yard, and began to keep house in one of the trees. At first the robins lived as before, but the strangers looked so terribly wise and so prodigiously solemn that by and by their chirps died away, and they all sat in awe upon their boughs, afraid to move for fear of displeasing their wise neighbors. "What good robins you have become," said an owl one day. "Only keep on, and you will be like we are. You must practice sleeping all day and keeping awake all night; feed upon mice, and, in short, be different in all points from what you are." Now, one day one of the robins gave a curious gasp. "What's up?" asked his neighbor. "I was trying to chirp," said the other, "but I have forgotten how!" "As for me," said the second, "I was trying to pretend that that hind leg of the mouse tasted good. Oh, for a worm, a smooth, fat, wriggling worm!" "Robins," cried a fourth, "come into court! I have something to propose." The owls looked very wise, but they were only asleep, so all the robins crowded their heads together.

"We are robins," said the fourth; "why should we try to be owls?" It was such a clear proposition that they saw it in a flash. And presently every robin had flown away. That night the owls found themselves the only occupants of the yard.

What do I mean by this story? Why, the yard represents a Children's Department in a paper. And the robins are the children; and the owls—but I shall not say who the owls are. Anyway, if the owls come flocking into our columns, away the robins will go! So all write to me, and don't forget that I live in Plattsburg, Mo.

Literature.

THE LAW OF PSYCHIC PHENOMENA: A working Hypothesis for the Systematic Study of Hypnotism, Spiritism and Mental Therapeutics. By Thomas J. Hudson, LL. D., Chicago. A. C. McClurg & Co., 1898.

The results of the investigation of the London Society for Psychical Research, whose branches extend throughout the civilized world, as they have been published from time to time, have awakened a new interest in a class of phenomena belonging to the borderland of mystery. Those who are acquainted with the results of these researches know that these strange and wonderful phenomena are as well attested as any facts can be. There has been a variety of theories as to the causes of these phenomena. This book, to which our attention was recently called by one of our readers, is an attempt, and we will add, a remarkable attempt, to formulate the law under which these phenomena occur. It is, so far as we know, the most satisfactory effort that has yet been made to account for the strange things connected with spiritism, hypnotism and the undisputed cures which have been effected under a variety of names, such as "mind cures," "faith healing," "magnetic healing," "Christian Science," etc.

Accepting as true what has been actually proven to have transpired, the author undertakes to find the underlying law of these psychological phenomena. The fundamental hypothesis of Mr. Hudson is that the mind of a man is dual; that is, that he possesses what he terms a subjective mind and an objective mind. Another proposition is that the subjective mind is constantly amenable to control by suggestion; and the third is that the subjective mind is incapable of inductive reasoning. He thus defines the difference between these two minds:

"The objective mind takes cognizance of the objective world. Its media of observation are five physical senses. It is the outgrowth of man's physical necessities. It is his guide in his struggle with his material environment. Its highest function is that of reasoning.

"The subjective mind takes cognizance of its environment by means independent of the physical senses. It perceives by intuition. It is the seat of the emotions and the storehouse of memory. It performs its highest functions when the objective senses are in abeyance. In a word, it is that intelligence which makes itself manifest in a hypnotic subject when he is in a state of somnambulism."

The subject of hypnotism is quite thoroughly treated, as is also that of telepathy. Most of the phenomena in Spiritism, according to the author's view, occur under the law of telepathy, or the power of thought-transference without any objective method of communication. The theory of Spiritists, that this class of phenomena are the result of communication with the spirits of the departed, is utterly rejected, and the author explains how the phenomena produced can be all accounted for without resorting to that hypothesis. The warning against the physical and moral effects of Spiritism is most sane and timely.

The question of psycho-therapeutics is treated quite at length, the author believing that there is a great deal in it of real hygenic value, and that if the matter is taken out of the hands of charlatans and given scientific investigation, it will yield results most beneficial to the human race.

In the closing chapters of the book, the author applies the principles of his theory to the physical manifestations and philosophy of Christ. He claims that all of Christ's miracles took place according to the latest and most scientific principles of psycho-therapeutics. He believes that he has furnished a scientific basis for belief in the New Testament record of all of Christ's works. While there is much that is suggestive in these last chapters, they are the least satisfactory part of the work, in our judgment, the author betraying the fact that he is a scientist rather than a Bible student. He is a firm believer, however, in Christ, and in the religion which he taught.

We have no doubt that this work will make it far easier for many to believe in the future existence of the soul and in our personal identity in the life to come, and in this way it will prove a great comfort to many minds. On the whole, it is not too much to say that it is a remarkable book and one that marks a distinct advance in the direction of a satisfactory solution of the promblem connected with these strange forces and phenomena about which so little has hitherto been known.

JUNIOR TOPICS OUTLINED. By Mrs. Ella N. Wood. Published by the United Society of Christian Endeavor, Boston and Chicago. Cloth. 5 x 7 1-2. Illustrated. 125 pages. Price, 50 cents.

In this new book for Junior workers every topic for 1899 is treated in a simple, practical way, and many suggestions for blackboard illustrations are given in pictures. No Junior superintendent will need resign or dread the meetings who has such a practical helper.

MAGAZINES.

The Anglo-Saxon is the title of a new monthly magazine that has just made its appearance in the literary world. This magazine is edited by Geo. E. Inglis, and published by the Anglo-Saxon Publishing Co., 6627 Washington Ave., Chicago, Ill., and is devoted to the identity of the Anglo-Saxon race with the House of Israel. Those interested in prophetic problems will find this a suggestive magazine of literature on that line of study.

The Century begins its new year with a brilliant cover in color by the well-known Parisian poster-artist, Grasset, who made the Napoleon poster for the Century. This time he pictures Alexander the Great on the famous Bucephalus. This is in connection with the magazine's new historical serial on Alexander, written by Prof. Benjamin Ide Wheeler, which will be one of the leading features for the coming year. The lessons from the career of the Macedonian conqueror are of particular interest in these days of empire-making projects. Aside from the archeological material that is pictured, the life is strikingly illustrated by Castaigne and Loeb. Captain Charles D. Sigsbee begins his "Personal Narrative of the *Maine*." This is the contribution of the commander of the battleship to the Century's New War Series, which will include articles by most of the leading officers in the land and naval operations in the recent war. Captain Sigsbee, in this paper, gives for the first time, and in a full and authoritative manner, the story of the ordering of the *Maine* to Havana, her arrival in the harbor, her reception by the Spanish officials, and the precautions that were taken to guard her safety. The article is fully illustrated from photographs that have not appeared elsewhere. The other articles are in keeping with the season, the times and the high standard of this mazazine.

With its November number St. Nicholas begins a new volume and celebrates its twenty-fifth birthday. In honor of this anniversary the magazine dons a special cover, bearing a birthday cake decorated with twenty-five candles. Notwithstanding its quarter of a century of existence, St. Nicolas is just as young as ever in spirit. A new Henty serial is begun, a tale of American history, that will be one of the features of the coming year. It is called "The Sole Survivors," and it deals with the struggles of an early Virginia colony with the Indians. E. H. House is to contribute a series of papers on "Bright Sides of History," dealing with amusing episodes in ancient and modern history. These are given in the course of a story, which tells of the sayings and doings of a party of clever boys and girls. Time would fail us to mention all the good things in this number which cannot but afford interest and pleasure to its readers these November days and nights.

The Preacher's Magazine for November is a Thanksgiving number. The leading sermon is entitled, "Sowing vs. Reaping," by the Ven. Archdeacon Colley. The Rev. James Weller contributes a sermon entitled, "Joy in Harvest," and Bishop Alexander King, D. D., a sermon entitled, "Growing till the Harvest." A most excellent article on "Pulpit Prayer" is contributed by Rev. Robert Wilson, Ph. D. The Homiletical Department contains a large number of outline sermons by various ministers, mostly relating to Thanksgiving Day. They are suggestive and helpful. The Children's Sermon is by the Rev. Martin Lewis. There are also various other articles relating to the day. The editor, William E. Ketcham, D. D., writes the Notes of the International Sunday-school Lessons, and the Outlines on the Golden Texts. The Rev. J. A. Clapperton continues his articles on "Pitfalls in Bible English," which have commanded so much attention. Wilbur B. Ketcham, Publisher, 7 and 9 West Eighteenth Street, New York.

The November Record of Christian Work, East Northfield, Mass., contains a number of unusually interesting and suggestive articles for the Bible student and Christian worker. Mr. Robert E. Speer, the well-known Bible teacher and secretary of the Presbyterian Board of Foreign Missions, contributes an article on "Practical Suggestions for Home Bible Study." Dr. J. R. Miller writes on "The Beatitude of Purity" in his series of articles, and Rev. Kenneth Mackenzie, Jr., contributes a specially interesting article on "The Transfiguration." The regular departments of the magazine are unusually strong, being edited by such men as Rev. C. I. Scofield, Rev. R. A. Torrey, D. L. Moody and D. W. Whittle.

Attention is drawn in The North American Review for November to the subject of "National Public Health Legislation," by U. O. B. Wingate, M. D., Secretary of the Wisconsin State Board of Health. Dr. Wingate is an earnest advocate of the so-called "Spooner Bill" which was presented to the Senate of the Fifty-fifth Congress, and which provides for the establishment of a commission composed of men actively engaged in sanitary work, whose sole object will be the bringing of all localities in the country into the best possible sanitary condition—an object whose attainment cannot be too highly estimated.

Every one should read Dr. Henry V. Noyes' article in the Missionary Review of the World for November, on "The Present Situation in

:he condi-
tical and
iteresting
. Allis, of
religious
Republic.
m photo-
is and the
agent of
y in those
Spaniard,
he inhab-
's clearly
upon the
Publish-

[ich., for
l striking
work for
iown the
the work
; a knight
ht of the
a banner
ross, and
te shield.
nment is
ooks and
the title
come the

ls getting
dition of

: Young
blishing a
l in Bible
itles are:
t Prayer
Spiritual
ind "The
lad to see
ain going
he young
rs of this
ew York

or.

ek, and
y, praise
ke a part
ended by
held in
however,
which is
igorating
o go into
or good,
for that
rd. The
if falleth
ver man

l for this
s, then,
out. He
iarvelous
arous to
not bar-
led, des-

we little thought, "Lord, thrust forth laborers into the harvest." Only let us be careful that we go forth weeping and not exulting, praising him and not praising ourselves, anxious for progress, civilization, enlightenment, and not for gain, colonies, pelf and plunder.

"For heathen heart that puts its trust
In reeking tube and iron shard,
All valiant dust that builds on dust,
And guarding calls not thee to guard,
For foolish boast, and frantic word,
Thy mercy on thy people, Lord!"

Forbid that we should glory, on this Thanksgiving Day, in aught save the cross of Christ! Let our nation humble itself beneath the Lord's hand, be led slowly out to new work, nor rush blindly boasting into untried fields

We have cause for thanksgiving this year, in the fact that all parts of our country are one to-day as they have never been before. There is no North, no South, no East, no West. The sons of those who wore the blue have with the sons of those who wore the gray, clasped hands above a buried difference, and we are all one.

We should praise God, too, for the fact that the difference between home and foreign missions, which we have so long tried in vain to ignore, has at last been broken down, and to-morrow we shall have home missionaries in the West Indies, the South Pacific and the other side of the world.

Once again, we cannot but feel glad and full of promise that so large a part of the body of soldiers and sailors of our country proved themselves true to the Lord of Lords, to the one who is their Master. The chaplains who followed their regiments self-sacrificingly to the field, the Y. M. C. A. forces that so carefully sought the welfare of the troops, the Endeavorers who, on land and sea, remained true to Christ and the church, the captains of the warships who dared to call upon the name of God in the face of hundreds of men in the time of marvelous victory—all these are worthy of undying praise, and they fill our hearts with thankfulness. Even to-day are there seven thousand in Israel, all knees that have not bowed to Baal, all lips that have not kissed him.

BETHANY C. E. READING COURSES.

[There are three courses: The Bible, Missions and the Disciples. The three handbooks for the *first* year are: "A Guide to Bible Study," "Handbook of Missions" and "Concerning the Disciples." The three handbooks for the *second* year are: "Life and Teachings of Jesus," "Missionary Fields and Forces of the Disciples" and "Sketches of our Pioneers." Three handbooks and the Bethany C. E. Bulletin, quarterly, sent to any address for one dollar. All orders should be addressed to the Bethany C. E. Company, 798 Republic St., Cleveland, O. Each course has a director: H. L. Willett is director of Bible study; W. J. Lhamon is the director of studies in Missions; F. D Power is director of studies Concerning the Disciples. This column is set apart to the use of these directors.]

Study of our Pioneers.

F. D. POWER, *Director*.

"The proper study of mankind is man," says Pope. We might amend by saying that divinity and humanity are the great studies. Yet man is himself a revelation of God. The man Christ Jesus came forth from the bosom of the Father and was the brightness of God's glory, the express image of his person. He was God manifest in the flesh, and every man is God's image manifested in the flesh.

Man is the sum-total of all the animals. "The true Shekinah is man," says Chrysostom. "We touch heaven when we lay hands on a human body," says Carlyle. "There is but one temple in the world, and that temple is the

some even smaller; some are
others in plain covers; som
subjects; some are romances,
some squibs; every one beg
page and closes with the "Fi

The great themes are most
of benefactors, lives that
blessings or foundations of
for the good of human kin
worthy of our imitation and
brance, deserve our first th
a Peter or a Paul; a Washing
a Gladstone; a Luther, Livin
Campbell: these stand out
amples, representatives of g
no intelligent person can aff
of their history. "The mem
blessed." "They that be te
as the firmament and they th
righteousness as the stars fo
"Honor to whom honor is d
differeth from another star in

Our readers are dealing
workers in the great religiou
which we are associated. Th
foundations; they belong to
they deserve to be rememb
templation of their labors an
virtues and achivements, mus
nobler endeavor. The little
"Sketches of our Pioneers,
textbook for the second year
in itself and we shall be di
brief information it contains
more extended investigation
history and to wider inform
the prominent figures that
hosts and blazed the way for
people need this study—the ol
memories and to kindle anew
great principles we advocate,
familiarize themselves with th
which they stand identified.

We are a peculiar people.
difference where a man stan
for what he stands. Before
sponsible for the measure of
his will and the measure of
Word. Learn where you sta
tion to reading. Acquaint y
Aquilas and Priscillas that
the way of the Lord more pe
ready always to give an an
that asketh you a reason of th
you with meekness and revere

Sunday School.

REPENTANCE UNDER PRESSURE.*

HERBERT L. WILLETT.

The closing years of Hezekiah's reign were not so glorious as his earlier career had promised. He was rich; but his wealth gave him an undue sense of pride. He had been measurably obedient to the divine will as voiced in the counsels of Isaiah, and this gave him an exaggerated idea of his own worth. The pride which comes from birth, or wealth, or education, and which removes one from sympathy with the life and struggle of other men, is foolish and offensive, and only one degree less obnoxious than the pride which grows out of a sense of righteousness, and is apt to cloak the worst Pharisaism. Both proceed from a nature tainted with selfishness. When sickness came to the king, and he learned that his end was near, he broke out into piteous laments at his fate, wondering how God could permit so good a man to die, and declaring that it would be better to let him live in order that he might continue to praise Jehovah! On his recovery he gave further expression to his pride by exhibiting to the envoys of Merodach Baladin, the pretender at Babylon, all the riches of his court, which called down on his head the indignant rebuke of Isaiah, who foresaw that alliance with the Babylonian rebel meant a new insult to the king of Assyria, from whose hand Hezekiah had escaped but yesterday. But these were blemishes upon an excellent life, and such blemishes as pride and selfishness will produce in any character.

Hezekiah was succeeded by his son, Manasseh. The name, originally belonging to one of the tribes of the Northern Kingdom, had become common since the downfall of Samaria and the extension of Hezekiah's kingkom in that direction. He was only twelve when he came to the throne, and the hour was one of peril. The heathen party, long in restraint during the ministry of Isaiah, "the keeper of the king's conscience," now sought the power they had lost. The swing of the pendulum was perpetual in Judah. At one time the prophetic party, including the priests, would control the court, and in such a period, the worship of Jehovah was in the ascendant. At another time the heathen party controlled, and when idolatry and every form of danger that intercourse with neighboring nations could bring, gained the day. Sometimes the change was wrought without reference to the king, who was a mere figurehead, plastic to the control of his advisers. At other times the king, while yet a youth, was secured by the party out of power, through instructors or associates, and then his majority saw the revolution. Such seems to have been the case with Manasseh. Confident of the future because he was secure in the present, Hezekiah left the training of his son, born later in his reign, to men who, outwardly conforming to the religion of the time, were quietly undermining his character and turning his mind away from the God of his fathers. No greater responsibility rests upon parents than the oversight of the education of their children. It is a mistake, wellnigh a crime, to permit the most sacred duty of life to be intrusted wholly to others in the confident belief that everything is all right, and the teachers provided by public school, college and university are always the proper instructors of the future race. Especially is this true in religious matters. A flippant and irreverent teacher may wreck the moral and spiritual life of a child reared in the most careful circle of Christian influence. Ceaseless vigilance is the price of liberty from such malign results.

*Sunday-school lesson for Nov. 20, 1898—Manasseh's Sin and Repentance (2 Chron. 33:9-16). Golden Text—If we confess our sins, he is faithful and just to forgive us our sins and to cleanse us from all unrighteousness (1 John 1:9). Lesson Outline—1. Sin and Obstinacy (9:10); 2. Affliction and Repentance (11, 12); 3. Restoration and Reform (13-16).

When Manasseh came to the throne the time was ripe for change. The heathen party that had been in retirement for years had profited by the carelessness of their rivals, and now came into power. The king threw himself into the religious reaction with vigor. He rebuilt the high places which his father had demolished. He brought in again the worship of Baal and Asherah. He reverted to the darkest sins of Ahaz, his grandfather, reviving the worship of the sun and planets, the incantations and necromancies, which have in every age fostered the delusion of Spiritism, and caused the blood of children, even those of his own family, to flow in sacrifice to his grotesque idols. Even in the very temple of God an image of the obscure Astarte was erected. All these were sins of darkest die, as viewed by the prophets, and their protests must have been frequent and loud. One wonders what the course of Isaiah was during this time, or whether he was yet alive. No record of his work runs beyond the great deliverance from Sennacherib in 701. Perhaps, as tradition has it, the aged prophet was brought to martyrdom in this reign, as a victim of that bloody persecution of the Jehovah worshipers, in which "much innocent blood" was shed (2 Kings 21:16). It has been thought that reference is made to the form of Isaiah's death in Heb. 11:37: "They were sawn asunder." But the protests of the prophets were received only as the indignant outcries of men who were losing power and position by the change. To the king it was not alone a question of religion, but of the whole state policy, and he chose to go with the heathen party. We may feel that such kings had no excuse for their conduct. But education has much to do in shaping one's ideas. And the light was not so bright by far as in our day. We may not and we should not find apology for their sins. But how small they were, considering the influences they met, as compared with ours, who live in the blaze of Christian intelligence and have no smallest excuse for our forgetfulness of God. We are tempted to hide our errors behind those of men who walked in the darkness, not in the light we enjoy.

But sin, whether ignorant, half-enlightened or intelligent, brings its sure results in disaster. Warnings had been unheeded. Trouble came. The prophets had spoken for God, but in vain. God must himself speak in judgments, a discipline like that of Samaria, a fate like that of the house of Ahab, alone remained. The king of Assyria, always the waiting scourge of Judah, came as the result of political complications of which we do not now have information. Esarhaddon (681-668) and Ashurbainpal (668-625) were the contemporaries of the long reign of Manasseh (686-641), but which of these kings invaded Judah we do not know. We have only the knowledge which the text furnishes, that the Asyrian forces overran the country and carried the king in chains to Babylon, which was at this time the capital of the empire. The fate of a captive king was by no means enviable. If his life was spared he was reduced to a wretched station, and kept as an exhibition of his master's power. Such a life was full of bitterness, not only the actual hardships of his situation, but the sad reflection upon the contrast between his present misery and his father's glory, and must have made Manasseh conscious that idolatry and hethenism did not pay. They had been his worst enemies. His heathen friends had been helpless in his hour of need. Such reflections brought the king to repentance. A slow and late repentance it was—a repentance under pressure. Many a man exhibits that sort, however. It is not so much a sorrow for sin; it is rather a desire to escape the consequences of sin. Never till sin is seen to be more awful than any of its results; never till one dreads moral bleakness mose than he fears the trouble it will bring, can a true vision of life be obtained. Let us ask ourselves why we do not commit this or that sin? Is it because we abhor the evil, or because we dread the scour[illegible] or the scandal? If the latter is the motive, l[illegible] us beware. Our house is built on sand.

But Manasseh's repentance was sufficient [illegible] bring good results. The earlier books say noth[illegible] ing of it. In the parallel narative in Kings it [illegible] not mentioned. Probably this is due to th[illegible] fact that the king was powerless to undo th[illegible] evil he had wrought. The remainder of h[illegible] reign was too short to permit any genuir[illegible] reformation in the kingdom. The closir[illegible] verses of the lesson record his public worl[illegible] and his efforts to restore the worship of Go[illegible] But the current of heathenism which had set [illegible] so strongly through the earlier years of h[illegible] long reign of more than half a century cou[illegible] not be checked in the few years that r[illegible] mained to him, and his son, Amon, was eve[illegible] more active as a supporter of heathenism tha[illegible] he himself had been. Manasseh's repentanc[illegible] like that of many other men, came too lat[illegible] He could not live to undo the disaster he h[illegible] worked. In spite of this brief record of h[illegible] afflictions and repentance, and the pray[illegible] attributed to him, recorded in the collection [illegible] Greek additions to the Old Testament (see t[illegible] Prayer of Manasseh it the Apocrypha), h[illegible] name will always be associated with one of t[illegible] most cruel persecutions of the faithful th[illegible] ever occurred in Judah, and stands at the hea[illegible] of the list of idolatrous kings of the Souther[illegible] Kingdom.

SUGGESTIONS EOR TEACHING.

Some men are pre-eminent only in evi[illegible] Warnings unheeded turn to bitter chastis[illegible] ments. Suffering is always useful if it lea[illegible] to reformation. Nothing can be more sad tha[illegible] the remembrance of a holy father to a d[illegible] graded son. Any repentance is better tha[illegible] none, but no repentance can ever bring ba[illegible] wasted years. Restoration to liberty a[illegible] former position is not restoration of sinles[illegible] ness. The prodigal is always received wit[illegible] welcome when he returns; but more blessed [illegible] the son who never strayed. It is beautiful [illegible] see one who has wasted time seeking to r[illegible] deem somewhat the dark past. But evil, li[illegible] good, is cumulative; what we have once do[illegible] we cannot recall; we may change our life, b[illegible] its deeds go on forever.

Berlin.

Marriages.

FURLONG—SPELL.—At the home of the bride, Halstead, Kan., James Furlong and Dora Spell were united in marriage Oct. 26, 1898, J. J. McLain officiating.

HAND—McCANDLESS.—At the home of the bride's parents, near Morgan, Ky., Oct. 19, 1898, Walter P. Jennings officiating, B. F. Hand and Ella McCandless.

JONES—GILBERT.—In Paris, Mo., Oct. 26, 1898, C. H. Strawn officiating, Mr. W. M. Jones to Miss Georgia E. Gilbert, both of Monroe County, Mo.

RICHARDS—CUTFORTH.—Oct. 23rd, at the Christian Parsonage, Payson, Ill., Mr. William Richards and Miss Kate Cutforth, both of Adams, Ill., Eld. C. Edwards officiating.

TRAILER—STATLER.—On Oct. 26th, at Deweese, Neb., Mr. James E. Trailer, of Cass County, Iowa, and Miss Allie May Statler, of Deweese, Neb., A. J. Barnes officiating.

Obituaries.

[One hundred words will be inserted free. Above one hundred words, one cent a word. Please send amount with each notice.]

BRENNEMAN.

Abraham H. Brenneman was born in Ralls County, Mo., December 18, 1848, and was killed at Virden, Ill., October 12, 1898. November 15, 1874, he was married to Rebecca M. Campbell, near Hannibal, Mo. To them were born nine children, six of whom, together with his faithful wife, mourn his untimely death. At the age of 18 years he obeyed the gospel under the preaching of Dr. Winthrop H. Hopson. He was a coal miner, and although filling an humble sphere he was a faithful man of God. Impelled by duty he obeyed the orders of the Miners' Union and went to Virden, and although unarmed and defenseless he was one of the first victims to fall during the unhappy riot of October 12. Funeral services were conducted by the writer on Friday, October 14, at 11 A. M., at the Christian Church, and he was laid to rest in the Girard cemetery to await the resurrection of the just.
GEO. L. PETERS.

INGRAM.

Chas. G. Ingram was born in Mississippi 23 years ago. He died here October 21, 1898. It was his supreme heart's desire to preach Christ in his native state. Death in singling him out robbed earth of a hero and Mississippi of a budding evangel of light. In the galaxy of redeemed departed he shines as a bright star. His expressed regret, "I hate to die when the world needs the gospel so bad," reveals his Christly character. He is dead, yet lives. May a double portion of his unselfish, consecrated spirit rest upon us all.
GEORGE B. EVANS.
Kimberlin Heights, Tenn.

IRVINE.

Brother J. J. Irvine died in the hospital at Norfolk, Va., at 2 A. M., Monday, Oct. 24th, 1898, after an illness of five days, from heart-failure, ensuing an operation for appendicitis, surrounded by his little family, attending surgeons and nurses and a large delegation from the church. Bro. Irvine was 38 years old and a native of Scotland, having come to the United States when 20 years of age, where he graduated from Kentucky University after a six years' course. He served the churches at Selma, Ala., and Jacksonville, Fla., and did a successful work as evangelist before locating with the church here, where he was asked to settle "for a *long* pastorate;" this I interpreted to mean for life. And, although he had preached but for three Lord's days, he had won the hearty co-operation and loyal esteem of the congregation and many of the people of the city, all of whom manifest the deepest sorrow at his death, and the untimely ending of the fine work he had so earnestly and wisely begun. His death was most triumphant and beautiful, and its lessons are deeply impressed upon all who witnessed his falling asleep. Truly was it "a sleep in Jesus —blessed sleep." The stricken church and many people attended his body to the wharf; and Dr. R. H. Walker, one of our deacons, was delegated to attend his remains and his family to Lexington, Ky., where the funeral was held on Wednesday, the 26th inst., and his body was laid to rest there. A memorial service in the church here was held last Lord's day evening. On every hand I hear Bro. Irvine's death spoken of as a triumph of faith. At his request I prepare this brief notice and convey to all his brethren his benediction and assurance that "all is well. His will be done."
C. Q. WRIGHT.
Norfolk, Va.

NALL.

Died of heart failure, Sept. 9, 1898, Mrs. Frances C. Nall, at the home of her daughter, in Adams County, Wash. The funeral services were conducted by Geo. H. Newman Sept. 10. Frances Cordelia Bohannan was born in Stoddard County, Mo., Nov. 27, 1832. She was married to Dr. J. Parks Nall, of Ironton, Mo., Dec. 29, 1852. Into this family were born eight children; five daughters are still living. Soon after her marriage mother heard the Christian faith preached, for the first time in her life, by Bro. Wilson, and soon after obeyed the gospel. She was faithful till death. Soon after the war she lost her husband, but with true motherly instinct and untiring industry she went bravely to work to provide for the wants of her family of little girls, and so raised them that they call her "Blessed" and deeply mourn her loss. But our loss is her gain. "He giveth his beloved sleep."
J. M. TURNER.

NEVINS.

Austin Sims Nevins was born in Tennessee, January 29th, 1816, and died in Girard, Macoupin County, Ill., October 15, 1898, in the 83rd year of his age. The greater part of his life was passed in this county, in the vicinity of Chapman's Point. He was the father of 13 children, 10 of whom, together with his faithful wife, survive. He became a Christian at an early age, and was faithful to his profession during a long life. He was a devoted husband and father, a true friend and kind neighbor. The funeral services were conducted at Oak Grove Church Sunday, October 16, by Rev. Galen Goode, assisted by Revs. Geo. L. Peters and W. H. Kindred. The body sleeps in the old churchyard awaiting the resurrection morn.
GEO. L. PETERS.

WETHERHOLD.

Lucy J. Reynolds was born in Macomb, Ill., July 30, 1861. Obeyed the gospel in her 11th year. Was b ptized by Bro. J. H. Smart. Was married to F. J. Wetherhold, June 8, 1891. Died in Macomb, Ill., Oct. 7, 1898. She was perfectly conscious to the last moment. Her last words, spoken just before her last breath, were, "In my Father's house are many mansions." Her sorrowing father would not take millions for these words now. Precious among the last words of the Savior! Precious as the last words of such a noble daughter. I, her father, could never be satisfied to close this obituary notice at this point. I must be permitted to tell some things that distinguished her among women. Her mother died 16 years ago. She, too, suffered for a long time. Lucy stayed with her, nursed her tenderly and lovingly to the end, thus exhibiting in deed as well as word, the highest possible degree of a daughter's love for her mother. She was her mother's comfort in all her afflictions. Then, when her mother was gone, with equal faithfulness she stayed with me, taking and filling a mother's place to the younger children until they were grown up. In all my labors she was my wise counselor, in my sickness my prudent, tender, loving nurse, in my griefs and sorrows my chiefest earthly comforter. To the last day of her life she manifested the same filial love to her father that she had so tenderly lavished upon her mother. She surely kept the law: "Honor thy father and thy mother," and obeyed the gospel injunction: "Children, obey your parents." She loved her sisters and her brothers, her nephews and nieces. She was a faithful wife, a model housekeeper, making a bright, pleasant, beautiful home for her husband and for her father. She was a woman of sound judgment, a wise woman in the best sense of the word. Her earth-life was spent in doing good, in toiling to make others comfortable and happy. Besides kindred she leaves many friends among the best of the people, both in Illinois and Missouri, who respected and loved her, whose hearts are saddened by her departure. A large concourse of people attended the funeral, many more than could get into the church. Bro. Bratton, pastor of the Presbyterian Church read appropriate Scripture lessons and offered a most excellent prayer. Bro. L. D. Goodwin, pastor of the Christian Church, preached an able and appropriate sermon from the text: "In my Father's house are many mansions," telling the audiedce that these were the last words spoken by Lucy Bro. J. S. Gash followed with tender, loving, comforting remarks. Then we bore her body away to the grave in beautiful Oakwood Cemetery and tenderly laid it to rest until the coming of the Lord. All that money could do, all that medical skill could do, was done to prolong her precious life. All that money could do to honor her in her burial was done by husband. I have one comfort: I fully believe that she occupies a beautiful *mansion* in the "Fathers house." I confidently believe that she will wear a crown of glory in the life eternal. Farewell, Lucy, my daughter! Oh, my daughter! my daugeter! my tears are flowing fast, my heart is broken; farewell! but not forever. I expect to meet you in the "Father's house," where there is no death. Blessed Savior, help me to live the few days left me so that I may meet my precious daughter in thy presence to dwell with thee forever and ever!
J. C. REYNOLDS.

SUBSCRIBERS' WANTS.

Miscellaneous wants and notices will be inserted in this department at the rate of two cents a word, each insertion, all words, large and small, to be counted, and two initials stand for one word. Please accompany notice with corresponding remittance to save book-keeping.

ATTENTION, STATE AND DISTRICT EVANGELISTS!—You can easily place a Christian Library in each community you evangelize, and thus give greater permanency to your work as well as largely increase your own salary. *Try it and see.* For fuller particulars address S. J. Phillips, Sugar Grove, Wis.

Publishers' Notes.

CHRISTIAN LESSON COMMENTARY FOR 1899.

For thirteen years this valuable publication has made its annual appearance and has reached a large circulation. The volume before us fully up to the high standard of its predecessors. Its pages are replete with notes, comments, illustrations, applications and suggestions, gathered from various sources, the design being to throw the best light possible on the Scripture text and assist the teacher and pupil to fix it in their minds and hide it in their hearts. We commend this commentary to all Sunday-school workers.—*The Plymouth Telescope, Dayton, O.*

The Gospel Call music books ordered have been promply received. Every one says these books are just what we want. One sister, in examining the book, began at the back, for as she said, "The good songs are always in the back of the book." When she had got about through the book she said, "I believe it has good songs all the way through."

F. E. BLANCHARD.

Barnard, Mo.

A CHRISTMAS CONCERT.

"The Wonderful Child," a new Christmas concert service, by W. W. Dowling. It is a pamphlet of 16 pages, embracing eight songs with music, numerous Scripture readings and between 15 and 20 poetical recitations, making an entertaining and instructive concert. It can be successfully rendered by the average Sunday-school. Those schools that expect to give an entertainment at Christmas should soon begin their preparation. Price of this concert is five cents per copy, or 50 cents per dozen, postpaid.

MARY ARDMORE, OR A TEST OF FAITH, by J. H. Stark, is just from our press. The story is based on the importance of having clearly defined religious convictions and then holding steadfastly to them until convinced of their error. The New Testament teaching of conversion and kindred subjects is brought out prominently and lucidly in this book. It is a book of 238 pages, very handsome in appearance, and the price is $1.00, postpaid.

QUEEN ESTHER.

I have just finished reading "Queen Esther," by M. M. Davis. My acquaintance with the author led me to expect something good in advance, but it was still a pleasant surprise. I know Bro. Davis as a preacher of sterling ability and a pastor of national repute, but had not until now known him as an author of splendid dramatic power. There are two especially strong features of this production, of which I wish to speak. The first is the dramatic power which clothes the main incident of the story so as to make it an epoch in the world's history, and brings its cheif actors so vividly before us that they seem to be living yet. The other is the application of the lessons to our own lives with such force that the question pierces the heart like a sword, but with such sympathy that one can feel the healing of the wound behind the passing of the blade. Buy it and read it, for it will stir your heart.

GRANVILLE JONES.

Midland, Tex.

PERSONAL MENTION.

At his own request, after two years' ministry at Benton, Ill., F. A. Sword was released by the church that he might accept a call from the church at Monticello, Ia., to which place he has gone with the love, esteem and commendation of the church at Benton.

Secretary B. S. Denny is in Corydon, Ia., with a view to permanently establishing a congregation.

Geo. A, Campbell, of Chicago, Ill., preached in Hampton, Ia., on Nov. 6th.

Jas. Small was at Fort Dodge, Ia., last Sunday. He begins his meeting in Keokuk, Nov. 12th.

B. W. Petitt preached at Oskaloosa, Ia., first Sunday in November.

F. M. Jordan, of Deer Lodge, Mont., was an Iowa visitor last week.

D. A. Wickizer, was called to Oskaloosa on Nov. 1st to conduct the funeral services of Sister Dixon, the mother of Mrs. Ben McCoy.

I. N. McCash conducted the funeral of one of his church officers last Thursday—Wm. Deitchman, formerly of Oskaloosa.

H. W. Everest, Dean of Drake University Bible Department, is slowly recovering from his slight paralytic stroke.

F. M. Bruner is still confined to his bed, but hopes to sit up soon. His great heart and masterly brain are not idle. He is constantly writing in spite of his years of confinement to his room and his bed. His home is University Place, Des Moines.

N. A. McConnell, of Cedar Rapids, Ia., is preaching almost every Sunday. On Oct. 30th at the Central City dedication, he delivered a sermon on the Lord's. Supper which will long be remembered by those who heard it.

A. M. Growden is engaged in a meeting at Russellville, Ky. He is open at present to engagements for a few meetings, or can be secured as pastor.

J. W. Lowber recently delivered a series of chapel talks on the first chapter of Genesis at the University of Texas, which attracted a good deal of attention.

J. H. Wright entered upon his second year's service with the Osceolo, Ia., church last Sunday, and reports two accessions by primary obedience and three by commendation recently. Bro. Wright will be recalled by many of our readers as a regular contributor to this journal for a number of years, often writing under the caption, "From an Easy Chair." He is favored regularly with one of the largest audiences in Iowa. The Osceola church has one of the most perfect and commodious auditoriums in the state, in which 900 can be comfortably seated.

Chas. A. Young, now engaged in lectures and Bible institute work in Virginia, writes that he has been unwell since at Chattanooga, but has not discontinued or omitted any of his work. He lectures at the State University at Charlottesville through the week and holds Bible institutes on Lord's days from city to city for the C. W. B. M. Concerning the field and the work of the University Bible Lectureship he says: "The churches are not strong in Virginia and I seldom secure more than fifty or a hundred dollars, but as Col. Cary's family have given us ten thousand dollars for the University of Virginia Bible Lectureship, I want to do everything I can to increase the amount to twenty-five thousand. Last Sunday I visited Gilboa, one of the oldest churches in Virginia, the home of W. K. Pendleton, and secured nearly one hundred dollars in cash and pledges for the work."

Robert T. Mathews has resigned the pastorate of the Broadway Church, Louisville, Ky., on account of the heavy financial obligations of the congregation in paying the debt on the new house of worship and will be open to a call elsewhere. Under his ministry of a year there have been about 30 additions and he succeeded in lifting a heavy current debt, and the contributions to missions and charities have exceeded $500. Under his counsel the church will endeavor to call a younger man on a smaller salary, who will find a church thoroughly united and noted for its appreciation of a devoted and efficient minister.

A. C. Hopkins, Canton, Mo., writes that he and his son and daughter are still engaged in the Chautauqua illustrated work, and that it benefits the church wherever held. This trio can also be secured to assist pastors and evangelists in protracted meetings.

C. B. Carlisle, late of Iowa, was appointe[d] and commissioned as chaplain in the arm[y] and was sent to Cuba. We have a letter fro[m] him bearing date of Oct. 18th, from Song[o] near Santiago, Cuba, saying: "I am her[e] hard at work, preaching, visiting the sic[k] giving out Red Cross supplies, feeding star[v]ing Cubans and doing the numberless litt[le] things the men cannot do for themselves. "Just now," he adds, "we are ordered [to] Holguin on the north side of this part of t[he] Island, where we are likely to put up our Chris[t]mas tree and hang thereon our stockings. He is making a study of the condition a[nd] needs of the people of the Island, and h[as] promised to write his impressions in futu[re] letters. Indeed, he will act as our Cub[an] correspondent. "The Catholic Church," [he] says, "has lost its hold on the masses, a[nd] they are awaiting the gospel message of t[he] Protestant Church. It will have to be simp[le] and plain—just as it is in the Christian Chur[ch] —Christ all in all." Bro. Carlisle has reques[t]ed the President to detach him to act as ci[ty] chaplain of Santiago, and if this request [is] granted he will take up the work in that ci[ty] of preaching the primitive gospel and seek [to] lead that priest-ridden people into a pur[er] faith and life.

THE CHRISTIAN-EVANGELIST.

A WEEKLY FAMILY AND RELIGIOUS JOURNAL.

ol. XXXV. November 17, 1898 No. 46

CONTENTS.

TORIAL:
urrent Events....................611
Give Thanks Unto the Lord........612
Divine Mission—What?..............612
volution Reversed 613
raise and Thanksgiving........ 613
ditor's Easy Chair......... 614
uestions and Answers... 614

GINAL CONTRIBUTIONS:
an I Love my Enemies—IV.—N. J. Aylsworth. 619

RESPONDENCE:
Vashington (D. C.) Letter...........620
ew York Letter.. 620
onstantinople Letter. 621
ur School Problem 622
ntroductory Letter...... 622
exas Letter...... 622
Bit of Dixie.........................623

ILY CIRCLE:
raise the Giver (poem)........ 630
armer Truesdall's Thanksgiving.....630
he Day Before Thanksgiving; or, the First Call for Volunteers 631
he Battle of the Heart (poem).. 633
od's Promises (poem)......... . . 633
ur First Thanksgiving..... 633
hort Stories.......... 634

CELLANEOUS:
urrent Religious Thought....... 615
ur Budget 616
ersonal Mention.......... 618
pen Parliament on Our National Conventions....... 624
otes and News.......................625
vangelistic..... 628
he Religious World................ 629
With the Children................ .. 635
unday-school.... 636
hristian Endeavor...................637
ethany C. E. Reading Courses 637
iterature.......... 638
arriages and Obituaries............638
issionary........ 639
ublishers' Notes.....................640

Subscription $1.75.

BENJ. L. SMITH,
CORRESPONDING SECRETARY AMERICAN CHRISTIAN MISSIONARY SOCIETY.

PUBLISHED BY

THE

CHRISTIAN - EVANGELIST

J. H. GARRISON, Editor.

W. W. HOPKINS, Assistant.

B. B. TYLER, J. J. HALEY,
EDITORIAL CONTRIBUTORS.

What We Plead For.

The Christian-Evangelist pleads for:

The Christianity of the New Testament, taught by Christ and his Apostles, versus the theology of the creeds taught by fallible men—the world's great need.

The divine confession of faith on which Christ built his church, versus human confessions of faith on which men have split the church.

The unity of Christ's disciples, for which he so fervently prayed, versus the divisions in Christ's body, which his apostles strongly condemned.

The abandonment of sectarian names and practices, based on human authority, for the common family name and the common faith, based on divine authority, versus the abandonment of scriptural names and usages for partisan ends.

The hearty co-operation of Christians in efforts of world-wide beneficence and evangelisation, versus petty jealousies and strifes in the struggle for denominational pre-eminence.

The fidelity to truth which secures the approval of God, versus conformity to custom to gain the favor of men.

The protection of the home and the destruction of the saloon, versus the protection of the saloon and the destruction of the home.

For the right against the wrong;
For the weak against the strong;
For the poor who've waited long
For the brighter age to be.
For the truth, 'gainst superstition,
For the faith, against tradition,
For the hope, whose glad fruition
Our waiting eyes shall see.

RATES OF SUBSCRIPTION.

Single subscriptions, new or old	$1.50 each
Ministers	1.00 "

All subscriptions payable in advance. Label shows the month up to the first day of which your subscription is paid. If an earlier date than the present is shown, you are in arrears. No paper discontinued without express orders to that effect. Arrears should be paid when discontinuance is ordered.

In ordering a change of post office, please give the OLD as well as the NEW address.

Do not send local check, but use Post office or Express Money Order, or draft on St. Louis, Chicago or New York, in remitting.

ADDRESS, CHRISTIAN PUBLISHING CO.,
1522 Locust St., St. Louis, Mo.

THE CHRISTIAN-EVANGELIST

"In faith, Unity; in opinion and methods, Liberty; in all things, Charity."

Vol. xxxv. St. Louis, Mo., Thursday, November 17, 1898. No. 46

CURRENT EVENTS.

The general outcome of last week's election, as regards national politics, is a strengthening of the Republican element in the Senate and of the Democratic element in the House of Representatives. Republican majorities were generally less than in 1896, but the decrease was less than their opponents had a right to expect on the basis of previous off-year elections. In at least seven states, Delaware, West Virginia, Wisconsin, New York, New Jersey, California and Indiana, the legislatures elected last week will elect Republican Senators to succeed their present Democratic Senators whose term expires March 4, 1899. It can not be doubted that there will be a clear majority of at least nine in the Senate to support the administration against all other elements combined. In the House, the expected Democratic gains made the continuance of Republican control a doubtful matter, but those gains were not enough to overcome the existing Republican majority in that body. During the latter half of his term, therefore, President McKinley will be backed by a Congress, both Houses of which are controlled by his own party, and which it may be fairly assumed is in substantial agreement with his policy. This is a noteworthy occurrence, in the first place, because of its rarity. Since the days of Andrew Jackson this is the first time that a congressional election in the middle of a Presidential term has given to the administration a Congress friendly in both its branches. But it is still more noteworthy because of the issues which are to be decided in the next two years. The Republican party has seen fit to conduct its campaign chiefly on the issues raised by the war. On these issues which are to be decided in the next two years. The Republican party has seen fit to conduct its campaign chiefly on the issues raised by the war. On these issues it has secured control of both Houses of Congress. In the presence of the problems which now confront us, it is no time for party politics in any petty sense; it is a time for statesmanship. But the burden of responsibility now rests upon the Republican party, and if that burden is not properly borne we shall know where to lay the blame.

The eyes of the nation were upon New York more than upon any other state in this election, perhaps, to see what would be the result of a fight between Roosevelt and Tammany. Roosevelt represented, in addition to general Republican principles, the popular hero of the late war, and, more important even than this, he represented sturdy, rugged and vigorous honesty in the administration of public affairs; Tammany represented—just what Tammany always represents. The result was a victory for Roosevelt, though not so overwhelming as it ought to have been. Greater New York gave Van Wyck a plurality of 84,000, but outside of the city, Tammany's candidate carried only five counties. Roosevelt's plurality was something less than 20,000 and Mr. Woodruff, candidate for lieutenant-governor, ran far behind that. If the interpretation of prominent Democrats is to be accepted, the mismanagement of the campaign by Croker and the boasts and threats by which he rendered himself generally disagreeable to his party, are alone responsible for the defeat of Van Wyck. If so, then Mr. Croker is for once deserving of our gratitude, though not of our admiration. So great is the dissatisfaction with the Crocker régime that there is talk of organizing another Democratic machine to take the place of Tammany, the chief mark of the new organization being the absence of Croker from its councils. It is an eloquent testimony to the strength of his grip upon Tammany that it is easier to let him have it, leave him alone with it and create a new organization without him, than to dislodge him from his position.

The Republican victory in the state campaign in Pennsylvania is as much of a disgrace as a Democratic victory would have been in New York. Croker and Tammany were defeated by a fair margin, but Quay and the disreputable machine which he controls carried the day in Pennsylvania. It was the old story of united rascality *versus* divided decency, organized corruption *versus* unorganized reformation. By the exercise of supreme political sagacity on the part of the astute Quay, the Republican machine was kept in active and harmonious operation and the vast majority of its habitual adherents were kept faithful to it, while the forces which naturally array themselves against such a machine were moved to divide their support between the regular Democratic ticket and that headed by Dr. Swallow, the Prohibition-Independent candidate for governor. There was a good showing of votes against the excellent work of Mr. Wanamaker in enlightening Pennsylvania voters as to the real characters and records of the men who control their state offices has, therefore, perhaps not been entirely wasted. But for the present there is no visible result. Quay still owns the state, has a special mortgage on the governor-elect, and has behind him a legislature which can be relied upon to return him to the Senate without raising any disturbance about it.

The state election in Illinois takes on some general interest from its bearing, even though indirect, upon the attitude of the voters of that state toward the recent extraordinary actions of their governor. The election in Illinois did not include the choice of a governor (the term of office in that state being four years), but there were a set of candidates who could fairly and clearly be called Tanner men, and Gov. Tanner himself took an active part in the campaign. Not only so, but he used as an important part of his campaign material a defense of his action in forbidding and preventing the importation of Southern laborers to take the places of the striking miners at Virden. We have already stated it as our opinion that, however much love of the laboring man and sympathy with the striker may have been in the heart of the governor as the motive to this action (and we hope it was that rather than a desire to manufacture campaign material for use among the working men), nevertheless the action was legally unjustifiable and might lead to very serious consequences. The general success of the Republican state ticket in Illinois under these circumstances may be taken as an indication that the people of Illinois either approve of the governor's act, which is the most significant thing he ever did, or at least that they do not think it worth while to administer a rebuke.

At Wilmington, North Carolina, the election has been the occasion of serious friction between whites and negroes. The latter have a majority of votes in the county, and have for years controlled the local government. The trouble arose out of an organized effort on the part of the whites to put an end to negro domination by fair means if possible, otherwise by any means which promised to be effective. There was less trouble than was anticipated on election day, for the negroes for the most part kept away from the polls, in consideration of the armed resistance which was ready to meet them. Wednesday a meeting of whites was held, with ex-Representative Waddell in the chair, to decide upon means for ridding the community more completely of negro influence. One measure approved was to encourage the plan of giving employment only to white labor, when possible. Another was to drive out of town a negro editor who had written and published objectionable articles. The negro editor left town during the night, but on Thursday the crowd enforced its edict by destroying his printing office and presses and burning the building. It was not a wild, excited mob, but the same crowd which had met the day before as a deliberative body with a chairman (and he an ex-Congressman) now exercising the function of the executive department of the government which it had set up. In the course of the day eight negroes were killed on the streets, and a few whites were wounded. The town government has been reorganized with Waddell as mayor, and comparative peace has been restored, but the instigators of the original trouble are now in command of the situation. They have struck their blow, and are very willing to increase the police force to preserve peace. To preserve peace in this case means to prevent retaliation for the deeds of violence which they have already committed.

It is a custom of long standing for the British Prime Minister to make a speech annually at the Lord Mayor's banquet, reviewing the political and diplomatic events of the year and making some specific statements as to the policy to be persued in the immediate future. Accordingly Lord Salisbury's speech at the Guild Hall, London, on Wesnesday night of last week, was looked forward to as the occasion for the solution of some mysteries which are troubling the public. Especially was the public anxious to know the meaning of Great Britain's present extraordinary preparations for war, and the general expectation was that this would be the occasion for the announcement of the establishment of a British protectorate over Egypt. But the public was disappointed. The definite statement was made that for the present no attempt would be made to establish a protectorate, since the rights and feelings of the other powers must be taken into consideration. The real cause of the vast military and naval preparations, which have been and still are on foot, is not satisfactorily explained. The premier declares that they do not mean a desire for war, much less the purpose of provoking war by any particular art of aggression, but only that Great Britain is "resolved to maintain the empire which Britons have received from their forefathers and to support the peace which is the glory and sustenance of our empire." If it means only this, one would suppose that the idea of maintaining the empire and supporting peace had just occurred to the administration, that it takes sudden steps to accomplish it. The general feeling is that the preparations are still unexplained. It may be very poor policy for England to neglect this opportunity for the establishment of a protectorate, and Lord Salisbury's announcement met with a very chilly reception among his own people, but outside of Great Britain there is a general feeling of relief at the thought that war is not so imminent as had been supposed.

According to recent statistical reports the farmers of the United States will receive during 1898 more money from abroad for their products than in any preceding year. A statement regarding the exports of principal agricultural products, just issued by the Treasury Bureau of Statistics, shows that in the item of breadstuffs alone the exports for the ten months ending October 31, 1898, amounted to $250,237,355, which is $65,000,000 greater than in the corresponding months of last year and $38,000'000 in excess of the exceptional year 1892. Provision exports also show a good record, being for the ten months of 1898, $162,830,643, against $146,607,039 in the corresponding months of last year and $123,508,568 in 1892. Cotton exports for the ten months are $13,-000,000 in excess of last year and the number of pounds is larger than in any corresponding period in the history of the country.

O GIVE THANKS UNTO THE LORD.

For the earth which has once more yielded its increase to supply the wants of all the living.

For the garnered treasures from the field and orchard and garden — gifts from Nature's bounteous hand.

For the product of mines, of looms, of shops and factories—the products of honest toil.

For the growing ranks in the army of industry, who find remunerative employment and the decreasing number of those who are idle.

For life continued to us with all its mighty hopes and possibilities and all its deathless aspirations.

For such a measure of physical health and mental sanity as have enabled us to make the best use of the life so graciously continued to us.

For the home, with all its sacred relationships and blessed influences, the oldest institution on earth as it is one of the divinest—a haven of rest for the weary, a refuge for the tempted, the persecuted and the forsaken.

For the church, with all its manifold agencies and instrumentalities, which has made increase during the year past, and which shows increasing signs of a desire to fulfill its divine mission in the world.

For the growing sense of brotherhood that is bringing the nations into closer relations, and emphasizing a solidarity of the race—the oneness of the human family.

For the increasing unity of believers and the awakening consciousnes of the church to the evils of our divisions and the necessity for unity and co-operation.

For the growth of colleges, universities and all educational interests, and for all the methods for the diffusion of light and knowledge.

For additional proofs of God in our national history, manifested in his outstretched arm during our late war for the freedom of Cuba.

For signal victories by land and by sea, and for the magnanimity as well as the bravery of our soldiers and our sailors towards their defeated foes.

For a united nation, which under stress of a national emergency closed its divided ranks and forever obliterated sectional lines that it might vindicate its flag and fulfill its mission.

For the new baptism in patriotism which has awakened a deeper love of country and a higher appreciation of the dignity and responsibility of American citizenship, prophesying political purification.

For all the forces of moral, social and political reform, which are seeking to elevate the standard of our political life and to show to the world the highest type of Christian civilization.

For the growth of missions; for the triumph of the gospel in all lands.

For the rising spirit of democracy among the oppressed peoples of the earth and for the waning power of tyrants.

For the advancement in science, in art, in invention, and for all the signs that we are building here on earth, the City of God.

For these, and the other numberless blessings that crown our lives and bless our age, let us give thanks unto the Lord.

A DIVINE MISSION—WHAT?

II.—LOYALTY.

It is a misfortune that liberty often de generates into license. Sometimes th cry of "liberty" has only a negativ meaning, signifying freedom from lawfu restraint and from the obligations growin out of certain beliefs. It should be ob served that the religious movement, con cerning whose divine mission we ar writing, contained no such conception of liberty as this. It was the liberty to be loyal to the truth and to Him who was Truth incarnate, which our fathers asserted. There is no conflict between Christian liberty and Christian loyalty, but there is an irrepressible conflict between an enslaved conscience and loyalty to God.

One who examines the history of the time in which this movement had its origin will discover two features existing side by side: a most pronounced emphasis on the necessity of theological soundness, with a scrupulous observance of the customs and traditions of the church, and along with that an almost total disregard of some of the plainest teachings of Christ and his apostles. It may perhaps be said in alleviation of this condition of things that this disobedience to Christ in the whole tenor and spirit of his teaching was largely unconscious. The minds of the people were so filled with false conceptions of Christianity that they were unable to understand its real nature and its claims upon them. Christ taught and exemplified a religion that emphasizes the Fatherhood of God and the brotherhood of man; a religion which melts away barriers that separate men from each other, and tends to draw them together in bonds of love and fraternity. The religion of the time was something very different in its emphasis and in its results.

It would seem clear from this condition of things that what the religious world needed was, not only liberation from the bondage of human creeds and traditions of men, but also a sublime emphasis and a constant insistence on the principle of unswerving loyalty to Jesus Christ as the Head of the church and as the King, as well as the Savior of men. This alone would prevent liberty from becoming anarchy. This alone would right the wrongs and correct the errors which prevailed in the religious world, and advance the kingdom of God among men. What these pioneers did, therefore, was not to make a new human creed with which to oppose the older ones; not to set forth another human leader whom they would pit against former religious leaders; in a word, it was not to oppose human authority in religion by the use of human authority. This would have been comparatively futile. It could at best have only ended in the origination of another sect, whose limitations would have been already fixed, and whose bondage to its own creed would soon have been as complete as that which existed under other human creeds.

What they did was something very different from that. They denied the right of any man or of any body of men to formulate a creed which should be the basis of fellowship and union among Christians. They claimed that this power resided in Christ alone, and was delegated only to his apostles, and that it wa province of all believers in Christ to abide loyally by the creed which he himself had given and which his apostles had elaborated and explained. They opposed human authority with divine authority. They opposed human traditions and practices by divine commandments and institutions. In a word, they exalted Christ above all human authority in religion, and refused to accept anything as binding that had not originated with Christ or his apostles.

This seemed at the time radical and revolutionary, as indeed it was, but nothing less than this would have been loyalty to Jesus Christ. Nothing less than this would have met the demands of the times. This was the thread which was to lead them out of the maze of denominational divisions and religious apostasy into the purity and unity of the original church. Hence, loyalty to Christ and loyalty to the Word of God, as the inspired expression of the will of Christ, became the keynote of this reformation. "Where the Bible speaks we speak; where the Bible is silent we are silent," became the motto of these early reformers. "What is your 'Thus saith the Lord?'" was the challenge with which they confronted every doctrinet ordinance and practice of the church. Whatsoever could not abide this test must go. This was the measuring reed by which the temple of God in the nineteenth century was to be measured.

It is only true to history to say that the pious Pedobaptist leaders in this movement did not see at first where this principle would lead them, and how much it would modify their own religious practice. They felt sure that it was right, however, and being right it ought to be followed. The sequel proved that they were not "disobedient to the heavenly vision." They fearlessly applied this test to their own previous religious beliefs and practices and changed them accordingly. This is the supreme test of a man's loyalty to truth. When one is willing to yield up his former convictions of truth and to abandon practices which he had become accustomed to regard as sacred, and in doing so to place himself out of sympathy and fellowship with all existing religious organizations, he has given the highest measure of proof of his fidelity to the truth that any mortal can give, unless it be martyrdom, which is only an intensified form of this same test.

It deserves to be held in continual remembrance by the younger generations, that from time to time come upon the scene, that this plea for religious reformation came to be what it is, in its principles, because our fathers opened their minds and their hearts to the truth of God, and resolved to be loyal to it, wheresoever it might lead them. They were free to follow the truth—to be loyal to the leadership of Christ. They became free that they might be loyal, and were loyal that they might continue to be free. If ever we lose this true and genuine spirit of religious reformation—the love of truth—or should consent to sacrifice it on the altar of a timid conservatism, or of a desire for popular favor, we should prove ourselves to be unworthy sons of noble sires. These two principles must be constantly kept in holy wedlock—liberty and loyalty. They cannot exist apart. They can only flourish as they live in union. To suppose that there is any antagonism between them, and to attempt to sacrifice the one for the other, would be a fatal mistake.

If the religious world has heard and has been influenced in any measure by our plea for Christian liberty or freedom from the bondage of human creeds, it has heard and has been no less influenced by the emphasis which we have laid upon the necessity of loyalty to the Word of God as the supreme and only test of religious faith, doctrine and practice. It was the moral tonic which the languid state of religion demanded, and the results show that it was God's remedy, not man's.

EVOLUTION REVERSED.

Henry Thomas Buckle, in his "History of Civilization in England," affirms the superiority of intellectual over moral truth, because the former is progressive and the latter is stationary. The eminent philosophical historian admits in this contention that moral and spiritual ideas are fixed and final, and have remained unchangeably the same in all ages of which we have any knowledge, while truths of the intellect and scientific truths are constantly changing in an effort towards improvement. Mr. Buckle reasons that progression and changeableness necessarily indicate superiority over that which is fixed and unchangeable. If I were asked to reason from these premises, my conclusion would be the reverse of his. The mutability of intellectual ideas proves their imperfection. That which is changeable is improvable, and that which is improvable is not perfect. When you change a thing you say by the act: "This thing is imperfect, it has not reached its highest state of development, it admits of further improvement." The improvability of our intellectual and scientifice conceptions shows them to be imperfect and inferior to our moral ideas which, being changeable, are in themselves improvable. Instead, then, of Mr. Buckle deciding in favor of the superiority of intellectual truth because it is in a constant state of flux and progress toward perfection, this is the very reason why he should have reversed his decision against the inferiority of the immutable moral relations that obtain in the universe of God, and the ground of their immutability is their basis in revelation.

Science, for example, acknowledges the imperfection of its conclusions by constantly changing its premises, while the histories of the Bible are steadily confirmed by modern research, and the spiritual truth which it teaches remains the same yesterday, to-day and forever. Its fundamental doctrines of sin and righteousness, of life and immortality, are as unchangeable as the nature of God, because they are the revelation of that nature. There is not a spiritual truth nor an idea of moral conduct now in the world that were not in it thousands of years ago. The inspired volume is the garnered treasure house of all the moral and spiritual truth in the world, and it changes not because, like its divine Author, the substance of its spiritual revelation, it is already perfect. Why do truths of the intellect, that pertain to the common affairs of life, change with the changing generations, while truths of the conscience and the heart remain the same in all ages and under all circumstances?

It is one of nature's rules that the highest develops last. We have first the inorganic or the dead world; then the organic or the living world; in this latter we have first the vegetable, then the animal, then the intellectual, then the moral, and lastly and highest, we have the spiritual. According to the ordinary course of things, and especially if the doctrine of evolution be true, moral and spiritual truths ought to have been the last to reach the stationary condition which perfection implies. But instead of this it reached its highest and most perfect form thousands of years before that which is next below it. Intellectual truth is still in its childhood—immature and uncertain—while moral and spiritual truth which, in the natural order of things, comes after it, has reached its maturity ages since. How is this to be explained? There is but one explanation. If man had been left to discover for himself, and by his unaided powers, those moral principles that form his character and regulate his conduct, as he has been left to make intellectual progress on his own account, the natural and usual order would have been followed and science would be ahead of morals in the certainty and maturity of its doctrines. The reverse of this is true because and only because God has spoken to man on the question of character and conduct, as these stand related to himself. The Bible contains a revelation from God in reference to these matters, and hence they reached a fixedness, a permanence and a perfection in the early ages of human history not otherwise possible. God has put himself on record in respect to human character and human salvation because these are matters of transcendent moment, leaving us for our own good to work out intellectual problems for ourselves. This is the reason, no doubt, why spiritual truth has taken precedence in its development towards perfection, while in all matters of purely scientific intellectual inquiry man has been left to work out his own salvation by slow degrees. It is hardly possible to give any other explanation, and thus explanation confirms the claim of the Bible to be a revelation from God. There is only one sense in which the Word is progressive and improvable, and that is in our understanding and application of its principles. We may apprehend it more clearly and practice it more faithfully, but we cannot improve the truth itself. Science and human wisdom may change, but the Word of the Lord endures forever.

J. J. H.

Hour of Prayer.

PRAISE AND THANKSGIVING.

(Mid-week Prayer-meeting Topic, Nov. 23rd.)

Enter into His gates with thanksgiving,
And into His courts with praise;
Give thanks unto Him, and bless His name.
—*Psa.* 100:4.

It is the eve of our National Thanksgiving Day. In accordance with the time-honored custom, the God-fearing and God-loving people of this nation will meet on the morrow at their accustomed places of worship to give thanks to Almighty God for the harvest that has crowned the labors of the year, for the rewards of industry in every department of human toil, for freedom from pestilence, and for all other national blessings. It is fitting, therefore, that on this prayer-meeting evening we should direct our minds toward the reasons we have for gratitude to God for his abundant mercies toward us. Ingratitude is one of the basest sins. It implies a nature hardened by selfishness and blinded by unbelief. Not to recognize our indebtedness to the Supreme Giver of all our gifts is to manifest a moral blindness and hardness of heart very sad to contemplate. The reason the psalmist assigns for giving thanks unto the Lord is that "He is good; his mercy endureth forever."

Let us think of the goodness of God to us during the year past. Let each one stop to enumerate, as far as possible, his individual blessings. Let us think of life, health, home and happiness which we have enjoyed during the year. If we stop to compare our lot with the more unfortunate of our race who are suffering from oppression, from hopeless disease, from abject poverty, from hunger and nakedness, we can the better realize the greatness of our own blessings and the measure of our indebtedness to God. "He forgiveth all our iniquities; he healeth all our diseases."

Our country as a whole has been blessed with an abundance from the products of the field, our mines have yielded their increase, a large number of our people have found remunerative employment, and all of the signs seem to point to an era of material prosperity.

But this is not the only nor even the greatest reason for thanksgiving. During the year past the nation has been engaged in war in behalf of an oppressed and long-suffering neighboring people. That war has been brought to a successful termination, accomplishing the purpose for which it was inaugurated.

In the prosecution of this war we have had signal evidences of the divine favor. Such remarkable victories, attended with so small a loss of life, are almost unparalleled in the history of modern warfare. They remind us of those ancient wars in which God interposed to deliver his people, and to show them that reliance upon his arm was greater security than all the munitions of war.

It is something to be grateful for that our nation has reached a point in its national development when it could wage war for so unselfish a purpose as the war in behalf of Cuba.

It is something to be grateful for that our nation has acquired additional power and prestige among the nations of the earth, not only for its signal victories on land and sea, but for the magnanimity and generosity it has displayed toward its defeated enemies.

It is something to be grateful for that the nation seems to have awakened to a new consciousness of its mission among the natious of the earth as a pro oter of peace and civilization and as a friend and helper of the oppressed and enslaved peoples of the earth.

It is something to be grateful for that so large a number of the people recognize the Divine Hand in our national history and the impulse which this recognition must give to national purity and righteousness.

For these reasons and many others let us

"Enter into His gates with thanksgiving,
And into His courts with praise."

Let us thank Him for all our individual and national blessings, and pray that His goodness may lead us, as individuals and as a nation, to repentance and to a better life.

PRAYER.

O, Thou who art the God of nations, we thank Thee that Thou didst plant in this New World a free and independent nation, whose citizens have been guaranteed the rights of civil and religious liberty. We thank Thee for Thy guiding Hand through more than a century of our national life, in which Thou hast made us a great nation, and given us wealth and power and civilization, and made us a beacon light and a source of inspiration to all the struggling peoples of earth. We thank Thee for the blessings of the year just closed and all the signal proofs of Thy divine favor which it has brought to us. May these tokens of Thy favor and care lead us to a renewed consecration to fulfill our national destiny and accomplish Thy gracious purposes on earth. Forgive our sins, individual and national, and bless our Chief Executive, his Cabinet and counselors, and all others who are in positions of influence and responsibility, to the end that Thy will may be done on earth as it is in Heaven. For Christ's sake. Amen!

Editor's Easy Chair.

The election has resulted in about the usual amount of disappointment and gratification. We feel sure that many, without regard to party lines, are gratified that Roosevelt, of New York, was elected governor of that state, on repeated declarations that he would enforce the law against all violators, whether high or low, rich or poor, and that he intended putting the Ten Commandments above his party fealty. The whole country will watch to see how well he carries out these pledges. It is a disappointment to all lovers of honesty in politics that Mr. Quay triumphed in Pennsylvania, over an independent effort to enforce in politics the command, "Thou shalt not steal." But the end is not yet.

During the election in this city we visited a polling-place where was standing a group of well-dressed citizens who had just voted. One of them said, "I voted for Mr. —— for sheriff." "Did you not know," we ventured to ask, "that you were voting for a man who has been connected with some of the worst political scandals of this city, and that he has been denounced in the press of his own party as notoriously corrupt?" "Oh, yes," he replied, "but the fellow who is running against him on the other ticket is still worse, and what can you do?" "Vote for neither, and preserve a good conscience at least," was our answer. But think of the condition of local politics when such men are nominated for office, and decent people are asked to vote for them! Where was the moral element of the city when these nominations were made? Perhaps this question should not be pressed, as it might disturb the "good conscience" of some of us who feel we have done our political duty if we go to the polls and vote on election day.

In reading, recently, Hattie Tying Griswold's "Personal Sketches of Recent Authors"—a delightful book, by the way—we were struck with a quotation which the author makes from Harriet Beecher Stowe. "Her lofty spirit," says the author, "is shown in the following words written in one of the darkest hours of defeat:"

"If this struggle is to be prolonged till there be not one home in the land where there is not one dead, till all the treasure amassed by the unpaid labor of the slave shall be wasted, till every drop of blood drawn by the lash shall be atoned by blood drawn by the sword, we can only bow and say, 'Just and true are thy ways, thou King of Saints.'"

This struck us as very much like a passage from Mr. Lincoln's second inaugural, and taking down from our library, the XXIII. Vol. of Charles Dudley Warner's "World's Best Literature," we read from that address of Mr. Lincoln the following:

"Fondly do we hope—fervently do we pray—that this mighty scourge of war may pass away. Yet if God wills that it continue until all the wealth piled by the bondman's two hundred and fifty years of unrequited toil shall be sunk and until every drop of blood drawn by the lash shall be paid by another drawn with the sword—as it was said three thousand years ago, so still it must be said, 'The judgments of the Lord are true and righteous altogether.'"

While Mr. Lincoln's language is more stately, and the whole passage is an improvement on that of Mrs. Stowe's, it is impossible not to believe that he had seen Mrs. Stowe's passage and had been impressed by it, although he was probably wholly unconscious of it at the time. The incident throws some light on the subject of unconscious plagiarism, which is not an unusual thing.

Questions and Answers.

What is signified by the expression, "Holy men of old spake as they were moved by the Holy Spirit?" *J. B. C.*

The expression signifies that the prophets of the Old Testament, to whom special reference is made, spake and wrote, not simply by the aid of their native genius or talents, but that the impulse which moved them was from the Holy Spirit. Of course the Holy Spirit used the faculties of these men, but did not obliterate their individual mental characteristics. God, by his Spirit, so illuminated their understanding and guided their utterances as to convey through them the truth which he desired to communicate to men, and to make such revelation of his will and his truth as would be a standard of doctrine and faith in all ages.

What bodies are signified by the phrase, "bodies terrestial?" (1 Cor. 15:40.)

W. H. P.

The trouble with some of the Corinthian members, as regards the resurrection, seems to have been that they were unable to conceive of any other kind of body than a material body like those we inhabit here on the earth. "How are the dead raised, and with what bodies do they come?" they asked. It was in answer to such questions that Paul told them that there are bodies celestial as well as bodies terrestial; that is, as we here have bodies adapted to the earth in which we live, so we shall have bodies adapted to the celestial world when we enter it. Even here on earth, he adds, there is a great variety of bodies, as of fish, birds, men, each having a body adapted to its environment. Why should it, then, be thought incredible that we should have new and spiritual bodies adapted to the spiritual world? The "terrestial bodies," we take it, include all forms of material bodies, in contrast with the "celestial bodies" of the spiritual realm.

What can be done in our local work to impress the membership with their responsibility to the larger work?

D. W. Moore.

This is an important question and may well engage the thought of every preacher. If the preacher improves the occasions of special collections for the different branches of our general work for the purpose of giving his congregation information concerning them it will do much to impress the responsibility of the larger work upon them. The most effective way of accomplishing this end, however, is to see to it that a good Christian paper that fosters these larger interests goes into the home of each family in the church. Nothing so widens one's sympathies and enlarges one's horizon as the weekly visits of a first-class religious journal.

Is it proper, or is it reprehensible for a pastor to refer to the church for which he may be preaching as "my" church, and to its officers as "my" officers? *S. M. M.*

There is nothing improper meant by the use of "my" in such cases. It is a short way of saying, "the church which I am serving, or the officers of the church of which I am the preacher." Ownership is not meant, but relationship. It is simply a question of taste, and we should say that the best taste would use the possessive case in such connection sparingly.

Current Religious Thought

The Herald and Presbyter offers the following wise counsel concerning the disposition of one's property by will. In the Oct. 12th issue it says:

In the disposition of property Christ should be taken into the account. In all our possessions we are simply stewards, and we are to hold ourselves and all that we are at his disposal. We are to honor him with our substance and with the first fruits of all our increase. We should put C rist in our daily lives, in our eating and drinking, in our earning and spending, in our living and dying. A certain prop rtion of what we expend during life should be for the upbuilding of his kingdom, and we are carefully to consider whether have not something to leave for this particular work when we con o die. In all our ways we are to acknowledge him, and in the direction which we give to the division of our estates may be a most reverent and loving and grateful acknowledgment of his goodness.

There are certain provisions for executing a will about which we do not intend to speak. They can be learned by each one who wishes to be informed, and differ somewhat in the various states. The form can readily be provided by the trusted counselor. The important matter is that one clearly understands what disposition he wishes to make, and that he does it in ample time, so that it cannot be called in question successfully by any one.

It is ordinarily best to administer one's own estate, so far as charitable bequests are concerned, by giving away during the lifetime what one wishes to go to the missionary board, the college or seminary, the hospital, the asylum or the church; but oftentimes this is not practicable. It may be possible to divert property in some such direction as indicated at death, while absolutely necessary to hold it during life. We have reason to believe, and to know, that many gifts are provided for in wills to-day for which religious, educational and missionary institutions will be the richer in years to come. And this is right. If one is able to do it he should, at some some time, help in some signal way the causes which are for the world's betterment, and, as far as he is able, help them a little all the time.

At the same time let all parents remember that the best egacy they can leave to the cause of Christ on earth is a family of children well trained and heartily interested in religious life and work. Through them their Christian influence may be perpetuated more potently and with greater promise than in any other way, for this is a means which may endure for many long generations. Parents should use most wise and careful efforts that the minds and hearts of their children be not embittered or alienated by being treated unjustly in the matter of bequests. As he would be most unwise and unjust who would, during his lifetime, leave his children to suffer because of his large gifts to causes which, in themsevles, are important and sacred, so he follows a sadly mistaken policy who, at death, diverts so much of his property to benevolent causes as to bring reproaches on his memory from his children who have been uncared for. The law of the tithe was meant to stir the selfish and also to restrain occasionally the enthusiast, and it might be well if, in gifts both before and after death, the divine intimation might be carefully considered.

The following estimate of the essentials to an efficient and successful pastorate and pastor by the Interior, recently, is not far short of the truth. It says:

The first requsite for imparting knowledge of any kind is to possess it. What is the secret of the variety and freshness of the truths and illustration with which the work of some speakers and writers teem? We answer that it comes of a habit of mind. The successful writer, at least, must form the habit of looking at everything he sees to see what there is in it for him as a writer. Our surroundings, the world and the universe are an infinite tapestry, the needlework of a single thread. Follow it as a clew from any point and it leads into an infinitude of interwoven truth and beauty. A thoughtful person in contemplative mood cannot see a little child upon the street, either dainty or dirty, without setting ajar and in motion a train of thought that is fresh, new and interesting. Those who cultivate, train and sharpen the perceptive faculties of the soul are oversupplied with truth—have more on any one subject than they can use, and all of it original and fresh.

A preacher to hold the attention of his people must be imbued with deep and sincere interest in their welfare, and in all that interests them—their health, domestic and social happines, the solution of their difficulties, the removal of their troubles, so far as he can, the assuagement of there griefs, the promotion of their hopes, especially for their children.

But not in this, no more than in his intellectual storehouse, can a pastor pour out without an inflowing stream. He becomes exhausted. Even sympathy must have sources or it will dry up. The pastor must have the close sympathy and affection of his people or he will fail. Pastors not unfrequently remark that as soon they fail to hold the sympathies of their people they will give up their pulpit, sometimes not seeming to know themselves why, except that they feel uncomfortable—are thirsty and hungry. They are dying, drying up, and if they remain will soon become nothing better than a sack of husks and dust—their "cured" people will stay, but the living ones will seek rain and dew elsewhere.

The preacher must draw from nature, providence, history, human experience—from every source for his intellectual supplies, but he must draw his spiritual supplies from his own people. Must he not draw them from God? Yes, ultimalety, but not directly That is not God's way of imparting spiritual wealth. He gives the single talent, and if we do not put it to use in the spiritual exchange it will not increas. What little there is of it will b lost. That was a good poem not long siace of a stylite hermit on his tower calling for God. "Where art thou, Lord?" he cried. "Down here among the people," came from the toiling masses below.

A spiritually poor congregation cannot have a good preacher. A spiritually poor preacher cannot have a good congregation. A good neighborhood cannot exist without both.

The need for more quietude and meditation in one's life is the moral of an excellent article in the Sunday-school Times, Oct. 15, by Hugo Macmillan, on "Stillness." The following is the concluding paragraph of the article:

This is an age of excitement. People are devoted to the pursuit of pleasure, and amusement is apt to become too engrossing, and even innocent play and healthy exercise are too often changed into serious pursuits, to which the whole attention is given up. There is a fever in people's souls—a fever of business, a haste to be rich and excell others, and to get on in the world. And this spirit is creeping into the church, and even our religious worship, which ought to rest our souls more than anything else, is apt to become se sational, and there is such a crowd of duties and services, even on the day of rest, that the object of it is in a large measure lost sight of, and there is no leisure or calmness of mind for spiritual meditation. Religious people of the calm East, such as Brahmins and Buddhists, have too much stillness. They sit for hours, or even days, together, silent, motionless, clearing their minds and hearts of all thought, emotion and desire, that, emptied of self, they may know God. Religious people in the busy West, on the other hand, are too active, and often keep God out of their lives by their restlessness about the very things of religion. For persons can be prevented from hearing the still small voice of Jesus knocking at the door of their heart, and seeking admittance, by the hurry and bustle of religious services on Sunday quite as much as by the noises and competition of the world during the week. You are all dragged more or less into this mighty whirlpool of excitement, and more and more you feel the force of it. It is necessary, therefore, that you should keep a sanctuary in your own souls, to which you can retreat from the noises and strifes of the world; that you should cultivate a calm and tranquil manner, cherish a quiet, meditative spirit, and find or make many opportunities of being alone with God, that you may think of things that belong to your peace. Doing this, you will be able more thoroughly to enjoy your innocent pleasures and perform your common duties. You will be calm and self-possessed when others are flustered, and you will know yourselves better, and God, too.

In view of the fact that the Emperor of Germany's visit to the Holy Land this month is exciting unusual attention, the following hint at the undercurrent interests from the New York Observer is not without interest in the case:

The ostensible purpose of the Kaiser in making the journey is to attend the dedication of the German church in Jerusalem, the site of which was presented by the Sultan, and to see the Holy Land and the German colonists settled there. The purpose is a laudable one, the Emperor, as a Christian sharing the desire of most Christians to visit, at least once in his life the scene of Christ's labor upon earth, and also to show his regard for the very numerous community in Syria which looks to him as its sovereign and protector. But though in the case of any other monarch there might thus seem little reason to attribute different motives to the journey, it is not surprising that in view of the Kaiser's known ambitions the European press should find it difficult to believe that the attraction of the Holy Places is all that takes him to Palestine. It is alleged, indeed, that the visit is undertaken in furtherance of a new idea of German expansion, that the Emperor sees in Asia Minor a field for German activity which would far surpass any that may be secured in Africa and the Far East. Nor in view of the condition of Turkey, and the foothold Germany has already acquired in that quarter, is the idea one so incapabl of realization as may at first appear, though attempt to realize it will, of course, arouse opposition on every hand. In the first place, German commercial interests in Asia Minor are already very large, a German company is building the railway which is ultimately to connect the Mediterranean with Bagdad, and the number of German settlers in Syria probably exceeds that in any purely German colony. Moreover, the influence of Germany at Constantinople is greater than that of any other power, owing to the assistance, political and material, rendered the Porte by Berlin; and though the Sultan would now no doubt like to release himself from dependance on the Kaiser, he has accepted too much to shake him off. Should, therefore, the Emperor follow the example of the powers elsewhere, and demand concessions in the outlying provinces of Turkey which would practically leave Germany in possession when the final break-up of the empire occurs, the Sultan might find it difficult to refuse. With so much in his favor, the idea of acquiring Syria, the territory between the Tigris and the Euphrates, and even Constantinople itself, may not seem to the Kaiser too unsubstantial for ultimate realization; and in any event, the notion of German possession of the Holy Land must appeal strongly to a mind like his. As we have said, the declaration of such a purpose would arouse opposition everywhere, as indeed the mere suspicion of it is already doing; for Russia would not quietly see the Holy Places pass into German hands, nor France give up her claims to Syria, nor Austria and Italy admit without adequate compensation the exclusive right of Germany to the most valuable portions of Asiatic Turkey. It may be, of course, that the Kaiser has no ulterior designs in his visit, that it is prompted only by desire to visit the cradle of Christianity, but it is certain that the rest of Europe will refuse to regard his tour as merely one of observation, and will grow more excited as it progresses.

Our Budget.

—Another bounteous harvest has been garnered.

—Let God be praised for his goodness unto the children of men.

—The original poems in our Family Circle this week are of special merit.

—Please notice what Benj. L. Smith has sent for this paper on Forefathers' Day and Children's Rally Day. One is past, the other is at hand.

—We are sorry to have to omit some interesting literature on C. W. B. M. Day, first Sunday in December, which came too late for this paper.

—The first edition of the special issue of the American Home Missionary on Children's Rally Day for America, we are told, is exhausted. The second is on the press. We are glad of the indication of success in this movement which this announcement affords. It will add enthusiasm to the cause of Home Missions in a way never felt before.

—The picture on our first page this week will immediately suggest the motto: "Home Missions to the Front," so thoroughly has Corresponding Secretary B. L. Smith identified himself with that good cause. It is not inappropriate that the picture appears along with our conference this week on the Jubilee Convention. Bro. Smith, as will be seen from his picture, is still a young man, and he may safely hope to live to see the fulfillment of his desires concerning Home Missions. The energy and wisdom displayed in the prosecution of this work under his joint administration shows that no mistake was made in his selection.

—See the announcement elsewhere concerning the educational conference at Moberly, Mo., Dec. 6th.

—Archbishop Ireland is trying to keep missionaries out of Cuba and Porto Rico by the "bluff" game. If they go, as they will, and fail, which they will not, the humiliation of the failure will not rest upon his shoulder nor the cost upon his purse; so why should he worry about their going on that account? We surmise that it is something else that troubles the Bishop.

—Special telegram:

Five Thousand Dollars from F. M. Drake for foreign missions. F. M. Rains.

This balances up the ex-Governor's home and foreign mission accounts nicely, making $5,000 to each. Here is an example which a few more brethren might follow. Gen. Drake has done great service by setting the pace for us. By the way, we are glad to see that our esteemed contemporary—the Christian Standard—has taken Bro. Drake back into its fellowship. But *why* is this thus?

—The article in this paper from J. Z. Tyler, calling the attention of our Endeavor Societies to the importance of a special effort on their part to an increased effort in the salvation of souls during the present missionary year, is worthy of special attention. This matter should be properly and effectively presented to each society at the earliest opportunity by the pastor, evangelist or other suitable person. In many instances the society alone would meet the expenses of a protracted meeting in some needy place, if not needed in its own church. Of course, where the church is making special effort to convert men and women to Christ the Endeavor Society of that congregation should do its utmost to assist it in the work. If the church is not making that effort then the Endeavor Society of that church should see that it is made. Remember that this basic principle of the Endeaver movement pledges you to the "support of your own church" and this you can best do by assisting in the conversion of men to Christ.

—With the November number the Third Christian Church Bulletin, Philadelphia, Pa., begins its fourth volume. No church local paper comes to us in better garb or with more cheering messages for its readers than this one from Philadelphia.

—The friends of Christian education among us may well feel gratified at the success which is attending the effort of Hiram College to greatly augment its endowment fund. We began to print the names of those who have agreed to pledge not less than $1 to said fund, but Pres. Zollars has overwhelmed us with his list of donors and we are compelled for lack of space to give this general acknowledgment instead of the list of names. The movement is taking on immense proportions and bids fair to become a popular subscription. What the people do for Hiram College they are likely to do for other institutions, and have proven themselves worthy when the time comes and the opportunity is offered.

—Nels P. Nelson, of Holbrook, Neb., wants the address of J. Hurd, or some of his relatives.

—The annual report of the Children's Home Society of Minnesota for 1898, an illustrated copy of which has just been received by us, is an excellent testimony to the practice of pure and undefiled religion in that state.

—The city of St. Louis now has a curfew ordinance to regulate the presence of boys and girls on the street after proper hours of the night. The record of this law where enforced in other cities bears evidence of being a healthful protective measure for children and the home, and we hope that such will be its fruits in this city. It should have the moral support of all wise parents and be strictly enforced by the authorities.

—The Kinsman, published at Salt Lake City, Utah, is a strong anti-Mormon magazine, published semimonthly under the editorial care and management of Rev. Wm. R. Campbell. The special mission of this journal, it says, is to secure the enforcement of the Federal law against polygamy and to undeceive the people on the claims and nature of this religious monstrosity.

—By order of the executive committee of the National Pure Food and Drug Congress a call has been issued for the second annual meeting to be held in Columbian University Hall, Washington, D. C., Jan. 18-21, 1899. This seems to us to be an important meeting, especially since its object is to secure legal protection against the adulteration of food and drugs. We ought for commercial, hygienic and moral reasons to have a law to prevent the adulteration and misbranding of products which enter into the consumption of mankind. The secretary of this committee very pertinently says: "Our boys are taught in the Sunday-schools and by their mothers to be honest above everything, and yet the minute they enter the store they are taught to deceive the customer and to sell misbranded products for the genuine article." Already this Congress has endorsed a bill before our National Congress known as the Faulkner Bill, No. 4144, in the Senate, and the Brosius Bill, No. 9154, in the House, which ought to be resolved into a law, and you can greatly assist in securing such an enactment by writing to your Senator and Representative on the subject. Or, better still, get up a petition with as many names as possible and send them for the next congressional session.

—R. H. Jesse, president of the University of Missouri, is right in insisting upon the abolishment of entrance and tuition fees in all departments of the University. This ought to be done at the next sitting of the legislature. There is no reason why the young men of other commonwealths should have advantages not open to the young men of Missouri, as is now the case. Nothing would have a happier effect upon the enrollment list of our State University than such a move. These fees are barriers t many young men who might otherwise be abl to secure a fine education within its courts an become useful men to the state. Let us hav an open University.

—To care for the health, and to emplo proper medical remedies, as the occasion de mands, is a Christian duty. A deliberate neg lect to do this amounts to self-murder. Th laws of health written deep in the physical con stitution of humanity are but the laws of God to be "obeyed and respected accordingly." *New York Observer.*

—The cost of the work of the Y. M. C. A Int. Com. for soldiers and sailors during th past summer and until the close of the year estimated at $80,000. The cost of the othe departments of the work of the Internation Committee will be a like sum, necessitating th securing of $160,000 before the close of th year to meet the expenses of the committee The associations take collections at one or othe of their meetings. The churches and unio meetings are asked to make a similar collec tion for the benefit of the committee, th amount thus secured to be forwarded to Mr. F B. Schenck, treasurer, 3 West Twenty-nint Street, New York.

—We have received a Bulletin of the Arm and Navy Department of the Y. M. C. Int. Com., issued November 1. It is an eight page publication, illustrated with a number o cuts of camp and army life, and is filled wit fresh and interesting news from the soldiers i the field and the sailors on our war vessels. detailed statement is made in regard to th work of the committee, and many interestin incidents are given. The work is strongly in dorsed by the President, the General of th Army, officers of all ranks, and soldiers an sailors. Any one can secure a copy of thi Bulletin by writing to the International Com mittee, 3 West Twenty-ninth Street, Ne York, sending a one-cent stamp for postage.

—The Actors' Society of America has issue a circular, calling upon the preachers an pastors of the churches to assist in their free dom from Sunday shows. The society has adopt ed strong resolutions against theatrical per formances at any hour of the day on Sunday and appeals to the clergy and all Christia people to assist in securing this liberty b proper legal enactment. There thus seems t be a tie in Sunday observance that binds al hearts in a common want and this commo demand must sooner or later be heeded by th lawmakers of our land. Let us have a weekl day of rest as demanded by the churches, th labor unions, the Actors' Society and othe organizations.

—The Missionary Intelligencer for Novem ber is an unusually large and interesting num ber. It contains the annual report of th Foreign Society for the missionary year, end ing Sept. 30, and should be kept for referenc during the present year. The information i contains covers the entire work of the Disciple of Christ in the foreign field.

—Are you aware of the fact that you have Roman Catholic pastor, no matter who you are what you are or where you live? If not, per haps the following paragraph from the Churc Progress will be news to you:

Such expressions as "Bishop of the Catholi diocese of so-and-so," or "Bishop of th Catholic Church in such-and-such a place," are incorrect and should be avoided. Th jurisdiction of a bishop is a strictly territoria one, and all persons within the boundaries o a diocese, whether Catholic or not, are subjec to it, especially if they are baptized. Th Non-Catholics living within the limits of parish belong to it, and its pastor and th bishop of the diocese in which it is are thei pastors, however unwilling they may be t recognize their authority. The proper expres sion in all cases is: The Bishop of N., etc.

—In this issue we publish an obituary of J B. Crane, who died at his home at Waynes boro, Va., on the 18th of October, of apoplexy The obituary was written by Rev. Cocke, th Presbyterian minister of Waynesboro, an personal friend of Bro. Crane. Bro. Crane kne e fathers of the Restoration personally, and recent years has been committing much of personal recollections of them and of the ginnings of the Restoration movement to iting. A number of his reminiscent articles peared in this paper during the last few ars and we still have a few unpublished icles. Bro. Crane has been an active serv-t of the Lord throughout his life and has ne to his rest with the honors of a veteran the Lord's army.

—Miss Mildred Franklin was last heard m at Port Said. There were twenty-five ssengers on the ship. Of these, nineteen re American missionaries. The time passes ickly and joyfully in such genial company.

—Dr. W. N. Hammond, 70 Yndustria St., vana, Cuba, wants five hundred Spanish-glish New Testaments. He is starting a nday-school in Havana and must have help order to secure any large success. The bans want to study English while studying eir Sunday-school lessons. Any one wishing contribute funds for this purpose may send e same to F. M. Rains, Box 750, Cincinnati,

—The following clipping is from the Canton ess of recent date, and has a bearing upon e forthcoming educational conference at oberly on Dec. 6th:

A delegation of nearly thirty persons went om Canton to Moberly Tuesday to attend the ucational conference in the interests of ristian University. The first session of the nference, not being largely attended from her parts of the state, was mainly prelimi-ry, and arranged for another meeting at e same place Dec. 6. It was proved that nton acted wisely in sending a delegation *rge enough to control* the organization and der for the next meeting, when the main sues are to be met! Joshua Alexander, an umnus of Christian University, was elected esident of the conference, and S. G. Clay, Fayette, another friend, was made secre-ry. It was resolved that the next meeting ould "consider and pass upon the propriety establishing and endowing one or more lleges in this state; and if this be approved, ays and means should then and there be pro-ded for this work." It will be necessary for anton to be *strongly represented* at that eeting, for her interests will be opposed by en having similar interests in other parts of e state. Every man that can be used should , Dec. 6th, to Moberly.

We hold no one responsible for the above t the Canton Press. It is needless for us to y that a conference, conducted in the spirit hich this clipping indicates, will amount to thing, no matter what its decisions may be. 'e take it that every fair-minded man in the ate desires that the educational conference, be held at Moberly, Dec. 6th, should be a presentative body of men, representing all r educational interests, and controlled by en whose vision is broad enough to take in r whole educational problem in the state. any local interest or any single institution ould undertake to make the conference serve s own particular interests without regard to her educational interests in the state, it would serve, and we hope it would receive, a prompt buke from the conference. As a friend of hristian University, who would rejoice in y successful effort to increase its endow-ent, and who stands ready to help it in every udable effort in that direction, we should gret exceedingly to know that the above lipping represents the spirit and method of e president, faculty and trustees of that stitution. We shall assume that it does not ntil developments prove the contrary.

—Prof. Charles W. Kent, in an article Missionary Tidings for November speaks ost encouragingly of the course of Bible which the gift of the $10,000 is made dependent. And so while lecturing at the university Dr. Young is visiting as many churches as possible in the interest of this work. Concerning the wisdom and the hope of this movement Prof. Kent says:

Our gratitude is elicited by our present success; our hopes are raised by this generous gift and the implied promise; our aim is high, for we are constrained to recognize the immense possibilities before us; our purpose should be well defined—to procure at once the remainder of the $25,000. Beyond even this is the vision of an endowment so enlarged as to raise the Lectureship to the dignity of a Chair put on the same plane as the languages and sciences. I could wish from the bottom of my heart that the University of Virginia might be the first institution to make the study of the English Bible in every respect co-ordinate with the study of Latin, or German, or Mathematics, or History, or any other course required for the Baccalaureate degree. If such a dream be realized it will be due to the wisdom and loyalty of the C. W. B. M.

—The Missionary Magazine for October contains the minutes of the 22nd annual convention of the churches of Christ in Missouri, held at Nevada, Sept. 26-29, 1898. Send to T. A. Abbott, 712 Commercial Bldg., this city, for copies. You need this number for study and reference.

—The acrostic form for a Bible reading, found elsewhere in this paper, by Sumner T. Martin, of Mason City, Ia., is worthy of your attention. It is commendable for its brevity, order and emphasis of the things to be brought out in the reading. We shall ask Bro. Martin to send us a few of these program readings that you may try them in your prayer-meetings. They, however, would not be difficult of preparation by any enterprising leader. Put this one on a blackboard before your meeting in the form given and note the effect.

—J. L. Darsie, financial agent for Bethany College, says that the report that this honored institution of learning was about to close its doors has greatly injured the college. He says that the situation is not one-half so bad as some people were led to believe and that she has no notion of suspending business. He also thinks that the report will so arouse her old friends that she will be immediately rescued from her present financial stress, and we trust that he rightly views the situation. Bro. Darsie is in the field to rally the friends of Bethany College to its present needs, and a better man for the place probably could not be found in or out of her alumni. We wish for Bro. Darsie the success that Bethany College rightfully expects of her friends. See an article from him in this paper on this subject.

Christ Our Model.

(A Bible Reading.)

Compassion:—1. For Sinners, Matt. 9:36. 2. For the Afflicted, Mark 1:40, 41. 3. For the Bereaved, Jno. 11:33-36.
Humility:—Jno. 13:1-17.
Righteousness:—Jno. 8:46; Heb. 4:15.
Industry:—Jno. 4:34; 9:4.
Self-control:—Jno. 18:10, 11, 22, 23.
Tender-hearted:—Matt. 18:21, 22; Luke 23:34.

Obedience:—1. To Parents, Luke 2:51, 52. 2. To Government, Matt. 22:21; 17:24-27. 3. To God Jno. 6:38; 17: 4.
Unselfishness:—Matt. 20:28; 16:24.
Religiousness:—1. As to Prayer, Luke 6:12; 22: 39-42.

Mercy:—Jno. 8:10, 11; 21:15-17.
Order:—Matt. 21:12, 13.
Dependence:—Matt. 26:40.
Earnestness:—Matt. 23:37.
Love:—Jno. 10:12, 13; 15:9, 12, 13.

Sumner T. Martin.

Mason City, Ia., Nov. 8, 1898.

The S. S., Endeavor and Prayer-meeting Departments.

In response to our note in our last issue relative to the utility of the departments above named, we have received the following responses:

I think the present arrangement of the Christian-Evangelist, so far as its various departments are concerned, is well-nigh perfect, and it is my candid opinion that the omission of any of these departments would be seriously detrimental both to the paper and to its large list of readers. C. J. Kimball.
St Louis, Mo., Nov. 14, 1898.

The Endeavor column by Bro. Jenkins and the Bible-school by Bro. Willett, and the "Quiet Hour" by the editor, are among the most valuable features of the paper. I am sure there would be a storm of protest if you dropped any one or all of these departments.
Yours, etc., W. S. Priest.
Lawrence, Kan., Nov. 12, 1898.

A well-known preacher in Missouri, who writes us privately, and whose name we therefore withhold, referring to the S. S., C. E. and prayer-meeting departments says he has inquired among the preachers and finds they do not read them. How far this applies to teachers, who generally have other means of preparing for their work we do not know. His own judgment in respect to the departments is as follows:

I believe they occupy space that can be put to better immediate service. I have been careful to inquire for months, especially of preachers, the utility of the work in consideration, and the answer has almost invariably been "I don't read them." So much S. S. matter is given in detail in papers devoted to that work that brief analyses are passed by. So of Endeavor lessons. But the prayer-meeting or midweek lessons are different. Those who use Christian Publishing Co. topics *need* what you say, and then for the *homiletics*, they are splendid. Let the S. S. and C. E. lessons go, but continue the midweek topics, and put on foot *uniform* midweek lesson.

If the prayer-meeting, Bible-school and the Christian Endeavor Society are useful means for advancing the cause of "Christ and the church," then surely their lessons should find a place in the columns of the Christian-Evangelist. We certainly have better prayer-meetings since we know the lesson theme a week in advance. I work in prayer-meeting, Bible-school and Christian Endeavor. Sometimes my lesson helps get misplaced, but the Christian-Evangelist, never.
Thos. R. Thornton.
Lee's Summit, Mo., Nov. 11, 1898.

Editor Christian-Evangelist: — I see a

most every subscriber with which I have conversed upon the subject say that these departments were among the leading reasons for continuing their subscriptio[illegible] to the paper. While every department is g[illegible]d, still these two live subjects demand full rec[illegible]ition, and the paper that fails to give them will lose many subscribers. E. C. ANDERSON.

Anniston, Ala., Nov. 12, 1898.

DEAR CHRISTIAN-EVANGELIST: — While 'tis true that all subscribers may not appreciate these columns, yet I am persuaded that there are none, however learned they may be, who cannot study them with profit. It is my judgment that anything which stimulates thought and helps the disciple to a more liberal and perfect understanding of the Word is worthy a place in our papers and a careful reading by the subscriber. CHAS. E. FREEMAN.

Springdale, Ark., Nov. 10, 1898.

THE CHRISTIAN - EVANGELIST: — Brethren, I arise to answer for myself about the various departments of a religious paper. I think it would be a serious mistake to leave off Endeavor Department, Sunday-school or any of those excellent departments. I see that some of our large secular dailies give an exposition of the Sunday-school lesson. Shall Christians be less wise? Maybe Bro. Ely would have the paper in *tracts*. These different helps go in to break up what might otherwise be monotony. Give us the CHRISTIAN - EVANGELIST with its "Current Events" to its "Publishers' Notes." Fraternally,

T. F. DRISKILL.

Corsicana, Tex., Nov. 12, 1898.

By all means continue the departments in the CHRISTIAN-EVANGELIST. Personally, I take great pleasure and receive much profit from the Sunday-school and Prayer-meeting columns. We use the topics in our midweek meetings. The CHRISTIAN-EVANGELIST becomes better with each year. I am proud of it. RUSSELL F. THRAPP.

Pittsfield, Ill. Nov. 10.

PERSONAL MENTION.

H. L. Willett writes that they are now nicely settled at Berlin, Germany, and greatly enjoying the surroundings.

B. F. Clay, the Western field secretary of the Foreign Missionary Society, called at this office while in the city last week. His home office is at Kansas City, Mo., but he expects to spend much time in the field in this the Jubilee Year of our missionary work.

A failure to make train connection at the Union Station, this city, last Thursday, gave us the pleasure of a call from W. S. Giltner, of Eminence, Ky. He was on his way to Jacksonville, Ill., where he expected to spend the Lord's day.

David Dick is attending St. Thomas Bible College, St. Thomas, Ontario, Canada.

L. W. Mulhall, evangelist, is stirring up the town of Centralia, Ill., all the churches and pastors co-operating.

D. L. Moody is now doing evangelistic work in Denver, Col., and is expected to begin work at Colorado Springs about Dec. 7th.

C. A. Young, who is delivering a course of Bible lectures at the University of Virginia, has been compelled to omit his Sunday work among the churches for a time, on account of ill health. This will account for the non-appearance of his letter.

W. W. Sniff, Gibson City, Ill., is in a very successful meeting with his congregation there, and Bro. Ferrall, of Watseka, is singing for them. There were 25 additions at last report.

J. B. Lehman and wife, of the Southern Christian Institute, Edwards, Miss., who have been refugees from the yellow fever for several weeks, have been visiting Bro. and Sister Sniff, at Gibson City, Ill. Mrs. Sniff and Mrs. Lehman are sisters. Bro. L. and wife returned to their work last week.

H. H. Peters has been unanimously called by the church at Rantoul Ill. for another year.

J. W. Lowber is delivering his fourth course of lectures at Grayson College, one of the affiliated colleges of the University of Texas.

Wallace Brockman, of Jacksonville, Ill., was recently married to Miss Fannie B. Kennedy, at Waverly, Ill., by Geo. L. Snively, pastor of the church at Jacksonville. They will reside at Jacksonville.

G. C. Ardrey has received a unanimous call from the church at Burton, Kan., for the third year of service there.

A. P. Cobb's permanent address is Decatur, Ill.

J. A. L. Romig has gone to Liverpool, England. He is to spend six months in evangelistic work among our English brethren.

M. P. Hayden, of Eureka, Ill., now engaged in evangelistic work, desires to locate as pastor of a church. He can begin work with the new year. Correspondence is solicited from churches seeking a pastor. Address as above.

Wm. Stanley has resigned his work as pastor of the church at Glasgow, Ky., and would like to locate with some church in Missouri or Texas. Bro. Stanley is a man of deep piety and ripe scholarship and leaves the church at Glasgow with its prayers and best wishes. Here is an opportunity for some church to secure an efficient preacher.

M. P. Hayden, of Eureka, Ill., has a highly commended lecture on "Phases of Physical Healing," which he is delivering wherever desired.

M. L. Anthony, since taking the work at Elkhart, Ill., has succeeded in stirring the church up in such a way that they have built a nice parsonage and made many other moves forward. They are now enjoying a good meeting with A. O. Hunsaker assisting in song.

F. N. Calvin has gone from Waco, Texas, to Milwaukee, Wis., instead of Kankakee, Ill., as stated in this column last week. He has accepted a temporary call at Milwaukee to begin December 1st.

M. Ingels, of Kansas, and L. O. Roath, of Missouri, have united for evangelistic work. They will make a strong gospel team. They are now at Fontana, Kan., and where also they may be addressed by other churches wanting a protracted meeting.

W. G. Smith has closed a successful pastorate of two years at New Castle, Ind., during which there were 74 additions. All the different activities of the church are reported greatly enlarged and his ministry. A fine report of his work was published in New Castle Press.

Thos. E. Jones, the evangelistic singer, who has been spending a little time in New York, under a distinguished vocal teacher, has returned to Chicago, and is ready once more to enter the evangelistic field. Bro. Jones is undoubtedly a singer of great power as well as a sincere, earnest Christian. He may be addressed care Christian Oracle, 358 Dearborn St., Chicago, Ill.

C. H. Trout has resigned his work at Mishawaka, Ind., on account of the financial condition of the church. During the past year there were 21 additions. Bro. Trout now desires correspondence with any church in need of a pastor. He leaves Mishawka with the good will of the church and commendation of its official board.

Elder George F. Assister, who has been acting as a supply pastor for the Christian Church at Chillicothe, Mo., for a number of months past, and who was on last Sunday called to the pastorate for the ensuing year, has announced his declination of the call and submitted his resignation, to take effect Dec. 21. At what point he will locate Elder Assister is not aware. He is a preacher of much ability as well as a careful, painstaking pastor, and is well calculated to do good work for the church whose call may prove acceptable to him.—*Chillicothe Daily Mail*.

G. W. Muckley has been on a trip out West and secured more than $500 for Church Extension on the church at Colorado Springs.

A. McLean has returned from a visit to Havana, Cuba, whither he went to look over the field with a view to missionary work in that city. The field seems ripe for Protestant missionaries, and especially those who will declare the pure, simple gospel of Christ.

CHANGES.

H. C. Shipley, Ionia to Jewell City, Kan.
R. Watson, Lebanon to Salem, Mo.
C. C. Waite, Glenville, O., to 4410 Division St., Pittsburg, Pa.
A. W. Gelner, Owasso to Hopedale, Ind.
S. H. Farrer, Ocoee to Orlando, Fla.
J. W. Garner, Beloit, Kan., to Perkins, Okla.
W. A. Meloan, Blandinsville to Media, Ill.
J. K. Reid, Bartow, Fla., to Louisville, Ky.
Glen McWilliams, Saratoga to Santa Clara, Cal.
W. W. Pew, Payette, Idaho, to Boise City, Ore.

Postponed.

DEAR BROTHER: — Owing to circumsta[illegible] we were unable to dedicate our new chu[illegible] building yesterday. We will dedicate the 2[illegible] Bro. B. S. Denny, our state secretary, [illegible] have charge of the services. The brethren [illegible] this part of the state are invited to be pres[illegible] and enjoy the services. Please announce i[illegible] this week's issue of your good paper.

Your brother, F. L. DAVI[illegible]

Dows, Ia., Nov. 14, 1898.

Nebraska Association.

The Nebraska Ministerial Association [illegible] hold a three days' session in Fairbury c[illegible] mencing Tuesday evening, Dec. 6th. [illegible] Christian ministers with their families [illegible] others interested in religious themes bot[illegible] the state and from adjacent states [illegible] cordially invited and will be entertained if they will send their names to me. An int[illegible] esting program is in preparation.

ALBERT BUXTON,

President Nebraska Christian Min. Ass[illegible]

Fairbury, Neb., Nov. 10.

SUBSCRIBERS' WANTS.

Miscellaneous wants and notices will be inserted [illegible] this department at the rate of two cents a word, ea[illegible] insertion, all words, large and small, to be count[illegible] and two initials stand for one word. Please acco[illegible] pany notice with corresponding remittance to sa[illegible] book-keeping.

ATTENTION, STATE AND DISTRICT EVANGELISTS [illegible] You can easily place a Christian Library in ea[illegible] community you evangelize, and thus give great[illegible] permanency to your work as well as largely increa[illegible] your own salary. *Try it and see.* For fuller partic[illegible] lars address S. J. Phillips, Sugar Grove, Wis.

I HAVE Harbingers and out-of-prints on hand, a[illegible] listed. Brethren, write me at Cardiff, Ark. Giv[illegible] me a list of what you have or want. J. F. Callahan.

A PREACHER of six years' experience attending o[illegible] of the colleges of this city desires correspond[illegible] ence with any church within one hundred miles [illegible] this city that needs a preacher. He ha[illegible] been ve[illegible] successful, is a young man, and bears testimonials [illegible] good character and good work. Address "A. B., care this office.

FOR SALE.—Two hundred and fifty (250) Ope[illegible] Chairs all in good order, very handsome seati[illegible] for Churches, Opera-houses, or Halls. Original cos[illegible] Five hundred dollars. Will be sold at a great sacrifi[illegible] Write to H E. Smith, Clerk of Christian Churc[illegible] Palmyra, Mo., if interested and desire a great ba[illegible] gain.

Original Contributions.

CAN I LOVE MY ENEMIES?

N. J. AYLSWORTH.

IV.

Our feelings are subject to a law of their own. We cannot love and hate at will. No command, even from heaven, can cause us to admire what is disgusting and loathsome. No command and no act of will can make beauty repulsive. It is a law of our nature that we shall love what is lovely and hate what is hateful. How, then, can we love an enemy whose conduct toward us is hateful? It does not seem unnatural that we should love our brethren. The mutual love of Christians resembles that of the family, and we can understand it. Why should not those having the same aim in life, the same hopes, the same Father, and possessing in various degrees the beauty of the Christian character, love each other? Nor does it seem strange that we should be moved by spectacles of suffering or feel a sympathy for the downtrodden and oppressed. Such things appeal to our pity, and in proportion to our tenderness of heart we are moved by them. That we should feel some sympathy for a brave enemy in war who has never borne us any ill-will, and whose gallantry challenges our admiration, seems possible. Is it not also possible to understand the compassion for the criminal, whose lot is so hard, and who, though an enemy to society, has never done us personally any wrong? And, under the quickening influence of Christianity, is it surprising that all these sympathies should grow very strong and fill life with the beauty of their ministries? But how can all this help us to love a personal enemy who stands before us in his hatefulness? On what principle shall we do ought but hate him? Must not the love of such an object contravene the fundamental law of our feelings? Is it not impossible? Is there anything in the nature of the human heart which will enable it to surmount such an obstacle, and bestow its love on the offender?

There are two terms in our language which yield us a very important suggestion at this point. The unconscious philosophy of human speech is generally correct. Words embody the common perception or average judgment of mankind, and this is seldom at fault.

When a man's selfishness manifests itself in trifling exactions in deal, we say that he is "small;" that is, extreme or refined selfishness is *smallness* of character. If this selfishness leads the tradesman to overreach or misrepresent, we say that he is "dishonest." The smallness is still there, but the breach of honesty strikes the imagination more forcibly, and thus gives the name to the act. Take away the dishonesty, which partially obscures the other quality, and the *smallness* stands out clearly to view. Extreme selfishness, as it manifests itself in deal, is seen by us to be *smallness*.

The smallness of selfishness will become still more apparent if we consider another term. If a man deals handsomely with his fellows; if he is slow to take offense, and overlooks many of the slights and injuries of others, and continues to bestow upon them kindness out of the abundance of his good-will, we say he is "magnanimous." This term is derived from the Latin words *magnus*, meaning great or large, and *animus*, mind. *Magnanimous*, therefore, means *large-minded*. Webster defines it as "great of mind." An abounding good-will, which flows out to all and is not turned aside by many of the little meannesses of men, we perceive to be *large-mindedness*. But this good-will, this benevolence, is but one of the degrees of that love of which we are speaking—the love of mankind. Love is largeness and selfishness is smallness of character. This is an intuitive perception of mankind, and has left its deposit in language. Webster defines *magnanimous* affirmatively as "great of mind," and negatively as "not selfish." Great-mindness is the opposite of selfishness; selfishness is smallness.

This has an important bearing on the question of resentment and retaliation. If, when passing on the street, a little dog runs out and barks and snaps at your feet, you do not get down on all fours and bark and snap at him! You do not *feel* like doing so. Yet this would be retaliation in kind. You do not feel like retaliating because you are a *man*, and your character is larger than the cur character, and you instietively feel that it would be beneath you. Your dignity and largeness of feeling stand in the way; and you snap your finger at the dog and call him pet names, and he trots along at your side pacified. This is what you *do*, and what you *feel* like doing. You feel above resentment; and because the cur has acted like a dog to you, you do not feel that you can afford to descend to his level and act like a dog to him. But you can afford to do this quite as well as you can afford to descend to the level of some small-minded person who, with the spirit of a cur, has said or done something mean to you, that you may say or do something mean in return. You cannot do this without first descending from your high-heartedness and getting his mean spirit.

There is a tendency for every spirit to beget its own likeness—for the angry word to call forth the angry word, and the hateful act to provoke a hateful act in return—but if you are to be a victim to all such influences your character is of very small proportions. A leaf may dam a rivulet, but not the mighty river. It causes scarcely a ripple on its surface, and then is borne along by the majesty of the flood. If the flow of your heart-life be large, deep and strong, the thousand little meannesses which you encounter in life will not turn it aside. Its magnificent good-will will override them, and you will feel that you cannot except from your benevolence those who are guilty. You will rather be moved to pity this littleness, and seek to lift them above it, than stoop to this level to retaliate.

Wherever we look we behold this actually taking place. The noble in character are ever moving above the littlenesses and meannesses of the small-hearted about them, and by reason of their very largeness, refusing to descend to the retaliations of life, are shedding their good-will like God's rain and sunshine on all. Wherever we find nobleness of character we find this tendency operating.

And here again, we reach the important truth that it is *natural* to love our enemies. This behavior of the noble-hearted is spontaneous. It would be contrary to their feelings to do otherwise. They scorn to be little. Resentment may be said to be natural to small, low nations; but surely these are not entitled to a monopoly of human nature. It is natural for the magnanimous—the large-hearted—to be unaffected by the entire brood of little hates and spites, and even to be drawn to those who harbor them by a pitying sympathy. Whether it be natural to hate or to love one's enemies is a question of smallness or largeness of character. As it is natural for small people to do small things and for great men to do great things; so is it natural for the small-hearted to resent and hate, and the great-hearted to bless and seek to benefit out of the abundance of their good-will. Tennyson speaks of "the little hearts that know not how to forgive." He who claims that one cannot love those who wrong him makes a humiliating confession, and reveals that he lacks experience in the higher manhood. In demanding that we shall love our enemies Christ is but calling us out of childhood into the manhood of the human heart. His command calls for nothing *extra*-human nature.

There may be a personal wrong so great and so aggravating as to stagger even a large noble-heartedness, and love's way of mastering in such a case will be considered in another place, but magnanimity or largeness of character—which all the forces of Christianity tend to foster—completely disposes of all the petty hates and resentments so common in the social relations of life.

Another fact which here comes into view is that the love of enemies is not a different affection from that by which we love our brethren, compassionate the suffering or seek to rescue the fallen. It calls for no new faculty, nor even for a different exercise of the same faculty; it is the same love triumphing over difficulties. He who loves his brethren with any considerable degree of strength has learned to love his enemies; and he who finds himself—like the the small-hearted about him—harboring grudges, feeling small resentments and engaging in little acts of retaliation, may well ask his heart some searching questions, and will then be likely to make an important discovery. He will find that his love, even toward his brethren, is *partial;* and this is a matter of great moment. For certain of his brethren whose stations in life correspond with his own, whose tastes and manners are congenial and pleasing, and whose society is enjoyable, he feels an attachment; but towards the rest he is indifferent. This is not brotherly love, but only the love of such brethren as please him, and is founded on characteristics quite other than that of brotherhood. Such love is little more than a form of selfishness. If we are drawn to others only in so far as they please us and minister to our enjoyment, our love moves wholly within the sphere of the selfish. This is a love which may be found in even the wickedest and most abjectly selfish of mankind. This mere love of complacency is not brotherly love. Take a brother to your heart, and into your society who is poor, ungainly in manner, ignorant, and who not only posses-ses no attractions of person or station, but has many trying and annoying faults to be overcome, and you have passed into another region. The love that does this is generous and self-bestowing in its nature; and such love, if it be strong, can surmount still another obstacle—resentment. He who is learning to love his brethren is learning the lesson of all noble love, including that of the enemy. The river which flows peacefully between its banks will also leap a barrier and form the cataract. The same forces which cause the one accomplish the other. If love in its gentle flow encounters a personal wrong or an act of hatred it receives a shock. There is commotion and a conflict of feeling, and perhaps a dash of resentment, but at last the rising tide of generous emotion rolls over it. It is love's Niagara. Such a flood was David's grief for Absalom, his enemy. It was hatred lost in love's deep agony. But this was only because parental love is a generous, self-sacrificing affection. All generous love, in proportion to its strength, will do the same. Since that mighty-hearted affection rolled over the death-agonies of the crucifixion in the words, "Father, forgive them!" love has known many Niagaras. They are the sublimest spectacles in human history. A rainbow spans Niagara; the light of heaven shines on these.

Even a brook will sift its silver over a rock, forming a little waterfall, and no very large amount of generous affection should be sufficient to surmount the petty resentments and little meannesses of life, and go on its way loving still. All generous love is enemy-loving in its nature. Let him who finds no such tendency in his heart beware! He has yet to learn Christ's first lesson in love.

It is unfortunate that a feeling which may dwell in the heart of the most adjectly selfish should go by the name of *love*. But as it does so it is of vital importance that the distinction should be made broad and clear between this fruitless sentiment and that generous affection which is enemy-loving in its very nature, and without which we must lack the fundamental virtue of the Christian character. And with every one the question should be asked searchingly, Am I living in the littleness of selfishness, or are my feelings too large and high for petty resentments?

Correspondence.

Washington (D. C.) Letter.

The sessions of the General Convention of the Protestant Episcopal Church excited more than ordinary interest in our city, accustomed as it is to great gatherings. The spectacular parade on the opening day, when seventy bishops, attired in their stately robes, filed into the Epiphany Church; the distinguished appearance of the six hundred clerical and lay delegates, the brilliant debates upon the floor of the House of Deputies, the dignity and orderliness which characterized the proceedings, tended to produce an exceptional and favorable impression.

As the convention proceeded to business I was reminded of a remark made by Dr. Charles H. Parkhurst, that "Christian union is in the air, it is in the thinking of men and in the deliberations of assemblies." The most important question which came before this convention was that relating to Christian unity. Rev. W. B. Huntington, of New York City, introduced the church unity amendment. After considerable discussion a substitute, proposed by Rev. J. J. Faude, of Minnesota, was adopted. This amendment to the constitution is as follows:

But the provision may be made by canon for the temporary use of other forms and directories of worship by congregations not already in union with this church who are willing to accept the spiritual oversight of the bishop of the diocese.

The purpose of this amendment, it is declared, is "to meet the case of certain congregations who, while they feel attracted to the doctrine and the form of worship of the EpiscopalChurch, and would gladly put themselves into relation with its ecclesiastical authorities are, nevertheless, not willing to accept all the forms of worship now prescribed. By allowing entire congregations to put themselves under the oversight of the bishop' it is hoped that they will gradually come to love the entire service of the church and will become in every sense members of the church."

The ultimate design is thus to unite all the Christians of this country into one great church of the American people.

The question of changing the canons of the church relating to marriage and divorce was the subject of prolonged debate. The present law of the church is that no minister shall solmnize the marriage of any person who has a divorced husband or wife still living, except in the case of the innocent party in a divorce for the cause of adultery. The committee to whom the matter had been referred proposed to omit this exception and make the marriage tie indissoluble. The convention decided by a small majority to adhere to the present canon. The question will be reopened at the next triennial convention, and it is thought that at that time the advocates of a change may triumph.

The principal event of the closing week was the unveiling of the Peace Cross on Mount St. Alboa, the site of the great cathedral which is yet to be built. The cross is twenty feet high and bears the date, the arms of the diocese of Washington, and the inscription, "Jesus Christ himself being the chief cornerstone." On the other face is a sentance from the Litany, "May it please thee to give to all nations unity, peace and concord."

Many of the Protestant pulpits were placed at the disposal of the Episcopal brethren, and some of the visiting clergymen accepted the invitations and made engagements to preach on Sunday. Bishop Satterlee, however, vetoed this and ordered the engagements canceled, giving as his reason that as Episcopal pulpits could not be opened to clergymen of other denominations, it would not be proper for his brethren to speak in their pulpits. The next convention will assemble in San Francisco.

Upon Wednesday, Nov. 2, at the residenc of the bride's parents, Miss Abigail Power only child of Bro. and Sister F. D. Power was united in marriage to Mr. J. Ernes Sparks, of Washington, D. C.

The Third church of this city has secured a option upon a valuable property in Soutl Washington. W. J. Wright, the energeti pastor, has $5,000 available, and if he can ar range to get $2,000 in addition will purchas the property.

J. R. Maxwell, who goes from Rockville, Md., to the Third Church, Richmond, is a man of excellent gifts. He had an exceptionally fine record among the Methodists during his fifteen years of service with that people. There is no better field on the Atlantic shore than East Richmond. We shall be surprised if we do not hear some good news from that quarter in the coming months.

W. R. Watkins, a late accession to our ranks, is with J. A. Hopkins in a meeting at Jerusalem, Hartford county, Md.

I expect to help Peter Ainslie in an evangelistic effort at the Calhoun St. Church, Baltimore, for two weeks in November.

EDWARD E. BAGBY.

New York Letter.

On Saturday, Nov. 5th, at eleven o'clock in the morning, two of our sisters, Dr. Olivia A. Baldwin, of Austin, Texas, and Miss Anna Lackey, of Fayetteville, Ark., sailed from this port on the good steamship "Etruria" of the Cunard Line, for their field of labor at Deoghur, India. A number of friends from our churches in New York saw them off at their pier, giving them many well-wishes and God-speeds on their long journey and in their great work among the heathen. They both attended our prayer-meeting on Wednesday evening, Nov. 2d, when Dr. Baldwin told in most fitting terms of her work in India and of the orphanage work she will take up on her return. Her descriptions of that people's condition and great needs touched all our hearts and caused us to feel that she was indeed the messenger of Christ unto them. She strengthened us very much by telling of the beautiful Christian character and blessed influence of one orphan girl who had grown up in our home in India. When she told us her name was Fulmona, we all immediately recognized her as the one our Mission Band in the 169th Street Church adopted and supported. This voluntary report did us much good and naturally causes us to hope that Mary Willis, the one our Band has adopted and now supports, may be as faithful to Christ as was Fulmona. Miss Lackey told us in her simple, girlish style of her joy in the Lord, now that she was on her way to this great work. Her words were truly heroic. These good sisters go out under the auspices of the Christian Woman's Board of Missions and will be a strong addition to their forces in that field. They expect to reach Bombay on the 9th of December.

***

On October 23d, Bro. G. A. Reinl and the congregation at Brockton, Mass., solemnly dedicated to the service of God their beautiful new church building. The church is located on Crescent Street, and is a two-story structure of Gothic architecture. The pulpit is arranged at the northerly end of the building, and at one side is the organ, and at either side of the pulpit small robing rooms are arranged. On the floor above is another large room which will be used for the primary department of the Bible-school. A small room is set aside there also for use as a library. The interior is finished in cypress wood and is tastefully furnished with carpets, nicely cushioned pews and a prettily draped pulpit. Everything about the building is thoroughly in keeping and it is a credit to those who have labored long and well to secure for themselves a house of worship. Bro. Roland A. Nicholas, of Worcester, preached the dedicatory sermon, and Bro. S. M. Hunt, of Springfield, raised $1,000 of the l,600 which the church owed, leaving an in-ebtedness of only $600. Bros. R. H. Bolton, ! Everett, and E. C. Davis, of Springfield, ook part in the services. The churches at Vorcester, Springfield, Taunton, Malden, Ev-rett and New Bedford, were all represented ι the services. In the afternoon ordination ervices were conducted, in which C. H. Everett and A. H. Barrows were set apart to he office of eldership, and J. F. Gardener and . F. Dunbar to that of the diaconate. It 'as a glorious day in the history of that noble and of Disciples of Christ at Brocton. This naterial prosperity represents much sacrifice nd devotion on the part of Bro. C. A. Reinl nd his faithful flock. May God richly bless hem and may this evidence of growth in-pire all New England to greater zeal for the ,ord.

***

A course of lectures on "The Religion of srael from the Earliest Times to the Exile" is eing delivered now at Union Theological Sem-nary in this city, under the auspices of the .merican Committee for the Study of Relig-ons. The lecturer is the Rev. Karl Budde,). D., Professor of Hebrew and Old Testa-nent Exegesis in the University of Strasburg. 'he program is an inviting one for the Bible tudent and is as follows: I. The Origin of he Religion of Yahweh. II. Yahweh and His Rivals. III. Priests, Prophets and Kings, he Champions of Yahweh. IV. Foreign Pow-rs and the Written Prophecies of the North-rn Kingdom. V. Similar Conflict in the outhern Kingdom. VI. Judah's Collapse nd the Basis of its Re-establishment. The Committee under whose auspices these lectures re given represent a number of the leading olleges, seminaries and universities of the East, and the lectures they provide will be epeated at several of them. This is the fourth eason of the Committee and also the fourth eries of lectures given to the public through hem. The first course was delivered by Prof. Rhyss Davids, on "Buddhism." Prof. T. K. Cheyne lectured last year. Judging from the rst of Dr. Budde's lectures the course will all out no little comment from critics and eligious editors. Some of his positions are ew and quite fascinating.

***

The Triennial Episcopal General Convention t Washington faced four questions of grave nportance to that community of believers. 'hey were: (1) The proposed canon on mar-iage and divorce; (2) The proposition to hange the name of their church; (3) The ad-isability of establishing missions in Roman Catholic countries; and (4) A proposition au-horizing bishops to take under their care and versight alien congregations not using in full he offices of the Prayer-book, but willing to ccept the spiritual oversight of the bishop. 'or many years Episcopal clergymen have per-ormed marriages for divorced parties if guilt-ess of the sin of adultery. This is allowable y an exception to the Church Canon. The xception to this law was the battle ground n the Washington Convention. Ultra High Churchmen wished it abolished, believing with Roman Catholics that divorce under any cir-umstances is un-Christian. The proposition vas so loaded with amendments that its pur-ose was practically changed and its friends oted it down, hoping to renew it three years ence. The proposition to change the name of he church was not a new one. Its summary lefeat, however, shows it is losing ground. 'he proposition came up in a form something ike this: "To designate the Church in the Constitution as the church known in law, as the Protestant Episcopal Church," etc. This ap-ealed to the humor of the convention and all nited in laughing it off the calendar. "We ook on the church as our mother," said one leputy, "but if this passes it will be our moth-r-in-law." A great daily of New York said ditorially:

For a Church numbering less than 700,000 ommunicants to call itself "the American Church," as has been proposed, would look like a piece of grotesque assumption to average people not biased by ecclesiasticism, and in the opinion of some of the wisest churchmen, the ridicule that it would provoke would paralyze the growth of the Church. It is not likely that the agitation will survive many years more.

The decision to establish missions in Roman Catholic countries was a radical step. The Episcopal missions in Mexico and Brazil were strongly opposed a few years since. The Convention reaffirmed the right of the Church to enter Roman Catholic countries whenever that church proved recreant to its trust. It has gone so far as to appoint a Bishop to Brazil and has taken measures looking toward establishing Episcopal propagandism in Cuba and Porto Rico. The adoption of Dr. Huntington's proposition (number 4 above) in an amended form marks a distinct change in the aloofness which hitherto characterized that church, and doubtless is a prophecy of even more liberal measures in the future. Taken altogether, it seems the Convention was a condemnation of High Churchmanship. It will not please the sectarian dogmatist, but it looks in the direction of American progress and individual liberty.

S. T. WILLIS.

1281 *Union Avenue.*

Constantinople Letter.

On September the first Mrs. Chapman and I left Greensburg, Ind., for our chosen field of labor in the Turkish Empire. On our way to New York we visited friends and relatives in Cincinnati, Claysville, Pa., and Washington, D. C. We set sail from New York September the tenth, on the "Aller," of the North German Lloyd Steamship Line. Our ship was a fine one, with every modern comfort and convenience. When it comes to the test, it is no easy matter to say good-bye to lifelong friends and native land, but believing that duty was before us, we kept back the tears and set our hearts upon Constantinople, our future home. As we sailed out of the harbor we saw the "Indiana" and the "Brooklyn," of the United States Navy, and while we long for the the time "when war shall be no more," still we felt that for years yet God will use the United States Navy to advance the cause of liberty and humanity throughout the world. In my inner pocket I carried our certificates of citizenship of the grandest nation on earth and among our baggage were several United States flags which shall adorn our home and henceforth be doubly beautiful to us.

It was all a new experience to us upon the "briny deep," and it is needless to say the voyage was full of interest and pleasure. The sea was smooth and the weather delightful. The only thing which marred the pleasure of voyage was seasickness, which takes all the spirit out of one and makes him very humble. When a man is seasick he wants the fact to be fully appreciated, though he rarely gets the sympathy that the circumstances demand. There were but twenty-eight cabin passengers on board our steamer, as there is comparatively little travel East across the Atlantic during August and September. In our company were an Italian baron and several of New York's "four hundred." While we were satisfied in being neither of Italian royal blood nor of the "four hundred," of New York, no doubt they felt sorry for the poor missionaries, of whom there were six on board, all bound for the Turkish Empire. We became very well acquainted with the four workers of the Americhn Board, whose company we enjoyed all the way to Constantinople.

As we approached Gibraltar the sun was setting, his last rays making glorious a scene well worth crossing the Atlantic to see. On one hand was old Spain with her mountain peaks running up into the clouds, on the other hand was Africa with her rocky cliffs and in front of us was the Rock Gibraltar, a grand and impregnable fortress where floats the "Union Jack." We spent a few hours ashore in the narrow streets among strange people—Moors, Spaniards and British redcoats — speaking different languages, of which Spanish seemed to be used the most, and saw the barracks where five thousand English soldiers are stationed.

We reached Naples in ten and one-half days after leaving New York. Naples is a very interesting city to travelers. It is full of beggars and rascals. When a stranger arrives it seems that the whole city combines in one grand effort to get his last cent. I have never seen more poorly dressed, deformed and degenerate people in one city than are to be found in Naples. We were compelled to remain a week in Italy before we could get our ship from Brindisi to Constantinople, and determined to make the best use of our delay, so after visiting the excavation at Pompeii, seeing the smoke and lava issuing from Mt. Vesuvius and visiting other points of interest in and about Naples, we took the train for Rome, a distance of one hundred and fifty miles.

Modern Rome is a city of five hundred thousand inhabitants and is a much cleaner and better city than Naples. In our limited time we could make only a hasty survey of the principal places of historic interest. The grand old ruins of the ancient city walls, the Colliseum, the Forum, Cæsar's palaces, the Baths of Caracalla and the obelisks—all speak of the "Rome which sat upon her seven hills and ruled the world." We took a drive out the Appian Way and thought of how Paul came to Rome, a prisioner in chains. We were in a dungeon which is confidently claimed to be the one in which Paul was confined, and saw the church said to stand over the place where "Paul spent two years in his own hired house." But after being shown two churches, one in Naples and the other in Rome, in each of which we were told Constantine was baptized, one is inclined to become skeptical as to the authenticity of current traditions. We also visited St. Peter's, St. Paul's, the Sancta Scala and the Catacombs. After seeing people kissing a vessel said to contain the blood of a saint who died fifteen hundred years ago, or kissing the toe of a bronze statue in St. Peter's, or climbing the Sancta Scala on their knees, saying a prayer on each step, one is strengthened in his conviction that the Roman Catholic Church is a great system of idolatry and superstition, with enough of the leaven of Christianity, we hope, to save many sincere but misguided souls.

We went from Naples to Brindisi by rail, passing through thirty-six tunnels on the way. At Brindisi we boarded the "Euterpe," of the Austrian Lloyd Steamship Line, and in two days reached Piræus. Here we had nine hours in which to visit Athens, four miles distant. We saw the Museum, the Cathredal, the Atrium, the Acropolis and stood on Mars' Hill, where Paul preached to the Stoics and Epicureans.

The next day we entered the Dardanelles. Fortifications are to be seen all along this narrow channel. No one less than a Dewey could reach the Bosphorus with a fleet against a hostile foe. Early Monday morning, October the second, we reached the capital of the Turkish Empire. A dense fog obscured our vision of the city and we were filled with disappointment, for we had heard so much of the magnificent view at the approach of the city. But at exactly the right time the morning sun arose above the Asian hills and scattered the fogs, and we beheld in its greatest beauty what is said to be one of the grandest views in all the world. If I could have put this scene on canvas or written it in a poem my fame would at once have been established, but unfortunately I had no canvas and my pen and ink were packed for landing and by the time I got through the Custom House my thoughts were all turned to prose and I am yet in obsucrity. "All is not gold that glitters," we found to be true upon entering the city. The streets are narrow and dirty, and the dogs—their name is legion! We were warmly greeted and welcomed by Bro. and Sister G. N. Shishmanian, at whose home we are at the present comfortably quartered.

We have begun the study of the language, the people, customs and situation. At another time I will write of our work and the needs of the field. The Lord has been very good to us in giving us a pleasant and prosperous voyage and a safe arrival. We hope to be useful in this part of the Lord's vineyard. "Brethern, pray for us." Very fraternally,

A. L. CHAPMAN.

Our School Problem.

DEAR BRO. GARRISON:—Permit me through the CHRISTIAN-EVANGELIST, to say a few words, in regard to the question which is now engaging the minds of many of our brethren, viz., schools, or higher education. I have been surprised at the spirit manifested by some in this matter. We as a people stand for union and unity. In theory we oppose all sects, while in practice we are divided among ourselves, and some are exceedingly sectarian. In the consideration of this important question we are not willing to lay aside personal interest and prejudice, but with the spirit of an iconoclast we set about to destroy whatever seems to conflict with our cherished theory or institution, and often in our attacks we make assertions which appear absurd to those who are acquainted with the facts in the case. No man ever accomplished a great work by *tearing down* a work of the same nature. Jealous divisions and bitter speeches are no less harmful in the educational world than in the purely religious. Now would it not be better to contemplate this question from a financial, intellectual and *Christian* standpoint, considering first of all the cause of Christ in its broad and most comprehensive sense? The field of the ministry offers the greatest opportunities, and we need men in that field who are equal to them. Goodness is absolutely necessary to be a true minister, but the time has passed when goodness is regarded as the only requisite. A minister must have preparation as well as piety; he must know men as well as mercy. I am in favor of an institution that will produce and develop all these requirements, be it what or where it may.

I want now to call attention to a statement which we often hear in connection with this question: "State Universities are hotbeds of infidelity; it is almost impossible to maintain faith in God in one of these institutions;" In the darker days, when every man was branded an heretic who ventured an opinion contrary to the religious traditions of his father, this saying had its birth, but I am surprised to hear a man in this age make such a statement. Please pardon a bit of personal experience. I spent five years in one of these State Universities, taking the regular classical course. During that time I met no infidel professors, although I was acquainted with about forty of the instructors in that institution. Each year I met and mingled with about five hundred young men and women and I can remember only one instance of a student having his faith shaken, and that young man found the literature which shook his faith in the library of one of our best ministers. There was no "Bible Chair" in connection with the institution while I was there, but I came out with my faith in Christ Jesus strengthened. I spent one year in one of "our own schools" and can truthfully say, I found as high a standard of morality, and as much genuine reverence for God in the State University as in "our own school" (and it was one of our best). Again, if we grant that the atmosphere of our Universities is not wholly religious, does that argue that we must withdraw all religious influence from them? Did Jesus teach that we are to take men entirely out of the world and its problems in order to prepare them to preach? If these are questions which are troubling the minds of my fellowmen, is it not my duty to grapple with those questions and assist in the solution of them? Sometime, somewhere, the minister must meet these questions which are engaging men's minds. Shall he face them and master them, or shall he "look upon them and pass by on the other side?" That we ought to have a GREAT SCHOOL, richly endowed, I readily admit; that we have none I sadly affirm. What is the best thing to do under the existing circumstances? is the question we must answer. I trust this question will be thought of, agitated and prayed over until it is solved in the spirit of the Christ, and settled in that manner which will be to the supreme interest of his kingdom.

I am sincerely,

C. A.

Introductory Letter.

As State Evangelist and Superintendent of Bible-schools and Endeavor Societies of Iowa, chosen for this work at our last State Convention, I feel that a few words by way of introduction will notbe out of place at this time. My work with the East Side Church in Des Moines did not close until the first of this month. Time has scarcely been sufficient, as yet, for adjustment to my new position. I am ready now to be a helper to all the churches, by whom I have been chosen, so far as time and ability will permit. If I can serve you in locating pastors, helping you to secure an evangelist, or assist you in a meeting personally, or to aid you in adjustment of difficulties, do not hesitate to call upon me; it is for this purpose you have chosen me. This is especially the time of the year that evangelistic work should be pushed to the front. Let as many meetings be held in Iowa this winter as possible. Remember, brethren, we have more than a million souls in this state, above the age of ten years that are non-Christian. There are about 30,000 in this state that have indicated their preference to be that of the Christian Church. These people are already converted to the plea we make and should soon be brought into full fellowship with it and us. Let the motto of every church in Iowa be, "Enlargement."

This will be impossible unless you come more largely to the help of the work than you have in the past. Do not fail to respond promptly to the communications sent you by our corresponding secretary, Bro. B. S. Denny. Iowa should raise at least $5,000 this year for state work. This would be less than ten cents per member. We have very few members who are not at least able to do this much, and these are many who will give many times more than this. This leads me to say some things to the

BIBLE-SCHOOLS AND ENDEAVOR SOCIETIES.

Last year there was practically nothing given for state work from these schools and societies. This year we expect to come to you and ask for your apportionment due the state. We hope to have such a liberal response from you that next year a man may be chosen whose entire time shall be given to this work. Your superintendent is planning together with his helpers, to arrange for four special days during the year. These will serve as rally days and will be of great service in building up your schools and societies. We want that these special days shall serve to build up your home work. Bro. W. Orr, of Clarenda, Iowa, is to have special charge of the arrangement of this program. He is the great rally man of Iowa.

He is now at work on the first program. At our last convention we were instructed to ask that our schools and societies contribute to state work "two cents per quarter" for each member. If this small amount is collected from this source it will give $2,800 to be used in the enlargement of the work in Iowa. Now all we ask of you is that upon these special days you take this offering for the state work.

I want that you shall become acquainted with Sister C. C. Rowlison, of Marshalltown, who was selected as superintendent of the primary work of our Bible-schools. If all the primary teachers and workers will secure a copy of "Instructions to Primary Workers" that is now being prepared by Sister Rowlison it will be of great help to them. We are expecting to have this and other helps for distribution this winter. Watch for the program which will soon be out for your first rally. Trusting that the Lord will bless you abundantly in your labors this year, while "trusting in the Lord Jesus Christ for strength," remember that your life should be: "For Christ and the Church." D. A. WICKIZER.

918 *East 12th St., Des Moines, Ia.*

Texas Letter.

Texas is just now indulging in a broad smile of pardonable pride. "Why?" you ask. The cause is a good one. At the Omaha Exposition the other day she took the prize for the best state exhibit. Is not that a good reason? Wouldn't your state smile, too, under similar circumstances? "Keep your eye on Texas."

Dallas, the Texas metropolis, is smiling, too, and why is that? Again, the cause is a good one. It is this: Within the last year she has gained about 5,000 in population, and now has 65,260 people within her corporate limits, and these limits are very small—so small that her suburbs, Oak Cliff and Fairland, are not included. "Keep your eye on Dallas."

Percy T. Carnes, after a stay of two years in New Mexico, comes back to Texas and locates at Italy, and our people are glad to have him return.

F. N. Calvin, as we feared, is to leave our state. He goes to the Far North, and takes up the work in that important city, Milwaukee, Wis. Thus we lose one of our very best men, and we want one as good in return. Calvin is systematic, energetic, polished and strong, both as pastor and preacher, and Milwaukee is to be congratulated.

B. B. Saunders has a fit closing of his work as an independent evangelist in the Terrell meeting. At this meeting there is intense interest and 30 additions, with more to follow. At the close of the meeting he takes the work of corresponding secretary of our state work.

J. W. Lowber is pushing things at Austin. The cornerstone of the new church will have been laid before this is in print. And he has been lecturing to the State University students on the first chapter of Genesis with good results.

John Ferguson has returned from Colorado, and is now at Taylor. He is ready for work either as pastor or evangelist, and our people know him too well for him to be idle very long.

J. B. Boen has received a call to the pastorate of the church at Guthrie, the capital of Oklahoma. We hope he will remain with us. He has been here so long, and has done so much work, that it would seem a little awkward to see him anywhere else. Boen is best known as an evangelist, but he is also a fine pastor.

Our meeting at the Central Church, with S. M. Martin as evangelist, is two weeks old, and seems to be steadily growing. All audiences are good, but those on Sunday are fine. His lectures on Sunday afternoons to men alone and women alone, alternately, are heard by immense crowds; and on Sunday evenings, after our 1,500 seats are filled, with many standing, hundreds are turned away.

M. M. Davis.

833 *Live Oak St., Dallas, Tex.*

A Bit of Dixie.

The General Christian Missionary Convention is over, and although it was even beyond the borders of our center of population, a host of Christian soldiers camped on the old battlefields of historic Chattanooga. Proverbial Tennessee hospitality was shown by our generous Chattanooga, from the mayor down to the ragged urchins, who sang out cheerily, "Times, sir; all about the convention!" We trust the convention impressed on all the ripeness of the Southern fields. Like the broad cotton plantations of Mississippi and Texas, "they are white unto the harvest." The South is a Macedonia calling for Pauls, "Come over and help us or we die."

We, the School of the Evangelists, were well represented at the convention. Our president, Dr. Johnson, and wife, together with twenty students, attended. Several have returned our call and others promised to visit the school later on. Our visitors last week were A. T. Fitts, state evangelist of South Carolina, Dr. Butchart, of China, A. F. Franklin and M. E. Dawson, of Milligan College, Tennessee, and a party of Ohioians. We hope others will visit the school if opportunity permits.

Christians who mean business and want to keep up to date are "conventionists." The progressive, push-ahead spirit permeating these gatherings gives momentum and stimulus for a year's onslought. Anti-ism begets a passiveness that at length stagnates spiritual growth. It builds about itself a Chinese wall of conservatism. It isolates itself from so many of God's blessings, placing them under the ban of "non-apostolic," that we cannot but pity such scriptural blindness. But I am off the subject.

Standing on Point Lookout, my fears kept whispering, "Lookout! Lookout!! Lookout!!!" Beneath was a precipitous fall of hundreds of feet, inviting death and destruction. We as a religious people stand on "point lookout" beneath which stretches out the kingdoms of the earth, all Christ's and ours, if we but make the strategic move; but halt! There yawns the chasm, "beware, Lookout!" One misstep may plunge us down, down, down!

Numbers of Tennessee's faithful preachers were at the convention. Among them we remember seeing A. I. Myhr, state evangelist; J. L. Haddock, traveling evangelist; R. M. Giddens, Paris; J. P. Holmes and J. E. Stewart, Knoxville; Dr. Johnson, Kimberlin Heights; A. R. Moore, Memphis, and of course Bro. Ellis, of Nashville. Let us get ready for Cincinnati next year and make it the Convention of conventions.

George B. Evans.

Kimberlin Heights, Tenn.

OPEN PARLIAMENT ON OUR NATIONAL CONVENTIONS.

The following questions have been sent to several brethren by way of opening the discussion. If others have suggestions let them be brief, as the following are, and to the point:

While the memory of our National Conventions is fresh in your mind will you please answer in about 200 words the following questions for the CHRISTIAN-EVANGELIST:

1. *What changes, if any, would you suggest in the manner of conducting our conventions?*

2. *What suggestions have you to offer as to the Jubilee Convention?*

An early reply will oblige

THE EDITOR.

In answer to your questions in regard to our National Conventions would say, *first* we have too many speeches and too little time for business. Change to one strong, well-prepared address for each half-day and night and give the rest of the time to the proper consideration of important business matters. Instead of giving wise and helpful direction to our national boards we are becoming ratification meetings only.

Second, let our Jubilee Convention become historic by unitizing our great missionary interests. The time has come when our state and national work should be one work; our foreign work should be our home work, the home, the foreign; the woman's work the men's work and the whole work one work. It would be a great blessing and an inspiration to our churches if we could unite all our forces and simplify our missionary machinery. Let the Jubilee Year become the beginning of this greatly desired end. G. A. HOFFMANN.

Columbia, Mo.

---

1. I have no suggestion as to the manner of conducting our missionary conventions.

2. As to the Jubilee Convention I have *two* things to suggest. One is that a whole session should be given to the business men of the convention. Not to handle new themes, however, but to handle the old themes. Let one give a business man's view of Foreign Missions, and another of Home Missions, and a third of Church Extension. Let a fourth tell how all our missionary methods may be improved, and let him criticise freely any faults in prevailing methods. In short, make up the entire program of the session from the ranks of business men, and don't let a single preacher have a word to say, even in pronouncing the benediction! It seems to me that it would be a most unique and helpful feature of the convention. The other suggestion, for the Jubilee Convention, is that two sessions (a morning and an afternoon session) be given to Christian Endeavor, and that the best Endeavor speakers and leaders in the United States, both among our own and other bodies, be engaged to speak. Make the program an *irresistible enticement*. Then run cheap excursions for that day on all the railroads going into Cincinnati, from 50 to 200 miles out, and get 3,000 Endeavor delegates into Music Hall. It can be done. The time is ripe for it. They can go in the morning and return in the evening. And it will be the grandest thing ever done at one of our conventions, to fill 3,000 enthusiastic Endeavorers chock full of zeal for our great work of Home and Foreign Missions. GEORGE DARSIE.

Frankfort, Ky., Nov. 7.

---

1. Our missionary conventions have all along been so ably, wisely and I think efficiently conducted, that I am unable to see wherein they can be improved upon.

2. The Jubilee Convention at Cincinnati will be the greatest event to occur in our religious history. The officers of the American Home Missionary Society, the Foreign Missionary Society, Society of Christian Endeavor, C. W. B. M., Church Extension—*all* organizations should commence at once through the Christian press, by circular and otherwise to awaken a deep interest in every quarter and locality where our membership exists. This work should be reinforced by all the Christian papers, by editorials and otherwise; and all the faithful and energetic Disciples should in season and out of season busy themselves in speaking of and encouraging the membership to increase their contributions and to attend the Jubilee Convention. This should be a recurring fire and kept up constantly to the time of holding the convention; then, these things being done and others which I know will be devised and suggested, the attendance will be immense and it will be indeed the year of jubilee. Yours fraternally, F. M. DRAKE.

As to changes in next year's program:

1. Let a board be organized, composed of an equal number from the three societies, to whom shall be referred several questions which now come to the convention.

2. Let one half-day session be broken into conferences and let as many be called as the various interests among us may demand.

3. Let a part of one afternoon, say from three to six, be given to sight-seeing under proper guides, that the session may not be broken from that cause.

4. At this Jubilee Convention let the best men in the brotherhood be on the program regardless of how lately they were on. But let none be on whose voices can not be heard in music hall (let the women make note).

Plans for a large convention:

1. Take note that Cincinnati is the liveliest place among the Disciples this year. No city is doing more aggressive missionary work than we are now.

2. Push every missionary work as never before.

3. Let the campaign for souls be such that every pastor will indeed become an evangelist.

4. Organize in every city or wherever we have a goodly number of Disciples and begin a campaign for delegates for the Jubilee Convention.

5. Put a speaker on every convention program this year who is awake to the needs of a great convention next year.

6. Let all secretaries and pastors have on their letter heads "Jubilee Convention, Cincinnati, '99, Oct. 12-20. 10,000 delegates; 10,000 souls for Christ; $1,000,000 for missions" (or at least time and place of convention).

7. Let all of our papers keep it constantly before the jubilee and at some time give us a special issue devoted largely to Jubilee Convention.

Brethren, it will be a great convention. Let us all have a part in making it such.

A. M. HARVUOT.

617 *Richmond St., Cincinnati, O.*

---

1. I think there might be a great improvement in our conventions by making the devotional part very pronounced and thorough. Well prepared short addresses on such subjects as Prayer, The Holy Spirit, Consecration, The presence of God, Feeding on the Word, The Spirit of Missions, Waiting on God, The Love of Christ, and so on, by men and women who are themselves full of the Holy Spirit and who speak out of deep and triumphant experiences, as well as according to the Scriptures, would be exceedingly profitable and inspiring. We ought to have the sweetest and most uplifting fellowship possible with our brethren and with our Heavenly Father. The addresses might be followed by earnest and specific prayers and a few choice hymns.

2. As to the Jubilee Convention, I think we should aim to secure a very large attendance, but *more particularly* to so infuse into all who attend the very Spirit of Christ that great fruits will necessarily and spontaneously result. In expecting and attempting great things we must depend upon the closest and fullest communion possible with the great, gracious and wonder-working God of Missions. *Special* prayers for the convention ought to be offered for a week or more preceding its first session. I. J. SPENCER.

Lexington, Ky.

---

1. That so many interests cannot be served best in the length of time given. I think conferences on Education, Benevolence, State Missions, Evangelism S. S. and C. E. work may be treated in separate meetings by those specially interested, but at hours which will not conflict with the business sessions of the missionary societies. I think those who are members of the several associations should have seats together, and in front, during the business sessions.

2. The Jubilee Convention ought to be made an object-lesson, emphasizing the great plea of the Disciples for Christian union, and showing that the Disciples of Christ are in fullest sympathy with the efforts of all other evangelical Christians to bring the whole world to a knowledge of Christ and his salvation, and this can be done by the attendance of multitudes, the reports of large offerings and enthusiastic addresses. The program should be prepared with unusual care and the papers should call frequent attention to it during the entire year. R. MOFFETT.

Cleveland, O., Nov 5.

Complying with your request of the 3rd inst.:

1. I would like to see greater deliberation in passing on important and far-reaching measures. We cannot afford to carry things by hand-clapping, nor in any way give room for the impression that business is being "put through" without time for sober judgment.

2. I think the business ought to be so brought before the brethren as to lead them more and more to feel that these are their affairs, and that they are perfectly competent to form independent judgments as to what they want done, without any effort to formulate their policy for them.

3. I believe our next convention ought to meet in sections for much of the business, only certain features to be presented before the whole convention. If we have as large a convention as I hope to see, this is the only practicable way to handle the business.

4. I believe there ought to be a more strict ruling as to the right to vote; or else let us hold only mass meetings, and not call them conventions of constitutional bodies.

5. Let the Jubilee Convention be made big enough to shake the country.

6. Make it a memorial of the pioneers.

J. H. HARDIN.

Eureka, Ill.

As to changes in our methods, I do not feel that any radical departures are called for. May be the following considerations are of some slight worth:

1. Much of the routine work of our conventions should be done through committees and the time now given to a perfunctory consideration of certain phases of the work be devoted to edifying and inspirational discussions.

2. Some way must be found to secure a larger representation of what we are pleased to term the "laity." Conventions of preachers are not representative. Our business men must be induced to come and both on platform and on committees should have largest place. Systematic and persistent effort must be made to bring our churches as churches, and not simply our preachers, into our convention work.

3. The interests of the convention are too large ever to be sacrificed to local needs. For the present at least central places should be chosen. World-wide interests must never be offered up upon the altar of a neighborhood need.

4. May it not be that biennial rather than annual conventions would accomplish the largest good?

As to our Jubilee Convention, whatever of worth there may be in above suggestions.

GEO. H. COMBS.

Kansas City, Mo.

Notes and News.

Any congregation desiring the services of a young student minister a part of the time at a small compensation is requested to address Box 191, Eureka, Ill.

The church at Burlington, Kan., Park C. Herbert, pastor, has issued a neat annual bulletin of its services, etc.

F. M. Phillips, of Hurricane, Ill, writes that the little band at that place is building a house of worship.

The Golden Jabileee of the Westport Christian Church, Kansas City, Mo., was observed on last Sunday with appropriate and impressive services. Thos. J. Dickson, pastor. About all of the Christian preachers of Kansas City seem to have been present.

The minutes of the 19th annual convention of the Missouri C. W. B. M., held at Nevada, Sept. 27, 28, 1898, are now in pamphlet form for distribution. Address Mrs. Virginia Hedges, Cor. Sec., Warrensburg, for as many copies as you need.

Dedication.

The new church house of the Disciples of Christ at Anita, Ia., will be dedicated Nov. 19th and 20th. The dedicatory sermon will be delivered by A. M. Haggard, Osakloosa. Ministers expected to be present and assist are E. H. Votaw, J. W. Neeley, J. McCauley, Geo. Herrick, ministers of Anita, and and J. T. Spurrier, Massena; W. E. Jones, Cumberland; E. E. Kneedy, Lewis; J. C. McInerry, Exira; J. D. Corbett, Bethel, and R. V. Leeson, Audubon.

First News from Missouri Day.

E. E. Merrill sends word that Troy observed the day and took collection. Simpson Ely, closing a meeting at Mound in Shelby County, observed the day, took up a collection and sent over $2 more than apportionment. Trenton, Plattsburg, Camden Point, Pattonsburg, Linneus, Rutledge, Wyaconda, Steffensville, New Bloomfield and Boydsville have reported. Who next? Missouri missions have the right of way.
T. A. Abbott.
4144 Westminster Place, St. Louis, Mo.

A Pastor Wanted.

I can put a church in correspondence with a pastor desirous of making a change, who is well educated, of excellent ability both as a worker and speaker, and whose wife is a helpmeet indeed, being a splendid musician and soloist. They are young and able to work. Salary, $800.
J. W. Vanderwolker,
Pastor Christian Church.
Sioux City, Ia., Nov. 11, 1898.

Dedication.

The writer was asked to dedicate the church at Mingo, Iowa, last Lord's day. The day was a beautiful one and the people came until many stood upon the outside. The brethren there number only about 30, but are full of zeal, and judging from their works their zeal has been according to knowledge. The building was one purchased from the Methodist people. Three lots were procured and the house moved upon them. It has been repainted on the inside and out, and also nicely papered. Has a seating capacity of more than 200. The money had been raised to meet all indebtedness previous to day of dedication except eight dollars. We asked the people for an offering of $50, and when the collection was taken it amounted to over $60, mostly cash.

The writer was locked out of this same building some three years ago while holding a meeting at Mingo. He was glad, however, to see the ones who were instrumental in the above at the dedicatorial services. The few brethren there are worthy of much credit for the sacrifice they have made to secure for themselves a church home. They expect to soon arrange for a series of meetings, after which they will arrange for regular preaching. Their work in securing the building has been accomplished without the aid of a minister. A consecrated people can accomplish much in the name of the Lord.
D. A. Wickizer.

Our Annual Rally.

November 6th was a great day with the church at this place. It had been set apart as the "Annual Rally Day" for the church. A pastoral letter had been sent to each member calling attention to the rally and urging an attendance. In each one of these letters a blank card was enclosed with the request that each member write his or her name thereon and bring it to the church on that day, when it would be taken up, thus enabling us to know just who were present. The attendance of the membership was the greatest it has been at a service for two years. The offering was the largest ever taken at a single service in the history of the church. We are following the rally with a meeting. Prof. C. E. Millard has charge of the music. The church and its minister are doing the preaching and praying that we may be used of God to his own glory.
W. W. Burks.
Parsons, Kan. Nov. 7' 1898.

Convention at Wayland, Mich.

The semi-annual convention of the third district of the state of Michigan will be held at Wayland, Thursday, Dec. 8th and continuing over Sunday. Every church in the district is requested to send delegates.
W. S. Muir, Sec.

A New Church at Tulip.

It was my pleasure to attend the dedicatory services of the new union church at Tulip, Monroe County, Mo., the last Sunday in October, and to preach the morning sermon and raise the money. It was my first work of this kind, but the money was all raised, and I was not sorry when the strain was over. After a short meeting I organized a church of 26 members. The Presbyterians and Methodists each have organized there. I expect to hold a short meeting for them as a present to the community and the Missouri State Board. The community is a good field for our brethren, and I expect to hear of good work done by our little band.
H. A. Denton.

Kansas District Convention.

The semi-annual district convention of the fifth district will be held at Abilene, Nov. 23-25, 1898. Let each church in the district be represented.
W. S. Lowe.
Manhattan, Kan.

Personal Benefits of the C. W. B. M.

A Christian woman should join the Auxiliary for her own sake, apart from all considerations respecting the advancement of Christ's cause at home or abroad. The benefits accruing from the Auxiliary to herself are neither few nor small. Her service in it will widen her intellectual horizon; it will deepen her spiritual life. She cannot help gaining a better knowledge of the world and its nations; she cannot help but be brought into closer fellowship with Christ. She will learn to pray in secret and in public. She will learn to write and to speak with power. There are thousands of women known to me whose lives have been enriched and ennobled by what they have done to help evangelize the world. If not a soul had been saved or helped through their efforts, the good that has come into their own lives is worth many times what it has cost them in time and thought and money. When, in addition to the cultural value of this relation, we think of the work that has been done by the missionaries, who are sustained by the Woman's Board, and the young men of the universities who have been saved from skepticism and agnosticism and materialism, it will be seen that there are sufficient reasons for uniting with the Auxiliary and working constantly and faithfully in it. The first Sunday in December should witness a great number of recruits.
A. McLean.
Cincinnati, Nov. 11, 1898.

Our Report.

We closed a four years' ministry, one-fourth time, with the church at Brooking, Clinton county, Mo., yesterday. During these years of, to us, pleasant ministry, 97 were added to the little congregation. They are in sympathy with missionary work and at peace among themselves. My successor will find this a pleasant field among whole-souled and sympathetic brethren. We are now open for engagement, part time, or protracted meetings. Address me at St. Joe, Station C.
J. B. Lockhart.
St. Joseph, Mo., Nov. 7, 1898.

Colorado Convention.

The theme of President Grant K. Lewis was "Some Responsibilities of the Churches." Dr. B. B. Tyler spoke on "Have we a Scriptural Eldership." The subject of Elmer W. Cole's address was "The Preacher of To-day—His Opportunities." Leonard G. Thompson delivered an address on "Fishers of Men," while R. B. Preston's theme was "Beginning at Jerusalem." The evening sermon of the second day was delivered by M. L. Streator on "The Coming of the Lord." There was a large number of preachers present. These items are hastily scratched from the Pueblo Chieftain, Nov. 3rd.

Important to Ministers.

THE LAST CALL.

If you don't think that it is important that your name and proper address shall appear in the OFFICIAL list, you need be at no pains to send either name or address for publication, or the twenty-five cents to pay for the magazine. But if you wish to avoid trouble when you apply for your railroad permit for 1899, my advice is that you write me at once, as the list MUST be in the hands of Mr. Caldwell by Dec. 1. This means *you*.

Yours in his name,
T. A. Abbott.
4144 Westminster Place, St. Louis, Mo.

Beloit (Kansas) Notes.

Here is a card received by Bro. O. L. Cook. Its contents give us a sample of the obstacles in the way of co-operation among our churches. From the tyranny of such men may the good Lord deliver our churches! Here is a text for a sermon on ignorance, egotism, prejudice and "bossism." We give the card verbatim, omitting name and place:

——Ks Sept 29

Bro Cook We cant hire the Bro. you sent here A good meny want him but som of us is opesed to him We dont want no preacher thats parts his hare in the midle. RULIN ELDER.

After the Willington convention the editor and his wife spent a week visiting old friends in Wichita. On Sunday, Oct. 9th, we worshiped with the Central Church and participated in the burning of the mortage that for so many years has been a burden to this congregation. The occasion was a happy one and we congratulate the church and its pastor, Bro. Dubber. May the Lord bless them and make his face to shine upon them. We feel great concern for their prosperity and happiness. Nowhere can there be found better, truer people than in the Central Church at Wichita.

Bro. Garner has returned from his trip to Kentucky. In the absence of the pastor he preached for the Beloit church, Oct. 9th. He showed his interest in the Kansas Evangelist by bringing a number of subscribers from Kentucky.

Bro. Drummond, of Smith Center, has been visiting his parents in Enid, O. T. A card just received from him says: "Have been preaching here a week. Three additions by letter and two by baptism."

Sister Hazelrigg writes from Plainville: "I will see that every family takes the paper if possisbe." W. T. HILTON.

Beloit, Kan.

Another Thousand Dollars.

A sister who has a deep interest in Foreign Missions, has just turned over $1,000 to the Foreign Society on the *Annuity plan*. She is well along in years. She will have no care about collecting interest, and will receive her annuity promptly every six months as long as she lives. We commend this plan to the friends of world-wide missions. There ought to be a number more to place money with the Society in this way. For full particulars, address F. M. RAINS, Treas.

Cincinnati, O.

Dedication.

Sunday, Oct. 30th the new house of worship at Shady, Johnson County, Tenn., was dedicated by the writer. There was a large attendance, dinner served on the ground, the necessary money made up and the brethren all happy in their no home. This is a small, young congregation and they are to be congratulated on their success and commended for their zeal and self-sacrificing spirit in the Lord's work. Two additions at Bristol recently. WM. BURLEIGH.

Bristol, Tenn., Nov. 3, 1898.

Convention at Carthage.

The fourth annual convention of the Christian churches of the Springfield district, Mo., will be held at Carthage, Nov. 28, 29 and 30, 1898. A good program has been prepared for this convention.

Come. All preachers in the district are especially requested to attend this convention.

An open parliament on the March offering will be held in connection with this convention.

W. A. OLDHAM, President.

Intensive vs. Extensive Education.

To the small college, after all, is due the credit of most successfully calling out all that is best in our young people. Intensity, thoroughness, individuality, self-reliance and self-assertion on the part of the student are the results thus best attained, while personal attention and the energizing power of the instructor in stimulating and inspiring his pupils is always best effected in small classes. The personal identity of the student is almost entirely lost in large classes where quantity rather than quality is the objective. Animals do not thrive or fare as well in large herds as they do in small companies, and students are intellectual animals, grazing in the fresh pastures of intellectual and moral achievement. This is one reason for the exceptional training and attainments of Bethany graduates. There is no shirking simply because there is no chance to shirk; no game of hide-and-go-seek with the professor, because each one is directly under his eye and has to stand the ordeal of the recitation room, where the question passes around and overtakes him much more frequently than once a week or once a fortnight. He has to run the gauntlet every day in classes large enough for such rivalry and spirit as will put him on his metal and keep his mind alert, while they are not too numerous to drown out his individuality.

There must be something in this kind of training when it produces men that are in demand to fill professorships in the foremost universities of our country, and when you can number them by the scores occupying similar positions in our own colleges and universities.

The intensive method is, in the end, bound to surpass the extensive. Men and women that can command all their abilities, and assert their best selves is what she strives to produce, and the history of Bethany's past shows how well she has succeeded. Could she do this if she were differently situated, or if she sought to be a great university in point of numbers and patronage? I doubt it. To be and to do what she has always sought to be, should still be her mission, and it is the duty of our great brotherhood to fully equip her for it. The start she has made, her history, her splendid traditions, her holy memories and her noble spirit can be reproduced in no other place or age. She is *sui generis*. She looks confidently to the future, as she can with satisfaction contemplate the past.

J. L. DARSIE.

Bethany, W. Va.

Hiram Jubilee Endowment Movement.

The great movement has started in earnest. Names are being collected as rapidly as we could hope for at this stage of the movement. About two hundred additional names appear in this week's issue and we expect these lists in the course of a few weeks to run to 500 or 1,000 per week.

One thing that we appreciate very greatly is the cordial sympathy and support that our colleges are showing. President Hopwood, of Milligan College, in Tennessee, sends us his name to be enrolled in the great Hiram army, President Coler, of the Bible Chair work in Michigan University, sends in his name, Chancellor W. Bayard Craig sends his name with words of approval, and Hiram VanKirk, of the Divinity House of Chicago, sends his name. All seems to recognize the fact that Hiram is not a rival, but simply a co-operative friend with other institutions of learning. We will reciprocate this kindly feeling in every way that we can.

E. V. ZOLLARS, President.

Hiram, O., Nov. 3, 1898.

Our Young People and the Evangelistic Campaign.

The Chattanooga Convention decided to signalize our Jubilee Year by an evangelistic movement all along the line. It seems fitting that while we are planning to increase our offerings for missions, both at home and abroad, there should be also an increase in our personal efforts to bring souls to a saving knowledge of Christ. There ought to be a deep and widespread movement to turn great multitudes to the Lord. There ought to be a great revival of genuine piety and a great deepening of the spiritual life among professed Christians. We need to learn the meaning and the joy and the power of a true consecration to Christ.

All our young people should be enlisted in this movement. Every Christian Endeavor Society should prove itself a great evangelistic force in its own community, and I call on every C. E. Society to *set apart the first Lord's day in December for the prayerful consideration of this matter*. Confer with pastors and church officers, with Sunday-school superintendents and teachers, concerning this matter, and invite them to attend this meeting. With the concurrence and co-operation of others, begin at once to plan for a genuine revival in your own church. Young people are especially favored as soul-winners, and so a special responsibility rests upon them in connection with this evangelistic advance. I put the bugle to my lips and blow a blast, which I hope every Christian Endeavorer among us will hear, calling them to rally and to march in the front ranks of this evangelistic forward movement.

J. Z. TYLER.

Cleveland, O., Nov. 8, 1898.

Educatioaal Conference Tuesday, December 6th, at Moberly.

By order of the Educational Conference, held at Moberly Nov. 1st, I call the attention of the Disciples of Missouri to the fact that there will be an Educational Conference held in the Central Christian Church, Moberly, Mo., Tuesday, December 6th, at 2 P. M., 1898. Every college, church and preacher in the state is urged to realize the importance of this conference and to be present by proper representation. Our educational interests are to be considered, and if possible some definite action taken that will render our educational affairs more efficient. The convention at Nevada, in September, ordered a conference to be held at Moberly, November 1. That conference met there at the time. The attendance being small and the representation being principally from one section of Missouri, the conference ordered another conference, or a reconvening of the same, at the Central Christian Church, Moberly, Mo., Tuesday, 2 P. M., December 6, 1898. It is earnestly hoped that all parts of the state will be represented there. The representation is as follows:

1 vote	to each	congregation of	200 or less.
2 votes	"	"	" 200 to 500.
3 "	"	"	" 500 or more.
2 "	"	college.	
1 vote	"	Missouri preacher in attendance.	

A commiitee of arrangements will announce in our papers about the entertainment.

S. G. CLAY, Secretary.

Fayette, Mo.

The Dedication at Virginia.

On Oct. 30 the new church house at Virginia, Ill., was dedicated. The day was ideal, the audience immense and the services deeply impressive and inspiring. A full-page report of the services, with cut of the old house and the new house and three preachers appeared in the Virginia Gazette, Nov. 4th, from which we gather the following facts. The new house cost $8,445.65:

Through C. W. Savage the building committee reported as follows: The total cost of the building complete, with the lot, was $9,050.00. The cost of the church alone was $8,445.65. Of this sum the insurance on the burned church, the furniture, etc., saved covered $3,159.53, leaving balance to raise of $5,260.12. $2,917.97 had been raised by subscription, etc., leaving $2,368.15, the net balance yet remaining unprovided for. Judge Scofield then took charge of the services in an endeavor to raise this last sum.

The address of Judge C. J. Scofield, at the evening service, was listened to with the deepest interest by the large audience. It is spoken of by many as being one of the strongest ever delivered in the city. His thought was taken from 1 Peter 2:4, 5.

The pulpit at the morning service was occupied by the pastor, G. F. Shields, Hon. C. J. Scofield, of Carthage and Rev. J. F. Humphrey, of the Methodist Episcopal Church and Rev. A. B. Welch, of the Cumberland Presbyterian Church.

Indiana Items.

We hear that L. L. Carpenter, of Wabash, is in a fine meeting in Gas City. The outlook is promising. His meetings are uniformly successful.

W. T. Brooks is conducting a successfu meeting at his home church in Ladoga. The meeting is gathering force each night, and 23 have been added; nine in one evening. C. M. Hughes, of Kentucky, leads the music.

A. M. Hootman is assisting G. W. Ford in a meeting in Poseyville. The Poseyville church is earnest and consecrated, and a good meeting is anticipated.

H. C. Patterson is doing his capable best to get the cause in Seymour in a good condition

been there
or a month
purchase a
nder way

has just
h 29 were
Louisville,
the meet-
fersonville

just com-
rch and it
Buskirk.
rovements
ates with

, has the
ip. It will
angelist T,
old them a

dedicated
flourishing
d-working

weeks ago
Cox is their

he meeting
he Central
entions are
the spirit of
s' conven-
Pritchard,
. K. Jones
diana pul-
community
may they
SCOVILLE.

the pastor-
ast and the
of a pastor,
man. The
education-
With dis-
passer-by
of a work-
We have
ation, but
e find the
ess of our
both con-
s a mining
kly output
in Joplin
last week.
ired.

ch Clerk.

. Bryan, at
tling. The
urces were
over $300.
ematics to
oon go into
ld find one
our hands.
the day for
churches.
the second
e fact that
the whole
of March,
ions; June,
ch Exten-
not simply
te Mission,
allowed to
not taken
he it next

January for this purpose. *One day in the year in all the churches ought to be set apart sacredly for State Missions.* On that day we ought to sing, talk, pray and give for this holy cause. The need is greater to-day than ever before for pushing this work. If we could bring before you all the evidence that we hear of need, urgent need, strong crying need for en-enlarged contributions to this work, we are sure that you would see it in such a way as to move you to assistance as never before. Here's my hand for the greatest year's work we have ever done. "If thy heart is as my heart, give me thine hand."

I am making a tour of the churches in the north part of the state, and I thank God that in every place the brethren are giving me a cordial, hearty welcome. Trenton, Plattsburg, Camden Point, Pattonsburg and Humpherys have already been visited. At the latter place I was snowed out and have to go on to Milan. May God bless the hearts loyal and true who respond so heartily to these appeals. REMEMBER NOVEMBER IS STATE MISSION MONTH.

Yours in his name,

T. A. ABBOTT.

Missouri Bible-school Notes.

The schools at Maryville, Tárkio, Mt. Cabanne and Mound City will introduce home departments immediately, while others are talking it up. Let us go up to Plattsburg next June with good reports of home department work.

The third Sunday in November is to be Children's Day for Home Missions, and while it was the candid judgment of your Bible-school board and last convention that one enthusiastically observed day would result in more funds for both Home and Foreign Missions, yet if you do not think so, do not forget Children's Day for Home Missions, third Sunday in November. Make it a great day.

The afternoons for Bible study under the auspices of the Bible Study Union, of St. Louis, with D. R. Dungan as leader, are seeing the large room in the Holland Building well filled with interested people. This is another indication of the growing interest in the Word of God, with a general desire to understand its teaching. No better selection for teacher could have been made.

Our evangelist, Geo. E. Prewitt, has lately had some experiences that tend to try one in a good work. At Dresden, where he went to help them reorganize their Bible-school he was advised to retrace his steps, as it was useless to undertake such a thing. At Beaman the people gave him their judgment of the situation by remaining at home.

Lexington has just secured a suitable assistant in their work, but even before he came E. M. McCausland remitted their quarterly payment to our Bible-school work, in which he is always interested and to which he always contributes.

Monroe City has grown in zeal and works, during M. J. Nicoson's stay with them, even more than in numbers. The Bible-school under J. T. Hickman is doing better than any other department of the church. The "O. T." (on time) badges are doing good work in bringing all grades more punctually, while the banner for attendance was held by a class of children just in their teens. In their offerings the school is growing, while in general deportment they are in advance of many of the larger schools in the state. One of their teachers, with his family, rides four miles and is always on time. The outlook for the work was never so bright in the history of the church. D. D. Boyle was with them in a meeting and was giving general satisfaction, as he does wherever he labors.

The cards going to our friends this week because of the emergency are made as appeal-ment is made immediately by which at least half of the pledges or apportionments are paid? You have never forsaken the work in the past and I appeal to you for the necessary help at this time. Some of the men are not paid for August, none of them for September nor October. Think of yourselves, brethren, think of your own loved ones, then ask your brethren to labor with us and offerings will come.

At Pleasant Grove, Monroe County, where many happy days' work were given with a people who loved their Master, and with whom this was my first institute, and from first to last the work and co-operation were enjoyable. In the examination on the "Land of the Book," taken from the Normal Instructor, the grades were high. Miss Alice Willis is superintendent, while her assistants were faithfully laboring to enable the school to do the best work for Christ. The only trouble at the Grove is neglect on the part of so many of the older members of the church. W. G. Surber, by ratification of the offiial action of the board, will be retained another year, all testifying to his efficient work. One cloud of apprehension from one of the workers of the church, a daughter of my dear old friend, J. R. Reavis, hung like a pall over every service, and our every prayer was that Israel's God would spare her to the church and home.

Rosendale, the home of our country Bible-school superintendent, Alvah Pettijohn, joins us in this work for Christ.

Louisiana, E. B. Rule superintendent, sends one half their apportionment promptly, and always will while E. J. Lampton is pastor.

Children's Day for Home Missions, third Sunday in November, ought to be a great day for the children in behalf of the gospel in the destitute parts of the United States.

F. L. Moore is giving all his time to the work at Fredericktown, with the understanding that the congregation is to allow him to help the struggling band at Marquand on the third Sunday night and the Monday night following in each month, and by this arrangement the little company at Marquand is getting stronger in numbers and faith.

The church at Dexter, years ago, met in a small one-room house, with room to spare, but now have a modern commodious building, with preaching every Lord's day, by E. E. Davidson, whose work is such that he has been called for another year.

No man in all this country is doing more gratuitous work than A. F. Holden, who labors one-half time at Charleston and one-fourth each at Marble Hill and Bertrand. Bro. Holden gave one-fonrth time last year to the church at Morley, for which he received twenty-three dollars.

Geo. F. McGee, who gives all his time to Poplar Bluff, also has arrangements by which he gives the Cedar Valley Church Sunday afternoon meetings, hoping thus to revive them again.

Eugene Burr, DeLassus, is preaching for Farmington, Silver Point, Flat River and Doe Run, much of it being a labor of love, for which God only compensates.

Reuben Taylor, Anniston, has just closed a meeting at Blodgett, organizing a congregation of twenty-four members, in a house built by others but turned over to us on the condition that our brethren would complete the same.

A. M. Harroll is giving all his time to the congregations at Piedmont and Mill Spring. But like the other watchmen of Zion in that territory he will help many of the weaker churches during his year's labors with the home churches. No class of men in the state are doing more purely mission work than the preachers of extreme South Missouri.

W. W. Harris, Cape Girardeau, also holds up the work at Jackson, the county seat.

Evangelistic.

TEXAS.

Ballinger.—There were two additions to our membership on the 6th, inst.; one young lady reclaimed and one made the good confession. We had large attendance at both morning and evening services. Our little church has completed a parsonage and the preacher and family will enjoy the pleasures of a nice new home. God be with you.—HENRY A. MAJOR.

KANSAS.

Pawnee Rock, Nov. 1.—Just closed a good meeting with 32 additions; 21 by confession and baptism and 11 by statement. The meeting was the result of a great spiritual awakening among our members.—CHAS. D. PURLEE, Evangelist, ELLIS PURLEE, Pastor.

Howard, Nov. 11. — Meeting closed at Cresco Wednesday evening. Ten days, 16 additions. Two confessions last night.—R. E. ROSENSTEIN.

Pawnee Rock, Nov. 1.—Just closed a good meeting with 32 additions; 21 by confession and baptism and 11 by statement. The meeting was the result of a great spiritual awakening among our members. Chas. D. Purlee, evangelist.—ELLIS PURLEE, pastor.

IOWA.

Dysart, Nov. 7.—Tabernacle meeting here is progressing nicely. Every corner was jammed and packed last night, and a good interest manifested. — WRIGHT AND MARTINDALE.

Irwin, Nov. 7.—We are in a meeting with our pastor, D. H. Bays, doing the preaching and presenting to us some most wholesome truths. Attendance large and good interest manifested. We expect the singing evangelist, Bro. Frank McVey, of Concordia, Kan., here in a few days to labor with us, and think we will have a grand meeting.—W. A. LESSENGER.

ARKANSAS.

Fayettville, Nov. 7.—There were three additions to the First Church last Sunday, one confession and two by letter.—N. M. RAGLAND.

Bald Knob, Nov. 9.—Seventeen additions, 16 baptisms at Harbor Schoolhouse three miles west of here. One-fourth the writer's time will be devoted to the cause at that place the coming year. Forty-eight young converts to be trained in the Master's service in this town and community around gives us pleasure and work.—M. A. SMITH.

UTAH.

Salt Lake City, Nov. 8.—Three added here since last report; one baptized and two by letter.—W. H. BAGBY.

KENTUCKY.

Stanford, Nov. 8.—There were 36 additions in our meeting, which is considered one of the best in every respect held here. We made no mistake in calling Bro. H. A. Northcutt to do the preaching, which he did most acceptably for nearly four weeks. Our success is no small compensation for missing the Chattanooga Convention.—FRANK W. ALLEN.

Stanford, Nov. 4.—We closed our meeting here last night with 37 additions. F. W. Allen is doing a fine work.—H. A. NORTHCUTT.

Russellville, Nov. 12.—Am in a splendid meeting here. Large audiences, deep interest. Nine accessions to date by confession. A. M. Growden, evangelist.—W. B. WRIGHT, pastor.

MISSOURI.

Canton, Nov. 5.—There have been nine added here during the month of October. The church seems to be taking on new life.—D. ERRETT.

Sheridan, Nov. 11.—Our meeting here is booming; 163 additions, six last night. T. W. Cottingham, district evangelist.—E. E. LOWE, pastor.

De Lassus, Nov. 9.—Three additions to the church at Flat River, Sunday; two from the United Brethren and one by baptism. Will begin a meeting this week.—EUGENE BURR.

Frankfort, Nov. 12.—Our meeting closed with five baptized and the church greatly blessed and edified. The preaching was begun by myself, but in a few days Bro. E. J. Lampton came to our rescue and gave us a series of grand discourses. He has few equals as a teacher of the Word. He preaches the pure gospel. For six years he has been at Louisiana and is greatly beloved by all. Jno. B. Corwine is now in a meeting there with him.—RAYTON S. BROOKS.

ILLINOIS.

Emden, Nov. 7.—Elder Evans, of Chrisman, has just closed a successful meeting at this place, resulting in 14 additions to the church, eight confessions and six reclaimed. The church was thoroughly aroused. Elder T T. Holton, pastor, assisted in the meeting. Elder Evans is a fearless expounder of the truth, and his great zeal in the cause of the Master, his great, loving heart filled with a longing desire to win souls to Christ, has won the confidence of the church at this place, and they unitedly wish him Godspeed in the great work of the ministry, and cheerfully commend him to the brethren in Christ who are in need of an evangelist. E. L. C.

Windsor, Nov. 8.—Closed a 10 days' meeting at the Smyser Church in Moultrie County last night; eight baptized and one by commendation. The church is doing excellent work under the regular ministry of W. S. Hermon, of Bethany. W. H. Waggoner, of Eureka, will follow the meeting with a Bible institute.
A. H. HARRELL.

Milford, Nov. 8.—Our work is progressing nicely at this place. The church and pastor have just closed a meeting with 16 accessions to the church. Others expected to follow soon. We hope to keep up the evangelistic spirit in our work. J. B. WRIGHT.

L. H. McCoy reports "two added lately by baptism, one at Pleasant Grove and one at Golden Gate." L. H. McCoy changes from Albion, Ill., to Flora, Ill.

Peoria, Nov. 8.—Marion Stevenson, pastor of the Edwards Street Christian Church, Decatur, Ill., is assisting J. P. McKnight, pastor of the Central Christian Church of Peoria, Ill., in a meeting. The meeting is just begun, but the present interest gives promise of a good meeting. J. P. MCKNIGHT.

Blandinsville, Nov. 7.—Two more additions to the Old Bedford Church. A. R. ADAMS.

PENNSYLVANIA.

Gipsy, Nov. 7.—Fourteen additions to date in a meeting of 12 days. 12 by obedience. Two restored. Eight at one meeting. We continue for a few days. Bro. Saum aad myself are doing the preaching.—C. E. SMITH.

INDIANA.

Franklin, Nov. 7.—Three were added yesterday. Two were buried with Christ in baptism; and one by letter.—WILLIS M. CUNNINGHAM.

Crawfordsville, Nov. 7.—Fifteen confessions at Scott's Prairie. Eight confessions and seven by relation at Waynetown. Meetiug still in progress.—A. L. CRUM.

Ladoga, Nov. 5.—Our meeting here closed last night with 23 additions; 19 by confession and baptism. This makes 45 additions to our membership in 10 months' work. One recent convert was a man 84 years old.—W. T. BROOKS.

KANSAS.

Agra.—Twelve days; 34 additions to date.—WILKISON & SLACK.

We are in a fine meeting at Fontana. If you want a good meeting write us here.—INGELS & ROUTH.

Atchison, Nov. 7.—Yesterday was a great day at the First Church in this city. Overflowing audiences. The Holy One present with power. Four added by letter and two by confession of faith.—W. S. P.

The Religious World.

The Y. M. C. A. of the University of Missouri is a valuable aid to its students who have to work their way through school. A committee canvasses the town of Columbia for work in their behalf. This association, President Jesse says, has a prayer-meeting every morning just before the regular University chapel service and one every Sunday afternoon. At the beginning of the session, when students are pouring in, every train is met by members of the association to help the new students to enter without inconvenience, to secure boarding-places, and where they need it to secure work. In many institutions the new students are met by hazing parties. In the State University there is no hazing, but the new student is met by a committee of Christian gentlemen that volunteer aid in making him happy in his new home.

The ninth annual conference of the Railroad Department of the Young Men's Christian Associations was held at Fort Wayne, Ind., October 20-23. More than 600 railroad delegates were present. All the meetings were largely attended and the gathering was one of the most spiritual conferences the associations have ever held. Strong indorsements of the work of the Railroad Department were presented by prominent officials from all parts of the country. The Railroad Department now has 130 associations, employing 145 secretaries and owning or using 51 buildings designed especially for their work, valued at nearly $800,000. In all of these buildings are reading rooms, libraries and other appliances common to Young Men's Christian Associations and in many of them lunch rooms and sleeping apartments. During the year an active evangelistic effort has been made in connection with the railroad associations, and large numbers of railroad men have been converted. It is a thoroughly practical as well as a spiritual work.

Tolstoy Fund.

Count Leo Tolstoy, whose seventieth birthday has recently been celebrated, writes to a correspondent in this country urging the raising of funds to aid in the emigration of the oppressed Doukhobortsi. These people—thrifty, industrious farmers, some ten thousand in number—form a Protestant sect whose tenets resemble those of the Quakers. Their only offense is their refusal from conscientious scruples to serve in the Russian army. For this reason they have been repeatedly exiled from one part of the empire to another, and so persecuted and maltreated by the government officials that their position in their own country has become intolerable. With much difficulty they have obtained permission to emigrate to foreign lands, and steps have been taken to settle them, temporarily at least, in the Island of Cyprus, but it is hoped that they may eventually reach America. There is urgent need of funds to enable them to take advantage of the privilege to emigrate which has been accorded to them. A committee has already been formed in London to raise money for this purpose, and the undersigned have been constituted a committee to co-operate with them in America. It seems appropriate that such money as is collected should be offered to the Doukhobortsi through Count Tolstoy, and that in honor of the seventieth anniversary of his birth it should be called the Tolstoy Fund. This cause lies close to the heart of the distinguished Russian and nothing could give him greater joy than its success. We appeal to all of our fellowcitizens who believe in liberty—in the freedom of man to abstain from taking up arms against his brother-man—to contribute as they may be able to this worthy object. Contributions in any amount may be sent to Isaac N. Seligman, Esq., Treasurer of the Committee, Mills Building, New York.

WILLIAM DEAN HOWELLS, New York;
JANE ADDAMS, Hull House, Chicago;
WILLIAM LLOYD GARRISON, Boston;
GEORGE DANA BOARDMAN, D. D. Phila.;
N. O. NELSON, St. Louis;
BOLTON HALL, New York;
ERNEST H. CROSBY, New York,
Committee.

New York, Oct. 25th, 1898.

Family Circle.

Praise the Giver!

EDWARD ORVILLE SHARPE.

I.

For the festival of glory.
In creation's ancient story,
When the morning stars were singing,
And those godlike voices ringing,
Told of wise and blessed power,
Loading earth with wondrous dower;
Bending bough and harvest golden
Ripening in Eden olden;
For such heritage of beauty,
Render love and praise and duty.

II.

For the heroes rare and saintly
Garbed and mannered all so quaintly;
Children they in faith and feeling,
Wayward oft, yet oft revealing
Tender hearts for heavenly trusting,
Wooed and won from earthly lusting;
For their praying and their toiling
Under burdens and reviling;
Men were they in mighty measure,
Rich are we in their soul-treasure;
While time flows to the Forever,
For such gifts O! praise the Giver.

III.

For the gift within the manger,
Rays of love and shades of danger;
Trace the way his feet have trodden,
Mark the soil his blood hath sodden,
Stand beside that flood of passion,
Crossed by none in such a fashion:
Since the tomb that tells the story
Of his conquest and his glory,
We may praise with hearts a-quiver,
For his throne and home forever.

IV.

For the message that is given
To all creatures under heaven;
Great the honor in its bearing
Through the world with faith unfearing,
Till mankind shall own its Master,
And shall wake to issues vaster:
For the victors gone before us,
And the triumph coming for us,
To our God be all praise given,
Here on earth and there in heaven!

Le Roy, Ill.

Farmer Truesdall's Thanksgiving.

BY THE EDITOR.

"Corn Holler" will not be found in the list of popular resorts. Its fame is purely local. It has no great scenic attractions, and it is a little off from the railroad and many miles removed from the hurry and bustle of city life. But the quiet beauty of the valley, hedged in by almost parallel lines of hills or low mountain ranges, has a charm all its own. Its rich soil made it famous in that part of the state for the yield of corn or Indian maize, which gave the valley its local designation as "Corn Holler." In addition to this, however, the valley produces an abundance of all manner of fruits and vegetables, which made its humble homes the abode of plenty.

Among the comfortable, well-to-do farmers living in "Corn Holler" was Samuel Truesdall, known familiarly as "Uncle Sam." His comfortable one-story house, with its cellar and a kitchen which had been added to the south side to meet the growing demands of the family, sat perched on the sloping hillside, surrounded by a picket fence and overlooking the farm and a good section of the valley. Samuel Truesdall's father had migrated from Kentucky to Missouri while the state was yet young and the country new, and had been attracted to this valley by the fertility of its soil, by the luxuriant forests of splendid trees that crowned the hills, and by a never-failing spring of pure water which gushed from the hillside. The elder Truesdall had long since been gathered to his fathers, and Samuel had fallen heir to the old homestead.

Twenty-five years had elapsed since Samuel Truesdall had led to his homestead his young bride, Elizabeth Langston, the daughter of a neighboring farmer. They had attended the same country school, where they had spelled together in the spelling matches, and had sung together in the old-fashioned singing schools of those early days. They had met at house-raisings and corn-huskings, when the men would come together to help each other, and the women to visit and quilt and perhaps to gossip in a harmless way. In addition to these opportunities for a mutual acquaintance and love-making, Samuel and Elizabeth had attended Sunday-school and church in the country meeting house, located in a grove not far from the spring above mentioned. In this plain church building some plain, honest country people met to worship God and to hear a plain man preach the simple gospel. The church was sometimes spoken of as a "Campbellite Church," in those rude times, but the people who worshiped there called themselves Christians, or Disciples of Christ. The elder Truesdall had brought with him from Kentucky the principles of the Reformation, which he had heard urged there by such men as Barton W. Stone, John A. Gano, John T. Johnson and others, and had become the leader in the church at "Corn Holler." Here Samuel and Elizabeth often went together, and here in their youthful years, each had confessed faith in Jesus Christ and had taken Him as Savior, Pattern and Guide.

Under these conditions it is not strange that their lives ran closer together until they were united in holy wedlock. By the aid of this simple faith they had led a peaceful, happy life, content with their lot, loving their neighbors and being loved and respected by them. Two children had blessed their home, a son and a daughter. The eldest was a daughter, Miranda, and she was still with them and was teaching the neighboring school. George Truesdall, the junior member of the family, though only in his twentieth year, had enlisted in the army when the first call for volunteers in the war with Spain had been made. The regiment to which he had belonged had been encamped at Chickamauga for some time, but word had been received from George that the regiment was being discharged, and that he expected to return home for Thanksgiving.

It was no wonder that the Truesdall homestead was astir earlier than usual on the day preceding Thanksgiving. Aunt Betty's face assumed something of its old-time color as she said to her husband that morning, "Do you remember, dear, that to-morrow is the 25th anniversary of our marriage?"

"I reckon I have not forgotten that we were spliced on Thanksgiving Day," replied Uncle Samuel; "but really, I didn't think it had been so long ago as that."

"Well, it has," said Aunt Betty, "and besides that, you know George is coming home to-morrow from the war to stay with us."

Uncle Samuel was quiet for a moment, and his eyes were moist with tears as his memory ran back over the years since he had with pride led pretty Lizzie Langston to his home as his young bride. And then the thought that George, their only boy, their brave soldier boy, was coming home, filled his heart too full for utterance. After a moment's silence, however, he said: "Well wife, I reckon we have got a good deal to be thankful for, and if you and Miranda say so we'll have such a Thanksgiving dinner to-morrow as George has never seen."

Aunt Betty and Miranda readily acceded to the proposition and signified their willingness to do their part in welcoming George home with a royal feast, and making the silver wedding a memorable occasion.

It was agreed that Uncle Sam should invade the barnyard and slay a sufficient number of fowls, including a large turkey that had been saved and fattened for the occasion, to meet all the demands of the feast, and that Miranda should send word around to a few of the young people to come in and meet George and welcome him home. And so the day before Thanksgiving was a busy day in the Truesdall homestead. Aunt Betty and Miranda found all they could do in those numerous preparations which thrifty housekeepers know so well how to make for such an occasion. While the women were engaged with these preparations, Farmer Truesdall, having beheaded the turkey and chickens and prepared the wood for the fire, strolled into the woods near by, but recently glorious in their autumnal tints, and gathered leaves and boughs of sumach with which to decorate the house. This done, he moved uneasily about the place, and was seen to cast frequent glances up the road that ran over the hill to Grantville, the nearest railroad station.

George had written his father that as he was not certain of the train he would arrive on he would come home on the Jonesville stage that ran in connection with the train in carrying mail and passengers between these two points. About five o'clock in the afternoon the stage coach came in view over the hill, and all eyes were fastened upon it to see if George were among the passengers. They were not long in suspense, for they soon saw a white handkerchief waving from the stage, and they readily divined that it was the signal of their soldier boy, Sergeant George Truesdall. Before the stage driver had brought his coach to a full stop George sprang from his seat to embrace the family that had met him at the gate. He was clothed in his soldier's uniform, with three stripes on his arms which marked his rank of sergeant. His face was tanned, and he looked the picture of robust health and manliness as he greeted his father and mother and sister, who joyfully welcomed him home again. As they passed down the walk together George cast glances hither and thither at familiar objects and scenes, and remarked, "After all, there is no place like home, and no neighborhood that is quite equal to 'Corn Holler.'" No sooner had he passed into the house than he saw evidences that unusual preparations were being made for Thanksgiving. "Mother," said George, "it looks as if you and Miranda were expecting company."

The Day Before Thanksgiving

or, The First Call for Volunteers.

By Robt C. Marquis.

I

is the day
before
nksgivin,
n old
n Holler
Aunt Betty
er knittin'-
nda-from the cellar
ood old
ner Truesdall
neat ax in his hand
n' toward the
block to view
atriot band
ster in the raw recruit,
Thanksgivin' Day
own boy that volunteered,
in' home to stay.

II

He turned around and saw a sight but few of us are used ter-
A comin' full tilt right down his tracks was the old bob-tailed rooster,
"I knew you'd be the first," said he, "But bless me what a crowd
Of turkeys, calves, pigs, lambs, ducks, geese, and even that peacock proud."
"I s'pose you'd be a brigadier, or maybe a commodore,
You're mighty good on dress parade, for eatin' mighty poor."

III

ur chest expansion's very fine, T. Gobblers is still better,
s back and front are quite in line, He'll never show white feather"
ou are enlisted, Gobbler, Sir, report at ten for duty,
l for the battle come prepared, "Miranda he's a beauty,"
table next day creaked and groaned 'neath that 'ere turkey gobbler,
And cakes and pies and puddings, and delicious apple cobbler.

a farmer, and that the crops had been especially fine in "Corn Holler," and he accompanied his son on his tour of inspection over the place.

The horses neighed a welcome to George, as he patted them lovingly on their necks, and even the cows and the pigs and the fowls seemed to recognize the presence of a familiar friend.

George surveyed the full barns and other signs of material prosperity with a good deal of pleasure, and slyly remarked to his father, that he was glad to know that he was able to get along so well without his assistance, as he had thought a little of beginning life on his own account. While looking at some of the fat porkers and fowls, George remarked that if he had had some of them at Chickamauga during the encampment there they would have been highly appreciated. At this point the supper-bell called them in to the evening meal, and it was a happy group that gathered around the table, a reunited family once more. George told of his experience in the army, intermingled with which were frequent expressions of appreciation of his mother's cooking. Plans for the morrow were also discussed during and after supper until bedtime.

It was during this conversation that the father repeated George's remark in the barn as to his thinking of beginning life for himself, and said he supposed it was merely a joke, as George was too young to think of marrying.

Miranda said she knew there had been a good deal of correspondence going on between George and his sweetheart, but she did not think the crisis was very near at hand; "besides," she added, "George, you must remember that I am older than you and my turn comes first."

"As to that, Miranda," said George, "if you can afford to turn down a young man like that dude drummer from St. Louis, you must not hold me responsible for leaving you behind in single blessedness." They all laughed at that good-natured sally, and George, looking more soberly, proceeded: "Yes, I may as well say to you that I have been corresponding a good deal with Myrtle during my absence in the army, and while it has been our purpose for some time to marry, we had not thought of fixing the date so early until within the last few weeks. In thinking over my return home on Thanksgiving day, and remembering that it was father's and mother's 'silver wedding,' I wrote Myrtle, suggesting that it would be very nice if we should marry on the 25th anniversary of my father's and mother's marriage. She thought this was short notice, but finally yielded her objections, and so it was decided that we would have an informal wedding. I understand we are to have services to-morrow at the church, and Bro. Wright has been notified that at the close of the service he is expected to pronounce the words that will make us husband and wife."

At this announcement, to which the family listened with open-eyed wonder, there were exclamtions of surprise, and Miranda went so far as to say that she thought he was "real mean" in not letting them know beforehand.

In explanation George said it was their purpose at first to give them a complete surprise, not letting any one but the minister know it until the close of the service, when the announcement would be made; but on reflection they had decided to let their families know the evening before in order that they may have on the "wedding garments."

Miranda replied, pettishly, that she had no "wedding garments," and she didn't know that she would attend the wedding; but said it in such a way as to mean that nothing could keep her away.

Uncle Sammy looked thoughtfully into the fire and said nothing.

Aunt Betty observed, with a sigh, "Of course, George, we hoped to have you with us a good while yet, but then you will not be going far away, and I can only hope that you and Myrtle may live as happily together as your father and I have these twenty-five years."

There was unusual tenderness and emotion in Uncle Sam's prayer that night before they retired.

At eleven o'clock the next day the whole neighborhood had gathered at the "Corn Holler" country church for the Thanksgiving service. A number of soldier boys had returned home, and it was noised around that there would be a sort of reunion of these and a good patriotic discourse by Elder Wright. After some special music Bro. Wright preached a very earnest discourse, in which he pointed out the reasons for thanksgiving, dwelling particularly upon the manifestations of divine favor during the late war with Spain, and upon the fact that a number of our own young men who responded to their country's call had returned safely to their homes. A song followed the sermon, during which the congregation arose. At the close the preacher asked the people to be seated, and said he had a very pleasant duty to perform before pronouncing the benediction. "One of our young friends," he remarked, "who left our community at the call of his country, has returned home and has decided to signalize his entrance once more upon the duties of civil life by forming a partnership for life with one of our esteemed young ladies in the neighborhood. Both of them are known to you all, and are esteemed by you all as most worthy members of this congregation." The closest attention was now given, and every eye was riveted upon the preacher. "The parties I refer to," the preacher went on to say, "are Mr. George Truesdall and Miss Myrtle Amesbury." At this announcement there was an audible expression of surprise and of gratification in the audience. The young couple were asked to come forward, and standing in front of the pulpit the preacher, in a few solemn words, pronounced them husband and wife, closing with an earnest prayer and benediction.

ι immediate rush to the front
., and greetings and con-
ι the happy pair were con-
ıe time. Aunt Betty, who
ng the first to extend her
lly remarked that it was
e hastening home, as the
dinner, which had been put
ι special cook for the day,
readiness for them. Elder
ıe Amesburys, and a few of
ys, and a number of other
.e on horseback and some in
heir way to Farmer Trues-
ıke of a bounteous repast
serve the double purpose
ving dinner and a wedding

ıd been lengthened out for
ıd it was a merry party that
nd it to partake of its
y were the sallies of wit and
ι back and forth while they
the dinner, and the unani-
was that no better Thanks-
had ever been spread in
than this one, and that no
al ever gathered than that
nbled at Farmer Truesdall's
g day to welcome home the
to celebrate Uncle Sam's
y's "silver wedding" and
f Sargeant Truesdall and
ry.

ttle of the Heart.

CE PEARL BRONAUGH.

ɔn the fields of war
ıave been won.
ıt battles rage afar
ɔf shell or gun!

rs amid the dead
d manly part;
ife must wage with dread
the heart.

ıd feels it just
ɔ prove;
; a woman must—
of her love.

ɔhes to the scene
may be wrought;
llows, close and keen,
ırch of thought.

is far less drear
r faith must cross;
ss a thing to fear
ess and loss!

lds the path he treads
ırk with fears,
ι of blood he sheds
thousand tears!

'atches with the brave,
ey may be,
ɔothe if not to save,
land or sea—

lent heart which fights
r with woe,
the hand which smites
ıf the foe.

whose feet must roam
dier's part!
ho fights at home
the heart!

God's Promises.

WILL H. DIXON.

Tho' the grass of the field may wither away,
And the earth's brightest flowers may crumble to dust,
And tho' all things on earth are passing away,
In God's blessed promises still may we trust.

O'er the week of all time His Word stands sublime.
Tho' its truthfulness many foes may assail,
Yet His Word shall stand fast tho' all may combine;
His blessed promises never can fail.

Tho' the earth and the heavens all pass away,
His Word shall forever and ever endure;
And tho' man's words and work shall pass to decay,
God's blessed promises forever are sure.

Rock Island, Ill., October, 1898.

Our First Thanksgiving.

BY ALICE CURTIS MOYER.

"The breaking waves dashed high
On a stern and rock-bound coast,
And the woods against a stormy sky
Their giant branches tossed;
And the heavy night hung dark
The hills and waters o'er,
When a band of exiles moored their bark
On the wild New England shore."

'Twas the following spring, 277 years ago—the gloomiest period in American history. Half the little "band of exiles" had died, among them being John Carver, their governor, and Rose Standish, the beautiful young wife of Capt. Standish, afterwards the wooer of Priscilla as told by Longfellow.

The winter had been one of intense suffering, and the spring had brought but little relief. But, undaunted, these Pilgrims, though weak and gaunt from hunger, cleared fields and planted corn, using every endeavor to make better the future. The graves of loved ones were included in the fields, that the Indians, of whom they lived in constant fear, might not discover how many of their number had succumbed.

Upon a certain morning of this desolate spring a sweet-faced Puritan maid stood in a cabin doorway, shading her eyes with her hand. Presently, espying a familiar form in the distance, she walked down the path in its direction. Seeing who it was that had come out to meet him, handsome John Chenoweth hastened forward and laid

"See how favored I have been, my love," said he, "though I went a long way. But why so sad? Do the mother and little sister still hunger? Did not the boy return shortly after we left—three days ago—with the clams and lobsters we procured while the tide was out? And yesterday, I sent you some birds; while to-day I return with as fine venison as the Plymouth regions can boast. Cheer up, my Agatha! As long as John Chenoweth is in possession of his two strong arms, a willing spirit and a warm heart that beats but for you, my loved one, you need have no fear." And he bared his head, taking in his own, the hand of the maiden before him.

"None realize more than I that what you say is true, John," replied she. "What should we have done during the long, hard winter but for you? My loved ones, however, will hunger no more; sufferings cannot now molest them."

"Then they are—"

"Yes; they passed peacefully away near the midnight hour of your first day of absence. The little one first, dear mother soon following. Last eve at sunset they were laid away just inside your field."

"My poor Agatha!"

"Nay, John! Do not pity me, unless because I could not go with them. Let us rather rejoice that they, at least, are out of sorrow's reach."

"I do rejoice for them, love. My regret is in your loneliness; but I cannot sorrow because you were not with them. I do so long, selfishly perhaps, to keep my Agatha on earth. My constant prayer throughout all has been that you might be spared. But I do not wonder that you do not care to live. These hardships are hard even for strong men to bear; so what must it be for women and tender little ones. If I could but shield you from it all!"

And heedless of the fact that they were in sight of the cabins, the Puritan maid was folded in the arms of her lover; and despite her belief that all great joy was sinful and must be attoned for, Agatha laid her head on John's broad shoulder, saying:

"Forgive me if I spoke repiningly. It was only becouse of the great emptiness that seemed to come to me when I kissed dear mother's lips. Feeling their marble

speak gentle words of sympathy and counsel. Far be it from me to shrink from any hardship. Did we not come here for conscience sake? With the shelter of your love I am content with my life on earth; and concerning the life to come I trust in God, the Father of all."

"Thank you, dear one. You say well. Rest assured, there are better times ahead. If faith and patience do not forsake us, neither will we be forsaken of God."

The deer was again placed upon the shoulder of the hunter, and side by side the lover went up the path, when suddenly they became aware that something unusual was going on—something exciting.

Hurrying forward, they soon joined their neighbors and became as excited as they, for Samoset had spoken his greeting of "Welcome" in English, and with the help of Squanto,* who acted as intrepreter, the Pilgrims were made to understand that a band of the dreaded Indians had come to make them a friendly visit. They were heartily received by the colonists, so devoutly thankful were they that their red neighbors had come in peace.

They had but little to offer them, and scant indeed would have been the fare, had not the Indians contributed to the feast by going into the wood and killing a number of deer.

It cannot be doubted that the fathers and mothers of this great republic were glad to join in what was not only the first Thanksgiving, but also the first American barbecue.

There were no religious observances, but there were games and pastimes. The feast lasted about a week and the "sad-faced Puritan women" and the squaws did the cooking. The treaty made with Massasoit, the chief, lasted for fifty years.

We have no authentic history for it, but doubtless John Chenoweth offered his deer as his part of the feast, and we can imagine with what zeal he joined in the games with the Indians, while his sweetheart, putting aside her grief, no doubt assisted with the cooking, for they had little time to grieve —had these earnest, sober-minded Pilgrims—and we have every reason to believe that the marriage solemnized on the last day of the feast had, for its contracting parties, John Chenoweth and Agatha Manning.

The influence of this people has been felt in every state. "Trusting to God to shape their destinies," resolving to brave all danger and any hardship, they had come to seek a home in the wilderness for the sake of conscience.

Two years after this "first Thanksgiving," the first religious Thanksgiving was held in the month of July. There had been a long drouth and nine hours of fasting and prayer was ordered. While they prayed, rain fell, and fasting gave place to thanksgiving.

Thanksgiving, however, was a long time being established as a holiday. For a long time its date was uncertain and neither did it always come on Thursday. Finally, however, there was a succession of good crops and the people wanted to give thanks; therefore, the fall of the year came to be Thanksgiving time, and then November came to be the month.

And thus it is that our national home holiday came about—growing out of small beginnings. The first Thanksgiving proclamation was issued in 1667, and now we all hasten to obey them, for we always have something to be thankful for. This is our great home-gathering holiday. Men will travel many miles to be with their families on that day. It is a time for family reunion; a time for both smiles and tears. It is the embodiment of the national idea, that "God is good" and "*his mercey endureth forever.*"

*An Indian who had been to England with Hunt in 1614.

Short Stories.

"Does this car go far as One Minute Street?" asked a passenger on a Market Street trolly. "Never heard of it," replied the conductor. "Well, then, Sixty-second Street," smiled the passenger. And the conductor coughed and said: "That's hour terminus.—*Philadelphia NorthAmerican.*

"Do you think it would be wrong for me to learn the noble art of self-defense?" a religiously-inclined young man inquired of his pastor.

"Certainly not," answered the minister. "I learnt it in youth myself, and I have found it of great value during my life."

"Indeed, sir! did you learn the old English system, or Sullivan's system?"

"Neither. I learned Solomon's system."

"Solomon's system?"

"Yes: you will find it laid down in the first verse of the fifteenth chapter of Proverbs: 'A soft answer turneth away wrath.' It is the best system of self-defense of which I know."—*Journal and Messenger.*

A great many foolish blunders are laid at the door of the negro preacher, many of them imaginary. The following is good enough to be true. It is said that an old colored man in reading a well-known hymn which contained the line, "Judge not the Lord by feeble sense," mistook "sense" for "saints," and gave this odd version, "Judge not the Lord by feeble saints." What a pity that people will judge the Lord by feeble saints! To what misconception and unhappy feelings it leads.—*The Evangel.*

A rich landlord once cruelly oppressed a poor widow. Her son, a little boy of eight years, witnessed it. He afterwards became a painter, and painted a life-likeness of the dark scene. Years afterwards he placed it where the man saw it. He turned pale, trembled in every joint, and offered a large sum to purchase it, that he might put it out of sight. Thus there is an invisible painter drawing on the canvas of the soul a life-likeness reflecting correctly all the passion, and actions of our spiritual history on earth. Eternity will reveal them to every man. We must meet our earth-life again, whether it has been good or evil.—*Christian Leader.*

"I understand that you were writing a book on the 'Beauties of Child-life.' Why did you never publish it?"

"Oh, our twins were born while I was writing the last chapter."

Young Doctor—My dear sir, you have a pronounced case of neurasthenia of the orbicularis palpebrarium.

Flynn—Pronounced, did yez say? Shure, an' I call it unpronounceable.

My dolly is from far Japan,
My gloves from banks of Seine,
My Leghorn hat's Italian,
My fan came straight from Spain,
From England is my muslin gown,
My hose from Germany.
My shoes were made in Boston town,
So when I'm dressed from toe to crown,
I'm Miss Geography!

With The Children.

CONDUCTED BY
J. BRECKENRIDGE ELLIS, PLATTSBURG, MO.

How it Began.

That evening George Weston came into his yard with a discontented expression, and although his football lay right in his path he did not stop to give it a kick. The neighbor's cat was on the fence, but George didn't scare her up the tree. The truth was, he was a discouraged boy. It was Saturday, and he had been playing from early morning; there had heen ten games of marbles, then a long game of "town ball," which had changed to "scrub," and at last degenerated into "tippy-up," there had been a band in town, and a free exhibition on a rope, stretched across Main Street, from the housetops. In the afternoon he had played "fox and hound" till his legs began to ache. So now George Weston was a discontented boy, because he was too tired to play longer. His spirit was willing, but his legs were weak.

His sister was sitting on the porch. "You hear those boys?" said George, dropping upon the steps, as a shout came from the distance. "They are going to play 'By-down.' Asked me to play. But I've got the legache. I wish *I* was my legs!" he added scornfully. "*I'd* show 'em about giving out just when there was going to be fun!"

Jennie langhed, "Well, since you are not your legs," she said, "and since your legs want to rest, why not join the Advacce Society?"

"What's that?" George asked.

"I have just been reading about it in the CHRISTIAN-EVANGELIST," replidd his sister. "There are five things you make up your mind to do, and that makes you a member."

"What good does it do to be a member?" returned George.

"That's where the fun comes in. But it does you a lot of good, besides the fun. The CHRISTIAN-EVANGELIST has just started a department for boys and girls, and the members of the Advance Society are to write for it on some subject given by the person who conducts it. And they are going to be such subjects as we are interested in, something children like to read about. And we will all talk in the column, just as if we were in a room together."

"Yes, I know that kind," interrupted George. "It's a column where the big people preach at us. Now, there's the Family Cultivator, and it has a Young Folks' Department. Well, I sometimes find pretty interesting reading in other parts of the paper. But I run from that Young Folks' Department as if it had the diphtheria! Why, the writers of it don't understand children, nor their ways. They think you've got to explain everything to them, and use little, soft words!"

"But *this* new department I was telling you about, is all different," said Jennie. "The boys and girls are to help to get it up, and we wil feel that its success depends on us. Here is the first general subject we to write on: 'The Funniest Thing that Ever Happened.'"

George laughed, "That sounds pretty lively for a children's column," he said, "I thought they always tried to make you solemn and sit around on benches! Why, there might be *fun* in that, after all."

"Of coursa there is. And I know something I am going to write about. The time Aunt Lizzie—"

"Oh, that time with the rat-trap," interrupted George, laughing. "That *was* funny! Why, Jennie, I believe I'll join that society. I never expected to hear of a children's column that would *amuse* me! What are those five things you have to do, to join?"

"Make up your mind to read a verse of the Bible every day."

"Well, I do that anyway," said George. "They do that in the Christian Endeavor, you know."

"Memorize a quotation from some famous author once a week."

"That's easy. Go ahead!"

"Read thirty lines of poetry a week."

"Don't like poetry," said George.

"I do," said Jennie.

"But that don't make me like it any better than I did before," observed her brother.

"But, George, how much poetry have you read?"

"Never read it," said George virtuously.

"Then how can you tell whether you like it or not. Just think how many of our great men have loved poetry, and how our wisest writers have written it. Even the novelists try their hands at it once in a while. Dickens wrote 'The Ivy Green,' and Thackeray, and Scott, and Stevenson —why you can't afford to dislike poetry when our greatest men have loved it! The fact is, it is the fashion to say, 'I don't like poetry,' nowadays. But I always think it's pretty hard on the people that say so. It doesn't hurt *poetry!*"

"Well, all right," cried George, I can stand it. It won't take but a few minutes to get over thirty lines—and, as you say, I don't know much about the stuff. But people don't talk poetry, so I never could see any sense in reading it. Suppose I were to say to you—

"Now, Jennie, dear, I'm getting hungry;
"Get me a piece of ham and—and—and"

—George began to laugh because he couldn't finish the rhyme. "I see I need poetry," he said, "go on!"

"And you must make up your mind to read five pages of history every week, and not in a schoolbook, either."

George whistled, "Five pages! Well, that isn't very much. I wish we had a vestpocket edition of some historian, the pages about two inches square. But I know I ought to read history. I told the teacher the other day that Chinese Gordon was the great New York editor. But she said I had mixed him up with James Gordon Bennett. I'm always mixing up facts. They are in a perfect mess in my brain, that's a fact! Now for the last thing!"

"Have a blank book, and write down what book you read in, and how much you read. It's a kind of a secretary book."

"That's fun!" cried George, rising. "Let's go and hunt up a blank book, and begin right now. But I wonder if we couldn't get some of the boys and girls to join? Then we could meet together once a week, and have a regular jolly time."

. . . . .

But I will have to wait until next week to tell about the way George and Jennie started their society. In the meantime, if my readers like the Advance Society idea, write to me, telling me they will join, and at the same time send me the funniest story they can write for this department.

Sunday School.

THE TWO PATHS.*

HERBERT L. WILLETT.

The Book of Proverbs is the national anthology of Israel. It is a collection of short, gem-like sayings, drawn from the experience of every-day life, and gathered into a book made up of widely diverse elements. The statements of the book are to the effect that it contains material from different periods, and the indications are clear that the proverbs gathered represent sayings coming from all classes of people through long periods of time. The process of proverb-making is common to all nations. Greek and Latin proverbs, Chinese and Indian proverbs, English proverbs, especially such as are found in the old ballads, and American proverbs in great variety are familiar to us. Such sayings as, "Honesty is the best policy," "It takes a thief to catch a thief," "A rolling stone gathers no moss" and "Its an ill wind that blows nobody good," are representatives of a great number of aphorisms, in which much sound experience has been packed into very few words. No one person made all these. People do not sit down, think hard and write proverbs. Rather such gems of wisdom as are found in brief form in all languages grow out of the thought and experience of all ranks and occupations. Sometimes a man comes to be noted for his sayings some of which live after him. Such a man was Benjamin Franklin. His "Poor Richard's Almanac" contained so many such sayings that to this day he is known as one whose utterances were likely to be terse and notable. When we come upon a good proverb we are accustomed to attribute it to him without knowing surely that he said it, but with a confidence that no one was more likely to utter it than he. Thus he is the common denominator for American proverbs.

Similar was Solomon's relation to the proverbs of Israel. He was known to have observed closely, to have been possessed of great practical sagacity and to have composed many sonnets and wise sayings (1 Kings 4:29-34). Collections of proverbs bearing his name circulated in the early period of the kingdom. To these additions were made, especially during the period of literary activity in the reign of Hezekiah, comprising proverbs that were found in common use at the time, and were therefore believed to be of Solomonic origin (Prov. 25:1). Other collections or fragments of collections came into circulation probably later, such as the oracle of Agur, the son of Jekah (Prov. 30:1) the words of King Lamuel (Prov. 31:1) and the anonymous acrostic in praise of the model woman (Prov. 31:1-31). It is probable that the man or circle of men who gathered all this material into our collection added chapters 1-9 as an introduction, dealing with the nature of wisdom and folly respectively, personifying them under the figure of two women, the one inviting to the choice of the good, the other soliciting to the pursuit of evil.

To the sages of Israel the man who followed good was a wise man, because goodness is in itself a possession richer than all one can obtain, and it brings every other real blessing. On the other hand, evil is of itself unprofitable when viewed from any rational ground. The bad man is not only a sinner—he is a fool. Perhaps this is the strongest appeal that can be made to some natures. There are people to whom it would be of no consequence if you could persuade them that they were doing wrong, but who would be very much disquieted by the thought that they were acting oddly, or foolishly, or in bad form. It is this class to which the wise men made their strongest appeal. "Do not be ill-mannered, do not do things that are in poor taste—be respectable." The man who does evil breaks all these rules of good society. One may object that this is not the highest appeal to make to people, but the teacher of ethics frequently finds it quite effective.

The common form of teaching in these first nine chapters of the Proverbs is paternal. They might fittingly be named "counsels of any father to any son." In the present lesson the contrast between the two ways of living is shown. This expression is itself a figure of speech, which has become common in all languages and serves to illustrate the truth that nearly all our phrases used to describe abstract ethical and spiritual truth are taken from some physical action or process. The prophets spoke of the return of Israel from Babylon upon the highway or road which God would construct for them through the desert. But only the righteous could travel by that path (Isa. 35), and so "the way of the righteous" (Psa. 1:6) came to be spoken of as descriptive no longer of an actual road, but of a method of life. This language is frequent in the New Testament. In John's preaching "the way" was the course of action marked out by the coming Messiah, and for this the Forerunner prepared, like a herald clearing the street before a king (Mk. 1:2). Hence in the apostolic days the favorite term for Christianity was "the way" (Acts 9:2; 22:4; 24:14). It has become so common in our speech that we easily forget that it is taken from the action of a traveler journeying upon a highway, where the choice between diverging paths is necessary and frequent. In the lesson the figure is constantly employed. The father has guided the son in the way of wisdom, has led him in paths that are straight. He goes, sometimes he runs. In one path he has difficulties and stumbles, in the other his progress is rapid. One path he is to enter, the other he must avoid. Our path grows broader and more attractive to the end, like the increasing light of morning to the glory of noon; the other path is dark and forbidding, and one is sure to stumble and fall in it.

It will be noticed that this description of the two paths seems in striking contrast to that of the Savior (Mk. 7:13-14), who advises his disciples to choose the narrow and difficult path rather than the one that is broad, easy and most frequented. But Jesus refers to the external aspects of the two paths, the wise men to their real character, as proved by experience. With Jesus we shall easily see that the road to evil is at first sight the more attractive; but with the sages we know that the other is the road affording real satisfaction.

The temperance application of the lesson is obvious. There is no father worth the name who would not counsel his son to avoid the habit of drinking any intoxicant as he would avoid serpents. Even fathers who are drinkers, and perhaps especially such, would warn their sons away from the awful results of such a practice. It brings one into the company of men whose whole purpose in life is depraved and vile. This is far more true to-day than it was then. At that time the people used fruit in great quantities, and its juice, fresh and unfermented, was a common article of drink. The older wine was also used and men often became drunken, but there was no class of people who made a business of seducing young men to drink, as do the saloonkeepers of the present day. Our quicker and more nervous life has made the ravages of drink far more terrible than in the slow and quiet East. And thus our drink problem of to-day is a hundredfold more complicated than was that of the writers of Proverbs. If they had cause to warn against such danger, how much more have we! If in an age when the greatest danger from serving drink consisted in the liability to occasional overindulgence, fathers had cause to take serious thought regarding the disaster and folly of drinking; then in our day, when ten thousand temptations wait at every turn, where our young men have to run the gauntlet of solicitation, not only from the organized representatives of the traffic, backed by the state, and from companions who have gone a step into self-destruction without being quite conscious of it, and without intending to do wrong, how much more have we! Not till the time when patriotism, regard for public welfare, the reign of conscience in politics and the supremacy of righteousness to every other interest shall arrive can we hope to be free from the curse of strong drink. But the struggle will go on, the field will be conquered slowly, new victories will be added to those already won and the newer generation will be taught self-respect and the love of God and purity as no other has been. Already the sky brightens along the horizon, and the signs of promise hang like the banners of God against the black-breasted night.

SUGGESTIONS FOR TEACHING.

No book contains more of wisdom for daily conduct than the Book of Proverbs; it was taught to children as the most valuable part of the Bible a century ago; Mr. Campbell was more familiar with it than with any other part of the Scriptures; it is not out of date yet. Those who know should teach what they have learned by experience; and happy is the child who learns from the life-lessons of his father. The rewards of right living are not alone in the future life, but here and now; an honest, self-respecting, clean and temperate man lives longer, is happier and brings a blessing on all he meets. It is worth everything to a child to be started in the right path by the faithful instructions of good parents and teachers. The advice and counsel of those we can trust are of greater value than all possessions. It is a terrible thought that some of our fellow human beings live by getting other people to do wrong; whose whole trade tends to bring misery to the world. In so far as we do what causes others to sin, are we not as bad as they? A life that seeks to follow the will of God grows happier all the time. If we are not happy, is it not because there is something wrong with us?

Berlin.

*Sunday-school lesson for Nov. 27, 1898—Temperance (Prov. 4:10-19). Golden Text—My son, if sinners entice thee, consent thou not (Prov. 1:10). Lesson Outline—1. Fatherly words (10-12); 2. Advice and warning (13-17); 3. The two paths (18, 19).

Christian Endeavor.

By Burris A. Jenkins.

TOPIC FOR NOV. 27.

ꞮEAT REFORMS THAT NEED OUR HELP.

(John 2:13-28.)

Ꞁhere is no business in the world requiring much patience as the reforming business. ıe mills of God grind slowly, but the refor-ɪrs want them to grind fast. Theo. Parker id, "The trouble is that God is not in a rry, and I am, and the defect of most re-·mers is that they get in too big a hurry." ›vertheless, if we consent to be patient and our reforms grow gradually we may be sure ɜy will grow. Christian Endeavorers can do ʒreat deal for the reform of current abuses. ıristian Endeavorers can influence the whole urch, and if the church would rise up in its wer it could run this country. Some of the ·orms to which we should give our attention ıy be mentioned.

Nearest at hand of all, perhaps, is dis-nesty in commercial transactions. A mer-ant declares he is going to have a sweep-out or le. Perhaps he puts a row of brooms up er his front window to indicate clearance; ɜn he doubles the price on everything and ls out to "bargain hunters." And we Chris-ıns encourage this kind of thing by running ·er "Cheap John" trade. A little two-year-l girl recently made believe that she was ıding the newspaper, and they all heard her ring, "bargains, bargains." Children are ınderful imitators. All this running after ɜ bargains is sure to corrupt merchants. If we ınt an article let us pay an honest price for ɔr do without.

Another reform could be carried on by Chris-n people in municipal affairs. In a great ıny cases, especially in smaller towns, a little itation would correct many abuses. Our vs are openly violated, saloons run after urs and other public resorts of the worst aracter are permitted in violation of the law d nobody does anything. In very many wns if some one honest Christian Endeavor- were to undertake the agitation he could an things out. Is your good citizenship nmittee awake?

Ꞁhere are reforms needed in the relation of ployer and employe. Labor reforms are ɜded, moreover, almost as much in the in-·est of the employer as that of the employe. or Illinois! How it reaches out its bleeding ıds to all of us and calls for reform. Men, mbers in our churches, too, are working ɜr hours, some of them fifteen hours out of enty-four, are scarcely permitted to see ɪir families, and are absolutely prohibited m entering their churches; and here, too, ·haps, a few words in some public print, or ittle private effort by some Christian En-ıvorer might inaugurate reform. If our ıng people once determine to grapple with 'h questions of social life much may gradual-be accomplished.

ınd what shall be said of the liquor reform? e necessity of it is plainly evident on all ıds; how to accomplish it, is the gravest ficulty, what steps should be taken, what ʒinning should be made, is puzzling many an ɟest, thinking man. Some great organized empts have been made, which have proved ıplete failures, and what to do next, the ıperance forces seem, at present, unable to ·ermine. Since the third party movement ɜ proved a failure, much as the third party vement proved a failure in abolition days, eems very much as if we should turn our at-tion, as was done in that very emergency, ɔne of the great parties. Does not history ·eat itself in reforms as in other matters? d is it not possible that if the Christian En-ıvorers should say to the political world, Whichever of the two great parties will first ɔpt a prohibition plank, we will vote for," might not the thing be accomplished? Ah, but we say that is turning a religious society into a political power. So be it; it is for a religious end. In the Breckenridge campaign, in Kentucky, every religious organization in the community was turned, for the time being, into a political organization. If ever we are to accomplish moral reforms we must begin in an organized and business manner, and then not be too impatient of results, but be willing to wait for God's own good time.

BETHANY C. E. READING COURSES.

[There are three courses: The Bible, Missions and the Disciples. The three handbooks for the *first* year are: "A Guide to Bible Study," "Handbook of Missions" and "Concerning the Disciples." The three handbooks for the *second* year are: "Life and Teachings of Jesus," "Missionary Fields and Forces of the Disciples" and "Sketches of our Pioneers." Three handbooks and the Bethany C. E. Bulletin, quarterly, sent to any address for one dollar. All orders should be addressed to the Bethany C. E. Company, 798 Republic St., Cleveland, O. Each course has a director: H. L. Willett is director of Bible study; W. J. Lhamon is the director of studies in Missions; F. D Power is director of studies Concerning the Disciples. This column is set apart to the use of these directors.]

Our Authority for Missions.

W. J. Lhamon, *Director*.

The introductory chapter to the second year-book on missions places especial emphasis on the risen Christ and his commission. This emphasis may well be redoubled in the present article. It is impossible to overstate the authority of Jesus in this beneficent work of seeking and saving the lost. If the primary meaning of the word missionary is "one sent," Jesus fulfilled that meaning wholly, for he is the one who is sent by the Father's love, that "whosoever believeth in him should not perish but have everlasting life." The authority for missions rests, therefore, not alone in the commission of the Savior, though that would have been abundantly sufficient for all who seek to obey him. But it rests in the very being of the Savior himself; he is the primal Christian missionary; his life is a missionary incarnation; his death is the pleading love of the missionary martyr; his resurrection is the assertion in miraculous form of his missionary triumph over sin and loss and death, and his commission is the logical and inevitable outcome of his whole career. There is no incongruity between the preaching and praying and dying Christ on the one hand and the risen and commanding Christ on the other. The commission is not an afterthought. All that it expresses Jesus from the first intended. The commission is the sublime conclusion and climax of a life that was sublime and climacteric. In it there is summed up the whole meaning of the Savior's presence on earth, and the whole force of his heavenly career in human form.

All the meaning of Christ's life, therefore, is enfolded in his commission, and is being unfolded age by age in the missions that are truly his. The presentation of Christ as Christ, by whomsoever, to whomsoever, whensoever, wheresoever and by whatsoever means that are Christly is a part of this unfolding.

To neglect, to refuse or to ignore this work is to stand in an attitude foreign to if not antagonistic to Christ. Such an attitude contradicts the profession of one's faith in Christ. Fundamentally, the confession of Jesus means the assumption of a missionary career. Baptism into Christ means baptism into the purposes of his life, and baptism into his purposes is baptism into his commission, and into his world-wide mission, and into all his missions. Every intelligently baptized Disciple arises from the water a missionary and is bound by all the sacredness of his baptismal vows to fulfill the commission according to his capabilities and opportunities. Otherwise, we cry, "Lord, Lord," and do not the thing he says.

Missionary societies are Christly expedients for the accomplishment of our bounden mission. They are Christly because they are brotherly, sisterly, simple, practical and di-

rected toward t
own life. For
scriptural. In
der the constra
his commission
are invited to s
course, the mis
forces of their
the progress of
cessions of int
work, and may
to the convictio
the conviction t
completion only
life with the pu

Literature.

BOOK NOTES.

"National Prosperity Through Christ" is the title of an exceedingly interesting tract of 48 pages, by Rev. T. M. C. Birmingham. Charles H. Kerr & Co., Chicago, publishers. Price ten cents.

Gladstone's popular book, "The Impregnable Rock of Ho y Scripture," formerly published at $1.00, is now issued in excellent form, paper covers, at the price of 15 cents, by John B. Alden, publisher, New York.

"Moody's Anecdotes," containing some of Moody's best stories used for sermon illustrations, have been published in book form, by the Bible Institute Colportage Association, 250 Lasalle Avenue, Chicago, Ill., for the Colportage Library. Paper covers, 126 pages, 15 cents.

MAGAZINES.

The November ReligiousReview of Reviews is a verv spiritual number and will not fail to particularly interest ministers. The contributed articles this month are from the pens of gifted and singularly successful writers, and the departments are rich in spiritual food. Published monthly. American Tract Society Building, New York.

The initial number of the Ledger Monthly comes to us in an autumn cover of very great beauty. A wistful, dreamy, beautiful woman looks out of a network of leaves in the brilliant colors of the October landscape. It is a symbolical picture of the American autumn, characteristic in color, form and expression. Rarely has anything more beautiful appeared in the popular art of to-day.

The Atlantic Monitor is the name of a new monthly eight-page journal published at Harper, Kan.

The Peace Commission in Paris is described and illustrated in the November Magazine number of the Outlook by a staff correspondent in Paris. Jacob A. Riis, the author of "How the Other Half Lives," contributes a graphic article concerning the "New York Police Department." Edward Everest Hale gives in this issue the eleventh installment of his "James Russell Lowell and His Friends," which will be concluded in the December magazine issue. Paul Bourget is the author of a story entitled "Antigone," which portrays a lofty personality. Among the illustrated articles in this number are a picturesque account of a visit to the country of Sitting Bull, by Rosa T. Shelton, and an article by Dr. Amory H. Bradford on Bunyan's "Pilgrim's Progress," with special reference to a beautiful new edition soon to be published, from which some remarkable illustrations are reproduced.

Marriages.

FAIRBANKS—COX.—On Thursday, Nov. 3, 1898, by W. M. Mayfield, at the residence of the bride, Samuel R. Fairbank and Jennie L. Cox, both of Soldier, Kan.

HUNT—MACK.—Married, at Springfield, Mo., Oct. 9, 1898, Walter H. Hunt and Luella L. Mack; D. W. Moore, pastor, officiating.

MOCKWART—MOFFETT.—At the home of the bride's parents, south of Milton, Nov. 3rd, 1898, Mr. E. E. Mockwart, of Muncie, Ind., and Miss Onea N. Moffett, of Wayne County, Ind.; Rev. T. A. Hall officiating.

PURLEE—BREWER.—Married, at the residence of the bride's parents, Wednesday evening, Oct. 26, 1898, Ellis Purlee and Maggie T. Brewer, both of Pawnee Rock, Kan.; C. D. Purlee officiating.

READ—ARNOLD.—At the home of the bride in Erie, Kan., Nov. 2, 1898, Mr. G. M. Read, pastor of the Christian Church at Arrowsmith, Ill., and Miss Lizzie M. Arnold; C. J. Saunders officiating.

SHOVE—WEST.—On Sunday, Nov. 6, 1828, at Havensville, Kan., by W. M. Mayfield, Luke Shove and Ella West, both of Havensville, Kan.

Obituaries.

[One hundred words will be inserted free. Above one hundred words, one cent a word. Please send amount with each notice.]

ARTZ.

Mr. Edwin Artz, of Augusta, Ill., died at his daughter's in Plattsburg, Mo., on the 30th of October, 1898, while on a visit there. He was born in Shipenburg, Penn., Dec. 24, 1837. Married to Miss Mary Helen Dixson in 1863. To them were born eight children, one of whom is dead. He and his wife were baptized by the writer in March, 1870, soon after he was chosen superintendent of the Sunday-school, which place he filled for over 28 years. His wife dying he married Miss Mary Helen Waldeck, who with his children mourn his departure. He filled in a large measure what is meant by father, husband, neighbor and Christian. At his home in Augusta, Ill., and in the presence of many friends, the funeral services were conducted by the undersigned on the 2nd of November. E. J. LAMPTON.

CRANE.

J. B. Crane, the honored subject of this sketch, was born at Mentz, Cayuga County, N. Y., September 21, 1822. He lived at the place of his birth until he was 18 years of age. He received a thorough education at Auburn, N. Y. When but 14 years of age he united with the church, and from that time on devoted the whole of his life to the cause of Christ. This he has accomplished with an eloquent tongue and a consecrated pen. He was an earnest, able and powerful preacher. He had deep convictions of truth, and yet held the truth in love for all his brethren in Christ. He kept abreast of the times and ready to aid in any movement to further the cause of his Savior. He was posted on all subjects and acquainted with many fields of investigation. He was liberal almost to a fault, and none ever asked a favor but it was granted. As a preacher his thought was rich, chaste and scriptural. Because of the natural bent of his mind he took delight in the profounder themes of our religion, treating them both from a philosophical and a scriptural point of view. He could soar to the heights of the noblest thoughts or descend to dig about the roots of any system of truth. He was well acquainted with the different systems of theology. He knew their limits and formative principles. He knew where they touched and where they diverged. He had clear convictions as to which was in accordance with the Holy Scriptures. He was learned in the different sciences. He took delight in the study of them all. From these wider fields of physical science he gathered a rich store of illustration and allusion which gave great wealth of resource when he came to speak or to write. He loved the natural sciences, and delighted to discuss the conflicting systems of metaphysics and ethics. No man had wider learning in these tracts of thought. He took hold of phrenology and mastered it as a branch of metaphysics. He found time to become a skillful physician. He took in both the alopathic and homœopathic systems, and could practice in either or combine in one treatment the good in both. He loved to use his pen. The last years of his life he spent in quiet and retirement preparing several books for pub cation, into which he has gathered the crea of his learning. It is to be hoped that th will soon be in the hands of the public, that may have the benefit of these mature labor He was a true friend. He never failed tho whom he loved, whether in his own hom which was enriched and beautified by his lov or in the community. No one could say th Dr. Crane ever tendered his friendship a then acted unworthy of the highest frien ship. His wife, with whom he had spe more than 50 happy years, mourns a gre loss. A daughter and son, whose affecti cheered him, abide on this side while he h crossed over. A grandson, upon whom h heart was centered, in young manhood r mains to follow him as he followed Chris The church has sustained a great loss in t death of this soldier of the cross.

A. A. COCKE, D. D.

Waynesboro, Va., Nov. 3rd, 1898.

MAC EL'REY.

In their home, Ninth Street, near Traine Deleware County, Pennsylvania, November 1898, Emma T., wife of Dr. Joseph H. M El'Rey, entered into immortality. She sai "There is no death. Death is but transition. Her life and character composed her ow proper eulogy.

PAGGETT.

Hiram Paggett died August 22, 1898. I was born April 4, 1804, near Livermor Maine. In 1818 he with his parents moved Ohio. In 1829 he was married to Jane Simop In 1850 he with his family moved to Iow where the remainder of his life was spen To the couple were born six sons and thr daughters, his wife and five children havi preceded him to the better land. He ear gave his life to Christ, and was an elder in t church for more than 50 years; has been reader and subscriber to the CHRISTIAN-EVA GELIST from the time of the first publicatio He was a grand man. None knew him but love him, and an association with him was make one better. None knew this better th did his grandchildren and great grandchildre who early learned to reverence so saintly person. KATE UPDIKE.

Missionary.

Echoes from Forefathers' Day.

Burlington, Ia.—We went to go on record as having observed Forefathers' Day and as being fully in sympathy with the work of Home Missions. MRS. S. S WALDO.

Edinburg, Ill.—We observed Forefathers' Day; it was our first attempt at any thing of the kind. We send our offering and our prayers. ETHEL PRATER.

Dowagiac, Mich.—We had a program that was profitable and instructive to our house full of attentive listeners. We are delighted with Forefathers' Day. H. A. GRENELL.

Liberty, Ind.—Our program was splendid and all enjoyed it. We thank you for the literature you sent. CORDA BARNES.

Indianapolis, Ind., Fourth Church.—We observed Forefathers' Day. The meeting was in charge of the missionary committee and was a grand success. We thank you for calling our attention to Forefather's Day.
WALTER LEGG.

Verdin, Neb.—We kept Forefathers' Day, delighting a large audience. We send our offering, regretting it is not larger.
H. A. PILASTER.

Webb City, Mo.—We thank you for the literature of Forefathers' Day; we had a delightful evening. MAY MARET.

Cleveland, O.—Enclosed please find New York draft for $25, the Forefathers' Day offering from the Y. P. S. C. E. of the Euclid Avenue Church. LYDIA O. PENNINGTON.

Toledo, O.—Enclosed find money order for $4, our offering for Forefather's Day. We had our program Sunday evening the 30th.
EVA F. HOUGH.

Norwood Ave. Church, Indianapolis, Ind.—The enclosed draft for $5 is the offering of the Central C. E. of Indianapolis, Ind., the Forefathers' Day offering to Home Missions. Our society has given more to Home Missions this year than ever before.
MRS. A. J. CLARK.

Wheeling, W. Va.—Enclosed find money order for $11, hoping that it may be in our power to celebrate Forefathers' Day next time with a still larger offering.
ELIZABETH BOYD.

Van Horn, Ia.—We have no Christian Church within twenty miles. I send three dollars from a few members who live here and five dollars and twenty-five cents from a Union Endeavor Society; we observed Forefathers' Day. We want to make our gift equal to one dollar per member for Home Missions, to set an example to our brethren.

Forefathers' Day is one of the most delightful days of the year when properly observed. If your society has not yet observed the day this year, plan to do so yet. Write us for literature, which we send free of cost.

If you have observed the day, please be prompt and send the offering, there is great need of it now.

Remember, this is our Jubilee Year and we are trying to raise $100,000 for Home Missions this year; the offerings from Forefathers' Day will help us in this great work.

BENJ. L. SMITH, C. C. SMITH, } Cor. Secs.
Y. M. C. A. Bldg., Cincinnati, O.

Concerning the Young People's Department of the C. W. B. M.

The receipts of this department during October, 1898, were $782.99; the corresponding month last year, $633.26. Much of the gain is in the orphanage fund. We are pleased to note that $149.60 was received for the children in the new orphanage at Deogbur.

The apportionment of shares of $10 each among the various states is as follows: Alabama, 1; Arkansas, 12; N. California, 12; S. California, 10; Colorado, 9; Connecticut, 4; District of Columbia, 3; Florida, 6; Georgia, 14; Idaho, 1; Illinois, 110; Indiana, 120; Indian Territory, 0; Iowa, 65; Kansas, 35; Kentucky, 110; Louisiana, 1; Maritime Provinces, 18; Maine, 2; Maryland, 12; Massachusetts, 4; Michigan, 18; Minnesota, 21; Mississippi, 1; Missouri, 75; Montana, 8; Nebraska, 25; New York, 12; North Carolina, 9; New Jersey, 0; Ohio, 120; Oklahoma, 2; Oregon, 10; Pennsylvania, 60; South Carolina, 3; South Dakota, 1; Tennessee, 2; Texas, 32; Vermont, 0; Virginia, 30; Washington, 10; West Virginia, 8; Wisconsin, 4.
MATTIE POUNDS, National Supt.

Children's Rally Day for America.

Here are some of the responses made to the call for Children's Rally for America:

Every superintendent, who seeks the best interests of his Sunday-school, will not fail to observe "Children's Rally Day for America," and take the best collection possible. The idea of thanksgiving and love of country unite naturally at this time, and rightly presented will draw large numbers, and there is no better way to utilize the enthusiasm awakened than to get all to give liberally to save America for Christ. I would observe this day for the school's sake if I had no interest in Home Missions. But this is an effort for missions not made last year, and let it not be feeble, but one that will count toward the $100,000 that must be raised for our Home Mission work this year.—A. M. HARVOUT, Cincinnati, Ohio.

Our Sunday-school will observe Children's Day for Home Missions. Please send to my address by return mail fifty copies of "Children's Rally for America."—J. E. J. WHITSLAR, Evansville, Ind.

I was glad to notice the plan for a "Children's Rally Day for America." I am on a committee for the Harvest Concert, and should like helps and suggestions. — MRS. NEWTON KNOW, Worcester, Mass.

Here came a call for the "Exercise" before the sample reached them: Have you any special exercise for Home Mission Rally Day in November? — H. E. HOWARD, Springfield, Mass.

Please send me twenty copies of programs for Thanksgiving Children's Day. Our school will observe the Rally Day.—J. H. HAZELRIGG, New Castle, Ind.

Please send me such suggestions and helps as you can to assist in the observance of Children's Rally Day for America.—W. A. SNIFF, Ardmore, I. T.

Your sample copy of the Home Missionary was received. Please send me two dozen copies.—MRS. L. O. KNIPP, Piqua, Ohio.

Your special issue of the American Home Missionary was received by our school, and we have decided to-day to observe the Rally.—J. W. GUY, Waupun, Pa.

Will you be kind enough to send us the "American Home Missionary," as I am sure it will greatly aid us in our Rally Day for Home Missions.—MRS. S. E. RIGGLE, Washington, Pa.

G. W. Muckley writes us that the Sunday-schools in Missouri are falling into line with great enthusiasm for Children's Rally Day for America.

We would like to have programs and necessary materials for Children's Thanksgiving Sunday.—CONRAD WOLF, Kokomo, Ind.

Our school will observe Rally Day in behalf of Home Missions, November 20th. Yours for a liberal collection. — CHARLES O. BENTON, Boxby, Ind.

Please send me seventy-five copies of Children's Rally for America. We have decided to use it.—W. H. WILSON, Prairie Depot, Ohio.

Please send us "Children's Rally for America." Our school will have the exercise. —W. Y. ALLEN, Elizabethtown, Ky.

BENJ. L. SMITH, Cor. Sec.
Cincinnati, Ohio.

Publishers' Notes.

We will be glad to send samples of all Sunday-school supplies to any superintendents who have not been using our Sunday-school literature. We believe it the most complete of any now offered, as it is adapted for use for all ages in the Sunday-school, from the primary class to the old folks' class. If not using our supplies, examine them before placing your order for the coming year. Address the Christian Publishing Co., St. Louis, Mo.

If your Sunday-school expects to greet Christmas with good cheer by rendering an appropriate concert, we would suggest that you send for our new Christmas exercise, "The Wonderful Child." This is the latest concert prepared by W. W. Dowling. It embraces songs, Scripture quotations and poetical recitations. The concert is not difficult to learn, and the average Sunday-school can render it in an acceptable manner.

The price is 5 cents per copy or 50 cents per dozen, postpaid.

Among the many books now appearing upon the subject of teaching it is both interesting and significant to find one devoted to the greatest teacher of all—"Jesus as a Teacher," by B. A. Hinsdale. Prof. Hinsdale is well fitted by training, experience and sympathy to write upon this subject. His broad knowledge of Jewish institutions and customs has enabled him to throw about his subject a charm and interest not usually found in books on teaching. The book is full of practical suggestions for the schoolroom work of to-day.—*The Inland Educator, Terre Haute, Ind.*

"Jesus as a Teacher" is a book of 330 pages, neatly bound in cloth, and the price is $1.25.

The Christian Lesson Commentary on the International Bible Studies for the year 1899, by W. W. Dowling, is fresh from the press. Besides the original matter it contains thoughts gathered from a large field of the best scholarship of the world, making it the cream of the best commentators. The Sunday-school teacher that will carefully study this work will be prepared to appear before his class as an *instructor*. We will be glad to mail *sample pages* of this commentary to any desiring to examine them. The book contains nearly 400 pages, and the price is $1.00 per copy, postpaid.

SUNDAY SCHOOL SUPPLIES

Reduced Price List

Quarterly Helps.

THE PRIMARY QUARTERLY.

A Lesson Magazine for the Youngest Classes. It contains Lesson Stories, Lesson Questions, Lesson Thoughts and Lesson Pictures, and never fails to interest the little ones.

TERMS.

Single copy, per quarter, 5 cents.

10 copies,	per quarter, $	.20;	per year, $	.75
25 copies,	"	.40;	"	1.50
50 "	"	.75;	"	3.00

THE YOUTH'S QUARTERLY.

A Lesson Magazine for the Junior Classes. The Scripture Text is printed in full, but an interesting Lesson Story takes the place of the usual explanatory notes.

TERMS—Single copy, per quarter, 5 cents; ten copies or more to one address, 2 1-2 cents each per quarter.

THE SCHOLAR'S QUARTERLY.

A Lesson Magazine for the Senior Classes. This Quarterly contains every help needed by the senior classes. Its popularity is shown by its immense circulation.

TERMS.

Single copy,	per quarter, $	.10;	per year, $	.30
10 copies,	"	.40;	"	1.25
25 "	"	.90;	"	3.00
50 "	"	1.60;	"	6.00
100 "	"	3.00;	"	12.00

THE BIBLE STUDENT.

A Lesson Magazine for the Advanced Classes, containing the Scripture Text in both the Common and Revised Versions, with Explanatory Notes, Helpful Readings, Practical Lessons, Maps, etc.

TERMS.

Single copy,	per quarter, $	.10;	per year, $	.40
10 copies,	"	.70;	"	2.50
25 "	"	1.60;	"	6.00
50 "	"	3.00;	"	10.50
100 "	"	5.50;	"	20.00

BIBLE LESSON PICTURE ROLL.

Printed in 8 colors. Each leaf, 26 by 37 inches, contains a picture illustrating one lesson. 13 leaves in a set. Price per set—one quarter—reduced to 75 cents.

CHRISTIAN PICTURE LESSON CARDS.

A reduced fac-simile of the large Bible Lesson Pictures, 13 cards in set, one for each Sunday in quarter. Price reduced to 2 1-2 cents per set.

Monthly.

CHRISTIAN BIBLE LESSON LEAVES.

These Lesson Leaves are especially for the use of Sunday-schools that may not be able to fully supply themselves with the Lesson Books or Quarterlies.

TERMS.

10 copies,	1 mo., $	.15;	3 mos., $	.30;	1 yr.,	$1.00
25 "	"	.25;	"	.60;	"	2.40
50 "	"	.45;	"	1.20;	"	4.60
100 "	"	.75;	"	2.10;	"	8.00

Weekly.

THE LITTLE ONES.

Printed in Colors.

This is a Weekly for the Primary Department in the Sunday-school and the Little Ones at Home, full of Charming Little Stories, Sweet Poems, Merry Rhymes and Jingles, Beautiful Pictures and Simple Lesson Talks. It is printed on fine tinted paper, and no pains or expense is spared to make it the prettiest and best of all papers for the very little people.

TERMS—Weekly, in clubs of not less than five copies to one address, 25 cents a copy per year.

THE SUNDAY-SCHOOL EVANGELIST.

This is a Weekly for the Sunday-school and Family, of varied and attractive contents, embracing Serial and Shorter Stories; Sketches; Incidents of Travel; Poetry; Field Notes; Lesson Talks, and Letters from the Children. Printed from clear type, on fine calendered paper, and profusely illustrated with new and beautiful engravings.

TERMS—Weekly, in clubs of not less than ten copies to one address, 30 cents a copy per year, or 8 cents per quarter.

OUR YOUNG FOLKS.

A Large Illustrated Weekly Magazine, devoted to the welfare and work of Our Young People, giving special attention to the Sunday-school and Young People's Society of Christian Endeavor. It contains wood-cuts and biographical sketches of prominent workers, Notes on the Sunday-school Lessons, and Endeavor Prayer-meeting Topics for each week, Outlines of Work, etc. This Magazine has called forth more commendatory notices than any other periodical ever issued by our people. The Sunday-school pupil or teacher who has this publication will need no other lesson help, and will be able to keep fully "abreast of the times" in the Sunday-school and Y. P. S. C. E. work.

TERMS—One copy, per year, 75 cents; in clubs of ten, 60 cents each; in packages of twenty-five or more to one name and address, only 50 cents each. Send for Sample.

CHRISTIAN PUBLISHING CO., St. Louis, Mo.

The Mormon—Christian War.

Bro. Chas. F. Richardson, pastor of the First Presbyterian Church, Ogden, Utah, writes:

Any way I can help you, will be glad to do it. I shall speak of you and your work and tracts in church papers. Keep your courage up; our sympathy and prayers are yours.

Bro. R. has no mean reputation as a "Mormon fighter" himself. He knows what it is to battle with a close organization within the shadow of its head temple and endowment house. A word of cheer is refreshing. I am certainly, as Bro. Garrison and others will testify, getting a free expression from "the other side," of what by no means could be called "sympathy or prayers" with or for me or my work. This I expected and expect. It is but a proof, and a good one, of the good work I am trying to do.

The following is the most *cents*ible communication I have received for a long time:

R. B. NEAL.—*Dear Sir:* Enclosed find $5.00 to help carry on your well begun work.

A UTAH SISTER.

That's all I know about it except that the $5.00 came in just when badly needed. To give some idea of the expense necessary to carry on this work I use the following letter, just received, as a text:

BRO. NEAL:—There are from two to four Mormon elders in each county in this state, and I wish to help expose their false teaching. They held a conference in Tallahutchie County in August, near where I was holding a meeting. There were forty elders in attendance. Some of them tramped one hundred and fifty miles to get there. . . . . . .

I am glad you are doing so much to expose their system. Hope that God will bless your efforts.

A. H. SMITH.

Denmark, Miss.

I was truly glad to get a letter on this from "a Smith." Lately I have been absorbed with the "Smith family" who gave this system to the world and who defend it.

I could only send this brother fifteen cents' worth of tracts. He ought to have a thousand to scatter. An average of 1,000 tracts to each county in the state of Mississippi would be small compared to the number Mormons scatter. Their elders are bound to leave a tract in every house. Put cost of tracts, at even one-half cent each for printing and postage, allow 1,000 for each county and multiply tracts and cost by number of counties in the state. This will give some idea of the money needed to wage a war as it should be fought. Would cost *hundreds of dollars* to tractize thoroughly each state. A *tract* ought to be put in the *tracks* of every Mormon elder.

I have the MS. of three more new and needed tracts ready to hand to a publisher, but lack funds. These tracts have been tested, or will be, by such men as F. D. Power, Russell Errett and Prof. I. B. Grubbs and others before sent out. I want, need, and must have, *partners* in this work. Fifty dollars now will put out the tract in good shape and large numbers. Bro. Power wrote this prediction over its front: "The author will soon be able to report to civilization in the immortal words of Bill Anthony, 'The ship is blown up and is sinking.'" What brother or sister or church will bear all or any part of the expense of this tract, now past due? I stand in hope if I sink in despair.

R. B. NEAL.

Grayson, Ky.

N-EVANGELIST.

MILY AND RELIGIOUS JOURNAL.

Iovember 24, 1898 No. 47.

THE

CHRISTIAN - EVANGELIST

J. H. GARRISON, EDITOR.

W. W. HOPKINS, ASSISTANT.

B. B. TYLER, J. J. HALEY,

EDITORIAL CONTRIBUTORS.

What We Plead For.

The Christian-Evangelist pleads for:

The Christianity of the New Testament, taught by Christ and his Apostles, versus the theology of the creeds taught by fallible men—the world's great need.

The divine confession of faith on which Christ built his church, versus human confessions of faith on which men have split the church.

The unity of Christ's disciples, for which he so fervently prayed, versus the divisions in Christ's body, which his apostles strongly condemned.

The abandonment of sectarian names and practices, based on human authority, for the common family name and the common faith, based on divine authority, versus the abandonment of scriptural names and usages for partisan ends.

The hearty co-operation of Christians in efforts of world-wide beneficence and evangelization, versus petty jealousies and strifes in the struggle for denominational pre-eminence.

The fidelity to truth which secures the approval of God, versus conformity to custom to gain the favor of men.

The protection of the home and the destruction of the saloon, versus the protection of the saloon and the destruction of the home.

For the right against the wrong;
For the weak against the strong;
For the poor who've waited long
For the brighter age to be.
For the truth, 'gainst superstition,
For the faith, against tradition,
For the hope, whose glad fruition
Our waiting eyes shall see.

RATES OF SUBSCRIPTION.

Single subscriptions, new or old .... $1.50 each
Ministers .... 1.00 "

All subscriptions payable in advance. Label shows the month up to the first day of which your subscription is paid. If an earlier date than the present is shown, you are in arrears. No paper discontinued without express orders to that effect. Arrears should be paid when discontinuance is ordered.

In ordering a change of post office, please give the OLD as well as the NEW address.

Do not send local check, but use Post office or Express Money Order, or draft on St. Louis, Chicago or New York, in remitting.

ADDRESS, CHRISTIAN PUBLISHING CO.,
1522 Locust St., St. Louis, Mo.

THE CHRISTIAN-EVANGEL

"In faith, Unity; in opinion and methods, Liberty; in all things, Charity.'

ol. xxxv. St. Louis, Mo., Thursday, November 24, 1898.

CURRENT EVENTS.

:he .work of the Spanish-American
ıce commissions in Paris is rapidly com-
: to a finish, in spite of the strenuous
ɔrts which the Spanish representatives
re made to avoid or postpone the inev-
ble. There has been much quibbling,
l many futile attempts to import side
ıes into thr discussion of the Philippine
estion. The delay has doubtless been
ɔmpted, not by any hope of winning con-
sions from our administration, but by
hope of exciting European sympathy
l interference, if possible, and the de-
e to have it known, both by the Spanish
ɔple and by Spain's creditors, that no
int had been yielded without resistance.
e definite demand made by the American
nmissioners includes the cession of the
ire Philippine group to the United
ıtes, in compensation for which Spain is
be reimbursed for her expenditures on
ernal improvements in the islands. The
anish protest to this demand is based on
phraseology of the protocol, which says
thing as to the *possession* of the Philip-
ıes,. but only leaves the *disposition* of
ɔm to be arranged by the joint commis-
n. The distinction between .the two
ms is subtle. The administration thinks
ıt it is fictitious. The diplomatic corre-
ɔndence which led up to the protocol
ɔws that there was a shrewd attempt on
part of the Spanish representatives to
ve some such loophole, but it also shows
ıt this design was detected and frus-
ted.

The text of the Spanish reply to the ex-
cit demands of our commissioners has
t yet been made public, but evidently it
s not an acceptance. Negotiations were
spended for a week while the government
Madrid was being consulted and the
ɔly was being framed. Judge Day and
colleagues are now at work on an
ıally elaborate reply to the reply, and
blic expectation will be disappointed if
s does not demand an immediate and
al answer, and demand it in such a tone
will indicate that further delay will be
ngerous. If correctly represented,
dge Day's reports to the President, al-
ɔugh brief and not couched in strong
ms, indicate a belief that Spain will
ld as soon as further delay is seen to be
possible. She would be insane to take
arbitration would savor somewhat of death-bed repentance. Saying nothing about the question whether or not we need the Philippines, or whether or not the Philippines need us, the obvious fact is that Spain is out of it to stay.

Kaiser Wilhelm's pilgrimage is about at an end. Every one will breathe a little easier when he is safely back in his own empire, for unquestionably it was a rather reckless procedure for him to leave the affairs of state just at this time to go rambling off through Syria. It would have been very awkward if anything had happened to him, and yet just now is the time when things are happening to princes and potentates with appalling frequency. The whole journey had a decidedly stage-y effect. A Protestant pilgrimage, under the patronage and protection of a Mohammedan monarch, and inaugurated with the approval of the Pope, must necessarily contain enough incongruities to make it picturesque. But William rendered it bizarre by the free exercise of his natural talent for attitudinizing in comic opera fashion. And for this reason, too, it will be a relief to know that it is all over and he is back at his capital. Much comment was aroused by the semi-official announcement that the return from Malta would be by way of Spain. Although it was well understood that the Kaiser would make his visit incognito, and although it was authoritatively stated that the only reason for choosing this route was the fear that the Empress' health might suffer from a too sudden transition from the climate of Palestine to that of Germany at this season, yet the public insisted on seeing in the plan an expression of sympathy with Spain and hostility to the United States. In view of this unanimous interpretation of the visit, and especially in view of the protests which came from the highest sources in his own government, the Emperor has abandoned this part of the plan and will return direct to Germany.

The powers of Europe are not swift in concerted action, but sometimes they bring something to pass in the course of time. Two years ago the Government of Crete seemed to demand immediate readjustment. Little Grece instantly interposed, and did her best. The world looked on with breathless interest, but the powers were not
have been turning all t
uation of Crete by the
been proceeding slowly
last week the troop shi
last Turkish soldiers a
Prince George of Gr
way to Crete to take
as the high commiss
ers. The autonomy
the supervision of the
thereby becomes a fact

Every new public ut
ish political leaders gi
the desire of that gove
understanding with th
the satisfaction which
fact that the Europe
plans and forecasts ar
the names of Great Br
States as two powers w
ally be expected to ac
each other and to pl
other's hands as agai
world. That this is the
gard to our relations wi
be no doubt. This is
which the world place
expansion. Lord Salis
Lord Mayor's banquet
topic, and Joseph Ch
last week at the Nation
Conference was even m
also to the relations b
France, Mr. Chambe
more explicit than th
and disappointing utte
The occupation of Fa
a number of unfriendl
has been committing
years, wherever and wl
offered. As another
and even more obvio
intent, we mention the
mands of France for
Newfoundland fisherie
in Mr. Chamberlain's
solely with a view to
policy in that quarter
terests there are a van
view of this disposit
France, Great Britai
upon her exclusive rig
ley are expected to ha
Mr. Chamberlain's
chronic state of un
France and England,

a resumption of the military occupation of the post, but that it is preliminary to an exploring expedition which Major Marchand will conduct in the region of some of the little-known tributaries of the Upper Nile. The original plan, of which Marchand's occupation of Fashoda formed a part, involved two military expeditions which were to meet at that point. One was to start in the French possessions in the Congo region and travel northeast to Fashoda, securing control of the territory passed over; this is the part which was accomplished by Major Marchand. The other was to start at the French station on the Coast of the Gulf of Aden and move northwest to Fashoda. The success of the two expeditions would have completed the chain of French influence across Africa from east to west and would thereby have foiled the British plan of long standing, to secure an unbroken line of possessions through the center of the continent from north to south. But the second of the two French expeditions was not successfully carried through. The plan failed and Major Marchand was left unsupported in an advanced position where he could have been at the mercy of the Dervishes, had not the timely victory of Gen. Kitchener removed that source of danger. The British victory in the Soudan, therefore, probably saved the French expedition from annihilation, but at the same time destroyed any lingering hope for its success. Major Marchand is now returning up the Nile to Fashoda, whence it is believed that he will proceed with his exploring expedition southeast to the French station on the Gulf of Aden; that is, he will follow roughly, in a reverse direction, the line of march laid out for the second military expedition, which should have joined him at Fashoda.

The latest word from the peace commissioners at Paris is that the Americans have informed the Spaniards that the United States must have the entire Philippine group of islands, and for a treaty cession of the same the United States will pay $20,000,000 to Spain and throw the islands open to the commerce of the world. Spain has been given until the 28th of the present month to accept these terms and the opinion seems to still prevail at Washington that she will accept without further delay. ——At this writing a terrible blizzard is raging throughout the entire northwestern quarter of the United States. In Kansas, Nebraska and Montana it is exceedingly severe. The storm broke upon this city on Monday afternoon and by Tuesday morning we had a genuine introduction to winter. The storm extends as far south as Texas, where freezing weather and fierce winds are reported.——The Trans-Mississippi Good Roads and Public Improvement Association of Missouri convened in this city Monday afternoon and will be in session two days. Every congressional district was well represented. About 350 delegates were present, representing pretty much all the busy occupations of life. The most important business transacted was the recommendation of new legislation and amendments to the Constitution, authorizing the levying of additional taxes for road improvement purposes.

EDUCATIONAL CONFERENCE.

We have already published a call for a conference on the subject of education, to be held at Moberly, beginning at three o'clock, Tuesday, Dec. 6. The circumstances under which this conference is called and the condition of our educational interests in the state make it a matter of very great importance that there be a good general representation at this meeting. It is important, not only to insure the doing of the right things, but to prevent any unwise action which might prove detrimental to the very cause it is intended to serve. What should be done? What can be done?

We can at least recognize the facts as they exist, and guide our course accordingly. To be more specific, here are some facts that must be faced:

1. We have such institutions in the state as Christian University, at Canton, Central Christian College, at Albany, the Orphan Schools at Camden and Fulton, and Christian College and the Missouri Bible College, at Columbia. Each one of these institutions feels the need of assistance, and is seeking to secure such financial aid as it can from the brotherhood of the state, particularly from that part of the state in which it is located.

2. No one of these institutions receives or has any right to hope for the unanimous support of the brotherhood of the state. The part of the state in which each of these schools is located would protest against subordinating its own interests to those of another institution situated in a different part of the state. Northeast Missouri, for instance, would repudiate any action of any conference that advised the cessation of all efforts on the part of the friends of Christian University to promote its endowment until Central Christian College was adequately endowed. The other institutions of the state would do the same thing under the same circumstances, and each of them, we believe, would be justified in such action. No one institution among us commands the co-operation of the entire brotherhood of the state nor is regarded by the brotherhood as having a first claim on its support. While the Bible College at Columbia, finds its supporters scattered throughout the state and is not limited to any locality, yet there are many brethren in the state who recognize the prior claims of some other institution, and who would not be coerced into supporting it by any resolution which an educational conference might pass.

3. There is not the slightest probability of the concentration of the entire brotherhood of the state in an effort to establish a new institution, in a different location, leaving uncared for the institutions that already exist. But, granted the consent, the means would not be forthcoming for its adequate equipment and endowment.

Now these are facts, *stubborn* facts, which it would be very unwise to ignore. What policy do they indicate? The answer seems very clear to us. There is but one thing which the educational conference at Moberly can do. When it has learned the condition and needs of these various schools, it may approve, or improve, if it can, any plan which any of these institutions may have devised for the increase of its endowment, or for its better equipment extend such advice as may seem wise to the various schools, and commend them to the brotherhood of the state. may, perhaps, in addition to this, appoi an educational board for the state to exe cise a general advisory influence over the various educational interests, throug which these several institutions may brin their claims before the brotherhood of th state.

Any attempt, as indicated by the resolu tion passed by the last conference, to sele one or two institutions on which to concer trate the support of the entire brotherhoo of the state, and to neglect all other inst tutions, would be futile. Such a resolutio if passed, would be a "dead letter," excep that it would serve to stir up antagonisn that need rather to be allayed. Speakir from the point of view of our entire educa tional interests in the state, we hope th no such action will be taken.

A DIVINE MISSION—WHAT?

III.—UNITY.

We have already characterized the ear part of the present century as a period intense sectarian strife and of most pr nounced denominationalism. The empha laid upon the denominational peculiariti was such as to excite the most bitt antagonism between the religious partie In this condition of things mutual c operation was out of the question. Tl characteristic of brotherly love, which w so marked a feature of the early Churc had been well-nigh obliterated by sectari animosities. It is scarcely necessary now point out how contrary all this was and to the express teaching of Christ and h apostles.

Imagine the effect of this state of feeling communities where various religious bodi were struggling for the supremacy, ar even in families which were often divide by religious differences. Not unfrequent husbands and wives belonging to differe denominations were not permitted to s together at the Lord's Table. Parents ar children were divided often in the san way. An attempt on the part of Thom Campbell, soon after his arrival in tl New World, to gather scattered membe of different branches of the Presbyteria Church in communion service in Weste Pennsylvania led to his arraignment befo the Presbyterian Synod for this irregularit Indeed, it was this fact, in connection wi the great need of closer religious sympatl and co-operation, that opened the eyes of Thomas and Alexander Campbell to tl evils of division.

We have also referred to the fact that i the early part of the present century infide ity was rampant, especially among the mo intelligent class of people. Is this fact to l wondered at in view of the type of Chri tianity which was presented to the world that time? Nothing could be more di tasteful to a man of culture and breadth sympathy than the narrow bigotry th characterized the religious thought an practice of the times. It was a consta stumblingblock in the way of people wl wanted to be religious and did not kno what church to join, and who did not desi to incur the displeasure and even animos ity of his neighbors by entering any one o the religious parties. It is not to be e pected that the human mind in its norm condition can be greatly interested in tl class of questions which were discussed much during that period.

In view of this condition of things and its fatal results upon missionary activity and the influence of the Church upon the social and political life of the time, it is not difficult to see, both in the light of the New Testament teaching and from the state of the Church, that unity must constitute a primary and fundamental principle in any program of reform which would meet the need of the age. If we are at all authorized in interpreting God's purposes in the light of history and of his revealed will, we are surely justified in saying that one of God's purposes in the raising up of this religious reformation was to call attention to the evils of divisions and to sound the note of unity among the divided people of God.

This it did in no uncertain tones. The Declaration and Address issued in 1809 deals very largely with the evils of a divided Church, and points out what its author believed to be the only remedy for these divisions. It claimed that these divisions were not only unscriptural and anti-scriptural, but that they were anti-natural, dividing asunder those who by the ties of a common spiritual kinship should be united. It claimed that the Church was "intentionally and constitutionally one," and consequently that any rupture of this unity was a violation of its constitution or organic law, and that the Church could never fulfill its mission in its divided condition, and that it must return to the organic law of its being and to its original unity in Christ before it could hope to enter upon an era of universal triumph.

It can readily be understood that this radical view, as it seemed at the time, excited great opposition. Religious people generally had come to accept denominationalism as the normal condition of the Church. That it would be possible for Christians to put away their divisions and their uncharitable contentions and live together in peace seemed to them utopian if not sacrilegious. Many specious arguments were resorted to to justify the existing divisions. It was said that if the Church were one we should have religious despotism; but this was, as was pointed out at the time, to mistake aggregation and ecclesiastical consolidation for unity. The primitive churches were one in their faith and ordinances, and yet there was no ecclesiasticism to threaten or curtail their liberty. Again it was said, "We cannot all see alike; men are differently constituted, mentally and temperamentally, and will always differ." To this it was replied that men differed in opinion, taste and temperament just as much in the early church as they do now, and yet, in spite of this difference, and in spite of bitter prejudices between Jew and Gentile, the Church was one in Christ, and that it is not necessary for men to all see alike on every question in order to be brethren and live together in peace; that Christian love makes it possible for people of various tastes and temperaments to dwell together in unity.

What has been the result of these nine decades of agitation on the subject of union? In the first place there has been a very large abatement of party feeling and sectarian strife. Members of different religious bodies now freely recognize each other as Christians, and, with few exceptions, can sit down together at the Lord's Table and express their common faith in a common Lord without fear of ecclesiastical interference with their right so to do. In the second place the evils of division and the desirability of a closer union are freely recognized and expressed by Christians of all religious bodies. As a result of this there has come to be very little emphasis placed on purely speculative opinions and beliefs, which make up the warp and woof of denominational distinctions, while there is decidedly more emphasis on vital and fundamental truth. Again, the multiplication of interdenominational organizations, in which Christians of different names and creeds work together harmoniously for the advancement of the kingdom of God, is an index of the growth of sentiment and unity and a prophecy of future triumph. The various religious bodies are co-operating in many ways, as in evangelical alliances, Y. M. C. A. organizations, Y. P. S. C. E. Society, international and interdenominational Sunday-school work, and in other ways for the advancement of the common cause of Christianity.

Are we not justified, in the light of the developments of the present century, and in the light of the express teaching of the New Testament, in understanding that one of God's purposes in our religious movement was to promote the cause of Christian unity? This is not saying, of course, that the change that has come over the religious world on the subject of unity is due entirely to the plea which we have made for unity; but that plea has certainly been an important factor, and the fact that there have been other factors working to the same end only goes to confirm the view that in urging our plea for unity we are working in harmony with the divine purpose.

COLORADO NOTES.

These notes are written in Colorado Springs. This place is about seventy-five miles south of Denver. It has a population of probably 25,000. Colorado College is located here. It has good buildings, a full faculty, well trained, and an endowment of about a quarter of a million of dollars. The library building would be an ornament to any city. The number of volumes in the library—which is called "the Coburn;" from the name of the gentleman who gave the building—is 27,000. There are as many students in Colorado College as can be accommodated. There is not an open saloon in this town. There is a clause in each title deed forbidding the use of the ground as a saloon site. Those who give tone to the town are generally New England people. Colorado Springs is a little Boston, located at the foot of Pike's Peak. The Young Men's Christian Association has a membership of almost 1,200. "The Yoke Fellow's Band" has been organized for Bible study. The general secretary, Mr. T. P. Day, says that if young men can be interested in the study of the Bible almost everything that is needed in the formation of character will follow. The acting pastor of the Christian Church will have charge of "The Worker's Training Class." Some of the topics to be studied are "Evidences of the Existence of God," "Necessity for a Revelation from God," "The Inspiration of the Bible," "The Theme of the Bible from Genesis to Revelation," "The Value of the Bible," "The Divisions of the Bible," "The Books of the Bible and Their Writers," "The Problem of Jesus: Who is He?" "The Nature of Christianity," etc.

The Presbyterian Church is the strongest body of Christians in Colorado Springs. The mayor of the city is a member of that church and an active Christian man. It is said he was elected to his office by the Christian Endeavorers. There is a strong Baptist Church here. This week—Nov. 13 19—the Association of Baptist Churches in the state of Colorado is in session here. The First Methodist Church is preparing to build a $60,000 house. The Christian Church in Colorado Springs has a standing with the strongest and the best. There is excellent material in it. A class of thirty has been organized for the systematic study of missions. The text-books are the Bible and McLean's and Lhamon's handbooks. The class has already learned that the Bible is *the* missionary handbook. The Old Testament contains a foregleam of world-wide missions. The four gospels give an accouut of the life and work of the Prince of foreign missionaries—Jesus of Nazareth, the Son of God. The Book of Acts is a record of the missionary activity of the disciples of Jesus during the first century of the Christian era. The epistles in the New Testament are letters written by missionaries to mission churches. The book of Revelation contains a prophetic account of the ultimate success of world-wide missions.

There is a fine Unitarian Church here. I is a center of culture—literary, musical social. The pastor meets with the evangelical ministers in their Monday morning conference. There are two Episcopal Churches in Colorado Springs. The rectors attend the weekly meetings of the pastors There is the utmost freedom of thought an speech, with entire good feeling. This is free country.

The South End Christian Church has become a mission of the First Christian Church. There are about sixty members W. T. Hunt was the preacher. He preache now in Craig, Colorado. He is a good man —full also of the Holy Spirit and of faith. His presence and that of his wife will be a blessing in any community. J. P. Lucas is pastor of the Christian Church in Colorado City. This place is four or five miles west of Colorado Springs, with which it is connected by steam and electricity. I is familiarly and locally known as "Old Town." Colorado City was in existence some years previous to the founding of Colorado Springs. It is one of the oldest if not *the* oldest town in the state. For a number of years Bro. Lucas was pastor in Colorado Springs. The beautiful house of worship in which the Disciples meet in this place is a monument to his ability. It was erected during his pastorate. He is held in affectionate remembrance here. There is a neat little house of worship in Colorado City and a church organization of probably seventy-five members.

The Board of the Colorado Christian Missionary Convention met in Denver Thursday, Nov. 10. The meeting was held in the office of B. O. Aylesworth, pastor of the Central Christian Church. Miss Lois A. White and G. W. Muckley were present, representing the Christian Woman's Board of Missions and the Board of Church Extension. The Christian Woman's Board has aided the work of evangelization in Colorado for a number of years. What they have done is appreciated. There are no warmer, friends of the Christian Woman's Board of Missions on earth than are to be found in Colorado. The president and corresponding secretary of the Colorado Christian Woman's Board are, *ex-officio*, members of the Board of the Colorado Christian Missionary Convention. And they are *members*—not merely figure-heads. The board determined to employ a state evangelist. There are about forty congregations of the Christian Church in the state, and possibly four thousand members. There are, however, not more than a dozen self-supporting congregations. At least 28 or 30 are in need of financial assistance. The Christian Woman's Board, in Indianapolis, will be asked to render aid. It is expected that they will do so. The Board of Church Extension has put about $7,000 in Colorado. The secretary recently spent a Lord's day morning in Colorado Springs. The Church Extension Fund, as a result, was increased more than five hundred dollars.

The annual meeting of the Christian Missionary Convention was held in Pueblo, Nov. 1-6. R. B. Preston is pastor of the Pueblo Christian Church. He is a good man, has a good wife and is doing an excellent work in Pueblo. He has been there about a year. Before he began to preach Bro. Preston was a lawyer and a business man. This experience increased his effectiveness in the pastorate. Among other good results of his work in Pueblo he has put the congregation in the way of paying a debt contracted a number of years ago. The hospitality of Pueblo was more than satisfactory to those who were at the convention.

The attendance was not large. There were less than one hundred delegates. The spirit was pre-eminently Christian. There is a fine body of preachers in Colorado. The ministers' meeting occupied one day. Grant K. Lewis, of the Highlands church, in Denver, was present. His address possessed superior merit. B. O. Aylesworth delivered an address that was a literary gem. He discussed a phase of the problem of union among Christians. All of the addresses possessed merit. They were of a high order. This remark ought also to be made concerning the addresses deliverek during the sessions of the missionary convention proper. The readers of the CHRISTIAN - EVANGELIST may have the pleasure ere long of reading one or two of them.

There is heroism on the part of those who represent the Master in the destitute regions of Colorado equal to the heroism of which we read displayed in heathen lands. There were times when there was not a dry eye in the Pueblo convention during the recital of experiences by mission workers. Miss White and Mr. Muckley attended this convention and added to its interest and value.

The meeting will be held next year in Denver, with the South Broadway congregation—the church of which S. B. Moore is pastor. B. O. Aylesworth was elected president of the convention; Leonard G. Thompson, Denver, is the corresponding secretary.

B. B. T.

—Deceit, dishonesty and disobedience are guideposts to destruction.

Editor's Easy Chair.

There is danger, we judge, from some indications, that we may rely too much, this Jubilee Year, upon noise and the clatter of machinery, and externalisms generally, rather than upon the presence and the power of God working in us and through us to accomplish the results which He desires. It is as true now as it was in the olden time that "not by might nor by power, but by my Spirit" that the work of the Lord must be carried on. The real thing that should concern us, this Jubilee Year, is not $100,000 for Home Missions, or $150,-000 for Foreign Missions, or 100,000 additions to the church. These would be desirable results, but they are secondary. The great aim during the present year, the completion of a half century of organized missionary work, should be the putting of ourselves and of all our resources at the service of the Lord; or, in other words, the consecration of our entire membership with all their gifts and resources to the advancement of the kingdom of God. It is a propitious time for ascertaining our spiritual needs, our shortcomings, our failures, and seeking to supply these needs and correct these faults. If we can only put ourselves in right relations with God and offer ourselves and our substance to Him to be used for the extension of His reign among men, the matter of missionary offerings and additions to the church will take care of themselves—not without our effort, of course, but the effort will be spontaneous and effective. We cannot begin on the outside and succeed. If we are to make any distinct advance in our missionary, educational and benevolent work, it must be as the result of an equally distinct advance in the spiritual condition of our churches, if the gain is to be permanent.

It would be a great mistake to lay chief emphasis upon the *size* of the next convention, and make it appear that the great object was to get 10,000 delegates present. It will not be difficult to do that, but we may do it and accomplish little by it. The thing to be sought for and aimed at is a convention of men and women who shall come together ready to offer themselves and their all in the service of God and humanity. Let there be a gathering of men and women coming together in this spirit, with hearts aglow with love to God and man and indwelt by the Spirit of God, and whether the convention numbers 1,000 or 10,000, it will be a remarkable convention, because of the power of God resting upon it. It is well enough, perhaps, to have some one in each city designated to organize delegations for the convention, but it is infinitely more important that some one in each church shall be stirred up by the Lord to stir up the congregation to more spiritual and unselfish living as the essential preparation for a victorious advance along all the lines of our work. Better 1,000 delegates animated by the Spirit of God, and gathering in humility to hear His word of command, and prepared to obey, than 10,000 or even 20,000 animated by motives less holy and unselfish. The lesson taught us in Gideon's victory has its application in our own time. This is not saying anything against organization, but it is a warning against relying upon that as the main thing.

If, as the result of the churches getting closer to God, putting away all unworldly methods and motives and ambitions, and seeking the glory of God and the salvation of men, 100,000 should be added to the Lord, it will indeed be a matter of rejoicing, both on earth and in heaven; and there can be no question but that this number and many more would be added if the church would purify itself of whatever displeases the Lord, and should both preach and practice the gospel of divine love for the redemption of man. But to add half-converted, worldly minded, prayerless members to the half-converted and unconsecrated membership we now have, would be no gain. What God needs to accomplish His great purposes on earth is, not numbers, but *quality*. He can take one consecrated soul and fill it with His Spirit and truth and love, and shake a whole continent with it. The great question we ought to face this Jubilee Year is, "Are we fit instruments to be used of God for the furtherance and ultimate success of so high and holy a plea as the restoration of the unity, the faith, the life and the victorious power of the Apostolic Church?" And the great *task* is, to put ourselves in readiness to be used for the accomplishment of His gracious purposes on earth. Then may we expect to see the banner of Christ exalted and his cause advancing by leaps and bounds.

And then, too, may we not hope that the spirit of boasting over numbers and growth and wealth and power and influence will be far from every one who speaks or writes during this Jubilee Year? Let us rather be filled with the spirit of humility which characterized our Lord, and, recognizing our own imperfections, and how far short we have come of accomplishing all that we might have accomplished had we been more faithful to our trust, let us in meekness seek to help one another and to win others from the dominion of Satan and from the allurements of the world, to give themselves unto loving service to Him who gave himself up for us. So shall we best represent to the world the Master whom we serve, and so shall we best recommend to thoughtful people everywhere the beauty and simplicity and divine character of the cause we plead. Again, let us say that we could adopt no better motto for the coming year than that to which we have referred: "Not by might, nor by power, but by my Spirit, saith the Lord."

The most favorable signs we could ask for, prophesying a great Jubilee Convention in '99, would be largely increased attendance on the prayer-meetings, and more earnest praying by those who attend, the rearing up of family altars which have been allowed to fall into ruin, more earnest, heart-searching preaching, from our pulpits, probing into the very core of the spiritual life, healing of church feuds, payment of back salaries to preachers and all other debts, a continuous spirit of revival in the churches, the growth of Sunday-schools, renewed interest in Bible study, more genuine consecration in the Endeavor Societies and a general attitude of expectancy of great blessings from God and the planning of large things for God. When you see these signs know ye that the day of triumph draws near.

fact that the Lord's Supper sets forth the central truth of Christianity and furnishes the most feasible and practical method of calling the attention of the people to this vital truth, and of enlisting them in public worship, would seem to argue the practical utility of its observance as part of the regular Lord's day worship.

Hour of Prayer.

THE LIGHT OF THE GENTILES.

(Midweek Prayer-meeting Topic, Nov. 30, 1898).

And nations shall come to thy light, and kings to the brightness of thy rising.—*Isa. 60: 3.*

So spake the great prophet of the Old Testament at a time of great national darkness. It is the glory of faith that in the hour of deepest adversity it is able to sing the note of future triumph. To the eye of mere sense or unbelief there was nothing that looked encouraging in the condition of the Jewish people at the time these words were spoken. Whether we consider them as uttered before the captivity or afterward, the condition was not such as to inspire the great hope expressed in this prophecy apart from faith in God's purpose. This great prophet had caught a vision of God's purpose in history, and especially in the history of his chosen people. He saw that God was working out his plans for the redemption of the race through his nation. Understanding this, he was able to foretell a brighter future for the cause of righteousness and for humanity.

To understand these words of the prophet we must identify, as they were identified in the prophet's mind, the faithful remnant of God's chosen people with that enlargement of the kingdom of God and of his righteousness which should come through Christ, the Messiah of the Jews. God's redemptive purpose is seen unfolding itself in the history of the Jewish people. This prophet foresees the time when God's chosen people, that is, the representatives of his cause and of his righteousness on earth, instead of being shrouded in darkness, oppressed, taken captive by the nations, shall be in the place of power and influence. "Nations shall come to thy light, and kings to the brightness of thy rising. Lift up thine eyes round about, and see; they all gather themselves together, they come to thee; thy sons shall come from far and thy daughters shall be carried in the arms. Then thou shalt see and be lightened, and thine heart shall tremble and be enlarged; because the abundance of the sea shall be turned unto thee, the wealth of the nations shall come unto thee" (vs. 3-5).

This is a magnificent future for this despised and persecuted people. From obscurity and captivity and persecution and darkness they are to come into power and glory and wealth. The secret of this wonderful change is stated thus: "The Lord shall arise upon thee, and his glory shall be seen upon thee" (v. 2). What do we see to-day as we lift up our eyes and look day the leading nations of the world? Take the Anglo-Saxon nations and peoples and consider their position and influence at the present time, and see a literal fulfillment of the prophecy. Is it not true that the United States and Great Britain may be said to hold in their power, very largely, under God, the future of the nations? In proportion as the glory of the Lord shall be seen upon them shall they become still more powerful in the years to come. Well will it be for these nations if they recognize the fact stated by the prophet, "For the name of the Lord thy God and for the Holy One of Israel," this power has come upon them.

There is a principle involved in this prophecy which may be universally applied. What matters it if some particular cause which we represent is weak in numbers and influence, and unpopular, provided it be a right cause? The Spirit that was in Isaiah is saying to us, "Arise, shine; for thy light is come, and the glory of the Lord is risen upon thee." It bids us take heart and hope in the darkest hours of misfortune and defeat, because—

"Right is right since God is God,
And right the day will win;
To doubt would be disloyalty,
To falter would be sin."

Apply it to the cause of temperance and the suppression of the liquor traffic. Is this a right cause? If so, the nations must ultimately accept it. The reign of time-serving politicians is only transient. Truth at last comes out victor. So with every other moral, social and religious reform. If they represent God's thought and are in harmony with God's purpose they will ultimately win, and the glory of the Lord shall rest upon them.

We need, sometimes, in our moments of despondency, when we feel discouraged with ourselves and with our progress, to comfort our own hearts with this truth. Darkness will give place to light, defeat to victory. Only let us be sure that we are right with God, and we can trust the future.

This prophecy of Isaiah is being progressively fulfilled. It is not yet completed. There are yet grander triumphs to crown the kingdom of God and the cause of righteousness. Christ is to be the light of all the nations, and their laws, constitutions, customs, and their entire civilization must be molded by the teaching and spirit of the Christ of prophecy and of history. We are coworkers with God in the fulfillment of this blessed prophecy. We labor in the assurance of certain triumph.

PRAYER.

O, Thou who art the God and Father of our Lord Jesus Christ, we thank Thee for the light which Thou hast shed upon the nations through the coming of Thy Son, our Savior, Jesus of Nazareth. We thank Thee that with His birth and life a new light has arisen upon the world, even the Sun of Righteousness with healing in His wings. We rejoice that the light of His life is shining more and more into the dark places of the earth, dispelling superstition

Our Budget.

—The Lord hath done great things for us.

—We of all people should praise the Lord for his goodness.

—Our thanksgiving should be expressed in deed as well as in word.

—The Chattanooga Convention motto for 1899 is being taken up with enthusiasm all along the ine.

—Our churches will make the greatest effort in their history during the coming year to go forward in every good work, especially in the evangelistic and missionary departments.

—Our readers must not forget our call for a few hundred dollars to assist Bro. Randall in securing a printing press and some type for his work in Jamaica. Up to this time only one brother has responded, but we take it that there must be a number of those who would be willing to make a small investment in the dissemination of gospel light on the Island of Jamaica. We hope our C. W. B. M. sisters especially will interest themselves in this matter and stir up the brethren.

—We desire to call special attention to the C. W. B. M. articles in this paper in the interest of C. W. B. M. Day, the first Sunday in December, which is now at hand. These are carefully written articles and in the interest of one of the most active and influential missionary agencies among the Disciples of Christ.

—As all of our readers are interested in the temperance work, the abstract of Mrs. Hunt's address before the National W. C. T. U. Convention, recently held at St. Paul, Minn., which appears in this paper, will be appreciated.

—The best way to inform yourself of the splendid record of our Church Extension work is to send to G. W. Muckley, Cor. Sec., Kansas City, Mo., for a copy of the October-December issue of Business in Christianity. No magazine of equal size could well contain more information on a given subject than does this one on Church Extension and its tenth annual report.

—The American Christian Missionary Convention, at Chattanooga, fixed the third Lord's day of Dcember (or the first Lord's day that the church may select thereafter if they can not do it on the day) as the time for taking the offerings for Ministerial Relief. Every church and preacher ought to make a Christmas gift to the veteran and disabled preachers and their wives.

—W. D. Humphrey, of Piedmont, Mo., writes us that he recently lost a son, a young man of 23 years, by typhoid fever. He now has but one of a family of four children left to him in his old age and feels greatly oppressed by this sorrow. But we pray that he may find that comfort which a loving Father in heaven can give only at such a time.

—Do not forget that the third Lord's day in December is the time for offerings to the Fund for Ministerial Relief. Every preacher and every church should remember this time and not neglect this offering. If any facts or information are needed concerning this work drop a postal card to D. R. Lucas, Indianapolis, Ind., and the matter wanted will be promptly forwarded to you.

—Valparaiso Day of the Chicago Ministerial Association of the Christian Church "was a great day," according to the program sent to us. There were two sessions, or practically an all-day meeting, with splendid addresses and devotional and social variations. John L. Brandt, of Valparaiso, Ind., is president of the Association.

—At our preachers' meeting in this office, on last Monday morning, the preachers listened to a very earnest address by F. O. Fannon, the pastor of the First Christian Church, of this city, on "How to Reach Young Men." In this address Bro. Fannon made a strong appeal for stronger religious influence in the home, which is evidently one of the great necessities of the hour.

—In a recent issue of the CHRISTIAN-EVANGELIST is a clipping from the Cumberland Presbyterian, with suitable comments, in regard to an elder in the Presbyterian Church, Ushigome, Tokyo, who was expelled for teaching immersion for baptism. The clipping is correct. It may add to its interest for the readers to know further particulars. The elder's name is Miyazaki San. He is the leading Christian poet of Japan, and is turning his attention to the translation of Christian hymns into Japanese. He is author of a popular work similar to Irving's Sketch Book and other works of merit. Last spring he was baptized by Bro. H. H. Gray, and at once openly taught his people his new convictions. He defended his case before the Presbyterian tribunals and boldly gave reasons for his faith. Eight months have passed. He may now be seen every Lord's day leading the singing and frequently preaching in the Christian Church of Koishikawa, Tokio, where he is now an elder and a zealous worker. He is the Japanese editor of our new paper, the Bible Way, and finds not a little comfort in reading and writing about Thomas Campbell.

FRANK H. MARSHALL.

Koishikawa, Tokio.

—The following "new game law," is credited to the Georgetown (Ky.) News. If it should appear *too* "game" to our readers it must be remembered that it comes from a "game" state. And yet one of our Missouri agents sends it to us, as if she thought it worthy of universal application:

Book agents may be killed from October 1 to September 1; spring poets from March 1 to June 1; scandal mongers, April 1 to February 1; umbrella borrowers, August 1 to November 1, and from February 1 to May 1, while every man who accepts a paper two years, but when the bill is presented says, "I never ordered it," may be killed on sight without reserve or relief from valuation or appraisement laws, and buried face downward, without benefit of clergy.

Secular journals may have readers who act in that way, but does any one suppose that subscribers to a *religious* paper would be capable of such a subterfuge? Perish the thought!

—I have a bit of rare good news which I would like to share with you and the readers of the CHRISTIAN-EVANGELIST. Mrs. A. M. Atkinson yesterday gave us one thousand dollars toward the English Bible Chair Endowment Fund. Was not that a beautiful gift for a worker in the Christian Woman's Board of Missions to make in this our silver anniversary year? We are thankful and happy for it, and hope it may inspire others whom God has made stewards of his riches to do likewise.

HELEN E. MOSES.

This is indeed "good news," and we congratulate our sisters on this liberal gift to one of the most important if not *the* most important branch of their work. It is like Sister A. to appreciate and help such a work in this generous way.

—Last week we stated that St. Louis had a curfew ordinance, but we now find that such is not the case. The Mayor vetoed the bill, and the city lawmakers refused to pass it over the veto. The bill had been so strongly supported by the city council before it went to the Mayor that we expected it to become a law, and so stated. The chief reason assigned by the Mayor for the veto of the bill was that it interfered with personal liberty, which if fully interpreted doubtless means, to the Mayor, interference with the saloons' opportunities to secure and educate customers for its traffic.

—In our reference to the Missionary Intelligencer for November last week we stated its information covered "the entire work of the Disciples of Christ in the foreign field." We should have added, done through our Foreign Missionary Society. The C. W. B. M. is doing a grand work in India and elsewhere, and a full account of their work may be had in the recent number of the Missionary Tidings. The C. W. B. M. Day, the first Lord's day in December, is at hand, and inasmuch as they have undertaken to greatly enlarge their offerings for 1899, we trust that the day will be more generally observed than ever before To this end we call special attention to the excellent articles on their work in this paper.

—Number four, Vol. five of Northfiel Echoes contains the addresses delivered at th Northfield Conference, Northfield, Mass., las summer. The two chief speakers were Rev G. Campbell Morgan and Rev. C. H. C. Mac Gregor, both of London, England. Thei addresses are upon living questions and highl charged with spiritual energy. There ar other addresses in this magazine also of grea value. D. L. Moody's "Problems of Churc Work" are especially interesting and practical. The article consists of Dr. Moody' replies to practical questions on church management and church work. No preache would regret the cost of this book nor the tim to read it.

—The list of persons who have killed themselves because they have been ruined by ru is a long one, and the list of those who hav killed themselves by rum is much longer Every day persons who have spent all thei money in buying rum hang themselves, c make way with themselves by other methods every day such persons are taken to the insan asylum, almhouses and prisons; every da they are discharged from situations; ever day they receive wounds without cause; ever day their wives and children, in some case their husbands and children, are mad wretched by the spectacle of their drunkenness. Nevertheless, the people of the Unite States look with favor upon the saloon, because they are shortsighted enough to thin that it keeps down taxes.—*The New Yor Christian Advocate.*

—The 39th annual meeting of the Providen Association, of this city, was held at the Firs Christian Church, Nov. 17th, at 8 P. M. Devotional exercises, select music, reports o officers and the election of the new board o directors made up the interesting program o the evening. The report of the general manager was especially interesting, and affords foo for reflection. The following figures from hi report will help to understand some of the conditions of metropolitan life and the scope of work done by an institution of this kind for the relief of distressed persons:

A summary of the statistical records shows that help in all departments and in various forms has been given to 14,202 different persons, 2,839 being homeless men, women and children, and has been given 68,211 times. Material relief in kind and amount was: Breadstuffs and groceries, 278,193 7-8 pounds; coal, 56,019 2-3 bushels; clothing, 12,928 pieces; shoes, 2,812 pairs; bedding, stoves and furniture, 481 articles; lodgings and meals supplied at the lodges for men and women and meals at the restaurant—lodging 6,077, and meals 134,440, of which 115,089 were served at the restaurant, 11,700 in midday dinners given to workers in the laundry and sewing rooms and 7,740 earned by labor at the woodyard. In the department for the special relief of the sick poor, care has been given in 1,185 cases, in which there have been 4,128 visits by the nurse; the attendance of 152 physicians has been secured; medicines supplied 1,113 times and hospital treatment for 126 patients, and there have been furnished sick diet 1,795 times, and 1,701 pieces of clothing for the bed and person. The statistics of relief by work show work given to 4,278 different persons, in all 22,556 times, and amounting to 19,674 1-2 days, and the value of earnings $11,922.26.

An important statistic is the number of cases not helped. Of the applications made for aid, 856 were found on visitation not needing or not deserving it; 718 not found and presumably giving false addresses, and by the labor test refusing work, 275 heads of families and 273 homeless men, making the number of applicants thus detected as not entitled to aid 1,404. How extensively as well as how thoroughly the applicants are investigated is shown by the visits at the homes of applicants numbering 7,270, and 4,798 calls made by the drivers of delivery wagons, which in important respects serve the uses of revisits.

—"The Success of Missions, or the Lowest Classes have been Reached," is the title of a 20-page tract by F. M. Rains, of the Foreign Society. This tract is one section of an address by him before the Chattanooga Convention, and which was ordered published in tract form by the convention. A one-cent postage stamp will secure a copy of the tract. Address the author, Cincinnati, Ohio.

The church is not the basis of truth in the se that it is its originator, or first cause, because it is truth's discoverer and interreter. Truth is not to be made to order by pe or a Mormon prophet, who convenient-possess themselves of a new decree or elation as suits their developing purpose. church cannot manufacture any truths any e than it can any souls *ex nihilo;* it cannot its hand upon any body of true doctrine affirm: ''This is my truth!'' but rather it declare: ''This is God's truth!'' What church can do is to discover the truth that ady is, to bring that to light and to notice, to apply it to the hearts and consciences of 1.—*The New York Observer*.

-All who have read ''On the Rock, or th Stranger than Fiction''—and who ong the Disciples have not?—will be glad to the face of its author, D. R. Dungan, ich we present on our first page this week. . Dungan is also the author of other popu- works, such as ''Modern Phases of Skepti- n,'' ''Rum, Ruin and the Remedy,'' Iermeneutics,'' etc., and is a frequent con- utor to our periodical literature. He has n connected with the Bible Departments of h Drake and Cotner Universities, and his iliarity with and knowledge of the Bible hardly second to that of any man in our ks. He is at present pastor of the Mt. anne Church in this city, and is conducting a on Bible class in the Holland Building every urday afternoon, for the study of the les- for the following day. This class, made largely of business men of various denomi- ions, who are teachers in the Sunday-school, utgrowing its quarters and is developing interest. Bro. Dungan was born in Noble nty, Ind., May 15, 1837, but has labored efly in the Northwest. He was twice nored with the chaplaincy of the Nebraska gislature, and was once candidate for gov- nor on the Prohibition ticket. He is still orous in mind and body and has the promise several years of further usefulness.

–The article from J. H. Mac El'Rey which publish elsewhere, furnishes the strongest oof of our willingness to ''hear the other le,'' and to permit the freest expression of inion on all living questions. Its defense of dern Spiritism will, we are sure, unsettle one's faith in Christ, and it may call out a ply that will serve to clear away some of the st that our correspondent throws upon the oject. Leaving to Mr. Lhamon's trenchant n to point out the inconsequential reasoning the article in question, we will only refer r readers to Hudson's recent work, ''The w of Psychical Phenomena,'' recently ticed in this paper, as a sufficient demon- ation of the truth that the phenomena of dern Spiritism have no connection with the rits of the departed.

e S. S., Endeavor and Prayer-meeting Departments.

n response to our note in a recent issue ative to the utility of the departments above med we have received the following ad- ional responses:

EDITOR CHRISTIAN-EVANGELIST:—I want to eak for myself and my friends in favor of aining the Christian Endeavor and Sunday- hool columns as a feature of your paper. thing else could be more helpful, we think.

L. E. MURRAY.

Ladoga, Ind., Nov. 15, 1898.

---

f. H. GARRISON—*Dear Brother:* I am 75 ars old to-day, have been a subscriber and der of the CHRISTIAN-EVANGELIST ever since was born, am an active worker in the En- avor, Sunday-school and prayer-meeting, d I want all of these departments continued in CHRISTIAN-EVANGELIST; they are a great lp to me. Your brother in Christ,

J. Q. HOLMES.

South Haven, Kan., Nov. 14, 1898.

---

notice in your paper an agitation concern- the Sunday-school and Christian Endeavor partments. As one of the young people and the sake of the young people I hope you l retain the Christian Endeavor Department. Not only is it of much help to us in our prayer-meetings, etc., but the very fact that such a paper as the CHRISTIAN-EVANGELIST so recognizes our work is a source of much encouragement and inspiration.

MINNIE BLAKE.

State Supt. of the C. E. of the Disciples of Christ for Colorado.

By all means continue ''special departments'' in CHRISTIAN EVANGELIST. Last week I read the entire article on the prayer-meeting topic, instead of making a speech myself. I have been in other prayer-meetings where I believe such procedure would be more edifying than what was offered.

C. M. FILLMORE.

Peru, Ind., Nov. 17, 1898.

I want to say that I am heartily in favor of continuing the Bible-school and Endeavor departments. Oftentimes that is the only commentary some church members have on the lessons and, like of myself, heartily enjoy it.

MRS. J. E. HODGE.

Fulton, Mo.

DEAR BRO. GARRISON:—I could perhaps get along without the C. E. and S. S. departments, as there is an abundance of literature on these topics, and yet I have read and enjoyed and have been profited by both these departments this year. But personally I could not well get on without the ''Hour of Prayer.'' I do not always use it in our prayer-meetings, but I invariably read it and would feel seriously the loss of it if it were taken out. I fear that we are not as much given to a cultivation of the devotional as we should be. Let us have more of it.

P. J. RICE.

Ft. Wayne, Ind., Nov. 18, 1898.

I write to record my vote for a *continuance* of the C. E. and B.-S. departments in the CHRISTIAN-EVANGELIST. While I take the best ''annual'' published, yet I always read with pleasure and profit Bro. Willett, and also Bro. Jenkins. But of the three departments, the C. E., B.-S. and Prayer-meeting. I think the Prayer the most valuable to the church The problem, how to get one of our religious papers in the home of each family in the church, with me is unsolved, but I am constantly working to that end. My work here is ''noiseless and peaceful.''

H. S. GILLIAM.

Hamilton, Mo.

As to the Sunday-school and Endeavor Departments, also the ''The Hour of Prayer,'' I think that a criticism that would be just and applicable to some papers would not apply to the CHRISTIAN-EVANGELIST. I have especially enjoyed ''The Hour of Prayer,'' and during a part of the year we used these as our subjects for midweek meetings and we should have continued if more of our brethren had been receiving the paper. [How would it do to increase the list of our subscribers at that point?—EDITOR.] The other two subjects look all right *to me*, and I only remember of hearing one criticism, in the eighteen months I have been here, coming from a regular reader. I don't see that you could dispense with any of these and thereby add to the paper, so long as they maintain their present tone. I desire to thank you personally for the comfort Mrs. Burks and I have received from your pen in ''The Hour of Prayer,'' ''Lake Musings'' and ''The Easy Chair.'' We have had some sad hours during this year.

Your brother,

W. W. BURKS.

Parsons, Kan., Nov. 11, 1898.

Value of a Church Paper.

Bro. R. H. Bateman preached one of the best sermons (a few weeks ago) on ''Christian Literature'' that I ever had the the pleasure of hearing, showing how important it is for every member of the Christian Church to have and read one or more of our church papers in order that they might know what the Christian Church was doing. Showing what a failure a a busines man would make if he did not post himself by reading up the journals of his profession. I wish that every member of the Christian Church who does not take a religious paper could have heard it. To-day he preached a splendid sermon on ''What Does the Christian Church Stand For?'' A good and appreciative audience. To-morrow Bro. B. commences a series of meetings for Bro. Ward, in Pasadena, and next Lord's day we expect a splendid sermon from Bro. H. E. Ward.

A. H. THOMAS.

Santa Ana, Cal., Oct. 23, 1898.

To be sure they have, and we are glad they are showing the wisdom to exercise that right. We shall be surprised if our wide-awake, enterprising Methodist brethren do not soon avail themselves of the same privilege. We have no monopoly of the plan if we were the first to adopt it, and as we said on the occasion of opening the work there, "Let them all come—the more the better." We have no disposition to deprive our religious neighbors of the benefit of a good thing, even though they did oppose it in the beginning.

PERSONAL MENTION.

W. G. Loucks is in a protracted meeting at Bright, Ind.

E. J. Fenstermacher has become the successor to G. M. Goode at Lexington, Mo.

Charles Darsie, pastor of the church at Collinwood, O., tendered his resignation to the church there, Nov. 13.

John Treloar has received and accepted a call to the chtrch at Huntingburgh, Ind., to the close of 1899.

J. S. Smith, of Ft. Recovery, O., a graduate of Hiram College, has accepted a call to preach for the church at Carrollton, Ill.

A number of our prominent preachers and others are arranging to go together on a tour to Egypt, Palestine and Europe. Going as a company will make it more pleasant as well as more economical. Write Bro. J. B. Sweeney, Waco, Tex., for itinerary and particulars.

The address of the president of the Missouri Ministerial Association, Clinton Lockhart, also president of Christian University, Canton, Mo., delivered at Carrollton, Mo., July 21, 1898, has been published in a pamphlet, for use by that Association. It is the first president's address of the Association and is worthy of this form for future use and preservation.

A farewell reception was tendered to H. C. Shipley by friends and members of the Christian Church in Carthage, S. D., Oct. 24, amid a Dakota snowstorm. Many were present and all had a good time. Bro. Shipley has accepted a call from the Christian Church in Jewell City, Kas.

H. A. Northcutt is now in a meeting with Geo. Coombs, at 6th and Prospect Ave., Kansas City, Mo.

A. M. Growden's meeting at Russellville has resulted in nine conversions up to date, besides others added otherwise. By invitation of the president of Bethel College (Baptist) he addressed the students of that institution on the 17th inst. He is open for engagements elsewhere to hold meetings or to locate as pastor of a congregation.

R. M. Messick has returned to Salem, Ore., where his family has been since his removal West some time ago. He has spent about 19 years of his life in ministerial work in the state of Missouri, laboring at Chillicothe, Trenton, Gallatin, Marshall, Carrollton, Higginsville, besides serving in the evangelistic field. He has the confidence and esteem of the brotherhood of Missouri, whose sentiments we only voice in commending him to the Christian love and confidence of the brethren in Washihgton, California and Oregon, or wherever he may desire to labor.

The resignation of J. S. Sweeney of Paris, Ky., closes one of the longest pastorates in our brotherhood, longer even than that of his brother, Z. T. Sweeney, at Columbus, Ind. Bro. J. S. Sweeney's health began to fail him last summer and it is, presumably, on this account that he resigns his work at Paris.

F. M. Kirkham has been ill since his arrival in San Francisco, but has recovered sufficiently to enter upon his work on the Pacific Christian.

J. C. Faulkender, of Joplin, Mo., writes that the church there is about closing arrangements for a preacher, and that further applications are unnecessary. This he says will also explain those applications received but not replied to.

Geo. F. Hall, pastor Christian Tabernacle, Decatur, Ill., recently delivered a lecture at Ft. Worth, Tex., being his second lecture trip to that city.

Joel Brown, field agent for the Christian Orphans' Home, called at this office last Monday. He seems to have been about the most successful agent in the field this fall in raising funds for the Orphans' Home. His heart is in the work and he is deeply in earnest in behalf of orphan children and their Home in this city.

Herbert L. Willett's address in Berlin, Germany, is Auhaltstrasse 15, until further notice.

The brethren and sisters of Cantrall, Ill., recently called at the parsonage unannounced, with liberal donations. U. N. Hieronymous is in his first pastorate and doing splendid work. Evangelist W. A. Meloan is expected to begin a revival about Dec. 1st.

J. D. Houston, of Georgetown, Ohio, would like to correspond with any church in need of a preacher for next year. He writes that he has been successful in evangelistic and pastoral work, is a graduate of the Bible College at Lexington, Ky., and has served some of our best churches.

CHANGES.

M. Pittman, Wilmington to E. City, N. C.
G. E. Shanklin, Slater to Stanbury, Mo.
E. T. Martin, Waverly, Ill., to Columbus, Ind.
J. W. Harris, Plymouth to Chickasaw, Miss.
E. J. Fenstermacher, Newport, Ky., to Lexington, Mo.
Wm. Mullendore, Somerset, Pa., to Terre Haute, Ind
J. W. Hewett, Aufaula to S. McAllister, I. T.
J. M. Blalock, Stanbury to Slater, Mo.
T. H. Bentley, Libscomb, Tex., to Moodyville, Kan.

Governor Tanner and the Miners.

DEAR EDITOR:—Let me say a word on the Virden strike through your columns.

Precedent and interpretation have long been so universally in favor of corporations and monopolies; authority has been so hard upon the *people* in case of differences (as witness the shooting at Hazelton, Penn.), that there is a fine justice in Gov. Tanner's brave stand for Virden strikers.

When an executive anticipates legislation in behalf of moral right and especially when it is the right of the masses, good people everywhere should see to it that their moral support makes up for possible lack of legal support.

Gen. Jackson paid two thousand dollars for the illegal arrest he made in New Orleans, but it helped to win him almost a bloodless victory, which victory closed the war of 1812. The nation has since voted his action "great." Posterity will so vote Gov. Tanner's defence of the "people whom the Lord loves." No rebuke, legal or personal, can take from this advanced step the honor of true patriotism. It must count, not only for the good of the Virden miners, but for the good of the poor colored men that were to supplant them—it must count for the good of all toilers throughout the lengte and breadth of the land. God strengthen the cause of the people!

EMMA E. PAGE.

Olympia, Wash., Oct. 31, 1898.

The foregoing is, as it seems to us, a misapprehension of the issue involved in the action of Gov. Tanner in his attempt to prevent the importation of miners from one state into another. We are wholly unable to appreciate the "fine justice" in the flagrant violation of the constitution which said action involves. There is no principle more clearly settled in our American policy than the freedom of laboring men to pass from one state to another in search of employment without let or hindrance from any governor or from any other source. We see nothing brave or heroic in Gov. Tanner's action. On the contrary, it seems to us he was "playing to the gallery" and seeking to make himself solid with the miners. We do not suppose that the poor colored men who, in seeking an opportunity to win bread for their families, were shot down at Virden, and the others who with them imperiled their lives, could be made to understand just how such action was in "defence of the people." They were a part of "the people," even though they were not in a condition to vote for Gov. Tanner. They were as much entitled to the protection of the law as the striking miners at Virden. They were seeking to exercise a right guaranteed by the constitution and laws of this land—a right which we all hold to be sacred. Gov. Tanner assumes the prerogative of denying to these men and to all others similarly situated the exercise of this right, and that without the semblance of law; and this attempt to override the constitution and trample upon the right of workingmen seeking employment under the protection of law our correspondent characterizes as an "advance step" to which must not be withheld "the honor of true patriotism." It will be a sad day for this country when the people come to regard such a step as entitled to either honor or respect. We can echo the prayer in the last sentence, "God strengthen the cause of the people!" and, we would add, "curtail the power of self-seeking and time-serving politicians, who do not scruple to violate law if they feel that they can thereby serve their personal interest."

Educational Spirit at Canton.

DEAR BRO. GARRISON:—Referring to an editorial item in the last CHRISTIAN-EVANGELIST, permit me to say, the attitude of Christian University toward all the other colleges in the state is most amicable; and there is no disposition in the University or among those who represent its claims to antagonize anything that is good, or to dominate in the educational conference in the spirit of rivalry, sectionalism or unfairness. We regard this cause as too holy, and the interests of the whole brotherhood here involved as too sacred for the seizure of any undue advantages.

The large delegation sent from here to the last conference was simply indicative of the high appreciation of the work of the University held by those who know it best. It is expected that many from here will attend the next conference, but I know that it is the disposition of all to favor every worthy suggestion that may be made, and to oppose nothing for merely local gain.

In evidence of this I may cite the broad spirit of the resolution adopted at the last conference in laying out the work of the next meeting, that it "shall discuss and pass upon the propriety of endowing and establishing *one or more colleges* in the state."

Further proof of this willingness to be fair and liberal toward the interests of all is seen in the earnest effort made from this place to call out a full delegation from every part of the state. The simple desire here is to compass the greatest possible good to the cause for all time to come.

CLINTON LOCKHART.

[If this spirit prevails in the Educational Conference all will be well.—EDITOR.]

Original Contributions.

"SPIRITISM OR WITCHCRAFT:" OTHER VIEWS.

JOSEPH R. MAC EL'REY

"The mortallest enemy unto knowledge, and that which hath done the greatest execution [injury] upon truth hath been a peremptory adhesion unto authority, or the establishing of our belief upon the dicta of antiquity.—*Sir Thomas Browne.*

"As there is no subject so fruitful of strife as the discussion of theological hypotheses, I have avoided as much as posible all bearings of original scientific inquiry upon religious opinions."—*G. Gore, LL., D., F.R.S.*, 1378.

I regret having to say of all this—

"'Tis true, and pity 'tis, 'tis true."

Scientists have noted those stigmas upon the faces of heterodox and orthodox religionists alike, inflicted upon each other from times beyond which the religious histories of man runneth not.

Each sect has worn them with
Fervid pride, transmitting them
As worthy trophies, ably won
On ardent, well-fought fields,
By valiant sire to champion son,
Who quarter to no comer yields.
Esprit de corps perpetuum
The sect must ever onward run.
Enthused by party zeal and full
Of words, rhapsodic, bold but weak,
He knowledge, reason, firm and cool,
With him to battle could not take.
A paper helmit, paper shield
And paper pavise he could wield.
Tricked out in these, to war he goes
'Gainst "ancient," midtime," "modern" foes.
"Spiritists," "witches," "sorcerers," sure
No Bible Christian can endure.
Hypnotists, psychists, seers to boot,
And what aught else "from the same root,"
"Like scallion, onion, cabbage, beet,"
Those "Christian Science healers" meet
As "cousins, kindred," on a level,
They all are children of the devil!

By "damning" very few of them "with faintest praise," Mr. Lhamon severely damns them all. He says, "Their aims, proposing to prove to us that the spirit lives after the body is gone, when they do not spring from mercenary motives are majestic." "But its efforts are not needed." This is remarkable language, and the conclusions drawn from it are more remarkable. If Spiritualism can and does prove what it proposes to do, why are the proofs not needed? Do the masses of the world implicitly believe that "the spirit lives after the body is gone?" But, if the masses do merely believe this, is verifiable proof of it now not desirable? What, whom, how can it hurt? Did it hurt when Jesus demonstrated it? Did it hurt the church? Did it hurt the priests? Every new thing has always hurt them. How can the priests demonstrate it now? Can Mr. Lhamon do it? By books? Can he demonstrate the books? In the nature of things can a book verify this? Tischendorf, the most celebrated evangelical man of this age, says in his "History of the Four Gospels," "The spirit of scepticism dominates this nineteenth century," etc.

"Spiritualist proof is not needed because Christ did his work without suspicion of mercenary taint." What connection can this allegation have with this question of the continuity of the spirit? Although not thinking of casting aspersion upon the character of "Christ," Jesus did proffer this world inducements for discipling with him. I think Mr. L. meant Jesus when he wrote it "Christ;" Jesus died, Christ did not die. Mr. L.'s knowledge of church history, past and present, should have admonished silence on matters of "mercenary taint" as a contrast against Spiritualists. Jesus commanded his hearers to give for benevolence tenths of all their possessions that they might be clean unto them. How implicitly do Jesus' disciples obey him in that item, even now? "Mercenary taint," indeed, one of the many stigmata upon the face of the despicable Spiritualists. It may be.

I am not defending or condemning *per se*. I am speaking from my sense of justice. Is not the whole church pockmarked and scarred all over by "mercenary taint?" Probably nine hundred and more in the thousand of those Mr. L. terms by the despicable names he would fasten upon them are pecuniarily poor people. But the benevolence of their public speakers will average as high as that of church preachers. Does Mr. L. know to the contrary? You know I might quote by the amount of the whole contents of the CHRISTIAN-EVANGELIST every week, the language of complaint, beseechment, gloomy, warning and closely impending and irreparable death, blotting out and condign punishment from God on the church if she neglect to bestow out of her abundance. What the church so sorely needs is to keep in pace with the progress of the world, etc., etc.

Why "Spiritism" did not always, and now, phenomenalize in ways to suit Mr. Lhamon, and why he has had only roundabout and indifferent experience "with his grandmother trotting herself off to some utter stranger and then wait for him to hire that stranger to give him an introduction to her," as he intimates was done, I am not able to tell. "Mediums" have told me that the clergy are generally very "mercenary" with them. They think that is because they get so many little favors; they do not expect to pay like other people, etc. Then, too, Mr. L. may have played "Peck's-bad-boy" games on his grandmother, therefore she may have preferred to meet him on her dignity.

Mr. L. objects to "so much Spiritualist machinery for their purposes." The Pietists, Quakers, some Disciples of Christ and many outsiders of all churches do the same, of those who build costly houses and mortgage them and their costly machinery, and hire high-priced choirs and attractive preachers and do questionable things to raise money to float all this, and then say it is all done to draw people of influence there, you know, to interest them in the interests of religion, etc., and to worship God—Spirit, Kurios, Adoni, Elohim, Yahweh—in spirit and in truth, for God seeketh such to worship. Many do seriously object to these things, because they savor of the spirit of materialism and not of the God-spirit, and that they are destructive of the spiritualism that prevailed in the church in the apostolic times, and often when displays much like those among Spiritualists and Christian Science healers in these days, were of frequent occurrence.

The stock reply for this is that "the days of miracles are gone, but miracles can be proved by the Bible." That is very risky now. Mr. L. says, "When Christ [he meant Jesus] came back from the dead he needed no medium to help him into the presence of the disciples." Indeed! How does he know? Were not the disciples mediums? Were they not Spirit-inspired? What does Mr. L. know about anything God or Jesus ever did without a medium? We are not discussing "the genera or species," but the fact of media. How does Mr. L. relate media if he makes any use of it in his salvation work? Does any spirit act without media? Without theory we could not have much philosophy. Mr. L. says, "It is neither fair nor honest to deny the phenomena to get rid of the theory." The preachers have done a vast amount of denying to get rid of both. Many of them now admit the facts and attempt to fit them to theories. They may find trouble and sorrow in fitting their theory of the Bible and the theory of the psychologists and the facts of spirit phenomena all into one.

Mr. Lhamon will, I think, now see his mistake in saying, "The Sybert Commission of the University of Pennsylvania made the most decisive report against Spiritualism ever given to the world." The secretary, Mr. Fullerton, of whom I have personal knowledge, was characteristically exact in his language. He said, "So far as it has shown itself before me, and I give no opinion beyond that, Spiritualism presents the melancholy spectacle of gross fraud perpetrated upon an uncritical portion of the community." There is no bias there. It is the verdict of facts—nothing more, nothing less.

No room or need for innuendo or insinuation without facts, which is the basest and last resort of a malicious, depraved person. The commission did not traverse beyond their case and make it a travesty. They had on their hands a company of persons claiming to be spirit mediums, who proved themselves to be, on no matter what grounds or causes, merely incompetents. Now on that basis alone—and that was sufficient—the work of the commissioner was carried to consummation. It was not a failure, because they reported what they found. They found incompetency in their mediums. Now it is the commonest thing to find in any incompetent professional the attempt to supplement incompetency by fraud in some kind of way. The commission found that and reported it. Their report did and meant no more. Many think they should have continued investigation with other mediums, and indefinitely, as many other companies of investigators have done. Prof. Robert Hare, of this university, investigated as an Atheist, and was convinced of the truth of spirit return and remained in that faith all his days. Sir William Crookes, the eminent scientist, said lately before the British Scientific Association, "I did not admire Spiritualism, but thought I would devote a few weeks to investigation of it. It lengthened into four or more years. I was then able to say as I say now, that I know the truth of spirit return."

The lists of eminent men who believe and know this are large, and are in every cultured country, in pulpits, universities, law, medicine, the sciences, governments, from England's Queen to our Lincoln, Rev. Canons Farrar, Wilberforce, W. Stainton, Moses-"Oxon," Editor Hall, London Art Journal, Editor Stead, Review of Reviews, Sir Alfred Tennyson, the

Brownings, Longfellow, the Wesley family for generations, Geo. Whitefield, Adam Clarke, Bishops Emery, George, McKendrey, J. P. Newman, Bishop Thompson, Bishop Clarke. Space will not permit the hundreds of most eminent names of men and women I can give verifying the truth of spirit return, not "from the dead," but from the spirit state back to this.

To me the one question comprehending the whole is this: How could the continuity of the soul—the spirit, the person—ever have been known but by the return of the spirit? How could immortality ever have been known by the mortal without manifestation of that fact to him in this earth-life? Admitting this fact, the substance of the whole great fact is admitted. The intervening space being passable, the only remaining question is, How many may pass to and fro? All pass from the mortal side. If none return, why not? No answer can be given because there is none to answer back. Back from where? Is there a where? and no answer from it? Absurd. A writing purporting to be an answer is no proof if there can be no communication. Thus we trace to its death the absurdity of saying we know the fact of immortality when we deny the fact of spirit-manifestation of it. We keep to the question of fact. The question of how is independent. It may or may not be capable of solution. Let us not mix these questions too soon. If they are worth public examination they should have as thorough searching as possible. The truth can never hurt the truth. Anything else than truth is only for those most easily injured by it.

CHRISTIAN ENDEAVOR.

W. T. HILTON.

Christian Endeavor stands for good citizenship. Here our young people find a broad field of usefulness. The need of activity in this department is urgent. The patriotism that this age demands at our hands is a civic rather than a military patriotism. We are cursed with three kinds of so-called patriots. The first is a patriot for revenue only. The second is the highly esteemed "good citizen," who is too busy with his private affairs to give any attention to civic duties; therefore he stays at home on election days and allows the "bosses" and their paymasters, the bar and whiskey ring, to dictate our legislation and the manner of executing our laws. The third is the partisan patriot. He is for party first, and country second. He delights to say that he never scratches the ticket. He will stand for the party nominees, though they be knaves and outlaws.

Now Christian Endeavor stands for a patriotism different from all these. The Christian Endeavor patriot says: "I am a citizen; I must perform the duties of citizenship. I have no right to neglect these obligations. My private interests must not interfere with them. I must act an unselfish part." As he drops his ballot in the box he says, "For my country and my God." While the partisan says, "I never scratch the ticket," the Christian Endeavor patriot says, "I always scratch it." Yes, Christian Endeavor is raising up a class of patriots that may very appropriately be called "ticket scratchers." They are good citizens in name and in fact. They do not neglect their duty; they do not permit party or selfish interests to turn them aside from doing what is for the highest good of their city, state or country.

Let Christian Endeavor train its members in good citizenship. It has undertaken no greater, grander, broader work than this.

Another open door for Christian Endeavor is the opportunity it has to foster unity among the people of God. I know that Christian unity is not a part of the Christian Endeavor idea. It stands for interdenominational fellowship rather than anti-denominational unity. This, however, should not deter us from giving sympathy and support to the movement. It does not ask for all that we plead for, but it is a step, and a very long one, in the right direction. The founders of Christian Endeavor built as well as they knew. They cut by the largest pattern they had. They sewed up the jacket and put it on, but already the young giant is beginning to burst out the seams. He is to be greater than those who gave him life. His fathers, with their religious training and environment, could not make a jacket larger than the one known as interdenominational fellowship. But, as the scientist would say, it was the nature of this youngster to evolve. As he grows he will embody principles greater than were ever dreamed of by those who gave him his start in life. We have seen this tendency of the Christian Endeavor movement, and for this reason it has found no great favor with us.

We want unity, organic unity. We believe that the spirit of unity is now in the air, and that it is taking possession of the hearts of men. We confidently look for the time when all the people of God shall be one. This unity may not come as we think it is going to come; perhaps not as we, seeing as we now do, would like to have it come. But we know that it will come. We have what we feel sure is the scriptural basis of Christian unity. One truth, however, we must learn: Fraternity must precede unity. Until we recognize in each other brethren we cannot be united, it matters not what basis of unity we may have. This very necessary truth Christian Endeavor is teaching us. While it stands for interdenominational fellowship, denominational walls are being broken down. Even now they are so low that we may look over and see that on the other side are those who love God. This, I say, is a necessary antecedent. The question is sometimes asked, Why not have wise and good men from all churches meet in council and decide upon some basis of unity? You had as well call a council of baboons to decide the question. It will never be settled in that way. We may formulate bases of unity, but we can never persuade or coax the people to accept our formulas. It cannot be done by legislation. Oneness among the people of God will be rather the result of growth. This truth gives Christian Endeavor its opportunity. It is a movement among young people of all denominations. It is bringing them into closer fellowship. They are learning the value of united effort in Christian work. They see the evils that grow out of division. Imperceptibly and unknown to themselves the desire for union grows upon them. Then, and not till then, will they be willing to consider the basis of unity.

These are some of the possibilities of Christian Endeavor. It represents the practical side of Christianity. It knows nothing about theology. Its mission is to teach us new methods in Christian activity. While it continues to do this it will be a growing force in the church. Its life depends upon its being up to date. If it becomes artificial and formal in its methods its influence will be at an end. Its course will have been run, and it will have to give place to some new movement.

We as a people have adopted it because it looks in the right direction. Its methods are practical, and it cares very little for metaphysical rubbish or theological jargon. Such a movement will always commend itself to us. While it does not ask for all that we ask for, it prepares the people to see the beauty and broadness of our great plea. As long as it continues to advocate the principles it now does and to do the great work it has done, it deserves and should receive our sympathy and our hearty approval.

Beloit, Kan.

CHRISTIANITY VERSUS CHURCHIANITY.

S. M. FOWLER.

More and more as the days go by am I impressed with the thought that we are making use of the word church never thought of in New Testament times. I can find no more evidence that Christ left what we call an organized church on earth, or that the apostles ever attempted such a thing, than that he or they gave us a systematic theology. He taught us great truths concerning God, his love and care of mankind, their condition and needs and destiny, exemplifying all he taught in his sinless, devoted life and victory over death, and told the disciples to tell it to the world.

The church was a confluence of homogeneous lives with a purpose, and left to the dictates of enlightened common sense to carry out that purpose. The measures they would adopt and the appointments they would make would necessarily be influenced by the habits of the people and apparent needs to be met, while a conformity of life to the divine image set before them was the mark ever in view to be gained.

A change in these measures and appointments with the expansion of thought and elevation of life would be as natural and necessary as the change in form from the blade to the full corn in the ear, or from the conduct of a struggling few for the acceptance of a divine principle to the application of that principle in a well-ordered community or a divinely regulated state.

Jesus' mission was to bring in the reign of God, or the kingdom of heaven, when the will of God would be done on earth as in heaven, done *freely*, done *cheerfully*, done *by all* and *all the time*. It was to be a growth, an unfolding, an ever-rising life. Hence Jesus forbade the backward look. The risen, glorified Christ, enthroned in the firmament of thought, was and is and ever will be an ideal above and before us to be reached. Christ in the heart, Christ in the home, Christ in the school and Christ in the state.

The first forms of the church work and life are no more adapted to its triumph and

the swaddling
full-grown man.
ıot organization,
ıut a devil in the
er be shunned or
on about orders
ınd their duties
nent precedents,
twaddle. There
recedent in New
is to adapt your-
now as best you
re.
congregations of
mprovement, co-
And when cer-
nd appointments
nd sought, that

organization is
and love of truth
benevolence and
ıstice to meet the
approval of our
s Christ's, and it
it Christ's con-
ch or congrega-
tian church or
onvention. Any
M. C. A., the
. C. E., or S. S.,
s the church of
specified way.
ıs as they came
ı of the Spirit of
ce and spirit of
t the best possi-
We will never
. John saw it
postasy through
l and is passing,
ophet had drop-
on had sunk to
Jerusalem had
heaven with its
ly gates, tree of
by the river of
rone of God and
rnacle of God is
nb its fadeless

'reflecting upon
is the whole of
knows him, the
eeing him knees
ss. More Chris-
ıity is the great

---

e World.
ıG.)

or. 6:14-18; Jno. 17:

, 19.
m. 12:2.
6:16; Phil. 2. 15, 16.
. 2:15-17; Jas. 4:4;

lark 16:15, 16; Matt.

-25; 2 Cor. 4:3, 4; 1

Matt. 12:22-32.
ss. 2:11, 12; 2 Peter

h. 2:1-3; 2 Peter 2:

JMNER T. MARTIN.
8.

Correspondence.

English Topics.

NEW ENGLISH BOOKS.

The great wonder of the literary world in England this season is the extraordinary number of splendid books of travel newly issued. I propose in this letter to devote my space to some of these fresh literary revelations, seeing that I have been feasting my own mind on some of them and should like to impart to my American friends some of my impressions after the enjoyment.

"THE KINGDOM OF THE YELLOW ROBE."

This is the title of a singularly interesting book on that ever-interesting country, Siam. It is from the pen of Ernest Young, late of the Educational Department, Siam. It is replete with religious as well as social, historical and political information. There is not a more romantic country on earth than Siam. Its wonderful capital, Bangkok, is the Venice of the East. A voyage on its lovely river, the Meinam, is evidently a progress through a veritable fairyland. And this country is crammed with religious associations, all pagan, but all fanatic, eccentric and utterly different from any of the systems of spiritual life of other lands. Here is one more country which will have to be opened up by our own missionaries, when our great Foreign Missionary Society—for great it is truly becoming—shall have the resources to expand its operations to that extent. Siam is Buddhist, but yet its Buddhism is *sui generis*. The people have made their religious life as picturesque and original as they are themselve. They are a kindly, laughing, *dolce non far niente* race, loving ease and pleasure, but sparkling with intelligence and vivacity, and only needing Christ and his Word to render them one of the foremost nations of the great East. We had last year the King of Siam, Chululingkorn, here amongst us in England. He spoke English perfectly, and created astonishment by his complete comprehension of all that he saw and his lively interest in everything that was worth noticing. The most wonderful thing about Siam is perhaps its child-life. The boys are perfectly free and independent. They remain unclothed as long as they can be called little boys; they scamper along the roads, driving young bullocks, sit on the backs of tame buffaloes as they plough the rice-fields, steal bananas, climb trees for cocoanuts, smoke enormous cigarettes, paddle their own canoes, never bother their heads about getting home in time for meals, lie about in shady places to rest, never read books, do not know the inside of a school, and spend the whole day according to their own idea of amusement. Yet any of these children who are sent to school make very bright pupils. Only a mere handful as yet attend any kind of school, but those have to do so who desire to obtain government employment. They learn English with remarkable rapidity in a very few months, which is much more than a Frenchman or a German could do. On the head of each child is allowed to grow a little tuft of hair in the center of a shaven crown. At the age of about fourteen this is removed with extraordinary religious rites. The "shaving of the topnot" is one of the most curious religious ceremonies practiced in the world. Mr. Ernest Young devotes a long and interesting chapter to its description.

THE SHAVING OF THE TOPNOT.

The ceremony of tonsure is a very ancient one, and is found existing in many countries widely separated from each other. The priests of Isis, the Hindu Siva, the Roman Catholic monks, the old Peruvian brothers all practiced it. According to Hindu legend there lies under the tuft in the center of the crown, which is reverenced as the summit of the human body, a microscopic aperture, through which the

human spirit finds entrance at bir
parts at death. When Ravana,
giant kings of Ceylon, once car
caressingly laid the tip of his finge
hair of the beautiful Vedavatti, sh
him in direst anger, declaring that
an outrageous insult life was no long
to her, and that she would speedily
abundant and outraged locks and t
in the flames before him. In Sia
earliest days the one tuft left afte
shaving is daily combed, twisted,
tied in a knot. A jeweled pin stuc
it, or a small wreath of flowers en
are its usual adornments. It is ne
off till it is finally removed with g
and ritual which lasts three days, du
time the Buddhist priests have m
with the boy or girl. On the mem
when the operation is to begin a gil
of Buddha is placed reverentially o
surrounded with candles, incense
flowers. Round this altar is formed
hollowed vessels of gold and silver
mystic conchshell and the shears an
Offerings of dainty food are placed o
plaited leaves, these being for th
deities of the place. On a throne
cloth, most curiously made, cov
curtains of gauze and gold, sits
candidate to be bathed with holy w
the topnot has been removed. But
is placed on the throne a nine-storie
of very frail but ornamental materi
nine stages of which are sweetmea
supposed to be delicious to the
Then begins a wonderful round of ce
prayers, offerings and feastings
friends and guests. Monks and pr
and go, gongs are ringing all the
each of the three days closes with
and joy. When the topnot has b
all the hairs are subjected to a variet
rites, all of which are supposed to
with different gods, demons and spir

THE FAITH OF IDOLATERS.

Why have I thought it worth whil
to these curious superstitions? Ju
they illustrate the truth that no nati
out its system of faith. And in the
is the unseen, is endless. There
evident that there is in countries lik
most promising soil for the planti
tree of the true faith. Here we have
fully clever people, who believe in
unrealities. Why not hasten to
something worthy of their faculty of
They are an affectionate and loveable
will take the truth with kindly readi
it is lovingly proclaimed to them.
the numerous Buddhist priests wo
what might injure their vested int
here is a land in which the youn
captured for Christ in mission scho
has been two long neglected. Not
beed attempted there by the great
Let us cast our eyes on that beautif
its wonderful opening for the gospel
not evangelize it the French will Ro
for they are the paramount power in
part of the country.

THE LAND THAT IS SHUT AGAINST THE

To my mind the most interesting
the world is Tibet, that heart of Asia
also sometimes called "the roof of th
This is now the one and only land in
world absolutely closed against the
the missionary for Christ. Encircle
mountain ramparts the Tibetans have
ally shut every avenue against W
ligious ideas. Here is the stron
Buddhism without a single mission
cross. Two books have been publ
year which have fascinated the En
ing public. The first was the thrilli
by Mr. Walter Savage Landor, of
perils and atrocious treatment in T
other, only a few weeks ago, is
Heden's great new book on his

journey towards Lhasa. About this extraordinary country you will some day be hearing from your own adventurous countryman, Mr. William Jameson Reid, who was interviewed in London in August. He arrived here from Boston on his way to Tibet, which he intends to penetrate from the western border of China. On Mr. Sven Heden's adventures I will not attemp to write, for I should be commencing to deal with a whole world of exciting travel. To us Christian people, however, there is a little book recently published in London, of far greater interest than those works of famous travelers which I have been describing. A work only costing eighteen pence, "Pioneering in Tibet," by Annie R. Taylor, tells that a young English missionary lady has made one of the most audacious and heroic attempts on record to penetrate this dark citadel of heathenism. This splendid Christian girl was filled with the desire to become a missionary at the early age of sixteen. For a time she worked in China, but she always felt that Tibet was to be the land of her adoption, and thither she eventually found her way. Miss Taylor went from Darjeeling into Sikkim, where for ten months she never saw a European. She lived in a hut near a Tibetan monostery and met with her faithful servant, Pontso, who has served her with such fidelity ever since. In September, 1892, she started on a remarkable journey. Over lofty mountains, amid snow and ice, through regions infested with brigands, facing hardships and dangers that would have quelled any but the stoutest heart, this heroine of the faith pressed on. "I went," she says, "in simple faith, believing that the Lord had called me." Her faith was rewarded, for in reading of her adventures, it seems as if she had led a charmed life. Robbed of her horses and goods, with several hair-breadth escapes from death, she yet succeeded in reaching within three days' ride of the capital, Lhasa, the furthest advance on to the forbidden ground hitherto attained by any European traveler. But her guide, a Chinaman, proved faithless, and going on ahead informed the officials of her coming. Consequently she was stopped by soldiers, who treated her respectfully, but assured her they would lose their lives if they allowed her to pass. Though turned back, her journey was not a fruitless one, for she was enabled to obtain a knowledge of the people, their land and their customs, which she could not in any other have secured. It is but a matter of time. When the central citadel of Asia's idolatry has once been captured for Jesus, then all the kingdoms of that mighty continent will become tributary to the Heavenly King. Will our churches of Christ send some of our noble young men and women to Tibet? How I should rejoice to see that day!

W. DURBAN.

43 *Park Road, South Tottenham, London, Nov.* 5, 1898.

Fredericksburg (Virginia) Letter.

From an appeal through the CHRISTIAN-EVANGELIST, some weeks ago, some dollars were added to our building fund for the new Christian Church at Fredericksburg, Va. One letter comes from our Bro. G. L. Wharton, in far-away India, enclosing an order on A. McLean for an amount for Fredericksburg. This comes from the Foreign Field to our Home work. To day we received a letter from Bro. M. McDonald, of Palmyra, Mo., enclosing a $10 check, who says: "I noticed your appeal in the CHRISTIAN-EVANGELIST for money to build for our brethren a house of worship in the old and historic town of Fredericksburg. This is highly commendable in you and I hope your efforts may be attended with abundant success. My old home was near Fredericksburg, and although I have lived here for over 35 years I have a warm spot in my heart for the old state and her dear people, never to be effaced. I trust that of the many brethren who read the CHRISTIAN-EVANGELIST quite a number have and others may see fit to answer your appeals."

The work was begun in this old historic town in 1832, sixty-six years ago, the present building being completed in 1833. For a few years prior to the Civil War the work grew and flourished and many of the best citizens of Fredericksburg endorsed the religious views of the then "Current Reformation." Such worthies as John Ferguson, J. G. Parrish, Jas. B. Goss, Peter Ainslie, Dr. Duvall, G. W. Abell, Silas Shelburne, Alexander Campbell and others were heard from the quaint old pulpit. And though the work here has long since gone to pieces—for more than thirty years not the sound of a Christian preacher's voice was heard from its pulpit—the memory of these great old men of pioneer days still remain with our town people. And our old building, plain, square-built, "squatty," dark and weather-beaten, battered and torn by shot and shell and the ravages of time, is yet held in some sort of respect and patriarchal veneration. Sight-seers to our town frequently call for the keys to "the old church," and both Northern and Southern visitors will drop a tear when they see the sad wreck of shot and shell, and remember the sixties when they were "tenting on the old came ground."

Brethren, this is our church home in the old historic city of Fredericksburg, Va. A real war relic, a souvenir of the Civil War that we have had on our hands since Dec. 1862 and that we are asking Uncle Sam to place in his list of "war claims." With whatsoever appearance it may now present, and with whatever title you may signifiy this ancient pile, you are on historic and sacred ground and should tread softly. The walls were laid in 1832, are still massive and contain many a once consecrated brick. In December, 1862, in the desperate battle of Fredericksburg, this old building stood right in the range of the Northern guns. For twelve hours of terrific bombardment a horrible deluge of leaden storm was poured upon the streets and houses of Fredericksburg.

The inhabitants fled for their lives from this terrible leaden storm that was beating their homes to pieces, and the town was left to the awful ravages of cruel war.

In "these scenes so awfully grand and terrible," on whose fields of battle more men have fallen than in any similar area in all the world, the old Fredericksburg Christian Church of 1833 met its doom. The building, besides being torn and and damaged by shot and shell, was, after the battles of Fredericksburg and the Wilderness, used as a hospital for Federal soldiers.

The large windows were torn out, the floors stained with blood, the benches made into coffins, the dead buried in the churchyard, the walls damaged, fences burned, stoves destroyed, the communion service carried off, and much other damage, together with the scattering of the membership, left the church completely disorganized. After several futile attempts to repair the building, the idea of its ever again being used as a house for the worship of God was totally abandoned, and for thirty-five years this "house of the Lord," was left unto its people desolate, the eyesore and common property of the town and a disgrace to the cause for which it was dedicated.

Come with me inside. You will find few changes. You are on the same blood-stained and uncarpeted floor, with some of the same benches on which dead soldiers lay. The walls are riddled with bullet holes from shot and shell that came through its broken panes. In one facing of the gallery may be seen two cannon ball holes. On the plain, square box pulpit rests the Bible that Campbell and other worthy pioneers read their lesson and text from sixty years ago; the plastering on the inside is giving way, and shows many ugly scars. An old-fashioned gallery runs two lengths of the building and the great plain windows have the upper sash boarded up. Not a stitch of carpeting on our floors, no chandeliers, no stained glass or ornamen
any description, plain pitcher and glass for
communion service, no baptistery.

Brethren, this is a fine field; with a l
money concentrated here a fine work coul
done and our cause firmly established in
section of Virginia. The point is strate
But we must build. We ought to have a g
house of worship here. We could afford
put $5,000 here, for every dollar we put h
will count in returns to the cause. If ev
brother Disciple who reads this article wo
send us *one dollar* we could build a splen
house of worship, and with a good chu
home a fine work can be done. The sacri
you would make in sending us a dollar wo
not mean muck to you, but very much to
cause and our Virginia work. The Frederic
burg work was freely discussed at our l
Virginia state convention. Our peo
generally feel the importance of the fi
and necessity of cultivating it, but recog
the fact that we ought and must have a be
building. I am raising a building fund. C
half the amount I started out to raise has b
subscrsbed and part paid in. Will you
emulate the example of Bro. McDonald
send us a donation? CEPHAS SHELBURNI

Iowa Letter.

Not long after the death of President Sch
fer, of the State University of Iowa, specu
tion as to his successor became rife. Am
the names made prominent so far stands t
of Chancellor W. B. Craig, of Drake Univ
sity. He is an alumnus of that school,
would prove himself competent for the pl
and immensely popular with the students.
quote from a letter just in from an educa
and church worker in Western Iowa: "H
rah for Chancellor Craig for Pres. S. U.
This would honor the Chancellor, but I s
above all things else, Drake University to
front!" Others who have been honored
the people of Iowa in this informal list of no
inees are Prof. Beardshear, of Ames Ag
cultural College; Mr. McLean, Dean of t
Law Department, S. U. I., and Homer See
ley, of the State Normal School. Iowa fe
proud of all four here mentioned, and wish
they could all be elected.

***

The Iowa contingent in the Minnesota Sta
University is of interest to me on sever
counts. It is composed of three persons
least. There may be others of which I do n
know. All these are members of our churche
No external church influences have contribut
to their preferment. Personal merit and fi
ness for the work has elevated them. Th
were all schoolmates of mine some years ag
One of them is my own brother. To stand
a man from his cradle, to see him in the han
of Providence, serving now here, now ther
and winning merited distinction, is always
inspitation. And when that man is yo
brother it means more yet. Another of th
trio is a sister of Bruce Shepherd, Dean of t
College of Letters in Drake, and the other
Willett Hayes, a brother of C. L. Hayes,
Eldora, Iowa. Prof. Hayes is well up in t
Agricultural Department. Dr. G. D. Ha
gard has just taken classes in the Medic
Department, and Miss Shepherd is an expe
in another department.

***

In two hours more the polls will close a
election day will have determined the fate
many men and not a few measures. It
interesting to an Iowa Prohibi ionist to no
the expressions of Iowa and Western pape
upon the prospects of Silas Swallow, of Pen
sylvania, in his contest with Matthew Qu
and the two machines he controls. Swallo
made his reputation as a Prohibitionist. H
is running now on that ticket, and is endors
by the Good Government Club and other r
form factions. It is amusing to see how ha
some of our papers strive to make themselv

.d the people believe that Prohibition is not it and that his victory, which is quite prob-·le, will mean nothing for Prohibition. ɘvertheless, his election would stand as a ndmark in the history of the party. It would an honor to his state, a blessing to the ıole nation and an omen of a brighter polit-al future.

***

Do extremes beget extremes? If so, may not account for "temperance fanatics?" ıey may by begotten by extreme blindness of .ti-Prohibitionists. In the November number the Review of Reviews the editor glories in hat Gen. Wood has done in administering .e Government of Santiago. And we should l glory in the achievements of this distin-ıished physician and renowned soldier. He ıs reduced the death rate 75 per cent. The litor in listing the means used never says one ord about one of the primary means to this ıd other good ends. Brig. Gen. Leonard 'ood shut up the rumshops. Why did the litor mention many minor means and pre-rve silence on this?

***

In the October number of the same Review r. Carroll Denham writes at length upon the Medical and Sanitary Aspects of the War." e contrasts the camp at Sibony, "where llow fever was gaining with immense ride," with Camp McCalla at Guantanamo, here there was not a case. In accounting for ıis he uses this significant sentence: "As ›on as they were in possession of the shore ›f Guantanamo) every hut on the beach was ırned (to destroy disease germs) and the ɜads were knocked out of all the casks of panish wine." Nothing is more cheering to student of the times than the new attitude of ıe most eminent physicians and surgeons on ıe alcohol question. With an increasing ımber it is no longer allowed a place among ·medial agents.

***

One of my classes in the Bible Department ! Drake University—a class of nineteen—upon ƙamination furnishes this interesting list of ıcts: They average eight years in the church; ıey can all repeat the so-called Lord's rayer; all but one can repeat the Ten Com-.andments and have read the New Testament; vo have read it ten times, one four times, ıree three times, five two times and two but ne time; seven have read the whole of the ld Testament, and four times is the most for ny one; three of the psalms is the most any ıe could repeat, and five were unable to ›peat one; but five were able to repeat the ·ve chapter in Paul's Corinthian Letters. his examination was taken without warning. lost of the class are first-year students. The ıme questions will be put and answered later ı the year and results reported. Why not ear from other college classes along similar nes?

***

A corrected list of Iowa delegates to our fational Conventions, Chattanooga, Tenn., is s follows: F. M. Drake, H. O. Breeden, W. V. Williams and daughter, Miss Jessie; S. '. Martin, B. H. Witmer, wife and daughter; .. F. Sanderson, G. T. Smith, Annette New-omber, Miss Kampkee, of Cedar Rapids; Irs. J. R. Davis and Mrs. C. S. Page, D.

Bethany.

"The History of Education among the Disciples" would be a fruitful theme for some gifted pen. Nor would it be wanting in some of the choicest elements of Christian heroism. It would have to relate how that Mr. Campbell, confronting as he did the tremendous possibilities that were opening up to a movement yet in its infancy, with prophetic vision saw that to successfully meet the future we must be an educated people; that with even the Bible in our hands, going forth to win the world away from sectism, we must make our appeal to the cultured thought of Christendom, as well as to unfold its pages to the simple in understanding; that our ministry, although humble and free from the spirit of priestcraft, must yet be able to stand before kings. Like Paul, while being all things to all men, they had to be the very best among the best of men, and how heroically Mr. Campbell arose to the situation and met the issue would be a part of the chronicle. Without means or resources for meeting this greater demand, except for his own masterful genius, back in the forest of a country then scarcely beyond the borders of civilization, he began to plant the enterprise that, under God, has been so efficient in molding and training the thought of our times.

The historian would have to relate how it was that he arose at four o'clock in the morning to build fires and to do the menial work of a janitor for his students; how, at six o'clock, the servant was transformed into the master, and the infant college met in the chapel for morning prayers; how, at eight o'clock, the work began in the recitation room, to continue for the remainder of the day; how that the president taught in every grade, in every kind, and in every variety and branch of knowledge, with the Bible above all and far in the forefront of all their work; how he reached out a helping hand to the poor boy that was willing to strive for an education and had not the means to acquire it, setting aside the profits of his publications to assist in this laudable work; how these boys, inspired by his own noble and indomitable spirit, "grasped the skirts of happy chance and grappled with their evil stars," growing in power and the accomplishments of higher training until they went forth to lead and compel the thought of their times.

But what might not the pen of the writer more say in relating the vicissitudes of this noble beginning as it advanced into the youth time and manhood of its larger life?. It would be necessary to relate how this grand man, studying sixteen hours a day, busy as an editor, debater, preacher, professor, farmer and man of affairs, yet had to command enough time and means to build and endow a college; how at the age of sixty, after the first building had been destroyed by fire, he went to the heroic task of laying the foundation of a larger building and a more extended work; how he appealed to the generosity of a young people, mostly situated in the rural districts; how nobly the South responded to his call and of their substance generously helped in this enterprise; how that, when the war came and swept it all away, and Mr. Campbell, now in done by any one. It would take many pages to relate how Mr. Pendleton struggled with the financial question, sacrificing his own means and struggling in ways only known to himself and his most intimate associates to keep the institution up to the measure of its past efficiency, and how nobly he succeeded amid much misunderstanding and unjust criticism; how Professor Loos taught the Latin, Greek, Hebrew, French and German languages and literatures, while at the same time he filled the pulpit of the church on Sunday, was secretary of the faculty, attended and took part in most of the important conventions of our brotherhood, was always busy with his pen as an editor, besides being useful in many other ways in the great work for which Mr. Campbell had trained him. This, and much more of these and many other heroes of whom they are fair specimens, our historian would call up in review were he to be true to the history of education among the Disciples.

The results of these struggles and sacrifices we are now enjoying with scarcely a thought of the source from whence they came. After the war had swept away Bethany's endowment, and sectional feeling had played havoc with her patronage, situated as she was in the anomalous position of being neither on the one side nor on the other, and yet a part of both, it required the rarest kind of skill and forbearance to tide her over those troublous times. The noblest and best things are born of adversity, and this our educational work is no exception, nor indeed is the work of education anywhere.

Out of reverses, misfortunes, struggles, sacrifices and untold labors, Bethany has had a splendid progeny in all the walks of life, who have come up through great tribulation. As matters now stand, by one more comparatively easy effort on the part of our people, she could be placed in a safe and secure position for all future time, and it would only be an act of gratitude for us to attend to this at once, while on the other hand it would be the basest ingratitude for us to let her die after what she has accomplished for us. Bethany is the crown of Mr. Campbell's great work, the tree of his own planting, and she is the only visible monument to his memory. What she *has* done is only a specimen of what she is now doing, and a promise of what she is yet able to do in the future. Success to all other educational enterprises among us! Bethany has always rejoiced in their prosperity, and lent them her sons. We need them all, but most of all we still need the old pioneer—the *Alma Mater* of all of our educational institutions, Bethany College.

J. L. DARSIE.

Bethany, W. Va.

A Time for Enlargement.

A great painter, having put the dream of his soul upon canvas, called in his master and asked for his criticisms. "Wider!" was the master's exhortation—"Wider!"

The work of the C. W. B. M. embodies the dream of a great sisterhood. It is beautiful with the beauty of self-sacrifice and warm with the coloring of love and sympathy. But our Master is not satisfied. Plainly he has written across the canvas, "Wider! Wider!"

auxiliary more fittingly mark the anniversary year than by the organization of a society in in some neighboring church or mission?

Larger offerings should be made. We have talked for these many years about "our dues," and through the payment of these habits of systematic giving have been established. But we should be going on from grace to grace. None who have the means at command for larger giving should be satisfied with the minimum. Other boards look to these two avenues of increase—the enlistment of new contributors and the growth in the offerings of those heretofore enlisted. The C. W. B. M. has not depended too much upon the former, but it must depend more and more each year upon the latter. We are asked for "A Silver Offering for the Silver Anniversary." This offering should run up into the tens of thousands of dollars; indeed, we have reason to believe that it will. Shall it not mark the beginning of a new era in all our giving?

Missionary forces should be strengthened and new fields entered. It seems trite to say that success is costly, but there are still many who do not seem to realize the truth of the saying. Success must be followed up by new outlays, if it is to be held. Opportunities improved bring insistent opportunities.

There should be a more complete consecration to the work. Our service to Christ should cease to be an incident in our lives, and become life itself. The years of the past have failed to leave with us their full lesson unless they have taught us our own need as well as the need of the world.

C. W. B. M. Day is upon us. Shall it not be a time for enlargement?

JESSIE BROWN POUNDS.

The Sign of a New Era.

The poet Lowell says:

"At the birth of each new era, with a recognizing start,
Nation wildly looks at nation, standing with mute lips apart."

Have we reached the dawn of such an era for the temperance cause? Three things indicate that we have.

The first is that the civilized nations of the earth are putting cause and effect together on the alcohol question as never before. In France, Switzerland and Belgium the increasing use of alcohol is recognized as the cause of a physical decline in stature that is filling those nations with alarm for their future. Close investigation is proving to the Kaiser that the beer drinking soldier has only about eighty per cent. of the endurance of the total abstainer, and economists are calling attention to the bad effects that increasing drink habits are having upon German industries. The young Czar of Russia, alarmed at the inroads which he sees alcohol making upon his army and people, is striving to stem the tide. Thoughtful Englishmen are saying that Britain's greatest enemy is alcohol. In our own country its effects upon our soldiers, in home camps and on the field, have been made sadly evident to the American people.

The second sign of the coming of a new era on the alcohol question is that the truth against alcohol is out. Everything that its advocates can say in its favor is controverted by the strongest scientific authorities of the world, who pronounce it a poison—the genius of degeneracy. Nothing can hide this truth from the people and their children whose heritage it is. Vain are the efforts to make the clock of the world move backward. Its great pendulum swings to the rythm of truth. In the fullness of time it strikes the death knell of error, and when that time comes no man can turn the hand back on the dial.

The third sign is that the per capita consumption of alcohol has begun to decline in this country, although its consumption is increasing in other nations. The New York Medical Record puts this decline during the last ten years at thirty per cent. Prior to that time there was a continual increase. During these years some of our prohibitory laws have been repealed, others have been weakened; less rather than more temperance platform work has been done, and more than four million people have come to us from foreign lands, bringing with them the alcoholic habits of the Old World. In the face of all these unfavorable conditions why has the per capita consumption of alcohol in this country decreased during this time, while previously it increased? Our English friends are doing as much church, society and band of hope work as we, and perhaps more, yet England's drink bill for 1897 ran up to $16,500,000 more than that of the preceding year.

The only new feature introduced into temperance work in this country during the past ten years so generally as to touch all sections, i the only method of importance in which temperance work differs from that of Engla is that of temperance education in the pu schools. It is this which is getting the tr to the people so generally as already to t fruit. It is this which is laying the foundat for the intelligent sobriety of the future Am ican. We would not for a moment question value of other temperance efforts which h helped to secure these results, but the figu show that such efforts without temperance e cation were inadequate to produce this decli

"Duty determines destiny," said Presid Mckinley in his Omaha speech. It is the le duty of nearly all the school boards and tea ers in this country to see that all pupils in schools are taught the nature and effects of

;oholic drinks, and other narcotics, together with other laws of health. The way in which that duty is performed during the next fifteen years will influence mightily the destiny of this nation.

New responsibilities have lately come to us as a people which we cannot shirk if we would. Unless I mistake the spirit of my countrymen, the motives which have led us on to this hour have been, not what we may gain for ourselves from Cuba, Porto Rico, Hawaii and the Philippines, but what we may be able to do for them as sharers of our civil and political liberties, our education, our freedom in religion and in the chance in life which is the American citizen's heritage. The liquor traffic represents unmitigated selfishness: it considers only what it can make for itself, without regard to the human ruin that follows every dollar of its gains. Its extension into our new possessions means the swift destruction of these peoples for whom our sons faced the Moloch of war.

The God of nations is calling us so to educate our people that this calamity may be averted from those for whom we are newly responsible, as we at the same time save our own children.

MARY H. HUNT.

Report of the Educational Conference Held at Moberly, Mo., Nov. 1st, 1898.

In pursuance of a motion adopted at the Missouri Christian Convention at Nevada in September for an Educational Conference to be held at Moberly, Mo., Nov. 1, a number of brethren met at the Central Christian Church, Moberly, Mo., Tuesday, Nov. 1, at 2:30 P. M. Bro. T. P. Haley was selected as chairman and S. G. Clay secretary of the meeting.

Some time was consumed in arriving at an understanding whether this meeting was a meeting of the special committee appointed by the convention, or of the Conference provided for at the adoption of the report of committee on schools and education. Upon motion of President C. Lockhart it was resolved that this assembly regard itself the Educational Conference called by the Nevada Convention of the Christian churches of Missouri.

Upon motion the chairman appointed a committee of five on order of business to report at the evening session. The names of committee are as follows: O. C. Clay, G. W. Barnett, Z. Moore, G. A. Hoffmann, U. I. Quigley. Conference adjourned till 7:30 P. M.

EVENING SESSION.

At 7:30 the chairman called the Conference to order, and C. H. Winders led in prayer.

Committee on order of business made the following report:

Your committee begs leave to report:

1. That each of the schools represented be requested to present the present conditions and work of their institutions, and that as much as twenty minutes be allowed to each speaker if he so desires.

2. And that when this Conference adjourns, it be to meet in Moberly, Tuesday, Dec. 6, 1898, at 3 P. M.

3. That in the next Conference each congregation represented having less than 200 members shall be entitled to one vote; each having 200 and less than 500, two votes; each having 500 or more, three votes; each college two votes, and each Missouri preacher present one vote.

4. That the secretary of this Conference be instructed to notify the churches and preachers of the next Conference.

5. That this meeting elect a permanent chairman and secretary to properly work up the attendance of the next Conference.

O. C. CLAY, Chairman.

G. A. HOFFMANN, Sec. of Com.

The Conference then heard the following brethren make reports of their respective schools:

Clinton Lockhart, president Christian University, Canton, spoke of the advantages and financial condition of his college. Value of property, $50,000; endowment, $17,000; debt, nothing.

J. B. Jones, president Christian Orphan School, Fulton, stated the condition and advantages of his school.

FINANCIAL STATEMENT.

ASSETTS.

Building, furniture and grounds	$15,000.00
Sixty acres of land	2,000.00
Other real estate	800.00
Notes	1,000.00
House and lot in Kansas City	20,000.00
Breckenringe Bequest	17,000.00
Total	$55,800.00

LIABILITIES.

Calloway county bank debt	$21,000.00
Other debts	6,000.00
Total	$30,000.00

ATTENDANCE FOR 1898.

Enrollment	112
Boarders	95
Day pupils	17

Z. Moore, Albany, represented Central Christian College.

FINANCIAL CONDITION.

Building and grounds worth	$30,000.00
Endowment notes	6,000.00
Subscription	4,500.00

Debt between $7,000 and $10,000.

C. H. Winders made a brief statement of Christial College, Columbia. Very prosperous.

T. P. Haley reported the growth and condition of the Bible College, Columbia.

FINANCIAL REPORT BY G. A. HOFFMANN.

Endowment in notes	$35,100.00
Real estate	15,000.00
Lot for building	3,000.00
Pledges	2,000 00
Total	$55,100.00

Short speeches were made by the following brethren in behalf of various colleges: G. A. Hoffmann, for Bible College; Davis Errett, for a college of our own for young men; H. A. Denton, for the Orphan School at Fulton; F. O. Norton, favoring centralizing our energies upon some great university for the education of our young men, but not to the neglect of our Orphan School.

Col. W. H. Dulaney spoke of the necessity of immediate care for the Orphan School at Fulton.

J. W. Alexander made a strong plea for the school at Canton.

T. P. Haley said we are confronted by conditions of having various school interests and asked that we do all we can to meet the conditions as they are. Stated the purpose of this Conference not to center our influence upon any one institution.

O. C. Clay, Canton, offered the following resolution, which after some discussion was adopted:

Resolved, That when this Conference shall reconvene on Tuesday, December the 6th, next, at Moberly, as directed by the order adopted this evening, it shall consider and pass upon the propriety of establishing and endowing one school or more in this state by our great brotherhood; and, if favorably acted upon by this Conference, that an honest effort be made, then and there, to provide the ways and means to accomplish this great and desirable object.

O. C. CLAY.

Upon motion of Davis Errett, J. W. Alexander, Gallatin, was elected permanent chairman of the Conference to be held in December. S. G. Clay elected secretary.

A committee of arrangements appointed consisting of D. H. Mounse, Moberly; R. B. Turner, Canton, and U. S. Quigley, Fulton.

It was moved and carried that the secretary have the minutes of this Conference published in our papers of the state.

Adjourned to meet in Moberly Tuesday, 3 P. M., Dec. 6.

T. P. HALEY, Chairman.

S. G. CLAY, Sec.

Notes and News.

A neat frame church house, costing $1,500, was recently dedicated at Eagleville, Mo., by Morgan Morgans, assisted by W. D. Bryant. Also by M. S. Gillidett, Brethren Alderman and Moore, of Albany, Mo. Bro. Morgans and daughter followed the service with a protracted meeting. He and daughter had previously closed a good meeting with the new church at Mt. Moriah. The Harrison County convention will be held in the new church at Eagleville in February next.

Dedication.

Our new church was dedicated Oct. 30th, and we now possess one of the best houses of worship in Virginia. It is built of brick, a handsome structure on the outside, while the inside is an artistic blending of colors which is exceeding lovely. Cost, $8,400. Total value of property, about $9,050. G. F. Shields is our pastor. ADAH TORREY HENDERSON.

Virginia, Ill.

Texas Work.

Our little band here is prospering. Began three years ago with eight or nine members and now we number over 75. I am keeping this place and two other points. Have paid our preacher and contributed to the F. C. M. and the A. C. M. all they asked of us. Called, inaugurated and entertained the great camp-meeting last July, which resulted in the formation of "the Northwest Texas Christian Assotion," with Elder G. T. Thomas, of Young County, as evangelist. He is now here in a meeting. We have quite a number (to use Texas phraseology) "staked out" for gospel subjects, but can't tell the results. All this is done without a house of worship of our own in our associational work. We are quite "progressive." We have an annual Y. P. S. C. E. Their annual meeting, next July, will be held in Young County. Also an annual C. W. B. M. meeting, and report results at the same meeting. The receipts at our July meeting amounted to something over $500. We paid for our tent and preacher and singer and all other expenses incident to it, and came off out of debt, and are now hoping to do still larger things another year. Pray for us.

THOS. G. NANCE.

Throckmorton, Tex.

Church Celebration.

Lake City Church celebrated their second anniversary in their new and elegant house Nov. 12th and 13th. The feast and rejoicing in fellowship on Saturday and special program on Sunday. The year has been a most prosperous one, the reports showing the net gain to be over one hundred souls and the financial condition good. Two additions two weeks ago.

F. H. LEMON.

Lake City, Ia.

Note This.

I am trying to so announce the next conference to be held at Moberly, Tuesday, Dec. 6th, as to secure a large attendance from all parts of the state; and I hope every school and college in the state will send delegates to the conference.

In this connection I will call attention to railroad rates. The Western Passenger Association has granted *one and one-third fare* on the *certificate plan* for the round trip, over all roads in the Association, upon the condition of 100 certificates for tickets costing more than 50 cents for regular fare one way. I will make a fuller announcement next week of this.

Delegates should send their names to D. H. Mounce, Moberly, Mo.

Hoping for a large attendance, I remain,

S. G. CLAY, Sec.

Red Oak.

The campaign has begun. God's Spirit is at work in the church. Bro. Brickert expects to commence a series of meetings soon. The congregations are increasing. Four accessions since last writing. Plans are being made for the advancement of the Lord's work here. Bro. Stark preached to us last Lord's day. Bro. Brickert has been delivering lectures at different places lately. Bro. Howard Furman has left for his home in Eldora; we are indeed sorry to lose so noble a young man. May God bless him, is our prayer. X. Y. Z.

The Cameron Church.

The cause at Cameron, Mo., moves gloriously onward under the efficient pastorate of Bro. S. J. White. The church is widening its influence, and how to do the most good is the one aim of all the plans discussed by our official board. During the past few months we have rearranged and much improved our galleries, put in a very convenient new baptistery, first-class new pipe organ, etc., spending in this way over $2,200. Our audiences are large and working forces in splendid condition. During our recent special meetings, conducted by Bro. White, there were 17 additions; 14 by conversion and two young men made the good confession at our regular services last Sunday evening. Present membership, 682. Good prospects for a continued ingathering.

WILL H. BROWN,
Clerk of Official Board.

Cameron, Mo., Nov. 15, 1898.

Clinton (Mo.) District.

It is composed of Jackson, Cass, Bates, Vernon, Barton, Cedar, St. Clair and Henry Counties. We have a strong, heatlhy brotherhood, which is amply able to do great work. I am sure that many are perfectly willing to aid in this work of the Lord. The place is Butler, Bates County, Mo. A splendid place for it. The time is Dec. 12, 13 and 14. This will be a good time. None are likely to be in a meeting. It commences Monday evening, Dec. 12th. We want and expect a great convention. Each church should at once appoint a delegate who will attend. There is an urgent demand that every preacher of the district be present. Don't fail. Bring some good business man from your congregation. Will not the preachers and superintendents announce the convention until all shall be impressed with it? Say—we want and expect *you* to come! You can assist in making this a success. Begin at once and keep at it until we have now a victory.

The following are the officers: Dr. B. E. Dawson, president; C. B. Lotspeich, treasurer; F. B. Elmore, evangelist; G. W. Webb, secretary.

The following are the committee on future work, and should report at convention: G. L. Bush, C. B. Lotspeich, J. H. Jones, A. C. McKeever, E. B. Woods, R. B. Coffey, W. B. Cochran. G. W. WEBB, Sec.

Milwaukee News.

The Milwaukee church, Wis., desires to announce to all who are interested that she has employed a pastor, my successor here, in the person of F. N. Calvin, of Waco, Texas, who will take up his work Dec. 1st. We account ourselves fortunate in securing the services of this eminent and successful man.

As for myself, I will continue to reside in Milwaukee and become state evangelist or state missionary. Wisconsin is enabled to undertake a vigorous work through her state board, by the assistance of our general boards, the A. C. M. S. and the C. W. B. M.

We fall into line and take up the new rally cry "100,000 souls for Christ in 1899." Wisconsin will have a joyous share in that glorious undertaking.

C. G. MCNEILL,
State Evangelist.

Annual Report.

Last fall and winter the Lindenwood Church claimed my further effort soliciting balance. March, 1898, I began traveling and soliciting support for the Christian Orphans' Home. I traveled 16,000 miles in that behalf, closing my engagement Nov. 1, 1898. The brotherhood is ready for a wide, strong movement in charitable work; articulating all we have and wisely expanding till benevolent care of the aged and the little ones shall be as well done with our people as among any religious body in the land. This tender theme of pure religion should have a half day in the national assembly of the brotherhood to unfold the inner life of the churches. Such an annual report of all our systematic benevolences will strengthen the educational and missionary interests of the conventions. Nothing in manifold interests would stir the hearts of the 10,000 or more attending the Jubilee Convention at Cincinnati next year than a full report and a most thrilling address on benevolences.

George Mueller's orphanages have cared for 10,000 of the wretched, needy ones. Dr. Barnardo has rescued in 31 years 30,000 homeless boys and girls. Some of the most prominent citizens in the West are the boys taken from New York City by Mr. Brace, through the Children's Aid Society. I could enlarge upon this one phase of benovolence through many columns. I hope the day will come soon when the prominent speakers in convention shall have more to say on benevolent institutions than either educational or missionary interests. The glory of the true Church of Christ is a sympathetic touch of a heartsome hand in its tender care of the aged and the orphan. My year's work has shown me the best side of our church life. I shall ever treasure the sweet memories of a year mingling with the best brethren and sisters of our brotherhood. God bless them all.

The first anniversary of the erection of the Lindenwood church was duly observed Nov. 6, at 2:30 P. M. Banks of potplants and flowers made the church charming. There was a deep gratitude expressed that the church is dedicated to God's service. Not a dollar of debt. It is the first church among us ever dedicated in St. Louis without soliciting a dollar.

I enter upon the pastorate of the Ellendale and Lindenwood churches. I am settled at Lindenwood to plead for South St. Louis and to work for our cause in so large a population.

W. B. YOUNG.

Lindenwood, St. Louis, Mo.

We learn that Bro. McClure, of Central College, Missouri, recently organized a church of 20 members at McFall, Mo., and that J. H. Coffey will preach for them one-fourth time. Other activities will be organized at the earliest opportunity.

What To Do.

I have not adopted the above caption to discuss Tolstoi's famous book. Although I have wandered far from home I am ever a Missourian, and therefore offer a few *practical* statements in answer to your question: "What ought the brotherhood in Missouri to undertake *now* to meet the educational demands that are made upon us?"

1. Let the "Educational Conference" be made a permanent institution, meeting about the same time the state convention meets, but distinct from the latter. "Agitate! agitate! agitate!" said a great Athenian. Talk *does* accomplish something. "In a multitude of counsel there is wisdom."

2. Undertake to advance the highest interests of *every educational plant in the state.* Every one, however small, is a center of Christian influence. Every one has a *local* patronage which others could not secure. Christian University is in a much more flourishing condition than it was when the Columbia College

plane with the best institutions of our land, but to be held there it must have more endowment. Now is the time. Let this great brotherhood unite in one supreme effort to place this time-honored institution upon a solid financial basis on the occasion of its 50th anniversary. We will be happier for having accomplished such a work. It will be an inspiration to all our colleges, and will be a great uplift to our brotherhood in their educational work.

E. V. ZOLLARS.

[Since our list of names published we have received 240 additional names from President Zollars, which we have not the room to publish. We shall, however, keep our readers posted as to the growth of this list.—EDITOR.]

Jamaica Printing Press.

In response to our appeal for help to purchase a printing press for Bro. Randall to take back to Jamaica with him, we have so far received but two responses, as follows:

Randolph Cook, Metropolis, Ill. $5.00
W. P. Keeler, Chicago, Ill. 1.00

In making his remittance Bro. Keeler suggests that we call for a popular subscription of $1.00, to which he thinks a sufficient number would respond to make up the necessary amount, which, Bro. Randall writes, will be about $400, including the necessary type, etc. Let us, then, have a large number of $1.00 donations to this enterprise.

Missouri C. W. B. M.

Several copies of the minutes of the Nevada convention have been sent to each auxiliary. If the officers failed to receive them they should notify me at once.

The quarterly letters were sent out in time

Sisters Richardson, Bradford, Day, Wilson and other auxiliary sisters received us as their guests and served a delightful repast in the church dining-room.

Sister Williams gave us a report of the Chattanooga Convention and an outline of the plan of work proposed for this year. It was the unanimous opinion of the board that the Missouri auxiliaries are well organized bodies, doing their work systematically and growing in knowledge and liberality. But it was also the opinion of the board that we ought to increase the number of auxiliaries and the membership.

Since the secretary is to be excused from field work she asks that a hundred dollars of her salary be paid for the work of organization. The board decided to do all in their power to increase the state fund so that we could employ an organizer for all of the time. The next question was a difficult one to decide—who will be the organizer? This woman must be able to present the work to any audience and to organize auxiliaries. She must attend district and county conventions, etc. There are many capable women in the Missouri C. W. B. M., but few are so situated that they can leave home at any time and remain in the field for weeks. We would be glad to receive letters from such sisters concerning future work.

Sisters Grant, Bantz, Spillman and Gilliam are able to do a grand work for Missouri if they could leave home for any great length of time. These sisters were all elected organizers and we hope they will undertake the work. Eastern Missouri will be the territory of Sisters Grant and Bantz. Western Missouri will belong to Sisters Spillman and Gilliam.

Last year Missouri secured 50 life memberships. This year we have set the mark for 50

Gethsemane Gleanings.

One young lady was baptized at Gethsemane last Sunday. All departments of the work are striving to keep pace with the demands of the times. "The Needs of the Hour," "The Race Problem" and "America's Opportunity," are some of the themes I have lately discussed in Gethsemane's pulpit.

Prof. Woodson Wilson, Ph.D., LL.D., of Princeton University, recently delivered five lectures at Richmond College. It was my privilege to hear two of them. In the first he discussed "Weights and Balances of our Government," reviewing the judiciary, legislative and executive branches, showing that while they were intended to counterbalance each other, the actual effect was frequently the reverse. He expressed the idea that the Constitution of the United States is one of restraint rather than action. That De Tocqueville said no people except those educated in law could understand it, while Bogehot, the English writer, said anybody could understand it. He said the secret of an equipoise in government is that we are a thinking poeple, not influenced by passion. Upon the question of expansion he said: "We are to compete with Germany and Russia. We are the power of light, they are the power of darkness. We must triumph. I did not want this business to start; I had nothing to do with starting it. It has started; let us keep up with the procession. If some one is to have all this world, let it be us." In our municipal government he said that in every instance we have failed.

In the next lecture he spoke of the "Organization of Congress." He contended that while it was popularly supposed that Congress was a deliberative body, there was really but one man in it, and that man the speaker. That all business is done through the committees, and he appoints the committees. That the Senate is fast becoming the most popular rich man's club in the country. That the President is a man of vast importance in the beginning of his term, but when the offices are filled he becomes a mere figurehead. One would think from this brief resume that the Professor was a pessimist of the darkest dye, but on the contrary he is one of the most optimistic men I ever saw. He merely pointed out the weak places in our governmental machinery, but seemed to think there was no reason why the American people should apprehend danger.

L. M. Omer, for five years the beloved pastor of the Third Church, Richmond, resigned a short time ago, and S. R. Maxwell has taken the work there, beginning his labors last Lord's day.

J. J. Irvine, who died of appendicitis, had begun to entwine himself about the hearts of the Norfolk saints when death struck him down. "Blessed are the dead which die in the Lord from henceforth. Yea, saith the Spirit, that they may rest from their labors, and their works do follow them." ALFRED BRUNK.

Newmans, Va., Nov. 10, 1898.

The church at Clay Center, Kan., recently paid its debt of $300. It has been a debt of 10 years' standing. Much credit is due to Mrs. Wilkison, the wife of the pastor, Otha Wilkison, for raising this sum by personal solicitations, and she had the pleasure of burning the mortgage before the church, preceded by appropriate services.

Organizing for Work.

The Eureka College Ministerial Association at its first meeting of the present college year elected C. W. Marlow and A. R. Spicer to the respective offices of president, and secretary and treasurer. The executive committee outlined a series of lectures for the coming year, which will cover the "Purpose and Scope of the Fathers' Plea." Also a series on "Evangelistic and Pastoral Labors." The association unanimously approved the recommendation of the Chattanooga Convention looking to a movement "all along the line." They propose to arrange and conduct, during the holidays, "A Schoolhouse and Deserted Field Campaign." We are in hearty sympathy with the "all-along-the-line" movement and trust that our effort may be heard from when the roll is called at the Jubilee Convention.

A. R. SPICER, Sec. E. C. M. A.

(Let others be incited to action by this splendid example.—EDITOR.]

Appeal to the Preachers.

The question of ministerial relief is one that appeals in a personal way to men who are devoting their lives to the preaching of the gospel. To them, in a great measure, is committed the honor and reputation of the church. "Like priest, like people," is an old proverb, and so far as the judgment of the world upon the church is concerned it is true. The world judges a church by the men who represent it in the pulpit. When the world looks on and sees an old preacher of the gospel in want and need on account of his devotion to the gospel, and his want is generally in proportion to his devotion to his work, they ask where is the boasted fellowship of his fellow-preachers, that they do not supply these wants? Their judgment in this case is so true that the thought is not a pleasing one. I need not make a long appeal to my preaching brethren, for the question resolves itself into a very simple problem. A preacher of the gospel who is disabled by reason of age, sickness or misfortune must be taken care of and his needs supplied. All will accept this and the responsibility of supplying this need rests upon their fellow-workers in the gospel. Then the query comes, How shall it be done? "Let their children take care of them," says one. Very well, if the children are able to do so they will very cheerfully accept the responsibility. But if the children be poor, or there are no children, what then? "Let them go to the poorhouse," says another. All right; these servants of the Lord can afford to go to the poorhouse, but alas! can we afford to let them go there? Are we ready to accept the disgrace that this method entails? When the Presbyterian Church, with no more preachers than we have, expends as it has this year $170,000 to care for its aged and indigent preachers, will it be a credit to us to allow our disabled preachers to be supported by the state? No! no! this will not do. Then, what shall be done? Let us take care of them. Two dollars per year from every active preacher and an offering from every church will supply a fund sufficient to enable the Board of Ministerial Relief to properly care for all who need and deserve our help. Brethren, this is the only practical, wise, scriptural and honorable method of doing this work. My faith in the good sense and honor of my brethren is such that I have not a doubt but they will help us in this work and see that it is done.

D. R. LUCAS.

Talks To Preachers.

I. *Do You Know* that the "preached Word," when accompanied by the "printed page," is rendered doubly effective in causing men to believe unto eternal life through Jesus' name? Compare Mark 16:15 with John 20:30,31.

II. *Do You Know* that your presentation of "our plea" may be greatly strengthened and its cardinal truths become more firmly fixed in the mind of your hearers, if aided by a careful reading of our best literature?

III. *Do You Know* that the Christian Library contains the best literature of the brotherhood on "our plea," and on the various phases of "the Current Reformation?"

IV. *Do You Know* that the placing of "a Christian library in every Christian Church" would so increase the missionary interest and zeal of our people that the motto of the Chattanooga Convention, "One hundred thousand accessions in 1899," would be much more easily realized? Finally,

V. *Do You Know* that it would aid you *spiritually, socially and financially* to assist the founder as many leading pastors and evangelists are doing?

"If You Know These Things Happy Are You If You Do Them." For fuller particulars address the founder, S. J. PHILLIPS.

Sugar Grove, Vernon County, Wis.

stic.

.

.—My meeting at
.st Thursday night
m the Baptists, one
imed, and 45 bap-

have just closed a
ke, Ky.; 12 were
ship will be erected
.—I. H. TEEL.
.—One made "the
hoolhouse appoint-
the 16th inst., and
20th.—J. A. WAL-

.

ing here, conducted
. M. McCurdy and
day night Nov. 13.
arge, but attentive
e meeting and the
interest and good
additions, but the
nevertheless. Our
gentlemen, preach
d up a high stand-
win many friends to
filed religion. We
the Harvest Home
ess them in other

meeting closed here
of additions, the
g order and a good
Sharon to-night.—

meeting continues;
D LANDRUM.
ng opened up here
ise and one confes-
Bro. Walters and
now to prepare for
ER.
re at work here for
sion on 6th and one
wife. 1 baptized
3th. The husband
wife about the same.
ion meeting in De-
a meeting in our
people are most no-
NNA.
eting here is a little
additions to date,
he kingdom. The
e all that could be
g for encouraging
ey, of Concordia,
singers of Israel,"
each evening are
ions. Pray for us.

-school increased
nth; six additions
e, and all depart-
We had Bro. E. C.
Lord's days. He
g. He is pushing
front all along the

nteen more added
were confessions.
ld. Scoville and
nd power.—E. R.

nd year with this
uring the first year
00 for all purposes.
ceived 70 into the
calls. The fortieth
ation of the church
when some friend
n address.—G. K.

.

e, one from the
etter; Aug. 7, one
r by letter; Sept.
from the Method-
one from the Ad-
m the Catholics;
copalians, one by
confession; Oct.
al, 24 to Oct. 16.
dle of March. The
n it upon itself to
urch building, and
e is nearing com-

work at Acampo
sperous condition.
ing evangelist in a
just held at Clay.

We had five confessions, the superintendent of the S. S. and others of the best people of the community. They will all take membership in the Elliott church. We baptized at the same time another most excellent young man from Elliott. The work goes forward. The town of Clay had a complete uplift. —J. DURHAM.

INDIANA.

Indianapolis, Nov. 14.—Fourteen additions at the North Park Church.—J. M. CANFIELD.

Morocco, Nov. 15.—One week ago last Lord's day there were 10 more baptisms. They were all received into the Christian Church at this place. We have secured the services of Bro. T. Z. Shuey and expect to hold our meeting in December, beginning with the first Lord's day.—R. L. CARTWRIGHT.

St Joe, Nov. 14.—I have been engaged in revival meetings at this place just three weeks to-day. We have had large audiences, good interest and 20 by baptism up to date; three of them from the Lutheran Church. Considering the weak and divided condition of the church at the beginning of the services, and the opposition encountered from the denominations, we feel that God has abundantly crowned our labors with success.—H. CLARK, pastor.

Franklin, Nov. 18.—Five made the good confession at Christian Chapel, three of whom confessed their Savior at the water. One father was 74 years old.—WILLIS M. CUNNINGHAM.

KANSAS.

Larned, Nov. 15.—Two confessions to this church. Interest fine. The writer will preach the union Thanksgiving service in the Presbyterian church.—C. H. HILTON.

Potwin, Nov. 14.—The church here is advancing all along the line. Two additions at regular services Nov. 14. We observed Forefathers' Day, taking a collection for Home Missions. Large numbers of young people attend our evening services.—K. W. WHITE.

Otha Wilkison, of Clay Center, assisted pastor Peter Slack in a three weeks' meeting at Agra, resulting in 40 additions, 39 baptisms. Meeting closed Nov. 13.

Fall River, Nov. 15.—For the past 10 or 12 days we have been enjoying a season of religious joy and refreshing. Bro. Daniel Trundle, of Eureka Springs, Ark., has been with us and by his labors has endeared himself to every heart. The central object in the meeting was to build up the church and cement all Christian hearts in fraternal love; in this effort our good brother was very successful. I have rarely if ever seen a better spirit pervade a meeting. We all feel that great good was accomplished. One good brother took membership with us.—W. BUTLER, pastor.

Halstead, Nov. 17.—I began a protracted meeting here last Saturdary evening. We had three accessions last night. Prospects are encouraging. The meeting will continue indefinitely. Bro. J. J. McClain is pastor and is a faithful worker.—L. B. COGGINS.

TEXAS.

Terrell, Nov. 8.—Have just closed a meeting here with 32 additions. The audiences were large and attentive and we trust much good has been done. Bro. Jewell Howard, the pastor of this church, will enter Add Ran University the first of January This church will continue to pay his salary until the first of January and give him the time intervening that he may visit churches in the surrounding country of Add Ran and make arrangements to preach on Sundays. This was a noble act on the part of the Terrell Church.—B. B. SANDERS, Cor. Sec. Texas Mission Work.

ILLINOIS.

Closed at Hoopston, Nov. 7th with 10 added the last night; 118 in all. Buchanan, Mich., next.—SCOVILLE AND SCOTT.

Watseka, Nov. 14.—Another added here yesterday. One week ago Sunday Dr. Hardin, of Eureka College, delivered a most interesting address to this people on Higher Education. He is always a welcame visitor.—B. S. FERRALL.

Albion, Nov. 16.—Bro. F. S. Haltom of Sumner, recently held a meeting of 16 days' at West Village with 16 additions to the church; 14 baptisms, two by relation. The church is very greatly benefited.—MORRIS COLYER.

Gibson City, Nov. 14.—We have just closed a meeting of a month's continuance. B. S. Ferrall, pastor of the church in Watseka and a most efficient song leader and soloist assisted us. Twenty-five were added to the church. The church seems to be making fine progress.—W. W. SNIFF, minister.

Just closed a meeting at McVey with eight additions; six confessions and two by letter. I begin a meeting at Boston Chapel this week; I am regularly employed for all my time with the following congregations: Atwater half time, McVey and Boston Chapel half time. I am for the present located with the congregation at Atwater, Ill.—H. J. HOSTETLER.

Henry, Nov. 13.—I am in a meeting h
Have preached one week. The three d
rain and snow storm last week nearly brok
our meeting. But worldly indifference
sectarian prejudice that abound here are w
than the bad weather. Expect to contine
other week at least.—M. P. HAYDEN.

Elkhart, Nov. 19.—Meeting here goe
with big crowds and excellent attent
Thirteen added to date. Will baptize
leading Methodists to-night. We cont
indefinitely.—ANTHONY AND HUNSAKER.

MISSOURI.

East Atchison, Nov. 15.—We have
closed a meeting here at Winthrop of t
weeks' duration, with 11 added to this chu
four by obedience, the rest by letter
restoration. On last Sunday we imme
three in the Missouri river; two of them
twin girls, and they were both immersed at
same time. We also organized a Y. P. S
E. of 28 members.—J. H. SPEER.

Kansas City, Nov. 14.—Closed an excel
meeting at our new mission, Ivanhoe,
Lord's day, with 29 additions, 19 of t
being heads of families. Had more tha
week of rain and snow, but the people
faithful. The outlook at this point is pro
ing. Bro. Ernest Forbes, the efficient su
intendent of the Sunday-school, and M
Rose Settle took charge of the music and d
with credit. At the Local Union rally of
C. E. Societies of the city last night, the
Street C. E. Society carried off the ban
Six members the past week, one associ
Our audiences at East 15th Street are incre
ing each Lord's day. City missions are c
stantly growing in favor with the churc
here.—FRANK L. BOWEN, city missionary.

Richmond, Nov. 17.—Just closed 12 da
meeting at Friendship church, near Richmo
with 32 additions; 24 confessions. The chu
feels strengthened in many ways.—R. L. W
SON.

Kearney, Nov. 16.—Our meeting starts
well. Six canfessions last night; 15 in
House packed at every service and inte
deepening. I go to Eureka, Kans., to dedic
their beautiful new house of worship on
fourth Lord's day in November. Correspo
ents will address me at 1048 Spruce St., To
ka, Kans.—D. D. BOYLE AND V. E. RIDENO
evangelists.

Civil Bend, Nov. 16.—We recently close
very interesting meeting at Fair Haven, H
rison County, Mo.; five additions, three
confession and baptism and two by stateme
We have just finished repairing our chu
building at Eagleville, Mo., and will be re
for the county meeting in February. We
now in a good meeting at Oak Ridge, Davi
County, and expect good results. Let us pr
—Z MITCHELL.

Cowgill, Nov. 19th.—We closed on the 1
at Princeton. Had fine interest and nine
ditions. This is a fine congregation, and
stay there was very pleasant. This chu
will ever occupy a warm place in our hear
Bro. Hunter has been employed to t
charge of the church.—MORGAN MORGANS A
DAUGHTER.

Higginsville.—Work here prosperous. C
confession last Sunday night.—ANDREW SCO

SUBSCRIBERS' WANTS.

Miscellaneous wants and notices will be inserte
this department at the rate of two cents a word, e
insertion, all words, large and small, to be count
and two initials stand for one word. Please acc
pany notice with corresponding remittance to s
book-keeping.

Literature.

THE MASTER'S BLESSEDS. By J. R. Miller, D.D. Fleming H. Revell, Chicago, Ill., publishers. Price, cloth, 182 pages, $1.00.

This book consists of a series of devotional chapters suggested by the beatitudes of Christ and cannot fail in its purpose of strengthening the inner man with its right supply of heavenly manna. After its reading the reader will have a greatly enlarged conception of the length, breadth, height and depth of the spiritual significance of the beatitudes and their better appreciation. The book itself is an ornament, and with its spiritual contents a gift that any friend of the Master would appreciate.

FRIENDSHIP. By Rev. Hugh Black, M. A. Fleming H. Revell Co., Chicago, publishers. Price, $1.25.

In an introduction to this new book, the Rev. W. Robertson Nicoll, D. D., says that Mr. Black "is now, we snppose, the most popular preacher in Scotland," and of the book, "It is full of good things winningly expressed; and though very simply written, is the result of real thought and experience. For young men especially this volume will be a golden possession, and it can hardly fail to affect their lives. Mr. Black says well that the subject of friendship is less thought of among us now than it was in the Old World." The book is handsomely printed in two colors, with original marginal and other decorations, by Mr. F. Berkeley Smith, while deckel-edge paper, and an elaborate cover design contribute further to the making of a gift book appropriate to all seasons and every occasion.

WAITING FOR THE KING, a poem by Richard Hayes McCartney. Fleming H. Revell Co., Chicago, Ill., publishers. Price, cloth, 150 pages, 50 cents.

THE SOWER. By John G. Woolley. The Church Press, Chicago. 50 cents.

Every reader who believes independent political action necessary to destroy the saloon will find in this volume the author's strongest arguments for such a course. These arguments are arrayed with consummate skill, and the arts of the publishers have been strikingly displayed in bringing out clearly the strong points. Mr. Woolley's terse, epigrammatic and figurative style was never exhibited at a better advantage. It is printed on very heavy deckel-edged paper, bound in cloth of dark maroon, with gilt top and title frontispiece.

PERSONAL SKETCHES OF RECENT AUTHORS. By Hattie Tyng Griswold, author of Home Life of Great Authors, etc. Chicago, A. C. McClurg & Co. $1.50.

If one wishes to spend a few days very pleasantly in the association of some of the men and women who have made their names famous in the world of literature, and would like to get a little closer to them and see more of their inner life than can be found in their own works, he will be delighted with this recent volume. The men whose lives are portrayed in these personal sketches are Alfred Tennyson, Ernest Renan, Charles Darwin, Matthew Arnold, George Du Maurier, Elizabeth Barrett Browning, John Ruskin, Thomas Henry Huxley, Harriet Beecher Stowe, Robert Louis Stevenson, William Dean Howell, Louisa May Alcott, Lyeff Tolstoi, Rudyard Kipling, Christina Rosetta, Henry David Thoreau, Bayard Taylor ane James Matthew Barrie. Our readers will agree that here are some delightful men and women, and it only remains for us to add that the sketches are drawn with a clever hand, with enough characteristic quotations from the various authors to throw light on the features of their characters which are treated. It is exceedingly interesting to note the early influences and surroundings which have helped to make these men and women what they became. One fact impressed us deeply as we read the volume, and that is that a great majority of these famous people in their earlier years had to struggle with poverty, and to do their work under what seemed to be most unfavorable conditions. One feels, when reading such a volume, that he has come into closer sympathy and touch with these writers, and is better prepared to appreciate their writings. To all lovers of books and of literature this volume will be thrice welcome. We feel safe in prophesying for it a wide reading both in the Old World and in the New.

THIRTEEN CHAPTERS ON FIRST-DAY OBSERVANCES. By John M. VanKirk, LL.B. Christian Index Co., DesMoines, Iowa, publishers. Price, cloth, 220 pages, $1; paper cover, 75 cents.

As the title indicates this book is a collection of evidences in support of the first day of the week as the day to be sacredly observed by Christian people. The author has treated his subject largely from the polemical standpoint, and has clearly made out a good case. No time is wasted with arguments negating Seventh-day observance. Considerable pains has been given to the first or Lord's day in history. The book is in large type and conveniently arranged both for reading and reference. The introduction is by Granville Snell, Trenton, Mo. The book is for sale by the author at Kalona, Iowa.

MAGAZINES.

Dr. William Elliot Griffis has written for the Sunday-school Times of November 19 a scholarly *resume* of the present conditions in that far-off land, which gives one an excellent idea of the factors that enter into the problem, from a missionary point of view. The author's long residence in and study of the Far East fit him peculiarly to treat of this subject.

Richard Harding Davis' "In the Rifle-pits," in the Christmas Scribner's, is a vivid presentation of that little exploited period from July 2 to July 15 when the army waited and suffered in the trenches before Santiago. Mr. Davis' short story, growing out of his war experiences, will appear in the January Scribner's, and he will continue to contribute frequently to that magazine throughout the year 1899.

The Ladies' Home Journal is about to publish six new, distinct series of articles which will include not less than 400 photographs presenting one hundred of the prettiest country homes in America, one hundred of the prettiest gardens, seventy churches decorated for festal occasions of all kinds, some forty of the prettiest girls' rooms in this country, twenty-five floral porches and vineclad houses, and the story of the native wild flowers in America, told in seventy-five photographs.

Marriages.

HOGAN—BARR.—Nov. 7th, at Kansas City, Mo., Mr. David P. Hogan and Miss Mamie Barr, both of Kansas City, Mo.; R. E. Lloyd, of the Church of Christ officiating.

LAWRENCE—MOORE.—Nov. 2nd, at the home of the bride's mother, Eld. C. Edwards, of Payson, officiating, Mr. Liba L. Lawrence and Miss Asceneth Moore.

LUMBECK—CRAIG.—In Malta Bend, Mo., Nov. 1, 1898, Harry Lumbeck, of Memphis, Tenn., and May Craig, of Malta Bend; Walter P. Jennings, of Lexington, Ky., officiating.

Obituaries.

[One hundred words will be inserted free. Above one hundred words, one cent a word. Please send amount with each notice.]

BACON.

Byron Bacon, son of Dr. C. W. and Mrs. Cora Bacon, of Pawnee, O. T., was born Aug. 11, 1897, and died Oct. 23, 1898. Byron was a bright, happy little soul, and drew all hearts to him. His death brings sorrow indeed to the fond parents. Sister Bacon wonders how mothers who do not trust in Christ can endure such trouble. But she and the Doctor know in whom they have believed. Faith and hope sustain them while they "pass under the rod." A FRIEND.

BOONE.

Departed this life in Jefferson City, Mo., Nov. 6, 1898, Mrs. Lucy A. Boone (*nee* Daly), relict of the late Elder C. Boone, for many years a citizen of Fayette, Howard County, Mo., and later of Jefferson City, where he passed away Jan. 17, 1885, in the 73rd year of his age. William C. Boone was born in Shelby County, Ky., and his wife, Lucy A. Daly, was born in Nicholasville, Ky. They came with their parents in an early day to Missouri, and were married in Fayette, June 10, 1834, by his brother, Rev. Hampton L. Boone, then a Methodist minister, afterwards a prominent preacher in the Christian Church. William C. Boone and his wife became members of the church in Fayette, and were baptized by Eld. Thomas M. Allen, that prince and peerless preacher of pioneer days. Mr. Boone was a prosperous man, and for many years was connected with the old Missouri State Bank at Fayette. His house was the preachers' home, and right royally were they always entertained. In her old age nothing delighted Mrs. Boone more than to talk of the great meetings held in Fayette and the grand, good men who shared their hospitality. Mrs. Boone was a woman of fine intellect, remarkable conversational powers and charming personality. She was familiar with the Holy Scriptures. She had unfaltering faith in God, and an abiding trust in Jesus, in whom alone she trusted. Her life was, therefore, calm and serene in the midst of all the trials through which she passed. The end was peaceful. As a child falls to sleep in the arms of its mother, so closed she her eyes and fell asleep in Jesus.

"Rest, weary head,
Lie down to slumber in the peaceful tomb.
Light from above has broken through its gloom
Here in the place where once thy Savior lay,
Where he shall awake thee on a future day,
Like a tired child upon its mother's breast.
Rest, sweetly rest!"

She was the mother of 11 children, seven sons and four daughters. Of these, four sons and four daughters survive her. All these were at her bedside when she passed away, save one, and he arrived in time for the funeral. Mrs. Alfred M. Long, of Jefferson City; Mrs. John I. Sears, of Kansas City; Mrs. Kirtley, of Columbia, and Mrs. Thompson, of Belleville, Ill., are her daughters. Dr. W. C. Boone, of New York; Dan Boone, of St. Louis; John Boone, of Kansas City, and Howard Boone, of Montana, are her sons, and never had mother more devoted children. There are 30 grandchildren and three great-grandchildren. Her daughters are Christians and walking in the footsteps of their now sainted mother. May her sons be won to Christ by her loving example. The writer, aided by Bro. J. P. Pinkerton, conducted the funeral services in the Christian Church, in the presence of a large congregation of her friends and neighbors. "And I heard a voice saying unto me: Write, Blessed are the dead which die in the Lord. Yes, from hence they do rest from their labors, and their works do follow them." T. P. HALEY.

Kansas City, Mo., Nov. 10, 1898.

LOWREY.

Henry N. Lowrey was born in Talmage, Summit County, O., Sept. 13, 1812, and died at his late home, 155 Charles St., Grand Rapids, Mich., Oct. 27, 1898, at the age of 86 years, one month and 14 days. He spent 51 years of his life in his native state. He married Jane A. Brittain, April 2nd, 1835, who was his faithful companion for nearly 56 years. From youth Bro. Lowrey was religiously inclined and in early life became a member of the M. E. Church. On New Year's day of 1850 he and his wife were baptized by Elder A. B. Green, and united with the congregation of Disciples at Stow, O., where he remained an active member until he moved to Cascade, Mich., in 1863. He was a charter member of the church at Cascade, which was organized in 1865. He was the first elder in this congregation and filled the office well for 10 years. In 1975 he moved to Grand Rapids, and was one of the faithful ones who assisted in bringing about an organization of the church in this city, where he held his membership until removed by death. He was a faithful man of God, always ready to perform the duties assigned him, from the most menial service to the pulpit, which he filled acceptably many times. Bro. Lowrey spent four years in Washington, in government employ, during which time he attended the Vermont Avenue Church under the ministration of Bro. Power. Since the death of his wife in 1891 he has had a pleasant home with his daughter and son-in-law, Mr. and Mrs. Baxter, where he lived till the death messenger came, and he sweetly fell asleep in Jesus. He leaves two daughters, one son, seven grandchildren and four great-grandchildren. By his own request the writer preached the funeral at his late home, which occured Oct. 29, 1898, attended by many relatives and friends who mourn, but not as those who have no hope. Bro. E. B. Widger, of Grand Rapids, assisted in the service. Now thanks be unto God, which always leadeth us in triumph in Christ. J. JAY FINLEY.

Cascade, Nov. 4, 1898.

MIDDLETON.

Lee Middlelon was born in Kentucky and died at his home in Hannibal, Mo., Nov. 6, 1898, aged 67 years. For 25 years he was a member of the Christian Church. Sixteen of these years he enjoyed with this church. He was naturally of a cheerful disposition. Misfortunes and ill health troubled him in later years. He was a kind husband, an affectionate and thoughtful father and a generous friend. He sympathized with others in financial misfortune to a degree that made his own burden too heavy. Many warm friends will miss him from his place in the life of the city. The funeral services were conducted by the writer, assisted by the pastor, Geo. Buckner, at the Christian Church, Clarksville, Mo. The family of wife and five children will miss his counsel and cheer. Two brothers and several sisters remain to cherish his memory. LEVI MARSHALL.

Hannibal, Mo.

SMITH.

On Friday, Oct. 21, there passed from earth the spirit of our brother, John O. Smith. Bro. Smith had passed his 90th year. He was born in 1808 in North Carolina. At the time of his death he was an elder of the Star Church. For 40 years he was an elder of the Lost Creek Church in Iowa. Funeral services were conducted by Bros. Garner and Fuller. Bro. N. A. McConnell, of Iowa, was expected to have conducted the services, but failed to get word in time. Bro. Smith was a good Christian, full of faith and of the Holy Spirit. G. W. GARNER.

Beloit, Kan., Nov. 7, 1898.

THOMAS.

On October 30th, 1898, Mrs. J. B. Thomas, of Atwook, Kan., departed this life at the age of 74 years. She had been a reader of the CHRISTIAN-EVANGELIST and its predecessor for 25 years. She died in the faith in which she had so long and faithfully lived. E.

Family Circle.

Woodland Message.

JOSEPHINE L. PEABODY.

I wandered through the woodland long;
I listened to the brooklet's song,
I paused beneath the sturdy oak.
I loved the silence all unbroke,
Save by the thrush's frequent trill.
I felt my soul within me thrill
With something never known before
It filled my heart and bubbled o'er.

I mused on nature's wondrous art
Until I felt within me start
The slumbering forces into life;
They rose in combat and in strife.
They seemed to grudge the short release;
They strove to snatch the hour of peace;
They wrestled there within my soul,
And each one strove to gain control.

Cried Unbelief, "And what are these?
That fragile flower, those sturdy trees,
This humble life, all have their day;
Their showers and sunshine then decay."
Then Doubt low whispered, "That seems so;
All nature is but clay, you know.
Those leaves of golden, green and red
Soon float on breezes brown and dead."

But Faith stepped forth to make her plea:
"Consider what these mean to thee.
They minister unto thy needs;
Through them thy Father intercedes."
And Hope called sweetly, "No frail flower
But has its little perfumed power,
Nor caught those leaves a gleam of gold
But they a loving message told."

Then Hate arose with livid face,
With words of scorn cursed all our race.
"Man holds unto his brother's lips
The deadly poison while he sips."
"Nay," answered Love, "Each human heart,
Must in its wee span do its part;
And heart to heart, and span to span,
Fulfill the Master Worker's plan.

"No hand so rough it cannot feel
A kindly touch in woe or weal,
Nor lips so stern they cannot smile.
No heart so hard, no soul so vile,
It can no gleam of pleasure gain
From dasied fields or falling rain.
Ne'er yet a man has passed his days
Without one sweet thought in his ways."

I listened to a mother bird
Chirp to her babes. With heart deep stirred
I plucked a flower that kissed my path,
Nor wondered at the brooklet's laugh
When stayed my hand its rapid flow.
God fashioned all this earth below.
Glad nature sings the song He taught.
MAN should rejoice in deed and thought.

Text Stories—XVII.
PRAYER.

BY ALICE CURTICE MOYER.

O, come, let us worship and bow down: let us kneel before the Lord, our maker.—*Psa.* 95:6.

The class had met at Bro. Jones' for the weekly study of the lesson. The subject was Prayer. At the close of the lesson study we were invited to ask questions or to offer suggestions that might be helpful.

After a moment of silence, in which no one responded, Bro. Jones, who is our teacher, said:

"Let us make this a sort of 'experience meeting' after the fashion of our Methodist brethren; let us testify as to what the word prayer means to us, and give our understanding of some of the terms and phrases concerning it, such as 'Pray without ceasing,' 'All things whatsoever ye ask,' 'Pray for them which despitefully use you,' 'But when thou prayest enter into thy closet,' etc. Bro. B.," turning to one of the eldest members of the class, "let us hear from you first on one of these phases of the subject."

Bro. B. rose and stood so as to face the class; he said:

"My friends, one of the most forcible passages concerning prayer, at least one that seems so to me is, 'But when thou prayest enter into thy closet, and when thou hast shut the door, pray to thy Father which is in secret.' I do not take this as implying that there should be no prayer in public—far from it—but it particularly emphasizes the need of private worship. Through prayer we maintain a personal relationship with our Heavenly Father. Daily communion with him is necessary to this relationship. I have made it a rule to rise a little earlier of mornings, rather than miss this quiet time of prayer; it helps so much to smooth out the wrinkles of the duties of the day; it strengthens me for the disappointments and worries and annoyances that do so often arise; it makes my sorrows lighter to tell God about them; it makes my joys greater to thank him for them; it helps me to love my friends and fellow-beings with a more Christlike love to ask that the Father's blessings may rest upon them. I want to urge upon you, my friends, this special need of the soul—this quiet hour of prayer and meditation—in this age of rush and unrest. Let us go to the Father in simple, childlike trust and listen for his voice in answer."

Bro. L. was the next to speak:

"I was made to think of this passage today: "All things whatsoever ye shall ask in prayer believing ye shall receive,' because of a conversation I overheard between two little bootblacks. Said one: 'Las' night I prayed that the first man I shined shoes for this morning would give me a dollar.' Said the other: 'And did it come to pass?' and the first answered: 'No; I knew it wouldn't.' His faith was similar to the faith of the dear old sister who wished the mound in her front yard taken away, and decided to pray for its removal. After spending a few moments on her knees she looked from her window, beheld the mound still there, and remarked resignedly: 'Just as I expected!' In both cases, however, there was a lack of understanding as well as of faith. God does hear and answer the prayer of the sincere, but we must approach the throne of grace intelligently. Of course, he may not always answer our prayers as we would like to have them answered, but rest assured he answers them in the way that is best for us. He will remove from our pathway mountains of difficulty and cast them into the sea Inability, where they cannot longer have power to hinder; he will make the crooked paths straight."

Sister H. now rose and said:

"One of the prayers that, it seems to me, must be most acceptable to God, is the prayer of thanksgiving. I have made it a rule, during life's journey, to find reasons why I should be thankful and not discontented, and until we look for such reasons we have no idea how many there are and how much there is for which we ought to give thanks."

Sister H., as we all knew, had had many crosses and much trouble, and we felt that if she could find reason to give thanks, surely we ought also to pray the prayer of thanksgiving.

Sister K. now spoke. She is a widow and has suffered wrongs at the hands of many. A most timid woman is she in public meetings—afraid of the sound of her own voice—but she seemed to forget her timidity as she said:

"The most difficult thing to do, yet in the doing of which I find greates comfort, is this command: 'Pray for them which despitefully use you and persecute you, that ye may be the children of your father which is in heaven.' It is easy to love those who love us and to pray for those whom we know have our welfare at heart, but when we can conquer any aversion we may feel toward our enemies and can pray for those who despitefully use us, we realize that it is a victory well worth battling for."

"When I was very young," began Bro. S. as Sister K. took her seat, "Pray without ceasing' was a sort of stumblingblock to me. 'How can we be continually on our knees?' I argued. 'But I have come to know that it means simply to be in a prayerful state of mind—a condition that tends so much to lift us above the petty annoyances of every-day life. I have found it to be a spirit well worth cultivating."

"One of the most beautiful things about prayer," said Bro. G., rising, "is that it gives us the pleasures of hope. We pray for the things that we do so want, and believing God's promises we have hope that our prayers will be granted. It is this hope that nourishes our aspirations and makes our morrow bright with the rosy hues of expectation. It unravels seeming mysteries and lifts us heavenward where Providence diffuses a sort of universal gladness over all the harsh dissonances of life, and unfolds to our view a future that is smiling and beckoning us onward to reap the satisfying harvest it has in store for us. This, it seems to me, is one of the most desirable effects of prayer; and the blessedness of it is, such a hope from such a source is not delusive."

"One of the tenderest things in this connection, it seems to me," said Bro. Jones, "is when the disciples said, 'Lord teach us to pray' they were told to say, 'Our Father.' Does not this give to us the privilege of coming to God, as the child comes to its earthly parent, and pour out to him our heart's desire, laying before him our wants and needs, knowing that he will not withhold his good gifts? There are few of us but know something of the protecting care of an earthly father; then how much more tender must be the care of the Heavenly Father to his children who, amid the trials and discouragements of life, can still say, 'Our Father,' knowing that he will not allow our burdens to be greater than we can bear."

We separated, each to his own home, realizing that the subject had been but partially covered, but feeling that we had spent a most profitable evening.

St. Louis, Mo.

so many fine, large trees of all kinds, and father was particular to point out the various kinds to us and teach us their names. We saw the squirrels jump from limb to limb of the trees and could watch droves of wild turkeys as they roamed through the pastures.

At noon we always stopped near a large spring for dinner; no picnic party ever enjoyed a dinner like we did the contents of that lunch basket. There was boiled ham, old-fashioned sweet corn bread, resembling our steamed brown bread of to-day, fried chicken, biscuits, pickles and preserves; besides these father would go to the nearest farm house and buy the hot "hoecake," which was always baked there for the noonday meal, get a pot of coffee and a pitcher of milk and cream, and there was a feast for a king.

The horses were unhitched and fed, while a few hours' rest was taken in the heat of the day. Sometimes a large rope was fastened to the limb of a tree and we enjoyed a fine swing. During the afternoon ride we became tired and sleepy and wished the journey was over; often we were refreshed by eating a large, red, ripe watermelon, still the road would stretch into many miles before evening; how eagerly we watched for the chimney of the old house. After awhile we would leave the main road to "go through" some neighbor's farm; the little darkey who opened the gates for us would bow and

the best of food was prepared, choice dainties were set out, each child was shown some special mark of attention, and love ruled in all hearts.

We gathered the eggs, drove the cow, peeled apples and peaches for drying, went to the fields for roasting ears and pole beans, or if late enough gathered hickory-nuts, walnuts and hazelnuts for the winter.

The large old-fashioned rooms, with rag carpets on the floors, woven in grandmother's loom, were neat and clean. The tall chimney mantel held the large clock and the vases filled with corn flowers, wild roses and asparagus branches; in the fall the huge fireplaces were filled with logs of wood and the bright, cheerful fire we then had is not equaled by anything in the home of to-day.

The old neighbors would come in to spend the day and such hurry and bustle as there would be to fix a "big dinner," such pies and custards as grandmother could make, such rolls of sweet, yellow butter and such good, hot biscuits to eat it on. There were dozens of chickens, turkeys, geese and guineafowls; the smokehouse contained the best and sweetest of old-fashioned hams, bacon and lard; the people lived on the fat of the land in those days and no "boughten stuff" filled the tables. Often father and the uncles and boys would take the partridge net and set it, with its wide wings, in some field and drive a whole covey of quail into it, which would

There was comfort and contentment everywhere and I have never seen happier people than those I remember in the home of my grandparents. To go back and spend one such day again with the dear, departed, loved ones, would be like going back to the Garden of Eden. L. S.

Warrensburg, Mo.

Sympathy.

BY IDA B. DAVIDSON.

The sad, tired world with all its busy cares,
Its voiceless sorrows and its throbbing pain,
Has such sore need of human sympathy,
To lesson with its kindly touch, the strain
Of daily living.

For human sympathy alone can thrill
The heart to glad, warm life and hope again;
Bearing the soul above the clouds of doubt
To join the chorus of a glad Amen!

Eureka, Ill.

Where a Nickel Was Lost.

BY DEWITT C. WING.

It was a cold morning in December, in a noisy business city; the streets were swarming with men, women and children —all classes, ages and sizes. An aged lady with only one arm, bent in form and weary in spirit, was plodding along the avenue, wending her way as best she could through the surging multitude. She was without means and poorly clad. Occasionally she stopped and peered about her and drew a long breath. Several times she asked for financial assistance, but all whom she asked said that cold and cruel No.

On the corner stood a well-dressed, genteel-looking young man awaiting the arrival of a street car. The poor old woman approached him and said: "Mister, will you please help me—please give me a nickel." "No," he said in a voice coarse and penetrating; "I haven't it to spare." She went on, her eye full of tears, meeting the same stone-hearted kind of people.

The young gentleman who had refused to help her was seen shortly thereafter going into a saloon, a den of evil, an endeavor society of the devil; investigation found that he had spent ten cents therein for rum, which amount was doubly detrimental to himself by reason of the fact that he had refused to give a half of it to a poor and needy old woman and spent it and another piece for drink!

The decrepid woman finally accosted a man of perhaps forty years of age and asked him for help; he opened his heart to her, and she was greatly cheered and encouraged.

I wonder which of the two men, the giver or refuser, stands right before God? No, I know there is no question about it. It is more blessed to give than receive; it is more blessed to give than not to give.

There are millions of opportunities offered every day for the proper distribution of charity; there are also many objects not deserving of charity. The case in question was and is.

Indianapolis, Ind.

"How Beautiful to be with God!"

As the shoreline of Time faded into the glad light of Eternity, and the sweet consciousness of the Infinite Presence filled the wonderful spirit of Frances Willard, she looked up with the calm of a soothed child, falling asleep in the golden glow of the eventime, and said:

"How beautiful to be with God!"

Like a benediction the words fell upon the ears of the listening world, and the message from the borderland of light floats back upon the pathway of turmoil and conflict, of sorrow and joy, and breathes the sweet fragrance of a higher hope into our hearts and lives.

"How beautiful to be with God!" We hear the glad echo of this last testimony, and a new realization of companionship with God comes up within us. The cares and responsibilities of every-day living throng us, their duties press and weary, but the harmony of heaven is ours, the beauty of its spirit touches with forgetfulness much of the hardship of the journey. In this full consciousness all life is transformed. The flowers spring up, the birds sing, the skies are blue; sad hearts cease their crying, because of the cup of comfort loving hands offer in unselfish thoughtfulness. Resentment dies out. Oppression is disarmed, the lash falls on the silent air, the stricken are tenderly lifted, the hungry fed. Strife is no more. "Peace on earth" swells out its joyful music to the tread of of the multitude, for the heart of man at last has found companionship with the Most High, the source of all that is noble and pure and holy, and feels with every heart-beat the Fatherhood of God, the brotherhood of man. Thus comes to pass the blessed words: "Behold, old things are passed away, all things are become new;" "Thy will be done upon earth, even as it is in heaven."—*Anna Wilson Simmons, in the New York Observer.*

Dedicated to the C. W. B. M.

BY ALFRED BRUNK.

Some ladies asked once on a time,
"Can women beat the men?"
Nor long they talked but with a dime,
Began their ardent fight with sin.

"Come, work, blest host, your mite
Can wondrous blessings mete;"
The call was heard, and with delight
Their sisters now the word repeat.

Consider well, be moved with love,
Carefully watch, be always meek.
Like serpents wise, kind as the dove,
Thus win the wanderers whom you seek.

Then, Christian, work where'er you dwell,
Let woman's prayer pierce through the sky,
Our Board will aid in mount or dell,
Of missions' fruits we'll sing on high.

Newmans, Va.

What We Should do as Girls.*

"Many young girls endowed with brilliant intellects, and capable of making the world better by a right use of the talents entrusted to their keeping, make a miserable failure of this thing called life."

They set forth upon the voyage under glowing skies and with faces turned to the eastward, where the dreamy splendor of the morning dawn throws its glamour over them, tinting all things with its fair delusions; even the long blue waves and the white sea-froth catch a glimmer of the golden tints, and break into sheens of sparkling beauty at their feet. It shuts from their sight the shadow of clouds that lower in the western horizon, and hushes from their ears the roar of distant breakers and the long, low, rolling thunder-note, premonitions of storms that must break sooner or later over every ship that sails the sea of life.

To-day *we*, a band of hopeful girls, are trimming our sails for the ocean of active life. To-day the shore is ours, to-morrow the ocean; and each feels if she does not ask the question: "How will my voyage end?"

We stand on the shore looking oceanward. The long waves break on the pebbly beach and kiss with lips of foam the eager, trembling feet, telling how tenderly the wavelets will caress our frail barks, and of the "lone sweet isles amid the sea where, when weary of toiling against wind and wave, we may rest secure from storm or flood."

But up from the heart of the waters a still, small voice is calling for earnest laborers in the fields of life. Our work in life is whatever we find ourselves competent to do.

We hear so much in these days of a public career for girls, in which may be gained fine plumage and notoriety, and in a very few instances fame. There are many ways in which a girl can perform her task in the work of this life without entering into the much-talked-of "public career." We must not undertake great things and neglect the many small duties that devolve upon us. "Seek to be good, but aim not to be great. A woman's noblest station is retreat; her fairest virtues fly from public sight."

We must remember we are not simply living in the present. The deeds we do now, the thoughts we think now, will yield a fruitage in the years to come. "Then we should be kind, be noble! Make our life one grand sweet song." "Drop kind words along our pathway. We will find them again, transformed into blue forget-me-nots, whose fragrance will welcome us as our feet near the verdant meads of the Glory-land."

We should be energetic, and this energy is but really the result of an educated will. By resolving to do all things well, and as quickly and gracefully as possible, even if the act be no greater than the pouring of a cup of tea, or the arranging of one's toilet, the will is gradually taught energy and its strength increases. Let us every one, therefore, lay aside all listlessness and "whatever our hands find to do, do it with a will." All the really strong characters in the world are they who are so by mere force of will. No gifts, even the most brilliant, are of much real worth without the will to use them.

The best and most enduring work is not done by the noisy persons who are forever calling attention to what they do. It is performed by those who, after their best performance, are conscious only that they have done those things which they ought to have done. Such workers are surprised when commended for what they accomplish. It has been said of Gen. Grant, and the words well describe the quiet, modest soldier:

"He came grim, silent, saw and did the deed
that was to do;
He slew our dragon, nor so seemed it knew;
He had done more than any simplest man
might do.
One of those still, plain men that do the
world's rough work."

So may we silently and willingly perform our duties, and cultivate each day those virtues—gentleness, kindness, modesty and purity—which are so admirable in the character of a young girl. For—

"As *pure* as a pearl,
And as perfect, is a noble and innocent girl."

*A graduating essay prepared and read by Miss Irene Johnson, Warrensburg, Mo.

With The Children.

CONDUCTED BY
J. BRECKENRIDGE ELLIS, PLATTSBURG, MO.

Getting Started.

After George and Jennie Weston had eaten their supper (oyster soup and pickles), they hastened to the bookcase to select the books which they intended to read in the Advance Society course. It was necessary to pick out a history or biography and a book containing poety.

"I am going to keep on reading Irving's Life of Washington," said Jennie, taking down the second volume, "I am very much interested in it, anyway, and you see it will count on the society work."

"*I'm* going to get the biggest history we've got," George announced. "I guess that Hume, up there, is about the thing; I see it's in six big fat volumes. I'm tired of seeing it take up so much space, and nobody ever reading it!"

"Oh, George!" exclaimed his sister, "I wouldn't begin on such a long history as *that*. Besides, I'm afraid you will tire of it, and then quit and leave me to be alone in our branch of the society. Get a book you will be interested in, like Southey's 'Life of Nelson,' or 'Dickens' History of England.'"

"No," said George. "Here, you hold this chair while I go after that Hume!" He mounted the baby's high chair, because that was the only way to reach the high shelf. "And don't you be afraid I'll quit. I'm going to be printed in the List of Honor. Look out! that chair's a-wobbling dreadful! Now I've got it!" He climbed down with his book, and they went to their study table where a lamp stood ready.

"First thing," said George, "let's get blank books to keep our record in."

"Hadn't we better make a record first?"

But George hunted up a notebook and spread it open before him ready to write down how much he had read as soon as he had done it. Then the children began to read and silence reigned in the room until Mr. Weston entered. That gentleman looked over George's shoulder. "Hume!" he exclaimed. "And Saturday night!" He felt his son's head. "Do you feel well, George?"

George said he was well, and his father departed with a perplexed expression. At last George finished his five pages, and he hurried to write in his book,

"Minutes of the Advance Society,
Kept by George Weston.
First week (Nov. 3-10, 1898).
History.—Hume's "England," Vol. I. 5 pp."

Then he looked at his sister, but she was reading steadily. After watching her awhile, he exclaimed, "Well, you *are* a show one!"

Jennie started. "Why! I have read an extra page without thinking!" she exclaimed.

"I stopped right in the middle of a sentence," said George, "at the end of the fifth page. Five pages are all you have to read."

"But I was interested and kept on. You ought to have gotten a book that would make you want to know what was going to happen."

"I didn't care what happened," said George. "My book said the Romans defeated Caractacus 'and took him prisoner and sent him to Rome where—' And I don't know 'where' *what*, because that ended the fifth page. But I can tell you, I feel big, reading that big history, and I would rather feel big than to feel interested! Now bring on your poetry."

There was a change of books (George cried, "Change cars!") and again silence reigned, till the boy demanded,

"Didn't Milton write a long time ago?"

"Why, yes, many, many years ago."

"I guess they didn't use periods, *then!*" said George, in an aggrieved tone. "At least I haven't run across one yet. Jennie, this is awful!"

"Why, George, what are you reading?"

"Paradise Lost. Jennie, I told you I couldn't stand poetry, and I'm afraid I am gone, now! I don't want to feel any bigger than Hume makes me feel. Now this thing—I don't any more know what they are doing here than—why, it ain't even about skies and birds and things, what they generally talk about in rhymes."

"Let me get you a book where the poetry tells little stories—here is Longfellow, and over here in his 'Tales of a Wayside Inn,' there are sure enough stories, only the lines rhyme."

"A story in poetry?"

"Why, of course. A lot of people meet at an inn, and each one tells a story to the rest; good stories, too!"

"Hand her over," said her brother. "But I wish I had been Longfellow; I'd have written all this out in prose, where the lines are even at the end! Poetry always looked to me like the lines were trying to trot." But he hunted out one of the tales, and read with a determined expression on his face. "Now that's over," he announced at last. "What are you reading, just keeping on and on, like you were wound up?"

"This is 'Gertrude of Wyoming,' by Campbell. It is about a little boy and girl and Indians, so far. The Indians killed the boy's parents, and a good chief slipped the boy away, and carried him through the woods to the girl's father. I expect they'll fall in love pretty soon."

"Yes, and die by and by," said George. "There is more dying in poetry than there is in the army! But come on, let's get our quotations. I want to do everything the same evening, and be free to do as I please the rest of the week. Here's what I'm going to learn, from Josh Billings." And George began to walk up and down the room declaiming in a loud voice, "Hope is a hen that lays more eggs than she can hatch. Hope is a hen that lays more eggs than she can hatch. Hope is a hen—" He stopped on seeing his father watching him from the doorway. Mr. Weston hurried away to his wife. "My dear," he said to her, "something is the matter with George. Awhile ago he had Hume, and now I don't know what he *has* got! But he is acting very queer."

So Mrs. Weston came in, looking pale, and her husband tiptoed behind her; they heard the words, "Hope is a hen that lays more eggs."

Mrs. Weston turned to her husband. "He is talking in his sleep," she whispered, looking alarmed. But at that Jennie and George laughed, and told them all about the Advance Society. "All you do to be members," they said, "Is to read every week thirty lines of poetry and five pages of history, memorize a quotation, read a verse of the Bible every day and keep account of what you do in your noteboc And if you keep at it twelve weeks, y are printed in the list of honor."

"I do believe I will join myself cried Mrs. Weston, when they talked abc it, and Mr. Weston had retreated to newspaper.

"You can't!" said George. "They s they didn't want any owls to be sole and scare us robbins away."

"Mamma is not an owl!" cried Jenn throwing her arms about her mother, "s is just a big robin, and of course she w join. Hurrah for the Advance Societ Here are three members. Let's get up big circle in the town!"

How Jennie and George started Advance Society circle will be told we after next, but next week we will give t true funny stories that have been sent i The Advance Society is growing with gre rapidity. Already many states are repr sented. We are very glad that not on children, from eight to eighteen ha joined, but a good number of older person All are welcome. I call upon the old ones to help make this department success. Send me stories such as childre like, or sketches that will amuse and ir struct. As for the children, I will giv them another general subject to write upc in our next issue. In the meantime I a always delighted to receive personal lette from the children, telling me about them selves. I intend to make up an artic from those letters I have already receive for a not distant day. Every mail brin new names for my roll-book. Do not b left out of this society, the only one of it kind in the world.

l.

Y.*

to question
aasseh pro-
ie religious
he reign of
features of
was in full
rown, and
kingdom.
proved by
surrection,
d, and re-
n, Josiah,

nportance,
s quite un-
eigned but
man gave
her's. In
rinces was
he case of
od of pros-
een left to
od work of
Here the
was grow-
ied the ac-
men who
imself and
important
h the high
phan, the
with Jere-
mily, and
vards des-
het of the
bable that
this small
to the king

ie prevail-
t Jehovah
hrow. The
y, and the
ad become
ofessional
interpret

but the central sanctuary, a principle never enunciated by the great lawgiver, who had sanctioned sacrifice at any spot where God should set his name; but in entire accord with the spirit of his teaching, since the true religion depended upon the centralizing of the worship at one place like the temple, where it could be supervised and controlled. It is not improbable, therefore, that the Book of Deuteronomy, at least in its essential features, was compiled sometime during the reigns of Manasseh and Amon, based upon the addresses of Moses in his farewell to the people; giving in the main the true principles of the Mosaic teaching, with the addition of the new law of centralization which the priests and prophets who co-operated in the work may well have felt sure Moses would have enjoined in the new day that had come. This new code could not be used in that time of trouble, and may have been laid away till happier days should dawn. They came at last with Josiah; the book was found, and its perusal wrought a transformation in the thought of the king and in the life of the nation.

Whatever may have been the origin of the book we may well discover its character from the effects produced. Comparing the reformation of Josiah and the great passover that he held with the regulations of Deuteronomy, we discover that they correspond closely. We may almost believe we can select the very portions of the book which were read, since it is hardly probable that the entire volume as we have it was read to a great popular assembly. Such sections as 6:4, 5, which Jesus called the great commandment; 12:2-7, enjoining the destruction of heathen symbols; 16:21, 22, prohibition of obelisks and stakes with sensual connotation; 18:9-15, prohibition of divination, and promise of a line of prophets, and the blessings and curses pronounced upon the obedient and disobedient respectively—these were undoubtedly some of the sections of the great code which brought terror to king and people.

For when the news was brouget to Josiah, and the book was read in his hearing, he recognized in it a message from God, yet one that neither he nor his fathers had known or observed. The very things freely tolerated were those on which severest condemnation was pronounced. He had already shown his zeal for

Here, as so often since, the d
covery of the Word of God wa
a great popular effort in behal
ness. Every religious reforma
turies has been supported by t
sage. Wherever the Bible is
buried in oblivion, or overlai
tion of men, there come days of
faith declines. Such were the ti
of Savonarola, of Wycliffe and
such in later times was the perio
To bring forth the Book, and ca
tion to it with trumpet voice
these men, and in similar time
the function of such prophets.

SUGGESTIONS FOR TEAC

When men are doing a good
be sure to find that which is
value. Quick response to the
Bible is proof of a soul open to t
discovery that we are doing wr
ways make us as profoundly di
Josiah. In a time of trouble th
of God through the prophetess;
through whom to go to God sa
It takes long years and many l
the truth that sin always brings
who bear the burden of grief ove
world are sharing the work of
discovery of the Bible in lands w
been known, in circles where
recognized, or in minds where
scured by neglect or tradition, is
of moral and spiritual regenerati
Berlin.

The Religious World.

An effort is being made in Australia to have D. L. Moody visit that country.

Last week was the Y. M. C. A. week of prayer for the deepening of the spiritual life of its active members, and for unsaved young men. We are glad to note this trend toward spiritual things and growing interest in the salvation of young men.

An Announcement to Ministers.

The Council of Seventy desire to announce that the Professional Reading Courses, to be conducted by the American Institute of Sacred Literature, was now fully in operation, two hundred ministers being already at work. It is significant that in so comparatively small a number the following variety of denominations is represented: Methodist Episcopal, Wesleyan Methodist, M. E. South, Presbyterian, Cumberland Presbyterian, Reformed Presbyterian, Southern Presbyterian, Disciples of Christ, Reformed, Lutheran, Evangelical Lutheran, Unitarian, Universalist, United Brethren and Pentecostal.

The subjects now ready as announced in June are (1) The Historical and Literary Origin of the Pentateuch; (2) The Old Testament Prophecy; (3) The Origin and Growth of the Hebrew Psalter; (4) The Life of the Christ; (5) The Apostolic Age; (6) The Problems Connected with the Gospel of John; (7) Christianity and Social Problems; (8) The Preparation of Sermons.

An average number of eight books has been placed upon each course. In the choice of these books every member of the Council of Seventy was invited to participate, and as a result forty distinct lists were sent, aggregating two hundred different books.

These lists were submitted to a committee, and under certain necessary conditions those books having the most votes were chosen. The lists therefore represent the composite decision of a body of seventy practical teachers of the Bible and kindred subjects in our leading universities and seminaries.

Except for payment of the annual membership fee, no restrictions are imposed upon those entering the Guild, either in time limit, choice of subject, report, etc. A carefully prepared review of each book is provided the reader. Every minister should at least inform himself concerning this opportunity for guidance and suggestion in the line of his professional reading. It is possible that by so doing he may find for himself a saving of his own time in looking up material and a stimulus toward work in some definite line of study and investigation.

All inquiries should be addressed to the American Institute of Sacred Literature, Hyde Park, Chicago, Ill.

Literature of the Disciples of Christ.

The literature of the Disciples of Christ marks a period of illumination in Christian thought, and no literature in the world transcends it in importance. It deals, not with reforming the modern Church, but restoring the Apostolic Church, and this is the most important theme since the close of the sacred canon. "Celebrated as the era of the Reformation is," said Alexander Campbell, "we doubt not that the era of the Restoration will as far transcend it in importance and fame, through the long and blissful millennium, as the New Testament transcends in simplicity, beauty, excellency and majesty the dogmas and notions of the creed of Westminster and the canons of the Assembly's Digest." Alexander Campbell broke the last clasp on the Bible and threw wide open its pages, and the literature of the Disciples of Christ is to keep them open, and bring men face to face with its eternal principles. Our motto has been and ever must be, "Let there be light." Our literature, consequently, has been destructive rather than constructive, building no fortress around divine truth, but, instead, burning the pallisade that a Christian philosophy and human theology had erected, and that weakened and obstructed truth. Our best books are "imperishable shrines, not of dead ashes, but of living souls." They are "the blood of master-spirits embalmed for a life beyond life." Alexander Campbell is still writing for the pages of the *Christian Baptist* and the *Millennial Harbinger*; J. T. Barclay is still taking notes in the "City of the Great King;" Isaac Errett is still writing his editorials for the *Christian Standard*, and B. W. Johnson is still working on his commentaries. We sit at the feet of these masters and enlarge their lives as we receive their wisdom and life.—*The Christian Tribune.*

man of God may be perfect, thoroughly furnished unto every good work; that the gospel should be preached in all ages as preached by the first authorized expounders and wise master-builders of the early church, the apostles of Jesus Christ; that the same answers should be given to inquiring penitents now as were given by the Spirit-sent and Spirit-filled teachers of primitive Christianity—Peter, Philip, Ananias and Paul—following this inevitable logic of their plea, the Campbells with their wives and a few others, were immersed June 1812, and the first congregation on this basis was formed.

There was no thought of creating another denomination. These men sought to reform abuses, to call men away from creeds, confessions, church standards, denominationalism, to a common Christianity. They proposed the union of all Christians on what was explicitly taught in the express letter of the infallible oracles. They contended if a man could be a Christian without believing in the Five Points of Calvinism or the five counterpoints of Arminianism, then these diverse doctrines were superadded to the Christianity of the New Testament—human additions—and ought not to be made tests of Christian fellowship and communion. They pleaded for the entire restoration of apostolic order to remove from Christianity the curse of sectarianism. They claimed the church should be emancipated from slavery to Augustine, Calvin, Luther, Wesley or any other man. They called men back beyond Geneva, beyond Wittenburg, beyond Oxford, beyond Constantinople, beyond Rome to Jerusalem. They said Jesus commanded, "Tarry in Jerusalem." "Preach the gospel among all nations beginning at Jerusalem," and back to Jerusalem we must go. It was a stern struggle. They lifted their battle-lit faces to the flashing of the guns of ridicule, calumny, denunciation, ostracism, but God was with them, and their blows shook hierarchs, prison doors flew open, and spiritual manacles dropped from souls that henceforth walked in the glorious liberty of the children of God, and even those who despised their movement have been swayed by their teachings.

Taking their position at Jerusalem, these men began their survey. They ran their baselines from the original stations. They taught the intelligibility of the Scriptures, that the original survey could be discovered and identified, and the bearings taken from the position of inspired men, and that in all the essentials of faith, every one could find the way of life. Beginning the survey here, settling their instruments and taking their bearings from this point, and directing their course by the old landmarks, they declared as essential to a divided and distracted Christendom, the only book that all Christians agree upon—the Bible; the only Leader and Sovereign that all agree in, and whose name is the only name they all may wear—Christ Jesus; the only faith they all regard as essential to salvation—faith in Jesus as the Christ, the Son of God and Savior of the world; the only baptism they all agree in—the immersion of the believer into the name of of fellowship they all believe in—obedience to Christ; the only church they all agreed upon—the Church of Christ, built upon the foundation of apostles and prophet, Jesus being the chief corner stone.

Italy (Lombardy).

The people of Lombardy, one of the northern divisions of Italy, are very different from the Italians of the South. Their part of the country was once inhabited by the Longabardi or Longbeards, from the north, who, uniting with the Italians, formed a people now possessing typical Italian grace and beauty, combined with the vigor and perseverance of the Germanic tribes.

In this division of Italy, famous for its well-cultivated land, the mulberry, grape and chestnut are successfully grown, and much silk and wine are produced.

The Singer Sewing-machine is almost universally in use by the thrifty people of Lombardy because of the simplicity of its mechanism, as well as the Company's liberal policy with its customers.

The photograph reproduction on another page shows an excellent type of Lombardy woman seated at a Singer sewing-machine. Her costume, much more quiet in tone and simple in design than that worn by Italian women of the South, is peculiar only in the shape and trimming of the bonnet which, set far back on the head, frames her face, and brings her strongly-marked features into bold relief.

Publishers' Notes.

Homer T. Wilson, pastor of Third Christian Church, Ft. Worth, Tex., and National Chaplain of the Traveler's Protective Association, and also well known as a popular lecturer in the South, has the following to say concerning M. M. Davis' recent book, "*Queen Esther:*"

"It is one of the most charming books I have ever read. It is a beautiful story, told in the author's own inimitable style. It is thrilling, pathetic, grand, and I most heartily commend it to all, and especially to young ladies. It is a household treasure."

"Queen Esther" is a book containing 132 pages, has appropriate illustrations, is bound in the latest style cloth, and the price is 75 cents, postpaid.

No teacher, be he or she a Christian or not, could fail of suggestion or inspiration in reading "Jesus as a Teacher," by Prof. B. A. Hinsdale, of the University of Michigan. Prof. Hinsdale has put into book form articles previously published and finds in Jesus the great Master of ethical method.

Teachers should never forget the great superiority of the new education to the old consists mainly in the farther advance that it has made along the path when the Great Teacher pioneered the way.

The above is an extract from a review of "Jesus as a Teacher," by the Religious Herald, of Hartfod, Conn. This work is worthy the attention of teachers in the university, the college and the public schools, as it is full of suggestions for the schoolroom of to-day.

It is a work of 330 pages, cloth bound, and the price is $1.25, postpaid.

"Mary Ardmore, or a Test of Faith," by J. H. Stark, is the new book that is rapidly gaining popular favor. It is written in the choicest terms, and will exert an elevating and refining influence on the minds of the readers. It is a book worthy a place in the family, and will interest both parents and children. Its thoughts will adorn the mind, and its beautiful illuminated bindings will please the eye. The long winter evenings can be profitably spent in reading this new book. It contains 328 pages, and the price is $1.00, postpaid.

The Religious Telescope, of Dayton, Ohio, is certainly excellent authority on the merits of Sunday-school literature. We are pleased to give our readers the following extract of a notice of our Lesson Commentary for 1899, as published in the Religious Telescope of Nov. 2nd, 1898:

"The Christian Lesson Commentary on the International Bible studies for 1899, by W. W. Dowling, has come to us. The volume before us is fully up to the high standard of its predecessors, and its pages are replete with notes, comments, illustrations, applications and suggestions gathered from various sources, the design being to throw the best light possible on the Scripture text, and assist the teacher and pupil to fix it upon the mind and hide it in the heart. We commend this commentary to all Sunday-school workers."

'In the Days of Jehu" and "King Saul" are two of our recent publications, the author of both being J. Breckenridge Ellis. A late issue of the Christian Oracle has the following notice of "King Saul:"

"The author gives it as his purpose to write a series of volumes which shall describe the various romantic narratives found in the Bible, and which, without altering or inventing one fact, shall develop these histories as if they were stories for the first time told. In this volume, as in the former, the author has succeeded admirably. This charming book has one of the volumes honored by being read 'out loud' in our household. It is a delightful task the author has set himself, and he is to be congratulated on his success."

"Mary Ardmore, or a Test of Faith," by J. H. Stark, author of "Hugh Carlin," etc., is claimed to be the best work that the author has yet written. It is a story showing the wonderful influence of a consecrated and pure woman. The heroine of this story is cultured and accomplished, and she uses these gifts to great advantage, leading all into a higher and better life with whom she mingles. Parents should place such books as "Mary Ardmore" in the hands of their sons and dauthters who are inclined to read novels. This book will influence their minds and lives for good. The price is $1, postpaid.

OPEN PARLIAMENT ON OUR NATIONAL CONVENTIONS.

The following questions have been sent to several brethren by way of opening the discussion. If others have suggestions let them be brief, as the following are, and to the point:

While the memory of our National Conventions is fresh in your mind will you please answer in about 200 words the following questions for the CHRISTIAN-EVANGELIST:

1. *What changes, if any, would you suggest in the manner of conducting our conventions?*
2. *What suggestions have you to offer as to the Jubilee Convention?*

An early reply will oblige

THE EDITOR.

Will you suffer a word from me on this very important subject? If I were to write a volume on the subject I could not express the whole matter in a better way than Bro. G. A. Hoffmann has expressed it in the CHRISTIAN-EVANGELIST before me (Nov. 17), and I do heartily pray that the time may soon come when there will be no separate organizations, but all of them combined in ONE, thus presenting "our plea" before the world in a practical way.

W. J. HUDSPDTH.

Little Rock, Ark.

The year 1899 will close the most wonderful century of human history.

The most important movement of this "age on ages telling," is the effort to restore the AUTHORITY OF THE CHRIST and THE WORD OF GOD and the UNITY OF THE CHURCH, so sought by the Disciples of Christ.

Scarcely less important than the rejection of human creeds and names for the divine creed and divine names was the organization of the isolated churches for mutual help and world-wide evangelization according to the spirit and example of the apostolic church.

Eighteen hundred and ninety-nine will be the jubilee of our world-wide missionary organization. The meeting in Cincinnati will probably be the largest missionary gathering of the century.

One hundred thousand dollars for Home Missions, no less for Foreign Missions, one hundred thousand conversions, advancement all alo g the line—this is a noble ambition, yet perhaps we ought to do more.

In regard to any changes in methods of holding conventions, it is self-evident we must have more time, or hold some sessions of the different conventions at the same hours. If the latter plan is adopted it will require great care to avoid depriving large numbers of some of the most interesting and important exercises.

If I am to give my conception of the most important interest it will be, "HOME-MISSIONS TO THE FRONT."

Care should be taken to rule every exercise within its own time. When this is full according to a program, there is a moral responsibility involved.

E. C. BROWNING.

Little Rock, Ark.

1. The entire interest of our conventions should center in the religious purpose which they represent. Sight-seeing, anythi g which draws the attention of the people from the consideration of the high and holy aims which they have met to further, is in my opinion detrimental to the work, and lowers in gree the spiritual level of the entire affai do not say that sight-seeing is wrong such circumstances, but that the two d harmonize.

The devotional seasons that have bee rich, and of marked power in some of our ventions, should be maintained at that level. It seems to me that these help to so fy and make permanent the convictions, lutions and tender emotions that are alway duced by the inspiring exercises of the con tion. They are too precious to be sacrific any god of expediency.

2. My heart is stirred to its depths ove possibilities of this jubilee year. May the a great ingathering of souls and of treasur the best cause in the world.

PERSIS L. CHRISTIA

Eureka Springs, Ark., Nov. 12.

1. I have not had the privilege of atten our National Conventions in recent year had better leave the suggestion of chang the manner of conducting them to others have been in a position to more closely obs them.

2. This Jubilee Convention and year o to be the greatest in our entire history. make it such I would suggest that work b gun in *every congregation of Disciples* thro out the land. Our brethren need to study a the religious movement with which we identified. The older brethren can have t hearts gladdened by a review of the glor past, and the younger ones should become quainted with the heroic efforts and elem that made up the history of the past. E cially should each congregation study the tory of these fifty years of organized and gressive missionary work. In connection this general study they should study the they, as congregations, have had in this w If this part has not been what it should b it stir us up to greater exertions than eve fore. Congregations should plan to have or more members at the convention. But should not go up to this convention e handed. Without a decided increase in our missionary offerings this Jubilee Con tion will be worse than a mistake—it w fatal to the great work of evangelizing the world in so far as our people are conce

Every minister should determine to do to increase the spirituality of the peopl whom he preaches and he should also see win as many souls to Christ as possible. this way the jubilee may be sounded ove the land.

The churches in our large cities should ganize for closer co-operation with our churc in Cincinnati to make this a great occasion.

B. F. CLAY

Kansas City, Mo., Nov. 17.

Concerning the Jubilee Convention, I ha suggestion to offer which may or may no found practical. It is about the attendanc the Endeavorers and others who can be th for only a short time. If the C. W. B. would give Saturday evening to the yo people (and C. W. B. M. work could be sented among other things to those prese let the Endeavor session be arranged for time. Then let excursions be seen f neighboring cities, such as Columbus, Lexi ton, Louisville, Indianapolis, etc., arrivin Cincinnati in time for the evening ses Saturday. Those who could not be th longer could thus be there on Sunday and c return on the early trains Monday in tim the week's business. Sunday will naturall the great day of the feast and as man possible should be there for the great c munion service, if they miss all else. S such plan will do much toward bringing attendance to the 10,000 mark. The detai such an idea can be worked out later.

JOHN E. POUND

Indianapolis, Ind.

1. More attention should be given to devotional feature. A great National vention ought to be an expression of that is best in our holy religion. Chan used to say that the House of Commons body had better taste than the man of the taste in it. So also a great assembly o Disciples of Christ should be more devout the most devout man in it. Such a conve would generate spiritual power as wel enthusiasm. The addresses should be ne so numerous nor so long. If there are two the same evening neither should oc more than thirty minutes. There should separate room—something like the cloak in the National Capitol—where delegates friends could meet and converse without turbing the convention. There should al some one—say a sergeant-at arms—to quietly about and assist the pres ding offic keeping order.

2. A speial effort should be made to hav the older generation of Disciples attend Jubilee Convention.

N. M. RAGLAN

Fayetteville, Ark.

THE
STIAN-EVANGELIST.

WEEKLY FAMILY AND RELIGIOUS JOURNAL.

December 1, 1898 No. 48.

S.

.............675
Vational Con-
........676
'...........676
for National
.............677
abored with
.. ..678
.... 678
... .679

xanderCamp-
.... 680

s..........685
....686
.............687
.............687
....688
.............688
ion of Sins..688
.............689
....689
'oreign Soci-
.............689

poem).......696
.............696
.............698
.............698
.............699

t...........682
... .683
... .684
.............691
....693
.............695
....700
.............701
.. ..702
'ourses 702
.............703
'ational Con-
.............704
.............704

$1.75.

J. W. McGARVEY,
PRESIDENT OF BIBLE COLLEGE, KENTUCKY UNIVERSITY.

PUBLISHED BY
ISTIAN PUBLISHING COMPANY

THE

CHRISTIAN - EVANGELIST

J. H. GARRISON, EDITOR.

W. W. HOPKINS, ASSISTANT.

B. B. TYLER, J. J. HALEY,

EDITORIAL CONTRIBUTORS.

What We Plead For.

The Christian-Evangelist pleads for:

The Christianity of the New Testament, taught by Christ and his Apostles, versus the theology of the creeds taught by fallible men—the world's great need.

The divine confession of faith on which Christ built his church, versus human confessions of faith on which men have split the church.

The unity of Christ's disciples, for which he so fervently prayed, versus the divisions in Christ's body, which his apostles strongly condemned.

The abandonment of sectarian names and practices, based on human authority, for the common family name and the common faith, based on divine authority, versus the abandonment of scriptural names and usages for partisan ends.

The hearty co-operation of Christians in efforts of world-wide beneficence and evangelization, versus petty jealousies and strifes in the struggle for denominational pre-eminence.

The fidelity to truth which secures the approval of God, versus conformity to custom to gain the favor of men.

The protection of the home and the destruction of the saloon, versus the protection of the saloon and the destruction of the home.

For the right against the wrong;
For the weak against the strong;
For the poor who've waited long
  For the brighter age to be.
For the truth, 'gainst superstition,
For the faith, against tradition,
For the hope, whose glad fruition
  Our waiting eyes shall see.

RATES OF SUBSCRIPTION.

Single subscriptions, new or old .... $1.50 each
Ministers ...... 1.00 "

All subscriptions payable in advance. Label shows the month up to the first day of which your subscription is paid. If an earlier date than the present is shown, you are in arrears. No paper discontinued without express orders to that effect. Arrears should be paid when discontinuance is ordered.

In ordering a change of post office, please give the OLD as well as the NEW address.

Do not send local check, but use Post office or Express Money Order, or draft on St. Louis, Chicago or New York, in remitting.

ADDRESS, CHRISTIAN PUBLISHING CO., 1522 Locust St., St. Louis, Mo.

THE CHRISTIAN-EVANGELIST

"In faith, Unity; in opinion and methods, Liberty; in all things, Charity."

Vol. xxxv. St. Louis, Mo., Thursday, December 1, 1898. No. 48

CURRENT EVENTS.

The commission appointed by the President to formulate and recommend a system of government for the Hawaiian Islands as a part of the United States, has returned from its tour of investigation in the islands. The details of the bill which it will present to Congress have not yet been announced, or even completely formulated. A meeting of the commission was held in Washington a few days ago to consider some of the items. It is understood that the commission will recommend a slightly modified form of the territorial government, including a governor and a legislature, but with certain necessary limitations to the right of suffrage.

In view of the approach of the date for the final evacuation of Cuba by the Spanish forces, preparations are being rapidly made for placing in the island a sufficient body of American troops to guarantee the preservation of order. One regiment has already sailed from Savannah for Neuvitas, Cuba, and others will soon be on the way. The time for the completion of Spanish arrangements for a permanent departure was extended, some weeks ago, from December 1 to January 1. Realizing that this is their last chance to grab anything in Cuba, the Spanish authorities are busily getting their hands on everything that is not red-hot or screwed down. Even the stone walls can scarcely be safely left out over night, now that the monument to Columbus which stood in Havana has been torn up by the roots and shipped back to Spain.

If the tide of gold importation is either an indication or a cause of commercial prosperity, the business men of America have at present no cause for complaint. The report of the Treasury Bureau of Statistics, shows that the amount of gold brought into the country during the first ten months of this year is more than twice that for the corresponding period in any preceding year in our history. Not only so, but there is also a vast preponderance of importation over exportation of gold. During the last sixty years the balance has been regularly the other way, with one or two exceptions. 1896 was the first year within the decade when there has been an excess of importations, and this year the excesses for the first ten months is raised from 37 to 129 millions. The ebb and current of the flow of gold are dependent upon causes which are hidden from us; but whatever those subtle influences are to which this sensitive current is subject, evidently those who control the matter perceive in the present situation satisfactory reasons for bringing gold into the country. We have but lately emerged from a condition of war and naturally our military leaders are the heroes of the hour, but there is no other commander by land or sea whose popularity can compare with that of Gen. Prosperity.

The international congress for the consideration of means for the suppression of anarchy held its first session at the Corsini Palace in Rome, Nov. 24. The program of the congress, as outlined by the Italian Minister of Justice, includes the following points: (1) To define a "criminal anarchist." (2) To classify anarchistic outbreaks as either political offenses or crimes against common law. (3) To consider special measures for restraining the press from encouraging anarchy. (4) To arrange for the summary extradition of fugitive anarchists. (5) To organize an international police service, or to make such modifications in the existing police systems as shall enable them to keep up international relations. Underlying all these particular topics is the fundamental question whether the mere profession of anarchistic sentiments is to be considered deserving of punishment, or whether it is necessary to wait until there shall have been some actual and overt violation of statute or common law. If anarchy is merely a political creed, then none of the nations of modern Europe would assert a right to suppress it, but would be forced to confine their repressive measures to the punishment of the individual crimes of which its adherents might be proved guilty. But if anarchy is a "cult of crime," an association with no other object than murder and outrage, then it can be suppressed without depending solely upon the conviction of individuals for specific criminal acts. In the latter case it would be regarded as criminal conspiracy and as such would be liable to punishment even in those cases where there was no opportunity for it to work itself out in actual crime. An interesting and pertinent parallel to this view is found in the attitude which the British Government took toward a religious sect in India known as the Thugs, the distinguishing feature of whose cult was indiscriminate assassination as a means of propitiating the goddess Vishnu. The government acted upon the hypothesis that such a cult as this was not religious, but criminal. Its devotees were, therefore, punished severely, without stopping to ascertain whether each individual had been guilty of actual murder. Similarly, is anarchy a political creed, or a criminal conspiracy?

The annual report of the Secretary of the Navy, which has just been made public, will be an important document for future historians of the Spanish-American war. There is nothing new in the Secretary's review of the naval operations during the war, but his statement has the advantage of being a final and authoritative summary. Still more important are the recommendations which the report contains. These indicate the lessons which the department has learned from its experience in this war. The most important of these recommendations are as follows: (1) That, in view of the inefficiency of the transport service during the late war, the transportation of troops by sea be hereafter under the control of the navy as it is in other countries. (2) That Congress shall devise and adopt some method of rewarding meritorious service in the navy other than the method now in use. By the present system, the reward of one officer may be and frequently is made at the expense of others who have rendered equally meritorious though less conspicuous service. (3) That the grades of Admiral and Vice-Admiral be revived temporarily, to be filled by such officers as the President shall nominate, with the advice and consent of the Senate. (4) That Congress authorize an increase of the enlisted force whenever necessary to 20,000 men and 2,500 apprentices. (5) That all smokeless power be used by the navy. (6) That Congress authorize the construction of three battleships of 13,500 tons, three armored cruisers of 12,000 tons, three protected cruisers of 6,000 tons, and six cruisers of 2,500 tons, the total estimated cost, exclusive of armor and armament, being $36,100,800.

The situation in the mining community at Pana, Ill., has become little, if any, less serious than was that at Virden. The operators at Pana succeeded in importing negro miners to take the places of the strikers before any steps could be taken to hinder them. The outcome of the affair at Virden encouraged the members of the union at Pana to make resistance again, and during the last ten days there has been a stormy time in that town. Martial law has been declared by Gov. Tanner, militia sent to Pana, and an attempt is being made to disarm both parties. Gov. Tanner has issued a statement explaining and defending his course of action in regard to the disturbances at Pana and Virden. In one case he did not attempt to prevent the importation of negro miners; in the other he did. The distinction between the two cases is that at Virden armed guards were brought with the negroes because it was known that the miners would resist. The employment of armed guards was, in Gov. Tanner's view, criminal, and made the whole proceeding criminal. He admits that the mere act of importing laborers, as at Pana, is not illegal. If so, it was his duty as governor to protect the company in the exercise of this right. If he had done so, there would have been no occasion for the employment of armed guards. He was asked to send troops to preserve the peace, but refused on the ground that the operators merely wanted to have the aid of the state in accomplishing their own designs, viz., the landing of the negro miners within the stockade. If, as he admits, they had a legal right to do this, it would appear that they had a right to expect the governor to preserve the peace so that they could do it without interference. Taking it all together, the conviction is forced upon us that the more Gov. Tanner says in defense of his course, the less defensible does that course appear.

Spain's Peace Commissioners at Paris, acting under instructions from Madrid, have yielded to the American demands, and cede the Philippine Archipelago, including Sulus and Visayas, to the United States, the latter agreeing to pay $20,000,000 in consideration of moneys expended by Spain for the improvement of these islands. It is reported that Spain agrees to sign the treaty, embodying this cession of territory, under protest. The secretaries of the two commissions have been instructed to put these agreements into treaty form, and this document is to be presented at a joint meeting of the commission during the present week. Except the formality of signing this treaty, which is also to embody an agreement concerning religious freedom in the Caroline Islands and certain commercial relations with Spain, this may be said to close the diplomatic part of our contest with Spain. The result is not pleasing to the statesmen, politicians and crowned heads of Continental Europe. They do not like to see this great Western Republic gaining a foothold in the East and becoming a factor, and, as they believe, a disturbing factor, in what is called the "Eastern question." While the Spanish press complains at the hard conditions exacted by the United States, there is no doubt but that it is the best possible solution of the problem, even from the Spanish point of view. The Daily Chronicle, of London, expresses the exact situation when it says: "So far as the decision to annex the Philippines goes, the United States, after some hesitation, has chosen the narrow path of duty, which always attracts the brave mind." This, we take it, expresses the true attitude of the United States to the whole question of annexation.

George Gould, it is said, has given $10,000 for the erection of a Y. M. C. A. Building at Texarkana, Ark. The T. P. and I. M. Railroads have given the lot and the building will be erected at once. All railroad men are to share the benefits of this refuge under the Y. M. C. A. management.

Owing to the hatred of the natives of the Philippine Islands toward the Roman Catholic Church Archbishop Kain is said to favor the annexing of those islands to the United States. He is, however, opposed to this movement on other grounds.

The Second Presbyterian Church of this city is almost ready to let the contract for its new $100,000 building, as $97,000 is already in hand and the remainder will be raised shortly. The building will be completed before the fall of 1899.

OPEN PARLIAMENT ON OUR NATIONAL CONVENTION.

We give this week another installment of our Open Parliament on our National Conventions, more particularly on our forthcoming Jubilee Convention. There will probably be more to follow. Several very good and practical suggestions have been received, which should, and no doubt will, receive the attention of the makers of the program for our next convention. It might be well to summarize some of the more important suggestions which have been made in this symposium.

1. The greater simplification and unification of our missionary methods and organizations, which has been suggested, is worthy of consideration. This is in the interest of economy in time and of distribution of interest in all departments of mission work. There has already been some progress made in that direction, and this tendency should be continued as far as it is found practicable. We have always believed, since both the home and foreign missionary work have been fully accepted by the brotherhood as alike necessary and important, that our entire missionary work could be carried forward under one organization, with the necessary number of boards.

2. The importance of having a larger number of business men in our conventions, and participating in their proceedings, will be universally recognized. It is a question of how best to secure this result. One way doubtless is to give them more work to do in the convention. The ministers also can do much to help bring about this result by urging the matter upon the business men of their respective congregations.

3. It seems to us that the suggestion for devoting one-half day to conferences on various interests is a wise one, as it would not only give these interests a hearing for such as are specially interested in them, but it would secure a full attendance for the other features of the program. This suggestion, in different forms, has been made by several brethren.

4. It will be noticed by our readers that there are two suggestions that seem to conflict. A number of the brethren urge the importance of more time for thorough deliberation and discussion of important matters, while others suggest that less time be spent on routine matters and more time allotted for short inspirational addresses. But, after all, there is no real conflict between these two suggestions. It is apparent that we *do* need more time for the discussion of such matters as are of importance, and concerning which the convention needs information to enable it to act intelligently. There are a great many other matters which are necessarily routine in their character, and may be disposed of very briefly. If committee reports are made in such a way as to facilitate action, there can be such a distribution of time as will permit a more thorough discussion of the matters needing discussion. And then *more* addresses can be secured by having *shorter* addresses, and we believe this change would meet with general approval. A wise chairman can do much to direct the convention in the proper course by having the program in mind, and hastening where haste can be safely made, and calling for discussion when discussion seems to be needed.

5. The suggestion that there should be a committee on credentials, to examine more carefully into the question as to who are entitled to vote than has been the custom heretofore, is eminently wise, if our convention is to be a deliberative body. This need not interfere with the presence of large numbers who are not delegates or entitled to a vote, but it will limit the voting of those who are entitled to this privilege, and will emphasize it as a privilege, and tend to increase the number of those who are authorized to vote. That these delegates should sit together in a body, toward the front as far as practicable, is also desirable.

6. No more important suggestion has been made, in our judgment, than that more time and attention should be given to the devotional feature of our conventions. If it be necessary to meet an hour earlier to secure this time, and devote the hour sometimes given to Bible lectures to purely devotional service, with such spiritual instruction intermingling as would feed the fires of devotion, many earnest souls could no doubt be gathered even at so early an hour as that. We cannot too much emphasize the truth stated by one of our writers in this Open Parliament that "in expecting and attempting great things we must depend upon the closest and fullest communion possible with the great, gracious and wonder-working God of missions." This is a most essential condition of the success of our Jubilee and all other National Conventions, as it is, indeed, of all work for God. Let this be a year of unusual prayerfulness and Bible-reading and consecration to God, and to the great work he has committed to us, and we shall undoubtedly have a convention of unusual power and of most gratifying results.

A DIVINE MISSION—WHAT?

IV.—CATHOLICITY.

The manifest necessity for a closer and more scriptural union among Christian people naturally led the fathers of this Reformation to consider the problem of how this union could be brought about. Their task was twofold: they had not only to convince the religious world of the evils of a divided Church and the necessity of union and co-operation, but also to point out a practicable remedy for the evils of division, or in other words, a scriptural basis of unity. The latter has proved to be the more difficult task.

It was clear enough, in the light of history, that these denominational divisions had their origin in an undue emphasis upon speculative beliefs about which good people differ, making these differences of opinion tests of fellowship; that is to say, the divisions arose, not so much about what was clearly revealed or clearly taught in the sacred Scriptures as on inferential reasoning and deductions. It was seen, too, that these differences did not, in most cases, relate to matters of vital importance, but were about matters concerning which people may differ and still be Christians. It was equally clear that if these divisions originated in an excessive emphasis of doctrinal opinions that were not vital, the remedy would likely be a change of emphasis, dropping into the background all unauthorized tests of fellowship, and bringing up into clear light the great fundamentals of Christian faith and duty.

viewing
ought of
the pro-
rity with
stles en-
that the
upon its
ions, not
or while
dence of
that they
of Christ
unques-
ity in all
w, there-
New Tes-
as a con-
y.
original
wer clear
hrist and
on of Je-
e Son of
further
faith in
e answer
urrender
and the
after his
with the
s is very
s well as
er to the
ne body,
ing, one
God and
through

licity in
e "unity
is either
the only
lent that
hristians
of Chris-
r been so
of Chris-
an creed
desirable
it would
, curtail
religious
en is al-
of relig-
of man-
nitations
them in
followers
us.
at there
formers,
plea for
the au-
urge the

Church was the very names worn by the followers of Christ. They were designated as disciples of Christ, as Christians, as brethren,.as saints, and their local congregations as churches simply, or Churches of God, or Churches of Christ. A tendency to follow human leadership and take on party names early manifested itself in the Corinthian church, but it was promptly and severely rebuked by the apostle Paul, who reminded them that such divisions come of the flesh, and that there is only one foundation, other than which no man can lay, even Jesus Christ. Who can doubt that the same apostle, animated by the same spirit, writing to the Churches to-day, would rebuke our party names, our party spirit, our party divisions and our party creeds? It was felt by the leaders in this Reformation that if they were to plead for unity among the followers of Christ they must place themselves upon a basis as broad and catholic as the New Testament itself, and that they must give up, not only their human creeds, which they had formerly acknowledged, but their party names also, and be willing to be designated as the original followers of Christ were designated in order that their name might furnish no obstacle in the way of unity.

Of course, this generous and magnanimous course in surrendering their denominational names in order to put themselves in a fraternal attitude toward all other Christians has been either ignorantly or purposely misconstrued as a claim for the exclusive right to the name Christian or Disciple of Christ. But this was to be expected. All who care to know the truth by this time, however, understand that there is nothing exclusive in the acceptance of these names, but that on the contrary, our hope and our prayer is that the time may soon come when all who revere the name of Christ will be content to wear his name, to be known as his disciples and to have his will as their only law of life.

The acceptance of the two ordinances, baptism and the Lord's Supper, in their original form and place was held to be necessary in order to a full restoration of New Testament catholicity. There was no controversy about these ordinances in their original form; the discussions have arisen about changes which have been made in them. But if we are to have union it must be on a basis which all acknowledge to be scriptural. This course, especially as regards baptism, has been a stumblingblock in the way of many who have otherwise been charmed by the manifest conformity to scriptural teaching of our position and plea for unity. We cannot enter into the discussion of it here and now further than

committed to us we do not see how
modify our course further than to
feel charitable and fraternal to t
differ from us, while we seek to b
our purpose in restoring the cath
the New Testament Church, in ord
restoration of its unity.

MORAL GROWTH A REASON
NATIONAL GRATITUDE

There are many, no doubt, wh
in the Amorite ascendency in this
and that the nation is on the do
morally. Perils there are, backs
have been, and evils exist in thr
forces, but God is not a failure,
devil is not a success, and Isr
possess the land. No person who
out of the United States during
thirty-five years can form any
conception of the tremendous dem
tion that followed in the wake of
Civil War. The whole tone and c
of our civilization was lowered by
ricidal strife, the spirit of lawlessn
reckless disregard of the value and
of human life filled the country with
and bloodshed, and to-day we ar
within fifty years of the end of th
consequences of that gigantic
and the national crime that precip
Lawlessness, worldliness and other
ruptured moral relations could no
out of the churches any more th
could be kept out of the families t
pose the nation. Evil forces gen
pandemonium let loose thirty ye
have got the start of us and their
tive momentum will be hard to
it may be said for the general en
ment, so far as both church and
concerned, that signs of reac
beginning to appear.

Some people think that democ
Christianity are doomed and that t
try is going to the dimnition boww
the facts do not report on their si
question. The fallacy of the whc
mistic argument lies in the sho
the periods that lie between its
comparison. Compare long perio
want to see how much the world
proved. Compare, if you please,
of the eighteenth with the clos
nineteenth century in the Unite
and behold the difference. Paine'
Reason was finally given to the
the year 1795. It was the most
book of the time. James Lane
his "Choir Invisible" represents a
the volumes of this work as sel
hot cakes on the streets of Lexing
a hundred years ago. When
Dwight took the presidency of

decency. There is less skepticism in the country than was ever known before.

In the beginning of the present century intemperance was common, the tippling habit was universal, and prohibition sentiment had never been heard of. Lyman Beecher says in his autobiography that the sideboard of a preacher, in his day, with its decanters, pitchers of water, tumblers, sugarbowl, nutmeg and spoons looked and smelled like the bar of a grogshop. In describing an ordination service he adds: "None of the Consociation were drunk; but that there was not, at times, a considerable amount of exhileretion, I cannot affirm." The traveling preacher carried it in one end of his saddlebags to balance the New Testament in the other end, and the potent, grave and reverent seniors of the official board of the church kept a barrel in the cellar. We are so far away from that time in Christian manners and morals that a preacher is scarcely allowed to smoke, and he has not the ghost of a chance for a decent pulpit if he is even suspected of unsoundness on the absolute prohibition of the liquor traffic. Less than a hundred years ago slavery was spreading its sable wings over half the continent and the church, both North and South, was silent on "the sum of all villainies." At the beginning of the century there wasn't a Protestant missionary society in the world, and the church was opposed to the evangelization of the heathen lands. There were no missionary organizations, home or foreign; and when first the attempt was made to organize a missionary society the preachers of that day protested against it as an irreverent attempt to interfere with the decrees of the Almighty. To-day the missionary organizations of Christendom are numbered by hundreds and their converts in heathen lands by millions, and no church is orthodox that neglects the first part of the Great Commission. One hundred years after Pentecost there was one Christian to every 150 of the world's population; to-day there are two to every five. It is a fact for congratulation and thankfulness that the religion of Jesus Christ is growing more rapidly in the United States than in any other country. The last census shows that the leading denominations increased their communicants in the last decade at the rate of 42 per cent., while the growth of the population was less than 25 per cent. It is claimed that 33 per cent. of our population are communicants of churches and that most of the other 67 per cent. are in some way connected or associated with the churches. It is estimated that the religious population of the United States embraces all but about five millions of its inhabitants.

And, thanks to modern investigation and criticism, which have taught us more about Jesus Christ and the Bible than we ever knew before, and to the great Endeavor movement and the increased missionary enthusiasm of the churches, the Christian world has begun to manifest symptoms of advance in spiritual power. The progress of interdenominational comity and courtesy and unity is even more remarkable than the advance in numerical expansion. Polemic religion is played out. Controversial Christianity is a back number except in the backwoods. Ascerbity and bitterness of the sectarian spirit is giving way to the sweetness and light of the gospel of the cross. We are learning to displace the metaphysics of the creeds with the ethics of the Sermon on the Mount. Fighting stress is now laid, not on the difference between tweedledum and tweedledee, but on the difference between a life of sin and a life of righteousness. We are learning the lesson that Christianity is a law, a life, a spirit and not shallow theories about trifles. Christianity is more Christian than it used to be, and for this reason the rising sun and the flowing tide are with us. Our convictions are deeper, our ideals are higher, our spirit is better, our faith is stronger, the united kingdom of God is at hand. I may be reminded that we have plenty of faults and sins and that gigantic evils threaten the future of our nation. Oh yes, but I am talking about the mercies that God Almighty has bestowed on this country, and I must remind you that evils and mercies do not belong to the same category.

J. J. H.

"THOSE WOMEN WHICH LABORED WITH ME."

Paul recognized the unity of the Lord's work. Those who had helped in his work were to be helped in theirs, for both he and they were workers together with the great Master of them all.

There has been too little of this spirit of reciprocity among the Disciples of Christ. One of the most serious hindrances to our missionary work has been a lack of unity in the means of administration. We have kept with almost scrupulous care to the lines dividing "foreign work," "home work" and "state work," and have distinguished almost as closely between the "Brethren's Boards" and the "Woman's Board," as if the sexes had different gospels.

One of the most encouraging latter-day signs is the tendency toward unification. The American Society is uniting the various State Boards in a closer co-operation than they have ever known before. Our secretaries have come to an understanding with regard to the times for special offerings, and for the presentation of their respective departments of work. This adjustment was much needed, and promises great good. Our churches need to be instructed concerning all of the enterprises of the brotherhood. They need to become familiar with the names of our missionaries, and to learn something concerning their work. Not only is the world the field of the church as a whole; the world should be the field of each local church and of every disciple of Christ. The work is one, and should be recognized as such.

The first Sunday in December will be observed as C. W. B. M. Day. Heretofore our women have usually held two public meetings in the course of the year—one on C. W. B. M. Day, in July, and one on Educational Day, in December. But the calendar has its limitations, and the Sundays of the year do not multiply with the multiplication of our missionary interests. It has been thought best, therefore, to celebrate but one day henceforth, and to present all the various departments of the work upon this occasion.

This is the silver anniversary year of the Christian Woman's Board of Missions. At our great Jubilee Convention at Cincinnati the sisters will celebrate the completion of twenty-five years of history. They are actively engaged in the effort to r
ninety thousand dollars as their offe
for the anniversary year. The inspira
for this offering, and for a large incr
in membership, should come through
public services of C. W. B. M. Day.

It seems reasonable to ask for the
operation of preachers and church offi
and workers everywhere, in order that
C. W. B. M. may have the forward imp
of a day thus fittingly observed.
women are contributors to all of the ge
al work of the church. They have sel
withheld their offerings from any c
board in order to give to the enterp
managed exclusively by their own.
large extent they have been sharers i
of the benevolences of the church.

Moreover, the work they are doing c
mends itself to our people. Their met
have been tested. About seventy th
and dollars were raised by them last y
This amount represents the contribut
of about forty thousand women.
means the enlistment of about forty th
and women as missionary givers, whi
a better result than an income twic
large from one-half the number of
tributors.

The calls from the field are insist
The work in India, in Jamaica an
Mexico, as it grows year by year, dem
a broader policy and increased sup
The needs of the home field are great,
it is especially desired that many v
points and weak states here in the h
land may this year be given the sl
temporary aid which will prepare the
support themselves and aid others.
unique work undertaken in connection
some of our State Universities this y
demands particular attention. In Virgi
the generous gift of $10,000 from the C
heirs makes almost imperative the duty
raising an additional sum from ot
sources within the state. The work
gathering together a modest endowm
for the work at Ann Arbor has b
undertaken, and should be carried to co
pletion within the present missionary y
The gift of $1,000 from Mrs. A. M. Atk
son to the English Bible Chair Endowm
Fund will, no doubt, cause others
make similar gifts.

Shall we not give encouragement to
work and the workers, and help th
women who have labored with us in
gospel of God's dear Son?

Hour of Prayer.

SOUL-WINNERS.

(Mid-week Prayer-meeting topic, Dec. 7th, 189

The fruit of the righteous is a tree of lif
And he that is wise winneth souls.
—*Prov.* 11:3

This is one of those sayings in which
crystallized the wisdom and experience o
nation which had been under the tuitio
God for many centuries. The two line
sentences quoted above have a very cl
connection, as will appear, being re
two ways of stating the the same truth
truth which commends itself to the rig
thought, the highest wisdom and the m
fruitful experience of the present age.

"The fruit of the righteous is a tre
life." This tree of life is doubtless s
gested by the tree of life which grew
the midst of the garden" of Eden, of wh

s, and shines forth with its im-
uty. The Christian may be a
in a fuller and higher degree
possible for any one to be, liv-
the time of Christ. The wise
he righteous man of to-day is
who accepts Christ and who is
s Spirit. The fruit of such an
ed, a "tree of life" to the hungry
ing ones of earth. It is also
ry such person that he "win-
" He may not preach, he may
ach in the Sunday-school, but if
ited from on high and be filled
irit of loving service and tender
the influence of his life and
will be such that men will be
to the religion which he pro-
to the Master which he serves.
responsibility that rests upon
stians, because of the influence
xert by our very characters,
inning men to Christ or in be-
umblingblocks in the way of
May the realization of this
ity lead each of us to a
honest examination of our
otives, as well as of our out-
ict, to the end that we may be
fe and not trees of death; that
n men to the service of God and
acles to keep them away from
e.

PRAYER.

who art the God of Abraham,
ac, and of Jacob, and who art
d and Father of our Lord Jesus
thank Thee that thou hast so
d endowed us that we may share
ure, that we may be filled with
and life, and so be agents of Thy
inistering life to the perishing
We thank Thee for the influence
hat may go out from our lives
ou dost dwell in us and Thy in-
go out through us to win others
rice. Make us to realize more
that Thou art speaking to the
igh the lives and characters of
profess Thy name, and may we
at the message which we deliver
what we are and by what we do,
by what we say, shall be such as
uls from the love and service of
ove and service of God, through
Lord. Amen!

or's Easy Chair.

achievement which would scarcely be credible now. Let us get ready for it.

A correspondent sends us the following lines from Lowell as expressing the same sentiment as that in those which stand at the head of our second page in our declaration of principles:

"They are slaves who fear to speak
For the fallen and the weak;
They are slaves who will not choose
Hatred, scoffing and abuse,
Rather than in silence shrink
From the truth they needs must think;
They are slaves who dare not be
In the right with two or three."

Our correspondent asks if we cannot say "amen" to these lines also. Indeed we can! There is not a fibre in our being that does not respond to the noble sentiment of these lines. We must regard him as a poor type of a Christian who does not indorse them, for Christ is the highest and noblest manifestation of the principle expressed in them. What this world needs, yea, what the church itself needs, is more of the moral heroism of Jesus of Nazareth, the Christ of God.

In the report of a sermon by J. M. Rudy, at Cedar Rapids, Ia., on "How Shall We Help Young Men?" as given in a local paper, occurs the following statement, which seems to us to cut down to the very core of the problem:

"Be the cause what it may, the average young man does not look upon 'being a man' as one and the same thing as 'being a Christian man.' The Christian is thought to be the abnormal, while the non-Christian is thought to be the normal man. The young man has come to feel that to be a man of real liberty and independence, he must not be found making a religious profession."

This is no doubt the feeling and the thought of the irreligious young men of our time. They have not been made to see that being a *man*, in the full and true meaning of the word, and being a *Christian* man is the same thing. In other words, they have never apprehended the true manliness of Christ and of Christianity. They have the pernicious idea, as false as it is pernicious, that it is manly to be non-Christian, to be skeptical, to reject the claims of God upon them and the demands of the moral law! We need a kind of

better to be going home than to be going in the opposite direction, in which there was plenty of room in the vacant cars. It occurred to us that the principle was capable of a broader application. Suppose our lot in life is a hard one, involving burdens to be borne, opposition to be overcome, poverty to be endured; at any rate the Christian may say: "I am going home!" He can often see how, by disregarding honor and truth and moral obligation, he might have an easier time, as it seems to him; but then that course would take him in the opposite direction from where he wishes to ultimately land. So, if he be wise, he decides that it is better to endure the pangs of poverty, and even persecution in behalf of the right, since that course leads homeward, where await him a welcome, rest and peace. One who had special opportunities for knowing both the afflictions of the present life and the joys of the life eternal, weighing the whole matter, said: "For I reckon that the sufferings of this present time are not worthy to be compared with the glory which shall be revealed to us-ward."

ARCHBISHOP PURCELL ON ALEXANDER CAMPBELL AND HIS WORK.

An Interview with the Catholic Prelate.

It is now some thirteen or fourteen years since I visited the city of Cincinnati in the pursuit of my calling. During a lengthened residence there, I had occasion one day to call upon John B. Purcell, the Archbishop of the Roman Catholic Church and by far the greatest man of which that church could boast in all America: a church which for many centuries towered above all other human institutions and still flourishes in undiminished grandeur in every portion of the globe. So old is it and so powerful that one is almost tempted to believe that it had indeed been planted by the hand of the Almighty and watered by the blood of its saints and martyrs.

I was then engaged in an occupation of little consequence and no emolument, but well suited to the mediocrity of my talents and my aspirations—an occupation that led me to call upon many of the highly literary and accomplished classes of men throughout the country. I had always been accustomed to the society of the best and most cultivated men, and felt that I might justly hold up my head in any assemblage into which I might be thrown. But as I approached this extraordinary man and mounted the steps of the palace, a strange and unaccountable feeling of timidity overcame me and led me to feel nervous and anxious about the kind of reception that would be accorded me by one who had reached so lofty a position in his grand old church and who had filled this position with unusual grace and dignity and honor.

Little did I dream of the kindness and courtesy with which I was to be met when ushered into the presence of this worthy prelate and begged to make myself welcome and entirely at home. Thus was I brought face to face with one of the most remarkable characters of the age—one high in position and powerful in intellect, and yet with manners as plain and simple and unaffected as those of the dear old man whom Sterne's magic pencil has graven on every heart and given a lodgement in every bosom. I entered the presence of this man a perfect stranger, without any letters of introduction, without any description of credentials whatever, dressed in the ordinary costume of a business man, or, to speak more properly, in a garb that reminded one of a combination of the gentleman, the trader and the backwoodsman. What reception was to be accorded to a person who entered a grand residence under all these circumstances and with all these drawbacks attaching to him? Ah! well I knew that here would come the test of the true gentleman.

In an instant I knew my man. I had taken the gauge and dimensions of his long head and of his big and manly heart. Upon the transaction of the business that had led me to make the call, we entered into a general conversation.

Observing a fine marble bust in his parlor, I asked whom it represented and if it had been executed in Italy. I then turned the conversation towards Greece and the Fine Arts and the age of Pericles. Here I was vastly more at home than His Grace, for this had been the talent of my family for generations and my own particular love and passion. Pretty soon we dropped down to the Pontificate of Leo the Xth, who was such a glorious patron of learning and the fine arts in the early days of Martin Luther and the Reformation. He seemed to gain new life and new energy when I commented largely on the munificent manner in which the Popes had befriended such men as Raphael and Michael Angelo, and had filled all the great galleries of Europe with the finest statuary and the most glorious paintings.

After the conversation had run on in this manner for sometime, the idea occurred to me to talk to His Grace about Mr. Campbell. So I boldly broached the subject and said: "Bishop, I am aware that you were once engaged in a debate with the greatest reformer of the nineteenth century, and one of the greatest men of any age."

"Oh!" said he, "you allude to Mr. Campbell, of course."

I said, "Yes, he is the man."

"Now," I went on, "I have, Bishop, many friends in Mr. Campbell's church who are persons of sterling worth and noble character, who would like very much to hear your opinion of that gentleman, of his work and his place in the history of the Christian Church and amongst the intellectual giants of the Protestant Reformation."

"Certainly," he responded, "I will glady talk with you about my worthy friend, Mr. Campbell. From the very first day of our acquaintance to the day of his death, I always entertained the kindliest feelings toward that gentleman. Oh! he was a most lovable character, indeed, and treated me in every way and on all occasions like a brother." Here the good man's eyes sparkled as he added:

"Was he not my brother in the Lord? Was he not like me a follower of the meek and lowly Jesus? Did he not believe in the resurrection of the dead and of the life beyond the grave where we shall all meet to part no more? Did he not kneel before the same cross in spirit and regard with reverence the Mother of Jesus and that poor woman who bathed his feet with her tears and wiped them with the hairs of her head, and of those other sweet and piou[s] women who followed the great Master i[n] his journeyings over the classic hills o[f] Judea and knelt beside his body whe[n] taken down from the cross and placed i[n] his narrow tomb?"

"It is true, we differed in some matters for instance, on church government, pray[-] ers for the departed, confessions of sin t[o] the priest, the celibacy of the clergy—wha[t] of that? These were all minor matters. In the essentials of Christianity we entirely agreed.

"In Mr. Campbell's church the form o[f] worship is very simple, as in the days of the apostles. He hoped always to keep it so. Here is where he was mistaken. It cannot be kept so. As the church becomes great in numbers, and rich and strong, it will lose its original simplicity. This is inevitable. We begin to see the change already in some of the richer congregations in the cities. Are not the advanced congregations already discarding congregational singing, and procuring fine organs and hired choirs? Are they not placing soft and luxurious cushions in their seats, and placing flowers in the pulpits and in the altars? Has not fine stained glass found its way into the lofty windows of their truly Gothic cathedrals? Surely, all these things have taken place, and very shortly they'll have representations of the apostles and the saints in these same windows, and fine frescoed ceilings, with scenes from sacred Scriptures represented thereon, as we have in the Sistine Chapel at Rome.

"I do not think that the Christian Church will introduce into their worship our incense-throwing, or our scarlet robes, or many other things that are peculiar to the Church of Rome. We have been many centuries in introducing all these forms into our worship. The church of Mr. Campbell is not one hundred years old. It is yet in its infancy, and a very lively brat it is, too! What forms it will adopt in its manner of worship in the future, what changes it will inaugurate in the next five hundred years, no one can tell. As I before intimated, the magnificent ritual of the Church of Rome has been the creation of ages and ages, until now it is as perfect, as imposing, and as impressive as it can possibly be made.

"Now, in the Jewish Church the same struggle is going on between the Reform Jews and the Orthodox. One represents the time of Moses and Joshua, the other modern civilization, science and progress. There is an irreconcilable conflict between these two wings of Judaism. Which will dominate? Of course, the more advanced. It is a case of the survival of the fittest and the wisest. So in the Christian Church. One section is opposed to choirs, fine music, splendid churches. The other just the reverse. One I call the backwoods church, the other the church of progress and of high moral and æsthetic culture. Now, I contend that the church is drifting, drifting away from the apostolic simplicity of which its founder dreamed, and has joined in the race which all Protestant churches are making toward something grander and more majestic.

"Do not imagine that I am saying that the church is losing any of its distinctive features—any of its fundamental doctrines. It has merely added something to them to make them more elegant and more attractive."

Said I, "Bishop, what do you think of the debate between Campbell and Rice?"

"Oh, as to that," said he, "I have never read the debate. It was very lengthy, you might say tedious. It ran through seventeen consecutive days, and each party claimed the victory, of course. One of the grand features of the debate was the presence of Henry Clay as a moderator. We Catholics felt no interest in the points at issue between these gentlemen. Take baptism, for instance, a subject on which both churches were very much exercised. We Romanists believe in the great, essential, absolute importance of the holy rite of baptism. In our church it is a sacrament like marriage. Beyond this we don't go one step. We care nothing about the style of baptism or the manner of administering it. We sprinkle, we pour, we immerse. We do precisely what the person to be baptized insists on. We generally sprinkle because it is most convenient.

"Pending the long debate between these two really great men my prayers were daily lifted up for Mr. Campbell. In his discussions with our clergy he had always been kind, affable, courteous; Rice quite the reverse. One was a gentleman; as to the other, what shall I say of him?"

"Bishop, how about your debate with Campbell?"

"Well, that only lasted a few days. Everything was conducted in decency and order, as St. Paul would say. Campbell was decidedly the very fairest man in debate I ever saw, as fair as you can possibly conceive. He never fought for victory, like Dr. Johnson. He seemed to be always fighting for the truth, or what he believed to be the truth. In this he differed from the other men. He never misrepresented his case nor that of his opponent; never tried to hide a weak point; never quibbled. He would have made a very poor lawyer, in the ordinary understanding of the term lawyer. Like his great friend, Henry Clay, he excelled in the clear statement of the case at issue. No dodging with him. He came right out fairly and squarely. He was what used to be called, in good old times, 'flat-footed.' Rather than force a victory by underhand or ignoble means, he preferred to encounter defeat. But whenever he fell, he fell like the Cavalier Bayard, with honor and a clear conscience.

"In our debate not a particle of ill-feeling or bitterness was mixed up. After the discussions were over we would meet and be just as friendly as if we both belonged to one and the same church. Oh, how I should like to have met this dear son of God socially and in private life, after age had whitened our locks and mellowed our tempers and dispositions!"

I said, "Bishop, what think you of his work?"

"Well," he said, "we Catholics do not think much of a church until it has existed fully a century. It must have passed its hundredth annual milestone. Hardly has this church seen its seventy-fifth birthday. But it is a lusty youth, and has certainly distanced all its rivals in the race for popular favor. Not even the Methodists, with their efficient itineracy and their sensational methods of worship, can hold their own with the Christian Church in the fierce struggle for proselytes and for supremacy. I see no signs of weakness, of decay, of decrepitude in this organization. Quite the contrary. It appears to be gathering new hope and courage and strength with each successive decade. Should this progress continue for the next quarter of a century, who will say what gigantic proportions it will assume? It has already passed away beyond the wildest dreams and hopes and expectations of its founder.

"Now as for Mr. Campbell's standing in future ages, I think it is quite within the bounds of truth to say that not ecclesiastical history alone, but profane history, will place him on the same pedestal with Luther and Calvin and Wesley, the peer of either of them. Had he lived in the early ages of Christendom and accomplished the wonderful amount of good with which he is justly credited he would after death have been sanctified and canonized and 'enrolled in the capitol' along with St. Chrysostom and St. Jerome as a father in the church, his name forever embalmed in its annals as a worthy successor of St. Peter and St. Paul. But alas! he missed these high honors by being born too late in the history of the world and in a prosaic age when money and power are more valued than piety and goodness and greatness."

"Bishop, what do you think of Calvin and his treatment of Servetus?"

"Oh! that was horrid—most horrid indeed. To allow his friends and tools in Switzerland to burn this man at the stake—this brother Reformer who had stood up so boldly against the mighty powers of Rome in defence of Protestants and Protestantism. Campbell could not possibly have done such a thing. It was not in his nature. No, not a single drop of cruel blood coursed through his veins.

"Still, no one can deny John Calvin's wonderful powers, his great supremacy as thinker, writer, reformer and metaphysician. A few of his works I have read with great pleasure and profit. He was the first of that long line of bold, learned divines who have immortalized the name of Presbyterianism and made it synonymous with talent and refinement. Numbers of these men have cut a large figure in the history of the world and distinguished themselves by their bold and resolute championship of human rights and of religious liberty.

"I believe Mr. Campbell got his fine education amongst the Presbyterians. He could not possibly have been trained in a better school for the great work that he had marked out for himself in early life. You know that his father, Thomas Campbell, was a Scotchman, and a very great Scotchman at that, and I believe that Alexander himself was born in that wonderful land and inherited the bold and rugged and resolute character that has always characterized the people of that charming country.*

"In early life he was a Baptist. But he was too bold and original a thinker to be hampered by Baptist rules and creeds and modes of thought. He was not born to travel in a beaten path. Nature never created him to follow any man. He was designed for a leader. He must blaze his own way through the forests of ecclesiastical traditions and heresies and contradictions, and right boldly and fearlessly and perseveringly he did, and, *Io triumphe*.

*Alexander Campbell was born in Ireland, though of Scotch descent.—EDITOR.

See the result—the creation of the 'Christian Church.' "

I said, "Bishop, do you not think it strange that Mr. Campbell's followers should be offended when called 'Campbellites'?"

At this he laughed very heartily and continued: "This was the very weakest and most foolish thing his people ever committed. Ashamed to be called 'Campbellites!' Fretted at being associated with the name of their noble founder! Strange! strange indeed! Do not the Germans call themselves Lutherans? Do not the accomplished Presbyterians glory in the name of Calvinist? Do not the Methodists shout at the name of their founder and sing themselves hoarse in loud hosannahs to the lasting glory of John Wesley? I do not know how others feel, but as for me, if I were a member of this persuasion, I should do myself the honor of calling myself a 'Campbellite,' and I should be proud of the name."

"Bishop, how did Mr. Campbell get such a start and succeed in founding so large, so respectable and so influential a church?"

"Oh! that is very easily accounted for. He was a born polemic—a theological debater or gladiator. He was, besides, very highly educated and thoroughly equipped for his work, well grounded in the general principles of theology. The Bible he knew by heart, and from a very diligent study and application of his powers had made himself thoroughly acquainted with the doctrines of all the leading churches of the country. Then he knew his power. He was fully conscious of his herculean strength. Hence he was always ready and anxious for a debate. It was his habit occasionally to pass through the southern portions of Ohio and Indiana and Illinois and through the fine bluegrass region of Kentucky and the rich farming sections of Missouri on both sides of the Missouri River where the farmers are and always have been exceedingly intelligent and rich and hospitable. Perhaps there is not a finer set of people on the face of the globe. These interesting pilgrimages began somewhere about 1824 or perhaps a little before that era and lasted perhaps for a quarter of a century with some intervals. His discourses attracted vast crowds of people who came from distant points and who listened to every word that fell from his lips and felt in their heart of hearts all the burning zeal of the devoted followers of Peter the Hermit. At that time the religious propensities of the people were very strong and there were few churches in the country and no places of amusement. People would ride fifty miles on horseback to attend a large baptizing, a camp meeting or a religious debate. Mr. Campbell was regarded as a kind of religious Goliath, and was met at every crossroads and at every toll-gate by well-intentioned, half-informed preachers of the different denominations and challenged to produce his credentials, to enter into a discussion in defence of his original and peculiar views. Our hero was nothing loth to do so. Such opportunities were precisely what he desired. A vast audience would gather together to hear what to them was vastly more attractive than a great battle to the death between two celebrated gladiators.

"These debates were brief and decisive. Campbell floored his opponents in a few moments. Their arguments fell to pieces as if they had no more strength than a potter's vessel. So quickly was this all accomplished that they could hardly realize their discomfiture. The people saw all this and it made Campbell thousands of proselytes; and their children and their children's children have to this day stuck to this church like grim death, and there they'll stick for generations to come. For certainly the members of the Christian Church are the most zealous and stubborn in their Prostestantism of all classes of Protestants.

"In thinking of the persistent and multifarious attacks upon Mr. Campbell by his puny adversaries, I was always strikingly reminded of the lines of the great dramatist in the play of Julius Cæsar:

'Why, man, he doth bestride
The world like a Colossus,
And we petty men
Creep between his huge legs
And peep about
To find ourselves dishonorable graves.'

"Again," said the Bishop, "of all the men that Campbell encountered in his long career Rice was by many odds the best equipped. In this discussion Campbell seemed to have forgotten the wise saying of Solomon: 'Oh, that mine enemy would write a book!' He had written and published largely. Rice had debated often and published almost nothing. Of course he had made a diligent study of all that the great Reformer had ever published and had all of his multifarious writings at his fingers' ends. Here was Rice's advantage. In traveling along the great high road of investigation Campbell had occasionally changed his views, as all wise men must do, and will do. To make his adversary contradict himself—to show where at one epoch he repudiated what he had advocated at another—this was Rice's strongest point.

"As I said before I have never read this remarkable debate."

Before bidding adieu to this venerable prelate, twelve or fifteen young men came into the parlor to pay their respects to this venerable father in Israel and to receive his blessing. They had (I presume) just finished their theological courses and were preparing to leave for the positions to which they had been assigned. Each of them kneeled before the good man and he placed his hands on their heads and muttered a low prayer as he did so; finally dismissing them all with a *Dominus vobis cum* as they filed out. The scene was very picturesque and affecting.

Then turning to me he begged pardon for the interruption and for his weakness (for tears glistened in his eyes) and with a kind look he bade me farewell. I. C.

Stop Stop! Stop!

When I made the announcement concerning preachers and their place of residence for the official list, I forgot two things: 1st. What a good advertising medium the CHRISTIAN-EVANGELIST is; 2nd. How wide its circulation. I meant simply *Missouri* preachers. But I am getting them from all over the land. I don't want anything outside of Missouri. But still there are ever so many Missouri preachers, some very close by, who are depending on the fact that I know them, yet my memory is very treacherous. If you are left out *don't blame the secretary*. Yours in his name,

T. A. ABBOTT.

4144 *Westminster Place, St. Louis, Mo.*

Current Religious Thought

Such teaching as the following, from the New York Observer, will go a long way toward relieving so many minds of that false notion which they have about the dryness, or fearlessness, or uselessness of prayer:

The purpose in prayer is not just to win something for ourselves, but to worship God for himself. Prayer may be communion, companionship, converse; the breathing of a sigh; the upward glancing of an eye; as it were the presence of an unseen hand in the darkness. There are prayers that do not need to be prayed, and that would spoil by being prayed, just as there are songs without words, and there may be love without a token. Such an intimacy of a worshipful divine communion was that enjoyed by the godly Bengel, whose devotions one night before retiring, after long study of God's Word, consisted simyly in his laying his head upon his folded arms and murmuring: "O Lord, thou knowest me. We are on the same old terms."

In all such prayer of a generally worshipful nature there is purpose, though it may not be the particular purpose of a definite petition. Yet, while the devout spirit may make of every place an oratory, may find each changing scene of life to be a Bethel, or House of God, there occurs many occasions in life when very special and urgent petitions must be offered, for the gift of some blessing or for escape from some calamity. Prayer in such a case cannot be too pointed or pressing. Such a petition was that of the dying Jacob, when he besought the Lord for Joseph's sons saying: "Bless the lads!" such an urgency that of Peter when sinking in the waters of Galilee he cried: "Lord save me!" Prayers of this purposeful, pressing nature when offered in faith never go unnoticed or unrewarded. Does God answer prayer? Of course he does. Why not? Turn the tables on your sceptic. Make him prove the impossibility of faith. If God could not answer prayer he would not be God, but the mere slave of his own creation. And if he would not answer prayer he could not be good, since then a hundred explicit promises of his would have to be unsaid, and more than one solemn covenant require to be broken. A God who can make a thousand worlds, or systems of worlds, can certainly answer a few stray prayers, that here and there thread their unwearied way in and out among the kindly stars until they reach his mighty yet merciful throne.

Dr. Gunsaulus, of Chicago, who last summer was near death's door, but now at his post again, is showing a marked tendency toward freedom from religious creeds and denominational restraints in the announcement of certain views of which he says: "With a great cost have I obtained this freedom. I reached these conclusions when I found myself nearest the celestial city, and in sight, as I believed, of the judgment bar of Christ. They bear the very atmosphere of those moments when, after months of enforced calm, I thought myself looking back on the end of my ministry in this world. I cannot forsake them; they are dearer to me than position or life." One of these views he has expressed in an article in a recent number of the Advance, as follows:

I am convinced that the first necessity for my laboring effectively at Plymouth Church, indeed the absolute requirement made by my heart and conscience, is the simplifying and strengthening of the articles of faith upon which the church sets up her banner and invites men and women to unite with her in the common task and hope of making this a better world. I would make our statement less theological and more religious. I would insist upon the orthodoxy which Christ had in mind when he said: "Not every one that sayeth, Lord, Lord, shall enter into the kingdom of heaven; but he that doeth the will of my Father which is in heaven." Entrance to the church ought to be simply saying: "By thy help, I will," in answer to the command of Jesus: "Follow me." A true sorrow that one has been wrong, an honest turning from wrong to right, desire to be like the Master, trust in him as one who has the right to guide and rule our lives, willingness to take his Spirit and put it into all our life and labor; these are the fundamental and ethical ideals I would emphasize; and I would substitute these for theological staten which, however true they may be, cern themselves with matters as yet unco ered by many truly Christian men and wo and may not be decisive at the springs of duct which Christ saw are, the fountain life.

The Observer, St. Louis, gets at merits of the question as to the origin basis of the religious dispositions of in the following paragraph from one of editorials:

There are indubitable evidences that faith of the primitive race was in one Supr Being. That faith has degenerated and its pristine force, but the belief in the su natural has, in all ages of the world, among all the races of the world, been a m force, and has stood for righteousness, e among savages. Men have lost sight of religion, but they have never been able divorce themselves entirely from God God's demands upon them. Even the Gr religion, with all its corruptions and imp ties, was on the side of moral order and m law. No religion has been wholly devoi moral power. However imperfect the religi beliefs of the ancients, the people held to sc kind of obligation to their gods. They rec nized their dependence on the deities rendered them service for their aid and p tection. The religion of our Lord is in acc with the deepest, most abiding and in structible convictions of the race. It could have been born of accident, nor of a m superstitious fancy. The soul of man did create its own immortal longings and aspi tions. The faith of man is correlated to Infinite, the Eternal and the Perfect. Sur the highest and purest and noblest sentime of the heart of man do net rest on a falsehoo The universe demands and explanation, a God is the only possible explanation of t universe. The human mind cannot rest co tent with the unreal and the false. God essential to man's needs, and it was he w implanted in the soul the religious instinct. it be true that man created his own God, it also true that he worships his own creatio Such is the persistence of the religious sen ment that it will not be satisfied without so object of worship. False religions give u mistakable evidence of the urgent demand the soul for the supernatural.

The Interior makes the visit of Emper William to Jerusalem the occasion fo bringing to light a trend of things in h empire that is fraught with great issues. says:

While the Emperor William is on his starrin tour to Palestine the social democrats at hom are working with intense energy with the pro agation of their doctrines and the extension their organization. Their ultimate success sure. It is a new Protestant Reformation wi added incentives. It is working from the bas of principles already ingrained in the people Protestantism—the Fatherhood of God, th brotherhood of man, and mutual responsibility Very many of the social democrats, repelled the union of the church with the monarchy, a unbelievers; but a notable change is appearin and its full accomplishment is inevitable. T socialists see the tremendous power they w by allying themselves with Christ as the leader, and have already abandoned Karl Ma and other rationalistic pioneers. The effect this is not only the very rapid extension of the principles, but the modification of those pri ciples to bring them into accord with the divi Teacher. In other words social democracy h reacted to conservatism, to the Christian r ligion in its well-guarded socialism. This what is rolling up its constantly and rapid increasing political ballot. What will th monarchy do? Not a very long time can elap before the monarch must choose. He has thr causes open—to submit, demit or fight. If h choose the latter Germany will become th theatre of a violence the end of which no ma can foresee.

New Study of the Revelation.

In order to encourage the new study of th Apocalypse of Patmos in ministerial circles will make a special inducement to Christia preachers if they will write to me that they a members of a pastor's association and would lik to encourage the reading of a paper and th discussion of the subject by their association.

Address J.S. HUGHES.

Station O, Chicago.

Our Budget.

—We are glad to hear the Michigan Evangelist say that its subscription list now almost supports the paper. The M. E. is now but one year old, but it has proven acceptable to the brethren of Michigan as a state organ, and they are thus showing their appreciation.

—The Hiram House Settlement has begun the publication of a bimonthly paper of twelve pages in the interest of its work. The name of this journal is the Hiram House Life. It is to be the exponent of the inner life of the Settlement.

—At Portland, First Church, in the third missionary district of Oregon, including about one-third of its population, a very profitable convention was held Nov. 8-10, and steps were taken to put an evangelist in the field all the time if funds can be secured.

—We learn from the Pacific Christian that the drouth in California is becoming a serious matter to its people and that the Roman Catholic and Episcopalian clergy have been called upon by their bishops to offer up prayers to God for rain. The P. C. asks also, "Why not all who profess to be Christians pray for rain" at such a time?

—Would it not be a good idea for the Bible-school superintendents and preachers to tell the children about the "Advance Society" organized and managed for their benefit by J. Breckenridge Ellis, of Plattsburg, Mo., of which he writes every week in our Family Circle Department. We feel sure that the children will be delighted with his plan for amusing and instructing them. At one church the preacher mentioned the matter and 14 children promised to join the society at once.

—The Board of Church Extension has just mailed its last annual report. The receipts this year are the best in the history of this important work, and the publication of the same in the annual report occupies over twenty pages. Illinois comes first in the amount contributed, having sent in $3,949.11; Ohio stands second with $2,996.47; Kentucky is third with $2,634; Indiana is fourth and Pennsylvania is fifth. In all departments there is shown a healthy increase. The list of life directors and life members show that the leading people among us are putting money into this fund. Besides the annual report, there is some very interesting information in regard to the work, embodied in such articles as "A Definition of the Fund," "Strengthen Thy Stakes," "Early on the Ground" and "The Plan and Management of the Fund." This report will be sent to any one who applies for it to G. W. Muckley, Cor. Sec., 600 Waterworks Building, Kansas City, Mo.

—Against the frequently made statement from Protestant sources to the effect that the state of civilization in any given country west of Asia declines in proportion to the dominance of the Roman Catholic Church therein, the Catholic News points to the condition of a large class of people in London who, it says, "are blessed with Anglo-Saxon civilization." This is evidently a shrewd way of meeting the argument aforesaid, but it only shows the more plainly how keenly the charge is felt and how difficult to meet. These same conditions not only obtain in large cities under Roman Catholic rule, but throughout the countries in which they are located. The basis of this argument should not rest upon the section of a city, but upon the intellectual and moral condition of the entire people of the nation in which that city is located.

—There must have been a strong regard in the Chattanooga Convention for the fitness of things when it fixed the third Lord's day in December for an offering for the Ministerial Relief Fund. How Christlike it is to contribute to the immediate relief of dependent ones at such a time! And how easy it will be to give under the influence of the giving spirit so characteristic of Christmas times.

—We have learned that F. H. Thompson was found frozen to death in the streets of Omaha, Neb., during the recent storm, but have no further particulars about his distressing death. He was at one time an agent for the Christian Publishing Co.

—We publish this week a very interesting and remarkable interview with Archbishop Purcell from the pen of one who had the privilege of a long and pleasant conversation with him. Our readers will no doubt be surprised to know the sentiments of the Archbishop in his later years toward Mr. Campbell, his whilom antagonist. It is a little strange that one who seems to have had such a keen insight into Mr. Campbell's character and motives should have been unable to understand the reasons which prompt his brethren and co-laborers in refusing to wear his name. Mr. Campbell's whole aim religiously as relates to the world was to bring men away from the dominion of creeds and party leaders and under the authority and leadership of Jesus Christ. It would, therefore, be very inconsistent, to call it by no harsher term, for them to accept the name of Mr. Campbell or of any other human leader. Our readers will, nevertheless, enjoy this remarkable interview and will thank us no doubt for having secured it for the CHRISTIAN-EVANGELIST.

—During the latter part of last summer we announced in these columns that a Congress of Disciples had been arranged for to meet in St. Louis sometime next spring. The committee having the matter in charge has about completed the program, which will be published soon. The time fixed for the meeting of the Congress is Tuesday, the 25th day of April next. The program embraces some of the leading questions of the time and a number of the ablest men in our ranks. Keep this matter in mind and arrange to attend.

—A brother from Indiana warns the churches against a "Ben Hurr" entertainment that is being imposed upon some of the churches of that state. He says it is immoral in its tendency and demoralizing to the young people who engage in it, besides proving generally a financial failure to the church. We knew nothing of this particular entertainment, but church officers can not be too cautious in looking into the character of these peripatetic shows, which propose to give an entertainment and divide proceeds with the church. All such devices for raising money are doubtful even when decent, but when their moral influence is bad no countenance whatever should be given to them.

—The brief message from A. M. Atkinson, calling the attention of the readers of the CHRISTIAN-EVANGELIST to the appointment by our last convention of the Lord's day before Christmas as the day for a general offering to the Ministerial Relief Fund will, we trust, attract the attention of all our preachers especially, and will lead them to make such preparation as is fitting and right, that the churches may acquit themselves honorably in reference to this beneficent work. Both the time and the object of the offering are such as to open the hearts of all to the demands of this tender ministry of love to our aged and needy veterans. Read what Bro. Atkinson says, for he says it as no one else can say it, and let his tender message find a response in all our hearts on the day mentioned.

—The Christian Oracle came out last week a renewed paper within and without. It is in new form, sixteen pages, and cover of unique design for the Thanksgiving number. New names appear at the head of its business and editorial departments—names that stand for business and for success. The editorial staff and promised correspondence are especially strong. The Oracle is evidently contemplating an era of growth and prosperity in its history.

—The Interior seems to be concerned about the inroad which Christian Science is making upon the churches, especially, as it says, upon Presbyterian and Baptist Churches. The remedy for this depleting malady, the Interior thinks, lies in better pastoral care for the flock. So far so good, we think, but this is not all. The people are conscious of a constant sense of bondage, captivity, oppression, burdens, etc., and are ready always to utilize every promise of deliverance, of liberty, of release, of rest. Jesus recognized these conditions and preached deliverance to the people, and since that time they have expected this assistance from the churches, which stand as his ambassadors. If the churches fail them in these ministrations they will seek relief elsewhere. Many of their troubles result from society and governments as now constituted, and true relief cannot come until these conditions are changed. A more earnest and sincere effort on the part of churches which stand for Christianity to better society and governments, and remove the real cause of their distress, is therefore needed as well as better pastoral care. Let the churches preach and practice real deliverance, and their pews will be crowded with hearers and seekers.

—Few things on this earth are better fitted to "stir a fever in the blood of age," even, and call out all the chivalrous sentiments of our nature, than the spectacle of a brave warrior standing in the face of a whole army of the foe, turning back the red tide of battle, bearing in his bosom the poisoned arrows of the enemy, when suddenly there advances from the reserve corps of the defensive enemy a stalwart son of Mars, with the sun's rays flashing from his shield, helmet and battle-axe, who takes his place beside his brother warrior, saying, "Thou shalt not fight alone, noble Ajax; I will stand by you, and we two shall scatter the armies of the alien and bring deliverance to those who are trembling before the advance of the invading host." Such a spectacle as that is visible just now in our current history to those who have eyes to see and hearts to appreciate the heroic and the sublime.

—One is sometimes surprised at the blunders of great scholars in their references to the Scriptures. The editor of the Expository Times says, "St. Paul's expression, 'the baptism of the Holy Ghost.'" This from the greatest critical paper in the English-speaking world! In the first place, there is no such expression in the Bible as "the baptism of the Holy Ghost." Neither Paul nor any other biblical writer uses it; and still worse, the idea it expresses is not in the Bible. In the second place, the phrase "baptize with the Holy Spirit," or more correctly speaking, "baptize in the Holy Spirit," is used in the Gospels and the Acts by John and Jesus, but is not employed by Paul. He uses the phrase "filled with the Spirit," but this is neither the expression nor the idea of the "baptism of the Holy Ghost."

—The following reasons for an interest in missions appeared in the Watchword and are worthy of careful study as they indicate the lines along which it is most profitable to work in our efforts to increase the interest of churches in missionary work:

In an open parliament on "How to Kindle and Keep Ablaze the Missionary Fire," conducted by J. Edgar Knipp, at the Miami Y. P. C. U. Convention, the question was asked, "What awakened in you an interest in missions?" Here are some of the answers in brief:

"Love for souls."
"Studying the subject of missions."
"The great Student Volunteer movement."
"The command of Jesus Christ."
"The study of God's Word."
"One of the first principles taught me by my mother."
"Giving to missions."
"Corresponding with a missionary in India."
"Personal acquaintance with missionaries."
"Contrast in the condition of heathen and Christian peoples."
"Reading the life of John G. Paton."
"The self-sacrificing spirit of Christ."

—After an absence of near two months the "Gospel Plea," published at Edwards, Miss., in the interest of Negro Education and Evangelization, has resumed its weekly visits. The break in its history was occasioned by the yellow fever epidemic.

—Dr. Whitsitt is said to have been heartily received by the General Association of the Baptist Churches in Virginia in session at Richmond, recently, and his speech on the work of the Seminary, with the utmost favor. The tide of persecution against Dr. Whitsitt seems to be subsiding and he may yet outlive its influence. Crusades against heretics are not popular religious movements in these days.

—It is altogether proper that the picture on our first page should have a place in our gallery of brethren whose position and work have made them known to a much larger circle than they have been permitted to come in personal contact with. President J. W. McGarvey, of the Bible College of Kentucky University, is widely known as a teacher, preacher, author and contributor to current literature. His name is a household word among the Disciples, and his likeness will become a household picture in thousands of homes through this issue of the CHRISTIAN-EVANGELIST. He was born in Hopkinsville, Ky., March 1st, 1829, and hence is now in his 70th year, but still well preserved and capable of doing a great deal of work. He graduated at Bethany College in 1850, and afterwards spent some time in Missouri both preaching and teaching. He is the author of a number of works, including Commentaries on Matthew, Mark, Acts of Apostles, "Lands of the Bible," "Text and Canon," "Credibility and Inspiration of the Bible." He is at present conducting a departmet of biblical criticism in the Christian Standard, of Cincinnati. One may not always agree with his critical views, but he will always be able to understand what he writes, which is more than can be said of many critics.

—J. Z. Tyler writes that he failed to receive Dr. Willett's article on the Bethany C. E. Reading Course, from Berlin this week, and in his stead supplies an article from his own ever-ready and lucid pen. We are sure that our readers can do a good work by calling attention to these articles and also by availing themselves of the benefits of these reading courses. This is a literary age of the world and those who will not read may expect to find themselves in the rear of the procession soon. Then they will be wondering what's the matter with the world and its people. Better fall in line and read up the history and outlook of the Disciples of Christ in this remarkable age of the world.

Educational Conference.

This will be our last opportunity to call attention to the educational conference which meets at Moberly on Tuesday next, Dec. 6th, at 3 P. M. Let the preachers and business brethren in Missouri, who feel an interest in this subject, be present to give their counsel as to the best course to pursue. If only the schools are represented by a few of their friends, little good will come of it. The conference has no legislative authority. Its power will be wholly moral and advisory. It is not even an adjourned meeting of the Missouri Christian Convention. If, however, the brethren who really represent the churches of the state are present in sufficient numbers, the advisory influence of the conference will be just as potent as that of the state convention. A thousand delegates from a single neighborhood, if they were all permitted to vote, could accomplish nothing. It is not a matter of votes except as those votes represent churches that will back up their votes with donations. Let the schools present to the conference some practical plan for self-help, and ask the co-operation of the brotherhood of the state.

Uniform Series of Prayer-meeting Topics.

The Uniform Series of Prayer-meeting Topics, arranged by the joint committee of seven, appointed by the Chattanooga Convention, has been carefully prepared, and is now in the printer's hand. The topics represent all our missionary interests and go into effect January first. No church can use them without improving its prayer-meeting, and there is no reason to doubt that they will come into immediate favor. There is something inspiring in the thought of a uniform topic for all our prayer-meetings throughout the land.

GEORGE DARSIE,
Chairman Committee.

The recent expressions of interest in the Hour of Prayer Department of the CHRISTIAN-EVANGELIST has been very gratifying, and many churches, we are glad to learn, have been using these topics, particularly during the past year. Now that a uniform series has been arranged, it may reasonably be hoped that our churches generally will adopt these topics, and that the prayer-meeting may assume a new interest and importance. There is something inspiring, as Bro. Darsie suggests, in the whole brotherhood using the same topics, studying the same Scriptures and directing their prayers to the same great objects. These topics will be found flexible enough to be adapted to special local needs, where such exist. There is no reason why the prayer-meeting should not be as much benefited by this uniform series of topics as the Sunday-school has been by the use of the international series of lessons. The topics arranged by the committee appointed by the national convention at Chattanooga come into use with the beginning of the New Year.

PERSONAL MENTION.

Granville Snell, of Trenton, Mo., preaches at Oskaloosa, Ia., Nov. 27th.

Sherman Hill preaches at Hampton, Ia., one Sunday in November.

I. N. McCash delivers an address, Nov. 28, at Creston, Ia., before a Ministerial Institute.

Prof. Hill M. Bell, of Drake, spent his Thanksgiving vacation in Chicago.

H. N. Dale, of Sioux City, Ia., spent a few days in Des Moines recently.

F. F. Grim, late of Iowa, now of Hamilton, Montana, has had 38 added under his ministry, the larger part being baptisms. Bro. G. has out a good tract on our beginnings as a people.

A synopsis of the sermon on "Make Your Calling and Election Sure," preached Nov. 13, by A. Sanders, pastor of the church at Newcastle, Wy., appeared in the Weston County Leader, published in that city.

C. McIntire has been unanimously called to preach for the church at Garden City, Minn., for one year. He has been with that church one month and praises their faith and loyalty to Christ very highly.

The Pacific Christian says that T. D. Garvin expect to close their work in Honolulu soon and will go to Australia where an inviting gospel field is said to be awaiting them or return to California.

An elder of the church at Brazil, Ind., says that Perry T. Martin, who has been with that church for two years, has been retained by the church as its pastor for an indefinite period of time. All debts of the church are paid and $400 on hand toward a church building.

Wm. Remphrey Hunt, writing from New York, says that he will sail for England on the 26th inst. and that he is returning to his place in the foreign field with delightful memories of the Chattanooga Convention and of the churches of our great brotherhood.

J. S. Smith preached the Union Thanksgiving sermon in the M. E. Church at Algonac, Mich.

C. K. Marshall, of Lexington, Ky., says that any congregation wishing to employ a faithful, energetic pastor, interested in all of the enterprises of the brotherhood would do well to write to R. H. Lampton, 248 E. 3rd St., Lexington, Ky. He is a graduate of the Bible College of that city.

Scott Cisco, clerk of the church at Wayneville, Ill., writes that the greatest meeting ever held in that community has just closed at Rock Creek Christian Church with 117 additions. R. Leland Brown, of Rockville, Ind., did the preaching.

Emma Bird, daughter of Mrs. Emily I Campbell, of New Cumberland, W. Va., w married to Charles Morell Watson, Nov. 24th 1898.

Bruce Wolverton, who recently returned Portland, Ore., from this city, writes that h has been kept very busy since his return. H is holding a meeting with the church at Fore Grove, Ore., and raising funds to pay off i floating debt. The leading school of the Con gregational Church in the Northwest is locate at Forest Grove. Bro. Wolverton writes als that he is asked to take the work of evangelis in the third district of Oregon, which is said t include about one-third of its population.

S. J. Phillips, of Sugar Grove, Wis., receiving some very earnest inquiries con cerning Christian Library for Bible-schools an Christian Endeavor Societies, about which h writes in this paper.

J. G. M. Luttenberger, of Dorchester, Ill. paid his respects to this office last week. Thoug not elected representative from his district Illinois in the last election, he is by no mean cast down over it. He still has on his wa paint and proposes to continue the battle in th interest of the Prohibition party and of tem perance. More lectures and better organiza tion is his motto for future work.

A young professor who has been teaching i the college here for four years, and who ha at the same time been preaching, desires t devote all his time to the ministry, and woul like to hear from churches who desire a pastor Salary, $800.

J. O. JOHNSON.

Des Moines, Ia.

CHANGES.

Grayson Hughes, Spickard to Breckenridge Mo.
M. S. Spear, Middleton to Plymouth, N. C
G. W. Henry, Angola to Warsaw, Ind.
E. E. Pierce, Lorain to Columbus, O.
B. S. Denny, Hampton to Des Moines, Ia.
J. R. Spencer, Ft. Madison, Ia., to Cold brook, Ill.
L. W. Welch, Hannibal to Kansas City, Mo
G. R. Maxwell, Rockville, Md., to Richmond, Va.
A. A. Honeywell, Rootstown to Brunswick, O.
W. H. Coleman, Carlisle, Ia., to Roseville, Ill.
Geo. Fowler, Spartinsburg, S. C., to St Thomas, Ont.
John Guthrie, Topeka to Paola, Kan.
J. W. Walker, Ashley to Dorchester, Neb.

SUBSCRIBERS' WANTS.

FLOWERS FOR WINTER.

Asparagus Spre geru. } Postpaid 12 cents each.
Calla Lily little gem. } Set of 3 for 30 cents.
Weeping Lantana. } 4 sets $1.00.

Send silver instead of stamps and get a Xmas gift free
Address, Roney Bros., Florists.
WEST GROVE, PA.

"ALL Is Not Gold That Glitters."—This charming song, for further introduction, will be sen to any address upon the receipt of 15 cts. (one fourt its regular price), by the author—leader of the Mt Cabanne Orchestry, and cornetist for the Choir o First Christian Church. Enthusiastically endorsed by Profs. Charles Humphrey, C. E. Millard, J. M. Dungan and many others. Address J. A. Dungan, 72 N. Kingshighway, St. Louis, Mo.

WANTED.—After nine years of successful work i this field I desire to locate elsewhere by th first or middle of January. Unquestionable refer ences furnished. Only churches that desire to pus forward in every good work need apply. F. L. Moore Fredericktown, Mo.

f peoples. When a nation passes into oblivion : leaves a graveyard behind. Posterity gathrs the contents of these graveyards into muэums. The gateway to a cemetery or the door f a tomb is of vast importance. They are oncrete ideas. The doors of Paris tombs reeal the most remarkable development, not lone from the standpoint of the architect, but s well from the religious and social point of iew. Here is a door, an iron one, without an perture except the keyhole; it is absolutely xpressionless; it is rusty. It is not alone; it ıas companions. Here are others, very numrous, with apertures in many forms—now a lover leaf, now a cross, now a star or circle. ?hey admit air, but not light. Another perıaps has a frameless transom; you see the dark pening; you have a sensation of fear and susicion. You could look over that door, but you lon't. The blank iron, the darkness, concealng the mysterious and unknown, seem to say, ?ass on. You flee. Still another door repulses rou in the same way, while being entirely different. It consists of iron bars crossing at right angles. It is a grate, that is to say, it is he door of a prison. It has a lock and chain. Such a tomb is a county jail and excites the same sensations. No common metal produces nore sympathetic feeling than bronze. These cemeteries are rich in tombs with bronze doors, the panels of which are decorated with graceful palm branches or bas-reliefs of a nature to attract and retain the attention and please the eye. The pannels are often in glass, which may or may not be protected with a light trellis. Such a door transforms completely the impression you have of such a tomb. It becomes a house. It loses its prison-like aspect. It represents the architecture of the avenue penetrating the graveyard. Architectural harmony may suffer somewhat, for you see cathedrals with dwelling house doors. In some rare instances a door is provided with a clean white curtain behind the glass. Perhaps the curtain is drawn obliquely wide, as in many a cottage door. The transformation is complete. In such a door you read the theology of the housewife. Such a portal arouses in you the most pleasant emotions, yet you no more think of looking in than you did before those iron doors. Back yonder it was fear, dread; here it is respect for the living which restrains you. This tomb is certainly inhabited. it is not a tomb at all; you cannot think of it as such. It is a tiny home. There is a woman behind that curtain. Such are your conclusions. The illusion, which the writer has often experienced, is rendered complete if, at this moment, the door quietly opens from within and a real person appears in the doorway, a pot of flowers in her hand, a lace bonnet on her head. In fact, these tombs require a great deal of attention all the year round. They are little houses which need to be kept; they have their keepers. The rich send their servants, their "bonnes," though doubtless many a mother or the daughters of well-to-do families perform with their own hands this sacred task. It is especially in the month of October that you see a great activity in the cemet-ries. The tombs are all cleaned and decorated for the feast of All Souls, which the French call *Toussaint*.

The apparition of a woman in the door has something of the effect of a Spiritualistic seance in broad daylight. You wish for a medium to stand between you and the vision and allow you

Another period; you turn again. You wonder why you asked such a stupid question in a cemetery. You reach a climax by asking a more stupid one; you want to know who *lives* in that splendid two-story house, with four marble statues at the corners, or what church that is at the corner of the same street, or who is the pastor.

The vision looks a little surprised but replies pleasantly: Nobody lives there, and that is not a church. These are tombs. This is the cemetery of Father Lachaise.

The housekeeper, to continue the illusion, locks the door gently and goes away when she has finished her task. You say to yourself: she has gone over to visit one of her neighbors.

The windows are no less varied, no less interesting, no less significant in the evolution of the tomb. All the modern doors correspond to windows, round, square or oblong, in the opposite wall. They exist also in the side walls of many tombs. In instances all four walls have disappeared, the corners have become columns. The tomb is glass. A bronze trellis protects it. Needless to say that such a sepulchre is without shadows. Yet it has just a little the air of a show case. The interior saves it from this degradation. But for the most part even the side windows are rare. In two or three new tombs in the cemetery of Montmarte, the entire rear wall has become glass devoted to splendid representations in colors. Two are the tombs of noted physicians. The rule is the single window in the rear wall. They are often without any design, many display the cross. The majority represent some holy scene, or reveal the portraits of some saint. Mary and Joseph are favorites as in the churches. In every cemetery there is a certain group of tombs which never have any picture whatever. Their windows bear a word in Hebrew characters. This is not an infallible mark of a Jewish tomb. The writer recalls a certain tomb in Montparnasse which had Hebrew characters in the window and a bust of Jesus in bronze on a Christian altar. A certain New Hampshire family has a tomb in the cemetery of Father Lachaise, in which the emblem of the United States is to be seen in the window. It is with the most joyful sensations that you stand before this open tomb, for it has no front wall, so full of the expression of nationality. To find in the window of a tomb, in a foreign land, the American eagle, the American flag in colors and the motto of American unity—what a surprise, what a pleasure! This tomb is neither a dungeon, nor a church, nor a home; it breathes but one thought—the nation; it awakens but one sensation—love of country and gratitude. It contains a beautiful marble statue. It is the Whitcomb tomb. In a few cases all such designs and representations are missing. The portrait of some child or the head of the family takes their place. t is full of significance, such a digression from the custom prevailing in all the others. It marks the triumph of an idea, the conquest of the tomb by the home. Nationality and religious feeling give way to the idea of the fireside, of the family. The expression family tomb gains a fullness of meaning which one raises in the others. In most cases the prison-like vault has developed into a church with stained windows and holy pictures. In but rare instances has the idea of the home conquered the church-like tomb. Nothing but the front door. If the reader ever

diance. It is the face of a happy father. He wears a gray coat. He has the appearance of a man at home in the midst of his family. It is the face of one who returns at close of day from a day's labor that has left no shadow over the features. Not a care. There is an expression of satisfaction, and toward the stranger who presses his face against the glass door, of welcome. You are glad you looked in, you do not want to go away. The sinking sun illumines that tomb, it increases the radiance of that face. At the hour when you flee from others because they are full of shadows you linger gladly here where the sunshine lingers. Why didn't you stay by yonder tomb? The sunshine was there, too, but it fell through the sad face of a saint. That tomb was a church, perhaps you paused a moment in silent prayer; but here the tomb is a home. When the sun sets you seek the fireside with its joyful blaze and merry voices.

One can imagine the family council where it was determined to make this deviation from public opinion. A tomb is always the occasion of a family reunion. There were probably friends present, probably also the priest. It was probably against the advice of all these that the home gained the victory over the gloom of the vault and the twilight of the cathedral. Perhaps some son, looking up at the father's picture on the sitting-room wall, said suddenly and cheerfully: "Let's put father's portrait in the tomb, it will make it more home-like." Irresistible suggestion of filial love! "The tomb will preserve what is lost from the home," he continues, "when we gather to change the flowers, or renew the wreaths, or to pray, his face will welcome us." May it not have been the mother, for whom the word home had become a hollow sound—for the motto of mothers is, "What is home without a father"—who added in assenting to the proposal of the son: "Yes; and when we all lie side by side beneath father's portrait it will seem so much like the family asleep at home." For the priest there remained nothing to do but to give his benediction to the holy decision.

With the sunlight streaming through door and window you venture to examine the interior of these habitations of the dead. This is no sacrilege, for the owners have rendered them public by giving them light. The glass pannel is often open, even the door on All Saint's day. The modern tombs are really hospitable. There are hospitable tombs just as there are hospitable homes in spite of the contradiction of terms. In a word, the interior is generally that of a miniature chapel, contains almost invariably an altar, a crucifix, some candles, and a prayer-chair or two. The tomb of the Rothschilds has a carpet. The walls are sometimes very rich, even mosaic. Marble statues are frequent. They are all full of thought and sentiment, gloomy enough in the case of the prison-like vaults. Yet happily modern ideas are prevailing. They excite your interest, your admiration, your enthusiasm. They make sorrow beautiful. You forget that death is sad, you forget that there is an invisible corridor which conducts from every tomb to a desolate hearth, you forget that the tomb is the complement of the home, that they are the products of human sorrow just as homes are the products of human happiness. Happy hearts plan homes, only the sad plan tombs. Yet it is a pleasure to forget that for every cradle there is a coffin, for every home a tomb, for every fireside a heap of ashes, humam ashes.

WM. H. MATLOCK.

Paris, Nov. 2.

Virginia Letter.

After a month of silence I resume the Virginia Letter. Many of the readers of the CHRISTIAN-EVANGELIST have learned from the Editor-in-Chief that a number of us were indisposed at the Read House in Chattanooga. Shortly after returning from the National Convention I visited several of the churches in Virginia. Having to drive some distance through the country in a driving rain, the effect was anything but salutary. It was simply the "last straw" of a series of unfortunate circumstances which compelled me to give up all my work for a couple of weeks. Hence my silence in the CHRISTIAN-EVANGELIST. The "Sunny South" is not always sunny. Two years ago, while Mrs. Young and I were in Athens, Ga., it rained for nearly three weeks, with scarcely any intermission, and since coming to Virginia the first of October, the rainy days have certainly equaled the days of sunshine, and a cold November rain in the South is, if anything, more apt to endanger one's health than a snowstorm in the North.

⁂

Since coming to Virginia I have visited only four of our churches during the past month; two of these are ministered to in word and work by Bro. Richard Bagby, whose home is Louisa, Va. Leaving Charlottesville on the Southern I visited Orange, where I was entertained in the home of Bro. Thomas Bond. There Bro. Bagby joined me and we drove twelve miles through the country to the Macedonia Church. This is one of the "mother" churches of Virginia. The present commodious brick building, in which the congregation worships, was erected before the war. Notwithstanding the terrible ravages of that severe struggle, the old church was uninjured, although the fierce battles of the Wilderness were fought hard by. Here the Caves were reared and began their Christian life. I met many of the relatives of Bro. R. L. Cave who, as college president at Christian University in Missouri, and now at Kentucky University, as well as for many years pastor of our leading church in Nashville, has faithfully served his Master and advanced the cause of the great brotherhood in which he is an honored worker. I was glad to learn that those who love Bro. Robert Cave were clear-visioned enough to regret the step he had taken, thus separating himself from the great movement with which he was formerly identified. I was entertained at the home of Bro. Jackson, who is a great sufferer from a wound he received in the Confederate army. It is but natural that he should have a warm place in his heart for his comrade in arms, but he is a loyal as well as humble follower of the Divine Master. I have ceased to be surprised at the high average of intelligence I find in many of our country churches, but the Macedonia congregation is far above mediocrity and has given to our brotherhood many other noble workers besides those above mentioned. One of these has become so widely known through his long and successful pastorate at the Walnut Street Church in Louisville that his life and ministry alone places our brotherhood under obligations to the Macedonia church. It was here that E. L. Powell, one of the purest spirits as well as clearest thinkers among us, confessed his faith in the Divine Savior when a barefooted boy of only twelve or fourteen summers. When reading the Easy Chair comments on the influences which shape a boy's life, having recently visited Macedonia Church, the contrast between the little towhead, attending Sunday-school at the church in the midst of a grove of outbranching oaks, and the noble Christian man whom I heard during the National Christian Endeavor Convention in San Francisco, as he held the intensest interest of a vast audience with his simple yet sublime thoughts concerning the heart of Christianity according to Christ, stood out vividly before my mind. Sunday-school teachers in the midst of your discouragements concerning that class of boys in the far-away country church or in the crowded city, trust God and take courage. You may be molding a noble benefactor of the race. Remember, we are told that when the dear Lord came to the last sad scenes of his earthly life, he loved his disciples "unto the end;" that is, he loved them for what they were to be under the developing power of the Christ-spirit. I shall long remember with pleasure my visit to the old Macedonia Church. Bro. Bagby is much loved and respected by all the members as a faithful, God-fearing follower of his Master.

At Unionville, the next point I visited, I also found quite a vigorous congregation. The large number of young men which came to church on horseback, wearing their leggins as in the colonial days, was especially noticeable. The leggins are frequently made of good leather, although generally made of canvas. The men stand around in groups outside of the church, talking politics, farming, etc., while quietly whittling sticks, until the services begin. These groups break up one by one and by the time the opening songs are sung, the long prayer has been offered and the sermon is well under way, most of the men have ranged themselves on one side of the church, frequently not even husbands sitting with their wives. These people are a little slow, but they are far above the average congregation in thoughfulness and appreciation.

The last Sunday in October I visited the old Gilboa Church, indeed one of the oldest in Virginia, as the first building was erected in 1834. This was the boyhood home of Bro. W. K. Pendleton, who was for many years intimately associated with Alexander Campbell as editor of the Millennial Harbinger and who was afterward for years president of Bethany College. Here Dr. Phil Pendleton, his brother, still lives, his residence now nearly a hundred years old, and his store, formerly the nucleus of the little village where, in the grove near by, the Gilboa Church is situated. Here again I found distinct evidences of culture and refinement above the average. There was no dust on the pews, as we frequently find in city churches, the lamps were all trimmed and bright, and between the two doors, by which the congregation entered the building, hangs a large and beautiful picture, symbolic of the Rock of Ages. I was entertained in the home of Mrs. Sarah E. Hankins, whose cultured daughter, Miss Mary, is an exception to the majority of young ladies who neglect their music after leaving college.

We had a delightful C. W. B. M. meeting in this consecrated, Christian home. Mr. Albert Hankins who, while a traveling man, takes every opportunity possible to preach Christ by a noble life, made his mother a life member of the C. W. B. M. The Gilboa Church has been ministered unto by many of our best preachers. Dr. Phil Pendleton informed me that Uriah Higginson was their first preacher, about 1834. Since then James Bagby, R. L. Coleman, R. C. Cave R. L. Cave, F. D. Power, I. J. Spencer and L. A. Cutler, besides others I have not space to mention, have served that congregation.

Here I found the memory of Col. John B. Cary held sacred, and nearly seventy-five dollars will be contributed this year, besides a number of pledges for the future, to the University of Virginia Bible Lectureship, founded by Col. John B. Cary. In my next letter I shall make mention of the frequent visits of Alexander Campbell to this section of Virginia.

⁂

Mr. Campbell's visits to Virginia were frequently in the interest of Bethany College, and it is but fitting that I should close this letter with a few serious statements in regard to that time-honored institution. It is now so generally known that early in October I was requested by the Board of Trustees of Bethany College to become its president that I do not hesitate to mention this fact publicly. The condition of Bethany College is well known to the public. Like many other institutions, Bethany has suffered from the inroads which the public system of education have made upon all distinctively Christian institutions, but the situation at Bethany is not hopeless. Reader, ask yourself this question: Can it be possible that our great brotherhood, which has grown to be more than a million strong and soon to control the heart of America religiously, will permit its oldest institution of learning to die? It is not a question of sentiment; it is not solely because Bethany was founded by Alexander Campbell that our brotherhood should rally to its support. We cannot afford to let any of our Christian colleges go down. Bethany College is in no worse condition to-day than other institutions which are doing good work. If the reader is interested in the future welfare of Bethany, will you please express such interest in a few lines? Address me at University Station, Charlottesville, Va.

CHARLES A. YOUNG.

A Sad Argument.

Died of cancer at the Poor Farm, Oct. 18, 1898, Elder ——— ——. While young he had united with the Christian Church and shortly after his marriage was ordained a minister of the gospel by that church, and followed preaching and school teaching in Ohio for twenty years. He was then called from Ohio to West Virginia, in which state he lived for fifteen years and devoted his entire time to the ministry. On account of failing health of himself and wife he gave up the ministry and came to Missouri and when —— was laid out he bought several lots and built the Commercial Hotel and run it for sometime, but was compelled on account of poor health to give up his business and rent the hotel out. In a few years he became so badly involved in debt on account of not being able to do anything to keep up his expenses that he sold most all his property to pay his indebtedness.

The good people of —— have been helping them for sometime, but their health got so bad that neither of them could care for the other and they were brought to the Poor Farm, July 24, last.

A few days before his death he called Mr. ——, the superintendent of the farm, to his bedside and requested that his body be not buried in the county cemetery on the farm, but buried in —— cemetery. Mr. —— carried out his wishes and buried him as requested.

The above was taken from a local newspaper which by mere chance came into my possession a few days ago. The article refers to a brother whom I know has done good service for the Master's cause in years gone by, and I venture to make public mention of the above because of the extreme sadness of the case. I mention it because it is one of the many sad cases in which brethren who have spent the best days of their lives in the work of the Master, when worn out in body and mind, have been cast upon the cold charities of an unfriendly world. This case would be indeed very sad if it were the only one of that nature ever known to happen within our brotherhood, but it is still more sad when we remember that there are existing among us many more such cases as this one.

The good wife of this good brother is still living and is an inmate of the same poor farm where he died. Is this the appreciation we have of those who have "borne the burden in the heat of the day?" These men were defenders and exponents in the Reformation when it meant hardships and denials of which the younger generations of preachers know nothing. Preaching was then hard and severe labor, with but little, if an any remuneration. Let us remember that we have not grown to over a million people without the most severe self-denial on the part of some one, and the severest of these denials and hardships fell upon the preachers of this brother's age.

This case is a sad and yet a very convincing argument in favor of the work of the Ministerial Aid Fund. It is a sad comment upon the liberality of a rich and prosperous people like the Church of Christ if we leave the treasury of this fund so depleted that Bros. Atkinson and Lucas shall be compelled to leave a single appeal for help unrelieved. It is not only shameful, but it is actual robbery to take the best years of a man's life for any cause, without giving him remuneration sufficient to provide for his immediate wants and leave enough for "old age" and then refuse to hold up and support the brethren who are trying to keep these "worn-out" brethren and their wives from the poor house in their last days. There are no doubt brethren who have known for a long time of the sad condition of this brother and his wife, but they were powerless to relieve them. Each church has its demands upon it and but few are able financially to undertake to wholly provide for such a case as this, and so they must in the end see those unfortunates become objects of public charity.

When we give to the Ministerial Aid Fund the support it should receive all difficulties will be obviated and our poor ministers and those depending upon them will never become objects of public charities. Let us all respond liberally to this work. It is a duty we owe the cause as well as to those individuals who are made recipients of these blessings.

HORACE SIBERELL.

Pickering, Mo.

C. W. B. M.

Ninety thousand dollars for '99, increase of membership, enlargement of work. Such is the purpose of the Woman's Board this Jubilee Year, which is larger with possibilities and brighter with promise than any we have known. It is heavier with responsibility. Responsibility is a divine inheritance. By discharging its obligations we grow in strength, grace and usefulness.

In our National Convention a year ago we set our aim for \$90,000 in '99. This rallying cry has been slowly growing in volume during the year, and at our late Convention at Chattanooga it was in the air. It had taken shape as a possibility and was repeated from the platform and in conversation. We may confidently hope to reach that amount if we have enough workers in the field to present the matter to the auxiliaries and the churches. The generous gift of \$10,000 from the wife of the late beloved John B. Cary comes also as a gift from God. It is an assurance that we shall reach the goal *if we work intelligently, systematically and continuously.*

Not only was \$90,000 for '99 in the air, but the larger thought: 90,000 members and the enlargement of the work in all departments. To reach \$90,000 this year, \$21,814.13 must be raised in advance of the actual receipts of 1898, which were \$68,185.87. Already has \$10,000 of this sum been received, leaving only \$11,814.13 increase to be made. This is easily within the possibilities so far as means are concerned. Our beloved president on hearing the good report from Chattanooga remarked: "Why not \$100,000?" And, indeed, why not?

⁂

The conditions of the West appeal strongly for generous appropriations. The East is a fruitful and crying field. City evangelization is a problem the church must solve successfully for the sake of both city and country. A generous endowment is needed *now* for the English Bible Chairs. The force of the Mexican mission needs to be increased. Jamaica needs buildings *now*, and more missionaries would strengthen that work. Deoghur, India, is in immediate need of buildings and a medical missionary. Dr. Olivia Baldwin and Miss Agnes Lackey are now on ther way to Deoghur to take charge of the orphanage to be established there. The one hundred children are orphans through the famine and are given the mission by the government. Every station in India is in need of funds with which to meet the growing demands in that land of universal need and boundless opportunity. Surely, we have a place in the ranks of the nation's workers, whom God is leading to the conquest of the world for righteousness.

In what spirit shall we come to this service? Shall it be the spirit of love and loyalty to Christ, and love for the humanity that Christ loved. The great commission, *Go*, was to every one who wears the name of Christ. "If ye love me ye will keep my commandments." An article, "Tennessee C. W. B. M.," in the CHRISTIAN-EVANGELIST of Nov. 10th, breathes the right spirit: "Can we afford to sit idly by when there is such a glorious opportunity for us to work in our Master's vineyard, when there is such an imperative call to be up and doing?" "Riginald Heber, after a day of toil in India, said to a friend: 'Gladly would I exchange years of common life for one such day as this.'" It proved his last day on earth, but it was a day of toil with Christ for the salvation of men. May we not have this spirit to some fuller degree and some such days of toil to mark this gracious year?

⁂

What we need and how to secure it—that is the question. Money and members are what we should work for at this time, in order that we may reach the ultimate object of all true missionary effort. The \$90,000 can be secured and the membership largely increased if the missionary facts and sentiments are generally presented to the churches. We have two agencies for doing this, auxiliaries and organizers. Each auxiliary can do its own part, and will be furnished programs, suggestions and instruction in the Tidings. State officers who will stimulate the auxiliaries to extra effort are in a very responsible position. On them very much depends, and they can and will accomplish much. We need, however, more field workers. Efficient organiners to canvass every state, and especially those where "our people" are numerous, and who would present the claims of universal missions thoroughly and patiently, would greatly forward the desired end. The National Board, I feel assured, would place a number of such in needy places should sufficient funds come to the treasury. What state is worthy of aid from the National Board in this way? Is it not the state which does its utmost to cultivate its own field? Every state that is behind in its own work can best forward the purpose of this year by making up its deficiencies. Let every auxiliary pay state dues, make an offering to state work, and so help its state officers to place an organizer in the field, if it be only for a short time. Pray and work to this end and there will be no failure. The situation calls for strict faithfulnesss from the National Board and throughout the ranks to the most indifferent member, and not only faithfulness, but generosity of means, time and labor.

To think of the good that might be done with $90,000, the weak churches made self-sustaining, the burdened hearts made joyful, the lives turned from sin and darkness unto the life of Christian joy and light, the joy there would be on earth and in heaven, makes the heart throb with grateful anticipation.

Let us work with patient, prayerful, persistent enthusiasm, and may God lead the Christian Woman's Board of Missions to the realization of its hope—$90,000 for '99, increrse of membership and enlargement of work for the Master. PERSIS L. CHRISTIAN.

Texas Letter.

O. Paget is president of the "Free Thinker's" Club, of this city, and he magnifies his office. He never lets an opportunity pass unimproved, of saying something mean about the church, and he seems fond of letting the "fellows of the baser sort" know that he is with them. The street car strike now on has given him his latest opportunity, and he improves it by urging the people to boycott the roads. He says, "Walk—don't ride. Go to your butcher, your grocer, your baker, your saloon man and say, 'If you ride I'll not patronize you.'' This classification shows his appreciation of different classes of men. The "saloon man" is ranked along with the "butcher," the "grocer" and the "baker." Is this the legitimate results of infidelity?

Our Lectureship just closed at Waxahachie was a great success. The attendance was large, the papers were good and the entertainment was nothing short of royal. Prof. McGarvey's presence added much to the profit of the meeting. His lectures were a rare treat. and he will be warmly welcomed should he ever come again within our borders. Our meeting prevented my attendance, and hence I cannot speak of it in detail. Pres. A. Clark is president next year, and we meet at Greenville.

G. Lyle Smith has resigned at Weatherford, and will leave there at the close of the year. Bro. Smith is one of our "gilt edge" men, and any church needing a pastor now has a rare opportunity of getting one.

T. D. Secrest, of Coleman, also tendered his resignation, but the church raised such a protest that he wisely reconsidered, and will remain with them.

J. B. Boen leaves us for Guthrie, Oklahoma, to assume pastoral charge in that important city. Boen feels the need of time for study, and hence he turns away, for the time being at least, from his favorite work of evangelizing. Our Texas people will follow him in love and prayers.

Geo. Van Pelt, under the auspices of the State Board, held a good meeting at Yoakum, with sixteen additions, and the appointment of a committee to buy the Baptist church house, an elegant new house, almost completed, and arrange to employ a pastor.

Mertens is shouting for joy, and well she may be, for Bro. Walling's twelve years' labor there is at last crowned with success. A church is now regularly organized and at work, and a house of worship is being erected.

Jewell Howard, after a successful pastorate at Terrell, resigns to re-enter Add-Ran University. He feels that no time is lost in thorough preparation for his work, and he is right.

Baxter Golightly has been very sick, but is now much better, and our people rejoice, for he is one of the best and most useful men.

C. L. Cole, has begun his twelfth year as pastor at Garland, and his work, like wine, grows better with age.

Tom Smith, one of the evangelists in the state work, has organized a church in South Waco, at a missionary point recently started by the Central Church.

Our meeting at the Central Church is four weeks old, with 31 additions. Bro. Martin's preaching is strong, and we are hopeful.

M. M. DAVIS.

833 *Live Oak St., Dallas, Tex.*

Lincoln Letter.

After three delightful years in Colorado we are in Nebraska again.

We closed our work at Manzanola, California, Oct. 14th, preaching five nights that week and baptizing four young women. Manzanola is one of the sunniest, fairests pots on earth, so far as we know, and the church, one of the best, is in need of a minister. For some consecrated godly young man that is a fruitful field for a life work among appreciative, loving hearts, who will always hold up his hands and help to plant "the Old Faith" in that sunny land. May the Lord richly bless Manzanola and her people, for they are worthy.

Since leaving we have received the sad news of the death of Sister Anna Eichling. As one of the "pure in heart" her presence in the house of the Lord was always an inspiration and she was always there if health permitted. With a face always full of sunshine and heart cheery and glad she was a great power in the Sunday-school as teacher of the infant class. During twelve years of pastoral work I have never known a sweeter Christian life. Such lives—the embodiment of a "peace that passeth understanding," and a "joy that is unspeakable and full of glory." John must have had in mind when he wrote, "And they do bring the glory and honor of the nations into it." May God bless and sustain Bro. Eichling and comfort the church.

Sunday, Oct. 16th, we passed in Denver with father and mother. It was a great delight to worship with them again in the house of the Lord.

We have located as pastor of the Bethany Church of Christ, worshiping at Cotner University. The church is in fine condition, and the former pastor, Bro. Bush, who still resides here, is held in high esteem.

The outlook for Cotner University is most hopeful, the attendance good, all lines of work prospering and the 25 or 26 young men in the Bible Department are of the highest order of intellect and Christian consecration.

Beloved of the Lord, we have no work of greater importance to-day than the maintaining and upbuilding of Cotner University. On the fertile plains and beautiful valleys of this trans-Mississippi empire (Kansas, Colorado, Nebraska and the Dakotas) will sometime be fought the Armageddon of our national destiny. A great tide of brain and brawn and young life is flowing from the Eastern and Central states and we owe to them and to God to lay broad and deep the foundations of better civilization here than the world has ever known.

We need to contend earnestly for that old faith once for all delivered to the saints, and to that end let us support our educational institutions.

Lincoln has been considerably stirred the last week by Mrs. Edholm, speaking for the "Rescue of Fallen Women," and the awful traffic in girls has been spoken of in a way that will do good. One case was instanced where a man who was skeptical as to "drugging, kidnaping," etc., having offered rewards for convincing proof was horrified to find his own daughter as the victim.

Dr. J. J. Lewis, of Boston, recently lectured to the students of Wesleyan University on the "Passion Play" of Oberamergan. This will be remembered as the play that was to purify the stage. This was years ago. Meanwhile the stage still lives to curse and cumber the ground. The way to purify the stage is to make Christianity so all-sufficient to humanity that the stage will be abolished for want of patrons. A. K. WRIGHT.

Lincoln, Neb.

Is Baptism for the Remission of Sins? No. 2.

When are the sins of the alien actually remitted? At what place, stage or time can the alien coming to Christ, and into his kingdom, have the assurance that his sins are forgiven?

If I read history aright, the fathers fought a great battle and won a great victory over this matter some half century ago. When the battle began there was not a question or matter prominent in religious circles and work more obscured.

It was a very common thing to find men and women who were searching and seeking for this knowledge in extreme agony of soul, and no man was found to stand forth and give the desired light. The rallying cry of the little band in Washington Co., Pa., "Where the Scriptures speak we will speak, and where the Scriptures are silent we will be silent," led the people adopting the sentiment to look into the Scriptures for the answer to every question, and to pledge themselves to accept and adopt that answer when found. These men had been born in the mist, and struggled gradually out of it into the light.

On the 18th day of November, 1827, at New Lisbon, Ohio, Walter Scott, who was the first man of his times to see the meaning of Acts 2:38, declared to the people assembled that God said, "Repent and be baptized, every one of you, in the name of Jesus Christ, for the remission of sins," and that God meant what he said, and that was the way to obtain remission of sins. He gave the invitation, and made it plain that all might understand it. William Amend was a devout Presbyterian. He had believed long years before. All that can be claimed for "faith" as a mental act, a heart condition, or spiritual attitude, had been his for many years. All that can be claimed for faith as an "attitude of the soul toward God," he had already. All that can be said of faith as a "subjective principle," William Amend had.

When he heard that invitation for the first time in his life from the lips of a preacher, he at once accepted it. The historian, the saintly Baxter of happy memory, says: "In the same day, in a beautiful, clear stream which flows on the southern border of the town, in the presence of a great multitude, he was baptized in the name of Jesus Christ for the remission of sins."

I cannot think that it would please the great explorer and discoverer, Scott, or the humble man of faith, Amend, to have leading men in the great movement for restoring the New Testament church in its teaching and practice, which they were then launching, seventy years later, employing such ambiguous language concerning this great matter as this: "In what *sense* baptism looks toward remission of sins is an open question." Or language that will be so uncertain that an inquiry is aroused as to whether baptism is for or because of remission of sins, which?

Was Walter Scott right? The men and women of faith who stood with him thought him to be right. The battle was fought on that ground. Mysticism, doubt, uncertainty and the mourner's bench system, and custom of experience telling, gave way before their cry: "God says to the believing soul, Repent and be baptized in the name of Jesus Christ for the remission of sins."

There was no hint that in baptism the believer had the assurance of forgiveness of sins already forgiven. They never employed the word actually, or really, in connection with remission. It was simply remission of sins. It meant just that. No more, no less. When the man whose heart was prepared for baptism was baptized, it was for the remission of sins, and his sins were then remitted. Up to that time they had not been remitted. It meant "absolving from guilt," and "included deliverance from the power and the habit of sin," and all this took place when the man was "baptized into Christ," wherein he is a new creature.

We have been before the world with this teaching more than half a century. Tens of thousands have accepted it. We have succeeded marvelously because we have offered to the people something definite—a sure thing. Whether we quote our writers word for word or not, we must deeply deplore the fact that their utterances have been such as to raise the question, Do we believe it? For the sake of the cause let us discuss no speculative or dim theories, and let us use no ambiguous language.

All of the revisions and translations of the Scriptures, and all of the efforts of those of the contrary part have failed to make the Holy Spirit say anything different from the declaration, "Repent and be baptized every one of you, in the name of Jesus Christ, for the remission of sins, and you shall receive the gift of the Holy Spirit." Brethren, let us preach it that way, and be true re-Peters.

E. L. FRAZIER.

Marion, Ind.

Indiana Items.

The Sunday before Christmas is set apart for an offering for the relief of our aged and disabled preachers and their families. Do not allow other and less important affairs to crowd this out of your memory, but rather lay aside a handsome gift for the good men who will otherwise fail to be made happy at the Christmastide.

⁂

I spent a few very pleasant hours to-day with A. M. Atkinson, in Wabash. He has had the cause of Ministerial Relief very close to his heart from its inception, and is anxious that every preacher present the matter to his people in December, and secure the heartiest and best gifts at all possible, as the needs are pressing and calls for aid are increasing. As the headquarters are in Indiana we ought not to fall behind in this gracious and noble work.

⁂

We have but few more spiritual or more successful pastors in Indiana than T. J. Clark, of Bloomington. He recently announced a brief season of prayer before the Lord's day morning service and invited any who were inclined to do so to attend. The service has been both well attended and most helpful to pastor and congregation. Why not try this everywhere? For many years the Valparaiso church officers have engaged in a brief season of prayer just before the Sunday morning sermon. These services are held in the lecture rooms.

⁂

It will be interesting to those who visited Chickamauga Park in October to know that at a meeting of the Grand Army and Confederate Posts at Chattanooga in 1885, Capt. I. P. Watts, of the 84th Indiana, proposed the purchase by the government of the Chickamauga battlefield. The proposition met with favor everywhere with the splendid outcome of the present park. Bro. Watts is one of our active and self-sacrificing Indiana preachers, residing at Winchester, and now donating part of his time to building up the broken walls in Swayzee, where he is doing excellent and much-needed work. May he meet with abundant success.

⁂

The church at Huntington has been rebuilding, and will reopen their house of worship on the 27th of November. L. L. Carpenter, the chief of dedicators, will have charge. Nearly all money necessary to pay for the improvements has been provided, and the services will be gladsome rather than goldsome. The house, with its new Sunday-school rooms, new tower and furnishings, windows, frescoings, seats, etc., will be the best church in the city. W. T. Wells is pastor, and is strong in his work and in the hearts of all the people. All departments of work are flourishing.

⁂

The Huntington church has sustained a great loss in the death of Dr. H. C. Grayston who, at the age of 76, passed to his eternal home a few days ago. The Doctor took great interest in the rebuilding of the church house, and every day went around to see how the work progressed. His absence will sadly mellow the reopening exercises. There are few men in any community like our noble Dr. Grayston. Of English birth and education, he and his good lady have been residents of Huntington for nearly a half century and represent the highest culture. I never knew a more perfect gentleman, and as a humble, gentle Christian he nobly impressed all with whom he came in contact. His sudden departure is a great loss.

⁂

In Ft. Wayne, P. J. Rice in the West Jefferson and Z. A. Harris in Creighton Avenue, are sustaining the gospel as but few men can. They both have the confidence of the people and will wield a splendid influence there for good. Bro. Rice has long held up the royal banner of Christ, and now in one of the handsomest edifices in Northern Indiana, will continue to build up a strong congregation. Bro. Harris comes from Hiram, O., and like Bro. Rice, is making genuine sacrifices for the cause they love.

⁂

E. L. Frazhier is pastor of both our churches in Marion, and has the hearty co-operation of both. This is prophetic of great good in that city.

The writer has engaged his time for every Lord's day in 1899. After the middle of December he and W. E. M. Hackleman will conduct the Indiana Christian. They now have the business formerly owned by W. T. Sellers, and handle all church, Sunday-school and Endeavor supplies that may be needed by Christian workers. They take subscriptions for all magazines and papers, and will supply any book of the Christian Church, or any popular book wherever published, at lowest rates. They are headquarters for all our Indiana people. 15 Virginia Ave., Indianapolis. Send to them at once for your Sunday-school supplies.

E. B. SCOFIELD.

Puerto Rico Letter.

J. H. GARRISON—*Dear Brother:* Your readers will doubtless be pleased to hear a word from this new U. S. territory.

We landed at Ponce Oct. 27th, remained there nearly a week and then began our journey across the country toward San Juan, the capital city of the island. Ponce is the largest of Puerto Rico's cities, and to a new comer one of great interest. New scenes upon every side meet the eye of a Kentuckian, or a resident of any part of the United States. A new order of vegetation appears. Even the grass, while it is grass, differs from that we have been accustomed to; where it is uncut or not eaten off it stands higher than my head, and that is six feet. The most striking thing among this sort are the stately cocoa palm trees that, although they have become common to my sight, are still a wonder and delight.

It is not my purpose in a letter to tell you my impressions of the country now. I have been traveling from place to place for over a week, have visited the Southeast Coast regions from Ponce to Guyama, thence to Cayey, an interior town of about five or six thousand, situated in a lonely valley between the southern and central range of mountains. The country round about is most picturesque and rich; indeed the whole country is rich, the very tops of the highest mountains are covered with a verdure almost as rank as the valleys, and every hill is crowned by numerous palm trees standing like silent sentries of the land. In the valleys, on the hillside and on the hilltops are farms with their little triangular and all kinds of angular fields of bananas, plantins, rice, corn (not very much corn, but in the valley it grows well, and we have some ears eight, ten and twelve inches long), and in the lowlands sugar plantations containing as much as 3,000 acres. Everywhere there is some kind of fruit to be seen, most of it used for food by the natives.

We are now at Coguas, another interior city in another rich valley. Coguas has ten or twelve thousand people. In all the important towns United States troops are stationed, and the streets of the city are patroled by a soldier bearing a Springfield or some other sort of gun. Some of these soldiers, by the way, are no recommendation to the American citizen. Some of them seem to think they are so far from home that there need be no restraint upon their actions.

Concerning the question that brought me to this country, viz., its religious condition and its need of the gospel, there can be but one answer: its religious condition is bad. I often wonder how, under the circumstances, the people are as good as they are. The Catholic Church is the only one here, except an Episcopal mission at Ponce, and they have no church buildings except in the larger towns as a rule. We travel twenty or more miles before we reach one, and that in the most densely populated districts, and these churches are the center and circumference of whatever religious influence there is good or bad. No wonder the people are faulty.

The gospel is needed, and I never saw the place where people were so anxious for something better than they have as they are here. They are eager to learn, schools are in demand and the common folk are most attentive to the story of Jesus. I do not speak Spanish well enough to preach to them in their own tongue, but Bro. W. H. Sloan, a Baptist missionary from the City of Mexico, is my traveling companion, and upon two occasions we have gathered a crowd to listen to the difference between Catholicism and Protestantism. At Aguirre about fifty gathered last Sunday evening, and Bro. Sloan told them that the Protestants were coming into the country; they ought to know what they believed and taught, and in a plain, kind way told them. They sat upon the ground or stood up for forty minutes and listened most attentively, and at the conclusion said they thanked us for bringing such good doctrine. The next morning as we were about to leave two came and wanted to be baptized, but we concluded they were not yet taught and told them to wait.

Upon several occasions in private houses, after a conversation with the family, the whole of them have expressed a desire to become Protestants. Of course they are not ready to take upon them discipleship, being untaught, but it shows how ready they are to leave Romanism. However ignorant they may be in other things, they do know that Romanism has done them no good, and are ready to leave it. We must give them the truth.

I am preparing two lectures to give upon my return, both to be illustrated by stereopticon views; one, "Puerto Rico," which will deal with the island physically, its climate, soil, production, vegetation, etc.; the other will be "The Puertoricans," dealing with the people, their homes, habits, occupations, religion and social environment generally. I hope through these to awaken an interest among our brethren in the evangelization of this island, to the extent that they will put money in the hands of the Home Board, who have undertaken this work, so as to enable them to begin a work here at once.

Yours, J. A. Erwin.

Coguas, Puerto Rico, Nov. 9, 1898.

Monthly Bulletin from the Foreign Society.

The Executive Committee met in the rooms in Cincinnati, Nov. 18th, 1898. Devotional services were conducted by J. A. Lord.

Finances.—The receipts for October amounted to $7,794.40. Some of this came from a bequest. Some was received on the Annuity plan. The regular receipts for the month are small.

Notes from the Field. India.—Mrs. Crisp writes from Mungeli that there have been three baptisms and that twenty men and women are inquiring about the way of salvation. Miss Mildred Franklin was heard from last at Port Said. There were twenty-five passengers; of these nineteen were American missionaries. Mr. McGavran is devoting the present cold season exclusively to village work. It is believed that as a result of the relief work in the time of famine multitudes are more willing to listen to the gospel than ever before. Mr. Louis Klopsch, of the Christian Herald, proposes to send $300 a year for three years to aid the work among the orphans in India. Dr. Drummond reports the arrival of a young missionary in his home.

China.—Dr. and Mrs. Osgood and Dr. Welpton reached Shanghai safely on the 28th of September. Dr. Welpton will spend the winter at Lu Cheo fu with Mr. and Mrs. Titus. Dr. and Mrs. Osgood go to Chu Cheo. They will be associated there with Mr. and Mrs. Arnold. Mr. Meigs writes that the work in Nankin is moving on finely. There are inquirers all the time. Mrs. Meigs expects to come home in the spring to recruit her health. Mr. Meigs will remain on the field for another year. James Ware has succeeded in getting a suitable place to work right in the heart of the mill district of Shanghai. At the first service the place was crowded. All the Christian women turned out and evinced great enthusiasm.

Japan.—C. E. Garst and H. H. Guy are devoting most of their time to evangelistic work. They find Japan everywhere open to the gospel. One man followed them a 100 miles to be immersed. He and his brother are very zealous. They are both developing considerable powers as exhorters. Mr. Guy is kept busy answering the questions of those who are studying Christianity. At Akozu, where we are carrying on quite a work, there has been great damage done by flood. This is the fourth year that they have been afflicted in this way.

Turkey.—Mr. and Mrs. Chapman arrived in Constantinople in good health. They have already begun the study of Armenian. There are ninety-four children in the school and there are others to go. Mr. Chapman has begun to preach by the aid of an interpreter. John Johnson, of Smyrna, needs a relief fund. In west Turkey the fig and grape crops have failed. Many of the people will suffer much during the winter. A little help will be of the greatest advantage to him. He is also preparing two or three leaflets for publication. He needs the funds to pay for printing these. His faith is in God and in the brethren.

Scandinavia.—Dr. Holck has requested th a strong man be sent to Norway to take char of the work in that fruitful field. He is n able to visit the churches there very ofte Some Norwegian man should be found to a these churches and to help in planting other The committee hopes to be able to send a m before the year closes.

England.—J. A. L. Romig has gone England to do evangelistic work. He expec to hold meetings in several of the churches a to open up work at several new points. L. Gow has resigned at Southampton.

Cuba.—The Executive Committee has deci ed to begin work in Cuba. At least two m should be sent to that field without delay. T sooner these men are sent, the better it will b The success of the work of Dr. Diaz sho what can be done in Cuba. Thousands of t people have broken with the establish church. Many of our own people will pour ir Cuba. The work in this field should be se supporting within two or three years.

A. McLean, Sec.

Notes and News.

Corresponding Secr.taries, Notice!

urch statistics for the *Yearbook* are e. Please make all corrections on the s' lists in your state to date and for- once to G. A. Hoffmann, Statistical y, Columbia, Mo.

G. A. HOFFMANN.

iram Jubilee Endowment.

iovement seems to be meeting with favor. Many words of encouragement ing to us from brethren in different the country. Names are not only :o us through the mails, but wherever trated lecture is presented it is enthu- ly received. Next week we will pub- of extracts from letters of prominent ., college men, editors and preachers. rewith submit our third list of names. ive not already sent in your name will do so at once? We want to get the olunteers at the earliest possible day.

E. V. ZOLLARS, President.

t of 106 names came to hand with the py.—EDITOR.]

Our New Home.

been here about one week and enjoyed ige from Northern Ohio. I am thank- favors from the Oracle and Christian ng Cos. En route I attended Sunday- nd meeting yesterday. Bro. Wallace, tor, insisted upon my preaching. I e hospitality and cabin service of Bro. Streator. We burn pine knots and tell ories. These candles of our forefathers hing brightly in the houses of many i who came here lately to secure timber d improve farms in a more mild clim- iere is room and welcome for more, but ply of choice bargains is limited. I secure a winter home at least for my- a few friends.

J. F. CALLAHAN.

ff, Ark., Nov. 21, 1898.

Acknowledgement.

'e to acknowledge a very gracious gift come to our Bible department library. the shape of about seventy volumes private library of our lamented Brother Skelton, donated by his brothers and Samuel, Frank and Will Skelton and hockley and Mrs. Ward. Bro. Leroy was of the class of '66 of Eureka . He died in '76 while pastor of the igton church, if I mistake not, and is the ie whose name is marked "deceased" oll of Eureka's alumni preachers. The ill be kept distinctly as a sweet savor memory. Are there not other useful ons among Eureka's friends that could consecrated to greater usefulness?

R. A. GILCREST.

the church at Volga, Nov. 20. He will preach in the Swedish language.

G. W. Elliott is in a successful meeting at Harold.

Several of our C. E. Societies report the observance of Forefathers' Day.

Good reports are received from the work of L. H. Humphreys at Sioux Falls.

Carthage and Romona are each pastorless at present.

There is a flourishing Bethany Reading Circle at Miller where E. W. Bowers ministers.

So far as we know, W. P. Shamhart, of Aberdeen, and M. D. Alexander, of Watertown, were our only representatives at Chattanooga.

Last year South Dakota sent $382.79 to the F. C. M. S. Even omitting the $100 annuity this is a very creditable gain over the $229.25 of 1897. However, we note with regret that only three of our C. E. Societies contributed to that work.

On Nov. 3 I had a funeral service at 1:30 and a wedding ceremony at 6. What is stranger still, on the same afternoon my M. E. colaborer had the same experience of officiating at a wedding and at a funeral.

A. H. SEYMOUR.

Arlington, S. D., Nov. 14, 1898.

Entertainment of Delegates at the Educational Conference.

All delegates going to the Educational Conference, Moberly, Dec. 6-8, 1898, should send a card to J. B. Briney, Moberly, Mo. Lodging will be furnished free at homes of the members of the church. Meals will be served at Central Christian Church at 25 cts. each. When you arrive at Moberly go to Central Christian Church. Those desiring hotel accommodations will report to D. H. Mounce, who will arrange for special rates for you.

S. G. CLAY, Sec.

Anent Dr. Mac El'Rey's Criticism.

EDITOR OF THE CHRISTIAN-EVANGELIST—

Dear Sir and Brother: Permit me to say that I had fully decided to take no note of Mr. Joseph H. Mac El'Rey's articles on Spiritism till my eye fell upon your editorial reference to the matter of their publication, and upon the expression of your desire that they might serve a useful purpose in calling out an article in response by myself. I have simply this to say: Mr. Mac El'Rey's logic is as lame as his rhetoric. His leading argument is the street urchin's retort, "You're another." His plural Latin coupled with English in the singular is quite distressing, but no more so than English plurals similarly outraged. When Mr. Mac El'Rey succeeds in parsing his productions I will attempt to answer them. As they stand they are unanswerable, being for the most part unintelligible. If you desire it, I shall seek to furnish you, as soon as I can command the leisure for its production, another article on this subject. I must ask you, however, to excuse me from making any further reference to Mr. Mac El'Rey's material-

Ministerial Relief.

The Lord's day before Christmas was appointed by the Chattanooga Convention for offerings by the churches to the cause of Ministerial Relief. The near approach of the day makes it important that the preachers begin at once suitable preparations for the offering. It is greatly desired that this, the first general offering to this tender and sacred ministry, shall be so generous as to reflect honor upon the church, and prove truly refreshing to the old veterans, whose closing days are full of sorrowful anxiety concerning their future comfort. We are seeking to awaken a deep and holy interest in the Cincinnati Jubilee Convention, which will be a most notable event in our history. What report shall we bear to that historic assembly, concerning our provision for the care of our old and needy preachers and their companions in service and affliction? The preachers hold the key to the situation, and it is confidently believed that they will not draw back from this holy duty. Brethren of the ministry, lead your churches into the blessed fellowship. They will hear your message with tearful interest and will find pleasure in the service your message reveals. It cannot be that this great brotherhood, so favored of the Lord, will knowingly permit any of their aged and needy preachers longer to suffer for the care which their long and faithful service so well deserves. Let us show our appreciation and gratitude for the heroic service of these messengers of our king, who pray and wait for the tokens of our remembrance. Let us not bring to their declining days the bitter pang of forgetfulness. Brethren, we entreat you in his name, make Dec. 25th a glad and notable day in our history.

If you have not received the last annual report, write Howard Cale, Indianapolis, Ind., and you will receive a copy.

A. M. Atkinson.

Wabash, Ind.

Oregon Notes.

Closed my work at North Yakima, Washington, Oct. 30th, 1898. During the year 83 were added to the church; 50 by baptism. Preached 133 sermons. Calls made, 562. Money raised for missions $152, paying in full all the apportionments of the different boards. For improvements, $250. Money raised for all purposes, $1,402. Personal pledges made for state work the coming year, $135. The church is in a prosperous condition and will continue to grow if a good man is secured for the pastorate. We will ever hold in grateful remembrance the faithful workers of the Yakima church, may the Lord who ruleth over all continue to bless them in their holy work.

Began work here, Nov. 6th, 1898, with bright prospects; two additions at the evening service. While the church has been without regular pastoral care for several months it is in good working order, better than some churches that have settled pastors. The church here is not very strong financially, but some of the best people of Corvallis are among its membership.

This is one of the important towns in the state. Corvallis is a beautiful little city, situated on the Willamette River 90 miles south of the city of Portland, with a population of 3,000. Here is located the Oregon Agricultural College, one of the leading institutions of learning in Oregon. The roll of students is made up largely from the farms of the state; many of them are members of the church and many others attend our services, thus making our influence more than local. We should have a strong, vigorus church here, and we hope that by the grace of God we will be able to wield a strong influence over our young men and women that come here for their education. To this end we need the prayers and sympathy of our great brotherhood.

L. F. Stephens.

Corvallis, Oregon.

Set in Order.

Bro. Routh and I found a weak church here—weak financially, numerically and spiritually. They were *distracted* by many personal difficulties. We have succeeded by the blessing of God in settling all these difficulties and in uniting the discordant elements. We have had four baptisms and one reclaimed. Splendid audiences. God interest. M. Ingels.

Fontana, Kan.

Talks to Churches—II.

I. *Are You Sure* that you are now doing the best work of which you are capable?

II. *Are You Sure* that the "preached Word," unaccompanied by the "printed page," is able to reach and convert the great "unchurched masses" of our country?

III. *Are You Sure* that "a Christian paper in every Christian home," and "a Christian library in every Christian Church," would not give our "reformatory movement" such an impetus *forward* as it has never had before?

IV. *Are You Sure* that "a rally all along the line," and "100,000 accessions in 1899" can be secured without the aid of such instrumentalities?

V. *Are You Sure* that if the founder of the Christian Library were kept busy during 1899, holding meetings and placing libraries, that the scattered members of many a church would not be "rallied" to the work again and that many "accessions" would not be added to the churches?

VI. *Are You Sure* that the delivery of his four lectures on "Paul and Ingersoll," "Is the Bibla a True Book?" "Our duty to Inquirers" and "Infidel versus Christian Literature," if given at the close of a two weeks' meeting, would not pay for both library and meeting?

If You Are Sure you want to *try it*, write the founder, S. J. Phillips.

Sugar Grove, Wis.

Concerning the Orphan Girls at Deoghur, India.

We have had a gratifying response to the call for individuals and organizations to assume the support of seventy-six girls given our missionaries by the British Government when it closed its orphanages. It is most gratifying that a large number of families have each promised to maintain a child. The majority of these families have small incomes. In some of them the payment of the $30 per year that is required will necessitate real self-denial. Our God will abide in such homes and richly bless them.

There are twenty-five or thirty girls for whom support has not yet been provided. They are now being maintained by our missionaries. We desire to assign them at once. Many persons hesitate about undertaking this work lest in future they may not be able to continue it. Those who prefer to do so can promise to support a child during this year, and at its close make a decision whether the work ought to be continued. Those willing to assist in this good work should write me at once.

Mattie Pounds.

306 *North Deleware St., Indianapolis, Ind.*

Cincinnati.

Judging from the number of additions reported in our preachers' meeting. the churches of Cincinnati are once more down to faithful and efficient work.

The Eastern Avenue congregation has called J. A. Pine as pastor. Lockland has secured a pastor in the person of W. O. Thomas. These brethren are consecrated, active young men, and constitute an important addition to the working force of Cincinnati.

Eighteen months ago J. S. Lawrence, seconded by less than a half-dozen workers, started a mission in a hall over a saloon, in Central Fairmount. They encountered many adversaries, but despite all of these, on last Sunday they dedicated to the service of the Lord a beautiful chapel which, aside from t lot on which it stands, cost $2,200. Br Lawrence and his coworkers have, in th achieved a great success and are deserving much praise. J. S. Lawrence is one of t most consecrated and energetic workers Cincinnati.

Isaac Selby, of Australia, one of our bret ren, has recently delivered a series of lectur in the Central Church of this city, in which handled skillfully many of the current issu between Christianity and the various forms modern infidelity and skepticism. At t close of these lectures the "Ohio Liber Society," through its representative, ch lenged him to a discussion, which Mr. Sel accepted. The discussion will be held in th city, Nov. 28th and 29th.

"Is Christianity the Religion of Humanity? Selby affirms; Blanchard, of Cleveland, O who represents the "Liberalists," denie "Is Evolution the True Doctrine of the Orig of Man and other Forms of Life?" Blancha affirms; Selby denies. It seems that some the brethren are inclined to return to the go old days of polemics and first principles; a why not? S. D. D.

Railroad Rates to Educational Confe ence, Moberly, Dec. 6-8, 1898.

All roads of the Western Passenger Associ tion have granted a rate of one and one thi fare for the round trip, to the Educatior Conference, Moberly, Mo., Dec. 6-8, '9 upon the following conditions: There must as many as 100 certificates or receipts for f regular fare going to Moberly at a cost of mo than fifty cents. You must ask your ho agent for a certificate, or receipt for tick purchused of him, if ticket costs more th fifty cents. If agent hasn't any certificate get a receipt from him for money paid for yo ticket. If you must go over two roads, g certificate over each road. Upon arrival the conference give your certificate to me to signed; and if there are 100 of them, th general agent at Moberly will stamp them an you will be entitled to one-third fare returning These rates only apply to persons buying *fu fare* tickets, costing *more* than fifty cents Tickets can be purchased three days before th conference and are good three days after Any one can have the advantage of thi rate who gets a certificate and has it signed b the secretary there. Don't forget two things to get a certificate or receipt, and to give it t me when you arrive at Moberly. Ask you home agent for any information you may need

Yours truly, S. G. Clay, Sec.

Evangelistic.

KANSAS.

Larned, Nov. 24.—Please to report three confessions to this church, our first contribution to the 100,000 for Christ. Everyone seems interested in the forward movement. This will be a glorious year for the Disciples. Church will grant me two meetings to help in this great work.—C. H. HILTON.

Sedgwick, Nov. 27.—Two additions to the church, with all lines of church work improving since I took the work here in July. Will send a list of subscribers by the first of January, 1899. Yours in faith.—A. M. McLAIN, pastor.

St. Francis, Nov. 25.—W. R. Gill just closed a four weeks' meeting here. The meetings were well attended, and the result of the labor was that 12 young people were baptized and taken into the church.—C. A.

ARKANSAS.

Little Rock, Nov. 25.—George R. Stainer has just closed a fine meeting in North Little Rock, with six additions. He is a fine man, and can be secured for a few meetings in Arkansas. Write him at Argenten, Ark. Care Dr. E. Meek.—W. J. HUDSPETH.

WASHINGTON.

Palouse, Nov. 21.—Two added by letter yesterday.—E. C. WIGMORE.

MICHIGAN.

Fife Lake, Nov. 26.—Meeting in new field two weeks old; 30 gathered ready to organize, and everything coming our way to unity in Christ.—S. BUTTERFIELD.

Buchanan, Nov. 21.—We had 21 more added here last night, and two at the A. M. service; 39 in two nights, and 51 to date.—SCOVILLE & SCOTT.

TEXAS.

Italy.—Percy T. Carnes, evangelist; B. B. Sanders, singer; five additions Nov. 20th; one by baptism.

San Antonio, Nov. 21.—One confession at our mid-week prayer-meeting Wednesday, 16th. Last night one of our Sunday-school boys stepped past his father and took a stand for Christ. The father followed. Then a young lady came. We had splendid audiences at all services. Many of the soldier boys attend, and our Endeavorers are doing all they can to help these boys who are removed from home influences, and their work is appreciated. Our G. A. S. is thriving. I took one confession at the city hospital yesterday.—GEO. B. RANSHAW.

IOWA.

Bedford.—R. A. Omer is assisting Pastor J. W. M. Walters in a meeting here.

Irwin.—D. H. Bays, author of Doctrines and Dogmas of Mormonism, reports nine added and the meeting continues. Frank McVey, of Concordia, Kans., is his singer.

Wintersett.—Pastor J. M. Lowe and singer. J. Will Landrum, have just closed a meeting with several added.

Laurens.—W. B. Cash, pastor, assisted by a student from Drake University, is in a meeting here.

Dysart.—Wright & Martindale are conducting a siege here.

Delta.—Pastor Fisher is holding our meeting here.

Mason City.—S. M. Martin, of California, will lead the great meeting here in January. Pastor Sumner T. Martin is already preparing for it.

Marshalltown.—Pastor C. C. Rowlison will exchange meetings with Frank G. Tyrrell, of St. Louis, Mo.

Exira.—D. A. Hunter is in a good meeting here. Full report later.

Marne.—J. T. Spurrier is organizing a new band here.

Central City.—D. A. Wickizer is in a good meeting at this place. Our expectations are high and the audiences are large.

Anita, Cass Co.—A. M. Haggard and pastor, C. A. Lockhart, are in a meeting here. Bro. H. preaches four nights and Bro. L. three each week. This enables Brother Haggard to teach his classes in Drake University.

Ninth & Shaw, Des Moines.—J. R. Speck is in a fine meeting here. We hope to report great results.

KENTUCKY.

Walton, Nov. 21.—W. J. Howe, of Centerville, Indiana, yesterday closed a good meeting at Newberg, Ky., with 15 additions; six by baptism, one reclaimed, and eight by statement. The preaching was strong and helpful. —J. W. ROGERS.

MASSACHUSETTS.

Everett, Nov. 21.—Yesterday baptized and fellowshipped two oonverts.—R. H. BOLTON, pastor.

NEBRASKA.

Lincoln, Nov. 22.—Closed a meeting at West Point on Lord's day with 15 additions. E. E. Francis is the untiring pastor. I now go to Rock Port, Mo. Churches desirous of a revival may address me there. Terms most reasonable.—S. W. GLASCOOK, evangelist.

OHIO.

Rutland, Nov. 21.—One confession and baptism at Orange yesterday.—T. L. LOWE.

Bellaire, Nov. 20.—Ten additions in last three weeks. Eight at regular services to-day. Five were by baptism. Two from the Baptists. —C. M. W.

INDIANA.

Rochester, Nov. 14.—One added to our number yesterday and two one week ago.—J. A. LYTLE.

North Madison, Nov. 25.—We had a good meeting at Liberty. Church revived. Ten additions by baptism. Church called me to remain next year. Have not accepted as yet. I begin a meeting at once at Concord Church. —C. D. MAPLE.

Fowler, Nov. 25.—Rev. Thomas J. Shuey, of Valparaiso, has just closed a three weeks' meeting for us here. Ten accessions were made to the church and the church was strengthened and deepened in spiritual life. Bro. Shuey is a strong preacher. All his sermons are good. He is wise and dignified in his work. He leaves the church on a higher plane.—LEE TINSLEY, pastor.

Nov. 24.—The work at Seymour progresses nicely. Work on the new house is being pushed and we hope to get it in closed by Dec. 20. The board desires me to remain there and take oversight of the work until January. I am one of the building committee with authority to push the work. I go to Keota, Ia., in January for a month and while I have more calls now than I can fill in a year, yet I would like another meeting in Iowa while I am there. Some of my greatest meetings have been in Iowa. Any church wanting me and my singer can address me at Irvington, Ind., for three weeks.—H. C. PATTERSON, state evangelist.

MISSOURI.

Canton, Nov. 25.—Meeting five days old. Six added and a growing interest. Pastor and people are holding the meeting.—D. ERRETT.

Kansas City, Nov. 24.—Eight additions to date in our meeting at Sixth and Prospect. —H. A. NORTHCUTT, evangelist; GEO. H. COMBS, pastor.

Albany, Nov. 22.—Prerched last Lord's day at Denver, Worth County; two additions. Will preach at same place on three Lord's days in next month.—A. D. WILLIAMS.

Lathrop, Nov. 21.—Yesterday was a great day for us at the Lathrop church, the Lord giving us four additions to the church, one at morning service and three at evening service. The work here will be in satisfactory condition when I leave, Jan. 1, 1899.—THOS. J. THOMPSON, pastor.

Breckinridge, Nov. 21.—Yesterday we began our work at this place. During the month of October we had three additions at Dawn and two additions at Mooresville.—GRAYSON HUGHES.

Grant City, Nov. 23.—Just closed a three weeks' meeting here with 26 additions. The meeting has been a very profitable one to the church. Bro. N. R. Davis, of Maryville, did the preaching. The brethren were delighted with the sermons. Bro. Davis has made many warm friends among our people. He is an earnest, logical speaker, and has sown seed while in our midst from which we confidently anticipate a great harvest.—W. H. HARRIS.

Plattsburg, Nov. 26.—At Agency, one of my regular preaching points, I have just closed a meeting of two weeks and two days with 30 additions; 25 confessions and baptisms, four from the denominations, one restored. This is my third meeting for this church. I

edifice will soon grace the little town of Fandon. Thanksgiving day was observed by union services held in the Christian church at Colchester. The discourse was delivered by Rev. Cromley, of the Free Methodist Church. After the services the brethren of the Christian Church repaired to the hall where a public thanksgiving dinner was served. Over 225 meals were served. The brethren and friends very gratefully remembered their pastor with a donation, among which was a baptismal suit. I began the work here last March and since that time have had 96 additions to the church.—F. M. BRANIC.

SOUTH DAKOTA.

Miller, Nov. 23.—Preached 29 sermons at Sunbeam schoolhouse. Nineteen additions; 15 confessions. Four from the Methodists, three from the Congregational and one from the Episcopal Churches.—E. W. BOWERS.

NEW YORK.

Syracuse.—Since our state convention, the first of September, I have held a short meeting at Pompey, with 31 added; another at Niagara Falls with 9 added; a longer one with the Jefferson St. Church, Buffalo, with 27 added. I have also spent two weeks among the churches. While at South Benton one night, there was one confession, 68 in all, and nearly all by obedience. The gospel ship can move on in the teeth of bad weather and political storms. Am beginning here with Bro. Edwords.—J. M. MORRIS, state evangelist.

Buffalo, Nov. 25.—The work of the Richmond Church of Christ opens up auspiciously. One addition last Lord's day. Eight additions on the 6th and seven accessions not previously reported. Only two of this number came by letter and all were added at our regular services without special effort. The Sunday-school has surpassed all previous records in its regular average attendance and the prayer-meeting averages more than 100 present every Wednesday evening. We expect to make a special effort for enlargement, beginning with the new year.—LLOYD DARSIE, 291 Ashland Ave.

Literature.

PRAYING IN THE HOLY GHOST. By Rev. G. H. C. Macgregor, M. A., author of "A Holy Life." Fleming H. Revell Company, New York and Chicago.

This volume of 139 pages, by a devout mind, will be certain to awaken a deeper interest in prayer in those who read it. The vital relation of the Holy Spirit to prayer is shown from many passages. It, therefore, not only emphasizes the value of prayer, but the importance of receiving the Holy Spirit, who is the inspiration of all true and prevailing prayer and of all Christian life and growth.

THE DREAM OF YOUTH. By Hugh Black, M. A., Pastor Free St. George's, Edinburgh. Fleming H. Revell Company, New York and Chicago, 1898. Price, 30 cents.

A small volume of 40 pages, a gem in mechanical beauty, in literary style and in nobility of thought. Every young person particularly should read it and catch the inspiration of high purpose that glows in its pages. It is based on three texts, one from Joel, one from Paul and one from Shakespeare, and are as follows:

"Your young men shall see visions."

"I was not disobedient to the heavenly vision."

"We are such stuff as dreams are made of."

To all young people who aspire to make the most of their lives our advice is to read "The Dream of Youth."

THE HOLMAN LINEAR PARALLEL TEACHERS' BIBLE. A. J. Holman, Philadelphia, Pub.

Infidels who boast that the Bible is played out, and is being superseded, should take some account of the enormous multiplication of the sacred book of Christians in these days of ours. Of the making of teachers' Bibles there is no end, and each succeeding book has points of advantage over all its predecessors. The last candidate for public favor in this ever-widening field of biblical teaching is the Holman S. S. Teachers' Bible, which combines the desirable features of linear, parallel and self-pronouncing, with a complete analytical concordance and beautiful maps of Bible lands in all the ages of Bible history. It meets a long-felt want with preachers and teachers. It is the book I have been looking for for a long time. Mr. Holman has given us a parallel Bible without remanding the new text to the margin, or putting it alongside the other in a separate column, doubling the size of the book. By this new arrangement both versions are immediately under the eye at the same time, making comparison easy and absolutely without trouble. There is a growing disposition among teachers and preachers especially to use the Revised Version, and yet there is a feeling that the old should not be entirely abandoned. The Holman Bible solves this problem admirably. The body of the text represents the two versions in common; the differences are printed in smaller letters in double lines one above the other; the upper line is the Common Version, and the lower line the Revised. This method brings the two texts at once under the eye for comparison. I use this Bible altogether in my studies and for purposes of teaching and exposition, because I find it the most convenient and useful in these lines. It does not supersede other Bibles, but is sure to prove itself well-nigh indispensable to intelligent Bible students of all classes. J. J. HALEY.

A BIRD'S-EYE VIEW OF OUR MISSIONS.—The title of the book is "Missionary Fields and Forces." The name of the writer is W. J. Lhamon. The number of pages is about one hundred and fifty. Its size is about five and one-half inches by four. It is one of the volumes of the Bethany Christian Endeavor Reading Courses. Address the Bethany Christian Endeavor Company, 798 Republic Street, Cleveland, Ohio. The frontispiece is a map on which is shown the geographical distribution of the Disciples. On the opposite page are notes on the map. The book contains twenty-one chapters. The first chapter is entitled, "The Primitive Gospel in Modern Missions." The second is a concise and clear statement of facts concerning the Foreign Christian Missionary Society. This is followed by chapters on our fields and forces in India, China, Japan, Turkey, Scandinavia, England and Africa. A half dozen chapters are devoted to Medical Missions. The story of the Christian Woman's Board of Missions is well told in a single chapter. The history and work of the American Christian Missionary Society is presented in about forty pages. The chapter on the Religious Conditions in England is a remarkably clear statement of the subject. The chapters on Hinduism, Confucianism and Mohammedanism are philosophical in character and reveal a remarkable breadth of view and an understanding of these religions unusually accurate. An appendix contains the names of all missionaries employed by the American Christian Missionary Society, the Christian Woman's Board of Missions and the Foreign Christian Missionary Society. Every Disciple ought to own a coyy of this wonderful little book as a *vade mecum*—a constant companion. W. J. Lhamon struck twelve when he wrote this book. The initial centence is worthy of quotation in this place as an example of the crisp style in which the book is written. It is as follows:

"The gospel is a revelation. Theology is an invention. It is the office of the followers of Jesus to proclaim the former. The commission of the Master does not include the latter. Christ is perfection, and his work a completion. He is God's last and best word to us; he is the 'fullness of him that filleth all in all;' he is 'man at his climax;' he is 'the moral miracle of history;' he is 'the surprise of the ages;' he is 'the Word made flesh,' and—'We have seen his glory, the glory of the only begotten of the Father, full of grace and truth.'"

Buy this book. Read it. Carry it in your pocket. Read passages in it to those who do not know what the Disciples are doing in the work of evangelizing the people at home and abroad. You will think better of the Disciples if you will accept and act on this advice. B. B. TYLER.

MAGAZINES.

The student of foreign missions will find the Record of Christian Work for December an unusually attractive number. Under the title of "The Awakening of China" are given three brief articles on the effect of the recent political changes upon missionary efforts, by Dr. Judson Smith, Mr. Robert Speer and Dr. A. B. Leonard. A letter from Dr. Arthur H. Smith, author of "Chinese Characteristics," presents still another phase of Christian work in China, while Rev. Henry W. Frost, of Toronto, describes the "Forward Movement" of the China Inland Mission in another article. In the same number, Dr. Hallock, of Rochester, calls attention to six "Joys that were Born into the World with Christ," and Dr. C. I. Scofield concludes his series of "Plain Papers on the Holy Spirit."

Rt. Hon. Joseph Chamberlain, British Colonial Secretary, in his remarkably frank article in the December Scribner's, makes very evident his views on America's relation to colonial expansion. In the course of them he says: "It can hardly be necessary to say that the British nation will cordially welcome the entrance of the United States into the field of colonial enterprise, so long and so successfully occupied by themselves. There would be no jealousy of the expansion of American enterprise and influence; on the contrary, every Englishman would heartily rejoice in the co-operation of the United States in the great work of tropical civilization. From the nations of the Continent of Europe he has nothing to learn except what to avoid. Their system, their objects and their ideals are entirely different from his; and, as he thinks, inferior."

In the first installment of his story of the "Merrimac," in the December Century, which is to be an unusually attractive number, Lieut. Hobson lays no claim to having originated the dea of blocking the channel at Santiago. The sinking of the collier had been ordered by Admiral Sampson, but the commanding offcer off Santiago had not executed the manœuver when the flagship arrived, and the working out of the plan, as well as its execution, was intrusted to Lieut. Hobson. The preliminary steps are detailed in this number of the magazine, and in later issues the story of the sinking of the ship and the capture and imprisonment of her crew will be given at first hand. This is the only account of his exploit that Mr. Hobson has written for publication.

The Christmas number of the Pall Mall Magazine splendidly sustains the reputation this magazine has won for its literary and artistic excellence. From one end to the other of its 160 pages it is filled with good things. Among the remarkable contents is a superb photogravure frontispiece, "The Virgin and Child," after the famous picture by Gerard David, and now published for the first time.

The prize poem, "Biopsis," a song of life in contrast to "Thanatopsis," a song of death, will take high rank among the living poems of the day. It was written by Prof. McBeath and is published in the Alkahest, Atlanta, Ga., for November. It is said to be the best poem in the language on life's Christian duties, and would be a blessing and an inspiration to be read many times a year during one's whole life.

MR. ALFRED AUSTIN, Lord Tennyson's successor in the laureateship of England, will contribute to the next volume of THE YOUTH'S COMPANION a poem based on an extremely dramatic and picturesque legend, which is singularly suited for recitation. The story itself is full of interest and color, and the metre is so fluent that even a child can recite the verses with ease and effect.

Family Circle.

"Keep Your Heart Warm."

EDWARD O. SHARPE.

There's a sweet line running in rhythmic, rhyming way,
Through my busy care and thinking, all the long and toilsome day;
It is pulsing, it is throbbing, on my soul's sad, lonesome shore.
Or, to use another figure, it's an angel at my door;
Now to give it due expression all my power bows and bends:
"Keep your heart warm to your old-time friends."

Blessed be the days of childhood with their joyous blossom ways:
See them o'er the shoulders in the past's dim, distant haze;
There our playmates circle round us in a gay and happy whirl,
Free and merry boyish comrades and one little sweetheart girl;
O! those years of harping laughter this blest benediction sends:
"Keep your heart warm to your old-time friends."

Many business cares perplex us—shop and field and pen and plow
Bend the form with heavy burdens, put the wrinkles on our brow;
Many friends come with the sunshine, fewer when the clouds arise,
And earth-voices mock our sorrows when the tears bedim our eyes.
Now I tell you what will help us and our trouble greatly mends:
"Keep your heart warm to your old-time friends."

I have seen (I grieve to say it) dearest friends drift wide apart;
Could it be the spot was vacant where there used to be a heart?
I can't do it. One I've loved once, you may know I cling to him
Through all miles and years between us till the sun and stars grow dim.
So I bid you still be loyal everywhere your pathway tends:
"Keep your heart warm to your old-time friends."

LeRoy, Ill.

Through Difficulties.

BY ALFRED BRUNK.

CHAPTER I.

INHUMANITY EXEMPLIFIED.

Mary Ashton was an orphan and lived with her uncle, Oliver Small, who was quite lenient with his own children, but very exacting with others. Her father had been killed on a grain thresher, and her mother died soon after. Mary and her brother Henry, who was some two years her junior, were thrown upon the world without home or means, as their father had been very poor. Mr. Small, their mother's brother, a well-to-do farmer, took the children to his own home. Richard, his second son, went West, taking Henry with him, and opened a small boot and shoe store in a growing town.

"Mary, why are you not out pickin' peas?" asked Mr. Small. "I do declare if you haint got on your go-to-meetin' dress! Whatever do you mean?"

"Why, Uncle Oliver, you told me I could go to school this fall, and it takes up this mornin', so I was gettin' ready to go," Mary answered, moving away from him.

"Yes, I know I did; but Sarah, and Sammy, and Billy all want to go, so you will have to stay at home and help do the work."

Mary burst into tears, but said nothing. She had learned long before how useless it was for her to say anything when her uncle had once made up his mind. She went upstairs to the little room she shared with Sarah, knelt down by the bed and gave way to a paroxysm of grief. When she became somewhat calmer she lifted up her heart to her Heavenly Father: "O, God, let me die! Life aint worth livin'; uncle scolds and whips me, and auntie takes my head off for nothin'; and I can't never see my own brother. O, God, if you are good like uncle says you are, then let me die!"

"What are you agroanin' here for?" asked a sharp voice near her. "Your uncle is a-stormin' around because you don't come on an' go to work. An' here you are, aint even got your workin' dress on yet! That's what folks git for havin' anything to do with other people's children. You would agone to the 'poorhouse,' both of you, if I could ahad my say."

Mary slipped into her working dress as quickly as she could and hastened into the field, glad to get away from her aunt's sharp tongue. The weather was excessively warm. The September sun poured down his torrid rays as if he were trying to set this old world on fire. But Mary labored on, regardless of the heat. At noon she was pale and nervous, and ate but little dinner.

"Mary," said her uncle, "I am goin' to the church meetin' this evenin', and I want you to get them peas all done by night. If there is a one left it won't be good for you, now I can tell you."

Mr. Small was a deacon of Dry Valley Church, was present at all the services, and never missed an officers' meeting. At this particular meeting one brother arose and said:

"Brethren, some of our young members have been disorderly. It has come to me from a reliable source that they have been robbing orchards in the neighborhood. Mr. Brown told me that if he caught them in his orchard again he would prosecute them. Now, brethren, I would suggest that we have a talk with the boys, and warn them—"

"I move that we turn 'em out," exclaimed Mr. Small. "Our young members are givin' us too much trouble. They know better, and I say put 'em out and be done with 'em."

"What are the names of the boys, Bro. Mangrove?" calmly asked the chairman of the meeting, a look of pain and vexation overspreading his face.

"Samuel Stone, Charles Wyman and Silas Small," replied Mr. Mangrove, and took his seat.

"It's a lie!" roared Mr. Small furiously. "I teach my children that it is almost as bad to steal as to murder, and I know Silas wouldn't do such a thing."

Just then the whole heavens were lighted up with glowing flame, a tremendous peal of thunder rocked the church and rain began to pour down in torrents. The church door flew open, and Silas himself burst into the room.

"Pa, come quick; Mary is dead!" he exclaimed.

For a few moments the wildest confusion prevailed, and Mr. Small, scarcely knowing what he did, mounted his horse and, followed by his son, started at a breakneck speed through the rain for home. He found Mary lying on a cot in the dining-room, and the family physician, Dr. Weightman, busy preparing ice to apply to his patient. He looked at Mr. Small sharply, and with withering scorn said:

"Is it possible, sir, that you, one of the wealthiest men in the valley, and a church officer, could be guilty of sending a delicate girl, and that girl your own sister's child, into the fields such torrid weather as to-day has been? If she dies nothing can save you from arrest for manslaughter."

After this tirade the doctor, half ashamed that he had permitted his feelings to so far master him as to cause him to cast professional dignity aside even for a moment, went to work energetically to save his patient. She had been prostrated by the heat, but thanks to Dr. Weightman's skill and to her own robust constitution, she rallied and in a few days was well on the way to health again.

"She will now get along first-rate," said the doctor to Mr. Small, "but she must on no account be permitted to labor in the sun when the weather is warm. Another prostration would mean death."

"There it is again," said Mr. Small. "When you take your poor kinfolks an' try to do a good part by 'em, they've got to go an' get sunstruck, an' be no account. But never you mind, Miss Mary, you can help me all the more in the house. An' I will see if you play off sick next summer like you have this."

Melville, Mr. Small's eldest son, resided in Booneville, the county-seat, which was a few miles away. He came to see Mary, and urged his parents to permit her to visit with him and his wife awhile. "The change of scene and air will do you good, and Laura is anxious for you to come."

Sammy then set up a howl, saying they had promised to let him go home with Melville, but his father ordered him to hold his peace in such a determined tone of voice that he slunk out of the house and said to the other boys that he wondered "what had come over pa."

CHAPTER II.

"WHERE THERE'S A WILL THERE'S A WAY."

Mary did go to Booneville, and while Melville's home was plainly furnished it was so much better than she had been accustomed to that Mary felt she had come to a palace. Melville's wife possessed a small organ, and it was her delight to listen to its harmonious tones. But especially was she delighted that she could attend church and hear her pastor, Mr. Sharon, preach; for he devoted one-half his time to Dry Valley Church and the remainder to Booneville, where he also resided.

"Mary," said he to her one day, "I am sorry you cannot attend school, for you have talents which should be developed. However, I have a number of schoolbooks which I shall be pleased to loan you, if you think you can use them. I shall also be pleased to assist you in your studies all I am able."

"Thank you," said Mary, bashfully, "you are too kind. I wanted to learn to teach school, but couldn't do much because I didn't have no books. Now may be I can learn." Mr. Sharon selected such as he thought would be useful to her.

A Little Child.

There is no wonder half so great
As is a little child;
Of such as he God's kingdom is,
So sweet and undefiled;
He has an angel's ministry,
And none can serve the world as he.

The wonder of a little child!
A thing of charm and grace;
God dwells with him, and he with God,
He sees the Father's face.
To him the secrets are revealed
That are from coarser natures sealed.

The wonder of a little child!
He smiles, and none knows why.
Perhaps he hears the angels speak,
And whispers his reply,
Perhaps his clear, heaven-lifted eyes,
See through the gate of Paradise.

The wonder of a little child!
He stirs the founts of love;
Hard hearts grow kind at sight of him,
He bears men's thoughts above.
There is no trouble in the bliss
That lingers in a baby's kiss.

Christ called to him a little child,
And held him to his breast,
And set him in the midst of men,
To teach them of life's best;
Who are the great? they asked. Christ smiled,
And pointed to the little child.
—*Marianne Farningham, in London Christian World.*

Choosing a King.

J. H. WRIGHT.

Fratricidal blood had stained the hands of Abimelech in his efforts to become king. His only surviving brother, Jonathan, challenged the justice of the men of Shechem and Millo in their choice of Abimelech. From a safe eminence he told them how "the trees went forth on a time to anoint a king over them." Some desired the olive, Judea's greatest blessing; others the fig, Judea's luxury, and still others the vine, "which cheereth God and man." Failing in these better selections, "then said all the trees unto the bramble, Come thou and rule over us." The first nominations could not be made unanimous; the last was—but what a nomination! King Bramble chosen to rule over the Cedars of Lebanon! He was a compromise candidate, selected in indifference, contempt and derision.

Something like this is seen occasionally in the political world. Good men of any given party may seek nomination. Friends stand by them, bitterness is engendered, stubbornness follows and a compromise candidate, often obscure or even worthless is selected.

It is true in social life. A man or woman places the heart's deepest affection upon one worthy of its love, but through some slanderous word doubt poisons the mind, love languishes, estrangement follows and in reaction or desperation a union is formed with some unworthy one, "just to get even," or to keep up appearances. Many a woman who loves a man worthy to be likened to the Olive or Fig or Vine turns around and in a moment's pique accepts a Bramble! Blessed be celibacy if its alternative be King Bramble to rule over the heart of man or woman!

Men sometimes make a similar choice in business life. Starting out with eye fixed upon honorable success, disappointed in their expectations, despite education, despite entreaties of loved ones, they choose the bramble of a degraded life. Well do I recall from among the faces I used often to see upon visits to a great asylum, one that attracted my attention and compelled me to ask his history. I learned that at one time he stood at the head of the bar in a great city. By a sinful course he lost standing, grew morose and at last was confined among the insane. What must have been his feelings in lucid moments! Did he not regret that he had chosen King Bramble?

CHOOSING THE REGNANT PRINCIPLES OF LIFE.

1. *Each chooses his king.* Good and evil are placed before us. Right principles or wrong may be our choice. Some choose deliberately between the Olive and the Bramble. Comparatively few may at first select the latter. It may come by slow stages and be the result of indifference or carelessness. And yet it is a choice. A fire or life insurance policy may demand renewal to-morrow. It is not necessary to deliberately say, "I will not renew it." Neglect is its equivalent, and if your house burns the loss is yours, or if you die the loss is your family's. And so it mat ers little whether it be from deliberate choice or not. If King Bramble reign, he is king.

2. *He who chooses King Bramble must suffer.* Jonathan prophesied that fire would come from the Bramble (Abimelech) and consume the men of Shechem, and it did. And so is it inevitably with all who choose evil. Nor is its converse the less true. Blessings flow from right choice. Strange is it, when men know the law of sowing and reaping, that they should act with such great indifference or vainly hope that while sowing to the flesh they may reap life everlasting.

But why should this be true? Why may not men do just as they please and be free from penalty? This brings in the inexorable law of responsibility. Restraint must be felt. It is everywhere. You may see a little bird fluttering in its cage and you say, "Poor little bird, I'll set you free." You open its cage, perchance in some great auditorium, and it joyously flits here and there and chirps, "I'm free, free, free," but you know it is not. By and by you open a window and out it goes and you and it sing, "Free, free!" Free from what? "From the cage and the house," you say. It is no longer a prisoner, it's free!" But it soars aloft till with weary wing it returns to earth again. Free? Yes, but there are bounds it cannot pass. And so, in some sense, is man free. No little prison may hold him; he may exult in his liberty, but all around him there is a circumscribed line that bounds the mighty domain of Right. Within is liberty, beyond is restraint or penalty.

The child first feels this restraint in the home, and a father's or mother's "no" tells him there is a boundary line.

Later on, in the schoolroom, the teacher checks, restrains, and again the boundary line is pointed out.

On the street he grows noisy, disturbs others, interferes with sacred privileges, and is surprised to learn that he is passing the boundary line of legal right, when the law's guardian says, "Stop, or come with me!"

Or he looks with longing upon some evil until a friend whispers, "Remember God's 'Thou shalt not!'" Again he learns that he is not free from restraint.

But the best of all forms of restraint is self-restraint. Toward this all home training, all schooling, all religious instruction should tend. Lead each individual to say, "Restraint is needful for my soul and the good of my fellows. God's 'Thou shalt not' shall be mine. I will choose the right, wherein is freedom. I will reject the evil, wherein is pain. King Bramble shall not reign over me."

3. He who chooses King Bramble *allies himself with the side of evil.* When even a man deliberately chooses evil instead of good, the Bramble instead of the Olive, he steps to the left and some blear-eyed sinner approaching to give him the hand of fellowship may say, "And so *you* are one of us!" No need to stand aloof. Your pride and self-respect may keep you from close association with such, but *you are on his side.* The only way of escape is by penitent return. Don't serve King Bramble just to be consistent!

4. However grand a man's nature may

umble will
tic Amer-
eagle in a
resented
of Ameri-
it. Once
n, seek its
ntain side,
igh storm
country's
loosed its
ht. For a
eparing to
own to eat
p! So do
of King
rless, the
ay and he
ble being.
Bramble's

onesty in-
ble king.
metal in-
contract
over me!"
dignity of
evil in his
!" Every
by human
rings, who
ts of "so-
l prevails
g!" Every
popularity,
speaking
he may
dias who
head on a
Olive, Fig
ny king!"

r Bramble
far coun-
ce in riot-
g Bramble
te us gods
this Moses
him," and
typical of
s crowned,
and Jesus
eware lest

?

e Christ-
Then shall
Mammon

Aimless People.

One of the saddest signs of the times is the large number of young men, and old ones, too, in our villages and towns who have no special aim in life more than to attend to immediate bodily necessities or gratifications. My attention was called to this lately while on my way to prayer-meeting. The streets were lined with men sauntering lazily along, ready to take part in the gossip of the day. Practically all were smoking cigars or cob pipes, and spitting. One may be taken as a type of all. He throws his hat back far enough to show that he parts his hair like a girl, leans against a post, shuts his eyes, scowls, crosses his legs and arm, wags his cigar back and forth like a dog's tail and imagines he's thinking! Chairs are taken out of the groceries and stores, placed on the sidewalk and filled with men who ought at least to be at home allowing their families to share the money spent for tobacco; but instead of that they puff their cigars, break off the ashes with the little finger, spit, grunt, close the eyes, twist around in their chairs, and so spend the evenings.

If any sign of our times is appalling, it is the almost universal use of tobacco by men and boys, and its almost inevitable concomitant of wine. I charge tobacco with a train of evils peculiar to itself, but also as being the vestibule to strong drink. Shame on a man who will burn up five cents in a cigar, and yet will not let his wife fumigate the house every day with

'50s; but that now seems to be all changed

I would by no means decry the result achieved by the laboring classes durin what we may call "working hours;" bu what I mostly desire is to suggest som plan whereby their unemployed time ma be turned to better account than to loaf o the street and rehash the gossip of th town. Every workingman should inforr himself in the higher departments of hi trade by reading books written by th masters of that craft, whatever it may be How many journeyman carpenters in thi country have studied architecture as science? and how many of them have nc had the opportunity to do so? How man of them know of the wonderful capabilitie of the steel square, aside from measurin inches and feet? How many of them coul be hired to read "Hodgson on the Square? How many printers have ever studie punctuation in all or any of its branches s as to make a sentence clear? Every trad is blessed with a magnificent literature c its own, and yet what a large proportion c the men and boys who work at them ar satisfied to pay no attention to their wor after the whistle blows!

If it be suggested that we can not alway be occupied by our work, and that we mus change, I will say that it is just what want. Instead of the plain drudgery c work, seek the higher ranks by followin the thoughts of those who have becom eminent in that line. Change upward.

Free public lectures, illustrated, for th

With The Children.

CONDUCTED BY

J. BRECKENRIDGE ELLIS, PLATTSBURG, MO.

True Funny Stories.

Here are the stories sent me by members of the Advance Society, when I called for the funniest stories they had ever heard, which they knew to be true. They are a credit to the children who wrote them, and I do not doubt many will be copied into other papers. Of course it is easy to make up a funny story—much easier than to make anybody laugh at it; and many things which seem very funny to us, seem to lose all the juice when we go to write about them. As Lily Gooch, of Ashland, Ill., says, after telling about a boy who tried to drag a calf to water, using rather strong English while he did so—the boy used the English, and not the calf—"It don't sound very funny to write it, but it *was* funny to see and hear it!" The same is true of a boy told about by Clara Moses, of the same place, who cleaned the joints of a pigtail, strung them on a string, and would make them curl up as if a pig were in front of the tail. The funniest thing that ever happened to Burleigh Cash, of Pennville, Ind., was at his Halloween party, where a jack o' lantern and a baby were the hero and heroine of the evening. And the funniest thing Bonnie Bell Blakey, of Williams, Ia., ever saw was at "Uncle Tom's Cabin," when two men, dressed in funny clothes, marched up and down the stage, saying, "Zig-zum-zig-zum, January, February, *March!*" Stella Linton, of Wilson, Wis., tells about four-year-old Charlie, who said he believed in immersion, much to the regret of his kitten, which he was baptizing, and which doubtless would have preferred to belong to another kind of church. Albert Davis, of Jacksonville, Mo., tells of an Indian who went to an Idaho city to buy a buggy. As they were all sold he bought a hearse, put his wife in it, and went pulling it out of town himself; said that was good enough for *him!*

My little friend was given a quarter to put in the contribution box. On her return from church her mother said, "Daughter, did you put in that money?" "No ma'am." "Why not?" "The sermon wasn't worth a quarter," returned the little girl.—(Roberta Broadhurst, Louisville, Ky.)

When my papa was a little boy, he had a friend named George Tyler. They started to school for the first time; both sat together. When the teacher asked papa his name, he pointed to his little friend and said: "There's George Tyler—*he* can tell!" The next day when they reached the school-yard a long line of boys perched on the fence began to drawl, "There's George Tyler—*he* can tell!" And for years after, whenever papa asked a question the scholars would sing: "There's George Tyler—*he* can tell!"—(E. Witmer Pardee, Snyder, N. Y.)

Some one gave our neighbor's little son a New Testament for a prize. He began to read it through. One day he was asked how far he had read. His answer was: "I have got as far as two-eyed Peter." (II Peter.)—(Ella Harness, Exline, Ia.)

Two little boys wearing white hats, got on the train with their mother. When they reached their destination one of the hats was lost. Suddenly one of the boys exclaimed: "There it is, over there!" His mother did not see it, but she said: "Well, get it, then." Now, an old gentleman was asleep on one of the seats, with his bald-head resting on the edge. This is what the little boy had seen. He made a lunge and grabbed the old gentleman by the head while the passengers roared with laughter. The old gentleman started up, stared about him and got his head on the other end of the seat.—(Nora Cunningham, Cloverdale, Kan.)

Little Jamie thought he would be great like George Washington, and as he didn't have a hatchet he took the carving-knife and hacked a nice young cherry-tree. Then he said to his grandfather: "Grandpa, *I* did it." But his grandfather didn't think he had done anything to be proud of and threatened to whip him if he did so again. Jamie burst out crying and sobbed: "What for, didn't George Washington's papa spank him?"—(Breckenridge Wayne, Reynolds, Ill.)

A little girl seeing the moon when it was just about half full, said to her mamma: "Now, now, moon's boke; but," she added, "Dod'll fix it." Another time, as she and her mamma were walking in the yard in the springtime, she asked, "What kind of a cute 'ittle see (tree) is this, mamma?" Her mamma said, "It is a little pine tree." Then I said, for I was this little girl, "Oh, we can have pine pie, can't we?"—(Minnie B. Snyder, Milton, Ky.)

A five-year-old girl asked her mother, "How will we get up to heaven when we die?" "I expect we will fly up." "Will we have wings?" "I guess so." "Will we have fevvers?"—(Myrtle Blanchard, Barnard, Mo.)

One day a little girl named Lavinia, seeing a man whose hair was getting gray said: "O, look at that man, nothing on his head but snow!" Then as she looked closer, she added, "Awful dirty snow, though." Lavinia's playthings were always on the floor. One day her grandma tied strings around the dolls' necks and hung them up, telling the little girl it did not hurt them. Sometime after, the grandmother exclaimed, "Well, child, you are always in the way!" Lavinia went up to her and said, "Hang me up grandma; hang me up!" Lavinia came in from play one day and said: "I saw the most pillow-slip bugs out there!" Her cousin, wondering what she meant, went out in the yard with her and found several gray caterpillars.—(Jessie L. Butler, Roseville, Ill.)

So there you are—thirteen funny stories. The story that is funny to one, sometimes doesn't seem funny to another. So if any of these don't seem funny to you, laugh twice as hard over those that do, and thus all the stories will get through. Up to last Monday week (the time of sending this to press) 66 had joined the Advance Society. By the time you see this the number will be climbing higher. This means that our society has succeeded. I thank you who have helped me to see its success. It makes me very happy to know that so many children, from New York to California, are spending a little time every week in improving their minds, and thus preparing themselves to more thoroughly enjoy life. For no people are so happy as those who have learned to love the higher kind of literature. It is fun to make battenburg, and fun to go fishing, too. But all this is nothing to the pleasure to be gotten from a good book when the fire burns bright and it looks cold and desolate outside the window.

Now the person who only cares to read trashy stories and the daily papers are like people who only care to associate with ignorant and idle company. Since it is the duty of every boy and girl to make the very most of himself, and make all the powers of the mind and soul grow, it will never do to neglect history and poetry, since they are steps to a higher kind of life. A boy or girl who isn't going to read the right kind of books because play seems more fun all the time, might as well have a watermelon for a soul, planted in August; if you know anything about watermelons, you know if they are planted in August they will never get red inside as a watermelon should. It is all well enough to say you will read history and poetry when you are grown, but you won't do it unless you begin young. And the person who grows up disliking this kind of literature has a soul with something lacking. Now I want to have a soul with all the parts there, and I am glad you do. I hope you will tell your friends about this society and ask them to join, and explain the five resolutions. It does look as if I were going to preach a sermon, doesn't it? and after all those funny stories, too!

Next week we will have another chapter of our continued story, telling how George and Jenny Weston started an Advance Society in their town. The week after our page will be devoted to letters I have received from our members, telling their names, ages and what they do and what they like; it will be an old-fashioned chat between us, and will seem like a family gathering.

Sunday School.

JEREMIAH'S ROLL DESTROYED.*

HERBERT L. WILLETT.

The reformation wrought by Josiah, beginning with the discovery of the law book in 621 B. C. completely changed the current of affairs in Judea. The heathen party was thrown out of all ability to accomplish its purpose, and idolatry was banished from royal recognition. This condition continued to the close of the reign, increasing in extent as the king widened the sway of the true religion, and destroyed the centers and symbols of the false. But just as in the case of Amon, his father, death cut short his career and left the hopes of the ruling party in ruins. With the death of Amon came the downfall of heathenism, with that of Josiah came its restoration; and to the prophetic party the blow was all the more difficult to bear because the tragedy was needless. The king should have lived many years yet to round out a rich and fruitful life. In the year 609 Josiah was firmly established on his throne and had about completed his work of reformation. He was the vassel of Assyria, whose king, Esarhaddon II., the Sardonapolus of the earlier historians, was but a weak successor to the great kings of former years. Nevertheless, Josiah held fast to his allegiance in faithfulness, and when Necho, the king of Egypt, started for the north to dispute the world's empire with Assyria, Josiah, relying on God and feeling the obligation to oppose an enemy of his master, threw his little army across the path of the Pharaoh at Megiddo. But disaster ended the attempt; he lost his life, either in battle, or as seems more likely from the account, in a parley with the Egyptians into which he was entrapped. The grief and despair of the faithful may well be imagined. The corpse of the king was brought to Jerusalem amid great lamentation and buried in the royal sepulchres, and a day of mourning for annual observance was established in memory of the tragic and mysterious event (2 Chron. 35:24, 25). Josiah's attempt to stop the Pharaoh had been a sumpreme example of trust in God; and yet God had abandoned him to death. Was this the reward of all his zeal in behalf of the true religion? It is often a hard lesson to learn, that presumption is not faith. Josiah had plunged into needless danger, and his expectation of safety and victory was nothing less than tempting God. Safety is promised only to those who "dwell in the secret place of the most high," and the command is evermore, "Thou shalt not tempt the Lord thy God." The death of Josiah brought corresponding satisfaction to the heathen party. It seemed to prove that the divine displeasure rested on the career of the king. A great reaction came, and heathenism once more lifted its head as the official cult of the land.

Meanwhile Jehoahaz, a son of Josiah, had been placed on the throne by the people, but the king of Egypt was not pleased by this arrangement and after three months deposed him and placed on the throne Eliakim, another son of the late king, changing his name to Jehoiakim and imposing on the country a heavy fine. The unhappy Jehoahaz he carried to Egypt where he died. The reign of Jehoiakim perpetuated the supremacy of the heathen party. In him Mananseh seemed to live again. His reign of eleven years (609-597) exhibited all the worst featuers of a weak, capricious, headstrong and dissolute monarch. Twoyears afterhis coronation the fall ofNinevah changed the map of the world. The Assyrian dominion gave place to the Babylonian under Nabopolassar, whose great son, Nebuchadrezzar, became as great a terror in the west lands as Tiglath Pileser had been in the days of Isaiah. In 604 B. C. the Pharaoh made a supreme effort to assert his power, but the Babylonian army completely overthrew him, and from that time on Egypt gave up its dreams of empire (2 Kings 24:7). But even after Nebuchadnezzar had asserted his sovereignty over the land the foolish Jehoiakim rebelled against him and brought upon himself and his land the horrors of war, though he himself seems not to have suffered as did his successors.

During all this period Jeremiah had been at work as a prophet. He was the son of a certain Hilkiah of Anathoth, a priest village not far from Jerusalem. He was one of that little company of men who formed the nucleus of better things in the opening of Josiah's reign and co-operated with the king in his great reforms. His call to the prophetic ministry came in 626 B. C., when he was still quite young (Jer. 6:1-6), and his earliest preaching (chs. 1-6) was devoted to denunciations of the moral condition of Judea, and warnings of an enemy from the north who would bring destruction for the national disobedience. At this early date Jeremiah clearly foresaw the Babylonian invasion and the distress that would fall upon Jerusalem. Then came the discovery of the book and Jeremiah's mission to preach "this covenant" throughout Judah (11:1-8). But he found much difficulty in persuading men to to obedience, and chiefly in his own town of Anathoth, where his life was threatened (11:9-12:6). In spite of all dangers these must have been happy years, for the prophet and the high priest were in close sympathy with the king, and their work was sure to triumph in the end. But the king's tragic death broke short all these hopes and left the reformers without a protector. Jeremiah might well play the part of chief mourner at the royal funeral (2 Chron. 35:24). Idolatry came back like a flood and the prophet bowed his head in sorrow, or uttered his voice in indignant protest against the folly of the time (chs. 7, 10, 26). From 608 to 604 he preached against the odds of popular disfavor using a drought as a sign of G d's anger, or a potter and his work as examples of divine selection; while the prophet himself more than once felt the touch of persecution in scourging and imprisonment (chs. 14, 15, 18, 19, 20). In 604, the first year of Nebuchadrezzar and the fourth of Jehoiakim, he predicted the seventy years of captivity in Babylon (ch. 25), and taught a significant lesson from the steadfastness of the temperate Rechabites (ch. 35). The battle of Carchemish, which occured a few months later, was described, together with the woes that should fall upon Egypt (ch. 46) and the other western nations through the Babylonian power (47-49). This point had been reached in the work of the prophet at the date of our lesson in 603 B. C.

It may be easily understood how difficult was the position of Jeremiah during the reign of such men as Jehoahaz and Jehoiakim. The death of Josiah left him to fight alone. Those who held fast to the true religion were probably numerous, but they could not contend against the royal will. Under such conditions the utterances of the prophet were in danger of being lost. He was accordingly directed to gather into a roll or book the substance of his preaching hitherto given. Baruch, his faithful servant, was set at the task and Jeremiah dictated to him the important utterances of the past years. It was unsafe for the prophet to show himself at the court or even in Jerusalem. He accordingly directed Baruch to stand in the temple corridors where the people assembled and read to them its contents. Not long after the celebration of a fast in December of the year 603 B. C. brought a great throng to Jerusalem, and Baruch seized the moment as favorable for the public reading of the roll. This brought it to the notice of some of the court officers favorably disposed to the faith, and they secured a special reading of the book by Baruch at the palace. The men who listened were terrified by the tidings and anxiously asked Baruch how the roll came into existence. When he told them Jeremiah had dictated it, they agreed, not without fear of the result, to bring the matter to the king's attention. The warnings of the roll should certainly be understood by Jehoiakim. But they knew his violent temper and cautioned Baruch to take care of himself and the prophet.

When the matter was told to the king he ordered the book to be read before him. Curiosity may have carried him so far. But when a few pages had been read and he understood their purport, he angrily drew his knife and slashed the parchments into fragments, casting them on the fire by which the hall was warmed during the rainy winter season. The reckless courtiers only laughed at the king's mad act, though the more serious had trembled at the reading by Baruch. Thus Jehoiakim thought to dispose of the prophet. He could not find the man; he could only destroy his roll. But not so do the messages of God fall to the ground. Another roll, in which all these utterances and many more were set down, was prepared by Baruch—a book which was probably the original of all the earlier portion of our book of Jeremiah.

Thus, as always, the effort to destroy the Divine Word was thwarted. Persecution, suppression, ridicule, rationalism have all been used in the assult on the Bible, but without avail. Men pass away, but it abides, for "all flesh is as grass, and all the goodness thereof is as a flower of the field. The grass withers, the flower fades; but the Word of our God shall stand forever."

SUGGESTIONS FOR TEACHING.

Even in a wicked court or city there are usually some good people who try to make conditions better. The king would not even listen to the words of the prophet; a few pages alone would he hear; so do many to-day refuse even to hear what might bring them life. The knife and the fire are the symbols of all those means by which men have tried to destroy God's Word. Bad companions always encourage one to sin against self and God. It is a noble thing to protest against evil, even if it seems to be without avail. Even if the king had found Jeremiah and killed him, the prophet would have been far better off than the wicked king. If one good thing is destroyed, others spring up in its place; it cannot perish. Men never escape the results of sin by denying them, or trying to destroy them. Whether the prophecy of Jeremiah against Jehoiakim was fulfilled in exact terms we are not told, but his state of soul was itself the most awful that could befall him. God's Word is destined to prevail and fill the earth.

Anhaltstrass 15, Berlin.

*Sunday-school lesson for Dec. 11, 1898—Trying to Destroy God's Word (Jer. 36:20-32). Golden Text—The Word of our God shall stand forever (Isa. 40:8). Lesson Outline—1. The roll destroyed (20-23): 2. The impious and the faithful (24-26); 3. The new roll (27-32).

Christian Endeavor.

By Burris A. Jenkins.

TOPIC FOR DEC. 11.

THE MINOR VIRTUES AND THEIR IMPORTANCE.

(Phil. 3:12-14; 4, 8; Matt. 5:48.)

It is difficult to say what virtues are minor and what are most important—quite as difficult as it is to say what sins are big and what are little. If the virtues spoken of by Paul in the Philippian letter may be considered minor, they are certainly nevertheless of vast importance. Let us consider them in their order.

Whatsoever things are true. He means true, not in the narrow sense of veracity, merely, but in the larger sense of the word. Men may not tell lies and still not be true, steadfast, firm; but he who is true in the wide sense of that term may be counted upon in all relationships of life and never vary. He is the same towards all and at all times; he is sincere, honest and upright; he is like the sun that shines with an unwavering light, like the stream that flows with an unchanging current, like the great balancewheel that revolves unswerving upon its axis.

Whatsoever things are honorable; reverend, the Greek word means. Things worthy of reverence; and alas, how lacking our average American is in this regard. "He flouts the law he makes, and makes the law he flouts." Sometimes he reveres neither God nor man; he sits in the house of God before the services begin—he or she—chattering like a magpie, moving about, shaking hands instead of reverencing a holy place and a holy time and preparing for the service of God.

"Whatsoever things are just." This word, too, is used in its larger sense of *righteousness*. Mere justice is not always a virtue; we may "miss the law of kindness, when we struggle to be just." Paul was not simply just, he was more; Jesus was not merely just, he was righteous and merciful; teaching all men (both Paul and Jesus), that righteousness was the aim of life.

Whatsoever things are pure, in the larger sense of stainless, not simply chaste. Purity of thought, purity of purpose, purity of motive, purity in business, purity in ambition, purity in church life, purity in all relationships and in all work, Paul means. We have narrowed the term too much. Christ said, "The pure in heart shall see God;" he meant those upon whose hearts no breath of tainted selfishness had fallen like a blurring mist, to hinder the vision of God which descends like light from above. Unselfish motives and deeds of every kind must be included under the name of purity.

Whatsoever things are lovely; that is, aimable, worthy of love, all those unnameable little deeds of kindness, of courtesy, of helpfulness which are wafted out from some lives like perfume from flowers. It is these of which the courteous and kindly apostle was thinking. Amiability may sometimes degenerate into insipidity, but it then becomes unlovely, it is no longer lovely. But when one thinks of the character of the amiable Master, with his kindliness, courtesy, strength and firmness, one realizes what was meant concerning him when he was called "The Lily of the Valley," "The Rose of Sharon," "The Chiefest of Ten Thousand," "The One Altogether Lovely." Renan calls him the "charming Rabbi."

Whatsoever things are of good report. Not "well spoken," "well reputed," but in the sense of fair speaking, winning and attractive. This word has very much the sense of the preceding one, lovely. There is not a strong distinction, but the thought of fair speaking is in itself a very attractive idea, one who always speaks well of every one, whose reports are good reports wherever it is possible to make them good, is surely a winning character.

Upon these six things, says Paul, we should think. It is on the very thoughts of these virtues that he lays emphasis. Virtue or vice may be a thing even of the thoughts.

BETHANY C. E. READING COURSES.

[There are three courses: The Bible, Missions and the Disciples. The three handbooks for the *first* year are: "A Guide to Bible Study," "Handbook of Missions" and "Concerning the Disciples." The three handbooks for the *second* year are: "Life and Teachings of Jesus," "Missionary Fields and Forces of the Disciples" and "Sketches of our Pioneers." Three handbooks and the Bethany C. E. Bulletin, quarterly, sent to any address for one dollar. All orders should be addressed to the Bethany C. E. Company, 798 Republic St., Cleveland, O. Each course has a director: H. L. Willett is director of Bible study; W. J. Lhamon is the director of studies in Missions; F. D Power is director of studies Concerning the Disciples. This column is set apart to the use of these directors.]

Reading the Bible by Books.

J. Z. TYLER.

The Bible is a unique library, composed of sixty-six unique booklets. These booklets were written centuries apart. They include law, history, poetry, proverbial philosophy, biography, prophecy and psalmody—almost every variety of literature. They were written by different men, at different times, under different specific purposes. And yet they are all bound together by such inward unity as to constitute one great book. It is not a mere aggregation of booklets, but a common spirit animates them all; great and growing common thoughts bind them together into a harmonious whole. These books came together, not through some human and external authority, but by an inward and spiritual affinity.

One of the best ways of studying the Bible is to take one of these booklets at a time. This is the plan pursued in our handbook prepared by President McGarvey and used during the first year of Bible study of our Bethany C. E. Reading Courses. After a few brief definitions, a brief general outline of the Old Testament and a brief sketch of the original text and its preservation, our handbook proceeds to consider each of the sixty-six booklets of the entire Bible. In each case the general characteristics and contents of the book are briefly but very clearly indicated. The historical thread running through the entire narrative is always kept in view. This handbook is not meant to be used as a substitute but, as its title indicates, it is to be used as "a guide to Bible study." The Bible itself is the object of our study and we make our first tour through the Bible, taking a book at a time.

Of course, it is impossible to make a critical study of these books. The purpose is to form an accurate acquaintance with them, to become somewhat familiar with the general scope and contents of each book, the main divisions of this divine literature and to gain a good bird's-eye view of the entire Bible. The study of special parts, of important persons, of fundamental doctrines, may be taken up later. Our first need is the need of an accurate general knowledge of the entire volume from Genesis to Revelation, and this we undertake to gain in our first year's study by rapic running over the entire sixty-six books, taki one at a time.

There are certain advantages in this metho First of all, it is the natural method. T Bible came into being by the production o book at a time, and each book still retains i own individuality. If we are, therefore, have an accurate understanding of the Bil just as it is, if we are to know what it clai for itself, we should pursue this natural meth of investigation. In the next place, it is t most interesting method. It makes the mc direct appeal to our intelligence, aiding very much in a rational understanding of t entire collection. No other book is treated such an irrational manner as is the Bible the average reader. To read it by chapte to dip in at one place to-day and another pla to-morrow, to read brief sections here a there without regard to the persons who wro them, the circumstances under which th were written, the purposes for which the were written, or the period in which they we written, is to misread the Bible. In all ou study of the Holy Scriptures we should neve forget that "God, having of old time spoke unto the fathers in the prophets by dive portions and in divers manners, hath at th end of these days spoken unto us in his Son' (Heb. 1:1).

This method of study enables us the better t apprehend the progress of revelation, and t understand that all portions are not of just th same worth to-day. The Bible is the record c a growing revelation that culminated in th gospel of Christ. Its progress is marked b larger, truer, higher ideas of God. In its re quirements it moves from the outward to th inward, from external restraints to inwar principles, from law to love. Its progres rises from the temporal to the eternal, fro the earthly to the heavenly. Its progress i broadly marked by three dispensations whic are generally designated as the Patriarchal the Jewish and the Christian. While thes three dispensations have fundamental principle in common, while each are divinely given, it i of great importance that we mark thei boundaries in our study of the Bible. Th failure to do this is the source of much con fusion. The Patriarchal dispensation, speak ing broadly, covers the entire period from th beginning down to Moses; the Jewish embrace the entire period from Moses to Christ; th Christian dispensation began with the corona tion of Christ and continues to the end c time. Its message is a message to all men All that went before was preparatory; this i final. The gospel is complete in itself. It ha its own Lawgiver, its Priesthood, its Mediator It establishes the long-promised kingdom on new foundation, with new subjects, new term of membership, a new name, a new life, a nev destiny.

These are some of the general features to b noted as we pass the sixty-six booklets of th Bible in rapid review.

Obituaries.

STACY.

S. S. Stacy was born at Cherry Hill, Pa., June 11, 1846. In childhood his parents moved to Northern Ohio, where he was married at Geneva, Nov. 13, 1867, to Miss Mary L. Brown. He was baptized by R. G. White in September, 1869, and united with the Church of Christ at Geneva. In the spring of 1870 he moved to Nebraska, which he made his home until the fall of 1894, when failing health led him to seek the warmer climate of Arizona, where he died on the second day of March, 1898, at his home near Phœnix. Bro. Stacy was a man of high ideals. In business life his conscience was tender beyond all customs usually considered just. In his dealings with men he let no matter rest until satisfied that he had obeyed the precepts embodied in the Golden Rule. Without regard to what some would have us believe he proved that honesty and at least a fair degree of prosperity can go hand in hand, and was ever found zealous in business, "fervent in spirit, serving the Lord." To him principle was the first consideration, and questions of policy seemed wholly outside his thought or care. While he had early received religious instruction, yet when he came to Nebraska our plea and actual church life and work were still new to him; but in a recently organized church, which he found at Bower, he had ample opportunities for work and development, into which he entered with devotion and faithfulness. Though still young, he was ere long chosen their deacon. To this trust he was most constant, and as this quality, as well as his foresight and judgment, became apparent to the little band he was in a few years chosen their sole elder. Now, more than before, the interests of the church became his interests; and his first thought and the main theme of his conversation was how to best advance the cause of Christ. Whether the distance to church was four miles; as for some time, or two miles, as at a later period, he was always at his post in attendance to duty. His *business* was to serve his Father, his secondary care to provide for earthly sustenance. In the latter duty he was ever industrious and careful. Using his earthly goods, however, rather as a trust than a possession, he did not tithe his giving; he could not stop with a tenth. Under his care and oversight, and of one who was later chosen to work with him, the attendance at services was increased from about 20 to over 100. A church and later a parsonage was built. Thus 15 years were passed, but death claimed some of the tried and older members and new men and methods displaced the workers of other years. Poor health now caused him to seek as a home a new location, which resulted in the selection of a farm six miles from Phœnix, Arizona. To this he with his family moved in September, 1894. Here, in spite of physical disadvantage his energy did not wane. Where little grew he left a green field of 160 acres, with trees of his own planting, now large and beautiful. Here, as elsewhere, he seemed needed, and though still a stranger confidence was at once reposed in him, and he was pressed into service for the public good. Soon selected as one of the school officers, he collected nearly all the money paid at the time of his death. A new schoolhouse was erected with extra room for church services. This was the last public work in which he served. Death came to him suddenly, almost instantly. As he was walking with his son in the road near his home he was taken with hemorrhage of the lungs, and only lived to call his son by name. The news came as a shock to the community as well as to his friends elsewhere. School was at once dismissed, and did not resume its sessions until the last respects had been paid. The funeral services were held from the home and were conducted by Bro. Cal Ogburn, of Phœnix. The Scripture lesson was read from 1 Cor. 15:46 57, and Rev. 21:1-7, and on the 3rd of March all that was mortal of Bro. Stacy was laid to rest. He leaves a wife, a son and daughter to mourn his absence, to miss the thoughtful love and care which had so long been theirs. Two small children have preceded him. The above tardy tribute gives but a brief outline of his life and services. Those who best knew him can in remembrance supply much of what is missing. Though the friendship and counsel of other years will be missed, we are still grateful for the pleasant memory, for the life, though not always understood, yet whose influence for integrity and faithfulness combined with charity can never be lost.

G.

Symposium on Our National Conventions.

The following additional contributions to our open parliament on our National Conventions have been received:

1. I would suggest that our conventions could be greatly improved by increasing the number of committees, and thus considering more carefully the reports of our boards and discussing more fully all questions pertaining to the interests of our missionary work. Instead of a half dozen committees with perhaps five persons to each committee, thirty or thirty-five delegates out of 500 or 1,000, there should be ten or twenty with from seven to fifteen members, enlisting a hundred or more delegates directly in the work of the conventions and subjecting every matter of importance to the most careful consideration on the part of our most thoughtful men and women. Our conventions are altogether overrun with speech-making. We must give more time to business. This can be done by distributing the work among wise committees and using the time now occupied with big speeches, symposiums, etc., for the discussion of committee reports. This will insure also a more regular attendance on the part of delegates because of their personal interest in the proceedings and a more enthusiastic support of all measures on their return to their home fields, for they can say in the words of Virgil, "I was a part of these things."

2. This suggestion applies to the Jubilee Conventions. Let us enlist the business men and the young people, the educational men, the pioneers, the literary folks, the musical element, the Sunday-school experts, those specially interested in charities and social settlement, the evangelists, the editors, all the different classes among us in features of the work which have special claims upon them. Let us give particular attention to our weak points. Let us have a just consideration of all our interests. Let us make special effort to enlist our brethren who are not in full sympathy with our missionary societies. Let us have a great big, brotherly thanksgiving feast and get all the family together and make them all happy and united in our glorious cause.

F. D. POWER.

Washington, D. C., Nov. 19, 1898.

The first question is that of our capacity to receive. Because Bellflower apples are superior in quality one should not be expected to eat a bushel in one day, nor to consume a barrel of allwheat flour in a week for the reason that that is the most nutritious food. The C. W. B. M. and the Foreign Society get through their work very well. The problem is to equitably set forth and adjust, in two and a half days of seven and nine sessions, all the interests represented by the Home Society. Every interest, including the Evangelistic, Church Extension, Negroes, Education, Christian Endeavor, Ministerial Relief, Sunday-school and Statistics, is entitled to time enough for the submission of the report and *one* formal address. All of these, except the general address, like that of George Darsie at Chattanooga, should be rigidly kept within thirty minutes' limit, some of them less than a half hour. If the special advocates of education, or Endeavor or any other interest, wish more time let him find it in separate or sectional conferences. To give an entire afternoon to Christian Endeavor is out of all proportion. The evangelistic work of the Home Society is entitled to the hearing of the whole convention. If different fields need emphasis that may be arranged for pending the motion for the adoption of report of committees on those fields.

N. S. HAYNES.

Eureka, Ill.

---

1. I would make the program so that each convention should have at least one meeting before the Lord's day. As it appears now the different conventions, C. W. B. M., Home and Foreign, have in some measure a different constituency and class of attendants. It should be so that all who attend the conventions would attend with equal interest all sessions. The evenings should be given to gospel sermons, at least a portion of them, for many attendants would like after a day of business a strong and helpful sermon at night.

2. An address on the convention of '49 should be made with a brief sketch of the leading characters of that time; in fact, of all of them as far as known. It might not be practical to deliver the whole address, but it could be printed.

D. R. LUCAS.

Indianapolis, Ind., Nov. 21.

I am very much in favor of the course advocated by Bro. G. A. Hoffmann, of Columbia, Mo., in reference to conducting our Jubilee Convention next year. Our two missionary societies should be in charge of the same head, and all moneys donated for missionary purposes should be equally divided, only when the donor specially requests it for one or the other. And the Ministerial Relief could be in the same hands and a part of the missionary funds appropriated to relief in that way. All funds that I should contribute I would be willing for an honest board to divide as they thought best for the interest of the *cause*.

F. M. GWALTNEY.

Prairie View, Ark, Nov.

Publishers' Notes.

"KING SAUL," by J. Brechenridge Ellis, is fresh from the press and contains a story that will be read with deep iuterest. It is a vivid recital of the history of the first king of Israel. The author begins his story by relating the marvelous manner in which Saul became the king of Israel, and the transition from the government by judges to that of kings. The wars, the appearance of David, the danger to the kingdom, the warnings of Samuel, Saul's debt to David for his life, the meeting with the witch at Endor and the battle of Gilboa are dramatically unfolded, and so interesting is the narrative that to begin a reading is to finish it.—*Octographic Revivw, Indianapolis, Ind.*

THE CHRISTIAN LESSON COMMENTARY for 1899, by W. W. Dowling, is not a whit behind its predecessors in the ability displayed in its preparation and in the clearness of its analysis of the lessons for this year. It is fitting volume to close the Sunday-school work of the century. Wonderful improvements have been made in Sunday school helps since the adoption of the uniform lessons in 1873. I am glad I was a delegate in that great and important convention, and had a little to do in starting the work, and since then in helping it along. The Christian Publishing Company has been fortunate in having men like B. W. Johnson and W. W. Dowling to superintend their Sunday-school publications. Their work has always been well done and in some respects superior to any other. The Commentary for 1899 is a valuable addition to the splendid series.

F. M. GREEN.

Kent, O.

THE CHRISTIAN LESSON COMMENTARY for 1899, edited by Rev. W. W. Dowling, is a beautifully bound and richly illustrated volume of over 400 pages. No Lesson Help fully and satisfactorily illustrates the lessons of the International series. In our preparation of the quarterlies no commentary gives us more satisfactory if equal aid. If the teacher wishes *best help* in his work, he will find it in Dowling's Commentary. Every teacher, where possible, should have a complete help in addition to his own church notes. We would be glad to see the *Christian Lesson Commentary* in the hands of all our teachers. With its aid we can hardly see how further help would be necessary on the line of commentary matter.—*Herald of Gospel Liberty, Dayton, O.*

The starry heavens are not more beautiful than on a clear, cold winter night. It is th that they seem to twinkle with more brillian and call forth the admiration of mankind. O late publication, "Wonders of the Sky, God's Glory Exhibited in the Heavens," W. J. Russell, is a beautiful little book, poin ing to the isles of light spread out on high, a then beyond to the Creator of all. The bo is bound in beautiful illuminated cloth, and t price is 50 cents, postpaid.

A CHRISTMAS PRESENT.

A very appropriate gift at Christmas times a good book. It is something enduring, and which the recipient can go for years wi pleasure and profit, and will be the means keeping the donor fresh in the mind of t party receiving such presents. Among o large list of publications may be found appr priate presents for ministers, Sunday-scho superintendents and teachers, officers a members of Endeavor Societies, and for ge eral use in the family circle. Write us for c catalogue and make your selections before t holiday rush.

IE

IAN-EVANGELIST

LY FAMILY AND RELIGIOUS JOURNAL.

December 8, 1898 No. 4

07
08
09
10
10
11
12
12
13
15
18
19
20
20
21
23
23
23
28
28
30
30
30
31
15
16
17
24
26
27
32
33
34
34
35
36
36
36

DR. W. K. PENDLETON.

PUBLISHED BY

AN PUBLISHING COMPANY

1522 Locust St., St. Louis.

THE

CHRISTIAN - EVANGELIST

J. H. GARRISON, EDITOR.

W. W. HOPKINS, ASSISTANT.

B. B. TYLER, J. J. HALEY,
EDITORIAL CONTRIBUTORS.

What We Plead For.

The Christian-Evangelist pleads for:

The Christianity of the New Testament, taught by Christ and his Apostles, versus the theology of the creeds taught by fallible men—the world's great need.

The divine confession of faith on which Christ built his church, versus human confessions of faith on which men have split the church.

The unity of Christ's disciples, for which he so fervently prayed, versus the divisions in Christ's body, which his apostles strongly condemned.

The abandonment of sectarian names and practices, based on human authority, for the common family name and the common faith, based on divine authority, versus the abandonment of scriptural names and usages for partisan ends.

The hearty co-operation of Christians in efforts of world-wide beneficence and evangelization, versus petty jealousies and strifes in the struggle for denominational pre-eminence.

The fidelity to truth which secures the approval of God, versus conformity to custom to gain the favor of men.

The protection of the home and the destruction of the saloon, versus the protection of the saloon and the destruction of the home.

For the right against the wrong;
For the weak against the strong;
For the poor who've waited long
For the brighter age to be.
For the truth, 'gainst superstition,
For the faith, against tradition,
For the hope, whose glad fruition
Our waiting eyes shall see.

RATES OF SUBSCRIPTION.

Single subscriptions, new or old	$1.50 each
Ministers	1.00 "

All subscriptions payable in advance. Label shows the month up to the first day of which your subscription is paid. If an earlier date than the present is shown, you are in arrears. No paper discontinued without express orders to that effect. Arrears should be paid when discontinuance is ordered.

In ordering a change of post office, please give the OLD as well as the NEW address.

Do not send local check, but use Post office or Express Money Order, or draft on St. Louis, Chicago or New York, in remitting.

ADDRESS, CHRISTIAN PUBLISHING CO.,
1522 Locust St., St. Louis, Mo.

CHRISTIAN-EVANGELI

n faith, Unity; in opinion and methods, Liberty; in all things, Charity."

St. Louis, Mo., Thursday, December 8, 1898.

EVENTS.

of the Secretary of
ıe Secretary of the
ıd importance as an
the history of 1898.
rt is a chronological
.ere is, of course, no
y of the administra-
of the department,
ı narrative presents a
tisfactorily managed
ssful issue.

ısent circumstances,
ın present a report
th the war or its re-
Agriculture, in his
ıpace to the consid-
ıroblems introduced
y the policy of ex-
pointed out that the
acquired possessions
ricultural, so far as
agriculture, at least,
prosperity depend.
ıate and other con-
are so various and
of the United States
oroughly studied at
ecommends to Con-
to defray the expense
scientific investiga-
resources and needs
ıo (Cuba), and the

ıe head of a commis-
Cuban Assembly,
eks ago, is now in
The purpose of the
t the President and
rom the standpoint
s, telling him what
United States and
are entitled to. Gen.
mself, both privately
nts for publication,
the freedom of the
.ny desire to annex
ates. He says that
to send a large army
a as the Spaniards
ı recognize the au-

A history of the operations at Santiago written by Admirable Sampson would be one story, and a history of those same operations written by General Shafter would be another. There would be some notable differences between the two. General Shafter believes that he is placed in a very bad light by Admiral Sampson's report and his official dispatches which have been published—and undoubtedly he is, but, since he confines his refutation chiefly to a denunciation of the whole account as "colored," there is little chance for independent judgment of the merits of the case. At the same time the testimonies which continue to come in to the Investigating Commission tend to confirm the belief that the land campaign was managed in a haphazard, impromptu, harum-scarum fashion which scarcely deserves the name of management at all. If this be true, then the victory only proves that there was worse mismanagement on the other side, or that the courage of the men atoned for all other defects. Col. Roosevelt's testimony was particularly interesting and vivid. He makes no complaints, but describes a condition of affairs in which food, medicine and other necessary supplies were obtained only by those who "rustled" for them. It happens that Col. Roosevelt's "rustling" faculty is highly developed, and consequently the Rough Riders had things which some other regiments lacked, which did not happen to be blessed with "rustling" colonels. However, as we have before suggested, General Shafter's own reports contain a sufficient array of facts which need to be explained, without going in search of more, and we hope, now that the election is over and all fear of political complications is or ought to be passed, the commission will proceed to come to the point.

The confederacy of Central American states, calling itself the Greater Republic of Central America, has collapsed, as is the custom of such confederacies. It was never more than the feeble embodiment of a yet feebler scheme, but it was hoped that it would add some stability to Central American politics. It now appears that the confederacy was, more than anything else, a

Salvador from the confedera
may have some bearing upon
Canal project. The present
the construction of the can
by the Nicaraguan Governm
feared that the Diet of the c
provokingly intractable bod
hand and hinder the renew
ing concessions. This was
in favor of returning to the
The downfall of the Great
Central America, if it has
improve the prospects for t
of the Nicaraguan Canal.

On December 2, Francis J
of Austria, and King of Hu
ted the fiftieth anniversary
to the throne of the dual
was no jubilee, and the cele
most entirely of a religious s
of the recent assassination o
All political prisoners were
many military and cival p
granted and decorations cc
object which the Emperor
in the administration of his
the more complete indicati
halves of his empire, Austri
The conclusion of a financia
cial agreement between then
fore the anniversary, was a
to the Emperor and, accord
statement, the most acce
could receive. There was m
on both sides, and the passa
ure was due chiefly to the
sonal desire for it. It is a
the loyalty and sympathetic
of his divided empire, now
reason both of its loyalty
this measure in which it
loyalty.

There are a dozen points
might break out in the
really surprising any one,
more than that many concei
for friction leading to wa
powers in the East. It is repo
is landing troops in Korea
sian aggression there, and

Since a pacific adjustment of Anglo-French relations on the Nile seeme assured, it is natural to turn to China to find a possible explanation of Great Britain's unusual preparations for war. There are some facts which lend color to the hypothesis that England is expecting a clash with France in the Yangtse valley. The outrages against foreigners in many parts of China during the past few weeks, since the party of reaction came into power, have called forth a chorus of diplomatic protests and demands for reparation. Taking occasion of this general situation, and of a case of violence offered to certain Frenchmen in the Yangtse district, France has been trying to extort from the Viceroy at Nanking, as indemnity for this outrage, a territorial concession near the mouth of the Yangtse river. This, however, is England's sphere of influence, and she has already begun to assume an attitude of defense to prevent its invasion by the French. The case has points of similarity to the situation in Egypt, and probably Great Britain would be as willing to fight to maintain her position on the Yangtse as on the Nile.

The President's annual message, read at the opening of the Fifty-fifth Congress on last Monday, only a synopsis of which we have seen at this writing, congratulates the country on the successful administration of its finances, the degree of business prosperity which prevails, and then turns to the war with Spain, which it briefly reviews. It congratulates the nation upon the successful prosecution of the war and its speedy termination. After mentioning by name some of the heroes of the war and some of the leading battles, he bears testimony to "the patriotism and devotion of the large portion of our army which, although eager to be ordered to posts of greatest exposure, fortunately was not requred outside the United States. They did their whole duty, and have earned the gratitude of the nation." The work of the Red Cross is gratefully acknowledged. Concerning issues which have grown out of the war, the President says that it would be inappropriate for him to discuss them until after the peace treaty is ratified. "In the meantime, and until Congress has legislated otherwise, it will be my duty to continue the military governments which have existed since our occupation, and give to the people and property protection and encouragement under a just and beneficent rule." Concerning Cuba he adds: "As soon as we are in possession of Cuba, and have pacified the island, it will be necessary to give aid and direction to its people to form a government for themselves." The message closes with recommending an appropriation for the centennial anniversary of the founding of the City of Washington, suggests an amendment to the alien contract law, "the rightful application of the eight-hour law for the benefit of labor and of the principle of arbitration," as matters needing the attention of Congress.

While Spain's acceptance of our demands in regard to the Philippines disposes of the most critical item in the peace negotiations, the final signature of a treaty of peace may be less imminent than was supposed a few days ago. There are many minor matters yet to be disposed of, such as the acquisition of one of the Carolines, and the guarantee of religious liberty to the entire group. Upon these points, not mentioned in the proctocol, we cannot make demands, but must proceed by more conciliatory and tedious processes. The plan of leaving these matters unsettled in the treaty, covering them only by a clause providing for another joint commission to discuss them, has the advantage of hastening the agreement upon the treaty, but the disadvantage of delaying the settlement of these particular points. It is feared by some, who wish for the contrary, that the treaty embodying this article in regard to the Philippines may not be able to command the two-thirds vote of the Senate necessary for ratification. In that case it can be held over until March 3, when the increase of Republican strength in the Senate would insure its ratification at a special session. Our offer of $20,000,000 for the Philippines has not met with great favor. Abroad it is not understood. Some think it a niggardly price to pay for the islands; others approve of our expansion, but consider it a piece of freakish and foolish generosity to have offered so much where so little was expected. The Spanish have accepted it ungraciously. The anti-expansionists at home oppose the expenditure of such a sum of good gold for a possession which may be of more harm than help to us. It is approved only by those who believe that we ought to have the Philippines, and that we have a right to them, and who understand that the twenty millions is not a purchase price, but a generous reimbursement of Spain for her expenditures for the improvement of the island.

The Tribune of Chicago has been securing an expression of sentiment from the senators as to their attitude on the subject of the ratification of the treaty with Spain on the conditions which it is understood have been agreed upon. A great majority of those expressing themselves declare in favor of ratification. Some decline to express an opinion until they see the treaty. Others express their decided opposition to what they call "annexation" or "imperialism." Some of the senators forget that the treaty with Spain decides nothing as to the future of the Philippines, except that they are not to be under Spain's dominion. The whole problem of their future disposition is one that is left to Congress to decide. The assumption on the part of some politicians, that the President has decided to make the Philippine Islands a part of the United States and its people amenable to our form of government, is without foundation. The condition in reference to the "Open Door" is wholly inconsistent with that view. They will, no doubt, be put under military government until such time as the people are capable of governing themselves. There is no departure from the fundamental principles of our government in such a policy.

Aguinaldo, the Philippine insurgent leader, it is reported on good authority, has renounced the Roman Catholic religion in an open proclamation to his followers and has espoused the cause of Protestantism. It is not improbable that this fact will have considerable influence in modifying the religious condition of these islands. It is not likely that any permanent improvement can come to the Philippines until there is a greater degree of religious as well as political enlightenment.

A DIVINE MISSION—WHAT?

V.—SIMPLICITY.

We use the term "simplicity" accordin
to its strict meaning, as indicating the con
dition of being unmixed or uncompounded
also freedom from excessive formality o
ostentation; also as indicating freedor
from abstruseness or subtlety; that is
clearness, intelligibility. The tendency o
religion to become overgrown or overlai
with elaborate ritual, with abstruse sub
tleties and gross superstitions is known t
every student of history. Another tendenc
which runs alongside of this is that c
multiplying ecclesiastical offices and creat
ing a hierarchy with rank above rank
culminating in ecclesiastical tyranny.

In saying, therefore, that the fathers wh
inaugurated this movement felt calle
upon, in view of the condition of th
religious world and of the plain teachin
of Scripture, to plead for the simplicity o
the gospel, we mean that they set them
selves to the task of freeing the gospe
from whatever accretions had gathere
about it, and the Church from those un
authorized additions to its officers an
their official prerogatives which were i
conflict with the freedom of individua
churches. This has always been a difficul
undertaking. Those who attack venerabl
errors and hoary superstitions which hav
been associated with religion are ofte
regarded as attacking religion itself, and
their efforts at reformation are regarded a
little less than sacrilegious, while th
effort to simplify Church organizations
and restore the essential equality tha
should prevail in the Church of God, i
sure to be fiercely resented by those wh
feel that their vested rights and thei
official prerogatives have been assailed
But reformers, who are called of God fo
their work and animated by His Spirit, d
not pause to take counsel of their fears o
to calculate the chances of success agains
powerful opposition, but proceed at once t
do the work to which God has called them
eaving the results with Him.

The whole process of conversion or New
Testament evangelism had become s
obscured and mystified by subtle definition
and false theories, which antagonized th
plain teaching of Scripture and the laws o
the human mind, that sincere, earnes
people, anxious to be Christians, were kep
in doubt and mental anxiety for year
because they could not find the way o
salvation. It would be impossible t
enumerate in the space at our command al
the particulars in which the once plain way
of salvation had become obscured by
human traditions. Among these, however
was the doctrine of "total hereditary
depravity," which was defined to mear
that man was so under the bondage o
original sin, and so utterly corrupt in his
whole nature, that he was wholly unabl
to think a worthy thought, or to perform a
worthy deed, or to do anything in th
direction of his own salvation until he wa
miraculously converted by the direct im-
pact of the Holy Spirit. Of course, thi
theory logically lays the responsibility fo
the non-conversion of the world upon God
Under its influence men waited for God's
"good time" when his Holy Spirit would
accomplish the work of their salvation
without their co-operation or consent
Faith, instead of being the act of an in-

mind based on evidence, was as something directly and mys- imparted to the human soul with- ıgency or co-operation. Repent- ı often confounded with sorrow ɔing, and feeling was made the ; of pardon and conversion. Bap- ɪng Protestants was relegated to of things indifferent and was not to have any connection with the ɔy which the unconverted were into a state of peace and recon- with God, or with a good con- vhile Catholics made it the channel rative grace.

state of things the doctrine that not so depraved as to rob him of ility, and that he had the power vay from his evil doings, to be- Christ and to surrender himself to rity, the Holy Spirit co-operating pel, in obedience, and in the lives to effect this change, seemed to e denying the necessity of regen- ıd the agency of the Holy Spirit.

that repentance was the actual f the soul to forsake sin, followed nation of life, and that baptism ıer a magical instrument to be he priesthood in the conversion of and adults nor a mere badge of tionalism which may or may not but is a solemn and significant act a penitent believer symbolizes his Christ and his purpose to lead a and receives the assurance of the of sins, looked to many pious "baptismal regeneration," which charged upon the early reform-

spite of all this opposition and entation, the presentation of the great object of faith, and not obedience to him and to his re- ts as the way of salvation, and upon his Word, and not upon ancies and feelings as the evidence ance, was everywhere hailed with earnest, seeking souls, who de- know the truth and to obey the t they might be saved. It was breaking out of the sun on a y, scattering the vapors and the ı the landscape and revealing all y in earth and sky. Thousands ing, troubled, anxious souls came into the church, claiming the mise, and rejoicing in the light of this simple, new-found truth. verts thus made, according to the method, were gathered in local ions, each one of which was self- , and all the members of which rded equally as "priests unto hout distinction of rank or au- Certain men of these congrega- account of their fitness, were teach these congregations, and look after their temporal inter- er on these congregations were at they were parts of one whole, to co-operate as sister churches rtberance of a common cause. e to be no popes, no cardinals, no ps, no archdeacons nor other cal officials, except bishops, pas- rseers, and deacons, in local con- , and evangelists. These congre- ay organize a general co-opera- missionary and other benevolent authority over the faith or the freedom of individuals or local churches.

This simplicity in evangelism and organization has commended itself by the remarkable success which has attended the plea urged by the present Reformation. It is a prime factor in that extraordinary growth which has puzzled the religious statisticians. In proportion as it obtains among the religious bodies of Christendom will we see the work of evangelizing the world go forward with something of that remarkable power and success which marked the apostolic age.

These five cardinal principles—Liberty, Loyalty, Unity, Catholicity and Simplicity—thus briefly stated, must serve as the skeleton which we shall endeavor to clothe with flesh and blood, and endow with life, at some time in the future. Our religious neighbors may call them "The Five Points of Campbellism." We prefer to regard them as Five Points that shall mark the church of the twentieth century.

AUTHORITY IN RELIGION.

The religion here spoken of is the Christian. The authority is that which is supreme. The inquiry relates to the seat of supreme or final authority in the religion of the Christ. The question is, What is the seat of ultimate authority in the Christian religion?

Good form now requires the discussion of this question in ministers' meetings. In such discussions the greatest variety of opinion is expressed. The replies to the question, strange as it may seem, are almost as various as the number of persons participating in the discussion.

In a recent ministerium, in which this question was considered, the following answers were given: "Conscience," "reason," "the Holy Spirit," "the Bible," "the church," "God" and "the Christ."

When Jesus concluded the Sermon on the Mount "the multitudes were astonished at his teaching: for he taught them as one having AUTHORITY."

On the Mount of Transfiguration a voice was heard from the cloud of glory, the voice of God, saying, "This is my beloved Son in whom I am well pleased; HEAR YE HIM." Moses was present, Elijah was also there. Under the circumstances the oracle meant that supreme authority belongs to Jesus as the Son of God. God did not say, Hear my Son and Buddha, hear my Son and Confucius, hear my Son and Mohammed, hear my Son and Moses, hear my Son and Elijah. Under the circumstances the oracle out of the cloud meant, HEAR MY SON ALONE. Supreme authority belongs to him. His message is the final, authoritative utterance on the subject of religion. Above him there is no one. He is now, in the Christian dispensation, regnant. Moses, Samuel, Isaiah, Elijah, Daniel, John the Baptist—all are superseded by Jesus the Christ. Conscience, reason, the Holy Spirit, the church—all are subordinate to the Christ. He is on the throne. The Holy Spirit by Paul says: "He must reign till." And again: "He is the Head of the body, the church."

The Christ claimed this position for himself.

When he was leaving the earth to return to heaven he said: "ALL AUTHORITY hath earth." If this language does not mean that Jesus is the seat of authority in the Christian religion it means nothing. The only question is, Did Jesus speak the truth when he said that all authority had been given to him? To those who believe in him as the Son of God this question is not considered—of course he spoke the truth.

Reason has a place in connection with the religion of the Christ. Jesus in his teaching appealed to reason. He sought to excite thought in the minds of men. He cited witnesses. He referred the people to the testimony of John the Baptist. His works, the works that the Father gave him to do, he said, sustained his Messianic claims. "The Father which hath sent me," he said, "hath borne witness of me." The Hebrew sacred writings, he claimed, also bore witness to him. Moses is called into court. Jesus said: "What THINK ye of Christ? Whose Son is he?" "If David called him Lord, how can he be David's Son?" Reason had its place in the teaching of Jesus. The men who were sent to arrest him reported to their superiors: "Never man so spake."

Reason had its place in the preaching of the apostles.

Peter reasoned with the people in Jerusalem on Pentecost Day and when he preached in Solomon's Porch. Again and again Paul reasoned with the Jews in their synagogue and elsewhere, out of their Scriptures, proving that Jesus is the Christ. "He reasoned of righteousness, temperance and the judgment to come," when he spoke in the presence of Felix, the Roman Governor. He reasoned with such power that "Felix was terrified," says the historian. To the saints in Rome Paul said: "Present your body a living sacrifice, . . . which is your reasonable service."

Men must reason about the Bible before they can intelligently receive it as from God. They must reason upon the claims of the Nazarene before they can intelligently believe on him as the Son of God and the Savior of lost men. Having decided that the Bible in the legitimate import of the word is inspired of God, they must receive its messages as true. Reason and learning may be called in to aid in deciding as to the import of a teaching or message—but the message is true whether its meaning is understood or not. This question has been settled in the settlement of the prior question. So also concerning the teaching of Jesus: Having decided that he is the Christ, his doctrine must be received as true. What thought he intended to convey by the use of certain words is a subject of legitimate inquiry. Here reason, again, and scholarship, have a place—but both are subordinate to him whom we call the Christ.

Conscience is an important factor. But conscience is neither an authoritative teacher nor guide. A man may be conscientious and exceedingly wicked. Saul of Tarsus was. He said when addressing the Sanhedrin after he became a Christian: "I have lived in all good conscience before God until this day." Whatever conscience is, it does not always cause a man to go in the right way or to do the right thing. It cannot, therefore, be regarded as *the* seat of authority.

Here the church is a word of admonition

He spoke of the effort that the church should make to win a man from the error of his ways. But besides this the church is worthy of respect when she speaks on any subject. Her age, her moral character, her origin, her divinely appointed mission, etc., should cause all men to give respectful attention to the church when she speaks on any subject. But the church is not infallible. Sometimes the church errs, and errs grievously. The church cannot, therefore, be the seat of authority in religion as the terms are above defined.

There is not space to consider the other suggestions—suggestions as to the Holy Spirit, the Bible, God.

When it is said that Jesus is the seat of authority he is thought of as a manifestation of Deity—he is thought of as God in human form.

The Holy Spirit is subordinate. He came to take the place of the Son of Man. The Holy Spirit was spoken of by the Christ as "*another* Comforter." "He shall not speak from himself; but what things soever he shall hear, these shall he speak." These words of the Master settle the question as to the place of the Holy Spirit—it is subordinate. The Christ alone is supreme. "HEAR YE HIM." B. B. T.

SPIRITUAL LIFE—HOW DEVELOPED.

I. WHAT IS SPIRITUAL LIFE?

It seems desirable first of all to get before our minds some definite conception by what is meant by spiritual life. Lexicons and dictionaries will not serve us here. We are indebted to the Bible for whatever knowledge we may possess on the subject, and to that source we must go for whatever metes and bounds the thing signified may have, and for those characteristics by which it may be identified.

The true starting-point for any adequate treatment of the subject it seems to us is the fundamental statement in Genesis, that "God created man in his own image, in the image of God created He him, male and female created He them." Without a true anthropology we cannot understand the nature of that life, which is the gift of God to men through Jesus Christ. Man is created in the image of God. God is spirit. Man is, therefore, essentially spirit. He has a material body, but he is a spiritual being. He was made like God in his mental, moral and volitional faculties. This image has been marred by sin. The object of the gospel is to restore man to the divine likeness.

If man is made in the image of God, it follows that he can never realize the end of his existence without living the life of God. In other words, it is only as man comes into fellowship with God and becomes partaker of the divine life, that he lives in the true sense of the word. Man alienated from God by wicked works and living in the flesh, following his appetites and passions, is said to be dead, morally, because he is not sharing in that life for which he was created—the life of God.

As the body is alive when it is in harmony with its environment and its organs are discharging their normal functions, and dies when this harmony is broken, so the spirit lives when it is in harmony with God, its spiritual environment, "in whom we live and move and have our being." The life of the body is, at its best, a temporal life, that ends in decay. The life of the spirit, on the contrary, is perpetual, and hence is called in the Scriptures "eternal life." It is eternal because it is the life of God and is shared by the soul that is in union with God.

If we are right thus far, then spiritual life is the life of the spirit that has come into vital relationship with God, through faith, and is sharing the divine life with Him. It is the life whose purpose, whose inspiration, whose likes and dislikes, whose principles and whose activities are all from God and are in harmony with His will. This is the true life, and because it is the true life it eternally persists.

Of course, there are degrees of spiritual life, ranging all the way from the highest type of consecrated manhood, where all the powers, energies, purposes and aspirations are in perfect harmony with God's will, as seen in the life of Christ, down to the weakest and frailest believer who has felt his sluggish moral nature quickened in the least degree by the recognition of God and of moral obligation. There is the same variety of type here that we find in the physical life, which ranges from the highest specimen of robust physical manhood or womanhood down along the descending scale to the hopeless invalid, to whom life is a burden. The question we are asked to answer is, How may this spiritual life, this life of God in the soul of man, be developed? This is indeed a most vital question. Time and space will only permit a few suggestions.

A primary and essential condition of growth in the spiritual life, we should say, is the *desire* for such growth and a willingness to do whatever is necessary to secure it. Without this the wheels of spiritual progress are effectually locked. Where there is no aspiration after a truer, fuller, richer life there can be no realization of spiritual growth. To create such discontent with the present spiritual attainments of the average church member and to awaken aspirations after something nobler and better is one of the difficult tasks of the Christian ministry; and yet, one that must not be neglected.

It is not enough to create a desire on the part of the people after a deeper spiritual life. There must be a definite *purpose* formed to strive to attain such a life. It is as true in spiritual growth as it is in the original acceptance of the gospel, that the will is supreme and that there must be a definite action on the part of the will to seek after spiritual things before they can be obtained. What proportion of our congregations have formed any such definite purpose would be a problem which each pastor may seek to solve for himself. It is to be feared that very many are living just as if there were no possibilities of Christian attainment before us for which it were worth while to struggle.

A closer study of Christ's life and the lives of those men and women who have been most Christlike, ought to reveal to the dullest mind marvelous possibilities of development in power and usefulness, unattained by the average Christian, and to awaken a hungering and thirsting after righteousness which must antedate all spiritual growth. Of a certain preacher among us it was once said by another distinguished preacher, "Bro. X's sermons always make me feel like I want to be a better man." A sermon that does not have this effect must be lacking in some of the elements of gospel preaching. Blessed is the preacher who can create in his congregation both the desire and purpose to live the Christ-life.

When one desires, not only life, but the *abundant* life, which Jesus said he came to give to man, and has formed a definite purpose in his mind to seek after such a life, the question still recurs as to how this desire and purpose may best be realized Another article will be devoted to that question.

Hour of Prayer.

THE HEAVENLY CITY.

(Midweek Prayer-meeting Topic, Dec. 14, 1898.)

And he carried me away in the Spirit to a mountain great and high, and showed me the Holy City Jerusalem coming down out of heaven from God, having the glory of God.—*Rev.* 21:10.

Who does not love the mountains? From our earliest recollection we have delighted to climb their rugged sides to the highest attainable peak, and look away over the surrounding country like a map spread out before us. We have stood upon some of the loftiest peaks of the Rockies, where perpetual snow glistened in the sunlight, and have looked over the series of peaks and foothills to the far-away plains of Colorado, when the scene was enchanting. We have ascended Mount Rigi, and from its serene heights looked down upon the beautiful Swiss lakes, over which the cloud-shadows were floating, and off to the great Alpine Range, whose summits were crowned with glaciers flashing like diamonds in the light of the sun. This, too, was grand.

But never was there another mountain scene like this which John describes. He was carried away in the Spirit to a "mountain great and high." Greatly to be pitied is he who has never been carried away in the Spirit to some lofty mount of vision, from which he could survey the past and look with clearer vision into the future. Such moments come to most of us at some time or other. It may be when, like John, we have been separated from the world, with its noise, its bustle, its feverish cares and vexing ambitions, and are alone in the midst of Nature's sublimities. Left to one's self, the soul turns its eye toward God, and in the midst of its meditations finds itself on some mountain top, where life takes on new meaning, and the path of duty seems clearer than ever before. Or this experience may come to us when disease has laid us low, and we approach the borderland where the flesh loses its dominancy and the spirit triumphs over it. In the calm and quietude of the solemn stillness eternity looms up before us and throws its light back upon our past life and our present condition. From this mount of vision we go back to the activities of life often with a new sense of responsibility and new incentives to endure suffering and affliction for the right.

It was a great moment in the life of this lonely seer on Patmos when he was carried away in the Spirit to this great and high mountain. John had no doubt been thinking about his isolation from his brethren, about the persecutions and trials to which they were subjected, and contrasting their weak and helpless condition with the great, haughty Roman Empire, then a hostile force. He needed a vision that would strengthen his heart and the hearts of his brethren in those fiery trials. What a magnificent scene burst upon his vision from that mountain top! He looked, and behold, "the Holy City, Jerusalem"—not the *old* City of Jerusalem, with its long, dark history of apostasy and retribution, but the *holy* city, the new Jerusalem, "coming down out of heaven from God, having the glory of God." This city, as the angel explained, was "the bride, the wife of the Lamb." Never prophet or seer looked upon a more inspiring scene than that. Two great and inspiring truths are taught us by this vision: (1) The power which is to transform this earth into more than its Edenic glory, and build the new Jerusalem, is from heaven; (2) the scene of its operations is here on earth. (See also Rev. 21:1-4.)

It was the perfected, redeemed, glorified Church of the living God, receiving its power and glory from heaven, and becoming the rightful habitation of man here on earth. It was the Church triumphant. It told John of the time when that divine society, of which he and his persecuted brethren were members, should be the dominant society on this earth. It prophesied a triumph of truth and righteousness under the reign of Jesus Christ, through whom this earth is to be transformed into an Eden, and humanity built into a city of God.

Glorious vision! Inspiring hope! Magnificent destiny! If any of us have caught such a vision of the future glory of the Church, let us seek to make it real through our lives and labors.

PRAYER.

We thank Thee, O God, for the visions of faith; that even on the barren islands of life the soul that is indwelt by Thy Spirit may have a vision of Thee and of Thy triumphant Church. We thank Thee for the witness borne by this faithful servant of old as to what he was permitted to see concerning the future times on that mountain top to which he was carried. We bless Thee for the hope inspired by such a vision, that this earth is yet to be the dwelling-place of God, and that righteousness is to prevail over sin and corruption. May this hope lead us to such self-purification and self-abnegation as shall enable us not only to share in that future glory, but to hasten its coming. In His name. Amen!

Editor's Easy Chair.

Few friendships are more lasting than those formed in our college life. Somehow we never forget the boys and girls with whom we recited Greek and La'in, and with whom we struggled in the literary societies to solve the great problems of the universe. They may have grown gray in the struggle of life, but to us they are boys and girls yet. It has not been our good fortune to meet very often with the sons and daugh-

traits and trend seen in college life, but it can never obliterate them. Sweet and holy are the friendships of youth, formed under conditions which exist in college life. Let the boys and girls who are in college to-day remember that and cultivate the friendship of the noble-hearted and true, and this shall be a tie that will bind them to worthy aims and ambitions all the days of their lives.

We are approaching the season of the year when people are accustomed to remember their friends and loved ones in some appropriate gift which is intended to be an expression of friendship or kindly feeling. It is one thing, however, to make a Christmas gift, and another to make an appropriate one. There are a few simple rules which should always be remembered in gift-making. To any one who is worthy to receive a gift, it is not the intrinsic value of the gift that counts for so much as the spirit in which the gift is made and its appropriateness. Costly gifts as a rule should be avoided. Gift-making should never become a burden, else it loses the very end sought to be gained. Gifts should never be made to persons from the motive that we expect or desire something from them in return. When the making of gifts becomes a sort of *quid pro quo* affair it has degenerated from its true purpose and ceases to be a token of friendship. It requires a little more time and thought in selecting or preparing appropriate gifts than many of us are able or willing to give to the subject. No doubt, thousands of our readers are now puzzling their heads as to what gifts they will make at Christmas time, and it is possible that a few of them, the younger ones, of course, are wondering what they will receive. We are sure the Easy Chair expresses the sentiment of its readers when it declares its preference for a pair of yarn mittens, given as an expression of love, to a gold watch given as an investment.

Some one has suggested—perhaps it was the pastor of the Garfi-ld Memorial Church at Washington—that we make this Jubilee Year an era of good feeling between progressives and conservatives, and between missionary and anti-missionary; or, perhaps we should say, between those who believe in missionary organizations and those who are opposed to such organizations, but believe in working it without organization other than local congregations. All right. Here is our hand to every man that believes in converting this world to Christ on any plan or without any plan. The anti-society brother who is doing his best to save men from sin either at home or abroad, shall have our prayers and our sympathies. We shall not require him, indeed, we never required him, to agree with us as to methods of missionary work in order that we may

those who are
this world in su

As to the con
these are relat
regarded as a
munity, while
ly progressive
this paper is
brethren as pr
conservative.
claim to be
or progressive
way you may
progress, but i
all truth and
kingdom of
difference bet
and stationary
President McG
there is an el
him as danger
consorting wit
the plea of the
to say of a ma
conservative, u
dard of conserv
is generally un
see organ of s
Garvey for hi
it, in turn, is
sheet for its
on rebaptism.

That there sh
among us, diff
servatism or pr
They are among
are in all polit
business relatio
ate this distinc
think and feel
an attempt to
same color and
between these t
charity. The c
that his more p
a view of any
cannot accept,
and become di
the progressive
has a new and b
his more conser
closing his eye
unwilling to re
stand the other
view as makes i
hold the posit
strictly loyal t
to treat each
will do away
though there w
tual friction, or
in religious thi
more liberal an
receive new id
Peter, but we w
pense with the
New Testament

Questions and Answers.

In the study of the life of Christ are we to separate his divine nature from his human nature? I have heard it said that Christ was wholly human until the time of his baptism, and from that time forth he has been divine. Is this correct? Enquirer.

No. It is a very unprofitable sort of speculation that seeks to analyze Christ's life, separating between the human and the divine. He was the divine embodied in the human, and lifting up the human to its ideal condition. His was the life of God manifested under human conditions and in human form. The statement concerning his being human before his baptism and divine afterwards is entirely unauthorized by the New Testament and by the facts in the life of Christ. The life he lived at Nazareth prior to his baptism was a sinless, ideal life, manifesting the qualities which set him apart as a unique personality. The life of God was manifest in him from the beginning, but of course, increasingly so as he came to the maturity of his human powers, entered upon his ministry and received the Holy Spirit without measure to fit him for his great work. There is evidence that at his baptism and the reception of the Spirit he came to a fuller consciousness of his Messianic mission than he had done before, but this is very different from dividing his life into two sections, from that point, making the first human and the latter divine. There is no phrase that so fitly expresses Christ's character and personality as the inspired phrase, "God manitest in the flesh," and this manifestation was throughout his entire life.

Does employing a preacher for a few months make him a member of a congregation without depositing a church letter or receiving the hand of fellowship of the congregation; and is he entitled to a church letter when he goes away?

G. O. Coburn.

We should say that no congregation should employ a preacher who does not present a letter showing his good standing in some local congregation. If they have satisfied themselves that he is in good standing, the mere matter of his depositing a church letter or receiving the hand of fellowship is not important. When he leaves the church, if his record has been good, there would be no objection to the church giving him a letter, stating as much and commending him to other congregations. If, however, his character has not been good, such letter should not be granted, even though he had deposited a letter with them and had received the hand of fellowship. The church letter is worth nothing, only so far as it states *facts*, and that a church letter should always do.

1. Is there anything in history sacred, or profane, that could be construed so as to indicate that the apostles practiced trine immersion?

2. When was the "Didache" written, and what bearing does it have on the subject? Duncan McFarlane.

1. There is not.

2. The "Didache," or Teaching of the Apostles, is a post-Apostolic production of the second century, and makes no claim to apostolic authority. Its direction concerning baptism shows that even at that early date the practice of baptizing into each of the three names of the Deity—Father, Son and Holy Spirit—had been introduced—a result, probably, of the trinitarian discussion of the time. This practice seemed to its advocates to emphasize the trinity of the Godhead. It does not seem to have occurred to them that it militates against the *unity* of the Godhead.

UNSECTARIAN CHRISTIANITY.*

M. E. HARLAN.

That which called my attention to the topic as discussed in this paper was an address delivered at Emporia at the State Convention of the Y. M. C. A., Nov. 10, 1898. The address was an address of welcome by Dr. Neel, in which he said, "We realize in the Y. M. C. A. better than in any other religious organization, perhaps, the exhibition of true Christian unity. This is what we need more of. The devil wants to see us divided. Nothing pleases him so much as to see dissensions among us, and the merest military tyro knows it is easier to defeat an opposing foe by attacking its ranks separately."

This, with the words quoted from the widely known, sweet-spirited, scholarly Alfred Barnes, the commentator, will constitute my text for this paper. I now quote from Barnes, in his comment on 1 Cor. 3:4-5, "For while one saith I am of Paul, and another I am of Apollos, are ye not carnal?"—"It was improper for the Corinthians to divide themselves into sects and to call themselves by the name of their teachers. We have here a rebuke to that spirit which has produced the existence of sects and parties. The practice of naming sects after certain men began early and was as early rebuked by apostolic authority. Would not the same apostolic authority now rebuke the spirit which calls one division of the church after the name of Calvin and another after the name of Arminius? Should not and will not all these divisions yet be merged in the high and holy name of Christian? Our Savior evidently supposed it possible that his church should be one (John 17:21:23), and Paul evidently supposed that the church at Corinth might be united. So the early churches were, and is it too much to hope that some way may yet be discovered which will break down the division into sects and unite Christians both in feeling and in name in spreading the gospel of the Redeemer everywhere? Does not every Christian desire it? Whose heart is not sickened at these contentions and strifes and whose soul will not breathe forth a pure desire to heaven that the time may come when the united hosts of God's elect shall go forth to subdue the world to the gospel o the Savior?"

These words suggested to me the above title, "Unsectarian Christianity." And what seeming contradictions in the very words! Surely our great Leader, as far as his followers were concerned, was unsectarian. What a contradiction of terms to call him a sectarian Christ! And yet, does not the Lord himself say that our true discipleship is conditioned on having a spirit as his? Such thoughts as these have led men like Neel and Parkhurst and Barnes and Gunsaulus to declare themselves as they have. And if for no other reason than that such men have declared themselves the subject has attached to it grave importance. I would not appeal to these men as final authority, for the ultimate test must lead to Christ's expressed will, and that will alone is final. What does he wish in the matter?

That he desired his people to be united I think no one will deny, for every figure used by him seems to indicate this. There is *individuality*, but *congregational* unity; e. g., he says, "I am the vine but ye" *individually* "are the branches." There is, then, that individuality, but vital unity, not between every church and Christ, but between every true disciple and Christ.

We propose to discuss the question from the following angles: 1st. Does the unity enjoined by Christ and the apostles now exist? 2nd. Is it desirable? 3rd. Is it possible?

I. To get before us clearly what the Savior and apostles meant by unity we must notice their language.

Let us now read John 17:21; 1. Cor. 1:10-11; 1 Cor. 3:3-5. That there is a deepening fraternity developing among religionists no one can deny, and we hail it with joy. Yet, to the mind of your essayist it has not yet reached the ideal state. From nature's great laboratory we learn the difference between adhesion and cohesion, between a mixture and a union. Different elements may mix, but they all will not unite. Chalk dust and sand mix, but they will not unite. Oxygen and hydrogen unite, and that combination in proper proportions produces water. That is union. So Paul argues that from the Jewish and Scythian and Greek elements there came a union and there was a new creation. While their political nationality was preserved there was religiously "neither male nor female, Jew nor Greek," but they were all one in Christ. To the extent we are Christians, to that extent the same relation or union will exist between members of his body, the church, as between himself and his individual members. With them the unity was so deep-seated that if Paul and James were pastors of two churches in Corinth or Jerusalem for a whole year they could exchange pastorates the next year without being called "turncoats." Surely that condition does not exist now. There is no doubt but that we mix better than we used to, but we have not yet reached the "promised land of unity." Some of us are afraid to venture. We say, "There are lions without and we will be slain in the streets." But to me it is clearly outlined up the sunlit slopes of the mountains of divine truth, and there above the mists of prejudice the laggard, dust-stained prilgrims will come at last and the church of God united will clasp glad hands and sing, "Behold how good and pleasant it is for brethren to dwell together in unity." It may not come *your* way, nor it may not come *my* way, but come it will in the providence of God, and when it does come it will come God's way.

II. Is it desirable? If I read present-day literature aright the great trend of thought is toward unity. The American Bible Society, the Bible-school Union, the Endeavor Society, have been prophets of

*Read before the Ministerial Association of Topeka, Kan., Nov. 21, 1898.

God in the wilderness crying, "Prepare ye the way of the Lord. Make his paths straight." While there have been some who desired to behead these John the Baptists they are still real vigorous corpses. Said Josiah Strong at the great Endeavor echo meeting last year at Los Angeles, California, "We have had the pan-American Congress and the pan-Presbyterian Congress, but," said he, "thank God the Endeavor movement is a pen large enough for all." Said the learned and eloquent Governor Bob Taylor, at Nashville, Tenn., last July, in welcoming the Endeavorers, "I see in the C. E. a lesson which at last, thank God, the churches are beginning to learn, that in the unity and harmony of Christian Endeavor lies the strength and power of the world. Let us all thank God that this idea of union has dawned on the church as well as the state." This was cheered to the echo by an audience of from six thousand to eight thousand people. Dr. George H. Corey, until about a year ago pastor of President McKinley's church in Washington, said in a paper before Washington ministers in July, 1897, "The Protestant church is so broken into fragments that are antagonistic in spirit and noncohesive in purpose, and nonco-operative in plan, that it can not be said to represent the true spirit of Christ. I do not believe Jesus Christ organized any of these little fragmentary eclesiastical institutions. It belittles him to think he did —his kingdom will eventually overmaster them all."

Dr. William B. Hale, of Massachusetts, in an article in the Forum, after mentioning a long list of silly and ludicrous entertainments to make money said, "The reason of these things is the fact that a hundred and forty sects have fastened themselves upon a people who cannot support them. The divided church is in humiliation and disgrace. Where now rival sects find it necessary to go to the masses with prize texts, bicycle runs for Christ and cyclone evangelist and lantern service, a united church, soberly engaged in its proper work, would find the masses eager to come to it."

The great and good Dr. A. J. Gordon says, "A church divided into sects is not the ideal church. It is not the church which he inaugurated nor for which he prayed in the end."

From my library I could multiply quotations like these at great length on Christian unity. Laughter is not argument and ridicule shall not stifle the voice of God. Can we not catch the trend of thought? The great unmothered, unchurched world to-day, wounded and bleeding at every pore, and yet strong in its sullen demand, is crying out against that bitter competition, that while it may seem to be the "life of trade," is often death to the trader. The battle is on, and when the smoke of the battle is cleared away you will see far up the slopes of Christian attainments, not "competition," but "co-operation," waving her scepter of peace over a people enslaved to Christ. It is not enough to say that "we must have division so that every one may be satisfied," for at least two reasons: 1. The first question that every devout disciple should ask is not, does it satisfy me? But does it satisfy Christ? Is it according to his plan? 2. The great religious unrest argues that division does not satisfy. We hold to our creeds only in form while in fact we do not magnify their tenets of faith. It is true to-day and can be easily demonstrated that you cannot tell what a man believes on credal questions by knowing what church he is with. With the great masses to-day it is not so much what you believe, but what you are.

Is uuion desirable? Ask our great evangelists. When they go into a place for revival work the first requsite is that they all sink their denominational peculiarities and work together that way as Christians. Question: If it is beneficent to work together that way for a month or six weeks, would it not be well to prolong the condition? Why do they desire to work in that way? They say the world must not see your differences or they will not be so easily reached. How like Christ such reasoning is, for did he not say "that these all may be one that the world may believe?" Christ closely associated the unity of his followers with the conversion of the world. If the working together as one church for one short meeting brings such marvelous results, think with what more than Pentecostal power we might sweep the whole earth if we were that way for a whole decade, a century.

Sometimes we laugh it off by saying, "Yes it is all right to have one church if you all will join my church." But while we laugh men die out of Christ and the question still is unanswered, "Is it desirable?"—not, "How shall it be done?" When once we allow the consuming desire to take hold on us the way will come. One thing is sure: you cannot force it over the wish of men. You can with saw and tackle in the very dead of winter take a pathway of ice off the great lakes, but that does not insure commerce. For as long as the frost-king reigns the way will close up again. But when the conditions are favorable and the sunlight falls like the kiss of tender morning, these icy chains that had clogged the way of commerce break up and again the crystalled beauty of the great blue deep sends a glad welcome to the hardy mariner. Thus the icebergs of selfishness and cold indifference to the will of God have menaced at times the way of our ship of Zion, but as we near the warm Gulf Stream of God's love these shall melt away at last. Brethren, it is true that to the extent that we are near Christ we are near each other, for he is not self-antagonistic or self-contradictory.

III. Is it possible? On this question let me read from Dr. Chas. H. Parkhurst, of New York. He who dared to face the Tammany tiger till it felt the sting of his piercing gaze and left in defeat, has been heard on this great question. He says, "If it is urged that denominations have their grounds in the inevitable differences which exist among men, it is sufficient to reply that these differences are no greater now than they were in the apostolic times when denominations had not begun to be thought of. And yet for Christians to group themselves on any other grounds than those laid down by Christ and to classify themselves under the leadership of an apostle is exactly what Paul rebuked when he forbade the Christians of Corinth to be known by the name of Paul or Apollos or Peter."

Do you say we need different churches to emphasize different truths? But why no emphasize all truth? A good friend said to me once, "We need the Baptists to emphasize baptism, the Methodists to emphasize fervor and the Salvation Army to emphazize lay preaching." But, brethren, baptism doesn't need to be emphasized by me more than by you. The Methodists have merited just praise for their fervor and their firm stand on all moral questions, and for one I thank God for it. But is it just for me to let them do all the emphasizing? That which is worth emphasizing my people need as much as theirs, and I do not regard myself a plagiarist when I insist that a godly, earnest life is necessary. And so we might go through the whole list. "The unity of the church is as certain as the final triumph of God in the earth and will precede it." Every time we pray, "Thy will be done in earth as in heaven," on the wings of that prayer is borne the bud of hope that is destined to bloom into fullest beauty when God's will is done. For none of us believe that there will be denominations or sects in heaven. Then, if we pray that his will shall be done here as there, why not work for the same great end?

Have all the toil and efforts in the past come to us in vain? "In faith, unity; in opinion, liberty; in all things, charity." Let us make these the three great pillars of our plea and let them stand out like the ancient pillars of Hercules. We commit a folly only when, like the ancients, we write upon these pillars, "No more beyond." The way beyond opens up into the Golden Gate of the resistless Pacific of completest victory. Let us make of each victory an Ebenezer with two faces like the Roman god, Janus, one face looking back and the other forward. None but the drone or fogy would be found gazing so intently on the past as to forget that there is a "yet to be." Out of the imperishable, glorious past comes voices that even age cannot make unfamiliar. These voices cry, "Onward, onward, forever!" Hear God and then apply what John says, "It doth not yet appear what we shall be." The crawling worm never dreams that it is to become the butterfly with the artist throwing into its wings the delicate tints of the rainbow, that as it rises will flash back gilded beauty. Thus becoming slaves to Christ's will we are but the chrysalis of what we may become under God.

CAN I LOVE MY ENEMIES?

N. J. AYLSWORTH.

V.

For him who would love his enemy there is help in yet another direction.

I believe Prof. John Fiske has said that cruelty is due to a lack of imagination. The explanation of this will appear by a moment's reflection.

Memory preserves for us much of the past. Reason enables us to anticipate much of the future, brings us into connection with the distant, and reveals to us much in the present which lies below the surface perception of the senses. But those *extra*-sensual perceptions are spectral and shadowy, and are feebly apprehended in comparison with the broad daylight of our sense perceptions. They do not seem real like the passing events of the moment in the midst of which we live. Especially do they fail to touch the feelings like objects which are clothed with the warmth and vitality of the present reality. And yet these things which lie beyond the ken of the senses may be of far greater importance than those actually before our eyes. Esau came home hungry; he smelled Jacob's pottage. These sense appeals took complete possession of him. He had a birthright, but it was away in the shadowy future. He sold it for the pottage, and committed a ghastly folly. Esau *knew*, but did not *realize* what he was doing.

To meet this defect in the apprehension of the unseen we are provided with a special faculty—the imagination. This is the *realizing* faculty, which clothes unseen things with vividness, with life, so that they seem to us real. It is a mistake to suppose that imagination is confined to poets, novelists, *et al.*, and that it is chiefly concerned with the unreal. It is possessed by all, and is necessary to our apprehension of the most important realities. It is chiefly the *realizing* faculty, and without it even the intellect would stagger and fail in its quest for truth.

The thought of Prof. Fiske would, therefore, be that, while in the infliction of cruelty the perpetrator is aware that he is causing pain, he has no adequate realization of the suffering he is producing; that he knows but does not *realize* what he is doing, and that if he did he would not do it. He lacks the power to put himself in the other's place, and consequently to feel for him. Just how far this is true I should not like to say, but it is pretty certain that if the suffering were fully realized it would banish much of the cruelty of the world.

Our imagination may often be quickened by the help of others, giving us a strong and living grasp on some unseen reality. No one influence did more to fire the heart of the North against slavery than "Uncle Tom's Cabin." It helped the imagination vividly to perceive slavery as it was. So of Hood's "Song of the Shirt" and Mrs. Browning's "Cry of the Children." Such also is the highest mission of the orator.

But what is most important for us now to consider is another remarkable fact. Our imagination is wont to realize in spots. Many things which lie easily within its grasp we do not realize, and thus go astray both in conduct and feeling. Perhaps I may be pardoned for presenting an illustration of this from my own life.

Childhood and youth were spent on a farm, near which there were woods with game and a small lake with an abundance of fish. When a mere boy I was supplied with a small fowling piece, and learned to shoot. The first fiction I ever read described the adventures of three boy hunters, and this lent an unspeakable charm to the pursuit of the hunter. City relatives visited us each summer to spend sometime in hunting and fishing. These were to me memorable and most delightful occasions. Under all these influences hunting became my most enjoyable pastime in a place where there were few amusements. After graduating from college and engaging in the pursuit of teaching, an occasional hunt was the favorite recreation. On starting upon one of those excursions a now aged preacher who was visiting us said, "Do you think it is right to kill things for sport?" Some commonplace reply was made, and I went; but those words haunted every moment of that day. They had not vividly portrayed the sufferings of those creatures "whose pains are hardly less than ours," but they had given that which set the imagination at work. From that day the pastime of hunting was forever ruined. It had its enjoyable features, but against these there always arose the counter question, How will the game enjoy it? It is sport on the one side; tragedy on the other—massacre, bereavement. Every boy should commit to memory the touching poem of Burns entitled, "The Wounded Hare."

During all these years I had seen the sufferings I was inflicting for my own diversion, but had never realized them because, strange to say, I had not distinctly thought about them. Their realization completely revolutionized my feeling on the subject.

How quickly our feelings of resentment undergo a change when we see our enemy cold in death! Our eyes have given us a new fact about him, and our hatreds fly like things of the night. We knew this would be, before: why did not our imagination make it real to us? Our feelings toward this enemy had left out half the facts.

One of two brothers was taken ill. A physician was summoned and said to the elder brother, who was watching, "I do not think Walter can live." In the night the sick man sprang from his bed, squared for a fight before his brother, and landed a blow. William's first impulse was to strike back, but he quickly thought, "Poor Walter is sick," and then he saw the white face in the coffin, aud could not strike. He put his strong arms around the struggling man and bore him to his bed and said with pathetic tenderness, "Ah! Walter, you see I have beat you this time. Wait till you get well and you can try it again." What became of William's impulse of retaliation when all the facts stood vividly before him?

A man has struck you. You raise your arm to return the blow, when lo! a voice: "The man is not himself. He is acting under the spell of a great blindness. His sin is sin, but it is still more a great calamity. Could you see its tragic end, it would break your heart. He has been sinned against more than sinning; and it is chiefly because of this that he is what he is. He has sorrows—sorrows which, could you know them, would touch you with sympathy. He has noble traits and aspirations for a better life, but they are shot down by tempters about him. He may become a noble man and dwell among the redeemed. I have died for him, and we here in heaven are following him with anxious solicitude. Do not strike him, but help us to save him." If you have within you any considerable degree of generous feeling you will be filled with a great compassion. Those who see you will say, "Behold! his face did shine;" and your enemy will go away smitten with a great astonishment. He has been wounded unto life. You have seen the white face in the coffin and you could not strike.

How does parental love master hatred? By dwelling on the erring child's misdeeds? No; it sees the cradle, the innocent face, hears the cherubic laughter, remembers noble traits and worthy acts, sees the tempter's snare, the struggle to overcome, witnesses the beguilement, hears the siren song, sees the spiritual assassination by the minions of evil—and then turns with bleeding heart to the piteous ruin. Yet, every sinner is a son, of whom some mother knows all this. Can you hate him in his calamity? Hatred moves in a great darkness which shuts out the facts.

How did Christ say, "Father, forgive them?" Listen! "FOR THEY KNOW NOT WHAT THEY DO." He does not say, *For they are very bad.* That would be unnatural. The heart does not work that way. He who could compassionate wickedness as such would not be divine, but only insane. He who could view it without righteous anger would be less than moral. Christ is gazing upon other aspects of that black deed. These men are the victims of a great darkness. They have been demoralized. Sons of God in possibility, what are they now? How awful the vision! how great the calamity! He is moved by the unspeakable piteousness of sin and cries aloud, "O, Father, forgive; they are not so bad as they seem." It is the mother's way. Does he see cradles? Perhaps. Does he hear innocent song and laughter? Perhaps. He *does* see the good in these men and what they might be, and then seeing what they are, his heart breaks with pity. What he saw in these sinners was a heart-moving spectacle; and what he saw was *true*.

God's love for the world is not without occasion. His feeling toward sinners is not a blind monstrosity of emotion. There is abundant reason for his feeling as he does, for sin is a most piteous business. It is sin, but it is above all a terrible calamity. Our little dark-closet hatreds do no honor to our manhood, much less to our Christianity.

Faith lets us behind the scenes—shows what God saw and what broke the heart of Christ. Let the whole tragedy of sin, first and last, stare upon you, and you cannot hate. The great tide of Christian love rolling over animosities, drowning wrongs and lifting up the suffering and sin-blackened in the arms of a healing compassion, is the only rational passion in view of all the facts. It is the only *natural* feeling, if we are to see things as they are. You can hate only by dropping from the heights of faith's clear vision, by allowing heaven's bliss and the awful doom of sin to swim from your sight, by forgetting human weakness and blindness and sorrow, and creeping down from manhood's high estate, with its broad sweep of vision, into the animal's little den of the present and seen, and with all else in eclipse, hugging in darkness your little revenge. The facts will storm the heart if you but see them, and take it captive with a yearning sorrow.

Will it be said that all these facts of the wider vision are, with most Christians, shadowy and indistinct—too spectral to touch the feelings or rain their fire into the heart? and that this is due to imaginative incapacity—a human limitation for which there is no remedy? Rather, it is due to imaginative *inadvertence*. The realizing imagination is the most affluent of all our endowments. It gets away with us in our sleep and wafts us through a thousand fairy worlds, filling us with delight or rending us with fear. Children see spectres in the dark. The vision of youth is a glorious apocalypse. How it kindles before him, and throws its magic spell upon his heart! The business man has his vision of success achieved. How he lives in it! It is his waking dream, and is more than a match for the toil of the present or the incitements to ease and pleasure. The bereaved mother finds a little shoe; and the scenes of the past are as of yesterday. She hears voices and sees forms long since vanished, and weeps with a fresh sorrow. The imagination is making a thousand things real to us that the eye does not see, and it can also make others. How many common souls have walked before God as seeing the invisible! The martyrs were not poets, yet the future world was more real to them than the present. What we dwell on with interest grows real to us, and we may "by the vision splendid be on our way attended." The palace is ours with its thousand ministries to the heart, if we will but rise above the kennel of the present and the seen. That vision waits on us, if we will but welcome it, that will fill us with a holy compassion and banish all the dark shadows of hate. If we see not these things, we are men of sense, not of faith. He who has a living faith can love his enemies, for he sees that which broke the heart of his Redeemer.

THE JOY OF THE CHRISTIAN MINISTRY.

G. A. RAGAN.

This subject suggests its opposite, the sorrow of the Christian ministry, which forms a proper background for the picture.

Like Christ, the true minister is a "man of sorrows and acquainted with grief." His duty continually takes him among unhappy, wretched and dying men. His path of service ever leads by pools of Bethesda, where suffering humanity lies waiting in the porches of disappointment, discouragement and despair. If he has the heart of Christ he will be "moved with compassion" and his sympathy will find expression in deeds of helpfulness and words of hope. Like Christ, he has wept over the lost, who seem to despise the goodness of God and will not respond to his infinite love.

Like Christ, many a minister has become poor, that through his poverty others might be enriched. Like Christ, he has been compelled to say: "'Foxes have holes and the birds of the air have nests,' but I have not where to lay my head as a permanent abiding-place." Many are foregoing the joys of a settled home that they may be ministers of the "manifold grace of God."

Many have to labor under adverse circumstances; fears and selfishness and strife and jealousies within; bitter opposition and dead indifference without; "spiritual wickedness in high places" and unblushing vice in low places.

But all the sorrows which may come to any faithful minister of Jesus Christ are not worthy to be compared with his joy here and his glory hereafter.

What are the bright lines which stand out so conspicuous against the dark background of the picture? What are the sweet ingredients in the cup of joy which the Master puts to the lips of his ministers?

1. The joy of unbroken communion with Christ. His work is such that whether in the study, in the pulpit or in pastoral visitation, he may have at all times a consciousness of "dwelling in the secret place of the Most High and abiding under the shadow of the Almighty."

Here he has learned to sing—

"In the secret of his presence how my soul delights to hide;
Oh, how precious are the lessons which I learn at Jesus' side!
Earthly cares can never vex me, nor trials lay me low,
For when Satan comes to tempt me, to the 'secret place' I go.

When my soul is faint and thirsty, 'neath the shadow of his wings
There is cool and pleasant shelter and refreshing crystal springs,
And my Savior rests beside me as we hold communion sweet.
If I should try I could not utter what he says when thus we meet."

2. The joy of active fellowship with Christ — partnership with him in the glorious work of saving the lost, realizing that God not only "works *in* us both to will and to do of his good pleasure," but *through* us to lift up the fallen and strengthen the weak. Here we feel that we are embassadors of Christ, by whom Infinite Love beseeches rebel sinners to be reconciled to the "Father of mercies."

In this relation we have a blessed sense of being channels of God's love and grace to our needy fellowmen. For this purpose Christ says to each of us: "Come *unto* me and abide *in* me that I may be *in you* a a well of water, springing up unto everlasting life," so that out of your Spirit-filled heart may flow "rivers of living water," at whose brink parched souls may quench their dying thirst and live.

3. The joy of unselfish service, the delight of going about "doing good," of ministering unto the needy rather than being ministered unto. "Whose I am and whom I serve," was the motto of Christ's greatest minister. He is the one who said: "To do good and to communicate, forget not." He interpreted, by his own joyful ministry, Christ's words at the well: "My meat is to do the will of him that sent me and to finish his work."

4. Finally the joy set before us, the joy of meeting the Master when he comes, and receiving from his pierced hands "the crown of glory that fadeth not away." What is this crown of glory? Paul said to those whom he had "turned to God from idols" in Thessalonica, "What is our hope or joy or crown of rejoicing? Are not even ye in the presence of our Lord Jesus Christ at his coming? For ye are our glory and joy." From his Roman prison he addressed his Philippian converts as "my joy and crown." In this, brother preachers, lies the greatest joy of the Christian ministry.

Illustrating this thought, Theodore Cuyler said in his valedictory sermon at the close of a public ministry of forty-four years: "What Lord Eldon from the bar, what Webster from the senate chamber, what Sir Walter Scott from the realms of romance, what Darwin from the field of science, what monarch from Wall Street or Lombard Street, can carry his laurels or his gold up to the judgment seat and say: 'These are my joy and crown?' The laurels and the gold will be dust—ashes. But if so humble a servant of Jesus Christ as your pastor can ever point to the gathered flock, arrayed in white before the celestial throne, then he may say, 'What is my hope, or joy, or crown of rejoicing? Are not even ye in the presence of Christ at his coming?' 'He that winneth souls is wise.' 'They that be wise shall shine as the brightness of the firmament and they that turn many to righteousness as the stars forever and ever.'"

In writing to his Corinthian converts Pastor Paul said: "I have espoused you unto one husband that I may present you as a chaste virgin unto Christ."

He looked forward to that great day when the clouds shall part and the glorified bridegroom shall come to take unto himself his bride. His clear eye saw the dead in Christ arise and join those who were living in Christ. He saw that blessed company, "clothed in fine linen," pure and spotless, with glorified bodies, ascend "to meet the Lord in the air and then to be forever with the Lord."

This vision was ever before him in his ministry. It throbbed and thrilled every fiber of his soul and filled him with joy unspeakable.

His is the "crown of glory which fadeth not away." This is the reward that the Chief Shephead will give his faithful pastors who have rescued his lost sheep and fed the flock of God. This is the crowning joy of the Christian ministry.

National Conference on our New Problems.

EDITOR CHRISTIAN-EVANGELIST:—Our people are beginning to realize that well-nigh all the questions of government—restrictions of suffrage, parochial versus public education, civil service reform, prohibition, the civil Sabbath, brutal amusements, the opium traffic, colonial government, monopolies, even slavery—have been thrust upon us by the acquisition of our new islands, and therefore a widespread interest has already been aroused by the announcement of a national conference on these themes in Washington, Dec. 13-15, during the second week of the new session of Congress, which promises to be the most interesting and momentous of any session since the Civil War. The speakers who have consented to discuss these themes in the convention include such specialists as Dr. Josiah Strong, Dr. Howard H. Russell, Anthony Comstock, Gen. C. H. Howard, Dr. Wilbur F. Crafts, Dr. M. D. Kneeland, Dr. Teunis W. Hamlin, Dr. Frank M. Bristol, Mrs. Mary H. Hunt, Mrs. Margaret D. Ellis, Mrs. E. M. Thacher, Mrs. E. B. Ingalls, with more to follow. The open discussions, where everybody who knows more than anybody, will contribute the statesmanship of the people to the solution of these problems, will be hardly less important than the more formal speeches. Mrs. Frances Graham, the sweetest soloist of the N. W. C. T. U., will make the music a feature of interest and power. For program and further particulars address W. F. CRAFTS.

210 Delaware Ave. & E., Washington, D. C.

A Plea for our Ministers.

The Chattanooga Convention fixed on the third Lord's day in December as the time for the offering for the Ministerial Relief Fund.

Knowing, as I do, the extreme suffering to which our aged ministers are exposed, I wish to enter my plea with the brethren everywhere, that in this happy Christmas time they remember those who are in bonds of poverty and need as bound with them, and that they double their own happiness by sharing with these needy servants of God.

May the Lord put it into the hearts of our brethren to send up to the Board of Ministerial Relief an offering for the poor saints of our Israel.

The Ministerial Relief Board will lack six hundred dollars of having enough on hand to to pay the January pledges to their beneficiaries.

Send all offerings to Howard Cale, 120 E. Market St., Indianapolis, Ind.; and may the deed be twice blessed, blessing him who gives as well as him who receives.

In the name of the King, BENJ. L. SMITH.
Cincinnati, O.

Our Budget.

—C. W. B. M. motto, $90,000 for '99.

—The F. C. M. S. motto, $150,000 for '99.

—The A. C. M. S. motto, $100,000 for '99.

—Their united war cry, 100,000 souls for Christ in '99.

—But the greatest of all wants is more spirituality in the church; more of Christ in the hearts and lives of its members.

—New York and Brooklyn have started an "open-church" movement. The plan proposes an open house every day in the year.

—The eye of the world will now be fixed upon our National Capital for a season.

—The recent storm on the Atlantic Coast was exceedingly destructive to life and property.

—A great fire in the heart of New York City on Sunday night destroyed thousands of dollars worth of property.

—Last Sunday was C. W. B. M. Day. If your auxiliary and church did not observe that day, for any reason, appoint another and aid the work.

—The Missionary Intelligencer for December, cogitating upon the record of church giving for Foreign Missions for 1898, says: "Missouri stands first in the number of contributing churches, 307. Kentucky stands first in the amount given by the churches as churches. Ohio stands first in the aggregate amount given, $14,492.62. Illinois stands first in the number of contributing Sunday-schools."

—A class in the study of missions has been organized in the First Christian Church at Colorado Springs, Col. It contains thirty members. There is a fine interest. The class is collecting a missionary library. Let a similar movement be inaugurated in other congregations.

—The St. Louis Christian Advocate now bears the name of an assistant editor, C. C. Woods, at its editorial head. Dr. Palmore is so in demand in different parts of the United States by the Methodist Episcopal Church South, that we can readily see the wisdom of a fixture in the home office.

—The third Sunday in this month is the day appointed for an offering for the Ministerial Relief Fund. The merits of this fund stand without the demonstration of argument, and the necessity for it is urgent. The appeal should not go unheeded. Pastors and evangelists who are growing old in the Lord's service should not be indifferent about bringing this grace also before the churches. Let there be due and timely consideration given to this subject and a liberal and general offering on that day.

—The new secretary of the Ministerial Relief Fund, D. R. Lucas, of Indianapolis, Ind., has furnished our readers with some interesting literature on that subject in this paper. The churches should not forget that the third Sunday in December will be the first opportunity they have had for a general offering for this ministry, and the united outpouring of love on that day should give courage to our dependent veterans in the Lord's army. Having worn out their lives in the Lord's service in the ministry of the heavenly things for the saints, it is but a small expression of their appreciation of this service to give to them of their earthly substance in return.

—The author of the interesting interview with Archbishop Purcell, in a note to the editor says concerning the Campbell and Purcell debate: "Many years ago I came across a copy of the book in an Indiana hotel and spent a delightful hour in perusing the same. I am surprised that it is not more generally circulated. No novel was half so interesting to me?" The demand for this book in recent years has been such as to justify the Christian Publishing Co. in issuing a new edition of the work, which will soon be ready. It is certainly one of the most notable discussions of the century, whether we consider the standing and ability of the two disputants or the nature of the themes discussed.

—The interview with Archbishop Purcell, which we published last week, has already awakened a good deal of interest. Two of our correspondents, however, referring to the matter, call attention to the fact that Archbishop Purcell died in 1883, the interview, which is said to have occurred thirteen years ago, must have taken place after his death. Either our correspondent, "I. C.," made a mistake in his dates or else the printer misinterpreted his chirography. The interview took place while the venerable prelate was yet in the body. We are asked also by others if the interview is a genuine one or whether it is a work of imagination. It purports to be a genuine interview by one whose social and religious standing entitles him to our credence. He is, we take it, a Presbyterian in faith, but an admirer of the ability and personal character of both Alexander Campbell and Archbishop Purcell. We presume he would not affirm under oath that this interview was a verbatim report of what was said on the occasion, but the author is sure that what is written fairly represents the sentiments of the Archbishop, and this is the only important matter. Whether the writer, whose initials are not "I. C.," but who wishes to remain strictly in cog., took notes at the time of the interview we do not know, but it is safe to presume that he would write concerning it and speak of it to others until the matter was very clearly fixed in his mind.

—The minutes of the 29th annual session of the Iowa Christian Convention, and 18th of the Iowa C. W. B. M., held at East Side Church, Des Moines, Iowa, Sept. 26-30, have been printed and bound for distribution, making a book of 100 pages. The care and extent of details given certainly indicate great care on the part of the secretaries of these societies and thoroughness of organization throughout the state. A copy of these minutes may be had by sending to B. S. Denny, Cor. Sec., Des Moines, Iowa.

—During the last few days what is known as the "Yale Missionary Band" have been holding meetings in this city in the interest of the cause of Foreign Missions in general. This band consists of five volunteer graduates from Yale '98 class, who have started out to devote one year to this work among the Y. P. S. C. E. Their mission is to awaken a deeper interest in Foreign Missions and a deeper interest in the support of college men who are willing to go into the foreign field as missionaries. It is said that under the "Student's Volunteer Movement" there are more than 3,500 students in America who have declared their purpose, if God permit, to become foreign missionaries. Much interest will, therefore, be taken in the work of the "Yale Missionary Band."

—I read N. J. Aylsworth's "Can I Love my Enemies—IV." to my congregation yesterday morning instead of my regular sermon, with comments. I think it is the best thing that can be said on the subject. "Can I Love my Enemies," should be given a permanent place in our literature. J. M. LOWE.

Winterset, Ia., Nov. 28.

—In an eloquent Thanksgiving sermon, delivered at a union service, Cedar Rapids, Ia., by J. M. Rudy, pastor of the Christian Church in that city, he gives the following prophetic reason for devout thanks to our Heavenly Father. We believe with Bro. Rudy that the doctrine "for humanity's sake" will become a rallying cry for the reformers of homeland conditions and the slogan that shall bruise the head of every oppressor and every organized evil in the land. "For Humanity's Sake" is the explanation of the doctrine and death of the Christ:

If the resources of a mighty army and the strength of a great navy are to be drawn upon for the sole purpose of setting common men and women free on a foreign island, we are more than justified in uttering the prophecy that this same doctrine will find a thousand preachers and expositors among the masses where it now has one. If this is our nation's estimate of human beings in a foreign land, why should we not plead for the same estimate of human beings at home? This will be done. The missionary of the cross who has been pleading the worth of life and the value of the soul is henceforth to be reinforced in his argument by the conduct of the United States army and navy, together with the explanation and interpretation of that conduct by great American statesmen.

Herein is the Christian's reason for giving thanks. You are to-day at the grave of the old and in the birth chamber of the new patriotism.

"My country, 'tis of thee,
Sweet land of liberty."

—The Union Signal, Chicago, for Dec. 1, contains a lengthy report of the recent W. C. T. U. National Convention at St. Paul, Minn., including the discussion of the report of the executive committee, in which the abandonment of the Temple was recommended. The vote on the report stood 285 yeas and 71 nays, which lost the Temple to the W. C. T. U. The result, however, created no surprise, as it had been anticipated for sometime previous to the convention. But Mrs. Carse, who has so long and so urgently championed the Temple movement, still hopes to redeem it from debt and make of it a monument still to Miss Willard.

—The Coming Age is the name of a new magazine which will be published at Boston (Pierce Bldg., Copley Square), beginning with 1899, under the editorship of B. O. Flower and Anna C. Reifsnider. It is to be "a magazine of constructive thought," and in this respect will differ somewhat from the Arena, the former magazine founded by Mr. Flower. The first volume of the new magazine is to contain a series of articles from leading men in the various religious bodies, giving the reason for their faith in them. We wish the new venture success.

—We clip the following from a Detroit paper:

GRAND RAPIDS, Mich., Nov. 28.—Special.—Rev. E. B. Widger, pastor of the Church of Christ, created a sensation in his high-toned church here yesterday by denouncing his congregation as the slowest he ever addressed. He said they had kept in one rut for twenty years and had made no progress in anything. The denomination is the third in the United States, but the local branch has not increased in membership in fifteen years. The pastor ended his talk by tendering his resignation.

Ex-Mayor Stow arose for the congregation and replied vigorously, and the discussion was red-hot. The pastor withdrew immediately after ending the services, and a committee is now considering a new pastor.

The above may or may not accurately represent the event to which it refers. We have no other notice of it. We do know, however, that the church at Grand Rapids is one of the best in the state, in the character of its membership, its reputation in the community and in its sympathy with all our co-operative work. It has had a series of excellent men as pastors, and while its growth has not been rapid, it has made substantial progress, and is a credit to the city and to the cause with which it is identified. Ex-Mayor Stow, who is said to have defended the congregation from the criticism of the retiring pastor, is himself an honor to any congregation of Christians, and a Christian man of moderation, of large-hearted generosity and of wisdom. We cannot believe that there was anything non decorous in the proceedings. No doubt the church will secure a good man for pastor and go forward in its career of usefulness.

That article by you on Governor Tanner is sound to the centre —J. V. COOMBS.

—The 33rd annual report of the Cincinnati Union Bethel, a copy of which just came to hand, shows a splendid record of work among river men and their families in their physical, moral, intellectual and spiritual interests and welfare. For a copy of this report send to Jas. F. Taylor Asst. Sec., Cincinnati, Ohio

—We have some reports of meetings that .re unsigned. Let those who report meetings, ›specially those who write high-sounding comnendations of preachers, not forget that their eports go for nought if unsigned.

—The responses from all quarters heartily ndorsing our word of caution as to the danger of diverting our enthusiasm this Jubilee Year nto wrong channels and seeking after contri›utions and numbers rather than seeking first he kingdom of God and his righteousness, is 'ery gratifying. We regret that we have not pace to quote from these letters. They show hat there is a widespread and deep conviction among the brethren that the deepest need of ›ur churches and membership, including the ninistry, is the putting away of the worldliess, selfishness and half-heartedness and whatever else has hindered the Lord's work in he past, and coming into a closer fellowship with God and with his Son Jesus Christ in an ffort to save the world.

—Word has reached this office indirectly of he murder of M. Baghdasarian, the Armenian rother whom the Iowa churches sent to Persia s a missionary. Can any of our readers conrm the report and furnish the particulars?

—According to the following recent telegram › B. L. Smith, Cincinnati, the offerings for Iome Missions are going forward by leaps and ounds. A few more such offerings as this will lmost create a landslide in the church for Iome Missions which would be a grand way to nemorialize this Jubilee Year. But here is the nessage. Read it:

"A Friend" sends us five thousand dollars or the Permanent Fund of Home Missions, the nterest of which is to be used to support a ome missionary all the time. Rejoice with s!

—Acting under the advice of his physician ›r. Abbott, the widely known pastor of the amous Plymouth Pulpit, recently surprised his ongregation and the religious world by anouncing his resignation. Dr. Abbott has been oing a vast amount of work as a preacher and ditor but it seems not to have been known that is physical strength was faltering under the ›ad. We trust that a partial release of his uties will permit the return of his vigor and xtend his years of usefulness in the world.

—Our first page this week presents the face f one who has occupied a prominent place mong the Disciples of Christ for over half a entury. A son-in-law of Alexander Campbell, e was also associated with him in the building p of Bethany College, being one of its profes›rs, and afterwards succeeding Mr. Campbell s its president. He was also associated with Ir. Campbell in the editorship of the Millenial Harbinger. He was a member of the West 'irginia Constitutional Convention, and for ›ur years State Superintendent of Public chools. The University of Virginia conferred pon him the degree of Doctor of Laws. Dr. 'endleton has had no superior among us as a raceful and scholarly writer. He has held an onored place in the councils of our brotherood for many years. He is a native of Louisa o., Va., is over fourscore years of age and s now enjoying that quietude which is so welome to age in his beautiful home at Eustis, la., where, amid his orange groves he keeps p his reading and remains abreast of the times. wo of his sons are associated with the Stand-rd Pub. Co., and all of them are following in interest, and we trust lead many to act in their behalf. The letter is signed by Helen E. Moses, C. W. B. M. secretary of their English Bible Work, to whom all communications should be sent. Her address is 306 W. Deleware St., Indianapolis, Ind.:

Our recent war with Spain is scattering the young men of our country throughout the nations; what is to be their mission, what the message of their lives in these lands? These are vital questions and are before us to-day for our consideration. A chaplain in the recent war, who had given the matter thorough and careful attention, says the highest per cent. of Christians he found in any company was fifty, while in one company numbering one hundred and four but two were members of any church. From such testimony, and there is much of it, we must conclude the Church of Christ will have much to do to meet the need for Bibles and Bible teachers. The Bible Societies and Missionary Boards are recognizing this, and are preparing for larger work than ever before. The women of the Church of Christ, through their organization, the Christian Woman's Board of Missions, have for several years been doing a work that goes to the very root of this need, and have been freely giving Bible teaching to the young men of this and other nations gathered in the universities of Michigan, Virginia and Georgia. Because of the permanent need of Bible teaching in the schools where are gathered hundreds, yes, thousands of the most promising young people of our land, it is the purpose of these Christian women to endow this work so that it may become a permanent memorial of their faith in the Word of God as the power given for the healing and saving of this and all nations. This year they propose to raise at least five thousand dollars toward this endowment, and ask a personal gift from you of one dollar, or as many more as you will give. Second, they ask you to do all you will toward urging the importance of Bible reading and teaching among those around you. Third, to send a list of names of those whom you think could, or should, be interested in this work.

PERSONAL MENTION.

W. H. Boles and daughter recently visited Burnside, Ill., with a series of lectures and entertainments that were greatly enjoyed.

E. B. Scofield, of Indianapolis, Ind., called at this office during a recent visit to this city. Scofield and Hackleman are successors to W. T. Sellars' book business, Indianapolis, Ind.

J. W. Hewett, South McAlister, I. T., desires to locate in the South and engage in pastoral work and solicits correspondence to that end.

Prof. W. E. Garrison, Chair of Hebrew and Church History in the Butler Bible College, Irvington, Ind., spent Thanksgiving with his parents in this city.

J. M. Rudy, pastor of the church at Cedar Rapids, Iowa, is planning for an aggressive work this winter, by thoroughly arousing the church to a keener sense of its privileges and powers.

J. T. Boone and wife recently spent a few days in this city visiting friends before starting for their new field of labor at Jacksonville, Fla. Bro. Boone reports the church at Memphis, his late pastorate, in a good, active state and well equipped for a forward movement.

A. West, assistant pastor West End Christian Church, this city, read a paper to our preachers last Monday on "Unity Among the Disciples of Christ." The paper suggested some very important facts for the consideration of his hearers.

Joel Brown, field agent of the Christian Orphans' Home, called at this office on last Monday. He is in the city to attend a meeting of the Orphans' Home Board. He tells us that Jesse McKnight, of Peoria, Ill., will dedicate the new church home at Scottville, Ill., the first Sunday in Jauary, 1899. He has a kind word to say of many of our churches upon

J. T. Thompson closes his work at Lathrop, Mo., Dec. 31, 1898. The elders of the church there commend him and his work in strong terms.

Charles A. Young has, we learn, conditionally accepted the presidency of Bethany College. If the condition—whatever it is—should be complied with, it is safe to predict a new lease of life to "Old Bethany, dear Bethany."

S. A. Strawn, pastor of the church at Lowell, Ind., has issued an annual circular letter to the members of his flock, recounting their progress through the closing year, and appealing to their Christian patriotism for greater things for the future, for Christ.

A. J. Ferguson has removed from Saybrook to Augusta, Ill., where he began work for the church Nov. 27th. He speaks encouragingly of the outlook at Augusta and is well impressed with the people he is to serve during the coming year.

R. R. Bulgin, of Scranton, Pa., has resigned his work for the church in that city that he may do the work of an evangelist more fully. The church at Scranton it is said has prospered greatly under his ministry and the brethren were loath to give him up.

A. W. Jones, of Roswell, New Mexico, who has been doing the work of an evangelist now desires the work of a pastor. He is 28 years old and gives excellent references. Churches in need of a pastor will please take note.

The Religious Review of Reviews for November contains a group tinted picture of the International Lesson Committee elected at the 8th International Sunday school Convention, Boston, to provide the uniform lessons for 1900 to 1905, in which group appears the familiar face of Dr. B. B. Tyler, of our editorial staff.

Ellis B. Harris, of Grant City, Mo., was recently ordained to the ministry of the gospel by the church at that place. N. R. Davis, of Skidmore, Mo., preached the ordination sermon and assisted the elders of the church in the ordination ceremony. E. B. Harris is thus following in the steps of his father, W. H. Harris, of Grant City, and begins life with bright prospects of great usefulness.

The cards are out announcing the wedding of Howard T. Cree, pastor of the church at Maysville, Ky., to Miss Lilly Bryan Thomas, daughter of Mr. and Mrs. Oswald Thomas, of Shelbyville, Ky. The ceremony will be performed in the Christian Church at Shelbyville, Thursday evening, Dec. 15, at 6 o'clock. With the aid of the "assistant pastor" the work at Maysville will doubtless be even more effective than heretofore. The CHRISTIAN-EVANGELIST extends its best wishes to the young couple for a useful and happy life.

CHANGES.

G. B. Martin, Mishawaka to Michigan City, Ind.
J. H. Painter, Plymouth, Ill., to Cozad, Neb.
S. J. Copher, Odessa to De Soto, Mo.
E. F. Mahan, Salem to Orleans, Ind.
A. J. Ferguson, Saybrook to Augusta, Ill.
R. B. Hayener, Windsor, Mo., to Mechanicsburg, Ill.
W. A. Coryea, Gervais, Ore., to Kelso, Wash.
C. E. Smith, Pineflats, Pa., to Bethany, W. Va.
O. A. Ishmael, Windsor to Drexel, Mo.
T. H. Kuhn, Kokomo to Irvington, Ind.
J. T. Boone, Memphis, Mo., to Jacksonville, Fla.
Sam'l Gregg, Cleveland to Le Sueur, Minn.

Correspondence.

English Topics.

A WONDERFUL AMERICAN BOOK.

These letters are upon English Topics and in writing them I rarely diverge from the usual path. At this moment I am tempted to treat on a matter primarily American, in order to show how a great American book strikes an Englishman. By the kindness of the St. Louis Christian Publishing Company I have received a copy of "Organic Evolution Considered," by Alfred Fairhurst, A. M., Professor of Natural Science in Kentucky University. I am in the middle of the volume and shall only slowly travel to the end. Every page is packed with either fact or argument. The facts are overwhelming and the logic is arrayed in tremendous batteries. I am perplexed to think how any student can read this volume and ever again give the smallest quarter to the Darwinians. The preliminary chapters on Matter, Force and the Method of Creation would form a capital little scientific handbook of themselves. Then follows a fine chapter of 22 pages on Natural Selection. The man who can read those 22 pages and not feel convinced that Darwin and Spencer are annihilated must be as difficult to teach as his simian ancestor according to those biologists. I was myself fully confirmed in my conviction that the Evolution theory was a hopeless fallacy, by carefully reading the great but beautifully simple French work of Quatrefages. That masterly philosopher curiously saved French modern science from the Darwinian deluge false hypotheses. Most people who know anything about modern thought in France are aware that French savants have not generally been carried away by Darwin, Huxley and Spencer, as the majority of English, German and American biologists have. This is about the only intellectual matter in which France has stood by the old theories. If Prof. Fairhurst's work could be circulated in England and if it were translated in German, it would vastly help to promote the flow of the tide which has already turned. Those sermons which Beecher preached shortly before his death, entirely in favor of Evolution from the Theistic standpoint were amongst the most flippantly specious of all his popular and beautiful discourses. They were swallowed with avidity by thousands of English readers. It is a singular fact that the sermons recently preached by Dr. Talmage and which I notice are castigated by the editor of the New York Christian Witness, are taken little notice of here. They are vehemently in condemnation of Darwinian doctrine and therefore they are persistently ignored. But they will quietly affect many minds. The New York Witness editor publishes the sermons and yet growls hideously at what he publishes, and I see he is fighting some of his astonished readers who stand up for Talmage. So the fight is only beginning. I am amused at the cool assumption of many who seem to imagine that nothing more is to be said; that man and the monkey have been indubitably proved to be the great-grandchildren of that disgusting creature, the arboreal tree-climbing quadruped of Darwin's imagination, with its hairy paletot, its big tail and its pointed ears. The truth is that the controversy is only in its incipient stage and therefore I am thankful for Prof. Fairhurst's contribution to the great discussion which can only have one end, that end being the funeral of the vaunted Darwinian doctrine.

THE ORIGIN OF MAN.

Perhaps the most important chapter in this remarkable book is that on the Origin of Man. This is the kind of chapter which would be enjoyed by the Duke of Argyll or Dr. Virchow, who has lately been amongst us from Berlin. Prof. Fairhurst shows that geologically man has but a brief existence. There has been no physical change in man during all the historic period. The oldest known skulls show no difference between primeval man and man as he is to day. According to Virchow, the missing link still remains a phantom. Virchow is the greatest scientist now living and if Germany had listened to his voice he would have saved that country from the blight of scientific as Quatrefages saved France. In this splendid chapter Prof. Fairhurst collates all the evidence on the subject of the Origin of Man worth having. A reader who masters this chapter needs nothing more. This writer seems to have read everything. Huxley, Romanes, Wallace, Dana, Max Mueller, Le Conte, are quoted with enlightening effect.

DARWIN AND THE CANNIBALS AND THE MISSIONARIES.

I am glad that Prof. Fairhurst calls up the story which should never be forgotten, which has often been related with great effect in English, of the relations of Darwin to missions amongst the heathen. When Darwin sailed past certain islands in the Pacific he found them inhabited by cannibals, whom he pronounced to be hopelessly beastial; but twenty-five years afterwards he found these same cannibals converted to Christianity and enjoying the blessings of civilization. In consequence of this astounding change wrought by Christian missionaries he gave annually to the day of his death a subscription of twenty-five pounds to the London Missionary Society. "How many years," asks Prof. Fairhurst, "would it take for even Christian missionaries to convert a tribe of gorillas into man-loving, God-fearing, self-conscious beings, capable of believing that they possessed immortal souls?"

ANARCHISTS IN ENGLAND.

All Americans know that we enjoy in England perfect liberty of the press. Anarchists and other wild revolutionists do not fail to take advantage of this freedom to set up their own various propaganda. But of mad and violent anarchism we have very little. What is more powerful and may some day assume great dimensions is that sort of anarchist communism which does not advocate assassination or any physical force, but openly protests against all forms of public authority and private property. There is a monthly journal called Freedom, now in its tenth volume, which is the organ of this party of which Prince Kropotkine is perhaps the best known leader. The true anarchist according to this journal is no enemy of society, but only of abuses. He is at war with all institutions and all habits which are based on the two principles of authority and property. The authority of man over man is a thing not to be accepted and submitted to, but to be resisted as essentially evil and wrong. "Property is theft," said Proudhon and all these anarchist communists proclaim themselves his disciples. Theoretically the English anarchist does not approve outrage, but it seems to me that he is very much like the Roman Catholics who theoretically does not approve of persecution. He very soon denies his own doctrine when it is put to actual test, when he has an opportunity of showing the wolf under the lambskin. It is quite evident that he has much more sympathy with the perpetrator of crime and of outrage than with the ordinary law-abiding citizen. The former is extolled as a devoted hero in the very same breath as he is called a homicidal maniac, while the latter is abused as a wretched groveler who must earn the contempt of high thinking men by his abject submission to injustice and wrong. Every now and then an English anarchist writer breaks out in bloodthirsty style. For instance, we have in London a revolutionary organ called the Commonweal, David Nicoll's paper, which all the time goes further than the average anarchists think prudent at present. In a recent issue this fiery editor says, "Have patience! From the blood, tears and pain of thousands shall arise an army that shall burn, slay, destroy. Though God would not save, yet shall he avenge them." Following this is a quotation from that arch-anarchist, Michael Bakounine. I will reproduce this, simply for the purpose of showing my American readers what fearful poison is being disseminated for the benefit of thousands of the masses here who are through the hardships of life only too eager to imbibe the venom of this hideous socialism.

"THE REVOLUTIONIST."

"The revolutionist is a man under a vow. He ought to have no personal interests, no business, no feelings, no property. He ought to be absorbed in one single interest, one single thought, one single passion—the revolution. . . . He has only one aim, one science—destruction; for that, and for nothing else, he studies mechanics, physics, chemistry and sometimes medicine. With the same object he observes men, characters, the situations and all the conditions of the existing social order. He hates and despises the existing morality. For him everything is moral that helps on the triumph of the revolution; everything is immoral and criminal that hinders it. Between him and society there is war—war to the death, incessant, irreconcilable. He ought to be ready to die, to endure torture, and, with his own hands, to kill all who place obstacles in the way of the revolution. So much the worse for him if he has any ties in the world—any ties of relationship, of friendship, of love! He is no true revolutionist if these attachments stay his arm. Nevertheless, he must live in the midst of society, feigning to be what he is not. He must penetrate everywhere—among the upper classes as well as among the middle, into the merchants' shops, into the church, into the government offices, into the army, into the literary world, into the detective force and into the imperial palace. . . . He must prepare a list of those that are condemned to death, and dispatch them in the order of their crimes. . . . All reasonings about the future are criminal, because they hinder destruction pure and simple and fetter the progress of the revolution. The brigand is the true revolutionist, the popular avenger, who acts without phrases taken from books. We must have a series of outrages and of audacious and even mad enterprises, striking terror into the powerful, and arousing the people till they believe in the triumph of the revolution."

So much for Michael Bakounine and his beautiful doctrine! Is it possible that seeds of this sort can be plentifully sown without producing a fearful crop? Unfortunately, socialism generally seems to tend in this direction for this reason, that the great majority of socialists are men and women who begin their ideas of reform by reforming God, Christ, the Bible and the church out of existence. I say this with regret, because I know some socialists who are splendid Christians, but are perplexed to know what to do under the present sectarian chaos and unable to see the right way out of it all. For the most part socialists in England cut the ground from under their own feet by their infidelity. W. DURBAN.

43 Park Road, South Tottenham, London, Nov. 18, 1898.

New York Letter.

Bro. C. M. Kreidler, pastor of the church at Troy, N. Y., paid our city a visit last week. His work in that city is in splendid condition. He has just entered upon his sixth year as pastor at Troy, and during the five years of his work there the membership of the church has grown from 170 to 563 and seventy have united with them within the past year. The prayer-meetings have outgrown the parlors and now are held in the lecture room, there being an average of about 200 in attendance. The working forces are thoroughly organized and are growing in efficiency all the time. A good index of this is in their missionary offerings. Five years ago they gave $78 for missions, last year they gave $430. They have recently organized a branch work in Lansingburg, a suburb of Troy, and hope to nurture it into a second church. Bro Kreidler reviewed the five years' work in a special discourse at the anniversary and indicated five forward steps which he says the church should take: Larger church attendance, including the children; enthusiastic evangelism in which every member should be engaged; greater interest upon the part of each member in directing aright the influence of the church; a deeper conscience in the matter of Christian stewardship, and more godly living. If these steps are taken greater prosperity will even attend the efforts of the Disciples in Troy.

***

The Church of Christ at Haverhill, Mass., under the pastoral care of Bro. E. M. Flinn, is greatly encouraged. They recently raised money and paid off a floating debt and this success together with enlarged attendance inspires pastor and people to go forward. They are planning to entertain the New England convention next June in its annual meeting. Here is a note, too, from the Church Leaflet (First Church, Philadelphia,) which has the right ring in it:

There is a growing sentiment among our members that a series of meetings should be held in the church this winter. It is a good sign. If the meetings should be held they will undoubtedly be conducted by the pastor himself, as his experience in conducting meetings would lead us to believe. He is also acquainted with one of the most prominent gospel singers in the United States, who, if we could obtain his services, would cause the church to be as crowded as it was in days gone by. It is earnestly hoped that this feeling will assume proportions that will make the meeting a necessity. Our pastor has been accustomed to conducting large meetings in the West, and we feel that his efforts here would meet with large results.

Bro. J. S. Myers, the pastor, in a personal note intimates that a growing sense of the need of greater achievements pervades the congregation. We hope this contemplated revival will materialize and result in the salvation of many souls.

***

The pastoral epistle from the Episcopal Bishops read in all churches of that faith in this country on the last Lord's day of October, among other things touches on three matter

centennial anniversary of the Book of Common Prayer. And we most earnestly ask that the day may be observed in our churches as commemorating an event which, more than any other single gift of God, has reversed the confusion of tongues by giving to the lips of countless worshipers the one "mouth" in which to show forth God's praise.

that it must be complemented and consecrated by more careful and definite training in religious truth in the family and in the Sunday-school, in church schools and colleges, and in the careful teaching of the clergy of the church.

It is good for us to know that the number of persons confirmed during the last three years

of the like preceding period by $1,150,104.70.

***

The strong tendency toward organization is one of the religious perils of our time. Almost every religious and moral sentiment, apparently, feels called upon to crystallize and have a president, a secretary and a treasurer. Mr. Theodore F. Seward has come to the front again; this time as the originator of the "Neighborhood Chain" movement. For a few years past he has worried himself, not to say other people also, in pushing his "Don't Worry Circle." His directions to candidates for admission to the order are as follows:

Write to three persons about reporting themselves as links, and ask each to write to three others, with a request that they also continue the work. When practicable, let the three persons spoken to be of a different religious faith from your own. Begin the practice of definitely and earnestly sending out thoughts of love, sympathy and helpfulness each day, if only for a very few minutes. Let loving wishes and prayers first go out to the whole round world, thus surrounding it with an invisible chain of love. Then turn the thought toward friends and acquaintances, especially toward those whom we cherish any unkind, envious or critical feeling. It is well to have a regular time for this daily exercise. There are already many thousand people throughout the world who follow the practice at the hour of noon. The sympathetic association with so many others in spiritual fellowship is an advantage.

This is all good in itself, but the church of Christ with the blessed gospel of God's grace in her hands, is doing or should be doing, this very thing. Why not use this widespread "organization" energy, in the name of Christ simply as members of his holy church?

***

Gen. Stewart L. Woodford, ex-Minister to Spain was the guest of honor at the Baptist Social Union at the Hotel Savoy a few evenings since, and in an address gave utterance to these words, which merit reading because of the speaker's high official position under our government in Spain:

"The truth," said he, "was told when it was said that I did everything to preserve peace between this country and Spain. I did it at the direction of the President of our country. Peace, I believe, is the purpose of the American people. When war did come, however, your President was as quick, as resolute and as sure in striking a decisive blow to Spain as he had been patient and forbearing before. I need not recount to you the victories that practically swept Spain's navy from the waters of the ocean or the rapid defeat of her troops on the land. But, now that peace has once more been restored, the American people are face to face with a grave question. What is to be done with the Philippines?

"This is a question we must consider intelligently and humanely. Porto Rico is ours by the action of the people of that island. Cuba is ours by r ght of conquest. We will retain it until, as we promised, a permanent, stable and free government is established by the people of the island. That, I fear, will be a much longer period than the President and Congress ever dreamed of when war was declared.

"War and crime have been the rule so long that I fear that before the conditions named can be fulfilled almost an entirely new set of people will have to be imported into the place.

"If we bring our highest courage to bear, and accept the responsibility regretfully but bravely, the same Providence that gave Dewey a victory at Manila Bay will give victory to the highest purpose of this nation, and result in a blessing, not only for our people, but for the entire civilized world." S. T. WILLIS.

1281 *Union Ave.*

Early Times in Indiana.

In the month of June, 1842, "the elders and brethren of the Church of Christ in Indiana" held a meeting in the city of Indianapolis, in which a general plan for the co-operation of the members and churches of this state was made for evangelistic work. The state was divided into four districts, "the first district to consist of that region of the country lying and being north of the national road and east of the meridian of Indianapolis; the second district to lie south of the first; the third to lie west of the second, bounded by the meridian of Indianapolis, and the national road on the north, and the fourth district to lie north of the third "

An evangelist was selected for each one of these districts and they were selected by ballot, namely, for the first district, Benjamin Franklin; second district, Ryland T. Brown; third district, James M. Mathes; fourth district, John O'Kane. The salaries for the evangelists were fixed at the sum of $460 for married men and $300 for unmarried, for their services for each year. They were expected to make their collections for their salaries at the meetings and by visiting the different churches for that purpose. An address was issued by that assembly with this title: "To the congregation associated on the foundation of the apostles and prophets and Jesus Christ the chief corner stone, throughout the state of Indiana." It was signed by Ryland T. Brown as chairman, and F. W. Emmons as secretary.

As we read this address we discovered that they saw very clearly the necessity for the co-operation of the churches, and the better support of their ministers. In that address we find these words:

"The day of miraculous gifts has passed; we cannot expect that our public laborers can command the stone to be made bread, or that the raven will feed them, like Elijah of old. If this were the case, the greater part of the brotherhood would be cut off from the glory of any active participation in the conversion of the world. But none are to be drones in the heavenly family. It is the duty of every Christian to labor in his appropriate sphere, and if we cannot preach ourselves we can aid in supplying the necessities of those who do, and so be joint laborers in the good cause. This is not only the rational feature of this subject, but it is the statute of heaven, signed, sealed and delivered by the Spirit of inspiration."

The next annual gathering was to be held at Noblesville, in Hamilton county, to commence on Friday before the second Lord's day in June, 1843, at which time the evangelists and delegates from the churches were to meet and report progress and deliberate for future operations. At that meeting in 1843 Barton W. Stone was present and preached his last sermon to the brethren in Indiana. His lovely character, his aged and fatherly advice, made him a unique figure at that meeting. He left there for his home in Jacksonville, Ill., where the next year he passed away to be with the Master and received the reward of his labors.

A venerable mother in Israel who was present at that meeting in 1843 gives many reminiscences of the historic characters among the Disciples attending that meeting. Benjamin Franklin had not yet gained the fame that afterwards made him so well known as a great gospel preacher throughout the entire country and as the editor of the American Christian Review. Dr. Ryland T. Brown, who afterwards became distinguished as a citizen of Indianapolis and as the man who knew more about more things and knew it well than any man in the state. All branches of science, and especially geology, were to him as an open book. He not only excelled in this field, but also in the clear understanding of the revelation that God gave to his people.

Another character at that meeting was John O'Kane, noted not only for his ability as a preacher, but also for his ever-abounding wit and good humor. He was six feet and one inch in height, very straight and slender, which gave him the appearance of being taller than he really was. In the style of the time, his hair was worn long and was black as a raven's wing. His eyes were black and set well back in the head, where at times they would sparkle with mirth, and at other times look out with the piercing glances that betokened woe to an opponent if an encounter should come on the field of polemics. With a swaggering air a preacher once refused to debate with him, at the same time observing that he would gladly discuss the doctrinal issues with Alexander Campbell, or some of the great leaders of the Reformation. Fixing his

keen eyes upon him, and pointing his long finger at him in the style of Randolph, O'Kane replied: "You, *you* debate with Alexander Campbell! Why, if one of his ideas got into your head it would explode like a bombshell!"

He was a man of sarcasm and irony, but with all, a man with a great and tender heart. The times in which he lived made men of conscience tenacious of what they believe to be the truth, and thus made them warriors and oftentimes harsh in dealing with their opposers. It was hard for O'Kane ever to permit an opportunity to go by without a retort if it were possible. A certain opposer of his once met him and extending his hand, said: "Well, Bro. John, I used to think that you were an unprofitable servant, but I think differently now." "Indeed," replied O'Kane, shaking his hand warmly, "that is precisely what I used to think of you, brother, but *I have never changed my mind!*"

D. R. LUCAS.

Colorado Convention.

It was held with the Central Church, Pueblo, Nov. 1-6. It was the seventeenth annual session. Seventy-four delegates and visitors were in attendance. B. O. Aylesworth opened the Ministerial Association with an address on "Some things Requisite to Christian Union." The address of the president, Grant K. Lewis, dealt with "Some Responsibilities of the Churches." L. B. Tyler answered the question, "Have we a Scriptural Eldership?" Elmer Ward Cole spoke of "The Preacher of To day—His Opportunities," Leonard G. Thompson on "Fishers of Men" and R. B. Preston on "Beginning at Jerusalem." M. L. Streator closed the association with an address on "The Coming of the Lord." The officers of the association for the year are Grant K. Lewis, president; J. E. Pickett, vice-president; Elmer Ward Cole, secretary, and R. B. Preston, treasurer.

In his address as president of the Colorado Christian Missionary Convention B. O. Aylesworth said that the last year in Colorado mission work was an illustrated souvenir of Christian heroism. The report of the corresponding secretary, Leonard G. Thompson, showed 40 churches with a membership of 4,208; 35 Sunday-schools with 3,602 members; 23 Young People's Societies of Christian Endeavor with 700 members, and 19 auxiliaries to the Christian Woman's Board of Missions with 338 members. Nine churches were assisted during the year out of the appropriations from the C. W. B. M., and from moneys raised within the state. Those nine churches raised an average of $11.06 per member for all purposes, and of 51 cents per member for missions. The 40 churches raised for all purposes $31,731.72. Of this sum $1,581.97 was spent for missions. This is an average of $7.54 per member for all purposes, and 37 1-2 cents per member for missions. Counting as the year-book counts we have 41 preachers in Colorado, but of these only 28 are preaching, and some of these only a part of the time. During the sessions of the missionary convention, J. E. Pickett spoke on ''Church Federation—What Is It?'' The convention address was delivered by Samuel B. Moore. He was followed by G. W. Muckley on Church Extension, and pledges aggregating $60 per year were taken.

The convention adopted the report of the committee on Plan of Work for the New Year to the effect that we raise $1,000 in Colorado this year for Colorado work, and that the state board apportion that amount among the churches; that a state evangelist be employed for Colorado; that each church support its pastor in at least one meeting during the year as missionary work at some needy point; that we attempt arrangements for meetings at needy places by Eastern pastors willing to do vacation work at the possible compensation; that capable, consecrated young men be sought—men who will succeed, who have succeeded, in the East—who are willing to devote their lives to Colorado work, content with meager support until their work bears fruit; that we appeal to the Christian Woman's Board of Missions for further help for those churches which cannot yet be self-sustaining.

The convention officers for the year are president, Samuel B. Moore; vice-president, J. E. Pickett; recording and corresponding secretary, Leonard G. Thompson; treasurer, A. E. Pierce; other members, B. O. Aylesworth, Grant K. Lewis, B. B. Tyler, R. B. Preston, Mrs. Laura B. Thompson, president of Colorado C. W. B. M., and Miss Sallie Barriger, secretary of C. W. B. M. The trustees are I. E. Barnum, H. Morse, Wm. A. Ellmore. The state board elects its own president and secretary. These offices are filled by B. O. Aylesworth and Grant K. Lewis.

The state C. W. B. M. occupied an afternoon and evening. The speakers in the afternoon were Mrs. Laura B. Thompson, president, Mrs. Kate Updyke and Mrs. F. D. Pettit. The report of the treasurer was presented by that officer, Mrs. M. L. Parks, who also read the report of the corresponding secretary, Mrs. Sallie B. Semones, the latter being absent. Mrs. M. L. Parks conducted ''A Model Auxiliary.'' Mrs. B. B. Tyler led the devotions. Miss Lois A. White spoke on ''Junior and Young People's Work.'' The convention address was delivered by Mrs. Minnie F. Boggess, who was followed by Miss White, outlining the mission fields and work of the C. W. B. M.

The Sunday-school Institute was conducted by Mrs. Belle V. Harbert, who spoke on ''The Scope of Sunday-school Work.'' Mrs. Lois [illegible] Bible Lesson,'' B. B. Tyler on ''How to have a Successful Teachers' Meeting'' and J. E. Pickett on ''The Value and Importance of Decision Day in the Sunday-school.''

In the Christian Endeavor session Leonard G. Thompson presided in the afternoon, in the absence of the state superintendent, E. F. Behr, and J. E. Pickett presided at night. Following the report and address of the state superintendent, which was read by the presiding officer of the afternoon, Mrs. Rose Nipher read a paper on ''How Develop the Individual?'' and Miss Minnie Brown one on ''What Should Christian Endeavorers Read?'' Grant K. Lewis presented the Bethany C. E. Reading Courses in detail, and Ernest Piper conducted a Parliament of Methods. At night the convention address was delivered by B. B. Tyler, the Christian Endeavor Pledge being his theme. Miss Minnie Blake, of Denver, was elected state superintendent of Christian Endeavor Societies for Colorado.

The Sunday services of the convention consisted of a sermon at 11 A. M., by Chas. A. Stevens, the Lord's Supper at 3 P. M., conducted by M. L. Streator, and a sermon at 8 P. M., by J. B. Johnson.

The music was inspiring throughout, being under the direction of C. C. Pomeroy, with the assistance of Miss Lizzie Noble as organist and a good force of singers from the Central Church. The hospitality of the Pueblo Disciples was abundant and hearty. In the judgment of the writer it was the best Colorado convention since that of 1892. Miss Lois A. White and G. W. Muckley were present for their first time in a Colorado convention, and with the exception of the visit of F. M. Rains, in 1893, it was the first visit of a national secretary to a Colorado convention. Colorado wishes the presence of more of our national secretaries at its conventions. Will they please remember the wish here expressed? The next convention meets with the South Broadway Church, Denver.

LEONARD G. THOMPSON.

Denver, Col.

Ministerial Relief Items.

The work of the Board of Ministerial Relief has been very properly called ''a ministry of love,'' for it is the spirit of love paying a debt she owes to those whose lives have been given to her service.

Every lover of Christ and his church is pleased at the growth in our missionary work and enterprises and hails with joy the increase in our missionary force at home and abroad. But the question arises, What is to be done in a few years more when these missionaries are compelled, on account of age or disability, to leave the mission field? There is only one way that seems practical to provide for them, and that is, by the Board of Ministerial Relief; a fund given to this board will always be a means of providing for their necessities.

The church must consider the question of her ministry that is to be, and the way she deals with the ministry she now has will settle in a large measure the character of her future ministry. Young men of ability will hesitate to devote their lives to the service of a church that neglects in any way its worn-out and disabled ministers.

One thing is certain to grow out of the work of the Board of Ministerial Relief, and that is a better understanding of the relation of the church to its ministry and of the ministry to the church. The mutual obligations of mutual service and care will make a stronger tie and bring them into a closer fellowship. Instead of the minister being, as many suppose him to be, a hireling working for wages alone, he will be a shepherd to the flock, while the flock will understand that he is simply eating the fruit of the flock.

The third Lord's day in December is the

It is near the Christmas time and the Christmas time is a time when the heart opens to the cry of the suffering and needy. Surely, this will be heard and heeded by all.

Neglect and forgetfulness are sometimes as great sins as actual deeds of wrong. Jesus says, ''The poor ye have always with you,'' and he makes them his representatives. Many a heart has longed as they have thought of the other days that they might have been in Judea to have ministered to the Christ. But every poor saint is a representative of his, for he himself hath said, ''Inasmuch as ye have done it unto the least of these, my disciples, ye have done it unto me.''

"Oh, sons of God, who wear his holy name,
  Are we in truth his children even yet?
Can we of these his servants say in lasting shame
  We dared forget?"

—*Jessie Brown Pounds.*

Twenty different states are represented among the beneficiaries of this society. We asked the missionary secretary of one state, who was sending us a list of the preachers of his state, to mark those whom he thought worthy, deserving and entitled to our aid, and were much gratified on receiving his list to find that without knowing anything of our work he had marked all those to whom we were extending relief in his state.

A minister who was called to attend the funeral of one of our beneficiaries after he had crossed the river, says:

''I realized this morning, as I stood by the coffined form of this aged brother, for the first time the great need of the work in which you are engaged. It is indeed a labor of love. I wish every minister of the Church of Christ could have stood with me this morning over the

Could this have been so, greater and more powerful appeals would be made in the aid of the cause you represent and for which you plead so earnestly, and you may rely on me to be one of the staunchest supporters of Ministerial Relief hereafter. I have been careless like many others and neglectful of this work, but will be so no more.''

Some persons who do not understand the conditions and circumstances attending the life of the minister of Christ, sometimes think and say that he ought to give more time and attention to looking after financial matters, so as to provide for himself in his old age. But it is a sad fact that the moment a minister begins to do this he loses his influence and power over the very class of men that thus criticised him. Let it once be considered in any way by the people that a minister is engaged in his work solely from financial considerations, and his power as a minister is gone. The fact is, to make money requires consecration and devotion to that work, and no man can be wholly consecrated to two great purposes at once. It would seem that Jesus settled that matter when he said, ''Ye cannot serve God and man.'' Hence, the only sensible way is for the minister to be consecrated to his work. Let the business man be consecrated to his, and let his supply be given to the minister in need. This is Christ's plan; this is the apostolic teaching.

''Well-nigh all our ministers have come from the ranks of the poor. If we go back, Moses was the son of a poor Levite; Gideon was a thrasher; David was a shepherd boy; the apostles were unlearned fishermen; Melancthon was a workman in an armorer's shop; Martin Luther was the child of a poor miner; Carey was a shoemaker of Northampton; Livingstone worked in cotton mills. Scores and hundreds of the best men who have filled the ranks of the Christian ministry have been poor boys with nothing to start upon when they entered upon the work to which God called them; often their salaries have been exceedingly meagre, barely enough having been paid them to keep themselves and their loved ones during their active years in the ministry; then all manner of charities and benevolences have appealed to them constantly. A score of calls for relief pressing upon the preacher, where one comes to the average church member.''—*F. D. Power*.

As a matter of fact there are many churches who are unable to pay a liberal salary to their minister. This being the fact the minister is compelled to make some sacrifice or give up the work, which in numberless instances they have always been ready to do. There are, in fact, very few churches in our land to-day who have not in their infancy been nurtured and cared for by the sacrifice of some preacher of the gospel. It is true, perhaps, that many churches do not pay what they really ought to pay their minister, but we are glad to say there is an inmprovent in this direction. The old story, however, is true perhaps even yet of some of them. A deacon in a prayer-meeting was very earnestly praying and in his prayer said:

''O, Lord, bless our pastor and keep him humble and poor.''

He was interrupted by another deacon, who said:

''Amen! that's right Lord, you keep him humble and we will keep him poor!''

Every young minister should carefully consider the question of insurance. At the of 25 years the expectancy of life is about 35 years or a little more. An endowment policy of insurance with a 35 year limit to a person of that age costs but very little more than what is called straight life insurance. One at the age of 25 years taking a 35 year endowment policy would thus receive at the age of 60 years the full face value of his policy. In the meantime, if his death should occur, the same amount would go to his family.

The soldier enlisted in the service of his country goes fearlessly forward, knowing that if he is in any way disabled by disease or wounds, the government that he serves will provide for his wants and see that he does not suffer in his old age. The church should certainly be animated by the same spirit in caring for the soldiers who are disabled in her service.

In the experience gained by a short canvass at the various conventions in behalf of the Ministerial Aid Fund, it has been highly gratifying the cordial and interested manner in which the people receive the message. All they need is to know the necessities of the case and they will supply the means to care for the Lord's poor ones.

It is recorded that when Knowles Shaw the the distinguished evangelist, was killed in a railroad accident, the last words that he had spoken to a companion minister by his side were these: ''It is a grand thing to rally men to the cause of Christ.'' These words sum up in a single sentence the great work of the minister of Christ. Devoted to this great work, enlarging the Master's kingdom, sowing the good seed in human hearts, it is certainly the duty of his brethren to sustain him in the active work, and also as well when he can no longer wield the Sword of the Spirit.

A minister once doing a good work for a congregation was not well supported. He got along for sometime, making a great sacrifice, but finally one Sunday he said:

''Brethren, you will have to pray the Lord to let down a Jacob's ladder from heaven each Sunday morning and evening so that I can go up to heaven in the evening of that day and come down in the morning. If you do not do this, one thing is certain, if I remain among you during the week, I must have something to eat.'' It is useless to say that after that his wants were well supplied. It is often carelessness and want of thought on the part of the congregation as to their duty.

Covetousness is a sin, but so also is prodigality. Many persons who would consider it wrong if they were charged with covetousness, at the same time spend great sums of money for things that are useless to say the least, and often harmful. In this age of ours the sin of prodigality is as great, perhaps, as that of covetousness.

Bernard de Palassy, the Huguenot potter, distinguished himself by his knowledge and talents. The French King, Henry III., said to him one day that he should be compelled to give him up to his enemies unless he changed his religion. ''You have often said to me sire,'' was his reply, ''that you pity me, but as for me, I pity you who have given utterance to such words as ''I shall be compelled.'' These are unkindly words and I say to you in royal phrase, neither the Guises nor all your people, nor yourself, are able to compel a humble manufacturer of earthenware to bend his knees before statues. I worship God alone.''

If you are going to do anything for the world, for humanity, for any good cause like that of Ministerial Relief, the time to do it is now. Alexander, being asked how he had conquered the world, replied, ''By not delaying,''

Despise not the day of small things, is an injunction of one of the old servants of the Lord. Small incidents sometimes lead to great results. After the battle of Gettysburg a soldier was found dead upon the field holding in his hand the picture of three small children. No clue to his name could be found. In the terrors of battle he had comforted himself with that picture. It was published and by this means the children were found in a village of Western New York. The sale of this picture resulted in the founding of the National Orphan Homestead at Gettysburg, where the Humiston children, the originals of the pictures, found a home, and where their mother was for many years matron.

It is a lamentable fact that some persons give that they may have the applause of their equals for their gifts, but it is best to remember to ''let the lips of the poor be the trumpet of thy gift.''

In the year 1776 the British Government, by an act of Parliement, placed a tax upon silver-plate. It was reported to the Commissoner of Revenue that John Wesley was evading the law. So they rather peremtorily demanded that he make a return. Mr. Wesley replied as follows: ''Sir, I have two silver teaspoons at London and two at Bristol. This is all the plate which I have at present and I shall not buy any more while so many around me want bread. I am, sir, your most humble servant, John Wesley.'' Perhaps there was never a more charitable man than Mr. Wesley. During his whole life he lived very economically and in the course of fifty years it has been supposed he gave away more than 30,000 pounds. What an example for the wealthy men of our times!

Among the men of our times who seem to rightly appreciate the use of the wealth they have been permitted to accumulate is that of Gen. F. M. Drake, ex-Governor of Iowa. At Chattanooga he gave $5,000 to the Home Missionary Society and since that has given $5,000 to the Foreign Missionary Society. He was the originator that gave $5,000 to the Church Extension Socicty; he has given over $100,000 to Drake University; he also gave $1,000 to the Ministerial Aid Fund; and his other benefactors are many, known only to those who have been recipients. The man who administers on his own estate while he lives will avoid the court and attorney's fees, that often at great cost attend the execution of a will.

Send all offerings to Howard Cale, 120 East Market St., Indianapolis, Ind.

D. R. LUCAS.

Kansas City Letter.

While the Christian world is uniting in thanksgiving for the manifold mercies of God upon his children, we need not think it strange if an occasional note of discord is heard, even in this favored land, where Providence has so lavishly scattered benefactions of every kind. We have been favored with such an exhibition of thanklessness here, on the part of Dr. J. E. Roberts, who styles himself "Minister of The Church of This World." Starting as a Baptist minister, Mr. Roberts soon drifted away from the secure anchorage of the Christian faith and became a Unitarian preacher. After several years' service in this capacity, first in Denver, and then in Kansas City, he became too radical for even that diluted form of religious liberalism, and resigned his pulpit, to the satisfaction of a portion of his congregation. Some of them, however, followed him into the "Church of This World," as he calls the loosely organized society that has gathered around him. He speaks every Sunday morning in the Coates Opera House, and his addresses are usually devoted to attacks upon the Christian faith and hope, such as will compare favably, in respect of brilliant rhetoric, skillful misrepresentation and appeal to prejudice and ignorance, with those of Col. Ingersoll. It is his special delight, on occasions when the followers of Christ are uniting in any service of gratitude and joy, such as Thanksgiving or Christmas, to vent his spleen in tirades of unusual bitterness against the particular cause of their happy remembrance. Last Sunday this gentleman delivered an anti-Thanksgiveng fulmination, which would have been quite funny, if it had not been so sadly untrue, unkind and irreverent. In the beginning of his address he declares that it is his purpose to continue his annual protest against this Thanksgiving custom, as long as he continues to be a public speaker. What he expects to accomplish by this he does not state, but probably his hopes are as high as were those of the ancient dame who wielded her broom against the inrushing waters, and fated to meet with the same degree of success, no doubt. But he presumes greatly upon the ignorance of his audience when he comes to state his first reason for opposing this custom, namely, that it is "totally un-American." Is he ignorant of the history of Thanksgiving? Does he not know that, since the year 1621, the very year after the landing of the Pilgrim Fathers upon the New England Coast, it has been the custom of our fathers to appoint frequent days of thanksgiving for what they believed to be special mercies from the hand of God? Does he not know that the Revolutionary Congress appointed several such days, and that the adoption of our Constitution, in 1789, was celebrated by a day of national thanksgiving, ordered by Congress, and duly proclaimed by Pres. George Washington? Does he not know that, since 1863, this annual Thanksgiving has been observed without the omission of a single year, and that it is as well established and universally observed as Christmas or the Fourth of July? Yes, doubtless he knows all this. But he thought that his audience would not know, so he was bold to say what he must have been aware was untrue to all history. If this nation is not a Christian nation, at least to the extent that justifies its observance of such memorial days as Thanksgiving and Christmas, then it has been sadly misunderstood by the statesmen who have been first to recognize the Divine Hand in our history.

But Mr. Roberts waxes very warm, as his address proceeds, perhaps because he feels somewhat the difficulty of imposing upon the public such manufactured history. He becomes very indignant at the thought that God is thanked for the results of our recent war with Spain, and demands that the credit of our glorious victories shall be given to Dewey and Sampson, and their fellow heroes, and to them alone. Then remembering, perhaps, that these brave men themselves were first to give to God the glory of our victories, he bursts out with this rare specimen of arrogant blasphemy: "I arise to demand that God Almighty be dismissed from the military and naval service!" Poor, ranting fool! Because he has dismissed God from his own heart and pulpit and church, he thinks to expel him from the hearts of our brave soldiers and sailors. Such madness is too pitiful for censure. Let us pray that this man's spiritual insanity may soon be dissipated, and that, like Nebuchadnezzar of old, he may come to realize again before he dies, that there is a God who ruleth in the heavens above and in the earth beneath.

W. F. RICHARDSON.

Kansas City, Mo., Nov. 25, 1898.

Cincinnati Letter.

EDITOR CHRISTIAN-EVANGELIST:—The great conventions meet here Oct. 13-20, 1899, and we are preparing for them.

The 10th missionary district, of Ohio, which includes Cincinnati, is awake to present opportunities. The church at Lockland which was organized last spring has called W. O. Thomas as pastor, and he starts well.

The new church at Norwood, where Bro. A. W. Taylor is pastor, and much beloved, is now in a fair meeting with our district evangelist, Bro. Allen Wilson, they have had 19 additions to date. Bro. J. A. Pine has lately come to Eastern Ave. and even now we have begun to love him. Last Sunday we dedicated a neat house at Fairmont, another suburb, where Bro. J. S. Lawrence and his faithful coworkers have conducted a Sunday-school for two years. The school averages about 125. Two confesssions within a week.

H. K. Pendleton and others are starting in their own "hired house," at Terrace Park. P. Y. Pendleton is now in a meeting at Monteray with five confessions thus far.

Bro. Lawman, of New Paris, expects to plant our cause at Campbellstown, the home of the parents of our Rose Oxer.

Bro. Seaman is in a meeting with the 4th Street Church, Covington, with 29 additions to date. The Central Church has started a misssion Sunday-school on Central Avanue and Walnut Street, each about a mile from the church. Stanley Spraggens superintendent of one and N. T. Purcell of the other. Mt. Auburn is calling for a Sunday-school, and there is a committee to report at the next board meeting what will be done in the rich suburb of Avondale, where we have several members.

Bro. Isaac Selby lately gave his series of lectures at the Central, at invitation of the Ministeral Association, and on Nov. 28 and 29, he is to debate with a representative of free thought from Cleveland. He is a champion, and our city churches should call him for a course of lectures. On Nov. 8th the Disciples of this vicinity held a banquet at the Grand Hotel, enjoying a pleasant evening. Reminiscences of days that are gone, work now being done and hopes for the future were brought before us in happy toasts. Our next monthly conference will be held at the Central Dec. 5th. Preachers' meeting at 10:30 A. M., lunch at 12; reception to our new preachers and wives at 1 P. M.; board meeting at 2 P. M., and at the same hour Sister Moses will address the women.

A. M. HARVOUT.

Cincinnati, Ohio.

Two Years More.

EDITOR CHRISTIAN-EVANGELIST: — In your issue Nov. 24th, page 672, in "Open Parliament on our National Conventions," Bro. E. C. Browning begins his remarks with: "The year 1899 will close the most wonderful century of human history." Stop and think a moment, Bro. B. It will not do to close this century of great things so soon as that. If the first century had closed with the year 99 there would have been only 99 years in the century. If the second century had closed with the year 199, there would have been only that many years in the two centuries. So also with this greatest of centuries, if you end it short of December 31, 1900, it will not be complete. For instance, Bro. B., if I were indebted to you $1,900, and would count out to you the dollars in payment and stop with the eighteen hundred and ninety-ninth dollar, you would surely say, "Come now, Bro. W., put up the other dollar." So also the 19th century owes us the full number of years, and must give us two more after 1898.

Fraternally yours, M. WETZEL.

Denver, Col.

Notes and News.

For the Boys.

EDITOR CHRISTIAN-EVANGELIST:—Rev. A. W. Conner, of Irvington, Ind., has moved our town to begin a good work for our boys. He makes an irresistible plea for the Young Prince. His work here is applauded by every one. Money castle is usually the last to surrender. Mr. Conner took it easily and nearly $1,000 was pledged to build a reading room and gymnasium for boys and young men in our town. Five directors were selected to direct the work. Every church should call for this plea. It will do you good.

Yours for the boys,
L. T. VAN CLEAVE.
Atlanta, Ill., Nov. 28, 1898.

Kentucky University and College of the Bible Graduates, Attention!

All graduates of Kentucky University and the College of the Bible who have changed their place of residence in the last three years will confer a favor by notifying me of same at once. Also all former students.

GEO. W. KEMPER,
President Society of Alumni.
181 *W. 3d St., Lexington, Ky.*

Evangelist Wanted.

The Iowa Central District Board which has for sometime been planning to employ a district evangelist now has matters in such shape that the right kind of a man should be able to secure a fair salary, and would be pleased to hear from men who feel capable of organizing, systematizing, "enthusing" and doing the work of an evangelist.

S. C. SLAYTON, Dist. Sec.
27th and Kingman Ave., Des Moines, Ia.

Dedication at Huntington, Indiana.

The Christian Church at Huntington, Ind., has just completed and dedicated a new and elegant church building.

Many years ago the church here, few in numbers and weak financially, built a small, unpretentious house where for many years they worshiped and laid the foundation for the good work that has been accomplished in these later years. Seventeen years ago, while the beloved and eloquent L. Berry Smith was pastor of the church, they built a brick house and worshiped in it until the present year. They have remodeled, and rebuilt it and made it one of the handsomest and most commodious church houses in the city. Bro. W. T. Wells is the hard-working and successful pastor at Huntington. He is in the hearts of the people both in and out of the church and is doing good, safe work.

Lord's day, Nov. 27th, was a day that will be remembered for a long time by the church here. It witnessed the formal opening and dedication of this beautiful edifice. After the sermon we asked for $3,600, the amount necessary to provide for all indebtedness. The giving was prompt and generous. Before the close of the night service the entire amount was raised and there was great joy in that city.

The church at Huntington starts on a new career of usefulness and has better facilities than ever before to do a great work for the Master.

L. L. CARPENTER.
Wabash, Ind.

A Good Convention.

Our district convention closed to-day. The attendance was about double what it was last year, but still a majority of the counties in the district were not represented. The papers read, however, and the sermons were of an unusually high order. Any of them would have been worthy of our National Convention. Brethren Clay, Davis and Abbott were present, and were the soul of the convention, as usual.

W. A. OLDHAM.
Carthage, Mo., Dec. 1, 1898.

A Note From England.

DEAR BROTHER GARRISON:—Arrived safe on Nov. 19th, and our work at Chester opens very encouragingly. Received a royal welcome from our good brethren here and we have every indication for a great harvest for the Master and a forward move all along the line of Christian work. We have had a large attendance and three confessions this first week of our work, while the general interest is deepening and widening rapidly.

Very truly yours in Him,
J. A. L. ROMIG.
21 *Seller St., Chester, Eng., Nov. 25, 1898.*

A Word from Oklahoma.

In reply to your request as to what the brethren think of the space occupied by notes and suggestions on Sunday-school Lessons, Midweek Prayer-meeting Topics, Christian Endeavor, Bethany Reading Courses, will say I have been delighted with them and prize them highly. To me they are highly instructive, and to my mind they are leading heavenward, bright lights here and there along the pathway as we journey to the heavenly Canaan. Their spirit is to lead to Christ and anything that will lead to "the Rock that is higher than I," I hail with joy. We need cheery words in this new country, and as we have but little preaching I love to hear the word of cheer in your paper and the success of the cause in other parts of the country, yet hoping and praying for increase of laborers here and the building up of the wilderness and waste places with the rose of Sharon until they may be called "Beulah." God being my helper I will toil on in the vineyard of the Lord as best I can by his assisting grace in the good work, praying that the brethren awake out of sleep.

Yours in the Lord,
J. H. TRACEY.
Thomas, Okla., Nov. 23, 1898.

Jamaica Printing Press.

TO THE EDITOR CHRISTIAN-EVANGELIST—*Dear Brother:* I am greatly indebted to you for your kind interest and help in obtaining a press to aid us in the work of our missions in Jamaica. At Chattanooga it appeared that the obtaining of the amount necessary for the purchase of the press would not be a matter of any difficulty. Approval of the undertaking was generally expressed. Hitherto I have not received nearly enough, and the response to your disinterested appeal has been small. As I intend to leave this country in another week, intended contributions should be promptly sent. We think the possession of this press will be an important auxiliary in carrying on our work. There will never be a better time for securing it than now. If friends who purposed sending will do so at once it will soon be done. I trust as many as possible will have a share in it.

Your truly,
C. E. RANDALL, Missionary in Jamaica.

It is Bro. Randall's purpose to start a small eight-page paper to be known as "The Jamaica Christian," on his return to Jamaica, if he succeeds in securing his press. This means an advanced step in that island, and those who contribute to this fund will be materially helping to make that step possible. Shall we not hear from a number in response to our call for $1.00 donations?—EDITOR.

Dedication at Eureka, Kan.

The dedication of the beautiful house of worship, recently finished in this city, passed off very pleasantly and successfully the 27th inst. By cash gifts and time pledges all debts are provided for. The day was cloudy and snow was falling, but the house was packed to its utmost capacity, there being by actual count over 700 seated. The music was very fine, the large choir being supported by an excellent orchestra. The giving was rapid and liberal. At 3:30 P. M. the house was filled and a delightful communion service was had. Preaching again at night, and I will stay over until Wednesday.

This splendid building and the great spiritual awakening is due, partly, to a meeting held by the writer last spring, but possibly more to the tireless efforts of the minister, W. E. Bobbitt, a young man of great promise. He closes his three years' work Jan. 1st, and will go to Drake for a few years. He is the most popular preacher in the city, and now has the satisfaction of having completed the largest and most beautiful church building in town. There are here, as there ever have been elsewhere, and ever must be anywhere, some noble men and women without whom no house would be built, preacher employed and paid, or missionary sent out to heathen lands.

The house is wooden, built of the best material and by first-class workmen; has two main rooms, class rooms, basement, good bell, and heated by hot air furnace. The pews and pulpit are of oak, and are very attractive and comfortable. The board have their eye on a man to follow Bro. Bobbitt, and we trust that there will be no break in the good work. There is a very bright future for the church in Eureka.

D. D. BOYD.
1048 *Spruce St., Topeka, Kan.*

Methods of Work.

DEAR BROTHER GARRISON:—I desire to add my words of commendation for the excellence of the CHRISTIAN-EVANGELIST as a religious paper. As I was thinking of its different departments it occurred to me that a regular department of "*Methods of Work*" would make an excellent column for your paper. The Church Economist, published in New York City, suggested this thought to me. In such a column as this might be recorded the new and varied methods of doing things used by the different ministers. I am sure that it would be very valuable and helpful to have such a clearing house of methods.

We have recently tried in our church a kindergartner department, conducted during the hour of services. A place at which parents, one of whom would otherwise have to stay at home, can leave children from the ages of two to six while they attend services. I think it is a capital idea. It affords the privileges of services to tired mothers, and is profitable to children as well.

Fraternally yours, J. E. LYNN.
Springfield, Ill.

[The idea suggested above is a capital one. Let us have from all our workers practical suggestions on how to do things. In this preachers, Sunday-school superintendents, Endeavor workers and others may help each other. If you have a good thing pass it around. Let us hear from others.—EDITOR.]

"Our National Conventions."

I cannot say that I am one of the "several brethren" of whom answers were asked, to the following questions:

1. *What changes, if any, would you suggest in the manner of conducting our conventions?*
2. *What suggestions have you to offer as to the Jubilee Convention?*

But I think that I can fairly respond with "others who have suggestions."

As to the *first* question, I hardly think it practicable to adopt any stereotyped program for conducting the annual business of the conventions. New occasions will bring new duties and each annual meeting must be considered from the standpoint of its own necessities. It is not likely that any method would suit all at all times.

As to the *second* question, it occurs to me that on the fiftieth anniversary of the American Christian Missionary Society all reports and papers, especially of a historical character, should be prepared with unusual care and published in a volume as a memorial of the occasion; this volume to include also the annual report of the corresponding secretaries for 1899. As far as possible each person who is living and has held the office of corresponding secretary in either the A. C. M. Society, the F. C. M. Society, or the C. W. B. Society should be asked to write the history of the society for his term of service These pages of history need not be read to the convention, but reported and published in the memorial volume. In order that this part of the work may be thoroughly done the various boards ought to take action soon.

F. M. GREEN.

Kent, Ohio.

[The suggestion about the publication of the proceedings, official reports and leading addresses of the Jubilee Convention, in a memorial volume, is a good one and one we have made to the secretaries, through whom the plan can best be carried out. The publication of such addresses in our religious journals does not answer the purpose, and they can hardly afford the space for them.—EDITOR.]

Missouri Bible-school Notes.

The results of John Giddens' work at Mountain View last spring are now manifest in the new church house nearing completion, in which their Bible-school will do regular work after January 1st, 1899.

In the work at home Hugh Puckett is growing constantly, so that the West Side school, Kansas City, is at its best to-day, while the superintendent is planning something new and good for the new year. In our work they heartily co-operate, while at home they are not slack in the better methods. Just right, they are.

At Holden I have just closed my first institute, and the interest was good from the first, while the work of all the membership was so much better than I had expected that I felt much encouraged by it. J. W. Boulton has done such work here as at Tarkio and the results are evident in every department of the church, especially in the Bible-school, in which my heart's interest centers. The examinations were such as gave me great satisfaction, while so many talked of the benefits which came to them. Their giving to our work was so generous that I ought to mention it, while their urgings to return caused some pride.

Thank the many friends for co-operation with us and for the prompt responses to the calls. It so happened this time, brethren, that your treasurer could not raise the money, or you would not have been so persistently dunned, but as it is I must ask that you help until we are caught up, and then I will bear the burden a while longer for you. Have you brought it before your school or church? Will you not do so right away? Now that State Mission Day is past, remember this las twork, permitting us to even up with all creditors by next week.

J. C. Henderson, the wide-awake superintendent of Pleasant Grove, near Cameron, is bringing their little school worthily to the front by keeping up with the advanced methods as he learns them, and while in this joins in sending the better plans into the weaker places of Missouri, accepting their apportionment and remitting one-half of same, and I believe every school in Missouri could easily do likewise if only some one would see that it was done.

In St. Clair, at Pape, the brethren keep their school going by constant work, but best of all are happy in it, with no complainings; and have just sent an offering to our work, as is done nearly every year, and it shall return, too.

The Home Department continues to grow in favor as tried, and if you have not begun such take it up immediately. The Monroe City school increased its membership nearly one hundred by it, and all are loud in their praises of its good.

We are nearing the annual changes, but let no school drop its superintendent just because he wants a change. Is he doing good work? Then let him make it better for 1899; so of all other workers. Make no changes except for cause.

Send to this office for the samples needed in your Home Department work.

The school at Clearmont, as also the school at Ham's Prairie, have given us to understand that their apportionments are accepted and will be paid, and we publicly thank them for it and ask, Will not others join the co-operation?

One of the happiest institutes in all my work has just closed at Lawson, a school that has elected their superintendent for life or good behavior, and A. W. Gross well deserves the honor. Every consideration was given to our work, all the time turned over to your servant, all the workers joined in heartily, and everything went merry as a marriage bell. In such happy work do not think your servant would ever tire. In compensation the brethren were most generous to us. The work of J. E. Dunn and E. J. Gantz is creditable to both, and now the church house is as attractive and inviting as it can be, and as it should be. Lawson is doing a great work in all that region, and are especially proud of their minister and his great work in all that territory.

At Pleasant View, Ray, another happy reception was given this work, while the brethren were exceedingly kind to the worker, urging that I come again, so that the storm which followed only sent me in home happy in the Lord. Thank you all.

H. F. DAVIS.

Commercial Building, St. Louis.

State Mission Notes.

Since the last notes I have visited Linneus, Rutledge, Nyaconda, Kahoka, Memphis, Downing, Lancaster, Antioch in Schuyler Co., Queen City and Piedmont. At each and all of these places I received a cordial welcome and met with a loving response to my appeals. The more I get acquainted with our ministerial force the more I am constrained to love them. It is the rarest thing, indeed, that one should turn a cold shoulder to me or to my work. True, I find some of the "loyal" brethren sometimes who give me their blessing as they see me go by. But they are learning better all the time. They are beginning to see that those whom they have stigmatized as being heretics of the worst kind are still lovers of God and can preach the old Jerusalem gospel fairly well.

And I do want to say for our churches that I have not yet found one that would refuse to give to the cause of state missions when it was properly placed before them. This leads me to have great hopes for the future of our work in the state. For I believe that the ministry yet more and more are going to be interested in this work, and in fact get so full of it that they will not let their people forget it, and the people will see to it that it is carried on.

I am afraid that the change of Missouri Day is going to work a hardship on our treasury, at least for this year. The churches had got in the habit of taking the collection in January, and to change it to November came on them so sudden that they were not prepared at all. Then it is the season of the year when many of the pastors are in protracted meetings and when the churches are either having or have just had or are preparing for their protracted effort. This often consumes all the ready money the congregations have, and they have none for outside work. We will, however, soon get adjusted to the new order of things, and we can go home from the state and General Conventions full of enthusiasm, and push the state mission collection to the front. In the meantime let no one pass the collection by. If you can't take it in November take it in December, or in the old month of January. The one thing to be sure of is that you take it, and take it at such a time as will bring the greatest good. I am led to say this because the treasurer writes to me that he has only recived $5 since the beginning of the month. You can see that we NEED money. We must have it, or else the men in the field will be called in. We have started to secure 100,000 additions in this land during this our Jubilee Year, and Missouri must do her part in this. It will not do to cut down the field force a single man. We want more men; they are ready to go if they can be assured of enough to keep wife and children from want while they are in the field. Brethren, let there be a unanimous response to this appeal. We need your help now.

Yours in his name,

T. A. ABBOTT.

4144 Westminster Place, St. Louis, Mo.

Missionary.

November Report.

Comparative statement of receipts to A. C. M. S. for *November*, 1897 and 1898:

No. of churches contributing ...	8	25	17
No. of C. E. S. contributing	32	110	71
" S.-S. "	.	44	44
" L. A. S. "	1	..	1x
" Individuals "	21	23	2
" other contributions..	2	1	1x
Amount contributed by churches	$28.02	$194.47	$166.45
Am't contributed by C. E.S.	91.37	329.85	238.28
" " " S.-S.	....	166.95	166.95
" " " Individuals	183.25	5,113,75	4,930.50
Am't contributed by L. A. S.	5.00		5.00x
" of other contributions	412.33	14.00	397 33x
Total	$718.97	$5,818.82	$5,099.35

Loss x.

Last year's amount included a bequest of $400, $200 of which was turned over immediately to the Church Extension Fnnd.

This year's amount includes a gift of $5,000 from F. M. Drake. The gain in collections is $499.85.

The Christmas time is coming. We have 70 missionaries under our employ. If there is any time in the whole year when the laborer should have his salary it is at this seeson of the year. This is especially true of those who labor for Christ. Our treasury is now empty. Will not those who owe on life memberships, or directorships, or on pledges, send us the money *now?* Or if any wish to send us a Jubilee offering, who have not a pledge, send it at once as a Christmas gift to our cause.

B. L. Smith,
C. C. Smith,
Cor. Secs.

Y. M. C. A. Bldg., Cincinnati, O.

C. W. B. M. District Convention.

The semiannial convention of the fifth missionary district of Nebraska met at Odell at 7 P. M., Tuesday, Nov. 15th, with a goodly number of delegates present, representing the different departments of our work. Devotional exercises and introductory remarks by our district president, Dr. Buxton, pastor of Fairbury Church. After the appointment of committees and a short and spicy address of welcome by G. A. Shadle, of Odell, and response by G. R. Dill, we were treated to an interesting, practical and helpful sermon by R. A. Schell, of Hebron, on "The Pyramid of Christian Character." Text 2 Peter 1:5, 6 and 7. The subject was well handled and we trust will bear fruit in many hearts.

The sunrise prayer-meeting of Wednesday, led by G. R. Dill, of Belvidere was well attended and interesting.

The Bible-school session occupied the forenoon, this was conducted by G. R. Dill, who is superintendent of this work in the district. The exercises opened at 9 o'clock with devotional services led by Miss Devore, of Bower, followed by an interesting talk on Sunday-school work by C. A. Phillips. Then followed report of the superintendent showing progress in the work. Answering the questions from the "Querry Box" occupied remainder of the session and proved interesting and profitable. One of the best sessions of the convention was held by our C. W. B. M. on Wednesday afternoon and evening, commencing at 2 o'clock. Devotionals were led by Mrs. Miller, of Diller. After appointing committees to report later Mrs. Younkin, district manager, made a few introductory remarks showing that the responsibility of our convention being profitable to us rests as well with the sisterhood of the 5th district as with the manager, as the carrying out of plans is as important as making them. Let us continue to be the banner district, having for our motto, "Whatever we do, do in the name of Christ and for his glory." Report of manager showed faithful work done with good results.

The symposium, "$90,000 for '99"—"What are your Auxiliaries Doing to Help Reach This?" was participated in by six of our ten auxiliaries in the district. These seemed to be almost unanimously working for an increase of forces by bringing our work more and more before the people. Our constitution does not debar the brotherhood from the privilege of working with us as members of our auxiliaries. The symposium was concluded by a paper, "Means to the End," written by Mrs. Dr. Andrews and read by Mrs. Dr. Buxton, of Fairbury, which met with hearty approval and was requested for publication.

Miss Griffith, our state secretary gave us a short talk, and among other good things suggested that Nebraska accept for her share of this work, "$2,500 for '99," and that we celebrate in our auxiliaries the silver anniversary of our C. W. B. M. with offerings of silver according to our several ability. Motion of Mrs. Cobbey, of Beatrice, that our district adopt an orphan aged five years, carried, and pledges from societies to raise the necessary $30 per year promptly made.

Then the children were asked to sing and gave us "India," the sweet little song composed by our dear Miss Frost, and in response to a hearty encore, "Come over and help us," and were tendered a unanimous vote of thanks by the rising audience.

In the evening, after report of committee on future work and a paper by Mrs. Cobbey, of Beatrice, "C. W. B. M.—Does it Pay?" which was so full of good things that a motion carried to have it published. The meeting was given over to the other departments of work, and a short time allowed a colored brother from Lincoln to present the cause of his people and ask for help to finish their church building, which is through persistent and hard labor nearly ready for occupancy, about $10 was collected from the audience who recognize in this earnest worker a brother in Christ.

The sermon of the evening was delivered by Dr. Buxton; text, Luke 17:33: "Whosoever shall seek to save his life," etc. Time and space would not permit me to tell of all the good things presented in this sermon, but I believe all were more than ever impressed with the great truth that we must die to self if we would live to Christ or any great usefulness in his service.

The forenoon session of Thursday was devoted to the business of the convention. Receipts from churches showed progress and improvement generally, if we except the one said to be "looking up" only because of lying so flat upon its back!

Election of officers resulted as follows:

President, A. Buxton, Fairbury.

Vice-president, Bro. John Rhodes, Beatrice.

Secretary and treasurer, Miss Sadie Cox, Bower.

Corresponding secretary, J. H. Moore, Diller.

Superintendent Y. P. S. C. E., R. H. Schell, Hebron.

Thursday P. M. was the C. E. session and was both profitable and interesting throughout, closing with a splendid paper by Mrs. G. A. Shadle, of Odell. The evening was devoted to consecration service and the address of corresponding secretary N. C. M. S., W. A. Baldwin, Ulyses, after which the convention adjourned to meet at Crete in May.

Mrs. M. E. King.

Fairbury, Neb.

Gift to Church Extension.

The Annuity plan for our Church Extension work seems to be growing in favor. Francis S. Smith, of Lock Haven, Pa., who was the first to give $500 to this fund on the Annuity plan, sent another $500 on Dec. 1st. He prefers to see his money work in the Church Extension Fund while he lives, at the same time earning him six per cent., which is as much as he could get elsewhere. He contemplated leaving money to the board in his will; being compelled to use the interest to live on, however, the Annuity plan furnishes him the present means of seeing his money building churches, while at the same time it gives him needed support. At his death the money will go directly into the Church Extension Fund, where he contemplated leaving it, and there will be no contest about it. It would be well for those who are expecting to leave money to this fund in their wills to put it into the fund now on the Annuity plan. An annuity bond will be given by the board, which will be the best of security. For information about the Annuity plan, write to G. W. Muckley, Cor. Sec., 600 Waterworks building, Kansas City, Mo Let it not be forgotten that the Board of Church Extension furnishes a catalogue of church plans which are up to date. This catalogue will be sent for 10 cents, and contains seventy-two modern designs, from a chapel costing $600 to a church costing $50,000. The catalogue also contains splendid advice for those who are building. If church plans are ordered from the board, two per cent. can be saved. For catalogue, address

G. W. Muckley, Cor. Sec.

600 *Waterworks Bldg., Kansas City, Mo.*

For a Forward Movement.

How can we raise $100,000 and save 100,000 souls for Christ in this the Jubilee Year?

Within the past three weeks I have noticed a great change in all our religious journals. The majority of our ablest preachers are agitating the movement "All Along the Line." While we preach an acceptable gospel which will no doubt add over one hundred thousand souls this coming year, we are compelled to raise $100,000 for Home Missions. This we must do systematically. According to Bro. G. A. Hoffmann, our statistical secretary's report, we have 1,085,615 church members in the United States. The amount given to Home Missions last year was $39,016 or less than 4 cents per member. I am sure we all ought to be able to give 15 cents per capita, which would mean $150,000 for the Jubilee Year. Then let us add another 10 cents per capita for Church Extension, which means $100,000 to assist in building houses of worship. People must be taught that the religion of Jesus Christ costs something. Free salvation, so commonly called, has a tendency toward infidelity and lacks practical sympathy in all our missionary work. Therefore, every disciple of Christ must teach, that "go ye into all the world" implies our money as well as our prayers and sympathy. Some Lord's day morning before communion ask yourself the following questions:

Am I a follower or disciple of Christ?

How much have I done for my congregation?

What have I done for state mission work?

Have I ever given toward the support of Home Missions?

What interest have I in the Missionary Society for Church Extension?

How much of my money have I given for Negro Education and Evangelization?

Do I ever remember our missionaries by giving to the Foreign C. M. S.?

Am I a member of the Christian Woman's Board of Missions? If not, why not?

How much interest do I take in building and endowment of schools?

Do I ever think of the Christian Church Widows' and Orphans' Home?

Do I ever remember the poor old ministers, by supporting the Ministerial Relief? If everybody would take as little intrrest in this God-ordained work, what would become and befall the church of which I claim to be a member in good standing? If we all would give and live more perfectly in line with those who make a living sacrifice the Jubilee Year would make room for a new era in the history of the United States. May God help us to win the victory, is my prayer. Jno. G. M. Luttenbergrr.

Dorchester, Ill.

Evangelistic.

ILLINOIS.

Monmouth, Dec. 3.—Knox P. Taylor has just closed a two weeks' Institute here that makes us all happier in the faith. We enjoyed two weeks of his work last year also, and feel like making the affair an annual appointment. The writer rounds out two years' service in the church ending 1898. We have accepted a continuous indefinite call to remain. W. H. Coleman, formerly of Carisle, Ia., has accepted and begun work at Roseville. Alexis church is growing under Bro. Hale's ministry. —C. H STEARNS.

Normal, Dec. 3.—Eight additions to the church at Oreana since Sept. 1st. The third Lord's day in November I preached for the brethren at Argenta, Ill., and ordained Bro. Frank Welton to the ministry.—D. H. SHANKLIN.

Ivan W. Ager, of Chapin, is in a promising meeting at Concord. He is soon to begin a meeting at Literberry.

A. O. Hunsaker is singing for W. H. Cannon in a meeting at Chapin.

Murphysboro, Dec. 1.—Two additions to the church last Lord's day; one by confession and one the widow of a Baptist minister. The work here is moving on nicely. Since I came here two months ago the church has taken on new life, and 85 have been added to the Endeavor in the last six weeks, and 15 to the church. The Sunday-school is growing. Our financial condition is better than it has been for four years. Our Thanksgiving dinner brought us $50, and an excellent program was given in the evening free.—W. H. WILLYARD, pastor.

Blandinsville, Nov. 28.—One more addition to the Old Bedford Church yesterday at regular service.—A. R. ADAMS.

Marshall, Nov. 28.—Our meeting here two two weeks old. Six additions, good interest; will continue one or two more weeks. I can be had for January; might assist in a short meeting after we close here.—C. M. HUGHES, singer.

Cuba.—Just closed our meeting here with 35 additions.—WM. DRUMMET, pastor of Christian Church.

Watseka, Nov. 28.—Another young man made the good confession here yesterday. At a recent midweek prayer-meeting our Junior Endeavorers were with us by invitation—and ere the service closed had a "*Scripture spelling bee*" to the delight and profit of all present. It took them almost one-half hour to spell down. See 2 Tim. 3:5.—B. S. FERRALL.

Roseville, Nov. 28.—The work here under our new pastor, Bro. W. H. Coleman, starts off nicely. We have a good attendance, excellent interest and five additions during the month of November. We are planning for a protracted meeting soon.—J. F. FISHER.

Pekin, Nov. 28.—Nov. 20th there were eight confessions, one reclaimed and one from the Baptists. One confession and one by letter last Lord's day. A total of 26 additions since last July.—FRED E. HAGIN.

IOWA.

Elliott, Dec. 3.—Began a series of meetings on Nov. 27, M. C. Johnson, of Henderson, Iowa, doing the preaching. We are moving right along; two by statement last evening; congregations fine. Bro. J. is a fine practical preacher of righteousness. Our cause in Southeast Iowa doing well so far as I know. I write on my way to Carson, Iowa, to fill his place.—T. J. REZNOR, pastor.

Modale, Nov. 28.—Our meeting increases in interest; 24 added to date; eight last night. Others to follow, we hope.—W. B. CREWDSON.

Ames, Nov. 30.—We began the work in Ames Nov. 6. During November there were five added by letter and one by confession. H. P. Williams left this church in good condition. The outlook for the winter is good. The five churches of the city begin a union revival meeting on Dec. 5, with Evangelist C. N. Hunt as leader.—JAMES R. MCINTIRE.

OKLAHOMA.

Thomas, Custer Co., Nov. 22.—B. C. Young, from Texas, has been laboring with us for over a week, commencing the 15th. The attendance good, and much interest manifested; three baptisms to date. The brethren much encouraged and built up in the faith. We need laborers in the field. Bro. Young says he will spend the winter in Custer County laboring at various points, where the brethren will help. He will commence a series of discourses in a new place, 10 miles northwest of this place, Nov. 27th. There are a few brethren there, but not organized. Your scribe may assist.—J. H. TRACY.

MINNESOTA.

Sharon.—Report five confessions for the Sharon meeting. Meeting just begun; good interest.—GREGG AND SWEETMAN, evangelists.

MISSOURI.

Ve Lassus, Nov. 28.—Just closed a meeting at Flat River with six additions. Had good attendance, and part of the time more than the church would hold. The meeting was held in the Baptist house. Our people are planning to build soon.—EUGENE BURR.

A. J. Carrick reports one addition to the church at Peakville recently.

Kansas City, Dec. 1.—We are having a good meeting in the 6th and Prospect Church. Thirty-six additions to date.—H. A. NORTHCUTT, evangelist; GEORGE H. COMBS, pastor.

Kansas City, Dec. 3.—J. J. Morgan, of Warrensburg, closed a short meeting with us last night, preaching 20 discourses with 20 added to the church. The results would have been doubled, doubtless, but for the blizzard through which we passed. Our people were greatly pleased with Bro. Morgan.—A. W. KOKENDOFFER, Forest Avenue Church.

Bethany, Nov. 28.—A. L. Jones, vice-president of Central Christian College of Albany, is making a canvass of the church of Harrison County, and is holding a meeting at the Mt. Olive Church, with nine additions to date.—ENOS S. OATMAN.

The preachers of this city reported 20 additions to the various churches last week.

INDIANA.

S. A Strawn, pastor of the church at Lowell, in his recount of the year's work just closed, says: "Our Sunday-school has held its own; Senior Endeavor grown from 13 to 47 and about $50 raised; a Junior Society numbering 42 and over $25 raised; Ladies' Aid several months since had raised $202 and still they are going forward. Our prayer-meeting has increased from 10 to 30 and 40, and growing spiritually. Our zeal in misssions is growing and we have given to our different missionary organizations over $102 and so far this year there has been 38 confessions and accessions.

Bloomfield, Dec. 2.—Closed a meeting at Paxton, Nov. 29 with 10 accessions. Bro. J. P. Davis, 605 South Fourth St., Terre Haute, did the preaching. He is sound in doctrine, scholarly, especially well versed in history and literature. He is a favorite with the young people and cultivates spirituality in the church. He might be obtained in a few meetings if written soon. Address him at 605 South Fourth St., Terre Haute, Ind.—T. A. COX.

Hopedale, Nov. 28.—Have recently closed a three weeks' meeting with the Spring Creek Church, White County Ind.; three confessions. —A. W. GEBRES.

Franklin, Nov. 27.—Yesterday at Mt. Gilead a noble young man was buried with Christ in baptism.—WILLIS M. CUNNINGHAM.

KANSAS.

Halstead, Dec. 3.—Our meeting is still in progress with 22 accessions to date. The meeting will continue indefinately. House is crowded every evening. The gospel is the power of God unto salvation.—L. B. COGGINS.

WASHINGTON.

Carson, Nov. 23.—W. V. Boltz, pastor of the Christian Church at The Dalles, Oregon, closed a protracted meeting on the 18th inst., that was the most successful that has ever been held in this valley. There were 21 that obeyed the gospel by confession and burial with Christ in baptism. In addition to the above we have seven Disciples that came here from other parts and that were members of other denominations that united with us, making in all a class of 31 Disciples as the result of Bro. Boltz's labors at this place. Bro. Boltz organized our little band by appointing elders, deacons and deaconesses. After giving us good and wholesome instructions for our future guidance he returned to The Dalles to make ready to take the field as an evangelist. We hope that Bro. Boltz will receive the hearty support and encouragement of the Disciples wherever he may go, as he is well equipped for the work possessing the essential qualifications of an evangelist in a high degree. He is strong, aggressive, logical, drawing conclusions and making deductions that carry conviction to the minds of those that hear him. He is also a very good singer and a very social fireside preacher. We heartily recommend Bro. Boltz to brethren desiring the services of an able evangelist.—C. C. WETHERELL, elder.

KENTTCKY.

Morganfield.—Wallace Tharp, of Crawford, Ind., has just closed a meeting with us which resulted in 36 added to the congregation. Twenty-five were by confession and baptism and 10 by letter and statement. Five were from the donominations. Bro. Tharp did the congregation much good and impressed the community at large as being an able, earnest preacher of the gospel. I have added to the congregation 25 in my regular work, making 61 during the year. This we have done with one-fourth of my time given to this congregation.—R. V. OMER.

KANSAS.

Indepenpence, Nov. 28.—Twelve accessions yesterday; nine confessions; 19 to date.—J. V. COOMBS.

Halstead, Nov. 28.—Our meetings still continue. Eight accessions to date. More to follow.—L. B. COGGINS.

I closed last night a short meeting with the Bethany Church, Parsons, with nine confessions. One deferred baptism until my next visit.

IOWA.

Newton, Nov. 25.—Our work here still grows. Two additions on Lord's day, Nov. 20, by letter, and the outlook for this congregation is brighter than ever before. We are hoping, praying and working, and must go forward.—J. C. HAMAN.

Winterset, Nov. 26.—Our meeting closed Nov. 22nd with 22 additions to the church; 11 confessions, three from Congregationalists, two from Baptists, two from Christian (New Light), one by statement, one from M. E.s, one from Presbyterians, one from Adventists. —LOWE & LANDRUN.

Humeston, Nov. 24.—Two baptisms and two by letter added recently to Humeston church. —H. P. DYER.

Sewal, Nov. 18th.—Just closed a series of meetings at this place, conducted by Bro. D. L. Ammons, of Seymour, Ia. The immediate result, five additions by baptism, four reclaimed and one from the U. B. Church. The Christian Church at Sewal was organized about four years ago by Elder H. Rice, of Seymour. We owe much to his excellent and untiring labors. For the past two years we have had the services of D. L. Ammons for one-fourth of his time. We have now engaged him for the third year. He is a sound and able workman. He is now called to his old home in West Virginia to conduct a series of meetings there before returning to his work at this place.—F. M. STEWART.

MICHIGAN.

Shepherd, Nov. 21.—Closed a meeting at Sumner last night with five additions. The Ferris church has hired Bro. H. M. Willis, and it is hoped that satisfactory arrangements can be made so that he can preach for the Sumner church. I go on to a new field tomorrow. Remember the fifth district M. C. M. S. at the throne.—MEADE E. DUETT, district evangelist.

ITALY (Florence).

Florence, La Bella, is a city of the Middle Ages, differing little to-day, except in the dress of its people, from the Florence beloved by Dante and the Della Robbias. It is famous for its palaces and for its collection of paintings, sculpture, and the manuscripts resulting from the genius, thought and power in Florence during the time of the Medicis.

Ruined by the vice and luxury of that reign, the Florentines have since made little progress. Their chief manufactures are of silk and plaited straw.

The photograph reproduced in another column shows a Florentine woman of the industrious middle class stitching a straw hat into shape by means of a Singer sewing machine. Although the average woman cannot correctly judge the comparative merits of different sewing machines, so far as mechanical construction is concerned, she has a nice appreciation of the difference in their work. The fact that Singer machines always turn out good work is the main reason why they are preferred by the women of all nations.

SUBSCRIBERS' WANTS.

Miscellaneous wants and notices will be inserted in this department at the rate of two cents a word, each insertion, all words, large and small, to be counted, and two initials stand for one word. Please accompany notice with corresponding remittance to save book-keeping.

WANTED.—After nine years of successful work in this field I desire to locate elsewhere by the first or middle of January. Unquestionable references furnished. Only churches that desire to push forward in every good work need apply. F. L. Moore, Fredericktown, Mo.

FOR SALE.—Brand New, High Grade Piano. Bargain if taken at once. For further particulars address Christian Pub. Co., 1522 Locust St., St. Louis.

Family Circle.

Rest.

MOLLIE H. TURNER.

An universal cry for rest
Goes ever upward sobbing,
From tortured nerves and weary brains
And hearts that ache with throbbing.

Amid life's trials, toils and tears,
We mutely bend and wonder;
Amid the wreck of cherished dreams,
We worry, shrink and ponder.

The demon Doubt doth stab our faith,
And leave it weak and bleeding;
We stagger blindly in the gloom,
God's promises unheeding.

The Prince and power of the air—
The Evil never dying—
Unceasing haunts our struggling steps,
And revel's o'er our crying.

While God seems far—so far away,
He can not hear our praying—
And in the dark our aching steps
From hope and Heaven are straying,

When lo! a voice steals on the ear,
Like Heaven's own music falling,
"Come unto me, despairing souls,"
The voice of Jesus calling.

"I'll fill your hearts with joy and peace.
All you so heavy laden—
Come unto me, I'll give you rest
From weariness and labor.

And take my yoke and learn of me,
For I am meek and lowly,
You shall find unto your souls,
With me the Pure and Holy."

Lexington, Ky.

Through Difficulties.

BY ALFRED BRUNK.

(CONCLUDED.)

"Hello, Ashton," cried a young man across the street; "remember to-night."

"What does that mean?" asked Mary.

"Oh, some of us boys are just going to have a little lark to-night," replied Henry, a little shamefacedly.

As they went along the street, Henry pointed out the places of interest, and dilated upon the wonderful growth of Westphalia, and predicted for it a great future. Stopping before a large, substantial frame building Henry said, "Here you are at last," and she was ushered into the home of Richard Small. Richard and his wife gave her a hearty greeting, and plied her with questions concerning the homeland.

"I would have sent the carriage to the depot for you, but Henry declared he knew you would enjoy the walk after so long a ride," said Richard.

"And so I did, immensely," said Mary. "What a thrifty, busy place this seems to be!" she added with enthusiasm.

"You are right," said Richard. "Everybody is making money. Two railroads have their roundhouses and shops here, and another road has been surveyed through the town. As for me, I am doing very well. My little boot and shoestore has grown into a large clothing and shoestore, and my mining property is panning out very well. But here, Mary, is some one you don't know," he added, as a little curly-headed girl, about four years of age, appeared in the doorway and rubbing her eyes as if she had been asleep.

"Come, Irma, and get acquainted with your new cousin," and Mrs. Small picked up the child and brought her toward Mary. Irma drew away bashfully.

"What a pretty child, Anna," said Mary, kissing the little girl, and in a short time the two were fast friends.

About two o'clock that night Mary was awakened out of a profound sleep by a heavy stride in the hall and, listening intently, she heard some muttered oath, in a voice which sounded much like her brother's. The next morning Henry slipped away to the store without meeting his sister. When he came home to supper he tried to evade her, but she was watching for him and demanded an explanation of the preceding night's affair.

"It wasn't anything, Mary; nothing at all," said he, but finally admitted that he and some of the young men had been on a drunken spree, and that that was not the first time. "But, Mary, what is a young fellow to do? All the boys here drink, and besides, it don't hurt a fellow if he don't take too much. Don't you be afraid that I will ever let it get the best of me." But his heart smote him when he saw the look of sadness upon her face.

On Sunday morning at the breakfast table she asked: "Where do you attend church?"

Richard looked confused, his wife blushed and Henry laughed outright. "Well, Mary, you are a tenderfoot, sure enough, to ask such a question as that in Westphalia," said he. "That will do for the slow, poky people back East, but we are progressive here, I can tell you."

"That's enough, Henry," said Richard, recovering himself. "There are some very good churches in town, but they don't reach the people, from some cause. We went a few times after we came here, but the services were so uninteresting that we quit going altogether. I wish it was otherwise, for saloons and gambling houses are multiplying, and some of our boys are getting pretty wild," and he looked significantly at Henry.

At Mary's request they went to one of the churches, and while there was considerable ostentation and pride, the services were lacking in heart-moving power, and Mary longed for the simple home services instead.

"Mary," said Richard, some days after her arrival, "I need a bookkeeper. Are you qualified for the position? If not, there is a good business college here which will prepare you for the work in a few months."

"No, I am not qualified, but will fit myself for the position without delay," said she.

Andrew Rogers was a young man of talent and refinement, who had come from New Orleans and opened a law office in Westphalia. Being on intimate terms with Richard Small, he became acquainted with Mary and was much impressed with her modest, unassuming ways, combined with an unconquerable spirit of independence.

"Miss Ashton, I have often wished that I were a Christian in the Bible sense of that term. In the course of my law studies I have examined the law of Moses thoroughly, also the sayings of Christ and the arguments of Paul. Moses is the basis of law in all civilized countries, Paul's closely knit arguments are unanswerable, and the life and sayings of Christ are unassailable. But the churches of to-day, or at least all that I know anything about, are builded upon dogma and human pride, and not upon Christ and the Bible; so instead of being attracted to them I am driven further and further away."

"I know nothing of law, and but little of churches," said Mary. "But I know a man who lives and preaches like Christ; I mean my old pastor, Mr. Sharon."

"I would love to hear him," said he, candidly, but believing in his heart that Mr. Sharon was only the ideal of a young and inexperienced lady, and that he would prove to be just like all others that he had heard.

After Mary had finished her business course and had been duly installed as bookkeeper in Mr. Small's store, she said to Mrs. Small one day: "Anna, Mr. Rogers has asked me to become his wife."

"And of course you told him you would," replied Mrs. Small.

"No; I told him I could wed no man who is not a Christian."

"Why, Mary, you are foolish. You will never get married here, if you take that stand. All the best and brightest young men here are out of the church."

"I can't help that. I will not marry out of the church," said Mary, decisively.

"Richard," she said one day, soon after this conversation, "I wrote Melville and asked him to see if Mr. Sharon would come and hold us a meeting. Here is his reply."

Richard took the letter and read as follows:

DEAR MARY:—Your letter in regard to the meeting was handed to Bro. Sharon, and he said that he would go, but would expect the people there to furnish a large hall or a tent of sufficient size to accommodate all who should desire to hear the gospel; that there must be no chance of a shut-down just as the people are becoming interested. Or, if lumber could be had, he could put up a temporary tabernacle, and would stay just as long as prospects were good for winning souls to Christ.

Your cousin,
MELVILLE SMALL.

"Hooray for the parson!" shouted Henry. "Now we will have long-faced sanctimoniousness, for sure."

"Well, it will cost a good deal, Mary," said Richard. "His fare must be paid, hall rent or a tent to be provided for, or a tabernacle must be built. Then there are lights, songbooks, organ and all that; I don't see how it can be done."

"Richard Small, I am ashamed of you!" she exclaimed, impetuously. "You are just like your father, only not so bad. What did you have when you came here? A little old boot and shoestand! Now you own the finest and largest store in town, have a fine home, have a large interest in the best paying mine in the state; blest with health, blest with fine prospects, could burn up thousands of dollars of money and scarcely miss it. Thousands of sinners here going to perdition, and my own brother among them, and you, poor, poverty-stricken tramp, can't do a thing to stem the awful tide of iniquity! God have mercy on your poor, stingy soul!" She turned away, and like an enraged queen, left the room.

"How's that?" asked Henry, as soon as he caught his breath. "Comes out mighty plain, seems to me. But I guess she's right. If I belonged to the gospel band I

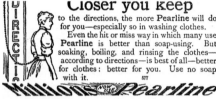

Mr. Rogers, who were near each other in the rear of the room. Mr. Rogers' face was firmly set, and he stood still as a statue of stone. She saw Henry glance anxiously toward him and start forward. Instinctively her hands dropped from the keys, she arose and met him, threw her arms about his neck and wept. Then remembering the occasion, she sat down and hid her face in her hands.

The meetings have closed. Henry and all others who confessed their faith in Christ have been baptized and the minister has returned home. One of the railway companies has given the church a fine lot in a beautiful section of the town, upon which to build a house of worship; the contract has been let and a substantial stone structure is reared; the new congregation has secured the services of Carl B. Brandlett, a scholarly young minister from Chicago, and popular sentiment is with them.

Mary is quiet and reserved, and performs her daily duties in a mechanical manner.

"Henry," said she to her brother one day, "you have a gift for public speaking; why don't you devote that gift to God and the church?"

"I have thought of it, Mary," said he, "but I tremble in view of the terrible responsiblity resting upon the minister of the gospel."

"Yes, Henry, there is a great responsibility, I know," she replied. "But who do you think will receive the greater reward, the one who knew his duty and performed it not, or the one who did the best he could, even if he did occasionally make a mistake?"

"Why he who did his duty, of course," Henry replied.

So he decided to enter a well-known Bible college that fall, and if he needed more funds than he possessed, his sister should assist him.

The time to dedicate the new house of worship in Westphalia is near. Mr. Sharon is on hand to preach the dedicatory sermon.

"Now, Mr. Sharon, what do you think is my duty under the circumstances?" asked Andrew Rogers in a confidential talk with Mr. Sharon.

"Why, sir, I think it is your imperative duty to obey the gospel. Let people make out of it what they will. If your motive is

"It shall be as you wish," said the faithful man of God, and informing Richard Small and wife, Mary and Henry, and a few others. The baptism was performed that very afternoon, but Mary was not present.

Some days after the dedication Mary astonished her friends by announcing that she was going to visit the old home again.

Everybody was delighted to see her back in Dry Valley, and surprised her not a little by making a heroine of her on account of the great work that had been done in Westphalia. After a pleasant stay of two months, she went to Booneville, expecting, after a few days' visit with Melville and his wife, to return to Westphalia. The next day after her arrival at Booneville she received a letter from Herny which was as follows:

"DEAR SIS:—I am off to-day for school. Sorry I could'nt see you before going away. I expect to hear from you often, for you know a fellow will get homesick. Just had a long talk with Rogers; he is the most practical Christian I ever saw; he didn't tell me, but he has paid the rent of several poor old women and sick and crippled men, and has done many other kind and charitable acts. But his talkwith me was about you; he said you were the best girl he ever knew, and of course I had to agree with him there. Then he said he could never love another as he has and does love you, and I like a simpleton said, 'Why don't you tell her so?' It seemed to shock him, and then he said, 'I will!' Give my love to uncle's folks and keep lots for yourself. Pray for your struggling brother, HENRY."

She looked up from the letter, her eyes swimming in tears, and saw—Andrew Rogers.

We will not stay to hear the conversation, but there can be no harm in going with them a few days later to the parsonage and seeing them married. After the ceremony the godly pastor and friend said:

"Mr. and Mrs. Rogers, your own lives illustrate the fact that all noble efforts ennoble and beautify our lives. Nor does this law end with earth, for its effects are clearly apparent in the home of the redeemed. Hence the immortal words concerning those who were arrayed in white robes: "These are they which came out of great tribulation and have washed their robes and made them white in the blood of the Lamb."

Do Your Best.

The signs are bad when folks commence
A-findin' fault with Providence,
And balkin' 'cause the earth don't shake
At every prancin' step they take.
No man is great till he can see
How less than little he would be
Ef stripped to self, and stark and bare,
He hung his sign out anywhere.

My doctern is to lay aside
Contentions and be satisfied;
Jest to do your best, and praise or blame
That follers, that counts jest the same.
I've allus noticed that success
Is mixed with trouble more or less,
And it's the man who does the best,
That gets more kicks than all the rest.

—*James Whitcomb Riley.*

A Trip to Programville.

A friend of mine was so put out because the convention did not go off to suit him that he concluded to make a trip down to Programville, to see if the fault lay there. He found all sorts of things being grown for the convention market, some good, some poor.

He learned that Farmer Hometalent never goes off his own farm for seed or stock. As a consequence his corn finally runs to nubbins, and his stock shrinks smaller and smaller until they become runts. The stuff that he takes to convention market would be much improved in quality if he would only exchange seedcorn with his neighbors and import new stock.

His neighbor, Farmer Catchall, goes to the other extreme of trying every new seed the agricultural department sends out, and every odd or fancy breed of stock advertised. He litters the convention market with all sorts of freaks and fads, from oratorical mushrooms to tropical parrots and musical sensitive plants. But he is very proud of the newest things because they are new.

Farmer Crowdtherow's idea of convention market is that it ought to be crammed so there's a continual strain and agony to get through it. He raises good stuff, but he always overloads his wagon and breaks down before he gets to market, or else does not arrive there until next day. He cannot be made to realize that there can be too much of a good thing, and that no one has yet found a way of packing more than sixty minutes in an hour.

Then there is Farmer Wisdomtooth who tests the new things on his own table before he takes them to market. He imports the best things from all parts of the globe, but keeps his accounts closely, and sticks to the staples that pay. His stall in the market is a delight to see, and if all Programville were like him, convention market would never be surfeited or stocked with trash. He says that his success is due to his looking at everything through two pairs of spectacles—prayer and common sense.

My friend is trying to persuade the agent for these spectacles to make a thorough canvass of Programville, in the interests of convention market.—*C. E. World.*

Thanksgiving Gifts—A Petition.

O, thou great and gracious God! Grant that none of us may ever forget that we are pensioners upon thy bounty; that it is from thy liberal hand and loving heart we receive our daily necessities and blessings. In answer to our daily prayer, "give us this day our daily bread," thou hast richly blessed us in basket and in store. Out of the fullness wherewith thou hast blessed us, help us in turn to bless those who to-day are struggling to keep the wolf from the door. May we not forget the words of Holy Writ: "Charge them that are rich in the world, that they do good, that they be rich in good works." May the words of our dear Lord come to us with renewed power to-day as he says: "Inasmuch as ye have done it unto one of the least of these my disciples, ye have done it unto me;" thus teaching us that he is identified with every child of woe and want, and that the outheld hand of the poor is his treasury awaiting our gifts. They are thine, O Lord, and we are thine, and in thy name we minister unto them. May the gift be blessed to us as well as to them. In this day of our fullness and gladness, we commend to thee *all* who travel the road—the *hard* road—of *poverty;* who sit around a scanty board and whose eyes rest pitifully upon children hungry and cold. May they not be forgotten of us as they are not forgotten of thee in heaven. Let the mercy and pity of the God of men, of families, of nations, rest upon the sick, the suffering, the sorrowing, the tempted, the troubled, the disappointed, the dying. Magnify thyself in the darkness to all such, and let thy grace be greater than all human want, and may souls buried in the depths of night know how much greater and sweeter is light than darkness. Dear Father, gather us all to thy heart, and make us to feel the presence of thy everlasting arms—arms that can crush the universe, yet in love supports and protects thy feeblest child. Hear, O Father, and grant us our petitions, we humbly beg in Jesus' name. Amen! FRANK W. ALLEN.

Some Literary Questions.

[To see the point and enjoy the wit of the following poem, observe carefully the play upon the last word in the name of each person.—EDITOR].

Is Thomas Hardy nowadays?
 Is Rider Haggard pale?
Is Minot Savage? Oscar Wilde?
 And Edward Everett Hale?

Was Lawrence Stern? Was Hermann Grimm?
 Was Edward Young? John Gay?
Jonathan Swift? and old John Bright?
 And why was Thomas Gray?

Was John Brown? and J. R. Green?
 Chief Justice Taney quite?
Is William Black? J. D. Blackmore?
 Mark Lemon? H. K. White?

Was Francis Bacon lean in streaks?
 John Suckling vealy? Pray?
Was Hogg much given to the pen?
 Are Lamb's Tales sold to-day?

Did Mary Mapes Dodge just in time?
 Did C. D. Warner? How?
At what did Andrew Marvel so?
 Does Edward Whymper now?

What goodies did Rose Terry Cooke?
 Or Richard Boyle beside?
What gave the wicked Thomas Paine?
 And made Mark Akenside?

Was Thomas Tickell-ish at all?
 Did Richard Steele, I ask?
Tell me, has George A. Sale suit?
 Did William Ware a mask?

Does Henry Cabot Lodge at home?
 John Horne Tooke what and when?
Is Gorden Cumming? Has G. W.
 Cabled his friends again?

—*Good Housekeeping.*

"Yes my friends," exclaimed a teetotal lecturer, "there are many excuses for the glass. The sick man says he must have his glass to make him well; the shivering cabman must have his glass to make him warm; the hard-working mechanic must have his glass to make him cool. But they lie, friends. Don't believe the workman who says he can't work without his glass. I defy any one to mention to me a workman who connot work as well, and better, without his glass than with it."

A voice at the back of the hall made itself audible: "I'll tell yer one."

"I defy you to do so," said the lecturer. "I defy you sir," he roared.

Then the voice observed: "The glazier can't do without his glass."

The lecturer continued that oration at a decided disadvantage.—*Golden Hours.*

With The Children.

CONDUCTED BY

J. BRECKENRIDGE ELLIS, PLATTSBURG, MO.

That Button.

"I have a plan," said Jennie Weston the next morning, which was Sunday, "that will help us to get up a little band, right in our town, of the Advance Society."

"Let's hear your plan," replied George.

"It is this: you and I, who are the only ones here who know of this society—except mamma, of course, but she don't count—"

"Why is it that mammas never *do* count?" inquired Mrs. Weston, who had overheard this remark.

"I mean," said Jennie, "you are quite an old lady, you know, and so of course you won't care to bother about us children."

"It is true I am quite old," replied the lady, "since I am almost thirty-eight. But even if I should live to be forty I never expect to lose interest in children. But I have a plan, too, and we will see which one does the most." Then she left the children alone.

"It is strange how mamma cares for the things we care for," observed Jennie. "I know when I am grown I will be so full of grown thoughts that I will forget I was ever young. It does take a terrible time to grow, don't it? Between you and me, George, I think children are nuisances, anyhow!"

George only laughed at her, because he was fond of being a boy, and was in no hurry for the time to come when he would have to sit on chairs half the time and be serious, and always look busy. But Jennie every once in a while had a state of feelings which, if they were not "the blues," were at least a pale indigo. Whenever she had these feelings, which happened after particularly trying and unpleasant events—she felt an insatiable longing to be grown. The reason she wished to be grown this morning was that she had broken her fine china saucer—a present from her grandmother, who lived in the country. "This is my plan," she said. "Let us both promise to ask some one to join the society; let us ask some one every day, until we get up a little band. Then we can meet, every once in awhile, and talk about what we are reading and about our department in the CHRISTIAN-EVANGELIST."

George agreed, and as it lacked some time till Sunday-school he stopped at Jim Dancy's house, to ask Jim to join; for he was in the habit of stopping for Jim, that they might go on to the church together. As he was a friend of the family he went around to the sitting room door, which was at the side of the house. "Come in," said the voice of Mr. Dancy.

George entered. Mrs. Dancy was reading a paperback novel. She looked up, smiled in a lost kind of way, and then continued to read. She kept her forefinger in her mouth, so it would be damp enough to turn over the pages just as quick as she was ready. Her hair was not done up, and she wore a wrapper. Mr. Dancy was seated in his rocking-chair, also reading a novel. He wore his high fur cap, which he always put on as soon as he had eaten his breakfast, whether he stayed in the house or not. The dining room door was partly open, and George could see that the dishes had not been touched since this literary pair left the table. The Dancys were old people, at least their hair was turning white, and they had gotten so used to novel-reading that when their son Jim was born, they didn't know what to do with him. So Jim had to learn to do a great many things for himself.

"Where is Jim?" asked George Weston.

Mr. Dancy laid his finger on the last word he had read, as if he were afraid it would get away, and then looked up. "I don't know where that boy is," he said, starting to scratch his head in perplexity. But finding his fur cap on his head, he changed his mind, and fell to reading again. Mrs. Dancy was very uneasy about the heroine of her story, because her buggy had just been upset, and she hadn't learned if the heroine had sprained her ankle, so the hero would have to carry her into her palatial residence. But she took time to say, "Did you look in the barn?"

George went to the barn and found Jim Dancy sitting on a sack of corn which he had dragged out on the smooth plank floor, so the sunlight would fall upon him and keep him warm. He was sewing a button on his Sunday suit. "Hello, George," he said, "going to Sunday-school?"

"Yes, I came by for you. I didn't know you sew—and on Sunday, too."

"I do when it's necessary," said Jim. "Which do you think is *wronger*, to stay at home, or sew on the button and go to church? Do you think I'm doing this because it's fun?"

George did not commit himself by deciding this question of ethics. He said, "I want you to join the Advance Society. Jennie and I belong. We are going to get a lot of boys and girls in it, and have a regular good time."

"Get out of my way while I thread this needle," said Jim. "All right, I guess I'll go in, if it will accommodate you. What do you have to do?"

"Why don't you run the thread through the hole?" inquired George, watching the process with much interest.

"Why wasn't I born a woman?" returned Jim Dancy. "You keep still, and I'll get this thread through before that hole knows what I'm after. Ha! There she is! What do you do in this society?"

"You become a member on agreeing to do five things; one is to read—"

"I'm not in," said Jim, prophetically.

"—five pages of history," persisted George.

"Nuck," said Jim, which was his way of replying in the negative. "If that society sewed on buttons or did something useful I might join. But I may as well tell you now, George Weston, that I don't believe in reading. I have seen too much of it in my time."

"May be you have seen the wrong kind of reading," suggested George Weston.

"It's all alike," interposed Jim Dancy. "You take a person that loves to read, and what does he do? I say to you, what does he do?"

"Well, what *does* he do?" demanded George.

"That's just it," said Jim. "He don't do nothin'—nothin' but read. If the house gets on fire—but you know what happened *here!*" Now, this is what Jim alluded to: One afternoon the flue caught on fire, and it seemed that nothing could save the house. The neighbors came from around, and carried buckets of water to the roof. The neighbors were n pleased when they found Mr. Dan perched on the garden fence, his cap on h head, and his novel in hand. But M Dancy was so near the end of a chapt that he could not lay down the book till l found how it was going to turn out.

"I've just thought of something!" cri George, slapping his knee. "You liste Jim Dancy. We're such good friends, it no use pretending your folks don't over the novel business. Now, a person a dicted to the novel habit is bored t history and poetry. Here's a schem Make your folks promise to read a amount of history and poetry every d before they get out their novels. Wh will happen? Why, they'll keep puttin off and putting off the solid reading, an in that way they will get to tending t things. 'Cours they'd rather sew on but tons than to read poetry. It'll work lik a charm!"

"How'll you make 'em promise? The would laugh at any such agreement. If w were to kidnap 'em, and ransom 'em o condition they read such stuff, it migh work. But how can a boy kidnap hi papa and mamma?"

"Keep still," said George Weston, "I' thinking!"

If you can't guess how this story "turn out," you can read the next part in tw weeks. Next week I am going to give th names of some of our members, with thei ages, the places where they live, and extracts from their letters. In this way you get acquainted. So look out for next week, and cut out the piece and paste it in a book; in this way you will get, after awhile, the names of all the members of our Advance Society. Monday before last there were 95 members. Growing, aren't we? Some true funny stories reached me too late to publish last week. But I am saving them. Now, I want every member to write to me at once on this subject: "Favorite Books and Authors." Name the ten books that you like best (you needn't name the Bible; I take for granted that stands first). And name your three favorite authors. If you are older than fourteen, name the books and authors you preferred before you became older. I hope every one who reads this will write to me upon this subject; I want to make an article out of the letters. Now, children, be fair with me, and name the books you really *like*, and not those you think you *ought* to like, such as Shakespeare. Get your parents to write out the list they preferred before they were fifteen, and send it with your list. If you have never read ten books, name as many as you have, that you think are best. I want to find out what kind of books children love—not the kind they think they *ought* to read, but the kind that makes them have a good time.

hool.

USALEM.

ETT.

the last notable
ah. The eleven
ked by a steady
f the country and
But there was a
extensive build-
o erected numer-
gs in Jerusalem.
patron of archi-
policy, however,
expense of great
ao were already
ly the enormous
ually. Jeremiah
his extravagance
aere building of
only of weaken-
operations were
(Jer. 22:13-19)
followed Josiah
reproof, warning
said that it was
l Josiah, but for
they well might
d away never to
came the reproof
ice has just been
e sentence upon
ext king, that he
sed thing, child-
30). In fact, the
continued only
B. C., scarcely
periences of the
a resulted in the
r of the princes
cluding the king
th many of the
Kings 24:8-16).
n, as were also
to were useful in
was the second
the first having
ing the reign of
; Dan. 1:1-2).
. the tottering
f Josiah, named
iachin, and his

e at a time when
s political fabric
seeds of politi-
corruption had
ruit was bitter.
would have been
y, and Zedekiah
ies which could
om. Like many
as a compound of
vas more favor-
a Jehoiakim had
two fires. The
prophe. with a
to the idea that
ng care of itself
it this false hope
Jeremiah to pro-
eing regarded as
Such predictions
Zedekiah's reign
kim in 27:1 is an
iah, as is shown
It was the con-
e that those al-
vity would soon
to be impossible
tter to the cap-
against the hope
d them to settle

ec. 18, 1898—The
Golden Text—Ye
e, when ye search

in their new homes and make the best of the situation (Jer. 29). The king was troubled by these opposing forces in his capital. He was afraid of offending the court party by appearing to regard Jeremiah with favor, and on the other hand he was alarmed by the prophet's evident certainty as to the fate of the city. Several times he sent to consult Jeremiah as to the probable outcome of the situation (Jer. 37:3; 38:14). When thus asked for his advice, Jeremiah frankly counseled the king to give up the city and go out and surrender himself into the hands of Nebuchadrezzar (Jer. 38.15 18). The king was half persuaded to follow the prophet's counsel, but fear of his court on the one hand and of ridicule by the Jews who were already in Babylon on the other held him in check, and thus halting between two opinions he disregarded Jeremiah's advice after having broken his oath of allegiance to the Babylonian king (2 Chron. 36: 11-13). It may well be imagined how difficult was the situation of Jeremiah during this time. The court party hated him bitterly because he was preaching the uselessness of defense. They claimed that he was weakening the hands of the men of war, and secured his imprisonment and well-nigh caused his death (Jer. 38). In all these perplexing experiences the prophet maintained supreme confidence in two facts: first, that Jerusalem was certain to fall into the hands of the Babylonians; and second, that it was just as certain to be restored after a period of desolation, when the exiles should return from Babylon and repossess the land. In this confidence he even purchased a piece of property to which he had the right of redemption in his ancestral city of Anathoth (Jer. 32: 6-15). The most serious danger that menanced Jeremiah resulted from his attempt to leave Jerusalem and visit his new possession. He was accused of desertion to the Babylonians, which received color from his whole attitude during this period. In vain did he protest his innocence. He was scourged, and put into prison, from which he was only rescued by the kindness of the king (Jer. 37:11-21). Thus the details of Jeremiah's tragic and fascinating story are gathered from the disarranged materials of the book which bears his name. Israel was umfaithful and her future could only bring purification through suffering. A new nation and a new covenant were necesary (Jer. 31). No repentance of serious nature could be expected now. Even the promise to liberate the slaves in Israel which had been made under the spur of fear when the seige began, was broken, and the slaves again put into service as soon as the pressing danger was over by the temporary withdrawal of the Babylonian troops. Jeremiah protested against this in vain (Jer. 34-8-22). The time of repentance was past; nothing remained but the final tragedy.

This tragedy is set forth in the lesson. The cup of Israel's transgression was full. A long course of sin brought at last its inevitable consequences. The seige of Jerusalem by Nebuchadrezzar was only one of a long series of similar transactions by which this king enlarged and established two kingdoms and terrified his enemies into obedience. But no similar deed of his was of equal importance in the religious history of the world. That ninth day of the fourth month, which was kept as a perpetual fast-day in the later life of the nation, was the final blow to the old national history and the ushering in of a new period. The attempt to escape on the part of the beseiged was only partially successful. The flight of the king toward the Jordan was intercepted and his few companions were dispersed. The king himself and his family were taken to Riblah, far to the north, where the princes were slain and the unhappy king was blinded and carried in chains to Babylon, where he came to an unhappy end. The horrors of the seige and the desolation which followed it are graphically told in the little book of Lamentations, which has ever been associated with the name of Jeremiah, though of its original authors nothing certain is known. The exultation of Judah's enemies, especially the Edomites, is remembered in many an indignant imperation of the Old Testament (Obadiah, Psalms 137:7), and the hope of the future was that a time of vengeance would come upon these triumphant and insulting foes (Isa. 63:1-6). The subsequent story of Jeremiah's life, as well as the fate of those who remained in Jerusalem where he chose to stay, is given to us in Jeremiah 40-43

Christian Endeavor.

BY BURRIS A. JENKINS.

TOPIC FOR DECEMBER 18.

HOW TO ENJOY OUR RELIGION.

(Neh. 8:8-12; 1 Peter 4:3, 12, 13.)

One of the first requisites of the enjoyment of religion is that the religion should be intelligent. Unless one understands his Bible, how can he enjoy reading it? Every Christian, then, should make all possible effort to get an insight into the true meaning of the Scriptures, should adopt what facilities are at his disposal for Bible study.

Again, in order thoroughly to enjoy religion it should never be made to go against reason. No one can be in a happy state of mind who is attempting to swallow some religious belief that is too big to be swallowed. God has given us reason, and by means of it he has taught us to test everything that comes before us. Let us, then, not be afraid to exercise that reason and to test religion as we test all things else.

Nor, again, should we ever offend the conscience, for if there is anything in our nature which it pains us more to offend than to offend reason, it is to offend conscience. How unhappy, how hard is the way of the transgressor! There can be no happiness, no joy, where the conscience is not at peace. Calamity cannot triumph over us; troubles outside ourselves cannot gain the victory over the indomitable soul, only one's conscience can make him unhappy and afraid. The one way to be happy in one's religion is to work at it. No one can merely profess a moral Christian standard without living up to it and be happy in the profession. To enjoy religion one must live up to its high standards.

This brings to our minds naturally the requisite of earnestness. Dr. Arnold gave his boys but one rule, "Be earnest." The Bible had already given that rule, "Do with thy might what thy hands find to do." It is only by thus throwing oneself with all one's power into his pursuits that he can truly enjoy life. James Whitcomb Riley said recently in a public address that all literary men he had ever known were men whose work to them was p ay. They did not work under the scourge and the spur; it was a joy to them to work. "They work," said he, "as amateurs, and not the business of their lives." Mr. Kipling calls it "the joy of the working." If only Christians would work at their Christianity as men work at their professions, it would add much to the joy of living. Earnestness, tension, attention, striving, pouring one's soul into one's religious life, will bring the joy.

Strange as it may sound, James tells us "to count it all joy when we fall into divers temptations." May we not, then, find something to enjoy in the very obstacles of the religious life? Obstacles add to the zest of life. Obstacles! To the well-trained hunting-horse, hedges, ditches and fences are there purposely for him to leap. Difficulties! They are but the pawns, knights and bishops with which the opponent plays his game. There would be no joy or zest to the playing without them. Who would be a jellyfish, floating about in every current and zephyr of the tropic seas? Who would not rather be a dolphin, dashing against the northwest storm, Gulf Streams or tidal waves, from end to end of ocean. Temptations, difficulty, will only add to the joy of our lives. The best things in the world to do are things that are hardest.

FRANK R. STOCKTON has written for THE YOUTH'S COMPANION an anecdotal article on new lines under the curious title of "The Wolf and the Wheelbarrow." There is not only an actual wolf and a real wheelbarrow in it, but lions, a lion tamer, a famous tragedian and some interesting ob'ects of natural history.

BETHANY C. E. READING COURSES.

[There are three courses: The Bible, Missions and the Disciples. The three handbooks for the *first* year are: "A Guide to Bible Study," "Handbook of Missions" and "Concerning the Disciples." The three handbooks for the *second* year are: "Life and Teachings of Jesus," "Missionary Fields and Forces of the Disciples" and "Sketches of our Pioneers." Three handbooks and the Bethany C. E. Bulletin, quarterly, sent to any address for one dollar. All orders should be addressed to the Bethany C. E. Company, 798 Republic St., Cleveland, O. Each course has a director: H. L. Willett is director of Bible study; W. J. Lhamon is the director of studies in Missions; F. D. Power is director of studies Concerning the Disciples. This column is set apart to the use of these directors.]

India, or the Land of the Trident.

W. J. LHAMON.

India has been called the "Land of the Trident," because in every Siva Temple there is a three-pronged fork, representing one of the Hindu triads. It has been called the "Wonderland of the East," and Mme. Ragozin is quoted as saying of it, "Another world; a world in itself. That is what India pre-eminently is, and therein lies the charm." It has been estimated that within its boundaries the United States, East of the Mississippi, minus Ohio and Indiana, could be placed twice over, and that the New England States would have to be nine and one-half times as large as they are to cover it. The majesty of its mountains and the beneficence of its rivers are unsurpassed. Mount Everest is "earth's highest measured elevation," and the River Ganges brings down annually "enough fertilizing mud to fill so many fifty-ton freight cars as would reach two and a half times around the world."

This land was peopled primarily by race cousins of ours. Two branches of the noble old Aryan family started from their ancestral home, one traveling West and North, the other East and South; the one becoming modern Europe, the other modern India. It is a strange and very interesting providence that after so many centuries, the Western Aryans in the persons of Englishmen should go back and conquer the Eastern Aryans in the persons of the Hindus, and that Europe and America should unite in carrying the gospel together with a Christian civilization to these ancient relatives.

Their need is great. Into this land there is crowded a population of not far from 300,000,000; 208,000,000 of whom are Hindus; 57,000,000 are Buddhists, and above 9,000,000 are animistic, attributing a personal soul to inanimate objects and to the forces of nature and worshiping the things so personified.

Relatively to our standard of living the conditions in India are dreadful. The houses of the poor are mud floors; they have no chimneys and usually no windows; they are as a rule not above twelve or fifteen feet square, and they cost from fifteen to eighteen dollars. The clothing of children up to eight years of age is conspicuous by reason of its absence. A Hindu proverb says, "Children and the legs of a stool do not feel the cold."

It is estimated that a man and his family can earn on an average five cents a day. "Food and grains can be bought at two pounds per penny; clothing is scanty and cheap; fuel costs nothing and house rent is scarcely known."

The Shastras define the position of the wife as follows: "A woman has no other god on earth than her husband. When in the presence of her husband a woman must not look on one side or on the other. She must keep her eyes on her master to be ready to receive his commands. When he speaks she must be quiet and listen to nothing besides. Let her words, her actions and her deportment give open assurance that she regards her husband as her god. Than shall she be honored of all men and shall be praised as a victorous and discreet woman."

Of the total populated of India only one man in every nine can read and write, and but one woman in a hundred and seventy-three can pass this double test. As regards letters they are a nation sitting in darkness.

The gods of India are more numerous than her people. Water and rivers and plants and mountains and animals and tools and jewelry and ancestors are worshiped. Nothing could be more sacred than snakes and monkeys, unless cows and ancestors. As to the gods most venerated, great differences seem to exist in the opinions of students. We are told that the worship of Ganesa, god of the demon host, is all but universal. Again we learn that the cow is the most sacred object in India. Again we are informed that ancestor worship in some form or another is the beginning, the middle and the end of what is known as Hindu worship.

The doctrine of transmigration has much to do with this teeming idolatry. "Even a flea may enclose the soul of some person who was a sage or a saint." This theosophic teaching has had all over India the baleful effect of degrading the human kind and not helping the animal kind.

The entire Brahmin caste is deemed divine, and the living members of it are objects of worship. A common saying is:

"All the world is subject to the gods;
The gods are subject to the holy texts;
The holy texts are subject to the Brahmins;
Therefore the Brahmin is my god."

Among the estimated 330,000,000 gods of India three are held in special reverence; Brahma the omnipotent, Vishnu the preserver and Siva the destroyer. The gods are worshiped through the mediation of priests with prayers, sacrifices, festivals, pilgrimages and offerings, and the whole system of religion is vitiated by the thought of merit and the spfrit of selfishness.

Of the doctrine of transmigration, named above, Mr. Beach says, in his excellent little book entitled, "The Cross in the Land of the Trident," "This doctrine of Hinduism pursues the soul after death. It is based upon the belief in immortality, and professes to explain the differing conditions of those born on the earth. One's lot is due to merit or demerit in previous stages of existence. Through 8,400,000 births one reaches at length the glad time when individual existence is absorbed in the divine. What wonder that a common saying is, "Existence is misery," or that a Hindu poet has said:

"How many births are past I cannot tell;
How many are to come no man can say;
But this alone I know and know full well,
That pain and grief embitter all the day."

Further information about the religion of the Hindus may be had from the chapter on Hinduism in the Handbook of Fields and Forces. Toward the teeming and idolatrous millions of India the hearts of many Christly people have been turned. Many missions have been opened and some of them have been eminently successful. The handbook will show what our own missions have done. Another quotation from Mr. Beach may be taken as a fitting conclusion of this essay. "Mr. Kidd urges from the standpoint of philanthropic altruism the administration of the affairs of India from the temperate zone. How much more ought the love of Christ constrain the American Christian to give himself to the spiritual welfare of the Hindu!"

ages.

–

.—At the residence of
ıelby City, Ky., Nov.
ley, of Stanford, and
ıbbs, by Frank W.

·Nelson Bugby and
ınited in marriage at
.ytle officiating.

: the residence of the
I. Crutcher, Sedalia,
November, 1898, Mr.
.d Miss Lora Lee, of

EET.—At the home of
ov. 17, 1898, C. H.
Louis E. Finnell to
ɔth of Monroe county,

LE.—In Denver, Col.,
el B. Moore, John F.
McIlmoyle, both of
dal party are manager
Gayest Manhattan''
rk.

On Nov. 16, 1898, Mr.
[rs. Lizzie Mobley, of
arried; A. L. Johnson

KLEY. — In Denver,
y Samuel B. Moore,
Cheyenne, Wyo., and
ınver.

INGS. — Nov. 23, in
A. Replogle to Mary
he pastor's youngest
ıgs officiating.

—Nov. 16, 1898, in
by C. H. Strawn, Mr.
Miss Sarah Alice Wil-
y, Mo.

.EY. — Married near
lbery to Miss Maggie
S. A. Strawn officiat-

N.—Nov. 30, 1898, in
Strawn, Mr. Eddie P.
B. Gritton, both of

nuel J. Yund and Miss
ted in marriage Nov.
J. A. Lytle.

ıries.

ɔe inserted free. Above
ɔt a word. Please send

–

SLEE.

; Cal., on Nov. 9th,
wife of H. B. Blakes-
.ths and 24 days. For
knew Sister Blakeslee
she with her husband
ful members of the
. Blakeslee will have
s of a great number of
w.

e heavy,
rength to bear,
ıe narrow way
ɔd from care.

organization, four years ago. Was born Jan. 5, 1832, married to Mary H. Hillyer, Feb. 12, 1859, united with the Christian Church, 1866. Funeral conducted Nov. 26, by the writer.

F. L. PETTIT.

Bethany, Neb.

DILLS.

Sister Elizabeth Dills died at her home near Armington, Ill., Nov. 8, 1898, in her 69th year. Her maiden name was Darnell. Born Jan. 3, 1830. At the age of 17 she gave her heart to Christ, with whom she walked in lowly fellowship 52 years. June 1, 1848, she was united in marriage to Thomas H. Dills. She was a true Christian, a devoted wife and beloved mother. She leaves a memory better than great riches. Her children rise up to call her blessed. An aged husband, two sons and four daughters and many friends mourn their loss. Through a lifetime of self-sacrifice this good woman has gone to her reward.

C. A. HECKEL.

ENGLAND.

At his home in Burrton, Kansas, September 11, 1898, of paralysis, S. J. England, at the ripe old age of 79 years and 4 months. He died with the blessed assurance of a home eternal, having been a member of the Christian Church 44 years. He was a devoted worker in the church in Kentucky, in Holton, Kansas, and in Burrton where his home has been for many years. His mother, who was Hannah Mershon, was one of the first converts to that church in Northeastern Kentucky and all her children, of whom he was the last, lived and died in that faith and he also lived to see all his children and many of his grandchildren brought into the fold. He was born in Bath County, Kentucky, married near Grayson, Carter County, to Clarinda Everman, Dec. 27, 1837, with whom he lived 60 years. She with seven children are left. He was quite a prominent character in Northeastern Kentucky, being a member of the state legislature at the beginning of the Civil War, where he cast one of the votes that kept Kentucky from seceding. In 1864 he moved to Girard, Illinois, where his son and two sons-in law, F. M. Jacobs and T. W. Ramey, all ministers, were preaching the gospel. In 1870 he moved to Kansas where he has since lived. He was one of the few remaining old-style Southern gentleman noted for generosity and hospitality, without an enemy, although active in public life and pronounced in his views on all subjects; in short, one of God's noblemen, whose life has made the world better. I cannot close this tribute to my dear old father's memory without alluding to the grand old songs of Zion which he loved so well and which find no place in our books of to-day, such as ''The Angels that Watched Round the Tomb,'' ''How Firm a Foundation,'' ''Come, Let Us Join our Friends Above,'' ''Why Should We Start and Fear to Die?'' ''Broad is the Road that Leads to Death,'' ''Time is Winging Us Away,'' and many others. Methinks I hear his voice now, so rich and full of pathos even in his old age, singing them as we so often did at home when they were no longer sung in the church, having been replaced by our modern music. So many of our songs seem frivolous in comparison. Sometimes it seems there is no place in the church for old people with the young people's societies and everything done to suit young ideas, but blessed be his holy name there is room for them in heaven. He was wholly prepared and waiting for the summons, as his health had been poor for three years. I close with one of his favorite quotations:

''Life is a scene of conquest, not of rest,
Man's is laborious happiness at best;
On this side of death his dangers never cease,
His joys are joys of conquest, not of peace.''

MRS. SARAH E. JARRETT.

cult to fill. The community has lost one who was always ready for every good work. A great host of friends attended the funeral in attestation of the high esteem in which this saintly woman was held.

''Dearest sister, thou hast left us,
Here thy loss we deeply feel,
But God that hath bereft us,
He can all our sorrows heal.''

A. W. HENRY.

About those Departments.

EDITOR CHRISTIAN-EVANGELIST:—I am sorry you did not state to your readers my reason for objecting to the Sunday-school and Christian Endeavor Departments in our papers. I have visited many Sunday-schools and Endeavor Societies, and I have failed to find any that were not well supplied with helpful literature. Such being the case, I do not see the necessity for filling the columns of our church papers with these departments. These special writers crowd out many other contributors who ought to be heard. Your own company furnishes literature to a vast number of schools and societies. Why the necessity of filling several columns in your paper with these departments? SIMPSON ELY.

We are not specially concerned with Bro. Ely's *reasons* for thinking these departments unnecessary, but with the *fact* of his so thinking. If our readers do not wish them, then we do not care to publish them, even though the reasons for not wanting them are not good. But, as Bro. E. has seen from the responses, allowing that those who have spoken represent those who have not spoken as well as themselves, a great majority of our readers do find them useful. We are grateful to Bro. E. for having called out these expressions, for they will encourage us to try to make these departments more useful than ever.

EDITOR CHRISTIAN-EVANGELIST:—I know that your Sunday school, Endeavor and Prayer-meeting departments are a great held to many isolated or shut-in Disciples, and hope they may continue in your highly valuable paper. If I were going to suggest anything it would be to keep the idea of thorough, systematic work in our Sunday-schools before our people more frequently.

MRS. M. L. ELLINGER.

Ottawa, Kan., Nov. 22.

EDITOR CHRISTIAN-EVANGELIST:—Relative to the discussion *pro* and *con.* the utility of your space, I beg leave to add my testimony to that already received. As to the Sunday-school department, the weekly lecture by Prof. Willett is like an oasis, sparkling with originality in the midst of a dreary desert of *commentaries.* His vigor of expression and pithy style would be surely missed if omitted from your columns. We have far too little of this originality as it is. Your (or let me say *our*) C. E. and Quiet Hour columns need no defense from my pen. The CHRISTIAN-EVANGELIST satisfies. D. C. TREMAINE.

Harrisville, N. Y., Nov. 19, 1898.

EDITOR CHRISTIAN-EVANGELIST:—By all means continue the departments in the CHRISTIAN-EVANGELIST. We work in prayer-meeting, Bible-school and Christian Endeavor and study these columns with much profit. We think the CHRISTIAN-EVANGELIST becomes better with each year.

LOU M. LANE.
MRS. J. T. GLASS.

Holden, Mo., Nov. 28, 1898.

Praised by the Soldiers.

The following appeared in the Times-Union, of Jacksonville, of Nov. 21:

Rev. T. H. Blenus, pastor of the Christian Church, of Jacksonville, who has been doing considerable and practical work among the sick soldiers has not been forgotten by them, a letter having been sent to President McKinley, a copy of which has been received here. The letter reads:

Jacksonville, Fla.

Second Division Hospital, Camp Cuba Libre, November, 1898.

To Hon. Wm. McKinley, President of the United States:

Dear Sir: On the departure of many of us from the Second Division hospital of this camp, where we have been under treatment, some of us for a number of weeks, we desire to express our appreciation of the kind treatment that we have received from those in charge of this hospital. Ample provision for our wants has been made, and we have had splendid and untiring attention from sergeons and nurses. While others have complained, we have had no reason to do so. The citizens of Jacksonville have shown the kindest and deepest concern for our welfare and have done very much for our comfort. Among many others we feel it our duty to mention one who has been unstinted in his visitations and untiring in his ministrations since last June, when the hospital was first opened here. We refer to the Rev. T. H. Blenus, pastor of the Christian Church at Jacksonville. This gentleman deserves the thanks of hundreds of our boys. In season and out of season he has ministered in love and kindness to the sick and dying, until his name has become common to all, and his presence in the hospital a source of encouragement. We cannot but feel that such continued and unselfish labors of love should call forth from us words of commendation and should be known to the Chief Magistrate of our beloved land.

[Signed] A number of the boys of the Second Division Hospital, Seventh Army Corps, Jacksonville, Fla.

The above copy of the original letter to the President was sent from Washington to T. H. Blenus by President McKinley, through the surgeon general.

Publishers' Notes.

The Christian Lesson Commentary for 1899 is on our table. It grows brighter and better as the years come and go. We have used it for thirteen years, and now start in for the fourteenth volume. It is pure in doctrine, full in explanation, pointed in application, and we trust international and general in circulation. —*The Christian Index, Des Moines, Iowa.*

Write to the Christian Publishing Co. for their catalogue, from which you can select an appropriate book for a Christmas present to your friends. A good book is "medicine for the soul" of the careful reader, and a gift of this kind is a constant reminder of the donor. A large number of good books are found published in this paper. Make your selection and send in your order before the holidays.

The study of the lives of Bible characters is both interesting and profitable. Important lessons can be gained from the careful study of such characters as King Saul, King Jehu and Queen Esther. We have recently published three books which deal with the lives of the above prominent characters. The authors and titles are as follows:

"In the Days of Jehu," by J. Breckenridge Ellis. 189 pages. Cloth. Price, 75 cents.

"King Saul," by J. Breckenridge Ellis. 281 pages. Cloth. Price, $1.

"Queen Esther," by M. M. Davis. 132 pages. Cloth. Price, 75 cents.

All of the above books are 12mo. in size and are bound in the latest style cloth binding. They are excellent books to place in the hands of the young. The minister can find in them material for sermons.

The Christian Lesson Commentary for 1899, by W. W. Dowling, has, in addition to the lessons for the year, three well-printed maps, the life of Jesus in regular chronological order, and a dictionary of proper names. Many of the lessons are illustrated by scenes from the times in which they were written. The book also contains very helpful opening services for the Bible-school. The lessons are well analyzed and presented in excellent form.

The author, W. W. Dowling, is so well known as the most experienced and capable writer on the Bible-school subjects and lesson commentaries that any new annual coming from his pen is always expected to excel. In this our great army of teachers will not be disappointed. It is certainly an excellent addition to the many volumes already produced —*Register-Review, Kansas City, Mo.*

All Sunday-school superintendents and teachers will be greatly assisted in their work by the study of our Lesson Commentary. In order that you may help them in their work and also show your appreciation of their effort in the Sunday-school, you should make them a Christmas present of the Christian Lesson Commentary for 1899, prepared by W. W. Dowling, and published by the Christian Publishing Co., St. Louis, Mo. In this book will be found the most thorough treatment of the Sunday-school lessons for 1899. All phases of the subject are discussed and the best scholarship of the world quoted. The Lesson Commentary for 1899 will be a helpful and appropriate Christmas present for any superintendent and teacher.

It is bound in dark green cloth, has red edges, contains over 400 pages and the price is $1, postpaid.

THE
ISTIAN-EVANGELIST.

A WEEKLY FAMILY AND RELIGIOUS JOURNAL.

December 15, 1898 No. 50.

NTS.

...............739
Work in Mis-
...............740
eveloped......741
. .. . 742
Men... 742
....743
s............. 743
:
Soul.—L. H.
...............744
of the Lord's
nus....... ...746

e, Kas........747
...............750
s 750
lleges.........751
.... 751
to Prayer. ..752
...............752
. ...753
...............753
...............754
ment..........754

...............758
of the Army...758
.. ..758
) 759
....759
(poem) 759
...............759
nfall...........760
Other There..761

...............746
ught..........747
....748
...............749
...............755
...............757
....762
...............763
....764
....765
ng Courses . .765
ries...........766

n $1.50

T. P. HALEY.

THE

CHRISTIAN - EVANGELIST

J. H. GARRISON, Editor.

W. W. HOPKINS, Assistant.

B. B. TYLER, J. J. HALEY,
EDITORIAL CONTRIBUTORS.

What We Plead For.

The Christian-Evangelist pleads for:

The Christianity of the New Testament, taught by Christ and his Apostles, versus the theology of the creeds taught by fallible men—the world's great need.

The divine confession of faith on which Christ built his church, versus human confessions of faith on which men have split the church.

The unity of Christ's disciples, for which he so fervently prayed, versus the divisions in Christ's body, which his apostles strongly condemned.

The abandonment of sectarian names and practices, based on human authority, for the common family name and the common faith, based on divine authority, versus the abandonment of scriptural names and usages for partisan ends.

The hearty co-operation of Christians in efforts of world-wide beneficence and evangelization, versus petty jealousies and strifes in the struggle for denominational pre-eminence.

The fidelity to truth which secures the approval of God, versus conformity to custom to gain the favor of men.

The protection of the home and the destruction of the saloon, versus the protection of the saloon and the destruction of the home.

For the right against the wrong;
For the weak against the strong;
For the poor who've waited long
For the brighter age to be.
For the truth, 'gainst superstition,
For the faith, against tradition,
For the hope, whose glad fruition
Our waiting eyes shall see.

RATES OF SUBSCRIPTION.

Single subscriptions, new or old .... $1.50 each
Ministers .... 1.00 "

All subscriptions payable in advance. Label shows the month up to the first day of which your subscription is paid. If an earlier date than the present is shown, you are in arrears. No paper discontinued without express orders to that effect. Arrears should be paid when discontinuance is ordered.

In ordering a change of post office, please give the OLD as well as the NEW address.

Do not send local check, but use Post office or Express Money Order, or draft on St. Louis, Chicago or New York, in remitting.

Address, CHRISTIAN PUBLISHING CO.,
1522 Locust St., St. Louis, Mo.

THE CHRISTIAN-EVANGELIST

"In faith, Unity; in opinion and methods, Liberty; in all things, Charity."

Vol. xxxv. St. Louis, Mo., Thursday, December 15, 1898. No. 50

CURRENT EVENTS.

The session of Congress which opened on Monday of last week has much to do and little time in which to do it. March 4th is the limit to the short session. There are certain matters of a more or less routine character which must be dealt with and appropriation bills must be passed. These will probably occupy most of the time and energies of the session. In addition to these, there will probably be legislation for the permanent increase of the army, this being considered by the administration as immediately necessary in view of the increase of our territory. Provision for the establishment of a permanent government for Hawaii may also be expected at an early day. These things must be done to avoid an extra session of Congress immediately after March 4th. There are other topics of importance to be considered, but, pressing as they are, they will not be allowed to interfere with the course of these necessary measures. An anti-scalping bill has already been passed by the House; a pooling bill will very likely be introduced; and the Nicaraguan Canal bill, according to Senator Morgan's promise, will be brought in early in the session. But it is not probable that Congress will in the present session undertake to deal with the complex problems of the organization of governments for our new possessions, Porto Rico and the Philippines.

Emperor William opened the new session of the Reichstag on Tuesday, Dec. 6th, the day after the opening of Congress. The Kaiser's speech from the throne touched cursorily upon several of the international topics of the day, calling attention to the speedy resumption of friendly relations between the United States and Spain and remarking upon the perfect neutrality which Germany had maintained between the two combatants. It is interesting to note at a single glance the Kaiser's warm approval of the Czar's proposals for disarmament, and the introduction into the Reichstag, with imperial sanction, of a bill providing for the increase of the German army on a peace footing slightly over half a million rank and file.

President McKinley's message has evoked a volume of comment commensurate with the importance of the topics with which it deals and the expectancy with which it was waited. The document makes no revelation of any unexpected general plan or policy on the part of the administration. Hence it has been received at home with approval or disapproval, according to the individual's preconceived approbation or disapprobation of the Presidential policy. The English papers generally approve of the message, considering it a clear, moderate and satisfactory statement of a wise policy, and seeing, in the declaration for an "open-door" policy in the East that America is "in line" with British purposes and will co-operate with them. Doubt is expressed only in regard to the clause referring to the Nicaraguan Canal, whether there is not a failure to recognize England's rights as guaranteed by the Clayton-Bulwer treaty. The French press, for the most part, expresses satisfaction and is not disposed to question our right to become a world-power, but it adverts, in the grieved tone of one who has lost confidence in humanity, to the fact that "as regards Cuba, the President's declaration is almost identical with the declaration of Great Britain when she entered Egypt, where she remains. Attention is called by the German papers to the fact that the President fails to reciprocate in any very definite fashion the warm expressions of desire for an Anglo-American alliance which have come from official sources in Great Britain.

As to the Nicaragua Canal, the President takes a decided position, that its construction has become a necessity and that "our national policy now more than ever calls for its control by this government." There is reported to be an understanding with Great Britain which prevents this from being construed as inimical to British interests. At any rate there has been no sign of anxiety on that point in any official quarter. Within less than a year the concession will expire which was granted by Nicaragua to the Maritime Company, through which the committee intends that the United States shall construct and control the canal. Other and conflicting concessions have been granted to a rival company which, if they hold good, would shut off the Maritime Company from the chance of renewal. The Senate committee has reported to the Senate its decision, that the second grant was illegal and that by it Nicaragua endangered its friendly relations with the United States.

The United States Army is quite sure to be reorganized, but it is not so sure whose plan will be adopted for the reorganization. General Miles has formulated a bill embodying his plan, which he has presented to Secretary Alger to be presented through the proper committee. This plan provides for the increase of the standing army to the ratio of one soldier for every thousand of population in the United States and two for every thousand in our foreign possessions, making a total of approximately 100,000 men. These are to be divided among the various arms of the service as follows: 15 regiments of cavalry, 14 regiments of seacoast artillery, two regiments of field artillery, two regiments of engineers and 50 regiments of infantry. The Miles bill proposes also the re-creation of the ranks of general and lieutenant-general, the former to be the rank of the military head of the entire army, the latter of the commander of each of the two army corps. The Hull army bill, formulated by the chairman of the House Committee on military affairs, is said to represent the views of the administration. It also provides for a total of 100,000 men, but differs from the Miles bill in several particulars; for example, in providing for only one lieutenant-general and no general, and in abandoning regimental formation for artillery. The latter bill has been introduced into the House.

The annual report of the Secretary of the Treasury contains a good many statistics, but they are not dry statistics. Such figures as the following have a deep significance as indicating the commercial activity and prosperity of our country during the past year in spite of the war. The statistics are for the fiscal year of 1898, the twelve months ending June 30. During this period, for the first time in our history, has the value of our exports of products of field and factory averaged more than one hundred millions per month. For the first time also we have exported more manufactured products than we have imported. The total exports for the year were more than double the total imports, leaving a balance of trade of over six hundred millions in our favor. The unprecedented excess of gold importations over exportations for the past year represents a part of the balance of trade. Foremost among Secretary Gage's recommendations is a repetition of his former suggestion for the gradual substitution of bank notes for greenbacks, by the retention of all the greenbacks which come into the treasury unless gold is offered in exchange for them. The same plan of monetary reform is commended by the President in his message.

A few evenings ago the British Ambassador at Paris, Sir Edmund Monson, took occasion in an after-dinner speech to make a general address to the French people, which was not marked by the customary diplomatic reserve. He assured the French people that England bore no grudge against them, but warned them against a continuance of their policy of nagging and irritation and against attempting to thwart British enterprise by petty maneuvers. He called attention to the Fashoda incident as disproving the familiar allegation that British diplomacy is noisy but ineffectual, and pointed out the fact that such exasperating though petty provocations as the plan of establishing French colleges as rivals of Gen. Kitchener's projected institution in the reconquered Soudan, might make it necessary for Great Britain to abandon her policy of forbearance—to the sorrow of France. The French papers at once resented the speech, and have become more furious about it, now that it appears that the ambassador's threatening words were not a mere "post-prandial indiscretion," but were inspired by his government. Lord Salisbury's responsibility for the speech is still, however, no more than a hypothesis. But Mr. Chamberlain, British Secretary for the Colonies, in a speech two days later, uttered a similar, almost identical warning to France against the "policy of exasperation." Mr. Chamberlain also announced the consummation of a definite understanding between Great Britain and Germany, comparable to that existing between France and Russia.

So far as can at present be ascertained the intention of the administration is to extend the United States tariff regulations to Porto Rico, but to maintain in the Philippines an open door for the commerce of all nations, giving ourselves no advantage over others. The justice and propriety of the former cause in regard to Porto Rico seems obvious enough. If it is to be really a part of the territory of the United States it must be joined to us by commercial as well as political bonds. With the Philippines the case is somewhat different. The example set by the other powers in the Orient, notably Great Britain, in granting equal privileges to the trades of all nations in the Chinese ports which they control, cannot wisely or courteously be ignored. It is true that our tenure of the Philippines will be of a different sort from the hold which England, for example, possesses on the Yangtse district of China, and will involve a more distinct right to a policy of commercial exclusiveness if we cared to inaugurate it. But if we are going to enter into the complex situation which constitutes the Eastern question, we cannot afford to appear as the champions of any narrower policy than Great Britain, whose plea for the commercial "open door" is the most hopeful feature in the mass of Oriental complications. The Spanish peace commissioners have asked that Spain be allowed equal commercial privileges with the United States in Porto Rico for a period of five years and in Cuba as long as we shall control it. The request is supported by the citation of the treaty by which Florida was transferred from Spanish to American hands, in which place equal trading privileges were granted for twelve years. There was a similar provision in the purchase of the Louisiana territory from Spain. A strong and plausible statement of the case has been made and the point is under consideration.

Gov. Tanner, of Illinois, has been indicted by grand jury on the charge of "willfu neglect of palpable duty as an officer and malfeasance in office." This indictment was made by the grand jury which has been sitting at Carlinville, Ill., since Nov. 9, investigating the causes of the riots at Virden, Oct. 12, and placing the blame for them. F. W. Lukins, manager of the Chicago-Virden Coal Co., is indicted for murder and manslaughter on three counts, and fifty-two other persons are charged with more or less seriously criminal participation in the disturbance. The indictment of the governor is based on the proved fact that the sheriff, foreseeing trouble, had asked for troops, that the manager had begged the governor to send troops to preserve the peace, and that the requests had been refused, although it was evident that order could not be maintained among the miners without militia. It was a close vote on the indictment of the governor, 13 to 10. The foreman of the jury is quoted as having uttered these words: "I considered Gov. Tanner the best friend to the laboring man in the state of Illinois, and I for one did not vote to indict him." We repeat our former statement, that the question is not as to the sincerity of Gov. Tanner's devotion to the interests of the laboring man, but relates solely to his obedience to the constitution under which he holds office. Few laboring men would care to assert that even their best friend could not conceivably exceed his authority or come short of his duty as an officer. The words of the foreman of the grand jury may or may not be a true estimate of Gov. Tanner's attitude toward organized labor, but in any case they are not pertinent to the question before the jury. The indictment has been made, but there is a considerable probability that the judicial machinery will slip a cog somewhere and that nothing will come of it.

UNITY IN EDUCATIONAL WORK IN MISSOURI.

The Educational Conference, which met in Moberly on the 6th inst., and adjourned at noon on the following day, came to a most happy termination. There was a feeling widespread among the brethren of the state that because of conflicting interests there could be no possible agreement on lines of educational work, and that the conference could have no other result than to accentuate the differences already existing on this question. The result, however, shows that the Missouri brethren are capable of better things. There do exist, no doubt, these differences of opinion concerning the most profitable lines of educational work, but there was enough of the spirit of unity and brotherly love among the brethren who convened at Moberly to triumph over individual differences and preferences, and to secure substantial unity of action.

The proceedings will, no doubt, be reported in our religious press by the secretary of the conference. It will suffice here to say that, after the preliminary matter of enrollment of delegates, numbering about 100, and the arrangement of an order of business, the first session closed and the conference adjourned to meet at 7 o'clock. At this meeting it was proposed to discuss and decide upon the wisdom of selecting one or more institutions upon which to concentrate our efforts at endowment until they had become adequately endowed. When the session had been opened by devotional exercises, a series of resolutions were introduced in the interest of unity and cooperation which had the happy effect of securing the unanimous approval, at last, of the entire conference. These resolutions set forth the fact that, while in the judgment of this conference it would be unwise to attempt to limit the benfactions of the brotherhood of the state to one or more institutions to the neglect of others, there were certain pressing needs which at present claim our attention.

The resolutions recommended, therefore, that an effort be made to secure a minimum sum of $50,000 for Christian University at Canton, in view of the work that it had done in the past and was capable of doing. This amount was subsequently changed to $100,000. It was further recommended, in view of the needs of the Bible College at Columbia, that an effort be made to erect a suitable building, as early as possible, upon the lot which had been purchased for its use, and this enterprise was commended to the liberality of the brotherhood of the state. It was still further recommended that the Female Orphan School at Fulton should be relieved from its financial misfortune as early as practicable and be otherwise aided in fulfilling its beneficent misssion.

An educational board, afterwards denominated as an executive committee, of seven brethren representing these various interests, was appointed to foster our educational interests in the state and to carry out, through and with the co-operation of the trustees of the institutions above mentioned, the foregoing recommendations, and to report to the next annual educational conference, which is to meet in connection with our next state convention.

Earnest and fraternal speeches were made by many brethren, setting forth the importance of these various educational interests, and the utmost liberality of spirit prevailed. President Lockhart made a ringing speech in behalf of the Bible College, at Columbia, while one of the steadfast friends of the Bible College not only upheld the claims of Christian University for recognition, but volunteered a pledge of $1,000 to its endowment fund on the basis of $100,000. In this sort of an atmosphere the spirit of sectionalism or local interests gave way to the larger conception of a united brotherhood working harmoniously together for the different departments of its one common work. It was not forgotten that we have other institutions in the state, such as the Camden Point Orphan School, which is out of debt and doing a good work, and Central Christian College, at Albany, which has a good building with a small debt, and Christian College, at Columbia, which under its present management has outgrown its old quarters and is planning for new and magnificent buildings. These are all factors in our educational work, and whatever can be done for them will be hailed with pleasure. But it was felt that for the time being the institutions previously referred to had the most pressing claims on the brotherhood of the state, and that our first duty was to look after their needs.

There was a morning session on Wednesday to talk over matters of detail and to agree on the members of the executive committee, all of which was harmoniously arranged. The closing moments of the conference were devoted to earnest thanksgiving to God for the manifestation of His presence and power over the hearts of the brethren, and invoking His blessing in carrying out the plans which had been agreed upon. The final song, "Praise God from whom all blessings flow," was sung with great spirit, and Hon. J. W. Alexander, the president of the conference, pronounced it adjourned.

This was a happier issue than any of us had dared to hope for, but no doubt there were earnest hearts that sought God's blessing and guidance upon this conference. It would be wrong to close this brief sketch of what we trust may prove a most important meeting without acknowledging a debt of gratitude due to the church at Moberly for its hospitality in furnishing lodgings for the delegates of the conference, and especially to the ladies for the splendid meals which they served in the church. Bro. Briney and his flock deserved the vote of thanks which they received from the conference for their kindness.

In conclusion, may we express the hope that the brethren who were not present at the conference may accept its conclusions in the same spirit of brotherly love and of magnanimity which marked its proceedings, and that we may all seek to carry out its purposes in the same spirit of unity and of earnest devotion to our educational interests in the state. We have never been in as good condition in Missouri as we are now for a great forward movement in the endowment and equipment of our schools. The brethren understand each other better than ever before. The importance and scope of the Bible College work at Columbia were never so fully understood nor its work so unanimously endorsed as at present. Christian University has never put itself into such close and sympathetic touch with the brotherhood of the state as it has done by its recent action. The disappointment and chagrin which many of the friends of the Orphan School at Fulton felt over its financial mismanagement in the past are giving place to the feeling that the school itself is not to blame for this, and that under wiser supervision, and with the purpose of holding it more steadfast to its original, benevolent aim, the institution must be relieved from indebtedness and helped forward in its Christlike mission.

We appeal, therefore, to the wealthy and well-to-do brethren and sisters in the state to help these institutions to do their work. Let us not trust our means to the legal technicalities of wills, but administer upon our own estates and see the work of God prospering under our liberality ere our eyes are totally eclipsed by the on-coming shadows of death.

SPIRITUAL LIFE—HOW DEVELOPED.*

II. PROCESS OF SPIRITUAL GROWTH.

Paul said concerning his own experience: "That life which I now live in the flesh I live in faith, the faith which is in the Son of God, who loved me and gave Himself up for me"(Gal.2:20). If there be any who say this life of which we speak cannot be lived here in the flesh, Paul asserts that it *can*, and that he lived it. He tells us, moreover *how* he lived it: "I live in faith, the faith which is in the Son of God." It can be lived in no other way. Faith is the soul's vision. It is only as the soul sees Christ, the Son of God, and yields itself to Him in loving obedience that it can share in that life which has been the wonder and admiration of all the ages. Faith perceives the royal qualities of Christ's character, the amazing love and grace which He offers to men, and lays hold on Him. We cannot expect the spiritual growth of our members without an increase of faith. This increase of faith can be secured only by being loyal to the conscience—the light which is in us—and conforming to every known requirement of duty; by a diligent study of God's Word and the daily efforts to practice it. The more one *practices* Christianity, the more he will believe in Christ, and the more he believes in Christ the larger measure of his power, grace and life he will receive.

The result of loyally following one's faith is to give to that faith a degree of certitude that amounts to knowledge. Hence Paul could say: "I *know* in whom I have *believed*." This harmonizes, too, with the words of Jesus who, in His great intercessory prayer, said: "And this is life e ernal, that they should know Thee, the only true God, and Him whom Thou has sent, even Jesus Christ" (Jno. 17:3).

The knowledge of God and of Christ referred to in this passage as "life eternal" is not, of course, a mere intellectual apprehension of God and of Christ. It is an experimental knowledge; that is, the knowledge that comes from hearing to God's voice, through faith, and loyally obeying that voice. This is perhaps the highest of all knowledge, because it is based upon the highest part of our nature and on the noblest activities of which the soul is capable—faith, hope and love.

There is one condition of spiritual growth that we feel needs to be emphasized because the neglect of it often leads to disastrous spiritual results. The note of *reality* should be in every religious experience, claim or profession. There should be the utmost harmony between our words and our actual religious desires, purposes and attainments. To profess more than we *feel*, and to claim more than we actually possess, religiously, is to play the part of a Pharisee, and may become a species of conscious or unconscious hypocrisy. There is the greater danger of this from the fact that our knowledge of what we ought to desire and purpose and be always runs ahead of what we do actually desire and purpose and are. There is no quality of Christian life more to be desired than *genuineness*. There is a temptation, of course, in some natures, to err in the opposite direction and to publicly discredit their spiritual state in a way that, if done by another, would subject him to the charge of slander. While avoiding all pretense of being better than we are, it is equally our duty, if we are to be genuine, to gratefully acknowledge any strength which God may have given us to achieve the victory over the evil that is within us and without us. If we will but recognize the source of all our spiritual blessings and power, and the true standard of spiritual measurement, there will be little danger of our falling into spiritual pride.

This heart-searching endeavor to be *genuine* and to rest on nothing but *reality* in religion is the best preparation for real, effective prayer, without which the soul can never rise to that spiritual altitude for which it was intended. Sincerity is as essential an element of prayer as faith is, and without it it is impossible that there should exist that consciousness of our spiritual needs which alone makes prayer possible. There is no better place in which to gauge the spiritual life of a church than at it prayer-meeting. It is not only in the *number* of prayers offered, but especially in the kind of praying, that we learn the real spiritual stateof the church. On what plane do these prayers move? What are the things for which the petitioners ask and for which they give thanks? What of the spontaneity in the prayers? What faith do they manifest in God's willingness to grant large spiritual blessings? What reaching out is there after higher and better things and greater victories in behalf of truth and righteousness? Is there in the prayers the genuine note of confession of sin and the spirit of repentance? A preacher should study the prayers of the membersof his congregation like a physician would note the symptoms of his patient by feeling his pulse, taking his temperature and examining his tongue, to ascertain his physical condition. Said Mr. Spurgeon, after talking with a minister for sometime, whom he had not met before, "Let us kneel down and pray, for I never feel that I know a man until I have heard him pray." Any one who has heard Mr. Spurgeon pray has never been in doubt as to the source of his wonderful power and success.

The problem of promoting the spiritual growth of a congregation, with which every conscientious minister has to deal, is largely the problem of how to get his members to pray more and to pray better. One of the ways of accomplishing this end is to get them to attempt some kind of religious work, for nothing discloses to one so clearly his spiritual needs as an effort to do some work for God, and this consciousness of spiritual need is one of the chief incentives to prayer. As we are more apt to pray genuinely and to make confession of our actual sins and ask God for the precise things that we need, when we pray alone, pastors would do well to insist on the importance of the "Quiet Hour," or at least a quiet *quarter* of an hour in each day, when the soul can be alone with God and with the great questions that affect its eternal destiny.

It is to be feared that in the hurry and bustle of our modern life the reading of God's Word and other religious reading is sadly neglected. The soul, like the body, must have its food in order to grow. Whatever can be done by ministers and others in getting our membership interested in Bible study and in the reading of religious journals that will acquaint them with the current work of the church today, will be most helpful in promoting their spiritual life.

Finally, the nature and value of worship should be impressed upon the minds of the members, and the whole order of church services should be so arranged as to develop reverence for God, and to cultivate the spirit of devotion. The music of the congregation, both as to the character of the songs and the character of the singing, and the prayers, and the observance of the Lord's Supper, the reading of God's Word, and even the receiving of the offerings of the people, all should be done with a view of promoting the spiritual life of the members.

But when all this is done we must be patient and wait for growth. It is in the spiritual as in the material world—"First the blade, then the corn, and then the full corn in the ear." We must be patient with ourselves and with each other. The

*This is the second part of a paper read by the editor before the St. Louis Christian Ministers' Meeting.

very mistakes which we make may be the rounds by which we ascend nearer to God, for it is on the stepping-stones of our dead selves that we rise to higher things. If we can only be sure that God is dealing with the soul, and the soul is responsive to God's dealings, we may wait for the rest.

Let us never doubt for a moment the divine purpose declared in the Word of God to conform us who believe to the image of Jesus Christ. This He will surely do if we yield ourselves to the leadings of God. "Beloved, now are we children of God, and it is not yet manifest what we shall be. We know that if He shall be manifested we shall be like Him, for we shall see Him as He is. And every one that hath this hope set on him purifieth himself even as He is pure."

THE MODERN PESSIMIST.

For many centuries the Devil declined to write his creed, or to express himself in books; but he has changed his mind of late years, and has commenced freely to paint pictures, write novels, and occasionally to to perpetrate a poem. He lends himself to the popular fiction of the pessimist school, puts himself forward in the form of decadent art, and has presumed to enter the lofty realm of poetry, hitherto devoted to good causes. His next literary effort will be the production of a Bible, or else he will expurgate and translate to suit himself, God's Bible. Satan is the author of pessimism, for no one but he could originate the idea that the life God created and the world he organized were failures. The philosopher who declared that this was the worst of all possible worlds was guilty of blasphemy, for he expressed the opinion that God was a failure and the Devil a success.

A typical pessimist is afflicted with mental strabismus, moral if not physical indigestion and a bad liver, or he is the victim of an incomplete development. He takes an exaggerated view of the worst side of life, unrelieved by the best side. Existence is hope unsatisfied, desire unfulfilled, joy unrealized, pleasures promised that melt like Dead Sea apples on the lips, or mock the vision like the mirage of an Eastern desert; life is pain, disaster and ultimate failure. This is an old view, because sin and Satan are old. An echo of it reaches us from the far distant age of the patriarchs, and it comes through a woman when her son had married against her will. When Esau married against her wishes Rebekah exclaimed: "I am weary of my life, what good shall my life do unto me." "My soul chooseth death rather than life," was the piteous plaint of Job in his troubles. "Let the day perish wherein I was born," said the afflicted patriarch. Further down and in times of higher knowledge, Elijah the prophet cried, "It is enough, now take away my life, for I am not better than my fathers." "I hate life," said the author of the book of Ecclesiastes, in one of his pessimistic moods. "Vanity of vanities, all is vanity, saith the preacher, and there is no profit under the sun," said he in the same frame of mind. There has been plenty of this feeling in literature and in history. "The happiest hour of life is the departure from it," said Calanus the Hindu companion of Alexander the Great. "Life is a continuation of misery," said Acosta the Portuguese. "I doubt," wrote Seneca, "if any one would accept life if he knew what it would cost him." "The blessings of life," wrote Pliny the elder, "are not equal to its ills, even though the number of the two were equal, nor can any pleasure compensate for the least pain." The great Oriental religions, professed by the majority of mankind, regard life as an intolerable burden of misery and sorrow, to be escaped from in the extinction of Nirvana, to be ended up after a long and weary succession of transmigrations through animals and degraded beings, in the absorption of the individual soul back into the essence of the universe. Hence the saying of Calanus the Hindu, "The happiest hour in life is the departure from it."

It is one of the strange things in these modern days of our Western life, in this New World of bouyant hope and abounding vigor, that philosophers, scientists, novelists and even poets are trying to bring back to mankind this old pagan night of Eastern pessimism, in their dolorous croakings on the dismal question: "Is life worth living?" The nasty French novel of the period, elaborately expounds this dank and dirty philosophy of animalism and negation. Grant Allen's New Hedonism, which is a revamp of the old pagan notion that pleasure is the chief end of life, is a quadrilateral, the four corners of which are Atheism, Pessimism, Free Love, and the denial of a Future Life. It is not singular that a philosophy which begins by making life all pleasure should end by making it all pain. After the fitful round of license and youthful indulgence, the pessimistic poet comes in thusly on the home stretch:

"What is the existence of man's life
But open war or slumberous strife?
Where sickness to his sense presents
The combat of the elements;
And never feels a perfect peace
Till Death's cold hand signs his release?

"It is a very weary interlude
Which doth short joys, long woes include.
The world, the stage; the prologue, tears;
The acts, vain hopes and varied fears;
The scene shuts up with loss of breath,
And leaves no epilogue but death."

Pessimism as a mood may be pardonably engendered by insupportable temporary conditions, as in the case of Job and Elijah; as a disease it has its roots in atheism; its essence is disbelief in God and in man. It sees the disorder in the world, and doubts the existence of an eternal order; it sees the lawlessness in society, and questions the reign of law; it sees confusion among men, and doubts the possibility of the higher unity. Its chief trouble is its superficiality for lack of insight. It sees evil, but has no eye for remedies. It can diagnose the world's disease, but can not see the remedial elements that the Maker of the world has provided for its cure. A theory of life based upon a perception of injustice and unrighteousness and prevailing wrong, that fails to recognize the means and possibilities of redemption, is deficient at the most essential point of a sound philosophy of human existence. A view so destitute of insight and sympathy, is destined to be smitten with permanent sterility. Some one has truly remarked that if Christ had been a pessimist, the mighty power which had flown from him to the ends of the earth would not have touched his nea follower. There is neither heart nor h nor help in pessimism, it is at best an its purest form a blind protest aga wrong.

The belief in a divine order being wor out in an imperfect world, in a div salvation being wrought out in a sin race, is the optimism of the Word of G The true optimist is often at one with pessimist in affirming that conditions, the time, could scarcely be worse; but stantly parts company with the pessimist adding that there is a power in the wo that can make them better, and a capac in man to co-operate with that pow The Christian view does not affirm t things are right and that man has no mo disease, but it does say that there i power in the universe, not ourselves, t makes for righteousness, that in view o reigning God and a supreme moral or and the capacity for recuperation in m wrong will be righted, sin destroyed a the world made a better place to live in.

J. J. H

Hour of Prayer.

THE VISIT OF THE WISE MEN.

(Midweek Prayer-meeting Topic, Dec. 21st, 18

And they came into the house and saw young child with Mary, his mother; and th fell down and worshiped him; and openi their treasures they offered unto him gif gold and frankincense and myrrh.—*Matt.* 2:

One of the pictures indelibly engrav upon the heart of humanity, never to effaced by the hand of Time, is that of t wonderful Babe of Bethlehem lying in manger, in the arms of his wonderi mother Mary, and visited by adoring she herds, and later by sages from the Ea who come to worship, and who lay ri gifts at his feet. It is a picture that strik the imagination, that touches the hea and quickens our whole religious natur It is a holy place and a holy time. Poe artists and historians have each sought interpret to us the wonderful significan of this scene. They see in it the meetin place of heaven and earth, the union humanity and divinity, God manifest the flesh. In this lesson we are special concerned with the visit of the wise m from the East.

Who were these wise men who ca from the East? We do not know. T important fact is that they were wise me who were studying the times in which th lived, and who were looking for the com ing of a King who, in wisdom and power, was to minister to the needs of t human race as no other king had ev ministered. There were many men, pe haps the great majority of men at th time, who were looking for no king prophet. They were satisfied with t world as it was, and were absorbed their little pursuits and ambitions a petty plans. But both in and out of Jud there were a few choice spirits waiting f the dawning of a new era for the rac This expectation was born both of the pr phetic word, which promised deliveranc and of the manifest need which they sa for the coming of a great Deliverer.

These men who came from the East we not of the Jewish race, but they had doub less heard, perhaps from captive Jews, it may be through portions of the sacre writings with which they had come in contact, that the world's great Prophet and Redeemer would be born among the Jews in Judea, and they came in search of this Child of promise and of hope. The incident shows that the expectation and the desire for a coming King was not limited to the Jews. There was a feeling that this coming King had a mission, not for the Jews alone, but for the entire race. These men who dwelt afar, gazing into the deep blue heavens by night in order to read in its sublime scroll the Will of the Supreme Mind, saw what they regarded as the star that was to guide them to the new-born King. Following its leading they were brought to where the young child lay.

The incident of Herod's jealousy, stirred up by their inquiry as to where the promised King of the Jews was to be born, and his scheme to murder this Child of promise, is in most striking contrast with the truly worshipful visit of the wise men from the East. Herod was looking after his crown and throne and power and position—his own selfish ends; but these wise men were looking for a new era, a brighter hope for humanity, and desired to worship at the shrine of Him who had come to introduce such an era. How different are the motives which actuate men in this life, and how truly men are measured by the motives which animate them!

Is it not true that from that first visit of the wise men from the East to the present time the truly wise in all nations and races have sought to find Christ, and having found Him, have offered Him worship? Why should the wise seek Christ and offer worship at His shrine? Because He is humanity's only hope. It is He that brought life and immortality to light. It was He that unbarred the tomb and made it the gateway of the life beyond. It was He that showed us the Father, illustrating in His own life and teaching the character of God. It was He that revealed to us the Father's will, and demonstrated in His own life the wonderful possibilities of humanity, indwelt by the Divine. It was His hand that turned back the dolorous tide of the ages, and brought in the new and brighter era of joy and hope and progress. It is He through whose atoning death and gracious intercession we receive forgiveness of sins and reconciliation with God. It is He who is binding men of all nations, races and languages of earth into a glorious brotherhood.

No wonder, then, the wise men of the East brought their gifts of gold and frankincense and myrrh, and what was even more precious—the tribute of adoring hearts. The marvel is that so many even yet, after nineteen centuries of glorious Christian history, neglect to seek Christ and bring to Him fragrant offerings of love and devotion. May this Christmastide, with its holy influences and hallowed memories, win many hearts, not simply to the Christ-child, but to the throned and sceptered Christ, who is to-day King of kings and Lord of lords.

PRAYER.

O, Thou who wert once the lowly Child in Bethlehem's manger, but who art now exalted above all thrones and principalities and powers, we come to Thee today with our incense of praise and thanksgiving and our heart's sincerest love and adoration. We thank Thee for Thy visit to this earth, for Thy lowly birth, for Thy poverty and suffering and tender ministries in our behalf, and Thy cruel death on the cross in order that we might have everlasting life. Accept the homage of our hearts to-day, dear Lord, and draw us into closer and sweeter fellowship with Thee in all Thy ministries of grace and truth to our sinning and sorrowing race. For Thy Name's sake. Amen!

Editor's Easy Chair.

Henry Watterson has been delivering an address to the Patria Club in New York City, in which he said some wise things; but about the wisest utterance in his speech was that concerning the danger of this country from the love of money. Mr. Watterson is not alarmed about expansion, but he says: "That which seems to me to bode real evil to the state, which is not affected by these new possessions, is that which comes from within, and passeth in show. The great menace is in one sentence—money. Not hard money or soft money, but simply money in its relation to the moral nature of the people. . . . . . It is the one thing universally used and abused, universally coveted and reviled." Further on he added: "Find out a nation's sin and you will find out its danger. The danger which hangs over us is the relation of money to the moral nature of the people. The advice: 'Put money in thy purse,' has become too much the gospel of the country. The trial of the trade-mark is over us all. Again, the statesmanship which is to lead us up the steep inclines to glory must ally traditions and progress and get closer and closer to the moral nature of the country."

Mr. Watterson shows himself something of a prophet in these utterances. The man who sees no danger to the country and no danger to the moral welfare of the people in the love of money, in the unscrupulous methods resorted to for getting it, as well as in the too general failure to use it wisely, even when honestly gained, cannot be credited with a very clear moral vision. The love of money is, as the apostle tells us, "a root of every evil." It is a root if not *the* root of the liquor traffic. It is a root of the social evil. It is a root of the gambling mania, of strikes, lockouts, industrial strifes, monopolies, political corruption, and whatever other evil afflicts the church and the state. It is not money in itself that is evil, but it is the *love* of it, for its own sake, and the bad use of it, that is doing all the mischief. Well it would be for the country if it would heed the voice of this political prophet as to the perils of wealth. The trade-mark is not the highest mark of national greatness, nor of social, intellectual or moral progress.

The Bible is full of warnings against covetousness, and its prophets and apostles admonish us faithfully on the subject. Christ's example and teaching leave no doubt as to what attitude He would have His followers assume toward money and money-getting. The principle of stewardship is clearly set forth by Him, according to which we are not to claim anything as our own. We are simply holding property in trust for God. We are required to use it for the benefit of mankind, and are taught that every man will be called into judgment and will be required to give an account of his stewardship. The imperative duty of every man of means, above the actual necessities of himself and family, is to begin at once to administer on his estate, and to use it for the furtherance of the interests of the kingdom of God. We have no right to die rich and take the chances of having the honest gainings of a lifetime squandered for unworthy objects. If God has blessed us in our business pursuits, He is thereby submitting us to one of the severest tests to which character can be put—the test of prosperity. He means to see whether we will be faithful in the "few things" He has committed to us here, so as to test our fitness for larger responsibilities in the life to come. Alas, how many have been "weighed in the balances and found wanting!"

Recurring again to Mr. Watterson's speech, he said concerning the changes brought about by the war: "Our new responsibilities will steady rather than endanger us." This is a hopeful view to take of the situation, and one that is not without support both in reason and experience. Many a young man has been made steady by having responsibilities laid upon him. The making of character lies not in shunning but in bearing responsibilities. We do not see why it should not be as true of nations as individuals, for a nation is but an aggregation of individuals. Dull, indeed, must be the moral susceptibilities of the American people if they do not understand that these larger responsibilities which have come upon us in consequence of the recent war, demand on our part a deeper sense of moral obligation and a greater effort at self-purification, in order that we may meet these new responsibilities that are upon us. We believe that this must necessarily be the effect, if the church of God is awake to its duty and its opportunity. It is a time in our national history when every moral force should be exerted in behalf of righteousness, of strict honesty and of political purity. Not only should preachers and teachers in the Sunday-school do this, but the great army of teachers in the public schools, colleges and universities, and editors of secular as well as religious journals, and statesmen all should unite their efforts in behalf of that righteousness which "exalteth a nation," and to the putting away of that sin which is a "reproach to any people."

Questions and Answers.

1. Does the Bible teach that when a sinner is converted to Christ and surrenders to him, it is impossible for such an one to ever fall?

2. Does the first ten verses of the 11th chapter of Isaiah refer to the second coming of Christ or to his first coming?

3. Tell us how Jesus was "three days and three nights in the heart of the earth," if buried Friday, and what does the "heart of the earth" signify? W. H. Barclay.

Crookston, Minn.

1. It does not. On the contrary, the Bible exactly harmonizes with human experience and observation on that subject. It does teach, however, that so long as one clings to Christ it is impossible for him to fall away. It is useless to refer to any passage in proof of this position, as we would cite the whole New Testament. Every command and every warning and every exhortation to steadfastness pre-

supposes the possibility of falling away from our first love.

2. We should say that the Scripture referred to has reference to the advent of Christ and the triumphs of his kingdom, including his whole reign and culminating in his complete triumph, or what is called the second coming.

3. The Jewish custom of referring to a part of the day as the whole of the day, or to any event occurring on the third day as having occurred after three days and nights, is sufficient to account for this scriptural phrase. "The heart of the earth" signifies simply the burial of his body in the earth, with perhaps a reference to the descent of Jesus in Hades, supposed by the ancients to be somewhere in the depths of the earth.

How are deacons and elders of the Christian Church made such in the state of Missouri? Do the churches keep up the practice of ordination as taught by Alexander Campbell? *R. E. Casey.*
Alamo, Tenn.

We fear that very many congregations in the state have no formal ordination of these officers. They are simply elected to these positions, and in many cases the election occurs annually. The practice of annual elections has had the effect of doing away in many places with the custom of ordination. The annual election has been resorted to to rid the congregation of undesirable material in its board of officers in the least objectionable way. When a church, however, has the men selected whom it feels sure are suitable for the positions to which they have been selected, it would be better for them to formally ordain them for these positions to hold office as long as it is mutually agreeable.

---

1. What is the prevalent view among the Disciples of Christ concerning the personality and the indwelling of the Holy Spirit?
2. What part or agency has the Holy Spirit in conversion? *J. C. Sargeant.*
Kimball, O.

1. The Disciples of Christ believe in and teach the personality of the Holy Spirit, and that it dwells in the heart of the Christian. The degree in which the Spirit guides and controls the life of the Christian depends upon the willingness of the believer to be so guided and his conformity to the will of Christ.

2. The Holy Spirit is the agent in every conversion under the gospel. "And when He is come He will convict the world in respect of sin, and of righteousness, and of judgment." The Holy Spirit operates through the gospel on the printed page, and especially as preached by men full of the Holy Spirit, and through the lives of Christian people, and perhaps in other ways that we know not of.

1. In what sense did Jesus ascend into heaven?
2. If as an embodied personality, and he shall so come again, how shall those on the side of this globe opposite to his appearing, behold him?
3. If heaven is not a substantial place, and Christ no longer an embodied personality, how are we to understand the Scriptures that so speak of him and the place of his abode? *Trouble Seeker.*

1. He assumed the glorified form and entered into that glory of which He had divested Himself in order to dwell in the flesh and manifest God to men.

2. This question presupposes that there will be an appearing of Jesus on one side of the globe different from that on another side. We know Christ is coming now all around the globe wherever His gospel is preached. We take it for granted that our glorified Lord will not be troubled by the rotundity of the earth in manifesting Himself to all who dwell upon the globe.

3. Heaven is, no doubt, a "substantial place," but it does not follow from that that every place where God rules supreme and where Christ's character is reproduced in the lives of the people may not become a part of heaven. May it not be that the "new Jerusalem," the Holy City, which John saw descending from God out of heaven, is to be built here on earth, and this is to be a part of the dwelling-place of God and filled with righteousness and glory? We may not know *where* we shall be any more than *what* we *shall* be, but it is enough to know that we shall be with Christ and be like Him.

THE NOONDAY OF THE SOUL.

L. H. STINE.

II. THE ÆSTHETICS OF LIGHT.

Light is beautiful wherever it is seen. Whether seen in the face of the refulgent moon, in the sparkle of the quenchless stars, in the unrivaled play of colors in the film of the soap-bubble, in the changing purple of the mother-of-pearl, in the gorgeous rays of the plumes of birds, in the gay tints of the evening cloud or in the spangles of the dewdrop trembling on the rosebud, light is always a "thing of beauty." Indeed, it is the "first of painters." Its pictures adorn with numerous "emblems of instructive duty," the walls of Nature's Temple. The flowers, that never come and go without a promise, form a beautiful picture of the "Children of Summer"—the favorites of heaven. They are beautiful because they are the guileless children of light. At this writing the trees are ladened with pendent cones of ice, and the dauntless beams of the declining sun are firing every twig, transforming the chaste crystals into gems of beauty, radiant as are the diamond and the ruby. Sporting with their precious jewels, they are richer far than blossoming trees. One can never know the immortal beauty an icicle conceals in its leaden-like core until a ray of sunlight smites it with a scourge of fire. The rainbow, bright pledge of peace, is a matchless work of art. A summer morning, the fairest sight in the realm of nature, "furrowing all the orient into gold," is a scene of thrilling beauty and is made so by the salute of the golden sun. Shelley sings of the beauty of night, through whose cold lustre rolls the cloudless moon, and it is Byron who, looking upon the snow-shining mountains when the stars are forth and the queen of night spreads her sacred mantle over the solemn scene, is enraptured with the "starry shade of dim and solitary loveliness," a vision beautiful enough for angels to behold, and there he learns the language of another world." Proud day, born out of eternity, calm and bright, like a "dove of heaven" bearing glad tidings from the last, fit emblem of the noonday of the soul and the exquisite prototype of "God's et nal day," is beautiful; because it is bles by the grace of sunshine.

Light is not only the painter that ma the world beautiful; it is also the undy artist that bestows its choicest gift beauty on the soul. Behold sweet char the bond of perfectness, the fine "virtu the heart" that renders "blessings curses;" the lowly man, "nameless worthy deeds," whose robe is "humility, mother of meekness" (Gregory of Nys and whose life grows out of the "ashe self-love and on the grave of pri (Rambach); the soft purple hue of the l ly violet "hid among its leaves and kn only by its fragrance;" the patient bearing with a calm and serene spirit lot assigned him, nor murmurs at the laid upon him; the benevolent man w soul feels a pleasure in voluntarily risl something to serve an honest man that gained one's heart; the sympathetic that lives not in himself alone, but fe himself related to another and is capa of suffering on account of the sufferings an enemy" (Cousin), and the merci man whose mercy, "nobility's true badg seasoning with lenity his spirit of justi "droppeth as the gentle rain from heave blessing alike "him that gives and l that takes." Here is the image of a sa at whose feet the pious heart reverer bows. He believed in the light and i he humbly walked, and with true alche power light of life transmuted the b materials of his nature into the pure si and gold of a radiant moral beauty.

It was light, the master painter, t working according to ancient desig produced the beautiful lives of There and of Francis of Assisi. The life of Joh the disciple "whom Jesus loved," at t time of the composition of the Four Gospel was woven of the tissues of t "Light of the World." It was the exce lent beauty of the "true light" that ma Madame Guyon an object of reverence a of admiration. It was the light of t coming glory that translated the life Paul out of its environment of prejudi and intolerance into the spiritual sove eignty of Christ's love and fashioned after the likeness of the Son of Man. T lives of John and Paul are masterpieces spiritual works of art. Their beau charms one's senses. One pauses to lo upon their brows inspired with lofty vie and to behold their upraised hands givi to God each flying moment, and sees their forms of surpassing beauty the ima of their divine Original.

"In order to arrive at this perfe beauty," says Plato, "it is necessary commence with the beauties of this low world, and the eyes being fixed upon t supreme beauty, to elevate ourselves u ceasingly toward it by passing, thus speak, through all the degrees of t scale, from a single beautiful body to tw from two to all others, from beauti bodies to beautiful sentiments, from bea tiful sentiments to beautiful though until from thought to thought we arrive the highest thought." One must beg with the beauties of the external world arrive at the beautiful of the soul. L one ask the morning star what report gives and one will discover in it a herald the gracious dispensation and the dawni of the day of unspeakable glory in hea

ror the glory of the Lord, are ed into the same image from glory, even as by the Lord the One is transformed from beautiter to beautiful character by be- a the perfect life of Jesus the character of the Lord. Plato in ophy of the beautiful, and Paul in ne of spiritual optics agree in ry of attaining the "beauty of

ith his harp tuned to the higher s, sings of "the beauty of the d Isaiah, borne on the wing of a vigorous hope, grows rapturous prospect of beholding the "King uty." God is the ideal of beauty. *par excellence*, the beautiful—for sfies more our faculties, our reaimagination, our heart! "He ofeason the highest idea, beyond ere is nothing more to seek, to on the most ravishing contem- the heart a sovereign object of ousin). The beauty of the Lord oubtless in the "combination of us attributes in one harmonious When seen in succession, the the rainbow are beautiful; but a "special beauty that, arising imple tint, is the result of their ge," and consists in their blended It is this harmonious blending tes that gives to the king his enbeauty. "The most probable f the beautiful," to quote again sin, "is that which composes it ntrary and equally necessary eleity and variety. Behold a beauer. Without doubt unity, order, n, symmetry even, are in it; for, hese qualities, reason would be om it, and all things are made rvelous reason. But, at the same t a diversity! How many shades or, what richness in the least de-

of the variety of the graces of [illegible]

wisdom and knowledge hidden." Jesus is the all-gifted one. Heaven is powerless to add another grace to his perfection, and the world finds all its best things represented in his comprehensive life.

Think, too, how perfect were the virtues of Jesus. His love was not mixed with the dross of remorseless hate. His faith was not stained with a single shadow of doubt. His purpose was transparent with conscious sincerity. His benevolence was purely disinterested as his humanity was without hypocrisy. Instead of being framed around a self-centred aim, his life was built around the needs of the human race. Every virtue was perfect in itself. It was free from defect.

Think, again, of the completeness of the life of Jesus. not a virtue was lacking, nor was there an abnormal development of a few virtues at the expense of all the others. The law of proportion was in full force in the building of the character of Jesus, and because it was a harmonious life it was a beautiful one.

Jesus is the only heroic person known in history of whom it can be said he was perfect and complete. "Noah was a righteous man and perfect in his generation," yet the indelible stain of a drunken debauch defiled his blameless life. Abraham was the incarnation of an illustrious faith, yet his surprising distrust of God showed itself in deliberate and premeditated equivocation and fraud. Moses was proverbial for his meekness, yet he was hasty and impassionate. David, the king, was a man after God's own heart, yet he was adequte to arts and strategems for cruelty and crime. Solomon, though he excelled all the other kings of the earth in moral wisdom, was a man of painful and fatal errors and became an old and foolish king. John, "the apostle of love," was the fervid disciple, yet his spirit was exclusive and he sought to accomplish the triumph of the kingdom of the Son of Man by a resort to cruel power. Peter, the impulsive disciple, was impetuous in his affections, yet he was

THE SPIRITUAL BENEFITS OF THE LORD'S SUPPER.

T. H. BLENUS.

The Author of our being has so constituted us as to feel certain impressions of mind at the sight of certain objects. The slightest circumstance recalls a departed friend, the smallest relic acquires a value. Around us the flowers of the field impress us with their beauty, and the wonderful magnificence of the stupendous works of God fill us with awe and admiration. Applying the same principle of our being to religion, our thoughts cannot be fixed upon evidences of infinite goodness and everlasting love without feelings of emotion. When we engage in the hallowed exercises of spiritual devotion we counterwork the power and influence of earthly objects, and retiring from the world and its temptations we shut out from the heart every intruding guest that would distract attention or disturb us in approaching our Heavenly Father. Like Moses of old we are made aware that we stand upon holy ground, and consequently put away from us all worldly affections and human desires. No act of divine worship in the Christian religion is more solemn or more sacred than that of the Lord's Supper. The most serious and solemn transactions in the plan of redemption are suggested by this institution. The occasion demands on the part of the participant a suitable frame of mind. It is no place for the touch of a profane hand. In this observance the Christian commemorates that scene in which the earth trembled and the sun veiled its face, as the Son of God became the world's Redeemer. It conveys to every faithful follower of Christ the grace of the New Covenant in view of which he is called upon to banish from heart and mind all worldly passions, unholy desires, feelings of anger and wrath, and with profound reverence and the deepest gratitude to sit at the table in a perpetual covenant never to be annulled. As the bow, bent by the Almighty hand, appears in the cloud as a memorial that the world has been saved from a deluge, and a signal that it shall be preserved from any other, so this commemorative institution in the church is a token of a divine covenant of eternal salvation. It is to be feared, and very much to be regretted, that with many persons this solemn and important privilege is looked upon more as a mere matter of form than an act of true, binding, faithful and consecrated devotion. To all such this bread is not the bread of life, nor this cup the cup of blessing. When Jesus wept at the grave of Lazarus the Jews exclaimed, when they saw the manifestation of his sorrow, "Behold how he laved him!" When the child of God comes to the Lord's Table he comes in contact with those emblems which represent his Lord, not shedding tears of sympathy alone, but shedding his blood for the lost and ruined of earth. We have much greater reason here to exclaim, "Behold how the Son of God loved humanity!" It is here that we remember the "Man of Sorrows." It is here we remember the cruel taunts and scourges of his persecutors. It is here we think of the patience and meekness of the Lamb of God. Here we thankfully acknowledge the work of the Savior in canceling the handwriting against us, fixing it to his cross and there leaving it as a trophy of his wonderful and complete victory. We see him sheathing the sword of the cherubim which turning every way guarded the tree of life, and we behold him opening to us the gates of heaven and landing us through the portals to eternal joy. Through this institution we enjoy the promise of a city which cannot be shaken, a kingdom which cannot be moved, and a crown that fadeth not away.

Jacksonville, Fla.

The Religious World.

Brotherhood of Andrew and Philip.

Three conventions were held in November. We note a few important matters developed by the conventions.

First. The desire for federation among the churches in undertaking this work for the men of the country. It was felt that no one denomination by itself is able fully to handle this problem. The hope for the future lies in united effort. The matter of federation was more specially mentioned because many independent Brotherhoods have been started largely copying the original society. It was felt to be a matter for congratulation that the success of the Brotherhood had put so many rival organizations into the field. Strong resolutions were adopted by these conventions urging all men's societies to come under the Brotherhood.

Second. The moral effect of the recent war and territorial expansion was noted. Again and again it was evident that the delegates looked upon the present period of national history as an ethical crisis of the highest moment. The hope was expressed that perhaps the Brotherhood could assemble the leading men of the 19 denominations in which it is found in a sort of national congress to discuss the situation.

Third. The internal matters of the chapters received due attention and encouraging reports were heard from every side. The two rules of prayer and service were again acknowledged as the basis for united action. Chapters were urged to pray, not only for unconverted men, but especially for their own pastors that men might be reached through the power of the preacher. The discussion of the Rule of Service was more valuable than ever. It was clearly shown that the great problem of all now to be solved by the churches of our country is, What shall the men of our churches do and how shall they do it? It was again pointed out that if the men who so largely control the wealth of the churches could be set on fire with the zeal for God's house many other problems would at once be solved. The rule of service in its broadest interpretation is respectfully submitted to pastors as quite likely to develop the desired zeal.

Fourth. Pastors of these denominations and of the churches generally were requested to inform themselves upon Brotherhood work by writing to the Rev. C. E. Wyckoff, Irvington, N. J., who mails literature upon application.

The National Christian Association is the title of an incorporated association which was organized in the city of Pittsburg, Pa., in 1868, by represe
seventeen orthodox denomination
that faith in Christ is the sole
acceptance with God; and that
ceived by faith is the sole power
eration. It believes, moreover, t
is the god of this world and the
false religions; and that the lod
denies Christ and worships Satan
ject is to keep the membersh
churches out of secret organiza
these among other reasons: 1.
they are declared to be organized
so necessarily broad as to exclud
of Christ as the world's only Red
Because they substitute in thei
and in the minds of many of th
bership, the secret society of the
church; 3. Because of the relati
obligation of these secret order
oaths and decisions of courts. The
tion has its principal place of bu
221 West Madison St., Chicago.

The recent meeting of the Bap
gress in Buffalo was not marked b
terest which has characterized s
vious sessions, and notably those
Chicago a year ago. The topics di
while important in and of themsel
involving in some instances the c
ation of fundamental truths, were
nature to awaken popular enthus
arouse emphatically expressed di
of opinion. While the views s
might be regarded in some quarters
vanced," there was such general ur
as to make the majority of session
tame. The Baptists of Buffalo f
reason did not feel attracted to t
gress in any great numbers, and
was a small attendance from outs
city the congregations were in
contrast with those of Chicago. We
sympathize with the opinion that t
gress has performed its mission an
well be allowed to rest under its mo
dedicated to past services. So long
are different views of doctrine and
held in the denomination by men
spiritual, scholarly and conscientiou
is reason for the maintenance of a p
for the discussion of these views,
elimination of discord and the se
the truth. The small attendance is
will be argued doubtless by some
due to the approaching collapse
Baptist Congress idea, but to a fa
give proper publicity to its meet
too rigid cutting out of popular s
and the failure to provide subject
which there may be the expression
scientiously divergent views.—*Th
dard.*

The missionary committee of the
ist Episcopal Church has just held
nual meeting in Providence, R. I.
port of the treasurer showed that
ceipts for both Home and Foreign M
from all sources, had been $1,181,789
the disbursements $1,196,802.61. The
priations to Foreign Missions had a
to $626,201.90; to Home Missions, in
"domestic," $447,615.21. The incide
penses, including $21,917,85 paid as i
amounted to $59,377.62; office ex
$10,968.94, Publication Fund, $22,
salaries of missionary bishops and
ries, $30,243.40. There had been an i
in the contributions amounting to $

66. The indebtedness at the close of the year, November 1, was $201,156.06. But this has since been reduced to less than $20,000, and it is expected that this balance will be provided for before December 1. The contributions of some of the states are as follows: Ohio, $97,765.74; Indiana, $51,-498.85: West Virginia, $9,320.56.—*Journal and Messenger.*

Special Help for the Sunday-school Teacher.

Among many other problems the Council of Seventy, working through the American Institute of Sacred Literature, is considering that of the needs of the Sunday-school teacher. Within a year several plans will be announced, all of which depend upon the willingness of the teacher to become himself a pupil under competent instruction. One of these plans is now ready, namely, a Correspondence Course in the Gospel of John. (The International Lessons are upon this Gospel from January to July, 1899.) The work will be conducted by a skilled instructor by means of weekly or fortnightly recitations, returned with corrections to the student. Only the most necessary books are required for the study—a Bible, a small commentary and a series of inductive studies. To those teachers who desire it the instructor will also give some special hints concerning methods of class work. The fee for tuition is as small as consistent with the work of an individual instructor. Every teacher and every Sunday-school superintendent should inform himself fully concerning this plan. Such information may be secured by addressing the American Institute of Sacred Literature, Hyde Park, Chicago, Ill.

Current Religious Thought

In discussing the "Task of the Modern Jew," in the Menorah, the Rev. Samuel Schulman says:

The task of the modern Jew, therefore, is to identify himself with the forces which make for better and a purer humanity. To whom, if not to him, ought any appeal for more social justice come with force? For his religion demands it of him, and he, least of all, if consistent, ought to shrink from the examination and conscientious study of every criticism that is made upon the absence of righteousness, upon the presence of undeserved suffering, upon the crying need in all civilization. Yes, the practicability of every religion will, in the future, be tested by the amount of encouragement it gives to its professors to solve the all-overshadowing problem of how to bring more justice and love between the classes of the human society, and judging from the past, judging from the feeling of responsibility that has been inculcated in every Jew for his brother, judging from the magnificent institutions of benevolence which Judaism has already called into life, the modern Jew is well prepared and educated to enter this field of work, and in co-operation with the noble men and women who are in the vanguard of all the churches, to vindicate the immortal truth and practical righteousness of his religion.

Prof. Clyde W. Votaw, Ph.D., of the University of Chicago, has an interesting article in a recent number of the independent from which we reprint the following introductory paragragphs:

The passing of religious denominationalism is no longer a matter of faith only. If the division of Christians into many sects, large and small, was the inevitable consequence of the Protestant Reformation, it has at any rate become clear that such division cannot continue. For all branches of Christianity are in essence Christian. The lines of seperation are, therefore, drawn upon things which are not essential. And it is the obvious duty of those who profess the Christian religion to subordinate unessentials in which they may not agree, in order that they may unite in the essentials upon which they do agree, for the building up of God's kingdom among men. We have come slowly and stubbornly to the realization that this is our duty, but now we know it. And the condemnation and extinction of denominationalism is sure.

Christendom is divided upon three main lines; government, worship and theology.

The several types of church government are the counterparts of the several types of political government which history has produced. From rigid monarchial government to thoroughgoing democracy is a long journey, but at each of the many stages along the way certain braches of the Christian brotherhood have taken up their stations; so that the Christian army is deployed in companies from one end of the route to the other.

Now the political ideal of mankind is government of, by and for the people—pure democracy, universal suffrage. Some nations are in process of realizing this ideal. Its counterpart in religious government is independence and self-management of the individual churches by the suffrage of the individual members. As political government becomes ever more democratic the world over, so ecclesiastical government passes increasingly into the hands of the church members as a whole. The future unquestionably has in store for us the ultimate triumph of true democracy, both in politics and religion. This means the extinction of every kind of church government which is not of, by and for the individual Christians. This will not bring exact uniformity, for popular government is capable of variation in method. But denominationalism, so far as it rests on different systems of government, will be done away with. The twentieth century will see wonderful advancement toward the popular control in state and church.

The following from Rev. John W. Chadwick in the Treasury for December is worthy of the most considerate attention, bearing as it does upon the present alarming manifestation of indifference toward public worship in the churches:

I do not believe that a great many people of intelligence and culture who are withdrawing in these times from the public ministration of religion are taking a line that will be altogether satisfactory to them as time goes on. Their own religious thought and feeling are enriched by many beautiful survivals of their early training—the faiths and hopes their parents cherished tenderly. It will be different with their children, who have been subjected to no such training, who have had no such inheritance. For them the earth and sky will still be beautiful, and daily work will have its noble stress, and love will shed its natural splendor on their hearts. But there will be no uplifts for them of heart and will to the supernal glory which is beyond the farthest stars, no thrill to the great names which heretofore have overtopped all others in the march of time. Or, what is likelier, discovering in themselves some void which is not filled by business or literature or art or social gayety or household cheer, they will illustrate that law of rhythm, of reaction, of which Mr. Spencer makes so much, and react from their negation in religion to something very positive—say, the Roman Catholic Church. The religious indifference of cultivated people is a kind of spiritual breeding tank to furnish converts to that or some other equally irrational system of belief. Their children are as soft as putty in the hands of the first man who comes along with any strenuous conviction or colossal fad.

Ministerial Relief Fund Needed.

EDITOR CHRISTIAN-EVANGELIST:—I have seen several notices of Dr. J. B. Crane's death. It pains me to hear of his death, for in 1888 my first year's ministry after having finished my course of study in the Kentucky Bible College, I was associated with him at Pierce City, Mo., and he was so much help to me. He gave me advice that I expect to heed through life, and I have books in my library purchased at his suggestion. I looked upon him as a man of rare learning and ability. He was a physician, preacher, author and poet in one. He graduated with Garfield and taught him and his wife French. Now what I want to say is this, that notwithstanding ths above, he told me that as a preacher he was a *failure*. That he could preach to the supreme satisfaction of all who heard him, but he could not get any *place* to preach. And when I knew him he was in abject poverty, *sleeping on the floor* and his great library, such as a close student would and could select in a long lifetime, had just been sold under the hammer for almost nothing, and it was only by his son and son-in-law working at the limekiln that they were enabled to buy bedsteads and *get up off the floor*. When such a thing is possible, there is something wrong. Now it is too late to assist Dr. Crane any, but we have many *living* elderly ministers who are English, Latin, Greek, Hebrew, German, French and especially Bible scholars, and good preachers who are upon the shelf because it may be that their hair is prematurely gray. We have what we call a ministerial relief fund and it is difficult to raise money for the same. Many of our elderly ministers are failing financially and if nothing is done will finally be subjects of the relief fund, are now abundantly able physically, mentally and spiritually to sustain themselves and possibly as long as they live, or lay up sufficient while they are able to keep them when they fail, provided they can *get places to preach*. The relief fund is indispensably necessary when they are not able to help themselves, but so long as they are able and want to help themselves, let's give them an opportunity. Their preaching may not be so full of zeal to excite people into the church who may be just as easily excited out, but their work, what they do, is broad, deep and permanent. Let's help the *living*, not wait till they are dead and laud them.

L. SWINDLE.

Glendora, Cal., Dec. 1, 1898.

The Cause at Lawrence, Kansas.

I have been in this beautiful university town a few days, assisting Bro. Charles M. Sharpe in a meeting. There have been so far about twenty additions to the church, mostly by confession. Bro. Sharpe is six months into the second term of service with the congregation, having been recalled to the pastorate from Illinois. He is a brilliant preacher, scholarly, chaste and effective. He graduated in June '97 from the university here, receiving his Master's degree, and is most highly commended by all the faculty and known by many of the students, who hear him with delight and profit. He has a large Bible class in Sunday-school, composed, for the most part, of university students, and just now he is taking them through a course of studies in the life of Christ.

I have had the pleasure of leading the chapel exercises at the university on two occasions. Here is a great school with 1,100 pupils enrolled. Here is where we ought to have a large and influential church. The possibilities of influencing a large number of students and indoctrinating them with a pure faith are great. We ought, by all means, to have a Bible Chair in connection with the university. The chancellor and faculty would favor such a movement. There is enough wealth among the Disciples of Christ in Kansas to establish a chair. Who will be the first to move in this matter. The church here numbers about 250 and has a fairly good building free from debt. The brethren are not rich, but are making an heroic effort to support Bro. Sharpe, who is generously laboring for much less than he is worth. It is his desire to make this the work of his life. I am just in from the union Thanksgiving services held in the Presbyterian Church. Bro. Sharpe preached the sermon, which was one of the best I ever heard on a similar occasion. It was unique. He is abundantly able to represent us among these cultured people. Upon him and the church I pray the continud blessings of heaven.

WALTER SCOTT PRIEST.

Lawrence, Kan., Thanksgiving Day.

—Christianity is the only religion that abounds in song. Atheism is songless; Agnosticism has nothing to sing about; the various forms of idolatry are not tuneful; but Judaism said, "Oh, come, let us sing unto the Lord;" and when Christ came the angels greeted his birth with a song, and since then Christian song has gained in fullness and strength of voice with each passing century.—*The Advance.*

Our Budget.

—Beautiful thoughts,

—Beautiful things,

—Beautiful songs,

—Beautiful deeds,

—These Christmas times.

—Remember Ministerial Relief Fund next Sunday.

—Our next issue will be our Christmas number.

—The reports from the field show that many successful protracted meetings are being held.

—The proposition to add at least 100,000 new members to the Church of Christ this year is being generally and heartily endorsed by both pastors and evangelists.

—At present there is every indication of an awakening of the Churches of Christ in the United States on missionary work this year that will make them one of the most active missionary people in the land.

—The program for the week of prayer appears in this paper.

—It is said that "not half a million copies of the Scriptures are yet in the hands of the twelve million of Mexicans." This shows to what extent the Roman Catholic priests are interested in circulating the Bible among their own people.

—The Missionary Voice for December and January rings with the jubilee spirit. Send for it and get a host of facts on Foreign Mission work.

—For a report of the 24th annual national convention of the C. W. B. M. see Missionary Tidings for December with its sixty pages of closely printed items. It is a veritable magazine of missionary information.

—We observe that some papers continue to write "Puerto Rico." Now that we have undertaken to Americanize that island, let all begin to write just plain Porto Rico. It is now an American island, you know.

—The American Home Missionary for November contains the minutes of the 49th annual convention of the American Christian Missionary Society, a copy of which every Disciple will of course have use for during the current year. Address B. L. Smith, Cincinnati, for a copy.

—The Practical Christian, Houston, Texas, is lengthening its cords and strengthening its stakes. The issue for December was a newsy one and the edition a large one.

—Sometime ago we received an unsigned report of a convention held by the Christian Churches of Harrison County, Iowa, at Mondamin, Sept. 16th, which we of course could not publish. We have since been given the name of the writer, but the report is now so far past the things related that it would not have the same interest it would have had when written, if we should publish it. It is but just to say that it is an excellent report of an excellent convention, and we regret that it could not have been published at the time. The addresses given are especially commended for their wisdom and practical value. All enjoyed the convention and went away with enlarged ideas of church work. They were also encouraged with the outlook of the cause in Harrison County for future work and usefulness.

—At a recent meeting of the City Mission Board of this city, having been promised aid from the American Christian Missionary Society, it was decided to employ an evangelist for this city. The question of city evangelization is one of the great questions of the day and one in which our home society is interesting itself as rapidly and extensively as its funds will permit. The churches of this city feel that by the aid of the Home Board an evangelist can be sustained in this city and the time for such a move has certainly come. St. Louis is an immense mission field of itself and the entire time of many evangelists could be constantly used if the means were at hand to support them, but more than one in the field at present will be impossible. The City Mission Board is now on the lookout for a suitable man and as soon as he can be found will be put in commission.

—The recent excellent musical entertainment held in the new Y. M. C. A. building, this city, for the benefit of the Christian Orphans' Home, we have learned netted about $200. This was appreciated as at this season of the year especially the Home is in great need for funds. And now that we have named it perhaps there are many who would like to remember this Home with a generous Christmas gift. If so it will be in order and greatly please the board. You can send the gift at any time to Mrs. O. C. Shedd, 4362 Pine Street.

—T. P. Haley, an excellent likeness of whom appears on our first page, this week, belongs to the "Old Guard" of Missouri. He is one of the strong men around whom our Missouri forces have rallied for more than a generation. And he is yet a young man, as his picture shows in spite of a few gray hairs. It would be difficult to overestimate the indebtedness of the Missouri brotherhood to him. Before the days of railroads, he traveled all over the state, preaching in courthouses, schoolhouses, rude church buildings and groves, baptizing believers and leaving communities with the principles of the Reformation. He is widely known outside of Missouri also, being a prominent actor in our national conventions. He has not written much outside of his work, "The Dawn of the Reformation in Missouri," except articles for our newspapers and quarterlies. He is a speaker rather than a writer, and before an audience he is a "master of assemblies." He lost his first wife, who was a sister of Bro. McGarvey, several years ago, and has since married a cultivated Christian woman, with whom he is living very happily in Kansas City, Mo., where he ministers to one of the weaker churches of that city. He is a member of the State Board of Charities, to which subject he has given much attention. Born in Fayette Co., Ky., in 1832, he is now in the 66th year of his age, but his mind was never more active nor more open to truth. Long may he be spared to the cause he has served so well.

—Our hearts are broken. Our dear little Florence has been suddenly taken from us. She died from scarlet fever Wednesday, Dec. 7, at 5 P. M. She was nearly nine years old, and was a member of the church. We wish the prayers of all that we may become reconciled. G. K. BERRY AND IDA V. BERRY.
Ionia, Mich., Dec. 9, 1898.

The foregoing announcement will call out the sympathy of a large circle of friends. Our brother and sister are indeed called upon to pass through the deep waters, but He who stilled the waves of Galilee will be with them, and his tender voice will still the tumult of their hearts and give them peace. Our sincerest condolence is tendered to our bereaved brother and sister in the shadows of this great affliction. "God is love."

—So far as we can learn from the Roman Catholic journals that reach our table the authorities of that great ecclesiasticism are terribly worried about the prospect of Protestant missionaries in the West Indies and Philippine islands and are trying to prevent them by very singular arguments—chiefly that the inhabitants of these islands are satisfied with their religion and the effort on the part of Protestants will be a futile waste of time and money It strikes us that if the Roman Catholic authorities are so confident of the religious convictions of their people in these islands they would not fear the influence of Protestant missionaries among them; and as to the waste of Protestant time and money—well, why should Roman Catholics grieve over such a thing as this any way?

—The Young People's Society of Christ Endeavor of the church at Tuxedo, Mo., Lut Moore pastor, have launched a home pa called, "The Tuxedo Church Visitor." It a neatly printed, lively edited monthly, cred able, and we trust will be useful to all int ested parties.

—A missionary institute is being held t week under the auspices of the Butler Bi College, in the Christian church at Irvingt Ind., and is conducted by the Christ Woman's Board of Missions and the Board Church Extension of the American Christ Missionary Society. An excellent progr has been arranged, a copy of which is bef us, consisting of addresses by such speak as G. W. Muckley, Mrs. Louise Kelly, M. Forrest, Lois A. White, Mrs. A. Atkinson, Mrs. Mattie Pounds and Mrs. Hel E. Moses. Each address is followed by question period to draw out what informati the speaker may have held in reserve. It is good idea to have these missionary institut in connection with our institutions of learnin

—A note from Bro. E. B. Widger, w recently resigned as pastor of the church Grand Rapids, Mich., says that the paragra which we clipped from the Detroit paper a published in last week's CHRISTIAN-EVANGE IST, concerning his resignation, does him a the church at Grand Rapids an injustice. says: "I have resigned as pastor, but I d this to my official board almost three mont ago, and on Nov. 27th announced same to tl congregation. There is the very best of fee ng between myself and the church. I did n 'score' or 'denounce' my church. There w not one word of discussion. There is but or reason for my resignation. I felt that wit our present location, church building an equipment for church work, we have n done and cannot do the work we ought to do i in a city." We are glad to publish this cor rection from Bro. Widger. We learned a goo while ago that newspaper reports are no always reliable, and so intimated in clipping this item from the Detroit paper. We ar glad to have given the pastor this opportunity of correcting the statements of the secular press.

—According to the Christian College Chronicle for November, Christian College is prospering in a way that should make its friends and the friends of education throughout the state rejoice. And what is being said of this institution at Columdia, Mo., by the secular and religious press of the state we are sure maketh glad the hearts of those upon whom the best interests of this college rest most heavily.

—The following pargraph clipped from the Bible Society Record of recent date is of special interest as a missionary outlook in the Philippine Islands, as against the freqent vehement utterances of Catholic bishops in the United States concerning the futility of Protestant missionary efforts in those islands:

From a private letter written at Manila, September 19, 1898, we are permitted to make the following extracts: "I have had sufficient time to feel the pulse and ascertain the temperature of the people here. *Make known to the missionary world that the harvest is ripe, and the laborers few.* While the people are thoroughly disgusted with a corrupt priesthood, they are not averse to a knowledge of the truth as it is in Christ Jesus. There is a wonderful opening for missionaries willing to teach English. That work can be made self-supporting from the start.

—A general call has been issued for a National Christian Citizenship Convention to be held at the First Presbyterian Church, Washington, D. C., this week. The object of this convention is to consider the nation's obligations to the newly acquired territories and certain moral reform measures of our own country likely to come before the present congressional session. Men eminent in reform movements are on the program to address this convention on the various measures to come up for discussion and their speeches and actions as an expression of the Christian sentiment of the land will not likely fail of good influence upon our present Congress.

—We acknowledge the receipt of a new and beautiful sacred solo, published by J. Fisher & Bro., 7 Bible House, New York, entitled "The New-born King."

Our subscription department is in receipt of a letter from Isaac Kello. If he will give us his post office address we will be better able to answer his communication.

—Mrs. Harmon A. Easton says she always reads Bible-school, Endeavor and Hour of Prayer departments in the CHRISTIAN-EVANGELIST whether she attends each service or not.

—The compilation of the minutes of the various missionary activities of the Churches of Christ in Montana in convention at Bozeman in September last makes a magazine of over 80 pages and contains information of great value to every Disciple in the West and of our entire brotherhood. This neatly printed magazine of information is dedicated to the C. W. B. M. and their auxiliaries through which the work in Montana was instituted and has since been so largely sustained. A copy of these minutes may be had by addressing a card to Edward Scharnikow, Rec. Sec., Deer Lodge, Mont.

—The Catholic News, New York, last week contained an editorial on "Does the Catholic Faith Impair a Nation's Vitality?" in which the editor seeks to dissipate the strength of the historic argument against Romanism based on the decay of the Latin nations. The editor's negative argument is very adroitly expressed but, as we think, misses entirely the real point. The decay of the Latin nations observed by Protestants, *et al.*, is merely an incidental phase of the subject. The real argument of Protestantism against Roman Catholicism, if the Catholic News wishes to put it in that way, is the failure of Roman Catholicism to energize its people with spiritual life and to stimulate them to spiritual activities, and hence their decaying condition.

—On Sunday, Dec. 2nd, the church at Hannibal, Mo., appropriately observed its sixtieth anniversary. The large auditorium was filled to overflowing and the services were deeply interesting and impressive. Upon the rostrum were seated fourteen of the pioneer members of the church, whose ages aggregate 929 years, as follows: Mrs. Weister, 80; Mrs. Norris, 74; Mrs. Fenner, 80; Mrs. Leonard, 66; Mr. and Mrs. Marseilles, 78 and 68 respectively; Mrs. Susan Morgan, 78; Mrs. Sarah Martin, 67; Mrs. Kate Bunch, 64; Mrs. Moore, 75; Mrs. Robinson, 63. The pastor read a brief history of the church which was published in full in the Hannibal Morning Journal, Dec. 3rd. The report is an interesting document, containing many interesting historic dates and reminiscences.

—The Orphan School Record, Fulton, Mo., continues its high standing as a college journal. It is edited on a plane of literature that would do credit to schools of much louder pretentions.

—Do not forget that next Sunday is the appointed day by the General Convention at Chattanooga for an offering for the Ministerial Relief Fund. The Secretary, D. R. Lucas, and others have shown the great need for immediate funds to keep those dependent on this fund from suffering during the present winter. Offerings should be made in all the churches on this day for this ministry and forwarded without delay to Howard Cale, 120 East Market St., Indianapolis, Ind.

—If we mistake not the CHRISTIAN-EVANGELIST is often accused of being on the fence on the critical issues of the day, while some have gone so far as to say it is in sympathy with the higher critics.—*Register-Review.*

We infer from the foregoing that the R. R. has mastered all the questions of higher criticism and is ready to pronounce final judgment concerning them. This is certainly an enviable position to occupy, but the CHRISTIAN-EVANGELIST is compelled to confess that there are several things within the realm of biblical criticism concerning which we are waiting for more light before reaching a final conclusion. None of these, however, affect the inspiration or authority of the Scriptures, or the divinity and Lordship of Jesus Christ. It must be lovely, however, to know everything without waiting for further facts.

—As we go to press a card from F. M. Rains, Cincinnati, Ohio, announces the receipt of $3,500 for Foreign Missions on the Annuity plan. We are glad to see money being thus consecrated to perpetual use in the Lord's work.

—F. G. Tyrrell, of this city, is to address the St. Louis Prohibition Union of Christian Men at the Compton Heights Christian Church, on Tuesday night of this week, in the interest of a stronger sentiment against the saloon, a better enforcement of present prohibition laws and a higher standard of citizenship in our nation. This seems like a sensible thing for prohibitionists to do under present conditions. A rigid enforcement of present prohibitory laws would go a long way toward the reduction of the saloon in the land.

—Lord Kitchener's request of the British people for a half million dollars to found a college at Khartum is not least among the surprising things of this surprising age of the world. Who would have thought of a demand or even of a prospective use for a college in the heart of Africa at this time? Surely are the deserts beginning to blossom and the waste places of the earth to bring forth fruit. A college in Central Africa under the control of Axglo-Saxon people means a new history for that old continent, and if followed up with proper missionary work it means new territory for the Master's kingdom.

PERSONAL MENTION.

F. A. Sheetz is in a meeting at Casey, Ia.

Sherman Hill is the newly elected pastor at Hampton, Ia.

Geo. E. Platt is the successor of J. A. Seaton at Marion, Ia.

B. D. Clark, of Larimore, Ia., has a new house ready for dedication on Dec. 25th.

Mrs. W. B. Craig is in Denver, Col., where she will spend part of the winter.

Geo. A. Jewett, one of the pillars of Des Moines Central Church has once more gone to Europe on a business trip.

W. F. Turner, of La Belle, Mo., has accepted a call from the church at Joplin, Mo., to begin Jan. 1st, 1899.

Prof. Ed Amherst Ott, of Drake University, is on the Pacific Coast delivering lectures. He will be at his post in January.

A. Clark, president of Add-Ran Christian University, has been called to succeed F. N. Calvin in the church at Waco, Texas.

We are informed that R. Watson, Salem, Mo.. will be an applicant for the chaplaincy of the State Senate at the ensuing term.

J. G. M. Luttenberger, who was present at the preachers' meeting, this city, last Monday, reports the church at Dorchester in a prosperous state.

Henry F. Davis was present at the preachers' meeting in this office on last Monday. He is a member of this association, but owing to his field work is not often present.

C. E. Smith has closed his work in Indiana County, Pa., and is now a student of Bethany College. The report of his work in the county named shows a fruitful ministry.

Ex-president Giltner, late of Eminence College, Kentucky, recently preached "two able sermons" to the church in Grant Cly, Mo., having been called to that city on business.

S. S. Lappin, for more than two years pastor at Paxton, Ill., has resigned to accept the work at LaFayette, Ind. The church at Paxton regret to see the change.

F. N. Calvin who recently began a specal work in Milwaukee, Wis., writes that the work is opening up encouragingly. His address is 235 Hanover St.

H. A. Easton who is assisting in a protracted meeting in Savannah, Ga., desires to correspond with any pastor or evangelist desiring a singer, in which work he is well and favorably known.

S. M. Martin has been in a protracted meeting with M. M. Davis at Central Christian Church, Dallas, Tex., for five weeks with about 30 additions to date.

Dr. W. Frank Ross recently lectured on "Religious Observations in Foreign Lands," to a thousand people in the Tabernacle at Decatur, Ill. He preached in Matton, Ill., last Sunday.

B. L. Kline, of Dallas, Ia., reports the new church house nearing completion. It will cost $1,600 and be dedicated by A. M. Haggard, acting Dean of the Bible College, Drake University.

Leanard G. Thompson, of Denver, has been engaged as state evangelist in Colorado. A better selection could not have been made. His address is 524, 38th Avenue, Denver, Colo.

G. A. Hoffmann, of Columbia, Mo., paid his respects to this office on last Monday. He was present at the preachers' meeting. He reports the school of Columbia as in a very prosperous state and the Register-Review outlook exceedingly bright.

J. E. Lynn, pastor of the church at Springfield, Ill., recently gave a banquet to the young men of the church, the occasion being the 28th anniversary of his birthday. It is said Bro. Lynn has the honor of being the youngest pastor in Springfield. About 60 men were present at the banquet and the time was occupied in a most delightful way.

Dr. W. A. Belding, of Troy N. Y., while enroute to South Gardiner, Maine, to hold a series of meetings, halted with us at our home one day and night and preached an excellent sermon for us. He is 82 years old, well preserved and a companionable brother. During sixty-odd years devoted to ministerial work he has immersed with his own hands between eleven and twelve thousand persons.—*New England Messenger.*

T. R. Hodkinson, of Clarksville, Iowa, who has been preaching and lecturing in Iowa, Kansas, Missouri, Colorado, Illinois and Wisconsin, desires now to locate with some church as pastor, or he would hold a few more church institutes on our principles if desired. He can furnish the highest testimonials, and his prices are moderate. Address him as above.

Dr. W. T. Moore, we regret to learn, is confined to his bed with a temporary illness. He attended and participated in the Moberly Educational Conference. We learn through him that Christian College is on such a boom that its trustees are planning to build a large and modern style building to accommodate its increasing patronrge. Mrs. Moore's ambition is to make it the Wellesley of the West. By the way, we have heard it hinted at that Sedalia has its eye on this institution, but Columbia would hardly permit its removal, we imagine.

CHANGES.

J. W. Taylor, Lexington, Ky., to Benton Harbor, Mich.

F. W. Collins, Kingsley to Kellogg, Ia.

A. M. Haggard, Oskaloosa to University Place, Des Moines, Ia.

H. L. Robinger, Shoun's Cross Roads, Tenn., to Mabel, N. C.

Z. E. Bates, Allegheny to Beaver, Pa.

G. E. Platt, Warsaw, Ind., to Marion, Ia.

R. E. McNight, Ashgrove to Springfield, Mo.

SUBSCRIBERS' WANTS.

Miscellaneous wants and notices will be inserted in this department at the rate of two cents a word, each insertion, all words, large and small, to be counted, and two initials stand for one word. Please accompany notice with corresponding remittance to save book-keeping.

Correspondence.

Cincinnati News.

On Monday, Dec. 5th, the tenth Ohio district monthly meeting was held in Central Christian Church, Cincinnati. Luncheon was served by the sisters of the church, which was also turned into a reception to the new preachers and their wives who have recently come to la or among us. These are A. W. Taylor, of the new church at Norwood; J. A. Pine, successor of Vernon Stauffer, of Eastern Ave.; W. O. Thomas, of the new church at Lockland, and Allan Wilson, our evangelist for the district.

The dinner was a joyful occasion, with its speeches and songs. About 150 present; A. M. Harvuot, toastmaster. J. A. Pine responded to "Why I Came to Cincinnati;" A. W. Taylor, "The Young Preacher;" Allen Wilson, "An Evangelist's View of the City's Needs;" A. McLean, "The Preachers' Wives;" J. A. Lord, "Preparation for the Convention in '99." While our people are already well organized for the physical care of all who come to the convention, the emphasis put upon the need of "spiritual preparation" on the part of the Cincinnati churches by Bro. Lord, met a hearty response. The spiritual activity of Cincinnati was never so great as it is to-day. We have planned this year the largest work ever yet undertaken. The coming of the Jubilee Convention is a great stimulus to us.

After dinner the C. W. B. M. Auxiliaries went into session to hear reports and plans, and to listen to an address by Sister Helen E. Moses. The tenth district board met in another room. Bro. Allen Wilson reported 32 additions in his meeting at Norwood. He continues there one more week. Attendance as large as the house will hold; at times people turned away. Every house in the suburb visited, and the people stirred up on religious matters. He goes to Walnut Hills Dec. 12th, to begin a meeting with Bro. Dutcher. The people at Walnut Hills are prepared for a meeting Bro. Dutcher has been using the question box of late with surprising interest.

Bro. A. W. Taylor has been visiting Madisonville on Sunday afternoons for a month, and the brethren, a small church, are anxious to begin a meeting. We expect Bro. Wilson to gather a good harvest there as soon as he is through at Walnut Hills.

A new house was dedicated at Central Fairmount, Nov. 20th. The district board is expecting to furnish them a regular pastor this month.

Bro. Pine, of Eastern Ave., has organized a Young Men's League of 18 members, who will assist him in bringing others to Christ. Last Sunday three young men made the good confession at Richmond St. Church, and Bro. Green will organize a Young Men's League this week, which will be a great help to him in seeking other young men for Christ.

An impressive memorial service was held in the Richmond St. Church, Nov. 20th, a tribute to the memory of Dr. H. N. Biddle, the fallen African missionary hero, who went out from this church. The house was filled with his friends and relatives. The speakers were Rev. J. S. Patton, an uncle and Baptist minister; Dr. P. T. Kilgour, his Sunday-school superintendent and medical college professor; Francis M. Biddle, his older brother, pastor of the Christian Church at Confluence, Pa.; A. McLean and Justin N. Green.

The Central Christian Church, with Bro. Harvuot as leader, is doing fine work in the city. They are running two mission schools, and are planning now for a protracted meeting to begin as soon as arrangements can be completed.

At Bellevue, just across the river, Bro. P. A. Cave, of Hagerstown, Md., is holding a meeting for Bro. Harding. Six additions to date. Bro. Seaman just closed a meeting at his church, Fourth St., Covington, with 30 additions. Bro. Geo. Miller, of the First Church, Covington, will begin a meeting January 15th, Bro. Isaac Selby preaching.

Bro. J. A. Erwin has just returned from Porto Rico. He reports a property boom there, and doubts the expediency of immediate investment. Brethren S. M. Cooper and F. M. Rains, just returned from Havana, Cuba, report the harvest ripe there for Christian reapers. The erstwhile Catholics of that country are convinced that there is a better religion than they have, and they are anxious for Americans to bring it to them.

By far the most interesting religious exercise we have had in Cincinnati for a long time was a series of lectures at the Central Christian Church by Isaac Selby, culminating in a debate with a notable infidel. Bro. Selby first lectured at Bro. Miller's church in Covington. The freethought people went to hear him. They were stirred up and talked to Bro. Miller about a debate. When Bro. Selby lectured in Cincinnati they came to hear him in greater numbers and plied him with questions. In the meantime they had secured the consent of Mr. C. Elton Blanchard, a freethought lecturer, and the editor of Current Thought, of Cleveland, to meet him. The arrangements were completed and the debate was held in the Auditorium, Monday and Tuesday evenings, Nov. 28th and 29th, Mr. Selby affirming that "Christianity is the Religion of Humanity," and Mr. Blanchard affirming that "Evolution is the True Doctrine of the Origin of Man and Other Forms of Life." To make a long and interesting story short, the Ohio Liberal League, for that is the society that challenged us, are a forlorn set of men, while the Christians who heard the debate, are the happiest people in Cincinnati. Bro. Miller, the chairman of our committe, has letters from the League secretary, acknowledging their discomfiture, saying their man disappointed them through lack of ability. They say that they want another meeting, with some other man to represent them. On the first evening of the debate about one-third of the audience were freethinkers; the second evening about one-sixth accounted for their side.

Let me say to the Christian brotherhood, that we ought to keep Bro. Selby in this country four or five years. He is pre-eminently fitted, both by nature and training, to show up the weakness of infidelity and the strength of Christianity. Having first been an honest infidel, spending ten years in its study and seven of activity in its defense, he understands that side of the question thoroughly. Among his many debates as an infidel he met a Christian preacher, in Australia, Bro. M. W. Green, who sowed the seeds of discontent with infidelity in his heart, from which he never recovered. He was afterwards led to a restudy of Christian evidences from the standpoint of the Disciples of Christ and is now an original, unique and powerful defender of the faith once for all delivered unto the saints. His artless, Christian manner and genuineness captures at once the hearts of his hearers. His work will always and everywhere do good. His time till next February is taken up. It is probable that he will lecture at a few points in Texas during February and March. Brethren in Texas, or other states wishing more particulars concerning his lectures and terms should write me at 119 West 6th St., Cincinnati, O.

J. H. FILLMORE.

The Latter-day Saints.

Many people coming to Salt Lake City for the first time are conscious of a feeling of surprise to find the Mormons looking, acting, speaking and dressing like ordinary mortals. This is due to the exaggerated ideas formed by us of those of whom we have heard much but seen nothing. As a matter of fact they differ in nothing from the classes and nationalities they represent. It is not uncommon to see on the streets men and women who look as though they had just stepped from one of Dickens' novels. I doubt not that it would be possible to find garments in this city still in use that date back to at least the last days of the styles in vogue in Dickens' time, and that were brought across the mountains and plains in the carts that were pushed by the hands of the women that wear them. Among them can be found as personable men and as beautiful women as can be found anywhere. They are the product of the recuperative power of the Anglo-Saxon races under favorable conditions. It is the sign of hope for the future. Civilization will refine the people, and once refined, they will revise the coarsness out of their creed. There are just three alternatives for a people who live in the midst of civilization and hold to tenets and indulge in practices that are obnoxious to that civilization, viz., reformation, emigration, extermination. A wise people will choose the first, and all the more certainly when revelations to meet the demands of every emergency can be had for the asking. Experience is a great teacher, and with the past for a key the future is not difficult to read.

The orders of the Mormon Church are apostles, presidents and patriarchs, high councils, seventies and lesser priests, teachers and deacons. The elders are the missionaries who compass the earth after converts. In theory they go without script or purse; in fact they get more than the average salary for such work of ministers of other churches, as the following facts and figures will show: There are 500 elders who have their headquarters at Chattanooga, Tenn. Through the money order department of that post office alone there is paid to Mormon elders an average of $300 per week, according to the statement made to me by the clerk of that department during the National Convention there. Just a little figuring reveals the fact that those elders who are ostensibly preaching the gospel (?) without money and without price are, as a matter of fact, receiving an average of $312 each which, with free lunch and lodging, isn't bad. This money is not sent by the church, but by relatives. In some cases it is a part of the regular income from the farm, mine or business of the individual; in others it represents the earnings of mothers, wives or sisters, or the proceeds of a dance given for the purpose, in one of the ward meeting houses.

Every city, town, village and community is organized into what is called a Stake of Zion, which is presided over by a stake president and two counselors. Salt Lake City is a stake of Zion. It is divided into twenty four wards. Each ward has a meeting house which is used for religious, social and political purposes. Each ward is presided over by a bishop. From 10 to 12 A. M. the Sunday-school is held in the ward meeting house, each family attending in its own ward, which embraces an area of nine square blocks, each block containing ten acres. At 2 P. M. the whole congregation of Israel is supposed to assemble at the tabernacle where two hours are spent in a service which embraces singing by the choir and talking (preaching) by those moved by the Spirit to do so. The first speaker is usually a returned elder who relates his experiences on the field and closes by adding his "testimuny to the truth of the gawspil." Then two or three of the apostles or presidents follow in long-drawn-out speeches, the substance of which si "great is Mormonism" and the effect of which is to make the people very tired. But they linger to hear the closing anthem by the choir, but for the singing of which but few would attend the tabernacle service. But for the tedious talkers the tabernacle would not begin to hold the people who would go to hear the choir. Such antiquated methods will be abandoned in time, but it will be after the time of the last lingering pioneer.

At 6 P. M. promptly, summer and winter, the Mutual Improvement Association, which answers to the C. E. Society, and of which there is one in each ward, meets in the ward meeting house and engages in exercises which are semi-religious and semi-secular in character. The solo is as apt to be a balad as a hymn. No mass assemblies are ever held in the temple. It is a building for ceremonies alone. In it marriages, baptisms for the dead, endowment ceremonies, etc., are performed.

My next will deal with the present status of polygamy in Utah as brought to light during the recent political campaign. It makes most interesting reading. W. H. BAGBY.

The Value of Small Colleges.

An institution of learning is only valuable as it gives opportunity, develops strength and uses these advantages to bring forth righteous conduct. The school which does not develop a truth-loving, truth-seeking spirit, with purpose of right living, does not fill out the mind of God in education.

An education must stand for the divinity in man—be a feeder and trainer of that inner self. It should bring man into fellowship with his race and make him loyal to his God.

Education must lead individuals or nations toward industry and economy that they may have to distribute, toward honest and justice that the strong may not oppress the weak, toward peace, righteousness and joy in the Holy Spirit that it may be used in the service of Christ.

No questions need be raised about technical, professional or practical education. These will follow. Let man be properly educated and have the spirit of righteousness with liberty to do, and material improvements will as naturally come as perfect fruits fall from a healthy tree.

A rightly educated people will as certainly think and work toward the beautiful and noble, as seeds bring forth after their kind.

To educate in this way does not depend so much upon the large college buildings, the limited or the rich endowment, as upon the men and the women who teach the classes and set the example in conduct. God speaks and acts through his people. "The heavens declare the glory of God," but man shows his life and character. The living teacher is the college power. Men and women through whom God can set forth ideals, inspire hopes and establish noble purposes, make the divinely ordered teachers. These may be found in the district school or in the university; and because small colleges are generally the work of idealists, founded on faith, upheld through self-denial and love, they are likely to have a larger proportion of active Christian teachers than institutions resting chiefly on intellectual force and upon money.

In small colleges the personal association between students and teachers is close and of high value. It gives encouragement, inspires confidence and begets in the young courage to undertake great works.

Students receive at first-hand the benefit of their teachers' experience and wisdom.

The lesser colleges distributed over the country give young people a start. They develop a desire for learning in the hearts of thousands who would otherwise never have aspirations toward higher education.

Except from the location of this college, and the personal work in leading young people to begin its curriculum, more than half of its one hundred and five graduates would never have taken up an educational course. As it is, nearly all of the number are in responsible and honorable places requiring higher education. And within the last three years eleven of these graduates have been students in some one of the great universities. Without the Missouri and the Ohio and other trbutaries there could be no Mississippi. If, instead of forty "little half-equipped colleges," the Disciples had one hundred, they would have material then to start one great university, or to furnish students for Bible colleges at the state universities.

When Bryce made his observations on the American Commonwealth, he found the wide distribution of small colleges to be one of the secrets of our country's greatness.

In Christian colleges students see wicked practices and evil customs abolished. They see frequent victories bearing toward the ideal and become established in a warfare for virtue; and hereby are sown the seeds of moral heroism. With all the blessings that come from great universities—and it is not denied that these are many—they are not strong at the point of establishing individual heroism and Christian ideality. These principles can be implanted in the student easier before he enters the university; hence the necessity for many small institutions.

Of students who turn to Christ during a course of study a much smaller proportion, even of the same age, come from the universities than from the small colleges.

In the universities they find fraternities, footballs and class honors of highest interest. They often meet their first skeptical associates or authors. At the end of their course they go out into the world unconverted, then fall under the temptations of money, ambition or appetite, and their influence to bring the world to Christ is lost.

Small colleges would have saved many of these and their lives would have blessed others. One has only to compare carefully the real Christian work done in half a dozen small institutions, having two hundred students each, with one state school having twelve hundred students, to appreciate the serious mistake of those who think "the day for small colleges" is passed.

Money, machinery and specialists, all, can not do the work of such institutions. These forces help; they give better form; but small colleges have their special function of developing a love of learning, raising ideals and bringing out personal character, which they will continue to do, while Christianity has in her folds independent, self-denying men to conduct them. JOSEPHUS HOPWOOD.

Milligan College, Tenn., Nov. 26, 1898.

New York Letter.

Our New York state evangelist, Bro. J. M. Morris, is doing excellent service. He has held a number of meetings since the state convention in September in which more than sixty persons have united with the churches. Among others he has held meetings with the churches at Niagara Falls and Jefferson St., Buffalo. Just now he is in a meeting with the church at Syracuse (E. R. Edwards pastor), with good hope of success. Some of his discourses are illustrated and will no doubt attract large congregations. Some of his illustrated sermons are "The New Creation," "Duty and Destiny," "The Word of God Rightly Divided" and "The Childhood and Manhood of the Church." This matter of illustrating sermons by means of the stereopticon, if wisely used may be very fruitful of good results. If magazines and books and lectures can profitably be illustrated, why not the sacred discourse? This is something about which many preachers might think.

***

At the twenty-third annual meeting of the Alumni Club of Union Theological Seminary, held at the St. Denis Hotel, the Rev. Samuel McComb, of Rutger's Riverside Presbyterian Church, spoke on "Browning as a Teacher for Our Time." He claimed Browning as the poet pre-eminently of the soul. With him the significance of life does not lie in outward circumstances, but in the inward development of the soul. Modern tendencies of thought combine to belittle the independent worth of man. We have a science which professes to find in the movements of the self-conscious spirit simply concomitants of nervous energy in the brain; a psychology which accounts for a Socrates by disorganized cellular matter, and for a St. Paul by an epileptic fit; a philosophy which while seeming to conserve moral freedom really entangles man in chains of necessity, forged by his past, and makes moral initiative impossible and repentance an absurdity. Browning lifts up his voice in protest in behalf of the soul. God has made it by emptying himself of a portion of his own causal activity, which he delegates to man that it may be used for free self-development. Further, God being thus the ground and cause of all souls, there is also a solid basis for an optimistic view of life. Browning is not like Mr. Hamertin's opitimist who conveniently shuts his eye to the evils of the world. The poet knows and dislikes sin and wrong with unparalleled disgust; but he sees in man's nature a divine endowment, nay, a differentiation of God himself. How, then, is the greatest criminal, Guitteau, a Francessetain or an Ottinia, deep buried beneath straits of evil to be viewed? Christ, we say, died for all; yes, for these, too, for he sees deep into the most sinful soul some hidden bud that bids the criminal to a divine order. Sin, however dark, does not exhaust the possibilities of personality. The preachers, who call men sinners, state but half the truth. The other half says they are sons of God, heirs of immortality. Here also Browning is the prophet of our time. Hope is the supreme need of the age. Melancholy, which is the fruit of imperfect knowledge, is also the creature of despair. The poet's message is a trumpet call that nerves all the powers of our being and makes a final surrender to evil impossible. Finally: Browning is the poet of love. No other poet has so glorified and enthroned this principle. It is the end of life, that for which life is given: "The charm o' the prize of beaming love." Nay, it is the life of God.

"A loving worm within its clod
Were diviner than a loveless god;
And his words I will dare to say."

This love has been embodied in Christ. He is at once the measure of man's being and the transcendent manifestation of God.

***

On Sunday evening Dec. 4th Mr. Samuel Colcord, of this city, gave his lecture, a "Reply to Ingersoll," in the 169th St. Church of the Disciples. In consequence of the extreme inclemency of the weather the audience was small, but deeply interested. Mr. Colcord gave the same lecture at Chickering Hall in the afternoon to a great audience, at which Mr. Ingersoll was present. The lecturer proposes to follow a week behind this notorious infidel all over the country answering his attack on Christianity. He came to New York City from his native Illinois at 26 years of age and on each Sunday afternoon for seven years drew large audiences to hear him lecture on the Claims of Christianity at Chickering Hall. Then in connection with that work he took the pastorate of the Puritan Congregational Church in Brooklyn, but this double duty soon impaired his health and forced him out of the ministry. He has since followed secular pursuits with marked success. Two years ago he visited Waco, Texas, and was induced to reply to a recent attack of Ingersoll on the Christian faith in that city and has been called to repeat it again and again. I have just read the proof-sheets of his lecture, "A Reply to Ingersoll," and am glad to say Mr. Colcord is fully equal to the task. His irony, his pathos, his skillful gathering up of the fruits of Christianity, all interwoven, make a lecture unusually fascinating and irresistible. If he comes your way you should hear him.

***

The Rev. Dr. Thomas C. Hall, son of the late Dr. John Hall, of this city, and until recently a pastor in Chicago, has just been called to the chair of Christian Ethics in Union Theological Seminary. It is of interest to note that he accepts a professorship in the very institution which his illustrious father could not bear to serve as trustee after the Briggs episode. In Presbyterian theology the father was a conservative; the son is a progressive, hence the latter agrees with Union, the former did not.

***

A series of special sermons is announced by the same institution, to be delivered on "The Holy Spirit." They are as follows: "The Holy Spirit as the Third Person of the Holy Trinity," Prof. W. N. Clark, Colgate University; "The Work of the Holy Spirit in Man Apart from the Church," Rev. Newman Smyth, New Haven; "Work of the Holy Spirit in Creation and Government of the World," Pres. W. D. Hyde, Bowdoin College; "The Holy Spirit's Advent at Pentecost," Pres. Henry A. Buttz, Drew Seminary; "The Holy Spirit Dwelling in the Church," Dean George Hodges, Cambridge; "The Holy Spirit and Holy Scripture," Rev. S. M. Hamilton, Louisville, Ky.; "Work of the Holy Spirit in Regeneration," Rev. George Alexander, New York; "The Holy Spirit Dwelling in the Christian, Rev. T. T. Munger, New Haven; "Holy Spirit the Guide into all Truth," Rev. W. R. Huntington, New York; "The Sanctifying Work of the Holy Spirit," Rev. Alexander McKenzie, Cambridge. These noted preachers handling such topics surely will cause this body of students to think, and if they will but send them afresh to the study of the New Testament, much good will result. S. T. WILLIS.

1281 Union Ave.

That Singular Answer to Prayer.

The CHRISTIAN-EVANGELIST of Nov. 10 contains an account of the suicide of a Mr. Fleiss, at Santa Cruz, Cal., taken from a daily of that city. It seems that R. L. McHatton, pastor of the Christian Church, in a public service prayed for means with which to complete their house of worship. Mr. Fleiss was present and heard the prayer. Soon afterward (we are not told how soon) Mr. Fleiss was found dead in his room and the circumstances gave evidence that he had suicided. A check good for $300 in favor of the Christian Church, Santa Cruz, Cal., properly signed and stamped, had been left by the suicide. An accompanying letter left no room to doubt that Mr. Fleiss intended the church named to have the benefit of the check.

The CHRISTIAN-EVANGELIST comments that "this was a singular answer to prayer. The answer, however, evidently did not come from heaven." The writer does not yet see the evidence that the answer was not from above. Bro. McHatton had asked God for means to enable them to finish their house of worship. Certainly a worthy subject for prayer. The means came. He who made out the check in the church's favor certainly had, as far as we can see, a perfect right to do so, though not a member of the church and, perhaps, not even a professed Christian. God often answers prayer through men and means. Who believing in God and prayer doubts this? And the men through whom he works are not always his believing children. Bro. McHatton had not, we feel sure, dictated to the Lord how, or through whom the desired means were to come. The fact that the donor did the wicked thing, if accountable, of taking his own life, was no necessary part of the answer to the prayer, and certainly had no place in the thought or petition of Bro. McHatton. The account of the sad incident shows what led the man to end his life. Bro. McHatton's prayer determined the disposition of his money—a very commendable one, surely.

Suppose a man to be taken dangerously ill. His wife prays earnestly for his recovery. A physician, having knowledge of the man's condition and also having heard the woman's prayer, volunteers his service and is allowed to prescribe. His directions are followed. The physician goes back to his office and executes what he has had in mind for some time—puts an end to his own life to get out of trouble into which he has fallen. The sick man speedily recovers. Is the CHRISTIAN-EVANGELIST prepared to say the woman's prayer was not answered, or that the answer was not from God? O. J. GIST,

Pastor Church of Christ.

Medford, Oregon.

[The CHRISTIAN-EVANGELIST did not question the perfect right of the church to the money above referred to. By saying that the answer to that prayer did not come from heaven, we simply meant that God did not move that man to suicide. And besides, the character of the letter which the suicide left does not indicate that he was impelled to make the gift from any moral or religious impulse. But it was well that so much of his money went to a church that had needed for it, instead of other probably less deserving and less needy places.—EDITOR.]

Canadian Letter.

The reports of offerings for the Home Mission work indicates some gain over last year. The new house for meeting at Selkirk was dedicated Thanksgiving Day. The meeting at Toronto Junction Church closed on the 13th inst., with the result of 11 confessions. Congregations are increasing at the Cecil St. Church, Toronto, and a goodly number of students from the different colleges are seen at all services. The collections for Home Missions was $37.72. The Toronto mission keeps up interest in all departments.

Marsville and Grand Valley, under the care of Bro. E. A. Cary, are doing well. Bro. Cary is working up a mission at South Luther. The church at Everton has had two confessions lately and is prospering. The Home Mission offering is $45 already and will, it is hoped, reach $50.

Mimosa Church recently held a S.-S. social which was largely attended and netted $25 for the work there. The Everton Church was greatly pleased to welcome back one of her sons last Lord's day, Bro. Robert Stewart and his bride (who is a sister-in-law of Bro. Baker, the former pastor here). Bro. Stewart is one of the seven sons of the church who are preaching the old Jerusalem gospel elsewhere, his father, Bro. David Stewart was preacher at Mimosa for 25 years and without any compensation therefor. Aylmer is still without a pastor. Bro. Harlow, a student, is supplying there. Bro. Sinclair has sent in his resignation to the church at Lobo.

The meeting house at Iona presents a very neat appearance with its new coat of paint and repairs.

The brethren at Hamilton are keeping well together and encouraging each other in the Lord, though still without a minister. They have called Bro. Pentmore from the United States. The collection at Hamilton was $32.

Bro. Sinclair has taken vigorous hold of the work at London and reports gain in all departments of the church there. Our watchword this year is $3,000 from the churches for the work in Ontario. W. R. S.

Everton, Ont., C. W.

Is the Prohibition Party a Failure?

In the CHRISTIAN-EVANGELIST of Nov. 17th Burris A. Jenkins makes the statement in his Christian Endeavor column that the Prohibition party has been a failure. This is surely a great mistake, and I am surprised at any one of the ability of Bro. Jenkins making such a statement as this. The facts do not justify this statement. Neither do they that the old Abolition party was a failure. It was a glorious success, and the abolition of slavery was as much due to the agitation carried on by Abolition leaders as to any other one thing. Without Birney, Lovejoy, Garrison and Phillips, Lincoln and his work could not have been possible.

And so with the Prohibition party. If the liquor traffic ever is abolished, as soon it must be, it will be largely due to the agitation carried on incessantly by the Prohibition party. A party does not necessarily have to come into power in order to be a success. It may accomplish its mission without this. The Prohibition party has already been a great success in this particular, and promises to be a much greater success, judging by the great increase in its vote this election. Christians, and especially Christian ministers, instead of crying out about the failure of the Prohibition party, should go into it and make it a glorious success. It is the only political party that stands for the suppression of the saloon. This would do the cause of Christ more good than anything that could now be done by this government. But as long as Christians continue to vote for and with political parties that favor and perpetuate this curse, we may expect it to continue to do its work of devastation, destruction and ruin. But when they vote against it the traffic will soon cease.

B. L. ALLEN,
State C. E. Supt. of Indiana.

Virginia Letter.

We have a noble band of Christian workers in the Charlottesville Church. Bernard P. Smith, the pastor, is an earnest young man, "full of faith and the Holy Spirit." The church has recently enjoyed a good meeting; Brother W. H. Book did the preaching. This "Book" is genuine, interesting and thoroughly original. There were a number of additions, and "the church was edified." Brother Book was called home when the meeting had reached its height, but before leaving he gave a lecture in the interest of the Piedmont Assembly which secured nearly fifty dollars. He also gave a number of afternoon Bible studies during the meeting on the "Person and Work of the Holy Spirit," which were greatly enjoyed by those who heard them. Brother Book is full of zeal and energy, unselfish and fearless. He has more calls for meetings than he can respond to, and yet he gives his best endeavors to the cause in Virginia. Like all the Milligan men I have met, he is a constant student of the Bible and thoroughly informed on all lines of missions. Several persons have united with the church since the meeting closed.

***

I recently spent a most delightful Lord's day with the church in Lynchburg, Va. In the Sermon on the Mount we read of "a city set a hill." Lynchburg is *on* a hill, *under* a hill and *all over* a hill. It is decidedly a hilly city. The old canal had its terminus here. It is one of the most prominent and prosperous cities of Virginia. The Glamorgan Pipe Works, of which the superintendent of our Lynchburg Sunday-school, Mr. Henry McWayne, is president, furnishes water pipes, hydrants, etc., to cities all over the East and South from Boston to New Orleans. Another member of the Christian Church in Lynchburg, who is a graduate of Bethany College, is business manager for the Lynchburg Plow Works. R. W. Lilly, who recently went to Lynchburg from Chicago, is doing excellent work. He was in the midst of a good meeting, doing the preaching himself. The church at Lynchburg, after a long struggle reaching back beyond the days when C. S. Lucas labored for them, is now free from de t and will soon be compelled to rebuild or enlarge their present building. The congregation under Brother Lilly's leadership will observe C. W. B. M. Day and secure one and perhaps several life memberships.

***

Thanksgiving Day and the day following, including the last Lord's day in November, were spent in Richmond, Va. They were delightful days of rest and spiritual fellowship spent in the Christian home of the late John B. Cary. Mrs. Young, "little Helen" and I enjoyed the hospitality of Sister Cary and her daughters, Mrs. Lizzie Daniel and Miss Gillie Cary. The visit afforded me the opportunity of having several satisfactory conferences with Mr. T. Archibald Cary in regard to our University of Virginia Bible work and also of seeing the excellent—I had almost said unprecedented—work which Brother Z. T. Sweeney is doing at the Seventh Street Church in Richmond. While the permanency of Brother Sweeney's engagement with the Richmond people is still *in statu quo*, it appears to one who sees the crowded audiences which fill the large church that the blessing of God is attending his labors in that important centre. In the letter of invitation which Miss Gillie Cary, her mother and sister extended us she wrote, "I shall not plan any institute work for you, but have planned to give you an absolute rest while visiting in our home." It was the most complete rest which I have enjoyed for several years, and Mrs. Young and Helen enjoy the visit equally as much as I did. We had the pleasure while in Richmond of breaking bread in the home of Mr. W. A. Crenshaw whose wife, Mrs. Lillian Moss Crenshaw, is the daughter of Brother David Moss, of Paris, Mo. They have a delightful home and Bro. Crenshaw is one of our good workers in the Seventh Street Church. We also dined with Mrs. Duke and family and with Bro. Maury and family. Although the weather was quite inclement, except one bright, sunshiny day, Miss Gillie Cary and Mrs. Daniel took Mrs. Young to see a number of the historic sights in Richmond. Probably no city in the South is the centre of more historic interest than Richmond. It was the capital of the Confederacy and the Confederate Museum is a collection of rare relics in the White House of the Confederacy. Old St. John's Episcopal Church, which was built in 1741, is still in an excellent state of preservation. It was here that Patrick Henry made his famous speech closing with the words, "Give me liberty or give me death!" In the Capital Square is an equestrian statue of Gen. Washington in bronze which is one of the finest works of art on the American Continent. Around the base of the statue in heroic size are figures of some of Virginia's most illustrious sons, such as John Marshall, Thomas Jefferson, *et al*. A few steps from Mr. Crenshaw's home is a noble equestrian statue of Robt. E. Lee, and just beyond one can still see the breastworks which tell of the struggle and suffering of the Virginia people during the Civil War.

***

Monday morning before leaving Richmond I attended the Christian ministers' meeting. At Bro. Sweeney's request I gave them a brief outline of the past and of the future prospects of our Bible teaching at the University of Virginia. Just before closing my remarks Dr. S. S. Laws, formerly president of the University of Missouri, entered the room and related his connection with the development of the Bible Chair idea. He expressed the hope that the great brotherhood of Missouri would speedily endow the Bible College at the University of Missouri. He commended the work which T. P. Haley and J. H. Garrison, with far reaching insight, have long championed. Brethren of Missouri, you have a great opportunity before you at Columbia. May God give you the consecration and wisdom to improve it. The pastors of all the Christian Churches in Richmond—Bros. Spencer, Maxwell, Garrison and Sweeney—expect to observe C. W. B. M. Day during the month of December. Bro. Maxwell has succeeded Bro. Omer at the Second Church. We shall long remember our visit to Richmond as one of the most pleasant experiences Mrs. Young and I have ever enjoyed.

***

In the cities of Virginia our churches are growing, but with rare exceptions, as at Gilboa and Macedonia, the country churches are languishing. It gave me great delight to see the Seventh Street Christian Church in Richmond crowded from the pulpit to the door and with chairs in the aisles. But the custom of having preaching only once each month has kept many of our Virginia churches from growing stronger. On the whole, however, the cause in Virginia is growing and taking on new life. As Sister Cary said to me, "God buries his workers, but he carries on his work." We have a number of young men who are coming forward to bear the responsibilities the older men are laying down. Over twenty years ago, when Col. Cary was traveling over the state of Virginia and struggling to support his family, he promised a book to the best Sunday-school scholar in a Sunday-school situated in Southwest Virginia. The boy who won the prize, Henry McWayne, is now superintendent of the Lynchburg Sunday-school and one of the most successful business men in Virginia. Brethren of Virginia, take courage. C. A. YOUNG.

Texas Letter.

N. M. Ragland preached his thirteenth anniversary sermon as pastor of the church at Fayetteville, Ark., on Nov. 20th. The good accomplished by this cultured and consecrated man during these years is beyond computation. His influence not only reaches his church and town, but through the University students it reaches every nook and corner of the state, and it will tell for good long after the pious author has gone home to his reward. The sermon, like all Bro. Ragland's productions, is chaste and eloquent, and it shows continued prosperity in his work. It was published in full by the city papers.

"The Success of Modern Missions," by F. M. Rains, shows that the gospel can reach and save the "lowest classes." It is a part of the address he delivered at the Chattanooga Convention. It is timely. More such literature in compact form, from those whose lives are lived in the missionary atmosphere, will do good. Let such men give it to us.

S. Y. Trice, who has been our Sunday-school superintendent in the Central Church for eleven years, was presented a handsome gold watch by the school, as a testimonial appreciation. It was a deserved compliment to one of the most faith workers I ever knew.

War, bloody war, a war of extermination,

is brewing in Texas. It is not a war with Spain or any other foreign foe. It is not a racial war between the whites and blacks. Neither is it a war on monopolies and trusts or labor unions. And it is not a war on the whisky traffic. But it is, nevertheless, a real war, and a war of vital importance. It is a war on the prairie dog. These little pests, by the hundreds and thousands and millions, feed upon the roots of the fine grass in the great "Pan-handle" region—a country as large as three ordinary states—where the cattle king flourishes in all his glory, and the land is about to become a barren waste. The people are thoroughly aroused, the papers are talking about it, and the legislature will soon be called on to enact laws to aid in this war of extermination. And all this is right. But the thing that strikes me as strange is the fact that men who will enlist in this war and do valiant service cannot be enlisted in the war against King Alcohol. They will fight the prairie dog, but not the saloon; they will fight for the cattle, but not for the boys.

President A. Clark, of Add-Ran University, will preach for the church at Waco until Bro. Calvin's successor is secured. This is a fortunate arrangement, for it does not interfere with Bro. Clark's college work and it gives the church the preaching of an unusually strong man.

R. B. Briney, son of J. B. Briney, of Missouri, locates with the church at Amarillo. We are glad to have this young man among us and hope he may prove himself a worthy son of so noble a sire.

C. E. Smootz comes to us from New York, strongly commended by the state board. He is at San Marcos with a delicate wife, and the churches of that region should give him work.

Our meeting at the Central Church, after a continuance of six weeks, has closed with 49 additions from all sources. We hoped for much larger results; but probably should not, as this seems to be an "off year" for large ingatherings. Bro. Martin will spend the holidays with his family in Oakland, Cal., after which he begins a meeting with his cousin, Sumner T. Martin. M. M. DAVIS.

833 Live Oak St., Dallas, Tex.

A Streak of Sunshine.

No life is all sunshine. The sky is more or less overhung with clouds for all of us. And the preacher's life is no exception to the rule. However faithful he may be he is not only "subject to like passions as we," but also to the same vicissitudes of fortune.

In our childhood days we used to chase the streak of sunshine and dance for joy in its yellow light as coming through the rift in the cloud it went like a passing smile over the earth. And now when our life's sky is clouded so much with the cares of life, its anxieties, its disappointments and toils, it gladdens our hearts so much when the bright spots come streaming through the clouds and show us how beautiful this world is after all when we "let the little sunsine in." God has been very gracious unto me and given me much of hope and gladness in my life. But one of these special streaks of sunshine has lately crossed my path, and I feel like acknowledging my gratitude for it.

I refer to the visit of our Bro. R. M. Messick to our church the forepart of this month. Bro. Messick is so large-hearted, good-natured and cheerful, his presence is like a burst of sunshine. But I do not refer to this alone. Fifteen years ago Bro. Messick, served this congregation as pastor for over three years. And now on his way to his far-off home in Oregon he stopped off to pay us a farewell visit. He intended to stay but a few days with us, but was detained two weeks for no other reason than that he could not get away from the entreaties of his brethren and friends. It was our lot to be with him much as he visited in the homes of our people. And it was in this experience that the "sunshine came in." He preached for us over Sunday and several nights while visiting with us during the day. And it made me think of the picture, "Daily in the temple and breaking bread from house to house did eat their meat with gladness and singleness of heart, praising God and having favor with all the people."

Brethren, if this is not a streak of sunshine in a preacher's life I cannot conceive what could bring one here on earth. Such love and fellowship is "better than gold." Though they gave him a nice present for this before he left. And it shows that faithful service will be appreciated and the servant held in esteem. Let those who will look at the dark side of a preacher's life, there is much to encourage in experiences like this. It may be our work is not usually remunerated as it ought to be, and as it is in other callings, yet there is no other life can show such blessed fellowship as this. Such a streak of sunshine does not cross the path of any other calling. And because of this I "thank God and take courage."

We were sorry to see Bro. Messick leave Missouri, and "sorrowing most of all for the words which he spoke, that they should see his face no more." But we look forward to the time when we shall "meet to part no more."

Though we hope many years of usefulness upon this earth are yet before Bro. Messick. He is still a good preacher of the Word. And one of the best fitted and most active and efficient men in pastoral work I ever saw. His visits in the home are a benediction. They were to us. And his coming to any church as its pastor will be a streak of sunshine cross their path. B. T. WHARTON.

Marshall, Mo., Nov. 30, 1898.

Hiram Jubilee Endowment.

A few of the many good words spoken in favor of the great Hiram Jubilee Endowment movement:

W. P. Aylesworth, Pres. Cotner University, Bethany, Neb.:—"Enclosed find card pledging $1.00 or more to your fund. I have not yet had an opportunity to place the matter before our faculty, but am sure they will feel, as I do, a deep interest in your 'Jubilee' movement. I am glad you have given other college men an opportunity to express their fellowship in this easy way. You have my fullest sympathy and best wishes."

J. H. Garrison, editor CHRISTIAN-EVANGELIST:—"We shall be glad to print what we can and to give the numbers that are responding, and otherwise help your good work along. I believe you are right in supposing that the success of your effort will prove beneficial to all other colleges.

Wishing you success in the enterprise, and authorizing you to use my name in the list of your donors for $1.00 and upwards, I am."

Mrs. Clara A. Sanborn, Londonville, O.:—"Count my name for this good work. Hiram holds first and warm place in my heart and I want to be one of the 50,000 to make the $1.00 donation and more if I can, when called upon to do so."

W. Bayard Craig, of Drake University, Des Moines, Ia.:—"Greeting to old Hiram. Count us in all things looking to the upbuilding of educational work among our people. We are not rivals, but co-operant friends."

J. Fraise Richard, Washington, D. C.:—"I have read with much interest your articles and appeal in behalf of Hiram College. I am pleased to see its work so successful. Hiram deserves to live and grow and exert an influence. It is in good soil and surrounded by good atmosphere."

G. P. Coler, Bible Chair, Ann Arbor, Mich.:—"I hope that your lectures may be profitable to you and helpful in promoting the cause of higher education among our people. I hope that your jubilee may be a great success. You may enroll me as one of the friends of Hiram College who will gladly contribute something to that fund."

J. W. Spayd, Owosso, Mich.:—"I have just read your letter in last week's Standard on 'Hiram's Jubilee Endowment.' I am partial to Hiram as you know, and desire to have a hand in that endowment. You may put me down on your list with a pledge of $5.00, payable next spring."

Dr. A. H. Flower, Boston, Mass.:—You have adopted a wise plan for raising the endowment fund of Hiram College. It will be a success. Add my name to your list."

C. Durant Jones and Ida Pickering Jones, Des Moines, Ia.:—"You may count on our names as two of that 50,000 who will make donations towards Hiram's endowment. We will join in the jubilee when the full amount is raised."

Mrs. Hattie Craig, Newman, Ill.:—"I have been reading of the endowment for Hiram and will gladly be a cheerful giver, though the amount be small."

Hiram Van Kirk, Divinity House, Chicago, Ill.:—"You may count me as one of the contributors to the Hiram Jubilee Endowment Fund. Use me if possible in your work for the endowment of Hiram. I like very much the plan of your lecture, and in case you are near Chicago be sure and visit us and we will have you give the same before an assembled gathering of the Divinity House and Hyde Park Church."

L. L. Carpenter, Wabash, Ind.:—"I desire to become one of the 50,000 persons to help endow Hiram College. Put my name on the list and I will do all that I can."

J. Hopwood, Pres Milligan College, Tenn.:—"I heartily approve of your efforts to endow Hiram College by popular subscription. Put my name on your list."

Simpson Ely, Kirksville, Mo.:—"Put my name down. I wish you abundant success. A bright day awaits Hiram College."

To the list of college men we are happy to add the names of S. M. Jefferson, Berkeley, Cal., Ashley S. Johnson, Kimberlin Heights, Tenn., and J. L. Darsie, Bethany, W. Va.

Notes and News.

The Outlook Improving.

We observed C. W. B. M. Day yesterday. In the forenoon Mrs. Fuller gave an address, and in the evening they had an open meeting, assisted by the Juniors. The work is on the up grade now. We will help some weak points in this county and Henry County in Institute work soon as the holidays are past.

J. H. FULLER.

Burlington, Ia., Dec. 5, 1898.

Nine Years of Service.

Rev. E. Jay Teagarden (pastor of the church at Danbury, Conn.) preached his ninth anniversary sermon at the morning service yesterday. It consisted of a careful review of the work of the past nine years and suggestions as to the work of the church during the year upon which they are just entering. At the time of the beginning of the present pastorate there were 280 members in the church. During the nine years 620 members have been added, an average of 69 each year; 350 of these have been added at the regular services, the remainder in special evangelistic services. There have been 59 deaths in the church. Letters have been granted to 74 members, who have united with other churches. Twenty have left the church without letter or have been dismissed from its membership. The present membership is 747. Of these 95 are non-resident and 72 are inactive. The working membership of the church is thus at present 580. During the nine years the pastor has preached 749 sermons in his own pulpit, has officiated at 151 funerals and performed the marriage ceremony 90 times, besides making over 5,000 pastoral calls. The church never had so large a force of workers nor so bright an outlook as at present. The pastor is organizing a committee of a hundred personal workers for the winter campaign, and he assured the members that if they second and assist his efforts as in the past, the present year will be the most successful of their united labors. He believes that no pastor ever had a heartier support from the entire membership of a church and that this is one of the greatest secrets of the success of the work. —*The Evening News.*

Dedication at Dows.

The First Church of Christ, at Dows, Ia., was dedicated Lord's day, Nov. 27, by Bro. B. S. Denny, secretary of the I. C. C.

The house is a beautiful little frame structure, with all modern conveniences. The auditorium is 26 by 46, with corner pulpit; Sunday-school room is 18 by 24; the dressing-rooms are 10 by 10, and are built onto the rear of the auditorium.

The house complete, as it now stands, cost $3,000. Of this amount there was $1,018.26 to be raised on dedication. Many of the brethren felt blue and were discouraged and afraid it could not be done. But Bro. Denny, in his kind and loving way, gave the call, and in response there was $1,129.70 pledged to meet the indebtedness, and there has been some more pledges since.

This is the first church Bro. Denny has dedicated since his election to the secretaryship of the I. C. C. He does his work in first-class order, picks up all odds and ends and leaves everything complete and every one rejoicing and happy. Brethren, don't be afraid to let Bro. Denny dedicate your church. I wish we had one for him to dedicate each Lord's day so long as he is our secretary.

This is a new church. It was organized last May at the close of a meeting held by Iowa's little giant, Bro. Lawrence Wright, with 52 members. Since the writer took up the work the 22d of May, there has been three additions (until the church was built).

The brethren deserve a great deal of credit and praise for their work. They built one of the most beautiful and convenient church buildings in this part of the country. And it was dedicated on the first Lord's day in the last six months of our year's labor with this people. It is not every congregation of only 54 or 55 members can or do accomplish that much in six short months. I feel proud of them. They did not make the mistake that many, many churches make, to organize and not build, but rent an old church or old deserted hall and continue to meet for a time and then go to pieces in a short time. It is sad to see so many churches do that very thing. And churches, too, that if taught to give would be able to build. I believe it is the making of a church to build a house the first year. They may not be able to build what they would like to have, but generally they are able to build something. After they have a building there is a greater degree of permanency about the work. There usually is a great many prophecies when one of our churches is organized regarding the life; such as, "Oh, that Campbellite Church won't last long; after the newness has worn off those folks will go back into the other churches," and many similar expressions. When they erect a building they feel as though they have something that is common to all, hence they are permanently organized. Brethren, be not afraid to build homes for the churches. It is pleasing to the One who gave us the church.

F. L. DAVIS.

An Anti-Mormon Monthly Magazine.

I am urged and encouraged to launch an anti-Mormon monthly magazine.

I favor an anti-Mormon magazine, for several reasons, and will consent to plant one on certain conditions.

REASONS FOR AN ANTI-MORMON PUBLICATION.

A magazine that is dedicated wholly and specifically to fighting this deadly and rapidly spreading "ism" *is needed.*

On such a publication the foes of the "ism" could and would *unite.* Mormonism is a common and deadly foe to all the church denominations in Christendom.

Such a publication would *supplement* and cheapen my tract work. Tract work cannot be *supplanted*, and ought not to be, if it could, by any other work.

CONDITIONS.

I have had a vast and a varied experience as a publisher and an editor. I propose to profit by that experience. It's a pleasant thing to *run a paper*, but when a paper *runs its editor and publisher*, I know of nothing more unpleasant or harrassing. I have been there.

1. I must have, with a goodly margin, enough pledged subscribers, in advance, to pay for blank paper and to pay the printer for one year.

2. The subscriptions pledged must be paid on receipt of the first copy of the monthly. With these returns I will buy the paper enough for one year and bank balance for the printers.

3. The price will be only fifty cents per year and only 1,200 subscribers will be needed to insure one year's run.

After the first year I think it will be a fixture. Those who have read my tracts and articles in various papers can judge of the style of magazine I will get out.

4. *All* exchanges of this paper are respectfully and urgently requested to publish this announcement.

If your heart is as my heart and you are willing to join hands with me in battling this monster fraud of the nineteenth century send in your name.

R. B. NEAL.

Grayson, Ky.

Kankakee (Ill.) Notes.

Bro. Geo. Hess, a young minister and school-teacher who is a member of this congregation, filled the pulpit very acceptably Lord's day morning, Nov. 27, in my absence. He expects soon to devote his entire time to the ministry.

Four added here recently in a short meeting held by Bro. J. T. Alsup. The conditions did not seem to be propitious, so we closed hoping to resume when the church gets *ready* for it.

The Sherburnville church expects to hold a revival meeting in January. The evangelist is not yet selected.

The Kankakee field is not as broad as many imagine. We have a population of about 14,000, but out of that there is not to exceed 3,500 American Protestants. The rest are foreign, mostly French Catholics. With nine Protestant churches the field is narrowed down considerably. And yet there is room and a fighting chance for building up a New Testament church of Christ here. It will be done.

In soliciting funds to pay off our lot debt our workers are often met with this objection: "There are too many churches in the city already, not room for any more to build up except at the expense of the others." But another one is gradually coming into view and is more and more being recognized as a factor in the city. Had we a church building and equipments we would grow rapidly.

"How to Read the Bible"......25 cts. per 100
"Baptism in Plain English"...." " " "
"What is Baptism For?"......" " " "
"Christian Union" ....30 " " "
"Teachings of the Christian Church" ...." " " "

I am publishing the above tracts, of which Sumner T. Martin, Mason City, Ia., says: "I have never seen a lot of tracts I like as well as these of yours. They have preached the gospel mightily these last three weeks, I assure you."

Two elders of the "Reorganized Church of Jesus Christ of Latter-day Saints" (Mormons) have been preaching at Sherburnville recently, but they had very little success in convincing the people that their doctrines are true. If you wish to post up on that form of heresy read D. H. Bays' book, "Doctrines and Dogmas of Mormonism," Christian Pub. Co., $1.50. It sweeps clean.

I have a full set (8 Vols.) of the "Nicene Fathers" in cloth, in splendid condition, that I will sell at a rare bargain. They cost me, new, $28.00, and will take $16.00 for them. Speak quick.

W. D. DEWEESE.

Kankakee, Ill.

From Butler County, Kansas.

The Butler County Co-operative Convention began its sessions here, in Augusta, at 7:30 P. M., Nov. 25, and closed the evening of Nov. 27. The addresses by the pastors and others were of a high order. Bro. E. E. Cowperthwait, of Eldorado, gave us a very excellent address the first evening of the convention. The second evening Bro. O. L. Cook, our state superintendent of missions, addressed us, also Lord's day, morning and evening, and at 3:30 P. M. he gave an illustrated address to a mass meeting of the children of the town. In the mind of him who knows the work that Bro. Cook does there can be no doubt as to the wisdom of our state board in selection him for the work to which they called him. The work that he accomplishes is a good illustration as to what consecrated scholarship and good judgment can accomplish. To say that the people of the church here and town, and of the entire convention, who heard him, were entertained, edified and drawn nearer the Master, would be speaking no more than the truth. To state the fact mildly and in short, his visit among was a complete success.

Now a word for the state work. How any one can say that the giving of money to the state work is a waste of money is a mystery, unless it be because of the ignorance of the work done, or because of covetousness. Bro. Cook, or a man who can do a similar work, is absoultely indispensable in any state where we would cause our work to succeed, at least this assertion is true of Kansas. The work done speaks for itself. This work in our state needs a stronger support than it is receiving. We are not doing for it what we are able to do. Let us give our board the $5,000 asked for, for this year, and many a word of praise will be spoken for the work done under the management of the state board that has not been heard hitherto because the support has not been sufficient to push the work according to the desire.

Brother preacher, give the state work your port, it is your true friend. Brethren in Christ in the State of Kansas and other states freely support it by your prayers and money for experience declares that under wise management of the money by the board that money is converted into a great moter-power that sends the gospel with a speed that could not be approached by a haphazzard, unorganized effort.

S. H. GIVLER.

Augusta, Kan., Nov. 28, 1898.

State Mission Notes.

One of the best workers in the field is J. B. Marley, of Piedmont, evangelist in Southeast Missouri. He has recently met with a severe loss in the destruction of his home by fire. This coming at the beginning of the winter season makes it doubly hard. By great good fortune the furniture was all saved, but in that broken and dilapidated condition so usual in case of fire.

The above item is my text, and I want to preach every friend of the cause in Missouri a short sermon. It is usual at state conventions to make a plea for funds, but you know that largely owing to my absence this was not done at Nevada. The money thus obtained was used to keep the work going for the first two months, in which but little money came in. Thus you see there was no provision for this time of scarcity this year. The convention kindly voted me a month's vacation, but when I discovered the true state of affairs I could not take it, but plunged right out into the field and have been working harder than I ever did in my life that the men in the field might have their funds.

I find that with all my individual effort we are running short. No one man can do the work of the office and obtain all the funds; he must have helpers. Brethren, this appeal is made to you and it is made with confidence that it will not fall upon deaf ears at all. Our growth in the state has been wonderful, and it has been such largely because of the efficiency of the state mission work. We are proud of the enlargement that God has given us, but let us look at it a moment.

During the last two years the mission work has put into the field 100,104 days' work, and preached 74,356 sermons and addresses, or to put it in another way, has crowned the life work of 20 efficient, enthusiastic preachers of the Word. What a mighty factor in our growth! There have been 600 churches organized in the last ten years and the mission forces have organized 424 of them. There has been a net increase of 75,740 in the last decade and in the same period the mission forces added 41,523.. Then who can tell how much of this other work has been inspired by the influence of their mighty evangelistic force at work in the state? We number 161,013 in the state, we have 1,575 churches; now substract the number of churches and additions that stand as the result of the mission work and what would have been our position as a people in the state but for this work?

What then? Shall we let go in any sense of this work? Surely not. Yet, it must lag unless the brotherhood shall rally to its support. Will not every preacher in the state take the above facts and present them to his people and ask for the apportionment? They will give it. They need only to be informed. Examples: L. J. Marshall presents the case at Palmira; their apportionment is $25, result collection $41.50; Simpson Ely goes to his people personally, in home, office and store and in three hours has the full amount of Kirksville's apportionment. Two different plans, but the result is the same. Su pppse each preacher in the state would do as well? One thing sure you would have a happy secretary. Try it. Our men are in want. Give us your help. Yours in His Name,

4144 *Westminster Place.* T. A. ABBOTT.

November a Great Month.

Comparing the receipts for *Foreign Missions* for the month of November with the corresponding month last year shows the following:

Contributing	1897	1898	Gain
Churches	8	16	8
Sunday-schools	18	7	Loss 11
Individuals	47	73	26
Endeavor Societies	11	10	Loss 1
Amount	$4,011.33	$9,392.03	$5,380.70

We are making a fine start on the new year. If the friends continue their liberality, we are sure of reaching $150,000 for Foreign Missions this year. The first two months of the new missionary year brought $17,186 43. Let us keep up these good returns all through the year.

F. M. RAINS, Treas.

Box 750 Cincinnati, O.

Evangelistic.

INDIANA.

The Daily Independent reports Evangelist Omer in a good meeting at Bedford.

TEXAS.

Percy T. Carnes reports seven additions to the church at Staly, Dec. 4.

TENNESSEE.

Springfield, Dec. 5.—I just closed a meeting at Grace Chapel, Montgomery county, with 15 additions, 12 by baptism. This makes 17 additions since the Chattanooga Convention. After a month's absence in evangelistic work I return to advance the spiritual interests of our home congregation.—LOUIS D. RIDDELL.

OHIO.

Hopedale.—Am in a meeting here with home forces. Two confessions to date and increasing interest.—P. H. WILSON.

IOWA.

Cherokee, Dec. 5.—Our meeting begins with 10 added. Interest and audience growing.—F. H. LEMON.

What Cheer, Dec. 7.—We are in a good meeting here, one week old. Six additions.—R. C. OGBURN.

Dows.—The meeting is one week old. The audiences are good. They pay good attention. The prospects are bright for a good meeting. We expect a singer this week. I would like to hear from some singers.—F. L. DAVIS.

Wm. E. Bute, of Stanhope, reports six additions Dec. 4. A protracted meeting was to begin on the 10th inst. Work on the new house likely to be postponed on account of cold weather. Will cost $1,800 when completed.

Elliott, Dec. 7.—I am assisting T. J. Reznor in a meeting, which is now 10 days old. Two added to the church by statement and four confessions. Crowded house and splendid interest.—M. C. JOHNSON.

We closed our first meeting a few days ago at Irwin, where I minister half time, with 10 additions to the church; eight confessions. The good effect of the meeting was further apparent in the manifest improvement in the spiritual condition of the membership of the church. Much of this interest is doubtless due to the excellent services of Bro. Frank McVey, our singer, who is one of the most excellent of Israel's sweet singers. Bro. McVey has kindly consented to help me in a few more meetings this winter, and any church in need of a good meeting at small cost may write me for particulars. Would like to commence immediately after the holidays.—D. H. BAYS.

Central City.—Twenty-three added in the D. A. Wickizer meeting.

Delta.—Pastor Fisher holds his own meeting and reports 25 added; all confessions and baptisms save three.

KANSAS.

Galena, Dec. 9.—One confession and one by letter on Dec. 4, and one confession and two by letter in November.—R. A. THOMPSON.

Parsons, Dec. 5.—Our meeting has resulted in much good; 14 added to date.—W. W. BURKS, pastor, C. E. MILLARD, singer.

Council Grove, Dec. 2.—Am in a meeting at Fairview S. H., 10 miles out in the country. Began 27th ult. One candidate for baptism.—J. A. WALTERS.

Chas. M. Sharpe reports 21 baptisms and nine additions otherwise at Lawrence in the 24 days' meeting, assisted by W. S. Priest.

Larned, Dec. 5.—Four were added to this church yesterday. C. W. B. M. Day a grand success. The writer has been elected county president of the Pawnee County Sunday-school Association for the ensuing year.—C. H. HILTON.

Newton, Dec. 3.—I am preaching at Mound Ridge, McPherson Co., half-time. The church is in good order. They have a good house well furnished and all paid for. Have just closed a three weeks' meeting here. Elder Hale, of Kingman, did the preaching. There were three additions by letter and nine confessions. A large majority of the settlement is Mennonite, but we will build up a very good church at that point. Bro. Hale is an excellent young man in every way and a good preacher.—AMMI FIKE.

MICHIGAN.

Buchanan, Dec 6.—Thirteen more added last night; 140 in all to date; will continue few days. Will dedicate the new church building at Antioch, O., Christmas Day and begin at Youngstown, O., Jan. 1st. Pastors would do well to write and ask Bro. E. R. Black, here, *how to prepare for a meeting*.—C. R. SCOVILLE.

PENNSYLVANIA.

Beaver, Dec. 6.—Two confessions at Beaver on last Lord's day evening. Just starting in my new field.—Z. E. BATES.

OREGON.

Eugene, Dec. 4.—Five confessions to-night; eight added first week. We continue.—MORTON L. ROSE.

OKLAHOMA TERRITORY.

Ponca, City, Dec. 6.—I began a meeting here Nov. 29th; have had four additions, two by confession. This is a new country and every opposition to Christian progress is exerted here. There are 14 saloons and four churches. Our church is the best location in town and our people are holding their own. They need a good pastor now. Mrs. Dora Short is clerk. Yours all along the line.—ELLIS PURLEE, Pawnee Rock, Kan.

MINNESOTA.

Sharon, Dec. 7.—We closed our meeting here with seven baptisms; some by statement and reclaimed. A good meeting. We begin a meeting at Ashland, Neb., the 15th inst.—GREGG AND SWEETMAN.

ILLINOIS.

Blandinsville, Dec. 4.—One addition to the Old Bedford Church last Sunday at regular service.—A. R. ADAMS.

Dixon, Dec. 5.—The Lord is certainly prospering our work here in Dixon. Seven during October, seven during November and six last Lord's day eve. Some every Sunday.—S. H. ZENDT, pastor.

Marshall, Dec. 7.—Our meeting here with J. I. Gunn and C. A. Burton closed Sunday night. We go from here to Metcalf, this state, to aid C. H. Berry in a meeting. Churches or evangelists desiring to make engagements with me for the new year can address me at Metcalf, Ill.—C. M. HUGHES, singing evangelist.

Elkhart, Dec. 6.—A good leader of song and soloist might address me at Elkhart, Ill. Am in a meeting at Latham at this writing for a few days.—M. L. ANTHONY, state evangelist.

Litchfield, Dec. 5.—After exceedingly hard work our meeting is being blessed of God; 14 added; congregation has decided to remodel their house and made it modern; have invited me to help them for three or four months in this work. If we do so will begin March 1st, 1899.—W. A. MELOAN.

Normal, Dec. 6.—Four added by letter recently.—E. B. BARNES.

Watseka, Dec. 5.—Yesterday was truly C. W. B. M Day with this congregation. The program carried out in the evening under the direction of our society was one of the best I ever heard. I am sure the large congregation present receive lasting good from it.—B. S. FERRALL, pastor.

Chapin, Dec. 10.—Meeting here with W. H. Cannon preaching continues; 11 days old with 11 accessions, five are young men.—A. O. HUNSAKER.

Blandinsville, Dec. 8.—Our meeting is in the second week with 15 added. Eight came forward last night. We hope for many more.—J. S. CLEMENTS.

Windsor, Dec. 8.—Our meeting of 18 days at Gays closed last night with 23 additions and a fine interest. Bro. Mark Sexton rendered valuable aid. Here is my hand for 100,000 additions in 1899.—A. H. HARRELL.

Peoria, Dec. 10.—Marion Stevenson, pastor of the Edwards Street Christian Church, Decatur, has just closed a meeting with the Central Christian, Peoria. The meeting resulted in 28 added to the church. Aside from the additions the church was greatly strengthened by Bro. Stevenson's work. He is pre-eminently a preacher of the "Word."—J. P. MCKNIGHT, pastor.

The church at Blue Mound, Ill., has secured J. R. Crank for its minister for the ensuing year.

MISSOURI.

Kansas City, Dec. 8.—A most delightful meeting of three weeks' duration at the 6th and Prospect Ave. Church; 40 added. Bro. H. A. Northcutt was with us, and his practical sermons, his tender, winsome heart-messages will live with us through all the days.—GEO. H. COMBS.

J. M. Tennison, writing from Lamar, Mo., says that since giving up his position with the National Orphans' Home of the Christian Church to go to his family in California, he has been without regular work. He says that he was never in better health than now or better capable of efficient pulpit or pastoral work, and would be glad to correspond with or visit if necessary any church or churches wishing his services. He desires an early engagement.

Kansas City, Dec. 6.—We closed a three weeks' meeting with the 6th and Prospect Church last night. There were 40 additions. The weather was bad all the time, but we had a fine meeting. This is a strong church. Brother Combs, who has been pastor here five years, is doing a great work. He is one of the best pastors I ever knew.—H. A. NORTHCUTT.

Bigelow, Dec. 5.—We are in a good meeting since Nov. 22nd. Five additions to date; four by confession, one reclaimed. Good audiences and good attention. F. E. Blanchard, of Barnard, is doing the preaching and doing it well.—J. R. HARLAN, pastor.

St. Louis.—First Church, eight additions; Compton Heights, nine additions; Fourth Church, three additions.

Sedalia, Dec. 5.—We have just closed our series of meetings for the year, resulting in 79 additions. We held meetings in the following places: Wheeling, Fulton County, Ark., Christian Union, Smithton, Calhoun, Sprague and Grand Pass. Quite a number were from the different denominations. We threw no rocks, but gathered the sharpest arrows from the quiver of divine truth and shot at the hearts of men and women.—J. I. ORRISON.

Cameron, Dec. 5.—Five additions at our regular services since last report; three yesterday and two Nov 27. We are closing up the year encouragingly in every way.—S. J. WHITE.

Center, Ralls County, Dec. 6.—Just closed a two weeks' meeting at Salt River Church, with seven confessions and two reclaimed. This was my fourth year's work there and my fourth meeting. They gave me a call for another year. One confession recently at Spaulding.—W. D. MCCULLEY.

Columbia.—We are in a vigorous campaign here through the leadership of Bro. Winders. He has his congregation thoroughly organized, and as a result the church is constantly growing numerically and spiritually. We had 10 confessions from Christian College girls last Lord's day at our usual service. Our house is crowded every Lord's day, and confessions are taken frequently.—J. W. MONSER.

Rock Port, Dec. 5.—Meeting eight days old. One addition to date; growing interest. Organized a Ladies' Aid Society. We are quite hopeful of progress all along the lines of church work.—S. W. GLASCOCK, evangelist.

Louisiana.—J. B. Corwine held us a meeting of 18 days, closing the 3rd of November. His sermons were as fine as I have ever listened to. Five confessed Christ, and the church was greatly helped by his earnest and faithful work.—E. J. LAMPTON.

Family Circle.

Communion.

STELLA CLANTON.

Whenever thou hast drawn apart
From all the cares and petty strife,
That vex the mind, and wring the heart,
To fit the soul for higher life;
Hast thou not felt within thy breast
A joy most holy and profound,
That quiets all the deep unrest,
And spreads a rapturous peace around?

Thou knowest it well. At evening close,
Thy labors ended for the day,
When humbly, ere thou sought repose,
Thou hast turned to God to pray;
Then, ere thy full petitions cease,
Over thy soul, before so sad,
Has stolen this sweet sense of peace,
And made thy drooping spirit glad.

'Tis God's own presence that we feel,
The presence of the Eternal One.
He draweth near when mortals kneel
To humbly say, Thy will be done.
Oh God, will all our life with Thee
Be like unto this taste of bliss?
Will all the years that are to be,
Be full of peacefulness like this?

Phœnix, Ar.

"The Greatest Enemy of the Army."

T. H. EDWARDS.

It would hardly see mnecessary in this sign of the coming of the "New Time" to accentuate the fact that the habit of indulging in intoxicants by any people or nation is deleterious to the general health, morals and intellect of an individual or nation; and especially to the physical development of the growing youth. Ask any of our most experienced, up-to-date, well read and close and observant physicians (who will answer *honestly*), and he will tell you alcohol, wine, beer or malt liquors are enervating and destructive to vital energy and to that development that should be attained in manhood, both physically and intellectually, say nothing of the moral degradation that it produces upon any people or nation who are known to indulge in the same as a beverage. The numerous testimonials of those who are the greatest experts of the day in *Materia Medica* and physical culture admit that the indulgence in the social glass, though a stimulant for the time being, soon causes the subjects given to such a habit to collapse and are less able to perform any arduous undertaking that takes mind or body.

The writer was a soldier for three and a quarter years in our Civil War who previous to his enlistment was a student and not a robust person, serving side by side with the mechanic and rugged farmer, but during his service of over three years did not indulge in any kind of intoxicants, yet came out whole, while those who drank and were much stronger physically broke down before serving out their terms of service, caused from dissipation due to drink and the evils that follow close upon such a course; they were the ones who paid little attention to the laws of hygiene, putting no restraint upon their inordinate desires and appetites; it was this class of soldiers who filled the hospitals, the last to rally from the disease and constituted the greatest number on the death roll; who did not serve their country so well while ving or fill out their three years of enlistment, nor were they any braver in facing the enemy, nor while in action kept their heads and nerves as well as those who abstained from the use of liquor; as a general rule I mean (I am speaking in the concrete as it were).

Let any one read Dickens' "Nicholas Nickleby," "Little Dorrit" and other of his works and he will see who were in the debtor's prison who were the imbeciles, who were the children brought into the world with appetites for the demon alcohol inherited from drunken parents whose bodies were poisoned and enfeebled by that which blights the intellect, dulls the moral sense and eats out the vitality of those who are its slaves like a cancer gnawat their vitals.

The allowing of the canteen system in the camps of our late army was a shame, a disgrace and a curse to the American army, a blot upon our national emblem that should bring a blush to the cheek of any true lover of our country, an injustice and an outrage against the feelings of the patriotic and virtuous mothers and fathers who sacrificed so much as they with ill forbodings of the dire calamities of war, with heavy hearts and prayers to God gave their sons to go forth and battle for humanity, for the rescue of the oppressed and the securing the rights of a down-trodden people.

No general that had the character of those young men from the fireside and influence of a Christian home at heart, with a true love of home and country in his soul, would have consented for a moment to have that enter into or allowed to follow in the wake of the army which is the downfall and cause of the destruction of his men, more than all the bullets of the enemy could possibly effect, and nothing but evil consequent upon such a permission; no commander of any moral standing—or a fool—would argue that the use of liquor would make a braver or more desirable soldier. Such a pretense could only issue from the mouth of a debauchee. I care not how high he ranks in military life, such reasoning is illogical and futile in this enlightened age. Why is it when the pugilist goes into training is forbidden to indulge in drinking and all other excess and special diet prepared for him if he is not thereby much better fitted to meet his antagonist? His trainer knows it, and he knows it, for he has reputation and his own and his friends' money at stake. "Wine, women and song" are not for him then, but regular and nutritious diet, regular hours for sleep and regular hours for hard work, that his eye may be clear, his heart beat regularly and his muscles become hard.

An officer who has so little respect for himself, his command or his country as to be found under the influence or drink with liquor should upon the first offence forfeit his commission and be dishonorably discharged.

We will never have an ideal army or navy until the moral character of an officer for promotion or retention in office shall be the first element in his make-up alongside of his being physically and intellectually competent. We want more characters like a Stonewall Jackson that the rank and file may emulate the bravery and virtues of all such commanders.

It is when the political trickster and dishonest schemer has no hold upon the public conscience, in our halls of Congress, legislature or our army will this nation stand forth as that of a truly God-fearing people, and this will come to pass when the masses vote for the *man* and not the *party;* when not money shall be the prime factor for lifting a man into office, but brains and honesty shall be the requisite attainments, then will the new time be.

Quincy, Ill.

Peleg.

BY F. M. GREEN.

The history of Peleg is as old as man, though he was not named for a great while after he was born. The real man Peleg was the son of Eber, and when he died he had tormented the world two hundred and thirty-nine years. Peleg means "Division," and if there is anything in a name, he made things lively. If he had lived as long as Methuselah there is no knowing what would have happened. But as a man he lived at the time of the transition from the antediluvian to the postdiluvian duration of life. Noah lived 950 years, Shem only 600, Arphaxed the first born of Shem after the deluge, only 438; and when we come to Peleg, who seems to have been contemporary with the dispersion, life is still shorter. Peleg lived 239 years, Reu his son 239 years, Serug, his grandson, 230 years, and Noah, his great-grandson, 148 years. He was born about 1,757 years before Christ was born in Bethlehem. Of his personal life only two or three sentences are spoken. Perhaps the reason for this is that his deeds would speak for themselves. The Peleg family is widely scattered. It has no particular country for its home, and if it had it would not live in it very long, for some would go to the left and some to the right, for is not their name "Division?"

Nations have their Pelegs, and it is a hard thing for the best of governments to keep them in line. They have their political wedges always ready for use and batter and storm until they lie down in their last sleep. To have a united country would be like purgatory to them—they are always for division.

The church has its Pelegs, and there is no congregation so small that some member of the family is not present. They divide and subdivide until only John and his wife are left, and then they apply for a divorce! The Pelegs somehow have great influence and the shadows of their giant forms cover some of the fairest portions of the earth as with a mantle. Their Gauls are divided into more than three parts. One strange characteristic of the Peleg family is that they are not satisfied in dividing the family, the neighborhood, the church, the nation or the world, but will even divide their own personalities so that a war is continually going on in their own members. No peacemaker, however blessed, has ever yet been able to absolutely conquer them. The ages have been compelled to endure their blighting influence and the prospect is that so long as "man is vile" the world will be pestered by their presence.

Kent, O.

Fishers of Men.

BY WILL H. DIXON.

Down by the *sea* of the mild *Galilee*,
The Savior passed time and again;
From the shore of the sea, He called, "Follow me
And I'll make you fishers of men."

He is calling to-day, in the same earnest *way;*
He is calling for fishers again;
And the brightest names *known* up around God's *throne*
Will be those who were fishers of men.

Rock Island, Ill., Oct. 25, 1898.

Prayer.

J. MCK. HODGE.

One of the most potent factors for the promotion of spirituality is prayer. We cannot hope to grow in grace without it. So often in the study of God's Word do we find it enjoined upon us in such passages as, "Pray without ceasing," "Men ought always to pray and not to faint."

As a child should go to an earthly parent with every sorrow, to thank him for his good gifts, tell what his further desires are, and ask his counsel and guidance in all things, so ought we to approach our Heavenly Father. Not with the self-righteousness of the Pharisee, but with the humility of the poor Publican.

Our blessed Master has given us this assurance: "If ye abide in me and my words abide in you, ye shall ask what ye will and it shall be granted unto you."

Fellow-Endeavorers, let u spray more in our Society. It is the current that connects our hearts with God, whereby the light of heaven enters our lives and is reflected upon the world. Let the current be uneven and our light sputters, but let it be broken, no prayers ascending, and our light goes out. Perhaps we say we know not *how* to pray. Christ has given us a model, let us examine it. Remember, we are not heard for our much speaking, for he warns us against using vain repetitions as the heathens do. Their cry from morning till noon to their false gods when warring against Elijah was, "O, Baal, hear us! O, Baal, hear us!" And the Ephesians, when exasperated against the apostles, cried out for two hours, "Great is Diana of the Ephesians!" In the Lord's prayer note its brevity, its simplicity, its *multum in parvo*, yet how wide a scope it embraces.

The Jews looked with awe upon any approach to the Divine Presence. 'Tis sweet to know that we can come as one family to that throne of mercy and say with Jesus, our elder brother, as he has taught us, "Our Father which art in heaven." None but a child who has left home, and felt that longing desire to return to its sheltering fold, can appreciate the depth of feeling expressed in that word, "heaven," the home every Christian expects to enjoy.

"Hallowed be thy name." Do we always breathe that name feeling that a halo of sacredness is encircling it, and like Moses when approaching the burning bush, do we heed the cry, "Take the sandals from off thy feet, for the ground whereon thou treadest is holy ground?"

"Thy kingdom come," we say, and yet sit with folded hands and idle brain, doing nothing for its advancement. When will this kingdom come? When every knee shall bow and every tongue confess that Jesus is *the Christ*. How many have ever exhorted by word or deed one fellow-traveler to bow the knee to him or make that good confession. Our motto, "For Christ and the Church," is but the thought expressed in other words. Let us never again pray, "Thy kingdom come," without some personal effort to extend it. About the hardest thing in this world to conquer is our stubborn wills. To be subservient to him in all things, amid whatever trials and afflictions we are called upon to bear, we are totally inconsistent if we cannot in meekness and resignation say, with all truthfulness, "Thy will be done." Three times in the garden of Gethsemane did our Savior utter these words in praying, that the cup of death might pass from him, but when called upon to drink it he did so, even to the bitter dregs, his expiring breath a prayer for his enemies: "Father, forgive them, for they know not what they do." What an example for us to emulate!

"Give us this day our daily bread," and because we do not receive poundcake we murmur and complain, forgetful of the fact that "whatsoever ye ask in my name, *believing*, ye shall receive." Of course daily bread, as here used, does not literally mean bodily sustenance, but every actual need, both physical and spiritual, of a child of God. We don't lay enough stress on believing. We ask too doubtingly. The most essential element in prayer is faith. The apostles were told that if they had faith no greater than a grain of mustard they would say to the mountains, "Be thou removed and planted in the sea, and it would be done." Let us say as the father of the demoniac child did, "Lord, I believe; help thou mine unbelief."

Another vital principle underlying all acceptable supplications to the divine Father is the forgiveness of our enemies or those who wrong us in any way. If God were as tardy in granting us forgiveness, who sin against him hourly, as we are some imaginary and trifling wrong of a neighbor, I am afraid our names would be blotted out of the Book of Life. He has promised faithfully to forgive us if we forgive others, and that there may be no misunderstanding he adds in the same connection, "But if you forgive not men their trespasses, neither will your Heavenly Father forgive your trespasses."

Oh yes, we know the Lord's Prayer by heart. "Lead us not into temptation, but deliver us from evil." Now, we know the Lord tempteth no man, yet we plunge boldly into the very midst of temptations. The poisonous tongue of envy and malice darting its venom at us, the serpent lurking in the wine cup, the fascinations of the mazy dance, the enchanting card table—we gaze on them all and say, "Deliver us from evil." But only the lion-hearted can stand the assailant's darts, and if we would come out unscathed we must heed the "Lead us not *into* temptation." See to it, then, that no vain petitions ascend and ascribe to him all the honor and glory for what we were and are and yet shall be.

"Teach Me Thy Paths."

IDA B. DAVISON.

Show me Thy ways, O Lord,
Teach me Thy paths, I pray:
That I may do Thy will—
Walk with Thee day by day.

Choose out my paths for me,
Thou knowest what is best;
Whether 'tis joy or pain
Makest my life most blessed.

Be Thou my light and guide,
I am so apt to stray.
Help me to follow Thee
When Thou hast shown the way.

Lead me in paths so plain
I may not go astray;
Whene'er Thou callest me
May I make no delay.

I am Thy child, dear Lord;
Order my steps in love.
Into the paths of peace,
That lead to Thee above.

Eureka, Ill.

The Christian Life.

Christian character is most severely tested by the little trials of life. It is easy to "feel good" when in a religious meeting or in the company of religious persons conversing about spiritual things. Perhaps the courage which moved the early confessors of Christ to face martyrdom was not of a higher or finer quality than that with which many a modern housekeeper confronts the daily perplexities of life. The man who is able to pass the inspection of the members of his own household is a pretty good Christian. So is the one whose business associates and employees thoroughly believe in him. No one can deceive those who are constantly brought into intimate association with him. The mother who makes a Christian profession must have the grace of God in her heart if she wishes her children to venerate her life and her servants to honor her and speak well of her. One reason why so much of our religion fails to impress the world is because it is superficial. The complaining father, the scolding mother, the tricky business man, the bitter-tongued gossip—these, to mention no others, bring discredit to the cause of Christ and tend to harden the hearts of worldlings. Sometimes a single case of sharp practice by a church member does great harm in an entire community.

Our Lord submitted with unfailing patience to all the ills of human life. There was nothing effeminate about him. On the contrary he was the manliest man that ever trod the earth. Yet he was also the kindliest, and in his acquiescence in the misfortunes that befell him became a pattern and an example for us all. Though his own disciples constantly misunderstood him and were unable to grasp the spiritual significance of his mission, he never manifested the least irritability. And it was to that disciple who had denied him on that memorable night, proclaiming with bitter oaths that he knew not the man, that he sent a special message of cheer after the resurrection. He has promished to give us his Spirit. Without the fulfillment of that promise our efforts to be good and do good will prove melancholy failures. But the grace of God can so change the heart and transform the life that even the scoffing world will notice it.—*Central Christian Advocate.*

The First Idealist.

A jelly-fish swam in a tropical sea,
And he said; "This world it consists of Me;
There's nothing above and nothing below
That a jelly-fish ever can possibly know,
Since we've got no sight, or hearing or smell,
Beyond what our single sense can tell.
Now, all that I learn from the sense of touch
Is the fact of my feelings, viewed as such;
But to think they have an external cause
Is an inference clean against logical laws.
Again, to suppose, as I've hitherto done,
There are other jelly-fish under the sun,
Is pure assumption that can't be backed
By a jot of proof, or a single fact.
In short, like Hume, I very much doubt
If there's anything else at all without.
So I come at last to the plain conclusion,
When the subject is fairly set free from confusion,
That the universe simply centers in me,
And if I were not, then nothing would be."

That minute a shark, who was strolling by,
Just gulped him down in the wink of an eye,
And he died, with a few convulsive twists—
But somehow the universe still exists.

—*The Sabbath Recorder.*

The Professor's Downfall.

There has not been in the last few years a more dramatic realization of the perversion of the moral nature under the influence of the spirit of revenge than that which has occurred in one of the well-known colleges of the country. The name of the college and the name of the criminal have already been given too much prominence in the daily press, and we will not mention them.

In 1893 a brilliant graduate of one of our leading universities was appointed instructor in ethics and logic in a smaller college. The young man began with great promise. He had made a most remarkable reputation in his college, and had taken a special course in the theological seminary. He had won enviable scholastic distinction and reward as a student of the science of reasoning, and it seemed as if no one could be better able to teach students the difference between right and wrong in human conduct than he.

After three years' teaching, the president decided that he would have to dispense with the services of the young professor. His method of teaching was not satisfactory, and he was notified that he would not be reappointed.

The announcement inflamed the young logician. Thinking he was right in his methods, and that the president was wrong, he conceived the idea that the president was jealous of his success, and was therefore trying to get rid of him. This idea completely mastered him, and from that hour he determined to ruin the man he considered his enemy.

In the meantime he was dismissed from his chair by the board of trustees, and left the town. His insubordination before he left ruined his reputation, so that he could not obtain employment anywhere else as a teacher. Imagining that the president was still working against him, his hatred for the dignitary increased. He began to plan a series of revenges. He first purposed to burn the great college hall that had been erected at an expense of three hundred thousand dollars, arguing that the president would be held responsible for the fire.

This building he fired one winter night, and no one suspected him. Only one wing was burned, and the fire was thought to be due to some student's carelessness. Balked in his purpose, the vindictive man successively ruined the chapel organ, cut the class vines on the building, threw hymnbooks and Bibles in the well, spread tar on the chapel seats, and perpetrated a series of such petty and malignant atrocities that it seemed as if only a maniac could have done them. The design of all these acts was to injure the president by showing that he was not popular with the students, and could not control them.

An investigation was set on foot, and the professor was suspected. He was arrested, and within a week confessed enough to send him to state prison for twenty years. In his confession he said:

"I thought I was doing the college a good by having the president removed. I considered him a hypocrite, and thought he ought to go."

But when he spoke of the desecration of the chapel, he burst into sobs. "To think," he said, "that I could desecrate the pulpit at which I used to pray and the Bible I used to read to the boys! God will never forgive me for doing this."

The pitiful history of moral destruction just related shows what comes of taking a single evil passion into the soul. One such example should be warning enough.—*Youth's Companion.*

We Shall Know Each Other There.

[The following article and poem was sent us without credit to the paper in which it was published.—EDITOR.]

The minister of a fashionable church preached a beautiful sermon on this subject: "Shall We Know Each Other There?" He drew the picture of a very beautiful heaven. We would walk in sunlit groves, by the music of waterfalls and gaze out upon amaranthine fields. And teen too "we shall know each other there," said the minister, "and there'll be no strangers in the New Jerusalem; we'll all be friends."

"Beautiful," said Deacon Sham, as he trotted down the aisle.

"A lovely sermon!" said Miss Simpkins as she put her bony hand into the minister's. She was stopped by a poor mechanic, who came up and addressed the preacher.

"Mr. ——, I am glad we shall recognize each other up there."

"Yes," said the minister, "it is one of the great consolations of our religion."

"Well, I'm right glad we shall know each other. It will be a great change, though, for I have attended your church for over four years, and none of the members of this society have recognized me yet. But—we shall know each other there."

What is it you say, pastor,
We shall know each other there,
In that grand and glorious country,
Land so bright and pure and fair,
When death's valley we have crossed—
Crossed its dark and surging tide—
And have entered into heaven,
Where the good and pure abide?

Rich and poor meet here, together,
Pass within the same church door,
Listening to God's holy Word,
As you read it o'er and o'er;
Plebian and patrician come,
All together bend the knee,
But no look of recognition
Scarcely ever do you see.

You speak of the Heavenly City,
Of its streets of pearl and gold,
But without love to our brother,
We can never it behold;
Love as did our forefathers,
In those grand and good old days,
And when they met together,
It was to give their Maker praise.

It was only a little log meeting house,
But love was the foundation,
And their song was Hallelujah
To the God of all creation!
They took each other by the hand,
In a kind and loving greeting,
That went far to pave rough ways,
Till the next Lord's day meeting.

Know each other, pastor, there?
When our robes are spotless, white,
Know each other over there,
In the land of endless light?
Then why not live here together,
As one great united band,
That we may have a glimpse of heaven
Before we enter the goodly land?

MRS. A. L. OWEN.

"What wonderfully magnificent teeth you have, Miss Ancient."

"You flatter me."

"Not at all. I was only admiring their fine workmanship."

* * *

She. Oh, this voting is perfectly lovely. I never did enjoy anything quite so much. Let's go around and vote at all the places.

He. Well, I guess not.

She. Oh, you mean thing.

With The Children.

CONDUCTED BY
J. BRECKENRIDGE ELLIS, PLATTSBURG, MO.

Some of Us.

For a long time I had been wondering if I could not get up a society for boys and girls that would help to make them happy, and at the same time improve and broaden their minds. I had noticed that the page devoted to children, as a rule, was filled with little letters in fine type, written by children, that other children did not care to read. They usually ran thus: "I am a little boy, nine years old. I go to school, and I have two white kittens. I like your paper very much." I wondered if I could not conduct a page that boys and girls would care for. The CHRISTIAN-EVANGELIST offered me a page. On the third of November appeared my first article, explaining the Advance Society. Any one could become a member who agreed to *try* to do five things: read five pages of history and 30 lines poetry every week; memorize a quotation from a well-known author once a week; read a verse of the Bible every day, and keep an account of what and how much is read in a notebook. I promised that the ones who were faithful for twelve weeks would have their names printed in our List of Honor. At the same time I explained that we would, from time to time, have general subjects upon which to write, and while I hoped each would write a short piece upon such subjects, nobody was compelled to do so. I stated that the first subject would be the funniest story known to any one, which must also be a true story. I would select the funniest from those sent me and publish in one article, giving credit to each writer.

Here was my plan. The piece was printed on the 3rd. I was very anxious for boys and girls everywhere to give a little time to history and to poetry and to memorizing, because I knew this would help to make them brighter and happier. But I did not know how the children would receive the idea. I was impatient to know if the scheme would fail, but I waited, because that was all I could do. Now, on the very next day after the page was published, two girls sat down and wrote me a letter; of course I knew nothing about it till Monday, when two letters came in by mail. The first one I opened was from Paris, Mo., and said: "I have read the article about your Advance Society; I want to join it.—Macie Randall, 12 years of age." The other letter was from Stronghurst, Ill., and read: "After carefully looking over your account of the Advance Society, I have a desire to join, and and therefore send my name. I am 11 years old, and have been a member of the Christian Church for three years.—Beulah A. Woodside." So these two were the first to join. At first I thought of calling them the Mothers of the Society, but perhaps this would not be fair, since the paper is longer in reaching some states than others.

On Tuesday I received seven new names; on Wednesday, 12; on Thursday, five more. Since then only three days have passed without bringing me a welcome letter. I usually receive three a day. Monday before last, the time of sending to press, there were 120 members. So we have succeeded, and I am now to tell you about the ones who have joined. Florence Waller Smith, Dameron, Mo., is 12; she says, "I think the Society will benefit all children." Stella Linton, Wilson, Wis., is 13. She sent one of our true funny stories. Della Taylor, of Lamonte, Mo., is eight. Nora Cunningham, Cloverdale, Kan., is 11. Florence Belle Beattie will be nine on Christmas day. I think they ought to hang her up on the Christmas tree, don't you?

Roberta Broadhurst, Louisville, Ky., says: "I am 12 years old, and have been a member of the church since I was nine. Strange to say, I made confession under the preaching of an Ellis—Bro. W. E. Ellis, of Nashville, Tenn. If you are fully as good as he, you are just the one for me!" To this I can only answer, "I am going to try to be fully as good as Bro. E." Lane and Errett Van Horn, 11 and 10, hail from Birmingham, Ala. I think it is delightful for two in the same family to join. Their little sister, Nell, is eight and afraid she is too young to join, but I don't think so, since Lane says, "We read a great deal at our house." Gladys Eubank, 11, is from Paris, Mo. She says that her mother does not approve of her reading novels. I congratulate Gladys upon having such a wise mother. There are only a few novels fit for children to read, and it is better to read none than to experiment with the wrong kind. Bonnie B. Blakely, Williams, Ia., is another member. Mrs. Carrie Smead and Mrs. F. M. Lowe, of Kansas City, with Frank M. Lowe (age, 10) come on a postal card. I am glad to have these ladies among our number. I would hate to be the only grown-up member of the Society. Mrs. Mattie Dever, Hume, Ill., sends her son's name, Gerald, and calls the Society "a good thing." Mabel and Ella Cash (13 and 11), of Litchfield, Ill., resolved to join Nov. 3rd. By the way, perhaps *these* are the Mothers of the Society. Julia and Lola Cox, of Cox, Mo., are 11 and eight. Both send true funny stories. This time I will give Lola's:

"When my sister was little she broke her doll. The first time she ever saw me *she* looked and said, 'Isn't she pretty, mamma? And she won't break a bit!'" Nina Martin, Hawthorn, Kan., furnishes a true funny story: Beulah Campbell, two years old, had seen her mother pick a chicken. Shortly afterward, seeing her grandfather shingle one of her little uncles' heads, she asked, "Grandpa, why don't you pick my other uncle's head?" Floyd Chastain Reid, Ft. Lyon, Mo., lives in the country. He is eight. He tells this funny story:

Floyd's little city cousin is visiting him; when he is riding and comes to a creek or pond he cries, "Oh, look at that bunch of water!" or, "See that pile of water!" Once when Floyd was telling him where a branch ran to, they came to a large "bunch of water," and the cousin asked what it was. Floyd explained that it was a pond. "And where does the pond run to?" asked his cousin.

Eltah J. Vince, of Ventura, Cal., used to live in Huntsville, Mo., which was named for her grandfather. Two of her uncles are preachers, Geo. Shanklin and Bartlett Anderson; and another uncle is Senator Anderson of Missouri. She is nine; she has a sister who is seven, and neither have missed a school day this year. She says, "We have no church in the country, but go to town (twelve miles away) twice a month to church. We live on the big blue ocean, and see the ships. It is warm here, and our yard is full of flowers and they bloom all winter, and the trees are full of oranges. I went in the yard and got some flowers for the table this morning. Tell your little girls to write to me." I hope some of the Society will do so. Perhaps Eltah will send you an orange seed; or she might go down to the seashore and catch an oyster and put it in her envelope. I wish I could give her a bucketful of snow for a bucketful of oranges. But perhaps they don't eat oranges in the South; you know in the country people don't drink cream—they save it for butter. I would hate to see all my trees full of oranges and know that all had to be shipped North to market!

Other members of the Society are Clarence L. Blakely (nine), Williams, Ia.; Alvin Burleigh Cash (10), Pennirille, Ind.; Mattie Wilson (18), Troy, Mo.; E. Witmer Pardee (11), Snyder, N. Y.; Elizabeth Valpey (10), Warm Springs, Cal.; Delight M. Shafer, Lebanon, Tex.; Jessie L. Butler (12), Roseville, Ill.; Madge Masters, Ozark, Ark., (12). Here is a little band in Harlan, Iowa: three sisters (17, 15 and 12). They are Maude, Grace and Ethel Taylor. "We are three," they write, "and all very fond of reading, history especially. We are reading the Bible through now. We all belong to the Christian Church. We hope to have our names on the Honor Roll in three months." Children, wouldn't you like to peep in on that circle of girls? Just think! there are enough in one family to play any reasonable kind of game, or sing three parts in a song; besides that, one can clean the dishes, one can sweep and one can sit up in the parlor and be company.

I haven't said anything about members in Plattsburg. You have heard that a prophet doesn't have much honor in his own country, but that is not the case with me; perhaps I am not a prophet. Any way, there are a lot of members in my town, but I cannot name any more this time, because if I took up the whole CHRISTIAN-EVANGELIST some of the other writers, who have great long pieces, might not like to be crowded out. Week after next I will tell you about other members. Next week you will have another chapter of the continued story. In the meantime I wish all would write me their ten favorite books, and three favorite authors; if you are fifteen, or older, write what were your favorites before you were fifteen. We are going to hold an election, and you are to vote; I will print a list of the books and authors who receive the biggest vote, also the names of those who come nearest to naming the most popular. Remember, the Bible is not counted in the ten books, because I take it for granted that is the favorite of all. And if any one has a true funny story, let's have it.

ure.

By H. F. Kletz-
: Bros., Naperville,
365 pages, $1.00.
it to catch the eye
le at once. It is a
ncidents, anecdotes
ig and impressing
ought to be known
. Its short biogra-
n and women are a
ture of the book.

ES.

utauquan Mr. John
ral News Staff of
tainingly of "The Im-
With statistics of its
and poverty is woven
ard to the municipal
ctions of the county
lections, the parks,
illustrations accom-

mond, the eminent
iases, has written for
outh's Companion an
est on the wonderful
ters, and shows that
e at least, is a sleep-
also announces arti-
m Jacobi on "The
quarantine methods
an.

as shrouded the sud-
n Prince of Austria,
in the December
on makes known for
he tragic story of the
heir to the Austrian
es this fragment of
ing touch of one who
the facts he relates,
is residence in that

of St. Nicholas is full
as times. The song
s, "My Little Jim
Siberia," "Football
and Geese," "An
and "The Dream of
teresting themes of
he illustrations are
ian Potthast and
among the popular
ted to the spirit and
.

ber of the American
ws some of the most
paintings of the life
ssot are reproduced.
on Tissot's life and

The Christmas number of Scribner's Magazine has several notable art features. The brilliant cover in silver, gold, and colors is from a prize design by Albert Herter. There are also sixteen pages of color-printing of an unusual kind—reproducing Maxfield Parrish's very original scheme of illustration and decoration, accompanying F. J. Stimson's poetical version of a scene from Wagner's "Rhine-Gold." In the article on "John Ruskin as a Painter," Mr. Spielmann has included reproductions of many unpublished paintings and sketches, secured only by reason of his long personal friendship with Ruskin. Another artistic feature is the frontispiece by the young

Sunday School.

THE PROSPERITY, DECLINE AND FALL OF JUDAH.*

HERBERT L. WILLETT.

The lessons of the quarter, of which this is a review, have dealt with the story of the kingdom of Judah, the smaller portion into which the kingdom of David and Solomon was divided at the death of the latter. The whole course of its history continued from 937 B. C., the date of the revolt of the ten tribes, to 586 B. C., the date of the downfall of Jerusalem and the beginning of the Babylonian captivity. During these centuries the condition of the kingdom rose and fell as the character of the government was weak or strong.

Judah shared with Israel its northern neighbor and rival the possession of the faith of the earlier prophets. But this religion in Judah was the normal and prescribed worship, while in the north it was scarcely to be called a national religion, but struggled from the beginning with foreign cults that were introduced and fostered by kings like Jeroboam and Ahab. It seems never to have been considered necessary that the monarch of the northern kingdom should be a supporter of the Jehovah worship. Prophets like Amos and Hosea, not to speak of Elijah, could only protest against these heathen faiths as impotent and degrading. But the national faith was esteemed dangerous for political reasons in the northern kingdom, as it brought the people into a unity of sentiment with their southern neighbors of Judah, and thus was likely to bring about a return of the Davidic dynasty to its supremacy over both kingdoms. In these facts will be seen the reason why in the northern kingdom the successful kings were always the opposers of the worship of Jehovah, and the periods of greatest prosperity were those of greatest religious decline; while in the southern kingdom the opposite was true—the greatest kings were those who supported the ancestral faith, repaired the temple, encouraged reformations and opposed idolatry.

Of such kings the most conspicuous were Asa and Jehosaphat, Joash, Uzziah, Hezekiah and Josiah, and under them all the kingdom reached a high period of prosperity and the religion centered at the temple was duly observed. Under such kings also prophecy was encouragad and the preaching of such men as Micah, Isaiah, Jeremiah and others was aided by the royal influence.

The quarter's lessons present phases of life in Judah which illustrate these various forces working in favor of or against religion and morality. First, there is the reformation under Asa, whose reign, with that of Jehosaphat, his son, presents features of special interest as an example of what can be accomplished by a ruler whose purposes are high. Likewise, in lesson three there is told the story of the loyalty of Joash to the interests of the temple and his gathering of funds for its repair. These are characteristic pictures of the best selections of the earlier history of Judah. Then comes the period of Isaiah, whose life covered the interval of forty years from the death of Uzziah in 739 to the invasion by Sennacherib in 701. The story of his call to service is told in lesson IV. The vision of the holiness of God which impressed the young man with his own sinfulness and led to his pardon and his self-devotion to the service of a prophet, together with the divine warning of the apparent failure of his work, are narrated. From the book which bears his name there is presented in lesson V. one of Isaiah's characteristic pictures of the future, the golden age of peace when the kingdom of God shall have come. The influence of Isaiah must have been strong and persistent at the court of Hezekiah, for we find that king becoming a reformer of religion in his realm and observing a great Passover, the like of which had not been known for centuries. The ministry of Isaiah closed with the remarkable fulfillment of his predictions of the seige of Jerusalem and the overthrow of the Assyrian forces.

The third period gives to us glimpses of the last days of Judah and some of the factors which led to its downfall. Lesson VIII. tells of Manasseh's sin which wrought such havoc among the believers in Jehovah, and brought in such a flood of idolatry and superstition that even the royal repentance produced but a temporary reaction in favor of the true faith. Lesson IX. is an intercalary lesson on temperance, illustrating from the Proverbs the choice and outcome of the two paths. Lesson X. tells of the finding of the lawbook in the reign of Josiah, under the influence of which a great reformation was wrought. Lesson XI. introduces to us a king of very different sort, though he was the son of Josiah. Jehoiakim was godless, extravagant, and a hater of all that pertained to the true faith, and when the writings of Jeremiah were brought to him and read he cut them up with a knife and threw them on a braisure of coals, thinking thus to destroy the prophet's work. Such reigns as this and such a condition of the kingdom as they produced could only have one result, and that was the downfall of Jerusalem, the punishment of her kings and the exile of her people, who were carried away into the distant regions of Babylon to remain under discipline until a new generation arose who could go back to the old home without danger of those political and commercial temptations which had wrought disaster in the earlier days. Thus in rapid outline the leading features of that national history, the most interesting in literature, are presented in the lessons of the past quarter.

SUGGESTIONS FOR TEACHING.

These lessons present numberless points of value to teachers and students. It is the first business of a ruler to reform what is deformed (I). The best of campaigns is one in which the people are educated to a new sense of responsibility and devotion. This Hezekiah accomplished by his messengers; this we can accomplish to-day by the preaching of the gospel and by Christian literature (II). The repair of what has fallen into neglect, not only in religious buildings, but in religious ideas, should be the effort of every lover of truth. This work of devotion to the service of God may be costly, but nothing that is good comes without effort and sacrifice (III). The call of service comes to every person as truly as it came to Isaiah. God needs servants and prophets to-day as much as ever, and they need the same preparation for their work, though it need not come in miraculous form (IV). The religions of the world point to a golden age long past. The true religion points to an age yet to be realized but already begun by the ministry of Jesus. The characteristics of that time of blessedness are peace and kindness (V). The observance of the ordinances of religion, though they are few and simple, is necessary to a loyal obedience to God (VI). Fearlessness in the face of danger is one of the characterics of those who trust in God (VII). Repentance is always the key that opens the door of blessing (VIII). Every child stands at the point where the ways divide. The choice of the right path is the secret of success (IX). The Bible is truly found when it is approached in a reverent spirit, when it is liberated from the superstitions and speculations of men, and when real satisfaction is found in its study (X). We do not need to burn nor cut to pieces the Bible in order to destroy it. It is destroyed to all intents and purposes by any one who neglects it (XI). The consequences of a course of conduct often reveal the character of the conduct itself. Sin may be discovered most surely in its results (XII).

Anhaltstrasse 15, *Berlin*.

*Sunday-school Lesson for December 25, 1898, Review Golden Text—Return unto me and I will return unto you, saith the Lord of hosts (Mal. 3:7). Lesson Outline—1. The earlier period, Lessons 1-3; 2. The period of Isaiah, Lessons 4-7; 3. Judah's decline and fall, Lessons 8-12.

Christian Endeavor.

By Burris A. Jenkins.

TOPIC FOR DECEMBER 25.

TRUTHS TAUGHT BY CHRISTMAS.

(LUKE 2:8-20.)

The old glad season of Christmas rolls round with all its lessons and its memories of other years. What old, old lessons they are, and all the sweeter and all the more needful for that they are so old. Some things humanity learns in childhood need ever to be learned again, and yet again, even to second childhood; even then, perhaps, we shall need to sit at the Great Teacher's feet, to hear them over still. Your little children love their old stories best, and so we grown up children never tire of learning our oldest sweet lessons; with their depths of unsounded truth and their reaches of unexplored thought, over and over again. Welcome happy Christmas, with lessons as old as Jesus' name, as old as motherhood, as old as birth and life and love! The older thou growest the dearer! The whiter thy hoary locks the welcomer!

Is it not the very mixture of the lessons, the mingled strains which make up the harmony, the blending of light and shade, the minor chords of joy and pain, that makes the message of Christmas doubly pleasant? Mixed with the joy and eagerness of the shepherds, with the song of the angels, "Behold, I bring you good tidings of great joy," is the subdued light of sadness in the mother's face, the hush and awe and wander of Joseph. This mixed message has been detected by the great artists and in their "Holy Nights" and their "Madonnas," they have, the best of them, echoed yet again the minor strains of its sweet harmony. For is there not harmony after all, in the mingling of joy and pain?

"We look before and after,
And pine for what is not,
E'en our sincerest laughter,
With some pain is fraught,
Our sweetest songs are those
Which tell of saddest thought."

Although, perhaps, that poem contains a trifle too much of the sadder element for Christmas, yet even this gladdest season of the year weaves together this double message of joy and pain, this interweaving of light and shade, which makes up the music and the beauty of life.

Once a year the whole world pauses, as if Joshua had again bidden the busy sun of this world's activities to stand still, while man, woman and child are forced to meditate, as the songs of joy fill the air, on that birth and its meaning. Joy is the prevailing note; deliverance, redemption, bounty, outpoured love, forgiveness, universal mercy—all these swell in the hearts of the more thoughtful, as the lessons of the day, while ever the smallest child in the poorest home sees something in this Christmas day, something different from all other days, with its sprig of green and its toy. The joy of the giving is perhaps the highest joy that comes, the father's and the mother's joy, the son's and the daughter's joy.

But besides all this chorus of sounding happiness steals into our lives also the shade of sadness that stole into Mary's heart as she foresaw the destiny of pain that awaited Him. How many a parent's heart well-nigh breaks as it sees how little it can do for the one it loves, how hindered by one circumstance or another, poverty, illness, some misfortune of the child itself—who knows what! And the season brings with it, then, its great mysterious lesson of the sword-thrust through the heart. But nevertheless, in that night of the nativity the stars shine, and best of all the Star of Bethlehem, while over the heart of all the weary and the sad and the lonely, the poor, the tempted, and even the forsaken, if they will all but open their hearts to His holy influence, will be poured the mingled message of Him who was born in Bethlehem: "Peace I leave with you; my peace I give unto you. Peace on earth, good will to men." O, we would not have the lesson to be one of unmixed and brazen joy! That most perfect mother's life had its iron in the soul. That most perfect Master's life had its Gethsemane and cross. How, then, can we fulfill his word, "Be ye perfect," unless we feel the iron of woe and the cross of sacrifice? Let us learn, then, in all the joy of this happiest time—and welcome all its sunshine, too, Endeavorers, with open hearts—the lesson of Mary, "Behold the handmaid of the Lord; be it unto me according to thy word," and the lesson of Jesus, "Not my will, but thine be done."

BETHANY C. E. READING COURSES.

[There are three courses: The Bible, Missions and the Disciples. The three handbooks for the *first* year are: "A Guide to Bible Study," "Handbook of Missions" and "Concerning the Disciples." The three handbooks for the *second* year are: "Life and Teachings of Jesus," "Missionary Fields and Forces of the Disciples" and "Sketches of our Pioneers." Three handbooks and the Bethany C. E. Bulletin, quarterly, sent to any address for one dollar. All orders should be addressed to the Bethany C. E. Company, 798 Republic St., Cleveland, O. Each course has a director: H. L. Willett is director of Bible study; W. J. Lhamon is the director of studies in Missions; F. D Power is director of studies Concerning the Disciples. This column is set apart to the use of these directors.]

The Gospels and the Life of Jesus.

HERBERT L. WILLETT, *Director*.

It is natural for the readers of the Gospels to think that the life of Jesus is quite fully contained in these four narratives; and yet nothing could be further from the fact. The Gospels are indeed scarcely more than brief tracts whose purpose was not to tell the story of Jesus' life, but to present some phases of it or some incidents from it which would prove convincing to those who read or heard. Perhaps in no particular do the Gospel narratives present more convincing proofs of the divine element in them than in the selection of material and the brevity of the accounts where so much must have impressed the writer as worthy of record. Out of the vast mass of sayings and doings of Jesus there have come to us what seem exceedingly scanty memorials of his life. And yet these are amply sufficient for all the purposes of the gospel.

We are also struck with the singular absence of attention to the order of events in the life of Jesus and the corresponding lack of notes regarding the times at which the various incidents took place. The writers seemed but little concerned with the sequences of events and made but little effort to connect them in regular manner, either with each other or with external events that would have given them an orderly setting. This is especially true in the Synoptic Gospels. The Gospel of John much more frequently refers to feasts held by the Jews (Ju. 5:1; 7:1-10; 12:1; 13:1), and a few times notes are found in Luke relating to the political history of Palestine (Luke 1:5; 2:1, 2; 3:1, 2). The order of events in Jesus' life seems to be most clearly presented in the Gospel of Mark, if we are at liberty to say that any of the Gospels attempt any regular arrangement. But this characteristic of Mark we should expect from the fact that he deals more with the external events of Jesus' life and less with his teachings. In general Matthew and Luke follow Mark's arrangement of material, but without any apparent effort to conform to any plan of time.

It is this fact which makes the task of producing a chronology of the life of Jesus so difficult. If the motive of the Gospel writers had been historical or chronological the task would have been comparatively easy; but their purpose was far other than this. And it is fortunate from every point of view, save that of the student of history, that the records were prepared just as they were. In the large sphere of the world's spiritual education we should have been the losers by any other plan than that which was followed. As it is the Gospels present four views of the life of Jesus, three of which stand closely connected with each other, and are yet quite independent of each other in spirit and purpose, and the fourth wholly unlike the other three. These four narratives present a composite picture of the Master which, though it omits many details which we should greatly desire to know, still preserves to us the leading characteristics of his person and his work, and thus gives to us the basis for our faith and hope.

It has been suggested by some of our readers who are taking the first year's course, that the Bible readings provided in the October Bulletin do not fit their course of reading, which is a general review of the Bible on the basis of the first handbook of last year, on Bible Study. It is therefore the purpose to present hereafter two sets of Bible readings, one for those taking the introductory year and one for those pursuing the current year's work, and in the January Bulletin this change will be made.

Marriages.

AZDELL—BERRY.—Married at the home of the bride's parents in Mexico, Mo., Oct. 19, 1898, Mr. J. E. Azdell and Miss Minnie E. Berry; J. D. Green officiating.

COBLE—MILLION.—At home of the bride, Hopedale, Ind., Oct. 19th, 6 P. M., Mr. Culver Coble and Miss Stella Million, by A. W. Gehres.

FREDERICK—DEHONY.—At the home of the bride's parents, four miles east of Mooresville, Ind., Nov. 27, 1898, Herman O. Frederick and Bertha Dehony; Willis M. Cunningham, of Franklin, Ind., officiating.

HENDERSON—RIVERS.—At the home of the bride near Providence, Ind., Celsaw B. Henderson and Lora D Rivers were united in marriage Nov. 9, 1898, by Willis M. Cunningham, of Franklin, Ind.

LEACH—PACKWOOD.—Married at Bethany Church, Parsons, Kan., on the evening of Nov. 23, 1898, at 8:30, by C. C. Deweese, Mr. Charles A. Leach and Miss Lucinda E. Packwood, both of Parsons, Kan.

REECE—DE VORE.—At the parsonage of the Christian Church, Thursday evening Nov. 17, 1898, Thos. Reece and Miss Sarah De Vore; A. W. Henry officiating.

Obituaries.

[One hundred words will be inserted free. Above one hundred words, one cent a word. Please send amount with each notice.]

GLENN.

Mrs. America Craig Glenn, born in Harrison Co., Ky., Oct. 19, 1818, died Nov. 24, 1898, aged 80 years, one month and five days. She was married Nov. 4, 1838, to Jno. M. Glenn, who died Aug. 25, 1876. To this union were orn ten children, eight of whom had crossed the silent river before her, five of them being grown before they died. She leaves two devoted sons—Pearl Glenn, of Paris, Mo, and French Glenn, of Nevada, Mo,—to mourn their loss in her departure. She was a true, practical Christian, a member of the Church of Christ for several years before exchanging the cross for her crown. In bereavement and cares she lived a noble life and has gone through much tribulation to a sorrowless shore.

C. H. STRAWN.

HARMISON.

Emma E. Tesler, the youngest daughter of Mr. and Mrs. Jacob Tesler, was born in Derry Township Jan. 15, 1863 and died Nov. 19, 1898. She was married to Jessie L. Harmison Oct. 31, 1883. She united with the Christian Church at El Dora, Ill., August, 1895. She has in every way proven herself to be a faithful and practical member of the church. She leaves a husband, two brothers and three sisters besides a host of relatives and friends to mourn their loss.

J. D. DARNEY.

El Dora, Ill.

LUCAS.

Albert Wilbraham Lucas, eldest son of Bro. and Sister J. P. Lucas, died in Colorado City, Col., the home of his parents, Monday morning, Nov. 28, 1898, aged 17 years, seven months and seven days. Albert was born in Vandalia, Michigan, April 21, 1881. He confessed Christ as his personal Savior and Lord in Emporia, Kansas, March 25, 1894, and was baptized by his father, who was at that time pastor of the Emporia Church of Christ. Albert was faithful in the discharge of his duties as a member of the church, Sunday-school and Society of Christian Endeavor. Bro. and Sister Lucas came to Colorado City from Creston, Iowa, last July, on account of the illness of their son. They hoped that this healthful climate would arrest the progress of the disease and prolong the life of their son, but it was too late. The dear boy made a heroic struggle for life, but in vain. He had an ambition to live that he might do good—especially that he might be helpful to his father in caring for the family. Albert was an unusually good boy. Though for months he was feeble, because of the disease which finally conquered him, he was not confined to his bed for a single day. He was sitting in his chair when the arrow of death smote him. He quietly fell asleep in Jesus as the bright rays of the morning sun were gilding the snow crowned summit of Pike's Peak, portentous of the dawning glory of that bright and eternal day that shall come to all such pure spirits through the mediation of the Son of God. Just nine months ago Bro. and Sister Lucas buried their eldest daughter, Nettie Glenn, in Bedford, Iowa, in which place Bro. Lucas served as pastor from 1883 to 1888. It was Albert's request that his body should be placed by the side of that of his sister. It was on the morning, therefore, of Nov. 29th that the grief-stricken father started to Bedford on the mournful journey. Albert leaves, besides his father and mother, one sister, Leona, and a younger brother, George, with a host of friends in Colorado Springs, Colorado City, and elsewhere, to mourn his departure. But they do not mourn as do those who have no hope through Jesus Christ our Lord. Albert and Nettie, hail and farewell! We shall meet you in the sweet by and by! J. P. Lucas is pastor of the Christian Church in Colorado City, and is greatly beloved by his people, and is highly esteemed in the community. The pastors of the Baptist and Methodist Churches assisted in the funeral services.

B. B. TYLER.

METZ.

On Oct. 15th, 1898, Lucinda Metz departed this life at the age of 74 years, five months and 13 days. She was born in Cincinnati, O. She died as she had lived with an abiding faith in Christ and was ready to go to the Savior. She leaves husband, three daughters and three sons. Mother of the writer.

A. D. METZ.

Wapella, Ill., Nov. 24, 1898.

MORIS.

Nelson Moris died at his residence near Fairfield, Wash., Nov. 22, 1898, at the extreme age of 82 years. He was born in Bucks Co., Pa., Dec. 27, 1816. When in his childhood his parents moved to Indiana where he spent his boyhood and early manhood, remaining there until 1863 when he crossed the plains and settled at the old homestead where he died. He was a kind and affectionate husband and father and a loyal citizen, but best of all he was a devoted Christian. He spent over a half century in the service of our Master. A wife and seven children survive him. The funeral services were conducted by the writer in the Mount Hope Church, at 12 o'clock on Thanksgiving Day. His remains were interred in the Mount Hope Cemetery. A large concourse of relatives and friends followed the remains to its last resting-place.

MELFORD W. SMITH.

PAGE.

Mrs. Flora Page French, youngest child of Moses P. Page, passed from death unto life, Nov. 6, '98, at Baker City, Oregon, where she was staid in the progress of an overland journey from Washington to Arizona, in search of healing air for her lungs. Her husband, Warren French, her sister, Mary Alice Page, and her three-year-old baby, Eugenie, were the only relatives beside her during her last earth-days, but strangers there were gracious friends, because one of Christ's own "was sick" they ministered unto her and, unto him. Life was sweet to Flora because there were those who loved her so, and whom she loved with joyfulness. She had a brave spirit and ever made a gallant stand against besetting hindrances to the realization of an ideal home here, but when her body fainted with its load of pain she leaned hard upon her Savior and longed to be at rest. All her asking was for the blessed Word and dear old hymns. And so she slept in peace, knowing that underneath were the everlasting arms. The earthly tabernacle was laid away, for the time, where her glad spirit had left it. So young, and already acquainted in two worlds! She was born in Illinois, Nov. 17, 1871, confessed Christ at the age of 13 in Allerton, married in Iowa, June 17, 1893, was a mother in 1895 and in 1898, saw "the King in his beauty in His ain countree."

P.

SILCOTT.

Mrs. A. J. Silcott was born in Holmes County, Ohio, Jan. 22, 1825; died Nov. 12, 1898. The deceased united with the Ripley Christian Church in 1846, and remained a faithful and zealous Christian till called to her reward. She leaves a husband, two daughters and a large circle of friends to mourn their loss. Funeral conducted by the writer.

M. GORSUCH.

STRUBINGER.

Burt F. Strubinger, son of Thomas C. and Sarah A. Strubinger, was born Oct. 25th, 1877, near El Dora, Ill., and died Nov. 21, 1898, at the home of his sister Mrs. Dr. Reynolds, of El Dora. He seemed to be in perfect health till Sunday when stricken with paralysis and lived only about 24 hours. He leaves a mother, three sisters and three brothers to mourn their loss He united with the Christian Church March 26th, 1898 and was a practical member of the church honoring his profession in social and business life. He will be greatly missed by us all.

J. D. DABNEY.

El Dora, Ill.

TAYLOR.

Mrs. Mary Jane Taylor, wife of Chas. G. Taylor, died in Fairfield, Iowa, Nov. 5, 1898, of typhoid fever. Sister Taylor made her confession of faith in Christ under the ministry of Bro J. B. Vawter and was baptized by him in 1877, and united with the church at Big Cedar, Iowa. She was an affectionate wife and daughter, gentle and kind in spirit and self-sacrificing in her work and care for others, and greatly beloved by all who knew her. She died comforted by her faith, and "was anxious to depart and be with Christ." Her husband and her aged parents are in great sorrow over their sore bereavement. The writer conducted the funeral obsequies, assisted by Bro. J. A. Raines.

LEANDER LANE.

THOMSON.

S. H. Thomson, 1335, 27th St., Des Moines, Ia., was found dead at the corner of 20th and Q Sts., Nov. 22nd. Bro. Thomson was employed by the Keystone View Co., of St. Louis. He was well dressed, but death, according to Dr. Furay, was plainly due to exposure in the storm with insufficient clothing. The remains were given in charge of G. H Bever Undertaking Co., South Omaha, Neb., who was ord red by relatives, on the 25th to send them to Joe Steellman, Dresden, Mo. Bro. Thomsom, whose home was in Missouri, had for many years been a resident of University Place, Des Moines, Ia., where he had been much of the time attending Drake University. Besides his school work, he had at Des Moines, at state and district conventions and on the road in Iowa and Missouri, represented the Christian Publishing Company, all of which gave him a very wide circle of acquaintances and as he was an earnest, Christian worker he had a great many warm personal friends. True to his custom, when he, several weeks ago, located in South Omaha he immediately identified himself with the work of the church there and was well known and much loved by the comgregation, who were making arrangements for his interment, if his friends had not been heard from. Bro. Thomson was, we believe, a member of the Volunteer Mission Band of Drake University and was planning to, at an early date, go to a mission field and he thought it more than probable that he would join his friend and fellowstudent, Bro. G. W. Coffman, Damo, C. P., India. Bro. Thomson's life was pure, he was a devoted follower of Christ and he leaves a wide circle of personal friends who will mourn his sudden takin away from life's industries in which he had high ambitions.

P.

TROUT.

Jeremiah Henson Trout was born in Trimble County, Ky., March 2, 1821 and died at his home in Waco County, Oregon, Oct. 23, 1898. Bro. Trout confessed Christ in his 19th year, and very earnestly and faithfully maintained his faith to the end. On his 27th birthday he married Mary Ewing, of Clark County, Mo. He lived in Warren County, Mo., from 1846 till 1863, then two years in Clark County, then 16 years in Scotland County, whence he moved to Oregon in 1881. He left a widow, one son and two daughters. Two children live in California, and one here.

P. P. UNDERWOOD.

Boyd, Ore., Nov. 23.

WIGHT.

John Morton Wight was born March 30, 1821, and passed to his rest Nov. 4, 1898, in his 78th year. He was born near Meadville, Pa., but spent 77 years in Andover, O. He studied law and was admitted to the bar from the law office of Senator Ben F. Wade. He became a Christian about 30 years ago, and was faithful to the last. His wife preceded him nearly three years and God made these, to him, blessed years of preparation. The last book he read was the Bible, and the Holy Spirit filled his soul with peace, patience, gentleness and love. He was an elder of the

Church of Christ at Padonaram as long as it existed. He leaves three sons and one daughter—William, of New York; Adelbert, of Salt Lake City; Frank, who was living with him when departed, and Iola, who is now living in Glendora, Cal. F. A. WIGHT.

WILLIAMS.

Died, Sister Minerva Jane Williams, whose maiden name was Lowery; was born Dec. 11, 1857. She was married to William C. Williams at the age of 27, Sept. 16, 1884. To this union was born seven children, five of whom are living; two boys and three girls. Sister Williams departed this life Nov. 18, 1898, age 41, living husband, five children, two sisters and one brother to mourn their loss. About one year ago the subject of this sketch became the victim of the dreaded disease, consumption, was confined to her room for many months. Her life grew more and more feeble, until at last her frail form succumbed to the inevitable. Sister Williams became a member of the Christian Church, being baptized by J. H. Coffee, Oct. 20, 1878. She lived a cc and was loved by all who kne her spirit took its flight she fr her ample preparations and excepting that she mourned i taken from her children. S benevolent disposition to Williams from earth that sl elysian abode of everlasting say in condolence to the bere trievable indeed is our loss!

Publishers' Notes.

The Christian Lesson Commentary for 1899, published by the Christian Publishing Co., St. Louis, Mo., is ready for delivery. It is ably written and contains maps and general helps for the study of the International Bible School Lessons. It is a commendable book. It has about 400 pages and is well bound.—*New England Messenger, Everett, Mass.*

Dr. I. Thayer, of New Castle, Pa., is a very competent judge of the merits of a book. He expresses his opinion of our Lesson Commentary for 1899 in the following manner:

"I have carefully examined the Christian Lesson Commentary for 1899. It shows painstaking scholarship and fidelity to the Word Its different methods of treating the text—expository, illustrative, applicatory and practical—with its suggestive questions and hints, opens the lesson fully to the understanding, and gives a wide range of thought. It is a rich storehouse from which a teacher can be fully equipped for teaching any grade of pupils. The numerous maps, illustrations, and the dictionary of Scripture proper names, with their pronunciation and meaning, are permanent and valuable features."

Send us your orders for "Christian Lesson Commentary" for 1899 *now*, that it may be in your hands before the beginning of the year. This would give ample time for the preparation of the lesson the first Sunday in the coming year. With the proper use of Christian Lesson Commentary for 1899 no teacher can fail to do proficient work as a Sunday-school teacher. It is a storehouse of thoughts on *all* phases of lesson text, and the busy teacher will find that much time and research can be saved by going each week to this book for preparation of the lesson to be taught. The appearance of the book makes it an ornament in the home and library. It contains over 400 pages, and is neatly bound in cloth, with red edges. The price is $1 00 per copy, postpaid, or $9.00 per dozen, not prepaid.

It is refreshing to find a writer so well versed in the history of the Jewish people as the author of "King Saul." J. Breckenridge Ellis proposes to write a number of volumes like this one on the historical characters of the Bible, and the ability he has shown for such a task is apparent in this volume as well as the one that preceded, "In the Days of Jehu." His ability is apparent, not only in the conception he has formed, the manner in which he portrays the characters, but also in his knowledge of the events in which these heroes were conspicuous figures. It is sincerely to be hoped that this series of historical sketches of Bible characters may find appreciative readers.—*Dr. H. Christopher, Editor Medical Herald, St. Joseph, Mo.*

I have just finished reading that delightful little book, "Queen Esther," by M. M. Davis, of Dallas, Texas, and what a refreshing and helpful thing it is! It is a charming bouquet of flowers beneath which you will find precious fruit. The author lifts the flowers at the close of each fragrant chapter and spreads the fruit before you, and you gratefully help yourself and are filled with heaven's own fullness. It should be read by both young and old. It is beautifully bound in cloth and illustrated. Price 75 cents.—*S. M. Martin.*

Write to the Christian Publishing Co. for their catalogue, from which you can select an appropriate book for a Christmas present to your friends. A good book is "medicine for the soul" of the careful reader, and a gift of this kind is a constant reminder of the donor. A large number of good books are found published in this paper. Make your selection and send in your order before the holidays.

Announcements.

Week of Prayer Program.

Topics suggested for the Week of Prayer by the Evangelical Alliance for the United States, January 1-8, 1899.

SUNDAY, JANUARY 1ST.—SERMONS.

Christian Unity: "I in them and thou in me, that they may be made perfect in one."—John 17:23.

MONDAY, JANUARY 2D.—PRAYERFUL CONFESSION.

In view of God's freely offered grace, too little welcomed and received; Christ's abiding presence, too little discerned and felt; the Spirit's guidance and power, too little desired and yielded to; the privilege and duty of Christians witnessing, too little prized and fulfilled. Matt. 7:11; Titus 2:11; Matt. 28:20; John 15:4, 5, 10; Joel 2:28, 29; John 16:7, 8, 13; John 1:41; Acts 1:8.

TUESDAY, JANUARY 3D.—THE CHURCH UNIVERSAL.

Prayer: That each member of the Church Universal, being born of the Spirit, may depart from all iniquity; may be fruitful in good works; may be faithful in prayer; may be filled with love for the brethren and for all men; and that the several branches of the Church Universal may live and work "in the unity of the Spirit and in the bond of peace."—2 Tim. 2:19; Phil. 4:8; Matt. 7:20; Matt. 6:9, 10; Luke 18:1; John 3:14; 1 Cor. 12:4-6; Eph. 4:3.

WEDNESDAY, JANUARY 4TH.—NATIONS AND THEIR RULERS.

Prayer: That all peoples may duly prize civil and religious freedom, and deserve to be thus free; may faithfully obey just laws and reverence righteous authority; may cherish the brotherhood which embraces all classes and conditions of men; and may hail Christ as their peaceful Prince. That rulers may rule in the love of God and man; may seek honorable peace and international good will; and may in all public affairs, apply the Christian principles which should guide individual conduct.—John 8:32; Prov. 14:34; Acts 17:26; Isa. 2:4.

THURSDAY, JANUARY 5TH.—FOREIGN MISSIONS.

Prayer: That individual Christians may render loyal obedience to their Savior's last command, and take fresh courage from his last promise. That our Foreign Missionary organizations may be filled with Christlike devotion, and Christlike love toward each other; and may ever be mindful of the new lessons which experience teaches. That our missionaries may be gloriously successful, being divinely enabled to recognize providential leadings, and to make full use of the witness to Himself which God has preserved in even heathen lands. And that, to save the lost, missionaries of the cross may speedily be sent to the very ends of the earth. Mark 16:15; Acts 10:34, 35; Acts 17:23; Rom. 2:15; 10:14, 15.

FRIDAY, JANUARY 6TH.—HOME MISSIONS.

Prayer: That individual Christians may feel their sacred obligations to do their utmost toward making their own land Immanuel's land; may realize the unity of the national welfare—the peril of one member being the peril of all; and may fully perceive that the exaltation of Christ in the home land advances His kingdom in all lands. That Home Missionary organizations may be endued with the Spirit of love and power; may worthily enjoy the complete confidence of the churches; and that they may severally move forward in practical Christian comity and mutual helpfulness. Ex. 35:20-29; Isa. 2:3; 41:6, 7; 52:8; 1 Cor. 12:4-6.

SATURDAY, JANUARY 7TH.—FAMILIES AND SCHOOLS.

Prayer: That the family may be reverenced as a divine institution; that all families may be held in the blessed bonds of mutual love and mutual honor; that, under God, parental affection may cherish childhood into joy, and parental example inspire to nobleness of life; and that whatever is against the Christian ideal of the family may be opposed and overcome. That all education may become nobly Christian; that such education may be more and more valued; that thus the highest well-being of both community and nation may be secured, and Christ be all and in all. Ps. 68:6; Isa. 8:18; Mal. 4:6; Eph. 3:15; Job 28:28; Eph. 3:10, 11.

SUNDAY, JANUARY 8TH.—SERMONS.

The power of united effort. "And five of you shall chase an hundred, and an hundred of you shall put ten thousand to flight."—Lev. 26:8. (Isa. 41:6, 7; Eccl. 4:12.)

Disciple Settlers Wanted.

DEAR BRO. GARRISON:—I wish to say a few things through the CHRISTIAN-EVANGELIST with reference to our congregation. We have a little country organization ten miles west and two miles south of Wellington, three and one-half miles from Mayfield. We have a good church building, number about 30 regular members with some delinquents. We have a fairly good Sunday-school and social meetings.

Bro. Frank Talmage visits us and preaches for us one Lord's day in each month. By emigration to the Strip at the opening and since we have been considerably weakened. As other churches are close around us and nearly every one is a member of one congregation or some of the contiguous denominations we do not stand much show to increase our membership in the near future from our present population.

We are anxious to get some good families of our brethren to come in and locate with us that we may be enabled to do greater good. We have some good farms close around that can be bought at very reasonable prices. Those who have continued farming here for some years have generally succeeded. I would like to correspond with some Disciples with the view of their locating with us and helping us built up the cause of Christ in this part of our country.

With the hope that some readers of the CHRISTIAN-EVANGELIST may read this and be inclined to come and locate with us, I have written these lines. J. J. WILLIAMS.

Milan, Kan., Dec. 5, 1898.

The Christian-Evangelist
Christmas
1898

THE

CHRISTIAN - EVANGELIST

J. H. GARRISON, EDITOR.

W. W. HOPKINS, ASSISTANT.

B. B. TYLER, J. J. HALEY,

EDITORIAL CONTRIBUTORS.

RATES OF SUBSCRIPTION.

Single subscriptions, new or old .... $1.50 each
Ministers .... 1.00 "

All subscriptions payable in advance. Label shows the month up to the first day of which your subscription is paid. If an earlier date than the present is shown, you are in arrears. No paper discontinued without express orders to that effect. Arrears should be paid when discontinuance is ordered.

In ordering a change of post office, please give the OLD as well as the NEW address.

Do not send local check, but use Post office or Express Money Order, or draft on St. Louis, Chicago or New York, in remitting.

ADDRESS, CHRISTIAN PUBLISHING CO.,
1522 Locust St., St. Louis, Mo.

CONTENTS.

EDITORIAL:
Current Events..........771
Christmas Chimes (poem)..........773
The Song and the Star..........773
The State University and the Christian College..........773
Looking Backward..........774
Editor's Easy Chair..........774

ORIGINAL CONTRIBUTIONS:
The Babe of Bethlehem.—Geo. T. Smith..775
Archbishop Purcell on Alexander Campbell.—J. H. Carter..........776

CORRESPONDENCE:
English Topics..........781
An Unfortunate Habit..........781
New York Letter..........781
Memories of Thomas Munnell..........782
Hiram College Jubilee Endowment..........784
The Moody Bible Institute..........784
Christian Science..........785
Centennial of Transylvania University....785
Methods of Work..........785
A Suggestion..........786
Schools of Thought Among the Disciples..786

FAMILY CIRCLE:
Ring, Bells, Ring! (poem)..........790
What Two Boys Did—I..........790
A Christmas Message..........792
Forgetting Self..........792
Illustrated Sermon..........793
A Plea for the Lord's Day (poem)..........794
All Things Work for Good..........794

MISCELLANEOUS:
The Religious World..........777
Current Religious Thought..........777
Our Budget..........778
Personal Mention..........780
Notes and News..........787
Evangelistic..........789
With the Children..........795
Sunday-school..........796
Christian Endeavor..........796
Literature..........798
Marriages and Obituaries..........799
Publisher's Notes..........800

Subscription $1.50

THE CHRISTIAN-EVANGELIST

"In faith, Unity; in opinion and methods, Liberty; in all things, Charity."

Vol. xxxv. St. Louis, Mo., Thursday, December 22, 1898. No. 51

CURRENT EVENTS.

The signing of the treaty of peace between the United States and Spain marked an important stage in the settlement of affairs between the two nations, and yet its significance is only that it formally records what was already a foregone conclusion. The Spanish Commissioners were not in a position to do anything but yield, and the Spanish Cortez, when it meets in special session in January to consider the treaty, will not be in a position to do anything but ratify it. While signing the treaty, the Spanish Commissioners filed a protest against it. In a measure, this was a justifiable and appropriate thing to do, for it is true that the treaty was not in any sense the result of their deliberation, but was something imposed upon them. But in their protest they do not succeed in showing that the United States took any unfair advantage of its victory. The exact terms of the treaty have not yet been made public, but, as they are generally understood, it touches only upon the matters mentioned in the protocol. There will be opportunity for considering the question of acquiring one of the Carolines and arranging a commercial treaty when diplomatic relations and friendly intercourse between the two nations have been restored.

The resignation of Sir William Harcourt from the leadership of the Liberal party has the appearance of a significant event in British politics, not that it will materially modify the policy of the government either at home or abroad, but that it indicates the drift of that policy, as Sir William understands it. It is reported that the immediate occasion of his resignation was the fact that the moneyed men, who have been in the habit of furnishing the sinews of war, consider him an enemy of capital and refuse to contribute to the party treasury so long as his leadership continues. Back of that lies the fact that Sir William considers the new liberalism, which is really "Roseberryite imperialism," as out of harmony with the established principles of the Liberal party. If the Liberal party wants to change its principles and enter upon a new career, well and good, but it cannot take him with it. Since Lord Roseberry represents this new Liberal imperialism, as expressed in his recent speeches touching upon the Fashoda incident and the relations of England and France in general, and represents it better than any one else, it is probable that he will, after due persuasion, accept the leadership which naturally belongs to him.

The Dreyfus case is progressing quite satisfactorily in the hands of the Court of Cassation; likewise the case of Col. Picquart has been brought up for a re-trial by this court. Col. Picquart was degraded and imprisoned after a court martial trial for nobody knows exactly what, except that while a member of the government he expressed a belief in the innocence of Dreyfus, and the civil trial will doubtless do him justice. The chief thing to be feared now is the indiscreet zeal of the friends of these men. Perhaps the whole French military administration is rotten to the core, but if so, the court will find it out and it will be more effectual for the friends or Dreyfus to wait for the court to proclaim it than to howl about it in the Chamber of Deptuies. Last week a member of that body made an inflammatory speech denouncing the army and the government in unmeasured terms. The immediate result was a fight on the floor of the house, but the more important consequence of the trial was the excitement of prejudice against the cause of reversion and of a disposition to stand by the army right or wrong. The government has done the right thing; *i. e.*, it has put the two cases into the hands of the supreme civil tribunal, and it deserves the vote of confidence which it received after this speech in the Chamber. Let us wait.

The resignation of Secretary Bliss from his position in the Cabinet has not yet been officially announced, but a report to that effect is generally credited. The reasons assigned are ill health and pressure of business. Mr. Bliss entered the Cabinet reluctantly and with no expectation of finishing the term. With a vacant Cabinet position and a vacant ambassadorship at the Court of St. James, the political gossips have ample scope for speculation and the President's seventy million unofficial advisers are overwhelming him with suggestions. One prediction among many is that the vacancy in the Cabinet will give an opportunity for the appointment of some Westerner in recognition of the cordial support which the administration has received from the states west of the Mississippi. The West being recognized in that way, Mr. Choate, of New York, could be appointed to the ambassadorship.

In 1803 the Louisiana Territory, extending from the Mississippi River to the Rocky Mountains, was ceded by France to the United States. It was the greatest attempt at "expansion" in our history and the century has justified the attempt. It is none too soon to begin now to plan for a celebration of the centenary of that event, which shall be on a scale commensurate with its historical importance. After much preliminary agitation, the governor of Missouri has issued a call to the fourteen other states, which were carved out of this territory, to send delegates to a conference to be held in St. Louis, Jan. 10, to consider plans for a World's Fair in 1903. It seems to be taken by general consent that this is the most desirable and practicable form of celebration and that St. Louis is the most appropriate location for an exposition in commemoration of the Louisiana purchase.

If the Nicaraguan Canal question fails of a speedy and satisfactory settlement it will not be for lack of congressional bills on that topic. There are now three bills before the House and two before the Senate, representing as many different plans for the construction of the canal. Besides these, Chairman Hepburn has yet another plan, magnificent in its simplicity and sublime in its utter disregard of present treaties, diplomatic probabilities and existing conditions generally. The plan is to persuade Nicaragua to cede absolutely to the United States a strip of land extending across the isthmus at the proper point, and there to dig the ditch. It is suggested that probably Mr. Hepburn's object, in proposing this as the most plausible scheme, is to defeat the project altogether. Senator Morgan has brought up his bill in the Senate, but probably the discussion will not become really serious until the commission, which has been investigating the case with the aid of engineers and experts during the last six months, makes its report, about the beginning of the year. The strong point of the Morgan bill, according to its own claims, is that it provides for the construction of the canal and for all the governmental control that is necessary or desirable, and yet, by leaving the enterprise in the hands of the Maritime Company, does not violate the Clayton-Bulwer treaty with England.

The visit of the Presidential party to the Peace Jubilee at Atlanta was the occasion of a mighty celebration, the dominant note of which was a joyful recognition of more complete reunion of the North and South as the outcome of the war. The President himself sounded this note in his speech by suggesting that the time had come when the nation ought to take under its care the graves of Confederate soldiers equally with those of Union soldiers. To carry out this suggestion it would be necessary only to transform the Confederate cemeteries into national cemeteries and relieve the Confederate associations of the expense of caring for them. It could be easily done with no considerable expenditure, and would be an appropriate manifestation of that closer unity of the nation which we all recognize as one of the most precious results of our foreign war.

In his speech at Savannah, Ga., President McKinley states the Philippine problem in a proper light when he asked the question: "If, following the clear precepts of duty, territory falls to us and the welfare of an alien people requires our guidance and protection, who will shrink from the responsibility, grave though it may be?" This is exactly the point of view which the CHRISTIAN-EVANGELIST has insisted on since Dewey's victory at Manila. There are politicians who do not look at the problem in this light, but who so far misconceive the spirit of their own government and of the people as to suppose that there is a disposition to ignore the rights and the best interests of the Filippinos for our own national gain. Nothing can be further, we are sure, from the feeling and purpose of the President and of the great mass of the American people whose wishes he correctly represents. The whole problem as to what is the best thing to be done for the welfare of these people is yet to be solved, but there is no solution in the turning of these people back under the rule of Spain, or in deserting them at once without giving such guidance and protection as they will surely need for a time. We do not doubt that American statesmanship will be equal to this emergency as it has proved itself equal to similar emergencies in the past.

The President's visit through the South seems to have supplied all that was lacking to obliterate the line of sectionalism between the North and the South. His speeches at Atlanta, at Montgomery and at Savannah were marked by such a spirit of broad Americanism and fraternity, and such sincere appreciation of the Southern people and the part which they played in the recent drama of war, as to quite win the hearts of the people of that section. His suggestion that the government should share in the duty of caring for the graves of the Confederate dead has awakened the profoundest feeling throughout the South, and as one of their leaders has expressed it, "has made them love the union once more." We have no doubt that in this suggestion the President voices the sentiment of the great body of the people of the North. The Southern people have demonstrated their loyalty to our common flag and their love of our common country, beyond all question, and it is but the part of a great and generous people to respect and honor the memory of brave men who died in what they believed to be the line of duty to their country. And this we say from the standpoint of one who followed the Stars and Stripes through four years of the war for the preservation of the Union.

Our Contributing Editor, B. B. Tyler, sends us the following paragraphs concerning Polygamy in Congress:

Shall Mr. Bingham H. Roberts, representative elect to Congress from Utah, be permitted to take his seat?

Why not? In the November election he was chosen, in an orderly manner, to represent a congressional district in the state of Utah in our National Legislature. His majority was more than six thousand. On the face of the returns it is clear that a large majority of the people of his district desire that he shall represent them in Congress. Why not?

It is not claimed that in his election the forms of the law were disregarded. So far as is known the election proceeded according to the requirements of the law applicable in such a case. There was no ballot box stuffing. There was no intimidation of electors. Why, then, raise the question concerning the seating of Mr. Roberts? Have not the people the right to choose whomsoever they will to represent them in the lawmaking body of the nation? If not, why not?

But this man is a Mormon! What if he is? Is not Utah a Mormon state? Is there anything in the constitution of the United States making it improper, unlawful or impossible for a Mormon to be a member of Congress?

But Mormonism is a fraud, a delusion, a false religion! Granted. What if it is? Does the constitution of the United States or our laws, declare in form or in effect that any men who profess the true religion are qualified to sit as members of Congress? The first amendment to the constitution declares that "Congress shall make no law respecting an establishment of religion, or prohibiting the free exercise thereof;" but if a man is disqualified from sitting as a representative in Congress because of the religion in which he professes to believe, then he, in effect, is not permitted to exercise freedom in his religious faith and practice! Why, then, raise the question concerning the eligibility of Mr. Roberts? The constitution is specific in setting forth the qualifications that must be possessed by members of Congress. It says that one to be a member of the House of Representatives must have been a citizen of the United States seven years, that he must be twenty-five years of age, and an inhabitant of the state in which he is chosen. All of these things are true of Mr. Roberts. He has been a citizen of the United States many times more than seven years. He is more than twenty-five years old. No one denies that he is an inhabitant of the state of Utah. Why not, then, permit him to take his seat in Congress as a member from Utah?

Brigham H. Roberts is a polygamist. He has three wives. This is known. He may have more. That he has three wives is not denied. One of Mr. Roberts' wives lives in Salt Lake City, and two in Centerville, ten miles North of Salt Lake. The ministers of the gospel in Salt Lake City protest against the seating of Roberts and allege these facts as containing the reasons for their protest. Twenty-four preachers sign the protest.

Mr. Roberts is editor of a magazine in which there appeared last spring a long editorial in which polygamy was defended.

Polygamy is not a part of the Mormon religion—not an *essential* part. One can be a Mormon and not be a polygamist. A special revelation, received many years ago, made polygamy an integral part of the faith and practice of the Church of Jesus Christ of Latter-day Saints. But even during the prevalence of that so-called revelation one could be a Mormon and not practice polygamy. The time never was when this faith and practice were essential to Mormonism.

The practice is now condemned by the highest authority in the church, and in the most solemn manner. After the passage of the Edmunds law in 1882, and when it was seen that the United States authorities were determined to enforce this law, a revelation was received setting aside the former communication from heaven on the subject of plural marriages. The Edmunds law made polygamy a crime, with appropriate punishments designated. This law was enforced under it in 1889. Brigham H. Roberts was condemned.

By the teaching of Mormonism, the ex*otric* teaching, Mr. Roberts, at this poin on this subject, is a sinner. By the laws c the United States he is a criminal. Thi is the reason why he should be denied seat in our National Legislature.

By the Edmunds law polygamists wer disfranchised. They are not permitted t vote nor to hold office. According to thi act of Congress Mr. Roberts has no righ to vote, and he cannot legally hold office If, in an election, Brigham H. Robert casts a vote he is guilty of an illegal act The law on all this is clear.

Mr. Cleveland and Mr. Harrison issue proclamations of amnesty in which pardo was expressly conditioned on the abandon ment of polygamy. Roberts has not aband oned his polygamous relations. One of hi wives gave birth to two children last Au gust.

In the magazine article above referred t Mr. Roberts says:

"'Joseph Smith received a commandmen from the Lord to introduce that order of mar riage into the church, and on the strength o that revelation, and not by reason of anythin that is written in the Jewish Scriptures, th Latter Day saints practiced plural marriage.'

"Polygamy is not adultery, for were it s considered, then Abraham, Jacob and th prophets, who practiced it, would not be al lowed an inheritance in the kingdom of heaven and if polygamy is not adultery, then it canno be classed as sin at all."

"It appears to the writer that modern Chris tians must either learn to tolerate polygamy or give up forever the glorious hope of resting in 'Abraham's bosom.'"

Thus Mr. Roberts thought and expresse himself in his magazine last spring Ought such a man to sit in the Congres of the United States? That his conduct o this subject is in harmony with his teach ing is not denied.

Utah was kept out of the union as a state for a number of years on acount of the recognition of polygamy by the Mormons. As the result of a solemn agreement to abstain from plural marriages Utah became a state in 1896. Brigham H. Roberts was a prominent actor in this matter. He seems to have no respect whatever for the terms of this solemn covenant. Ought such a man to be recognized as a member of Congress? He is now in rebellion against the laws passed by the National Legislature and approved by the President—laws to which he *especially* agreed to be obedient.

It looks as if the election of this man to Congress was a deliberate defiance of the United States Government by the Mormons. They seem in this affair to say to Congress and the President: "We defy you. We will see if you will enforce the laws relating to plural marriages. We are now a sovereign state. We will do as we please. Help yourselves if you can. We deliberately trample your laws under our feet. What will you do about it?"

There are a few people in the United States who fear that Roman Catholics will destroy our free American institutions; but there is far greater danger from Mormons; they are planting themselves in some of the states in which a few voters, comparatively, will hold the balance of power. The representation in the Senate from one of these states is equal to that of the most populous state in the Union. The time is apparently not far distant when the Mormons will be able to control the election of United States senators. They can also control electoral votes in a Presidential election, and there is no valid reason why they may not in a closely contested campaign determine the election of the President.

Now is the time to meet the issue. The gauntlet has been thrown down. What will we do?

Christmas Chimes.

(See first page illustration.)

Chime on, sweet bells of Christmas, chime,
Your music breathes a hope sublime,
Your silvery tones on wintry air
Drive back the clouds of dark despair.

Ring out from steeple, dome and tower,
Proclaim to list'ning ears the hour
When Heaven stooped down to kiss the earth,
And Love, incarnate, came to birth.

O, bells of Christmas! loud and clear
Ring out your notes of hope and cheer!
Till all the world with joy shall sing,
For Bethlehem's Babe is Christ, our King.

Chime on, sweet bells of Christmas, chime,
Through every land, in every clime,
Till Heaven and earth united be,
And Jesus reigns o'er land and sea.

E. DITOR.

THE SONG AND THE STAR

"There's a song on the air,
There's a star in the sky,
There's a mother's deep prayer,
There's a babe's tender cry.
And the star rains its fire
While the Beautiful sing,
For the manger of Bethlehem
Cradles a King."

That song that broke the stillness of the night on the Judean hills, in the long ago, is reverberating still throughout the earth. That star that rained its fire to guide the course of the wise men, has become a Sun that lights the whole world to Christ. That "mother's deep prayer" finds its response in the mother-hearts of all the world. That "babe's tender cry" has made sacred the childhood of all succeeding ages.

The song that was sung that first Christmas night by the Chorus Choir of Heaven was the Gloria in Excelsis, looking Godward, and on its earthward side it was "peace among men in whom He is well pleased." These are the two notes in the great Anthem of Redemption—Glory to God in the highest, on earth peace among men with whom God is pleased. The anthem would be incomplete without either of these notes. This angel-song means that Christ's mission on earth was to exalt God among the nations, and promote peace among men by bringing them into accord with the Divine Will.

These two purposes run parallel with each other and the ages have witnessed their mutual progress. God has, indeed, been exalted by a fuller revelation of His grace and truth through Jesus Christ. When Jesus called Him our Heavenly Father He gave Him the highest place in human thought and adoration; and just in proportion as humanity has been brought into harmony with the Will of God has peace prevailed. In the divine plan Peace and Righteousness go together; in Christ they meet and kiss each other. There is no use in organizing a Peace Society unless we organize a Society of Righteousness by the side of it. There will never be universal peace until there is universal righteousness.

Such is the purport of that angel-song. May its melody find a response thoughout all Christendom this Christmas-tide! May there be the burying of old strifes and feuds, and the putting away of all alienations and bitterness, to the end that God may be well pleased with us, and that His peace may fill our minds and hearts. May the nations learn the lesson that peace can only be maintained in righteousness. This is one of the lessons emphasized by the events of the present year.

That star which guided the wise men to the cradle of the new-born King is now filling the earth with its light, every beam of which points toward the Christ of Bethlehem, of Calvary and of Olivet. Science, art, philosophy, government, social progress, history — what are all these but luminous rays of light that direct the candid inquirer toward Him who is the Light of the world? Christ is the key to history, and the only solution of the enigma of human life. He it is who transforms chaos into kosmos. As He is "the Light of the world," so every ray of light followed to its source leads to Him.

Let us, then, carried on the wings of imagination, visit once more these far-away scenes. Let us listen to the song of the angels that floated out on the midnight air. Let us gaze at the star that rained its fire and, following its light, let us, kneel with the adoring shepherds and with the wise men from the East, and offer our gifts of gold and frankincense and myrrh to this new-born King. Let us enter into the spirit of this great anniversary. Let us realize something of the nearness of heaven to earth which the shepherds must have felt on that memorable night, when angel-wings beat the air above their heads. Let us open our hearts to all the holy influences of the season, and above all, let us receive into them the Christ who was born in a manger because there was no room in the inn. May He be born anew in all our hearts this Christmas season!

THE STATE UNIVERSITY AND THE CHRISTIAN COLLEGE.

Under a grant made by the United States Government several years ago many of the states have established what are known as State Universities, which are generally recognized as the crown and apex of our system of public education. One of the most remarkable phenomena in the educational world is the steady and rapid growth of these State Universities. Without exception, so far as we know, the attendance of these state institutions is steadily increasing, while the facilities they afford for educational purposes are being constantly multiplied. They have served a good purpose, too, in making the Western and Middle States more independent of the East than they would have been.

These facts raise a question which thoughtful people, interested in the welfare of the country, cannot ignore. What should be the attitude of the great body of Christian people of this country toward these State Universities? We can think of only three attitudes which Christian people may assume toward them. One is that of active opposition to them on the ground that their support by the state is a species of paternalism, or on the ground that they are not subserving the public good; or they may assume an attitude of indifference, as if the problem were not worthy of consideration; or, recognizing in these State Universities great possibilities of good and potent agencies for disseminating light and truth among the people, they may assume a sympathetic relation to these schools, seek to remove them as far as possible from the control of merely partisan politics, correct whatever evil tendencies there may be in connection with them, and supplement their teaching by the establishment of Bible Chairs or schools in proximity to them so as to give their students the benefit of biblical instruction.

As a matter of fact some religious people have opposed the universities on one or the other of the grounds mentioned, but this has generally been done in the interest of some denominational school. As to the charge of "paternalism," it will have more force when the people who raise that cry offer the funds which are necessary to carry on the educational work. Our public-school system is one of the glories of our nation, and the university seems to be the logical outgrowth of this national system of education. If we should join in with our Roman Catholic citizens in opposing the idea of education by the state, and should succeed in destroying this system of education, which the generosity of the people of the United States have built up, we should see a retrograde movement in general intelligence and education, which would in time bring us to a level with some of the Roman Catholic countries.

It must be said, however, that the attitude of indifference is the one which has been most geuerally assumed by the Christian people toward these universities, and it is the least defensible of all possible attitudes. If the State University is not a good thing, it is a very bad thing, and should be opposed. The attitude of indifference is unworthy of intelligent citizens.

The third attitude which we have mentioned is manifestly, as we think, the right one for an intelligent Christian people to assume. Here are these State Universities, which already have millions of dollars invested in them. They command the best teaching ability of the country. They afford facilities for instruction equaled only by a few of the Eastern Universities. They have a larger and more rapidly increasing patronage than our denominational schools. This is not only because they have better educational facilities than the average denominational school; the very fact that they are not controlled by any religious body makes them more acceptable to many. In all human probability these Universities are here to remain, and are destined to increase in patronage and power. Is it not, then, a part of wisdom and prudent foresight to so surround these institutions with religious influence and biblical instruction as to make them centers, not only of intellectual training, but of moral and religious influence? A more manifest duty than this we cannot conceive of.

We believe the movement inaugurated among us in recent years to associate Bible teaching with these State Universities is one of the most important educational ideas of modern times, and is destined to exert a far-reaching influence both upon the character of these institutions and upon the church itself. The plan seems to be a part of that larger conception of the kingdom of God which is now being accepted by intelligent Christians everywhere, which regards the state itself as a part of the divine order, and which would apply Christianity to all the functions of our social and political life. For this reason the State Universities are welcoming this biblical instruction, seeing that it is an essential part of a complete education. By the wise action of the church in relation to these State Universities they may be made important agencies for the advancement of the kingdom of God. An opposite course, which would divorce them from Christian sympathy and co-operation, would prove a calamity, the evil influence of which it would be difficult to exaggerate.

But what of our Christian or distinctly religious institutions of learning? Have they a future? We think they have not come into being without reason, and the causes that brought them into being have not ceased to operate. What should be the relation of these institutions to the State Universities? In cases where individual munificence has endowed and equipped institutions that can cope with the State Universities in the scope and thoroughness of their work, their relation should be that of generous and fraternal rivalry. In cases where the religious institution is able only to give the college course, it should undertake to do no more than that, but put itself into such articulation with the universities as will enable their graduates to pursue any postgraduate studies they may wish to pursue in these universities.

But it should be understood that if our religious institutions are to exist and flourish, their friends must endow and equip them so that their work, *as far as it goes*, will be as thorough as in the universities. The time has past when we can rely on denominational zeal as a substitute for proper endowment in sustaining these schools. If we believe in the mission of Christian colleges we must endow them and enable them to cope with other schools in the quality of their work and in the advantages they offer. Granted that they have special advantages over state schools, which we quite freely grant, we must see to it that these advantages are not more than offset by the disadvantages growing out of the lack of proper support. *We must endow our Christian schools or witness their steady but sure decay.*

There is much truth in the following words from Max O'Rell's article on Cheerfulness in the North American Review for December:

The world is full of joy, full of beauty, and we want the great thinkers to make us discover it. We do not want Carlyles to scold us; we do not want prelates, with incomes of $100,000 a year, to lecture on thrift to poor factory girls sweated on three dollars a week. The masses of the people hear a good deal of the joys that await them in the next world. By and by, they will want a bit of heaven on this earth. They will ask for it, nay, they will demand it, and, believe me, they will get it.

Hour of Prayer.

LOOKING BACKWARD.

(Midweek Prayer Meeting Topic, Dec. 28th, 1898.)

Many, O Lord my God, are the wonderful works which thou hast done,
And thy thoughts which are to us-ward:
They cannot be set in order unto thee;
If I would declare and speak of them,
They are more than can be numbered.
—*Psa.* 40:5.

There are some people, doubtless, who are disposed to look backward too much to the neglect of present duties and responsibilities. But there are times and seasons when it would seem to be pre-eminently proper to turn our minds back to the past, and learn the lessons which it has for us. It is, indeed, greatly wise that we should hold converse with our past hours, and let them teach us concerning the future. It is especially necessary that we should recall, in thoughtful moments, God's dealings with us in the past and remember His mercies to us-ward. In such a mood was the psalmist when he wrote the psalm of which the above text is a part.

The close of the year especially would seem to be a fit time for thinking over the past. It is a time for "memory and for tears." The dying year inevitably reminds us of the rapid flight of time and the brevity of human life. This is the last midweek prayer meeting of the old year. It is fitting that we look backward over the year that is closing, and ask ourselves two questions at least: What has God done for me? and what have I done for God? When the psalmist looked back over God's dealings with him and his nation, he exclaimed: "Many, O Lord my God, are the wonderful works which thou hast done." It is the nature of faith to recognize the hand of God in all the providences of our lives. In how many ways has God's love manifested itself toward us during the year past! Who can number them? The psalmist mentions a few things that the Lord had done for him:

(1) "He inclined unto me and heard my cry" (v. 1). How many of us can say the same thing to-night concerning our prayers? Surely, many of us. We called upon Him in our troubles and He lightened our hearts.

(2) "He brought me up also out of an horrible pit, out of the miry clay;
And He set my feet upon a rock, and established my goings" (v. 2).

Have none of us felt our feet in the miry clay of sin, or in the slippery way of evil doers, during the year past? And have we turned to God and felt His strong arm lifting us up and setting our feet upon a rock? If so, then we can join with the psalmist in another experience which he describes as follows:

(3) "And He hath put a new song into my mouth, even praise unto our God" (v. 3). Have we not been able to sing some new song of praise to God in view of His mercies to us, and our deliverance from sin, or from sickness, or from some other earthly calamity? It is wonderful how the recognition of God's mercies fills our mouths with songs of praise, and puts the spirit of music in our hearts. "Let those refuse to sing who never knew our God."

(4) The influence of the psalmist's changed life upon others was another reason for his gratitude:

"Many see it, and fear,
And shall trust in the Lord" (v. 3).

He was not only grateful, on his own account, for what the Lord had done for him, but the good influence which this would have upon others, leading them to "trust in the Lord," was reason for further gratitude. Have any of us the consolation, in looking back over our lives to-night, of feeling that our example during the year has been helpful to others in leading them to trust in the Lord? We may not be conscious of any direct results of the influence of our lives, but we may be sure that, if we have "walked with God" until our faces have caught something of the light of His countenance and the joy of His peace, others have been stimulated by our example to leading better lives.

It is comforting to know, too, that while we have occasionally thought of God He has been thinking of us continually. Of both God's works and God's "thoughts which are to us-ward" the psalmist exclaims:

"They cannot be set in order unto thee;
If I would declare and speak of them,
They are more than can be numbered."

We love to know that our friends think of us, but it is a wonderful thought that the great and good God, who holds the universe in balance, thinks of us individually, and has a plan for each life. He has been watching us during the year to see what response we would make to His mercies and to all His tender appeals. If we have grieved our Heavenly Father by our forgetfulness of Him, and by our failure to respond to His calls upon us for service and for growth in the divine life, let this last prayer-meeting of the year be an occasion of sincere repentance and the seeking of God's pardoning grace and love. Thus strengthened and renewed, we may turn our faces resolutely and hopefully to the responsibilities of the year to come.

PRAYER.

O Thou Father of infinite mercies, how great is Thy kindness to the children of men! How tenderly Thou hast dealt with us during the year that is now drawing to a close! Thy hand has led us, and fed us, and upheld us; and "like as a father pitieth his children," Thou hast pitied us and cared for us during all the experiences of the year. As we recount all Thy wonderful acts of kindness toward us, and are reminded of Thy thought concerning us, we must confess that we have not responded as fully as we should have done to these manifestations of Thy love. We confess our faults before Thee, and humbly ask Thy pardon through the merits of our Lord Jesus Christ, through whom, also, we implore Thy rich grace to live better and more fruitful lives the coming year than we have ever done in the past. And when our earthly lives are closed, may it be that Eternity shall open up for us higher and nobler spheres of activity where we may serve and praise Thee forever. Amen!

Editor's Easy Chair.

It is natural that Christmas should be pre-eminently the children's festival. It calls up the Babe of Bethlehem and the manger-cradle. The Christ-child is an object of profoundest interest both to heaven and earth. The birth of every child is a mystery, but the birth of this wonderful Child of Prophecy, of Promise and of Hope—how much mystery clusters about that event! If we are wise we have long since ceased to try to understand the mystery, and are content to accept the fact so full of significance for the race. Childhood can do that; a philosopher can do no more

And so Christmas has become, of all the days of the year, Children's Day. They look forward to it with anticipations of joy, mingled somewhat with awe, and its coming is hailed with delight by all the juveniles of Christendom. Welcome, Christmas, for the children's sake!

But, after all, it would be difficult to tell who are happier these days preceding Christmas, the children or their parents, and the older brothers and sisters and the uncles and aunts. How many precious little packages are stored away in secret places, some of them wrought by loving hands, some of them purchased by hard-earned wages, in order to make the children happy on Christmas! Nothing, perhaps, brings so much joy to the human heart as the effort to make somebody else's life brighter and happier. Hence it is that the faces of the old, as well as the young, take on a brighter and happier look these ante-Christmas days. The saddest of all hearts just now are the hearts of loving, toiling parents who, by reason of misfortune or sickness or lack of work, feel that they can make no presents to their little ones. But the great mass of people, it is pleasant to believe, will find something by which to make the Christmas season a little brighter for their loved ones, and it is this *giving* and *preparing* to give to others that brings happiness. And so we add—Welcome, Christmas, for the sake of the old people!

It is a blessed thing that it does not take much to convey an expression of love and friendship. Many a child in the homes of the poor will be filled with delight with some simple little toy which others, it may be, have cast away, or some simple little dish to which they have not been accustomed, or a little game—anything that will mean to them that Christmas has come and they are remembered. It would be a mistake to suppose that the largest amount of happiness on Christmas Day will be found in the homes of the rich and the well-to-do. If any one believes this, let him make a series of visits Christmas morning to the homes of the poor, and he will find bright eyes sparkling and little hearts exulting in happiness over simple little dolls or toys that wealthier children would despise. There will be as much joy and happiness even in the cabins of the poor, on Christmas Day, where actual want does not exist, as in the palaces of the rich. We are glad that this is so. Welcome, Christmas, for the sake of the poor!

The writer can recall a humble Missouri cottage home, silhouetted against a wintry sky in the mellow light of memory, in which there were no purchased gifts exchanged. Everything given or received was of the rudest or simplest nature, and was made by loving hands. He remembers, yet, the yule-log on Christmas eve, the large fire-place and the bright, blazing fire. The boys and girls that gathered around that hearthstone had never a sigh on account of poverty. There were apples and nuts, and innocent games and laughter, and the light of a mothers's love-lit eyes. These were enough. Little did we know or care about rich and costly gifts such as are lavished so freely on loved ones in the homes of the rich. It would be difficult to find boys and girls with happier hearts than those we call to mind in that humble cabin home of the long ago. The very youngest of that circle has grandchildren now, but all of them remember those early Christmas days, in the old home, with a warmth in the heart and a mist in the eye. No, it is not wealth that makes Christmas, but love. For the sake of childhood memories, we welcome Christmas!

One of the delightful features of Christmas is the home-gathering. It is true in a special sense, at Christmas, that "there is no place like home." If the boys and girls who have married, or who have left the old home are not separated from us by too great a distance we expect them to come home and shelter under the rooftree with the "old folks at home." And if, in addition, there come also the prattle of childish voices and the patter of shildish feet of little ones who come to visit "grandpapa" and "grandmamma," the home-coming is doubly welcome, and Christmas has an added charm. Let the fire burn brightly on the hearthstones. Bring in the guitar, the mandolin, the banjo and all the rest of the stringed instruments, and let music lend its mellowing influence to the happy circle. Who knows when they will all meet again? Let our homes echo once more with the music of the old songs this Christmastide. For the sake of our homes and the glad home-coming, we welcome thee, O merrry Christmas!

THE BABE OF BETHLEHEM.

GEORGE T. SMITH.

God experiments. He tests men and systems. Certain postulates, held by men of to-day, have been tested on a world-wide scale and through centuries. One is, nature is ample for man's instruction and guidance: the other, man can obey the right and save himself without the cross. All objections to the gospel ultimately rest on one or the other of these assumptions.

In the mighty experiment of the ages God chose the Gentiles to test the first, the Jews to decide the second.

The Gentiles were richly endowed for their mission. Most of the earth was theirs. Time ample was given; indeed, in non-Christian lands the experiment is yet in progress. The love of beauty of the Japanese, the patience and industry of the Chinese, the subtlety of the Hindoos, the longing for purity of the Persians are, in Occidental eyes, the small change of the capital of this prodigal son.

The eagle eye to discern law, the right arm to enforce it and the firm heel to stamp the nations with the seal of one empire, were the wealth of the Romans. The love of domestic virtues, the perseverance, the chastity of the Teutonic sons of the hardy North equipped them for the search. Above all, the intellectual acuteness and supremacy of the Greek was the crown of glory of that ancient world. Brilliant with gems, twenty centuries have not eclipsed their radiance, nor exhausted their light. Smaller than Rhode Island was Attica, 84,000 was her free population, yet for hundreds of years that soil produced the most remarkable galaxy of men whose talents ever adorned the race.

Warriors on land and sea, statesmen, sculptors, painters, orators, poets, dramatists, philosophers and historians shone as lucid gems. The Draper and Buckle school derive all results from environment. Greece has the same happy days, the same sunny skies, the same Marathon looking on the mountains and the mountains on the sea, but Salamis and Porch are dead. That God gave abnormal brain power to the Hellenic race admits of no doubt to the student of the long steps of the Governor of nations.

The Mighty Ruler also determined the bounds of the nations, the periods of their history, that they might seek him, though, in truth, he is ever near.

The pre-Socratic school studied the philosophy of nature; the Socratic school, the philosophy of mind; the post-Socratic, the philosophy of life. They all looked for God, but they all landed in agnosticism and despair.

True, you may read some fine thoughts about God, especially in Plato, but, if Justin Martyr's testimony be valid, Plato gleaned these from Jewish writings, and through fear of the judges withheld the source. If we award the merit of originality to Xenophanes and the Socratic trinity, the case is worse. For in such an etherial atmosphere of exalted truth, the discoverers were unable to remain for any length of time. They did not hold it consistently, they never made it practical, they could not impart it to their disciples, still less transmit it a single link. It was a Jew who on Mars' Hill revealed to them their unknown God. Such was the paucity of their knowledge that he identified the true God with their Zeus, the Jupiter of the Romans, a shady character, whose morals would not stand the light of day, so he made the night twice as long. He was no more the father of gods and men than other deities to whom the lively Greeks gave the same title.

The experiment was complete, saying nothing of the Oriental world, wearied and worn out in the hopeless struggle, subjugated to the arts of smaller but more virile people. When the Babe lay in the manger the world had tested its riches to the full and had reached aching despair.

The philosophers openly taught (R. G. Ingersoll has echoed it) that the best thing in the power of man was to take his own life. The reason is plain. Fiery youth may revel in seasual pleasures, but satiety is soon reached. Against a blank wall, with the rays of a pitiless sun beating upon him, with a raging thirst which nothing can quench, the devotee of pleasure soon finds himself. God is the source of our being, the end of our quest. Without him the spirit cannot rest. Knowledge divorced from God is valueless.

Failure, weariness, disgust, were the deadly blossoms of the nightshade which grew out of the polluted soil of unrestrained appetite. Their noisome fetor poisoned society, destroyed the sanctity of home and undermined the state.

So revolting is the picture drawn by Paul of the condition of the Gentile world, we shrink from reading the first chapter of Romans in public. So true is it that its horrible revelations have startled Chinamen into saying: "You wrote that after you came to our country," yet so moderate that worse things may be gathered from the stern Tacitus, the loose Sallust and the vacillating Seneca of Paul's time. Martial tells the name of a woman married and divorced ten times in a month! This is a straw in the stream of moral rottenness when Rome worshiped the emperor as a god, and beheaded Christians.

Let a modern papan sing of that day:

> "On that hard pagan world disgust
> And secret loathing fell;
> Deep weariness and sated lust
> Made human life a hell."

We sometimes think that if everybody around us were doing right it would be easy for us. Perhaps. The Jewish people were cemented together as no other people. They had a common blood, a mutual history, the same religion. In the furnace of Egypt and the desert they were fused into one body. Separated from all other nations by these bonds of sympathy, by their geographical position, with a law covering every detail of life, they had the best possible opportunity to show that a man can save himself through obedience to a law of justice.

The law was divine. It was just and good. Theirs was the only theocracy the world ever saw. God was their king. His erpetual hand was upon them, bringing punishment when they departed from the way and pouring down prosperity on the obedient. The law was plain: The man who doeth these things shall live by them. They failed. Not a Jew was justified by the law. It made no provision for even one small transgression. Mercy alone can do that. Justice is blind.

Exact compliance alone meets the case. No Jew, no legalist of to-day, could live without a flaw.

After fifteen hundred years of experiment, long after idolatry had been burned out of the nation by the Babylonian furnace, John the Baptist first, then Jesus, made terrific accusations against the people.

This gigantic experiment bankrupted man. He was silent. Three propositions were indubitably established in the minds of the wise: That man is ignorant, that he is sinful, that he is helpless. The redeemer of this lost and despairing race must be infinite in wisdom, infinite in power. God's answer to this desire of nations lay in a manger at Bethlehem. Weak and ignorant as any babe, poorer than most, fleeing from Herod's thirsty sword, carried to Nazareth from fear of Archelaus, this Babe of Bethlehem was the hope of the world for deliverance from all its woes.

"Jesus" means savior. "Christ" means anointed. Three classes of men, viz., prophets, priests and kings, were anointed in the earlier dispensation. Jesus is God's anointed Prophet, Priest and King. As a prophet he is a teacher. He is *the* teacher. "He taught nothing but himself," is the pregnant saying of Renan. So doing, he taught God. Wonderful teacher is he. No man ever thus spoke. His school takes no recess, has no vacation, sends out no graduates. The centuries sit at his feet; nations have slowly learned to spell under him. None can read.

By his adorable sacrifice of love he has entranced the hearts of those whom he cleanses from all guilt. His blood suffices.

As the mighty Captain of our salvation he redeems. His the broken tomb. He the Resurrection and the Life.

Thus as the Christ of God he meets precisely the needs of man. No real want is left without provision. Ignorant, guilty, helpless are we; the Babe of Bethlehem comes to our relief. It was love among the hateful; virtue in the midst of hypocrisy; humility in the presence of scornful pride; self-immolation before cruel self-seeeking. He loved himself last. Into that seething mass of fierce and brutal sensuality, that cynical, sneering agnosticism, that repellant formalism and hypocrisy the tiny babe came. What a marvelous change! Goethe's lamp in the fisherman's hut turned into silver. The Babe of Bethlehem called angel voices from the heavens and exalted motherhood to the skies. Out of the mire and the stony rock he plucked pellucid gems for his crown. He transformed the young tiger, breathing out threatenings and slaughter, into the lamblike apostle, branded with many Philippian stripes. He satisfied Justin Martyr's mind, wearied in a search which had beggared philosophy. He subdued the strong and undisciplined nature of Augustine, richly endowing and inspiring him to show the folly and weakness of all that attempts to rival the peerless Babe. But time would fail to tell of the Norbets, the Gardiners, the Billy Brays who have worshiped with the wise men and with redeemed lives.

Scorned at first, then feared by the rabbis who rejoiced over that grave at the foot of Calvary, malighed as a perverse, malefic and destructive superstition by Tacitus, Suetonius and Pliny the younger, the religion which sprang from that cradle grappled with the sullen despair, the torpid conscience, the enthroned diabolism, the deified lust of a callous or sneering world, and in spite of venomous hate swept away the mass of rotten idolatry, abolished the degrading worship of the emperor, sheathed the gladiatorial sword, made home possible and soared above the eagles of Rome.

Weakened by the results of the conversion of Constantine, it was buried beneath the repeated inundations of barbaric mud. Still it overcame and humanized the barbarians, it planted beneficent institutions wherever they are known, it purified and enriched the language, cleansed the customs and transformed the face of Europe. Rising triumphant from beneath the debris with which the weakness and wickedness of papal superstition had covered it from the sight of men it rushed forward to new and permanent victories. The nations which have nourished it have marched to the front rank of all that is good and powerful among men. In this land it has magnified human nature till its dignity, its incomparable value even when in ruins, fills us with awe and makes us restless for the inexpressible blessings held out to the nation whose God is the Lord.

Not in these lies his chief praise. After man's long and weary search by the candle of reason and the torch of nature, after the vain attempt to live so that justice would not cut him down, the Jewish shepherd, the Persian Magi worship at the cradle whose tiny hands are yet to lift the centuries out of the rut of cruelty and sensuality and place them upon the highways of holiness. He comes to the eyes that are heavy with long waiting, he gives the clear knowledge that in revealing God makes nature, man and history naked and open before the wondering eyes. To the prodigal defeated in temptation, mortified over deep guilt, he discloses the sole fountain that renews the man, by cleansing from all sin. To the weak, beaten by the world's fierce greed and bankrupt in hope, facing bitter and black death, he comes pointing to Joseph's shattered tomb and the radiant light which streams in golden tints along the path of him who has abolished death.

He has wiped away the tears from eyes pained by weeping, he has given the weary sweet rest, he has assuaged the grief of hearts which knew no other consolation, he has opened the heavens to the dying, disclosing rapturous scenes of beauty, he has gilded the sorrow of those remaining by the unquenchable hope that the parting is only till the morning.

About forty years before that hallowed night, Virgil wrote of a babe. He was to crush the Serpent and usher in a new birth of centuries. That babe, when a youth was imprisoned by the brutal emperor and died accomplishing nothing. Gibbon calls attention to Virgil's verse. They form an acrostic, viz., Jesus the Christ. He, dying while a young man has crippled the Serpent, ushered in a few new series of ages. No wonder that while all other religions have spent their youthful force and are descending into the valley, while agnosticism is pessimistic the religion of this Child is aggressive, energetic, youthful and the heir of the future.

Wise men bow before that cradle, and no such royal gifts reach any earthly monarch as the human hearts so freely give in the passionate enthusiasm of their love for this peerless Babe.

Albia, Ia., Dec. 6, 1898.

ARCHBISHOP PURCELL ON ALEXANDER CAMPBELL.

J. H. CARTER.

In common with many others I read with much interest the alleged interview with Archbishop Purcell on Alexander Campbell. If I may judge from the reference to the interview contained in the CHRISTIAN-EVANGELIST, of this week (under "Our Budget"), the genuineness of it seems to have been questioned. This does not seem to me to be very strange. There certainly appears to be one remarkable inconsistency between the views of the Archbishop as published in the interview, and those expressed in the debate with Mr. Campbell.

In the second column of the interview the Archbishop is reported as saying: "Did he [Alexander Campbell] not kneel before the same cross in spirit, *and regard with reverence the Mother of Jesus?*" Observe carefully the words of this quotation which I have italicised.

Now let us turn to the Campbell and Purcell debate. Mr. Campbell, in his opening speech said:

> "Are we, then, to understand her [the Catholic Church] as the immutable, universal, ancient, primitive, apostolic Church of Christ? Are we to understand this by the Roman Catholic Church of the nineteenth century, with her popes, her cardinals, her patriarch, primates, metropolitans, archbishops, archdeacons, monks, friars, nuns, etc., etc., teaching and preaching the use and worship of images, relics, penances, invocations of departed men and women, *veneration for some being whom they call the 'Mother of God?'* " P. 12 (italics mine.)

Archbishop (then Bishop) Purcell, in his first reply, referred to Mr. Campbell's lan-

l to the Virgin Mary in the
.ent passage:

an says he will use no language
an opprobrious meaning. * *
merating the various doctrines
:hurch, I was shocked to hear
guage, 'some being called the
' Great God! didst thou not
rld thy Son, Jesus Christ, to
aan, and didst thou not select
ughters of Eve to be the moth-
of benediction, and was not
one, to whose care was com-
.ncy, and to whom he was
she not the chosen one
whom its archangel was sent
aication, 'Hail, full of Grace,'
Protestant version—'Thou that
:d—the Lord is with thee,' and
her stigmatized in such lan-
lgnated as 'some being called
od?' '' (Campbell and Purcell
.

:he debate Purcell so severely
'. Campbell for "stigmatiz-
some being called the Moth-
is represented in the inter-
ig: "Did he [Alexander
regard with reverence the
s?"

supposed that Archbishop
:hat Mr. Campbell accepted
of the Catholic Church, but
in common with all Chris-
'enced Mary, the mother of
ighest type of womanhood
of God for so high an of-
no question as to the "gen-
ie interview; it certainly oc-
nly a question of how faith-

tional endowments, and debts and one-half for charitable uses. The bishops make an interesting inventory of Methodist financial capabilities, saying that they hold church property having a total value of $116,000,000, educational property worth $28,000,000, give $23,000,000 each year for support and extension of Christian work under Methodist control and have individual incomes aggregating $500,000,000 a year. The appeal has been out but a short time, but already individual trustees, conferences and other official bodies are acting in the matter. There has been some opposition to the plan, but it is melted away. Methodists are welcoming the suggestion very generally.

In Utah the Congregationalist and Presbyterian missionaries have joined hands against the Mormons. They are also trying to inaugurate a campaign in Eastern cities against the religious monstrosity of the West. The tale which these missionaries tell is a most doleful one. They charge Mormons with the most nefarious designs, and say many new schemes have been added since the death of the late president and the election of the new official head of the Mormon Church. The charge is made, with proof, that polygamy is more common than ever. Some ministers in the East are much exercised over the matter, and the Presbyteries and other church bodies are taking action. It is charged that no fewer than 2,000 Mormon missionaries are at work in this country and in Europe proselyting for their doctrine, and all of them serving without financial remuneration.

Current Religious

Of the joys born into t
Christ, Rev. G. B. F. Ha
Record of Christian Work
mentions the following:

Christ is the Christmas giver
richest and sweetes joys huma
perience were born in the wo
was born. Let us name a few
I. One is the joy of knowi
God. Christ was Immanuel—
near that we could see and
know him. Before the coming
ideas of God were most haz
and even crude. In a true sen

"Love came down at Chri
Love of all lovely, Lov
Love was born at Christm
Star and angels gave t

The incarnation is simply a gr
of God's love.. He loved befo
men that he loved and how
II. Another is the joy of pos
human Mediator. Before Chri
seemed distant and difficult
separating was man's sense of
came "that he might be a me
ful high priest in things perta
make reconciliation for the
ple." This office he executet
up of himself a sacrifice to s
tice and reconcile us to God
continual intercession for us
that we know the way of par
accepted it, carry about wit
abiding sense of calm and pea
assurance and the privilege
came largely with the birth of
III. Still another is the j
adoption into God's family.
himself to us as our brother.
to be children of his Father.
we have adoption, whereby
into the number of God's cl
name put upon us, the Spiri
unto us, have his fatherly ca
tions, are admitted to all t
privileges of the sons of Go
of all the promises and fe
Christ in glory. These priv
realized by men until after
Christ.

Our Budget.

—A "Merry Christmas" to all our readers!

—This means greetings to a hundred thousand appreciative readers, located in every state and territory in the Union, and in many foreign lands.

—This number will not reach some of our readers until after Christmas is passed, but they may know when they do receive it that they are included in our Christmas greetings.

—The unforgetting Christ accounts for the unforgotten Savior.

—The unforgotten Christ authenticates the historic Jesus of Nazareth.

—The unforgotten Jesus of Nazareth accounts for the decay and downfall of heathen nations now observable in the world.

—The mystery of the incarnation widens, broadens and deepens with the increase of Christ's government in the world.

—The fullness of the Godhead in Christ Jesus becomes more and more apparent as the results of his influence over men, nations and ages, pass to the historic page.

—Men will never tire of hearing the glad song of that angelic choir, sung for the first time to the humble shepherds of Bethlehem, on the night of Jesus' birth. "Glory to God in the highest, and on earth peace among men in whom he is well pleased" was the glad refrain that burst upon the ear of those shepherds on that joyful night.

—Remember the Ministerial Relief Fund before the old year dies, if possible; but at any rate remember it soon.

—We had intended making this a Jubilee number, but on account of the extra demands of the Christmas season will make our next issue—the last issue of the year—our Jubilee number.

—The program for the Congress of the Disciples has been received, but is of necessity laid over till next week. Look out for it. It contains the promise of a rich feast.

—"Through Difficulties," by Alfred Brunk, is an interesting story begun in this paper.

—Our original article on the "Babe of Bethlehem" will bear close reading. Its broad sweep of the forces and philosophies of the world strongly emphasize its orthodox conclusions concerning the Christ.

—Christmas customs encourage the spirit of "good will" and thus honors Christ even when and where it is not immediately intended or his name mentioned; and it s a fact that "good will" exists among men that pleases our Heavenly Father and his Son, who became flesh for us. It would be well in every possible way to bring the mind of children and parents to think of Christ in every Christmas gift and Christmas service or entertainment, but let us not complain at the manifestations of "good will toward men" manifested in other forms and ways, even among indifferent and religiously careless people. Any gift given in "good will" is a religious act and does credit to the soul of man, and, let us say, pleases God. May God bless every giver and gift-receiver and every heart in which the gift spirit prevails, whether they have the ability to give or not. Every heart so inspired has been touched with the finger of God's love.

—The Foreign Christian Missionary has published a folding circular, book-size pages, for circulation in the interest of the Jubilee Year and convention. The circular is filled with historic information and facts and illuminated with a large globe in blue and white with red stars to indicate the location of our missionary stations in foreign lands. This circular is one of the neatest and most attractive missionary documents for hand-to-hand work that we have yet seen. Let them circulate by the thousands.

—Our Christmas story, "Forgetting Self," is a beautiful illustration of the true Christian spirit.

—The Christmas poems in this paper are of excellent spirit and order, and you will enjoy reading them.

—The St. Joseph Daily News, St. Joseph, Mo., Dec. 12, contains a sermon, so called, in which the preacher, "Rev. Mr. Jackson," gives twenty reasons for the practice of sprinkling and pouring for Christ's baptism. Aside from the painful display of ignorance, or what is worse, the willful perversion of Scripture, we are amazed at his acceptance of immersion as Christian baptism after having so completely disproved, as he supposes, even the shadow of its appearance in the New Testament. But probably being so accustomed to the practice of unscriptural things in his religion, he was not aware of this glaring inconsistency in his sermon.

—Buffalo, N. Y., Dec. 9, 1898.—DEAR BRO. GARRISON: The CHRISTIAN-EVANGELIST, which I have read from my childhood, deserves the gratitude of its readers rather than criticisms for the Sunday-school and Christian Endeavor Departments. I should never have thought of such criticisms. Yours for continuance,
LOWELL C. MCPHERSON.

—The Foreign Society has found a medical missionary for the Upper Congo country, Africa, to succeed the late H. N. Biddle. His name is Dr. R. J. Dye, of Ionia, Mich. He has been in New York for nearly four years, making special prepartion for his work, and is said to be one of the best equipped missionaries the society has ever appointed. It is important that some one join E. E. Faris at Bolengi at once. Dr. Dye will sail early in January.

—Some of the German as well as English papers are publishing and commenting on J. W. Lowber's lecture on "Genesis and Geology," at Grayson College and at the University of Texas. Pres. J. W. McGarvey fully endorsed this lecture in his review at the Texas Lectureship, and the secular press made a mistake in stating the contrary.

—We are living in an age in which the name of Jesus is above every other name on this earth. Like the morning sun it has been steadily ascending so that it now shines out full and clear above the highest mountain peak of personal fame and power in oriental or occidental lands. The names of the founders of oriental religions are fast losing their splendor and power under the increasing light of the Sun of Righteousness and the smaller lights are paling into insignificance. We do not yet see all things put under the authority of Christ, but we do see his fame and his glory filling the earth, his spirit possessing the nations of the earth, his gospel leavening the world and his disciples multiplying in all lands. To day his is "the sweetest name on mortal tongue, the sweetest carol ever sung."

—The election of a "socialist" for mayor of Haverhill, Mass., at the last election, has created considerable interest in the East, and his administration will be watched with no small degree of anxiety in the minds of many people. On the day of his induction in office he was literally besieged with newspaper reporters from leading journals East and West, anxious to know what his policy was to be. But in so far as the mayor expressed himself there are no indications of revolutionary steps to be taken, at least in the near future. The mayor believes in the referendum doctrine, and will endeavor to give the people an opportunity to test its merits. Some of the things which the mayor with his supporters will try to realize under his administration, as indicated in the above interview are, co-operative production and distribution; municipal ownership of street railways, gas and electric plants; an eight-hour day for laborers with a minimum of $2 per day; the abolition of grade crossings; a more equal distribution of taxes; and the city to furnish shoes and clothing to poor children, when necessary, to sen them to school. If this mayor succeeds ir realizing his official hopes the city of Haverhill is to become the leader in real municipa reforms in this country. But we shall have to wait and watch for the new era until it comes.

—Xmas as an abbreviation for Christmas arose in this way: X is the initial letter of the Greek name for Christ, Xristos, and the coincidence of its cruciform shape led early to its adoption as a figure and symbol of Christ. In the Catacombs X is frequently found to stand for Christ. The early Christian artists, when making a representation of the Trinity, would place either a cross or an X beside the Father and the Holy Ghost.—*Sunday Magazine*.

—The Central Christian Church, Indianapolis, Ind., has adopted the individual communion cup system. The outfit is said to have cost $100 and was made a gift to the church by Charles T. Whitsitt, of that city. This is the first of our people—the Disciples of Christ—to adopt the individual cup system, to our knowledge.

—Few joys are more refined, pure, elevating and heavenly than the joy of giving presents to our friends in Christmas times. It is at such times that we feel like emptying ourselves for others, even as Christ emptied himself for us. How common to hear the wish for more money at such times to make more people happy. And how the heart of the true disciple of Christ swells with anxiety for the poor at such times lest they be unremembered. What a blessed feeling to have toward our fellowmen, and what a sense of "good will;" what a recognition of the tie of brotherhood. But why these blessed thoughts and this good will at Christmas times chiefly? Why should there not be the same joy in giving good gifts unto men at all times? Why not retain the Christmas spirit from one year to another? To the soul in full fellowship with Christ we believe there is the same joy in giving, the same feeling of "good will toward men" and the same spirit from year to year. The Christmas spirit never leaves such persons. The answer to all these questions, then, depends upon our fellowship with Christ. In him time becomes one continual Christmas.

—The Independent is now in its Jubilee Year and appropriately observed the beginning of it with historic articles from some of its prominent correspondents in the number dated Dec. 8th. The Independent was founded at a time in our national history when the people were agitating great social, political and religious questions and when the mutterings of an approaching Civil War could be heard. On these great questions the Independent generally took the side of liberty and the larger life of the people and nation. It was at first a Congregationalist organ, but under the editorial management of Mr. Beecher it became and has since remained largely an undenominational journal. The Independent has always been ably edited, and some of the most brilliant minds of the nation have contributed to its pages. We wish the Independent another half century of usefulness in the world's social, political and religious history.

—L. H. Batchelder, A. M., in an article in the Chautauqua for December, on "The Central Element of Organized Matter," emphasizes his theme by the use of the following quotation: "There is not a living thing, from the minutest microscopic life to the highest mammal, from the tiniest cryptogram to the huge California redwood, which does not contain carbon as an essential element." What an eloquent illustration of what Christianity ought to be in the organized moral universe! There is not a human being from the poorest peasant to the wealthiest monarch, not a social organism from the humblest home to the mightiest empire, but that should contain Christianity as an essential element. Anything in the moral universe that will not unite with Christianity has no right to exist. Christ is the center of the moral universe and his light should penetrate everything; everything should absorb and retain his nature as its central element. There can be no organic life without carbon; neither can there be spiritual life without Christ.

—The Educational Forum, Chicago, says that the number of colleges and universities unable to find presidents is increasing and mentions Amherst, Brown, Cincinnati, Colegate, Oberlin, Rochester and the state universities of Iowa and California among the list of those without presidents. This is a somewhat surprising statement. Can it be the lack of funds, or is it because of a dearth of suitable men for these positions? If the latter, then the fact ought to be an inspiration to young men for the higher education.

—A close observer of the times and undercurrents cannot fail to see in various ways and places a trend of things toward a higher sense of justice and a broader sympathy for the masses. In some respects these conditions are coming about through the agitation of direct reform measures while in others they are the results of the abuses of trusts and the perversion of public rights. That was a significant warning in ex-President Harrison's Washington Day address, in Chicago, when he said that the systematic evasion of the law taxing personal property was bound to produce a widespread demand for retaliatory legislation in the shape of income and legacy taxes, and well illustrates how good sometimes results from evils carried to excess. The people are coming to understand that the public as well as the individual has rights and that public officials have no right to barter these away to private use at any price. Public rights should be the first sources of revenue for governmental purposes, and not until these have proven inadequate should the tax on industry and personal possessions be levied.

—In this paper will be found an article under the heading, "A Day of Prayer," from Benj. L. Smith, Cor. Sec. of the A. C. M. S., and A. McLean, Cor. Sec. F. C. M. S., requesting that the churches throughout the land observe January 15, 1899, as a day of prayer for fruitful blessings during the Jubilee Year and that pastors and evangelists preach upon these things on that day. This certainly indicates the spirit in which the churches should work this year, and cannot fail of good results if humbly and earnestly observed.

—I read "Farmer Truesdall's Thanksgiving," by the editor, with a great deal of interest. I hope the editor will continue to do so.

ALFRED BRUNK.

This brother is to be credited with unusual literary ability, as he seems to be the only reader of the CHRISTIAN-EVANGELIST who was able to discover the latent merit of the story referred to. We are encouraged.

—EDITOR CHRISTIAN-EVANGELIST:—In your paper of Dec. 1st there appears a very remarkable article, entitled "Archbishop Purcell on Alexander Campbell and His Work," by "I. C."

I take the liberty of asking you if you vouch for the genuineness of this article. If it be truly a "real" interview, it is certainly well worth preserving. Not knowing "I. C.," or whether you stand back of the articles you publish, I venture to make this inquiry.

We have but lately begun to take your paper and are very much pleased with it.

Respectfully,

J. H. DARLING.

Joliet, Ill., Dec. 9,

The article to which our correspondent refers is certainly "genuine" and the interview is "genuine." How accurately the interview represents the conversation which actually took place is a matter which depends upon the memory of the writer and the means he has taken to preserve a record of the interview. In other words, it is the *authenticity* of the document, and not its *genuineness*, that is called in question. The author aims, no doubt, to fairly represent the Archbishop. Dr. W.T. Moore told us recently that he called on the Bishop, in 1868, to get a letter of introduction from him, when he was about to visit Rome, thinking it might be of benefit to him in exploring the "Eternal City," and that he had a conversation with him, in which the Bishop expressed views concerning Mr. Campbell quite similar to those expressed in the interview to which our correspondent refers.

—The word church applies, first, to the universal body of believers in Christ, no matter where found. They constitute the church built upon the great truth put forth by Peter in his confession, "Thou art the Christ, the Son of the living God."—*Journal and Messenger*.

It isn't strange, in the light of such a statement as the above, that the American Baptist Flag is for turning the Journal and Messenger out of the Baptist fold. The above is a clear case of "Campbellite" heresy.

—The author of the interview with Archbishop Purcell, which has created a great deal of interest and some inquiry, in a personal letter to the editor referring to the question of his reliability refers us to Rev. Willis G. Craig, Professor in McCormick Theological Seminary at Chicago, Judge Ira Julian, of Frankfort, Ky., and a number of other distinguished people. He is a graduate of Center College, Kentucky, later of the Law School at Harvard, and after that was a student of the Sorborne, Paris. There can be no question either as to his ability or reliability.

—It is strange how different human nature is among Baptists from what it is among us, "as a people!" Just read what the Journal and Messenger says of some of their preachers:

It is a great strain on human nature when a pastor who, because of his great dignity and high mightiness, does absolutely nothing for the increase of subscriptions in his church, asks us, either directly or indirectly, to publish long accounts of his sayings and doings, or, what is the same, the sayings and possible doings of his church. It takes a large amount of editorial grace to overcome the feeling that if the pastor really thinks that space in the Journal and Messenger is worth so much to him, he ought to see to it that more of his members read what it prints.

—C. A. Young writes us a letter from Charlottesville, Va., where he is engaged in his Bible lectures, and pours out his homesickness for his native state in the following poetic quotation:

"We love thee Missouri!
  Thy sweet rustic grace,
Thy plain homespun manners,
  And broad, honest face.
While the star-spangled banner
  In triumph shall wave
O'er the land of the free
  And the home of the brave,
'Twill shelter no prouder,
  No nobler than thee!
Missouri! Missouri!
  Bright home of the free!"

It may be that Missouri will find a niche for Bro. Young if the rest of creation will let him alone.

—S. R. Ezzell, Ferris, Texas, sends us "An Old Preacher's Final Statement," in which, after reciting a series of financial misfortunes during his 46 years' ministry, including the failure of insurance company and losses by "rascals and dishonest churches," he says:

I am now drooping near my 64th milepost, too poor in this world's goods to pay my burial expenses; but "rich in faith and an heir of the kingdom which God hath promised to them that love him." As a conscientious Christian, believing it to be due me and mine, also my debtors and my creditors and the sacred cause of my Master; and believing I shall be the better satisfied living and dying, I do hereby solemnly make and respectfully submit this true, brief, frank statement for the aforesaid reasons. This, the 24th day of June, A. D., 1898.

S. R. EZZELL.

Ferris, Ellis County, Tex.

P. S.—I intend to keep striving to pay every cent I owe.

S. R. E.

—Alvah H. Doty, M.D., health officer of the port of New York, in an exceedingly interesting article on the scientific prevention of yellow fever, says some things which all men and especially all health officers would do well to consider. Dr. Doty thinks that the yellow fever infection always in some way starts from Cuba and says:

"No other place in the world to-day offers such a menace to the public health of this country as the Cuban seaports, notably Havana." And yet, inasmuch as yellow fever, according to Dr. Doty, "is not contagious in the strict sense; that is, it is not communicated from person to person as is smallpox or scarlet fever," even this overshadowing danger can be dissipated. Dr. Doty thinks yellow fever the legitimate product of unsanitary conditions and limited by altitudes and temperatures to certain localities, and that even within its congenial sphere it may be prevented or killed by proper sanitary regulations. Even Havana, the hotbed of fever germs, he says, may be freed from the pest by proper sewerage and sanitary regulations, and that no improvement in the prevention of the infection in this and other countries can be had until new and modern systems of sewerage shall be thoroughly installed in all the seaports of Cuba.

—Considerable interest has been created in the recent successes of Hertz, Brauly, Marconi, Clarke, Tesla, *et al.*, in space telegraphy and as in all new and wonderful achievements of science great things have been predicted of it. For instance, the destruction of a war-ship, military fort or city, at the will of a distant invisible agent, and other equally startling and revolutionary things are predicted of it. That space telegraphy is a wonderful achievement, and within a limited sphere may do wonderful things, is not to be doubted, but that it will ever be available for destructive uses at long range, as stated above, cannot be believed by any one who will take the pains to inquire into the things and conditions essential to its existence. In so far as yet possible the discovery is limited to a very narrow field because of essential conditions and inherent dispositions, and it is therefore not likely to become a war weapon or agency in the very near future. Messages have been sent by space telegraphy over a distance of 18 miles, but the difficulties multiply very rapidly with increasing miles from the transmitting instrument. The present known practical uses of the discovery thus far are intercommunication between ships at sea, moving trains and signal purposes. No doubt other uses for it will be found, but as the invention now stands its capacity for general practical purposes is likely to remain as now indefinitely.

—Christmas brings trying times to many people. Some see others with plenty of money buying beautiful presents for their friends while their friends, whom they love just as dearly, must go without these sweet tokens of love and friendship for lack of money to purchase them. These are great trials, trials which those who have plenty know not of, and to keep a sweet spirit and cheerful heart under such circumstances is a great personal achievement—a gain worth more than all the Christmas gifts that could be bestowed. But those who have and to spare ought to think of the thousands of people in the land who have dear ones, but no money with which to buy them even the smallest gift for Christmas, and in some way help to bear their burden. But let not those who are short of money to supply their friends with the number and quality of presents desired become sour and embittered against those who can give if they do not share with you in these joys. Let the world be just as cheerful as possible. Let good will prevail. Let the peace of God reign supreme in the heart and the end will be one of joy. No money is required for these blessings. God's gifts to men are without money and without price.

—EDITOR CHRISTIAN-EVANGELIST:—I would dislike very much to have your Sunday-school and Endeavor departments discontinued. They are a great help to me, as we seldom see any of our Sunday-school publications, and I am but one of a great many, especially in this new country. C. J. CHASTAIN.

Yukon, Okla., Dec. 11, 1898.

—The CHRISTIAN-EVANGELIST almost every week gives, on its first page, a splendid picture of some one of our prominent preachers and workers. These pictures add to the attractivenes and interest of the paper.—*The Christian.*

We are glad to hear this word of appreciation from our esteemed brother of St. Johns, N. B., and believe that it voices the appreciation of all our readers. This effort to please our readers in good things is not without much additional cost to the publishers, but the readers of the CHRISTIAN-EVANGELIST know that we do not stop an expense when the way to increase the merits of the paper becomes apparent. Those who will be at pains to cut out these half-tone pictures will soon find themselves the possessors of excellent picture albums of our prominent preachers. Another good way by which to express appreciation of the CHRISTIAN-EVANGELIST would be to send us new names for our subscription list. And when you do this remember that you are working in your own interest and that your home, your neighbors and the church as well as that of our own. And now that we are at the threshold of a new year it would be a good time to send us a few names at once for our list.

A Word of Congratulation.

MY DEAR BRO. GARRISON:—I hasten to congratulate the brotherhood of Missouri on the happy issue of the Educational Conference, as indicated in your editorial of this week. It is, I think, just what ought to have been done, and what I urged in principle at the first Conference. I shall be glad to co-operate with my brethren in trying to make the plan indicated helpful to all our schools. Let me urge patience on the part of all concerned. The work proposed will not be done in a day nor in a year, but with the faithful co-operation of all our preachers much can be done, and confidence and hope inspired on all lines. Would that all our brethren whom God has blessed with means could see their opportunity, and feel their responsibility just now. Let us pray that they may. I regretted my inability to attend the Conference. I was just at that time in the service of the great state of Missouri trying to guard the interest of the helpless blind children in the Blind School of your city. At the close of the protracted investigation I was completely prostrated, and was not able to attend the Conference. It is perhaps just as well.

Allow me to thank you for the picture and the all-too-flattering notice of myself in the CHRISTIAN-EVANGELIST this week. In looking back over a ministry of forty-five years in Missouri I can see many mistakes and some failures, but I can conscientiously say that I have always done and said what I thought to be true and right at the time.

I have loved our cause and plea as I have loved my life, and never more than I love it to-day. I count myself happy to have been associated with the grand men who have so nobly wrought on Missouri soil, and it is a great joy and cause of constant thankfulness that I am so preserved in mind and body that I count the last years of my life the happiest I have known. If there is the appearance of egotism in this letter, lay the blame on yourself, for what youth of 66 summers would not be a little spoiled by your words of commendation?

I have wanted for sometime to say that the CHRISTIAN-EVANGELIST improves with each issue and every passing year. Who knows how many rocks and shoals our good ship of Zion has cleared by reason of its wise counsel and sweet spirit? Do all our preachers read it and commend it to the churches? I hope they do. T. P. HALEY.

Kansas City, Mo., Dec. 16.

Jamaica Printing Press and the Advance Society.

Little Gerald Dever, of Hume, Ill., sends us $1 for the Jamaica printing press, and says: "Mamma told me about the printing press for Jamaica. I belong to the Advance Society, and want to do something to help for Jesus' sake, so I send you $1 for the printing press." His mother adds in a postscript: "I believe if an appeal were made to the Advance Society each member would respond with $1 or more." This Advance Society has a good name, and evidently believes in *advancing*, and they recognize in the printing press one of the *ways* to advance. Bro. Ellis is doing a capital work among the young folks, and they are all in a buzz about it all over the country. Have you read about the Advance Society in the CHRISTIAN-EVANGELIST? We should be glad to hear from as many members of the Advance Society as feel interested in helping to purchase a printing press for Bro. Randall in Jamaica. It is a little remarkable that the contributions so far have come from Illinois exclusively. Let us hear from some of the other states also.

PERSONAL MENTION.

J. M. Morris is meeting with fine success as state evangelist in New York.

S. W. Glascock, has become the pastor of the church at Rock Port, Mo.

H. W. Everest, of Des Moines, Ia., has gone to Conroe, Tex., for a season.

V. E. Ridenour will assist H. C. Patterson in a meeting at Keota, Ia., beginning Jan. 1.

G. M. Weimer, of Huntington, W. Va., has accepted a call to preach for the church at Vincennes, Ind.

R. E. Lloyd, of Kansas City, Mo., asks churches wanting a meeting or a preacher to correspond with him.

N. R. Davis, who recently ordained E. B. Harris, of Grant City, Mo., to the work of the ministry, commends him highly in every way.

Leander Lane has accepted a call to become the pastor of the church at Fairfield, Ia., where he has been preaching for four months.

N. J. Nichols will remain at Tina, Mo., another year. It is said that he has done a good work there.

C. M. Chilton, of St. Joseph, Mo., is to aid pastor Gresham in a meeting at Savannah, Mo., in January next.

O. P. Speigel, Cor. Sec., says that the Alabama Christian Missionary Convention will be held in Selma, Jan. 10-12, 1899.

J. B. Jeans, of Hamilton, Mo., has been called to preach for the church at Sumner, Mo., where he recently held a successful meeting.

M. C. Johnson, of Elliot, Iowa, would like to hold a protracted meeting for some church in January next. He has just closed a good meeting at Elliot.

B. B. Tyler has had a call to Honolulu, Hawaii, but writes us that he feels it his duty to remain at Colorado Springs for the present. D. L. Moody, the evangelist, is stirring up that place with a series of revival services.

J. T. Ogle, pastor of the church at Carrollton, Mo., invites all former pastors of that church to the celebration of its 53rd anniversary Dec. 21st.

The full text of A. E. Ewell's sermon at the courthouse, Wichita Falls, Tex., on Thanksgiving Day, appeared in the Wichita Weekly Times of that city, Dec. 9th. A. E. Ewell is the pastor of the Christian Church at Wichita Falls, Tex.

The name of J. L. Parsons, New Albany, Ind., now appears on the Christian Guide as a contributing editor. Bro. Parsons has written for a number of our papers and is widely known as a writer and preacher.

J. P. Adcock, of Ft. Scott, Kas., who spent last summer in evangelistic work with tent and singer in Oklahoma and Texas, and who wishes to do a similar work next summer, desires work for some church or a few protracted meetings to occupy his time until spring.

Evangelists Scoville and Scott have recently closed a meeting at Buchanan, Mich., with 205 additions; 32 came the last night. Bro. Scoville reports 1,240 additions this year in his meetings, not counting about four months in which they did not work. The Buchanan meeting is reported at length by another in this paper.

T. S. Noblitt, of Ellendale, N. Dak., has been called to the principalship of the academy at Middle Grove, Mo. He has accepted and writes that he will also be able to do some preaching at adjacent points. He will be at Middle Grove Jan. 1, 1899. The church at Ellendale, N. Dak., is in good condition, he writes, and in want of a preacher for 1899.

D. R. Dungan, pastor of Mt. Cabanne Christian Church, this city, spent four days of last week at Columbus, Mo., during which time he delivered four lectures to the Christian Bible College on "Sacred Geography." He was also in demand at Christian College for chapel exercises and talks, and of course greatly enjoyed the visit.

CHANGES.

Richard Bagby, Charlottesville to Louisa, Va.

J. H. Speer, East Atchison, Mo., to North Topeka, Kan.

J. P. Adcock, Mead, I. T., to Ft. Scott, Kan.

J. G. Williams, Tower Hill to Assumption, Ill.

W. G. Smith, New Castle to Delphi, Ind.

H. W. Everest, Des Moines, Ia., to Conroe, Tex.

H. W. Stewart, St. John, N. B., to Winston, N. C.

I. M. Boswell, Junction City, Ky., to Meridian, Miss.

G. M. Weimer, Huntington, W. Va., to Vincennes, Ind.

W. H. McGinnis, Athens to Waverly, Ill.

SUBSCRIBERS' WANTS.

Miscellaneous wants and notices will be inserted in this department at the rate of two cents a word, each insertion, all words, large and small, to be counted, and two initials stand for one word. Please accompany notice with corresponding remittance to save book-keeping.

FOR SALE.—Brand New, High Grade Piano. Bargain if taken at once. For further particulars address Christian Pub. Co., 1522 Locust St., St. Louis.

ence.

cs.

EAT:

.e first portion of
r of interesting
saying only a few
pulpit power in
tainly Dr. Park-
seems to be in
whom American
loctor has of late
erous sickness of
one of the most
and is famous for
for years has con-
ered solos which
s services at the
Dr. Parker been
ich has involved
ion, that he has
een unable to ap-
er's wife, who is
h more to do with
ost congregations
wives of preach-
appreciation till it
be of any avail.
abernacle, lately
mas Spurgeon is
in the restored
tructed on an im-
cannot again be-
ill the Tabernacle
considerable time

about our work,
more interesting
er affairs in the
our churches in
opeful spirit than
period. The re-
the best results
as arrived and has
campaign from
ngs. He will do

whether American or British. Molland posted us up in all the old history of China. We knew after his talk the origin of Chinese paganism. Saw enchanted us by his graphic accounts of his own observations. Hearndèn made us feel as if we had actually been in China. Arnold made us feel as if we all ought at once to go and conquer China for God. Hunt and his wife electrified us with proofs of marvelous success in the whole of the Chinese mission field. There is something of vivid and impassioned earnestness, zeal and sincerity in our own missionaries which distinguishes them from the agents of the sectarian societies, excellent and devoted as many of them are. We have no "returned empties," as the Church of England people in irony dub their Colonial and Missionary Bishops when they come home.

THE GOLD PLATE AT ST. PAUL'S CATHEDRAL.

At a cost of 7,500 pounds in English money the now notorious Mr. Ernest Terah Hooley about two years ago presented a service of solid gold communion plate to St. Paul's Cathedral. Bitterly have the dean and chapter of the great cathederal regretted their acceptance of this gift from the arch mammon-worshiper whose doings have sent so many thrills of consternation through English society. Hooley was one of the mushroom millionaires produced in these days of feverish speculation and reckless gambling in the money market. He rigged up syndicates which gave millions for such concerns as the Dunlop Cycle Company. Into these companies, which bore his stamp of sanction or proprietorship, thousands of covetous people rushed fo invest their all on earth with the expectation of bursting suddenly into wealth without working any more. Thousands of others joined in mere simplicity, and and ruined in the host of impoverished victims. Suddenly Hooley became the biggest bankrupt of modern times. He then adopted the plan of making what he called "revelations" as to the doings of his confederates and friends, many of whom are great people, some being earls, some baronets and some members of the House of Commons. There has been a panic in all directions. The authorities at St. Paul's

it is the safest thing to say. England will no more be able to give up her hold on Egypt than America will be able to abandon the Philippines. Either surrender would be a crime amounting to high treason to the interests of humanity. It would have been a mercy to the human race if the United States had seized every colony that Spain possessed. Of course, this could not be done. But as before long England may have trouble about Egypt of the most perilous nature, I will as an Englishman try in my small way to influence in the interests of righteousness and justice the valued opinion of all our American friends. Americans now in England are forcibly struck with the affectionate sympathy felt and displayed through all classes for the American people and the American foreign policy. The proof that this is genuine national feeling is that it characterizes all classes alike. Those who disagree on many other matters of party are all agreed here. Britain would have fought for America had there been recent need of it. Every man and woman I know expresses just that opinion. Now, if Egypt be deserted to please France, then ruin for Egypt is a certainty. I am watching current continental literature, and I easily preceive that a strong and malignant feeling prevails against the whole Anglo-Saxon policy of liberty and progress. The great governments which are crushing their populations under the autocratic burdens of militarism—Germany, Austria and Russia—are plotting busily against the fast-developing predominance in the world of America and Britain. And France, bewitched by her dreams of recovering her military glory, and tortued between priestcraft amongst the women and atheism amongst the men, is about to make herself the base tool of the triple tyranny. A crisis is not very far off. Instead of the disarmament dreamed about by the good-natured young Tsar, of Russia, there will be a frantic haste to arm for the coming Armageddon. The ministers of the Tsar have humored and encouraged him, because they know Russia needs time. The archangel of the coming mischief will be the Kaiser. That timely rescuer, who has fortunately appeared on the scene, "providentially," to counteract the mistakes, and the lack of wisdom, and the sins of omission and commission of the departed one. Our new pastor sees but little good that has been accomplished, and of course has no word of approval for anything. He notifies the brethren at large that it will take him a long time to straighten matters in his new and hitherto unfortunate field, and hence not much news of advance is to be expected from him for sometime to come. In some of his remarks and insinuations Christian humility and righteous forbearance are entirely lost to sight, and accusations of sinister motives are mentioned often without apology.

Nihil est quin male narrando passit depravari, and so it is with the type of man we write of. Suppressing all that may be good, a case is soon made out, and the new pastor enters upon his duties bidding for a sympathy almost akin to commiseration. We are glad to believe that this unfortunate, unministerial, unbrotherly and unchristian habit belongs only to a very limited class. It is a habit that should be frowned upon by the churches, and I believe is discountenanced by every preacher who is not a mere place-seeker. Such a characteristic is by no manner of means an evidence of superiority, but is rather a mark of narrowness of soul and of inferior ability. No broad-minded Christian worker ever stoops to elavate himself by any such questionable methods.

T. H. BLENUS.

New York Letter.

Knowing that our beloved corresponding secretary of the Foreign Christian Missionary Society had just returned from a tour of inspection in Cuba, I dropped him a note asking a few questions, with the view of giving our readers his impressions of Cuba as a mission field. I also asked Bro. McLean to state what has been done by Catholics and Protestants in that island, and what, in his opinion, are the best methods to be employed in effective work there. As the interest in Cuba's present condition and in her prospects is international, I am certain all would like to read Bro. McLean's words. He says:

1. In my opinion Cuba is a fruitful missionary field. The priests as a rule are Spaniards. Naturally, their sympathies were with the Spaniards in the recent struggle. I was told by reputable people that they did not think the Cubans had any more rights than beasts. The archbishop of Cuba offered the Spanish Government $20,000,000, in the last days of the war, to build four battleships. He proposed to ge this money by stripping the saints in the churches of their crowns and jewels. For these reasons the church has in large measure lost its influence over the people.

Churches abound, masses are said every day in the week, the confessional is open, gifts are made to the saints, but the people are ignorant and degraded. At no time has the church done much for the moral and spiritual well-being of the Cubans. Lottery tickets are for sale everywhere, bullfights are as popular as they are in Spain. Sunday is like other days; most of the business houses are open; tradesmen of all kinds carry on their work.

Americans are all but worshiped. The Cubans have begun to lift up their heads and to look for their redemption. They believe that the day of civil and religious liberty is at hand.

2. You ask me to state what I think should be done. I think that Bibles and New Testaments should be sent to Cuba by the thousands. These should be in Spanish and in English. Most of the people that I saw want to be able to read and to talk English. They regard English as the language of freedom. Day-schools and Sunday-schools should be opened. The gospel should be preached to the people in their own tongue. Church buildings should be erected. There is nothing that will do so much to stir up the priests to reform their own lives and to do their best work as to have Protestant churches planted throughout Cuba.

3. The Southern Baptists have been at work in Cuba for some twelve years. They bought a theater for $60,000 and transformed it into a church. The location is a capital one. This building will seat about 1,200 people. Dr. Alberto J. Diaz is the chief worker in Havana. He told me that he baptized 3,000 people with his own hands. About half that number are living and remain. He planted seven churches. There are only two left. His converts have been killed in war. The churches in the suburbs have been destroyed. Dr. Diaz has been in prison six times. He was set at liberty on the condition that he should leave the country. For three years and a half he has been in Mexico. Recently he has returned and has reopened his church. This is the only Protestant church in Havana. I was told that there was no other Protestant church on the island. The Sunday evening I was in Havana Dr. Diaz spoke. I think there were at least 800 people present. Being a Cuban and speaking the Spanish language fluently he naturally commands the attention of the people and secures good audiences. His work has been marvelously successful.

4. The Americans are pouring into Cuba. The people in Havana expect at least 20,000 Americans within the next six months. Protestant churches must be planted troughout the island. These churches in a little while will be self-supporting. Meanwhile, the Cubans are poor. They need healp. The island has been desolated by war. With the return of peace and the establishment of good government Cuba will be one of the richest countries in the world. The land will yield three or four crops in a year.

***

Lyman Abbott, pastor of the Plymouth Congregational Church, Brooklyn, read to his congregation yesterday morning (the 27th) a letter resigning the pastorate of that historic church. He is now sixty-three years old and has begun to feel the burden of advancing age. His physician has warned him that he must either give up his editorial work on the Outlook or the pastorate of Plymouth. He does the later. Abbott has made quite a stir now and then by what has been termed "reckless utterances" in his pulpit, especially so in the recent series of discourses he preached on the Bible. It was reported at the time that his congregation lustily cheered his assaults on the trustworthiness of certain parts of the Scriptures. It is apparent, according to what has come through certain personal channels, from within the ring, that the Doctor found it necessary to try certain "attractions" to get a respectable hearing, at least on Sunday evenings. One season, high-class music was tried and failed. So they thought best to try the old Bible in Plymouth Church. Judging from Lyman Abbott's "Pantheism," and "Evolution," and "Socialism," and "Destructive Criticism" which seem to be uppermost in his reported sermonic and editorial thought, it is safe to infer that the preaching of the simple gospel in Plymouth pulpit is somewhat rare. Curiosity brought the "crowds" out to hear the lecturer attack the Bible. I say *lecturer* because he is pre-eminently a lecturer, and not a preacher in the New Testament sense of that holy office—to proclaim Christ as the Savior of lost men. Dr. Abbott has a great hearing throughout the weekly issue of the Outlook, and it is to be regretted that the simple, beautiful, and only divine plan of salvation through Christ is not more prominently set forth by him in that journal.

***

Bro. J. S. Sweeney, who recently resigned at Paris, Ky., after a pastorate of twenty-eight years, is perhaps one of the ablest defenders of the Christian faith in America. He has held between eighty and ninety religious discussions in various parts of this country, having met with wonderful skill Infidels, Agaostics, Universalists, Spiritualists, Baptists and Pedobaptists. He has received into the First Christian Church (Disciples of Christ) over 3,000 members during his pastorate. His church has now about 1,500 members, and through its social, intellectual and financial standing dominates in a large measure Bourbon County, and to a great extent controls the sentiment of Central Kentucky. His father, a minister, is still living at the age of 93, and his three brothers were able ministers of the Word, one of whom, Z. T. Sweeney, was consul general to Constantinople under President Harrison. Bro. Sweeney's purpose in resigning is to lecture in many places on the evidences of Christianity.

Bro. F. M. Rains' tract, "The Success of Modern Missions," ought to be read by every preacher in the land, and sowed broadcast through all our congregations. It is surcarged with vital power and inspiration. It will put a quietus on objections to Christian missions.

Let every pastor see to it that the young people of his flock organize themselves into a Bethany Reading Circle, or better still, let the pastor, if possible, lead the courses of study himself. These three books, "Sketches of the Pioneers," "The Life and Teaching of Jesus" and "Our Mission Fields" are gems. The good brerhren Power, Willett and Lhamon, who wrote them, put their very best into these books. The proper training of our young people is one of the great needs of our time, and these three lines of study are the very ones most needed. Bro. J. Z. Tyler, Cleveland, Ohio, will give all desired information about this work. May God guide and bless this important enterprise and sustain our noble national superintendent in his great labor of love.

S. T. WILLIS.

1281 *Union Avenue.*

Memories of Thomas Munnell.

Thomas Munnell, of happy memory, was as those intimately acquainted with him well know, a man of much more than ordinary ability and excellence of character.

Some of his articles in our quarterlies and best weeklies bear the marks of scholarship and much thought. And while he never followed in the wake of any human being, he never aspired to become a leader. What he did with his pen and tongue he did, as I am convinced, in order to accomplish good. And while the reader of his clear, trenchant articles could not always agree with him in premise or conclusion, one thing he was compelled to admit—the manliness, earnestness and sincerity of the writer.

This Reformation or this Restoration movement, in letter and spirit, he had studied thoroughly. He well understood that the central personage, the one in whom all must believe who approach the Father seeking salvation, was and is and must ever be Jesus the Christ the Son of the living God, and that thus believing with all the heart, many cherished opinions become matters of indifference in serving God the Father through the Crucified One.

Some writers are startling—if not that, they

extract from a sketch prepared by Bro. Munnell for a book I propose giving to the public by and by. It is concerning Moses E. Lard as thinker, speaker, writer: "Much of his [Bro. Lard's] time he walked in the shadows, but w walking heavenward all the same. Sometimes he was joyful, almost ecstatic, especially when the wings of his imagination and matchless pathos swept him up almost in sight of heaven; at such moments he saw and felt himself surrounded with all the verities of the upper world: you heard his first burst of glorious surprise in meeting his mother, his own family and the many he loved on earth. You would see him looking back on old earth again, and noting the 'little undulations' in the ground whence their bodies had recently sprung; then turning to them again all around him, you would hear that strange shrill voice of tumultuous joy as he seemed to take the whole situation in. Many ministers can stir the soul to transient ecstasy, but who was ever able to so disturb the deep waters and cause the sea to roll on so long after the sermon was ended?"

What greetings on the "shining shore," in that world of light, life and immortality!

W. C. ROGERS.

Cameron, Mo.

Hiram College Jubilee Endowment.

1. A CONSPICUOUS YEAR.

The year 1900 is conspicuous as the closing year of the nineteenth century—the most remarkable century of the Christian era. It is safe to say that the race has made more progress in all lines of development, both material and intellectual, than during any ten centuries of the world's history. Ought not this closing year of this wonderful century to be signalized by the greatest achievements of any year of the century? The eyes of all are turned upon the coming year. All benevolent and philanthropic enterprises are already beginning to plan for great things during the year that is soon to be ushered in. This is as it should be. Let all awake to the occasion and its opportunities. The year 1900 may indeed be an epoch-making year in every benevolent enterprise.

2. A STRIKING FACT.

It is worthy of note that the closing year of the century is Hiram's Jubilee Year. Fifty years of history will be completed at the Commencement in June, 1900. The students of Hiram, the friends of Hiram, the friends of education, have a double incentive for doing great things for Hiram College in this conspicuous year. $250,000 is a small amount to ask the friends of this institution to give it. No institution is considered adequately endowed in this day that has less than half a million dollars. If Hiram shall receive $250,000 as an addition to its present endowment, it will enter upon the twentieth century with almost boundless possibilities for good in the line of Christian education.

3. THE RELATIVE IMPORTANCE OF OUR EDUCATIONAL INSTITUTIONS.

The Methodist Church has decided to signalize the close of the century by raising twenty millions of dollars for the general purposes of the church. Ten millions of this will go to the cause of education, the other ten million to missionary and other general interests of the church. It will be seen that the Methodist Church regards education as equal in importance to all other general interests combined, including its missionary work, and are they wrong in this? Is not education fundamental to everything? Certainly this will not be denied by any thoughtful man. May not the Disciples as a people learn a lesson from the Methodists? Has not the time come when education should come to the front and occupy the most prominent place in the eyes of our brotherhood until at least we have a few adequately endowed colleges? With the fullest sympathy for all our institutions of learning and without any desire to monopolize the attention of the brotherhood, Hiram calls upon the Disciples of Christ to join together in one supreme effort to give the institution such an endowment as will enable it to hold a place among the leading colleges of the country.

4. THE NECESSITY FOR COLLEGE ENDOWMENT.

If any fail to see the necessity for college endowment they have but to consider the history of all colleges, to be convinced of its importance. Schools of academic grade that teach a comparatively small curriculum of study and consequently do the work with few teachers, run without endowment; but there is not a college in our land that maintains the average college standard and does work of the average quality that can run without endowment. If colleges had to be supporred by tuition fees the expenses would be so great that three-fourths of the young people of the country would be cut off from collegiate training. Furthermore it is useless to talk about endowing colleges with one hundred or even two hundred thousand dollars in this day of advancing standards, when the field of education has broadened so rapidly. Hiram college teaches twice as many classes as it did twenty years ag and it must do it to meet the demands upon it and compete successfully with other institutions. The same thing is true in a general way of other institutions. This means that colleges must have twice as much endowment as was necessary twenty years ago.

5. HOW TO HOLD OUR YOUNG PEOPLE.

A great deal is said about our young people attending state and denominational colleges. It is urged as a duty upon our brethren to patronize our own colleges. I am in sympathy with this demand, but I am fully convinced that we cannot hold our young people in our own colleges unless we make our colleges equal in advantages offered to those of other religious bodies. If we will endow our colleges properly, increase their courses of instruction in number and strength until they are at least up to the average, we will hold our young people. In other words, when we give our young people what they want and what they can get elsewhere, we will have no trouble in keeping them in our own schools. People will not patronize colleges simply as a matter of duty to the college or religious body with which they are connected. They must have what they want, what the age demands and what is furnished elsewhere, and when this is done no argument will be necessary to induce our young people to patronize our schools.

6. A POPULAR ENDORSEMENT.

Why cannot a college be endowed by the people by a great popular movement? Why cannot at least 50,000 persons join heart and hand to the endowment of Hiram College on the occasion of its fiftieth anniversary? 50,000 people who would average $5.00 apiece would give Hiram the $250,000 that it needs to insure its perpetuity and enlarged usefulness. Hiram has been a college of the people. Hundreds ot young men and women who have been educated at Hiram never could have had the advantage of a collegiate training had it not been for Hiram College. Expenses have been kept marvelously low for the purpose of bringing higher education within the reach of young people of very limited means. More than half of the young people in Hiram to-day are self-supporting students. Such an institution has a right to call upon the people to endow it. Will not the people respond?

HIRAM COLLEGE JUBILEE ENLISTMENT CARD.

Whereas, the friends of Hiram College are uniting in a movement to add $250,000 to the endowment of that institution on the occasion of its fiftieth anniversary in June of the year 1900; and whereas, an effort is now being made to secure the names of 50,000 persons, more or less, who will make a donation of from one dollar to one thousand dollars each for that purpose, I hereby agree to join this movement by promising to pay one dollar or more and will name the definite amount of my donation and the time of payment when called upon to do so.

Name ....

Post Office............... ......

Street & Number....... ....

Date............189..

Do not wait. Send in your name. A very encouraging beginning has been made, but names must begin to come in before long by the thousand to accomplish the desired result. Let all the friends of education join together in one supreme effort to accomplish this most important result.

E. V. Z.

The Moody Bible Institute.

In daily life, in all parts of the country, I find that there are hundreds of consecrated men and women with an intense love for souls who feel called of God to do his work. All they lack to do effective service for him is a systematic knowledge of the Bible.

The question asked me hundreds of times by young people convicted by a direct call of God for evangelistic work, or where they could be used for his glory, was, "Where can I obtain this knowledge?" This question started the Bible Institute in Chicago as a training school for Home and Foreign Missions ten years ago.

I have been convinced the way to reach the masses is to reach them—that is, to go after them. I have not announced "Hold the Fort" in my meetings for years; the time for holding the fort is past, and now we must go out of the fort and fight hand to hand with the powers of evil. The Bible Institute at Chicago aims to equip workers who can fight this way—hand to hand.

The school is open the year round, and as the course is in a circle of two years students may enter at any time.

is no reality in disease, for God only

u follow the same treatment of exhortation for every disease?''
ıme in every case. The whisper of he mortal mind will bring relief. nd death have no foundation in

ence is neither scientific nor Chris- l it is a matter of regret that any of legislatures should permit these practice their theories at the bed- e sick. It is a kind of conglomera- taphysics, paganism and Christian- ıs wage war against it, and cast out d those possessed of familiar spirits. ›n, Mormonism and soothsayers go together. WM. H. KNOTTS.
le, Ind.

---

ial of Transylvania University.

ımittees appointed by the Executive of the Board of Curators of Ken- versity and by the society of Alumni titution acting together, have decid- erve the 100th anniversary of the f Transylvania University by suitable in Lexington on Sunday, Jan. 1, ch is the anniversary day and also commencement week, which begins th day of June next.
ıngements for the commemoration on roximo have been almost completed. e religious denominations which have n Lexington were represented among ents of Transylvania University and all of them among the benefactors, erality sustained the university in ıbious times. For these reasons the e of Arrangements has suggested to ers of Lexington that they recognize ersary in connection with the morn- ses of that day in such way and to at as they may severally think best.
commemorative exercises will be e evening in Morrison Chapel, which ppropriately decorated for the occa- e living Alumni of Transylvania Uni- Bacon College and Kentucky Univer-

A Suggestion.

I read with appreciation "Early Times in Indiana," in a late number of the CHRISTIAN-EVANGELIST, written by D. R. Lucas. I like such themes. They help to bind this active rushing age to the blessed memories of the past. I readily recall the features of Eld. John O'Kane whose portrait I painted nearly a score of years ago for his widow in Pike County, Mo. I could easily discern those traits ascribed to him by Bro. Lucas, in the lineaments of the small picture from which I worked. I love to dwell on the old times in Missouri and the early struggles of the workers, for our plea in Monroe and adjoining counties have a special charm for me because that was, and is yet, home. (My suggestion will come later.)

Although I am just now nearing the half century mark I can see that the old faces that beamed with religious enthusiasm and zeal at the old meetings have about all "passed over the river" and the next generation is growing gray. I can well remember in old Middlegrove vicinity having old Bro. Bassett (who passed away since I have been in Washington, at about ninety-two) pointed out to me the place in the white oak forest down the creek, where the first old log church of our people in that section was built. My good old grandfather helped in that noble work.

Later that rude old building was torn down and moved to the eastern edge of the village. In about 1855, that gave way to our first frame building, which in turn gave place to the present building in about 1883. In these first two old church buildings T. M. Allen, Alfred Wilson and others of like character proclaimed the primitive gospel to an appreciative people. I like to recall what was said of these stalwart old laborers for the Master's cause. That was before my old teacher, Bro. J. A. Berry, now of Ashland, Mo., I believe, came to our home village to take charge of the "Academy" and to preach too in our church. Another thing I remember was that of hearing about the young Haleys who "were making preachers of themselves" over about old Antioch some half a dozen miles away in the edge of Randolph County. Our beloved T. P. is one of those boys. Bro. Alex. Procter's early home was there too and Bro. W. M. Featherston, who took my confession and baptized me over thirty years ago, was raised in that nest of coming religious giants and drove oxen and rode wild colts with the rest of them. Dear indeed must be to them the hallowed memories associated with old Antioch neighborhood. The characteristics of several of those old pioneers who labored before these last named I can remember and Bro. Lucas' narrative brings up several of such to my mind both interesting and amusing. But consideration of space forbids me to narrate them and my suggestion is, cannot some good brother with a genius for gathering data, incidents, experiences, etc., collect and put into book form a history of our early church in Missouri? I would suggest that it embrace only our growth up to say 1860, not too much given to explanations of our plea or other theological subjects now already voluminously written and spoken upon, but filled with the common every-day experiences of our people in their first efforts to establish New Testament Christianity. The advent of every John the Baptist or first evangelist into each and every community I would have recorded. I would like too to have related some experiences in each locality, facts recalled, which would enable us to go back, as it were, and keep step with these our venerated pathfinders and sympathize with them in their joys and sorrows, successes and failures, and thus as near as possible follow or go with them up to the beginning of the Civil War. To attempt to bring it up to the present date would necessitate so much condensation that it would fail to fulfill my idea of an actual history combined with personal reminiscences at once interesting, entertaining and instructive. I would also have it illustrated as much as possible with portraits of our first workers and their houses, if means could be obtained to do so. I hope I've been sufficiently explicit in my suggestion, and if there is no such book can we not have one?

R. J. TYDINGS.

Washington, D. C., Dec. 14, 1898.

Schools of Thought Among the Disciples.

It is not to be expected that all will think alike in any religious community, nor is it to be desired. The toleration of opinion in matters of expediency, and the tenacity of belief in matters of fundamental importance, has always been the boast of the Disciples. This has given wide range and liberty of view, while it has conserved the body and unified its faith. Even in the first century there was this same divergence of opinion, as the result of provincialisms.

Among us just now there are at least five distinct schools of thought.

(1) There are our "*sound brethren*," who call themselves Old School Disciples, and are often nicknamed "antis" (a term of reproach which should be discarded), who are often so *very perpendicular* that some of them actually lean over to the side of sectarianism and schism. No more sincere people ever lived than are found among this class of brethren who, too often, have allowed the moss to accumulate on their backs and the kinks to get into their theological wigs. Bless them, they will see things differently some day when they get out of the woods into the open air of larger privilege and opportunity!

(2) Then there are those of the opposite extreme, who are so *awfully liberal* that they have almost lost their balance and are ready to plunge headlong into the lap of free-thought and latitudinarianism. It is easy to let go of some of the old-fashioned ideas of the past, because they are out of style, but where to stop is the serious question; so that the safe course is to hold fast to the homely old ideas, while scrutinizing with jealous care the new forms of thought lest, perchance, one's equilibrium may be endangered.

(3) Another class are the critics. Our Current Reformation always had a bountiful supply of critics, both high and low. Since my boyhood days they have always been a curious study to me. These chaps that go about with such a complacent air of scholastic importance—how Mr. Campbell used to take them off with his fine sarcasm! They remind one of Dr. Thomas Chalmers and the scientists, in his astronomical sermons. But we need critics, and plenty of them, to be sure, if they will only come to us in the garments of humility. These are the people who go on before the procession and blaze the way into the realms of advanced thought. If, at times, they wander off too far and lose their bearings, by heroically sounding the alarm they will come back again to camp, and start off anew on another scent.

(4) Then there is a class who, while holding on to the conservative teachings of our people, on the one hand, cast longing eyes towards systematic theology, denominational fellowship and ecclesiastical authority *et id omnes gen.* I confess a sympathy for this tendency myself. Have we not been advocating for nearly a century a plea for the union of God's people? And if, in our anxiety for its consummation, we are tempted to meet the people more than half way, will we not be forgiven for this trifling iniquity? What if we do carry interdenominational fellowship a little too far, and even forget some of our peculiar ideas? To be frank about this matter, however, we need to be on our guard a trifle, right here, and keep a firmer attitude on the position we as a people have so long held.

(5) How shall I speak of a school of thought among us, that is intensely conservative, somewhat narrow, always safe and sound, plodding along with slow and steady gait, like a sturdy old ox, good-natured, cynical at times, cultured, refined and ever on the alert to defend the faith once for all delivered to the saints? How this school has laid down the law on church polity, exploited in many an arena on the music question, in days long since, and even yet maintains a position of "masterly inactivity," watching with ever jealous eye the religious horoscope of our times! Bless their stars! like the Old Guard, they are always to be relied on when the fight rages and the battle waxes hot! Finally, the highest type of a Disciple of Christ among us for this wonderful day in which we live, would be a blending of all the better elements of these various schools. If a composite picture could gather all of their features into one likeness, and our people could use it as a type, it would be suggestive, at least, of what we *really are*, and how much we have yet to achieve in order to be fashioned unto the likeness of the Lord Jesus Christ.

J. L. DARSIE.

Bethany, W. Va.

Notes and News.

"Michigan Grains."

I was at Ionia on Lord's day last, and had a pleasant visit with the brethren. Brother Berry preached two excellent discourses. He is doing fine work there, and is loved by all.

The brethren in Ionia are walking in love, and therefore have a bright prospect before them. Their splendid membership is increasing.

The church at Yale will give their pastor, Bro. McColl, a donation and supper on the 23rd. He enters upon the work of the fourth year with the brethren there. He recently baptized a Methodist minister and his wife. Brother and Sister Manley will now be disciples only.

The brethren at Yale will hold a series of meetings in the near future, with a bright prospect of success, as the field is apparently ripe for the harvest.

Brother Spayd lately baptized two promising young men at Owasso. He begins a series of meetings next Lord's day evening, as he closes his fourth year of service there. He has resigned his work there, his resignation taking effect the 31st of December. There is a chance now for some church to secure a good pastor with a good record. It will not be long before he is engaged again, for only when he was engaged as state evangelist has he been without a pastorate. He is just in his prime.

Brother Smith has resigned at Algonac.

Muir is yet without a pastor. "The harvest is plenty, but the laborers are few."

Three have lately been baptized at High Banks, where Bro. Jeffrey labors.

R. BRUCE BROWN.

The Indianapolis Co-operation.

The churches in the Hoosier capital have inaugurated a movement that may prove a most wholesome departure. We have been needing a departure ever since we came upon the stage of action; and, long ago, we ought to have learned a lesson from our *sectarian* neighbors that would have added the element of common sense to our numerous elements of uncommon sense.

The movement is in the way of organized co-operation. There are, in all, fourteen congregations (and five or six *incompatibles*) in the city. They (excusing the incompatibles) have undertaken to evangelize the municipality. All recognize the fact that the city is growing faster than the church; and it is clear that something must be done or the church will fail to keep up with the duty it has undertaken. While the incompatibles are assembling in little squads and discussing the usefulness of good music, of activity among the young people, and advocating the *apostolic authority* of the eldership, these fourteen congregations are trying to plan for the salvation of the people.

Haughville is a suburb on the west side of the river. Several years ago a congregation was founded in this then rural section, and its little meeting-house has now come to be at the very center of a thriving population. Not stopping to discuss the causes, we have to record the sad fact that the church has failed to grow as the field has grown. In fact, "Judah" is lower there than he was a dozen years ago. The harmony of spirit has been diminished, and the activity of the body is correspondingly reduced. The short way to tell the story is to say their title to the house is in imminent danger, and they plead inability to hold it.

The co-operation is engaged upon the problem of saving the cause in Haughville. The title has been made over to a properly authorized committee of this body, and the co-operation has undertaken to pay off the indebtedness. The plan is to receive from the membership their regular weekly contributions, whereby they have been supporting their preacher, and devote every dollar of it to the debt. Of the many ministers in the co-operation there will always be one ready and willing to supply the pulpit with preaching; and when anything is to be paid the co-operation will furnish the money to pay it.

We are watching this experiment with great interest; for, if it succeeds, it will be a good thing to try elsewhere.

Who knows but that this may be the beginning of what we so sadly need—a plan? If, without any planning, we have surprised the world by a growth to over a million in 80 years, what may we not do with an orderly plan? Long ago we should have been hitting upon something. We have many hundred preachers, and some good ones at that, who are out of employment, and there is more than a congregation for every such preacher which languishes in spiritual inactivity for the want of ministerial service.

Methodism, Presbyterianism, Lutheranism, Catholicism, is better than that. I dare anybody to answer me! WALTER S. SMITH.

Arlington, Ind., Dec. 4.

Michigan's Greatest Meeting.

By far the greatest meeting among the Disciples of Christ in America this season, and the best ever held in the Wolverine state, has just closed in Buchanan, Mich., with 205 additions; 32 came last night. We parted only "at midnight," praising God and humbled under his mighty hand.

When in a town of 2,000 inhabitants, with eight denominational churches, such a victory is attained we must exclaim, "What hath God wrought!" For powerful, persistent, patient, pointed, plain preaching of the New Testament doctrine in pulpit and from "house to house," evangelists Scoville and Scott are without peers in their heaven-sanctioned work.

Pastors, listen! Chas. Reign Scoville will preach more "old Jerusalem gospel" in a month's meeting than most of us do in ten years, and it is preached with a simplicity and force few possess. Bro. Scott is a most efficient personal worker and chorister. Their faith in God, in Christ, in the gospel and in men inspires every hearer to do his best. Their work is absolutely free from sensationalism and catchy methods, but their enthusiasm, earnestness and faith are—well—*tremendous*.

Editors, doctors, college and high-school teachers, graduates, tradesmen, men and women of talent and culture have come to "Jesus and the Bible;" many whole families are now united in Christ. Denominationalism received a terrible blow, creeds and doctrines of men were not dragged into the pulpit, but the Bible was held up so high that men and women by the score just ran to the blessed Book. The isms of churchianity were not exposed to ridicule, but Christ was so exalted that people saw "no man save Jesus only," and they forsook human names for "the only name." At every baptismal service this subject was briefly presented with a clearness that won every person to the truth of the "one baptism."

Cards and tracts on "Our Position," "Baptism," "Christian Unity," etc., were placed in every home. Our evangelists are humble as John, daring as Daniel, earnest as Paul and dependent on God, *giving all praise always to him.*

They drew men to Christ, not to themselves. Converts know whom they believe and why. No, we are not afraid of their falling away as much as we would be of the few converts who came in an ordinary meeting. "Christian unity" was preached with mighty emphasis and won the very best people from the denominations. Charts, banners, blackboards, helped much in teaching the people. The opposition and persecution of the churches of the town greatly helped us and the truth. The spirit of the martyrs was inspired by the preacher and possessed the converts. Some few were kept from obedience by ungodly or sectarian parents. We had a noble church to begin with and "every man stood in his place." Like the Spanish-American war, this meeting means to us "enlargement" in every way.

May God help us to be true to our trust and may God long spare these noble evangelists and continue to use them for his glory.

E. R. BLACK, Pastor.

Buchanan, Mich., Dec. 12, 1898.

Missouri Bible-school Notes.

At Oregon, with my friend, Clyde Darsie and the army of assistants, we had one of the pleasant and happy institutes of the year, the only shadow being caused by the fact that the minister would soon leave them for a post-graduate course at Chicago, and the church was feeling as if the place would not soon be filled. Quite a compliment to a young man in virtually his first work, but it was worthily bestowed. The sessions were all well attended while the Sunday work was very heavy on all of us, but was happily and so profitably spent. Oregon is one of the schools that in all its labors never forgets others. A message of love and sympathy was sent to Bro. Hugh Benton, sick in the Philadelphia hospital, one of the devoted boys of the school and church.

Oakland (Boone) has for years had a constant effort to carry on the Master's work on account of removals, deaths and reverses, but in the band remaining a few are determined to continue honoring the Christ by helping the poor, hence their giving to this work, more or less, every year.

At New Franklin our work was under circumstances similar to Oregon, for W. T. Henson had resigned against the wish of all and could not be persuaded to recall the resignation. J. M. Settle continues as superintendent, while our brother, Col. Estill, continues the main support of the church and was in the past most kind and generous to our work.

In the new year's work, hear of but few changes in the superintendents of the state, which speaks well for the superintendents and good for the schools.

At Huntington, Alfred Munyon, one of the host of Canton boys, mentioned our work, asking the church to help the faithful in the school by paying the pledge, and the secretary now remits. Thanks to such friends as Alfred, who is doing such a successful work for Christ while qualifying himself for even better things.

Four young misses did us great favor last summer at Merwin, but by some mistake it did not reach this office, so the school sends us another offering for the children and Christ, and it goes to-day to John Giddens who is so faithful and devoted in all this good work, and who never consults ought save the work.

At Dover we had the Lafayette County Bible-school Rally, but the severe weather cut off the attendance, but for interest it was fine. Brethren Scott, of Higginsville, and Fenstermacher, of Lexington, were ever helping in our counsels, while W. H. Cook, the preacher, never missed a session. Mrs. E. L. Peddicord is our county superintendent, and one more faithful is not in the state. My home with Bro. and Sister Harwood was delightfully pleasant, thanks to good Christian friends. But my association with that genial scholar, Geo. W. Plattenburg, ws indeed a feast in every sense. Quiet and unpretentious, yet well versed in biblical lore, I always court such opportunities and associations as his. Wish such men never grew old. Geo. B. Gordon, the school superintendent, seemed right in his element with us, while he gave me the dues from Dover to date, as he always does. The Lord bless such.

Good reports are coming in from the home department, but more schools ought to enjoy its blessings. Have you ever tried it in your school? If not, then you are losing an opportunity to help the school, the home, the church. Do you want to try it, and can I help you in it? That is mywork and I am glad to do it.

W. H. Hawkins, county superintendent in Nodaway, writes for the apportionments of all the schools of the county and he means to be one that has a Teacher's Bible at Plattsburg convention. Good. Who else of the county superintendents will?

To the many friends, especially the preachers who helped us in our fanancial straits, thank you all, and God bless you for it, is the prayer of H. F. DAVIS.

Commercial Building, St. Louis, Mo.

Arkansas Mission Notes for November.

Bro. M. A. Smith has had 45 additions to the church at Bald Knob and vicinity during the last few months. He is "a workman that needeth not to be ashamed." Arrangements have been made to retain him in that field at a better support. The writer spent a few days with them.

Bro. Crutcher is doing a fine work at Pine Bluff.

Proper energy and appreciation of responsibility by the few members of Lonoke and vicinity can secure a house of worship and a live congregation in that important center—the county-seat of Lonoke county.

W. R. Johnson, who has done valiant service at Atkins and in a number of churches near by, talks of going to Texas. His praise is heard from all.

Van Buren is arranging for a preacher to begin with the beginning of the year. This is a very important point.

Bro. T. N. Kincaid gives a most excellent report of three months' work at Hot Springs. Sermons, 23; pastoral visits, 300; money raised on salary, $120; current expenses, $23; missions, $2.80; total, $143,80. Bro. Kincaid, if he can be supported, will bring the Hot Springs church to the front.

Bro. Clark presents his report of good work during the month in the Southwest District. Report is not at hand at this writing, being left on file. His work has been interfered with the last two months by ill health.

Mena has called F. F. Wyatt, of Kansas City, Kas. This place must be helped. To neglect it would be the loss of the most sacrificing work that has been done in the state.

The state convention of the colored Disciples will meet Dec. 15, at Pea Ridge, in Lonoke county.

A SUGGESTION.—Is there a man, or a congregation, or several combined, that would like to select Hot Spring, Mena, or any one of the three other cities in Arkansas, where $100 in addition to what can be raised in the field will keep a good preacher for one year, or who will put $50 or $100 into any one of the three missionary districts, where it will enable a good evangelist to work? This would enable you to see just what your money is accomplishing. This may not be better than putting it into the general fund—probably not—but it would be much better than not doing the work. The churches in our own state that are not making prompt payments are preventing success.

Brethren, let us have all arrearages paid before Jan. 1, 1899. Happy holidays and increase of the Christ-spirit to all.

E. C. BROWNING.

Little Rock, Ark.

The Christian Library—Questions and Answers.

DEAR BRO. PHILLIPS:—What is the Christian Library of which you write in the CHRISTIAN-EVANGELIST and how can one be obtained? If it would not be too much trouble I would like a few particulars of your peculiar plan of work.

Yours, E. M. HAILE.

Kingman, Kan., Dec. 3, 1896.

REPLY.—The above card is a fair sample of of what we are daily receiving, and the publication of the following reply may serve for the enlightenment of others as well.

As its name implies, the Christian Library is a superb collection (ninety-one volumes) of the very best books of the Christian Church. They cover every possible phase ofthe "Current Reformation"—*history, doctrine* and *work*. Included in this collection is the celebrated "Christian Sunday-school Library" (forty volumes), a full line of C. E. works, the leading debates of our brethren, our best commentaries and works of reference, a number of missionary books and books of travel, and the best productions of our story-writers. In short, it is just such a library as every Christian Church, S. S. and C. E. ought to have.

My "peculiar plan of work" is to visit a church (when invited), hold a two weeks' meeting and endeavor by every means in my power to lead men to Christ. After each invitation I shall talk briefly on the Christian Library work, and endeavor to organize a library club of at least fifty members. To each of these members the CHRISTIAN-EVANGELIST will be sent one year free.

At the close of the meeting proper, a series of four popular lectures will be given, at popular prices. In this way we shall endeavor to secure enough money to average $2.75 per club member, and also to pay my traveling expenses.

If this fails, other methods will be tried until success is assured.

After the library is secured, a "reading circle" is formed, a competent instructor selected and a systematic study of the books begun. Each circle will be allowed to arrange its own courses of reading if desired. The purpose of the library is threefold: 1. To thoroughly *inform* the brotherhood; 2. The sectarian brethren; 3. The outside world, as to our doctrine and work. If after such meeting the library is not placed I shall only ask the brethren to pay me at the rate of $12.50 per week and bear my traveling expenses.

I am arranging to visit Kansas and Missouri immediately after the holidays, and shall be glad to hear at once from all churches in that part of the country wanting meetings and library. Address the founder,

S. J. PHILLIPS.

Sugar Grove, Wis.

A Day of Prayer.

A Jubilee shall that fiftieth year be unto you. —Lev. 25:11.

Without me ye can do nothing.—Jesus, John 15:5.

I can do all things through Christ which strengtheneth me.—Paul, Phil. 4:13.

I have planted, Apollos watered; but God gave the increase. So, then, neither is he that planteth anything, neither he that watereth; but God that giveth the increase.—1 Cor. 3: 6, 7.

Bring ye all the tithes into the storehouse, that there may be meat in mine house, and prove me now herewith, saith the Lord of hosts, if I will not open you the windows of heaven, and pour you out a blessing, that there shall not be room enough to receive it.— Mal. 3:10.

I say unto you, that if two of you shall agree on earth as touching anything that they shall ask, it shall be done for them of my Father which is in heaven.—Matt. 18:19.

There is manifest intense activity of thought and feeling pervading the church; the hearts of all true lovers of God's cause are full of earnest hopes and expectation for great things to be done for God's cause in this, the Jubilee Year of the American Christian Missionary Society. The friends of missions are stirred to intense interest in the hope that our missionary work is to be lifted to a higher plane than ever before.

Believing that all this is well-pleasing to God, and knowing that without his help all human plans must fail, we earnestly ask our churches and our brethren everywhere to observe Lord's day, Jan. 15, as a day of prayer to the Head of the Church, that this Jubilee Year will be a blessing to the churches, and that souls may come into the kingdom as doves fly to their windows, and that our missionary work may be blessed of God.

We suggest that a sermon along these lines would be a help to the work of the churches.

BENJ. L. SMITH, Cor. Sec. A. C. M. S.
A. MCLEAN, Cor. Sec. F. C. M. S.

Evangelistic.

ENGLAND.

Chester, 21 Seller St., Dec. 10.—Our work nere continues most favorable, with 17 added first three weeks; 16 by confession, and the interest and attendance growing. We expect to open on a larger scale in our next meeting where we can reach the masses, and fully expect the same measure then as God has given us in America.—J. A. L. ROMIG.

UTAH.

Salt Lake City, Dec. 12.—One added here by letter yesterday.—W. H. BAGBY.

SOUTH DAKOTA.

Miller, Dec. 12.—One confession at Sunbeam.—E. W. BOWERS.

KENTUCKY.

Lexington, Dec. 15.—A. P. Finley closed a two week's meeting at the South Side Church, Dec. 11, with 16 additions. The interest was good throughout. Bro. Finley did splendid preaching.—WARD RUSSELL.

OHIO.

Shreve, Dec. 13.—Closed a very successful meeting in Loudonville last Sunday night, resulting in an organization of 35 members, 20 of whom were added during the meeting. It was a hard-fought battle, but the truth was victorious. The inspiring solos of Miss Mary A. Sanborn contributed much to the success of the meeting.—G. F. CRITES.

Mapleton, Dec. 16.—We closed a meeting with our home church (Indian Run) last Lord's day with seven confessions. Bro. A. Baker, of Malvern, did most of the preaching and did it well. He is a true man, faithful to God and his Word.—R. L. LOTZ, pastor.

KANSAS.

Halstead, Dec. 12.—Our meeting still in progress; 45 accesssons to date. Organized a Y. P. S. C. E. last night with 32 active members.—L. B. COGGINS.

La Crosse, Dec. 12.—Closed a three weeks' meeting at Alexander with 19 confessions. We have 27 members at that place.—A. NEESE.

Council Grove, Dec. 10.—Eight persons responded to the gospel invitation in our Fairview, S.H. meeting 10 miles out in the country. Will continue over the 11th and maybe the 18th inst.—J. A. WALTERS.

Fall River, Dec. 16.—Just closed a good meeting six miles southeast of Fall River. I labored five weeks and organized a church with 30 members; one from the Catholics, six from the Methodists, the rest from the world. Many others are abcut ready to come in with us.—S. JONES.

NEBRASKA.

Fairfield, Dec. 12.—Six additions at regular appointment at Randall Schoolhouse; five by confession. I have been preaching one-fourth time for the last four months. My work at Oxford is moving on nicely.—E. W. YOCUM.

Beatrice, Dec. 12.—Closed a short meeting here last night; 13 additions, 12 by baptism. Church in good working shape.—F. A. BRIGHT, pastor.

Fairfield, Dec. 12.—Yesterday closed my engagement with the church here, having been here two years. The church has received quite a number of additions during that period and has also lost by removal quite a number. Found the church in debt and leave it entirely free from debt and with surplus in treasury, besides having paid for Home and Foreign Missions $100 the last year. Two additions yesterday by letter and one baptized since last report.—GEO. LOBINGIER.

IOWA.

Bedford, Dec. 11.—Thirty-two accessions to date; interest increasing. Will continue indefinitely.—R. A. OMER AND WALTERS.

Meeting at Elliott two weeks old. Six added by obedience, four by letter and statement. Crowded houses.—M. C. JOHNSON, evangelist.

Lenox, Dec. 12.—Just closed a meeting of four weeks with 16 accessions. The greatest revival was among the church members. Those who were cold and indifferent are now enthusiastic in the work.—W. D. RYAN, pastor.

Sloan, Dec. 12.—Meeting, three weeks. Evangelist, pastor J. R. Mowry preaching; closed. Six baptisms; two husbands and wives, two ladies. Bro. Mowry is a faithful man of God, a plain, practical, pungent preacher.—WM. B. CLEMER, pastor.

Keokuk, Dec. 15th.—One confession last Sunday at Elsbury, Mo., where I have been called to preach one-fourth time. Paynesville, Mo., has recalled me to serve them for another year for half time, and Lin Knoll, Mo., takes one-fourth. I am continuing my studies in medicine and surgery in the Keokuk Medical College, and long to re-enter the missionary field as soon after I graduate as possible. Yours very truly.—W. W. RUMSEY.

WISCONSIN.

West Lima, Dec. 12.—Closed a short meeting at Wesley with four additions, two by obedience and two from the Christian (New Light) Church. We have a noble band of workers who are working hard to build up primitive Christianity in that part of the state.—D. G. WAGNER.

INDIANA.

Columbus, Dec. 14.—Closed a three weeks' meeting at East Columbus with 53 additions. Begin at Walesboro to-night.—EUGENE T. MARTIN, evangelist.

Peru, Dec. 12.—Two accessions yesterday; 300 enrolled yesterday since I organized the congregation a little over five years ago.—CHAS. M. FILLMORE.

NEW YORK.

Syracuse, Dec. 12.—State Evangelist J. M. Morris just closed a series of meetings with the church here of 16 days with 12 baptisms and one by letter. Our church passed a resolution commending our evangelist for his fidelity to the truth. He is a good man for the pioneer work needed in this state.—E. RICHARD EDWARDS, pastor.

Buffalo, Dec. 16.—Four persons united with the Richmond Ave. Church of Christ last Lord's day evening; three by confession and one by baptism. Two of these were heads of families. Our work moves along most encouragingly.—FLOYD DARSIE.

KANSAS.

Kansas City, Dec. 12.—Just closed a four weeks' meeting at the Tabernacle, 7th and Gar Ave., Kansas City. with 23 additions. W. E. Harlow and his singer, Miss Murphy, conducted the services, and they certainly make a strong team.—C. M. WICKHAM, pastor.

Pawnee Rock, Dec. 14.—Just closed a two weeks' meeting at Ponca City, O. T., with six added; three confessions. Our church is the best location in town and they are much in need of a good young preacher and can support the right man. The population of Ponca City is about 3,000 and our plea ought to be well presented. Mrs. Dora Short is church clerk.—ELLIS PURLEE.

ARKANSAS.

Eureka Springse Dec. 12.—We are assisting Bro. Daniel Trundle in a meeting here. Meeting four days old with four additions. Good interest and large audiences. Last night the M. E. and Presbyterian preachers dismissed their audiences and attended our services. Our short but pleasant meeting at Cowgill, Mo., did not result in many additions, but believe it did much good. This is a grand church. Bro. J. T. Shreve has done a good work there. He goes to Milan, Mo.—MORGANS AND DAUGHTER.

Eureka Springs, Dec. 10.—Nine additions to date. Meeting one week old. Morgan Morgans is doing the preaching and his daughter, Mary, leads the singing. Bro. M. is an expositor of God's Word. His arguments are clear-cut and strong, his language good and his manner reverential. He is wise in presenting controvertial themes, where so many fail because of tact, kindness or fairness to the position of others.—DANIEL TRUNDLE, pastor.

ILLINOIS.

Blandinsville, Dec. 12.—Two additions to the Old Bedford Church yesterday at our regular service.—A. R. ADAMS.

The church in East. Louis recently reported one addition. W. R. Jinnett is the pastor. The church is in a prosperous condition.

Atwater.—Closed our meeting of three weeks' at Boston Chapel with 12 additions; nine confessions, one by letter and two reclaimed. Good interest and order prevailed. It is to be hoped that the fruits of this meeting may last for years and that there will be other fruits follow as the result of the seed sown in this meeting. God be the praise for the gospel of love.—H. J. HOSTETLER.

Pekin, Dec. 14.—Just closed a two weeks' meeting at the Malone Christian Church, six miles southwest of Green Valley, with nine confessions and 14 reclaimed. B. L. Wray, of Eureka, has rendered efficient work and will continue to supply the pulpit twice a month.—FRED E. HAGIN.

Two confessions Sunday night. Audiences large and interest good. Geo. T. Purves and the writer are doing a little outside work at Lost Creek, Wever and Niota, the last-named in Illinois. The prospect of a new church house is bright.—R. H. INGRAM.

Watseka, Dec. 12.—Four added since last report; two by letter and one by obedience at our mission point in Watseka and another at Pitwood, where I spoke last Saturday evening. The work throughout the county seems to be progressing.—B. S. FERRALL, pastor.

Pittsfield, Dec. 16.—Meeting at Chapin resulted in 27 additions; 16 baptized. A. O. Hunsaker had charge of the singing.—W. H. CANNON.

Springfield, Dec. 12.—Six added to the church here at regular services Sunday, Dec. 4th. We raised $1,000 Sunday morning, Dec. 11th, for changes we expect to make in the church building and to pay for a new furnace just put in. Fraternaly yours.—J. E. LYNN.

MISSOURI.

Ham's Prairie, Dec. 12.—Two added by statement at Cedar City, last Lord's day. The church is very weak there. J. D. Greer is to hold them a meeting in January, and we are working and praying that they may be mightily built up.—FRANK J. NICHOLS.

Sumner, Dec. 13.—J. B. Jeans, of Hamilton, recently finished a three weeks' meeting in Sumner, with 21 additions. Those added are the best citizens of the community; some whole families made the confession.—J. W. W.

Closed a short meeting at Summit with 17 added; 10 of these are new to us. They want a pastor one-fourth or one-half time. Address Joe Wilson, Mound City, Mo. The meeting paid off $65 church indebtedness. I am now at Hackberry, near Savannah, Mo. Prospects good for a meeting.—T. W. COTTINGHAM.

Lockwood, Dec. 14.—Closed a two weeks' meeting at Newport, where V. B. Burr is preaching once a month, with five added; three by baptism and two by recommendation. Bro. Burr was with me a part of the time. He also preaches at Center Point and Round Prairie; also Antioch in Dade County. I am now ready to take evangelistic work or one or more churches as pastor.—DANIEL E. PALMER.

St. Louis.—There were three additions at West End Christian Chu-ch recently, not formerly reported.—O. A. BARTHOLOMEW.

St. Louis.—One week ago the First Church of this city reported eight additions, and the Compton Heights Church nine additions.

Carrollton, Dec. 12.—Just closed a two weeks' meeting here with 13 additions; two from M. E.s, five by letter and six by baptism. Yesterday at our regular services there were five more confessions, as a result of the meeting, and one by letter. It was a glorious day. This makes 19 additions to the church here recently.—J. T. OGLE.

Schell City, Dec. 16.—I have just closed a meeting of 36 days at Buffalo, with 56 additions. The minister, J. D. Babb, is a good, true man. I was glad to have the presence and help of F. J. Yokeley, S. E. Hendrickson and T. S. Tinsley. The church has been greatly blessed, I think, in the work done during the meeting.—E. WILKES, California, Mo.

Bigelow, Dec. 16.—A three weeks' meeting at this place just closed, conducted by J. R. Hardan, our pastor, assisted by T. E. Blanchard, of Barnard, resulting in 12 additions; six by baptism.—A. W. CHUNING, superintendent Bigelow Bible-school.

Family Circle.

Ring, Bells, Ring!

NELIA MCGAVACK.

Oh, bells, in the steeple old and gray,
With joyful motion swing and sway,
Ring out glad peals for Christmas Day,
Ring, bells, ring!

And bells in the steeples fair and new,
With holy joy thrill through and through,
Ring out *your* Christmas message, too,
Ring, bells, ring!

Ring, bells, all over this listening earth,
With one glad peal our planet girth,
Ring the news of the Savior's birth,
Ring, bells, ring!

Ring till earth shall with gladness say:
"Dear Lord, I bring my gift to-day,
My life at thy feet I lay."
Ring, bells, ring!

Colfax, Ill.

What Two Boys Did—I.

BY ALFRED BRUNK.

"Hooray!" shouted Harry Latham, as he came into the dining room on Christmas morning and beheld a fine sled with his name plainly written upon a tag which was fastened to the sled. "I don't know of anything I wanted so bad as a sled. I have a fine pair of skates and Christmas books by the dozen. Now for a fine ride down the hill." He was opening the outside door when his father came downstairs and called him.

"Where are you going, my son?"

"Just out to the hill to try my new sled," he replied.

"No, Harry, not now. We must have our morning devotions, and after breakfast you and Myrtle must hasten to the church for the last practice on the anthem you are to sing to-day."

Harry hung his head sullenly, but made no reply. Just then Myrtle bounded into the room and in the exurberance of her joy she threw her arms about Harry's neck. "Oh, Harry, look! Just see what I got for Christmas! A mandolin! I am going to play it for the poor children at the mission." She was a beautiful child, with golden curls and eyes which reflected heaven's own blue. Mrs. Latham entered the room and after their prayer and praise service they all sat down to breakfast.

Mr. Latham was a prosperous wholesale and retail grocer in the seaport city of Worthington, and was an elder in the Cedar Avenue Church, which was one of the most wealthy and popular churches in the city. Mr. Hollingbrook, a learned and eloquent preacher, was the pastor, and in addition to his Cedar Avenue work had established a mission among the tenement dwellers on Breaker Street.

At the close of the Christmas services at the church, Harry went home and had lunch, after which he repaired to the hill with his new sled. Just beyond the foot of the hill the railroad had thrown up quite a grade, cutting away the lower part of the hill. A telegraph pole stood on the hill near the cutaway. The boys would coast down the hill and let their sleds jump over the cutaway. A large crowd had already gathered when Harry arrived.

"Here comes Hank Latham, now," shouted one of the boys.

It was a motley crowd. Representatives of almost every grade of society were there, from the gamin of the streets to the aristocracy of Cedar Avenue. They had a wide pathway beaten down in the snow and were going over the cutaway with many a shout, and sometimes an oath. Harry was soon in the midst of the sport with his new sled which was one of the finest on the hill. Many of the boys had no sleds and depended on the generosity of the more fortunate ones, and some of the most reckless would wait until a rider was fairly under way and then jump on behind him, which created no little confusion, and caused an occasional fight. Among the onlookers was Fred Gotleib, the only son of his widowed mother and who was familiarly known among the boys as "Dutchy." He watched the exciting chases down the hill with a longing, hungry look in his eyes.

"Why don't you take a hand, Dutchy?" asked Solly Hughes.

"Vell, I aindt got no shled, so you see I candt ride, don't it?" replied Fred.

"Maybe Harry Latham will let you have his," said Solly, with a sneer on his lips.

"No, I vouldn't ags him. He vas too high alreaty," answered Fred.

"Say Harry, Dutchy wants to take a ride on your sled," said Solly, as Harry came puffing up the hill.

"Well, he can't have it, if does," snapped Harry. "If you wan't him to ride so bad why don't you give him your sled?"

"Because I thought you would be glad to let him have yours, seeing as his mother washes for your folks and gets her pay in wormy cheese and stale butter."

"Take care, Solly Hughes," said Harry, drawing back his arm and doubling his fist.

"Oh, I'm not afraid of you nor any of your folks," said Solly; "but if you won't let him have your sled he shall have mine. Here Dutchy, take my sled and ride. I am tired and will rest awhile. Look out for telegraph pole!"

Fred thanked him and taking the sled went on up the hill, and carefully seating himself started down the slope. As he came opposite Solly and Harry, the latter gave the sled a vicious kick, which turned it from its course and it made straight for the telegraph pole. Fred had lost all control of it, and sat with his head bent slightly forward and held on with all his strength. Several of the boys saw Harry's act and watched the sled in breathless expectation as it sped down the hill. With terrific force it struck the pole and was smashed into ruins. Fred, with some of the pieces still in his hands, passed the pole and tumbled over the cutaway.

"Harry, what did you do that for?" asked Solly, as they all started in a run down the hill. "You have killed him and broke my sled. I'll have yours in place of it."

Harry said nothing but his heart smote him. They found Fred at the bottom of the cutaway unconscious.

"Its knocked him sensible," said one of the boys.

"He's passed his checks," said another one.

"Yaas, he's kicked the bucket this time, you bet," said one.

"Look ahere, boys, Dutchy's done for and we can't help him none, now, so I say let's put him in the brush over there and go ahead with our play," said Bobby Simpkins.

"Tut, tut, Bob, we can't do that. The correner's got to see him and tell what's the matter with him," said Solly.

Harry edged his way to Fred. "Boys," said he, "I was too rash and am sorry for it. I will pay Solly for his sled; but first something must be done with Fred. He may not be dead after all. So let's take him to our house and get a doctor."

The sentiment which had been strongly against Harry now turned in his favor, and more than one ragged boy in that group shouted, "Hurrah for Harry Latham!"

Fred was gently lifted up the cutaway, placed on Harry's sled and with much care was taken to Mr. Latham's. On the way he returned to consciousness and began groaning with pain.

"See! boys, he aint dead after all!" exclaimed Solly.

When they reached the house Harry told the servant that he wished to see his parents, whereupon they came to the door accompained by Myrtle.

"Father, Fred Gotleib got hurt and we brought him here to see what is the matter with him. Where can we put him?"

"You had better take him in little Willie's room and get a doctor."

"I'll go for the doctor," said Solly.

"Get Dr. Markham," said Mr. Latham, and Solly was off like a shot, followed by a dozen of his companions.

"No, not in there," said Mrs. Latham.

"Why not, wife?" asked her husband. "Willie always wanted to do good to everybody and I know it would please him if he could know."

"You are right, and I suppose it was a feeling of selfishness on my part to wish to keep a poor wounded boy out of my dear baby's room. I know he always wanted to help some one."

Fred was taken into the room which had been Willie's and placed upon the little bed. On the wall opposite hung a large picture of a fair, bright-eyed boy, apparently about eight years of age. It was the picture of Willie, who had gone to live with the angels.

Dr. Markham came in and made a careful examination. "Ahem! bones broken above the knee. Nerves somewhat shattered by fright. Must be kept very quiet and should have a skilled nurse. If you can let him remain here it will be an act of humanity, Mr. Latham, as it might endanger his life to remove him now."

"Certainly, he shall remain here doctor. He is the son of our washerwoman and we could not think of turning him out."

"Ah! well, I am glad to know that he will have good treatment. You had better get Eva Steadwell to nurse him, if she can be had, as she is the best in the city, and in a few days if he improves his mother may come and remain with him. Let him be kept quiet."

The boys all went back to the hill and continued their sport, and just before they left for their homes, Harry took his sled to Solly and said: "Here, Solly, take my sled for the one I broke for you."

Solly hesitated, but Harry urged him and he finally took it.

Harry treated Fred like a brother and he did all he could to repay him for the pain he had caused him. When Fred had fully regained his health and strength, Mr. Latham employed him in the retail department of his great store. The two boys now began the study of the Bible. The life of ras especially fascinating to Fred. going over the scenes of the trials cifixion, for the first time, his frame with anger:

hadeful Chews! undt dey kildt Shust like 'em. Dere ish dot Luben- it lies so aboud your vader. I shust e hat a hand in id do."

y laughed. "No, Fred, this happen- years ago in Palestine. Lubenstein t living then and he is not from ne anyway, he is from Russia."

nd gare, he vas shust mean enough ildt him if he could a godt dere ," replied Fred.

Hollingbrook began a series of meet- t the mission, and one night Harry red went forward. Myrtle was a member of Cedar Avenue and it was expected that the boys ake membership there after being d, but they decided to cast their h the mission.

Latham, I have come to the con- that I am not cut out for a business and shall leave your service when ble with you," said Fred one day to ployer. He now spoke good Eng- it with a strong German accent.

n dispense with your services now," r. Latham with some warmth, "but I y that I never had man or boy who re faithfully his work." He turned desk and wrote a few lines upon a paper.

a have been very kind to me sir, and sorry to leave you, but I wish to ake a work among my own people her foreigners here in the city. I een very much impressed with their and am going to do what I can for ,

y, my boy, your ambition is a le one, but you can't do a work like ithout money."

e," replied Fred, "but I believe the rill open the hearts of his people and ey will furnish the necessary money. I will do what I can, and perhaps one in years to come will see the ance of the work and carry it forward ess."

, father, and I am going in with nd we are going to teach them not he gospel, but how to save their , to keep out of saloons, how to keep house and bodies clean, and we will the children to read and write and grow up good Christian, American s."

ll," said Mr. Latham, "you have set task before you and a worthy one, arry I was thinking it is time you earning business. So you must let try his experiment alone, while you our place in the firm of Latham &

ll, father, I will not disobey you, had my heart set on joining Fred in ission. We have already rented a entry and closed the account. The boys then went away with sadness depicted in their countenances and sorrow in their hearts.

(TO BE CONTINUED.)

What a Boy Thinks About Santa Claus.

BY JOHN. S. MARTIN.

I'm but a very little boy,
And once I had a funny toy
Which mamma said was brought to me
By Santa Claus who roams so free;
That every year when Christmas comes
He somehow visits all our homes,
And fills our stockings full of toys
And things that's nice for girls and boys.
And mamma says he comes at night
When all the doors are locked up tight;
That through the chimney open wide
Is how he makes his way inside.
But I could never see just how
He gets through one that we have now;
For it is scarcely big enough
To hold my sisters little muff.
Another thing I cannot see—
And one that always puzzles me—
Is how he travels in a sleigh
When all the snow has gone away.
(Sometimes you know it happens so,
When Christmas comes there is no snow.)
But mamma says that Santa Claus
Can travel even though it thaws.
And if the roads be mud or snow
They're never so he cannot go.
And all because his team so queer
Is made of ten tiny raindeer,
That skip with Santa and his load,
No matter what the kind of road.
And when he taps them with his lash
They're off at once just like a flash,
With such a rattling, clashing noise,
You'd think they were a lot of boys.
But I'm not sure if it be true
That that's the way they always do,
For I have lain awake at night,
But never yet have caught a sight
Of Santa Claus, nor heard the bells,
Of which my mamma often tells.
And so I've thought that good old St. Nick,
Who travels o'er the earth so quick,
Must pass throughout the sleeping town
With no more noise than thistle down.
And when he gets into the house
Keeps just as still's a little mouse.

Jessie's Experience.

(A CHRISTMAS STORY FOR LITTLE

STELLA STRAWN.

Jessie and Beulah were cousins, come to spend Christmas with gran

The day before Christmas grand privately to each girl, "I am goi out this afternoon. I trust while I you will not go in my room. Don't a little box which is on my bureau.'

Beaulah said, "Of course not, gr and thought no more about it. Bu was different. She wondered wha the box. The more she thought more she wanted to see it.

"It would not hurt to see what k box it is," she thought, but when the box, it was only a little thread-

How Jessie wished to know the of that box.

And alas! She slipped softly took the cover off the box.

Jessie looked all around and then in. There was nothing in the bc little note. Jessie with eager haste note and opened it. A ring drop such a lovoly ring, with white a sets in the gold ring. The note s the little granddaughter who does in the box. A Christmas gift from ma."

Jessie put the ring and note b shut the box, and went down into ting room where Beulah was readi

Just then grandma came in an Jessie left the room.

"Beulah," said grandma, "did in the box?"

"Why, of course not, grandm Beulah, "didn't you trust me?"

"Oh yes," said grandma, "I w be sure, was all."

Grandma left the room and met the hall. Grandma delayed Jessie "Jessie, did you look into the box?

Jessie hung her head, but tho was meddlesome, she would not tell she said, "Yes, grandma, but, I' Will you forgive me, though you the ring to Beulah?"

A Christmas Message.

BY L. R. HORNISH.

I thought, as I stood by a manger,
Where the cattle were munching their hay,
Secured from the storm-cloud or danger,
Of the Babe that at Bethlehem lay.

I thought of the poor and the friendless,
The hungry, the sick and the lame;
The burdens of life seemed so endless,
And then—I recalled his dear name.

And I knew the light that, gleaming
On the shepherds in times long ago,
All bright o'er earth, was still beaming
And shedding its Christmas glow.

And faces bowed down and saddened,
White, on pillows of pain,
Were lifted, lightened and gladdened
By music of angels again.

And I said, all this is well in his keeping,
And he who the sparrows doth feed,
Will dry the tears of the weeping
And care for his world in its need.

Washington, Ill.

Forgetting Self.

BY ALICE CURTICE MOYER.

The post office building loomed up proudly. It towered high above the great white snowdrifts, and looked down with supreme disdain upon all minor buildings, as though it knew and gloried in its reputation—that of being the finest building in the little city.

Inside this proud edifice was a beelike business. The heavy Eastern mail had just arrived and all hands were busy sorting and distributing.

Miss Ennis, of the stamp department, wore a frown on her face. 'Twas the week before Christmas, and all morning she had sold stamps and weighed packages till her head swam, and somehow the faces that had looked in at her window had in them so much joyous expression, the forerunner of Christmas happiness, that envy stole in and took possession of her heart, and then, as she reflected upon the, to her, joyous holidays, discontent came in to keep envy company.

"Seek out some one who is less fortunate than yourself and make his burdens lighter," the pastor's wife had ventured to advise when Miss Ennis once complained of her cheerless life.

The words of the pastor's wife came back to her to-day, "but," she argued to herself, "there can be none more miserable than I. Christmas is a most appropriate time for doing good and the poor we have with us always, but—what is the use! I have seen washerwomen and ragpickers whom I have envied," and the frown deepened.

"How cross she is!" said Miss Deane, of the money order department, to her pretty assistant, as they met the stamp clerk in the hall, going out to luncheon.

"Like a bear," answered the pretty assistant.

"She's good though—"

"Certainly. Old maids usually do make conspicuous some admirable quality," giggled the pretty assistant.

—"That is," resumed Miss Deane, not noticing the interruption, "she's a great church worker, but she impresses me as being one who—well—one who finds no soul-satisfying happiness in a Christian life. But people say her life was embittered long ago when the lover of her youth went West to seek a fortune and died of thirst on the plains. Then her parents died soon after and she was left alone in the world. She owns a cozy home, but nobody is ever invited there; she just lives alone and broods over her troubles. No wonder she is disagreeable at times," and Miss Deane and her pretty assistant passed on, quite unmindful that the subject of their conversation, having forgotten her gloves, had turned to retrace her steps and heard every word.

For a moment she stood thoughtfully at her desk and drew on the returned-for articles. Then she took up and read for the second time as odd a little missive as she had ever seen. It was addressd to Santa Claus, and ran thus:

"Deer Santy Klos my papa is dead and my dear mama is sick, but I will hang up my stocking and I know you will come. I thot I would rite early and give you plenty of time to make up your mind what you will bring to me. I will put down the number so you can find the plais it is 425 maple street. I send you a kis dear santy and if you will let me se you i will give you one of my curls this letter is from Zoe."

Dropping it upon her desk, Miss Ennis went out to a restaurant, but somehow that plaintive little letter was before her. All afternoon she thought of it, and upon retiring that night she thought of it again.

"I wonder if the little thing will be disappointed. I've a notion"—and then she tried to go to sleep.

Two hours later she sat straight up in bed and said aloud:

I'll do it. I'm a cross, selfish old maid, but I'll make a call on Maple Street before I come home to-morrow evening," and then sleep came.

Next evening a well-wrapped figure turned down a narrow street and knocked at 425.

A little blue-eyed maiden of six years or thereabouts opened the door—a fair sweet little thing was she, with curls all about her dainty face and shoulders.

"The author of the letter," thought Miss Ennis, and then she asked:

"May I come in?"

"The little girl opened wide the door, motioned her visitor in and brought a chair before she spoke in a low tone:

"My mamma's asleep and we must not talk loud."

"Is your mamma any better to-day?" asked Miss Ennis, feeling her heart warm toward the thoughtful little daughter.

The blue eyes filled with tears and the little lips trembled:

"I'm afraid she isn't."

"Does the doctor come to see her often?"

"He does not come now because dear mamma has no more money for him. She has no money at all, now, for she gave the last to the man who brought the coal to-day. But mamma says that God's children will never be forsaken."

"How old are you, dear?" asked Miss Ennis.

"Six. Mamma calls me her little lady."

"Zoe! Zoe!" called a faint voice from the other room, and the little girl ran to answer.

"To whom are you talking, little daughter?"

"A lady who has come to see us, mamma," and then Miss Ennis was shown into the sick room.

It took but a glance to see that little Zoe would soon be left motherless.

Miss Ennis sat down beside the bed. She could be charming when she chose, and somehow she felt her heart go out to the mother just as it had to the little daughter, and soon the invalid was pouring into sympathetic ears a story which brought tears to the eyes of the listener. The death of the husband and father had occurred two years before, leaving wife and child almost penniless; but with an energy beyond her strength the widow had earned a living for herself and child, until six months before, when a severe cold hastened the disease which had been slowly creeping upon her. For the past two months she had been bedfast the greater portion of the time. "And would you believe it," said she, "my little Zoe has been my principal nurse, for indeed I could afford no other. You would be surprised to see how helpful she is, and so hopeful, too. She wrote a letter to Santa Claus yesterday, and I have been wondering how I can save her from a bitter disappointment, but—"

"Never mind," interposed Miss Ennis gently. "I will see to it, if you will allow me. I've nobody to care for, and it will give me great pleasure to make little Zoe happy."

The invalid looked searchingly into the face of her visitor.

"Give me your hand, dear friend," said she. "All night long I prayed God to send a friend to my little one, and I know my prayer is answered. I can read it in your face. I could not leave her until he sent you, but now—I—am—ready—".

And little Zoe was motherless.

A week later — Christmas Eve — Miss Ennis sat in her cozy parlor, but not alone. A little head nestled against her breast, the curls of which she caressed lovingly as she spoke in soothing, loving tones:

"Yes, my little Zoe, your mamma is so happy up in heaven, that she wants to see her little daughter happy, too. So close your eyes, my precious, and dream of what Santa Claus and the fairies will bring you to-night."

Then softly:

"Dear Lord, I thank thee that thou hast given to me this sacred trust, this little one who has broken down old barriers, has opened up the fountains of my heart and has saved me from my old bitter self. And I do thank thee, that in my heart to-night there is peace, and toward my fellowmen there is naught save good-will. Oh, the joy of *forgetting self!*"

CHRISTMAS
CAROL.
Robt. C. Marquis.
in the air, There's a star in the sky; There's a
of the star Lie the a-ges impearled, And that
And a ba-by's low cry; There's a tu-mult of joy O'er the
swept o-ver the world. We re-joice in the light And we
the vir-gin's sweet Boy Is the
comes down thro' the night from the
Lord of the Earth. And the star sheds its beams While the
heav-en-ly throng. Ev-'ry hearth is a-flame, And the
For the
In the
man-ger of Beth-le-hem Cra-dles a King! Aye! the
homes of the na-tions that Je-sus is King! Aye! we
nd the beau-ti-ful sing; For the man-ger of Beth-le-hem
E-van-gel they bring And we greet in His cra-dle our
Rit.
Cra-dles a King!
Sav-ior and King!

A Plea for the Lord's Day.

BY WILL H. DIXON.

God's day well *spent* will bring *content*,
And sweetest peace afford,
To every *man* throughout his *span*,
Who strives to serve his Lord.

The day most *blest* of peace and *rest*,
Which God to us hath given,
Should find each *one* at set of *sun*,
A little nearer heaven.

Rock Island, Ill., Oct., 1898.

All Things Work for Good.

BY ALBERT SCHWARTZ.

All things work together for good to them who love God, to them who are the called according to his purpose.—*Rom.* 8:28.

Glorious thought! Oh, message sweet! Words heaven-inspired and full of brightest hope!

I.

All things work for good?

Yea, verily, "to them who *love God*." He is the master workman, infinite, kind and loving; "all things" are but his tools, while "those who love" are the blessed recipients of the Heavenly Father's ever-present, ever-needed watch-care and mercy.

II.

All things work for good?

Truly, to "the called according to his purpose," to those who have heard and heeded the pleadings of tender love and mercy as they call from the wounded hands and feet and side of the crucified, yet triumphant and glorified Savior. As the Father freely gave his beloved Son, will he not much rather fulfill to us this sweet promise? *Trust* him, then. Let no doubt abide. Do joys and pleasures gladden the way? They are the Father's sweet gifts to make his children nobler. Do clouds overshadow? Murmur not. All sunshine may spoil the fruitage of the soul. The Father knows best "how much of joy and how much of sorrow" we may need. Be sure no evil can harm the soul that trusts in him. Though he may permit the course of life to be changed suddenly and violently—changed from sunlight to darkness, from sweet gladness to bitter sadness, from cherished plans and hopes to unwelcome and unplanned tasks and conditions—trust even then. *"Though he slay me, yet will I trust him."*

III.

All things work for good?

Yes, for so the inspired soldier of the God of battles says. Then "let courage rise with danger," let it brave the hardships and trials of life. The good soldier bravely endures a thousand hardships and willingly faces danger, nor shrinks he back from the greatest sacrifice. His life is ready for the altar.

Though along with every trial and every sorrow, with every joy and every responsibility comes some new conflict with Satan's hosts, let us faint not; for "the Captain of our salvation will lead into no useless battle, nor will he ever allow defeat to come if we keep ever at his side. Let the drooping heart revive. Let tears and sorrows drive us to the fray; for unless there first be tears, trials and battles there can be no victor's reward and crown.

IV.

All things work for good?

Yes, unless the *Word* may fail. Then what ceaseless thanksgiving should flow from the heart! Yet, unless joy-bells gayly ring, unless sweet and easy fortune breathes its benediction upon us, unless the circle of friends is unbroken we mortals—selfish and weak—find it exceedingly hard to be grateful. Indeed, when adversity, heavy affliction, sore trial, loneliness, crushed hopes and desolating death cast their deep shadows and cause the fount of tears to flow, we find it hard even to *accept* them, harder yet to *trust*, and hardest of all to be *thankful* while enduring them. But as our Father is the master workman and as he knows our needs completely, why not look up 'midst pain and tears and say, "We thank thee, Father?"

V.

All things work for good?

Without such assurance, how could patience be maintained? Whom God loves he chastens, and all chastening is grievous.

Without patience we would fall out by the way or possibly rebel, but patience would die except for heavenly assurance. Knowing that chastening is "for our profit that we may partake of the holiness," we patiently endure. We have seen men ruined by prosperity and pleasure. We have also seen fellow-travelers on life's highway made more noble, lovely, useful and godlike through suffering and sorrow borne with patient spirit. Shall we, then, shrink back and rebel against those things which may, likewise refine us, fit us for nobler service to God and man, and unlock for us God's storehouse of truest and everlasting honor? Would we be pure gold? If so, we cannot avoid the refiner's fire. Would we be Christlike? He was made perfect through suffering.

Abundant reason, indeed, why we should "let patience have her perfect work!" And if tears must fall, behold how beautifully God adorns them with the bright bow of his promise that "all things work together for good to them that love God!" "I am persuaded that neither death, nor life, nor angels, nor principalities, nor things present, nor things to come, nor powers, nor height, nor depth, nor any other creature shall be able to separate us from the love of God, which is in Christ Jesus our Lord."

Galesburg, Ill.

With The Children.

CONDUCTED BY

J. BRECKENRIDGE ELLIS, PLATTSBURG, MO.

Grote.

George Weston got to Sunday-school a little late, on account of thinking out a plan by which Jim Dancy's parents might be made to promise to read history and poetry before their novels. But that didn't matter, because the Sunday-school was a little late in beginning, since the teachers wouldn't come at half past nine. It was a way of theirs. Jennie Weston was already in her place. Jennie's teacher was a splendid young lady, very much loved by her pupils, because she was so kind and explained the lessons so clearly. There was only one serious objection to her as a teacher: she was hardly ever at Sunday-school. She was not present this morning, and Jennie was disappointed, because this is the one she had meant to ask to join the Advance Society. "I wish I was grown!" she whispered to herself; this is the way she always expressed her disappointments.

There was a faithful member of the church, Bro. Putt, that the superintendent always got to take the place of an absent teacher. Not that Bro. Putt could teach, but he was willing to try, and was always so cheerful and modest, saying, "You know I am no teacher," which was very true. So he came over to Jennie's class, and held tightly to his lesson book, and had the scholars read the verses aloud, as if it were a reading class, and he asked the questions that are answered right under the verses in black letters and they answered as if they were still in a reading class. Since each knew which verse was coming, she hunted up her answer and sat with her finger on it, as if she were trying to keep it warm. Once Bro. Putt skipped a girl, but the next girl said, "That ain't my verse, Bro. Putt," and he said, "Sure enough," and looked disturbed.

Between the time Sunday-school let's out and church begins, the younger people sometimes take a walk on the broad sidewalk before the building. During this walk, Jennie asked a girl to join the Advance Society. "Who belongs?" asked the girl. Jennie answered that she was the first one asked to join. "I'll belong if the girls of my set do," said the other. "You ask Linnie Breezely. If Linnie Breezely joins, *I'll* join." Most of the girls in Mizzouryville belong to "sets," as if they were china cups or water-pitchers. Linnie Breezely was the ruler of one of these circles. Jennie decided to hunt up Linnie the next day at school and win her over.

That evening George Weston drew his father aside and unfolded his plan. "You know how Mr. and Mrs. Dancy spend all their time in reading novels," he said. "If it wasn't for novels, Mr. Dancy would tend to his jewlery business, instead of taking people's watches to regulate, and then putting them away somewhere and forgetting about them. And people never know when he will be in his office. So he is losing all his trade. And if it wasn't for novels, Mrs. Dancy would clean up, you know, and get to church and keep buttons sewed on and be like other women."

"This is all very true," said Mr. Weston, "and if Dancy wasn't my old schoolmate,"—

"But here is a plan to stop it all!" and George explained it with great eagerness. Then he added, "in this way, you can make them promise to do anything reasonable. So you bear down on them hard and say to them, 'Unless you promise to read twenty pages of history every day, and 200 lines of poetry, and a chapter of the Bible, and memorize a quotation, all before you pick up a single novel, you may know what to expect!' Then what will happen? Why, rather than read all that, they will tend to their work, and Jim won't be an orphan with a living father and mother!"

"Do you have to read all that to belong to your society?" asked Mr. Weston, looking very much amused.

"Oh, no! We only have five pages of history a *week* and thirty lines of poetry with just a *verse* of the Bible a day and a quotation to learn once a week. But this is a bad case and you must try a bad medicine. Ain't that a proverb? Will you do it papa? And hunt out the dryest history you can find and the poetry with the least sense in it!"

"I'll see," said Mr. Weston, who never told his children whether or not he would do a thing. But the next day, as he went to town to his office after dinner, Mr. Weston stopped at the Dancy's. Jim was hurrying off to school with a big piece of cornbread in his hand, because Mrs. Dancy had been so fascinated by the love passages in "Her Own True Love," that she had not noticed the time of day, and so failed to get any dinner. Mr. Weston had to stand at the front door a long time, while strange and hurried noises came from the interior. At last Mr. Dancy opened the door in a breathless state, his fur cap fixed on his head, and his pocket bulging with a book which he had crowded into it. Mr. Weston followed him into the parlor where Mrs. Dancy presently came, with an annoyed look which she tried to cover up with a large smile. She was wondering if the heroine of her novel fainted on Theodore's shoulder, or whether he sank beside her and chafed her hands. Theodore was the young man in the story.

"Just a minute to stay," said Mr. Weston, briskly. "Here's a package of four books I have brought to lend you." The Dancys brightened up, but looked rueful when they saw the first volume of Grote's "History of Greece", and Hallam's "Middle Ages," side by side with a translation of the "Iliad" and Milton's "Samson Agonistes."

"Dancy," said Mr. Weston suddenly, looking quite stern, "you know I've let the time run on that mortgage, till I couldn't make back my interest if I sold you out to-day, and all because you were my old chum in school. But I need the money, and I'm sorry to tell you I must give you notice that I shall foreclose!"

Mr. and Mrs. Dancy forgot all about their novels in a moment. "Weston," said Dancy with a troubled look, "I know you've been uncommon kind; but I haven't got the money and I don't seem to be getting along well, anyhow. And if you foreclose the mortgage, I'm a ruined man!"

Mr. Weston paced up and down the floor. "I'd be sorry to ruin you, Dancy. In fact, it is you who have ruined yourself, by giving your time to novels when—but it's no use to touch on *that*. You would never listen to me. This is a business affair. I must foreclose!"

Mrs. Dancy began to cry. Mr. Dancy pulled off his fur cap and looked at it with a frowning brow, as if he would say, "Where did *you* come from?"

"On one condition," said Mr. Weston slowly, "I will extend the time." Then he told about reading the history, poetry and Bible every day before they began on the novels. Of course they were glad to make the required promise, which he drew up in writing for them to sign. Then he went away. The Dancys hurried back to their sitting room, and Mrs. Dancy took off her Sunday dress and put on her wrapper. With a sigh of relief she was going after the heroine and Theodore, when she remembered her promise. She took up Hallam; Mr. Dancy got Grote. For a while silence reigned in the room. Presently Mrs. Dancy yawned. Then her husband said, "I believe I'll go up town and fix that watch of Bob Anderson's; I declare, I've had that watch on hand three weeks!" He laid Grote carefully away on the shelf, as if he did not expect to need him for sometime. Not long after he had left the house, Mrs. Weston, looking from her side window, was surprised to see the Dancy bedding stretched along the top of the garden fence in the sun, while the yard was filled with furniture. Mrs. Dancy was giving her house a "thorough cleaning."

I want to find out what kind of books children love to read. I believe you will be glad to know what other children like. I invite all to send me a list of their ten favorite books (not counting the Bible) and three favorite authors. If older than 14, tell what you preferred before you became 15. When a grown-up person knew I had asked this of our members, he laughed and said not many children had read ten books before they were 15. What do you think of that? Why, I have already received some answers. But if you haven't read ten books, send those you have read, or that have been read to you, that you liked—if you can only name two. Were you not interested in the letters of our members last week? Next week we will have another page of them, full of bright, interesting facts about other members' with funny stories, etc. Then the next week our continued story again, which will describe the school life of the Westons.

And, children, Sunday is Christmas! Maybe you had forgotten it. What are you going to give? More than you get, I hope. How? By returning love and smiles and kind words for your presents, and by being kind to some one less happy. I hope every one of the Advance Society (and we now hail from 18 states and from Canada) will take Christmas into somebody's life. Wherever you may be, there are others not as happy as you. Share with them a little of your happiness. Don't give everything you have to your kinfolks. Save a smile for the poor, and a loving word for the sorrowing, and a thought, deep and tender, full of gratitude and love for the Christ of Christmas.

Sunday School.

THE PROLOGUE.*

HERBERT L. WILLETT.

The lessons for 1898 were occupied for six months with the life of Christ, and for the remainder of the year with the story of the two kingdoms of Israel and Judah. Those for 1899 will deal with the life of Jesus as recorded in the Gospel of John, which will occupy the first six months, and will then return to the narrative of the last period of Old Testament history as recorded in the book of Ezra and Nehemiah, with side lights from the prophetic books of that age.

The Gospel of John is unquestionably the most important book in the Bible. If there were nothing else to make it an interesting volume, the fact that it grows out of the experiences of the disciple dearest to our Lord would give it this value. But the contents of the book are of supreme importance, expressing as they do the latest thought of the New Testament age regarding our Savior. The life of John is, perhaps, the most notable example of the uplifting influence of the companionship and teachings of Jesus and the quickening power of the Holy Spirit which the Scriptures record. He was by no means the quiet, calm, spiritual man of whom we usually think, when he began his acquaintance with Jesus at the Jordan. The picture presented by the four Gospels is that of a young man of Galilean characteristics, sharing the ardent Messianic hopes of the time; impulsive and fiery; an eager follower of the stern and prophetic ministry of John the Baptist, a man to whom, with his brother, Jesus gave the significant title, "Sons of Thunder;" a man displaying at times intolerance, anger and ambition (Lu. 9:49-56; Mk. 10:35 f), qualities hardly to be expected in a disciple "whom Jesus loved." Yet there was in him the promise of a noble spiritual manhood, and the discipline of Jesus' ministry was the beginning of that long process of education which led up to the mature and unique qualities which voice themselves in the Gospel and the first Epistle. He was never so conspicuous a member of the apostolic group as was Peter, and in the book of Acts plays a wholly minor part, disappearing almost entirely soon after Pentecost. Of the second period of his life, that marked by the great persecution at Rome and the destruction of Jerusalem, we have only the memorials furnished by the Apocalypse, which seems to date from this period, about 68 A. D., and to show that the spiritual education of John was still incomplete, though at the time he was the sole survivor of the apostolic circle. The closing years of his life, after his return from Patmos to Ephesus, brought him the full responsibilities of the only living representative of Jesus' personal ministry, and completed the rich character which has always been the charm of John's personality as expressed in his Gospel and his Epistles, the first of which is probably the closing word of the New Testament.

The Gospel of John is thus the product of the latest portion of the first Christian century. It is not an attempt to tell the story of Jesus' life, for the Synoptic Gospels were already in circulation and John had no need to tell their message afresh. His work is rather that of an interpreter who presents the message of those events of which the others had spoken, and interprets to us the meaning of Jesus as the incarnation of God in the flesh, his self-expression or "word" (logos) in the terms of human life. It is a special privilege to be permitted to study this book for the next six months. It is not so easy to understand as the other Gospels, but it is the mountain peak of New Testament thought and the mature utterance of one whose spiritual vision grew brighter and brighter unto the perfect day.

There is no more splendid utterance in the Scripture than the prologue to John's Gospel, contained in John 1:1-18, the whole of which should have been included in the present lesson. It takes us at once into the clear white light of eternity and shows us the place of Jesus in the life of the universe. Its first utterance is full of the profoundest meaning. The whole life of God is a process of self-disclosure to men. From the very beginning has he uttered himself; therefore, in the beginning was the Word. This Word was with God, nay indeed it was God. The first thought of the writer is not that of the personality of the Word, but rather that God's revelation of himself was not a recent thing but an eternal process. Then swiftly follows the emphasis upon the personality of this representative or expression of God. The Word is not merely personified, though personification is a common method with the Bible writers, especially of the Old Testament. Nor is there in the use of the word "logos" the adoption of the meaning which Philo associated with that word. The attempt to make John's phrase synonymous with the speculations of the Alexandrian school is not convincing. This expression of God, this Word, was the instrument of creation; which not only signifies the fact that creation itself is a method of expressing God's thoughts, but as well that the Word was the Creator. Thus in creation as in redemption the Father is the designer, the Son is the executor, and the Holy Spirit is the finisher. Nothing is planned without God; nothing is created without the Christ; nothing is completed without the Holy Spirit. The element which was especially Christ's to impart was life. "That which hath been made in him was life," seems to be the better rendering of the words in verses 3, 4. Both in creation and in redemption it is the work of our Savior to impart life. He came "to give life and to give it more abundantly;" without him there can be no life worth the name, for that life is the light of men, the only principle which can enlighten. But this life which was the light of the world and was first of all personalized in himself came into human society and was totally unrecognized. The world was darkness, and it did not perceive the light that was in its midst.

But the light did not come unheralded. A man sent from God came to announce the coming of that light and to bear witness of his approach. This was John, who in the fourth Gospel is never called John the Baptist, since the writer never names himself, and refers the name John only to the prophet of the Jordan. He plainly said that he was not the expected one, but only a witness; and the process of witness which was begun by John was continued by men of every class who saw Jesus.

But while John was preaching the light was already "coming into the world." This seems to be the meaning of the words in verse 9. The true light which lighteth every man had been coming into the world through the Old Testament dispensation, which was a preparation for his full disclosure. This gradual process of the coming of the light into the world was consummated when Jesus manifested the Father in his life. But still the world did not know him. He came to his own possessions, but they who were his own, that is, the Jewish people whose preparation had been so long under way, would not receive him. But there were those who received him and to them he gave the right to be the children of God, as that right had been possessed hitherto only by the children of Abraham. Nor was this relation one of human birth, but spiritual. And thus the Word was embodied in flesh and dwelt in the world full of grace and truth, and his glory was seen by his believing followers. The Incarnation is thus the most significant fact of the centuries; a fact eternal in its outreaches and significance. The Gospel of John is the Gospel of the Incarnation.

Anhaltstrasse 15, Berlin.

*Sunday-school lesson for Jan. 1, 1899—Christ the True Light John (1:1-18). Golden Text—In him was life and he was the light of men (John 1:4). Lesson Outline—1. The Eternal Word (1-5); 2. John the Witness (6-8); 3. The Incarnation (9-14).

Christian Endeavor.

BY BURRIS A. JENKINS.

TOPIC FOR JANUARY 1, 1899.

THE ANGEL PRESENCE FOR THE NEW YEAR.

(Ex. 23:20-25.)

The dangers were thick about Israel as the people crossed over the Jordan into the land that had long been their destiny. And precious indeed must have been the promise that an angel should guide their steps amid all snares and pitfalls, that he who so long had guided them in the wilderness would be with them yet, lest they forget.

Our own nation at the dawn of this last year in the old century is facing perils such as it has never known before. The long safe sojourn in the wilderness of national seclusion, where we have been fed by the manna and guided by the Presence, has come to an end. We have crossed the Rubicon, the Jordan, we have burned our ships, England's splendid isolation has been ended by the end of ours, and unknown reaches lie before us. Grant, O God, thine angel to be with us yet, and guide us aright!

So, in the lives of some of us there is doubtless dawning a new year of perils and of opportunities. We have left behind us the old days with their guidance and their safety, we are crossing into the untried regions of the future years. We can see only far enough ahead to perceive a way crowded with enemies, possibly thick with ambuscades. Precious to us, then, is God's ever-living promise, "I will not leave thee nor forsake thee, I will guide thee with mine eye, I will send an angel before thee to keep thee in the way."

It was a beautiful idea, that thought of Israel, that each had his guardian angel, which always watched before the Father. And is it not in all essentials a true thought, too? Our Savior put the stamp of his approval upon it. Knowing, then, that in each of our dangers some sweet messenger of certain knowledge wings its way to the Father's heart, that in every joy somehow the throbbing pulse of our exultation reaches him, that in all our doings, if we will but trust him, he guards us more carefully than he does the sparrow or the wide-winged waterfowl, how secure ought we to rest in his care!

Special Providence? Why, of course we should believe in it. There is no other kind of Providence. All of it is special Providence. Does he not care for nations? Does he not care for men? Those who put their trust in him are never forsaken, provided they do their best to do his will. Trust God, and exert thy strength, O Sampson! Trust God and blow your trumpets, Gideonites. Trust God and pay your debts, Christians. Trust God and keep dry powder, soldiers of the Lord. Trust God and work hard, missionaries of the Lord's kingdom here on earth.

It would seem that if one of the Lord's own should become so beset with enemies that his life is actually in danger and finally is lost, it is the greatest evidence that he has been forsaken of the Lord. But such was the case with Jesus, his own Son. In those darkest of dangers the Lord's presence was with his Son. Not at any time was his comfort withdrawn. In the dark hours of the garden the angel of God spake in various ways the sustaining message to his heart. Sydney Lanier has beautifully fancied it thus:

"Into the woods my Master went
Clear forespent, forespent.
Into the woods my Master came,
Forespent with love and shame.
But the olives they were not blind to him,
The little gray leaves were kind to him,
And the thorn tree had a mind to him,
When into the woods he came.

"Out from the woods my Master went,
And he was well content.
Out from the woods my Master came,
Content with death and shame.

When death and shame would woo him last
From under the trees they drew him last,
'Twas on a tree they slew him last,
When out from the woods he came.''

The Lord did not forsake him at any time, though even the Master himself once thought that God had forsaken him. But he did not think it long. In a few moments only he saw the everlasting arms reached out to him, and into those hands he commended his spirit.

BETHANY C. E. READING COURSES.

Genesis of the Disciples of Christ.

F. D. POWER.

Taking the New Testament as the special authoritative rule of faith and practice for Christians, the Campbells were consistent. They recognized in a practical way the distinction between the law and the gospel, the Old and the New Testament. They said: Let men inquiring the way of salvation no longer be referred to Job and the Psalms, Isaiah or the Proverbs. God's revelation is progressive; first the family, then the tribe or nation, then the world—the Patriarchal, Jewish and Christian dispensations. We are no longer under Moses, but under Christ. The New Testament involves the abrogation of the Old. ''In that he saith a new covenant, he hath made the first old.'' The old had its purpose. The moon has its uses, so has the sun; the night is worthy, so is the joyous and glorious day. The old covenant, the old order, circumcision, the Sabbath, have passed away. ''The law came by Moses, but grace and truth came by Jesus Christ.'' ''Go into all the world and preach the gospel to every creature.''

Here, they said, are four books—Mathew, Mark, Luke and John—to produce faith in Christ. ''Many other signs truly did Jesus that are not written in this book; but these are written that ye might believe that Jesus is the Christ, the Son of God; and that believing, ye might have life through his name.''

Here in the Acts of the Apostles, showing how the gospel was preached to all classes and conditions of men; and that the apostles treated all as possessed of reason, capable of understanding and believing, of hearing and doing the will of God.

Here are the Epistles, written to Christians to show them how they should live as subjects of the kingdom; and here is the Apocalypse, or Revelation of John, casting light upon the fortunes and destinies of the church.

Going thus to the original sources of Christianity, these men declared: We must take the names given to the followers of Christ in the New Testament—Christians or Disciples of Christ. We do not read here of the church of Rome, or of Luther, or of Wesley, but the ''Church of Christ.'' ''The disciples were men called Christians.'' Party names divide God's people. Divisions hinder the progress of the kingdom. Christ prayed that his people might be one, that the world might believe.

Sects say: ''Lo, here is Christ, and lo' there.'' There is not an Arminian Christ and a Calvinistic Christ. God's people are sinning when they say: ''I am of Paul, and I of Apollos, and I of Cephas, and I of Christ.''

The party hatchet must be buried, party shibboleths given up, party banners furled and party names abandoned; and together, elbows touching, faces lifted in one direction, keeping step to the same music and advancing under the one banner of the Messiah, the church must move to the conquest of the world.

Accepting only the names of the New Testament, they took the ordinances also. Here is the Lord's Supper, they said, observed on every Lord's day as a solemn memorial feast. We must so observe it. Here is the institution of baptism, administered to believing penitents, by an immersion in water, in the name of Father, Son and Holy Spirit. Walking in the old paths, we must so practice it. Of this ordinance, what is apostolic? they asked. What bears the stamp of catholicity? What is the practice of the Greek Church? What does all scholarship agree to have been the primitive practice? What do the founders of the religious bodies, Luther, Calvin, Wesley and the Roman Catholic, honestly admit to have been the exclusive practice of the apostles?

Show us the way of the book. We are tired of big popes and of little popes. We want no man's system of belief. Let us know what Jesus says, and the men authorized by him to speak. The world is sick of the rabid and venomous conflicts of sectarianism, of mind-shackling and soul-crushing human creeds. Thousands are wandering in the night with no stars to light them, with no sunlight, their barks driven by every storm, tossed on every billow, whirled in every eddy, praying for some one to guide them to a haven of safety and peace.

Let us bring the restless world back to the old foundations. Let us restore Christianity as in the beginning. How far these men succeeded, let the world judge. At first they were like—

"An infant crying in the night,
An infant crying for the light,
And with no language but a cry."

To-day millions hear the voice. It will not do to reform the clergy. We must go to the original preachers—Christ and the apostles. It will not do to reform the creeds; one creed is as good as another. We must go to the Word of God.

A New Feature in the Reading Courses.

It has been suggested that the value of the Bethany C. E. Reading Courses might be greatly increased if they would adopt the method of University Extension. I am favorably inclined to the suggestion, but wish the advice of those who are interested in this effort to instruct and indoctrinate our young people.

The method, as I understand it, would be something like this: Selecting those points throughout the country where the Disciples are strongest as radiating centers, specially equipped men and women could be sent out to weaker points to give courses of popular lectures on our three chosen lines of study. As these lines of study are of interest to the church, the Sunday-school and the C. W. B. M., as well as to the Christian Endeavor Societies, all these could be united in awakening a public interest in these special lectures on Bible study, on world-wide missions and on the fundamental principles and history of our own plea. It seems to me that three courses of lectures given by picked persons would be of far greater value to many communities than the average revival service. They would awaken thought, start inquiry, set the people to reading and develop an intelligent, uplifting and abiding religious influence.

The expenses would be comparatively light and could easily be provided by the sale of tickets for the entire course. With proper enterprise, these tickets could be placed at a price within the reach of the poorest, and in many cases well-to-do persons would be glad to supply to the less fortunate this means of self-improvement. These lectures might be given in close succession as at an institute, or they may be distributed throughout the season. Local considerations would determine this.

This method would enable us to utilize quite a good deal of our very best talent now only partially employed. It would enable us to bring to bear directly upon the masses of our people and in connection with the most fundamental subjects, very much of the unused treasures of knowlege. It would do much to disseminate among the masses the valuable results of scholarly research. I am sufficiently radical to believe that our treasures of learning as well as all other treasures, are to be held in trust under Christ for the greatest possible good of the greatest possible number of people. All our treasures and our talents are for use to the very utmost. This is my conception of Christian service and out of this conviction the Bethany C. E. Reading Courses were born. It now seems to me that the suggestion to apply University Extension methods to these courses opens the way by which we may utilize the best among us for the systematic instruction of the masses of our people. It seems to me that the application of this method would do very much to make all our people intelligent concerning the evangelization of the world and concerning our plea to divided Christendom. It seems to me that there is thus opened before us a vast and most inviting field.

Will every one who reads this please write me a line that I may know how the suggestion strikes our thoughtful people?

J. Z. TYLER.

768 *Republic St., Cleveland O., Dec.* 3, 1898.

[We do not see why the foregoing suggestion is not entirely practicable and why this extension method should not form a feature of our Jubilee activities. If found to produce desirable results, as it would, no doubt, it might become a permanent method of educational work along religious lines. We hope that many of our readers will write Bro. Tyler, giving their opinions as to the feasibility of the plan.—EDITOR.]

Literature.

JERUSALEM, THE HOLY. A brief History of Ancient Jerusalem, with an account of the Modern City and its conditions, Political, Religious and Social, by Edwin Sherman Wallace, late United States Consul for Palestine. Price, $1.50. Fleming H. Revell Co., Chicago, New York and Toronto. 1898.

Perhaps no other city in the world has passed through quite so many changes, and been the scene of so many important events, as the far-famed City of Jerusalem. This volume gives perhaps all that is known to date concerning this wonderful city and its strange history, the author having availed himself of the latest scientific investigations and best works, including Prof. Sayce's "Patriarchal Palestine," Edersheim's "Jesus the Messiah," Dr. Robinson's "Biblical Researches," Williams' "Holy City" and Barclay's "City of the Great King." It contains illustrations and maps that serve the better to set forth the facts and conditions of the city, past and present. The author says in his preface that "some fifty years ago the appearance of Williams' 'Holy City' and Barclay's 'City of the Great King' gave the English public two real histories of Jerusalem." He adds, however, that the greater length of these excellent works has confined them mainly to the shelves of large libraries, while the growth in knowledge has thrown fresh light on many phases of the subject; hence this volume. Any one anticipating a visit to this ancient city, the Mecca of both Jews and Christians, and desiring an accurate knowledge of the history and present condition of the city, certainly cannot do better than to possess himself of this work, and give it careful study before making the journey. It is a volume of 359 pages, aside from the preface and index, and the mechanical quality of the book adds to its value.

THE POST-APOSTOLIC AGE. By Lucius Waterman, D. D., with an introduction, by Henry Codman Potter, D. D., LL. D., Bishop of New York. Chas. Scribner & Sons. 1898.

This is Volume II. of the Ten Epochs of Christian History, edited by Jno. Fulton, D. D., LL. D. The author of this volume professes to have written the work in the true spirit of scientific investigation, and the work itself bears evidence of this feature so far as we have examined it, though, like all authors, he, of course, is influenced largely by his point of view. He says, however, "For those readers in particular who have never trodden this way before, I have tried to be an honest guide, fairly indicating to them the places where another might guide them altogether differently." A review of this work will be given when we have had time to examine it more fully. Meantime, we simply call the attention of our readers to the appearance of this volume.

"MISSIONS AND POLITICS IN ASIA." By Robert E. Speer. Fleming H. Revell Co., Chicago, publishers. Price, $1.00; cloth binding, 270 pages.

"The lectures composing this volume were suggested by the studies and observation of an entended tour in Asia, in the years 1896 and 1897. They are printed substantially as they were delivered to the faculty and students of Princeton Theological Seminary in February, 1898. Their object was to sketch in broad outline the spirit of the Eastern peoples, the present making of history in Asia and the part therein of Christian missions. They are at once the fruit and the ground of the conviction, vindicated by the obvious facts of history and of life, that Christ is the present Lord and King of all life and history, and their certain goal."

"DOCTRINE AND LIFE." By Iowa writers. Edited by G. L. Brokaw, A. M., editor Christian Index, and published by the Christian Index Co., Des Moines, Iowa. Cloth binding, 504 pages. No price given.

This is a book of 28 sermons, by Iowa preachers. It also contains a half-tone cut and biographical sketch of each preacher. Themes of the sermons or addresses in this book indicate a strong grip upon gospel truth and present-day issues, and is worthy of a place in every preacher's library.

AMERICAN REVISED BIBLE. Being the Revised Version set forth in A. D. 1881-1885. With the Readings and Renderings preferred by the American Revision Companies incorporated in the Text and with Copyright Marginal References. Printed for the Universities of Oxford and Cambridge. New York, American Branch, 91 and 93 Fifth Ave., 1898.

This is the Bible many have been waiting for. It has incorporated in the text the preferred readings and renderings of the American committee, all of which, in our judgment, add to the value of this version. "In" is substituted for "with" in connection with baptism, "Jehovah" is substituted for "Lord" throughout the Old Testament, *pneuma* is rendered by "Spirit" instead of "Ghost," and many other equally important changes are made. The references made for this version are a valuable addition. The typography and print are all that could be desired. We welcome this version and hope it may prevail over all others.

"THE LIFE AND TEACHING OF JESUS." By Dr. H. L. Willett.

This book is the finest compendium of the facts in the life of Jesus, and the chief characteristics of his teaching, which we believe to be in print. Its condensation is only equaled by its lucidity of style. To master this little volume is to have a very clear knowledge of the history of Jesus and of his doctrine. It is divided into two parts, the first part dealing with the life and the second with the teaching of Jesus. Following is the list of the chapter headings in the two parts:

Part I. I. The The Gospel Records. II. Birth and Early Life. III. The Opening of Jesus' Ministry. IV. The Period of Public Ministry and Success. V. The Climax of Jesus' Ministry. VI. The Week of Tragedy and Triumph.

Part II. I. Characteristics of Jesus' Teaching. II. Jesus' Teaching Regarding God. III. Jesus' Teaching Regarding Himself. IV. The Kingdom of God. V. Jesus' Teaching Regarding Man. VI. Jesus and Judaism. VII. Jesus' Teaching about the Holy Spirit. VIII. Jesus' Teaching Regarding the Future.

This volume belongs to the series of books issued by the committee for the Bethany C. E. Reading Courses. It would be a good thing to enlist the whole membership of our churches in the study of such books as this and others of the series, as indeed is done in a few instances. They contain the very information which our membership need most at present.

"WHY I AM A VEGETARIAN." By J. Howard Moore, Frances L. Dusenberry, Chicago, publisher. Paper cover, 48 pages, price 25 cents.

This is the address delivered before the Chicago Vegetarian Society, by J. Howard Moore, and is now in its seventh thousand edition. It is in strong language and intended to carry conviction at first reading.

IN CHRIST JESUS, OR THE SPHERE OF THE BELIEVER'S LIFE. By Arthur T. Pierson. Funk & Wagnals Co., New York, Publishers. 196 pages.

This book contains a treatise on each of the Epistles of Paul to the early Christians in which the new man and the new life in Christ Jesus is ever-apparent and well-defined, developed and emphasized theme of the writer. The careful reading of this book cannot fail to enlarge the believer's conception of his privileges and blessings in Christ Jesus.

THE SAMBO BOOK. By Isaac Coale, Jr. Williams & Wilkins Co., Baltimore, Publishers. 96 pages, large size primer type.

Sambo's stories make interesting Christmas reading for children. A good Christmas gift book for juvenile readers.

PROFESSOR SHALER, the eminent geologist, predicts that in the distant future the great lakes will cease to pour over Niagara, and that the four upper lakes will find their outlet at Chicago. He gives his reasons in a most interesting article, which he has written for the next volume of THE YOUTH'S COMPANION. Professor Shaler has written another article for the same periodical on "Klondikes, Old and New."

Marriages.

BAYNE—WALKER.—Dec. 5, at Kansas City, Mo., Mr. Arthur Bayne and Miss Emma Walker, both of Kansas City, Mo.; R. E. Lloyd, of the Church of Christ, officiating.

HAMILTON—BROWNING.—Nov. 23, at the Christian parsonage, Payson, Ill., Mrs Samuel Hamilton and Mrs. Sylvia Browning; Eld. C. Edwards officiating.

REYNOLDS—LEACH.—At the residence of the bride's aunt, Mrs. Harriet Lipe, in Macomb, Ill., Mr. James Nathanael Reynolds and Miss Anna Blanch Leach: J. C. Reynolds officiating, Oct 24, 1898. The writer also married the bride's father and mother many years ago. The bridegroom is his youngest son.

Obituaries.

[One hundred words will be inserted free. Above one hundred words, one cent a word. Please send amount with each notice.]

BRYAN.

Bro. Walter J. Bryan's death occurred at the Bryan residence in this city, Dec. 3, 1898, aged 18 years. He died in the triumph of a living faith, and has entered into his rest. Though this is the old home of John A. Logan, the people could not have honored him any more than they did this our friend and brother whose future was so bright and hopeful. The funeral occurred Sunday afternoon from the Christian Church. The writer conducted the funeral services. The church was crowded and many were unable to get in. The casket was literally covered with floral designs sent by friends. From the church to the cemetery Grear's Concert Band, of which the deceased was a member, played a funeral march, and a long procession followed. Peaceto his ashes, and rest to his soul. W. H. WILLYARD.

Murphysboro, Ill., Dec. 16, 1898.

CLARK.

Nicholas S. Clark, born Nov. 9, 1832, at Glasgow, Howard county, Mo., died at Fortuna, Humboldt county, Cal., Nov. 16, 1898. He came to the Pacific Coast in 1853, and to Humboldt county in 1886. He was the father of nine children, seven of whom are living, and with the mother all were present at his death except one daughter. Though not a Christian, his wife was an honorable one. Funeral services at the Christian Church conducted by the writer. A. B. MARKLE.

CLARK.

Dr. John H. Clark died at the home of his son the Hon. Champ Clark, of Bowling Green, Mo., on Nov. 26th, in the 86th year of his age. He was born in New Jersey, near where Atlantic City now stands, on March 6th, 1813. Somewhere in the forties he went to Kentucky, settled down at Lawrenceburg, and was married to Althea Jane Beauchamp, a woman of rare beauty, refinement and education. After seven brief years of happiness, she was called up higher, but he ever fondly cherished her memory, regarded her children as a sacred trust from her, and looked forward always to meeting her in the better land. He was the grandson of a Quaker preacher. In early life he had been a Methodist, but more than fifty years ago had cast in his lot with the Disciples of Christ, and from then till the day of his death he remained an ardent advocate of the truth, as he understood it. He had a fine original mind, was fond of reading and well informed, and so long as he lived never considered himself too old to learn anything. He had not only the mind to understand, but the deft hand that executes, and all of the Eastern man's versatility, and so it came to pass that in the course of his life, he had worked at many things and did them all well: carriage building, clock-making, plough-making, singing, teaching and dentistry. After the death of his beloved wife, he removed to Washington Co., Ky., where for thirty years he successfully practiced the profession of dentistry. He left two children, the Hon. Champ Clark, of Bowling Green, Mo., and Mrs. J. J. Haley, of Cynthiana, Ky. Two things he had loved supremely: his church and his country, and he lived to see his son recognized as one of the most brilliant and able congressmen of his beloved Democratic party, and his daughter an efficient and earnest worker in the church, both in this country and in foreign lands. Seldom has there been a more earnest student of the Bible; to earnestly study it, to examine its truths, to write out his understanding of its teachings had been the delight and occupation of his old age. After his death there were reams of manuscript found amongst his effects, all relating to the Scriptures. Even during the last two years of feebleness and infirmity, his Bible was his daily companion. He died from a shock to his system, the result of a fall caused by a slight touch of paralysis. After three days of unconsciousness, he passed quietly into that "sun-bright clime, undimmed by sorrow, unhurt by time," of which he had delighted to sing. No one that saw his peaceful face, could doubt but he had entered with joy into the presence of his Master—

"Where those angel faces smile,
Which he had loved long since, and lost awhile."

H.

JONES.

Died, Dec. 3, aged 30, Myrtie, daughter of Wm. Jones and wife, granddaughter of Harrison Jones. She united with the church at 16 and she was one of the pure ones of earth. She will be greatly missed by the church and community and especially at her home. Her presence was always a blessing. While it is hard to have the tender ties of earth broken, yet heaven means more to us when we realize that our sister has taken her abode in the city where God shall wipe away all tears from our eyes. J. D. JOHNSON.

Canton, O.

PARRY.

Sister Eliza Ann Parry died Nov. 23rd, 1898, in the 53rd year of her age. She was born near Cherry Tree, Pa. On Sept. 27, 1866, she was married to Bro. Wm. H. Parry, who departed this life Sept. 6, 1886. Subsequently removed to near Pineflats, Pa., where she resided to the time of her death. Her life was one of quiet peacefulness with her friends and neighbors, and was a consistent member of the Pineflats Church of Christ, and though she was hindered by ill health from attending worship during the last few months of her life, her conversation showed that she was in active sympathy with the cause of Christ. She leaves two sons and two daughters to mourn their loss. The funeral was conducted by the writer at Pineflats, Pa. CHARLES E. SMITH.

REAVIS.

Miss Lucy J. Reavis, born in Boone County, Ky., July 26, 1841, passed from her home on earth to her home in heaven, Dec. 2, 1888, aged 57 years, four months and six days. Sister Lucy united with the Church of Christ at Pleasant Grove, Monroe Cou ty, Mo., about 36 years ago, since which she has been a quiet, inoffensive and devoted Christian. She seemed to make two objects the primary aims of her life—to do right and to make others happy. Her mother died several years ago, since which she has been a ministering angel to her aged father who lingers to long for the summons to follow across the silent river. She leves also three sisters and two brothers to mourn her departure. Her funeral was conducted by C. H. Strawn in the church where she so long had met fo worship.

C. H. STRAWN.

THE SPANISH WOMAN.

It has been said that every native Spanish woman is energetic; whether she be from Andalusia or Asturias, the South or the North, she has none of the creole languor of Spanish-descended women of Cuba, Mexico and tropical America.

In the current number of the Singer series of national costume illustrations a typical picture is presented, showing a man and woman of Seville, where the orignal photograph was taken in 1891.

How characteristic are the accessories! The woman is industrious, and regards with an air of distinct disapproval the weak-faced individual before her with his guitar and glass of wine.

Because of the war, many a Spanish woman would now be driven to hard straits were it not for the Singer sewing machine, which is furnished to her on the most liberal terms of payment; thus she easily becomes self-supporting. Singer machines are almost universally used in Spain because of their simplicity, great range of work, and superior construction. They are "built like a watch," and never bother their fair operators, whether in Spain or elsewhere.

Publishers' Notes.

THE UNIFORM SERIES OF PRAYER-MEETING TOPICS FOR 1899.—Seventh consecutive year—are ready and being sent out in large numbers. Every church should follow these Topics during the coming year, as very many of the foremost churches have for years past. The first Topic in each month provides for a Concert of Prayer for Missions in harmony with the resolution adopted at the Chattanooga Convention. The Topics are published by the Christian Pub. Co., and sent postpaid at the rate of 25 cents per hundred.

TOPICAL OUTLINES is a neat Booklet of 32 pages containing a careful analysis of the Mid-week Church Prayer-meeting Topics—uniform series—with copious Scripture references that will serve as a guide to the leader and as an aid to the members in taking a prompt and intelligent part in the service. Every member should have a copy. Only 25 cents per dozen. Published by Christian Pub. Co.

COMPETENT WITNESSES TESTIFY

Concerning: *Christian Lesson Commentary* for 1899:

It is a fitting volume with which to close the Sunday-school work of the century. The Christian Publishing Co. is fortunate in having W. W. Dowling to superintend their Sunday-school publications. His work has always been done well and in some respects superior to any other. The very best that could be found has been annually and intelligently laid before the teachers in our Sunday-schools. The Commentary for 1899 is a valuable addition to the splendid series.—*F. M. Green, Kent, O.*

I have examined *Christian Lesson Commentary* for 1899, by W. W. Dowling. Whatever other commentaries we may have, he will find something in this one additional to all and which he needs. I know of no other which in itself will so fully prepare one for teaching the lesson, if all of its sections are carefully and thoroughly mastered.—*Chas. M. Fillmore, Peru, Ind.*

Christian Lesson Commentary for 1899 is on our table. It grows brighter and better as the years come and go. We have used it for thirteen years and now start in for the fourteenth volume. It is pure in doctrine, full in explanation, pointed in application and we trust international and general in circulation. It is well arranged, the notes are full and the illustrations are helpful.—*Christian Index, Des Moines, Ia.*

Christian Lesson Commentary for 1899, by W. W. Dowling, is an 8vo. volume of 413 pages. For thirteen years this valuable publication has made its annual appearance. The volume before us is fully up to the high standard of its predecessors, and its pages are replete with notes, comments, illustrations, applications and suggestions gathered from various sources, the designs being to throw the best light possible on the Scripture text. We commend this commentary to all Sunday-school workers.—*The Religious Telescope.*

The Christian Lesson Commentary for 1899, edited by W. W. Dowling, is a beautifully bound and richly illustrated volume of over 400 pages. No Lesson Help more fully and satisfactorily illustrates the lessons of the International Series. In our preparation of the Quarterlies no commentary gives us more satisfactory, if equal, aid. If the teacher wishes best help in his work, he will find it in Dowling's Commentary. We would be glad to see the Christian Lesson Commentary in the hands of all our teachers. With its aid we can hardly see how further help would be necessary in the line of commentary matter.—*Herald of Gospel Liberty*, Dayton, Ohio.

The Christian Lesson Commentary for 1899 contains 414 pages, and from title-page to the end is loaded with good things. It presents the best plan for the study of the lesson that I have yet found. If carefully and intelligently followed for preparation it will thoroughly equip any thoughtful teacher to helpfully and efficiently teach the lesson. The preliminary helps, the lesson analysis, the expositions, the illustrative material, the truths to be applied, the practical lessons to be emphasized, the suggestive material provided, certainly furnish, in rich abundance, all that any intelligent person requires to make him a teacher "that needs not to be ashamed," properly teaching his class. J. H. MACNEILL,
Pastor Christian Church.
Muncie, Ind.

The price of *Christian Lesson Commentary* for 1999, by W. W. Dowling, is $1 per copy postpaid, or $9 per dozen copies not prepaid. The book is printed on *good* paper, with red edges and bound in a splendid quality of dark-green cloth. Address Christian Publishing Co., 1522 Locust St., St. Louis, Mo.

Expansion.

This is the paramount question of the day. We believe in expanding—the list of readers of the CHRISTIAN-EVANGELIST. Do you?

We believe in it, because in increasing the number of the readers of the CHRISTIAN-EVANGELIST—

(1) More minds will be enlightened concerning the achievements and needs of the cause;

(2) More hearts will be warmed with love for others of our race less fortunately situated than ourselves;

(3) More charity of opinions and more unity of action will obtain among us because our zeal in a common purpose, kindled by knowledge and love, and—

(4) The kingdom of Christ will thereby be rapidly extended and the will of God be more nearly done on earth.

Will the CHRISTIAN-EVANGELIST be useful in bringin these desirable things to pass? Well, we think—but never mind, here are a few opinions from others.

"The CHRISTIAN-EVANGELIST is an ably edited paper and sound to the core." CEPHAS SHELBURNE, Fredericksburg, Va.

"I consider the CHRISTIAN-EVANGELIST one of our very best religious papers. I admire its Christian spirit and am sure it is doing much in advancing the cause of our blessed Master." H. C. SAUM, Decker's Point, Pa.

"I think I have neglected a duty in not expressing sooner my continued delight in the broad, liberal Christian tone of the CHRISTIAN-EVANGELIST. I left one of the leading denominations twelve years ago in search of "Liberty *with* Loyalty," and shall ever be thankful that I became acquainted with the Disciples of Christ. Sometimes, however, in my six years' rambling in your great country, I have seen occasionally the bitterest kind of sectarianism amongst even the Disciples. Your paper will save the grand cause from crystallizing into Ishmaelites on the hand and Sadducees on the other." T. R. HODKINSON, Clarksville, Ia.

Once in awhile I find something in your paper that I do not heartily approve, but after all necessary abatements have been made I think that in the moderation of its temper, in the substantial value of its discussions and its general literary excellency it incontestibly leads, by an ample space, all of our weekly publications. This is the opinion of one after the "Old Methods." GEO. PLATTENBURG, Dover, Mo.

THE CHRISTIAN-EVANGELIST.

A WEEKLY FAMILY AND RELIGIOUS JOURNAL.

Vol. XXXV. December 29, 1898 No. 52.

CONTENTS.

EDITORIAL:

Current Events....................803
Thirty Years an Editor....................804
The Year of Jubilee.................... 804
Ebenezer 805
Are We Pagans?....................805
The Secret of All Thankfulness........806
Editor's Easy Chair.............. ..807
The Christian Portrait Gallery... 807
Nine Decades of History....... 807

CORRESPONDENCE:

Kansas City Letter............. 817
Texas Letter....................817
Brigham H. Roberts....................818
Nebraska Missionary Notes.. 818
Notes from the Foreign Field........ .818
A Visit to Columbia 818
Christian Institute, Shanghai, China..819
The Churches of Christ in St. Louis,..819
Iowa Letter....................820
Circular Letter to the Board of Education 820

FAMILY CIRCLE:

A Song of Peace (poem)... 824
What Two Boys Did—II...............824
The Prodigal Girl (poem)............ 825
Sunrise on the Desert (poem)..........826
The Family Altar....................826

MISCELLANEOUS:

Our Budget.................... 808
Personal Mention....... 810
Origin, History and Needs of the Amer-Christian Missionary Society........811
Notes and News....................821
Evangelistic 822
Publisher's Notes 823
With the Children........ 827
Sunday-school........ 828
Christian Endeavor....................829
Bethany C. E. Reading Courses.... 829
Literature.................... 830
Marriages and Obituaries.............831
Announcements.......... 832

Subscription $1.50

W. F. RICHARDSON.

PUBLISHED BY

CHRISTIAN PUBLISHING COMPANY

1522 Locust St., St. Louis.

THE

CHRISTIAN - EVANGELIST

J. H. GARRISON, EDITOR.

W. W. HOPKINS, ASSISTANT.

B. B. TYLER, J. J. HALEY,
EDITORIAL CONTRIBUTORS.

What We Plead For.

The Christian-Evangelist pleads for:

The Christianity of the New Testament, taught by Christ and his Apostles, versus the theology of the creeds taught by fallible men—the world's great need.

The divine confession of faith on which Christ built his church, versus human confessions of faith on which men have split the church.

The unity of Christ's disciples, for which he so fervently prayed, versus the divisions in Christ's body, which his apostles strongly condemned.

The abandonment of sectarian names and practices, based on human authority, for the common family name and the common faith, based on divine authority, versus the abandonment of scriptural names and usages for partisan ends.

The hearty co-operation of Christians in efforts of world-wide beneficence and evangelization, versus petty jealousies and strifes in the struggle for denominational pre-eminence.

The fidelity to truth which secures the approval of God, versus conformity to custom to gain the favor of men.

The protection of the home and the destruction of the saloon, versus the protection of the saloon and the destruction of the home.

For the right against the wrong;
For the weak against the strong;
For the poor who've waited long
For the brighter age to be.
For the truth, 'gainst superstition,
For the faith, against tradition,
For the hope, whose glad fruition
Our waiting eyes shall see.

RATES OF SUBSCRIPTION.

Single subscriptions, new or old ....$1.50 each
Ministers .... 1.00 "

All subscriptions payable in advance. Label shows the month up to the first day of which your subscription is paid. If an earlier date than the present is shown, you are in arrears. No paper discontinued without express orders to that effect. Arrears should be paid when discontinuance is ordered.

In ordering a change of post office, please give the OLD as well as the NEW address.

Do not send local check, but use Post office or Express Money Order, or draft on St. Louis, Chicago or New York, in remitting.

ADDRESS, CHRISTIAN PUBLISHING CO.,
1522 Locust St., St. Louis, Mo.

THE CHRISTIAN-EVANGELIST

"In faith, Unity; in opinion and methods, Liberty; in all things, Charity."

Vol. xxxv. St. Louis, Mo., Thursday, December 29, 1898. No. 52

CURRENT EVENTS.

Ethen Allen Hitchcock, at present United States Ambassador at St. Petersburg, has been appointed successor of Mr. Bliss as Secretary of the Interior. Mr. Hitchcock is a native of Alabama, but has been for many years a resident of St. Louis. Now, for the third time in the last twenty-five years, a citizen of St. Louis becomes Secretary of the Interior. It is believed that the original appointment would have fallen to Mr. Hitchcock instead of Mr. Bliss had not considerations of geographical distribution of Cabinet positions demanded that a New Yorker be put in the place. The first part of the prophecy quoted last week has already been fulfilled in the appointment of a Western man to the vacancy in the Cabinet. The way is now clear for the fulfillment of the second part by the appointment of Mr. Choate, of New York, or some other Eastern man, as Ambassador to the court of St. James. There have been an extraordinary number of changes in the McKinley Cabinet. During its less than two years of existence, Secretaries Sherman, Day, McKenna, Gary and Bliss have resigned their positions, either to retire or to accept other places.

A recent cartoon, referring to the Czar's proposition for disarmament, pictures the Czar in crown and gown standing upon the shore of a boisterous sea whose waves threaten to engulf him. The waves of this sea are labeled "Survival of the Fittest," "Natural Selection," "Selfishness," and against these the monarch waves a scepter labled "Peace Proposition." Below is the inscription, "*A Modern Canute.*" So the Czars's attempt to stay the tide and still the waves of selfishness with a proposal for peace, is characterized as a vain and foolish attempt to avert the inevitable and resist the irresistable. We remember that there was one, who once sailed the Sea of Galilee, in whose mouth the word "peace" was potent for the stilling of waves, and who combated human selfishness with this same weapon—peace. Contemporary satirists might have depicted his method in some such cartoon as that described above. Perhaps the Czar's position is not consistent and perhaps he is but a dreamer of dreams. But one cannot believe in the final triumph of the principles of Jesus without seeing in this suggestion of a victory of peace over selfishness, not an idle dream, but a vision, distant perhaps, but true.

The War Inquiry Board goes on with its investigation. Last week it had a series of prominent witnesses, including Generals Miles, Shafter, Merritt and Howard. Gen. Shafter was inclined to dismiss all criticisms with the sweeping generalization that "hindsights are always better than foresights," a remark which contains some truth, to be sure, but not enough to justify an army officer in a failure to exercise foresight. One of Gen. Miles' most striking statements was his condemnation of the refrigerated beef, which was furnished to the army to the extent of 327 tons, which he said might better be called "embalmed beef." Frequent complaints were made to the commissary-general, but he seemed to insist that it should be used. The canned fresh beef, of which about 100 tons were supplied, was also condemned by the officers whose commands used it. The statements to the board the next day by Adjutant-General Corbin do not accord with those of General Miles, and the differences still remain to be reconciled.

The details have been arranged for the transfer of the sovereignty of Cuba from Spain to the United States. At noon, Jan. 1, the Spanish flag on Morro Castle and the public buildings of Havana will be hauled down, and the American flag will be raised. At the same time the government will be surrendered to the American evacuation commissioners and by them to Maj. Gen. Brooke. The American commissioners have done good service in hastening the departure of the Spanish troops, but the evacuation will not be complete on the day of the surrender. The articles, which have been agreed upon to govern the transfer of sovereignty make liberal provision for the rights and privileges of the Spanish soldiers pending their embarkation, but at the same time guarantee, as well as any agreement can, that they shall not be able in any way to obstruct the work of the American Government in purifying and civilizing Cuba.

We are told that there is imminent danger of a Cabinet crisis at Madrid, and we are not disposed to doubt the report. When, during the past two years, has that danger not existed? When affairs are in such a condition that they can't become worse, any change is apt to be acceptable, and Cabinets have with difficulty kept their places in this situation. It has been said that Gen. Weyler is not in sympathy with the Sagasta ministry and will try to overthrow it. He himself denies this report in a signed statement in which he proclaims his complete reconciliation with the Liberal party. As he acutely remarks, the issue upon which he separated from the party, viz., the administration of Spanish sovereignty in Cuba, is now a dead issue. We should say it was. It is just as dead as Spanish colonial sovereignty is, and nothing could be more conspicuously defunct than that.

We believe that, in the end, justice will be done in the Dreyfus case, but it is sometimes hard to keep up that faith. As our readers well know, the case is being retried by the Court of Cassation, the highest civil tribunal in France. The most important document in the original trial was the "dossier," said to have been the chief item in the conviction of Dreyfus. Its contents were so dangerous to the safety of the state that it was necessary to observe absolute secrecy. Consequently, the accused was convicted upon evidence which was never presented to any but his accusers. The important question in the new trial is, what shall be done with the dossier. The Minister of War refused to submit the documents to the Court of Cassation without a guarantee that their secrecy would be preserved, *i. e.*, that they would not be shown to the council for the defense. The court very properly declined to accept them upon these terms. Still, Dreyfus could never be completely cleared and restored to his former standing in the army unless these documents were examined and pronounced spurious. Such is their confidence that the dossier is a forgery, that the council for the defense has waived the right of examining the documents. In the present trial, then, as in the court martial, the chief evidence will be of a sort against which no defense is possible. The difference is that in this case the court is not especially interested in the condemnation of the prisoner.

Senator Frye, a member of the Peace Commission, now lately returned from Paris, has made a statement in regard to the future of the Philippines, which is highly significant, coming as it does from one so thoroughly acquainted with the matter so far as it is affected by the treaty of peace. The fact of chief importance which he emphasizes is that the treaty settles nothing in regard to the Philippines except that Spain is not to have them. We have not bought them for twenty millions, but have agreed to pay Spain tnat amount to leave. The future ownership of the islands is still to be determined, though obviously it must be determined by us. Senator Frye says: "The suggestion that we could sell these islands is one not likely to be considered by self-respecting Americans. But the ratification of the treaty will leave us free to do as we please, and whatever the people desire will probably be done." This view of the significance of the treaty is gaining ground and will probably completely nullify the opposition to ratification. Further, Senator Frye says: "I believe we will retain the Philippines, and that the people of this country would not consent to their abandonment. I think that with patience and wisdom in government—by treating the people of the Philippines justly—that nearly the entire population of the Philippine Islands will be an intelligent, industrious, prosperous, self-sustaining and contented people."

THIRTY YEARS AN EDITOR.

Three decades have elapsed since the editor of this paper wrote his editorial salutatory. This is not a long period. We used to think it was, but it is not. It hardly seems possible that so many years have come and gone between that editorial and this; and yet it is a matter of simple substraction: 1899—1869=30. This testimony of figures is confirmed by a glance in the mirror. And so in the mouth of two witnesses — arithmetic and the looking-glass—the truth is established.

In January, 1869, the aforesaid salutatory appeared. It was written with gre trepidation, but with abounding hope Here is the closing paragraph:

"Our bark is ready. Carefully, hopefully, prayerfully, we commit it to the great sea of religious literature. Her sails are unfurled. Our colors float proudly from the summit of the mast. With our hands on the helm and our eyes steadily fixed on Bethlehem's Star, a 'God bless you' and a 'Happy New Year' to all, and we make our editorial bow."

Alas! little did we then know of the storms that blow upon the sea of religious journalism. It is needless to say that the sails fanned by those early zephyrs were long since blown into shreds and displaced by steam, and that we no longer rely upon vagrant winds to waft our bark into port. And even with this change, the deck of our noble bark, now enlarged to a ship, has often been under water as our vessel has "listed" under stress of fierce opposing winds and heavy seas. Sometimes timid passengers have thought us a little reckless in encountering such gales, and have advised a change of direction in order to reach an easier port; but so far the good ship has, by the grace of God, kept its prow turned steadfastly toward the Star of Bethlehem, in spite of wind and wave. In other words, it has aimed to be true to the light of Christ as it has been able to see and to receive that light.

Dropping now the nauticalfigure, we have witnessed many changes—social, political and religious—during our editorial career, and of course have encountered some opposition, as any man or any paper is sure to do that seeks to know the truth and to be loyal to the truth. But of this we do not complain, seeing that we "have not yet resisted unto blood" nor suffered as our fathers suffered for the cause they loved. In looking back over these thirty years of editorial experience we can see many evidences of God's goodness and forbearance, and recall many pleasant reminiscences along the way. Among these are the friendships and confidences and kind and helpful words of many of God's faithful ones, many of whom remain with us; but some have joined the great Majority. There have been shadows, of course, but they have only served to make us appreciate the sunshine all the more. The work has been arduous and the burdens have been heavy, and sometimes the way has been exceedingly difficult, but God's hand has led us on, and to Him is due the praise and gratitude for whatever good has been accomplished by the paper through all these years.

Our own religious brotherhood has undergone many changes in these thirty years. The change in leadership has been almost complete. The men who were then bearing the heavy responsibilities of leadership, and to whom the brotherhood looked for counsel and guidance—where are they? Many of them have passed on to the holier fellowships and more glorious activities of the life beyond, while most of those who remain are resting in the quietude of old age, waiting for the great change when they shall join their comrades who have gone before. Isaac Errett was then but just entering well upon his brilliant editorial career, so full of promise and blessing for the cause he loved; O. A. Burgess was in the full zenith of his splendid manhood, vindicating the claims of the Bible against the attacks of infidelity and standing as a mighty leader among the hosts of his brethren; Thos. Munnell, patient, resourceful, liberal - minded, was leading on our missionary columns; A. I. Hobbs, a prince in Israel, was attracting wide attention by his ability and zeal; Dr. Hopson was in the zenith of his fame as a pulpit orator; D. P. Henderson's silvery voice was still ringing out in musical tones as he urged his brethren to fidelity and plead with sinners to turn to God; G. W. Longan, with pen and voice was seeking to bring his brethren into larger life and liberty; Moses E. Lard had scarcely reached the meridian of his splendid powers, and was holding vast audiences by the spell of his genius and writing wonderful articles in his quarterly; R. M. Bishop stood as a pillar in our missionary work, and the lamented Garfield was already rising into national fame. But time would fail us to tell of other stalwart leaders who stood with these men in those days, but who have been called to the experiences of the life unseen. But others, true and tried, have been raised up to fill their places. "God buries His workmen, but carries on His work."

There has been a great change in numbers, in strength and in our organized activities. Our membership has more than doubled within that period, and the position we now occupy in the estimation of the religious world is very different from what it was thirty years ago. Then newspaper and pulpit misrepresentations of our teaching and position was almost the rule, instead of being the exception as at present. We have witnessed a vast abatement of partisan bitterness and sectarian illiberality within this period. There has been no little growth among ourselves in this respect. While we are not less loyal to what we call "Our Plea" now than we were at the beginning of this period, we are coming to appreciate more the religious work that has been done and is being done by others, and to have a kindlier feeling of fellowship to all who love Christ and are seeking to advance his kingdom in the world. We have come to a clearer understanding of our place and our mission among the religious forces of Christendom, and to recognize more clearly that this mission can only be fulfilled in the spirit of the largest catholicity and Christian charity.

Another change among us is that of greater charity toward each other in our differences of opinion. There was the flavor of intolerance in many of the discussions of those days which only lingers yet in exceptional cases. Education is the enemy of dogmatism. The air of infallibility is not so manifest now in our newspaper controversies, and it is not so easy, as it formerly was, to down a man with tl simple cry, "Unsound!" We are learnir to differ as brethren. There is more roo among us than there was thirty years ag for differences of opinion.

It is not for us to say how much the CHRISTIAN-EVANGELIST has done to bring about these changes. Our readers will bear us testimony, however, that we have stood as the steadfast champion of the fullest Christian liberty, and of the largest charity, through all these years. We may be permitted to add, also, that hundreds of brethren have attributed their escape from the bondage of a narrow legalism into the larger and freer life of the gospel and a wider comprehension of our plea for Christian unity, to the ministry of the CHRISTIAN-EVANGELIST.

Here we raise our Ebenezer. Hitherto the Lord hath helped us. We trust Him for the future. We go forward, not knowing what awaits us. Nor are we anxious. It is not probable that there remain to us thirty years more for service of any kind, but what remains shall be given to Him whom we love with an increasing passion as the years go by.

THE YEAR OF JUBILEE.

The Year of Jubilee was a year of joy among the Jews because it was the year in which Hebrew slaves were ransomed, and alienated estates came back into the possession of their original owners. It must have been a year, therefore, to which toiling bondsmen, imprisoned captives and landless tenants looked forward with joyful anticipation. It was a year of joy, of liberty and of gracious favor from God.

We have called this our Jubilee Year, as it is the fiftieth year of our organized missionary work. It ought, therefore, to be a year of liberation from bondage to false prejudices, to low ideals, to injurious customs, and of our entrance into the larger life and liberty of the gospel. Jewish promises were mainly temporal; those to the Christian are chiefly spiritual. The spiritual antitypes of those temporal blessings which the Year of Jubilee brought to the Jew are a larger measure of spiritual liberty, of release from error and superstition, and entering upon our spiritual inheritance.

What are some of the false ideas in which many among us have been in bondage? One of these is that the Bible furnishes a prescribed method of missionary work, and that we are compelled to carry on our missionary work according to such method. This is a misconception of the Bible, particularly of the New Testament, which is our rule of faith and practice, and fails to appreciate the liberty which we have in Christ. This view has done much to provoke controversy, to stifle missionary zeal, to prevent co-operation of churches, and so to hinder progress in missionary work. It would be a glorious thing if during this Jubilee Year those who have been imprisoned by that misconception of the gospel could be liberated and enabled to rejoice in the liberty wherewith Christ has made us free.

Some of us have been held captive by the idea that if we meet the demands of our local congregations or, at least, of our city, neighborhood or state, we have done all that duty requires at our hands. This, too, is an utter misconception of the obligations which rest upon us as disciples of Christ, whose marching orders are: "Go into all the world and preach the gospel to every creature." It is not enough that we give the gospel to our own community or neighborhood, while nations and tribes are languishing for the "bread of life." O, that men's ideas of their obligations could be enlarged this Year of Jubilee!

Another false notion to which many churches and preachers have been in bondage is that the more they do for the general work of missions, the less they will have for local work. If our fifty years of experience in missionary work has shattered any false idea it has certainly destroyed that. The churches that do most for general Home Missions and Foreign Missions are those that do the most work in their immediate localities. The reflex influence of mission work has enriched all the churches that have engaged in it, enlarging their gifts and their spiritual power. The poorest church is the one that contents itself with caring for itself.

There is an inheritance from which many of us have been shut out these many years, into which we ought to enter this Jubilee Year. It is the supreme joy that comes from the consecration of our time, our talents and our resources to Christ and the demands of his cause. Many of us have not known the peculiar joy and the deep spiritual peace which have come to our missionaries, because we have made no adequate sacrifices to the Lord's cause. What a splendid thing it would be if thousands of our able, well-to-do brethren should decide this Jubilee Year to give a larger portion of their earthly goods for the welfare of humanity, and should thereby enter into an inheritance of blessedness and of Christian peace of which they have hitherto known little or nothing.

Finally, this Jubilee Year should remind us that there is an inheritance of unattained Christian life into which it is our privilege to enter. Said Joshua to the hesitating tribes at Shiloh: "How long are ye slack to go in to possess the land which the Lord, the God of your fathers, hath given you?" How long, oh, faltering, hesitating Disciples of Christ, will ye be slack to go forward and possess the rich spiritual inheritance which Christ hath provided for us through his death and resurrection from the dead? There are spiritual Sierras before us, on whose glowing heights our feet may stand, if we but press forward courageously under the heroic leadership of Jesus Christ our Guide. "We have not yet already attained, nor have we apprehended that for which we have been apprehended of Christ Jesus." Let us go forward with joyful strides to the realization of this sublime purpose and make this year a Year of Jubilee indeed.

EBENEZER.

Memorials are pleasing to God and profitable to men. Because God believed in memorials he gave many to the Jews, and the crowning one was the Jubilee ushered in by trumpets, releasing every Jew from the burden of indebtedness, restoring to every Jewish family its patrimony, and to every bondslave his freedom; the Jubilee was the gladdest festival in all the Jewish economy.

We are coming into the Jubilee of our organized mission work, that of the American Christian Missionary Society; it is well for us to look to some of the reasons of our rejoicing and ask ourselves whether and why we should raise our Ebenezer.

The American Christian Missionary Society was organized in 1849; it is the mother of all general organized work among us. What is there in our history and in God's dealings with us that we should rejoice in the retrospect in this Jubilee Year?

We might well say that we will build our Ebenezer because of our high calling in the great plea he has given us to make before the world. The plea for Christian union on the basis of God's Word alone, with no test of fellowship but what God's Word makes a test of salvation, is the grandest, the simplest and the freest plea made under heaven among men. God has honored us in permitting us to make this great plea.

We could raise an Ebenezer for God's providence in our movement; our location as a rural people, yet in the heart of this great country, is a cause of thanksgiving. As leaven in the meal, as the lungs and heart in the body, as the religious mother in the home—so God has placed us in the midst of this good land.

We can raise an Ebenezer for the men whom God gave us to lead this great movement. Grant that we may have idealized them, yet we have a roll of worthies of which the roll of members of our 1849 convention is a part; men who loved the truth and loved the Word of God better than they loved houses or homes or lands or earthly store; who labored and sacrificed for the spread of the simple gospel of the New Testament. We are entered into their labors and reaping that which they sowed with so many toils and tears. We can say, "Hitherto the Lord has led us." Their names are written in the Lamb's Book of Life. When we think of their eloquent voices, of their hopeful hearts and their devoted lives, we honor them and thank God for the men who led us to this good year.

We can raise an Ebenezer as we study the great increase which God has given us. The highest estimate of the number of our brethren when the American Society was organized is one hundred thousand; to-day the lowest is one million, who stand upon the simple platform of New Testament faith. Far beyond our membership has gone the leavening influence of our plea, and the whole religious tone and thought and practice of American Protestantism have been influenced by the teaching and practice of our movement.

The Lord has given us good reason for our Ebenezer in the success which has attended our organized mission work. The statistics do not tell the whole story, but some items make us to rejoice. The organization of 2,185 churches as the result of missionary effort is a result over which all good men will rejoice in this country. Eighty-five thousand souls baptized into Christ is a result that brings joy into heaven itself.

So now let us build our Ebenezer, and with thankful hearts help the American Christian Missionary Society celebrate its Jubilee with thankfulness in the works of our King.

ARE WE PAGANS?

Henry Watterson, quoted in last week's CHRISTIAN-EVANGELIST, said in a recent issue of the Courier-Journal, that paganism was a matter of faith, not of morals. While this is the practical distinction of paganism, it has much in every way to do with immorals. In common with Christianity it recognizes an unseen power behind phenomena, ruling the world, but it has never occurred even to pagan theology to connect this power in any vital sense with moral conduct and character. Paganism is religion minus morality. Christianity is religion plus morality. The power not ourselves is one that makes for righteousness. I once heard George Adam Smith remark that the God of Israel was a God with a character. Pagan deities are gods without character and their devotees, in consequence, are people without morals. Pagan religion consists of ceremonies and sacrifices to appease the wrath of an offended deity bent on the destruction of his people. Worship with paganism is an end, with Christianity it is a means. Churches, creeds, doctrines, theologies, ministries, ordinances and organizations are not ends with the religion of Christ, but means that contribute to the redemption of humanity and the making of character. The supreme end Christ had in view in coming here was to make men. No doctrine or institution is an end in Christianity, character alone occupies that position. Realization of the ideal in Christ, perfection of manhood after the likeness of the Son of Man, is the essential end and purpose that Christianity is working to achieve in the history of humanity. Paganism lives in the flesh and seeks to avert the displeasure of fickle and non-existent gods.

The religion of Israel was consecration to God, and the expression of that consecration by separation from the world. It knew from the perfection of Jehovah's character that righteousness and holiness belonged to the people. The Christian religion is separation from the world, and union with God in love and righteousness that goes out to save the world from sin. Does the pagan consciousness still survive and dominate in the control of human affairs? How many still regard Christianity as dogma, creed, ritual, sacrament, officialism and church as an end in itself; and while admiring the life of Christ as unique and beautiful, look upon it as ideal and wholly impracticable under existing conditions? How many agree with the dictum of Archbishop McGee, that no government could stand a week if it undertook in hard earnest to carry out the principles of the sermon on the Mount? How many have realized the significance of the fact that an ethical sermon and not a theological creed is placed in the forefront of the teaching of Jesus? What proportion of the male members of Evangelical churches understand that the ethics of the gospel must of necessity control politics, business, social relations and the common life of men? Is our mode of celebrating the anniversary of the world's Redeemer indicative of a Christian or a pagan civilization? How far have we got in these nineteen centuries toward making the question, "What would Jesus do?" the basis of our own individual and corporate action? How much of New Testament

Christianity have we restored to our churches, to say nothing of the world at large?

Nothing so forcibly reminds us of the dominance of paganism as the Christmas festivities through which we are now passing, professedly in observance of the birth of Christ. The paganism just under the skin breaks out in a violent eruption of frolic and revelry, drunkenness and social dissipation, unequaled by any other season of the year; and no doubt a visitant from another world, if he should honor us with his presence, would unite with the decent denizens of the earth in profound surprise that a Christian nation should thus celebrate the birth of its Savior. Our heathen convivialities are painful reminders of the fact that too many have the motto of the wild-eyed, long-haired German socialist who exclaimed, "This world is my paradise and in it I will revel and not rot." The dear Dutchman missed it, however, by a single conjunction. According to fact and logical sequence, the declaration should have been: This world is my paradise and in it I will revel and rot.

Modern society is built on the mud foundation of the pagan philosophy of life. Its devotees live for pleasure, for amusement, for excitement and for the indulgence of its lackadaisical propensities. Strip life of its moral aims and it becomes mere animal existence of eat, drink and be merry, and this has been the bane of the world's society from the beginning. Pleasure is both the means and the end of its existence. Dress, fashion, cards, social amusement, an incessant whirl of pastimes and gayeties constitute the beau ideal of the social pagan. The intellect is dwarfed and there seems to be no consciousness of the spiritual nature at all. Greed of gain was never more rampant and voracious than it is to-day; not that men love gain merely for the sake of gain, but for the sake of the pleasure and power and luxury that gain will purchase. Ages of wealth and leisure become materialistic and morally decadent, and this means the ultimate degeneracy of a nation's manhood and the near approach of the end, as it did with pagan Rome. This is yet a vigorous and virile nation, but there is too much of this death-dealing paganism in our blood to bode well for the future of our civilization.

I am not ignorant of the fact that there is a legitimate element of pleasure in all healthy life. Relaxation from strain and pressure of work makes a certain amount of enjoyment and even amusement essential. This would be a gloomy world if there were nothing diverting or pleasurable in it. The world is not all tragic and humdrum. The comic is a part of the cosmic. All social relaxations in the way of diversion must not be indiscriminately condemned, if they do not wholly disregard the moral elements of life. While extremes should be avoided in this direction, it must be borne in mind that the diversions of life must be subordinated to the serious aims and fundamental purposes of existence. As we have long since learned from Longfellow's familiar verses:

"Not enjoyment and not sorrow
Is our destined end or way,
But to act, that each to-morrow
Find us farther than to-day."

J. J. H.

Hour of Prayer.

THE SECRET OF ALL FRUITFULNESS.*

(John 15:1-10; Matt. 7:16-20.)

CENTRAL TRUTH: *Right doing depends upon right being; conduct upon character; the outward act upon the inward life.*

With this topic, the first for the New Year, we begin the uniform topics, which have been arranged by a committee appointed by the Chattanooga Convention. We sincerely request all who may read or use these Prayer Meeting lessons to pray for God's guidance in their preparation and His blessing upon their use in the prayer meetings.

It is altogether meet that in this first prayer meeting of the New Year, with all the mighty responsibilities of the year confronting us, we should turn our thoughts to the secret of that fruitfulness which Christ expects in all his followers. First of all, read prayerfully and thoughtfully the Scripture citations above given. They are the words of the Master Himself. Notice, first, the *importance* of fruit-bearing. If the "chief end of man" is to "glorify God and to enjoy him forever," the question as to how we may best glorify God is exceedingly important. Let the answer to this question be read in John 15:8: "Herein is my Father glorified, that ye bear much fruit." Let it be noticed that it is not enough to simply bear fruit; the Master expects *much* fruit. Fruit-bearing, then, is the way to glorify our Father. Furthermore, it is the test of discipleship: "And so shall ye be my disciples."

There can be no question about what the Master means by fruit-bearing. He refers to the good deeds and good influences that go out from our human lives to the blessing of other lives. By noble, pure, unselfish deeds of kindness and of service, we glorify our Father in heaven and furnish the only test of our discipleship which either heaven or earth will recognize. The missions of the church are among its noblest fruit.

But the *secret* of this fruitfulness—what is it? "Abide in me and I in you. As the branch cannot bear fruit of itself except it abide in the vine, so neither can ye except ye abide in me" (v. 4). Union with Christ is an essential and unalterable condition of fruitfulness. As the branch draws its life force from the vine by which it produces fruit, so we derive from God, through union with Christ, the life which manifests itself in "*good* fruit" and "*much* fruit." How vain it is, then, for any individual or for any church to depart from the divine method in order to enjoy spiritual prosperity. The only way for a church or an individual to be fruitful, to enjoy real genuine prosperity, is through a close and vital union with Jesus Christ, pursuing His work in His spirit and with His unselfish motive.

Another condition of increased fruitfulness is spiritual cleansing: "And every branch that beareth fruit, He cleanseth it that it may bear more fruit" (v. 2). This process of spiritual cleansing cannot be neglected by one who desires his life to be abundantly fruitful. This cleansing or pruning process is not always agreeable to us, but the Master sees that it is necessary in order that our fruit-bearing capacity be increased. Are we able to pray, "Cleanse me, O Lord, that I may bear more fruit to the glory of our Heavenly Father?"

*Midweek Prayer Meeting Topic, Jan. 4th, 1899 (Concert of Prayer for Missions).

The words of Jesus, as given by Matthew in the passage above cited, deal more particularly with fruit-bearing as a test of charcter. He is giving His disciples instruction as to how they may detect false prophets, who come among them in sheep's clothing. The principle, however, applies universally: "By their fruits ye shall know them" (Matt. 7:16). Not by their professions, not by their reputations, not by their letters of commendation even, for even bad men sometimes manage to get letters of commendation, but by their *fruits*—by their lives and conduct—you shall know them. Not only are we to judge each other by this rule, but Christ will, no doubt, judge us by this same standard in the great day: "Inasmuch as ye have done it unto one of the least of these ye have done it unto me" (Matt. 25:41).

The great central truth, then, that Jesus is teaching us in this lesson is that the *heart* of man must be made right, the character changed from evil to good, before the life can be transformed and abound in good deeds. This emphasizes, beyond all mere human words, the absolute importance of spiritual renovation in order to success in Christian work. Then, in order to continuous fruit-bearing, we must *abide* in Christ—live daily in conscious fellowship with him. It is not enough to "put on Christ." We must *walk* in him.

Are we to make this a great missionary year, in which many thousand souls are to be brought to Christ? Are we to increase our missionary offerings until other messengers of the cross shall be sent into the dark places of the earth with the message of light and salvation? This must come about by such a spiritual change as will bring us into accord with the mind of Christ, and the putting away of all evil from our lives that hinders our receiving the fullness of the divine love and blessing. This is the supreme duty, as it is the supreme privilege, that confronts us.

PRAYER.

O Lord, we thank Thee that Thou hast called us out of the world unto Thyself, and hath cleansed us by Thy Word, and hath brought us into union with Thyself, to the end that our lives may be fruitful unto the glory of our Father who art in heaven. And yet, we must acknowledge that we have not surrendered ourselves fully to Thy will, and have not been thoroughly cleansed from all our evil ways. Draw us closer to Thee, we beseech Thee, O Lord, and help us to put away every evil desire and false ambition from our hearts, and every evil practice from our lives, that we may receive the full measure of that abundant life which Thou didst bring into the world, and receiving which we may abound unto all fruitfulness in every good word and work. And grant, we beseech Thee, that this fresh consecration of our lives, at the dawn of the New Year, may enable us to do more the coming year than we have ever done before for the spread of Thy gospel and for the salvation of our fellowmen. For thy Name's sake. Amen!

Rev. J. M. Campbell, Congregational minister, Lombard, Ill., writes us follows:

I think that the space given to the S. S. department in the CHRISTIAN-EVANGELIST is most profitably filled. Prof. Willett's articles are like himself, fresh, modern and interesting. He has a wonderful faculty for investing old scenes with movement and life, and of making Old Testament worthies who had become mere names stand out before us as men of flesh and blood like ourselves, but the main charm in his articles is their sweet, spiritual tone.

Editor's Easy Chair.

Just a glance backward along the track of the old year before we cross over the line into the new will not be amiss. It has been a wonderful year. Do our readers fully appreciate that fact? We believe the future historian of the republic will treat the year 1898 as a turning-point in our national history. The year opened portentously, with ominous mutterings of a coming storm, our relations with Spain growing more estranged every day. Prospects of Spain's putting down the insurrection in Cuba had completely vanished, and it was becoming clear that something must be done to end the sad drama. Spain was deaf to the appeals of the United States and refused our good offices in behalf of peace. A state of intense excitement and suspense existed both in this country and in Spain. The elements of war were in solution in the political atmosphere. What would precipitate them?

Then came an explosion in Havana Harbor, February 15, and 250 of our brave sailor boys were hurled into eternity, and one of the proudest battleships of the United States, wrecked and ruined, sank in Spanish waters. That was the precipitant. Things hastened to a crisis rapidly. March 9, Congress appropriated fifty millions for national defense. On the 19th of April Congress passed intervention resolutions. The President's ultimatum went to Madrid on April 20th, and was haughtily rejected. On the 25th war was declared to exist between Spain and the United States. The North American fleet, under command of Commodore Sampson, was sent to blockade Cuba, and the Asiatic fleet at Hong Kong, under command of Commodore Dewey, was ordered to capture or destroy the Spanish fleet in the Philippine Islands. Nine days later, on the last day of April, Dewey sailed through the channel into Manila Harbor, and on the morning of May 1st attacked and destroyed the Spanish fleet and raised the American flag on Fort Cavite, and the nation had entered upon a new epoch of history.

Events followed each other in rapid succession until, with the destruction of Cervera's fleet at Santiago, July 3d, and the capture of that city by the United States troops a few days later, Spain was brought to her knees asking for terms of peace. Then came the protocol, the peace commission, and but recently the completed Treaty of Peace, ceding Porto Rico, the Philippine Islands, the Island of Guam in the Ladrones, and relinquishing Cuba to work out her destiny under the protection and guidance of the United States. The war was short, sharp and decisive. The victories at Manila and Santiago were almost unparalleled in the annals of history. The campaign about Santiago attested once more the valor of our American volunteers and regulars. The war loan and the swift response to the call for volunteers have revealed the deep patriotism of the American people, and astonished the world.

What are some of the results of these stupendous events? Cuba is free from her long-time oppressors, and has the opportunity of establishing a republic of her own, after the pattern of her deliverer. Ten millions of people in the Philippines are freed from Spanish tyranny, and the people are guaranteed civil and religious liberty, and will be permitted, under the fostering care of a liberty-loving people, to work out for themselves such a destiny as they may choose. Our own nation is united as it has not been before in its history, and has a prestige throughout the world that it never had before. It has been born anew, as it were, to the consciousness of its high mission as a great civilizing agency in the world, and can never again go back to the narrower ideas that prevailed before the war. Bonds of sympathy and friendship have been woven between Great Britain and the United States which will unite in closer unity these two great branches of the Anglo-Saxon family in spreading freedom and Christian civilization throughout the world. These results are so magnificent in their importance and far-reaching influence that it is yet too early to estimate them. It will take some future historian to rightly value their influence upon the future history of the world.

One thing stands out in clear light as we glance back over the history of the year, and that is that God is still the Ruler of nations. His hand has been mightily manifested in all the events of the year. Who can doubt but that out of these events have come wider scope for the gospel and a freer course for the kingdom of God? It would be cowardly and unworthy of a great people with a great destiny to shrink from the responsibilities which God has laid upon us in the wonderful events of this wonderful year. Rather let us, cleansing ourselves from all our national sins and girding ourselves for the mighty tasks that are before us, go forward unfalteringly to accomplish our national destiny, and to aid in bringing in the universal reign of righteousness and peace over all the earth.

THE CHRISTIAN PORTRAIT GALLERY.

Early in the year the Christian Publishing Company will begin the publication of a quarterly magazine of 32 pages, 8vo, containing the pictures of the leading men and women who have been connected with the history of our Reformation from the beginning to the present time, together with historical sketches of the same. It is believed to be due to the memory of the heroic men who have devoted their lives to the cause of religious reformation, that their work, their names and their faces should be made familiar to the present and coming generations, and that these should be put in a form for permanent preservation. This is believed to be due, not only to these persons of the past and of the present, but to the cause to which they have and are giving their lives.

Some of the special features of the Portrait Gallery will be special numbers devoted to men who have been associated together, more or less, in their work. There will be, for instance, one or more numbers of the pioneers; perhaps another of their successors. Another number will contain our missionaries; another, perhaps, men associated with our missionary organizations. Another number, one or more, will consist of our college men; another, perhaps, of the publishers, editors, etc. In this way we will put it in the power of the brotherhood to become familiar with the faces and features, the names and characters of the men and women who have contributed most to make our cause what it is.

The price of this quarterly publication is put at $1 per year in order to bring it within the reach of all. The first number of the Christian Portrait Gallery will appear in February. Subscriptions should be forwarded at once in order that we may form an idea as to the number of the first edition. Address Christian Publishing Company, 1522 Lucas Place, St. Louis.

NINE DECADES OF HISTORY.

The CHRISTIAN-EVANGELIST for 1899 will contain a notable series of historical sketches of the great Restoration Movement of the nineteenth century, by a number of the ablest writers in our ranks. These articles will begin in January, and will probably run through the entire volume. As this is our Jubilee Year in organized missionary work, the primary object is to furnish a somewhat condensed but clear historical outline of these fifty years from 1849 to 1899. But in order to furnish the proper background for this history there will, first of all, be a series of articles covering the ground briefly from the inauguration of the movement in 1809 until the organization of the American Christian Missionary Society in 1849, a period of forty years. Prof. C. L. Loos, of Kentucky University, will be the historian for this period, covering such events as the Declaration and Address, the organization of the first church, the connection with the Baptists, the Mahoning Association, founding of Bethany College, the Christian Baptist and Millennial Harbinger, and other events leading up to the Convention of 1849. The Jubilee period is divided as follows:

Period I.—From the organization of the American Christian Missionary Society to the outbreak of the Civil War in 1861. The historian for this period is B. B. Tyler, a student of our earlier history.

Period II.—Covers the years of the Civil War, and ends with the death of Alexander Campbell in 1866. Historian, Dr. W. T. Moore, Dean of the Bible College, Columbia, Mo., whose memory covers these stirring years.

Period III.—Is bounded by the death of Mr. Campbell on the one side and the organization of the Foreign Christian Missionary Society in 1875. Historian, T. W. Grafton, pastor of the church at Rock Island, Ill., author of the Life of Alexander Campbell.

Period IV.—Covers the ground from 1875 to 1899, and will be treated by two historians, A. McLean writing the history of the Foreign Society, and B. L. Smith the history of the American Christian Missionary Society from that date until the present. Their special fitness for this work will be apparent.

The purpose of each of these writers will be to give a sort of bird's-eye view of the period which he treats, including the leading men, most important events and measures, and whatever else may furnish the reader a clear view of the Reformation in the different stages of its progress. By this means the CHRISTIAN-EVANGELIST hopes to make this Jubilee Year the occasion of acquainting the rank and file of the brotherhood with the leading events, the leading men and the leading principles of the Current Reformation.

We feel justified, in view of the extra outlay involved in this and other striking features of the CHRISTIAN-EVANGELIST for 1899, together with the reduction of the price of the paper to $1.50 per year, in asking the co-operation of all our readers in greatly extending the circulation of the paper. They can do this by calling the attention of their friends to this remarkable historical series and urging them to subscribe at once.

Our Budget.

—Exit 1898, *annis mirabilis*.

—Enter 1899, which may be another wonderful year.

—How rapidly the century hastens to its close —this glorious, much-vaunted 19th century!

—Two years more and the doors of the 20th century will be flung wide open, and the world will march on through it toward the nearing dawn of the Millennium.

—Not only do the years fly swiftly, but history is being made with greater rapidity than in any previous age of the world. It will take a large volume to contain the events of the year 1898 and their logical consequences.

—Jubilee number.

—For the C. W. B. M. this year $90,000.

—For the A. C. M. S. this year $100,000.

—For the F. C. M. S. this year $150,000.

—For our combined missionary societies this year $340,000. This is a modest sum for a people a million strong to raise.

—An awakened people a million strong could easily raise one-half million dollars this year for missionary purposes.

—Being at the threshold of a new century ought to be an additional reason for a much larger offering for missions this year than ever before by our people.

—The year 1899 ought to witness vast progress in our own religious movement, being as it is, the Jubilee Year of our co-operative missionary work. All the signs point to such progress, culminating in a great Jubilee Convention at Cincinnati in October.

—We scarcely need call attention to the pages especially devoted in this number to a historical review of the American Christian Missionary Society and the notes of preparation for the Jubilee Convention. Our readers could scarcely miss this feature of the paper, in this closing number of the year.

—A glance at the faces of the men of the past and of the preseut, whose pictures are presented in this number, cannot but impress our minds with the fact that men live in history in proportion as they give themselves unselfishly to the highest and holiest of causes. These men of the past are not dead. They live in the affectionate remembrance of those who love the cause they served so well.

—The program, so far as it is completed, of the Congress of the Christian Churches, or Disciples of Christ, will be found elsewhere, and we think will in itself beget interest in the minds of all who are interested in our future growth and development. We hope those who are interested in such discussions as are contemplated in this Congress will give publicity to this announcement and assist us in making it an occasion of great interest and profit. St. Louis never fails to extend a cordial welcome to its guests.

—One of the handsomest Christmas numbers of any of our religious exchanges is the Christmas number of the Christian Oracle, and its contents are quite in keeping with its beautiful exterior appearance. The Oracle is showing great enterprise and vigor under its new management and bids fair to forge to the front in our religious journalism. The older religious papers must look to their laurels.

—See list of the Uniform Series of Midweek Prayer Meeting Topics for 1899, which we print elsewhere. These will be furnished on topic cards, at a nominal charge, on application. See advertisement of same in this number. The coming year should be marked by its great prayer meetings. The uniform topics will help the churches in making good prayer meetings. They will be commented on in the various papers of the brotherhood, and in that way interest will be stimulated in the weekly prayer meeting. An examination of these topics will show that the committee has given a good deal of thought to their selection. As it is another step in the direction of closer unity, we hope all our churches will adopt the uniform series.

—The extension of the Master's kingdom in the world at home or abroad means the salvation of souls, and the salvation of men by conversion to Christ at home or abroad means the extension of the Master's kingdom in the world. So whether we aregiving for missions or converting men to Christ we are working for the Master.

—Next October will probably witness the largest representative convention of the Disciples of Christ in their history. This year is the half-century milepost of our missionary endeavors and the event will stimulate unusual activities in every way. Greater ingatherings into the churches, greater offerings for Home and Foreign Missions, greater diligence in preaching the Word and greater growth in spiritual things are some of the blessings anticipated for the year, and if realized will produce such an outpouring of delegates and of praise at our next convention as we have not yet seen. The churches of Cincinnati are already preparing for the feast and the leaven of a great convention is at work already. Let there be such an awakening of the spirit of primitive Christianity that its circular waves will not cease until they shall have encompassed the earth.

—For a church to increase in numerical strength is good, but at best is not the best of church growth; to grow in grace and in knowledge of the truth is better. We should then strive this Jubilee Year to bring about a spiritual awakening in all the churches. The year should abound in refreshing showers of spirituality from the presence of God. Should there be a large ingathering of souls in the churches without a corresponding growth in spirituality the results of our Jubilee efforts will be of short duration. Let the devotional spirit, then, be more diligently cultivated in every Endeavor and Junior Society, every Bible-school, every prayer meeting and every public service of the church throughout the year.

—I have read nothing better for quite a time than the article in a recent issue of the CHRISTIAN-EVANGELIST on "Archbishop Purcell on Alexander Campbell and His Work." Why not tract it? It seems that it would be especially useful to hand to those who "have never heard of the Disciples." You know we still meet a few of this kind. You may put me down for 100 copies, at whatever may be the cost of the article in tract form. The CHRISTIAN-EVANGELIST is a welcome visitor to me and is read with pleasure and always with profit. Hoping that you can give us this tract,

I remain fraternally yours,

ROBT. G. FRANK.

Nicholasville, Ky.

—It is an inspiration to any true church of Christ to see men accepting Christ and falling into ranks in the Lord's army. In this sense every church is a recruiting station and during this Jubilee Year should witness the enlistment of many soldiers under the banner of the cross. In this work every activity of the church can and should engage from the pulpit to the pew; from the Bible-school to the Junior Endeavorers. The sweet invitation of Christ should be kindly and earnestly urged upon the weary and the heavy laden. Let men everywhere know that "to-day is the day of salvation" and urge upon them to accept God's forgiving mercies at once. There is danger in delays; there is death in negligence. This Jubilee Year should witness the addition of at least 100,000 souls to the Lord's army under the ministry of the Disciples of Christ.

—The Reform Bureau, Washington, D. C., exists for the promotion of those Christian reforms on which the churches sociologically unite while theologically differing. It proffers co-operation to all associations that stand for the defense of the Sabbath and purity; for the suppression of intemperance, gambling and political corruption; for the substitution of arbitration and conciliation for both industrial and international wars. The Rev. Wilbur F. Crafts, is the superintendent and treasurer, and F. D. Power, pastor Vermont Avenue Christian Church, secretary. The work of this bureau is sustained by membership fees and by voluntary contributions. The bureau now has a number of reform measures before the present Congress and is urging the people everywhere to urge their congressman by letters and by petitions to support these measures. Some of these are the Hoar bil prohibiting the pictorial reproduction of prize fights, the Ellis bill to prohibit the sale of liquor in canteens and in government buildings, the Gillett bill forbidding inter state gambling by telegraph or telephone and others, eleven in all. Whatever influence you can bring to bear on your congressman and on congress to insure the passage of these bills will be a step toward a purer and higher national life and a protection for home and childhood. Wilbur F. Crafts well says at the close of an address in behalf of these bills: "Whole trainloads went hundreds of miles to see Candidate Mckinley in the interest of 'sound money.' Shall we not be willing, a few of us, to go to the next street or the next town to see our congressman or senator in behalf of 'sound morals?' "

—The Y. M. C. A. Educational Council of this city is planning to secure an excellent Christian reference library of ten thousand volumes or more. The council desires that the learned men of the city as well as the young men who are starting in life shall be able to find in this already well-equipped moral, religious and literary home just the books they need. This sort of a library will greatly enhance the power of this association for good in this city, and it is to be hoped that every public-spirited man in St. Louis will take a pride in this movement and also assist to create the library designed by the council.

—There seems to be more or less uneasiness in W. C. T. U. circles about the outcome of the Temple controversy, and its bearing on the Union, notwithstanding their action at their late national convention at St. Paul. A circular has recently been issued stating at some length the financial condition of the Temple as a reason for the action of the convention. Without going into details of the figures given, it appears that if the Union had succeeded in raising the $300,000, to meet certain bonds of like amount, as Mrs. Carse was trying to do, they would still be a long way from owning the Temple, or even from having secured the control of it, as there was a first mortgage on it of $600,000 building bonds, besides a later floating debt. After reviewing assests and liabilities of the Temple, the circular says: "The fact that since the sum of only $49,400 is available for the Temple (all other sums named at any time being prospective or speculative), it would at this writing still require $1,215,600 to pay in full for the Temple. These, and many other considerations, including the fact that up to the last year only 7 1-2 per cent. of the money given to buy the Temple had gone for that purpose, while 92 1-2 had been eaten up by the expenses, made it plain to all who investigated, that the National W. C. T. U. must free itself from the responsibility of encouraging the enterprise, and that there was nothing left but to discontinue the Temple as an affiliated interest of the National W. C. T. U."

—We have just been informed that the Board of Church Extension has recently received $833 on the Annuity plan and an unexpected gift of $500 on a named loan fund. The receipts of this board since October 1, 1898, are over $9,000, being one-third as much as was received for Church Extension last year. This is a fine opening for the Jubilee Year, and we trust this is an index of the enlargement of our work along all lines that shall take place during the year.

—The Anti-saloon League, of Des Moines, is not a mere sentimental society. As its name implies it is in actual war with saloons and other lawbreakers of that city. Foremost in the crusade recently inaugurated against lawbreaking in that city by saloonkeepers, druggists and gamblers, is the Rev. H. H. Abrams and I. N. McCash, both of whom opened fire on these men from their pulpits. A recent sermon by I. N. McCash, pastor of University Place Christian Church, prevented an ex-saloonkeeper from becoming the city's assessor. Detectives have been employed by the League and seventeen drugstores and wine saloons were found to be selling liquors in violation of the law. Considerable gambling, especially of the slot-machine type, was also found. Great interest has been awakened and will result in a higher respect for existing laws. We are glad to hear of these crusades against lawbreakers and hope that the decent element of other cities may catch the contagion and do some more cleaning along similar lines.

—A dispatch from New York, of the 17th inst., to the Globe-Democrat, says:

The American Missionary Association has appointed one of its secretaries, the Rev. A. F. Beard, D. D., and Hon. Lucien M. Warner, of Bridgeport, Conn., as a special delegation to visit Porto Rico and investigate concerning the initiation of religious work there on behalf of the association, which represents the Congregational Churches of the United States. The association is believed to be the first religious organization in the United States to take the initiatory steps for work in Porto Rico, resulting from the island coming into possession of the United States. The association has also made a special appropriation for Chinese work in Portland, Ore.

We would not rob our Congregational brethren of any credit due them for religious enterprise, but the truth of history compells us to state that the American Christian Missionary Society, representing the Christian Churches or Disciples of Christ, sent a representation from the Chattanooga Convention in October last, to Porto Rico to spy out the land, and the same issue of the Globe-Democrat that contained the above dispatch contained a report sent to the President by our missionary, J. A. Erwin, who also reported in the CHRISTIAN-EVANGELIST several weeks ago. As to the Chinse work in Portland, we are ahead of them several years. Let us provoke one another to love and to good wsrks.

—The contributed articles in this paper on our work for the Jubilee Year properly lay great stress on raising $100,000 for Home Missions, $150,000 for the foreign field and adding 100,000 souls to the church. This is a very modest sum for so large a body of people, with such wealth as they have, to raise this year. And 100,000 conversions ought not to be a difficult task. But light as these burdens are they will not be carried to their destination without hearty co-operation, liberal giving, earnest praying, sound preaching, much exhortation and, above all, great diligence on the part of every awakened Disciple of Christ. In short, it means work, and work that is greatly needed. Let every interested Disciple of Christ—for there are many who are not interested in these matters—take a personal interest in these things and do personal work in order to make sure of their accomplishment this Jubilee Year.

—One of the apparent and practical ways of increasing the blessing of our Jubilee Year and the Jubilee Convention is to increase the circulation of our church papers. In this way the spiritual life of every church and each of its activities may be greatly stimulated. Church papers have come to be about as effective an agency in the development of spirituality in the individual, the home and the church as either watching, praying or preaching. They help the Christian to watch, they help him to pray and they often reach the heart with sermons when no other food is accessible, to say nothing of the advantage of having the best thought of the age on the living topics of the day. There should then be an effort made by every Disciple of Christ to extend the circulation of our church papers this year. This is one of the things that should not be omitted.

—Strange, isn't it, that some people and even some preachers will say, "You can't tell what the Campbellites believe because they have no creed," and yet these same folks will declare on tiptoe by all that's good and bad that they "believe in baptismal regeneration!"

—While we are all anxious to see men and women bowing to the authority of Jesus of Nazareth and being added to the church, let us not forget Paul's injunction to the church at Corinth, "Let every man take heed how he buildeth." Preachers especially should scrupulously observe this rule. It will not strengthen the church, neither the cause of righteousnses, to persuade men into the church on compromise terms. There should be a full surrender to Christ. Men must not be induced nor inducted into the church other than by the door—Christ. They must be converted to Christ, not to a doctrine; neither to men. To do this the Word of God must be preached, and only such other influences brought to bear upon men and women as are consistent with its teaching. To take heed how one builds is to have due regard for the tools that God has put in our hands therefor and the care and thoroughness with which we do the work.

—It is proper, in this Jubilee number of the paper, that the first page should be occupied with the picture of the man who is to preside over the Jublee Convention. W. F. Richardson, pastor of the First Christian Church, of Kansas City, though comparatively a young man, is widely known throughout the brotherhood, having served some of our leading churches as pastor, and being a regular contributor to our current religious literature. He was not present in the Chattanooga Convention, being confined at home by a lame knee, but he was chosen unanimously as president of the next convention without any knowledge on his part that he was being considered for that position. Bro. Richardson was born in the year 1852, and graduated in Eureka College in the year 1876. In a letter to a friend recently, referring to the Jubilee Convention, he wrote as follows, without any thought that the editor of this paper would ever see it or that it would ever be printed:

Before receiving your letter, I was thinking of the Jubilee Convention and my own part in it, and the conviction was strongly forced upon my mind and heart that the convention was in some danger of being diverted to a mere cyclone of enthusiasm which would leave little of real result, other than hurtful, in its wake. It seemed to be borne in upon me that it must be made an occasion of deep, spiritual exaltation for our people, and must have, as one of its direct results, that of bringing our churches and ministry into closer contact with the Lord himself, and into a more entire subjection to his will. The very next day came the letters of yourself and Bro. D. And, as if to emphasize the coincidence, the next number of the CHRISTIAN-EVANGELIST contained a strong editorial by Bro. J. H. Garrison, which read as if he had just talked the matter over with you, so familiar was the sentiment expressed. These and other facts seem to me to indicate that our people are already beginning to look toward the Jubilee Convention as an occasion for a spiritual advance of all our churches. The Lord grant it may be so!

This extract is a better indication of the type of man he is than any description which we could give. We are glad to give our readers an excellent likeness of this popular preacher and pastor.

—Ashley S. Johnson, LL.D., founder and president of School of Evangelists, Kimberlin Heights, Tenn., has compiled and arranged a self-interpreting New Testament. The unique feature of this commentary is that the explanatory comments are simply other Scriptures bearing on the same subject. The idea is a good one and we see no reason why such a book would not be of great service to preachers. The Scriptures explain themselves, is a common remark with the Disciples of Christ, and this book is constructed on this theory. A copy of this Self-interpreting New Testament may be had or further information about it may be obtained by addressing the author a letter at Kimberlin Heights, Tenn. The book will be sold as are all of his publications to advance the interests of the School of Evangelists, to which he is devoting his life. This new book is the result, as he states, of twenty-one years of patient study and will doubtless be duly appreciated by Bible readers and students.

—Since the minutes of the American Home Missionary convention at Chattanooga can be had in full in the November number of the American Home Missionary it would be much more satisfactory for the reader to send to Benj. L. Smith, Cor. Sec., Cincinnati, Ohio, for a copy than to read a review of the same in any paper. There are so many things of interest and so much said on each thing that a review would fail to impress the mind of the vastness of the work done in our land by this society last year. And now that it is the Jubilee Year of this society this magazine will furnish you excellent material for kindling a fire in your heart and church that will not fail to bring renewed life and blessings. We should be glad to know that there was a copy of these minutes in the home of every Disciple of Christ in the land.

—The Church Progress, this city, last week, in speaking of the proposed Protestant missions in Cuba and the Philippines, said: "In spite of warning from some of their own ministers they persist in wasting money in fields where they simply sow tares and reap thistles." This reminds us that the Roman Catholic journals just as persistently waste their words in trying to resist these missions. The only difference is that wind is cheaper than money. In another paragraph the same paper says: "There are ten million Catholics in this country, and we will see to it that Protestant missionary enterprise doesn't repeat its nefarious practices in the Philippines." What manner of threat is this, we should like to know? But all the same, neither bluffs nor threats will keep Protestant missionaries out of Cuba and the Philippines. Then, if after hearing these missionaries, the natives prefer to retain their present religion, they can do so. Coercion will not be used to change them, but Roman Catholicism will be put upon its merits as a moral and religious force.

—On the first day after the signing of the treaty of peace, the representatives of eleven great reform societies met in national convention in Washington, D. C., to discuss new problems and responsibilities that have been thrust upon this nation by its war with Spain and to strengthen the backbone of the present Congress. The eloquent addresses of the able men and women who came before the convention kept it at a high pitch of enthusiasm from first to last and the sentiment expressed was strongly against the return of any of Spain's surrendered islands to oppression. The convention favored the immediate introduction of every moral force of our nation into those islands. The spoils system in governments was strongly condemned and the need for increased Christian influence upon congressmen and Congress was as strongly urged. The drink problem received a large share of the time and attention of the convention. That the strong speeches made in this convention on the burning questions of the day will greatly strengthen the public conscience in favor of a higher standard of morals in our national life cannot be doubted and we are glad to note that another convention of a similar character is to be held next year to complete the federation against the saloon and to discuss the issues that may then be before Congress.

—The program of the Missouri Christian Lectureship, to be held at Huntsville, March 20-22, appears in this paper.

—We are compelled to omit a great many news items and condense others this week, by the demands of the Jubilee matter.

—Great interest is reported in the meeting at Austin, Minn., by Miller & Givens, evangelists. Crowds are too great for the seating capacity. Meeting will continue till Jan. 1, when the new building will be dedicated.

—The church at Carrollton, Mo., has just celebrated its 53rd anniversary. Bro. J. T. Ogle, pastor, writes: "It was a delightful occasion. Letters were read from several former pastors." It is a good thing for churches as well as individuals to observe these birthday anniversaries.

—EDITOR CHRISTIAN-EVANGELIST: —I have just finished reading your Christmas number, and I unhesitatingly pronounce it the best of the year. It is certainly like sitting down to a feast of good things. May the Lord long continue and bless the CHRISTIAN-EVANGELIST.

FRANK E. JONES.

Galva, Kan., Dec., 24.

—If any class of people are debtors to our church papers it is our preachers and our missionary secretaries. In how many ways this is true may be known without mention here. We presume that not a preacher nor a missionary secretary could be found among us that would not at once acknowledge the truth of this statement. Now this debt they can easily pay by preaching at least one sermon, each, this Jubilee Year, on the merits of church papers and their usefulness in the individual, home, church and mission life. Church papers preach the gospel, stimulate the mind for spiritual things, and encourage every good work, and they are the chief sources of information concerning the state and progress of the work in other places. They are not rivals of the preacher and the secretary, but their best aids. Should not they, therefore, be at pains to increase the demand for church papers in their respective congregations this Jubilee Year? There is ample room in the merits of a good church paper for a splendid and useful sermon, and the time should be found to preach it.

—One of the characteristics of the Disciples of Christ this Jubilee Year should be prayerfulness. We could not better observe this glad year than to make it a year of prayer. Not only should there be more prayer meetings and prayer circles held, but more closet devotions; more constancy of the spirit of prayer in our hearts from day to day. Not only should there be more praying, but our prayers should have more purpose in them. The things that the church and the world most need should be well defined in our minds, most earnestly desired in our hearts and most importunately asked of God. And, withal, our own wants, coldness and indifference to spiritual things should have a large place in our prayers. Let this, then, not be a day or a week, but a year of prayer. We need it, the church needs it, the ministers of the church need it, our missionaries need it and the world needs it.

—The Wesleyan Methodist Church, of England, proposes to raise $5,000,000 for a 20th century special fund. The Methodists of this country have proposed a $20,000,000 fund. This is liberal giving and means much for Methodism in the next century. Why could not a people a million strong raise an extra million dollars for educational, church and missionary purposes for the elevation of our plea nearer to its proper place in the 20th century?

—We hear most favorable reports of our Children's Department, conducted by J. Breckenridge Ellis, of Plattsburg, Mo., and of the "Advance Society," of which he is the founder. No child can belong to this society without profit and enjoyment, and the influences for good that will go out from it are incalculable. We again ask parents, preachers and all adult readers of the CHRISTIAN-EVANGELIST to call the attention of children to this department. The briefs of children's etters and stories are especially interesting, and we have heard of older people who read this department with decided relish. Brother Ellis has a way of putting things that makes them attractive and interesting alike to old and young.

—The Ministerial Association, of Salt Lake City, has put in shape for circulation throughout theUnitedStates an address calling upon the people to join with them in their protest against Hon. B. H. Roberts being allowed to take the place in Congress to which he has been elected. The address presents the undeniable evidence of Mr. Roberts' polygamous belief and life, declaring that he at this time has not fewer than three wives. The address further states that Mr. Roberts nor his friends denied the charge of having a plurality of wives during the campaign, and claims that he is not even a citizen capable of exercising the privileges of citizenship. The address holds that this is a bold attempt by Mormon leaders to compel the national recognition of poligamy by the quiet recognition of Mr. Roberts as a member of Congress, which thing would bring reproach upon the commowealth of Utah and the fair name of the United States, hence its call upon the people everywhere to resent the insult, by using their influence to prevent his seating in the next Congress. The document, withal, is a strong presentation of a great moral issue, thus revived, and is worthy of careful consideration by every lover of purity and holiness in the home and in public life. We should be glad, if space permitted, to publish the address in full, but such an issue as it raises, which we have stated, is alone sufficient to arouse all our readers to a sense of the danger attending the seating of such a man in the highest legislative body of our country.

—The following paragraph from an interview with Archbishop Chappelle, papal delegate to the West Indies, reported in a recent number of the Catholic News, would be amusing if not so threatening. Singular that the Archbishop said nothing about the religious reconstruction of those islands. But perhaps it is in this direction that the President of the United States can be of assistance to the Archbishop and thus return the unasked favor. But here is what Archbishop Chappelle is reported to have said:

"My mission," said the Archbishop to a reporter while in Washington, "is one of a priest and an American citizen as well. While striving to watch over the religious interests of the Catholic Church, helping the bishops in the work of reorganization, I shall use my utmost influence to help the Government of the United States to succeed in the work of political and social reconstruction. I am, indeed, profoundly convinced that upon that will depend in large measure the social, political and economic welfare of the inhabitants of these islands.

PERSONAL MENTION.

T. T. Holton, of Lincoln, Ill., can be had for a protracted meeting immediately after Christmas.

J. S. Hughes, Station O, Chicago, offers to Christian people everywhere his new lecture on "Dowilism and Christian Science."

A line from L. H. Stine, Quincy, Ill., informs us that his work in that city is opening up in a most encouraging way, and they hope to have a part in the 100,000 souls for Christ this Jubilee Year.

C. G. Le Masters is to preach for the church at Tillamook, Ore., during 1899, and will be the first pastor the church has yet had.

The high altitude of Ogden, Utah, compelled J. H. Bauserman to seek another field of labor. He is now at Valley Falls, Kan.

Without a dissenting voice I. C. Thompson, of Toronto, has been retained at Ulman, Mo., for the eighth year of his ministry in that place.

C. W. Cooper, of Carthage, Mo., writes that he has been disabled from preaching for six or eight years, but is now able for work again and would like to correspond with some church in need of a preacher.

J. P. Lichtenberger, pastor of the church at Canton, Ill., writes encouragingly of the work in that city. His official card is a simple yet comprehensive statement of the peculiarties of the people for whom he preaches.

A. O. Hunsaker will sing for C. D. Purlee at Princeton, Ill., beginning, Jan. 1st.

B L. Allen, managing editor of the Indiana Christian, published at Indianapolis, announces that he will retire from that position Jan. 1, 1899. The Indiana Christian seems to have grown rapidly under his administration.

G. F. Assiter, late pastor of the church at Chillicothe, has accepted calls from the church at Boonville and that at New Franklin, Mo., dividing his time between the two churches. His address after Jan. 1 will be New Franklin, Mo.

B. F. Daily, for three years pastor of the Christian Church at Greenfield, Ind., recently accepted a call to the church at Somerset, Pa., and will begin work there Feb. 1st, 1899. He has done a good work at Greenfield.

W. A. Gardener, for many years pastor of the West Side Church at San Francisco, a brother widely known and highly esteemed, not only in California, but in Missouri, his former home, has accepted a call of the church in Honolulu, Hawaii, and as he orders his paper changed to that island, we take it that he makes the change at once. Bro. Garnder has but recently recovered from a severe illness, and we trust that this change will inure to his health, as we are sure it will to the prosperity of our cause in Honolulu. Our best wishes go with him to this western precinct of our American territory.

T. A. Meredith, evangelist and singer, Howard Lake, Minn., writes: "I am ready to engage with any church for meetings upon terms that will prove easy for them to meet. Have had several years' experience as pastor, evangelist and singer and have been successful. Correspondents will receive prompt answer.

In its report of the Chattanooga Convention, the Record of Christian Work, East Northfield, Mass., pays the following excellent tribute to a few of our prominent preachers, as follows: "The Rev. F. D. Power, of Washington City, who presided over the Home Convention, was the pastor of President Garfield and preached his funeral sermon. Through twenty-four years of work in Washington, he has built up a splendid church, which has planted and fostered two other congregations in that city. His presidential address on "The Holy Spirit in Missions" was a marvelous speech of power. The Rev. W. J. Wright, of the same city, fanned the zeal of the convention into a flame with his address, "Missions the Heart of Church Life;" and the Rev. Geo. H. Combs, of Kansas City, in a discourse, "The Preacher's Responsibility in World-wide Evangelism," gave the ministers an eloquent and much-needed lesson. The Rev. Geo. Darsie, of Frankfort, Ky., took the convention, in thought, up on the mount of inspiration and showed them the beauty and glory of America and led them to see the importance of taking it for Christ. President E. V. Zollars, of Hiram College, in an address on "Christian Education," made all feel the great need of thorough mental training for efficient Christian service."

CHANGES.

G. Lyle Smith, Weatherford to Terrall, Texas.

Sherman Hill, Mankato, Minn., to Hampton, Ia.

W. W. Witmer, Terre Haute, Ind., to West Rupert, Vt.

R. J. Avriett, Jewell, Ark., to Galion, Ia.

J. R. Crank, Mendon to Blue Mound, Ill.

J. J. Kathcart, Bushnell to Springfield, Ill.

J. H. Bauserman, Ogden, Utah, to Valley Falls, Kan.

Origin, History and Needs of the American Christian Missionary Society

Jubilee Year.

Call to remembrance the former days.—*Heb. 10:34.*

Memorial feasts are pleasing to God and profitable to men. God ordained that Israel should have her Sabbath, her Passover, her Penticost, her Feast of the Tabernacles, her Sabbath year and her Jubilee; and of all these the chiefest was the Jubilee. It was the fiftieth year, all captives were free, all debts were remitted, and every one returned to the possession of his patrimony. It celebrated God's goodness and noted God's care for Israel.

Into such a Jubilee Year the American Christian Missionary Society has entered. Organized in 1849, it completes its fifty years of history in October, 1899.

How shall we fitly celebrate this glad year? By thanksgiving and thanksliving; by calling to remembrance the former years and noting God's care; by lifting the work of the American Christian Missionary Society to the front of all the enterprises of the brotherhood; by winning 100,000 souls to Christ this year; by giving at least $100,000 for Home Missions this year.

May God give us wisdom and knowledge, zeal and courage; may he cause his face to shine upon our work and give the increase!

BENJ. L. SMITH, Cor. Sec.

Cincinnati, O.

David S. Burnet, the Father of our Co-operative Work.

I have laid the foundation and another buildeth thereon.—*1 Cor. 3:10.*

Honor to whom honor is due is a just saying. As we approach the Jubilee of the American Christian Missionary Society, there will be a renewed study into the beginnings of our organized mission work.

D. S. BURNET.

The men of the pioneer period can be arrayed into three groups:

1. Those opposed to all co-operative work, a very small but noisy group.

2. The middle group, those who believed in missionary work, but who did not wish to be too aggressive in pushing it on. This was a large group in the decade between 1840 and 1850.

4. The third group, a respectable number of men who saw clearly that if our plea was to win victories, it was to be by organized effort. These said, (1) we can do nothing in distributing the Bible abroad without co-operation; (2) we can do comparatively little in the great missionary field of the world, either at home or abroad, without co-operation; (3) we cannot concentrate the tens of thousands of our Israel in any great Christian effort without co-operation.

Relying upon these self-evident truths, this band of men pressed it home upon the heart of the church that a meeting must be held and the church of God organized into a great committee to work and plan and pray and pay for the advance of Christ's kingdom in the hearts of men. Foremost among this group is David S. Burnet. When others hesitated, Burnet pressed on; when others halted, he stopped not; while other consulted their fears, he counseled only with conscience and courage, and urged and pleaded with his brethren to organize for aggressive work. When the brethren of Cincinnati and vicinity organized in 1845 a Bible Society, D. S. Burnet was selected as its president. In the time of hesitancy between 1845 and 1849, it was Burnet's voice that sounded clear and strong for organization and co-operation.

The pages of the Christian Age will show his devotion and leadership in this work. When the convention was called it was D. S. Burnet's name that was signed to the call. When the convention met and Alexander Campbell remained away on account of illness, D. S. Burnet was the unanimous choice for president of the first general convention, and guided its deliberations to a successful issue. Of course, with Mr. Campbell standing so high among us, no other name than his was thought of for president of the new society, but D. S. Burnet was the first vice-president and afterwards served the society for many years as corresponding secretary, without pay. He was distinguished as an organizer, and our present organized work owes its origin to his efforts more than to those of any other man. Of it he wrote, "I consider the inauguration of our society system, which I vowed to urge upon the brethren if God raised me from my protracted illness in 1845, as one of the most important acts of my career."

It is thought that he wrote the constitution of the society; it is certain that he was the father of co-operative mission work among our people, and as such deserves to be honored.

BENJ. L. SMITH, Cor. Sec.

Cincinnati, O.

Its History.

The American Christian Missionary Society was organized in Cincinnati, O., Oct. 26th, 1849. D. S. Burnet presided over the convention out of which came this society.

Alexander Campbell was elected the first president and remained such until his death in 1868.

The society is organized to preach the gospel in this and other lands. The first missionary was Dr. James T. Barclay, to Jerusalem. The first work at home was the church at Steubenville, O. In 1853 Alexander Crane, a liberated slave, was sent to Africa as a missionary; soon after reaching the field he died of African fever—our first martyr missionary. In 1858 J. O. Beardslee and family went to Jamaica to found a mission; that work continues to this day. It is now under the care of the Christian Woman's Board of Missions.

The work in the home field began in 1853. Chicago was helped in 1854, B. F. Hall planting our cause there. The Central Church was the outgrowth of his work. D. S. Burnet was supported as missionary pastor of the First Church in Philadelphia, Pa.

Since 1849 the missionaries of the society have organized 2,192 churches; baptized 87,547

WALNUT HILLS CHURCH BUILDING.

believers; churches have been helped in their infancy and weakness; state and district missionary societies have been formed and guided into useful service; state boards of missions have been supported and invigorated into fruitfulness; a missionary atmosphere has been created; a missionary conscience educated. If a tree is known by its fruits, the American Christian Missionary Society will stand the test.

Its history is a glorious one. It came into being from the feeling that we must unite our efforts to win larger victories. Its career has been with the best of the church in all these years.

In 1857 its income dropped to $405.85—the lowest amount ever reached. Then came the work of Isaac Errett as corresponding secretary, and it was lifted to $16,000, which remained the highest amount until Robert Moffett brought the sum to $24,000, which was the standard for many years. Last year its income went beyond $41,000, and now in the preparation for its Jubilee Year it is asking $100,000 as the least sum that can be asked as a fit celebration of its Jubilee. BENJ. L. SMITH, Cor. Sec.

Cincinnati, O.

The First President of the Society.

So he fed them in the integrity of his heart, and guided them by the skillfulness of his hands.—*Psa 78:72.*

The man who stood head and shoulders above his brethren, and was the only suggested name to be president of the newly organized missionary society, was Alexander Campbell, born Sept. 12th, 1788, in the north of Ireland, of Seceder Presbyterian lineage. He moved to America in 1809. He began to preach at an early age and took up his father's plea for the union of all God's people, on the basis of the Word of God as the only rule of faith and practice. His father, Thomas Campbell, was the man of talent who suggested the motto, "Where the Scriptures speak, we speak; where the Scriptures are silent, we are silent." The son, Alexander Campbell, was the man of genius, and took up the cry of Christian union given him by his father, and by his commanding talents compelled a hearing and pressed it with convincing force and power upon the hearts of thousands of persons in various parts of the land.

In the Christian Baptist from 1823-1830 he used the weapon of criticism with telling power, it was the battle of the giants, the hand of all were raised against one, the hand of one against them all. Alexander Campbell conquered a peace, and the right of the Christian union movement to live.

In the Millennial Harbinger his work is more constructive and less general, less critical and more suggestive, and in the Harbinger, in line and precept, he taught the duty of organization and co-operation in the upbuilding of the cause.

ALEXANDER CAMPBELL.

David S. Burnet suggested the organization of the missionary society, but Alexander Campbell was its first president and remained such until his death in 1866.

Mr. Campbell was absent from the first convention, "owing to indisposition." He was made a life director of the society by E. B. Howels, of Cincinnati, paying $100, and was at once elected president of the society. Mr. Campbell was not a liberal giver as compared with others, but as president he gave the work his advocacy. He presided over nearly every convention, in later years, calling to his assistance one of the vice-presidents. He delived the annual addresses, and by his commanding influence brought many wavering ones to the support of the work. The last convention over which he presided was in October, 1863, at Cincinnati; he was very feeble and called to his assistance R. M. Bishop, vice-president. He was a great theologian, a great teacher, rather than an organizer. By the weight of his character, the greatness of his intellect and the momentum of his goodness, he rose to leadership, and all this endowment of power he gave to the American Christian Missionary Society in the days of its littleness and weakness. BENJ. L. SMITH, Cor. Sec.

Our Work Among the Colored People.

Soon after the war the attention of our people was called to the Christian duty of educating and Christianizing the negroes of the South. As early as 1871 a committee was appointed on "Preaching the Gospel to the Freedmen," consisting of L. L. Pinkerton, T. M. Harris and J. C. Goodrich. Two of the members of this committee were raised in the midst of slavery. The introduction of the report contains the following: "It would be difficult to exaggerate the spiritual destitution of the colored people of the Southern states. They need education in the popular meaning of the word; they need instruction in the most elementary principles of the doctrine of Christ; they need instruction in the economy of human life; in a word, they need instruction in everything." And one of the resolutions adopted was: "That all colored ministers employed by this society be required to frequently call the attention of their people to the subject of education and to urge upon their people the paramount duty of providing schools for their children." How clearly they saw the true need! The first recommendation of the committee, however, was: "That the churches be requested to take at least one collection annually for the support of evangelical work among the freedmen, and to send the money so collected to the General Christian Missionary Convention." There was a motion to strike this from the report—ayes, 27; noes, 35.

In 1873 Thomas Munnell made extended mention of the donations for and work among the freedmen. His report also contained the report of Wm. Baily, secretary of the local board, in regard to the establishing of a school for the education of colored men for the ministry. The school was established at Louisville, Kentucky—P. H. Morse as teacher. This school was continued till 1876 when, for lack of support, it was discontinued. We have frequently heard this effort called a failure, yet H. J. Brayboy, of Lowndes Co., Alabama, of the class of '75, has been a true leader of this people for nearly a quarter of a century, and I have found others doing good work for the salvation of their race who had received all their education there. They knew not how well they wrought. It was during the administration of Thomas Munnell that special emphasis was given to this work in his reports. Committees were appointed and special schemes set on foot to do educational and evangelistic work among the negroes. As he closed his earthly labors just the year before our Jubilee, it is only fitting that we call attention to his invaluable labors for this race. I have carefully gone through the minutes during his administration and find that he gave heart and life and labor abundant to the advancement of this cause. It was during this period that the Southern Christian Institute was established (an account of which will appear in this issue), and evangelistic work was done in Georgia, Alabama and Mississippi.

For some years after this little was done by our General Convention. About he year 1888 a school was started at New Castle, Kentucky, and a property was purchased, the money for which came largely from the churches in Kentucky. This school, like the one at Louisville, was not sufficiently supported, and in 1891 the property was sold and the proceeds, $2,500, given to the Board of Negro Education and Evangelization.

In 1889 the convention at Louisville appointed a committee on work among the negroes. J. W. Jenkins was chosen agent to represent this work in the field, and did valuable work both in raising money and in studying into the needs of the work.

At the National Convention held at Des Moines in 1890, according to the recommendation of J. W. Jenkins, the Board of Negro Education and Evangelization was appointed. The members of the board were J. T. Hawkins, president; W. J. Loos, secretary; E. L. Powell, vice-president; H. L. Stone, treasurer; J. W. McGarvey, W. S. Giltner and Joseph I. Irwin—all but one (J. I. Irwin) were of Kentucky. Four members of the board, then chosen, remain as members until the present time. For one year this board searched for a corresponding secretary in the South, and at the convention at Allegheny in 1891 W. J. Loos reported. This was one of the greatest reports ever made in our history, considering that no progress had been made.

It was in the fall of 1891 that C. C. Smith was chosen corresponding secretary, and commenced his labors Jan. 1st, 1892. Since then a place has been given, in each convention, to the consideration of this work. During the seven years since the calling of a secretary this board has raised and expended $68,737.09, or almost ten thousand dollars a year. It has, during most of the time, maintained three schools: one at Louisville, Kentucky; one at Edwards, Mississippi, and one at Lum, Alabama. It has each year maintained from three to six evangelists in the field. It has by improvements made at the Southern Christian Institute added to its value at least $10,000. It has built a school building at Lum, Alabama. It has laid aside $4,000 for the purchase of a home for the Louisville Bible School. Last January this work was made one with the American Christian Missionary Society for the raising of funds, the Board of Negro Education and Evangelization to receive twenty per cent. of all funds after the expenses of raising are deducted. C. C. SMITH, Cor. Sec.

Cincinnati, Ohio.

Credentials for the Jubilee Convention.

The Jubilee Convention of our people will be held at Cincinnati, O., October 13-20, 1899. It is expected that ten thousand delegates will be present. In addition to the regular feature of our conventions there will be special features celebrating the Jubilee; studying our history, learning lessons from our past and drinking inspirations for our future.

THOMAS CAMPBELL.

On account of size, during some of the ses-

o sec-
e con-

ı Mis-
siness
egular
siness
as fol-

ctors,
egates
from
of the
rector
eneral
annual
yment
an an-
y con-
be en-
ting of
e Mis-
a divi-
ects of
egates
ociety,
ry five
hurch,
n as-
te an-
ership
iation
to be-
a per-
hat no
eneral
at the
Christ.
rch of
ings of
Society
libera-

ple ex-
ovide a
are the
to the

ificate:

....
church
General
at Cin-

....
urch.
Direc-
o enroll

careful
es the

Sec.

bration
adapted

ublime
dream-

rld are

',
ntains;
shake,
moun-

eation,
,
on.
r-found

aming,
urled,
stward

But worldly thrift outstript their utmost zeal,
  And throngs impelling throngs were past them driven,
To whom the Sabbath bell made no appeal,
  Nor holy text inspired the hopes of heaven.

Though not, as on Pentecostal Day,
  With cloven tongues endowed, a heavenly token,
The mingling tribes of earth that hither stray,
  In their own tongue hear God's great wonders spoken.

Burnet loved the fields that met his anxious eyes;
  How few, alas, the reapers thither hasting!
Lo, all around he heard imploring cries
  To gather sheaves already ripe and wasting.

How *Challen* planned, and *Scott* did cheer!
  The consecrated *Errett* still is living,
As from his sainted grave we hear
  His voice proclaim the blessedness of giving.

We had our consecrated *Bishop*, too,
  And loved his gentle sway and Christlike spirit;
To bring this land to Christ, how brave, how true—
  God grant such bishops we may oft inherit!

With all his armor on, and flushed with zeal;
  "This land for Christ," *Munnell* did call—
And ere the echoes died of his appeal,
  He rallied churches one and all.

When some grew faint, and drew the helping hand,
  And sad perplexities made our faith decline,
Then *Moffett* came to lead our band;
  His clarion voice sounds all along the line.

Then *Hardin* comes, and *Smith* him follows;
  "*Home Missions to the front*" is now the cry;
The holy cross before them all is glowing—
  A holy symbol to guide the people's eye.

O, glorious *Cross!* thy outstretched arms ex-

In the Millennial Harbinger his work is more constructive and less general, less critical and more suggestive, and in the Harbinger, in line and precept, he taught the duty of organ-

ALEXANDER CAMPBELL.

ization and co-operation in the upbuilding of the cause.

David S. Burnet suggested the organization of the missionary society, but Alexander Campbell was its first president and remained such until his death in 1866.

Mr. Campbell was absent from the first convention, "owing to indisposition." He was made a life director of the society by E. B. Howels, of Cincinnati, paying $100, and was at once elected president of the society. Mr. Campbell was not a liberal giver as compared with others, but as president he gave the work his advocacy. He presided over nearly every convention, in later years, calling to his assistance one of the vice-presidents. He delivered the annual addresses, and by his commanding influence brought many wavering ones to the support of the work. The last convention over which he presided was in October, 1863, at Cincinnati; he was very feeble and called to his assistance R. M. Bishop, vice-president. He was a great theologian, a great teacher, rather than an organizer. By the weight of his character, the greatness of his intellect and the momentum of his goodness, he rose to leadership, and all this endowment of power he gave to the American Christian Missionary Society in the days of its littleness and weakness. BENJ. L. SMITH, Cor. Sec.

Our Work Among the Colored People.

Soon after the war the attention of our people was called to the Christian duty of educating and Christianizing the negroes of the South. As early as 1871 a committee was appointed on "Preaching the Gospel to the Freedmen," consisting of L. L. Pinkerton, T. M. Harris and J. C. Goodrich. Two of the members of this committee were raised in the midst of slavery. The introduction of the report contains the following: "It would be difficult to exaggerate the spiritual destitution of the colored people of the Southern states. They need education in the popular meaning of the word; they need instruction in the most elementary principles of the doctrine of Christ; they need instruction in the economy of human life; in a word, they need instruction in everything." And one of the resolutions adopted was: "That all colored ministers employed by this society be required to frequently call the attention of their people to the subject of education and to urge upon their people the paramount duty of providing schools for their children." How clearly they saw the true need! The first recommendation of the committee, however, was: "That the churches be requested to take at least one collection annually for the support of evangelical work among the freedmen, and to send the money so collected to the General Christian Missionary Convention." There was a motion to strike this from the report—ayes, 27; noes, 35.

In 1873 Thomas Munnell made extended mention of the donations for and work among the freedmen. His report also contained the report of Wm. Baily, secretary of the local board, in regard to the establishing of a school for the education of colored men for the ministry. The school was established at Louisville, Kentucky—P. H. Morse as teacher. This school was continued till 1876 when, for lack of support, it was discontinued. We have frequently heard this effort called a failure, yet H. J. Brayboy, of Lowndes Co., Alabama, of the class of '75, has been a true leader of this people for nearly a quarter of a century, and I have found others doing good work for the salvation of their race who had received all their education there. They knew not how well they wrought. It was during the administration of Thomas Munnell that special emphasis was given to this work in his reports. Committees were appointed and special schemes set on foot to do educational and evangelistic work among the negroes. As he closed his earthly labors just the year before our Jubilee, it is only fitting that we call attention to his invaluable labors for this race. I have carefully gone through the minutes during his administration and find that he gave heart and life and labor abundant to the advancement of this cause. It was during this period that the Southern Christian Institute was established (an account of which will appear in this issue), and evangelistic work was done in Georgia, Alabama and Mississippi.

For some years after this little was done by our General Convention. About he year 1888 a school was started at New Castle, Kentucky, and a property was purchased, the money for which came largely from the churches in Kentucky. This school, like the one at Louisville, was not sufficiently supported, and in 1891 the property was sold and the proceeds, $2,500, given to the Board of Negro Education and Evangelization.

In 1889 the convention at Louisville appointed a committee on work among the negroes. J. W. Jenkins was chosen agent to represent this work in the field, and did valuable work both in raising money and in studying into the needs of the work.

At the National Convention held at Des Moines in 1890, according to the recommendation of J. W. Jenkins, the Board of Negro Education and Evangelization was appointed. The members of the board were J. T. Hawkins, president; W. J. Loos, secretary; E. L. Powell, vice-president; H. L. Stone, treasurer; J. W. McGarvey, W. S. Giltner and Joseph I. Irwin—all but one (J. I. Irwin) were of Kentucky. Four members of the board, then chosen, remain as members until the present time. For one year this board searched for a corresponding secretary in the South, and at the convention at Allegheny in 1891 W. J. Loos reported. This was one of the greatest reports ever made in our history, considering that no progress had been made.

It was in the fall of 1891 that C. C. Smith was chosen corresponding secretary, and commenced his labors Jan. 1st, 1892. Since then a place has been given, in each convention, to the consideration of this work. During the seven years since the calling of a secretary this board has raised and expended $68,737.09, or almost ten thousand dollars a year. It has, during most of the time, maintained three schools: one at Louisville, Kentucky; one at Edwards, Mississippi, and one at Lum, Alabama. It has each year maintained from three to six evangelists in the field. It has by improvements made at the Southern Christian Institute added to its value at least $10,000. It has built a school building at Lum, Alabama. It has laid aside $4,000 for the purchase of a home for the Louisville Bible School. Last January this work was made one with the American Christian Missionary Society for the raising of funds, the Board of Negro Education and Evangelization to receive twenty per cent. of all funds after the expenses of raising are deducted. C. C. SMITH, Cor. Sec.

Cincinnati, Ohio.

Credentials for the Jubilee Convention.

The Jubilee Convention of our people will be held at Cincinnati, O., October 13-20, 1899. It is expected that ten thousand delegates will

THOMAS CAMPBELL.

be present. In addition to the regular feature of our conventions there will be special features celebrating the Jubilee; studying our history, learning lessons from our past and drinking inspirations for our future.

On account of size, during some of the ses-ns the convention will be divided into secns, meeting in different places for the coneration of different subjects.

he business of the American Christian Misnary Society will be transacted at a business sion, properly announced at the regular urs. Those who can vote in this business sion are designated by the constitution as fols, Art. 3:

ts members shall consist of Life Directors, fe Members, Annual Members, Delegates m Churches of Christ and Delegates from ates as follows, viz.: Any member of the urch of Christ may become a Life Director the Society and a member of the General ard by the payment of $100, in five annual stallments; a Life Member by the payment $50, in five annual installments; or an anal member by the payment of $5. Any conegation contributing $10 or more shall be enled to one delegate in the annual meeting of is society for that year; and any State Misnary Board or Society contributing a divind from its State Treasury for the objects of is society, shall be entitled to two delegates the annual meeting of the General Society, d to one additional delegate for every five ousand Disciples in the state; any church, nday-school, or other local Christian asciation, shall be permitted one delegate anally for ten years for each Life Membership Life Directorship taken by the Association such; or such Association may elect to beow a memberseip or directorship upon a pern to be named by them; provided that no rson shall be entitled to a seat in the General oard, or General Society, who is not at the me time a member of the Church of Christ. By-law.—All members of the Church of hrist who may attend the annual meetings of e American Christian Missionary Society all be entitled to participate in its deliberaons, but not vote.

On account of the great number of people excted at our convention we shall provide a mmittee on credentials to decide who are the *ters* of the convention according to to the ove constitutional provision.

The following form will do for a certificate:

CERTIFICATE.

This is to certify that......................... as been appointed a delegate from the church t.................................to the General Convention of the Christian Church at Cinnati, O., Oct. 13-20, 1899.

Signed.................................

Clerk of Church.

The names of Life Members and Life Direcors are on record; they need only to enroll heir names.

Secretaries of state boards will be careful his year to give delegates from states the roper credentials.

BENJ. L. SMITH, Cor. Sec.

Cincinnati, Ohio.

Jubilee Poem.

BY SIDNEY DYER, PH.D.

[This poem was written for the Jubilee Celebration the Baptist Church. The last verses are adapted our work and workers.—BENJ. L. SMITH.]

PATRIA NOSTRA CHRISTO.

, wondrous land! thy onward march sublime
Has far outstript the prophet's wildest dreaming!
'he miracle of all historic time;
Thy name and fame o'er all the world are beaming!

. land complete in all its map and make,
With paradisal vales and gushing fountains;
Vhose cataracts the deep foundations shake,
And heaven itself seems pillared on its mountains.

Jehovah was our guide across the sea;
He gave us half the world, his best creation,
'o build a state where all left truly free,
Would yet in union from a model nation.

When first Columbus touched the new-found world,
The *terra firma* seen in wondrous dreaming,
The cross-emblazoned flag he there unfurled,
And swift its orient beams shot Westward streaming.

Ere long the Pilgrims in his footsteps trod;
To spread their rigid faith they did not falter,
But everywhere, that they might worship God,
They reared a holy shrine, and built their altar.

But worldly thrift outstript their utmost zeal,
And throngs impelling throngs were past them driven,
To whom the Sabbath bell made no appeal,
Nor holy text inspired the hopes of heaven.

Though not, as on Pentecostal Day,
With cloven tongues endowed, a heavenly token,
The mingling tribes of earth that hither stray,
In their own tongue hear God's great wonders spoken.

Burnet loved the fields that met his anxious eyes;
How few, alas, the reapers thither hasting!
Lo, all around he heard imploring cries
To gather sheaves already ripe and wasting.

How *Challen* planned, and *Scott* did cheer!
The consecrated *Errett* still is living,
As from his sainted grave we hear
His voice proclaim the blessedness of giving.

A fitting man was he, commissioned first;
Forth to his work, his faith not burning darkly;
Far to the East his voice prophetic burst—
A captain of the host, our beloved *Barclay*.

We had our consecrated *Bishop*, too,
And loved his gentle sway and spirit;
To bring this land to Christ, how b true—
God grant such bishops we may oft

With all his armor on, and flushed wi
"This land for Christ," *Munnell* d
And ere the echoes died of his appeal
He rallied churches one and all.

When some grew faint, and drew th hand,
And sad perplexities made our faith
Then *Moffett* came to lead our band;
His clarion voice sounds all along t

Then *Hardin* comes, and *Smith* him
"*Home Missions to the front*" is cry;
The holy cross before them all is glow
A holy symbol to guide the people's

O, glorious *Cross!* thy outstretched cite
To holy zeal and ceaseless consecra
Until, like thee, arrayed in spotless
Our blest Redeemer claims his ran tion!

A Voice from Arizona.

A voice from Arizona crying, Arizona for Christ! Arizona for the religion of Christ, as Christ taught it and as Christ had it taught and as Christ wants it taught. Yes, better still, America for Christ! Why not? America for Christ means the world evangelized. The English language is to be the commercial language of the world. Freight it with the pure gospel and it will be borne around the world. "Home Missions to the front" is the true idea. It will harm none. It means good to all. One hundred thousand dollars for Home Missions. Shall we have it by the "Jubilee Convention?" (1) We are able to give it. (2) The Lord demands it. (3) The field is ripe for the harvest. (4) There is a rich reward for the faithful. Let us have it then. I want to attend that convention and hear it read aloud and see the joy and witness the enthusiasm.

R. A. HOPPER.

Tempe, Ariz.

Out of Love for Christ.

One hundred thousand dollars this year? Yes, because it is our Jubilee Year and we should have this sum to express our joy. We have the unmixed gospel and it is more in demand than ever before, while creeds are rapidly losing power. We are the only people who give the full apostolic answer to the question, "What shall I do to be saved," and every inquirer in the United States has a right to this answer. It having been given to us shall we not give it to others? People are growing tired of divisions now existing between God's people, and as we are the only ones proposing unity upon common and scriptural ground shall we not press this proposition upon all believing hearts? There are the great cities that must be taken for God or they will take the country for the devil. One hundred thousand dollars would help to enter these centres where the gospel will be heard and obeyed. By all means let us have this sum out of our love for Christ and his cause.

J. FRED JONES, Sec. I. C. M. C.

Stanford, Ill.

A Great Idea.

A great idea once lodged in the brain and dermeating the entire nature makes the ordinary seem insignificant and the extraordinary altogether possible. The Chattanooga Convention gave us a great idea—the worthy celebration of the Jubilee of the A. C. M. S. What we *have* done immediately sinks into littleness and only something great can melt the demands of this kingly thought. To properly and adequately honor the fifty years' history of noble organization means that we should have such a gathering in Cincinnati as our people have never before known—a gathering whose rejoicing shall be heard round the world. It means, too, that there shall be poured into the treasury of this society a sum that shall harmonize with the greatness of the occasion. Would we not be ashamed of less than one hundred thousand dollars? The very thought of less would chill and kill the enthusiasm of a magnificent anniversary. Our songs would go halting and our speeches would give forth no flash or fire. It is imparative that Home Missions receive unusual emphasis in the coming months—that our people be roused to the mighty possibilities of this work and that every congregation lend a hand—a hand that shall push the work with might and main, a hand that shall cleave unto the task, a hand that shall be turned in receptive attitude until it shall be full and then empied with prayer and praise into the treasury of the A. C. M. S.

E. L. POWELL.

Louisville, Ky.

The Divinest Pleasure.

The pleasure of giving was the divinest pleasure our Master had. He gave himself. We cannot well refuse our smaller gifts.

By all means let us raise $100,000 for Home Missions this year. Men who never gave before should do so this time if the Jubilee is to be any joy to them.

Those who fail to do so can have no part in the great "Hallelujah" that will echo to the throne when the $100,000 mark is passed.

I suggest a general day of prayer for this great undertaking.

C. G. MCNEILL.

Milwaukee, Wis.

One Hundred Thousand for Home Missions.

Is this too much to ask of one million Disciples? A "Jubilee Year" should let the world know that we have faith in our plea and in our country, and that we are a people whose hearts are in the right place on this missionary question—the growing question of this and the next decades. "By their fruits ye shall know them." The world is coming more and more to appreciate service. Theology, like faith, is dead without works—works that tell how we have learned of God. Our neglect of Home Missions is a great shame, and the more so because the needs of the fields and our opportunities to enter them with every promise of success were never greater. The American missionary may reach people of almost every nationality on American soil. America for Christ means the world for Christ. There are yet whole sections of our great land which have not heard the gospel as preached by the apostles. There are visions of great and populous sections where a few earnest missionaries sent early into the field established churches which became a light and a power for these growing communities. If our brethren could only see what a little money will do now, and that if we delay we may almost be shut out from the opportunity to establish the cause that is dear to all who love the Lord, they would surely come forward with liberal hands for this work. We need, too, to enter our great cities. We cannot do this successfully without large appropriations. We can enter the towns that are to be great cities with a small sum, and this the board has been doing; but we need to plant a score of churches in our New Yorks, Bostons and Chicagos. Let us get ready to sing, "The Year of Jubilee has come."

R. MOFFETT.

Cleveland, O.

JOHN SMITH.

An Easy Task.

When will we begin to be logical and work forwards instead of backwards. Our foreign enterprises are leading our Home Missions by six times. In order to have a due money product for the foreign fields we should cultivate the home fields, which are in the very nature of the case the base of supplies for Foreign Missions. "Home Missions to the front" would mean millions for Foreign Missions. Enlarge the base of supply!

Here is a suggestion: We have over 5,000 ministers in the United States. Let every preacher make ready to give $5 in the May offering to Home Missions this Jubilee Year; 5,000x$5=$25,000, or one-fourth of the $100,000 asked.

Every $300 spent in Home Missions may as well mean three new congregations, 150 new members and money raised to support three new ministers.

In like ratio, $100,000 may as well mean 335 new congregations, 50,250 new members, and 335 new ministers at work in new fields.

We have one city in Oregon, Portland (100,000), in which we could profitably invest the $100,000 to get started in its evangelization. And there are some other cities of our nation almost as large and important as Portland, that ought soon after to have the attention of the brotherhood. How much, indeed, have we to do to bring Home Missions to the front?

One million people are charged from the Lord to save the world. The United States is their base of supplies for missionaries and means.

Every state secretary and every preacher should begin at once to sound the note of $100,000 for Home Missions in this Jubilee Year, declaring with emphasis for the broadening of our base.

Oregon ought to raise $2,222 and stand full 6 ft., 2 in., with form erect, beside her sister states, hearing the holy mission from above and moving with diligence and compassion to save our nation and a lost world.

J. B. LISTER.

Eugene, Oregon.

A Great Work.

This will be truly a Jubilee Year, long to be remembered by us, if we save one hundred thousand souls for Christ and raise one hundred thousand dollars for our home work. We can then more vigorously enter our great cities and have during the next fifty years a larger base of supplies for all our missionary work. Too long we have neglected the opportunities at our very doors. The plea we have reaches the cities at this time as no other can do. Doubtless for such a time as this God has raised us up, and if we fail to do our duty others will arise more worthy than we. Home Missions to the front, with one hundred thousand dollars for the Jubilee Year, is our watchword.

GEO. A. MILLER.

Covington, Ky.

Special Claims Upon the People.

The A. C. M. S. has special claims which should commend it to the earnest co-operation of every church in the land.

1. It is the mother society. And as such its rightful position is at the front. It can point with pride to forty-nine years of meritorious work. It has sought the glory of God and the salvation of souls. It has wrought according to apostolic and scriptural methods. It has disseminated apostolic and Bible truth. Its missionaries have organized churches and Sunday-schools in destitute places all over the West. It is the mother of all our missionary societies. Next to the Bible itself, it has contributed to the unity and strength of the brotherhood, and every lover of pure and primitive Christianity should recognize its great service and rally with might and main to its bugle call of "$100,000 for Jubilee Year

2. Every dollar given to its work calls out three or four other dollars from local fields, that would not have been available but for the dollar given. A man quadruples his money the moment he gives it. So it is that $300 from the society will support on evangelist in the field. And very often less than that sum will station a pastor with a poor, struggling church to water and cultivate it, and make it the pillar and ground of all our work. But it is a well-authenticated fact that to build up one true gospel missionary church in any needy section North, East, South or West, is to lay the foundations, not only for the conversion of scores and hundreds of our fellowcitizens, but of thousands in the regions beyond. What a mighty impetus to our cause, then, would $100,000 be in the hands of the A. C. M. S. Let us give it, and rejoice to give it.

3. That America is ripe as a mission field, goes without saying. In free and enlightened America people are searching for a free and enlightening gospel. And the A. C. M. S. will assist mightily in giving it to them, with $100,000 at its disposal. Nor will it lose sight of the thirty millions of the people of our country who never attend church. And it will look after the three-fourths of our Western farmers who are without church privileges. Golden opportunities have already been lost by the niggardliness of our giving and the half-heartedness of our support. And it becomes us as a great and growing religious body to in a measure atone for our woeful negligence by handing over to the A. C. M. S. the small sum of $100,000 for its stupendous undertaking of evangelizing the ripest mission field of the globe.

4. Intelligent self-interest should prompt every state to respond liberally to the call for $100,000, for the A. C. M. S. is right now working hand in hand with twenty-nine state boards. That it does not co-operate with more is due to its hands being tied for lack of funds. $100,000, for the A. C. M. S. means more money for the work in the various states of the Union.

5. $100,000 will enable the society to move upon the cities in a manner hitherto unknown. If, as Bishop McCabe has said, a million dollars were at his disposal, he would put every cent of it in Chicago, we need have no fear of oversupplying our society with funds. And if with the limited amount at its command so great and so glorious a work in the cities has been accomplished, what may we not expect from $100,000 at its disposal this year, and an ever-increasing amount in the years to come?

X.

A Real Jubilee.

One hundred thousand dollars should be the minimum and not the maximum of the gifts of Disciples of Christ for the cause of Home Missions. The calls that are coming to our secretaries asking help in spreading the great plea of the Current Reformation, East, West, North and South, should stir our hearts and touch our pocketbooks, until we shall give more rather than less than $100,000 for the "Jubilee Year." With such an income as this we could enter the cities, and to enter these city fields with well-equipped men, with sufficient financial backing, means to take the cities for *primitive Christianity*. $100,000 for Home Missions and the rally all along the line will bring us up to the Jubilee Convention at Cincinnati, '99, with 100,000 souls for Jesus Christ, and then it will be a Jubilee indeed as well as in name.

H. F. MACLANE.

Toledo. O.

A Birthday Jubilee League.

Next year we are going to celebrate the Golden Jubilee of our good old mother, A. C. M. S., who has done so much for our beloved family of God. Has added over 2,000 churches to our brotherhood, baptized over 87,000 believers into Christ, and last year organized more than one church every week. And besides this she has encouraged, helped forward and mothered every good enterprise of our people from fifty years ago until now.

Let us all begin now to get ready to attend the birthday Jubilee next October. And especially let us go to work now to get up a special gift for the good old mother. And then whether we go or not she will know we thought of her and cared for her, and it will make her glad, and the heart of our whole brotherhood will rejoice.

I am one who is willing to join a "Birthday Jubillee League," agreeing to give one dollar as a special birthday gift to mother A. C. M. S. We ought to have a hundred thousand others to join it. And then would be solved the problem of "One Hundred Thousand Dollars in 1899."

I am yours for raising it,

B. T. WHARTON.

Marshall, Mo., Nov. 30, 1898.

Must Work for it.

"One hundred thousand dollars for the Jubilee of the American Christian Missionary Society!" We can get it if the *preachers* work for it. We must get it if the home board is to undertake aggressive work in our large cities. The cities are increasing in population very much more rapidly than the country, owing to the continual and ever-increasing movement of population from rural to urban districts and to accessions of large bodies of aliens. We must plant churches where the people are. We must engage the enemy in his own stronghold. We have been skirmishing long enough; let us celebrate the Jubilee Year by entering into the thickest of the fight with the determination to give no quarter.

A. C. GRAY.

Mt. Healthy, O.

A Wise Decision.

The Chattanooga Convention decided that this offering should be $100,000, and we must see that it is not a cent less. The A. C. M. S. is now fifty years old, far enough removed from youth to shield her from foolish and hurtful mistakes, and sufficiently far from old age to protect her from decrepitude. She is just in the zenith of her power, rich in health, experience and holy ambition. Her field is America, the fairest land under the sun and the pivot of the world, and her people are Anglo-Saxon, the race designed to rule the world. But this field, as we all know, has been neglected and this Jubilee Year is the time to rectify the wrong. Twenty-nine states receive from her a helping hand, and just as fast as she is able others will be helped. And better still: Give her this $100,000 and she will enter our great cities.

M. M. DAVIS.

Dallas, Tex.

Must Reach the Mark.

We must reach the one hundred thousand dollar mark for Home Missions in ninety-nine. Because (1) it will be the fiftieth anniversary of the American Christian Missionary Society. A less amount would not justify a Jubilee Convention of so great a people as we are.

(2) We have confessed our neglect of Home Missions in the past, and must promptly make amends.

(3) It is the best cause among the greatest and best people in the world.

(4) America is a ripe harvest field. A little money invested here yields a larger and quicker return than in any other field.

(5) Owing to her location, the character of her people and institutions and her inexhaustible resources, she is now and is destined to be the base of supply for the evangelization of the world.

One hundred thousand dollars would enable our home board to promptly enter many of the great cities of our country and take them for Christ The Lord help us to see and grasp this strategic moment of our opportunity! Let every preacher, church and Disciple take up the cry, "Home Missions to the front!" and make the parent society occupy on her fiftieth anniversary that place she so richly deserves. Then we shall have a Jubilee Convention indeed.

S. D. DUTCHER.

Cincinnati, O.

The Everlasting Commandment.

As a body, the Disciples have not yet fully awakened to the supreme importance of the everlasting command, "*Go ye!*" We have not yet come to see clearly the sublime fact, that the *primary object* of our organic existence is to convert the whole world to Christ. Self-culture is, indeed, desirable, but self-culture, in the gospel sense, without the recognition of the supremacy of the missionary, is to have a body without a spirit. Every Christian is a *sent* messenger to the unsaved world. When he ceases to follow up the mission which he is in the world to pursue, he ceases at that very point to be Christlike—he is not any longer a "Christian."

A congregation is simply a body of *sent* messengers, with the same everlasting command behind them—"*Go ye!*" Losing sight of this is to forget the gospel idea of a church on earth. Your primary obligation is *not* to simply exist as a congregation, but to *save mankind*. By so doing, you feed your own life. Ceasing in this, the sap of spiritual vitality ceases to flow in your veins, and death speedily ensues.

Think not of missions as a kind of supplementary to the gospel life. It is not. Missions, or "the gospel of Christ for *all*," is *the* gospel of Christ. He died for *all*. "Go into *all* the world," and "teach *all* nations," and "preach my gospel to *every* creature," are directions that cannot escape the notice of the lively conscience.

Each year this central truth, like a bright star, ascends higher toward the zenith of the Church of Christ in this country. Brothers, help to spread the truth. Help to rouse *all* the congregations to Christ's own ideal. Let not one phase of this divine work be lost sight of. If you cannot go, send some one who can go.

W. BEDALL.

Flora, Ill.

Saying and Doing.

"What more could I say than to you hath been said" regarding the Home Mission work for the present year? This is not the question I should ask, but what more can I *do* than I have already done? would be the better interrogation. Brethren, we must come to a realization of the fact that it is not the *saying*, but the *doing*, that counts in the Lord's work.

The home board said just what was needed when it raised the cry, $100,000 for Home Missions for the Jubilee Year. Now it is left with the brethren in the field as to whether the work will be fully accomplished. If those of us who have this responsibility resting upon us will sit in our libraries and write "up-to-date" articles for publication we will do well. Those of us who write these articles and then with loving hearts and willing hands, in the love of God and for his glory, put into practice our own suggestions, will raise the "$100,000 for Home Missions this year" and will do our part to "win 100,000 souls for Christ."

F. F. DAWSON, Cor. Sec.
N. C. C. Missionary Convention.
Washington, N. C., Nov. 18, 1898.

The Beginning of Wonders.

One hundred thousand dollars for Home Missions! One hundred thousand conversions! Century of wonders! Times both hopeful and portentous! Holy ambition!

One thousand years' progress compressed into one hundred; a continent settled; the nations made neighbors; language printed on the lightning's wing and dropped on listening ears in every city of the earth; the air vocal with the voices of far-away neighbors, and all the world opened to the gospel and the march of civilization.

Most important issues of the century—the *the authority of the Christ* and the *Word of God* and the *unity of the church* as represented or intended by the Disciples of Christ.

The problem must be decided in America. She is the source of supply. "HOME MISSIONS TO THE FRONT!"

Put one hundred thousand dollars in the Home Mission field to help the weak places this year, and take no backward steps hereafter, and the Disciples will soon be the first in strength and influence in our country and among the most active in the foreign fields. It is wonderful what a little means will accomplish. We must reach this wide domain and penetrate the dense population of the cities. Let us place our material things at the feet of our Captain and King and enter the twentieth century fully equipped with the armor of God. Lord help us to discern the signs of the times and our part in the living issues!

E. C. BROWNING.
Little Rock, Ark.

Chattanooga's Contribution to the 100,000 for 1899.

The meeting at the Walnut Street Church closed last Friday night. In many respects this is the greatest meeting this church has ever had. It has stirred the entire city and produced a profound impression. After three weeks in the church we built a tabernacle on Market Street with a seating capacity of 700. This was filled from the start. It was here our success was achieved. There were about 70 additions to the church; 52 by primary obedience. The church has been greatly strengthened and encouraged. We can now see a bright outlook for the cause here. Not many years hence we shall have one of the strongest churches in the city. A word should be said of the preacher and his singer. J. V. Updike is an up-to-date evangelist. A long and successful experience has admirably fitted him for his work. He understands the gospel and can preach it with power. He is in earnest and has a warm, sympathetic heart. He preaches the truth in love, but he *preaches* it. During the entire meeting there was the heartiest co-operation and sympathy between him and the regular minister. Not a hitch or misunderstanding occurred; each respected the other's wishes and opinions, and shoulder to shoulder we worked together. Prof. H. A. Easton, the singer, was in charge of the music. He understands well his part and performs it with strict fidelity. The singing was the best we have ever had in a similar meeting. I must not omit "honorable mention" of the church itself. Its members prayed and gave and labored earnestly and faithfully. Never did a church more loyally support such a work, and they deserve much credit for the splendid results. Many gave up their business almost entirely to work for the meeting. Such sacrifice is as rare as it was genuine.

M. D. CLUBB.
Chattanooga, Tenn.

Food for Reflection.

The November number of the American Home Missionary contains the report of the Chattanooga Convention, and is filled with facts which furnish food for reflection. To give even an epitome of its contents would require more space than I can expect to have allotted to me, hence I shall cull a few interesting facts and figures from it, and hope that after tasting the delicious fruit, my readers will not be content until they have secured and devoured and digested the entire lot.

First, we have some encouraging facts. The total income for the year closing Oct. 1, 1898, was $41,345.67, a gain of $3,446.40 over last year. There was an increase of 316 in the number of contributing churches. The average per member for Home Missions was 23 cents. In this respect we hold the fourth place among the leading Protestant bodies. 234 churches were reorganized during the year; this being by far the largest number organized by any Protestant body from which reports could be had. The work of city evangelization has moved forward with an amazing rapidity—and its success in the past is an earnest of what can be done in the future—if only the money is forthcoming, or better yet, *if the money comes forth*. We must take America through its cities and must take the world through America. Let us give united thanks unto God for what he has helped us to do.

Second, we have some thought-provoking acts. There are only 37 churches that gave as much as $100 for Home Missions during the year. "Despise not the day of small things" does not mean, "Be satisfied with it."

There is an almost innumerable foreign population among which we have done little or no work. "I am debtor both to the Greek and to the *barbarian*." Let us hasten to make it possible that each of them shall hear the mighty Word of God in his own tongue. On pages 28 and 29 we have some heart-searching "cries of need." Listen: "We must build or die." "Please do not refuse us." "Please help me preach the primitive gospel to my Scandinavian brethren." From every quarter comes the "Macedonian call;" let us not turn a deaf ear to it.

These facts are gathered from the report of the acting board. The department reports, such as that of the superintendent of C. E., etc., are equally interesting. We have already entered upon our Jubilee Year and should lend every energy to make it a year of magnificent achievement.

Send a request for the November number of the Home Missionary to Benj. L. Smith, Y. M. C. A. Building, Cincinnati, O., and then read it when it comes, and pass it on to some one else.

ROBT. G. FRANK.
Nicholasville, Ky., Dec. 12, 1898.

Eugene Divinity School.

Wednesday, December 14th, was a day of great rejoicing among the many friends of the Eugene Divinity School in Oregon. It was occasioned by paying the last dollar of indebtedness on the building and its fixtures. The school property now represents $7,000, all of which has been raised by the ceaseless efforts of the dean, E. C. Sanderson, A. M., D. D.

The Jubilee Thanksgiving service was well attended and was a highly spiritual affair. Those who took part in the program were Rev. M. L. Rose, pastor of the Eugene Church, J. A. Bushnell, president of the Board of Regents, President Chapman, of the University of Oregon, Rev. Edwin Beaudreau, Rev. J. J. Handsaker and superintendent of missions, Rev. William F. Cowden. The students recited the one-hundredth psalm and furnished special music. The dean closed with words of encouragement. "We are now financially free, but we yet owe much to God. May none of us feel that we are to cease working, but let us realize that we have larger fields and new responsibilities."

The remarks of all were encouraging and full of praise. The president of the University of Oregon closed his remarks by saying, "Glory to God and his servant who has been instrumental in doing all this."

The evening was spent at the home of Dean and sister Sanderson, where a most delightful social time was had and a delicious dinner was served.

Rev. William F. Cowden spent the week with the school and delivered a number of lectures on practical church work. It is needless to say that these were grand. They seemed to be the cream of a life of rich experience in the work of the Lord.

HARRY BENTON.

Correspondence.

Kansas City Letter.

Kansas City has for some time gloried in her reputation as the leading city of the great Mississippi Valley in many particulars. Not only has her growth been remarkably rapid and substantial, but in two respects she has outstripped even the cities of the first class. As a railway center and a stock market, she leads the whole country. Her trunk lines radiate in every direction, while her stock-yards and packing houses employ enough men to make in themselves, with their families, a respectable little city. As a wholesale market for all the staple commodities of commerce, she is taking front rank. Her churches and schools, hospitals and benevolent homes, are cause for just pride. But in one thing she was lacking; and the proud head of the boasting Kansas Cityan was brought low in the presence of a visitor from St. Louis or Cincinnati, by the question, "Where is your great assembly hall, like ours, where thousands can gather for purposes political, religious, musical or otherwise?" She endured this humiliation as long as possible and then set to work to surpass other cities in this, as she has done in other respects; and is now completing her convention hall, which is said to be the finest structure and most complete in the whole West. If this statement is called in question, and we are asked to prove it, we reply that we do not wait for proof, we simply admit it! This building, which has a seating capacity of fifteen thousand, will be opened to the people with a popular concert at the beginning of the new year, and when opened will be absolutely free from debt.

All this is good, and seems worthy of praise. But there is a fly in the ointment. Many of the good people of this city have been sadly disappointed and grieved, during the past few weeks, by the action taked by the directors of this building, for the raising of the paltry sum needed to finish and furnish it. When the report was made that a few thousand dollars were still required to prepare the hall for occupancy, the gifts began coming in with the generosity which has ever marked the people of this city in public enterprises. In a few days half the sum had been promised and the whole would shortly have been in hand. But, when Mr. K. B. Armour gave a splendid cow from his magnificent herd of blooded cattle, to be sold for the fund, somebody suggested that any such gifts received be used as prizes for ticket-holders for the opening concert. The idea took like wildfire, and soon a full-fledged lottery was in operation on our streets. Many gifts of stock, jewelry, merchandise of all kinds and other vendable articles came pouring in, until it is estimated that there will be fifteen thousand prizes. The papers have "boomed" it daily, and a hundred and sixty thousand tickets have already been sold, with demands for more. The city and surrounding country have gone daft on the subject, and men, women and children have been crowding the office of the directors, eagerly snatching for the chances of gain.

It is needless to say that this whole affair has been a most demoralizing one. Not only has it consumed the earnings of many poor men and women, and boys and girls, who could illy spare the quarters they paid for these tickets. This is the least of its evil results. It has given the vice of gambling a public recognition in this city which it has not had for many years; and if we do not reap the fruit of this sowing in an increase of the vice among all classes of our people, it will only be because its evils are so plainly manifest as to forbid that any but those already victims to the awful habit should be led away by this spasm of indulgence. Another result which is to be deplored is the toleration with which it makes many good people look upon an act which is absolutely wrong, judged either by the law of God or of state and the city. Although this sale of chances has all the marks of an ordinary lottery, and differs from it only in the purpose of its institution, there are many excellent people, doubtless, who feel that it is entirely harmless. "It is for the good cause, you know!" But we must not forget what Paul says of the principle of "doing evil that good may come." The most deplorable result of this infatuation on the part of our people, it seems to me, is its effect on the young. It will be difficult for their parents, after purchasing for them chances in this drawing, to persuade them that there is any special harm or danger in repeating the act on other occasions. Many a youth will have the first tiny flame of the passion for unearned gain kindled in his heart this convention hall drawing. May God in his mercy avert from our city and people the most serious of the results of this unfortunate affair and purge the hearts and clarify the vision of us all, till we shall be careful, in civic as in religious life to void the very appearance of evil.

Turning for a moment to a more pleasant theme, I am glad to report that the Sixth and Prospect and Forest Avenue Churches of this city have recently closed revival meetings, which were marked with good interest and gratifying results. Bro. H. A. Northcutt helped Bro. Combs at the former church, and Bro. J. J. Morgan, of Warrensburg, assisted Bro. Kokendoffer at the latter. Their labors were highly appreciated by the brethren. Bro. Carey E. Morgan, of Minneapolis, is to assist me in a meeting with the First Church in January. We are hoping for a season of rich refreshing from the Lord.

W. F. RICHARDSON.

Kansas City, Mo., Dec. 15, 1898.

Texas Letter.

Booker T. Washington, the Moses of the negroes of the South, made a great speech at Ft. Worth recently before the Farmer's National Congress, every word of which is worthy a place in the CHRISTIAN-EVANGELIST, but for want of space only a few sentences can be given. He said:

"The negro problem in the South is fast passing from a question of sentiment into one of business, and one of commercial and industrial values. In working out a solution of this problem, it is well to bear in mind that the mere fact of law could not make a dependent man an independent man, could not make an ignorant voter an intelligent voter, could not make one citizen respect another. These results come to the negro as to all races, by beginning at the bottom and working gradually up toward the highest civilization and accomplishments. The negro will find himself valued and appreciated as a citizen in proportion as he learns to do something as well or better than any one else. I have just finished reading a little pamphlet written by a well-educated colored man, Mr. Geo. W. Carver, giving the results of his experiments in raising sweet potatoes this year. He shows in plain, simple language, based on scientific principles, how he has raised 266 bushels on a single acre of common land and made a net profit of $121. The average yield of sweet potatoes to the acre in the section of the South where this experiment was tried is 37 bushels. This same colored man is now preparing to make the same land produce 500 bushels of potatoes. If I were to write a volume, I do not think I could state the case of the negro more strongly than this illustration puts it. No race that makes itself permanently felt in building up the country is long left without proper reward and recognition. The most important problem now confronting the negro and the negro's friend, is the turning of the force of the negro's education in the direction that it will contribute most to the betterment of the country and the negro himself. Recurring again to the instance of the colored man who made his education felt in raising sweet potatoes, I would say if we had a hundred such men in each county in the South there would soon be no race problem to discuss. But how are we to get such men? Those interested in the education of the negro must look facts and conditions in the face. Too great a gap has been left between the negro's real condition and the position for which we have tried to fit him through the medium of text-books. Much that the negro has studied presupposes conditions which do not exist. There has been almost no thought of connecting the educated brain with the educated hand. Education of the head increases wants, and unless the hands are educated at the same time so as to supply these increased wants, in many cases you will find an individual of little benefit to society. It is almost a crime to take young men from the farming district and educate them, as is often done, in every subject except agriculure, the one subject which they should know most about. The result is that the young man, instead of being educated to love agriculture, is educated out of sympathy with it and instead of returning to his old father's farm and showing him how to raise more produce with less labor, he is often tempted to go into the town or city and live by his wits.

"Immediately after the war it would have been wiser if some of the time spent in trying to go to Congress, and in making political speeches, had been spent in trying to become the leading real estate dealers, or carpenters, or in starting dairy farms and truck gardens. When a person eats another person's food, wears another's clothes and lives in another's house, it is pretty hard to tell how to vote, or whether he votes at all. In Alabama we find it a hard thing to make a good Christian out of a hungry negro. It is said we will be hewers of wood and drawers of water, but we will be more; we will turn the wood into implements of agriculture and the water into steam, and thus make a bond of friendship between the two races in a way to make us realize anew that God hath made of one blood all people to dwell on the face of the earth."

B. B. Sanders, state evangelist, holds his first meeting under the board at New Hope, with good results and a church of 28 members organized.

W. C. Dimmitt, one of our oldest and most honorable preachers, has the sympathy of us all in the death of his daughter, Miss Sallie, which occurred at Benjamin, Nov. 24.

John Logan, late state evangelist of New York, has been employed by our board to begin work Jan. 1. Bro. Logan is one of the best preachers in the South. E. M. Douthit has also been employed as singer. Now with Sanders, Logan and Douthit in the field we cofidently look for a great work.

S. K. Hallam resigns at McKinney and it is said he will probably go to New Mexico as an evangelist under the home board. We regret much to lose men like Hallam, Boen and Calvin, but are comforted in the thought that others will be blessed by their labors.

G. Lyle Smith begins work at Terrell, Jan. 1. Bro. Smith, by common consent, is one of the best men in our ranks and Terrell is an important place, so we are happy.

The President's Atlanta speech has stirred the hearts of the South to its center. Never since Grant's immortal sentence, "Let us have peace," have our people been so aroused. And well they may be, for his words are pathetic, patriotic and fraternal. "Sectional lines no longer mar the map of the United States. Sectional feelings no longer hold back the love we bear each other. Fraternity is the national anthem sung by a chorus of forty-five states and our territories at home and beyond the seas. The union is once more the common altar of our love and loyalty, our devotion and sacrifice. The old flag again waves over us in peace, with new glories which your sons and ours have this year added to its sacred folds. Every soldier's grave made during the Civil War is a tribute to American valor. And while when the graves were made we differed widely about the future of this government, the time has now come in the evolution of sentiment and feeling under the providence of God, when in the spirit of fraternity we should share with you in the care of the graves of the Confederate soldiers."

Speeches like this, in spite of partisan prejudice, from men like McKinley, will soon bridge the "bloody chasm" and make us one again. M. M. DAVIS.

833 Live Oak St., Dallas, Tex.

Brigham H. Roberts.

Anent the agitation over the recent election of the above-named gentleman to a seat in the Lower House of our National Congress, a statement of the case as it appears to one on the ground will not be out of place in the columns of the CHRISTIAN-EVANGELIST. It is very difficult for one to talk intelligently on a subject with which he is not familiar, or about conditions from which he is far removed. This accounts in part at least for some very foolish talk that has been indulged in by different parties in the East, who are not under the necessity of weighing their words before uttering them. Let it be understood that successful opposition to the seating of Roberts can not be based on theological grounds. The fact that he believes in an Adam God cuts no figure any more than Mariolatry. It is his constitutional right to believe in such a god if he chooses to do so. To make the fight on such grounds is to prejudice our own cause, for politicians will say that it is a sectarian agitation pure and simple and they will pay no attention to it.

If Roberts is kept out of the seat to which he is elected, it must be on the ground of constitutional ineligibility. It must be shown that he is not a citizen of the United States, or that he is a criminal in the eyes of the land. This is what is attempted to be done in the circular issued by the Ministerial Alliance of Salt Lake City. The United States Government granted amnesty to only such as abandoned polygamous relations permanently. B. H. Roberts, by the charge of the governor of the state, who is a Mormon and the child of a plural wife, and his own admission, is cohabiting with at least three women who bear his name and are known as his wives. He is a good Latter-day Saint, which in its last analysis means a present-day polygamist, not only in theory, but in practice. It is a fact that the Mormon people as firmly and as generally believe in the doctrine of plural marriage as they ever did. There have always been some among them who repudiated it in practice. But it still forms a part of the vital faith of the church, as is evidenced by its retention in the book of "Doctrines and Covenants" and the public teaching by the leaders, both from the pulpit and in their literature. It is not dead, nor does it sleep. It is abandoned as saloons are closed on Sunday. The sidedoor is open. It is only in a state of partial suspension. They confidently look forward to the time when the practice will be fully restored. And this is perfectly natural. Believing themselves to be the chosen people of God, they expect him to open up the way for them to obey his commandments, of which plural marriage is one of the most important. They confidently expect to be the dominant power, not only in Utah, but in the whole world in time. Believing this and that it is a heaven-imposed duty to marry more than one wife, it is not strange that individuals dare the slight danger of prosecution since statehood, and continue to live in the old relations. It would be passing strange if it were otherwise. Given the premise of the past history and present faith of Mormonism and it is simply impossible to reach any other conclusion than the present existence of polygamous relations among them. But we are not left to a process of reasoning to establish the fact. It is before our eyes. It stalks abroad at noonday. It is safe to affirm that there is not a sane person, man or woman, in Salt Lake City who is not perfectly satisfied that Roberts is guilty as charged. Yet, in spite of this conviction, that amounts to knowledge, Mr. Roberts was elected by Gentile as well as Mormon votes. The fact that Gentiles voted for him does not prove the innocence of the candidate, but the indifference of the voter. In Utah as elsewhere there are too many voters who ask but one question when asked to vote for any individual, viz., "Is he the regular nominee of my party?" If he is, though he be a Herr Most, he gets the vote of him who puts party above purity.

It is not a surprising thing that Mr. Roberts should have been elected to Congress from Utah. He is the most popular speaker and writer in the church, and the literal exponent, so to speak, of its teachings. It will be a surprising thing as well as a disgraceful thing for him to be seated in the Congress of the United States. Not that morally he is not as good as some who have been there, but because he is the subject of an ecclesiasticism that is organically antagonistic to all government save its own, and whose teachings and practices are utterly subversive of the very foundations of civilization, to say nothing of Christianity. If, as is possible, by some technicality of law, he gains his seat, then in the interest of civilization and decency the constitution should be so amended as to make marriage monogamy. This would be in the interest of the happiness of Mormon wives, for if the pathos of polygamy could be told it would melt the mountains to tears. W. H. BAGBY.

Salt Lake City, Dec. 21, 1898.

Nebraska Missionary Notes.

The state board of the Nebraska Christian Missionary Society met at Lincoln Tuesday, December 13th. Everything is looking reasonably hopeful. The large debt which we have been carrying for so many years is now down to less than $250. Receipts are coming slower than we had hoped, but we expect an increase soon. A goodly amount of evangelistic work is being done. Two new churches have been organized this year by the evangelists of the state board, Schuyler and Beulah. Each of these fields are very hopeful. The state board is planning to do some work in districts eight and nine in the near future. Good meetings are in progress at Wilber and Seward. These places were organized last year, and will be aided a little this year in sustaining their work. A. K. Wright and Miss Austin are in the meeting at Seward, and Lemon and Travis at Wilber. These brethren are soon to commence a meeting at Wymore. We hope for great things from that meeting. J. H. Moore is in a good meeting at Diller, where he is the regular pastor for one-half time.

The Ministerial Convention held at Fairbury last week, though not largely attended, was a most profitable meeting. District No. 6 held its convention at York the latter part of the same week. District No. 8 will hold its convention at Arapahoe the last of this month.

Our secretary, W. A. Baldwin, has been doing some figuring lately. He finds that according to our membership we are giving more liberally to our missionary cause than many of our older states. But we are not satisfied yet; we want to do still greater things for God. We expect to make this Jubilee Year the best year in the history of our work; a larger contribution for missions, more souls for Christ and a greater spiritual growth among our members. We need more pastors in the state; men of faith and good works; men who will be able to lead the churches into higher and better things. This is bound to be a great state in the years to come. Its resources are almost limitless along the lines of agriculture.

The greatest trouble with our work here is that of continual changing of preachers. I came into the state two years and one-half ago, and there are now only two pastors in the state who occupy the same pulpits they were in at that time. We must have an improvement along this line. Preachers and churches also are too restless. Every time a condition arises that is not just congenial the first thought is, I will change places or, We must get another preacher; when they ought in the spirit of the Master try to better the condition. I know just how it is. I am tempted to do the same thing many times. Brethren, let us cease being children along these lines. Let us become brave, earnest, consecrated men and women for God. Let us do our duty in faith and loving kindness, and the Master will take care of the results.

Fraternally, F. A. BRIGHT,
Pres. of Nebraska Christian Missionary Society.

Notes from the Foreign Field.

The receipts for the last month amount to $9,392.03. This is a gratifying gain over the corresponding month a year ago.

Mr. and Mrs. E. M. Gordon expect to spend the month of February visiting the churches. After February Mr. Gordon expects to return to his work in India.

John G. McGavran and G. L. Wharton are preaching and camping among the villages.

G. W. Coffman writes about the holy men in India. Some are especially holy, having held their arms up above their heads so long that they have withered and become useless. Some of the marks of holiness are absence of clothing, long and matted hair ashes and paint on face and body. Some claim that they never sit down, others sit on spikes, others wear long nails, sometimes having caused the nails to grow through the hand by clinching the fist. These are the chief signs among the Hindus of holiness.

Nathoo Lall recently had four baptisms at Charwa, India. Two were baptized in Hurda the last month.

H. H. Guy, of Japan, writes that the time is ripe for the preaching of the gospel. The different missionaries understand this and are doing more direct preaching than they have ever done in the past.

Two young men were immersed in Akozu, Japan. Another convert is 89 years of age. The indications for a large increase this year are good.

Teizo Kawai has reached Japan. He will locate in Akita and carry on work there.

R. L. Pruett and F. H. Marshall have been preaching around Shizuoka. They have been preaching a part of the time where the gospel had never been preached. When they told them of the true God and of his wonderful love to poor sinners, two of them worshiped the preachers.

M. B. Madden reports two baptisms at Izuno and three at Fukushima. He reports two new stations opened and thirty copies of the Scriptures sold.

T. J. Arnold writes that on the ship on which he returned to China were twenty-five other missionaries. They represented seven societies and six nations.

A. L. Chapman is greatly pleased with his new field. Were it not for the opposition of the Turkish Goverement this would be one of the most fruitful fields in the world. In the Custom House five of his books were confiscated. The authorities were afraid that these books might incite the people to revolution.

Dr. Garabed Kavorkian writes of the tour he has been making among the churches of Turkey. The Turkish Governor and the American consul gave good heed to his message.

Dr. R. J. Dye has been appointed to go to Africa as a medical missionary. He will sail from New York about the 14th of January. He will take the place left vacant by the death of Dr. Biddle.

The Society is looking for two men for Cuba. If men able to speak Spanish can be found the expense of starting the work will be materially lessened.

A Visit to Columbia.

It was my place to deliver four lectures to the students and friends of Bible College, in Columbia, sometime during the month of April, 1899, but as Bro. Richardson, who was to lecture in December 1898, was unable to fill his engagement, I exchanged times with him. So I spoke there beginning December 13. Bro. Moore was not sufficiently recovered yet to be at his post. I would have gladly taken care of the classes while there, but they had been dismissed till their professor could be with them. The subject of "Sacred Geogrpahy" was hardly appreciated, as the first evening there were less than forty persons present. After that the gain was rapid; the second evening there were 140 present and 300 the third evening. Chapel service at the State University the morning I was there was small, only thirty-five being in the seats, and but one professor. Religion seemed to be used with great economy. They have about five hundred students, all told, in the University. They have ample accommodations for two thousand. And yet, so far as I know of their classroom work, it is good. I met with a number of young men competent to speak on the subject, and they gave a good report of the work done in the university.

I attended chapel service at Christian College, over which Sister Moore presides, and took tea there one evening. That school is crowded. They would have had many more if they could have furnished the room. The work done there is excellent. This can be made a great institution. And in the hands of Sister Moore the cultus will be the very best and the work of education thorough.

As to the Bible College, in my opinion we need a building and at least 100,000 dollars endowment. The lot that has been purchased is in the right place. No better selection could have been made. Let some whole-hearted brother now come forward and place a good building on it. They would, perhaps, give him the name of the hall, and thus perpetuate the record of his good deed. Two able men should be there all the time, with as much ability as the men who are employed in the State University. I was treated very kindly while there and will remember my visit with great pleasure.

D. R. DUNGAN.

Christian Institute, Shanghai, China.

Dedicated Day, Nov. 6, 1898. Contains (1) chapel, for church services; (2) li rary; (3) preaching hall; (4) office and study; (5) two school rooms; (6) preacher's (Chinese) home; (7) baptistery and dressing rooms; (8) room

for women's work. Cost, with lot, $3,700. Located in the center of the American settlement. The occasion was indeed an important one for the work in China. Congratulations pour in from all sides. The idea akin to that of the "institutional church"—has awakened a good deal of interest here already, as this is the first attempt of the kind in the East, as far as I know. Concerning our work here the N.-C. Daily News, this city, Nov. 8th, says:

Yesterday afternoon the dedicatory services of a new building to be used in connection with the uplifting and Christianizing of the Chinese were held, a large number of foreign and native guests being present.

The Institute is situated at the angle of Miller and Hanbury Roads and is somewhat original in plan, resembling in some particulars the "institutional churches" of the United States. At present there is only one building which includes a preaching hall, chapel, library, two class rooms, a baptistery and quarters for a native preacher, also a study and office. Every department is well furnished and the institute is already in working order, most of the rooms being now used for the purposes for which they were intended. At present this building will be the headquarters of native work of the peculiar character which the institute undertakes to do, but it is confidently hoped that this building will be but the forerunner of several such institutes in other parts of the Settlements and around.

The cost of the land, building, etc., has reached roughly $7,300 (mex.) largely subscribed by a few friends especially interested in mission work in Shanghai. The property, however, is in the name of the Foreign Christian Missionary Society of the United States. There is a day school for boys, night classes for teaching English, a girls' day-school in another building and work among women will be carried on here for the present. Operations are now in progress for the formation of a literary society, which is expected to do incalculably good work.

The number of church members is now 34, but a material increase is looked for.

Shortly, the aim of the institute is to enlighten and help as many natives as passible of all classes and of all ages, with the ultimate object of converting them to Christianity.

The work has begun well and there are not wanting signs of its future success.

At the service held yesterday afternoon commendatory addresses were given by Rev. G. F. Fitch, of the Presbyterian Mission Press, and Rev. G. R. Loehr, of the Southern Methodist Mission, U. S. A., whilst Rev. W. P. Bentley, the principal, gave a most interesting account of the history and objects of the work.

The signs of success are not few. We had three confessions and immersions last week. This event and the advent of a son into our home, makes this a memorable week in our lives.

W. P. BENTLEY.

The Churches of Christ in St. Louis.

First Christian, 3126 Locust St., F. O. Fannon, pastor.
Second Christian, 11th and Tyler Sts., W. W. Hopkins, supply pastor.
Central Christian, 3619 Finney Ave., F. G. Tyrrell, pastor.
Fourth Christian, 1501 Penrose St., W. H. Kern, pastor.
Fifth Christian, 3331 South 7th St., W. F. Hamann, pastor.
Mount Cabanne, King's Highway and Morgan St., D. R. Dungan, pastor.
Compton Heights, 2800 St. Vincent Ave., S. B. Moore, pastor.
Beulah, Marcus and Hammett Pl., E. M. Smith, pastor.
West End, Plymouth and Hamilton Aves., O. A. Bartholomew, pastor.
Lindenwood, Lindenwood suburb, W. B. Young, pastor.
Ellendale, Lanham and Hewett Aves., W. B. Young, pastor.
Tuxedo, Tuxedo suburb, Luther Moore, pastor.
Carondelet, Pennsylvania and Upton, John Strange, pastor.
First Christian, East St. Louis, Ill., W. R. Jinnett, pastor.

Total Church Enrollment, 3,175.
" Bible school Enrollment, 2,541.
" Christian Endeavor Enrollment, 487.
" Seating Capacity of Buildings, 4,450.
" Value of Church Property, $142,200.
" Amount of Church Debt, $33,800.
" Annual Collections, $24,191 42.
" Given to Foreign Missions, $933.22.
" Given to Home Missions, $526.12.
" Given to City Missions, $323.90.
" No. of Additions, 635.
" No. Baptisms, 331.
" No. of Deaths, 14.
" No. of Removals, 251.
" Gain for Year, 452.
" Average Bible-school Attendance, 1,712.
" Average C. E. Attendance, 388.
" Average Prayer-meeting Attendance, 469.
" State work, $135.
" Church Extension, $209.

Of the above churches Carondelet is without a house. Of the items of state work and Church Extension it should be said that the

Central Christian Church is the only one that reported these items separately. What other churches may have given to these missionary departments is either included in other items or not reported. We regret that the Junior Societies and Christian Orphans' Home and other church activities were not included in this report. In our next general report we shall try to include every feature of church work. This is our first attempt at anything like a full report from all the churches including that of East St. Louis, Ill.

Respectfully submitted by
W. W. HOPKINS,
Secretary City Mission Board.

Iowa Letter.

It is not often that Iowa daily papers keep any religious body of people before their readers for weeks and months. For sometime the Episcopalians have been greatly exercised over the election of a bishop for Iowa. The outcome was the election of a Chicago man, and the defeat of Dr. Green, of Cedar Rapids, Iowa. Dr. Green had many Iowa papers against him. As to the merits of his case, I will venture no statement. But all know that the daily papers took up the matter, and for weeks kept it up, because of the sensational elements in the contest. The absence of the Spirit of Christ in religious gatherings insures many columns of advertising in our papers.

The Iowa colleges have a state oratorical association, in which they contest annually for state honors. From this annual contest the winner represents the state in an interstate contest. Drake University has twice won in the state contest and sent her man to the interstate gathering, and Oskaloosa College once did the same. The victors in these cases were Joseph Dyer, Miss Ethel (Brown) Garrett, now in China, and Leslie Morgan. Drake University wishes to add another name to this list as soon as possible. On December 8th she selected by home contest her delegate for the state contest in February, 1899, at Mt. Vernon, Ia. Miss Susie K. Glaspell, of Davenport, Ia., was the winner. M. A. Thompson, recently of the 51st Iowa Volunteers, carries second honors, and F. E. Knowles was third. Miss Glaspell has the enthusiasm of the whole school with her in her effort at the state contest. Mr. Knowles won second place in thought and composition. Other contestants were M. G. E. Bennett, T. T. Thompson and D. N. Gillett.

Dean Everest has greatly improved in health, but his physicians advised a milder climate for the winter. He has left for Texas where he will devote the winter to completing his forthcoming book on ethics. The writer has been selected by Dean Everest to meet his classes in the Bible College to the close of the school year in June. Until that time address me at University Place, Des Moines, Ia.

On Dec. 5th and 6th, C. C. Rowlison, of Marshalltown, Ia., with his wife, was in Des Moines. He delivered two lectures at the Central Church for Pastor H. O. Breeden. His theme was Church History and his work was a part of the institutional program for the winter. He will come again on Dec. 19th and 20th and again on Jan. 9th and 10th. The students in chapel gave Bro. Rowlison a hearty reception.

G. L. Brokaw, of the Christian Index, has just issued a vlume of sermons by Iowa writers. It is a book of 500 pages and entitled, very appropriately, "Doctrine and Life." There are twenty-eight sermons and as many portraits and biographical sketches. Among the names I mention Dean Everest, B. S. Denny, D. A. Wickizer, Chacellor Craig, I. N. McCash, Sumner T. Martin, James Small and H. O. Breeden. A copious index adds to the volume of the book. Barring some slight typographical errors the book is a credit to its publisher and to the contributors to its pages. The writer has sent out ten copies as Christmas presents.

A. M. HAGGARD.

Circular Letter of the Board of Education.

RECOMMENDATIONS OF THE CHATTANOOGA CONVENTION.

1. That the churches be requested to observe Educational Day, the first Lords day in July—no offerings to be called for—the purpose of this observance to create and foster a general interest in the work of our colleges, and specially the department devoted to educating young men for the ministry of the Word.

2. That the state organizations be requested to devote a part of the program of the annual convention to the subject of collegiate education, and call attention to the importance of giving ample support to our colleges.

3. That the next annual program of this society devote one session, or its equivalent, to this important suject.

STATION N, CHICAGO, Nov. 18, 1898.

DEAR BROTHER:—We call your attention to the above recommendations and earnestly beg your co-operation in the campaign for EDUCATION ON THE CAUSE OF EDUCATION which has been committed to our charge.

1. We believe—

(1) That our colleges ought to be put on a financial basis.

(2) That the children of our own families ought to attend our own schools, at least as far as the courses given will carry them.

(3) That the standard of our colleges should be made equal to any competing institutions.

(4) That these things can and will be done if the attention of our brethren is called to this problem, and if this cause be laid to the hearts of the people all along the line.

2. For this campaign the American Christian Missionary Society has granted that one session of their valuable time be given to our colleges in which they shall present their work and claims for support. An educational secretary is to be appointed in every state and addresses on education among the Disciples are to be given at the various state conventions. The *first Lords day* in *July* has been set apart as Educational Day in all the churches. Preachers are asked to preach on *education*, its relation to the Christian life, its necessity for the work of the Christian minister and missionary, etc. Godly men are to be exhorted that supplications, prayers, intercessions and thanksgivings be made for all presidents, professors and students who are in high places of opportunity, that they may lead a righteous and godly life, that God may lead them into all the truth, that they may send out many messengers of light and salvation to this needy world. It is to be hoped that the thanksgiving will be, not in word only, but in deed, in all liberality as God hath prospered every one. But a general collection is not asked for by the Educational Board. It is hoped that these services will prepare the way for the visits of the presidents, financial secretaries and other representatives of our colleges and schools that they will be received gladly, heard with interest and sent on their way rejoicing at the opening of the Lord of the hearts and purses of his people.

3. For this an extended literature will be issued from time to time by the Board of Education.

The Educational Bulletin is to be continued under the valuable oversight of Mrs. A. A. Forrest, of Irvington, Indiana, as editor. This will contain during the year—

(a) The address of President E. V. Zollars, "Education, its Impartance and Status among the Disciples," given at the National Convention at Chattanooga.

(b) The address of President J. H. Hardin on "College Endowment," to be given at the Congress of Disciples at St. Louis, April next.

(c) "Short History of Education among the Disciples." A booklet by Mrs. A. A. Forrest.

(d) "Outlines of Sermons," on education among the Disciples, by Professor J. B. Sweeney.

(e) Articles are to appear from time to time in the papers which have so kindly opened their columns to this work. These will be written by men on the field and acquainted with the claims of each institution.

Besides the above work of publication the Board of Education acts as a distributing center for the common literature of our colleges. The above pamphlets will be mailed to every preacher in the country for use on Educational Day. Also a circular of each college will be enclosed, which will set forth the particular history and work. Statistics are being gathered which will show the facts and condition of our schools.

The Board of Education will act as a clearing house for all matters in common between the colleges, as far as is desired, in the correlation of courses, in the interchange of students, in the advocacy of a common cause before the general public.

4. For this most valuable work the Board of Education consisting of the following representatives of the several institutions:

J. H. Herdin, President, Eureka; Hiram Van Kirk, Secretary and Treasurer Disciples' Divinity House, University of Chicago; Mrs. A. A. Forrest, General Editor, Irvington, Ind.; E. V. Zollars, Hiram; B. C. Deweese, Kentucky University; O. T. Morgan, Drake; J. B. Sweeney, Add-Ran, donate their services. The only expense of the board will be that of publication and correspondence. These will not exceed $400. Last year without any public appeal *friends* of the educational cause gave $126.78. We ask the same to continue their support this year. Many others will doubtless be glad to send us personal offerings of from $1 to $10. Many churches will also kindly give us a portion of their missionary offerings. Five per cent. of the whole amount given for outside work could be used by this board in as advantageous a way as possible. Other churches may be pleased to make us a special offering. Above all we covet your sympathy and co-operation.

Send all moneys and communications to

HIRAM VAN KIRK, Sec. and Treas.
Station N, Chicago, Ill.

Notes and News.

The Mason City (Ia.) auxiliary observed C. W. B. M. Day in a public program Lord's day morning, Dec. 11' occupying the regular preaching hour. Our apportionment of $15 was raised and our membership increased. The society now numbers 107.

JOSEPHINE PRUSIA, Sec.

We are about completing the remodeling of our church at a cost of about 600, under the pastorate of Bro. A. J. Ellis, who has helped us raise this money and also a church debt of $200. Churches needing a pastor who can also help them would do well to write to him at Blanchard, Ia. W. S. WOOD, Clerk.

Another beautiful church edifice has been opened for worship. The dedication of the new church at Ligonier, Ind., took place Nov. 20. The pastor, Geo. Musson, was assisted in the dedicatory services by E. V. Zollars, president of Hiram College. The choir was composed of singers from all the churches of the city, and Miss Anna Sack presided at the piano. Elder Musson, pastor of the church, directed the services and had full charge of the meeting, while Prof. Peters had charge of the choir and directed the music. The church was filled to its utmost capacity, the audience being composed of the best people of the city and surrounding country. The yearly meeting having just been held on the two days previous, there were also many visitors from the principal towns in the surrounding country. Other pastors of the city made short addresses at the evening service. The occasion was an enjoyable one and long to be remembered. It is said that there is now but one better church building in Ligonier.

Relief Fund Remembered.

Dear Brethren:—The church here sent $4.54 for ministerial aid. Hurrah for a forward movement *all* along the line.

G. M. REED, Pastor.

Murray, Neb., Dec. 19, 1898.

Church Prosperity.

Three hundred and fourty-three in Sunday-school yesterday. Work in all departments moving forward. Would like to correspond with a singer for January, beginning about Jan. 7th. Send lowest terms. R. F. THRAPP.

Pittsfield, Ill., Dec. 19, 1898.

Church Anniversary.

The Church of Christ in East Smithfield, Pa., will observe the 30th anniversary of the dedication of its present edifice, and the 68th anniversary of the organization of the church, together with the annual roll call service and silver offering on the 14th day of January, 1899. Dinner served at noon.

S. C. HUMPHREY, Pastor.

C. W. B. M. Notes.

Chas. A. Young closed a successful term of three months' Bible teaching at the University of Virginia Dec. 16. After holding an institute at Martinsville, Va., he will begin work at Athens, Ga., in the University of Georgia.

C. W. B. M. Day was largely observed in the churches, although the storm greatly hindered the attendance and lessened the collection.

Ann Arbor, Mich., reports a collection of $60 on C. W. B. M. Day.

Mrs. Helen E. Moses has been quite ill since her visit to Cincinnati, O., and Ann Arbor, Mich. She has canceled future appointments for the winter.

The Missionary Inst ·it·s, Dec. 13-15, under the auspices of the Bible College at Irvington, Ind., was very well attended and profitable. The severe cold weather and poor heating of the Downey Ave. Church necessitated the sessions being held in the Y. M. C. A. room in Butler College building. It was greatly regretted that Mrs. Helen E. Moses was unable to be present and deliver her address.

Letters have been received in this country from Olivia A. Baldwin, M. D., and Annie Agnes Lackey, mailed at Marseilles, France. These sisters are en route to India under appointment by the Christian Woman's Board of Missions.

Miss Ada McNeil, M. D., arrived safely in Bombay, India., after a pleasant voyage. She spent a few days visiting places of interest in Bombay, then stopped at Hurda with the missionaries. She is to be associated with Bro. N. Mitchell and wife at Bina.

LOIS A. WHITE, Cor. Sec.

State Mission Notes.

"*One hundred thousand additions this year.*"

This is the motto of the General Home Society for this year. Missouri's quota of this number is about 10,000. I said in my notes a few weeks back that we ought to do this, and from every part of the state has come the hearty response, "We can and we will." If you have studied carefully the figures presented in the last "Notes" I am sure that you can't help but see that one of the surest means to the accomplishment of this purpose is to keep our state mission work to the very highest point of efficiency.

If we are in earnest in this matter we will not be content with well *wishing*, but will go to the fullest possible well *doing*. The wishing is all right if it leads to the doing, otherwise it is mere sentimentality. Will you believe me if I say that we never have had such opportunities for aggressive successful work in all our history as now? God is proving us by the presentation of these opportunities. Will he find us wanting as he thus tests us?

We are limited, cramped, curbed by the awful want of funds. This coming month, January, is the old month for the taking of the state mission collection and the raising of the apportionment. Many who have been observing Mission Day did not in November because the notice was so short. Let such remember that it is always in order to work, watch and pray, yes and pay, too, for state missions. What better gift can you bestow than to make a New Year's gift for bringing Missouri to Christ?

Let us have a generous, hearty response.

Yours in his name, T. A. ABBOTT.

4144 *Westminster Place, St. Louis.*

Missouri C. W. B. M.

As Christmas is drawing near it is an appropriate time for all of the auxiliaries to send in their quarterly dues and thankofferings and C. W. B. M. Day collections. If any auxiliary failed to observe the 4th of December with a special service, let a program be prepared and rendered as soon as possible.

Two of the fifty auxiliaries that we desire to organize during the missionary year have been organized. The credit of the organization at Savannah is given to Sisters Dew and Williams —two loyal workers who reside there. Sister Goode writes that they have organized an auxiliary at Wyatt Park Church. There are now two good auxiliaries in St. Joseph.

Miss Mattie Burgess has returned to Missouri from India and is now caring for her afflicted mother at her home near St. Joseph. Will many of our women write her letters of loving sympathy?

Mrs. Sarah H. Jenkins, of Kansas City, the former treasurer of the Missouri C. W. B. M., has been quite ill for the last three months. We earnestly hope that she may soon be restored to health. She has spent many years in Christ's service and has ever been a liberal contributor to the support of the cause. She has been identified with the C. W. B. M. from the beginning and has made generous donations every year. We missed her in the fall conventions and the board meeting, and her absence was deeply deplored. The lovely Christian character of Sister Jenkins would add strength to the work of any cause.

VIRGINIA HEDGES.

Warrensburg, Mo., Dec. 19, 1898.

Ministerial Items.

Returns from the offerings for Ministerial Relief are beginning to come in and it is expected that every church and preacher will take this offering.

If you did not take the offering at the time appointed let it be done yet.

This Jubilee Year must be the beginning of greater things for the ministry. When you read this let your next duty be to send your offering to Howard Cale, Indianapolis, Indiana.

The January remittances to most of our beneficaries were made in time for Christmas and more than eighty of the "Lord's poor ones" made happy in the remembrance of the fellowship of their brethren.

If you have not a part in this it is a mistake. Your Christmas will be happier if you help this work.

A brother from Illinois writes:

I send my congratulation to Ministerial Relief. It is but a mite, $2.00, but it is all that I am able to give. I am past earning anything, being an old man, almost 79 years old, and with very limited means.

I hope and pray that our brotherhood will respond to the call liberally.

A correspondent suggests that all of our papers put in a standing announcement of the name and address of each representative of the different associations authorized to receive donations, as he could find none of their addresses in the papers. A good idea.

D. R. LUCAS.

Evangelistic.

OHIO.

Massillon, Dec. 23.—There have been 25 added here since my last report.—F. H. SIMPSON.

PENNSYLVANIA.

Beaver, Dec. 19.—One confession and baptism; two by statement from the Baptists yesterday.—Z. B. BATES, pastor.

TEXAS.

Galveston, Dec. 18.—Three added to-day; five the past month; 12 the past two months. Our West End mission is thriving; we now have regular preaching there. We are recovering from the war and quarantine scare. The work is growing.—JESSE B. HASTON.

ARKANSAS.

Eureka Springs, Dec. 23.—There have been 32 so far in the meeting; 24 by baptism and no let up to the interest. We will close, if we possibly can, and spend holidays at home. Our next meeting will be at Pierce City, Mo., near home.—MORGAN MORGANS AND DAUGHTER.

NEBRASKA.

Nebraska City, Dec. 23.—The writer just closed a meeting at Guid Rock, resulting in 19 additions; 11 by baptism.—J. T. SMITH.

Ashland, Dec. 24.—Our meeting here is starting nicely. Good attendance. Interest growing. Bro. Gregg is preaching practical discourses. We expect to do something here. —F. HOWARD SWEETMAN, singer.

INDIANA.

Indianapolis, Dec. 21.—At the North Park Church, five additions since last report.—J. M. CANFIELD.

Liberty Christian Church, Dec. 18.—Bro. Wm. Mondy, of Ohio, began a series of meetings here one week ago to-day. Bro. Ward, of Irvington, is here to-day. Seventeen confessions to date. Meetings will continue.—W. E. LISHER, elder.

Indianapolis, Dec. 26.—There were six additions at the North Park Church, of this city yesterday.—J. M. CANFIELD.

MISSOURI.

Civil Bend, Dec. 20.—We recently closed a meeting at Oak Ridge, Daviess county, with 13 additions; nine by baptism and four otherwise. We are now in a meeting at Eagleville. Bro. A. L. Johnson is with us and renders valuable aid to our work. We have the promise of M. S. Gillidett, who will come to our aid also.—Z. MITCHELL.

Spickard, Dec. 19.—J. P. Schooler just closed a very fine meeting here with 40 additions to the church and the church cemented together in love and full accord one to another.—WESLEY BROWN.

Our work at Mechanicsburg starts off very nicely; good audiences, and one confession Sunday night. We are planning for a meeting to begin with the new year.—R. B. HAVENER.

Buffalo, Dec. 13.—Sunday night closed the fifth week of our meeting conducted by Edmond Wilkes, of California, Mo. Through his efficient teaching there were 56 additions. We enter the new year in "full force" with J. D. Babb, leader. He has served us as pastor one year, and it is the unanimous voice of the church that he stay with us another year.—WM. A. COY.

St. Joseph, Dec. 23.—Fifty-six additions in our meeting at First Church.—C. M. CHILTON.

ILLINOIS.

Chauncey, Dec. 19.—Recently held a meeting at Young's, Marion county. Nine conversions; one by letter.—JAS. F. ROSBOROUGH.

Illiopolis, Dec. 21.—We have closed a short meeting; 10 added. Bro. G. M. Goode, of Lexington, Mo., did the preaching. Began my sixth year here yesterday.—S. F. ROGERS.

Arcola, Dec. 19.—I have been here and at Humbolt, Ill., 10 months. Have been able to say there have been added to the Arcola list 38 names and to the Humboldt nine names. Expect to give my whole time to Arcola next year. Yours for the "100,000 for Christ in '99."—J. T. CLEMENS.

Camp Point, Dec. 21.—Meeting at Bedford, Ia., closed with '54 accessions. Bro. Walters is doing a most excellent work at Bedford and is held in very high esteem. Our work was crippled for want of room. The brethren will probably build during the coming year. My next meeting will be at Leon, Ia., commencing Jan. 1.—R. A. OMER.

Irving, Dec. 24.—Our meeting at Chapin with W. H. Cannon closed with 27 added. Many were men and women of prominence and influence.—A. O. HUNSAKER.

Watseka, Dec. 26.—Two more made the ood confession here yesterday and one was added by letter. Have been preaching a few nights at Pitwood and have been rewarded by hearing several own Jesus as Lord and Savior. Bro. King is their pastor and is beloved by all. —B. S. FERRALL, pastor.

IOWA.

Our work is prospering. Improvements have been made on our church property to the extent of $700, making our building the best in this county. One confession recently.

Fraternally, C. P. LEACH.

Moulton, Ia.

Ft. Madison, Dec. 19.—One confession and one by statement last night. J. Carroll Stark, of Hamilton, Ill., Sundayed with us and preached two excellent sermons.—R. H. INGRAM.

Keosauqua, Dec. 17.—Bro. Hendrickson closed a five weeks' meeting at this place with 10 additions. Considering the weather and sickness in our vicinity the results were all that could be expected.—A. G. FELLOWS, clerk.

KANSAS.

Winfield, Dec. 19.—I held a short meeting at Walnut with four additions and pledges made to save the church from being sold; work in Winfield gradually improving and a move on foot to pay off the entire church debt of six or seven hundred dollars.—W. T. ADAMS.

Halstead, Dec. 17.—Our meeting closed Dec. 18 after five weeks with 46 additions. L. B. Coggins, of Mt. Hope, Sedgwick County, did the preaching. Bro. C. is a very able man and he has a warm place in the hearts of the people of Halstead.—D. W. THOMPSON.

The Christian Church at Parsons has just closed a six weeks' special meeting. The whole church has its influence and each individual member made to feel a deeper seuse of consecration and spirituality. The meeting was conducted by the pastor, W. W. Burks. assisted by Prof. C. E. Millard, as soloist. Bro. Burks in this special effort has preached some masterful sermons, which prove him to be both a scholar and a student. He is a strong preacher and has done much for the Parsons church and for the Christian cause in the state of Kansas. The singing of Prof. Millard added much to the success of the meeting. Prof. Millard won the hearts of the audience in the great convention at Chattanooga, where he recently sang. The Parsons church felt indeed fortunate to be able through their pastor to secure him.—A. M.

Erie, Dec. 21.—Ten additions since last report; three at Shaw, three at Rush Schoolhouse (eight miles north of Erie), four at Erie, and three to be baptized at Erie soon.—C. J. SANDERS.

Halstead, Dec. 22.—The series of meetings held by Bro. L. B. Coggins lasted five weeks. Closed last Sunday, 18th. The number of those uniting were 32 by baptism; 11 by statement and three by letter, making a total of 46. The house was crowded nearly every evening, notwithstanding the bad weather.—T. L. EVANS, clerk.

Galena, Dec. 23.—Two additions by letter and two baptisms in December.—R. A. THOMPSON.

Publishers' Notes.

I am highly pleased with the *Christian Lesson Commentary* for 1899. The preliminary notes are instructive, the expository comments well chosen; the lesson analysis suggestive, and the practical lessons and suggestive hints to student and teacher are helpful if thoughtfully used. I frankly say that I know of no better aid to the teachers and advanced scholars than *Christian Lesson Commentary*.

H. C. GARRISON.

Richmond, Va.

Christian Lesson Commentary, the handsomely bound volume of more than 400 pages, leaves little to be dsired in the way of aids to the study of the Sunday-school lessons for the year 1899. A glance at the pages shows that vast labor has been employed in its preparation. One who will pursue the daily readings which immediately precede each lesson, and will study the lesson in the light of the very copious and appropriate notes and suggestions accompanying it, must become intelligent in the Scriptures covered by these lessons.

We have for several years given the volumes of this series, as they appeared, a permanent place in our library, and we prize them very highly as commentaries on the Scriptures. Every teacher and advanced student in our Sunday-schools should have this book.—*Christian Courier, Dallas, Tex.*

Christian Lesson Commentary for 1899, edited by W. W. Dowling, is before me. Like its predecessors, it has the marks of thoroughness. The editor of this work never allows anything of vital interest in the text to escape his attention. In every lesson what needs to be said is well and amply said. Teachers and students in the Sunday-school who secure this commentary will find it replete in needed analysis, exposition and other treatment of the lessons. The editor and publishers deserve much praise for what they in this book have so well done.

W. O. MOORE.

Indianapolis, Ind.

I have carefully examined the Christian Lesson Commentary for 1899. It shows painstaking scholarship and fidelity to the work. Its different methods of treating the text—expository, illustrative, applicatory and practical—with its suggestive questions and hints on teaching it, opens the lesson fully to the understanding and gives a wide range of thought. It is a rich storehouse from which a teacher can be thoroughly equipped for teaching any grade of pupils. The numerous maps and illustrations, and the dictionary of Scripture proper names, with their pronunciation and meaning, are prominent and valuable features.—*I. A. Thayer, New Castle, Pa.*

The Christian Lesson Commentary for 1899, by Rev. W. W. Dowling, is published by the Christian Publishing Co., St. Louis. This is an attractive and interesting commentary on the international Sunday-school lessons for 1899 and is well worthy a place in the library of Sunday-school workers. It is richly illustrated and has many attractive features. It is practical, spiritual and exegetical, and will be found very valuable to all Sunday-school teachers and students.—*The Central Methodist, Louisville, Ky.*

Expansion.

Expansion of knowledge.
Expansion of zeal.
Expansion of charity.
Expansion of ideas.
Expansion of numbers.
Expansion of influence.
Expansion of the circulation of religious literature in order that the other expansions may be brought to pass.

The past week has certainly been one of expansion for the CHRISTIAN-EVANGELIST. Our friends have been kind; and better than that, they have added to their kindess *activity*. From all directions we have added many new subscribers, even renewing one from far-away Kailua, North Kona, Hawaii.

Nor do we fail to appreciate the renewals of our old subscribers so tried and true in their faithfulness.

Their subscriptions are fully as helpful and really more encouraging because they *know*, and by renewing *approve* the quality of the CHRISTIAN-EVANGELIST.

We would like to acknowledge the assistance of each one, but we cannot justify ourselves in taking much space and thereby excluding things which will be more helpful to our readers. We will say that the aid of every one of our subscribers is solicited and when extended is thoroughly appreciated by us.

We plead for the *best cause*, let us have the *best paper* in Christendom. Continue to encourage us and you will see that result.

"I thought I wrote a card asking that my CHRISTIAN-EVANGELIST be changed from Memphis, Mo., to Jacksonville, Fla. I have not, however, received a copy since coming here. I am getting right hungry to see the dear good paper once more."

J. T. BOONE.

Jacksonville, Fla.

The card was received and change of address made at once. The next issue was mailed promptly, but having missed the last one to Memphis, Bro. Boone's very commendable appetite was not disposed to be patient. It is only when we miss blessings that we really appreciate them. While we are on the subject, let us say that we will be obliged to our readers to report to this office any failure to receive the CHRISTIAN-EVANGELIST *regularly and promptly*.

Do you know that T. W. Grafton's Life of Alexander Campbell contains a clear and comprehensive account of the chief events in the life of the great reformer, that it is a neat cloth bound volume of 234 pages and that while it sells for One Dollar we offer it with one year's subscription to the CHRISTIAN-EVANGELIST to old and new subscribers, for Two Dollars? "Think on these things," but don't think *too long;* act while the opportunity is yours.

"I wish to renew my subscription to the CHRISTIAN-EVANGELIST and to thank you for the "Easy Chair" items. My sentiments exactly; "A pair of yarn mittens given as an expression of love, far preferable to a gold watch given as an investment."

BETTY BROWN ARMER.

Richmond, Ky.

The gems of thought and words of encouragement in the practical affairs of life, that appear in the Easy Chair each week, are the occasion of our receiving many letters of thanks and commendation.

It is proper to caution our readers not to confuse the Bible which we are offering in connection with the CHRISTIAN-EVANGELIST with the many inferior editions on the market. Ours is the *genuine* Oxford Self-pronouncing Teacher's Bible. The type is Bourgeois, 8vo. The Bible measures 8 1-8 x 5 1-2 inches, and in the pasteboard box weighs two pounds and twelve ounces. It is guaranteed to please.

For $2.50 we send the Bible and the CHRISTIAN-EVANGELIST for one year. This offer is subject to withdrawal at any time without notice.

"I have been a subscriber to the CHRISTIAN-EVANGELIST for twenty-two or twenty-three years, and as for me and my house, we will continue to serve the Lord by renewing our subscription for another year.

"Yours for progress in the divine life,"

T. C. HAMBLETON.

Jeffersonville, Ill.

Family Circle.

A Song of Peace.

I.

Peace in the sunlight, and peace in the rain;
Peace where in meadows the wild doves complain;
Peace on the fields that were red with the slain—
Peace in God's country forever!

II.

Peace where the great ships have roared with their guns—
Where the battle smoke darkened all stars and all suns;
Peace in the hearts of the patriot ones—
Peace in God's country forever!

III.

Peace where the lightnings from heaven are buried;
Where the loved flag of Freedom forever's unfurled—
Where the red stripes of glory shall garland the world—
Peace in God's country forever!

—Atlanta Constitution.

What Two Boys Did—II.

BY ALFRED BRUNK.

(CONTINUED FROM LAST WEEK.)

Mr. Latham's office was situated so he could oversee the selling departments of both the wholesale and retail branches of his establishment. As he watched the busy scene below him, saw the people come and go, strange thoughts passed through his mind. He thought of Jesus who, "though he was rich yet for your (our) sakes he became poor," of Paul trudging all over the country giving his life freely that the gospel might run and have free course; "as poor, yet making many rich." He laid back in his chair and closed his eyes. Visions of wealth floated before him. Merchandise, jewels, silver and gold were heaped upon his right hand and upon his left. A bright angel approached him and with a magic wand showed him the poverty, squalor and degradation of earth's millions and pointing to the wealth surrounding him said, "Whose shall these things be?" The angel turned away and vanished. Ravishing music greeted his ear. Mammoth temples were unlocked and their gorgeous wealth was stacked about him. Higher and higher rose the pyramid until he was completely shut in by the glittering array. The air became close and stifling; he tried to shake down the huge mass that he might extricate himself from his prison. He succeeded so well that the different articles fell upon him, and he was pinned to the earth. A mocking laugh greeted his ear; the wealth was brushed aside and he was raised to his feet, and stood facing the most horrible looking object he ever saw. "Whose shall these thing be?" asked the hideous one. "Well, not yours; they were given you in trust, and you have used them as if they were your own. Come with me." He gave a quick jerk and pulled himself loose from the grinning monster.

"Ha, Bro. Latham, I caught you napping this time," said Mr. Hollingbrook, shaking him by the hand. "No; I haven't time to sit down. Just called to tell you of a poor family of Swedes down on Wharf Street. Bad circumstances; no money, no work, drinks I suspect, two children quite sick. I called to see if you would permit Myrtle to go with me to their quarters and play the mandolin and sing for them. I will, of course, take good care of her till she gets home."

Myrtle! Myrtle again! What did it mean?

"Did you say they were very poor? and sickness in the family?" He pressed an electric button. Soon a young man stood before him. "John, send a barrel of flour, the best, to—to—what number, Bro. Hollingbrook? Oh, yes, 54 Wharf Street, fifth floor; and, yes, two hams, five dozen eggs and—and—what else, pastor?"

"Some oatmeal," suggested Mr. Hollingbrook, much surprised at the turn of affairs.

"Yes, a dozen groats, and have Dr. Markham call at once, and have Clover Dairy furnish them a gallon of milk daily till further notice."

The young man withdrew, and Mr. Latham turned to his pastor.

"Sit down," he said, "I must talk with you about a serious problem," then he repeated what the boys had told him. They conferred together for sometime and agreed upon a plan which they both deemed wise. That night Mr. Latham called the two boys and Myrtle into his presence.

"Boys," said he slowly, "I have carefully thought over your remarks and have arrived at this conclusion: You may try your mission work for one year; I shall interfere with none of your plans. All I ask is that you consult with Bro. Hollingbrook in all important matters. Myrtle can go with you when her mother or pastor or some other reliable person can be there to protect her. That is all I have to say."

For answer Harry and Myrtle both fell upon his neck, while Fred was so happy he knew not whether to laugh or cry, and compromised by looking as solemn as an owl.

The boys began their work with great enthusiasm. It created no little gossip among Mr. Latham's friends to know that his son had gone into mission work with a poor German boy, among the worst class of foreigners in the city, and that his daughter assisted them. For the work, in the nature of things, became so well known that several of the Cedar Avenue members went to all the meetings, thus making it possible for Myrtle to attend. The boys soon found that it was no small task which they had undertaken. While some would attend the meetings and give good attention, the majority were very unruly, and the boys could do very little with them. They would listen very respectfully to Myrtle's playing or singing, but would make all kinds of hideous noises when Fred or Harry attempted to speak to them. Fred won upon them, however, as the months passed, and they learned to love him. Before the year was ended the two boys appeared before Mr. Latham, and Harry said:

"Father, I am convinced that I would never be a good missionary. I am ready to take my place in the store."

"But what of Fred and the mission?" asked his father.

"He is going to keep it up, although it does get discouraging at times; but he is getting to be the best hand to keep them quiet I ever saw. Why, they all just love him," said Harry, proudly looking at Fred.

"The worst trouble, Mr. Latham, is that they ask me so many questions that I can't answer," said Fred. "I thought as they were poor and ignorant that I could get along all right, but I find I was mistaken."

"That's just it," said Harry," and I am going to work hard in the store and send Fred to school, and then he will be a match for any of them."

"How is this, Fred?" asked Mr. Latham.

"Why, Harry said that as he couldn't be a missionary and I could, he would take the money God gave him and send me to school, and he would be preaching the gospel through me. I didn't want to do it at all, sir, but he believes it is the Lord's will."

"Fred, suppose I were to loan you the money to pay your way through school, when do you think you could pay it back?" asked Mr. Latham.

"I couldn't take it that way, sir, for as I expect to be a poor missionary it is not likely I should ever be able to repay you."

Mr. Latham again consulted his pastor. "Bro. Latham, I will be frank with you. You are blessed with wealth, and it is rapidly increasing. Your son has been given back to you and may, perhaps, continue the business after you are gone. Fred has the proper material in him and will make his mark in the world if he is given an opportunity. You may do untold good by educating him and it may return upon your own head in a way you little suspect now." Mr. Hollingbrook saw what the father did not see.

"Fred," said Mr. Latham a few days after this conversation, "I have made up my mind to educate you if you will permit me to do so, and I do this unconditionally. That is, you are not to bind yourself to follow any particular course in life. The only thing I shall insist upon is, that you attend the university at Prairie Centre."

Fred thanked him heartily, but demurred at leaving Worthington. He would be compelled to give up his mission; but upon that point Mr. Latham was inexorable, and Fred consented to abandon the mission for the time being, and went to Prairie Centre. There he remained for five years. Being of quick perception he learned rapidly, especially in the languages, several of which he mastered. Harry worked hard in the store, conquering all difficulties, and was general manager of the business by the time Fred had completed his university course. Myrtle not only attended school, but perfected herself in music. One day Harry was busy in the store when in walked a tall young man with handsome, classical features.

"Why, Fred, how do you do!" said Harry. "How you have grown. And so you are through school at last. I am so glad, for I have missed you every day you were away."

"Yes, I am glad to get back. You, too, have grown, but not so much as I have. How are—are all you people?"

That evening Fred took dinner with the Lathams, and it was a happy group that surrounded the table. Mr. Latham, proud of the part he had taken in the development of Fred; Mrs. Latham, the genial, smiling hostess; hale, hearty Harry, happy at the return of his friend; Myrtle, accomplished and beautiful as a rose from celestial gardens; Fred himself, stately, 'tis true, but with a heart filled with love for all the world.

"Well, Mr. Gotleib, what are your plans now?" asked Mr. Latham.

"They are in a chaotic state at present, Mr. Latham," replied Fred. I thought I would rest and recuperate for a few days before beginning active operations."

"Quite right," said Mr. Latham.

During the course of the dinner Harry saw what his father and mother did not see, and he rejoiced in his heart. After dinner the gentlemen retired to the library.

"Fred," said Harry, "I have not labored all these years for naught, and of my available funds I have set aside a considerable portion for our mission work. This I place in your possession, not as a gift or charity, but as my part of our work. You are to use it as seems best to you."

"And I supplement it with a like amount," said Mr. Latham.

"I can accept this money upon one condition only; which is, that it is not mine, but the Lord's, and to be used for his glory and for the salvation of souls."

"Certainly," said Mr. Latham, "only you are to use it as your judgment dictates."

"Then I will accept the trust as the Lord's steward," said Fred.

"Say, Fred, before reopening the mission would it not be a good idea for you to visit the different cities and churches this summer, and look into the actual condition of things over the country and wind up with the General Convention?"

"I would like to do so, Harry, and doubt not I would gather up many practical suggestions, but I doubt the propriety of using this money for that purpose."

"No, no, Mr. Gotleib, you are entirely mistaken; this money is the Lord's, it is true, but you are to use it as your judgment dictates. If you deem it best to travel and look into existing conditions, it is yours for that purpose; if you feel that God will be honored by spending a portion of it upon your own person, then it is your duty to do so; and in fact this is necessary, as you must have food and clothing."

"I am glad that you look at it in that light, and I shall follow your suggestion without the fear that you and Harry will think I am wasting your money."

"As I expect to go to the convention, we we will come home together," said Mr. Latham.

Fred traveled for more than three months, visiting the principal cities of the country, being gladly welcomed by the brethren everywhere. As a large portion of the time was vacation season he preached in many of the pulpits in various cities, and could also note the condition of the poor who were compelled to remain at their posts through the hottest season as well as at all other times.

"Father," said Harry one day, "that money we turned over to Fred—is it his money, or is it the Lord's money?"

"Why, it is the Lord's money, to be sure."

"How, then, can he travel all over the country and spend it sight-seeing?"

"Why it is this way, Harry: We gave him the money upon the single condition that he use it for that which, in his judgment, would best advance the cause of God, and this has a wide application. We know that out of this money his personal expenses must be met. Suppose we had told him that one stipulation was, that under no circumstances should he pay more than $15.00 for a suit of clothes. Had he accepted the money with that condition attached, he would have been under obligations to fulfill it to the letter, but as it now is, if he can best glorify God by wearing the best of clothes, it is his duty to buy the best; but if he can advance the cause better by wearing the cheapest clothing, then it is his duty to get it. As to his traveling, if it were for the purpose of personal gratification it would be a wrong use of the money; but if it be for the purpose of disseminating the light of Christianity, it is perfectly right and proper."

"Then, father, the money is his to use for the Lord's glory and for the salvation of souls."

"It is."

"And it would be the same if it were houses, or lands, or goods, would it not?"

"Yes, the same principle would govern," replied his father.

"Then, father, why does not this store and all other wealth belong to God, just the same as Fred's money does?"

"Why, there is a great deal of difference, my son. We gave Fred this money upon a certain condition. He is in duty bound to comply with that condition. As to our property, we earned it by our own hard work, without any conditions whatever."

"I am not so sure of that, father. Doesn't the Bible plainly say that 'the earth is the Lord's and the fullness thereof?' And that being the case, whose is all this property? It evidently is not ours, for we cannot take any of it away with us when we die; and as God is eminently just he would not deprive us of that which is ours. If it does not belong to us, then whose is it? Not our neighbors', for God has given it into our temporary keeping. No, father, it is not ours, in any absolute sense at all. It is ours only that we may use it for God's glory and for the salvation of souls."

"Why, Harry, you are quite a polemic. I have known for sometime that you were something of a dreamer, but I did not know you could argue your case so well."

Nevertheless, it set him to thinking, and when a man will think there is some hope for him.

At the convention Fred was an interested listener to all that was said. He was especially taken with the motto, "The world for Christ," and eagerly drank in everything which bore upon the "how" the world is to be won for Christ.

Mr. Latham was there, and he and Fred returned to Worthington together.

(CONCLUDED NEXT WEEK.)

The Prodigal Girl.

BY SOUTH G. PRESTON.

How oft have you heard of the Prodigal Son,
From pulpit, from platform and press,
A story of love, repentance and woe,
First told by the Immaculate One.
But say: "Did you ever in all this world—
This world where every thing goes in a whirl—
Did you ever," I say, "Hear a loving, kind word,
In pity spoken, to a Prodigal Girl?"
Spurned by womankind, from society driven;
A helpless wanderer, forlorn and alone:
Not a friend in the world—Is there none in heaven,
Who pities, while she reaps in sorrow the sown?

There's a welcome at home for the Prodigal Son,
For the world rejoices and loves its own—
Receives the libertine in its mansions of pearl,
While it scorns the name of the Prodigal Girl.

I saw a young maiden both lovely and fair,
As she dwelt in a city of the world—
She was modest and pure and of noble birth;
Was Genivieve Brown, with graces rare.
I saw her again; but short months had flown;
People gazed on her as she passed along,
The woeful victim of a slanderous tongue—
An innocent sufferer of a terrible wrong.
The maiden went on, little dreaming of the fate
That would carry her down to the depths in a whirl:
She saw at last, when it was too late—
That her mother's only child, was a Prodigal Girl.

I saw her again as she tried to rise
Above the suspicion of friends—
But there was none to love, or sympathize,
She found no friend, beneath the skies.
In the House of the Lord, there was none to hear
Her cry of sorrow—her wail of despair;
For no one in that vast and fashionable throng,
Had ever err'd, or committed a wrong.
When they led her out of the elegant pew,
The Angelic Host in sorrow withdrew—
And the tears of repentance that fell from her eyes,
Were carried by angels above the skies.

I saw the gentleman that caused her shame,
As he knelt in his cushioned pew;
The trial was over: "He wasn't to blame!"
And the ministering angels again withdrew.
The church for him the battle had fought;
While he gazed unmoved on the ruin he'd wrought.

I saw her again; saddest scene of all,
In the Chamber of Death, alone;
Her beautiful spirit from earth had flown—
In obedience to her Savior's call.
God had forgiven her—not so the world—
The world, that turns with a dizzy whirl—
On earth she heard no loving, kind word,
In heaven was a welcome for the Prodigal Girl.
Loved by the angels, safe at home in heaven;
A redeemed spirit, in the City of Pearl—
No longer from joy and happiness driven;
But a guardian angel for some Prodigal Girl.

Sunrise on the Desert.

BY STELLA CLANTON.

All night beneath the cloudless summer sky,
Not with effeminate draperies drawn round,
But in unfettered majesty as warriors lie,
The naked desert lay in sleep profound.

No sound, no touch disturbed its slumbers deep;
No trees could whisper on its bare brown breast,
No sound from man could interrupt its sleep;
No breath of flowers disturb its peaceful rest.

Deep stillness reigned; and when a streak of gray,
Fast deepening into a rosy red,
Announced the coming of the royal day,
I walked forth in the silence with bowed head.

My feet were in the barren desert sand,
But o'er me and around me the Most High
Proclaimed his presence, as with lavish hand
He spread his splendid glories in the sky.

The east grew brighter; with no cloud in sight
To take the brilliant beauty for its own,
The wealth of color in the sun's rich light
Was given to the calm, clear sky alone.

The sun arose above the level of the land,
Its rising hidden by no bush or tree;
It spread its slanting rays across the sand,
And changed the desert to a golden sea.

I marvel not that untaught man should kneel
And groping blindly for the Holy One;
That he the presence of a God should feel,
When bursts upon his sight the rising sun.

Phœnix, Ariz.

The Family Altar.

BY F. BURGE GRISWOOD.

To those of us who have the blessedness to recall the habitual gathering around this sacred home centre in the days of our early childhood and youth, it is a great sorrow to observe the sad decadence in these modern times of so worthy a practice.

Even among professing Christians, the habit of family prayers has largely fallen into disuse and the individual members of many households are left to irregular and solitary devotions.

If parents could fully realize the influence for good that follows the daily assembling of the family group, for the recognition of God's gracious mercies, and for prayer for a continuance of his loving care and protection, they would not readily give up, or neglect such potent means of grace and blessing for themselves and their children.

Especially during the summer outings, when both young and old are more or less absorbed in worldly recreations, are the wonted times for hallowed devotions relinquished, and desultory readings of the Scriptures and hurried communion with God take the place of the sweet home hour of prayer and praise. In the midst of these sad reflections, there has come to me so beautiful an instance of faithfulness to Christian duty, that I feel impelled to speak of it as a worthy example for the imitation of those who have proved remiss in the obligations to our holy religion.

In a summer watering-place in a large and fashionable hotel, a venerable mother, with her sons and daughters and their wives, husbands and children, to the number of thirty souls, is spending a month or more. Every day she makes it a rule to assemble the whole party for reading of God's Holy Book, and for prayer and thanksgiving to the Author of all good. Wherever this earnest Christian woman goes she takes with her the faith and love which should govern the children of the Most High in every phase of life. To her there is nothing so important as her promised allegiance to the King of kings. No joy so sweet as the service which he permits and the communion which he grants.

Who will say that every pleasure on earth is not enhanced in tenfold degree by the hour daily consecrated to God and heaven.
—*Christian Intelligencer.*

STANDING or kneeling on the sidewalk were a group of boys intent upon a game of marbles. One little urchin, with knuckles on the chalked line, suddenly raised his head to call out to a companion:

"Stand but o' my sunshine, can't ye? I can't half see what I'm aimin' at when you shut off the light."

We went on our way with a wish that his admonition could reach a wider circle. For in the great game of life that busies us all there are so many who are barring the light. They watch the work that is going on around them, and by chilling indifference or contemptuous comment shut out the sunlight, and so spoil many an aim that might else be true.

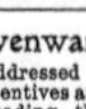

With The Children.

CONDUCTED BY
J. BRECKENRIDGE ELLIS, PLATTSBURG, MO.

More of Us.

Well, children, are you about done with 1898? I am going to get me a bran-new year in a few days, a year nice and clean without any mistakes or sorrows in it. Just think! None of us have done anything wrong or wasted any time in 1899. What are you going to do with this year? Wouldn't it be a fine thing to celebrate this 1899 by keeping all the resolutions of the Advance Society? One year in which we read a verse of the Bible every day! That would be something to be proud of! And a quotation each week from a celebrated author; and remember that five pages of history a week and 30 lines of poetry amount to 1,525 pages and 10,950 lines for the year, if I haven't multiplied wrong. That's the way to store your minds with bright and useful thoughts and give you something to talk about, so when you are in company you won't have to sit dumb like hens.

I have already told you about 35 of our members. Before I tell of others I had better begin with Plattsburg, because I live here, you know, and if I left any of these out, they wouldn't have so far to come to "get me." Our preacher is Bro. T. H. Capp. He told his Junior Endeavor Society about our society, and I made a speech—I am sorry you were not there to hear me—and when Bro. Capp said he was going to join, we got 14; his children, Resa, Nannie and Frank; and Cordie Harris, Irene Walker, Rose Blethro, Millie and Bessie Imbler, Ruth Rea, Beryl Marshall, Don and Fanny Hockaday, Perry Crafton. And the next Sunday we got some more; but since we had to wait a week to get them, I am going to wait before giving their names. Because if this piece was nothing but a string of names, it wouldn't be very exciting. That's so with fishes, you know. It's fun getting them, but taking them home on the string is only mildly amusing. Miss Kate Barnes also joined, because how are you going to do anything great without a few older persons? And the ages of all these average about 11 and 12. Why couldn't our members get their preacher to do this in their towns? Are you afraid of your preachers? I hope not. Frank M. Reid (12), Madison, Cal., says, "I read about the Advance Society and thought it was just fine!" His father is the minister at that place. Here is a chance for Frank's father. Florence Belle Beattie lives in Dover, Mo., Minnie B. Snyder (11), in Milton, Ky.

"I am a lttle girl," writes Della E. Durham, from Arbela, Mo., "that would like to join the Advance Society. I am eight; my mother died about three years ago. I came from the Christian Orphans' Home, to live with papa and mamma Searight. My five brothers and sisters have homes in different places of this state." Children, it is a blessed thing to have a home of our own, but there is one thing sweeter—to make a home for somebody else. From Raytown, Mo., come Roy Greene and Homer Slaughter. Mattie Maxfield (12), New City, Ill., says, "I like continued stories and then I am always anxious for the next paper." Laura Belle Campbell (12) is from Dayton.

Lena Collins (12), Benton, City, Mo., tells this story: Sunday-school Teacher—"Who killed Abel?" Little Girl—"I don't know, ma'am; I just moved here from Arkansas." The funniest thing Emily B. Riley (9), Kearney, Mo., ever saw, was some seals beating a drum. She doesn't say where she saw them, but I suspect it must have been at some entertainment, for I've been in Kearney and saw no seals. Helen Ross (8), lives in Independence, Mo.; Jessie B. Shafer (12), in Nilewood, Ill.; Emily Rice (13), Enfield, Ill., tells this true incident: "One Sunday morning at Sunday-school, two little ducks came waddling in and went straight up to our superintendent, Miss Johnson, who picked them up and carried them out. This caused much fun for the time being."

Mary Emma Keithley (8), Center, Mo., sends a true funny story: "Once while some people were being baptized, a little boy—whose grandma had been dipping her old hens in water to break them from sitting—looked up at his papa and said, 'I guess they won't set any more, will they, papa?' " Lina Pike, Nevada, Mo., (10) kept our resolutions three weeks before sending her name; she wanted to test herself. Henry Grady Maxwell (9), New City, Ill., is a pretty busy boy. He goes to school, helps feed the chickens and pigs. Every day he shucks his little wagon full of corn and hauls it to his pet pigs. He says, "I wish I could do something to make these columns a success." He can—by showing the paper to others and talking about it.

Here are a little boy and girl from Mt. Vernon, Ill.—possibly a brother and sister. The lad writes, "I am a little child just 54 years old and weigh 185 pounds. I want to join your society, and wonder if I can really and truly keep all of the pledges." —(F. P. Scott.) The little girl says, "I am delighted with your Advance Society and want to be a member. My papa still calls me his little girl; I am one of the children yet, for my big boy loves to play with his 'little mother,' and my baby grandchild delights to pull my glasses from my eyes, and we all have a happy time. I am not an owl, and I don't believe you could make an owl of a happy little robin if it lived a hundred years."—(Mrs. Scott.) I wish we had more children like these. They are not grown people, but growing people. Lots of people quit growing at about thirty-five, and they spend the rest of their lives in creaky boots and serious faces, saying, "Make less noise, children!" I know a physician who is seventy-nine, and who just began to study Hebrew last fall—isn't grown yet!

Virginia Winn (12), Dover, Mo., says, "I am trying to get up a circle here; I've gotten one member." Here is a little band in Essex, Ia.: Hazel Gilmore (7), Lola Gilmore (12), Myrtle Seward (12). Kate Keith (11), Lexington, Ky., is a "native of the Golden West;" she went to school three years in California. Grace Doolittle (9), Cozad, Neb.; E. Maude Kimler (17), Davis Mo.; Effie Smith, Church Hill, Tenn.; Mabel Ragland (12), Newton, Kas.; Ruth L. Gorham, Hudson, O.; Bessie Bacon, Overton, Tex.; Grace Stewart, (14), Santa Paula, Cal.; Irvin Stewart Mill Grove, Ind.; Ralph (13) and Lois O. Perry (10), Thomas, Okla.; Cecil (12) and Mildred Hughes (9), Davenport, Wash.

An amusing story comes from Canada: Marion and Dorrit, two little cousins, were on their way home one night, after they had been out to tea. They were sleepy and fussy, so Marion's mother told them to watch their shadows. Marion was greatly pleased. But little Dorrit was frightened by hers and tried to run away from it. When she found she could not do this she cried, "Take it away! take it away!"—(Grace G. Flaglor, St. Johns, N. B.) Ruth L. Gorham is ten, and lives in Hudson, O. She got her teacher, Miss Mattie M. Douds, to join our society. C. Ellis Younger, Lebanon, Mo., is twenty.

But I must wait for another time te name others. Don't be afraid you are forgotten. am very grateful for the kind things that have been written me, but I can't repeat them here, because you couldn't see me sitting in my corner and blushing, and you might think me vain. Several have said they never cared to read till our society started. The kind words have made me quite happy, although I have a lot of other things to make me happy, too; plenty of candy—chocolate is my specialty—and good books, and a great big turkey that we can eat the hash of ever so long after he—for it is a gobbler—has been warmed over for dinners. I don't say this to brag, but to remind you if your kind words please me, who have all I need, what will they do for those who have not so much! Lots of people—big people, too, and church members—never try to be friendly to others, but stand up stiff, like little wooden animals waiting for somebody to come along and put in their little yellow ark with its red roof and blue windows. I just punch such ones in the back, and when they turn about in surprise, I grapple their hand, somehow, before they know it. It does 'em good. Well, there are many children who are shy and friendless, who would like to be noticed, but don't know how to ask you to like them.

Do you like to read? Then you like to talk about your books. This is the last week I can give you for sending your ten favorite books and three favorite authors. Many votes are already in. So far, the books that have the largest vote is "Little Women," and "Robinson Crusoe;" it is a tie between them. The favorite author is Miss Alcott, and Longfellow comes close behind. Next two weeks will be devoted to our continued story. A new character is introduced, and if you haven't read the other chapters, you can get along all right anyway. Good-by, children; I send you all New Year's greeting, and may you have a very happy year, and I would like to send you all a present, but there are 140 of you now, and besides, if I am posted up in my Delineator, presents are not the fashion this year, anyhow.

Sunday School.

THE FIRST RECRUITS.*

HERBERT L. WILLETT.

In the Gospel of John the ministry of Jesus begins with a week of interesting experiences. After the prologue the first day's incidents are described in 1:19-28. This was probably on Thursday, counting back from the end of the week on which the wedding in Cana occurred. The first day was signalized by the arrival of a deputation of Jews who asked John the Baptist concerning himself and his work, and drew from him the reply that he was not the expected Messiah, but only a voice preparing his way. The second day (29-34) was seemingly the moment of Jesus' return from the temptation, of which occasion John took advantage to bear witness to him as the Lamb of God and to speak of the signs by which this fact had been confirmed at the baptism of Jesus. The third and a portion of the fourth day's incidents are chronicled in the lesson.

On the third day John the Baptist was in the company of two of his disciples. Like the prophets of the Old Testament he had gathered about himself a group of men who had listened with enthusiasm to his preaching, and perhaps carried it later on into wider regions. They were his disciples, and to them he gave instructions, teaching them to fast and to pray, and conforming more or less to the religious customs of the time. But John was not ambitious to be the center of a group of admirers, and when Jesus appeared he gladly welcomed his arrival as the moment when the real work of the kingdom was to be inaugurated. His own ministry had been but preparatory. As Jesus passed by John pointed him out to the two disciples as the Lamb of God. By this phrase he seems to gather up the most sacred meanings of Old Testament history. The significance of the term does not seem to lie so much in the fact of its relation to the animal offerings of the Old Testament, for of the coming death of Jesus John probably knew nothing. His ideas of the Messiah were not those of a suffering servant. More closely does his thought seem to relate itself to the new covenant of which Jeremiah had spoken, by which sin was to be taken away. In the patriarchal age covenants were ratified between the divided parts of a lamb, and thus were made sacred. The lamb stood as the symbol of the covenant, the sign of obligation upon both parties to keep its terms. Jesus came to give himself to this work of rebinding men to God, and his life and death alike were the expression of the sacredness of the covenant. In his death particularly lay the full expression of his ministry, and his blood as the sign of his life became "the blood of the everlasting covenant" (Heb. 13:20).

Of the two disciples to whom John spoke one was Andrew. Whether or not the other was John it is impossible to know with certainty, but this has been conjectured. Both were interested by the words of their master, and followed with curiosity to know more of the purposes of Jesus. He saw them following him and turned about to encourage them in their questioning. He gave them just the encouragement they needed. He invited them to come and see where he lived, for he was probably enjoying the hospitality of some citizen of Bethany beyond Jordan, where lay the ministry of John at this time. It was four o'clock in the afternoon when Jesus and the two disciples of John went to his abode. How much of that night was spent in converse we do not know, but the result is shown in the conduct of one of those men immediately after. This was Andrew, who is known chiefly as the brother of Peter, but who, it must be remembered, was a disciple before his brother. It was to Peter he now went as soon as occasion offered, and assured him that the Messiah was at last in their midst. What Jesus had said proved his Messiahship to their minds. Andrew needed nothing further to start him upon the career of a disciple of Jesus. This work he began at once by going to the one nearest, who was his brother.

How interesting must have been the first interview of our Savior with Simon, who was afterward to play so important a part as the leading disciple. When Jesus looked upon him he understood at once his characteristics, and gave him a name which was not only expressive of the latent character of the man, but became the name by which he was known in the group of disciples—Cephas, the Hebrew equivalent of the Greek name Peter. This word certainly did not express Peter's character at that time, but rather was the prophecy of what he was to become—a man of rock in later days in defense of the truth.

On the fourth day of this memorable week Jesus started for Galilee to spend a brief time with his mother and relatives in the northern provinces before he returned to Judea to begin his active ministry. Two of the disciples whom Jesus had called to his side, Andrew and Peter, lived in the little town of Bethsaida near the Sea of Galilee, and another townsman of that place, Philip by name, had likewise come to listen to John's preaching. Jesus found him and invited him to follow him. Philip at once sought his friend Nathanael and brought him to the Master with the assurance that he of whom Moses and the prophets had written was found in the person of Jesus, who was supposed to be the son of Joseph of Nazareth. Nathanael was surprised that one who lived in such an obscure place should be thought the Messiah. He was to come of the royal family of David and to carry on a kingly campaign, ending in the destruction of Israel's enemies and a reign of peace and power. Certainly this teacher from Nazareth bore no resemblance to the popular idea, but between the lines we must read the story of Philip's conviction, growing out of an unrecorded conversation with Jesus, and to the question of his friend he had the best of all replies that can be made to any scepticism regarding the claims of our Savior—"Come and see."

The remainder of the chapter should be carefully studied in connection with the lesson. That which convinced Nathanael of the character of Jesus was the word with which he met him, recalling to him some recent meditation of his under a fig tree, where he had probably been thinking of the vision of Jacob at Bethel with its upreaching ladder. Jesus called him an Israelite in whom there was no guile, an Israel out of whom the Jacob had departed; and when Nathanael, perceiving his knowledge of his nature and of his recent meditation, confessed in astonishment that he was the Son of God, the King of Israel, Jesus assured him that he would see more marvelous things than these, and that soon; nay indeed, from henceforth he should see the vision of Jacob realized in the opening of heaven to earth and the ascending and descending angels bearing the messages of the Son of Man.

SUGGESTIONS FOR TEACHING.

The work of every Christian, like that of John the Baptist, is to point men to Christ. It is also the work of every teacher to hand over his pupils to the higher teacher when they have completed their training with him. Jesus is eternally the Lamb of God, the indispensable means of redemption, the one whose blood has sealed the everlasting covenant between God and men. The considerateness of Jesus' conduct toward the inquiring disciples illustrates how anxious we should be to encourage those who are timid seekers after our Master. Where does Christ abide? The answer to all scepticism is the answer of Jesus to the disciples, and of Philip to Nathanael, "Come and see." One need not argue where the facts are so abundant. If men once come to Jesus with true hearts they will not only abide with him, but will at once seek to bring others. Jesus knows what is in men and seeks those for service who can best perform it. Unpromising persons and places are not to be despised. Personal work with those nearest us is most effective in fulfilling our work of saving men.

Anhaltstrasse 15, Berlin.

*Sunday-school lesson for Jan. 8, 1899—Christ's First Disciples (John 1:35-46). Golden Text—Behold the Lamb of God (John 1:36). Lesson Outline—1. John and the two disciples (35-39); 2. Andrew brings Peter (40-42); 3. Philip brings Nathanael (40-46).

Lightning Source UK Ltd.
Milton Keynes UK
UKHW011957201118
332601UK00012B/1986/P

9 780483 517271